CONSTITUTIONAL LAW

ASPEN CASEBOOK SERIES

CONSTITUTIONAL LAW
Fourth Edition

Erwin Chemerinsky

Dean and Distinguished Professor of Law
University of California, Irvine, School of Law

Wolters Kluwer
Law & Business

Wolters Kluwer Law & Business serves customers worldwide with CCH, Aspen Publishers, and Kluwer Law International products. (www.wolterskluwerlb.com)

No part of this publication may be reproduced or transmitted in any form or by any means, electronic or mechanical, including photocopy, recording, or utilized by any information storage or retrieval system, without written permission from the publisher. For information about permissions or to request permissions online, visit us at www.wolterskluwerlb.com, or a written request may be faxed to our permissions department at 212-771-0803.

To contact Customer Service, e-mail customer.service@wolterskluwer.com, call 1-800-234-1660, fax 1-800-901-9075, or mail correspondence to:

Wolters Kluwer Law & Business
Attn: Order Department
PO Box 990
Frederick, MD 21705

Printed in the United States of America.

1 2 3 4 5 6 7 8 9 0

ISBN 978-1-4548-1753-6

Library of Congress Cataloging-in-Publication Data

Chemerinsky, Erwin.
    Constitutional law/Erwin Chemerinsky, Dean and Distinguished Professor of Law, University of California, Irvine, School of Law. — Fourth Edition.
        pages cm. — (Aspen casebook series)
    Includes index.
    ISBN 978-1-4548-1753-6
    1. Constitutional law — United States. I. Title.
    KF4550.C429 2013
    342.73 — dc23
                                                                                            2013010433

Certified Chain of Custody
Promoting Sustainable Forestry

www.sfiprogram.org
SFI-01042

SFI label applies to the text stock

About Wolters Kluwer Law & Business

Wolters Kluwer Law & Business is a leading global provider of intelligent information and digital solutions for legal and business professionals in key specialty areas, and respected educational resources for professors and law students. Wolters Kluwer Law & Business connects legal and business professionals as well as those in the education market with timely, specialized authoritative content and information-enabled solutions to support success through productivity, accuracy and mobility.

Serving customers worldwide, Wolters Kluwer Law & Business products include those under the Aspen Publishers, CCH, Kluwer Law International, Loislaw, Best Case, ftwilliam .com and MediRegs family of products.

CCH products have been a trusted resource since 1913, and are highly regarded resources for legal, securities, antitrust and trade regulation, government contracting, banking, pension, payroll, employment and labor, and healthcare reimbursement and compliance professionals.

Aspen Publishers products provide essential information to attorneys, business professionals and law students. Written by preeminent authorities, the product line offers analytical and practical information in a range of specialty practice areas from securities law and intellectual property to mergers and acquisitions and pension/benefits. Aspen's trusted legal education resources provide professors and students with high-quality, up-to-date and effective resources for successful instruction and study in all areas of the law.

Kluwer Law International products provide the global business community with reliable international legal information in English. Legal practitioners, corporate counsel and business executives around the world rely on Kluwer Law journals, looseleafs, books, and electronic products for comprehensive information in many areas of international legal practice.

Loislaw is a comprehensive online legal research product providing legal content to law firm practitioners of various specializations. Loislaw provides attorneys with the ability to quickly and efficiently find the necessary legal information they need, when and where they need it, by facilitating access to primary law as well as state-specific law, records, forms and treatises.

Best Case Solutions is the leading bankruptcy software product to the bankruptcy industry. It provides software and workflow tools to flawlessly streamline petition preparation and the electronic filing process, while timely incorporating ever-changing court requirements.

ftwilliam.com offers employee benefits professionals the highest quality plan documents (retirement, welfare and non-qualified) and government forms (5500/PBGC, 1099 and IRS) software at highly competitive prices.

MediRegs products provide integrated health care compliance content and software solutions for professionals in healthcare, higher education and life sciences, including professionals in accounting, law and consulting.

Wolters Kluwer Law & Business, a division of Wolters Kluwer, is headquartered in New York. Wolters Kluwer is a market-leading global information services company focused on professionals.

This book is dedicated to my students —
past, present, and future.

SUMMARY OF CONTENTS

CONTENTS

CHAPTER 2

CHAPTER 3

THE FEDERAL EXECUTIVE POWER	**317**

CHAPTER 4

LIMITS ON STATE REGULATORY AND TAXING POWER   431

CHAPTER 5

THE STRUCTURE OF THE CONSTITUTION'S PROTECTION OF CIVIL RIGHTS AND CIVIL LIBERTIES — 517

CHAPTER 6

ECONOMIC LIBERTIES   601

CHAPTER 9

CHAPTER 10

FIRST AMENDMENT: RELIGION **1673**

PREFACE

This book is dedicated to my students and is a product of having listened to their views about constitutional law casebooks over the past 33 years. Although I have used several different books, my students always have voiced the desire for a more straightforward, student-friendly text. With the encouragement and support of Carol McGeehan at Aspen Publishers, that is what I have tried to provide.

Concerns that my students have raised have influenced every aspect of this book. They have expressed a desire for a book that does not pose countless rhetorical questions, leaving them uncertain about what to focus on in their studying. This book assumes that each teacher will ask the questions that are of greatest interest to him or her. (An accompanying teacher's manual offers suggestions, based on the questions that I focus on in teaching the cases.)

My students also have communicated experiencing difficulty with passages from excerpted law review articles. They have indicated that often the excerpts are so brief and so removed from the context of the original article that they are difficult to understand. They also have expressed the desire for a book that provides more context for understanding the cases.

This book attempts to address these concerns by presenting, almost without exception, just three types of material: major cases, secondary cases that are more heavily edited, and author-written essays. My essays are meant to provide a context for the cases, to provide historical background, to describe the development of the law in areas where the cases are not directly presented, and to summarize scholarly debates on various topics. Throughout the book, my goal is to provide students the material I would want them to read before class on a particular topic. Unlike virtually every other constitutional law casebook, there are no numbered notes following cases.

I am not attempting to provide a reference book that is comprehensive in presenting every related case or citations to every major law review article. Instead, my hope is to provide a casebook that gives students the basic material to study and understand constitutional law. Professors desiring to expose their students to the rich scholarly literature on the topic may supplement this book with one of the many excellent constitutional law readers that are available.

The book follows a simple, fairly traditional organization. I realize, however, that every teacher has a preferred structure for the course. I never have followed the organization of any casebook that I have used. Also, I know that the structure and organization of constitutional law courses vary widely across the country. Therefore, I have written this book so that it will be easy for teachers to use in any order. Except for references to make clear where particular topics are covered, I have tried to avoid referring to material in other chapters in a way that assumes students have read the book in order.

The book is organized in ten chapters. Chapter 1 focuses on the federal judicial power. After presenting the cases on the authority for judicial review, Chapter 1 focuses on the method of constitutional interpretation, congressional control over Supreme Court jurisdiction, and the justiciability doctrines as constraints on the judicial power. Apart from the justiciability doctrines, other constitutional and prudential limits on the federal judicial power, such as the abstention doctrines, are omitted because they usually are covered in federal courts courses rather than in constitutional law. The one exception to this is that Chapter 2, which discusses congressional power, includes a subsection on Congress's ability to authorize suits against state governments. This includes discussion of the Eleventh Amendment and recent sovereign immunity cases.

Chapter 2 focuses on the federal legislative power, particularly in relation to the scope of Congress's power and the extent to which concern for state sovereignty should limit such power. The chapter begins by considering McCulloch v. Maryland and then examines, in detail, several specific congressional powers: the Commerce Clause, the spending power, §5 of the Fourteenth Amendment, and the authority to authorize suits against state governments. In each area, the focus is on the breadth of congressional authority and the extent to which concern for states should cause it to be interpreted narrowly or should restrict it through the Tenth Amendment.

Chapter 3 examines the federal executive power, particularly in relation to executive-legislative conflicts. Thus, as a matter of organization, the focus of Chapter 2 is Congress's power relative to state authority, and the focus of Chapter 3 is issues arising in conflicts between Congress and the executive branch. The chapter begins by considering whether the president may exercise inherent authority and its application to the area of executive privilege. Next, the chapter looks at the constitutional problems of administrative agencies, including the nondelegation doctrine; the legislative veto; and other ways of holding agencies accountable, such as the appointment and removal powers. The chapter then considers the president's powers in foreign affairs and in the war on terror. Finally, the chapter considers ways of holding the executive accountable, such as through civil suits or impeachment.

Chapter 4 focuses on federalism as a limit on state and local power. The chapter begins by examining the issue of preemption and then considers the dormant Commerce Clause and the Privileges and Immunities Clause of Article IV. The chapter concludes with a short discussion of state taxation of interstate commerce.

Chapter 5 is titled "The Structure of the Constitution's Protection of Civil Rights and Civil Liberties." It attempts to present material concerning every part of the Constitution dealing with individual liberties and civil rights. Specifically, the central theme of the chapter concerns to whom the Constitution applies. The chapter examines the application of the Bill of Rights to the states (incorporation) and the application of the Constitution's protections to private actors (the state action doctrine).

Chapter 6 looks at the Constitution's protection of economic liberties. Freedom of contract under the Due Process Clause; the Contracts Clause of Article I, §10; and the Takings Clause are all considered. I have chosen this approach for many reasons. The various doctrines concerning economic liberties are best understood, of course, when studied together, but it is useful for students to see how the Supreme Court treated economic rights over the course of the twentieth century and to contrast this treatment with its protection of other individual rights in the same period.

Chapter 7 looks at equal protection. After an introduction to the concept of equal protection, the chapter presents the material on rational basis review and then considers discrimination based on race and national origin, gender, alienage, parents' marital status, age, disability, wealth, and sexual orientation.

Chapter 8 examines the Constitution's protection of individual rights, other than the First Amendment. The chapter presents the law concerning rights of privacy and personhood, the right to travel, the right to vote, and the right of access to the courts. The chapter concludes by examining procedural due process rights. The chapter thus covers individual rights protected under each of the clauses of the Fourteenth Amendment: the Due Process, Equal Protection, and Privileges or Immunities Clauses. Although the chapter is clear about where each right was found and is protected, its unifying theme is its focus on the rights possessed by individuals.

Chapter 9 focuses on the First Amendment's protection of freedom of expression. This is the longest chapter of the book, and I recognize that courses vary in how they cover this topic. Some schools, such as my own, have an entire course devoted to the First Amendment's protection of speech and religion. For such courses, I have been fairly comprehensive in covering these topics, so that the book has enough material in these two chapters to be used for an entire course. However, I also recognize that some constitutional law courses cover the First Amendment as a smaller part of a broader survey course. I therefore tried to be careful to construct the chapter so that it could be used in whole or in part, in any order, and still be comprehensible.

The chapter begins by considering the Court's method in examining freedom of speech, exploring topics such as the distinctions between content-based and content-neutral government regulation, prior restraints, vagueness and overbreadth, what is "speech," and what is an infringement of speech. The chapter then considers the categories of unprotected and less-protected speech, such as incitement, sexual speech, commercial speech, defamation, and so on. Next the chapter examines the availability of property for speech and concludes by considering, in turn, freedom of association and freedom of the press.

Finally, Chapter 10 looks at the Religion Clauses: the Free Exercise Clause and the Establishment Clause. Again, the goal is to provide sufficient material to allow use of the book in a course specializing in the First Amendment or to allow excerption for a constitutional law survey course.

In the years since the third edition, there have been major decisions in virtually every area of constitutional law, including standing, congressional power, presidential power and the war on terror, preemption, school desegregation, abortion rights and voting rights, and First Amendment issues concerning speech and religion. There is substantial coverage of all of these new developments. One disquieting trend has been the significant increase in the length of Supreme Court opinions. I have erred on the side of completeness to give students a full sense of the arguments on both sides. But I also felt that the book simply could not get any longer. Thus, in some areas I have substituted essays for older or less important cases.

Two other prefatory comments are necessary. When I began this book, my goal was to edit the cases less than most constitutional law casebooks. Reading the original decisions convinces me that for virtually every case, important material inevitably has been excised. However, as I worked on the book, I discovered that producing a text of reasonable length necessitates far more editing than I wish were necessary. I agonized over how to cut the cases and always ended up editing far more than I wanted. For the sake of readability, I have not indicated with ellipses where I have cut. Providing ellipses does not tell the reader anything about what was omitted, and constant ellipses are distracting. However, additions to the Court's language, even of a word, are indicated in brackets. I generally omitted the Court's citations, except where they seemed important to communicate something specific about the authority relied on.

The other prefatory comment concerns the relationship of this book to my one-volume treatise, *Constitutional Law: Principles and Policies*. The books are quite different in their goals and presentation. This is a casebook designed to present the major cases of constitutional law along with sufficient additional material to provide context and a basis for class discussions. The treatise is meant to be a reference work that summarizes the law and describes competing policy considerations.

Of course, there are places where I am saying essentially the same thing, such as in providing context and historical background. Initially, I was determined not to repeat anything I said in the treatise. This proved impossible and, I think, unnecessary. I often could not think of other ways to communicate the same material. Thus, sometimes the same language, and even the same paragraphs, appear in both books. My hope is that this will in no way diminish the usefulness of my treatise, even for students using this casebook. The books are so different in their focus and presentation that occasional overlap should not be a problem.

This fourth edition follows the same approach as the first three editions but has the benefit of many helpful comments and suggestions I received from users of the book. In some places, the cases are less edited.

This fourth edition is current through the end of the Supreme Court's October 2011 term, which ended on June 28, 2012. I will continue to prepare annual supplements and a new edition every four years. I welcome suggestions from students and teachers using this book.

Erwin Chemerinsky

April 2013

ACKNOWLEDGMENTS

I am very grateful to the many people who made this book possible. First and foremost, I thank Carol McGeehan, who suggested that I write this book and who helped me in formulating its approach. As always, Aspen Publishers has been everything an author could hope for and more.

Second, I am grateful for all the institutional support I received in completing the first edition of this book at the University of Southern California Law School and the second edition at Duke University School of Law. At USC, Deans Scott Bice and Matthew Spitzer were enormously supportive of this book and of my work. Darin Fox provided terrific computer assistance, and my assistant, Margaret Miller, was invaluable in helping me complete this book and supporting me in all my professional endeavors for 15 years. At Duke, Dean Katherine Bartlett was wonderfully supportive of my work, including this book. I prepared the third and fourth editions in my current institutional home, the University of California, Irvine, School of Law. I am very grateful to Chancellor Michael Drake and Provost Michael Gottfredson (now president of the University of Oregon) for all of their support and encouragement.

Third, many friends provided excellent comments and suggestions that are reflected throughout the book. Barry Friedman and Bill Marshall helped me develop the concept of the book and played an early key role in my writing it. Larry Simon and Marcy Strauss read chapters and provided useful suggestions. I am also very grateful to John Eastman, James Kushner, Sheldon Nahmod, Chris Schroeder, Neil Siegel, Stephen Siegel, Marcy Strauss, Len Strickman, and Nadine Strossen for their helpful comments on the first three editions. Doug Laycock and Evan Lee provided invaluable suggestions as I was completing this edition.

Fourth, I am very appreciative of my research assistants. I received great assistance from Robin Bechtold, Diara Fleming, and Amy Kreutner on the first edition; from Chris Baird, David Breau, Leslie Cooley, Sarah Kline, and Michelle Riskind on the second edition; from Kara Kapp and Jonathan Tam on the third edition; and from Francisco Balderamma and Tina Salvato on this edition.

Finally, and most important, I thank my family: my wife, Catherine Fisk, and my children, Jeff, Adam, Alex, and Mara, and my wonderful daughter-in-law, Kim. Their love, support, and encouragement mean more than words can ever express.

THE CONSTITUTION OF THE UNITED STATES

We the People of the United States, in Order to form a more perfect Union, establish justice, insure domestic Tranquility, provide for the common defence, promote the general Welfare, and secure the Blessings of Liberty to ourselves and our Posterity, do ordain and establish this Constitution for the United States of America.

ARTICLE I

Section 1. All legislative Powers herein granted shall be vested in a Congress of the United States which shall consist of a Senate and House of Representatives.

Section 2. [1] The House of Representatives shall be composed of Members chosen every second Year by the People of the several States, and the Electors in each State shall have the Qualifications requisite for Electors of the most numerous Branch of the State Legislature.

[2] No Person shall be a Representative who shall not have attained to the Age of twenty five Years, and been seven Years a Citizen of the United States, and who shall not, when elected, be an Inhabitant of that State in which he shall be chosen.

[3] Representatives and direct Taxes shall be apportioned among the several States which may be included within this Union, according to their respective Numbers, which shall be determined by adding to the whole Number of free Persons, including those bound to Service for a Term of Years, and excluding Indians not taxed, three fifths of all other Persons. The actual Enumeration shall be made within three Years after the first meeting of the Congress of the United States, and within every subsequent Term of ten Years, in such Manner as they shall by Law direct. The Number of Representatives shall not exceed one for every thirty Thousand, but each State shall have at Least One Representative; and until such enumeration shall be made, the State of New Hampshire shall be entitled to chuse three, Massachusetts eight, Rhode Island and Providence Plantations one, Connecticut five, New York six, New Jersey four, Pennsylvania eight, Delaware one, Maryland six, Virginia ten, North Carolina five, South Carolina five, and Georgia three.

[4] When vacancies happen in the Representation from any State, the Executive Authority thereof shall issue Writs of Election to fill such Vacancies.

[5] The House of Representatives shall chuse their Speaker and other Officers; and shall have the sole Power of Impeachment.

Section 3. [1] The Senate of the United States shall be composed of two Senators from each State, chosen by the Legislature thereof, for six Years; and each Senator shall have one Vote.

[2] Immediately after they shall be assembled in Consequence of the first Election, they shall be divided as equally as may be into three Classes. The Seats of the Senators of the first Class shall be vacated at the Expiration of the second Year, of the second Class at the Expiration of the fourth Year, and of the third Class at the Expiration of the sixth Year, so that one third may be chosen every second Year; and if Vacancies happen by Resignation, or otherwise, during the Recess of the Legislature of any State, the Executive thereof may make temporary Appointments until the next Meeting of the Legislature, which shall then fill such Vacancies.

[3] No Person shall be a Senator who shall not have attained to the Age of thirty Years, and been nine Years a Citizen of the United States, and who shall not, when elected, be an Inhabitant of that State for which he shall be chosen.

[4] The Vice President of the United States shall be President of the Senate, but shall have no Vote, unless they be equally divided.

[5] The Senate shall chuse their other Officers, and also a President pro tempore, in the absence of the Vice President, or when he shall exercise the Office of President of the United States.

[6] The Senate shall have the sole Power to try all Impeachments. When sitting for that Purpose, they shall be on Oath or Affirmation. When the President of the United States is tried, the Chief Justice shall preside: And no Person shall be convicted without the Concurrence of two thirds of the Members present.

[7] Judgment in Cases of Impeachment shall not extend further than to removal from Office, and disqualification to hold and enjoy any Office of honor, Trust or Profit under the United States: but the Party convicted shall nevertheless be liable and subject to Indictment, Trial, judgment and Punishment, according to Law.

Section 4. [1] The Times, Places and Manner of holding Elections for Senators and Representatives, shall be prescribed in each State by the Legislature thereof; but the Congress may at any time by law make or alter such Regulations, except as to the Places of chusing Senators.

[2] The Congress shall assemble at least once in every Year, and such Meeting shall be on the first Monday in December, unless they shall by Law appoint a different Day.

Section 5. [1] Each house shall be the Judge of the Elections, Returns and Qualifications of its own members, and a Majority of each shall constitute a Quorum to do Business; but a smaller Number may adjourn from day to day, and may be authorized to compel the Attendance of absent members, in such Manner, and under such Penalties as each House may provide.

[2] Each House may determine the Rules of its Proceedings, punish its Members for disorderly Behavior, and, with the Concurrence of two thirds, expel a Member.

[3] Each House shall keep a Journal of its Proceedings, and from time to time publish the same, excepting such Parts as may in their Judgment require Secrecy; and the Yeas and Nays of the Members of either House on any question shall, at the Desire of one fifth of those Present, be entered on the Journal.

[4] Neither House, during the Session of Congress, shall, without the Consent of the other, adjourn for more than three days, nor to any other Place than that in which the two Houses shall be sitting.

Section 6. [1] The Senators and Representatives shall receive a Compensation for their Services, to be ascertained by Law, and paid out of the Treasury of the United States. They shall in all Cases, except Treason, Felony and Breach of the Peace, be privileged from Arrest during their Attendance at the Session of their respective Houses, and in going to and returning from the same; and for any Speech or Debate in either House, they shall not be questioned in any other Place.

[2] No Senator or Representative shall, during the time for which he was elected, be appointed to any civil Office under the Authority of the United States, which shall have been created, or the Emoluments whereof shall have been encreased during such time; and no Person holding any office under the United States, shall be a Member of either House during his Continuance in Office.

Section 7. [1] All Bills for raising Revenue shall originate in the House of Representatives; but the Senate may propose or concur with Amendments as on other Bills.

[2] Every Bill which shall have passed the House of Representatives and the Senate, shall, before it becomes a Law, be presented to the President of the United States; If he approve he shall sign it, but if not he shall return it, with his Objections to the House in which it shall have originated, who shall enter the Objections at large on their Journal, and proceed to reconsider it. If after such Reconsideration two thirds of that House shall agree to pass the Bill, it shall be sent, together with the Objections, to the other House, by which it shall likewise be reconsidered, and if approved by two thirds of that House, it shall become a Law. But in all such Cases the Votes of both Houses shall be determined by Yeas and Nays, and the Names of the Persons voting for and against the Bill shall be entered on the Journal of each House respectively. If any Bill shall not be returned by the President within ten Days (Sundays excepted) after it shall have been presented to him, the Same shall be a Law, in like Manner as if he had signed it, unless the Congress by their Adjournment prevents its Return, in which Case it shall not be a Law.

[3] Every Order, Resolution, or Vote to Which the Concurrence of the Senate and House of Representatives may be necessary (except on a question of Adjournment) shall be presented to the President of the United States; and before the Same shall take Effect, shall be approved by him, or being disapproved by him, shall be repassed by two thirds of the Senate and House of Representatives, according to the Rules and Limitations prescribed in the Case of a Bill.

Section 8. [1] The Congress shall have Power To lay and collect Taxes, Duties, Imposts and Excises, to pay the Debts and provide for the common Defence and general Welfare of the United States; but all Duties, Imposts and Excises shall be uniform throughout the United States;

[2] To borrow money on the credit of the United States;

[3] To regulate Commerce with foreign Nations, and among the several States, and with the Indian Tribes;

[4] To establish an uniform Rule of Naturalization, and uniform Laws on the subject of Bankruptcies throughout the United States;

[5] To coin Money, regulate the Value thereof, and of foreign Coin, and fix the Standard of Weights and Measures;

[6] To provide the Punishment of counterfeiting the Securities and current Coin of the United States;

[7] To establish Post Offices and post Roads;

[8] To promote the Progress of Science and useful Arts, by securing for limited Times to Authors and Inventors the exclusive Right to their respective Writings and Discoveries;

[9] To constitute Tribunals inferior to the supreme Court;

[10] To define and punish Piracies and Felonies committed on the high Seas, and Offenses against the Law of Nations;

[11] To declare War, grant Letters of Marque and Reprisal, and make Rules concerning Captures on Land and Water;

[12] To raise and support Armies, but no Appropriation of Money to that Use shall be a longer Term than two Years;

[13] To provide and maintain a Navy;

[14] To make Rules for the Government and Regulation of the land and naval Forces;

[15] To provide for calling forth the Militia to execute the Laws of the Union, suppress Insurrections and repel Invasions;

[16] To provide for organizing, arming, and disciplining, the Militia, and for governing such Part of them as may be employed in the Service of the United States, reserving to the States respectively, the Appointment of the Officers, and the Authority of training the Militia according to the discipline prescribed by Congress;

[17] To exercise exclusive Legislation in all Cases whatsoever, over such District (not exceeding ten Miles square) as may, by Cession of particular States, and the Acceptance of Congress, become the Seat of the Government of the United States, and to exercise like Authority over all Places purchased by the Consent of the Legislature of the State in which the Same shall be, for the Erection of Forts, Magazines, Arsenals, dock-Yards, and other needful Buildings; — And

[18] To make all Laws which shall be necessary and proper for carrying into Execution the foregoing Powers, and all other Powers vested by this Constitution in the Government of the United States, or in any Department or Officer thereof.

Section 9. [1] The Migration or Importation of such Persons as any of the States now existing shall think proper to admit, shall not be prohibited by the Congress prior to the Year one thousand eight hundred and eight, but a Tax or duty may be imposed on such Importation, not exceeding ten dollars for each Person.

[2] The privilege of the Writ of Habeas Corpus shall not be suspended, unless when in Cases of Rebellion or Invasion the public Safety may require it.

[3] No Bill of Attainder or ex post facto Law shall be passed.

[4] No Capitation, or other direct, Tax shall be laid, unless in Proportion to the Census or Enumeration herein before directed to be taken.

[5] No Tax or Duty shall be laid on articles exported from any State.

[6] No Preference shall be given by any Regulation of Commerce or Revenue to the Ports of one State over those of another: nor shall Vessels bound to, or from, one State, be obliged to enter, clear, or pay Duties in another.

[7] No Money shall be drawn from the Treasury, but in Consequence of Appropriations made by Law; and a regular Statement and Account of the Receipts and Expenditures of all public Money shall be published from time to time.

[8] No title of Nobility shall be granted by the United States: And no Person holding any Office of Profit or Trust under them, shall, without the Consent of the Congress, accept of any present, Emolument, Office, or Title, of any kind whatever, from any King, Prince, or foreign State.

Section 10. [1] No State shall enter into any Treaty, Alliance, or Confederation; grant Letters of Marque and Reprisal; coin Money; emit Bills of Credit; make any Thing but gold and silver Coin a Tender in Payment of Debts; pass any Bill of Attainder, ex post facto Law, or Law impairing the Obligation of Contracts, or grant any title of Nobility.

[2] No State shall, without the Consent of the Congress, lay any Imposts or Duties on Imports or Exports, except what may be absolutely necessary for executing its inspection Laws: and the net Produce of all Duties and Imposts, laid by any State on Imports or Exports, shall be for the Use of the Treasury of the United States; and all such Laws be subject to the Revision and Controul of the Congress.

[3] No State shall, without the Consent of Congress, lay any Duty of Tonnage, keep Troops, or Ships of War in time of Peace, enter into any Agreement or Compact with another State, or with a foreign Power, or engage in War, unless actually invaded, or in such imminent Danger as will not admit of delay.

ARTICLE II

Section 1. [1] The executive Power shall be vested in a President of the United States of America. He shall hold his Office during the Term of four Years, and, together with the Vice President, chosen for the same Term, be elected, as follows:

[2] Each State shall appoint, in such Manner as the Legislature thereof may direct, a Number of Electors, equal to the whole Number of Senators and Representatives to which the State may be entitled in the Congress: but no Senator or Representative, or Person holding an Office of Trust or Profit under the United States, shall be appointed an Elector.

[3] The Electors shall meet in their respective States, and vote by Ballot for two Persons, of whom one at least shall not be an Inhabitant of the same State with themselves. And they shall make a List of all the Persons voted for, and of the Number of Votes for each; which List they shall sign and certify, and transmit sealed to the Seat of the Government of the United States, directed to the President of the Senate. The President of the Senate shall, in the Presence of the Senate and House of Representatives, open all the Certificates, and the Votes shall then be counted. The Person having the greatest Number of Votes shall be the President, if such Number be a Majority of the whole Number of Electors appointed; and if there be more than one who have such Majority, and have an equal Number of Votes, then the House of Representatives shall immediately chuse by Ballot one of them for President; and if no Person have a Majority, then

from the five highest on the List the said House shall in like Manner chuse the President. But in chusing the President, the Votes shall be taken by States, the Representation from each State having one vote; a quorum for this Purpose shall consist of a Member or Members from two thirds of the States, and a Majority of all the States shall be necessary to a Choice. In every Case, after the Choice of the President, the Person having the Greatest Number of Votes of the Electors shall be the Vice President. But if there should remain two or more who have equal Votes, the Senate shall chuse from them by Ballot the Vice President.

[4] The Congress may determine the Time of chusing the Electors, and the Day on which they shall give their Votes; which Day shall be the same throughout the United States.

[5] No person except a natural born Citizen, or a Citizen of the United States, at the time of the Adoption of this Constitution, shall be eligible to the Office of President; neither shall any Person be eligible to that Office who shall not have attained to the Age of thirty five Years, and been fourteen Years a Resident within the United States.

[6] In case of the removal of the President from Office, or of his Death, Resignation, or Inability to discharge the Powers and Duties of the said Office, the Same shall devolve on the Vice President, and the Congress may by Law provide for the Case of Removal, Death, Resignation or Inability, both of the President and Vice President, declaring what Officer shall then act as President, and such Officer shall act accordingly, until the Disability be removed, or a President shall be elected.

[7] The President shall, at stated Times, receive for his Services, a Compensation, which shall neither be increased nor diminished during the Period for which he shall have been elected, and he shall not receive within that Period any other Emolument from the United States, or any of them.

[8] Before he enter on the Execution of his Office, he shall take the following Oath or Affirmation: "I do solemnly swear (or affirm) that I will faithfully execute the Office of President of the United States, and will to the best of my Ability, preserve, protect and defend the Constitution of the United States."

Section 2. [1] The President shall be Commander in Chief of the Army and Navy of the United States, and of the Militia of the several States, when called into the actual Service of the United States; he may require the Opinion, in writing, of the principal Officer in each of the executive Departments, upon any subject relating to the Duties of their respective Offices, and he shall have Power to grant Reprieves and Pardons for Offenses against the United States, except in Cases of Impeachment.

[2] He shall have Power, by and with the Advice and Consent of the Senate, to make Treaties, provided two thirds of the Senators present concur; and he shall nominate, and by and with the Advice and Consent of the Senate, shall appoint Ambassadors, other public Ministers and Consuls, Judges of the supreme Court, and all other Officers of the United States, whose Appointments are not herein otherwise provided for, and which shall be established by Law: but the Congress may by Law vest the Appointment of such inferior Officers, as they think proper, in the President alone, to the Courts of Law, or in the Heads of Departments.

[3] The President shall have Power to fill up all Vacancies that may happen during the Recess of the Senate by granting Commissions which shall expire at the End of their next Session.

Section 3. He shall from time to time give to the Congress Information of the State of the Union, and recommend to their Consideration such Measures as he shall judge necessary and expedient; he may, on extraordinary Occasions, convene both Houses, or either of them, and in Case of Disagreement between them, with Respect to the time of Adjournment, he may adjourn them to such Time as he shall think proper; he shall receive Ambassadors and other public Ministers; he shall take Care that the Laws be faithfully executed, and shall Commission all the Officers of the United States.

Section 4. The President, Vice President and all civil Officers of the United States, shall be removed from Office on Impeachment for, and Conviction of, Treason, Bribery, or other high Crimes and Misdemeanors.

ARTICLE III

Section 1. The judicial Power of the United States, shall be vested in one supreme Court, and in such inferior Courts as the Congress may from time to time ordain and establish. The Judges, both of the supreme and inferior Courts, shall hold their Offices during good Behaviour, and shall, at stated Times, receive for their Services a Compensation, which shall not be diminished during their Continuance in Office.

Section 2. [1] The Judicial Power shall extend to all Cases, in Law and Equity, arising under this Constitution, the Laws of the United States, and Treaties made, or which shall be made, under their Authority; — to all Cases affecting Ambassadors, other public Ministers and Consuls; — to all Cases of admiralty and maritime Jurisdiction; — to Controversies to which the United States shall be a Party; — to Controversies between two or more States; between a State and Citizens of another State; — between Citizens of different States; — between Citizens of the same State claiming Lands under Grants of different States, and between a State, or the Citizens thereof, and foreign States, Citizens or Subjects.

[2] In all cases affecting Ambassadors, other public Ministers and Consuls, and those in which a State shall be Party, the supreme Court shall have original Jurisdiction. In all the other Cases before mentioned, the supreme Court shall have appellate Jurisdiction, both as to Law and Fact, with such Exceptions, and under such Regulations as the Congress shall make.

[3] The trial of all Crimes, except in Cases of Impeachment, shall be by Jury; and such Trial shall be held in the State where the said Crimes shall have been committed; but when not committed within any State, the Trial shall be at such Place or Places as the Congress may by Law have directed.

Section 3. [1] Treason against the United States, shall consist only in levying War against them, or in adhering to their Enemies, giving them Aid and Comfort. No person shall be convicted of Treason unless on the Testimony of two Witnesses to the same over Act, or on Confession in open Court.

[2] The Congress shall have Power to declare the Punishment of Treason, but no Attainder of Treason shall work Corruption of Blood, or Forfeiture except during the Life of the Person attainted.

ARTICLE IV

Section 1. Full Faith and Credit shall be given in each State to the public Acts, Records, and judicial Proceedings of every other State. And the Congress may by general Laws prescribe the Manner in which such Acts, Records and Proceedings shall be proved, and the Effect thereof.

Section 2. [1] The Citizens of each State shall be entitled to all Privileges and Immunities of Citizens in the several States.

[2] A Person charged in any State with Treason, Felony, or other Crime, who shall flee from Justice, and be found in another State, shall on demand of the executive Authority of the State from which he fled, be delivered up, to be removed to the State having Jurisdiction of the Crime.

[3] No Person held to Service or Labour in one State, under the Laws thereof, escaping into another, shall, in Consequence of any Law or Regulation therein, be discharged from such Service or Labour, but shall be delivered up on Claim of the Party to whom such Service or Labour may be due.

Section 3. [1] New States may be admitted by the Congress into this Union; but no new State shall be formed or erected within the Jurisdiction of any other State; nor any State be formed by the Junction of two or more States, or Parts of States, without the Consent of the Legislatures of the States concerned as well as of the Congress.

[2] The Congress shall have Power to dispose of and make all needful Rules and Regulations respecting the Territory or other Property belonging to the United States; and nothing in this Constitution shall be so construed as to Prejudice any Claims of the United States, or of any particular State.

Section 4. The United States shall guarantee to every State in this Union a Republican Form of Government, and shall protect each of them against Invasion; and on Application of the Legislature, or of the Executive (when the Legislature cannot be convened) against domestic Violence.

ARTICLE V

The Congress, whenever two thirds of both Houses shall deem it necessary, shall propose Amendments to this Constitution, or, on the Application of the Legislatures of two thirds of the several States, shall call a Convention for proposing Amendments, which, in either Case, shall be valid to all Intents and Purposes, as part of this Constitution, when ratified by the Legislatures of three fourths of the several States, or by Conventions in three fourths thereof, as the one or the other Mode of Ratification may be proposed by the Congress; Provided that no Amendment which may be made prior to the Year One thousand eight hundred and eight shall in any Manner affect the first and fourth Clauses in the Ninth Section of the first Article; and that no State, without its Consent, shall be deprived of its equal Suffrage in the Senate.

ARTICLE VI

[1] All Debts contracted and Engagements entered into, before the Adoption of this Constitution, shall be as valid against the United States under this Constitution, as under the Confederation.

[2] This Constitution, and the Laws of the United States which shall be made in Pursuance thereof; and all Treaties made, or which shall be made, under the Authority of the United States, shall be the supreme Law of the Land; and the Judges in every State shall be bound thereby, any Thing in the Constitution or Laws of any State to the Contrary notwithstanding.

[3] The Senators and Representatives before mentioned, and the Members of the several State Legislatures, and all executive and judicial Officers, both of the United States and of the several States, shall be bound by Oath or Affirmation, to support this Constitution; but no religious Test shall ever be required as a Qualification to any Office or public Trust under the United States.

ARTICLE VII

The Ratification of the Conventions of nine States shall be sufficient for the Establishment of this Constitution between the States so ratifying the Same.

Done in Convention by the Unanimous Consent of the States present the Seventeenth Day of September in the Year of our Lord one thousand seven hundred and Eighty seven and of the Independence of the United States of America the Twelfth.

ARTICLES IN ADDITION TO, AND AMENDMENT OF, THE CONSTITUTION OF THE UNITED STATES OF AMERICA, PROPOSED BY CONGRESS, AND RATIFIED BY THE LEGISLATURES OF THE SEVERAL STATES, PURSUANT TO THE FIFTH ARTICLE OF THE ORIGINAL CONSTITUTION.

AMENDMENT I [1791]

Congress shall make no law respecting an establishment of religion, or prohibiting the free exercise thereof; or abridging the freedom of speech, or of the press; or the right of the people peaceably to assemble, and to petition the Government for a redress of grievances.

AMENDMENT II [1791]

A well regulated Militia, being necessary to the security of a free State, the right of the people to keep and bear Arms, shall not be infringed.

AMENDMENT III [1791]

No Soldier shall, in time of peace be quartered in any house, without the consent of the Owner, nor in time of war, but in a manner to be prescribed by law.

AMENDMENT IV [1791]

The right of the people to be secure in their persons, houses, papers, and effects, against unreasonable searches and seizures, shall not be violated, and no Warrants shall issue, but upon probable cause, supported by Oath or affirmation, and particularly describing the place to be searched, and the persons or things to be seized.

AMENDMENT V [1791]

No person shall be held to answer for a capital, or otherwise infamous crime, unless on a presentment or indictment of a Grand Jury, except in cases arising in the land or naval forces, or in the Militia, when in actual service in time of War or public danger; nor shall any person be subject for the same offence to be twice put in jeopardy of life or limb; nor shall be compelled in any criminal case to be a witness against himself, nor be deprived of life, liberty, or property, without due process of law; nor shall private property be taken for public use, without just compensation.

AMENDMENT VI [1791]

In all criminal prosecutions, the accused shall enjoy the right to a speedy and public trial, by an impartial jury of the State and district wherein the crime shall have been committed, which district shall have been previously ascertained by law, and to be informed of the nature and cause of the accusation; to be confronted with the witnesses against him; to have compulsory process for obtaining witnesses in his favor, and to have the Assistance of Counsel for his defence.

AMENDMENT VII [1791]

In Suits at common law, where the value in controversy shall exceed twenty dollars, the right of trial by jury shall be preserved, and no fact tried by a jury, shall be otherwise reexamined in any Court of the United States, than according to the rules of the common law.

AMENDMENT VIII [1791]

Excessive bail shall not be required, nor excessive fines imposed, nor cruel and unusual punishments inflicted.

AMENDMENT IX [1791]

The enumeration in the Constitution, of certain rights, shall not be construed to deny or disparage others retained by the people.

AMENDMENT X [1791]

The powers not delegated to the United States by the Constitution, nor prohibited by it to the States, are reserved to the States respectively, or to the people.

AMENDMENT XI [1798]

The Judicial power of the United States shall not be construed to extend to any suit in law or equity, commenced or prosecuted against one of the United States by Citizens of another State, or by Citizens or Subjects of any Foreign State.

AMENDMENT XII [1804]

The Electors shall meet in their respective states and vote by ballot for President and Vice-President, one of whom, at least, shall not be an inhabitant of the same state with themselves; they shall name in their ballots the person voted for as President, and in distinct ballots the person voted for as Vice-President, and they shall make distinct lists of all persons voted for as President, and of all persons voted for as Vice-President, and of the number of votes for each, which lists they shall sign and certify, and transmit sealed to the seat of the government of the United States, directed to the President of the

Senate;—The President of the Senate shall, in the presence of the Senate and House of Representatives, open all the certificates and the votes shall then be counted;—The person having the greatest number of votes for President, shall be the President, if such number be a majority of the whole number of Electors appointed; and if no person have such majority, then from the persons having the highest numbers not exceeding three on the list of those voted for as President, the House of Representatives shall choose immediately, by ballot, the President. But in choosing the President, the votes shall be taken by states, the representation from each state having one vote; a quorum for this purpose shall consist of a member or members from two-thirds of the states, and a majority of all the states shall be necessary to a choice. And if the House of Representatives shall not choose a President whenever the right of choice shall devolve upon them, before the fourth day of March next following, then the Vice-President shall act as President, as in the case of the death or other constitutional disability of the President.—The person having the greatest number of votes as Vice-President, shall be the Vice-President, if such number be a majority of the whole number of Electors appointed, and if no person have a majority, then from the two highest numbers on the list, the Senate shall choose the Vice-President; a quorum for the purpose shall consist of two-thirds of the whole number of Senators, and a majority of the whole number shall be necessary to a choice. But no person constitutionally ineligible to the office of President shall be eligible to that of Vice-President of the United States.

AMENDMENT XIII [1865]

Section 1. Neither slavery nor involuntary servitude, except as a punishment for crime whereof the party shall have been duly convicted, shall exist within the United States, or any place subject to their jurisdiction.

Section 2. Congress shall have power to enforce this article by appropriate legislation.

AMENDMENT XIV [1868]

Section 1. All persons born or naturalized in the United States, and subject to the jurisdiction thereof, are citizens of the United States and of the State wherein they reside. No State shall make or enforce any law which shall abridge the privileges or immunities of citizens of the United States; nor shall any State deprive any person of life, liberty, or property, without due process of law; nor deny to any person within its jurisdiction the equal protection of the laws.

Section 2. Representatives shall be apportioned among the several States according to their respective numbers, counting the whole number of persons in each State, excluding Indians not taxed. But when the right to vote at any election for the choice of electors for President and Vice-President of the United States, Representatives in Congress, the Executive and Judicial officers of a State, or the members of the Legislature thereof, is denied to any of the male inhabitants of such State, being twenty-one years of age, and citizens of the United States, or in any way abridged, except for participation in rebellion, or other crime, the basis of representation therein shall be reduced in the proportion which the number of such male citizens shall bear to the whole number of male citizens twenty-one years of age in such State.

Section 3. No person shall be a Senator or Representative in Congress, or elector of President and Vice-President, or hold any office, civil or military, under the United States, or under any State, who, having previously taken an oath, as a member of Congress, or as an officer of the United States, or as a member of any State legislature, or as an executive or judicial officer of any State, to support the Constitution of the United States, shall have engaged in insurrection or rebellion against the same, or given aid or comfort to the enemies thereof. But Congress may by a vote of two-thirds of each House, remove such disability.

Section 4. The validity of the public debt of the United States, authorized by law, including debts incurred for payment of pensions and bounties for services in suppressing insurrection or rebellion, shall not be questioned. But neither the United States nor any State shall assume or pay any debt or obligation incurred in aid of insurrection or rebellion against the United States, or any claim for the loss of emancipation of any slave; but all such debts, obligations and claims shall be held illegal and void.

Section 5. The Congress shall have power to enforce, by appropriate legislation, the provisions of this article.

AMENDMENT XV [1870]

Section 1. The right of citizens of the United States to vote shall not be denied or abridged by the United States or by any State on account of race, color, or previous condition of servitude.

Section 2. The Congress shall have power to enforce this article by appropriate legislation.

AMENDMENT XVI [1913]

The Congress shall have power to lay and collect taxes on incomes, from whatever source derived, without apportionment among the several States, and without regard to any census or enumeration.

AMENDMENT XVII [1913]

[1] The Senate of the United States shall be composed of two Senators from each State, elected by the people thereof, for six years, and each Senator shall have one vote. The electors in each State shall have the qualifications requisite for electors of the most numerous branch of the State legislatures.

[2] When vacancies happen in the representation of any State in the Senate, the executive authority of such State shall issue writs of election to fill such vacancies: *Provided*, That the legislature of any State may empower the executive thereof to make temporary appointments until the people fill the vacancies by election as the legislature may direct.

[3] This amendment shall not be so construed as to affect the election or term of any Senator chosen before it becomes valid as part of the Constitution.

AMENDMENT XVIII [1919]

Section 1. After one year from the ratification of this article the manufacture, sale, or transportation of intoxicating liquors within, the importation thereof into, or the exportation thereof from the United States and all territory subject to the jurisdiction thereof for beverage purposes is hereby prohibited.

Section 2. The Congress and the several States shall have concurrent power to enforce this article by appropriate legislation.

Section 3. This article shall be inoperative unless it shall have been ratified as an amendment to the Constitution by the legislatures of the several States, as provided in the Constitution, within seven years from the date of the submission hereof to the States by the Congress.

AMENDMENT XIX [1920]

[1] The right of citizens of the United States to vote shall not be denied or abridged by the United States or by any State on account of sex.

[2] Congress shall have power to enforce this article by appropriate legislation.

AMENDMENT XX [1933]

Section 1. The terms of the President and Vice President shall end at noon on the 20th day of January, and the terms of Senators and Representatives at noon on the 3d day of January, of the years in which such terms would have ended if this article had not been ratified; and the terms of their successor shall then begin.

Section 2. The Congress shall assemble at least once in every year, and such meeting shall begin at noon on the 3d day of January, unless they shall by law appoint a different day.

Section 3. If, at the time fixed for the beginning of the term of the President, the President elect shall have died, the Vice President elect shall become President. If a President shall not have been chosen before the time fixed for the beginning of his term, or if the President elect shall have failed to qualify, then the Vice President elect shall act as President until a President shall have qualified; and the Congress may by law provide for the case wherein neither a President elect nor a Vice President elect shall have qualified, declaring who shall then act as President, or the manner in which one who is to act shall be selected, and such person shall act accordingly until a President or Vice President shall have qualified.

Section 4. The Congress may by law provide for the case of the death of any of the persons from whom the House of Representatives may choose a President whenever the right of choice shall have devolved upon them, and for the case of the death of any of the persons from whom the Senate may choose a Vice President whenever the right of choice shall have devolved upon them.

Section 5. Sections 1 and 2 shall take effect on the 15th day of October following the ratification of this article.

Section 6. This article shall be inoperative unless it shall have been ratified as an amendment to the Constitution by the legislatures of three-fourths of the several States within seven years from the date of its submission.

AMENDMENT XXI [1933]

Section 1. The eighteenth article of amendment to the Constitution of the United States is hereby repealed.

Section 2. The transportation or importation into any State, Territory, or possession of the United States for delivery or use therein of intoxicating liquors, in violation of the laws thereof, is hereby prohibited.

Section 3. This article shall be inoperative unless it shall have been ratified as an amendment to the Constitution by conventions in the several States, as provided in the Constitution, within seven years from the date of the submissions hereof to the States by the Congress.

AMENDMENT XXII [1951]

Section 1. No person shall be elected to the office of the President more than twice, and no person who has held the office of President, or acted as President, for more than two years of a term to which some other person was elected President shall be elected to the office of the President more than once. But this Article shall not apply to any person holding the office of President when this Article was proposed by the Congress, and shall not prevent any person who may be holding the office of President, or acting as President, during the term within which the Article becomes operative from holding the office of President or acting as President during the remainder of such term.

Section 2. This article shall be inoperative unless it shall have been ratified as an amendment to the Constitution by the legislatures of three-fourths of the several States within seven years from the date of its submission to the States by the Congress.

AMENDMENT XXIII [1961]

Section 1. The District constituting the seat of Government of the United States shall appoint in such manner as the Congress may direct:

A number of electors of President and Vice President equal to the whole number of Senators and Representatives in Congress to which the District would be entitled if it were a State, but in no event more than the least populous State; they shall be in addition to those appointed by the States, but they shall be considered, for the purposes of the election of President and Vice President, to be electors appointed by a State; and they shall meet in the District and perform such duties as provided by the twelfth article of amendment.

Section 2. The Congress shall have power to enforce this article by appropriate legislation.

AMENDMENT XXIV [1964]

Section 1. The right of citizens of the United States to vote in any primary or other election for President or Vice President for electors for President or Vice President, or for Senator or Representative in Congress, shall not be denied or abridged by the United States or any State by reason of failure to pay any poll tax or other tax.

Section 2. The Congress shall have power to enforce this article by appropriate legislation.

AMENDMENT XXV [1967]

Section 1. In case of the removal of the President from office or of his death or resignation, the Vice President shall become President.

Section 2. Whenever there is a vacancy in the office of the Vice President, the President shall nominate a Vice President who shall take office upon confirmation by a majority vote of both Houses of Congress.

Section 3. Whenever the President transmits to the President pro tempore of the Senate and the Speaker of the House of Representatives his written declaration that he is unable to discharge the powers and duties of his office, and until he transmits to them a written declaration to the contrary, such powers and duties shall be discharged by the Vice President as Acting President.

Section 4. Whenever the Vice President and a Majority of either the principal officers of the executive departments or of such other body as Congress may by law provide, transmit to the President pro tempore of the Senate and the Speaker of the House of Representatives their written declaration that the President is unable to discharge the powers and duties of his office, the Vice President shall immediately assume the powers and duties of the office as Acting President.

Thereafter, when the President transmits to the President pro tempore of the Senate and the Speaker of the House of Representatives his written declaration that no inability exists, he shall resume the powers and duties of his office unless the Vice President and a majority of either the principal officers of the executive department or of such other body as Congress may by law provide, transmit within four days to the President pro tempore of the Senate and the Speaker of the House of Representatives their written declaration that the President is unable to discharge the powers and duties of his office. Thereupon Congress shall decide the issue, assembling within forty-eight hours for that purpose if not in session. If the Congress, within twenty-one days after receipt of the latter written declaration, or, if Congress is not in session, within twenty-one days after Congress is required to assemble, determined by two-thirds vote of both Houses that the President is unable to discharge the powers and duties of his office, the Vice President shall continue to discharge the same as Acting President; otherwise, the President shall resume the powers and duties of his office.

AMENDMENT XXVI [1971]

Section 1. The right of citizens of the United States, who are eighteen years of age or older, to vote shall not be denied or abridged by the United States or by any State on account of age.

Section 2. The Congress shall have power to enforce this article by appropriate legislation.

AMENDMENT XXVII [1992]

Section 1. No law, varying the Compensation for the services of the Senators and Representatives, shall take effect, unless an election of Representatives shall have intervened.

CONSTITUTIONAL LAW

CHAPTER

1

THE FEDERAL JUDICIAL POWER

A. THE AUTHORITY FOR JUDICIAL REVIEW

In studying constitutional law, you will be reading countless Supreme Court cases deciding the constitutionality of federal, state, and local laws and executive actions. Surprisingly, the Constitution is silent as to whether the Supreme Court and other federal courts have the authority to engage in such judicial review. In England, for example, both in 1787 and today, no English court has the authority to invalidate an act of Parliament. In 1787, the framers of the United States Constitution, in Philadelphia, did not discuss whether the federal judiciary should have the power of judicial review.

The authority for judicial review was first announced by the Supreme Court in Marbury v. Madison in 1803.[1] *Marbury* establishes the authority for judicial review of both federal executive and legislative acts. The historical background of the case is important in understanding the decision that follows. In November 1800, the incumbent president, John Adams, lost in a hotly contested election. Thomas Jefferson received a majority of the popular vote but tied in the Electoral College vote with Aaron Burr. Jefferson ultimately prevailed, based on a vote in the House of Representatives.

Adams was a Federalist, and the Federalists were determined to exercise their influence before the Republican, Jefferson, took office. In January 1801, Adams's secretary of state, John Marshall, was named to serve as the third chief justice of the U.S. Supreme Court. Throughout the remainder of Adams's presidency, Marshall served as both secretary of state and chief justice.

On February 13, 1801, Congress enacted the Circuit Judge Act, which reduced the number of Supreme Court justices from six to five, decreasing the opportunity for Republican control of the Court. The Act also eliminated the Supreme Court Justices' duty to serve as circuit judges and created 16 new judgeships on the circuit courts. However, this change was short-lived; in 1802, Congress repealed this statute, restoring the practice of circuit riding by Supreme Court Justices and eliminating the newly created circuit court judgeships. The constitutionality of congressional abolition of judgeships was not tested in the courts.

---

1. For excellent, in-depth analysis of Marbury v. Madison, *see* James A. O'Fallon, *Marbury*, 44 Stan. L. Rev. 219 (1992); William W. Van Alstyne, *A Critical Guide to Marbury v. Madison*, 1969 Duke L.J. 1.

On February 27, 1801, less than a week before the end of Adams's term, Congress adopted the Organic Act of the District of Columbia, which authorized the president to appoint 42 justices of the peace. Adams announced his nominations on March 2, and on March 3, the day before Jefferson's inauguration, the Senate confirmed the nominees. Immediately, Secretary of State (and Chief Justice) John Marshall signed the commissions for these individuals and dispatched his brother, James Marshall, to deliver them. A few commissions, including one for William Marbury, were not delivered before Jefferson's inauguration. President Jefferson instructed his secretary of state, James Madison, to withhold the undelivered commissions.

William Marbury filed suit in the U.S. Supreme Court seeking a writ of mandamus to compel Madison, as secretary of state, to deliver the commission. A writ of mandamus is a petition to a court asking it to order a government officer to perform a duty. Marbury claimed that the Judiciary Act of 1789 authorized the Supreme Court to grant mandamus in a proceeding filed initially in the Supreme Court. Although Marbury's petition was filed in December 1801, the Supreme Court did not hear the case until 1803 because Congress, by statute, abolished the June and December 1802 Terms of the Supreme Court.

In reading Marbury v. Madison, it will be useful to focus on the following questions: (1) How does the Court justify judicial review of executive actions, and, according to the Court, when is such judicial review available and when is it unavailable? (2) Why does the Court find the Judiciary Act of 1789 unconstitutional? (3) How does the Court justify judicial review of legislative acts?

MARBURY v. MADISON
5 U.S. (1 Cranch) 137 (1803)

Mr. Chief Justice MARSHALL delivered the opinion of the court.
The following questions have been considered and decided.

1. Has the applicant a right to the commission he demands?
2. If he has a right, and that right has been violated, do the laws of his country afford him a remedy?
3. If they do afford him a remedy, is it a mandamus issuing from this court?

The first object of inquiry is,
1. Has the applicant a right to the commission he demands?
This is an appointment made by the president, by and with the advice and consent of the senate, and is evidenced by no act but the commission itself. In such a case therefore the commission and the appointment seem inseparable; it being almost impossible to show an appointment otherwise than by proving the existence of a commission: still the commission is not necessarily the appointment; though conclusive evidence of it.

In considering this question, it has been conjectured that the commission may have been assimilated to a deed, to the validity of which, delivery is essential.

It has also occurred as possible, and barely possible, that the transmission of the commission, and the acceptance thereof, might be deemed necessary to complete the right of the plaintiff. The transmission of the commission is a practice directed by convenience, but not by law.

It is therefore decidedly the opinion of the court, that when a commission has been signed by the president, the appointment is made; and that the commission is complete when the seal of the United States has been affixed to it by the secretary of state.

To withhold the commission, therefore, is an act deemed by the court not warranted by law, but violative of a vested legal right.

2. If he has a right, and that right has been violated, do the laws of his country afford him a remedy?

The very essence of civil liberty certainly consists in the right of every individual to claim the protection of the laws, whenever he receives an injury. One of the first duties of government is to afford that protection.

The government of the United States has been emphatically termed a government of laws, and not of men. It will certainly cease to deserve this high appellation, if the laws furnish no remedy for the violation of a vested legal right. It behooves us then to inquire whether there be in its composition any ingredient which shall exempt from legal investigation, or exclude the injured party from legal redress.

Is it in the nature of the transaction? Is the act of delivering or withholding a commission to be considered as a mere political act belonging to the executive department alone, for the performance of which entire confidence is placed by our constitution in the supreme executive; and for any misconduct respecting which, the injured individual has no remedy?

It follows then that the question, whether the legality of an act of the head of a department be examinable in a court of justice or not, must always depend on the nature of that act. If some acts be examinable, and others not, there must be some rule of law to guide the court in the exercise of its jurisdiction.

By the constitution of the United States, the president is invested with certain important political powers, in the exercise of which he is to use his own discretion, and is accountable only to his country in his political character, and to his own conscience. To aid him in the performance of these duties, he is authorized to appoint certain officers, who act by his authority and in conformity with his orders.

In such cases, their acts are his acts; and whatever opinion may be entertained of the manner in which executive discretion may be used, still there exists, and can exist, no power to control that discretion. The subjects are political. They respect the nation, not individual rights, and being entrusted to the executive, the decision of the executive is conclusive. The application of this remark will be perceived by adverting to the act of congress for establishing the department of foreign affairs. This officer, as his duties were prescribed by that act, is to conform precisely to the will of the president. He is the mere organ by whom that will is communicated. The acts of such an officer, as an officer, can never be examinable by the courts.

But when the legislature proceeds to impose on that officer other duties; when he is directed peremptorily to perform certain acts; when the rights of individuals are dependent on the performance of those acts; he is so far the officer of the law; is amenable to the laws for his conduct; and cannot at his discretion sport away the vested rights of others.

The conclusion from this reasoning is, that where the heads of departments are the political or confidential agents of the executive, merely to execute the will of the president, or rather to act in cases in which the executive possesses a constitutional or legal discretion, nothing can be more perfectly clear than that their acts are only politically examinable. But where a specific duty is assigned by law, and individual rights depend upon the performance of that duty, it seems equally clear that the individual who considers himself injured has a right to resort to the laws of his country for a remedy.

The question whether a right has vested or not, is, in its nature, judicial, and must be tried by the judicial authority. If, for example, Mr. Marbury had taken the oaths of a magistrate, and proceeded to act as one; in consequence of which a suit had been instituted against him, in which his defence had depended on his being a magistrate; the validity of his appointment must have been determined by judicial authority.

So, if he conceives that by virtue of his appointment he has a legal right either to the commission which has been made out for him or to a copy of that commission, it is equally a question examinable in a court, and the decision of the court upon it must depend on the opinion entertained of his appointment.

It remains to be inquired whether,

3. He is entitled to the remedy for which he applies. This depends on,

1. The nature of the writ applied for. And,
2. The power of this court.

1.   THE NATURE OF THE WRIT

This writ, if awarded, would be directed to an officer of government, and its mandate to him would be, to use the words of Blackstone, "to do a particular thing therein specified, which appertains to his office and duty, and which the court has previously determined or at least supposes to be consonant to right and justice." These circumstances certainly concur in this case.

Still, to render the mandamus a proper remedy, the officer to whom it is to be directed, must be one to whom, on legal principles, such writ may be directed; and the person applying for it must be without any other specific and legal remedy.

The province of the court is, solely, to decide on the rights of individuals, not to inquire how the executive, or executive officers, perform duties in which they have a discretion. Questions, in their nature political, or which are, by the constitution and laws, submitted to the executive, can never be made in this court.

If one of the heads of departments commits any illegal act, under colour of his office, by which an individual sustains an injury, it cannot be pretended that his office alone exempts him from being sued in the ordinary mode of proceeding, and being compelled to obey the judgment of the law. How then can his office exempt him from this particular mode of deciding on the legality of his conduct, if the case be such a case as would, were any other individual the party complained of, authorize the process?

It is not by the office of the person to whom the writ is directed, but the nature of the thing to be done, that the propriety or impropriety of issuing a mandamus is to be determined. Where he is directed by law to do a certain act affecting the absolute rights of individuals, in the performance of which he is not placed under the particular direction of the president, [mandamus is appropriate].

This, then, is a plain case of a mandamus, either to deliver the commission, or a copy of it from the record; and it only remains to be inquired.

Whether it can issue from this court.

The act to establish the judicial courts of the United States authorizes the supreme court "to issue writs of mandamus, in cases warranted by the principles and usages of law, to any courts appointed, or persons holding office, under the authority of the United States."

The secretary of state, being a person, holding an office under the authority of the United States, is precisely within the letter of the description; and if this court is not authorized to issue a writ of mandamus to such an officer, it must be because the law is unconstitutional, and therefore absolutely incapable of conferring the authority, and assigning the duties which its words purport to confer and assign.

In the distribution of this power it is declared that "the supreme court shall have original jurisdiction in all cases affecting ambassadors, other public ministers and consuls, and those in which a state shall be a party. In all other cases, the supreme court shall have appellate jurisdiction."

It has been insisted at the bar, that as the original grant of jurisdiction to the supreme and inferior courts is general, and the clause, assigning original jurisdiction to the supreme court, contains no negative or restrictive words; the power remains to the legislature to assign original jurisdiction to that court in other cases than those specified in the article which has been recited; provided those cases belong to the judicial power of the United States.

If it had been intended to leave it in the discretion of the legislature to apportion the judicial power between the supreme and inferior courts according to the will of that body, it would certainly have been useless to have proceeded further than to have defined the judicial power, and the tribunals in which it should be vested. The subsequent part of the section is mere surplusage, is entirely without meaning, if such is to be the construction. If congress remains at liberty to give this court appellate jurisdiction, where the constitution has declared their jurisdiction shall be original; and original jurisdiction where the constitution has declared it shall be appellate; the distribution of jurisdiction made in the constitution, is form without substance.

It cannot be presumed that any clause in the constitution is intended to be without effect; and therefore such construction is inadmissible, unless the words require it.

When an instrument organizing fundamentally a judicial system, divides it into one supreme, and so many inferior courts as the legislature may ordain and establish; then enumerates its powers, and proceeds so far to distribute them, as to define the jurisdiction of the supreme court by declaring the cases in which it shall take original jurisdiction, and that in others it shall take appellate jurisdiction, the plain import of the words seems to be, that in one class of cases its jurisdiction is original, and not appellate; in the other it is appellate, and not original. If any other construction would render the clause inoperative, that is an additional reason for rejecting such other construction, and for adhering to the obvious meaning.

It is the essential criterion of appellate jurisdiction, that it revises and corrects the proceedings in a cause already instituted, and does not create that case. Although, therefore, a mandamus may be directed to courts, yet to issue such a writ to an officer for the delivery of a paper, is in effect the same as to sustain an original action for that paper, and therefore seems not to belong to appellate, but to original jurisdiction. Neither is it necessary in such a case as this, to enable the court to exercise its appellate jurisdiction.

The authority, therefore, given to the supreme court, by the act establishing the judicial courts of the United States, to issue writs of mandamus to public officers, appears not to be warranted by the constitution; and it becomes necessary to inquire whether a jurisdiction, so conferred, can be exercised.

The question, whether an act, repugnant to the constitution, can become the law of the land, is a question deeply interesting to the United States; but, happily, not of an intricacy proportioned to its interest. It seems only necessary to recognise certain principles, supposed to have been long and well established, to decide it.

This original and supreme will organizes the government, and assigns to different departments their respective powers. It may either stop here; or establish certain limits not to be transcended by those departments.

The government of the United States is of the latter description. The powers of the legislature are defined and limited; and that those limits may not be mistaken or forgotten, the constitution is written. To what purpose are powers limited, and to what purpose is that limitation committed to writing; if these limits may, at any time, be passed by those intended to be restrained? The distinction between a government with limited and unlimited powers is abolished, if those limits do not confine the persons on whom they are imposed, and if acts prohibited and acts allowed are of equal obligation. It is a proposition too plain to be contested, that the constitution controls any legislative act repugnant to it; or, that the legislature may alter the constitution by an ordinary act.

Between these alternatives there is no middle ground. The constitution is either a superior, paramount law, unchangeable by ordinary means, or it is on a level with ordinary legislative acts, and like other acts, is alterable when the legislature shall please to alter it.

If the former part of the alternative be true, then a legislative act contrary to the constitution is not law: if the latter part be true, then written constitutions are absurd attempts, on the part of the people, to limit a power in its own nature illimitable.

Certainly all those who have framed written constitutions contemplate them as forming the fundamental and paramount law of the nation, and consequently the theory of every such government must be, that an act of the legislature repugnant to the constitution is void.

This theory is essentially attached to a written constitution, and is consequently to be considered by this court as one of the fundamental principles of our society. It is not therefore to be lost sight of in the further consideration of this subject.

If an act of the legislature, repugnant to the constitution, is void, does it, notwithstanding its invalidity, bind the courts and oblige them to give it effect? Or, in other words, though it be not law, does it constitute a rule as operative as if it was a law? This would be to overthrow in fact what was established in theory; and would seem, at first view, an absurdity too gross to be insisted on. It shall, however, receive a more attentive consideration.

It is emphatically the province and duty of the judicial department to say what the law is. Those who apply the rule to particular cases, must of necessity expound and interpret that rule. If two laws conflict with each other, the courts must decide on the operation of each.

So if a law be in opposition to the constitution: if both the law and the constitution apply to a particular case, so that the court must either decide that case conformably to the law, disregarding the constitution; or conformably to the constitution, disregarding the law: the court must determine which of these conflicting rules governs the case. This is of the very essence of judicial duty.

If then the courts are to regard the constitution; and the constitution is superior to any ordinary act of the legislature; the constitution, and not such ordinary act, must govern the case to which they both apply.

Those then who controvert the principle that the constitution is to be considered, in court, as a paramount law, are reduced to the necessity of maintaining that courts must close their eyes on the constitution, and see only the law.

This doctrine would subvert the very foundation of all written constitutions. It would declare that an act, which, according to the principles and theory of our government, is entirely void, is yet, in practice, completely obligatory. It would declare, that if the legislature shall do what is expressly forbidden, such act, notwithstanding the express prohibition, is in reality effectual. It would be giving to the legislature a practical and real omnipotence with the same breath which professes to restrict their powers within narrow limits. It is prescribing limits, and declaring that those limits may be passed at pleasure.

That it thus reduces to nothing what we have deemed the greatest improvement on political institutions — a written constitution, would of itself be sufficient, in America where written constitutions have been viewed with so much reverence, for rejecting the construction. But the peculiar expressions of the constitution of the United States furnish additional arguments in favour of its rejection.

The judicial power of the United States is extended to all cases arising under the constitution.

Could it be the intention of those who gave this power, to say that, in using it, the constitution should not be looked into? That a case arising under the constitution should be decided without examining the instrument under which it arises? This is too extravagant to be maintained.

In some cases then, the constitution must be looked into by the judges. And if they can open it at all, what part of it are they forbidden to read, or to obey?

There are many other parts of the constitution which serve to illustrate this subject.

The constitution declares that "no bill of attainder or ex post facto law shall be passed." If, however, such a bill should be passed and a person should be prosecuted under it, must the court condemn to death those victims whom the constitution endeavours to preserve?

"No person," says the constitution, "shall be convicted of treason unless on the testimony of two witnesses to the same overt act, or on confession in open court." Here the language of the constitution is addressed especially to the courts. It prescribes, directly for them, a rule of evidence not to be departed from. If the legislature should change that rule, and declare one witness, or a confession out of court, sufficient for conviction, must the constitutional principle yield to the legislative act?

From these and many other selections which might be made, it is apparent, that the framers of the constitution contemplated that instrument as a rule for the government of courts, as well as of the legislature.

Why otherwise does it direct the judges to take an oath to support it? This oath certainly applies, in an especial manner, to their conduct in their official character. How immoral to impose it on them, if they were to be used as the instruments, and the knowing instruments, for violating what they swear to support!

Why does a judge swear to discharge his duties agreeably to the constitution of the United States, if that constitution forms no rule for his government, if it is closed upon him and cannot be inspected by him?

It is also not entirely unworthy of observation, that in declaring what shall be the supreme law of the land, the constitution itself is first mentioned; and not the laws of the United States generally, but those only which shall be made in pursuance of the constitution, have that rank.

Thus, the particular phraseology of the constitution of the United States confirms and strengthens the principle, supposed to be essential to all written constitutions, that a law repugnant to the constitution is void, and that courts, as well as other departments, are bound by that instrument.

NOTES ON MARBURY v. MADISON

Marbury v. Madison establishes a number of key propositions that continue to this day. First, it creates the authority for judicial review of executive actions. The Court draws a distinction between areas in which there are individual rights, and therefore government duties, and those in which the executive has discretion as to how to act. In the latter, the Court says that only the political process is the check on the executive branch.

Second, *Marbury* establishes that Article III is the ceiling of federal court jurisdiction. The precise holding is that Congress cannot expand the original jurisdiction of the Supreme Court. More generally, *Marbury* stands for the proposition that Article III authorizes the maximum jurisdiction of the federal courts. As a result, Congress cannot authorize federal courts to hear cases beyond what is specified in Article III, and federal courts cannot gain jurisdiction by consent.

Third, *Marbury* establishes the authority for judicial review of legislative acts. This, of course, is what Marbury v. Madison is most renowned for establishing. *Marbury* does this by declaring unconstitutional a provision of a federal law, the Judiciary Act of 1789, which the Court interprets as authorizing the Supreme Court to exercise mandamus on original jurisdiction. Yet a careful reading of that provision makes it questionable whether the provision authorizes this. The relevant portion of section 13 of the Judiciary Act stated:

> The Supreme Court shall also have appellate jurisdiction from the circuit courts and courts of the several states, in the cases hereinafter specially provided for; . . . and shall have power to issue writs of prohibition . . . to the district courts, when proceeding as courts of admiralty and maritime jurisdiction, and writs of mandamus, in cases warranted by the principles and usages of law, to any court appointed, or persons holding office, under the authority of the United States.

The statute seems to be about appellate jurisdiction and not original jurisdiction. If the Court had interpreted the law this way, *Marbury* would have lost on jurisdictional grounds and the Court never would have had occasion to reach the issue of whether the Supreme Court can review the constitutionality of federal laws.

That, of course, is part of the brilliance of Marbury v. Madison: Chief Justice John Marshall established judicial review while declaring unconstitutional a statute that he read as expanding the Court's powers. Politically, Marshall had no choice but to deny Marbury relief; the Jefferson administration surely would have refused to comply with a court order to deliver the commission. In addition, there was a real possibility that Jefferson might seek the impeachment of the Federalist justices in an attempt to gain Republican control of the judiciary. One judge, albeit a clearly incompetent jurist, already had been impeached, and not long after his removal, the House of Representatives impeached Justice Samuel Chase on the grounds that he had made electioneering statements from the bench and had criticized the repeal of the 1801 Circuit Court Act. Yet John Marshall did more than simply rule in favor of the Jefferson administration; he used the occasion of deciding Marbury v. Madison to establish the power of the judiciary and to articulate a role for the federal courts that survives to this day.

The Supreme Court did not declare another federal statute unconstitutional until 1857 in the infamous case of Dred Scott v. Sandford, 60 U.S. (19 How.) 393 (1857), which invalidated the Missouri Compromise and helped to precipitate the Civil War.[2] By then, the power of the Court to consider the constitutionality of federal laws was an accepted part of American government.

Marbury v. Madison has been invoked by the Supreme Court in some of the most important cases in American history. For example, in Cooper v. Aaron, 358 U.S. 1 (1958), the Supreme Court responded to Arkansas's refusal to obey a federal court order desegregating the Little Rock public schools by relying on the authority of Marbury v. Madison. In an unusual opinion, signed individually by each justice, the Court rejected Arkansas's position and emphatically declared: "Article VI of the Constitution makes the Constitution 'the supreme Law of the Land.' . . . Marbury v. Madison . . . declared the basic principle that the federal judiciary is supreme in the exposition of the law of the Constitution, and that principle has ever since been respected by this Court and the Country as a permanent and indispensable feature of our constitutional system. . . . Every state legislator and executive and judicial officer is solemnly committed by oath . . . 'to support this Constitution.'"

Similarly, in United States v. Nixon, 418 U.S. 683 (1974), the Supreme Court ordered President Richard Nixon to produce tapes of White House conversations in connection with the Watergate investigation. In response to the president's claims that he alone should determine the scope of executive privilege, Chief Justice Warren Burger, writing for the Court, stated: "The President's counsel . . . reads the Constitution as providing an absolute privilege of confidentiality for all Presidential communications. Many decisions of this Court, however, have unequivocally reaffirmed the holding of Marbury v. Madison that '[i]t is emphatically the province and duty of the judicial department to say what the law is.'"

Marbury v. Madison thus provides the foundation for American constitutional law by establishing the authority for judicial review of executive and legislative acts.

---

2. *Dred Scott* is discussed in Chapter 7, which focuses on equal protection.

AUTHORITY FOR JUDICIAL REVIEW OF STATE JUDGMENTS

Marbury v. Madison establishes only the authority for judicial review of federal executive and legislative actions. The authority for judicial review of state court decisions was established in two decisions early in the nineteenth century: Martin v. Hunter's Lessee and Cohens v. Virginia.

MARTIN v. HUNTER'S LESSEE, 14 U.S. (1 Wheat.) 304 (1816): There were two competing claims to certain land within the state of Virginia. Martin claimed title to the land based on inheritance from Lord Fairfax, a British citizen who owned the property. The United States and England had entered into two treaties protecting the rights of British citizens to own land in the United States. However, Hunter claimed that Virginia had taken the land before the treaties came into effect and, hence, Martin did not have a valid claim to the property.

The Virginia Court of Appeals ruled in favor of Hunter and, in essence, in favor of the state's authority to have taken and disposed of the land. The U.S. Supreme Court issued a writ of error and reversed the Virginia decision. The Supreme Court held that the federal treaty was controlling and that it established Lord Fairfax's ownership and thus the validity of inheritance pursuant to his will. The Virginia Court of Appeals, however, declared that the Supreme Court lacked the authority to review state court decisions. The Virginia court stated that the "Courts of the United States, therefore, belonging to one sovereignty, cannot be appellate Courts in relation to the State Courts, which belong to a different sovereignty—and, of course, their commands or instructions impose no obligation."

The U.S. Supreme Court again granted review and declared the authority to review state court judgments. Justice Joseph Story wrote the opinion for the Court. Chief Justice John Marshall did not participate because he and his brother had contracted to purchase a large part of the Fairfax estate that was at issue in the litigation.

Justice Story argued that the structure of the Constitution presumes that the Supreme Court may review state court decisions. Story argued that the Constitution creates a Supreme Court and gives Congress discretion whether to create lower federal courts. But if Congress chose not to establish such tribunals, then the Supreme Court would be powerless to hear any cases, except for the few fitting within its original jurisdiction, unless it could review state court rulings.

Additionally, Justice Story explained the importance of Supreme Court review of state courts. Justice Story said that although he assumed that "judges of the state courts are, and always will be, of as much learning, integrity, and wisdom as those of courts of the United States," the Constitution is based on a recognition that "state attachments, state prejudices, state jealousies, and state interests might sometimes obstruct, or control, or be supposed to obstruct or control, the regular administration of justice." Furthermore, Justice Story observed that Supreme Court review is essential to ensure uniformity in the interpretation of federal law. Justice Story concluded that the very nature of the Constitution, the contemporaneous understanding of it, and many years of experience all established the Supreme Court's authority to review state court decisions.

COHENS v. VIRGINIA, 19 U.S. (6 Wheat.) 264 (1821): Two brothers were convicted in Virginia state court of selling District of Columbia lottery tickets in violation of Virginia law. The defendants sought review in the United States Supreme Court because they claimed the Constitution prevented their prosecution for selling tickets authorized by Congress. Virginia argued: (1) in general, the Supreme Court had no authority to review state court decisions; and (2) in particular, review was not allowed in criminal cases and in cases where a state government was a party.

The Supreme Court, in an opinion by Chief Justice John Marshall, reaffirmed the constitutionality of §25 of the Judiciary Act and the authority of the Supreme Court to review state court judgments. The Court emphasized that state courts often could not be trusted to adequately protect federal rights because "[i]n many States the judges are dependent for office and for salary on the will of the legislature." The Court thus declared that criminal defendants could seek Supreme Court review when they claimed that their conviction violated the Constitution.

B. LIMITS ON THE FEDERAL JUDICIAL POWER

The judicial power to say what the law is gives to unelected federal judges great authority. There thus has been an ongoing, unresolved debate over how this power is constrained and whether the limits on judicial authority are sufficient. Three primary limits exist: interpretive limits, congressional limits, and justiciability limits. Interpretive limits raise the question of how the Constitution should be interpreted; some approaches seek to greatly narrow the judicial power, while others accord judges broad latitude in deciding the meaning of the Constitution. Congressional limits refer to the ability of Congress to restrict federal court jurisdiction. Justiciability limits refer to a series of judicially created doctrines that limit the types of matters that federal courts can decide.

1. *Interpretive Limits*

Much of the Constitution is written in broad, open-textured language. How should the Court, or anyone seeking to interpret the Constitution, give meaning to these words? What weight should be given to the text, to the framers' intent, to the practices at the time the constitutional provision was adopted, to tradition, to social policy needs? There is no agreement among Justices or scholars as to the appropriate method of constitutional interpretation. Yet the resolution of every issue of constitutional law turns on this question.

The issue of how courts should interpret the Constitution is particularly controversial and, of course, at the core of the issues discussed throughout this book. On the one hand, some believe that it is essential that the Court's discretion in interpreting the Constitution be narrowly circumscribed to limit the judicial power. They argue that democracy means rule by electorally accountable officials and that judicial review by unelected federal judges is inconsistent with this. The late Yale law professor Alexander Bickel said that judicial review is a "deviant institution in American democracy" because it permits unelected judges to overturn the decisions of popularly accountable officials.[3] Robert Bork similarly remarked that a "Court that makes rather than implements value choices cannot be squared with the presuppositions of a democratic society."[4]

Those adopting this approach seek to constrain courts interpreting the Constitution. Some argue, for example, that the Court is justified in protecting constitutional rights only if they are clearly stated in the text or intended by the framers. Those who adopt this theory, often called originalism, defend it as a desirable way to limit unelected judges in a democratic society.[5] Originalism is the view that "judges deciding constitutional issues should confine themselves to enforcing norms that are stated or clearly implicit in the written Constitution."[6]

Others disagree with these theories and argue that it is desirable for the Court to have substantial discretion in determining the meaning of the Constitution. Often called "nonoriginalists," they argue that it is important that the Constitution evolve by interpretation and not only by amendment. Nonoriginalism is the "view that courts should go beyond that set of references and enforce norms that cannot be discovered within the four corners of the document."[7] The claim is that nonoriginalist review is essential so that the Constitution does not remain virtually static, so that it can evolve to meet the needs of a society that is advancing technologically and morally.

Nonoriginalists argue, for example, that equal protection in the second half of the twentieth century must mean that government-mandated racial segregation is unacceptable; yet there is strong evidence that the framers of the Fourteenth Amendment approved this practice. The drafters of the Equal Protection Clause did not intend to protect women from discrimination, but it is widely accepted that the clause should apply to gender discrimination. Indeed, the argument is made that under originalism it would be unconstitutional to elect a woman as president or vice president because the Constitution refers to these office holders with the word "he," and the framers clearly intended that they be male.

Originalists believe that the Court should find a right to exist in the Constitution only if it is expressly stated in the text or was clearly intended by its framers. If the Constitution is silent, originalists say it is for the legislature, unconstrained by the courts, to decide the law. Nonoriginalists think that it is permissible for the Court to interpret the Constitution to protect rights that are not expressly stated or clearly intended. Originalists believe that the Constitution should evolve solely by amendment; nonoriginalists believe that the Constitution's meaning can evolve by amendment and by interpretation.

But within these theories there is a wide range of different approaches. Some originalists argue that the framers' specific intent must be followed, while others maintain that only the framers' abstract intent is controlling. Justice Scalia has argued that the focus should not be on the framers' intentions, but on the meaning of the Constitution as evidenced by the text and the practices at the time the Constitution was ratified. Similarly, among nonoriginalists there are

---

3. Alexander Bickel, *The Least Dangerous Branch* 18 (1962).
4. Robert Bork, *Neutral Principles and Some First Amendment Problems*, 47 Ind. L.J. 1, 6 (1971).
5. *See, e.g.*, Raoul Berger, *Ely's Theory of Judicial Review*, 42 Ohio St. L.J. 87, 87 (1981).
6. John Hart Ely, *Democracy and Distrust* 1 (1980).
7. *Id.*

those who emphasize tradition, those who stress natural law principles, those who say constitutional law should be about improving the processes of government, those who emphasize contemporary values, and other variants too. Often, the Supreme Court has looked to tradition in deciding whether a right is protected by the Constitution.[8]

The debate over how the Constitution should be interpreted—and the extent to which the method of interpretation should limit the judiciary—arises in all areas of constitutional law.

HOW SHOULD THE CONSTITUTION BE INTERPRETED? THE SECOND AMENDMENT AS AN EXAMPLE

In thinking about the debate over the appropriate method of interpretation, consider, as an example, the meaning of the Second Amendment, which states: "A well regulated Militia, being necessary to the security of a free State, the right of the people to keep and bear Arms, shall not be infringed." There is a heated debate among scholars, as well as in society, about the proper interpretation of the Second Amendment. On the one hand, some believe that the Second Amendment safeguards a right of individuals to keep and own firearms. From this perspective, laws that infringe this right are at least presumptively unconstitutional. On the other hand, some believe that the Second Amendment means only that there is a right to have guns for militia service.

The underlying issue, of course, is how should the Supreme Court—or a lower court or a member of Congress or you—decide the proper meaning of the Second Amendment. In June 2008, for the first time in U.S. history, the Supreme Court invalidated a law as violating the Second Amendment and held that the Second Amendment protects a right to have guns apart from militia service.

In reading District of Columbia v. Heller, focus on the interpretive methodology used by the majority and the dissents. What sources do they look to? What should they consider?

DISTRICT OF COLUMBIA v. HELLER

554 U.S. 570 (2008)

Justice SCALIA delivered the opinion of the Court.

We consider whether a District of Columbia prohibition on the possession of usable handguns in the home violates the Second Amendment to the Constitution.

---

8. *Compare* Bowers v. Hardwick, 478 U.S. 186 (1986) (refusing to find constitutional protection for a right to engage in private consensual homosexual activity, in part, because of the lack of a tradition of providing such protection), *with* Moore v. City of East Cleveland, Ohio, 431 U.S. 494 (1977) (finding constitutional protection for the right of an extended family to live together because of the tradition of protecting such families). Both cases are presented in Chapter 8.

I

The District of Columbia generally prohibits the possession of handguns. It is a crime to carry an unregistered firearm, and the registration of handguns is prohibited. See D.C.Code §§7-2501.01(12), 7-2502.01(a), 7-2502.02(a)(4) (2001). Wholly apart from that prohibition, no person may carry a handgun without a license, but the chief of police may issue licenses for 1-year periods. See §§22-4504(a), 22-4506. District of Columbia law also requires residents to keep their lawfully owned firearms, such as registered long guns, "unloaded and dissembled or bound by a trigger lock or similar device" unless they are located in a place of business or are being used for lawful recreational activities. See §7-2507.02.[9]

Respondent Dick Heller is a D.C. special police officer authorized to carry a handgun while on duty at the Federal Judicial Center. He applied for a registration certificate for a handgun that he wished to keep at home, but the District refused. He thereafter filed a lawsuit in the Federal District Court for the District of Columbia seeking, on Second Amendment grounds, to enjoin the city from enforcing the bar on the registration of handguns, the licensing requirement insofar as it prohibits the carrying of a firearm in the home without a license, and the trigger-lock requirement insofar as it prohibits the use of "functional firearms within the home."

II

We turn first to the meaning of the Second Amendment.

A

The Second Amendment provides: "A well regulated Militia, being necessary to the security of a free State, the right of the people to keep and bear Arms, shall not be infringed." In interpreting this text, we are guided by the principle that "[t]he Constitution was written to be understood by the voters; its words and phrases were used in their normal and ordinary as distinguished from technical meaning."

The two sides in this case have set out very different interpretations of the Amendment. Petitioners and today's dissenting Justices believe that it protects only the right to possess and carry a firearm in connection with militia service. Respondent argues that it protects an individual right to possess a firearm unconnected with service in a militia, and to use that arm for traditionally lawful purposes, such as self-defense within the home.

The Second Amendment is naturally divided into two parts: its prefatory clause and its operative clause. The former does not limit the latter grammatically, but rather announces a purpose. The Amendment could be rephrased, "Because a well regulated Militia is necessary to the security of a free State, the right of the people to keep and bear Arms shall not be infringed." Although this structure of the Second Amendment is unique in our Constitution, other legal

---

9. There are minor exceptions to all of these prohibitions, none of which is relevant here. [Footnote by the Court.]

documents of the founding era, particularly individual-rights provisions of state constitutions, commonly included a prefatory statement of purpose.

Logic demands that there be a link between the stated purpose and the command. The Second Amendment would be nonsensical if it read, "A well regulated Militia, being necessary to the security of a free State, the right of the people to petition for redress of grievances shall not be infringed." But apart from that clarifying function, a prefatory clause does not limit or expand the scope of the operative clause.

1.   Operative Clause

a. "Right of the People." The first salient feature of the operative clause is that it codifies a "right of the people." The unamended Constitution and the Bill of Rights use the phrase "right of the people" two other times, in the First Amendment's Assembly-and-Petition Clause and in the Fourth Amendment's Search-and-Seizure Clause. The Ninth Amendment uses very similar terminology. All three of these instances unambiguously refer to individual rights, not "collective" rights, or rights that may be exercised only through participation in some corporate body.

What is more, in all six other provisions of the Constitution that mention "the people," the term unambiguously refers to all members of the political community, not an unspecified subset. This contrasts markedly with the phrase "the militia" in the prefatory clause. As we will describe below, the "militia" in colonial America consisted of a subset of "the people" — those who were male, able bodied, and within a certain age range. Reading the Second Amendment as protecting only the right to "keep and bear Arms" in an organized militia therefore fits poorly with the operative clause's description of the holder of that right as "the people."

We start therefore with a strong presumption that the Second Amendment right is exercised individually and belongs to all Americans.

b. "Keep and bear Arms." We move now from the holder of the right — "the people" — to the substance of the right: "to keep and bear Arms."

Before addressing the verbs "keep" and "bear," we interpret their object: "Arms." The 18th-century meaning is no different from the meaning today. The 1773 edition of Samuel Johnson's dictionary defined "arms" as "weapons of offence, or armour of defence." 1 Dictionary of the English Language 107 (4th ed.) (hereinafter Johnson). Timothy Cunningham's important 1771 legal dictionary defined "arms" as "any thing that a man wears for his defence, or takes into his hands, or useth in wrath to cast at or strike another." 1 A New and Complete Law Dictionary (1771). The term was applied, then as now, to weapons that were not specifically designed for military use and were not employed in a military capacity.

Some have made the argument, bordering on the frivolous, that only those arms in existence in the 18th century are protected by the Second Amendment. We do not interpret constitutional rights that way. Just as the First Amendment protects modern forms of communications, and the Fourth Amendment applies to modern forms of search, the Second Amendment extends, prima facie, to all instruments that constitute bearable arms, even those that were not in existence at the time of the founding.

We turn to the phrases "keep arms" and "bear arms." Johnson defined "keep" as, most relevantly, "[t]o retain; not to lose," and "[t]o have in custody."

Webster defined it as "[t]o hold; to retain in one's power or possession." No party has apprised us of an idiomatic meaning of "keep Arms." Thus, the most natural reading of "keep Arms" in the Second Amendment is to "have weapons."

The phrase "keep arms" was not prevalent in the written documents of the founding period that we have found, but there are a few examples, all of which favor viewing the right to "keep Arms" as an individual right unconnected with militia service.

From our review of founding-era sources, we conclude that this natural meaning was also the meaning that "bear arms" had in the 18th century. In numerous instances, "bear arms" was unambiguously used to refer to the carrying of weapons outside of an organized militia. The most prominent examples are those most relevant to the Second Amendment: Nine state constitutional provisions written in the 18th century or the first two decades of the 19th, which enshrined a right of citizens to "bear arms in defense of themselves and the state" or "bear arms in defense of himself and the state." It is clear from those formulations that "bear arms" did not refer only to carrying a weapon in an organized military unit.

Justice Stevens places great weight on James Madison's inclusion of a conscientious-objector clause in his original draft of the Second Amendment: "but no person religiously scrupulous of bearing arms, shall be compelled to render military service in person." He argues that this clause establishes that the drafters of the Second Amendment intended "bear Arms" to refer only to military service. It is always perilous to derive the meaning of an adopted provision from another provision deleted in the drafting process. In any case, what Justice Stevens would conclude from the deleted provision does not follow. It was not meant to exempt from military service those who objected to going to war but had no scruples about personal gunfights. Quakers opposed the use of arms not just for militia service, but for any violent purpose whatsoever — so much so that Quaker frontiersmen were forbidden to use arms to defend their families, even though "[i]n such circumstances the temptation to seize a hunting rifle or knife in self-defense . . . must sometimes have been almost overwhelming." Thus, the most natural interpretation of Madison's deleted text is that those opposed to carrying weapons for potential violent confrontation would not be "compelled to render military service," in which such carrying would be required.

Finally, Justice Stevens suggests that "keep and bear Arms" was some sort of term of art, presumably akin to "hue and cry" or "cease and desist." This suggestion usefully evades the problem that there is no evidence whatsoever to support a military reading of "keep arms." And even if "keep and bear Arms" were a unitary phrase, we find no evidence that it bore a military meaning. Although the phrase was not at all common (which would be unusual for a term of art), we have found instances of its use with a clearly nonmilitary connotation.

c. Meaning of the Operative Clause. Putting all of these textual elements together, we find that they guarantee the individual right to possess and carry weapons in case of confrontation. This meaning is strongly confirmed by the historical background of the Second Amendment. We look to this because it has always been widely understood that the Second Amendment, like the First and Fourth Amendments, codified a pre-existing right. The very text of the Second Amendment implicitly recognizes the pre-existence of the right and declares only that it "shall not be infringed."

There seems to us no doubt, on the basis of both text and history, that the Second Amendment conferred an individual right to keep and bear arms. Of course the right was not unlimited, just as the First Amendment's right of free speech was not. Thus, we do not read the Second Amendment to protect the right of citizens to carry arms for any sort of confrontation, just as we do not read the First Amendment to protect the right of citizens to speak for any purpose. Before turning to limitations upon the individual right, however, we must determine whether the prefatory clause of the Second Amendment comports with our interpretation of the operative clause.

2. *Prefatory Clause*

The prefatory clause reads: "A well regulated Militia, being necessary to the security of a free State. . . ."

a. "Well-Regulated Militia." In United States v. Miller (1939), we explained that "the Militia comprised all males physically capable of acting in concert for the common defense." That definition comports with founding-era sources.

Petitioners take a seemingly narrower view of the militia, stating that "[m]ilitias are the state- and congressionally-regulated military forces described in the Militia Clauses (art. I, §8, cls. 15-16)." Although we agree with petitioners' interpretive assumption that "militia" means the same thing in Article I and the Second Amendment, we believe that petitioners identify the wrong thing, namely, the organized militia. Unlike armies and navies, which Congress is given the power to create ("to raise . . . Armies"; "to provide . . . a Navy," Art. I, §8, cls. 12-13), the militia is assumed by Article I already to be in existence. Congress is given the power to "provide for calling forth the militia," §8, cl. 15; and the power not to create, but to "organiz[e]" it — and not to organize "a" militia, which is what one would expect if the militia were to be a federal creation, but to organize "the" militia, connoting a body already in existence, ibid., cl. 16. This is fully consistent with the ordinary definition of the militia as all able-bodied men.

Finally, the adjective "well-regulated" implies nothing more than the imposition of proper discipline and training.

b. "Security of a Free State." The phrase "security of a free state" meant "security of a free polity," not security of each of the several States as the dissent below argued. There are many reasons why the militia was thought to be "necessary to the security of a free state." First, of course, it is useful in repelling invasions and suppressing insurrections. Second, it renders large standing armies unnecessary — an argument that Alexander Hamilton made in favor of federal control over the militia. Third, when the able-bodied men of a nation are trained in arms and organized, they are better able to resist tyranny.

3. *Relationship between Prefatory Clause and Operative Clause*

We reach the question, then: Does the preface fit with an operative clause that creates an individual right to keep and bear arms? It fits perfectly, once one knows the history that the founding generation knew and that we have described above. That history showed that the way tyrants had eliminated a militia consisting of all the able-bodied men was not by banning the militia but simply by taking away the people's arms, enabling a select militia or standing army to suppress political opponents. This is what had occurred in England that prompted codification of the right to have arms in the English Bill of Rights.

It is therefore entirely sensible that the Second Amendment's prefatory clause announces the purpose for which the right was codified: to prevent elimination of the militia. The prefatory clause does not suggest that preserving the militia was the only reason Americans valued the ancient right; most undoubtedly thought it even more important for self-defense and hunting. But the threat that the new Federal Government would destroy the citizens' militia by taking away their arms was the reason that right — unlike some other English rights — was codified in a written Constitution. Justice Breyer's assertion that individual self-defense is merely a "subsidiary interest" of the right to keep and bear arms is profoundly mistaken. He bases that assertion solely upon the prologue — but that can only show that self-defense had little to do with the right's codification; it was the central component of the right itself.

B

Our interpretation is confirmed by analogous arms-bearing rights in state constitutions that preceded and immediately followed adoption of the Second Amendment. Four States adopted analogues to the Federal Second Amendment in the period between independence and the ratification of the Bill of Rights. Two of them — Pennsylvania and Vermont — clearly adopted individual rights unconnected to militia service.

North Carolina also codified a right to bear arms in 1776. Many colonial statutes required individual arms-bearing for public-safety reasons — such as the 1770 Georgia law that "for the security and defence of this province from internal dangers and insurrections" required those men who qualified for militia duty individually "to carry fire arms" "to places of public worship."

The 1780 Massachusetts Constitution presented another variation on the theme: "The people have a right to keep and to bear arms for the common defence...." Once again, if one gives narrow meaning to the phrase "common defence" this can be thought to limit the right to the bearing of arms in a state-organized military force. But once again the State's highest court thought otherwise. Writing for the court in an 1825 libel case, Chief Justice Parker wrote: "The liberty of the press was to be unrestrained, but he who used it was to be responsible in cases of its abuse; like the right to keep fire arms, which does not protect him who uses them for annoyance or destruction."

We therefore believe that the most likely reading of all four of these pre-Second Amendment state constitutional provisions is that they secured an individual right to bear arms for defensive purposes.

Between 1789 and 1820, nine States adopted Second Amendment analogues. The historical narrative that petitioners must endorse would thus treat the Federal Second Amendment as an odd outlier, protecting a right unknown in state constitutions or at English common law, based on little more than an overreading of the prefatory clause.

C

Justice Stevens relies on the drafting history of the Second Amendment — the various proposals in the state conventions and the debates in Congress. It is dubious to rely on such history to interpret a text that was widely understood to codify a preexisting right, rather than to fashion a new one. But even assuming that this legislative history is relevant, Justice Stevens flatly misreads the historical record.

It is true, as Justice Stevens says, that there was concern that the Federal Government would abolish the institution of the state militia. That concern found expression, however, not in the various Second Amendment precursors proposed in the State conventions, but in separate structural provisions that would have given the States concurrent and seemingly nonpreemptible authority to organize, discipline, and arm the militia when the Federal Government failed to do so.

D

We now address how the Second Amendment was interpreted from immediately after its ratification through the end of the 19th century. Three important founding-era legal scholars interpreted the Second Amendment in published writings. All three understood it to protect an individual right unconnected with militia service. We have found only one early 19th-century commentator who clearly conditioned the right to keep and bear arms upon service in the militia — and he recognized that the prevailing view was to the contrary.

The 19th-century cases that interpreted the Second Amendment universally support an individual right unconnected to militia service. Many early 19th-century state cases indicated that the Second Amendment right to bear arms was an individual right unconnected to militia service, though subject to certain restrictions.

In the aftermath of the Civil War, there was an outpouring of discussion of the Second Amendment in Congress and in public discourse, as people debated whether and how to secure constitutional rights for newly free slaves. Since those discussions took place 75 years after the ratification of the Second Amendment, they do not provide as much insight into its original meaning as earlier sources. Yet those born and educated in the early 19th century faced a widespread effort to limit arms ownership by a large number of citizens; their understanding of the origins and continuing significance of the Amendment is instructive.

Blacks were routinely disarmed by Southern States after the Civil War. Those who opposed these injustices frequently stated that they infringed blacks' constitutional right to keep and bear arms. Needless to say, the claim was not that blacks were being prohibited from carrying arms in an organized state militia. It was plainly the understanding in the post-Civil War Congress that the Second Amendment protected an individual right to use arms for self-defense. Every late-19th-century legal scholar that we have read interpreted the Second Amendment to secure an individual right unconnected with militia service.

E

We now ask whether any of our precedents forecloses the conclusions we have reached about the meaning of the Second Amendment. Justice Stevens places overwhelming reliance upon this Court's decision in United States v. Miller (1939). *Miller* did not hold that and cannot possibly be read to have held that. The judgment in the case upheld against a Second Amendment challenge two men's federal convictions for transporting an unregistered short-barreled shotgun in interstate commerce, in violation of the National Firearms Act. It is entirely clear that the Court's basis for saying that the Second Amendment did not apply was not that the defendants were "bear[ing] arms" not "for . . . military purposes" but for "nonmilitary use." Rather, it was that the type of weapon at issue was not eligible for Second Amendment protection. Beyond that, the opinion provided no explanation of the content of the right.

This holding is not only consistent with, but positively suggests, that the Second Amendment confers an individual right to keep and bear arms (though only arms that "have some reasonable relationship to the preservation or efficiency of a well regulated militia"). Had the Court believed that the Second Amendment protects only those serving in the militia, it would have been odd to examine the character of the weapon rather than simply note that the two crooks were not militiamen. *Miller* stands only for the proposition that the Second Amendment right, whatever its nature, extends only to certain types of weapons.

It is particularly wrongheaded to read *Miller* for more than what it said, because the case did not even purport to be a thorough examination of the Second Amendment. The respondent made no appearance in the case, neither filing a brief nor appearing at oral argument; the Court heard from no one but the Government.

We conclude that nothing in our precedents forecloses our adoption of the original understanding of the Second Amendment.

III

Like most rights, the right secured by the Second Amendment is not unlimited. From Blackstone through the 19th-century cases, commentators and courts routinely explained that the right was not a right to keep and carry any weapon whatsoever in any manner whatsoever and for whatever purpose. For example, the majority of the 19th-century courts to consider the question held that prohibitions on carrying concealed weapons were lawful under the Second Amendment or state analogues. Although we do not undertake an exhaustive historical analysis today of the full scope of the Second Amendment, nothing in our opinion should be taken to cast doubt on longstanding prohibitions on the possession of firearms by felons and the mentally ill, or laws forbidding the carrying of firearms in sensitive places such as schools and government buildings, or laws imposing conditions and qualifications on the commercial sale of arms.

We also recognize another important limitation on the right to keep and carry arms. *Miller* said, as we have explained, that the sorts of weapons protected were those "in common use at the time." We think that limitation is fairly supported by the historical tradition of prohibiting the carrying of "dangerous and unusual weapons."

It may be objected that if weapons that are most useful in military service — M-16 rifles and the like — may be banned, then the Second Amendment right is completely detached from the prefatory clause. But as we have said, the conception of the militia at the time of the Second Amendment's ratification was the body of all citizens capable of military service, who would bring the sorts of lawful weapons that they possessed at home to militia duty. It may well be true today that a militia, to be as effective as militias in the 18th century, would require sophisticated arms that are highly unusual in society at large. Indeed, it may be true that no amount of small arms could be useful against modern-day bombers and tanks. But the fact that modern developments have limited the degree of fit between the prefatory clause and the protected right cannot change our interpretation of the right.

IV

We turn finally to the law at issue here. As we have said, the law totally bans handgun possession in the home. It also requires that any lawful firearm in the home be disassembled or bound by a trigger lock at all times, rendering it inoperable.

As the quotations earlier in this opinion demonstrate, the inherent right of self-defense has been central to the Second Amendment right. The handgun ban amounts to a prohibition of an entire class of "arms" that is overwhelmingly chosen by American society for that lawful purpose. The prohibition extends, moreover, to the home, where the need for defense of self, family, and property is most acute. Under any of the standards of scrutiny that we have applied to enumerated constitutional rights, banning from the home "the most preferred firearm in the nation to 'keep' and use for protection of one's home and family," would fail constitutional muster.

Justice Breyer moves on to make a broad jurisprudential point: He criticizes us for declining to establish a level of scrutiny for evaluating Second Amendment restrictions. He proposes, explicitly at least, none of the traditionally expressed levels (strict scrutiny, intermediate scrutiny, rational basis), but rather a judge-empowering "interest-balancing inquiry" that "asks whether the statute burdens a protected interest in a way or to an extent that is out of proportion to the statute's salutary effects upon other important governmental interests."

We know of no other enumerated constitutional right whose core protection has been subjected to a freestanding "interest-balancing" approach. The very enumeration of the right takes out of the hands of government—even the Third Branch of Government—the power to decide on a case-by-case basis whether the right is really worth insisting upon. A constitutional guarantee subject to future judges' assessments of its usefulness is no constitutional guarantee at all. Constitutional rights are enshrined with the scope they were understood to have when the people adopted them, whether or not future legislatures or (yes) even future judges think that scope too broad. We would not apply an "interest-balancing" approach to the prohibition of a peaceful neo-Nazi march through Skokie. The First Amendment contains the freedom-of-speech guarantee that the people ratified, which included exceptions for obscenity, libel, and disclosure of state secrets, but not for the expression of extremely unpopular and wrong-headed views. The Second Amendment is no different. Like the First, it is the very product of an interest-balancing by the people—which Justice Breyer would now conduct for them anew. And whatever else it leaves to future evaluation, it surely elevates above all other interests the right of law-abiding, responsible citizens to use arms in defense of hearth and home.

Justice Breyer chides us for leaving so many applications of the right to keep and bear arms in doubt, and for not providing extensive historical justification for those regulations of the right that we describe as permissible. But since this case represents this Court's first in-depth examination of the Second Amendment, one should not expect it to clarify the entire field. And there will be time enough to expound upon the historical justifications for the exceptions we have mentioned if and when those exceptions come before us.

In sum, we hold that the District's ban on handgun possession in the home violates the Second Amendment, as does its prohibition against rendering any lawful firearm in the home operable for the purpose of immediate self-defense. Assuming that Heller is not disqualified from the exercise of Second Amendment rights, the District must permit him to register his handgun and must issue him a license to carry it in the home.

We are aware of the problem of handgun violence in this country, and we take seriously the concerns raised by the many amici who believe that prohibition of handgun ownership is a solution. The Constitution leaves the District of Columbia a variety of tools for combating that problem, including some measures regulating handguns. But the enshrinement of constitutional rights necessarily takes certain policy choices off the table. These include the absolute prohibition of handguns held and used for self-defense in the home. Undoubtedly some think that the Second Amendment is outmoded in a society where our standing army is the pride of our Nation, where well-trained police forces provide personal security, and where gun violence is a serious problem. That is perhaps debatable, but what is not debatable is that it is not the role of this Court to pronounce the Second Amendment extinct.

Justice STEVENS, with whom Justice SOUTER, Justice GINSBURG, and Justice BREYER join, dissenting.

The question presented by this case is not whether the Second Amendment protects a "collective right" or an "individual right." Surely it protects a right that can be enforced by individuals. But a conclusion that the Second Amendment protects an individual right does not tell us anything about the scope of that right.

Guns are used to hunt, for self-defense, to commit crimes, for sporting activities, and to perform military duties. The Second Amendment plainly does not protect the right to use a gun to rob a bank; it is equally clear that it does encompass the right to use weapons for certain military purposes. Whether it also protects the right to possess and use guns for nonmilitary purposes like hunting and personal self-defense is the question presented by this case. The text of the Amendment, its history, and our decision in United States v. Miller (1939), provide a clear answer to that question.

The Second Amendment was adopted to protect the right of the people of each of the several States to maintain a well-regulated militia. It was a response to concerns raised during the ratification of the Constitution that the power of Congress to disarm the state militias and create a national standing army posed an intolerable threat to the sovereignty of the several States. Neither the text of the Amendment nor the arguments advanced by its proponents evidenced the slightest interest in limiting any legislature's authority to regulate private civilian uses of firearms. Specifically, there is no indication that the Framers of the Amendment intended to enshrine the common-law right of self-defense in the Constitution.

In 1934, Congress enacted the National Firearms Act, the first major federal firearms law. Upholding a conviction under that Act, this Court held that, "[i]n the absence of any evidence tending to show that possession or use of a 'shotgun having a barrel of less than eighteen inches in length' at this time has some reasonable relationship to the preservation or efficiency of a well regulated militia, we cannot say that the Second Amendment guarantees the right to keep and bear such an instrument." United States v. Miller. The view of the Amendment we took in *Miller*—that it protects the right to keep and bear arms for certain military purposes, but that it does not curtail the Legislature's power to regulate the nonmilitary use and ownership of weapons—is both the most natural reading of the Amendment's text and the interpretation most faithful to the history of its adoption.

Since our decision in *Miller*, hundreds of judges have relied on the view of the Amendment we endorsed there; we ourselves affirmed it in 1980. See Lewis v. United States (1980). No new evidence has surfaced since 1980 supporting the view that the Amendment was intended to curtail the power of Congress to regulate civilian use or misuse of weapons. Indeed, a review of the drafting history of the Amendment demonstrates that its Framers rejected proposals that would have broadened its coverage to include such uses.

Even if the textual and historical arguments on both sides of the issue were evenly balanced, respect for the well-settled views of all of our predecessors on this Court, and for the rule of law itself, would prevent most jurists from endorsing such a dramatic upheaval in the law.

In this dissent I shall first explain why our decision in *Miller* was faithful to the text of the Second Amendment and the purposes revealed in its drafting history. I shall then comment on the postratification history of the Amendment, which makes abundantly clear that the Amendment should not be interpreted as limiting the authority of Congress to regulate the use or possession of firearms for purely civilian purposes.

I

The text of the Second Amendment is brief. It provides: "A well regulated Militia, being necessary to the security of a free State, the right of the people to keep and bear Arms, shall not be infringed."

Three portions of that text merit special focus: the introductory language defining the Amendment's purpose, the class of persons encompassed within its reach, and the unitary nature of the right that it protects.

"A well regulated Militia, being necessary to the security of a free State"

The preamble to the Second Amendment makes three important points. It identifies the preservation of the militia as the Amendment's purpose; it explains that the militia is necessary to the security of a free State; and it recognizes that the militia must be "well regulated." In all three respects it is comparable to provisions in several State Declarations of Rights that were adopted roughly contemporaneously with the Declaration of Independence. Those state provisions highlight the importance members of the founding generation attached to the maintenance of state militias; they also underscore the profound fear shared by many in that era of the dangers posed by standing armies.

The preamble thus both sets forth the object of the Amendment and informs the meaning of the remainder of its text. Such text should not be treated as mere surplusage, for "[i]t cannot be presumed that any clause in the constitution is intended to be without effect." Marbury v. Madison (1803).

The Court today tries to denigrate the importance of this clause of the Amendment by beginning its analysis with the Amendment's operative provision and returning to the preamble merely "to ensure that our reading of the operative clause is consistent with the announced purpose." That is not how this Court ordinarily reads such texts, and it is not how the preamble would have been viewed at the time the Amendment was adopted.

"The right of the people"

The centerpiece of the Court's textual argument is its insistence that the words "the people" as used in the Second Amendment must have the same meaning, and protect the same class of individuals, as when they are used in the First and Fourth Amendments. According to the Court, in all three provisions — as well as the Constitution's preamble, "the term unambiguously refers to all members of the political community, not an unspecified subset." But the Court itself reads the Second Amendment to protect a "subset" significantly narrower than the class of persons protected by the First and Fourth Amendments; when it finally drills down on the substantive meaning of the Second Amendment, the Court limits the protected class to "law-abiding, responsible citizens." But the class of persons protected by the First and Fourth Amendments is not so limited; for even felons (and presumably irresponsible citizens as well) may invoke the protections of those constitutional provisions. The Court offers no way to harmonize its conflicting pronouncements.

"To keep and bear Arms"

Although the Court's discussion of these words treats them as two "phrases" — as if they read "to keep" and "to bear" — they describe a unitary right: to possess arms if needed for military purposes and to use them in conjunction with military activities.

The term "bear arms" is a familiar idiom; when used unadorned by any additional words, its meaning is "to serve as a soldier, do military service, fight." 1 Oxford English Dictionary 634 (2d ed. 1989). It is derived from the Latin arma ferre, which, translated literally, means "to bear [ferre] war equipment [arma]."

The Amendment's use of the term "keep" in no way contradicts the military meaning conveyed by the phrase "bear arms" and the Amendment's preamble. To the contrary, a number of state militia laws in effect at the time of the Second Amendment's drafting used the term "keep" to describe the requirement that militia members store their arms at their homes, ready to be used for service when necessary. The Virginia military law, for example, ordered that "every one of the said officers, non-commissioned officers, and privates, shall constantly keep the aforesaid arms, accoutrements, and ammunition, ready to be produced whenever called for by his commanding officer." "[K]eep and bear arms" thus perfectly describes the responsibilities of a framing-era militia member.

When each word in the text is given full effect, the Amendment is most naturally read to secure to the people a right to use and possess arms in conjunction with service in a well-regulated militia. So far as appears, no more than that was contemplated by its drafters or is encompassed within its terms. Even if the meaning of the text were genuinely susceptible to more than one interpretation, the burden would remain on those advocating a departure from the purpose identified in the preamble and from settled law to come forward with persuasive new arguments or evidence. The textual analysis offered by respondent and embraced by the Court falls far short of sustaining that heavy burden.

Indeed, not a word in the constitutional text even arguably supports the Court's overwrought and novel description of the Second Amendment as "elevat[ing] above all other interests" "the right of law-abiding, responsible citizens to use arms in defense of hearth and home."

II

The proper allocation of military power in the new Nation was an issue of central concern for the Framers. The compromises they ultimately reached, reflected in Article I's Militia Clauses and the Second Amendment, represent quintessential examples of the Framers' "splitting the atom of sovereignty."

It is strikingly significant that Madison's first draft omitted any mention of nonmilitary use or possession of weapons. Rather, his original draft repeated the essence of the two proposed amendments sent by Virginia, combining the substance of the two provisions succinctly into one, which read: "The right of the people to keep and bear arms shall not be infringed; a well armed, and well regulated militia being the best security of a free country; but no person religiously scrupulous of bearing arms, shall be compelled to render military service in person."

Madison's decision to model the Second Amendment on the distinctly military Virginia proposal is therefore revealing, since it is clear that he considered and rejected formulations that would have unambiguously protected civilian uses of firearms. When Madison prepared his first draft, and when that draft was debated and modified, it is reasonable to assume that all participants in the drafting process were fully aware of the other formulations that would have protected civilian use and possession of weapons and that their choice to craft the Amendment as they did represented a rejection of those alternative formulations.

Madison's initial inclusion of an exemption for conscientious objectors sheds revelatory light on the purpose of the Amendment. It confirms an intent to describe a duty as well as a right, and it unequivocally identifies the military character of both. The objections voiced to the conscientious-objector clause only confirm the central meaning of the text.

The history of the adoption of the Amendment thus describes an overriding concern about the potential threat to state sovereignty that a federal standing army would pose, and a desire to protect the States' militias as the means by which to guard against that danger. But state militias could not effectively check the prospect of a federal standing army so long as Congress retained the power to disarm them, and so a guarantee against such disarmament was needed. As we explained in *Miller*: "With obvious purpose to assure the continuation and render possible the effectiveness of such forces the declaration and guarantee of the Second Amendment were made. It must be interpreted and applied with that end in view." The evidence plainly refutes the claim that the Amendment was motivated by the Framers' fears that Congress might act to regulate any civilian uses of weapons. And even if the historical record were genuinely ambiguous, the burden would remain on the parties advocating a change in the law to introduce facts or arguments "'newly ascertained[]'"; the Court is unable to identify any such facts or arguments.

[IV]

The Court concludes its opinion by declaring that it is not the proper role of this Court to change the meaning of rights "enshrine[d]" in the Constitution. But the right the Court announces was not "enshrined" in the Second Amendment by the Framers; it is the product of today's law-changing decision. The majority's exegesis has utterly failed to establish that as a matter of text or history, "the right of law-abiding, responsible citizens to use arms in defense of hearth and home" is "elevate[d] above all other interests" by the Second Amendment.

Until today, it has been understood that legislatures may regulate the civilian use and misuse of firearms so long as they do not interfere with the preservation of a well-regulated militia. The Court's announcement of a new constitutional right to own and use firearms for private purposes upsets that settled understanding, but leaves for future cases the formidable task of defining the scope of permissible regulations. Today judicial craftsmen have confidently asserted that a policy choice that denies a "law-abiding, responsible citize[n]" the right to keep and use weapons in the home for self-defense is "off the table." Given the presumption that most citizens are law abiding, and the reality that the need to defend oneself may suddenly arise in a host of locations outside the home, I fear that the District's policy choice may well be just the first of an unknown number of dominoes to be knocked off the table.

I do not know whether today's decision will increase the labor of federal judges to the "breaking point" envisioned by Justice Cardozo, but it will surely give rise to a far more active judicial role in making vitally important national policy decisions than was envisioned at any time in the 18th, 19th, or 20th centuries.

The Court properly disclaims any interest in evaluating the wisdom of the specific policy choice challenged in this case, but it fails to pay heed to a far more important policy choice — the choice made by the Framers themselves. The Court would have us believe that over 200 years ago, the Framers made a choice to limit the tools available to elected officials wishing to regulate civilian uses of weapons, and to authorize this Court to use the common-law process of case-by-case judicial lawmaking to define the contours of acceptable gun control policy. Absent compelling evidence that is nowhere to be found in the Court's opinion, I could not possibly conclude that the Framers made such a choice.

Justice BREYER, with whom Justice STEVENS, Justice SOUTER, and Justice GINSBURG join, dissenting.

We must decide whether a District of Columbia law that prohibits the possession of handguns in the home violates the Second Amendment. The majority, relying upon its view that the Second Amendment seeks to protect a right of personal self-defense, holds that this law violates that Amendment. In my view, it does not.

I

The majority's conclusion is wrong for two independent reasons. The first reason is that set forth by Justice Stevens — namely, that the Second Amendment protects militia-related, not self-defense-related, interests. These two interests are sometimes intertwined. To assure 18th-century citizens that they could keep arms for militia purposes would necessarily have allowed them to keep arms that they could have used for self-defense as well. But self-defense alone, detached from any militia-related objective, is not the Amendment's concern.

The second independent reason is that the protection the Amendment provides is not absolute. The Amendment permits government to regulate the interests that it serves. Thus, irrespective of what those interests are — whether they do or do not include an independent interest in self-defense — the majority's view cannot be correct unless it can show that the District's regulation is unreasonable or inappropriate in Second Amendment terms. This the majority cannot do.

In respect to the first independent reason, I agree with Justice Stevens, and I join his opinion. In this opinion I shall focus upon the second reason. I shall show that the District's law is consistent with the Second Amendment even if that Amendment is interpreted as protecting a wholly separate interest in individual self-defense. That is so because the District's regulation, which focuses upon the presence of handguns in high-crime urban areas, represents a permissible legislative response to a serious, indeed life-threatening, problem.

Thus I here assume that one objective (but, as the majority concedes, not the primary objective) of those who wrote the Second Amendment was to help assure citizens that they would have arms available for purposes of self-defense. Even so, a legislature could reasonably conclude that the law will advance goals of great public importance, namely, saving lives, preventing injury, and reducing crime. The law is tailored to the urban crime problem in that it is local in scope and thus affects only a geographic area both limited in size and entirely urban; the law concerns handguns, which are specially linked to urban gun deaths and injuries, and which are the overwhelmingly favorite weapon of armed criminals; and at the same time, the law imposes a burden upon gun owners that seems proportionately no greater than restrictions in existence at the time the Second Amendment was adopted. In these circumstances, the District's law falls within the zone that the Second Amendment leaves open to regulation by legislatures.

[II]

I therefore begin by asking a process-based question: How is a court to determine whether a particular firearm regulation (here, the District's restriction on handguns) is consistent with the Second Amendment? What kind of constitutional standard should the court use? How high a protective hurdle does the Amendment erect?

The question matters. The majority is wrong when it says that the District's law is unconstitutional "[u]nder any of the standards of scrutiny that we have applied to enumerated constitutional rights." How could that be? It certainly would not be unconstitutional under, for example, a "rational basis" standard, which requires a court to uphold regulation so long as it bears a "rational relationship" to a "legitimate governmental purpose." The law at issue here, which in part seeks to prevent gun-related accidents, at least bears a "rational relationship" to that "legitimate" life-saving objective.

Respondent proposes that the Court adopt a "strict scrutiny" test, which would require reviewing with care each gun law to determine whether it is "narrowly tailored to achieve a compelling governmental interest." But the majority implicitly, and appropriately, rejects that suggestion by broadly approving a set of laws — prohibitions on concealed weapons, forfeiture by criminals of the Second Amendment right, prohibitions on firearms in certain locales, and governmental regulation of commercial firearm sales — whose constitutionality under a strict scrutiny standard would be far from clear.

Indeed, adoption of a true strict-scrutiny standard for evaluating gun regulations would be impossible. That is because almost every gun-control regulation will seek to advance (as the one here does) a "primary concern of every government — a concern for the safety and indeed the lives of its citizens." The Court has deemed that interest, as well as "the Government's general interest in preventing crime," to be "compelling," and the Court has in a wide variety of constitutional contexts found such public-safety concerns sufficiently forceful to justify restrictions on individual liberties. Thus, any attempt in theory to apply strict scrutiny to gun regulations will in practice turn into an interest-balancing inquiry, with the interests protected by the Second Amendment on one side and the governmental public-safety concerns on the other, the only question being whether the regulation at issue impermissibly burdens the former in the course of advancing the latter.

I would simply adopt such an interest-balancing inquiry explicitly. The fact that important interests lie on both sides of the constitutional equation suggests that review of gun-control regulation is not a context in which a court should effectively presume either constitutionality (as in rational-basis review) or unconstitutionality (as in strict scrutiny). Rather, "where a law significantly implicates competing constitutionally protected interests in complex ways," the Court generally asks whether the statute burdens a protected interest in a way or to an extent that is out of proportion to the statute's salutary effects upon other important governmental interests. Any answer would take account both of the statute's effects upon the competing interests and the existence of any clearly superior less restrictive alternative. Contrary to the majority's unsupported suggestion that this sort of "proportionality" approach is unprecedented, the Court has applied it in various constitutional contexts, including election-law cases, speech cases, and due process cases.

In applying this kind of standard the Court normally defers to a legislature's empirical judgment in matters where a legislature is likely to have greater expertise and greater institutional factfinding capacity. Nonetheless, a court, not a legislature, must make the ultimate constitutional conclusion, exercising its "independent judicial judgment" in light of the whole record to determine whether a law exceeds constitutional boundaries.

[III]

A

No one doubts the constitutional importance of the statute's basic objective, saving lives. But there is considerable debate about whether the District's statute helps to achieve that objective.

First, consider the facts as the legislature saw them when it adopted the District statute. As stated by the local council committee that recommended its adoption, the major substantive goal of the District's handgun restriction is "to reduce the potentiality for gun-related crimes and gun-related deaths from occurring within the District of Columbia." The committee concluded, on the basis of "extensive public hearings" and "lengthy research," that "[t]he easy availability of firearms in the United States has been a major factor contributing to the drastic increase in gun-related violence and crime over the past 40 years." It reported to the Council "startling statistics," regarding gun-related crime, accidents, and deaths, focusing particularly on the relation between handguns and crime and the proliferation of handguns within the District.

The committee informed the Council that guns were "responsible for 69 deaths in this country each day," for a total of "[a]pproximately 25,000 gun-deaths . . . each year," along with an additional 200,000 gun-related injuries. Three thousand of these deaths, the report stated, were accidental. A quarter of the victims in those accidental deaths were children under the age of 14. And according to the committee, "[f]or every intruder stopped by a homeowner with a firearm, there are 4 gun-related accidents within the home."

In respect to local crime, the committee observed that there were 285 murders in the District during 1974 — a record number. The committee report further-more presented statistics strongly correlating handguns with crime. Of the 285 murders in the District in 1974, 155 were committed with handguns. Ibid. This did not appear to be an aberration, as the report revealed that "handguns [had been] used in roughly 54% of all murders" (and 87% of murders of law enforce-ment officers) nationwide over the preceding several years. Nor were handguns only linked to murders, as statistics showed that they were used in roughly 60% of robberies and 26% of assaults. "A crime committed with a pistol," the commit-tee reported, "is 7 times more likely to be lethal than a crime committed with any other weapon." The committee furthermore presented statistics regarding the availability of handguns in the United States, and noted that they had "be-come easy for juveniles to obtain," even despite then-current District laws pro-hibiting juveniles from possessing them.

Next, consider the facts as a court must consider them looking at the matter as of today. Petitioners, and their amici, have presented us with more recent sta-tistics that tell much the same story that the committee report told 30 years ago. At the least, they present nothing that would permit us to second-guess the Council in respect to the numbers of gun crimes, injuries, and deaths, or the role of handguns.

From 1993 to 1997, there were 180,533 firearm-related deaths in the United States, an average of over 36,000 per year. Over that same period there were an additional 411,800 nonfatal firearm-related injuries treated in U.S. hospitals, an average of over 82,000 per year. Of these, 62% resulted from assaults, 17% were unintentional, 6% were suicide attempts, 1% were legal interventions, and 13% were of unknown causes.

The statistics are particularly striking in respect to children and adolescents. In over one in every eight firearm-related deaths in 1997, the victim was someone under the age of 20. Firearm-related deaths account for 22.5% of all injury deaths between the ages of 1 and 19. More male teenagers die from firearms than from all natural causes combined. Persons under 25 accounted for 47% of hospital-treated firearm injuries between June 1, 1992, and May 31, 1993.

Handguns are involved in a majority of firearm deaths and injuries in the United States. From 1993 to 1997, 81% of firearm-homicide victims were killed by handgun. In the same period, for the 41% of firearm injuries for which the weapon type is known, 82% of them were from handguns. Firearm Injury and Death From Crime 4. And among children under the age of 20, handguns account for approximately 70% of all unintentional firearm-related injuries and deaths. In particular, 70% of all firearm-related teenage suicides in 1996 involved a handgun.

Handguns also appear to be a very popular weapon among criminals. In a 1997 survey of inmates who were armed during the crime for which they were incarcerated, 83.2% of state inmates and 86.7% of federal inmates said that they were armed with a handgun. Statistics further suggest that urban areas, such as the District, have different experiences with gun-related death, injury, and crime, than do less densely populated rural areas. A disproportionate amount of violent and property crimes occur in urban areas, and urban criminals are more likely than other offenders to use a firearm during the commission of a violent crime.

Finally, the linkage of handguns to firearms deaths and injuries appears to be much stronger in urban than in rural areas. "[S]tudies to date generally support the hypothesis that the greater number of rural gun deaths are from rifles or shotguns, whereas the greater number of urban gun deaths are from handguns."

Finally, consider the claim of respondent's amici that handgun bans cannot work; there are simply too many illegal guns already in existence for a ban on legal guns to make a difference. In a word, they claim that, given the urban sea of pre-existing legal guns, criminals can readily find arms regardless. Nonetheless, a legislature might respond, we want to make an effort to try to dry up that urban sea, drop by drop. And none of the studies can show that effort is not worthwhile.

In a word, the studies to which respondent's amici point raise policy-related questions. They succeed in proving that the District's predictive judgments are controversial. But they do not by themselves show that those judgments are incorrect; nor do they demonstrate a consensus, academic or otherwise, supporting that conclusion.

Thus, it is not surprising that the District and its amici support the District's handgun restriction with studies of their own. One in particular suggests that, statistically speaking, the District's law has indeed had positive life-saving effects. See Loftin, McDowall, Weirsema, & Cottey, Effects of Restrictive Licensing of Handguns on Homicide and Suicide in the District of Columbia, 325 New England J. Med. 1615 (1991). Others suggest that firearm restrictions as a general matter reduce homicides, suicides, and accidents in the home. Still others suggest that the defensive uses of handguns are not as great in number as respondent's amici claim.

Respondent and his amici reply to these responses; and in doing so, they seek to discredit as methodologically flawed the studies and evidence relied upon by the District. The upshot is a set of studies and counterstudies that, at most, could leave a judge uncertain about the proper policy conclusion. But from respondent's perspective any such uncertainty is not good enough. That is because legislators, not judges, have primary responsibility for drawing policy conclusions from empirical fact. And, given that constitutional allocation of decision-making responsibility, the empirical evidence presented here is sufficient to allow a judge to reach a firm legal conclusion.

In particular this Court, in First Amendment cases applying intermediate scrutiny, has said that our "sole obligation" in reviewing a legislature's "predictive judgments" is "to assure that, in formulating its judgments," the legislature "has drawn reasonable inferences based on substantial evidence." And judges, looking at the evidence before us, should agree that the District legislature's predictive judgments satisfy that legal standard. That is to say, the District's judgment, while open to question, is nevertheless supported by "substantial evidence."

There is no cause here to depart from [that] standard for the District's decision represents the kind of empirically based judgment that legislatures, not courts, are best suited to make. In fact, deference to legislative judgment seems particularly appropriate here, where the judgment has been made by a local legislature, with particular knowledge of local problems and insight into appropriate local solutions.

For these reasons, I conclude that the District's statute properly seeks to further the sort of life-preserving and public-safety interests that the Court has called "compelling."

B

I next assess the extent to which the District's law burdens the interests that the Second Amendment seeks to protect. Respondent and his amici, as well as the majority, suggest that those interests include: (1) the preservation of a "well regulated Militia"; (2) safeguarding the use of firearms for sporting purposes, e.g., hunting and marksmanship; and (3) assuring the use of firearms for self-defense. For argument's sake, I shall consider all three of those interests here.

1

The District's statute burdens the Amendment's first and primary objective hardly at all. As previously noted, there is general agreement among the Members of the Court that the principal (if not the only) purpose of the Second Amendment is found in the Amendment's text: the preservation of a "well regulated Militia." What scant Court precedent there is on the Second Amendment teaches that the Amendment was adopted "[w]ith obvious purpose to assure the continuation and render possible the effectiveness of [militia] forces" and "must be interpreted and applied with that end in view."

2

The majority briefly suggests that the "right to keep and bear Arms" might encompass an interest in hunting. But in enacting the present provisions, the District sought "to take nothing away from sportsmen." And any inability of District residents to hunt near where they live has much to do with the jurisdiction's exclusively urban character and little to do with the District's firearm laws. For reasons similar to those I discussed in the preceding subsection — that the District's law does not prohibit possession of rifles or shotguns, and the presence of opportunities for sporting activities in nearby States — I reach a similar conclusion, namely, that the District's law burdens any sports-related or hunting-related objectives that the Amendment may protect little, or not at all.

3

The District's law does prevent a resident from keeping a loaded handgun in his home. And it consequently makes it more difficult for the householder to use the handgun for self-defense in the home against intruders, such as burglars. As the Court of Appeals noted, statistics suggest that handguns are the most popular weapon for self defense. To that extent the law burdens to some degree an interest in self-defense that for present purposes I have assumed the Amendment seeks to further.

C

In weighing needs and burdens, we must take account of the possibility that there are reasonable, but less restrictive alternatives. Are there other potential measures that might similarly promote the same goals while imposing lesser restrictions? Here I see none.

The reason there is no clearly superior, less restrictive alternative to the District's handgun ban is that the ban's very objective is to reduce significantly the number of handguns in the District, say, for example, by allowing a law enforcement officer immediately to assume that any handgun he sees is an illegal handgun. And there is no plausible way to achieve that objective other than to ban the guns.

D

The upshot is that the District's objectives are compelling; its predictive judgments as to its law's tendency to achieve those objectives are adequately supported; the law does impose a burden upon any self-defense interest that the Amendment seeks to secure; and there is no clear less restrictive alternative. I turn now to the final portion of the "permissible regulation" question: Does the District's law disproportionately burden Amendment-protected interests? Several considerations, taken together, convince me that it does not.

First, the District law is tailored to the life-threatening problems it attempts to address. The law concerns one class of weapons, handguns, leaving residents free to possess shotguns and rifles, along with ammunition. The area that falls within its scope is totally urban. That urban area suffers from a serious handgun-fatality problem. The District's law directly aims at that compelling problem. And there is no less restrictive way to achieve the problem-related benefits that it seeks.

Second, the self-defense interest in maintaining loaded handguns in the home to shoot intruders is not the primary interest, but at most a subsidiary interest, that the Second Amendment seeks to serve. The Second Amendment's language, while speaking of a "Militia," says nothing of "self-defense."

Further, any self-defense interest at the time of the Framing could not have focused exclusively upon urban-crime related dangers. Two hundred years ago, most Americans, many living on the frontier, would likely have thought of self-defense primarily in terms of outbreaks of fighting with Indian tribes, rebellions such as Shays' Rebellion, marauders, and crime-related dangers to travelers on the roads, on footpaths, or along waterways. Insofar as the Framers focused at all on the tiny fraction of the population living in large cities, they would have been aware that these city dwellers were subject to firearm restrictions that their rural counterparts were not. They are unlikely then to have thought of a right to keep loaded handguns in homes to confront intruders in urban settings as central. And the subsequent development of modern urban police departments, by diminishing the need to keep loaded guns nearby in case of intruders, would have moved any such right even further away from the heart of the amendment's more basic protective ends.

Nor, for that matter, am I aware of any evidence that handguns in particular were central to the Framers' conception of the Second Amendment. The lists of militia-related weapons in the late 18th-century state statutes appear primarily to refer to other sorts of weapons, muskets in particular.

Third, irrespective of what the Framers could have thought, we know what they did think. Samuel Adams, who lived in Boston, advocated a constitutional amendment that would have precluded the Constitution from ever being "construed" to "prevent the people of the United States, who are peaceable citizens, from keeping their own arms." And he doubtless knew that Massachusetts law prohibited Bostonians from keeping loaded guns in the house. So how could Samuel Adams have advocated such protection unless he thought that the protection was consistent with local regulation that seriously impeded urban residents from using their arms against intruders? It seems unlikely that he meant to deprive the Federal Government of power (to enact Boston-type weapons regulation) that he kn[e]w Boston had and (as far as we know) he would have thought constitutional under the Massachusetts Constitution.

Fourth, a contrary view, as embodied in today's decision, will have unfortunate consequences. The decision will encourage legal challenges to gun regulation throughout the Nation. Because it says little about the standards used to evaluate regulatory decisions, it will leave the Nation without clear standards for resolving those challenges. And litigation over the course of many years, or the mere specter of such litigation, threatens to leave cities without effective protection against gun violence and accidents during that time. As important, the majority's decision threatens severely to limit the ability of more knowledgeable, democratically elected officials to deal with gun-related problems. But I cannot understand how one can take from the elected branches of government the right to decide whether to insist upon a handgun-free urban populace in a city now facing a serious crime problem and which, in the future, could well face environmental or other emergencies that threaten the breakdown of law and order.

For these reasons, I conclude that the District's measure is a proportionate, not a disproportionate, response to the compelling concerns that led the District to adopt it.[10]

2. *Congressional Limits*

Article III of the Constitution provides that the "Supreme Court shall have appellate jurisdiction, both as to Law and Fact, with such Exceptions, and under such Regulations as the Congress shall make." May Congress use this authority to restrict Supreme Court jurisdiction to hear particular types of cases so as to effectively overrule Supreme Court decisions? There is no definitive answer to this question, although many proposals have been

---

10. District of Columbia v. Heller involved only whether a federal law was unconstitutional. Two years later, in McDonald v. City of Chicago, 130 S. Ct. 3020 (2010), the Court held that the Second Amendment applies to state and local governments. *McDonald*, and more generally the application of the Bill of Rights to state and local governments, is presented in Chapter 5. [Footnote by casebook author.]

introduced into Congress in an attempt to restrict jurisdiction to change the substantive law.

For example, during the 1950s, the Supreme Court invalidated some loyalty oaths for government workers and attorneys.[11] In response, the Jennings-Butler Bill was introduced in the U.S. Senate to prevent review of State Board of Bar Examiners' decisions concerning who could practice law in a state.[12] Altogether, since the 1940s, more than 100 proposals were introduced in Congress to restrict federal court jurisdiction over particular topics.[13] During the 1980s, there were proposals in Congress to prevent federal courts from hearing cases involving challenges to state laws permitting school prayers or state laws restricting access to abortions.[14] More recently, in June 2004, the House of Representatives passed a bill to prevent the Supreme Court or lower federal courts from interpreting or hearing challenges to the Defense of Marriage Act.[15] And in September 2004, the House passed a bill to preclude judicial review of the constitutionality of the Pledge of Allegiance.[16]

In large part, the debate centers on two major constitutional issues: What does the language of Article III mean when it says that Supreme Court jurisdiction exists subject to such "exceptions and regulations" as Congress shall make? Does separation of powers limit the ability of Congress to restrict Supreme Court jurisdiction?

THE EXCEPTIONS AND REGULATIONS CLAUSE

Even after more than 200 years of American history, there is no consensus as to what the Constitution means when it provides that the Supreme Court possesses appellate jurisdiction "both as to Law and Fact, with such Exceptions, and under such Regulations as the Congress shall make." On one side of the debate are those who believe that this provides Congress with broad powers to remove matters from the Supreme Court's purview. The argument, in part, is that the framers of the Constitution intended such congressional control as a check on the judiciary's power.[17] Evidence of this intent, it is argued, is found in the fact that the first Congress did not vest the Supreme Court with appellate jurisdiction over all of the types of cases and controversies enumerated in Article III. For example, under the Judiciary Act of 1789, the Supreme Court had authority only to review decisions of a state's highest court that ruled against a federal constitutional claim.[18] It was not until the twentieth century that the Supreme

---

11. *See, e.g.,* Schware v. Board of Bar Examiners, 353 U.S. 232 (1957); Konigsberg v. State Bar, 353 U.S. 252 (1957).

12. S. 3386, 85th Cong., 2d Sess. (1958).

13. Paul Bator, Daniel Meltzer, Paul Mishkin, & David Shapiro, *Hart & Wechsler's The Federal Courts and the Federal System* 377 (3d ed. 1988).

14. *See, e.g.,* S. 158, 97th Cong., 1st Sess. (1981); H.R. 3225, 97th Cong., 1st Sess. (1981) (bills restricting federal court jurisdiction in abortion cases); S. 481, 97th Cong., 1st Sess. (1981); H.R. 4756, 97th Cong., 1st Sess. (1981) (bills restricting federal court jurisdiction over cases that involve voluntary school prayers).

15. H.R. 3313, 108th Cong., 2d Sess. (2004).

16. H.R. 2023, 108th Cong., 2d Sess. (2004).

17. *See, e.g.,* Herbert Wechsler, *The Courts and the Constitution*, 65 Colum. L. Rev. 1001, 1005-1006 (1965).

18. Act of Sept. 24, 1789, 1 Stat. 73; *see* Peter W. Low & John Jeffries, Jr., *Federal Courts and the Law of Federal-State Relations* 171 (3d ed. 1994).

Court was accorded power to review decisions of a state court that ruled in favor of a constitutional right.[19]

On the other side of the debate are those who believe that Congress is limited in its ability to control Supreme Court jurisdiction. Some argue that the term "Exceptions" in Article III was intended to modify the word "Fact."[20] The contention is that the framers were concerned about the Supreme Court's ability to overturn fact-finding by lower courts, especially when done by juries. Under this view, Congress could create an exception to the Supreme Court's jurisdiction for review of matters of fact, but Congress could not eliminate the Court's appellate jurisdiction for issues of law.

Alternatively, it is argued that even though Congress is given authority to limit Supreme Court jurisdiction under the text of Article III, this power—like all congressional powers—cannot be used in a manner that violates the Constitution. Opponents of jurisdiction restriction contend that congressional preclusion of Supreme Court review of particular topics would violate other parts of the Constitution.[21]

The primary Supreme Court case interpreting the Exceptions and Regulations Clause is Ex parte McCardle. In reading *McCardle*, consider whether it is precedent for a federal law precluding Supreme Court review of particular types of cases or whether it is distinguishable.

EX PARTE McCARDLE

74 U.S. 506 (1868)

[McCardle was a newspaper editor in Vicksburg, Mississippi, who was arrested by federal officials for writing a series of newspaper articles that were highly critical of Reconstruction and especially of the military rule of the South following the Civil War. McCardle filed a petition for a writ of habeas corpus pursuant to a statute adopted in 1867 that permitted federal courts to grant habeas corpus relief to anyone held in custody in violation of the Constitution or laws of the United States by either a state government or the federal government. Before 1867, under the Judiciary Act of 1789, which was supplemented but not replaced by the 1867 law, federal courts could hear habeas petitions only of those who were held in federal custody.

McCardle contended that the Military Reconstruction Act was unconstitutional in that it provided for military trials for civilians. He also claimed that his prosecution violated specific Bill of Rights' provisions, including the First, Fifth, and Sixth Amendments. The U.S. government argued that the federal courts lacked jurisdiction to grant habeas corpus to McCardle under the 1867 act. The federal government read the 1867 statute, despite its language to the contrary, as providing federal court relief only for state prisoners. The Supreme Court rejected this contention and set the case for argument on the merits of

---

19. Act of Dec. 23, 1914, 38 Stat. 790.

20. *See* Raoul Berger, *Congress v. The Supreme Court* 285-296 (1969).

21. *See, e.g.,* Leonard G. Ratner, *Congressional Power over the Appellate Jurisdiction of the Supreme Court,* 109 U. Pa. L. Rev. 157 (1960); Lawrence Gene Sager, *Foreword: Constitutional Limitations on Congress' Authority to Regulate the Jurisdiction of the Federal Courts,* 95 Harv. L. Rev. 17 (1981); Laurence A. Tribe, *Jurisdictional Gerrymandering: Zoning Disfavored Rights out of the Federal Courts,* 16 Harv. C.R.-C.L. L. Rev. 129 (1981).

McCardle's claim that the Military Reconstruction Act and his prosecution were unconstitutional.

On March 9, 1868, the Supreme Court held oral arguments on McCardle's constitutional claims. Three days later, on March 12, 1868, Congress adopted a rider to an inconsequential tax bill that repealed that part of the 1867 statute that authorized Supreme Court appellate review of writs of habeas corpus. Members of Congress stated that their purpose was to remove the *McCardle* case from the Supreme Court's docket and thus prevent the Court from potentially invalidating Reconstruction. Representative Wilson declared that the "amendment [repealing Supreme Court authority under the 1867 act is] aimed at striking at a branch of the jurisdiction of the Supreme Court . . . thereby sweeping the [*McCardle*] case from the docket by taking away the jurisdiction of the Court."

On March 25, 1868, President Andrew Johnson vetoed the attempted repeal of Supreme Court jurisdiction. This was five days before the Senate was scheduled to begin its impeachment trial of President Johnson and the grounds for impeachment focused solely on his alleged obstruction of Reconstruction. Congress immediately overrode President Johnson's veto on March 27, 1868.

The Supreme Court then considered whether it had jurisdiction to hear McCardle's constitutional claims in light of the recently adopted statute denying it authority to hear appeals under the 1867 act that was the basis for jurisdiction in McCardle's petition.]

Chief Justice CHASE delivered the opinion of the court.

The first question necessarily is that of jurisdiction; for, if the act of March, 1868, takes away the jurisdiction defined by the act of February, 1867, it is useless, if not improper, to enter into any discussion of other questions.

It is quite true, as was argued by the counsel for the petitioner, that the appellate jurisdiction of this court is not derived from acts of Congress. It is, strictly speaking, conferred by the Constitution. But it is conferred "with such exceptions and under such regulations as Congress shall make."

It is unnecessary to consider whether, if Congress had made no exceptions and no regulations, this court might not have exercised general appellate jurisdiction under rules prescribed by itself. The exception to appellate jurisdiction in the case before us, however, is not an inference from the affirmation of other appellate jurisdiction. It is made in terms. The provision of the act of 1867, affirming the appellate jurisdiction of this court in cases of habeas corpus is expressly repealed. It is hardly possible to imagine a plainer instance of positive exception.

We are not at liberty to inquire into the motives of the legislature. We can only examine into its power under the Constitution; and the power to make exceptions to the appellate jurisdiction of this court is given by express words.

What, then, is the effect of the repealing act upon the case before us? We cannot doubt as to this. Without jurisdiction the court cannot proceed at all in any cause. Jurisdiction is power to declare the law, and when it ceases to exist, the only function remaining to the court is that of announcing the fact and dismissing the cause. And this is not less clear upon authority than upon principle.

It is quite clear, therefore, that this court cannot proceed to pronounce judgment in this case, for it has no longer jurisdiction of the appeal; and judicial duty is not less fitly performed by declining ungranted jurisdiction than in exercising firmly that which the Constitution and the laws confer.

Counsel seem to have supposed, if effect be given to the repealing act in question, that the whole appellate power of the court, in cases of habeas corpus, is denied. But this is an error. The act of 1868 does not except from that jurisdiction any cases but appeals from Circuit Courts under the act of 1867. It does not affect the jurisdiction which was previously exercised.

NOTES ON EX PARTE McCARDLE

Less than a year after its decision in *McCardle,* the Supreme Court in Ex parte Yerger, 75 U.S. (8 Wall.) 85 (1868), held that it had authority to review habeas corpus decisions of lower federal courts under the Judiciary Act of 1789. Like *McCardle, Yerger* involved a newspaper editor's challenge to the constitutionality of the Military Reconstruction Act. After the Supreme Court upheld its jurisdiction to decide Yerger's constitutional claims, the federal military authorities dismissed all charges against him, thereby again preventing Supreme Court review of the constitutionality of Reconstruction.

SEPARATION OF POWERS AS A LIMIT ON CONGRESS'S AUTHORITY

To what extent does separation of powers limit the ability of Congress to exercise control over Supreme Court decision making? The primary Supreme Court decision finding a federal law unconstitutional on the grounds that it violates separation of powers is United States v. Klein. In reading *Klein,* consider what limits it imposes on Congress's ability to control or restrict Supreme Court jurisdiction.

UNITED STATES v. KLEIN
80 U.S. 128 (1871)

[In 1863, Congress adopted a statute providing that individuals whose property was seized during the Civil War could recover the property, or compensation for it, upon proof that they had not offered aid or comfort to the enemy during the war. The Supreme Court subsequently held that a presidential pardon fulfilled the statutory requirement of demonstrating that an individual was not a supporter of the rebellion.

In response to this decision and frequent pardons issued by the president, Congress quickly adopted a statute providing that a pardon was inadmissible as evidence in a claim for return of seized property. Moreover, the statute provided that a pardon, without an express disclaimer of guilt, was proof that the person aided the rebellion and would deny the federal courts jurisdiction over the claims. The statute declared that upon "proof of such pardon . . . the jurisdiction of the court in the case shall cease, and the court shall forthwith dismiss the suit of such claimant."]

Chief Justice CHASE delivered the opinion of the court.

The substance of this enactment is that an acceptance of a pardon, without disclaimer, shall be conclusive evidence of the acts pardoned, but shall be null and void as evidence of the rights conferred by it, both in the Court of Claims and in this court on appeal.

It was urged in argument that the right to sue the government in the Court of Claims is a matter of favor; but this seems not entirely accurate. It is as much the duty of the government as of individuals to fulfil its obligations. Before the establishment of the Court of Claims claimants could only be heard by Congress. That court was established in 1855 for the triple purpose of relieving Congress, and of protecting the government by regular investigation, and of benefiting the claimants by affording them a certain mode of examining and adjudicating upon their claims. It was required to hear and determine upon claims founded upon any law of Congress, or upon any regulation of an executive department, or upon any contract, express or implied, with the government of the United States.

Undoubtedly the legislature has complete control over the organization and existence of that court and may confer or withhold the right of appeal from its decisions. And if this act did nothing more, it would be our duty to give it effect. If it simply denied the right of appeal in a particular class of cases, there could be no doubt that it must be regarded as an exercise of the power of Congress to make "such exceptions from the appellate jurisdiction" as should seem to it expedient.

But the language of the proviso shows plainly that it does not intend to withhold appellate jurisdiction except as a means to an end. Its great and controlling purpose is to deny to pardons granted by the President the effect which this court had adjudged them to have. The proviso declares that pardons shall not be considered by this court on appeal. We had already decided that it was our duty to consider them and give them effect, in cases like the present, as equivalent to proof of loyalty. It provides that whenever it shall appear that any judgment of the Court of Claims shall have been founded on such pardons, without other proof of loyalty, the Supreme Court shall have no further jurisdiction of the case and shall dismiss the same for want of jurisdiction. The proviso further declares that every pardon granted to any suitor . . . if accepted in writing without disclaimer of the fact recited, be taken as conclusive evidence in that court and on appeal, of the act recited; and on proof of pardon or acceptance, summarily made on motion or otherwise, the jurisdiction of the court shall cease and the suit shall be forthwith dismissed.

It is evident from this statement that the denial of jurisdiction to this court, as well as to the Court of Claims, is founded solely on the application of a rule of decision, in causes pending, prescribed by Congress. The court has jurisdiction of the cause to a given point; but when it ascertains that a certain state of things exists, its jurisdiction is to cease and it is required to dismiss the cause for want of jurisdiction.

It seems to us that this is not an exercise of the acknowledged power of Congress to make exceptions and prescribe regulations to the appellate power.

The court is required to ascertain the existence of certain facts and thereupon to declare that its jurisdiction on appeal has ceased, by dismissing the bill. What is this but to prescribe a rule for the decision of a cause in a particular way? In the case before us, the Court of Claims has rendered judgment for the claimant and an appeal has been taken to this court. We are directed to dismiss the appeal, if we find that the judgment must be affirmed, because of a pardon granted to the intestate of the claimants. Can we do so without allowing one party to the controversy to decide it in its own favor? Can we do so without allowing that the legislature may prescribe rules of decision to the Judicial Department of the government in cases pending before it?

We must think that Congress has inadvertently passed the limit which separates the legislative from the judicial power. It is of vital importance that these powers be kept distinct. The Constitution provides that the judicial power of the United States shall be vested in one Supreme Court and such inferior courts as the Congress shall from time to time ordain and establish. The same instrument, in the last clause of the same article, provides that in all cases other than those of original jurisdiction, "the Supreme Court shall have appellate jurisdiction both as to law and fact, with such exceptions and under such regulations as the Congress shall make."

Congress has already provided that the Supreme Court shall have jurisdiction of the judgments of the Court of Claims on appeal. Can it prescribe a rule in conformity with which the court must deny to itself the jurisdiction thus conferred, because and only because its decision, in accordance with settled law, must be adverse to the government and favorable to the suitor? This question seems to us to answer itself.

The rule prescribed is also liable to just exception as impairing the effect of a pardon, and thus infringing the constitutional power of the Executive. It is the intention of the Constitution that each of the great co-ordinate departments of the government — the Legislative, the Executive, and the Judicial — shall be, in its sphere, independent of the others. To the executive alone is intrusted the power of pardon; and it is granted without limit. Pardon includes amnesty. It blots out the offence pardoned and removes all its penal consequences. It may be granted on conditions. In these particular pardons, that no doubt might exist as to their character, restoration of property was expressly pledged, and the pardon was granted on condition that the person who availed himself of it should take and keep a prescribed oath.

NOTES ON UNITED STATES v. KLEIN

There have been many occasions in which Congress has reacted to a Supreme Court decision interpreting a statute by adopting a law effectively overruling the Court's ruling. In essence, Congress is directing the results in future cases. The key question is whether this is distinguishable from *Klein*. The Supreme Court distinguished *Klein* in the following more recent case.

ROBERTSON v. SEATTLE AUDUBON SOCIETY, 503 U.S. 429 (1992): The Department of Interior and Related Agencies Appropriations Act of 1990 required the Bureau of Land Management to offer specified land for sale and also imposed restrictions on harvesting from other land. Additionally, the act expressly noted two pending cases and said that "Congress hereby determines and directs that management of areas according to subsections (b)(3) and (b)(5) of this section on [the specified lands] is adequate consideration for the purpose of meeting the statutory requirements that are the basis for [the two lawsuits]."

The Supreme Court rejected the argument that Congress was directing the outcome of the pending litigation. The Supreme Court held that Congress had changed the law itself and did not direct findings or results under the old law. The Court said that *Klein* applies in a situation where Congress directs the judiciary as to decision making under an existing law and does not apply when Congress adopts a new law. The Court found that as a new law the statute was constitutional.

These cases establish no clear principles as to what the phrase "exceptions and regulations" means or when separation of powers prevents Congress from changing the law in response to a Supreme Court decision interpreting a statute. Ultimately, the arguments about Congress's ability to check the federal judiciary, like so many areas of constitutional law, turn on disputes about the meaning of the Constitution's language, the intent of its framers, and the competing policy considerations.

3. Justiciability Limits

Article III, §2 authorizes federal courts to hear several types of "cases" and "controversies." The Supreme Court has interpreted these words as giving rise to a series of limits on the federal judicial power. These limits are frequently referred to as justiciability doctrines. The justiciability doctrines are all judicially created limits on the matters that can be heard in federal courts. The Supreme Court has declared that some of these are "constitutional," meaning that Congress by statute cannot override them. The Court also has said that some of the doctrines are "prudential," meaning that they are based on prudent judicial administration and can be overridden by Congress since they are not constitutional requirements.

All of the justiciability doctrines raise basic policy questions about the proper role of the federal judiciary in a democratic society. As Chief Justice Warren explained, the "words [cases and controversies] define the role assigned to the judiciary in a tripartite allocation of power to assure that the federal courts will not intrude into areas committed to the other branches of government."[22] The justiciability doctrines also are intended to improve judicial decision making by providing the federal courts with concrete controversies best suited for judicial resolution. The Supreme Court explained that the requirement for cases and controversies "limit[s] the business of federal courts to questions presented in an adversary context and in a form historically viewed as capable of resolution through the judicial process."[23] Moreover, the justiciability doctrines, by limiting the availability of federal court review, conserve judicial resources.

There are five major justiciability doctrines: the prohibition against advisory opinions, standing, ripeness, mootness, and the political question doctrine. All must be met for any federal court, at any level, to hear a case.[24]

In addition to the justiciability doctrines, the Supreme Court has said that it would follow certain "principles of avoidance" to ensure that it will reach

---

22. Flast v. Cohen, 392 U.S. 83, 95 (1968).
23. *Id.*
24. There are other constitutional limits on the federal judicial power in addition to the justiciability doctrines. One of the most important is the Eleventh Amendment which has been interpreted as barring suits against states in federal court by states' own citizens and citizens of other states. The complex body of Eleventh Amendment law generally is covered in Federal Courts classes and not Constitutional Law courses and so is beyond the scope of this book. However, the Court has had occasion to discuss the Eleventh Amendment in considering the scope of Congress's powers under §5 of the Fourteenth Amendment. These cases are presented in Chapter 2. For a discussion of the Eleventh Amendment, *see* Erwin Chemerinsky, *Federal Jurisdiction,* Chapter 7 (6th ed. 2012).

constitutional questions only when necessary. The most famous articulation of these "avoidance principles" was by Justice Louis Brandeis in a concurring opinion in Ashwander v. Tennessee Valley Authority.[25] Justice Brandeis wrote:

> Considerations of propriety, as well as long-established practice, demand that we refrain from passing upon the constitutionality of an act of Congress unless obliged to do so in the proper performance of our judicial function, when the question is raised by a party whose interests entitle him to raise it. The Court developed, for its own governance in the cases confessedly within its jurisdiction, a series of rules under which it has avoided passing upon a large part of all the constitutional questions pressed upon it for decision. They are:
>
> 1. The Court will not pass upon the constitutionality of legislation in a friendly, nonadversary, proceeding, declining because to decide such questions "is legitimate only in the last resort, and as a necessity in the determination of real, earnest, and vital controversy between individuals. It never was the thought that, by means of a friendly suit, a party beaten in the legislature could transfer to the courts an inquiry as to the constitutionality of the legislative act."
>
> 2. The Court will not "anticipate a question of constitutional law in advance of the necessity of deciding it." "It is not the habit of the court to decide questions of a constitutional nature unless absolutely necessary to a decision of the case."
>
> 3. The Court will not "formulate a rule of constitutional law broader than is required by the precise facts to which it is to be applied."
>
> 4. The Court will not pass upon a constitutional question although properly presented by the record, if there is also present some other ground upon which the case may be disposed of. This rule has found most varied application. Thus, if a case can be decided on either of two grounds, one involving a constitutional question, the other a question of statutory construction or general law, the Court will decide only the latter. Appeals from the highest court of a state challenging its decision of a question under the Federal Constitution are frequently dismissed because the judgment can be sustained on an independent state ground.
>
> 5. The Court will not pass upon the validity of a statute upon complaint of one who fails to show that he is injured by its operation. Among the many applications of this rule, none is more striking than the denial of the right of challenge to one who lacks a personal or property right. Thus, the challenge by a public official interested only in the performance of his official duty will not be entertained.
>
> 6. The Court will not pass upon the constitutionality of a statute at the instance of one who has availed himself of its benefits.
>
> 7. "When the validity of an act of the Congress is drawn in question, and even if a serious doubt of constitutionality is raised, it is a cardinal principle that this Court will first ascertain whether a construction of the statute is fairly possible by which the question may be avoided."

Some of these requirements overlap with the justiciability doctrines discussed below. Some are additional principles of restraint. As you examine the five justiciability doctrines — prohibition of advisory opinions, standing, ripeness, mootness, and the political question doctrine — consider the extent to which they embody Brandeis's principles of judicial restraint in constitutional cases.

---

25. 297 U.S. 288 (1936). For an excellent discussion of these avoidance principles, *see* Lisa A. Kloppenberg, Avoiding Constitutional Questions, 35 B.C.L. Rev. 1003 (1994).

a. Prohibition of Advisory Opinions

The core of Article III's requirement for cases and controversies is that federal courts cannot issue advisory opinions. What are the characteristics that must be present in a lawsuit to avoid being an advisory opinion? First, there must be an actual dispute between adverse litigants.

OPINION OF THE JUSTICES, reprinted in Richard H. Fallon et al., *Hart and Wechsler's The Federal Courts and the Federal System* 92-93 (4th ed. 1996): Early in American history, a conflict occurred between France and England. The United States adopted a position of neutrality. Secretary of State Thomas Jefferson asked the Supreme Court for its answers to a long list of questions concerning America's conduct as a neutral party. In his letter to the Justices, Jefferson said that "[t]he President therefore would be much relieved if he found himself free to refer questions of this description to the opinions of the judges of the [Court], whose knowledge of the subject would secure us against errors dangerous to the peace of the United States." For example, Jefferson asked the Justices, "May we, within our own ports, sell ships to both parties, prepared merely for merchandise? May they be pierced for guns?"

The Justices wrote back to President Washington and declined to answer the questions asked. The Justices, in their letter, stated: "[The] three departments of the government . . . being in certain respects checks upon each other, and our being judges of a court in the last resort, are considerations which afford strong arguments against the propriety of our extra-judicially deciding the questions alluded to." The Justices concluded their letter: "We exceedingly regret every event that may cause embarrassment to your administration, but we derive consolation from the reflection that your judgment will discern what is right, and that your usual prudence, decision, and firmness will surmount every obstacle to the preservation of the rights, peace, and dignity of the United States."

Second, in order for a case to be justiciable and not an advisory opinion, there must be a substantial likelihood that a federal court decision in favor of a claimant will bring about some change or have some effect. This requirement also dates back to the Supreme Court's earliest days.

HAYBURN'S CASE, 2 U.S. (2 Dall.) 409 (1792): Congress adopted a law permitting Revolutionary War veterans to file pension claims in the U.S. Circuit Courts. The judges of these courts were to inform the secretary of war of the nature of the claimant's disability and the amount of benefits to be paid. The secretary could refuse to follow the court's recommendation.

Five Supreme Court justices, while sitting as circuit judges, found this approach unconstitutional. The justices explained that the duty of making recommendations regarding pensions was "not of a judicial nature." They said that it would violate separation of powers because the judicial actions might be "revised and controuled by the legislature, and by an officer in the executive department. Such revision and controul we deemed radically inconsistent with the independence of that judicial power which is vested in the courts."

Consider the application of this principle in a more recent context in the following case:

PLAUT v. SPENDTHRIFT FARM, INC.

514 U.S. 211 (1995)

[In 1991, the Court ruled that actions brought under the securities laws, specifically §10(b) and Rule 10(b)(5), had to be brought within one year of discovering the facts giving rise to the violation and three years of the violation. Congress then amended the law to allow cases that were filed before this decision to go forward if they could have been brought under the prior law. The effect of the statute was to reopen actions that had been dismissed under the Court's prior ruling.]

Justice Scalia delivered the opinion of the Court.

Our decisions to date have identified two types of legislation that require federal courts to exercise the judicial power in a manner that Article III forbids. The first appears in United States v. Klein (1872), where we refused to give effect to a statute that was said "[to] prescribe rules of decision to the Judicial Department of the government in cases pending before it." Whatever the precise scope of *Klein*, however, later decisions have made clear that its prohibition does not take hold when Congress "amend[s] applicable law." Robertson v. Seattle Audubon Soc. (1992). Section 27A(b) indisputably does set out substantive legal standards for the Judiciary to apply, and in that sense changes the law (even if solely retroactively). The second type of unconstitutional restriction upon the exercise of judicial power identified by past cases is exemplified by Hayburn's Case, 2 Dall. 409 (1792), which stands for the principle that Congress cannot vest review of the decisions of Article III courts in officials of the Executive Branch. Yet under any application of §27A(b) only courts are involved; no officials of other departments sit in direct review of their decisions. Section 27A(b) therefore offends neither of these previously established prohibitions.

We think, however, that §27A(b) offends a postulate of Article III just as deeply rooted in our law as those we have mentioned. Article III establishes a "judicial department" with the "province and duty . . . to say what the law is" in particular cases and controversies. Marbury v. Madison (1803). The record of history shows that the framers crafted this charter of the judicial department with an expressed understanding that it gives the Federal Judiciary the power, not merely to rule on cases, but to decide them, subject to review only by superior courts in the Article III hierarchy — with an understanding, in short, that "a judgment conclusively resolves the case" because "a 'judicial Power' is one to render dispositive judgments." By retroactively commanding the federal courts to reopen final judgments, Congress has violated this fundamental principle.

Section 27A(b) effects a clear violation of the separation-of-powers principle we have just discussed. It is, of course, retroactive legislation, that is, legislation that prescribes what the law was at an earlier time, when the act whose effect is controlled by the legislation occurred — in this case, the filing of the initial Rule 10b-5 action in the District Court.

It is true, as petitioners contend, that Congress can always revise the judgments of Article III courts in one sense: When a new law makes clear that it is retroactive, an appellate court must apply that law in reviewing judgments still on appeal that were rendered before the law was enacted, and must alter the outcome accordingly. But a distinction between judgments from which all appeals have been forgone or completed, and judgments that remain on appeal (or subject to being appealed), is implicit in what Article III creates: not a batch of unconnected courts, but a judicial department composed of "inferior Courts" and "one supreme Court." Within that hierarchy, the decision of an inferior court is not (unless the time for appeal has expired) the final word of the department as a whole. It is the obligation of the last court in the hierarchy that rules on the case to give effect to Congress's latest enactment, even when that has the effect of overturning the judgment of an inferior court, since each court, at every level, must "decide according to existing laws." Having achieved finality, however, a judicial decision becomes the last word of the judicial department with regard to a particular case or controversy, and Congress may not declare by retroactive legislation that the law applicable to that very case was something other than what the courts said it was.

To be sure, a general statute such as this one may reduce the perception that legislative interference with judicial judgments was prompted by individual favoritism; but it is legislative interference with judicial judgments nonetheless. Not favoritism, nor even corruption, but power is the object of the separation-of-powers prohibition. The prohibition is violated when an individual final judgment is legislatively rescinded for even the very best of reasons, such as the legislature's genuine conviction (supported by all the law professors in the land) that the judgment was wrong; and it is violated 40 times over when 40 final judgments are legislatively dissolved.

We know of no previous instance in which Congress has enacted retroactive legislation requiring an Article III court to set aside a final judgment, and for good reason. The Constitution's separation of legislative and judicial powers denies it the authority to do so. Section 27A(b) is unconstitutional to the extent that it requires federal courts to reopen final judgments entered before its enactment. The judgment of the Court of Appeals is affirmed.

NOTES ON ADVISORY OPINIONS

Many of the other justiciability doctrines implement the prohibition against advisory opinions. For instance, the standing requirement for an injury, the need that a case be ripe, and that it not be moot, all seek to ensure that there is an actual dispute between adverse litigants. Similarly, the standing requirement that the plaintiff demonstrate that the defendant is the cause of the injury so that a favorable court decision will remedy the harm seeks to ensure that a federal court ruling will make a difference.

Earlier in this century, courts expressed concern over whether requests for declaratory judgments were advisory opinions. Initially, the Supreme Court expressed doubts about whether suits for declaratory judgments could be justiciable. *See* Piedmont & Northern Ry. Co. v. United States, 280 U.S. 469 (1930); Willing v. Chicago Auditorium Assn., 277 U.S. 274 (1928). Subsequently, the Supreme Court said that suits for declaratory judgments are justiciable as long as they meet the requirements for judicial review.

NASHVILLE, C. & ST. L. RY. v. WALLACE, 288 U.S. 249 (1933): A company sought a declaratory judgment that a tax was an unconstitutional burden on interstate commerce. The Supreme Court explained that because the matter would have been justiciable as a request for an injunction, the suit for a declaratory judgment was capable of federal court adjudication. Justice Stone, writing for the majority, explained, "The Constitution does not require that the case or controversy should be presented by traditional forms of procedure, invoking only traditional remedies. [Article III] did not crystallize into changeless form the procedure of 1789 as the only possible means for presenting a case or controversy." The Court emphasized that the focus was on "substance" and "not with form" and that the case was justiciable "so long as the case retains the essentials of an adversary proceeding, involving a real, not a hypothetical, controversy."

b.   Standing

Standing is the second major justiciability requirement. Indeed, the Supreme Court has declared that standing is the most important justiciability requirement. Standing is the determination of whether a specific person is the proper party to bring a matter to the court for adjudication. The Supreme Court has declared: "In essence the question of standing is whether the litigant is entitled to have the court decide the merits of the dispute or of particular issues." Warth v. Seldin, 422 U.S. 490 (1975).

There are several requirements that must be met in order for a plaintiff to have standing.[26] Although all are judicially created, the Court has said that some are based on its interpretation of Article III, and thus constitutionally required, while others are prudential. There are three constitutional standing requirements. First, the plaintiff must allege that he or she has suffered or imminently will suffer an injury. Second, the plaintiff must allege that the injury is fairly traceable to the defendant's conduct. Third, the plaintiff must allege that a favorable federal court decision is likely to redress the injury. In addition to these constitutional requirements, the Court also has identified two major prudential standing principles. Unlike constitutional barriers, Congress may override prudential limits by statute. First, a party generally may assert only his or her own rights and cannot raise the claims of third parties not before the court. Second, a plaintiff may not sue as a taxpayer who shares a grievance in common with all other taxpayers.

i.   *Constitutional Standing Requirements*

The following two cases, Allen v. Wright and Massachusetts v. Environmental Protection Agency, are major rulings concerning the meaning of the three constitutional standing requirements: injury, causation, and redressability. In reading these cases, consider what types of injuries are sufficient for standing;

---

26. There is a rich literature on the standing doctrines. *See, e.g.,* Susan Bandes, *The Idea of a Case,* 42 Stan. L. Rev. 227 (1990); William A. Fletcher, *The Structure of Standing,* 98 Yale L.J. 221, 223 (1988).

what must a plaintiff allege in order to meet the causation and redressability requirements? Underlying these cases is the question of whether the standing doctrine is appropriately applied to properly limit the role of the federal judiciary or whether the Court has unduly prevented the federal courts from fulfilling their responsibility of enforcing the Constitution and federal laws.

ALLEN v. WRIGHT
468 U.S. 737 (1984)

Justice O'CONNOR delivered the opinion of the Court.

Parents of black public school children allege in this nation-wide class action that the Internal Revenue Service (IRS) has not adopted sufficient standards and procedures to fulfill its obligation to deny tax-exempt status to racially discriminatory private schools. They assert that the IRS thereby harms them directly and interferes with the ability of their children to receive an education in desegregated public schools. The issue before us is whether plaintiffs have standing to bring this suit. We hold that they do not.

I

The IRS denies tax-exempt status under the Internal Revenue Code, and hence eligibility to receive charitable contributions deductible from income taxes to racially discriminatory private schools. The IRS policy requires that a school applying for tax-exempt status show that it "admits the students of any race to all the rights, privileges, programs, and activities generally accorded or made available to students at that school and that the school does not discriminate on the basis of race in administration of its educational policies, admissions policies, scholarship and loan programs, and athletic and other school-administered programs." To carry out this policy, the IRS has established guidelines and procedures for determining whether a particular school is in fact racially nondiscriminatory. Failure to comply with the guidelines "will ordinarily result in the proposed revocation of" tax-exempt status.

In 1976 respondents challenged these guidelines and procedures in a suit filed in Federal District Court against the Secretary of the Treasury and the Commissioner of Internal Revenue. The plaintiffs named in the complaint are parents of black children who, at the time the complaint was filed, were attending public schools in seven States in school districts undergoing desegregation. They brought this nationwide class action "on behalf of themselves and their children, and . . . on behalf of all other parents of black children attending public school systems undergoing, or which may in the future undergo, desegregation pursuant to court order [or] HEW regulations and guidelines, under state law, or voluntarily." They estimated that the class they seek to represent includes several million persons.

Respondents allege in their complaint that many racially segregated private schools were created or expanded in their communities at the time the public schools were undergoing desegregation. According to the complaint, many such private schools, including 17 schools or school systems identified by name in the complaint (perhaps some 30 schools in all), receive tax exemptions either directly or through the tax-exempt status of "umbrella" organizations that operate or support the schools. Respondents allege that the challenged Government conduct harms them in two ways. The challenged conduct

> (a) constitutes tangible federal financial aid and other support for racially segregated educational institutions, and
> (b) fosters and encourages the organization, operation and expansion of institutions providing racially segregated educational opportunities for white children avoiding attendance in desegregating public school districts and thereby interferes with the efforts of federal courts, HEW and local school authorities to desegregate public school districts which have been operating racially dual school systems.

Thus, respondents do not allege that their children have been the victims of discriminatory exclusion from the schools whose tax exemptions they challenge as unlawful. Indeed, they have not alleged at any stage of this litigation that their children have ever applied or would ever apply to any private school. Rather, respondents claim a direct injury from the mere fact of the challenged Government conduct and, as indicated by the restriction of the plaintiff class to parents of children in desegregating school districts, injury to their children's opportunity to receive a desegregated education. The latter injury is traceable to the IRS grant of tax exemptions to racially discriminatory schools, respondents allege, chiefly because contributions to such schools are deductible from income taxes under §§170(a)(1) and (c)(2) of the Internal Revenue Code and the "deductions facilitate the raising of funds to organize new schools and expand existing schools in order to accommodate white students avoiding attendance in desegregating public school districts."

II

A

Article III of the Constitution confines the federal courts to adjudicating actual "cases" and "controversies." As the Court explained in Valley Forge Christian College v. Americans United for Separation of Church and State, Inc. (1982), the "case or controversy" requirement defines with respect to the Judicial Branch the idea of separation of powers on which the Federal Government is founded. The several doctrines that have grown up to elaborate that requirement are "founded in concern about the proper—and properly limited—role of the courts in a democratic society." Warth v. Seldin (1975). The case-or-controversy doctrines state fundamental limits on federal judicial power in our system of government.

The Art. III doctrine that requires a litigant to have "standing" to invoke the power of a federal court is perhaps the most important of these doctrines. "In essence the question of standing is whether the litigant is entitled to have the court decide the merits of the dispute or of particular issues." Standing doctrine embraces several judicially self-imposed limits on the exercise of federal jurisdiction, such as the general prohibition on a litigant's raising another person's legal rights, the rule barring adjudication of generalized grievances more appropriately addressed in the representative branches, and the requirement that a plaintiff's complaint fall within the zone of interests protected by the law invoked. The requirement of standing, however, has a core component derived directly from the Constitution. A plaintiff must allege personal injury fairly traceable to the defendant's allegedly unlawful conduct and likely to be redressed by the requested relief.

Like the prudential component, the constitutional component of standing doctrine incorporates concepts concededly not susceptible of precise definition. The injury alleged must be, for example, "'distinct and palpable,'" and not "abstract" or "conjectural" or "hypothetical." The injury must be "fairly" traceable to the challenged action, and relief from the injury must be "likely" to follow from a favorable decision. These terms cannot be defined so as to make application of the constitutional standing requirement a mechanical exercise.

More important, the law of Art. III standing is built on a single basic idea— the idea of separation of powers. It is this fact which makes possible the gradual clarification of the law through judicial application. Of course, both federal and state courts have long experience in applying and elaborating in numerous contexts the pervasive and fundamental notion of separation of powers.

Determining standing in a particular case may be facilitated by clarifying principles or even clear rules developed in prior cases. Typically, however, the standing inquiry requires careful judicial examination of a complaint's allegations to ascertain whether the particular plaintiff is entitled to an adjudication of the particular claims asserted. Is the injury too abstract, or otherwise not appropriate, to be considered judicially cognizable? Is the line of causation between the illegal conduct and injury too attenuated? Is the prospect of obtaining relief from the injury as a result of a favorable ruling too speculative? These questions and any others relevant to the standing inquiry must be answered by reference to the Art. III notion that federal courts may exercise power only "in the last resort, and as a necessity," and only when adjudication is "consistent with a system of separated powers and [the dispute is one] traditionally thought to be capable of resolution through the judicial process."

B

Respondents allege two injuries in their complaint to support their standing to bring this lawsuit. First, they say that they are harmed directly by the mere fact of Government financial aid to discriminatory private schools. Second, they say that the federal tax exemptions to racially discriminatory private schools in their communities impair their ability to have their public schools desegregated.

We conclude that neither suffices to support respondents' standing. The first fails under clear precedents of this Court because it does not constitute judicially cognizable injury. The second fails because the alleged injury is not fairly traceable to the assertedly unlawful conduct of the IRS.[27]

---

27. The "fairly traceable" and "redressability" components of the constitutional standing inquiry were initially articulated by this Court as "two facets of a single causation requirement." To the extent there is a difference, it is that the former examines the causal connection between the assertedly unlawful conduct and the alleged injury and the judicial relief requested. Cases such as this, in which the relief requested goes well beyond the violation of law alleged, illustrate why it is important to keep the inquiries separate if the "redressability" component is to focus on the requested relief. Even if the relief respondents request might have a substantial effect on the desegregation of public schools, whatever deficiencies exist in the opportunities for desegregated education for respondents' children might not be traceable to IRS violations of law — grants of tax exemptions to racially discriminatory schools in respondents' communities. [Footnote by the Court.]

Respondents' first claim of injury can be interpreted in two ways. It might be a claim simply to have the Government avoid the violation of law alleged in respondents' complaint. Alternatively, it might be a claim of stigmatic injury, or denigration, suffered by all members of a racial group when the Government discriminates on the basis of race. Under neither interpretation is this claim of injury judicially cognizable.

This Court has repeatedly held that an asserted right to have the Government act in accordance with law is not sufficient, standing alone, to confer jurisdiction on a federal court. In Schlesinger v. Reservists Committee to Stop the War (1974), for example, the Court rejected a claim of citizen standing to challenge Armed Forces Reserve commissions held by Members of Congress as violating the Incompatibility Clause of Art. I, §6, of the Constitution. As citizens, the Court held, plaintiffs alleged nothing but "the abstract injury in nonobservance of the Constitution. . . ." More recently, in Valley Forge, supra, we rejected a claim of standing to challenge a Government conveyance of property to a religious institution. Insofar as the plaintiffs relied simply on "their shared individuated right" to a Government that made no law respecting an establishment of religion, we held that plaintiffs had not alleged a judicially cognizable injury. "[A]ssertion of a right to a particular kind of Government conduct, which the Government has violated by acting differently, cannot alone satisfy the requirements of Art. III without draining those requirements of meaning." Respondents here have no standing to complain simply that their Government is violating the law.

Neither do they have standing to litigate their claims based on the stigmatizing injury often caused by racial discrimination. There can be no doubt that this sort of noneconomic injury is one of the most serious consequences of discriminatory government action and is sufficient in some circumstances to support standing. Our cases make clear, however, that such injury accords a basis for standing only to "those persons who are personally denied equal treatment" by the challenged discriminatory conduct.

The consequences of recognizing respondents' standing on the basis of their first claim of injury illustrate why our cases plainly hold that such injury is not judicially cognizable. If the abstract stigmatic injury were cognizable, standing would extend nationwide to all members of the particular racial groups against which the Government was alleged to be discriminating by its grant of a tax exemption to a racially discriminatory school, regardless of the location of that school. All such persons could claim the same sort of abstract stigmatic injury respondents assert in their first claim of injury. A black person in Hawaii could challenge the grant of a tax exemption to a racially discriminatory school in Maine. Recognition of standing in such circumstances would transform the federal courts into "no more than a vehicle for the vindication of the value interests of concerned bystanders." United States v. SCRAP (1973). Constitutional limits on the role of the federal courts preclude such a transformation.

It is in their complaint's second claim of injury that respondents allege harm to a concrete, personal interest that can support standing in some circumstances. The injury they identify — their children's diminished ability to receive an education in a racially integrated school — is, beyond any doubt, not only judicially cognizable but, one of the most serious injuries recognized in our legal system. Despite the constitutional importance of curing the injury alleged by respondents, however, the federal judiciary may not redress it unless standing requirements are met. In this case, respondents' second claim of injury cannot support standing because the injury alleged is not fairly traceable to the Government conduct respondents challenge as unlawful.

The illegal conduct challenged by respondents is the IRS's grant of tax exemptions to some racially discriminatory schools. The line of causation between that conduct and desegregation of respondents' schools is attenuated at best. From the perspective of the IRS, the injury to respondents is highly indirect and "results from the independent action of some third party not before the court."

The diminished ability of respondents' children to receive a desegregated education would be fairly traceable to unlawful IRS grants of tax exemptions only if there were enough racially discriminatory private schools receiving tax exemptions in respondents' communities for withdrawal of those exemptions to make an appreciable difference in public school integration. Respondents have made no such allegation. It is, first, uncertain how many racially discriminatory private schools are in fact receiving tax exemptions. Moreover, it is entirely speculative, as respondents themselves conceded in the Court of Appeals, whether withdrawal of a tax exemption from any particular school would lead the school to change its policies. It is just as speculative whether any given parent of a child attending such a private school would decide to transfer the child to public school as a result of any changes in educational or financial policy made by the private school once it was threatened with loss of tax-exempt status. It is also pure speculation whether, in a particular community, a large enough number of the numerous relevant school officials and parents would reach decisions that collectively would have a significant impact on the racial composition of the public schools.

The links in the chain of causation between the challenged Government conduct and the asserted injury are far too weak for the chain as a whole to sustain respondents' standing. In Simon v. Eastern Kentucky Welfare Rights Org., the Court held that standing to challenge a Government grant of a tax exemption to hospitals could not be founded on the asserted connection between the grant of tax-exempt status and the hospitals' policy concerning the provision of medical services to indigents. The causal connection depended on the decisions hospitals would make in response to withdrawal of tax-exempt status, and those decisions were sufficiently uncertain to break the chain of causation between the plaintiffs' injury and the challenged Government action. The chain of causation is even weaker in this case. It involves numerous third parties (officials of racially discriminatory schools receiving tax exemptions and the parents of children attending such schools) who may not even exist in respondents' communities and whose independent decisions may not collectively have a significant effect on the ability of public school students to receive a desegregated education.

The idea of separation of powers that underlies standing doctrine explains why our cases preclude the conclusion that respondents' alleged injury "fairly can be traced to the challenged action" of the IRS. That conclusion would pave the way generally for suits challenging, not specifically identifiable Government violations of law, but the particular programs agencies establish to carry out their legal obligations. Such suits, even when premised on allegations of several instances of violations of law, are rarely if ever appropriate for federal-court adjudication.

When transported into the Art. III context, that principle, grounded as it is in the idea of separation of powers, counsels against recognizing standing in a case brought, not to enforce specific legal obligations whose violation works a direct harm, but to seek a restructuring of the apparatus established by the Executive Branch to fulfill its legal duties. The Constitution, after all, assigns to the Executive Branch, and not to the Judicial Branch, the duty to "take Care that the Laws be faithfully executed." U.S. Const., Art. II, §3. We could not recognize respondents' standing in this case without running afoul of that structural principle.

Justice STEVENS, with whom Justice BLACKMUN joins, dissenting. Three propositions are clear to me: (1) respondents have adequately alleged "injury in fact"; (2) their injury is fairly traceable to the conduct that they claim to be unlawful; and (3) the "separation of powers" principle does not create a jurisdictional obstacle to the consideration of the merits of their claim.

I

Respondents, the parents of black school-children, have alleged that their children are unable to attend fully desegregated schools because large numbers of white children in the areas in which respondents reside attend private schools which do not admit minority children. This kind of injury may be actionable whether it is caused by the exclusion of black children from public schools or by an official policy of encouraging white children to attend nonpublic schools. A subsidy for the withdrawal of a white child can have the same effect as a penalty for admitting a black child.

II

In final analysis, the wrong respondents allege that the Government has committed is to subsidize the exodus of white children from schools that would otherwise be racially integrated. The critical question in these cases, therefore, is whether respondents have alleged that the Government has created that kind of subsidy.

In answering that question, we must of course assume that respondents can prove what they have alleged. Furthermore, at this stage of the litigation we must put to one side all questions about the appropriateness of a nationwide class action. The controlling issue is whether the causal connection between the injury and the wrong has been adequately alleged.

We have held that when a subsidy makes a given activity more or less expensive, injury can be fairly traced to the subsidy for purposes of standing analysis because of the resulting increase or decrease in the ability to engage in the activity. Indeed, we have employed exactly this causation analysis in the same context at issue here — subsidies given private schools that practice racial discrimination.

This causation analysis is nothing more than a restatement of elementary economics: when something becomes more expensive, less of it will be purchased. Sections 170 and 501(c)(3) are premised on that recognition. If racially discriminatory private schools lose the "cash grants" that flow from the operation of the statutes, the education they provide will become more expensive and hence less of their services will be purchased. Conversely, maintenance of these tax benefits makes an education in segregated private schools relatively more attractive, by decreasing its cost. Accordingly, without tax-exempt status, private schools will either not be competitive in terms of cost, or have to change their admissions policies, hence reducing their competitiveness for parents seeking "a racially segregated alternative" to public schools, which is what respondents have alleged many white parents in desegregating school districts seek.

III

Considerations of tax policy, economics, and pure logic all confirm the conclusion that respondents' injury in fact is fairly traceable to the Government's allegedly wrongful conduct. The Court therefore is forced to introduce the concept of "separation of powers" into its analysis. The Court writes that the separation of powers "explains why our cases preclude the conclusion" that respondents' injury is fairly traceable to the conduct they challenge.

The Court could mean one of three things by its invocation of the separation of powers. First, it could simply be expressing the idea that if the plaintiff lacks Art. III standing to bring a lawsuit, then there is no "case or controversy" within the meaning of Art. III and hence the matter is not within the area of responsibility assigned to the Judiciary by the Constitution. While there can be no quarrel with this proposition, in itself it provides no guidance for determining if the injury respondents have alleged is fairly traceable to the conduct they have challenged.

Second, the Court could be saying that it will require a more direct causal connection when it is troubled by the separation of powers implications of the case before it. That approach confuses the standing doctrine with the justiciability of the issues that respondents seek to raise. The purpose of the standing inquiry is to measure the plaintiff's stake in the outcome, not whether a court has the authority to provide it with the outcome it seeks.

Third, the Court could be saying that it will not treat as legally cognizable injuries that stem from an administrative decision concerning how enforcement resources will be allocated. This surely is an important point. Respondents do seek to restructure the IRS's mechanisms for enforcing the legal requirement that discriminatory institutions not receive tax-exempt status. Such restructuring would dramatically affect the way in which the IRS exercises its prosecutorial discretion. The Executive requires latitude to decide how best to enforce the law, and in general the Court may well be correct that the exercise of that discretion, especially in the tax context, is unchallengeable.

However, as the Court also recognizes, this principle does not apply when suit is brought "to enforce specific legal obligations whose violation works a direct harm." For example, despite the fact that they were challenging the methods used by the Executive to enforce the law, citizens were accorded standing to challenge a pattern of police misconduct that violated the constitutional constraints on law enforcement activities in Allee v. Medrano (1974). Here, respondents contend that the IRS is violating a specific constitutional limitation on its enforcement discretion. There is a solid basis for that contention.

MASSACHUSETTS v. ENVIRONMENTAL PROTECTION AGENCY

549 U.S. 497 (2007)

Justice Stevens delivered the opinion of the Court.

A well-documented rise in global temperatures has coincided with a significant increase in the concentration of carbon dioxide in the atmosphere. Respected scientists believe the two trends are related. For when carbon dioxide is released into the atmosphere, it acts like the ceiling of a greenhouse, trapping solar energy and retarding the escape of reflected heat. It is therefore a species — the most important species — of a "greenhouse gas."

Calling global warming "the most pressing environmental challenge of our time," a group of States, local governments, and private organizations, alleged in a petition for certiorari that the Environmental Protection Agency (EPA) has abdicated its responsibility under the Clean Air Act to regulate the emissions of four greenhouse gases, including carbon dioxide. Specifically, petitioners asked us to answer two questions concerning the meaning of §202(a)(1) of the Act: whether EPA has the statutory authority to regulate greenhouse gas emissions from new motor vehicles; and if so, whether its stated reasons for refusing to do so are consistent with the statute.

In response, EPA, supported by 10 intervening States and six trade associations, correctly argued that we may not address those two questions unless at least one petitioner has standing to invoke our jurisdiction under Article III of the Constitution.

Article III of the Constitution limits federal-court jurisdiction to "Cases" and "Controversies." Those two words confine "the business of federal courts to questions presented in an adversary context and in a form historically viewed as capable of resolution through the judicial process." The parties' dispute turns on the proper construction of a congressional statute, a question eminently suitable to resolution in federal court. Congress has moreover authorized this type of challenge to EPA action. See 42 U.S.C. §7607(b)(1). That authorization is of critical importance to the standing inquiry: "Congress has the power to define injuries and articulate chains of causation that will give rise to a case or controversy where none existed before." "In exercising this power, however, Congress must at the very least identify the injury it seeks to vindicate and relate the injury to the class of persons entitled to bring suit." We will not, therefore, "entertain citizen suits to vindicate the public's nonconcrete interest in the proper administration of the laws."

EPA maintains that because greenhouse gas emissions inflict widespread harm, the doctrine of standing presents an insuperable jurisdictional obstacle. We do not agree. At bottom, "the gist of the question of standing" is whether petitioners have "such a personal stake in the outcome of the controversy as to assure that concrete adverseness which sharpens the presentation of issues upon which the court so largely depends for illumination." *Baker v. Carr* (1962).

To ensure the proper adversarial presentation, *Lujan v. Defenders of Wildlife* (1992) holds that a litigant must demonstrate that it has suffered a concrete and particularized injury that is either actual or imminent, that the injury is fairly traceable to the defendant, and that it is likely that a favorable decision will redress that injury. However, a litigant to whom Congress has "accorded a procedural right to protect his concrete interests," — here, the right to challenge agency action unlawfully withheld, §7607(b)(1) — "can assert that right without meeting all the normal standards for redressability and immediacy." When a litigant is vested with a procedural right, that litigant has standing if there is some possibility that the requested relief will prompt the injury-causing party to reconsider the decision that allegedly harmed the litigant.

Only one of the petitioners needs to have standing to permit us to consider the petition for review. We stress here, the special position and interest of Massachusetts. It is of considerable relevance that the party seeking review here is a sovereign State and not, as it was in *Lujan*, a private individual.

Well before the creation of the modern administrative state, we recognized that States are not normal litigants for the purposes of invoking federal jurisdiction. That Massachusetts does in fact own a great deal of the "territory alleged to be affected" only reinforces the conclusion that its stake in the outcome of this case is sufficiently concrete to warrant the exercise of federal judicial power.

When a State enters the Union, it surrenders certain sovereign prerogatives. Massachusetts cannot invade Rhode Island to force reductions in greenhouse gas emissions, it cannot negotiate an emissions treaty with China or India, and in some circumstances the exercise of its police powers to reduce in-state motor-vehicle emissions might well be pre-empted.

These sovereign prerogatives are now lodged in the Federal Government, and Congress has ordered EPA to protect Massachusetts (among others) by prescribing standards applicable to the "emission of any air pollutant from any class or classes of new motor vehicle engines, which in [the Administrator's] judgment cause, or contribute to, air pollution which may reasonably be anticipated to endanger public health or welfare." Congress has moreover recognized a concomitant procedural right to challenge the rejection of its rulemaking petition as arbitrary and capricious. Given that procedural right and Massachusetts' stake in protecting its quasi-sovereign interests, the Commonwealth is entitled to special solicitude in our standing analysis.

With that in mind, it is clear that petitioners' submissions as they pertain to Massachusetts have satisfied the most demanding standards of the adversarial process. EPA's steadfast refusal to regulate greenhouse gas emissions presents a risk of harm to Massachusetts that is both "actual" and "imminent." There is, moreover, a "substantial likelihood that the judicial relief requested" will prompt EPA to take steps to reduce that risk.

The Injury

The harms associated with climate change are serious and well recognized. Indeed, the NRC Report itself—which EPA regards as an "objective and independent assessment of the relevant science[]," — identifies a number of environmental changes that have already inflicted significant harms, including "the global retreat of mountain glaciers, reduction in snow-cover extent, the earlier spring melting of rivers and lakes, [and] the accelerated rate of rise of sea levels during the 20th century relative to the past few thousand years. . . ."

Petitioners allege that this only hints at the environmental damage yet to come. According to the climate scientist Michael MacCracken, "qualified scientific experts involved in climate change research" have reached a "strong consensus" that global warming threatens (among other things) a precipitate rise in sea levels by the end of the century, "severe and irreversible changes to natural ecosystems," a "significant reduction in water storage in winter snowpack in mountainous regions with direct and important economic consequences," and an increase in the spread of disease. He also observes that rising ocean temperatures may contribute to the ferocity of hurricanes.

That these climate-change risks are "widely shared" does not minimize Massachusetts' interest in the outcome of this litigation. The severity of that injury will only increase over the course of the next century: If sea levels continue to rise as predicted, one Massachusetts official believes that a significant fraction of coastal property will be "either permanently lost through inundation or temporarily lost through periodic storm surge and flooding events." Remediation costs alone, petitioners allege, could run well into the hundreds of millions of dollars.

Causation

EPA does not dispute the existence of a causal connection between man-made greenhouse gas emissions and global warming. At a minimum, therefore, EPA's refusal to regulate such emissions "contributes" to Massachusetts' injuries.

EPA nevertheless maintains that its decision not to regulate greenhouse gas emissions from new motor vehicles contributes so insignificantly to petitioners' injuries that the agency cannot be haled into federal court to answer for them. For the same reason, EPA does not believe that any realistic possibility exists that the relief petitioners seek would mitigate global climate change and remedy their injuries. That is especially so because predicted increases in greenhouse gas emissions from developing nations, particularly China and India, are likely to offset any marginal domestic decrease.

But EPA overstates its case. Its argument rests on the erroneous assumption that a small incremental step, because it is incremental, can never be attacked in a federal judicial forum. Yet accepting that premise would doom most challenges to regulatory action. Agencies, like legislatures, do not generally resolve massive problems in one fell regulatory swoop. They instead whittle away at them over time, refining their preferred approach as circumstances change and as they develop a more-nuanced understanding of how best to proceed. That a first step might be tentative does not by itself support the notion that federal courts lack jurisdiction to determine whether that step conforms to law.

And reducing domestic automobile emissions is hardly a tentative step. Even leaving aside the other greenhouse gases, the United States transportation sector emits an enormous quantity of carbon dioxide into the atmosphere—according to the MacCracken affidavit, more than 1.7 billion metric tons in 1999 alone. That accounts for more than 6% of worldwide carbon dioxide emissions. To put this in perspective: Considering just emissions from the transportation sector, which represent less than one-third of this country's total carbon dioxide emissions, the United States would still rank as the third-largest emitter of carbon dioxide in the world, outpaced only by the European Union and China. Judged by any standard, U.S. motor-vehicle emissions make a meaningful contribution to greenhouse gas concentrations and hence, according to petitioners, to global warming.

THE REMEDY

While it may be true that regulating motor-vehicle emissions will not by itself reverse global warming, it by no means follows that we lack jurisdiction to decide whether EPA has a duty to take steps to slow or reduce it. Because of the enormity of the potential consequences associated with man-made climate change, the fact that the effectiveness of a remedy might be delayed during the (relatively short) time it takes for a new motor-vehicle fleet to replace an older one is essentially irrelevant. Nor is it dispositive that developing countries such as China and India are poised to increase greenhouse gas emissions substantially over the next century: A reduction in domestic emissions would slow the pace of global emissions increases, no matter what happens elsewhere.

[Justice Stevens then went on to hold that the EPA had statutory authority to promulgate regulations dealing with global warming and either had to do so or justify not doing so.]

Chief Justice ROBERTS, with whom Justice SCALIA, Justice THOMAS, and Justice ALITO join, dissenting.

Global warming may be a "crisis," even "the most pressing environmental problem of our time." Indeed, it may ultimately affect nearly everyone on the planet in some potentially adverse way, and it may be that governments have done too little to address it. It is not a problem, however, that has escaped the attention of policymakers in the Executive and Legislative Branches of our Government, who continue to consider regulatory, legislative, and treaty-based means of addressing global climate change.

Apparently dissatisfied with the pace of progress on this issue in the elected branches, petitioners have come to the courts claiming broad-ranging injury, and attempting to tie that injury to the Government's alleged failure to comply with a rather narrow statutory provision. I would reject these challenges as non-justiciable. Such a conclusion involves no judgment on whether global warming exists, what causes it, or the extent of the problem. Nor does it render petitioners without recourse. This Court's standing jurisprudence simply recognizes that redress of grievances of the sort at issue here "is the function of Congress and the Chief Executive," not the federal courts.

I

Our modern framework for addressing standing is familiar: "A plaintiff must allege personal injury fairly traceable to the defendant's allegedly unlawful conduct and likely to be redressed by the requested relief." Applying that standard here, petitioners bear the burden of alleging an injury that is fairly traceable to the Environmental Protection Agency's failure to promulgate new motor vehicle greenhouse gas emission standards, and that is likely to be redressed by the prospective issuance of such standards.

Before determining whether petitioners can meet this familiar test, however, the Court changes the rules. It asserts that "States are not normal litigants for the purposes of invoking federal jurisdiction," and that given "Massachusetts' stake in protecting its quasi-sovereign interests, the Commonwealth is entitled to special solicitude in our standing analysis."

Relaxing Article III standing requirements because asserted injuries are pressed by a State, however, has no basis in our jurisprudence, and support for any such "special solicitude" is conspicuously absent from the Court's opinion.

II

It is not at all clear how the Court's "special solicitude" for Massachusetts plays out in the standing analysis, except as an implicit concession that petitioners cannot establish standing on traditional terms. But the status of Massachusetts as a State cannot compensate for petitioners' failure to demonstrate injury in fact, causation, and redressability.

When the Court actually applies the three-part test, it focuses on the State's asserted loss of coastal land as the injury in fact. If petitioners rely on loss of land as the Article III injury, however, they must ground the rest of the standing analysis in that specific injury. That alleged injury must be "concrete and particularized," and "distinct and palpable." Central to this concept of "particularized" injury is the requirement that a plaintiff be affected in a "personal and individual way," and seek relief that "directly and tangibly benefits him" in a manner distinct from its impact on "the public at large."

The very concept of global warming seems inconsistent with this particularization requirement. Global warming is a phenomenon "harmful to humanity at large," and the redress petitioners seek is focused no more on them than on the public generally — it is literally to change the atmosphere around the world.

If petitioners' particularized injury is loss of coastal land, it is also that injury that must be "actual or imminent, not conjectural or hypothetical," "real and immediate," and "certainly impending."

As to "actual" injury, the Court observes that "global sea levels rose somewhere between 10 and 20 centimeters over the 20th century as a result of global warming" and that "[t]hese rising seas have already begun to swallow Massachusetts' coastal land." But none of petitioners' declarations supports that connection. One declaration states that "a rise in sea level due to climate change is occurring on the coast of Massachusetts, in the metropolitan Boston area," but there is no elaboration. And the declarant goes on to identify a "significan[t]" non-global-warming cause of Boston's rising sea level: land subsidence. Thus, aside from a single conclusory statement, there is nothing in petitioners' 43 standing declarations and accompanying exhibits to support an inference of actual loss of Massachusetts coastal land from 20th century global sea level increases. It is pure conjecture.

The Court's attempts to identify "imminent" or "certainly impending" loss of Massachusetts coastal land fares no better. One of petitioners' declarants predicts global warming will cause sea level to rise by 20 to 70 centimeters *by the year 2100.* Another uses a computer modeling program to map the Commonwealth's coastal land and its current elevation, and calculates that the high-end estimate of sea level rise would result in the loss of significant state-owned coastal land. But the computer modeling program has a conceded average error of about 30 centimeters and a maximum observed error of 70 centimeters. As an initial matter, if it is possible that the model underrepresents the elevation of coastal land to an extent equal to or in excess of the projected sea level rise, it is difficult to put much stock in the predicted loss of land. But even placing that problem to the side, accepting a century-long time horizon and a series of compounded estimates renders requirements of imminence and immediacy utterly toothless. "Allegations of possible future injury do not satisfy the requirements of Art. III. A threatened injury must be certainly impending to constitute injury in fact."

III

Petitioners' reliance on Massachusetts's loss of coastal land as their injury in fact for standing purposes creates insurmountable problems for them with respect to causation and redressability. To establish standing, petitioners must show a causal connection between that specific injury and the lack of new motor vehicle greenhouse gas emission standards, and that the promulgation of such standards would likely redress that injury. As is often the case, the questions of causation and redressability overlap. And importantly, when a party is challenging the Government's allegedly unlawful regulation, or lack of regulation, of a third party, satisfying the causation and redressability requirements becomes "substantially more difficult."

Petitioners view the relationship between their injuries and EPA's failure to promulgate new motor vehicle greenhouse gas emission standards as simple and direct: Domestic motor vehicles emit carbon dioxide and other greenhouse gases. Worldwide emissions of greenhouse gases contribute to global warming and therefore also to petitioners' alleged injuries. Without the new vehicle standards, greenhouse gas emissions — and therefore global warming and its attendant harms — have been higher than they otherwise would have been; once EPA changes course, the trend will be reversed.

The Court ignores the complexities of global warming, and does so by now disregarding the "particularized" injury it relied on in step one, and using the dire nature of global warming itself as a bootstrap for finding causation and redressability. First, it is important to recognize the extent of the emissions at issue here. Because local greenhouse gas emissions disperse throughout the atmosphere and remain there for anywhere from 50 to 200 years, it is global emissions data that are relevant. According to one of petitioners' declarations, domestic motor vehicles contribute about 6 percent of global carbon dioxide emissions and 4 percent of global greenhouse gas emissions. The amount of global emissions at issue here is smaller still; §202(a)(1) of the Clean Air Act covers only *new* motor vehicles and *new* motor vehicle engines, so petitioners' desired emission standards might reduce only a fraction of 4 percent of global emissions.

This gets us only to the relevant greenhouse gas emissions; linking them to global warming and ultimately to petitioners' alleged injuries next requires consideration of further complexities.

Petitioners are never able to trace their alleged injuries back through this complex web to the fractional amount of global emissions that might have been limited with EPA standards. In light of the bit-part domestic new motor vehicle greenhouse gas emissions have played in what petitioners describe as a 150-year global phenomenon, and the myriad additional factors bearing on petitioners' alleged injury — the loss of Massachusetts coastal land — the connection is far too speculative to establish causation.

IV

Redressability is even more problematic. To the tenuous link between petitioners' alleged injury and the indeterminate fractional domestic emissions at issue here, add the fact that petitioners cannot meaningfully predict what will come of the 80 percent of global greenhouse gas emissions that originate outside the United States. As the Court acknowledges, "developing countries such as China and India are poised to increase greenhouse gas emissions substantially over the next century," so the domestic emissions at issue here may become an increasingly marginal portion of global emissions, and any decreases produced by petitioners' desired standards are likely to be overwhelmed many times over by emissions increases elsewhere in the world.

The Court's sleight-of-hand is in failing to link up the different elements of the three-part standing test. What must be likely to be redressed is the particular injury in fact. The injury the Court looks to is the asserted loss of land. The Court contends that regulating domestic motor vehicle emissions will reduce carbon dioxide in the atmosphere, and therefore redress Massachusetts's injury. But even if regulation does reduce emissions — to some indeterminate degree, given events elsewhere in the world — the Court never explains why that makes it likely that the injury in fact — the loss of land — will be redressed. School-children know that a kingdom might be lost "all for the want of a horseshoe nail," but "likely" redressability is a different matter. The realities make it pure conjecture to suppose that EPA regulation of new automobile emissions will likely prevent the loss of Massachusetts coastal land.

The good news is that the Court's "special solicitude" for Massachusetts limits the future applicability of the diluted standing requirements applied in this case. The bad news is that the Court's self-professed relaxation of these Article III requirements has caused us to transgress "the proper — and properly limited — role of the courts in a democratic society."

I respectfully dissent.

NOTES ON CONSTITUTIONAL STANDING REQUIREMENTS: INJURY, CAUSATION, AND REDRESSABILITY

Injury

In both of these cases, the Supreme Court emphasizes that injury is a core requirement of Article III in order for there to be a case or controversy. The cases discuss, at length, what types of injuries are sufficient to meet the standing requirement. The cases also are clear that it must be an injury that the plaintiff personally has suffered or imminently will suffer. In connection with this requirement, consider the following two cases, in which the Supreme Court rejected standing on the ground that the plaintiff failed to adequately demonstrate a personally suffered injury. In each, consider whether you agree with the Court's conclusion that the injury requirement was not fulfilled. Compare these cases to the third decision in which the Court found standing.

CITY OF LOS ANGELES v. LYONS, 461 U.S. 95 (1983): Justice WHITE delivered the opinion of the court:

Adolph Lyons filed a complaint for damages, injunction, and declaratory relief against the City of Los Angeles and four of its police officers. The complaint alleged that on October 6, 1976, at 2 A.M., Lyons was stopped by the defendant officers for a traffic or vehicle code violation and that although Lyons offered no resistance or threat whatsoever, the officers, without provocation or justification, seized Lyons and applied a "chokehold" rendering him unconscious and causing damage to his larynx.

Originally, Lyons's complaint alleged that at least two deaths had occurred as a result of the application of chokeholds by the police. His first amended complaint alleged that 10 chokehold-related deaths had occurred. By May, 1982, there had been five more such deaths.

Lyons has failed to demonstrate a case or controversy with the City that would justify the equitable relief sought. Lyons's standing to seek the injunction requested depended on whether he was likely to suffer future injury from the use of the chokeholds by police officers. Count V of the complaint alleged the traffic stop and choking incident five months before. That Lyons may have been illegally choked by the police on October 6, 1976, while presumably affording Lyons standing to claim damages against the individual officers and perhaps against the City, does nothing to establish a real and immediate threat that he would again be stopped for a traffic violation, or for any other offense, by an officer or officers who would illegally choke him into unconsciousness without any provocation or resistance on his part. The additional allegation in the complaint that the police in Los Angeles routinely apply chokeholds in situations where they are not threatened by the use of deadly force falls far short of the allegations that would be necessary to establish a case or controversy between these parties.

In order to establish an actual controversy in this case, Lyons would have had not only to allege that he would have another encounter with the police but also to make the incredible assertion either, (1) that all police officers in Los Angeles always choke any citizen with whom they happen to have an encounter, whether for the purpose of arrest, issuing a citation or for questioning or, (2) that the City ordered or authorized police officers to act in such manner. Although Count V alleged that the City authorized the use of the control holds in situations where deadly force was not threatened, it did not indicate why Lyons might be realistically threatened by police officers who acted within the strictures of the City's policy. If, for example, chokeholds were authorized to be used only to counter resistance to an arrest by a suspect, or to thwart an effort to escape, any future threat to Lyons from the City's policy or from the conduct of police officers would be no more real than the possibility that he would again have an encounter with the police and that either he would illegally resist arrest or detention or the officers would disobey their instructions and again render him unconscious without any provocation.

Absent a sufficient likelihood that he will again be wronged in a similar way, Lyons is no more entitled to an injunction than any other citizen of Los Angeles; and a federal court may not entertain a claim by any or all citizens who no more than assert that certain practices of law enforcement officers are unconstitutional.

Justice MARSHALL, with whom Justice BRENNAN, Justice BLACKMUN, and Justice STEVENS join, dissenting.

The District Court found that the City of Los Angeles authorizes its police officers to apply life-threatening chokeholds to citizens who pose no threat of violence, and that respondent, Adolph Lyons, was subjected to such a choke-hold. The Court today holds that a federal court is without power to enjoin the enforcement of the City's policy, no matter how flagrantly unconstitutional it may be. Since no one can show that he will be choked in the future, no one — not even a person who, like Lyons, has almost been choked to death — has standing to challenge the continuation of the policy. The City is free to continue the policy indefinitely as long as it is willing to pay damages for the injuries and deaths that result. I dissent from this unprecedented and unwarranted approach to standing.

LUJAN v. DEFENDERS OF WILDLIFE, 504 U.S. 555 (1992): Justice SCALIA delivered the opinion of the court.

A challenge was brought to a rule promulgated by the Secretary of the Interior interpreting Section 7 of the Endangered Species Act concerning when the federal government could comply with the Endangered Species Act. Under the rule, the federal government would comply with the Act only for actions taken in the United States or on the high seas. Citizens brought a suit challenging the new regulation, having standing, in part, on a provision in the Act authorizing citizen standing.

Respondents' claim to injury is that the lack of consultation with respect to certain funded activities abroad "increas[es] the rate of extinction of endangered and threatened species." Of course, the desire to use or observe an animal species, even for purely esthetic purposes, is undeniably a cognizable interest for purpose of standing. "But the 'injury in fact' test requires more than an injury to a cognizable interest. It requires that the party seeking review be himself among the injured." To survive the Secretary's summary judgment motion, respondents had to submit affidavits or other evidence showing, through specific facts, not only that listed species were in fact being threatened by funded activities abroad, but also that one or more of respondents' members would thereby be "directly" affected apart from their "'special interest' in th[e] subject." With respect to this aspect of the case, the Court of Appeals focused on the affidavits of two Defenders' members — Joyce Kelly and Amy Skilbred. Ms. Kelly stated that she traveled to Egypt in 1986 and "observed the traditional habitat of the endangered [N]ile crocodile there and intend[s] to do so again, and hope[s] to observe the crocodile directly," and that she "will suffer harm in fact as the result of [the] American . . . role . . . in overseeing the rehabilitation of the Aswan High Dam on the Nile . . . and [in] develop[ing] . . . Egypt's . . . Master Water Plan." Ms. Skilbred averred that she traveled to Sri Lanka in 1981 and "observed th[e] habitat" of "endangered species such as the Asian elephant and the leopard" at what is now the site of the Mahaweli project funded by the Agency for International Development (AID), although she "was unable to see any of the endangered species"; "this development project," she continued, "will seriously reduce endangered, threatened, and endemic species habitat including areas that I visited . . . [, which] may severely shorten the future of these species"; that threat, she concluded, harmed her because she "intend[s] to return to Sri Lanka in the future and hope[s] to be more fortunate in spotting at least the endangered elephant and leopard." When Ms. Skilbred was asked at a subsequent deposition if and when she had any plans to return to Sri Lanka, she reiterated that "I intend to go back to Sri Lanka," but confessed that she had no current plans: "I don't know [when]. There is a civil war going on right now. I don't know. Not next year, I will say. In the future."

We shall assume for the sake of argument that these affidavits contain facts showing that certain agency-funded projects threaten listed species — though that is questionable. They plainly contain no facts, however, showing how damage to the species will produce "imminent" injury to Mses. Kelly and Skilbred. That the women "had visited" the areas of the projects before the projects commenced proves nothing. As we have said in a related context, "'Past exposure to illegal conduct does not in itself show a present case or controversy regarding injunctive relief . . . if unaccompanied by any continuing, present adverse effects.'" And the affiants' profession of an "inten[t]" to return to the places they had visited before — where they will presumably, this time, be deprived of the opportunity to observe animals of the endangered species — is simply not enough. Such "some day" intentions — without any description of concrete plans, or indeed even any specification of when the some day will be — do not support a finding of the "actual or imminent" injury that our cases require.

Besides relying upon the Kelly and Skilbred affidavits, respondents propose a series of novel standing theories. The first, inelegantly styled "ecosystem nexus," proposes that any person who uses any part of a "contiguous ecosystem" adversely affected by a funded activity has standing even if the activity is located a great distance away. This approach is inconsistent with our opinion in *National Wildlife Federation*, which held that a plaintiff claiming injury from environmental damage must use the area affected by the challenged activity and not an area roughly "in the vicinity" of it. It makes no difference that the general-purpose section of the ESA states that the Act was intended in part "to provide a means whereby the ecosystems upon which endangered species and threatened species depend may be conserved." To say that the Act protects ecosystems is not to say that the Act creates (if it were possible) rights of action in persons who have not been injured in fact, that is, persons who use portions of an ecosystem not perceptibly affected by the unlawful action in question.

Respondents' other theories are called, alas, the "animal nexus" approach, whereby anyone who has an interest in studying or seeing the endangered animals anywhere on the globe has standing; and the "vocational nexus" approach, under which anyone with a professional interest in such animals can sue. Under these theories, anyone who goes to see Asian elephants in the Bronx Zoo, and anyone who is a keeper of Asian elephants in the Bronx Zoo, has standing to sue because the Director of the Agency for International Development (AID) did not consult with the Secretary regarding the AID-funded project in Sri Lanka. This is beyond all reason. Standing is not "an ingenious academic exercise in the conceivable," but as we have said requires, at the summary judgment stage, a factual showing of perceptible harm. It is clear that the person who observes or works with a particular animal threatened by a federal decision is facing perceptible harm, since the very subject of his interest will no longer exist. It is even plausible — though it goes to the outermost limit of plausibility — to think that a person who observes or works with animals of a particular species in the very area of the world where that species is threatened by a federal decision is facing such harm, since some animals that might have been the subject of his interest will no longer exist. It goes beyond the limit, however, and into pure speculation and fantasy, to say that anyone who observes or works with an endangered species, anywhere in the world, is appreciably harmed by a single project affecting some portion of that species with which he has no more specific connection.

Besides failing to show injury, respondents failed to demonstrate redressability. Instead of attacking the separate decisions to fund particular projects allegedly causing them harm, respondents chose to challenge a more generalized level of Government action (rules regarding consultation), the invalidation of which would affect all overseas projects. This programmatic approach has obvious practical advantages, but also obvious difficulties insofar as proof of causation or redressability is concerned. As we have said in another context, "suits challenging, not specifically identifiable Government violations of law, but the particular programs agencies establish to carry out their legal obligations . . . [are], even when premised on allegations of several instances of violations of law, . . . rarely if ever appropriate for federal-court adjudication." Allen v. Wright.

The most obvious problem in the present case is redressability. Since the agencies funding the projects were not parties to the case, the District Court could accord relief only against the Secretary: He could be ordered to revise his regulation to require consultation for foreign projects. But this would not remedy respondents' alleged injury unless the funding agencies were bound by the Secretary's regulation, which is very much an open question. Whereas in other contexts the ESA is quite explicit as to the Secretary's controlling authority, *see, e.g.*, 16 U.S.C. §1533(a)(1) ("The Secretary shall" promulgate regulations determining endangered species); §1535(d)(1) ("The Secretary is authorized to provide financial assistance to any State"), with respect to consultation the initiative, and hence arguably the initial responsibility for determining statutory necessity, lies with the agencies, *see* §1536(a)(2) ("Each Federal agency shall, in consultation with and with the assistance of the Secretary, insure that any" funded action is not likely to jeopardize endangered or threatened species). When the Secretary promulgated the regulation at issue here, he thought it was binding on the agencies. The Solicitor General, however, has repudiated that position here, and the agencies themselves apparently deny the Secretary's authority. The agencies were not parties to the suit, and there is no reason they should be obliged to honor an incidental legal determination the suit produced.

A further impediment to redressability is the fact that the agencies generally supply only a fraction of the funding for a foreign project. AID, for example, has provided less than 10% of the funding for the Mahaweli project. Respondents have produced nothing to indicate that the projects they have named will either be suspended, or do less harm to listed species, if that fraction is eliminated. It is entirely conjectural whether the nonagency activity that affects respondents will be altered or affected by the agency activity they seek to achieve. There is no standing.

Justice BLACKMUN, with whom Justice O'CONNOR joins, dissenting.

Were the Court to apply the proper standard for summary judgment, I believe it would conclude that the sworn affidavits and deposition testimony of Joyce Kelly and Amy Skilbred advance sufficient facts to create a genuine issue for trial concerning whether one or both would be imminently harmed by the Aswan and Mahaweli projects. In the first instance, as the Court itself concedes, the affidavits contained facts making it at least "questionable" (and therefore within the province of the factfinder) that certain agency-funded projects threaten listed species. The only remaining issue, then, is whether Kelly and Skilbred have shown that they personally would suffer imminent harm.

I think a reasonable finder of fact could conclude from the information in the affidavits and deposition testimony that either Kelly or Skilbred will soon return to the project sites, thereby satisfying the "actual or imminent" injury standard. The Court dismisses Kelly's and Skilbred's general statements that they intended to revisit the project sites as "simply not enough." But those statements did not stand alone. A reasonable finder of fact could conclude, based not only upon their statements of intent to return, but upon their past visits to the project sites, as well as their professional backgrounds, that it was likely that Kelly and Skilbred would make a return trip to the project areas. Contrary to the Court's contention that Kelly's and Skilbred's past visits "prov[e] nothing," the fact of their past visits could demonstrate to a reasonable factfinder that Kelly and Skilbred have the requisite resources and personal interest in the preservation of the species endangered by the Aswan and Mahaweli projects to make good on their intention to return again.

By requiring a "description of concrete plans" or "specification of when the some day [for a return visit] will be," the Court, in my view, demands what is likely an empty formality. No substantial barriers prevent Kelly or Skilbred from simply purchasing plane tickets to return to the Aswan and Mahaweli projects. This case differs from other cases in which the imminence of harm turned largely on the affirmative actions of third parties beyond a plaintiff's control. To be sure, a plaintiff's unilateral control over his or her exposure to harm does not necessarily render the harm nonspeculative. Nevertheless, it suggests that a finder of fact would be far more likely to conclude the harm is actual or imminent, especially if given an opportunity to hear testimony and determine credibility.

I fear the Court's demand for detailed descriptions of future conduct will do little to weed out those who are genuinely harmed from those who are not. More likely, it will resurrect a code-pleading formalism in federal court summary judgment practice, as federal courts, newly doubting their jurisdiction, will demand more and more particularized showings of future harm. Just to survive summary judgment, for example, a property owner claiming a decline in the value of his property from governmental action might have to specify the exact date he intends to sell his property and show that there is a market for the property, lest it be surmised he might not sell again. A nurse turned down for a job on grounds of her race had better be prepared to show on what date she was prepared to start work, that she had arranged daycare for her child, and that she would not have accepted work at another hospital instead. And a Federal Tort Claims Act plaintiff alleging loss of consortium should make sure to furnish this Court with a "description of concrete plans" for her nightly schedule of attempted activities.

In conclusion, I cannot join the Court on what amounts to a slash-and-burn expedition through the law of environmental standing. In my view, "[t]he very essence of civil liberty certainly consists in the right of every individual to claim the protection of the laws, whenever he receives an injury." Marbury v. Madison (1803).

I dissent.

UNITED STATES v. HAYS, 515 U.S. 737 (1995): Justice O'CONNOR delivered the opinion of the court:

We held in Shaw v. Reno (1993), that a plaintiff may state a claim for relief under the Equal Protection Clause of the Fourteenth Amendment by alleging that a State "adopted a reapportionment scheme so irrational on its face that it can be understood only as an effort to segregate voters into separate voting districts because of their [race] and that the separation lacks sufficient justification." Appellees Ray Hays, Edward Adams, Susan Shaw Singleton, and Gary Stokley claim that the State of Louisiana's congressional districting plan is such a "racial gerrymander," and that it violates the Fourteenth Amendment. But appellees do not live in the district that is the primary focus of their racial gerrymandering claim, and they have not otherwise demonstrated that they, personally, have been subjected to a racial classification. For that reason, we conclude that appellees lack standing to bring this lawsuit.

Demonstrating the individualized harm our standing doctrine requires may not be easy in the racial gerrymandering context, as it will frequently be difficult to discern why a particular citizen was put in one district or another. Where a plaintiff resides in a racially gerrymandered district, however, the plaintiff has been denied equal treatment because of the legislature's reliance on racial criteria, and therefore has standing to challenge the legislature's action. Voters in such districts may suffer the special representational harms racial classifications can cause in the voting context. On the other hand, where a plaintiff does not live in such a district, he or she does not suffer those special harms, and any inference that the plaintiff has personally been subjected to a racial classification would not be justified absent specific evidence tending to support that inference. Unless such evidence is present, that plaintiff would be asserting only a generalized grievance against governmental conduct of which he or she does not approve.

FEDERAL ELECTION COMMN. v. AKINS, 524 U.S. 11 (1998): Justice BREYER delivered the opinion of the Court:

The Court held that Congress, by statute, could create a right to information and that the denial of such information was an injury sufficient to satisfy Article III. A group of voters brought suit challenging a decision by the Federal Election Commission that the American Israel Public Affairs Committee is not a "political committee" subject to regulation and reporting requirements under the Federal Election Campaign Act of 1971. A federal statute authorizes suit by any person "aggrieved" by a Federal Election Commission Decision.

The Court granted standing and concluded that Congress had created a right to information about political committees and that the plaintiffs were denied the information by virtue of the Federal Election Commission's decision. The Court explained: "The 'injury in fact' that respondents have suffered consists of their inability to obtain information — lists of AIPAC donors . . . and campaign-related contributions and expenditures — that on respondents' view of the law, the statute requires that AIPAC make public." In other words, the statute created a right to information, albeit a right that would not exist without the statute, and the alleged infringement of that statutory right was deemed sufficient to meet Article III and to allow standing under the broad citizen suit provision for any aggrieved person.

Causation and Redressability

Allen and *Lujan* also make clear that there are two other constitutional requirements for standing: The plaintiff must allege and prove that the defendant caused the harm, so that it is likely that a favorable court decision will remedy the injury. Although the cases express that causation and redressability are distinct constitutional requirements, they are obviously interrelated.

The causation/redressability standing requirement has been more controversial than the injury requirement. On the one hand, it can be argued that this requirement simply implements the prohibition against advisory opinions; if a federal court decision will have little effect, if it will not redress the injuries, then it is an advisory opinion. On the other hand, it can be argued that causation and redressability are inappropriate determinations to make on the basis of the pleadings. All decisions about standing initially are made on the basis of the pleadings, assuming all allegations within them to be true. The criticism is that redressability is inherently a factual question — how likely it is that a favorable court decision will have a particular effect — that should not be made at the outset of a lawsuit. Traditionally, courts consider whether equitable relief will have the desired effect at the remedy stage, after there has been an opportunity for discovery and a hearing on the merits.

To appraise these competing views, and to understand the requirements, it is useful to consider the major cases, in addition to *Allen* and *Lujan*, where the Court has applied causation and redressability.

LINDA R. S. v. RICHARD D., 410 U.S. 614 (1973): An unwed mother sued to have the father of her child prosecuted for failure to pay child support. The mother challenged the Texas policy of prosecuting fathers of legitimate children for not paying required child support but not prosecuting fathers of illegitimate children. The Supreme Court dismissed the case for lack of standing, explaining that an injunction commanding state prosecutions would not ensure that the mother would receive any additional child support money. Justice Thurgood Marshall, writing for the Court, stated, "[I]f appellant were granted the requested relief, it would result only in the jailing of the child's father. The prospect that prosecution, at least in the future, will result in payment of support can, at best, be termed only speculative."

WARTH v. SELDIN, 422 U.S. 490 (1975): Several plaintiffs challenged the constitutionality of zoning practices in Penfield, New York, a suburb of Rochester. The plaintiffs included Rochester residents who wanted to live in Penfield but claimed that they could not because of the zoning practices that prevented construction of multifamily dwellings and low-income housing. Also, an association of home builders that wanted to construct such housing joined as plaintiffs in the suit.

The Supreme Court held that these plaintiffs lacked standing because they could not demonstrate that appropriate housing would be constructed without the exclusionary zoning ordinances. The Court felt that the low-income residents seeking to live in Penfield might not be able to afford to live there even if the town's zoning ordinances were invalidated. Also, the builders might not choose to construct new housing in Penfield, regardless of the outcome of the lawsuit. Justice Powell, writing for the Court, stated, "But the record is devoid of any indication that these projects, or other like projects, would have satisfied petitioners' needs at prices they could afford, or that, were the court to remove the obstructions attributable to respondents, such relief would benefit petitioners."

SIMON v. EASTERN KENTUCKY WELFARE RIGHTS ORGANIZATION, 426 U.S. 26 (1976): A federal law required that hospitals provide free care to indigents in order to receive tax-exempt status. The plaintiffs were individuals who claimed that they requested and were denied needed medical care by tax-exempt hospitals. The plaintiffs challenged an Internal Revenue Service revision of a Revenue Ruling limiting the amount of free medical care that hospitals receiving tax-exempt status were required to provide. Whereas previously tax-exempt charitable hospitals had to provide free care for indigents, under the new provisions only emergency medical treatment of indigents was required.

The Supreme Court denied standing, concluding that it was "purely speculative" whether the new Revenue Ruling was responsible for the denial of medical services to the plaintiffs and that "the complaint suggests no substantial likelihood that victory in this suit would result in respondents' receiving the hospital treatment they desire."

DUKE POWER CO. v. CAROLINA ENVIRONMENTAL STUDY GROUP, INC., 438 U.S. 59 (1978): Forty individuals and two organizations challenged the constitutionality of the Price-Anderson Act, which limits the liability of utility companies in the event of a nuclear reactor accident. The claim was that the Price-Anderson Act violated the Due Process Clause because it allowed injuries to occur without compensation.

The defendant moved to dismiss the case on the ground that the injury was purely speculative: No catastrophic nuclear accident had occurred, no one had been denied compensation, and perhaps no one ever would suffer the injury. The Supreme Court found standing to exist because the construction of a nuclear reactor in the plaintiffs' area subjected them to many injuries, including exposure to radiation, thermal pollution, and fear of a major nuclear accident. The Court concluded that the causation and redressability tests were met because *but for* the Price-Anderson Act the reactor would not be built and the plaintiffs would not suffer these harms. After finding standing, the Court held that the Price-Anderson Act was constitutional.

ii. Prudential Standing Requirements

There are two major prudential standing requirements: the prohibition of third-party standing and the prohibition of generalized grievances.[28] Like the

---

28. There is a third prudential standing requirement that arises almost exclusively in the administrative law context: the rule that the plaintiff seeking standing must be within the zone of interests protected by the statute in question. This requirement applies when a person is challenging an administrative agency regulation that does not directly control the person's actions. The Supreme Court has stated that the plaintiff must allege that "the interest sought to be protected by the complainant is arguably within the zone of interests to be protected or regulated by the statute or constitutional guarantee in question." Association of Data Processing Serv. Orgs., Inc. v. Camp, 397 U.S. 150, 153 (1970). In other words, if a plaintiff is suing pursuant to a statutory provision, in order

constitutional standing requirements of injury, causation, and redressability, the prudential requirements are judicially created. The difference, though, is that Congress, by statute, can overrule the prudential requirements because they are derived not from the Constitution but instead from the Court's view of prudent judicial administration.

THE PROHIBITION OF THIRD-PARTY STANDING

The Supreme Court has stated that "even when the plaintiff has alleged injury sufficient to meet the 'case or controversy' requirement, the Court has held that the plaintiff generally must assert his own legal rights and interests, and cannot rest his claim to relief on the legal rights or interests of third parties."[29] A plaintiff can assert only injuries that he or she has suffered; a plaintiff cannot present the claims of third parties who are not part of the lawsuit.

The Supreme Court, however, has recognized exceptions to this requirement. These are situations where a plaintiff who meets the other standing requirements may present the claims of a third party. The following case explains the prohibition of third-party standing and the exceptions to this rule.[30]

SINGLETON v. WULFF

428 U.S. 106 (1976)

Justice BLACKMUN delivered the opinion of the Court:

This case involves a claim of a State's unconstitutional interference with the decision to terminate pregnancy. The particular object of the challenge is a Missouri statute excluding abortions that are not "medically indicated" from the purposes for which Medicaid benefits are available to needy persons. In its present posture, however, the case presents [an issue] not going to the merits of this dispute: whether the plaintiff-appellees, as physicians who perform nonmedically indicated abortions, have standing to maintain the suit, to which we answer that they do.

I

The suit was filed in the United States District Court for the Eastern District of Missouri by two Missouri-licensed physicians. Each plaintiff avers, in an affidavit filed in opposition to a motion to dismiss, that he "has provided, and anticipates providing abortions to welfare patients who are eligible for Medicaid payments."

---

to have standing the plaintiff must be part of the group intended to benefit from the law. Although the Court's statement of the test includes its application to constitutional provisions, the zone of interests requirement is used only in statutory cases, usually involving administrative law issues.

29. Warth v. Seldin, 422 U.S. at 499. *See also* United Food and Commercial Workers v. Brown Group, 517 U.S. 544 (1996) (discussing the bar against third-party standing as prudential).

30. In addition to the two exceptions discussed in *Singleton*, there is a third exception: the overbreadth doctrine. A defendant to whom a law constitutionally may be applied may challenge a law as regulating substantially more speech than the Constitution allows to be regulated. Overbreadth is discussed in Chapter 9, which examines freedom of speech.

The plaintiffs further allege in their affidavits that all Medicaid applications filed in connection with abortions performed by them have been refused by the defendant, who is the responsible state official, in reliance on the challenged statutory provision. In any event, each plaintiff states that he anticipates further refusals by the defendant to fund nonmedically indicated abortions.

II

Two distinct standing questions are presented. First, whether the plaintiff-respondents allege "injury in fact," that is, a sufficiently concrete interest in the outcome of their suit to make it a case or controversy subject to a federal court's Art. III jurisdiction, and, second, whether, as a prudential matter, the plaintiff-respondents are proper proponents of the particular legal rights on which they base their suit.

A. The first of these questions needs little comment for there is no doubt now that the respondent-physicians suffer concrete injury from the operation of the challenged statute. Their complaint and affidavits allege that they have performed and will continue to perform operations for which they would be reimbursed under the Medicaid program, were it not for the limitation of reimbursable abortions to those that are "medically indicated." If the physicians prevail in their suit to remove this limitation, they will benefit, for they will then receive payment for the abortions. The State (and Federal Government) will be out of pocket by the amount of the payments. The relationship between the parties is classically adverse, and there clearly exists between them a case or controversy in the constitutional sense.

B. The question of what rights the doctors may assert in seeking to resolve that controversy is more difficult. Federal courts must hesitate before resolving a controversy, even one within their constitutional power to resolve, on the basis of the rights of third persons not parties to the litigation. The reasons are two. First, the courts should not adjudicate such rights unnecessarily, and it may be that in fact the holders of those rights either do not wish to assert them, or will be able to enjoy them regardless of whether the in-court litigant is successful or not. Second, third parties themselves usually will be the best proponents of their own rights. The courts depend on effective advocacy, and therefore should prefer to construe legal rights only when the most effective advocates of those rights are before them. The holders of the rights may have a like preference, to the extent they will be bound by the courts' decisions under the doctrine of Stare decisis. These two considerations underlie the Court's general rule: "Ordinarily, one may not claim standing in this Court to vindicate the constitutional rights of some third party."

Like any general rule, however, this one should not be applied where its underlying justifications are absent. With this in mind, the Court has looked primarily to two factual elements to determine whether the rule should apply in a particular case. The first is the relationship of the litigant to the person whose right he seeks to assert. If the enjoyment of the right is inextricably bound up with the activity the litigant wishes to pursue, the court at least can be sure that its construction of the right is not unnecessary in the sense that the right's enjoyment will be unaffected by the outcome of the suit. Furthermore, the relationship between the litigant and the third party may be such that the former is fully, or very nearly, as effective a proponent of the right as the latter.

The other factual element to which the Court has looked is the ability of the third party to assert his own right. Even where the relationship is close, the reasons for requiring persons to assert their own rights will generally still apply. If there is some genuine obstacle to such assertion, however, the third party's absence from court loses its tendency to suggest that his right is not truly at stake, or truly important to him, and the party who is in court becomes by default the right's best available proponent.

Application of these principles to the present case quickly yields its proper result. The closeness of the relationship is patent, as it was in *Griswold* and in *Doe*. A woman cannot safely secure an abortion without the aid of a physician, and an impecunious woman cannot easily secure an abortion without the physician's being paid by the State. The woman's exercise of her right to an abortion, whatever its dimension, is therefore necessarily at stake here. Moreover, the constitutionally protected abortion decision is one in which the physician is intimately involved. Aside from the woman herself, therefore, the physician is uniquely qualified to litigate the constitutionality of the State's interference with, or discrimination against, that decision.

As to the woman's assertion of her own rights, there are several obstacles. For one thing, she may be chilled from such assertion by a desire to protect the very privacy of her decision from the publicity of a court suit. A second obstacle is the imminent mootness, at least in the technical sense, of any individual woman's claim. Only a few months, at the most, after the maturing of the decision to undergo an abortion, her right thereto will have been irrevocably lost, assuming, as it seems fair to assume, that unless the impecunious woman can establish Medicaid eligibility she must forgo abortion. It is true that these obstacles are not insurmountable. Suit may be brought under a pseudonym, as so frequently has been done. A woman who is no longer pregnant may nonetheless retain the right to litigate the point because it is "'capable of repetition yet evading review.'" And it may be that a class could be assembled, whose fluid membership always included some women with live claims. But if the assertion of the right is to be "representative" to such an extent anyway, there seems little loss in terms of effective advocacy from allowing its assertion by a physician.

For these reasons, we conclude that it generally is appropriate to allow a physician to assert the rights of women patients as against governmental interference with the abortion decision.

Singleton v. Wulff focuses on two factors in determining whether a plaintiff can sue on behalf of a third party: the closeness of the relationship between the plaintiff and the injured third party, and the likelihood that the third party can sue on its own behalf. Consider how these factors were applied in the following cases:

BARROWS v. JACKSON, 346 U.S. 249 (1953): Barrows, a white person who had signed a racially restrictive covenant, was sued for breach of contract for allowing nonwhites to occupy the property. As a defense, Barrows raised the rights of blacks, who were not parties to the lawsuit, to be free from discrimination. The Court allowed third-party standing, permitting the white defendant to raise the interests of blacks to rent and own property in the community. The Court stated that "it would be difficult if not impossible for the persons whose rights are asserted to present their grievance before any court." Because blacks were not parties to the covenant, they had no legal basis for participating in the breach of contract suit. (The suit occurred before open housing laws were enacted that would have allowed African Americans to challenge the covenants as impermissible discrimination.)

CRAIG v. BOREN, 429 U.S. 190 (1976): Oklahoma law permitted women to buy 3.2 percent beer at age 18, but said that men could not do so until age 21.[31] A bartender challenged the law on behalf of male customers between the ages of 18 and 21. The bartender suffered economic loss from the law, thus fulfilling the injury requirement. The Court allowed the bartender standing to assert the rights of his customers and explained "that vendors and those in like positions have been uniformly permitted to resist efforts at restricting their operations by acting as advocates for the rights of third parties who seek access to their market or function."

GILMORE v. UTAH, 429 U.S. 1012 (1976): Gary Gilmore was sentenced to death in the state of Utah but chose not to pursue habeas corpus relief in federal court. His mother sued for a stay of execution on his behalf. In a five-to-four decision, the Court refused to hear his mother's claim. The Court's *per curiam* opinion said that the defendant had waived his rights by not pursuing them.

Chief Justice Burger, in a concurring opinion, said that the mother should be denied standing: "When the record establishing a knowing and intelligent waiver of Gary Mark Gilmore's right to seek appellate review is combined with the December 8 written response submitted to this Court, it is plain that the Court is without jurisdiction to entertain the 'next friend' application filed by Bessie Gilmore. This Court has jurisdiction pursuant to Art. III of the Constitution only over 'cases and controversies,' and we can issue stays only in aid of our jurisdiction. There is no dispute, presently before us, between Gary Mark Gilmore and the State of Utah, and the application of Bessie Gilmore manifestly fails to meet the statutory requirements to invoke this Court's power to review the action of the Supreme Court of Utah. No authority to the contrary has been brought to our attention, and nothing suggested in dissent bears on the threshold question of jurisdiction."

In 2004, the Court returned to the issue of third-party standing in a high-profile case concerning whether the words "under God" in the Pledge of Allegiance are constitutional. The Court dismissed the case on standing grounds. In Elk Grove Unified School District v. Newdow, 542 U.S. 1 (2004), the Court held that a father lacked standing to sue on behalf of his daughter because he lacked legal custody for the girl and the mother who had legal custody did not want to sue. Justice Stevens wrote, "In our view, it is improper for the federal courts to entertain a claim by a plaintiff whose standing to sue is founded on family law rights that are in dispute when prosecution of the lawsuit may have an adverse effect on the person who is the source of the plaintiff's claimed standing. When hard questions of domestic relations are sure to affect the outcome, the prudent course is for the federal court to stay its hand rather than reach out to resolve a

---

31. The equal protection issues in this case are presented in Chapter 7.

weighty question of federal constitutional law. There is a vast difference between Newdow's right to communicate with his child — which both California law and the First Amendment recognize — and his claimed right to shield his daughter from influences to which she is exposed in school despite the terms of the custody order. We conclude that, having been deprived under California law of the right to sue as next friend, Newdow lacks prudential standing to bring this suit in federal court." Yet why is Newdow's ability to sue based on who has custody of the girl? Does he not have a claim that his own right to control the religious upbringing of his daughter is infringed by the requirement of "under God" in the Pledge of Allegiance?

THE PROHIBITION OF GENERALIZED GRIEVANCES

The prohibition against generalized grievances prevents individuals from suing if their only injury is as a citizen or a taxpayer concerned with having the government follow the law. The Court has said that the prohibition against generalized grievances is a "prudential principle" preventing standing "when the asserted harm is a generalized grievance shared in a substantially equal measure by all or a large class of citizens."[32]

In understanding and appraising the prohibition of generalized grievances, consider the following major case, which articulated and applied the rule.

UNITED STATES v. RICHARDSON

418 U.S. 166 (1974)

Chief Justice BURGER delivered the opinion of the Court.

We granted certiorari in this case to determine whether the respondent has standing to bring an action as a federal taxpayer alleging that certain provisions concerning public reporting of expenditures under the Central Intelligence Agency Act of 1949, violate Art. I, §9, cl. 7, of the Constitution which provides:

> No Money shall be drawn from the Treasury, but in Consequence of Appropriations made by Law; and a regular Statement and Account of the Receipts and Expenditures of all public Money shall be published from time to time.

In Frothingham v. Mellon (1923), the plaintiff sought to enjoin enforcement of the Federal Maternity Act of 1921, which provided for financial grants to States with programs for reducing maternal and infant mortality. She alleged violation of the Fifth Amendment's Due Process Clause on the ground that the legislation encroached on an area reserved to the States. In *Frothingham,* the injury alleged was that the congressional enactment challenged as unconstitutional would, if implemented, increase the complainant's future federal income taxes. Denying standing, the *Frothingham* Court rested on the "comparatively minute[,] remote, fluctuating and uncertain," impact on the taxpayer, and the failure to allege the kind of direct injury required for standing.

---

32. Warth v. Seldin, 422 U.S. 490, 499 (1975).

In Flast v. Cohen (1968), this Court explained: "The 'gist of the question of standing' is whether the party seeking relief has 'alleged such a personal stake in the outcome of the controversy as to assure that concrete adverseness . . . upon which the court so largely depends for illumination of difficult constitutional questions." The Court then announced a two-pronged standing test which requires allegations: (a) challenging an enactment under the Taxing and Spending Clause of Art. I, §8, of the Constitution; and (b) claiming that the challenged enactment exceeds specific constitutional limitations imposed on the taxing and spending power. While the "impenetrable barrier to suits against Acts of Congress brought by individuals who can assert only the interest of federal taxpayers," had been slightly lowered, the Court made clear it was reaffirming the principle of *Frothingham* precluding a taxpayer's use of "a federal court as a forum in which to air his generalized grievances about the conduct of government or the allocation of power in the Federal System."

The mere recital of the respondent's claims and an examination of the statute under attack demonstrate how far he falls short of the standing criteria of *Flast* and how neatly he falls within the *Frothingham* holding left undisturbed. Although the status he rests on is that he is a taxpayer, his challenge is not addressed to the taxing or spending power, but to the statutes regulating the CIA, specifically 50 U.S.C. §403j(b). That section provides different accounting and reporting requirements and procedures for the CIA, as is also done with respect to other governmental agencies dealing in confidential areas.

Respondent makes no claim that appropriated funds are being spent in violation of a "specific constitutional limitation upon the . . . taxing and spending power. . . ." Rather, he asks the courts to compel the Government to give him information on precisely how the CIA spends its funds. Thus there is no "logical nexus" between the asserted status of taxpayer and the claimed failure of the Congress to require the Executive to supply a more detailed report of the expenditures of that agency. The question presented thus is simply and narrowly whether these claims meet the standards for taxpayer standing set forth in *Flast;* we hold they do not. Respondent is seeking "to employ a federal court as a forum in which to air his generalized grievances about the conduct of government."

The respondent's claim is that without detailed information on CIA expenditures — and hence its activities — he cannot intelligently follow the actions of Congress or the Executive, nor can he properly fulfill his obligations as a member of the electorate in voting for candidates seeking national office.

This is surely the kind of a generalized grievance described in both *Frothingham* and *Flast* since the impact on him is plainly undifferentiated and "common to all members of the public." While we can hardly dispute that this respondent has a genuine interest in the use of funds and that his interest may be prompted by his status as a taxpayer, he has not alleged that, as a taxpayer, he is in danger of suffering any particular concrete injury as a result of the operation of this statute.

Ex parte Levitt is especially instructive. There Levitt sought to challenge the validity of the commission of a Supreme Court Justice who had been nominated and confirmed as such while he was a member of the Senate. Levitt alleged that the appointee had voted for an increase in the emoluments provided by Congress for Justices of the Supreme Court during the term for which he was last elected to the United States Senate. The claim was that the appointment violated the explicit prohibition of Art. I, §6, cl. 2, of the Constitution. The Court disposed of Levitt's claim, stating: "'It is an established principle that to entitle a private individual to invoke the judicial power to determine the validity of executive or legislative action he must show that he has sustained or is immediately in danger of sustaining a direct injury as the result of that action and it is not sufficient that he has merely a general interest common to all members of the public.'"

Of course, if Levitt's allegations were true, they made out an arguable violation of an explicit prohibition of the Constitution. Yet even this was held insufficient to support standing because, whatever Levitt's injury, it was one he shared with "all members of the public."

It can be argued that if respondent is not permitted to litigate this issue, no one can do so. In a very real sense, the absence of any particular individual or class to litigate these claims gives support to the argument that the subject matter is committed to the surveillance of Congress, and ultimately to the political process. The Constitution created a representative Government with the representatives directly responsible to their constituents at stated periods of two, four, and six years; that the Constitution does not afford a judicial remedy does not, of course, completely disable the citizen who is not satisfied with the "ground rules" established by the Congress for reporting expenditures of the Executive Branch. Lack of standing within the narrow confines of Art. III jurisdiction does not impair the right to assert his views in the political forum or at the polls. Slow, cumbersome, and unresponsive though the traditional electoral process may be thought at times, our system provides for changing members of the political branches when dissatisfied citizens convince a sufficient number of their fellow electors that elected representatives are delinquent in performing duties committed to them.

Justice STEWART, with whom Justice MARSHALL joins, dissenting.

The Court's decisions in Flast v. Cohen (1968), and Frothingham v. Mellon (1923), throw very little light on the question at issue in this case. For, unlike the plaintiffs in those cases, Richardson did not bring this action asking a court to invalidate a federal statute on the ground that it was beyond the delegated power of Congress to enact or that it contravened some constitutional prohibition. Richardson's claim is of an entirely different order. It is that Art. I, §9, cl. 7, of the Constitution, the Statement and Account Clause, gives him a right to receive, and imposes on the Government a corresponding affirmative duty to supply, a periodic report of the receipts and expenditures "of all public Money." In support of his standing to litigate this claim, he has asserted his status both as a taxpayer and as a citizen-voter. Whether the Statement and Account Clause imposes upon the Government an affirmative duty to supply the information requested and whether that duty runs to every taxpayer or citizen are questions that go to the substantive merits of this litigation. Those questions are not now before us, but I think that the Court is quite wrong in holding that the respondent was without standing to raise them in the trial court.

Seeking a determination that the Government owes him a duty to supply the information he has requested, the respondent is in the position of a traditional Hohfeldian plaintiff. He contends that the Statement and Account Clause gives him a right to receive the information and burdens the Government with a correlative duty to supply it. Courts of law exist for the resolution of such right-duty disputes. When a party is seeking a judicial determination that a defendant owes him an affirmative duty, it seems clear to me that he has standing to litigate the issue of the existence vel non of this duty once he shows that the defendant has declined to honor his claim. If the duty in question involved the payment of a sum of money, I suppose that all would agree that a plaintiff asserting the duty would have standing to litigate the issue of his entitlement to the money upon a showing that he had not been paid. I see no reason for a different result when the defendant is a Government official and the asserted duty relates not to the payment of money, but to the disclosure of items of information.

In a companion case, decided the same day, Schlesinger v. Reservists Committee to Stop the War, 418 U.S. 208 (1974), the Court also denied citizen and taxpayer standing. The plaintiffs sued to enjoin members of Congress from serving in the military reserves. Article 1, §6 of the Constitution prevents a senator or representative from holding civil office. As in *Richardson*, standing was denied because the plaintiff alleged injury only as a citizen or taxpayer with an interest in having the government follow the law and not a violation of a specific constitutional right. The Court stated: "Respondents seek to have the Judicial Branch compel the Executive Branch to act in conformity with the Incompatibility Clause, an interest shared by all citizens. . . . Our system of government leaves many crucial decisions to the political processes. The assumption that if respondents have no standing to sue, no one would have standing, is not a reason to find standing."

In both *Richardson* and *Schlesinger*, the Court recognizes that denying taxpayer and citizen standing likely will mean that no one could bring a lawsuit challenging the allegedly unconstitutional conduct. The crucial issue, then, is whether it is desirable that some constitutional provisions be left entirely to the political branches for their interpretation and enforcement. On the one hand, the Court's majority argues that the absence of judicial review confirms that these are matters best left to the political process. On the other hand, critics argue that it is essential that the judiciary be available to enforce all of the Constitution or it can be effectively rendered a nullity. The same issue, with the same competing views, arises below in connection with the political question doctrine.

The Supreme Court has recognized only one exception where taxpayer standing is permitted: to challenge government expenditures as violating the Establishment Clause of the First Amendment, the provision that prohibits Congress from making any law respecting the establishment of religion. The key case is Flast v. Cohen, discussed in *Richardson* and presented below:

FLAST v. COHEN
392 U.S. 83 (1968)

Chief Justice WARREN delivered the opinion of the Court.

In Frothingham v. Mellon (1923), this Court ruled that a federal taxpayer is without standing to challenge the constitutionality of a federal statute. That ruling has stood for 45 years as an impenetrable barrier to suits against Acts of Congress brought by individuals who can assert only the interest of federal taxpayers. In this case, we must decide whether the *Frothingham* barrier should be lowered when a taxpayer attacks a federal statute on the ground that it violates the Establishment and Free Exercise Clauses of the First Amendment.

Appellants filed suit in the United States District Court for the Southern District of New York to enjoin the allegedly unconstitutional expenditure of federal funds under Titles I and II of the Elementary and Secondary Education Act of 1965. The complaint alleged that the seven appellants had as a common attribute that "each pay[s] income taxes of the United States," and it is clear from the complaint that the appellants were resting their standing to maintain the action solely on their status as federal taxpayers. The gravamen of the appellants' complaint was that federal funds appropriated under the Act were being used to finance instruction in reading, arithmetic, and other subjects in religious schools, and to purchase textbooks and other instructional materials for use in such schools. Such expenditures were alleged to be in contravention of the Establishment and Free Exercise Clauses of the First Amendment.

The question of standing is related only to whether the dispute sought to be adjudicated will be presented in an adversary context and in a form historically viewed as capable of judicial resolution. It is for that reason that the emphasis in standing problems is on whether the party invoking federal court jurisdiction has "a personal stake in the outcome of the controversy," and whether the dispute touches upon "the legal relations of parties having adverse legal interests." A taxpayer may or may not have the requisite personal stake in the outcome, depending upon the circumstances of the particular case. Therefore, we find no absolute bar in Article III to suits by federal taxpayers challenging allegedly unconstitutional federal taxing and spending programs. There remains, however, the problem of determining the circumstances under which a federal taxpayer will be deemed to have the personal stake and interest that impart the necessary concrete adverseness to such litigation so that standing can be conferred on the taxpayer qua taxpayer consistent with the constitutional limitations of Article III.

The nexus demanded of federal taxpayers has two aspects to it. First, the taxpayer must establish a logical link between that status and the type of legislative enactment attacked. Thus, a taxpayer will be a proper party to allege the unconstitutionality only of exercises of congressional power under the taxing and spending clause of Art. I, §8, of the Constitution. It will not be sufficient to allege an incidental expenditure of tax funds in the administration of an essentially regulatory statute. Secondly, the taxpayer must establish a nexus between that status and the precise nature of the constitutional infringement alleged. Under this requirement, the taxpayer must show that the challenged enactment exceeds specific constitutional limitations imposed upon the exercise of the congressional taxing and spending power and not simply that the enactment is generally beyond the powers delegated to Congress by Art. I, §8. When both nexuses are established, the litigant will have shown a taxpayer's stake in the outcome of the controversy and will be a proper and appropriate party to invoke a federal court's jurisdiction.

The taxpayer-appellants in this case have satisfied both nexuses to support their claim of standing under the test we announce today. Their constitutional challenge is made to an exercise by Congress of its power under Art. I, §8, to spend for the general welfare, and the challenged program involves a substantial expenditure of federal tax funds. In addition, appellants have alleged that the challenged expenditures violate the Establishment and Free Exercise Clauses of the First Amendment. Our history vividly illustrates that one of the specific evils feared by those who drafted the Establishment Clause and fought for its adoption was that the taxing and spending power would be used to favor one religion over another or to support religion in general. James Madison, who is generally recognized as the leading architect of the religion clauses of the First Amendment, observed in his famous Memorial and Remonstrance Against Religious Assessments that "the same authority which can force a citizen to contribute three pence only of his property for the support of any one establishment, may force him to conform to any other establishment in all cases whatsoever." The concern of Madison and his supporters was quite clearly that religious liberty ultimately would be the victim if government could employ its taxing and spending powers to aid one religion over another or to aid religion in general. The Establishment Clause was designed as a specific bulwark against such potential abuses of governmental power, and that clause of the First Amendment operates as a specific constitutional limitation upon the exercise by Congress of the taxing and spending power conferred by Art. I, §8.

Mr. Justice HARLAN, dissenting.

The Court's analysis consists principally of the observation that the requirements of standing are met if a taxpayer has the "requisite personal stake in the outcome" of this suit. This does not, of course, resolve the standing problem; it merely restates it. The Court implements this standard with the declaration that taxpayers will be "deemed" to have the necessary personal interest if their suits satisfy two criteria: first, the challenged expenditure must form part of a federal spending program, and not merely be "incidental" to a regulatory program; and second, the constitutional provision under which the plaintiff claims must be a "specific limitation" upon Congress' spending powers. The difficulties with these criteria are many and severe, but it is enough for the moment to emphasize that they are not in any sense a measurement of any plaintiff's interest in the outcome of any suit. As even a cursory examination of the criteria will show, the Court's standard for the determination of standing and its criteria for the satisfaction of that standard are entirely unrelated.

It is surely clear that a plaintiff's interest in the outcome of a suit in which he challenges the constitutionality of a federal expenditure is not made greater or smaller by the unconnected fact that the expenditure is, or is not, "incidental" to an "essentially regulatory" program. An example will illustrate the point. Assume that two independent federal programs are authorized by Congress, that the first is designed to encourage a specified religious group by the provision to it of direct grants-in-aid, and that the second is designed to discourage all other religious groups by the imposition of various forms of discriminatory regulation. Equal amounts are appropriated by Congress for the two programs. If a taxpayer challenges their constitutionality in separate suits, are we to suppose, as evidently does the Court, that his "personal stake" in the suit involving the second is necessarily smaller than it is in the suit involving the first, and that he should therefore have standing in one but not the other?

The Court's second criterion is similarly unrelated to its standard for the determination of standing. The intensity of a plaintiff's interest in a suit is not measured, even obliquely, by the fact that the constitutional provision under which he claims is, or is not, a "specific limitation" upon Congress' spending powers. I am quite unable to understand how, if a taxpayer believes that a given public expenditure is unconstitutional, and if he seeks to vindicate that belief in a federal court, his interest in the suit can be said necessarily to vary according to the constitutional provision under which he states his claim.

It seems to me clear that public actions, whatever the constitutional provisions on which they are premised, may involve important hazards for the continued effectiveness of the federal judiciary. Although I believe such actions to be within the jurisdiction conferred upon the federal courts by Article III of the Constitution, there surely can be little doubt that they strain the judicial function and press to the limit judicial authority. There is every reason to fear that unrestricted public actions might well alter the allocation of authority among the three branches of the Federal Government. It is not, I submit, enough to say that the present members of the Court would not seize these opportunities for abuse, for such actions would, even without conscious abuse, go far toward the final transformation of this Court into the Council of Revision which, despite Madison's support, was rejected by the Constitutional Convention. I do not doubt that there must be "some effectual power in the government to restrain or correct the infractions" of the Constitution's several commands, but neither can I suppose that such power resides only in the federal courts. We must as judges recall that, as Mr. Justice Holmes wisely observed, the other branches of the Government "are ultimate guardians of the liberties and welfare of the people in quite as great a degree as the courts." The powers of the federal judiciary will be adequate for the great burdens placed upon them only if they are employed prudently, with recognition of the strengths as well as the hazards that go with our kind of representative government.

Flast never has been overruled: Taxpayers have standing to challenge government expenditures as violating the Establishment Clause. But *Flast* also never has been extended. Even in the context of the Establishment Clause, the Supreme Court has refused to extend *Flast* beyond challenges to expenditures. In Valley Forge Christian College v. Americans United for Separation of Church and State, Inc., 454 U.S. 464 (1982), the Court held that taxpayers lacked standing to challenge the federal government's decision to grant property or its power to dispose of property under Article IV, §3. The Court held that taxpayers have standing only to challenge *expenditures* under Congress's Article I, §8 spending power as violating the Establishment Clause.

In Hein v. Freedom from Religion Foundation, 551 U.S. 587 (2007), the Court further limited Flast v. Cohen and held that taxpayers lacked standing to challenge expenditures from general executive revenue as violating the Establishment Clause. President George W. Bush created the Faith-Based and Community Initiatives program to allow faith-based programs, such as churches, synagogues, and mosques, to receive federal funds. A challenge was brought to conferences and speeches that were done in conjunction with the program. The Court noted that "Congress did not specifically authorize the use of federal funds to pay for the conferences or speeches that the plaintiffs challenged. Instead, the conferences and speeches were paid for out of general Executive Branch appropriations."

The Court denied standing. Justice Alito wrote a plurality opinion joined by Chief Justice Roberts and Justice Kennedy and said that Flast v. Cohen was distinguishable: "The expenditures at issue in *Flast* were made pursuant to an express congressional mandate and a specific congressional appropriation. . . . The . . . link between congressional action and constitutional violation that supported taxpayer standing in *Flast* is missing here. Respondents do not challenge any specific congressional action or appropriation; nor do they ask the Court to invalidate any congressional enactment or legislatively created program as unconstitutional. That is because the expenditures at issue here were not made pursuant to any Act of Congress. Rather, Congress provided general appropriations to the Executive Branch to fund its day-to-day activities. These appropriations did not expressly authorize, direct, or even mention the expenditures of which respondents complain. Those expenditures resulted from executive discretion, not congressional action. We have never found taxpayer standing under such circumstances."

Justices Scalia and Thomas concurred in the judgment and would have overruled Flast v. Cohen: "If this Court is to decide cases by rule of law rather than show of hands, we must surrender to logic and choose sides: Either *Flast v. Cohen* (1968) should be applied to (at a minimum) all challenges to the governmental expenditure of general tax revenues in a manner alleged to violate a constitutional provision specifically limiting the taxing and spending power, or *Flast* should be repudiated. For me, the choice is easy. *Flast* is wholly irreconcilable with the Article III restrictions on federal-court jurisdiction that this Court has repeatedly confirmed are embodied in the doctrine of standing."

Justice Souter wrote a dissenting opinion joined by Justices Stevens, Ginsburg, and Breyer and would have allowed standing under Flast v. Cohen. Justice Souter wrote, "[T]he controlling opinion closes the door on these taxpayers because the Executive Branch, and not the Legislative Branch, caused their injury. I see no basis for this distinction in either logic or precedent, and respectfully dissent. . . . Here, there is no dispute that taxpayer money in identifiable amounts is funding conferences, and these are alleged to have the purpose of promoting religion. The taxpayers therefore seek not to "extend" *Flast*, but merely to apply it. When executive agencies spend identifiable sums of tax money for religious purposes, no less than when Congress authorizes the same thing, taxpayers suffer injury."

Finally, most recently in Arizona School Tuition Organization v. Winn, 131 S. Ct. 1436 (2011), the Court ruled five to four that taxpayers lacked standing to challenge an Arizona law that allowed taxpayers to obtain tax credits tax of up to $500 per person and $1,000 per married couple for contributions to school tuition organizations (STOs). The record demonstrated that the vast majority of funds from these STOs went to religious schools. Justice Kennedy, in an opinion joined by Chief Justice Roberts and Justices Scalia, Thomas, and Alito, distinguished Flast v. Cohen and said that there is a difference between government expenditures and tax credits, even when both benefit religion:

> The distinction between governmental expenditures and tax credits refutes respondents' assertion of standing. When Arizona taxpayers choose to contribute to STOs, they spend their own money, not money the State has collected from respondents or from other taxpayers. Arizona's §43-1089 does not "extrac[t] and

spen[d]" a conscientious dissenter's funds in service of an establishment, or "'force a citizen to contribute three pence only of his property'" to a sectarian organization. On the contrary, respondents and other Arizona taxpayers remain free to pay their own tax bills, without contributing to an STO. Respondents are likewise able to contribute to an STO of their choice, either religious or secular. And respondents also have the option of contributing to other charitable organizations, in which case respondents may become eligible for a tax deduction or a different tax credit. The STO tax credit is not tantamount to a religious tax or to a tithe and does not visit the injury identified in *Flast.* It follows that respondents have neither alleged an injury for standing purposes under general rules nor met the *Flast* exception. Finding standing under these circumstances would be more than the extension of *Flast* "to the limits of its logic." It would be a departure from *Flast*'s stated rationale.

Justice Kagan wrote for the four dissenters and argued that there is no meaningful difference between government expenditures that assist religion and tax credits that do so. She wrote:

Since its inception, the Arizona private-school-tuition tax credit has cost the State, by its own estimate, nearly $350 million in diverted tax revenue. . . . Beginning in *Flast v. Cohen* (1968), and continuing in case after case for over four decades, this Court and others have exercised jurisdiction to decide taxpayer-initiated challenges not materially different from this one. Today, the Court breaks from this precedent by refusing to hear taxpayers' claims that the government has unconstitutionally subsidized religion through its tax system. These litigants lack standing, the majority holds, because the funding of religion they challenge comes from a tax credit, rather than an appropriation. A tax credit, the Court asserts, does not injure objecting taxpayers, because it "does not extract and spend [their] funds in service of an establishment.

This novel distinction in standing law between appropriations and tax expenditures has as little basis in principle as it has in our precedent. Cash grants and targeted tax breaks are means of accomplishing the same government objective — to provide financial support to select individuals or organizations. Taxpayers who oppose state aid of religion have equal reason to protest whether that aid flows from the one form of subsidy or the other. Either way, the government has financed the religious activity. And so either way, taxpayers should be able to challenge the subsidy. Precisely because appropriations and tax breaks can achieve identical objectives, the government can easily substitute one for the other. Today's opinion thus enables the government to end-run *Flast*'s guarantee of access to the Judiciary. From now on, the government need follow just one simple rule — subsidize through the tax system — to preclude taxpayer challenges to state funding of religion.

Suppose a State desires to reward Jews — by, say, $500 per year — for their religious devotion. Should the nature of taxpayers' concern vary if the State allows Jews to claim the aid on their tax returns, in lieu of receiving an annual stipend? Or assume a State wishes to subsidize the ownership of crucifixes. It could purchase the religious symbols in bulk and distribute them to all takers. Or it could mail a reimbursement check to any individual who buys her own and submits a receipt for the purchase. Or it could authorize that person to claim a tax credit equal to the price she paid. Now, really — do taxpayers have less reason to complain if the State selects the last of these three options? The Court today says they do, but that is wrong. The effect of each form of subsidy is the same, on the public fisc and on those who contribute to it. Regardless of which mechanism the State uses, taxpayers have an identical stake in ensuring that the State's exercise of its taxing and spending power complies with the Constitution.

c. Ripeness

The third major justiciability doctrine is ripeness. Ripeness, like mootness (discussed in the next section), is a justiciability doctrine determining when review is appropriate. While standing is concerned with who is a proper party to litigate a particular matter, ripeness and mootness determine when that litigation may occur. Specifically, the ripeness doctrine seeks to separate matters that are premature for review because the injury is speculative and never may occur, from those cases that are appropriate for federal court action.

There is an obvious overlap with the injury requirement in the standing doctrine. In order to have standing, the plaintiff must demonstrate that an injury has occurred or imminently will occur. In order for the case to be ripe, the plaintiff must show that review is not premature; that is, the plaintiff must demonstrate that a harm has occurred or imminently will occur.

To the extent that the substantive requirements overlap and the result will be the same regardless of whether the issue is characterized as ripeness or standing, little turns on the choice of the label. Ripeness, though, usually is used to ask a more specific question: When may a party seek pre-enforcement review of a statute or regulation? Customarily, a person can challenge the legality of a statute or regulation when he or she is prosecuted for violating it. There is an unfairness, however, to requiring a person to violate a law in order to challenge it. A person might unnecessarily obey an unconstitutional law, refraining from the prohibited conduct, rather than risk criminal punishments. Alternatively, a person might violate a statute or regulation, confident that it will be invalidated, only to be punished when the law is upheld. A primary purpose of the Declaratory Judgment Act was to permit people to avoid this choice and obtain pre-enforcement review of statutes and regulations. Ripeness, then, is best understood as the determination of whether a federal court can grant pre-enforcement review; for example, when may a court hear a request for a declaratory judgment, or when must it decline review?

In evaluating ripeness, consider the following case in which the Court denied review by finding that the challenge was not ripe for review.

POE v. ULLMAN
367 U.S. 497 (1961)

Mr. Justice FRANKFURTER announced the judgment of the Court and an opinion in which the Chief Justice, Mr. Justice CLARK and Mr. Justice WHITTAKER join.

These appeals challenge the constitutionality, under the Fourteenth Amendment, of Connecticut statutes which, as authoritatively construed by the Connecticut Supreme Court of Errors, prohibit the use of contraceptive devices and the giving of medical advice in the use of such devices. In proceedings seeking declarations of law, not on review of convictions for violation of the statutes, that court has ruled that these statutes would be applicable in the case of married couples and even under claim that conception would constitute a serious threat to the health or life of the female spouse.

No. 60 combines two actions brought in a Connecticut Superior Court for declaratory relief. The complaint in the first alleges that the plaintiffs, Paul and

Pauline Poe, are a husband and wife, thirty and twenty-six years old respectively, who live together and have no children. Mrs. Poe has had three consecutive pregnancies terminating in infants with multiple congenital abnormalities from which each died shortly after birth. Plaintiffs have consulted Dr. Buxton, an obstetrician and gynecologist of eminence, and it is Dr. Buxton's opinion that the cause of the infants' abnormalities is genetic, although the underlying "mechanism" is unclear. In view of the great emotional stress already suffered by plaintiffs, the probable consequence of another pregnancy is psychological strain extremely disturbing to the physical and mental health of both husband and wife. Plaintiffs know that it is Dr. Buxton's opinion that the best and safest medical treatment which could be prescribed for their situation is advice in methods of preventing conception. Dr. Buxton knows of drugs, medicinal articles and instruments which can be safely used to effect contraception. Medically, the use of these devices is indicated as the best and safest preventive measure necessary for the protection of plaintiffs' health. Plaintiffs, however, have been unable to obtain this information for the sole reason that its delivery and use may or will be claimed by the defendant State's Attorney (appellee in this Court) to constitute offenses against Connecticut law.

The second action in No. 60 is brought by Jane Doe, a twenty-five-year-old housewife. Mrs. Doe, it is alleged, lives with her husband, they have no children; Mrs. Doe recently underwent a pregnancy which induced in her a critical physical illness — two weeks' unconsciousness and a total of nine weeks' acute sickness which left her with partial paralysis, marked impairment of speech, and emotional instability. Another pregnancy would be exceedingly perilous to her life. She, too, has consulted Dr. Buxton, who believes that the best and safest treatment for her is contraceptive advice.

In No. 61, also a declaratory judgment action, Dr. Buxton is the plaintiff. Setting forth facts identical to those alleged by Jane Doe, he asks that the Connecticut statutes prohibiting his giving of contraceptive advice to Mrs. Doe be adjudged unconstitutional, as depriving him of liberty and property without due process.

The Connecticut law prohibiting the use of contraceptives has been on the State's books since 1879. During the more than three-quarters of a century since its enactment, a prosecution for its violation seems never to have been initiated, save in State v. Nelson. The circumstances of that case, decided in 1940, only prove the abstract character of what is before us. There, a test case was brought to determine the constitutionality of the Act as applied against two doctors and a nurse who had allegedly disseminated contraceptive information. After the Supreme Court of Errors sustained the legislation on appeal from a demurrer to the information, the State moved to dismiss the information. Neither counsel nor our own researchers have discovered any other attempt to enforce the prohibition of distribution or use of contraceptive devices by criminal process. The unreality of these law suits is illumined by another circumstance. We were advised by counsel for appellants that contraceptives are commonly and notoriously sold in Connecticut drug stores. Yet no prosecutions are recorded; and certainly such ubiquitous, open, public sales would more quickly invite the attention of enforcement officials than the conduct in which the present appellants wish to engage — the giving of private medical advice by a doctor to his individual patients, and their private use of the devices prescribed.

Insofar as appellants seek to justify the exercise of our declaratory power by the threat of prosecution, facts which they can no more negative by complaint and demurrer than they could by stipulation preclude our determining their appeals on the merits. It is clear that the mere existence of a state penal statute would constitute insufficient grounds to support a federal court's adjudication of its constitutionality in proceedings brought against the State's prosecuting officials if real threat of enforcement is wanting. The fact that Connecticut has not chosen to press the enforcement of this statute deprives these controversies of the immediacy which is an indispensable condition of constitutional adjudication. This Court cannot be umpire to debates concerning harmless, empty shadows. To find it necessary to pass on these statutes now, in order to protect appellants from the hazards of prosecution, would be to close our eyes to reality.

Justice DOUGLAS, dissenting.

If there is a case where the need for this remedy in the shadow of a criminal prosecution is shown, it is this one. Plaintiffs in No. 60 are two sets of husband and wife. One wife is pathetically ill, having delivered a stillborn fetus. If she becomes pregnant again, her life will be gravely jeopardized. This couple have been unable to get medical advice concerning the "best and safest" means to avoid pregnancy from their physician, plaintiff in No. 61, because if he gave it he would commit a crime. The use of contraceptive devices would also constitute a crime. And it is alleged — and admitted by the State — that the State's Attorney intends to enforce the law by prosecuting offenses under the laws.

A public clinic dispensing birth-control information has indeed been closed by the State. Doctors and a nurse working in that clinic were arrested by the police and charged with advising married women on the use of contraceptives. That litigation produced State v. Nelson, which upheld these statutes. That same police raid on the clinic resulted in the seizure of a quantity of the clinic's contraception literature and medical equipment and supplies.

What are these people — doctor and patients — to do? Flout the law and go to prison? Violate the law surreptitiously and hope they will not get caught? By today's decision we leave them no other alternatives. It is not the choice they need have under the regime of the declaratory judgment and our constitutional system. It is not the choice worthy of a civilized society. A sick wife, a concerned husband, a conscientious doctor seek a dignified, discrete, orderly answer to the critical problem confronting them. We should not turn them away and make them flout the law and get arrested to have their constitutional rights determined. They are entitled to an answer to their predicament here and now.

The Connecticut law was subsequently declared unconstitutional five years later in Griswold v. Connecticut, 381 U.S. 479 (1965). The director of a Planned Parenthood clinic and Dr. Buxton openly violated the Connecticut law and were prosecuted. As a defense, they challenged the constitutionality of the statute. The Court declared the law unconstitutional as violating the right to privacy. Griswold is presented in Chapter 8 in connection with the discussion of privacy and reproductive autonomy. The underlying question is whether waiting for an actual prosecution was appropriate restraint by the Supreme Court or whether it was undesirable avoidance of an important constitutional issue.

Although Poe v. Ullman discusses ripeness, it does not articulate any clear criteria for courts to use in evaluating whether a case is ripe. The following case, Abbott Laboratories v. Gardner, announces criteria that often have been used in evaluating ripeness.

ABBOTT LABORATORIES v. GARDNER
387 U.S. 136 (1967)

Mr. Justice HARLAN delivered the opinion of the Court.

In 1962 Congress amended the Federal Food, Drug, and Cosmetic Act, to require manufacturers of prescription drugs to print the "established name" of the drug "prominently and in type at least half as large as that used thereon for any proprietary name or designation for such drug," on labels and other printed material. The "established name" is one designated by the Secretary of Health, Education, and Welfare; the "proprietary name" is usually a trade name under which a particular drug is marketed. The underlying purpose of the 1962 amendment was to bring to the attention of doctors and patients the fact that many of the drugs sold under familiar trade names are actually identical to drugs sold under their "established" or less familiar trade names at significantly lower prices.

The present action was brought by a group of 37 individual drug manufacturers and by the Pharmaceutical Manufacturers Association, of which all the petitioner companies are members, and which includes manufacturers of more than 90% of the Nation's supply of prescription drugs. They challenged the regulations on the ground that the Commissioner exceeded his authority under the statute by promulgating an order requiring labels, advertisements, and other printed matter relating to prescription drugs to designate the established name of the particular drug involved every time its trade name is used anywhere in such material.

The injunctive and declaratory judgment remedies are discretionary, and courts traditionally have been reluctant to apply them to administrative determinations unless these arise in the context of a controversy "ripe" for judicial resolution. Without undertaking to survey the intricacies of the ripeness doctrine it is fair to say that its basic rationale is to prevent the courts, through avoidance of premature adjudication, from entangling themselves in abstract disagreements over administrative policies, and also to protect the agencies from judicial interference until an administrative decision has been formalized and its effects felt in a concrete way by the challenging parties. The problem is best seen in a twofold aspect, requiring us to evaluate both the fitness of the issues for judicial decision and the hardship to the parties of withholding court consideration.

As to the former factor, we believe the issues presented are appropriate for judicial resolution at this time. [A]ll parties agree that the issue tendered is a purely legal one: whether the statute was properly construed by the Commissioner to require the established name of the drug to be used every time the proprietary name is employed.

This is also a case in which the impact of the regulations upon the petitioners is sufficiently direct and immediate as to render the issue appropriate for judicial review at this stage. These regulations purport to give an authoritative interpretation of a statutory provision that has a direct effect on the day-to-day business of all prescription drug companies; its promulgation puts petitioners in a dilemma that it was the very purpose of the Declaratory Judgment Act to ameliorate. As the District Court found on the basis of uncontested allegations, "Either they must comply with the every time requirement and incur the costs of changing over their promotional material and labeling or they must follow their present course and risk prosecution." If petitioners wish to comply they must change all their labels, advertisements, and promotional materials; they must destroy stocks of printed matter; and they must invest heavily in new printing type and new supplies. The alternative to compliance — continued use of material which they believe in good faith meets the statutory requirements, but which clearly does not meet the regulation of the Commissioner — may be even more costly. That course would risk serious criminal and civil penalties for the unlawful distribution of "misbranded" drugs.

In light of the criteria articulated in Abbott Laboratories v. Gardner, consider the following cases and whether the claim should have been deemed ripe for review.

UNITED PUBLIC WORKERS v. MITCHELL, 330 U.S. 75 (1947): A lawsuit was filed challenging the constitutionality of the Hatch Act of 1940, which prevented federal employees from taking "any active part in political management or political campaigns." The plaintiffs sought a declaratory judgment that the law violated their First Amendment rights and provided detailed affidavits listing the activities they wished to engage in. The Court found their claims to be not ripe. The Court said that the plaintiffs "seem clearly to seek advisory opinions upon broad claims. . . . A hypothetical threat is not enough. We can only speculate as to the kinds of political activity the appellants desire to engage in or as to the contents of their proposed public statements or the circumstances of their publication."[33]

INTERNATIONAL LONGSHOREMEN'S & WAREHOUSEMEN'S UNION, LOCAL 37 v. BOYD, 347 U.S. 222 (1954): The case arose before Alaska became a state. For many years, some resident aliens in the United States went to work in Alaska during the summer. The aliens sued to ensure that they would be able to return to the United States after leaving to go to Alaska. The aliens sued to enjoin immigration officers from preventing their return to the United States. The aliens argued that without a declaratory judgment as to their ability to return they would be forced to choose between giving up a job or risking permanent exclusion from the country. Because the case arose before Alaska became a state, the Supreme Court, in an opinion by Justice Frankfurter, held that their suit was not ripe. The Court found that the situation was "hypothetical" and concluded that "[d]etermination of the scope and constitutionality of

---

33. In a subsequent case, U.S. Civil Service Commn. v. National Assn. of Letter Carriers, AFL-CIO, 413 U.S. 548 (1973), the Court found a challenge to the Hatch Act to be ripe because the plaintiffs alleged that they desired to engage in specific political activity. The Court held that the Hatch Act does not violate the First Amendment.

legislation in advance of its immediate adverse effect in the context of a concrete case involves too remote and abstract an inquiry for the proper exercise of the judicial function."

REGIONAL RAIL REORGANIZATION ACT CASES, 419 U.S. 102 (1974): Eight major railroads brought a lawsuit challenging the conveyance of their property to Conrail. The district court found the case not justiciable on ripeness grounds because the reorganization plan had not yet been formulated and a special court had not yet ordered the reconveyances. But the Supreme Court held that the case was ripe, concluding, "Where the inevitability of the operation of a statute against certain individuals is patent, it is irrelevant to the existence of a justiciable controversy that there will be a time delay before the disputed provisions will come into effect."

LAKE CARRIERS ASSN. v. MacMULLAN, 406 U.S. 498 (1972): A state law prohibited discharge of sewage from boats. Plaintiffs challenged the statute's validity. State officials had announced that they would not enforce the law until land-based pumpout facilities would be available, a construction process that would take a substantial amount of time. Although enforcement was many years in the future, the Court found that the suit was ripe because it was inevitable that the law would be enforced and that as a result the boat owners had to begin installing new facilities on their boats in anticipation of the time when the law was implemented.

d. Mootness

A plaintiff must present a live controversy at all stages of federal court litigation. If anything occurs while a lawsuit is pending to end the plaintiff's injury, the case is to be dismissed as moot. For example, a case is moot if a criminal defendant dies during the appeals process or if a civil plaintiff dies where the cause of action does not survive death.[34] Also, if the parties settle the matter, a live controversy obviously no longer exists.[35] If a challenged law is repealed or expires, the case is moot.[36]

The Supreme Court frequently has explained that the mootness doctrine is derived from Article III's prohibition against federal courts issuing advisory opinions.[37] If a case is moot, there no longer is an actual controversy between

---

34. Dove v. United States, 423 U.S. 325 (1976).

35. *See, e.g.*, United Airlines, Inc. v. McDonald, 432 U.S. 385, 400 (1977) (Powell, J., dissenting) ("The settlement of an individual claim typically moots any issues associated with it."). Settlement must be distinguished from a situation in which the defendant voluntarily agrees to refrain from a practice, but is free to resume it at any time. As discussed below, the latter does not moot the case.

36. *See, e.g.*, Burke v. Barnes, 479 U.S. 361 (1987) (bill expired during pendency of appeal, rendering moot the question of whether the president's pocket veto prevented bill from becoming law); United States Dept. of Treasury v. Galioto, 477 U.S. 556 (1986) (amendment to federal statute rendered the case moot); Kremens v. Bartley, 431 U.S. 119, 128 (1977) (statutes providing for commitment of minors to institutions were repealed, rendering the case moot); *but see* City of Mesquite v. Aladdin's Castle, Inc., 455 U.S. 283 (1982) (repeal of a city ordinance was not moot where the city was likely to reenact it after completion of legal proceedings), discussed below.

37. *See, e.g.*, SEC v. Medical Comm. for Human Rights, 404 U.S. 403, 406 (1972); Hall v. Beals, 396 U.S. 45, 48 (1969). *But see* Honig v. Doe, 484 U.S. 305, 330 (1988) (Rehnquist, C.J., concurring) (arguing that mootness doctrine is primarily prudential and not constitutionally based).

adverse litigants. Also, if events subsequent to the initiation of the lawsuit have resolved the matter, then a federal court decision is not likely to have any effect.

The Supreme Court has applied the mootness doctrine in a less strict manner than other justiciability doctrines, such as standing. Indeed, the Court has spoken of "the flexible character of the Article III mootness doctrine."[38] This flexibility is manifested in three exceptions to the mootness doctrine.[39]

One exception to the mootness doctrine is for "wrongs capable of repetition but evading review." Some injuries are of such short duration that inevitably they are over before the federal court proceedings are completed. A case is not dismissed, even though it is moot, if there is an injury likely to recur in the future and it is possible that it could happen to the plaintiff again, and it is of such a short duration that it likely always will evade review. Consider and compare the following three cases that discussed this exception to the mootness doctrine:

MOORE v. OGILVIE, 394 U.S. 814 (1969): Illinois law required that a petition to nominate candidates for the general election for a new political party be signed by at least 25,000 qualified voters, including 200 qualified voters from each of at least 50 counties. In 1968, the plaintiffs filed petitions for inclusion on the ballot but were denied this because they did not meet the requirement for the number of signatures in each county. They immediately filed suit, but, of course, the election was over by the time the Supreme Court heard the case.

The Court said, "[Defendants] urged in a motion to dismiss that since the November 5, 1968, election has been held, there is no possibility of granting any relief to appellants and that the appeal should be dismissed. But while the 1968 election is over, the burden allowed to be placed on the nomination of candidates for statewide offices remains and controls future elections, as long as Illinois maintains her present system as she has done since 1935. The problem is therefore 'capable of repetition, yet evading review.' The need for its resolution thus reflects a continuing controversy in the federal-state area where our 'one man, one vote' decisions have thrust."

ROE v. WADE, 410 U.S. 113 (1973): Roe was a pregnant woman in Texas who filed a lawsuit seeking a declaratory judgment that the Texas law prohibiting abortion was unconstitutional and an injunction restraining the defendant from enforcing the law. At the time she filed her suit in 1970, she alleged that she was in the first trimester of her pregnancy and seeking an abortion. Obviously, when the Supreme Court decided her case in 1973, she was no longer pregnant. The defendant moved to dismiss on mootness grounds.[40]

---

38. U.S. Parole Commn. v. Geraghty, 445 U.S. 388, 400 (1980).

39. Additionally, it should be remembered that a case is not moot if the plaintiff has some ongoing injury, even if other injuries are over. For example, a challenge to a criminal conviction is not moot, even after the defendant has completed the sentence and is released from custody, when the defendant continues to face adverse consequences of the criminal conviction. *See* Sibron v. New York, 392 U.S. 40 (1968). Similarly, a plaintiff seeking both injunctive relief and money damages can continue to pursue the case, even after the request for an equitable remedy is rendered moot. Havens Realty Corp. v. Coleman, 455 U.S. 363, 370-371 (1982) (case not moot because plaintiffs would each be entitled to $400 in liquidated damages if defendants were found liable).

40. The parts of the opinion concerning the Constitution's protection of the right to abortion are discussed in Chapter 8.

The Court stated, "Viewing Roe's case as of the time of its filing and thereafter until as late as May, there can be little dispute that it then presented a case or controversy and that, wholly apart from the class aspects, she, as a pregnant single woman thwarted by the Texas criminal abortion laws, had standing to challenge those statutes. The usual rule in federal cases is that an actual controversy must exist at all stages of appellate or certiorari review, and not simply at the date the action is initiated.

"But when, as here, pregnancy is a significant fact in the litigation, the normal 266-day human gestation period is so short that the pregnancy will come to term before the usual appellate process is complete. If that termination makes a case moot, pregnancy litigation seldom will survive much beyond the trial stage, and appellate review will be effectively denied. Our law should not be that rigid. Pregnancy often comes more than once to the same woman, and in the general population, if man is to survive, it will always be with us. Pregnancy provides a classic justification for a conclusion of nonmootness. It truly could be 'capable of repetition, yet evading review.'

"We, therefore, agree with the District Court that Jane Roe had standing to undertake this litigation, that she presented a justiciable controversy, and that the termination of her 1970 pregnancy has not rendered her case moot."

DEFUNIS v. ODEGAARD, 416 U.S. 312 (1974): Marco DeFunis, a white male, was denied admission to the University of Washington Law School. He filed suit challenging his denial of admission on the ground that the university's affirmative action program denied him equal protection. The case was not filed as a class action suit. He received a preliminary injunction and was allowed to attend law school while the suit was pending. By the time the case reached the Supreme Court, DeFunis was a third-year law student. The university stated that he would be allowed to finish school no matter what the Court's ruling.

The Court explained, "The starting point for analysis is the familiar proposition that 'federal courts are without power to decide questions that cannot affect the rights of litigants in the case before them.' The inability of the federal judiciary 'to review moot cases derives from the requirement of Art. III of the Constitution under which the exercise of judicial power depends upon the existence of a case or controversy.'

"It might be suggested that this case presents a question that is 'capable of repetition, yet evading review,' and is thus amenable to federal adjudication even though it might otherwise be considered moot. But DeFunis will never again be required to run the gauntlet of the Law School's admission process, and so the question is certainly not 'capable of repetition' so far as he is concerned. Moreover, just because this particular case did not reach the Court until the eve of the petitioner's graduation from Law School, it hardly follows that the issue he raises will in the future evade review. If the admissions procedures of the Law School remain unchanged, there is no reason to suppose that a subsequent case attacking those procedures will not come with relative speed to this Court, now that the Supreme Court of Washington has spoken. This case, therefore, in no way presents the exceptional situation in which the doctrine might permit a departure from '[t]he usual rule in federal cases . . . that an actual controversy must exist at all stages of appellate or certiorari review, and not simply at the date the action is initiated.'

"Because the petitioner will complete his law school studies at the end of the term for which he has now registered regardless of any decision this Court might reach on the merits of this litigation, we conclude that the Court cannot, consistently with the limitations of Art. III of the Constitution, consider the substantive constitutional issues tendered by the parties."

A second major exception to the mootness doctrine is for voluntary cessation. A case is not to be dismissed as moot if the defendant voluntarily ceases the allegedly improper behavior but is free to return to it at any time. Only if there is no reasonable chance that the defendant could resume the offending behavior is a case deemed moot on the basis of voluntary cessation. Consider the following recent case, which applied this exception.

FRIENDS OF THE EARTH, INC. v. LAIDLAW ENVIRONMENTAL SERVICES
528 U.S. 167 (2000)

[Environmental groups brought a lawsuit pursuant to a citizen suit provision of Clean Water Act (CWA) against the holder of a National Pollutant Discharge Elimination System (NPDES) permit, alleging that it was violating mercury discharge limits. The plaintiffs sought declaratory and injunctive relief, civil penalties, costs, and attorney fees.]

Justice GINSBURG delivered the opinion of the Court.

The only conceivable basis for a finding of mootness in this case is Laidlaw's voluntary conduct—either its achievement by August 1992 of substantial compliance with its NPDES permit or its more recent shutdown of the Roebuck facility. It is well settled that "a defendant's voluntary cessation of a challenged practice does not deprive a federal court of its power to determine the legality of the practice." "[I]f it did, the courts would be compelled to leave '[t]he defendant . . . free to return to his old ways.'" In accordance with this principle, the standard we have announced for determining whether a case has been mooted by the defendant's voluntary conduct is stringent: "A case might become moot if subsequent events made it absolutely clear that the allegedly wrongful behavior could not reasonably be expected to recur." The "heavy burden of persua[d-ing]" the court that the challenged conduct cannot reasonably be expected to start up again lies with the party asserting mootness.

[A] defendant claiming that its voluntary compliance moots a case bears the formidable burden of showing that it is absolutely clear the allegedly wrongful behavior could not reasonably be expected to recur. By contrast, in a lawsuit brought to force compliance, it is the plaintiff's burden to establish standing by demonstrating that, if unchecked by the litigation, the defendant's allegedly wrongful behavior will likely occur or continue, and that the "threatened injury [is] certainly impending."

Standing doctrine functions to ensure, among other things, that the scarce resources of the federal courts are devoted to those disputes in which the parties have a concrete stake. In contrast, by the time mootness is an issue, the case has been brought and litigated, often (as here) for years. To abandon the case at an advanced stage may prove more wasteful than frugal. This argument from sunk costs does not license courts to retain jurisdiction over cases in which one or both of the parties plainly lacks a continuing interest, as when the parties have settled or a plaintiff pursuing a nonsurviving claim has died.

Laidlaw also asserts, in a supplemental suggestion of mootness, that the closure of its Roebuck facility, which took place after the Court of Appeals issued its decision, mooted the case. The facility closure, like Laidlaw's earlier achievement of substantial compliance with its permit requirements, might moot the case, but—we once more reiterate—only if one or the other of these events made it absolutely clear that Laidlaw's permit violations could not reasonably be expected to recur. The effect of both Laidlaw's compliance and the facility closure on the prospect of future violations is a disputed factual matter. FOE points out, for example—and Laidlaw does not appear to contest—that Laidlaw retains its NPDES permit. These issues have not been aired in the lower courts; they remain open for consideration on remand.

The third and final exception to the mootness doctrine is for class action suits. The Supreme Court has held that a properly certified class action suit may continue even if the named plaintiff's claims are rendered moot. The Court has reasoned that the "class of unnamed persons described in the certification acquired a legal status separate from the interest asserted by [the plaintiff]," and thus as long as the members of the class have a live controversy the case can continue.[41] The following case describes and applies this exception.

UNITED STATES PAROLE COMMISSION v. GERAGHTY
445 U.S. 388 (1980)

[A federal prisoner, after twice being denied parole from a federal prison, brought suit challenging the validity of the U.S. Parole Commission's Parole Release Guidelines. The district court denied respondent's request for certification of the suit as a class action on behalf of a class of "all federal prisoners who are or who will become eligible for release on parole," and granted summary judgment for petitioners on the merits. Respondent was released from prison while his appeal to the court of appeals was pending.]

Mr. Justice BLACKMUN delivered the opinion of the Court.

This case raises the question whether a trial court's denial of a motion for certification of a class may be reviewed on appeal after the named plaintiff's personal claim has become "moot."

It is clear that the controversy over the validity of the Parole Release Guidelines is still a "live" one between petitioners and at least some members of the class respondent seeks to represent. This is demonstrated by the fact that prisoners currently affected by the guidelines have moved to be substituted, or to intervene, as "named" respondents in this Court.

---

41. Sosna v. Iowa, 419 U.S. 393, 399 (1975).

On several occasions the Court has considered the application of the "personal stake" requirement in the class-action context. In Sosna v. Iowa (1975), it held that mootness of the named plaintiff's individual claim after a class has been duly certified does not render the action moot. It reasoned that "even though appellees . . . might not again enforce the Iowa durational residency requirement against [the class representative], it is clear that they will enforce it against those persons in the class that appellant sought to represent and that the District Court certified." The Court stated specifically that an Art. III case or controversy "may exist . . . between a named defendant and a member of the class represented by the named plaintiff, even though the claim of the named plaintiff has become moot."

When, however, there is no chance that the named plaintiff's expired claim will reoccur, mootness still can be avoided through certification of a class prior to expiration of the named plaintiff's personal claim. E.g., Franks v. Bowman Transportation Co. (1976). Some claims are so inherently transitory that the trial court will not have even enough time to rule on a motion for class certification before the proposed representative's individual interest expires.

These cases demonstrate the flexible character of the Art. III mootness doctrine. As has been noted in the past, Art. III justiciability is "not a legal concept with a fixed content or susceptible of scientific verification." "[T]he justiciability doctrine [is] one of uncertain and shifting contours."

As noted above, the purpose of the "personal stake" requirement is to assure that the case is in a form capable of judicial resolution. The imperatives of a dispute capable of judicial resolution are sharply presented issues in a concrete factual setting and self-interested parties vigorously advocating opposing positions. We conclude that these elements can exist with respect to the class certification issue notwithstanding the fact that the named plaintiff's claim on the merits has expired. The question whether class certification is appropriate remains as a concrete, sharply presented issue. In Sosna v. Iowa it was recognized that a named plaintiff whose claim on the merits expires after class certification may still adequately represent the class. Implicit in that decision was the determination that vigorous advocacy can be assured through means other than the traditional requirement of a "personal stake in the outcome." Respondent here continues vigorously to advocate his right to have a class certified.

We therefore hold that an action brought on behalf of a class does not become moot upon expiration of the named plaintiff's substantive claim, even though class certification has been denied. The proposed representative retains a "personal stake" in obtaining class certification sufficient to assure that Art. III values are not undermined. If the appeal results in reversal of the class certification denial, and a class subsequently is properly certified, the merits of the class claim then may be adjudicated pursuant to the holding in *Sosna*.

e. The Political Question Doctrine

i. *The Political Question Doctrine Defined*

The political question doctrine refers to allegations of constitutional violations that federal courts will not adjudicate, and that the Supreme Court deems to be inappropriate for judicial review. The Court has held that some constitutional provisions are left to the political branches of government to interpret and enforce. Although there is an allegation that the Constitution has been violated, cases brought under these provisions are dismissed as non-justiciable political questions.

The underlying question is whether there should be a political question doctrine. Critics of the political question doctrine argue that it is wrong to leave some constitutional provisions solely to the political branches to interpret and enforce.[42] The argument is that the Constitution is meant to insulate matters from the political process and therefore it is wrong to leave constitutional provisions to the elected branches of government to interpret and enforce.

But the political question doctrine is defended on separation of powers grounds; the Constitution is seen as assigning certain provisions to the other branches of government. Moreover, defenders of the political question doctrine argue that it minimizes judicial intrusion into the operations of the other branches of government and that it allocates decisions to the branches of government that have superior expertise in particular areas. For example, some argue that the Court rightly has treated many constitutional issues concerning foreign policy to be political questions because of the greater information and expertise of the other branches of government.[43]

WHAT IS A POLITICAL QUESTION? THE ISSUES OF MALAPPORTIONMENT AND PARTISAN GERRYMANDERING

The Supreme Court has applied the political question doctrine almost throughout American history. Baker v. Carr, below, is the most famous articulation of the criteria for determining what is a political question. *Baker* involves the question of whether an equal protection challenge to malapportionment of state legislatures is a nonjusticiable political question. To understand *Baker*, it is important to know that the Court rejected an earlier challenge to malapportionment based on the "Guaranty Clause." This clause is found in Article IV, §4 of the Constitution: "The United States shall guarantee to every State in this Union a Republican Form of Government, and shall protect each of them against Invasion; and on Application of the Legislature, or of the Executive (when the Legislature cannot be convened) against domestic Violence." In Colegrove v. Green, in 1946, the Court held that challenges to malapportionment under this provision are a nonjusticiable political question.[44]

Indeed, the Supreme Court long has refused to find cases under the Guaranty Clause justiciable. In Luther v. Borden, in 1849, the Court refused to hear a challenge to the Rhode Island government under the Guaranty Clause[45] after the voters of Rhode Island adopted a new state constitution, in part in response to significant malapportionment in the state legislature. After this enactment, the existing government, which was sure to lose power under the new document,

---

42. *See, e.g.,* Martin H. Redish, *Judicial Review and the "Political Question,"* 79 Nw. U. L. Rev. 1031 (1985).

43. *See, e.g.,* Fritz Scharpf, *Judicial Review and the Political Question: A Functional Analysis,* 75 Yale L.J. 517, 567 (1966).

44. 328 U.S. 549 (1946).

45. 48 U.S. (7 How.) 1 (1849).

enacted a law prohibiting the constitution from going into effect. Nonetheless, elections were held — even though the existing government had declared voting in them to be a crime. Relatively few people participated, but a new government was chosen, led by Thomas Dorr, who was elected governor. Dorr's government met for two days in an abandoned foundry and then disbanded.

In April 1842, a sheriff, L. Borden, broke into the house of one of the election commissioners, Martin Luther, to search for evidence of illegal participation in the prohibited election. Luther sued Borden for trespass. Borden claimed that the search was a lawful exercise of government power. Luther, however, contended that Borden acted pursuant to an unconstitutional government's orders; he maintained that the Rhode Island government violated the Republican Form of Government Clause.

The Supreme Court held that the case posed a political question that could not be decided by a federal court. The Court stated: "Under this article of the Constitution it rests with Congress to decide what government is the established one in a State. For as the United States guarantee to each State a republican government, Congress must necessarily decide what government is established in the State before it can determine whether it is republican or not." The Court also explained that the case posed a political question because if the state's government was declared unconstitutional, then all of its actions would be invalidated, creating chaos in Rhode Island.

The Supreme Court never has varied from this holding: Cases under the Guaranty Clause are nonjusticiable. Colegrove v. Green followed this in refusing to adjudicate a challenge to malapportionment under the Guaranty Clause. The issue in Baker v. Carr is whether the same challenge is justiciable when brought under equal protection. As you read Baker v. Carr, compare the views of the majority and dissenting opinions as to the appropriate role of the judiciary.

BAKER v. CARR

369 U.S. 186 (1962)

Justice BRENNAN delivered the opinion of the Court.

Of course the mere fact that the suit seeks protection of a political right does not mean it presents a political question. Such an objection "is little more than a play upon words." Rather, it is argued that apportionment cases, whatever the actual wording of the complaint, can involve no federal constitutional right except one resting on the guaranty of a republican form of government, and that complaints based on that clause have been held to present political questions which are nonjusticiable.

We hold that the claim pleaded here neither rests upon nor implicates the Guaranty Clause and that its justiciability is therefore not foreclosed by our decisions of cases involving that clause. [I]n the Guaranty Clause cases and in the other "political question" cases, it is the relationship between the judiciary and the coordinate branches of the Federal Government, and not the federal judiciary's relationship to the States, which gives rise to the "political question."

We have said that "In determining whether a question falls within (the political question) category, the appropriateness under our system of government of attributing finality to the action of the political departments and also the lack of satisfactory criteria for a judicial determination are dominant considerations." The nonjusticiability of a political question is primarily a function of the separation of powers. Much confusion results from the capacity of the "political question" label to obscure the need for case-by-case inquiry. Deciding whether a matter has in any measure been committed by the Constitution to another branch of government, or whether the action of that branch exceeds whatever authority has been committed, is itself a delicate exercise in constitutional interpretation, and is a responsibility of this Court as ultimate interpreter of the Constitution.

It is apparent that several formulations which vary slightly according to the settings in which the questions arise may describe a political question, although each has one or more elements which identify it as essentially a function of the separation of powers. Prominent on the surface of any case held to involve a political question is found a textually demonstrable constitutional commitment of the issue to a coordinate political department; or a lack of judicially discoverable and manageable standards for resolving it; or the impossibility of deciding without an initial policy determination of a kind clearly for nonjudicial discretion; or the impossibility of a court's undertaking independent resolution without expressing lack of the respect due coordinate branches of government; or an unusual need for unquestioning adherence to a political decision already made; or the potentiality of embarrassment from multifarious pronouncements by various departments on one question.

[After describing the cases under the Guaranty Clause, the Court explained:] But because any reliance on the Guaranty Clause could not have succeeded it does not follow that appellants may not be heard on the equal protection claim which in fact they tender. True, it must be clear that the Fourteenth Amendment claim is not so enmeshed with those political question elements which render Guaranty Clause claims nonjusticiable as actually to present a political question itself. But we have found that not to be the case here.

We conclude then that the nonjusticiability of claims resting on the Guaranty Clause which arises from their embodiment of questions that were thought "political," can have no bearing upon the justiciability of the equal protection claim presented in this case. Finally, we emphasize that it is the involvement in Guaranty Clause claims of the elements thought to define "political questions," and no other feature, which could render them nonjusticiable. Specifically, we have said that such claims are not held nonjusticiable because they touch matters of state governmental organization.

Since, as has been established, the equal protection claim tendered in this case does not require decision of any political question, and since the presence of a matter affecting state government does not render the case nonjusticiable, [w]e conclude that the complaint's allegations of a denial of equal protection present a justiciable constitutional cause of action upon which appellants are entitled to a trial and a decision. The right asserted is within the reach of judicial protection under the Fourteenth Amendment.

Justice FRANKFURTER, whom Mr. Justice HARLAN joins, dissenting.

The Court today reverses a uniform course of decision established by a dozen cases, including one by which the very claim now sustained was unanimously rejected only five years ago. The impressive body of rulings thus cast aside reflected the equally uniform course of our political history regarding the relationship between population and legislative representation — a wholly different matter from denial of the franchise to individuals because of race, color, religion or sex. Such a massive repudiation of the experience of our whole past in asserting destructively novel judicial power demands a detailed analysis of the role of this Court in our constitutional scheme.

Disregard of inherent limits in the effective exercise of the Court's "judicial Power" not only presages the futility of judicial intervention in the essentially political conflict of forces by which the relation between population and representation has time out of mind been and now is determined. It may well impair the Court's position as the ultimate organ of "the supreme Law of the Land" in that vast range of legal problems, often strongly entangled in popular feeling, on which this Court must pronounce. The Court's authority — possessed of neither the purse nor the sword — ultimately rests on sustained public confidence in its moral sanction. Such feeling must be nourished by the Court's complete detachment, in fact and in appearance, from political entanglements and by abstention from injecting itself into the clash of political forces in political settlements.

For this Court to direct the District Court to enforce a claim to which the Court has over the years consistently found itself required to deny legal enforcement and at the same time to find it necessary to withhold any guidance to the lower court how to enforce this turnabout, new legal claim, manifests an odd — indeed an esoteric — conception of judicial propriety. Even assuming the indispensable intellectual disinterestedness on the part of judges in such matters, they do not have accepted legal standards or criteria or even reliable analogies to draw upon for making judicial judgments. To charge courts with the task of accommodating the incommensurable factors of policy that underlie these mathematical puzzles is to attribute, however flatteringly, omnicompetence to judges. The framers of the Constitution persistently rejected a proposal that embodied this assumption and Thomas Jefferson never entertained it.

In effect, today's decision empowers the courts of the country to devise what should constitute the proper composition of the legislatures of the fifty States. If state courts should for one reason or another find themselves unable to discharge this task, the duty of doing so is put on the federal courts or on this Court, if State views do not satisfy this Court's notion of what is proper districting.

In this situation, as in others of like nature, appeal for relief does not belong here. Appeal must be to an informed, civically militant electorate. In a democratic society like ours, relief must come through an aroused popular conscience that sears the conscience of the people's representatives. In any event there is nothing judicially more unseemly nor more self-defeating than for this Court to make in terrorem pronouncements, to indulge in merely empty rhetoric, sounding a word of promise to the ear, sure to be disappointing to the hope. This is the latest in the series of cases in which the Equal Protection and Due Process Clauses of the Fourteenth Amendment have been invoked in federal courts as restrictions upon the power of the States to allocate electoral weight among the voting populations of their various geographical subdivisions.

The present case involves all of the elements that have made the Guarantee Clause cases non-justiciable. It is, in effect, a Guarantee Clause claim masquerading under a different label. To find such a political conception legally enforceable in the broad and unspecific guarantee of equal protection is to rewrite the Constitution. Certainly, "equal protection" is no more secure a foundation for judicial judgment of the permissibility of varying forms of representative government than is "Republican Form."

Subsequently, the Court held that apportionment must meet the standard of one person, one vote; that is, all districts must be approximately equal in population size.[46] These cases are discussed in Chapter 8.

The Court also had occasion to consider justiciability in the election context in deciding whether challenges to political gerrymandering constitute a political question. In Davis v. Bandemer, the plaintiffs contended that the Republican-controlled Indiana legislature gerrymandered the drawing of election districts to maximize the election of Republican representatives.[47] While careful to preserve one person, one vote and to avoid racial discrimination, the state legislature tried to divide the Democrats into separate districts where possible and to combine Republican voters into districts where they would be the majority. The result was that Democrats obtained a majority of the popular vote in the state in legislative elections but only won a minority of the seats in the legislature. The plaintiff claimed that this was a violation of equal protection.

The Supreme Court held that the claim was justiciable. The Court explained that "the standards that we set forth here for adjudicating this political gerrymandering claim are [no] less manageable than the standards that have been developed for racial gerrymandering claims." Accordingly, the Court held that "political gerrymandering cases are properly justiciable under the Equal Protection Clause."

In 2004, the Court reconsidered whether challenges to partisan gerrymandering is a political question. In reading Vieth v. Jubelirer, notice there is no majority opinion. In light of this, in reading the case consider whether such challenges are now justiciable and, if so, when.

VIETH v. JUBELIRER
541 U.S. 267 (2004)

Justice SCALIA announced the judgment of the Court and delivered an opinion, in which the Chief Justice, Justice O'CONNOR, and Justice THOMAS join.

Plaintiffs-appellants Richard Vieth, Norma Jean Vieth, and Susan Furey challenge a map drawn by the Pennsylvania General Assembly establishing districts for the election of congressional Representatives, on the ground that the districting constitutes an unconstitutional political gerrymander. In Davis v. Bandemer (1986), this Court held that political gerrymandering claims are justiciable,[48] but could not agree upon a standard to adjudicate them. The present

---

46. *See* Reynolds v. Sims, 377 U.S. 533 (1964) (articulating the one-person, one-vote standard).

47. 478 U.S. 109 (1986).

48. The term "political gerrymander" has been defined as "[t]he practice of dividing a geographical area into electoral districts, often of highly irregular shape, to give one political party an unfair advantage by diluting the opposition's voting strength." Black's Law Dictionary 696 (7th ed. 1999). [Footnote by the Court.]

appeal presents the questions whether our decision in *Bandemer* was in error, and, if not, what the standard should be.

I

The facts, as alleged by the plaintiffs, are as follows. The population figures derived from the 2000 census showed that Pennsylvania was entitled to only 19 Representatives in Congress, a decrease in two from the Commonwealth's previous delegation. Pennsylvania's General Assembly took up the task of drawing a new districting map. At the time, the Republican party controlled a majority of both state Houses and held the Governor's office. Prominent national figures in the Republican Party pressured the General Assembly to adopt a partisan redistricting plan as a punitive measure against Democrats for having enacted pro-Democrat redistricting plans elsewhere. The Republican members of Pennsylvania's House and Senate worked together on such a plan. On January 3, 2002, the General Assembly passed its plan, which was signed into law by Governor Schweiker as Act 1.

Plaintiffs, registered Democrats who vote in Pennsylvania, brought suit in the United States District Court for the Middle District of Pennsylvania, seeking to enjoin implementation of Act 1.

[II]

As Chief Justice Marshall proclaimed two centuries ago, "[i]t is emphatically the province and duty of the judicial department to say what the law is." Marbury v. Madison (1803). Sometimes, however, the law is that the judicial department has no business entertaining the claim of unlawfulness — because the question is entrusted to one of the political branches or involves no judicially enforceable rights. In Baker v. Carr (1962), we set forth six independent tests for the existence of a political question: "[1] a textually demonstrable constitutional commitment of the issue to a coordinate political department; or [2] a lack of judicially discoverable and manageable standards for resolving it; or [3] the impossibility of deciding without an initial policy determination of a kind clearly for nonjudicial discretion; or [4] the impossibility of a court's undertaking independent resolution without expressing lack of the respect due coordinate branches of the government; or [5] an unusual need for unquestioning adherence to a political decision already made; or [6] the potentiality of embarrassment from multifarious pronouncements by various departments on one question." . . .

These tests are probably listed in descending order of both importance and certainty. The second is at issue here, and there is no doubt of its validity. . . .

Over the dissent of three Justices, the Court held in Davis v. Bandemer that, since it was "not persuaded that there are no judicially discernible and manageable standards by which political gerrymander cases are to be decided," such cases were justiciable. The clumsy shifting of the burden of proof for the premise (the Court was "not persuaded" that standards do not exist, rather than "persuaded" that they do) was necessitated by the uncomfortable fact that the six-Justice majority could not discern what the judicially discernable standards might be. There was no majority on that point. Nor can it be said that the lower courts have, over 18 years, succeeded in shaping the standard that this Court was initially unable to enunciate. They have simply applied the standard set forth in *Bandemer*'s four-Justice plurality opinion. This might be thought to prove that the four-Justice plurality standard has met the test of time — but for the fact that its application has almost invariably produced the same result (except for the incurring of attorney's fees) as would have obtained if the question were nonjusticiable: judicial intervention has been refused. As one commentary has put it, "[t]hroughout its subsequent history, *Bandemer* has served almost exclusively as an invitation to litigation without much prospect of redress."

Eighteen years of judicial effort with virtually nothing to show for it justify us in revisiting the question whether the standard promised by *Bandemer* exists. As the following discussion reveals, no judicially discernible and manageable standards for adjudicating political gerrymandering claims have emerged. Lacking them, we must conclude that political gerrymandering claims are nonjusticiable and that *Bandemer* was wrongly decided. . . .

[III]

Justice Kennedy recognizes that we have "demonstrat[ed] the shortcomings of the other standards that have been considered to date." He acknowledges, moreover, that we "lack . . . comprehensive and neutral principles for drawing electoral boundaries"; and that there is an "absence of rules to limit and confine judicial intervention." From these premises, one might think that Justice Kennedy would reach the conclusion that political gerrymandering claims are nonjusticiable. Instead, however, he concludes that courts should continue to adjudicate such claims because a standard may one day be discovered.

Justice Kennedy asserts that to declare nonjusticiability would be incautious. Our rush to such a holding after a mere 18 years of fruitless litigation "contrasts starkly" he says, "with the more patient approach" that this Court has taken in the past. We think not. When it has come to determining what areas fall beyond our Article III authority to adjudicate, this Court's practice, from the earliest days of the Republic to the present, has been more reminiscent of Hannibal than of Hamlet.

But the conclusive refutation of Justice Kennedy's position is the point we first made: it is not an available disposition. We can affirm because political districting presents a nonjusticiable question; or we can affirm because we believe the correct standard which identifies unconstitutional political districting has not been met; we cannot affirm because we do not know what the correct standard is. Reduced to its essence, Justice Kennedy's opinion boils down to this: "As presently advised, I know of no discernible and manageable standard that can render this claim justiciable. I am unhappy about that, and hope that I will be able to change my opinion in the future." What are the lower courts to make of this pronouncement? We suggest that they must treat it as a reluctant fifth vote against justiciability at district and statewide levels — a vote that may change in some future case but that holds, for the time being, that this matter is nonjusticiable.

[IV]

We conclude that neither Article I, §2, nor the Equal Protection Clause, nor (what appellants only fleetingly invoke) Article I, §4, provides a judicially enforceable limit on the political considerations that the States and Congress may take into account when districting.

Justice KENNEDY, concurring in the judgment.

A decision ordering the correction of all election district lines drawn for partisan reasons would commit federal and state courts to unprecedented intervention in the American political process. The Court is correct to refrain from directing this substantial intrusion into the Nation's political life. While agreeing with the plurality that the complaint the appellants filed in the District Court must be dismissed, and while understanding that great caution is necessary when approaching this subject, I would not foreclose all possibility of judicial relief if some limited and precise rationale were found to correct an established violation of the Constitution in some redistricting cases.

When presented with a claim of injury from partisan gerrymandering, courts confront two obstacles. First is the lack of comprehensive and neutral principles for drawing electoral boundaries. No substantive definition of fairness in districting seems to command general assent. Second is the absence of rules to limit and confine judicial intervention. With uncertain limits, intervening courts — even when proceeding with best intentions — would risk assuming political, not legal, responsibility for a process that often produces ill will and distrust.

In my view, however, the arguments are not so compelling that they require us now to bar all future claims of injury from a partisan gerrymander. It is not in our tradition to foreclose the judicial process from the attempt to define standards and remedies where it is alleged that a constitutional right is burdened or denied. Nor is it alien to the Judiciary to draw or approve election district lines. Courts, after all, already do so in many instances. A determination by the Court to deny all hopes of intervention could erode confidence in the courts as much as would a premature decision to intervene. Our willingness to enter the political thicket of the apportionment process with respect to one-person, one-vote claims makes it particularly difficult to justify a categorical refusal to entertain claims against this other type of gerrymandering.

That no such standard has emerged in this case should not be taken to prove that none will emerge in the future. Where important rights are involved, the impossibility of full analytical satisfaction is reason to err on the side of caution. Allegations of unconstitutional bias in apportionment are most serious claims, for we have long believed that "the right to vote" is one of "those political processes ordinarily to be relied upon to protect minorities."

If suitable standards with which to measure the burden a gerrymander imposes on representational rights did emerge, hindsight would show that the Court prematurely abandoned the field. That is a risk the Court should not take. Instead, we should adjudicate only what is in the papers before us.

Because, in the case before us, we have no standard by which to measure the burden appellants claim has been imposed on their representational rights, appellants cannot establish that the alleged political classifications burden those same rights.

Where it is alleged that a gerrymander had the purpose and effect of imposing burdens on a disfavored party and its voters, the First Amendment may offer a sounder and more prudential basis for intervention than does the Equal Protection Clause. The First Amendment analysis concentrates on whether the legislation burdens the representational rights of the complaining party's voters for reasons of ideology, beliefs, or political association. The analysis allows a pragmatic or functional assessment that accords some latitude to the States.

The ordered working of our Republic, and of the democratic process, depends on a sense of decorum and restraint in all branches of government, and in the citizenry itself. Here, one has the sense that legislative restraint was abandoned. That should not be thought to serve the interests of our political order. Nor should it be thought to serve our interest in demonstrating to the world how democracy works. Whether spoken with concern or pride, it is unfortunate that our legislators have reached the point of declaring that, when it comes to apportionment, "We are in the business of rigging elections."

Still, the Court's own responsibilities require that we refrain from intervention in this instance. The failings of the many proposed standards for measuring the burden a gerrymander imposes on representational rights make our intervention improper. If workable standards do emerge to measure these burdens, however, courts should be prepared to order relief. With these observations, I join the judgment of the plurality.

Justice STEVENS, dissenting.

The central question presented by this case is whether political gerrymandering claims are justiciable. Although our reasons for coming to this conclusion differ, five Members of the Court are convinced that the plurality's answer to that question is erroneous. Moreover, as is apparent from our separate writings today, we share the view that, even if these appellants are not entitled to prevail, it would be contrary to precedent and profoundly unwise to foreclose all judicial review of similar claims that might be advanced in the future. That we presently have somewhat differing views — concerning both the precedential value of some of our recent cases and the standard that should be applied in future cases — should not obscure the fact that the areas of agreement set forth in the separate opinions are of far greater significance.

The concept of equal justice under law requires the State to govern impartially. In my view, when partisanship is the legislature's sole motivation — when any pretense of neutrality is forsaken unabashedly and all traditional districting criteria are subverted for partisan advantage — the governing body cannot be said to have acted impartially.

Although we reaffirm the central holding of the Court in Davis v. Bandemer (1986), we have not reached agreement on the standard that should govern partisan gerrymandering claims. I would decide this case on a narrow ground. State action that discriminates against a political minority for the sole and unadorned purpose of maximizing the power of the majority plainly violates the decisionmaker's duty to remain impartial.

In sum, in evaluating a challenge to a specific district, I would apply the standard set forth in the [race] cases and ask whether the legislature allowed partisan considerations to dominate and control the lines drawn, forsaking all neutral principles. Under my analysis, if no neutral criterion can be identified to justify the lines drawn, and if the only possible explanation for a district's bizarre shape is a naked desire to increase partisan strength, then no rational basis exists to save the district from an equal protection challenge. Such a narrow test would cover only a few meritorious claims, but it would preclude extreme abuses, and it would perhaps shorten the time period in which the pernicious effects of such a gerrymander are felt. This test would mitigate the current trend under which partisan considerations are becoming the be-all and end-all in apportioning representatives.

Justice SOUTER, with whom Justice GINSBURG joins, dissenting.

The Constitution guarantees both formal and substantial equality among voters. For 40 years, we have recognized that lines dividing a State into voting districts must produce divisions with equal populations: one person, one vote. Reynolds v. Sims (1964). Otherwise, a vote in a less populous district than others carries more clout.

Creating unequally populous districts is not, however, the only way to skew political results by setting district lines. The choice to draw a district line one way, not another always carries some consequence for politics, save in a mythical State with voters of every political identity distributed in an absolutely gray uniformity. The spectrum of opportunity runs from cracking a group into impotent fractions, to packing its members into one district for the sake of marginalizing them in another. However equal districts may be in population as a formal matter, the consequence of a vote cast can be minimized or maximized, and if unfairness is sufficiently demonstrable, the guarantee of equal protection condemns it as a denial of substantial equality.

I

The notion of fairness assumed to be denied in these cases has been described as "each political group in a State [having] the same chance to elect representatives of its choice as any other political group," and as a "right to 'fair and effective representation.'" It is undeniable that political sophisticates understand such fairness and how to go about destroying it, although it cannot possibly be described with the hard edge of one person, one vote. The difficulty has been to translate these notions of fairness into workable criteria, as distinct from mere opportunities for reviewing courts to make episodic judgments that things have gone too far, the sources of difficulty being in the facts that some intent to gain political advantage is inescapable whenever political bodies devise a district plan, and some effect results from the intent. Thus, the issue is one of how much is too much, and we can be no more exact in stating a verbal test for too much partisanship than we can be in defining too much race consciousness when some is inevitable and legitimate. Instead of coming up with a verbal formula for too much, then, the Court's job must be to identify clues, as objective as we can make them, indicating that partisan competition has reached an extremity of unfairness.

II

Since this Court has created the problem no one else has been able to solve, it is up to us to make a fresh start. There are a good many voices saying it is high time that we did, for in the years since *Davis,* the increasing efficiency of partisan redistricting has damaged the democratic process to a degree that our predecessors only began to imagine.

I would therefore preserve *Davis*'s holding that political gerrymandering is a justiciable issue, but otherwise start anew. For a claim based on a specific single-member district, I would require the plaintiff to make out a prima facie case with five elements. First, the resident plaintiff would identify a cohesive political group to which he belonged, which would normally be a major party, as in this case and in *Davis*. There is no reason in principle, however, to rule out a claimant from a minor political party (which might, if it showed strength, become the target of vigorous hostility from one or both major parties in a State) or from a different but politically coherent group whose members engaged in bloc voting, as a large labor union might do.

Second, a plaintiff would need to show that the district of his residence, paid little or no heed to those traditional districting principles whose disregard can be shown straightforwardly: contiguity, compactness, respect for political subdivisions, and conformity with geographic features like rivers and mountains. Because such considerations are already relevant to justifying small deviations from absolute population equality, and because compactness in particular is relevant to demonstrating possible majority-minority districts under the Voting Rights Act of 1965, there is no doubt that a test relying on these standards would fall within judicial competence.

Third, the plaintiff would need to establish specific correlations between the district's deviations from traditional districting principles and the distribution of the population of his group. For example, one of the districts to which appellants object most strongly in this case is District 6, which they say "looms like a dragon descending on Philadelphia from the west, splitting up towns and communities throughout Montgomery and Berks Counties." To make their claim stick, they would need to point to specific protuberances on the draconian shape that reach out to include Democrats, or fissures in it that squirm away from Republicans. They would need to show that when towns and communities were split, Democrats tended to fall on one side and Republicans on the other.

Fourth, a plaintiff would need to present the court with a hypothetical district including his residence, one in which the proportion of the plaintiff's group was lower (in a packing claim) or higher (in a cracking one) and which at the same time deviated less from traditional districting principles than the actual district. This hypothetical district would allow the plaintiff to claim credibly that the deviations from traditional districting principles were not only correlated with, but also caused by, the packing or cracking of his group. Drawing the hypothetical district would, of course, necessarily involve redrawing at least one contiguous district, and a plaintiff would have to show that this could be done subject to traditional districting principles without packing or cracking his group (or another) worse than in the district being challenged.

Fifth, and finally, the plaintiff would have to show that the defendants acted intentionally to manipulate the shape of the district in order to pack or crack his group. In substantiating claims of political gerrymandering under a plan devised by a single major party, proving intent should not be hard, once the third and fourth (correlation and cause) elements are established, politicians not being politically disinterested or characteristically naive. I would, however, treat any showing of intent in a major-party case as too equivocal to count unless the entire legislature were controlled by the governor's party (or the dominant legislative party were vetoproof).

If the affected group were not a major party, proof of intent could, admittedly, be difficult. It would be possible that a legislature might not even have had the plaintiff's group in mind, and a plaintiff would naturally have a hard time show-ing requisite intent behind a plan produced by a bipartisan commission.

A plaintiff who got this far would have shown that his State intentionally acted to dilute his vote, having ignored reasonable alternatives consistent with tradi-tional districting principles. I would then shift the burden to the defendants to justify their decision by reference to objectives other than naked partisan advantage. They might show by rebuttal evidence that districting objectives could not be served by the plaintiff's hypothetical district better than by the district as drawn, or they might affirmatively establish legitimate objectives bet-ter served by the lines drawn than by the plaintiff's hypothetical. The State might, for example, posit the need to avoid racial vote dilution. It might plead one person, one vote, a standard compatible with gerrymandering but in some places perhaps unattainable without some lopsided proportions. The State might adopt the object of proportional representation among its political parties through its districting process.

Justice BREYER, dissenting.

The use of purely political considerations in drawing district boundaries is not a "necessary evil" that, for lack of judicially manageable standards, the Consti-tution inevitably must tolerate. Rather, pure politics often helps to secure con-stitutionally important democratic objectives. But sometimes it does not. Sometimes purely political "gerrymandering" will fail to advance any plausible democratic objective while simultaneously threatening serious democratic harm. And sometimes when that is so, courts can identify an equal protection violation and provide a remedy. Because the plaintiffs could claim (but have not yet proved) that such circumstances exist here, I would reverse the District Court's dismissal of their complaint.

[There is] at least one circumstance where use of purely political boundary-drawing factors can amount to a serious, and remediable, abuse, namely the unjustified use of political factors to entrench a minority in power. By entrench-ment I mean a situation in which a party that enjoys only minority support among the populace has nonetheless contrived to take, and hold, legislative power. By unjustified entrenchment I mean that the minority's hold on power is purely the result of partisan manipulation and not other factors. These "other" factors that could lead to "justified" (albeit temporary) minority entrenchment include sheer happenstance, the existence of more than two major parties, the unique constitutional requirements of certain representa-tional bodies such as the Senate, or reliance on traditional (geographic, com-munities of interest, etc.) districting criteria.

The democratic harm of unjustified entrenchment is obvious. Where unjus-tified entrenchment takes place, voters find it far more difficult to remove those responsible for a government they do not want; and these democratic values are dishonored.

Courts need not intervene often to prevent the kind of abuse I have described, because those harmed constitute a political majority, and a majority normally can work its political will. Where a State has improperly gerrymandered legislative or congressional districts to the majority's disadvantage, the majority should be able to elect officials in statewide races — particularly the Governor — who may help to undo the harm that districting has caused the majority's party, in the next round of districting if not sooner. And where a State has improperly gerrymandered congressional districts, Congress retains the power to revise the State's districting determinations.

Moreover, voters in some States, perhaps tiring of the political boundary-drawing rivalry, have found a procedural solution, confiding the task to a commission that is limited in the extent to which it may base districts on partisan concerns. According to the National Conference of State Legislatures, 12 States currently give "first and final authority for [state] legislative redistricting to a group other than the legislature." A number of States use a commission for congressional redistricting: Arizona, Hawaii, Idaho, Montana, New Jersey, and Washington, with Indiana using a commission if the legislature cannot pass a plan and Iowa requiring the district-drawing body not to consider political data.

But we cannot always count on a severely gerrymandered legislature itself to find and implement a remedy. The party that controls the process has no incentive to change it. And the political advantages of a gerrymander may become ever greater in the future. The availability of enhanced computer technology allows the parties to redraw boundaries in ways that target individual neighborhoods and homes, carving out safe but slim victory margins in the maximum number of districts, with little risk of cutting their margins too thin. By redrawing districts every two years, rather than every 10 years, a party might preserve its political advantages notwithstanding population shifts in the State. The combination of increasingly precise map-drawing technology and increasingly frequent map drawing means that a party may be able to bring about a gerrymander that is not only precise, but virtually impossible to dislodge. Thus, court action may prove necessary.

When it is necessary, a court should prove capable of finding an appropriate remedy. Courts have developed districting remedies in other cases. The bottom line is that courts should be able to identify the presence of one important gerrymandering evil, the unjustified entrenching in power of a political party that the voters have rejected. They should be able to separate the unjustified abuse of partisan boundary-drawing considerations to achieve that end from their more ordinary and justified use. And they should be able to design a remedy for extreme cases. . . . [49]

The political question doctrine is best understood by considering areas where it has been applied. In addition to the election cases described above, below are presented three of the more important areas where it has been applied: (1) challenges to restrictions on congressional membership—where the political question doctrine was rejected, (2) challenges to the president's conduct of foreign policy, and (3) challenges to the impeachment process—where the political question doctrine was applied. As you read these cases, consider whether these constitutional provisions and constitutional controversies are best deemed nonjusticiable political questions or whether they should have been decided on the merits by the courts.

---

49. In League of United American Citizens v. Perry, 548 U.S. 399 (2006), the court dismissed a challenge to partisan gerrymandering in Texas. Again, the court was split five to four and again there was no majority opinion. [Footnote by casebook author.]

ii.   The Political Question Doctrine Applied: Congressional Self-Governance

POWELL v. McCORMACK
395 U.S. 486 (1969)

Chief Justice WARREN delivered the opinion of the Court.

In November 1966, petitioner Adam Clayton Powell, Jr., was duly elected from the 18th Congressional District of New York to serve in the United States House of Representatives for the 90th Congress. However, pursuant to a House resolution, he was not permitted to take his seat. Powell (and some of the voters of his district) then filed suit in Federal District Court, claiming that the House could exclude him only if it found he failed to meet the standing requirements of age, citizenship, and residence contained in Art. I, §2, of the Constitution — requirements the House specifically found Powell met — and thus had excluded him unconstitutionally.

During the 89th Congress, a Special Subcommittee on Contracts of the Committee on House Administration conducted an investigation into the expenditures of the Committee on Education and Labor, of which petitioner Adam Clayton Powell, Jr., was chairman. The Special Subcommittee issued a report concluding that Powell and certain staff employees had deceived the House authorities as to travel expenses. The report also indicated there was strong evidence that certain illegal salary payments had been made to Powell's wife at his direction. No formal action was taken during the 89th Congress. However, prior to the organization of the 90th Congress, the Democratic members-elect met in caucus and voted to remove Powell as chairman of the Committee on Education and Labor.

When the 90th Congress met to organize in January 1967, Powell was asked to step aside while the oath was administered to the other members-elect. [After a Committee investigation and report, the House voted to exclude Powell and directed that the Speaker notify the Governor of New York that the seat was vacant.]

[W]e turn to the question whether the case is justiciable.

Respondents' first contention is that this case presents a political question because under Art. I, §5, there has been a "textually demonstrable constitutional commitment" to the House of the "adjudicatory power" to determine Powell's qualifications. Thus it is argued that the House, and the House alone, has power to determine who is qualified to be a member.

In order to determine whether there has been a textual commitment to a coordinate department of the Government, we must interpret the Constitution. In other words, we must first determine what power the Constitution confers upon the House through Art. I, §5, before we can determine to what extent, if any, the exercise of that power is subject to judicial review. Respondents maintain that the House has broad power under §5, and, they argue, the House may determine which are the qualifications necessary for membership. On the other hand, petitioners allege that the Constitution provides that an elected representative may be denied his seat only if the House finds he does not meet one of the standing qualifications expressly prescribed by the Constitution.

In order to determine the scope of any "textual commitment" under Art. I, §5, we necessarily must determine the meaning of the phrase to "be the Judge of the Qualifications of its own Members." Petitioners argue that the records of the debates during the Constitutional Convention; available commentary from the post-Convention, pre-ratification period; and early congressional applications of Art. I, §5, support their construction of the section. Our examination of the relevant historical materials leads us to the conclusion that petitioners are correct and that the Constitution leaves the House without authority to exclude any person, duly elected by his constituents, who meets all the requirements for membership expressly prescribed in the Constitution.

[After reviewing English history, debates at the Constitutional Convention, and subsequent practices, the Court concluded:] Had the intent of the framers emerged from these materials with less clarity, we would nevertheless have been compelled to resolve any ambiguity in favor of a narrow construction of the scope of Congress' power to exclude members-elect. A fundamental principle of our representative democracy is, in Hamilton's words, "that the people should choose whom they please to govern them." As Madison pointed out at the Convention, this principle is undermined as much by limiting whom the people can select as by limiting the franchise itself. In apparent agreement with this basic philosophy, the Convention adopted his suggestion limiting the power to expel. To allow essentially that same power to be exercised under the guise of judging qualifications, would be to ignore Madison's warning, borne out in the *Wilkes* case and some of Congress's own post-Civil War exclusion cases, against "vesting an improper & dangerous power in the Legislature." Moreover, it would effectively nullify the Convention's decision to require a two-thirds vote for expulsion. Unquestionably, Congress has an interest in preserving its institutional integrity, but in most cases that interest can be sufficiently safeguarded by the exercise of its power to punish its members for disorderly behavior and, in extreme cases, to expel a member with the concurrence of two-thirds. In short, both the intention of the framers, to the extent it can be determined, and an examination of the basic principles of our democratic system persuade us that the Constitution does not vest in the Congress a discretionary power to deny membership by a majority vote.

For these reasons, we have concluded that Art. I, §5, is at most a "textually demonstrable commitment" to Congress to judge only the qualifications expressly set forth in the Constitution. Therefore, the "textual commitment" formulation of the political question doctrine does not bar federal courts from adjudicating petitioners' claims.

In United States Term Limits, Inc. v. Thornton, 514 U.S. 779 (1975), the Supreme Court applied *Powell* and held that states cannot set term limits for members of Congress. The Court ruled that Article I sets the only permissible qualifications for members of Congress and that it is unconstitutional for a state law to create term limits by keeping candidates for congressional office from being listed on the ballot after they serve a set number of terms.

iii. The Political Question Doctrine Applied: Foreign Policy

Although the Supreme Court has declared that "it is error to suppose that every case or controversy which touches foreign relations lies beyond judicial cognizance,"[50] the Court also frequently has held that cases presenting issues related to the conduct of foreign affairs pose political questions.[51] In Oetjen v. Central Leather Co., in 1918, the Court declared: "The conduct of the foreign relations of our Government is committed by the Constitution to the Executive and Legislature 'the political' Departments of the Government, and the propriety of what may be done in the exercise of this political power is not subject to judicial inquiry or decision."[52]

Over the past few decades, there have been several challenges to the president's use of troops in foreign countries. For example, during the Vietnam War, several dozen cases were filed in the federal courts arguing that the war was unconstitutional because there was no congressional declaration of war. Although the Supreme Court did not rule in any of these cases, either as to justiciability or on the merits, most of the lower courts deemed that the challenges to the war do constitute a political question.[53] In the same way, the political question doctrine was used by lower courts to dismiss challenges to the constitutionality of the president's military activities in El Salvador,[54] U.S. involvement in the Persian Gulf War,[55] and U.S. participation in the bombing of Yugoslavia in 1999.[56]

The underlying issue, as with all areas of the political question doctrine, is whether this is appropriate judicial deference or unwarranted judicial abdication on an important constitutional issue. The Supreme Court last addressed the political question doctrine in the context of foreign policy in Goldwater v. Carter. Most recently, a federal court of appeals affirmed a dismissal and a challenge to the constitutionality of the Iraq War on political question grounds.[57]

GOLDWATER v. CARTER

444 U.S. 996 (1979)

[President Jimmy Carter rescinded the United States' treaty with Taiwan as part of recognizing the People's Republic of China. Senator Barry Goldwater

---

50. Baker v. Carr, 369 U.S. 186, 211 (1962).

51. For a defense of this use of the political question doctrine, *see* Theodore Blumoff, *Judicial Review, Foreign Affairs, and Legislative Standing*, 25 Ga. L. Rev. 227 (1991).

52. 246 U.S. 297, 302 (1918). *See also* Chicago & S. Air Lines v. Waterman S.S. Corp., 333 U.S. 103, 111 (1948).

53. *See, e.g.*, Holtzman v. Schlesinger, 484 F.2d 1307, 1309 (2d Cir. 1973), *cert. denied*, 416 U.S. 936 (1974); DaCasta v. Laird, 471 F.2d 1146, 1147 (2d Cir. 1973); Sarnoff v. Connally, 457 F.2d 809, 810 (9th Cir. 1972), *cert. denied*, 409 U.S. 929 (1972); Orlando v. Laird, 443 F.2d 1039, 1043 (2d Cir. 1971), *cert. denied*, 404 U.S. 869 (1971); Simmons v. United States, 406 F.2d 456, 460 (5th Cir. 1969), *cert. denied*, 395 U.S. 982 (1969); *see also* Anthony D'Amato & Robert M. O'Neil, *The Judiciary and Vietnam* 51-58 (1972) (description of cases concerning the Vietnam War as a political question); Louis Henkin, *Vietnam in the Courts of the United States: Political Questions*, 63 Am. J. Intl. L. 284 (1969).

54. *See, e.g.*, Crockett v. Reagan, 720 F.2d 1355 (D.C. Cir. 1983), *cert. denied*, 467 U.S. 1251 (1984); Sanchez-Espinoza v. Reagan, 770 F.2d 202 (D.C. Cir. 1985); Lowry v. Reagan, 676 F. Supp. 333 (D.D.C. 1987); *but cf.* Ramirez de Arellano v. Weinberger, 745 F.2d 1500 (D.C. Cir. 1984) (holding justiciable a claim by a U.S. citizen that the federal government had taken his property in Honduras for the purpose of using it as a military training site; no challenge to the legality of the military activities was present).

55. *See, e.g.*, Ange v. Bush, 752 F. Supp. 509 (D.D.C. 1990).

56. Campbell v. Clinton, 52 F. Supp. 2d 34 (D.D.C. 1999).

57. Doe v. Bush, 322 F.3d 109 (1st Cir. 2003).

brought a constitutional challenge arguing that the Senate must rescind a treaty, just as the Senate must ratify the making of a treaty.]

Justice REHNQUIST, with whom the Chief Justice, Mr. Justice STEWART, and Mr. Justice STEVENS join, concurring in the judgment.

I am of the view that the basic question presented by the petitioners in this case is "political" and therefore nonjusticiable because it involves the authority of the President in the conduct of our country's foreign relations and the extent to which the Senate or the Congress is authorized to negate the action of the President.

[T]he controversy in the instant case is a nonjusticiable political dispute that should be left for resolution by the Executive and Legislative Branches of the Government. Here, while the Constitution is express as to the manner in which the Senate shall participate in the ratification of a treaty, it is silent as to that body's participation in the abrogation of a treaty.

In light of the absence of any constitutional provision governing the termination of a treaty, and the fact that different termination procedures may be appropriate for different treaties, the instant case in my view also "must surely be controlled by political standards."

I think that the justifications for concluding that the question here is political in nature are compelling because it involves foreign relations — specifically a treaty commitment to use military force in the defense of a foreign government if attacked. Having decided that the question presented in this action is nonjusticiable, I believe that the appropriate disposition is for this Court to vacate the decision of the Court of Appeals and remand with instructions for the District Court to dismiss the complaint.

Justice POWELL, concurring.

Although I agree with the result reached by the Court, I would dismiss the complaint as not ripe for judicial review. This Court has recognized that an issue should not be decided if it is not ripe for judicial review. Prudential considerations persuade me that a dispute between Congress and the President is not ready for judicial review unless and until each branch has taken action asserting its constitutional authority. Differences between the President and the Congress are commonplace under our system. The differences should, and almost invariably do, turn on political rather than legal considerations. The Judicial Branch should not decide issues affecting the allocation of power between the President and Congress until the political branches reach a constitutional impasse. Otherwise, we would encourage small groups or even individual Members of Congress to seek judicial resolution of issues before the normal political process has the opportunity to resolve the conflict.

Justice BRENNAN [concurring in the judgment and dissenting].

In this case, a few Members of Congress claim that the President's action in terminating the treaty with Taiwan has deprived them of their constitutional role with respect to a change in the supreme law of the land. Congress has taken no official action. In the present posture of this case, we do not know whether there ever will be an actual confrontation between the Legislative and Executive Branches. Although the Senate has considered a resolution declaring that Senate approval is necessary for the termination of any mutual defense treaty, no final vote has been taken on the resolution. Moreover, it is unclear whether the resolution would have retroactive effect. It cannot be said that either the Senate or the House has rejected the President's claim. If the Congress chooses not to confront the President, it is not our task to do so. I therefore concur in the dismissal of this case.

Justice Rehnquist suggests, however, that the issue presented by this case is a nonjusticiable political question which can never be considered by this Court. I cannot agree. In my view, reliance upon the political-question doctrine is inconsistent with our precedents. As set forth in the seminal case of Baker v. Carr, 369 U.S. 186 (1962), the doctrine incorporates three inquiries: (i) Does the issue involve resolution of questions committed by the text of the Constitution to a coordinate branch of Government? (ii) Would resolution of the question demand that a court move beyond areas of judicial expertise? (iii) Do prudential considerations counsel against judicial intervention? In my opinion the answer to each of these inquiries would require us to decide this case if it were ready for review.

First, the existence of "a textually demonstrable constitutional commitment of the issue to a coordinate political department," turns on an examination of the constitutional provisions governing the exercise of the power in question. No constitutional provision explicitly confers upon the President the power to terminate treaties. Further, Art. II, §2, of the Constitution authorizes the President to make treaties with the advice and consent of the Senate. Article VI provides that treaties shall be a part of the supreme law of the land. These provisions add support to the view that the text of the Constitution does not unquestionably commit the power to terminate treaties to the President alone.

Second, there is no "lack of judicially discoverable and manageable standards for resolving" this case; nor is a decision impossible "without an initial policy determination of a kind clearly for nonjudicial discretion." We are asked to decide whether the President may terminate a treaty under the Constitution without congressional approval. Resolution of the question may not be easy, but it only requires us to apply normal principles of interpretation to the constitutional provisions at issue. The present case involves neither review of the President's activities as Commander in Chief nor impermissible interference in the field of foreign affairs. Such a case would arise if we were asked to decide, for example, whether a treaty required the President to order troops into a foreign country. But "it is error to suppose that every case or controversy which touches foreign relations lies beyond judicial cognizance." Baker v. Carr.

Finally, the political-question doctrine rests in part on prudential concerns calling for mutual respect among the three branches of Government. Thus, the Judicial Branch should avoid "the potentiality of embarrassment [that would result] from multifarious pronouncements by various departments on one question." Similarly, the doctrine restrains judicial action where there is an "unusual need for unquestioning adherence to a political decision already made."

If this case were ripe for judicial review, none of these prudential considerations would be present. Interpretation of the Constitution does not imply lack of respect for a coordinate branch. If the President and the Congress had reached irreconcilable positions, final disposition of the question presented by this case would eliminate, rather than create, multiple constitutional interpretations. The specter of the Federal Government brought to a halt because of the mutual intransigence of the President and the Congress would require this Court to provide a resolution pursuant to our duty "'to say what the law is.'" Quoting Marbury v. Madison.

In my view, the suggestion that this case presents a political question is incompatible with this Court's willingness on previous occasions to decide whether one branch of our Government has impinged upon the power of another. Under the criteria enunciated in Baker v. Carr, we have the responsibility to decide whether both the Executive and Legislative Branches have constitutional roles to play in termination of a treaty. If the Congress, by appropriate formal action, had challenged the President's authority to terminate the treaty with Taiwan, the resulting uncertainty could have serious consequences for our country. In that situation, it would be the duty of this Court to resolve the issue.

iv. The Political Question Doctrine Applied: Impeachment and Removal

In 1999, the House of Representatives voted articles of impeachment against President Bill Clinton.[58] The question often was raised as to whether any aspects of the impeachment procedure could be subjected to judicial review. The leading Supreme Court case on the subject was decided just six years earlier, and it indicates that the challenges to impeachment and removal are not justiciable.

NIXON v. UNITED STATES
506 U.S. 224 (1993)

Chief Justice Rehnquist delivered the opinion of the Court.

Petitioner Walter L. Nixon, Jr., asks this Court to decide whether Senate Rule XI, which allows a committee of Senators to hear evidence against an individual who has been impeached and to report that evidence to the full Senate, violates the Impeachment Trial Clause, Art. I, §3, cl. 6. That Clause provides that the "Senate shall have the sole Power to try all Impeachments." But before we reach the merits of such a claim, we must decide whether it is "justiciable," that is, whether it is a claim that may be resolved by the courts. We conclude that it is not.

Nixon, a former Chief Judge of the United States District Court for the Southern District of Mississippi, was convicted by a jury of two counts of making false statements before a federal grand jury and sentenced to prison. The grand jury investigation stemmed from reports that Nixon had accepted a gratuity from a Mississippi businessman in exchange for asking a local district attorney to halt the prosecution of the businessman's son. Because Nixon refused to resign from his office as a United States District Judge, he continued to collect his judicial salary while serving out his prison sentence.

On May 10, 1989, the House of Representatives adopted three articles of impeachment for high crimes and misdemeanors. The first two articles charged

---

58. The issue of impeachment and the Clinton impeachment proceedings are discussed more fully in Chapter 3.

Nixon with giving false testimony before the grand jury and the third article charged him with bringing disrepute on the Federal Judiciary.

After the House presented the articles to the Senate, the Senate voted to invoke its own Impeachment Rule XI, under which the presiding officer appoints a committee of Senators to "receive evidence and take testimony." Senate Impeachment Rule XI. The Senate committee held four days of hearings, during which 10 witnesses, including Nixon, testified. Pursuant to Rule XI, the committee presented the full Senate with a complete transcript of the proceeding and a Report stating the uncontested facts and summarizing the evidence on the contested facts. Nixon and the House impeachment managers submitted extensive final briefs to the full Senate and delivered arguments from the Senate floor during the three hours set aside for oral argument in front of that body. Nixon himself gave a personal appeal, and several Senators posed questions directly to both parties. The Senate voted by more than the constitutionally required two-thirds majority to convict Nixon on the first two articles. The presiding officer then entered judgment removing Nixon from his office as United States District Judge.

Nixon thereafter commenced the present suit, arguing that Senate Rule XI violates the constitutional grant of authority to the Senate to "try" all impeachments because it prohibits the whole Senate from taking part in the evidentiary hearings. See Art. I, §3, cl. 6. Nixon sought a declaratory judgment that his impeachment conviction was void and that his judicial salary and privileges should be reinstated.

In this case, we must examine Art. I, §3, cl. 6, to determine the scope of authority conferred upon the Senate by the framers regarding impeachment. It provides:

> The Senate shall have the sole Power to try all Impeachments. When sitting for that Purpose, they shall be on Oath or Affirmation. When the President of the United States is tried, the Chief Justice shall preside: And no Person shall be convicted without the Concurrence of two thirds of the Members present.

The language and structure of this Clause are revealing. The first sentence is a grant of authority to the Senate, and the word "sole" indicates that this authority is reposed in the Senate and nowhere else. The next two sentences specify requirements to which the Senate proceedings shall conform: The Senate shall be on oath or affirmation, a two-thirds vote is required to convict, and when the President is tried the Chief Justice shall preside.

We think that the word "sole" is of considerable significance. Indeed, the word "sole" appears only one other time in the Constitution — with respect to the House of Representatives' "sole Power of Impeachment." Art. I, §2, cl. 5. The common-sense meaning of the word "sole" is that the Senate alone shall have authority to determine whether an individual should be acquitted or convicted. If the courts may review the actions of the Senate in order to determine whether that body "tried" an impeached official, it is difficult to see how the Senate would be "functioning . . . independently and without assistance or interference."

There are two additional reasons why the Judiciary, and the Supreme Court in particular, were not chosen to have any role in impeachments. First, the framers recognized that most likely there would be two sets of proceedings for individuals who commit impeachable offenses — the impeachment trial and a separate criminal trial. In fact, the Constitution explicitly provides for two separate proceedings. See Art. I, §3, cl. 7. The framers deliberately separated the two forums to avoid raising the specter of bias and to ensure independent judgments. Certainly judicial review of the Senate's "trial" would introduce the same risk of bias as would participation in the trial itself.

Second, judicial review would be inconsistent with the framers' insistence that our system be one of checks and balances. In our constitutional system, impeachment was designed to be the only check on the Judicial Branch by the Legislature. Judicial involvement in impeachment proceedings, even if only for purposes of judicial review, is counterintuitive because it would eviscerate the "important constitutional check" placed on the Judiciary by the framers. Nixon's argument would place final reviewing authority with respect to impeachments in the hands of the same body that the impeachment process is meant to regulate.

Nevertheless, Nixon argues that judicial review is necessary in order to place a check on the Legislature. Nixon fears that if the Senate is given unreviewable authority to interpret the Impeachment Trial Clause, there is a grave risk that the Senate will usurp judicial power. The framers anticipated this objection and created two constitutional safeguards to keep the Senate in check. The first safeguard is that the whole of the impeachment power is divided between the two legislative bodies, with the House given the right to accuse and the Senate given the right to judge. The second safeguard is the two-thirds supermajority vote requirement. Hamilton explained that "[a]s the concurrence of two-thirds of the senate will be requisite to a condemnation, the security to innocence, from this additional circumstance, will be as complete as itself can desire."

In addition to the textual commitment argument, we are persuaded that the lack of finality and the difficulty of fashioning relief counsel against justiciability. We agree with the Court of Appeals that opening the door of judicial review to the procedures used by the Senate in trying impeachments would "expose the political life of the country to months, or perhaps years, of chaos." This lack of finality would manifest itself most dramatically if the President were impeached. The legitimacy of any successor, and hence his effectiveness, would be impaired severely, not merely while the judicial process was running its course, but during any retrial that a differently constituted Senate might conduct if its first judgment of conviction were invalidated. Equally uncertain is the question of what relief a court may give other than simply setting aside the judgment of conviction. Could it order the reinstatement of a convicted federal judge, or order Congress to create an additional judgeship if the seat had been filled in the interim?

Justice WHITE, with whom Justice BLACKMUN joins, concurring in the judgment.

Petitioner contends that the method by which the Senate convicted him on two articles of impeachment violates Art. I, §3, cl. 6, of the Constitution, which mandates that the Senate "try" impeachments. The Court is of the view that the Constitution forbids us even to consider his contention. I find no such prohibition and would therefore reach the merits of the claim. I concur in the judgment because the Senate fulfilled its constitutional obligation to "try" petitioner.

The majority states that the question raised in this case meets two of the criteria for political questions set out in Baker v. Carr. Of course the issue in the political question doctrine is not whether the constitutional text commits exclusive responsibility for a particular governmental function to one of the political branches. There are numerous instances of this sort of textual commitment, e.g., Art. I, §8, and it is not thought that disputes implicating these provisions are nonjusticiable. Rather, the issue is whether the Constitution has given one of the political branches final responsibility for interpreting the scope and nature of such a power.

Even if the Impeachment Trial Clause is read without regard to its Companion clause, the Court's willingness to abandon its obligation to review the constitutionality of legislative acts merely on the strength of the word "sole" is perplexing. Consider, by comparison, the treatment of Art. I, §1, which grants "All legislative powers" to the House and Senate. As used in that context "all" is nearly synonymous with "sole"—both connote entire and exclusive authority. Yet the Court has never thought it would unduly interfere with the operation of the Legislative Branch to entertain difficult and important questions as to the extent of the legislative power. Quite the opposite, we have stated that the proper interpretation of the Clause falls within the province of the Judiciary.

Justice SOUTER, concurring in the judgment.

I agree with the Court that this case presents a nonjusticiable political question. Because my analysis differs somewhat from the Court's, however, I concur in its judgment by this separate opinion.

As the Court observes, judicial review of an impeachment trial would under the best of circumstances entail significant disruption of government. One can, nevertheless, envision different and unusual circumstances that might justify a more searching review of impeachment proceedings. If the Senate were to act in a manner seriously threatening the integrity of its results, convicting, say, upon a coin toss, or upon a summary determination that an officer of the United States was simply "a bad guy," judicial interference might well be appropriate. In such circumstances, the Senate's action might be so far beyond the scope of its constitutional authority, and the consequent impact on the Republic so great, as to merit a judicial response despite the prudential concerns that would ordinarily counsel silence. "The political question doctrine, a tool for maintenance of governmental order, will not be so applied as to promote only disorder."

CHAPTER

2

THE FEDERAL
LEGISLATIVE POWER

A. INTRODUCTION: CONGRESS AND THE STATES

When may Congress act? What laws may Congress adopt? A basic principle of American government is that Congress may act only if there is express or implied authority in the Constitution, whereas states may act unless the Constitution prohibits the action. Article I of the Constitution, which creates the federal legislative power, begins by stating, "All legislative powers herein granted shall be vested in a Congress of the United States which shall consist of a Senate and House of Representatives." Additionally, the Tenth Amendment declares, "The powers not delegated to the United States by the Constitution, nor prohibited by it to the States, are reserved to the States respectively, or to the people."

In evaluating the constitutionality of any act of Congress, there are always two questions. First, does Congress have the authority under the Constitution to legislate? This requires defining the scope of the powers granted to Congress, particularly in Article I, §8 of the Constitution. Second, if so, does the law violate another constitutional provision or doctrine, such as by infringing separation of powers or interfering with individual liberties?

In answering both of these questions the issue has arisen throughout American history as to the extent to which concern for state governments and their prerogatives should matter. During some eras of constitutional history, such as between the late nineteenth century and 1937 and again in the past decade, concern for state governments has profoundly answered how the Court has dealt with both of these questions. The Court during these times limited congressional power to leave areas of governance to state governments. During these times, the Court also directly protected state sovereignty, concluding that even valid exercises of legislative power are unconstitutional when they infringe state sovereignty. The Court has used the Tenth Amendment as the basis for this protection of state governments from federal encroachment.

During other times of American history, however, the Court has refused to use concern over state governments either as a basis for narrowly interpreting the scope of Congress's powers or as a limit through the Tenth Amendment on the reach of federal legislation. From the 1930s until the 1990s, the Court broadly defined the scope of Congress's authority under Article I of the Constitution and refused to use the Tenth Amendment as a limit on federal power. Since the 1990s, the Court again has invalidated laws as exceeding the scope of Congress's powers and as violating the Tenth Amendment.

In other words, throughout American history, Congress's powers have been defined relative to the states. Some of the most important political battles in American history — abolition of slavery, Reconstruction, progressive labor legislation, the New Deal, the civil rights movement — have been fought over how power should be allocated between the federal and state governments.

The division of power between Congress and the states is the focus of this chapter. The chapter considers how Congress's powers enumerated in the Constitution should be defined. It also considers whether and when the Tenth Amendment, and its protection of state governments, is and should be a limit on congressional power.

The chapter begins with McCulloch v. Maryland, an enormously important case concerning the relationship between federal and state governments. Following *McCulloch*, the issue is raised as to the values to be gained and lost by safeguarding state government entities. As part of this discussion, the Court's most recent federalism decision — National Federation of Independent Business v. Sebelius (2012), concerning the constitutionality of the Patient Protection and Affordable Care Act — is presented. It concerns issues examined in the following sections concerning the Necessary and Proper Clause, the Commerce Clause, the Spending Power, and the Tenth Amendment. Rather than divide the case and the dissents among the sections on this topic, it is presented as a whole, and each aspect can be considered in the context of the particular areas of federalism law. Subsequent sections of this chapter examine then particular federal powers, including the Necessary and Proper Clause (section B), especially Congress's Commerce Clause authority (section C), its taxing and spending power (section D), its authority under §5 of the Fourteenth Amendment (section E), and its power to authorize suits against state governments (section F).

THE FRAMEWORK FOR ANALYSIS: McCULLOCH v. MARYLAND

McCulloch v. Maryland is the most important Supreme Court decision in American history defining the scope of Congress's powers and delineating the relationship between the federal government and the states. The issue in *McCulloch* is whether it is constitutional for the State of Maryland to tax the Bank of the United States.

Some historical background is likely to be useful in understanding the decision. The controversy over the Bank of the United States began early in George Washington's presidency, in 1790, with a major dispute in both Congress and the executive branch as to whether Congress had the authority to create such a bank.[1] Secretary of the Treasury Alexander Hamilton strongly favored creating a Bank of the United States, but he was opposed by Secretary of State Thomas Jefferson and Attorney General Edmund Randolph. Both Jefferson and Randolph argued that Congress lacked the authority under the Constitution to create such a

---

1. A thorough discussion of the history of the Bank of the United States can be found in 1 Charles Warren, *The Supreme Court in United States History* 499-540 (1st ed. 1922).

bank and that doing so would usurp state government prerogatives. Ultimately, Hamilton persuaded President George Washington to support creating the bank, but the debate continued in Congress. James Madison, then in the House of Representatives, echoed the views of Jefferson and Randolph, and opposed the bank. Despite this opposition, Congress created the first Bank of the United States.

The bank existed for 21 years until its charter expired in 1811. However, after the War of 1812, the country experienced serious economic problems, and the Bank of the United States was re-created in 1816. In fact, although he had opposed such a bank a quarter of a century earlier, President James Madison endorsed its re-creation. The U.S. government actually owned only 20 percent of the new bank.

The Bank of the United States did not solve the country's economic problems and, indeed, many blamed the bank's monetary policies for aggravating a serious depression. State governments were particularly angry at the bank because the bank called in loans owed by the states. Several states adopted laws designed to limit the operation of the bank. Some states adopted laws prohibiting its operation within their borders. Others, such as Maryland, taxed it. The Maryland law required that any bank not chartered by the state pay either an annual tax of $15,000 or a tax of 2 percent on all of its notes that needed to be on special stamped paper.

The bank refused to pay the Maryland tax, and John James sued for himself and the State of Maryland in the County Court of Baltimore to recover the money owed under the tax. The defendant, McCulloch, was the cashier of that branch of the Bank of the United States. The trial court rendered judgment in favor of the plaintiffs, James, and the State of Maryland, and the Maryland Court of Appeals affirmed.

McCULLOCH v. MARYLAND

17 U.S. (4 Wheat.) 316 (1819)

MARSHALL, Ch. J., delivered the opinion of the court.

In the case now to be determined, the defendant, a sovereign state, denies the obligation of a law enacted by the legislature of the Union, and the plaintiff, on his part, contests the validity of an act which has been passed by the legislature of that state. The constitution of our country, in its most interesting and vital parts, is to be considered; the conflicting powers of the government of the Union and of its members, as marked in that constitution, are to be discussed; and an opinion given, which may essentially influence the great operations of the government. No tribunal can approach such a question without a deep sense of its importance, and of the awful responsibility involved in its decision. But it must be decided peacefully, or remain a source of hostile legislation, perhaps, of hostility of a still more serious nature; and if it is to be so decided, by this tribunal alone can the decision be made. On the supreme court of the United States has the constitution of our country devolved this important duty.

[I]

The first question made in the cause is — has congress power to incorporate a bank? It has been truly said, that this can scarcely be considered as an open question, entirely unprejudiced by the former proceedings of the nation respecting it. The principle now contested was introduced at a very early period of our history, has been recognised by many successive legislatures, and has been acted upon by the judicial department, in cases of peculiar delicacy, as a law of undoubted obligation.

It will not be denied, that a bold and daring usurpation might be resisted, after an acquiescence still longer and more complete than this. But it is conceived, that a doubtful question, one on which human reason may pause, and the human judgment be suspended, in the decision of which the great principles of liberty are not concerned, but the respective powers of those who are equally the representatives of the people, are to be adjusted; if not put at rest by the practice of the government, ought to receive a considerable impression from that practice. An exposition of the constitution, deliberately established by legislative acts, on the faith of which an immense property has been advanced, ought not to be lightly disregarded.

The power now contested was exercised by the first congress elected under the present constitution. The bill for incorporating the Bank of the United States did not steal upon an unsuspecting legislature, and pass unobserved. Its principle was completely understood, and was opposed with equal zeal and ability. After being resisted, first, in the fair and open field of debate, and afterwards, in the executive cabinet, with as much persevering talent as any measure has ever experienced, and being supported by arguments which convinced minds as pure and as intelligent as this country can boast, it became a law. The original act was permitted to expire; but a short experience of the embarrassments to which the refusal to revive it exposed the government, convinced those who were most prejudiced against the measure of its necessity, and induced the passage of the present law. It would require no ordinary share of intrepidity, to assert that a measure adopted under these circumstances, was a bold and plain usurpation, to which the constitution gave no countenance.

In discussing this question, the counsel for the state of Maryland have deemed it of some importance, in the construction of the constitution, to consider that instrument, not as emanating from the people, but as the act of sovereign and independent states. The powers of the general government, it has been said, are delegated by the states, who alone are truly sovereign; and must be exercised in subordination to the states, who alone possess supreme dominion. It would be difficult to sustain this proposition. The convention which framed the constitution was indeed elected by the state legislatures. But the instrument, when it came from their hands, was a mere proposal, without obligation, or pretensions to it. It was reported to the then existing congress of the United States, with a request that it might "be submitted to a convention of delegates, chosen in each state by the people thereof, under the recommendation of its legislature, for their assent and ratification."

This mode of proceeding was adopted; and by the convention, by congress, and by the state legislatures, the instrument was submitted to the people. They acted upon it in the only manner in which they can act safely, effectively and wisely, on such a subject, by assembling in convention. It is true, they assembled in their several states — and where else should they have assembled? No political dreamer was ever wild enough to think of breaking down the lines which separate the states, and of compounding the American people into one common mass. Of consequence, when they act, they act in their states. But the measures they adopt do not, on that account, cease to be the measures of the people themselves, or become the measures of the state governments.

From these conventions, the constitution derives its whole authority. The government proceeds directly from the people; is "ordained and established," in the name of the people; and is declared to be ordained, "in order to form a more perfect union, establish justice, insure domestic tranquillity, and secure the blessings of liberty to themselves and to their posterity." The assent of the states, in their sovereign capacity, is implied, in calling a convention, and thus submitting that instrument to the people. But the people were at perfect liberty to accept or reject it; and their act was final. It required not the affirmance, and could not be negatived, by the state governments. The constitution, when thus adopted, was of complete obligation, and bound the state sovereignties.

It has been said, that the people had already surrendered all their powers to the state sovereignties, and had nothing more to give. But, surely, the question whether they may resume and modify the powers granted to government, does not remain to be settled in this country. Much more might the legitimacy of the general government be doubted, had it been created by the states. The powers delegated to the state sovereignties were to be exercised by themselves, not by a distinct and independent sovereignty, created by themselves. To the formation of a league, such as was the confederation, the state sovereignties were certainly competent. But when, "in order to form a more perfect union," it was deemed necessary to change this alliance into an effective government, possessing great and sovereign powers, and acting directly on the people, the necessity of referring it to the people, and of deriving its powers directly from them, was felt and acknowledged by all. The government of the Union, then (whatever may be the influence of this fact on the case), is, emphatically and truly, a government of the people. In form, and in substance, it emanates from them. Its powers are granted by them, and are to be exercised directly on them, and for their benefit.

This government is acknowledged by all, to be one of enumerated powers. The principle, that it can exercise only the powers granted to it, would seem too apparent, to have required to be enforced by all those arguments, which its enlightened friends, while it was depending before the people, found it necessary to urge; that principle is now universally admitted. But the question respecting the extent of the powers actually granted, is perpetually arising, and will probably continue to arise, so long as our system shall exist. In discussing these questions, the conflicting powers of the general and state governments must be brought into view, and the supremacy of their respective laws, when they are in opposition, must be settled.

If any one proposition could command the universal assent of mankind, we might expect it would be this — that the government of the Union, though limited in its powers, is supreme within its sphere of action. This would seem to result, necessarily, from its nature. It is the government of all; its powers are delegated by all; it represents all, and acts for all. Though any one state may be willing to control its operations, no state is willing to allow others to control them. The nation, on those subjects on which it can act, must necessarily bind its component parts. But this question is not left to mere reason: the people have, in express terms, decided it, by saying, "this constitution, and the laws of the United States, which shall be made in pursuance thereof," "shall be the supreme law of the land," and by requiring that the members of the state legislatures, and the officers of the executive and judicial departments of the states, shall take the oath of fidelity to it. The government of the United States, then, though limited in its powers, is supreme; and its laws, when made in pursuance of the constitution, form the supreme law of the land, "anything in the constitution or laws of any state to the contrary notwithstanding."

Among the enumerated powers, we do not find that of establishing a bank or creating a corporation. But there is no phrase in the instrument which, like the articles of confederation, excludes incidental or implied powers; and which requires that everything granted shall be expressly and minutely described. Even the 10th amendment, which was framed for the purpose of quieting the excessive jealousies which had been excited, omits the word "expressly," and declares only, that the powers "not delegated to the United States, nor prohibited to the states, are reserved to the states or to the people;" thus leaving the question, whether the particular power which may become the subject of contest, has been delegated to the one government, or prohibited to the other, to depend on a fair construction of the whole instrument. The men who drew and adopted this amendment had experienced the embarrassments resulting from the insertion of this word in the articles of confederation, and probably omitted it, to avoid those embarrassments. A constitution, to contain an accurate detail of all the subdivisions of which its great powers will admit, and of all the means by which they may be carried into execution, would partake of the prolixity of a legal code, and could scarcely be embraced by the human mind. It would, probably, never be understood by the public. Its nature, therefore, requires, that only its great outlines should be marked, its important objects designated, and the minor ingredients which compose those objects, be deduced from the nature of the objects themselves. That this idea was entertained by the framers of the American constitution, is not only to be inferred from the nature of the instrument, but from the language. Why else were some of the limitations, found in the 9th section of the 1st article, introduced? It is also, in some degree, warranted, by their having omitted to use any restrictive term which might prevent its receiving a fair and just interpretation. In considering this question, then, we must never forget that it is a constitution we are expounding.

Although, among the enumerated powers of government, we do not find the word "bank" or "incorporation," we find the great powers, to lay and collect taxes; to borrow money; to regulate commerce; to declare and conduct a war; and to raise and support armies and navies. The sword and the purse, all the external relations, and no inconsiderable portion of the industry of the nation, are intrusted to its government. It can never be pretended, that these vast powers draw after them others of inferior importance, merely because they are inferior. Such an idea can never be advanced. But it may with great reason be contended, that a government, intrusted with such ample powers, on the due execution of which the happiness and prosperity of the nation so vitally depends, must also be intrusted with ample means for their execution. The power being given, it is the interest of the nation to facilitate its execution. It can never be their interest, and cannot be presumed to have been their intention, to clog and embarrass its execution, by withholding the most appropriate means. Can we adopt that construction (unless the words imperiously require it), which would impute to the framers of that instrument, when granting these powers for the public good, the intention of impeding their exercise, by withholding a choice of means? If, indeed, such be the mandate of the constitution, we have only to obey; but that instrument does not profess to enumerate the means by which the powers it confers may be executed; nor does it prohibit the creation of a corporation, if the existence of such a being be essential, to the beneficial exercise of those powers. It is, then, the subject of fair inquiry, how far such means may be employed.

It is not denied, that the powers given to the government imply the ordinary means of execution. That, for example, of raising revenue, and applying it to national purposes, is admitted to imply the power of conveying money from place to place, as the exigencies of the nation may require, and of employing the usual means of conveyance. The government which has a right to do an act, and has imposed on it, the duty of performing that act, must, according to the dictates of reason, be allowed to select the means; and those who contend that it may not select any appropriate means, that one particular mode of effecting the object is excepted, take upon themselves the burden of establishing that exception.

But the constitution of the United States has not left the right of congress to employ the necessary means, for the execution of the powers conferred on the government, to general reasoning. To its enumeration of powers is added, that of making "all laws which shall be necessary and proper, for carrying into execution the foregoing powers, and all other powers vested by this constitution, in the government of the United States, or in any department thereof." The counsel for the state of Maryland have urged various arguments, to prove that this clause, though, in terms, a grant of power, is not so, in effect; but is really restrictive of the general right, which might otherwise be implied, of selecting means for executing the enumerated powers. In support of this proposition, they have found it necessary to contend, that this clause was inserted for the purpose of conferring on congress the power of making laws. That, without it, doubts might be entertained, whether congress could exercise its powers in the form of legislation.

But the argument on which most reliance is placed, is drawn from that peculiar language of this clause. Congress is not empowered by it to make all laws, which may have relation to the powers confered on the government, but such only as may be "necessary and proper" for carrying them into execution. The word "necessary" is considered as controlling the whole sentence, and as limiting the right to pass laws for the execution of the granted powers, to such as are indispensable, and without which the power would be nugatory. That it excludes the choice of means, and leaves to congress, in each case, that only which is most direct and simple.

Is it true, that this is the sense in which the word "necessary" is always used? Does it always import an absolute physical necessity, so strong, that one thing to which another may be termed necessary, cannot exist without that other? We think it does not. If reference be had to its use, in the common affairs of the world, or in approved authors, we find that it frequently imports no more than that one thing is convenient, or useful, or essential to another. To employ the means necessary to an end, is generally understood as employing any means calculated to produce the end, and not as being confined to those single means, without which the end would be entirely unattainable. Such is the character of human language, that no word conveys to the mind, in all situations, one single definite idea; and nothing is more common than to use words in a figurative sense. Almost all compositions contain words, which, taken in a their rigorous sense, would convey a meaning different from that which is obviously intended. It is essential to just construction, that many words which import something excessive, should be understood in a more mitigated sense — in that sense which common usage justifies. The word "necessary" is of this description. It has not a fixed character, peculiar to itself. It admits of all degrees of comparison; and is often connected with other words, which increase or diminish the impression the mind receives of the urgency it imports. A thing may be necessary, very necessary, absolutely or indispensably necessary. To no mind would the same idea be conveyed by these several phrases. This word, then, like others, is used in various senses; and, in its construction, the subject, the context, the intention of the person using them, are all to be taken into view.

Let this be done in the case under consideration. The subject is the execution of those great powers on which the welfare of a nation essentially depends. It must have been the intention of those who gave these powers, to insure, so far as human prudence could insure, their beneficial execution. This could not be done, by confiding the choice of means to such narrow limits as not to leave it in the power of congress to adopt any which might be appropriate, and which were conducive to the end. This provision is made in a constitution, intended to endure for ages to come, and consequently, to be adapted to the various crises of human affairs. To have prescribed the means by which government should, in all future time, execute its powers, would have been to change, entirely, the character of the instrument, and give it the properties of a legal code. It would have been an unwise attempt to provide, by immutable rules, for exigencies which, if foreseen at all, must have been seen dimly, and which can be best provided for as they occur. To have declared, that the best means shall not be used, but those alone, without which the power given would be nugatory, would have been to deprive the legislature of the capacity to avail itself of experience, to exercise its reason, and to accommodate its legislation to circumstances.

So, with respect to the whole penal code of the United States: whence arises the power to punish, in cases not prescribed by the constitution? All admit, that the government may, legitimately, punish any violation of its laws; and yet, this is not among the enumerated powers of congress. The right to enforce the observance of law, by punishing its infraction, might be denied, with the more plausibility, because it is expressly given in some cases.

Take, for example, the power "to establish post-offices and post-roads." This power is executed, by the single act of making the establishment. But, from this has been inferred the power and duty of carrying the mail along the post-road, from one post-office to another. And from this implied power, has again been inferred the right to punish those who steal letters from the post-office, or rob the mail. It may be said, with some plausibility, that the right to carry the mail, and to punish those who rob it, is not indispensably necessary to the establishment of a post-office and post-road. This right is indeed essential to the beneficial exercise of the power, but not indispensably necessary to its existence. So, of the punishment of the crimes of stealing or falsifying a record or process of a court of the United States, or of perjury in such court. To punish these offences, is certainly conducive to the due administration of justice. But courts may exist, and may decide the causes brought before them, though such crimes escape punishment.

In ascertaining the sense in which the word "necessary" is used in this clause of the constitution, we may derive some aid from that with which it it is associated. Congress shall have power "to make all laws which shall be necessary and proper to carry into execution" the powers of the government. If the word "necessary" was used in that strict and rigorous sense for which the counsel for the state of Maryland contend, it would be an extraordinary departure from the usual course of the human mind, as exhibited in composition, to add a word, the only possible effect of which is, to qualify that strict and rigorous meaning; to present to the mind the idea of some choice of means of legislation, not strained and compressed within the narrow limits for which gentlemen contend.

We think so for the following reasons: 1st. The clause is placed among the powers of congress, not among the limitations on those powers. 2d. Its terms purport to enlarge, not to diminish the powers vested in the government. It purports to be an additional power, not a restriction on those already granted. No reason has been, or can be assigned, for thus concealing an intention to narrow the discretion of the national legislature, under words which purport to enlarge it. The framers of the constitution wished its adoption, and well knew that it would be endangered by its strength, not by its weakness. Had they been capable of using language which would convey to the eye one idea, and, after deep reflection, impress on the mind, another, they would rather have disguised the grant of power, than its limitation. If, then, their intention had been, by this clause, to restrain the free use of means which might otherwise have been implied, that intention would have been inserted in another place, and would have been expressed in terms resembling these. "In carrying into execution the foregoing powers, and all others," &c., "no laws shall be passed but such as are necessary and proper." Had the intention been to make this clause restrictive, it would unquestionably have been so in form as well as in effect.

We admit, as all must admit, that the powers of the government are limited, and that its limits are not to be transcended. But we think the sound construction of the constitution must allow to the national legislature that discretion, with respect to the means by which the powers it confers are to be carried into execution, which will enable that body to perform the high duties assigned to it, in the manner most beneficial to the people. Let the end be legitimate, let it be within the scope of the constitution, and all means which are appropriate, which are plainly adapted to that end, which are not prohibited, but consist with the letter and spirit of the constitution, are constitutional.

Should congress, in the execution of its powers, adopt measures which are prohibited by the constitution; or should congress, under the pretext of executing its powers, pass laws for the accomplishment of objects not intrusted to the government; it would become the painful duty of this tribunal, should a case requiring such a decision come before it, to say, that such an act was not the law of the land. But where the law is not prohibited, and is really calculated to effect any of the objects intrusted to the government, to undertake here to inquire into the decree of its necessity, would be to pass the line which circumscribes the judicial department, and to tread on legislative ground. This court disclaims all pretensions to such a power.

[II]

Whether the state of Maryland may, without violating the constitution, tax that branch? That the power of taxation is one of vital importance; that it is retained by the states; that it is not abridged by the grant of a similar power to the government of the Union; that it is to be concurrently exercised by the two governments—are truths which have never been denied. But such is the paramount character of the constitution, that its capacity to withdraw any subject from the action of even this power, is admitted. The states are expressly forbidden to lay any duties on imports or exports, except what may be absolutely necessary for executing their inspection laws. If the obligation of this prohibition must be conceded — if it may restrain a state from the exercise of its taxing power on imports and exports — the same paramount character would seem to restrain, as it certainly may restrain, a state from such other exercise of this power, as is in its nature incompatible with, and repugnant to, the constitutional laws of the Union. A law, absolutely repugnant to another, as entirely repeals that other as if express terms of repeal were used.

On this ground, the counsel for the bank place its claim to be exempted from the power of a state to tax its operations. There is no express provision for the case, but the claim has been sustained on a principle which so entirely pervades the constitution, is so intermixed with the materials which compose it, so interwoven with its web, so blended with its texture, as to be incapable of being separated from it, without rending it into shreds. This great principle is, that the constitution and the laws made in pursuance thereof are supreme; that they control the constitution and laws of the respective states, and cannot be controlled by them. From this, which may be almost termed an axiom, other propositions are deduced as corollaries, on the truth or error of which, and on their application to this case, the cause has been supposed to depend. These are, 1st. That a power to create implies a power to preserve: 2d. That a power to destroy, if wielded by a different hand, is hostile to, and incompatible with these powers to create and to preserve: 3d. That where this repugnancy exists, that authority which is supreme must control, not yield to that over which it is supreme.

The power of congress to create, and of course, to continue, the bank, was the subject of the preceding part of this opinion; and is no longer to be considered as questionable. That the power of taxing it by the states may be exercised so as to destroy it, is too obvious to be denied. But taxation is said to be an absolute power, which acknowledges no other limits than those expressly prescribed in the constitution, and like sovereign power of every other description, is intrusted to the discretion of those who use it. But the very terms of this argument admit, that the sovereignty of the state, in the article of taxation itself, is subordinate to, and may be controlled by the constitution of the United States. How far it has been controlled by that instrument, must be a question of construction. In making this construction, no principle, not declared, can be admissible, which would defeat the legitimate operations of a supreme government. It is of the very essence of supremacy, to remove all obstacles to its action within its own sphere, and so to modify every power vested in subordinate governments, as to exempt its own operations from their own influence. This effect need not be stated in terms. It is so involved in the declaration of supremacy, so necessarily implied in it, that the expression of it could not make it more certain. We must, therefore, keep it in view, while construing the constitution. The argument on the part of the state of Maryland, is, not that the states may directly resist a law of congress, but that they may exercise their acknowledged powers upon it, and that the constitution leaves them this right, in the confidence that they will not abuse it. Before we proceed to examine this argument, and to subject it to test of the constitution, we must be permitted to bestow a few considerations on the nature and extent of this original right of taxation, which is acknowledged to remain with the states. It is admitted, that the power of taxing the people and their property, is essential to the very existence of government, and may be legitimately exercised on the objects to which it is applicable, to the utmost extent to which the government may choose to carry it. The only security against the abuse of this power, is found in the structure of the government itself. In imposing a tax, the legislature acts upon its constituents. This is, in general, a sufficient security against erroneous and oppressive taxation.

The people of a state, therefore, give to their government a right of taxing themselves and their property, and as the exigencies of government cannot be limited, they prescribe no limits to the exercise of this right, resting confidently on the interest of the legislator, and on the influence of the constituent over their representative, to guard them against its abuse. But the means employed by the government of the Union have no such security, nor is the right of a state to tax them sustained by the same theory. Those means are not given by the people of a particular state, not given by the constituents of the legislature, which claim the right to tax them, but by the people of all the states. They are given by all, for the benefit of all — and upon theory, should be subjected to that government only which belongs to all.

It may be objected to this definition, that the power of taxation is not confined to the people and property of a state. It may be exercised upon every object brought within its jurisdiction. The sovereignty of a state extends to everything which exists by its own authority, or is introduced by its permission; but does it extend to those means which are employed by congress to carry into execution powers conferred on that body by the people of the United States? We think it demonstrable, that it does not. Those powers are not given by the people of a single state. They are given by the people of the United States, to a government whose laws, made in pursuance of the constitution, are declared to be supreme. Consequently, the people of a single state cannot confer a sovereignty which will extend over them.

That the power to tax involves the power to destroy; that the power to destroy may defeat and render useless the power to create; that there is a plain repugnance in conferring on one government a power to control the constitutional measures of another, which other, with respect to those very measures, is declared to be supreme over that which exerts the control, are propositions not to be denied. But all inconsistencies are to be reconciled by the magic of the word confidence. Taxation, it is said, does not necessarily and unavoidably destroy. To carry it to the excess of destruction, would be an abuse, to presume which, would banish that confidence which is essential to all government. But is this a case of confidence? Would the people of any one state trust those of another with a power to control the most insignificant operations of their state government? We know they would not. Why, then, should we suppose, that the people of any one state should be willing to trust those of another with a power to control the operations of a government to which they have confided their most important and most valuable interests? In the legislature of the Union alone, are all represented. The legislature of the Union alone, therefore, can be trusted by the people with the power of controlling measures which concern all, in the confidence that it will not be abused. This, then, is not a case of confidence, and we must consider it is as it really is.

If we apply the principle for which the state of Maryland contends, to the constitution, generally, we shall find it capable of changing totally the character of that instrument. We shall find it capable of arresting all the measures of the government, and of prostrating it at the foot of the states. The American people have declared their constitution and the laws made in pursuance thereof, to be supreme; but this principle would transfer the supremacy, in fact, to the states. If the states may tax one instrument, employed by the government in the execution of its powers, they may tax any and every other instrument. They may tax the mail; they may tax the mint; they may tax patent-rights; they may tax the papers of the custom-house; they may tax judicial process; they may tax all the means employed by the government, to an excess which would defeat all the ends of government. This was not intended by the American people. They did not design to make their government dependent on the states.

The court has bestowed on this subject its most deliberate consideration. The result is a conviction that the states have no power, by taxation or otherwise, to retard, impede, burden, or in any manner control, the operations of the constitutional laws enacted by congress to carry into execution the powers vested in the general government. This is, we think, the unavoidable consequence of that supremacy which the constitution has declared. We are unanimously of opinion, that the law passed by the legislature of Maryland, imposing a tax on the Bank of the United Sates, is unconstitutional and void.

WHAT ROLE SHOULD CONCERN OVER PROTECTING STATES HAVE IN DEFINING CONGRESS'S POWERS?

Throughout American history, a central issue has been the extent to which concern over protecting the prerogatives and institutions of state governments should matter in defining the scope of Congress's legislative power. Should Congress's authority, under provisions such as the Commerce Clause and the spending power and §5 of the Fourteenth Amendment, be narrowly interpreted to leave more governance solely to the states? Or should Congress's powers be broadly defined without concern for preserving areas for state control? Should the Tenth Amendment be enforced by the judiciary as a limit on Congress's powers so as to protect state governments? Or should the Tenth Amendment be seen simply as a reminder that Congress can act only if it has express or implied authority, while states can act unless the Constitution prohibits their conduct?

These are the central questions throughout this chapter, and they are some of the most important in all of constitutional law. As alluded to earlier and as will be evident in the cases to follow, the Court has answered the questions differently at varying points in American history.

In considering these questions and how the Supreme Court has answered them, it is important to recognize that there are two key underlying normative issues.[2] First, how important is the protection of state sovereignty and federalism? Second, should it be the role of the judiciary to protect state prerogatives or should this be left to the political process?

As to the former question, those who oppose judicial protection of states as a limit on Congress's power argue that national legislation is needed to deal with national problems. From this perspective, the Court should not circumscribe

---

2. For excellent discussions of this issue, *see* David Shapiro, *Federalism: A Dialogue* (1995); Edward L. Rubin & Malcolm Feeley, *Federalism: Some Notes on a National Neurosis*, 41 UCLA L. Rev. 903 (1994).

the scope of Congress's authority or use the Tenth Amendment to invalidate federal laws. On the other side, those who favor judicial use of federalism as a constraint on Congress's power usually identify three benefits of protecting state governments: decreasing the likelihood of federal tyranny, enhancing democratic rule by providing government that is closer to the people, and allowing states to be laboratories for new ideas.

The first justification for protecting states from federal intrusions is that the division of power vertically, between federal and state governments, lessens the chance of federal tyranny.[3] The framers thought that the possibility of federal abuses could be limited by restricting the authority of the federal government.[4] Moreover, the danger of tyranny at the federal level is much more ominous than autocratic rule at the state or local level. Professor Rapczynski continues, "Should the federal government ever be captured by an authoritarian movement or assert itself as a special cohesive interest, the resulting oppression would almost certainly be much more severe and durable than any state would be capable."[5]

Yet others argue that the notion of radically limited federal powers seems anachronistic in the face of a modern national market economy and decades of extensive federal regulations. Additionally, there has been a major shift over time as to how abusive government is best controlled. Now it is thought that if a federal action intrudes upon individual liberties the federal judiciary will invalidate it as unconstitutional. Judicial review is seen as an important check against tyrannical government actions.

A second frequently invoked value of federalism is that states are closer to the people and thus more likely to be responsive to public needs and concerns.[6] Professor David Shapiro summarizes this argument when he writes, "[O]ne of the stronger arguments for a decentralized political structure is that, to the extent that the electorate is small, and elected representatives are thus more immediately accountable to individuals and their concerns, government is brought closer to the people and democratic ideals are more fully realized."[7] However, there is a danger that the greater responsiveness increases the dangers of government tyranny. There is a greater danger of special interests capturing government at smaller and more local levels. James Madison wrote of the danger of "factions" in Federalist 10 and modern political science literature offers support for his fears.[8]

Moreover, it is not clear what size of government unit is necessary for such responsiveness. For example, is a state the size of California, or for that matter a city the size of Los Angeles, sufficiently more homogeneous in its interests as to increase the likelihood of responsive government? Professor Shapiro writes, "[T]he goal of realizing democratic values to the maximum extent feasible may not be significantly enhanced by reducing the relevant polity from one of some 280,000,000 (the United States) to one of, say 30,000,000 (the State of California)."[9]

3. Andrzej Rapczynski, *From Sovereignty to Process: The Jurisprudence of Federalism After Garcia*, 1985 Sup. Ct. Rev. 641, 380.

4. Alexander Hamilton explained that "[the] necessity of local administration for local purposes would be a complete barrier against the oppressive use of such power." Federalist No. 32 (Alexander Hamilton), *Federalist Papers* at 137 (C. Rossiter Ed. 1961).

5. Rapczynski, *supra* note 3, at 388.

6. *Id.* at 391.

7. David Shapiro, *Federalism: A Dialogue* 92 (1995).

8. James Madison, Federalist No. 10, *The Federalist Papers* (C. Rossiter ED. 1961).

9. Shapiro, *supra* note 7, at 93.

A final argument that is frequently made for protecting federalism is that states can serve as laboratories for experimentation. Justice Brandeis apparently first articulated this idea when he declared: "To stay experimentation in things social and economic is a grave responsibility. Denial of the right to experiment might be fraught with serious consequences to the Nation. It is one of the happy incidents of the federal system that a single courageous State may, if its citizens choose, serve as a laboratory; and try novel social and economic experiments without risk to the rest of the country."[10] Justice O'Connor stated that the "Court's decision undermines the most valuable aspects of our federalism. Courts and commentators frequently have recognized that the 50 states serve as laboratories for the development of new social, economic, and political ideas."[11]

However, any federal legislation preempting state or local laws limits experimentation. Indeed, the application of constitutional rights to the states limits their experimenting with providing fewer safeguards of individual liberties. The key questions are when is it worth experimenting and when is experimentation to be rejected because of a need to impose a national mandate?

There also is a related process question: Who is in the best position to decide when further experimentation is warranted or when there is enough knowledge to justify federal actions? Critics of judicial protection of states argue that the desire for using states as laboratories is a policy argument to be made to Congress against federal legislation and not a judicial argument that should be used to invalidate particular federal laws on the grounds that they unduly limit experimentation. Additionally, Congress and even federal agencies can design experiments and try differing approaches in varying parts of the country.[12]

The second major question in evaluating judicial protection of states from federal encroachment is whether it should be the role of the judiciary to enforce the Tenth Amendment and protect state sovereignty or whether this is an issue that should be left to the political process. One view is that judicial enforcement of federalism as a limit on Congress is unnecessary because the political process will adequately protect state government interests. Professor Herbert Wechsler, in a landmark article, provided the intellectual foundation for this approach.[13] Wechsler argued that the interests of the states are represented in the national political process and that the nature of that process provides sufficient protection of state sovereignty, thus making it unnecessary for the courts to enforce federalism as a limit on Congress.[14]

But the assumption that states' interests are adequately represented in the national political process is questionable.[15] At the time the Constitution was written, states chose senators and thus were directly represented in Congress. Today, in contrast, with popular election of senators, it is harder to argue that

---

10. New State Ice Co. v. Liebman, 285 U.S. 262, 311 (1932) (Brandeis, J., dissenting).

11. Federal Energy Regulatory Commission v. Mississippi, 456 U.S. 742, 787-788 (1982) (O'Connor, J., dissenting).

12. Rubin & Feeley, *supra* note 2, at 925.

13. Herbert Wechsler, *The Political Safeguards of Federalism: The Role of the States in the Composition and Selection of the National Government*, 54 Colum. L. Rev. 543 (1954).

14. Professor Jesse Choper has advanced a similar thesis. *See* Jesse Choper, *Judicial Review and the National Political Process* (1980).

15. Professor Larry Kramer makes a strong argument that the interests of the states are protected through mechanisms such as administrative bureaucracies and political parties. Larry Kramer, *Understanding Federalism*, 47 Vand. L. Rev. 1485 (1994), offers a subtle account of the way in which the interests of the states are protected in the political process.

the states' interests as states are adequately protected in Congress.[16] It seems unlikely that the voters, in choosing representatives and senators, weigh heavily the extent to which the individual legislator votes in a manner that serves the interests of the state as an entity.

The remaining material in this chapter concerns how the Supreme Court has defined the scope of Congress's powers under three crucial constitutional provisions: the commerce power, the spending power, and §5 of the Fourteenth Amendment. Other issues concerning Congress's powers, such as the authority to delegate power to administrative agencies and Congress's role in foreign policy, are discussed in the next chapter.

In examining Congress's commerce power, its spending power, its authority under §5 of the Fourteenth Amendment, and its power to authorize suits against state governments, consider how in different time periods the Court has evaluated the importance of protecting state governments and the judicial role in this regard. During some periods, the Court has expansively defined Congress's authority and refused to use the Tenth Amendment as a limit. During other times, including now, the Court has limited the scope of Congress's powers and viewed the Tenth Amendment as a constraint on Congress's authority.

The Court's most recent decision concerning federalism was National Federation of Independent Business v. Sebelius, which addresses the constitutionality of the Patient Protection and Affordable Care Act. In it, the justices consider issues concerning the meaning of the Necessary and Proper Clause, the Commerce Clause, the Spending Power, and the Tenth Amendment. It is presented here, at the beginning of the chapter, with the expectation that each aspect can be considered in connection with the examination of each of these topics in the subsequent sections.

NATIONAL FEDERATION OF INDEPENDENT BUSINESS v. SEBELIUS
131 S. Ct. 2566 (2012)

Chief Justice ROBERTS announced the judgment of the Court and delivered the opinion of the Court with respect to Parts I, II, and III-C, an opinion with respect to Part IV, in which Justice BREYER and Justice KAGAN join, and an opinion with respect to Parts III-A, III-B, and III-D.

Today we resolve constitutional challenges to two provisions of the Patient Protection and Affordable Care Act of 2010: the individual mandate, which requires individuals to purchase a health insurance policy providing a minimum level of coverage; and the Medicaid expansion, which gives funds to the States on the condition that they provide specified health care to all citizens whose income falls below a certain threshold. We do not consider whether the Act embodies sound policies. That judgment is entrusted to the Nation's elected leaders. We ask only whether Congress has the power under the Constitution to enact the challenged provisions.

---

16. *See* Andrzej Rapczynski, *From Sovereignty to Process: The Jurisprudence of Federalism After* Garcia, 1985 Sup. Ct. Rev. 341, 393.

In our federal system, the National Government possesses only limited powers; the States and the people retain the remainder. In this case we must again determine whether the Constitution grants Congress powers it now asserts, but which many States and individuals believe it does not possess. Resolving this controversy requires us to examine both the limits of the Government's power, and our own limited role in policing those boundaries.

This case concerns two powers that the Constitution does grant the Federal Government, but which must be read carefully to avoid creating a general federal authority akin to the police power. The Constitution authorizes Congress to "regulate Commerce with foreign Nations, and among the several States, and with the Indian Tribes." Our precedents read that to mean that Congress may regulate "the channels of interstate commerce," "persons or things in interstate commerce," and "those activities that substantially affect interstate commerce." The power over activities that substantially affect interstate commerce can be expansive.

Congress may also "lay and collect Taxes, Duties, Imposts and Excises, to pay the Debts and provide for the common Defence and general Welfare of the United States." Put simply, Congress may tax and spend. This grant gives the Federal Government considerable influence even in areas where it cannot directly regulate. The Federal Government may enact a tax on an activity that it cannot authorize, forbid, or otherwise control. And in exercising its spending power, Congress may offer funds to the States, and may condition those offers on compliance with specified conditions. These offers may well induce the States to adopt policies that the Federal Government itself could not impose.

The reach of the Federal Government's enumerated powers is broader still because the Constitution authorizes Congress to "make all Laws which shall be necessary and proper for carrying into Execution the foregoing Powers." We have long read this provision to give Congress great latitude in exercising its powers: "Let the end be legitimate, let it be within the scope of the constitution, and all means which are appropriate, which are plainly adapted to that end, which are not prohibited, but consist with the letter and spirit of the constitution, are constitutional."

Our permissive reading of these powers is explained in part by a general reticence to invalidate the acts of the Nation's elected leaders. "Proper respect for a coordinate branch of the government" requires that we strike down an Act of Congress only if "the lack of constitutional authority to pass [the] act in question is clearly demonstrated." Members of this Court are vested with the authority to interpret the law; we possess neither the expertise nor the prerogative to make policy judgments. Those decisions are entrusted to our Nation's elected leaders, who can be thrown out of office if the people disagree with them. It is not our job to protect the people from the consequences of their political choices.

Our deference in matters of policy cannot, however, become abdication in matters of law. "The powers of the legislature are defined and limited; and that those limits may not be mistaken, or forgotten, the constitution is written." Marbury v. Madison (1803).

I

In 2010, Congress enacted the Patient Protection and Affordable Care Act. The Act aims to increase the number of Americans covered by health insurance and decrease the cost of health care. The Act's 10 titles stretch over 900 pages and contain hundreds of provisions. This case concerns constitutional challenges to two key provisions, commonly referred to as the individual mandate and the Medicaid expansion.

The individual mandate requires most Americans to maintain "minimum essential" health insurance coverage. The mandate does not apply to some individuals, such as prisoners and undocumented aliens. Many individuals will receive the required coverage through their employer, or from a government program such as Medicaid or Medicare. But for individuals who are not exempt and do not receive health insurance through a third party, the means of satisfying the requirement is to purchase insurance from a private company.

Beginning in 2014, those who do not comply with the mandate must make a "[s]hared responsibility payment" to the Federal Government. That payment, which the Act describes as a "penalty," is calculated as a percentage of household income, subject to a floor based on a specified dollar amount and a ceiling based on the average annual premium the individual would have to pay for qualifying private health insurance. In 2016, for example, the penalty will be 2.5 percent of an individual's household income, but no less than $695 and no more than the average yearly premium for insurance that covers 60 percent of the cost of 10 specified services (e.g., prescription drugs and hospitalization). The Act provides that the penalty will be paid to the Internal Revenue Service with an individual's taxes, and "shall be assessed and collected in the same manner" as tax penalties, such as the penalty for claiming too large an income tax refund. The Act, however, bars the IRS from using several of its normal enforcement tools, such as criminal prosecutions and levies. And some individuals who are subject to the mandate are nonetheless exempt from the penalty— for example, those with income below a certain threshold and members of Indian tribes.

On the day the President signed the Act into law, Florida and 12 other States filed a complaint in the Federal District Court for the Northern District of Florida. Those plaintiffs—who are both respondents and petitioners here, depending on the issue—were subsequently joined by 13 more States, several individuals, and the National Federation of Independent Business.

The second provision of the Affordable Care Act directly challenged here is the Medicaid expansion. Enacted in 1965, Medicaid offers federal funding to States to assist pregnant women, children, needy families, the blind, the elderly, and the disabled in obtaining medical care. In order to receive that funding, States must comply with federal criteria governing matters such as who receives care and what services are provided at what cost. By 1982 every State had chosen to participate in Medicaid. Federal funds received through the Medicaid program have become a substantial part of state budgets, now constituting over 10 percent of most States' total revenue.

The Affordable Care Act expands the scope of the Medicaid program and increases the number of individuals the States must cover. For example, the Act requires state programs to provide Medicaid coverage to adults with incomes up to 133 percent of the federal poverty level, whereas many States now cover adults with children only if their income is considerably lower, and do not cover childless adults at all. The Act increases federal funding to cover the States' costs in expanding Medicaid coverage, although States will bear a portion of the costs on their own. If a State does not comply with the Act's new coverage requirements, it may lose not only the federal funding for those requirements, but all of its federal Medicaid funds.

II

Before turning to the merits, we need to be sure we have the authority to do so. The Anti-Injunction Act provides that "no suit for the purpose of restraining the assessment or collection of any tax shall be maintained in any court by any person, whether or not such person is the person against whom such tax was assessed." This statute protects the Government's ability to collect a consistent stream of revenue, by barring litigation to enjoin or otherwise obstruct the collection of taxes. Because of the Anti-Injunction Act, taxes can ordinarily be challenged only after they are paid, by suing for a refund.

The Anti-Injunction Act applies to suits "for the purpose of restraining the assessment or collection of any *tax*." Congress, however, chose to describe the "[s]hared responsibility payment" imposed on those who forgo health insurance not as a "tax," but as a "penalty." There is no immediate reason to think that a statute applying to "any tax" would apply to a "penalty."

The Affordable Care Act does not require that the penalty for failing to comply with the individual mandate be treated as a tax for purposes of the Anti-Injunction Act. The Anti-Injunction Act therefore does not apply to this suit, and we may proceed to the merits.

III

The Government advances two theories for the proposition that Congress had constitutional authority to enact the individual mandate. First, the Government argues that Congress had the power to enact the mandate under the Commerce Clause. Under that theory, Congress may order individuals to buy health insurance because the failure to do so affects interstate commerce, and could undercut the Affordable Care Act's other reforms. Second, the Government argues that if the commerce power does not support the mandate, we should nonetheless uphold it as an exercise of Congress's power to tax. According to the Government, even if Congress lacks the power to direct individuals to buy insurance, the only effect of the individual mandate is to raise taxes on those who do not do so, and thus the law may be upheld as a tax.

A

The Government's first argument is that the individual mandate is a valid exercise of Congress's power under the Commerce Clause and the Necessary and Proper Clause. According to the Government, the health care market is characterized by a significant cost-shifting problem. Everyone will eventually need health care at a time and to an extent they cannot predict, but if they do not have insurance, they often will not be able to pay for it. Because state and federal laws nonetheless require hospitals to provide a certain degree of care to individuals without regard to their ability to pay, hospitals end up receiving compensation for only a portion of the services they provide. To recoup the losses, hospitals pass on the cost to insurers through higher rates, and insurers, in turn, pass on the cost to policy holders in the form of higher premiums. Congress estimated that the cost of uncompensated care raises family health insurance premiums, on average, by over $1,000 per year.

In the Affordable Care Act, Congress addressed the problem of those who cannot obtain insurance coverage because of preexisting conditions or other health issues. It did so through the Act's "guaranteed-issue" and "community-rating" provisions. These provisions together prohibit insurance companies from denying coverage to those with such conditions or charging unhealthy individuals higher premiums than healthy individuals.

The guaranteed-issue and community-rating reforms do not, however, address the issue of healthy individuals who choose not to purchase insurance to cover potential health care needs. In fact, the reforms sharply exacerbate that problem, by providing an incentive for individuals to delay purchasing health insurance until they become sick, relying on the promise of guaranteed and affordable coverage. The reforms also threaten to impose massive new costs on insurers, who are required to accept unhealthy individuals but prohibited from charging them rates necessary to pay for their coverage. This will lead insurers to significantly increase premiums on everyone.

The individual mandate was Congress's solution to these problems. By requiring that individuals purchase health insurance, the mandate prevents cost-shifting by those who would otherwise go without it. In addition, the mandate forces into the insurance risk pool more healthy individuals, whose premiums on average will be higher than their health care expenses. This allows insurers to subsidize the costs of covering the unhealthy individuals the reforms require them to accept. The Government claims that Congress has power under the Commerce and Necessary and Proper Clauses to enact this solution.

1

The Government contends that the individual mandate is within Congress's power because the failure to purchase insurance "has a substantial and deleterious effect on interstate commerce" by creating the cost-shifting problem. The path of our Commerce Clause decisions has not always run smooth, but it is now well established that Congress has broad authority under the Clause. We have recognized, for example, that "[t]he power of Congress over interstate commerce is not confined to the regulation of commerce among the states," but extends to activities that "have a substantial effect on interstate commerce." Congress's power, moreover, is not limited to regulation of an activity that by itself substantially affects interstate commerce, but also extends to activities that do so only when aggregated with similar activities of others.

The Constitution grants Congress the power to "*regulate* Commerce." The power to *regulate* commerce presupposes the existence of commercial activity to be regulated. If the power to "regulate" something included the power to create it, many of the provisions in the Constitution would be superfluous. For example, the Constitution gives Congress the power to "coin Money," in addition to the power to "regulate the Value thereof." And it gives Congress the power to "raise and support Armies" and to "provide and maintain a Navy," in addition to the power to "make Rules for the Government and Regulation of the land and naval Forces." If the power to regulate the armed forces or the value of money included the power to bring the subject of the regulation into existence, the specific grant of such powers would have been unnecessary. The language of the Constitution reflects the natural understanding that the power to regulate assumes there is already something to be regulated.

Our precedent also reflects this understanding. As expansive as our cases construing the scope of the commerce power have been, they all have one thing in common: They uniformly describe the power as reaching "activity." It is nearly impossible to avoid the word when quoting them.

The individual mandate, however, does not regulate existing commercial activity. It instead compels individuals to *become* active in commerce by purchasing a product, on the ground that their failure to do so affects interstate commerce. Construing the Commerce Clause to permit Congress to regulate individuals precisely *because* they are doing nothing would open a new and potentially vast domain to congressional authority. Every day individuals do not do an infinite number of things. In some cases they decide not to do something; in others they simply fail to do it. Allowing Congress to justify federal regulation by pointing to the effect of inaction on commerce would bring countless decisions an individual could *potentially* make within the scope of federal regulation, and—under the Government's theory—empower Congress to make those decisions for him.

Indeed, the Government's logic would justify a mandatory purchase to solve almost any problem. To consider a different example in the health care market, many Americans do not eat a balanced diet. That group makes up a larger percentage of the total population than those without health insurance. The failure of that group to have a healthy diet increases health care costs, to a greater extent than the failure of the uninsured to purchase insurance. Those increased costs are borne in part by other Americans who must pay more, just as the uninsured shift costs to the insured. Congress addressed the insurance problem by ordering everyone to buy insurance. Under the Government's theory, Congress could address the diet problem by ordering everyone to buy vegetables.

Everyone will likely participate in the markets for food, clothing, transportation, shelter, or energy; that does not authorize Congress to direct them to purchase particular products in those or other markets today. The Commerce Clause is not a general license to regulate an individual from cradle to grave, simply because he will predictably engage in particular transactions. Any police power to regulate individuals as such, as opposed to their activities, remains vested in the States.

2

The Government next contends that Congress has the power under the Necessary and Proper Clause to enact the individual mandate because the mandate is an "integral part of a comprehensive scheme of economic regulation"—the guaranteed-issue and community-rating insurance reforms. Under this argument, it is not necessary to consider the effect that an individual's inactivity may have on interstate commerce; it is enough that Congress regulate commercial activity in a way that requires regulation of inactivity to be effective.

Applying these principles, the individual mandate cannot be sustained under the Necessary and Proper Clause as an essential component of the insurance reforms. Each of our prior cases upholding laws under that Clause involved exercises of authority derivative of, and in service to, a granted power. The individual mandate, by contrast, vests Congress with the extraordinary ability to create the necessary predicate to the exercise of an enumerated power.

Just as the individual mandate cannot be sustained as a law regulating the substantial effects of the failure to purchase health insurance, neither can it be upheld as a "necessary and proper" component of the insurance reforms. The commerce power thus does not authorize the mandate.

B

That is not the end of the matter. Because the Commerce Clause does not support the individual mandate, it is necessary to turn to the Government's second argument: that the mandate may be upheld as within Congress's enumerated power to "lay and collect Taxes."

Under the mandate, if an individual does not maintain health insurance, the only consequence is that he must make an additional payment to the IRS when he pays his taxes. That, according to the Government, means the mandate can be regarded as establishing a condition — not owning health insurance — that triggers a tax — the required payment to the IRS. Under that theory, the mandate is not a legal command to buy insurance. Rather, it makes going without insurance just another thing the Government taxes, like buying gasoline or earning income. And if the mandate is in effect just a tax hike on certain taxpayers who do not have health insurance, it may be within Congress's constitutional power to tax.

The question is not whether that is the most natural interpretation of the mandate, but only whether it is a "fairly possible" one. As we have explained, "every reasonable construction must be resorted to, in order to save a statute from unconstitutionality." The Government asks us to interpret the mandate as imposing a tax, if it would otherwise violate the Constitution. Granting the Act the full measure of deference owed to federal statutes, it can be so read, for the reasons set forth below.

C

The exaction the Affordable Care Act imposes on those without health insurance looks like a tax in many respects. The "[s]hared responsibility payment," as the statute entitles it, is paid into the Treasury by "taxpayer[s]" when they file their tax returns. It does not apply to individuals who do not pay federal income taxes because their household income is less than the filing threshold in the Internal Revenue Code. For taxpayers who do owe the payment, its amount is determined by such familiar factors as taxable income, number of dependents, and joint filing status. The requirement to pay is found in the Internal Revenue Code and enforced by the IRS, which — as we previously explained — must assess and collect it "in the same manner as taxes." This process yields the essential feature of any tax: it produces at least some revenue for the Government. Indeed, the payment is expected to raise about $4 billion per year by 2017.

It is of course true that the Act describes the payment as a "penalty," not a "tax." But while that label is fatal to the application of the Anti-Injunction Act, it does not determine whether the payment may be viewed as an exercise of Congress's taxing power. It is up to Congress whether to apply the Anti-Injunction Act to any particular statute, so it makes sense to be guided by Congress's choice of label on that question. That choice does not, however, control whether an exaction is within Congress's constitutional power to tax.

None of this is to say that the payment is not intended to affect individual conduct. Although the payment will raise considerable revenue, it is plainly designed to expand health insurance coverage. But taxes that seek to influence conduct are nothing new. Some of our earliest federal taxes sought to deter the purchase of imported manufactured goods in order to foster the growth of domestic industry. That §5000A seeks to shape decisions about whether to buy health insurance does not mean that it cannot be a valid exercise of the taxing power.

Our precedent demonstrates that Congress had the power to impose the exaction in §5000A under the taxing power, and that §5000A need not be read to do more than impose a tax. That is sufficient to sustain it. The "question of the constitutionality of action taken by Congress does not depend on recitals of the power which it undertakes to exercise."

Even if the taxing power enables Congress to impose a tax on not obtaining health insurance, any tax must still comply with other requirements in the Constitution. Plaintiffs argue that the shared responsibility payment does not do so, citing Article I, §9, clause 4. That clause provides: "No Capitation, or other direct, Tax shall be laid, unless in Proportion to the Census or Enumeration herein before directed to be taken." This requirement means that any "direct Tax" must be apportioned so that each State pays in proportion to its population. According to the plaintiffs, if the individual mandate imposes a tax, it is a direct tax, and it is unconstitutional because Congress made no effort to apportion it among the States.

Even when the Direct Tax Clause was written it was unclear what else, other than a capitation (also known as a "head tax" or a "poll tax"), might be a direct tax. A tax on going without health insurance does not fall within any recognized category of direct tax. It is not a capitation. Capitations are taxes paid by every person, "without regard to property, profession, or *any other circumstance*." The whole point of the shared responsibility payment is that it is triggered by specific circumstances — earning a certain amount of income but not obtaining health insurance. The payment is also plainly not a tax on the ownership of land or personal property. The shared responsibility payment is thus not a direct tax that must be apportioned among the several States.

The Affordable Care Act's requirement that certain individuals pay a financial penalty for not obtaining health insurance may reasonably be characterized as a tax. Because the Constitution permits such a tax, it is not our role to forbid it, or to pass upon its wisdom or fairness.

D

Justice Ginsburg questions the necessity of rejecting the Government's commerce power argument, given that §5000A can be upheld under the taxing power. But the statute reads more naturally as a command to buy insurance than as a tax, and I would uphold it as a command if the Constitution allowed it. It is only because the Commerce Clause does not authorize such a command that it is necessary to reach the taxing power question. And it is only because we have a duty to construe a statute to save it, if fairly possible, that §5000A can be interreted as a tax. Without deciding the Commerce Clause question, I would find no basis to adopt such a saving construction.

The Federal Government does not have the power to order people to buy health insurance. Section 5000A would therefore be unconstitutional if read as a command. The Federal Government does have the power to impose a tax on those without health insurance. Section 5000A is therefore constitutional, because it can reasonably be read as a tax.

IV

A

The States also contend that the Medicaid expansion exceeds Congress's authority under the Spending Clause. They claim that Congress is coercing the States to adopt the changes it wants by threatening to withhold all of a State's Medicaid grants, unless the State accepts the new expanded funding and complies with the conditions that come with it. This, they argue, violates the basic principle that the "Federal Government may not compel the States to enact or administer a federal regulatory program."

There is no doubt that the Act dramatically increases state obligations under Medicaid. Congress may use its spending power to create incentives for States to act in accordance with federal policies. But when "pressure turns into compulsion," the legislation runs contrary to our system of federalism. "[T]he Constitution simply does not give Congress the authority to require the States to regulate." That is true whether Congress directly commands a State to regulate or indirectly coerces a State to adopt a federal regulatory system as its own.

Permitting the Federal Government to force the States to implement a federal program would threaten the political accountability key to our federal system. "[W]here the Federal Government directs the States to regulate, it may be state officials who will bear the brunt of public disapproval, while the federal officials who devised the regulatory program may remain insulated from the electoral ramifications of their decision." Spending Clause programs do not pose this danger when a State has a legitimate choice whether to accept the federal conditions in exchange for federal funds. In such a situation, state officials can fairly be held politically accountable for choosing to accept or refuse the federal offer. But when the State has no choice, the Federal Government can achieve its objectives without accountability. Indeed, this danger is heightened when Congress acts under the Spending Clause, because Congress can use that power to implement federal policy it could not impose directly under its enumerated powers.

The States, however, argue that the Medicaid expansion is far from the typical case. They object that Congress has "crossed the line distinguishing encouragement from coercion," in the way it has structured the funding: Instead of simply refusing to grant the new funds to States that will not accept the new conditions, Congress has also threatened to withhold those States' existing Medicaid funds. The States claim that this threat serves no purpose other than to force unwilling States to sign up for the dramatic expansion in health care coverage effected by the Act.

Given the nature of the threat and the programs at issue here, we must agree. We have upheld Congress's authority to condition the receipt of funds on the States' complying with restrictions on the use of those funds, because that is the means by which Congress ensures that the funds are spent according to its view of the "general Welfare." Conditions that do not here govern the use of the funds, however, cannot be justified on that basis. When, for example, such conditions take the form of threats to terminate other significant independent grants, the conditions are properly viewed as a means of pressuring the States to accept policy changes.

In this case, the financial "inducement" Congress has chosen is much more than "relatively mild encouragement" — it is a gun to the head. Section 1396c of the Medicaid Act provides that if a State's Medicaid plan does not comply with the Act's requirements, the Secretary of Health and Human Services may declare that "further payments will not be made to the State." A State that opts out of the Affordable Care Act's expansion in health care coverage thus stands to lose not merely "a relatively small percentage" of its existing Medicaid funding, but *all* of it. Medicaid spending accounts for over 20 percent of the average State's total budget, with federal funds covering 50 to 83 percent of those costs. The threatened loss of over 10 percent of a State's overall budget, in contrast, is economic dragooning that leaves the States with no real option but to acquiesce in the Medicaid expansion.

Here, the Government claims that the Medicaid expansion is properly viewed merely as a modification of the existing program because the States agreed that Congress could change the terms of Medicaid when they signed on in the first place. The Medicaid expansion, however, accomplishes a shift in kind, not merely degree. The original program was designed to cover medical services for four particular categories of the needy: the disabled, the blind, the elderly, and needy families with dependent children. Previous amendments to Medicaid eligibility merely altered and expanded the boundaries of these categories. Under the Affordable Care Act, Medicaid is transformed into a program to meet the health care needs of the entire nonelderly population with income below 133 percent of the poverty level. It is no longer a program to care for the neediest among us, but rather an element of a comprehensive national plan to provide universal health insurance coverage.

B

Nothing in our opinion precludes Congress from offering funds under the Affordable Care Act to expand the availability of health care, and requiring that States accepting such funds comply with the conditions on their use. What Congress is not free to do is to penalize States that choose not to participate in that new program by taking away their existing Medicaid funding.

The Affordable Care Act is constitutional in part and unconstitutional in part. The individual mandate cannot be upheld as an exercise of Congress's power under the Commerce Clause. That Clause authorizes Congress to regulate interstate commerce, not to order individuals to engage in it. In this case, however, it is reasonable to construe what Congress has done as increasing taxes on those who have a certain amount of income, but choose to go without health insurance. Such legislation is within Congress's power to tax.

As for the Medicaid expansion, that portion of the Affordable Care Act violates the Constitution by threatening existing Medicaid funding. Congress has no authority to order the States to regulate according to its instructions. Congress may offer the States grants and require the States to comply with accompanying conditions, but the States must have a genuine choice whether to accept the offer. The States are given no such choice in this case: They must either accept a basic change in the nature of Medicaid, or risk losing all Medicaid funding. The remedy for that constitutional violation is to preclude the Federal

Government from imposing such a sanction. That remedy does not require striking down other portions of the Affordable Care Act.

The Framers created a Federal Government of limited powers, and assigned to this Court the duty of enforcing those limits. The Court does so today. But the Court does not express any opinion on the wisdom of the Affordable Care Act. Under the Constitution, that judgment is reserved to the people.

Justice GINSBURG, with whom Justice SOTOMAYOR joins, and with whom Justice BREYER and Justice KAGAN join as to Parts I, II, III, and IV, concurring in part, concurring in the judgment in part, and dissenting in part.

I

According to the Chief Justice, the Commerce Clause does not permit that preservation. This rigid reading of the Clause makes scant sense and is stunningly retrogressive.

Since 1937, our precedent has recognized Congress' large authority to set the Nation's course in the economic and social welfare realm. The Chief Justice's crabbed reading of the Commerce Clause harks back to the era in which the Court routinely thwarted Congress' efforts to regulate the national economy in the interest of those who labor to sustain it. It is a reading that should not have staying power.

A

In enacting the Patient Protection and Affordable Care Act (ACA), Congress comprehensively reformed the national market for health-care products and services. By any measure, that market is immense. Collectively, Americans spent $2.5 trillion on health care in 2009, accounting for 17.6% of our Nation's economy. Within the next decade, it is anticipated, spending on health care will nearly double.

The health-care market's size is not its only distinctive feature. Unlike the market for almost any other product or service, the market for medical care is one in which all individuals inevitably participate. Virtually every person residing in the United States, sooner or later, will visit a doctor or other health-care professional. Most people will do so repeatedly.

Although every U.S. domiciliary will incur significant medical expenses during his or her lifetime, the time when care will be needed is often unpredictable. An accident, a heart attack, or a cancer diagnosis commonly occurs without warning. Inescapably, we are all at peril of needing medical care without a moment's notice.

To manage the risks associated with medical care — its high cost, its unpredictability, and its inevitability — most people in the United States obtain health insurance. Not all U.S. residents, however, have health insurance. In 2009, approximately 50 million people were uninsured, either by choice or, more likely, because they could not afford private insurance and did not qualify for government aid. As a group, uninsured individuals annually consume more than $100 billion in healthcare services, nearly 5% of the Nation's total. Over 60% of those without insurance visit a doctor's office or emergency room in a given year.

B

The large number of individuals without health insurance, Congress found, heavily burdens the national health-care market. As just noted, the cost of emergency care or treatment for a serious illness generally exceeds what an individual can afford to pay on her own. Unlike markets for most products, however, the inability to pay for care does not mean that an uninsured individual will receive no care. Federal and state law, as well as professional obligations and embedded social norms, require hospitals and physicians to provide care when it is most needed, regardless of the patient's ability to pay.

As a consequence, medical-care providers deliver significant amounts of care to the uninsured for which the providers receive no payment. In 2008, for example, hospitals, physicians, and other health-care professionals received no compensation for $43 billion worth of the $116 billion in care they administered to those without insurance.

Health-care providers do not absorb these bad debts. Instead, they raise their prices, passing along the cost of uncompensated care to those who do pay reliably: the government and private insurance companies. In response, private insurers increase their premiums, shifting the cost of the elevated bills from providers onto those who carry insurance. The net result: Those with health insurance subsidize the medical care of those without it. As economists would describe what happens, the uninsured "free ride" on those who pay for health insurance.

The size of this subsidy is considerable. Congress found that the cost-shifting just described "increases family [insurance] premiums by on average over $1,000 a year." Higher premiums, in turn, render health insurance less affordable, forcing more people to go without insurance and leading to further cost-shifting.

The failure of individuals to acquire insurance has other deleterious effects on the health-care market. Because those without insurance generally lack access to preventative care, they do not receive treatment for conditions—like hypertension and diabetes—that can be successfully and affordably treated if diagnosed early on. When sickness finally drives the uninsured to seek care, once treatable conditions have escalated into grave health problems, requiring more costly and extensive intervention. The extra time and resources providers spend serving the uninsured lessens the providers' ability to care for those who do have insurance.

C

States cannot resolve the problem of the uninsured on their own. Like Social Security benefits, a universal health-care system, if adopted by an individual State, would be "bait to the needy and dependent elsewhere, encouraging them to migrate and seek a haven of repose." States that undertake health-care reforms on their own thus risk "placing themselves in a position of economic disadvantage as compared with neighbors or competitors." Facing that risk, individual States are unlikely to take the initiative in addressing the problem of the uninsured, even though solving that problem is in all States' best interests. Congress' intervention was needed to overcome this collective-action impasse.

D

To ensure that individuals with medical histories have access to affordable insurance, Congress devised a three-part solution. First, Congress imposed a "guaranteed issue" requirement, which bars insurers from denying coverage to any person on account of that person's medical condition or history. Second, Congress required insurers to use "community rating" to price their insurance policies. Community rating, in effect, bars insurance companies from charging higher premiums to those with preexisting conditions.

But these two provisions, Congress comprehended, could not work effectively unless individuals were given a powerful incentive to obtain insurance. In the 1990's, several States — including New York, New Jersey, Washington, Kentucky, Maine, New Hampshire, and Vermont — enacted guaranteed-issue and community-rating laws without requiring universal acquisition of insurance coverage. The results were disastrous. "All seven states suffered from skyrocketing insurance premium costs, reductions in individuals with coverage, and reductions in insurance products and providers."

3

In sum, Congress passed the minimum coverage provision as a key component of the ACA to address an economic and social problem that has plagued the Nation for decades: the large number of U.S. residents who are unable or unwilling to obtain health insurance. Whatever one thinks of the policy decision Congress made, it was Congress' prerogative to make it. Reviewed with appropriate deference, the minimum coverage provision, allied to the guaranteed-issue and community-rating prescriptions, should survive measurement under the Commerce and Necessary and Proper Clauses.

II

Until today, this Court's pragmatic approach to judging whether Congress validly exercised its commerce power was guided by two familiar principles. First, Congress has the power to regulate economic activities "that substantially affect interstate commerce." This capacious power extends even to local activities that, viewed in the aggregate, have a substantial impact on interstate commerce. Second, we owe a large measure of respect to Congress when it frames and enacts economic and social legislation.

Straightforward application of these principles would require the Court to hold that the minimum coverage provision is proper Commerce Clause legislation. Beyond dispute, Congress had a rational basis for concluding that the uninsured, as a class, substantially affect interstate commerce. Those without insurance consume billions of dollars of health-care products and services each year. Those goods are produced, sold, and delivered largely by national and regional companies who routinely transact business across state lines. The uninsured also cross state lines to receive care. Some have medical emergencies while away from home. Others, when sick, go to a neighboring State that provides better care for those who have not prepaid for care.

Not only do those without insurance consume a large amount of health care each year; critically, as earlier explained, their inability to pay for a significant portion of that consumption drives up market prices, foists costs on other consumers, and reduces market efficiency and stability. Given these far-reaching effects on interstate commerce, the decision to forgo insurance is hardly inconsequential or equivalent to "doing nothing"; it is, instead, an economic decision Congress has the authority to address under the Commerce Clause.

The minimum coverage provision, furthermore, bears a "reasonable connection" to Congress' goal of protecting the health-care market from the disruption caused by individuals who fail to obtain insurance. By requiring those who do not carry insurance to pay a toll, the minimum coverage provision gives individuals a strong incentive to insure. This incentive, Congress had good reason to believe, would reduce the number of uninsured and, correspondingly, mitigate the adverse impact the uninsured have on the national health-care market.

Congress also acted reasonably in requiring uninsured individuals, whether sick or healthy, either to obtain insurance or to pay the specified penalty. As earlier observed, because every person is at risk of needing care at any moment, all those who lack insurance, regardless of their current health status, adversely affect the price of health care and health insurance. Moreover, an insurance-purchase requirement limited to those in need of immediate care simply could not work. Insurance companies would either charge these individuals prohibitively expensive premiums, or, if community-rating regulations were in place, close up shop.

Rather than evaluating the constitutionality of the minimum coverage provision in the manner established by our precedents, the Chief relies on a newly minted constitutional doctrine. The commerce power does not, the Chief Justice announces, permit Congress to "compe[l] individuals to become active in commerce by purchasing a product."

The Chief Justice's novel constraint on Congress' commerce power gains no force from our precedent and for that reason alone warrants disapprobation. But even assuming, for the moment, that Congress lacks authority under the Commerce Clause to "compel individuals not engaged in commerce to purchase an unwanted product," such a limitation would be inapplicable here. Everyone will, at some point, consume health-care products and services. Thus, if the Chief Justice is correct that an insurance-purchase requirement can be applied only to those who "actively" consume health care, the minimum coverage provision fits the bill.

Nor is it accurate to say that the minimum coverage provision "compel[s] individuals . . . to purchase an unwanted product," or "suite of products." Virtually everyone, I reiterate, consumes health care at some point in his or her life. Health insurance is a means of paying for this care, nothing more. In requiring individuals to obtain insurance, Congress is therefore not mandating the purchase of a discrete, unwanted product. Rather, Congress is merely defining the terms on which individuals pay for an interstate good they consume: Persons subject to the mandate must now pay for medical care in advance (instead of at the point of service) and through insurance (instead of out of pocket). Establishing payment terms for goods in or affecting interstate commerce is quintessential economic regulation well within Congress' domain.

In concluding that the Commerce Clause does not permit Congress to regulate commercial "inactivity," and therefore does not allow Congress to adopt the practical solution it devised for the health-care problem, the Chief Justice views the Clause as a "technical legal conception," precisely what our case law tells us not to do. These line-drawing exercises were untenable, and the Court long ago abandoned them.

Underlying the Chief Justice's view that the Commerce Clause must be confined to the regulation of active participants in a commercial market is a fear that the commerce power would otherwise know no limits. This concern is unfounded. As several times noted, the unique attributes of the health-care market render everyone active in that market and give rise to a significant free-riding problem that does not occur in other markets.

Nor would the commerce power be unbridled, absent the Chief Justice's "activity" limitation. Congress would remain unable to regulate noneconomic conduct that has only an attenuated effect on interstate commerce and is traditionally left to state law.

An individual's decision to self-insure, I have explained, is an economic act with the requisite connection to interstate commerce. Other choices individuals make are unlikely to fit the same or similar description.

Other provisions of the Constitution also check congressional overreaching. A mandate to purchase a particular product would be unconstitutional if, for example, the edict impermissibly abridged the freedom of speech, interfered with the free exercise of religion, or infringed on a liberty interest protected by the Due Process Clause.

Supplementing these legal restraints is a formidable check on congressional power: the democratic process. As the controversy surrounding the passage of the Affordable Care Act attests, purchase mandates are likely to engender political resistance. This prospect is borne out by the behavior of state legislators. Despite their possession of unquestioned authority to impose mandates, state governments have rarely done so.

III

For the reasons explained above, the minimum coverage provision is valid Commerce Clause legislation. When viewed as a component of the entire ACA, the provision's constitutionality becomes even plainer.

The Necessary and Proper Clause "empowers Congress to enact laws in effectuation of its [commerce] powe[r] that are not within its authority to enact in isolation." Hence, "[a] complex regulatory program . . . can survive a Commerce Clause challenge without a showing that every single facet of the program is independently and directly related to a valid congressional goal. . . . The relevant question is simply whether the means chosen are 'reasonably adapted' to the attainment of a legitimate end under the commerce power."

Recall that one of Congress' goals in enacting the Affordable Care Act was to eliminate the insurance industry's practice of charging higher prices or denying coverage to individuals with preexisting medical conditions. The commerce power allows Congress to ban this practice, a point no one disputes. But even assuming there were "practicable" alternatives to the minimum coverage provision, "we long ago rejected the view that the Necessary and Proper Clause demands that an Act of Congress be '*absolutely* necessary' to the exercise of an enumerated power." The minimum coverage provision meets this requirement.

IV

In the early 20th century, this Court regularly struck down economic regulation enacted by the peoples' representatives in both the States and the Federal

Government. The Chief Justice Commerce Clause opinion, and even more so the joint dissenters' reasoning, bear a disquieting resemblance to those long-overruled decisions.

Ultimately, the Court upholds the individual mandate as a proper exercise of Congress' power to tax and spend "for the . . . general Welfare of the United States." I concur in that determination, which makes the Chief Justice's Commerce Clause essay all the more puzzling. Why should the Chief Justice strive so mightily to hem in Congress' capacity to meet the new problems arising constantly in our ever-developing modern economy? I find no satisfying response to that question in his opinion.

V

Through Medicaid, Congress has offered the States an opportunity to furnish health care to the poor with the aid of federal financing. The question posed by the 2010 Medicaid expansion, then, is essentially this: To cover a notably larger population, must Congress take the repeal/reenact route, or may it achieve the same result by amending existing law? The answer should be that Congress may expand by amendment the classes of needy persons entitled to Medicaid benefits. A ritualistic requirement that Congress repeal and reenact spending legislation in order to enlarge the population served by a federally funded program would advance no constitutional principle and would scarcely serve the interests of federalism. To the contrary, such a requirement would rigidify Congress' efforts to empower States by partnering with them in the implementation of federal programs.

The Chief Justice acknowledges that Congress may "condition the receipt of [federal] funds on the States' complying with restrictions on the use of those funds," but nevertheless concludes that the 2010 expansion is unduly coercive. His conclusion rests on three premises, each of them essential to his theory. First, the Medicaid expansion is, in the Chief Justice's view, a new grant program, not an addition to the Medicaid program existing before the ACA's enactment. Second, the expansion was unforeseeable by the States when they first signed on to Medicaid. Third, the threatened loss of funding is so large that the States have no real choice but to participate in the Medicaid expansion. The Chief Justice therefore — *for the first time ever* — finds an exercise of Congress' spending power unconstitutionally coercive.

Medicaid, as amended by the ACA, however, is not two spending programs; it is a single program with a constant aim — to enable poor persons to receive basic health care when they need it. Given past expansions, plus express statutory warning that Congress may change the requirements participating States must meet, there can be no tenable claim that the ACA fails for lack of notice. Moreover, States have no entitlement to receive any Medicaid funds; they enjoy only the opportunity to accept funds on Congress' terms. Future Congresses are not bound by their predecessors' dispositions; they have authority to spend federal revenue as they see fit. The Federal Government, therefore, is not, as the Chief Justice charges, threatening States with the loss of "existing" funds from one spending program in order to induce them to opt into another program. Congress is simply requiring States to do what States have long been required to do to receive Medicaid funding: comply with the conditions Congress prescribes for participation.

Congress' authority to condition the use of federal funds is not confined to spending programs as first launched. The legislature may, and often does, amend the law, imposing new conditions grant recipients henceforth must meet in order to continue receiving funds.

The Chief Justice ultimately asks whether "the financial inducement offered by Congress . . . pass[ed] the point at which pressure turns into compulsion." The financial inducement Congress employed here, he concludes, crosses that threshold: The threatened withholding of "existing Medicaid funds" is "a gun to the head" that forces States to acquiesce. When future Spending Clause challenges arrive, as they likely will in the wake of today's decision, how will litigants and judges assess whether "a State has a legitimate choice whether to accept the federal conditions in exchange for federal funds"? Are courts to measure the number of dollars the Federal Government might withhold for noncompliance? The portion of the State's budget at stake? And which State's — or States' — budget is determinative: the lead plaintiff, all challenging States (26 in this case, many with quite different fiscal situations), or some national median? Does it matter that Florida, unlike most States, imposes no state income tax, and therefore might be able to replace foregone federal funds with new state revenue? Or that the coercion state officials in fact fear is punishment at the ballot box for turning down a politically popular federal grant?

At bottom, my colleagues' position is that the States' reliance on federal funds limits Congress' authority to alter its spending programs. This gets things backwards: Congress, not the States, is tasked with spending federal money in service of the general welfare. And each successive Congress is empowered to appropriate funds as it sees fit. When the 110th Congress reached a conclusion about Medicaid funds that differed from its predecessors' view, it abridged no State's right to "existing," or "pre-existing," funds. For, in fact, there are no such funds. There is only money States *anticipate* receiving from future Congresses.

For the reasons stated, I agree with the Chief Justice that, as to the validity of the minimum coverage provision, the judgment of the Court of Appeals for the Eleventh Circuit should be reversed. In my view, the provision encounters no constitutional obstruction. Further, I would uphold the Eleventh Circuit's decision that the Medicaid expansion is within Congress' spending power.

Justice SCALIA, Justice KENNEDY, Justice THOMAS, and Justice ALITO, dissenting.

Congress has set out to remedy the problem that the best health care is beyond the reach of many Americans who cannot afford it. It can assuredly do that, by exercising the powers accorded to it under the Constitution. The question in this case, however, is whether the complex structures and provisions of the Patient Protection and Affordable Care Act (Affordable Care Act or ACA) go beyond those powers. We conclude that they do.

This case is in one respect difficult: it presents two questions of first impression. The first of those is whether failure to engage in economic activity (the purchase of health insurance) is subject to regulation under the Commerce Clause. Failure to act does result in an effect on commerce, and hence might be said to come under this Court's "affecting commerce" criterion of Commerce Clause jurisprudence. But in none of its decisions has this Court extended the Clause that far. The second question is whether the congressional power to tax and spend, permits the conditioning of a State's continued receipt of all funds under a massive state-administered federal welfare program upon its acceptance of an expansion to that program. Several of our opinions have suggested that the power to tax and spend cannot be used to coerce state administration of a federal program, but we have never found a law enacted under the spending power to be coercive. Those questions are difficult.

The case is easy and straightforward, however, in another respect. What is absolutely clear, affirmed by the text of the 1789 Constitution, by the Tenth Amendment ratified in 1791, and by innumerable cases of ours in the 220 years since, is that there are structural limits upon federal power — upon what it can prescribe with respect to private conduct, and upon what it can impose upon the sovereign States. Whatever may be the conceptual limits upon the Commerce Clause and upon the power to tax and spend, they cannot be such as will enable the Federal Government to regulate all private conduct and to compel the States to function as administrators of federal programs.

The Act before us here exceeds federal power both in mandating the purchase of health insurance and in denying nonconsenting States all Medicaid funding. These parts of the Act are central to its design and operation, and all the Act's other provisions would not have been enacted without them. In our view it must follow that the entire statute is inoperative.

I THE INDIVIDUAL MANDATE

Article I, §8, of the Constitution gives Congress the power to "regulate Commerce . . . among the several States." The Individual Mandate in the Act commands that every "applicable individual shall for each month beginning after 2013 ensure that the individual, and any dependent of the individual who is an applicable individual, is covered under minimum essential coverage." If this provision "regulates" anything, it is the *failure* to maintain minimum essential coverage. One might argue that it regulates that failure by requiring it to be accompanied by payment of a penalty. But that failure — that abstention from commerce — is not "Commerce." To be sure, *purchasing* insurance *is* "Commerce"; but one does not regulate commerce that does not exist by compelling its existence.

We do not doubt that the buying and selling of health insurance contracts is commerce generally subject to federal regulation. But when Congress provides that (nearly) all citizens must buy an insurance contract, it goes beyond "adjust[ing] by rule or method," Johnson, *supra,* or "direct[ing] according to rule"; it directs the creation of commerce.

A

First, the Government submits that §5000A is "integral to the Affordable Care Act's insurance reforms" and "necessary to make effective the Act's core reforms." Here, however, Congress has impressed into service third parties, healthy individuals who could be but are not customers of the relevant industry, to offset the undesirable consequences of the regulation. Congress' desire to force these individuals to purchase insurance is motivated by the fact that they are further removed from the market than unhealthy individuals with pre-existing conditions, because they are less likely to need extensive care in the near future. If Congress can reach out and command even those furthest removed from an interstate market to participate in the market, then the Commerce

Clause becomes a font of unlimited power, or in Hamilton's words, "the hideous monster whose devouring jaws . . . spare neither sex nor age, nor high nor low, nor sacred nor profane." The Federalist No. 33, p. 202 (C. Rossiter ed. 1961).

The case upon which the Government principally relies to sustain the Individual Mandate under the Necessary and Proper Clause is *Gonzales v. Raich* (2005), [which held that Congress under its commerce power could prohibit the cultivation and possession of small amounts of marijuana for medicinal purposes]. *Raich* is far different from the Individual Mandate in another respect. The Court's opinion in *Raich* pointed out that the growing and possession prohibitions were the only practicable way of enabling the prohibition of interstate traffic in marijuana to be effectively enforced. With the present statute, by contrast, there are many ways other than this unprecedented Individual Mandate by which the regulatory scheme's goals of reducing insurance premiums and ensuring the profitability of insurers could be achieved. For instance, those who did not purchase insurance could be subjected to a surcharge when they do enter the health insurance system. Or they could be denied a full income tax credit given to those who do purchase the insurance.

The Government's second theory in support of the Individual Mandate is that §5000A is valid because it is actually a "regulat[ion of] activities having a substantial relation to interstate commerce, . . . *i.e.*, . . . activities that substantially affect interstate commerce." The primary problem with this argument is that §5000A does not apply only to persons who purchase all, or most, or even any, of the health care services or goods that the mandated insurance covers. Indeed, the main objection many have to the Mandate is that they have no intention of purchasing most or even any of such goods or services and thus no need to buy insurance for those purchases.

The Government responds that the health-care market involves "essentially universal participation." The principal difficulty with this response is that it is, in the only relevant sense, not true. It is true enough that everyone consumes "health care," if the term is taken to include the purchase of a bottle of aspirin. But the health care "market" that is the object of the Individual Mandate not only includes but principally consists of goods and services that the young people primarily affected by the Mandate *do not purchase*. They are quite simply not participants in that market, and cannot be made so (and thereby subjected to regulation) by the simple device of defining participants to include all those who will, later in their lifetime, probably purchase the goods or services covered by the mandated insurance. Such a definition of market participants is unprecedented, and were it to be a premise for the exercise of national power, it would have no principled limits.

II THE TAXING POWER

As far as §5000A is concerned, we would stop there. Congress has attempted to regulate beyond the scope of its Commerce Clause authority, and §5000A is therefore invalid.

In answering that question we must, if "fairly possible," construe the provision to be a tax rather than a mandate-with-penalty, since that would render it constitutional rather than unconstitutional. But we cannot rewrite the statute to be what it is not. Our cases establish a clear line between a tax and a penalty:

"'[A] tax is an enforced contribution to provide for the support of government; a penalty . . . is an exaction imposed by statute as punishment for an unlawful act.'"

So the question is, quite simply, whether the exaction here is imposed for violation of the law. It unquestionably is. The minimum-coverage provision is found in 26 U.S.C. §5000A, entitled *"Requirement* to maintain minimum essential coverage." It commands that every "applicable individual *shall* . . . ensure that the individual . . . is covered under minimum essential coverage." And the immediately following provision states that, "[i]f . . . an applicable individual . . . fails to meet the *requirement* of subsection (a) . . . there is hereby imposed . . . a *penalty.*"

Quite separately, the fact that Congress (in its own words) "imposed . . . a penalty," 26 U.S.C. §5000A(b)(1), for failure to buy insurance is alone sufficient to render that failure unlawful. It is one of the canons of interpretation that a statute that penalizes an act makes it unlawful: "[W]here the statute inflicts a penalty for doing an act, although the act itself is not expressly prohibited, yet to do the act is unlawful, because it cannot be supposed that the Legislature intended that a penalty should be inflicted for a lawful act."

We never have classified as a tax an exaction imposed for violation of the law, and so too, we never have classified as a tax an exaction described in the legislation itself as a penalty. But we have never — *never* — treated as a tax an exaction which faces up to the critical difference between a tax and a penalty, and explicitly denominates the exaction a "penalty." Eighteen times in §5000A itself and elsewhere throughout the Act, Congress called the exaction in §5000A(b) a "penalty."

For all these reasons, to say that the Individual Mandate merely imposes a tax is not to interpret the statute but to rewrite it. Judicial tax-writing is particularly troubling. Taxes have never been popular, and in part for that reason, the Constitution requires tax increases to originate in the House of Representatives. That is to say, they must originate in the legislative body most accountable to the people, where legislators must weigh the need for the tax against the terrible price they might pay at their next election, which is never more than two years off. We have no doubt that Congress knew precisely what it was doing when it rejected an earlier version of this legislation that imposed a tax instead of a requirement-with-penalty. Imposing a tax through judicial legislation inverts the constitutional scheme, and places the power to tax in the branch of government least accountable to the citizenry.

Finally, we must observe that rewriting §5000A as a tax in order to sustain its constitutionality would force us to confront a difficult constitutional question: whether this is a direct tax that must be apportioned among the States according to their population. Perhaps it is not (we have no need to address the point); but the meaning of the Direct Tax Clause is famously unclear, and its application here is a question of first impression that deserves more thoughtful consideration than the lick-and-a-promise accorded by the Government and its supporters.

IV THE MEDICAID EXPANSION

We now consider respondents' second challenge to the constitutionality of the ACA, namely, that the Act's dramatic expansion of the Medicaid program exceeds Congress' power to attach conditions to federal grants to the States.

The ACA does not legally compel the States to participate in the expanded Medicaid program, but the Act authorizes a severe sanction for any State that refuses to go along: termination of all the State's Medicaid funding. For the average State, the annual federal Medicaid subsidy is equal to more than one-fifth of the State's expenditures. A State forced out of the program would not only lose this huge sum but would almost certainly find it necessary to increase its own health-care expenditures substantially, requiring either a drastic reduction in funding for other programs or a large increase in state taxes. And these new taxes would come on top of the federal taxes already paid by the State's citizens to fund the Medicaid program in other States.

This practice of attaching conditions to federal funds greatly increases federal power. "[O]bjectives not thought to be within Article I's enumerated legislative fields, may nevertheless be attained through the use of the spending power and the conditional grant of federal funds." This formidable power, if not checked in any way, would present a grave threat to the system of federalism created by our Constitution.

Recognizing this potential for abuse, our cases have long held that the power to attach conditions to grants to the States has limits. When federal legislation gives the States a real choice whether to accept or decline a federal aid package, the federal-state relationship is in the nature of a contractual relationship. If a federal spending program coerces participation the States have not "exercise[d] their choice" — let alone made an "informed choice." Coercing States to accept conditions risks the destruction of the "unique role of the States in our system." Congress effectively engages in this impermissible compulsion when state participation in a federal spending program is coerced, so that the States' choice whether to enact or administer a federal regulatory program is rendered illusory.

Once it is recognized that spending-power legislation cannot coerce state participation, two questions remain: (1) What is the meaning of coercion in this context? (2) Is the ACA's expanded Medicaid coverage coercive? We now turn to those questions.

D

The answer to the first of these questions — the meaning of coercion in the present context — is straightforward. As we have explained, the legitimacy of attaching conditions to federal grants to the States depends on the voluntariness of the States' choice to accept or decline the offered package. Therefore, if States really have no choice other than to accept the package, the offer is coercive, and the conditions cannot be sustained under the spending power. And as our decision in South Dakota v. Dole makes clear, theoretical voluntariness is not enough.

In South Dakota v. Dole, we considered whether the spending power permitted Congress to condition 5% of the State's federal highway funds on the State's adoption of a minimum drinking age of 21 years. The question whether a law enacted under the spending power is coercive in fact will sometimes be difficult, but where Congress has plainly "crossed the line distinguishing encouragement from coercion," a federal program that coopts the States' political processes must be declared unconstitutional.

The Federal Government's argument in this case at best pays lip service to the anticoercion principle. The Federal Government suggests that it is sufficient if States are "free, *as a matter of law,* to turn down" federal funds.

This argument ignores reality. When a heavy federal tax is levied to support a federal program that offers large grants to the States, States may, as a practical matter, be unable to refuse to participate in the federal program and to substitute a state alternative. Even if a State believes that the federal program is ineffective and inefficient, withdrawal would likely force the State to impose a huge tax increase on its residents, and this new state tax would come on top of the federal taxes already paid by residents to support subsidies to participating States.

E

Whether federal spending legislation crosses the line from enticement to coercion is often difficult to determine, and courts should not conclude that legislation is unconstitutional on this ground unless the coercive nature of an offer is unmistakably clear. In this case, however, there can be no doubt. In structuring the ACA, Congress unambiguously signaled its belief that every State would have no real choice but to go along with the Medicaid Expansion. If the anticoercion rule does not apply in this case, then there is no such rule.

Medicaid has long been the largest federal program of grants to the States. In 2010, the Federal Government directed more than $552 billion in federal funds to the States. Of this, more than $233 billion went to pre-expansion Medicaid. *This amount equals nearly 22% of all state expenditures combined.* The States devote a larger percentage of their budgets to Medicaid than to any other item.

The States are far less reliant on federal funding for any other program. After Medicaid, the next biggest federal funding item is aid to support elementary and secondary education, which amounts to 12.8% of total federal outlays to the States, and equals only 6.6% of all state expenditures combined.

For these reasons, the offer that the ACA makes to the States — go along with a dramatic expansion of Medicaid or potentially lose all federal Medicaid funding — is quite unlike anything that we have seen in a prior spending-power case.

What the statistics suggest is confirmed by the goal and structure of the ACA. In crafting the ACA, Congress clearly expressed its informed view that no State could possibly refuse the offer that the ACA extends.

The Federal Government does not dispute the inference that Congress anticipated 100% state participation, but it argues that this assumption was based on the fact that ACA's offer was an "exceedingly generous" gift. This characterization of the ACA's offer raises obvious questions. If that offer is "exceedingly generous," as the Federal Government maintains, why have more than half the States brought this lawsuit, contending that the offer is coercive? And why did Congress find it necessary to threaten that any State refusing to accept this "exceedingly generous" gift would risk losing all Medicaid funds? Congress could have made just the *new* funding provided under the ACA contingent on acceptance of the terms of the Medicaid Expansion. Congress took such an approach in some earlier amendments to Medicaid, separating new coverage requirements and funding from the rest of the program so that only new funding was conditioned on new eligibility extensions.

In sum, it is perfectly clear from the goal and structure of the ACA that the offer of the Medicaid Expansion was one that Congress understood no State could refuse. The Medicaid Expansion therefore exceeds Congress' spending power and cannot be implemented.

V

The Court today decides to save a statute Congress did not write. It rules that what the statute declares to be a requirement with a penalty is instead an option subject to a tax. And it changes the intentionally coercive sanction of a total cut-off of Medicaid funds to a supposedly noncoercive cut-off of only the incremental funds that the Act makes available.

The Court regards its strained statutory interpretation as judicial modesty. It is not. It amounts instead to a vast judicial overreaching. It creates a debilitated, inoperable version of health-care regulation that Congress did not enact and the public does not expect. It makes enactment of sensible health-care regulation more difficult, since Congress cannot start afresh but must take as its point of departure a jumble of now senseless provisions, provisions that certain interests favored under the Court's new design will struggle to retain. And it leaves the public and the States to expend vast sums of money on requirements that may or may not survive the necessary congressional revision.

The values that should have determined our course today are caution, minimalism, and the understanding that the Federal Government is one of limited powers. But the Court's ruling undermines those values at every turn. In the name of restraint, it overreaches. In the name of constitutional avoidance, it creates new constitutional questions. In the name of cooperative federalism, it undermines state sovereignty.

The Constitution, though it dates from the founding of the Republic, has powerful meaning and vital relevance to our own times. The constitutional protections that this case involves are protections of structure. Structural protections — notably, the restraints imposed by federalism and separation of powers — are less romantic and have less obvious a connection to personal freedom than the provisions of the Bill of Rights or the Civil War Amendments. Hence they tend to be undervalued or even forgotten by our citizens. It should be the responsibility of the Court to teach otherwise, to remind our people that the Framers considered structural protections of freedom the most important ones, for which reason they alone were embodied in the original Constitution and not left to later amendment. The fragmentation of power produced by the structure of our Government is central to liberty, and when we destroy it, we place liberty at peril. Today's decision should have vindicated, should have taught, this truth; instead, our judgment today has disregarded it.

For the reasons here stated, we would find the Act invalid in its entirety.

B.   THE NECESSSARY AND PROPER CLAUSE

In McCulloch v. Maryland, the Court interprets the "necessary and proper clause" in Article I, §8 as a grant of power to Congress, not a limitation. The Court says that Congress has the power to use any means, not prohibited by the Constitution, to carry outs its authority. In National Federation of Independent Business v. Sebelius, five justices rejected the argument that the individual mandate in the Affordable Care Act is a constitutional exercise of Congress's authority under the Necessary and Proper Clause.

There have been relatively few decisions in American history interpreting and applying the Necessary and Proper Clause. The recent decision in United States v. Comstock does so.

UNITED STATES v. COMSTOCK
130 S. Ct. 1949 (2010)

Justice BREYER delivered the opinion of the Court.

A federal civil-commitment statute authorizes the Department of Justice to detain a mentally ill, sexually dangerous federal prisoner beyond the date the prisoner would otherwise be released. We have previously examined similar statutes enacted under state law to determine whether they violate the Due Process Clause. See *Kansas v. Hendricks* (1997); *Kansas v. Crane* (2002). But this case presents a different question. Here we ask whether the Federal Government has the authority under Article I of the Constitution to enact this federal civil-commitment program or whether its doing so falls beyond the reach of a government "of enumerated powers." McCulloch v. Maryland (1819). We conclude that the Constitution grants Congress the authority to enact §4248 as "necessary and proper for carrying into Execution" the powers "vested by" the "Constitution in the Government of the United States."

I

The federal statute before us allows a district court to order the civil commitment of an individual who is currently "in the custody of the [Federal] Bureau of Prisons," if that individual (1) has previously "engaged or attempted to engage in sexually violent conduct or child molestation," (2) currently "suffers from a serious mental illness, abnormality, or disorder," and (3) "as a result of" that mental illness, abnormality, or disorder is "sexually dangerous to others," in that "he would have serious difficulty in refraining from sexually violent conduct or child molestation if released."

In order to detain such a person, the Government (acting through the Department of Justice) must certify to a federal district judge that the prisoner meets the conditions just described, *i.e.,* that he has engaged in sexually violent activity or child molestation in the past and that he suffers from a mental illness that makes him correspondingly dangerous to others. When such a certification is filed, the statute automatically stays the individual's release from prison, thereby giving the Government an opportunity to prove its claims at a hearing through psychiatric (or other) evidence. The statute provides that the prisoner "shall be represented by counsel" and shall have "an opportunity" at the hearing "to testify, to present evidence, to subpoena witnesses on his behalf, and to confront and cross-examine" the Government's witnesses.

If the Government proves its claims by "clear and convincing evidence," the court will order the prisoner's continued commitment in "the custody of the Attorney General," who must "make all reasonable efforts to cause" the State where that person was tried, or the State where he is domiciled, to "assume responsibility for his custody, care, and treatment." If either State is willing to assume that responsibility, the Attorney General "shall release" the individual "to the appropriate official" of that State. But if, "notwithstanding such efforts, neither such State will assume such responsibility," then "the Attorney General shall place the person for treatment in a suitable [federal] facility."

Confinement in the federal facility will last until either (1) the person's mental condition improves to the point where he is no longer dangerous (with or without appropriate ongoing treatment), in which case he will be released; or (2) a State assumes responsibility for his custody, care, and treatment, in which case he will be transferred to the custody of that State. The statute establishes a system for ongoing psychiatric and judicial review of the individual's case, including judicial hearings at the request of the confined person at six-month intervals.

In November and December 2006, the Government instituted proceedings in the Federal District Court for the Eastern District of North Carolina against the five respondents in this case. Three of the five had previously pleaded guilty in federal court to possession of child pornography, and the fourth had pleaded guilty to sexual abuse of a minor. With respect to each of them, the Government claimed that the respondent was about to be released from federal prison, that he had engaged in sexually violent conduct or child molestation in the past, and that he suffered from a mental illness that made him sexually dangerous to others. During that same time period, the Government instituted similar proceedings against the fifth respondent, who had been charged in federal court with aggravated sexual abuse of a minor, but was found mentally incompetent to stand trial. Each of the five respondents moved to dismiss the civil-commitment proceeding on constitutional grounds.

II

The question presented is whether the Necessary and Proper Clause, Art. I, §8, cl. 18, grants Congress authority sufficient to enact the statute before us. In resolving that question, we assume, but we do not decide, that other provisions of the Constitution — such as the Due Process Clause — do not prohibit civil commitment in these circumstances. In other words, we assume for argument's sake that the Federal Constitution would permit a State to enact this statute, and we ask solely whether the Federal Government, exercising its enumerated powers, may enact such a statute as well. On that assumption, we conclude that the Constitution grants Congress legislative power sufficient to enact §4248. We base this conclusion on five considerations, taken together.

First, the Necessary and Proper Clause grants Congress broad authority to enact federal legislation. Nearly 200 years ago, this Court stated that the Federal "[G]overnment is acknowledged by all to be one of enumerated powers," *McCulloch*, which means that "[e]very law enacted by Congress must be based on one or more of" those powers. But, at the same time, "a government, entrusted with such" powers "must also be entrusted with ample means for their execution." Accordingly, the Necessary and Proper Clause makes clear that the Constitution's grants of specific federal legislative authority are accompanied by broad power to enact laws that are "convenient, or useful" or "conducive" to the authority's "beneficial exercise." "Let the end be legitimate, let it be within the scope of the constitution, and all means which are appropriate, which are plainly adapted to that end, which are not prohibited, but consist with the letter and spirit of the constitution, are constitutional."

We have since made clear that, in determining whether the Necessary and Proper Clause grants Congress the legislative authority to enact a particular federal statute, we look to see whether the statute constitutes a means that is rationally related to the implementation of a constitutionally enumerated power.

Thus, the Constitution, which nowhere speaks explicitly about the creation of federal crimes beyond those related to "counterfeiting," "treason," or "Piracies and Felonies committed on the high Seas" or "against the Law of Nations," nonetheless grants Congress broad authority to create such crimes. And Congress routinely exercises its authority to enact criminal laws in furtherance of, for example, its enumerated powers to regulate interstate and foreign commerce, to enforce civil rights, to spend funds for the general welfare, to establish federal courts, to establish post offices, to regulate bankruptcy, to regulate naturalization, and so forth.

Similarly, Congress, in order to help ensure the enforcement of federal criminal laws enacted in furtherance of its enumerated powers, "can cause a prison to be erected at any place within the jurisdiction of the United States, and direct that all persons sentenced to imprisonment under the laws of the United States shall be confined there." Moreover, Congress, having established a prison system, can enact laws that seek to ensure that system's safe and responsible administration by, for example, requiring prisoners to receive medical care and educational training, and can also ensure the safety of the prisoners, prison workers and visitors, and those in surrounding communities by, for example, creating further criminal laws governing entry, exit, and smuggling, and by employing prison guards to ensure discipline and security.

Neither Congress' power to criminalize conduct, nor its power to imprison individuals who engage in that conduct, nor its power to enact laws governing prisons and prisoners, is explicitly mentioned in the Constitution. But Congress nonetheless possesses broad authority to do each of those things in the course of "carrying into Execution" the enumerated powers "vested by" the "Constitution in the Government of the United States."

Second, the civil-commitment statute before us constitutes a modest addition to a set of federal prison-related mental-health statutes that have existed for many decades. Here, Congress has long been involved in the delivery of mental health care to federal prisoners, and has long provided for their civil commitment. In 1855 it established Saint Elizabeth's Hospital in the District of Columbia to provide treatment to "the insane of the army and navy . . . and of the District of Columbia." In 1857 it provided for confinement at Saint Elizabeth's of any person within the District of Columbia who had been "charged with [a] crime" and who was "insane" or later became "insane during the continuance of his or her sentence in the United States penitentiary." In 1874, expanding the geographic scope of its statutes, Congress provided for civil commitment in federal facilities (or in state facilities if a State so agreed) of "*all* persons who have been or shall be convicted of any offense in *any* court of the United States" and who are or "shall become" insane "during the term of their imprisonment." And in 1882 Congress provided for similar commitment of those "*charged*" with federal offenses who become "insane" while in the "custody" of the United States. Thus, over the span of three decades, Congress created a national, federal civil-commitment program under which any person who was either charged with or convicted of any federal offense in any federal court could be confined in a federal mental institution.

In 2006, Congress enacted the particular statute before us. It differs from earlier statutes in that it focuses directly upon persons who, due to a mental illness, are sexually dangerous. Notably, many of these individuals were likely already subject to civil commitment under §4246, which, since 1949, has authorized the postsentence detention of federal prisoners who suffer from a mental illness and who are thereby dangerous (whether sexually or otherwise). Aside from its specific focus on sexually dangerous persons, §4248 is similar to the provisions first enacted in 1949. In that respect, it is a modest addition to a longstanding federal statutory framework, which has been in place since 1855.

Third, Congress reasonably extended its longstanding civil-commitment system to cover mentally ill and sexually dangerous persons who are already in federal custody, even if doing so detains them beyond the termination of their criminal sentence. For one thing, the Federal Government is the custodian of its prisoners. As federal custodian, it has the constitutional power to act in order to protect nearby (and other) communities from the danger federal prisoners may pose. If a federal prisoner is infected with a communicable disease that threatens others, surely it would be "necessary and proper" for the Federal Government to take action, pursuant to its role as federal custodian, to refuse (at least until the threat diminishes) to release that individual among the general public, where he might infect others. And if confinement of such an individual is a "necessary and proper" thing to do, then how could it not be similarly "necessary and proper" to confine an individual whose mental illness threatens others to the same degree?

Moreover, §4248 is "reasonably adapted," to Congress' power to act as a responsible federal custodian. Congress could have reasonably concluded that federal inmates who suffer from a mental illness that causes them to "have serious difficulty in refraining from sexually violent conduct," would pose an especially high danger to the public if released. And Congress could also have reasonably concluded (as detailed in the Judicial Conference's report) that a reasonable number of such individuals would likely *not* be detained by the States if released from federal custody, in part because the Federal Government itself severed their claim to "legal residence in any State" by incarcerating them in remote federal prisons.

Fourth, the statute properly accounts for state interests. Respondents and the dissent contend that §4248 violates the Tenth Amendment because it "invades the province of state sovereignty" in an area typically left to state control. But the Tenth Amendment's text is clear: "The powers *not delegated to the United States* by the Constitution, nor prohibited by it to the States, are reserved to the States respectively, or to the people." The powers "delegated to the United States by the Constitution" include those specifically enumerated powers listed in Article I along with the implementation authority granted by the Necessary and Proper Clause. Virtually by definition, these powers are not powers that the Constitution "reserved to the States."

Nor does this statute invade state sovereignty or otherwise improperly limit the scope of "powers that remain with the States." To the contrary, it requires *accommodation* of state interests.

Fifth, the links between §4248 and an enumerated Article I power are not too attenuated. Neither is the statutory provision too sweeping in its scope. Indeed even the dissent acknowledges that Congress has the implied power to criminalize any conduct that might interfere with the exercise of an enumerated power, and also the additional power to imprison people who violate those (inferentially authorized) laws, and the additional power to provide for the safe and reasonable management of those prisons, and the additional power to regulate the prisoners' behavior even after their release. And the same enumerated power that justifies the creation of a federal criminal statute, and that justifies the additional implied federal powers that the dissent considers legitimate, justifies civil commitment under §4248 as well. Thus, we must reject respondents' argument that the Necessary and Proper Clause permits no more than a single step between an enumerated power and an Act of Congress.

Nor need we fear that our holding today confers on Congress a general "police power, which the Founders denied the National Government and reposed in the States." As the Solicitor General repeatedly confirmed at oral argument, §4248 is narrow in scope. It has been applied to only a small fraction of federal prisoners. Thus, far from a "general police power," §4248 is a reasonably adapted and narrowly tailored means of pursuing the Government's legitimate interest as a federal custodian in the responsible administration of its prison system.

We take these five considerations together. They include: (1) the breadth of the Necessary and Proper Clause, (2) the long history of federal involvement in this arena, (3) the sound reasons for the statute's enactment in light of the Government's custodial interest in safeguarding the public from dangers posed by those in federal custody, (4) the statute's accommodation of state interests, and (5) the statute's narrow scope. Taken together, these considerations lead us to conclude that the statute is a "necessary and proper" means of exercising the federal authority that permits Congress to create federal criminal laws, to punish their violation, to imprison violators, to provide appropriately for those imprisoned, and to maintain the security of those who are not imprisoned but who may be affected by the federal imprisonment of others. The Constitution consequently authorizes Congress to enact the statute.

We do not reach or decide any claim that the statute or its application denies equal protection of the laws, procedural or substantive due process, or any other rights guaranteed by the Constitution. Respondents are free to pursue those claims on remand, and any others they have preserved.

Justice Thomas, with whom Justice Scalia joins, dissenting.

The Court holds today that Congress has power under the Necessary and Proper Clause to enact a law authorizing the Federal Government to civilly commit "sexually dangerous person[s]" beyond the date it lawfully could hold them on a charge or conviction for a federal crime. I disagree. The Necessary and Proper Clause empowers Congress to enact only those laws that "carr[y] into Execution" one or more of the federal powers enumerated in the Constitution. Because §4248 "Execut[es]" no enumerated power, I must respectfully dissent.

[I]

No enumerated power in Article I, §8, expressly delegates to Congress the power to enact a civil-commitment regime for sexually dangerous persons, nor does any other provision in the Constitution vest Congress or the other branches of the Federal Government with such a power. Accordingly, §4248 can be a valid exercise of congressional authority only if it is "necessary and proper for carrying into Execution" one or more of those federal powers actually enumerated in the Constitution.

Section 4248 does not fall within any of those powers. The Government identifies no specific enumerated power or powers as a constitutional predicate for §4248, and none are readily discernable. Indeed, not even the Commerce Clause—the enumerated power this Court has interpreted most expansively, can justify federal civil detention of sex offenders. Under the Court's precedents, Congress may not regulate noneconomic activity (such as sexual violence) based solely on the effect such activity may have, in individual cases or in the aggregate, on interstate commerce. That limitation forecloses any claim that §4248 carries into execution Congress' Commerce Clause power, and the Government has never argued otherwise.

This Court, moreover, consistently has recognized that the power to care for the mentally ill and, where necessary, the power "to protect the community from the dangerous tendencies of some" mentally ill persons, are among the numerous powers that remain with the States. As a consequence, we have held that States may "take measures to restrict the freedom of the dangerously mentally ill"—including those who are sexually dangerous—provided that such commitments satisfy due process and other constitutional requirements.

Section 4248 closely resembles the involuntary civil-commitment laws that States have enacted under their *parens patriae* and general police powers. To be sure, protecting society from violent sexual offenders is certainly an important end. Sexual abuse is a despicable act with untold consequences for the victim personally and society generally. But the Constitution does not vest in Congress the authority to protect society from every bad act that might befall it.

In my view, this should decide the question. Section 4248 runs afoul of our settled understanding of Congress' power under the Necessary and Proper Clause. Congress may act under that Clause only when its legislation "carr[ies] into Execution" one of the Federal Government's enumerated powers. Section 4248 does not execute *any* enumerated power. Section 4248 is therefore unconstitutional.

[II]

The Court perfunctorily genuflects to *McCulloch*'s framework for assessing Congress' Necessary and Proper Clause authority, and to the principle of dual sovereignty it helps to maintain, then promptly abandons both in favor of a novel five-factor test supporting its conclusion that §4248 is a "necessary and proper" adjunct to a jumble of *unenumerated* "authorit[ies]." The Court's newly minted test cannot be reconciled with the Clause's plain text or with two centuries of our precedents interpreting it. It also raises more questions than it answers. Must each of the five considerations exist before the Court sustains future federal legislation as proper exercises of Congress' Necessary and Proper Clause authority? What if the facts of a given case support a finding of only four considerations? Or three? And if three or four will suffice, *which* three or four are imperative? At a minimum, this shift from the two-step *McCulloch* framework to this five-consideration approach warrants an explanation as to why *McCulloch* is no longer good enough and which of the five considerations will bear the most weight in future cases, assuming some number less than five suffices. (Or, if not, why all five are required.) The Court provides no answers to these questions.

Not long ago, this Court described the Necessary and Proper Clause as "the last, best hope of those who defend ultra vires congressional action." Regrettably, today's opinion breathes new life into that Clause, and — the Court's protestations to the contrary notwithstanding — comes perilously close to transforming the Necessary and Proper Clause into a basis for the federal police power that "we *always* have rejected." In so doing, the Court endorses the precise abuse of power Article I is designed to prevent — the use of a limited grant of authority as a "pretext . . . for the accomplishment of objects not intrusted to the government."

C. THE COMMERCE POWER

Article I, §8 states, "The Congress shall have the power . . . [t]o regulate Commerce with foreign Nations, and among the several States, and with the Indian Tribes." Practically speaking, this provision has been the authority for a broad array of federal legislation, ranging from criminal statutes to securities laws to civil rights laws to environmental laws. From the perspective of constitutional law, the Commerce Clause has been the focus of the vast majority of Supreme Court decisions that have considered the scope of congressional power and federalism.

There have been roughly four eras of Commerce Clause jurisprudence. During the initial era, from early in American history until the 1890s, the commerce power was broadly defined but minimally used. In a period from the 1890s until 1937, the Court narrowly defined the scope of Congress's commerce power and used the Tenth Amendment as a limit. The era from 1937 until the 1990s was a time when the Court expansively defined the scope of the commerce power and refused to apply the Tenth Amendment as a limit. Since the 1990s, the Court has again narrowed the scope of the commerce power and revived the Tenth Amendment as an independent, judicially enforceable limit on federal actions.

Throughout these eras, the Court is considering three questions. First: What is "commerce"? Is it one stage of business, or does it include all aspects of business — even life in the United States? Second: What does "among the several states" mean? Is it limited to instances where there is a direct effect on interstate commerce, or does any effect on interstate activities suffice? And third: Does the Tenth Amendment limit Congress? If Congress is acting within the scope of its commerce power, can a law be declared unconstitutional as violating the Tenth Amendment?

1. *The Initial Era: Gibbons v. Ogden Defines the Commerce Power*

The New York legislature granted a monopoly to Robert Fulton and Robert Livingston for operating steamboats in New York waters. Fulton and Livingston licensed Aaron Ogden to operate a ferryboat between New York City and Elizabethtown Port in New Jersey. Thomas Gibbons operated a competing ferry service and thus violated the exclusive rights given to Fulton and Livingston, and their licensee Ogden, under the monopoly. Gibbons maintained that he had the right to operate his ferry because it was licensed under a federal law as "vessels in the coasting trade." Nonetheless, Ogden successfully sued for an injunction in the New York state courts.

The Supreme Court considered the scope of Congress's powers and then whether the New York grant of a monopoly was constitutional. The latter aspect of the case, the permissibility of the state law, is discussed in Chapter 4. Below is the Court's discussion of the scope of Congress's commerce power.

GIBBONS v. OGDEN
22 U.S. (9 Wheat.) 1 (1824)

Chief Justice MARSHALL delivered the opinion of the Court.

As preliminary to the very able discussions of the constitution, which we have heard from the bar, and as having some influence on its construction, reference has been made to the political situation of these States, anterior to its formation. It has been said, that they were sovereign, were completely independent, and were connected with each other only by a league. This is true. But, when these allied sovereigns converted their league into a government, when they converted their Congress of Ambassadors, deputed to deliberate on their common concerns, and to recommend measures of general utility, into a Legislature, empowered to enact laws on the most interesting subjects, the whole character in which the States appear, underwent a change, the extent of which must be determined by a fair consideration of the instrument by which that change was effected.

This instrument contains an enumeration of powers expressly granted by the people to their government. It has been said, that these powers ought to be construed strictly. But why ought they to be so construed? Is there one sentence in the constitution which gives countenance to this rule? In the last of the enumerated powers, that which grants, expressly, the means for carrying all others into execution, Congress is authorized "to make all laws which shall be necessary and proper" for the purpose.

The words are, "Congress shall have power to regulate commerce with foreign nations, and among the several States, and with the Indian tribes." The subject to be regulated is commerce; and our constitution being one of enumeration, and not of definition, to ascertain the extent of the power, it becomes necessary to settle the meaning of the word. The counsel for the appellee would limit it to traffic, to buying and selling, or the interchange of commodities, and do not admit that it comprehends navigation. This would restrict a general term, applicable to many objects, to one of its significations. Commerce, undoubtedly, is traffic, but it is something more: it is intercourse. It describes the commercial intercourse between nations, and parts of nations, in all its branches, and is regulated by prescribing rules for carrying on that intercourse. The mind can scarcely conceive a system for regulating commerce between nations, which shall exclude all laws concerning navigation, which shall be silent on the admission of the vessels of the one nation into the ports of the other, and be confined to prescribing rules for the conduct of individuals, in the actual employment of buying and selling, or of barter.

If commerce does not include navigation, the government of the Union has no direct power over that subject, and can make no law prescribing what shall constitute American vessels, or requiring that they shall be navigated by American seamen. Yet this power has been exercised from the commencement of the government, has been exercised with the consent of all, and has been understood by all to be a commercial regulation. All America understands, and has uniformly understood, the word "commerce," to comprehend navigation. It was so understood, and must have been so understood, when the constitution was framed. The power over commerce, including navigation, was one of the primary objects for which the people of America adopted their government, and must have been contemplated in forming it. The convention must have used the word in that sense, because all have understood it in that sense; and the attempt to restrict it comes too late.

The word used in the constitution, then, comprehends, and has been always understood to comprehend, navigation within its meaning; and a power to regulate navigation, is as expressly granted, as if that term had been added to the word "commerce."

To what commerce does this power extend? The constitution informs us, to commerce "with foreign nations, and among the several States, and with the Indian tribes."

It has, we believe, been universally admitted, that these words comprehend every species of commercial intercourse between the United States and foreign nations. No sort of trade can be carried on between this country and any other, to which this power does not extend. It has been truly said, that commerce, as the word is used in the constitution, is a unit, every part of which is indicated by the term.

The subject to which the power is next applied, is to commerce "among the several States." The word "among" means intermingled with. A thing which is among others, is intermingled with them. Commerce among the States, cannot stop at the external boundary line of each State, but may be introduced into the interior.

It is not intended to say that these words comprehend that commerce, which is completely internal, which is carried on between man and man in a State, or between different parts of the same State, and which does not extend to or affect other States. Such a power would be inconvenient, and is certainly unnecessary.

Comprehensive as the word "among" is, it may very properly be restricted to that commerce which concerns more States than one. The phrase is not one which would probably have been selected to indicate the completely interior traffic of a State, because it is not an apt phrase for that purpose; and the enumeration of the particular classes of commerce, to which the power was to be extended, would not have been made, had the intention been to extend the power to every description. The enumeration presupposes something not enumerated; and that something, if we regard the language or the subject of the sentence, must be the exclusively internal commerce of a State. The genius and character of the whole government seem to be, that its action is to be applied to all the external concerns of the nation, and to those internal concerns which affect the States generally; but not to those which are completely within a particular State, which do not affect other States, and with which it is not necessary to interfere, for the purpose of executing some of the general powers of the government. The completely internal commerce of a State, then, may be considered as reserved for the State itself.

But, in regulating commerce with foreign nations, the power of Congress does not stop at the jurisdictional lines of the several States. It would be a very useless power, if it could not pass those lines. The commerce of the United States with foreign nations, is that of the whole United States. Every district has a right to participate in it. The deep streams which penetrate our country in every direction, pass through the interior of almost every State in the Union, and furnish the means of exercising this right. If Congress has the power to regulate it, that power must be exercised whenever the subject exists. If it exists within the States, if a foreign voyage may commence or terminate at a port within a State, then the power of Congress may be exercised within a State.

We are now arrived at the inquiry—What is this power?

It is the power to regulate; that is, to prescribe the rule by which commerce is to be governed. This power, like all others vested in Congress, is complete in itself, may be exercised to its utmost extent, and acknowledges no limitations, other than are prescribed in the constitution. If, as has always been understood, the sovereignty of Congress, though limited to specified objects, is plenary as to those objects, the power over commerce with foreign nations, and among the several States, is vested in Congress as absolutely as it would be in a single government, having in its constitution the same restrictions on the exercise of the power as are found in the constitution of the United States. The wisdom and the discretion of Congress, their identity with the people, and the influence which their constituents possess at elections, are, in this, as in many other instances, as that, for example, of declaring war, the sole restraints on which they have relied, to secure them from its abuse. They are the restraints on which the people must often rely, in all representative governments.

———————

During the remainder of the nineteenth century, until the 1890s, there were relatively few cases considering the scope of Congress's Commerce Clause power. In the years after *Gibbons* and before the Civil War, the Supreme Court rarely considered challenges to federal legislation adopted under Congress's Commerce Clause authority. After the Civil War, there were a few cases concerning the scope of the commerce power. Some of the cases continued *Gibbons*'s expansive definition of commerce. For example, in *The Daniel Ball,* 77 U.S. (1 Wall.) 557 (1871), the Court accorded Congress broad authority to license ships, even those operating entirely intrastate, as long as the boats were carrying goods that had come from another state or that ultimately would go to another state. The Court explained that unsafe ships in intrastate commerce could affect and harm ships in interstate commerce.

Yet there also were a few cases that departed from *Gibbons* and invalidated federal legislation as exceeding the scope of the commerce power. The first case to overturn a federal law in this way was United States v. Dewitt, 76 U.S. (9 Wall.) 41 (1869), in 1870. A federal law outlawed the sale of naphtha and other illuminating oils that could ignite at less than 110 degrees Fahrenheit. The Court held that the law was "a police regulation, relating exclusively to the internal trade of the States." In a precursor to decisions that followed after the 1890s, the Court declared the law unconstitutional because it was "a virtual denial of any power to interfere with the internal trade and business of the separate States."

In *The Trademark Cases*, 100 U.S. (10 Otto) 82 (1878), the Court invalidated the federal law that established a federal system for registering trademarks. The Court concluded that the law was unconstitutional because it applied to wholly intrastate businesses and business transactions and therefore "is obviously the exercise of a power not confided to Congress."

2. *The 1890s-1937: A Limited Federal Commerce Power*

In the late nineteenth century, concurrent with the Industrial Revolution and the growth of the national economy, Congress began using the Commerce Clause much more extensively to regulate businesses. The Interstate Commerce Act in 1887 was largely meant to provide for federal regulation of railroads, and the Sherman Antitrust Act in 1890 was intended to combat monopolies and restraints of trade.

Beginning in the 1890s, the Supreme Court narrowly interpreted the scope of Congress's commerce power and used the Tenth Amendment as an independent constraint on congressional authority. Between the late nineteenth century and 1937, the Court was controlled by conservative justices deeply committed to laissez-faire economics and strongly opposed to government economic regulations. Many federal laws were invalidated as exceeding the scope of Congress's commerce power or as violating the Tenth Amendment and the zone of activities reserved to the states. Many state laws were invalidated as interfering with freedom of contract, which the Court found to be protected as a fundamental right under the liberty of the Due Process Clause.[17] So, for example, a federal law requiring a minimum wage during this period would be invalidated as exceeding the scope of Congress's power and as usurping states' prerogatives;[18] a state law requiring a minimum wage would be invalidated as impermissibly interfering with freedom of contract.[19]

This era of constitutional law is extremely important. It was the first time that the Supreme Court aggressively used its power of judicial review to invalidate federal and state laws. Constitutional law since 1937 has very much been a reaction to this earlier era. The Court did not invalidate another law as exceeding the scope of the Commerce Clause until 1995[20] and has generally very much deferred to federal and state economic regulations.

Although appreciating and understanding constitutional law in this era requires looking at all of these cases together, this chapter focuses solely on the decisions concerning the scope of Congress's power. The Court's use of freedom of contract during this time period as a limit on state power is discussed in Chapter 6.

17. These cases are discussed in Chapter 6.
18. *See, e.g.*, Carter v. Carter Coal Co., 298 U.S. 238 (1936) (invalidating the wage and hour provisions of the Bituminous Coal Conservation Act of 1935).
19. *See, e.g.*, Morehead v. New York ex rel. Tipaldo, 298 U.S. 587 (1936) (invalidating a state minimum wage law for women).
20. United States v. Lopez, 514 U.S. 549 (1995), presented below.

Between the late nineteenth century and 1937, the Court espoused a philosophy often termed "dual federalism." Dual federalism was the view that the federal and state governments were separate sovereigns, that each had separate zones of authority, and that it was the judicial role to protect the states by interpreting and enforcing the Constitution to protect the zone of activities reserved to the states.

Dual federalism was embodied in three important doctrines that the Court developed and followed during this time period. First, the Court narrowly defined the meaning of *commerce* so as to leave a zone of power to the states. Specifically, as described below, the Court held that commerce was one stage of business, distinct from earlier phases such as mining, manufacturing, or production. Under this view, only commerce itself could be regulated by Congress; the others were left for state regulation.

Second, the Court restrictively defined *among the states* as allowing Congress to regulate only when there was a substantial effect on interstate commerce. In all other areas, regulation again was left to the states.

Finally, the Court held that the Tenth Amendment reserved a zone of activities to the states and that even federal laws within the scope of the commerce clause were unconstitutional if they invaded that zone. For example, the Court held that regulation of production was left to the states, and therefore a federal law that prohibited shipment in interstate commerce of goods made by child labor was unconstitutional, even though it was limited to interstate commerce, because it violated the Tenth Amendment.[21]

Each of these three doctrines requires further elaboration. However, it should be noted at the outset that the Court was not completely consistent in applying these principles. The Court was most likely to follow them when considering federal economic regulations; the Court was least likely to adhere to them, and most willing to uphold federal laws, when they concerned federal morals regulation. Thus, as described below, the Court invalidated federal antitrust laws[22] and employment regulation statutes[23] but upheld federal laws prohibiting lotteries[24] and regulating sexual behavior.[25] Perhaps a principled distinction between these cases can be articulated, or more likely, the decisions were simply a product of the Court's particular brand of conservatism—economically conservative and thus aggressive in striking down economic regulations, morally conservative and thus deferential to laws directed at what was perceived as sin.

a. What Is "Commerce"?

The three doctrines described above created a powerful limit on the scope of Congress's power. First, the Court held that *commerce* was to be narrowly defined as one stage of business, separate and distinct from earlier phases such as mining, manufacturing, and production. In United States v. E.C. Knight, 156 U.S. 1

---

21. Hammer v. Dagenhart (*The Child Labor Case*), 247 U.S. 251 (1918), discussed below.
22. United States v. E.C. Knight Co., 156 U.S. 1 (1895), discussed below.
23. *See, e.g.*, Carter v. Carter Coal Co., 298 U.S. 238 (1936).
24. Champion v. Ames, 188 U.S. 321 (1902).
25. *See, e.g.*, Hoke v. United States, 227 U.S. 308 (1913); Caminetti v. United States, 242 U.S. 470 (1917) (upholding the Mann Act, which made it a crime to take a woman across state lines for immoral purposes).

(1895), toward the beginning of this era, the Court held that the Sherman Antitrust Act could not be used to stop a monopoly in the sugar refining industry because the Constitution did not allow Congress to regulate manufacturing. The U.S. government attempted to use the Sherman Antitrust Act to block the American Sugar Refining Company from acquiring four competing refineries. The acquisition would have given the company control of over 98 percent of the sugar refining industry.

Nonetheless, the Court held that federal law could not be applied because the monopoly was in the production of sugar, not in its commerce. The Court flatly declared, "Commerce succeeds to manufacture, and is not a part of it." The Court was clear that this rigid distinction was based on a need for preserving a zone of activities to the states. The Court explained that although the commerce power was one of the "strongest bond[s] of the union, . . . the preservation of the autonomy of the States [w]as required by our dual form of government."

This distinction between manufacturing and commerce seems arbitrary; a company would desire a monopoly in production because it would benefit from monopoly profits in commerce. The Court acknowledged this but said that the relationship was too indirect to allow federal regulation under the commerce power. The Court said that it would be "far-reaching" to allow Congress to act "whenever interstate or international commerce may be ultimately affected." The Court explained that the effect on commerce was only "indirect" and thus outside the scope of federal power.

This very limited definition of commerce continued throughout this era until 1937. For example, in Carter v. Carter Coal Co., 298 U.S. 238 (1936), the Court declared unconstitutional the Bituminous Coal Conservation Act of 1935. The law contained detailed findings as to the relationship between coal and the national economy and declared that the production of coal directly affected interstate commerce. The law provided for local coal boards to be established to determine prices for coal and to determine, after collective bargaining by unions and employers, wages and hours for employees. A shareholder in the Carter Coal Company sued it to stop it from complying with the law.

The Supreme Court, in an opinion by Justice Sutherland, declared the law unconstitutional. The Court focused on the unconstitutionality of federal regulation of wages and hours. The Court stated:

> [C]ommerce is the equivalent of the phrase "intercourse for the purposes of trade." Plainly, the incidents leading up to and culminating in the mining of coal do not constitute such intercourse. The employment of men, the fixing of their wages, hours of labor and working conditions, the bargaining in respect of these things — whether carried on separately or collectively — each and all constitute intercourse for the purposes of production, not of trade. . . . Mining brings the subject matter of commerce into existence. Commerce disposes of it.

The Court again emphasized that this narrow definition of commerce was essential to protect the states. The Court lamented, "Every journey to a forbidden end begins with the first step; and the danger of such a step by the federal government in the direction of taking over the powers of the states is that the end of the journey may find the states so despoiled of their powers, or — what may amount to the same thing — so relieved of responsibilities . . . as to reduce them to little more than geographic subdivisions of the national domain."

Decisions such as *E.C. Knight* and *Carter* rest on many assumptions: that it makes sense to distinguish commerce from other stages of business, that the Constitution requires that a rigid zone of activities be left to the states, and that it is the judicial role to protect this zone. From the late nineteenth century until 1937, these premises were fervently accepted by the Supreme Court.

b. What Does "Among the States" Mean?

The second major aspect of the Court's approach to the Commerce Clause during this era was the requirement that there be a direct effect on interstate commerce. For example, in the *Shreveport Rate Cases*, 234 U.S. 342 (1914), the Court upheld the ability of the Interstate Commerce Commission to set intrastate railroad rates because of their direct impact on interstate commerce. Specifically, a railroad was ordered to charge the same rates for shipments to Marshall, Texas, whether from Shreveport, Louisiana, or from Dallas, Texas. The Court upheld the federal regulation and held that "Congress in the exercise of its paramount power may prevent the common instrumentalities of interstate and intrastate commercial intercourse from being used in their intrastate operations to the injury of interstate commerce." The Court said that Congress "does possess the power to foster and protect interstate commerce, and to take all measures necessary or appropriate to that end, although intrastate transactions of interstate carriers may thereby be controlled."

The distinction between direct and indirect effects is inherently elusive and difficult to draw. In contrast to the *Shreveport Rate Cases*, A.L.A. Schecter Poultry Corp. v. United States, 295 U.S. 495 (1935), often referred to as the "sick chickens" case, declared a federal law unconstitutional based on an insufficient effect on interstate commerce. The National Industrial Recovery Act, a key piece of New Deal legislation, authorized the president to approve "codes of fair competition" developed by boards of various industries. Pursuant to this law, the president approved a Live Poultry Code for New York City. In part, the code was designed to ensure quality poultry by preventing sellers from requiring buyers to purchase the entire coop of chickens, including sick ones. The code also regulated employment by requiring collective bargaining, prohibiting child labor, and establishing a 40-hour workweek and a minimum wage.

The Supreme Court declared the code unconstitutional because there was not a sufficiently "direct" relationship to interstate commerce. Although the Court acknowledged that virtually all of the poultry in New York was shipped from other states, the Court said that the code was not regulating the interstate transactions; rather, the code concerned the operation of businesses within New York. The Court emphasized that Congress only could regulate when there was a direct effect on interstate commerce. The Court explained, "In determining how far the federal government may go in controlling intrastate transactions upon the ground that they 'affect' interstate commerce, there is a necessary and well-established distinction between direct and indirect effects." The federal government has the authority to regulate when there are direct effects on commerce, "[b]ut where the effect of intrastate transactions upon interstate commerce is merely indirect, such transactions remain within the domain of state power."

The Court once again explained that this distinction was essential to protect state governments and ultimately the American system of government. The Court stated, "If the commerce clause were construed to reach all enterprises and transactions which could be said to have an indirect effect upon interstate commerce, the federal authority would embrace practically all the activities of the people and the authority of the State over its domestic concerns would exist only by sufferance of the federal government." The Court thus declared that enforcing the distinction between direct and indirect effects on commerce "must be recognized as . . . essential to the maintenance of our constitutional system."

The difficulty, of course, is in drawing a meaningful and useful distinction between direct and indirect effects. The Court struggled with this throughout the era. One approach that the Court often used was to allow Congress to regulate to protect the stream of commerce. The Court initially articulated this approach in Swift & Co. v. United States, 196 U.S. 375 (1905), which upheld the application of the Sherman Antitrust Act to an agreement among meat dealers to fix the price at which they would purchase meat from stockyards. Although the stockyard was intrastate, the Court stressed how it was only a temporary stop for the cattle. Justice Holmes, writing for the Court, explained that the stockyards were in "a current of commerce among the States, and the purchase of the cattle is a part and incident of such commerce."

Likewise, in Stafford v. Wallace, 258 U.S. 495 (1922), for example, the Court upheld the Packers and Stockyards Act of 1921, which authorized the secretary of commerce to regulate rates and prescribe standards for the operation of stockyards where livestock was kept. The law was designed to protect consumers by lessening collusion between stockyard managers and packers and also by decreasing the ability of packers to set prices for livestock. The Supreme Court upheld the federal law emphasizing that the stockyards are in the stream of commerce. Chief Justice Taft, writing for the Court, explained that the "stockyards are but a throat through which the current flows, and the transactions which occur therein are only incident to this current from the West to the East, and from one State to another. Such transactions can not be separated from the movement to which they contribute and necessarily take on its character."

The Court relied on this stream of commerce approach to allow Congress to prohibit the sale of impure or adulterated food or drugs,[26] to require retail labeling for items traveling in interstate commerce,[27] and to restrict the sale of intoxicating beverages to Indians.[28]

The Court, however, did not consistently apply its stream of commerce approach. For example, in Railroad Retirement Board v. Alton R.R. Co., 295 U.S. 330 (1935), the Court declared unconstitutional the Railroad Retirement Act of 1934, which provided a pension system for railroad workers. Railroads obviously were part of the stream of interstate commerce, and the Court had upheld other federal regulations of railroads. In Southern Railway v. United States, 222 U.S. 20 (1911), the Court upheld the Federal Safety Appliance Acts, which regulated couplers on railroad cars. In Baltimore & Ohio Railroad

---

26. Hipolite Egg. Co. v. United States, 220 U.S. 31 (1911).
27. McDermott v. Wisconsin, 228 U.S. 115 (1913).
28. United States v. Nice, 241 U.S. 591 (1916).

Co. v. Interstate Commerce Commission, 221 U.S. 612 (1911), the Court upheld a federal law that set maximum hours for railroad workers.

Yet in the *Alton R.R. Co.* case the Court struck down the requirement for a pension for railroad workers and distinguished the other cases as concerning the safety or efficiency of the railroads. The Court said that Congress could not use its commerce power to require a pension program for railroad employees because the law was only to help "the social welfare of the worker, and therefore [was] remote from any regulation of commerce."

The key point is that the Court interpreted "among the states" as requiring a direct effect on interstate commerce. Yet the Court never formulated a clear or consistent way to distinguish direct from indirect effects. Why did intrastate railroad rates have a direct effect on interstate commerce, while regulations designed to limit the shipment of sick chickens in interstate commerce have only an indirect effect? The stream of commerce approach was sometimes used during this era to evaluate whether an activity was among the states. Yet the Court was no more consistent in applying this test. Why are prices at stockyards in the stream of commerce but practices at poultry farms not part of that stream?

c. Does State Sovereignty Limit Congressional Power?

Finally, the Court held that even if an activity was commerce and was among the states, Congress still could not regulate if it was intruding into the zone of activities reserved to the states. The Court concluded that the Tenth Amendment reserved control of activities such as mining, manufacturing, and production to the states. Even federal laws regulating commerce among the states were unconstitutional if they sought to control mining, manufacturing, and production.

The Child Labor Case (Hammer v. Dagenhart), 247 U.S. 251 (1918), was the most significant decision to use the Tenth Amendment in this way. A federal law prohibited the shipment in interstate commerce of goods produced in factories that employed children under age 14 or employed children between the ages of 14 and 16 for more than eight hours per day or six days a week. Although the law only regulated goods in interstate commerce, the Court declared it unconstitutional because it controlled production. The Court declared that "[t]he grant of power to Congress over the subject of interstate commerce was to enable it to regulate such commerce, and not to give it authority to control the States in their exercise of the police power over local trade and manufacture." The Court said that regulating the hours of labor of children was entrusted "purely [to] state authority." The Court expressly rejected the argument that federal legislation was necessary to prevent unfair competition; states that wanted to outlaw child labor would find it difficult to do so as long as other states allowed child labor.

Indeed, the Court spoke in apocalyptic terms as to the consequences if Congress was accorded such regulatory power: "The far reaching result of upholding the act cannot be more plainly indicated than by pointing out that if Congress can thus regulate matters entrusted to local authority by prohibition of the movement of commodities in interstate commerce, all freedom of commerce will be at an end, and the power of the States over local matters may be eliminated, and thus our system of government be practically destroyed."

The Child Labor Case can be contrasted to another decision from that era, *The Lottery Case* (Champion v. Ames), 188 U.S. 321 (1903), in which the Court upheld a federal law prohibiting the interstate shipment of lottery tickets. In both *The Child Labor Case* and *The Lottery Case*, the federal law prohibited the shipment of a specified item — goods made by child labor or lottery tickets — in interstate commerce. In both, Congress obviously was seeking to stop intrastate activities: the use of child labor and gambling in lotteries. Yet in the former the Court declared the federal law unconstitutional, whereas in the latter the Court upheld the federal law.

In *The Lottery Case*, the Court made it clear that the power to regulate interstate commerce includes the ability to prohibit items from being in interstate commerce. The Court concluded that it was within Congress's Commerce Clause power to stop lottery tickets from being a part of interstate commerce. The Court declared, "If a State, when considering legislation for the suppression of lotteries within its own limits, may properly take into view the evils that inhere in the raising of money, in that mode, why may not Congress, invested with power to regulate commerce among the several States, provide that such commerce shall not be polluted by the carrying of lottery tickets from one State to another?"

The Court explicitly rejected the argument that the federal law violated the Tenth Amendment and intruded on state government prerogatives. Also, the Court rejected the argument that according Congress such power would give Congress seemingly limitless authority and would endanger the constitutional structure. The Court simply said, "[T]he possible abuse of a power is not an argument against its existence."

Thus, the Court did not consistently define the zone of activities reserved to the states. Yet the Court during this era clearly believed in dual sovereignty and used it to limit federal power.

Perhaps there are principled distinctions between these cases, or perhaps they simply reflect a conservative Court much more willing to defer to morals laws than to economic regulations. Whatever the cause, these three doctrines — the narrow definition of commerce, the restrictive interpretation of among the states, and the use of state sovereignty as a constraint on congressional power — all advanced dual federalism and all limited the scope of Congress's authority under the Commerce Clause.

3. *1937-1990s: Broad Federal Commerce Power*

By the mid-1930s, there were enormous pressures for a change in the Supreme Court's narrow approach to defining the scope of Congress's power. It must be remembered that during this time the Court also was narrowly interpreting the scope of other congressional powers, such as the spending power (discussed below), and greatly restricting the ability of state governments to regulate the economy by protecting freedom of contract under substantive due process (discussed in Chapter 6).

The economic crisis caused by the Depression made the Supreme Court's hostility to economic regulation and its commitment to a laissez-faire economy seem anachronistic and harmful. Unemployment was widespread, and the wages of those with jobs were low. Business failure was endemic, and production was substantially lessened. Foreclosures of home and farm mortgages were common.

Strong political pressure developed for change. President Franklin Roosevelt won a landslide reelection victory in 1936 and saw this as a strong endorsement for the New Deal programs that the Court was invalidating, such as in Carter v. Carter Coal and Schechter Poultry v. United States. In March 1937, Roosevelt proposed that Congress adopt legislation to increase the size of the Supreme Court.[29] Under the proposal, one justice would be added to the Court for each justice over age 70, up to a maximum of 15 justices. In light of the ages of the justices then on the Court, Roosevelt would have been able to add six new justices and thus secure a majority on the Court to uphold the New Deal programs.

Roosevelt's Court-packing plan drew intense opposition, even from some supporters of New Deal programs, on the ground that it was a threat to the independence of the federal judiciary. It is worth noting, however, that nothing in the Constitution mandated or even suggested a number of justices for the Court. The first Judiciary Act prescribed a Court of six. This was temporarily reduced to five in 1801 and increased back to six in 1802. The number of justices was increased to seven in 1807, to nine in 1837, and to ten in 1864. Generally, the increase in the size of the Court was a result of the addition of a new federal circuit court of appeals. Supreme Court justices were responsible for "riding circuit" and sitting as federal appeals court judges; an additional justice was created each time the country expanded and a new circuit was added.

In 1866, with unpopular President Andrew Johnson in the White House, Congress reduced the size of the Supreme Court to seven. This kept Johnson from filling an existing vacancy on the Court and meant that the next two vacancies also would go unfilled in order to bring the Court's size down from ten to seven. In 1869, after Ulysses Grant became president, the number on the Court was increased to nine, where it has been ever since.

Although the number of justices was not specified in the Constitution, Roosevelt's Court-packing plan was intensely opposed as a threat to judicial independence. In 1937, Justice Owen Roberts changed his position and was the fifth to uphold two laws of the type that previously had been invalidated: a state minimum wage law for women and a federal law regulating labor relations.[30] There is a debate over whether Roberts was influenced by the political pressure of the Court-packing plan or whether he planned to change his vote prior to Roosevelt's proposal. Whatever the cause, Roberts's change in sentiment will forever be known as "the switch in time that saved nine."

KEY DECISIONS CHANGING THE COMMERCE CLAUSE DOCTRINE

Three decisions—NLRB v. Jones & Laughlin Steel Corp. in 1937, United States v. Darby in 1941, and Wickard v. Filburn in 1942—overruled the earlier era of decisions and expansively defined the scope of Congress's commerce power. Indeed, because of these three decisions, from 1937 until 1995, not one federal law was declared unconstitutional as exceeding the scope of

---

29. The "Court packing" proposal is discussed in detail in Robert Jackson, *The Struggle for Judicial Supremacy* (1941).

30. West Coast Hotel v. Parish, 300 U.S. 379 (1937) (upholding a state minimum wage law for women), discussed in Chapter 6; NLRB v. Jones & Laughlin Steel Corp., 301 U.S. 1 (1937) (upholding federal regulation of the steel industry), discussed below.

Congress's commerce power. These three key rulings are presented and then followed by consideration of how the Court defined "commerce among the states" after these decisions and how the Court treated the Tenth Amendment prior to the 1990s.

NLRB v. JONES & LAUGHLIN STEEL CORP.
301 U.S. 1 (1937)

Chief Justice Hughes delivered the opinion of the Court.

In a proceeding under the National Labor Relations Act of 1935 the National Labor Relations Board found that the respondent, Jones & Laughlin Steel Corporation, had violated the act by engaging in unfair labor practices affecting commerce. The unfair labor practices charged were that the corporation was discriminating against members of the union with regard to hire and tenure of employment, and was coercing and intimidating its employees in order to interfere with their self-organization. The discriminatory and coercive action alleged was the discharge of certain employees.

The facts as to the nature and scope of the business of the Jones & Laughlin Steel Corporation have been found by the Labor Board, and, so far as they are essential to the determination of this controversy, they are not in dispute. The corporation is organized under the laws of Pennsylvania and has its principal office at Pittsburgh. It is engaged in the business of manufacturing iron and steel in plants situated in Pittsburgh and nearby Aliquippa, Pa. It manufactures and distributes a widely diversified line of steel and pig iron, being the fourth largest producer of steel in the United States. With its subsidiaries—nineteen in number—it is a completely integrated enterprise, owning and operating ore, coal and limestone properties, lake and river transportation facilities and terminal railroads located at its manufacturing plants. It owns or controls mines in Michigan and Minnesota. It operates four ore steamships on the Great Lakes, used in the transportation of ore to its factories. It owns coal mines in Pennsylvania. It operates towboats and steam barges used in carrying coal to its factories. It owns limestone properties in various places in Pennsylvania and West Virginia. It owns the Monongahela connecting railroad which connects the plants of the Pittsburgh works and forms an interconnection with the Pennsylvania, New York Central and Baltimore & Ohio Railroad systems. It owns the Aliquippa & Southern Railroad Company, which connects the Aliquippa works with the Pittsburgh & Lake Erie, part of the New York Central system. Much of its product is shipped to its warehouses in Chicago, Detroit, Cincinnati and Memphis, — to the last two places by means of its own barges and transportation equipment. In Long Island City, New York, and in New Orleans it operates structural steel fabricating shops in connection with the warehousing of semifinished materials sent from its works. Through one of its wholly-owned subsidiaries it owns, leases, and operates stores, warehouses, and yards for the distribution of equipment and supplies for drilling and operating oil and gas wells and for pipe lines, refineries and pumping stations. It has sales offices in twenty cities in the United States and a wholly-owned subsidiary which is devoted exclusively to distributing its product in Canada. Approximately 75 percent of its product is shipped out of Pennsylvania.

Summarizing these operations, the Labor Board concluded that the works in Pittsburgh and Aliquippa "might be likened to the heart of a self-contained, highly integrated body. They draw in the raw materials from Michigan, Minnesota, West Virginia, Pennsylvania in part through arteries and by means controlled by the respondent; they transform the materials and then pump them out to all parts of the nation through the vast mechanism which the respondent has elaborated."

To carry on the activities of the entire steel industry, 33,000 men mine ore, 44,000 men mine coal, 4,000 men quarry limestone, 16,000 men manufacture coke, 343,000 men manufacture steel, and 83,000 men transport its product. Respondent has about 10,000 employees in its Aliquippa plant, which is located in a community of about 30,000 persons.

The act is challenged in its entirety as an attempt to regulate all industry, thus invading the reserved powers of the States over their local concerns. It is asserted that the references in the act to interstate and foreign commerce are colorable at best; that the act is not a true regulation of such commerce or of matters which directly affect it, but on the contrary has the fundamental object of placing under the compulsory supervision of the federal government all industrial labor relations within the nation.

If this conception of terms, intent and consequent inseparability were sound, the act would necessarily fall by reason of the limitation upon the federal power which inheres in the constitutional grant, as well as because of the explicit reservation of the Tenth Amendment. The authority of the federal government may not be pushed to such an extreme as to destroy the distinction, which the commerce clause itself establishes, between commerce "among the several States" and the internal concerns of a state. That distinction between what is national and what is local in the activities of commerce is vital to the maintenance of our federal system.

We think it clear that the National Labor Relations Act may be construed so as to operate within the sphere of constitutional authority. There can be no question that the commerce thus contemplated by the act (aside from that within a Territory or the District of Columbia) is interstate and foreign commerce in the constitutional sense. The act also defines the term "affecting commerce": "The term 'affecting commerce' means in commerce, or burdening or obstructing commerce or the free flow of commerce, or having led or tending to lead to a labor dispute burdening or obstructing commerce or the free flow of commerce."

This definition is one of exclusion as well as inclusion. The grant of authority to the Board does not purport to extend to the relationship between all industrial employees and employers. Its terms do not impose collective bargaining upon all industry regardless of effects upon interstate or foreign commerce. It purports to reach only what may be deemed to burden or obstruct that commerce and, thus qualified, it must be construed as contemplating the exercise of control within constitutional bounds. It is a familiar principle that acts which directly burden or obstruct interstate or foreign commerce, or its free flow, are within the reach of the congressional power. Acts having that effect are not rendered immune because they grow out of labor disputes. It is the effect upon commerce, not the source of the injury, which is the criterion.

Respondent says that, whatever may be said of employees engaged in interstate commerce, the industrial relations and activities in the manufacturing department of respondent's enterprise are not subject to federal regulation. The argument rests upon the proposition that manufacturing in itself is not commerce.

The congressional authority to protect interstate commerce from burdens and obstructions is not limited to transactions which can be deemed to be an essential part of a "flow" of interstate or foreign commerce. Burdens and obstructions may be due to injurious action springing from other sources. The fundamental principle is that the power to regulate commerce is the power to enact "all appropriate legislation" for its "protection or advancement"; to adopt measures "to promote its growth and insure its safety"; "to foster, protect, control, and restrain." That power is plenary and may be exerted to protect interstate commerce "no matter what the source of the dangers which threaten it." Although activities may be intrastate in character when separately considered, if they have such a close and substantial relation to interstate commerce that their control is essential or appropriate to protect that commerce from burdens and obstructions, Congress cannot be denied the power to exercise that control.

The close and intimate effect which brings the subject within the reach of federal power may be due to activities in relation to productive industry although the industry when separately viewed is local. It is thus apparent that the fact that the employees here concerned were engaged in production is not determinative. The question remains as to the effect upon interstate commerce of the labor practice involved.

Giving full weight to respondent's contention with respect to a break in the complete continuity of the "stream of commerce" by reason of respondent's manufacturing operations, the fact remains that the stoppage of those operations by industrial strife would have a most serious effect upon interstate commerce. In view of respondent's far-flung activities, it is idle to say that the effect would be indirect or remote. It is obvious that it would be immediate and might be catastrophic. We are asked to shut our eyes to the plainest facts of our national life and to deal with the question of direct and indirect effects in an intellectual vacuum. Because there may be but indirect and remote effects upon interstate commerce in connection with a host of local enterprises throughout the country, it does not follow that other industrial activities do not have such a close and intimate relation to interstate commerce as to make the presence of industrial strife a matter of the most urgent national concern. When industries organize themselves on a national scale, making their relation to interstate commerce the dominant factor in their activities, how can it be maintained that their industrial labor relations constitute a forbidden field into which Congress may not enter when it is necessary to protect interstate commerce from the paralyzing consequences of industrial war?

Experience has abundantly demonstrated that the recognition of the right of employees to self-organization and to have representatives of their own choosing for the purpose of collective bargaining is often an essential condition of industrial peace. Refusal to confer and negotiate has been one of the most prolific causes of strife.

Justice McREYNOLDS delivered the following dissenting opinion.
Justice Van Devanter, Justice Sutherland, Justice Butler and I are unable to agree with the decisions just announced. The Court as we think departs from

well-established principles followed in Schechter Poultry Corporation v. United States, and Carter v. Carter Coal Co. In each cause the Labor Board formulated and then sustained a charge of unfair labor practices towards persons employed only in production. It ordered restoration of discharged employees to former positions with payment for losses sustained. These orders were declared invalid below upon the ground that respondents while carrying on production operations were not thereby engaging in interstate commerce; that labor practices in the course of such operations did not directly affect interstate commerce; consequently respondents' actions did not come within congressional power.

The wide sweep of the statute will more readily appear if consideration be given to the Board's proceedings against the smallest and relatively least important — the Clothing Company. If the act applies to the relations of that Company to employees in production, of course it applies to the larger respondents with like business elements although the affairs of the latter may present other characteristics. Though differing in some respects, all respondents procure raw materials outside the state where they manufacture, fabricate within and then ship beyond the state. Manifestly that view of congressional power would extend it into almost every field of human industry.

UNITED STATES v. DARBY
312 U.S. 100 (1941)

Justice STONE delivered the opinion of the Court.

The two principal questions raised by the record in this case are, first, whether Congress has constitutional power to prohibit the shipment in interstate commerce of lumber manufactured by employees whose wages are less than a prescribed minimum or whose weekly hours of labor at that wage are greater than a prescribed maximum, and, second, whether it has power to prohibit the employment of workmen in the production of goods "for interstate commerce" at other than prescribed wages and hours.

The Fair Labor Standards Act set up a comprehensive legislative scheme for preventing the shipment in interstate commerce of certain products and commodities produced in the United States under labor conditions as respects wages and hours which fail to conform to standards set up by the Act. Its purpose is to exclude from interstate commerce goods produced for the commerce and to prevent their production for interstate commerce, under conditions detrimental to the maintenance of the minimum standards of living necessary for health and general well-being; and to prevent the use of interstate commerce as the means of competition in the distribution of goods so produced, and as the means of spreading and perpetuating such substandard labor conditions among the workers of the several states.

Section 15 of the statute prohibits certain specified acts and punishes willful violation of it by a fine of not more than $10,000 and punishes each conviction after the first by imprisonment of not more than six months or by the specified fine or both. Section 15(a)(1) makes unlawful the shipment in interstate commerce of any goods "in the production of which any employee was employed in violation of section 6(206) or section 7(207)," which provide, among other things, that during the first year of operation of the Act a minimum wage of

25 cents per hour shall be paid to employees "engaged in [interstate] commerce or in the production of goods for [interstate] commerce," and that the maximum hours of employment for employees "engaged in commerce or in the production of goods for commerce" without increased compensation for overtime, shall be forty-four hours a week.

The indictment charges that appellee is engaged, in the state of Georgia, in the business of acquiring raw materials, which he manufactures into finished lumber with the intent, when manufactured, to ship it in interstate commerce to customers outside the state, and that he does in fact so ship a large part of the lumber so produced.

While manufacture is not of itself interstate commerce the shipment of manufactured goods interstate is such commerce and the prohibition of such shipment by Congress is indubitably a regulation of the commerce. The power to regulate commerce is the power "to prescribe the rule by which commerce is to be governed." The power of Congress over interstate commerce "is complete in itself, may be exercised to its utmost extent, and acknowledges no limitations, other than are prescribed by the constitution." Gibbons v. Ogden. Congress, following its own conception of public policy concerning the restrictions which may appropriately be imposed on interstate commerce, is free to exclude from the commerce articles whose use in the states for which they are destined it may conceive to be injurious to the public health, morals or welfare, even though the state has not sought to regulate their use.

Such regulation is not a forbidden invasion of state power merely because either its motive or its consequence is to restrict the use of articles of commerce within the states of destination and is not prohibited unless by other Constitutional provisions. It is no objection to the assertion of the power to regulate interstate commerce that its exercise is attended by the same incidents which attend the exercise of the police power of the states. Whatever their motive and purpose, regulations of commerce which do not infringe some constitutional prohibition are within the plenary power conferred on Congress by the Commerce Clause. Subject only to that limitation, presently to be considered, we conclude that the prohibition of the shipment interstate of goods produced under the forbidden substandard labor conditions is within the constitutional authority of Congress.

In the more than a century which has elapsed since the decision of Gibbons v. Ogden, these principles of constitutional interpretation have been so long and repeatedly recognized by this Court as applicable to the Commerce Clause, that there would be little occasion for repeating them now were it not for the decision of this Court twenty-two years ago in Hammer v. Dagenhart. Hammer v. Dagenhart has not been followed. The distinction on which the decision was rested that Congressional power to prohibit interstate commerce is limited to articles which in themselves have some harmful or deleterious property — a distinction which was novel when made and unsupported by any provision of the Constitution — has long since been abandoned.

The conclusion is inescapable that Hammer v. Dagenhart, was a departure from the principles which have prevailed in the interpretation of the commerce clause both before and since the decision and that such vitality, as a precedent, as it then had has long since been exhausted. It should be and now is overruled.

There remains the question whether such restriction on the production of goods for commerce is a permissible exercise of the commerce power. The power of Congress over interstate commerce is not confined to the regulation of commerce among the states. It extends to those activities intrastate which so affect interstate commerce or the exercise of the power of Congress over it as to make regulation of them appropriate means to the attainment of a legitimate end, the exercise of the granted power of Congress to regulate interstate commerce.

Congress, having by the present Act adopted the policy of excluding from interstate commerce all goods produced for the commerce which do not conform to the specified labor standards, it may choose the means reasonably adapted to the attainment of the permitted end, even though they involve control of intrastate activities.

Our conclusion is unaffected by the Tenth Amendment which provides: "The powers not delegated to the United States by the Constitution, nor prohibited by it to the States, are reserved to the States respectively, or to the people." The amendment states but a truism that all is retained which has not been surrendered. There is nothing in the history of its adoption to suggest that it was more than declaratory of the relationship between the national and state governments as it had been established by the Constitution before the amendment or that its purpose was other than to allay fears that the new national government might seek to exercise powers not granted, and that the states might not be able to exercise fully their reserved powers.

From the beginning and for many years the amendment has been construed as not depriving the national government of authority to resort to all means for the exercise of a granted power which are appropriate and plainly adapted to the permitted end.

WICKARD v. FILBURN

317 U.S. 111 (1942)

Justice JACKSON delivered the opinion of the Court.

The appellee for many years past has owned and operated a small farm in Montgomery County, Ohio, maintaining a herd of dairy cattle, selling milk, raising poultry, and selling poultry and eggs. It has been his practice to raise a small acreage of winter wheat, sown in the Fall and harvested in the following July; to sell a portion of the crop; to feed part to poultry and livestock on the farm, some of which is sold; to use some in making flour for home consumption; and to keep the rest for the following seeding. The intended disposition of the crop here involved has not been expressly stated.

In July of 1940, pursuant to the Agricultural Adjustment Act of 1938, as then amended, there were established for the appellee's 1941 crop a wheat acreage allotment of 11.1 acres and a normal yield of 20.1 bushels of wheat an acre. He was given notice of such allotment in July of 1940 before the Fall planting of his 1941 crop of wheat, and again in July of 1941, before it was harvested. He sowed, however, 23 acres, and harvested from his 11.9 acres of excess acreage 239 bushels, which under the terms of the Act as amended on May 26, 1941, constituted farm marketing excess, subject to a penalty of 49 cents a bushel, or $117.11 in all.

The general scheme of the Agricultural Adjustment Act of 1938 as related to wheat is to control the volume moving in interstate and foreign commerce in order to avoid surpluses and shortages and the consequent abnormally low or high wheat prices and obstructions to commerce. Within prescribed limits and by prescribed standards the Secretary of Agriculture is directed to ascertain and proclaim each year a national acreage allotment for the next crop of wheat, which is then apportioned to the states and their counties, and is eventually broken up into allotments for individual farms.

It is urged that under the Commerce Clause of the Constitution, Article I, §8, clause 3, Congress does not possess the power it has in this instance sought to exercise. The question would merit little consideration since our decision in United States v. Darby, sustaining the federal power to regulate production of goods for commerce except for the fact that this Act extends federal regulation to production not intended in any part for commerce but wholly for consumption on the farm. Appellee says that this is a regulation of production and consumption of wheat. Such activities are, he urges, beyond the reach of Congressional power under the Commerce Clause, since they are local in character, and their effects upon interstate commerce are at most "indirect."

We believe that a review of the course of decision under the Commerce Clause will make plain, however, that questions of the power of Congress are not to be decided by reference to any formula which would give controlling force to nomenclature such as "production" and "indirect" and foreclose consideration of the actual effects of the activity in question upon interstate commerce.

Once an economic measure of the reach of the power granted to Congress in the Commerce Clause is accepted, questions of federal power cannot be decided simply by finding the activity in question to be "production" nor can consideration of its economic effects be foreclosed by calling them "indirect." Whether the subject of the regulation in question was "production," "consumption," or "marketing" is, therefore, not material for purposes of deciding the question of federal power before us. But even if appellee's activity be local and though it may not be regarded as commerce, it may still, whatever its nature, be reached by Congress if it exerts a substantial economic effect on interstate commerce and this irrespective of whether such effect is what might at some earlier time have been defined as "direct" or "indirect."

The parties have stipulated a summary of the economics of the wheat industry. Commerce among the states in wheat is large and important. The effect of consumption of homegrown wheat on interstate commerce is due to the fact that it constitutes the most variable factor in the disappearance of the wheat crop. Consumption on the farm where grown appears to vary in an amount greater than 20 percent of average production. The total amount of wheat consumed as food varies but relatively little, and use as seed is relatively constant.

The maintenance by government regulation of a price for wheat undoubtedly can be accomplished as effectively by sustaining or increasing the demand as by limiting the supply. The effect of the statute before us is to restrict the amount which may be produced for market and the extent as well to which one may forestall resort to the market by producing to meet his own needs. That appellee's own contribution to the demand for wheat may be trivial by itself is not enough to remove him from the scope of federal regulation where, as here, his contribution, taken together with that of many others similarly situated, is far from trivial.

It is well established by decisions of this Court that the power to regulate commerce includes the power to regulate the prices at which commodities in that commerce are dealt in and practices affecting such prices. One of the primary purposes of the Act in question was to increase the market price of wheat and to that end to limit the volume thereof that could affect the market. It can hardly be denied that a factor of such volume and variability as home-consumed wheat would have a substantial influence on price and market conditions. This may arise because being in marketable condition such wheat overhangs the market and if induced by rising prices tends to flow into the market and check price increases. But if we assume that it is never marketed, it supplies a need of the man who grew it which would otherwise be reflected by purchases in the open market. Home-grown wheat in this sense competes with wheat in commerce. The stimulation of commerce is a use of the regulatory function quite as definitely as prohibitions or restrictions thereon. This record leaves us in no doubt that Congress may properly have considered that wheat consumed on the farm where grown if wholly outside the scheme of regulation would have a substantial effect in defeating and obstructing its purpose to stimulate trade therein at increased prices.

These three cases adopt broad definitions of "commerce" and "among the states" and reject the Tenth Amendment as a limit on Congress's Commerce Clause power. Commerce includes all stages of business; no longer is a distinction drawn between commerce and other stages of business such as mining, manufacture, and production. Congress can regulate any activity, intrastate or interstate, that has a substantial effect on interstate commerce. Indeed, Congress can regulate activities that themselves have little effect on interstate commerce if the activity, looked at cumulatively throughout the country, has a substantial effect on commerce. The Tenth Amendment, as *Darby* states, is simply a reminder that for Congress to legislate it must point to express or implied power. The Tenth Amendment is no longer seen as reserving a zone of activities for exclusive state control.

This expansive definition of Congress's commerce power continued from 1937 until the 1990s. From 1937 until 1992, not one federal law was invalidated as exceeding the scope of Congress's Commerce Clause authority and only once was a federal law found to violate the Tenth Amendment, and that case was expressly overruled less than a decade later. In describing the law after *Jones Laughlin*, *Darby*, and *Wickard*, initially the cases concerning the meaning of "commerce among the states" are described, followed by an examination of cases concerning the Tenth Amendment during this time period.

THE MEANING OF "COMMERCE AMONG THE STATES"

Consider three areas where the Court had the occasion to consider the meaning of "commerce among the states" after 1937: civil rights laws, regulatory laws, and criminal laws.

Civil Rights Laws

The Civil Rights Act of 1964 is among the most important federal laws enacted during the twentieth century. The law prohibits private employment discrimination based on race, gender, or religion, and forbids racial discrimination by places of public accommodation such as hotels and restaurants. Congress enacted this legislation under its Commerce Clause power.

Logically, it might seem that the civil rights law would be most easily justified under Congress's authority pursuant to §5 of the Fourteenth Amendment. However, the Supreme Court, in *The Civil Rights Cases,* 109 U.S. 3 (1883), held that Congress, pursuant to §5, only could regulate government conduct and could not regulate private behavior under the Fourteenth Amendment.[31] Therefore in 1964, it was uncertain whether Congress could use its Fourteenth Amendment power to outlaw private discrimination in employment and public accommodations. Congress thus chose the Commerce Clause as the authority for this landmark legislation.[32]

HEART OF ATLANTA MOTEL, INC. v. UNITED STATES

379 U.S. 241 (1964)

Justice CLARK delivered the opinion of the Court.

This is a declaratory judgment action, attacking the constitutionality of Title II of the Civil Rights Act of 1964. The case comes here on admissions and stipulated facts. Appellant owns and operates the Heart of Atlanta Motel which has 216 rooms available to transient guests. The motel is located on Courtland Street, two blocks from downtown Peachtree Street. It is readily accessible to interstate highways 75 and 85 and state highways 23 and 41. Appellant solicits patronage from outside the State of Georgia through various national advertising media, including magazines of national circulation; it maintains over 50 billboards and highway signs within the State, soliciting patronage for the motel; it accepts convention trade from outside Georgia and approximately 75% of its registered guests are from out of State. Prior to passage of the Act the motel had followed a practice of refusing to rent rooms to Negroes, and it alleged that it intended to continue to do so. In an effort to perpetuate that policy this suit was filed.

The appellant contends that Congress in passing this Act exceeded its power to regulate commerce. The appellees counter that the unavailability to Negroes of adequate accommodations interferes significantly with interstate travel, and that Congress, under the Commerce Clause, has power to remove such obstructions and restraints.

The sole question posed is, therefore, the constitutionality of the Civil Rights Act of 1964 as applied to these facts.

Our study of the legislative record has brought us to the conclusion that Congress possessed ample power in this regard. While the Act as adopted carried no congressional findings the record of its passage through each house is replete with evidence of the burdens that discrimination by race or color places upon

---

31. The scope of Congress's §5 power is considered below in this chapter. In United States v. Morrison, 529 U.S. 598 (2000), the Court reaffirmed this aspect of the *Civil Rights Cases.* The *Civil Rights Cases* are presented in Chapter 5 in considering the requirement for government action for the Constitution to apply.

32. Earlier cases had upheld the ability of Congress to prohibit discrimination in the channels of interstate commerce. *See, e.g.,* Morgan v. Virginia, 328 U.S. 373 (1946); Boynton v. Virginia, 364 U.S. 454 (1960).

interstate commerce. This testimony included the fact that our people have become increasingly mobile with millions of people of all races traveling from State to State; that Negroes in particular have been the subject of discrimination in transient accommodations, having to travel great distances to secure the same; that often they have been unable to obtain accommodations and have had to call upon friends to put them up overnight, and that these conditions had become so acute as to require the listing of available lodging for Negroes in a special guidebook which was itself "dramatic testimony to the difficulties" Negroes encounter in travel. These exclusionary practices were found to be nationwide, the Under Secretary of Commerce testifying that there is "no question that this discrimination in the North still exists to a large degree" and in the West and Midwest as well. This testimony indicated a qualitative as well as quantitative effect on interstate travel by Negroes. The former was the obvious impairment of the Negro traveler's pleasure and convenience that resulted when he continually was uncertain of finding lodging. As for the latter, there was evidence that this uncertainty stemming from racial discrimination had the effect of discouraging travel on the part of a substantial portion of the Negro community.

The same interest in protecting interstate commerce which led Congress to deal with segregation in interstate carriers and the white-slave traffic has prompted it to extend the exercise of its power to gambling, *Lottery Case* (Champion v. Ames); to criminal enterprises, Brooks v. United States (1925); to deceptive practices in the sale of products, Federal Trade Comm. v. Mandel Bros., Inc. (1959); to fraudulent security transactions, Securities & Exchange Comm. v. Ralston Purina Co. (1953); to misbranding of drugs, Weeks v. United States (1918); to wages and hours, United States v. Darby (1941); to members of labor unions, National Labor Relations Board v. Jones & Laughlin Steel Corp. (1937); to crop control, Wickard v. Filburn (1942); to discrimination against shippers, United States v. Baltimore & Ohio R. Co. (1948); to the protection of small business from injurious price cutting, Moore v. Mead's Fine Bread Co. (1954); to resale price maintenance, Hudson Distributors, Inc. v. Eli Lilly & Co. (1964); to professional football, Radovich v. National Football League (1957); and to racial discrimination by owners and managers of terminal restaurants, Boynton v. Com. of Virginia, 364 U.S. 454 (1960).

That Congress was legislating against moral wrongs in many of these areas rendered its enactments no less valid. In framing Title II of this Act Congress was also dealing with what it considered a moral problem. But that fact does not detract from the overwhelming evidence of the disruptive effect that racial discrimination has had on commercial intercourse. It was this burden which empowered Congress to enact appropriate legislation, and, given this basis for the exercise of its power, Congress was not restricted by the fact that the particular obstruction to interstate commerce with which it was dealing was also deemed a moral and social wrong.

It is said that the operation of the motel here is of a purely local character. But, assuming this to be true, "[i]f it is interstate commerce that feels the pinch, it does not matter how local the operation which applies the squeeze." Thus the power of Congress to promote interstate commerce also includes the power to regulate the local incidents thereof, including local activities in both the States of origin and destination, which might have a substantial and harmful effect upon that commerce. One need only examine the evidence which we have discussed above to see that Congress may—as it has—prohibit racial discrimination by motels serving travelers, however "local" their operations may appear.

We, therefore, conclude that the action of the Congress in the adoption of the Act as applied here to a motel which concededly serves interstate travelers is within the power granted it by the Commerce Clause of the Constitution, as interpreted by this Court for 140 years. It may be argued that Congress could have pursued other methods to eliminate the obstructions it found in interstate commerce caused by racial discrimination. But this is a matter of policy that rests entirely with the Congress not with the courts. How obstructions in commerce may be removed—what means are to be employed—is within the sound and exclusive discretion of the Congress. It is subject only to one caveat—that the means chosen by it must be reasonably adapted to the end permitted by the Constitution. We cannot say that its choice here was not so adapted. The Constitution requires no more.

Justice DOUGLAS, concurring.

Though I join the Court's opinions, I am somewhat reluctant here, to rest solely on the Commerce Clause. My reluctance is not due to any conviction that Congress lacks power to regulate commerce in the interests of human rights. It is rather my belief that the right of people to be free of state action that discriminates against them because of race, like the "right of persons to move freely from State to State," "occupies a more protected position in our constitutional system than does the movement of cattle, fruit, steel and coal across state lines." [T]he result reached by the Court is for me much more obvious as a protective measure under the Fourteenth Amendment than under the Commerce Clause. For the former deals with the constitutional status of the individual not with the impact on commerce of local activities or vice versa.

Hence I would prefer to rest on the assertion of legislative power contained in §5 of the Fourteenth Amendment. A decision based on the Fourteenth Amendment would have a more settling effect, making unnecessary litigation over whether a particular restaurant or inn is within the commerce definitions of the Act or whether a particular customer is an interstate traveler. Under my construction, the Act would apply to all customers in all the enumerated places of public accommodation. And that construction would put an end to all obstructionist strategies and finally close one door on a bitter chapter in American history.

KATZENBACH v. McCLUNG, SR. & McCLUNG, JR.

379 U.S. 294 (1964)

Justice CLARK delivered the opinion of the Court.

Ollie's Barbecue is a family-owned restaurant in Birmingham, Alabama, specializing in barbecued meats and homemade pies, with a seating capacity of 220 customers. It is located on a state highway 11 blocks from an interstate one and a somewhat greater distance from railroad and bus stations. The restaurant caters to a family and white-collar trade with a take-out service for Negroes. It employs 36 persons, two-thirds of whom are Negroes.

In the 12 months preceding the passage of the Act, the restaurant purchased locally approximately $150,000 worth of food, $69,683 or 46% of which was meat that it bought from a local supplier who had procured it from outside the State. The District Court expressly found that a substantial portion of the food served in the restaurant had moved in interstate commerce. The restaurant has refused to serve Negroes in its dining accommodations since its original opening in 1927, and since July 2, 1964, it has been operating in violation of the Act. The court below concluded that if it were required to serve Negroes it would lose a substantial amount of business.

The basic holding in *Heart of Atlanta Motel*, answers many of the contentions made by the appellees. There we outlined the overall purpose and operations plan of Title II and found it a valid exercise of the power to regulate interstate commerce insofar as it requires hotels and motels to serve transients without regard to their race or color. In this case we consider its application to restaurants which serve food a substantial portion of which has moved in commerce.

Ollie's Barbecue admits that it is covered by the Act. The Government makes no contention that the discrimination at the restaurant was supported by the State of Alabama. There is no claim that interstate travelers frequented the restaurant. The sole question, therefore, narrows down to whether Title II, as applied to a restaurant annually receiving about $70,000 worth of food which has moved in commerce, is a valid exercise of the power of Congress.

We believe that [the extensive] testimony [before Congress about the effects of discrimination by restaurants] afforded ample basis for the conclusion that established restaurants in such areas sold less interstate goods because of the discrimination, that interstate travel was obstructed directly by it, that business in general suffered and that many new businesses refrained from establishing there as a result of it. Hence the District Court was in error in concluding that there was no connection between discrimination and the movement of interstate commerce.

It goes without saying that, viewed in isolation, the volume of food purchased by Ollie's Barbecue from sources supplied from out of state was insignificant when compared with the total foodstuffs moving in commerce. But, as our late Brother Jackson said for the Court in Wickard v. Filburn: "That appellee's own contribution to the demand for wheat may be trivial by itself is not enough to remove him from the scope of federal regulation where, as here, his contribution, taken together with that of many others similarly situated, is far from trivial."

Much is said about a restaurant business being local but "even if appellee's activity be local and though it may not be regarded as commerce, it may still, whatever its nature, be reached by Congress if it exerts a substantial economic effect on interstate commerce. . . ." Wickard v. Filburn. The activities that are beyond the reach of Congress are "those which are completely within a particular State, which do not affect other States, and with which it is not necessary to interfere, for the purpose of executing some of the general powers of the government." Gibbons v. Ogden. This rule is as good today as it was when Chief Justice Marshall laid it down almost a century and a half ago.

This Court has held time and again that this power extends to activities of retail establishments, including restaurants, which directly or indirectly burden or obstruct interstate commerce. Here, Congress has determined for itself that refusals of service to Negroes have imposed burdens both upon the interstate flow of food and upon the movement of products generally. Of course, the mere fact that Congress has said when particular activity shall be deemed to affect commerce does not preclude further examination by this Court. But where we find that the legislators, in light of the facts and testimony before them, have a rational basis for finding a chosen regulatory scheme necessary to the protection of commerce, our investigation is at an end. The only remaining question — one answered in the affirmative by the court below — is whether the particular restaurant either serves or offers to serve interstate travelers or serves food a substantial portion of which has moved in interstate commerce.

Confronted as we are with the facts laid before Congress, we must conclude that it had a rational basis for finding that racial discrimination in restaurants had a direct and adverse effect on the free flow of interstate commerce. The power of Congress in this field is broad and sweeping; where it keeps within its sphere and violates no express constitutional limitation it has been the rule of this Court, going back almost to the founding days of the Republic, not to interfere. The Civil Rights Act of 1964, as here applied, we find to be plainly appropriate in the resolution of what the Congress found to be a national commercial problem of the first magnitude. We find it in no violation of any express limitations of the Constitution and we therefore declare it valid.

Regulatory Laws

HODEL v. INDIANA, 452 U.S. 314 (1981): The Court upheld a federal law that regulated strip mining and required reclamation of strip-mined land.

The Court found that this law was within the scope of Congress's Commerce Clause authority and described this power in expansive terms. The Court declared, "A court may invalidate legislation enacted under the Commerce Clause only if it is clear that there is no rational basis for a congressional finding that the regulated activity affects interstate commerce, or that there is no reasonable connection between the regulatory means selected and the asserted ends."

It is worth noting that not all of the Justices agreed with this broad definition of the commerce power. Justice Rehnquist, in a companion case, wrote: "It would be a mistake to conclude that Congress's power to regulate . . . is unlimited. Some activities may be so private or local in nature that they may not be in commerce. . . . [The] Court asserts that regulation will be upheld if Congress had a rational basis for finding that the regulated activity affects interstate commerce. . . . [But] it has long been established that . . . [t]here must instead be a showing that the regulated activity has a *substantial effect* on that commerce."[33]

Criminal Laws

PEREZ v. UNITED STATES, 402 U.S. 146 (1971): Justice Douglas wrote the opinion for the Court.

---

33. Hodel v. Virginia Surface Mining & Reclamation Assn., Inc., 452 U.S. 264, 310-312 (1981) (Rehnquist, J., concurring in the judgment).

The question in this case is whether Title II of the Consumer Credit Protection Act, is a permissible exercise by Congress of its powers under the Commerce Clause of the Constitution. Petitioner is one of the species commonly known as "loan sharks" which Congress found are in large part under the control of "organized crime." "Extortionate credit transactions" are defined as those characterized by the use or threat of the use of "violence or other criminal means" in enforcement. There was ample evidence showing petitioner was a "loan shark" who used the threat of violence as a method of collection.

The constitutional question is a substantial one. The Commerce Clause reaches, in the main, three categories of problems. First, the use of channels of interstate or foreign commerce which Congress deems are being misused, as, for example, the shipment of stolen goods or of persons who have been kidnapped. Second, protection of the instrumentalities of interstate commerce, as for example, the destruction of an aircraft, or persons or things in commerce, as, for example, thefts from interstate shipments. Third, those activities affecting commerce. It is with this last category that we are here concerned.

Extortionate credit transactions, though purely intrastate, may in the judgment of Congress affect interstate commerce. The findings by Congress are quite adequate on that ground. The McDade Amendment in the House, was the one ultimately adopted. As stated by Congressman McDade it grew out of a "profound study of organized crime, its ramifications and its implications." The results of that study were included in a report, The Urban Poor and Organized Crime, submitted to the House on August 29, 1967, which revealed that "organized crime takes over $350 million a year from America's poor through loan-sharking alone." Congressman McDade also relied on The Challenge of Crime in a Free Society, A Report by the President's Commission on Law Enforcement and Administration of Justice (February 1967) which stated that loan sharking was "the second largest source of revenue for organized crime," and is one way by which the underworld obtains control of legitimate businesses.

The essence of all these reports and hearings was summarized and embodied in formal congressional findings. They supplied Congress with the knowledge that the loan shark racket provides organized crime with its second most lucrative source of revenue, exacts millions from the pockets of people, coerces its victims into the commission of crimes against property, and causes the takeover by racketeers of legitimate businesses.

We have mentioned in detail the economic, financial, and social setting of the problem as revealed to Congress. We do so not to infer that Congress need make particularized findings in order to legislate. We relate the history of the Act in detail to answer the impassioned plea of petitioner that all that is involved in loan sharking is a traditionally local activity. It appears, instead, that loan sharking in its national setting is one way organized interstate crime holds its guns to the heads of the poor and the rich alike and syphons funds from numerous localities to finance its national operations.

Justice STEWART, dissenting.

Congress surely has power under the Commerce Clause to enact criminal laws to protect the instrumentalities of interstate commerce, to prohibit the misuse of the channels or facilities of interstate commerce, and to prohibit or regulate those intrastate activities that have a demonstrably substantial effect on interstate commerce. But under the statute before us a man can be convicted without any proof of interstate movement, of the use of the facilities of interstate commerce, or of facts showing that his conduct affected interstate commerce. I think the framers of the Constitution never intended that the National Government might define as a crime and prosecute such wholly local activity through the enactment of federal criminal laws.

In order to sustain this law we would, in my view, have to be able at the least to say that Congress could rationally have concluded that loan sharking is an activity with interstate attributes that distinguish it in some substantial respect from other local crime. But it is not enough to say that loan sharking is a national problem, for all crime is a national problem. It is not enough to say that some loan sharking has interstate characteristics, for any crime may have an interstate setting. And the circumstance that loan sharking has an adverse impact on interstate business is not a distinguishing attribute, for interstate business suffers from almost all criminal activity, be it shoplifting or violence in the streets.

Because I am unable to discern any rational distinction between loan sharking and other local crime, I cannot escape the conclusion that this statute was beyond the power of Congress to enact. The definition and prosecution of local, intrastate crime are reserved to the States under the Ninth and Tenth Amendments.

THE TENTH AMENDMENT BETWEEN 1937 AND THE 1990S

In United States v. Darby, above, the Court declared that the Tenth Amendment is "but a truism," simply a reminder that for Congress to act it must have authority under the Constitution. This approach to the Tenth Amendment was followed without exception until 1976, when the Court invalidated a federal law for violating the Tenth Amendment.

In National League of Cities v. Usery, 426 U.S. 833 (1976), the Court, by a five-to-four margin, declared unconstitutional the application of the Fair Labor Standards Act, which required payment of the minimum wage to state and local employees. The Court began with the premise that "there are limits upon the power of Congress to override state sovereignty, even when exercising its otherwise plenary powers to tax or to regulate commerce." The Court found that requiring states to pay their employees the minimum wage violated the Tenth Amendment because the law "operate[s] to directly displace the States' freedom to structure integral operations in areas of traditional governmental functions."

The Court explained that forcing state and local governments to pay their employees the minimum wage would require that they either raise taxes or cut other services to pay these costs. The Court said that this would displace decisions traditionally left to the states and "may substantially restructure traditional ways in which the local governments have arranged their affairs." In other words, National League of Cities v. Usery held that Congress violates the Tenth Amendment when it interferes with traditional state and local government functions. The Court, however, did not attempt to define what is such a traditional function; the Court only held that forcing payment of the minimum wage was unconstitutional.

Justice Harry Blackmun wrote a concurring opinion that said that he saw the majority as adopting "a balancing approach [that] . . . does not outlaw federal power in areas such as environmental protection, where the federal interest is demonstrably greater and where state facility compliance with imposed federal standards would be essential."

Justice William Brennan wrote for the four dissenters and lamented the Court's use of the Tenth Amendment as a limit on congressional power: "My Brethren thus have today manufactured an abstraction without substance, founded neither in the words of the Constitution nor on precedent. . . . Today's repudiation of this unbroken line of precedents that firmly reject my Brethren's ill-conceived abstraction can only be regarded as a transparent cover for invalidating a congressional judgment with which they disagree. The only analysis even remotely resembling that adopted today is found in a line of opinions dealing with the Commerce Clause and the Tenth Amendment that ultimately provoked a constitutional crisis for the Court in the 1930s."

In the decade after *National League of Cities*, the Supreme Court rejected Tenth Amendment challenges to several other federal laws and continually narrowed the Tenth Amendment protection provided in that decision. In each case, Justice Blackmun voted with the majority, often as the crucial fifth vote refusing to extend or apply National League of Cities v. Usery.

In Hodel v. Virginia Surface Mining & Reclamation Association, 452 U.S. 264 (1981), the Court made it clear that *Usery* only applied when Congress was regulating state governments, not when Congress was regulating private conduct. In *Hodel*, the Court upheld a federal law that regulated strip mining and required reclamation of strip-mined land. The Court clarified its test for the Tenth Amendment in light of *Usery*. The Court said that for a federal law to violate the Tenth Amendment, it needed to regulate "the States as States"; it must "address matters that are indisputably attribute[s] of state sovereignty"; it must directly impair the States' ability to "structure integral operations in areas of traditional governmental functions"; and it must not be such that "the nature of the federal interest . . . justifies state submission." The Court in *Hodel* found that the law, the Surface Mining Control and Reclamation Act of 1977, was constitutional because it did not regulate the states as states. In several other cases, the Court also rejected Tenth Amendment challenges to federal laws.[34]

In 1985, the Court expressly overruled *National League of Cities*.

GARCIA v. SAN ANTONIO METROPOLITAN TRANSIT AUTHORITY

469 U.S. 528 (1985)

Justice BLACKMUN delivered the opinion of the Court.

We revisit in these cases an issue raised in National League of Cities v. Usery. In that litigation, this Court, by a sharply divided vote, ruled that the Commerce Clause does not empower Congress to enforce the minimum-wage and overtime provisions of the Fair Labor Standards Act (FLSA) against the States "in areas of

---

34. United Transportation Union v. Long Island R.R. Co., 455 U.S. 678 (1982) (application of the Railway Labor Act to a state-owned railroad did not violate the Tenth Amendment); Federal Energy Regulatory Commission (FERC) v. Mississippi, 456 U.S. 742 (1982) (rejecting a challenge to the Public Utilities Regulatory Policies Act of 1978, which required that state utility commissions consider FERC proposals); Equal Employment Opportunity Commission v. Wyoming, 460 U.S. 226 (1983) (upholding a federal law forcing states to comply with the Age Discrimination in Employment Act violated the Tenth Amendment).

traditional governmental functions." Although *National League of Cities* supplied some examples of "traditional governmental functions," it did not offer a general explanation of how a "traditional" function is to be distinguished from a "nontraditional" one. Since then, federal and state courts have struggled with the task, thus imposed, of identifying a traditional function for purposes of state immunity under the Commerce Clause.

Our examination of this "function" standard applied in these and other cases over the last eight years now persuades us that the attempt to draw the boundaries of state regulatory immunity in terms of "traditional governmental function" is not only unworkable but is also inconsistent with established principles of federalism and, indeed, with those very federalism principles on which *National League of Cities* purported to rest. That case, accordingly, is overruled.

Thus far, this Court itself has made little headway in defining the scope of the governmental functions deemed protected under *National League of Cities*. Many constitutional standards involve "undoubte[d] . . . gray areas," and, despite the difficulties that this Court and other courts have encountered so far, it normally might be fair to venture the assumption that case-by-case development would lead to a workable standard for determining whether a particular governmental function should be immune from federal regulation under the Commerce Clause.

We believe, however, that there is a more fundamental problem at work here, a problem that explains why an attempt to draw distinctions with respect to federal regulatory authority under *National League of Cities* is unlikely to succeed regardless of how the distinctions are phrased. The problem is that neither the governmental/proprietary distinction nor any other that purports to separate out important governmental functions can be faithful to the role of federalism in a democratic society. The essence of our federal system is that within the realm of authority left open to them under the Constitution, the States must be equally free to engage in any activity that their citizens choose for the common weal, no matter how unorthodox or unnecessary anyone else — including the judiciary — deems state involvement to be. Any rule of state immunity that looks to the "traditional," "integral," or "necessary" nature of governmental functions inevitably invites an unelected federal judiciary to make decisions about which state policies it favors and which ones it dislikes.

We therefore now reject, as unsound in principle and unworkable in practice, a rule of state immunity from federal regulation that turns on a judicial appraisal of whether a particular governmental function is "integral" or "traditional." Any such rule leads to inconsistent results at the same time that it disserves principles of democratic self-governance, and it breeds inconsistency precisely because it is divorced from those principles. If there are to be limits on the Federal Government's power to interfere with state functions — as undoubtedly there are — we must look elsewhere to find them.

The central theme of *National League of Cities* was that the States occupy a special position in our constitutional system and that the scope of Congress's authority under the Commerce Clause must reflect that position. Of course, the Commerce Clause by its specific language does not provide any special limitation on Congress's actions with respect to the States.

What has proved problematic is not the perception that the Constitution's federal structure imposes limitations on the Commerce Clause, but rather the nature and content of those limitations. We doubt that courts ultimately can identify principled constitutional limitations on the scope of Congress's Commerce Clause powers over the States merely by relying on a priori definitions of state sovereignty. In part, this is because of the elusiveness of objective criteria for "fundamental" elements of state sovereignty, a problem we have witnessed in the search for "traditional governmental functions."

Apart from the limitation on federal authority inherent in the delegated nature of Congress's Article I powers, the principal means chosen by the framers to ensure the role of the States in the federal system lies in the structure of the Federal Government itself.[35] It is no novelty to observe that the composition of the Federal Government was designed in large part to protect the States from overreaching by Congress. The framers thus gave the States a role in the selection both of the Executive and the Legislative Branches of the Federal Government. The States were vested with indirect influence over the House of Representatives and the Presidency by their control of electoral qualifications and their role in Presidential elections. U.S. Const., Art. I, §2, and Art. II, §1. They were given more direct influence in the Senate, where each State received equal representation and each Senator was to be selected by the legislature of his State. Art. I, §3. The significance attached to the States' equal representation in the Senate is underscored by the prohibition of any constitutional amendment divesting a State of equal representation without the State's consent. Art. V.

The extent to which the structure of the Federal Government itself was relied on to insulate the interests of the States is evident in the views of the framers. James Madison explained that the Federal Government "will partake sufficiently of the spirit [of the States], to be disinclined to invade the rights of the individual States, or the prerogatives of their governments." The Federalist No. 46.

The effectiveness of the federal political process in preserving the States' interests is apparent even today in the course of federal legislation. On the one hand, the States have been able to direct a substantial proportion of federal revenues into their own treasuries in the form of general and program-specific grants in aid. The federal role in assisting state and local governments is a long-standing one; Congress provided federal land grants to finance state governments from the beginning of the Republic, and direct cash grants were awarded as early as 1887 under the Hatch Act. In the past quarter-century alone, federal grants to States and localities have grown from $7 billion to $96 billion. As a result, federal grants now account for about one-fifth of state and local government expenditures. The States have obtained federal funding for such services as police and fire protection, education, public health and hospitals, parks and recreation, and sanitation. Moreover, at the same time that the States have exercised their influence to obtain federal support, they have been able to exempt themselves from a wide variety of obligations imposed by Congress under the Commerce Clause.

We realize that changes in the structure of the Federal Government have taken place since 1789, not the least of which has been the substitution of

---

35. *See, e.g.,* J. Choper, Judicial Review and the National Political Process 175-184 (1980); Wechsler, The Political Safeguards of Federalism: The Role of the States in the Composition and Selection of the National Government, 54 Colum. L. Rev. 543 (1954); La Pierre, the Political Safeguards of Federalism Redux: Intergovernmental Immunity and the States as Agents of the Nation, 60 Wash. U. L.Q. 779 (1982). [Footnote by the Court.]

popular election of Senators by the adoption of the Seventeenth Amendment in 1913, and that these changes may work to alter the influence of the States in the federal political process. Nonetheless, against this background, we are convinced that the fundamental limitation that the constitutional scheme imposes on the Commerce Clause to protect the "States as States" is one of process rather than one of result. Any substantive restraint on the exercise of Commerce Clause powers must find its justification in the procedural nature of this basic limitation, and it must be tailored to compensate for possible failings in the national political process rather than to dictate a "sacred province of state autonomy."

Insofar as the present cases are concerned, then, we need go no further than to state that we perceive nothing in the overtime and minimum-wage requirements of the FLSA, as applied to SAMTA, that is destructive of state sovereignty or violative of any constitutional provision. SAMTA faces nothing more than the same minimum-wage and overtime obligations that hundreds of thousands of other employers, public as well as private, have to meet.

Of course, we continue to recognize that the States occupy a special and specific position in our constitutional system and that the scope of Congress's authority under the Commerce Clause must reflect that position. But the principal and basic limit on the federal commerce power is that inherent in all congressional action — the built-in restraints that our system provides through state participation in federal governmental action. The political process ensures that laws that unduly burden the States will not be promulgated. In the factual setting of these cases the internal safeguards of the political process have performed as intended.

National League of Cities v. Usery is overruled.

Justice POWELL, with whom the Chief Justice, Justice REHNQUIST, and Justice O'CONNOR join, dissenting.

The Court today, in its 5-4 decision, overrules National League of Cities v. Usery, a case in which we held that Congress lacked authority to impose the requirements of the Fair Labor Standards Act on state and local governments. Because I believe this decision substantially alters the federal system embodied in the Constitution, I dissent.

There are, of course, numerous examples over the history of this Court in which prior decisions have been reconsidered and overruled. There have been few cases, however, in which the principle of stare decisis and the rationale of recent decisions were ignored as abruptly as we now witness. The reasoning of the Court in *National League of Cities*, and the principle applied there, have been reiterated consistently over the past eight years.

Whatever effect the Court's decision may have in weakening the application of stare decisis, it is likely to be less important than what the Court has done to the Constitution itself. A unique feature of the United States is the federal system of government guaranteed by the Constitution and implicit in the very name of our country. Despite some genuflecting in the Court's opinion to the concept of federalism, today's decision effectively reduces the Tenth Amendment to meaningless rhetoric when Congress acts pursuant to the Commerce Clause.

To leave no doubt about its intention, the Court renounces its decision in *National League of Cities* because it "inevitably invites an unelected federal judiciary to make decisions about which state policies it favors and which ones it dislikes." In other words, the extent to which the States may exercise their authority, when Congress purports to act under the Commerce Clause, henceforth is to be determined from time to time by political decisions made by members of the Federal Government, decisions the Court says will not be subject to judicial review. I note that it does not seem to have occurred to the Court that it — an unelected majority of five Justices — today rejects almost 200 years of the understanding of the constitutional status of federalism. In doing so, there is only a single passing reference to the Tenth Amendment. Nor is so much as a dictum of any court cited in support of the view that the role of the States in the federal system may depend upon the grace of elected federal officials, rather than on the Constitution as interpreted by this Court.

The Court finds that the test of state immunity approved in *National League of Cities* and its progeny is unworkable and unsound in principle. In finding the test to be unworkable, the Court begins by mischaracterizing *National League of Cities* and subsequent cases. In concluding that efforts to define state immunity are unsound in principle, the Court radically departs from long-settled constitutional values and ignores the role of judicial review in our system of government.

Today's opinion does not explain how the States' role in the electoral process guarantees that particular exercises of the Commerce Clause power will not infringe on residual state sovereignty. Members of Congress are elected from the various States, but once in office they are Members of the Federal Government. Although the States participate in the Electoral College, this is hardly a reason to view the President as a representative of the States' interest against federal encroachment. We noted recently "[t]he hydraulic pressure inherent within each of the separate Branches to exceed the outer limits of its power. . . ." INS v. Chadha (1983). The Court offers no reason to think that this pressure will not operate when Congress seeks to invoke its powers under the Commerce Clause, notwithstanding the electoral role of the States.

The Court apparently thinks that the State's success at obtaining federal funds for various projects and exemptions from the obligations of some federal statutes is indicative of the "effectiveness of the federal political process in preserving the States' interests. . . ." But such political success is not relevant to the question whether the political processes are the proper means of enforcing constitutional limitations. The fact that Congress generally does not transgress constitutional limits on its power to reach state activities does not make judicial review any less necessary to rectify the cases in which it does do so. The States' role in our system of government is a matter of constitutional law, not of legislative grace. "The powers not delegated to the United States by the Constitution, nor prohibited by it to the States, are reserved to the States, respectively, or to the people." U.S. Const., Amdt. 10.

More troubling than the logical infirmities in the Court's reasoning is the result of its holding, i.e., that federal political officials, invoking the Commerce Clause, are the sole judges of the limits of their own power. This result is inconsistent with the fundamental principles of our constitutional system. See, e.g., The Federalist No. 78 (Hamilton). At least since Marbury v. Madison (1803), it has been the settled province of the federal judiciary "to say what the law is" with respect to the constitutionality of Acts of Congress. In rejecting the role of the judiciary in protecting the States from federal overreaching, the Court's opinion offers no explanation for ignoring the teaching of the most famous case in our history.

[T]he Court today propounds a view of federalism that pays only lipservice to the role of the States. Although it says that the States "unquestionably do 'retai[n] a significant measure of sovereign authority,'" it fails to recognize the broad, yet specific areas of sovereignty that the framers intended the States to retain. Indeed, the Court barely acknowledges that the Tenth Amendment exists. Indeed, the Court's view of federalism appears to relegate the States to precisely the trivial role that opponents of the Constitution feared they would occupy.

Justice REHNQUIST, dissenting.

I join both Justice Powell's and Justice O'Connor's thoughtful dissents. [U]nder any one of these approaches the judgment in these cases should be affirmed, and I do not think it incumbent on those of us in dissent to spell out further the fine points of a principle that will, I am confident, in time again command the support of a majority of this Court.

4. 1990s-???: Narrowing of the Commerce Power and Revival of the Tenth Amendment as a Constraint on Congress

In the 1990s, the Supreme Court once more changed course with regard to the scope of Congress's powers under the Commerce Clause and whether the Tenth Amendment is a limit on federal power. In 1995, in United States v. Lopez, the Supreme Court for the first time in almost 60 years found that a federal law exceeded Congress's Commerce Clause authority. *Lopez* led to challenges to literally dozens of federal laws. In 2000, the Court reaffirmed *Lopez* in United States v. Morrison. Additionally, in 1992, in New York v. United States and in 1997, in Printz v. United States, the Court again used the Tenth Amendment to protect state governments from federal encroachments. All of these cases are presented below. Additionally, of course, both the commerce power and the Tenth Amendment are discussed in National Federation of Independent Business v. Sebelius, which is presented above.

In reading these recent decisions concerning the Commerce Clause and the Tenth Amendment, it will be helpful to focus on two questions, one descriptive and one normative. Descriptively, what principles does the Court articulate as to when Congress exceeds the scope of its Commerce Clause authority and when Congress violates the Tenth Amendment? Normatively, does the Court persuasively justify the desirability of these limits on federal powers?

a. What Is Congress's Authority to Regulate "Commerce Among the States"?

UNITED STATES v. LOPEZ
514 U.S. 549 (1995)

Chief Justice REHNQUIST delivered the opinion of the Court.

In the Gun-Free School Zones Act of 1990, Congress made it a federal offense "for any individual knowingly to possess a firearm at a place that the individual knows, or has reasonable cause to believe, is a school zone." 18 U.S.C. §922(q)(1)(A). The Act neither regulates a commercial activity nor contains a requirement that the possession be connected in any way to interstate commerce. We hold that the Act exceeds the authority of Congress "[t]o regulate Commerce . . . among the several States. . . ."

On March 10, 1992, respondent, who was then a 12th-grade student, arrived at Edison High School in San Antonio, Texas, carrying a concealed .38-caliber handgun and five bullets. Acting upon an anonymous tip, school authorities confronted respondent, who admitted that he was carrying the weapon. He was arrested and charged under Texas law with firearm possession on school premises. The next day, the state charges were dismissed after federal agents charged respondent by complaint with violating the Gun-Free School Zones Act of 1990. The term "school zone" is defined as "in, or on the grounds of, a public, parochial or private school" or "within a distance of 1,000 feet from the grounds of a public, parochial or private school."

Respondent waived his right to a jury trial. The District Court conducted a bench trial, found him guilty, and sentenced him to six months' imprisonment and two years' supervised release.

We start with first principles. The Constitution creates a Federal Government of enumerated powers. As James Madison wrote: "The powers delegated by the proposed Constitution to the federal government are few and defined. Those which are to remain in the State governments are numerous and indefinite." The Federalist No. 45. This constitutionally mandated division of authority "was adopted by the framers to ensure protection of our fundamental liberties." "Just as the separation and independence of the coordinate branches of the Federal Government serve to prevent the accumulation of excessive power in any one branch, a healthy balance of power between the States and the Federal Government will reduce the risk of tyranny and abuse from either front."

[The Court then reviewed the history of Commerce Clause decisions from Gibbons v. Ogden through the early 1940s.] *Jones & Laughlin Steel, Darby*, and *Wickard* ushered in an era of Commerce Clause jurisprudence that greatly expanded the previously defined authority of Congress under that Clause. In part, this was a recognition of the great changes that had occurred in the way business was carried on in this country. Enterprises that had once been local or at most regional in nature had become national in scope. But the doctrinal change also reflected a view that earlier Commerce Clause cases artificially had constrained the authority of Congress to regulate interstate commerce. But even these modern-era precedents which have expanded congressional power under the Commerce Clause confirm that this power is subject to outer limits.

Consistent with this structure, we have identified three broad categories of activity that Congress may regulate under its commerce power. First, Congress may regulate the use of the channels of interstate commerce. See, e.g., *Darby; Heart of Atlanta Motel.* Second, Congress is empowered to regulate and protect the instrumentalities of interstate commerce, or persons or things in interstate commerce, even though the threat may come only from intrastate activities. See, e.g., *Shreveport Rate Cases* (1914); *Southern R. Co. v. United States* (1911) (upholding amendments to Safety Appliance Act as applied to vehicles used in intrastate commerce). Finally, Congress's commerce authority includes the power to regulate those activities having a substantial relation to interstate commerce, *Jones & Laughlin Steel*, i.e., those activities that substantially affect interstate commerce.

Within this final category, admittedly, our case law has not been clear whether an activity must "affect" or "substantially affect" interstate commerce in order to be within Congress's power to regulate it under the Commerce Clause. We conclude, consistent with the great weight of our case law, that the proper test requires an analysis of whether the regulated activity "substantially affects" interstate commerce.

We now turn to consider the power of Congress, in the light of this framework, to enact §922(q). The first two categories of authority may be quickly disposed of: §922(q) is not a regulation of the use of the channels of interstate commerce, nor is it an attempt to prohibit the interstate transportation of a commodity through the channels of commerce; nor can §922(q) be justified as a regulation by which Congress has sought to protect an instrumentality of interstate commerce or a thing in interstate commerce. Thus, if §922(q) is to be sustained, it must be under the third category as a regulation of an activity that substantially affects interstate commerce.

First, we have upheld a wide variety of congressional Acts regulating intrastate economic activity where we have concluded that the activity substantially affected interstate commerce. Section 922(q) is a criminal statute that by its terms has nothing to do with "commerce" or any sort of economic enterprise, however broadly one might define those terms. Section 922(q) is not an essential part of a larger regulation of economic activity, in which the regulatory scheme could be undercut unless the intrastate activity were regulated. It cannot, therefore, be sustained under our cases upholding regulations of activities that arise out of or are connected with a commercial transaction, which viewed in the aggregate, substantially affects interstate commerce.

Second, §922(q) contains no jurisdictional element which would ensure, through case-by-case inquiry, that the firearm possession in question affects interstate commerce. For example, in United States v. Bass (1971), the Court interpreted former 18 U.S.C. §1202(a), which made it a crime for a felon to "receiv[e], posses[s], or transpor[t] in commerce or affecting commerce . . . any firearm." The Court interpreted the possession component of §1202(a) to require an additional nexus to interstate commerce both because the statute was ambiguous and because "unless Congress conveys its purpose clearly, it will not be deemed to have significantly changed the federal-state balance." Unlike the statute in *Bass*, §922(q) has no express jurisdictional element which might limit its reach to a discrete set of firearm possessions that additionally have an explicit connection with or effect on interstate commerce.

Although as part of our independent evaluation of constitutionality under the Commerce Clause we of course consider legislative findings, and indeed even congressional committee findings, regarding effect on interstate commerce, the Government concedes that "[n]either the statute nor its legislative history contain[s] express congressional findings regarding the effects upon interstate commerce of gun possession in a school zone." We agree with the Government that Congress normally is not required to make formal findings as to the substantial burdens that an activity has on interstate commerce. But to the extent that congressional findings would enable us to evaluate the legislative judgment that the activity in question substantially affected interstate commerce, even though no such substantial effect was visible to the naked eye, they are lacking here.

The Government's essential contention, is that we may determine here that §922(q) is valid because possession of a firearm in a local school zone does indeed substantially affect interstate commerce. The Government argues that possession of a firearm in a school zone may result in violent crime and that violent crime can be expected to affect the functioning of the national economy in two ways. First, the costs of violent crime are substantial, and, through the mechanism of insurance, those costs are spread throughout the population. Second, violent crime reduces the willingness of individuals to travel to areas within the country that are perceived to be unsafe. The Government also argues that the presence of guns in schools poses a substantial threat to the educational process by threatening the learning environment. A handicapped educational process, in turn, will result in a less productive citizenry. That, in turn, would have an adverse effect on the Nation's economic well-being. As a result, the Government argues that Congress could rationally have concluded that §922(q) substantially affects interstate commerce.

We pause to consider the implications of the Government's arguments. The Government admits, under its "costs of crime" reasoning, that Congress could regulate not only all violent crime, but all activities that might lead to violent crime, regardless of how tenuously they relate to interstate commerce. Similarly, under the Government's "national productivity" reasoning, Congress could regulate any activity that it found was related to the economic productivity of individual citizens: family law (including marriage, divorce, and child custody), for example. Under the theories that the Government presents in support of §922(q), it is difficult to perceive any limitation on federal power, even in areas such as criminal law enforcement or education where States historically have been sovereign. Thus, if we were to accept the Government's arguments, we are hard pressed to posit any activity by an individual that Congress is without power to regulate.

Although Justice Breyer argues that acceptance of the Government's rationales would not authorize a general federal police power, he is unable to identify any activity that the States may regulate but Congress may not. Justice Breyer posits that there might be some limitations on Congress's commerce power, such as family law or certain aspects of education. These suggested limitations, when viewed in light of the dissent's expansive analysis, are devoid of substance.

For instance, if Congress can, pursuant to its Commerce Clause power, regulate activities that adversely affect the learning environment, then, a fortiori, it also can regulate the educational process directly. Congress could determine that a school's curriculum has a "significant" effect on the extent of classroom learning. As a result, Congress could mandate a federal curriculum for local elementary and secondary schools because what is taught in local schools has a significant "effect on classroom learning," and that, in turn, has a substantial effect on interstate commerce.

Admittedly, a determination whether an intrastate activity is commercial or noncommercial may in some cases result in legal uncertainty. But, so long as Congress's authority is limited to those powers enumerated in the Constitution, and so long as those enumerated powers are interpreted as having judicially enforceable outer limits, congressional legislation under the Commerce Clause always will engender "legal uncertainty." The Constitution mandates this uncertainty by withholding from Congress a plenary police power that would authorize enactment of every type of legislation.

These are not precise formulations, and in the nature of things they cannot be. But we think they point the way to a correct decision of this case. The possession of a gun in a local school zone is in no sense an economic activity that might, through repetition elsewhere, substantially affect any sort of inter-state commerce. Respondent was a local student at a local school; there is no indication that he had recently moved in interstate commerce, and there is no requirement that his possession of the firearm have any concrete tie to interstate commerce.

To uphold the Government's contentions here, we would have to pile infer-ence upon inference in a manner that would bid fair to convert congressional authority under the Commerce Clause to a general police power of the sort retained by the States. Admittedly, some of our prior cases have taken long steps down that road, giving great deference to congressional action. The broad language in these opinions has suggested the possibility of additional expansion, but we decline here to proceed any further. To do so would require us to conclude that the Constitution's enumeration of powers does not presup-pose something not enumerated, and that there never will be a distinction between what is truly national and what is truly local. This we are unwilling to do.

Justice KENNEDY, with whom Justice O'CONNOR joins, concurring.

The history of the judicial struggle to interpret the Commerce Clause during the transition from the economic system the Founders knew to the single, national market still emergent in our own era counsels great restraint before the Court determines that the Clause is insufficient to support an exercise of the national power. That history gives me some pause about today's decision, but I join the Court's opinion with these observations on what I conceive to be its necessary though limited holding.

The history of our Commerce Clause decisions contains at least two lessons of relevance to this case. The first, as stated at the outset, is the imprecision of content-based boundaries used without more to define the limits of the Com-merce Clause. The second, related to the first but of even greater consequence, is that the Court as an institution and the legal system as a whole have an immense stake in the stability of our Commerce Clause jurisprudence as it has evolved to this point. Stare decisis operates with great force in counseling us not to call in question the essential principles now in place respecting the congressional power to regulate transactions of a commercial nature. That fundamental restraint on our power forecloses us from reverting to an understanding of commerce that would serve only an 18th-century economy, dependent then upon production and trading practices that had changed but little over the preceding centuries; it also mandates against returning to the time when congressional authority to regulate undoubted commercial activities was limited by a judicial determination that those matters had an insufficient con-nection to an interstate system. Congress can regulate in the commercial sphere on the assumption that we have a single market and a unified purpose to build a stable national economy.

It would be mistaken and mischievous for the political branches to forget that the sworn obligation to preserve and protect the Constitution in maintaining the federal balance is their own in the first and primary instance. At the same time, the absence of structural mechanisms to require those officials to undertake this principled task, and the momentary political convenience often attendant upon their failure to do so, argue against a complete renunciation of the judicial role. Although it is the obligation of all officers of the Government to respect the constitutional design, the federal balance is too essential a part of our constitutional structure and plays too vital a role in securing freedom for us to admit inability to intervene when one or the other level of Government has tipped the scales too far.

The statute before us upsets the federal balance to a degree that renders it an unconstitutional assertion of the commerce power, and our intervention is required. As the Chief Justice explains, unlike the earlier cases to come before the Court here neither the actors nor their conduct has a commercial character, and neither the purposes nor the design of the statute has an evident commercial nexus. The statute makes the simple possession of a gun within 1,000 feet of the grounds of the school a criminal offense. In a sense any conduct in this interdependent world of ours has an ultimate commercial origin or consequence, but we have not yet said the commerce power may reach so far. If Congress attempts that extension, then at the least we must inquire whether the exercise of national power seeks to intrude upon an area of traditional state concern.

An interference of these dimensions occurs here, for it is well established that education is a traditional concern of the States. Milliken v. Bradley (1974); Epperson v. Arkansas (1968). The proximity to schools, including of course schools owned and operated by the States or their subdivisions, is the very premise for making the conduct criminal. In these circumstances, we have a particular duty to ensure that the federal-state balance is not destroyed.

While it is doubtful that any State, or indeed any reasonable person, would argue that it is wise policy to allow students to carry guns on school premises, considerable disagreement exists about how best to accomplish that goal. In this circumstance, the theory and utility of our federalism are revealed, for the States may perform their role as laboratories for experimentation to devise various solutions where the best solution is far from clear.

If a State or municipality determines that harsh criminal sanctions are necessary and wise to deter students from carrying guns on school premises, the reserved powers of the States are sufficient to enact those measures. Indeed, over 40 States already have criminal laws outlawing the possession of firearms on or near school grounds.

Other, more practicable means to rid the schools of guns may be thought by the citizens of some States to be preferable for the safety and welfare of the schools those States are charged with maintaining. These might include inducements to inform on violators where the information leads to arrests or confiscation of the guns; programs to encourage the voluntary surrender of guns with some provision for amnesty; penalties imposed on parents or guardians for failure to supervise the child; laws providing for suspension or expulsion of gun-toting students.

The statute now before us forecloses the States from experimenting and exercising their own judgment in an area to which States lay claim by right of history and expertise, and it does so by regulating an activity beyond the realm of commerce in the ordinary and usual sense of that term. The tendency of this statute to displace state regulation in areas of traditional state concern is evident from its territorial operation. There are over 100,000 elementary and secondary schools in the United States. Each of these now has an invisible federal zone extending 1,000 feet beyond the (often irregular) boundaries of the school property. Yet throughout these areas, school officials would find their own programs for the prohibition of guns in danger of displacement by the federal authority unless the State chooses to enact a parallel rule.

Absent a stronger connection or identification with commercial concerns that are central to the Commerce Clause, that interference contradicts the federal balance the framers designed and that this Court is obliged to enforce.

Justice THOMAS, concurring.

The Court today properly concludes that the Commerce Clause does not grant Congress the authority to prohibit gun possession within 1,000 feet of a school, as it attempted to do in the Gun-Free School Zones Act of 1990. Although I join the majority, I write separately to observe that our case law has drifted far from the original understanding of the Commerce Clause. In a future case, we ought to temper our Commerce Clause jurisprudence in a manner that both makes sense of our more recent case law and is more faithful to the original understanding of that Clause.

While the principal dissent concedes that there are limits to federal power, the sweeping nature of our current test enables the dissent to argue that Congress can regulate gun possession. But it seems to me that the power to regulate "commerce" can by no means encompass authority over mere gun possession, any more than it empowers the Federal Government to regulate marriage, littering, or cruelty to animals, throughout the 50 States. Our Constitution quite properly leaves such matters to the individual States, notwithstanding these activities' effects on interstate commerce. Any interpretation of the Commerce Clause that even suggests that Congress could regulate such matters is in need of reexamination.

In an appropriate case, I believe that we must further reconsider our "substantial effects" test with an eye toward constructing a standard that reflects the text and history of the Commerce Clause without totally rejecting our more recent Commerce Clause jurisprudence.

Today, however, I merely support the Court's conclusion with a discussion of the text, structure, and history of the Commerce Clause and an analysis of our early case law. My goal is simply to show how far we have departed from the original understanding and to demonstrate that the result we reach today is by no means "radical." I also want to point out the necessity of refashioning a coherent test that does not tend to "obliterate the distinction between what is national and what is local and create a completely centralized government."

At the time the original Constitution was ratified, "commerce" consisted of selling, buying, and bartering, as well as transporting for these purposes. See 1 S. Johnson, A Dictionary of the English Language 361 (4th ed. 1773) (defining commerce as "Intercour[s]e; exchange of one thing for another; interchange of any thing; trade; traffick"); N. Bailey, An Universal Etymological English Dictionary (26th ed. 1789) ("trade or traffic"); T. Sheridan, A Complete Dictionary of the English Language (6th ed. 1796) ("Exchange of one thing for another; trade, traffick"). As one would expect, the term "commerce" was used in contradistinction to productive activities such as manufacturing and agriculture.

Moreover, interjecting a modern sense of commerce into the Constitution generates significant textual and structural problems. For example, one cannot replace "commerce" with a different type of enterprise, such as manufacturing. When a manufacturer produces a car, assembly cannot take place "with a foreign nation" or "with the Indian Tribes." Parts may come from different States or other nations and hence may have been in the flow of commerce at one time, but manufacturing takes place at a discrete site. Agriculture and manufacturing involve the production of goods; commerce encompasses traffic in such articles.

The Constitution not only uses the word "commerce" in a narrower sense than our case law might suggest, it also does not support the proposition that Congress has authority over all activities that "substantially affect" interstate commerce. The Commerce Clause does not state that Congress may "regulate matters that substantially affect commerce with foreign Nations, and among the several States, and with the Indian Tribes."

Put simply, much if not all of Art. I, §8 (including portions of the Commerce Clause itself), would be surplusage if Congress had been given authority over matters that substantially affect interstate commerce. An interpretation of cl. 3 that makes the rest of §8 superfluous simply cannot be correct. Yet this Court's Commerce Clause jurisprudence has endorsed just such an interpretation: The power we have accorded Congress has swallowed Art. I, §8.

Indeed, if a "substantial effects" test can be appended to the Commerce Clause, why not to every other power of the Federal Government? There is no reason for singling out the Commerce Clause for special treatment. Accordingly, Congress could regulate all matters that "substantially affect" the Army and Navy, bankruptcies, tax collection, expenditures, and so on. In that case, the Clauses of §8 all mutually overlap, something we can assume the Founding Fathers never intended.

I am aware of no cases prior to the New Deal that characterized the power flowing from the Commerce Clause as sweepingly as does our substantial effects test. My review of the case law indicates that the substantial effects test is but an innovation of the 20th century.

As recently as 1936, the Court continued to insist that the Commerce Clause did not reach the wholly internal business of the States. See Carter v. Carter Coal Co. (1936); see also A.L.A. Schechter Poultry Corp. v. United States (1935). The Federal Government simply could not reach such subjects regardless of their effects on interstate commerce.

These cases all establish a simple point: From the time of the ratification of the Constitution to the mid-1930's, it was widely understood that the Constitution granted Congress only limited powers, notwithstanding the Commerce Clause. Moreover, there was no question that activities wholly separated from business, such as gun possession, were beyond the reach of the commerce power. If anything, the "wrong turn" was the Court's dramatic departure in the 1930's from a century and a half of precedent.

Apart from its recent vintage and its corresponding lack of any grounding in the original understanding of the Constitution, the substantial effects test suffers from the further flaw that it appears to grant Congress a police power over the Nation. The substantial effects test suffers from this flaw, in part, because of its "aggregation principle." Under so-called "class of activities" statutes, Congress can regulate whole categories of activities that are not themselves either "interstate" or "commerce." In applying the effects test, we ask whether the class of activities as a whole substantially affects interstate commerce, not whether any specific activity within the class has such effects when considered in isolation.

The aggregation principle is clever, but has no stopping point. Suppose all would agree that gun possession within 1,000 feet of a school does not substantially affect commerce, but that possession of weapons generally (knives, brass knuckles, nunchakus, etc.) does. Under our substantial effects doctrine, even though Congress cannot single out gun possession, it can prohibit weapon possession generally. But one always can draw the circle broadly enough to cover an activity that, when taken in isolation, would not have substantial effects on commerce. Under our jurisprudence, if Congress passed an omnibus "substantially affects interstate commerce" statute, purporting to regulate every aspect of human existence, the Act apparently would be constitutional. Even though particular sections may govern only trivial activities, the statute in the aggregate regulates matters that substantially affect commerce.

Unless the dissenting Justices are willing to repudiate our long-held understanding of the limited nature of federal power, I would think that they, too, must be willing to reconsider the substantial effects test in a future case. If we wish to be true to a Constitution that does not cede a police power to the Federal Government, our Commerce Clause's boundaries simply cannot be "defined" as being "commensurate with the national needs" or self-consciously intended to let the Federal Government "defend itself against economic forces that Congress decrees inimical or destructive of the national economy." Such a formulation of federal power is no test at all: It is a blank check.

At an appropriate juncture, I think we must modify our Commerce Clause jurisprudence. Today, it is easy enough to say that the Clause certainly does not empower Congress to ban gun possession within 1,000 feet of a school.

Justice STEVENS, dissenting.

The welfare of our future "Commerce with foreign Nations, and among the several States," U.S. Const., Art. I, §8, cl. 3, is vitally dependent on the character of the education of our children. I therefore agree entirely with Justice Breyer's explanation of why Congress has ample power to prohibit the possession of firearms in or near schools—just as it may protect the school environment from harms posed by controlled substances such as asbestos or alcohol. I also agree with Justice Souter's exposition of the radical character of the Court's holding and its kinship with the discredited, pre-Depression version of substantive due process.

Guns are both articles of commerce and articles that can be used to restrain commerce. Their possession is the consequence, either directly or indirectly, of commercial activity. In my judgment, Congress's power to regulate commerce in firearms includes the power to prohibit possession of guns at any location because of their potentially harmful use; it necessarily follows that Congress may also prohibit their possession in particular markets. The market for the possession of handguns by school-age children is, distressingly, substantial. Whether or not the national interest in eliminating that market would have justified federal legislation in 1789, it surely does today.

Justice SOUTER, dissenting.

In reviewing congressional legislation under the Commerce Clause, we defer to what is often a merely implicit congressional judgment that its regulation addresses a subject substantially affecting interstate commerce "if there is any rational basis for such a finding." Hodel v. Virginia Surface Mining & Reclamation Assn., Inc. (1981). If that congressional determination is within the realm of reason, "the only remaining question for judicial inquiry is whether 'the means chosen by Congress [are] reasonably adapted to the end permitted by the Constitution.'"

The practice of deferring to rationally based legislative judgments "is a paradigm of judicial restraint." In judicial review under the Commerce Clause, it reflects our respect for the institutional competence of the Congress on a subject expressly assigned to it by the Constitution and our appreciation of the legitimacy that comes from Congress's political accountability in dealing with matters open to a wide range of possible choices.

It was not ever thus, however, as even a brief overview of Commerce Clause history during the past century reminds us. The modern respect for the competence and primacy of Congress in matters affecting commerce developed only after one of this Court's most chastening experiences, when it perforce repudiated an earlier and untenably expansive conception of judicial review in derogation of congressional commerce power. A look at history's sequence will serve to show how today's decision tugs the Court off course, leading it to suggest opportunities for further developments that would be at odds with the rule of restraint to which the Court still wisely states adherence.

There is today, however, a backward glance at both the old pitfalls, as the Court treats deference under the rationality rule as subject to gradation according to the commercial or noncommercial nature of the immediate subject of the challenged regulation. The distinction between what is patently commercial and what is not looks much like the old distinction between what directly affects commerce and what touches it only indirectly. And the act of calibrating the level of deference by drawing a line between what is patently commercial and what is less purely so will probably resemble the process of deciding how much interference with contractual freedom was fatal. Thus, it seems fair to ask whether the step taken by the Court today does anything but portend a return to the untenable jurisprudence from which the Court extricated itself almost 60 years ago. The answer is not reassuring. To be sure, the occasion for today's decision reflects the century's end, not its beginning. But if it seems anomalous that the Congress of the United States has taken to regulating school yards, the Act in question is still probably no more remarkable than state regulation of bake shops 90 years ago. In any event, there is no reason to hope that the Court's qualification of rational basis review will be any more successful than the efforts at substantive economic review made by our predecessors as the century began. Taking the Court's opinion on its own terms, Justice Breyer has explained both the hopeless porosity of "commercial" character as a ground of Commerce Clause distinction in America's highly connected economy, and the inconsistency of this categorization with our rational basis precedents from the last 50 years.

Justice BREYER, with whom Justice STEVENS, Justice SOUTER, and Justice GINSBURG join, dissenting.

The issue in this case is whether the Commerce Clause authorizes Congress to enact a statute that makes it a crime to possess a gun in, or near, a school. In my view, the statute falls well within the scope of the commerce power as this Court has understood that power over the last half century.

In reaching this conclusion, I apply three basic principles of Commerce Clause interpretation. First, the power to "regulate Commerce . . . among the several States," U.S. Const., Art. I, §8, cl. 3, encompasses the power to regulate local activities insofar as they significantly affect interstate commerce. See, e.g., Gibbons v. Ogden (1824); Wickard v. Filburn. As the majority points out, the Court, in describing how much of an effect the Clause requires, sometimes has used the word "substantial" and sometimes has not.

Second, in determining whether a local activity will likely have a significant effect upon interstate commerce, a court must consider, not the effect of an individual act (a single instance of gun possession), but rather the cumulative effect of all similar instances (i.e., the effect of all guns possessed in or near schools). See, e.g., *Wickard.*

Third, the Constitution requires us to judge the connection between a regulated activity and interstate commerce, not directly, but at one remove. Courts must give Congress a degree of leeway in determining the existence of a significant factual connection between the regulated activity and interstate commerce — both because the Constitution delegates the commerce power directly to Congress and because the determination requires an empirical judgment of a kind that a legislature is more likely than a court to make with accuracy. The traditional words "rational basis" capture this leeway. Thus, the specific question before us, as the Court recognizes, is not whether the "regulated activity sufficiently affected interstate commerce," but, rather, whether Congress could have had "a rational basis" for so concluding.

Applying these principles to the case at hand, we must ask whether Congress could have had a rational basis for finding a significant (or substantial) connection between gun-related school violence and interstate commerce. Or, to put the question in the language of the explicit finding that Congress made when it amended this law in 1994: Could Congress rationally have found that "violent crime in school zones," through its effect on the "quality of education," significantly (or substantially) affects "interstate" or "foreign commerce"? As long as one views the commerce connection, not as a "technical legal conception," but as "a practical one," the answer to this question must be yes. Numerous reports and studies — generated both inside and outside government — make clear that Congress could reasonably have found the empirical connection that its law, implicitly or explicitly, asserts.

For one thing, reports, hearings, and other readily available literature make clear that the problem of guns in and around schools is widespread and extremely serious. These materials report, for example, that four percent of American high school students (and six percent of inner-city high school students) carry a gun to school at least occasionally, Centers for Disease Control 2342; Sheley, McGee, & Wright 679; that 12 percent of urban high school students have had guns fired at them; that 20 percent of those students have been threatened with guns; and that, in any 6-month period, several hundred thousand schoolchildren are victims of violent crimes in or near their schools, U.S. Dept. of Justice 1 (1989); House Select Committee Hearing 15 (1989). And, they report that this widespread violence in schools throughout the Nation significantly interferes with the quality of education in those schools. See, e.g., House Judiciary Committee Hearing 44 (1990) (linking school violence to dropout rate); U.S. Dept. of Health 118-119 (1978) (school-violence victims suffer academically). Based on reports such as these, Congress obviously could have thought that guns and learning are mutually exclusive. Congress could therefore have found a substantial educational problem — teachers unable to teach, students unable to learn — and concluded that guns near schools contribute substantially to the size and scope of that problem.

Having found that guns in schools significantly undermine the quality of education in our Nation's classrooms, Congress could also have found, given the effect of education upon interstate and foreign commerce, that gun-related violence in and around schools is a commercial, as well as a human, problem. Education, although far more than a matter of economics, has long been inextricably intertwined with the Nation's economy.

In recent years the link between secondary education and business has strengthened, becoming both more direct and more important. [T]here is evidence that, today more than ever, many firms base their location decisions upon the presence, or absence, of a work force with a basic education.

Specifically, Congress could have found that gun-related violence near the classroom poses a serious economic threat (1) to consequently inadequately educated workers who must endure low paying jobs, and (2) to communities and businesses that might (in today's "information society") otherwise gain, from a well-educated work force, an important commercial advantage, of a kind that location near a railhead or harbor provided in the past. Congress might also have found these threats to be no different in kind from other threats that this Court has found within the commerce power, such as the threat that loan sharking poses to the "funds" of "numerous localities," Perez v. United States, and that unfair labor practices pose to instrumentalities of commerce. As I have pointed out, Congress has written that "the occurrence of violent crime in school zones" has brought about a "decline in the quality of education" that "has an adverse impact on interstate commerce and the foreign commerce of the United States." The violence-related facts, the educational facts, and the economic facts, taken together, make this conclusion rational. And, because under our case law, the sufficiency of the constitutionally necessary Commerce Clause link between a crime of violence and interstate commerce turns simply upon size or degree, those same facts make the statute constitutional.

To hold this statute constitutional is not to "obliterate" the "distinction between what is national and what is local," . . . ; nor is it to hold that the Commerce Clause permits the Federal Government to "regulate any activity that it found was related to the economic productivity of individual citizens," to regulate "marriage, divorce, and child custody," or to regulate any and all aspects of education. First, this statute is aimed at curbing a particularly acute threat to the educational process — the possession (and use) of life-threatening firearms in, or near, the classroom. The empirical evidence that I have discussed above unmistakably documents the special way in which guns and education are incompatible. Second, the immediacy of the connection between education and the national economic well-being is documented by scholars and accepted by society at large in a way and to a degree that may not hold true for other social institutions. It must surely be the rare case, then, that a statute strikes at conduct that (when considered in the abstract) seems so removed from commerce, but which (practically speaking) has so significant an impact upon commerce.

The majority's holding—that §922 falls outside the scope of the Commerce Clause—creates three serious legal problems. First, the majority's holding runs contrary to modern Supreme Court cases that have upheld congressional actions despite connections to interstate or foreign commerce that are less significant than the effect of school violence.

The second legal problem the Court creates comes from its apparent belief that it can reconcile its holding with earlier cases by making a critical distinction between "commercial" and noncommercial "transaction[s]." That is to say, the Court believes the Constitution would distinguish between two local activities, each of which has an identical effect upon interstate commerce, if one, but not the other, is "commercial" in nature. As a general matter, this approach fails to heed this Court's earlier warning not to turn "questions of the power of Congress" upon "formula[s]" that would give "controlling force to nomenclature such as 'production' and 'indirect' and foreclose consideration of the actual effects of the activity in question upon interstate commerce."

The third legal problem created by the Court's holding is that it threatens legal uncertainty in an area of law that, until this case, seemed reasonably well settled. Congress has enacted many statutes (more than 100 sections of the United States Code), including criminal statutes (at least 25 sections), that use the words "affecting commerce" to define their scope, see, e.g., 18 U.S.C. §844(i) (destruction of buildings used in activity affecting interstate commerce), and other statutes that contain no jurisdictional language at all, see, e.g., 18 U.S.C. §922(o)(1) (possession of machineguns). Do these, or similar, statutes regulate noncommercial activities? If so, would that alter the meaning of "affecting commerce" in a jurisdictional element?

Upholding this legislation would do no more than simply recognize that Congress had a "rational basis" for finding a significant connection between guns in or near schools and (through their effect on education) the interstate and foreign commerce they threaten.

UNITED STATES v. MORRISON

529 U.S. 598 (2000)

Chief Justice REHNQUIST delivered the opinion of the Court.

In these cases we consider the constitutionality of 42 U.S.C. §13981, which provides a federal civil remedy for the victims of gender-motivated violence. The United States Court of Appeals for the Fourth Circuit, sitting en banc, struck down §13981 because it concluded that Congress lacked constitutional authority to enact the section's civil remedy. [W]e affirm.

I

Petitioner Christy Brzonkala enrolled at Virginia Polytechnic Institute (Virginia Tech) in the fall of 1994. In September of that year, Brzonkala met respondents Antonio Morrison and James Crawford, who were both students at Virginia Tech and members of its varsity football team. Brzonkala alleges that, within 30 minutes of meeting Morrison and Crawford, they assaulted and repeatedly raped her. After the attack, Morrison allegedly told Brzonkala, "You better not have any ... diseases." In the months following the rape, Morrison also allegedly announced in the dormitory's dining room that he "like[d] to get girls drunk and...." The omitted portions, quoted verbatim in the briefs on file with this Court, consist of boasting, debased remarks about what Morrison would do to women, vulgar remarks that cannot fail to shock and offend.

Brzonkala alleges that this attack caused her to become severely emotionally disturbed and depressed. She sought assistance from a university psychiatrist, who prescribed antidepressant medication. Shortly after the rape Brzonkala stopped attending classes and withdrew from the university.

In early 1995, Brzonkala filed a complaint against respondents under Virginia Tech's Sexual Assault Policy. During the school-conducted hearing on her complaint, Morrison admitted having sexual contact with her despite the fact that she had twice told him "no." After the hearing, Virginia Tech's Judicial Committee found insufficient evidence to punish Crawford, but found Morrison guilty of sexual assault and sentenced him to immediate suspension for two semesters.

Virginia Tech's dean of students upheld the judicial committee's sentence. However, in July 1995, Virginia Tech informed Brzonkala that Morrison intended to initiate a court challenge to his conviction under the Sexual Assault Policy. University officials told her that a second hearing would be necessary to remedy the school's error in prosecuting her complaint under that policy, which had not been widely circulated to students. Following this second hearing the Judicial Committee again found Morrison guilty and sentenced him to an identical 2-semester suspension. This time, however, the description of Morrison's offense was, without explanation, changed from "sexual assault" to "using abusive language."

Morrison appealed his second conviction through the university's administrative system. On August 21, 1995, Virginia Tech's senior vice president and provost set aside Morrison's punishment. After learning from a newspaper that Morrison would be returning to Virginia Tech for the fall 1995 semester, she dropped out of the university.

In December 1995, Brzonkala sued Morrison, Crawford, and Virginia Tech in the United States District Court for the Western District of Virginia. Section 13981 was part of the Violence Against Women Act of 1994. It states that "[a]ll persons within the United States shall have the right to be free from crimes of violence motivated by gender." To enforce that right, subsection (c) declares: "A person (including a person who acts under color of any statute, ordinance, regulation, custom, or usage of any State) who commits a crime of violence motivated by gender and thus deprives another of the right declared in subsection (b) of this section shall be liable to the party injured, in an action for the recovery of compensatory and punitive damages, injunctive and declaratory relief, and such other relief as a court may deem appropriate." Section 13981 defines a "crim[e] of violence motivated by gender" as "a crime of violence committed because of gender or on the basis of gender, and due, at least in part, to an animus based on the victim's gender."

[II]

Due respect for the decisions of a coordinate branch of Government demands that we invalidate a congressional enactment only upon a plain showing that

Congress has exceeded its constitutional bounds. With this presumption of constitutionality in mind, we turn to the question whether §13981 falls within Congress's power under Article I, §8, of the Constitution. Brzonkala and the United States rely upon the third clause of the Article, which gives Congress power "[t]o regulate Commerce with foreign Nations, and among the several States, and with the Indian Tribes."[36]

As we discussed at length in *Lopez*, our interpretation of the Commerce Clause has changed as our Nation has developed. As we observed in *Lopez*, modern Commerce Clause jurisprudence has "identified three broad categories of activity that Congress may regulate under its commerce power." "First, Congress may regulate the use of the channels of interstate commerce." "Second, Congress is empowered to regulate and protect the instrumentalities of interstate commerce, or persons or things in interstate commerce, even though the threat may come only from intrastate activities." "Finally, Congress's commerce authority includes the power to regulate those activities having a substantial relation to interstate commerce, . . . i.e., those activities that substantially affect interstate commerce."

Petitioners do not contend that these cases fall within either of the first two of these categories of Commerce Clause regulation. They seek to sustain §13981 as a regulation of activity that substantially affects interstate commerce. Given §13981's focus on gender-motivated violence wherever it occurs (rather than violence directed at the instrumentalities of interstate commerce, interstate markets, or things or persons in interstate commerce), we agree that this is the proper inquiry.

Both petitioners and Justice Souter's dissent downplay the role that the economic nature of the regulated activity plays in our Commerce Clause analysis. But a fair reading of *Lopez* shows that the noneconomic, criminal nature of the conduct at issue was central to our decision in that case.

With these principles underlying our Commerce Clause jurisprudence as reference points, the proper resolution of the present cases is clear. Gender-motivated crimes of violence are not, in any sense of the phrase, economic activity. While we need not adopt a categorical rule against aggregating the effects of any noneconomic activity in order to decide these cases, thus far in our Nation's history our cases have upheld Commerce Clause regulation of intrastate activity only where that activity is economic in nature.

Like the Gun-Free School Zones Act at issue in *Lopez*, §13981 contains no jurisdictional element establishing that the federal cause of action is in pursuance of Congress's power to regulate interstate commerce. In contrast with the lack of congressional findings that we faced in *Lopez*, §13981 is supported by numerous findings regarding the serious impact that gender-motivated violence has on victims and their families. But the existence of congressional findings is not sufficient, by itself, to sustain the constitutionality of Commerce Clause legislation. As we stated in *Lopez*, "[S]imply because Congress may conclude that a particular activity substantially affects interstate commerce does not necessarily make it so."

---

36. The Court also considered the constitutionality of the Violence Against Women Act as an exercise of Congress's power under §5 of the Fourteenth Amendment. This aspect of *Morrison* is presented below. [Footnote by casebook author.]

In these cases, Congress's findings are substantially weakened by the fact that they rely so heavily on a method of reasoning that we have already rejected as unworkable if we are to maintain the Constitution's enumeration of powers. Congress found that gender-motivated violence affects interstate commerce "by deterring potential victims from traveling interstate, from engaging in employment in interstate business, and from transacting with business, and in places involved in interstate commerce; . . . by diminishing national productivity, increasing medical and other costs, and decreasing the supply of and the demand for interstate products." H.R. Conf. Rep. No. 103-711.

The reasoning that petitioners advance seeks to follow the but-for causal chain from the initial occurrence of violent crime (the suppression of which has always been the prime object of the States' police power) to every attenuated effect upon interstate commerce. If accepted, petitioners' reasoning would allow Congress to regulate any crime as long as the nationwide, aggregated impact of that crime has substantial effects on employment, production, transit, or consumption. Indeed, if Congress may regulate gender-motivated violence, it would be able to regulate murder or any other type of violence since gender-motivated violence, as a subset of all violent crime, is certain to have lesser economic impacts than the larger class of which it is a part. Petitioners' reasoning, moreover, will not limit Congress to regulating violence but may, as we suggested in *Lopez*, be applied equally as well to family law and other areas of traditional state regulation since the aggregate effect of marriage, divorce, and childrearing on the national economy is undoubtedly significant. Given these findings and petitioners' arguments, the concern that we expressed in *Lopez* that Congress might use the Commerce Clause to completely obliterate the Constitution's distinction between national and local authority seems well founded.

We accordingly reject the argument that Congress may regulate noneconomic, violent criminal conduct based solely on that conduct's aggregate effect on interstate commerce. The Constitution requires a distinction between what is truly national and what is truly local. In recognizing this fact we preserve one of the few principles that has been consistent since the Clause was adopted.

Justice THOMAS, concurring.

The majority opinion correctly applies our decision in United States v. Lopez (1995), and I join it in full. I write separately only to express my view that the very notion of a "substantial effects" test under the Commerce Clause is inconsistent with the original understanding of Congress's powers and with this Court's early Commerce Clause cases. By continuing to apply this rootless and malleable standard, however circumscribed, the Court has encouraged the Federal Government to persist in its view that the Commerce Clause has virtually no limits. Until this Court replaces its existing Commerce Clause jurisprudence with a standard more consistent with the original understanding, we will continue to see Congress appropriating state police powers under the guise of regulating commerce.

Justice SOUTER, with whom Justice STEVENS, Justice GINSBURG, and Justice BREYER join, dissenting.

Our cases, which remain at least nominally undisturbed, stand for the following propositions. Congress has the power to legislate with regard to activity that, in the aggregate, has a substantial effect on interstate commerce. The fact of such a substantial effect is not an issue for the courts in the first instance, but for the Congress, whose institutional capacity for gathering evidence and taking testimony far exceeds ours. By passing legislation, Congress indicates its conclusion, whether explicitly or not, that facts support its exercise of the commerce power. The business of the courts is to review the congressional assessment, not for soundness but simply for the rationality of concluding that a jurisdictional basis exists in fact. Any explicit findings that Congress chooses to make, though not dispositive of the question of rationality, may advance judicial review by identifying factual authority on which Congress relied.

Applying those propositions in these cases can lead to only one conclusion. One obvious difference from United States v. Lopez, is the mountain of data assembled by Congress, here showing the effects of violence against women on interstate commerce. Passage of the Act in 1994 was preceded by four years of hearings. Congress thereby explicitly stated the predicate for the exercise of its Commerce Clause power. Is its conclusion irrational in view of the data amassed? True, the methodology of particular studies may be challenged, and some of the figures arrived at may be disputed. But the sufficiency of the evidence before Congress to provide a rational basis for the finding cannot seriously be questioned. Indeed, the legislative record here is far more voluminous than the record compiled by Congress and found sufficient in two prior cases upholding Title II of the Civil Rights Act of 1964 against Commerce Clause challenges.

While Congress did not, to my knowledge, calculate aggregate dollar values for the nationwide effects of racial discrimination in 1964, in 1994 it did rely on evidence of the harms caused by domestic violence and sexual assault, citing annual costs of $3 billion in 1990. Equally important, though, gender-based violence in the 1990's was shown to operate in a manner similar to racial discrimination in the 1960's in reducing the mobility of employees and their production and consumption of goods shipped in interstate commerce. Like racial discrimination, "[g]ender-based violence bars its most likely targets—women—from full partic[ipation] in the national economy."

Why is the majority tempted to reject the lesson so painfully learned in 1937? If we now ask why the formalistic economic/noneconomic distinction might matter today, after its rejection in *Wickard*, the answer is not that the majority fails to see causal connections in an integrated economic world. The answer is that in the minds of the majority there is a new animating theory that makes categorical formalism seem useful again. Just as the old formalism had value in the service of an economic conception, the new one is useful in serving a conception of federalism.

It is the instrument by which assertions of national power are to be limited in favor of preserving a supposedly discernible, proper sphere of state autonomy to legislate or refrain from legislating as the individual States see fit. The legitimacy of the Court's current emphasis on the noncommercial nature of regulated activity, then, does not turn on any logic serving the text of the Commerce Clause or on the realism of the majority's view of the national economy.

The Court finds it relevant that the statute addresses conduct traditionally subject to state prohibition under domestic criminal law, a fact said to have some heightened significance when the violent conduct in question is not itself aimed directly at interstate commerce or its instrumentalities. Again, history seems to be recycling, for the theory of traditional state concern as grounding a limiting principle has been rejected previously, and more than once.

All of this convinces me that today's ebb of the commerce power rests on error, and at the same time leads me to doubt that the majority's view will prove to be enduring law. There is yet one more reason for doubt. Although we sense the presence of *Carter Coal, Schechter,* and *Usery* once again, the majority embraces them only at arm's-length. Where such decisions once stood for rules, today's opinion points to considerations by which substantial effects are discounted. Cases standing for the sufficiency of substantial effects are not overruled; cases overruled since 1937 are not quite revived. As our predecessors learned then, the practice of such ad hoc review cannot preserve the distinction between the judicial and the legislative, and this Court, in any event, lacks the institutional capacity to maintain such a regime for very long. This one will end when the majority realizes that the conception of the commerce power for which it enter-tains hopes would inevitably fail the test expressed in Justice Holmes's statement that "[t]he first call of a theory of law is that it should fit the facts." O. Holmes, The Common Law 167 (Howe ed. 1963). The facts that cannot be ignored today are the facts of integrated national commerce and a political relationship between States and Nation much affected by their respective treasuries and constitutional modifications adopted by the people. The federalism of some earlier time is no more adequate to account for those facts today than the theory of laissez-faire was able to govern the national economy 70 years ago.

In two cases, the Court has narrowly construed federal laws to avoid the question of whether they exceed the scope of Congress's commerce power. In United States v. Jones, 529 U.S. 848 (2000), the Supreme Court unanimously held that the federal Arson Act does not apply to arson of a dwelling. The Court, in an opinion by Justice Ginsburg, said that applying the Arson Act to arson of a private residence would raise serious constitutional issues concerning Con-gress's power under the Commerce Clause. As a result, the Court said to avoid "constitutional doubts" it would interpret the law to not apply to such acts.

The Court took the same approach, although in a much more closely divided decision, in Solid Waste Agency of Northern Cook County v. United States Army Corps of Engineers, 531 U.S. 159 (2001). The issue was whether the Clean Water Act, which applies to "navigable waters," could be applied to intrastate waters because of the presence of migratory birds. The Court, five to four, said no, holding that it would interpret the statute this way so as to avoid constitutional doubts.

Chief Justice Rehnquist, working for the Court, stated:

> Where an administrative interpretation of a statute invokes the outer limits of Congress' power, we expect a clear indication that Congress intended that result. This requirement stems from our prudential desire not to needlessly reach constitutional issues and our assumption that Congress does not casually authorize administrative agencies to interpret a statute to push the limit of congressional authority. This concern is heightened where the administrative interpretation alters the federal-state framework by permitting federal encroachment upon a traditional state power. Thus, "where an otherwise acceptable construction of a statute would raise serious constitutional problems, the Court will construe the statute to avoid such problems unless such construction is plainly contrary to the intent of Congress."

Twice in the past six years we have reaffirmed the proposition that the grant of authority to Congress under the Commerce Clause, though broad, is not unlimited. See United States v. Morrison (2000); United States v. Lopez (1995). Respondents argue that the "Migratory Bird Rule" falls within Congress' power to regulate intrastate activities that "substantially affect" interstate commerce. They note that the protection of migratory birds is a "national interest of very nearly the first magnitude," Missouri v. Holland (1920), and that, as the Court of Appeals found, millions of people spend over a billion dollars annually on recreational pursuits relating to migratory birds. These arguments raise significant constitutional questions. For example, we would have to evaluate the precise object or activity that, in the aggregate, substantially affects interstate commerce. This is not clear, for although the Corps has claimed jurisdiction over petitioner's land because it contains water areas used as habitat by migratory birds, respondents now focus upon the fact that the regulated activity is petitioner's municipal landfill, which is "plainly of a commercial nature." But this is a far cry, indeed, from the "navigable waters" and "waters of the United States" to which the statute by its terms extends.

These are significant constitutional questions raised by respondents' application of their regulations, and yet we find nothing approaching a clear statement from Congress that it intended §404(a) to reach an abandoned sand and gravel pit such as we have here. Permitting respondents to claim federal jurisdiction over ponds and mudflats falling within the "Migratory Bird Rule" would result in a significant impingement of the States' traditional and primary power over land and water use. We thus read the statute as written to avoid the significant constitutional and federalism questions raised by respondents' interpretation, and therefore reject the request for administrative deference.

Justice Stevens, writing for the four dissenting justices, argued that the Army Corps of Engineers had the authority to apply the Clean Water Act to intrastate waters because of the presence of migratory birds. He wrote:

> Contrary to the Court's suggestion, the Corps' interpretation of the statute does not "encroac[h]" upon "traditional state power" over land use. "Land use planning in essence chooses particular uses for the land; environmental regulation, at its core, does not mandate particular uses of the land but requires only that, however the land is used, damage to the environment is kept within prescribed limits." California Coastal Comm'n v. Granite Rock Co. (1987). The CWA is not a land-use code; it is a paradigm of environmental regulation. Such regulation is an accepted exercise of federal power. Hodel v. Virginia Surface Mining & Reclamation Assn., Inc. (1981).
>
> The Corps' exercise of its §404 permitting power over "isolated" waters that serve as habitat for migratory birds falls well within the boundaries set by this Court's Commerce Clause jurisprudence. In United States v. Lopez (1995), this Court identified "three broad categories of activity that Congress may regulate under its commerce power": (1) channels of interstate commerce; (2) instrumentalities of interstate commerce, or persons and things in interstate commerce; and (3) activities that "substantially affect" interstate commerce. The migratory bird rule at issue here is properly analyzed under the third category. In order to constitute a proper exercise of Congress' power over intrastate activities that "substantially affect" interstate commerce, it is not necessary that each individual instance of the activity substantially affect commerce; it is enough that, taken in the aggregate, the class of activities in question has such an effect.
>
> The activity being regulated in this case (and by the Corps' §404 regulations in general) is the discharge of fill material into water. The Corps did not assert

jurisdiction over petitioner's land simply because the waters were "used as habitat by migratory birds." It asserted jurisdiction because petitioner planned to discharge fill into waters "used as habitat by migratory birds." Had petitioner intended to engage in some other activity besides discharging fill (i.e., had there been no activity to regulate), or, conversely, had the waters not been habitat for migratory birds (i.e., had there been no basis for federal jurisdiction), the Corps would never have become involved in petitioner's use of its land. There can be no doubt that, unlike the class of activities Congress was attempting to regulate in United States v. Morrison (2000) ("[g]ender-motivated crimes"), and *Lopez* (possession of guns near school property), the discharge of fill material into the Nation's waters is almost always undertaken for economic reasons.

Moreover, no one disputes that the discharge of fill into "isolated" waters that serve as migratory bird habitat will, in the aggregate, adversely affect migratory bird populations. Nor does petitioner dispute that the particular waters it seeks to fill are home to many important species of migratory birds, including the second-largest breeding colony of Great Blue Herons in northeastern Illinois, and several species of waterfowl protected by international treaty and Illinois endangered species laws.

The power to regulate commerce among the several States necessarily and properly includes the power to preserve the natural resources that generate such commerce. Moreover, the protection of migratory birds is a well-established federal responsibility. As Justice Holmes noted in Missouri v. Holland, the federal interest in protecting these birds is of "the first magnitude." Because of their transitory nature, they "can be protected only by national action."

During the last few years of the Rehnquist Court, two challenges to federal laws as exceeding the scope of the commerce power were rejected. One, Pierce County, Washington v. Guillen, was unanimous and did not engender controversy. The other, Gonzales v. Raich, was enormously controversial and led some commentators to argue that the Court was shifting away from significant limits on Congress's commerce power.

In Pierce County, Washington v. Guillen, 537 U.S. 129 (2003), the Court unanimously reaffirmed broad authority for Congress to legislate concerning road safety as part of its power to regulate the channels of interstate commerce. A federal statute provides that if a local government does a traffic study as part of applying for federal funds, that study is not discoverable. Congress's concern was that local governments would refrain from conducting such investigations if they could be used as evidence against them in suits arising from automobile accidents.

Guillen involved two separate accidents at intersections in the state of Washington, and the local governments had recently conducted studies of traffic conditions at both locations. The plaintiffs sued the local governments and sought access to the traffic studies. The Washington Supreme Court declared unconstitutional the federal law that exempted these studies from discovery. The U.S. Supreme Court, in an opinion by Justice Clarence Thomas, unanimously reversed and upheld the federal law. Justice Thomas explained that "[i]t is well established that the Commerce Clause gives Congress authority to regulate the use of the channels of interstate commerce. . . . [The statutes] can be viewed as legislation aimed at improving safety in the channels of interstate commerce and increasing protection for the instrumentalities of interstate commerce. As such, they fall within Congress' Commerce Clause power."

GONZALES v. RAICH
545 U.S. 1 (2005)

Justice STEVENS delivered the opinion of the Court.

California is one of at least nine States that authorize the use of marijuana for medicinal purposes. The question presented in this case is whether the power vested in Congress by Article I, §8, of the Constitution "[t]o make all Laws which shall be necessary and proper for carrying into Execution" its authority to "regulate Commerce with foreign Nations, and among the several States" includes the power to prohibit the local cultivation and use of marijuana in compliance with California law.

I

California has been a pioneer in the regulation of marijuana. In 1913, California was one of the first States to prohibit the sale and possession of marijuana, and at the end of the century, California became the first State to authorize limited use of the drug for medicinal purposes. In 1996, California voters passed Proposition 215, now codified as the Compassionate Use Act of 1996. The proposition was designed to ensure that "seriously ill" residents of the State have access to marijuana for medical purposes, and to encourage Federal and State Governments to take steps towards ensuring the safe and affordable distribution of the drug to patients in need. The Act creates an exemption from criminal prosecution for physicians, as well as for patients and primary caregivers who possess or cultivate marijuana for medicinal purposes with the recommendation or approval of a physician.

Respondents Angel Raich and Diane Monson are California residents who suffer from a variety of serious medical conditions and have sought to avail themselves of medical marijuana pursuant to the terms of the Compassionate Use Act. They are being treated by licensed, board-certified family practitioners, who have concluded, after prescribing a host of conventional medicines to treat respondents' conditions and to alleviate their associated symptoms, that marijuana is the only drug available that provides effective treatment. Both women have been using marijuana as a medication for several years pursuant to their doctors' recommendation, and both rely heavily on cannabis to function on a daily basis. Indeed, Raich's physician believes that forgoing cannabis treatments would certainly cause Raich excruciating pain and could very well prove fatal.

On August 15, 2002, county deputy sheriffs and agents from the federal Drug Enforcement Administration (DEA) came to Monson's home. After a thorough investigation, the county officials concluded that her use of marijuana was entirely lawful as a matter of California law. Nevertheless, after a 3-hour standoff, the federal agents seized and destroyed all six of her cannabis plants. Respondents thereafter brought this action against the Attorney General of the United States and the head of the DEA seeking injunctive and declaratory relief prohibiting the enforcement of the federal Controlled Substances Act (CSA) to the extent it prevents them from possessing, obtaining, or manufacturing cannabis for their personal medical use.

The case is made difficult by respondents' strong arguments that they will suffer irreparable harm because, despite a congressional finding to the contrary, marijuana does have valid therapeutic purposes. The question before us, however, is not whether it is wise to enforce the statute in these circumstances; rather, it is whether Congress' power to regulate interstate markets for medicinal substances encompasses the portions of those markets that are supplied with drugs produced and consumed locally. Well-settled law controls our answer. The CSA is a valid exercise of federal power, even as applied to the troubling facts of this case. We accordingly vacate the judgment of the Court of Appeals.

II

Shortly after taking office in 1969, President Nixon declared a national "war on drugs." As the first campaign of that war, Congress set out to enact legislation that would consolidate various drug laws on the books into a comprehensive statute, provide meaningful regulation over legitimate sources of drugs to prevent diversion into illegal channels, and strengthen law enforcement tools against the traffic in illicit drugs. That effort culminated in the passage of the Comprehensive Drug Abuse Prevention and Control Act of 1970.

[Subsequently, Congress enacted the CSA and] Congress devised a closed regulatory system making it unlawful to manufacture, distribute, dispense, or possess any controlled substance except in a manner authorized by the CSA. The CSA categorizes all controlled substances into five schedules. The drugs are grouped together based on their accepted medical uses, the potential for abuse, and their psychological and physical effects on the body. Each schedule is associated with a distinct set of controls regarding the manufacture, distribution, and use of the substances listed therein. The CSA and its implementing regulations set forth strict requirements regarding registration, labeling and packaging, production quotas, drug security, and recordkeeping.

In enacting the CSA, Congress classified marijuana as a Schedule I drug. Schedule I drugs are categorized as such because of their high potential for abuse, lack of any accepted medical use, and absence of any accepted safety for use in medically supervised treatment.

III

Respondents in this case do not dispute that passage of the CSA, as part of the Comprehensive Drug Abuse Prevention and Control Act, was well within Congress' commerce power. Nor do they contend that any provision or section of the CSA amounts to an unconstitutional exercise of congressional authority. Rather, respondents' challenge is actually quite limited; they argue that the CSA's categorical prohibition of the manufacture and possession of marijuana as applied to the intrastate manufacture and possession of marijuana for medical purposes pursuant to California law exceeds Congress' authority under the Commerce Clause.

In assessing the validity of congressional regulation, none of our Commerce Clause cases can be viewed in isolation. As charted in considerable detail in *United States v. Lopez*, our understanding of the reach of the Commerce Clause, as well as Congress' assertion of authority thereunder, has evolved over time.

Cases decided during that "new era," which now spans more than a century, have identified three general categories of regulation in which Congress is authorized to engage under its commerce power. First, Congress can regulate the channels of interstate commerce. Second, Congress has authority to regulate and protect the instrumentalities of interstate commerce, and persons or things in interstate commerce. Third, Congress has the power to regulate activities that substantially affect interstate commerce. Only the third category is implicated in the case at hand.

Our case law firmly establishes Congress' power to regulate purely local activities that are part of an economic "class of activities" that have a substantial effect on interstate commerce. See, e.g., *Wickard v. Filburn* (1942). As we stated in *Wickard*, "even if appellee's activity be local and though it may not be regarded as commerce, it may still, whatever its nature, be reached by Congress if it exerts a substantial economic effect on interstate commerce." We have never required Congress to legislate with scientific exactitude. When Congress decides that the "total incidence" of a practice poses a threat to a national market, it may regulate the entire class. In this vein, we have reiterated that when "a general regulatory statute bears a substantial relation to commerce, the de minimis character of individual instances arising under that statute is of no consequence."

Our decision in *Wickard* is of particular relevance. In *Wickard*, we upheld the application of regulations promulgated under the Agricultural Adjustment Act of 1938, which were designed to control the volume of wheat moving in interstate and foreign commerce in order to avoid surpluses and consequent abnormally low prices. *Wickard* thus establishes that Congress can regulate purely intrastate activity that is not itself "commercial," in that it is not produced for sale, if it concludes that failure to regulate that class of activity would undercut the regulation of the interstate market in that commodity.

The similarities between this case and *Wickard* are striking. Like the farmer in *Wickard*, respondents are cultivating, for home consumption, a fungible commodity for which there is an established, albeit illegal, interstate market. Just as the Agricultural Adjustment Act was designed "to control the volume [of wheat] moving in interstate and foreign commerce in order to avoid surpluses . . ." and consequently control the market price, a primary purpose of the CSA is to control the supply and demand of controlled substances in both lawful and unlawful drug markets. In *Wickard*, we had no difficulty concluding that Congress had a rational basis for believing that, when viewed in the aggregate, leaving home-consumed wheat outside the regulatory scheme would have a substantial influence on price and market conditions. Here too, Congress had a rational basis for concluding that leaving home-consumed marijuana outside federal control would similarly affect price and market conditions.

More concretely, one concern prompting inclusion of wheat grown for home consumption in the 1938 Act was that rising market prices could draw such wheat into the interstate market, resulting in lower market prices. The parallel concern making it appropriate to include marijuana grown for home consumption in the CSA is the likelihood that the high demand in the interstate market will draw such marijuana into that market. While the diversion of homegrown wheat tended to frustrate the federal interest in stabilizing prices by regulating the volume of commercial transactions in the interstate market, the diversion of homegrown marijuana tends to frustrate the federal interest in eliminating commercial transactions in the interstate market in their entirety. In both cases, the regulation is squarely within Congress' commerce power because production of the commodity meant for home consumption, be it wheat or marijuana, has a substantial effect on supply and demand in the national market for that commodity.[37]

In assessing the scope of Congress' authority under the Commerce Clause, we stress that the task before us is a modest one. We need not determine whether respondents' activities, taken in the aggregate, substantially affect interstate commerce in fact, but only whether a "rational basis" exists for so concluding. Given the enforcement difficulties that attend distinguishing between marijuana cultivated locally and marijuana grown elsewhere, 21 U.S.C. §801(5), and concerns about diversion into illicit channels, we have no difficulty concluding that Congress had a rational basis for believing that failure to regulate the intrastate manufacture and possession of marijuana would leave a gaping hole in the CSA. Thus, as in *Wickard*, when it enacted comprehensive legislation to regulate the interstate market in a fungible commodity, Congress was acting well within its authority to "make all Laws which shall be necessary and proper" to "regulate Commerce . . . among the several States." U.S. Const., Art. I, §8. That the regulation ensnares some purely intrastate activity is of no moment. As we have done many times before, we refuse to excise individual components of that larger scheme.

IV

To support their contrary submission, respondents rely heavily on two of our more recent Commerce Clause cases. In their myopic focus, they overlook the larger context of modern-era Commerce Clause jurisprudence preserved by those cases. Moreover, even in the narrow prism of respondents' creation, they read those cases far too broadly. Those two cases, of course, are *United States v. Lopez* (1995) and *United States v. Morrison* (2000). As an initial matter, the statutory challenges at issue in those cases were markedly different from the challenge respondents pursue in the case at hand. Here, respondents ask us to excise individual applications of a concededly valid statutory scheme. In contrast, in both *Lopez* and *Morrison*, the parties asserted that a particular statute or provision fell outside Congress' commerce power in its entirety. This distinction is pivotal for we have often reiterated that "[w]here the class of activities is regulated and that class is within the reach of federal power, the courts have no power 'to excise, as trivial, individual instances' of the class."

Unlike those at issue in *Lopez* and *Morrison*, the activities regulated by the CSA are quintessentially economic. "Economics" refers to "the production, distribution, and consumption of commodities." Webster's Third New International Dictionary (1966). The CSA is a statute that regulates the production, distribution, and consumption of commodities for which there is an established,

---

37. To be sure, the wheat market is a lawful market that Congress sought to protect and stabilize, whereas the marijuana market is an unlawful market that Congress sought to eradicate. This difference, however, is of no constitutional import. It has long been settled that Congress' power to regulate commerce includes the power to prohibit commerce in a particular commodity. [Footnote by the Court.]

and lucrative, interstate market. Prohibiting the intrastate possession or manufacture of an article of commerce is a rational (and commonly utilized) means of regulating commerce in that product. Such prohibitions include specific decisions requiring that a drug be withdrawn from the market as a result of the failure to comply with regulatory requirements as well as decisions excluding Schedule I drugs entirely from the market. Because the CSA is a statute that directly regulates economic, commercial activity, our opinion in *Morrison* casts no doubt on its constitutionality.

V

Respondents also raise a substantive due process claim and seek to avail themselves of the medical necessity defense. These theories of relief were set forth in their complaint but were not reached by the Court of Appeals. We therefore do not address the question whether judicial relief is available to respondents on these alternative bases. We do note, however, the presence of another avenue of relief. As the Solicitor General confirmed during oral argument, the statute authorizes procedures for the reclassification of Schedule I drugs. But perhaps even more important than these legal avenues is the democratic process, in which the voices of voters allied with these respondents may one day be heard in the halls of Congress.

Justice SCALIA, concurring in the judgment.

I agree with the Court's holding that the Controlled Substances Act (CSA) may validly be applied to respondents' cultivation, distribution, and possession of marijuana for personal, medicinal use. I write separately because my understanding of the doctrinal foundation on which that holding rests is, if not inconsistent with that of the Court, at least more nuanced.

Since *Perez v. United States* (1971), our cases have mechanically recited that the Commerce Clause permits congressional regulation of three categories: (1) the channels of interstate commerce; (2) the instrumentalities of interstate commerce, and persons or things in interstate commerce; and (3) activities that "substantially affect" interstate commerce. The first two categories are self-evident, since they are the ingredients of interstate commerce itself. The third category, however, is different in kind, and its recitation without explanation is misleading and incomplete.

It is misleading because, unlike the channels, instrumentalities, and agents of interstate commerce, activities that substantially affect interstate commerce are not themselves part of interstate commerce, and thus the power to regulate them cannot come from the Commerce Clause alone. Rather, Congress's regulatory authority over intrastate activities that are not themselves part of interstate commerce (including activities that have a substantial effect on interstate commerce) derives from the Necessary and Proper Clause. And the category of "activities that substantially affect interstate commerce" is incomplete because the authority to enact laws necessary and proper for the regulation of interstate commerce is not limited to laws governing intrastate activities that substantially affect interstate commerce. Where necessary to make a regulation of interstate commerce effective, Congress may regulate even those intrastate activities that do not themselves substantially affect interstate commerce.

Today's principal dissent objects that, by permitting Congress to regulate activities necessary to effective interstate regulation, the Court reduces *Lopez* and *Morrison* to "little more than a drafting guide." I think that criticism unjustified. Unlike the power to regulate activities that have a substantial effect on interstate commerce, the power to enact laws enabling effective regulation of interstate commerce can only be exercised in conjunction with congressional regulation of an interstate market, and it extends only to those measures necessary to make the interstate regulation effective. As *Lopez* itself states, and the Court affirms today, Congress may regulate noneconomic intrastate activities only where the failure to do so "could . . . undercut" its regulation of interstate commerce. This is not a power that threatens to obliterate the line between "what is truly national and what is truly local."

Lopez and *Morrison* affirm that Congress may not regulate certain "purely local" activity within the States based solely on the attenuated effect that such activity may have in the interstate market. But those decisions do not declare noneconomic intrastate activities to be categorically beyond the reach of the Federal Government. Neither case involved the power of Congress to exert control over intrastate activities in connection with a more comprehensive scheme of regulation. To dismiss this distinction as "superficial and formalistic," . . . (O'Connor, J., dissenting), is to misunderstand the nature of the Necessary and Proper Clause, which empowers Congress to enact laws in effectuation of its enumerated powers that are not within its authority to enact in isolation. See *McCulloch v. Maryland* (1819).

And there are other restraints upon the Necessary and Proper Clause authority. As Chief Justice Marshall wrote in *McCulloch v. Maryland*, even when the end is constitutional and legitimate, the means must be "appropriate" and "plainly adapted" to that end. Moreover, they may not be otherwise "prohibited" and must be "consistent with the letter and spirit of the constitution." These phrases are not merely hortatory.

The application of these principles to the case before us is straightforward. In the CSA, Congress has undertaken to extinguish the interstate market in Schedule I controlled substances, including marijuana. The Commerce Clause unquestionably permits this. The power to regulate interstate commerce "extends not only to those regulations which aid, foster and protect the commerce, but embraces those which prohibit it." To effectuate its objective, Congress has prohibited almost all intrastate activities related to Schedule I substances — both economic activities (manufacture, distribution, possession with the intent to distribute) and noneconomic activities (simple possession). That simple possession is a noneconomic activity is immaterial to whether it can be prohibited as a necessary part of a larger regulation. Rather, Congress's authority to enact all of these prohibitions of intrastate controlled-substance activities depends only upon whether they are appropriate means of achieving the legitimate end of eradicating Schedule I substances from interstate commerce.

By this measure, I think the regulation must be sustained. Not only is it impossible to distinguish "controlled substances manufactured and distributed intrastate" from "controlled substances manufactured and distributed interstate," but it hardly makes sense to speak in such terms. Drugs like marijuana are fungible commodities. As the Court explains, marijuana that is grown at home and possessed for personal use is never more than an instant from the interstate market—and this is so whether or not the possession is for medicinal use or lawful use under the laws of a particular State. Congress need not accept on faith that state law will be effective in maintaining a strict division between a lawful market for "medical" marijuana and the more general marijuana market.

I thus agree with the Court that, however the class of regulated activities is subdivided, Congress could reasonably conclude that its objective of prohibiting marijuana from the interstate market "could be undercut" if those activities were excepted from its general scheme of regulation. That is sufficient to authorize the application of the CSA to respondents.

Justice O'CONNOR, with whom the Chief Justice and Justice THOMAS join as to all but Part III, dissenting.

We enforce the "outer limits" of Congress' Commerce Clause authority not for their own sake, but to protect historic spheres of state sovereignty from excessive federal encroachment and thereby to maintain the distribution of power fundamental to our federalist system of government. *United States v. Lopez* (1995). One of federalism's chief virtues, of course, is that it promotes innovation by allowing for the possibility that "a single courageous State may, if its citizens choose, serve as a laboratory; and try novel social and economic experiments without risk to the rest of the country." *New State Ice Co. v. Liebmann* (1932) (Brandeis, J., dissenting).

This case exemplifies the role of States as laboratories. The States' core police powers have always included authority to define criminal law and to protect the health, safety, and welfare of their citizens. Exercising those powers, California (by ballot initiative and then by legislative codification) has come to its own conclusion about the difficult and sensitive question of whether marijuana should be available to relieve severe pain and suffering. Today the Court sanctions an application of the federal Controlled Substances Act that extinguishes that experiment, without any proof that the personal cultivation, possession, and use of marijuana for medicinal purposes, if economic activity in the first place, has a substantial effect on interstate commerce and is therefore an appropriate subject of federal regulation. In so doing, the Court announces a rule that gives Congress a perverse incentive to legislate broadly pursuant to the Commerce Clause—nestling questionable assertions of its authority into comprehensive regulatory schemes—rather than with precision. That rule and the result it produces in this case are irreconcilable with our decisions in *Lopez* and *Morrison*. Accordingly I dissent.

The Court's principal means of distinguishing *Lopez* from this case is to observe that the Gun-Free School Zones Act of 1990 was a "brief, single-subject statute," whereas the CSA is "a lengthy and detailed statute creating a comprehensive framework for regulating the production, distribution, and possession of five classes of 'controlled substances.'" Thus, according to the Court, it was possible in *Lopez* to evaluate in isolation the constitutionality of criminalizing local activity (there gun possession in school zones), whereas the local activity that the CSA targets (in this case cultivation and possession of marijuana for personal medicinal use) cannot be separated from the general drug control scheme of which it is a part.

Today's decision allows Congress to regulate intrastate activity without check, so long as there is some implication by legislative design that regulating intrastate activity is essential (and the Court appears to equate "essential" with "necessary") to the interstate regulatory scheme. Seizing upon our language in *Lopez* that the statute prohibiting gun possession in school zones was "not an essential part of a larger regulation of economic activity, in which the regulatory scheme could be undercut unless the intrastate activity were regulated," the Court appears to reason that the placement of local activity in a comprehensive scheme confirms that it is essential to that scheme. If the Court is right, then *Lopez* stands for nothing more than a drafting guide: Congress should have described the relevant crime as "transfer or possession of a firearm anywhere in the nation" — thus including commercial and noncommercial activity, and clearly encompassing some activity with assuredly substantial effect on interstate commerce. Had it done so, the majority hints, we would have sustained its authority to regulate possession of firearms in school zones. Furthermore, today's decision suggests we would readily sustain a congressional decision to attach the regulation of intrastate activity to a pre-existing comprehensive (or even not-so-comprehensive) scheme. If so, the Court invites increased federal regulation of local activity even if, as it suggests, Congress would not enact a new interstate scheme exclusively for the sake of reaching intrastate activity. I cannot agree that our decision in *Lopez* contemplated such evasive or overbroad legislative strategies with approval. Until today, such arguments have been made only in dissent. If the Court always defers to Congress as it does today, little may be left to the notion of enumerated powers.

A number of objective markers are available to confine the scope of constitutional review here. Both federal and state legislation — including the CSA itself, the California Compassionate Use Act, and other state medical marijuana legislation — recognize that medical and nonmedical (i.e., recreational) uses of drugs are realistically distinct and can be segregated, and regulate them differently. Respondents challenge only the application of the CSA to medicinal use of marijuana. Moreover, because fundamental structural concerns about dual sovereignty animate our Commerce Clause cases, it is relevant that this case involves the interplay of federal and state regulation in areas of criminal law and social policy, where "States lay claim by right of history and expertise." Under our precedents, the conduct is economic and, in the aggregate, substantially affects interstate commerce. Even if intrastate cultivation and possession of marijuana for one's own medicinal use can properly be characterized as economic, and I question whether it can, it has not been shown that such activity substantially affects interstate commerce. Similarly, it is neither self-evident nor demonstrated that regulating such activity is necessary to the interstate drug control scheme.

The Court's definition of economic activity is breathtaking. It defines as economic any activity involving the production, distribution, and consumption of commodities. And it appears to reason that when an interstate market for a commodity exists, regulating the intrastate manufacture or possession of that commodity is constitutional either because that intrastate activity is itself economic, or because regulating it is a rational part of regulating its market. Putting to one side the problem endemic to the Court's opinion — the shift in focus from the activity at issue in this case to the entirety of what the CSA regulates — the Court's definition of economic activity for purposes of Commerce Clause jurisprudence threatens to sweep all of productive human activity into federal regulatory reach.

Even assuming that economic activity is at issue in this case, the Government has made no showing in fact that the possession and use of homegrown marijuana for medical purposes, in California or elsewhere, has a substantial effect on interstate commerce. Similarly, the Government has not shown that regulating such activity is necessary to an interstate regulatory scheme. Whatever the specific theory of "substantial effects" at issue (i.e., whether the activity substantially affects interstate commerce, whether its regulation is necessary to an interstate regulatory scheme, or both), a concern for dual sovereignty requires that Congress' excursion into the traditional domain of States be justified.

That is why characterizing this as a case about the Necessary and Proper Clause does not change the analysis significantly. Congress must exercise its authority under the Necessary and Proper Clause in a manner consistent with basic constitutional principles. Likewise, that authority must be used in a manner consistent with the notion of enumerated powers — a structural principle that is as much part of the Constitution as the Tenth Amendment's explicit textual command. Accordingly, something more than mere assertion is required when Congress purports to have power over local activity whose connection to an intrastate market is not self-evident. Otherwise, the Necessary and Proper Clause will always be a back door for unconstitutional federal regulation. Indeed, if it were enough in "substantial effects" cases for the Court to supply conceivable justifications for intrastate regulation related to an interstate market, then we could have surmised in *Lopez* that guns in school zones are "never more than an instant from the interstate market" in guns already subject to extensive federal regulation, recast *Lopez* as a Necessary and Proper Clause case, and thereby upheld the Gun-Free School Zones Act of 1990.

There is simply no evidence that homegrown medicinal marijuana users constitute, in the aggregate, a sizable enough class to have a discernable, let alone substantial, impact on the national illicit drug market — or otherwise to threaten the CSA regime.

The Government has not overcome empirical doubt that the number of Californians engaged in personal cultivation, possession, and use of medical marijuana, or the amount of marijuana they produce, is enough to threaten the federal regime. Nor has it shown that Compassionate Use Act marijuana users have been or are realistically likely to be responsible for the drug's seeping into the market in a significant way. The Government does cite one estimate that there were over 100,000 Compassionate Use Act users in California in 2004, but does not explain, in terms of proportions, what their presence means for the national illicit drug market.

Relying on Congress' abstract assertions, the Court has endorsed making it a federal crime to grow small amounts of marijuana in one's own home for one's own medicinal use. This overreaching stifles an express choice by some States, concerned for the lives and liberties of their people, to regulate medical marijuana differently. If I were a California citizen, I would not have voted for the medical marijuana ballot initiative; if I were a California legislator I would not have supported the Compassionate Use Act. But whatever the wisdom of California's experiment with medical marijuana, the federalism principles that have driven our Commerce Clause cases require that room for experiment be protected in this case. For these reasons I dissent.

Justice THOMAS, dissenting.

Respondents Diane Monson and Angel Raich use marijuana that has never been bought or sold, that has never crossed state lines, and that has had no demonstrable effect on the national market for marijuana. If Congress can regulate this under the Commerce Clause, then it can regulate virtually anything — and the Federal Government is no longer one of limited and enumerated powers.

Respondents' local cultivation and consumption of marijuana is not "Commerce . . . among the several States." By holding that Congress may regulate activity that is neither interstate nor commerce under the Interstate Commerce Clause, the Court abandons any attempt to enforce the Constitution's limits on federal power. The majority supports this conclusion by invoking, without explanation, the Necessary and Proper Clause. Regulating respondents' conduct, however, is not "necessary and proper for carrying into Execution" Congress' restrictions on the interstate drug trade. Thus, neither the Commerce Clause nor the Necessary and Proper Clause grants Congress the power to regulate respondents' conduct.

As I explained at length in *United States v. Lopez* (1995), the Commerce Clause empowers Congress to regulate the buying and selling of goods and services trafficked across state lines. The Clause's text, structure, and history all indicate that, at the time of the founding, the term "'commerce' consisted of selling, buying, and bartering, as well as transporting for these purposes." Commerce, or trade, stood in contrast to productive activities like manufacturing and agriculture.

Certainly no evidence from the founding suggests that "commerce" included the mere possession of a good or some purely personal activity that did not involve trade or exchange for value. In the early days of the Republic, it would have been unthinkable that Congress could prohibit the local cultivation, possession, and consumption of marijuana.

More difficult, however, is whether the CSA is a valid exercise of Congress' power to enact laws that are "necessary and proper for carrying into Execution" its power to regulate interstate commerce. The Necessary and Proper Clause is not a warrant to Congress to enact any law that bears some conceivable connection to the exercise of an enumerated power. Nor is it, however, a command to Congress to enact only laws that are absolutely indispensable to the exercise of an enumerated power.

Respondents are not regulable simply because they belong to a large class (local growers and users of marijuana) that Congress might need to reach, if they also belong to a distinct and separable subclass (local growers and users of state-authorized, medical marijuana) that does not undermine the CSA's interstate ban. California's Compassionate Use Act sets respondents' conduct apart from other intrastate producers and users of marijuana.

In sum, neither in enacting the CSA nor in defending its application to respondents has the Government offered any obvious reason why banning medical marijuana use is necessary to stem the tide of interstate drug trafficking. Congress' goal of curtailing the interstate drug trade would not plainly be thwarted if it could not apply the CSA to patients like Monson and Raich. That is, unless Congress' aim is really to exercise police power of the sort reserved to the States in order to eliminate even the intrastate possession and use of marijuana.

The majority prevents States like California from devising drug policies that they have concluded provide much-needed respite to the seriously ill. It does so without any serious inquiry into the necessity for federal regulation or the propriety of "displac[ing] state regulation in areas of traditional state concern." The majority's rush to embrace federal power "is especially unfortunate given the importance of showing respect for the sovereign States that comprise our Federal Union." Our federalist system, properly understood, allows California and a growing number of other States to decide for themselves how to safeguard the health and welfare of their citizens. I would affirm the judgment of the Court of Appeals.

b. Does the Tenth Amendment Limit Congress's Authority?

The first indication of the revival of the Tenth Amendment occurred in Gregory v. Ashcroft, 501 U.S. 452 (1991). State court judges in Missouri challenged a provision of the Missouri Constitution that set a mandatory retirement age as violating the federal Age Discrimination in Employment Act. The Supreme Court held that a federal law will be applied to important state government activities only if there is a clear statement from Congress that the law was meant to apply. The Court did not use the Tenth Amendment to invalidate the federal law on its face or as applied. Instead, the Court used the Tenth Amendment and federalism considerations as a rule of construction. The Court ruled that a federal law that imposes a substantial burden on a state government will be applied only if Congress clearly indicated that it wanted the law to apply. The Age Discrimination in Employment Act lacks such a clear statement, and hence the Court refused to apply it to preempt the Missouri mandatory retirement age. Justice O'Connor, writing for the Court, discussed the importance of autonomous state governments as a check on possible federal tyranny and stressed the significance of the Tenth Amendment as a constitutional protector of state sovereignty.

There have been two decisions following Gregory v. Ashcroft that used the Tenth Amendment to invalidate federal laws: New York v. United States and Printz v. United States.

NEW YORK v. UNITED STATES
505 U.S. 144 (1992)

Justice O'CONNOR delivered the opinion of the Court.

These cases implicate one of our Nation's newest problems of public policy and perhaps our oldest question of constitutional law. The public policy issue involves the disposal of radioactive waste: In these cases, we address the constitutionality of three provisions of the Low-Level Radioactive Waste Policy Amendments Act of 1985. The constitutional question is as old as the Constitution: It consists of discerning the proper division of authority between the Federal Government and the States. We conclude that while Congress has substantial power under the Constitution to encourage the States to provide for the disposal of the radioactive waste generated within their borders, the Constitution does not confer upon Congress the ability simply to compel the States to do so.

I

We live in a world full of low level radioactive waste. Radioactive material is present in luminous watch dials, smoke alarms, measurement devices, medical fluids, research materials, and the protective gear and construction materials used by workers at nuclear power plants. Low level radioactive waste is generated by the Government, by hospitals, by research institutions, and by various industries. The waste must be isolated from humans for long periods of time, often for hundreds of years. Millions of cubic feet of low level radioactive waste must be disposed of each year.

The 1985 Act was based largely on a proposal submitted by the National Governors' Association. The Act provides three types of incentives to encourage the States to comply with their statutory obligation to provide for the disposal of waste generated within their borders. [The Court described the first two as monetary incentives to encourage opening waste sites and access incentives, allowing states without sites to be denied access to other states' sites. The focus of the case is on the third type of incentive.]

The take title provision. The third type of incentive is the most severe. The Act provides:

> If a State (or, where applicable, a compact region) in which low-level radioactive waste is generated is unable to provide for the disposal of all such waste generated within such State or compact region by January 1, 1996, each State in which such waste is generated, upon the request of the generator or owner of the waste, shall take title to the waste, be obligated to take possession of the waste, and shall be liable for all damages directly or indirectly incurred by such generator or owner as a consequence of the failure of the State to take possession of the waste as soon after January 1, 1996, as the generator or owner notifies the State that the waste is available for shipment.

II

A

The task of ascertaining the constitutional line between federal and state power has given rise to many of the Court's most difficult and celebrated cases.

These questions can be viewed in either of two ways. In some cases the Court has inquired whether an Act of Congress is authorized by one of the powers delegated to Congress in Article I of the Constitution. See, e.g., Perez v. United States (1971); McCulloch v. Maryland (1819). In other cases the Court has sought to determine whether an Act of Congress invades the province of state sovereignty reserved by the Tenth Amendment. See, e.g., Garcia v. San Antonio Metropolitan Transit Authority (1985). In a case like these, involving the division of authority between federal and state governments, the two inquiries are mirror images of each other. If a power is delegated to Congress in the Constitution, the Tenth Amendment expressly disclaims any reservation of that power to the States; if a power is an attribute of state sovereignty reserved by the Tenth Amendment, it is necessarily a power the Constitution has not conferred on Congress.

Congress exercises its conferred powers subject to the limitations contained in the Constitution. Thus, for example, under the Commerce Clause Congress may regulate publishers engaged in interstate commerce, but Congress is constrained in the exercise of that power by the First Amendment. The Tenth Amendment likewise restrains the power of Congress, but this limit is not derived from the text of the Tenth Amendment itself, which, as we have discussed, is essentially a tautology. Instead, the Tenth Amendment confirms that the power of the Federal Government is subject to limits that may, in a given instance, reserve power to the States. The Tenth Amendment thus directs us to determine, as in this case, whether an incident of state sovereignty is protected by a limitation on an Article I power.

B

Petitioners do not contend that Congress lacks the power to regulate the disposal of low level radioactive waste. Space in radioactive waste disposal sites is frequently sold by residents of one State to residents of another. Regulation of the resulting interstate market in waste disposal is therefore well within Congress's authority under the Commerce Clause. Petitioners likewise do not dispute that under the Supremacy Clause Congress could, if it wished, pre-empt state radioactive waste regulation. Petitioners contend only that the Tenth Amendment limits the power of Congress to regulate in the way it has chosen. Rather than addressing the problem of waste disposal by directly regulating the generators and disposers of waste, petitioners argue, Congress has impermissibly directed the States to regulate in this field.

Most of our recent cases interpreting the Tenth Amendment have concerned the authority of Congress to subject state governments to generally applicable laws. This litigation presents no occasion to apply or revisit the holdings of any of these cases, as this is not a case in which Congress has subjected a State to the same legislation applicable to private parties.

This litigation instead concerns the circumstances under which Congress may use the States as implements of regulation; that is, whether Congress may direct or otherwise motivate the States to regulate in a particular field or a particular way. Our cases have established a few principles that guide our resolution of the issue.

1

As an initial matter, Congress may not simply "commandee[r] the legislative processes of the States by directly compelling them to enact and enforce a federal regulatory program." While Congress has substantial powers to govern the Nation directly, including in areas of intimate concern to the States, the Constitution has never been understood to confer upon Congress the ability to require the States to govern according to Congress's instructions.

Indeed, the question whether the Constitution should permit Congress to employ state governments as regulatory agencies was a topic of lively debate among the framers. In providing for a stronger central government, therefore, the framers explicitly chose a Constitution that confers upon Congress the power to regulate individuals, not States. As we have seen, the Court has consistently respected this choice. We have always understood that even where Congress has the authority under the Constitution to pass laws requiring or prohibiting certain acts, it lacks the power directly to compel the States to require or prohibit those acts. The allocation of power contained in the Commerce Clause, for example, authorizes Congress to regulate interstate commerce directly; it does not authorize Congress to regulate state governments' regulation of interstate commerce.

2

This is not to say that Congress lacks the ability to encourage a State to regulate in a particular way, or that Congress may not hold out incentives to the States as a method of influencing a State's policy choices. Our cases have identified a variety of methods, short of outright coercion, by which Congress may urge a State to adopt a legislative program consistent with federal interests. Two of these methods are of particular relevance here.

First, under Congress's spending power, "Congress may attach conditions on the receipt of federal funds." South Dakota v. Dole (1986). Such conditions must (among other requirements) bear some relationship to the purpose of the federal spending; otherwise, of course, the spending power could render academic the Constitution's other grants and limits of federal authority. Where the recipient of federal funds is a State, as is not unusual today, the conditions attached to the funds by Congress may influence a State's legislative choices.

Second, where Congress has the authority to regulate private activity under the Commerce Clause, we have recognized Congress's power to offer States the choice of regulating that activity according to federal standards or having state law pre-empted by federal regulation. This arrangement, which has been termed "a program of cooperative federalism," is replicated in numerous federal statutory schemes. These include the Clean Water Act; the Occupational Safety and Health Act of 1970; the Resource Conservation and Recovery Act of 1976, and the Alaska National Interest Lands Conservation Act.

By either of these methods, as by any other permissible method of encouraging a State to conform to federal policy choices, the residents of the State retain the ultimate decision as to whether or not the State will comply. If a State's citizens view federal policy as sufficiently contrary to local interests, they may elect to decline a federal grant. If state residents would prefer their government to devote its attention and resources to problems other than those deemed important by Congress, they may choose to have the Federal Government rather than the State bear the expense of a federally mandated regulatory program, and they may continue to supplement that program to the extent state law is not pre-empted. Where Congress encourages state regulation rather than compelling it, state governments remain responsive to the local electorate's preferences; state officials remain accountable to the people.

By contrast, where the Federal Government compels States to regulate, the accountability of both state and federal officials is diminished. If the citizens of New York, for example, do not consider that making provision for the disposal of radioactive waste is in their best interest, they may elect state officials who share their view. That view can always be pre-empted under the Supremacy Clause if it is contrary to the national view, but in such a case it is the Federal Government that makes the decision in full view of the public, and it will be federal officials that suffer the consequences if the decision turns out to be detrimental or unpopular. But where the Federal Government directs the States to regulate, it may be state officials who will bear the brunt of public disapproval, while the federal officials who devised the regulatory program may remain insulated from the electoral ramifications of their decision. Accountability is thus diminished when, due to federal coercion, elected state officials cannot regulate in accordance with the views of the local electorate in matters not pre-empted by federal regulation.

With these principles in mind, we turn to the three challenged provisions of the Low-Level Radioactive Waste Policy Amendments Act of 1985.

III

[The Court upheld the monetary and access incentives created by Congress for states to open waste sites. The Court found that the former was permissible as an exercise of the spending power. The Court found the second was permissible under Congress's authority to encourage compacts among the states.]

C

The take title provision is of a different character. In this provision, Congress has crossed the line distinguishing encouragement from coercion.

The take title provision offers state governments a "choice" of either accepting ownership of waste or regulating according to the instructions of Congress. Respondents do not claim that the Constitution would authorize Congress to impose either option as a freestanding requirement. On one hand, the Constitution would not permit Congress simply to transfer radioactive waste from generators to state governments. Such a forced transfer, standing alone, would in principle be no different than a congressionally compelled subsidy from state governments to radioactive waste producers. The same is true of the provision requiring the States to become liable for the generators' damages. Standing alone, this provision would be indistinguishable from an Act of Congress directing the States to assume the liabilities of certain state residents. Either type of federal action would "commandeer" state governments into the service of federal regulatory purposes, and would for this reason be inconsistent with the Constitution's division of authority between federal and state governments. On the other hand, the second alternative held out to state governments — regulating pursuant to Congress's direction — would, standing alone, present a simple command to state governments to implement legislation enacted by Congress. As we have seen, the Constitution does not empower Congress to subject state governments to this type of instruction.

Because an instruction to state governments to take title to waste, standing alone, would be beyond the authority of Congress, and because a direct order to regulate, standing alone, would also be beyond the authority of Congress, it follows that Congress lacks the power to offer the States a choice between the two. A choice between two unconstitutionally coercive regulatory techniques is no choice at all. Either way, "the Act commandeers the legislative processes of the States by directly compelling them to enact and enforce a federal regulatory program," Hodel v. Virginia Surface Mining & Reclamation Assn., Inc., an outcome that has never been understood to lie within the authority conferred upon Congress by the Constitution.

Respondents emphasize the latitude given to the States to implement Congress's plan. The Act enables the States to regulate pursuant to Congress's instructions in any number of different ways. States may avoid taking title by contracting with sited regional compacts, by building a disposal site alone or as part of a compact, or by permitting private parties to build a disposal site. States that host sites may employ a wide range of designs and disposal methods, subject only to broad federal regulatory limits. This line of reasoning, however, only underscores the critical alternative a State lacks: A State may not decline to administer the federal program. No matter which path the State chooses, it must follow the direction of Congress.

The take title provision appears to be unique. No other federal statute has been cited which offers a state government no option other than that of implementing legislation enacted by Congress. Whether one views the take title provision as lying outside Congress's enumerated powers, or as infringing upon the core of state sovereignty reserved by the Tenth Amendment, the provision is inconsistent with the federal structure of our Government established by the Constitution.

The United States argues that the Constitution's prohibition of congressional directives to state governments can be overcome where the federal interest is sufficiently important to justify state submission. But whether or not a particularly strong federal interest enables Congress to bring state governments within the orbit of generally applicable federal regulation, no Member of the Court has ever suggested that such a federal interest would enable Congress to command a state government to enact state regulation. No matter how powerful the federal interest involved, the Constitution simply does not give Congress the authority to require the States to regulate. The Constitution instead gives Congress the authority to regulate matters directly and to pre-empt contrary state regulation. Where a federal interest is sufficiently strong to cause Congress to legislate, it must do so directly; it may not conscript state governments as its agents. The sited state respondents focus their attention on the process by which the Act was formulated. They correctly observe that public officials representing the State of New York lent their support to the Act's enactment. Respondents note that the Act embodies a bargain among the sited and unsited States, a compromise to which New York was a willing participant and from which New York has reaped much benefit. Respondents then pose what appears at first to be a troubling question: How can a federal statute be found an unconstitutional infringement of state sovereignty when state officials consented to the statute's enactment?

The answer follows from an understanding of the fundamental purpose served by our Government's federal structure. The Constitution does not protect the sovereignty of States for the benefit of the States or state governments as abstract political entities, or even for the benefit of the public officials governing the States. To the contrary, the Constitution divides authority between federal and state governments for the protection of individuals. State sovereignty is not just an end in itself: "Rather, federalism secures to citizens the liberties that derive from the diffusion of sovereign power. Just as the separation and independence of the coordinate branches of the Federal Government serves to prevent the accumulation of excessive power in any one branch, a healthy balance of power between the States and the Federal Government will reduce the risk of tyranny and abuse from either front." Gregory v. Ashcroft (1991).

Where Congress exceeds its authority relative to the States, therefore, the departure from the constitutional plan cannot be ratified by the "consent" of state officials. An analogy to the separation of powers among the branches of the Federal Government clarifies this point. The Constitution's division of power among the three branches is violated where one branch invades the territory of another, whether or not the encroached-upon branch approves the encroachment. State officials thus cannot consent to the enlargement of the powers of Congress beyond those enumerated in the Constitution.

States are not mere political subdivisions of the United States. State governments are neither regional offices nor administrative agencies of the Federal Government. The positions occupied by state officials appear nowhere on the Federal Government's most detailed organizational chart. The Constitution instead "leaves to the several States a residuary and inviolable sovereignty," The Federalist No. 39, reserved explicitly to the States by the Tenth Amendment. Whatever the outer limits of that sovereignty may be, one thing is clear: The Federal Government may not compel the States to enact or administer a federal regulatory program. The Constitution permits both the Federal Government and the States to enact legislation regarding the disposal of low level radioactive waste. The Constitution enables the Federal Government to pre-empt state regulation contrary to federal interests, and it permits the Federal Government to hold out incentives to the States as a means of encouraging them to adopt suggested regulatory schemes. It does not, however, authorize Congress simply to direct the States to provide for the disposal of the radioactive waste generated within their borders. While there may be many constitutional methods of achieving regional self-sufficiency in radioactive waste disposal, the method Congress has chosen is not one of them.

Justice WHITE, with whom Justice BLACKMUN and Justice STEVENS join, concurring in part and dissenting in part.

The Court today affirms the constitutionality of two facets of the Low-Level Radioactive Waste Policy Amendments Act of 1985 (1985 Act). These provisions include the monetary incentives from surcharges collected by States with low-level radioactive waste storage sites, and the "access incentives," which deny access to disposal sites for States that fail to meet certain deadlines for low-level radioactive waste disposal management. The Court strikes down and severs a third component of the 1985 Act, the "take title" provision, which requires a noncomplying State to take title to or to assume liability for its low-level radioactive waste if it fails to provide for the disposal of such waste by January 1, 1996. The Court deems this last provision unconstitutional under principles of federalism. Because I believe the Court has mischaracterized the essential inquiry, misanalyzed the inquiry it has chosen to undertake, and undervalued the effect the seriousness of this public policy problem should have on the constitutionality of the take title provision, I respectfully dissent from [this aspect] of its opinion.

I

My disagreement with the Court's analysis begins at the basic descriptive level of how the legislation at issue in these cases came to be enacted. The Court goes some way toward setting out the bare facts, but its omissions cast the statutory context of the take title provision in the wrong light. To read the Court's version of events, one would think that Congress was the sole proponent of a solution to the Nation's low-level radioactive waste problem. Not so. The Low-Level Radioactive Waste Policy Act of 1980 (1980 Act), and its amendatory 1985 Act, resulted from the efforts of state leaders to achieve a state-based set of remedies to the waste problem. They sought not federal pre-emption or intervention, but rather congressional sanction of interstate compromises they had reached.

The two signal events in 1979 that precipitated movement toward legislation were the temporary closing of the Nevada disposal site in July 1979, after several serious transportation-related incidents, and the temporary shutting of the Washington disposal site because of similar transportation and packaging problems in October 1979. At that time the facility in Barnwell, South Carolina, received approximately three-quarters of the Nation's low-level radioactive waste, and the Governor ordered a 50 percent reduction in the amount his State's plant would accept for disposal. The Governor of Washington threatened to shut down the Hanford, Washington, facility entirely by 1982 unless "some meaningful progress occurs toward" development of regional solutions to the waste disposal problem. Only three sites existed in the country for the disposal of low-level radioactive waste, and the "sited" States confronted the undesirable alternatives either of continuing to be the dumping grounds for the entire Nation's low-level waste or of eliminating or reducing in a constitutional manner the amount of waste accepted for disposal.

The imminence of a crisis in low-level radioactive waste management cannot be overstated. Accordingly, the National Governors' Association Task Force urged that "each state should accept primary responsibility for the safe disposal of low-level radioactive waste generated within its borders" and that "the states should pursue a regional approach to the low-level waste disposal problem."

A movement thus arose to achieve a compromise between the sited and the unsited States, in which the sited States agreed to continue accepting waste in exchange for the imposition of stronger measures to guarantee compliance with the unsited States' assurances that they would develop alternative disposal facilities. The bill that in large measure became the 1985 Act "represent[ed] the diligent negotiating undertaken by" the National Governors' Association and "embodied" the "fundamentals of their settlement."

Unlike legislation that directs action from the Federal Government to the States, the 1980 and 1985 Acts reflected hard-fought agreements among States as refereed by Congress. The distinction is key, and the Court's failure properly to characterize this legislation ultimately affects its analysis of the take title provision's constitutionality.

II

Even were New York not to be estopped from challenging the take title provision's constitutionality, I am convinced that, seen as a term of an agreement entered into between the several States, this measure proves to be less constitutionally odious than the Court opines. First, the practical effect of New York's position is that because it is unwilling to honor its obligations to provide in-state storage facilities for its low-level radioactive waste, other States with such plants must accept New York's waste, whether they wish to or not. Otherwise, the many economically and socially beneficial producers of such waste in the State would have to cease their operations. The Court's refusal to force New York to accept responsibility for its own problem inevitably means that some other State's sovereignty will be impinged by it being forced, for public health reasons, to accept New York's low-level radioactive waste. I do not understand the principle of federalism to impede the National Government from acting as referee among the States to prohibit one from bullying another.

Moreover, it is utterly reasonable that, in crafting a delicate compromise between the three overburdened States that provided low-level radioactive waste disposal facilities and the rest of the States, Congress would have to ratify some punitive measure as the ultimate sanction for noncompliance. The take title provision, though surely onerous, does not take effect if the generator of the waste does not request such action, or if the State lives up to its bargain of providing a waste disposal facility either within the State or in another State pursuant to a regional compact arrangement or a separate contract.

III

The Court announces that it has no occasion to revisit such decisions as Gregory v. Ashcroft (1991); South Carolina v. Baker (1988); Garcia v. San Antonio Metropolitan Transit Authority (1985); EEOC v. Wyoming (1983); and National League of Cities v. Usery (1976). Although this statement sends the welcome signal that the Court does not intend to cut a wide swath through our recent Tenth Amendment precedents, it nevertheless is unpersuasive. I have several difficulties with the Court's analysis in this respect: It builds its rule around an insupportable and illogical distinction in the types of alleged incursions on state sovereignty; it derives its rule from cases that do not support its analysis; it fails to apply the appropriate tests from the cases on which it purports to base its rule; and it omits any discussion of the most recent and pertinent test for determining the take title provision's constitutionality.

The Court's distinction between a federal statute's regulation of States and private parties for general purposes, as opposed to a regulation solely on the activities of States, is unsupported by our recent Tenth Amendment cases. In no case has the Court rested its holding on such a distinction. Moreover, the Court makes no effort to explain why this purported distinction should affect the analysis of Congress's power under general principles of federalism and the Tenth Amendment. The distinction, facilely thrown out, is not based on any defensible theory. An incursion on state sovereignty hardly seems more constitutionally acceptable if the federal statute that "commands" specific action also applies to private parties. The alleged diminution in state authority over its own affairs is not any less because the federal mandate restricts the activities of private parties.

Given the scanty textual support for the majority's position, it would be far more sensible to defer to a coordinate branch of government in its decision to devise a solution to a national problem of this kind. Certainly in other contexts, principles of federalism have not insulated States from mandates by the National Government. The Court has upheld congressional statutes that impose clear directives on state officials, including those enacted pursuant to the Extradition Clause, see, e.g., Puerto Rico v. Branstad (1987), the post-Civil War Amendments, see, e.g., South Carolina v. Katzenbach (1966), as well as congressional statutes that require state courts to hear certain actions, see, e.g., Testa v. Katt (1947).

IV

Though I disagree with the Court's conclusion that the take title provision is unconstitutional, I do not read its opinion to preclude Congress from adopting a similar measure through its powers under the Spending or Commerce Clauses. The Court makes clear that its objection is to the alleged "commandeer[ing]" quality of the take title provision. The spending power offers a means of enacting a take title provision under the Court's standards. Congress could, in other words, condition the payment of funds on the State's willingness to take title if it has not already provided a waste disposal facility.

Similarly, should a State fail to establish a waste disposal facility by the appointed deadline (under the statute as presently drafted, January 1, 1996) Congress has the power pursuant to the Commerce Clause to regulate directly the producers of the waste. Thus, as I read it, Congress could amend the statute to say that if a State fails to meet the January 1, 1996, deadline for achieving a means of waste disposal, and has not taken title to the waste, no low-level radioactive waste may be shipped out of the State of New York. This background suggests that the threat of federal pre-emption may suffice to induce States to accept responsibility for failing to meet critical time deadlines for solving their low-level radioactive waste disposal problems, especially if that federal intervention also would strip state and local authorities of any input in locating sites for low-level radioactive waste disposal facilities. And should Congress amend the statute to meet the Court's objection and a State refuse to act, the National Legislature will have ensured at least a federal solution to the waste management problem.

Finally, our precedents leave open the possibility that Congress may create federal rights of action in the generators of low-level radioactive waste against persons acting under color of state law for their failure to meet certain functions designated in federal-state programs.

V

The ultimate irony of the decision today is that in its formalistically rigid obeisance to "federalism," the Court gives Congress fewer incentives to defer to the wishes of state officials in achieving local solutions to local problems. By invalidating the measure designed to ensure compliance for recalcitrant States, such as New York, the Court upsets the delicate compromise achieved among the States and forces Congress to erect several additional formalistic hurdles to clear before achieving exactly the same objective. Because the Court's justifications for undertaking this step are unpersuasive to me, I respectfully dissent.

Justice STEVENS, concurring in part and dissenting in part.

Under the Articles of Confederation, the Federal Government had the power to issue commands to the States. Because that indirect exercise of federal power proved ineffective, the framers of the Constitution empowered the Federal Government to exercise legislative authority directly over individuals within the States, even though that direct authority constituted a greater intrusion on state sovereignty. Nothing in that history suggests that the Federal Government may not also impose its will upon the several States as it did under the Articles. The Constitution enhanced, rather than diminished, the power of the Federal Government.

The notion that Congress does not have the power to issue "a simple command to state governments to implement legislation enacted by Congress," is incorrect and unsound. There is no such limitation in the Constitution. The Tenth Amendment surely does not impose any limit on Congress's exercise of the powers delegated to it by Article I. Nor does the structure of the constitutional order or the values of federalism mandate such a formal rule. To the contrary, the Federal Government directs state governments in many realms. The Government regulates state-operated railroads, state school systems, state prisons, state elections, and a host of other state functions. Similarly, there can be no doubt that, in time of war, Congress could either draft soldiers itself or command the States to supply their quotas of troops. I see no reason why Congress may not also command the States to enforce federal water and air quality standards or federal standards for the disposition of low-level radioactive wastes.

PRINTZ v. UNITED STATES

521 U.S. 898 (1997)

Justice SCALIA delivered the opinion of the Court.

The question presented in these cases is whether certain interim provisions of the Brady Handgun Violence Prevention Act, commanding state and local law enforcement officers to conduct background checks on prospective handgun purchasers and to perform certain related tasks, violate the Constitution.

I

The Gun Control Act of 1968 (GCA), establishes a detailed federal scheme governing the distribution of firearms. In 1993, Congress amended the GCA by enacting the Brady Act. The Act requires the Attorney General to establish a national instant background check system by November 30, 1998, and immediately puts in place certain interim provisions until that system becomes operative. Under the interim provisions, [state and local law enforcement personnel must do background checks before issuing permit for firearms].

Petitioners Jay Printz and Richard Mack, the chief law enforcement officers [CLEOs] for Ravalli County, Montana, and Graham County, Arizona, respectively, filed separate actions challenging the constitutionality of the Brady Act's interim provisions.

II

From the description set forth above, it is apparent that the Brady Act purports to direct state law enforcement officers to participate, albeit only temporarily, in the administration of a federally enacted regulatory scheme. Regulated firearms dealers are required to forward Brady Forms not to a federal officer or employee, but to the CLEOs, whose obligation to accept those forms is implicit in the duty imposed upon them to make "reasonable efforts" within five days to determine whether the sales reflected in the forms are lawful. While the CLEOs are subjected to no federal requirement that they prevent the sales determined to be unlawful (it is perhaps assumed that their state-law duties will require prevention or apprehension), they are empowered to grant, in effect, waivers of the federally prescribed 5-day waiting period for handgun purchases by notifying the gun dealers that they have no reason to believe the transactions would be illegal.

The petitioners here object to being pressed into federal service, and contend that congressional action compelling state officers to execute federal laws is unconstitutional. Because there is no constitutional text speaking to this precise question, the answer to the CLEOs' challenge must be sought in historical understanding and practice, in the structure of the Constitution, and in the jurisprudence of this Court. We treat those three sources, in that order, in this and the next two sections of this opinion.

Petitioners contend that compelled enlistment of state executive officers for the administration of federal programs is, until very recent years at least, unprecedented. The Government contends, to the contrary, that "the earliest Congresses enacted statutes that required the participation of state officials in the implementation of federal laws," Brief for United States 28. The Government's contention demands our careful consideration, since early congressional enactments "provid[e] 'contemporaneous and weighty evidence' of the Constitution's meaning," Bowsher v. Synar (1986). Indeed, such "contemporaneous legislative exposition of the Constitution . . . , acquiesced in for a long term of years, fixes the construction to be given its provisions." Myers v. United States (1926) (citing numerous cases). Conversely if, as petitioners contend, earlier Congresses avoided use of this highly attractive power, we would have reason to believe that the power was thought not to exist.

The Government observes that statutes enacted by the first Congresses required state courts to record applications for citizenship, to transmit abstracts of citizenship applications and other naturalization records to the Secretary of State, and to register aliens seeking naturalization and issue certificates of registry. It may well be, however, that these requirements applied only in States that authorized their courts to conduct naturalization proceedings.

These early laws establish, at most, that the Constitution was originally understood to permit imposition of an obligation on state judges to enforce federal prescriptions, insofar as those prescriptions related to matters appropriate for the judicial power. [W]e do not think the early statutes imposing obligations on state courts imply a power of Congress to impress the state executive into its service. Indeed, it can be argued that the numerousness of these statutes, contrasted with the utter lack of statutes imposing obligations on the States' executive (notwithstanding the attractiveness of that course to Congress), suggests an assumed absence of such power.

Not only do the enactments of the early Congresses, as far as we are aware, contain no evidence of an assumption that the Federal Government may command the States' executive power in the absence of a particularized constitutional authorization, they contain some indication of precisely the opposite assumption. On September 23, 1789 — the day before its proposal of the Bill of Rights, see 1 Annals of Congress 912-913 — the First Congress enacted a law aimed at obtaining state assistance of the most rudimentary and necessary sort for the enforcement of the new Government's laws: the holding of federal prisoners in state jails at federal expense. Significantly, the law issued not a command to the States' executive, but a recommendation to their legislatures. Moreover, when Georgia refused to comply with the request,

Congress's only reaction was a law authorizing the marshal in any State that failed to comply with the Recommendation of September 23, 1789, to rent a temporary jail until provision for a permanent one could be made.

To complete the historical record, we must note that there is not only an absence of executive-commandeering statutes in the early Congresses, but there is an absence of them in our later history as well, at least until very recent years. The Government points to a number of federal statutes enacted within the past few decades that require the participation of state or local officials in implementing federal regulatory schemes. Some of these are connected to federal funding measures, and can perhaps be more accurately described as conditions upon the grant of federal funding than as mandates to the States; others, which require only the provision of information to the Federal Government, do not involve the precise issue before us here, which is the forced participation of the States' executive in the actual administration of a federal program. For deciding the issue before us here, they are of little relevance. Even assuming they represent assertion of the very same congressional power challenged here, they are of such recent vintage that they are no more probative than the statute before us of a constitutional tradition that lends meaning to the text.

III

The constitutional practice we have examined above tends to negate the existence of the congressional power asserted here, but is not conclusive. We turn next to consideration of the structure of the Constitution, to see if we can discern among its "essential postulate[s]," a principle that controls the present cases.

A

It is incontestible that the Constitution established a system of "dual sovereignty." Gregory v. Ashcroft (1991). Although the States surrendered many of their powers to the new Federal Government, they retained "a residuary and inviolable sovereignty," The Federalist No. 39 (J. Madison). This is reflected throughout the Constitution's text, including (to mention only a few examples) the prohibition on any involuntary reduction or combination of a State's territory, Art. IV, §3; the Judicial Power Clause, Art III, §2, and the Privileges and Immunities Clause, Art. IV, §2, which speak of the "Citizens" of the States; the amendment provision, Article V, which requires the votes of three-fourths of the States to amend the Constitution; and the Guarantee Clause, Art. IV, §4, which "presupposes the continued existence of the states and . . . those means and instrumentalities which are the creation of their sovereign and reserved rights." Residual state sovereignty was also implicit, of course, in the Constitution's conferral upon Congress of not all governmental powers, but only discrete, enumerated ones, Art. I, §8, which implication was rendered express by the Tenth Amendment's assertion that "[t]he powers not delegated to the United States by the Constitution, nor prohibited by it to the States, are reserved to the States respectively, or to the people."

The framers' experience under the Articles of Confederation had persuaded them that using the States as the instruments of federal governance was both ineffectual and provocative of federal-state conflict. See The Federalist No. 15.

Preservation of the States as independent political entities being the price of union, and "[t]he practicality of making laws, with coercive sanctions, for the States as political bodies" having been, in Madison's words, "exploded on all hands," 2 Records of the Federal Convention of 1787, p. 9 (M. Farrand ed. 1911), the framers rejected the concept of a central government that would act upon and through the States, and instead designed a system in which the state and federal governments would exercise concurrent authority over the people—who were, in Hamilton's words, "the only proper objects of government," The Federalist No. 15, at 109.

This separation of the two spheres is one of the Constitution's structural protections of liberty. "Just as the separation and independence of the coordinate branches of the Federal Government serve to prevent the accumulation of excessive power in any one branch, a healthy balance of power between the States and the Federal Government will reduce the risk of tyranny and abuse from either front."

B

We have thus far discussed the effect that federal control of state officers would have upon the first element of the "double security" alluded to by Madison: the division of power between State and Federal Governments. It would also have an effect upon the second element: the separation and equilibration of powers between the three branches of the Federal Government itself. The Constitution does not leave to speculation who is to administer the laws enacted by Congress; the President, it says, "shall take Care that the Laws be faithfully executed," Art. II, §3, personally and through officers whom he appoints (save for such inferior officers as Congress may authorize to be appointed by the "Courts of Law" or by "the Heads of Departments" who are themselves presidential appointees), Art. II, §2. The Brady Act effectively transfers this responsibility to thousands of CLEOs in the 50 States, who are left to implement the program without meaningful Presidential control (if indeed meaningful Presidential control is possible without the power to appoint and remove). The insistence of the framers upon unity in the Federal Executive—to insure both vigor and accountability—is well known. That unity would be shattered, and the power of the President would be subject to reduction, if Congress could act as effectively without the President as with him, by simply requiring state officers to execute its laws.

IV

Finally, and most conclusively in the present litigation, we turn to the prior jurisprudence of this Court. When we were at last confronted squarely with a federal statute that unambiguously required the States to enact or administer a federal regulatory program, our decision should have come as no surprise. At issue in New York v. United States (1992) were the so-called "take title" provisions of the Low-Level Radioactive Waste Policy Amendments Act of 1985, which required States either to enact legislation providing for the disposal of radioactive waste generated within their borders, or to take title to, and possession of the waste. We concluded that Congress could constitutionally require the States to do neither. "The Federal Government," we held, "may not compel the States to enact or administer a federal regulatory program."

The Government contends that New York is distinguishable on the following ground: unlike the "take title" provisions invalidated there, the background-check provision of the Brady Act does not require state legislative or executive officials to make policy, but instead issues a final directive to state CLEOs.

The Government's distinction between "making" law and merely "enforcing" it, between "policymaking" and mere "implementation," is an interesting one. Executive action that has utterly no policymaking component is rare, particularly at an executive level as high as a jurisdiction's chief law-enforcement officer. Is it really true that there is no policymaking involved in deciding, for example, what "reasonable efforts" shall be expended to conduct a background check?

Even assuming, moreover, that the Brady Act leaves no "policymaking" discretion with the States, we fail to see how that improves rather than worsens the intrusion upon state sovereignty. Preservation of the States as independent and autonomous political entities is arguably less undermined by requiring them to make policy in certain fields than by "reduc[ing] [them] to puppets of a ventriloquist Congress." It is an essential attribute of the States' retained sovereignty that they remain independent and autonomous within their proper sphere of authority. It is no more compatible with this independence and autonomy that their officers be "dragooned" into administering federal law, than it would be compatible with the independence and autonomy of the United States that its officers be impressed into service for the execution of state laws.

Finally, the Government puts forward a cluster of arguments that can be grouped under the heading: "The Brady Act serves very important purposes, is most efficiently administered by CLEOs during the interim period, and places a minimal and only temporary burden upon state officers." Assuming all the mentioned factors were true, they might be relevant if we were evaluating whether the incidental application to the States of a federal law of general applicability excessively interfered with the functioning of state governments. But where, as here, it is the whole object of the law to direct the functioning of the state executive, and hence to compromise the structural framework of dual sovereignty, such a "balancing" analysis is inappropriate. It is the very principle of separate state sovereignty that such a law offends, and no comparative assessment of the various interests can overcome that fundamental defect.

We adhere to that principle today, and conclude categorically, as we concluded categorically in *New York*: "The Federal Government may not compel the States to enact or administer a federal regulatory program." The mandatory obligation imposed on CLEOs to perform background checks on prospective handgun purchasers plainly runs afoul of that rule.

We held in *New York* that Congress cannot compel the States to enact or enforce a federal regulatory program. Today we hold that Congress cannot circumvent that prohibition by conscripting the State's officers directly. The Federal Government may neither issue directives requiring the States to address particular problems, nor command the States' officers, or those of their political subdivisions, to administer or enforce a federal regulatory program. It matters not whether policymaking is involved, and no case-by-case weighing of the burdens or benefits is necessary; such commands are fundamentally incompatible with our constitutional system of dual sovereignty.

Justice STEVENS, with whom Justice SOUTER, Justice GINSBURG, and Justice BREYER join, dissenting.

When Congress exercises the powers delegated to it by the Constitution, it may impose affirmative obligations on executive and judicial officers of state and local governments as well as ordinary citizens. This conclusion is firmly supported by the text of the Constitution, the early history of the Nation, decisions of this Court, and a correct understanding of the basic structure of the Federal Government.

These cases do not implicate the more difficult questions associated with congressional coercion of state legislatures addressed in New York v. United States (1992). Nor need we consider the wisdom of relying on local officials rather than federal agents to carry out aspects of a federal program, or even the question whether such officials may be required to perform a federal function on a permanent basis. The question is whether Congress, acting on behalf of the people of the entire Nation, may require local law enforcement officers to perform certain duties during the interim needed for the development of a federal gun control program. It is remarkably similar to the question, heavily debated by the framers of the Constitution, whether the Congress could require state agents to collect federal taxes. Or the question whether Congress could impress state judges into federal service to entertain and decide cases that they would prefer to ignore.

Indeed, since the ultimate issue is one of power, we must consider its implications in times of national emergency. Matters such as the enlistment of air raid wardens, the administration of a military draft, the mass inoculation of children to forestall an epidemic, or perhaps the threat of an international terrorist, may require a national response before federal personnel can be made available to respond. If the Constitution empowers Congress and the President to make an appropriate response, is there anything in the Tenth Amendment, "in historical understanding and practice, in the structure of the Constitution, [or] in the jurisprudence of this Court," that forbids the enlistment of state officers to make that response effective? More narrowly, what basis is there in any of those sources for concluding that it is the Members of this Court, rather than the elected representatives of the people, who should determine whether the Constitution contains the unwritten rule that the Court announces today?

Perhaps today's majority would suggest that no such emergency is presented by the facts of these cases. But such a suggestion is itself an expression of a policy judgment. And Congress's view of the matter is quite different from that implied by the Court today.

The Brady Act was passed in response to what Congress described as an "epidemic of gun violence." H. Rep. No. 103-344, 103rd Cong. 1st Sess. 1985. The Act's legislative history notes that 15,377 Americans were murdered with firearms in 1992, and that 12,489 of these deaths were caused by handguns. Congress expressed special concern that "[t]he level of firearm violence in this country is, by far, the highest among developed nations." The partial solution contained in the Brady Act, a mandatory background check before a handgun may be purchased, has met with remarkable success. Between 1994 and 1996, approximately 6,600 firearm sales each month to potentially dangerous persons were prevented by Brady Act checks; over 70% of the rejected purchasers were convicted or indicted felons. Whether or not the evaluation reflected in the enactment of the Brady Act is correct as to the extent of the danger and the efficacy of the legislation, the congressional decision surely warrants more respect than it is accorded in today's unprecedented decision.

I

The text of the Constitution provides a sufficient basis for a correct disposition of this case. Article I, §8, grants the Congress the power to regulate commerce among the States. Putting to one side the revisionist views expressed by Justice Thomas, there can be no question that provision adequately supports the regulation of commerce in handguns effected by the Brady Act. Moreover, the additional grant of authority in that section of the Constitution "[t]o make all Laws which shall be necessary and proper for carrying into Execution the foregoing Powers" is surely adequate to support the temporary enlistment of local police officers in the process of identifying persons who should not be entrusted with the possession of handguns. In short, the affirmative delegation of power in Article I provides ample authority for the congressional enactment.

Unlike the First Amendment, which prohibits the enactment of a category of laws that would otherwise be authorized by Article I, the Tenth Amendment imposes no restriction on the exercise of delegated powers. Using language that plainly refers only to powers that are "not" delegated to Congress, it provides: "The powers not delegated to the United States by the Constitution, nor prohibited by it to the States, are reserved to the States respectively, or to the people." The Amendment confirms the principle that the powers of the Federal Government are limited to those affirmatively granted by the Constitution, but it does not purport to limit the scope or the effectiveness of the exercise of powers that are delegated to Congress.

There is not a clause, sentence, or paragraph in the entire text of the Constitution of the United States that supports the proposition that a local police officer can ignore a command contained in a statute enacted by Congress pursuant to an express delegation of power enumerated in Article I.

II

Under the Articles of Confederation the National Government had the power to issue commands to the several sovereign states, but it had no authority to govern individuals directly. Thus, it raised an army and financed its operations by issuing requisitions to the constituent members of the Confederacy, rather than by creating federal agencies to draft soldiers or to impose taxes.

That method of governing proved to be unacceptable, not because it demeaned the sovereign character of the several States, but rather because it was cumbersome and inefficient. The basic change in the character of the government that the framers conceived was designed to enhance the power of the national government, not to provide some new, unmentioned immunity for state officers.

Indeed, the historical materials strongly suggest that the Founders intended to enhance the capacity of the federal government by empowering it — as a part of the new authority to make demands directly on individual citizens — to act through local officials. Hamilton made clear that the new Constitution, "by extending the authority of the federal head to the individual citizens of the several States, will enable the government to employ the ordinary magistracy of each, in the execution of its laws." The Federalist No. 27, at 180. Hamilton's meaning was unambiguous; the federal government was to have the power to demand that local officials implement national policy programs.

More specifically, during the debates concerning the ratification of the Constitution, it was assumed that state agents would act as tax collectors for the federal government. The Court's response to this powerful historical evidence is weak. The majority suggests that "none of these statements necessarily implies . . . Congress could impose these responsibilities without the consent of the States." No fair reading of these materials can justify such an interpretation. As Hamilton explained, the power of the government to act on "individual citizens"—including "employ[ing] the ordinary magistracy" of the States—was an answer to the problems faced by a central government that could act only directly "upon the States in their political or collective capacities." The Federalist, No. 27.

More importantly, the fact that Congress did elect to rely on state judges and the clerks of state courts to perform a variety of executive functions, is surely evidence of a contemporary understanding that their status as state officials did not immunize them from federal service. The majority's description of these early statutes is both incomplete and at times misleading.

III

The Court's "structural" arguments are not sufficient to rebut that presumption. The fact that the framers intended to preserve the sovereignty of the several States simply does not speak to the question whether individual state employees may be required to perform federal obligations, such as registering young adults for the draft, creating state emergency response commissions designed to manage the release of hazardous substances, collecting and reporting data on underground storage tanks that may pose an environmental hazard, and reporting traffic fatalities, and missing children, to a federal agency.

As we explained in Garcia v. San Antonio Metropolitan Transit Authority (1985): "[T]he principal means chosen by the framers to ensure the role of the States in the federal system lies in the structure of the Federal Government itself. It is no novelty to observe that the composition of the Federal Government was designed in large part to protect the States from overreaching by Congress." Given the fact that the Members of Congress are elected by the people of the several States, with each State receiving an equivalent number of Senators in order to ensure that even the smallest States have a powerful voice in the legislature, it is quite unrealistic to assume that they will ignore the sovereignty concerns of their constituents. It is far more reasonable to presume that their decisions to impose modest burdens on state officials from time to time reflect a considered judgment that the people in each of the States will benefit therefrom.

Recent developments demonstrate that the political safeguards protecting Our Federalism are effective. The majority expresses special concern that were its rule not adopted the Federal Government would be able to avail itself of the services of state government officials "at no cost to itself." But this specific problem of federal actions that have the effect of imposing so-called "unfunded mandates" on the States has been identified and meaningfully addressed by Congress in recent legislation. See Unfunded Mandates Reform Act of 1995, Pub.L. 104-4, 109 Stat. 48.

Nor is there force to the assumption undergirding the Court's entire opinion that if this trivial burden on state sovereignty is permissible, the entire structure of federalism will soon collapse. These cases do not involve any mandate to state legislatures to enact new rules. When legislative action, or even administrative rulemaking, is at issue, it may be appropriate for Congress either to pre-empt the State's lawmaking power and fashion the federal rule itself, or to respect the State's power to fashion its own rules. But this case, unlike any precedent in which the Court has held that Congress exceeded its powers, merely involves the imposition of modest duties on individual officers. The Court seems to accept the fact that Congress could require private persons, such as hospital executives or school administrators, to provide arms merchants with relevant information about a prospective purchaser's fitness to own a weapon; indeed, the Court does not disturb the conclusion that flows directly from our prior holdings that the burden on police officers would be permissible if a similar burden were also imposed on private parties with access to relevant data. A structural problem that vanishes when the statute affects private individuals as well as public officials is not much of a structural problem.

The provision of the Brady Act that crosses the Court's newly defined constitutional threshold is more comparable to a statute requiring local police officers to report the identity of missing children to the Crime Control Center of the Department of Justice than to an offensive federal command to a sovereign state. If Congress believes that such a statute will benefit the people of the Nation, and serve the interests of cooperative federalism better than an enlarged federal bureaucracy, we should respect both its policy judgment and its appraisal of its constitutional power.

In Reno v. Condon the Supreme Court rejected a Tenth Amendment challenge to the federal Driver's Privacy Protection Act that prohibits state departments of motor vehicles from releasing personal information such as home addresses and Social Security numbers. Strikingly, Reno v. Condon was a unanimous decision by the Supreme Court. As you read the decision, it is important to focus on how the Court distinguishes New York v. United States and Printz v. United States and what principles thus emerge for when Congress can and cannot regulate state governments.

RENO v. CONDON

528 U.S. 141 (2000)

Chief Justice REHNQUIST delivered the opinion of the Court.

The Driver's Privacy Protection Act of 1994 (DPPA or Act) regulates the disclosure of personal information contained in the records of state motor vehicle departments (DMVs). We hold that in enacting this statute Congress did not run afoul of the federalism principles enunciated in New York v. United States (1992) and Printz v. United States (1997).

The DPPA regulates the disclosure and resale of personal information contained in the records of state DMVs. State DMVs require drivers and automobile owners to provide personal information, which may include a person's name, address, telephone number, vehicle description, Social Security number, medical information, and photograph, as a condition of obtaining a driver's license or registering an automobile. Congress found that many States, in turn, sell this personal information to individuals and businesses. These sales generate significant revenues for the States.

The DPPA establishes a regulatory scheme that restricts the States' ability to disclose a driver's personal information without the driver's consent. The DPPA generally prohibits any state DMV, or officer, employee, or contractor thereof, from "knowingly disclos[ing] or otherwise mak[ing] available to any person or entity personal information about any individual obtained by the department in connection with a motor vehicle record." The DPPA defines "personal information" as any information "that identifies an individual, including an individual's photograph, Social Security number, driver identification number, name, address (but not the 5-digit zip code), telephone number, and medical or disability information," but not including "information on vehicular accidents, driving violations, and driver's status."

The DPPA's provisions do not apply solely to States. The Act also regulates the resale and redisclosure of drivers' personal information by private persons who have obtained that information from a state DMV. The DPPA establishes several penalties to be imposed on States and private actors that fail to comply with its requirements.

South Carolina law conflicts with the DPPA's provisions. Under that law, the information contained in the State's DMV records is available to any person or entity that fills out a form listing the requester's name and address and stating that the information will not be used for telephone solicitation.

Following the DPPA's enactment, South Carolina and its Attorney General, respondent Condon, filed suit in the United States District Court for the District of South Carolina, alleging that the DPPA violates the Tenth and Eleventh Amendments to the United States Constitution.

We of course begin with the time-honored presumption that the DPPA is a "constitutional exercise of legislative power." The United States asserts that the DPPA is a proper exercise of Congress's authority to regulate interstate commerce under the Commerce Clause. The United States bases its Commerce Clause argument on the fact that the personal, identifying information that the DPPA regulates is a "thin[g] in interstate commerce," and that the sale or release of that information in interstate commerce is therefore a proper subject of congressional regulation. United States v. Lopez (1995). We agree with the United States' contention. The motor vehicle information which the States have historically sold is used by insurers, manufacturers, direct marketers, and others engaged in interstate commerce to contact drivers with customized solicitations. The information is also used in the stream of interstate commerce by various public and private entities for matters related to interstate motoring. Because drivers' information is, in this context, an article of commerce, its sale or release into the interstate stream of business is sufficient to support congressional regulation.

But the fact that drivers' personal information is, in the context of this case, an article in interstate commerce does not conclusively resolve the constitutionality of the DPPA. In *New York* and *Printz*, we held federal statutes invalid, not because Congress lacked legislative authority over the subject matter, but because those statutes violated the principles of federalism contained in the Tenth Amendment.

South Carolina contends that the DPPA violates the Tenth Amendment because it "thrusts upon the States all of the day-to-day responsibility for administering its complex provisions," and thereby makes "state officials the unwilling implementors of federal policy." South Carolina emphasizes that the DPPA requires the State's employees to learn and apply the Act's substantive restrictions, which are summarized above, and notes that these activities will consume the employees' time and thus the State's resources. South Carolina further notes that the DPPA's penalty provisions hang over the States as a potential punishment should they fail to comply with the Act.

We agree with South Carolina's assertion that the DPPA's provisions will require time and effort on the part of state employees, but reject the State's argument that the DPPA violates the principles laid down in either *New York* or *Printz*. We think, instead, that this case is governed by our decision in South Carolina v. Baker (1988). In *Baker*, we upheld a statute that prohibited States from issuing unregistered bonds because the law "regulate[d] state activities," rather than "seek[ing] to control or influence the manner in which States regulate private parties." We further noted:

> The NGA [National Governor's Association] nonetheless contends that §310 has commandeered the state legislative and administrative process because many state legislatures had to amend a substantial number of statutes in order to issue bonds in registered form and because state officials had to devote substantial effort to determine how best to implement a registered bond system. Such "commandeering" is, however, an inevitable consequence of regulating a state activity. Any federal regulation demands compliance. That a State wishing to engage in certain activity must take administrative and sometimes legislative action to comply with federal standards regulating that activity is a commonplace that presents no constitutional defect.

Like the statute at issue in *Baker*, the DPPA does not require the States in their sovereign capacity to regulate their own citizens. The DPPA regulates the States as the owners of databases. It does not require the South Carolina Legislature to enact any laws or regulations, and it does not require state officials to assist in the enforcement of federal statutes regulating private individuals. We accordingly conclude that the DPPA is consistent with the constitutional principles enunciated in *New York* and *Printz*.

As a final matter, we turn to South Carolina's argument that the DPPA is unconstitutional because it regulates the States exclusively. The essence of South Carolina's argument is that Congress may only regulate the States by means of "generally applicable" laws, or laws that apply to individuals as well as States. But we need not address the question whether general applicability is a constitutional requirement for federal regulation of the States, because the DPPA is generally applicable. The DPPA regulates the universe of entities that participate as suppliers to the market for motor vehicle information —

the States as initial suppliers of the information in interstate commerce and private resellers or redisclosers of that information in commerce.

D.   THE TAXING AND SPENDING POWER

Article I, §8 states that "Congress shall have Power to lay and collect Taxes, Duties, Imposts and Excises, to pay the Debts and provide for the common Defence and general Welfare of the United States; but all Duties, Imposts and Excises shall be uniform throughout the United States." Under the Articles of Confederation, the limited federal government had no taxing power and therefore no revenue to spend. Obviously, in the twentieth century, the power to tax and spend is one of the most important of all Congressional powers.

FOR WHAT PURPOSES MAY CONGRESS TAX AND SPEND?

A basic question concerns the purposes for which Congress may tax and spend. Is Congress limited to taxing and spending only to carry out other powers specifically enumerated in Article I, or does Congress have broad authority to tax and spend for the general welfare? The Court adopted the latter, much more expansive view in United States v. Butler, below.

In reading *Butler*, it is important to distinguish two issues: the scope of Congress's taxing and spending power, and whether the Tenth Amendment is a limit on it. *Butler*'s holding as to the former remains good law, but its ruling as to the Tenth Amendment is no longer followed. It is certainly possible, though, that the reemergence of the Tenth Amendment in decisions such as New York v. United States and Printz v. United States, presented above, may lead the Court to impose some limits on the spending power in the future.

UNITED STATES v. BUTLER
297 U.S. 1 (1936)

Justice ROBERTS delivered the opinion of the Court.

In this case we must determine whether certain provisions of the Agricultural Adjustment Act, 1933, conflict with the Federal Constitution. [The Agricultural Adjustment Act declared that because of a crisis in agricultural production, the Secretary of Agriculture, among other powers, could set limits on production of certain crops and impose taxes on production in excess of these limits. The Act also authorized grants to farmers to control production and thus regulate prices.]

There should be no misunderstanding as to the function of this court in such a case. It is sometimes said that the court assumes a power to overrule or control the action of the people's representatives. This is a misconception. The Constitution is the supreme law of the land ordained and established by the people. All legislation must conform to the principles it lays down. When an act of Congress is appropriately challenged in the courts as not conforming to the constitutional mandate, the judicial branch of the government has only one duty; to lay the article of the Constitution which is invoked beside the statute which is challenged and to decide whether the latter squares with the former. All the court does, or can do, is to announce its considered judgment upon the question.

Article 1, §8, of the Constitution, vests sundry powers in the Congress. The clause thought to authorize the legislation, the first, confers upon the Congress power "to lay and collect Taxes, Duties, Imposts and Excises, to pay the Debts and provide for the common Defence and general Welfare of the United States." It is not contended that this provision grants power to regulate agricultural production upon the theory that such legislation would promote the general welfare. The government concedes that the phrase "to provide for the general welfare" qualifies the power "to lay and collect taxes."

The Congress is expressly empowered to lay taxes to provide for the general welfare. Since the foundation of the nation, sharp differences of opinion have persisted as to the true interpretation of the phrase. Madison asserted it amounted to no more than a reference to the other powers enumerated in the subsequent clauses of the same section; that, as the United States is a government of limited and enumerated powers, the grant of power to tax and spend for the general national welfare must be confined to the enumerated legislative fields committed to the Congress. In this view the phrase is mere tautology, for taxation and appropriation are or may be necessary incidents of the exercise of any of the enumerated legislative powers. Hamilton, on the other hand, maintained the clause confers a power separate and distinct from those later enumerated and is not restricted in meaning by the grant of them, and Congress consequently has a substantive power to tax and to appropriate, limited only by the requirement that it shall be exercised to provide for the general welfare of the United States. Each contention has had the support of those whose views are entitled to weight. This court has noticed the question, but has never found it necessary to decide which is the true construction. Mr. Justice Story, in his Commentaries, espouses the Hamiltonian position. We shall not review the writings of public men and commentators or discuss the legislative practice. Study of all these leads us to conclude that the reading advocated by Mr. Justice Story is the correct one. While, therefore, the power to tax is not unlimited, its confines are set in the clause which confers it, and not in those of section 8 which bestow and define the legislative powers of the Congress. It results that the power of Congress to authorize expenditure of public moneys for public purposes is not limited by the direct grants of legislative power found in the Constitution.

But the adoption of the broader construction leaves the power to spend subject to limitations. We are not now required to ascertain the scope of the phrase "general welfare of the United States" or to determine whether an appropriation in aid of agriculture falls within it. Wholly apart from that question, another principle embedded in our Constitution prohibits the enforcement of the Agricultural [A]djustment Act. The act invades the reserved rights of the states. It is a statutory plan to regulate and control agricultural production, a matter beyond the powers delegated to the federal government. The tax, the appropriation of the funds raised, and the direction for their disbursement, are but parts of the plan. They are but means to an unconstitutional end.

Congress has no power to enforce its commands on the farmer to the ends sought by the Agricultural Adjustment Act. It must follow that it may not indirectly accomplish those ends by taxing and spending to purchase compliance. The Constitution and the entire plan of our government negative any such use of the power to tax and to spend as the act undertakes to authorize. It does not help to declare that local conditions throughout the nation have created a situation of national concern; for this is but to say that whenever there is a widespread similarity of local conditions, Congress may ignore constitutional limitations upon its own powers and usurp those reserved to the states. If, in lieu of compulsory regulation of subjects within the states' reserved jurisdiction, which is prohibited, the Congress could invoke the taxing and spending power as a means to accomplish the same end, clause 1 of section 8 of article 1 would become the instrument for total subversion of the governmental powers reserved to the individual states.

Since, as we have pointed out, there was no power in the Congress to impose the contested exaction, it could not lawfully ratify or confirm what an executive officer had done in that regard.

Justice STONE (dissenting).

I think the judgment should be reversed.

The present stress of widely held and strongly expressed differences of opinion of the wisdom of the Agricultural Adjustment Act makes it important, in the interest of clear thinking and sound result, to emphasize at the outset certain propositions which should have controlling influence in determining the validity of the act. They are:

1. The power of courts to declare a statute unconstitutional is subject to two guiding principles of decision which ought never to be absent from judicial consciousness. One is that courts are concerned only with the power to enact statutes, not with their wisdom. The other is that while unconstitutional exercise of power by the executive and legislative branches of the government is subject to judicial restraint, the only check upon our own exercise of power is our own sense of self-restraint. For removal of unwise laws from the statute books appeal lies, not to the courts, but to the ballot and to the processes of democratic government.

2. The constitutional power of Congress to levy an excise tax upon the processing of agricultural products is not questioned.

3. As the present depressed state of agriculture is nation wide in its extent and effects, there is no basis for saying that the expenditure of public money in aid of farmers is not within the specifically granted power of Congress to levy taxes to "provide for the . . . general welfare." The opinion of the Court does not declare otherwise.

4. No question of a variable tax fixed from time to time by fiat of the Secretary of Agriculture, or of unauthorized delegation of legislative power, is now presented.

It is with these preliminary and hardly controverted matters in mind that we should direct our attention to the pivot on which the decision of the Court is made to turn. It is that a levy unquestionably within the taxing power of Congress may be treated as invalid because it is a step in a plan to regulate agricultural production and is thus a forbidden infringement of state power. The levy is not any the less an exercise of taxing power because it is intended to defray an expenditure for the general welfare rather than for some other support of government. Nor is the levy and collection of the tax pointed to as effecting the regulation. While all federal taxes inevitably have some influence on the internal economy of the states, it is not contended that the levy of a processing tax upon manufacturers using agricultural products as raw material has any perceptible regulatory effect upon either their production or manufacture.

Subsequent cases affirmed Congress's expansive authority under the taxing and spending clauses.

CHAS. C. STEWARD MACH. CO. v. DAVIS, 301 U.S. 548 (1937): Justice CARDOZO delivered the opinion of the Court.

The validity of the tax imposed by the Social Security Act on employers of eight or more is here to be determined. The tax, which is described in the statute as an excise, is laid with uniformity throughout the United States as a duty, an impost, or an excise upon the relation of employment.

We are told that the relation of employment is one so essential to the pursuit of happiness that it may not be burdened with a tax. Appeal is made to history.

As to the argument from history: Doubtless there were many excises in colonial days and later that were associated, more or less intimately, with the enjoyment or the use of property. This would not prove, even if no others were then known, that the forms then accepted were not subject to enlargement. But in truth other excises were known, and known since early times.

The historical prop failing, the prop or fancied prop of principle remains. We learn that employment for lawful gain is a "natural" or "inherent" or "inalienable" right, and not a "privilege" at all. But natural rights, so called, are as much subject to taxation as rights of less importance. It extends to vocations or activities pursued as of common right. What the individual does in the operation of a business is amenable to taxation just as much as what he owns, at all events if the classification is not tyrannical or arbitrary.

The subject-matter of taxation open to the power of the Congress is as comprehensive as that open to the power of the states, though the method of apportionment may at times be different. "The Congress shall have Power to lay and collect Taxes, Duties, Imposts and Excises." Article 1, §8. If the tax is a direct one, it shall be apportioned according to the census or enumeration. If it is a duty, impost, or excise, it shall be uniform throughout the United States. Together, these classes include every form of tax appropriate to sovereignty. The statute books of the states are strewn with illustrations of taxes laid on occupations pursued of common right. We find no basis for a holding that the power in that regard which belongs by accepted practice to the Legislatures of the states, has been denied by the Constitution to the Congress of the nation.

In other cases, the Court construed the spending power broadly in upholding other aspects of the Social Security Act. In Steward Machine Co. v. Davis, 301 U.S. 548 (1937), the Court upheld provisions of the Social Security Act that provide unemployment compensation, and in Helvering v. Davis, 301 U.S. 619 (1937), the Court upheld the provisions of the Social Security Act that provide for an old-age pension program. In both cases, the Court emphasized the broad scope of Congress's spending power.

Many commentators have speculated that the Rehnquist Court's revival of federalism as a limit on federal powers will cause it to restrict the scope of Congress's spending power. Although this still may occur, it has not yet taken place and, in Sabri v. United States, the Court reaffirmed a broad scope for Congress's authority under the spending clause.

SABRI v. UNITED STATES

541 U.S. 600 (2004)

Justice SOUTER delivered the opinion of the Court.

The question is whether 18 U.S.C. §666(a)(2), proscribing bribery of state, local, and tribal officials of entities that receive at least $10,000 in federal funds, is a valid exercise of congressional authority under Article I of the Constitution. We hold that it is.

I

Petitioner Basim Omar Sabri is a real estate developer who proposed to build a hotel and retail structure in the city of Minneapolis. Sabri lacked confidence, however, in his ability to adapt to the lawful administration of licensing and zoning laws, and offered three separate bribes to a city councilman, Brian Herron, according to the grand jury indictment that gave rise to this case. At the time the bribes were allegedly offered (between July 2, 2001, and July 17, 2001), Herron served as a member of the Board of Commissioners of the Minneapolis Community Development Agency (MCDA), a public body created by the city council to fund housing and economic development within the city.

The charges were brought under 18 U.S.C. §666(a)(2), which imposes federal criminal penalties on anyone who "corruptly gives, offers, or agrees to give anything of value to any person, with intent to influence or reward an agent of an organization or of a State, local or Indian tribal government, or any agency thereof, in connection with any business, transaction, or series of transactions of such organization, government, or agency involving anything of value of $5,000 or more." For criminal liability to lie, the statute requires that "the organization, government, or agency receiv[e], in any one year period, benefits in excess of $10,000 under a Federal program involving a grant, contract, subsidy, loan, guarantee, insurance, or other form of Federal assistance." In 2001, the City Council of Minneapolis administered about $29 million in federal funds paid to the city, and in the same period, the MCDA received some $23 million of federal money.

Before trial, Sabri moved to dismiss the indictment on the ground that §666(a)(2) is unconstitutional on its face for failure to require proof of a connection between the federal funds and the alleged bribe, as an element of liability. The Government responded that "even if an additional nexus between the bribery conduct and the federal funds is required, the evidence in this case will easily meet such a standard" because Sabri's alleged actions related to federal dollars. Although Sabri did not contradict this factual claim, the District Court agreed with him that the law was facially invalid. A divided panel of the Eighth Circuit reversed, holding that there was nothing fatal in the absence of an express requirement to prove some connection between a given bribe and federally pedigreed dollars, and that the statute was constitutional under the Necessary and Proper Clause in serving the objects of the congressional spending power.

II

Sabri raises what he calls a facial challenge to §666(a)(2): the law can never be applied constitutionally because it fails to require proof of any connection between a bribe or kickback and some federal money. It is fatal, as he sees it, that the statute does not make the link an element of the crime, to be charged in the indictment and demonstrated beyond a reasonable doubt.

We can readily dispose of this position that, to qualify as a valid exercise of Article I power, the statute must require proof of connection with federal money as an element of the offense. We simply do not presume the unconstitutionality of federal criminal statutes lacking explicit provision of a jurisdictional hook, and there is no occasion even to consider the need for such a requirement where there is no reason to suspect that enforcement of a criminal statute would extend beyond a legitimate interest cognizable under Article I, §8.

Congress has authority under the Spending Clause to appropriate federal monies to promote the general welfare, Art. I, §8, cl. 1, and it has corresponding authority under the Necessary and Proper Clause, Art. I, §8, cl. 18, to see to it that taxpayer dollars appropriated under that power are in fact spent for the general welfare, and not frittered away in graft or on projects undermined when funds are siphoned off or corrupt public officers are derelict about demanding value for dollars. See generally McCulloch v. Maryland (1819). Congress does not have to sit by and accept the risk of operations thwarted by local and state improbity. Section 666(a)(2) addresses the problem at the sources of bribes, by rational means, to safeguard the integrity of the state, local, and tribal recipients of federal dollars.

It is true, just as Sabri says, that not every bribe or kickback offered or paid to agents of governments covered by §666(b) will be traceably skimmed from specific federal payments, or show up in the guise of a quid pro quo for some dereliction in spending a federal grant. But this possibility portends no enforcement beyond the scope of federal interest, for the reason that corruption does not have to be that limited to affect the federal interest. Money is fungible, bribed officials are untrustworthy stewards of federal funds, and corrupt contractors do not deliver dollar-for-dollar value. Liquidity is not a financial term for nothing; money can be drained off here because a federal grant is pouring in there. And officials are not any the less threatening to the objects behind federal spending just because they may accept general retainers. It is certainly enough that the statutes condition the offense on a threshold amount of federal dollars defining the federal interest, such as that provided here, and on a bribe that goes well beyond liquor and cigars.

Justice THOMAS, concurring in the judgment.

I write further because I find questionable the scope the Court gives to the Necessary and Proper Clause as applied to Congress's authority to spend. In particular, the Court appears to hold that the Necessary and Proper Clause authorizes the exercise of any power that is no more than a "rational means" to effectuate one of Congress's enumerated powers. This conclusion derives from the Court's characterization of the seminal case McCulloch v. Maryland (1819), as having established a "means-ends rationality" test, a characterization that I am not certain is correct.

But the Court did not then conclude that the Necessary and Proper Clause gives unrestricted power to the Federal Government. Rather, it set forth the following test: "Let the end be legitimate, let it be within the scope of the constitution, and all means which are appropriate, which are plainly adapted to that end, which are not prohibited, but consist with the letter and spirit of the constitution, are constitutional." "[A]ppropriate" and "plainly adapted" are hardly synonymous with "means-end rationality." Indeed, "plain" means "evident to the mind or senses: obvious," "clear," and "characterized by simplicity: not complicated." Webster's Ninth New Collegiate Dictionary 898 (1991). A statute can have a "rational" connection to an enumerated power without being obviously or clearly tied to that enumerated power. To show that a statute is "plainly adapted" to a legitimate end, then, one must seemingly show more than that a particular statute is a "rational means," to safeguard that end; rather, it would seem necessary to show some obvious, simple, and direct relation between the statute and the enumerated power. Under the McCulloch formulation, I have doubts that §666(a)(2) is a proper use of the Necessary and Proper Clause as applied to Congress's power to spend. All that is necessary for §666(a)(2) to apply is that the organization, government, or agency in question receives more than $10,000 in federal benefits of any kind, and that an agent of the entity is bribed regarding a substantial transaction of that entity. No connection whatsoever between the corrupt transaction and the federal benefits need be shown.

The Court does a not-wholly-unconvincing job of tying the broad scope of §666(a)(2) to a federal interest in federal funds and programs. But simply noting that "[m]oney is fungible," for instance, does not explain how there could be any federal interest in "prosecut[ing] a bribe paid to a city's meat inspector in connection with a substantial transaction just because the city's parks department had received a federal grant of $10,000." United States v. Santopietro (C.A.2 1999). It would be difficult to describe the chain of inferences and assumptions in which the Court would have to indulge to connect such a bribe to a federal interest in any federal funds or programs as being "plainly adapted" to their protection.

Because I would decide this case on the Court's Commerce Clause jurisprudence, I do not ultimately decide whether Congress's power to spend combined with the Necessary and Proper Clause could authorize the enactment of §666(a)(2). But regardless of the particular outcome of this case under the correct test, the Court's approach seems to greatly and improperly expand the reach of Congress's power under the Necessary and Proper Clause. Accordingly, I concur in the judgment.

CONDITIONS ON GRANTS TO STATE GOVERNMENTS

One important issue concerning the spending power concerns the ability of Congress to place conditions on grants to state and local governments. The Court has held that Congress may place strings on such grants, as long as the conditions are expressly stated and as long as they have some relationship to the purpose of the spending program.

In Oklahoma v. Civil Service Commission, 330 U.S. 127 (1947), the Court upheld a provision of the federal Hatch Act which granted federal funds to state governments on the condition that the states adopt civil service systems and limit the political activities of many categories of government workers. The Court explained that Congress has broad power to set conditions for the receipt of federal funds even as to areas that Congress might otherwise not be able to regulate. The Court stated: "While the United States is not concerned with, and has no power to regulate, local political activities as such of state officials, it does have power to fix the terms upon which its money allotments to states shall be disbursed."

In South Dakota v. Dole, the Court upheld conditions on grants to state and local governments but also explained the conditions that must be met.

SOUTH DAKOTA v. DOLE
483 U.S. 203 (1987)

Chief Justice REHNQUIST delivered the opinion of the Court.

Petitioner South Dakota permits persons 19 years of age or older to purchase beer containing up to 3.2% alcohol. In 1984 Congress enacted 23 U.S.C. §158, which directs the Secretary of Transportation to withhold a percentage of federal highway funds otherwise allocable from States "in which the purchase or public possession . . . of any alcoholic beverage by a person who is less than twenty-one years of age is lawful." The State sued in United States District Court seeking a declaratory judgment that §158 violates the constitutional limitations on congressional exercise of the spending power and violates the Twenty-first Amendment to the United States Constitution.

The Constitution empowers Congress to "lay and collect Taxes, Duties, Imposts, and Excises, to pay the Debts and provide for the common Defence and general Welfare of the United States." Incident to this power, Congress may attach conditions on the receipt of federal funds, and has repeatedly employed the power "to further broad policy objectives by conditioning receipt of federal moneys upon compliance by the recipient with federal statutory and administrative directives."

The spending power is of course not unlimited, Pennhurst State School and Hospital v. Halderman (1981), but is instead subject to several general restrictions articulated in our cases. The first of these limitations is derived from the language of the Constitution itself: the exercise of the spending power must be in pursuit of "the general welfare." In considering whether a particular expenditure is intended to serve general public purposes, courts should defer substantially to the judgment of Congress. Second, we have required that if Congress desires to condition the States' receipt of federal funds, it "must do so unambiguously . . . , enabl[ing] the States to exercise their choice knowingly, cognizant of the consequences of their participation." Third, our cases have suggested (without significant elaboration) that conditions on federal grants might be illegitimate if they are unrelated "to the federal interest in particular national projects or programs." Finally, we have noted that other constitutional provisions may provide an independent bar to the conditional grant of federal funds.

South Dakota does not seriously claim that §158 is inconsistent with any of the first three restrictions mentioned above. We can readily conclude that the provision is designed to serve the general welfare. The conditions upon which States receive the funds, moreover, could not be more clearly stated by Congress. Indeed, the condition imposed by Congress is directly related to one of the main purposes for which highway funds are expended — safe interstate travel.

We have also held that a perceived Tenth Amendment limitation on congressional regulation of state affairs did not concomitantly limit the range of conditions legitimately placed on federal grants. Our decisions have recognized that in some circumstances the financial inducement offered by Congress might be so coercive as to pass the point at which "pressure turns into compulsion." Here, however, Congress has directed only that a State desiring to establish a minimum drinking age lower than 21 lose a relatively small percentage of certain federal highway funds. Petitioner contends that the coercive nature of this program is evident from the degree of success it has achieved. We cannot conclude, however, that a conditional grant of federal money of this sort is unconstitutional simply by reason of its success in achieving the congressional objective.

When we consider, for a moment, that all South Dakota would lose if she adheres to her chosen course as to a suitable minimum drinking age is 5% of the funds otherwise obtainable under specified highway grant programs, the argument as to coercion is shown to be more rhetoric than fact.

Justice BRENNAN, dissenting.

I agree with Justice O'Connor that regulation of the minimum age of purchasers of liquor falls squarely within the ambit of those powers reserved to the States by the Twenty-first Amendment. Since States possess this constitutional power, Congress cannot condition a federal grant in a manner that abridges this right. The Amendment, itself, strikes the proper balance between federal and state authority. I therefore dissent.

Justice O'CONNOR, dissenting.

The Court today upholds the National Minimum Drinking Age Amendment, as a valid exercise of the spending power conferred by Article I, §8. But §158 is not a condition on spending reasonably related to the expenditure of federal funds and cannot be justified on that ground. Rather, it is an attempt to regulate the sale of liquor, an attempt that lies outside Congress's power to regulate commerce because it falls within the ambit of §2 of the Twenty-first Amendment.

My disagreement with the Court is relatively narrow on the spending power issue: it is a disagreement about the application of a principle rather than a disagreement on the principle itself. I agree with the Court that Congress may attach conditions on the receipt of federal funds to further "the federal interest in particular national projects or programs."

But the Court's application of the requirement that the condition imposed be reasonably related to the purpose for which the funds are expended is cursory and unconvincing. We have repeatedly said that Congress may condition grants under the spending power only in ways reasonably related to the purpose of the federal program. In my view, establishment of a minimum drinking age of 21 is not sufficiently related to interstate highway construction to justify so conditioning funds appropriated for that purpose.

When Congress appropriates money to build a highway, it is entitled to insist that the highway be a safe one. But it is not entitled to insist as a condition of the use of highway funds that the State impose or change regulations in other areas of the State's social and economic life because of an attenuated or tangential relationship to highway use or safety. Indeed, if the rule were otherwise, the Congress could effectively regulate almost any area of a State's social, political, or economic life on the theory that use of the interstate transportation system is somehow enhanced. If, for example, the United States were to condition highway moneys upon moving the state capital, I suppose it might argue that interstate transportation is facilitated by locating local governments in places easily accessible to interstate highways — or, conversely, that highways might become overburdened if they had to carry traffic to and from the state capital. In my mind, such a relationship is hardly more attenuated than the one which the Court finds supports, §158.

Both the majority and the dissent in South Dakota v. Dole discuss Pennhurst State School and Hospital v. Halderman, 451 U.S. 1 (1981), in which the Supreme Court held that Congress may place strings on grants to state and local governments as long as the conditions are expressly stated. The Developmentally Disabled Assistance and Bill of Rights Act of 1975 created a federal grant program for state governments to provide for better care for the developmentally disabled. The act included a "bill of rights" for the developmentally disabled. The Pennhurst State School and Hospital, a facility run by the State of Pennsylvania, was sued for violating the bill of rights contained in the act.

The Court ruled in favor of the state, holding that "if Congress intends to impose a condition on the grant of federal moneys it must do so unambiguously." The Court explained that conditions must be clearly stated so that states will know the consequences of their choosing to take federal funds. The Court concluded that the act failed to require that states meet the bill of rights as a condition for accepting federal money.

In National Federation of Independent Business v. Sebelius, presented above, the Court for the first time found conditions on federal spending to be unconstitutional as unduly coercive.

E.   CONGRESS'S POWERS UNDER
THE POST-CIVIL WAR AMENDMENTS

After the Civil War, three extremely important amendments were added to the Constitution. The Thirteenth Amendment, adopted in 1865, prohibits slavery and involuntary servitude, except as a punishment for a crime, and also provides in §2, "Congress shall have power to enforce this article by appropriate legislation." The Fourteenth Amendment, adopted in 1868, provides that all persons born or naturalized in the United States are citizens and that no state can abridge the privileges or immunities of such citizens; nor may states deprive any person of life, liberty, or property without due process of law or deny any person of equal protection of the laws. Section 5 of the Fourteenth Amendment states, "[T]he Congress shall have power to enforce, by appropriate legislation, the provisions of this article."

The Fifteenth Amendment declares that "[t]he right of citizens of the United States to vote shall not be denied or abridged by the United States or by any State on account of race, color, or previous condition of servitude." Section 2 again provides that Congress has the power to enforce it by appropriate legislation.

The three Reconstruction-era amendments thus contain provisions that empower Congress to enact civil rights legislation. Two major questions arise concerning the scope of this power. First, may Congress regulate private conduct under this authority, or is Congress limited to regulating only government actions? Second, what is the scope of Congress's power under these amendments?

1.   Whom May Congress Regulate Under the Post-Civil War Amendments?

In the *Civil Rights Cases*, 109 U.S. 3 (1883), the Court held that Congress, pursuant to §2 of the Thirteenth Amendment and §5 of the Fourteenth Amendment, may regulate only state and local government actions, not private conduct.[38] The Civil Rights Act of 1875 provided that all persons were "entitled to the full and equal enjoyment of the accommodations, advantages, facilities and privileges of inns, public conveyances, on land or water, theatres, and other places of public amusement; subject only to the conditions and limitations established by law, and applicable to citizens of every race and color, regardless of any previous condition of servitude." In other words, the law broadly prohibited private racial discrimination by hotels, restaurants, transportation, and other public accommodations.

By an eight-to-one decision, the Court held that the act was unconstitutional and adopted a restrictive view as to the power of Congress to use these provisions to regulate private behavior. As to the Thirteenth Amendment, the Court recognized that it applies to private conduct; it prohibits people from being or owning slaves. The Court, however, said that Congress's power was limited to ensuring an end to slavery; Congress could not use this power to eliminate discrimination. The Court explained that "[i]t would be running the slavery

---

38. The *Civil Rights Cases* are presented in Chapter 5.

argument into the ground to make it apply to every act of discrimination which a person may see fit to make as to the guests he will entertain, or as to the people he will take into his coach or cab or car, or admit to his concert or theatre, or deal with in other matters of intercourse or business." Indeed, the Court stated that Congress could abolish "all badges and incidents of slavery," but it could not use its power under the Thirteenth Amendment to "adjust what may be called the social rights of men and races in the community."

The Court, writing less than 20 years after the Civil War, said that slavery was a thing of the past and that there was little need for civil rights legislation to protect blacks. Justice Bradley, writing for the Court, stated, "When a man has emerged from slavery, and by the aid of beneficent legislation has shaken off the inseparable concomitants of that state, there must be some stage in the progress of his elevation when he takes the rank of a mere citizen and ceases to be the special favorite of the laws, and when his rights as a citizen, or a man, are to be protected in the ordinary modes by which other men's rights are protected."

The Court also held that Congress lacked the authority to enact the law under the Fourteenth Amendment. In fact, the Court broadly declared that the Fourteenth Amendment only applies to government action and that therefore it cannot be used by Congress to regulate private behavior. The Court stated that "the fourteenth amendment is prohibitory . . . upon the states. [Individual] invasion of individual rights is not the subject matter of the amendment." The Court made it clear that Congress's authority was only over state and local governments and their officials, not over private conduct: "It does not authorize Congress to create a code of municipal law for the regulation of private rights; but to provide modes of redress against the operation of State laws, and the actions of State officers."

Now, however, it is well established that Congress, pursuant to §2 of the Thirteenth Amendment, may prohibit private racial discrimination. In Jones v. Alfred H. Mayer Co., 392 U.S. 409 (1968), the Court held that Congress could prohibit private discrimination in selling and leasing property. The case involved a private real estate developer who refused to sell housing or land to African Americans. An African American couple sued under 42 U.S.C. §1982, which provides that all citizens have "the same right, in every State and Territory, as is enjoyed by white citizens thereof to inherit, purchase, lease, sell, hold and convey real and personal property."

The Court held that §1982 applies to prohibit private discrimination and that Congress had the authority under the Thirteenth Amendment to adopt the law. The Court said that Congress has broad legislative power under the Thirteenth Amendment: "Congress has the power under the Thirteenth Amendment rationally to determine what are the badges and incidents of slavery, and the authority to translate that determination into effective legislation."

Similarly, in Runyon v. McCrary, 427 U.S. 160 (1976), the Court held that 42 U.S.C. §1981 applies to prohibit discrimination in private contracting and that this is within the scope of Congress's power under §2 of the Thirteenth Amendment. Section 1981 provides that "[a]ll persons within the jurisdiction of the United States shall have the same right in every State and Territory to make and enforce contracts, to sue, be parties, give evidence, and to the full and equal benefit of all laws and proceedings for the security of persons and property as is enjoyed by white citizens." *Runyon* raised the question of whether §1981 prohibits private schools from excluding qualified African American children solely because of their race.

The Supreme Court saw no basis for distinguishing Jones v. Alfred H. Mayer Co and concluded "that §1981, like §1982, reaches private conduct." The Court unanimously reaffirmed this conclusion in 1989 in Patterson v. McLean Credit Union, 491 U.S. 164 (1989).

However, the Supreme Court recently reaffirmed that Congress cannot regulate private behavior under the Fourteenth Amendment. In United States v. Guest, 383 U.S. 745 (1966), five Justices, although not in a single opinion, concluded that Congress may outlaw private discrimination pursuant to §5 of the Fourteenth Amendment. *Guest* involved the federal law that makes it a crime for two or more persons to go "in disguise on the highway, or on the premises of another, with intent to prevent or hinder his free exercise or enjoyment of any right or privilege." 18 U.S.C. §241. The Court held that interference with the use of facilities in interstate commerce violated the law, whether or not motivated by a racial animus.

The majority opinion did not reach the question of whether Congress could regulate private conduct under §5 of the Fourteenth Amendment. However, six of the justices—three in a concurring opinion and three in a dissenting opinion—expressed the view that Congress could prohibit private discrimination under its §5 powers. Justice Tom Clark, in a concurring opinion joined by Justices Hugo Black and Abe Fortas, said that "the specific language of §5 empowers the Congress to enact laws punishing all conspiracies—with or without state action—that interfere with Fourteenth Amendment rights." Likewise, Justice William Brennan in an opinion that concurred in part and dissented in part, and that was joined by Chief Justice Earl Warren and Justice William Douglas, concluded that Congress may prohibit private discrimination pursuant to §5. However, the Supreme Court recently overruled *Guest* and held that Congress cannot regulate private behavior under §5.

UNITED STATES v. MORRISON
529 U.S. 598 (2000)

[The case is presented above in connection with the Commerce Clause. The issue is the constitutionality of the civil damages provision of the Violence Against Women Act. The case involves a woman who, while a freshman at Virginia Tech University, was allegedly raped by football players. She sued under the civil remedies provision of the act. In the first part of the majority opinion, the Court held that it exceeded the scope of Congress's Commerce Clause authority.[39] In the alternative, the government argued that the law was constitutional as an exercise of Congress's power under §5 of the Fourteenth Amendment.]

Chief Justice REHNQUIST delivered the opinion of the Court:

Because we conclude that the Commerce Clause does not provide Congress with authority to enact §13981, we address petitioners' alternative argument

---

39. The portion of the opinion concerning the Commerce Clause is presented above in section B of this chapter. [Footnote by casebook author.]

that the section's civil remedy should be upheld as an exercise of Congress's remedial power under §5 of the Fourteenth Amendment. As noted above, Congress expressly invoked the Fourteenth Amendment as a source of authority to enact §13981.

Petitioners' §5 argument is founded on an assertion that there is pervasive bias in various state justice systems against victims of gender-motivated violence. This assertion is supported by a voluminous congressional record.

The principles governing an analysis of congressional legislation under §5 are well settled. [T]he language and purpose of the Fourteenth Amendment place certain limitations on the manner in which Congress may attack discriminatory conduct. These limitations are necessary to prevent the Fourteenth Amendment from obliterating the framers' carefully crafted balance of power between the States and the National Government.

Foremost among these limitations is the time-honored principle that the Fourteenth Amendment, by its very terms, prohibits only state action. "[T]he principle has become firmly embedded in our constitutional law that the action inhibited by the first section of the Fourteenth Amendment is only such action as may fairly be said to be that of the States. That Amendment erects no shield against merely private conduct, however discriminatory or wrongful." Shelley v. Kraemer (1948).

Shortly after the Fourteenth Amendment was adopted, we decided two cases interpreting the Amendment's provisions, United States v. Harris (1883), and the *Civil Rights Cases* (1883). We concluded that th[e] law[s] exceeded Congress's §5 power because the law was "directed exclusively against the action of private persons, without reference to the laws of the State, or their administration by her officers." The force of the doctrine of stare decisis behind these decisions stems not only from the length of time they have been on the books, but also from the insight attributable to the Members of the Court at that time. Every Member had been appointed by President Lincoln, Grant, Hayes, Garfield, or Arthur — and each of their judicial appointees obviously had intimate knowledge and familiarity with the events surrounding the adoption of the Fourteenth Amendment.

Petitioners rely on United States v. Guest (1966), for the proposition that the rule laid down in the *Civil Rights Cases* is no longer good law. In *Guest,* the Court reversed the construction of an indictment under 18 U.S.C. §241, saying in the course of its opinion that "we deal here with issues of statutory construction, not with issues of constitutional power." Three Members of the Court, in a separate opinion by Justice Brennan, expressed the view that the *Civil Rights Cases* were wrongly decided, and that Congress could under §5 prohibit actions by private individuals. Three other Members of the Court, who joined the opinion of the Court, joined a separate opinion by Justice Clark which in two or three sentences stated the conclusion that Congress could "punis[h] all conspiracies — with or without state action — that interfere with Fourteenth Amendment rights."

Though these three Justices saw fit to opine on matters not before the Court in *Guest,* the Court had no occasion to revisit the *Civil Rights Cases* and *Harris,* having determined "the indictment [charging private individuals with conspiring to deprive blacks of equal access to state facilities] in fact contain[ed] an express allegation of state involvement."

Section 13981 is not aimed at proscribing discrimination by officials which the Fourteenth Amendment might not itself proscribe; it is directed not at any State or state actor, but at individuals who have committed criminal acts motivated by gender bias. In the present cases, for example, §13981 visits no consequence whatever on any Virginia public official involved in investigating or prosecuting Brzonkala's assault. The section is, therefore, unlike any of the §5 remedies that we have previously upheld.

Petitioner Brzonkala's complaint alleges that she was the victim of a brutal assault. But Congress's effort in §13981 to provide a federal civil remedy can be sustained neither under the Commerce Clause nor under §5 of the Fourteenth Amendment. If the allegations here are true, no civilized system of justice could fail to provide her a remedy for the conduct of respondent Morrison. But under our federal system that remedy must be provided by the Commonwealth of Virginia, and not by the United States.

Justice BREYER dissenting.

Given my conclusion on the Commerce Clause question, I need not consider Congress's authority under §5 of the Fourteenth Amendment. Nonetheless, I doubt the Court's reasoning rejecting that source of authority. The Court points out that in United States v. Harris (1883), and the *Civil Rights Cases* (1883), the Court held that §5 does not authorize Congress to use the Fourteenth Amendment as a source of power to remedy the conduct of private persons. That is certainly so. The Federal Government's argument, however, is that Congress used §5 to remedy the actions of state actors, namely, those States which, through discriminatory design or the discriminatory conduct of their officials, failed to provide adequate (or any) state remedies for women injured by gender-motivated violence—a failure that the States, and Congress, documented in depth.

But why can Congress not provide a remedy against private actors? Those private actors, of course, did not themselves violate the Constitution. But this Court has held that Congress at least sometimes can enact remedial "[l]egislation . . . [that] prohibits conduct which is not itself unconstitutional." It intrudes little upon either States or private parties. It may lead state actors to improve their own remedial systems, primarily through example. It restricts private actors only by imposing liability for private conduct that is, in the main, already forbidden by state law. Why is the remedy "disproportionate"? And given the relation between remedy and violation—the creation of a federal remedy to substitute for constitutionally inadequate state remedies—where is the lack of "congruence"?

Despite my doubts about the majority's §5 reasoning, I need not, and do not, answer the §5 question, which I would leave for more thorough analysis if necessary on another occasion. Rather, in my view, the Commerce Clause provides an adequate basis for the statute before us. And I would uphold its constitutionality as the "necessary and proper" exercise of legislative power granted to Congress by that Clause.

2.   What Is the Scope of Congress's Power?

There are two different views as to the scope of Congress's power under the post-Civil War Amendments and particularly under §5 of the Fourteenth

Amendment. One approach is narrow and accords Congress only authority to prevent or provide remedies for violations of rights recognized by the Supreme Court; under this view, Congress cannot expand the scope of rights or provide additional rights. An alternative approach also accords Congress authority to interpret the Fourteenth Amendment to expand the scope of rights or even to create new rights. Under this view, Congress may create rights by statute where the Court has not found them in the Constitution, but Congress cannot dilute or diminish constitutional rights.

The choice between these two views is in part about a textual argument concerning what §5 means when it empowers Congress "to enforce" the amendment by appropriate legislation. Those who take the narrower view contend that Congress is not "enforcing" if it is creating new rights. But those who take the broader view argue that Congress is enforcing the amendment by creating greater protections than those found by the Court.

The dispute over these two views also is about the appropriate roles of the Court and Congress in deciding the substantive content of rights. Those who take the narrow position see it as solely the Court's role to decide the rights protected under the Constitution; Congress's role is limited to enacting laws to prevent and remedy violations. But those who adopt the broader view of Congress's §5 power see both Congress and the Court as having authority to recognize and protect rights under the Constitution.

As with all of the material in this chapter, there also is an important underlying issue concerning the allocation of power between the federal and state governments. Advocates of the narrow view see it as limiting federal power, reserving more governance for the states, and lessening the instances in which the federal government can regulate state and local actions. In contrast, supporters of the broader approach defend it as creating needed national power to protect civil rights and civil liberties.

In Katzenbach v. Morgan, the first case presented, the Court seemed to adopt the broader approach and accord Congress expansive authority under §5 of the Fourteenth Amendment. In three recent cases, City of Boerne v. Flores, Florida Prepaid v. College Savings Bank, and Kimel v. Florida Board of Regents, the Court clearly chose the narrow view and limited Congress's power under §5.

KATZENBACH v. MORGAN & MORGAN

384 U.S. 641 (1966)

Justice BRENNAN delivered the opinion of the Court.

These cases concern the constitutionality of §4(e) of the Voting Rights Act of 1965. That law, in the respects pertinent in these cases, provides that no person who has successfully completed the sixth primary grade in a public school in, or a private school accredited by, the Commonwealth of Puerto Rico in which the language of instruction was other than English shall be denied the right to vote in any election because of his inability to read or write English. Appellees, registered voters in New York City, brought this suit to challenge the constitutionality of §4(e) insofar as it pro tanto prohibits the enforcement of the election laws of New York requiring an ability to read and write English as a condition of voting.

The Attorney General of the State of New York argues that an exercise of congressional power under §5 of the Fourteenth Amendment that prohibits the enforcement of a state law can only be sustained if the judicial branch determines that the state law is prohibited by the provisions of the Amendment that Congress sought to enforce. More specifically, he urges that §4(e) cannot be sustained as appropriate legislation to enforce the Equal Protection Clause unless the judiciary decides — even with the guidance of a congressional judgment — that the application of the English literacy requirement prohibited by §4(e) is forbidden by the Equal Protection Clause itself. We disagree. Neither the language nor history of §5 supports such a construction. A construction of §5 that would require a judicial determination that the enforcement of the state law precluded by Congress violated the Amendment, as a condition of sustaining the congressional enactment, would depreciate both congressional resourcefulness and congressional responsibility for implementing the Amendment. It would confine the legislative power in this context to the insignificant role of abrogating only those state laws that the judicial branch was prepared to adjudge unconstitutional, or of merely informing the judgment of the judiciary by particularizing the "majestic generalities" of §1 of the Amendment.

Thus our task in this case is not to determine whether the New York English literacy requirement as applied to deny the right to vote to a person who successfully completed the sixth grade in a Puerto Rican school violates the Equal Protection Clause. Accordingly, our decision in Lassiter v. Northampton County Bd. of Election, sustaining the North Carolina English literacy requirement as not in all circumstances prohibited by the first sections of the Fourteenth and Fifteenth Amendments, is inapposite. *Lassiter* did not present the question before us here: Without regard to whether the judiciary would find that the Equal Protection Clause itself nullifies New York's English literacy requirement as so applied, could Congress prohibit the enforcement of the state law by legislating under §5 of the Fourteenth Amendment? In answering this question, our task is limited to determining whether such legislation is, as required by §5, appropriate legislation to enforce the Equal Protection Clause.

By including §5 the draftsmen sought to grant to Congress, by a specific provision applicable to the Fourteenth Amendment, the same broad powers expressed in the Necessary and Proper Clause, Art. I, §8, cl. 18. We therefore proceed to the consideration whether §4(e) is "appropriate legislation" to enforce the Equal Protection Clause, that is, under the McCulloch v. Maryland standard, whether §4(e) may be regarded as an enactment to enforce the Equal Protection Clause, whether it is "plainly adapted to that end" and whether it is not prohibited by but is consistent with "the letter and spirit of the [C]onstitution."[40]

There can be no doubt that §4(e) may be regarded as an enactment to enforce the Equal Protection Clause. Congress explicitly declared that it

---

40. Contrary to the suggestion of the dissent, infra, §5 does not grant Congress power to exercise discretion in the other direction and to enact "statutes so as in effect to dilute equal protection and due process decisions of this Court." We emphasize that Congress's power under §5 is limited to adopting measures to enforce the guarantees of the Amendment; §5 grants Congress no power to restrict, abrogate, or dilute these guarantees. Thus, for example, an enactment authorizing the States to establish racially segregated systems of educaion would not be — as required by §5 — a measure "to enforce" the Equal Protection Clause since that clause of its own force prohibits such state laws. [Footnote by the Court.]

enacted §4(e) "to secure the rights under the [F]ourteenth [A]mendment of persons educated in American-flag schools in which the predominant classroom language was other than English." The persons referred to include those who have migrated from the Commonwealth of Puerto Rico to New York and who have been denied the right to vote because of their inability to read and write English, and the Fourteenth Amendment rights referred to include those emanating from the Equal Protection Clause. More specifically, §4(e) may be viewed as a measure to secure for the Puerto Rican community residing in New York nondiscriminatory treatment by government—both in the imposition of voting qualifications and the provision or administration of governmental services, such as public schools, public housing and law enforcement.

Section 4(e) may be readily seen as "plainly adapted" to furthering these aims of the Equal Protection Clause. The practical effect of §4(e) is to prohibit New York from denying the right to vote to large segments of its Puerto Rican community. Congress has thus prohibited the State from denying to that community the right that is "preservative of all rights." This enhanced political power will be helpful in gaining nondiscriminatory treatment in public services for the entire Puerto Rican community. Section 4(e) thereby enables the Puerto Rican minority better to obtain "perfect equality of civil rights and the equal protection of the laws." It was well within congressional authority to say that this need of the Puerto Rican minority for the vote warranted federal intrusion upon any state interests served by the English literacy requirement. It was for Congress, as the branch that made this judgment, to assess and weigh the various conflicting considerations. It is not for us to review the congressional resolution of these factors. It is enough that we be able to perceive a basis upon which the Congress might resolve the conflict as it did. There plainly was such a basis to support §4(e) in the application in question in this case. Any contrary conclusion would require us to be blind to the realities familiar to the legislators.

Since Congress undertook to legislate so as to preclude the enforcement of the state law, and did so in the context of a general appraisal of literacy requirements for voting, to which it brought a specially informed legislative competence, it was Congress's prerogative to weigh these competing considerations. Here again, it is enough that we perceive a basis upon which Congress might predicate a judgment that the application of New York's English literacy requirement to deny the right to vote to a person with a sixth grade education in Puerto Rican schools in which the language of instruction was other than English constituted an invidious discrimination in violation of the Equal Protection Clause.

We therefore conclude that §4(e), in the application challenged in this case, is appropriate legislation to enforce the Equal Protection Clause and that the judgment of the District Court must be and hereby is reversed.

Justice HARLAN, whom Justice STEWART joins, dissenting.

Worthy as its purposes may be thought by many, I do not see how §4(e) of the Voting Rights Act of 1965, can be sustained except at the sacrifice of fundamentals in the American constitutional system—the separation between the legislative and judicial function and the boundaries between federal and state political authority. By the same token I think that the validity of New York's literacy test, a question which the Court considers only in the context of the federal statute, must be upheld. It will conduce to analytical clarity if I discuss the second issue first.

Any analysis of this problem must begin with the established rule of law that the franchise is essentially a matter of state concern, subject only to the overriding requirements of various federal constitutional provisions dealing with the franchise, e.g., the Fifteenth, Seventeenth, Nineteenth, and Twenty-fourth Amendments, and, as more recently decided, to the general principles of the Fourteenth Amendment.

In 1959, in Lassiter v. Northampton Election Bd., this Court dealt with substantially the same question and resolved it unanimously in favor of the legitimacy of a state literacy qualification. There a North Carolina English literacy test was challenged. We held that there was "wide scope" for State qualifications of this sort. I believe the same interests recounted in *Lassiter* indubitably point toward upholding the rationality of the New York voting test.

The pivotal question in this instance is what effect the added factor of a congressional enactment has on the straight equal protection argument dealt with above. The Court declares that since §5 of the Fourteenth Amendment gives to the Congress power to "enforce" the prohibitions of the Amendment by "appropriate" legislation, the test for judicial review of any congressional determination in this area is simply one of rationality; that is, in effect, was Congress acting rationally in declaring that the New York statute is irrational? Although §5 most certainly does give to the Congress wide powers in the field of devising remedial legislation to effectuate the Amendment's prohibition on arbitrary state action, I believe the Court has confused the issue of how much enforcement power Congress possesses under §5 with the distinct issue of what questions are appropriate for congressional determination and what questions are essentially judicial in nature.

When recognized state violations of federal constitutional standards have occurred, Congress is of course empowered by §5 to take appropriate remedial measures to redress and prevent the wrongs. But it is a judicial question whether the condition with which Congress has thus sought to deal is in truth an infringement of the Constitution, something that is the necessary prerequisite to bringing the §5 power into play at all.

Section 4(e), however, presents a significantly different type of congressional enactment. The question here is not whether the statute is appropriate remedial legislation to cure an established violation of a constitutional command, but whether there has in fact been an infringement of that constitutional command, that is, whether a particular state practice or, as here, a statute is so arbitrary or irrational as to offend the command of the Equal Protection Clause of the Fourteenth Amendment. That question is one for the judicial branch ultimately to determine. Were the rule otherwise, Congress would be able to qualify this Court's constitutional decisions under the Fourteenth and Fifteenth Amendments let alone those under other provisions of the Constitution, by resorting to congressional power under the Necessary and Proper Clause. In view of this Court's holding in *Lassiter*, that an English literacy test is a permissible exercise of state supervision over its franchise, I do not think it is open to Congress to limit the effect of that decision as it has undertaken to do by §4(e). In effect the Court reads §5 of the Fourteenth Amendment as giving Congress the power to define the substantive scope of the Amendment. If that indeed be the true reach of §5, then I do not see why Congress should not be able as well to exercise its §5 "discretion" by enacting statutes so as in effect to dilute equal protection and due process decisions of this Court. In all such cases there is room for reasonable men to differ as to whether or not a denial of equal protection or due process has occurred, and the final decision is one of judgment. Until today this judgment has always been one for the judiciary to resolve.

To deny the effectiveness of this congressional enactment is not of course to disparage Congress's exertion of authority in the field of civil rights; it is simply to recognize that the Legislative Branch like the other branches of federal authority is subject to the governmental boundaries set by the Constitution. To hold, on this record, that §4(e) overrides the New York literacy requirement seems to me tantamount to allowing the Fourteenth Amendment to swallow the State's constitutionally ordained primary authority in this field. For if Congress by what, as here, amounts to mere ipse dixit can set that otherwise permissible requirement partially at naught I see no reason why it could not also substitute its judgment for that of the States in other fields of their exclusive primary competence as well.

In City of Boerne v. Flores, the Court appeared to adopt a very different view of the scope of Congress's authority under §5 of the Fourteenth Amendment than that taken by a majority in *Katzenbach*. To understand *City of Boerne*, which follows, a bit of background is necessary. In Employment Div., Dept. of Human Resources of Oregon v. Smith, 494 U.S. 872 (1990), the Supreme Court significantly narrowed the scope of the Free Exercise Clause.[41] Oregon law prohibited the consumption of peyote, a hallucinogenic substance. Native Americans challenged this law claiming that it infringed free exercise of religion because their religious rituals required the use of peyote. Under prior Supreme Court precedents, government actions burdening religion are upheld only if they are necessary to achieve a compelling government purpose. The Supreme Court, in *Smith*, changed the law and held that the Free Exercise Clause cannot be used to challenge neutral laws of general applicability. The Oregon law prohibiting consumption of peyote was deemed neutral because it was not motivated by a desire to interfere with religion and it was a law of general applicability.

In response to this decision, in 1993, Congress overwhelmingly adopted the Religious Freedom Restoration Act, which was signed into law by President Clinton. The Religious Freedom Restoration Act was express in stating that its goal was to overturn *Smith* and restore the test that was followed before that decision. The act requires courts considering free exercise challenges, including to neutral laws of general applicability, to uphold the government's actions only if they are necessary to achieve a compelling purpose. In City of Boerne v. Flores, the Court declared the Religious Freedom Restoration Act unconstitutional.

CITY OF BOERNE v. FLORES
521 U.S. 507 (1997)

Justice KENNEDY delivered the opinion of the Court.

A decision by local zoning authorities to deny a church a building permit was challenged under the Religious Freedom Restoration Act of 1993 (RFRA). The

------

41. Employment Division v. Smith is presented in Chapter 10 in the discussion of free exercise of religion.

case calls into question the authority of Congress to enact RFRA. We conclude the statute exceeds Congress's power.

I

Situated on a hill in the city of Boerne, Texas, some 28 miles northwest of San Antonio, is St. Peter Catholic Church. Built in 1923, the church's structure replicates the mission style of the region's earlier history. The church seats about 230 worshippers, a number too small for its growing parish. Some 40 to 60 parishioners cannot be accommodated at some Sunday masses. In order to meet the needs of the congregation the Archbishop of San Antonio gave permission to the parish to plan alterations to enlarge the building.

A few months later, the Boerne City Council passed an ordinance authorizing the city's Historic Landmark Commission to prepare a preservation plan with proposed historic landmarks and districts. Under the ordinance, the Commission must preapprove construction affecting historic landmarks or buildings in a historic district.

Soon afterwards, the Archbishop applied for a building permit so construction to enlarge the church could proceed. City authorities, relying on the ordinance and the designation of a historic district (which, they argued, included the church), denied the application. The Archbishop brought this suit challenging the permit denial in the United States District Court for the Western District of Texas. The complaint contained various claims, but to this point the litigation has centered on RFRA and the question of its constitutionality. The Archbishop relied upon RFRA as one basis for relief from the refusal to issue the permit.

II

Congress enacted RFRA in direct response to the Court's decision in Employment Div., Dept. of Human Resources of Oregon v. Smith (1990). RFRA prohibits "[g]overnment" from "substantially burden[ing]" a person's exercise of religion even if the burden results from a rule of general applicability unless the government can demonstrate the burden "(1) is in furtherance of a compelling governmental interest; and (2) is the least restrictive means of furthering that compelling governmental interest."

III

A

The parties disagree over whether RFRA is a proper exercise of Congress's §5 power "to enforce" by "appropriate legislation" the constitutional guarantee that no State shall deprive any person of "life, liberty, or property, without due process of law" nor deny any person "equal protection of the laws."

All must acknowledge that §5 is "a positive grant of legislative power" to Congress, Katzenbach v. Morgan (1966). Legislation which deters or remedies constitutional violations can fall within the sweep of Congress's enforcement power even if in the process it prohibits conduct which is not itself unconstitutional and intrudes into "legislative spheres of autonomy previously reserved to the States." We have also concluded that other measures protecting voting rights are within Congress's power to enforce the Fourteenth and Fifteenth Amendments, despite the burdens those measures placed on the States.

It is also true, however, that "[a]s broad as the congressional enforcement power is, it is not unlimited." In assessing the breadth of §5's enforcement power, we begin with its text. Congress has been given the power "to enforce" the "provisions of this article." We agree with respondent, of course, that Congress can enact legislation under §5 enforcing the constitutional right to the free exercise of religion. The "provisions of this article," to which §5 refers, include the Due Process Clause of the Fourteenth Amendment.

Congress's power under §5, however, extends only to "enforc[ing]" the provisions of the Fourteenth Amendment. The Court has described this power as "remedial." The design of the Amendment and the text of §5 are inconsistent with the suggestion that Congress has the power to decree the substance of the Fourteenth Amendment's restrictions on the States. Legislation which alters the meaning of the Free Exercise Clause cannot be said to be enforcing the Clause. Congress does not enforce a constitutional right by changing what the right is. It has been given the power "to enforce," not the power to determine what constitutes a constitutional violation. Were it not so, what Congress would be enforcing would no longer be, in any meaningful sense, the "provisions of [the Fourteenth Amendment]."

While the line between measures that remedy or prevent unconstitutional actions and measures that make a substantive change in the governing law is not easy to discern, and Congress must have wide latitude in determining where it lies, the distinction exists and must be observed. There must be a congruence and proportionality between the injury to be prevented or remedied and the means adopted to that end. Lacking such a connection, legislation may become substantive in operation and effect. History and our case law support drawing the distinction, one apparent from the text of the Amendment.

1

The Fourteenth Amendment's history confirms the remedial, rather than substantive, nature of the Enforcement Clause. The Joint Committee on Reconstruction of the 39th Congress began drafting what would become the Fourteenth Amendment in January 1866. The objections to the Committee's first draft of the Amendment, and the rejection of the draft, have a direct bearing on the central issue of defining Congress's enforcement power. In February, Republican Representative John Bingham of Ohio reported the following draft amendment to the House of Representatives on behalf of the Joint Committee: "The Congress shall have power to make all laws which shall be necessary and proper to secure to the citizens of each State all privileges and immunities of citizens in the several States, and to all persons in the several States equal protection in the rights of life, liberty, and property."

The proposal encountered immediate opposition, which continued through three days of debate. Members of Congress from across the political spectrum criticized the Amendment, and the criticisms had a common theme: The proposed Amendment gave Congress too much legislative power at the expense of the existing constitutional structure. Democrats and conservative Republicans argued that the proposed Amendment would give Congress a power to intrude into traditional areas of state responsibility, a power inconsistent with the federal design central to the Constitution.

Section 1 of the new draft Amendment imposed self-executing limits on the States. Section 5 prescribed that "[t]he Congress shall have power to enforce, by appropriate legislation, the provisions of this article." Under the revised Amendment, Congress's power was no longer plenary but remedial. Congress was granted the power to make the substantive constitutional prohibitions against the States effective. Representative Bingham said the new draft would give Congress "the power . . . to protect by national law the privileges and immunities of all the citizens of the Republic . . . whenever the same shall be abridged or denied by the unconstitutional acts of any State." Representative Stevens described the new draft Amendment as "allow[ing] Congress to correct the unjust legislation of the States."

The design of the Fourteenth Amendment has proved significant also in maintaining the traditional separation of powers between Congress and the Judiciary. The first eight Amendments to the Constitution set forth self-executing prohibitions on governmental action, and this Court has had primary authority to interpret those prohibitions. The Bingham draft, some thought, departed from that tradition by vesting in Congress primary power to interpret and elaborate on the meaning of the new Amendment through legislation. Under it, "Congress, and not the courts, was to judge whether or not any of the privileges or immunities were not secured to citizens in the several States." The power to interpret the Constitution in a case or controversy remains in the Judiciary.

2

The remedial and preventive nature of Congress's enforcement power, and the limitation inherent in the power, were confirmed in our earliest cases on the Fourteenth Amendment. In the Civil Rights Cases (1883), the Court invalidated sections of the Civil Rights Act of 1875 which prescribed criminal penalties for denying to any person "the full enjoyment of" public accommodations and conveyances, on the grounds that it exceeded Congress's power by seeking to regulate private conduct. The Enforcement Clause, the Court said, did not authorize Congress to pass "general legislation upon the rights of the citizen, but corrective legislation; that is, such as may be necessary and proper for counteracting such laws as the States may adopt or enforce, and which, by the amendment, they are prohibited from making or enforcing. . . ." Although the specific holdings of these early cases might have been superseded or modified, see, e.g., Heart of Atlanta Motel, Inc. v. United States (1964); United States v. Guest (1966), their treatment of Congress's §5 power as corrective or preventive, not definitional, has not been questioned.

3

Any suggestion that Congress has a substantive, non-remedial power under the Fourteenth Amendment is not supported by our case law. If Congress could define its own powers by altering the Fourteenth Amendment's meaning, no longer would the Constitution be "superior paramount law, unchangeable by ordinary means." It would be "on a level with ordinary legislative acts, and, like other acts, . . . alterable when the legislature shall please to alter it." Marbury v. Madison. Under this approach, it is difficult to conceive of a principle that would limit congressional power. Shifting legislative majorities could change the Constitution and effectively circumvent the difficult and detailed amendment process contained in Article V.

We now turn to consider whether RFRA can be considered enforcement legislation under §5 of the Fourteenth Amendment.

B

Respondent contends that RFRA is a proper exercise of Congress's remedial or preventive power. The Act, it is said, is a reasonable means of protecting the free exercise of religion as defined by *Smith*. It prevents and remedies laws which are enacted with the unconstitutional object of targeting religious beliefs and practices. If Congress can prohibit laws with discriminatory effects in order to prevent racial discrimination in violation of the Equal Protection Clause, then it can do the same, respondent argues, to promote religious liberty.

While preventive rules are sometimes appropriate remedial measures, there must be a congruence between the means used and the ends to be achieved. The appropriateness of remedial measures must be considered in light of the evil presented. Strong measures appropriate to address one harm may be an unwarranted response to another, lesser one.

A comparison between RFRA and the Voting Rights Act is instructive. In contrast to the record which confronted Congress and the judiciary in the voting rights cases, RFRA's legislative record lacks examples of modern instances of generally applicable laws passed because of religious bigotry. The history of persecution in this country detailed in the hearings mentions no episodes occurring in the past 40 years. Regardless of the state of the legislative record, RFRA cannot be considered remedial, preventive legislation, if those terms are to have any meaning. RFRA is so out of proportion to a supposed remedial or preventive object that it cannot be understood as responsive to, or designed to prevent, unconstitutional behavior. It appears, instead, to attempt a substantive change in constitutional protections. Preventive measures prohibiting certain types of laws may be appropriate when there is reason to believe that many of the laws affected by the congressional enactment have a significant likelihood of being unconstitutional.

RFRA is not so confined. Sweeping coverage ensures its intrusion at every level of government, displacing laws and prohibiting official actions of almost every description and regardless of subject matter. RFRA's restrictions apply to every agency and official of the Federal, State, and local Governments. RFRA applies to all federal and state law, statutory or otherwise, whether adopted before or after its enactment. RFRA has no termination date or termination mechanism. Any law is subject to challenge at any time by any individual who alleges a substantial burden on his or her free exercise of religion. The reach and scope of RFRA distinguish it from other measures passed under Congress's enforcement power, even in the area of voting rights.

The stringent test RFRA demands of state laws reflects a lack of proportionality or congruence between the means adopted and the legitimate end to be achieved. If an objector can show a substantial burden on his free exercise, the State must demonstrate a compelling governmental interest and show that the law is the least restrictive means of furthering its interest. Claims that a law substantially burdens someone's exercise of religion will often be difficult to contest. Requiring a State to demonstrate a compelling interest and show that it has adopted the least restrictive means of achieving that interest is the most demanding test known to constitutional law. Laws valid under *Smith* would fall under RFRA without regard to whether they had the object of stifling or punishing free exercise. We make these observations not to reargue the position of the majority in *Smith* but to illustrate the substantive alteration of its holding attempted by RFRA. Even assuming RFRA would be interpreted in effect to mandate some lesser test, say one equivalent to intermediate scrutiny, the statute nevertheless would require searching judicial scrutiny of state law with the attendant likelihood of invalidation. This is a considerable congressional intrusion into the States' traditional prerogatives and general authority to regulate for the health and welfare of their citizens.

The substantial costs RFRA exacts, both in practical terms of imposing a heavy litigation burden on the States and in terms of curtailing their traditional general regulatory power, far exceed any pattern or practice of unconstitutional conduct under the Free Exercise Clause as interpreted in *Smith*. Simply put, RFRA is not designed to identify and counteract state laws likely to be unconstitutional because of their treatment of religion. In most cases, the state laws to which RFRA applies are not ones which will have been motivated by religious bigotry. If a state law disproportionately burdened a particular class of religious observers, this circumstance might be evidence of an impermissible legislative motive.

Our national experience teaches that the Constitution is preserved best when each part of the government respects both the Constitution and the proper actions and determinations of the other branches. When the Court has interpreted the Constitution, it has acted within the province of the Judicial Branch, which embraces the duty to say what the law is. Marbury v. Madison. When the political branches of the Government act against the background of a judicial interpretation of the Constitution already issued, it must be understood that in later cases and controversies the Court will treat its precedents with the respect due them under settled principles, including stare decisis, and contrary expectations must be disappointed. RFRA was designed to control cases and controversies, such as the one before us; but as the provisions of the federal statute here invoked are beyond congressional authority, it is this Court's precedent, not RFRA, which must control.

Broad as the power of Congress is under the Enforcement Clause of the Fourteenth Amendment, RFRA contradicts vital principles necessary to maintain separation of powers and the federal balance. The judgment of the Court of Appeals sustaining the Act's constitutionality is reversed.

Justice O'CONNOR, with whom Justice BREYER joins except as to a portion of Part I, dissenting.

I dissent from the Court's disposition of this case. I agree with the Court that the issue before us is whether the Religious Freedom Restoration Act (RFRA) is a proper exercise of Congress's power to enforce §5 of the Fourteenth Amendment. But as a yardstick for measuring the constitutionality of RFRA, the Court uses its holding in Employment Div., Dept. of Human Resources of Oregon v. Smith (1990), the decision that prompted Congress to enact RFRA, as a means of more rigorously enforcing the Free Exercise Clause. I remain of the view that *Smith* was wrongly decided, and I would use this case to reexamine the Court's holding there. Therefore, I would direct the parties to brief the question whether *Smith* represents the correct understanding of the Free Exercise Clause and set the case for reargument. If the Court were to correct the misinterpretation of the Free Exercise Clause set forth in *Smith,* it would simultaneously put our First Amendment jurisprudence back on course and allay the legitimate concerns of a majority in Congress who believed that *Smith* improperly restricted religious liberty. We would then be in a position to review RFRA in light of a proper interpretation of the Free Exercise Clause.

Since *Boerne,* the Supreme Court has had occasion to consider the scope of Congress's §5 power in several cases that involve the authority of Congress to authorize suits against state governments. Each of these decisions is presented below in the final section of the chapter, which examines the authority of Congress to authorize suits against state governments.

As discussed below, the Supreme Court has held that Congress can authorize suits against state governments pursuant to §5 of the Fourteenth Amendment but not under any other congressional power. The Court thus has had to consider whether federal laws authorizing suits against state governments for patent infringement are within the scope of Congress's §5 power. These cases apply City of Boerne v. Flores and provide further elaboration of its restrictive view of Congress's §5 authority. They are presented below because they arise in the context of Congress's power to authorize suits against state governments.[42]

F.　CONGRESS'S POWER TO AUTHORIZE SUITS AGAINST STATE GOVERNMENTS

1.　*Background on the Eleventh Amendment and State Sovereign Immunity*

The Eleventh Amendment states, "The Judicial power of the United States shall not be construed to extend to any suit in law or equity, commenced or prosecuted against one of the United States by Citizens of another State, or by Citizens or Subjects of any foreign state." The Eleventh Amendment was intended to strike from the Constitution clauses of Article III, §2 of the Constitution which states that the judicial power of the United States extends to suits "between a State and Citizens of another State" and "between a State, or the Citizens thereof, and foreign States, Citizens or subjects."

---

42. The Court also was asked to consider the scope of Congress's powers under §5 of the Fourteenth Amendment and under §2 of the Fifteenth Amendment in deciding whether the extension §5 of the Voting Rights Act for 25 years is constitutional. Section 5 applies to states with a history of race discrimination in voting and requires that a significant change in the election system be preapproved (precleared) by either the Attorney General of the United States or a three-judge federal court in Washington, D.C. In Northwest Austin Municipal District v. Holder, 557 U.S. 193 (2009), the Court raised serious questions about whether this is constitutional but interpreted the statute to avoid the constitutional issue. In 2013, the Court has this constitutional issue again before it in Shelby County, Alabama v. Holder.

More specifically, the Eleventh Amendment was adopted to overrule the Supreme Court's decision in Chisholm v. Georgia, 2 U.S. (2 Dall.) 419 (1793). *Chisholm* involved an attempt by a South Carolina citizen to recover money owed by the State of Georgia. He sued in federal court pursuant to the language of Article III that expressly allows federal courts to hear suits against state governments by citizens of other states. The State of Georgia claimed that it had sovereign immunity and could not be sued without its consent. The Supreme Court, in a four-to-one decision, ruled in Chisholm's favor. They concluded that the clear language of Article III authorized suits against a state by citizens of another state.

State legislators and governors were outraged by the Supreme Court's decision in Chisholm v. Georgia. Georgia adopted a statute declaring that anyone attempting to enforce the Supreme Court's decision is "hereby declared to be guilty of a felony, and shall suffer death, without the benefit of clergy by being hanged."[43] The intense reaction to *Chisholm* is reflected in the speed with which a constitutional amendment to overturn the decision was adopted. The Supreme Court decided *Chisholm* on February 14, 1794. By March 4, 1794, less than three weeks later, both houses of Congress had approved the Eleventh Amendment. Within a year, the requisite number of states ratified it, although it was three more years until the president issued a proclamation declaring the Eleventh Amendment to have been properly ratified.

In 1890, in Hans v. Louisiana, 134 U.S. 1 (1890), the Court held that the Eleventh Amendment also bars suits against a state by its own citizens. Although the terms of the amendment only prohibit suits against a state by citizens of other states and foreign countries, Hans v. Louisiana held that it would be "anomalous" to allow states to be sued by their own citizens. Thus, since *Hans*, states have been immune to suits both by their own citizens and by citizens of other states.

There is great disagreement among scholars and Justices as to the proper interpretation of the Eleventh Amendment. Some, including a majority of the current Court, believe that sovereign immunity creates a constitutional restriction on federal court subject matter jurisdiction for all suits against state governments. By this view, the Eleventh Amendment is part of a broader constitutional limitation on federal court jurisdiction created by sovereign immunity.[44]

A second view of the Eleventh Amendment treats it as restricting only the diversity jurisdiction of federal courts.[45] The language of the Eleventh Amendment clearly is directed at modifying this latter provision. In fact, the amendment simply states, "The Judicial Power of the United States shall not be construed to extend to any suit . . . against one of the United States by Citizens of another state." Because *Chisholm* only involved this latter part of Article III, it makes sense to view the Eleventh Amendment as restricting only diversity suits against state governments. Therefore, according to this view, the Eleventh

---

43. Peter W. Low & John C. Jeffries, Jr., *Federal Courts and the Law of Federal-State Relations* 810 (4th ed. 1998).

44. *See, e.g.*, Alden v. Maine, 527 U.S. 706 (1999), presented below.

45. *See* John J. Gibbons, *The Eleventh Amendment and State Sovereign Immunity: A Reinterpretation*, 83 Colum. L. Rev. 1889 (1983); William A. Fletcher, *A Historical Interpretation of the Eleventh Amendment: A Narrow Construction of an Affirmative Grant of Jurisdiction Rather than a Prohibition Against Jurisdiction*, 35 Stan. L. Rev. 1033 (1983).

Amendment does not bar suits against states based on other parts of Article III. Most notably, the amendment does not preclude suits based on federal question jurisdiction. Thus, all claims of state violations of the U.S. Constitution or federal laws could be heard in federal courts. Four justices on the current Court accept this view.

The Eleventh Amendment, under the former view adopted by a majority of the current Court, creates a major hurdle for those seeking to enforce federal laws against state governments.[46] States cannot be sued in federal court, even for egregious violations of federal rights. There are three ways around the Eleventh Amendment to hold state governments accountable in federal court.

One is that state officers may be sued in federal court, even when state governments cannot be sued. The Eleventh Amendment does not preclude suits against state officers for injunctive relief, even when the remedy will enjoin the implementation of an official state policy. Ex parte Young, 209 U.S. 123 (1908), is widely credited with establishing this principle. Simply stated, state officers may be sued for injunctive relief or for damages to be paid by them, but state officers cannot be sued where it is the state treasury that will be paying damages to compensate for past wrongs.[47]

Second, states may waive their Eleventh Amendment immunity and may consent to be sued in federal court. Although allowing such waivers seems inconsistent with viewing the Eleventh Amendment as a restriction on the federal courts' subject matter jurisdiction, it is firmly established that "if a State waives its immunity and consents to suit in federal court, the Eleventh Amendment does not bar the action."[48] If a state waives its Eleventh Amendment immunity, then it may be sued directly in federal court, even for retroactive relief to be paid out of the state treasury. However, the Court has stated clearly that the "test for determining whether a state has waived its [Eleventh Amendment] immunity from federal-court jurisdiction is a stringent one."[49] The Court has held that waivers must be explicit; there is no doctrine of implied or constructive waiver of the Eleventh Amendment.[50]

Third, the Supreme Court has held that Congress, acting pursuant to §5 of the Fourteenth Amendment, may authorize suits against state governments. This authority is established in the cases in the next section. Following the cases creating this authority, the three recent Supreme Court decisions construing the scope of Congress's §5 power are presented. Finally, the section concludes by presenting the Supreme Court's recent decision in Alden v. Maine, holding that Congress cannot authorize suits against state governments in state courts.

---

46. The Supreme Court has held that the Eleventh Amendment does not bar suits against local governments. Mt. Healthy City School Dist. Bd. of Educ. v. Doyle, 429 U.S. 274 (1977); Lincoln County v. Luning, 133 U.S. 529 (1890).

47. There is a large body of law as to when suits against state officers are allowed and when they are not permitted. For a discussion of this law, *see* Erwin Chemerinsky, *Federal Jurisdiction* (6th ed. 2012), Chapter 7.

48. Atascadero State Hosp. v. Scanlon, 473 U.S. 234, 238 (1985).

49. Atascadero State Hosp. v. Scanlon, 473 U.S. at 241. Most recently, in Sossamon v. Texas, 131 S. Ct. 1651 (2011), the Court held that a state could not be sued for money damages under a statutory provision (in the Religious Land Use and Institutionalized Persons Act), which authorized "appropriate relief against a government" that received federal funds. The Court said that this was not sufficiently specific in authorizing monetary relief to be a waiver of sovereign immunity.

50. College Savings Bank v. Florida Prepaid Postsecondary Educ. Expense Bd., 527 U.S. 666 (1999).

Alden held that state governments have sovereign immunity and cannot be sued in state courts without their consent even for violations of federal laws.

2.   Congress's Power to Authorize Suits Against State Governments

a.   The Basic Rule: Congress May Authorize Suits Against States Pursuant Only to §5 of the Fourteenth Amendment

The Supreme Court has considered the ability of Congress to override sovereign immunity and authorize suits against state governments. Fitzpatrick v. Bitzer was a key initial case.

FITZPATRICK v. BITZER
427 U.S. 445 (1976)

Justice REHNQUIST delivered the opinion of the Court.

In the 1972 Amendments to Title VII of the Civil Rights Act of 1964, Congress, acting under section 5 of the Fourteenth Amendment, authorized federal courts to award money damages in favor of a private individual against a state government found to have subjected that person to employment discrimination on the basis of "race, color, religion, sex, or national origin." The principal question presented by these cases is whether, as against the shield of sovereign immunity afforded the State by the Eleventh Amendment, Congress has the power to authorize Federal courts to enter such an award against the State as a means of enforcing the substantive guarantees of the Fourteenth Amendment.

The impact of the Fourteenth Amendment upon the relationship between the Federal Government and the States, and the reach of congressional power under §5, were examined at length by this Court in Ex parte State of Virginia (1880). A state judge had been arrested and indicted under a federal criminal statute prohibiting the exclusion on the basis of race of any citizen from service as a juror in a state court. The judge claimed that the statute was beyond Congress's power to enact under either the Thirteenth or the Fourteenth Amendment. The Court first observed that these Amendments "were intended to be, what they really are, limitations of the power of the States and enlargements of the power of Congress." It then addressed the relationship between the language of §5 and the substantive provisions of the Fourteenth Amendment:

> The prohibitions of the Fourteenth Amendment are directed to the States, and they are to a degree restrictions of State power. It is these which Congress is empowered to enforce, and to enforce against State action, however put forth, whether that action be executive, legislative, or judicial. Such enforcement is no invasion of State sovereignty. No law can be, which the people of the States have, by the Constitution of the United States, empowered Congress to enact.

It is true that none of these previous cases presented the question of the relationship between the Eleventh Amendment and the enforcement power granted to Congress under §5 of the Fourteenth Amendment. But we think that the Eleventh Amendment, and the principle of state sovereignty which it embodies, see Hans v. Louisiana (1890), are necessarily limited by the enforcement provisions of §5 of the Fourteenth Amendment. In that section Congress is expressly granted authority to enforce "by appropriate legislation" the substantive provisions of the Fourteenth Amendment, which themselves embody significant limitations on state authority. When Congress acts pursuant to §5, not only is it exercising legislative authority that is plenary within the terms of the constitutional grant, it is exercising that authority under one section of a constitutional Amendment whose other sections by their own terms embody limitations on state authority. We think that Congress may, in determining what is "appropriate legislation" for the purpose of enforcing the provisions of the Fourteenth Amendment, provide for private suits against States or state officials which are constitutionally impermissible in other contexts.

In Pennsylvania v. Union Gas Co., 491 U.S. 1 (1989), the Supreme Court held five to four that Congress may override the Eleventh Amendment and authorize suits against state governments pursuant to any of its constitutional powers, as long as the law in its text expressly authorizes such suits. In the case, the Supreme Court confronted two questions: (1) Does the Comprehensive Environmental Response, Compensation, and Liability Act of 1980 (CERCLA), as amended by the Superfund Amendments and Reauthorization Act of 1986 (SARA), authorize suits against state governments in federal court? (2) If so, does Congress, when legislating pursuant to the Commerce Clause, have the authority to create such state government liability?

The Court answered both questions affirmatively. However, the Court did so without a majority opinion and was very splintered. There were five votes that CERCLA permits states to be sued for monetary liability in federal court: Justices Brennan, Marshall, Blackmun, Stevens, and Scalia. There also were five votes that Congress, acting pursuant to its Commerce Clause authority, can create such federal court jurisdiction: Justices Brennan, Marshall, Blackmun, Stevens, and White.

Between 1989, when Pennsylvania v. Union Gas was decided, and 1996, when Seminole Tribe v. Florida was decided, there was a significant change in the composition of the Supreme Court. Four of the justices in majority in Pennsylvania v. Union Gas had left the Court—Justices Brennan, Marshall, Blackmun, and White. All four of the dissenters in Pennsylvania v. Union Gas remained on the Court. They were joined by Justice Clarence Thomas and overruled Pennsylvania v. Union Gas by a five-to-four margin.

SEMINOLE TRIBE OF FLORIDA v. FLORIDA

517 U.S. 44 (1996)

Chief Justice REHNQUIST delivered the opinion of the Court.

The Indian Gaming Regulatory Act provides that an Indian tribe may conduct certain gaming activities only in conformance with a valid compact between the tribe and the State in which the gaming activities are located. The Act, passed by Congress under the Indian Commerce Clause, U.S. Const., Art. I, §8, cl. 3, imposes upon the States a duty to negotiate in good faith with an Indian tribe toward the formation of a compact and authorizes a tribe to bring suit in federal court against a State in order to compel performance of that duty. We hold that notwithstanding Congress's clear intent to abrogate the States' sovereign immunity, the Indian Commerce Clause does not grant Congress that power, and therefore §2710(d)(7) cannot grant jurisdiction over a State that does not consent to be sued.

I

Congress passed the Indian Gaming Regulatory Act in 1988 in order to provide a statutory basis for the operation and regulation of gaming by Indian tribes. [The act requires that states negotiate in "good faith" with Indian tribes to permit gambling on Native American reservations and authorizes suits against state governments to enforce the law.]

In September 1991, the Seminole Tribe of Florida, petitioner, sued the State of Florida and its Governor, Lawton Chiles, respondents. Invoking jurisdiction under 25 U.S.C. §2710(d)(7)(A), as well as 28 U.S.C. §§1331 and 1362, petitioner alleged that respondents had "refused to enter into any negotiation for inclusion of [certain gaming activities] in a tribal-state compact," thereby violating the "requirement of good faith negotiation" contained in §2710(d)(3). Respondents moved to dismiss the complaint, arguing that the suit violated the State's sovereign immunity from suit in federal court.

II

Petitioner argues that Congress through the Act abrogated the States' immunity from suit. In order to determine whether Congress has abrogated the States' sovereign immunity, we ask two questions: first, whether Congress has "unequivocally expresse[d] its intent to abrogate the immunity"; and second, whether Congress has acted "pursuant to a valid exercise of powers."

A

Congress's intent to abrogate the States' immunity from suit must be obvious from "a clear legislative statement." This rule arises from a recognition of the important role played by the Eleventh Amendment and the broader principles that it reflects. Here, we agree with the parties, with the Eleventh Circuit in the decision below, and with virtually every other court that has confronted the question that Congress has in §2710(d)(7) provided an "unmistakably clear" statement of its intent to abrogate. Section 2710(d)(7)(A)(i) vests jurisdiction in "[t]he United States district courts . . . over any cause of action . . . arising from the failure of a State to enter into negotiations . . . or to conduct such negotiations in good faith."

B

Having concluded that Congress clearly intended to abrogate the States' sovereign immunity through §2710(d)(7), we turn now to consider whether the Act was passed "pursuant to a valid exercise of power." [O]ur inquiry into whether Congress has the power to abrogate unilaterally the States' immunity from suit is narrowly focused on one question: Was the Act in question passed pursuant to a constitutional provision granting Congress the power to abrogate? See, e.g., Fitzpatrick v. Bitzer (1976). Previously, in conducting that inquiry, we have found authority to abrogate under only two provisions of the Constitution. In *Fitzpatrick*, we recognized that the Fourteenth Amendment, by expanding federal power at the expense of state autonomy, had fundamentally altered the balance of state and federal power struck by the Constitution. We noted that §1 of the Fourteenth Amendment contained prohibitions expressly directed at the States and that §5 of the Amendment expressly provided that "The Congress shall have power to enforce, by appropriate legislation, the provisions of this article." We held that through the Fourteenth Amendment, federal power extended to intrude upon the province of the Eleventh Amendment and therefore that §5 of the Fourteenth Amendment allowed Congress to abrogate the immunity from suit guaranteed by that Amendment.

In only one other case has congressional abrogation of the States' Eleventh Amendment immunity been upheld. In Pennsylvania v. Union Gas Co. (1989), a plurality of the Court found that the Interstate Commerce Clause, Art. I, §8, cl. 3, granted Congress the power to abrogate state sovereign immunity, stating that the power to regulate interstate commerce would be "incomplete without the authority to render States liable in damages." Justice White added the fifth vote necessary to the result in that case, but wrote separately in order to express that he "[did] not agree with much of [the plurality's] reasoning."

The Court in *Union Gas* reached a result without an expressed rationale agreed upon by a majority of the Court. We have already seen that Justice Brennan's opinion received the support of only three other Justices. Of the other five, Justice White, who provided the fifth vote for the result, wrote separately in order to indicate his disagreement with the plurality's rationale, and four Justices joined together in a dissent that rejected the plurality's rationale. Since it was issued, *Union Gas* has created confusion among the lower courts that have sought to understand and apply the deeply fractured decision.

The plurality's rationale also deviated sharply from our established federalism jurisprudence and essentially eviscerated our decision in Hans v. Lousiana (1890). Never before the decision in *Union Gas* had we suggested that the bounds of Article III could be expanded by Congress operating pursuant to any constitutional provision other than the Fourteenth Amendment. Indeed, it had seemed fundamental that Congress could not expand the jurisdiction of the federal courts beyond the bounds of Article III. Marbury v. Madison (1803).

In the five years since it was decided, *Union Gas* has proved to be a solitary departure from established law. Reconsidering the decision in *Union Gas*, we conclude that none of the policies underlying stare decisis require our continuing adherence to its holding. The decision has, since its issuance, been of questionable precedential value, largely because a majority of the Court expressly disagreed with the rationale of the plurality. The case involved the interpretation of the Constitution and therefore may be altered only by constitutional amendment or revision by this Court. Finally, both the result in *Union Gas* and the plurality's rationale depart from our established understanding of the Eleventh Amendment and undermine the accepted function of Article III. We feel bound to conclude that *Union Gas* was wrongly decided and that it should be, and now is, overruled.

In overruling *Union Gas* today, we reconfirm that the background principle of state sovereign immunity embodied in the Eleventh Amendment is not so ephemeral as to dissipate when the subject of the suit is an area, like the regulation of Indian commerce, that is under the exclusive control of the Federal Government. Even when the Constitution vests in Congress complete law-making authority over a particular area, the Eleventh Amendment prevents congressional authorization of suits by private parties against unconsenting States. The Eleventh Amendment restricts the judicial power under Article III, and Article I cannot be used to circumvent the constitutional limitations placed upon federal jurisdiction. Petitioner's suit against the State of Florida must be dismissed for a lack of jurisdiction.

Justice Stevens, dissenting.

This case is about power — the power of the Congress of the United States to create a private federal cause of action against a State, or its Governor, for the violation of a federal right. [I]n a sharp break with the past, today the Court holds that with the narrow and illogical exception of statutes enacted pursuant to the Enforcement Clause of the Fourteenth Amendment, Congress has no such power.

The importance of the majority's decision to overrule the Court's holding in Pennsylvania v. Union Gas Co. cannot be overstated. The majority's opinion does not simply preclude Congress from establishing the rather curious statutory scheme under which Indian tribes may seek the aid of a federal court to secure a State's good-faith negotiations over gaming regulations. Rather, it prevents Congress from providing a federal forum for a broad range of actions against States, from those sounding in copyright and patent law, to those concerning bankruptcy, environmental law, and the regulation of our vast national economy.

There may be room for debate over whether, in light of the Eleventh Amendment, Congress has the power to ensure that such a cause of action may be enforced in federal court by a citizen of another State or a foreign citizen. There can be no serious debate, however, over whether Congress has the power to ensure that such a cause of action may be brought by a citizen of the State being sued. Congress's authority in that regard is clear.

The fundamental error that continues to lead the Court astray is its failure to acknowledge that its modern embodiment of the ancient doctrine of sovereign immunity "has absolutely nothing to do with the limit on judicial power contained in the Eleventh Amendment." It rests rather on concerns of federalism and comity that merit respect but are nevertheless, in cases such as the one before us, subordinate to the plenary power of Congress.

Justice Souter, with whom Justice Ginsburg and Justice Breyer join, dissenting.

In holding the State of Florida immune to suit under the Indian Gaming Regulatory Act, the Court today holds for the first time since the founding of the Republic that Congress has no authority to subject a State to the jurisdiction of a federal court at the behest of an individual asserting a federal right.

The fault I find with the majority today is not in its decision to reexamine *Union Gas*, for the Court in that case produced no majority for a single rationale supporting congressional authority. Instead, I part company from the Court because I am convinced that its decision is fundamentally mistaken, and for that reason I respectfully dissent.

It is useful to separate three questions: (1) whether the States enjoyed sovereign immunity if sued in their own courts in the period prior to ratification of the National Constitution; (2) if so, whether after ratification the States were entitled to claim some such immunity when sued in a federal court exercising jurisdiction either because the suit was between a State and a nonstate litigant who was not its citizen, or because the issue in the case raised a federal question; and (3) whether any state sovereign immunity recognized in federal court may be abrogated by Congress.

The answer to the first question is not clear, although some of the framers assumed that States did enjoy immunity in their own courts. The second question was not debated at the time of ratification, except as to citizen-state diversity jurisdiction; there was no unanimity, but in due course the Court in Chisholm v. Georgia (1793), answered that a state defendant enjoyed no such immunity. As to federal-question jurisdiction, state sovereign immunity seems not to have been debated prior to ratification, the silence probably showing a general understanding at the time that the States would have no immunity in such cases.

The adoption of the Eleventh Amendment soon changed the result in *Chisholm*, not by mentioning sovereign immunity, but by eliminating citizen-state diversity jurisdiction over cases with state defendants. I will explain why the Eleventh Amendment did not affect federal-question jurisdiction, a notion that needs to be understood for the light it casts on the soundness of *Hans*'s holding that States did enjoy sovereign immunity in federal-question suits. The *Hans* Court erroneously assumed that a State could plead sovereign immunity against a noncitizen suing under federal-question jurisdiction, and for that reason held that a State must enjoy the same protection in a suit by one of its citizens. The error of *Hans*'s reasoning is underscored by its clear inconsistency with the Founders' hostility to the implicit reception of common-law doctrine as federal law, and with the Founders' conception of sovereign power as divided between the States and the National Government for the sake of very practical objectives.

The Court's answer today to the third question is likewise at odds with the Founders' view that common law, when it was received into the new American legal system, was always subject to legislative amendment. In ignoring the reasons for this pervasive understanding at the time of the ratification, and in holding that a non-textual common-law rule limits a clear grant of congressional power under Article I, the Court follows a course that has brought it to grief before in our history, and promises to do so again.

The doctrine of sovereign immunity comprises two distinct rules, which are not always separately recognized. The one rule holds that the King or the Crown, as the font of law, is not bound by the law's provisions; the other provides that the King or Crown, as the font of justice, is not subject to suit in its own courts. The one rule limits the reach of substantive law; the other, the jurisdiction of the courts. We are concerned here only with the latter rule, which took its common-law form in the high Middle Ages.

The significance of this doctrine in the nascent American law is less clear, however, than its early development and steady endurance in England might suggest. While some colonial governments may have enjoyed some such immunity, the scope (and even the existence) of this governmental immunity in pre-Revolutionary America remains disputed.

Whatever the scope of sovereign immunity might have been in the Colonies, however, or during the period of Confederation, the proposal to establish a National Government under the Constitution drafted in 1787 presented a prospect unknown to the common law prior to the American experience: [T]he States would become parts of a system in which sovereignty over even domestic matters would be divided or parcelled out between the States and the Nation, the latter to be invested with its own judicial power and the right to prevail against the States whenever their respective substantive laws might be in conflict.

The history and structure of the Eleventh Amendment convincingly show that it reaches only to suits subject to federal jurisdiction exclusively under the Citizen-State Diversity Clauses. In precisely tracking the language in Article III providing for citizen-state diversity jurisdiction, the text of the Amendment does, after all, suggest to common sense that only the Diversity Clauses are being addressed. If the framers had meant the Amendment to bar federal-question suits as well, they could not only have made their intentions clearer very easily, but could simply have adopted the first post-*Chisholm* proposal, introduced in the House of Representatives by Theodore Sedgwick of Massachusetts on instructions from the Legislature of that Commonwealth. Its provisions would have had exactly that expansive effect:

> [N]o state shall be liable to be made a party defendant, in any of the judicial courts, established, or which shall be established under the authority of the United States, at the suit of any person or persons, whether a citizen or citizens, or a foreigner or foreigners, or of any body politic or corporate, whether within or without the United States.

Three critical errors in Hans v. Louisiana weigh against constitutionalizing its holding as the majority does today. The first we have already seen: the *Hans* Court misread the Eleventh Amendment. It also misunderstood the conditions under which common-law doctrines were received or rejected at the time of the founding, and it fundamentally mistook the very nature of sovereignty in the young Republic that was supposed to entail a State's immunity to federal-question jurisdiction in a federal court. While I would not, as a matter of stare decisis, overrule *Hans* today, an understanding of its failings on these points will show how the Court today simply compounds already serious error in taking *Hans* the further step of investing its rule with constitutional inviolability against the considered judgment of Congress to abrogate it.

Because neither text, precedent, nor history supports the majority's abdication of our responsibility to exercise the jurisdiction entrusted to us in Article III, I would reverse the judgment of the Court of Appeals.

b.   Cases Denying Congress Authority to Act Under §5 to Authorize Suits Against State Governments

After *Seminole Tribe*, it is clear that Congress may authorize suits against state governments only when it is acting pursuant to §5 of the Fourteenth Amendment. Therefore, the scope of Congress's power under this provision becomes crucial. If a law is within that authority, then states can be sued for violating it. If a law is not within that authority, then states cannot be sued for violating it.[51] In three decisions between 1999 and 2001, the Court found that federal statutes could not be used to sue state governments because the laws did not fit within the scope of Congress's §5 power.

FLORIDA PREPAID POSTSECONDARY EDUCATION EXPENSE BOARD v. COLLEGE SAVINGS BANK & UNITED STATES, 527 U.S. 627 (1999): Chief Justice REHNQUIST delivered the opinion of the Court.

In 1992, Congress amended the patent laws and expressly abrogated the States' sovereign immunity from claims of patent infringement. Respondent College Savings then sued the State of Florida for patent infringement, and the Court of Appeals held that Congress had validly abrogated the States' sovereign immunity from infringement suits pursuant to its authority under §5 of the Fourteenth Amendment. We hold that, under City of Boerne v. Flores (1997), the statute cannot be sustained as legislation enacted to enforce the guarantees of the Fourteenth Amendment's Due Process Clause.

Since 1987, respondent College Savings Bank, a New Jersey chartered savings bank located in Princeton, New Jersey, has marketed and sold certificates of deposit known as the CollegeSure CD, which are essentially annuity contracts for financing future college expenses. College Savings obtained a patent for its financing methodology, designed to guarantee investors sufficient funds to cover the costs of tuition for colleges. Petitioner Florida Prepaid Postsecondary Education Expenses Board (Florida Prepaid) is an entity created by the State of Florida that administers similar tuition prepayment contracts available to Florida residents and their children. College Savings claims that, in the course of administering its tuition prepayment program, Florida Prepaid directly and indirectly infringed College Savings' patent.

College Savings brought an infringement action under 35 U.S.C. §271(a) against Florida Prepaid in the United States District Court for the District of New Jersey in November 1994. By the time College Savings filed its suit, Congress had already passed the Patent and Plant Variety Protection Remedy Clarification Act (Patent Remedy Act), 35 U.S.C. §§271(h), 296(a). Congress enacted the Patent Remedy Act to "clarify that States, instrumentalities of States, and officers and employees of States acting in their official capacity, are subject to suit in Federal court by any person for infringement of patents and plant variety protections."

> Any State, any instrumentality of a State, and any officer or employee of a State or instrumentality of a State acting in his official capacity, shall not be immune, under the eleventh amendment of the Constitution of the United States or under any other doctrine of sovereign immunity, from suit in Federal court by any person . . . for infringement of a patent under section 271, or for any other violation under this title.

Relying on these provisions, College Savings alleged that Florida Prepaid had willfully infringed its patent under §271, as well as contributed to and induced infringement.

---

51. The only exception is that the Supreme Court has held that sovereign immunity does not apply in bankruptcy proceedings. Central Virginia Community College v. Katz, 546 U.S. 346 (2006).

After this Court decided Seminole Tribe of Fla. v. Florida (1996), Florida Prepaid moved to dismiss the action on the grounds of sovereign immunity. Florida Prepaid argued that the Patent Remedy Act was an unconstitutional attempt by Congress to use its Article I powers to abrogate state sovereign immunity. College Savings responded that Congress had properly exercised its power pursuant to §5 of the Fourteenth Amendment to enforce the guarantees of the Due Process Clause in §1 of the Amendment.

College Savings and the United States nonetheless contend that Congress's enactment of the Patent Remedy Act validly abrogated the States' sovereign immunity. To determine the merits of this proposition, we must answer two questions: "first, whether Congress has 'unequivocally expresse[d] its intent to abrogate the immunity,' . . . and second, whether Congress has acted 'pursuant to a valid exercise of power.'" We agree with the parties and the Federal Circuit that in enacting the Patent Remedy Act, Congress has made its intention to abrogate the States' immunity "'unmistakably clear in the language of the statute.'" Indeed, Congress's intent to abrogate could not have been any clearer.

Whether Congress had the power to compel States to surrender their sovereign immunity for these purposes, however, is another matter. Congress justified the Patent Remedy Act under three sources of constitutional authority: the Patent Clause, Art. I, §8, cl. 8; the Interstate Commerce Clause, Art. I, §8, cl. 3; and §5 of the Fourteenth Amendment. In *Seminole Tribe*, of course, this Court overruled the plurality opinion in Pennsylvania v. Union Gas Co. (1989). *Seminole Tribe* makes clear that Congress may not abrogate state sovereign immunity pursuant to its Article I powers; hence the Patent Remedy Act cannot be sustained under either the Commerce Clause or the Patent Clause.

Instead, College Savings and the United States argue that the Federal Circuit properly concluded that Congress enacted the Patent Remedy Act to secure the Fourteenth Amendment's protections against deprivations of property without due process of law. While reaffirming the view that state sovereign immunity does not yield to Congress's Article I powers, this Court in *Seminole Tribe* also reaffirmed its holding in Fitzpatrick v. Bitzer (1976), that Congress retains the authority to abrogate state sovereign immunity pursuant to the Fourteenth Amendment.

College Savings and the United States are correct in suggesting that "appropriate" legislation pursuant to the Enforcement Clause of the Fourteenth Amendment could abrogate state sovereignty. Congress itself apparently thought the Patent Remedy Act could be so justified.

But the legislation must nonetheless be "appropriate" under §5 as that term was construed in *City of Boerne*. Can the Patent Remedy Act be viewed as remedial or preventive legislation aimed at securing the protections of the Fourteenth Amendment for patent owners? Following *City of Boerne*, we must first identify the Fourteenth Amendment "evil" or "wrong" that Congress intended to remedy, guided by the principle that the propriety of any §5 legislation "must be judged with reference to the historical experience . . . it reflects." The underlying conduct at issue here is state infringement of patents and the use of sovereign immunity to deny patent owners compensation for the invasion of their patent rights. It is this conduct then — unremedied patent infringement by the States — that must give rise to the Fourteenth Amendment violation that Congress sought to redress in the Patent Remedy Act.

In enacting the Patent Remedy Act, however, Congress identified no pattern of patent infringement by the States, let alone a pattern of constitutional violations. Unlike the undisputed record of racial discrimination confronting Congress in the voting rights cases, Congress came up with little evidence of infringing conduct on the part of the States. The House Report acknowledged that "many states comply with patent law" and could provide only two examples of patent infringement suits against the States. The Federal Circuit in its opinion identified only eight patent-infringement suits prosecuted against the States in the 110 years between 1880 and 1990.

Testimony before the House Subcommittee in favor of the bill acknowledged that "states are willing and able to respect patent rights. The fact that there are so few reported cases involving patent infringement claims against states underlies the point." Even the bill's sponsor conceded that "[w]e do not have any evidence of massive or widespread violation of patent laws by the States either with or without this State immunity." The Senate Report, as well, contains no evidence that unremedied patent infringement by States had become a problem of national import. At most, Congress heard testimony that patent infringement by States might increase in the future.

Though patents may be considered "property" for purposes of our analysis, the legislative record still provides little support for the proposition that Congress sought to remedy a Fourteenth Amendment violation in enacting the Patent Remedy Act. [U]nder the plain terms of the Clause and the clear import of our precedent, a State's infringement of a patent, though interfering with a patent owner's right to exclude others, does not by itself violate the Constitution. Instead, only where the State provides no remedy, or only inadequate remedies, to injured patent owners for its infringement of their patent could a deprivation of property without due process result. See Parratt v. Taylor (1981).

Congress, however, barely considered the availability of state remedies for patent infringement and hence whether the States' conduct might have amounted to a constitutional violation under the Fourteenth Amendment. It did hear a limited amount of testimony to the effect that the remedies available in some States were uncertain. Congress itself said nothing about the existence or adequacy of state remedies in the statute or in the Senate Report, and made only a few fleeting references to state remedies in the House Report, essentially repeating the testimony of the witnesses.

The legislative record thus suggests that the Patent Remedy Act does not respond to a history of "widespread and persisting deprivation of constitutional rights" of the sort Congress has faced in enacting proper prophylactic §5 legislation. *City of Boerne.* Instead, Congress appears to have enacted this legislation in response to a handful of instances of state patent infringement that do not necessarily violate the Constitution. Though the lack of support in the legislative record is not determinative, identifying the targeted constitutional wrong or evil is still a critical part of our §5 calculus because "[s]trong measures appropriate to address one harm may be an unwarranted response to another, lesser one." Here, the record at best offers scant support for Congress's conclusion that States were depriving patent owners of property without due process of law by pleading sovereign immunity in federal-court patent actions.

The historical record and the scope of coverage therefore make it clear that the Patent Remedy Act cannot be sustained under §5 of the Fourteenth

Amendment. The examples of States avoiding liability for patent infringement by pleading sovereign immunity in a federal-court patent action are scarce enough, but any plausible argument that such action on the part of the State deprived patentees of property and left them without a remedy under state law is scarcer still. The statute's apparent and more basic aims were to provide a uniform remedy for patent infringement and to place States on the same footing as private parties under that regime. These are proper Article I concerns, but that Article does not give Congress the power to enact such legislation after *Seminole Tribe.*

Justice STEVENS, with whom Justice SOUTER, Justice GINSBURG, and Justice BREYER join, dissenting.

The Constitution vests Congress with plenary authority over patents and copyrights. Nearly 200 years ago, Congress provided for exclusive jurisdiction of patent infringement litigation in the federal courts. In 1992 Congress clarified that jurisdictional grant by an amendment to the patent law that unambiguously authorizes patent infringement actions against States, state instrumentalities, and any officer or employee of a State acting in his official capacity. Given the absence of effective state remedies for patent infringement by States and the statutory pre-emption of such state remedies, the 1992 Patent and Plant Variety Protection Remedy Clarification Act (Patent Remedy Act) was an appropriate exercise of Congress's power under §5 of the Fourteenth Amendment to prevent state deprivations of property without due process of law.

This Court's recent decision in City of Boerne v. Flores (1997), amply supports congressional authority to enact the Patent Remedy Act, whether one assumes that States seldom infringe patents, or that patent infringements potentially permeate an "unlimited range of state conduct." Today the Court first acknowledges that the "need for uniformity in the construction of patent law is undoubtedly important," but then discounts its significance as merely "a factor which belongs to the Article I patent-power calculus, rather than to any determination of whether a state plea of sovereign immunity deprives a patentee of property without due process of law." But the "Article I patent-power calculus," is directly relevant to this case because it establishes the constitutionality of the congressional decision to vest exclusive jurisdiction over patent infringement cases in the federal courts. That basic decision was unquestionably appropriate. It was equally appropriate for Congress to abrogate state sovereign immunity in patent infringement cases in order to close a potential loophole in the uniform federal scheme, which, if undermined, would necessarily decrease the efficacy of the process afforded to patent holders.

As the Court recognizes, Congress's authority under §5 of the Fourteenth Amendment extends to enforcing the Due Process Clause of that Amendment. Congress decided, and I agree, that the Patent Remedy Act was a proper exercise of this power. The Court acknowledges, as it must, that patents are property.

As I read the Court's opinion, its negative answer to that question has nothing to do with the facts of this case. Instead, it relies entirely on perceived deficiencies in the evidence reviewed by Congress before it enacted the clarifying amendment. "In enacting the Patent Remedy Act . . . Congress identified no pattern of patent infringement by the States, let alone a pattern of constitutional violations."

It is quite unfair for the Court to strike down Congress's Act based on an absence of findings supporting a requirement this Court had not yet articulated.

The legislative history of the Patent Remedy Act makes it abundantly clear that Congress was attempting to hurdle the then-most-recent barrier this Court had erected in the Eleventh Amendment course — the "clear statement" rule.

Nevertheless, Congress did hear testimony about inadequate state remedies for patent infringement when considering the Patent Remedy Act. Congress heard other general testimony that state remedies would likely be insufficient to compensate inventors whose patents had been infringed. The Acting Commissioner of Patents stated: "If States and their instrumentalities were immune from suit in federal court for patent infringement, patent holders would be forced to pursue uncertain, perhaps even non-existent, remedies under State law." The legislative record references several cases of patent infringement involving States. In addition, Congress found that state infringement of patents was likely to increase. Furthermore, States and their instrumentalities are heavily involved in the federal patent system. The United States Patent and Trademark Office issued more than 2,000 patents to universities (both public and private) in 1986 alone. Royalty earnings from licenses at United States universities totaled $273.5 million in 1995, a 12% increase over the prior year.

Even if [state] remedies might be available in theory, it would have been "appropriate" for Congress to conclude that they would not guarantee patentees due process in infringement actions against state defendants. State judges have never had the exposure to patent litigation that federal judges have experienced for decades, and, unlike infringement actions brought in federal district courts, their decisions would not be reviewable in the Court of Appeals for the Federal Circuit. Surely this Court would not undertake the task of reviewing every state court decision that arguably misapplied patent law.

Finally, this Court has never mandated that Congress must find "widespread and persisting deprivation of constitutional rights," in order to employ its §5 authority. It is not surprising, therefore, that Congress did not compile an extensive legislative record analyzing the due process (or lack thereof) that each State might afford for a patent infringement suit retooled as an action in tort. In 1992, Congress had no reason to believe it needed to do such a thing; indeed, it should not have to do so today.

For these reasons, I am convinced that the 1992 Act should be upheld even if full respect is given to the Court's recent cases cloaking the States with increasing protection from congressional legislation. I do, however, note my continuing dissent from the Court's aggressive sovereign immunity jurisprudence; today, this Court once again demonstrates itself to be the champion of States' rights. In this case, it seeks to guarantee rights the States themselves did not express any particular desire in possessing: during Congress's hearings on the Patent Remedy Act, although invited to do so, the States chose not to testify in opposition to the abrogation of their immunity.

KIMEL v. FLORIDA BOARD OF REGENTS, 528 U.S. 62 (2000): Justice O'Connor delivered the opinion of the Court.

The Age Discrimination in Employment Act of 1967, makes it unlawful for an employer, including a State, "to fail or refuse to hire or to discharge any individual or otherwise discriminate against any individual . . . because of such individual's age." In these cases, three sets of plaintiffs filed suit under the Act, seeking money damages for their state employers' alleged discrimination on the basis of age. In these cases, we are asked to consider whether the

ADEA contains a clear statement of Congress's intent to abrogate the States' Eleventh Amendment immunity and, if so, whether the ADEA is a proper exercise of Congress's constitutional authority. We conclude that the ADEA does contain a clear statement of Congress's intent to abrogate the States' immunity, but that the abrogation exceeded Congress's authority under §5 of the Fourteenth Amendment.

To determine whether a federal statute properly subjects States to suits by individuals, we apply a "simple but stringent test: 'Congress may abrogate the States' constitutionally secured immunity from suit in federal court only by making its intention unmistakably clear in the language of the statute.'" We agree with petitioners that the ADEA satisfies that test. The ADEA clearly provides for suits by individuals against States. The Act authorizes employees to maintain actions for back pay "against any employer (including a public agency) in any Federal or State court of competent jurisdiction. . . ." Read as a whole, the plain language of these provisions clearly demonstrates Congress's intent to subject the States to suit for money damages at the hands of individual employees.

In *Seminole Tribe*, we held that Congress lacks power under Article I to abrogate the States' sovereign immunity. Section 5 of the Fourteenth Amendment, however, does grant Congress the authority to abrogate the States' sovereign immunity. In Fitzpatrick v. Bitzer (1976), we recognized that "the Eleventh Amendment, and the principle of state sovereignty which it embodies, are necessarily limited by the enforcement provisions of §5 of the Fourteenth Amendment."

As we recognized most recently in City of Boerne v. Flores (1997), §5 is an affirmative grant of power to Congress. "It is for Congress in the first instance to 'determin[e] whether and what legislation is needed to secure the guarantees of the Fourteenth Amendment,' and its conclusions are entitled to much deference." Congress's §5 power is not confined to the enactment of legislation that merely parrots the precise wording of the Fourteenth Amendment. Rather, Congress's power "to enforce" the Amendment includes the authority both to remedy and to deter violation of rights guaranteed thereunder by prohibiting a somewhat broader swath of conduct, including that which is not itself forbidden by the Amendment's text.

Nevertheless, we have also recognized that the same language that serves as the basis for the affirmative grant of congressional power also serves to limit that power. For example, Congress cannot "decree the substance of the Fourteenth Amendment's restrictions on the States. . . . It has been given the power 'to enforce,' not the power to determine what constitutes a constitutional violation." The ultimate interpretation and determination of the Fourteenth Amendment's substantive meaning remains the province of the Judicial Branch.

Applying the same "congruence and proportionality" test in these cases, we conclude that the ADEA is not "appropriate legislation" under §5 of the Fourteenth Amendment. Initially, the substantive requirements the ADEA imposes on state and local governments are disproportionate to any unconstitutional conduct that conceivably could be targeted by the Act. We have considered claims of unconstitutional age discrimination under the Equal Protection Clause three times. See Gregory v. Ashcroft (1991); Vance v. Bradley (1979); Massachusetts Bd. of Retirement v. Murgia (1976) (per curiam). In all three cases, we held that the age classifications at issue did not violate the Equal

Protection Clause. Age classifications, unlike governmental conduct based on race or gender, cannot be characterized as "so seldom relevant to the achievement of any legitimate state interest that laws grounded in such considerations are deemed to reflect prejudice and antipathy." Older persons, again, unlike those who suffer discrimination on the basis of race or gender, have not been subjected to a "history of purposeful unequal treatment." Old age also does not define a discrete and insular minority because all persons, if they live out their normal life spans, will experience it. Accordingly, as we recognized in *Murgia*, *Bradley*, and *Gregory*, age is not a suspect classification under the Equal Protection Clause.

States may discriminate on the basis of age without offending the Fourteenth Amendment if the age classification in question is rationally related to a legitimate state interest. The rationality commanded by the Equal Protection Clause does not require States to match age distinctions and the legitimate interests they serve with razorlike precision. As we have explained, when conducting rational basis review "we will not overturn such [government action] unless the varying treatment of different groups or persons is so unrelated to the achievement of any combination of legitimate purposes that we can only conclude that the [government's] actions were irrational." In contrast, when a State discriminates on the basis of race or gender, we require a tighter fit between the discriminatory means and the legitimate ends they serve. Under the Fourteenth Amendment, a State may rely on age as a proxy for other qualities, abilities, or characteristics that are relevant to the State's legitimate interests. The Constitution does not preclude reliance on such generalizations. That age proves to be an inaccurate proxy in any individual case is irrelevant.

Judged against the backdrop of our equal protection jurisprudence, it is clear that the ADEA is "so out of proportion to a supposed remedial or preventive object that it cannot be understood as responsive to, or designed to prevent, unconstitutional behavior." *City of Boerne*. The Act, through its broad restriction on the use of age as a discriminating factor, prohibits substantially more state employment decisions and practices than would likely be held unconstitutional under the applicable equal protection, rational basis standard.

That the ADEA prohibits very little conduct likely to be held unconstitutional, while significant, does not alone provide the answer to our §5 inquiry. Difficult and intractable problems often require powerful remedies, and we have never held that §5 precludes Congress from enacting reasonably prophylactic legislation. Our task is to determine whether the ADEA is in fact just such an appropriate remedy or, instead, merely an attempt to substantively redefine the States' legal obligations with respect to age discrimination. One means by which we have made such a determination in the past is by examining the legislative record containing the reasons for Congress's action. "The appropriateness of remedial measures must be considered in light of the evil presented. Strong measures appropriate to address one harm may be an unwarranted response to another, lesser one."

Our examination of the ADEA's legislative record confirms that Congress's 1974 extension of the Act to the States was an unwarranted response to a perhaps inconsequential problem. Congress never identified any pattern of age discrimination by the States, much less any discrimination whatsoever that rose to the level of constitutional violation. The evidence compiled by petitioners to demonstrate such attention by Congress to age discrimination by the States falls well short of the mark. That evidence consists almost entirely of isolated sentences clipped from floor debates and legislative reports.

Finally, the United States' argument that Congress found substantial age discrimination in the private sector, is beside the point. Congress made no such findings with respect to the States. Although we also have doubts whether the findings Congress did make with respect to the private sector could be extrapolated to support a finding of unconstitutional age discrimination in the public sector, it is sufficient for these cases to note that Congress failed to identify a widespread pattern of age discrimination by the States.

A review of the ADEA's legislative record as a whole, then, reveals that Congress had virtually no reason to believe that state and local governments were unconstitutionally discriminating against their employees on the basis of age. Although that lack of support is not determinative of the §5 inquiry, Congress's failure to uncover any significant pattern of unconstitutional discrimination here confirms that Congress had no reason to believe that broad prophylactic legislation was necessary in this field. In light of the indiscriminate scope of the Act's substantive requirements, and the lack of evidence of widespread and unconstitutional age discrimination by the States, we hold that the ADEA is not a valid exercise of Congress's power under §5 of the Fourteenth Amendment. The ADEA's purported abrogation of the States' sovereign immunity is accordingly invalid.

Our decision today does not signal the end of the line for employees who find themselves subject to age discrimination at the hands of their state employers. We hold only that, in the ADEA, Congress did not validly abrogate the States' sovereign immunity to suits by private individuals. State employees are protected by state age discrimination statutes, and may recover money damages from their state employers, in almost every State of the Union. Those avenues of relief remain available today, just as they were before this decision.

Justice STEVENS, with whom Justice SOUTER, Justice GINSBURG, and Justice BREYER join, dissenting in part and concurring in part.

Congress's power to regulate the American economy includes the power to regulate both the public and the private sectors of the labor market. Federal rules outlawing discrimination in the workplace, like the regulation of wages and hours or health and safety standards, may be enforced against public as well as private employers. In my opinion, Congress's power to authorize federal remedies against state agencies that violate federal statutory obligations is coextensive with its power to impose those obligations on the States in the first place. Neither the Eleventh Amendment nor the doctrine of sovereign immunity places any limit on that power.

The application of the ancient judge-made doctrine of sovereign immunity in cases like these is supposedly justified as a freestanding limit on congressional authority, a limit necessary to protect States' "dignity and respect" from impairment by the National Government. The framers did not, however, select the Judicial Branch as the constitutional guardian of those state interests. Rather, the framers designed important structural safeguards to ensure that when the National Government enacted substantive law (and provided for its enforcement), the normal operation of the legislative process itself would adequately defend state interests from undue infringement. See generally Wechsler, The Political Safeguards of Federalism: The Role of the States in the Composition and Selection of the National Government, 54 Colum. L. Rev. 543 (1954).

Federalism concerns do make it appropriate for Congress to speak clearly when it regulates state action. But when it does so, as it has in these cases, we can safely presume that the burdens the statute imposes on the sovereignty of the several States were taken into account during the deliberative process leading to the enactment of the measure. Those burdens necessarily include the cost of defending against enforcement proceedings and paying whatever penalties might be incurred for violating the statute. In my judgment, the question whether those enforcement proceedings should be conducted exclusively by federal agencies, or may be brought by private parties as well, is a matter of policy for Congress to decide. In either event, once Congress has made its policy choice, the sovereignty concerns of the several States are satisfied, and the federal interest in evenhanded enforcement of federal law, explicitly endorsed in Article VI of the Constitution, does not countenance further limitations. There is not a word in the text of the Constitution supporting the Court's conclusion that the judge-made doctrine of sovereign immunity limits Congress's power to authorize private parties, as well as federal agencies, to enforce federal law against the States. The importance of respecting the framers' decision to assign the business of lawmaking to the Congress dictates firm resistance to the present majority's repeated substitution of its own views of federalism for those expressed in statutes enacted by the Congress and signed by the President.

The Eleventh Amendment simply does not support the Court's view. As has been stated before, the Amendment only places a textual limitation on the diversity jurisdiction of the federal courts. Here, however, private petitioners did not invoke the federal courts' diversity jurisdiction; they are citizens of the same State as the defendants and they are asserting claims that arise under federal law. Thus, today's decision (relying as it does on *Seminole Tribe*) rests entirely on a novel judicial interpretation of the doctrine of sovereign immunity, which the Court treats as though it were a constitutional precept. It is nevertheless clear to me that if Congress has the power to create the federal rights that these petitioners are asserting, it must also have the power to give the federal courts jurisdiction to remedy violations of those rights, even if it is necessary to "abrogate" the Court's "Eleventh Amendment" version of the common-law defense of sovereign immunity to do so. That is the essence of the Court's holding in Pennsylvania v. Union Gas Co. (1989).

I remain convinced that *Union Gas* was correctly decided and that the decision of five Justices in *Seminole Tribe* to overrule that case was profoundly misguided. Despite my respect for stare decisis, I am unwilling to accept *Seminole Tribe* as controlling precedent. The kind of judicial activism manifested in cases like *Seminole Tribe*, Alden v. Maine, Florida Prepaid Postsecondary Ed. Expense Bd. v. College Savings Bank, represents such a radical departure from the proper role of this Court that it should be opposed whenever the opportunity arises.

BOARD OF TRUSTEES, UNIVERSITY OF ALABAMA v. GARRETT, 531 U.S. 356 (2001): Chief Justice Rehnquist delivered the opinion of the Court.

We decide here whether employees of the State of Alabama may recover money damages by reason of the State's failure to comply with the provisions of Title I of the Americans with Disabilities Act of 1990 (ADA or Act). We hold that such suits are barred by the Eleventh Amendment.

The ADA prohibits certain employers, including the States, from "discriminat[ing] against a qualified individual with a disability because of the disability of such individual in regard to job application procedures, the hiring, advancement, or discharge of employees, employee compensation, job training, and other terms, conditions, and privileges of employment." To this end, the Act requires employers to "mak[e] reasonable accommodations to the known physical or mental limitations of an otherwise qualified individual with a disability who is an applicant or employee, unless [the employer] can demonstrate that the accommodation would impose an undue hardship on the operation of the [employer's] business."

Respondent Patricia Garrett, a registered nurse, was employed as the Director of Nursing, OB/Gyn/Neonatal Services, for the University of Alabama in Birmingham Hospital. In 1994, Garrett was diagnosed with breast cancer and subsequently underwent a lumpectomy, radiation treatment, and chemotherapy. Garrett's treatments required her to take substantial leave from work. Upon returning to work in July 1995, Garrett's supervisor informed Garrett that she would have to give up her Director position. Garrett then applied for and received a transfer to another, lower paying position as a nurse manager.

We have recognized, however, that Congress may abrogate the States' Eleventh Amendment immunity when it both unequivocally intends to do so and "act[s] pursuant to a valid grant of constitutional authority." The first of these requirements is not in dispute here. See 42 U.S.C. §12202 ("A State shall not be immune under the eleventh amendment to the Constitution of the United States from an action in [a] Federal or State court of competent jurisdiction for a violation of this chapter"). The question, then, is whether Congress acted within its constitutional authority by subjecting the States to suits in federal court for money damages under the ADA.

Congress may not, of course, base its abrogation of the States' Eleventh Amendment immunity upon the powers enumerated in Article I. In Fitzpatrick v. Bitzer (1976), however, we held that "the Eleventh Amendment, and the principle of state sovereignty which it embodies, are necessarily limited by the enforcement provisions of §5 of the Fourteenth Amendment." As a result, we concluded, Congress may subject nonconsenting States to suit in federal court when it does so pursuant to a valid exercise of its §5 power. Our cases have adhered to this proposition. Accordingly, the ADA can apply to the States only to the extent that the statute is appropriate §5 legislation.

Congress is not limited to mere legislative repetition of this Court's constitutional jurisprudence. "Rather, Congress's power 'to enforce' the Amendment includes the authority both to remedy and to deter violation of rights guaranteed thereunder by prohibiting a somewhat broader swath of conduct, including that which is not itself forbidden by the Amendment's text."

City of Boerne v. Flores also confirmed, however, the long-settled principle that it is the responsibility of this Court, not Congress, to define the substance of constitutional guarantees. Accordingly, §5 legislation reaching beyond the scope of §1's actual guarantees must exhibit "congruence and proportionality between the injury to be prevented or remedied and the means adopted to that end."

The first step in applying these now familiar principles is to identify with some precision the scope of the constitutional right at issue. Here, that inquiry requires us to examine the limitations §1 of the Fourteenth Amendment places upon States' treatment of the disabled. We look to our prior decisions under the Equal Protection Clause dealing with this issue.

In Cleburne v. Cleburne Living Center, Inc. (1985), we considered an equal protection challenge to a city ordinance requiring a special use permit for the operation of a group home for the mentally retarded. We conclud[ed] that such legislation incurs only the minimum "rational-basis" review applicable to general social and economic legislation. In a statement that today seems quite prescient, we explained that "if the large and amorphous class of the mentally retarded were deemed quasi-suspect for the reasons given by the Court of Appeals, it would be difficult to find a principled way to distinguish a variety of other groups who have perhaps immutable disabilities setting them off from others, who cannot themselves mandate the desired legislative responses, and who can claim some degree of prejudice from at least part of the public at large. One need mention in this respect only the aging, the disabled, the mentally ill, and the infirm. We are reluctant to set out on that course, and we decline to do so."

Under rational-basis review, where a group possesses "distinguishing characteristics relevant to interests the State has the authority to implement," a State's decision to act on the basis of those differences does not give rise to a constitutional violation. "Such a classification cannot run afoul of the Equal Protection Clause if there is a rational relationship between the disparity of treatment and some legitimate governmental purpose." Heller v. Doe (1993).

Thus, the result of *Cleburne* is that States are not required by the Fourteenth Amendment to make special accommodations for the disabled, so long as their actions towards such individuals are rational. They could quite hardheadedly — and perhaps hardheartedly — hold to job-qualification requirements which do not make allowance for the disabled. If special accommodations for the disabled are to be required, they have to come from positive law and not through the Equal Protection Clause.[52]

Once we have determined the metes and bounds of the constitutional right in question, we examine whether Congress identified a history and pattern of unconstitutional employment discrimination by the States against the disabled. Just as §1 of the Fourteenth Amendment applies only to actions committed "under color of state law," Congress's §5 authority is appropriately exercised only in response to state transgressions. The legislative record of the ADA, however, simply fails to show that Congress did in fact identify a pattern of irrational state discrimination in employment against the disabled.

Congress made a general finding in the ADA that "historically, society has tended to isolate and segregate individuals with disabilities, and, despite some improvements, such forms of discrimination against individuals with disabilities continue to be a serious and pervasive social problem." The record assembled by Congress includes many instances to support such a finding. But the great majority of these incidents do not deal with the activities of States.

Several of these incidents undoubtedly evidence an unwillingness on the part of state officials to make the sort of accommodations for the disabled required by the ADA. Whether they were irrational under our decision in *Cleburne* is more debatable, particularly when the incident is described out of context. But even if it were to be determined that each incident upon fuller examination showed unconstitutional action on the part of the State, these incidents taken together

52. It is worth noting that by the time that Congress enacted the ADA in 1990, every State in the Union had enacted such measures. [Footnote by the Court.]

fall far short of even suggesting the pattern of unconstitutional discrimination on which §5 legislation must be based. Congress, in enacting the ADA, found that "some 43,000,000 Americans have one or more physical or mental disabilities." In 1990, the States alone employed more than 4.5 million people. It is telling, we think, that given these large numbers, Congress assembled only such minimal evidence of unconstitutional state discrimination in employment against the disabled.

Justice Breyer maintains that Congress applied Title I of the ADA to the States in response to a host of incidents representing unconstitutional state discrimination in employment against persons with disabilities. A close review of the relevant materials, however, undercuts that conclusion. Justice Breyer's Appendix C consists not of legislative findings, but of unexamined, anecdotal accounts of "adverse, disparate treatment by state officials."[53] Of course, as we have already explained, "adverse, disparate treatment" often does not amount to a constitutional violation where rational-basis scrutiny applies. These accounts, moreover, were submitted not directly to Congress but to the Task Force on the Rights and Empowerment of Americans with Disabilities, which made no findings on the subject of state discrimination in employment. And, had Congress truly understood this information as reflecting a pattern of unconstitutional behavior by the States, one would expect some mention of that conclusion in the Act's legislative findings. There is none.

Even were it possible to squeeze out of these examples a pattern of unconstitutional discrimination by the States, the rights and remedies created by the ADA against the States would raise the same sort of concerns as to congruence and proportionality as were found in *City of Boerne*. For example, whereas it would be entirely rational (and therefore constitutional) for a state employer to conserve scarce financial resources by hiring employees who are able to use existing facilities, the ADA requires employers to "mak[e] existing facilities used by employees readily accessible to and usable by individuals with disabilities." The ADA does except employers from the "reasonable accommodatio[n]" requirement where the employer "can demonstrate that the accommodation would impose an undue hardship on the operation of the business of such covered entity." However, even with this exception, the accommodation duty far exceeds what is constitutionally required in that it makes unlawful a range of alternate responses that would be reasonable but would fall short of imposing an "undue burden" upon the employer. The Act also makes it the employer's duty to prove that it would suffer such a burden, instead of requiring (as the Constitution does) that the complaining party negate reasonable bases for the employer's decision.

The ADA's constitutional shortcomings are apparent when the Act is compared to Congress's efforts in the Voting Rights Act of 1965 to respond to a serious pattern of constitutional violations. In South Carolina v. Katzenbach (1966), we considered whether the Voting Rights Act was "appropriate" legislation to enforce the Fifteenth Amendment's protection against racial discrimination in voting. Concluding that it was a valid exercise of Congress's enforcement power under §2 of the Fifteenth Amendment, we noted that

---

53. Justice Breyer attached a 39-page appendix to his opinion (Appendix C) that listed references in the legislative history to government discrimination against the disabled. [Footnote by casebook author.]

"[b]efore enacting the measure, Congress explored with great care the problem of racial discrimination in voting."

In that Act, Congress documented a marked pattern of unconstitutional action by the States. State officials, Congress found, routinely applied voting tests in order to exclude African-American citizens from registering to vote. Congress also determined that litigation had proved ineffective and that there persisted an otherwise inexplicable 50-percentage-point gap in the registration of white and African-American voters in some States. Congress's response was to promulgate in the Voting Rights Act a detailed but limited remedial scheme designed to guarantee meaningful enforcement of the Fifteenth Amendment in those areas of the Nation where abundant evidence of States' systematic denial of those rights was identified.

The contrast between this kind of evidence, and the evidence that Congress considered in the present case, is stark. Congressional enactment of the ADA represents its judgment that there should be a "comprehensive national mandate for the elimination of discrimination against individuals with disabilities." Congress is the final authority as to desirable public policy, but in order to authorize private individuals to recover money damages against the States, there must be a pattern of discrimination by the States which violates the Fourteenth Amendment, and the remedy imposed by Congress must be congruent and proportional to the targeted violation. Those requirements are not met here, and to uphold the Act's application to the States would allow Congress to rewrite the Fourteenth Amendment law laid down by this Court in *Cleburne*. Section 5 does not so broadly enlarge congressional authority.[54]

Justice BREYER, with whom Justice STEVENS, Justice SOUTER, and Justice GINSBURG join, dissenting.

Reviewing the congressional record as if it were an administrative agency record, the Court holds the statutory provision before us unconstitutional. The Court concludes that Congress assembled insufficient evidence of unconstitutional discrimination, that Congress improperly attempted to "re-write" the law we established in Cleburne v. Cleburne Living Center, Inc. (1985), and that the law is not sufficiently tailored to address unconstitutional discrimination.

Section 5, however, grants Congress the "power to enforce, by appropriate legislation" the Fourteenth Amendment's equal protection guarantee. As the Court recognizes, state discrimination in employment against persons with disabilities might "run afoul of the Equal Protection Clause" where there is no "rational relationship between the disparity of treatment and some legitimate governmental purpose." In my view, Congress reasonably could have concluded that the remedy before us constitutes an "appropriate" way to enforce this basic equal protection requirement. And that is all the Constitution requires.

The Court says that its primary problem with this statutory provision is one of legislative evidence. It says that "Congress assembled only . . . minimal evidence

54. Our holding here that Congress did not validly abrogate the States' sovereign immunity from suit by private individuals for money damages under Title I does not mean that persons with disabilities have no federal recourse against discrimination. Title I of the ADA still prescribes standards applicable to the States. Those standards can be enforced by the United States in actions for money damages, as well as by private individuals in actions for injuctive relief under Ex parte Young (1908). In addition, state laws protecting the rights of persons with disabilities in employment and other aspects of life provide independent avenues of redress. [Footnote by the Court.]

of unconstitutional state discrimination in employment." In fact, Congress compiled a vast legislative record documenting "massive, society-wide discrimination" against persons with disabilities. S. Rep. No. 101-116, pp. 8-9 (1989). In addition to the information presented at 13 congressional hearings and its own prior experience gathered over 40 years during which it contemplated and enacted considerable similar legislation, Congress created a special task force to assess the need for comprehensive legislation. That task force held hearings in every State, attended by more than 30,000 people, including thousands who had experienced discrimination firsthand. The task force hearings, Congress's own hearings, and an analysis of "census data, national polls, and other studies" led Congress to conclude that "people with disabilities, as a group, occupy an inferior status in our society, and are severely disadvantaged socially, vocationally, economically, and educationally." As to employment, Congress found that "[t]wo-thirds of all disabled Americans between the age of 16 and 64 [were] not working at all," even though a large majority wanted to, and were able to, work productively. S. Rep. No. 101-116, at 9. And Congress found that this discrimination flowed in significant part from "stereotypic assumptions" as well as "purposeful unequal treatment."

The powerful evidence of discriminatory treatment throughout society in general, including discrimination by private persons and local governments, implicates state governments as well, for state agencies form part of that same larger society. There is no particular reason to believe that they are immune from the "stereotypic assumptions" and pattern of "purposeful unequal treatment" that Congress found prevalent. The Court claims that it "make[s] no sense" to take into consideration constitutional violations committed by local governments. But the substantive obligation that the Equal Protection Clause creates applies to state and local governmental entities alike. Local governments often work closely with, and under the supervision of, state officials, and in general, state and local government employers are similarly situated. Nor is determining whether an apparently "local" entity is entitled to Eleventh Amendment immunity as simple as the majority suggests — it often requires a "detailed examination of the relevant provisions of [state] law."

In any event, there is no need to rest solely upon evidence of discrimination by local governments or general societal discrimination. There are roughly 300 examples of discrimination by state governments themselves in the legislative record. I fail to see how this evidence "fall[s] far short of even suggesting the pattern of unconstitutional discrimination on which §5 legislation must be based."

The congressionally appointed task force collected numerous specific examples, provided by persons with disabilities themselves, of adverse, disparate treatment by state officials. They reveal, not what the Court describes as "half a dozen" instances of discrimination, but hundreds of instances of adverse treatment at the hands of state officials — instances in which a person with a disability found it impossible to obtain a state job, to retain state employment, to use the public transportation that was readily available to others in order to get to work, or to obtain a public education, which is often a prerequisite to obtaining employment. State-imposed barriers also frequently made it difficult or impossible for people to vote, to enter a public building, to access important government services, such as calling for emergency assistance, and to find a place to live due to a pattern of irrational zoning decisions similar to the discrimination that we held unconstitutional in *Cleburne.*

Regardless, Congress expressly found substantial unjustified discrimination against persons with disabilities. The evidence in the legislative record bears out Congress's finding that the adverse treatment of persons with disabilities was often arbitrary or invidious in this sense, and thus unjustified. For example, one study that was before Congress revealed that "most . . . governmental agencies in [one State] discriminated in hiring against job applicants for an average period of five years after treatment for cancer," based in part on coworkers' misguided belief that "cancer is contagious." A school inexplicably refused to exempt a deaf teacher, who taught at a school for the deaf, from a "listening skills" requirement. A State refused to hire a blind employee as director of an agency for the blind — even though he was the most qualified applicant. Certain state agencies apparently had general policies against hiring or promoting persons with disabilities. A zoo turned away children with Downs Syndrome "because [the zookeeper] feared they would upset the chimpanzees." There were reports of numerous zoning decisions based upon "negative attitudes" or "fear," such as a zoning board that denied a permit for an obviously pretextual reason after hearing arguments that a facility would house "deviants" who needed "room to roam." Congress could have reasonably believed that these examples represented signs of a widespread problem of unconstitutional discrimination.

The Court argues in the alternative that the statute's damage remedy is not "congruent" with and "proportional" to the equal protection problem that Congress found. The Court suggests that the Act's "reasonable accommodation" requirement, and disparate impact standard, "far excee[d] what is constitutionally required." But we have upheld disparate impact standards in contexts where they were not "constitutionally required."

And what is wrong with a remedy that, in response to unreasonable employer behavior, requires an employer to make accommodations that are reasonable? Of course, what is "reasonable" in the statutory sense and what is "unreasonable" in the constitutional sense might differ. In other words, the requirement may exceed what is necessary to avoid a constitutional violation. But it is just that power — the power to require more than the minimum — that §5 grants to Congress, as this Court has repeatedly confirmed.

c.   Congress's Greater Authority to Legislate Concerning Types of Discrimination and Rights That Receive Heightened Scrutiny

As is discussed in subsequent chapters concerning individual rights and equal protection, the Supreme Court uses "heightened scrutiny" for some types of discrimination and for fundamental rights. For example, discrimination based on race or infringement of fundamental rights must meet strict scrutiny; that is, it must be necessary to achieve a compelling government purpose. Some types of discrimination must meet "intermediate scrutiny"; that is, they must be substantially related to achieving a substantial government purpose.

In two very recent cases, the Supreme Court has held that Congress has more authority to act under §5 when dealing with types of discrimination and rights that trigger heightened scrutiny. In reading these cases, consider why the Court concluded that Congress's power under §5 varies depending on the level of scrutiny used.

NEVADA DEPARTMENT OF HUMAN RESOURCES v. HIBBS, 538 U.S. 721 (2003): Chief Justice REHNQUIST delivered the opinion of the Court.

The Family and Medical Leave Act of 1993 (FMLA or Act) entitles eligible employees to take up to 12 work weeks of unpaid leave annually for any of several reasons, including the onset of a "serious health condition" in an employee's spouse, child, or parent. The Act creates a private right of action to seek both equitable relief and money damages "against any employer (including a public agency) in any Federal or State court of competent jurisdiction," should that employer "interfere with, restrain, or deny the exercise of" FMLA rights. We hold that employees of the State of Nevada may recover money damages in the event of the State's failure to comply with the family-care provision of the Act.

Petitioners include the Nevada Department of Human Resources (Department) and two of its officers. Respondent William Hibbs (hereinafter respondent) worked for the Department's Welfare Division. In April and May 1997, he sought leave under the FMLA to care for his ailing wife, who was recovering from a car accident and neck surgery. The Department granted his request for the full 12 weeks of FMLA leave and authorized him to use the leave intermittently as needed between May and December 1997. Respondent did so until August 5, 1997, after which he did not return to work. In October 1997, the Department informed respondent that he had exhausted his FMLA leave, that no further leave would be granted, and that he must report to work by November 12, 1997. Respondent failed to do so and was terminated. Respondent sued petitioners in the United States District Court seeking damages and injunctive and declaratory relief.

For over a century now, we have made clear that the Constitution does not provide for federal jurisdiction over suits against nonconsenting States. Congress may, however, abrogate such immunity in federal court if it makes its intention to abrogate unmistakably clear in the language of the statute and acts pursuant to a valid exercise of its power under §5 of the Fourteenth Amendment. The clarity of Congress's intent here is not fairly debatable. The Act enables employees to seek damages "against any employer (including a public agency) in any Federal or State court of competent jurisdiction," and Congress has defined "public agency" to include both "the government of a State or political subdivision thereof and any agency of . . . a State, or a political subdivision of a State."

This case turns, then, on whether Congress acted within its constitutional authority when it sought to abrogate the States' immunity for purposes of the FMLA's family-leave provision.

The FMLA aims to protect the right to be free from gender-based discrimination in the workplace. We have held that statutory classifications that distinguish between males and females are subject to heightened scrutiny. For a gender-based classification to withstand such scrutiny, it must "serv[e] important governmental objectives," and "the discriminatory means employed [must be] substantially related to the achievement of those objectives." The State's justification for such a classification "must not rely on overbroad generalizations about the different talents, capacities, or preferences of males and females." We now inquire whether Congress had evidence of a pattern of constitutional violations on the part of the States in this area.[55]

The history of the many state laws limiting women's employment opportunities is chronicled in — and, until relatively recently, was sanctioned by — this Court's own opinions. The long and extensive history of sex discrimination prompted us to hold that measures that differentiate on the basis of gender warrant heightened scrutiny; here, the persistence of such unconstitutional discrimination by the States justifies Congress' passage of prophylactic §5 legislation.

As the FMLA's legislative record reflects, a 1990 Bureau of Labor Statistics (BLS) survey stated that 37 percent of surveyed private-sector employees were covered by maternity leave policies, while only 18 percent were covered by paternity leave policies. The corresponding numbers from a similar BLS survey the previous year were 33 percent and 16 percent, respectively. While these data show an increase in the percentage of employees eligible for such leave, they also show a widening of the gender gap during the same period. Thus, stereotype-based beliefs about the allocation of family duties remained firmly rooted, and employers' reliance on them in establishing discriminatory leave policies remained widespread. Congress also heard testimony that "[p]arental leave for fathers . . . is rare. Even . . . [w]here child-care leave policies do exist, men, both in the public and private sectors, receive notoriously discriminatory treatment in their requests for such leave." Fifteen States provided women up to one year of extended maternity leave, while only four provided men with the same. This and other differential leave policies were not attributable to any differential physical needs of men and women, but rather to the pervasive sex-role stereotype that caring for family members is women's work. Evidence pertaining to parenting leave is relevant here because state discrimination in the provision of both types of benefits is based on the same gender stereotype: that women's family duties trump those of the workplace. Justice Kennedy's dissent (hereinafter the dissent) ignores this common foundation that, as Congress found, has historically produced discrimination in the hiring and promotion of women. Consideration of such evidence does not, as the dissent contends, expand our §5 inquiry to include "general gender-based stereotypes in employment." To the contrary, because parenting and family leave address very similar situations in which work and family responsibilities conflict, they implicate the same stereotypes.

Finally, Congress had evidence that, even where state laws and policies were not facially discriminatory, they were applied in discriminatory ways. It was aware of the "serious problems with the discretionary nature of family leave," because when "the authority to grant leave and to arrange the length of that leave rests with individual supervisors," it leaves "employees open to discretionary and possibly unequal treatment." H.R. Rep. No. 103-8, pt. 2, pp. 10-11 (1993). Testimony

---

55. The text of the Act makes this clear. Congress found that "due to the nature of the roles of men and women in our society, the primary responsibility for family caretaking often falls on women, and such responsibility affects the working lives of women more than it affects the working lives of men." In response to this finding, Congress sought "to accomplish the [Act's other] purposes . . . in a manner that . . . minimizes the potential for employment discrimination on the basis of sex by ensuring generally that leave is available . . . on a gender-neutral basis[,] and to promote the goal of equal employment opportunity for women and men." [Footnote by the Court.]

supported that conclusion, explaining that "[t]he lack of uniform parental and medical leave policies in the work place has created an environment where [sex] discrimination is rampant."

In sum, the States' record of unconstitutional participation in, and fostering of, gender-based discrimination in the administration of leave benefits is weighty enough to justify the enactment of prophylactic §5 legislation.

We reached the opposite conclusion in *Garrett* and *Kimel.* In those cases, the §5 legislation under review responded to a purported tendency of state officials to make age- or disability-based distinctions. Under our equal protection case law, discrimination on the basis of such characteristics is not judged under a heightened review standard, and passes muster if there is "a rational basis for doing so at a class-based level, even if it 'is probably not true' that those reasons are valid in the majority of cases." Thus, in order to impugn the constitutionality of state discrimination against the disabled or the elderly, Congress must identify, not just the existence of age- or disability-based state decisions, but a "widespread pattern" of irrational reliance on such criteria. We found no such showing with respect to the ADEA and Title I of the Americans with Disabilities Act of 1990 (ADA). Here, however, Congress directed its attention to state gender discrimination, which triggers a heightened level of scrutiny. Because the standard for demonstrating the constitutionality of a gender-based classification is more difficult to meet than our rational-basis test — it must "serv[e] important governmental objectives" and be "substantially related to the achievement of those objectives," it was easier for Congress to show a pattern of state constitutional violations. Congress was similarly successful in South Carolina v. Katzenbach (1966), where we upheld the Voting Rights Act of 1965: Because racial classifications are presumptively invalid, most of the States' acts of race discrimination violated the Fourteenth Amendment.

The impact of the discrimination targeted by the FMLA is significant. Congress determined: "Historically, denial or curtailment of women's employment opportunities has been traceable directly to the pervasive presumption that women are mothers first, and workers second. This prevailing ideology about women's roles has in turn justified discrimination against women when they are mothers or mothers-to-be." Stereotypes about women's domestic roles are reinforced by parallel stereotypes presuming a lack of domestic responsibilities for men. Because employers continued to regard the family as the woman's domain, they often denied men similar accommodations or discouraged them from taking leave. These mutually reinforcing stereotypes created a self-fulfilling cycle of discrimination that forced women to continue to assume the role of primary family caregiver, and fostered employers' stereotypical views about women's commitment to work and their value as employees. Those perceptions, in turn, Congress reasoned, lead to subtle discrimination that may be difficult to detect on a case-by-case basis.

We believe that Congress's chosen remedy, the family-care leave provision of the FMLA, is "congruent and proportional to the targeted violation." By creating an across-the-board, routine employment benefit for all eligible employees, Congress sought to ensure that family-care leave would no longer be stigmatized as an inordinate drain on the workplace caused by female employees, and that employers could not evade leave obligations simply by hiring men. By setting a minimum standard of family leave for all eligible employees, irrespective of gender, the FMLA attacks the formerly state-sanctioned stereotype that only women are responsible for family caregiving, thereby reducing employers' incentives to engage in discrimination by basing hiring and promotion decisions on stereotypes.

We also find significant the many other limitations that Congress placed on the scope of this measure. The FMLA requires only unpaid leave, and applies only to employees who have worked for the employer for at least one year and provided 1,250 hours of service within the last 12 months. Employees in high-ranking or sensitive positions are simply ineligible for FMLA leave; of particular importance to the States, the FMLA expressly excludes from coverage state elected officials, their staffs, and appointed policymakers. Employees must give advance notice of foreseeable leave, and employers may require certification by a health care provider of the need for leave. In choosing 12 weeks as the appropriate leave floor, Congress chose "a middle ground, a period long enough to serve 'the needs of families' but not so long that it would upset 'the legitimate interests of employers.'" Moreover, the cause of action under the FMLA is a restricted one: The damages recoverable are strictly defined and measured by actual monetary losses, and the accrual period for backpay is limited by the Act's 2-year statute of limitations (extended to three years only for willful violations).

For the above reasons, we conclude that §2612(a)(1)(C) is congruent and proportional to its remedial object, and can "be understood as responsive to, or designed to prevent, unconstitutional behavior."

Justice SCALIA, dissenting.

I join Justice Kennedy's dissent, and add one further observation: The constitutional violation that is a prerequisite to "prophylactic" congressional action to "enforce" the Fourteenth Amendment is a violation by the State against which the enforcement action is taken. There is no guilt by association, enabling the sovereignty of one State to be abridged under §5 of the Fourteenth Amendment because of violations by another State, or by most other States, or even by 49 other States.

Today's opinion for the Court does not even attempt to demonstrate that each one of the 50 States covered by 29 U.S.C. §2612(a)(1)(C) was in violation of the Fourteenth Amendment. It treats "the States" as some sort of collective entity which is guilty or innocent as a body. "[T]he States' record of unconstitutional participation in, and fostering of, gender-based discrimination," it concludes, "is weighty enough to justify the enactment of prophylactic §5 legislation." This will not do. Prophylaxis in the sense of extending the remedy beyond the violation is one thing; prophylaxis in the sense of extending the remedy beyond the violator is something else.

Justice KENNEDY, with whom Justice SCALIA and Justice THOMAS join, dissenting.

The Court is unable to show that States have engaged in a pattern of unlawful conduct which warrants the remedy of opening state treasuries to private suits. The inability to adduce evidence of alleged discrimination, coupled with the inescapable fact that the federal scheme is not a remedy but a benefit program, demonstrate the lack of the requisite link between any problem Congress has identified and the program it mandated.

The relevant question, as the Court seems to acknowledge, is whether, notwithstanding the passage of Title VII and similar state legislation, the States continued to engage in widespread discrimination on the basis of gender in the provision of family leave benefits. If such a pattern were shown, the Eleventh Amendment would not bar Congress from devising a congruent and proportional remedy. The evidence to substantiate this charge must be far more specific, however, than a simple recitation of a general history of employment discrimination against women. When the federal statute seeks to abrogate state sovereign immunity, the Court should be more careful to insist on adherence to the analytic requirements set forth in its own precedents. Persisting overall effects of gender-based discrimination at the workplace must not be ignored; but simply noting the problem is not a substitute for evidence which identifies some real discrimination the family leave rules are designed to prevent. Respondents fail to make the requisite showing. The Act's findings of purpose are devoid of any discussion of the relevant evidence.

As the Court seems to recognize, the evidence considered by Congress concerned discriminatory practices of the private sector, not those of state employers.

The statistical information compiled by the Bureau of Labor Statistics (BLS), which are the only factual findings the Court cites, surveyed only private employers. Ante, at 1979. While the evidence of discrimination by private entities may be relevant, it does not, by itself, justify the abrogation of States' sovereign immunity.

Even if there were evidence that individual state employers, in the absence of clear statutory guidelines, discriminated in the administration of leave benefits, this circumstance alone would not support a finding of a state-sponsored pattern of discrimination. The evidence could perhaps support the charge of disparate impact, but not a charge that States have engaged in a pattern of intentional discrimination prohibited by the Fourteenth Amendment. The federal-state equivalence upon which the Court places such emphasis is a deficient rationale at an even more fundamental level, however, for the States appear to have been ahead of Congress in providing gender-neutral family leave benefits. Thirty States, the District of Columbia, and Puerto Rico had adopted some form of family-care leave in the years preceding the Act's adoption.

The Court acknowledges that States have adopted family leave programs prior to federal intervention, but argues these policies suffered from serious imperfections. Even if correct, this observation proves, at most, that programs more generous and more effective than those operated by the States were feasible. That the States did not devise the optimal programs is not, however, evidence that the States were perpetuating unconstitutional discrimination. Given that the States assumed a pioneering role in the creation of family leave schemes, it is not surprising these early efforts may have been imperfect. This is altogether different, however, from purposeful discrimination.

The Court's lengthy discussion of the allegedly deficient state policies falls short of meeting this standard. A great majority of these programs exhibit no constitutional defect and, in fact, are authorized by this Court's precedent. The Court points out that seven States adopted leave provisions applicable only to women. Yet it must acknowledge that three of these schemes concerned solely pregnancy disability leave. Our cases make clear that a State does not violate the Equal Protection Clause by granting pregnancy disability leave to women without providing for a grant of parenting leave to men. Geduldig v. Aiello (1974).

Considered in its entirety, the evidence fails to document a pattern of unconstitutional conduct sufficient to justify the abrogation of States' sovereign immunity. The few incidents identified by the Court "fall far short of even suggesting the pattern of unconstitutional discrimination on which §5 legislation must be based." Juxtaposed to this evidence is the States' record of addressing gender-based discrimination in the provision of leave benefits on their own volition.

Our concern with gender discrimination, which is subjected to heightened scrutiny, as opposed to age- or disability-based distinctions, which are reviewed under rational standard, does not alter this conclusion. The application of heightened scrutiny is designed to ensure gender-based classifications are not based on the entrenched and pervasive stereotypes which inhibit women's progress in the workplace. This consideration does not divest respondents of their burden to show that "Congress identified a history and pattern of unconstitutional employment discrimination by the States." The Court seems to reaffirm this requirement. In my submission, however, the Court does not follow it. Given the insufficiency of the evidence that States discriminated in the provision of family leave, the unfortunate fact that stereotypes about women continue to be a serious and pervasive social problem would not alone support the charge that a State has engaged in a practice designed to deny its citizens the equal protection of the laws.

It bears emphasis that, even were the Court to bar unconsented federal suits by private individuals for money damages from a State, individuals whose rights under the Act were violated would not be without recourse. The Act is likely a valid exercise of Congress's power under the Commerce Clause, and so the standards it prescribes will be binding upon the States. The United States may enforce these standards in actions for money damages; and private individuals may bring actions against state officials for injunctive relief under Ex parte Young (1908). What is at issue is only whether the States can be subjected, without consent, to suits brought by private persons seeking to collect moneys from the state treasury. Their immunity cannot be abrogated without documentation of a pattern of unconstitutional acts by the States, and only then by a congruent and proportional remedy. There has been a complete failure by respondents to carry their burden to establish each of these necessary propositions. I would hold that the Act is not a valid abrogation of state sovereign immunity and dissent with respect from the Court's conclusion to the contrary.

TENNESSEE v. LANE, 541 U.S. 509 1978 (2004): Justice STEVENS delivered the opinion of the Court.

Title II of the Americans with Disabilities Act of 1990 (ADA or Act) provides that "no qualified individual with a disability shall, by reason of such disability, be excluded from participation in or be denied the benefits of the services, programs or activities of a public entity, or be subjected to discrimination by any such entity." The question presented in this case is whether Title II exceeds Congress's power under §5 of the Fourteenth Amendment.

I

In August 1998, respondents George Lane and Beverly Jones filed this action against the State of Tennessee and a number of Tennessee counties, alleging past and ongoing violations of Title II. Respondents, both of whom are paraplegics who use wheelchairs for mobility, claimed that they were denied access to, and the services of, the state court system by reason of their disabilities. Lane alleged that he was compelled to appear to answer a set of criminal charges on the second floor of a county courthouse that had no elevator. At his first appearance, Lane crawled up two flights of stairs to get to the courtroom. When Lane returned to the courthouse for a hearing, he refused to crawl again or to be carried by officers to the courtroom; he consequently was arrested and jailed for failure to appear. Jones, a certified court reporter, alleged that she has not been able to gain access to a number of county courthouses, and, as a result, has lost both work and an opportunity to participate in the judicial process. Respondents sought damages and equitable relief.

II

The ADA was passed by large majorities in both Houses of Congress after decades of deliberation and investigation into the need for comprehensive legislation to address discrimination against persons with disabilities. In the years immediately preceding the ADA's enactment, Congress held 13 hearings and created a special task force that gathered evidence from every State in the Union. The conclusions Congress drew from this evidence are set forth in the task force and Committee Reports, described in lengthy legislative hearings, and summarized in the preamble to the statute. Central among these conclusions was Congress's finding that "individuals with disabilities are a discrete and insular minority who have been faced with restrictions and limitations, subjected to a history of purposeful unequal treatment, and relegated to a position of political powerlessness in our society, based on characteristics that are beyond the control of such individuals and resulting from stereotypic assumptions not truly indicative of the individual ability of such individuals to participate in, and contribute to, society." Invoking "the sweep of congressional authority, including the power to enforce the Fourteenth Amendment and to regulate Commerce," the ADA is designed "to provide a clear and comprehensive national mandate for the elimination of discrimination against individuals with disabilities." It forbids discrimination against persons with disabilities in three major areas of public life: employment, which is covered by Title I of the statute; public services, programs, and activities, which are the subject[s] of Title II; and public accommodations, which are covered by Title III.

Title II prohibits any public entity from discriminating against "qualified" persons with disabilities in the provision or operation of public services, programs, or activities. The Act defines the term "public entity" to include state and local governments, as well as their agencies and instrumentalities.

III

Our cases have also held that Congress may abrogate the State's Eleventh Amendment immunity. To determine whether it has done so in any given case, we "must resolve two predicate questions: first, whether Congress unequivocally expressed its intent to abrogate that immunity; and second, if it did, whether Congress acted pursuant to a valid grant of constitutional authority."

The first question is easily answered in this case. The Act specifically provides: "A State shall not be immune under the eleventh amendment to the Constitution of the United States from an action in Federal or State court of competent jurisdiction for a violation of this chapter." The question, then, is whether Congress had the power to give effect to its intent. . . .

IV

The first step of the *Boerne* inquiry requires us to identify the constitutional right or rights that Congress sought to enforce when it enacted Title II. In University of Alabama v. Garrett (2001), we observed [that] classifications based on disability violate that constitutional command if they lack a rational relationship to a legitimate governmental purpose. Title II, like Title I, seeks to enforce this prohibition on irrational disability discrimination. But it also seeks to enforce a variety of other basic constitutional guarantees, infringements of which are subject to more searching judicial review. *See, e.g.,* Dunn v. Blumstein (1972) [right to vote]; Shapiro v. Thompson (1969) [right to travel]; Skinner v. Oklahoma ex rel. Williamson (1942) [right to procreate]. These rights include some, like the right of access to the courts at issue in this case, that are protected by the Due Process Clause of the Fourteenth Amendment. The Due Process Clause and the Confrontation Clause of the Sixth Amendment, as applied to the States via the Fourteenth Amendment, both guarantee to a criminal defendant such as respondent Lane the "right to be present at all stages of the trial where his absence might frustrate the fairness of the proceedings." Faretta v. California (1975). The Due Process Clause also requires the States to afford certain civil litigants a "meaningful opportunity to be heard" by removing obstacles to their full participation in judicial proceedings.

Whether Title II validly enforces these constitutional rights is a question that "must be judged with reference to the historical experience which it reflects." While §5 authorizes Congress to enact reasonably prophylactic remedial legislation, the appropriateness of the remedy depends on the gravity of the harm it seeks to prevent. "Difficult and intractable problems often require powerful remedies," but it is also true that "[s]trong measures appropriate to address one harm may be an unwarranted response to another, lesser one."

With respect to the particular services at issue in this case, Congress learned that many individuals, in many States across the country, were being excluded from courthouses and court proceedings by reason of their disabilities. A report before Congress showed that some 76% of public services and programs housed in state-owned buildings were inaccessible to and unusable by persons with disabilities, even taking into account the possibility that the services and programs might be restructured or relocated to other parts of the buildings. Congress itself heard testimony from persons with disabilities who described the physical inaccessibility of local courthouses. And its appointed task force heard numerous examples of the exclusion of persons with disabilities from state judicial services and programs, including exclusion of persons with visual impairments and hearing impairments from jury service, failure of state and local governments to provide interpretive services for the hearing impaired, failure to permit the testimony of adults with developmental disabilities in abuse cases, and failure to make courtrooms accessible to witnesses with physical disabilities.[56]

The conclusion that Congress drew from this body of evidence is set forth in the text of the ADA itself: "[D]iscrimination against individuals with disabilities persists in such critical areas as . . . education, transportation, communication, recreation, institutionalization, health services, voting, and access to public services." This finding, together with the extensive record of disability discrimination that underlies it, makes clear beyond peradventure that inadequate provision of public services and access to public facilities was an appropriate subject for prophylactic legislation.

V

The only question that remains is whether Title II is an appropriate response to this history and pattern of unequal treatment. Petitioner urges us both to examine the broad range of Title II's applications all at once, and to treat that breadth as a mark of the law's invalidity. According to petitioner, the fact that Title II applies not only to public education and voting-booth access but also to seating at state-owned hockey rinks indicates that Title II is not appropriately tailored to serve its objectives. But nothing in our case law requires us to consider Title II, with its wide variety of applications, as an undifferentiated whole. Whatever might be said about Title II's other applications, the question presented in this case is not whether Congress can validly subject the States to private suits for money damages for failing to provide reasonable access to hockey rinks, or even to voting booths, but whether Congress had the power under §5 to enforce the constitutional right of access to the courts. Because we find that Title II unquestionably is valid §5 legislation as it applies to the class of cases implicating the accessibility of judicial services, we need go no further.

Congress's chosen remedy for the pattern of exclusion and discrimination described above, Title II's requirement of program accessibility, is congruent and proportional to its object of enforcing the right of access to the courts. The unequal treatment of disabled persons in the administration of judicial services has a long history, and has persisted despite several legislative efforts to remedy the problem of disability discrimination. Faced with considerable evidence of the shortcomings of previous legislative responses, Congress was justified in concluding that this "difficult and intractable proble[m]" warranted "added prophylactic measures in response."

The remedy Congress chose is nevertheless a limited one. Recognizing that failure to accommodate persons with disabilities will often have the same practical effect as outright exclusion, Congress required the States to take

---

56. The Chief Justice dismisses as "irrelevant" the portions of this evidence that concern the conduct of nonstate governments. This argument rests on the mistaken premise that a valid exercise of Congress's §5 power must always be predicated solely on evidence of constitutional violations by the States themselves. To operate on that premise in this case would be particularly inappropriate because this case concerns the provision of judicial services, an area in which local governments are typically treated as "arm[s] of the State" for Eleventh Amendment purposes, and thus enjoy precisely the same immunity from unconsented suit as the States. In any event, our cases have recognized that evidence of constitutional violations on the part of nonstate governmental actors is relevant to the §5 inquiry. [Footnote by the Court.]

reasonable measures to remove architectural and other barriers to accessibility. But Title II does not require States to employ any and all means to make judicial services accessible to persons with disabilities, and it does not require States to compromise their essential eligibility criteria for public programs. It requires only "reasonable modifications" that would not fundamentally alter the nature of the service provided, and only when the individual seeking modification is otherwise eligible for the service. As Title II's implementing regulations make clear, the reasonable modification requirement can be satisfied in a number of ways. This duty to accommodate is perfectly consistent with the well-established due process principle that, "within the limits of practicability, a State must afford to all individuals a meaningful opportunity to be heard" in its courts. Judged against this backdrop, Title II's affirmative obligation to accommodate persons with disabilities in the administration of justice cannot be said to be "so out of proportion to a supposed remedial or preventive object that it cannot be understood as responsive to, or designed to prevent, unconstitutional behavior." It is, rather, a reasonable prophylactic measure, reasonably targeted to a legitimate end.

Justice GINSBURG, with whom Justice SOUTER and Justice BREYER join, concurring.

For the reasons stated by the Court, and mindful of Congress' objective in enacting the Americans with Disabilities Act — the elimination or reduction of physical and social structures that impede people with some present, past, or perceived impairments from contributing, according to their talents, to our Nation's social, economic, and civic life — I join the Court's opinion.

Legislation calling upon all government actors to respect the dignity of individuals with disabilities is entirely compatible with our Constitution's commitment to federalism, properly conceived. It seems to me not conducive to a harmonious federal system to require Congress, before it exercises authority under §5 of the Fourteenth Amendment, essentially to indict each State for disregarding the equal-citizenship stature of persons with disabilities. (But see Scalia, J., dissenting: "Congress may impose prophylactic §5 legislation only upon those particular States in which there has been an identified history of relevant constitutional violations.") Members of Congress are understandably reluctant to condemn their own States as constitutional violators, complicit in maintaining the isolated and unequal status of persons with disabilities. I would not disarm a National Legislature for resisting an adversarial approach to law-making better suited to the courtroom.

As the Court's opinion documents, Congress considered a body of evidence showing that in diverse parts of our Nation, and at various levels of government, persons with disabilities encounter access barriers to public facilities and services. That record, the Court rightly holds, at least as it bears on access to courts, sufficed to warrant the barrier-lowering, dignity-respecting national solution the People's representatives in Congress elected to order.

Chief Justice REHNQUIST, with whom Justice KENNEDY and Justice THOMAS join, dissenting.

In Board of Trustees of Univ. of Ala. v. Garrett (2001), we held that Congress did not validly abrogate States' Eleventh Amendment immunity when it enacted Title I of the Americans with Disabilities Act of 1990 (ADA). Today, the Court concludes that Title II of that Act, §§12131-12165, does validly abrogate that immunity, at least insofar "as it applies to the class of cases implicating the fundamental right of access to the courts." Because today's decision is irreconcilable with *Garrett* and the well-established principles it embodies, I dissent.

Rather than limiting its discussion of constitutional violations to the due process rights on which it ultimately relies, the majority sets out on a wide-ranging account of societal discrimination against the disabled. This digression recounts historical discrimination against the disabled through institutionaliza-tion laws, restrictions on marriage, voting, and public education, conditions in mental hospitals, and various other forms of unequal treatment in the admin-istration of public programs and services. Some of this evidence would be rel-evant if the Court were considering the constitutionality of the statute as a whole; but the Court rejects that approach in favor of a narrower "as-applied" inquiry. We discounted much the same type of outdated, generalized evidence in *Garrett* as unsupportive of Title I's ban on employment discrimination. The evidence here is likewise irrelevant to Title II's purported enforcement of Due Process access-to-the-courts rights.

Even if it were proper to consider this broader category of evidence, much of it does not concern unconstitutional action by the States. The bulk of the Court's evidence concerns discrimination by nonstate governments, rather than the States themselves. We have repeatedly held that such evidence is irrelevant to the inquiry whether Congress has validly abrogated Eleventh Amendment immunity, a privilege enjoyed only by the sovereign States. Moreover, the majority today cites the same congressional task force evidence we rejected in *Garrett*. As in *Garrett*, this "unexamined, anecdotal" evidence does not suffice. Most of the brief anecdotes do not involve States at all, and those that do are not sufficiently detailed to determine whether the instances of "unequal treatment" were irrational, and thus unconstitutional under our decision in *Cleburne*. There-fore, even outside the "access to the courts" context, the Court identifies few, if any, constitutional violations perpetrated by the States against disabled persons.

With respect to the due process "access to the courts" rights on which the Court ultimately relies, Congress's failure to identify a pattern of actual constitutional violations by the States is even more striking. Indeed, there is nothing in the legislative record or statutory findings to indicate that disabled persons were systematically denied the right to be present at criminal trials, denied the meaningful opportunity to be heard in civil cases, unconstitutionally excluded from jury service, or denied the right to attend criminal trials.

Even if the anecdotal evidence and conclusory statements relied on by the majority could be properly considered, the mere existence of an architecturally "inaccessible" courthouse — i.e., one a disabled person cannot utilize without assistance — does not state a constitutional violation. A violation of due process occurs only when a person is actually denied the constitutional right to access a given judicial proceeding. We have never held that a person has a constitutional right to make his way into a courtroom without any external assistance. Indeed, the fact that the State may need to assist an individual to attend a hearing has no bearing on whether the individual successfully exercises his due process right to be present at the proceeding. Nor does an "inaccessible" courthouse violate the Equal Protection Clause, unless it is irrational for the State not to alter the courthouse to make it "accessible." But financial considerations almost always furnish a rational basis for a State to decline to make those alterations. Thus, evidence regarding inaccessible courthouses, because it is not evidence of constitutional violations, provides no basis to abrogate States' sovereign immunity.

The near-total lack of actual constitutional violations in the congressional record is reminiscent of *Garrett*, wherein we found that the same type of minimal anecdotal evidence "f[e]ll far short of even suggesting the pattern of unconstitutional [state action] on which §5 legislation must be based." The barren record here should likewise be fatal to the majority's holding that Title II is valid legislation enforcing due process rights that involve access to the courts. Accordingly, Title II can only be understood as a congressional attempt to "rewrite the Fourteenth Amendment law laid down by this Court," rather than a legitimate effort to remedy or prevent state violations of that Amendment.

Justice Scalia, dissenting.

I joined the Court's opinion in *Boerne* with some misgiving. I have generally rejected tests based on such malleable standards as "proportionality," because they have a way of turning into vehicles for the implementation of individual judges' policy preferences. Even so, I signed on to the "congruence and proportionality" test in *Boerne*, and adhered to it in later cases.

I yield to the lessons of experience. The "congruence and proportionality" standard, like all such flabby tests, is a standing invitation to judicial arbitrariness and policy-driven decisionmaking. Worse still, it casts this Court in the role of Congress's taskmaster. Under it, the courts (and ultimately this Court) must regularly check Congress's homework to make sure that it has identified sufficient constitutional violations to make its remedy congruent and proportional. As a general matter, we are ill advised to adopt or adhere to constitutional rules that bring us into constant conflict with a coequal branch of Government. And when conflict is unavoidable, we should not come to do battle with the United States Congress armed only with a test ("congruence and proportionality") that has no demonstrable basis in the text of the Constitution and cannot objectively be shown to have been met or failed.

I would replace "congruence and proportionality" with another test—one that provides a clear, enforceable limitation supported by the text of §5. Section 5 grants Congress the power "to enforce, by appropriate legislation," the other provisions of the Fourteenth Amendment. *Morgan* notwithstanding, one does not, within any normal meaning of the term, "enforce" a prohibition by issuing a still broader prohibition directed to the same end. One does not, for example, "enforce" a 55-mile-per-hour speed limit by imposing a 45-mile-per-hour speed limit—even though that is indeed directed to the same end of automotive safety and will undoubtedly result in many fewer violations of the 55-mile-per-hour limit. And one does not "enforce" the right of access to the courts at issue in this case, by requiring that disabled persons be provided access to all of the "services, programs, or activities" furnished or conducted by the State. That is simply not what the power to enforce means—or ever meant.

Thus, principally for reasons of stare decisis, I shall henceforth apply the permissive *McCulloch* standard to congressional measures designed to remedy racial discrimination by the States. I would not, however, abandon the requirement that Congress may impose prophylactic §5 legislation only upon those particular States in which there has been an identified history of relevant constitutional violations. I would also adhere to the requirement that the prophylactic remedy predicated upon such state violations must be directed against the States or state actors rather than the public at large. And I would not, of course, permit any congressional measures that violate other provisions of the Constitution. When those requirements have been met, however, I shall leave it to Congress, under constraints no tighter than those of the Necessary and Proper Clause, to decide what measures are appropriate under §5 to prevent or remedy racial discrimination by the States.

I shall also not subject to "congruence and proportionality" analysis congressional action under §5 that is not directed to racial discrimination. Rather, I shall give full effect to that action when it consists of "enforcement" of the provisions of the Fourteenth Amendment, within the broad but not unlimited meaning of that term I have described above. When it goes beyond enforcement to prophylaxis, however, I shall consider it ultra vires. The present legislation is plainly of the latter sort.

In United States v. Georgia, the Court held that a prisoner who alleged unconstitutional state behavior could sue the state because Congress under §5 of the Fourteenth Amendment can provide a remedy for unconstitutional state conduct. Thus, it appears after United States v. Georgia, in considering whether a state government can be sued for violating a federal law that authorizes such suits, the initial question is whether the plaintiff alleges a constitutional violation. If so, a state can be sued. If not, the question becomes whether the statute is dealing with a type of discrimination that receives heightened scrutiny or a fundamental right, in which case the lawsuit against the state likely can go forward. But if the plaintiff is not alleging a constitutional violation and the case does not involve a type of discrimination or a right receiving heightened scrutiny, the state can be sued only if Congress finds pervasive unconstitutional state conduct.

UNITED STATES v. GEORGIA

546 U.S. 151 (2006)

Justice SCALIA delivered the opinion of the Court.

We consider whether a disabled inmate in a state prison may sue the State for money damages under Title II of the Americans with Disabilities Act of 1990.

Tony Goodman is a paraplegic inmate in the Georgia prison system who, at all relevant times, was housed at the Georgia State Prison in Reidsville. Goodman's pro se complaint and subsequent filings in the District Court included many allegations, both grave and trivial, regarding the conditions of his confinement in the Reidsville prison. Among his more serious allegations, he claimed that he was confined for 23-to-24 hours per day in a 12-by-3-foot cell in which he could not turn his wheelchair around. He alleged that the lack of accessible facilities rendered him unable to use the toilet and shower without assistance, which was often denied. On multiple occasions, he asserted, he had injured himself in attempting to transfer from his wheelchair to the shower or toilet on his own, and, on several other occasions, he had been forced to sit in his own feces and urine while prison officials refused to assist him in cleaning up the waste. He also claimed that he had been denied physical therapy and medical treatment, and denied access to virtually all prison programs and services on account of his disability.

While the Members of this Court have disagreed regarding the scope of Congress's "prophylactic" enforcement powers under §5 of the Fourteenth Amendment, no one doubts that §5 grants Congress the power to "enforce . . . the provisions" of the Amendment by creating private remedies against the States for actual violations of those provisions. "Section 5 authorizes Congress to create a cause of action through which the citizen may vindicate his Fourteenth Amendment rights." This enforcement power includes the power to abrogate state sovereign immunity by authorizing private suits for damages against the States. Thus, insofar as Title II creates a private cause of action for damages against the States for conduct that actually violates the Fourteenth Amendment, Title II validly abrogates state sovereign immunity. The Eleventh Circuit erred in dismissing those of Goodman's Title II claims that were based on such unconstitutional conduct.

From the many allegations in Goodman's pro se complaint and his subsequent filings in the District Court, it is not clear precisely what conduct he intended to allege in support of his Title II claims. Because the Eleventh Circuit did not address the issue, it is likewise unclear to what extent the conduct underlying Goodman's constitutional claims also violated Title II. It is therefore unclear whether Goodman's amended complaint will assert Title II claims premised on conduct that does not independently violate the Fourteenth Amendment. Once Goodman's complaint is amended, the lower courts will be best situated to determine in the first instance, on a claim-by-claim basis, (1) which aspects of the State's alleged conduct violated Title II; (2) to what extent such misconduct also violated the Fourteenth Amendment; and (3) insofar as such misconduct violated Title II but did not violate the Fourteenth Amendment, whether Congress's purported abrogation of sovereign immunity as to that class of conduct is nevertheless valid.

3. Congress's Power to Authorize Suits Against State Governments in State Courts

The Eleventh Amendment has been interpreted to bar suits against state governments in federal court. The consequence of this was thought to be that suits barred by the Eleventh Amendment had to be litigated in state court instead of in a federal forum. However, in Alden v. Maine, in 1999, the Court held that Congress cannot authorize suits against state governments in state court. State governments may not be sued in state court, even on federal claims, without their consent.

ALDEN v. MAINE
527 U.S. 706 (1999)

Justice KENNEDY delivered the opinion of the Court.

In 1992, petitioners, a group of probation officers, filed suit against their employer, the State of Maine, in the United States District Court for the District of Maine. The officers alleged the State had violated the overtime provisions of the Fair Labor Standards Act of 1938 (FLSA) and sought compensation and liquidated damages. While the suit was pending, this Court decided Seminole Tribe of Fla. v. Florida (1996), which made it clear that Congress lacks power under Article I to abrogate the States' sovereign immunity from suits commenced or prosecuted in the federal courts. Upon consideration of *Seminole Tribe*, the District Court dismissed petitioners' action, and the Court of Appeals affirmed. Petitioners then filed the same action in state court. The state trial court dismissed the suit on the basis of sovereign immunity, and the Maine Supreme Judicial Court affirmed.

We hold that the powers delegated to Congress under Article I of the United States Constitution do not include the power to subject nonconsenting States to private suits for damages in state courts. We decide as well that the State of Maine has not consented to suits for overtime pay and liquidated damages under the FLSA. On these premises we affirm the judgment sustaining dismissal of the suit.

I

The Eleventh Amendment makes explicit reference to the States' immunity from suits "commenced or prosecuted against one of the United States by Citizens of another State, or by Citizens or Subjects of any Foreign State." We have, as a result, sometimes referred to the States' immunity from suit as "Eleventh Amendment immunity." The phrase is convenient shorthand but something of a misnomer, for the sovereign immunity of the States neither derives from nor is limited by the terms of the Eleventh Amendment. Rather, as the Constitution's structure, and its history, and the authoritative interpretations by this Court make clear, the States' immunity from suit is a fundamental aspect of the sovereignty which the States enjoyed before the ratification of the Constitution, and which they retain today (either literally or by virtue of their admission into the Union upon an equal footing with the other States) except as altered by the plan of the Convention or certain constitutional Amendments.

A

Although the Constitution establishes a National Government with broad, often plenary authority over matters within its recognized competence, the founding document "specifically recognizes the States as sovereign entities." Various textual provisions of the Constitution assume the States' continued existence and active participation in the fundamental processes of governance. Any doubt regarding the constitutional role of the States as sovereign entities is removed by the Tenth Amendment, which, like the other provisions of the Bill of Rights, was enacted to allay lingering concerns about the extent of the national power.

B

The generation that designed and adopted our federal system considered immunity from private suits central to sovereign dignity. When the Constitution was ratified, it was well established in English law that the Crown could not be sued without consent in its own courts. See Chisholm v. Georgia (1793) (Iredell, J., dissenting) (surveying English practice). Although the American people had rejected other aspects of English political theory, the doctrine that a sovereign could not be sued without its consent was universal in the States when the Constitution was drafted and ratified.

The ratification debates, furthermore, underscored the importance of the States' sovereign immunity to the American people. Grave concerns were raised by the provisions of Article III which extended the federal judicial power to controversies between States and citizens of other States or foreign nations. The leading advocates of the Constitution assured the people in no uncertain terms that the Constitution would not strip the States of sovereign immunity.

Despite the persuasive assurances of the Constitution's leading advocates and the expressed understanding of the only state conventions to address the issue in explicit terms, this Court held, just five years after the Constitution was adopted, that Article III authorized a private citizen of another State to sue the State of Georgia without its consent. Chisholm v. Georgia (1793). The Court's decision "fell upon the country with a profound shock." 1 C. Warren, The Supreme Court in United States History 96 (rev. ed. 1926). The States, in particular, responded with outrage to the decision. It might be argued that the Chisholm decision was a correct interpretation of the constitutional design and that the Eleventh Amendment represented a deviation from the original understanding. This, however, seems unsupportable. The text and history of the Eleventh Amendment also suggest that Congress acted not to change but to restore the original constitutional design.

Given the outraged reaction to Chisholm, as well as Congress's repeated refusal to otherwise qualify the text of the Amendment, it is doubtful that if Congress meant to write a new immunity into the Constitution it would have limited that immunity to the narrow text of the Eleventh Amendment. The more natural inference is that the Constitution was understood, in light of its history and structure, to preserve the States' traditional immunity from private suits. As the Amendment clarified the only provisions of the Constitution that anyone had suggested might support a contrary understanding, there was no reason to draft with a broader brush.

Although the dissent attempts to rewrite history to reflect a different original understanding, its evidence is unpersuasive. The handful of state statutory and constitutional provisions authorizing suits or petitions of right against States only confirms the prevalence of the traditional understanding that a State could not be sued in the absence of an express waiver, for if the understanding were otherwise, the provisions would have been unnecessary.

In short, the scanty and equivocal evidence offered by the dissent establishes no more than what is evident from the decision in Chisholm—that some members of the founding generation disagreed with Hamilton, Madison, Marshall, Iredell, and the only state conventions formally to address the matter. The events leading to the adoption of the Eleventh Amendment, however, make clear that the individuals who believed the Constitution stripped the States of their immunity from suit were at most a small minority.

Not only do the ratification debates and the events leading to the adoption of the Eleventh Amendment reveal the original understanding of the States' constitutional immunity from suit, they also underscore the importance of sovereign immunity to the founding generation. Simply put, "The Constitution never would have been ratified if the States and their courts were to be stripped of their sovereign authority except as expressly provided by the Constitution itself."

C

The Court has been consistent in interpreting the adoption of the Eleventh Amendment as conclusive evidence "that the decision in *Chisholm* was contrary to the well-understood meaning of the Constitution," and that the views expressed by Hamilton, Madison, and Marshall during the ratification debates, and by Justice Iredell in his dissenting opinion in *Chisholm*, reflect the original understanding of the Constitution. As a consequence, we have looked to "history and experience, and the established order of things," rather than "[a]dhering to the mere letter" of the Eleventh Amendment, in determining the scope of the States' constitutional immunity from suit.

Following this approach, the Court has upheld States' assertions of sovereign immunity in various contexts falling outside the literal text of the Eleventh Amendment. In Hans v. Louisiana, the Court held that sovereign immunity barred a citizen from suing his own State under the federal-question head of jurisdiction. Later decisions rejected similar requests to conform the principle of sovereign immunity to the strict language of the Eleventh Amendment in holding that nonconsenting States are immune from suits brought by federal corporations, Smith v. Reeves (1900), foreign nations, *Principality of Monaco*, or Indian tribes, Blatchford v. Native Village of Noatak (1991), and in concluding that sovereign immunity is a defense to suits in admiralty, though the text of the Eleventh Amendment addresses only suits "in law or equity," Ex parte New York (1921).

These holdings reflect a settled doctrinal understanding, consistent with the views of the leading advocates of the Constitution's ratification, that sovereign immunity derives not from the Eleventh Amendment but from the structure of the original Constitution itself.

II

In this case we must determine whether Congress has the power, under Article I, to subject nonconsenting States to private suits in their own courts. As the foregoing discussion makes clear, the fact that the Eleventh Amendment by its terms limits only "[t]he Judicial power of the United States" does not resolve the question.

A

Petitioners contend the text of the Constitution and our recent sovereign immunity decisions establish that the States were required to relinquish this portion of their sovereignty. We turn first to these sources.

1

Article I, §8 grants Congress broad power to enact legislation in several enumerated areas of national concern. The Supremacy Clause, furthermore, provides: "This Constitution, and the Laws of the United States which shall be made in Pursuance thereof . . . , shall be the supreme Law of the Land; and the Judges in every State shall be bound thereby, any Thing in the Constitution or Laws of any state to the Contrary notwithstanding." It is contended that, by virtue of these provisions, where Congress enacts legislation subjecting the States to suit, the legislation by necessity overrides the sovereign immunity of the States.

As is evident from its text, however, the Supremacy Clause enshrines as "the supreme Law of the Land" only those federal Acts that accord with the constitutional design. See *Printz*. Appeal to the Supremacy Clause alone merely raises the question whether a law is a valid exercise of the national power. The Constitution, by delegating to Congress the power to establish the supreme law of the land when acting within its enumerated powers, does not foreclose a State from asserting immunity to claims arising under federal law merely because that law derives not from the State itself but from the national power. A contrary view could not be reconciled with Hans v. Louisiana, which sustained Louisiana's immunity in a private suit arising under the Constitution itself. Nor can we conclude that the specific Article I powers delegated to Congress necessarily include, by virtue of the Necessary and Proper Clause or otherwise, the incidental authority to subject the States to private suits as a means of achieving objectives otherwise within the scope of the enumerated powers.

Although the sovereign immunity of the States derives at least in part from the common-law tradition, the structure and history of the Constitution make clear that the immunity exists today by constitutional design. The dissent has provided no persuasive evidence that the founding generation regarded the States' sovereign immunity as defeasible by federal statute.

2

Whether Congress has authority under Article I to abrogate a State's immunity from suit in its own courts is, then, a question of first impression. In determining whether there is "compelling evidence" that this derogation of the States' sovereignty is "inherent in the constitutional compact," we continue our discussion of history, practice, precedent, and the structure of the Constitution.

We believe, that the founders' silence is best explained by the simple fact that no one, not even the Constitution's most ardent opponents, suggested the document might strip the States of the immunity. In light of the overriding concern regarding the States' war-time debts, together with the well known creativity, foresight, and vivid imagination of the Constitution's opponents, the silence is most instructive. It suggests the sovereign's right to assert immunity from suit in its own courts was a principle so well established that no one conceived it would be altered by the new Constitution.

In light of the language of the Constitution and the historical context, it is quite apparent why neither the ratification debates nor the language of the Eleventh Amendment addressed the States' immunity from suit in their own courts. The concerns voiced at the ratifying conventions, the furor raised by *Chisholm*, and the speed and unanimity with which the Amendment was adopted, moreover, underscore the jealous care with which the founding generation sought to preserve the sovereign immunity of the States. To read this history as permitting the inference that the Constitution stripped the States of immunity in their own courts and allowed Congress to subject them to suit there would turn on its head the concern of the founding generation — that Article III might be used to circumvent state-court immunity. In light of the historical record it is difficult to conceive that the Constitution would have been adopted if it had been understood to strip the States of immunity from suit in their own courts and cede to the Federal Government a power to subject nonconsenting States to private suits in these fora.

Our historical analysis is supported by early congressional practice, which provides "contemporaneous and weighty evidence of the Constitution's meaning." Although early Congresses enacted various statutes authorizing federal suits in state court, we have discovered no instance in which they purported to authorize suits against nonconsenting States in these fora.

The theory and reasoning of our earlier cases suggest the States do retain a constitutional immunity from suit in their own courts. We have often described the States' immunity in sweeping terms, without reference to whether the suit was prosecuted in state or federal court. We have said on many occasions, furthermore, that the States retain their immunity from private suits prosecuted in their own courts. We have also relied on the States' immunity in their own courts as a premise in our Eleventh Amendment rulings.

Our final consideration is whether a congressional power to subject nonconsenting States to private suits in their own courts is consistent with the structure of the Constitution. We look both to the essential principles of federalism and to the special role of the state courts in the constitutional design.

Although the Constitution grants broad powers to Congress, our federalism requires that Congress treat the States in a manner consistent with their status as residuary sovereigns and joint participants in the governance of the Nation. The principle of sovereign immunity preserved by constitutional design "thus accords the States the respect owed them as members of the federation."

Petitioners contend that immunity from suit in federal court suffices to preserve the dignity of the States. Private suits against nonconsenting States, however, present "the indignity of subjecting a State to the coercive process of judicial tribunals at the instance of private parties," regardless of the forum. Not only must a State defend or default but also it must face the prospect of being thrust, by federal fiat and against its will, into the disfavored status of a debtor, subject to the power of private citizens to levy on its treasury or perhaps even government buildings or property which the State administers on the public's behalf.

In some ways, of course, a congressional power to authorize private suits against nonconsenting States in their own courts would be even more offensive to state sovereignty than a power to authorize the suits in a federal forum. Although the immunity of one sovereign in the courts of another has often depended in part on comity or agreement, the immunity of a sovereign in its own courts has always been understood to be within the sole control of the sovereign itself. A power to press a State's own courts into federal service to coerce the other branches of the State, furthermore, is the power first to turn the State against itself and ultimately to commandeer the entire political machinery of the State against its will and at the behest of individuals. Such plenary federal control of state governmental processes denigrates the separate sovereignty of the States.

It is unquestioned that the Federal Government retains its own immunity from suit not only in state tribunals but also in its own courts. In light of our constitutional system recognizing the essential sovereignty of the States, we are reluctant to conclude that the States are not entitled to a reciprocal privilege.

Underlying constitutional form are considerations of great substance. Private suits against nonconsenting States — especially suits for money damages — may threaten the financial integrity of the States. It is indisputable that, at the time of the founding, many of the States could have been forced into insolvency but for their immunity from private suits for money damages. Even today, an unlimited congressional power to authorize suits in state court to levy upon the treasuries of the States for compensatory damages, attorney's fees, and even punitive damages could create staggering burdens, giving Congress a power and a leverage over the States that is not contemplated by our constitutional design. The potential national power would pose a severe and notorious danger to the States and their resources.

A general federal power to authorize private suits for money damages would place unwarranted strain on the States' ability to govern in accordance with the will of their citizens. Today, as at the time of the founding, the allocation of scarce resources among competing needs and interests lies at the heart of the political process. While the judgment creditor of the State may have a legitimate claim for compensation, other important needs and worthwhile ends compete for access to the public fisc. Since all cannot be satisfied in full, it is inevitable that difficult decisions involving the most sensitive and political of judgments must be made. If the principle of representative government is to be preserved to the States, the balance between competing interests must be reached after deliberation by the political process established by the citizens of the State, not by judicial decree mandated by the Federal Government and invoked by the private citizen.

III

The constitutional privilege of a State to assert its sovereign immunity in its own courts does not confer upon the State a concomitant right to disregard the Constitution or valid federal law. The States and their officers are bound by obligations imposed by the Constitution and by federal statutes that comport with the constitutional design. We are unwilling to assume the States will refuse to honor the Constitution or obey the binding laws of the United States. The good faith of the States thus provides an important assurance that "[t]his Constitution, and the Laws of the United States which shall be made in Pursuance thereof . . . shall be the supreme Law of the Land." U.S. Const., Art. VI.

Sovereign immunity, moreover, does not bar all judicial review of state compliance with the Constitution and valid federal law. Rather, certain limits are implicit in the constitutional principle of state sovereign immunity. The first of these limits is that sovereign immunity bars suits only in the absence of consent. Many States, on their own initiative, have enacted statutes consenting to a wide variety of suits. Nor, subject to constitutional limitations, does the Federal Government lack the authority or means to seek the States' voluntary consent to private suits. The States have consented, moreover, to some suits pursuant to the plan of the Convention or to subsequent constitutional amendments. In ratifying the Constitution, the States consented to suits brought by other States or by the Federal Government.

We have held also that in adopting the Fourteenth Amendment, the people required the States to surrender a portion of the sovereignty that had been preserved to them by the original Constitution, so that Congress may authorize private suits against nonconsenting States pursuant to its §5 enforcement power.

The second important limit to the principle of sovereign immunity is that it bars suits against States but not lesser entities. The immunity does not extend to suits prosecuted against a municipal corporation or other governmental entity which is not an arm of the State. Nor does sovereign immunity bar all suits against state officers.

The principle of sovereign immunity as reflected in our jurisprudence strikes the proper balance between the supremacy of federal law and the separate sovereignty of the States. Established rules provide ample means to correct ongoing violations of law and to vindicate the interests which animate the Supremacy Clause.

[IV]

This case at one level concerns the formal structure of federalism, but in a Constitution as resilient as ours form mirrors substance. Congress has vast power but not all power. When Congress legislates in matters affecting the States, it may not treat these sovereign entities as mere prefectures or corporations. Congress must accord States the esteem due to them as joint participants in a federal system, one beginning with the premise of sovereignty in both the central Government and the separate States. Congress has ample means to ensure compliance with valid federal laws, but it must respect the sovereignty of the States.

Justice SOUTER, with whom Justice STEVENS, Justice GINSBURG, and Justice BREYER join, dissenting.

In Seminole Tribe of Fla. v. Florida (1996), a majority of this Court invoked the Eleventh Amendment to declare that the federal judicial power under Article III of the Constitution does not reach a private action against a State, even on a federal question. In the Court's conception, however, the Eleventh Amendment was understood as having been enhanced by a "background principle" of state sovereign immunity (understood as immunity to suit), that operated beyond its limited codification in the Amendment, dealing solely with federal citizen-state diversity jurisdiction. To the *Seminole Tribe* dissenters, of whom I was one, the Court's enhancement of the Amendment was at odds with constitutional history and at war with the conception of divided sovereignty that is the essence of American federalism.

On each point the Court has raised it is mistaken, and I respectfully dissent from its judgment.

I

The Court rests its decision principally on the claim that immunity from suit was "a fundamental aspect of the sovereignty which the States enjoyed before the ratification of the Constitution," an aspect which the Court understands to have survived the ratification of the Constitution in 1788 and to have been "confirm[ed]" and given constitutional status by the adoption of the Tenth Amendment in 1791. If the Court truly means by "sovereign immunity" what that term meant at common law, its argument would be insupportable. While sovereign immunity entered many new state legal systems as a part of the common law selectively received from England, it was not understood to be indefeasible or to have been given any such status by the new National Constitution, which did not mention it. Had the question been posed, state sovereign immunity could not have been thought to shield a State from suit under federal law on a subject committed to national jurisdiction by Article I of the Constitution. Congress exercising its conceded Article I power may unquestionably abrogate such immunity.

There is almost no evidence that the generation of the framers thought sovereign immunity was fundamental in the sense of being unalterable. Whether one looks at the period before the framing, to the ratification controversies, or to the early republican era, the evidence is the same. Some framers thought sovereign immunity was an obsolete royal prerogative inapplicable in a republic; some thought sovereign immunity was a common-law power defeasible, like other common-law rights, by statute; and perhaps a few thought, in keeping with a natural law view distinct from the common-law conception, that immunity was inherent in a sovereign because the body that made a law could not logically be bound by it Natural law thinking on the part of a doubtful few will not, however, support the Court's position.

A

The American Colonies did not enjoy sovereign immunity, that being a privilege understood in English law to be reserved for the Crown alone; "antecedent to the Declaration of Independence, none of the colonies were, or pretended to be, sovereign states," 1 J. Story, Commentaries on the Constitution §207, p. 149 (5th ed. 1891). Several colonial charters, including those of Massachusetts, Connecticut, Rhode Island, and Georgia, expressly specified that the corporate body established thereunder could sue and be sued. If a colonial lawyer had looked into Blackstone for the theory of sovereign immunity, as indeed many did, he would have found nothing clearly suggesting that the Colonies as such enjoyed any immunity from suit.

B

Starting in the mid-1760s, ideas about sovereignty in colonial America began to shift as Americans argued that, lacking a voice in Parliament, they had not in any express way consented to being taxed. The story of the subsequent development of conceptions of sovereignty is complex and uneven; here, it is enough to say that by the time independence was declared in 1776, the locus of sovereignty was still an open question, except that almost by definition, advocates of independence denied that sovereignty with respect to the American Colonies remained with the King in Parliament.

As the concept of sovereignty was unsettled, so was that of sovereign immunity. Some States appear to have understood themselves to be without immunity from suit in their own courts upon independence. Connecticut and Rhode Island adopted their pre-existing charters as constitutions, without altering the provisions specifying their suability. Other new States understood themselves to be inheritors of the Crown's common-law sovereign immunity and so enacted statutes authorizing legal remedies against the State parallel to those available in England.

C

At the Constitutional Convention, the notion of sovereign immunity, whether as natural law or as common law, was not an immediate subject of debate, and the sovereignty of a State in its own courts seems not to have been mentioned. This comes as no surprise, for although the Constitution required state courts to apply federal law, the framers did not consider the possibility that federal law might bind States, say, in their relations with their employees. In the subsequent ratification debates, however, the issue of jurisdiction over a State did emerge in the question whether States might be sued on their debts in federal court, and on this point, too, a variety of views emerged and the diversity of sovereign immunity conceptions displayed itself.

From a canvass of this spectrum of opinion expressed at the ratifying conventions, one thing is certain. No one was espousing an indefeasible, natural law view of sovereign immunity. The controversy over the enforceability of state debts subject to state law produced emphatic support for sovereign immunity from eminences as great as Madison and Marshall, but neither of them indicated adherence to any immunity conception outside the common law.

At the close of the ratification debates, the issue of the sovereign immunity of the States under Article III had not been definitively resolved, and in some instances the indeterminacy led the ratification conventions to respond in ways that point to the range of thinking about the doctrine. Several state ratifying conventions proposed amendments and issued declarations that would have exempted States from subjection to suit in federal court.

II

The Court's rationale for today's holding based on a conception of sovereign immunity as somehow fundamental to sovereignty or inherent in statehood fails for the lack of any substantial support for such a conception in the thinking of the founding era. The Court cannot be counted out yet, however, for it has a second line of argument looking not to a clause-based reception of the natural law conception or even to its recognition as a "background principle," but to a structural basis in the Constitution's creation of a federal system. Immunity, the Court says, "inheres in the system of federalism established by the Constitution," its "contours [being] determined by the founders' understanding, not by the principles or limitations derived from natural law."

A

The National Constitution formally and finally repudiated the received political wisdom that a system of multiple sovereignties constituted the "great solecism of an imperium in imperio." Once "the atom of sovereignty" had been split, U.S. Term Limits, Inc. v. Thornton (1995) (Kennedy, J., concurring), the general scheme of delegated sovereignty as between the two component governments of the federal system was clear.

Hence the flaw in the Court's appeal to federalism. The State of Maine is not sovereign with respect to the national objective of the FLSA. Nor can it be argued that because the State of Maine creates its own court system, it has authority to decide what sorts of claims may be entertained there, and thus in effect to control the right of action in this case. Maine has created state courts of general jurisdiction; once it has done so, the Supremacy Clause of the Constitution, Art. VI, cl. 2, which requires state courts to enforce federal law and state-court judges to be bound by it, requires the Maine courts to entertain this federal cause of action.

B

It is symptomatic of the weakness of the structural notion proffered by the Court that it seeks to buttress the argument by relying on "the dignity and respect afforded a State, which the immunity is designed to protect," and by invoking the many demands on a State's fisc. It would be hard to imagine anything more inimical to the republican conception, which rests on the understanding of its citizens precisely that the government is not above them, but of them, its actions being governed by law just like their own. Whatever justification there may be for an American government's immunity from private suit, it is not dignity.

It is equally puzzling to hear the Court say that "federal power to authorize private suits for money damages would place unwarranted strain on the States' ability to govern in accordance with the will of their citizens." So long as the citizens' will, expressed through state legislation, does not violate valid federal law, the strain will not be felt; and to the extent that state action does violate federal law, the will of the citizens of the United States already trumps that of the citizens of the State: the strain then is not only expected, but necessarily intended.

Least of all does the Court persuade by observing that "other important needs" than that of the "judgment creditor" compete for public money. The "judgment creditor" in question is not a dunning bill-collector, but a citizen whose federal rights have been violated, and a constitutional structure that stints on enforcing federal rights out of an abundance of delicacy toward the States has substituted politesse in place of respect for the rule of law.

The Court might respond that the United States may bring suit in federal court against a State for damages under the FLSA. It is true, of course, that the FLSA does authorize the Secretary of Labor to file suit seeking damages, but unless Congress plans a significant expansion of the National Government's litigating forces to provide a lawyer whenever private litigation is barred by today's decision and *Seminole Tribe,* the allusion to enforcement of private rights by the National Government is probably not much more than whimsy. Facing reality, Congress specifically found, as long ago as 1974, "that the enforcement capability of the Secretary of Labor is not alone sufficient to provide redress in all or even a substantial portion of the situations where compliance is not forthcoming voluntarily." One hopes that such voluntary compliance will prove more popular than it has in Maine, for there is no reason today to suspect that enforcement by the Secretary of Labor alone would likely prove adequate to assure compliance with this federal law in the multifarious circumstances of some 4.7 million employees of the 50 States of the Union.

The point is not that the difficulties of enforcement should drive the Court's decision, but simply that where Congress has created a private right to damages, it is implausible to claim that enforcement by a public authority without any incentive beyond its general enforcement power will ever afford the private right a traditionally adequate remedy. No one would think the remedy adequate if private tort claims against a State could only be brought by the National Government: the tradition of private enforcement, as old as the common law itself, is the benchmark. But wage claims have a lineage of private enforcement just as ancient, and a claim under the FLSA is a claim for wages due on work performed. Denying private enforcement of an FLSA claim is thus on par with closing the courthouse door to state tort victims unaccompanied by a lawyer from Washington.

The resemblance of today's state sovereign immunity to the *Lochner* era's industrial due process is striking. The Court began this century by imputing immutable constitutional status to a conception of economic self-reliance that was never true to industrial life and grew insistently fictional with the years, and the Court has chosen to close the century by conferring like status on a conception of state sovereign immunity that is true neither to history nor to the structure of the Constitution. I expect the Court's late essay into immunity doctrine will prove the equal of its earlier experiment in laissez-faire, the one being as unrealistic as the other, as indefensible, and probably as fleeting.

———————————

In Federal Maritime Commission v. South Carolina State Port Authority, 535 U.S. 743 (2002), the Court followed and applied Alder v. Maine to hold that states cannot be sued in federal agency proceedings without their consent. Justice Thomas, writing for the majority in a five-to-four decision, declared:

> The preeminent purpose of state sovereign immunity is to accord States the dignity that is consistent with their status as sovereign entities. Given both this interest in protecting States' dignity and the strong similarities between [Federal Maritime Commission (FMC)] proceedings and civil litigation, we hold that state sovereign immunity bars the FMC from adjudicating complaints filed by a private party against a nonconsenting State. Simply put, if the Framers thought it an impermissible affront to a State's dignity to be required to answer the complaints of private parties in federal courts, we cannot imagine that they would have found it acceptable to compel a State to do exactly the same thing before the administrative tribunal of an agency, such as the FMC. The affront to a State's dignity does not lessen when an adjudication takes place in an administrative tribunal as opposed to an Article III court. In both instances, a State is required to defend itself in an adversarial proceeding against a private party before an impartial federal officer. Moreover, it would be quite strange to prohibit Congress from exercising its Article I powers to abrogate state sovereign immunity in Article III judicial proceedings, see Seminole Tribe v. Florida (1996), but permit the use of those same Article I powers to create court-like administrative tribunals where sovereign immunity does not apply.

Justice Breyer wrote a dissenting opinion, joined by Justices Stevens, Souter, and Ginsburg. He said:

> The Court holds that a private person cannot bring a complaint against a State to a federal administrative agency where the agency (1) will use an internal adjudicative process to decide if the complaint is well founded, and (2) if so, proceed to court to enforce the law. Where does the Constitution contain the principle of law that the Court enunciates? I cannot find the answer to this question in any text, in any tradition, or in any relevant purpose. In saying this, I do not simply reiterate the dissenting views set forth in many of the Court's recent sovereign immunity decisions. For even were I to believe that those decisions properly stated the law—which I do not—I still could not accept the Court's conclusion here.

The Court cannot justify today's decision in terms of its practical consequences. The decision, while permitting an agency to bring enforcement actions against States, forbids it to use agency adjudication in order to help decide whether to do so. Consequently the agency must rely more heavily upon its own informal staff investigations in order to decide whether a citizen's complaint has merit. The natural result is less agency flexibility, a larger federal bureaucracy, less fair procedure, and potentially less effective law enforcement. And at least one of these consequences, the forced growth of unnecessary federal bureaucracy, undermines the very constitutional objectives the Court's decision claims to serve.

These consequences are not purely theoretical. The Court's decision may undermine enforcement against state employers of many laws designed to protect worker health and safety. See, e.g., 42 U.S.C. §7622 (Clean Air Act); 33 U.S.C. §1367 (Clean Water Act); 15 U.S.C. §2622 (Toxic Substances Control Act); 42 U.S.C. §6971 (Solid Waste Disposal Act). And it may inhibit the development of federal fair, rapid, and efficient, informal non-judicial responses to complaints, for example, of improper medical care (involving state hospitals).

CHAPTER

3

THE FEDERAL EXECUTIVE POWER

This chapter examines the powers of the presidency and the executive branch. It particularly focuses on the tensions between the executive and legislative powers. The previous chapter examines the federal legislative power in relationship to state governments. This chapter, in contrast, centers on the relationship between two branches of the federal government.

Six topics are examined. First, section A focuses on the issue of inherent presidential power and the question of when, if at all, the president may act without constitutional or statutory authority. The issue of executive privilege is considered as an example of this controversy. Second, section B looks at the ability of Congress to expand presidential powers beyond those enumerated in the Constitution, specifically examining the Supreme Court's recent decision in the line-item veto case.

Third, section C considers the constitutional problems posed by administrative agencies. The section begins by considering the nondelegation doctrine and its demise and then examines the legislative veto as a possible alternative check on administrative agencies. In light of the demise of the legislative veto, the chapter then considers other alternative checks on agencies, including the use of the removal power.

Fourth, section D looks at the allocation of decision-making authority in the area of foreign policy. In particular, responsibilities with regard to treaties and war powers are considered. Fifth, section E examines executive power and the war on terrorism.

Finally, section F concludes by examining checks on the executive, including civil suits for money damages and impeachment.

A. INHERENT PRESIDENTIAL POWER

When, if ever, may the president act without express constitutional or statutory authorization? If the president has explicit constitutional authority for particular conduct, then the issues are solely whether the president is acting within the scope of the granted power and whether the president is violating some other constitutional provision. If there is a statute authorizing the president's conduct, then the question is whether that law is constitutional. But what if there is neither constitutional nor statutory authority?

The debate over this question began in the earliest days of the nation and had impeccable authorities on each side of the dispute. Early in the presidency of George Washington, Alexander Hamilton and James Madison clashed over this issue and whether the president could issue a neutrality proclamation as to a war occurring between England and France. Alexander Hamilton argued that the difference in the wording of Articles I and II reveals the framers' intention to create inherent presidential powers.[1] Article I initially states, "All legislative Powers herein granted shall be vested in a Congress of the United States." Article II of the Constitution begins, "The executive Power shall be vested in a President of the United States of America." Because Article II does not limit the president to powers "herein granted," Hamilton argued that the president has authority not specifically delineated in the Constitution.

Others, beginning with James Madison,[2] have disputed this interpretation of Article II, contending that the opening language of Article II was "simply to settle the question whether the executive branch should be plural or single and to give the executive a title."[3] According to this position, the president has no powers that are not enumerated in Article II and, indeed, such unenumerated authority would be inconsistent with a Constitution creating a government of limited authority.

The leading Supreme Court decision concerning this issue is Youngstown Sheet & Tube Co. v. Sawyer. In reading this decision, focus on how each of the opinions would answer the question of when the president may act without express constitutional or statutory authority. Following this case, a specific, important example is presented: When, if at all, may the president claim executive privilege?

YOUNGSTOWN SHEET & TUBE CO. v. SAWYER
343 U.S. 579 (1952)

Justice BLACK delivered the opinion of the Court.

We are asked to decide whether the President was acting within his constitutional power when he issued an order directing the Secretary of Commerce to take possession of and operate most of the Nation's steel mills. The mill owners argue that the President's order amounts to lawmaking, a legislative function which the Constitution has expressly confided to the Congress and not to the President. The Government's position is that the order was made on findings of the President that his action was necessary to avert a national catastrophe which would inevitably result from a stoppage of steel production, and that in meeting this grave emergency the President was acting within the aggregate of his constitutional powers as the Nation's Chief Executive and the

1. Alexander Hamilton, First Letter of *Pacificus* (June 29, 1793), reprinted in William M. Goldsmith, *The Growth of Presidential Power: A Documented History* 398, 401 (1974).

2. James Madison, The First letter of *Helvidius*, reprinted in W. Goldsmith, *supra* note 1, at 405.

3. Edward S. Corwin, *The Steel Seizure Case: A Judicial Brick Without Straw*, 53 Colum. L. Rev. 53, 53 (1953).

Commander in Chief of the Armed Forces of the United States. The issue emerges here from the following series of events:

In the latter part of 1951, a dispute arose between the steel companies and their employees over terms and conditions that should be included in new collective bargaining agreements. Long-continued conferences failed to resolve the dispute. On December 18, 1951, the employees' representative, United Steelworkers of America, C.I.O., gave notice of an intention to strike when the existing bargaining agreements expired on December 31. The Federal Mediation and Conciliation Service then intervened in an effort to get labor and management to agree. This failing, the President on December 22, 1951, referred the dispute to the Federal Wage Stabilization Board to investigate and make recommendations for fair and equitable terms of settlement. This Board's report resulted in no settlement. On April 4, 1952, the Union gave notice of a nationwide strike called to begin at 12:01 A.M. April 9. The indispensability of steel as a component of substantially all weapons and other war materials led the President to believe that the proposed work stoppage would immediately jeopardize our national defense and that governmental seizure of the steel mills was necessary in order to assure the continued availability of steel. Reciting these considerations for his action, the President, a few hours before the strike was to begin, issued Executive Order 10340. The order directed the Secretary of Commerce to take possession of most of the steel mills and keep them running. The Secretary immediately issued his own possessory orders, calling upon the presidents of the various seized companies to serve as operating managers for the United States. They were directed to carry on their activities in accordance with regulations and directions of the Secretary. The next morning the President sent a message to Congress reporting his action. Twelve days later he sent a second message. Congress has taken no action.

Obeying the Secretary's orders under protest, the companies brought proceedings against him in the District Court. Their complaints charged that the seizure was not authorized by an act of Congress or by any constitutional provisions.

The President's power, if any, to issue the order must stem either from an act of Congress or from the Constitution itself. There is no statute that expressly authorizes the President to take possession of property as he did here. Nor is there any act of Congress to which our attention has been directed from which such a power can fairly be implied. Indeed, we do not understand the Government to rely on statutory authorization for this seizure. There are two statutes which do authorize the President to take both personal and real property under certain conditions. However, the Government admits that these conditions were not met and that the President's order was not rooted in either of the statutes.

Moreover, the use of the seizure technique to solve labor disputes in order to prevent work stoppages was not only unauthorized by any congressional enactment; prior to this controversy, Congress had refused to adopt that method of settling labor disputes. When the Taft-Hartley Act was under consideration in 1947, Congress rejected an amendment which would have authorized such governmental seizures in cases of emergency. Apparently it was thought that the technique of seizure, like that of compulsory arbitration, would interfere with the process of collective bargaining. Consequently, the plan Congress adopted in that Act did not provide for seizure under any circumstances. Instead, the plan sought to bring about settlements by use of the customary devices of mediation, conciliation, investigation by boards of inquiry, and public reports. In some instances temporary injunctions were authorized to provide cooling-off periods. All this failing, unions were left free to strike after a secret vote by employees as to whether they wished to accept their employers' final settlement offer.

It is clear that if the President had authority to issue the order he did, it must be found in some provisions of the Constitution. And it is not claimed that express constitutional language grants this power to the President. The contention is that presidential power should be implied from the aggregate of his powers under the Constitution. Particular reliance is placed on provisions in Article II which say that "the executive Power shall be vested in a President . . ."; that "he shall take Care that the Laws be faithfully executed"; and that he "shall be Commander in Chief of the Army and Navy of the United States."

The order cannot properly be sustained as an exercise of the President's military power as Commander in Chief of the Armed Forces. The Government attempts to do so by citing a number of cases upholding broad powers in military commanders engaged in day-to-day fighting in a theater of war. Such cases need not concern us here. Even though "theater of war" be an expanding concept, we cannot with faithfulness to our constitutional system hold that the Commander in Chief of the Armed Forces has the ultimate power as such to take possession of private property in order to keep labor disputes from stopping production. This is a job for the Nation's lawmakers, not for its military authorities.

Nor can the seizure order be sustained because of the several constitutional provisions that grant executive power to the President. In the framework of our Constitution, the President's power to see that the laws are faithfully executed refutes the idea that he is to be a lawmaker. The Constitution limits his functions in the lawmaking process to the recommending of laws he thinks wise and the vetoing of laws he thinks bad. And the Constitution is neither silent nor equivocal about who shall make laws which the President is to execute.

The Founders of this Nation entrusted the lawmaking power to the Congress alone in both good and bad times. It would do no good to recall the historical events, the fears of power and the hopes for freedom that lay behind their choice. Such a review would but confirm our holding that this seizure order cannot stand.

Mr. Justice JACKSON, concurring in the judgment and opinion of the Court.

That comprehensive and undefined presidential powers hold both practical advantages and grave dangers for the country will impress anyone who has served as legal adviser to a President in time of transition and public anxiety. A judge, like an executive adviser, may be surprised at the poverty of really useful and unambiguous authority applicable to concrete problems of executive power as they actually present themselves. Just what our forefathers did envision, or would have envisioned had they foreseen modern conditions, must be divined from materials almost as enigmatic as the dreams Joseph was called upon to interpret for Pharaoh. A century and a half of partisan debate and scholarly speculation yields no net result but only supplies more or less apt quotations from respected sources on each side of any question. They largely cancel each other. And court decisions are indecisive because of the judicial practice of dealing with the largest questions in the most narrow way.

We may well begin by a somewhat over-simplified grouping of practical situations in which a President may doubt, or others may challenge, his powers, and by distinguishing roughly the legal consequences of this factor of relativity.

1. When the President acts pursuant to an express or implied authorization of Congress, his authority is at its maximum, for it includes all that he possesses in his own right plus all that Congress can delegate. In these circumstances, and in these only, may he be said (for what it may be worth), to personify the federal sovereignty. If his act is held unconstitutional under these circumstances, it usually means that the Federal Government as an undivided whole lacks power. A seizure executed by the President pursuant to an Act of Congress would be supported by the strongest of presumptions and the widest latitude of judicial interpretation, and the burden of persuasion would rest heavily upon any who might attack it.

2. When the President acts in absence of either a congressional grant or denial of authority, he can only rely upon his own independent powers, but there is a zone of twilight in which he and Congress may have concurrent authority, or in which its distribution is uncertain. Therefore, congressional inertia, indifference or quiescence may sometimes, at least as a practical matters, enable, if not invite, measures of independent presidential responsibility. In this area, any actual test of power is likely to depend on the imperatives of events and contemporary imponderables rather than on abstract theories of law.

3. When the President takes measures incompatible with the expressed or implied will of Congress, his power is at its lowest ebb, for then he can rely only upon his own constitutional powers minus any constitutional powers of Congress over the matter. Courts can sustain exclusive Presidential control in such a case only by disabling the Congress from acting upon the subject. Presidential claim to a power at once so conclusive and preclusive must be scrutinized with caution, for what is at stake is the equilibrium established by our constitutional system.

Into which of these classifications does this executive seizure of the steel industry fit? It is eliminated from the first by admission, for it is conceded that no congressional authorization exists for this seizure. That takes away also the support of the many precedents and declarations which were made in relation, and must be confined, to this category.

Can it then be defended under flexible tests available to the second category? It seems clearly eliminated from that class because Congress has not left seizure of private property an open field but has covered it by three statutory policies inconsistent with this seizure.

This leaves the current seizure to be justified only by the severe tests under the third grouping, where it can be supported only by any remainder of executive power after subtraction of such powers as Congress may have over the subject. In short, we can sustain the President only by holding that seizure of such strike-bound industries is within his domain and beyond control by Congress. Thus, this Court's first review of such seizures occurs under circumstances which leave Presidential power most vulnerable to attack and in the least favorable of possible constitutional postures.

The clause on which the Government relies is that "The President shall be Commander in Chief of the Army and Navy of the United States. . . ." These cryptic words have given rise to some of the most persistent controversies in our constitutional history. Assuming that we are in a war de facto, whether it is or is not a war de jure, does that empower the Commander-in-Chief to seize industries he thinks necessary to supply our army? The Constitution expressly places in Congress power "to raise and support Armies" and "to provide and maintain a Navy." This certainly lays upon Congress primary responsibility for supplying the armed forces. Congress alone controls the raising of revenues and their appropriation and may determine in what manner and by what means they shall be spent for military and naval procurement. I suppose no one would doubt that Congress can take over war supply as a Government enterprise. On the other hand, if Congress sees fit to rely on free private enterprise collectively bargaining with free labor for support and maintenance of our armed forces, can the Executive because of lawful disagreements incidental to that process, seize the facility for operation upon Government-imposed terms?

There are indications that the Constitution did not contemplate that the title Commander-in-Chief of the Army and Navy will constitute him also Commander-in-Chief of the country, its industries and its inhabitants. He has no monopoly of "war powers," whatever they are. While Congress cannot deprive the President of the command of the army and navy, only Congress can provide him an army or navy to command. That military powers of the Commander-in-Chief were not to supersede representative government of internal affairs seems obvious from the Constitution and from elementary American history.

The executive action we have here originates in the individual will of the President and represents an exercise of authority without law. No one, perhaps not even the President, knows the limits of the power he may seek to exert in this instance and the parties affected cannot learn the limit of their rights. We do not know today what powers over labor or property would be claimed to flow from Government possession if we should legalize it, what rights to compensation would be claimed or recognized, or on what contingency it would end. With all its defects, delays and inconveniences, men have discovered no technique for long preserving free government except that the Executive be under the law, and that the law be made by parliamentary deliberations. Such institutions may be destined to pass away. But it is the duty of the Court to be last, not first, to give them up.

Justice DOUGLAS, concurring.

There can be no doubt that the emergency which caused the President to seize these steel plants was one that bore heavily on the country. But the emergency did not create power; it merely marked an occasion when power should be exercised. And the fact that it was necessary that measures be taken to keep steel in production does not mean that the President, rather than the Congress, had the constitutional authority to act. The Congress, as well as the President, is trustee of the national welfare. The President can act more quickly than the Congress. The President with the armed services at his disposal can move with force as well as with speed. All executive power — from the reign of ancient kings to the rule of modern dictators — has the outward appearance of efficiency.

Legislative power, by contrast, is slower to exercise. There must be delay while the ponderous machinery of committees, hearings, and debates is put into motion. That takes time; and while the Congress slowly moves into action, the emergency may take its toll in wages, consumer goods, war production, the standard of living of the people, and perhaps even lives. Legislative action may indeed often be cumbersome, time-consuming, and apparently inefficient. But as Mr. Justice Brandeis stated in his dissent in Myers v. United States:

> The doctrine of the separation of powers was adopted by the Convention of 1787 not to promote efficiency but to preclude the exercise of arbitrary power. The

purpose was not to avoid friction, but, by means of the inevitable friction incident to the distribution of the governmental powers among three departments, to save the people from autocracy.

We therefore cannot decide this case by determining which branch of government can deal most expeditiously with the present crisis. The answer must depend on the allocation of powers under the Constitution. That in turn requires an analysis of the conditions giving rise to the seizure and of the seizure itself.

The legislative nature of the action taken by the President seems to me to be clear. When the United States takes over an industrial plant to settle a labor controversy, it is condemning property. The seizure of the plant is a taking in the constitutional sense. A permanent taking would amount to the nationalization of the industry. A temporary taking falls short of that goal. But though the seizure is only for a week or a month, the condemnation is complete and the United States must pay compensation for the temporary possession.

The President has no power to raise revenues. That power is in the Congress by Article I, Section 8 of the Constitution. The President might seize and the Congress by subsequent action might ratify the seizure. But until and unless Congress acted, no condemnation would be lawful. The branch of government that has the power to pay compensation for a seizure is the only one able to authorize a seizure or make lawful one that the President had effected. That seems to me to be the necessary result of the condemnation provision in the Fifth Amendment. It squares with the theory of checks and balances expounded by Mr. Justice BLACK in the opinion of the Court in which I join.

Justice FRANKFURTER, concurring.

We must therefore put to one side consideration of what powers the President would have had if there had been no legislation whatever bearing on the authority asserted by the seizure, or if the seizure had been only for a short, explicitly temporary period, to be terminated automatically unless Congressional approval were given. These and other questions, like or unlike, are not now here. I would exceed my authority were I to say anything about them.

The question before the Court comes in this setting. Congress has frequently—at least 16 times since 1916—specifically provided for executive seizure of production, transportation, communications, or storage facilities. In every case it has qualified this grant of power with limitations and safeguards. The power to seize has uniformly been given only for a limited period or for a defined emergency, or has been repealed after a short period. Its exercise has been restricted to particular circumstances such as "time of war or when war is imminent," the needs of "public safety" or of "national security or defense," or "urgent and impending need." The period of governmental operation has been limited, as, for instance, to "sixty days after the restoration of productive efficiency." Congress also has not left to implication that just compensation be paid: it has usually legislated in detail regarding enforcement of this litigation-breeding general requirement.

Congress in 1947 was again called upon to consider whether governmental seizure should be used to avoid serious industrial shutdowns. Congress decided against conferring such power generally and in advance, without special congressional enactment to meet each particular need. Under the urgency of telephone and coal strikes in the winter of 1946, Congress addressed itself to the problems raised by "national emergency" strikes and lockouts. The termination of wartime seizure powers on December 31, 1946, brought these matters to the attention of Congress with vivid impact. A proposal that the President be given powers to seize plants to avert a shutdown where the "health or safety" of the nation was endangered, was thoroughly canvassed by Congress and rejected. No room for doubt remains that the proponents as well as the opponents of the bill which became the Labor Management Relations Act of 1947 clearly understood that as a result of that legislation the only recourse for preventing a shutdown in any basic industry, after failure of mediation, was Congress. Authorization for seizure as an available remedy for potential dangers was unequivocally put aside. An amendment presented in the House providing that where necessary "to preserve and protect the public health and security" the President might seize any industry in which there is an impending curtailment of production, was voted down after debate, by a vote of more than three to one.

[N]othing can be plainer than that Congress made a conscious choice of policy in a field full of perplexity and peculiarly within legislative responsibility for choice. In formulating legislation for dealing with industrial conflicts, Congress could not more clearly and emphatically have withheld authority than it did in 1947. Perhaps as much so as is true of any piece of modern legislation, Congress acted with full consciousness of what it was doing and in the light of much recent history. Previous seizure legislation had subjected the powers granted to the President to restrictions of varying degrees of stringency. Instead of giving him even limited powers, Congress in 1947 deemed it wise to require the President, upon failure of attempts to reach a voluntary settlement, to report to Congress if he deemed the power of seizure a needed shot for his locker. The President could not ignore the specific limitations of prior seizure statutes. No more could he act in disregard of the limitation put upon seizure by the 1947 Act.

It cannot be contended that the President would have had power to issue this order had Congress explicitly negated such authority in formal legislation. Congress has expressed its will to withhold this power from the President as though it had said so in so many words.

Deeply embedded traditional ways of conducting government cannot supplant the Constitution or legislation, but they give meaning to the words of a text or supply them. It is an inadmissibly narrow conception of American constitutional law to confine it to the words of the Constitution and to disregard the gloss which life has written upon them. In short, a systematic, unbroken, executive practice, long pursued to the knowledge of the Congress and never before questioned, engaged in by Presidents who have also sworn to uphold the Constitution, making as it were such exercise of power part of the structure of our government, may be treated as a gloss on "executive Power" vested in the President by §1 of Art. II. Down to the World War II period, then, the record is barren of instances comparable to the one before us.

A scheme of government like ours no doubt at times feels the lack of power to act with complete, all-embracing, swiftly moving authority. No doubt a government with distributed authority, subject to be challenged in the courts of law, at least long enough to consider and adjudicate the challenge, labors under restrictions from which other governments are free. It has not been our tradition to envy such governments. In any event our government was designed to have such restrictions. The price was deemed not too high in view of the safeguards which these restrictions afford.

Chief Justice VINSON, with whom Justice REED and Justice MINTON join, dissenting.

The President of the United States directed the Secretary of Commerce to take temporary possession of the Nation's steel mills during the existing emergency because "a work stoppage would immediately jeopardize and imperil our national defense and the defense of those joined with us in resisting aggression, and would add to the continuing danger of our soldiers, sailors and airmen engaged in combat in the field."

In passing upon the question of Presidential powers in this case, we must first consider the context in which those powers were exercised. Those who suggest that this is a case involving extraordinary powers should be mindful that these are extraordinary times. A world not yet recovered from the devastation of World War II has been forced to face the threat of another and more terrifying global conflict.

In 1950, when the United Nations called upon member nations "to render every assistance" to repel aggression in Korea, the United States furnished its vigorous support. For almost two full years, our armed forces have been fighting in Korea, suffering casualties of over 108,000 men. Hostilities have not abated. The "determination of the United Nations to continue its action in Korea to meet the aggression" has been reaffirmed. Congressional support of the action in Korea has been manifested by provisions for increased military manpower and equipment and for economic stabilization, as hereinafter described. Alert to our responsibilities, which coincide with our own self preservation through mutual security, Congress has enacted a large body of implementing legislation. As an illustration of the magnitude of the over-all program, Congress has appropriated $130 billion for our own defense and for military assistance to our allies since the June, 1950, attack in Korea.

The President has the duty to execute the foregoing legislative programs. Their successful execution depends upon continued production of steel and stabilized prices for steel. Accordingly, when the collective bargaining agreements between the Nation's steel producers and their employees, represented by the United Steel Workers, were due to expire on December 31, 1951, and a strike shutting down the entire basic steel industry was threatened, the President acted to avert a complete shutdown of steel production.

One is not here called upon even to consider the possibility of executive seizure of a farm, a corner grocery store or even a single industrial plant. Such considerations arise only when one ignores the central fact of this case — that the Nation's entire basic steel production would have shut down completely if there had been no Government seizure. Even ignoring for the moment whatever confidential information the President may possess as "the Nation's organ for foreign affairs," the uncontroverted affidavits in this record amply support the finding that "a work stoppage would immediately jeopardize and imperil our national defense."

Plaintiffs do not remotely suggest any basis for rejecting the President's finding that any stoppage of steel production would immediately place the Nation in peril. At the time of seizure there was not, and there is not now, the slightest evidence to justify the belief that any strike will be of short duration. The Union and the steel companies may well engage in a lengthy struggle. Plaintiff's counsel tells us that "sooner or later" the mills will operate again. That may satisfy the steel companies and, perhaps, the Union. But our soldiers and our allies will hardly be cheered with the assurance that the ammunition upon which their lives depend will be forthcoming — "sooner or later," or, in other words, "too little and too late."

Accordingly, if the President has any power under the Constitution to meet a critical situation in the absence of express statutory authorization, there is no basis whatever for criticizing the exercise of such power in this case.

A review of executive action demonstrates that our Presidents have on many occasions exhibited the leadership contemplated by the framers when they made the President Commander in Chief, and imposed upon him the trust to "take Care that the Laws be faithfully executed." With or without explicit statutory authorization, Presidents have at such times dealt with national emergencies by acting promptly and resolutely to enforce legislative programs, at least to save those programs until Congress could act. Congress and the courts have responded to such executive initiative with consistent approval.

Focusing now on the situation confronting the President on the night of April 8, 1952, we cannot but conclude that the President was performing his duty under the Constitution to "take Care that the Laws be faithfully executed" — a duty described by President Benjamin Harrison as "the central idea of the office." The President reported to Congress the morning after the seizure that he acted because a work stoppage in steel production would immediately imperil the safety of the Nation by preventing execution of the legislative programs for procurement of military equipment. And, while a shutdown could be averted by granting the price concessions requested by plaintiffs, granting such concessions would disrupt the price stabilization program also enacted by Congress. Rather than fail to execute either legislative program, the President acted to execute both.

Much of the argument in this case has been directed at straw men. We do not now have before us the case of a President acting solely on the basis of his own notions of the public welfare. Nor is there any question of unlimited executive power in this case. The President himself closed the door to any such claim when he sent his Message to Congress stating his purpose to abide by any action of Congress, whether approving or disapproving his seizure action. Here, the President immediately made sure that Congress was fully informed of the temporary action he had taken only to preserve the legislative programs from destruction until Congress could act.

Faced with the duty of executing the defense programs which Congress had enacted and the disastrous effects that any stoppage in steel production would have on those programs, the President acted to preserve those programs by seizing the steel mills. There is no question that the possession was other than temporary in character and subject to congressional direction — either approving, disapproving or regulating the manner in which the mills were to be administered and returned to the owners. The President immediately informed Congress of his action and clearly stated his intention to abide by the legislative will. No basis for claims of arbitrary action, unlimited powers or dictatorial usurpation of congressional power appears from the facts of this case. On the contrary, judicial, legislative and executive precedents throughout our history demonstrate that in this case the President acted in full conformity with his duties under the Constitution.

THE SCOPE OF INHERENT POWER:
THE ISSUE OF EXECUTIVE PRIVILEGE

The issue of when the president may exercise inherent power arises in many contexts. For example, in section C below, there is discussion of the president's authority to remove executive officials, a power nowhere mentioned in the Constitution.

One of the most important issues concerning the inherent power of the president is whether and under what circumstances the president can invoke executive privilege. Executive privilege refers to the ability of the president to keep secret conversations with or memoranda to or from advisors. The Constitution does not mention such authority, but presidents have claimed it throughout American history. Presidents have contended that executive privilege is necessary for them to receive candid advice. Also, executive privilege is defended as important to protect national security; diplomacy is regarded as requiring secrecy.

The Supreme Court did not expressly consider the constitutionality and scope of executive privilege until 1974 in the landmark case of United States v. Nixon. Some factual background will help in understanding the case that follows. On June 17, 1972, a burglary occurred at the Democratic National Headquarters in the Watergate building in Washington, D.C. Over the course of the next year, it was discovered that the burglars were connected to the Committee for the Reelection of the President and that high-level White House officials were involved in a cover-up.[4] The year was filled with reporters finding evidence linking the burglary and cover-up to high officials, the president and his aides angrily denying the evidence and attacking the media, and then reporters finding further evidence and making additional allegations against the White House.

In the summer of 1973, Senator Sam Ervin from North Carolina chaired closely watched hearings of the Senate Select Committee on Watergate. One of the dramatic moments occurred when a presidential aide, Alexander Butterfield, revealed that there was a secret taping system in the Oval Office and that presidential conversations were routinely recorded.

Because top Justice Department officials, including former Attorney General John Mitchell, were suspected of involvement in the cover-up, there was political pressure for an independent investigation. Attorney General Elliot Richardson appointed Harvard law professor Archibald Cox to serve as a special prosecutor.

Cox subpoenaed tapes of White House conversations, and the president challenged the subpoena in courts. On October 12, 1973, the U.S. Court of Appeals for the District of Columbia sided with the special prosecutor and gave the president one week to file an appeal. On October 19, the president announced that he would turn over edited transcripts of the tapes and that he would ask Senator John Stennis (who was reported to be quite hard of hearing) to listen to the tapes and verify their accuracy. President Nixon also announced

---

4. For a fascinating account of the discovery of this information, *see* Carl Bernstein & Bob Woodward, *All the President's Men* (1974).

that he would comply with no additional subpoenas and turn over no additional tapes.

On Saturday, October 20, Special Prosecutor Archibald Cox declared Nixon's position unacceptable; there was a court order to turn over tapes, not transcripts. More important, he would seek whatever tapes he needed. President Nixon ordered Attorney General Richardson to fire Cox; Richardson refused and resigned. Nixon then asked the Justice Department's number-two official to fire Cox; William Ruckelshaus also refused and resigned. The request was then made to the number-three person in the Justice Department, Solicitor General Robert Bork. Bork then fired Cox in what came to be known as the Saturday Night Massacre.[5]

The first resolutions calling for Richard Nixon's impeachment were introduced into the House of Representatives and intense political pressure caused the appointment of a new special prosecutor, Leon Jaworski. On March 1, 1974, a grand jury for the U.S. District Court for the District of Columbia indicted seven top officials of the Nixon administration and the Committee for the Reelection of the President for obstruction of justice and conspiracy to defraud. President Nixon was named an "unindicted co-conspirator." The grand jury said that it would have indicted him for being part of the conspiracy, but did not know if it had the authority to indict a sitting president.

On April 18, 1974, a subpoena duces tecum (a subpoena to produce documents) was issued, at the request of the special prosecutor, for the president to turn over tapes and other materials to use as possible evidence in the upcoming criminal trial. On April 30, President Nixon announced that he was disclosing edited transcripts of 43 conversations, including 20 that were the subject of the subpoena. On May 1, the president moved to quash the subpoena. On May 20, the U.S. District Court denied the motion to quash and directed the president to provide all of the items that had been subpoenaed. The Supreme Court granted review prior to consideration by the Court of Appeals.

Meanwhile, the House Judiciary Committee was considering articles of impeachment against President Nixon. Impeachment hearings were held in July 1974, while the *Nixon* case was pending before the Supreme Court. The Supreme Court announced its decision in *Nixon* on July 25, 1974, and unanimously ruled that Nixon had to comply with the subpoena. The House Judiciary Committee voted its first article of impeachment on July 25 for obstruction of justice in connection with the Watergate break-in and cover-up. On July 29 and 30, the Committee voted two additional articles of impeachment for abuse of power and for failure to comply with a judiciary committee subpoena.

On August 6, 1974, President Nixon complied with the subpoena and made the transcripts of the tapes available to the public. The tapes showed that President Nixon clearly had obstructed justice by ordering the Federal Bureau of Investigation not to investigate the Watergate matter. Three days later, on Thursday, August 9, 1974, President Nixon became the only president in history to resign.

---

5. For a detailed account of this incident and its aftermath, *see* Theodore H. White, *Breach of Faith: The Fall of Richard Nixon* (1975).

UNITED STATES v. RICHARD M. NIXON,
PRESIDENT OF THE UNITED STATES

418 U.S. 683 (1974)

Chief Justice BURGER delivered the opinion of the Court

This litigation presents for review the denial of a motion, filed in the District Court on behalf of the President of the United States, in the case of United States v. Mitchell et al. to quash a third-party subpoena duces tecum issued by the United States District Court for the District of Columbia, pursuant to Fed. Rule Crim. Proc. 17(c). The subpoena directed the President to produce certain tape recordings and documents relating to his conversations with aides and advisers. The court rejected the President's claims of absolute executive privilege, of lack of jurisdiction, and of failure to satisfy the requirements of Rule 17(c).

THE CLAIM OF PRIVILEGE

A

[W]e turn to the claim that the subpoena should be quashed because it demands "confidential conversations between a President and his close advisors that it would be inconsistent with the public interest to produce." The first contention is a broad claim that the separation of powers doctrine precludes judicial review of a President's claim of privilege. The second contention is that if he does not prevail on the claim of absolute privilege, the court should hold as a matter of constitutional law that the privilege prevails over the subpoena duces tecum.

In the performance of assigned constitutional duties each branch of the Government must initially interpret the Constitution, and the interpretation of its powers by any branch is due great respect from the others. The President's counsel, as we have noted, reads the Constitution as providing an absolute privilege of confidentiality for all Presidential communications. Many decisions of this Court, however, have unequivocally reaffirmed the holding of Marbury v. Madison (1803), that "[i]t is emphatically the province and duty of the judicial department to say what the law is."

Our system of government "requires that federal courts on occasion interpret the Constitution in a manner at variance with the construction given the document by another branch." Powell v. McCormack. Notwithstanding the deference each branch must accord the others, the "judicial Power of the United States" vested in the federal courts by Art. III, §1, of the Constitution can no more be shared with the Executive Branch than the Chief Executive, for example, can share with the Judiciary the veto power, or the Congress share with the Judiciary the power to override a Presidential veto. Any other conclusion would be contrary to the basic concept of separation of powers and the checks and balances that flow from the scheme of a tripartite government. We therefore reaffirm that it is the province and duty of this Court "to say what the law is" with respect to the claim of privilege presented in this case. Marbury v. Madison.

B

In support of his claim of absolute privilege, the President's counsel urges two grounds, one of which is common to all governments and one of which is peculiar to our system of separation of powers. The first ground is the valid need for protection of communications between high Government officials and those who advise and assist them in the performance of their manifold duties; the importance of this confidentiality is too plain to require further discussion. Human experience teaches that those who expect public dissemination of their remarks may well temper candor with a concern for appearances and for their own interests to the detriment of the decisionmaking process. Whatever the nature of the privilege of confidentiality of Presidential communications in the exercise of Art. II powers, the privilege can be said to derive from the supremacy of each branch within its own assigned area of constitutional duties. Certain powers and privileges flow from the nature of enumerated powers; the protection of the confidentiality of Presidential communications has similar constitutional underpinnings.

The second ground asserted by the President's counsel in support of the claim of absolute privilege rests on the doctrine of separation of powers. Here it is argued that the independence of the Executive Branch within its own sphere, insulates a President from a judicial subpoena in an ongoing criminal prosecution, and thereby protects confidential Presidential communications.

However, neither the doctrine of separation of powers, nor the need for confidentiality of high-level communications, without more, can sustain an absolute, unqualified Presidential privilege of immunity from judicial process under all circumstances. The President's need for complete candor and objectivity from advisers calls for great deference from the courts. However, when the privilege depends solely on the broad, undifferentiated claim of public interest in the confidentiality of such conversations, a confrontation with other values arises. Absent a claim of need to protect military, diplomatic, or sensitive national security secrets, we find it difficult to accept the argument that even the very important interest in confidentiality of Presidential communications is significantly diminished by production of such material for in camera inspection with all the protection that a district court will be obliged to provide.

The impediment that an absolute, unqualified privilege would place in the way of the primary constitutional duty of the Judicial Branch to do justice in criminal prosecutions would plainly conflict with the function of the courts under Art. III. In designing the structure of our Government and dividing and allocating the sovereign power among three co-equal branches, the framers of the Constitution sought to provide a comprehensive system, but the separate powers were not intended to operate with absolute independence.

To read the Art. II powers of the President as providing an absolute privilege as against a subpoena essential to enforcement of criminal statutes on no more than a generalized claim of the public interest in confidentiality of nonmilitary and non-diplomatic discussions would upset the constitutional balance of "a workable government" and gravely impair the role of the courts under Art. III.

C

Since we conclude that the legitimate needs of the judicial process may outweigh Presidential privilege, it is necessary to resolve those competing interests in a manner that preserves the essential functions of each branch.

In this case the President challenges a subpoena served on him as a third party requiring the production of materials for use in a criminal prosecution; he does so on the claim that he has a privilege against disclosure of confidential communications. He does not place his claim of privilege on the ground they are military or diplomatic secrets. As to these areas of Art. II duties the courts have traditionally shown the utmost deference to Presidential responsibilities.

No case of the Court, however, has extended this high degree of deference to a President's generalized interest in confidentiality. Nowhere in the Constitution, as we have noted earlier, is there any explicit reference to a privilege of confidentiality, yet to the extent this interest relates to the effective discharge of a President's powers, it is constitutionally based.

The right to the production of all evidence at a criminal trial similarly has constitutional dimensions. The Sixth Amendment explicitly confers upon every defendant in a criminal trial the right "to be confronted with the witnesses against him" and "to have compulsory process for obtaining witnesses in his favor." Moreover, the Fifth Amendment also guarantees that no person shall be deprived of liberty without due process of law. It is the manifest duty of the courts to vindicate those guarantees, and to accomplish that it is essential that all relevant and admissible evidence be produced.

In this case we must weigh the importance of the general privilege of confidentiality of Presidential communications in performance of the President's responsibilities against the inroads of such a privilege on the fair administration of criminal justice. The interest in preserving confidentiality is weighty indeed and entitled to great respect. However, we cannot conclude that advisers will be moved to temper the candor of their remarks by the infrequent occasions of disclosure because of the possibility that such conversations will be called for in the context of a criminal prosecution.

On the other hand, the allowance of the privilege to withhold evidence that is demonstrably relevant in a criminal trial would cut deeply into the guarantee of due process of law and gravely impair the basic function of the courts. A President's acknowledged need for confidentiality in the communications of his office is general in nature, whereas the constitutional need for production of relevant evidence in a criminal proceeding is specific and central to the fair adjudication of a particular criminal case in the administration of justice. Without access to specific facts a criminal prosecution may be totally frustrated. The President's broad interest in confidentiality of communications will not be vitiated by disclosure of a limited number of conversations preliminarily shown to have some bearing on the pending criminal cases.

We conclude that when the ground for asserting privilege as to subpoenaed materials sought for use in a criminal trial is based only on the generalized interest in confidentiality, it cannot prevail over the fundamental demands of due process of law in the fair administration of criminal justice. The generalized assertion of privilege must yield to the demonstrated, specific need for evidence in a pending criminal trial.

For the first time since United States v. Nixon 30 years ago, in Cheney v. U.S. District Court for the District of Columbia, 124 S. Ct. 2576 (2004), the Supreme Court considered an issue of executive privilege. The case arose in an unusual procedural context. A lawsuit was filed claiming that an energy task force, chaired by Vice President Dick Cheney, violated the Federal Advisory Committee Act by holding secret meetings. The plaintiffs sought and received a discovery order. The defendants then sought a writ of mandamus from the Court of

Appeals to stop enforcement of the discovery order. The Court of Appeals denied the writ of mandamus. In the context of considering whether the Court of Appeals should have issued a writ of mandamus, the Supreme Court discussed executive privilege and when it is to be considered. The Court did not resolve whether executive privilege applied here, or even whether mandamus should be issued. The Court remanded the case for further consideration. In discussing executive privilege, the Court, in an opinion by Justice Kennedy, distinguished United States v. Nixon, and stated:

> [S]eparation-of-powers considerations should inform a court of appeals' evaluation of a mandamus petition involving the President or the Vice President. The Court of Appeals dismissed these separation-of-powers concerns. Relying on United States v. Nixon, it held that even though respondents' discovery requests are overbroad and "go well beyond FACA's requirements," the Vice President and his former colleagues on the NEPDG "shall bear the burden" of invoking privilege with narrow specificity and objecting to the discovery requests with "detailed precision."
>
> This analysis, however, overlooks fundamental differences in the two cases. *Nixon* cannot bear the weight the Court of Appeals puts upon it. First, unlike this case, which concerns respondents' requests for information for use in a civil suit, *Nixon* involves the proper balance between the Executive's interest in the confidentiality of its communications and the "constitutional need for production of relevant evidence in a criminal proceeding." The distinction *Nixon* drew between criminal and civil proceedings is not just a matter of formalism. As the Court explained, the need for information in the criminal context is much weightier because "our historic[al] commitment to the rule of law . . . is nowhere more profoundly manifest than in our view that 'the twofold aim [of criminal justice] is that guilt shall not escape or innocence suffer.'" The need for information for use in civil cases, while far from negligible, does not share the urgency or significance of the criminal subpoena requests in *Nixon*. As *Nixon* recognized, the right to production of relevant evidence in civil proceedings does not have the same "constitutional dimensions."
>
> Contrary to the District Court's and the Court of Appeals' conclusions, *Nixon* does not leave them the sole option of inviting the Executive Branch to invoke executive privilege while remaining otherwise powerless to modify a party's overly broad discovery requests. Executive privilege is an extraordinary assertion of power "not to be lightly invoked." Once executive privilege is asserted, coequal branches of the Government are set on a collision course. The Judiciary is forced into the difficult task of balancing the need for information in a judicial proceeding and the Executive's Article II prerogatives. This inquiry places courts in the awkward position of evaluating the Executive's claims of confidentiality and autonomy, and pushes to the fore difficult questions of separation of powers and checks and balances. These "occasion[s] for constitutional confrontation between the two branches" should be avoided whenever possible.
>
> As we discussed at the outset, under principles of mandamus jurisdiction, the Court of Appeals may exercise its power to issue the writ only upon a finding of "exceptional circumstances amounting to a judicial 'usurpation of power,'" or "a clear abuse of discretion." As this case implicates the separation of powers, the Court of Appeals must also ask, as part of this inquiry, whether the District Court's actions constituted an unwarranted impairment of another branch in the performance of its constitutional duties.
>
> We decline petitioners' invitation to direct the Court of Appeals to issue the writ against the District Court. [M]atters bearing on whether the writ of mandamus should issue should also be addressed, in the first instance, by the Court of Appeals after considering any additional briefs and arguments as it deems appropriate. We

note only that all courts should be mindful of the burdens imposed on the Executive Branch in any future proceedings. Special considerations applicable to the President and the Vice President suggest that the courts should be sensitive to requests by the Government for interlocutory appeals to reexamine, for example, whether the statute embodies the de facto membership doctrine.

B. THE AUTHORITY OF CONGRESS TO INCREASE EXECUTIVE POWER

The prior section focused on the power of the president to act without express constitutional or statutory authority. This section focuses on the power of Congress to enhance the powers of the president by conferring authority not contained in the Constitution. Underlying this issue are two different views of separation of powers. One approach sees separation of powers as appropriately resolved, whenever possible, between the president and Congress; if the two branches agree, the courts only rarely should invalidate their actions. The other view sees separation of powers as constitutionally mandated and therefore envisions a crucial judicial role in enforcing its requirements.

The issue of Congress's authority to increase executive power arises again, importantly, in the next section, which focuses on the ability of Congress to delegate legislative power to administrative agencies. Here the focus is on a recent Supreme Court decision, Clinton v. City of New York, which involved the constitutionality of a federal statute that created the line-item veto. The statute empowered the president to veto (or, more precisely, to "cancel") particular parts of appropriation bills while allowing the rest to go into effect.

WILLIAM J. CLINTON, PRESIDENT
OF THE UNITED STATES v. CITY OF NEW YORK
524 U.S. 417 (1998)

Justice STEVENS delivered the opinion of the Court.

The Line Item Veto Act (Act), was enacted in April 1996 and became effective on January 1, 1997.

I

We begin by reviewing the canceled items that are at issue in these cases. Title XIX of the Social Security Act, as amended, authorizes the Federal Government to transfer huge sums of money to the States to help finance medical care for the indigent. In 1991, Congress directed that those federal subsidies be reduced by the amount of certain taxes levied by the States on health care providers. In 1994, the Department of Health and Human Services (HHS) notified the State of New York that 15 of its taxes were covered by the 1991 Act, and that as of June 30, 1994, the statute therefore required New York to return $955 million to the United States. New York turned to Congress for relief. On August 5, 1997,

Congress enacted a law that resolved the issue in New York's favor. Section 4722(c) of the Balanced Budget Act of 1997 identifies the disputed taxes and provides that they "are deemed to be permissible health care related taxes and in compliance with the requirements" of the relevant provisions of the 1991 statute.

On August 11, 1997, the President sent identical notices to the Senate and to the House of Representatives canceling "one item of new direct spending," specifying §4722(c) as that item, and stating that he had determined that "this cancellation will reduce the Federal budget deficit." He explained that §4722(c) would have permitted New York "to continue relying upon impermissible provider taxes to finance its Medicaid program" and that "[t]his preferential treatment would have increased Medicaid costs, would have treated New York differently from all other States, and would have established a costly precedent for other States to request comparable treatment."

A person who realizes a profit from the sale of securities is generally subject to a capital gains tax. In §968 of the Taxpayer Relief Act of 1997, Congress amended §1042 of the Internal Revenue Code to permit owners of certain food refiners and processors to defer the recognition of gain if they sell their stock to eligible farmers' cooperatives. The purpose of the amendment, as repeatedly explained by its sponsors, was "to facilitate the transfer of refiners and processors to farmers' cooperatives." The amendment to §1042 was one of the 79 "limited tax benefits" authorized by the Taxpayer Relief Act of 1997 and specifically identified in Title XVII of that Act as "subject to [the] line item veto."

On the same date that he canceled the "item of new direct spending" involving New York's health care programs, the President also canceled this limited tax benefit. In his explanation of that action, the President endorsed the objective of encouraging "value-added farming through the purchase by farmers' cooperatives of refiners or processors of agricultural goods," but concluded that the provision lacked safeguards and also "failed to target its benefits to small- and medium-size cooperatives."

II

Appellees filed two separate actions against the President and other federal officials challenging these two cancellations. The plaintiffs in the first case are the City of New York, two hospital associations, one hospital, and two unions representing health care employees. The plaintiffs in the second are a farmers' cooperative consisting of about 30 potato growers in Idaho and an individual farmer who is a member and officer of the cooperative.

The Line Item Veto Act gives the President the power to "cancel in whole" three types of provisions that have been signed into law: "(1) any dollar amount of discretionary budget authority; (2) any item of new direct spending; or (3) any limited tax benefit." It is undisputed that the New York case involves an "item of new direct spending" and that the Snake River case involves a "limited tax benefit" as those terms are defined in the Act. It is also undisputed that each of those provisions had been signed into law pursuant to Article I, §7, of the Constitution before it was canceled.

The Act requires the President to adhere to precise procedures whenever he exercises his cancellation authority. In identifying items for cancellation he must consider the legislative history, the purposes, and other relevant information about the items. He must determine, with respect to each cancellation, that it will "(i) reduce the Federal budget deficit; (ii) not impair any essential Government functions; and (iii) not harm the national interest." Moreover, he must transmit a special message to Congress notifying it of each cancellation within five calendar days (excluding Sundays) after the enactment of the canceled provision. It is undisputed that the President meticulously followed these procedures in these cases.

A cancellation takes effect upon receipt by Congress of the special message from the President. If, however, a "disapproval bill" pertaining to a special message is enacted into law, the cancellations set forth in that message become "null and void." The Act sets forth a detailed expedited procedure for the consideration of a "disapproval bill," but no such bill was passed for either of the cancellations involved in these cases. A majority vote of both Houses is sufficient to enact a disapproval bill. The Act does not grant the President the authority to cancel a disapproval bill, but he does, of course, retain his constitutional authority to veto such a bill.

In both legal and practical effect, the President has amended two Acts of Congress by repealing a portion of each. "[R]epeal of statutes, no less than enactment, must conform with Art. I." INS v. Chadha (1983). There is no provision in the Constitution that authorizes the President to enact, to amend, or to repeal statutes.

Both Article I and Article II assign responsibilities to the President that directly relate to the lawmaking process, but neither addresses the issue presented by these cases. The President "shall from time to time give to the Congress Information on the State of the Union, and recommend to their Consideration such Measures as he shall judge necessary and expedient. . . ." Art. II, §3. Thus, he may initiate and influence legislative proposals. Moreover, after a bill has passed both Houses of Congress, but "before it become[s] a Law," it must be presented to the President. If he approves it, "he shall sign it, but if not he shall return it, with his Objections to that House in which it shall have originated, who shall enter the Objections at large on their Journal, and proceed to reconsider it." Art. I, §7, cl. 2. His "return" of a bill, which is usually described as a "veto," is subject to being overridden by a two-thirds vote in each House.

There are important differences between the President's "return" of a bill pursuant to Article I, §7, and the exercise of the President's cancellation authority pursuant to the Line Item Veto Act. The constitutional return takes place before the bill becomes law; the statutory cancellation occurs after the bill becomes law. The constitutional return is of the entire bill; the statutory cancellation is of only a part. Although the Constitution expressly authorizes the President to play a role in the process of enacting statutes, it is silent on the subject of unilateral Presidential action that either repeals or amends parts of duly enacted statutes.

There are powerful reasons for construing constitutional silence on this profoundly important issue as equivalent to an express prohibition. The procedures governing the enactment of statutes set forth in the text of Article I were the product of the great debates and compromises that produced the Constitution itself. Familiar historical materials provide abundant support for the conclusion that the power to enact statutes may only "be exercised in accord with a single, finely wrought and exhaustively considered, procedure." Our first President understood the text of the Presentment Clause as requiring that he either "approve all the parts of a Bill, or reject it in toto."

What has emerged in these cases from the President's exercise of his statutory cancellation powers, however, are truncated versions of two bills that passed both Houses of Congress. They are not the product of the "finely wrought" procedure that the framers designed.

[III]

[W]e express no opinion about the wisdom of the procedures authorized by the Line Item Veto Act. Many members of both major political parties who have served in the Legislative and the Executive Branches have long advocated the enactment of such procedures for the purpose of "ensur[ing] greater fiscal accountability in Washington." H.R. Conf. Rep. 104-491, p. 15 (1996). The text of the Act was itself the product of much debate and deliberation in both Houses of Congress and that precise text was signed into law by the President. We do not lightly conclude that their action was unauthorized by the Constitution.

If there is to be a new procedure in which the President will play a different role in determining the final text of what may "become a law," such change must come not by legislation but through the amendment procedures set forth in Article V of the Constitution.

Justice KENNEDY, concurring.

A nation cannot plunder its own treasury without putting its Constitution and its survival in peril. The statute before us, then, is of first importance, for it seems undeniable the Act will tend to restrain persistent excessive spending. Nevertheless, for the reasons given by Justice Stevens in the opinion for the Court, the statute must be found invalid. Failure of political will does not justify unconstitutional remedies.

I write to respond to my colleague Justice Breyer, who observes that the statute does not threaten the liberties of individual citizens, a point on which I disagree. The argument is related to his earlier suggestion that our role is lessened here because the two political branches are adjusting their own powers between themselves. To say the political branches have a somewhat free hand to reallocate their own authority would seem to require acceptance of two premises: first, that the public good demands it, and second, that liberty is not at risk. The former premise is inadmissible. The Constitution's structure requires a stability which transcends the convenience of the moment. The latter premise, too, is flawed. Liberty is always at stake when one or more of the branches seek to transgress the separation of powers. Separation of powers was designed to implement a fundamental insight: concentration of power in the hands of a single branch is a threat to liberty.

Justice BREYER, with whom Justice O'CONNOR and Justice SCALIA join, dissenting.

[I]

I approach the constitutional question before us with three general considerations in mind. First, the Act represents a legislative effort to provide the President with the power to give effect to some, but not to all, of the expenditure and revenue-diminishing provisions contained in a single massive appropriations bill. And this objective is constitutionally proper.

When our Nation was founded, Congress could easily have provided the President with this kind of power. In that time period, our population was less than four million, federal employees numbered fewer than 5,000, annual federal budget outlays totaled approximately $4 million, and the entire operative text of Congress's first general appropriations law [was two sentences long]. At that time, a Congress, wishing to give a President the power to select among appropriations, could simply have embodied each appropriation in a separate bill, each bill subject to a separate Presidential veto.

Today, however, our population is about 250 million, the Federal Government employs more than four million people, the annual federal budget is $1.5 trillion, and a typical budget appropriations bill may have a dozen titles, hundreds of sections, and spread across more than 500 pages of the Statutes at Large. Congress cannot divide such a bill into thousands, or tens of thousands, of separate appropriations bills, each one of which the President would have to sign, or to veto, separately. Thus, the question is whether the Constitution permits Congress to choose a particular novel means to achieve this same, constitutionally legitimate, end.

Second, the case in part requires us to focus upon the Constitution's generally phrased structural provisions, provisions that delegate all "legislative" power to Congress and vest all "executive" power in the President. The Court, when applying these provisions, has interpreted them generously in terms of the institutional arrangements that they permit.

Third, we need not here referee a dispute among the other two branches. And, as the majority points out, "'When this Court is asked to invalidate a statutory provision that has been approved by both Houses of the Congress and signed by the President, particularly an Act of Congress that confronts a deeply vexing national problem, it should only do so for the most compelling constitutional reasons.'" (quoting Bowsher v. Synar (1986) (Stevens, J., concurring in judgment)).

These three background circumstances mean that, when one measures the literal words of the Act against the Constitution's literal commands, the fact that the Act may closely resemble a different, literally unconstitutional, arrangement is beside the point. To drive exactly 65 miles per hour on an interstate highway closely resembles an act that violates the speed limit. But it does not violate that limit, for small differences matter when the question is one of literal violation of law. No more does this Act literally violate the Constitution's words.

[II]

The Court believes that the Act violates the literal text of the Constitution. A simple syllogism captures its basic reasoning:

Major Premise: The Constitution sets forth an exclusive method for enacting, repealing, or amending laws.

Minor Premise: The Act authorizes the President to "repea[l] or amen[d]" laws in a different way, namely by announcing a cancellation of a portion of a previously enacted law.

Conclusion: The Act is inconsistent with the Constitution.

I find this syllogism unconvincing, however, because its Minor Premise is faulty. When the President "canceled" the two appropriation measures now before us, he did not repeal any law nor did he amend any law. He simply followed the law, leaving the statutes, as they are literally written, intact.

To take a simple example, a legal document, say a will or a trust instrument, might grant a beneficiary the power (a) to appoint property "to Jones for his life, remainder to Smith for 10 years so long as Smith . . . etc., and then to Brown," or (b) to appoint the same property "to Black and the heirs of his body," or (c) not to exercise the power of appointment at all. To choose the second or third of these alternatives prevents from taking effect the legal consequences that flow from the first alternative, which the legal instrument describes in detail. Any such choice, made in the exercise of a delegated power, renders that first alternative language without "legal force or effect." But such a choice does not "repeal" or "amend" either that language or the document itself. The will or trust instrument, in delegating the power of appointment, has not delegated a power to amend or to repeal the instrument; to the contrary, it requires the delegated power to be exercised in accordance with the instrument's terms.

These features of the law do not mean that the delegated power is, or is just like, a power to appoint property. But they do mean that it is not, and it is not just like, the repeal or amendment of a law, or, for that matter, a true line item veto (despite the Act's title). Because one cannot say that the President's exercise of the power the Act grants is, literally speaking, a "repeal" or "amendment," the fact that the Act's procedures differ from the Constitution's exclusive procedures for enacting (or repealing) legislation is beside the point. The Act itself was enacted in accordance with these procedures, and its failure to require the President to satisfy those procedures does not make the Act unconstitutional.

C. THE CONSTITUTIONAL PROBLEMS OF THE ADMINISTRATIVE STATE

One of the most dramatic changes in American government since the Constitution was written in 1787 has been the growth of administrative agencies. Although federal agencies and departments have existed in some form since the beginning of American history, it is only in the last century that Congress has routinely delegated its legislative power to executive agencies. The creation of the Interstate Commerce Commission in 1887 ushered in a new era for the federal government: the creation of federal administrative agencies with broad powers. Over the course of the next century, a vast array of federal agencies were created, such as the Federal Communications Commission, the Securities and Exchange Commission, the Food and Drug Administration, the Environmental Protection Agency, the Nuclear Regulatory Commission, and countless more.

These agencies exercise all of the powers of government: legislative, executive, and judicial. Administrative agencies generally have legislative power, as they possess the authority to promulgate rules that have the force of law. Administrative agencies also have executive power, because they are responsible for bringing enforcement actions against those who violate the relevant federal laws and regulations. Finally, administrative agencies frequently have judicial power in that they employ administrative law judges who hear cases brought by agency officials against those accused of violating the agency's regulations.

The combination of legislative, executive, and judicial power in the same hands is troubling. James Madison wrote, "The accumulation of all powers, legislative, executive, and judiciary, in the same hands . . . may justly be pronounced the very definition of tyranny." The Federalist No. 47, p. 301 (Clinton Rossiter ed., 1961). More generally, controlling and checking administrative agencies poses an important constitutional problem, unaddressed by the text or the framers' intent.

Subsection 1 considers the nondelegation doctrine, the principle that Congress cannot delegate legislative power, and its demise. The existence of broad delegations of legislative authority to administrative agencies is part of the constitutional problem posed by administrative agencies. One possible check on administrative agencies is the "legislative veto": Congress, acting pursuant to statutory authorization, invalidates an agency's action by a resolution that is not presented to the President for a possible veto. However, as presented in Subsection 2, the Supreme Court declared this tool unconstitutional. Subsection 3 then examines other checks on administrative agencies, including the appointment and removal power, judicial review, and Congress delegating authority to itself.

The tension explored throughout this section is on how to reconcile the practical need for administrative agencies in the complex, modern world with basic principles of separation of powers and checks and balances.

1. The Nondelegation Doctrine and Its Demise

One solution to the constitutional problems posed by administrative agencies is the non-delegation doctrine: the principle that Congress may not delegate its legislative power to administrative agencies. The nondelegation doctrine forces a politically accountable Congress to make the policy choices, rather than leaving this to unelected administrative officials.

The height of the Court's enforcement of the nondelegation doctrine was in the mid-1930s in two decisions that invalidated New Deal legislation. The National Industrial Recovery Act, a key piece of New Deal legislation, authorized the president to approve "codes of fair competition" developed by boards of various industries.

A.L.A. SCHECHTER POULTRY CORP. v. UNITED STATES

295 U.S. 495 (1935)

[The A.L.A. Schechter Poultry Corporation was indicted for an alleged conspiracy and for violations of the Code of Fair Competition for the Live Poultry Industry of the metropolitan area in and about the city of New York. The Code of Fair Competition prescribed labor standards for poultry businesses and many aspects of how such businesses could operate. The code was created by a business group delegated this authority by a federal law, the National Industrial Recovery Act.]

Chief Justice HUGHES delivered the opinion of the Court.[6]

The question, then, turns upon the authority which section 3 of the Recovery Act vests in the President to approve or prescribe. If the codes have standing as penal statutes, this must be due to the effect of the executive action. But Congress cannot delegate legislative power to the President to exercise an unfettered discretion to make whatever laws he thinks may be needed or advisable for the rehabilitation and expansion of trade or industry.

Accordingly we turn to the Recovery Act to ascertain what limits have been set to the exercise of the President's discretion: First, the President, as a condition of approval, is required to find that the trade or industrial associations or groups which propose a code "impose no inequitable restrictions on admission to membership" and are "truly representative." That condition, however, relates only to the status of the initiators of the new laws and not to the permissible scope of such laws. Second, the President is required to find that the code is not "designed to promote monopolies or to eliminate or oppress small enterprises and will not operate to discriminate against them." And to this is added a proviso that the code "shall not permit monopolies or monopolistic practices." But these restrictions leave virtually untouched the field of policy envisaged by section 1, and, in that wide field of legislative possibilities, the proponents of a code, refraining from monopolistic designs, may roam at will, and the President may approve or disapprove their proposals as he may see fit. That is the precise effect of the further finding that the President is to make — that the code "will tend to effectuate the policy of this title."

Section 3 of the Recovery Act is without precedent. It supplies no standards for any trade, industry, or activity. It does not undertake to prescribe rules of conduct to be applied to particular states of fact determined by appropriate administrative procedure. Instead of prescribing rules of conduct, it authorizes the making of codes to prescribe them. For that legislative undertaking, section 3 sets up no standards, aside from the statement of the general aims of rehabilitation, correction, and expansion described in section 1. In view of the scope of that broad declaration and of the nature of the few restrictions that are imposed, the discretion of the President in approving or prescribing codes, and thus enacting laws for the government of trade and industry throughout the country, is virtually unfettered. We think that the code-making authority thus conferred is an unconstitutional delegation of legislative power.

---

6. The Court also found the law unconstitutional as exceeding the scope of Congress's Commerce Clause authority. This aspect of the decision is discussed in Chapter 2. [Footnote by casebook author.]

PANAMA REFINING CO. v. RYAN

293 U.S. 388 (1935)

[A provision of the National Industrial Recovery Act authorized the president to prohibit transportation in interstate and foreign commerce of petroleum produced in excess of the amount permitted by state.]

Chief Justice Hughes delivered the opinion of the Court.

On July 11, 1933, the President, by Executive Order No. 6199 prohibited "the transportation in interstate and foreign commerce of petroleum and the products thereof produced or withdrawn from storage in excess of the amount permitted to be produced or withdrawn from storage by any State law or valid regulation or order prescribed thereunder, by any board, commission, officer, or other duly authorized agency of a State." This action was based on section 9(c) of title 1 of the National Industrial Recovery Act of June 16, 1933.

[The federal law] contains nothing as to the circumstances or conditions in which transportation of petroleum or petroleum products should be prohibited — nothing as to the policy of prohibiting or not prohibiting the transportation of production exceeding what the states allow.

It is no answer to insist that deleterious consequences follow the transportation of "hot oil" — oil exceeding state allowances. The Congress did not prohibit that transportation. The Congress did not undertake to say that transportation of "hot oil" was injurious. The Congress did not say that transportation of that oil was "unfair competition." The Congress did not declare in what circumstances that transportation should be forbidden, or require the President to make any determination as to any facts or circumstances. Among the numerous and diverse objectives broadly stated, the President was not required to choose. The President was not required to ascertain and proclaim the conditions prevailing in the industry which made the prohibition necessary. The Congress left the matter to the President without standard or rule, to be dealt with as he pleased.

The Constitution provides that "All legislative Powers herein granted shall be vested in a Congress of the United States, which shall consist of a Senate and House of Representatives." And the Congress is empowered "To make all Laws which shall be necessary and proper for carrying into Execution" its general powers. The Congress manifestly is not permitted to abdicate or to transfer to others the essential legislative functions with which it is thus vested. Undoubtedly legislation must often be adapted to complex conditions involving a host of details with which the national Legislature cannot deal directly. The Constitution has never been regarded as denying to the Congress the necessary resources of flexibility and practicality, which will enable it to perform its function in laying down policies and establishing standards, while leaving to selected instrumentalities the making of subordinate rules within prescribed limits and the determination of facts to which the policy as declared by the Legislature is to apply. Without capacity to give authorizations of that sort we should have the anomaly of a legislative power which in many circumstances calling for its exertion would be but a futility. But the constant recognition of the necessity and validity of such provisions and the wide range of administrative authority which has been developed by means of them cannot be allowed to obscure the limitations of the authority to delegate, if our constitutional system is to be maintained.

If section 9(c) were held valid, it would be idle to pretend that anything would be left of limitations upon the power of the Congress to delegate its lawmaking function. The reasoning of the many decisions we have reviewed would be made vacuous and their distinctions nugatory. Instead of performing its lawmaking function, the Congress could at will and as to such subjects as it chooses transfer that function to the President or other officer or to an administrative body. The question is not of the intrinsic importance of the particular statute before us, but of the constitutional processes of legislation which are an essential part of our system of government.

In the almost 70 years since *Panama Oil* and *Schechter*, not a single federal law has been declared an impermissible delegation of legislative power by the Supreme Court. Although these decisions have not been expressly overruled, they never have been followed either. All delegations, no matter how broad, have been upheld. Although the Court says that when Congress delegates its legislative power it must provide criteria to guide the agency's exercise of discretion,[7] all delegations, even without any criteria, have been upheld. Undoubtedly, this reflects a judicial judgment that broad delegations were necessary in the complex world of the late twentieth century and that the judiciary is ill equipped to draw meaningful lines. For example, in Mistretta v. United States, 488 U.S. 361 (1989), the Supreme Court upheld the Federal Sentencing Reform Act, which created the United States Sentencing Commission, an agency located in the judicial branch with broad discretion to promulgate sentencing guidelines to determine the punishments for those convicted of federal crimes.

Many have predicted a revival of the nondelegation doctrine, but it has not happened, as illustrated by the Supreme Court's decision in Whitman v. American Trucking Association, Inc.

WHITMAN v. AMERICAN TRUCKING ASSOCIATION, INC.
531 U.S. 457 (2001)

Justice SCALIA delivered the opinion of the Court.

These cases present the question [w]hether §109(b)(1) of the Clean Air Act (CAA) delegates legislative power to the Administrator of the Environmental Protection Agency (EPA).

Section 109(a) of the CAA requires the Administrator of the EPA to promulgate [National Ambient Air Quality Standards] NAAQS for each air pollutant for which "air quality criteria" have been issued. Once a NAAQS has been promulgated, the Administrator must review the standard (and the criteria on which it is based) "at five-year intervals" and make "such revisions . . . as may be appropriate." These cases arose when, on July 18, 1997, the Administrator revised the NAAQS for particulate matter (PM) and ozone.

The District of Columbia Circuit agreed with the respondents that §109(b)(1) delegated legislative power to the Administrator in contravention

---

7. *See, e.g.*, National Cable Television Assn. v. United States, 415 U.S 336 (1974).

of the United States Constitution, Art. I, §1, because it found that the EPA had interpreted the statute to provide no "intelligible principle" to guide the agency's exercise of authority. The court thought, however, that the EPA could perhaps avoid the unconstitutional delegation by adopting a restrictive construction of §109(b)(1), so instead of declaring the section unconstitutional the court remanded the NAAQS to the agency.

Section 109(b)(1) of the CAA instructs the EPA to set "ambient air quality standards the attainment and maintenance of which in the judgment of the Administrator, based on [the] criteria [documents of §108] and allowing an adequate margin of safety, are requisite to protect the public health." The Court of Appeals held that this section as interpreted by the Administrator did not provide an "intelligible principle" to guide the EPA's exercise of authority in setting NAAQS. "[The] EPA," it said, "lack[ed] any determinate criteria for drawing lines. It has failed to state intelligibly how much is too much." The court hence found that the EPA's interpretation (but not the statute itself) violated the nondelegation doctrine. We disagree.

In a delegation challenge, the constitutional question is whether the statute has delegated legislative power to the agency. Article I, §1, of the Constitution vests "[a]ll legislative Powers herein granted . . . in a Congress of the United States." This text permits no delegation of those powers, and so we repeatedly have said that when Congress confers decision-making authority upon agencies Congress must "lay down by legislative act an intelligible principle to which the person or body authorized to [act] is directed to conform." We have never suggested that an agency can cure an unlawful delegation of legislative power by adopting in its discretion a limiting construction of the statute. The idea that an agency can cure an unconstitutionally standardless delegation of power by declining to exercise some of that power seems to us internally contradictory. The very choice of which portion of the power to exercise — that is to say, the prescription of the standard that Congress had omitted — would itself be an exercise of the forbidden legislative authority. Whether the statute delegates legislative power is a question for the courts, and an agency's voluntary self-denial has no bearing upon the answer.

We agree with the Solicitor General that the text of §109(b)(1) of the CAA at a minimum requires that "[f]or a discrete set of pollutants and based on published air quality criteria that reflect the latest scientific knowledge, [the] EPA must establish uniform national standards at a level that is requisite to protect public health from the adverse effects of the pollutant in the ambient air." Requisite, in turn, "mean[s] sufficient, but not more than necessary." These limits on the EPA's discretion are strikingly similar to the ones we approved in Touby v. United States (1991), which permitted the Attorney General to designate a drug as a controlled substance for purposes of criminal drug enforcement if doing so was "necessary to avoid an imminent hazard to the public safety." They also resemble the Occupational Safety and Health Act provision requiring the agency to "set the standard which most adequately assures, to the extent feasible, on the basis of the best available evidence, that no employee will suffer any impairment of health" — which the Court upheld in Industrial Union Dept., AFL-CIO v. American Petroleum Institute (1980), and which even then-Justice Rehnquist, who alone in that case thought the statute violated the nondelegation doctrine, would have upheld if, like the statute here, it did not permit economic costs to be considered.

The scope of discretion §109(b)(1) allows is in fact well within the outer limits of our non-delegation precedents. In the history of the Court we have found the requisite "intelligible principle" lacking in only two statutes, one of which provided literally no guidance for the exercise of discretion, and the other of which conferred authority to regulate the entire economy on the basis of no more precise a standard than stimulating the economy by assuring "fair competition." *See* Panama Refining Co. v. Ryan (1935); A.L.A. Schechter Poultry Corp. v. United States (1935). We have, on the other hand, upheld the validity of §11(b)(2) of the Public Utility Holding Company Act of 1935, which gave the Securities and Exchange Commission authority to modify the structure of holding company systems so as to ensure that they are not "unduly or unnecessarily complicate[d]" and do not "unfairly or inequitably distribute voting power among security holders." American Power & Light Co. v. SEC (1946). We have approved the wartime conferral of agency power to fix the prices of commodities at a level that "will be generally fair and equitable and will effectuate the [in some respects conflicting] purposes of th[e] Act." Yakus v. United States (1944). And we have found an "intelligible principle" in various statutes authorizing regulation in the "public interest." *See, e.g.*, National Broadcasting Co. v. United States (1943) (FCC's power to regulate airwaves); New York Central Securities Corp. v. United States (1932) (ICC's power to approve railroad consolidations). In short, we have "almost never felt qualified to second-guess Congress regarding the permissible degree of policy judgment that can be left to those executing or applying the law."

[E]ven in sweeping regulatory schemes we have never demanded, as the Court of Appeals did here, that statutes provide a "determinate criterion" for saying "how much [of the regulated harm] is too much." It is therefore not conclusive for delegation purposes that, as respondents argue, ozone and particulate matter are "nonthreshold" pollutants that inflict a continuum of adverse health effects at any airborne concentration greater than zero, and hence require the EPA to make judgments of degree. "[A] certain degree of discretion, and thus of lawmaking, inheres in most executive or judicial action." Mistretta v. United States (Scalia, J., dissenting). Section 109(b)(1) of the CAA, which to repeat we interpret as requiring the EPA to set air quality standards at the level that is "requisite"—that is, not lower or higher than is necessary—to protect the public health with an adequate margin of safety, fits comfortably within the scope of discretion permitted by our precedent. We therefore reverse the judgment of the Court of Appeals.

2. The Legislative Veto and Its Demise

In light of the demise of the nondelegation doctrine, the issue arises as to how the power of administrative agencies will be checked and controlled. Congress, of course, could enact a law overturning an agency's rule, but requiring legislative action obviously limits the circumstances in which Congress can or will exercise its checking function.

Therefore, in the 1930s, not coincidentally corresponding to the time of great growth in federal administrative agencies, Congress created the "legislative veto" as a check on the actions of administrative agencies. Congress included in statutes provisions authorizing Congress or one of its houses or committees to overturn an agency's action by doing something less than adopting a new law. A typical form of a legislative veto provision authorized Congress to overturn an agency's decision by a resolution of one house of Congress. Legislative vetoes also took the form of overturning agency rules by resolution of both houses of Congress or even by action of a congressional committee. Nearly 200 federal laws contained legislative veto provisions.[8]

In Immigration and Naturalization Service (INS) v. Chadha, the Supreme Court declared unconstitutional the legislative veto.

IMMIGRATION & NATURALIZATION SERVICE v. JAGDISH RAI CHADHA

462 U.S. 919 (1983)

Chief Justice BURGER delivered the opinion of the Court.

[The case] presents a challenge to the constitutionality of the provision in §244(c)(2) of the Immigration and Nationality Act, authorizing one House of Congress, by resolution, to invalidate the decision of the Executive Branch, pursuant to authority delegated by Congress to the Attorney General of the United States, to allow a particular deportable alien to remain in the United States.

I

Chadha is an East Indian who was born in Kenya and holds a British passport. He was lawfully admitted to the United States in 1966 on a nonimmigrant student visa. His visa expired on June 30, 1972. On October 11, 1973, the District Director of the Immigration and Naturalization Service ordered Chadha to show cause why he should not be deported for having "remained in the United States for a longer time than permitted." Pursuant to §242(b) of the Immigration and Nationality Act (Act), a deportation hearing was held before an immigration judge on January 11, 1974. Chadha conceded that he was deportable for overstaying his visa and the hearing was adjourned to enable him to file an application for suspension of deportation under §244(a)(1) of the Act.

After Chadha submitted his application for suspension of deportation, the deportation hearing was resumed on February 7, 1974. On the basis of evidence adduced at the hearing, affidavits submitted with the application, and the results of a character investigation conducted by the INS, the immigration judge, on June 25, 1974, ordered that Chadha's deportation be suspended. The immigration judge found that Chadha met the requirements of §244(a)(1): he had resided continuously in the United States for over seven years, was of good moral character, and would suffer "extreme hardship" if deported.

Pursuant to §244(c)(1) of the Act, the immigration judge suspended Chadha's deportation and a report of the suspension was transmitted to Congress. Once the Attorney General's recommendation for suspension of Chadha's deportation was conveyed to Congress [by resolution of either the Senate or

---

8. INS v. Chadha, 462 U.S. 919, 967 (1983) (White, J., dissenting).

the House of Representatives], Congress had the power under §244(c)(2) of the Act to veto the Attorney General's determination that Chadha should not be deported.

On December 12, 1975, Representative Eilberg, Chairman of the Judiciary Subcommittee on Immigration, Citizenship, and International Law, introduced a resolution opposing "the granting of permanent residence in the United States to [six] aliens," including Chadha. The resolution was referred to the House Committee on the Judiciary. On December 16, 1975, the resolution was discharged from further consideration by the House Committee on the Judiciary and submitted to the House of Representatives for a vote. The resolution had not been printed and was not made available to other Members of the House prior to or at the time it was voted on. So far as the record before us shows, the House consideration of the resolution was based on Representative Eilberg's statement from the floor that "[i]t was the feeling of the committee, after reviewing 340 cases, that the aliens contained in the resolution [Chadha and five others] did not meet these statutory requirements, particularly as it relates to hardship; and it is the opinion of the committee that their deportation should not be suspended." The resolution was passed without debate or recorded vote. Since the House action was pursuant to §244(c)(2), the resolution was not treated as an Article I legislative act; it was not submitted to the Senate or presented to the President for his action.

II

A

We turn now to the question whether action of one House of Congress under §244(c)(2) violates strictures of the Constitution. We begin, of course, with the presumption that the challenged statute is valid. By the same token, the fact that a given law or procedure is efficient, convenient, and useful in facilitating functions of government, standing alone, will not save it if it is contrary to the Constitution. Convenience and efficiency are not the primary objectives — or the hallmarks — of democratic government and our inquiry is sharpened rather than blunted by the fact that Congressional veto provisions are appearing with increasing frequency in statutes which delegate authority to executive and independent agencies: "Since 1932, when the first veto provision was enacted into law, 295 congressional veto-type procedures have been inserted in 196 different statutes as follows: from 1932 to 1939, five statutes were affected; from 1940-49, nineteen statutes; between 1950-59, thirty-four statutes; and from 1960-69, forty-nine. From the year 1970 through 1975, at least one hundred sixty-three such provisions were included in eighty-nine laws."

Explicit and unambiguous provisions of the Constitution prescribe and define the respective functions of the Congress and of the Executive in the legislative process. Since the precise terms of those familiar provisions are critical to the resolution of this case, we set them out verbatim. Art. I provides:

> "All legislative Powers herein granted shall be vested in a Congress of the United States, which shall consist of a Senate and a House of Representatives." "Every Bill which shall have passed the House of Representatives and the Senate, shall, before it becomes a Law, be presented to the President of the United States; . . ." "Every

Order, Resolution, or Vote to which the Concurrence of the Senate and House of Representatives may be necessary (except on a question of Adjournment) shall be presented to the President of the United States; and before the Same shall take Effect, shall be approved by him, or being disapproved by him, shall be repassed by two thirds of the Senate and House of Representatives, according to the Rules and Limitations prescribed in the Case of a Bill."

These provisions of Art. I are integral parts of the constitutional design for the separation of powers. The very structure of the articles delegating and separating powers under Arts. I, II, and III exemplify the concept of separation of powers and we now turn to Art. I.

B.   THE PRESENTMENT CLAUSES

The records of the Constitutional Convention reveal that the requirement that all legislation be presented to the President before becoming law was uniformly accepted by the framers. Presentment to the President and the Presidential veto were considered so imperative that the draftsmen took special pains to assure that these requirements could not be circumvented.

The decision to provide the President with a limited and qualified power to nullify proposed legislation by veto was based on the profound conviction of the framers that the powers conferred on Congress were the powers to be most carefully circumscribed. It is beyond doubt that lawmaking was a power to be shared by both Houses and the President. The President's role in the lawmaking process also reflects the framers' careful efforts to check whatever propensity a particular Congress might have to enact oppressive, improvident, or ill-considered measures.

C.   BICAMERALISM

The bicameral requirement of Art. I, §1, 7 was of scarcely less concern to the framers than was the Presidential veto and indeed the two concepts are interdependent. By providing that no law could take effect without the concurrence of the prescribed majority of the Members of both Houses, the framers reemphasized their belief, already remarked upon in connection with the Presentment Clauses, that legislation should not be enacted unless it has been carefully and fully considered by the Nation's elected officials.

However familiar, it is useful to recall that apart from their fear that special interests could be favored at the expense of public needs, the framers were also concerned, although not of one mind, over the apprehensions of the smaller states. Those states feared a commonality of interest among the larger states would work to their disadvantage; representatives of the larger states, on the other hand, were skeptical of a legislature that could pass laws favoring a minority of the people. It need hardly be repeated here that the Great Compromise, under which one House was viewed as representing the people and the other the states, allayed the fears of both the large and small states.

We see therefore that the framers were acutely conscious that the bicameral requirement and the Presentment Clauses would serve essential constitutional functions. The President's participation in the legislative process was to protect the Executive Branch from Congress and to protect the whole people from improvident laws. The division of the Congress into two distinctive bodies assures that the legislative power would be exercised only after opportunity for full study and debate in separate settings. The President's unilateral veto power, in turn, was limited by the power of two thirds of both Houses of Congress to overrule a veto thereby precluding final arbitrary action of one person. It emerges clearly that the prescription for legislative action in Art. I, §1, 7 represents the framers' decision that the legislative power of the Federal government be exercised in accord with a single, finely wrought and exhaustively considered, procedure.

[III]

[W]e must establish that the challenged action under §244(c)(2) is of the kind to which the procedural requirements of Art. I, §7 apply. Not every action taken by either House is subject to the bicameralism and presentment requirements of Art. I. Whether actions taken by either House are, in law and fact, an exercise of legislative power depends not on their form but upon "whether they contain matter which is properly to be regarded as legislative in its character and effect." S. Rep. No. 1335, 54th Cong., 2d Sess., 8 (1897).

Examination of the action taken here by one House pursuant to §244(c)(2) reveals that it was essentially legislative in purpose and effect. In purporting to exercise power defined in Art. I, §8, cl. 4 to "establish an uniform Rule of Naturalization," the House took action that had the purpose and effect of altering the legal rights, duties and relations of persons, including the Attorney General, Executive Branch officials and Chadha, all outside the legislative branch. Section 244(c)(2) purports to authorize one House of Congress to require the Attorney General to deport an individual alien whose deportation otherwise would be canceled under §244. The one-House veto operated in this case to overrule the Attorney General and mandate Chadha's deportation; absent the House action, Chadha would remain in the United States. Congress has acted and its action has altered Chadha's status.

The nature of the decision implemented by the one-House veto in this case further manifests its legislative character. After long experience with the clumsy, time consuming private bill procedure, Congress made a deliberate choice to delegate to the Executive Branch, and specifically to the Attorney General, the authority to allow deportable aliens to remain in this country in certain specified circumstances. It is not disputed that this choice to delegate authority is precisely the kind of decision that can be implemented only in accordance with the procedures set out in Art. I. Disagreement with the Attorney General's decision on Chadha's deportation — that is, Congress's decision to deport Chadha — no less than Congress's original choice to delegate to the Attorney General the authority to make that decision, involves determinations of policy that Congress can implement in only one way; bicameral passage followed by presentment to the President. Congress must abide by its delegation of authority until that delegation is legislatively altered or revoked.

Finally, we see that when the framers intended to authorize either House of Congress to act alone and outside of its prescribed bicameral legislative role, they narrowly and precisely defined the procedure for such action. There are but four provisions in the Constitution, explicit and unambiguous, by which one House may act alone with the unreviewable force of law, not subject to the President's veto:

(a) The House of Representatives alone was given the power to initiate impeach-ments. Art. I, §2, cl. 6;

(b) The Senate alone was given the power to conduct trials following im-peachment on charges initiated by the House and to convict following trial. Art. I, §3, cl. 5;

(c) The Senate alone was given final unreviewable power to approve or to disapprove presidential appointments. Art. II, §2, cl. 2;

(d) The Senate alone was given unreviewable power to ratify treaties negotiated by the President. Art. II, §2, cl. 2.

Clearly, when the Draftsmen sought to confer special powers on one House, independent of the other House, or of the President, they did so in explicit, unambiguous terms. These carefully defined exceptions from presentment and bicameralism underscore the difference between the legislative functions of Congress and other unilateral but important and binding one-House acts provided for in the Constitution. These exceptions are narrow, explicit, and separately justified; none of them authorize the action challenged here. On the contrary, they provide further support for the conclusion that Congressional authority is not to be implied and for the conclusion that the veto provided for in §244(c)(2) is not authorized by the constitutional design of the powers of the Legislative Branch.

Since it is clear that the action by the House under §244(c)(2) was not within any of the express constitutional exceptions authorizing one House to act alone, and equally clear that it was an exercise of legislative power, that action was subject to the standards prescribed in Article I. The bicameral requirement, the Presentment Clauses, the President's veto, and Congress's power to override a veto were intended to erect enduring checks on each Branch and to protect the people from the improvident exercise of power by mandating certain pre-scribed steps. To preserve those checks, and maintain the separation of powers, the carefully defined limits on the power of each Branch must not be eroded. To accomplish what has been attempted by one House of Congress in this case requires action in conformity with the express procedures of the Constitution's prescription for legislative action: passage by a majority of both Houses and presentment to the President.

The choices we discern as having been made in the Constitutional Conven-tion impose burdens on governmental processes that often seem clumsy, ineffi-cient, even unworkable, but those hard choices were consciously made by men who had lived under a form of government that permitted arbitrary governmen-tal acts to go unchecked. There is no support in the Constitution or decisions of this Court for the proposition that the cumbersomeness and delays often encountered in complying with explicit Constitutional standards may be avoided, either by the Congress or by the President. With all the obvious flaws of delay, untidiness, and potential for abuse, we have not yet found a better way to preserve freedom than by making the exercise of power subject to the care-fully crafted restraints spelled out in the Constitution.

Justice POWELL, concurring in the judgment.

The Court's decision, based on the Presentment Clauses, Art. I, §7, cls. 2 and 3, apparently will invalidate every use of the legislative veto. The breadth of this holding gives one pause. Congress has included the veto in literally hundreds of statutes, dating back to the 1930s. Congress clearly views this procedure as essential to controlling the delegation of power to administrative agencies. One reasonably may disagree with Congress' assessment of the veto's utility, but the respect due its judgment as a coordinate branch of Government cautions that our holding should be no more extensive than necessary to decide this case. In my view, the case may be decided on a narrower ground. When Congress finds that a particular person does not satisfy the statutory criteria for permanent residence in this country it has assumed a judicial function in violation of the principle of separation of powers. Accordingly, I concur only in the judgment.

Functionally, the doctrine [of separation of powers] may be violated in two ways. One branch may interfere impermissibly with the other's performance of its constitutionally assigned function. *See* Nixon v. Administrator of General Services (1977); United States v. Nixon (1974). Alternatively, the doctrine may be violated when one branch assumes a function that more properly is entrusted to another. *See* Youngstown Sheet & Tube Co. v. Sawyer. This case presents the latter situation.

On its face, the House's action appears clearly adjudicatory. The House did not enact a general rule; rather it made its own determination that six specific persons did not comply with certain statutory criteria. It thus undertook the type of decision that traditionally has been left to other branches. Even if the House did not make a de novo determination, but simply reviewed the Immigration and Naturalization Service's findings, it still assumed a function ordinarily entrusted to the federal courts. Where, as here, Congress has exercised a power "that cannot possibly be regarded as merely in aid of the legislative function of Congress," the decisions of this Court have held that Congress impermissibly assumed a function that the Constitution entrusted to another branch.

The impropriety of the House's assumption of this function is confirmed by the fact that its action raises the very danger the framers sought to avoid — the exercise of unchecked power. In deciding whether Chadha deserves to be deported, Congress is not subject to any internal constraints that prevent it from arbitrarily depriving him of the right to remain in this country. Unlike the judiciary or an administrative agency, Congress is not bound by established substantive rules. Nor is it subject to the procedural safeguards, such as the right to counsel and a hearing before an impartial tribunal, that are present when a court or an agency adjudicates individual rights. The only effective constraint on Congress's power is political, but Congress is most accountable politically when it prescribes rules of general applicability. When it decides rights of specific persons, those rights are subject to "the tyranny of a shifting majority."

In my view, when Congress undertook to apply its rules to Chadha, it exceeded the scope of its constitutionally prescribed authority. I would not reach the broader question whether legislative vetoes are invalid under the Presentment Clauses.

Justice WHITE, dissenting.

Today the Court not only invalidates §244(c)(2) of the Immigration and Nationality Act, but also sounds the death knell for nearly 200 other statutory provisions in which Congress has reserved a "legislative veto." For this reason, the Court's decision is of surpassing importance. And it is for this reason that the Court would have been well-advised to decide the case, if possible, on the narrower grounds of separation of powers, leaving for full consideration the constitutionality of other congressional review statutes operating on such varied matters as war powers and agency rulemaking, some of which concern the independent regulatory agencies.

The prominence of the legislative veto mechanism in our contemporary political system and its importance to Congress can hardly be overstated. It has become a central means by which Congress secures the accountability of executive and independent agencies. Without the legislative veto, Congress is faced with a Hobson's choice: either to refrain from delegating the necessary authority, leaving itself with a hopeless task of writing laws with the requisite specificity to cover endless special circumstances across the entire policy landscape, or in the alternative, to abdicate its law-making function to the executive branch and independent agencies. To choose the former leaves major national problems unresolved; to opt for the latter risks unaccountable policymaking by those not elected to fill that role. Accordingly, over the past five decades, the legislative veto has been placed in nearly 200 statutes. The device is known in every field of governmental concern: reorganization, budgets, foreign affairs, war powers, and regulation of trade, safety, energy, the environment and the economy.

[T]he legislative veto is more than "efficient, convenient, and useful." It is an important if not indispensable political invention that allows the President and Congress to resolve major constitutional and policy differences, assures the accountability of independent regulatory agencies, and preserves Congress' control over lawmaking. Perhaps there are other means of accommodation and accountability, but the increasing reliance of Congress upon the legislative veto suggests that the alternatives to which Congress must now turn are not entirely satisfactory.

The history of the legislative veto also makes clear that it has not been a sword with which Congress has struck out to aggrandize itself at the expense of the other branches — the concerns of Madison and Hamilton. Rather, the veto has been a means of defense, a reservation of ultimate authority necessary if Congress is to fulfill its designated role under Article I as the nation's lawmaker. While the President has often objected to particular legislative vetoes, generally those left in the hands of congressional committees, the Executive has more often agreed to legislative review as the price for a broad delegation of authority. To be sure, the President may have preferred unrestricted power, but that could be precisely why Congress thought it essential to retain a check on the exercise of delegated authority.

For all these reasons, the apparent sweep of the Court's decision today is regrettable. The Court's Article I analysis appears to invalidate all legislative vetoes irrespective of form or subject. Because the legislative veto is commonly found as a check upon rulemaking by administrative agencies and upon broad-based policy decisions of the Executive Branch, it is particularly unfortunate that the Court reaches its decision in a case involving the exercise of a veto over deportation decisions regarding particular individuals. Courts should always be wary of striking statutes as unconstitutional; to strike an entire class of statutes based on consideration of a somewhat atypical and more-readily indictable exemplar of the class is irresponsible.

The reality of the situation is that the constitutional question posed today is one of immense difficulty over which the executive and legislative branches —

as well as scholars and judges — have understandably disagreed. That disagreement stems from the silence of the Constitution on the precise question: The Constitution does not directly authorize or prohibit the legislative veto. Thus, our task should be to determine whether the legislative veto is consistent with the purposes of Art. I and the principles of Separation of Powers which are reflected in that Article and throughout the Constitution. We should not find the lack of a specific constitutional authorization for the legislative veto surprising, and I would not infer disapproval of the mechanism from its absence. From the summer of 1787 to the present the government of the United States has become an endeavor far beyond the contemplation of the framers. Only within the last half century has the complexity and size of the Federal Government's responsibilities grown so greatly that the Congress must rely on the legislative veto as the most effective if not the only means to insure their role as the nation's lawmakers. But the wisdom of the framers was to anticipate that the nation would grow and new problems of governance would require different solutions. Accordingly, our Federal Government was intentionally chartered with the flexibility to respond to contemporary needs without losing sight of fundamental democratic principles.

The power to exercise a legislative veto is not the power to write new law without bicameral approval or presidential consideration. The veto must be authorized by statute and may only negative what an Executive department or independent agency has proposed. On its face, the legislative veto no more allows one House of Congress to make law than does the presidential veto confer such power upon the President.

The central concern of the presentation and bicameralism requirements of Article I is that when a departure from the legal status quo is undertaken, it is done with the approval of the President and both Houses of Congress — or, in the event of a presidential veto, a two-thirds majority in both Houses. This interest is fully satisfied by the operation of §244(c)(2). The President's approval is found in the Attorney General's action in recommending to Congress that the deportation order for a given alien be suspended. The House and the Senate indicate their approval of the Executive's action by not passing a resolution of disapproval within the statutory period. Thus, a change in the legal status quo — the deportability of the alien — is consummated only with the approval of each of the three relevant actors. The disagreement of any one of the three maintains the alien's pre-existing status: the Executive may choose not to recommend suspension; the House and Senate may each veto the recommendation. The effect on the rights and obligations of the affected individuals and upon the legislative system is precisely the same as if a private bill were introduced but failed to receive the necessary approval.

Thus understood, §244(c)(2) fully effectuates the purposes of the bicameralism and presentation requirements. I regret that I am in disagreement with my colleagues on the fundamental questions that this case presents. But even more I regret the destructive scope of the Court's holding. It reflects a profoundly different conception of the Constitution than that held by the Courts which sanctioned the modern administrative state. Today's decision strikes down in one fell swoop provisions in more laws enacted by Congress than the Court has cumulatively invalidated in its history. I fear it will now be more difficult "to insure that the fundamental policy decisions in our society will be made not by an appointed official but by the body immediately responsible to the people," Arizona v. California (1963) (Harlan, J., dissenting). I must dissent.

Chadha involved a legislative veto of an adjudicatory proceeding; Congress, by resolution of the House of Representatives, overturned an immigration judge's decision to allow Chadha to remain in the country. Almost immediately after *Chadha*, the Court extended its holding to preclude legislative vetoes of agency rules. *See, e.g.*, Process Gas Consumers Group v. Consumers Energy Council of America, 463 U.S. 1216 (1983). It is thus clearly established that if Congress wants to overturn an executive action there must be bicameralism, passage by both houses of Congress, and presentment, giving the bill to the President for signature or veto. Anything less is a legislative veto and legislative vetoes are unconstitutional.

3.   Checking Administrative Power

What other mechanisms exist to check administrative agencies and are they sufficient? Congress can control administrative agencies through statutes. For instance, laws can be enacted directing agencies to perform certain tasks or denying them authority in particular areas. Also, Congress can overturn agency decisions by statute, following the prescribed procedures for bicameralism and presentment. The president, of course, can veto such statutes, requiring that Congress act by a two-thirds vote to effectuate such a check.

Furthermore, Congress controls the budget of administrative agencies and can use this to exercise an important check on their work. Congressional committees that oversee particular agencies often play a key role in monitoring and controlling agency actions.

Another important check on agencies is the appointment and removal power. The president's authority to select members of agencies, subject to confirmation by the Senate, often directs the conduct of the agencies. Also, the president's power to remove agency officials is another check. The appointment and removal power have generated many constitutional issues concerning separation of powers and are worth examining.

THE APPOINTMENT POWER

Article II, §2 provides that the president "shall nominate, and by and with the Advice and Consent of the Senate, shall appoint Ambassadors, other public Ministers and Consuls, Judges of the Supreme Court, and all other Officers of the United States, whose Appointments are not herein otherwise provided for, and which shall be established by Law: but the Congress may by Law vest the Appointment of such inferior Officers, as they think proper, in the President alone, to the Courts of Law, or in the Heads of Departments."

The key constitutional issue here concerns who may possess the appointment power. Morrison v. Olson is the leading case dealing with this issue.

ALEXIA MORRISON, INDEPENDENT
COUNSEL v. THEODORE B. OLSON

487 U.S. 654 (1988)

Chief Justice Rehnquist delivered the opinion of the Court.

This case presents us with a challenge to the independent counsel provisions of the Ethics in Government Act of 1978. We hold today that these provisions of the Act do not violate the Appointments Clause of the Constitution, the limitations of Article III, nor do they impermissibly interfere with the President's authority under Article II in violation of the constitutional principle of separation of powers.

I

Briefly stated, Title VI of the Ethics in Government Act allows for the appointment of an "independent counsel" to investigate and, if appropriate, prosecute certain high-ranking Government officials for violations of federal criminal laws. The Act requires the Attorney General, upon receipt of information that he determines is "sufficient to constitute grounds to investigate whether any person [covered by the Act] may have violated any Federal criminal law," to conduct a preliminary investigation of the matter. When the Attorney General has completed this investigation, or 90 days has elapsed, he is required to report to a special court (the Special Division) created by the Act "for the purpose of appointing independent counsels." If the Attorney General determines that "there are no reasonable grounds to believe that further investigation is warranted," then he must notify the Special Division of this result. In such a case, "the division of the court shall have no power to appoint an independent counsel."

If, however, the Attorney General has determined that there are "reasonable grounds to believe that further investigation or prosecution is warranted," then he "shall apply to the division of the court for the appointment of an independent counsel." Upon receiving this application, the Special Division "shall appoint an appropriate independent counsel and shall define that independent counsel's prosecutorial jurisdiction."

With respect to all matters within the independent counsel's jurisdiction, the Act grants the counsel "full power and independent authority to exercise all investigative and prosecutorial functions and powers of the Department of Justice, the Attorney General, and any other officer or employee of the Department of Justice." Under §594(a)(9), the counsel's powers include "initiating and conducting prosecutions in any court of competent jurisdiction, framing and signing indictments, filing informations, and handling all aspects of any case, in the name of the United States."

Two statutory provisions govern the length of an independent counsel's tenure in office. The first defines the procedure for removing an independent counsel. Section 596(a)(1) provides: "An independent counsel appointed under this chapter may be removed from office, other than by impeachment and conviction, only by the personal action of the Attorney General and only for good cause, physical disability, mental incapacity, or any other condition that substantially impairs the performance of such independent counsel's duties."

If an independent counsel is removed pursuant to this section, the Attorney General is required to submit a report to both the Special Division and the Judiciary Committees of the Senate and the House "specifying the facts found and the ultimate grounds for such removal." Under the current version of the Act, an independent counsel can obtain judicial review of the Attorney General's action by filing a civil action in the United States District Court for the District of Columbia. The reviewing court is authorized to grant reinstatement or "other appropriate relief."

The other provision governing the tenure of the independent counsel defines the procedures for "terminating" the counsel's office. Under §596(b)(1), the office of an independent counsel terminates when he or she notifies the Attorney General that he or she has completed or substantially completed any investigations or prosecutions undertaken pursuant to the Act. In addition, the Special Division, acting either on its own or on the suggestion of the Attorney General, may terminate the office of an independent counsel at any time if it finds that "the investigation of all matters within the prosecutorial jurisdiction of such independent counsel . . . have been completed or so substantially completed that it would be appropriate for the Department of Justice to complete such investigations and prosecutions."

Finally, the Act provides for congressional oversight of the activities of independent counsel. An independent counsel may from time to time send Congress statements or reports on his or her activities.

[II]

The Appointments Clause of Article II reads as follows:

> [The President] shall nominate, and by and with the Advice and Consent of the Senate, shall appoint Ambassadors, other public Ministers and Consuls, Judges of the Supreme Court, and all other Officers of the United States, whose Appointments are not herein otherwise provided for, and which shall be established by Law: but the Congress may by Law vest the Appointment of such inferior Officers, as they think proper, in the President alone, in the Courts of Law, or in the Heads of Departments.

U.S. Const., Art. II, §2, cl. 2.

The parties do not dispute that "[t]he Constitution for purposes of appointment . . . divides all its officers into two classes." As we stated in Buckley v. Valeo (1976): "[P]rincipal officers are selected by the President with the advice and consent of the Senate. Inferior officers Congress may allow to be appointed by the President alone, by the heads of departments, or by the Judiciary." The initial question is, accordingly, whether appellant is an "inferior" or a "principal" officer. If she is the latter, as the Court of Appeals concluded, then the Act is in violation of the Appointments Clause.

The line between "inferior" and "principal" officers is one that is far from clear, and the framers provided little guidance into where it should be drawn. We need not attempt here to decide exactly where the line falls between the two types of officers, because in our view appellant clearly falls on the "inferior officer" side of that line. Several factors lead to this conclusion.

First, appellant is subject to removal by a higher Executive Branch official. Although appellant may not be "subordinate" to the Attorney General (and the President) insofar as she possesses a degree of independent discretion to exercise the powers delegated to her under the Act, the fact that she can be removed by the Attorney General indicates that she is to some degree "inferior" in rank and authority. Second, appellant is empowered by the Act to perform only certain, limited duties. An independent counsel's role is restricted primarily to investigation and, if appropriate, prosecution for certain federal crimes. Admittedly, the Act delegates to appellant "full power and independent authority to exercise all investigative and prosecutorial functions and powers of the Department of Justice," but this grant of authority does not include any authority to formulate policy for the Government or the Executive Branch, nor does it give appellant any administrative duties outside of those necessary to operate her office. The Act specifically provides that in policy matters appellant is to comply to the extent possible with the policies of the Department.

Third, appellant's office is limited in jurisdiction. Not only is the Act itself restricted in applicability to certain federal officials suspected of certain serious federal crimes, but an independent counsel can only act within the scope of the jurisdiction that has been granted by the Special Division pursuant to a request by the Attorney General. Finally, appellant's office is limited in tenure. There is concededly no time limit on the appointment of a particular counsel. Nonetheless, the office of independent counsel is "temporary" in the sense that an independent counsel is appointed essentially to accomplish a single task, and when that task is over the office is terminated, either by the counsel herself or by action of the Special Division. Unlike other prosecutors, appellant has no ongoing responsibilities that extend beyond the accomplishment of the mission that she was appointed for and authorized by the Special Division to undertake. In our view, these factors relating to the "ideas of tenure, duration . . . and duties" of the independent counsel are sufficient to establish that appellant is an "inferior" officer in the constitutional sense.

Justice SCALIA, dissenting.

That is what this suit is about. Power. The allocation of power among Congress, the President, and the courts in such fashion as to preserve the equilibrium the Constitution sought to establish — so that "a gradual concentration of the several powers in the same department," Federalist No. 51 (J. Madison), can effectively be resisted. Frequently an issue of this sort will come before the Court clad, so to speak, in sheep's clothing: the potential of the asserted principle to effect important change in the equilibrium of power is not immediately evident, and must be discerned by a careful and perceptive analysis. But this wolf comes as a wolf.

To repeat, Article II, §1, cl. 1, of the Constitution provides: "The executive Power shall be vested in a President of the United States."

This does not mean some of the executive power, but all of the executive power. It seems to me, therefore, that the decision of the Court of Appeals invalidating the present statute must be upheld on fundamental separation-of-powers principles if the following two questions are answered affirmatively: (1) Is the conduct of a criminal prosecution (and of an investigation to decide whether to prosecute) the exercise of purely executive power? (2) Does the statute deprive the President of the United States of exclusive control over the exercise of that power? Surprising to say, the Court appears to concede an affirmative answer to both questions, but seeks to avoid the inevitable conclusion that since the statute vests some purely executive power in a person who is not the President of the United States it is void.

The Court concedes that "[t]here is no real dispute that the functions performed by the independent counsel are 'executive,'" though it qualifies that concession by adding "in the sense that they are law enforcement functions that typically have been undertaken by officials within the Executive Branch." The qualifier adds nothing but atmosphere. In what other sense can one identify "the executive Power" that is supposed to be vested in the President (unless it includes everything the Executive Branch is given to do) except by reference to what has always and everywhere — if conducted by government at all — been conducted never by the legislature, never by the courts, and always by the executive. There is no possible doubt that the independent counsel's functions fit this description. She is vested with the "full power and independent authority to exercise all investigative and prosecutorial functions and powers of the Department of Justice [and] the Attorney General." Governmental investigation and prosecution of crimes is a quintessentially executive function.

As for the second question, whether the statute before us deprives the President of exclusive control over that quintessentially executive activity: The Court does not, and could not possibly, assert that it does not. That is indeed the whole object of the statute. Instead, the Court points out that the President, through his Attorney General, has at least some control. That concession is alone enough to invalidate the statute, but I cannot refrain from pointing out that the Court greatly exaggerates the extent of that "some" Presidential control. "Most important[t]" among these controls, the Court asserts, is the Attorney General's "power to remove the counsel for 'good cause.'" This is somewhat like referring to shackles as an effective means of locomotion.

The utter incompatibility of the Court's approach with our constitutional traditions can be made more clear, perhaps, by applying it to the powers of the other two branches. Is it conceivable that if Congress passed a statute depriving itself of less than full and entire control over some insignificant area of legislation, we would inquire whether the matter was "so central to the functioning of the Legislative Branch" as really to require complete control, or whether the statute gives Congress "sufficient control over the surrogate legislator to ensure that Congress is able to perform its constitutionally assigned duties"? Of course we would have none of that. Once we determined that a purely legislative power was at issue we would require it to be exercised, wholly and entirely, by Congress. Or to bring the point closer to home, consider a statute giving to non-Article III judges just a tiny bit of purely judicial power in a relatively insignificant field, with substantial control, though not total control, in the courts — perhaps "clear error" review, which would be a fair judicial equivalent of the Attorney General's "for cause" removal power here. Is there any doubt that we would not pause to inquire whether the matter was "so central to the functioning of the Judicial Branch" as really to require complete control, or whether we retained "sufficient control over the matters to be decided that we are able to perform our constitutionally assigned duties"? We would say that our "constitutionally assigned duties" include complete control over all exercises of the judicial power. We should say here that the President's constitutionally assigned duties include complete control over investigation and prosecution of violations of the law, and that the inexorable command of Article II is clear and definite: the executive power must be vested in the President of the United States.

Is it unthinkable that the President should have such exclusive power, even when alleged crimes by him or his close associates are at issue? No more so than that Congress should have the exclusive power of legislation, even when what is at issue is its own exemption from the burdens of certain laws. No more so than that this Court should have the exclusive power to pronounce the final decision on justiciable cases and controversies, even those pertaining to the constitutionality of a statute reducing the salaries of the Justices. A system of separate and coordinate powers necessarily involves an acceptance of exclusive power that can theoretically be abused. As we reiterate this very day, "[i]t is a truism that constitutional protections have costs." While the separation of powers may prevent us from righting every wrong, it does so in order to ensure that we do not lose liberty.

In sum, this statute does deprive the President of substantial control over the prosecutory functions performed by the independent counsel, and it does substantially affect the balance of powers. That the Court could possibly conclude otherwise demonstrates both the wisdom of our former constitutional system, in which the degree of reduced control and political impairment were irrelevant, since all purely executive power had to be in the President; and the folly of the new system of standardless judicial allocation of powers we adopt today.

The authority for creating an Independent Counsel, the Ethics in Government Act, expired in 1999. After the investigation of President Bill Clinton by Independent Counsel Kenneth Starr, described more fully in the last section of this chapter, Congress simply let the Act expire and did not renew the authority for the creation of an Independent Counsel. Some believe that this is a vindication for the views expressed by Justice Scalia in his dissent in Morrison v. Olson, while others contend that the expiration of the authority for an Independent Counsel is a serious mistake that will be regretted when there are future scandals involving the President or high-level executive officials.

The Court has imposed one important limit on who may possess the appointment power: The Court has held that Congress cannot give the appointment power to itself or to its officers. Article II specifies several possibilities as to who may possess the appointment power; Congress is not among them. In Buckley v. Valeo, 424 U.S. 1 (1976), the Court held unconstitutional a federal law that empowered the Speaker of the House of Representatives and the President Pro Tempore of the Senate to appoint four of the six members of the Federal Election Commission.

The Court emphasized the text of Article II, which specifies who may possess the appointment power. The Court said that under Article II, Congress could vest the appointment power for inferior offices in the President, the heads of departments, or the lower federal courts. The Speaker of the House and the President Pro Tem of the Senate are obviously none of these and therefore the Court found that they could not possess the appointment power.

THE REMOVAL POWER

There is no provision of the Constitution concerning the president's authority to remove executive branch officials. The principle that has emerged from the cases is that, in general, the president may remove executive officials unless removal is limited by statute. Congress, by statute, may limit removal both if it is an office where independence from the president is desirable and if the law does not prohibit removal but, rather, limits removal to instances where good cause is shown.

No single case has clearly articulated this principle. Rather it comes from the experience of Andrew Johnson's impeachment and from five Supreme Court decisions that have considered the removal power, all reviewed below. The section then concludes by describing the law concerning the removal power that emerges from this authority.

THE IMPEACHMENT OF ANDREW JOHNSON

Consideration of the removal power must begin with an incident that was never directly reviewed in the courts: the impeachment of President Andrew Johnson for firing the secretary of war in violation of a federal law that prohibited the removal.[9] After the assassination of President Abraham Lincoln, there was great consternation that a Southerner, Andrew Johnson from Tennessee, was the president at the end of the Civil War. The perception was that Johnson's sympathies were with the South and that he was obstructing reconstruction and the North's claiming the benefits of its victory. Congress passed the Tenure in Office Act of 1867 to prevent him from removing key members of the cabinet.

Secretary of War Edwin Stanton openly challenged the president's authority, and Johnson fired Stanton, even though that violated the Tenure in Office Act. The House of Representatives voted articles of impeachment based almost entirely on this removal. The vote in the Senate, however, was one short of the two-thirds necessary for removal, and thus Johnson completed his term as president.

MYERS v. UNITED STATES, 272 U.S. 52 (1926): Chief Justice TAFT delivered the opinion of the Court.

This case presents the question whether under the Constitution the President has the exclusive power of removing executive officers of the United States whom he has appointed by and with the advice and consent of the Senate.

Myers, appellant's intestate, was on July 21, 1917, appointed by the President, by and with the advice and consent of the Senate, to be a postmaster of the first class at Portland, Or., for a term of four years. On January 20, 1920, Myers' resignation was demanded. He refused the demand. On February 2, 1920, he was removed from office by order of the Postmaster General, acting by direction of the President. He protested to the department against his removal, and continued to do so until the end of his term. He pursued no other occupation and drew compensation for no other service during the interval. On April 21, 1921, he brought this suit in the Court of Claims for his salary from the date of his removal, which, as claimed by supplemental petition filed after July 21, 1921, the end of his term, amounted to $8,838.71.

---

9. For a detailed description of the facts of this impeachment, *see* Raoul Berger, *Impeachment: The Constitutional Problem* (1973).

The question where the power of removal of executive officers appointed by the President by and with the advice and consent of the Senate was vested, was presented early in the first session of the First Congress. There is no express provision respecting removals in the Constitution, except as section 4 of article 2, above quoted, provides for removal from office by impeachment. The subject was not discussed in the Constitutional Convention.

The power to prevent the removal of an officer who has served under the President is different from the authority to consent to or reject his appointment. When a nomination is made, it may be presumed that the Senate is, or may become, as well advised as to the fitness of the nominee as the President, but in the nature of things the defects in ability or intelligence or loyalty in the administration of the laws of one who has served as an officer under the President are facts as to which the President, or his trusted subordinates, must be better informed than the Senate, and the power to remove him may therefore be regarded as confined for very sound and practical reasons, to the governmental authority which has administrative control. The power of removal is incident to the power of appointment, not to the power of advising and consenting to appointment, and when the grant of the executive power is enforced by the express mandate to take care that the laws be faithfully executed, it emphasizes the necessity for including within the executive power as conferred the exclusive power of removal.

It is reasonable to suppose also that had it been intended to give to Congress power to regulate or control removals in the manner suggested, it would have been included among the specifically enumerated legislative powers in Article 1, or in the specified limitations on the executive power in Article 2. The difference between the grant of legislative power under Article 1 to Congress which is limited to powers therein enumerated, and the more general grant of the executive power to the President under Article 2 is significant. The fact that the executive power is given in general terms strengthened by specific terms where emphasis is appropriate, and limited by direct expressions where limitation is needed, and that no express limit is placed on the power of removal by the executive is a convincing indication that none was intended.

HUMPHREY'S EXECUTOR v. UNITED STATES, 295 U.S. 602 (1935): Justice SUTHERLAND delivered the opinion of the Court.

Plaintiff brought suit in the Court of Claims against the United States to recover a sum of money alleged to be due the deceased for salary as a Federal Trade Commissioner from October 8, 1933, when the President undertook to remove him from office, to the time of his death on February 14, 1934. William E. Humphrey, the decedent, on December 10, 1931, was nominated by President Hoover to succeed himself as a member of the Federal Trade Commission, and was confirmed by the United States Senate. He was duly commissioned for a term of seven years, expiring September 25, 1938; and, after taking the required oath of office, entered upon his duties. On July 25, 1933, President Roosevelt addressed a letter to the commissioner asking for his resignation, on the ground "that the aims and purposes of the Administration with respect to the work of the Commission can be carried out most effectively with personnel of my own selection," but disclaiming any reflection upon the commissioner personally or upon his services. The commissioner replied, asking time to consult his friends. The commissioner declined to resign; and on October 7, 1933, the President wrote him: "Effective as of this date you are hereby removed from the office of Commissioner of the Federal Trade Commission."

The provisions of section 1 of the Federal Trade Commission Act, stat[e] that "any commissioner may be removed by the President for inefficiency, neglect of duty, or malfeasance in office." The question first to be considered is whether, by the provisions of section 1 of the Federal Trade Commission Act already quoted, the President's power is limited to removal for the specific causes enumerated therein.

The commission is to be nonpartisan; and it must, from the very nature of its duties, act with entire impartiality. It is charged with the enforcement of no policy except the policy of the law. Its duties are neither political nor executive, but predominantly quasi judicial and quasi legislative. Like the Interstate Commerce Commission, its members are called upon to exercise the trained judgment of a body of experts "appointed by law and informed by experience."

The legislative reports in both houses of Congress clearly reflect the view that a fixed term was necessary to the effective and fair administration of the law. The debates in both houses demonstrate that the prevailing view was that the Commission was not to be "subject to anybody in the government but . . . only to the people of the United States"; free from "political domination or control" or the "probability or possibility of such a thing"; to be "separate and apart from any existing department of the government — not subject to the orders of the President."

Thus, the language of the act, the legislative reports, and the general purposes of the legislation as reflected by the debates, all combine to demonstrate the congressional intent to create a body of experts who shall gain experience by length of service; a body which shall be independent of executive authority, except in its selection, and free to exercise its judgment without the leave or hindrance of any other official or any department of the government. To the accomplishment of these purposes, it is clear that Congress was of opinion that length and certainty of tenure would vitally contribute. And to hold that, nevertheless, the members of the commission continue in office at the mere will of the President, might be to thwart, in large measure, the very ends which Congress sought to realize by definitely fixing the term of office.

To support its contention that the removal provision of section 1, as we have just construed it, is an unconstitutional interference with the executive power of the President, the government's chief reliance is Myers v. United States.

The office of a postmaster is so essentially unlike the office now involved that the decision in the Myers Case cannot be accepted as controlling our decision here. A postmaster is an executive officer restricted to the performance of executive functions. He is charged with no duty at all related to either the legislative or judicial power. The actual decision in the Myers Case finds support in the theory that such an officer is merely one of the units in the executive department and, hence, inherently subject to the exclusive and illimitable power of removal by the Chief Executive, whose subordinate and aid he is. It goes no farther; much less does it include an officer who occupies no place in the executive department and who exercises no part of the executive power vested by the Constitution in the President.

The Federal Trade Commission is an administrative body created by Congress to carry into effect legislative policies embodied in the statute in accordance with the legislative standard therein prescribed, and to perform other specified duties as a legislative or as a judicial aid. Such a body cannot in any proper sense be characterized as an arm or as an eye of the executive. Its duties are performed without executive leave and, in the contemplation of the statute, must be free from executive control. In administering the provisions of the statute in respect of "unfair methods of competition," that is to say, in filling in and administering the details embodied by that general standard, the commission acts in part quasi legislatively and in part quasi judicially. In making investigations and reports thereon for the information of Congress under section 6, in aid of the legislative power, it acts as a legislative agency. Under section 7, which authorizes the commission to act as a master in chancery under rules prescribed by the court, it acts as an agency of the judiciary. To the extent that it exercises any executive function, as distinguished from executive power in the constitutional sense, it does so in the discharge and effectuation of its quasi legislative or quasi judicial powers, or as an agency of the legislative or judicial departments of the government.

We think it plain under the Constitution that illimitable power of removal is not possessed by the President in respect of officers of the character of those just named. The authority of Congress, in creating quasi legislative or quasi judicial agencies, to require them to act in discharge of their duties independently of executive control cannot well be doubted; and that authority includes, as an appropriate incident, power to fix the period during which they shall continue, and to forbid their removal except for cause in the meantime. For it is quite evident that one who holds his office only during the pleasure of another cannot be depended upon to maintain an attitude of independence against the latter's will.

WIENER v. UNITED STATES, 357 U.S. 349 (1958): Justice FRANKFURTER delivered the opinion of the Court.

This is a suit for back pay, based on petitioner's alleged illegal removal as a member of the War Claims Commission. The facts are not in dispute. By the War Claims Act of 1948, Congress established that Commission with "jurisdiction to receive and adjudicate according to law," claims for compensating internees, prisoners of war, and religious organizations, who suffered personal injury or property damage at the hands of the enemy in connection with World War II. The Commission was to be composed of three persons, at least two of whom were to be members of the bar, to be appointed by the President, by and with the advice and consent of the Senate. The Commission was to wind up its affairs not later than three years after the expiration of the time for filing claims. This limit on the Commission's life was the mode by which the tenure of the Commissioners was defined, and Congress made no provision for removal of a Commissioner.

Having been duly nominated by President Truman, the petitioner was confirmed on June 2, 1950, and took office on June 8, following. On his refusal to heed a request for his resignation, he was, on December 10, 1953, removed by President Eisenhower.

[T]he most reliable factor for drawing an inference regarding the President's power of removal in our case is the nature of the function that Congress vested in the War Claims Commission. What were the duties that Congress confided to this Commission? And can the inference fairly be drawn from the failure of Congress to provide for removal that these Commissioners were to remain in office at the will of the President? For such is the assertion of power on which petitioner's removal must rest. The ground of President Eisenhower's removal of petitioner was precisely the same as President Roosevelt's removal of Humphrey. Both Presidents desired to have Commissioners, one on the Federal Trade Commission, the other on the War Claims Commission, "of my own selection." They wanted these Commissioners to be their men. The terms of removal in the two cases are identical and express the assumption that the agencies of which the two Commissioners were members were subject in the discharge of their duties to the control of the Executive. An analysis of the Federal Trade Commission Act left this Court in no doubt that such was not the conception of Congress in creating the Federal Trade Commission. The terms of the War Claims Act of 1948 leave no doubt that such was not the conception of Congress regarding the War Claims Commission.

The history of this legislation emphatically underlines this fact. The Commission was established as an adjudicating body with all the paraphernalia by which legal claims are put to the test of proof, with finality of determination "not subject to review by any other official of the United States or by any court by mandamus or otherwise." The claims were to be "adjudicated according to law," that is, on the merits of each claim, supported by evidence and governing legal considerations, by a body that was "entirely free from the control or coercive influence, direct or indirect," Humphrey's Executor v. United States, either the Executive or the Congress. If, as one must take for granted, the War Claims Act precluded the President from influencing the Commission in passing on a particular claim, a fortiori must it be inferred that Congress did not wish to have hang over the Commission the Damocles' sword of removal by the President for no reason other than that he preferred to have on that Commission men of his own choosing.

For such is this case. We have not a removal for cause involving the rectitude of a member of an adjudicatory body, nor even a suspensory removal until the Senate could act upon it by confirming the appointment of a new Commissioner or otherwise dealing with the matter. Judging the matter in all the nakedness in which it is presented, namely, the claim that the President could remove a member of an adjudicatory body like the War Claims Commission merely because he wanted his own appointees on such a Commission, we are compelled to conclude that no such power is given to the President directly by the Constitution, and none is impliedly conferred upon him by statute simply because Congress said nothing about it. The philosophy of *Humphrey's Executor*, in its explicit language as well as its implications, precludes such a claim.

BOWSHER v. SYNAR, 478 U.S 714 (1986): Chief Justice Burger delivered the opinion of the Court.

The question presented by these appeals is whether the assignment by Congress to the Comptroller General of the United States of certain functions under the Balanced Budget and Emergency Deficit Control Act of 1985 violates the doctrine of separation of powers.

On December 12, 1985, the President signed into law the Balanced Budget and Emergency Deficit Control Act of 1985, popularly known as the "Gramm-Rudman-Hollings Act." The purpose of the Act is to eliminate the federal budget deficit. To that end, the Act sets a "maximum deficit amount" for federal spending for each of fiscal years 1986 through 1991. The size of that maximum deficit amount progressively reduces to zero in fiscal year 1991. If in any fiscal year the federal budget deficit exceeds the maximum deficit amount by more than a specified sum, the Act requires across-the-board cuts in federal spending to reach the targeted deficit level, with half of the cuts made to defense programs and the other half made to nondefense programs. The Act exempts certain priority programs from these cuts.

The Constitution does not contemplate an active role for Congress in the supervision of officers charged with the execution of the laws it enacts. We conclude that Congress cannot reserve for itself the power of removal of an officer charged with the execution of the laws except by impeachment. To permit the execution of the laws to be vested in an officer answerable only to Congress would, in practical terms, reserve in Congress control over the execution of the laws.

To permit an officer controlled by Congress to execute the laws would be, in essence, to permit a congressional veto. Congress could simply remove, or threaten to remove, an officer for executing the laws in any fashion found to be unsatisfactory to Congress. This kind of congressional control over the execution of the laws, *Chadha* makes clear, is constitutionally impermissible.

The dangers of congressional usurpation of Executive Branch functions have long been recognized. "[T]he debates of the Constitutional Convention, and the Federalist Papers, are replete with expressions of fear that the Legislative Branch of the National Government will aggrandize itself at the expense of the other two branches." Buckley v. Valeo (1976). Indeed, we also have observed only recently that "[t]he hydraulic pressure inherent within each of the separate Branches to exceed the outer limits of its power, even to accomplish desirable objectives, must be resisted." With these principles in mind, we turn to consideration of whether the Comptroller General is controlled by Congress.

The critical factor lies in the provisions of the statute defining the Comptroller General's office relating to removability. Although the Comptroller General is nominated by the President from a list of three individuals recommended by the Speaker of the House of Representatives and the President pro tempore of the Senate, and confirmed by the Senate, he is removable only at the initiative of Congress. He may be removed not only by impeachment but also by joint resolution of Congress "at any time" resting on any one of the following bases: "(i) permanent disability; (ii) inefficiency; (iii) neglect of duty; (iv) malfeasance; or (v) a felony or conduct involving moral turpitude."

It is clear that Congress has consistently viewed the Comptroller General as an officer of the Legislative Branch. Over the years, the Comptrollers General have also viewed themselves as part of the Legislative Branch. By placing the responsibility for execution of the Balanced Budget and Emergency Deficit Control Act in the hands of an officer who is subject to removal only by itself, Congress in effect has retained control over the execution of the Act and has intruded into the executive function. The Constitution does not permit such intrusion.

MORRISON v. OLSON, 487 U.S. 654 (1988): The case involved the constitutionality of the provisions of the Ethics in Government Act, which provide for the appointment of an independent counsel to investigate alleged wrongdoing by the president and other high-level executive officials. The portion of the opinion concerning the constitutionality of the act's having appointment of the independent counsel done by federal court judges is presented above. This is the part of the opinion concerning the removal power.

Chief Justice REHNQUIST delivered the opinion of the Court:

We now turn to consider whether the Act is invalid under the constitutional principle of separation of powers. The first is whether the provision of the Act restricting the Attorney General's power to remove the independent counsel to only those instances in which he can show "good cause," taken by itself, impermissibly interferes with the President's exercise of his constitutionally appointed functions.

Unlike both *Bowsher* and *Myers*, this case does not involve an attempt by Congress itself to gain a role in the removal of executive officials other than its established powers of impeachment and conviction. The Act instead puts the removal power squarely in the hands of the Executive Branch; an independent counsel may be removed from office, "only by the personal action of the Attorney General, and only for good cause." There is no requirement of congressional approval of the Attorney General's removal decision, though the decision is subject to judicial review. In our view, the removal provisions of the Act make this case more analogous to Humphrey's Executor v. United States (1935), and Wiener v. United States (1958), than to *Myers* or *Bowsher*.

Appellees contend that *Humphrey's Executor* and *Wiener* are distinguishable from this case because they did not involve officials who performed a "core executive function." They argue that our decision in *Humphrey's Executor* rests on a distinction between "purely executive" officials and officials who exercise "quasi-legislative" and "quasi-judicial" powers. In their view, when a "purely executive" official is involved, the governing precedent is *Myers*, not *Humphrey's Executor*. And, under *Myers*, the President must have absolute discretion to discharge "purely" executive officials at will.

We undoubtedly did rely on the terms "quasi-legislative" and "quasi-judicial" to distinguish the officials involved in *Humphrey's Executor* and *Wiener* from those in *Myers*, but our present considered view is that the determination of whether the Constitution allows Congress to impose a "good cause"-type restriction on the President's power to remove an official cannot be made to turn on whether or not that official is classified as "purely executive." The analysis contained in our removal cases is designed not to define rigid categories of those officials who may or may not be removed at will by the President, but to ensure that Congress does not interfere with the President's exercise of the "executive power" and his constitutionally appointed duty to "take care that the laws be faithfully executed" under Article II. *Myers* was undoubtedly correct in its holding, and in its broader suggestion that there are some "purely executive" officials who must be removable by the President at will if he is to be able to accomplish his constitutional role.

At the other end of the spectrum from *Myers*, the characterization of the agencies in *Humphrey's Executor* and *Wiener* as "quasi-legislative" or "quasi-judicial" in large part reflected our judgment that it was not essential to the President's proper execution of his Article II powers that these agencies be headed up by individuals who were removable at will. We do not mean to suggest that an analysis of the functions served by the officials at issue is irrelevant. But the real question is whether the removal restrictions are of such a nature that they impede the President's ability to perform his constitutional duty, and the functions of the officials in question must be analyzed in that light.

Considering for the moment the "good cause" removal provision in isolation from the other parts of the Act at issue in this case, we cannot say that the imposition of a "good cause" standard for removal by itself unduly trammels on executive authority. Although the counsel exercises no small amount of discretion and judgment in deciding how to carry out his or her duties under the Act, we simply do not see how the President's need to control the exercise of that discretion is so central to the functioning of the Executive Branch as to require as a matter of constitutional law that the counsel be terminable at will by the President.

Nor do we think that the "good cause" removal provision at issue here impermissibly burdens the President's power to control or supervise the independent counsel, as an executive official, in the execution of his or her duties under the Act. This is not a case in which the power to remove an executive official has been completely stripped from the President, thus providing no means for the President to ensure the "faithful execution" of the laws. Rather, because the independent counsel may be terminated for "good cause," the Executive, through the Attorney General, retains ample authority to assure that the counsel is competently performing his or her statutory responsibilities in a manner that comports with the provisions of the Act. Although we need not decide in this case exactly what is encompassed within the term "good cause" under the Act, the legislative history of the removal provision also makes clear that the Attorney General may remove an independent counsel for "misconduct." We do not think that this limitation as it presently stands sufficiently deprives the President of control over the independent counsel to interfere impermissibly with his constitutional obligation to ensure the faithful execution of the laws.

FREE ENTERPRISE FUND v. PUBLIC COMPANY ACCOUNTING OVERSIGHT BOARD, 130 S. Ct. 3138 (2010): The case involved a provision of the Sarbanes-Oxley Act of 2002. Among other measures, the act introduced tighter regulation of the accounting industry under a new Public Company Accounting Oversight Board. The board is composed of five members, appointed to staggered five-year terms by the Securities and Exchange Commission. The Securities and Exchange Commission can remove members of the board only "for good cause shown," "in accordance with" certain procedures. The members of the Securities and Exchange Commission can be removed by the president only for "good cause."

Chief Justice ROBERTS delivered the opinion of the Court:

May the President be restricted in his ability to remove a principal officer, who is in turn restricted in his ability to remove an inferior officer, even though that inferior officer determines the policy and enforces the laws of the United States?

We hold that such multilevel protection from removal is contrary to Article II's vesting of the executive power in the President. The President cannot "take Care that the Laws be faithfully executed" if he cannot oversee the faithfulness of the officers who execute them. Here the President cannot remove an officer who enjoys more than one level of good-cause protection, even if the President determines that the officer is neglecting his duties or discharging them improperly. That judgment is instead committed to another officer, who may or may not agree with the President's determination, and whom the President cannot remove simply because that officer disagrees with him. This contravenes the President's "constitutional obligation to ensure the faithful execution of the laws."

[W]e have previously upheld limited restrictions on the President's removal power. In those cases, however, only one level of protected tenure separated the President from an officer exercising executive power. It was the President—or a subordinate he could remove at will—who decided whether the officer's conduct merited removal under the good-cause standard.

The Act before us does something quite different. It not only protects Board members from removal except for good cause, but withdraws from the President any decision on whether that good cause exists. That decision is vested instead in other tenured officers—the Commissioners—none of whom is subject to the President's direct control. The result is a Board that is not accountable to the President, and a President who is not responsible for the Board.

A second level of tenure protection changes the nature of the President's review. Now the Commission cannot remove a Board member at will. The President therefore cannot hold the Commission fully accountable for the Board's conduct, to the same extent that he may hold the Commission accountable for everything else that it does. The Commissioners are not responsible for the Board's actions. They are only responsible for their own determination of whether the Act's rigorous good-cause standard is met. And even if the President disagrees with their determination, he is powerless to intervene—unless that determination is so unreasonable as to constitute "inefficiency, neglect of duty, or malfeasance in office."

This novel structure does not merely add to the Board's independence, but transforms it. Neither the President, nor anyone directly responsible to him, nor even an officer whose conduct he may review only for good cause, has full control over the Board. The President is stripped of the power our precedents have preserved, and his ability to execute the laws—by holding his subordinates accountable for their conduct—is impaired.

That arrangement is contrary to Article II's vesting of the executive power in the President. Without the ability to oversee the Board, or to attribute the Board's failings to those whom he *can* oversee, the President is no longer the judge of the Board's conduct. He is not the one who decides whether Board members are abusing their offices or neglecting their duties. He can neither ensure that the laws are faithfully executed, nor be held responsible for a Board member's breach of faith. This violates the basic principle that the President "cannot delegate ultimate responsibility or the active obligation to supervise that goes with it," because Article II "makes a single President responsible for the actions of the Executive Branch."

Justice BREYER wrote a dissenting opinion, joined by Justices STEVENS, GINSBURG, and SOTOMAYOR.

Congress and the President had good reason for enacting the challenged "for cause" provision. First and foremost, the Board adjudicates cases. This Court has long recognized the appropriateness of using "for cause" provisions to protect the personal independence of those who even only sometimes engage in adjudicatory functions.

Moreover, in addition to their adjudicative functions, the Accounting Board members supervise, and are themselves, technical professional experts. This Court has recognized that the "difficulties involved in the preparation of" sound auditing reports require the application of "scientific accounting principles." And this Court has recognized the constitutional legitimacy of a justification that rests agency independence upon the need for technical expertise. Here, the justification for insulating the "technical experts" on the Board from fear of losing their jobs due to political influence is particularly strong. Congress deliberately sought to provide that kind of protection.

We should ask one further question. Even if the "for cause" provision before us does not itself significantly interfere with the President's authority or aggrandize Congress' power, is it nonetheless necessary to adopt a bright-line rule forbidding the provision lest, through a series of such provisions, each itself upheld as reasonable, Congress might undercut the President's central constitutional role? The answer to this question is that no such need has been shown. Moreover, insofar as the Court seeks to create such a rule, it fails. And in failing it threatens a harm that is far more serious than any imaginable harm this "for cause" provision might bring about.

The Court begins to reveal the practical problems inherent in its double for-cause rule when it suggests that its rule may not apply to "the civil service." But even if I assume that the majority categorically excludes the competitive service from the scope of its new rule, the exclusion would be insufficient. Reading the criteria above as stringently as possible, I still see no way to avoid sweeping hundreds, perhaps thousands of high level government officials within the scope of the Court's holding, putting their job security and their administrative actions and decisions constitutionally at risk. To make even a conservative estimate, one would have to begin by listing federal departments, offices, bureaus and other agencies whose heads are by statute removable only "for cause." I have found 48 such agencies. Then it would be necessary to identify the senior officials in those agencies (just below the top) who themselves are removable only "for cause." I have identified 573 such high-ranking officials. This list is a conservative estimate because it consists only of career appointees in the Senior Executive Service (SES). The potential list of those whom today's decision affects is yet larger. [A]dministrative law judges (ALJs) "are all executive officers." My research reflects that the Federal Government relies on 1,584 ALJs to adjudicate administrative matters in over 25 agencies

In my view the Court's decision is wrong—very wrong. Its rule of decision is both imprecise and overly broad. In light of the present imprecision, it must either narrow its rule arbitrarily, leaving it to apply virtually alone to the Accounting Board, or it will have to leave in place a broader rule of decision applicable to many other "inferior officers" as well. In doing the latter, it will undermine the President's authority. And it will create an obstacle, indeed pose a serious threat, to the proper functioning of that workable Government that the Constitution seeks to create—in provisions this Court is sworn to uphold.

———————————

Together, these cases seem to establish that the president may fire any executive official. Congress, however, can limit removal by statute if it is an office for which independence from the president is desirable, the statute does not prohibit removal but limits it to where there is good cause, and the statute does not keep the president from firing executive branch officials where there is good cause.

Ultimately the question is whether these mechanisms for controlling administrative agencies—statutes, budget, informal committee controls, appointment, and removal—are sufficient. Some justices have suggested that it would be desirable to revive the nondelegation doctrine. Justice Scalia seemed to be arguing for this in his dissent in Morrison v. Olson, above. Additionally, in the early 1980s, Justice Rehnquist took a similar position. In Industrial Union Dept., AFL-CIO v. American Petroleum Institute, 448 U.S. 607 (1980), the Court upheld provisions of the Occupational Safety and Health Act that authorized the secretary of labor to adopt standards that are "reasonably necessary or appropriate to provide safe or healthful employment" and to "set the standard which most adequately assures, to the extent feasible, on the basis of the best available evidence, that no employee will suffer material impairment of health." Justice Rehnquist, in a dissenting opinion, argued that these provisions should have been invalidated as an excessive delegation of legislative power. He wrote, "When fundamental policy decisions underlying important legislation about to be enacted are to be made, the buck stops with Congress and the President insofar as he exercises his constitutional role in the legislative process." If the Court were to follow the views of Rehnquist and Scalia, the issue then would become how to distinguish permissible from impermissible delegations of power.

D. SEPARATION OF POWERS AND FOREIGN POLICY

The Constitution says very little about foreign policy decision making. Article I, §8 grants Congress the power to regulate commerce with foreign nations, "[t]o declare War, grant letters of Marque and Reprisal, and make Rules concerning Captures on Land and Water," to raise and support armies, and to "define and punish Piracies and Felonies committed on the high Seas, and Offenses against the Law of Nations." Article II says that the "President shall be Commander in Chief of the Army and Navy of the United States, and of the Militia of the several States, when called into the actual Service of the United States." Article II also provides that the president "shall have Power, by and with Advice and Consent of the Senate, to make Treaties, provided two thirds of the Senators present concur."

These relatively few provisions raise many difficult and important issues. For example, what is the relationship between Congress's power to declare war and the president's authority as commander in chief? When may the president use troops, including in war situations, without a congressional declaration of war? Another illustration of the Constitution's ambiguity is whether the president can use executive agreements instead of treaties in dealing with foreign countries. Is this an appropriate exercise of the power of the chief executive or is it an unconstitutional usurpation of the Senate's power?

This is an area of constitutional law where reliance on the framers' intent is particularly difficult. A world of instantaneous communications, missiles that can be sent across the world in minutes, and troops that can be sent anywhere within hours is vastly different from that which existed in 1787.

This area of constitutional law is different in another way as well: the relative absence of judicial decisions. As described in Chapter 1, the Supreme Court frequently has declared that issues concerning foreign policy are nonjusticiable political questions — matters for the executive and legislature to resolve without judicial review. *See, e.g.,* Goldwater v. Carter, 444 U.S. 996 (1979) (holding nonjusticiable a challenge to the president's rescission of the U.S. treaty with Taiwan) (included in Chapter 1).

This section considers three issues. First, are foreign policy and domestic affairs different under the Constitution? Does the president have more inherent authority regarding foreign policy than as to domestic affairs? Second, what are the constitutional limits on agreements with foreign nations? In particular, may the president use executive agreements rather than treaties? Finally, how is decision-making authority over war powers allocated?

1.   Are Foreign Policy and Domestic Affairs Different?

Do the same principles of separation of powers apply in foreign policy as in domestic affairs? Should the Constitution be interpreted as according the president more inherent powers as to foreign policy? The leading case supporting this view is United States v. Curtiss-Wright Export Corp. The issue in the case is the constitutionality of a congressional delegation of power to the president in the area of foreign policy. As you read the decision, it is important to remember that the Supreme Court was aggressively enforcing the nondelegation doctrine — the principle that Congress cannot delegate legislative power to executive agencies — at the time the case was decided.

UNITED STATES v. CURTISS-WRIGHT EXPORT CORP.
299 U.S. 304 (1936)

Justice SUTHERLAND delivered the opinion of the Court.

Congress passed a resolution authorizing the President to stop sales of arms to countries involved in the Chaco border dispute. President Roosevelt immediately issued an order prohibiting munitions sales to the warring nations in the Chaco border dispute.

On January 27, 1936, an indictment was returned in the court below, the first count of which charges that appellees, beginning with the 29th day of May, 1934, conspired to sell in the United States certain arms of war, namely, fifteen machine guns, to Bolivia, a country then engaged in armed conflict in the Chaco, in violation of the Joint Resolution of Congress approved May 28, 1934, and the provisions of a proclamation issued on the same day by the President of the United States pursuant to authority conferred by section 1 of the resolution.

Whether, if the Joint Resolution had related solely to internal affairs, it would be open to the challenge that it constituted an unlawful delegation of legislative power to the Executive, we find it unnecessary to determine. The whole aim of the resolution is to affect a situation entirely external to the United States, and falling within the category of foreign affairs. The determination which we are called to make, therefore, is whether the Joint Resolution, as applied to that situation, is vulnerable to attack under the rule that forbids a delegation of the lawmaking power. In other words, assuming (but not deciding) that the challenged delegation, if it were confined to internal affairs, would be invalid, may it nevertheless be sustained on the ground that its exclusive aim is to afford a remedy for a hurtful condition within foreign territory?

It will contribute to the elucidation of the question if we first consider the differences between the powers of the federal government in respect of foreign or external affairs and those in respect of domestic or internal affairs. That there are differences between them, and that these differences are fundamental, may not be doubted.

The two classes of powers are different, both in respect of their origin and their nature. The broad statement that the federal government can exercise no powers except those specifically enumerated in the Constitution, and such implied powers as are necessary and proper to carry into effect the enumerated powers, is categorically true only in respect of our internal affairs. In that field, the primary purpose of the Constitution was to carve from the general mass of legislative powers then possessed by the states such portions as it was thought desirable to vest in the federal government, leaving those not included in the enumeration still in the states. That this doctrine applies only to powers which the states had is self-evident. And since the states severally never possessed international powers, such powers could not have been carved from the mass of state powers but obviously were transmitted to the United States from some other source. During the Colonial period, those powers were possessed exclusively by and were entirely under the control of the Crown.

It results that the investment of the federal government with the powers of external sovereignty did not depend upon the affirmative grants of the Constitution. The powers to declare and wage war, to conclude peace, to make treaties, to maintain diplomatic relations with other sovereignties, if they had never been mentioned in the Constitution, would have vested in the federal government as necessary concomitants of nationality.

Not only, as we have shown, is the federal power over external affairs in origin and essential character different from that over internal affairs, but participation in the exercise of the power is significantly limited. In this vast external realm, with its important, complicated, delicate and manifold problems, the President alone has the power to speak or listen as a representative of the nation. He makes treaties with the advice and consent of the Senate; but he alone negotiates. Into the field of negotiation the Senate cannot intrude; and Congress itself is powerless to invade it. As Marshall said in his great argument of March 7, 1800, in the House of Representatives, "The President is the sole organ of the nation in its external relations, and its sole representative with foreign nations."

It is important to bear in mind that we are here dealing not alone with an authority vested in the President by an exertion of legislative power, but with such an authority plus the very delicate, plenary and exclusive power of the President as the sole organ of the federal government in the field of international relations—a power which does not require as a basis for its exercise an act of Congress, but which, of course, like every other governmental power, must be exercised in subordination to the applicable provisions of the Constitution. It is quite apparent that if, in the maintenance of our international relations, embarrassment—perhaps serious embarrassment—is to be avoided and success for our aims achieved, congressional legislation which is to be made effective through negotiation and inquiry within the international field must often accord to the President a degree of discretion and freedom from statutory restriction which would not be admissible were domestic affairs alone involved. Moreover, he, not Congress, has the better opportunity of knowing the conditions which prevail in foreign countries, and especially is this true in time of war. He has his confidential sources of information. He has his agents in the form of diplomatic, consular and other officials. Secrecy in respect of information gathered by them may be highly necessary, and the premature disclosure of it productive of harmful results.

NOTES ON CURTISS-WRIGHT

Justice Sutherland's broad interpretation of presidential power in foreign affairs has been challenged by constitutional scholars. First, some contend that his view is inconsistent with a written Constitution that contains provisions concerning foreign policy. If Sutherland's view were correct, there would have been no reason for the Constitution to enumerate any powers in the area of foreign affairs; all powers would exist automatically as part of national sovereignty. The detailing of authority for conducting foreign policy rebuts the assumption that the president has complete control over foreign affairs simply by virtue of being chief executive.[10]

Second, many have criticized the historical account that is the foundation for Justice Sutherland's opinion. Professor Charles Lofgren notes that the "history on which [*Curtiss-Wright*] rest[s] is 'shockingly inaccurate'" and not based on either the text of the Constitution or the framers' intent.[11] In his view, the framers intended that the president, like all branches of the federal government, have limited powers, not the expansive inherent authority described in *Curtiss-Wright*.

If the President has broad inherent power in foreign policy as indicated in *Curtiss-Wright*, does this mean that congressional actions to limit the president in this realm are unconstitutional? The issue arose during the 1980s in connection with an attempt by the Reagan administration to circumvent a federal law prohibiting aid to the contras in Nicaragua. The Boland Amendment to the appropriation bills barred any "agency or entity of the United States involved in intelligence activities" from spending funds "to support military or paramilitary operations in Nicaragua."[12]

Some high-level members of the Reagan administration intentionally violated the Boland Amendment by raising funds from third parties to fund the contras and by selling arms to Iran to fund the contras.[13] Some have defended these actions on the ground that the Boland Amendment was an impermissible restriction on the president's power to conduct foreign policy. For example, a Republican minority report to a House Committee report declared, "[The] Constitution gives the President some power to act on his own in foreign affairs. . . . Congress may not use its control over appropriations, including

10. *See* David M. Levitan, *The Foreign Relations Power: An Analysis of Mr. Justice Sutherland's Theory*, 55 Yale L.J. 467, 493-494 (1946).
11. Charles A. Lofgren, *United States v. Curtiss-Wright Export Corp.: A Historical Reassessment*, 83 Yale L.J. 1, 32 (1973).
12. 101 Stat. 1011 (1987).
13. *See* Lawrence E. Walsh, *Final Report of the Independent Counsel for Iran/Contra Matters* (1993); Michael Arthur Ledeen, *Perilous Statecraft: An Insider's Account of the Iran-Contra Affair* (1988).

salaries, to prevent the executive or judiciary from fulfilling Constitutionally mandated obligations."[14]

Others, including the Democratic majority on the House Committee, argued that Congress controls the power of the purse and therefore should be able to control government spending. The Boland Amendment was a restriction on expenditures. Moreover, Article I gives Congress the power to regulate foreign commerce. Thus, supporters of the Boland Amendment contended that it was constitutional and the president has no authority to disobey a constitutional statute in the conduct of foreign or domestic affairs.

The Boland Amendment thus poses a relatively recent example concerning the scope of the President's powers in foreign policy and the ability of Congress to impose limits.

2.   Treaties and Executive Agreements

Article II, §2 states that the president "shall have Power, by and with the Advice and Consent of the Senate, to make Treaties, provided two thirds of the Senators present concur." The major constitutional issue that has arisen concerns the authority of the president to use executive agreements rather than treaties for foreign policy commitments. A treaty is an agreement between the United States and a foreign country that is negotiated by the president and is effective when ratified by the Senate.[15] An executive agreement, in contrast, is an agreement between the United States and a foreign country that is effective when signed by the president and the head of the other government. In other words, if the document is labeled "treaty," Senate approval is required. If the document is titled "executive agreement," no Senate ratification is necessary.

Although the Constitution does not mention executive agreements, it is well established that such agreements are constitutional. Indeed, based on past experience, it appears that executive agreements can be used for any purpose; that is, anything that can be done by treaty can be done by executive agreement. Never in American history has the Supreme Court declared an executive agreement unconstitutional as usurping the Senate's treaty-approving function. Even major foreign policy commitments have been implemented through executive agreements. For example, in 1940, the "Destroyer-Bases Agreement" substantially expanded American involvement in World War II when President Roosevelt agreed to loan Great Britain 50 naval destroyers in exchange for the United States receiving free 99-year leases to develop military bases on several sites in the Caribbean and Newfoundland.[16]

The Court has sided with the president each time there has been a challenge to an executive agreement. In United States v. Pink[17] and United States v.

---

14. Report of the Congressional Committees Investigating the Iran-Contra Affair, S. Rep. No. 100-216, H. Rep. No. 100-433 (1987) at 473 (minority report).

15. For an argument that there is a new form of presidential-congressional international agreement, approved by both houses of Congress but not requiring approval of two-thirds of the Senate, *see* Bruce Ackerman & David Golove, *Is NAFTA Constitutional?* 108 Harv. L. Rev. 799 (1995); *but see* Laurence H. Tribe, *Taking Text and Structure Seriously: Reflections on Free-Form Method in Constitutional Interpretation*, 108 Harv. L. Rev. 1221 (1995) (strongly objecting to such an approach).

16. Richard W. Leopold, *The Growth of American Foreign Policy*, 565-566 (1962).

17. 315 U.S. 203 (1942).

Belmont,[18] the Supreme Court upheld an executive agreement, the Litvinov Agreement, whereby the United States recognized the Soviet Union in exchange for the Soviet Union assigning to the United States its interests in a Russian insurance company in New York. The Soviet Union had nationalized the interest in this insurance company in 1918 and 1919. The United States would use these assets to pay claims that it and others had against the Soviet Union.[19]

The Court upheld the executive agreement and explained that because it was not a treaty, Senate approval was not required. New York courts had refused to enforce the Litvinov Agreement, but the Court ruled that states must comply with executive agreements. Executive agreements, like treaties, prevail over state law and policy. Justice Douglas, writing for the Court in *Pink*, explained, "A treaty is a 'Law of the Land' under the supremacy clause [of Article VI] of the Constitution. Such international compacts and agreements as the Litvinov Assignment have a similar dignity."[20] Similarly, in United States v. Belmont, the Court stated that "in the case of all international compacts and agreements . . . complete power over international affairs is in the national government and is not and cannot be subject to any curtailment or interference on the part of the several states."[21]

A more recent example of the Supreme Court upholding an executive agreement was Dames & Moore v. Regan in 1981.

DAMES & MOORE v. REGAN, SECRETARY OF THE TREASURY
453 U.S. 654 (1981)

Justice REHNQUIST delivered the opinion of the Court.

The questions presented by this case touch fundamentally upon the manner in which our Republic is to be governed. Throughout the nearly two centuries of our Nation's existence under the Constitution, this subject has generated considerable debate. We have had the benefit of commentators such as John Jay, Alexander Hamilton, and James Madison writing in The Federalist Papers at the Nation's very inception, the benefit of astute foreign observers of our system such as Alexis de Tocqueville and James Bryce writing during the first century of the Nation's existence, and the benefit of many other treatises as well as more than 400 volumes of reports of decisions of this Court. As these writings reveal it is doubtless both futile and perhaps dangerous to find any epigrammatical explanation of how this country has been governed. Indeed, as Justice Jackson noted, "[a] judge . . . may be surprised at the poverty of really useful and unambiguous authority applicable to concrete problems of executive power as they actually present themselves."

18. 301 U.S. 324 (1937).

19. In *Pink*, the Court also rejected a claim that the agreement was an impermissible taking of property without just compensation in violation of the Fifth Amendment. The Court noted that the Litvinov Agreement did not bar compensation for claims, although it did give the United States priority as a creditor.

20. 315 U.S. at 230.

21. 301 U.S. at 331.

I

On November 4, 1979, the American Embassy in Tehran was seized and our diplomatic personnel were captured and held hostage. In response to that crisis, President Carter, acting pursuant to the International Emergency Economic Powers Act (hereinafter IEEPA) declared a national emergency on November 14, 1979, and blocked the removal or transfer of "all property and interests in property of the Government of Iran, its instrumentalities and controlled entities and the Central Bank of Iran which are or become subject to the jurisdiction of the United States. . . ." Exec. Order No. 12170.

On January 20, 1981, the Americans held hostage were released by Iran pursuant to an Agreement entered into the day before and embodied in two Declarations of the Democratic and Popular Republic of Algeria. The Agreement stated that "[i]t is the purpose of [the United States and Iran] . . . to terminate all litigation as between the Government of each party and the nationals of the other, and to bring about the settlement and termination of all such claims through binding arbitration." In furtherance of this goal, the Agreement called for the establishment of an Iran-United States Claims Tribunal which would arbitrate any claims not settled within six months. Awards of the Claims Tribunal are to be "final and binding" and "enforceable . . . in the courts of any nation in accordance with its laws." Under the Agreement, the United States is obligated "to terminate all legal proceedings in United States courts involving claims of United States persons and institutions against Iran and its state enterprises, to nullify all attachments and judgments obtained therein, to prohibit all further litigation based on such claims, and to bring about the termination of such claims through binding arbitration."

On April 28, 1981, petitioner filed this action in the District Court for declaratory and injunctive relief against the United States and the Secretary of the Treasury, seeking to prevent enforcement of the Executive Orders and Treasury Department regulations implementing the Agreement with Iran. In its complaint, petitioner alleged that the actions of the President and the Secretary of the Treasury implementing the Agreement with Iran were beyond their statutory and constitutional powers and, in any event, were unconstitutional to the extent they adversely affect petitioner's final judgment against the Government of Iran and the Atomic Energy Organization, its execution of that judgment in the State of Washington, its prejudgment attachments, and its ability to continue to litigate against the Iranian banks.

Not infrequently in affairs between nations, outstanding claims by nationals of one country against the government of another country are "sources of friction" between the two sovereigns. United States v. Pink (1942). To resolve these difficulties, nations have often entered into agreements settling the claims of their respective nationals. As one treatise writer puts it, international agreements settling claims by nationals of one state against the government of another "are established international practice reflecting traditional international theory." L. Henkin, Foreign Affairs and the Constitution 262 (1972). Consistent with that principle, the United States has repeatedly exercised its sovereign authority to settle the claims of its nationals against foreign countries. Though those settlements have sometimes been made by treaty, there has also been a longstanding practice of settling such claims by executive agreement without the advice and consent of the Senate. Under such agreements, the President has agreed to renounce or extinguish claims of United States nationals against foreign governments in return for lump-sum payments or the establishment of arbitration procedures. It is clear that the practice of settling claims continues today. Since 1952, the President has entered into at least 10 binding settlements with foreign nations, including an $80 million settlement with the People's Republic of China.

Crucial to our decision today is the conclusion that Congress has implicitly approved the practice of claim settlement by executive agreement. This is best demonstrated by Congress' enactment of the International Claims Settlement Act of 1949. The Act had two purposes: (1) to allocate to United States nationals funds received in the course of an executive claims settlement with Yugoslavia, and (2) to provide a procedure whereby funds resulting from future settlements could be distributed. To achieve these ends Congress created the International Claims Commission, now the Foreign Claims Settlement Commission, and gave it jurisdiction to make final and binding decisions with respect to claims by United States nationals against settlement funds. By creating a procedure to implement future settlement agreements, Congress placed its stamp of approval on such agreements. Indeed, the legislative history of the Act observed that the United States was seeking settlements with countries other than Yugoslavia and that the bill contemplated settlements of a similar nature in the future.

Over the years Congress has frequently amended the International Claims Settlement Act to provide for particular problems arising out of settlement agreements, thus demonstrating Congress' continuing acceptance of the President's claim settlement authority. In addition to congressional acquiescence in the President's power to settle claims, prior cases of this Court have also recognized that the President does have some measure of power to enter into executive agreements without obtaining the advice and consent of the Senate. In United States v. Pink (1942), for example, the Court upheld the validity of the Litvinov Assignment, which was part of an Executive Agreement whereby the Soviet Union assigned to the United States amounts owed to it by American nationals so that outstanding claims of other American nationals could be paid.

Finally, we re-emphasize the narrowness of our decision. We do not decide that the President possesses plenary power to settle claims, even as against foreign governmental entities. But where, as here, the settlement of claims has been determined to be a necessary incident to the resolution of a major foreign policy dispute between our country and another, and where, as here, we can conclude that Congress acquiesced in the President's action, we are not prepared to say that the President lacks the power to settle such claims.

During the 1940s and 1950s, Senator Bricker proposed a constitutional amendment, known as the Bricker Amendment, that would have prevented the use of executive agreements. The Amendment never was passed by Congress, but it reflects deep concern over the President's ability to circumvent the treaty ratification process by using executive agreements instead.

3. War Powers

The Constitution is an invitation for a struggle between the president and Congress over control of the war power. The Constitution, in Article I, grants

Congress the power to declare war and the authority to raise and support the army and the navy. Article II makes the president the commander in chief.

Basic, unresolved questions exist concerning these powers. First, what constitutes a declaration of war? Must it be a formal declaration of war, such as was adopted by Congress after the bombing of Pearl Harbor to authorize America's entry into World War II? Or may it be less explicit? For example, was the Gulf of Tonkin Resolution, which authorized the use of military force in Southeast Asia, sufficient to constitute a declaration of war for the Vietnam War? Might even repeated congressional approval of funding for a war be regarded as sufficient even without passage of a resolution explicitly approving the war?

Second, when may the president use American troops in hostilities without congressional approval? To what extent does the president's power as commander in chief authorize the use of troops in foreign countries without a formal declaration of war? Neither of these questions ever has been clearly answered by the Supreme Court. In fact, given the Court's view that such foreign policy disputes constitute a political question, answers are unlikely to come from the judiciary.

Thus, the Supreme Court rarely has spoken as to the constitutionality of the president using troops in a war or warlike circumstances without congressional approval. In fact, the only Supreme Court case to address the issue was in the unique context of the Civil War and the actions of the president to deal with the rebellion. In the *Prize Cases*, the Court ruled that the president had the power to impose a blockade on Southern states without a congressional declaration of war.[22] No other Supreme Court case has addressed the constitutionality of presidential war making without a congressional declaration of war. Therefore, little exists in the way of law regarding the circumstances in which the president may use troops without congressional approval or as to what Congress may do to suspend American involvement in a war.

In 1973, Congress adopted the War Powers Resolution to address these two questions.[23] The War Powers Resolution was a response to the Vietnam War in which two presidents, Lyndon Johnson and Richard Nixon, fought a highly unpopular war with great cost in lives and dollars without a formal declaration of war from Congress.

TITLE 50. WAR AND NATIONAL DEFENSE;
CHAPTER 33—WAR POWERS RESOLUTION

§1541. Purpose and Policy

(a) Congressional declaration

It is the purpose of this chapter to fulfill the intent of the framers of the Constitution of the United States and insure that the collective judgment of

---

22. 67 U.S. (2 Black) 635 (1862).
23. 50 U.S.C. §1541. Although it is called "The War Powers Resolution," it is a properly adopted federal statute.

both the Congress and the President will apply to the introduction of United States Armed Forces into hostilities, or into situations where imminent involvement in hostilities is clearly indicated by the circumstances, and to the continued use of such forces in hostilities or in such situations.

(b) Congressional legislative power under necessary and proper clause

Under article I, section 8, of the Constitution, it is specifically provided that the Congress shall have the power to make all laws necessary and proper for carrying into execution, not only its own powers but also all other powers vested by the Constitution in the Government of the United States, or in any department or officer thereof.

(c) Presidential executive power as Commander-in-Chief; limitation

The constitutional powers of the President as Commander-in-Chief to introduce United States Armed Forces into hostilities, or into situations where imminent involvement in hostilities is clearly indicated by the circumstances, are exercised only pursuant to (1) a declaration of war, (2) specific statutory authorization, or (3) a national emergency created by attack upon the United States, its territories or possessions, or its armed forces.

§1542. Consultation; Initial and Regular Consultations

The President in every possible instance shall consult with Congress before introducing United States Armed Forces into hostilities or into situations where imminent involvement in hostilities is clearly indicated by the circumstances, and after every such introduction shall consult regularly with the Congress until United States Armed Forces are no longer engaged in hostilities or have been removed from such situations.

§1543. Reporting Requirement

(a) Written report; time of submission; circumstances necessitating submission; information reported

In the absence of a declaration of war, in any case in which United States Armed Forces are introduced —

(1) into hostilities or into situations where imminent involvement in hostilities is clearly indicated by the circumstances;

(2) into the territory, airspace or waters of a foreign nation, while equipped for combat, except for deployments which relate solely to supply, replacement, repair, or training of such forces; or

(3) in numbers which substantially enlarge United States Armed Forces equipped for combat already located in a foreign nation

the President shall submit within 48 hours to the Speaker of the House of Representatives and to the President pro tempore of the Senate a report, in writing, setting forth —

(A) the circumstances necessitating the introduction of United States Armed Forces;

(B) the constitutional and legislative authority under which such introduction took place; and

(C) the estimated scope and duration of the hostilities or involvement.

(b) Other information reported

The President shall provide such other information as the Congress may request in the fulfillment of its constitutional responsibilities with respect to committing the Nation to war and to the use of United States Armed Forces abroad.

(c) Periodic reports; semiannual requirement

Whenever United States Armed Forces are introduced into hostilities or into any situation described in subsection (a) of this section, the President shall, so long as such armed forces continue to be engaged in such hostilities or situation, report to the Congress periodically on the status of such hostilities or situation as well as on the scope and duration of such hostilities or situation, but in no event shall he report to the Congress less often than once every six months.

§1544. Congressional Action

(a) Transmittal of report and referral to Congressional committees; joint request for convening Congress

Each report submitted pursuant to section 1543(a)(1) of this title shall be transmitted to the Speaker of the House of Representatives and to the President pro tempore of the Senate on the same calendar day.

(b) Termination of use of United States Armed Forces; exceptions; extension period

Within sixty calendar days after a report is submitted or is required to be submitted pursuant to section 1543(a)(1) of this title, whichever is earlier, the President shall terminate any use of United States Armed Forces with respect to which such report was submitted (or required to be submitted), unless the Congress (1) has declared war or has enacted a specific authorization for such use of United States Armed Forces, (2) has extended by law such sixty-day period, or (3) is physically unable to meet as a result of an armed attack upon the United States. Such sixty-day period shall be extended for not more than an additional thirty days if the President determines and certifies to the Congress in writing that unavoidable military necessity respecting the safety of United States Armed Forces requires the continued use of such armed forces in the course of bringing about a prompt removal of such forces.

(c) Concurrent resolution for removal by President of United States Armed Forces

Notwithstanding subsection (b) of this section, at any time that United States Armed Forces are engaged in hostilities outside the territory of the United States, its possessions and territories without a declaration of war or specific statutory authorization, such forces shall be removed by the President if the Congress so directs by concurrent resolution.

§1547. Interpretation of Joint Resolution

(a) Inferences from any law or treaty

Authority to introduce United States Armed Forces into hostilities or into situations wherein involvement in hostilities is clearly indicated by the circumstances shall not be inferred—

(1) from any provision of law (whether or not in effect before November 7, 1973), including any provision contained in any appropriation Act, unless such provision specifically authorizes the introduction of United States Armed Forces into hostilities or into such situations and states that

it is intended to constitute specific statutory authorization within the meaning of this chapter; or

(2) from any treaty heretofore or hereafter ratified unless such treaty is implemented by legislation specifically authorizing the introduction of United States Armed Forces into hostilities or into such situations and stating that it is intended to constitute specific statutory authorization within the meaning of this chapter.

(b) Joint headquarters operations of high-level military commands

Nothing in this chapter shall be construed to require any further specific statutory authorization to permit members of United States Armed Forces to participate jointly with members of the armed forces of one or more foreign countries in the headquarters operations of high-level military commands which were established prior to November 7, 1973, and pursuant to the United Nations Charter or any treaty ratified by the United States prior to such date.

(c) Introduction of United States Armed Forces

For purposes of this chapter, the term "introduction of United States Armed Forces" includes the assignment of members of such armed forces to command, coordinate, participate in the movement of, or accompany the regular or irregular military forces of any foreign country or government when such military forces are engaged, or there exists an imminent threat that such forces will become engaged, in hostilities.

(d) Constitutional authorities or existing treaties unaffected; construction against grant of Presidential authority respecting use of United States Armed Forces

Nothing in this chapter—

(1) is intended to alter the constitutional authority of the Congress or of the President, or the provisions of existing treaties; or

(2) shall be construed as granting any authority to the President with respect to the introduction of United States Armed Forces into hostilities or into situations wherein involvement in hostilities is clearly indicated by the circumstances which authority he would not have had in the absence of this chapter.

§1548. Separability of Provisions
If any provision of this chapter or the application thereof to any person or circumstance is held invalid, the remainder of the chapter and the application of such provision to any other person or circumstance shall not be affected thereby.

The constitutionality of the War Powers Resolution has not been tested. In 1999, Representative Tom Campbell brought a lawsuit arguing that the bombing of Yugoslavia was in violation of the War Powers Resolution. The United States District Court for the District of Columbia dismissed the case for lack of standing and the United States Court of Appeals for the District of

Columbia Circuit affirmed. Campbell v. Clinton, 52 F. Supp. 2d 34 (D.D.C. 1999), *aff'd* 203 F.3d 19 (D.C. Cir. 2000). In 2003, a lawsuit was brought to have the impending war in Iraq declared unconstitutional. It, too, was dismissed as nonjusticiable. Doe v. Bush, 323 F.3d 133 (1st Cir. 2003). It is quite possible that every challenge to a president's actions as violating the War Powers Resolution will be dismissed on justiciability grounds, either for lack of standing or as a political question.

Nonetheless, the underlying constitutional issue remains: Is the War Powers Resolution an unconstitutional intrusion on the president's powers as commander in chief? Or is the War Powers Resolution a permissible effort by Congress to interpret the Constitution and ensure checks and balances?

E.   PRESIDENTIAL POWER AND THE WAR ON TERRORISM

The tragic events of September 11, 2001, have led to many government actions that will raise important difficult constitutional questions: Is the indefinite detention of "unlawful combatants" constitutional? Are secret deportation proceedings constitutional? Is it permissible for the government to hold individuals indefinitely as "material witnesses"? Are provisions of the USA Patriot Act, which include expanded authorization for electronic eavesdropping by the government, constitutional?

The materials below consider two issues: When may the executive detain U.S. enemy combatants, and when, if at all, are military tribunals constitutional?

1.   Detentions

In June 2004, the Supreme Court decided three major cases concerning civil liberties and the war on terrorism. Two were resolved largely on nonconstitutional grounds. In Rasul v. Bush, 542 U.S. 466 (2004), the Supreme Court held that detainees being held at Guantanamo Bay, Cuba, had a right to have their habeas corpus petition heard in a federal court. In Padilla v. Rumsfeld, 542 U.S. 426 (2004), the Court held that an American citizen, apprehended in the United States and held as an enemy combatant in a military prison in South Carolina, could not present a habeas corpus petition in federal court in New York, where he was earlier held. Rather, the habeas petition needed to be refiled in South Carolina.

But in Hamdi v. Rumsfeld, below, the Court considered whether an American citizen apprehended in a foreign country could be indefinitely detained as an enemy combatant without any form of due process. By a five-to-four margin, though without a majority opinion, the Court ruled that there was sufficient legal authority to detain Hamdi as an enemy combatant. But the Court, by an eight-to-one margin, concluded that Hamdi must be accorded due process, including a meaningful factual hearing. In October 2004, Hamdi was released from custody after agreeing to renounce his U.S. citizenship, not take up arms against the United States, and not to return to this country.

HAMDI v. RUMSFELD
542 U.S. 507 (2004)

Justice O'CONNOR announced the judgment of the Court and delivered an opinion, in which the Chief Justice, Justice KENNEDY, and Justice BREYER join.

At this difficult time in our Nation's history, we are called upon to consider the legality of the Government's detention of a United States citizen on United States soil as an "enemy combatant" and to address the process that is constitutionally owed to one who seeks to challenge his classification as such. The United States Court of Appeals for the Fourth Circuit held that petitioner's detention was legally authorized and that he was entitled to no further opportunity to challenge his enemy-combatant label. We now vacate and remand. We hold that although Congress authorized the detention of combatants in the narrow circumstances alleged here, due process demands that a citizen held in the United States as an enemy combatant be given a meaningful opportunity to contest the factual basis for that detention before a neutral decisionmaker.

I

On September 11, 2001, the al Qaeda terrorist network used hijacked commercial airliners to attack prominent targets in the United States. Approximately 3,000 people were killed in those attacks. One week later, in response to these "acts of treacherous violence," Congress passed a resolution authorizing the President to "use all necessary and appropriate force against those nations, organizations, or persons he determines planned, authorized, committed, or aided the terrorist attacks" or "harbored such organizations or persons, in order to prevent any future acts of international terrorism against the United States by such nations, organizations or persons." Soon thereafter, the President ordered United States Armed Forces to Afghanistan, with a mission to subdue al Qaeda and quell the Taliban regime that was known to support it.

This case arises out of the detention of a man whom the Government alleges took up arms with the Taliban during this conflict. His name is Yaser Esam Hamdi. Born an American citizen in Louisiana in 1980, Hamdi moved with his family to Saudi Arabia as a child. By 2001, the parties agree, he resided in Afghanistan. At some point that year, he was seized by members of the Northern Alliance, a coalition of military groups opposed to the Taliban government, and eventually was turned over to the United States military. The Government asserts that it initially detained and interrogated Hamdi in Afghanistan before transferring him to the United States Naval Base in Guantanamo Bay in January 2002. In April 2002, upon learning that Hamdi is an American citizen, authorities transferred him to a naval brig in Norfolk, Virginia, where he remained until a recent transfer to a brig in Charleston, South Carolina. The Government contends that Hamdi is an "enemy combatant," and that this status justifies holding him in the United States indefinitely—without formal charges or proceedings—unless and until it makes the determination that access to counsel or further process is warranted.

II

The threshold question before us is whether the Executive has the authority to detain citizens who qualify as "enemy combatants." There is some debate as to the proper scope of this term, and the Government has never provided any court with the full criteria that it uses in classifying individuals as such. It has made clear, however, that, for purposes of this case, the "enemy combatant" that it is seeking to detain is an individual who, it alleges, was "'part of or supporting forces hostile to the United States or coalition partners'" in Afghanistan and who "'engaged in an armed conflict against the United States'" there. We therefore answer only the narrow question before us: whether the detention of citizens falling within that definition is authorized.

The Government maintains that no explicit congressional authorization is required, because the Executive possesses plenary authority to detain pursuant to Article II of the Constitution. We do not reach the question whether Article II provides such authority, however, because we agree with the Government's alternative position, that Congress has in fact authorized Hamdi's detention.

Our analysis on that point, set forth below, substantially overlaps with our analysis of Hamdi's principal argument for the illegality of his detention. He posits that his detention is forbidden by 18 U.S.C. §4001(a). Section 4001(a) states that "[n]o citizen shall be imprisoned or otherwise detained by the United States except pursuant to an Act of Congress." Congress passed §4001(a) in 1971 as part of a bill to repeal the Emergency Detention Act of 1950, which provided procedures for executive detention, during times of emergency, of individuals deemed likely to engage in espionage or sabotage. Congress was particularly concerned about the possibility that the Act could be used to reprise the Japanese internment camps of World War II.

The Government again presses two alternative positions. First, it argues that §4001(a) applies only to "the control of civilian prisons and related detentions," not to military detentions. Second, it maintains that §4001(a) is satisfied, because Hamdi is being detained "pursuant to an Act of Congress"—the [Authorization for Use of Military Force]. Again, because we conclude that the Government's second assertion is correct, we do not address the first. In other words, for the reasons that follow, we conclude that the AUMF is explicit congressional authorization for the detention of individuals in the narrow category we describe (assuming, without deciding, that such authorization is required), and that the AUMF satisfied §4001(a)'s requirement that a detention be "pursuant to an Act of Congress" (assuming, without deciding, that §4001(a) applies to military detentions).

The AUMF authorizes the President to use "all necessary and appropriate force" against "nations, organizations, or persons" associated with the September 11, 2001, terrorist attacks. There can be no doubt that individuals who fought against the United States in Afghanistan as part of the Taliban, an organization known to have supported the al Qaeda terrorist network responsible for those attacks, are individuals Congress sought to target in passing the AUMF. We conclude that detention of individuals falling into the limited category we are considering, for the duration of the particular conflict in which they were captured, is so fundamental and accepted an incident to war as to be an exercise of the "necessary and appropriate force" Congress has authorized the President to use.

The capture and detention of lawful combatants and the capture, detention, and trial of unlawful combatants, by "universal agreement and practice," are "important incident[s] of war." *Ex parte Quirin.* The purpose of detention is to prevent captured individuals from returning to the field of battle and taking up arms once again. [I]t is of no moment that the AUMF does not use specific language of detention. Because detention to prevent a combatant's return to the battlefield is a fundamental incident of waging war, in permitting the use of "necessary and appropriate force," Congress has clearly and unmistakably authorized detention in the narrow circumstances considered here.

Hamdi contends that the AUMF does not authorize indefinite or perpetual detention. Certainly, we agree that indefinite detention for the purpose of interrogation is not authorized. Further, we understand Congress's grant of authority for the use of "necessary and appropriate force" to include the authority to detain for the duration of the relevant conflict, and our understanding is based on longstanding law-of-war principles. If the practical circumstances of a given conflict are entirely unlike those of the conflicts that informed the development of the law of war, that understanding may unravel. But that is not the situation we face as of this date. Active combat operations against Taliban fighters apparently are ongoing in Afghanistan. The United States may detain, for the duration of these hostilities, individuals legitimately determined to be Taliban combatants who "engaged in an armed conflict against the United States." If the record establishes that United States troops are still involved in active combat in Afghanistan, those detentions are part of the exercise of "necessary and appropriate force," and therefore are authorized by the AUMF.

Ex parte Milligan (1866) does not undermine our holding about the Government's authority to seize enemy combatants, as we define that term today. In that case, the Court made repeated reference to the fact that its inquiry into whether the military tribunal had jurisdiction to try and punish Milligan turned in large part on the fact that Milligan was not a prisoner of war, but a resident of Indiana arrested while at home there. That fact was central to its conclusion. Had Milligan been captured while he was assisting Confederate soldiers by carrying a rifle against Union troops on a Confederate battlefield, the holding of the Court might well have been different. The Court's repeated explanations that Milligan was not a prisoner of war suggest that had these different circumstances been present he could have been detained under military authority for the duration of the conflict, whether or not he was a citizen.[24]

---

24. Here the basis asserted for detention by the military is that Hamdi was carrying a weapon against American troops on a foreign battlefield; that is, that he was an enemy combatant. The legal category of enemy combatant has not been elaborated upon in great detail. The permissible bounds of the category will be defined by the lower courts as subsequent cases are presented to them. [Footnote by the Court.]

III

Even in cases in which the detention of enemy combatants is legally authorized, there remains the question of what process is constitutionally due to a citizen who disputes his enemy-combatant status. Hamdi argues that he is owed a meaningful and timely hearing and that "extra-judicial detention [that] begins and ends with the submission of an affidavit based on third-hand hearsay" does not comport with the Fifth and Fourteenth Amendments. The Government counters that any more process than was provided below would be both unworkable and "constitutionally intolerable." Our resolution of this dispute requires a careful examination both of the writ of habeas corpus, which Hamdi now seeks to employ as a mechanism of judicial review, and of the Due Process Clause, which informs the procedural contours of that mechanism in this instance.

A

Though they reach radically different conclusions on the process that ought to attend the present proceeding, the parties begin on common ground. All agree that, absent suspension, the writ of habeas corpus remains available to every individual detained within the United States. Only in the rarest of circumstances has Congress seen fit to suspend the writ. All agree suspension of the writ has not occurred here. Thus, it is undisputed that Hamdi was properly before an Article III court to challenge his detention.

First, the Government urges the adoption of the Fourth Circuit's holding below — that because it is "undisputed" that Hamdi's seizure took place in a combat zone, the habeas determination can be made purely as a matter of law, with no further hearing or factfinding necessary. This argument is easily rejected. As the dissenters from the denial of rehearing en banc noted, the circumstances surrounding Hamdi's seizure cannot in any way be characterized as "undisputed," as "those circumstances are neither conceded in fact, nor susceptible to concession in law, because Hamdi has not been permitted to speak for himself or even through counsel as to those circumstances." Further, the "facts" that constitute the alleged concession are insufficient to support Hamdi's detention. Under the definition of enemy combatant that we accept today as falling within the scope of Congress's authorization, Hamdi would need to be "part of or supporting forces hostile to the United States or coalition partners" and "engaged in an armed conflict against the United States" to justify his detention in the United States for the duration of the relevant conflict. The habeas petition states only that "[w]hen seized by the United States Government, Mr. Hamdi resided in Afghanistan." An assertion that one *resided* in a country in which combat operations are taking place is not a concession that one was "*captured* in a zone of active combat operations in a foreign theater of war," and certainly is not a concession that one was "part of or supporting forces hostile to the United States or coalition partners" and "engaged in an armed conflict against the United States." Accordingly, we reject any argument that Hamdi has made concessions that eliminate any right to further process.

The Government's second argument requires closer consideration. This is the argument that further factual exploration is unwarranted and inappropriate in light of the extraordinary constitutional interests at stake. Under the Government's most extreme rendition of this argument, "[r]espect for separation of powers and the limited institutional capabilities of courts in matters of military decision-making in connection with an ongoing conflict" ought to eliminate entirely any individual process, restricting the courts to investigating only whether legal authorization exists for the broader detention scheme. At most, the Government argues, courts should review its determination that a citizen is an enemy combatant under a very deferential "some evidence" standard. Under this review, a court would assume the accuracy of the Government's articulated basis for Hamdi's detention, as set forth in the Mobbs Declaration, and assess only whether that articulated basis was a legitimate one.

In response, Hamdi emphasizes that this Court consistently has recognized that an individual challenging his detention may not be held at the will of the Executive without recourse to some proceeding before a neutral tribunal to determine whether the Executive's asserted justifications for that detention have basis in fact and warrant in law.

Both of these positions highlight legitimate concerns. And both emphasize the tension that often exists between the autonomy that the Government asserts is necessary in order to pursue effectively a particular goal and the process that a citizen contends he is due before he is deprived of a constitutional right. The ordinary mechanism that we use for balancing such serious competing interests, and for determining the procedures that are necessary to ensure that a citizen is not "deprived of life, liberty, or property, without due process of law," is the test that we articulated in Mathews v. Eldridge (1976). *Mathews* dictates that the process due in any given instance is determined by weighing "the private interest that will be affected by the official action" against the Government's asserted interest, "including the function involved" and the burdens the Government would face in providing greater process. The *Mathews* calculus then contemplates a judicious balancing of these concerns, through an analysis of "the risk of an erroneous deprivation" of the private interest if the process were reduced and the "probable value, if any, of additional or substitute safeguards." We take each of these steps in turn.

1

It is beyond question that substantial interests lie on both sides of the scale in this case. Hamdi's "private interest . . . affected by the official action," is the most elemental of liberty interests — the interest in being free from physical detention by one's own government. Nor is the weight on this side of the *Mathews* scale offset by the circumstances of war or the accusation of treasonous behavior, for "[i]t is clear that commitment for *any* purpose constitutes a significant deprivation of liberty that requires due process protection," and at this stage in the *Mathews* calculus, we consider the interest of the *erroneously* detained individual. Indeed, as *amicus* briefs from media and relief organizations emphasize, the risk of erroneous deprivation of a citizen's liberty in the absence of sufficient process here is very real. Moreover, as critical as the Government's interest may be in detaining those who actually pose an immediate threat to the national security of the United States during ongoing international conflict, history and common sense teach us that an unchecked system of detention carries the potential to become a means for oppression and abuse of others who do not present that sort of threat. We reaffirm today the fundamental nature of a citizen's right to be free from involuntary confinement by his own government without due process of law, and we weigh the opposing governmental interests against the curtailment of liberty that such confinement entails.

2

On the other side of the scale are the weighty and sensitive governmental interests in ensuring that those who have in fact fought with the enemy during a war do not return to battle against the United States. As discussed above, the law of war and the realities of combat may render such detentions both necessary and appropriate, and our due process analysis need not blink at those realities. Without doubt, our Constitution recognizes that core strategic matters of war-making belong in the hands of those who are best positioned and most politically accountable for making them.

The Government also argues at some length that its interests in reducing the process available to alleged enemy combatants are heightened by the practical difficulties that would accompany a system of trial-like process. In its view, military officers who are engaged in the serious work of waging battle would be unnecessarily and dangerously distracted by litigation half a world away, and discovery into military operations would both intrude on the sensitive secrets of national defense and result in a futile search for evidence buried under the rubble of war. To the extent that these burdens are triggered by heightened procedures, they are properly taken into account in our due process analysis.

3

Striking the proper constitutional balance here is of great importance to the Nation during this period of ongoing combat. But it is equally vital that our calculus not give short shrift to the values that this country holds dear or to the privilege that is American citizenship. It is during our most challenging and uncertain moments that our Nation's commitment to due process is most severely tested; and it is in those times that we must preserve our commitment at home to the principles for which we fight abroad.

We therefore hold that a citizen-detainee seeking to challenge his classification as an enemy combatant must receive notice of the factual basis for his classification, and a fair opportunity to rebut the Government's factual assertions before a neutral decision maker. These essential constitutional promises may not be eroded.

At the same time, the exigencies of the circumstances may demand that, aside from these core elements, enemy-combatant proceedings may be tailored to alleviate their uncommon potential to burden the Executive at a time of ongoing military conflict. Hearsay, for example, may need to be accepted as the most reliable available evidence from the Government in such a proceeding. Likewise, the Constitution would not be offended by a presumption in favor of the Government's evidence, so long as that presumption remained a rebuttable one and fair opportunity for rebuttal were provided. Thus, once the Government puts forth credible evidence that the habeas petitioner meets the enemy-combatant criteria, the onus could shift to the petitioner to rebut that evidence with more persuasive evidence that he falls outside the criteria. A burden-shifting scheme of this sort would meet the goal of ensuring that the errant tourist, embedded journalist, or local aid worker has a chance to prove military error while giving due regard to the Executive once it has put forth meaningful support for its conclusion that the detainee is in fact an enemy combatant. In the words of *Mathews*, process of this sort would sufficiently address the "risk of erroneous deprivation" of a detainee's liberty interest while eliminating certain procedures that have questionable additional value in light of the burden on the Government.

We think it unlikely that this basic process will have the dire impact on the central functions of warmaking that the Government forecasts. The parties agree that initial captures on the battlefield need not receive the process we have discussed here; that process is due only when the determination is made to *continue* to hold those who have been seized.

D

In so holding, we necessarily reject the Government's assertion that separation of powers principles mandate a heavily circumscribed role for the courts in such circumstances. Indeed, the position that the courts must forgo any examination of the individual case and focus exclusively on the legality of the broader detention scheme cannot be mandated by any reasonable view of separation of powers, as this approach serves only to *condense* power into a single branch of government. We have long since made clear that a state of war is not a blank check for the President when it comes to the rights of the Nation's citizens. Whatever power the United States Constitution envisions for the Executive in its exchanges with other nations or with enemy organizations in times of conflict, it most assuredly envisions a role for all three branches when individual liberties are at stake. Thus, while we do not question that our due process assessment must pay keen attention to the particular burdens faced by the Executive in the context of military action, it would turn our system of checks and balances on its head to suggest that a citizen could not make his way to court with a challenge to the factual basis for his detention by his government, simply because the Executive opposes making available such a challenge. Absent suspension of the writ by Congress, a citizen detained as an enemy combatant is entitled to this process.

Because we conclude that due process demands some system for a citizen detainee to refute his classification, the proposed "some evidence" standard is inadequate. Any process in which the Executive's factual assertions go wholly unchallenged or are simply presumed correct without any opportunity for the alleged combatant to demonstrate otherwise falls constitutionally short.

Justice SOUTER, with whom Justice GINSBURG joins, concurring in part, dissenting in part, and concurring in the judgment.

The plurality accept[s] the Government's position that if Hamdi's designation as an enemy combatant is correct, his detention (at least as to some period) is authorized by an Act of Congress as required by §4001(a), that is, by the Authorization for Use of Military Force. Here, I disagree and respectfully dissent. The Government has failed to demonstrate that the Force Resolution authorizes the detention complained of here even on the facts the Government claims. If the Government raises nothing further than the record now shows, the Non-Detention Act entitles Hamdi to be released.

[I]

The threshold issue is how broadly or narrowly to read the Non-Detention Act, the tone of which is severe: "No citizen shall be imprisoned or otherwise detained by the United States except pursuant to an Act of Congress." Should the severity of the Act be relieved when the Government's stated factual justification for incommunicado detention is a war on terrorism, so that the Government may be said to act "pursuant" to congressional terms that fall short of explicit authority to imprison individuals? With one possible though important qualification, the answer has to be no. For a number of reasons, the prohibition within §4001(a) has to be read broadly to accord the statute a long reach and to impose a burden of justification on the Government.

First, the circumstances in which the Act was adopted point the way to this interpretation. The provision superseded a cold-war statute, the Emergency Detention Act of 1950, which had authorized the Attorney General, in time of emergency, to detain anyone reasonably thought likely to engage in espionage or sabotage. That statute was repealed in 1971 out of fear that it could authorize a repetition of the World War II internment of citizens of Japanese ancestry; Congress meant to preclude another episode like the one described in Korematsu v. United States (1944). The fact that Congress intended to guard against a repetition of the World War II internments when it repealed the 1950 statute and gave us §4001(a) provides a powerful reason to think that §4001(a) was meant to require clear congressional authorization before any citizen can be placed in a cell. Congress's understanding of the need for clear authority before citizens are kept detained is itself therefore clear, and §4001(a) must be read to have teeth in its demand for congressional authorization.

Finally, even if history had spared us the cautionary example of the internments in World War II, there would be a compelling reason to read §4001(a) to demand manifest authority to detain before detention is authorized. The defining character of American constitutional government is its constant tension between security and liberty, serving both by partial helpings of each. In a government of separated powers, deciding finally on what is a reasonable degree of guaranteed liberty whether in peace or war (or some condition in between) is not well entrusted to the Executive Branch of Government, whose particular responsibility is to maintain security. For reasons of inescapable human nature, the branch of the Government asked to counter a serious threat is not the branch on which to rest the Nation's entire reliance in striking the balance between the will to win and the cost in liberty on the way to victory; the responsibility for security will naturally amplify the claim that security legitimately raises. A reasonable balance is more likely to be reached on the judgment of a different branch, just as Madison said in remarking that "the constant aim is to divide and arrange the several offices in such a manner as that each may be a check on the other — that the private interest of every individual may be a sentinel over the public rights." The Federalist No. 51. Hence the need for an assessment by Congress before citizens are subject to lockup, and likewise the need for a clearly expressed congressional resolution of the competing claims.

Since the Government has given no reason either to deflect the application of §4001(a) or to hold it to be satisfied, I need to go no further; the Government hints of a constitutional challenge to the statute, but it presents none here. I will, however, stray across the line between statutory and constitutional territory just far enough to note the weakness of the Government's mixed claim of inherent, extrastatutory authority under a combination of Article II of the Constitution and the usages of war. It is in fact in this connection that the Government developed its argument that the exercise of war powers justifies the detention, and what I have just said about its inadequacy applies here as well. Beyond that, it is instructive to recall Justice Jackson's observation that the President is not Commander in Chief of the country, only of the military. Youngstown Sheet & Tube Co. v. Sawyer (1952) (concurring opinion) (presidential authority is "at its lowest ebb" where the President acts contrary to congressional will).

There may be room for one qualification to Justice Jackson's statement, however: in a moment of genuine emergency, when the Government must act with no time for deliberation, the Executive may be able to detain a citizen if there is reason to fear he is an imminent threat to the safety of the Nation and its people (though I doubt there is any want of statutory authority). This case, however, does not present that question, because an emergency power of necessity must at least be limited by the emergency; Hamdi has been locked up for over two years.

Whether insisting on the careful scrutiny of emergency claims or on a vigorous reading of §4001(a), we are heirs to a tradition given voice 800 years ago by Magna Carta, which, on the barons' insistence, confined executive power by "the law of the land."

[II]

Because I find Hamdi's detention forbidden by §4001(a) and unauthorized by the Force Resolution, I would not reach any questions of what process he may be due in litigating disputed issues in a proceeding under the habeas statute or prior to the habeas enquiry itself. For me, it suffices that the Government has failed to justify holding him in the absence of a further Act of Congress, criminal charges, a showing that the detention conforms to the laws of war, or a demonstration that §4001(a) is unconstitutional.

Since this disposition does not command a majority of the Court, however, the need to give practical effect to the conclusions of eight members of the Court rejecting the Government's position calls for me to join with the plurality in ordering remand on terms closest to those I would impose. Although I think litigation of Hamdi's status as an enemy combatant is unnecessary, the terms of the plurality's remand will allow Hamdi to offer evidence that he is not an enemy combatant, and he should at the least have the benefit of that opportunity.

Justice SCALIA, with whom Justice STEVENS joins, dissenting.

Petitioner, a presumed American citizen, has been imprisoned without charge or hearing in the Norfolk and Charleston Naval Brigs for more than two years, on the allegation that he is an enemy combatant who bore arms against his country for the Taliban. His father claims to the contrary, that he is an inexperienced aid worker caught in the wrong place at the wrong time. This case brings into conflict the competing demands of national security and our citizens' constitutional right to personal liberty. Although I share the Court's evident unease as it seeks to reconcile the two, I do not agree with its resolution.

Where the Government accuses a citizen of waging war against it, our constitutional tradition has been to prosecute him in federal court for treason or some other crime. Where the exigencies of war prevent that, the Constitution's Suspension Clause, Art. I, §9, cl. 2, allows Congress to relax the usual protections temporarily. Absent suspension, however, the Executive's assertion of military exigency has not been thought sufficient to permit detention without charge. No one contends that the congressional Authorization for Use of Military Force, on which the Government relies to justify its actions here, is an implementation of the Suspension Clause. Accordingly, I would reverse the decision below.

The very core of liberty secured by our Anglo-Saxon system of separated powers has been freedom from indefinite imprisonment at the will of the Executive. The allegations here, of course, are no ordinary accusations of criminal activity. Yaser Esam Hamdi has been imprisoned because the Government believes he participated in the waging of war against the United States. The relevant question, then, is whether there is a different, special procedure for imprisonment of a citizen accused of wrongdoing *by aiding the enemy in wartime.*

Justice O'Connor, writing for a plurality of this Court, asserts that captured enemy combatants (other than those suspected of war crimes) have traditionally been detained until the cessation of hostilities and then released. That is probably an accurate description of wartime practice with respect to enemy *aliens.* The tradition with respect to American citizens, however, has been quite different. Citizens aiding the enemy have been treated as traitors subject to the criminal process.

There are times when military exigency renders resort to the traditional criminal process impracticable. English law accommodated such exigencies by allowing legislative suspension of the writ of habeas corpus for brief periods. Our Federal Constitution contains a provision explicitly permitting suspension, but limiting the situations in which it may be invoked: "The privilege of the Writ of Habeas Corpus shall not be suspended, unless when in Cases of Rebellion or Invasion the public Safety may require it." The Suspension Clause was by design a safety valve, the Constitution's only "express provision for exercise of extraordinary authority because of a crisis."

Several limitations give my views in this matter a relatively narrow compass. They apply only to citizens, accused of being enemy combatants, who are detained within the territorial jurisdiction of a federal court. This is not likely to be a numerous group; currently we know of only two, Hamdi and Jose Padilla. Where the citizen is captured outside and held outside the United States, the constitutional requirements may be different. Moreover, even within the United States, the accused citizen-enemy combatant may lawfully be detained once prosecution is in progress or in contemplation. The Government has been notably successful in securing conviction, and hence long-term custody or execution, of those who have waged war against the state.

I frankly do not know whether these tools are sufficient to meet the Government's security needs, including the need to obtain intelligence through interrogation. It is far beyond my competence, or the Court's competence, to determine that. But it is not beyond Congress's. If the situation demands it, the Executive can ask Congress to authorize suspension of the writ—which can be made subject to whatever conditions Congress deems appropriate, including even the procedural novelties invented by the plurality today. To be sure, suspension is limited by the Constitution to cases of rebellion or invasion. But whether the attacks of September 11, 2001, constitute an "invasion," and whether those attacks still justify suspension several years later, are questions for Congress rather than this Court. If civil rights are to be curtailed during wartime, it must be done openly and democratically, as the Constitution requires, rather than by silent erosion through an opinion of this Court.

Justice THOMAS, dissenting.

The Executive Branch, acting pursuant to the powers vested in the President by the Constitution and with explicit congressional approval, has determined that Yaser Hamdi is an enemy combatant and should be detained. This detention falls squarely within the Federal Government's war powers, and we lack the expertise and capacity to second-guess that decision. As such, petitioner's habeas challenge should fail, and there is no reason to remand the case. The plurality reaches a contrary conclusion by failing adequately to consider basic principles of the constitutional structure as it relates to national security and foreign affairs and by using the balancing scheme of Mathews v. Eldridge (1976). I do not think that the Federal Government's war powers can be balanced away by this Court. Arguably, Congress could provide for additional procedural protections, but until it does, we have no right to insist upon them. But even if I were to agree with the general approach the plurality takes, I could not accept the particulars. The plurality utterly fails to account for the Government's compelling interests and for our own institutional inability to weigh competing concerns correctly. I respectfully dissent.

Although the President very well may have inherent authority to detain those arrayed against our troops, I agree with the plurality that we need not decide that question because Congress has authorized the President to do so. The Authorization for Use of Military Force (AUMF) authorizes the President to "use all necessary and appropriate force against those nations, organizations, or persons he determines planned, authorized, committed, or aided the terrorist attacks" of September 11, 2001. But I do not think that the plurality has adequately explained the breadth of the President's authority to detain enemy combatants, an authority that includes making virtually conclusive factual findings. In my view, the structural considerations discussed above, as recognized in our precedent, demonstrate that we lack the capacity and responsibility to second-guess this determination.

The Government's asserted authority to detain an individual that the President has determined to be an enemy combatant, at least while hostilities continue, comports with the Due Process Clause. As these cases also show, the Executive's decision that a detention is necessary to protect the public need not and should not be subjected to judicial second-guessing. Indeed, at least in the context of enemy-combatant determinations, this would defeat the unity, secrecy, and dispatch that the Founders believed to be so important to the warmaking function.

Accordingly, I conclude that the Government's detention of Hamdi as an enemy combatant does not violate the Constitution. By detaining Hamdi, the President, in the prosecution of a war and authorized by Congress, has acted well within his authority. Hamdi thereby received all the process to which he was due under the circumstances. I therefore believe that this is no occasion to balance the competing interests, as the plurality unconvincingly attempts to do.

Undeniably, Hamdi has been deprived of a serious interest, one actually protected by the Due Process Clause. Against this, however, is the Government's overriding interest in protecting the Nation. If a deprivation of liberty can be justified by the need to protect a town, the protection of the Nation, *a fortiori*, justifies it.

In October 2006, Congress passed and President Bush signed the Military Commission Act of 2006. Among other things, the act provides that noncitizens held as enemy combatants shall not have access to federal court via a writ of habeas corpus. Instead, they must go through military proceedings and then seek review in the United States Court of Appeals for the District of Columbia Circuit. The D.C. Circuit is limited to hearing claims under the Constitution and federal statutes; it cannot hear claims under treaties such as the Geneva Accords. The Military Commission Act creates express statutory authority for military commissions and defines their procedures.

Boumediene v. Bush held that the denial of access to habeas corpus is an unconstitutional suspension of the writ of habeas corpus. Underlying the majority and the dissenting opinions are very different views about the appropriate role of the judiciary in the war on terror.

BOUMEDIENE v. BUSH
553 U.S. 723 (2008)

Justice KENNEDY delivered the opinion of the Court.

Petitioners are aliens designated as enemy combatants and detained at the United States Naval Station at Guantanamo Bay, Cuba. There are others detained there, also aliens, who are not parties to this suit.

Petitioners present a question not resolved by our earlier cases relating to the detention of aliens at Guantanamo: whether they have the constitutional privilege of habeas corpus, a privilege not to be withdrawn except in conformance with the Suspension Clause, Art. I, §9, cl. 2. We hold these petitioners do have the habeas corpus privilege. Congress has enacted a statute, the Detainee Treatment Act of 2005 (DTA), that provides certain procedures for review of the detainees' status. We hold that those procedures are not an adequate and effective substitute for habeas corpus. Therefore §7 of the Military Commissions Act of 2006 (MCA) operates as an unconstitutional suspension of the writ. We do not address whether the President has authority to detain these petitioners nor do we hold that the writ must issue. These and other questions regarding the legality of the detention are to be resolved in the first instance by the District Court.

I

Under the Authorization for Use of Military Force (AUMF), the President is authorized "to use all necessary and appropriate force against those nations, organizations, or persons he determines planned, authorized, committed, or aided the terrorist attacks that occurred on September 11, 2001, or harbored such organizations or persons, in order to prevent any future acts of international terrorism against the United States by such nations, organizations or persons."

In Hamdi v. Rumsfeld (2004), five Members of the Court recognized that detention of individuals who fought against the United States in Afghanistan "for the duration of the particular conflict in which they were captured, is so fundamental and accepted an incident to war as to be an exercise of the 'necessary and appropriate force' Congress has authorized the President to use." After *Hamdi*, the Deputy Secretary of Defense established Combatant Status Review Tribunals (CSRTs) to determine whether individuals detained at Guantanamo were "enemy combatants," as the Department defines that term. A later memorandum established procedures to implement the CSRTs. The Government maintains these procedures were designed to comply with the due process requirements identified by the plurality in *Hamdi*.

Interpreting the AUMF, the Department of Defense ordered the detention of these petitioners, and they were transferred to Guantanamo. Some of these individuals were apprehended on the battlefield in Afghanistan, others in places as far away from there as Bosnia and Gambia. All are foreign nationals, but none is a citizen of a nation now at war with the United States. Each denies he is a member of the al Qaeda terrorist network that carried out the September 11 attacks or of the Taliban regime that provided sanctuary for al Qaeda. Each petitioner appeared before a separate CSRT; was determined to be an enemy combatant; and has sought a writ of habeas corpus in the United States District Court for the District of Columbia.

The first actions commenced in February 2002. We granted certiorari and reversed, holding that 28 U.S.C. §2241 extended statutory habeas corpus jurisdiction to Guantanamo. See Rasul v. Bush (2004). After *Rasul*, petitioners' cases were consolidated and entertained in two separate proceedings. In the first set of cases, Judge Richard J. Leon granted the Government's motion to dismiss, holding that the detainees had no rights that could be vindicated in a habeas corpus action. In the second set of cases Judge Joyce Hens Green reached the opposite conclusion, holding the detainees had rights under the Due Process Clause of the Fifth Amendment.

While appeals were pending from the District Court decisions, Congress passed the DTA. Subsection (e) of §1005 of the DTA amended 28 U.S.C. §2241 to provide that "no court, justice, or judge shall have jurisdiction to hear or consider . . . an application for a writ of habeas corpus filed by or on behalf of an alien detained by the Department of Defense at Guantanamo Bay, Cuba." Section 1005 further provides that the Court of Appeals for the District of Columbia Circuit shall have "exclusive" jurisdiction to review decisions of the CSRTs.

In Hamdan v. Rumsfeld (2006), the Court held this provision did not apply to cases (like petitioners') pending when the DTA was enacted. Congress responded by passing the MCA.

II

As a threshold matter, we must decide whether MCA §7 denies the federal courts jurisdiction to hear habeas corpus actions pending at the time of its enactment. We hold the statute does deny that jurisdiction, so that, if the statute is valid, petitioners' cases must be dismissed.

As amended by the terms of the MCA, 28 U.S.C.A. §2241(e) now provides:

> (1) No court, justice, or judge shall have jurisdiction to hear or consider an
> application for a writ of habeas corpus filed by or on behalf of an alien detained by

the United States who has been determined by the United States to have been properly detained as an enemy combatant or is awaiting such determination.

(2) Except as provided in [§1005(e)(2) and (e)(3) of the DTA] no court, justice, or judge shall have jurisdiction to hear or consider any other action against the United States or its agents relating to any aspect of the detention, transfer, treatment, trial, or conditions of confinement of an alien who is or was detained by the United States and has been determined by the United States to have been properly detained as an enemy combatant or is awaiting such determination.

Section 7(b) of the MCA provides the effective date for the amendment of §2241(e). It states: "The amendment made by [MCA §7(a)] shall take effect on the date of the enactment of this Act, and shall apply to all cases, without exception, pending on or after the date of the enactment of this Act which relate to any aspect of the detention, transfer, treatment, trial, or conditions of detention of an alien detained by the United States since September 11, 2001."

If this ongoing dialogue between and among the branches of Government is to be respected, we cannot ignore that the MCA was a direct response to *Hamdan*'s holding that the DTA's jurisdiction-stripping provision had no application to pending cases. The Court of Appeals was correct to take note of the legislative history when construing the statute, and we agree with its conclusion that the MCA deprives the federal courts of jurisdiction to entertain the habeas corpus actions now before us.

III

In deciding the constitutional questions now presented we must determine whether petitioners are barred from seeking the writ or invoking the protections of the Suspension Clause either because of their status, i.e., petitioners' designation by the Executive Branch as enemy combatants, or their physical location, i.e., their presence at Guantanamo Bay. The Government contends that noncitizens designated as enemy combatants and detained in territory located outside our Nation's borders have no constitutional rights and no privilege of habeas corpus. Petitioners contend they do have cognizable constitutional rights and that Congress, in seeking to eliminate recourse to habeas corpus as a means to assert those rights, acted in violation of the Suspension Clause.

The Framers viewed freedom from unlawful restraint as a fundamental precept of liberty, and they understood the writ of habeas corpus as a vital instrument to secure that freedom. Experience taught, however, that the common-law writ all too often had been insufficient to guard against the abuse of monarchial power. That history counseled the necessity for specific language in the Constitution to secure the writ and ensure its place in our legal system.

That the Framers considered the writ a vital instrument for the protection of individual liberty is evident from the care taken to specify the limited grounds for its suspension: "The Privilege of the Writ of Habeas Corpus shall not be suspended, unless when in Cases of Rebellion or Invasion the public Safety may require it." Art. I, §9, cl. 2. The word "privilege" was used, perhaps, to avoid mentioning some rights to the exclusion of others. (Indeed, the only mention of the term "right" in the Constitution, as ratified, is in its clause giving Congress the power to protect the rights of authors and inventors. See Art. I, §8, cl. 8.) Surviving accounts of the ratification debates provide additional evidence that the Framers deemed the writ to be an essential mechanism in the separation-of-powers scheme.

In our own system the Suspension Clause is designed to protect against these cyclical abuses. The Clause protects the rights of the detained by a means consistent with the essential design of the Constitution. It ensures that, except during periods of formal suspension, the Judiciary will have a time-tested device, the writ, to maintain the "delicate balance of governance" that is itself the surest safeguard of liberty. The Clause protects the rights of the detained by affirming the duty and authority of the Judiciary to call the jailer to account.

IV

Drawing from its position that at common law the writ ran only to territories over which the Crown was sovereign, the Government says the Suspension Clause affords petitioners no rights because the United States does not claim sovereignty over the place of detention.

Guantanamo Bay is not formally part of the United States. And under the terms of the lease between the United States and Cuba, Cuba retains "ultimate sovereignty" over the territory while the United States exercises "complete jurisdiction and control." Under the terms of the 1934 Treaty, however, Cuba effectively has no rights as a sovereign until the parties agree to modification of the 1903 Lease Agreement or the United States abandons the base.

The United States contends, nevertheless, that Guantanamo is not within its sovereign control. This was the Government's position well before the events of September 11, 2001. And in other contexts the Court has held that questions of sovereignty are for the political branches to decide. Even if this were a treaty interpretation case that did not involve a political question, the President's construction of the lease agreement would be entitled to great respect.

We therefore do not question the Government's position that Cuba, not the United States, maintains sovereignty, in the legal and technical sense of the term, over Guantanamo Bay. But this does not end the analysis. Our cases do not hold it is improper for us to inquire into the objective degree of control the Nation asserts over foreign territory. Accordingly, for purposes of our analysis, we accept the Government's position that Cuba, and not the United States, retains de jure sovereignty over Guantanamo Bay. As we did in *Rasul*, however, we take notice of the obvious and uncontested fact that the United States, by virtue of its complete jurisdiction and control over the base, maintains de facto sovereignty over this territory.

Were we to hold that the present cases turn on the political question doctrine, we would be required first to accept the Government's premise that de jure sovereignty is the touchstone of habeas corpus jurisdiction. This premise, however, is unfounded. For the reasons indicated above, the history of common-law habeas corpus provides scant support for this proposition; and, for the reasons indicated below, that position would be inconsistent with our precedents and contrary to fundamental separation-of-powers principles.

A

The Court has discussed the issue of the Constitution's extraterritorial application on many occasions. These decisions undermine the Government's argument that, at least as applied to noncitizens, the Constitution necessarily stops where de jure sovereignty ends.

Practical considerations weighed heavily as well in Johnson v. Eisentrager (1950), where the Court addressed whether habeas corpus jurisdiction extended to enemy aliens who had been convicted of violating the laws of war. The prisoners were detained at Landsberg Prison in Germany during the Allied Powers' postwar occupation. The Court stressed the difficulties of ordering the Government to produce the prisoners in a habeas corpus proceeding. It "would require allocation of shipping space, guarding personnel, billeting and rations" and would damage the prestige of military commanders at a sensitive time.

True, the Court in *Eisentrager* denied access to the writ, and it noted the prisoners "at no relevant time were within any territory over which the United States is sovereign, and [that] the scenes of their offense, their capture, their trial and their punishment were all beyond the territorial jurisdiction of any court of the United States." The Government seizes upon this language as proof positive that the *Eisentrager* Court adopted a formalistic, sovereignty-based test for determining the reach of the Suspension Clause. We reject this reading for three reasons.

First, we do not accept the idea that the above-quoted passage from *Eisentrager* is the only authoritative language in the opinion and that all the rest is dicta. The Court's further determinations, based on practical considerations, were integral to Part II of its opinion and came before the decision announced its holding.

Second, because the United States lacked both de jure sovereignty and plenary control over Landsberg Prison, it is far from clear that the *Eisentrager* Court used the term sovereignty only in the narrow technical sense and not to connote the degree of control the military asserted over the facility. The Justices who decided *Eisentrager* would have understood sovereignty as a multifaceted concept. That the Court devoted a significant portion of Part II to a discussion of practical barriers to the running of the writ suggests that the Court was not concerned exclusively with the formal legal status of Landsberg Prison but also with the objective degree of control the United States asserted over it. Even if we assume the *Eisentrager* Court considered the United States' lack of formal legal sovereignty over Landsberg Prison as the decisive factor in that case, its holding is not inconsistent with a functional approach to questions of extraterritoriality. The formal legal status of a given territory affects, at least to some extent, the political branches' control over that territory. De jure sovereignty is a factor that bears upon which constitutional guarantees apply there.

Third, if the Government's reading of *Eisentrager* were correct, the opinion would have marked not only a change in, but a complete repudiation of, the Insular Cases' functional approach to questions of extraterritoriality. We cannot accept the Government's view. Nothing in *Eisentrager* says that de jure sovereignty is or has ever been the only relevant consideration in determining the geographic reach of the Constitution or of habeas corpus.

B

The Government's formal sovereignty-based test raises troubling separation-of-powers concerns as well. The political history of Guantanamo illustrates the deficiencies of this approach. The United States has maintained complete and uninterrupted control of the bay for over 100 years. Yet the Government's view is that the Constitution had no effect there, at least as to noncitizens, because the United States disclaimed sovereignty in the formal sense of the term. The necessary implication of the argument is that by surrendering formal sovereignty over any unincorporated territory to a third party, while at the same time entering into a lease that grants total control over the territory back to the United States, it would be possible for the political branches to govern without legal constraint.

Our basic charter cannot be contracted away like this. Even when the United States acts outside its borders, its powers are not "absolute and unlimited" but are subject "to such restrictions as are expressed in the Constitution." Abstaining from questions involving formal sovereignty and territorial governance is one thing. To hold the political branches have the power to switch the Constitution on or off at will is quite another. The former position reflects this Court's recognition that certain matters requiring political judgments are best left to the political branches. The latter would permit a striking anomaly in our tripartite system of government, leading to a regime in which Congress and the President, not this Court, say "what the law is." Marbury v. Madison (1803).

These concerns have particular bearing upon the Suspension Clause question in the cases now before us, for the writ of habeas corpus is itself an indispensable mechanism for monitoring the separation of powers. The test for determining the scope of this provision must not be subject to manipulation by those whose power it is designed to restrain.

C

In addition to the practical concerns discussed above, the *Eisentrager* Court found relevant that each petitioner:

> (a) is an enemy alien; (b) has never been or resided in the United States; (c) was captured outside of our territory and there held in military custody as a prisoner of war; (d) was tried and convicted by a Military Commission sitting outside the United States; (e) for offenses against laws of war committed outside the United States; (f) and is at all times imprisoned outside the United States.

Based on this language from *Eisentrager*, and the reasoning in our other extra-territoriality opinions, we conclude that at least three factors are relevant in determining the reach of the Suspension Clause: (1) the citizenship and status of the detainee and the adequacy of the process through which that status determination was made; (2) the nature of the sites where apprehension and then detention took place; and (3) the practical obstacles inherent in resolving the prisoner's entitlement to the writ.

Applying this framework, we note at the onset that the status of these detainees is a matter of dispute. The petitioners, like those in *Eisentrager*, are not American citizens. But the petitioners in *Eisentrager* did not contest, it seems, the Court's assertion that they were "enemy alien[s]." In the instant cases, by contrast, the detainees deny they are enemy combatants. They have been afforded some process in CSRT proceedings to determine their status; but, unlike in *Eisentrager*, there has been no trial by military commission for violations of the laws of war. The difference is not trivial. The records from the *Eisentrager* trials suggest that, well before the petitioners brought their case to this Court, there had been a rigorous adversarial process to test the legality of their detention. The *Eisentrager* petitioners were charged by a bill of particulars that made detailed factual allegations against them. To rebut the accusations, they were entitled to representation by counsel, allowed to introduce evidence on their own behalf, and permitted to cross-examine the prosecution's witnesses.

In comparison the procedural protections afforded to the detainees in the CSRT hearings are far more limited, and, we conclude, fall well short of the procedures and adversarial mechanisms that would eliminate the need for habeas corpus review. Although the detainee is assigned a "Personal Representative" to assist him during CSRT proceedings, the Secretary of the Navy's memorandum makes clear that person is not the detainee's lawyer or even his "advocate." The Government's evidence is accorded a presumption of validity. The detainee is allowed to present "reasonably available" evidence, but his ability to rebut the Government's evidence against him is limited by the circumstances of his confinement and his lack of counsel at this stage. And although the detainee can seek review of his status determination in the Court of Appeals, that review process cannot cure all defects in the earlier proceedings.

As to the second factor relevant to this analysis, the detainees here are similarly situated to the *Eisentrager* petitioners in that the sites of their apprehension and detention are technically outside the sovereign territory of the United States. As noted earlier, this is a factor that weighs against finding they have rights under the Suspension Clause. But there are critical differences between Landsberg Prison, circa 1950, and the United States Naval Station at Guantanamo Bay in 2008. Unlike its present control over the naval station, the United States' control over the prison in Germany was neither absolute nor indefinite. Like all parts of occupied Germany, the prison was under the jurisdiction of the combined Allied Forces. Guantanamo Bay, on the other hand, is no transient possession. In every practical sense Guantanamo is not abroad; it is within the constant jurisdiction of the United States.

As to the third factor, we recognize, as the Court did in *Eisentrager*, that there are costs to holding the Suspension Clause applicable in a case of military detention abroad. Habeas corpus proceedings may require expenditure of funds by the Government and may divert the attention of military personnel from other pressing tasks. While we are sensitive to these concerns, we do not find them dispositive. Compliance with any judicial process requires some incremental expenditure of resources. Yet civilian courts and the Armed Forces have functioned along side each other at various points in our history. The Government presents no credible arguments that the military mission at Guantanamo would be compromised if habeas corpus courts had jurisdiction to hear the detainees' claims. And in light of the plenary control the United States asserts over the base, none are apparent to us.

The situation in *Eisentrager* was far different, given the historical context and nature of the military's mission in post-War Germany. When hostilities in the European Theater came to an end, the United States became responsible for an occupation zone encompassing over 57,000 square miles with a population of 18 million. In addition to supervising massive reconstruction and aid efforts the American forces stationed in Germany faced potential security threats from a defeated enemy. In retrospect the post-War occupation may seem uneventful. But at the time *Eisentrager* was decided, the Court was right to be concerned about judicial interference with the military's efforts to contain "enemy elements, guerilla fighters, and 'were-wolves.'"

Similar threats are not apparent here; nor does the Government argue that they are. The United States Naval Station at Guantanamo Bay consists of 45 square miles of land and water. The base has been used, at various points, to house migrants and refugees temporarily. At present, however, other than the detainees themselves, the only long-term residents are American military personnel, their families, and a small number of workers. The detainees have been deemed enemies of the United States. At present, dangerous as they may be if released, they are contained in a secure prison facility located on an isolated and heavily fortified military base.

There is no indication, furthermore, that adjudicating a habeas corpus petition would cause friction with the host government. No Cuban court has jurisdiction over American military personnel at Guantanamo or the enemy combatants detained there. While obligated to abide by the terms of the lease, the United States is, for all practical purposes, answerable to no other sovereign for its acts on the base. Were that not the case, or if the detention facility were located in an active theater of war, arguments that issuing the writ would be "impracticable or anomalous" would have more weight. Under the facts presented here, however, there are few practical barriers to the running of the writ. To the extent barriers arise, habeas corpus procedures likely can be modified to address them.

We hold that Art. I, §9, cl. 2, of the Constitution has full effect at Guantanamo Bay. If the privilege of habeas corpus is to be denied to the detainees now before us, Congress must act in accordance with the requirements of the Suspension Clause.

V

In light of this holding the question becomes whether the statute stripping jurisdiction to issue the writ avoids the Suspension Clause mandate because Congress has provided adequate substitute procedures for habeas corpus.

The gravity of the separation-of-powers issues raised by these cases and the fact that these detainees have been denied meaningful access to a judicial forum for a period of years render these cases exceptional.

Our case law does not contain extensive discussion of standards defining suspension of the writ or of circumstances under which suspension has occurred. This simply confirms the care Congress has taken throughout our Nation's history to preserve the writ and its function. Indeed, most of the major legislative enactments pertaining to habeas corpus have acted not to contract the writ's protection but to expand it or to hasten resolution of prisoners' claims.

We do not endeavor to offer a comprehensive summary of the requisites for an adequate substitute for habeas corpus. We do consider it uncontroversial, however, that the privilege of habeas corpus entitles the prisoner to a meaningful opportunity to demonstrate that he is being held pursuant to "the erroneous application or interpretation" of relevant law. And the habeas court must have the power to order the conditional release of an individual unlawfully detained—though release need not be the exclusive remedy and is not the appropriate one in every case in which the writ is granted.

Where a person is detained by executive order, rather than, say, after being tried and convicted in a court, the need for collateral review is most pressing.

A criminal conviction in the usual course occurs after a judicial hearing before a tribunal disinterested in the outcome and committed to procedures designed to ensure its own independence. These dynamics are not inherent in executive detention orders or executive review procedures. In this context the need for habeas corpus is more urgent. The intended duration of the detention and the reasons for it bear upon the precise scope of the inquiry. Habeas corpus proceedings need not resemble a criminal trial, even when the detention is by executive order. But the writ must be effective. The habeas court must have sufficient authority to conduct a meaningful review of both the cause for detention and the Executive's power to detain.

To determine the necessary scope of habeas corpus review, therefore, we must assess the CSRT process, the mechanism through which petitioners' designation as enemy combatants became final. Whether one characterizes the CSRT process as direct review of the Executive's battlefield determination that the detainee is an enemy combatant—as the parties have and as we do—or as the first step in the collateral review of a battlefield determination makes no difference in a proper analysis of whether the procedures Congress put in place are an adequate substitute for habeas corpus. What matters is the sum total of procedural protections afforded to the detainee at all stages, direct and collateral.

Petitioners identify what they see as myriad deficiencies in the CSRTs. The most relevant for our purposes are the constraints upon the detainee's ability to rebut the factual basis for the Government's assertion that he is an enemy combatant. As already noted, at the CSRT stage the detainee has limited means to find or present evidence to challenge the Government's case against him. He does not have the assistance of counsel and may not be aware of the most critical allegations that the Government relied upon to order his detention. The detainee can confront witnesses that testify during the CSRT proceedings. But given that there are in effect no limits on the admission of hearsay evidence—the only requirement is that the tribunal deem the evidence "relevant and helpful,"—the detainee's opportunity to question witnesses is likely to be more theoretical than real.

Even if we were to assume that the CSRTs satisfy due process standards, it would not end our inquiry. Habeas corpus is a collateral process that exists, in Justice Holmes' words, to "cu[t] through all forms and g[o] to the very tissue of the structure. It comes in from the outside, not in subordination to the proceedings, and although every form may have been preserved opens the inquiry whether they have been more than an empty shell." Even when the procedures authorizing detention are structurally sound, the Suspension Clause remains applicable and the writ relevant.

Although we make no judgment as to whether the CSRTs, as currently constituted, satisfy due process standards, we agree with petitioners that, even when all the parties involved in this process act with diligence and in good faith, there is considerable risk of error in the tribunal's findings of fact. And given that the consequence of error may be detention of persons for the duration of hostilities that may last a generation or more, this is a risk too significant to ignore.

For the writ of habeas corpus, or its substitute, to function as an effective and proper remedy in this context, the court that conducts the habeas proceeding must have the means to correct errors that occurred during the CSRT proceedings. This includes some authority to assess the sufficiency of the Government's evidence against the detainee. It also must have the authority to admit and consider relevant exculpatory evidence that was not introduced during the earlier proceeding. Federal habeas petitioners long have had the means to supplement the record on review, even in the postconviction habeas setting. Here that opportunity is constitutionally required.

The extent of the showing required of the Government in these cases is a matter to be determined. We need not explore it further at this stage. We do hold that when the judicial power to issue habeas corpus properly is invoked the judicial officer must have adequate authority to make a determination in light of the relevant law and facts and to formulate and issue appropriate orders for relief, including, if necessary, an order directing the prisoner's release.

C

We now consider whether the DTA allows the Court of Appeals to conduct a proceeding meeting these standards. The DTA does not explicitly empower the Court of Appeals to order the applicant in a DTA review proceeding released should the court find that the standards and procedures used at his CSRT hearing were insufficient to justify detention. This is troubling. Yet, for present purposes, we can assume congressional silence permits a constitutionally required remedy. The absence of a release remedy and specific language allowing AUMF challenges are not the only constitutional infirmities from which the statute potentially suffers, however. The more difficult question is whether the DTA permits the Court of Appeals to make requisite findings of fact. Assuming the DTA can be construed to allow the Court of Appeals to review or correct the CSRT's factual determinations, as opposed to merely certifying that the tribunal applied the correct standard of proof, we see no way to construe the statute to allow what is also constitutionally required in this context: an opportunity for the detainee to present relevant exculpatory evidence that was not made part of the record in the earlier proceedings.

On its face the statute allows the Court of Appeals to consider no evidence outside the CSRT record.

Under the DTA the Court of Appeals has the power to review CSRT determinations by assessing the legality of standards and procedures. This implies the power to inquire into what happened at the CSRT hearing and, perhaps, to remedy certain deficiencies in that proceeding. But should the Court of Appeals determine that the CSRT followed appropriate and lawful standards and procedures, it will have reached the limits of its jurisdiction. There is no language in the DTA that can be construed to allow the Court of Appeals to admit and consider newly discovered evidence that could not have been made part of the CSRT record because it was unavailable to either the Government or the detainee when the CSRT made its findings. This evidence, however, may be critical to the detainee's argument that he is not an enemy combatant and there is no cause to detain him.

By foreclosing consideration of evidence not presented or reasonably available to the detainee at the CSRT proceedings, the DTA disadvantages the detainee by limiting the scope of collateral review to a record that may not be accurate or complete.

Although we do not hold that an adequate substitute must duplicate §2241 in all respects, it suffices that the Government has not established that the detainees' access to the statutory review provisions at issue is an adequate substitute for the writ of habeas corpus. MCA §7 thus effects an unconstitutional suspension of the writ. In view of our holding we need not discuss the reach of the writ with respect to claims of unlawful conditions of treatment or confinement.

VI

The real risks, the real threats, of terrorist attacks are constant and not likely soon to abate. The ways to disrupt our life and laws are so many and unforeseen that the Court should not attempt even some general catalogue of crises that might occur. Certain principles are apparent, however. Practical considerations and exigent circumstances inform the definition and reach of the law's writs, including habeas corpus. The cases and our tradition reflect this precept.

In cases involving foreign citizens detained abroad by the Executive, it likely would be both an impractical and unprecedented extension of judicial power to assume that habeas corpus would be available at the moment the prisoner is taken into custody. If and when habeas corpus jurisdiction applies, as it does in these cases, then proper deference can be accorded to reasonable procedures for screening and initial detention under lawful and proper conditions of confinement and treatment for a reasonable period of time. Domestic exigencies, furthermore, might also impose such onerous burdens on the Government that here, too, the Judicial Branch would be required to devise sensible rules for staying habeas corpus proceedings until the Government can comply with its requirements in a responsible way. Here, as is true with detainees apprehended abroad, a relevant consideration in determining the courts' role is whether there are suitable alternative processes in place to protect against the arbitrary exercise of governmental power.

The cases before us, however, do not involve detainees who have been held for a short period of time while awaiting their CSRT determinations. Were that the case, or were it probable that the Court of Appeals could complete a prompt review of their applications, the case for requiring temporary abstention or exhaustion of alternative remedies would be much stronger. These qualifications no longer pertain here. In some of these cases six years have elapsed without the judicial oversight that habeas corpus or an adequate substitute demands. And there has been no showing that the Executive faces such onerous burdens that it cannot respond to habeas corpus actions. To require these detainees to complete DTA review before proceeding with their habeas corpus actions would be to require additional months, if not years, of delay. The detainees in these cases are entitled to a prompt habeas corpus hearing.

Our decision today holds only that the petitioners before us are entitled to seek the writ; that the DTA review procedures are an inadequate substitute for habeas corpus; and that the petitioners in these cases need not exhaust the review procedures in the Court of Appeals before proceeding with their habeas actions in the District Court. The only law we identify as unconstitutional is MCA §7. Accordingly, both the DTA and the CSRT process remain intact. Our holding with regard to exhaustion should not be read to imply that a habeas court should intervene the moment an enemy combatant steps foot in a territory where the writ runs. The Executive is entitled to a reasonable period of time to determine a detainee's status before a court entertains that detainee's habeas corpus petition.

In considering both the procedural and substantive standards used to impose detention to prevent acts of terrorism, proper deference must be accorded to the political branches. There are further considerations, however. Security subsists, too, in fidelity to freedom's first principles. Chief among these are freedom from arbitrary and unlawful restraint and the personal liberty that is secured by adherence to the separation of powers. It is from these principles that the judicial authority to consider petitions for habeas corpus relief derives.

Our opinion does not undermine the Executive's powers as Commander in Chief. On the contrary, the exercise of those powers is vindicated, not eroded, when confirmed by the Judicial Branch. Within the Constitution's separation-of-powers structure, few exercises of judicial power are as legitimate or as necessary as the responsibility to hear challenges to the authority of the Executive to imprison a person. Some of these petitioners have been in custody for six years with no definitive judicial determination as to the legality of their detention. Their access to the writ is a necessity to determine the lawfulness of their status, even if, in the end, they do not obtain the relief they seek.

Because our Nation's past military conflicts have been of limited duration, it has been possible to leave the outer boundaries of war powers undefined. If, as some fear, terrorism continues to pose dangerous threats to us for years to come, the Court might not have this luxury. This result is not inevitable, however. The political branches, consistent with their independent obligations to interpret and uphold the Constitution, can engage in a genuine debate about how best to preserve constitutional values while protecting the Nation from terrorism.

It bears repeating that our opinion does not address the content of the law that governs petitioners' detention. That is a matter yet to be determined. We hold that petitioners may invoke the fundamental procedural protections of habeas corpus. The laws and Constitution are designed to survive, and remain in force, in extraordinary times. Liberty and security can be reconciled; and in our system they are reconciled within the framework of the law. The Framers decided that habeas corpus, a right of first importance, must be a part of that framework, a part of that law.

Justice SOUTER, with whom Justice GINSBURG and Justice BREYER join, concurring.

I join the Court's opinion in its entirety and add this afterword only to emphasize two things one might overlook after reading the dissents.

Four years ago, this Court in Rasul v. Bush (2004) held that statutory habeas jurisdiction extended to claims of foreign nationals imprisoned by the United States at Guantanamo Bay, "to determine the legality of the Executive's potentially indefinite detention" of them. Subsequent legislation eliminated the statutory habeas jurisdiction over these claims, so that now there must be constitutionally based jurisdiction or none at all. But no one who reads the Court's opinion in *Rasul* could seriously doubt that the jurisdictional question must be answered the same way in purely constitutional cases, given the Court's reliance on the historical background of habeas generally in answering the statutory question.

A second fact insufficiently appreciated by the dissents is the length of the disputed imprisonments, some of the prisoners represented here today having been locked up for six years. Hence the hollow ring when the dissenters suggest that the Court is somehow precipitating the judiciary into reviewing claims that the military (subject to appeal to the Court of Appeals for the District of Columbia Circuit) could handle within some reasonable period of time. These suggestions of judicial haste are all the more out of place given the Court's realistic acknowledgment that in periods of exigency the tempo of any habeas review must reflect the immediate peril facing the country. After six years of sustained executive detentions in Guantanamo, subject to habeas jurisdiction but without any actual habeas scrutiny, today's decision is no judicial victory, but an act of perseverance in trying to make habeas review, and the obligation of the courts to provide it, mean something of value both to prisoners and to the Nation.

Chief Justice ROBERTS, with whom Justice SCALIA, Justice THOMAS, and Justice ALITO join, dissenting.

Today the Court strikes down as inadequate the most generous set of procedural protections ever afforded aliens detained by this country as enemy combatants. The political branches crafted these procedures amidst an ongoing military conflict, after much careful investigation and thorough debate. The Court rejects them today out of hand, without bothering to say what due process rights the detainees possess, without explaining how the statute fails to vindicate those rights, and before a single petitioner has even attempted to avail himself of the law's operation. And to what effect? The majority merely replaces a review system designed by the people's representatives with a set of shapeless procedures to be defined by federal courts at some future date. One cannot help but think, after surveying the modest practical results of the majority's ambitious opinion, that this decision is not really about the detainees at all, but about control of federal policy regarding enemy combatants.

The majority is adamant that the Guantanamo detainees are entitled to the protections of habeas corpus—its opinion begins by deciding that question. I regard the issue as a difficult one, primarily because of the unique and unusual jurisdictional status of Guantanamo Bay. I nonetheless agree with Justice Scalia's analysis of our precedents and the pertinent history of the writ, and accordingly join his dissent. The important point for me, however, is that the Court should have resolved these cases on other grounds. Habeas is most fundamentally a procedural right, a mechanism for contesting the legality of executive detention. The critical threshold question in these cases, prior to any inquiry about the writ's scope, is whether the system the political branches designed protects whatever rights the detainees may possess. If so, there is no need for any additional process, whether called "habeas" or something else.

Congress entrusted that threshold question in the first instance to the Court of Appeals for the District of Columbia Circuit, as the Constitution surely allows Congress to do. But before the D.C. Circuit has addressed the issue, the Court cashiers the statute, and without answering this critical threshold question itself. The Court does eventually get around to asking whether review under the DTA is, as the Court frames it, an "adequate substitute" for habeas, but even then its opinion fails to determine what rights the detainees possess and whether the DTA system satisfies them. The majority instead compares the undefined DTA process to an equally undefined habeas right—one that is to be given shape only in the future by district courts on a case-by-case basis. This whole approach is misguided.

It is also fruitless. How the detainees' claims will be decided now that the DTA is gone is anybody's guess. But the habeas process the Court mandates will most likely end up looking a lot like the DTA system it replaces, as the district court judges shaping it will have to reconcile review of the prisoners' detention with the undoubted need to protect the American people from the terrorist threat — precisely the challenge Congress undertook in drafting the DTA. All that today's opinion has done is shift responsibility for those sensitive foreign policy and national security decisions from the elected branches to the Federal Judiciary.

I believe the system the political branches constructed adequately protects any constitutional rights aliens captured abroad and detained as enemy combatants may enjoy. I therefore would dismiss these cases on that ground. With all respect for the contrary views of the majority, I must dissent.

The majority's overreaching is particularly egregious given the weakness of its objections to the DTA. Simply put, the Court's opinion fails on its own terms. The majority strikes down the statute because it is not an "adequate substitute" for habeas review, but fails to show what rights the detainees have that cannot be vindicated by the DTA system.

The majority is equally wrong to characterize the CSRTs as part of that initial determination process. They are instead a means for detainees to challenge the Government's determination. The Executive designed the CSRTs to mirror Army Regulation 190-8, the very procedural model the plurality in *Hamdi* said provided the type of process an enemy combatant could expect from a habeas court. The CSRTs operate much as habeas courts would if hearing the detainee's collateral challenge for the first time: They gather evidence, call witnesses, take testimony, and render a decision on the legality of the Government's detention. If the CSRT finds a particular detainee has been improperly held, it can order release.

The majority insists that even if "the CSRTs satisf[ied] due process standards," full habeas review would still be necessary, because habeas is a collateral remedy available even to prisoners "detained pursuant to the most rigorous proceedings imaginable." This comment makes sense only if the CSRTs are incorrectly viewed as a method used by the Executive for determining the prisoners' status, and not as themselves part of the collateral review to test the validity of that determination. The majority can deprecate the importance of the CSRTs only by treating them as something they are not.

In short, the *Hamdi* plurality concluded that this type of review would be enough to satisfy due process, even for citizens. Congress followed the Court's lead, only to find itself the victim of a constitutional bait and switch.

Given the statutory scheme the political branches adopted, and given *Hamdi*, it simply will not do for the majority to dismiss the CSRT procedures as "far more limited" than those used in military trials, and therefore beneath the level of process "that would eliminate the need for habeas corpus review." The question is not how much process the CSRTs provide in comparison to other modes of adjudication. The question is whether the CSRT procedures — coupled with the judicial review specified by the DTA — provide the "basic process" *Hamdi* said the Constitution affords American citizens detained as enemy combatants.

To what basic process are these detainees due as habeas petitioners? We have said that "at the absolute minimum," the Suspension Clause protects the writ "'as it existed in 1789.'" The majority admits that a number of historical authorities suggest that at the time of the Constitution's ratification, "common-law courts abstained altogether from matters involving prisoners of war." If this is accurate, the process provided prisoners under the DTA is plainly more than sufficient — it allows alleged combatants to challenge both the factual and legal bases of their detentions.

Assuming the constitutional baseline is more robust, the DTA still provides adequate process, and by the majority's own standards. The DTA system — CSRT review of the Executive's determination followed by D.C. Circuit review for sufficiency of the evidence and the constitutionality of the CSRT process — meets these criteria.

All told, the DTA provides the prisoners held at Guantanamo Bay adequate opportunity to contest the bases of their detentions, which is all habeas corpus need allow. The DTA provides more opportunity and more process, in fact, than that afforded prisoners of war or any other alleged enemy combatants in history.

Despite these guarantees, the Court finds the DTA system an inadequate habeas substitute, for one central reason: Detainees are unable to introduce at the appeal stage exculpatory evidence discovered after the conclusion of their CSRT proceedings. The Court hints darkly that the DTA may suffer from other infirmities, but it does not bother to name them, making a response a bit difficult. As it stands, I can only assume the Court regards the supposed defect it did identify as the gravest of the lot.

If this is the most the Court can muster, the ice beneath its feet is thin indeed. As noted, the CSRT procedures provide ample opportunity for detainees to introduce exculpatory evidence — whether documentary in nature or from live witnesses — before the military tribunals. And if their ability to introduce such evidence is denied contrary to the Constitution or laws of the United States, the D.C. Circuit has the authority to say so on review.

For all its eloquence about the detainees' right to the writ, the Court makes no effort to elaborate how exactly the remedy it prescribes will differ from the procedural protections detainees enjoy under the DTA. The Court objects to the detainees' limited access to witnesses and classified material, but proposes no alternatives of its own. Indeed, it simply ignores the many difficult questions its holding presents. What, for example, will become of the CSRT process? The majority says federal courts should generally refrain from entertaining detainee challenges until after the petitioner's CSRT proceeding has finished. But to what deference, if any, is that CSRT determination entitled?

There are other problems. Take witness availability. What makes the majority think witnesses will become magically available when the review procedure is labeled "habeas"? Will the location of most of these witnesses change — will they suddenly become easily susceptible to service of process? Or will subpoenas issued by American habeas courts run to Basra? And if they did, how would they be enforced? Speaking of witnesses, will detainees be able to call active-duty military officers as witnesses? If not, why not?

The majority has no answers for these difficulties. What it does say leaves open the distinct possibility that its "habeas" remedy will, when all is said and done, end up looking a great deal like the DTA review it rejects.

The majority rests its decision on abstract and hypothetical concerns. Step back and consider what, in the real world, Congress and the Executive have actually granted aliens captured by our Armed Forces overseas and found to be enemy combatants:

- The right to hear the bases of the charges against them, including a summary of any classified evidence.

- The ability to challenge the bases of their detention before military tribunals modeled after Geneva Convention procedures. Some 38 detainees have been released as a result of this process.
- The right, before the CSRT, to testify, introduce evidence, call witnesses, question those the Government calls, and secure release, if and when appropriate.
- The right to the aid of a personal representative in arranging and presenting their cases before a CSRT.
- Before the D.C. Circuit, the right to employ counsel, challenge the factual record, contest the lower tribunal's legal determinations, ensure compliance with the Constitution and laws, and secure release, if any errors below establish their entitlement to such relief.

In sum, the DTA satisfies the majority's own criteria for assessing adequacy. This statutory scheme provides the combatants held at Guantanamo greater procedural protections than have ever been afforded alleged enemy detainees—whether citizens or aliens—in our national history.

So who has won? Not the detainees. The Court's analysis leaves them with only the prospect of further litigation to determine the content of their new habeas right, followed by further litigation to resolve their particular cases, followed by further litigation before the D.C. Circuit—where they could have started had they invoked the DTA procedure. Not Congress, whose attempt to "determine—through democratic means—how best" to balance the security of the American people with the detainees' liberty interests, has been unceremoniously brushed aside. Not the Great Writ, whose majesty is hardly enhanced by its extension to a jurisdictionally quirky outpost, with no tangible benefit to anyone. Not the rule of law, unless by that is meant the rule of lawyers, who will now arguably have a greater role than military and intelligence officials in shaping policy for alien enemy combatants. And certainly not the American people, who today lose a bit more control over the conduct of this Nation's foreign policy to unelected, politically unaccountable judges.

Justice SCALIA, with whom the Chief Justice, Justice THOMAS, and Justice ALITO join, dissenting.

Today, for the first time in our Nation's history, the Court confers a constitutional right to habeas corpus on alien enemies detained abroad by our military forces in the course of an ongoing war. The Chief Justice's dissent, which I join, shows that the procedures prescribed by Congress in the Detainee Treatment Act provide the essential protections that habeas corpus guarantees; there has thus been no suspension of the writ, and no basis exists for judicial intervention beyond what the Act allows. My problem with today's opinion is more fundamental still: The writ of habeas corpus does not, and never has, run in favor of aliens abroad; the Suspension Clause thus has no application, and the Court's intervention in this military matter is entirely ultra vires.

I shall devote most of what will be a lengthy opinion to the legal errors contained in the opinion of the Court. Contrary to my usual practice, however, I think it appropriate to begin with a description of the disastrous consequences of what the Court has done today.

America is at war with radical Islamists. The enemy began by killing Americans and American allies abroad: 241 at the Marine barracks in Lebanon, 19 at the

Khobar Towers in Dhahran, 224 at our embassies in Dar es Salaam and Nairobi, and 17 on the USS Cole in Yemen. On September 11, 2001, the enemy brought the battle to American soil, killing 2,749 at the Twin Towers in New York City, 184 at the Pentagon in Washington, D.C., and 40 in Pennsylvania. It has threatened further attacks against our homeland; one need only walk about buttressed and barricaded Washington, or board a plane anywhere in the country, to know that the threat is a serious one. Our Armed Forces are now in the field against the enemy, in Afghanistan and Iraq. Last week, 13 of our countrymen in arms were killed.

The game of bait-and-switch that today's opinion plays upon the Nation's Commander in Chief will make the war harder on us. It will almost certainly cause more Americans to be killed. That consequence would be tolerable if necessary to preserve a time-honored legal principle vital to our constitutional Republic. But it is this Court's blatant abandonment of such a principle that produces the decision today. The President relied on our settled precedent in Johnson v. Eisentrager (1950), when he established the prison at Guantanamo Bay for enemy aliens. Citing that case, the President's Office of Legal Counsel advised him "that the great weight of legal authority indicates that a federal district court could not properly exercise habeas jurisdiction over an alien detained at [Guantanamo Bay]." Memorandum from Patrick F. Philbin and John C. Yoo, Deputy Assistant Attorneys General, Office of Legal Counsel, to William J. Haynes II, General Counsel, Dept. of Defense (Dec. 28, 2001). Had the law been otherwise, the military surely would not have transported prisoners there, but would have kept them in Afghanistan, transferred them to another of our foreign military bases, or turned them over to allies for detention. Those other facilities might well have been worse for the detainees themselves.

In the long term, then, the Court's decision today accomplishes little, except perhaps to reduce the well-being of enemy combatants that the Court ostensibly seeks to protect. In the short term, however, the decision is devastating. At least 30 of those prisoners hitherto released from Guantanamo Bay have returned to the battlefield. See S.Rep. No. 110-90, pt. 7, p. 13 (2007) (Minority Views of Sens. Kyl, Sessions, Graham, Cornyn, and Coburn) (hereinafter Minority Report). Some have been captured or killed. See also Mintz, Released Detainees Rejoining the Fight, Washington Post, Oct. 22, 2004, pp. A1, A12. But others have succeeded in carrying on their atrocities against innocent civilians. In one case, a detainee released from Guantanamo Bay masterminded the kidnapping of two Chinese dam workers, one of whom was later shot to death when used as a human shield against Pakistani commandoes. Another former detainee promptly resumed his post as a senior Taliban commander and murdered a United Nations engineer and three Afghan soldiers. Still another murdered an Afghan judge. It was reported only last month that a released detainee carried out a suicide bombing against Iraqi soldiers in Mosul, Iraq. See White, Ex-Guantanamo Detainee Joined Iraq Suicide Attack, Washington Post, May 8, 2008, p. A18.

These, mind you, were detainees whom the military had concluded were not enemy combatants. Their return to the kill illustrates the incredible difficulty of assessing who is and who is not an enemy combatant in a foreign theater of operations where the environment does not lend itself to rigorous evidence collection. Astoundingly, the Court today raises the bar, requiring military officials to appear before civilian courts and defend their decisions under procedural and evidentiary rules that go beyond what Congress has specified. As The Chief Justice's dissent makes clear, we have no idea what those procedural and evidentiary rules are, but they will be determined by civil courts and (in the Court's contemplation at least) will be more detainee-friendly than those now applied, since otherwise there would no reason to hold the congressionally prescribed procedures unconstitutional. If they impose a higher standard of proof (from foreign battlefields) than the current procedures require, the number of the enemy returned to combat will obviously increase.

But even when the military has evidence that it can bring forward, it is often foolhardy to release that evidence to the attorneys representing our enemies. And one escalation of procedures that the Court is clear about is affording the detainees increased access to witnesses (perhaps troops serving in Afghanistan?) and to classified information. During the 1995 prosecution of Omar Abdel Rahman, federal prosecutors gave the names of 200 unindicted co-conspirators to the "Blind Sheik's" defense lawyers; that information was in the hands of Osama Bin Laden within two weeks. In another case, trial testimony revealed to the enemy that the United States had been monitoring their cellular network, whereupon they promptly stopped using it, enabling more of them to evade capture and continue their atrocities.

And today it is not just the military that the Court elbows aside. A mere two Terms ago in Hamdan v. Rumsfeld (2006), when the Court held (quite amazingly) that the Detainee Treatment Act of 2005 had not stripped habeas jurisdiction over Guantanamo petitioners' claims, four Members of today's five-Justice majority joined an opinion saying the following: "Nothing prevents the President from returning to Congress to seek the authority [for trial by military commission] he believes necessary."

Turns out they were just kidding. For in response, Congress, at the President's request, quickly enacted the Military Commissions Act, emphatically reasserting that it did not want these prisoners filing habeas petitions. It is therefore clear that Congress and the Executive—both political branches—have determined that limiting the role of civilian courts in adjudicating whether prisoners captured abroad are properly detained is important to success in the war that some 190,000 of our men and women are now fighting. As the Solicitor General argued, "the Military Commissions Act and the Detainee Treatment Act . . . represent an effort by the political branches to strike an appropriate balance between the need to preserve liberty and the need to accommodate the weighty and sensitive governmental interests in ensuring that those who have in fact fought with the enemy during a war do not return to battle against the United States."

But it does not matter. The Court today decrees that no good reason to accept the judgment of the other two branches is "apparent." "The Government," it declares, "presents no credible arguments that the military mission at Guantanamo would be compromised if habeas corpus courts had jurisdiction to hear the detainees' claims." What competence does the Court have to second-guess the judgment of Congress and the President on such a point? None whatever. But the Court blunders in nonetheless. Henceforth, as today's opinion makes unnervingly clear, how to handle enemy prisoners in this war will ultimately lie with the branch that knows least about the national security concerns that the subject entails.

Today the Court warps our Constitution in a way that goes beyond the narrow issue of the reach of the Suspension Clause, invoking judicially brainstormed separation-of-powers principles to establish a manipulable "functional" test for the extraterritorial reach of habeas corpus (and, no doubt, for the extraterritorial reach of other constitutional protections as well). It blatantly misdescribes important precedents, most conspicuously Justice Jackson's opinion for the Court in Johnson v. Eisentrager. It breaks a chain of precedent as old as the common law that prohibits judicial inquiry into detentions of aliens abroad absent statutory authorization. And, most tragically, it sets our military commanders the impossible task of proving to a civilian court, under whatever standards this Court devises in the future, that evidence supports the confinement of each and every enemy prisoner.

The Nation will live to regret what the Court has done today. I dissent.

2. *Military Tribunals*

In November 2001, President Bush issued an order for military tribunals. The order for military tribunals raises many basic questions: Does the president, as commander in chief, have the authority to create military tribunals or is creating courts entirely a congressional power under the Constitution? Can the government suspend provisions of the Bill of Rights in trying noncitizens accused of terrorism or supporting terrorism? More generally, how should the Constitution be interpreted during wartime?

There is one major Supreme Court decision concerning military tribunals prior to the current era: *Ex parte Quirin*, from World War II.

EX PARTE QUIRIN, 317 U.S. 1 (1942): Chief Justice STONE delivered the opinion of the Court.

The question for decision is whether the detention of petitioners by respondent for trial by Military Commission, appointed by Order of the President of July 2, 1942, on charges preferred against them purporting to set out their violations of the law of war and of the Articles of War, is in conformity to the laws and Constitution of the United States.

After denial of their applications by the District Court, petitioners asked leave to file petitions for habeas corpus in this Court. In view of the public importance of the questions raised by their petitions and of the duty which rests on the courts, in time of war as well as in time of peace, to preserve unimpaired the constitutional safeguards of civil liberty, and because in our opinion the public interest required that we consider and decide those questions without any avoidable delay, we directed that petitioners' applications be set down for full oral argument at a special term of this Court, convened on July 29, 1942.

The following facts appear from the petitions or are stipulated. Except as noted they are undisputed. All the petitioners were born in Germany; all have lived in the United States. All returned to Germany between 1933 and 1941. All except petitioner Haupt are admittedly citizens of the German Reich, with which the United States is at war. Haupt came to this country with his parents when he was five years old; it is contended that he became a citizen of the United States by virtue of the naturalization of his parents during his minority and that he has not since lost his citizenship. The Government, however, takes the position that on attaining his majority he elected to maintain German allegiance and citizenship or in any case that he has by his conduct renounced or abandoned his United States citizenship. For reasons presently to be stated we do not find it necessary to resolve these contentions.

After the declaration of war between the United States and the German Reich, petitioners received training at a sabotage school near Berlin, Germany, where they were instructed in the use of explosives and in methods of secret writing. Thereafter petitioners, with a German citizen, Dasch, proceeded from Germany to a seaport in Occupied France, where petitioners Burger, Heinck and Quirin, together with Dasch, boarded a German submarine which proceeded across the Atlantic to Amagansett Beach on Long Island, New York. The four were there landed from the submarine in the hours of darkness, on or about June 13, 1942, carrying with them a supply of explosives, fuses and incendiary and timing devices. While landing they wore German Marine Infantry uniforms or parts of uniforms. Immediately after landing they buried their uniforms and the other articles mentioned and proceeded in civilian dress to New York City.

The remaining four petitioners at the same French port boarded another German submarine, which carried them across the Atlantic to Ponte Vedra Beach, Florida. On or about June 17, 1942, they came ashore during the hours of darkness wearing caps of the German Marine Infantry and carrying with them a supply of explosives, fuses, and incendiary and timing devices. They immediately buried their caps and the other articles mentioned and proceeded in civilian dress to Jacksonville, Florida, and thence to various points in the United States. All were taken into custody in New York or Chicago by agents of the Federal Bureau of Investigation. All had received instructions in Germany from an officer of the German High Command to destroy war industries and war facilities in the United States, for which they or their relatives in Germany were to receive salary payments from the German Government. They also had been paid by the German Government during their course of training at the sabotage school and had received substantial sums in United States currency, which were in their possession when arrested. The currency had been handed to them by an officer of the German High Command, who had instructed them to wear their German uniforms while landing in the United States.

The President, as President and Commander in Chief of the Army and Navy, by Order of July 2, 1942, appointed a Military Commission and directed it to try petitioners for offenses against the law of war and the Articles of War, and prescribed regulations for the procedure on the trial and for review of the record of the trial and of any judgment or sentence of the Commission. On the same day, by Proclamation, the President declared that "all persons who are subjects, citizens or residents of any nation at war with the United States or who give obedience to or act under the direction of any such nation, and who during time of war enter or attempt to enter the United States . . . through coastal or boundary defenses, and are charged with committing or attempting or preparing to commit sabotage, espionage, hostile or warlike acts, or violations of the law of war, shall be subject to the law of war and to the jurisdiction of military tribunals."

The Proclamation also stated in terms that all such persons were denied access to the courts. Pursuant to direction of the Attorney General, the Federal Bureau of Investigation surrendered custody of petitioners to respondent, Provost

Marshal of the Military District of Washington, who was directed by the Secretary of War to receive and keep them in custody, and who thereafter held petitioners for trial before the Commission.

On July 3, 1942, the Judge Advocate General's Department of the Army prepared and lodged with the Commission the following charges against petitioners, supported by specifications:

1.   Violation of the law of war.
2.   Violation of Article 81 of the Articles of War, defining the offense of relieving or attempting to relieve, or corresponding with or giving intelligence to, the enemy.
3.   Violation of Article 82, defining the offense of spying.
4.   Conspiracy to commit the offenses alleged in charges 1, 2 and 3.

The Commission met on July 8, 1942, and proceeded with the trial, which continued in progress while the causes were pending in this Court. On July 27th, before petitioners' applications to the District Court, all the evidence for the prosecution and the defense had been taken by the Commission and the case had been closed except for arguments of counsel. It is conceded that ever since petitioners' arrest the state and federal courts in Florida, New York, and the District of Columbia, and in the states in which each of the petitioners was arrested or detained, have been open and functioning normally.

Petitioners' main contention is that the President is without any statutory or constitutional authority to order the petitioners to be tried by military tribunal for offenses with which they are charged; that in consequence they are entitled to be tried in the civil courts with the safeguards, including trial by jury, which the Fifth and Sixth Amendments guarantee to all persons charged in such courts with criminal offenses. In any case it is urged that the President's Order, in prescribing the procedure of the Commission and the method for review of its findings and sentence, and the proceedings of the Commission under the Order, conflict with Articles of War adopted by Congress and are illegal and void.

The Government challenges each of these propositions. But regardless of their merits, it also insists that petitioners must be denied access to the courts, both because they are enemy aliens or have entered our territory as enemy belligerents, and because the President's Proclamation undertakes in terms to deny such access to the class of persons defined by the Proclamation, which aptly describes the character and conduct of petitioners. It is urged that if they are enemy aliens or if the Proclamation has force no court may afford the petitioners a hearing. But there is certainly nothing in the Proclamation to preclude access to the courts for determining its applicability to the particular case. And neither the Proclamation nor the fact that they are enemy aliens forecloses consideration by the courts of petitioners' contentions that the Constitution and laws of the United States constitutionally enacted forbid their trial by military commission. [W]e have resolved those questions by our conclusion that the Commission has jurisdiction to try the charge preferred against petitioners. There is therefore no occasion to decide contentions of the parties unrelated to this issue. We pass at once to the consideration of the basis of the Commission's authority.

We are not here concerned with any question of the guilt or innocence of petitioners. Constitutional safeguards for the protection of all who are charged with offenses are not to be disregarded in order to inflict merited punishment on some who are guilty. But the detention and trial of petitioners — ordered by the President in the declared exercise of his powers as Commander in Chief of the Army in time of war and of grave public danger — are not to be set aside by the courts without the clear conviction that they are in conflict with the Constitution or laws of Congress constitutionally enacted.

Congress and the President, like the courts, possess no power not derived from the Constitution. But one of the objects of the Constitution, as declared by its preamble, is to "provide for the common defence." As a means to that end the Constitution gives to Congress the power to "provide for the common Defence," Art. I, §8, cl. 1; "To raise and support Armies," "To provide and maintain a Navy," Art. I, §8, cls. 12, 13; and "To make Rules for the Government and Regulation of the land and naval Forces," Art. I, §8, cl. 14. Congress is given authority "To declare War, grant Letters of Marque and Reprisal, and make Rules concerning Captures on Land and Water," Art. I, §8, cl. 11; and "To define and punish Piracies and Felonies committed on the high Seas, and Offenses against the Law of Nations," Art. I, §8, cl. 10. And finally the Constitution authorizes Congress "To make all Laws which shall be necessary and proper for carrying into Execution the foregoing Powers, and all other Powers vested by this Constitution in the Government of the United States, or in any Department or Officer thereof." Art. I, §8, cl. 18.

The Constitution confers on the President the "executive Power," Art II, §1, cl. 1, and imposes on him the duty to "take Care that the Laws be faithfully executed." Art. II, §3. It makes him the Commander in Chief of the Army and Navy, Art. II, §2, cl. 1, and empowers him to appoint and commission officers of the United States. Art. H, §3, cl. 1.

By the Articles of War, Congress has provided rules for the government of the Army. It has provided for the trial and punishment, by courts martial, of violations of the Articles by members of the armed forces and by specified classes of persons associated or serving with the Army. Arts. 1, 2. But the Articles also recognize the "military commission" appointed by military command as an appropriate tribunal for the trial and punishment of offenses against the law of war not ordinarily tried by court martial. *See* Arts. 12, 15. Articles 38 and 46 authorize the President, with certain limitations, to prescribe the procedure for military commissions. Articles 81 and 82 authorize trial, either by court martial or military commission, of those charged with relieving, harboring or corresponding with the enemy and those charged with spying. And Article 15 declares that "the provisions of these articles conferring jurisdiction upon courts-martial shall not be construed as depriving military commission . . . or other military tribunals of concurrent jurisdiction in respect of offenders or offenses that by statute or by the law of war may be triable by such military commissions . . . or other military tribunals." Article 2 includes among those persons subject to military law the personnel of our own military establishment. But this, as Article 12 provides, does not exclude from that class "any other person who by the law of war is subject to trial by military tribunals" and who under Article 12 may be tried by court martial or under Article 15 by military commission.

From the very beginning of its history this Court has recognized and applied the law of war as including that part of the law of nations which prescribes, for the conduct of war, the status, rights and duties of enemy nations as well as of enemy individuals. By the Articles of War, and especially Article 15, Congress has explicitly provided, so far as it may constitutionally do so, that military tribunals shall have jurisdiction to try offenders or offenses against the law of war in appropriate cases. Congress, in addition to making rules for the government of our Armed Forces, has thus exercised its authority to define and punish offenses against the law of nations by sanctioning, within constitutional limitations, the jurisdiction of military commissions to try persons for offenses which, according to the rules and precepts of the law of nations, and more particularly the law of war, are cognizable by such tribunals. And the President, as Commander in Chief, by his Proclamation in time of war has invoked that law. By his Order creating the present Commission he has undertaken to exercise the authority conferred upon him by Congress, and also such authority as the Constitution itself gives the Commander in Chief, to direct the performance of those functions which may constitutionally be performed by the military arm of the nation in time of war.

An important incident to the conduct of war is the adoption of measures by the military command not only to repel and defeat the enemy, but to seize and subject to disciplinary measures those enemies who in their attempt to thwart or impede our military effort have violated the law of war. It is unnecessary for present purposes to determine to what extent the President as Commander in Chief has constitutional power to create military commissions without the support of Congressional legislation. For here Congress has authorized trial of offenses against the law of war before such commissions. We are concerned only with the question whether it is within the constitutional power of the national government to place petitioners upon trial before a military commission for the offenses with which they are charged. We must therefore first inquire whether any of the acts charged is an offense against the law of war cognizable before a military tribunal, and if so whether the Constitution prohibits the trial. We may assume that there are acts regarded in other countries, or by some writers on international law, as offenses against the law of war which would not be triable by military tribunal here, either because they are not recognized by our courts as violations of the law of war or because they are of that class of offenses constitutionally triable only by a jury. It was upon such grounds that the Court denied the right to proceed by military tribunal in *Ex parte Milligan*, supra. But as we shall show, these petitioners were charged with an offense against the law of war which the Constitution does not require to be tried by jury.

It is no objection that Congress in providing for the trial of such offenses has not itself undertaken to codify that branch of international law or to mark its precise boundaries, or to enumerate or define by statute all the acts which that law condemns. An Act of Congress punishing "the crime of piracy as defined by the law of nations" is an appropriate exercise of its constitutional authority, Art. I, §8, cl. 10, "to define and punish" the offense since it has adopted by reference the sufficiently precise definition of international law. Similarly by the reference in the 15th Article of War to "offenders or offenses that . . . by the law of war may be triable by such military commissions," Congress has incorporated by reference, as within the jurisdiction of military commissions, all offenses which are defined as such by the law of war and which may constitutionally be included within that jurisdiction. Congress had the choice of crystallizing in permanent form and in minute detail every offense against the law of war, or of adopting the system of common law applied by military tribunals so far as it should be recognized and deemed applicable by the courts. It chose the latter course.

By universal agreement and practice the law of war draws a distinction between the armed forces and the peaceful populations of belligerent nations and also between those who are lawful and unlawful combatants. Lawful combatants are subject to capture and detention as prisoners of war by opposing military forces. Unlawful combatants are likewise subject to capture and detention, but in addition they are subject to trial and punishment by military tribunals for acts which render their belligerency unlawful. The spy who secretly and without uniform passes the military lines of a belligerent in time of war, seeking to gather military information and communicate it to the enemy, or an enemy combatant who without uniform comes secretly through the lines for the purpose of waging war by destruction of life or property, are familiar examples of belligerents who are generally deemed not to be entitled to the status of prisoners of war, but to be offenders against the law of war subject to trial and punishment by military tribunals.

Such was the practice of our own military authorities before the adoption of the Constitution, and during the Mexican and Civil Wars. During the Civil War the military commission was extensively used for the trial of offenses against the law of war. By a long course of practical administrative construction by its military authorities, our Government has likewise recognized that those who during time of war pass surreptitiously from enemy territory into our own, discarding their uniforms upon entry, for the commission of hostile acts involving destruction of life or property, have the status of unlawful combatants punishable as such by military commission. This precept of the law of war has been so recognized in practice both here and abroad, and has so generally been accepted as valid by authorities on international law that we think it must be regarded as a rule or principle of the law of war recognized by this Government by its enactment of the Fifteenth Article of War.

This specification so plainly alleges violation of the law of war as to require but brief discussion of petitioners' contentions. As we have seen, entry upon our territory in time of war by enemy belligerents, including those acting under the direction of the armed forces of the enemy, for the purpose of destroying property used or useful in prosecuting the war, is a hostile and war-like act. It subjects those who participate in it without uniform to the punishment prescribed by the law of war for unlawful belligerents. It is without significance that petitioners were not alleged to have borne conventional weapons or that their proposed hostile acts did not necessarily contemplate collision with the Armed Forces of the United States. Paragraphs 351 and 352 of the Rules of Land Warfare, already referred to, plainly contemplate that the hostile acts and purposes for which unlawful belligerents may be punished are not limited to assaults on the Armed Forces of the United States. Modern warfare is directed at the destruction of enemy war supplies and the implements of their production and transportation quite as much as at the armed forces. Every consideration which makes the unlawful belligerent punishable is equally applicable whether his objective is the one or the other. The law of war cannot rightly treat those agents of enemy armies who enter our territory, armed with explosives intended for the destruction of war industries and supplies, as any the less belligerent enemies than are agents similarly entering for the purpose of destroying fortified places or our Armed Forces. By passing our boundaries for such purposes without uniform or other emblem signifying their belligerent status, or by discarding that means of identification after entry, such enemies become unlawful belligerents subject to trial and punishment.

Citizenship in the United States of an enemy belligerent does not relieve him from the consequences of a belligerency which is unlawful because in violation of the law of war. Citizens who associate themselves with the military arm of the enemy government, and with its aid, guidance and direction enter this country bent on hostile acts are enemy belligerents within the meaning of the Hague Convention and the law of war. It is as an enemy belligerent that petitioner Haupt is charged with entering the United States, and unlawful belligerency is the gravamen of the offense of which he is accused.

Nor are petitioners any the less belligerents if, as they argue, they have not actually committed or attempted to commit any act of depredation or entered the theatre or zone of active military operations. The argument leaves out of account the nature of the offense which the Government charges and which the Act of Congress, by incorporating the law of war, punishes. It is that each petitioner, in circumstances which gave him the status of an enemy belligerent, passed our military and naval lines and defenses or went behind those lines, in civilian dress and with hostile purpose. The offense was complete when with that purpose they entered — or, having so entered, they remained upon — our territory in time of war without uniform or other appropriate means of identification. For that reason, even when committed by a citizen, the offense is distinct from the crime of treason defined in Article III, §3 of the Constitution, since the absence of uniform essential to one is irrelevant to the other.

But petitioners insist that even if the offenses with which they are charged are offenses against the law of war, their trial is subject to the requirement of the Fifth Amendment that no person shall be held to answer for a capital or otherwise infamous crime unless on a presentment or indictment of a grand jury, and that such trials by Article III, §2, and the Sixth Amendment must be by jury in a civil court. Before the Amendments, §2 of Article III, the Judiciary Article, had provided: "The Trial of all Crimes, except in Cases of Impeachment, shall be by Jury," and had directed that "such Trial shall be held in the State where the said Crimes shall have been committed."

Presentment by a grand jury and trial by a jury of the vicinage where the crime was committed were at the time of the adoption of the Constitution familiar parts of the machinery for criminal trials in the civil courts. But they were procedures unknown to military tribunals, which are not courts in the sense of the Judiciary Article, and which in the natural course of events are usually called upon to function under conditions precluding resort to such procedures. As this Court has often recognized, it was not the purpose or effect of §2 of Article III, read in the light of the common law, to enlarge the then existing right to a jury trial. The object was to preserve unimpaired trial by jury in all those cases in which it had been recognized by the common law and in all cases of a like nature as they might arise in the future, but not to bring within the sweep of the guaranty those cases in which it was then well understood that a jury trial could not be demanded as of right. The Fifth and Sixth Amendments, while guaranteeing the continuance of certain incidents of trial by jury which Article III, §2 had left unmentioned, did not enlarge the right to jury trial as it had been established by that Article.

All these are instances of offenses committed against the United States, for which a penalty is imposed, but they are not deemed to be within the provisions of the Fifth and Sixth Amendments relating to "crimes" and "criminal prosecutions." In the light of this long-continued and consistent interpretation we must conclude that §2 of Article III and the Fifth and Sixth Amendments cannot be taken to have extended the right to demand a jury to trials by military commission, or to have required that offenses against the law of war not triable by jury at common law be tried only in the civil courts. It has not hitherto been challenged, and so far as we are advised it has never been suggested in the very extensive literature of the subject that an alien spy, in time of war, could not be tried by military tribunal without a jury.

The exception from the Amendments of "cases arising in the land or naval forces" was not aimed at trials by military tribunals, without a jury, of such offenses against the law of war. Its objective was quite different—to authorize the trial by court martial of the members of our Armed Forces for all that class of crimes which under the Fifth and Sixth Amendments might otherwise have been deemed triable in the civil courts. The cases mentioned in the exception are not restricted to those involving offenses against the law of war alone, but extend to trial of all offenses, including crimes which were of the class traditionally triable by jury at common law.

We cannot say that Congress in preparing the Fifth and Sixth Amendments intended to extend trial by jury to the cases of alien or citizen offenders against the law of war otherwise triable by military commission, while withholding it from members of our own armed forces charged with infractions of the Articles of War punishable by death. It is equally inadmissible to construe the Amendments— whose primary purpose was to continue unimpaired presentment by grand jury and trial by petit jury in all those cases in which they had been customary—as either abolishing all trials by military tribunals, save those of the personnel of our own armed forces, or what in effect comes to the same thing, as imposing on all such tribunals the necessity of proceeding against unlawful enemy belligerents only on presentment and trial by jury. We conclude that the Fifth and Sixth Amendments did not restrict whatever authority was conferred by the Constitution to try offenses against the law of war by military commission, and that petitioners, charged with such an offense not required to be tried by jury at common law, were lawfully placed on trial by the Commission without a jury.

Accordingly, we conclude that Charge I, on which petitioners were detained for trial by the Military Commission, alleged an offense which the President is authorized to order tried by military commission; that his Order convening the Commission was a lawful order and that the Commission was lawfully constituted; that the petitioners were held in lawful custody and did not show cause for their discharge.

In June 2006, in Hamdan v. Rumsfeld, 548 U.S. 557 (2006), the Court ruled, by a 5-3 margin, that the military tribunals provided pursuant to an Executive Order by President Bush were invalid. The Court found that the procedures violated the Uniform Code of Military Justice and the Geneva Accords. The Court did not consider the constitutional issues raised. Congress responded by enacting the Military Commission Act of 2006. The procedures ordered under it have not yet been ruled upon by the Supreme Court, though the Court invalidated the restrictions on habeas corpus in the Act in Boumediene v. Bush, above.

F. CHECKS ON THE PRESIDENT

How can the president be held accountable? Undoubtedly, some of the most important mechanisms are informal, such as through the pressure of public opinion and checks by Congress, such as through the budget process. Two primary formal mechanisms exist: civil suits and criminal proceedings against the president, and impeachment.

1. Suing and Prosecuting the President

When may the president of the United States be civilly sued? There have been two Supreme Court cases dealing with this issue, Nixon v. Fitzgerald and Clinton v. Jones. The former established absolute immunity—complete protection from civil suit—for a president for all official actions while in office. The latter rejected any immunity for acts that occur before a president takes office.

RICHARD NIXON v. A. ERNEST FITZGERALD
457 U.S. 731 (1982)

Justice POWELL delivered the opinion of the Court.

The plaintiff in this lawsuit seeks relief in civil damages from a former President of the United States. The claim rests on actions allegedly taken in the former President's official capacity during his tenure in office. The issue before us is the scope of the immunity possessed by the President of the United States.

I

In January 1970 the respondent A. Ernest Fitzgerald lost his job as a management analyst with the Department of the Air Force. Fitzgerald's dismissal occurred in the context of a departmental reorganization and reduction in force, in which his job was eliminated. In announcing the reorganization, the Air Force characterized the action as taken to promote economy and efficiency in the Armed Forces.

Respondent's discharge attracted unusual attention in Congress and in the press. Fitzgerald had attained national prominence approximately one year earlier, during the waning months of the Presidency of Lyndon B. Johnson. On November 13, 1968, Fitzgerald appeared before the Subcommittee on Economy in Government of the Joint Economic Committee of the United States Congress. To the evident embarrassment of his superiors in the Department of Defense, Fitzgerald testified that cost-overruns on the C-5A transport plane could approximate $2 billion. He also revealed that unexpected technical difficulties had arisen during the development of the aircraft.

Fitzgerald's proposed reassignment encountered resistance within the administration. In an internal memorandum of January 20, 1970, White House aide Alexander Butterfield reported to Haldeman that "'Fitzgerald is no doubt a top-notch cost expert, but he must be given very low marks in loyalty; and after all, loyalty is the name of the game.'" Butterfield therefore recommended that "'[W]e should let him bleed, for a while at least.'" There is no evidence of White House efforts to reemploy Fitzgerald subsequent to the Butterfield memorandum.

At a news conference on January 31, 1973, the President was asked about [Fitzgerald's firing]. Mr. Nixon took the opportunity to assume personal responsibility for Fitzgerald's dismissal:

> I was totally aware that Mr. Fitzgerald would be fired or discharged or asked to resign. I approved it and Mr. Seamans must have been talking to someone who had discussed the matter with me. No, this was not a case of some person down the line deciding he should go. It was a decision that was submitted to me. I made it and I stick by it.

A day later, however, the White House press office issued a retraction of the President's statement. According to a press spokesman, the President had confused Fitzgerald with another former executive employee.

[II]

This case now presents the claim that the President of the United States is shielded by absolute immunity from civil damages liability. In the case of the President the inquiries into history and policy, though mandated independently by our cases, tend to converge. Because the Presidency did not exist through most of the development of common law, any historical analysis must draw its evidence primarily from our constitutional heritage and structure. Historical inquiry thus merges almost at its inception with the kind of "public policy" analysis appropriately undertaken by a federal court. This inquiry involves policies and principles that may be considered implicit in the nature of the President's office in a system structured to achieve effective government under a constitutionally mandated separation of powers.

Here a former President asserts his immunity from civil damages claims of two kinds. He stands named as a defendant in a direct action under the Constitution and in two statutory actions under federal laws of general applicability. In neither case has Congress taken express legislative action to subject the President to civil liability for his official acts.

Applying the principles of our cases to claims of this kind, we hold that petitioner, as a former President of the United States, is entitled to absolute immunity from damages liability predicated on his official acts. We consider this immunity a functionally mandated incident of the President's unique office, rooted in the constitutional tradition of the separation of powers and supported by our history.

The President occupies a unique position in the constitutional scheme. Article II, §1, of the Constitution provides that "[t]he executive Power shall be vested in a President of the United States. . . ." This grant of authority establishes the President as the chief constitutional officer of the Executive Branch, entrusted with supervisory and policy responsibilities of utmost discretion and sensitivity. These include the enforcement of federal law—it is the President who is charged constitutionally to "take Care that the Laws be faithfully executed"; the conduct of foreign affairs — a realm in which the Court has recognized that "[i]t would be intolerable that courts, without the relevant information, should review and perhaps nullify actions of the Executive taken on information properly held secret"; and management of the Executive Branch — a task for which "imperative reasons requir[e] an unrestricted power [in the President] to remove the most important of his subordinates in their most important duties."

In arguing that the President is entitled only to qualified immunity, the respondent relies on cases in which we have recognized immunity of this scope for governors and cabinet officers. We find these cases to be inapposite. The President's unique status under the Constitution distinguishes him from other executive officials.

Because of the singular importance of the President's duties, diversion of his energies by concern with private lawsuits would raise unique risks to the effective functioning of government. As is the case with prosecutors and judges — for whom absolute immunity now is established — a President must concern himself with matters likely to "arouse the most intense feelings." Yet, as our decisions have recognized, it is in precisely such cases that there exists the greatest public interest in providing an official "the maximum ability to deal fearlessly and impartially with" the duties of his office. This concern is compelling where the officeholder must make the most sensitive and far-reaching decisions entrusted to any official under our constitutional system. Nor can the sheer prominence of the President's office be ignored. In view of the visibility of his office and the effect of his actions on countless people, the President would be an easily identifiable target for suits for civil damages. Cognizance of this personal vulnerability frequently could distract a President from his public duties, to the detriment of not only the President and his office but also the Nation that the Presidency was designed to serve.

A rule of absolute immunity for the President will not leave the Nation without sufficient protection against misconduct on the part of the Chief Executive. There remains the constitutional remedy of impeachment. In addition, there are formal and informal checks on Presidential action that do not apply with equal force to other executive officials. The President is subjected to constant scrutiny by the press. Vigilant oversight by Congress also may serve to deter Presidential abuses of office, as well as to make credible the threat of impeachment. Other incentives to avoid misconduct may include a desire to earn reelection, the need to maintain prestige as an element of Presidential influence, and a President's traditional concern for his historical stature.

The existence of alternative remedies and deterrents establishes that absolute immunity will not place the President "above the law." For the President, as for judges and prosecutors, absolute immunity merely precludes a particular private remedy for alleged misconduct in order to advance compelling public ends.

Justice WHITE, with whom Justice BRENNAN, Justice MARSHALL, and Justice BLACKMUN join, dissenting.

In Marbury v. Madison (1803), the Court, speaking through the Chief Justice, observed that while there were "important political powers" committed to the President for the performance of which neither he nor his appointees were accountable in court, "the question, whether the legality of an act of the head of a department be examinable in a court of justice or not, must always depend on the nature of that act." The Court nevertheless refuses to follow this course with respect to the President. It makes no effort to distinguish categories of Presidential conduct that should be absolutely immune from other categories of conduct that should not qualify for that level of immunity. The Court instead concludes that whatever the President does and however contrary to law he knows his conduct to be, he may, without fear of liability, injure federal employees or any other person within or without the Government.

Attaching absolute immunity to the Office of the President, rather than to particular activities that the President might perform, places the President above the law. It is a reversion to the old notion that the King can do no wrong. Until now, this concept had survived in this country only in the form of sovereign immunity. That doctrine forecloses suit against the Government itself and against Government officials, but only when the suit against the latter actually seeks relief against the sovereign. Suit against an officer, however, may be maintained where it seeks specific relief against him for conduct contrary to his statutory authority or to the Constitution. Now, however, the Court clothes the Office of the President with sovereign immunity, placing it beyond the law.

In Marbury v. Madison, the Chief Justice, speaking for the Court, observed: "The government of the United States has been emphatically termed a government of laws, and not of men. It will certainly cease to deserve this high appellation, if the laws furnish no remedy for the violation of a vested legal right." Until now, the Court has consistently adhered to this proposition. In Scheuer v. Rhodes (1974), a unanimous Court held that the Governor of a State was entitled only to a qualified immunity.

Unfortunately, the Court now abandons basic principles that have been powerful guides to decision. It is particularly unfortunate since the judgment in this case has few, if any, indicia of a judicial decision; it is almost wholly a policy choice, a choice that is without substantial support and that in all events is ambiguous in its reach and import.

WILLIAM JEFFERSON CLINTON v. PAULA CORBIN JONES
520 U.S. 681 (1997)

Justice STEVENS delivered the opinion of the Court.

This case raises a constitutional and a prudential question concerning the Office of the President of the United States. Respondent, a private citizen, seeks to recover damages from the current occupant of that office based on actions allegedly taken before his term began. The President submits that in all but the most exceptional cases the Constitution requires federal courts to defer such litigation until his term ends and that, in any event, respect for the office warrants such a stay. Despite the force of the arguments supporting the President's submissions, we conclude that they must be rejected.

I

Petitioner, William Jefferson Clinton, was elected to the Presidency in 1992, and reelected in 1996. His term of office expires on January 20, 2001. In 1991 he was the Governor of the State of Arkansas. Respondent, Paula Corbin Jones, is a resident of California. In 1991 she lived in Arkansas, and was an employee of the Arkansas Industrial Development Commission.

On May 6, 1994, she commenced this action in the United States District Court for the Eastern District of Arkansas by filing a complaint naming petitioner and Danny Ferguson, a former Arkansas State Police officer, as defendants. As the case comes to us, we are required to assume the truth of the detailed — but as yet untested — factual allegations in the complaint.

Those allegations principally describe events that are said to have occurred on the afternoon of May 8, 1991, during an official conference held at the Excelsior Hotel in Little Rock, Arkansas. The Governor delivered a speech at the conference; respondent — working as a state employee — staffed the registration desk. She alleges that Ferguson persuaded her to leave her desk and to visit the Governor in a business suite at the hotel, where he made "abhorrent" sexual advances that she vehemently rejected. She further claims that her superiors at work subsequently dealt with her in a hostile and rude manner, and changed her duties to punish her for rejecting those advances. Respondent seeks actual damages of $75,000, and punitive damages of $100,000.

II

In response to the complaint, petitioner promptly advised the District Court that he intended to file a motion to dismiss on grounds of Presidential immunity, and requested the court to defer all other pleadings and motions until after the immunity issue was resolved.

Petitioner's principal submission — that "in all but the most exceptional cases," the Constitution affords the President temporary immunity from civil damages litigation arising out of events that occurred before he took office — cannot be sustained on the basis of precedent.

Only three sitting Presidents have been defendants in civil litigation involving their actions prior to taking office. Complaints against Theodore Roosevelt and Harry Truman had been dismissed before they took office; the dismissals were affirmed after their respective inaugurations. Two companion cases arising out of an automobile accident were filed against John F. Kennedy in 1960 during the Presidential campaign. After taking office, he unsuccessfully argued that his status as Commander in Chief gave him a right to a stay under the Soldiers' and Sailors' Civil Relief Act of 1940. The motion for a stay was denied by the District Court, and the matter was settled out of court. Thus, none of those cases sheds any light on the constitutional issue before us.

The principal rationale for affording certain public servants immunity from suits for money damages arising out of their official acts is inapplicable to unofficial conduct. In cases involving prosecutors, legislators, and judges we have repeatedly explained that the immunity serves the public interest in enabling such officials to perform their designated functions effectively without fear that a particular decision may give rise to personal liability.

This reasoning provides no support for an immunity for unofficial conduct. As we explained in *Fitzgerald*, "the sphere of protected action must be related closely to the immunity's justifying purposes." Because of the President's broad responsibilities, we recognized in that case an immunity from damages claims arising out of official acts extending to the "outer perimeter of his authority." But we have never suggested that the President, or any other official, has an immunity that extends beyond the scope of any action taken in an official capacity.

Petitioner's effort to construct an immunity from suit for unofficial acts grounded purely in the identity of his office is unsupported by precedent. Petitioner's strongest argument supporting his immunity claim is based on the text and structure of the Constitution. He does not contend that the occupant of the Office of the President is "above the law," in the sense that his conduct is entirely immune from judicial scrutiny. The President argues merely for a postponement of the judicial proceedings that will determine whether he violated any law. His argument is grounded in the character of the office that was created by Article II of the Constitution, and relies on separation of powers principles that have structured our constitutional arrangement since the founding.

As a starting premise, petitioner contends that he occupies a unique office with powers and responsibilities so vast and important that the public interest demands that he devote his undivided time and attention to his public duties. He submits that—given the nature of the office—the doctrine of separation of powers places limits on the authority of the Federal Judiciary to interfere with the Executive Branch that would be transgressed by allowing this action to proceed.

We have no dispute with the initial premise of the argument. Former presidents, from George Washington to George Bush, have consistently endorsed petitioner's characterization of the office. It does not follow, however, that separation of powers principles would be violated by allowing this action to proceed. The doctrine of separation of powers is concerned with the allocation of official power among the three co-equal branches of our Government.

Rather than arguing that the decision of the case will produce either an aggrandizement of judicial power or a narrowing of executive power, petitioner contends that—as a by-product of an otherwise traditional exercise of judicial power—burdens will be placed on the President that will hamper the performance of his official duties. Petitioner's predictive judgment finds little support in either history or the relatively narrow compass of the issues raised in this particular case. As we have already noted, in the more than 200-year history of the Republic, only three sitting Presidents have been subjected to suits for their private actions. If the past is any indicator, it seems unlikely that a deluge of such litigation will ever engulf the Presidency. As for the case at hand, if properly managed by the District Court, it appears to us highly unlikely to occupy any substantial amount of petitioner's time.

In sum, "[i]t is settled law that the separation-of-powers doctrine does not bar every exercise of jurisdiction over the President of the United States." If the Judiciary may severely burden the Executive Branch by reviewing the legality of the President's official conduct, and if it may direct appropriate process to the President himself, it must follow that the federal courts have power to determine the legality of his unofficial conduct. The burden on the President's time and energy that is a mere by-product of such review surely cannot be considered as onerous as the direct burden imposed by judicial review and the occasional invalidation of his official actions. We therefore hold that the doctrine of separation of powers does not require federal courts to stay all private actions against the President until he leaves office.

We add a final comment on two matters that are discussed at length in the briefs: the risk that our decision will generate a large volume of politically motivated harassing and frivolous litigation, and the danger that national security concerns might prevent the President from explaining a legitimate need for a continuance.

We are not persuaded that either of these risks is serious. Most frivolous and vexatious litigation is terminated at the pleading stage or on summary judgment, with little if any personal involvement by the defendant. See Fed. Rules Civ. Proc. 12, 56. Moreover, the availability of sanctions provides a significant deterrent to litigation directed at the President in his unofficial capacity for purposes of political gain or harassment. History indicates that the likelihood that a significant number of such cases will be filed is remote. Although scheduling problems may arise, there is no reason to assume that the District Courts will be either unable to accommodate the President's needs or unfaithful to the tradition — especially in matters involving national security — of giving "the utmost deference to Presidential responsibilities." Several Presidents, including petitioner, have given testimony without jeopardizing the Nation's security. In short, we have confidence in the ability of our federal judges to deal with both of these concerns.

If Congress deems it appropriate to afford the President stronger protection, it may respond with appropriate legislation. As petitioner notes in his brief, Congress has enacted more than one statute providing for the deferral of civil litigation to accommodate important public interests.

The Federal District Court has jurisdiction to decide this case. Like every other citizen who properly invokes that jurisdiction, respondent has a right to an orderly disposition of her claims.

No case has addressed whether a sitting President can be criminally prosecuted. In March 1974, a federal grand jury considered indicting then-President Richard Nixon and decided instead to declare him an unindicted co-conspirator because it was unsure whether it could indict a sitting President. During the Clinton presidency, there was much discussion as to whether he could be criminally indicted for perjury while in office. This did not occur, either because the Independent Counsel believed that the President had immunity from criminal prosecution or because of a judgment about the merits of the case.

On the one hand, there is a strong argument that impeachment and removal should be the sole remedy against a President. The danger is that criminal prosecution inevitably would interfere with the President's ability to perform and that the impeachment process is the appropriate remedy for wrongdoing. On the other hand, no principle is more basic than that no person is above the law. This justifies allowing the President, like all others, to be charged and tried for crimes.

2. Impeachment

The ultimate check on presidential power is impeachment and removal. Article II, §4 of the Constitution provides, "The President, Vice President and all civil Officers of the United States, shall be removed from Office on Impeachment for, and Conviction of, Treason, Bribery, or other high Crimes and

Misdemeanors." Article I, §2 provides that the House of Representatives has the sole power to impeach. If there is an impeachment by the House, then a trial is held in the Senate. Article I, §3 gives the Senate the sole power to try impeachments and prescribes that "no Person shall be convicted without the Concurrence of two thirds of the Members present."

Two major issues remain unresolved concerning these provisions. First, what are "high Crimes and Misdemeanors"? At one end of the spectrum is the view that these are limited to acts that violate the criminal law and that can be deemed a serious threat to society.[25] At the opposite pole is the statement of Gerald Ford, who was a congressman from Michigan when he proposed the impeachment of Supreme Court Justice William Douglas largely because of Douglas's liberal views: "[A]n impeachable offense is whatever a majority of the House of Representatives considers [it] to be."[26]

Second, what procedures must be followed when there is an impeachment and removal proceeding? For example, is it permissible for the Senate to have a committee hear the evidence and make a recommendation to the entire body, or must the Senate sit as a tribunal to hear the case?

There is no definitive answer to either of these questions.[27] There is no Supreme Court case addressing either. In fact, none is likely in the future because the Supreme Court has held that challenges to the impeachment and removal process pose nonjusticiable political questions.[28]

Although there are not judicial precedents to guide Congress, there is historical experience. Three times there have been serious efforts to impeach the president, and two presidents have been impeached.

Andrew Johnson was the first president to be impeached. He was impeached in 1867 for firing Secretary of War Edwin Stanton in violation of the Tenure in Office Act.[29] After the end of the Civil War, Congress became increasingly frustrated with Johnson, a Southerner from Tennessee, presiding over Reconstruction. Congress adopted the Tenure in Office Act of 1867 to keep Johnson from firing Lincoln's cabinet. The act declared that such a firing would be deemed a "high misdemeanor," indicating that Congress was considering the possibility of impeachment from the outset. The Supreme Court subsequently held that the Tenure in Office Act violated separation of powers.[30] Nonetheless, the House impeached and Johnson avoided removal by just one vote in the Senate.

The second serious attempt to impeach a president occurred in 1974 and was directed against Richard Nixon. The House Judiciary Committee voted three articles of impeachment. One was for obstruction of justice in connection with the Watergate cover-up; one was for using government agencies, such as the FBI

25. *See* Charles L. Black, Jr., *Impeachment: A Handbook* 39-40 (1974) (a violation of the criminal law is not essential, but a good indicator of a high crime or misdemeanor).

26. 116 Cong. Rec. 11913 (1970).

27. For an excellent scholarly treatment of these and other issues surrounding impeachment, *see* Michael J. Gerhardt, *The Federal Impeachment Process* (2d ed. 2000).

28. *See* Nixon v. United States, 506 U.S. 224 (1993) (dismissing as a political question a suit brought by federal district court Judge Walter Nixon objecting to the Senate assigning a committee the responsibility of hearing the evidence against him following impeachment by the House of Representatives).

29. *See, e.g.*, Michael Les Benedict, *The Impeachment and Trial of Andrew Johnson* (1973); Milton Lomask, *Andrew Johnson: President on Trial* (1973); Gene Smith, *High Crimes and Misdemeanors: The Impeachment and Trial of Andrew Johnson* (1977); Gerhardt, *supra* note 27, at 10 n.30.

30. Myers v. United States, 272 U.S. 52 (1926) (included earlier in this chapter).

and the IRS, for political advantages; and the final article was for failing to comply with subpoenas. Before the matter could be considered by the entire House, Nixon resigned.

Most recently, of course, President Bill Clinton was impeached by the House of Representatives in 1998, but the Senate did not convict him. A short version of a long story begins after the Supreme Court decided Clinton v. Jones, above, and allowed Paula Jones's civil suit against Bill Clinton to proceed. The U.S. District Court then allowed Jones's attorney to depose President Clinton and permitted questions to be asked about Clinton's other sexual relationships.

Monica Lewinsky, a former White House aide, had described to her friend Linda Tripp a sexual relationship that Lewinsky had with the president that included many phone calls, private meetings, phone sex, and oral sex. Tripp informed Jones's lawyers of this, and on the eve of Clinton's deposition in the *Jones* case, Tripp secretly met for hours with lawyers for Jones and briefed them about Lewinsky.

On January 17, 1998, Clinton's deposition was taken and he was asked about Lewinsky. Below is the key part of Clinton's statement during the deposition:

Q. Did you have an extramarital sexual affair with Monica Lewinsky?
Clinton: No.
Q. If she told someone that she had a sexual affair with you beginning in November of 1995, would that be a lie?
Clinton: It's certainly not the truth. It would not be the truth.
Q. I think I used the term "sexual affair." And so the record is completely clear, have you ever had sexual relations with Monica Lewinsky, as that term is defined in Deposition Exhibit 1, as modified by the Court?
Bennett: I object because I don't know that he can remember —
J. Wright: Well, it's real short. He can — I will permit the question and you may show the witness definition number one.
Clinton: I have never had sexual relations with Monica Lewinsky. I've never had an affair with her.

The possibility that the president had committed perjury was brought to the attention of Attorney General Janet Reno. She authorized Independent Counsel Kenneth Starr, who was investigating the Whitewater land scandal for possible presidential involvement, to broaden his investigation to consider whether the president had committed perjury or obstructed justice. Starr conducted a lengthy investigation, including having the president testify before a grand jury.

On August 17, 1998, Clinton testified before the grand jury. His testimony later became the basis for a separate accusation of perjury. In his grand jury testimony, President Clinton refused to answer any specific questions of a sexual nature about his relationship with Monica Lewinsky; instead, he read and referred to the following prepared statement:

When I was alone with Ms. Lewinsky on certain occasions in early 1996 and once in early 1997, I engaged in conduct that was wrong. These encounters did not consist of sexual intercourse; they did not constitute "sexual relations" as I understood that term to be defined at my January 17, 1998, deposition; but they did involve inappropriate intimate contact. These inappropriate encounters ended, at my insistence, in early 1997. . . .

While I will provide the grand jury whatever other information I can, because of privacy considerations affecting my family, myself, and others, and in an effort to preserve the dignity of the Office I hold, this is all I will say about the specifics of these particular matters.

President Clinton did engage in extended hypothetical and definitional discussions as to what would or would not constitute sexual relations or fall within his definition of the term "sexual relations." The following was the most important exchange, with Clinton answering the questions:

A. You are free to infer that my testimony is that I did not have sexual relations, as I understood this term to be defined.
Q. Including touching her breast, kissing her breast, or touching her genitalia?
A. That's correct.

In the fall of 1998, Independent Counsel Kenneth Starr released a very detailed report documenting the relationship between Monica Lewinsky and Bill Clinton. The report described the progress of their relationship, many phone calls over a long period of time, sexual touchings, and oral sex. The House Judiciary Committee then conducted impeachment hearings and voted four articles of impeachment against the president. The vote in the House Judiciary Committee was entirely along partisan lines, with all of the Republican members voting for impeachment and the Democrats voting against.

The first article of the articles of impeachment stated:

> In his conduct while President of the United States, William Jefferson Clinton, in violation of his constitutional oath faithfully to execute the office of President of the United States and, to the best of his ability, preserve, protect, and defend the Constitution of the United States . . . has willfully corrupted and manipulated the judicial process of the United States for his personal gain and exoneration, impeding the administration of justice [through his perjury before the grand jury concerning this prior relationship with an intern and his prior sworn testimony]. . . .
>
> In doing this, William Jefferson Clinton has undermined the integrity of his office, has brought disrepute on the Presidency, has betrayed his trust as President, and has acted in a manner subversive of the rule of law and justice, to the manifest injury of the people of the United States.[31]

Article Two stated:

> In his conduct while President of the United States, William Jefferson Clinton, in violation of his constitutional oath faithfully to execute the office of President of the United States and, to the best of his ability, preserve, protect, and defend the Constitution of the United States, and in violation of his constitutional duty to take care that the laws be faithfully executed, has willfully corrupted and manipulated the judicial process of the United States for his personal gain and exoneration, impeding the administration of justice [through acts of deception and perjury]. . . .[32]

---

31. H.R. Res. 611, 105th Cong. (1998) (enacted), reprinted in 144 Cong. Rec. H11, 11774 (daily ed. Dec. 18, 1998). The second paragraph was repeated in each of the four articles of impeachment.

32. *Id.*, reprinted in 144 Cong. Rec. H11, 11774 (daily ed. Dec. 18, 1998).

Article Three stated:

> In his conduct while President of the United States, William Jefferson Clinton, in violation of his constitutional oath faithfully to execute the office of President of the United States and, to the best of his ability, preserve, protect, and defend the Constitution of the United States, and in violation of his constitutional duty to take care that the laws be faithfully executed, has prevented, obstructed, and impeded the administration of justice, and has to that end engaged personally, and through his subordinates and agents, in a course of conduct or scheme designed to delay, impede, cover up, and conceal the existence of evidence and testimony related to a Federal civil rights action brought against him in a duly instituted judicial proceeding. . . .[33]

Article Four stated:

> Using the powers and influence of the office of President of the United States, William Jefferson Clinton, in violation of his constitutional oath faithfully to execute the office of President of the United States and, to the best of his ability, preserve, protect, and defend the Constitution of the United States, and in disregard of his constitutional duty to take care that the laws be faithfully executed, has engaged in conduct that resulted in misuse and abuse of his high office, impaired the due and proper administration of justice and the conduct of lawful inquiries, and contravened the authority of the legislative branch and the truth seeking purpose of a coordinate investigative proceeding, in that, as President, William Jefferson Clinton refused and failed to respond to certain written requests for admission and willfully made perjurious, false and misleading sworn statements in response to certain written requests for admission propounded to him as part of the impeachment inquiry. . . .[34]

On December 19, 1998, the House of Representatives passed two articles of impeachment. The first article passed by a vote of 228-206, with five Democrats defecting to vote for impeachment and five Republicans defecting to vote against impeachment. Article Three passed by a vote of 221-212, with five Democrats defecting to vote for impeachment and five Republicans defecting to vote against impeachment. On Article Two, alleging perjury in the civil deposition, 28 Republicans crossed party lines to vote against the article, defeating the article 205-229. On Article Four, alleging perjury in the president's answer to Congress, 81 Republicans crossed party lines in favor of the president, while one Democrat crossed party lines in favor of Article Four, for a final vote of 148-285.

The U.S. Senate then conducted a trial of President Clinton on the two articles of impeachment. The chief justice of the United States, as prescribed by the Constitution, presided. In accord with Senate rules, the senators' deliberations were entirely in closed session. Neither article of impeachment received the two-thirds vote needed to remove the president.

It is unclear what lesson is to be learned from any of these experiences concerning what constitutes "high crimes and misdemeanors." All of these instances were highly partisan, and all raise the fundamental question of what should be regarded as an impeachable offense.

---

33. *Id.*, reprinted in 144 Cong. Rec. H11, 11774-11775 (daily ed. Dec. 18, 1998).
34. *Id.*, reprinted in 144 Cong. Rec. H11, 11774-11775 (daily ed. Dec. 18, 1998).

CHAPTER

4

LIMITS ON STATE REGULATORY AND TAXING POWER

This chapter focuses on limits on state power that derive from the existence of a national government and of other states. There are two possibilities when considering whether a state or local law is invalidated because of these restrictions. One situation is where Congress has acted. If Congress has passed a law and it is a lawful exercise of congressional power, the question is whether the federal law preempts state or local law. Article VI of the Constitution provides that the "Constitution, and the Laws of the United States which shall be made in Pursuance thereof; and all Treaties made, or which shall be made, under the Authority of the United States, shall be the Supreme Law of the Land." Because of the Supremacy Clause, if there is a conflict between federal law and state or local law, the latter is deemed preempted.

The other situation is where Congress has not acted—or at least the judiciary decides that federal law does not preempt state or local law. Nonetheless, even though there is not preemption, state and local laws can be challenged under two principles: the dormant Commerce Clause and the Privileges and Immunities Clause. The dormant Commerce Clause, or as it sometimes called, "the negative Commerce Clause," is the principle that state and local laws are unconstitutional if they place an undue burden on interstate commerce. The Supreme Court has inferred this limit on state regulatory power from the grant of power to Congress to regulate commerce among the states. Even if Congress has not acted, even if its commerce power lies dormant, state and local governments cannot place an undue burden on interstate commerce.

Another basis for attacking state and local laws in the absence of preemption is the Privileges and Immunities Clause of Article IV, §2. This provision states, "The Citizens of each State shall be entitled to all Privileges and Immunities of Citizens in the several States." The Supreme Court has interpreted the Privileges and Immunities Clause as limiting the ability of states to discriminate against out-of-staters with regard to constitutional rights or important economic activities. Almost all of the recent Supreme Court cases applying the Privileges and Immunities Clause have involved challenges to state and local laws that discriminate against out-of-staters with regard to their ability to earn a livelihood.

A central issue throughout this chapter is the appropriate degree of judicial oversight or of judicial deference to state and local governments. At one extreme, it is possible to argue that state and local governments should be unfettered by the federal government as much as possible. From this view, preemption should be restricted to those situations where Congress has expressly preempted state and local laws. Also from this view, there should be no dormant Commerce Clause or only a very narrow one. State and local regulation generally should be limited only if Congress clearly precludes state and local actions.

At the other extreme, some argue that it is essential for the judiciary to preserve the federal nature of American government. From this perspective, preemption is not something to avoid; rather, preemption should be found whenever doing so will better effectuate the interests of federal law and of the federal government. Likewise, the dormant Commerce Clause is an essential restriction on abuses by state governments so as to preserve a free flow of goods and services throughout the economy.

Thus, the material in this chapter is very much about federalism. What is the appropriate and desirable allocation of power between the federal government and the states and also among the state governments? What is the proper role of the judiciary in reviewing state and local regulations?

A. PREEMPTION OF STATE AND LOCAL LAWS

As described above, Article VI of the Constitution contains the Supremacy Clause, which provides that the Constitution, and laws and treaties made pursuant to it, are the supreme law of the land. If there is a conflict between federal and state law, the federal law controls and the state law is invalidated because federal law is supreme. In Gibbons v. Ogden, 22 U.S. (9 Wheat.) 1, 211 (1824), Chief Justice John Marshall said, "[A]cts of the State Legislatures ... [that] interfere with, or are contrary to the laws of Congress [are to be invalidated because][i]n every such case, the act of Congress ... is supreme; and the law of State, though enacted in the exercise of powers not controverted, must yield to it." Much more recently the Supreme Court declared, "[U]nder the Supremacy Clause, from which our pre-emption doctrine is derived, 'any state law, however clearly within a State's acknowledged power, which interferes with or is contrary to federal law, must yield.'" Gade v. National Solid Wastes Management Association (1992).

The difficulty, of course, is in deciding whether a particular state or local law is preempted by a specific federal statute or regulation. As in so many other areas of constitutional law, there is no clear rule for deciding whether a state or local law should be invalidated on preemption grounds. The Supreme Court once remarked that there is not "an infallible constitutional test or an exclusive constitutional yardstick. In the final analysis, there can be no one crystal clear distinctly marked formula."[1]

Traditionally, the Supreme Court has identified two major situations where preemption occurs. One is where a federal law expressly preempts state or local law. The other situation is where preemption is implied by a clear congressional intent to preempt state or local law.

---

1. Hines v. Davidowitz, 312 U.S. 52, 67 (1941).

In Gade v. National Solid Wastes Management Assn., the Court summarized the tests for preemption:

> Pre-emption may be either express or implied, and is compelled whether Congress' command is explicitly stated in the statute's language or implicitly contained in its structure and purpose. Absent explicit pre-emptive language, we have recognized at least two types of implied pre-emption: field pre-emption, where the scheme of federal regulation is so pervasive as to make reasonable the inference that Congress left no room for the States to supplement it, and conflict pre-emption, where compliance with both federal and state regulations is a physical impossibility, or where state law stands as an obstacle to the accomplishment and execution of the full purposes and objectives of Congress.

Although these categories, or minor variations, are frequently used, they are not distinct. For example, even if there is statutory language expressly preempting state law, Congress rarely is clear about the scope of what is preempted or how particular situations should be handled. Courts must decide what is preempted, and this inevitably leads to an inquiry into congressional intent. Conversely, implied preemption is often a function of both perceived congressional intent and the language used in the statute or regulation.

The Supreme Court has recognized that in both express and implied preemption the issue is discerning congressional intent. The Court has said that "[t]he question whether a certain state action is pre-empted by federal law is one of congressional intent."[2] It has remarked that "'[t]he purpose of Congress is the ultimate touchstone' in every preemption case."[3] The problem, of course, is that Congress's intent, especially as to the scope of preemption, is rarely expressed or clear. Therefore, although the Court purports to be finding congressional intent, it often is left to make guesses about purpose based on fragments of statutory language, random statements in the legislative history, and the degree of detail of the federal regulation.

For the sake of clarity, this section is organized parallel to the test for preemption articulated by the Supreme Court in Gade v. National Solid Wastes Management that is quoted above and that has been frequently repeated by the Court.[4] There are two major situations where preemption is found. First, express preemption occurs where there is explicit preemptive language. Second, there is implied preemption. The Court has identified three types of implied preemption, though the categories are not always kept distinct by the Court. One type of implied preemption is where there is a conflict between federal and state law. For example, even if federal law does not expressly preempt state law, preemption will be found where "compliance with both federal and state regulations is a physical impossibility."[5]

Second, implied preemption also will be found if state law impedes the achievement of a federal objective. Even if federal and state law are not mutually exclusive and even if there is no congressional expression of a desire to preempt state law,

2. Gade v. National Soild Wastes Management Assn., 505 U.S. 88, 96 (1992) (citations omitted).

3. See Medtronic Inc. v. Lohr, 518 U.S. 470, 485 (1996), quoting Retail Clerks v. Schermerhorn, 375 U.S. 96, 103 (1963).

4. 505 U.S. at 96. See, e.g., Freightliner Corp. v. Myrick, 514 U.S. 208, 287 (1995); Wisconsin Public Intervenor v. Mortier, 501 U.S. 597, 604-605 (1991).

5. Florida Lime & Avocado Growers, Inc. v. Paul, 373 U.S. 132, 142-143 (1963).

preemption will be found if state law "stands as an obstacle to the accomplishment and execution of the full purposes and objectives of Congress."[6]

A final type of implied preemption is termed "field preemption" — where the scheme of federal law and regulation is "so pervasive as to make reasonable the inference that Congress left no room for the States to supplement it."[7]

For each of these types of preemption, the Court has said that the ultimate question is the intent behind the federal law or regulation. The problem is that the intent often is not expressed or is subject to many different plausible characterizations.

Ultimately, preemption doctrines are about allocating governing authority between the federal and state governments. A broad view of preemption leaves less room for governance by state and local governments. It is for this reason that, at times, the Court has declared that the preemption analysis "start[s] with the assumption that the historic powers of the States [are] not to be superseded by . . . Federal Act unless that [is] the clear and manifest purpose of Congress."[8] But a very narrow preemption doctrine minimizes the reach of federal law and risks undermining the federal objectives.

The basic question is how willing courts should be to find preemption. Should there be a strong presumption against a court concluding that there is preemption? If so, what should be sufficient to overcome this presumption? Or should courts be willing to find preemption whenever doing so would effectuate the purposes of federal law?

1. Express Preemption

Whenever Congress has the authority to legislate, Congress can make federal law exclusive in a field. The clearest way for Congress to do this is to expressly preclude state or local regulation in an area. Thus, some federal laws contain clauses that expressly preempt state and local laws. For example, the federal Employee Retirement Income Security Act of 1974 (ERISA) states that it "supersede[s] any and all State laws insofar as they may now or hereafter relate to any employee benefit plan."[9] The following case is illustrative of the issues that arise when courts deal with issues of express preemption.

LORILLARD TOBACCO CO. v. REILLY
533 U.S. 525 (2001)

O'CONNOR, J., delivered the opinion of the Court, Parts I, II-C, and II-D of which were unanimous; Parts II-A, II-B of which were joined by REHNQUIST, C.J., and SCALIA, KENNEDY, and THOMAS, JJ.

In January 1999, the Attorney General of Massachusetts promulgated comprehensive regulations governing the advertising and sale of cigarettes, smokeless tobacco, and cigars. The first question presented for our review is

6. Hines v. Davidowitz, 312 U.S. 52, 67 (1941).
7. Rice v. Santa Fe Elevator Corp., 331 U.S. 218, 230 (1947).
8. *Id.*
9. 29 U.S.C. §1144(a).

whether certain cigarette advertising regulations are pre-empted by the Federal Cigarette Labeling and Advertising Act (FCLAA).

I

In January 1999, pursuant to his authority to prevent unfair or deceptive practices in trade, the Massachusetts Attorney General (Attorney General) promulgated regulations governing the sale and advertisement of cigarettes, smokeless tobacco, and cigars. The purpose of the regulations is "to eliminate deception and unfairness in the way tobacco products are marketed, sold and distributed in Massachusetts in order to address the incidence of tobacco use by children under legal age . . . [and] in order to prevent access to such products by underage consumers."

The cigarette and smokeless tobacco regulations being challenged before this Court provide:

(2) Retail Outlet Sales Practices. Except as otherwise provided, it shall be an unfair or deceptive act or practice for any person who sells or distributes cigarettes or smokeless tobacco products through a retail outlet located within Massachusetts to engage in any of the following retail outlet sales practices:

(c) Using self-service displays of cigarettes or smokeless tobacco products;

(d) Failing to place cigarettes and smokeless tobacco products out of the reach of all consumers, and in a location accessible only to outlet personnel.

(5) Advertising Restrictions. Except as provided, it shall be an unfair or deceptive act or practice for any manufacturer, distributor or retailer to engage in any of the following practices:

(a) Outdoor advertising, including advertising in enclosed stadiums and advertising from within a retail establishment that is directed toward or visible from the outside of the establishment, in any location that is within a 1,000 foot radius of any public playground, playground area in a public park, elementary school or secondary school;

(b) Point-of-sale advertising of cigarettes or smokeless tobacco products any portion of which is placed lower than five feet from the floor of any retail establishment which is located within a one thousand foot radius of any public playground, playground area in a public park, elementary school or secondary school, and which is not an adult-only retail establishment.

II

Before reaching the First Amendment issues, we must decide to what extent federal law pre-empts the Attorney General's regulations. The cigarette petitioners contend that the FCLAA pre-empts the Attorney General's cigarette advertising regulations.

A

In the FCLAA, Congress has crafted a comprehensive federal scheme governing the advertising and promotion of cigarettes. The FCLAA's pre-emption provision provides:

(a) Additional statements

No statement relating to smoking and health, other than the statement required by section 1333 of this title, shall be required on any cigarette package.

(b) State regulations

No requirement or prohibition based on smoking and health shall be imposed under State law with respect to the advertising or promotion of any cigarettes the packages of which are labeled in conformity with the provisions of this chapter.

The FCLAA's pre-emption provision does not cover smokeless tobacco or cigars.

In this case, our task is to identify the domain expressly pre-empted, because "an express definition of the pre-emptive reach of a statute . . . supports a reasonable inference . . . that Congress did not intend to pre-empt other matters." Congressional purpose is the "ultimate touchstone" of our inquiry. Because "federal law is said to bar state action in [a] fiel[d] of traditional state regulation," namely, advertising, we "wor[k] on the assumption that the historic police powers of the States [a]re not to be superseded by the Federal Act unless that [is] the clear and manifest purpose of Congress." In the pre-emption provision, Congress unequivocally precludes the requirement of any additional statements on "cigarette packages beyond those provided in [the statute]." Congress further precludes States or localities from imposing any requirement or prohibition based on smoking and health with respect to the advertising and promotion of cigarettes. Without question, the second clause is more expansive than the first; it employs far more sweeping language to describe the state action that is pre-empted. We must give meaning to each element of the pre-emption provision. We are aided in our interpretation by considering the predecessor pre-emption provision and the circumstances in which the current language was adopted.

In 1964, the groundbreaking Report of the Surgeon General's Advisory Committee on Smoking and Health concluded that "[c]igarette smoking is a health hazard of sufficient importance in the United States to warrant appropriate remedial action." In 1965, Congress enacted the FCLAA as a proactive measure in the face of impending regulation by federal agencies and the States. The purpose of the FCLAA was twofold: to inform the public adequately about the hazards of cigarette smoking, and to protect the national economy from interference due to diverse, nonuniform, and confusing cigarette labeling and advertising regulations with respect to the relationship between smoking and health. The FCLAA prescribed a label for cigarette packages. Section 5 of the FCLAA included a pre-emption provision in which "Congress spoke precisely and narrowly." Subsection 5(a) prohibited any requirement of additional statements on cigarette packaging. Subsection 5(b) provided that "[n]o statement relating to smoking and health shall be required in the advertising of any cigarettes the packages of which are labeled in conformity with the provisions of this Act."

In 1969, House and Senate committees held hearings about the health effects of cigarette smoking and advertising by the cigarette industry. The bill that emerged from the House of Representatives strengthened the warning and maintained the pre-emption provision. The Senate amended that bill, adding the ban on radio and television advertising, and changing the pre-emption language to its present form.

The final result was the Public Health Cigarette Smoking Act of 1969, in which Congress, following the Senate's amendments, made three significant changes to the FCLAA. First, Congress drafted a new label that read: "Warning: The Surgeon General Has Determined That Cigarette Smoking Is Dangerous to Your Health." Second, Congress declared it unlawful to advertise cigarettes on any medium of electronic communication subject to the jurisdiction of the FCC. Finally, Congress enacted the current pre-emption provision, which proscribes any "requirement or prohibition based on smoking and health . . . imposed under State law with respect to the advertising or promotion" of cigarettes. The new subsection 5(b) did not pre-empt regulation by federal agencies, freeing the FTC to impose warning requirements in cigarette advertising. The new pre-emption provision, like its predecessor, only applied to cigarettes, and not other tobacco products.

In 1984, Congress again amended the FCLAA in the Comprehensive Smoking Education Act. The purpose of the Act was to "provide a new strategy for making Americans more aware of any adverse health effects of smoking, to assure the timely and widespread dissemination of research findings and to enable individuals to make informed decisions about smoking." The Act established a series of warnings to appear on a rotating basis on cigarette packages and in cigarette advertising, and directed the Health and Human Services Secretary to create and implement an educational program about the health effects of cigarette smoking.

The FTC has continued to report on trade practices in the cigarette industry. In 1999, the first year since the master settlement agreement, the FTC reported that the cigarette industry expended $8.24 billion on advertising and promotions, the largest expenditure ever. Substantial increases were found in point-of-sale promotions, payments made to retailers to facilitate sales, and retail offers such as buy one, get one free, or product giveaways. Substantial decreases, however, were reported for outdoor advertising and transit advertising.

The scope and meaning of the current pre-emption provision become clearer once we consider the original pre-emption language and the amendments to the FCLAA. Without question, "the plain language of the pre-emption provision in the 1969 Act is much broader." Rather than preventing only "statements," the amended provision reaches all "requirement[s] or prohibition[s] . . . imposed under State law." And, although the former statute reached only statements "in the advertising," the current provision governs "with respect to the advertising or promotion" of cigarettes. Congress expanded the pre-emption provision with respect to the States, and at the same time, it allowed the FTC to regulate cigarette advertising. Congress also prohibited cigarette advertising in electronic media altogether. Viewed in light of the context in which the current pre-emption provision was adopted, we must determine whether the FCLAA pre-empts Massachusetts' regulations governing outdoor and point-of-sale advertising of cigarettes.

B

Turning first to the language in the pre-emption provision relied upon by the Court of Appeals, we reject the notion that the Attorney General's cigarette advertising regulations are not "with respect to" advertising and promotion. The Attorney General argues that the cigarette advertising regulations are not "based on smoking and health," because they do not involve health-related content in cigarette advertising but instead target youth exposure to cigarette advertising. To be sure, Members of this Court have debated the precise meaning of "based on smoking and health," but we cannot agree with the Attorney General's narrow construction of the phrase.

As Congress enacted the current pre-emption provision, Congress did not concern itself solely with health warnings for cigarettes. In the 1969 amendments, Congress not only enhanced its scheme to warn the public about the hazards of cigarette smoking, but also sought to protect the public, including youth, from being inundated with images of cigarette smoking in advertising. In pursuit of the latter goal, Congress banned electronic media advertising of cigarettes. And to the extent that Congress's contemplated additional targeted regulation of cigarette advertising, it vested that authority in the FTC.

The context in which Congress crafted the current pre-emption provision leads us to conclude that Congress prohibited state cigarette advertising regulations motivated by concerns about smoking and health. Massachusetts has attempted to address the incidence of underage cigarette smoking by regulating advertising, much like Congress's ban on cigarette advertising in electronic media. At bottom, the concern about youth exposure to cigarette advertising is intertwined with the concern about cigarette smoking and health. Thus the Attorney General's attempt to distinguish one concern from the other must be rejected.

The Attorney General next claims that the State's outdoor and point-of-sale advertising regulations for cigarettes are not pre-empted because they govern the location, and not the content, of advertising. This is also Justice Stevens' main point with respect to pre-emption.

The content versus location distinction has some surface appeal. The pre-emption provision immediately follows the section of the FCLAA that prescribes warnings. The pre-emption provision itself refers to cigarettes "labeled in conformity with" the statute. But the content/location distinction cannot be squared with the language of the pre-emption provision, which reaches all "requirements" and "prohibitions" "imposed under State law." A distinction between the content of advertising and the location of advertising in the FCLAA also cannot be reconciled with Congress' own location-based restriction, which bans advertising in electronic media, but not elsewhere. We are not at liberty to pick and choose which provisions in the legislative scheme we will consider, but must examine the FCLAA as a whole.

Justice Stevens maintains that Congress did not intend to displace state regulation of the location of cigarette advertising. There is a critical distinction, however, between generally applicable zoning regulations, and regulations targeting cigarette advertising. The latter type of regulation, which is inevitably motivated by concerns about smoking and health, squarely contradicts the FCLAA. The FCLAA's comprehensive warnings, advertising restrictions, and pre-emption provision would make little sense if a State or locality could simply target and ban all cigarette advertising.

In sum, we fail to see how the FCLAA and its pre-emption provision permit a distinction between the specific concern about minors and cigarette advertising and the more general concern about smoking and health in cigarette advertising, especially in light of the fact that Congress crafted a legislative solution for those very concerns. We also conclude that a distinction between state regulation of the location as opposed to the content of cigarette advertising has no foundation in the text of the pre-emption provision. Congress pre-empted state cigarette advertising regulations like the Attorney General's because they would upset federal legislative choices to require specific warnings and to impose the ban on cigarette advertising in electronic media in order to address concerns about smoking and health. Accordingly, we hold that the Attorney General's outdoor and point-of-sale advertising regulations targeting cigarettes are pre-empted by the FCLAA.

Justice STEVENS, with whom Justices SOUTER, GINSBURG, and BREYER join, dissenting [on the preemption issue].

As the majority acknowledges, under prevailing principles, any examination of the scope of a preemption provision must "'start with the assumption that the historic police powers of the States [are] not to be superseded by . . . Federal Act unless that [is] the clear and manifest purpose of Congress.'" Cipollone v. Liggett Group, Inc. (1992). As the regulations at issue in this suit implicate two powers that lie at the heart of the States' traditional police power—the power to regulate land usage and the power to protect the health and safety of minors—our precedents require that the Court construe the preemption provision "narrow[ly]." If Congress's intent to preempt a particular category of regulation is ambiguous, such regulations are not preempted.

The text of the preemption provision must be viewed in context, with proper attention paid to the history, structure, and purpose of the regulatory scheme in which it appears. An assessment of the scope of a preemption provision must give effect to a "reasoned understanding of the way in which Congress intended the statute and its surrounding regulatory scheme to affect business, consumers, and the law."

This task, properly performed, leads inexorably to the conclusion that Congress did not intend to preempt state and local regulations of the location of cigarette advertising when it adopted the provision at issue in this suit. In both 1965 and 1969, Congress made clear the purposes of its regulatory endeavor, explaining with precision the federal policies motivating its actions. According to the acts, Congress adopted a "comprehensive Federal program to deal with cigarette labeling and advertising with respect to any relationship between smoking and health," for two reasons: (1) to inform the public that smoking may be hazardous to health and (2) to ensure that commerce and the interstate economy not be "impeded by diverse, nonuniform, and confusing cigarette labeling and advertising regulations with respect to any relationship between smoking and health."

In order to serve the second purpose it was necessary to preempt state regulation of the content of both cigarette labels and cigarette advertising. If one State required the inclusion of a particular warning on the package of cigarettes while another State demanded a different formulation, cigarette manufacturers would have been forced into the difficult and costly practice of producing different packaging for use in different States. To foreclose the waste of resources that would be entailed by such a patchwork regulatory system, Congress expressly precluded other regulators from requiring the placement on cigarette packaging of any "statement relating to smoking and health." Similar concerns applied to cigarette advertising. If different regulatory bodies required that different warnings or statements be used when cigarette manufacturers advertised their products, the text and layout of a company's ads would have had to differ from locale to locale. The resulting costs would have come with little or no health benefit. Moreover, given the nature of publishing, it might well have been the case that cigarette companies would not have been able to advertise in national publications without violating the laws of some jurisdictions. In response to these concerns, Congress adopted a parallel provision preempting state and local regulations requiring inclusion in cigarette advertising of any "statement relating to smoking and health."

There was, however, no need to interfere with state or local zoning laws or other regulations prescribing limitations on the location of signs or billboards. Laws prohibiting a cigarette company from hanging a billboard near a school in Boston in no way conflict with laws permitting the hanging of such a billboard in other jurisdictions. Nor would such laws even impose a significant administrative burden on would-be advertisers, as the great majority of localities impose general restrictions on signage, thus requiring advertisers to examine local law before posting signs whether or not cigarette-specific laws are preempted.

The legislative history of the provision also supports such a reading. The record does not contain any evidence that Congress intended to expand the scope of preemption beyond content restrictions. To the contrary, the Senate Report makes it clear that the changes merely "clarified" the scope of the original provision. Even as amended, Congress perceived the provision as "narrowly phrased" and emphasized that its purpose is to "avoid the chaos created by a multiplicity of conflicting regulations." According to the Senate Report, the changes "in no way affect the power of any state or political subdivision of any state with respect to . . . the sale of cigarettes to minors . . . or similar police regulations."

I am firmly convinced that, when Congress amended the preemption provision in 1969, it did not intend to expand the application of the provision beyond content regulations. I, therefore, find the conclusion inescapable that the zoning regulation at issue in this suit is not a "requirement or prohibition . . . with respect to . . . advertising" within the meaning of the 1969 Act. Even if I were not so convinced, however, I would still dissent from the Court's conclusion with regard to preemption, because the provision is, at the very least, ambiguous. The historical record simply does not reflect that it was Congress's "'clear and manifest purpose,'" to preempt attempts by States to utilize their traditional zoning authority to protect the health and welfare of minors. Absent such a manifest purpose, Massachusetts and its sister States retain their traditional police powers.

Another case concerning the scope of an express preemption provision was Riegel v. Medtronic, 552 U.S. 312 (2008). The Medical Devices Amendments of 1976, 21 U.S.C. §360k, preempt states from imposing "requirements" different from federal law after the Food and Drug Administration approves a medical device. The Court held, eight to one, that this preempts state tort liability against manufacturers for devices approved by the FDA. The Court reasoned that tort liability, like regulation, changes behavior and essentially creates requirements. Justice Ginsburg was alone in dissent and stressed that there should be a presumption against preemption. She said that if Congress wanted to preempt tort liability, it could do so, but that this law only preempted states from imposing "requirements."

More recently, in Chamber of Commerce v. Whiting, 131 S. Ct. 1968 (2011), the Court considered a provision of federal immigration law that expressly preempts "any State or local law imposing civil or criminal sanctions (other than through licensing and similar laws) upon those who employ . . . unauthorized aliens." An Arizona statute — the Legal Arizona Workers Act — provides that the licenses of state employers that knowingly or intentionally employ unauthorized aliens may be, and in certain circumstances must be, suspended or revoked.[10]

The Court, in a five-to-three decision, concluded that the Arizona law was not preempted. Chief Justice Roberts, writing for the majority, explained, "Because we conclude that the State's licensing provisions fall squarely within the federal statute's savings clause and that the Arizona regulation does not otherwise conflict with federal law, we hold that the Arizona law is not preempted. When a federal law contains an express preemption clause, we 'focus on the plain wording of the clause, which necessarily contains the best evidence of Congress' preemptive intent.' [Federal law] expressly preempts States from imposing 'civil or criminal sanctions' on those who employ unauthorized aliens, 'other than through licensing and similar laws.' The Arizona law, on its face, purports to impose sanctions through licensing laws. The state law authorizes state courts to suspend or revoke an employer's business licenses if that employer knowingly or intentionally employs an unauthorized alien."

Justices Breyer and Sotomayor each wrote a dissenting opinion arguing that Congress had a much narrower intent and did not intend to give states the authority to revoke a corporation's ability to do business in the state.

2. Implied Preemption

a. Conflicts Preemption

If a federal and a state law are mutually exclusive, so that a person cannot comply with both, the state law is deemed preempted. This is called "conflicts preemption." The difficulty often lies in determining whether the laws actually conflict. For example, if the federal government sets a standard for air pollution control, but a state sets a stricter standard, is there conflicts preemption? It depends entirely on the intent of the federal government. If the federal government made the express decision to allow pollution above that level, then a stricter state regulation is in conflict with the federal law. But if the federal government was just setting the minimum standard, the floor of regulation, then a stricter state law is not in conflict with the federal law and would not be preempted. The following case raises exactly this issue.

FLORIDA LIME & AVOCADO GROWERS, INC. v. PAUL, DIRECTOR,
DEPARTMENT OF AGRICULTURE OF CALIFORNIA

373 U.S. 132 (1963)

Justice BRENNAN delivered the opinion of the Court.

Section 792 of California's Agricultural Code, which gauges the maturity of avocados by oil content, prohibits the transportation or sale in California of avocados which contain "less than 8 per cent of oil, by weight excluding the

---

10. This is a different law from Arizona's SB 1070, which authorizes aggressive law enforcement to decrease the presence in Arizona of those who are not lawfully in the United States. That law and the decision concerning it (Arizona v. United States (2012)) are presented below.

skin and seed." In contrast, federal marketing orders approved by the Secretary of Agriculture gauge the maturity of avocados grown in Florida by standards which attribute no significance to oil content. This case presents the question of the constitutionality of the California statute insofar as it may be applied to exclude from California markets certain Florida avocados which, although certified to be mature under the federal regulations, do not uniformly meet the California requirement of 8% of oil.

We consider first appellants' challenge under the Supremacy Clause. That the California statute and the federal marketing orders embody different maturity tests is clear. However, this difference poses, rather than disposes of the problem before us.

A holding of federal exclusion of state law is inescapable and requires no inquiry into congressional design where compliance with both federal and state regulations is a physical impossibility for one engaged in interstate commerce. That would be the situation here if, for example, the federal orders forbade the picking and marketing of any avocado testing more than 7% oil, while the California test excluded from the State any avocado measuring less than 8% oil content. No such impossibility of dual compliance is presented on this record, however. As to those Florida avocados of the hybrid and Guatemalan varieties which were actually rejected by the California test, the District Court indicated that the Florida growers might have avoided such rejections by leaving the fruit on the trees beyond the earliest picking date permitted by the federal regulations, and nothing in the record contradicts that suggestion. Nor is there a lack of evidentiary support for the District Court's finding that the Florida varieties marketed in California "attain or exceed 8% oil content while in a prime commercial marketing condition," even though they may be "mature enough to be acceptable prior to the time that they reach that content." Thus the present record demonstrates no inevitable collision between the two schemes of regulation, despite the dissimilarity of the standards.

b. Preemption Because State Law Impedes the Achievement of a Federal Objective

Preemption also can be found if a state or local law is deemed to impede the achievement of a federal objective. In other words, even if the federal and state laws are not mutually exclusive, preemption will be found if the state or local law interferes with attaining a federal legislative goal. In applying this type of preemption, the courts must determine the federal objective and must decide the point at which state regulation unduly interferes with achieving the goal. The following cases illustrate this inquiry.

PACIFIC GAS & ELECTRIC CO. v. STATE ENERGY RESOURCES CONSERVATION & DEVELOPMENT COMMISSION
461 U.S. 190 (1983)

Justice WHITE delivered the opinion of the Court.

The turning of swords into plowshares has symbolized the transformation of atomic power into a source of energy in American society. To facilitate this development the federal government relaxed its monopoly over fissionable materials and nuclear technology, and in its place, erected a complex scheme to promote the civilian development of nuclear energy, while seeking to safeguard the public and the environment from the unpredictable risks of a new technology. Early on, it was decided that the states would continue their traditional role in the regulation of electricity production. The interrelationship of federal and state authority in the nuclear energy field has not been simple; the federal regulatory structure has been frequently amended to optimize the partnership.

This case emerges from the intersection of the federal government's efforts to ensure that nuclear power is safe with the exercise of the historic state authority over the generation and sale of electricity. At issue is whether provisions in the 1976 amendments to California's Warren-Alquist Act, which condition the construction of nuclear plants on findings by the State Energy Resources Conservation and Development Commission that adequate storage facilities and means of disposal are available for nuclear waste, are preempted by the Atomic Energy Act of 1954.

I

A nuclear reactor must be periodically refueled and the "spent fuel" removed. This spent fuel is intensely radioactive and must be carefully stored. The general practice is to store the fuel in a water-filled pool at the reactor site. For many years, it was assumed that this fuel would be reprocessed; accordingly, the storage pools were designed as short-term holding facilities with limited storage capacities. As expectations for reprocessing remained unfulfilled, the spent fuel accumulated in the storage pools, creating the risk that nuclear reactors would have to be shut down. This could occur if there were insufficient room in the pool to store spent fuel and also if there were not enough space to hold the entire fuel core when certain inspections or emergencies required unloading of the reactor. In recent years, the problem has taken on special urgency. Some 8,000 metric tons of spent nuclear fuel have already accumulated, and it is projected that by the year 2000 there will be some 72,000 metric tons of spent fuel. Government studies indicate that a number of reactors could be forced to shut down in the near future due to the inability to store spent fuel.

There is a second dimension to the problem. Even with water-pools adequate to store safely all the spent fuel produced during the working lifetime of the reactor, permanent disposal is needed because the wastes will remain radioactive for thousands of years. A number of long-term nuclear waste management strategies have been extensively examined. These range from sinking the wastes in stable deep seabeds, to placing the wastes beneath ice sheets in Greenland and Antarctica, to ejecting the wastes into space by rocket. The greatest attention has been focused on disposing of the wastes in subsurface geologic repositories such as salt deposits. Problems of how and where to store nuclear wastes has engendered considerable scientific, political, and public debate. There are both safety and economic aspects to the nuclear waste issue: first, if not properly stored, nuclear wastes might leak and endanger both the environment and human health; second, the lack of a long-term disposal option increases the risk that the insufficiency of interim storage space for spent fuel will lead to reactor-shutdowns, rendering nuclear energy an unpredictable and uneconomical adventure.

The California laws at issue here are responses to these concerns. Two [provisions] are before us. Section 25524.1(b) provides that before additional nuclear plants may be built, the Energy Commission must determine on a case-by-case basis that there will be "adequate capacity" for storage of a plant's spent fuel rods "at the time such nuclear facility requires such . . . storage." The law also requires that each utility provide continuous, on-site, "full core reserve storage capacity" in order to permit storage of the entire reactor core if it must be removed to permit repairs of the reactor.

Section 25524.2 deals with the long-term solution to nuclear wastes. This section imposes a moratorium on the certification of new nuclear plants until the Energy Commission "finds that there has been developed and that the United States through its authorized agency has approved and there exists a demonstrated technology or means for the disposal of high-level nuclear waste." "Disposal" is defined as a "method for the permanent and terminal disposition of high-level nuclear waste. . . ." Such a finding must be reported to the state legislature, which may nullify it.

[II]

Petitioners, the United States, and supporting amici, present three major lines of argument as to why §25524.2 is preempted. First, they submit that the statute — because it regulates construction of nuclear plants and because it is allegedly predicated on safety concerns — ignores the division between federal and state authority created by the Atomic Energy Act, and falls within the field that the federal government has preserved for its own exclusive control. Second, the statute, and the judgments that underlie it, conflict with decisions concerning the nuclear waste disposal issue made by Congress and the Nuclear Regulatory Commission. Third, the California statute frustrates the federal goal of developing nuclear technology as a source of energy. We consider each of these contentions in turn.

A

Even a brief perusal of the Atomic Energy Act reveals that, despite its comprehensiveness, it does not at any point expressly require the States to construct or authorize nuclear power plants or prohibit the States from deciding, as an absolute or conditional matter, not to permit the construction of any further reactors. Instead, petitioners argue that the Act is intended to preserve the federal government as the sole regulator of all matters nuclear, and that §25524.2 falls within the scope of this impliedly preempted field. But as we view the issue, Congress, in passing the 1954 Act and in subsequently amending it, intended that the federal government should regulate the radiological safety aspects involved in the construction and operation of a nuclear plant, but that the States retain their traditional responsibility in the field of regulating electrical utilities for determining questions of need, reliability, cost, and other related state concerns.

Need for new power facilities, their economic feasibility, and rates and services, are areas that have been characteristically governed by the States. [This] is not particularly controversial. But deciding how §25524.2 is to be construed and classified is a more difficult proposition. At the outset, we emphasize that the statute does not seek to regulate the construction or operation of a nuclear powerplant. It would clearly be impermissible for California to attempt to do so, for such regulation, even if enacted out of non-safety concerns, would nevertheless directly conflict with the NRC's exclusive authority over plant construction and operation. Respondents appear to concede as much. Respondents do broadly argue, however, that although safety regulation of nuclear plants by states is forbidden, a state may completely prohibit new construction until its safety concerns are satisfied by the federal government. We reject this line of reasoning. State safety regulation is not preempted only when it conflicts with federal law. Rather, the federal government has occupied the entire field of nuclear safety concerns, except the limited powers expressly ceded to the states. A state moratorium on nuclear construction grounded in safety concerns falls squarely within the prohibited field. Moreover, a state judgment that nuclear power is not safe enough to be further developed would conflict directly with the countervailing judgment of the NRC, that nuclear construction may proceed notwithstanding extant uncertainties as to waste disposal. A state prohibition on nuclear construction for safety reasons would also be in the teeth of the Atomic Energy Act's objective to insure that nuclear technology be safe enough for widespread development and use — and would be preempted for that reason.

That being the case, it is necessary to determine whether there is a non-safety rationale for §25524.2. California has maintained, and the Court of Appeals agreed, that §25524.2 was aimed at economic problems, not radiation hazards. The California Assembly Committee on Resources, Land Use, and Energy, which proposed a package of bills including §25524.2, reported that the waste disposal problem was "largely economic or the result of poor planning, not safety related." Without a permanent means of disposal, the nuclear waste problem could become critical leading to unpredictably high costs to contain the problem or, worse, shutdowns in reactors.

B

Petitioners' second major argument concerns federal regulation aimed at the nuclear waste disposal problem itself. It is contended that §25524.2 conflicts with federal regulation of nuclear waste disposal, with the NRC's decision that it is permissible to continue to license reactors, notwithstanding uncertainty surrounding the waste disposal problem, and with Congress' recent passage of legislation directed at that problem.

Pursuant to its authority under the Act, the AEC, and later the NRC, promulgated extensive and detailed regulations concerning the operation of nuclear facilities and the handling of nuclear materials. The NRC's imprimatur, however, indicates only that it is safe to proceed with such plants, not that it is economically wise to do so. Because the NRC order does not and could not compel a utility to develop a nuclear plant, compliance with both it and §25524.2 are possible. Moreover, because the NRC's regulations are aimed at insuring that plants are safe, not necessarily that they are economical, §25524.2 does not interfere with the objective of the federal regulation.

C

Finally, it is strongly contended that §25524.2 frustrates the Atomic Energy Act's purpose to develop the commercial use of nuclear power. It is well established that state law is preempted if it "stands as an obstacle to the accomplishment of the full purposes and objectives of Congress." Hines v. Davidowitz (1941).

There is little doubt that a primary purpose of the Atomic Energy Act was, and continues to be, the promotion of nuclear power. The Act itself states that it is a program "to encourage widespread participation in the development and utilization of atomic energy for peaceful purposes to the maximum extent consistent with the common defense and security and with the health and safety of the public."

The Court of Appeals is right, however, that the promotion of nuclear power is not to be accomplished "at all costs." The elaborate licensing and safety provisions and the continued preservation of state regulation in traditional areas belie that. Moreover, Congress has allowed the States to determine — as a matter of economics — whether a nuclear plant vis-à-vis a fossil fuel plant should be built. The decision of California to exercise that authority does not, in itself, constitute a basis for preemption. Therefore, while the argument of petitioners and the United States has considerable force, the legal reality remains that Congress has left sufficient authority in the states to allow the development of nuclear power to be slowed or even stopped for economic reasons. Given this statutory scheme, it is for Congress to rethink the division of regulatory authority in light of its possible exercise by the states to undercut a federal objective. The courts should not assume the role which our system assigns to Congress.

In two recent cases, the Court considered implied preemption in the context of whether drug companies can be sued for the failure to warn patients of potential side effects, even though the Food and Drug Administration approved the warning labels. In Wyeth v. Levine, 555 U.S. 555 (2009), the Court held that a drug company could be sued on a failure to warn theory even though its warning label had been approved by the FDA. The Court, in a six-to-three decision, held that there is no conflict between allowing such tort liability and federal law; drug companies always can engage in more speech to warn consumers of side effects. The Court said that allowing liability would further, not undermine, the federal regulatory goal of drug safety and well-informed patients and physicians.

However, in PLIVA v. Mensing, 131 S. Ct. 2567 (2011), the Supreme Court held that makers of generic drugs may not be sued on a failure to warn theory. Justice Thomas, writing for the majority in a five-to-four decision, concluded that the Hatch-Waxman Amendments to the Food and Drug Act allow generic drugs to be sold as long as they are the equivalent of nongeneric drugs and as long as they have the same warning label as the FDA has approved for nongeneric drugs. The Court said that this precludes makers of generic drugs from changing their labels and thus preempts state tort suits for failure to warn. Justice Sotomayor wrote for the dissenters and objected that it makes no sense to allow liability for a nongeneric drug and preempt liability for the generic version of the same product. She argued that the holding in Wyeth v. Levine should apply to both generic and nongeneric drugs.

c. Preemption Because Federal Law Occupies the Field

A final form of implied preemption is where federal law wholly occupies a field. Even though federal law does not expressly preempt state law, preemption will be found if there is a clear congressional intent to have federal law occupy a particular area of law. The most important example of this is immigration law.

Hines v. Davidowitz, 312 U.S. 52 (1941), is a classic example of preemption of state regulation in the field of immigration. A Pennsylvania law required aliens to register with the state, carry a state-issued registration card, and pay a small registration fee. The Supreme Court deemed this law preempted by emphasizing that alien registration "is in a field which affects international relations, the one aspect of our government that from the first has been most generally conceded imperatively to demand broad national authority."

The Court stressed the extensive federal regulation in the area, including a "broad and comprehensive plan describing the terms and conditions upon which aliens may enter this country, how they may acquire citizenship, and the manner in which they may be deported." Indeed, a federal law specifically required alien registration with the federal government.

Two aspects of *Hines* are particularly noteworthy. First, the Court found preemption of a state law that complemented the federal law; the state law in no way interfered with the federal law or its implementation. The Court said that states cannot "contradict or complement" federal immigration law.

Second, the Court found field preemption in *Hines* even in the absence of express preemptive language in the federal statute. Congress certainly could have explicitly preempted state alien registration in the federal law that required aliens to register. But Congress did not do this. The dissent in *Hines* emphasized this point.

The Court relied on *Hines* in its recent decision concerning preemption of Arizona's immigration law, SB 1070.

ARIZONA v. UNITED STATES

132 S. Ct. 2492 (2012)

Justice KENNEDY delivered the opinion of the Court.

To address pressing issues related to the large number of aliens within its borders who do not have a lawful right to be in this country, the State of Arizona in 2010 enacted a statute called the Support Our Law Enforcement and Safe Neighborhoods Act. The law is often referred to as S.B. 1070, the version introduced in the state senate. Its stated purpose is to "discourage and deter the unlawful entry and presence of aliens and economic activity by persons unlawfully present in the United States." The law's provisions establish an official state policy of "attrition through enforcement." The question before the Court is whether federal law preempts and renders invalid four separate provisions of the state law.

I

The United States filed this suit against Arizona, seeking to enjoin S.B. 1070 as preempted. Four provisions of the law are at issue here. Two create new state offenses. Section 3 makes failure to comply with federal alien-registration requirements a state misdemeanor. Section 5, in relevant part, makes it a misdemeanor for an unauthorized alien to seek or engage in work in the State; this provision is referred to as §5(C). Two other provisions give specific arrest authority and investigative duties with respect to certain aliens to state and local law enforcement officers. Section 6 authorizes officers to arrest without a warrant a person "the officer has probable cause to believe . . . has committed any public offense that makes the person removable from the United States." Section 2(B) provides that officers who conduct a stop, detention, or arrest must in some circumstances make efforts to verify the person's immigration status with the Federal Government.

II

A

The Government of the United States has broad, undoubted power over the subject of immigration and the status of aliens. This authority rests, in part, on the National Government's constitutional power to "establish an uniform Rule of Naturalization," and its inherent power as sovereign to control and conduct relations with foreign nations.

The federal power to determine immigration policy is well settled. Immigration policy can affect trade, investment, tourism, and diplomatic relations for the entire Nation, as well as the perceptions and expectations of aliens in this country who seek the full protection of its laws. Perceived mistreatment of aliens in the United States may lead to harmful reciprocal treatment of American citizens abroad.

It is fundamental that foreign countries concerned about the status, safety, and security of their nationals in the United States must be able to confer and communicate on this subject with one national sovereign, not the 50 separate States. This Court has reaffirmed that "[o]ne of the most important and delicate of all international relationships . . . has to do with the protection of the just rights of a country's own nationals when those nationals are in another country." *Hines v. Davidowitz* (1941).

Federal governance of immigration and alien status is extensive and complex. Congress has specified which aliens may be removed from the United States and the procedures for doing so.

Discretion in the enforcement of immigration law embraces immediate human concerns. Unauthorized workers trying to support their families, for example, likely pose less danger than alien smugglers or aliens who commit a serious crime. The equities of an individual case may turn on many factors, including whether the alien has children born in the United States, long ties to the community, or a record of distinguished military service. Some discretionary decisions involve policy choices that bear on this Nation's international relations. Returning an alien to his own country may be deemed inappropriate even where he has committed a removable offense or fails to meet the criteria for admission. The foreign state may be mired in civil war, complicit in political persecution, or enduring conditions that create a real risk that the alien or his family will be harmed upon return. The dynamic nature of relations with other countries requires the Executive Branch to ensure that enforcement policies are consistent with this Nation's foreign policy with respect to these and other realities.

B

The pervasiveness of federal regulation does not diminish the importance of immigration policy to the States. Arizona bears many of the consequences of unlawful immigration. Hundreds of thousands of deportable aliens are apprehended in Arizona each year. Unauthorized aliens who remain in the State comprise, by one estimate, almost six percent of the population. And in the State's most populous county, these aliens are reported to be responsible for a disproportionate share of serious crime.

Statistics alone do not capture the full extent of Arizona's concerns. Accounts in the record suggest there is an "epidemic of crime, safety risks, serious property damage, and environmental problems" associated with the influx of illegal migration across private land near the Mexican border.

[III]

Section 3

Section 3 of S.B. 1070 creates a new state misdemeanor. It forbids the "willful failure to complete or carry an alien registration document . . . in violation of 8 United States Code section 1304(e) or 1306(a)." In effect, §3 adds a state-law penalty for conduct proscribed by federal law. The United States contends that this state enforcement mechanism intrudes on the field of alien registration, a field in which Congress has left no room for States to regulate.

The Court discussed federal alien-registration requirements in *Hines v. Davidowitz.* The Court found that Congress intended the federal plan for registration to be a "single integrated and all-embracing system." Because this "complete scheme . . . for the registration of aliens" touched on foreign relations, it did not allow the States to "curtail or complement" federal law or to "enforce additional or auxiliary regulations."

The framework enacted by Congress leads to the conclusion here, as it did in *Hines,* that the Federal Government has occupied the field of alien registration. The federal statutory directives provide a full set of standards governing alien registration, including the punishment for noncompliance. Where Congress occupies an entire field, as it has in the field of alien registration, even complementary state regulation is impermissible. Field preemption reflects a congressional decision to foreclose any state regulation in the area, even if it is parallel to federal standards.

Arizona contends that §3 can survive preemption because the provision has the same aim as federal law and adopts its substantive standards. This argument not only ignores the basic premise of field preemption—that States may not enter, in any respect, an area the Federal Government has reserved for itself—but also is unpersuasive on its own terms. Permitting the State to impose its own penalties for the federal offenses here would conflict with the careful framework Congress adopted. Were §3 to come into force, the State would have the power to bring criminal charges against individuals for violating a federal law even in circumstances where federal officials in charge of the comprehensive scheme determine that prosecution would frustrate federal policies.

As it did in *Hines,* the Court now concludes that, with respect to the subject of alien registration, Congress intended to preclude States from "complement[ing] the federal law, or enforc[ing] additional or auxiliary regulations." Section 3 is preempted by federal law.

Section 5(C)

Unlike §3, which replicates federal statutory requirements, §5(C) enacts a state criminal prohibition where no federal counterpart exists. The provision makes it a state misdemeanor for "an unauthorized alien to knowingly apply for work, solicit work in a public place or perform work as an employee or independent contractor" in Arizona. Violations can be punished by a $2,500 fine and incarceration for up to six months. The United States contends that the provision upsets the balance struck by the Immigration Reform and Control Act of 1986 (IRCA) and must be preempted as an obstacle to the federal plan of regulation and control.

Congress enacted IRCA as a comprehensive framework for "combating the employment of illegal aliens." The law makes it illegal for employers to knowingly hire, recruit, refer, or continue to employ unauthorized workers. It also requires every employer to verify the employment authorization status of prospective employees. These requirements are enforced through criminal penalties and an escalating series of civil penalties tied to the number of times an employer has violated the provisions.

This comprehensive framework does not impose federal criminal sanctions on the employee side (*i.e.*, penalties on aliens who seek or engage in unauthorized work). Under federal law some civil penalties are imposed instead.

The legislative background of IRCA underscores the fact that Congress made a deliberate choice not to impose criminal penalties on aliens who seek, or engage in, unauthorized employment. In the end, IRCA's framework reflects a considered judgment that making criminals out of aliens engaged in unauthorized work — aliens who already face the possibility of employer exploitation because of their removable status — would be inconsistent with federal policy and objectives.

The ordinary principles of preemption include the well-settled proposition that a state law is preempted where it "stands as an obstacle to the accomplishment and execution of the full purposes and objectives of Congress." Under §5(C) of S.B. 1070, Arizona law would interfere with the careful balance struck by Congress with respect to unauthorized employment of aliens. Section 5(C) is preempted by federal law.

Section 6

Section 6 of S.B. 1070 provides that a state officer, "without a warrant, may arrest a person if the officer has probable cause to believe . . . [the person] has committed any public offense that makes [him] removable from the United States." The United States argues that arrests authorized by this statute would be an obstacle to the removal system Congress created.

As a general rule, it is not a crime for a removable alien to remain present in the United States. If the police stop someone based on nothing more than possible removability, the usual predicate for an arrest is absent. When an alien is suspected of being removable, a federal official issues an administrative document called a Notice to Appear. The form does not authorize an arrest. Instead, it gives the alien information about the proceedings, including the time and date of the removal hearing. If an alien fails to appear, an *in absentia* order may direct removal.

The federal statutory structure instructs when it is appropriate to arrest an alien during the removal process. For example, the Attorney General can exercise discretion to issue a warrant for an alien's arrest and detention "pending a decision on whether the alien is to be removed from the United States." And if an alien is ordered removed after a hearing, the Attorney General will issue a warrant. In both instances, the warrants are executed by federal officers who have received training in the enforcement of immigration law.

Section 6 attempts to provide state officers even greater authority to arrest aliens on the basis of possible removability than Congress has given to trained federal immigration officers. Under state law, officers who believe an alien is removable by reason of some "public offense" would have the power to conduct an arrest on that basis regardless of whether a federal warrant has issued or the alien is likely to escape. This state authority could be exercised without any input from the Federal Government about whether an arrest is warranted in a particular case. This would allow the State to achieve its own immigration policy. The result could be unnecessary harassment of some aliens (for instance, a veteran, college student, or someone assisting with a criminal investigation) whom federal officials determine should not be removed.

This is not the system Congress created. Federal law specifies limited circumstances in which state officers may perform the functions of an immigration officer. A principal example is when the Attorney General has granted that authority to specific officers in a formal agreement with a state or local government.

By authorizing state officers to decide whether an alien should be detained for being removable, §6 violates the principle that the removal process is entrusted to the discretion of the Federal Government. A decision on removability requires a determination whether it is appropriate to allow a foreign national to continue living in the United States. Decisions of this nature touch on foreign relations and must be made with one voice.

Section 2(B)

Section 2(B) of S.B. 1070 requires state officers to make a "reasonable attempt . . . to determine the immigration status" of any person they stop, detain, or arrest on some other legitimate basis if "reasonable suspicion exists that the person is an alien and is unlawfully present in the United States." The law also provides that "[a]ny person who is arrested shall have the person's immigration status determined before the person is released." The accepted way to perform these status checks is to contact ICE, which maintains a database of immigration records.

Three limits are built into the state provision. First, a detainee is presumed not to be an alien unlawfully present in the United States if he or she provides a valid Arizona driver's license or similar identification. Second, officers "may not consider race, color or national origin . . . except to the extent permitted by the United States [and] Arizona Constitution[s]." Third, the provisions must be "implemented in a manner consistent with federal law regulating immigration, protecting the civil rights of all persons and respecting the privileges and immunities of United States citizens."

Consultation between federal and state officials is an important feature of the immigration system. Congress has made clear that no formal agreement or special training needs to be in place for state officers to "communicate with the [Federal Government] regarding the immigration status of any individual, including reporting knowledge that a particular alien is not lawfully present in the United States." And Congress has obligated ICE to respond to any request made by state officials for verification of a person's citizenship or immigration status.

Congress has done nothing to suggest it is inappropriate to communicate with ICE in these situations, however. Indeed, it has encouraged the sharing of information about possible immigration violations. The federal scheme thus leaves room for a policy requiring state officials to contact ICE as a routine matter.

Some who support the challenge to §2(B) argue that, in practice, state officers will be required to delay the release of some detainees for no reason other than to verify their immigration status. Detaining individuals solely to verify their immigration status would raise constitutional concerns. And it would disrupt the federal framework to put state officers in the position of holding aliens in custody for possible unlawful presence without federal direction and supervision. The program put in place by Congress does not allow state or local officers to adopt this enforcement mechanism.

The nature and timing of this case counsel caution in evaluating the validity of §2(B). The Federal Government has brought suit against a sovereign State to challenge the provision even before the law has gone into effect. There is a basic uncertainty about what the law means and how it will be enforced. At this stage, without the benefit of a definitive interpretation from the state courts, it would be inappropriate to assume §2(B) will be construed in a way that creates a conflict with federal law. As a result, the United States cannot prevail in its current challenge. This opinion does not foreclose other preemption and constitutional challenges to the law as interpreted and applied after it goes into effect.

[IV]

Immigration policy shapes the destiny of the Nation. The history of the United States is in part made of the stories, talents, and lasting contributions of those who crossed oceans and deserts to come here.

The National Government has significant power to regulate immigration. With power comes responsibility, and the sound exercise of national power over immigration depends on the Nation's meeting its responsibility to base its laws on a political will informed by searching, thoughtful, rational civic discourse. Arizona may have understandable frustrations with the problems caused by illegal immigration while that process continues, but the State may not pursue policies that undermine federal law.

Justice SCALIA, concurring in part and dissenting in part.

The United States is an indivisible "Union of sovereign States." Today's opinion, approving virtually all of the Ninth Circuit's injunction against enforcement of the four challenged provisions of Arizona's law, deprives States of what most would consider the defining characteristic of sovereignty: the power to exclude from the sovereign's territory people who have no right to be there. Neither the Constitution itself nor even any law passed by Congress supports this result. I dissent.

I

As a sovereign, Arizona has the inherent power to exclude persons from its territory, subject only to those limitations expressed in the Constitution or constitutionally imposed by Congress.

In light of the predominance of federal immigration restrictions in modern times, it is easy to lose sight of the States' traditional role in regulating immigration — and to overlook their sovereign prerogative to do so. I accept as a given that State regulation is excluded by the Constitution when (1) it has been prohibited by a valid federal law, or (2) it conflicts with federal regulation — when, for example, it admits those whom federal regulation would exclude, or excludes those whom federal regulation would admit.

Possibility (1) need not be considered here: there is no federal law prohibiting the States' sovereign power to exclude (assuming federal authority to enact such a law). The mere existence of federal action in the immigration area — and the so-called field preemption arising from that action, upon which the Court's opinion so heavily relies, cannot be regarded as such a prohibition. We are not talking here about a federal law prohibiting the States from regulating bubble-gum advertising, or even the construction of nuclear plants. We are talking about a federal law going to the *core* of state sovereignty: the power to exclude. Like elimination of the States' other inherent sovereign power, immunity from suit, elimination of the States' sovereign power to exclude requires that "Congress . . . unequivocally expres[s] its intent to abrogate." Implicit "field preemption" will not do.

Nor can federal power over illegal immigration be deemed exclusive because of what the Court's opinion solicitously calls "foreign countries['] concern[s] about the status, safety, and security of their nationals in the United States." Even in its international relations, the Federal Government must live with the inconvenient fact that it is a Union of independent States, who have their own sovereign powers.

What this case comes down to, then, is whether the Arizona law conflicts with federal immigration law — whether it excludes those whom federal law would admit, or admits those whom federal law would exclude. It does not purport to do so. It applies only to aliens who neither possess a privilege to be present under federal law nor have been removed pursuant to the Federal Government's inherent authority. I proceed to consider the challenged provisions in detail.

§2(B)

The Government has conceded that "even before Section 2 was enacted, state and local officers had state-law authority to inquire of DHS [the Department of Homeland Security] about a suspect's unlawful status and otherwise cooperate with federal immigration officers." That concession, in my view, obviates the need for further inquiry. The Court therefore properly rejects the Government's challenge, recognizing that, "[a]t this stage, without the benefit of a definitive interpretation from the state courts, it would be inappropriate to assume §2B will be construed in a way that creates a conflict with federal law."

§6

This provision of S.B. 1070 expands the statutory list of offenses for which an Arizona police officer may make an arrest without a warrant. If an officer has probable cause to believe that an individual is "removable" by reason of a public offense, then a warrant is not required to make an arrest. The Government's primary contention is that §6 is pre-empted by federal immigration law because it allows state officials to make arrests "without regard to federal priorities."

Of course on this pre-enforcement record there is no reason to assume that Arizona officials will ignore federal immigration policy (unless it be the questionable policy of not wanting to identify illegal aliens who have committed offenses that make them removable). As Arizona points out, federal law expressly provides that state officers may "cooperate with the Attorney General in the identification, apprehension, detention, or removal of aliens not lawfully present in the United States," and "cooperation" requires neither identical efforts nor prior federal approval. It is consistent with the Arizona statute, and with the "cooperat[ive]" system that Congress has created, for state officials to arrest a removable alien, contact federal immigration authorities, and follow their lead on what to do next. And it is an assault on logic to say that identifying a removable alien and holding him for federal determination of whether he should be removed "violates the principle that the removal process is entrusted to the discretion of the Federal Government." The State's detention does not represent commencement of the removal process unless the Federal Government makes it so.

But that is not the most important point. The most important point is that, as we have discussed, Arizona is *entitled* to have "its own immigration policy" — including a more rigorous enforcement policy — so long as that does not conflict with federal law.

§3

It is beyond question that a State may make violation of federal law a violation of state law as well. We have held that to be so even when the interest protected is a distinctively federal interest, such as protection of the dignity of the national flag, or protection of the Federal Government's ability to recruit soldiers. The Court points out, however, that in some respects the state law exceeds the punishments prescribed by federal law: It rules out probation and pardon, which are available under federal law. The answer is that it makes no difference. Illegal immigrants who violate §3 violate *Arizona* law. It is one thing to say that the Supremacy Clause prevents Arizona law from excluding those whom federal law admits. It is quite something else to say that a violation of Arizona law cannot be punished more severely than a violation of federal law. Especially where (as here) the State is defending its own sovereign interests, there is no precedent for such a limitation. The sale of illegal drugs, for example, ordinarily violates state law as well as federal law, and no one thinks that the state penalties cannot exceed the federal. As I have discussed, moreover, "field preemption" cannot establish a prohibition of additional state penalties in the area of immigration.

§5(C)

The Court concludes that §5(C) "would interfere with the careful balance struck by Congress," (another field pre-emption notion, by the way) but that is easy to say and impossible to demonstrate. The Court relies primarily on the fact that "[p]roposals to make unauthorized work a criminal offense were debated and discussed during the long process of drafting [the Immigration Reform and Control Act of 1986 (IRCA)]," "[b]ut Congress rejected them." There is no more reason to believe that this rejection was expressive of a desire that there be no sanctions on employees, than expressive of a desire that such sanctions be left to the States. To tell the truth, it was most likely expressive of what inaction ordinarily expresses: nothing at all. It is a "naïve assumption that the failure of a bill to make it out of committee, or to be adopted when reported to the floor, is the same as a congressional rejection of what the bill contained."

[II]

The brief for the Government in this case asserted that "the Executive Branch's ability to exercise discretion and set priorities is particularly important because of the need to allocate scarce enforcement resources wisely." Of course there is no reason why the Federal Executive's need to allocate *its* scarce enforcement resources should disable Arizona from devoting *its* resources to illegal immigration in Arizona that in its view the Federal Executive has given short shrift. Must Arizona's ability to protect its borders yield to the reality that Congress has provided inadequate funding for federal enforcement—or, even worse, to the Executive's unwise targeting of that funding?

Are the sovereign States at the mercy of the Federal Executive's refusal to enforce the Nation's immigration laws? A good way of answering that question is to ask: Would the States conceivably have entered into the Union if the Constitution itself contained the Court's holding? Today's judgment surely fails that test.

As is often the case, discussion of the dry legalities that are the proper object of our attention suppresses the very human realities that gave rise to the suit. Arizona bears the brunt of the country's illegal immigration problem. Its citizens feel themselves under siege by large numbers of illegal immigrants who invade their property, strain their social services, and even place their lives in jeopardy. Federal officials have been unable to remedy the problem, and indeed have recently shown that they are unwilling to do so. Thousands of Arizona's estimated 400,000 illegal immigrants—including not just children but men and women under 30—are now assured immunity from enforcement, and will be able to compete openly with Arizona citizens for employment.

Arizona has moved to protect its sovereignty—not in contradiction of federal law, but in complete compliance with it. The laws under challenge here do not extend or revise federal immigration restrictions, but merely enforce those restrictions more effectively. If securing its territory in this fashion is not within the power of Arizona, we should cease referring to it as a sovereign State. I dissent.

B. THE DORMANT COMMERCE CLAUSE

The "dormant Commerce Clause" is the principle that state and local laws are unconstitutional if they place an undue burden on interstate commerce. There is no constitutional provision that expressly declares that states may not burden interstate commerce. Rather, the Supreme Court has inferred this from the grant of power to Congress in Article I, §8 to regulate commerce among the states.

If Congress has legislated, the issue is whether the federal law preempts the state or local law — the issue discussed above. But even if Congress has not acted or no preemption is found, the state or local law can be challenged on the ground that it excessively burdens commerce among the states. In other words, even if Congress has not acted — even if its commerce power lies dormant, state and local laws still can be challenged as unduly impeding interstate commerce. As Felix Frankfurter explained, "[T]he doctrine [is] that the Commerce Clause, by its own force and without national legislation, puts it into the power of the Court to place limits on state authority."[11]

The Commerce Clause thus has two distinct functions. One is an authorization for congressional actions. The scope of Congress's power to legislate under the Commerce Clause is discussed in Chapter 2. The other function of the Commerce Clause is in limiting state and local regulation. This is the dormant or "negative" Commerce Clause.

The dormant Commerce Clause is not the only way of challenging state laws that burden interstate commerce, especially if the state or local law discriminates against out-of-staters. For example, if the state or local government discriminates against out-of-staters with regard to a fundamental right or important economic activities, a challenge can be brought under the Privileges and Immunities Clause of Article IV, §2. The Privileges and Immunities Clause is discussed in the next subsection. Also, laws that discriminate against out-of-staters can be challenged under the Equal Protection Clause of the Fourteenth Amendment.

The discussion of the dormant Commerce Clause begins in subsection 1 of this section by examining whether there should be a dormant Commerce Clause. Understanding the policies underlying the dormant Commerce Clause is important in considering the cases that follow. Also, there is a debate among justices and scholars as to whether there should be a dormant Commerce Clause and under what circumstances courts should use it.

Subsection 2 then describes the Court's nineteenth-century dormant Commerce Clause cases. These older precedents often are invoked in modern decisions, even though the tests used in contemporary cases are quite different from those used in the nineteenth century.

Subsection 3 presents the key cases concerning the contemporary dormant Commerce Clause. The central question in dormant Commerce Clause analysis is whether the state or local law discriminates against out-of-staters or whether it treats in-staters and out-of-staters alike. If a law is found to discriminate, it is very likely to be declared unconstitutional. If a law is deemed nondiscriminatory, the law is likely to be upheld. Therefore, subsection 3 proceeds in three steps: First, how is it determined whether a law is discriminatory? Second, what is the analysis for laws that are discriminatory? And finally, what is the analysis for laws that are not discriminatory?

Subsection 4 then considers exceptions to the dormant Commerce Clause — that is, situations in which laws that otherwise would violate the dormant Commerce Clause will be allowed. One exception is if Congress approves the state or local action. Congress has plenary power to regulate commerce among the states

---

11. Felix Frankfurter, *The Commerce Clause under Marshall, Taney, and Waits* 18 (1937).

and may authorize laws that otherwise would violate the dormant Commerce Clause. The other major exception is termed "the market participant exception." Under the market participant exception, a state or local government may favor its own citizens in receiving benefits from state or local governments or in dealing with government-owned businesses.

1.   Why a Dormant Commerce Clause?

Congress always has the authority under its commerce power to preempt state or local regulation of commerce. Therefore, Congress could invalidate any state or local law that it deems to place an undue burden on interstate commerce. The crucial issue with regard to the dormant Commerce Clause is whether the judiciary, in the absence of congressional action, should invalidate state and local laws because they place an undue burden on interstate commerce.

The Supreme Court explains the justifications for the dormant Commerce Clause in the following case.

H.P. HOOD & SONS, INC. v. DU MOND, COMMISSIONER OF AGRICULTURE & MARKETS OF NEW YORK

336 U.S. 525 (1949)

Justice JACKSON delivered the opinion of the Court.

This case concerns the power of the State of New York to deny additional facilities to acquire and ship milk in interstate commerce where the grounds of denial are that such limitation upon interstate business will protect and advance local economic interests.

H.P. Hood & Sons, Inc., a Massachusetts corporation, has long distributed milk and its products to inhabitants of Boston. That city obtains about 90% of its fluid milk from states other than Massachusetts. Dairies located in New York State since about 1900 have been among the sources of Boston's supply, their contribution having varied but during the last ten years approximately 8%.

The controversy concerns a proposed additional plant for the same kind of operation at Greenwich, New York [which the state seeks to deny to the Massachusetts company].

Our decision in a milk litigation most relevant to the present controversy deals with the converse of the present situation. Baldwin v. G. A. F. Seelig, Inc. In that case, New York placed conditions and limitations on the local sale of milk imported from Vermont designed in practical effect to exclude it, while here its order proposes to limit the local facilities for purchase of additional milk so as to withhold milk from export. The State agreed then, as now, that the Commerce Clause prohibits it from directly curtailing movement of milk into or out of the State. This Court unanimously rejected the State's contention in the *Seelig* case and held that the Commerce Clause, even in the absence of congressional action, prohibits such regulations for such ends. The opinion was by Mr. Justice Cardozo, experienced in the milk problems of New York and favorably disposed toward the efforts of the State to control the industry. It recognized, as do we, broad power in the State to protect its inhabitants against perils to health or safety, fraudulent traders and highway hazards even by use of measures which bear adversely upon interstate commerce. But it laid repeated emphasis upon the principle that the State may not promote its own economic advantages by curtailment or burdening of interstate commerce.

The Constitution, said Mr. Justice Cardozo for the unanimous Court, "was framed upon the theory that the peoples of the several states must sink or swim together, and that in the long run prosperity and salvation are in union and not division." He reiterated that the economic objective, as distinguished from any health, safety and fair-dealing purpose of the regulation, was the root of its invalidity. The action of the State would "neutralize the economic consequences of free trade among the states." "Such a power, if exerted, will set a barrier to traffic between one state and another as effective as if customs duties, equal to the price differential, had been laid upon the thing transported." "If New York, in order to promote the economic welfare of her farmers, may guard them against competition, with the cheaper prices of Vermont, the door has been opened to rivalries and reprisals that were meant to be averted by subjecting commerce between the states to the power of the nation." And again, "Neither the power to tax nor the police power may be used by the state of destination with the aim and effect of establishing an economic barrier against competition with the products of another state or the labor of its residents. Restrictions so contrived are an unreasonable clog upon the mobility of commerce. They set up what is equivalent to a rampart of customs duties designed to neutralize advantages belonging to the place of origin. They are thus hostile in conception as well as burdensome in result."

This distinction between the power of the State to shelter its people from menaces to their health or safety and from fraud, even when those dangers emanate from interstate commerce, and its lack of power to retard, burden or constrict the flow of such commerce for their economic advantage, is one deeply rooted in both our history and our law.

When victory relieved the Colonies from the pressure for solidarity that war had exerted, a drift toward anarchy and commercial warfare between states began. "[E]ach state would legislate according to its estimate of its own interests, the importance of its own products, and the local advantages or disadvantages of its position in a political or commercial view." This came "to threaten at once the peace and safety of the Union." Story, The Constitution. The sole purpose for which Virginia initiated the movement which ultimately produced the Constitution was "to take into consideration the trade of the United States; to examine the relative situations and trade of the said states; to consider how far a uniform system in their commercial regulation may be necessary to their common interest and their permanent harmony" and for that purpose the General Assembly of Virginia in January of 1786 named commissioners and proposed their meeting with those from other states. The desire of the Forefathers to federalize regulation of foreign and interstate commerce stands in sharp contrast to their jealous preservation of power over their internal affairs. No other federal power was so universally assumed to be necessary, no other state power was so readily relinquished.

The necessity of centralized regulation of commerce among the states was so obvious and so fully recognized that the few words of the Commerce Clause were little illuminated by debate. But the significance of the clause was not lost and its effect was immediate and salutary.

The material success that has come to inhabitants of the states which make up this federal free trade unit has been the most impressive in the history of commerce, but the established interdependence of the states only emphasizes the necessity of protecting interstate movement of goods against local burdens and repressions. We need only consider the consequences if each of the few states that produce copper, lead, high-grade iron ore, timber, cotton, oil or gas should decree that industries located in that state shall have priority. What fantastic rivalries and dislocations and reprisals would ensue if such practices were begun! Or suppose that the field of discrimination and retaliation be industry. May Michigan provide that automobiles cannot be taken out of that State until local dealers' demands are fully met? Would she not have every argument in the favor of such a statute that can be offered in support of New York's limiting sales of milk for out-of-state shipment to protect the economic interests of her competing dealers and local consumers? Could Ohio then pounce upon the rubber-tire industry, on which she has a substantial grip, to retaliate for Michigan's auto monopoly?

Our system, fostered by the Commerce Clause, is that every farmer and every craftsman shall be encouraged to produce by the certainty that he will have free access to every market in the Nation, that no home embargoes will withhold his export, and no foreign state will by customs duties or regulations exclude them. Likewise, every consumer may look to the free competition from every producing area in the Nation to protect him from exploitation by any. Such was the vision of the Founders; such has been the doctrine of this Court which has given it reality.

The State, however, insists that denial of the license for a new plant does not restrict or obstruct interstate commerce, because petitioner has been licensed at its other plants without condition or limitation as to the quantities it may purchase. Hence, it is said, all that has been denied petitioner is a local convenience — that of being able to buy and receive at Greenwich, quantities of milk it is free to buy at Eagle Bridge and Salem. It suggests that, by increased efficiency or enlarged capacity at its other plants, petitioner might sufficiently increase its supply through those facilities.

The weakness of this contention is that a buyer has to buy where there is a willing seller, and the peculiarities of the milk business necessitate location of a receiving and cooling station for nearby producers. The Commissioner has not made and there is nothing to persuade us that he could have made findings that petitioner can obtain such additional supplies through its existing facilities; indeed he found that "applicant has experienced some difficulty during the flush season because of the inability of the plant facilities to handle the milk by 9 A.M.," the time its receipt is required by Boston health authorities unless it is cooled by the farmer before delivery, and a substantial part of it is not.

The Court in Hood & Sons v. Du Mond presents the traditional arguments for having a dormant Commerce Clause. First, there is a historical argument for the dormant Commerce Clause: The framers intended to prevent state laws that interfered with interstate commerce. Second, there is an economic justification for the dormant Commerce Cause: The economy is better off if state and local laws impeding interstate commerce are invalidated. Third, there is a political justification for the dormant Commerce Clause: States and their citizens should not be harmed by laws in other states where they lack political representation. In McCulloch v. Maryland, the Supreme Court invalidated Maryland's tax on the Bank of the United States, in part, because it was a tax that ultimately would be borne by those in other states that obviously did not have representation in the Maryland political process.[12] Similarly, the political process cannot be trusted when a state is helping itself at the expense of out-of-staters who have no representation. Justice Stone explained: "Underlying the stated rule has been the thought, often expressed in judicial opinion, that when the regulation is of such a character that its burden falls principally upon those without the state, legislative action is not likely to be subjected to those political restraints which are normally exerted on legislation where it affects adversely some interests within the state."[13]

But others argue against the existence of a dormant Commerce Clause. The strongest recent criticism of the existence of the dormant Commerce Clause was by Justice Clarence Thomas in a dissenting opinion in Camps Newfound/Owatonna, Inc. v. Town of Harrison, 520 U.S. 564 (1997). The majority of the Supreme Court declared unconstitutional on dormant Commerce Clause grounds a state property tax because its exemption for property owned by charitable institutions excluded organizations operated principally for the benefit of nonresidents.

Justice Thomas dissented and strongly criticized the dormant Commerce Clause, especially in instances where the state does not discriminate against out-of-staters. Thomas wrote:

> The negative Commerce Clause has no basis in the text of the Constitution, makes little sense, and has proved virtually unworkable in application. In one fashion or another, every Member of the current Court and a goodly number of our predecessors have at least recognized these problems, if not been troubled by them.
>
> To cover its exercise of judicial power in an area for which there is no textual basis, the Court has historically offered two different theories in support of its negative Commerce Clause jurisprudence. The first theory posited was that the Commerce Clause itself constituted an exclusive grant of power to Congress. See, e.g., Passenger Cases (1849). The "exclusivity" rationale was likely wrong from the outset, however. And, in any event, the Court has long since "repudiated" the notion that the Commerce Clause operates as an exclusive grant of power to Congress, and thereby forecloses state action respecting interstate commerce. Freeman v. Hewit (1946) (Rutledge, J., concurring). Indeed, the Court's early view that the Commerce Clause, on its own, prohibited state impediments to interstate commerce such that "Congress cannot re-grant, or in any manner reconvey to the states that power," Cooley v. Board of Wardens of Port of Philadelphia ex rel. Soc. for Relief of Distressed Pilots (1852), quickly proved untenable. And, as this Court's definition of the scope of congressional authority under the positive Commerce Clause has expanded, the exclusivity rationale has moved from untenable to absurd.
>
> The second theory offered to justify creation of a negative Commerce Clause is that Congress, by its silence, pre-empts state legislation. See Robbins v. Shelby County Taxing Dist. (1887) (asserting that congressional silence evidences congressional intent that there be no state regulation of commerce). In other words,

---

12. 17 U.S. (4 Wheat.) 316, 429-430 (1819), presented in Chapter 2.
13. South Carolina State Highway Department v. Barnwell Brothers, Inc., 303 U.S. 177, 185 (1938).

we presumed that congressional "inaction" was "equivalent to a declaration that inter-State commerce shall be free and untrammelled." Welton v. Missouri (1876). To the extent that the "pre-emption-by-silence" rationale ever made sense, it, too, has long since been rejected by this Court in virtually every analogous area of the law.

Even were we wrongly to assume that congressional silence evidenced a desire to pre-empt some undefined category of state laws, and an intent to delegate such policy-laden categorization to the courts, treating unenacted congressional intent as if it were law would be constitutionally dubious.

In sum, neither of the Court's proffered theoretical justifications — exclusivity or pre-emption-by-silence — currently supports our negative Commerce Clause jurisprudence, if either ever did. Despite the collapse of its theoretical foundation, I suspect we have nonetheless adhered to the negative Commerce Clause because we believed it necessary to check state measures contrary to the perceived spirit, if not the actual letter, of the Constitution.

Moreover, our negative Commerce Clause jurisprudence has taken us well beyond the invalidation of obviously discriminatory taxes on interstate commerce. We have used the Clause to make policy-laden judgments that we are ill equipped and arguably unauthorized to make. Any test that requires us to assess (1) whether a particular statute serves a "legitimate" local public interest; (2) whether the effects of the statute on interstate commerce are merely "incidental" or "clearly excessive in relation to the putative benefits"; (3) the "nature" of the local interest; and (4) whether there are alternative means of furthering the local interest that have a "lesser impact" on interstate commerce, and even then makes the question "one of degree," surely invites us, if not compels us, to function more as legislators than as judges. Moreover, our open-ended balancing tests in this area have allowed us to reach different results based merely "on differing assessments of the force of competing analogies."

In my view, none of this policy-laden decisionmaking is proper. Rather, the Court should confine itself to interpreting the text of the Constitution, which itself seems to prohibit in plain terms certain of the more egregious state taxes on interstate commerce described above, and leaves to Congress the policy choices necessary for any further regulation of interstate commerce.

The argument against the dormant Commerce Clause is, in part, textual. The drafters of the Constitution could have included a provision prohibiting states from interfering with interstate commerce. Also, opponents of the dormant Commerce Clause argue that the Constitution gives Congress the power to regulate commerce and Congress can act to invalidate state laws that unduly burden interstate commerce. The argument is that this should not be a task for an unelected federal judiciary. Thus, this is an argument based partially on separation of powers (the task of reviewing state laws should be done by Congress and not by the courts) and partially on federalism (minimizing the instances where state and local laws are invalidated).

In reading the cases that follow, consider these competing policy considerations, whether there should be a dormant Commerce Clause, and especially when it should apply.

2. The Dormant Commerce Clause Before 1938

The dormant Commerce Clause can be traced back to Gibbons v. Ogden, 22 U.S. (9 Wheat.) 1 (1824). The issue in *Gibbons* was whether the state of New York could grant an exclusive monopoly for operating steamboats in New York waters and thereby prevent a person with a federal license from operating in New York. As presented in Chapter 2, Chief Justice John Marshall, writing for the Court, used *Gibbons* as the occasion for broadly defining the scope of Congress's power under the Commerce Clause. Marshall said that "commerce" refers to all stages of business and that "among the states" includes matters that affect more than one state and are not purely internal. Chief Justice John Marshall also used *Gibbons* for considering the Commerce Clause as an independent limit on state power, even where Congress has not acted. Marshall explained that "when a State proceeds to regulate commerce with foreign nations, or among the several states, it is exercising the very power that is granted to Congress, and is doing the very thing which Congress is authorized to do." This argument would seem to imply that Congress's commerce power is exclusive; that any state regulation of commerce is inconsistent with federal power. The idea appears to be that the power to regulate commerce is the authority to decide that commerce should not be regulated and that states therefore should not be able to act with regard to commerce unless specifically authorized by Congress.

Chief Justice Marshall, however, did not go nearly this far in limiting state authority. Rather, Marshall drew a distinction between a state's exercise of its police power and a state exercising the federal power over commerce. Marshall said, for example, that state inspection laws are constitutional even though they may have a "considerable influence on commerce" because they are a "portion of that great immense of legislation, which embraces every thing within the territory of a State, not surrendered to the general government; all which can be most advantageously exercised by the States themselves. Inspection laws, quarantine laws, health laws of every description, as well as laws for regulating the internal commerce of a State, and those which respect turnpike roads, ferries, etc., are component parts of this mass."

In several cases following *Gibbons*, the Court applied this approach in evaluating state laws under the Commerce Clause. For example, in Willson v. The Black Bird Creek Marsh Co., 27 U.S. (2 Pet.) 245 (1829), the Court considered whether a state could construct a dam that obstructed an interstate waterway. The Court rejected a challenge by the owner of a federally licensed ship, because construction of the dam was a permissible exercise of the state's police power. Similarly, in Mayor, Aldermen, and Commonalty of New York v. Miln, 36 U.S. (11 Pet.) 102 (1837), the Court upheld a state law requiring passenger identification lists for all ships arriving from other states or countries. The Court said that the law was "not a regulation of commerce but of police," apparently because it was based on a desire to protect public safety by guarding against the arrival of undesirables.

The Court has struggled ever since *Gibbons* with attempting to articulate criteria for when state laws burdening commerce should be upheld as valid exercises of the police power and when they should be invalidated as violating the dormant Commerce Clause.[14] Cooley v. Board of Wardens is a particularly important case in which the Court drew a distinction between subject matter that is national, in which case state laws are invalidated under the dormant

---

14. *See, e.g.*, The Passenger Cases, 48 U.S. (7 How.) 283 (1849), where the Court split five to four, with every justice writing a separate opinion, and invalidated a state law requiring every incoming passenger to pay for the costs of health inspections and treatment; *see also The License Cases*, 46 U.S. (5 How.) 504 (1847).

Commerce Clause, and subject matter that is local, in which case state laws are allowed.

AARON B. COOLEY v. THE BOARD OF WARDENS OF THE PORT OF PHILADELPHIA

53 U.S. (12 How.) 299 (1851)

[A Pennsylvania law required all ships entering or leaving the Port of Philadelphia to use a local pilot or pay a fine that went to support retired pilots.]

We think this particular regulation concerning half-pilotage fees, is an appropriate part of a general system of regulations of this subject. Testing it by the practice of commercial states and countries legislating on this subject, we find it has usually been deemed necessary to make similar provisions.

[We] cannot pronounce a law which does this, to be so far removed from the usual and fit scope of laws for the regulation of pilots and pilotage, as to be deemed, for this cause, a covert attempt to legislate upon another subject under the appearance of legislating on this one. It is urged that the second section of the act of the Legislature of Pennsylvania, of the 11th of June, 1832, proves that the state had other objects in view than the regulation of pilotage.

It must be remembered, that the fair objects of a law imposing half-pilotage when a pilot is not received, may be secured, and at the same time some classes of vessels exempted from such charge. Thus the very section of the act of 1803, now under consideration, does not apply to coasting vessels of less burden than seventy-five tons, not to those bound to, or sailing from, a port in the river Delaware. The purpose of the law being to cause masters of such vessels as generally need a pilot, to employ one, and to secure to the pilots a fair remuneration for cruising in search of vessels, or waiting for employment in port, there is an obvious propriety in having reference to the number, size, and nature of employment of vessels frequenting the port; and it will be found, by an examination of the different systems of these regulations, which have from time to time been made in this and other countries, that the legislative discretion has been constantly exercised in making discriminations, founded on differences both in the character of the trade, and the tonnage of vessels engaged therein.

We do not perceive anything in the nature or extent of this particular discrimination in favor of vessels engaged in the coal trade, which would enable us to declare it to be other than a fair exercise of legislative discretion, acting upon the subject of the regulation of the pilotage of this port of Philadelphia, with a view to operate upon the masters of those vessels, who, as a general rule, ought to take a pilot, and with the further view of relieving from the charge of half-pilotage, such vessels as from their size, or the nature of their employment, should be exempted from contributing to the support of pilots, except so far as they actually receive their services.

The Act of 1789 contains a clear and authoritative declaration by the first Congress that the nature of this subject is such that it should be left to the legislation of the states; that it is local and not national; that it is likely to be the best provided for, not by one system or plan for regulations, but by as many as the legislative discretion of the several states should deem applicable to the local peculiarities of the parts within their limits.

Many cases applied the *Cooley* test throughout the nineteenth century and into the twentieth century. In Welton v. Missouri, 91 U.S. (1 Otto) 275 (1875), the Court used the *Cooley* approach to invalidate a law that required peddlers of out-of-state merchandise to pay a tax and obtain a license, whereas no similar requirements existed for in-state merchants. The Court said that "transportation and exchange of commodities is of national importance, and admits and requires uniformity of regulation." Similarly, in Wabash, St. Louis & Pacific Ry. Co. v. Illinois, 118 U.S. 557 (1886), the Court used the *Cooley* approach to invalidate a state law that regulated railway rates for goods brought to or from other states. The Court emphasized that there would be enormous burdens on interstate commerce if all states adopted such laws and thus concluded that it was an area that required national uniformity and not local regulation.

But during this same time the Court upheld other state laws on the ground that they were in areas where diverse regulation was desirable. For instance, in Smith v. Alabama, 124 U.S. 465 (1888), the Court upheld a state law requiring that all locomotive engineers operating in the state be licensed by a state board of examiners. Likewise, in Erb v. Morasch, 177 U.S. 584 (1900), the Court upheld a city's ordinance that restricted train speed within the city. In Atchinson Topeka & Santa Fe Ry. Co. v. Railroad Commn., 283 U.S. 380 (1931), the Court upheld a state law that required electric headlights of prescribed brightness on all trains operating within the state.

3.   The Contemporary Test for the Dormant Commerce Clause

a.   The Shift to a Balancing Approach

The nineteenth century's approaches summarized above — the police power/commerce power test of *Gibbons* and the local/national subject matter test of *Cooley* — attempted to draw rigid categories of areas where federal law was exclusive and those where states could regulate. The modern approach is based not on rigid categories, but rather on courts balancing the benefits of a law against the burdens that it imposes on interstate commerce. It should be noted, however, that the Court never has expressly overruled any of the earlier tests and sometimes invokes them in explaining a particular result.

The Court's shift to a balancing approach for the dormant Commerce Clause is evident from comparing two cases, South Carolina State Highway Dept. v. Barnwell Bros. and Southern Pacific Co. v. Arizona.

SOUTH CAROLINA STATE HIGHWAY DEPARTMENT v.
BARNWELL BROS., INC.

303 U.S. 177 (1938)

Justice STONE delivered the opinion of the Court.

Act No. 259 of the General Assembly of South Carolina, of April 28, 1933, prohibits use on the state highways of motor trucks and "semitrailer motortrucks" whose width exceeds 90 inches, and whose weight including load exceeds 20,000 pounds. For purposes of the weight limitation, section 2 of the statute provides that a semitrailer motortruck, which is a motor propelled truck with a trailer whose front end is designed to be attached to and supported by the truck, shall be considered a single unit. The principal question for decision is whether these prohibitions impose an unconstitutional burden upon interstate commerce.

South Carolina has built its highways and owns and maintains them. It has received from the federal government, in aid of its highway improvements, money grants which have been expended upon the highways to which the injunction applies. But appellees do not challenge here the ruling of the District Court that Congress has not undertaken to regulate the weight and size of motor vehicles in interstate motor traffic and has left undisturbed whatever authority in that regard the states have retained under the Constitution.

The Commerce Clause by its own force, prohibits discrimination against interstate commerce, whatever its form or method, and the decisions of this Court have recognized that there is scope for its like operation when state legislation nominally of local concern is in point of fact aimed at interstate commerce, or by its necessary operation is a means of gaining a local benefit by throwing the attendant burdens on those without the state. It was to end these practices that the Commerce Clause was adopted. The Commerce Clause has also been thought to set its own limitation upon state control of interstate rail carriers so as to preclude the subordination of the efficiency and convenience of interstate traffic to local service requirements.

Few subjects of state regulation are so peculiarly of local concern as is the use of state highways. There are few, local regulation of which is so inseparable from a substantial effect on interstate commerce. Unlike the railroads, local highways are built, owned, and maintained by the state or its municipal subdivisions. The state has a primary and immediate concern in their safe and economical administration. The present regulations, or any others of like purpose, if they are to accomplish their end, must be applied alike to interstate and intrastate traffic both moving in large volume over the highways. The fact that they affect alike shippers in interstate and intrastate commerce in large number within as well as without the state is a safeguard against their abuse.

[O]ur decisions [have held] that a state may impose nondiscriminatory restrictions with respect to the character of motor vehicles moving in interstate commerce as a safety measure and as a means of securing the economical use of its highways. [C]ourts do not sit as Legislatures, either state or national. They cannot act as Congress does when, after weighing all the conflicting interests, state and national, it determines when and how much the state regulatory power shall yield to the larger interests of a national commerce. And in reviewing a state highway regulation where Congress has not acted, a court is not called upon, as are state Legislatures, to determine what, in its judgment, is the most suitable restriction to be applied of those that are possible, or to choose that one which in its opinion is best adapted to all the diverse interests affected.

Since the adoption of one weight or width regulation, rather than another, is a legislative, not a judicial, choice, its constitutionality is not to be determined by weighing in the judicial scales the merits of the legislative choice and rejecting it if the weight of evidence presented in court appears to favor a different standard. The choice of a weight limitation based on convenience of application and consequent lack of need for rigid supervisory enforcement is for the Legislature, and we cannot say that its preference for the one over the other is in any sense arbitrary or unreasonable. The choice is not to be condemned because the Legislature prefers a workable standard, less likely to be violated than another under which the violations will probably be increased but more easily detected. It is for the Legislature to say whether the one test or the other will in practical operation better protect the highways from the risk of excessive loads. The regulatory measures taken by South Carolina are within its legislative power. They do not infringe the Fourteenth Amendment, and the resulting burden on interstate commerce is not forbidden.

SOUTHERN PACIFIC CO. v. ARIZONA ex rel. SULLIVAN, ATTORNEY GENERAL

325 U.S. 761 (1945)

Chief Justice STONE delivered the opinion of the Court.

The Arizona Train Limit Law of May 16, 1912 makes it unlawful for any person or corporation to operate within the state a railroad train of more than fourteen passenger or seventy freight cars, and authorizes the state to recover a money penalty for each violation of the Act.

Although the Commerce Clause conferred on the national government power to regulate commerce, its possession of the power does not exclude all state power of regulation. Ever since Willson v. Black-Bird Creek Marsh Co., and Cooley v. Board of Wardens, it has been recognized that, in the absence of conflicting legislation by Congress, there is a residuum of power in the state to make laws governing matters of local concern which nevertheless in some measure affect interstate commerce or even, to some extent, regulate it. When the regulation of matters of local concern is local in character and effect, and its impact on the national commerce does not seriously interfere with its operation, and the consequent incentive to deal with them nationally is slight, such regulation has been generally held to be within state authority.

In the application of these principles some enactments may be found to be plainly within and others plainly without state power. But between these extremes lies the infinite variety of cases in which regulation of local matters may also operate as a regulation of commerce, in which reconciliation of the conflicting claims of state and national power is to be attained only by some appraisal and accommodation of the competing demands of the state and national interests involved. Hence the matters for ultimate determination here are the nature and extent of the burden which the state regulation of interstate trains, adopted as a safety measure, imposes on interstate commerce, and whether the relative weights of the state and national interests involved are such as to make inapplicable the rule, generally observed, that the free flow of interstate commerce and its freedom from local restraints in matters requiring uniformity of regulation are interests safeguarded by the Commerce Clause from state interference.

The findings show that the operation of long trains, that is trains of more than fourteen passenger and more than seventy freight cars, is standard practice over the main lines of the railroads of the United States, and that, if the length of trains is to be regulated at all, national uniformity in the regulation adopted, such as only Congress can prescribe, is practically indispensable to the operation of an efficient and economical national railway system. On many railroads passenger trains of more than fourteen cars and freight trains of more than seventy cars are operated, and on some systems freight trains are run ranging from one hundred and twenty-five to one hundred and sixty cars in length. Outside of Arizona, where the length of trains is not restricted, appellant runs a substantial proportion of long trains. In 1939 on its comparable route for through traffic through Utah and Nevada from 66 to 85% of its freight trains were over 70 cars in length and over 43% of its passenger trains included more than fourteen passenger cars. In Arizona, approximately 93% of the freight traffic and 95% of the passenger traffic is interstate. Because of the Train Limit Law appellant is required to haul over 30% more trains in Arizona than would otherwise have been necessary.

The record shows a definite relationship between operating costs and the length of trains, the increase in length resulting in a reduction of operating costs per car. The additional cost of operation of trains complying with the Train Limit Law in Arizona amounts for the two railroads traversing that state to about $1,000,000 a year. The reduction in train lengths also impedes efficient operation. More locomotives and more manpower are required; the necessary conversion and reconversion of train lengths at terminals and the delay caused by breaking up and remaking long trains upon entering and leaving the state in order to comply with the law, delays the traffic and diminishes its volume moved in a given time, especially when traffic is heavy.

The unchallenged findings leave no doubt that the Arizona Train Limit Law imposes a serious burden on the interstate commerce conducted by appellant. It materially impedes the movement of appellant's interstate trains through that state and interposes a substantial obstruction to the national policy proclaimed by Congress, to promote adequate, economical and efficient railway transportation service. Enforcement of the law in Arizona, while train lengths remain unregulated or are regulated by varying standards in other states, must inevitably result in an impairment of uniformity of efficient railroad operation because the railroads are subjected to regulation which is not uniform in its application. Compliance with a state statute limiting train lengths requires interstate trains of a length lawful in other states to be broken up and reconstituted as they enter each state according as it may impose varying limitations upon train lengths. The alternative is for the carrier to conform to the lowest train limit restriction of any of the states through which its trains pass, whose laws thus control the carriers' operations both within and without the regulating state.

If one state may regulate train lengths, so may all the others, and they need not prescribe the same maximum limitation. The practical effect of such regulation is to control train operations beyond the boundaries of the state exacting it because of the necessity of breaking up and reassembling long trains at the nearest terminal points before entering and after leaving the regulating state. The serious impediment to the free flow of commerce by the local regulation of train lengths and the practical necessity that such regulation, if any, must be prescribed by a single body having a nation-wide authority are apparent.

The trial court found that the Arizona law had no reasonable relation to safety, and made train operation more dangerous. Examination of the evidence and the detailed findings makes it clear that this conclusion was rested on facts found which indicate that such increased danger of accident and personal injury as may result from the greater length of trains is more than offset by the increase in the number of accidents resulting from the larger number of trains when train lengths are reduced.

We think, as the trial court found, that the Arizona Train Limit Law, viewed as a safety measure, affords at most slight and dubious advantage, if any, over unregulated train lengths, because it results in an increase in the number of trains and train operations and the consequent increase in train accidents of a character generally more severe than those due to slack action. Its undoubted effect on the commerce is the regulation, without securing uniformity, of the length of trains operated in interstate commerce, which lack is itself a primary cause of preventing the free flow of commerce by delaying it and by substantially increasing its cost and impairing its efficiency.

In recent years, some justices, most notably Rehnquist, Scalia, and Thomas, have objected to this balancing test and have argued in favor of upholding all state laws that are deemed nondiscriminatory. Justice Scalia contended, "This process is ordinarily called 'balancing,' but the scale analogy is not really appropriate, since the interests on both sides are incommensurate. It is more like judging whether a particular line is longer than a particular rock is heavy. . . . Weighing the governmental interests of a State against the needs of interstate commerce is, by contrast, a task squarely within the responsibility of Congress, and ill suited to the judicial function."[15] As quoted above, Justice Thomas also has been very critical of the balancing test in dormant Commerce Clause cases.[16]

The question, of course, is what should replace the balancing test. The categorical approaches that preceded it were not useful in deciding whether a particular law violated the dormant Commerce Clause. Justice Scalia's answer is to eliminate dormant Commerce Clause review where the state is not discriminating against out-of-staters. Scalia wrote, "I would therefore abandon the balancing approach to these negative Commerce Clause cases . . . and leave essentially legislative judgments to the Congress. . . . In my view, a state statute is invalid under the Commerce Clause if, and only if, it accords discriminatory treatment to interstate commerce in a respect not required to achieve a lawful state purpose."[17]

The question that Justices Scalia and Thomas raise is whether there should be any dormant Commerce Clause review when a state law is deemed nondiscriminatory.

On the one hand, assuring a free flow of commerce among the states is best achieved by eliminating burdens on interstate commerce. On the other hand, there is no reason to distrust the political process when it is treating in-staters and out-of-staters alike. Limiting the scope of the dormant Commerce Clause has the benefits of minimizing the judicial role and maximizing the deference paid to state and local governments.

15. Bendix Autolite Corp. v. Midwesco Enterprises, Inc., 486 U.S. 888 (1988) (Scalia, J., dissenting).

16. Camps Newfound/Owatonna, Inc. v. Town of Harrison, 520 U.S. 564 (1997) (Thomas, J., dissenting), quoted above.

17. Bendix Autolite Corp. v. Midwesco Enterprises, Inc., 486 U.S. 888 (1988) (Scalia, J., dissenting).

b.   Determining Whether a Law Is Discriminatory

The balancing prescribed by the Supreme Court is not the same in all dormant Commerce Clause cases, but instead varies depending upon whether the state or local law discriminates against out-of-staters or treats in-staters and out-of-staters alike. As discussed below, if the Court concludes that a state is discriminating against out-of-staters, then there is a strong presumption against the law and it will be upheld only if it is necessary to achieve an important purpose. In contrast, if the Court concludes that the law is nondiscriminatory, then the presumption is in favor of upholding the law, and it will be invalidated only if it is shown that the law's burdens on interstate commerce outweigh its benefits.

Thus, the threshold question is determining whether the state law is discriminatory against out-of-staters. This makes sense in light of the purposes of the dormant Commerce Clause. The framers were most concerned about stopping protectionist state legislation, where a state would discriminate against out-of-staters to benefit its citizens at the expense of out-of-staters. Also, it is thought that protectionist laws are most likely to interfere with the economy. Besides, if a law applies to in-staters and out-of-staters equally, then at least some of those affected by the law are represented in the political process.

Sometimes laws are facially discriminatory against out-of-staters; that is, the laws in their very terms draw a distinction between in-staters and out-of-staters. Other times, laws are facially neutral, but might be motivated by a desire to help in-staters at the expense of out-of-staters or might have a discriminatory impact against those from other states. The first set of cases presented below involves facial discrimination; then presented are cases involving claims of facially neutral laws with discriminatory purpose or impact. After these cases, the next subsection looks at the analysis used when a law is deemed discriminatory; following this is a subsection examining the analysis for when a law is deemed not discriminatory.

FACIALLY DISCRIMINATORY LAWS

Sometimes, a law clearly favors in-staters over out-of-staters. For example, in Granholm v. Heald, 544 U.S. 460 (2005), the Court struck down state laws that allowed in-state wineries, but not out-of-state wineries, to sell wine directly to consumers through the mail. In recent years, many of the cases before the Supreme Court involving the dormant Commerce Clause have involved challenges to state and local environmental regulations. Below are three important Supreme Court decisions considering local laws designed to deal with solid-waste disposal problems.

CITY OF PHILADELPHIA v. NEW JERSEY

437 U.S. 617 (1978)

Justice STEWART delivered the opinion of the Court.

A New Jersey law prohibits the importation of most "solid or liquid waste which originated or was collected outside the territorial limits of the

State. . . ." In this case we are required to decide whether this statutory prohibition violates the Commerce Clause of the United States Constitution.

I

The statutory provision in question is ch. 363 of 1973 N.J. Laws, which took effect in early 1974. In pertinent part it provides: "No person shall bring into this State any solid or liquid waste which originated or was collected outside the territorial limits of the State, except garbage to be fed to swine in the State of New Jersey, until the commissioner [of the State Department of Environmental Protection] shall determine that such action can be permitted without endangering the public health, safety and welfare and has promulgated regulations permitting and regulating the treatment and disposal of such waste in this State."

Immediately affected by these developments were the operators of private landfills in New Jersey, and several cities in other States that had agreements with these operators for waste disposal. They brought suit against New Jersey and its Department of Environmental Protection in state court, attacking the statute and regulations on a number of state and federal grounds.

All objects of interstate trade merit Commerce Clause protection; none is excluded by definition at the outset. Hence, we reject the state court's suggestion that the banning of "valueless" out-of-state wastes by ch. 363 implicates no constitutional protection. Just as Congress has power to regulate the interstate movement of these wastes, States are not free from constitutional scrutiny when they restrict that movement.

[II]

Although the Constitution gives Congress the power to regulate commerce among the States, many subjects of potential federal regulation under that power inevitably escape congressional attention "because of their local character and their number and diversity." South Carolina State Highway Dept. v. Barnwell Bros., Inc. (1939). In the absence of federal legislation, these subjects are open to control by the States so long as they act within the restraints imposed by the Commerce Clause itself.

The opinions of the Court through the years have reflected an alertness to the evils of "economic isolation" and protectionism, while at the same time recognizing that incidental burdens on interstate commerce may be unavoidable when a State legislates to safeguard the health and safety of its people. Thus, where simple economic protectionism is effected by state legislation, a virtually per se rule of invalidity has been erected. The clearest example of such legislation is a law that overtly blocks the flow of interstate commerce at a State's borders.

The crucial inquiry, therefore, must be directed to determining whether ch. 363 is basically a protectionist measure, or whether it can fairly be viewed as a law directed to legitimate local concerns, with effects upon interstate commerce that are only incidental.

The purpose of ch. 363 is set out in the statute itself as follows: "The Legislature finds and determines that . . . the volume of solid and liquid waste continues to rapidly increase, that the treatment and disposal of these wastes continues to pose an even greater threat to the quality of the environment of New Jersey, that the available and appropriate land fill sites within the State are being diminished, that the environment continues to be threatened by the treatment and disposal of waste which originated or was collected outside the State, and that the public health, safety and welfare require that the treatment and disposal within this State of all wastes generated outside of the State be prohibited."

[I]t does not matter whether the ultimate aim of ch. 363 is to reduce the waste disposal costs of New Jersey residents or to save remaining open lands from pollution, for we assume New Jersey has every right to protect its residents' pocketbooks as well as their environment. And it may be assumed as well that New Jersey may pursue those ends by slowing the flow of all waste into the State's remaining landfills, even though interstate commerce may incidentally be affected. But whatever New Jersey's ultimate purpose, it may not be accomplished by discriminating against articles of commerce coming from outside the State unless there is some reason, apart from their origin, to treat them differently. Both on its face and in its plain effect, ch. 363 violates this principle of nondiscrimination.

The Court has consistently found parochial legislation of this kind to be constitutionally invalid, whether the ultimate aim of the legislation was to assure a steady supply of milk by erecting barriers to allegedly ruinous outside competition, or to create jobs by keeping industry within the State, or to preserve the State's financial resources from depletion by fencing out indigent immigrants. In each of these cases, a presumably legitimate goal was sought to be achieved by the illegitimate means of isolating the State from the national economy.

The New Jersey law at issue in this case falls squarely within the area that the Commerce Clause puts off limits to state regulation. On its face, it imposes on out-of-state commercial interests the full burden of conserving the State's remaining landfill space. The New Jersey law blocks the importation of waste in an obvious effort to saddle those outside the State with the entire burden of slowing the flow of refuse into New Jersey's remaining landfill sites. That legislative effort is clearly impermissible under the Commerce Clause of the Constitution. Today, cities in Pennsylvania and New York find it expedient or necessary to send their waste into New Jersey for disposal, and New Jersey claims the right to close its borders to such traffic. Tomorrow, cities in New Jersey may find it expedient or necessary to send their waste into Pennsylvania or New York for disposal, and those States might then claim the right to close their borders. The Commerce Clause will protect New Jersey in the future, just as it protects her neighbors now, from efforts by one State to isolate itself in the stream of interstate commerce from a problem shared by all.

Justice Rehnquist, with whom the Chief Justice joins, dissenting.

A growing problem in our Nation is the sanitary treatment and disposal of solid waste. For many years, solid waste was incinerated. Because of the significant environmental problems attendant on incineration, however, this method of solid waste disposal has declined in use in many localities, including New Jersey. "Sanitary" landfills have replaced incineration as the principal method of disposing of solid waste. In ch. 363 of the 1973 N.J. Laws, the State of New Jersey legislatively recognized the unfortunate fact that landfills also present extremely serious health and safety problems. First, in New Jersey, "virtually all sanitary landfills can be expected to produce leachate, a noxious and highly polluted liquid which is seldom visible and frequently pollutes . . . ground and surface waters." The natural decomposition process which occurs in landfills also produces large quantities of methane and thereby presents a significant explosion hazard. Landfills can also generate "health hazards caused by rodents, fires and scavenger birds" and, "needless to say, do not help New Jersey's aesthetic appearance nor New Jersey's noise or water or air pollution problems."

The health and safety hazards associated with landfills present appellees with a currently unsolvable dilemma. Other, hopefully safer, methods of disposing of solid wastes are still in the development stage and cannot presently be used. But appellees obviously cannot completely stop the tide of solid waste that its citizens will produce in the interim. For the moment, therefore, appellees must continue to use sanitary landfills to dispose of New Jersey's own solid waste despite the critical environmental problems thereby created.

The question presented in this case is whether New Jersey must also continue to receive and dispose of solid waste from neighboring States, even though these will inexorably increase the health problems discussed above. The Court answers this question in the affirmative. New Jersey must either prohibit all landfill operations, leaving itself to cast about for a presently nonexistent solution to the serious problem of disposing of the waste generated within its own borders, or it must accept waste from every portion of the United States, thereby multiplying the health and safety problems which would result if it dealt only with such wastes generated within the State. Because past precedents establish that the Commerce Clause does not present appellees with such a Hobson's choice, I dissent.

Many cases involving facially discriminatory laws have dealt with attempts by state and local governments to conserve their natural resources for use by their own residents. The following case is illustrative of such a state law that facially discriminates in this way.

HUGHES v. OKLAHOMA
441 U.S. 322 (1979)

Justice BRENNAN delivered the opinion of the Court.

The question presented for decision is whether [an] Oklahoma Statute violates the Commerce Clause, of the United States Constitution, insofar as it provides that "[n]o person may transport or ship minnows for sale outside the state which were seined or procured within the waters of this state. . . ."

The burden to show discrimination rests on the party challenging the validity of the statute, but "[w]hen discrimination against commerce . . . is demonstrated, the burden falls on the State to justify it both in terms of the local benefits flowing from the statute and the unavailability of non-discriminatory alternatives adequate to preserve the local interests at stake." Furthermore, when considering the purpose of a challenged statute, this Court is not bound by the name, description or characterization given it by the legislature or the courts of the State, but will determine for itself the practical impact of the law.

Section 4-115(B) on its face discriminates against interstate commerce. It forbids the transportation of natural minnows out of the State for purposes of sale, and thus "overtly blocks the flow of interstate commerce at [the] State's borders." Such facial discrimination by itself may be a fatal defect, regardless of the State's purpose, because "the evil of protectionism can reside in legislative means as well as legislative ends." At a minimum such facial discrimination invokes the strictest scrutiny of any purported legitimate local purpose and of the absence of nondiscriminatory alternatives.

Oklahoma argues that §4-115(B) serves a legitimate local purpose in that it is "readily apparent as a conservation measure." The State's interest in maintaining the ecological balance in state waters by avoiding the removal of inordinate numbers of minnows may well qualify as a legitimate local purpose. We consider the States' interests in conservation and protection of wild animals as legitimate local purposes similar to the States' interests in protecting the health and safety of their citizens. But the fiction of state ownership may no longer be used to force those outside the State to bear the full costs of "conserving" the wild animals within its borders when equally effective nondiscriminatory conservation measures are available. Far from choosing the least discriminatory alternative, Oklahoma has chosen to "conserve" its minnows in the way that most overtly discriminate against interstate commerce. The State places no limits on the numbers of minnows that can be taken by licensed minnow dealers; nor does it limit in any way how these minnows may be disposed of within the State. Yet it forbids the transportation of any commercially significant number of natural minnows out of the State for sale. Section 4-115(B) is certainly not a "last ditch" attempt at conservation after nondiscriminatory alternatives have proved unfeasible. It is rather a choice of the most discriminatory means even though nondiscriminatory alternatives would seem likely to fulfill the State's purported legitimate local purpose more effectively.

The Court has held that reciprocity requirements — a state allows out-of-staters to have access to markets or resources only when the out-of-staters are from states that grant similar benefits — are facially discriminatory. For instance, in Great A&P Tea Co. v. Cottrell, 424 U.S. 366 (1976), the Court unanimously invalidated a Mississippi law that provided that milk could be shipped into Mississippi from another state only if it had a public health certificate and only if the other state would accept milk from Mississippi on a reciprocal basis. Likewise, in Sporhase v. Nebraska, 458 U.S. 941 (1982), the Court found that a state law was discriminatory when it denied a permit to draw and use water for use in another state unless that state granted reciprocal rights to draw water for use in Nebraska.

FACIALLY NEUTRAL LAWS

The Supreme Court has held that facially neutral laws can be found to be discriminatory if they either have the purpose or the effect of discriminating against out-of-staters. The Court has declared: "A court may find that a state law constitutes 'economic protectionism' on proof either of discriminatory effect or of discriminatory purpose." Minnesota v. Clover Leaf Creamery Co., 450 U.S. 1027 (1981). This is very different from analysis under the Equal Protection Clause, discussed in Chapter 7, where a facially neutral law is deemed discriminatory only if there is both a discriminatory purpose and a discriminatory effect.

The difficulty for courts is in deciding whether a particular law has a discriminatory purpose or a legitimate nondiscriminatory objective and whether a law should be deemed to have a discriminatory impact. This difficulty is illustrated by comparing the following cases. In the first case presented, Hunt v. Washington State Apple Advertising Commn., the Court found that discriminatory impact is sufficient for a law to be deemed discriminatory and concluded that the state's statute was impermissibly discriminatory in its effects. In the second case, Exxon Corp. v. Governor of Maryland, the Court found that the law was not discriminatory and upheld its constitutionality. As you read these cases, compare their discriminatory effects and consider whether there is a meaningful difference in this regard between the decisions.

HUNT, GOVERNOR OF THE STATE OF NORTH CAROLINA v. WASHINGTON STATE APPLE ADVERTISING COMMISSION

432 U.S. 333 (1977)

Chief Justice BURGER delivered the opinion of the Court.

Washington State is the Nation's largest producer of apples, its crops accounting for approximately 30% of all apples grown domestically and nearly half of all apples shipped in closed containers in interstate commerce. As might be expected, the production and sale of apples on this scale is a multimillion dollar enterprise which plays a significant role in Washington's economy. Because of the importance of the apple industry to the State, its legislature has undertaken to protect and enhance the reputation of Washington apples by establishing a stringent, mandatory inspection program, administered by the State's Department of Agriculture, which requires all apples shipped in interstate commerce to be tested under strict quality standards and graded accordingly. In all cases, the Washington State grades, which have gained substantial acceptance in the trade, are the equivalent of, or superior to, the comparable grades and standards adopted by the United States Department of Agriculture (USDA). Compliance with the Washington inspection scheme costs the State's growers approximately $1 million each year.

In 1973, North Carolina enacted a statute which required all closed containers of apples sold, offered for sale, or shipped into the State to bear "no grade other than the applicable U.S. grade or standard." State grades were expressly prohibited. In addition to its obvious consequence prohibiting the display of Washington State apple grades on containers of apples shipped into North Carolina, the regulation presented the Washington apple industry with a marketing problem of potentially nationwide significance. Washington apple growers annually ship in commerce approximately 40 million closed containers of apples, nearly 500,000 of which eventually find their way into North Carolina, stamped with the applicable Washington State variety and grade. It is the industry's practice to purchase these containers preprinted with the various apple varieties and grades, prior to harvest. After these containers are filled with apples of the appropriate type and grade, a substantial portion of them are placed in cold-storage warehouses where the grade labels identify the product and facilitate its handling. These apples are then shipped as needed throughout the year; after February 1 of each year, they constitute approximately two-thirds of all apples sold in fresh markets in this country. Since the ultimate destination of these apples is unknown at the time they are placed in storage, compliance with North Carolina's unique regulation would have required Washington growers to obliterate the printed labels on containers shipped to North Carolina, thus giving their product a damaged appearance. Alternatively, they could have changed their marketing practices to accommodate the needs of the North Carolina market, i.e., repack apples to be shipped to North Carolina in containers bearing only the USDA grade, and/or store the estimated portion of the harvest destined for that market in such special containers. As a last resort, they could discontinue the use of the preprinted containers entirely. None of these costly and less efficient options was very attractive to the industry. Moreover, in the event a number of other States followed North Carolina's lead, the resultant inability to display the Washington grades could force the Washington growers to abandon the State's expensive inspection and grading system which their customers had come to know and rely on over the 60-odd years of its existence.

As the District Court correctly found, the challenged statute has the practical effect of not only burdening interstate sales of Washington apples, but also discriminating against them. This discrimination takes various forms. The first, and most obvious, is the statute's consequence of raising the costs of doing business in the North Carolina market for Washington apple growers and dealers, while leaving those of their North Carolina counterparts unaffected. As previously noted, this disparate effect results from the fact that North Carolina apple producers, unlike their Washington competitors, were not forced to alter their marketing practices in order to comply with the statute. They were still free to market their wares under the USDA grade or none at all as they had done prior to the statute's enactment. Obviously, the increased costs imposed by the statute would tend to shield the local apple industry from the competition of Washington apple growers and dealers who are already at a competitive disadvantage because of their great distance from the North Carolina market.

Second, the statute has the effect of stripping away from the Washington apple industry the competitive and economic advantages it has earned for itself through its expensive inspection and grading system. The record demonstrates that the Washington apple-grading system has gained nationwide acceptance in the apple trade.

Third, by prohibiting Washington growers and dealers from marketing apples under their State's grades, the statute has a leveling effect which insidiously operates to the advantage of local apple producers. As noted earlier, the Washington State grades are equal or superior to the USDA grades in all corresponding categories. Hence, with free market forces at work, Washington sellers would normally enjoy a distinct market advantage vis-à-vis local producers in those categories where the Washington grade is superior. However, because of the statute's operation, Washington apples which would otherwise qualify for and be sold under the superior Washington grades will now have to be marketed under their inferior USDA counterparts. Such "downgrading" offers the North Carolina apple industry the very sort of protection against competing out-of-state products that the Commerce Clause was designed to prohibit. At worst, it will have the effect of an embargo against those Washington apples in the superior grades as Washington dealers withhold them from the North Carolina market. At best, it will deprive Washington sellers of the market premium that such apples would otherwise command.

When discrimination against commerce of the type we have found is demonstrated, the burden falls on the State to justify it both in terms of the local benefits flowing from the statute and the unavailability of nondiscriminatory alternatives adequate to preserve the local interests at stake. Dean Milk Co. v. Madison (1951). North Carolina has failed to sustain that burden on both scores. The several States unquestionably possess a substantial interest in protecting their citizens from confusion and deception in the marketing of foodstuffs, but the challenged statute does remarkably little to further that laudable goal at least with respect to Washington apples and grades. The statute, as already noted, permits the marketing of closed containers of apples under no grades at all. Such a result can hardly be thought to eliminate the problems of deception and confusion created by the multiplicity of differing state grades; indeed, it magnifies them by depriving purchasers of all information concerning the quality of the contents of closed apple containers. Moreover, although the statute is ostensibly a consumer protection measure, it directs its primary efforts, not at the consuming public at large, but at apple wholesalers and brokers who are the principal purchasers of closed containers of apples. And those individuals are presumably the most knowledgeable individuals in this area. Since the statute does nothing at all to purify the flow of information at the retail level, it does little to protect consumers against the problems it was designed to eliminate.

In addition, it appears that nondiscriminatory alternatives to the outright ban of Washington State grades are readily available. For example, North Carolina could effectuate its goal by permitting out-of-state growers to utilize state grades only if they also marked their shipments with the applicable USDA label. In that case, the USDA grade would serve as a benchmark against which the consumer could evaluate the quality of the various state grades.

EXXON CORP. v. GOVERNOR OF MARYLAND

437 U.S. 117 (1978)

Justice STEVENS delivered the opinion of the Court.

A Maryland statute provides that a producer or refiner of petroleum products (1) may not operate any retail service station within the State, and (2) must extend all "voluntary allowances" uniformly to all service stations it supplies.

The Maryland statute is an outgrowth of the 1973 shortage of petroleum. In response to complaints about inequitable distribution of gasoline among retail stations, the Governor of Maryland directed the State Comptroller to conduct a market survey. The results of that survey indicated that gasoline stations operated by producers or refiners had received preferential treatment during the period of short supply. The Comptroller therefore proposed legislation which was "designed to correct the inequities in the distribution and pricing of gasoline reflected by the survey."

The essential facts alleged in the complaint are not in dispute. All of the gasoline sold by Exxon in Maryland is transported into the State from refineries located elsewhere. Although Exxon sells the bulk of this gas to wholesalers and independent retailers, it also sells directly to the consuming public through 36 company-operated stations. Exxon uses these stations to test innovative marketing concepts or products. Focusing primarily on the Act's requirement that it discontinue its operation of these 36 retail stations, Exxon's complaint challenged the validity of the statute.

Plainly, the Maryland statute does not discriminate against interstate goods, nor does it favor local producers and refiners. Since Maryland's entire gasoline supply flows in interstate commerce and since there are no local producers or refiners, such claims of disparate treatment between interstate and local commerce would be meritless. Appellants, however, focus on the retail market arguing that the effect of the statute is to protect in-state independent dealers from out-of-state competition. They contend that the divestiture provisions "create a protected enclave for Maryland independent dealers. . . ." As support for this proposition, they rely on the fact that the burden of the divestiture requirements falls solely on interstate companies. But this fact does not lead, either logically or as a practical matter, to a conclusion that the State is discriminating against interstate commerce at the retail level.

As the record shows, there are several major interstate marketers of petroleum that own and operate their own retail gasoline stations. These interstate dealers, who compete directly with the Maryland independent dealers, are not affected by the Act because they do not refine or produce gasoline. In fact, the Act creates no barriers whatsoever against interstate independent dealers; it does not prohibit the flow of interstate goods, place added costs upon them, or distinguish between in-state and out-of-state companies in the retail market. The absence of any of these factors fully distinguishes this case from those in which a State has been found to have discriminated against interstate commerce. See, e.g., Hunt v. Washington Apple Advertising Commn. For instance, the Court in *Hunt* noted that the challenged state statute raised the cost of doing business for out-of-state dealers, and, in various other ways, favored the in-state dealer in the local market. No comparable claim can be made here. While the refiners will no longer enjoy their same status in the Maryland market, in-state independent dealers will have no competitive advantage over out-of-state dealers. The fact that the burden of a state regulation falls on some interstate companies does not, by itself, establish a claim of discrimination against interstate commerce.

Appellants argue, however, that this fact does show that the Maryland statute impermissibly burdens interstate commerce. They point to evidence in the record which indicates that, because of the divestiture requirements, at least three refiners will stop selling in Maryland, and which also supports their claim that the elimination of company-operated stations will deprive the consumer of certain special services. Even if we assume the truth of both assertions, neither warrants a finding that the statute impermissibly burdens interstate commerce. Some refiners may choose to withdraw entirely from the Maryland market, but there is no reason to assume that their share of the entire supply will not be promptly replaced by other interstate refiners. The source of the consumers' supply may switch from company-operated stations to independent dealers, but interstate commerce is not subjected to an impermissible burden simply because an otherwise valid regulation causes some business to shift from one interstate supplier to another.

Appellants claim that the statute "will surely change the market structure by weakening the independent refiners. . . ." We cannot, however, accept appellants' underlying notion that the Commerce Clause protects the particular structure or methods of operation in a retail market. [T]he Clause protects the interstate market, not particular interstate firms, from prohibitive or burdensome regulations. It may be true that the consuming public will be injured by the loss of the high-volume, low-priced stations operated by the independent refiners, but again that argument relates to the wisdom of the statute, not to its burden *on* commerce.

Justice BLACKMUN, dissenting.

I dissent from the Court's opinion because it fails to condemn impermissible discrimination against interstate commerce in *retail* gasoline marketing. The divestiture provisions preclude out-of-state competitors from retailing gasoline within Maryland. The effect is to protect in-state retail service station dealers from the competition of the out-of-state businesses. This protectionist discrimination is not justified by any legitimate state interest that cannot be vindicated by more evenhanded regulation. [The law,] therefore, violate[s] the Commerce Clause.

In Maryland the retail marketing of gasoline is interstate commerce, for all petroleum products come from outside the State. Retailers serve interstate travelers. To the extent that particular retailers succeed or fail in their businesses, the interstate wholesale market for petroleum products is affected.

The Commerce Clause forbids discrimination against interstate commerce, which repeatedly has been held to mean that States and localities may not discriminate against the transactions of out-of-state actors in interstate markets. The discrimination need not appear on the face of the state or local regulation. "The Commerce Clause forbids discrimination, whether forthright or ingenious. In each case it is our duty to determine whether the statute under attack, whatever its name may be, will in its practical operation work discrimination against interstate commerce." The state or local authority need not intend to discriminate in order to offend the policy of maintaining a free-flowing national economy. As demonstrated in *Hunt*, a statute that on its face restricts both intrastate and interstate transactions may violate the Clause by having the "practical effect" of discriminating in its operation. If discrimination results from a statute, the burden falls upon the state or local government to demonstrate legitimate local benefits justifying the inequality and to show that less discriminatory alternatives cannot protect the local interests.

With this background, the unconstitutional discrimination in the Maryland statute becomes apparent. No facial inequality exists; §§(b) and (c) preclude all refiners and producers from marketing gasoline at the retail level. But given the structure of the retail gasoline market in Maryland, the effect of §§(b) and (c) is to exclude a class of predominantly out-of-state gasoline retailers while providing protection from competition to a class of nonintegrated retailers that is overwhelmingly composed of local businessmen.

In 1974, of the 3,780 gasoline service stations in the State, 3,547 were operated by nonintegrated local retail dealers. Of the 233 company-operated stations, 197 belonged to out-of-state integrated producers or refiners. Thirty-four were oper-ated by nonintegrated companies that would not have been affected imme-diately by the Maryland statute. The only in-state integrated petroleum firm, Crown Central Petroleum, Inc., operated just two service stations. Of the class of stations statutorily insulated from the competition of the out-of-state inte-grated firms, then, more than 99% were operated by local business interests. Of the class of enterprises excluded entirely from participation in the retail gasoline market, 95% were out-of-state firms, operating 98% of the stations in the class.

The discrimination suffered by the out-of-state integrated producers and refi-ners is significant. Five of the excluded enterprises, Ashland Oil, Inc., BP Oil, Inc., Kayo Oil Co., Petroleum Marketing Corp., and Southern States Coopera-tive, Inc., market nonbranded gasoline through price competition rather than through brand recognition. Of the 98 stations marketing gasoline in this man-ner, all but 6 are company operated. The record also contains testimony that the discrimination will burden the operations of major branded companies, such as appellants Exxon, Phillips, Shell, and Gulf, all of which are out-of-state firms. Most importantly, §§(b) and (c) will preclude these companies, as well as those mentioned in the previous paragraph, from competing directly for the profits of retail marketing.

[T]he State appears to be concerned about unfair competitive behavior such as predatory pricing or inequitable allocation of petroleum products by the integrated firms. These are the only examples of specific misconduct asserted in the State's answers. But none of the concerns support the discrimination in §§(b) and (c). There is no proof in the record that any significant portion of the class of out-of-state firms burdened by the divestiture sections has engaged in such misconduct. Furthermore, predatory pricing and unfair allocation already have been prohibited by both state and federal law. Less discriminatory legisla-tion, which would regulate the leasing of all service stations, not just those owned by the out-of-state integrated producers and refiners, could prevent whatever evils arise from short-term leases.

The Court also found discrimination based on the disparate impact of a facially neutral law in C&A Carbone, Inc. v. Town of Clarkstown, 511 U.S. 383 (1994). A city adopted an ordinance that required all nonhazardous solid waste in the town to be deposited at a transfer station. The law allowed recyclers to continue to receive solid waste, but they had to bring their nonrecyclables to the transfer station. In other words, the companies could not ship nonrecyclable waste itself and they had to pay a fee at the transfer station even if it had already sorted the waste.

The ordinance was facially neutral and applied to both in-state and out-of-state companies. Nonetheless, the Court deemed the law discriminatory because of its effect on out-of-staters: "While the immediate effect of the ordinance is to direct local transport of solid waste to a designated site within the local jurisdic-tion, its economic effects are interstate in reach. . . . [T]he flow control ordi-nance discriminates, for it allows only the favored operator to process waste that is within the limits of the town. The ordinance is no less discriminatory because in-state or in-town processors are also covered by the prohibition."

By contrast, in United Haulers Assn. v. Oneida-Herkimer Solid Waste Management Authority, 550 U.S. 330 (2007), the Court found constitutional an ordinance very similar to that which it struck down in *C&A Carbone*. In *C&A Carbone*, the city had a "flow control ordinance" for trash that required haulers to bring it to a private facility, whereas in *United Haulers*, the ordinance required that the trash be brought to a state-created public benefit corporation.

The Court found that this distinction was crucial. Chief Justice Roberts, writing for the Court, explained, "We find this difference constitutionally significant. Disposing of trash has been a traditional government activity for years, and laws that favor the government in such areas — but treat every private business, whether in-state or out-of-state, exactly the same — do not discriminate against interstate commerce for purposes of the Commerce Clause. Applying the Commerce Clause test reserved for regulations that do not discriminate against interstate commerce, we uphold these ordinances because any incidental burden they may have on interstate commerce does not outweigh the benefits they confer on the citizens of Oneida and Herkimer Counties."

But the dissent by Justice Alito, joined by Justices Stevens and Kennedy, saw this as a distinction without a difference. It was still the government discriminating in favor of in-state businesses at the expense of out-of-state businesses by requiring that trash be brought to the in-state facility. For this dissent, this discrimination was enough to trigger strict scrutiny and invalidate the ordinance.

Facially neutral laws also can be found to be discriminatory if they were enacted for a protectionist purpose: helping in-staters at the expense of out-of-staters. Although the following two cases involve discussion of both purpose and effect, in the former, West Lynn Creamery, Inc. v. Healy, the Court invalidated a state law largely because of its discriminatory purpose, but in the latter case, Minnesota v. Clover Leaf Creamery Co., the Court upheld the law by finding that the law did not have a discriminatory objective.

WEST LYNN CREAMERY, INC. v. HEALY, COMMISSIONER OF MASSACHUSETTS DEPARTMENT OF FOOD & AGRICULTURE

512 U.S. 186 (1994)

Justice STEVENS delivered the opinion of the Court.

A Massachusetts pricing order imposes an assessment on all fluid milk sold by dealers to Massachusetts retailers. About two-thirds of that milk is produced out of State. The entire assessment, however, is distributed to Massachusetts dairy farmers. The question presented is whether the pricing order unconstitutionally discriminates against interstate commerce. We hold that it does.

Petitioner West Lynn Creamery, Inc., is a milk dealer licensed to do business in Massachusetts. It purchases raw milk, which it processes, packages, and sells to wholesalers, retailers, and other milk dealers. About 97% of the raw milk it purchases is produced by out-of-state farmers. Petitioner LeComte's Dairy, Inc., is also a licensed Massachusetts milk dealer. It purchases all of its milk from West Lynn and distributes it to retail outlets in Massachusetts.

In the 1980s and early 1990s, Massachusetts dairy farmers began to lose market share to lower cost producers in neighboring States. In response, the

Governor of Massachusetts appointed a Special Commission to study the dairy industry. The commission found that many producers had sold their dairy farms during the past decade and that if prices paid to farmers for their milk were not significantly increased, a majority of the remaining farmers in Massachusetts would be "forced out of business within the year."

On January 28, 1992, relying on the commission's report, the Commissioner of the Massachusetts Department of Food and Agriculture (respondent) declared a State of Emergency. [T]he Massachusetts order requires dealers to make payments into a fund that is disbursed to farmers on a monthly basis. The assessments, however, are only on Class I sales and the distributions are only to Massachusetts farmers.

The Commerce Clause also limits the power of the Commonwealth of Massachusetts to adopt regulations that discriminate against interstate commerce. "This 'negative' aspect of the Commerce Clause prohibits economic protectionism — that is, regulatory measures designed to benefit in-state economic interests by burdening out-of-state competitors. . . . Thus, state statutes that clearly discriminate against interstate commerce are routinely struck down . . . unless the discrimination is demonstrably justified by a valid factor unrelated to economic protectionism. . . ." New Energy Co. of Ind. v. Limbach (1988).

Respondent's principal argument is that, because "the milk order achieves its goals through lawful means," the order as a whole is constitutional. He argues that the payments to Massachusetts dairy farmers from the Dairy Equalization Fund are valid, because subsidies are constitutional exercises of state power, and that the order premium which provides money for the fund is valid, because it is a nondiscriminatory tax. Therefore the pricing order is constitutional, because it is merely the combination of two independently lawful regulations. In effect, respondent argues, if the State may impose a valid tax on dealers, it is free to use the proceeds of the tax as it chooses; and if it may independently subsidize its farmers, it is free to finance the subsidy by means of any legitimate tax.

Even granting respondent's assertion that both components of the pricing order would be constitutional standing alone, the pricing order nevertheless must fall. A pure subsidy funded out of general revenue ordinarily imposes no burden on interstate commerce, but merely assists local business. The pricing order in this case, however, is funded principally from taxes on the sale of milk produced in other States. By so funding the subsidy, respondent not only assists local farmers, but burdens interstate commerce. The pricing order thus violates the cardinal principle that a State may not "benefit in-state economic interests by burdening out-of-state competitors."

More fundamentally, respondent errs in assuming that the constitutionality of the pricing order follows logically from the constitutionality of its component parts. By conjoining a tax and a subsidy, Massachusetts has created a program more dangerous to interstate commerce than either part alone. Nondiscriminatory measures, like the evenhanded tax at issue here, are generally upheld, in spite of any adverse effects on interstate commerce, in part because "[t]he existence of major in-state interests adversely affected . . . is a powerful safeguard against legislative abuse." Minnesota v. Clover Leaf Creamery Co. (1981). However, when a nondiscriminatory tax is coupled with a subsidy to one of the groups hurt by the tax, a State's political processes can no longer be relied upon to prevent legislative abuse, because one of the in-state interests which would otherwise lobby against the tax has been mollified by the subsidy.

So, in this case, one would ordinarily have expected at least three groups to lobby against the order premium, which, as a tax, raises the price (and hence lowers demand) for milk: dairy farmers, milk dealers, and consumers. But because the tax was coupled with a subsidy, one of the most powerful of these groups, Massachusetts dairy farmers, instead of exerting their influence against the tax, were in fact its primary supporters.

More fundamentally, respondent ignores the fact that Massachusetts dairy farmers are part of an integrated interstate market. [T]he purpose and effect of the pricing order are to divert market share to Massachusetts dairy farmers. This diversion necessarily injures the dairy farmers in neighboring States. Preservation of local industry by protecting it from the rigors of interstate competition is the hallmark of the economic protectionism that the Commerce Clause prohibits.

STATE OF MINNESOTA v. CLOVER LEAF CREAMERY CO.

449 U.S. 456 (1981)

Justice BRENNAN delivered the opinion of the Court.

In 1977, the Minnesota Legislature enacted a statute banning the retail sale of milk in plastic nonreturnable, nonrefillable containers, but permitting such sale in other nonreturnable, nonrefillable containers, such as paperboard milk cartons. The purpose of the Minnesota statute is set out as §1: "The legislature finds that the use of nonreturnable, nonrefillable containers for the packaging of milk and other milk products presents a solid waste management problem for the state, promotes energy waste, and depletes natural resources. The legislature therefore determines that the use of nonreturnable, nonrefillable containers for packaging milk and other milk products should be discouraged and that the use of returnable and reusable packaging for these products is preferred and should be encouraged." Proponents of the legislation argued that it would promote resource conservation, ease solid waste disposal problems, and conserve energy. Relying on the results of studies and other information, they stressed the need to stop introduction of the plastic nonreturnable container before it became entrenched in the market.

After the Act was passed, respondents filed suit in Minnesota District Court, seeking to enjoin its enforcement. The court further found that, contrary to the statement of purpose in §1, the "actual basis" for the Act "was to promote the economic interests of certain segments of the local dairy and pulpwood industries at the expense of the economic interests of other segments of the dairy industry and the plastics industry." The court therefore declared the Act "null, void, and unenforceable."

When legislating in areas of legitimate local concern, such as environmental protection and resource conservation, States are nonetheless limited by the Commerce Clause. If a state law purporting to promote environmental purposes is in reality "simple economic protectionism," we have applied a "virtually per se rule of invalidity." Philadelphia v. New Jersey (1978). Even if a statute regulates "even-handedly," and imposes only "incidental" burdens on interstate commerce, the courts must nevertheless strike it down if "the burden imposed on such commerce is clearly excessive in relation to the putative local benefits."

Pike v. Bruce Church, Inc. (1970). Moreover, "the extent of the burden that will be tolerated will of course depend on the nature of the local interest involved, and on whether it could be promoted as well with a lesser impact on interstate activities."

A court may find that a state law constitutes "economic protectionism" on proof either of discriminatory effect or of discriminatory purpose. Respondents advance a "discriminatory purpose" argument, relying on a finding by the District Court that the Act's "actual basis was to promote the economic interests of certain segments of the local dairy and pulpwood industries at the expense of the economic interests of other segments of the dairy industry and the plastics industry."

Minnesota's statute does not effect "simple protectionism," but "regulates even-handedly" by prohibiting all milk retailers from selling their products in plastic, nonreturnable milk containers, without regard to whether the milk, the containers, or the sellers are from outside the State. This statute is therefore unlike statutes discriminating against interstate commerce, which we have consistently struck down. E.g., Hughes v. Oklahoma (1979); Philadelphia v. New Jersey [(1978)]; Hunt v. Washington Apple Advertising Comm'n [(1977)]. Since the statute does not discriminate between interstate and intrastate commerce, the controlling question is whether the incidental burden imposed on interstate commerce by the Minnesota Act is "clearly excessive in relation to the putative local benefits." We conclude that it is not.

The burden imposed on interstate commerce by the statute is relatively minor. Milk products may continue to move freely across the Minnesota border, and since most dairies package their products in more than one type of container, the inconvenience of having to conform to different packaging requirements in Minnesota and the surrounding States should be slight. Within Minnesota, business will presumably shift from manufacturers of plastic nonreturnable containers to producers of paperboard cartons, refillable bottles, and plastic pouches, but there is no reason to suspect that the gainers will be Minnesota firms, or the losers out-of-state firms. Indeed, two of the three dairies, the sole milk retailer, and the sole milk container producer challenging the statute in this litigation are Minnesota firms.

Pulpwood producers are the only Minnesota industry likely to benefit significantly from the Act at the expense of out-of-state firms. Respondents point out that plastic resin, the raw material used for making plastic nonreturnable milk jugs, is produced entirely by non-Minnesota firms, while pulpwood, used for making paperboard, is a major Minnesota product. Nevertheless, it is clear that respondents exaggerate the degree of burden on out-of-state interests, both because plastics will continue to be used in the production of plastic pouches, plastic returnable bottles, and paperboard itself, and because out-of-state pulpwood producers will presumably absorb some of the business generated by the Act. Even granting that the out-of-state plastics industry is burdened relatively more heavily than the Minnesota pulpwood industry, we find that this burden is not "clearly excessive" in light of the substantial state interest in promoting conservation of energy and other natural resources and easing solid waste disposal problems, which we have already reviewed in the context of equal protection analysis. We find these local benefits ample to support Minnesota's decision under the Commerce Clause. Moreover, we find no approach with "a lesser impact on interstate activities."

c. Analysis If a Law Is Deemed Discriminatory

The cases presented above demonstrate that the crucial initial inquiry in dormant Commerce Clause cases is whether the law is discriminatory against out-of-staters. In City of Philadelphia v. New Jersey, the Court said "where simple economic protectionism is effected by state legislation, a virtually per se rule of invalidity has been erected." In C&A Carbone, Inc. v. Town of Clarkstown, the Court declared, "Discrimination against interstate commerce in favor of local business or investment is per se invalid, save in a narrow class of cases in which the municipality can demonstrate, under rigorous scrutiny, that it has no other means to advance a legitimate local interest." In Hunt v. Washington State Apple Advertising Commission, the Court stated, "When discrimination against commerce of the type we have found is demonstrated, the burden falls on the State to justify it both in terms of the local benefits flowing from the statute and the unavailability of nondiscriminatory alternatives adequate to preserve the local interests at stake."

The initial case, Dean Milk Co. v. City of Madison, Wisconsin, illustrates the rigorous scrutiny used when laws are deemed discriminatory. Following it is Maine v. Taylor, the only case thus far in which the Supreme Court has upheld a discriminatory state law challenged under the dormant Commerce Clause.

DEAN MILK CO. v. CITY OF MADISON, WISCONSIN
340 U.S. 349 (1951)

This appeal challenges the constitutional validity of [a] section of an ordinance of the City of Madison, Wisconsin, regulating the sale of milk and milk products within the municipality's jurisdiction. [The] section in issue makes it unlawful to sell any milk as pasteurized unless it has been processed and bottled at an approved pasteurization plant within a radius of five miles from the central square of Madison. Appellant is an Illinois corporation engaged in distributing milk and milk products in Illinois and Wisconsin. It contended below, as it does here, that both the five-mile limit on pasteurization plants and the twenty-five-mile limit on sources of milk violate the Commerce Clause and the Fourteenth Amendment to the Federal Constitution.

The City of Madison is the county seat of Dane County. Within the county are some 5,600 dairy farms with total raw milk production in excess of 600,000,000 pounds annually and more than ten times the requirements of Madison. Aside from the milk supplied to Madison, fluid milk produced in the county moves in large quantities to Chicago and more distant consuming areas, and the remainder is used in making cheese, butter and other products.

Appellant purchases and gathers milk from approximately 950 farms in northern Illinois and southern Wisconsin, none being within twenty-five miles of Madison. Its pasteurization plants are located at Chemung and Huntley, Illinois, about 65 and 85 miles respectively from Madison. Appellant was denied a license to sell its products within Madison solely because its pasteurization plants were more than five miles away. It is conceded that the milk which appellant seeks to sell in Madison is supplied from farms and processed in plants licensed and inspected by public health authorities of Chicago, and is labeled

"Grade A" under the Chicago ordinance which adopts the rating standards recommended by the United States Public Health Service.

Upon these facts we find it necessary to determine only the issue raised under the Commerce Clause, for we agree with appellant that the ordinance imposes an undue burden on interstate commerce. [T]his regulation in practical effect excludes from distribution in Madison wholesome milk produced and pasteurized in Illinois. In thus erecting an economic barrier protecting a major local industry against competition from without the State, Madison plainly discriminates against interstate commerce. This it cannot do, even in the exercise of its unquestioned power to protect the health and safety of its people, if reasonable nondiscriminatory alternatives, adequate to conserve legitimate local interests, are available. It is immaterial that Wisconsin milk from outside the Madison area is subjected to the same proscription as that moving in interstate commerce.

It appears that reasonable and adequate alternatives are available. If the City of Madison prefers to rely upon its own officials for inspection of distant milk sources, such inspection is readily open to it without hardship for it could charge the actual and reasonable cost of such inspection to the importing producers and processors. Moreover, appellee Health Commissioner of Madison testified that as proponent of the local milk ordinance he had submitted the provisions here in controversy and an alternative proposal based on the Model Milk Ordinance recommended by the United States Public Health Service. The model provision imposes no geographical limitation on location of milk sources and processing plants but excludes from the municipality milk not produced and pasteurized conformably to standards as high as those enforced by the receiving city. In implementing such an ordinance, the importing city obtains milk ratings based on uniform standards and established by health authorities in the jurisdiction where production and processing occur. The receiving city may determine the extent of enforcement of sanitary standards in the exporting area by verifying the accuracy of safety ratings of specific plants or of the milkshed in the distant jurisdiction through the United States Public Health Service, which routinely and on request spot checks the local ratings.

To permit Madison to adopt a regulation not essential for the protection of local health interests and placing a discriminatory burden on interstate commerce would invite a multiplication of preferential trade areas destructive of the very purpose of the Commerce Clause. Under the circumstances here presented, the regulation must yield to the principle that "one state in its dealings with another may not place itself in a position of economic isolation."

MAINE v. TAYLOR & UNITED STATES

477 U.S. 131 (1986)

Justice BLACKMUN delivered the opinion of the Court.

Once again, a little fish has caused a commotion. See Hughes v. Oklahoma (1979); TVA v. Hill (1978). The fish in this case is the golden shiner, a species of minnow commonly used as live bait in sport fishing. Appellee Robert J. Taylor operates a bait business in Maine. Despite a Maine statute prohibiting the importation of live baitfish, he arranged to have 158,000 live golden shiners delivered to him from outside the State. The shipment was intercepted, and a federal grand jury in the District of Maine indicted Taylor for violating and conspiring to violate the Lacey Act Amendments of 1981. Section 3(a)(2)(A) of those Amendments makes it a federal crime "to import, export, transport, sell, receive, acquire, or purchase in interstate or foreign commerce . . . any fish or wildlife taken, possessed, transported, or sold in violation of any law or regulation of any State or in violation of any foreign law."

Taylor moved to dismiss the indictment on the ground that Maine's import ban unconstitutionally burdens interstate commerce and therefore may not form the basis for a federal prosecution under the Lacey Act. Maine intervened to defend the validity of its statute, arguing that the ban legitimately protects the State's fisheries from parasites and nonnative species that might be included in shipments of live baitfish.

Maine's statute restricts interstate trade in the most direct manner possible, blocking all inward shipments of live baitfish at the State's border. Still, this fact alone does not render the law unconstitutional. The limitation imposed by the Commerce Clause on state regulatory power "is by no means absolute," and "the States retain authority under their general police powers to regulate matters of 'legitimate local concern,' even though interstate commerce may be affected." In determining whether a State has overstepped its role in regulating interstate commerce, this Court has distinguished between state statutes that burden interstate transactions only incidentally, and those that affirmatively discriminate against such transactions. While statutes in the first group violate the Commerce Clause only if the burdens they impose on interstate trade are "clearly excessive in relation to the putative local benefits," Pike v. Bruce Church, Inc. (1970), statutes in the second group are subject to more demanding scrutiny. The Court explained in Hughes v. Oklahoma, that once a state law is shown to discriminate against interstate commerce "either on its face or in practical effect," the burden falls on the State to demonstrate both that the statute "serves a legitimate local purpose," and that this purpose could not be served as well by available nondiscriminatory means.

[At] the evidentiary hearing [in] the District Court, [t]hree scientific experts testified for the prosecution and one for the defense. The prosecution experts testified that live baitfish imported into the State posed two significant threats to Maine's unique and fragile fisheries. First, Maine's population of wild fish — including its own indigenous golden shiners — would be placed at risk by three types of parasites prevalent in out-of-state baitfish, but not common to wild fish in Maine. Second, nonnative species inadvertently included in shipments of live baitfish could disturb Maine's aquatic ecology to an unpredictable extent by competing with native fish for food or habitat, by preying on native species, or by disrupting the environment in more subtle ways. The prosecution experts further testified that there was no satisfactory way to inspect shipments of live baitfish for parasites or commingled species. According to their testimony, the small size of baitfish and the large quantities in which they are shipped made inspection for commingled species "a physical impossibility." Parasite inspection posed a separate set of difficulties because the examination procedure required destruction of the fish.

Although the proffered justification for any local discrimination against interstate commerce must be subjected to "the strictest scrutiny," Hughes v. Oklahoma, the empirical component of that scrutiny, like any other form of factfinding, is the basic responsibility of district courts, rather than appellate courts. After reviewing the expert testimony presented to the Magistrate, however, we cannot say that the District Court clearly erred in finding that substantial scientific uncertainty surrounds the effect that baitfish parasites and nonnative species could have on Maine's fisheries. Moreover, we agree with the District Court that Maine has a legitimate interest in guarding against imperfectly understood environmental risks, despite the possibility that they may ultimately prove to be negligible. The constitutional principles underlying the Commerce Clause cannot be read as requiring the State of Maine to sit idly by and wait until potentially irreversible environmental damage has occurred or until the scientific community agrees on what disease organisms are or are not dangerous before it acts to avoid such consequences.

Justice STEVENS, dissenting.

There is something fishy about this case. Maine is the only State in the Union that blatantly discriminates against out-of-state baitfish by flatly prohibiting their importation. Although golden shiners are already present and thriving in Maine (and, perhaps not coincidentally, the subject of a flourishing domestic industry), Maine excludes golden shiners grown and harvested (and, perhaps not coincidentally sold) in other States. This kind of stark discrimination against out-of-state articles of commerce requires rigorous justification by the discriminating State. "When discrimination against commerce of the type we have found is demonstrated, the burden falls on the State to justify it both in terms of the local benefits flowing from the statute and the unavailability of nondiscriminatory alternatives adequate to preserve the local interests at stake." Hunt v. Washington State Apple Advertising Comm'n (1977).

Like the District Court, the Court concludes that uncertainty about possible ecological effects from the possible presence of parasites and nonnative species in shipments of out-of-state shiners suffices to carry the State's burden of proving a legitimate public purpose. The Court similarly concludes that the State has no obligation to develop feasible inspection procedures that would make a total ban unnecessary. It seems clear, however, that the presumption should run the other way. Since the State engages in obvious discrimination against out-of-state commerce, it should be put to its proof. Ambiguity about dangers and alternatives should actually defeat, rather than sustain, the discriminatory measure.

This is not to derogate the State's interest in ecological purity. But the invocation of environmental protection or public health has never been thought to confer some kind of special dispensation from the general principle of non-discrimination in interstate commerce. If Maine wishes to rely on its interest in ecological preservation, it must show that interest, and the infeasibility of other alternatives, with far greater specificity. Otherwise, it must further that asserted interest in a manner far less offensive to the notions of comity and cooperation that underlie the Commerce Clause. Maine's unquestionable natural splendor notwithstanding, the State has not carried its substantial burden of proving why it cannot meet its environmental concerns in the same manner as other States with the same interest in the health of their fish and ecology. I respectfully dissent.

d. Analysis If a Law Is Deemed Nondiscriminatory

If the court concludes that a state's law is not discriminatory — that is, it treats in-staters and out-of-staters alike — then it is subjected to a much less demanding test. Nondiscriminatory laws are upheld as long as the benefits to the government outweigh the burdens on interstate commerce. As presented earlier, it should be remembered that some justices—most notably Chief Justice Rehnquist and Justices Scalia and Thomas—object to the subjectivity of this balancing test and even question whether the dormant Commerce Clause should apply in the absence of state discrimination against out-of-staters. Their arguments should be considered during the reading of the following cases.

The initial case presented below, Pike v. Bruce Church, is the decision most frequently cited as establishing the test used in analyzing laws that are not discriminatory.

LOREN J. PIKE v. BRUCE CHURCH, INC.

397 U.S. 137 (1970)

Justice STEWART delivered the opinion of the Court.

The appellee is a company engaged in extensive commercial farming operations in Arizona and California. The appellant is the official charged with enforcing the Arizona Fruit and Vegetable Standardization Act. A provision of the Act requires that, with certain exceptions, all cantaloupes grown in Arizona and offered for sale must "be packed in regular compact arrangement in closed standard containers approved by the supervisor. . . ." Invoking his authority under that provision, the appellant issued an order prohibiting the appellee company from transporting uncrated cantaloupes from its Parker, Arizona, ranch to nearby Blythe, California, for packing and processing. The company then brought this action in a federal court to enjoin the order as unconstitutional.

The facts are not in dispute, having been stipulated by the parties. The appellee company has for many years been engaged in the business of growing, harvesting, processing, and packing fruits and vegetables at numerous locations in Arizona and California for interstate shipment to markets throughout the Nation. One of the company's newest operations is at Parker, Arizona, where, pursuant to a 1964 lease with the Secretary of the Interior, the Colorado River Indian Agency, and the Colorado River Indian Tribes, it undertook to develop approximately 6,400 acres of uncultivated, arid land for agricultural use. The company has spent more than $3,000,000 in clearing, leveling, irrigating, and otherwise developing this land. The company began growing cantaloupes on part of the land in 1966, and has harvested a large cantaloupe crop there in each subsequent year. The cantaloupes are considered to be of higher quality than those grown in other areas of the State. Because they are highly perishable, cantaloupes must upon maturity be immediately harvested, processed, packed, and shipped in order to prevent spoilage. The processing and packing operations can be performed only in packing sheds. Because the company had no such facilities at Parker, it transported its 1966 Parker cantaloupe harvest in bulk loads to Blythe, California, 31 miles away, where it operated centralized and efficient packing shed facilities. There the melons were sorted, inspected, packed, and shipped. In 1967 the company again sent its Parker cantaloupe crop to Blythe for sorting, packing, and shipping. In 1968, however, the appellant entered the order here in issue, prohibiting the company from shipping its cantaloupes out of the State unless they were packed in containers in a manner and of a kind approved by the appellant. Because cantaloupes in the quantity involved can be so packed only in packing sheds, and because no such facilities were available to the company at Parker or anywhere else nearby in Arizona, the company faced imminent loss of its anticipated 1968 cantaloupe crop in the gross amount of $700,000.

Although the criteria for determining the validity of state statutes affecting interstate commerce have been variously stated, the general rule that emerges can be phrased as follows: Where the statute regulates even-handedly to effectuate a legitimate local public interest, and its effects on interstate commerce are only incidental, it will be upheld unless the burden imposed on such commerce is clearly excessive in relation to the putative local benefits. If a legitimate local purpose is found, then the question becomes one of degree. And the extent of the burden that will be tolerated will of course depend on the nature of the local interest involved, and on whether it could be promoted as well with a lesser impact on interstate activities.

We are not dealing here with "state legislation in the field of safety where the propriety of local regulation has long been recognized," or with an Act designed to protect consumers in Arizona from contaminated or unfit goods. Its purpose and design are simply to protect and enhance the reputation of growers within the State. These are surely legitimate state interests.

But the State's tenuous interest in having the company's cantaloupes identified as originating in Arizona cannot constitutionally justify the requirement that the company build and operate an unneeded $200,000 packing plant in the State. The nature of that burden is, constitutionally, more significant than its extent. For the Court has viewed with particular suspicion state statutes requiring business operations to be performed in the home State that could more efficiently be performed elsewhere. Even where the State is pursuing a clearly legitimate local interest, this particular burden on commerce has been declared to be virtually per se illegal.

While the order issued under the Arizona statute does not impose such rigidity on an entire industry, it does impose just such a straitjacket on the appellee company with respect to the allocation of its interstate resources. Such an incidental consequence of a regulatory scheme could perhaps be tolerated if a more compelling state interest were involved. But here the State's interest is minimal at best — certainly less substantial than a State's interest in securing employment for its people. If the Commerce Clause forbids a State to require work to be done within its jurisdiction to promote local employment, then surely it cannot permit a State to require a person to go into a local packing business solely for the sake of enhancing the reputation of other producers within its borders.

The following two cases, Bibb v. Navajo Freight Lines and Consolidated Freightways Corp. v. Kassell, are examples of where the Court has used the balancing test to find nondiscriminatory laws unconstitutional.

BIBB, DIRECTOR, DEPARTMENT OF PUBLIC SAFETY OF ILLINOIS v. NAVAJO FREIGHT LINES, INC.

359 U.S. 520 (1959)

Justice DOUGLAS delivered the opinion of the Court.

We are asked in this case to hold that an Illinois statute requiring the use of a certain type of rear fender mudguard on trucks and trailers operated on the highways of that State conflicts with the Commerce Clause of the Constitution. The statutory specification for this type of mudguard provides that the guard shall contour the rear wheel, with the inside surface being relatively parallel to the top 90 degrees of the rear 180 degrees of the whole surface. The surface of the guard must extend downward to within 10 inches from the ground when the truck is loaded to its maximum legal capacity. The guards must be wide enough to cover the width of the protected tire, must be installed not more than 6 inches from the tire surface when the vehicle is loaded to maximum capacity, and must have a lip or flange on its outer edge of not less than 2 inches.

Appellees, interstate motor carriers holding certificates from the Interstate Commerce Commission, challenged the constitutionality of the Illinois Act. A specially constituted three-judge District Court concluded that it unduly and unreasonably burdened and obstructed interstate commerce, because it made the conventional or straight mudflap, which is legal in at least 45 States, illegal in Illinois, and because the statute, taken together with a Rule of the Arkansas Commerce Commission requiring straight mudflaps, rendered the use of the same motor vehicle equipment in both States impossible. The statute was declared to be violative of the Commerce Clause and appellants were enjoined from enforcing it.

The power of the State to regulate the use of its highways is broad and pervasive. We have recognized the peculiarly local nature of this subject of safety, and have upheld state statutes applicable alike to interstate and intrastate commerce, despite the fact that they may have an impact on interstate commerce. South Carolina State Highway Dept. v. Barnwell Bros. (1939).

These safety measures carry a strong presumption of validity when challenged in court. If there are alternative ways of solving a problem, we do not sit to determine which of them is best suited to achieve a valid state objective. Policy decisions are for the state legislature, absent federal entry into the field. Unless we can conclude on the whole record that "the total effect of the law as a safety measure in reducing accidents and casualties is so slight or problematical as not to outweigh the national interest in keeping interstate commerce free from interferences which seriously impede it," we must uphold the statute.

The District Court found that "since it is impossible for a carrier operating in interstate commerce to determine which of its equipment will be used in a particular area, or on a particular day, or days, carriers operating into or through Illinois . . . will be required to equip all their trailers in accordance with the requirements of the Illinois Splash Guard statute." With two possible exceptions the mudflaps required in those States which have mudguard regulations would not meet the standards required by the Illinois statute. The cost of installing the contour mudguards is $30 or more per vehicle. The District Court found that the initial cost of installing those mudguards on all the trucks owned by the appellees ranged from $4,500 to $45,840. There was also evidence in the record to indicate that the cost of maintenance and replacement of these guards is substantial.

Illinois introduced evidence seeking to establish that contour mudguards had a decided safety factor in that they prevented the throwing of debris into the faces of drivers of passing cars and into the windshields of a following vehicle. But the District Court in its opinion stated that it was "conclusively shown that the contour mud flap possesses no advantages over the conventional or straight mud flap previously required in Illinois and presently required in most of the states," and that "there is rather convincing testimony that use of the contour flap creates hazards previously unknown to those using the highways." These hazards were found to be occasioned by the fact that this new type of mudguard tended to cause an accumulation of heat in the brake drum, thus decreasing the effectiveness of brakes, and by the fact that they were susceptible of being hit and bumped when the trucks were backed up and of falling off on the highway.

An order of the Arkansas Commerce Commission requires that trailers operating in that State be equipped with straight or conventional mudflaps. Vehicles equipped to meet the standards of the Illinois statute would not comply with Arkansas standards, and vice versa. Thus if a trailer is to be operated in both States, mudguards would have to be interchanged, causing a significant delay in an operation where prompt movement may be of the essence. It was found that from two to four hours of labor are required to install or remove a contour mudguard. Moreover, the contour guard is attached to the trailer by welding and if the trailer is conveying a cargo of explosives (e.g., for the United States Government) it would be exceedingly dangerous to attempt to weld on a contour mudguard without unloading the trailer.

It was also found that the Illinois statute seriously interferes with the "interline" operations of motor carriers—that is to say, with the interchanging of trailers between an originating carrier and another carrier when the latter serves an area not served by the former. These "interline" operations provide a speedy through-service for the shipper. Interlining contemplates the physical transfer of the entire trailer; there is no unloading and reloading of the cargo. The interlining process is particularly vital in connection with shipment of perishables, which would spoil if unloaded before reaching their destination, or with the movement of explosives carried under seal. Of course, if the originating carrier never operated in Illinois, it would not be expected to equip its trailers with contour mudguards. Yet if an interchanged trailer of that carrier were hauled to or through Illinois, the statute would require that it contain contour guards. Since carriers which operate in and through Illinois cannot compel the originating carriers to equip their trailers with contour guards, they may be forced to cease interlining with those who do not meet the Illinois requirements. Over 60 percent of the business of 5 of the 6 plaintiffs is interline traffic. For the other it constitutes 30 percent. All of the plaintiffs operate extensively in interstate commerce, and the annual mileage in Illinois of none of them exceeds 7 percent of total mileage.

We deal not with absolutes but with questions of degree. The state legislatures plainly have great leeway in providing safety regulations for all vehicles—interstate as well as local. Our decisions so hold. Yet the heavy burden which the Illinois mudguard law places on the interstate movement of trucks and trailers seems to us to pass the permissible limits even for safety regulations.

CONSOLIDATED FREIGHTWAYS CORP. OF DELAWARE v.
RAYMOND KASSEL

455 U.S. 329 (1981)

Justice POWELL announced the judgment of the Court and delivered an opinion, in which Justice WHITE, Justice BLACKMUN, and Justice STEVENS joined.

The question is whether an Iowa statute that prohibits the use of certain large trucks within the State unconstitutionally burdens interstate commerce.

I

Appellee Consolidated Freightways Corporation of Delaware (Consolidated) is one of the largest common carriers in the country. It offers service in 48 States under a certificate of public convenience and necessity issued by the Interstate Commerce Commission. Among other routes, Consolidated carries commodities through Iowa on Interstate 80, the principal east-west route linking New York, Chicago, and the west coast, and on Interstate 35, a major north-south route.

Consolidated mainly uses two kinds of trucks. One consists of a three-axle tractor pulling a 40-foot two-axle trailer. This unit, commonly called a single, or "semi," is 55 feet in length overall. Such trucks have long been used on the Nation's highways. Consolidated also uses a two-axle tractor pulling a single-axle trailer which, in turn, pulls a single-axle dolly and a second single-axle trailer. This combination, known as a double, or twin, is 65 feet long overall. Many trucking companies, including Consolidated, increasingly prefer to use doubles to ship certain kinds of commodities. Doubles have larger capacities, and the trailers can be detached and routed separately if necessary. Consolidated would like to use 65-foot doubles on many of its trips through Iowa.

The State of Iowa, however, by statute restricts the length of vehicles that may use its highways. Unlike all other States in the West and Midwest, Iowa generally prohibits the use of 65-foot doubles within its borders. Instead, most truck combinations are restricted to 55 feet in length. Doubles, mobile homes, trucks carrying vehicles such as tractors and other farm equipment, and singles hauling livestock, are permitted to be as long as 60 feet. Notwithstanding these restrictions, Iowa's statute permits cities abutting the state line by local ordinance to adopt the length limitations of the adjoining State. Where a city has exercised this option, otherwise oversized trucks are permitted within the city limits and in nearby commercial zones.

Because of Iowa's statutory scheme, Consolidated cannot use its 65-foot doubles to move commodities through the State. Instead, the company must do one of four things: (i) use 55-foot singles; (ii) use 60-foot doubles; (iii) detach the trailers of a 65-foot double and shuttle each through the State separately; or (iv) divert 65-foot doubles around Iowa. Dissatisfied with these options, Consolidated filed this suit in the District Court averring that Iowa's statutory scheme unconstitutionally burdens interstate commerce. Iowa defended the law as a reasonable safety measure enacted pursuant to its police power. The State asserted that 65-foot doubles are more dangerous than 55-foot singles and, in any event, that the law promotes safety and reduces road wear within the State by diverting much truck traffic to other States.

In a 14-day trial, both sides adduced evidence on safety, and on the burden on interstate commerce imposed by Iowa's law. On the question of safety, the District Court found that the "evidence clearly establishes that the twin is as safe as the semi." For that reason, "there is no valid safety reason for barring twins from Iowa's highways because of their configuration. The evidence convincingly, if not overwhelmingly, establishes that the 65-foot twin is as safe as, if not safer than, the 60-foot twin and the 55-foot semi. . . . Twins and semis have different characteristics. Twins are more maneuverable, are less sensitive to wind, and create less splash and spray. However, they are more likely than semis to jackknife or upset. They can be backed only for a short distance. The negative characteristics are not such that they render the twin less safe than semis overall. Semis are more stable but are more likely to 'rear end' another vehicle."

In light of these findings, the District Court applied the standard we enunciated in Raymond Motor Transportation, Inc. v. Rice (1978), and concluded that the state law impermissibly burdened interstate commerce.

We conclude that the Iowa truck-length limitations unconstitutionally burden interstate commerce. In Raymond Motor Transportation, Inc. v. Rice, the Court held that a Wisconsin statute that precluded the use of 65-foot doubles violated the Commerce Clause. This case is *Raymond* revisited. Here, as in *Raymond*, the State failed to present any persuasive evidence that 65-foot doubles are less safe than 55-foot singles. Moreover, Iowa's law is now out of step with the laws of all other Midwestern and Western States. Iowa thus substantially burdens the interstate flow of goods by truck. In the absence of congressional action to set uniform standards, some burdens associated with state safety regulations must be tolerated. But where, as here, the State's safety interest has been found to be illusory, and its regulations impair significantly the federal interest in efficient and safe interstate transportation, the state law cannot be harmonized with the Commerce Clause.

Iowa made a more serious effort to support the safety rationale of its law than did Wisconsin in *Raymond*, but its effort was no more persuasive. As noted above, the District Court found that the "evidence clearly establishes that the twin is as safe as the semi." The record supports this finding.

The trial focused on a comparison of the performance of the two kinds of trucks in various safety categories. The evidence showed, and the District Court found, that the 65-foot double was at least the equal of the 55-foot single in the ability to brake, turn, and maneuver. The double, because of its axle placement, produces less splash and spray in wet weather. And, because of its articulation in the middle, the double is less susceptible to dangerous "off-tracking," and to wind.

Consolidated, meanwhile, demonstrated that Iowa's law substantially burdens interstate commerce. Trucking companies that wish to continue to use 65-foot doubles must route them around Iowa or detach the trailers of the doubles and ship them through separately. Alternatively, trucking companies must use the smaller 55-foot singles or 60-foot doubles permitted under Iowa law. Each of these options engenders inefficiency and added expense. The record shows that Iowa's law added about $12.6 million each year to the costs of trucking companies. Consolidated alone incurred about $2 million per year in increased costs.

In addition to increasing the costs of the trucking companies (and, indirectly, of the service to consumers), Iowa's law may aggravate, rather than ameliorate, the problem of highway accidents. Fifty-five foot singles carry less freight than 65-foot doubles. Either more small trucks must be used to carry the same quantity of goods through Iowa, or the same number of larger trucks must drive longer distances to bypass Iowa. In either case, as the District Court noted, the restriction requires more highway miles to be driven to transport the same quantity of goods. Other things being equal, accidents are proportional to distance traveled. Thus, if 65-foot doubles are as safe as 55-foot singles, Iowa's law tends to increase the number of accidents, and to shift the incidence of them from Iowa to other States. Because Iowa has imposed this burden without any significant countervailing safety interest, its statute violates the Commerce Clause.

Justice Rehnquist, with whom Chief Justice Burger and Justice Stewart join, dissenting.

The result in this case suggests, to paraphrase Justice Jackson, that the only state truck-length limit "that is valid is one which this Court has not been able to get its hands on." Although the plurality opinion and the opinion concurring in the judgment strike down Iowa's law by different routes, I believe the analysis in both opinions oversteps our limited authority to review state legislation under the Commerce Clause and seriously intrudes upon the fundamental right of the States to pass laws to secure the safety of their citizens. Accordingly, I dissent.

It is necessary to elaborate somewhat on the facts as presented in the plurality opinion to appreciate fully what the Court does today. Iowa's action in limiting the length of trucks which may travel on its highways is in no sense unusual. Every State in the Union regulates the length of vehicles permitted to use the public roads. Nor is Iowa a renegade in having length limits which operate to exclude the 65-foot doubles favored by Consolidated. These trucks are prohibited in other areas of the country as well, some 17 States and the District of Columbia, including all of New England and most of the Southeast. While pointing out that Consolidated carries commodities through Iowa on Interstate 80, "the principal east-west route linking New York, Chicago, and the west coast," the plurality neglects to note that both Pennsylvania and New Jersey, through which Interstate 80 runs before reaching New York, also ban 65-foot doubles. In short, the persistent effort in the plurality opinion to paint Iowa as an oddity standing alone to block commerce carried in 65-foot doubles is simply not supported by the facts.

A determination that a state law is a rational safety measure does not end the Commerce Clause inquiry. A "sensitive consideration" of the safety purpose in relation to the burden on commerce is required. When engaging in such a consideration the Court does not directly compare safety benefits to commerce costs and strike down the legislation if the latter can be said in some vague sense to "outweigh" the former. Such an approach would make an empty gesture of the strong presumption of validity accorded state safety measures, particularly those governing highways. It would also arrogate to this Court functions of forming public policy, functions which, in the absence of congressional action, were left by the framers of the Constitution to state legislatures. These admonitions are peculiarly apt when, as here, the question involves the difficult comparison of financial losses and "the loss of lives and limbs of workers and people using the highways."

The purpose of the "sensitive consideration" referred to above is rather to determine if the asserted safety justification, although rational, is merely a pretext for discrimination against interstate commerce. We will conclude that it is if the safety benefits from the regulation are demonstrably trivial while the burden on commerce is great. Iowa defends its statute as a highway safety regulation. There can be no doubt that the challenged statute is a valid highway safety regulation and thus entitled to the strongest presumption of validity against Commerce Clause challenges.

One particular type of nondiscriminatory law is worth noting: The Court has consistently declared unconstitutional state laws that regulate the out-of-state conduct of businesses. In Edgar v. MITE Corp., 457 U.S. 624 (1982), the Court declared unconstitutional an Illinois law that required the Secretary of State to adjudicate the fairness of tender offers for the purchase of corporate stock and to reject the transaction if the offer was inequitable or would work a fraud on the sellers. The Court said that the law was a "direct restraint on interstate commerce" because the state was controlling "conduct beyond the boundaries of the state." The state law regulated sales of stock that occurred outside of Illinois. The Court applied the balancing test and found that the law was unconstitutional because it substantially burdened interstate commerce by "hindering the reallocation of economic resources to their highest-valued use," but there was "nothing to be weighed in the balance to sustain the law."

Similarly, Brown-Forman Distillers Corp. v. New York State Liquor Authority, 476 U.S. 573 (1986), involved a New York law that required liquor distillers selling wholesale in the state to file a monthly price schedule, to sell at those prices in New York, and to sell at the lowest prices the distiller charged wholesale in any other state for the same month. The Court found the latter provision to violate the dormant Commerce Clause because it had the "practical effect of . . . control[ling] liquor prices in other states." The Court explained, "While New York may regulate the sale of liquor within its borders, and may seek low prices for its residents, it may not project its legislation into other States by regulating the price to be paid for liquor in those states."

In Healy v. The Beer Institute, 491 U.S. 324 (1989), the Court declared unconstitutional a Connecticut law that required beer companies to post their prices each month and to attest that the prices were not higher than their prices in the four states bordering Connecticut. The Court noted that "the Commerce Clause . . . precludes the application of a state statute to commerce that takes place wholly outside the State's borders, whether or not the commerce has effects within the State." The Court said therefore that "[t]he critical inquiry is whether the practical effect of the regulation is to control conduct beyond the boundaries of the State." The Connecticut law was declared unconstitutional because it affected the prices charged out of the state.

SUMMARY

State laws that discriminate against out-of-staters are almost always declared unconstitutional. Such a law will be allowed only if it is proven that the law is necessary — the least restrictive means — to achieve a nonprotectionist purpose. If a law does not discriminate against out-of-staters, the Court balances its burdens on interstate commerce against its benefits. The inquiry is fact dependent and the outcome obviously turns on how the Court appraises the burdens and the benefits.

e. Exceptions to the Dormant Commerce Clause

There are two exceptions where laws that otherwise would violate the dormant Commerce Clause will be allowed. One exception is if Congress approves the state law. Even a clearly unconstitutional, discriminatory state law will be allowed if approved by Congress because Congress has plenary power to regulate commerce among the states. The second exception is termed the "market participant exception": A state may favor its own citizens in receiving benefits from government programs or in dealing with government-owned businesses. Each exception is presented in turn.

CONGRESSIONAL APPROVAL

The Supreme Court consistently has held that the Constitution empowers Congress to regulate commerce among the states and that therefore state laws burdening commerce are permissible, even when they otherwise would violate the dormant Commerce Clause, if they have been approved by Congress. The Court thus declared, "If Congress ordains that the States may freely regulate an aspect of interstate commerce, any action taken by a State within the scope of the congressional authorization is rendered invulnerable to Commerce Clause challenge."[18] This means that Congress may "[confer] . . . upon the States an ability to restrict the flow of interstate commerce that they would not otherwise enjoy."[19]

This principle has long been followed. For example, in In re Rahrer, 140 U.S. 545 (1891), the Court upheld a state law restricting the importation and sale of alcoholic beverages. Earlier, the Court had declared unconstitutional an almost identical law from another state,[20] but Congress then adopted a law expressly permitting such state regulation of alcoholic beverages. In light of the new federal statute, the Court shifted positions and allowed the state law. The Court said that "[t]he power to regulate is solely in the general government, and it is an essential part of that regulation to prescribe the regular means for accomplishing the introduction and incorporation of articles into and with the mass of property in the country or State."

Of course, if Congress has acted, the commerce power no longer is dormant. The issue would be whether the federal law is a constitutional exercise of the commerce power; if so, the law must be followed even if it means upholding laws that otherwise would violate the dormant Commerce Clause. It is interesting that this is one of the few areas where Congress has the clear authority to overrule a Supreme Court decision interpreting the Constitution. If the Court deems

---

18. Western & Southern Life Insurance Co. v. State Board of Equalization of California, 451 U.S. 648, 652-653 (1981).
19. Lewis v. BT Investment Managers, Inc., 447 U.S. 27, 44 (1980).
20. Leisy v. Hardin, 135 U.S. 100 (1890).

a matter to violate the dormant Commerce Clause, Congress can respond by enacting a law approving the action and thereby effectively overruling the Supreme Court. However, although the law will not violate the dormant Commerce Clause, it still can be challenged under other constitutional provisions, such as equal protection or the Privileges and Immunities Clause of Article IV.

One of the most important areas where the Supreme Court has found congressional approval to authorize state laws that otherwise would violate the dormant Commerce Clause concerns regulation of the insurance industry.

WESTERN & SOUTHERN LIFE INSURANCE CO. v. STATE BOARD OF EQUALIZATION OF CALIFORNIA

451 U.S. 648 (1981)

Justice BRENNAN delivered the opinion of the Court.

Section 685 of the California Insurance Code imposes a retaliatory tax on out-of-state insurers doing business in California, when the insurer's State of incorporation imposes higher taxes on California insurers doing business in that State than California would otherwise impose on that State's insurers doing business in California. This case presents the question of the constitutionality of retaliatory taxes assessed by the State of California against appellant Western & Southern Life Insurance Co., an Ohio corporation, and paid under protest for the years 1965 through 1971.

In a long line of cases stretching back to the early days of the Republic, however, this Court has recognized that the Commerce Clause contains an implied limitation on the power of the States to interfere with or impose burdens on interstate commerce. Even in the absence of congressional action, the courts may decide whether state regulations challenged under the Commerce Clause impermissibly burden interstate commerce.

Our decisions do not, however, limit the authority of Congress to regulate commerce among the several States as it sees fit. In the exercise of this plenary authority, Congress may "confe[r] upon the States an ability to restrict the flow of interstate commerce that they would not otherwise enjoy." Lewis v. BT Investment Managers, Inc. (1980). If Congress ordains that the States may freely regulate an aspect of interstate commerce, any action taken by a State within the scope of the congressional authorization is rendered invulnerable to Commerce Clause challenge.

Congress removed all Commerce Clause limitations on the authority of the States to regulate and tax the business of insurance when it passed the McCarran-Ferguson Act. Nevertheless, Western & Southern, joined by the Solicitor General as amicus curiae, argues that the McCarran-Ferguson Act does not permit "anticompetitive state taxation that discriminates against out-of-state insurers." We find no such limitation in the language or history of the Act.

Section 1 of the Act contains a declaration of policy: "Congress declares that the continued regulation and taxation by the several States of the business of insurance is in the public interest, and that silence on the part of the Congress shall not be construed to impose any barrier to the regulation or taxation of such business by the several States." Section 2 declares: "The business of insurance . . . shall be subject to the laws of the several States which relate to the regulation or taxation of such business."

The unequivocal language of the Act suggests no exceptions. We must therefore reject Western & Southern's Commerce Clause challenge to the California retaliatory tax: the McCarran-Ferguson Act removes entirely any Commerce Clause restriction upon California's power to tax the insurance business.

Similarly, in Prudential Insurance Co. v. Benjamin, 328 U.S. 408 (1946), the Court said that Congress could approve state taxes that discriminate against interstate commerce and that otherwise would be unconstitutional. A state imposed a tax on insurance companies, but exempted in-state companies. The Court said that the federal McCarran Act "was a determination by Congress that state taxes, which in its silence might be held invalid as discriminatory, do not place on interstate insurance business a burden which it is unable generally to bear or should not bear in the competition with local business." The Court declared that Congress's "broad authority" over commerce means that if Congress acts, "limitations imposed for the preservation of their powers become inoperative."

However, it must be remembered that although a law will not violate the dormant Commerce Clause if there is congressional approval, it still can be challenged under other constitutional provisions. Congressional approval does not excuse a violation of equal protection, or the Privileges and Immunities Clause, or other constitutional provisions besides the dormant Commerce Clause. For instance, in Metropolitan Life Insurance Co. v. Ward, 470 U.S. 869 (1985), the Court found that a state tax that discriminated against out-of-state insurance companies violated the Equal Protection Clause, even though a federal law permitted such discriminatory taxes and thus there was not a violation of the dormant Commerce Clause.

THE MARKET PARTICIPANT EXCEPTION

The market participant exception provides that a state may favor its own citizens in dealing with government-owned business and in receiving benefits from government programs. In other words, if the state is literally a participant in the market, such as with a state-owned business, and not a regulator, the dormant Commerce Clause does not apply. Discrimination against out-of-staters is allowed that otherwise would be impermissible.

The Court initially articulated the market participant exception in Hughes v. Alexandria Scrap Corp., 426 U.S. 794 (1976). In *Hughes*, the Court upheld a Maryland law designed to rid the state of abandoned automobiles by having the state pay for the destruction of inoperable cars. The state required minimal documentation of ownership from in-state scrap processors, but required more elaborate proof from out-of-state scrap processors through either a certificate of title, a police certificate vesting title, or a bill of sale from a police auction. The Court said that the state was a market participant as it was purchasing the cars, and therefore its discriminatory actions against out-of-staters did not violate the dormant Commerce Clause. The Court declared, "Nothing in the purposes animating the Commerce Clause prohibits a State, in the absence of congressional action, from participating in the market and exercising the right to favor its own citizens over others."

The following case is an application of the market participant exception and includes a discussion in both the majority and the dissenting opinions as to whether this exception should exist.

REEVES, INC. v. WILLIAM STAKE
447 U.S. 429 (1980)

Justice BLACKMUN delivered the opinion of the Court.

The issue in this case is whether, consistent with the Commerce Clause, the State of South Dakota, in a time of shortage, may confine the sale of the cement it produces solely to its residents.

I

In 1919, South Dakota undertook plans to build a cement plant. The project, a product of the State's then prevailing Progressive political movement, was initiated in response to recent regional cement shortages that "interfered with and delayed both public and private enterprises," and that were "threatening the people of this state." In 1920, the South Dakota Cement Commission anticipated "[t]hat there would be a ready market for the entire output of the plant within the state." The plant, however, located at Rapid City, soon produced more cement than South Dakotans could use. Over the years, buyers in no less than nine nearby States purchased cement from the State's plant. Between 1970 and 1977, some 40% of the plant's output went outside the State.

The plant's list of out-of-state cement buyers included petitioner Reeves, Inc. Reeves is a ready-mix concrete distributor organized under Wyoming law and with facilities in Buffalo, Gillette, and Sheridan, Wyoming. From the beginning of its operations in 1958, and until 1978, Reeves purchased about 95% of its cement from the South Dakota plant. In 1977, its purchases were $1,172,000.

As the 1978 construction season approached, difficulties at the plant slowed production. Meanwhile, a booming construction industry spurred demand for cement both regionally and nationally. The plant found itself unable to meet all orders. Faced with the same type of "serious cement shortage" that inspired the plant's construction, the Commission "reaffirmed its policy of supplying all South Dakota customers first and to honor all contract commitments, with the remaining volume allocated on a first come, first served basis."

Reeves, which had no pre-existing long-term supply contract, was hit hard and quickly by this development. On June 30, 1978, the plant informed Reeves that it could not continue to fill Reeves' orders, and on July 5, it turned away a Reeves truck. Unable to find another supplier, Reeves was forced to cut production by 76% in mid-July. On July 19, Reeves brought this suit against the Commission, challenging the plant's policy of preferring South Dakota buyers, and seeking injunctive relief.

The basic distinction between States as market participants and States as market regulators makes good sense and sound law. The Commerce Clause responds principally to state taxes and regulatory measures impeding free private trade in the national marketplace. There is no indication of a constitutional plan to limit the ability of the States themselves to operate freely in the free market.

Restraint in this area is also counseled by considerations of state sovereignty, the role of each State "'as guardian and trustee for its people,'" and "the long recognized right of trader or manufacturer, engaged in an entirely private business, freely to exercise his own independent discretion as to parties with whom he will deal." Moreover, state proprietary activities may be, and often are, burdened with the same restrictions imposed on private market participants. Even-handedness suggests that, when acting as proprietors, States should similarly share existing freedoms from federal constraints, including the inherent limits of the Commerce Clause.

Finally, as this case illustrates, the competing considerations in cases involving state proprietary action often will be subtle, complex, politically charged, and difficult to assess under traditional Commerce Clause analysis. Given these factors, the adjustment of interests in this context is a task better suited for Congress than this Court.

South Dakota, as a seller of cement, unquestionably fits the "market participant" label more comfortably than a State acting to subsidize local scrap processors.

Justice POWELL, with whom Mr. Justice BRENNAN, Mr. Justice WHITE, and Mr. Justice STEVENS join, dissenting.

The South Dakota Cement Commission has ordered that in times of shortage the state cement plant must turn away out-of-state customers until all orders from South Dakotans are filled. This policy represents precisely the kind of economic protectionism that the Commerce Clause was intended to prevent. The Court, however, finds no violation of the Commerce Clause, solely because the State produces the cement. I agree with the Court that the State of South Dakota may provide cement for its public needs without violating the Commerce Clause. But I cannot agree that South Dakota may withhold its cement from interstate commerce in order to benefit private citizens and businesses within the State.

The need to ensure unrestricted trade among the States created a major impetus for the drafting of the Constitution. "The power over commerce . . . was one of the primary objects for which the people of America adopted their government. . . ." Gibbons v. Ogden (1824). Indeed, the Constitutional Convention was called after an earlier convention on trade and commercial problems proved inconclusive. C. Beard, An Economic Interpretation of the Constitution 61-63 (1935).

The application of the Commerce Clause to this case should turn on the nature of the governmental activity involved. If a public enterprise undertakes an "integral operatio[n] in areas of traditional governmental functions," National League of Cities v. Usery (1976), the Commerce Clause is not directly relevant. If, however, the State enters the private market and operates a commercial enterprise for the advantage of its private citizens, it may not evade the constitutional policy against economic Balkanization.

This distinction derives from the power of governments to supply their own needs and from the purpose of the Commerce Clause itself, which is designed to protect "the natural functioning of the interstate market." In procuring goods and services for the operation of government, a State may act without regard to the private marketplace and remove itself from the reach of the Commerce

Clause. But when a State itself becomes a participant in the private market for other purposes, the Constitution forbids actions that would impede the flow of interstate commerce. These categories recognize no more than the "constitutional line between the State as government and the State as trader." New York v. United States (1946).

I share the Court's desire to preserve state sovereignty. But the Commerce Clause long has been recognized as a limitation on that sovereignty, consciously designed to maintain a national market and defeat economic provincialism. The Court today approves protectionist state policies. In the absence of contrary congressional action, those policies now can be implemented as long as the State itself directly participates in the market.

By enforcing the Commerce Clause in this case, the Court would work no unfairness on the people of South Dakota. They still could reserve cement for public projects and share in whatever return the plant generated. They could not, however, use the power of the State to furnish themselves with cement forbidden to the people of neighboring States.

The creation of a free national economy was a major goal of the States when they resolved to unite under the Federal Constitution. The decision today cannot be reconciled with that purpose.

WHITE v. MASSACHUSETTS COUNCIL OF CONSTRUCTION EMPLOYERS, INC., 460 U.S. 204 (1983): Justice REHNQUIST delivered the opinion of the Court.

In 1979 the mayor of Boston, Massachusetts, issued an executive order which required that all construction projects funded in whole or in part by city funds, or funds which the city had the authority to administer, should be performed by a work force consisting of at least half bona fide residents of Boston.

We hold that on the record before us the application of the mayor's executive order to the contracts in question did not violate the Commerce Clause of the United States Constitution. Insofar as the city expended only its own funds in entering into construction contracts for public projects, it was a market participant and entitled to be treated as such. Insofar as the mayor's executive order was applied to projects funded in part with funds obtained from the federal programs described above, the order was affirmatively sanctioned by the pertinent regulations of those programs.

The above decisions are the major Supreme Court cases announcing and applying the market participant exception. In the following case, the Supreme Court imposed a limit on how far a state or local government can go in discriminating under the market participant exception.

SOUTH-CENTRAL TIMBER DEVELOPMENT, INC. v.
COMMISSIONER, DEPARTMENT OF NATURAL RESOURCES OF ALASKA
467 U.S. 82 (1984)

Justice WHITE announced the judgment of the Court and delivered the opinion of the Court with respect to Parts I and II, and an opinion with respect to

Parts III and IV, in which Justice BRENNAN, Justice BLACKMUN, and Justice STEVENS joined.

In September 1980, the Alaska Department of Natural Resources published a notice that it would sell approximately 49 million board-feet of timber in the area of Icy Cape, Alaska, on October 23, 1980. The notice of sale, the prospectus, and the proposed contract for the sale all provided that "[p]rimary manufacture within the State of Alaska will be required as a special provision of the contract." Under the primary-manufacture requirement, the successful bidder must partially process the timber prior to shipping it outside of the State. The requirement is imposed by contract and does not limit the export of unprocessed timber not owned by the State. The stated purpose of the requirement is to "protect existing industries, provide for the establishment of new industries, derive revenue from all timber resources, and manage the State's forests on a sustained yield basis." Governor's Policy Statement. When it imposes the requirement, the State charges a significantly lower price for the timber than it otherwise would.

Petitioner, South-Central Timber Development, Inc., is an Alaska corporation engaged in the business of purchasing standing timber, logging the timber, and shipping the logs into foreign commerce, almost exclusively to Japan. It does not operate a mill in Alaska and customarily sells unprocessed logs. When it learned that the primary-manufacture requirement was to be imposed on the Icy Cape sale, it brought an action in Federal District Court seeking an injunction, arguing that the requirement violated the negative implications of the Commerce Clause.

Our cases make clear that if a State is acting as a market participant, rather than as a market regulator, the dormant Commerce Clause places no limitation on its activities. The precise contours of the market-participant doctrine have yet to be established, however, the doctrine having been applied in only three cases of this Court to date. See White v. Massachusetts Council of Construction Employers, Inc. (1983); Reeves, Inc. v. Stake (1980); Hughes v. Alexandria Scrap Corp. (1976).

The State of Alaska contends that its primary-manufacture requirement fits squarely within the market-participant doctrine, arguing that "Alaska's entry into the market may be viewed as precisely the same type of subsidy to local interests that the Court found unobjectionable in *Alexandria Scrap*." However, when Maryland became involved in the scrap market it was as a purchaser of scrap; Alaska, on the other hand, participates in the timber market, but imposes conditions downstream in the timber-processing market. Alaska is not merely subsidizing local timber processing in an amount "roughly equal to the difference between the price the timber would fetch in the absence of such a requirement and the amount the state actually receives."

[I]t is clear that the State is more than merely a seller of timber. In the commercial context, the seller usually has no say over, and no interest in, how the product is to be used after sale; in this case, however, payment for the timber does not end the obligations of the purchaser, for, despite the fact that the purchaser has taken delivery of the timber and has paid for it, he cannot do with it as he pleases. Instead, he is obligated to deal with a stranger to the contract after completion of the sale.

If the State directly subsidized the timber-processing industry by such an amount, the purchaser would retain the option of taking advantage of the subsidy by processing timber in the State or forgoing the benefits of the subsidy and exporting unprocessed timber. Under the Alaska requirement, however, the choice is made for him: if he buys timber from the State he is not free to take the timber out of state prior to processing.

The market-participant doctrine permits a State to influence "a discrete, identifiable class of economic activity in which [it] is a major participant." White v. Massachusetts Council of Construction Workers, Inc. Contrary to the State's contention, the doctrine is not carte blanche to impose any conditions that the State has the economic power to dictate, and does not validate any requirement merely because the State imposes it upon someone with whom it is in contractual privity.

The limit of the market-participant doctrine must be that it allows a State to impose burdens on commerce within the market in which it is a participant, but allows it to go no further. The State may not impose conditions, whether by statute, regulation, or contract, that have a substantial regulatory effect outside of that particular market. Unless the "market" is relatively narrowly defined, the doctrine has the potential of swallowing up the rule that States may not impose substantial burdens on interstate commerce even if they act with the permissible state purpose of fostering local industry.

[D]ownstream restrictions have a greater regulatory effect than do limitations on the immediate transaction. Instead of merely choosing its own trading partners, the State is attempting to govern the private, separate economic relationships of its trading partners; that is, it restricts the post-purchase activity of the purchaser, rather than merely the purchasing activity. In contrast to the situation in *White*, this restriction on private economic activity takes place after the completion of the parties' direct commercial obligations, rather than during the course of an ongoing commercial relationship in which the city retained a continuing proprietary interest in the subject of the contract. In sum, the State may not avail itself of the market-participant doctrine to immunize its downstream regulation of the timber-processing market in which it is not a participant.

Justice REHNQUIST, with whom Justice O'CONNOR joins, dissenting.

In my view, the line of distinction drawn in the plurality opinion between the State as market participant and the State as market regulator is both artificial and unconvincing. The plurality draws this line "simply as a matter of intuition," but then seeks to bolster its intuition through a series of remarks more appropriate to antitrust law than to the Commerce Clause. For example, the plurality complains that the State is using its "leverage" in the timber market to distort consumer choice in the timber-processing market, a classic example of a tying arrangement. And the plurality cites the common-law doctrine of restraints on alienation and the antitrust limits on vertical restraints in dismissing the State's claim that it could accomplish exactly the same result in other ways.

The plurality does offer one other reason for its demarcation of the boundary between these two concepts. "[D]ownstream restrictions have a greater regulatory effect than do limitations on the immediate transaction. Instead of merely choosing its own trading partners, the State is attempting to govern the private, separate economic relationships of its trading partners; that is, it restricts the post-purchase activity of the purchaser, rather than merely the purchasing activity." But, of course, this is not a "reason" at all, but merely a restatement of the conclusion. The line between participation and regulation is what we are trying to determine. To invoke that very distinction in support of the line drawn is merely to fall back again on intuition.

Alaska is merely paying the buyer of the timber indirectly, by means of a reduced price, to hire Alaska residents to process the timber. Under existing precedent, the State could accomplish that same result in any number of ways. For example, the State could choose to sell its timber only to those companies that maintain active primary-processing plants in Alaska. Reeves, Inc. v. Stake (1980). Or the State could directly subsidize the primary-processing industry within the State. Hughes v. Alexandria Scrap Corp. (1976). The State could even pay to have the logs processed and then enter the market only to sell processed logs. It seems to me unduly formalistic to conclude that the one path chosen by the State as best suited to promote its concerns is the path forbidden it by the Commerce Clause.

The underlying policy question is whether there should be a market participant exception. The market participant exception can be criticized on several grounds.[21] First, the dormant Commerce Clause is meant to stop protectionist actions by state governments; protectionism should not be allowed regardless of whether the state is acting in a proprietary or a regulatory capacity. Second, there is not a clear distinction between situations where the government is acting as a regulator and when it is a market participant.

On the other hand, the market participant exception can be defended as allowing citizens in a state to recoup the benefits of the taxes that they pay. Professor Tribe says that the exception is justified by "[t]he sense of fairness in allowing a community to retain the public benefits created by its own public investment."[22] The market participant exception also is defended on the ground that "state spending programs are less coercive than regulatory programs or taxes with similar purposes" and they "seem less hostile to other states and less inconsistent with the concept of union than discriminatory regulation or taxation."[23]

C.   THE PRIVILEGES AND IMMUNITIES CLAUSE OF ARTICLE IV, §2

1.   Introduction

Another provision that limits state and local regulation is the Privileges and Immunities Clause found in Article IV, §2. The provision states, "The Citizens

---

21. For a criticism of the market participant exception, *see* Karl Manheim, *New-Age Federalism and the Market Participant Doctrine*, 22 Ariz. St. L.J. 559 (1990).

22. Laurence Tribe, *Constitutional Choices* 145 (1985).

23. Donald Regan, *The Supreme Court and State Protectionism: Making Sense of the Dormant Commerce Clause*, 84 Mich. L. Rev. 1091, 1194 (1986).

of each State shall be entitled to all Privileges and Immunities of Citizens in the several States." The Supreme Court has interpreted this provision as limiting the ability of a state to discriminate against out-of-staters with regard to fundamental rights or important economic activities. The Court has said that "[t]he section, in effect, prevents a State from discriminating against citizens of other States in favor of its own."[24] As presented below, most cases under the Privileges and Immunities Clause involve challenges to state and local laws that discriminate against out-of-staters with regard to their ability to earn a livelihood.[25] Such discrimination will be allowed only if it is substantially related to achieving a substantial state interest.[26]

Discrimination against citizens of other states is a prerequisite for application of the Privileges and Immunities Clause.[27] The Supreme Court long has held that the term "citizen" in the Privileges and Immunities Clause is limited to individuals who are United States citizens.[28] Thus, corporations cannot sue under the Privileges and Immunities Clause because, by definition, they are not citizens.[29] Nor can aliens sue under the Privileges and Immunities Clause.

The dormant Commerce Clause and the Privileges and Immunities Clause overlap: Both can be used to challenge state and local laws that discriminate against out-of-staters. In fact, the Supreme Court has spoken of the "mutually reinforcing relationship" between the dormant Commerce Clause and the Privileges and Immunities Clause.[30]

There are, however, some key differences. First, the Privileges and Immunities Clause can be used only if there is discrimination against out-of-staters. The dormant Commerce Clause, as explained above, can be used to challenge state and local laws that burden interstate commerce regardless of whether they discriminate against out-of-staters. However, under the dormant Commerce Clause, laws that discriminate are much more likely to be invalidated.

Second, corporations and aliens can sue under the dormant Commerce Clause, but not the Privileges and Immunities Clause. The Privileges and Immunities Clause is expressly limited to "citizens," whereas no such limitation exists with regard to the dormant Commerce Clause.

Third, there are two exceptions to the dormant Commerce Clause that do not apply to the Privileges and Immunities Clause. If Congress approves state laws, then they do not violate the dormant Commerce Clause; if Congress has acted, its commerce power no longer is dormant. But congressional approval does not

24. Hague v. Committee for Industrial Organization, 307 U.S. 496, 511 (1939).

25. For an excellent discussion of the Clause and its purposes, *see* Jonathan Varat, *State "Citizenship" and Interstate Equality*, 48 U. Chi. L. Rev. 487 (1981).

26. *See* United Building & Construction Trades Council v. Mayor & Council of Camden, 465 U.S. 208 (1984).

27. *See* Zobel v. Williams, 457 U.S. 55, 59 n.5 (1982) (finding that an Alaskan law that gave refunds based on duration of state residence did not violate the Privileges and Immunities Clause. The Court said that the law did not discriminate between citizens and noncitizens but among citizens based on duration of residence. The Court did find that the law violated equal protection.).

28. The Court has held that in determining whether a person is a citizen of a state, residency in the state is synonymous with state citizenship. *See* United Building & Construction Trades Council v. Mayor & Council of Camden, 465 U.S. 208, 216 (1984) ("[I]t is now established that the terms 'citizen' and 'resident' are essentially 'interchangeable' for purposes of analysis of most cases under the Privileges and Immunities Clause.") (citations omitted).

29. Blake v. McClung, 172 U.S. 239 (1898); Paul v. Virginia, 75 U.S. (8 Wall.) 168 (1868); *see also* Hemphill v. Orloff, 277 U.S. 537 (1928) (trust cannot sue under the Privileges and Immunities Clause because of its corporate form).

30. Hicklin v. Orbeck, 437 U.S. 518, 531 (1978).

excuse a law that violates the Privileges and Immunities Clause. Also, as described above, there is a market participant exception to the dormant Commerce Clause that allows states to favor their own citizens in receiving benefits from government programs and in dealing with government-owned businesses. No such exception exists for the Privileges and Immunities Clause. Thus, in White v. Massachusetts Council of Construction Employers, Inc., presented above, the Court found that a city law requiring that 50 percent of those hired to work on city construction projects be residents of the city did not violate the dormant Commerce Clause because of the market participant exception.[31] But a year later, in United Building & Construction Trades Council v. Mayor & Council of Camden, presented below, the Court declared unconstitutional a city's ordinance requiring that at least 40 percent of the employees on city projects be city residents. The Court found that the law violated the Privileges and Immunities Clause and explained that the market participant exception applies only with regard to dormant Commerce Clause challenges.

2. Analysis Under the Privileges and Immunities Clause

When a challenge is brought under the Privileges and Immunities Clause, there are two basic questions.[32] First, has the state discriminated against out-of-staters with regard to privileges and immunities that it accords its own citizens? Second, if there is such discrimination, is there a sufficient justification for the discrimination? The Privileges and Immunities Clause is not absolute, but it creates a strong presumption against state and local laws that discriminate against out-of-staters with regard to fundamental rights or important economic activities. Both of these issues are discussed in most of the cases below. However, the first set of cases focus primarily on the former issue; the second set of decisions especially discuss the latter question.

WHAT ARE THE "PRIVILEGES AND IMMUNITIES OF CITIZENSHIP"?

The classic statement of the meaning of the phrase "privileges and immunities" of citizenship was provided by Justice Bushrod Washington in Corfield v. Coryell, 6 F. Cas. 546, 551, 4 Wash. C.C. 371, No. 3230 (Cir. Ct. E.D. Pa. 1823), when he said that the clause protects interests that "are fundamental; which belong, of right, to the citizens of all free governments. [They] may be comprehended under the following general heads: Protection by the government, the enjoyment of life and liberty, with the right to acquire and possess property of every kind, and to pursue and obtain happiness and safety; subject nevertheless to such restraints as the government may justly prescribe for the general good of the whole."[33]

---

31. 460 U.S. 204 (1983).

32. The Supreme Court has expressly referred to this as "a two-step inquiry." United Building & Construction Trades Council v. Mayor & Council of Camden, 465 U.S. 208, 218 (1984).

33. In *Corfield*, the court of appeals upheld a New Jersey law that prevented nonresidents from gathering clams from state waters. The court said that clams were the property of the state. Subsequently, the Supreme Court has rejected the view that natural resources, such as animals, are property and not items of commerce. *See, e.g.,* Hughes v. Oklahoma, 441 U.S. 222 (1979).

More recently, the Court said that the Clause applies "[o]nly with respect to those privileges and immunities bearing upon the vitality of the Nation as a single entity."[34] The Court also has said that the issue is whether the interest is "sufficiently fundamental to the promotion of interstate harmony."[35]

Yet these and similar statements are abstract and provide relatively little guidance in identifying what are the "privileges and immunities of citizens" under Article IV. It is well settled that the Privileges and Immunities Clause is meant to limit the ability of states to discriminate against citizens from other states, but it is not at all clear as to what constitutes the area — privileges and immunities — where discrimination is forbidden. Indeed, the Supreme Court has acknowledged that "the contours of [the Clause] are not well developed."[36]

Examining the cases concerning the Privileges and Immunities Clause reveals that the Court primarily has applied it in two contexts: (1) when a state is discriminating against out-of-staters with regard to constitutional rights and (2) when a state is discriminating against out-of-staters with regard to important economic activities. The latter almost always arises in the context of a state discriminating against out-of-staters with regard to their ability to earn a livelihood. The Court has refused to apply the Privileges and Immunities Clause in situations where the discrimination against out-of-staters has involved neither constitutional rights nor important economic activities.

The rights enumerated in the Bill of Rights seem the most obvious and the most basic "privileges and immunities of citizenship."[37] Generally, however, there is no need to use the Privileges and Immunities Clause to protect constitutionally guaranteed rights. If a state were to prevent out-of-staters from engaging in religious worship, a challenge certainly could be brought under the Privileges and Immunities Clause. Most likely, though, the suit would be brought under the First Amendment as applied to the states through the Fourteenth Amendment.

Although such cases arise only relatively rarely, the Privileges and Immunities Clause can be used to challenge state and local laws that discriminate against out-of-staters with regard to the exercise of constitutional rights. For example, in Doe v. Bolton, 410 U.S. 179 (1973), the Supreme Court concluded that a state could not limit the ability of out-of-staters to obtain abortions in the state. *Doe* was a companion case to Roe v. Wade[38] and involved a Georgia law that allowed residents to obtain an abortion if a physician determined that continuing the pregnancy would endanger a woman's life or health, the fetus would be born with a serious defect, or the pregnancy resulted from rape. The Court declared the law unconstitutional and invalidated the residency requirement based on the Privileges and Immunities Clause. The Court said, "Just as the Privileges and Immunities Clause . . . protects persons who enter other States to ply their trade, so must it protect persons who enter Georgia seeking the medical services that

---

34. Baldwin v. Fish & Game Commission of Montana, 436 U.S. 371, 383 (1978) (citations omitted).

35. United Buliding & Construction Trades Council v. Mayor & Council of the City of Camden, 465 U.S. at 218.

36. Baldwin v. Montana Fish and Game Commission, 436 U.S. at 380.

37. *See* Duncan v. Louisiana, 391 U.S. 145, 166 (1968) (Black, J., concurring) ("What more precious 'privilege' of American citizenship could there be than that privilege to claim the protections of our great Bill of Rights?").

38. 410 U.S. 113 (1973).

are available there. A contrary holding would mean that a State could limit to its own residents the general medical care available within its borders. This we could not approve."

The vast majority of cases under the Privileges and Immunities Clause involve states discriminating against out-of-staters with regard to their ability to earn their livelihood. The following cases are key instances in which the Supreme Court has considered the Privileges and Immunities Clause in this context.

TOOMER v. WITSELL

334 U.S. 385 (1948)

Chief Justice VINSON delivered the opinion of the Court.

This is a suit to enjoin as unconstitutional the enforcement of several South Carolina statutes governing commercial shrimp fishing in the three-mile maritime belt off the coast of that State. The statutes appellants challenge relate to shrimping during the open season in the three-mile belt: Section 3300 of the South Carolina Code provides that the waters in that area shall be "a common for the people of the State for the taking of fish." Section 3379, as amended in 1947, requires payment of a license fee of $25 for each shrimp boat owned by a resident, and of $2,500 for each one owned by a non-resident.

Appellants, who initiated the action, are five individual fishermen, all citizens and residents of Georgia, and a non-profit fish dealers' organization incorporated in Florida. The purpose and effect of this statute, they contend, is not to conserve shrimp, but to exclude non-residents and thereby create a commercial monopoly for South Carolina residents. As such, the statute is said to violate the Privileges and Immunities Clause of Art. IV, §2, of the Constitution and the equal protection clause of the Fourteenth Amendment.

The primary purpose of this clause, like the clauses between which it is located — those relating to full faith and credit and to interstate extradition of fugitives from justice — was to help fuse into one Nation a collection of independent, sovereign States. It was designed to insure to a citizen of State A who ventures into State B the same privileges which the citizens of State B enjoy. For protection of such equality the citizen of State A was not to be restricted to the uncertain remedies afforded by diplomatic processes and official retaliation. Indeed, without some provision of the kind removing from the citizens of each State the disabilities of alienage in the other States, and giving them equality of privilege with citizens of those States, the Republic would have constituted little more than a league of States; it would not have constituted the Union which now exists. In line with this underlying purpose, it was long ago decided that one of the privileges which the clause guarantees to citizens of State A is that of doing business in State B on terms of substantial equality with the citizens of that State.

Like many other constitutional provisions, the Privileges and Immunities Clause is not an absolute. It does bar discrimination against citizens of other States where there is no substantial reason for the discrimination beyond the mere fact that they are citizens of other States. But it does not preclude disparity of treatment in the many situations where there are perfectly valid independent reasons for it. Thus the inquiry in each case must be concerned with whether such reasons do exist and whether the degree of discrimination bears a close relation to them. The inquiry must also, of course, be conducted with due regard for the principle that the States should have considerable leeway in analyzing local evils and in prescribing appropriate cures.

With these factors in mind, we turn to a consideration of the constitutionality of §3379. By that statute South Carolina plainly and frankly discriminates against non-residents, and the record leaves little doubt but what the discrimination is so great that its practical effect is virtually exclusionary. As justification for the statute, appellees urge that the State's obvious purpose was to conserve its shrimp supply, and they suggest that it was designed to head off an impending threat of excessive trawling. The record casts some doubt on these statements. But in any event, appellees' argument assumes that any means adopted to attain valid objectives necessarily squares with the Privileges and Immunities Clause. It overlooks the purpose of that clause, which, as indicated above, is to outlaw classifications based on the fact of non-citizenship unless there is something to indicate that non-citizens constitute a peculiar source of the evil at which the statute is aimed. Thus, §3379 must be held unconstitutional.

UNITED BUILDING & CONSTRUCTION TRADES COUNCIL OF CAMDEN COUNTY v. MAYOR & COUNCIL OF THE CITY OF CAMDEN

465 U.S. 208 (1984)

Justice REHNQUIST delivered the opinion of the Court

A municipal ordinance of the city of Camden, New Jersey requires that at least 40% of the employees of contractors and subcontractors working on city construction projects be Camden residents. Appellant, the United Building and Construction Trades Council of Camden and Vicinity (the Council), challenges that ordinance as a violation of the Privileges and Immunities Clause, Article IV, §2, of the United States Constitution.

We first address the argument, accepted by the Supreme Court of New Jersey, that the Clause does not even apply to a municipal ordinance such as this. Two separate contentions are advanced in support of this position: first, that the Clause only applies to laws passed by a State and, second, that the Clause only applies to laws that discriminate on the basis of state citizenship. The first argument can be quickly rejected. The fact that the ordinance in question is a municipal, rather than a state, law does not somehow place it outside the scope of the Privileges and Immunities Clause. First of all, one cannot easily distinguish municipal from state action in this case: the municipal ordinance would not have gone into effect without express approval by the State Treasurer. More fundamentally, a municipality is merely a political subdivision of the State from which its authority derives. It is as true of the Privileges and Immunities Clause as of the Equal Protection Clause that what would be unconstitutional if done directly by the State can no more readily be accomplished by a city deriving its authority from the State.

The second argument merits more consideration. The New Jersey Supreme Court concluded that the Privileges and Immunities Clause does not apply to an ordinance that discriminates solely on the basis of municipal residency. The Clause is phrased in terms of state citizenship and was designed "to place the citizens of each State upon the same footing with citizens of other States, so far as the advantages resulting from citizenship in those States are concerned." Paul v. Virginia (1869).

Municipal residency classifications, it is argued, simply do not give rise to the same concerns. We cannot accept this argument. We have never read the Clause so literally as to apply it only to distinctions based on state citizenship. A person who is not residing in a given State is ipso facto not residing in a city within that State. Thus, whether the exercise of a privilege is conditioned on state residency or on municipal residency he will just as surely be excluded. Given the Camden ordinance, an out-of-state citizen who ventures into New Jersey will not enjoy the same privileges as the New Jersey citizen residing in Camden. It is true that New Jersey citizens not residing in Camden will be affected by the ordinance as well as out-of-state citizens. And it is true that the disadvantaged New Jersey residents have no claim under the Privileges and Immunities Clause. But New Jersey residents at least have a chance to remedy at the polls any discrimination against them. Out-of-state citizens have no similar opportunity and they must "not be restricted to the uncertain remedies afforded by diplomatic processes and official retaliation." Toomer v. Witsell (1948). We conclude that Camden's ordinance is not immune from constitutional review at the behest of out-of-state residents merely because some in-state residents are similarly disadvantaged.

Application of the Privileges and Immunities Clause to a particular instance of discrimination against out-of-state residents entails a two-step inquiry. As an initial matter, the court must decide whether the ordinance burdens one of those privileges and immunities protected by the Clause. As a threshold matter, then, we must determine whether an out-of-state resident's interest in employment on public works contracts in another State is sufficiently "fundamental" to the promotion of interstate harmony so as to "fall within the purview of the Privileges and Immunities Clause." Certainly, the pursuit of a common calling is one of the most fundamental of those privileges protected by the Clause. Many, if not most, of our cases expounding the Privileges and Immunities Clause have dealt with this basic and essential activity.

The conclusion that Camden's ordinance discriminates against a protected privilege does not, of course, end the inquiry. It does not preclude discrimination against citizens of other States where there is a "substantial reason" for the difference in treatment. The city of Camden contends that its ordinance is necessary to counteract grave economic and social ills. Spiralling unemployment, a sharp decline in population, and a dramatic reduction in the number of businesses located in the city have eroded property values and depleted the city's tax base. The resident hiring preference is designed, the city contends, to increase the number of employed persons living in Camden and to arrest the "middle class flight" currently plaguing the city. The city also argues that all non-Camden residents employed on city public works projects, whether they reside in New Jersey or Pennsylvania, constitute a "source of the evil at which the statute is aimed." That is, they "live off" Camden without "living in" Camden. Camden contends that the scope of the discrimination practiced in the ordinance, with its municipal residency requirement, is carefully tailored to alleviate this evil without unreasonably harming nonresidents, who still have access to 60% of the available positions.

Nonetheless, we find it impossible to evaluate Camden's justification on the record as it now stands. No trial has ever been held in the case. No findings of fact have been made. The Supreme Court of New Jersey certified the case for direct appeal after the brief administrative proceedings that led to approval of the ordinance by the State Treasurer. It would not be appropriate for this Court either to make factual determinations as an initial matter or to take judicial notice of Camden's decay. We, therefore, deem it wise to remand the case to the New Jersey Supreme Court. That court may decide, consistent with state procedures, on the best method for making the necessary findings.

In Toomer v. Witsell and United Building & Construction Trades Council v. Mayor & Council of Camden, the Court stated that discrimination against out-of-staters with regard to their ability to earn their livelihood violated the Privileges and Immunities Clause. In the following case, the Court made it clear that the clause is limited to protecting this economic interest and civil liberties; discrimination against out-of-staters in other areas is not prohibited by the Privileges and Immunities Clause of Article IV.

LESTER BALDWIN v. FISH & GAME COMMISSION OF MONTANA
436 U.S. 371 (1978)

Justice BLACKMUN delivered the opinion of the Court.

This case presents issues under the Privileges and Immunities Clause of the Constitution's Art. IV, §2, as to the constitutional validity of disparities, as between residents and nonresidents, in a State's hunting license system. For the 1975 hunting season, a Montana resident could purchase a license solely for elk for $4. The nonresident, however, in order to hunt elk, was required to purchase a combination license at a cost of $151; this entitled him to take one elk and two deer. For the 1976 season, the Montana resident could purchase a license solely for elk for $9. The nonresident, in order to hunt elk was required to purchase a combination license at a cost of $225; this entitled him to take one elk, one deer, one black bear, and game birds, and to fish with hook and line. A resident was not required to buy any combination of licenses, but if he did, the cost to him of all the privileges granted by the nonresident combination license was $30. The nonresident thus paid 7 1/2 times as much as the resident, and if the nonresident wished to hunt only elk, he paid 25 times as much as the resident.

Appellant Lester Baldwin is a Montana resident. He also is an outfitter holding a state license as a hunting guide. The majority of his customers are nonresidents who come to Montana to hunt elk and other big game. Appellants Carlson, Huseby, Lee and Moris are residents of Minnesota. They have hunted big game, particularly elk, in Montana in past years and wish to continue to do so.

In 1975, the five appellants, disturbed by the difference in the kinds of Montana elk-hunting licenses available to nonresidents, as contrasted with those available to residents of the State, and by the difference in the fees the nonresident and the resident must pay for their respective licenses, instituted the present federal suit for declaratory and injunctive relief and for reimbursement, in part, of fees already paid.

Appellants strongly urge here that the Montana licensing scheme for the hunting of elk violates the Privileges and Immunities Clause of Art. IV §2, of our Constitution. That Clause is not one the contours of which have been precisely shaped by the process and wear of constant litigation and judicial interpretation over the years since 1789.

When the Privileges and Immunities Clause has been applied to specific cases, it has been interpreted to prevent a State from imposing unreasonable burdens on citizens of other States in their pursuit of common callings within the State; in the ownership and disposition of privately held property within the State; and in access to the courts of the State.

It has not been suggested, however, that state citizenship or residency may never be used by a State to distinguish among persons. Suffrage, for example, always has been understood to be tied to an individual's identification with a particular State. No one would suggest that the Privileges and Immunities Clause requires a State to open its polls to a person who declines to assert that the State is the only one where he claims a right to vote. The same is true as to qualification for an elective office of the State. Some distinctions between residents and nonresidents merely reflect the fact that this is a Nation composed of individual States, and are permitted; other distinctions are prohibited because they hinder the formation, the purpose, or the development of a single Union of those States. Only with respect to those "privileges" and "immunities" bearing upon the vitality of the Nation as a single entity must the State treat all citizens, resident and nonresident, equally. Here we must decide into which category falls a distinction with respect to access to recreational big-game hunting. Does the distinction made by Montana between residents and nonresidents in establishing access to elk hunting threaten a basic right in a way that offends the Privileges and Immunities Clause? Merely to ask the question seems to provide the answer. We repeat much of what already has been said above: Elk hunting by nonresidents in Montana is a recreation and a sport. In itself—wholly apart from license fees—it is costly and obviously available only to the wealthy nonresident or to the one so taken with the sport that he sacrifices other values in order to indulge in it and to enjoy what it offers. It is not a means to the nonresident's livelihood. The mastery of the animal and the trophy are the ends that are sought; appellants are not totally excluded from these. The elk supply, which has been entrusted to the care of the State by the people of Montana, is finite and must be carefully tended in order to be preserved.

Appellants' interest in sharing this limited resource on more equal terms with Montana residents simply does not fall within the purview of the Privileges and Immunities Clause. Equality in access to Montana elk is not basic to the maintenance or well-being of the Union. Appellants do not—and cannot—contend that they are deprived of a means of a livelihood by the system or of access to any part of the State to which they may seek to travel. Whatever rights or activities may be "fundamental" under the Privileges and Immunities Clause, we are persuaded, and hold, that elk hunting by nonresidents in Montana is not one of them.

WHAT JUSTIFICATIONS ARE SUFFICIENT TO PERMIT DISCRIMINATION?

The Court repeatedly has stated that the Privileges and Immunities Clause is not absolute. There is discussion in the above cases as to what interests are sufficient to permit discrimination. The Court's most detailed consideration of this issue is in the following decision.

SUPREME COURT OF NEW HAMPSHIRE v. KATHRYN A. PIPER

470 U.S. 274 (1985)

Justice POWELL delivered the opinion of the Court.

The Rules of the Supreme Court of New Hampshire limit bar admission to state residents. We here consider whether this restriction violates the Privileges and Immunities Clause of the United States Constitution, Art. IV, §2.

Kathryn Piper lives in Lower Waterford, Vermont, about 400 yards from the New Hampshire border. In 1979, she applied to take the February 1980 New Hampshire bar examination. Piper submitted with her application a statement of intent to become a New Hampshire resident. Following an investigation, the Board of Bar Examiners found that Piper was of good moral character and met the other requirements for admission. She was allowed to take, and passed, the examination. Piper was informed by the Board that she would have to establish a home address in New Hampshire prior to being sworn in.

Derived, like the Commerce Clause, from the fourth of the Articles of Confederation, the Privileges and Immunities Clause was intended to create a national economic union. It is therefore not surprising that this Court repeatedly has found that "one of the privileges which the Clause guarantees to citizens of State A is that of doing business in State B on terms of substantial equality with the citizens of that State." Toomer v. Witsell. There is nothing in [prior decisions] suggesting that the practice of law should not be viewed as a "privilege" under Art. IV, §4, 6. Like the occupations considered in our earlier cases, the practice of law is important to the national economy.

The lawyer's role in the national economy is not the only reason that the opportunity to practice law should be considered a "fundamental right." We believe that the legal profession has a noncommercial role and duty that reinforce the view that the practice of law falls within the ambit of the Privileges and Immunities Clause. Out-of-state lawyers may—and often do—represent persons who raise unpopular federal claims. In some cases, representation by nonresident counsel may be the only means available for the vindication of federal rights.

The conclusion that Rule 42 deprives nonresidents of a protected privilege does not end our inquiry. The Court has stated that "[l]ike many other constitutional provisions, the Privileges and Immunities Clause is not an absolute." The Clause does not preclude discrimination against nonresidents where (i) there is a substantial reason for the difference in treatment; and (ii) the discrimination practiced against nonresidents bears a substantial relationship to the State's objective. In deciding whether the discrimination bears a close or substantial relationship to the State's objective, the Court has considered the availability of less restrictive means.

The Supreme Court of New Hampshire offers several justifications for its refusal to admit nonresidents to the bar. It asserts that nonresident members would be less likely (i) to become, and remain, familiar with local rules and procedures; (ii) to behave ethically; (iii) to be available for court proceedings;

and (iv) to do pro bono and other volunteer work in the State. We find that none of these reasons meets the test of "substantiality," and that the means chosen do not bear the necessary relationship to the State's objectives.

There is no evidence to support appellant's claim that nonresidents might be less likely to keep abreast of local rules and procedures. Nor may we assume that a nonresident lawyer — anymore than a resident — would disserve his clients by failing to familiarize himself with the rules. As a practical matter, we think that unless a lawyer has, or anticipates, a considerable practice in the New Hampshire courts, he would be unlikely to take the bar examination and pay the annual dues of $125.

New Hampshire's "simple residency" requirement is underinclusive as well, because it permits lawyers who move away from the State to retain their membership in the bar. There is no reason to believe that a former resident would maintain a more active practice in the New Hampshire courts than would a nonresident lawyer who had never lived in the State.

We also find the appellant's second justification to be without merit, for there is no reason to believe that a nonresident lawyer will conduct his practice in a dishonest manner. The nonresident lawyer's professional duty and interest in his reputation should provide the same incentive to maintain high ethical standards as they do for resident lawyers. A lawyer will be concerned with his reputation in any community where he practices, regardless of where he may live. Furthermore, a nonresident lawyer may be disciplined for unethical conduct.

There is more merit to the appellant's assertion that a nonresident member of the bar at times would be unavailable for court proceedings. In the course of litigation, pretrial hearings on various matters often are held on short notice. At times a court will need to confer immediately with counsel. Even the most conscientious lawyer residing in a distant State may find himself unable to appear in court for an unscheduled hearing or proceeding. Nevertheless, we do not believe that this type of problem justifies the exclusion of nonresidents from the state bar. One may assume that a high percentage of nonresident lawyers willing to take the state bar examination and pay the annual dues will reside in places reasonably convenient to New Hampshire. Furthermore, in those cases where the nonresident counsel will be unavailable on short notice, the State can protect its interests through less restrictive means. The trial court, by rule or as an exercise of discretion, may require any lawyer who resides at a great distance to retain a local attorney who will be available for unscheduled meetings and hearings.

The final reason advanced by appellant is that nonresident members of the state bar would be disinclined to do their share of pro bono and volunteer work. Perhaps this is true to a limited extent, particularly where the member resides in a distant location. We think it is reasonable to believe, however, that most lawyers who become members of a state bar will endeavor to perform their share of these services. This sort of participation, of course, would serve the professional interest of a lawyer who practices in the State. Furthermore, a nonresident bar member, like the resident member, could be required to represent indigents and perhaps to participate in formal legal-aid work.

In summary, appellant neither advances a "substantial reason" for its discrimination against nonresident applicants to the bar, nor demonstrates that the discrimination practiced bears a close relationship to its proffered objectives.

Our holding in this case does not interfere with the ability of the States to regulate their bars. The nonresident who seeks to join a bar, unlike the pro hac vice applicant, must have the same professional and personal qualifications required of resident lawyers. Furthermore, the nonresident member of the bar is subject to the full force of New Hampshire's disciplinary rules.

Justice REHNQUIST, dissenting.

Today the Court holds that New Hampshire cannot decide that a New Hampshire lawyer should live in New Hampshire. This may not be surprising to those who view law as just another form of business frequently practiced across state lines by interchangeable actors; the Privileges and Immunities Clause of Art. IV, §2, has long been held to apply to States' attempts to discriminate against nonresidents who seek to ply their trade interstate. The decision will be surprising to many, however, because it so clearly disregards the fact that the practice of law is — almost by definition — fundamentally different from those other occupations that are practiced across state lines without significant deviation from State to State. The fact that each State is free, in a large number of areas, to establish independently of the other States its own laws for the governance of its citizens, is a fundamental precept of our Constitution that, I submit, is of equal stature with the need for the States to form a cohesive union. What is at issue here is New Hampshire's right to decide that those people who in many ways will intimately deal with New Hampshire's self-governance should reside within that State.

[A] State has a very strong interest in seeing that its legislators and its judges come from among the constituency of state residents, so that they better understand the local interests to which they will have to respond. Unlike the Court, I would recognize that the State also has a very "substantial" interest in seeing that its lawyers also are members of that constituency.

My belief that the practice of law differs from other trades and businesses for Art. IV, §2, purposes is not based on some notion that law is for some reason a superior profession. The reason that the practice of law should be treated differently is that law is one occupation that does not readily translate across state lines. Certain aspects of legal practice are distinctly and intentionally nonnational; in this regard one might view this country's legal system as the antithesis of the norms embodied in the Art. IV Privileges and Immunities Clause. Put simply, the State has a substantial interest in creating its own set of laws responsive to its own local interests, and it is reasonable for a State to decide that those people who have been trained to analyze law and policy are better equipped to write those state laws and adjudicate cases arising under them. The State therefore may decide that it has an interest in maximizing the number of resident lawyers, so as to increase the quality of the pool from which its lawmakers can be drawn. A residency law such as the one at issue is the obvious way to accomplish these goals. Since at any given time within a State there is only enough legal work to support a certain number of lawyers, each out-of-state lawyer who is allowed to practice necessarily takes legal work that could support an in-state lawyer, who would otherwise be available to perform various functions that a State has an interest in promoting.

In addition, I find the Court's "less restrictive means" analysis both ill-advised and potentially unmanageable. Initially I would note, as I and other Members of this Court have before, that such an analysis, when carried too far, will ultimately lead to striking down almost any statute on the ground that the Court could think of another "less restrictive" way to write it. This approach to judicial review, far more than the usual application of a standard of review, tends to place courts in the position of second-guessing legislators on legislative matters. Surely this is not a consequence to be desired. In any event, I find the less-restrictive-means analysis, which is borrowed from our First Amendment jurisprudence, to be out of place in the context of the Art. IV Privileges and Immunities Clause.

There is yet another interest asserted by the State that I believe would justify a decision to limit membership in the state bar to state residents. The State argues that out-of-state bar members pose a problem in situations where counsel must be available on short notice to represent clients on unscheduled matters. The Court brushes this argument aside, speculating that "a high percentage of nonresident lawyers willing to take the state bar examination and pay the annual dues will reside in places reasonably convenient to New Hampshire," and suggesting that in any event the trial court could alleviate this problem by requiring the lawyer to retain local counsel. Assuming that the latter suggestion does not itself constitute unlawful discrimination under the Court's test, there nevertheless may be good reasons why a State or a trial court would rather not get into structuring attorney-client relationships by requiring the retention of local counsel for emergency matters. The situation would have to be explained to the client, and the allocation of responsibility between resident and nonresident counsel could cause as many problems as the Court's suggestion might cure.

Nor do I believe that the problem can be confined to emergency matters. The Court admits that even in the ordinary course of litigation a trial judge will want trial lawyers to be available on short notice; the uncertainties of managing a trial docket are such that lawyers rarely are given a single date on which a trial will begin; they may be required to "stand by"—or whatever the local terminology is—for days at a time, and then be expected to be ready in a matter of hours, with witnesses, when the case in front of them suddenly settles. A State reasonably can decide that a trial court should not have added to its present scheduling difficulties the uncertainties and added delays fostered by counsel who might reside 1,000 miles from New Hampshire. If there is any single problem with state legal systems that this Court might consider "substantial," it is the problem of delay in litigation—a subject that has been profusely explored in the literature over the past several years. Surely the State has a substantial interest in taking steps to minimize this problem.

Thus, I think that New Hampshire had more than enough "substantial reasons" to conclude that its lawyers should also be its residents. I would hold that the Rule of the New Hampshire Supreme Court does not violate the Privileges and Immunities Clause of Art. IV.

CHAPTER
5

THE STRUCTURE OF THE CONSTITUTION'S PROTECTION OF CIVIL RIGHTS AND CIVIL LIBERTIES

A. INTRODUCTION

The text of the Constitution, apart from the Bill of Rights, contains few provisions concerning individual liberties. Article I, §9, which places limits on Congress's powers, declares that "[t]he privilege of the Writ of Habeas Corpus shall not be suspended, unless when in Cases of Rebellion or Invasion, the public Safety may require it." Article I, §9 also states, "No Bill of Attainder or ex post facto Law shall be passed." Article I, §10, which contains limits on state government powers, similarly provides, "No State shall . . . pass any Bill of Attainder, ex post facto Law, or law impairing the Obligation of Contracts."

Article III, §2 states that "[t]he trial of all Crimes, except in Cases of Impeachment, shall be by jury; and such Trial shall be held in the State where the said Crimes shall have been committed." Article III, §3 also provides, "Treason against the United States, shall consist only in levying War against them or, in adhering to their Enemies, giving them Aid and Comfort. No person shall be convicted of Treason unless on the Testimony of two Witnesses to the same overt Act, or on Confession in open Court." Section 3 concludes by declaring that although Congress may prescribe the punishment for treason, there shall be no "Corruption of Blood, or Forfeiture except during the Life of the Person attained." In other words, only the traitor can be punished; family members and future generations cannot be sanctioned because of someone else's wrongdoing.

Finally, Article VI concludes that "no religious Test shall ever be required as a Qualification to any Office of public Trust under the United States." In Torcaso v. Watkins, 367 U.S. 488 (1961), the Supreme Court used the Free Exercise Clause of the First Amendment to impose a similar requirement on state governments. In *Torcaso*, the Supreme Court declared unconstitutional a state constitutional provision that required a declaration of a belief in God as a prerequisite to taking public office.

Although these provisions are not trivial, they are minor compared with the protection of liberties found in the Bill of Rights. The seven Articles of the Constitution are primarily about the structure of government and not individual rights.

Why is there so little in the text of the Constitution about individual liberties? In part, this was because the framers thought that an enumeration of rights was unnecessary in that they had created a government with limited powers and thus without the authority to violate basic liberties. In part, too, the framers were concerned that the enumeration of some rights in the text of the Constitution inevitably would be incomplete and thus would deny protection to those not listed. The Ninth Amendment was added to address this latter concern and provides, "The enumeration in the Constitution, of certain rights, shall not be construed to deny or disparage others retained by the people."

Several states, however, were concerned about the absence of an enumeration of rights and ratified the Constitution with a request that it would be amended to add a Bill of Rights. In the first Congress, James Madison drafted 16 amendments; 12 were ratified by Congress and 10 by the states. These became known as the Bill of Rights.

Section B considers the application of the Bill of Rights to states. As discussed below, the Supreme Court initially concluded that the Bill of Rights applied only to the federal government.[1] The Fourteenth Amendment's clause, that "No State shall make or enforce any law which shall abridge the privileges or immunities of citizens of the United States," might have been a basis for applying the Bill of Rights to the states. However, in the *Slaughter-House Cases*, in 1872, the Supreme Court interpreted the clause in an extremely narrow manner and thus precluded its use as a vehicle for applying the Bill of Rights to the states.[2] In the twentieth century, the Supreme Court applied most of the Bill of Rights to the states by finding that the provisions were incorporated into the Due Process Clause of the Fourteenth Amendment.

Section C examines the application of constitutional rights to private entities and individuals. The basic rule, often termed "the state action doctrine," is that such rights only apply to the government; private entities and individuals are not required to comply with the Constitution. The rationale for this doctrine and its exceptions are considered in detail in section C.

B. THE APPLICATION OF THE BILL OF RIGHTS TO THE STATES

1. The Rejection of Application Before the Civil War

The Bill of Rights, of course, is the first ten amendments to the Constitution. The first eight amendments detail protection of individual rights. Some, such as the First Amendment's protection of freedom of speech and religion and the

---

1. Barron v. Mayor & City Council of Baltimore, 32 U.S. (7 Pet.) 243 (1833), discussed in Chapter 6.
2. 83 U.S. (16 Wall.) 36 (1872), discussed hereafter.

criminal procedure protections of the Fourth, Fifth, and Sixth Amendments, are the subject of frequent litigation. Others, such as the Third Amendment's right against having soldiers quartered in a person's home, have no contemporary significance. The Ninth Amendment provides, "The enumeration in the Constitution, of certain rights, shall not be construed to deny or disparage others retained by the people." The Tenth Amendment, discussed in detail in Chapter 2, states, "The powers not delegated to the United States by the Constitution, nor prohibited by it to the States, are reserved to the States respectively, or to the people."

The issue arose early in American history as to whether the Bill of Rights applies to state and local governments. The Supreme Court definitively answered that question in the following case.

BARRON v. MAYOR & CITY COUNCIL OF BALTIMORE

32 U.S. (7 Pet.) 243 (1833)

[Barron sued the city for taking property without just compensation in violation of the Fifth Amendment. He contended that the city ruined his wharf by diverting streams and thereby made the water too shallow for boats. The issue was whether the Takings Clause of the Fifth Amendment applied to the city.]

Chief Justice MARSHALL delivered the opinion of the Court.

The plaintiff in error contends that the fifth amendment to the constitution, which inhibits the taking of private property for public use without just compensation [has been violated]. He insists, that this amendment being in favor of the liberty of the citizen, ought to be so construed as to restrain the legislative power of a state, as well as that of the United States.

The question thus presented is, we think, of great importance, but not of much difficulty. The constitution was ordained and established by the people of the United States for themselves, for their own government, and not for the government of the individual states. Each state established a constitution for itself, and in that constitution, provided such limitations and restrictions on the powers of its particular government, as its judgment dictated. The people of the United States framed such a government for the United States as they supposed best adapted to their situation and best calculated to promote their interests. The powers they conferred on this government were to be exercised by itself; and the limitations on power, if expressed in general terms, are naturally, and, we think, necessarily, applicable to the government created by the instrument. They are limitations of power granted in the instrument itself; not of distinct governments, framed by different persons and for different purposes.

If these propositions be correct, the fifth amendment must be understood as restraining the power of the general government, not as applicable to the states. In their several constitutions, they have imposed such restrictions on their respective governments, as their own wisdom suggested; such as they deemed most proper for themselves. It is a subject on which they judge exclusively, and with which others interfere no further than they are supposed to have a common interest.

But it is universally understood, it is a part of the history of the day, that the great revolution which established the constitution of the United States, was not effected without immense opposition. Serious fears were extensively entertained, that those powers which the patriot statesmen, who then watched over the interests of our country, deemed essential to union, and to the attainment of those unvaluable objects for which union was sought, might be exercised in a manner dangerous to liberty. In almost every convention by which the constitution was adopted, amendments to guard against the abuse of power were recommended. These amendments demanded security against the apprehended encroachments of the general government—not against those of the local governments. In compliance with a sentiment thus generally expressed, to quiet fears thus extensively entertained, amendments were proposed by the required majority in congress, and adopted by the states.

These amendments contain no expression indicating an intention to apply them to the state governments. This court cannot so apply them.

We are of opinion, that the provision in the fifth amendment to the constitution, declaring that private property shall not be taken for public use, without just compensation, is intended solely as a limitation on the exercise of power by the government of the United States, and is not applicable to the legislation of the states.

From a late-twentieth-century perspective, it is troubling that state and local governments were free to violate basic constitutional rights. Yet, at the time of its decision, *Barron* made sense because of faith in state constitutions and because of the shared understanding that the Bill of Rights was meant to apply only to the federal government. As Professor John Hart Ely noted, "In terms of the original understanding, *Barron* was almost certainly decided correctly."[3]

2. *A False Start in Applying the Bill of Rights to the States: The Privileges or Immunities Clause and the* Slaughter-House Cases

The Fourteenth Amendment, adopted after the Civil War, declares, "No State shall make or enforce any law which shall abridge the privileges or immunities of citizens of the United States." It might be argued that this provision was meant to apply the Bill of Rights to the states; the Bill of Rights would seem to be the most basic "privileges or immunities" of citizenship. Indeed, Justice Hugo Black declared that "the words 'No State shall make or enforce any law which shall abridge the privileges or immunities of citizens of the United States' seem to me an eminently reasonable way of expressing the idea that henceforth the Bill of Rights shall apply to the States."[4]

The historical accuracy of Justice Black's claim concerning the Privileges or Immunities Clause is uncertain. On the one hand, the choice of the words "privileges" and "immunities" suggests that the framers intended to protect fundamental rights from state and local interference. The words "privileges" and "immunities" were already a part of the Constitution in Article IV, §2

---

3. John Hart Ely, *Democracy and Distrust* 196 n.58 (1980).
4. Duncan v. Louisiana, 391 U.S. 145, 166 (1968) (Black, dissenting).

(discussed in Chapter 4), which prevents a state from denying citizens of other states the privileges and immunities it accords its own citizens. More than 40 years before the adoption of the Fourteenth Amendment, Justice Washington stated that the Privileges and Immunities Clause in Article IV protected rights "which are, in their nature, fundamental; which belong, of right, to the citizens of all free governments."[5]

During the congressional debate over the Fourteenth Amendment, representatives and senators said that the Fourteenth Amendment Privileges or Immunities Clause was meant to protect basic rights from state interference. Senator Howard, for example, quoted Justice Washington's earlier statement as to the meaning of privileges and immunities and declared, "Such is the character of the privileges and immunities spoken of in the second section of the fourth article of the Constitution. To these privileges and immunities . . . should be added the personal rights guaranteed and secured by the first eight amendments of the Constitution."[6] Likewise, Representative Bingham, who is credited with drafting the provision, stated that "the privileges and immunities of citizens of the United States [are] chiefly defined in the first eight amendments to the Constitution."[7]

Yet the historical claim that the Privileges or Immunities Clause was meant to apply the Bill of Rights to the states is very much disputed. Charles Fairman, in an exhaustive study of the framers' intent on this issue, concluded, "[The theory that the] privileges or immunities clause incorporated Amendments I to VIII found no recognition in the practice of Congress, or the action of state legislatures, constitutional conventions, or courts. . . . Congress would not have attempted such a thing, the country would not have stood for it, the legislatures would not have ratified."[8]

As is so often the case in discussing the framers' intent, there probably was not a single view within the Congress that passed the Fourteenth Amendment or the states that ratified it as to whether the Privileges or Immunities Clause was meant to apply the Bill of Rights to the states.[9] Some of the members of Congress and the state legislatures probably believed that the Privileges or Immunities Clause included the Bill of Rights; some probably didn't think so; and many probably didn't consider the question.

Apart from claims based on the framers' intent, a strong argument can be made that the Privileges or Immunities Clause should be interpreted as applying the Bill of Rights to the states. The claim would be that the provisions of the Bill of Rights are the basic "privileges" and "immunities" possessed by all citizens. That argument, however, was foreclosed in the first Supreme Court case to interpret the Fourteenth Amendment: the *Slaughter-House Cases.*

---

5. Corfield v. Coryell, 6 F. Cas. 546, 551 (C.C.E.D. Pa. 1823) (No. 3,230).

6. Cong. Globe, 39th Cong., 1st Sess. 2765 (1866).

7. Cong. Globe, 42d Cong., 1st Sess. App. 84 (1871).

8. Charles Fairman, *Does the Fourteenth Amendment Incorporate the Bill of Rights,* 2 Stan. L. Rev. 132, 137 (1949).

9. *See* Timothy S. Bishop, Comment, *The Privileges or Immunities Clause of the Fourteenth Amendment: The Original Intent,* 79 Nw. U.L. Rev. 142, 174 (1984) (supporting the view that there was a range of intentions in Congress concerning the meaning of the Privileges or Immunities Clause). For an excellent criticism of both Justice Black and Professor Fairman's historical arguments, *see* Alfred H. Kelly, *Clio and the Court: An Illicit Love Affair,* 1965 Sup. Ct. Rev. 119, 132-134.

SLAUGHTER-HOUSE CASES:
BUTCHERS' BENEVOLENT ASSOCIATION OF NEW ORLEANS v.
CRESCENT CITY LIVESTOCK LANDING & SLAUGHTER-HOUSE CO.

83 U.S. (16 Wall.) 36 (1872)

[Seeing a huge surplus of cattle in Texas, the Louisiana legislature gave a monopoly in the livestock landing and the slaughterhouse business for the city of New Orleans to the Crescent City Livestock Landing and Slaughter-House Company. The law required that the company allow any person to slaughter animals in the slaughterhouse for a fixed fee. Several butchers brought suit challenging the grant of the monopoly. They argued that the state law impermissibly violated their right to practice their trade. The butchers invoked many of the provisions of the recently adopted constitutional amendments. They argued that the restriction created involuntary servitude, deprived them of their property without due process of law, denied them equal protection of the laws, and abridged their privileges or immunities as citizens.]

Justice MILLER delivered the opinion of the Court.

These cases arise out of the efforts of the butchers of New Orleans to resist the Crescent City Live-Stock Landing and Slaughter-House Company in the exercise of certain powers conferred by the charter which created it, and which was granted by the legislature of that State.

It is not, and cannot be successfully controverted, that it is both the right and the duty of the legislative body — the supreme power of the State or municipality — to prescribe and determine the localities where the business of slaughtering for a great city may be conducted. To do this effectively it is indispensable that all persons who slaughter animals for food shall do it in those places and nowhere else. It cannot be denied that the statute under consideration is aptly framed to remove from the more densely populated part of the city, the noxious slaughter-houses, and large and offensive collections of animals necessarily incident to the slaughtering business of a large city, and to locate them where the convenience, health, and comfort of the people require they shall be located.

The plaintiffs in error allege that the statute is a violation of the Constitution of the United States in these several particulars: That it creates an involuntary servitude forbidden by the thirteenth article of amendment; That it abridges the privileges and immunities of citizens of the United States; That it denies to the plaintiffs the equal protection of the laws; and, That it deprives them of their property without due process of law; contrary to the provisions of the first section of the fourteenth article of amendment.

This court is thus called upon for the first time to give construction to these articles. We do not conceal from ourselves the great responsibility which this duty devolves upon us. No questions so far-reaching and pervading in their consequences, so profoundly interesting to the people of this country, and so important in their bearing upon the relations of the United States, and of the several States to each other and to the citizens of the States and of the United States, have been before this court during the official life of any of its present members. Fortunately that history is fresh within the memory of us all, and its leading features, as they bear upon the matter before us, free from doubt.

[*Thirteenth Amendment*]: The institution of African slavery, as it existed in about half the States of the Union, and the contests pervading the public mind for many years, between those who desired its curtailment and ultimate extinction and those who desired additional safeguards for its security and perpetuation, culminated in the effort, on the part of most of the States in which slavery existed, to separate from the Federal government, and to resist its authority. This constituted the war of the rebellion, and whatever auxiliary causes may have contributed to bring about this war, undoubtedly the overshadowing and efficient cause was African slavery.

In that struggle slavery, as a legalized social relation, perished. It perished as a necessity of the bitterness and force of the conflict.

When the armies of freedom found themselves upon the soil of slavery they could do nothing less than free the poor victims whose enforced servitude was the foundation of the quarrel. And when hard pressed in the contest these men (for they proved themselves men in that terrible crisis) offered their services and were accepted by thousands to aid in suppressing the unlawful rebellion, slavery was at an end wherever the Federal government succeeded in that purpose. The proclamation of President Lincoln expressed an accomplished fact as to a large portion of the insurrectionary districts, when he declared slavery abolished in them all. But the war being over, those who had succeeded in re-establishing the authority of the Federal government were not content to permit this great act of emancipation to rest on the actual results of the contest or the proclamation of the Executive, both of which might have been questioned in after times, and they determined to place this main and most valuable result in the Constitution of the restored Union as one of its fundamental articles. Hence the thirteenth article of amendment of that instrument.

To withdraw the mind from the contemplation of this grand yet simple declaration of the personal freedom of all the human race within the jurisdiction of this government—a declaration designed to establish the freedom of four millions of slaves—and with a microscopic search endeavor to find in it a reference to servitudes, which may have been attached to property in certain localities, requires an effort, to say the least of it.

The word servitude is of larger meaning than slavery, as the latter is popularly understood in this country, and the obvious purpose was to forbid all shades and conditions of African slavery. It was very well understood that in the form of apprenticeship for long terms, as it had been practiced in the West India Islands, on the abolition of slavery by the English government, or by reducing the slaves to the condition of serfs attached to the plantation, the purpose of the article might have been evaded, if only the word slavery had been used. And it is all that we deem necessary to say on the application of that article to the statute of Louisiana, now under consideration.

[*Fourteenth Amendment*]: [N]otwithstanding the formal recognition by those States of the abolition of slavery, the condition of the slave race would, without further protection of the Federal government, be almost as bad as it was before. Among the first acts of legislation adopted by several of the States in the legislative bodies which claimed to be in their normal relations with the Federal government, were laws which imposed upon the colored race onerous disabilities and burdens, and curtailed their rights in the pursuit of life, liberty, and property to such an extent that their freedom was of little value, while they had lost the protection which they had received from their former owners from motives both of interest and humanity.

They were in some States forbidden to appear in the towns in any other character than menial servants. They were required to reside on and cultivate the soil without the right to purchase or own it. They were excluded from many occupations of gain, and were not permitted to give testimony in the courts in any case where a white man was a party. It was said that their lives were at the mercy of bad men, either because the laws for their protection were insufficient or were not enforced.

We repeat, then, in the light of this recapitulation of events, almost too recent to be called history, but which are familiar to us all; and on the most casual examination of the language of these amendments, no one can fail to be impressed with the one pervading purpose found in them all, lying at the foundation of each, and without which none of them would have been even suggested; we mean the freedom of the slave race, the security and firm establishment of that freedom, and the protection of the newly-made freeman and citizen from the oppressions of those who had formerly exercised unlimited dominion over him. It is true that only the fifteenth amendment, in terms, mentions the negro by speaking of his color and his slavery. But it is just as true that each of the other articles was addressed to the grievances of that race, and designed to remedy them as the fifteenth.

We do not say that no one else but the negro can share in this protection. Both the language and spirit of these articles are to have their fair and just weight in any question of construction. Undoubtedly while negro slavery alone was in the mind of the Congress which proposed the thirteenth article, it forbids any other kind of slavery, now or hereafter. If Mexican peonage or the Chinese coolie labor system shall develop slavery of the Mexican or Chinese race within our territory, this amendment may safely be trusted to make it void. And so if other rights are assailed by the States which properly and necessarily fall within the protection of these articles, that protection will apply, though the party interested may not be of African descent. But what we do say, and what we wish to be understood is, that in any fair and just construction of any section or phrase of these amendments, it is necessary to look to the purpose which we have said was the pervading spirit of them all, the evil which they were designed to remedy.

The language is, "No State shall make or enforce any law which shall abridge the privileges or immunities of citizens of the United States." It is a little remarkable, if this clause was intended as a protection to the citizen of a State against the legislative power of his own State, that the word citizen of the State should be left out when it is so carefully used, and used in contradistinction to citizens of the United States, in the very sentence which precedes it. It is too clear for argument that the change in phraseology was adopted understandingly and with a purpose.

Of the privileges and immunities of the citizen of the United States, and of the privileges and immunities of the citizen of the State, and what they respectively are, we will presently consider; but we wish to state here that it is only the former which are placed by this clause under the protection of the Federal Constitution, and that the latter, whatever they may be, are not intended to have any additional protection by this paragraph of the amendment.

If, then, there is a difference between the privileges and immunities belonging to a citizen of the United States as such, and those belonging to the citizen of the State as such the latter must rest for their security and protection where they have heretofore rested; for they are not embraced by this paragraph of the amendment.

[I]n section two of the fourth article [of the Constitution], in the following words: "The citizens of each State shall be entitled to all the privileges and immunities of citizens of the several States." Fortunately we are not without judicial construction of this clause of the Constitution. The first and the leading case on the subject is that of Corfield v. Coryell, decided by Mr. Justice Washington in the Circuit Court for the District of Pennsylvania in 1823. "The inquiry," he says, "is, what are the privileges and immunities of citizens of the several States? We feel no hesitation in confining these expressions to those privileges and immunities which are fundamental; which belong of right to the citizens of all free governments, and which have at all times been enjoyed by citizens of the several States which compose this Union, from the time of their becoming free, independent, and sovereign. What these fundamental principles are, it would be more tedious than difficult to enumerate. They may all, however, be comprehended under the following general heads: protection by the government, with the right to acquire and possess property of every kind, and to pursue and obtain happiness and safety, subject, nevertheless, to such restraints as the government may prescribe for the general good of the whole."

[T]he entire domain of the privileges and immunities of citizens of the States, as above defined, lay within the constitutional and legislative power of the States, and without that of the Federal government. Was it the purpose of the fourteenth amendment, by the simple declaration that no State should make or enforce any law which shall abridge the privileges and immunities of citizens of the United States, to transfer the security and protection of all the civil rights which we have mentioned, from the States to the Federal government? And where it is declared that Congress shall have the power to enforce that article, was it intended to bring within the power of Congress the entire domain of civil rights heretofore belonging exclusively to the States?

All this and more must follow, if the proposition of the plaintiffs in error be sound. For not only are these rights subject to the control of Congress whenever in its discretion any of them are supposed to be abridged by State legislation, but that body may also pass laws in advance, limiting and restricting the exercise of legislative power by the States, in their most ordinary and usual functions, as in its judgment it may think proper on all such subjects. And still further, such a construction followed by the reversal of the judgments of the Supreme Court of Louisiana in these cases, would constitute this court a perpetual censor upon all legislation of the States, on the civil rights of their own citizens, with authority to nullify such as it did not approve as consistent with those rights, as they existed at the time of the adoption of this amendment. But when, as in the case before us, these consequences are so serious, so far-reaching and pervading, so great a departure from the structure and spirit of our institutions; when the effect is to fetter and degrade the State governments by subjecting them to the control of Congress, in the exercise of powers heretofore universally conceded to them of the most ordinary and fundamental character; when in fact it radically changes the whole theory of the relations of the State and Federal governments to each other and of both these governments to the people; the argument has a force that is irresistible, in the absence of language which expresses such a purpose too clearly to admit of doubt.

We are convinced that no such results were intended by the Congress which proposed these amendments, nor by the legislatures of the States which ratified them. Having shown that the privileges and immunities relied on in the argument are those which belong to citizens of the States as such, and that they are left to the State governments for security and protection, and not by this article placed under the special care of the Federal government, we may hold ourselves excused from defining the privileges and immunities of citizens of the United States which no State can abridge, until some case involving those privileges may make it necessary to do so.

But lest it should be said that no such privileges and immunities are to be found if those we have been considering are excluded, we venture to suggest some which owe their existence to the Federal government, its National character, its Constitution, or its laws. One of these is well described in the case of Crandall v. Nevada. It is said to be the right of the citizen of this great country, protected by implied guarantees of its Constitution, "to come to the seat of government to assert any claim he may have upon that government, to transact any business he may have with it, to seek its protection, to share its offices, to engage in administering its functions. He has the right of free access to its seaports, through which all operations of foreign commerce are conducted, to the subtreasuries, land offices, and courts of justice in the several States." But it is useless to pursue this branch of the inquiry, since we are of opinion that the rights claimed by these plaintiffs in error, if they have any existence, are not privileges and immunities of citizens of the United States within the meaning of the clause of the fourteenth amendment under consideration.

[*Due process*]: The argument has not been much pressed in these cases that the defendant's charter deprives the plaintiffs of their property without due process of law. We are not without judicial interpretation, therefore, both State and National, of the meaning of this clause. And it is sufficient to say that under no construction of that provision that we have ever seen, or any that we deem admissible, can the restraint imposed by the State of Louisiana upon the exercise of their trade by the butchers of New Orleans be held to be a deprivation of property within the meaning of that provision.

[*Equal protection*]: "Nor shall any State deny to any person within its jurisdiction the equal protection of the laws." In the light of the history of these amendments, and the pervading purpose of them, which we have already discussed, it is not difficult to give a meaning to this clause. The existence of laws in the States where the newly emancipated negroes resided, which discriminated with gross injustice and hardship against them as a class, was the evil to be remedied by this clause, and by it such laws are forbidden.

We doubt very much whether any action of a State not directed by way of discrimination against the negroes as a class, or on account of their race, will ever be held to come within the purview of this provision. It is so clearly a provision for that race and that emergency, that a strong case would be necessary for its application to any other.

Justice FIELD, dissenting:

The first clause of the fourteenth amendment recognizes in express terms, if it does not create, citizens of the United States, and it makes their citizenship dependent upon the place of their birth, or the fact of their adoption, and not upon the constitution or laws of any State or the condition of their ancestry. A citizen of a State is now only a citizen of the United States residing in that State.

The fundamental rights, privileges, and immunities which belong to him as a free man and a free citizen, now belong to him as a citizen of the United States, and are not dependent upon his citizenship of any State. The exercise of these rights and privileges, and the degree of enjoyment received from such exercise, are always more or less affected by the condition and the local institutions of the State, or city, or town where he resides. They are thus affected in a State by the wisdom of its laws, the ability of its officers, the efficiency of its magistrates, the education and morals of its people, and by many other considerations. This is a result which follows from the constitution of society, and can never be avoided, but in no other way can they be affected by the action of the State, or by the residence of the citizen therein. They do not derive their existence from its legislation, and cannot be destroyed by its power.

The amendment does not attempt to confer any new privileges or immunities upon citizens, or to enumerate or define those already existing. It assumes that there are such privileges and immunities which belong of right to citizens as such, and ordains that they shall not be abridged by State legislation. If this inhibition has no reference to privileges and immunities of this character, but only refers, as held by the majority of the court in their opinion, to such privileges and immunities as were before its adoption specially designated in the Constitution or necessarily implied as belonging to citizens of the United States, it was a vain and idle enactment, which accomplished nothing, and most unnecessarily excited Congress and the people on its passage. With privileges and immunities thus designated or implied no State could ever have interfered by its laws, and no new constitutional provision was required to inhibit such interference. The supremacy of the Constitution and the laws of the United States always controlled any State legislation of that character. But if the amendment refers to the natural and inalienable rights which belong to all citizens, the inhibition has a profound significance and consequence.

I am unable to agree with the majority of the court in these cases.

The *Slaughter-House Cases* narrowly interpreted each part of section one of the Fourteenth Amendment. The Supreme Court's narrow interpretation of the Due Process Clause was overruled relatively quickly. The Court rejected the application of the Due Process Clause to protect a right to practice one's trade, with its declaration, without elaboration or explanation, that "it is sufficient to say that under no construction of that provision that we have ever seen, or any that we deem admissible, can the restraint imposed by the State of Louisiana upon the exercise of their trade by the butchers of New Orleans be held to be a deprivation of property within the meaning of that provision." Yet, as presented in Chapter 6, by the late nineteenth century and in the first third of the twentieth century, the Court found that the Due Process Clause did protect a right to practice a person's trade or profession. As presented in Chapter 8, throughout the twentieth century the Court has used the Due Process Clause to safeguard privacy and autonomy rights such as the right to marry, the right to custody of one's children, the right to purchase and use contraceptives, and the right to abortion.

The Court's narrow interpretation of the Equal Protection Clause lasted until well into the twentieth century. The Court said that the Equal Protection Clause only was meant to protect blacks and offered the prediction that "[w]e doubt very much whether any action of a State not directed by way of discrimination against the negroes as a class, or on account of their race, will ever be held to come within the purview of this provision." This prediction obviously proved false, and the Equal Protection Clause has been applied to prevent discrimination based on characteristics such as gender, alienage, and legitimacy.

However, the Supreme Court's extremely narrow interpretation of the Privileges or Immunities Clause lasted until very recently. The Court's declaration that the Privileges or Immunities Clause was not meant to provide a basis for invalidating state and local laws precluded the use of that provision to apply the Bill of Rights to the states. Indeed, the Court was explicit that "privileges and immunities . . . are left to the State governments for security and protection, and not by this article placed under the special care of the federal government." This means that the Privileges or Immunities Clause is removed as a basis for applying the Bill of Rights to the states or for protecting any rights from state interference.

Professor Corwin remarked that "[u]nique among constitutional provisions, the privileges and immunities clause of the Fourteenth Amendment enjoys the distinction of having been rendered a practical nullity by a single decision of the Supreme Court rendered within five years after its ratification."[10] Until 1999, only once in the 130 years since the ratification of the Fourteenth Amendment has a law been declared unconstitutional as violating the Privileges or Immunities Clause, and that case was overruled five years later.[11]

Interestingly, many scholars, including prominent conservatives, such as Clarence Thomas (prior to being appointed to the Supreme Court), have urged a resurrection of the Privileges or Immunities Clause.[12] The words of the clause suggest that it clearly protects rights — those that can be deemed privileges or immunities of citizenship — from state interference.

In 1999, for essentially the first time in American history, the Supreme Court used the Privileges or Immunities Clause to invalidate a state law.[13]

SAENZ v. ROE
526 U.S. 489 (1999)

Justice STEVENS delivered the opinion of the Court.

In 1992, California enacted a statute limiting the maximum welfare benefits available to newly arrived residents. The scheme limits the amount payable to a

10. Legislative Reference Service, Library of Congress, *The Constitution of the United States of America* 965 (Edward S. Corwin ed., 1953).

11. In Colgate v. Harvey, 296 U.S. 404 (1935), the Supreme Court invalidated a state tax that applied solely to income and dividends earned outside the state. In part, the Court said that this was unconstitutional because it infringed a "privilege . . . attributable to national citizenship." *Id.* at 430. However, four years later, the Court overruled *Colgate* in Madden v. Kentucky, 309 U.S. 83 (1940). Also, in Edwards v. California, 314 U.S. 160 (1941), four justices relied on the Privileges or Immunities Clause as creating a right to interstate travel and as a basis for invalidating a California law that made it a crime to bring an indigent person into the state.

12. Clarence Thomas, *The Higher Law Background of the Privileges or Immunities Clause*, 12 Harv. J.L. & Pub. Poly. 63, 68 (1989); Philip B. Kurland, *The Privileges or Immunities Clause: "Its Hour Come Round at Last"?*, 1972 Wash. U. L.Q. 405, 418-420.

13. The case is presented here for its discussion of the Privileges or Immunities Clause of the Fourteenth Amendment. The right to travel is discussed in detail in Chapter 8.

family that has resided in the State for less than 12 months to the amount payable by the State of the family's prior residence.

What is at issue in this case is the right of the newly arrived citizen to the same privileges and immunities enjoyed by other citizens of the same State. That right is protected not only by the new arrival's status as a state citizen, but also by her status as a citizen of the United States. That additional source of protection is plainly identified in the opening words of the Fourteenth Amendment: "All persons born or naturalized in the United States, and subject to the jurisdiction thereof, are citizens of the United States and of the State wherein they reside. No State shall make or enforce any law which shall abridge the privileges or immunities of citizens of the United States. . . ."

Despite fundamentally differing views concerning the coverage of the Privileges or Immunities Clause of the Fourteenth Amendment, most notably expressed in the majority and dissenting opinions in the *Slaughter-House Cases*, it has always been common ground that this Clause protects the third component of the right to travel. Writing for the majority in the *Slaughter-House Cases*, Justice Miller explained that one of the privileges conferred by this Clause "is that a citizen of the United States can, of his own volition, become a citizen of any State of the Union by a bona fide residence therein, with the same rights as other citizens of that State."

That newly arrived citizens "have two political capacities, one state and one federal," adds special force to their claim that they have the same rights as others who share their citizenship. Neither mere rationality nor some intermediate standard of review should be used to judge the constitutionality of a state rule that discriminates against some of its citizens because they have been domiciled in the State for less than a year.

Because this case involves discrimination against citizens who have completed their interstate travel, the State's argument that its welfare scheme affects the right to travel only "incidentally" is beside the point. Were we concerned solely with actual deterrence to migration, we might be persuaded that a partial withholding of benefits constitutes a lesser incursion on the right to travel than an outright denial of all benefits. But since the right to travel embraces the citizen's right to be treated equally in her new State of residence, the discriminatory classification is itself a penalty.

These classifications may not be justified by a purpose to deter welfare applicants from migrating to California. First, although it is reasonable to assume that some persons may be motivated to move for the purpose of obtaining higher benefits, the empirical evidence reviewed by the District Judge, which takes into account the high cost of living in California, indicates that the number of such persons is quite small — surely not large enough to justify a burden on those who had no such motive. Second, California has represented to the Court that the legislation was not enacted for any such reason.

Chief Justice Rehnquist, with whom Justice Thomas joins, dissenting.

The Court today breathes new life into the previously dormant Privileges or Immunities Clause of the Fourteenth Amendment—a Clause relied upon by this Court in only one other decision, Colgate v. Harvey (1935), overruled five years later by Madden v. Kentucky (1940). It uses this Clause to strike down what I believe is a reasonable measure falling under the head of a "good-faith residency requirement." Because I do not think any provision of the Constitution—and surely not a provision relied upon for only the second time since its enactment 130 years ago — requires this result, I dissent.

Justice THOMAS, with whom the Chief Justice joins, dissenting.

I write separately to address the majority's conclusion that California has violated "the right of the newly arrived citizen to the same privileges and immunities enjoyed by other citizens of the same State." In my view, the majority attributes a meaning to the Privileges or Immunities Clause that likely was unintended when the Fourteenth Amendment was enacted and ratified.

[I]t comes as quite a surprise that the majority relies on the Privileges or Immunities Clause at all in this case. That is because the *Slaughter-House Cases* sapped the Clause of any meaning. Although the majority appears to breathe new life into the Clause today, it fails to address its historical underpinnings or its place in our constitutional jurisprudence.

Because I believe that the demise of the Privileges or Immunities Clause has contributed in no small part to the current disarray of our Fourteenth Amendment jurisprudence, I would be open to reevaluating its meaning in an appropriate case. Before invoking the Clause, however, we should endeavor to understand what the framers of the Fourteenth Amendment thought that it meant. We should also consider whether the Clause should displace, rather than augment, portions of our equal protection and substantive due process jurisprudence. The majority's failure to consider these important questions raises the specter that the Privileges or Immunities Clause will become yet another convenient tool for inventing new rights, limited solely by the "predilections of those who happen at the time to be Members of this Court." Moore v. East Cleveland (1977).

I respectfully dissent.

3.   The Incorporation of the Bill of Rights into the Due Process Clause of the Fourteenth Amendment

Because of the *Slaughter-House Cases*, the application of the Bill of Rights to the states could not be through the Privileges or Immunities Clause. In the early twentieth century, the Supreme Court suggested an alternate approach: finding that at least some of the Bill of Rights provisions are part of the liberty protected from state interference by the Due Process Clause of the Fourteenth Amendment.

In 1897, in Chicago, Burlington & Quincy Railroad Co. v. City of Chicago, 166 U.S. 226 (1897), the Supreme Court ruled that the Due Process Clause of the Fourteenth Amendment prevents states from taking property without just compensation. Although the Court did not speak explicitly of the Fourteenth Amendment incorporating the Takings Clause, that was the practical effect of the decision.

In Twining v. New Jersey, 211 U.S. 78 (1908), the Supreme Court first expressly discussed applying the Bill of Rights to the states through the process of finding a right to be "incorporated" into the Due Process Clause of the Fourteenth Amendment. *Twining* involved whether a jury in state court could be instructed that it could draw a negative inference against a criminal defendant who did not testify. The Court had previously ruled that this violated the Fifth Amendment's privilege against self-incrimination. The issue was whether this right applied in state court.

The Supreme Court held that it did not (something later reversed), but the Court said that "it is possible that some of the personal rights safeguarded by the first eight Amendments against national action may also be safeguarded against state action, because a denial of them would be a denial of due process of law. If this is so, it is not because those rights are enumerated in the first eight Amendments, but because they are of such a nature that they are included in the conception of due process of law."

The Court then considered how to determine whether a right is included in due process of law: "What is due process of law may be ascertained by an examination of those settled usages and modes of proceedings existing in the common and statute law of England before the emigration of our ancestors, and shown not to have been unsuited to their civil and political condition by having been acted on by them after the settlement of this country."

The Court concluded that the privilege against self-incrimination was not incorporated into due process (a holding that was later reversed): "We inquire whether the exemption from self-incrimination is of such a nature that it must be included in the conception of due process. Is it a fundamental principle of liberty and justice which inheres in the very idea of free government and is the inalienable right of a citizen of such a government? If it is, and if it is of a nature that pertains to process of law, this court has declared it to be essential to due process of law. Even if the historical meaning of due process of law and the decisions of this court did not exclude the privilege from it, it would be going far to rate it as an immutable principle of justice which is the inalienable possession of every citizen of a free government. Salutary as the principle may seem to the great majority, it cannot be ranked with the right to hearing before condemnation, the immunity from arbitrary power not acting by general laws, and the inviolability of private property."

Twining expressly opened the door to the Supreme Court applying provisions of the Bill of Rights to the states by finding them to be included — incorporated — into the Due Process Clause of the Fourteenth Amendment. Soon the Court began to use this door. In Gitlow v. New York, 268 U.S. 652 (1925), the Court for the first time said that the First Amendment's protection of freedom of speech applies to the states through its incorporation into the Due Process Clause of the Fourteenth Amendment. The Court declared, "For present purposes we may and do assume that freedom of speech and of the press — which are protected by the First Amendment from abridgment by Congress — are among the fundamental personal rights and liberties protected by the Due Process Clause of the Fourteenth Amendment from impairment by the States." In *Gitlow*, the Court actually rejected the constitutional challenge to a state law that made it a crime to advocate the violent overthrow of government by force or violence. Two years later, in Fiske v. Kansas, 274 U.S. 380 (1927), the Court for the first time found that a state law regulating speech violated the Due Process Clause of the Fourteenth Amendment.

In 1933, in Powell v. Alabama, 287 U.S. 45 (1932), the Court found that a state's denial of counsel in a capital case denied due process, thereby in essence applying the Sixth Amendment to the states in capital cases. The infamous Scottsboro trial involved two African American men who were convicted of rape without the assistance of an attorney at trial and with a jury from which all blacks had been excluded. The Supreme Court concluded that the Due Process Clause of the Fourteenth Amendment protects fundamental rights from state interference and that this can include Bill of Rights provisions. But the Court said that "[i]f this is so, it is not because those rights are enumerated in the first eight Amendments, but because they are of such a nature that they are included in the 'conception of due process of law.'" The Court held that in a capital case, "it [is] clear that the right to the aid of counsel is of this fundamental character."

THE DEBATE OVER INCORPORATION

Once the Court found that the Due Process Clause of the Fourteenth Amendment protected fundamental rights from state infringement, there was a major debate over which liberties are safeguarded. For many years, this debate raged among justices and commentators. On the one side, there were the total incorporationists who believed that all of the Bill of Rights should be deemed to be included in the Due Process Clause of the Fourteenth Amendment. Justices Black and Douglas were the foremost advocates of this position.[14]

On the other side, there were the selective incorporationists who believed that only some of the Bill of Rights were sufficiently fundamental to apply to state and local governments. Justice Cardozo, for example, wrote that "[t]he process of absorption . . . [applied to rights where] neither liberty nor justice would exist if they were sacrificed."[15] Justice Cardozo said that the Due Process Clause included "principles of justice so rooted in the tradition and conscience of our people as to be ranked as fundamental" and that were therefore "implicit in the concept of ordered liberty."[16] Justice Frankfurter said that due process precludes those practices that "offend those canons of decency and fairness which express the notions of justice of English-speaking peoples."[17]

The debate between total and selective incorporation was obviously extremely important because it determined the reach of the Bill of Rights and the extent to which individuals could turn to the federal courts for protection from state and local governments. The following two cases were particularly important in that debate.

PALKO v. CONNECTICUT, 302 U.S. 319 (1937): Justice CARDOZO delivered the opinion of the Court.

A statute of Connecticut permitting appeals in criminal cases to be taken by the state is challenged by appellant as an infringement of the Fourteenth Amendment of the Constitution of the United States.

The argument for appellant is that whatever is forbidden by the Fifth Amendment is forbidden by the Fourteenth also. The Fifth Amendment, which is not directed to the States, but solely to the federal government, creates immunity from double jeopardy. No person shall be "subject for the same offense to be twice put in jeopardy of life or limb." The Fourteenth Amendment ordains,

---

14. *See, e.g.*, Adamson v. California, 332 U.S. 46, 71-72 (1947) (Black, J., dissenting).
15. Palko v. Connecticut, 302 U.S. 319, 326 (1937).
16. *Id.* at 325.
17. Adamson v. California, 332 U.S. 46, 67 (1947) (Frankfurter, J., concurring).

"nor shall any State deprive any person of life, liberty, or property, without due process of law." To retry a defendant, though under one indictment and only one, subjects him, it is said, to double jeopardy in violation of the Fifth Amendment, if the prosecution is one on behalf of the United States. From this the consequence is said to follow that there is a denial of life or liberty without due process of law, if the prosecution is one on behalf of the people of a state.

We have said that in appellant's view the Fourteenth Amendment is to be taken as embodying the prohibitions of the Fifth. His thesis is even broader. Whatever would be a violation of the original bill of rights (Amendments 1 to 8) if done by the federal government is now equally unlawful by force of the Fourteenth Amendment if done by a state. There is no such general rule. The Fifth Amendment provides, among other things, that no person shall be held to answer for a capital or otherwise infamous crime unless on presentment or indictment of a grand jury. This court has held that, in prosecutions by a state, presentment or indictment by a grand jury may give way to informations at the instance of a public officer. Hurtado v. California (1884). This court has ruled that consistently with those amendments trial by jury may be modified by a state or abolished altogether.

The right to trial by jury and the immunity from prosecution except as the result of an indictment may have value and importance. Even so, they are not of the very essence of a scheme of ordered liberty. To abolish them is not to violate a "principle of justice so rooted in the traditions and conscience of our people as to be ranked as fundamental." Few would be so narrow or provincial as to maintain that a fair and enlightened system of justice would be impossible without them.

Is [allowing the State to appeal the] kind of double jeopardy to which the statute has subjected him a hardship so acute and shocking that our policy will not endure it? Does it violate those "fundamental principles of liberty and justice which lie at the base of all our civil and political institutions"? The answer surely must be "no." There is here no seismic innovation. The edifice of justice stands. The conviction of appellant is not in derogation of any privileges or immunities that belong to him as a citizen of the United States.

ADAMSON v. CALIFORNIA, 332 U.S. 46 (1947): Justice REED delivered the opinion of the Court.

The appellant, Adamson, was convicted, without recommendation for mercy, by a jury in a Superior Court of the State of California of murder in the first degree. The provisions of California law permit the failure of a defendant to explain or to deny evidence against him to be commented upon by court and by counsel and to be considered by court and jury. The defendant did not testify. As the trial court gave its instructions and the District Attorney argued the case in accordance with the constitutional and statutory provisions just referred to, we have for decision the question of their constitutionality in these circumstances under the limitations of §1 of the Fourteenth Amendment.

It is settled law that the clause of the Fifth Amendment, protecting a person against being compelled to be a witness against himself, is not made effective by the Fourteenth Amendment as a protection against state action on the ground that freedom from testimonial compulsion is a right of national citizenship, or because it is a personal privilege or immunity secured by the Federal Constitution as one of the rights of man that are listed in the Bill of Rights. The reasoning that leads to those conclusions starts with the unquestioned premise that the Bill of Rights, when adopted, was for the protection of the individual against the federal government and its provisions were inapplicable to similar actions done by the states.

[A]ppellant argues, the Due Process Clause of the Fourteenth Amendment protects his privilege against self-incrimination. The Due Process Clause of the Fourteenth Amendment, however, does not draw all the rights of the federal Bill of Rights under its protection. That contention was made and rejected in Palko v. Connecticut. Specifically, the Due Process Clause does not protect, by virtue of its mere existence the accused's freedom from giving testimony by compulsion in state trials that is secured to him against federal interference by the Fifth Amendment. Twining v. New Jersey. For a state to require testimony from an accused is not necessarily a breach of a state's obligation to give a fair trial.

The Due Process Clause forbids compulsion to testify by fear of hurt, torture or exhaustion. It forbids any other type of coercion that falls within the scope of due process. California follows Anglo-American legal tradition in excusing defendants in criminal prosecutions from compulsory testimony. So our inquiry is directed, not at the broad question of the constitutionality of compulsory testimony from the accused under the Due Process Clause, but to the constitutionality of the provision of the California law that permits comment upon his failure to testify.

The purpose of due process is not to protect an accused against a proper conviction but against an unfair conviction. When evidence is before a jury that threatens conviction, it does not seem unfair to require him to choose between leaving the adverse evidence unexplained and subjecting himself to impeachment through disclosure of former crimes. Indeed, this is a dilemma with which any defendant may be faced. If facts, adverse to the defendant, are proven by the prosecution, there may be no way to explain them favorably to the accused except by a witness who may be vulnerable to impeachment on cross-examination. The defendant must then decide whether or not to use such a witness. The fact that the witness may also be the defendant makes the choice more difficult but a denial of due process does not emerge from the circumstances.

Justice FRANKFURTER (concurring).

For historical reasons a limited immunity from the common duty to testify was written into the Federal Bill of Rights, and I am prepared to agree that, as part of that immunity, comment on the failure of an accused to take the witness stand is forbidden in federal prosecutions. It is so, of course, by explicit act of Congress. But to suggest that such a limitation can be drawn out of "due process" in its protection of ultimate decency in a civilized society is to suggest that the Due Process Clause fastened fetters of unreason upon the States.

Between the incorporation of the Fourteenth Amendment into the Constitution and the beginning of the present membership of the Court—a period of 70 years—the scope of that Amendment was passed upon by 43 judges. Of all these judges, only one, who may respectfully be called an eccentric exception, ever indicated the belief that the Fourteenth Amendment was a shorthand summary of the first eight Amendments theretofore limiting only the Federal Government, and that due process incorporated those eight Amendments as restrictions upon the powers of the States. Among these judges were not only those who would have to be included among the greatest in the history of the Court, but — it is especially relevant to note — they included those whose services in the cause of human rights and the spirit of freedom are the most conspicuous in our history. It is not invidious to single out Miller, Davis, Bradley, Waite, Matthews, Gray, Fuller, Holmes, Brandeis, Stone and Cardozo (to speak only of the dead) as judges who were alert in safeguarding and promoting the interests of liberty and human dignity through law. But they were also judges mindful of the relation of our federal system to a progressively democratic society and therefore duly regardful of the scope of authority that was left to the States even after the Civil War.

A construction which gives to due process no independent function but turns it into a summary of the specific provisions of the Bill of Rights would, as has been noted, tear up by the roots much of the fabric of law in the several States, and would deprive the States of opportunity for reforms in legal process designed for extending the area of freedom.

Justice BLACK, dissenting.

The appellant was tried for murder in a California state court. He did not take the stand as a witness in his own behalf. The prosecuting attorney, under purported authority of a California statute, argued to the jury that an inference of guilt could be drawn because of appellant's failure to deny evidence offered against him. The appellant's contention in the state court and here has been that the statute denies him a right guaranteed by the Federal Constitution.

The first 10 amendments were proposed and adopted largely because of fear that Government might unduly interfere with prized individual liberties. The people wanted and demanded a Bill of Rights written into their Constitution. The amendments embodying the Bill of Rights were intended to curb all branches of the Federal Government in the fields touched by the amendments — Legislative, Executive, and Judicial.

My study of the historical events that culminated in the Fourteenth Amendment, and the expressions of those who sponsored and favored, as well as those who opposed its submission and passage, persuades me that one of the chief objects that the provisions of the Amendment's first section, separately, and as a whole, were intended to accomplish was to make the Bill of Rights applicable to the states. With full knowledge of the import of the *Barron* decision, the framers and backers of the Fourteenth Amendment proclaimed its purpose to be to overturn the constitutional rule that case had announced. This historical purpose has never received full consideration or exposition in any opinion of this Court interpreting the Amendment.[18]

---

18. In Griffin v. California, 380 U.S. 609 (1965), the Supreme Court overruled *Adamson* and held that the Due Process Clause of the Fourteenth Amendment was violated by a prosecutor's comments on a defendant's silence. [Footnote by casebook author.]

The debate over incorporation centered primarily on three issues.[19] First, the debate was over history and whether the framers of the Fourteenth Amendment intended it to apply the Bill of Rights to the states. Both sides of the debate claimed that history supported their view.

Second, the incorporation debate was over federalism. Applying the Bill of Rights to the states imposes a substantial set of restrictions on state and local governments. Not surprisingly, opponents of total incorporation argued based on federalism: the desirability of preserving state and local governing autonomy by freeing state and local governments from application of the Bill of Rights. Defenders of total incorporation responded that federalism is not a sufficient reason for tolerating violations of fundamental liberties.

Third, the debate was over the appropriate judicial role. In contrast, advocates of selective incorporation denied that this allowed subjective choices by justices. They maintained that total incorporation would mean more judicial oversight of state and local actions and thus less room for democracy to operate.

THE CURRENT LAW AS TO WHAT'S INCORPORATED

The selective incorporationists prevailed in this debate in that the Supreme Court never has accepted the total incorporationist approach. However, from a practical perspective, the total incorporationists largely succeeded in their objective because, one by one, the Supreme Court found almost all of the provisions to be incorporated. This is reflected in the following case, which summarizes the many decisions, particularly of the Warren Court during the 1950s and 1960s, finding almost all of the Bill of Rights to be incorporated.

DUNCAN v. LOUISIANA
391 U.S. 145 (1968)

Justice WHITE delivered the opinion of the Court.

Appellant, Gary Duncan, was convicted of simple battery in the Twenty-fifth Judicial District Court of Louisiana. Under Louisiana law simple battery is a misdemeanor, punishable by a maximum of two years' imprisonment and a $300 fine. Appellant sought trial by jury, but because the Louisiana Constitution grants jury trials only in cases in which capital punishment or imprisonment at hard labor may be imposed, the trial judge denied the request. Appellant was convicted and sentenced to serve 60 days in the parish prison and pay a fine of $150.

The Fourteenth Amendment denies the States the power to "deprive any person of life, liberty, or property, without due process of law." In resolving conflicting claims concerning the meaning of this spacious language, the Court has looked increasingly to the Bill of Rights for guidance; many of the rights guaranteed by the first eight Amendments to the Constitution have been

19. For a detailed description of the debate and the issues, *see* Jerold L. Israel, *Selective Incorporation Revisited*, 71 Geo. L.J. 253, 336-338 (1982).

held to be protected against state action by the Due Process Clause of the Fourteenth Amendment. That clause now protects the right to compensation for property taken by the State, Chicago, B. & Q.R. Co. v. City of Chicago (1897); the rights of speech, press, and religion covered by the First Amendment, see, e.g., Fiske v. State of Kansas (1927); the Fourth Amendment rights to be free from unreasonable searches and seizures and to have excluded from criminal trials any evidence illegally seized, Mapp v. State of Ohio (1961); the right guaranteed by the Fifth Amendment to be free of compelled self-incrimination, Malloy v. Hogan (1964); and the Sixth Amendment rights to counsel, Gideon v. Wainwright (1963); to a speedy, Klopfer v. State of North Carolina (1967), and public trial, In re Oliver (1948); to confrontation of opposing witnesses, Pointer v. State of Texas (1965); and to compulsory process for obtaining witnesses, Washington v. State of Texas (1967).

The test for determining whether a right extended by the Fifth and Sixth Amendments with respect to federal criminal proceedings is also protected against state action by the Fourteenth Amendment has been phrased in a variety of ways in the opinions of this Court. The question has been asked whether a right is among those "fundamental principles of liberty and justice which lie at the base of all our civil and political institutions," Powell v. State of Alabama, (1932); whether it is "basic in our system of jurisprudence," In re Oliver (1948); and whether it is "a fundamental right, essential to a fair trial," Gideon v. Wainwright (1963).

The claim before us is that the right to trial by jury guaranteed by the Sixth Amendment meets these tests. The position of Louisiana, on the other hand, is that the Constitution imposes upon the States no duty to give a jury trial in any criminal case, regardless of the seriousness of the crime or the size of the punishment which may be imposed. Because we believe that trial by jury in criminal cases is fundamental to the American scheme of justice, we hold that the Fourteenth Amendment guarantees a right of jury trial in all criminal cases which— were they to be tried in a federal court—would come within the Sixth Amendment's guarantee.

The guarantees of jury trial in the Federal and State Constitutions reflect a profound judgment about the way in which law should be enforced and justice administered. A right to jury trial is granted to criminal defendants in order to prevent oppression by the Government. Providing an accused with the right to be tried by a jury of his peers gave him an inestimable safeguard against the corrupt or overzealous prosecutor and against the compliant, biased, or eccentric judge. If the defendant preferred the common-sense judgment of a jury to the more tutored but perhaps less sympathetic reaction of the single judge, he was to have it. Beyond this, the jury trial provisions in the Federal and State Constitutions reflect a fundamental decision about the exercise of official power—a reluctance to entrust plenary powers over the life and liberty of the citizen to one judge or to a group of judges. Fear of unchecked power, so typical of our State and Federal Governments in other respects, found expression in the criminal law in this insistence upon community participation in the determination of guilt or innocence. The deep commitment of the Nation to the right of jury trial in serious criminal cases as a defense against arbitrary law enforcement qualifies for protection under the Due Process Clause of the Fourteenth Amendment, and must therefore be respected by the States.

Justice BLACK, with whom Justice DOUGLAS joins, concurring.

The Court today holds that the right to trial by jury guaranteed defendants in criminal cases in federal courts by Art. III of the United States Constitution and by the Sixth Amendment is also guaranteed by the Fourteenth Amendment to defendants tried in state courts. With this holding I agree for reasons given by the Court.

I am very happy to support this selective process through which our Court has since the *Adamson* case held most of the specific Bill of Rights' protections applicable to the States to the same extent they are applicable to the Federal Government. All of these holdings making Bill of Rights' provisions applicable as such to the States mark, of course, a departure from the *Twining* doctrine holding that none of those provisions were enforceable as such against the States.

My view has been and is that the Fourteenth Amendment, as a whole, makes the Bill of Rights applicable to the States. This would certainly include the language of the Privileges and Immunities Clause, as well as the Due Process Clause. I can say only that the words "No State shall make or enforce any law which shall abridge the privileges or immunities of citizens of the United States" seem to me an eminently reasonable way of expressing the idea that henceforth the Bill of Rights shall apply to the States. What more precious "privilege" of American citizenship could there be than that privilege to claim the protections of our great Bill of Rights? I suggest that any reading of "privileges or immunities of citizens of the United States" which excludes the Bill of Rights' safeguards renders the words of this section of the Fourteenth Amendment meaningless. Senator Howard, who introduced the Fourteenth Amendment for passage in the Senate, certainly read the words this way.

Finally I want to add that I am not bothered by the argument that applying the Bill of Rights to the States "according to the same standards that protect those personal rights against federal encroachment," interferes with our concept of federalism in that it may prevent States from trying novel social and economic experiments. I have never believed that under the guise of federalism the States should be able to experiment with the protections afforded our citizens through the Bill of Rights.

In closing I want to emphasize that I believe as strongly as ever that the Fourteenth Amendment was intended to make the Bill of Rights applicable to the States. I have been willing to support the selective incorporation doctrine, however, as an alternative, although perhaps less historically supportable than complete incorporation. The selective incorporation process, if used properly, does limit the Supreme Court in the Fourteenth Amendment field to specific Bill of Rights' protections only and keeps judges from roaming at will in their own notions of what policies outside the Bill of Rights are desirable and what are not. And, most importantly for me, the selective incorporation process has the virtue of having already worked to make most of the Bill of Rights' protections applicable to the States.

The Supreme Court's most recent decision concerning incorporation was in 2010, in McDonald v. City of Chicago. In District of Columbia v. Heller (2008) (presented in Chapter 1), the Supreme Court held that the Second Amendment is not limited to protecting a right to have firearms for militia service; it protects an individual's right to have guns, at least for self-protection in the home. Because the District of Columbia is a part of the federal government, the Court had no occasion to consider whether the Second Amendment applies to state and local governments. In *McDonald*, the Court addressed this and held five to four that the Second Amendment applies to state and local governments. Justice Alito, writing for a plurality of four, used incorporation into the Due Process Clause to accomplish this. Justice Thomas, concurring and concurring in the judgment, would have used the Privileges or Immunities Clause of the Fourteenth Amendment.

McDONALD v. CITY OF CHICAGO

130 S. Ct. 3020 (2010)

Justice Alito announced the judgment of the Court

Two years ago, in *District of Columbia v. Heller* (2008), we held that the Second Amendment protects the right to keep and bear arms for the purpose of self-defense, and we struck down a District of Columbia law that banned the possession of handguns in the home. The city of Chicago (City) and the village of Oak Park, a Chicago suburb, have laws that are similar to the District of Columbia's, but Chicago and Oak Park argue that their laws are constitutional because the Second Amendment has no application to the States. We have previously held that most of the provisions of the Bill of Rights apply with full force to both the Federal Government and the States. Applying the standard that is well established in our case law, we hold that the Second Amendment right is fully applicable to the States.

[I]

Petitioners argue that we should overrule [earlier] decisions and hold that the right to keep and bear arms is one of the "privileges or immunities of citizens of the United States." In petitioners' view, the Privileges or Immunities Clause protects all of the rights set out in the Bill of Rights, as well as some others, but petitioners are unable to identify the Clause's full scope. Nor is there any consensus on that question among the scholars who agree that the *Slaughter-House Cases'* interpretation is flawed.

We see no need to reconsider that interpretation here. For many decades, the question of the rights protected by the Fourteenth Amendment against state infringement has been analyzed under the Due Process Clause of that Amendment and not under the Privileges or Immunities Clause. We therefore decline to disturb the *Slaughter-House* holding.

[The Court then reviewed the history of incorporation in detail.]

[II]

With this framework in mind, we now turn directly to the question whether the Second Amendment right to keep and bear arms is incorporated in the concept of due process. In answering that question, as just explained, we must decide whether the right to keep and bear arms is fundamental to *our* scheme of ordered liberty, or as we have said in a related context, whether this right is "deeply rooted in this Nation's history and tradition."

Our decision in *Heller* points unmistakably to the answer. Self-defense is a basic right, recognized by many legal systems from ancient times to the present day, and in *Heller*, we held that individual self-defense is "the *central component*" of the Second Amendment right. Explaining that "the need for defense of self, family, and property is most acute" in the home, we found that this right applies to handguns because they are "the most preferred firearm in the nation to 'keep' and use for protection of one's home and family." Thus, we concluded, citizens must be permitted "to use [handguns] for the core lawful purpose of self-defense."

Heller makes it clear that this right is "deeply rooted in this Nation's history and tradition." *Heller* explored the right's origins, noting that the 1689 English Bill of Rights explicitly protected a right to keep arms for self-defense, and that by 1765, Blackstone was able to assert that the right to keep and bear arms was "one of the fundamental rights of Englishmen." Blackstone's assessment was shared by the American colonists. As we noted in *Heller*, King George III's attempt to disarm the colonists in the 1760's and 1770's "provoked polemical reactions by Americans invoking their rights as Englishmen to keep arms."

The right to keep and bear arms was considered no less fundamental by those who drafted and ratified the Bill of Rights. "During the 1788 ratification debates, the fear that the federal government would disarm the people in order to impose rule through a standing army or select militia was pervasive in Antifederalist rhetoric." Federalists responded, not by arguing that the right was insufficiently important to warrant protection but by contending that the right was adequately protected by the Constitution's assignment of only limited powers to the Federal Government. Thus, Antifederalists and Federalists alike agreed that the right to bear arms was fundamental to the newly formed system of government.

This understanding persisted in the years immediately following the ratification of the Bill of Rights. In addition to the four States that had adopted Second Amendment analogues before ratification, nine more States adopted state constitutional provisions protecting an individual right to keep and bear arms between 1789 and 1820.

After the Civil War, many of the over 180,000 African Americans who served in the Union Army returned to the States of the old Confederacy, where systematic efforts were made to disarm them and other blacks. The laws of some States formally prohibited African Americans from possessing firearms. Union Army commanders took steps to secure the right of all citizens to keep and bear arms, but the 39th Congress concluded that legislative action was necessary. Its efforts to safeguard the right to keep and bear arms demonstrate that the right was still recognized to be fundamental. The Civil Rights Act of 1866, which was considered at the same time as the Freedmen's Bureau Act, sought to protect the right of all citizens to keep and bear arms.

In debating the Fourteenth Amendment, the 39th Congress referred to the right to keep and bear arms as a fundamental right deserving of protection. Senator Samuel Pomeroy described three "indispensable" "safeguards of liberty under our form of Government." One of these, he said, was the right to keep and bear arms. Even those who thought the Fourteenth Amendment unnecessary believed that blacks, as citizens, "have equal right to protection, and to keep and bear arms for self-defense." Evidence from the period immediately following the ratification of the Fourteenth Amendment only confirms that the right to keep and bear arms was considered fundamental.

In sum, it is clear that the Framers and ratifiers of the Fourteenth Amendment counted the right to keep and bear arms among those fundamental rights necessary to our system of ordered liberty.

[III]

Municipal respondents' remaining arguments are at war with our central holding in *Heller*: that the Second Amendment protects a personal right to keep and bear arms for lawful purposes, most notably for self-defense within the home. Municipal respondents, in effect, ask us to treat the right recognized in *Heller* as a second-class right, subject to an entirely different body of rules than the other Bill of Rights guarantees that we have held to be incorporated into the Due Process Clause.

Municipal respondents submit that the Due Process Clause protects only those rights "recognized by all temperate and civilized governments, from a deep and universal sense of [their] justice." According to municipal respondents, if it is possible to imagine *any* civilized legal system that does not recognize a particular right, then the Due Process Clause does not make that right binding on the States. Therefore, the municipal respondents continue, because such countries as England, Canada, Australia, Japan, Denmark, Finland, Luxembourg, and New Zealand either ban or severely limit handgun ownership, it must follow that no right to possess such weapons is protected by the Fourteenth Amendment.

This line of argument is, of course, inconsistent with the long-established standard we apply in incorporation cases. And the present-day implications of municipal respondents' argument are stunning. For example, many of the rights that our Bill of Rights provides for persons accused of criminal offenses are virtually unique to this country. If *our* understanding of the right to a jury trial, the right against self-incrimination, and the right to counsel were necessary attributes of *any* civilized country, it would follow that the United States is the only civilized Nation in the world.

Municipal respondents maintain that the Second Amendment differs from all of the other provisions of the Bill of Rights because it concerns the right to possess a deadly implement and thus has implications for public safety. And they note that there is intense disagreement on the question whether the private possession of guns in the home increases or decreases gun deaths and injuries.

The right to keep and bear arms, however, is not the only constitutional right that has controversial public safety implications. All of the constitutional provisions that impose restrictions on law enforcement and on the prosecution of crimes fall into the same category.

In *Heller*, we held that the Second Amendment protects the right to possess a handgun in the home for the purpose of self-defense. Unless considerations of *stare decisis* counsel otherwise, a provision of the Bill of Rights that protects a right that is fundamental from an American perspective applies equally to the

Federal Government and the States. We therefore hold that the Due Process Clause of the Fourteenth Amendment incorporates the Second Amendment right recognized in *Heller*.

Justice SCALIA, concurring.

I join the Court's opinion. Despite my misgivings about Substantive Due Process as an original matter, I have acquiesced in the Court's incorporation of certain guarantees in the Bill of Rights "because it is both long established and narrowly limited." This case does not require me to reconsider that view, since straightforward application of settled doctrine suffices to decide it.

Justice THOMAS, concurring in part and concurring in the judgment.

Applying what is now a well-settled test, the plurality opinion concludes that the right to keep and bear arms applies to the States through the Fourteenth Amendment's Due Process Clause because it is "fundamental" to the American "scheme of ordered liberty," and "deeply rooted in this Nation's history and tradition." I agree with that description of the right. But I cannot agree that it is enforceable against the States through a clause that speaks only to "process." Instead, the right to keep and bear arms is a privilege of American citizenship that applies to the States through the Fourteenth Amendment's Privileges or Immunities Clause.

The meaning of §1's next sentence has divided this Court for many years. That sentence begins with the command that "[n]o State shall make or enforce any law which shall abridge the privileges or immunities of citizens of the United States." On its face, this appears to grant the persons just made United States citizens a certain collection of rights — i.e., privileges or immunities — attributable to that status.

The notion that a constitutional provision that guarantees only "process" before a person is deprived of life, liberty, or property could define the substance of those rights strains credulity for even the most casual user of words. Moreover, this fiction is a particularly dangerous one. The one theme that links the Court's substantive due process precedents together is their lack of a guiding principle to distinguish "fundamental" rights that warrant protection from nonfundamental rights that do not. Today's decision illustrates the point.

To be sure, the plurality's effort to cabin the exercise of judicial discretion under the Due Process Clause by focusing its inquiry on those rights deeply rooted in American history and tradition invites less opportunity for abuse than the alternatives. But any serious argument over the scope of the Due Process Clause must acknowledge that neither its text nor its history suggests that it protects the many substantive rights this Court's cases now claim it does.

I cannot accept a theory of constitutional interpretation that rests on such tenuous footing. This Court's substantive due process framework fails to account for both the text of the Fourteenth Amendment and the history that led to its adoption, filling that gap with a jurisprudence devoid of a guiding principle. I believe the original meaning of the Fourteenth Amendment offers a superior alternative, and that a return to that meaning would allow this Court to enforce the rights the Fourteenth Amendment is designed to protect with greater clarity and predictability than the substantive due process framework has so far managed.

I acknowledge the volume of precedents that have been built upon the substantive due process framework, and I further acknowledge the importance of *stare decisis* to the stability of our Nation's legal system. But *stare decisis* is only an "adjunct" of our duty as judges to decide by our best lights what the Constitution means. Moreover, as judges, we interpret the Constitution one case or controversy at a time. The question presented in this case is not whether our entire Fourteenth Amendment jurisprudence must be preserved or revised, but only whether, and to what extent, a particular clause in the Constitution protects the particular right at issue here. With the inquiry appropriately narrowed, I believe this case presents an opportunity to reexamine, and begin the process of restoring, the meaning of the Fourteenth Amendment agreed upon by those who ratified it.

"It cannot be presumed that any clause in the constitution is intended to be without effect." Because the Court's Privileges or Immunities Clause precedents have presumed just that, I set them aside for the moment and begin with the text. The text examined demonstrates three points about the meaning of the Privileges or Immunities Clause in §1. First, "privileges" and "immunities" were synonyms for "rights." Second, both the States and the Federal Government had long recognized the inalienable rights of their citizens. Third, Article IV, §2 of the Constitution protected traveling citizens against state discrimination with respect to the fundamental rights of state citizenship.

I agree with the Court that the Second Amendment is fully applicable to the States. I do so because the right to keep and bear arms is guaranteed by the Fourteenth Amendment as a privilege of American citizenship.

Justice STEVENS, dissenting.

In *District of Columbia v. Heller* (2008), the Court answered the question whether a federal enclave's "prohibition on the possession of usable handguns in the home violates the Second Amendment to the Constitution." The question we should be answering in this case is whether the Constitution "guarantees individuals a fundamental right," enforceable against the States, "to possess a functional, personal firearm, including a handgun, within the home." That is a different — and more difficult — inquiry than asking if the Fourteenth Amendment "incorporates" the Second Amendment. The so-called incorporation question was squarely and, in my view, correctly resolved in the late 19th century.

I agree with the plurality's refusal to accept petitioners' primary submission. Their briefs marshal an impressive amount of historical evidence for their argument that the Court interpreted the Privileges or Immunities Clause too narrowly in the *Slaughter-House Cases* (1873). But the original meaning of the Clause is not as clear as they suggest — and not nearly as clear as it would need to be to dislodge 137 years of precedent. The burden is severe for those who seek radical change in such an established body of constitutional doctrine. Moreover, the suggestion that invigorating the Privileges or Immunities Clause will reduce judicial discretion, strikes me as implausible, if not exactly backwards. "For the very reason that it has so long remained a clean slate, a revitalized Privileges or Immunities Clause holds special hazards for judges who are mindful that their proper task is not to write their personal views of appropriate public policy into the Constitution."

The question in this case, then, is not whether the Second Amendment right to keep and bear arms (whatever that right's precise contours) applies to the

States because the Amendment has been incorporated into the Fourteenth Amendment. It has not been. The question, rather, is whether the particular right asserted by petitioners applies to the States because of the Fourteenth Amendment itself, standing on its own bottom. And to answer that question, we need to determine, first, the nature of the right that has been asserted and, second, whether that right is an aspect of Fourteenth Amendment "liberty." Even accepting the Court's holding in *Heller*, it remains entirely possible that the right to keep and bear arms identified in that opinion is not judicially enforceable against the States, or that only part of the right is so enforceable. It is likewise possible for the Court to find in this case that some part of the *Heller* right applies to the States, and then to find in later cases that other parts of the right also apply, or apply on different terms.

First, firearms have a fundamentally ambivalent relationship to liberty. Just as they can help homeowners defend their families and property from intruders, they can help thugs and insurrectionists murder innocent victims. The threat that firearms will be misused is far from hypothetical, for gun crime has devastated many of our communities. *Amici* calculate that approximately one million Americans have been wounded or killed by gunfire in the last decade. Urban areas such as Chicago suffer disproportionately from this epidemic of violence. Handguns contribute disproportionately to it. Just as some homeowners may prefer handguns because of their small size, light weight, and ease of operation, some criminals will value them for the same reasons. In recent years, handguns were reportedly used in more than four-fifths of firearm murders and more than half of all murders nationwide.

Hence, in evaluating an asserted right to be free from particular gun-control regulations, liberty is on both sides of the equation. Guns may be useful for self-defense, as well as for hunting and sport, but they also have a unique potential to facilitate death and destruction and thereby to destabilize ordered liberty. *Your* interest in keeping and bearing a certain firearm may diminish *my* interest in being and feeling safe from armed violence. And while granting you the right to own a handgun might make you safer on any given day — assuming the handgun's marginal contribution to self-defense outweighs its marginal contribution to the risk of accident, suicide, and criminal mischief — it may make you and the community you live in less safe overall, owing to the increased number of handguns in circulation. It is at least reasonable for a democratically elected legislature to take such concerns into account in considering what sorts of regulations would best serve the public welfare.

Second, the right to possess a firearm of one's choosing is different in kind from the liberty interests we have recognized under the Due Process Clause. Despite the plethora of substantive due process cases that have been decided in the post-*Lochner* century, I have found none that holds, states, or even suggests that the term "liberty" encompasses either the common-law right of self-defense or a right to keep and bear arms. I do not doubt for a moment that many Americans feel deeply passionate about firearms, and see them as critical to their way of life as well as to their security. Nevertheless, it does not appear to be the case that the ability to own a handgun, or any particular type of firearm, is critical to leading a life of autonomy, dignity, or political equality: The marketplace offers many tools for self-defense, even if they are imperfect substitutes, and neither petitioners nor their *amici* make such a contention.

Third, the experience of other advanced democracies, including those that share our British heritage, undercuts the notion that an expansive right to keep and bear arms is intrinsic to ordered liberty. Many of these countries place restrictions on the possession, use, and carriage of firearms far more onerous than the restrictions found in this Nation. That the United States is an international outlier in the permissiveness of its approach to guns does not suggest that our laws are bad laws. It does suggest that this Court may not need to assume responsibility for making our laws still more permissive.

Admittedly, these other countries differ from ours in many relevant respects, including their problems with violent crime and the traditional role that firearms have played in their societies. But they are not so different from the United States that we ought to dismiss their experience entirely. The fact that our oldest allies have almost uniformly found it appropriate to regulate firearms extensively tends to weaken petitioners' submission that the right to possess a gun of one's choosing is fundamental to a life of liberty. While the "American perspective" must always be our focus, it is silly—indeed, arrogant—to think we have nothing to learn about liberty from the billions of people beyond our borders.

Furthermore, and critically, the Court's imposition of a national standard is still more unwise because the elected branches have shown themselves to be perfectly capable of safeguarding the interest in keeping and bearing arms. The strength of a liberty claim must be assessed in connection with its status in the democratic process. And in this case, no one disputes "that opponents of [gun] control have considerable political power and do not seem to be at a systematic disadvantage in the democratic process," or that "the widespread commitment to an individual right to own guns . . . operates as a safeguard against excessive or unjustified gun control laws." Indeed, there is a good deal of evidence to suggest that, if anything, American lawmakers tend to *under* regulate guns, relative to the policy views expressed by majorities in opinion polls. If a particular State or locality has enacted some "improvident" gun-control measures, as petitioners believe Chicago has done, there is no apparent reason to infer that the mistake will not "eventually be rectified by the democratic process."

In *McDonald,* Justice Alito's opinion recognized that there are still four provisions of the Bill of Rights that never have been incorporated and do not apply to state and local governments. First, the Third Amendment right to not have soldiers quartered in a person's home never has been deemed incorporated. The reason almost certainly is that a Third Amendment case presenting the incorporation question never has reached the Supreme Court. If ever such a case would arise, the Supreme Court surely would find this provision applies to the states.[20]

Second, the Court has held that the Fifth Amendment's right to a grand jury indictment in criminal cases is not incorporated.[21] Thus, states need not use

---

20. *See* Engblom v. Carey, 677 F.2d 957 (2d Cir. 1982) (finding that the Third Amendment is incorporated).

21. Hurtado v. California, 110 U.S. 516 (1884).

grand juries and can choose alternatives such as preliminary hearings and prosecutorial informations.

Third, the Court has ruled that the Seventh Amendment right to jury trial in civil cases is not incorporated.[22] States therefore can eliminate juries in some or even all civil suits without violating the United States Constitution.

Finally, the Court never has ruled as to whether the prohibition of excessive fines in the Eighth Amendment is incorporated.[23]

The remainder of the Bill of Rights, as detailed above, has been deemed incorporated. Technically, the Bill of Rights still applies directly only to the federal government; Barron v. Mayor & City Council of Baltimore never has been expressly overruled. Therefore, whenever a case involves a state or local violation of a Bill of Rights provision, to be precise, it involves that provision as applied to the states through the Due Process Clause of the Fourteenth Amendment.

But the issue of incorporation of the other provisions may arise again. In Zelman v. Simmons-Harris, 536 U.S. 639 (2002), Justice Thomas, in a concurring opinion, argued that the Establishment Clause of the First Amendment should not have the same content when applied to the states as applied to the federal government. Justice Thomas's concurring opinion, and the decision in *Zelman* approving vouchers, is presented at length in Chapter 10. As to incorporation, Justice Thomas said:

> The Establishment Clause of the First Amendment states that "Congress shall make no law respecting an establishment of religion." On its face, this provision places no limit on the States with regard to religion. The Establishment Clause originally protected States, and by extension their citizens, from the imposition of an established religion by the Federal Government. Whether and how this Clause should constrain state action under the Fourteenth Amendment is a more difficult question.
>
> When rights are incorporated against the States through the Fourteenth Amendment they should advance, not constrain, individual liberty. Consequently, in the context of the Establishment clause, it may well be that state action should be evaluated on different terms than similar action by the Federal Government. "States, while bound to observe strict neutrality, should be freer to experiment with involvement [in religion] — on a neutral basis — than the Federal Government." Thus, while the Federal Government may "make no law respecting an establishment of religion," the States may pass laws that include or touch on religious matters so long as these laws do not impede free exercise rights or any other individual religious liberty interest. By considering the particular religious liberty right alleged to be invaded by a State, federal courts can strike a proper balance between the demands of the Fourteenth Amendment on the one hand and the federalism prerogatives of States on the other.
>
> Whatever the textual and historical merits of incorporating the Establishment Clause, I can accept that the Fourteenth Amendment protects religious liberty rights. But I cannot accept its use to oppose neutral programs of school choice through the incorporation of the Establishment Clause. There would be a tragic irony in converting the Fourteenth Amendment's guarantee of individual liberty into a prohibition on the exercise of educational choice.

22. Minneapolis & St. Louis Railroad Co. v. Bombolis, 241 U.S. 211 (1916).
23. Browning-Ferris Industries of Vt., Inc. v. Kelco Disposal, Inc., 492 U.S. 257, 262, 276 n.2 (1989).

THE CONTENT OF INCORPORATED RIGHTS

If a provision of the Bill of Rights applies to the states, is its content identical as to when it is applied to the federal government? Or as it is sometimes phrased, does the Bill of Rights provision apply "jot for jot"?[24]

The Supreme Court has not consistently answered these questions. In some cases, the Court has expressly stated that the Bill of Rights provision applied in exactly the same manner whether it is a federal or a state government action. For example, the Supreme Court has declared that it is "firmly embedded in our constitutional jurisprudence . . . that the several States have no greater power to restrain the individual freedoms protected by the First Amendment than does the Congress of the United States."[25] Similarly, the Court has said that "the guarantees of the First Amendment, the prohibition of unreasonable searches and seizures of the Fourth Amendment, and the right to counsel guaranteed by the Sixth Amendment, are all to be enforced against the States under the Fourteenth Amendment according to the same standards that protect those personal rights against federal encroachment."[26] The Court said that it "rejected the notion that the Fourteenth Amendment applies to the states only a 'watered-down, subjective version of the individual guarantees of the Bill of Rights.'"[27]

However, in other instances, the Court has ruled that some Bill of Rights provisions apply differently to the states than to the federal government. In Williams v. Florida, 399 U.S. 78 (1970), the Supreme Court held that states need not use 12-person juries in criminal cases, even though that is the practice for federal trials. The Court upheld the constitutionality of six-person juries in state criminal trials and explained that the jury of 12 was "a historical accident, unnecessary to effect the purposes of the jury system."

In Apodaca v. Oregon, 406 U.S. 404 (1972), and Johnson v. Louisiana, 406 U.S. 356 (1972), the Supreme Court held that states may allow non-unanimous jury verdicts in criminal cases. Although the Sixth Amendment has been interpreted to require unanimous juries in federal criminal trials, the Supreme Court ruled that states may allow convictions based on 11-1 or 10-2 jury votes. However, the Court has ruled that conviction by a nonunanimous six-person jury violates due process.[28]

From a practical perspective, except for the requirements of a 12-person jury and a unanimous verdict, the Bill of Rights provisions that have been incorporated apply to the states exactly as they apply to the federal government. This might be criticized on federalism grounds as unduly limiting the states. But rights such as freedom of speech are fundamental liberties and there is no reason why their content should vary depending on the level of government.

---

24. *See* Duncan v. Louisiana, 391 U.S. at 145, 181 (1968) (Harlan, J., dissenting) (using the "jot-for-jot" language).

25. Wallace v. Jaffree, 472 U.S. 38, 48-49 (1985). *Wallace* involved a First Amendment Establishment Clause challenge to school prayers. Some justices, at times, have suggested that they believed that the First Amendment's protection of freedom of speech apply differently to states than to the federal government. *See, e.g.,* Roth v. United States, 354 U.S. 476 (1957) (Harlan, J., concurring); Beauharnais v. Illinois, 343 U.S. 250 (1952) (Jackson, J., dissenting).

26. Malloy v. Hogan, 378 U.S. 1, 10 (1964).

27. *Id.* at 10-11 (citations omitted).

28. Burch v. Louisiana, 441 U.S. 130 (1979).

Although the debate over incorporation raged among Justices and scholars during the 1940s, 1950s, and 1960s, now the issue seems settled. Except for the few provisions mentioned above, the Bill of Rights provisions do apply to state and local governments and, in almost all instances, with the same content regardless of whether the challenge is a challenge to federal, state, or local actions.

C.   THE APPLICATION OF THE BILL OF RIGHTS AND THE CONSTITUTION TO PRIVATE CONDUCT

1.   *The Requirement for State Action*

The Constitution's protections of individual liberties and its requirement for equal protection apply only to the government. Private conduct generally does not have to comply with the Constitution. This is often referred to as the "state action" doctrine, although "state action" is something of a misnomer. The Constitution applies to government at all levels, federal, state, and local, and to the actions of government officers at all levels. The Constitution, however, generally does not apply to private entities or actors. The following decision — the *Civil Rights Cases* — is generally regarded as the initial articulation of the state action doctrine.

THE CIVIL RIGHTS CASES: UNITED STATES v. STANLEY
109 U.S. 3 (1883)

BRADLEY, J.

These cases are all founded on the first and second sections of the act of congress known as the "Civil Rights Act," passed March 1, 1875, entitled "An act to protect all citizens in their civil and legal rights." The sections of the law referred to provide as follows:

> Section 1. That all persons within the jurisdiction of the United States shall be entitled to the full and equal enjoyment of the accommodations, advantages, facilities, and privileges of inns, public conveyances on land or water, theaters, and other places of public amusement; subject only to the conditions and limitations established by law, and applicable alike to citizens of every race and color, regardless of any previous condition of servitude.
>
> Sec. 2. That any person who shall violate the foregoing section by denying to any citizen, except for reasons by law applicable to citizens of every race and color, and regardless of any previous condition of servitude, the full enjoyment of any of the accommodations, advantages, facilities, or privileges in said section enumerated, or by aiding or inciting such denial, shall, for every such offense, forfeit and pay the sum of $500 to the person aggrieved thereby, to be recovered in an action of debt, with full costs; and shall, also, for every such offense, be deemed guilty of a misdemeanor, and upon conviction thereof shall be fined not less than $500 nor more than $1,000, or shall be imprisoned not less than 30 days nor more than one year.

Two of the cases, those against Stanley and Nichols, are indictments for deny-ing to persons of color the accommodations and privileges of an inn or hotel; two of them, those against Ryan and Singleton, are, one an information, the other an indictment, for denying to individuals the privileges and accommoda-tions of a theater, the information against Ryan being for refusing a colored person a seat in the dress circle of Maguire's theater in San Francisco; and the indictment against Singleton being for denying to another person, whose color is not stated, the full enjoyment of the accommodations of the theater known as the Grand Opera House in New York, "said denial not being made for any reasons by law applicable to citizens of every race and color, and regardless of any previous condition of servitude."

Has congress constitutional power to make such a law? Of course, no one will contend that the power to pass it was contained in the constitution before the adoption of the last three amendments. The first section of the fourteenth amendment,—which is the one relied on,—after declaring who shall be citi-zens of the United States, and of the several states, is prohibitory in its character, and prohibitory upon the states. It is state action of a particular character that is prohibited. Individual invasion of individual rights is not the subject-matter of the amendment.

[T]he last section of the amendment invests congress with power to enforce it by appropriate legislation. To enforce what? To enforce the prohibition. To adopt appropriate legislation for correcting the effects of such prohibited state law and state acts, and thus to render them effectually null, void, and innocuous. This is the legislative power conferred upon congress, and this is the whole of it. It does not invest congress with power to legislate upon subjects which are within the domain of state legislation; but to provide modes of relief against state legislation, or state action, of the kind referred to. It does not authorize congress to create a code of municipal law for the regulation of private rights; but to provide modes of redress against the operation of state laws, and the action of state officers, executive or judicial, when these are subversive of the fundamental rights specified in the amendment. Positive rights and privileges are undoubtedly secured by the fourteenth amendment; but they are secured by way of prohibition against state laws and state proceedings affecting those rights and privileges, and by power given to congress to legislate for the purpose of carrying such prohibition into effect; and such legislation must necessarily be predicated upon such supposed state laws or state proceedings, and be directed to the correction of their operation and effect.

And so in the present case, until some state law has been passed, or some state action through its officers or agents has been taken, adverse to the rights of citizens sought to be protected by the fourteenth amendment, no legislation of the United States under said amendment, nor any proceeding under such leg-islation, can be called into activity, for the prohibitions of the amendment are against state laws and acts done under state authority.

An inspection of the law shows that it makes no reference whatever to any supposed or apprehended violation of the fourteenth amendment on the part of the states. It is not predicated on any such view. It does not profess to be corrective of any constitutional wrong committed by the states; it does not make its operation to depend upon any such wrong committed. In other words, it steps into the domain of local jurisprudence, and lays down rules for the conduct of individuals in society towards each other, and imposes sanctions for the enforcement of those rules, without referring in any manner to any supposed action of the state or its authorities. If this legislation is appropriate for enforcing the prohibitions of the amendment, it is difficult to see where it is to stop.

HARLAN, J., dissenting.

The opinion in these cases proceeds, as it seems to me, upon grounds entirely too narrow and artificial. The substance and spirit of the recent amendments of the constitution have been sacrificed by a subtle and ingenious verbal criticism. "It is not the words of the law but the internal sense of it that makes the law. The letter of the law is the body; the sense and reason of the law is the soul." Constitutional provisions, adopted in the interest of liberty, and for the purpose of securing, through national legislation, if need be, rights inhering in a state of freedom, and belonging to American citizenship, have been so construed as to defeat the ends the people desired to accomplish, which they attempted to accomplish, and which they supposed they had accomplished by changes in their fundamental law. By this I do not mean that the determination of these cases should have been materially controlled by considerations of mere expediency or policy. I mean only, in this form, to express an earnest conviction that the court has departed from the familiar rule requiring, in the interpretation of constitutional provisions, that full effect be given to the intent with which they were adopted.

The blanket rule that the Constitution only applies to the government must be qualified in a few respects. First, the Thirteenth Amendment to the Constitution is the one provision that directly regulates private conduct. Section 1 of the Thirteenth Amendment states, "Neither slavery nor involuntary servitude, except as a punishment for crime whereof the party shall have been duly convicted, shall exist within the United States, or any place subject to their jurisdiction." In other words, the Thirteenth Amendment forbids people from being or owning slaves. For example, the Supreme Court has said that the Thirteenth Amendment forbids compelling a person to work for another individual to repay a debt.[29]

Second, statutes, both federal and state, can apply constitutional norms to private conduct. The state action doctrine provides that the Constitution only applies to the government. But the government can enact laws that require that private conduct meet the same standards that the Constitution requires of the government. For example, the constitutional requirement for equal protection applies just to the government. Congress, however, has enacted laws, such as the

---

29. United States v. Reynolds, 235 U.S. 133 (1914); *see also* Bailey v. Alabama, 219 U.S. 219 (1911) (it is unconstitutional to imprison a person for failure to pay debt). However, the Supreme Court has held that injunctions to halt labor disputes do not violate the Thirteenth Amendment. *See* International Union v. Wisconsin Employment Relations Bd., 336 U.S. 245 (1949). The Court also has ruled that the military draft does not violate the Thirteenth Amendment, Arver v. United States, 245 U.S. 366, 390 (1918), and that it does not violate the Thirteenth Amendment for a state to require that all able-bodied men between the ages of 21 and 45 work on road construction for a period of time. Butler v. Perry, 240 U.S. 328 (1916).

Civil Rights Act of 1964, that prohibit private discrimination by private employ-ers and by places of public accommodation.[30] Another illustration is a California law that requires that private schools and universities provide the same protec-tion of speech that students would receive at a public school or university.[31] Actions, of course, are brought directly under such statutes and are governed by the terms of the laws; the Constitution still does not apply.

Finally, there are exceptions to the state action requirement; situations where private conduct has to comply with the Constitution. These exceptions are pre-sented in detail below.

In evaluating the Supreme Court cases below that concern the exceptions to the state action doctrine, it is important to consider the costs and benefits of having such a rule. Obviously, those who believe that the disadvantages of the state action doctrine outweigh its advantages want broad exceptions to the doc-trine and those who think the reverse want very narrow exceptions.

There are serious costs to the state action requirement: Absent statutory restrictions, private conduct can infringe or trample even the most basic rights. Freedom of speech, privacy, and equality—this society's most cherished values—can be violated without any redress in the courts. Private infringements of basic freedoms can be just as harmful as government violations. Speech can be lost or chilled just as much through private sanctions as through public ones. Private discrimination causes and perpetuates social inequalities at least as per-nicious as those caused by government actions.

On the other hand, the state action doctrine is defended as desirable on the grounds that it preserves a zone of private autonomy and that it advances fed-eralism. The Supreme Court has explained that the state action requirement "preserves an area of individual freedom by limiting the reach of federal law and federal judicial power."[32] The state action doctrine means that private actors have the freedom to ignore the Constitution and the limits contained within it. A vast array of private actions might be constrained and challenged in the courts if there were not a state action requirement for the application of the Constitution.

Also, the Supreme Court says that the state action doctrine enhances feder-alism by preserving a zone of state sovereignty.[33] The *Civil Rights Cases* held that federal constitutional rights do not govern individual behavior and, further-more, that Congress lacks the authority to apply them to private conduct.[34] Structuring the legal relationships of private citizens was for the state, not for the national government.

In considering the exceptions to the state action doctrine, it is important to consider these competing policy considerations in evaluating whether the Court has properly defined the exceptions or whether they are too broad or too narrow.

---

30. Congress's authority to adopt such laws is discussed in Chapter 2.

31. Cal. Educ. Code §48950(a) ("School districts operating one or more high schools and private secondary schools shall not make or enforce any rule subjecting any high school pupil to disciplinary sanctions solely on the basis of conduct that is speech or other communication that, when engaged in outside the campus, is protected by governmental restriction by the First Amend-ment to the United States Constitution or Section 2 of Article I of the California Constitution."). *See also* §94367(a) (identical provision applied to private post-secondary schools).

32. Lugar v. Edmondson Oil Co., 457 U.S. 922, 936 (1982).

33. *Id.* at 936.

34. 109 U.S. at 11.

2.   The Exceptions to the State Action Doctrine

There are two exceptions to the state action doctrine; that is, situations where private conduct must comply with the Constitution. One is the "public functions exception," which says that a private entity must comply with the Constitution if it is performing a task that has been traditionally, exclusively done by the government. The other is the "entanglement exception," which says that private conduct must comply with the Constitution if the government has authorized, encouraged, or facilitated the unconstitutional conduct.

At the outset in examining the exceptions to the state action doctrine it must be recognized that the cases do not neatly fit together. Some of the decisions seem clearly inconsistent with one another and the Court often has made little effort to reconcile them. Cases concerning these exceptions have been called a "conceptual disaster area"[35] and even the Supreme Court has admitted that the "cases deciding when private action might be deemed that of the state have not been a model of consistency."[36]

There are several explanations for this inconsistency. In part, it reflects inherent problems with state action; the government always has the power to regulate private behavior and there never can be a clear line for when the failure to do so constitutes state action and a constitutional violation. Likewise, the government is involved, to some extent, in almost every activity. It is difficult, if not impossible, to draw a meaningful line as to the point where the involvement is great enough to require the private action to comply with the Constitution.

The inconsistencies also reflect the way in which some of the state action decisions were written and decided. As explained below, cases with regard to both of the exceptions articulated broad principles that could make a wide range of private conduct actionable under the Constitution. Because those cases have not been overruled, but also not always followed, there is tension among the decisions.

The inconsistencies also reflect social realities. From the late 1940s through the 1960s, the Court expansively defined what constitutes state action as part of trying to combat racial discrimination. These decisions understandably articulated broad principles that could make a great deal of private conduct reviewable under the Constitution. Since the 1960s, especially in cases involving other constitutional provisions, the Court has applied a much narrower definition of state action. There are inconsistencies among the cases that the Court never has acknowledged or resolved.

In fact, a review of the decisions indicates that the Court has been much more likely to apply the exceptions in cases involving race discrimination than in cases involving other constitutional claims. Indeed, the United States Court of Appeals for the Second Circuit expressly held that the scope of the exceptions to the state action doctrine turns on whether it is a claim of race discrimination or another constitutional right.[37] Yet this distinction seems difficult to defend. State action is about whether the Constitution should apply because of the

---

35. Charles L. Black, Jr., *Foreword: "State Action," Equal Protection, and California's Proposition 14*, 81 Harv. L. Rev. 69, 95 (1967).

36. Edmondson v. Leesville Concrete Co., 500 U.S. 614, 632 (1991).

37. *See* Lebron v. National Railroad Passenger Corp. (Amtrack), 12 F.3d 388, 392 (2d Cir. 1993), *rev'd on other grounds*, 513 U.S. 374 (1995).

government's involvement or because the act is one that is traditionally governmental in nature. It is unclear why this inquiry depends at all on the particulars of the constitutional claim.

The inconsistency among the cases also reflects the reduced need to rely on the Constitution to reach private racial discrimination. The adoption of the Civil Rights Act of 1964, which prohibited private discrimination by places of public accommodation and private employers, greatly lessened the need for constitutional litigation to end discrimination. For example, prior to the 1964 Civil Rights Act, the Court had to consider whether there was state action when the government leased premises to a restaurant that racially discriminated.[38] But after the 1964 Civil Rights Act, the state action inquiry would have been unnecessary because the law prohibited the restaurant from racially discriminating even if there was no government involvement.

The two exceptions — the public functions exception and the entanglement exception — are discussed, in turn, below. It should be noted that many cases involve discussion of both exceptions and therefore are considered below under each of the exceptions. Also, in some cases, the Court is not clear as to which exception it is discussing. This, too, contributes to the doctrinal confusion concerning the state action doctrine.

a.   The Public Functions Exception

There is a sharp contrast between how the Court defined the public functions exception in the following two cases: Marsh v. Alabama and Jackson v. Metropolitan Edison Co. *Marsh* is expansive in its definition and could be used to find a great deal of private conduct to be state action. *Jackson* is quite narrow and makes it very difficult to find that private actors are performing a public function. After these contrasting cases, two important areas where the Court has considered the public functions exception are presented: elections and private property used for public purposes.

MARSH v. ALABAMA

326 U.S. 501 (1946)

Justice BLACK delivered the opinion of the Court.

In this case we are asked to decide whether a State, consistently with the First and Fourteenth Amendments, can impose criminal punishment on a person who undertakes to distribute religious literature on the premises of a company-owned town contrary to the wishes of the town's management. The town, a suburb of Mobile, Alabama, known as Chickasaw, is owned by the Gulf Shipbuilding Corporation. Except for that it has all the characteristics of any other American town.

The property consists of residential buildings, streets, a system of sewers, a sewage disposal plant and a "business block" on which business places are situated. A deputy of the Mobile County Sheriff, paid by the company, serves

---

38. Burton v. Wilmington Parking Authority, 365 U.S. 715 (1961), discussed later.

as the town's policeman. Merchants and service establishments have rented the stores and business places on the business block and the United States uses one of the places as a post office from which six carriers deliver mail to the people of Chickasaw and the adjacent area. The town and the surrounding neighborhood, which can not be distinguished from the Gulf property by anyone not familiar with the property lines, are thickly settled, and according to all indications the residents use the business block as their regular shopping center. To do so, they now, as they have for many years, make use of a company-owned paved street and sidewalk located alongside the store fronts in order to enter and leave the stores and the post office. There is nothing to stop highway traffic from coming onto the business block and upon arrival a traveler may make free use of the facilities available there. In short the town and its shopping district are accessible to and freely used by the public in general and there is nothing to distinguish them from any other town and shopping center except the fact that the title to the property belongs to a private corporation.

Appellant, a Jehovah's Witness, came onto the sidewalk we have just described, stood near the post-office and undertook to distribute religious literature. In the stores the corporation had posted a notice which read as follows: "This Is Private Property, and Without Written Permission, No Street, or House Vendor, Agent or Solicitation of Any Kind Will Be Permitted." Appellant was warned that she could not distribute the literature without a permit and told that no permit would be issued to her. She protested that the company rule could not be constitutionally applied so as to prohibit her from distributing religious writings. When she was asked to leave the sidewalk and Chickasaw she declined. The deputy sheriff arrested her and she was charged in the state court with violating the 1940 Alabama Code which makes it a crime to enter or remain on the premises of another after having been warned not to do so. Appellant contended that to construe the state statute as applicable to her activities would abridge her right to freedom of press and religion contrary to the First and Fourteenth Amendments to the Constitution. This contention was rejected and she was convicted.

Had the title to Chickasaw belonged not to a private but to a municipal corporation and had appellant been arrested for violating a municipal ordinance rather than a ruling by those appointed by the corporation to manage a company-town it would have been clear that appellant's conviction must be reversed. Under our decision[s], neither a state nor a municipality can completely bar the distribution of literature containing religious or political ideas on its streets, sidewalks and public places.

Our question then narrows down to this: Can those people who live in or come to Chickasaw be denied freedom of press and religion simply because a single company has legal title to all the town? For it is the state's contention that the mere fact that all the property interests in the town are held by a single company is enough to give that company power, enforceable by a state statute, to abridge these freedoms.

We do not agree that the corporation's property interests settle the question. The State urges in effect that the corporation's right to control the inhabitants of Chickasaw is coextensive with the right of a homeowner to regulate the conduct of his guests. We can not accept that contention. Ownership does not always mean absolute dominion. The more an owner, for his advantage, opens up his property for use by the public in general, the more do his rights become circumscribed by the statutory and constitutional rights of those who use it.

Whether a corporation or a municipality owns or possesses the town the public in either case has an identical interest in the functioning of the community in such manner that the channels of communication remain free. As we have heretofore stated, the town of Chickasaw does not function differently from any other town. The "business block" serves as the community shopping center and is freely accessible and open to the people in the area and those passing through. The managers appointed by the corporation cannot curtail the liberty of press and religion of these people consistently with the purposes of the Constitutional guarantees, and a state statute, as the one here involved, which enforces such action by criminally punishing those who attempt to distribute religious literature clearly violates the First and Fourteenth Amendments to the Constitution.

Many people in the United States live in company-owned towns. These people, just as residents of municipalities, are free citizens of their State and country. Just as all other citizens they must make decisions which affect the welfare of community and nation. To act as good citizens they must be informed. In order to enable them to be properly informed their information must be uncensored. There is no more reason for depriving these people of the liberties guaranteed by the First and Fourteenth Amendments than there is for curtailing these freedoms with respect to any other citizen.

When we balance the Constitutional rights of owners of property against those of the people to enjoy freedom of press and religion, as we must here, we remain mindful of the fact that the latter occupy a preferred position. In our view the circumstance that the property rights to the premises where the deprivation of liberty, here involved, took place, were held by others than the public, is not sufficient to justify the State's permitting a corporation to govern a community of citizens so as to restrict their fundamental liberties and the enforcement of such restraint by the application of a State statute. Insofar as the State has attempted to impose criminal punishment on appellant for undertaking to distribute religious literature in a company town, its action cannot stand.

JACKSON v. METROPOLITAN EDISON CO.

419 U.S. 345 (1974)

Justice REHNQUIST delivered the opinion of the Court.

Respondent Metropolitan Edison Co. is a privately owned and operated Pennsylvania corporation which holds a certificate of public convenience issued by the Pennsylvania Public Utility Commission empowering it to deliver electricity to a service area which includes the city of York, Pa. As a condition of holding its certificate, it is subject to extensive regulation by the Commission. Under a provision of its general tariff filed with the Commission, it has the right to discontinue service to any customer on reasonable notice of nonpayment of bills.

Petitioner Catherine Jackson is a resident of York, who has received electricity in the past from respondent. Until September 1970, petitioner received electric service to her home in York under an account with respondent in her own name.

When her account was terminated because of asserted delinquency in payments due for service, a new account with respondent was opened in the name of one James Dodson, another occupant of the residence, and service to the residence was resumed. There is a dispute as to whether payments due under the Dodson account for services provided during this period were ever made. In August 1971, Dodson left the residence. Service continued thereafter but concededly no payments were made. Petitioner states that no bills were received during this period.

On October 6, 1971, employees of Metropolitan came to the residence and inquired as to Dodson's present address. Petitioner stated that it was unknown to her. On the following day, another employee visited the residence and informed petitioner that the meter had been tampered with so as not to register amounts used. She disclaimed knowledge of this and requested that the service account for her home be shifted from Dodson's name to that of Robert Jackson, later identified as her 12-year-old son. Four days later on October 11, 1971, without further notice to petitioner, Metropolitan employees disconnected her service.

Mrs. Jackson argues that under the Due Process Clause of the Fourteenth Amendment she cannot be deprived of this entitlement to utility service without adequate notice and a hearing before an impartial body: until these are completed, her service must continue. The Due Process Clause of the Fourteenth Amendment provides: "(N)or shall any State deprive any person of life, liberty, or property, without due process of law." In 1883, this Court in the Civil Rights Cases (1883) affirmed the essential dichotomy set forth in that Amendment between deprivation by the State, subject to scrutiny under its provisions, and private conduct, "however discriminatory or wrongful," against which the Fourteenth Amendment offers no shield.

While the principle that private action is immune from the restrictions of the Fourteenth Amendment is well established and easily stated, the question whether particular conduct is "private," on the one hand, or "state action," on the other, frequently admits of no easy answer.

Here the action complained of was taken by a utility company which is privately owned and operated, but which in many particulars of its business is subject to extensive state regulation. The mere fact that a business is subject to state regulation does not by itself convert its action into that of the State for purposes of the Fourteenth Amendment. Nor does the fact that the regulation is extensive and detailed, as in the case of most public utilities, do so. It may well be that acts of a heavily regulated utility with at least something of a governmentally protected monopoly will more readily be found to be "state" acts than will the acts of an entity lacking these characteristics. But the inquiry must be whether there is a sufficiently close nexus between the State and the challenged action of the regulated entity so that the action of the latter may be fairly treated as that of the State itself.

Petitioner first argues that "state action" is present because of the monopoly status allegedly conferred upon Metropolitan by the State of Pennsylvania. As a factual matter, it may well be doubted that the State ever granted or guaranteed Metropolitan a monopoly. But assuming that it had, this fact is not determinative in considering whether Metropolitan's termination of service to petitioner was "state action" for purposes of the Fourteenth Amendment.

Petitioner next urges that state action is present because respondent provides an essential public service required to be supplied on a reasonably continuous basis by [Pennsylvania law] and hence performs a "public function." We have, of course, found state action present in the exercise by a private entity of powers traditionally exclusively reserved to the State. *See, e.g.,* Nixon v. Condon (1932) (election); Terry v. Adams (1953) (election); Marsh v. Alabama (1946) (company town); Evans v. Newton (1966) (municipal park). If we were dealing with the exercise by Metropolitan of some power delegated to it by the State which is traditionally associated with sovereignty, such as eminent domain, our case would be quite a different one. But while the Pennsylvania statute imposes an obligation to furnish service on regulated utilities, it imposes no such obligation on the State. The Pennsylvania courts have rejected the contention that the furnishing of utility services is either a state function or a municipal duty.

Perhaps in recognition of the fact that the supplying of utility service is not traditionally the exclusive prerogative of the State, petitioner invites the expansion of the doctrine of this limited line of cases into a broad principle that all businesses "affected with the public interest" are state actors in all their actions. We decline the invitation. Doctors, optometrists, lawyers, and grocery selling a quart of milk are all in regulated businesses, providing arguably essential goods and services, "affected with a public interest." We do not believe that such a status converts their every action, absent more, into that of the State.

All of petitioner's arguments taken together show no more than that Metropolitan was a heavily regulated, privately owned utility, enjoying at least a partial monopoly in the providing of electrical service within its territory, and that it elected to terminate service to petitioner in a manner which the Pennsylvania Public Utility Commission found permissible under state law. Under our decision this is not sufficient to connect the State of Pennsylvania with respondent's action so as to make the latter's conduct attributable to the State for purposes of the Fourteenth Amendment.

We conclude that the State of Pennsylvania is not sufficiently connected with respondent's action in terminating petitioner's service so as to make respondent's conduct in so doing attributable to the State for purposes of the Fourteenth Amendment.

Justice MARSHALL, dissenting.

The Metropolitan Edison Co. provides an essential public service to the people of York, Pa. It is the only entity, public or private, that is authorized to supply electric service to most of the community. As a part of its charter to the company, the State imposes extensive regulations, and it cooperates with the company in myriad ways. Additionally, the State has granted its approval to the company's mode of service termination — the very conduct that is challenged here. Taking these factors together, I have no difficulty finding state action in this case. As the Court concluded in Burton v. Wilmington Parking Authority (1961), the State has sufficiently "insinuated itself into a position of interdependence with (the company) that it must be recognized as a joint participant in the challenged activity."

Our state-action cases have repeatedly relied on several factors clearly presented by this case: a state-sanctioned monopoly; an extensive pattern of cooperation between the "private" entity and the State; and a service uniquely public in nature. Today the Court takes a major step in repudiating this line of authority and adopts a stance that is bound to lead to mischief when applied to problems beyond the narrow sphere of due process objections to utility terminations.

I disagree with the majority's position on three separate grounds. First, the suggestion that the State would have to "put its own weight on the side of the proposed practice by ordering it" seems to me to mark a sharp departure from our previous state-action cases. [W]e have consistently indicated that state authorization and approval of "private" conduct would support a finding of state action. Second, I question the wisdom of giving such short shrift to the extensive interaction between the company and the State, and focusing solely on the extent of state support for the particular activity under challenge. Finally, it seems to me in any event that the State has given its approval to Metropolitan Edison's termination procedures. The State Utility Commission approved a tariff provision under which the company reserved the right to discontinue its service on reasonable notice for nonpayment of bills.

The fact that the Metropolitan Edison Co. supplies an essential public service that is in many communities supplied by the government weighs more heavily for me than for the majority. The Court concedes that state action might be present if the activity in question were "traditionally associated with sovereignty," but it then undercuts that point by suggesting that a particular service is not a public function if the State in question has not required that it be governmentally operated. This reads the "public function" argument too narrowly. The whole point of the "public function" cases is to look behind the State's decision to provide public services through private parties. In my view, utility service is traditionally identified with the State through universal public regulation or ownership to a degree sufficient to render it a "public function."

Marsh and *Jackson* use very different tests for the public function test. *Marsh* uses a balancing test and looks to whether the private property is used for a public purpose. *Jackson* focuses on whether it is an activity that has been traditionally, exclusively done by the government. Cases involving two different areas in which the Court has applied the public functions test follow: one dealing with elections (Terry v. Adams) and one dealing with private property used for public purposes (Evans v. Newton). In examining these cases, consider the approach to the public functions doctrine used in each.

TERRY v. ADAMS
345 U.S. 461 (1953)

Mr. Justice BLACK announced the judgment of the Court.

In Smith v. Allwright (1944), we held that rules of the Democratic Party of Texas excluding Negroes from voting in the party's primaries violated the Fifteenth Amendment. This case raises questions concerning the constitutional power of a Texas county political organization called the Jaybird Democratic Association or Jaybird Party to exclude Negroes from its primaries on racial grounds. The Jaybirds deny that their racial exclusions violate the Fifteenth Amendment. They contend that the Amendment applies only to elections or primaries held under state regulation, that their association is not regulated by the state at all, and that it is not a political party but a self-governing voluntary club.

The Jaybird Association or Party was organized in 1889. Its membership was then and always has been limited to white people; they are automatically members if their names appear on the official list of county voters. It has been run like other political parties with an executive committee named from the county's voting precincts. Expenses of the party are paid by the assessment of candidates for office in its primaries. Candidates for county offices submit their names to the Jaybird Committee in accordance with the normal practice followed by regular political parties all over the country. Advertisements and posters proclaim that these candidates are running subject to the action of the Jaybird primary. While there is no legal compulsion on successful Jaybird candidates to enter Democratic primaries they have nearly always done so and with few exceptions since 1889 have run and won without opposition in the Democratic primaries and the general elections that followed. Thus the party has been the dominant political group in the county since organization, having endorsed every county-wide official elected since 1889.

It is apparent that Jaybird activities follow a plan purposefully designed to exclude Negroes from voting and at the same time to escape the Fifteenth Amendment's command that the right of citizens to vote shall neither be denied nor abridged on account of race. These were the admitted party purposes according to the testimony of the Jaybird's president.

The Fifteenth Amendment provides as follows: "The right of citizens of the United States to vote shall not be denied or abridged by the United States or by any State on account of race, color, or previous condition of servitude." The Amendment bans racial discrimination in voting by both state and nation. It thus establishes a national policy, obviously applicable to the right of Negroes not to be discriminated against as voters in elections to determine public governmental policies or to select public officials, national, state, or local.

It is significant that precisely the same qualifications as those prescribed by Texas entitling electors to vote at county-operated primaries are adopted as the sole qualifications entitling electors to vote at the county-wide Jaybird primaries with a single proviso — Negroes are excluded. Everyone concedes that such a proviso in the county-operated primaries would be unconstitutional. The Jaybird Party thus brings into being and holds precisely the kind of election that the Fifteenth Amendment seeks to prevent. When it produces the equivalent of the prohibited election, the damage has been done.

For a state to permit such a duplication of its election processes is to permit a flagrant abuse of those processes to defeat the purposes of the Fifteenth Amendment. The use of the county-operated primary to ratify the result of the prohibited election merely compounds the offense. It violates the Fifteenth Amendment for a state, by such circumvention, to permit within its borders the use of any device that produces an equivalent of the prohibited election.

The only election that has counted in this Texas county for more than fifty years has been that held by the Jaybirds from which Negroes were excluded. The Democratic primary and the general election have become no more than the perfunctory ratifiers of the choice that has already been made in Jaybird elections from which Negroes have been excluded. It is immaterial that the state does not control that part of this elective process which it leaves for the Jaybirds to manage. The Jaybird primary has become an integral part, indeed the only effective part, of the elective process that determines who shall rule and govern in the county. The effect of the whole procedure, Jaybird primary plus Democratic primary plus general election, is to do precisely that which the Fifteenth Amendment forbids — strip Negroes of every vestige of influence in selecting the officials who control the local county matters that intimately touch the daily lives of citizens.

EVANS v. NEWTON

382 U.S. 296 (1966)

Justice DOUGLAS delivered the opinion of the Court.

In 1911 United States Senator Augustus O. Bacon executed a will that devised to the Mayor and Council of the City of Macon, Georgia, a tract of land which, after the death of the Senator's wife and daughters, was to be used as "a park and pleasure ground" for white people only, the Senator stating in the will that while he had only the kindest feeling for the Negroes he was of the opinion that "in their social relations the two races (white and negro) should be forever separate." The will provided that the park should be under the control of a Board of Managers of seven persons, all of whom were to be white. The city kept the park segregated for some years but in time let Negroes use it, taking the position that the park was a public facility which it could not constitutionally manage and maintain on a segregated basis.

Thereupon, individual members of the Board of Managers of the park brought this suit in a state court against the City of Macon and the trustees of certain residuary beneficiaries of Senator Bacon's estate, asking that the city be removed as trustee and that the court appoint new trustees, to whom title to the park would be transferred. The city answered, alleging it could not legally enforce racial segregation in the park. The other defendants admitted the allegation and requested that the city be removed as trustee. Several Negro citizens of Macon intervened, alleging that the racial limitation was contrary to the laws and public policy of the United States, and asking that the court refuse to appoint private trustees. Moreover, other heirs of Senator Bacon intervened and they and the defendants other than the city asked for reversion of the trust property to the Bacon estate in the event that the prayer of the petition were denied. Thereafter the city resigned as trustee and amended its answer accordingly.

The Georgia court accepted the resignation of the city as trustee and appointed three individuals as new trustees, finding it unnecessary to pass on the other claims of the heirs. On appeal by the Negro intervenors, the Supreme Court of Georgia affirmed, holding that Senator Bacon had the right to give and bequeath his property to a limited class, that charitable trusts are subject to supervision of a court of equity, and that the power to appoint new trustees so that the purpose of the trust would not fail was clear.

There are two complementary principles to be reconciled in this case. One is the right of the individual to pick his own associates so as to express his preferences and dislikes, and to fashion his private life by joining such clubs and groups as he chooses. The other is the constitutional ban in the Equal Protection

Clause of the Fourteenth Amendment against state-sponsored racial inequality, which of course bars a city from acting as trustee under a private will that serves the racial segregation cause. A private golf club, however, restricted to either Negro or white membership is one expression of freedom of association. But a municipal golf course that serves only one race is state activity indicating a preference on a matter as to which the State must be neutral.

What is "private" action and what is "state" action is not always easy to determine. "Only by sifting facts and weighing circumstances" can we determine whether the reach of the Fourteenth Amendment extends to a particular case. The range of government activities is broad and varied, and the fact that government has engaged in a particular activity does not necessarily mean that an individual entrepreneur or manager of the same kind of undertaking suffers the same constitutional inhibitions.

If a testator wanted to leave a school or center for the use of one race only and in no way implicated the State in the supervision, control, or management of that facility, we assume arguendo that no constitutional difficulty would be encountered. This park, however, is in a different posture. For years it was an integral part of the City of Macon's activities. From the pleadings we assume it was swept, manicured, watered, patrolled, and maintained by the city as a public facility for whites only, as well as granted tax exemption. The momentum it acquired as a public facility is certainly not dissipated ipso facto by the appointment of "private" trustees. So far as this record shows, there has been no change in municipal maintenance and concern over this facility. Whether these public characteristics will in time be dissipated is wholly conjectural. If the municipality remains entwined in the management or control of the park, it remains subject to the restraints of the Fourteenth Amendment. We only hold that where the tradition of municipal control had become firmly established, we cannot take judicial notice that the mere substitution of trustees instantly transferred this park from the public to the private sector.

This conclusion is buttressed by the nature of the service rendered the community by a park. The service rendered even by a private park of this character is municipal in nature. It is open to every white person, there being no selective element other than race. Golf clubs, social centers, luncheon clubs, schools such as Tuskegee was at least in origin, and other like organizations in the private sector are often racially oriented. A park, on the other hand, is more like a fire department or police department that traditionally serves the community. Mass recreation through the use of parks is plainly in the public domain; and state courts that aid private parties to perform that public function on a segregated basis implicate the State in conduct proscribed by the Fourteenth Amendment. Like the streets of the company town in Marsh v. State of Alabama, and the elective process of Terry v. Adams, the predominant character and purpose of this park are municipal.

Under the circumstances of this case, we cannot but conclude that the public character of this park requires that it be treated as a public institution subject to the command of the Fourteenth Amendment, regardless of who now has title under state law.

The Supreme Court has considered the application of the public function doctrine in deciding whether there is a First Amendment right to use privately owned shopping centers for speech purposes. The Court initially analogized shopping centers to the company town in Marsh v. Alabama and concluded that there is a First Amendment right of access. The Court then qualified this right and finally it overturned its initial ruling and held that there is no First Amendment right to use private shopping centers for speech purposes.

AMALGAMATED FOOD EMPLOYEES UNION LOCAL 590 v. LOGAN VALLEY PLAZA, INC.

391 U.S. 308 (1968)

Justice MARSHALL delivered the opinion of the Court.

This case presents the question whether peaceful picketing of a business enterprise located within a shopping center can be enjoined on the ground that it constitutes an unconsented invasion of the property rights of the owners of the land on which the center is situated.

Logan Valley Plaza, Inc. (Logan), one of the two respondents herein, owns a large, newly developed shopping center complex, known as the Logan Valley Mall, located near the City of Altoona, Pennsylvania. At the time of the events in this case, Logan Valley Mall was occupied by two businesses, Weis Markets, Inc. (Weis), the other respondent herein, and Sears, Roebuck and Co. (Sears), although other enterprises were then expected and have since moved into the center. Weis operates a supermarket and Sears operates both a department store and an automobile service center.

On December 8, 1965, Weis opened for business, employing a wholly non-union staff of employees. A few days after it opened for business, Weis posted a sign on the exterior of its building prohibiting trespassing or soliciting by anyone other than its employees on its porch or parking lot. On December 17, 1965, members of Amalgamated Food Employees Union, Local 590, began picketing Weis. They carried signs stating that the Weis market was nonunion and that its employees were not "receiving union wages or other union benefits." The picketing continued until December 27, during which time the number of pickets varied between four and 13 and averaged around six. The picketing was carried out almost entirely in the parcel pickup area and that portion of the parking lot immediately adjacent thereto. Although some congestion of the parcel pickup area occurred, such congestion was sporadic and infrequent.

We start from the premise that peaceful picketing carried on in a location open generally to the public is, absent other factors involving the purpose or manner of the picketing, protected by the First Amendment. Thornhill v. State of Alabama (1940). The case squarely presents, therefore, the question whether Pennsylvania's generally valid rules against trespass to private property can be applied in these circumstances to bar petitioners from the Weis and Logan premises. It is clear that if the shopping center premises were not privately owned but instead constituted the business area of a municipality, which they to a large extent resemble, petitioners could not be barred from exercising their First Amendment rights there on the sole ground that title to the property was in the municipality.

This Court has also held, in Marsh v. State of Alabama (1946), that under some circumstances property that is privately owned may, at least for First Amendment purposes, be treated as though it were publicly held. The similarities between the business block in *Marsh* and the shopping center in the present case are striking. The perimeter of Logan Valley Mall is a little less than 1.1 miles. Inside the mall were situated, at the time of trial, two substantial commercial enterprises with numerous others soon to follow. The general public has unrestricted access to the mall property. The shopping center here is clearly the functional equivalent of the business district of Chickasaw involved in *Marsh*.

We see no reason why access to a business district in a company town for the purpose of exercising First Amendment rights should be constitutionally required, while access for the same purpose to property functioning as a business district should be limited simply because the property surrounding the "business district" is not under the same ownership. Here the roadways provided for vehicular movement within the mall and the sidewalks leading from building to building are the functional equivalents of the streets and sidewalks of a normal municipal business district. The shopping center premises are open to the public to the same extent as the commercial center of a normal town.

All we decide here is that because the shopping center serves as the community business block "and is freely accessible and open to the people in the area and those passing through," Marsh v. State of Alabama, the State may not delegate the power, through the use of its trespass laws, wholly to exclude those members of the public wishing to exercise their First Amendment rights on the premises in a manner and for a purpose generally consonant with the use to which the property is actually put.

We do not hold that respondents, and at their behest the State, are without power to make reasonable regulations governing the exercise of First Amendment rights on their property. Certainly their rights to make such regulations are at the very least co-extensive with the powers possessed by States and municipalities, and recognized in many opinions of this Court, to control the use of public property. Even where municipal or state property is open to the public generally, the exercise of First Amendment rights may be regulated so as to prevent interference with the use to which the property is ordinarily put by the State. In addition, the exercise of First Amendment rights may be regulated where such exercise will unduly interfere with the normal use of the public property by other members of the public with an equal right of access to it.

[But] "[o]wnership does not always mean absolute dominion. The more an owner, for his advantage, opens up his property for use by the public in general, the more do his rights become circumscribed by the statutory and constitutional rights of those who use it." Logan Valley Mall is the functional equivalent of a "business block" and for First Amendment purposes must be treated in substantially the same manner.

LLOYD CORP. v. TANNER

407 U.S. 551 (1972)

Justice POWELL delivered the opinion of the Court.

This case presents the question reserved by the Court in Amalgamated Food Employees Union Local 590 v. Logan Valley Plaza, Inc. (1968), as to the right of a privately owned shopping center to prohibit the distribution of handbills on its property when the handbilling is unrelated to the shopping center's operations. Lloyd Corp., Ltd. (Lloyd) owns a large, modern retail shopping center in Portland, Oregon. Lloyd Center embraces altogether about 50 acres, including some 20 acres of open and covered parking facilities which accommodate more than 1,000 automobiles. It has a perimeter of almost one and one-half miles, bounded by four public streets. It is crossed in varying degrees by several other public streets, all of which have adjacent public sidewalks. Lloyd owns all land and buildings within the Center, except these public streets and sidewalks. There are some 60 commercial tenants, including small shops and several major department stores.

The Center embodies a relatively new concept in shopping center design. The stores are all located within a single large, multi-level building complex sometimes referred to as the "Mall." Within this complex, in addition to the stores, there are parking facilities, malls, private sidewalks, stairways, escalators, gardens, an auditorium, and a skating rink. Some of the stores open directly on the outside public sidewalks, but most open on the interior privately owned malls. Some stores open on both. There are no public streets or public sidewalks within the building complex, which is enclosed and entirely covered except for the landscaped portions of some of the interior malls.

The distribution of the handbills occurred in the malls. They are a distinctive feature of the Center, serving both utilitarian and esthetic functions. Essentially, they are private, interior promenades with 10-foot sidewalks serving the stores, and with a center strip 30 feet wide in which flowers and shrubs are planted, and statuary, fountains, benches, and other amenities are located. There is no vehicular traffic on the malls.

The Center had been in operation for some eight years when this litigation commenced. Throughout this period it had a policy, strictly enforced, against the distribution of handbills within the building complex and its malls. On November 14, 1968, the respondents in this case distributed within the Center handbill invitations to a meeting of the "Resistance Community" to protest the draft and the Vietnam war. The distribution, made in several different places on the mall walkways by five young people, was quiet and orderly, and there was no littering. There was a complaint from one customer. Security guards informed the respondents that they were trespassing and would be arrested unless they stopped distributing the handbills within the Center.

Logan Valley was decided on the basis of its factual situation, and the facts in this case are significantly different. The holding in *Logan Valley* was not dependent upon the suggestion that the privately owned streets and sidewalks of a business district or a shopping center are the equivalent, for First Amendment purposes, of municipally owned streets and sidewalks. No such expansive reading of the opinion of the Court is necessary or appropriate. The opinion was carefully phrased to limit its holding to the picketing involved, where the picketing was "directly related in its purpose to the use to which the shopping center property was being put," and where the store was located in the center of a large private enclave with the consequence that no other reasonable opportunities for the pickets to convey their message to their intended audience were available. Neither of these elements is present in the case now before the Court.

The handbilling by respondents in the malls of Lloyd Center had no relation to any purpose for which the center was built and being used. The message sought to be conveyed by respondents was directed to all members of the public, not solely to patrons of Lloyd Center or of any of its operations. Respondents could have distributed these handbills on any public street, on any public sidewalk, in any public park, or in any public building in the city of Portland.

A further fact, distinguishing the present case from *Logan Valley*, is that the Union pickets in that case would have been deprived of all reasonable opportunity to convey their message to patrons of the Weis store had they been denied access to the shopping center. The situation at Lloyd Center was notably different. The central building complex was surrounded by public sidewalks, totaling 66 linear blocks. All persons who enter or leave the private areas within the complex must cross public streets and sidewalks, either on foot or in automobiles. When moving to and from the privately owned parking lots, automobiles are required by law to come to a complete stop. Handbills may be distributed conveniently to pedestrians, and also to occupants of automobiles, from these public sidewalks and streets. Indeed, respondents moved to these public areas and continued distribution of their handbills after being requested to leave the interior malls. It would be an unwarranted infringement of property rights to require them to yield to the exercise of First Amendment rights under circumstances where adequate alternative avenues of communication exist. Such an accommodation would diminish property rights without significantly enhancing the asserted right of free speech. In ordering this accommodation the courts below erred in their interpretation of this Court's decisions in *Marsh* and *Logan Valley*.

The basic issue in this case is whether respondents, in the exercise of asserted First Amendment rights, may distribute handbills on Lloyd's private property contrary to its wishes and contrary to a policy enforced against all handbilling. In addressing this issue, it must be remembered that the First and Fourteenth Amendments safeguard the rights of free speech and assembly by limitations on state action, not on action by the owner of private property used nondiscriminatorily for private purposes only. Nor does property lose its private character merely because the public is generally invited to use it for designated purposes. Few would argue that a free-standing store, with abutting parking space for customers, assumes significant public attributes merely because the public is invited to shop there. Nor is size alone the controlling factor. The essentially private character of a store and its privately owned abutting property does not change by virtue of being large or clustered with other stores in a modern shopping center. We hold that there has been no such dedication of Lloyd's privately owned and operated shopping center to public use as to entitle respondents to exercise therein the asserted First Amendment rights.

HUDGENS v. NATIONAL LABOR RELATIONS BOARD

424 U.S. 507 (1976)

Justice STEWART delivered the opinion of the Court.

A group of labor union members who engaged in peaceful primary picketing within the confines of a privately owned shopping center were threatened by an agent of the owner with arrest for criminal trespass if they did not depart. The petitioner, Scott Hudgens, is the owner of the North DeKalb Shopping Center, located in suburban Atlanta, Ga. The center consists of a single large building with an enclosed mall. Surrounding the building is a parking area which can accommodate 2,640 automobiles. The shopping center houses 60 retail stores leased to various businesses. One of the lessees is the Butler Shoe Co. Most of the stores, including Butler's, can be entered only from the interior mall.

In January 1971, warehouse employees of the Butler Shoe Co. went on strike to protest the company's failure to agree to demands made by their union in contract negotiations. The strikers decided to picket not only Butler's warehouse but its nine retail stores in the Atlanta area as well, including the store in the North DeKalb Shopping Center. On January 22, 1971, four of the striking warehouse employees entered the center's enclosed mall carrying placards which read: "Butler Shoe Warehouse on Strike, AFL-CIO, Local 315." The general manager of the shopping center informed the employees that they could not picket within the mall or on the parking lot and threatened them with arrest if they did not leave. The employees departed but returned a short time later and began picketing in an area of the mall immediately adjacent to the entrances of the Butler store. After the picketing had continued for approximately 30 minutes, the shopping center manager again informed the pickets that if they did not leave they would be arrested for trespassing. The pickets departed.

It is, of course, a commonplace that the constitutional guarantee of free speech is a guarantee only against abridgment by government, federal or state. Thus, while statutory or common law may in some situations extend protection or provide redress against a private corporation or person who seeks to abridge the free expression of others, no such protection or redress is provided by the Constitution itself. This elementary proposition is little more than a truism.

It matters not that some Members of the Court may continue to believe that the *Logan Valley* case was rightly decided. Our institutional duty is to follow until changed the law as it now is, not as some Members of the Court might wish it to be. And in the performance of that duty we make clear now, if it was not clear before, that the rationale of *Logan Valley* did not survive the Court's decision in the *Lloyd* case. [T]he ultimate holding in *Lloyd* amounted to a total rejection of the holding in *Logan Valley*.

If a large self-contained shopping center is the functional equivalent of a municipality, as *Logan Valley* held, then the First and Fourteenth Amendments would not permit control of speech within such a center to depend upon the speech's content. For while a municipality may constitutionally impose reasonable time, place, and manner regulations on the use of its streets and sidewalks for First Amendment purposes, and may even forbid altogether such use of some of its facilities, what a municipality may not do under the First and Fourteenth Amendments is to discriminate in the regulation of expression on the basis of the content of that expression. "[A]bove all else, the First Amendment means that government has no power to restrict expression because of its message, its ideas, its subject matter, or its content." Police Dept. of Chicago v. Mosley. It conversely follows, therefore, that if the respondents in the *Lloyd* case did not have a First Amendment right to enter that shopping center to distribute handbills concerning Vietnam, then the pickets in the present case did not have a First Amendment right to enter this shopping center for the purpose of advertising their strike against the Butler Shoe Co. We conclude, in short, that under the present state of the law the constitutional guarantee of free expression has no part to play in a case such as this.

b. The Entanglement Exception

The other major exception to the state action doctrine is termed the "entanglement exception." Under this exception, the Constitution applies if the government affirmatively authorizes, encourages, or facilitates private conduct that violates the Constitution. Either the government must cease its involvement with the private actor or the private entity must comply with the Constitution.

The key question, then, is what degree of government involvement is sufficient to make the Constitution applicable? What types of government encouragement are sufficient for state action? Unfortunately, the entanglement exception cases are even more inconsistent than those concerning the public function exception.

The entanglement exception cases have arisen primarily in four areas: judicial and law enforcement actions, government licensing and regulation, government subsidies, and voter initiatives permitting discrimination. These categories are admittedly arbitrary in that many cases involve all or most of these government activities, just as cases often involve both the public functions and the entanglement exception. Nonetheless, the categories at least provide useful groupings for considering the cases.

JUDICIAL AND LAW ENFORCEMENT ACTIONS

SHELLEY v. KRAEMER
334 U.S. 1 (1948)

Chief Justice VINSON delivered the opinion of the Court.

These cases present for our consideration questions relating to the validity of court enforcement of private agreements, generally described as restrictive covenants, which have as their purpose the exclusion of persons of designated race or color.

On February 16, 1911, thirty out of a total of thirty-nine owners of property fronting both sides of Labadie Avenue between Taylor Avenue and Cora Avenue in the city of St. Louis, signed an agreement, which was subsequently recorded, providing in part: . . . "the said property is hereby restricted to the use and occupancy for the term of Fifty (50) years from this date, so that it shall be a condition all the time and whether recited and referred to as [sic] not in subsequent conveyances and shall attach to the land, as a condition precedent to the sale of the same, that hereafter no part of said property or any portion thereof shall be, for said term of Fifty-years, occupied by any person not of the Caucasian race, it being intended hereby to restrict the use of said property for said period of time against the occupancy as owners or tenants of any portion of said property for resident or other purpose by people of the Negro or Mongolian Race."

The entire district described in the agreement included fifty-seven parcels of land. The thirty owners who signed the agreement held title to forty-seven parcels, including the particular parcel involved in this case. At the time the agreement was signed, five of the parcels in the district were owned by Negroes. One of those had been occupied by Negro families since 1882, nearly thirty years before the restrictive agreement was executed.

On August 11, 1945, pursuant to a contract of sale, petitioners Shelley, who are Negroes, for valuable consideration received from one Fitzgerald a warranty deed to the parcel in question. The trial court found that petitioners had no actual knowledge of the restrictive agreement at the time of the purchase. On October 9, 1945, respondents, as owners of other property subject to the terms of the restrictive covenant, brought suit in Circuit Court of the city of St. Louis praying that petitioners Shelley be restrained from taking possession of the property and that judgment be entered divesting title out of petitioners Shelley and revesting title in the immediate grantor or in such other person as the court should direct.

It cannot be doubted that among the civil rights intended to be protected from discriminatory state action by the Fourteenth Amendment are the rights to acquire, enjoy, own and dispose of property. Equality in the enjoyment of property rights was regarded by the framers of that Amendment as an essential pre-condition to the realization of other basic civil rights and liberties which the Amendment was intended to guarantee. It is clear that restrictions on the right of occupancy of the sort sought to be created by the private agreements in these cases could not be squared with the requirements of the Fourteenth Amendment if imposed by state statute or local ordinance.

But the present cases do not involve action by state legislatures or city councils. Here the particular patterns of discrimination and the areas in which the restrictions are to operate, are determined, in the first instance, by the terms of agreements among private individuals. Participation of the State consists in the enforcement of the restrictions so defined. The crucial issue with which we are here confronted is whether this distinction removes these cases from the operation of the prohibitory provisions of the Fourteenth Amendment.

Since the decision of this Court in the Civil Rights Cases (1883), the principle has become firmly embedded in our constitutional law that the action inhibited by the first section of the Fourteenth Amendment is only such action as may fairly be said to be that of the States. That Amendment erects no shield against merely private conduct, however discriminatory or wrongful.

But here there was more. These are cases in which the purposes of the agreements were secured only by judicial enforcement by state courts of the restrictive terms of the agreements. The respondents urge that judicial enforcement of private agreements does not amount to state action; or, in any event, the participation of the State is so attenuated in character as not to amount to state action within the meaning of the Fourteenth Amendment.

That the action of state courts and of judicial officers in their official capacities is to be regarded as action of the State within the meaning of the Fourteenth Amendment, is a proposition which has long been established by decisions of this Court. That principle was given expression in the earliest cases involving the construction of the terms of the Fourteenth Amendment. Thus, in Commonwealth of Virginia v. Rives (1880) this Court stated: "It is doubtless true that a

State may act through different agencies, — either by its legislative, its executive, or its judicial authorities; and the prohibitions of the amendment extend to all action of the State denying equal protection of the laws, whether it be action by one of these agencies or by another." Similar expressions, giving specific recognition to the fact that judicial action is to be regarded as action on the State for the purposes of the Fourteenth Amendment, are to be found in numerous cases which have been more recently decided.

But the examples of state judicial action which have been held by this Court to violate the Amendment's commands are not restricted to situations in which the judicial proceedings were found in some manner to be procedurally unfair. It has been recognized that the action of state courts in enforcing a substantive common-law rule formulated by those courts, may result in the denial of rights guaranteed by the Fourteenth Amendment, even though the judicial proceedings in such cases may have been in complete accord with the most rigorous conceptions of procedural due process.

The short of the matter is that from the time of the adoption of the Fourteenth Amendment until the present, it has been the consistent ruling of this Court that the action of the States to which the Amendment has reference, includes action of state courts and state judicial officials. Although, in construing the terms of the Fourteenth Amendment, differences have from time to time been expressed as to whether particular types of state action may be said to offend the Amendment's prohibitory provisions, it has never been suggested that state court action is immunized from the operation of those provisions simply because the act is that of the judicial branch of the state government.

Against this background of judicial construction, extending over a period of some three-quarters of a century, we are called upon to consider whether enforcement by state courts of the restrictive agreements in these cases may be deemed to be the acts of those States; and, if so, whether that action has denied these petitioners the equal protection of the laws which the Amendment was intended to insure. We have no doubt that there has been state action in these cases in the full and complete sense of the phrase.

These are not cases, as has been suggested, in which the States have merely abstained from action, leaving private individuals free to impose such discriminations as they see fit. Rather, these are cases in which the States have made available to such individuals the full coercive power of government to deny to petitioners, on the grounds of race or color, the enjoyment of property rights in premises which petitioners are willing and financially able to acquire and which the grantors are willing to sell. The difference between judicial enforcement and nonenforcement of the restrictive covenants is the difference to petitioners between being denied rights of property available to other members of the community and being accorded full enjoyment of those rights on an equal footing. We hold that in granting judicial enforcement of the restrictive agreements in these cases, the States have denied petitioners the equal protection of the laws and that, therefore, the action of the state courts cannot stand.

Although *Shelley* long has been controversial,[39] there seems little doubt that judges are government actors and that judicial remedies are state action. It was also not controversial when the Supreme Court held in New York Times Co. v. Sullivan, 376 U.S. 254 (1964), 15 years after *Shelley,* that the common law of libel is state action that must comply with the First Amendment.[40] The Court said that although the defamation action was a "civil lawsuit between private parties, the Alabama courts have applied a state rule of law which [allegedly] . . . impose[s] invalid restrictions on their constitutional freedoms. . . . It matters not that the law has been applied in a civil action and that it is common law only. . . . The test is not the form in which state power has been applied but, whatever the form, whether such power has in fact been exercised."

From this perspective, *Shelley* seems unremarkable: A branch of the government, the judiciary, was enforcing the law of the state, albeit the common law, to enforce racial discrimination by enforcing the discriminatory covenants.

Yet *Shelley* remains controversial because ultimately everything can be made state action under it. If any decision by a state court represents state action, then ultimately all private actions must comply with the Constitution. Anyone who believes that his or her rights have been violated can sue in state court. If the court dismisses the case because the state law does not forbid the violation, there is state action sustaining the infringement of the right, just as there would have been state action had the court dismissed the case in *Shelley.* All private violations of rights exist because state law allows them. It is difficult to imagine anything that cannot potentially be transformed into state action under this reasoning.

The Court, of course, never has taken *Shelley* this far; nor has it articulated any clear limiting principles. In fact, the Court only rarely has applied *Shelley* as a basis for finding state action.[41] There are two major areas in which the Court has considered judicial enforcement as state action: use of courts for prejudgment attachment and the use of peremptory challenges at trials.

Example: Prejudgment Attachment

LUGAR v. EDMONDSON OIL CO.

457 U.S. 922 (1982)

Justice WHITE delivered the opinion of the Court.

In 1977, petitioner, a lessee-operator of a truckstop in Virginia, was indebted to his supplier, Edmondson Oil Co., Inc. Edmondson sued on the debt in Virginia state court. Ancillary to that action and pursuant to state law, Edmondson sought prejudgment attachment of certain of petitioner's property. The

---

39. *See, e.g.,* Herbert Wechsler, *Toward Neutral Principles of Constitutional Law,* 73 Harv. L. Rev. 1, 29 (1959) (criticizing *Shelley*).

40. This is discussed in detail in Chapter 9.

41. In Pennsylvania v. Board of Directors of City Trust of the City of Philadelphia, 353 U.S. 230 (1957), the Court, without expressly citing *Shelley,* found that there was state action when public officials ran a private trust, for a school for orphans, in a racially discriminatory manner. *See also* Evans v. Newton, 382 U.S. 296 (1966) (finding state action when the city delegated running a private park, segregated pursuant to the terms of a will, to a private entity that racially discriminated), presented earlier.

procedure required only that Edmondson allege, in an ex parte petition, a belief that petitioner was disposing of or might dispose of his property in order to defeat his creditors. Acting upon that petition, a Clerk of the state court issued a writ of attachment, which was then executed by the County Sheriff. This effectively sequestered petitioner's property, although it was left in his possession. Pursuant to the statute, a hearing on the propriety of the attachment and levy was later conducted. Thirty-four days after the levy, a state trial judge ordered the attachment dismissed because Edmondson had failed to establish the statutory grounds for attachment alleged in the petition.

Petitioner subsequently brought this action under 42 U.S.C. §1983 against Edmondson and its president. His complaint alleged that in attaching his property respondents had acted jointly with the State to deprive him of his property without due process of law.

If a defendant debtor in state-court debt collection proceedings can successfully challenge, on federal due process grounds, the plaintiff creditor's resort to the procedures authorized by a state statute, it is difficult to understand why that same behavior by the state-court plaintiff should not provide a cause of action under §1983. If the creditor-plaintiff violates the debtor-defendant's due process rights by seizing his property in accordance with statutory procedures, there is little or no reason to deny to the latter a cause of action under the federal statute, §1983, designed to provide judicial redress for just such constitutional violations.

As a matter of substantive constitutional law the state-action requirement reflects judicial recognition of the fact that most rights secured by the Constitution are protected only against infringement by governments. Careful adherence to the "state action" requirement preserves an area of individual freedom by limiting the reach of federal law and federal judicial power. It also avoids imposing on the State, its agencies or officials, responsibility for conduct for which they cannot fairly be blamed. A major consequence is to require the courts to respect the limits of their own power as directed against state governments and private interests. Whether this is good or bad policy, it is a fundamental fact of our political order.

Our cases have accordingly insisted that the conduct allegedly causing the deprivation of a federal right be fairly attributable to the State. These cases reflect a two-part approach to this question of "fair attribution." First, the deprivation must be caused by the exercise of some right or privilege created by the State or by a rule of conduct imposed by the state or by a person for whom the State is responsible. Second, the party charged with the deprivation must be a person who may fairly be said to be a state actor. This may be because he is a state official, because he has acted together with or has obtained significant aid from state officials, or because his conduct is otherwise chargeable to the State. Without a limit such as this, private parties could face constitutional litigation whenever they seek to rely on some state rule governing their interactions with the community surrounding them.

Turning to this case, the first question is whether the claimed deprivation has resulted from the exercise of a right or privilege having its source in state authority. The second question is whether, under the facts of this case, respondents, who are private parties, may be appropriately characterized as "state actors." While private misuse of a state statute does not describe conduct that can be attributed to the State, the procedural scheme created by the statute obviously is the product of state action. This is subject to constitutional restraints and properly may be addressed in a §1983 action, if the second element of the state-action requirement is met as well. [W]e have consistently held that a private party's joint participation with state officials in the seizure of disputed property is sufficient to characterize that party as a "state actor" for purposes of the Fourteenth Amendment.

The Court of Appeals erred in holding that in this context "joint participation" required something more than invoking the aid of state officials to take advantage of state-created attachment procedures. That holding is contrary to the conclusions we have reached as to the applicability of due process standards to such procedures. Whatever may be true in other contexts, this is sufficient when the State has created a system whereby state officials will attach property on the ex parte application of one party to a private dispute. In summary, petitioner was deprived of his property through state action; respondents were, therefore, acting under color of state law in participating in that deprivation.

Lugar can be contrasted to the Supreme Court's earlier decision in Flagg Brothers v. Brooks, 436 U.S. 149 (1978). In *Flagg Brothers*, the Supreme Court held that a private creditor's self-help repossession did not constitute state action and thus due process was not required prior to the sale of her belongings. After an individual was evicted from her home, the sheriff arranged for storage of her possessions at a warehouse. The warehouse demanded that she pay the storage fees or it would sell her property. The customer claimed a right to due process before the sale, but the Supreme Court concluded that since the warehouse company was privately owned the Constitution did not apply.

The customer's primary contention was that the State of New York "delegated" to the company "a power 'traditionally exclusively reserved to the State.'" The customer argued that resolving disputes is a traditional function of government and that the government had delegated this task to the creditor by giving it the authority to sell the goods to pay the debt. The Supreme Court expressly rejected this argument and said that there were many ways in which the dispute could have been resolved: The debtor could have sought a waiver of the creditor's rights to sell her goods, the debtor could have sought to replevy her goods under state law, and the debtor had a statutory damages action available for violations of the law. The Supreme Court said that in light of all these options, it could not be said that the government delegated to the creditor "an exclusive prerogative of the sovereign."

The key difference between *Lugar* and *Flagg Brothers* was the direct involvement of a state officer, the sheriff, in the former case, while the latter was entirely private self-help. Yet, in both cases, state law provided the procedures for the debtors' action. In *Lugar*, state law provided the procedure for prejudgment attachment; in *Flagg Brothers*, state law provided for the self-help action. In fact, in *Flagg Brothers* involvement of the sheriff was unnecessary precisely because the state's law allowed the repossession action without assistance of the sheriff.

Example: Peremptory Challenges

The other major area where the Court has considered court involvement to be state action concerns the exercise of peremptory challenges. Peremptory challenges are the ability of a litigant to excuse prospective jurors without showing cause.

In Batson v. Kentucky, 476 U.S. 79 (1986), the Supreme Court held that equal protection prohibits prosecutors from using peremptory challenges in a discriminatory fashion in criminal cases. The issue then arose as to whether *Batson* should be applied when private litigants — such as parties in private civil litigation or even criminal defendants — exercise peremptory challenges in a discriminatory fashion.

EDMONSON v. LEESVILLE CONCRETE CO.

500 U.S. 614 (1991)

Justice KENNEDY delivered the opinion of the Court.

We must decide in the case before us whether a private litigant in a civil case may use peremptory challenges to exclude jurors on account of their race. Recognizing the impropriety of racial bias in the courtroom, we hold the race-based exclusion violates the equal protection rights of the challenged jurors.

Thaddeus Donald Edmonson, a construction worker, was injured in a jobsite accident at Fort Polk, Louisiana, a federal enclave. Edmonson sued Leesville Concrete Company for negligence in the United States District Court for the Western District of Louisiana, claiming that a Leesville employee permitted one of the company's trucks to roll backward and pin him against some construction equipment. Edmonson invoked his Seventh Amendment right to a trial by jury.

During voir dire, Leesville used two of its three peremptory challenges authorized by statute to remove black persons from the prospective jury. Citing our decision in Batson v. Kentucky (1986), Edmonson, who is himself black, requested that the District Court require Leesville to articulate a race-neutral explanation for striking the two jurors. The District Court denied the request on the ground that *Batson* does not apply in civil proceedings. As empaneled, the jury included 11 white persons and 1 black person. The jury rendered a verdict for Edmonson, assessing his total damages at $90,000. It also attributed 80% of the fault to Edmonson's contributory negligence, however, and awarded him the sum of $18,000.

In Powers v. Ohio (1991), we held that a criminal defendant, regardless of his or her race, may object to a prosecutor's race-based exclusion of persons from the petit jury. [W]e made clear that a prosecutor's race-based peremptory challenge violates the equal protection rights of those excluded from jury service.

[D]iscrimination on the basis of race in selecting a jury in a civil proceeding harms the excluded juror no less than discrimination in a criminal trial. In either case, race is the sole reason for denying the excluded venireperson the honor and privilege of participating in our system of justice.

That an act violates the Constitution when committed by a government official, however, does not answer the question whether the same act offends constitutional guarantees if committed by a private litigant or his attorney. The Constitution's protections of individual liberty and equal protection apply in general only to action by the government.

We begin our discussion within the framework for state-action analysis set forth in *Lugar*. There we considered the state-action question in the context of a due process challenge to a State's procedure allowing private parties to obtain prejudgment attachments. We asked first whether the claimed constitutional deprivation resulted from the exercise of a right or privilege having its source in state authority, and second, whether the private party charged with the deprivation could be described in all fairness as a state actor.

There can be no question that the first part of the *Lugar* inquiry is satisfied here. By their very nature, peremptory challenges have no significance outside a court of law. Their sole purpose is to permit litigants to assist the government in the selection of an impartial trier of fact. While we have recognized the value of peremptory challenges in this regard, particularly in the criminal context, there is no constitutional obligation to allow them. Peremptory challenges are permitted only when the government, by statute or decisional law, deems it appropriate to allow parties to exclude a given number of persons who otherwise would satisfy the requirements for service on the petit jury. Legislative authorizations, as well as limitations, for the use of peremptory challenges date as far back as the founding of the Republic; and the common-law origins of peremptories predate that.

Today in most jurisdictions, statutes or rules make a limited number of peremptory challenges available to parties in both civil and criminal proceedings. In the case before us, the challenges were exercised under a federal statute that provides, "In civil cases, each party shall be entitled to three peremptory challenges." 28 U.S.C. §1870. Without this authorization, granted by an Act of Congress itself, Leesville would not have been able to engage in the alleged discriminatory acts.

Given that the statutory authorization for the challenges exercised in this case is clear, the remainder of our state-action analysis centers around the second part of the *Lugar* test, whether a private litigant in all fairness must be deemed a government actor in the use of peremptory challenges. Our precedents establish that, in determining whether a particular action or course of conduct is governmental in character, it is relevant to examine the following: the extent to which the actor relies on governmental assistance and benefits, whether the actor is performing a traditional governmental function, and whether the injury caused is aggravated in a unique way by the incidents of governmental authority. Based on our application of these three principles to the circumstances here, we hold that the exercise of peremptory challenges by the defendant in the District Court was pursuant to a course of state action.

Although private use of state-sanctioned private remedies or procedures does not rise, by itself, to the level of state action, our cases have found state action when private parties make extensive use of state procedures with "the overt, significant assistance of state officials." It cannot be disputed that, without the overt, significant participation of the government, the peremptory challenge system, as well as the jury trial system of which it is a part, simply could not exist.

A private party could not exercise its peremptory challenges absent the overt, significant assistance of the court. The government summons jurors, constrains their freedom of movement, and subjects them to public scrutiny and examination. The party who exercises a challenge invokes the formal authority of the court, which must discharge the prospective juror, thus effecting the "final and practical denial" of the excluded individual's opportunity to serve on the petit jury. Without the direct and indispensable participation of the judge, who beyond all question is a state actor, the peremptory challenge system would serve no purpose. By enforcing a discriminatory peremptory challenge, the court "has not only made itself a party to the [biased act], but has elected to place its power, property and prestige behind the [alleged] discrimination." Burton v. Wilmington Parking Authority (1961). In so doing, the government has "create[d] the legal framework governing the [challenged] conduct," National Collegiate Athletic Assn. v. Tarkanian (1989), and in a significant way has involved itself with invidious discrimination.

In Georgia v. McCollum, 505 U.S. 42 (1992), the Court considered "whether a criminal defendant's exercise of a peremptory challenge constitutes state action for purposes of the Equal Protection Clause." If any one is the antithesis of the government, it is a criminal defendant who is being prosecuted. Yet, for purposes of jury selection, the Court found that a criminal defendant is a state actor in exercising peremptory challenges. The Court followed exactly the same reasoning as in *Edmonson*: Laws create peremptory challenges and jury selection is a government function accomplished through the power of the state and overseen by a judge.

GOVERNMENT REGULATION

The Court also has considered the entanglement exception in instances when the government licenses or regulates an activity. In general, government licensing or regulating is insufficient for a finding of state action, unless there is other government encouraging or facilitating of unconstitutional conduct. Yet here, too, the cases are not easily reconciled.

Burton v. Wilmington Parking Authority, presented below, is the key case where government licensing and regulation was deemed sufficient for state action. The subsequent case, Moose Lodge v. Irvis, distinguishes and narrows *Burton*. The underlying question is whether there is a meaningful distinction among these cases in terms of the degree of government involvement.

BURTON v. WILMINGTON PARKING AUTHORITY

365 U.S. 715 (1961)

Justice CLARK delivered the opinion of the Court.

In this action for declaratory and injunctive relief it is admitted that the Eagle Coffee Shoppe, Inc., a restaurant located within an off-street automobile parking building in Wilmington, Delaware, has refused to serve appellant food or drink solely because he is a Negro. The parking building is owned and operated by the Wilmington Parking Authority, an agency of the State of Delaware, and the restaurant is the Authority's lessee. On the merits we have concluded that the exclusion of appellant under the circumstances shown to be present here was discriminatory state action in violation of the Equal Protection Clause of the Fourteenth Amendment.

The Authority was created by the City of Wilmington pursuant to the Delaware Code. It is "a public body corporate and politic, exercising public powers of the State as an agency thereof." Its statutory purpose is to provide adequate parking facilities for the convenience of the public and thereby relieve the "parking crisis, which threatens the welfare of the community." To this end the Authority is granted wide powers including that of constructing or acquiring by lease, purchase or condemnation, lands and facilities, and that of leasing "portions of any of its garage buildings or structures for commercial uses by the lessee, where, in the opinion of the Authority, such leasing is necessary and feasible for the financing and operation of such facilities."

The first project undertaken by the Authority was the erection of a parking facility on Ninth Street in downtown Wilmington. Before it began actual construction of the facility, the Authority was advised by its retained experts that the anticipated revenue from the parking of cars and proceeds from sale of its bonds would not be sufficient to finance the construction costs of the facility. Moreover, the bonds were not expected to be marketable if payable solely out of parking revenues. To secure additional capital needed for its "debt-service" requirements, and thereby to make bond financing practicable, the Authority decided it was necessary to enter long-term leases with responsible tenants for commercial use of some of the space available in the projected "garage building." The public was invited to bid for these leases. In April 1957 such a private lease, for 20 years and renewable for another 10 years, was made with Eagle Coffee Shoppe, Inc., for use as a "restaurant, dining room, banquet hall, cocktail lounge and bar and for no other use and purpose."

Other portions of the structure were leased to other tenants, including a bookstore, a retail jeweler, and a food store. Upon completion of the building, the Authority located at appropriate places thereon official signs indicating the public character of the building, and flew from mastheads on the roof both the state and national flags.

In August 1958 appellant parked his car in the building and walked around to enter the restaurant by its front door on Ninth Street. Having entered and sought service, he was refused it. Thereafter he filed this declaratory judgment action.

The Civil Rights Cases (1883) "embedded in our constitutional law" the principle "that the action inhibited by the first section (Equal Protection Clause) of the Fourteenth Amendment is only such action as may fairly be said to be that of the States." That Amendment erects no shield against merely private conduct, however discriminatory or wrongful. Only by sifting facts and weighing circumstances can the nonobvious involvement of the State in private conduct be attributed its true significance.

The land and building were publicly owned. As an entity, the building was dedicated to "public uses" in performance of the Authority's "essential governmental functions." The costs of land acquisition, construction, and maintenance are defrayed entirely from donations by the City of Wilmington, from loans and revenue bonds and from the proceeds of rentals and parking services out of which the loans and bonds were payable. Upkeep and maintenance of the building, including necessary repairs, were responsibilities of the Authority and were payable out of public funds. It cannot be doubted that the peculiar relationship of the restaurant to the parking facility in which it is located confers on each an incidental variety of mutual benefits. Guests of the restaurant are afforded a convenient place to park their automobiles, even if they cannot enter the restaurant directly from the parking area. Similarly, its convenience for diners may well provide additional demand for the Authority's parking facilities. Neither can it be ignored, especially in view of Eagle's affirmative allegation that for it to serve Negroes would injure its business, that profits earned by discrimination not only contribute to, but also are indispensable elements in, the financial success of a governmental agency.

Addition of all these activities, obligations and responsibilities of the Authority, the benefits mutually conferred, together with the obvious fact that the restaurant is operated as an integral part of a public building devoted to a public parking service, indicates that degree of state participation and involvement in discriminatory action which it was the design of the Fourteenth Amendment to condemn. It is irony amounting to grave injustice that in one part of a single building, erected and maintained with public funds by an agency of the State to serve a public purpose, all persons have equal rights, while in another portion, also serving the public, a Negro is a second-class citizen, offensive because of his race, without rights and unentitled to service, but at the same time fully enjoys equal access to nearby restaurants in wholly privately owned buildings.

[I]n its lease with Eagle the Authority could have affirmatively required Eagle to discharge the responsibilities under the Fourteenth Amendment imposed upon the private enterprise as a consequence of state participation. But no State may effectively abdicate its responsibilities by either ignoring them or by merely failing to discharge them whatever the motive may be. By its inaction, the Authority, and through it the State, has not only made itself a party to the refusal of service, but has elected to place its power, property and prestige behind the admitted discrimination. The State has so far insinuated itself into a position of interdependence with Eagle that it must be recognized as a joint participant in the challenged activity, which, on that account, cannot be considered to have been so "purely private" as to fall without the scope of the Fourteenth Amendment.

Specifically defining the limits of our inquiry, what we hold today is that when a State leases public property in the manner and for the purpose shown to have been the case here, the proscriptions of the Fourteenth Amendment must be complied with by the lessee as certainly as though they were binding covenants written into the agreement itself.

MOOSE LODGE NO. 107 v. IRVIS

407 U.S. 163 (1972)

Justice REHNQUIST delivered the opinion of the Court.

Appellee Irvis, a Negro (hereafter appellee), was refused service by appellant Moose Lodge, a local branch of the national fraternal organization located in

Harrisburg, Pennsylvania. Appellee then brought this action under 42 U.S.C. §1983 for injunctive relief in the United States District Court for the Middle District of Pennsylvania. He claimed that because the Pennsylvania liquor board had issued appellant Moose Lodge a private club license that authorized the sale of alcoholic beverages on its premises, the refusal of service to him was "state action" for the purposes of the Equal Protection Clause of the Fourteenth Amendment. He named both Moose Lodge and the Pennsylvania Liquor Authority as defendants, seeking injunctive relief that would have required the defendant liquor board to revoke Moose Lodge's license so long as it continued its discriminatory practices.

Moose Lodge is a private club in the ordinary meaning of that term. It is a local chapter of a national fraternal organization having well-defined requirements for membership. It conducts all of its activities in a building that is owned by it. It is not publicly funded. Only members and guests are permitted in any lodge of the order; one may become a guest only by invitation of a member or upon invitation of the house committee.

Appellee, while conceding the right of private clubs to choose members upon a discriminatory basis, asserts that the licensing of Moose Lodge to serve liquor by the Pennsylvania Liquor Control Board amounts to such state involvement with the club's activities as to make its discriminatory practices forbidden by the Equal Protection Clause of the Fourteenth Amendment.

The Court has never held, of course, that discrimination by an otherwise private entity would be violative of the Equal Protection Clause if the private entity receives any sort of benefit or service at all from the State, or if it is subject to state regulation in any degree whatever. Since state-furnished services include such necessities of life as electricity, water, and police and fire protection, such a holding would utterly emasculate the distinction between private as distinguished from state conduct set forth in The Civil Rights Cases, and adhered to in subsequent decisions. Our holdings indicate that where the impetus for the discrimination is private, the State must have "significantly involved itself with invidious discriminations," Reitman v. Mulkey (1967), in order for the discriminatory action to fall within the ambit of the constitutional prohibition.

Our prior decisions dealing with discriminatory refusal of service in public eating places are significantly different factually from the case now before us.

Here there is nothing approaching the symbiotic relationship between lessor and lessee that was present in *Burton*, where the private lessee obtained the benefit of locating in a building owned by the state-created parking authority, and the parking authority was enabled to carry out its primary public purpose of furnishing parking space by advantageously leasing portions of the building constructed for that purpose to commercial lessees such as the owner of the Eagle Restaurant. Unlike *Burton*, the Moose Lodge building is located on land owned by it, not by any public authority. Far from apparently holding itself out as a place of public accommodation, Moose Lodge quite ostentatiously proclaims the fact that it is not open to the public at large. Nor is it located and operated in such surroundings that although private in name, it discharges a function or performs a service that would otherwise in all likelihood be performed by the State. In short, while Eagle was a public restaurant in a public building, Moose Lodge is a private social club in a private building.

With the exception hereafter noted, the Pennsylvania Liquor Control Board plays absolutely no part in establishing or enforcing the membership or guest policies of the club that it licenses to serve liquor. There is no suggestion in this record that Pennsylvania law, either as written or as applied, discriminates against minority groups either in their right to apply for club licenses themselves or in their right to purchase and be served liquor in places of public accommodation.

However detailed the regulation may be in some particulars, it cannot be said to in any way foster or encourage racial discrimination. Nor can it be said to make the State in any realistic sense a partner or even a joint venturer in the club's enterprise. We therefore hold that the operation of the regulatory scheme enforced by the Pennsylvania Liquor Control Board does not sufficiently implicate the State in the discriminatory guest policies of Moose Lodge to make the latter "state action" within the ambit of the Equal Protection Clause of the Fourteenth Amendment.

Justice DOUGLAS, with whom Justice MARSHALL joins, dissenting.

[T]he fact that a private club gets some kind of permit from the State or municipality does not make it ipso facto a public enterprise or undertaking, any more than the grant to a householder of a permit to operate an incinerator puts the householder in the public domain. We must, therefore, examine whether there are special circumstances involved in the Pennsylvania scheme which differentiate the liquor license possessed by Moose Lodge from the incinerator permit.

Pennsylvania has a state store system of alcohol distribution. Resale is permitted by hotels, restaurants, and private clubs which all must obtain licenses from the Liquor Control Board. The scheme of regulation is complete and pervasive; and the state courts have sustained many restrictions on the licensees. Once a license is issued the licensee must comply with many detailed requirements or risk suspension or revocation of the license. Among these requirements is Regulation §113.09 which says: "Every club licensee shall adhere to all of the provisions of its Constitution and By-laws." This regulation means, as applied to Moose Lodge, that it must adhere to the racially discriminatory provision of the Constitution of its Supreme Lodge that "[t]he membership of lodges shall be composed of male persons of the Caucasian or White race above the age of twenty-one years, and not married to someone of any other than the Caucasian or White race, who are of good moral character, physically and mentally normal, who shall profess a belief in a Supreme Being."

[W]e have held that "a State is responsible for the discriminatory act of a private party when the State, by its law, has compelled the act." It is irrelevant whether the law is statutory, or an administrative regulation. And it is irrelevant whether the discriminatory act was instigated by the regulation, or was independent of it. The result, as I see it, is the same as though Pennsylvania had put into its liquor licenses a provision that the license may not be used to dispense liquor to blacks, browns, yellows — or atheists or agnostics. Regulation §113.09 is thus an invidious form of state action.

Were this regulation the only infirmity in Pennsylvania's licensing scheme, I would perhaps agree with the majority that the appropriate relief would be a decree enjoining its enforcement. But there is another flaw in the scheme not so easily cured. Liquor licenses in Pennsylvania, unlike driver's licenses, or marriage licenses, are not freely available to those who meet racially neutral qualifications. There is a complex quota system. What the majority neglects to say is that the quota for Harrisburg, where Moose Lodge No. 107 is located, has been full for many years. No more club licenses may be issued in that city.

This state-enforced scarcity of licenses restricts the ability of blacks to obtain liquor, for liquor is commercially available only at private clubs for a significant portion of each week. Access by blacks to places that serve liquor is further limited by the fact that the state quota is filled. A group desiring to form a nondiscriminatory club which would serve blacks must purchase a license held by an existing club, which can exact a monopoly price for the transfer. The availability of such a license is speculative at best, however, for, as Moose Lodge itself concedes, without a liquor license a fraternal organization would be hard pressed to survive. Thus, the State of Pennsylvania is putting the weight of its liquor license, concededly a valued and important adjunct to a private club, behind racial discrimination.

GOVERNMENT SUBSIDIES

A third type of government entanglement is government financial support. Here, too, there are some cases indicating that this can be used as a basis for finding state action. But later decisions make it highly doubtful that subsidies by themselves, no matter how large, could justify applying the Constitution.

NORWOOD v. HARRISON
413 U.S. 455 (1973)

A three-judge District Court sustained the validity of a Mississippi statutory program under which textbooks are purchased by the State and lent to students in both public and private schools, without reference to whether any participating private school has racially discriminatory policies.

Appellants, who are parents of four schoolchildren in Tunica County, Mississippi, filed a class action on behalf of students throughout Mississippi to enjoin in part the enforcement of the Mississippi textbook lending program. The complaint alleged that certain of the private schools excluded students on the basis of race and that, by supplying textbooks to students attending such private schools, appellees, acting for the State, have provided direct state aid to racially segregated education. It was also alleged that the textbook aid program thereby impeded the process of fully desegregating public schools, in violation of appellants' constitutional rights.

Private schools in Mississippi have experienced a marked growth in recent years. As recently as the 1963-1964 school year, there were only 17 private schools other than Catholic schools; the total enrollment was 2,362 students. In these nonpublic schools 916 students were Negro, and 192 of these were enrolled in special schools for retarded, orphaned, or abandoned children. By September 1970, the number of private non-Catholic schools had increased to 155 with a student population estimated at 42,000, virtually all white. Appellees do not challenge the statement, which is fully documented in appellants' brief, that "the creation and enlargement of these [private] academies occurred simultaneously with major events in the desegregation of public schools. . . ."

This case does not raise any question as to the right of citizens to maintain private schools with admission limited to students of particular national origins, race, or religion or of the authority of a State to allow such schools. See Pierce v. Society of Sisters (1925). The narrow issue before us, rather, is a particular form of tangible assistance the State provides to students in private schools in common with all other students by lending textbooks under the State's 33-year-old program for providing free textbooks to all the children of the State. The program dates back to a 1940 appeal for improved educational facilities by the Governor of Mississippi to the state legislature.

The appellees intimate that the State must provide assistance to private schools equivalent to that which it provides to public schools without regard to whether the private schools discriminate on racial grounds. Clearly, the State need not.

This Court has consistently affirmed decisions enjoining state tuition grants to students attending racially discriminatory private schools. A textbook lending program is not legally distinguishable from the forms of state assistance foreclosed by the prior cases. Free textbooks, like tuition grants directed to private school students, are a form of financial assistance inuring to the benefit of the private schools themselves. An inescapable educational cost for students in both public and private schools is the expense of providing all necessary learning materials. When, as here, that necessary expense is borne by the State, the economic consequence is to give aid to the enterprise; if the school engages in discriminatory practices the State by tangible aid in the form of textbooks thereby gives support to such discrimination. Racial discrimination in state-operated schools is barred by the Constitution and it is also axiomatic that a state may not induce, encourage or promote private persons to accomplish what it is constitutionally forbidden to accomplish.

The recurring theme of appellees' argument is a sympathetic one — that the State's textbook loan program is extended to students who attend racially segregated private schools only because the State sincerely wishes to foster quality education for all Mississippi children, and, to that end, has taken steps to insure that no sub-group of schoolchildren will be deprived of an important educational tool merely because their parents have chosen to enroll them in segregated private schools. We need not assume that the State's textbook aid to private schools has been motivated by other than a sincere interest in the educational welfare of all Mississippi children. But good intentions as to one valid objective do not serve to negate the State's involvement in violation of a constitutional duty. "The existence of a permissible purpose cannot sustain an action that has an impermissible effect." The Equal Protection Clause would be a sterile promise if state involvement in possible private activity could be shielded altogether from constitutional scrutiny simply because its ultimate end was not discrimination but some higher goal. A State's constitutional obligation requires it to steer clear, not only of operating the old dual system of racially segregated schools, but also of giving significant aid to institutions that practice racial or other invidious discrimination.

In Gilmore v. City of Montgomery, Alabama, 417 U.S. 556 (1974), the Supreme Court held that a city could not give racially segregated private schools exclusive use of public recreational facilities. Montgomery, Alabama, allowed segregated private schools to have exclusive possession of football stadiums, baseball diamonds, basketball courts, and tennis courts for athletic contests and other school-sponsored events. The Court found state action because the "city's actions significantly enhanced the attractiveness of segregated private schools, formed in reaction against the federal court school order, by enabling them to offer complete athletic programs."

Norwood and *Gilmore* both involved challenges to state government assistance to segregated private schools in Mississippi and Alabama, states with a long history of school segregation. Outside this context, however, the Court has been unwilling to find government subsidy to be a basis for finding state action. Indeed, the following two more recent cases expressly reject the argument that government subsidy is sufficient for a finding of state action.

RENDELL-BAKER v. KOHN
457 U.S. 830 (1982)

Chief Justice Burger delivered the opinion of the Court.

We granted certiorari to decide whether a private school, whose income is derived primarily from public sources and which is regulated by public authorities, acted under color of state law when it discharged certain employees.

I

Respondent Kohn is the director of the New Perspectives School, a nonprofit institution located on privately owned property in Brookline, Massachusetts. The school was founded as a private institution and is operated by a board of directors, none of whom are public officials or are chosen by public officials. The school specializes in dealing with students who have experienced difficulty completing public high schools; many have drug, alcohol, or behavioral problems, or other special needs. In recent years, nearly all of the students at the school have been referred to it by the Brookline or Boston School Committees, or by the Drug Rehabilitation Division of the Massachusetts Department of Mental Health. The school issues high school diplomas certified by the Brookline School Committee.

When students are referred to the school by Brookline or Boston under Chapter 766 of the Massachusetts Acts of 1972, the School Committees in those cities pay for the students' education. The school also receives funds from a number of other state and federal agencies. In recent years, public funds have accounted for at least 90%, and in one year 99%, of respondent school's operating budget. There were approximately 50 students at the school in those years and none paid tuition.

To be eligible for tuition funding under Chapter 766, the school must comply with a variety of regulations, many of which are common to all schools. The State has issued detailed regulations concerning matters ranging from recordkeeping to student-teacher ratios. Concerning personnel policies, the Chapter 766 regulations require the school to maintain written job descriptions and written statements describing personnel standards and procedures, but they impose few specific requirements. The school is also regulated by Boston and Brookline as a result of its Chapter 766 funding.

Rendell-Baker was discharged by the school in January 1977, and the five other petitioners were discharged in June 1978. Rendell-Baker's discharge resulted from a dispute over the role of a student-staff council in making hiring decisions. A dispute arose when some students presented a petition to the school's board of directors in December 1976, seeking greater responsibilities for the student-staff council. Director Kohn opposed the proposal, but Rendell-Baker supported it and so advised the board. On December 13, Kohn notified the State Committee on Criminal Justice, which funded Rendell-Baker's position, that she intended to dismiss Rendell-Baker and employ someone else. Kohn notified Rendell-Baker of her dismissal in January 1977.

In the spring of 1978, students and staff voiced objections to Kohn's policies. The five petitioners other than Rendell-Baker, who were all teachers at the school, wrote a letter to the board of directors urging Kohn's dismissal. When the board affirmed its confidence in Kohn, students from the school picketed the home of the president of the board. The students were threatened with suspension; a local newspaper then ran a story about the controversy at the school. In response to the story, the five petitioners wrote a letter to the editor in which they stated that they thought the prohibition of picketing was unconstitutional. On the day the letter to the editor appeared, the five teachers told the president of the board that they were forming a union. Kohn discharged the teachers the next day. They brought suit against the school and its directors in December 1978.

Petitioners allege that respondents violated 42 U.S.C. §1983 by discharging them because of their exercise of their First Amendment right of free speech and without the process due them under the Fourteenth Amendment. The core issue presented in this case is not whether petitioners were discharged because of their speech or without adequate procedural protections, but whether the school's action in discharging them can fairly be seen as state action. If the action of the respondent school is not state action, our inquiry ends.

The school is not fundamentally different from many private corporations whose business depends primarily on contracts to build roads, bridges, dams, ships, or submarines for the government. Acts of such private contractors do not become acts of the government by reason of their significant or even total engagement in performing public contracts.

Here the decisions to discharge the petitioners were not compelled or even influenced by any state regulation. Indeed, in contrast to the extensive regulation of the school generally, the various regulators showed relatively little interest in the school's personnel matters. The most intrusive personnel regulation promulgated by the various government agencies was the requirement that the Committee on Criminal Justice had the power to approve persons hired as vocational counselors. Such a regulation is not sufficient to make a decision to discharge, made by private management, state action.

[Petitioners] assert that the school is a state actor [in] that it performs a "public function." However, our holdings have made clear that the relevant question is not simply whether a private group is serving a "public function."

We have held that the question is whether the function performed has been "traditionally the exclusive prerogative of the State." Jackson v. Metropolitan Edison Co. There can be no doubt that the education of maladjusted high school students is a public function, but that is only the beginning of the inquiry. Chapter 766 of the Massachusetts Acts of 1972 demonstrates that the State intends to provide services for such students at public expense. That legislative policy choice in no way makes these services the exclusive province of the State. Indeed, the Court of Appeals noted that until recently the State had not undertaken to provide education for students who could not be served by traditional public schools. That a private entity performs a function which serves the public does not make its acts state action.

Justice MARSHALL, with whom Justice BRENNAN joins, dissenting.

Petitioners in these consolidated cases, former teachers and a counselor at the New Perspectives School in Brookline, Mass., were discharged by the school's administrators when they criticized certain school policies. The Court today holds that their suits must be dismissed because the school did not act "under color" of state law. According to the majority, the decision of the school to discharge petitioners cannot fairly be regarded as a decision of the Commonwealth of Massachusetts. In my view, this holding simply cannot be justified. The State has delegated to the New Perspectives School its statutory duty to educate children with special needs. The school receives almost all of its funds from the State, and is heavily regulated. This nexus between the school and the State is so substantial that the school's action must be considered state action. I therefore dissent.

The decisions of this Court clearly establish that where there is a symbiotic relationship between the State and a privately owned enterprise, so that the State and a privately owned enterprise are participants in a joint venture, the actions of the private enterprise may be attributable to the State. "Conduct that is formally 'private' may become so entwined with governmental policies or so impregnated with a governmental character" that it can be regarded as governmental action. Evans v. Newton.

The New Perspectives School receives virtually all of its funds from state sources. This financial dependence on the State is an important indicium of governmental involvement. The school's very survival depends on the State. If the State chooses, it may exercise complete control over the school's operations simply by threatening to withdraw financial support if the school takes action that it considers objectionable.

The school is heavily regulated and closely supervised by the State. This fact provides further support for the conclusion that its actions should be attributed to the State. When an entity is not only heavily regulated and funded by the State, but also provides a service that the State is required to provide, there is a very close nexus with the State. Under these circumstances, it is entirely appropriate to treat the entity as an arm of the State. Here, since the New Perspectives School exists solely to fulfill the State's obligations under Chapter 766, I think it fully reasonable to conclude that the school is a state actor.

The majority repeatedly compares the school to a private contractor that "depends primarily on contracts to build roads, bridges, dams, ships, or submarines for the government." The New Perspectives School can be readily distinguished, however. Although shipbuilders and dambuilders, like the school, may be dependent on government funds, they are not so closely supervised by the government. And unlike most private contractors, the school is performing a statutory duty of the State.

Even though there are myriad indicia of state action in this case, the majority refuses to find that the school acted under color of state law when it discharged petitioners. The decision in this case marks a return to empty formalism in state action doctrine. Because I believe that the state action requirement must be given a more sensitive and flexible interpretation than the majority offers, I dissent.

BLUM v. YARETSKY

457 U.S. 991 (1982)

Justice REHNQUIST delivered the opinion of the Court.

Respondents represent a class of Medicaid patients challenging decisions by the nursing homes in which they reside to discharge or transfer patients without notice or an opportunity for a hearing. The question is whether the State may be held responsible for those decisions so as to subject them to the strictures of the Fourteenth Amendment.

I

Congress established the Medicaid program in 1965 as Title XIX of the Social Security Act, to provide federal financial assistance to States that choose to reimburse certain medical costs incurred by the poor. As a participating State, New York provides Medicaid assistance to eligible persons who receive care in private nursing homes, which are designated as either "skilled nursing facilities" (SNFs) or "health related facilities" (HRFs). The latter provide less extensive, and generally less expensive, medical care than the former. Nursing homes chosen by Medicaid patients are directly reimbursed by the State for the reasonable cost of health care services.

An individual must meet two conditions to obtain Medicaid assistance. He must satisfy eligibility standards defined in terms of income or resources and he must seek medically necessary services. To assure that the latter condition is satisfied, federal regulations require each nursing home to establish a utilization review committee (URC) of physicians whose functions include periodically assessing whether each patient is receiving the appropriate level of care, and thus whether the patient's continued stay in the facility is justified. If the URC determines that the patient should be discharged or transferred to a different level of care, either more or less intensive, it must notify the state agency responsible for administering Medicaid assistance.

At the time their complaint was filed, respondents Yaretsky and Cuevas were patients in the American Nursing Home, an SNF located in New York City. Both were recipients of assistance under the Medicaid program. In December 1975 the nursing home's URC decided that respondents did not need the care they were receiving and should be transferred to a lower level of care in an HRF. New York City officials, who were then responsible for administering the Medicaid program in the city, were notified of this decision and prepared to reduce or terminate payments to the nursing home for respondents' care. Following administrative hearings, state social service officials affirmed the decision to discontinue benefits unless respondents accepted a transfer to an HRF providing a reduced level of care.

Respondents then commenced this suit, acting individually and on behalf of a class of Medicaid-eligible residents of New York nursing homes. Named as defendants were the Commissioners of the New York Department of Social Services and the Department of Health. Respondents alleged in part that the defendants had not afforded them adequate notice either of URC decisions and the reasons supporting them or of their right to an administrative hearing to challenge those decisions. Respondents maintained that these actions violated their rights under state and federal law and under the Due Process Clause of the Fourteenth Amendment. They sought injunctive relief and damages.

[II]

Faithful adherence to the "state action" requirement of the Fourteenth Amendment requires careful attention to the gravamen of the plaintiff's complaint. In this case, respondents objected to the involuntary discharge or transfer of Medicaid patients by their nursing homes without certain procedural safeguards. They have named as defendants state officials responsible for administering the Medicaid program in New York. These officials are also responsible for regulating nursing homes in the State, including those in which respondents were receiving care. But respondents are not challenging particular state regulations or procedures, and their arguments concede that the decision to discharge or transfer a patient originates not with state officials, but with nursing homes that are privately owned and operated. Their lawsuit, therefore, seeks to hold state officials liable for the actions of private parties, and the injunctive relief they have obtained requires the State to adopt regulations that will prohibit the private conduct of which they complain.

This case is obviously different from those cases in which the defendant is a private party and the question is whether his conduct has sufficiently received the imprimatur of the State so as to make it "state" action for purposes of the Fourteenth Amendment. It also differs from other "state action" cases in which the challenged conduct consists of enforcement of state laws or regulations by state officials who are themselves parties in the lawsuit; in such cases the question typically is whether the private motives which triggered the enforcement of those laws can fairly be attributed to the State.

First, although it is apparent that nursing homes in New York are extensively regulated, "[t]he mere fact that a business is subject to state regulation does not by itself convert its action into that of the State for purposes of the Fourteenth Amendment." Jackson v. Metropolitan Edison Co. The complaining party must also show that "there is a sufficiently close nexus between the State and the challenged action of the regulated entity so that the action of the latter may be fairly treated as that of the State itself." The purpose of this requirement is to assure that constitutional standards are invoked only when it can be said that the State is responsible for the specific conduct of which the plaintiff complains.

The importance of this assurance is evident when, as in this case, the complaining party seeks to hold the State liable for the actions of private parties.

Second, although the factual setting of each case will be significant, our precedents indicate that a State normally can be held responsible for a private decision only when it has exercised coercive power or has provided such significant encouragement, either overt or covert, that the choice must in law be deemed to be that of the State. Flagg Bros., Inc. v. Brooks. Mere approval of or acquiescence in the initiatives of a private party is not sufficient to justify holding the State responsible for those initiatives under the terms of the Fourteenth Amendment.

Third, the required nexus may be present if the private entity has exercised powers that are "traditionally the exclusive prerogative of the State." Jackson v. Metropolitan Edison Co.

Analyzed in the light of these principles, the Court of Appeals' finding of state action cannot stand. The court reasoned that state action was present in the discharge or transfer decisions implemented by the nursing homes because the State responded to those decisions by adjusting the patient's Medicaid benefits. Respondents, however, do not challenge the adjustment of benefits, but the discharge or transfer of patients to lower levels of care without adequate notice or hearings. That the State responds to such actions by adjusting benefits does not render it responsible for those actions. The decisions about which respondents complain are made by physicians and nursing home administrators, all of whom are concededly private parties. There is no suggestion that those decisions were influenced in any degree by the State's obligation to adjust benefits in conformity with changes in the cost of medically necessary care.

Respondents do not rest on the Court of Appeals' rationale, however. They argue that the State "affirmatively commands" the summary discharge or transfer of Medicaid patients who are thought to be inappropriately placed in their nursing facilities. Were this characterization accurate, we would have a different question before us. However, our review of the statutes and regulations identified by respondents does not support respondents' characterization of them. [R]espondents' complaint is about nursing home decisions to discharge or transfer, not to admit, Medicaid patients. But we are not satisfied that the State is responsible for those decisions either. Those decisions ultimately turn on medical judgments made by private parties according to professional standards that are not established by the State.

We conclude that respondents have failed to establish "state action" in the nursing homes' decisions to discharge or transfer Medicaid patients to lower levels of care. Consequently, they have failed to prove that petitioners have violated rights secured by the Fourteenth Amendment.

Justice BRENNAN, with whom Justice MARSHALL joins, dissenting.

If the Fourteenth Amendment is to have its intended effect as a restraint on the abuse of state power, courts must be sensitive to the manner in which state power is exercised. In an era of active government intervention to remedy social ills, the true character of the State's involvement in, and coercive influence over, the activities of private parties, often through complex and opaque regulatory frameworks, may not always be apparent. But if the task that the Fourteenth Amendment assigns to the courts is thus rendered more burdensome, the courts' obligation to perform that task faithfully, and consistently with the constitutional purpose, is rendered more, not less, important. In deciding whether "state action" is present in the context of a claim brought under 42 U.S.C. §1983, the ultimate determination is simply whether the §1983 defendant has brought the force of the State to bear against the §1983 plaintiff in a manner the Fourteenth Amendment was designed to inhibit. Where the defendant is a government employee, this inquiry is relatively straightforward. But in deciding whether "state action" is present in actions performed directly by persons other than government employees, what is required is a realistic and delicate appraisal of the State's involvement in the total context of the action taken.

The Court's analysis in this case is simple, but it is also demonstrably flawed, for it proceeds upon a premise that is factually unfounded. The Court first describes the decision to transfer a nursing home resident from one level of care to another as involving nothing more than a physician's independent assessment of the appropriate medical treatment required by that resident. Building upon that factual premise, the Court has no difficulty concluding that the State plays no decisive role in the transfer decision: By reducing the resident's benefits to meet the change in treatment prescribed, the State is simply responding to "medical judgments made by private parties according to professional standards that are not established by the State." If this were an accurate characterization of the circumstances of this case, I too would conclude that there was no "state action" in the nursing home's decision to transfer.

But the level-of-care decisions at issue in this case, even when characterized as the "independent" decision of the nursing home, have far less to do with the exercise of independent professional judgment than they do with the State's desire to save money. To be sure, standards for implementing the level-of-care scheme established by the Medicaid program are framed with reference to the underlying purpose of that program — to provide needed medical services. And not surprisingly, the State relies on doctors to implement this aspect of its Medicaid program. But the idea of two mutually exclusive levels of care — skilled nursing care and intermediate care — embodied in the federal regulatory scheme and implemented by the State, reflects no established medical model of health care. On the contrary, the two levels of long-term institutionalized care enshrined in the Medicaid scheme are legislative constructs, designed to serve governmental cost-containment policies.

From a purely medical standpoint, the idea of shifting nursing home residents from a "higher level of care" to a "lower level of care," which almost invariably involves transfer from one facility to another, rarely makes sense. As one commentator has observed: "These transfers eject helpless, disoriented people from the places they have lived for months or even years to facilities, not of their own choosing, that they have never seen before. The evidence is overwhelming that, without extraordinary preparatory efforts that are hardly ever made, any move is harmful for the preponderance of the frail elderly." B. Vladeck, Unloving Care 140 (1980).

Ignoring the State's fiscal interest in the level-of-care determination, the Court proceeds to a cursory, and misleading, discussion of the State's involvement in the assignment of residents to particular levels of care. In my view, an accurate and realistic appraisal of the procedures actually employed in the State of New York leaves no doubt that not only has the State established the system of treatment levels and utilization review in order to further its own fiscal goals, but that the State prescribes with as much precision as is possible the standards by which individual determinations are to be made. There can thus be little doubt that in the vast majority of cases, decisions as to "level of treatment" in the admission process are made according to the State's specified criteria.

The degree of interdependence between the State and the nursing home is far more pronounced than it was between the State and the private entity in Burton v. Wilmington Parking Authority (1961). The State subsidizes practically all of the operating and capital costs of the facility, and pays the medical expenses of more than 90% of its residents. And, in setting reimbursement rates, the State generally affords the nursing homes a profit as well. Even more striking is the fact that the residents of those homes are, by definition, utterly dependent on the State for their support and their placement. For many, the totality of their social network is the nursing home community. Within that environment, the nursing home operator is the immediate authority, the provider of food, clothing, shelter, and health care, and, in every significant respect, the functional equivalent of a State. Surely, in this context we must be especially alert to those situations in which the State "has elected to place its power, property and prestige behind" the actions of the nursing home owner. See Burton v. Wilmington Parking Authority.

INITIATIVES ENCOURAGING VIOLATIONS OF RIGHTS

A fourth circumstance in which the entanglement exception has been applied is when voters have approved an initiative that encourages violation of rights. Reitman v. Mulkey, which follows, is the leading case in this regard.

REITMAN v. MULKEY
387 U.S. 369 (1967)

Justice WHITE delivered the opinion of the Court.

The question here is whether Art. I, §26, of the California Constitution denies "to any person . . . the equal protection of the laws" within the meaning of the Fourteenth Amendment of the Constitution of the United States. Section 26 of Art. I, an initiated measure submitted to the people as Proposition 14 in a statewide ballot in 1964, provides in part as follows: "Neither the State nor any subdivision or agency thereof shall deny, limit or abridge, directly or indirectly, the right of any person, who is willing or desires to sell, lease or rent any part or all of his real property, to decline to sell, lease or rent such property to such person or persons as he, in his absolute discretion, chooses." The real property covered by §26 is limited to residential property and contains an exception for state-owned real estate.

In Mulkey v. Reitman, the Mulkeys who are husband and wife and respondents here, sued under §51 and §52 of the California Civil Code alleging that petitioners had refused to rent them an apartment solely on account of their race. Petitioners moved for summary judgment on the ground that §§51 and 52, insofar as they were the basis for the Mulkeys' action, had been rendered null and void by the adoption of Proposition 14 after the filing of the complaint.

Proposition 14 was enacted, [with the] immediate design and intent, the California court said, . . . "to overturn state laws that bore on the right of private sellers and lessors to discriminate," and "to forestall future state action that might circumscribe this right." This aim was successfully achieved: the adoption of Proposition 14 "generally nullifies both the [State's anti-discrimination laws] as they apply to the housing market," and establishes "a purported constitutional right to privately discriminate on grounds which admittedly would be unavailable under the Fourteenth Amendment should state action be involved."

[The California Supreme Court] conceded that the State was permitted a neutral position with respect to private racial discriminations and that the State was not bound by the Federal Constitution to forbid them. But, because a significant state involvement in private discriminations could amount to unconstitutional state action, Burton v. Wilmington Parking Authority (1961), the court deemed it necessary to determine whether Proposition 14 invalidly involved the State in racial discriminations in the housing market. Its conclusion was that it did.

Petitioners contend that the California court has misconstrued the Fourteenth Amendment since the repeal of any statute prohibiting racial discrimination, which is constitutionally permissible, may be said to "authorize" and "encourage" discrimination because it makes legally permissible that which was formerly proscribed. But, as we understand the California court, it did not posit a constitutional violation on the mere repeal of the Unruh and Rumford Acts. It did not read either our cases or the Fourteenth Amendment as establishing an automatic constitutional barrier to the repeal of an existing law prohibiting racial discriminations in housing; nor did the court rule that a State may never put in statutory form an existing policy of neutrality with respect to private discriminations. What the court below did was first to reject the notion that the State was required to have a statute prohibiting racial discriminations in housing. Second, it held the intent of §26 was to authorize private racial discriminations in the housing market, to repeal [existing antidiscrimination laws] and to create a constitutional right to discriminate on racial grounds in the sale and leasing of real property. Hence, the court dealt with §26 as though it expressly authorized and constitutionalized the private right to discriminate. Third, the court assessed the ultimate impact of §26 in the California environment and concluded that the section would encourage and significantly involve the State in private racial discrimination contrary to the Fourteenth Amendment.

The California court could very reasonably conclude that §26 would and did have wider impact than a mere repeal of existing statutes. Section 26 announced the constitutional right of any person to decline to sell or lease his real property to anyone to whom he did not desire to sell or lease. [Existing antidiscrimination laws] were thereby repealed. But the section struck more deeply and more widely. Private discriminations in housing were now not only free from Rumford and Unruh but they also enjoyed a far different status than was true before the passage of those statutes. The right to discriminate, including the right to discriminate on racial grounds, was now embodied in the State's basic charter, immune from legislative, executive, or judicial regulation at any level of the state government. Those practicing racial discriminations need no longer rely solely on their personal choice. They could now invoke express constitutional authority, free from censure or interference of any kind from official sources. All individuals, partnerships, corporations and other legal entities, as well as their agents and representatives, could now discriminate with respect to their residential real property, which is defined as any interest in real property of any kind or quality, "irrespective of how obtained or financed," and seemingly irrespective of the relationship of the State to such interests in real property.

Here the California court, armed as it was with the knowledge of the facts and circumstances concerning the passage and potential impact of §26, and familiar with the milieu in which that provision would operate, has determined that the provision would involve the State in private racial discriminations to an unconstitutional degree. We accept this holding of the California court.

Justice HARLAN, whom Justice BLACK, Justice CLARK, and Justice STEWART join, dissenting.

I consider that this decision, which cuts deeply into state political processes, is supported neither by anything "found" by the Supreme Court of California nor by any of our past cases decided under the Fourteenth Amendment. In my view today's holding, salutary as its result may appear at first blush, may in the long run actually serve to handicap progress in the extremely difficult field of racial concerns. I must respectfully dissent.

The facts of this case are simple and undisputed. The legislature of the State of California has in the last decade enacted a number of statutes restricting the right of private landowners to discriminate on the basis of such factors as race in the sale or rental of property. These laws aroused considerable opposition, causing certain groups to organize themselves and to take advantage of procedures embodied in the California Constitution permitting a "proposition" to be presented to the voters for a constitutional amendment. "Proposition 14" was thus put before the electorate in the 1964 election and was adopted by a vote of 4,526,460 to 2,395,747.

In the case at hand California, acting through the initiative and referendum, has decided to remain "neutral" in the realm of private discrimination affecting the sale or rental of private residential property; in such transactions private owners are now free to act in a discriminatory manner previously forbidden to them. In short, all that has happened is that California has effected a pro tanto repeal of its prior statutes forbidding private discrimination. This runs no more afoul of the Fourteenth Amendment than would have California's failure to pass any such antidiscrimination statutes in the first instance. The fact that such repeal was also accompanied by a constitutional prohibition against future enactment of such laws by the California Legislature cannot well be thought to affect, from a federal constitutional standpoint, the validity of what California has done. The Fourteenth Amendment does not reach such state constitutional action any more than it does a simple legislative repeal of legislation forbidding private discrimination.

The Court attempts to fit §26 within the coverage of the Equal Protection Clause by characterizing it as in effect an affirmative call to residents of California to discriminate. The main difficulty with this viewpoint is that it depends upon a characterization of §26 that cannot fairly be made. The provision is neutral on its face. A state enactment, particularly one that is simply permissive of private decision-making rather than coercive and one that has been adopted in this most democratic of processes, should not be struck down by the judiciary under the Equal Protection Clause without persuasive evidence of an invidious purpose or effect.

A moment of thought will reveal the far-reaching possibilities of the Court's new doctrine, which I am sure the Court does not intend. Every act of private discrimination is either forbidden by state law or permitted by it. There can be little doubt that such permissiveness—whether by express constitutional or statutory provision, or implicit in the common law—to some extent "encourages" those who wish to discriminate to do so. Under this theory "state action" in the form of laws that do nothing more than passively permit private discrimination could be said to tinge all private discrimination with the taint of unconstitutional state encouragement.

This type of alleged state involvement, simply evincing a refusal to involve itself at all, is of course very different from that illustrated in [prior] cases where the Court found active involvement of state agencies and officials in specific acts of discrimination. It is also quite different from cases in which a state enactment could be said to have the obvious purpose of fostering discrimination. I believe the state action required to bring the Fourteenth Amendment into operation must be affirmative and purposeful, actively fostering discrimination. Only in such a case is ostensibly "private" action more properly labeled "official." I do not believe that the mere enactment of §26, on the showing made here, falls within this class of cases.

I think that this decision is not only constitutionally unsound, but in its practical potentialities short-sighted. Opponents of state antidiscrimination statutes are now in a position to argue that such legislation should be defeated because, if enacted, it may be unrepealable. More fundamentally, the doctrine underlying this decision may hamper, if not preclude, attempts to deal with the delicate and troublesome problems of race relations through the legislative process. The lines that have been and must be drawn in this area, fraught as it is with human sensibilities and frailties of whatever race or creed, are difficult ones. The drawing of them requires understanding, patience, and compromise, and is best done by legislatures rather than by courts. When legislation in this field is unsuccessful there should be wide opportunities for legislative amendment, as well as for change through such processes as the popular initiative and referendum. This decision, I fear, may inhibit such flexibility. Here the electorate itself overwhelmingly wished to overrule and check its own legislature on a matter left open by the Federal Constitution. By refusing to accept the decision of the people of California, and by contriving a new and ill-defined constitutional concept to allow federal judicial interference, I think the Court has taken to itself powers and responsibilities left elsewhere by the Constitution.

The Court has invalidated other initiatives that overturned antidiscrimination laws. In Hunter v. Erickson, 393 U.S. 385 (1969), the Supreme Court declared unconstitutional an initiative in Akron, Ohio, that repealed open housing laws and required voter approval of any such future law. The Court found that the initiative was an "explicitly racial classification treating racial housing matters differently from other racial and housing matters."

In Washington v. Seattle School Dist. No. 1, 458 U.S. 457 (1982), the Supreme Court declared unconstitutional a Washington initiative that provided that no school board could require any student to attend a school other than the school geographically nearest or next nearest the student's place of residence. The initiative precluded pupils from being assigned for purposes of desegregation and this goal — frustrating desegregation — made the initiative unconstitutional.

The Court distinguished the companion case of Crawford v. Board of Education, 458 U.S. 527 (1982), where the Court upheld a California initiative that provided that state courts could not order mandatory assignment or transportation of students unless a federal court would do so to remedy a violation of the Fourteenth Amendment. The Court found that there was no racial classification in the law and the repeal of remedies not required by the Constitution is permissible.

Distinguishing *Crawford* from the other cases is difficult. There was not a racial classification within the California initiative and it only limited remedies not required by the Constitution. Yet the initiative in *Crawford* had as its objective limiting busing just as the initiatives in *Reitman* and *Hunter* sought to limit open housing laws and as the initiative in *Washington* also aimed to decrease busing. The point at which the state's encouragement of discrimination becomes unconstitutional is never clearly defined in these cases.

Most recently, in Romer v. Evans, 517 U.S. 620 (1996), the Court declared unconstitutional a Colorado initiative that repealed laws prohibiting discrimination against gays, lesbians, and bisexuals and preventing future laws to protect such individuals.[42] The Court found that the law was motivated by animus against gays and lesbians and that it violated equal protection to preclude these groups from using the political process in the manner available to all other groups in the state.

Inevitably, the determination of state action is inextricably linked to the Court's view as to whether there is a violation of equal protection. In *Reitman*, *Hunter*, *Washington*, and *Romer*, the Court saw the initiatives as being motivated by impermissible discriminatory purposes and found denials of equal protection. Thus, the question of when initiatives permitting private discrimination constitute state action inevitably turns on whether the Court views the initiative as denying equal protection.

ENTWINEMENT

As the preceding material indicates, the Supreme Court has recognized two narrow exceptions to the state action requirement: the public functions exception, which provides that private conduct must comply with the Constitution when it is performing a task that has traditionally been done exclusively by the government; and the entanglement exception, in which the government affirmatively authorizes, encourages, or facilitates unconstitutional conduct. In Brentwood Academy v. Tennessee Secondary School Athletic Assn., the Court finds that a private entity is a state actor based on its "entwinement" with the government. The key question, not answered by the Court, is how "entwinement" relates to "entanglement." Is this a new exception to the state action

---

42. Romer v. Evans is presented in detail in Chapter 7, "Equal Protection."

requirement? If so, how is it different? Is it that entanglement requires government encouragement, but entwinement does not? None of these questions is addressed by the Court, but they will undoubtedly be litigated in the future and are thus ones to consider as you read this decision.

BRENTWOOD ACADEMY v. TENNESSEE SECONDARY SCHOOL ATHLETIC ASSOCIATION

531 U.S. 288 (2001)

Justice SOUTER delivered the opinion of the Court.

The issue is whether a statewide association incorporated to regulate interscholastic athletic competition among public and private secondary schools may be regarded as engaging in state action when it enforces a rule against a member school. The association in question here includes most public schools located within the State, acts through their representatives, draws its officers from them, is largely funded by their dues and income received in their stead, and has historically been seen to regulate in lieu of the State Board of Education's exercise of its own authority. We hold that the association's regulatory activity may and should be treated as state action owing to the pervasive entwinement of state school officials in the structure of the association, there being no offsetting reason to see the association's acts in any other way.

I

Respondent Tennessee Secondary School Athletic Association (Association) is a not-for-profit membership corporation organized to regulate interscholastic sport among the public and private high schools in Tennessee that belong to it. No school is forced to join, but without any other authority actually regulating interscholastic athletics, it enjoys the memberships of almost all the State's public high schools (some 290 of them or 84% of the Association's voting membership), far outnumbering the 55 private schools that belong. A member school's team may play or scrimmage only against the team of another member, absent a dispensation.

The Association's rulemaking arm is its legislative council, while its board of control tends to administration. The voting membership of each of these nine-person committees is limited under the Association's bylaws to high school principals, assistant principals, and superintendents elected by the member schools, and the public school administrators who so serve typically attend meetings during regular school hours. Although the Association's staff members are not paid by the State, they are eligible to join the State's public retirement system for its employees. Member schools pay dues to the Association, though the bulk of its revenue is gate receipts at member teams' football and basketball tournaments, many of them held in public arenas rented by the Association.

The constitution, bylaws, and rules of the Association set standards of school membership and the eligibility of students to play in interscholastic games. Each school, for example, is regulated in awarding financial aid, most coaches must have a Tennessee state teaching license, and players must meet minimum academic standards and hew to limits on student employment. Under the bylaws, "in all matters pertaining to the athletic relations of his school," the principal is responsible to the Association, which has the power "to suspend, to fine, or otherwise penalize any member school for the violation of any of the rules of the Association or for other just cause."

Ever since the Association was incorporated in 1925, Tennessee's State Board of Education (State Board) has (to use its own words) acknowledged the corporation's functions "in providing standards, rules and regulations for interscholastic competition in the public schools of Tennessee." Specifically, in 1972, it went so far as to adopt a rule expressly "designat[ing]" the Association as "the organization to supervise and regulate the athletic activities in which the public junior and senior high schools in Tennessee participate on an interscholastic basis." [O]n several occasions over the next 20 years, the State Board reviewed, approved, or reaffirmed its approval of the recruiting Rule at issue in this case. In 1996, however, the State Board dropped the original Rule expressly designating the Association as regulator; it substituted a statement "recogniz[ing] the value of participation in interscholastic athletics and the role of [the Association] in coordinating interscholastic athletic competition," while "authoriz[ing] the public schools of the state to voluntarily maintain membership in [the Association]."

The action before us responds to a 1997 regulatory enforcement proceeding brought against petitioner, Brentwood Academy, a private parochial high school member of the Association. The Association's board of control found that Brentwood violated a rule prohibiting "undue influence" in recruiting athletes, when it wrote to incoming students and their parents about spring football practice. The Association accordingly placed Brentwood's athletic program on probation for four years, declared its football and boys' basketball teams ineligible to compete in playoffs for two years, and imposed a $3,000 fine. When these penalties were imposed, all the voting members of the board of control and legislative council were public school administrators.

Brentwood sued the Association and its executive director in federal court under 42 U.S.C. §1983, claiming that enforcement of the Rule was state action and a violation of the First and Fourteenth Amendments.

II

A

Our cases try to plot a line between state action subject to Fourteenth Amendment scrutiny and private conduct (however exceptionable) that is not. The judicial obligation is not only to "'preserv[e] an area of individual freedom by limiting the reach of federal law' and avoi[d] the imposition of responsibility on a State for conduct it could not control," but also to assure that constitutional standards are invoked "when it can be said that the State is responsible for the specific conduct of which the plaintiff complains." If the Fourteenth Amendment is not to be displaced, therefore, its ambit cannot be a simple line between States and people operating outside formally governmental organizations, and the deed of an ostensibly private organization or individual is to be treated sometimes as if a State had caused it to be performed. Thus, we say that state action may be found if, though only if, there is such a "close nexus between the

State and the challenged action" that seemingly private behavior "may be fairly treated as that of the State itself."

What is fairly attributable is a matter of normative judgment, and the criteria lack rigid simplicity. From the range of circumstances that could point toward the State behind an individual face, no one fact can function as a necessary condition across the board for finding state action; nor is any set of circumstances absolutely sufficient, for there may be some countervailing reason against attributing activity to the government.

Our cases have identified a host of facts that can bear on the fairness of such an attribution. We have, for example, held that a challenged activity may be state action when it results from the State's exercise of "coercive power," when the State provides "significant encouragement, either overt or covert," or when a private actor operates as a "willful participant in joint activity with the State or its agents." We have treated a nominally private entity as a state actor when it is controlled by an "agency of the State," when it has been delegated a public function by the State, when it is "entwined with governmental policies" or when government is "entwined in [its] management or control."

Amidst such variety, examples may be the best teachers, and examples from our cases are unequivocal in showing that the character of a legal entity is determined neither by its expressly private characterization in statutory law, nor by the failure of the law to acknowledge the entity's inseparability from recognized government officials or agencies.

NCAA v. Tarkanian (1989) arose when an undoubtedly state actor, the University of Nevada, suspended its basketball coach, Tarkanian, in order to comply with rules and recommendations of the National Collegiate Athletic Association (NCAA). The coach charged the NCAA with state action, arguing that the state university had delegated its own functions to the NCAA, clothing the latter with authority to make and apply the university's rules, the result being joint action making the NCAA a state actor.

To be sure, it is not the strict holding in *Tarkanian* that points to our view of this case, for we found no state action on the part of the NCAA. We could see, on the one hand, that the university had some part in setting the NCAA's rules, and the Supreme Court of Nevada had gone so far as to hold that the NCAA had been delegated the university's traditionally exclusive public authority over personnel. But on the other side, the NCAA's policies were shaped not by the University of Nevada alone, but by several hundred member institutions, most of them having no connection with Nevada, and exhibiting no color of Nevada law. Since it was difficult to see the NCAA, not as a collective membership, but as surrogate for the one State, we held the organization's connection with Nevada too insubstantial to ground a state action claim.

But dictum in *Tarkanian* pointed to a contrary result on facts like ours, with an organization whose member public schools are all within a single State. "The situation would, of course, be different if the [Association's] membership consisted entirely of institutions located within the same State, many of them public institutions created by the same sovereign."

B

Just as we foresaw in *Tarkanian*, the "necessarily fact-bound inquiry," leads to the conclusion of state action here. The nominally private character of the Association is overborne by the pervasive entwinement of public institutions and public officials in its composition and workings, and there is no substantial reason to claim unfairness in applying constitutional standards to it.

The Association is not an organization of natural persons acting on their own, but of schools, and of public schools to the extent of 84% of the total. Under the Association's bylaws, each member school is represented by its principal or a faculty member, who has a vote in selecting members of the governing legislative council and board of control from eligible principals, assistant principals and superintendents.

In sum, to the extent of 84% of its membership, the Association is an organization of public schools represented by their officials acting in their official capacity to provide an integral element of secondary public schooling. There would be no recognizable Association, legal or tangible, without the public school officials, who do not merely control but overwhelmingly perform all but the purely ministerial acts by which the Association exists and functions in practical terms. Only the 16% minority of private school memberships prevents this entwinement of the Association and the public school system from being total and their identities totally indistinguishable.

To complement the entwinement of public school officials with the Association from the bottom up, the State of Tennessee has provided for entwinement from top down. State Board members are assigned ex officio to serve as members of the board of control and legislative council, and the Association's ministerial employees are treated as state employees to the extent of being eligible for membership in the state retirement system.

Justice THOMAS, with whom the Chief Justice, Justice SCALIA, and Justice KENNEDY join, dissenting.

We have never found state action based upon mere "entwinement." Until today, we have found a private organization's acts to constitute state action only when the organization performed a public function; was created, coerced, or encouraged by the government; or acted in a symbiotic relationship with the government. The majority's holding — that the Tennessee Secondary School Athletic Association's (TSSAA) enforcement of its recruiting rule is state action — not only extends state-action doctrine beyond its permissible limits but also encroaches upon the realm of individual freedom that the doctrine was meant to protect. I respectfully dissent.

I

Like the state-action requirement of the Fourteenth Amendment, the state-action element of 42 U.S.C. §1983 excludes from its coverage "merely private conduct, however discriminatory or wrongful." "Careful adherence to the 'state action' requirement" thus "preserves an area of individual freedom by limiting the reach of federal law and federal judicial power." The state-action doctrine also promotes important values of federalism, "avoid[ing] the imposition of responsibility on a State for conduct it could not control." Although we have used many different tests to identify state action, they all have a common purpose. Our goal in every case is to determine whether an action "can fairly be attributed to the State."

A

Regardless of these various tests for state action, common sense dictates that the TSSAA's actions cannot fairly be attributed to the State, and thus cannot constitute state action. The TSSAA was formed in 1925 as a private corporation to organize interscholastic athletics and to sponsor tournaments among its member schools. Any private or public secondary school may join the TSSAA by signing a contract agreeing to comply with its rules and decisions. Although public schools currently compose 84% of the TSSAA's membership, the TSSAA does not require that public schools constitute a set percentage of its membership, and, indeed, no public school need join the TSSAA. The TSSAA's rules are enforced not by a state agency but by its own board of control, which comprises high school principals, assistant principals, and superintendents, none of whom must work at a public school. Of course, at the time the recruiting rule was enforced in this case, all of the board members happened to be public school officials. However, each board member acts in a representative capacity on behalf of all the private and public schools in his region of Tennessee, and not simply his individual school.

The State of Tennessee did not create the TSSAA. The State does not fund the TSSAA and does not pay its employees. In fact, only 4% of the TSSAA's revenue comes from the dues paid by member schools; the bulk of its operating budget is derived from gate receipts at tournaments it sponsors. The State does not permit the TSSAA to use state-owned facilities for a discounted fee, and it does not exempt the TSSAA from state taxation. No Tennessee law authorizes the State to coordinate interscholastic athletics or empowers another entity to organize interscholastic athletics on behalf of the State. The only state pronouncement acknowledging the TSSAA's existence is a rule providing that the State Board of Education permits public schools to maintain membership in the TSSAA if they so choose.

Moreover, the State of Tennessee has never had any involvement in the particular action taken by the TSSAA in this case: the enforcement of the TSSAA's recruiting rule prohibiting members from using "undue influence" on students or their parents or guardians "to secure or to retain a student for athletic purposes." There is no indication that the State has ever had any interest in how schools choose to regulate recruiting. In fact, the TSSAA's authority to enforce its recruiting rule arises solely from the voluntary membership contract that each member school signs, agreeing to conduct its athletics in accordance with the rules and decisions of the TSSAA.

B

Even approaching the issue in terms of any of the Court's specific state-action tests, the conclusion is the same: The TSSAA's enforcement of its recruiting rule against Brentwood Academy is not state action. The TSSAA has not performed a function that has been "traditionally exclusively reserved to the State." Jackson v. Metropolitan Edison Co. (1974). The organization of interscholastic sports is neither a traditional nor an exclusive public function of the States. Widespread organization and administration of interscholastic contests by schools did not begin until the 20th century. Indeed, no one claims that the State of Tennessee played any role in the creation of the TSSAA as a private corporation in 1925. The TSSAA was designed to fulfill an objective — the organization of interscholastic athletic tournaments — that the government had not contemplated, much less pursued. And although the board of control currently is composed of public school officials, and although public schools currently account for the majority of the TSSAA's membership, this is not required by the TSSAA's constitution.

In addition, the State of Tennessee has not "exercised coercive power or . . . provided such significant encouragement [to the TSSAA], either overt or covert," that the TSSAA's regulatory activities must in law be deemed to be those of the State. The State has not promulgated any regulations of interscholastic sports, and nothing in the record suggests that the State has encouraged or coerced the TSSAA in enforcing its recruiting rule. To be sure, public schools do provide a small portion of the TSSAA's funding through their membership dues, but no one argues that these dues are somehow conditioned on the TSSAA's enactment and enforcement of recruiting rules. Likewise, even if the TSSAA were dependent on state funding to the extent of 90%, instead of less than 4%, mere financial dependence on the State does not convert the TSSAA's actions into acts of the State.

Finally, there is no "symbiotic relationship" between the State and the TSSAA. Contrary to the majority's assertion, the TSSAA's "fiscal relationship with the State is not different from that of many contractors performing services for the government." The TSSAA provides a service — the organization of athletic tournaments — in exchange for membership dues and gate fees, just as a vendor could contract with public schools to sell refreshments at school events. Certainly the public school could sell its own refreshments, yet the existence of that option does not transform the service performed by the contractor into a state action. Also, there is no suggestion in this case that, as was the case in *Burton*, the State profits from the TSSAA's decision to enforce its recruiting rule.

Because I do not believe that the TSSAA's action of enforcing its recruiting rule is fairly attributable to the State of Tennessee, I would affirm.

II

Although the TSSAA's enforcement activities cannot be considered state action as a matter of common sense or under any of this Court's existing theories of state action, the majority presents a new theory. Under this theory, the majority holds that the combination of factors it identifies evidences "entwinement" of the State with the TSSAA, and that such entwinement converts private action into state action. The majority does not define "entwinement," and the meaning of the term is not altogether clear. But whatever this new "entwinement" theory may entail, it lacks any support in our state-action jurisprudence. There is no case in which we have rested a finding of state action on entwinement alone.

Because the majority never defines "entwinement," the scope of its holding is unclear. If we are fortunate, the majority's fact-specific analysis will have little bearing beyond this case. But if the majority's new entwinement test develops in future years, it could affect many organizations that foster activities, enforce rules, and sponsor extracurricular competition among high schools — not just in athletics, but in such diverse areas as agriculture, mathematics, music, marching bands, forensics, and cheerleading. Indeed, this entwinement test may extend to other organizations that are composed of, or controlled by, public officials or public entities, such as firefighters, policemen, teachers, cities, or counties. I am not prepared to say that any private organization that permits public entities and public officials to participate acts as the State in anything or everything it does, and our state-action jurisprudence has never reached that far. The state-action doctrine was developed to reach only those actions that are truly attributable to the State, not to subject private citizens to the control of federal courts hearing §1983 actions. I respectfully dissent.

CHAPTER

6

ECONOMIC LIBERTIES

A. INTRODUCTION

Some constitutional rights can be grouped together under the category of "economic liberties." Economic liberties generally refer to constitutional rights concerning the ability to enter into and enforce contracts; to pursue a trade or profession; and to acquire, possess, and convey property.

For example, the Contracts Clause found in Article I, §10 of the Constitution provides that "[n]o State shall . . . pass any . . . Law impairing the Obligation of Contracts." Also, several constitutional provisions protect property rights. The Fifth Amendment's Takings Clause states "nor shall private property be taken for public use without just compensation." The Fifth and Fourteenth Amendments, respectively, provide that neither the federal nor state governments can take a person's property (or life or liberty) without due process of law. At times, the Court also has used the Due Process Clause to protect other economic liberties such as freedom of contract, freedom to pursue a livelihood, and freedom to practice a trade or profession.

This chapter focuses on all of these economic liberties. Throughout this chapter the key normative issue concerns the appropriate degree of judicial protection for economic liberties. How important are the rights of property and contracting? What was the framers' intent concerning these rights? Does the legislature have a special expertise concerning these rights that justifies a greater degree of judicial deference compared to when the Court deals with political and civil liberties, such as freedom of speech and the right to vote? What, if anything, was wrong with the Court's decisions in the first third of the twentieth century aggressively protecting economic rights? Since 1937, has the Court unduly or appropriately deferred to government economic regulations?

HISTORICAL OVERVIEW

The framers obviously were concerned about protecting economic rights and thus included in the Constitution provisions such as the Contracts Clause and the Takings Clause. Indeed, Charles Beard, in a famous book published early in the twentieth century, argued that the primary impetus for the Constitution was a desire to protect property and wealth.[1] Although later historians have challenged Beard's analysis and conclusions,[2] there is no doubt that the framers intended to protect economic rights.

The Supreme Court's protection of economic liberties has varied enormously over time. In the early nineteenth century, the Court invoked natural law principles to protect property rights.[3] Also, throughout the nineteenth century, the Court aggressively used the Contracts Clause to limit the ability of states to interfere with existing contractual obligations.

Beginning in the late nineteenth century and continuing until 1937, the Court found that freedom of contract was a basic right under the liberty and property provisions of the Due Process Clause. During this period of constitutional history, sometimes referred to as the *Lochner* era,[4] the Court aggressively protected economic rights under the Due Process Clause. Many state laws, such as minimum wage and maximum hour statutes, were declared unconstitutional as violating the Fourteenth Amendment by impermissibly interfering with freedom of contract. The Contracts Clause was not used often during this era; the protection of freedom of contract under the Due Process Clause made the Contracts Clause superfluous. Freedom of contract under the Due Process Clause limited the government's ability both to impair existing contracts and to regulate the content of future contracts; the Contracts Clause always has been confined to the former.

It is extremely important to note that during this same era the Court used federalism to limit the ability of Congress to regulate the economy. From the late nineteenth century until 1937, the Court narrowly defined the scope of Congress's powers under the Commerce Clause and it also found that the Tenth Amendment reserved a zone of authority exclusively to the states. In other words, if a state adopted a minimum wage or a maximum hour law, it likely would have been invalidated for violating the Due Process Clause of the Fourteenth Amendment. But if the federal government adopted the same law, it would have been declared unconstitutional as exceeding the scope of Congress's powers or as violating states' rights and the Tenth Amendment. The decisions during this era concerning the scope of Congress's powers are presented in Chapter 2. Although the doctrines used were different, they were inspired by the same philosophy: a strong commitment to a laissez-faire economy and to protecting business from government regulations.

After 1937, the law changed dramatically and the Court adopted a policy of great deference to government economic regulations. No longer did the Court protect freedom of contract under the liberty of the Due Process Clause. Nor did the Court impose limits on Congress's ability to regulate the economy based on federalism or on narrow definitions of federal powers.

This reluctance to protect economic liberties also has manifested itself in cases under the Contracts Clause. Only twice since 1937 has the Court found

---

1. Charles A. Beard, *An Economic Interpretation of the Constitution of the United States* (1913).
2. *See, e.g.*, Forrest McDonald, *We the People: The Economic Origins of the Constitution* (1958).
3. Fletcher v. Peck, 10 U.S. (6 Cranch.) 87 (1810); Calder v. Bull, 3 U.S. (3 Dall.) 386 (1798).
4. The label comes from the decision in Lochner v. New York, 198 U.S. 45 (1905) (invalidating a maximum hours law for bakers), which is regarded as a paradigm case in the era. *Lochner* is presented below.

that any law violates the Contracts Clause in Article I, §10.[5] However, especially in the last two decades, the Court has used the Takings Clause to protect property rights.

ORGANIZATION OF THE CHAPTER

Section B examines economic substantive due process. Specifically, as discussed below, the focus is on the Court's interpretation of the word "liberty" in the Due Process Clause to protect freedom of contract as a fundamental right. The discussion of substantive due process is placed first simply because it has dominated the Court's approach to economic liberties in this century. In the first third of the twentieth century, the Court's use of substantive due process to protect economic rights made most of the other constitutional provisions in the area unnecessary. Since 1937, however, the Court's tremendous reluctance to use economic substantive due process has been paralleled by a general unwillingness to safeguard economic liberties.

Section C focuses on the Contracts Clause. It briefly describes the Court's active use of this provision in the nineteenth century and then examines contemporary decisions limiting the scope of this Clause.

Finally, section D discusses the Takings Clause. Four major questions are considered: What is a "taking"? What is "property"? When is a taking for "public use"? And what is the requirement for "just compensation"?

B. ECONOMIC SUBSTANTIVE DUE PROCESS

1. Introduction

The Fifth and Fourteenth Amendments provide, respectively, that neither the federal nor the state governments can deprive any person of life, liberty, or property without due process of law. The Due Process Clauses have been interpreted to provide two different types of protection. One is termed "procedural due process." As the phrase implies, this refers to the procedures that government must follow when it takes away a person's life, liberty, or property. For example, procedural due process often focuses on what kind of notice and what type of a hearing the government must provide when it deprives a person of life, liberty, or property. Procedural due process is presented in detail in Chapter 8.

The other use of the Due Process Clause is called "substantive due process." Substantive due process asks whether the government has an adequate reason for taking away a person's life, liberty, or property. In other words, the focus is on the sufficiency of the justification for the government's action, not on the procedures the government has followed. For example, when a right under the Due Process Clause is deemed fundamental by the Supreme Court, the government must prove that its action is necessary to achieve a compelling purpose.

---

5. Allied Structural Steel Co. v. Spannaus, 438 U.S. 234 (1978); United States Trust Co. v. New Jersey, 431 U.S. 1 (1977). These cases are presented in Section C of this chapter.

A simple example contrasts procedural and substantive due process. The Supreme Court has held that the word "liberty" in the Due Process Clause protects a fundamental right of parents to the custody of their children. The Court has said that "procedural due process" requires notice and a hearing — procedures — before termination of custody. By comparison, "substantive due process" requires that the government show a compelling reason for terminating custody, such as by proving parental abuse or neglect.

Over the course of American history, substantive due process has been used primarily in two areas: protecting economic liberties and safeguarding privacy. The former is the focus of this section. The latter, on privacy and autonomy rights, is discussed in Chapter 8.

In presenting economic substantive due process, this section next describes the early history of the doctrine. Then it presents the economic substantive due process cases in the late nineteenth century through 1937, when the Supreme Court aggressively used this doctrine to invalidate government economic regulations. Finally, the section concludes by examining the economic substantive due process decisions since 1937, a time of great judicial deference to government economic regulations.

2. The Early History of Economic Substantive Due Process

The Supreme Court rejected the first attempts to use the Due Process Clause to protect economic rights from government interference. In Murray v. Hoboken Land & Improvement Co.,[6] the Court denied a due process challenge to an attempt by the government to collect delinquent taxes. The Court emphasized that due process is met as long as the government's *procedures* are in accordance with the law.

In the *Slaughter-House Cases*, 83 U.S. (16 Wall.) 36 (1872), the Court expressly rejected a substantive due process claim.[7] The *Slaughter-House Cases* involved a challenge to a Louisiana law that granted a private company a 25-year monopoly in the livestock landing and slaughterhouse business. The law also required that the company allow any person to use the facilities to slaughter animals for a fixed fee.

Several butchers brought a lawsuit challenging the constitutionality of the grant of a monopoly. In addition to arguing that the law was involuntary servitude in violation of the Thirteenth Amendment, that it violated the Privileges or Immunities Clause, and that it violated the Equal Protection Clauses of the Fourteenth Amendment, the plaintiffs contended that it denied their right to practice their trade and thus violated the Due Process Clause. The Supreme Court rejected all of these arguments. As to due process, the Court emphasized that this Clause concerned the procedures that government must follow and thus could not be used to challenge the law for interfering with the right of butchers to practice their trade. Indeed, the Court said that "under no construction of that provision that we have ever seen, or any that we deem admissible, can the restraint imposed by the State of Louisiana upon the exercise of their trade by the butchers of New Orleans be held to be a deprivation of property within

6. 59 U.S. (18 How.) 272 (1855).
7. The *Slaughter-House Cases* are presented in detail in Chapter 5.

the meaning of that provision."[8] The Court flatly rejected the idea that the Due Process Clause could be used to safeguard a right to practice a trade or profession from arbitrary government interference.

Justices Field and Bradley strongly dissented. In addition to disagreeing with the majority as to the meaning of the Privileges or Immunities Clause, Field and Bradley also differed as to the content of the Due Process Clause. They saw the Due Process Clause as limiting the ability of states to adopt arbitrary laws, especially ones that interfered with natural rights. Justice Bradley, for example, declared, "[T]he individual citizen, as a necessity, must be left free to adopt such calling, profession, or trade as may seem to him most conducive to that end. Without this right he cannot be a freeman. This right to choose one's calling is an essential part of that liberty which it is the object of government to protect; and a calling, when chosen, is a man's property and right. Liberty and property are not protected where these rights are arbitrarily assailed." In other words, Justice Bradley interpreted the words liberty and property in the Due Process Clause as protecting a right to practice a trade or profession and believed that arbitrary interference with these rights violated the Fourteenth Amendment. Although this position was rejected by a majority of the Court in the *Slaughter-House Cases*, it soon became the majority view of the Supreme Court.

Beginning in the 1870s, government regulation significantly increased as industrialization changed the nature of the economy. Simultaneously, businesses turned to the courts to have the new regulatory laws declared unconstitutional. At the same time, over these decades, scholars and judges increasingly espoused a belief in a laissez-faire, unregulated economy. In part, this was based on a philosophy of social Darwinism, which professed that society would thrive with the least government regulation interference, allowing the "best" to advance and prosper.[9] Additionally, this view was based on a belief that government regulations unduly interfered with the natural rights of people to own and use their property and with a basic liberty interest in freedom of contract.[10] Furthermore, support for a laissez-faire philosophy simply reflected hostility by businesses to the increased government regulation designed to protect workers, unions, consumers, and competitors.

Loan Association v. Topeka, 87 U.S. (20 Wall.) 655 (1874), decided one year after the *Slaughter-House Cases*, is regarded as one of the first instances of the Court's using natural law principles to limit government regulatory power. In Loan Association v. Topeka, the Court invalidated a city law that imposed a tax to fund bonds to attract private businesses to Topeka. Without expressly referring to the Constitution because the case arose as a diversity suit, the Court invalidated the law as "purely in aid of private or personal [objects] beyond the legislative power, and an unauthorized invasion of private right."

Over the next two decades, in a series of cases, the Supreme Court rejected due process challenges to government economic regulations. Yet, in these cases, Supreme Court dicta indicated that it would invalidate laws as violating due

---

8. 83 U.S. (16 Wall.) at 81.

9. A widely cited work advocating this view was Herbert Spencer, *Social Statics* (1851).

10. Leading proponents of this view were Thomas M. Cooley, *Constitutional Limitations* (1878), and Christopher G. Tiedeman, *A Treatise on the Limitations of the Police Power in the United States* (1886).

process if they interfered with natural principles of justice. Although these cases articulated the principles of substantive economic due process, the Court did not use them to declare laws unconstitutional.

For example, in Munn v. Illinois, 94 U.S. 113 (1876), the Court upheld a state law that set maximum rates for grain-storage warehouses. The Court indicated, however, that "under some circumstances" regulation of business would be found to violate due process. The Court said that the central question was whether the "private property is 'affected with a public interest,' . . . [because] when one devotes his property to a use in which the public has an interest, he, in effect, grants to the public an interest in that use, and must submit to be controlled by the public for the common good." The Court expressly declared that it was for the judiciary to evaluate the reasonableness of state regulations. The Court stated, "Undoubtedly, in mere private contracts, relating to matters in which the public has no interest, what is reasonable must be ascertained judicially."

In the *Railroad Commission Cases*, 116 U.S. 307 (1886), the Court upheld a state law regulating railroad rates, but the Court indicated that due process could be used to challenge such rates in the future. The Court stated that the "power to regulate is not a power to destroy. Under pretence of regulating fares and freights, the State cannot require a railroad corporation to carry persons or property without reward; neither can it do that which in law amounts to a taking of private property for public use without just compensation, or without due process of law." Indeed, just a few years later, the Court found a state railroad regulation to violate the Due Process Clause and held that "[t]he question of the reasonableness of a rate of charge for transportation by a railroad company is eminently a question for judicial investigation, requiring due process of law for its determination."[11]

In Mugler v. Kansas, 123 U.S. 623 (1887), the Court upheld as constitutional a state law that prohibited the sale of alcoholic beverages. But the Court strongly indicated that state laws would be invalidated as violating due process unless they truly were an exercise of the state's police power. The Court said that if "a statute purporting to have been enacted to protect the public health, the public morals, or the public safety, has no real or substantial relation to those objects, or is a palpable invasion of rights secured by the fundamental law, it is the duty of the courts so to adjudge, and thereby give effect to the Constitution."

Munn v. Illinois, the *Railroad Commission Cases*, and Mugler v. Kansas were important for articulating that due process was a limit on the government's regulatory power, even though in each of these cases the Court ruled in favor of the government. The Court expressed the philosophy that was to dominate constitutional law for the first third of the twentieth century. Moreover, at about the same time, in 1886, the Supreme Court held that corporations were "persons" under the Due Process and Equal Protection Clauses.[12] This meant, of course, that corporations could use the Constitution and the philosophy expressed in cases such as *Munn*, the *Railroad Commission Cases*, and *Mugler* to challenge government regulations.

---

11. Chicago, Milwaukee & St. Paul Railway Co. v. Minnesota, 134 U.S. 418, 458 (1890).
12. Santa Clara County v. Southern Pacific R.R. Co., 118 U.S. 394 (1886).

3. Substantive Due Process of the Lochner Era

The above cases suggested the Court's willingness to use the Due Process Clause to invalidate government economic regulations as interfering with freedom of contract. The Court did so in Allgeyer v. Louisiana.

ALLGEYER v. LOUISIANA
165 U.S. 578 (1897)

Justice PECKHAM delivered the opinion of the Court.

A conditional prohibition in regard to foreign insurance companies doing business within the state of Louisiana is to be found in article 236 of the constitution of that state, which reads as follows: "No foreign corporation shall do any business in this state without having one or more known places of business and an authorized agent or agents in the state upon whom process may be served."

There is no doubt of the power of the state to prohibit foreign insurance companies from doing business within its limits. The state can impose such conditions as it pleases upon the doing of any business by those companies within its borders, and unless the conditions be complied with the prohibition may be absolute.

In this case, [however], the only act which it is claimed was a violation of the statute in question consisted in sending the letter through the mail notifying the company of the property to be covered by the policy already delivered. We have, then, a contract which it is conceded was made outside and beyond the limits of the jurisdiction of the state of Louisiana, being made and to be performed within the state of New York, where the premiums were to be paid, and losses, if any, adjusted. The letter of notification did not constitute a contract made or entered into within the state of Louisiana. It was but the performance of an act rendered necessary by the provisions of the contract already made between the parties outside of the state. It was a mere notification that the contract already in existence would attach to that particular property. In any event, the contract was made in New York, outside of the jurisdiction of Louisiana, even though the policy was not to attach to the particular property until the notification was sent.

The supreme court of Louisiana says that the act of writing within that state the letter of notification was an act therein done to effect an insurance on property then in the state, in a marine insurance company which had not complied with its laws, and such act was therefore prohibited by the statute. As so construed, we think the statute is a violation of the fourteenth amendment of the federal constitution, in that it deprives the defendants of their liberty without due process of law. The statute which forbids such act does not become due process of law, because it is inconsistent with the provisions of the constitution of the Union. The "liberty" mentioned in that amendment means, not only the right of the citizen to be free from the mere physical restraint of his person, as by incarceration, but the term is deemed to embrace the right of the citizen to be free in the enjoyment of all his faculties; to be free to use them in all lawful ways; to live and work where he will; to earn his livelihood by any lawful calling; to pursue any livelihood or avocation; and for that purpose to enter into all contracts which may be proper, necessary, and essential to his carrying out to a successful conclusion the purposes above mentioned.

Has not a citizen of a state, under the provisions of the federal constitution above mentioned, a right to contract outside of the state for insurance on his property, — a right of which state legislation cannot deprive him? We are not alluding to acts done within the state by an insurance company or its agents doing business therein, which are in violation of the state statutes. When we speak of the liberty to contract for insurance or to do an act to effectuate such a contract already existing, we refer to and have in mind the facts of this case, where the contract was made outside the state, and as such was a valid and proper contract. The act done within the limits of the state, under the circumstances of this case and for the purpose therein mentioned, we hold a proper act, — one which the defendants were at liberty to perform, and which the state legislature had no right to prevent, at least with reference to the federal constitution. To deprive the citizen of such a right as herein described without due process of law is illegal. Such a statute as this in question is not due process of law, because it prohibits an act which under the federal constitution the defendants had a right to perform. This does not interfere in any way with the acknowledged right of the state to enact such legislation in the legitimate exercise of its police or other powers as to it may seem proper. In the exercise of such right, however, care must be taken not to infringe upon those other rights of the citizen which are protected by the federal constitution.

The Atlantic Mutual Insurance Company of New York has done no business of insurance within the state of Louisiana, and has not subjected itself to any provisions of the statute in question. It had the right to enter into a contract in New York with citizens of Louisiana for the purpose of insuring the property of its citizens, even if that property were in the state of Louisiana, and correlatively the citizens of Louisiana had the right without the state of entering into contract with an insurance company for the same purpose. Any act of the state legislature which should prevent the entering into such a contract, or the mailing within the state of Louisiana of such a notification as is mentioned in this case, is an improper and illegal interference with the conduct of the citizen, although residing in Louisiana, in his right to contract and to carry out the terms of a contract validly entered into outside and beyond the jurisdiction of the state. For these reasons we think the statute in question was a violation of the federal constitution.

Eight years after *Allgeyer*, the Supreme Court followed its reasoning and used substantive due process to invalidate a state law protecting workers in Lochner v. New York. *Lochner* is the most famous case of the era, in part because it so clearly expressed the themes followed by the Court in using freedom of contract under the Due Process Clause to limit government economic regulations.

LOCHNER v. NEW YORK

198 U.S. 45 (1905)

Justice PECKHAM delivered the opinion of the Court.

[T]he defendant [was convicted] of a misdemeanor [for violating the following law]:

> Hours of labor in bakeries and confectionery establishments. No employee shall be required or permitted to work in a biscuit, bread, or cake bakery or confectionery establishment more than sixty hours in any one week, or more than ten hours in any one day, unless for the purpose of making a shorter work day on the last day of the week; nor more hours in any one week than will make an average of ten hours per day for the number of days during such week in which such employee shall work.

The statute necessarily interferes with the right of contract between the employer and employees, concerning the number of hours in which the latter may labor in the bakery of the employer. The general right to make a contract in relation to his business is part of the liberty of the individual protected by the 14th Amendment of the Federal Constitution. Allgeyer v. Louisiana. Under that provision no state can deprive any person of life, liberty, or property without due process of law. The right to purchase or to sell labor is part of the liberty protected by this amendment, unless there are circumstances which exclude the right.

There are, however, certain powers, existing in the sovereignty of each state in the Union, somewhat vaguely termed police powers, the exact description and limitation of which have not been attempted by the courts. Those powers, broadly stated, and without, at present, any attempt at a more specific limitation, relate to the safety, health, morals, and general welfare of the public. Both property and liberty are held on such reasonable conditions as may be imposed by the governing power of the state in the exercise of those powers, and with such conditions the 14th Amendment was not designed to interfere. Mugler v. Kansas.

The state, therefore, has power to prevent the individual from making certain kinds of contracts, and in regard to them the Federal Constitution offers no protection. If the contract be one which the state, in the legitimate exercise of its police power, has the right to prohibit, it is not prevented from prohibiting it by the 14th Amendment. Contracts in violation of a statute, either of the Federal or state government, or a contract to let one's property for immoral purposes, or to do any other unlawful act, could obtain no protection from the Federal Constitution, as coming under the liberty of person or of free contract. Therefore, when the state, by its legislature, in the assumed exercise of its police powers, has passed an act which seriously limits the right to labor or the right of contract in regard to their means of livelihood between persons who are both employer and employee, it becomes of great importance to determine which shall prevail — the right of the individual to labor for such time as he may choose, or the right of the state to prevent the individual from laboring, or from entering into any contract to labor, beyond a certain time prescribed by the state.

This court has recognized the existence and upheld the exercise of the police powers of the states in many cases. Among the later cases where the state law has been upheld by this court is that of Holden v. Hardy. A provision in the act of the legislature of Utah was there under consideration, the act limiting the employment of workmen in all underground mines or workings, to eight hours per day, "except in cases of emergency, where life or property is in imminent danger." It also limited the hours of labor in smelting and other institutions for the reduction or refining of ores or metals to eight hours per day, except in like cases of emergency. The act was held to be a valid exercise of the police powers of the state. It was held that the kind of employment, mining, smelting, etc., and the character of the employees in such kinds of labor, were such as to make it reasonable and proper for the state to interfere to prevent the employees from being constrained by the rules laid down by the proprietors in regard to labor.

It must, of course, be conceded that there is a limit to the valid exercise of the police power by the state. There is no dispute concerning this general proposition. Otherwise the 14th Amendment would have no efficacy and the legislatures of the states would have unbounded power, and it would be enough to say that any piece of legislation was enacted to conserve the morals, the health, or the safety of the people; such legislation would be valid, no matter how absolutely without foundation the claim might be. The claim of the police power would be a mere pretext, — become another and delusive name for the supreme sovereignty of the state to be exercised free from constitutional restraint. This is not contended for. In every case that comes before this court, therefore, where legislation of this character is concerned, and where the protection of the Federal Constitution is sought, the question necessarily arises: Is this a fair, reasonable, and appropriate exercise of the police power of the state, or is it an unreasonable, unnecessary, and arbitrary interference with the right of the individual to his personal liberty, or to enter into those contracts in relation to labor which may seem to him appropriate or necessary for the support of himself and his family? Of course the liberty of contract relating to labor includes both parties to it. The one has as much right to purchase as the other to sell labor.

This is not a question of substituting the judgment of the court for that of the legislature. If the act be within the power of the state it is valid, although the judgment of the court might be totally opposed to the enactment of such a law. But the question would still remain: Is it within the police power of the state? and that question must be answered by the court.

The question whether this act is valid as a labor law, pure and simple, may be dismissed in a few words. There is no reasonable ground for interfering with the liberty of person or the right of free contract, by determining the hours of labor, in the occupation of a baker. There is no contention that bakers as a class are not equal in intelligence and capacity to men in other trades or manual occupations, or that they are not able to assert their rights and care for themselves without the protecting arm of the state, interfering with their independence of judgment and of action. They are in no sense wards of the state. Viewed in the light of a purely labor law, with no reference whatever to the question of health, we think that a law like the one before us involves neither the safety, the morals, nor the welfare, of the public, and that the interest of the public is not in the slightest degree affected by such an act. The law must be upheld, if at all, as a law pertaining to the health of the individual engaged in the occupation of a baker. It does not affect any other portion of the public than those who are engaged in that occupation. Clean and wholesome bread does not depend upon whether the baker works but ten hours per day or only sixty hours a week. The limitation of the hours of labor does not come within the police power on that ground.

It is a question of which of two powers or rights shall prevail, the power of the state to legislate or the right of the individual to liberty of person and freedom of contract. The mere assertion that the subject relates, though but in a remote degree, to the public health, does not necessarily render the enactment valid. The act must have a more direct relation, as a means to an end, and the end itself must be appropriate and legitimate, before an act can be held to be valid which interferes with the general right of an individual to be free in his person and in his power to contract in relation to his own labor.

It is unfortunately true that labor, even in any department, may possibly carry with it the seeds of unhealthiness. But are we all, on that account, at the mercy of legislative majorities? A printer, a tinsmith, a locksmith, a carpenter, a cabinet-maker, a dry goods clerk, a bank's, a lawyer's, or a physician's clerk, or a clerk in almost any kind of business, would all come under the power of the legislature, on this assumption. No trade, no occupation, no mode of earning one's living, could escape this all-pervading power, and the acts of the legislature in limiting the hours of labor in all employments would be valid, although such limitation might seriously cripple the ability of the laborer to support himself and his family.

It is also urged, pursuing the same line of argument, that it is to the interest of the state that its population should be strong and robust, and therefore any legislation which may be said to tend to make people healthy must be valid as health laws, enacted under the police power. If this be a valid argument and a justification for this kind of legislation, it follows that the protection of the Federal Constitution from undue interference with liberty of person and freedom of contract is visionary, wherever the law is sought to be justified as a valid exercise of the police power. Scarcely any law but might find shelter under such assumptions, and conduct, properly so called, as well as contract, would come under the restrictive sway of the legislature. Not only the hours of employees, but the hours of employers, could be regulated, and doctors, lawyers, scientists, all professional men, as well as athletes and artisans, could be forbidden to fatigue their brains and bodies by prolonged hours of exercise, lest the fighting strength of the state be impaired. We mention these extreme cases because the contention is extreme. We do not believe in the soundness of the views which uphold this law.

On the contrary, we think that such a law as this, although passed in the assumed exercise of the police power, and as relating to the public health, or the health of the employees named, is not within that power, and is invalid. The act is not, within any fair meaning of the term, a health law, but is an illegal interference with the rights of individuals, both employers and employees, to make contracts regarding labor upon such terms as they may think best, or which they may agree upon with the other parties to such contracts. Statutes of the nature of that under review, limiting the hours in which grown and intelligent men may labor to earn their living, are mere meddlesome interferences with the rights of the individual, and they are not saved from condemnation by the claim that they are passed in the exercise of the police power and upon the subject of the health of the individual whose rights are interfered with, unless there be some fair ground, reasonable in and of itself, to say that there is material danger to the public health, or to the health of the employees, if the hours of labor are not curtailed. This interference on the part of the legislatures of the several states with the ordinary trades and occupations of the people seems to be on the increase. It is impossible for us to shut our eyes to the fact that many of the laws of this character, while passed under what is claimed to be the police power for the purpose of protecting the public health or welfare, are, in reality, passed from other motives. We are justified in saying so when, from the character of the law and the subject upon which it legislates, it is apparent that the public health or welfare bears but the most remote relation to the law. Under such circumstances the freedom of master and employee to contract with each other in relation to their employment, and in defining the same, cannot be prohibited or interfered with, without violating the Federal Constitution.

Justice HOLMES, dissenting.

I regret sincerely that I am unable to agree with the judgment in this case, and that I think it my duty to express my dissent.

This case is decided upon an economic theory which a large part of the country does not entertain. If it were a question whether I agreed with that theory, I should desire to study it further and long before making up my mind. But I do not conceive that to be my duty, because I strongly believe that my agreement or disagreement has nothing to do with the right of a majority to embody their opinions in law.

It is settled by various decisions of this court that state constitutions and state laws may regulate life in many ways which we as legislators might think as injudicious, or if you like as tyrannical, as this, and which, equally with this, interfere with the liberty to contract. Sunday laws and usury laws are ancient examples. The liberty of the citizen to do as he likes so long as he does not interfere with the liberty of others to do the same, which has been a shibboleth for some well-known writers, is interfered with by school laws, by the Postoffice, by every state or municipal institution which takes his money for purposes thought desirable, whether he likes it or not. The 14th Amendment does not enact Mr. Herbert Spencer's Social Statics.

[A] Constitution is not intended to embody a particular economic theory, whether of paternalism and the organic relation of the citizen to the state or of laissez faire. It is made for people of fundamentally differing views, and the accident of our finding certain opinions natural and familiar, or novel, and even shocking, ought not to conclude our judgment upon the question whether statutes embodying them conflict with the Constitution of the United States.

I think that the word "liberty," in the 14th Amendment, is perverted when it is held to prevent the natural outcome of a dominant opinion, unless it can be said that a rational and fair man necessarily would admit that the statute proposed would infringe fundamental principles as they have been understood by the traditions of our people and our law. It does not need research to show that no such sweeping condemnation can be passed upon the statute before us. A reasonable man might think it a proper measure on the score of health. Men whom I certainly could not pronounce unreasonable would uphold it as a first instalment of a general regulation of the hours of work. Whether in the latter aspect it would be open to the charge of inequality I think it unnecessary to discuss.

Justice Harlan, with whom Justice White and Justice Day join, dissenting.

While this court has not attempted to mark the precise boundaries of what is called the police power of the state, the existence of the power has been uniformly recognized, equally by the Federal and State courts. All the cases agree that this power extends at least to the protection of the lives, the health, and the safety of the public against the injurious exercise by any citizen of his own rights.

I take it to be firmly established that what is called the liberty of contract may, within certain limits, be subjected to regulations designed and calculated to promote the general welfare, or to guard the public health, the public morals, or the public safety. The rule is universal that a legislative enactment, Federal or state, is never to be disregarded or held invalid unless it be, beyond question, plainly and palpably in excess of legislative power.

Let these principles be applied to the present case. It is plain that this statute was enacted in order to protect the physical well-being of those who work in bakery and confectionery establishments. It must be remembered that this statute does not apply to all kinds of business. It applies only to work in bakery and confectionery establishments, in which, as all know, the air constantly breathed by workmen is not as pure and healthful as that to be found in some other establishments or out of doors.

Professor Hirt in his treatise on the "Diseases of the Workers" has said: "The labor of the bakers is among the hardest and most laborious imaginable, because it has to be performed under conditions injurious to the health of those engaged in it." Another writer says: "The constant inhaling of flour dust causes inflammation of the lungs and of the bronchial tubes. The eyes also suffer through this dust, which is responsible for the many cases of running eyes among the bakers. The long hours of toil to which all bakers are subjected produce rheumatism, cramps, and swollen legs." Nearly all bakers are palefaced and of more delicate health than the workers of other crafts, which is chiefly due to their hard work and their irregular and unnatural mode of living, whereby the power of resistance against disease is greatly diminished. The average age of a baker is below that of other workmen; they seldom live over their fiftieth year, most of them dying between the ages of forty and fifty. During periods of epidemic diseases the bakers are generally the first to succumb to the disease, and the number swept away during such periods far exceeds the number of other crafts in comparison to the men employed in the respective industries.

We are not to presume that the state of New York has acted in bad faith. Nor can we assume that its legislature acted without due deliberation, or that it did not determine this question upon the fullest attainable information and for the common good. We cannot say that the state has acted without reason, nor ought we to proceed upon the theory that its action is a mere sham. Our duty, I submit, is to sustain the statute as not being in conflict with the Federal Constitution, for the reason — and such is an all-sufficient reason — it is not shown to be plainly and palpably inconsistent with that instrument. Let the state alone in the management of its purely domestic affairs, so long as it does not appear beyond all question that it has violated the Federal Constitution. This view necessarily results from the principle that the health and safety of the people of a state are primarily for the state to guard and protect.

Lochner v. New York thus announced three themes that were followed until 1937: Freedom of contract was a right protected by the Due Process Clauses of the Fifth and Fourteenth Amendments; the government could interfere with freedom of contract only to serve a valid police purpose of protecting public health, public safety, or public morals; and the judiciary would carefully scrutinize legislation to ensure that it truly served such a police purpose. This is classic substantive due process: The Due Process Clause was used not to ensure that the government followed proper procedures but to ensure that laws served an adequate purpose. The Court scrutinized both the ends served by the legislation, to ensure that there really was a valid police purpose, and the means, for the law to sufficiently achieve its purported goal.

Over the next three decades, the Court followed the principles articulated in *Lochner*, finding many laws unconstitutional as interfering with freedom of contract. It is estimated that almost 200 state laws were declared unconstitutional as violating the Due Process Clause of the Fourteenth Amendment.[13] Yet, during this time, the Court upheld many state and federal economic regulations as sufficiently related to a valid police purpose. It is difficult to reconcile some of the decisions from this era. The cases, reviewed below, concerned statutes protecting unions, setting maximum hours, requiring a minimum wage, regulating prices, and safeguarding consumers.

LAWS PROTECTING UNIONIZING

In the early part of the twentieth century, as workers attempted to unionize, many states and the federal government adopted laws to facilitate unionization by prohibiting employers from insisting, as a condition of employment, that employees agree not to join a union. The Supreme Court declared the laws unconstitutional as impermissibly infringing freedom of contract. In Adair v. United States, 208 U.S. 161 (1908), the Court declared unconstitutional such a federal law and said in an opinion by Justice Harlan, "While, as already suggested, the right of liberty and property guaranteed by the Constitution against deprivation without due process of law is subject to such reasonable restraints as the common good or the general welfare may require, it is not within the functions of government — at least, in the absence of contract between the parties — to compel any person in the course of his business and against his will to accept or retain the personal services of another, or to compel any person, against his will, to perform personal services for another. The right of a person to sell his labor upon such terms as he deems proper is, in its essence, the same as the right of the purchaser of labor to prescribe the conditions upon which he will accept such labor from the person offering to sell it. So the right of the employee to quit the service of the employer, for whatever reason, is the same as the right of the employer, for whatever reason, to dispense with the services of such employee."

13. Benjamin F. Wright, *The Growth of American Constitutional Law* 154 (1942) (159 Supreme Court cases found state laws to violate due process and equal protection; 25 more were found to violate due process and another constitutional provision). It should be remembered that the Court's commitment to laissez-faire economics also caused it to invalidate federal economic regulations as exceeding the scope of the Commerce Clause or as violating the Tenth Amendment (discussed in Chapter 2).

In Coppage v. Kansas, 236 U.S. 1 (1915), the Court declared unconstitutional a state law and in an opinion by Justice Pitney stated:

> Granted the equal freedom of both parties to the contract of employment, has not each party the right to stipulate upon what terms only he will consent to the inception, or to the continuance, of that relationship? And may he not insist upon an express agreement, instead of leaving the terms of the employment to be implied? Supposing an employer is unwilling to have in his employ one holding membership in a labor union, and has reason to suppose that the man may prefer membership in the union to the given employment without it—we ask, can the legislature oblige the employer in such case to refrain from dealing frankly at the outset? Approaching the matter from a somewhat different standpoint, is the employee's right to be free to join a labor union any more sacred, or more securely founded upon the Constitution, than his right to work for whom he will, or to be idle if he will?
>
> These queries answer themselves. The answers, as we think, lead to a single conclusion: Under constitutional freedom of contract, whatever either party has the right to treat as sufficient ground for terminating the employment, where there is no stipulation on the subject, he has the right to provide against by insisting that a stipulation respecting it shall be a sine qua non of the inception of the employment, or of its continuance if it be terminable at will.
>
> Included in the right of personal liberty and the right of private property—partaking of the nature of each—is the right to make contracts for the acquisition of property. Chief among such contracts is that of personal employment, by which labor and other services are exchanged for money or other forms of property. If this right be struck down or arbitrarily interfered with, there is a substantial impairment of liberty in the long-established constitutional sense. The right is as essential to the laborer as to the capitalist, to the poor as to the rich; for the vast majority of persons have no other honest way to begin to acquire property, save by working for money.
>
> An interference with this liberty so serious as that now under consideration, and so disturbing of equality of right, must be deemed to be arbitrary, unless it be supportable as a reasonable exercise of the police power of the state. [N]othing of that sort is involved in this case.
>
> To ask a man to agree, in advance, to refrain from affiliation with the union while retaining a certain position of employment, is not to ask him to give up any part of his constitutional freedom. He is free to decline the employment on those terms, just as the employer may decline to offer employment on any other; for "it takes two to make a bargain."

MAXIMUM HOURS LAWS

In *Lochner*, the Court declared unconstitutional a state law setting maximum hours for bakers. The Court's opinion in *Lochner* distinguished Holden v. Hardy, 169 U.S. 366 (1898), in which the Court had upheld a maximum hours law for coal miners. The legislature sought to protect the health of miners by limiting their exposure to coal dust. In *Lochner*, the Court distinguished *Holden* as a legitimate exercise of the police power of the state and concluded that there "is nothing in Holden v. Hardy which covers the case now before us."

Three years after *Lochner*, in Muller v. Oregon, the Court upheld a maximum hours law for women. *Muller* is especially famous because attorney and later Supreme Court Justice Louis Brandeis wrote a detailed 113-page brief purporting to document that women's reproductive health required limiting nondomestic work. After *Lochner* held that there had to be proof that a law was closely related to advancing public health, public safety, or public morals, attorneys began filing detailed briefs, filled with social science data, seeking to show the need for the law. Often termed the "Brandeis brief" because of what Louis Brandeis filed in *Muller*, these documents used social science data to demonstrate the need for a particular law.

MULLER v. OREGON

208 U.S. 412 (1908)

Justice BREWER delivered the opinion of the Court.

On February 19, 1903, the legislature of the state of Oregon passed an act, the first section of which is in these words:

> Sec. 1. That no female (shall) be employed in any mechanical establishment, or factory, or laundry in this state more than ten hours during any one day. The hours of work may be so arranged as to permit the employment of females at any time so that they shall not work more than ten hours during the twenty-four hours of any one day.

The single question is the constitutionality of the statute under which the defendant was convicted, so far as it affects the work of a female in a laundry. It may not be amiss, in the present case, before examining the constitutional question, to notice the course of legislation, as well as expressions of opinion from other than judicial sources. In the brief filed by Mr. Louis D. Brandeis for the defendant in error is a very copious collection of all these matters. [The brief presents] extracts from over ninety reports of committees, bureaus of statistics, commissioners of hygiene, inspectors of factories, both in this country and in Europe, to the effect that long hours of labor are dangerous for women, primarily because of their special physical organization. The matter is discussed in these reports in different aspects, but all agree as to the danger. It would, of course, take too much space to give these reports in detail. Perhaps the general scope and character of all these reports may be summed up in what an inspector for Hanover says: "The reasons for the reduction of the working day to ten hours — (a) the physical organization of women, (b) her maternal functions, (c) the rearing and education of the children, (d) the maintenance of the home — are all so important and so far reaching that the need for such reduction need hardly be discussed."

It is undoubtedly true, as more than once declared by this court, that the general right to contract in relation to one's business is part of the liberty of the individual, protected by the 14th Amendment to the Federal Constitution; yet it is equally well settled that this liberty is not absolute and extending to all contracts, and that a state may, without conflicting with the provisions of the 14th Amendment, restrict in many respects the individual's power of contract.

That woman's physical structure and the performance of maternal functions place her at a disadvantage in the struggle for subsistence is obvious. This is especially true when the burdens of motherhood are upon her. Even when they are not, by abundant testimony of the medical fraternity continuance for a long time on her feet at work, repeating this from day to day, tends to injurious effects upon the body, and, as healthy mothers are essential to vigorous offspring, the physical well-being of woman becomes an object of public interest and care in order to preserve the strength and vigor of the race.

Still again, history discloses the fact that woman has always been dependent upon man. He established his control at the outset by superior physical strength. [T]his control in various forms, with diminishing intensity, has continued to the present. As minors, though not to the same extent, she has been looked upon in the courts as needing especial care that her rights may be preserved. Education was long denied her, and while now the doors of the schoolroom are opened and her opportunities for acquiring knowledge are great, yet even with that and the consequent increase of capacity for business affairs it is still true that in the struggle for subsistence she is not an equal competitor with her brother. Though limitations upon personal and contractual rights may be removed by legislation, there is that in her disposition and habits of life which will operate against a full assertion of those rights. She will still be where some legislation to protect her seems necessary to secure a real equality of right. Doubtless there are individual exceptions, and there are many respects in which she has an advantage over him; but looking at it from the viewpoint of the effort to maintain an independent position in life, she is not upon an equality. Differentiated by these matters from the other sex, she is properly placed in a class by herself, and legislation designed for her protection may be sustained, even when like legislation is not necessary for men, and could not be sustained.

It is impossible to close one's eyes to the fact that she still looks to her brother and depends upon him. Even though all restrictions on political, personal, and contractual rights were taken away, and she stood, so far as statutes are concerned, upon an absolutely equal plane with him, it would still be true that she is so constituted that she will rest upon and look to him for protection; that her physical structure and a proper discharge of her maternal functions — having in view not merely her own health, but the well-being of the race — justify legislation to protect her from the greed as well as the passion of man. The limitations which this statute places upon her contractual powers, upon her right to agree with her employer as to the time she shall labor, are not imposed solely for her benefit, but also largely for the benefit of all. Many words cannot make this plainer. The two sexes differ in structure of body, in the functions to be performed by each, in the amount of physical strength, in the capacity for long continued labor, particularly when done standing, the influence of vigorous health upon the future well-being of the race, the self-reliance which enables one to assert full rights, and in the capacity to maintain the struggle for subsistence. This difference justifies a difference in legislation, and upholds that which is designed to compensate for some of the burdens which rest upon her.

For these reasons, and without questioning in any respect the decision in Lochner v. New York, we are of the opinion that it cannot be adjudged that the act in question is in conflict with the Federal Constitution.

A decade later, in Bunting v. Oregon, 243 U.S. 426 (1917), the Court upheld a maximum hours law for men and women in manufacturing jobs. The state established a ten-hour workday for those involved in manufacturing positions. The Supreme Court found that the law was a valid exercise of the state's police power because it was needed to protect the health of employees in these industries.

MINIMUM WAGE LAWS

Although in Muller v. Oregon the Court upheld maximum hour laws for women, it declared unconstitutional minimum wage laws for women.

ADKINS v. CHILDREN'S HOSPITAL
261 U.S. 525 (1923)

Justice SUTHERLAND delivered the opinion of the Court.

The question presented for determination by these appeals is the constitutionality of the Act of September 19, 1918, providing for the fixing of minimum wages for women and children in the District of Columbia.

The statute now under consideration is attacked upon the ground that it authorizes an unconstitutional interference with the freedom of contract included within the guaranties of the Due Process Clause of the Fifth Amendment. That the right to contract about one's affairs is a part of the liberty of the individual protected by this clause is settled by the decisions of this court and is no longer open to question. Within this liberty are contracts of employment of labor. In making such contracts, generally speaking, the parties have an equal right to obtain from each other the best terms they can as the result of private bargaining.

There is, of course, no such thing as absolute freedom of contract. It is subject to a great variety of restraints. But freedom of contract is, nevertheless, the general rule and restraint the exception, and the exercise of legislative authority to abridge it can be justified only by the existence of exceptional circumstances. Whether these circumstances exist in the present case constitutes the question to be answered.

[T]he ancient inequality of the sexes, otherwise than physical, as suggested in the Muller Case has continued "with diminishing intensity." In view of the great — not to say revolutionary — changes which have taken place since that utterance, in the contractual, political, and civil status of women, culminating in the Nineteenth Amendment, it is not unreasonable to say that these differences have now come almost, if not quite, to the vanishing point. In this aspect of the matter, while the physical differences must be recognized in appropriate cases, and legislation fixing hours or conditions of work may properly take them into account, we cannot accept the doctrine that women of mature age require or may be subjected to restrictions upon their liberty of contract which could not lawfully be imposed in the case of men under similar circumstances. To do so would be to ignore all the implications to be drawn from the present day trend of legislation, as well as that of common thought and usage, by which woman is accorded emancipation from the old doctrine that she must be given special protection or be subjected to special restraint in her contractual and civil relationships. In passing, it may be noted that the instant statute applies in the case of a woman employer contracting with a woman employee as it does when the former is a man.

What is sufficient to supply the necessary cost of living for a woman worker and maintain her in good health and protect her morals is obviously not a precise or unvarying sum—not even approximately so. The amount will depend upon a variety of circumstances: The individual temperament, habits of thrift, care, ability to buy necessaries intelligently, and whether the woman live alone or with her family. To those who practice economy, a given sum will afford comfort, while to those of contrary habit the same sum will be wholly inadequate. The relation between earnings and morals is not capable of standardization. It cannot be shown that well-paid women safeguard their morals more carefully than those who are poorly paid. Morality rests upon other considerations than wages, and there is, certainly, no such prevalent connection between the two as to justify a broad attempt to adjust the latter with reference to the former. As a means of safeguarding morals the attempted classification, in our opinion, is without reasonable basis.

The law takes account of the necessities of only one party to the contract. It ignores the necessities of the employer by compelling him to pay not less than a certain sum, not only whether the employee is capable of earning it, but irrespective of the ability of his business to sustain the burden, generously leaving him, of course, the privilege of abandoning his business as an alternative for going on at a loss.

The law is not confined to the great and powerful employers but embraces those whose bargaining power may be as weak as that of the employee. It takes no account of periods of stress and business depression, of crippling losses, which may leave the employer himself without adequate means of livelihood. To the extent that the sum fixed exceeds the fair value of the services rendered, it amounts to a compulsory exaction from the employer for the support of a partially indigent person, for whose condition there rests upon him no peculiar responsibility, and therefore, in effect, arbitrarily shifts to his shoulders a burden which, if it belongs to anybody, belongs to society as a whole.

The feature of this statute, which perhaps more than any other, puts upon it the stamp of invalidity, is that it exacts from the employer an arbitrary payment for a purpose and upon a basis having no causal connection with his business, or the contract or the work the employee engages to do. It follows, from what has been said, that the act in question passes the limit prescribed by the Constitution.

The Court reaffirmed *Adkins* in 1936, in Morehead v. New York ex rel. Tipaldo, 298 U.S. 587 (1936), which also declared unconstitutional a state minimum wage law for women. In *Morehead*, as in *Adkins*, the Court found that the minimum wage law impermissibly interfered with freedom of contract because it did not serve a valid state police purpose.

CONSUMER PROTECTION LEGISLATION

Another type of legislation that was invalidated was consumer protection legislation. The following case is illustrative.

WEAVER v. PALMER BROS. CO.
270 U.S. 402 (1926)

Justice BUTLER delivered the opinion of the Court.

The question for decision is whether the provision purporting absolutely to forbid the use of shoddy in comfortables violates the Due Process Clause or the Equal Protection Clause.

Appellee makes approximately 3,000,000 comfortables [bedcovers] annually, and about 750,000 of these are filled with materials defined by the act as shoddy. New material from which appellee makes shoddy consists of clippings and pieces of new cloth obtained from cutting tables in garment factories; secondhand shoddy is made of secondhand garments, rags, and the like. Comfortables made of secondhand shoddy sell at lower prices than those filled with other materials.

There is no controversy between the parties as to whether shoddy may be rendered harmless by disinfection or sterilization. While it is sometimes made from filthy rags, and from other materials that have been exposed to infection, it stands undisputed that all dangers to health may be eliminated by appropriate treatment at low cost.

There was no evidence that any sickness or disease was ever caused by the use of shoddy, and the record contains persuasive evidence, and by citation discloses the opinions of scientists eminent in fields related to public health that the transmission of disease-producing bacteria is almost entirely by immediate contact with, or close proximity to, infected persons; that such bacteria perish rapidly when separated from human or animal organisms; and that there is no probability that such bacteria or vermin likely to carry them survive after the period usually required for the gathering of the materials, the production of shoddy, and the manufacture and the shipping of comfortables. This evidence tends strongly to show that in the absence of sterilization or disinfection there would be little, if any, danger to the health of the users of comfortables filled with shoddy, new or secondhand; and confirms the conclusion that all danger from the use of shoddy may be eliminated by sterilization.

Here it is established that sterilization eliminates the dangers, if any, from the use of shoddy. As against that fact, the provision in question cannot be sustained as a measure to protect health; and the fact that the act permits the use of numerous materials, prescribing sterilization if they are secondhand, also serves to show that the prohibition of the use of shoddy, new or old, even when sterilized, is unreasonable and arbitrary.

Justice HOLMES (dissenting).

If the Legislature of Pennsylvania was of opinion that disease is likely to be spread by the use of unsterilized shoddy in comfortables I do not suppose that this Court would pronounce the opinion so manifestly absurd that it could not be acted upon. If we should not, then I think that we ought to assume the opinion to be right for the purpose of testing the law. The Legislature may have been of opinion further that the actual practice of filling comfortables with unsterilized shoddy gathered from filthy floors was wide spread, and this again we must assume to be true. It is admitted to be impossible to distinguish the innocent from the infected product in any practicable way, when it is made up into the comfortables. On these premises, if the Legislature regarded the danger as very great and inspection and tagging as inadequate remedies, it seems to me that in order to prevent the spread of disease it constitutionally could forbid any use of shoddy for bedding and upholstery.

Another type of consumer protection legislation considered by the Court was price regulations. Laws setting the maximum prices for theater tickets,[14] employment agencies,[15] and gasoline[16] were declared unconstitutional as interfering with freedom of contract. The Court repeatedly distinguished Munn v. Illinois, which had upheld price controls for grain storage on the ground that it affected the public interest.[17] The Court stressed the importance of freedom of contract and narrowly defined the permissible scope of the government's police power.

However, toward the end of the *Lochner* era, in 1934, the Court upheld price regulations for milk in Nebbia v. New York.

NEBBIA v. NEW YORK
291 U.S. 502 (1934)

Justice ROBERTS delivered the opinion of the Court.

The Legislature of New York established by chapter 158 of the Laws of 1933, a Milk Control Board with power, among other things to "fix minimum and maximum . . . retail prices to be charged by . . . stores to consumers for consumption off the premises where sold." The board fixed nine cents as the price to be charged by a store for a quart of milk. Nebbia, the proprietor of a grocery store in Rochester, sold two quarts and a 5-cent loaf of bread for 18 cents; and was convicted for violating the board's order.

The question for decision is whether the Federal Constitution prohibits a state from so fixing the selling price of milk. We first inquire as to the occasion for the legislation and its history.

During 1932 the prices received by farmers for milk were much below the cost of production. The decline in prices during 1931 and 1932 was much greater than that of prices generally. The situation of the families of dairy producers had

---

14. Tyson & Brother v. Banton, 273 U.S. 418 (1927).
15. Ribnik v. McBride, 277 U.S. 350 (1928).
16. Williams v. Standard Oil Co., 278 U.S. 235 (1929).
17. 94 U.S. 113 (1876), discussed above. In some cases, the Court did uphold price regulations. *See* Block v. Hirsh, 256 U.S. 135 (1921) (price controls for rental housing); German Alliance Insurance Co. v. Lewis, 233 U.S. 389 (1914) (price controls for fire insurance).

become desperate and called for state aid similar to that afforded the unemployed, if conditions should not improve.

Milk is an essential item of diet. It cannot long be stored. It is an excellent medium for growth of bacteria. These facts necessitate safeguards in its production and handling for human consumption which greatly increase the cost of the business. Failure of producers to receive a reasonable return for their labor and investment over an extended period threaten a relaxation of vigilance against contamination.

The question is whether the enforcement of section 312(e) denied the appellant the due process secured to him by the Fourteenth Amendment. Save the conduct of railroads, no business has been so thoroughly regimented and regulated by the State of New York as the milk industry. Legislation controlling it in the interest of the public health was adopted in 1862 and subsequent statutes, have been carried into the general codification known as the Agriculture and Markets Law. A perusal of these statutes discloses that the milk industry has been progressively subjected to a larger measure of control.

Under our form of government the use of property and the making of contracts are normally matters of private and not of public concern. The general rule is that both shall be free of governmental interference. But neither property rights nor contract rights are absolute; for government cannot exist if the citizen may at will use his property to the detriment of his fellows, or exercise his freedom of contract to work them harm. Equally fundamental with the private right is that of the public to regulate it in the common interest. Thus has this court from the early days affirmed that the power to promote the general welfare is inherent in government.

The milk industry in New York has been the subject of long-standing and drastic regulation in the public interest. The legislative investigation of 1932 was persuasive of the fact that for this and other reasons unrestricted competition aggravated existing evils and the normal law of supply and demand was insufficient to correct maladjustments detrimental to the community. The inquiry disclosed destructive and demoralizing competitive conditions and unfair trade practices which resulted in retail price cutting and reduced the income of the farmer below the cost of production.

We do not understand the appellant to deny that in these circumstances the Legislature might reasonably consider further regulation and control desirable for protection of the industry and the consuming public. That body believed conditions could be improved by preventing destructive price-cutting by stores which, due to the flood of surplus milk, were able to buy at much lower prices than the larger distributors and to sell without incurring the delivery costs of the latter. In the order of which complaint is made the Milk Control Board fixed a price of 10 cents per quart for sales by a distributor to a consumer, and 9 cents by a store to a consumer, thus recognizing the lower costs of the store, and endeavoring to establish a differential which would be just to both. In the light of the facts the order appears not to be unreasonable or arbitrary, or without relation to the purpose to prevent ruthless competition from destroying the wholesale price structure on which the farmer depends for his livelihood, and the community for an assured supply of milk.

So far as the requirement of due process is concerned, and in the absence of other constitutional restriction, a state is free to adopt whatever economic policy may reasonably be deemed to promote public welfare, and to enforce that policy by legislation adapted to its purpose. The courts are without authority either to declare such policy, or, when it is declared by the legislature, to override it. If the laws passed are seen to have a reasonable relation to a proper legislative purpose, and are neither arbitrary nor discriminatory, the requirements of due process are satisfied. Tested by these considerations we find no basis in the Due Process Clause of the Fourteenth Amendment for condemning the provisions of the Agriculture and Markets Law here drawn into question.

4. Economic Substantive Due Process Since 1937

PRESSURES FOR CHANGE

By the mid-1930s, enormous pressures were mounting for the Court to abandon the laissez-faire philosophy of the *Lochner* era. The Depression created a widespread perception that government economic regulations were essential. With millions unemployed and with wages incredibly low for those with jobs, employees had no realistic chance of bargaining in the workplace.

The intellectual foundations of the *Lochner* era also were under attack. *Lochner* rested on the assumption that freedom of contract and related property rights were part of the natural liberties possessed by individuals. Legal realists attacked this premise and persuasively argued that the law reflected political choices; using freedom of contract to invalidate state laws was a political choice that favored employers over employees and corporations over consumers.[18] As such, the Supreme Court's decision in *Lochner* and its progeny could not be regarded as "restoring the natural order which had been upset by the legislature ... [because] [t]here was no 'natural' economic order to upset or restore."[19] If the law merely reflected political choices, there was no reason for the Court to overturn the decisions made by the political process.

At the same time, there were strong political pressures for change. After Franklin Roosevelt was elected to a second term as president in 1936, he proposed a "Court-packing plan," in which the president could appoint one additional justice for every justice on the Court who was over age 70, up to a maximum of 15 justices.[20] Roosevelt was particularly upset that the Court had invalidated several key pieces of New Deal legislation as part of its commitment to a laissez-faire philosophy.[21]

---

18. *See, e.g.,* Roscoe Pound, *The Call for a Realist Jurisprudence,* 44 Harv. L. Rev. 697 (1931); Ray A. Brown, *Due Process of Law, Police Power, and the Supreme Court,* 40 Harv. L. Rev. 943 (1927); Thomas Reed Powell, *The Judiciality of Minimum-Wage Legislation,* 37 Harv. L. Rev. 545 (1924). For a discussion of the importance of legal realist writings in undermining the intellectual foundations of Lochnerism, *see* Howard Gillman, *The Constitution Beseiged: The Rise and Demise of Lochner Era Police Powers Jurisprudence* (1993); Morton J. Horwitz, *The Transformation of American Law, 1870-1960: The Crisis of Legal Orthodoxy* (1992).

19. Laurence Tribe, *American Constitutional Law* 579 (2d ed. 1988).

20. The Court-packing plan and the reactions to it are discussed in Chapter 2.

21. These cases are discussed in Chapter 2.

THE END OF LOCHNERISM

In 1937, in two cases — one involving substantive due process and one involving the scope of Congress's commerce power — Justice Owen Roberts switched sides and cast the fifth vote to uphold the statutes. Perhaps this was a reaction to the Court-packing plan or perhaps he made up his mind in these cases before even learning about that threat. Regardless, in these two decisions, the Court signaled the end of the laissez-faire jurisprudence that had dominated constitutional law for several decades.

In West Coast Hotel v. Parrish, below, the Court signaled the end of substantive economic due process; the Court upheld a state law that required a minimum wage for women employees and expressly overruled Adkins v. Children's Hospital and Morehead v. Tipaldo.

WEST COAST HOTEL CO. v. PARRISH

300 U.S. 379 (1937)

Chief Justice HUGHES delivered the opinion of the Court.

This case presents the question of the constitutional validity of the minimum wage law of the state of Washington. The act, entitled "Minimum Wages for Women," authorizes the fixing of minimum wages for women and minors.

The appellant conducts a hotel. The appellee Elsie Parrish was employed as a chambermaid and (with her husband) brought this suit to recover the difference between the wages paid her and the minimum wage fixed pursuant to the state law. The minimum wage was $14.50 per week of 48 hours. The appellant challenged the act as repugnant to the Due Process Clause of the Fourteenth Amendment of the Constitution of the United States.

The importance of the question, in which many states having similar laws are concerned, the close division by which the decision in the *Adkins* case was reached, and the economic conditions which have supervened, and in the light of which the reasonableness of the exercise of the protective power of the state must be considered, make it not only appropriate, but we think imperative, that in deciding the present case the subject should receive fresh consideration.

[T]he violation alleged by those attacking minimum wage regulation for women is deprivation of freedom of contract. What is this freedom? The Constitution does not speak of freedom of contract. It speaks of liberty and prohibits the deprivation of liberty without due process of law. In prohibiting that deprivation, the Constitution does not recognize an absolute and uncontrollable liberty. Liberty in each of its phases has its history and connotation. But the liberty safeguarded is liberty in a social organization which requires the protection of law against the evils which menace the health, safety, morals, and welfare of the people. Liberty under the Constitution is thus necessarily subject to the restraints of due process, and regulation which is reasonable in relation to its subject and is adopted in the interests of the community is due process.

This power under the Constitution to restrict freedom of contract has had many illustrations. That it may be exercised in the public interest with respect to contracts between employer and employee is undeniable. In dealing with the relation of employer and employed, the Legislature has necessarily a wide field of discretion in order that there may be suitable protection of health and safety, and that peace and good order may be promoted through regulations designed to insure wholesome conditions of work and freedom from oppression.

We think that the decision in the *Adkins* case was a departure from the true application of the principles governing the regulation by the state of the relation of employer and employed. With full recognition of the earnestness and vigor which characterize the prevailing opinion in the *Adkins* case, we find it impossible to reconcile that ruling with these well-considered declarations. What can be closer to the public interest than the health of women and their protection from unscrupulous and overreaching employers? And if the protection of women is a legitimate end of the exercise of state power, how can it be said that the requirement of the payment of a minimum wage fairly fixed in order to meet the very necessities of existence is not an admissible means to that end? The Legislature of the state was clearly entitled to consider the situation of women in employment, the fact that they are in the class receiving the least pay, that their bargaining power is relatively weak, and that they are the ready victims of those who would take advantage of their necessitous circumstances. The Legislature was entitled to adopt measures to reduce the evils of the "sweating system," the exploiting of workers at wages so low as to be insufficient to meet the bare cost of living, thus making their very helplessness the occasion of a most injurious competition. The Legislature had the right to consider that its minimum wage requirements would be an important aid in carrying out its policy of protection. The adoption of similar requirements by many states evidences a deepseated conviction both as to the presence of the evil and as to the means adapted to check it. Legislative response to that conviction cannot be regarded as arbitrary or capricious and that is all we have to decide. Even if the wisdom of the policy be regarded as debatable and its effects uncertain, still the Legislature is entitled to its judgment.

There is an additional and compelling consideration which recent economic experience has brought into a strong light. The exploitation of a class of workers who are in an unequal position with respect to bargaining power and are thus relatively defenseless against the denial of a living wage is not only detrimental to their health and well being, but casts a direct burden for their support upon the community. What these workers lose in wages the taxpayers are called upon to pay. The bare cost of living must be met. We may take judicial notice of the unparalleled demands for relief which arose during the recent period of depression and still continue to an alarming extent despite the degree of economic recovery which has been achieved. It is unnecessary to cite official statistics to establish what is of common knowledge through the length and breadth of the land. While in the instant case no factual brief has been presented, there is no reason to doubt that the state of Washington has encountered the same social problem that is present elsewhere. The community is not bound to provide what is in effect a subsidy for unconscionable employers. The community may direct its law-making power to correct the abuse which springs from their selfish disregard of the public interest.

One year after West Coast Hotel v. Parrish, the Supreme Court reaffirmed its holding and the new policy of judicial deference to government economic regulations. In United States v. Carolene Products Co., below, the Court upheld the Filled Milk Act of 1923 that prohibited "filled milk," a substance obtained by mixing milk and vegetable oil. *Carolene Products* is perhaps most famous for a footnote within it — footnote 4 — that proclaims a need for judicial deference to government economic regulations, with more aggressive judicial review reserved for cases involving fundamental rights and "discrete and insular minorities."

UNITED STATES v. CAROLENE PRODUCTS CO.
304 U.S. 144 (1938)

Justice Stone delivered the opinion of the Court.

The question for decision is whether the "Filled Milk Act" of Congress of March 4, 1923, which prohibits the shipment in interstate commerce of skimmed milk compounded with any fat or oil other than milk fat, so as to resemble milk or cream, infringes the Fifth Amendment.

Appellee was indicted in the District Court for Southern Illinois for violation of the act by the shipment in interstate commerce of certain packages of "Milnut," a compound of condensed skimmed milk and coconut oil made in imitation or semblance of condensed milk or cream. The indictment states, in the words of the statute, that Milnut "is an adulterated article of food, injurious to the public health," and that it is not a prepared food product of the type excepted from the prohibition of the act.

The prohibition of shipment of appellee's product in interstate commerce does not infringe the Fifth Amendment. Twenty years ago this Court, in Hebe Co. v. Shaw, held that a state law which forbids the manufacture and sale of a product assumed to be wholesome and nutritive, made of condensed skimmed milk, compounded with coconut oil, is not forbidden by the Fourteenth Amendment. The power of the Legislature to secure a minimum of particular nutritive elements in a widely used article of food and to protect the public from fraudulent substitutions, was not doubted; and the Court thought that there was ample scope for the legislative judgment that prohibition of the offending article was an appropriate means of preventing injury to the public.

We see no persuasive reason for departing from that ruling here, where the Fifth Amendment is concerned; and since none is suggested, we might rest decision wholly on the presumption of constitutionality. But affirmative evidence also sustains the statute. In twenty years evidence has steadily accumulated of the danger to the public health from the general consumption of foods which have been stripped of elements essential to the maintenance of health. The Filled Milk Act was adopted by Congress after committee hearings, in the course of which eminent scientists and health experts testified. An extensive investigation was made of the commerce in milk compounds in which vegetable oils have been substituted for natural milk fat, and of the effect upon the public health of the use of such compounds as a food substitute for milk. There is nothing in the Constitution which compels a Legislature, either national or state, to ignore such evidence, nor need it disregard the other evidence which amply supports the conclusions of the Congressional committees that the danger is greatly enhanced where an inferior product, like appellee's, is indistinguishable from a valuable food of almost universal use, thus making fraudulent distribution easy and protection of the consumer difficult.

Even in the absence of such aids, the existence of facts supporting the legislative judgment is to be presumed, for regulatory legislation affecting ordinary commercial transactions is not to be pronounced unconstitutional unless in the light of the facts made known or generally assumed it is of such a character as to preclude the assumption that it rests upon some rational basis within the knowledge and experience of the legislators.[22]

Where the existence of a rational basis for legislation whose constitutionality is attacked depends upon facts beyond the sphere of judicial notice, such facts may properly be made the subject of judicial inquiry, and the constitutionality of a statute predicated upon the existence of a particular state of facts may be challenged by showing to the court that those facts have ceased to exist. But by their very nature such inquiries, where the legislative judgment is drawn in question, must be restricted to the issue whether any state of facts either known or which could reasonably be assumed affords support for it.

Here the demurrer challenges the validity of the statute on its face and it is evident from all the considerations presented to Congress, and those of which we may take judicial notice, that the question is at least debatable whether commerce in filled milk should be left unregulated, or in some measure restricted, or wholly prohibited. As that decision was for Congress, neither the finding of a court arrived at by weighing the evidence, nor the verdict of a jury can be substituted for it.

ECONOMIC SUBSTANTIVE DUE PROCESS SINCE 1937

Since 1937, not one state or federal economic regulation has been found unconstitutional as infringing liberty of contract as protected by the Due Process Clauses of the Fifth and Fourteenth Amendments. The Court has made it clear that economic regulations—laws regulating business and employment practices—will be upheld when challenged under the Due Process Clause as long as they are rationally related to a legitimate government purpose.

---

22. There may be narrower scope for operation of the presumption of constitutionality when legislation appears on its face to be within a specific prohibition of the Constitution, such as those of the first ten Amendments, which are deemed equally specific when held to be embraced within the Fourteenth.

It is unnecessary to consider now whether legislation which restricts those political processes which can ordinarily be expected to bring about repeal of undesirable legislation, is to be subjected to more exacting judicial scrutiny under the general prohibitions of the Fourteenth Amendment than are most other types of legislation. On restrictions upon the right to vote, see Nixon v. Herndon; on restraints upon the dissemination of information, see Near v. Minnesota; on interferences with political organizations, see Stromberg v. California; as to prohibition of peaceable assembly, see De Jonge v. Oregon.

Nor need we enquire whether similar considerations enter into the review of statutes directed at particular religious, Pierce v. Society of Sisters; or racial minorities, Nixon v. Herndon; whether prejudice against discrete and insular minorities may be a special condition, which tends seriously to curtail the operation of those political processes ordinarily to be relied upon to protect minorities, and which may call for a correspondingly more searching judicial inquiry. Compare McCulloch v. Maryland; South Carolina State Highway Department v. Barnwell Bros. [Footnote (4) by Court.]

The government's purpose can be any goal not prohibited by the Constitution. In fact, it does not need to be proven that the asserted purpose was the legislature's actual objective. Any conceivable purpose is sufficient. The law only need seem to be a reasonable way of attaining the end; it did not need to be narrowly tailored to achieving the goal.

The reality is that virtually any law can meet this very deferential requirement. The following case, Williamson v. Lee Optical of Oklahoma, Inc., often is referred to as a paradigm example of post-1937 judicial deference to government economic regulations.

WILLIAMSON v. LEE OPTICAL OF OKLAHOMA, INC.
348 U.S. 483 (1955)

Justice DOUGLAS delivered the opinion of the Court.

This suit was instituted in the District Court to have an Oklahoma law declared unconstitutional and to enjoin state officials from enforcing it, for the reason that it allegedly violated various provisions of the Federal Constitution.

The District Court held unconstitutional under the Due Process Clause of the Fourteenth Amendment the portions of §2 which make it unlawful for any person not a licensed optometrist or ophthalmologist to fit lenses to a face or to duplicate or replace into frames lenses or other optical appliances, except upon written prescriptive authority of an Oklahoma licensed ophthalmologist or optometrist.

An ophthalmologist is a duly licensed physician who specializes in the care of the eyes. An optometrist examines eyes for refractive error, recognizes (but does not treat) diseases of the eye, and fills prescriptions for eyeglasses. The optician is an artisan qualified to grind lenses, fill prescriptions, and fit frames.

The effect of §2 is to forbid the optician from fitting or duplicating lenses without a prescription from an ophthalmologist or optometrist. In practical effect, it means that no optician can fit old glasses into new frames or supply a lens, whether it be a new lens or one to duplicate a lost or broken lens, without a prescription. The District Court conceded that it was in the competence of the police power of a State to regulate the examination of the eyes. But it rebelled at the notion that a State could require a prescription from an optometrist or ophthalmologist "to take old lenses and place them in new frames and then fit the completed spectacles to the face of the eyeglass wearer." It held that such a requirement was not "reasonably and rationally related to the health and welfare of the people." The court found that through mechanical devices and ordinary skills the optician could take a broken lens or a fragment thereof, measure its power, and reduce it to prescriptive terms.

The Oklahoma law may exact a needless, wasteful requirement in many cases. But it is for the legislature, not the courts, to balance the advantages and disadvantages of the new requirement. It appears that in many cases the optician can easily supply the new frames or new lenses without reference to the old written prescription. It also appears that many written prescriptions contain no directive data in regard to fitting spectacles to the face. But in some cases the directions contained in the prescription are essential, if the glasses are to be fitted so as to correct the particular defects of vision or alleviate the eye condition. The legislature might have concluded that the frequency of occasions when a prescription is necessary was sufficient to justify this regulation of the fitting of eyeglasses.

Likewise, when it is necessary to duplicate a lens, a written prescription may or may not be necessary. But the legislature might have concluded that one was needed often enough to require one in every case. Or the legislature may have concluded that eye examinations were so critical, not only for correction of vision but also for detection of latent ailments or diseases, that every change in frames and every duplication of a lens should be accompanied by a prescription from a medical expert. To be sure, the present law does not require a new examination of the eyes every time the frames are changed or the lenses duplicated. For if the old prescription is on file with the optician, he can go ahead and make the new fitting or duplicate the lenses. But the law need not be in every respect logically consistent with its aims to be constitutional. It is enough that there is an evil at hand for correction, and that it might be thought that the particular legislative measure was a rational way to correct it.

The day is gone when this Court uses the Due Process Clause of the Fourteenth Amendment to strike down state laws, regulatory of business and industrial conditions, because they may be unwise, improvident, or out of harmony with a particular school of thought. See Nebbia v. People of State of New York; West Coast Hotel Co. v. Parrish. We emphasize again what Chief Justice Waite said in Munn v. State of Illinois, "For protection against abuses by legislatures the people must resort to the polls, not to the courts."

Several other cases, like *Williamson*, reveal how unlikely it is that any economic regulation will be found to violate due process. In Lincoln Federal Labor Union v. Northwestern Iron & Metal Co., 335 U.S. 525 (1949), the Court unanimously upheld a state "right to work" law, which mandated that no person could be denied a job for failure to join a union. The Court stressed that it had long repudiated the "*Allgeyer-Lochner-Adair-Coppage* constitutional doctrine." The Court said that states could legislate against "injurious practices in their internal commercial and business affairs, so long as their laws do not run afoul of some specific federal constitutional prohibition, or of some valid federal law."

In Ferguson v. Skrupa, 372 U.S. 726 (1963), the Court upheld a Kansas law that made it unlawful for a person to engage in the business of debt adjusting, except incident to the practice of law. A debt adjustor would make a deal with a debtor to pay money to the adjustor on a regular basis, and the adjustor would then distribute it to the debtor's creditors based on an agreed-on plan. The effect of the Kansas law was to put debt adjusters, who were not lawyers, out of business.

Justice Black, writing for the Court, said, "Under the system of government created by our Constitution, it is up to legislatures, not courts, to decide on the wisdom and utility of legislation. There was a time when the Due Process Clause was used by this Court to strike down laws which were thought unreasonable, that is, unwise or incompatible with some particular economic or social philosophy. . . . [That doctrine] has long since been discarded. . . . It is now settled that States have power to legislate against what are found to be injurious practices in their internal commercial and business affairs, so long as their laws do not run afoul of some specific federal constitutional prohibition, or some valid federal law."

Ferguson shows that the Court no longer interpreted the Due Process Clause to protect a right to practice a trade or profession or even freedom of contract. The Kansas law undoubtedly was an anticompetitive measure to give lawyers a monopoly in debt adjustments. Nonetheless, the Court proclaimed deference to the legislature and upheld the law.

THE REBIRTH OF ECONOMIC DUE PROCESS? CONSTITUTIONAL LIMITS ON PUNITIVE DAMAGES

Although no law has been invalidated on economic substantive due process grounds since 1937, the following recent cases involve the Supreme Court invalidating large punitive damage awards as violating due process. These cases, of course, also involve economic substantive due process: the Court using the Due Process Clause to declare unconstitutional a government action, here by state courts, as not sufficiently justified. To this point, there have been three Supreme Court decisions elaborating *constitutional* limits on punitive damages.

BMW OF NORTH AMERICA, INC. v. GORE
517 U.S. 559 (1996)

Justice STEVENS delivered the opinion of the Court.

The Due Process Clause of the Fourteenth Amendment prohibits a State from imposing a "grossly excessive" punishment on a tortfeasor. TXO Production Corp. v. Alliance Resources Corp. (1993). The wrongdoing involved in this case was the decision by a national distributor of automobiles not to advise its dealers, and hence their customers, of predelivery damage to new cars when the cost of repair amounted to less than 3 percent of the car's suggested retail price. The question presented is whether a $2 million punitive damages award to the purchaser of one of these cars exceeds the constitutional limit.

I

In January 1990, Dr. Ira Gore, Jr. (respondent), purchased a black BMW sports sedan for $40,750.88 from an authorized BMW dealer in Birmingham, Alabama. After driving the car for approximately nine months, and without noticing any flaws in its appearance, Dr. Gore took the car to "Slick Finish," an independent detailer, to make it look "'snazzier than it normally would appear.'" Mr. Slick, the proprietor, detected evidence that the car had been repainted. Convinced that he had been cheated, Dr. Gore brought suit against petitioner BMW of North America (BMW), the American distributor of BMW automobiles. Dr. Gore alleged that the failure to disclose that the car had been repainted constituted suppression of a material fact. The complaint prayed for $500,000 in compensatory and punitive damages, and costs.

At trial, BMW acknowledged that it had adopted a nationwide policy in 1983 concerning cars that were damaged in the course of manufacture or transportation. If the cost of repairing the damage exceeded 3 percent of the car's suggested retail price, the car was placed in company service for a period of time and then sold as used. If the repair cost did not exceed 3 percent of the suggested retail price, however, the car was sold as new without advising the dealer that any repairs had been made. Because the $601.37 cost of repainting Dr. Gore's car was only about 1.5 percent of its suggested retail price, BMW did not disclose the damage or repair to the Birmingham dealer.

Dr. Gore asserted that his repainted car was worth less than a car that had not been refinished. To prove his actual damages of $4,000, he relied on the testimony of a former BMW dealer, who estimated that the value of a repainted BMW was approximately 10 percent less than the value of a new car that had not been damaged and repaired. To support his claim for punitive damages, Dr. Gore introduced evidence that since 1983 BMW had sold 983 refinished cars as new, including 14 in Alabama, without disclosing that the cars had been repainted before sale at a cost of more than $300 per vehicle. Using the actual damage estimate of $4,000 per vehicle, Dr. Gore argued that a punitive award of $4 million would provide an appropriate penalty for selling approximately 1,000 cars for more than they were worth.

The jury returned a verdict finding BMW liable for compensatory damages of $4,000. In addition, the jury assessed $4 million in punitive damages, based on a determination that the nondisclosure policy constituted "gross, oppressive or malicious" fraud.

On appeal, the Alabama Supreme Court also rejected BMW's claim that the award exceeded the constitutionally permissible amount. The Alabama Supreme Court did, however, rule in BMW's favor on one critical point: The court found that the jury improperly computed the amount of punitive damages by multiplying Dr. Gore's compensatory damages by the number of similar sales in other jurisdictions. Having found the verdict tainted, the court held that "a constitutionally reasonable punitive damages award in this case is $2,000,000," and therefore ordered a remittitur in that amount.

II

Punitive damages may properly be imposed to further a State's legitimate interests in punishing unlawful conduct and deterring its repetition. In our federal system, States necessarily have considerable flexibility in determining the level of punitive damages that they will allow in different classes of cases and in any particular case. Most States that authorize exemplary damages afford the jury similar latitude, requiring only that the damages awarded be reasonably necessary to vindicate the State's legitimate interests in punishment and deterrence.

Only when an award can fairly be categorized as "grossly excessive" in relation to these interests does it enter the zone of arbitrariness that violates the Due Process Clause of the Fourteenth Amendment. For that reason, the federal excessiveness inquiry appropriately begins with an identification of the state interests that a punitive award is designed to serve. We therefore focus our attention first on the scope of Alabama's legitimate interests in punishing BMW and deterring it from future misconduct.

No one doubts that a State may protect its citizens by prohibiting deceptive trade practices and by requiring automobile distributors to disclose presale repairs that affect the value of a new car. But the States need not, and in fact do not, provide such protection in a uniform manner.

We may assume, arguendo, that it would be wise for every State to adopt Dr. Gore's preferred rule, requiring full disclosure of every presale repair to a car, no matter how trivial and regardless of its actual impact on the value of the car. But while we do not doubt that Congress has ample authority to enact such a policy for the entire Nation, it is clear that no single State could do so, or even impose its own policy choice on neighboring States. Similarly, one State's power to impose burdens on the interstate market for automobiles is not only subordinate to the federal power over interstate commerce, Gibbons v. Ogden (1824), but is also constrained by the need to respect the interests of other States.

We think it follows from these principles of state sovereignty and comity that a State may not impose economic sanctions on violators of its laws with the intent of changing the tortfeasors' lawful conduct in other States. Before this Court Dr. Gore argued that the large punitive damages award was necessary to induce BMW to change the nationwide policy that it adopted in 1983. But by attempting to alter BMW's nationwide policy, Alabama would be infringing on the policy choices of other States. To avoid such encroachment, the economic penalties that a State such as Alabama inflicts on those who transgress its laws, whether the penalties take the form of legislatively authorized fines or judicially imposed punitive damages, must be supported by the State's interest in protecting its own consumers and its own economy. Alabama may insist that BMW adhere to a particular disclosure policy in that State. Alabama does not have the power, however, to punish BMW for conduct that was lawful where it occurred and that had no impact on Alabama or its residents. Nor may Alabama impose sanctions on BMW in order to deter conduct that is lawful in other jurisdictions.

III

Elementary notions of fairness enshrined in our constitutional jurisprudence dictate that a person receive fair notice not only of the conduct that will subject him to punishment, but also of the severity of the penalty that a State may impose. Three guideposts, each of which indicates that BMW did not receive adequate notice of the magnitude of the sanction that Alabama might impose for adhering to the nondisclosure policy adopted in 1983, lead us to the conclusion that the $2 million award against BMW is grossly excessive: the degree of reprehensibility of the nondisclosure; the disparity between the harm or potential harm suffered by Dr. Gore and his punitive damages award; and the difference between this remedy and the civil penalties authorized or imposed in comparable cases.

DEGREE OF REPREHENSIBILITY

Perhaps the most important indicium of the reasonableness of a punitive damages award is the degree of reprehensibility of the defendant's conduct.

As the Court stated nearly 150 years ago, exemplary damages imposed on a defendant should reflect "the enormity of his offense." Day v. Woodworth (1852).

In this case, none of the aggravating factors associated with particularly reprehensible conduct is present. The harm BMW inflicted on Dr. Gore was purely economic in nature. The presale refinishing of the car had no effect on its performance or safety features, or even its appearance for at least nine months after his purchase. BMW's conduct evinced no indifference to or reckless disregard for the health and safety of others. To be sure, infliction of economic injury, especially when done intentionally through affirmative acts of misconduct, or when the target is financially vulnerable, can warrant a substantial penalty. But this observation does not convert all acts that cause economic harm into torts that are sufficiently reprehensible to justify a significant sanction in addition to compensatory damages.

RATIO

The second and perhaps most commonly cited indicium of an unreasonable or excessive punitive damages award is its ratio to the actual harm inflicted on the plaintiff. The principle that exemplary damages must bear a "reasonable relationship" to compensatory damages has a long pedigree.

In Pacific Mutual Insurance v. Haslip (1991) we concluded that even though a punitive damages award of "more than 4 times the amount of compensatory damages" might be "close to the line," it did not "cross the line into the area of constitutional impropriety." TXO v. Alliance Resource Corp. (1993), following dicta in *Haslip*, refined this analysis by confirming that the proper inquiry is "'whether there is a reasonable relationship between the punitive damages award and the harm likely to result from the defendant's conduct as well as the harm that actually has occurred.'"

The $2 million in punitive damages awarded to Dr. Gore by the Alabama Supreme Court is 500 times the amount of his actual harm as determined by the jury. Moreover, there is no suggestion that Dr. Gore or any other BMW purchaser was threatened with any additional potential harm by BMW's nondisclosure policy. The disparity in this case is thus dramatically greater than those considered in *Haslip* and *TXO*. In most cases, the ratio will be within a constitutionally acceptable range, and remittitur will not be justified on this basis. When the ratio is a breathtaking 500 to 1, however, the award must surely "raise a suspicious judicial eyebrow."

SANCTIONS FOR COMPARABLE MISCONDUCT

Comparing the punitive damages award and the civil or criminal penalties that could be imposed for comparable misconduct provides a third indicium of excessiveness. In this case the $2 million economic sanction imposed on BMW is substantially greater than the statutory fines available in Alabama and elsewhere for similar malfeasance.

The maximum civil penalty authorized by the Alabama Legislature for a violation of its Deceptive Trade Practices Act is $2,000; other States authorize more severe sanctions, with the maxima ranging from $5,000 to $10,000. None of these statutes would provide an out-of-state distributor with fair notice that the first violation — or, indeed the first 14 violations — of its provisions might subject an offender to a multimillion dollar penalty. Moreover, at the time

BMW's policy was first challenged, there does not appear to have been any judicial decision in Alabama or elsewhere indicating that application of that policy might give rise to such severe punishment.

The sanction imposed in this case cannot be justified on the ground that it was necessary to deter future misconduct without considering whether less drastic remedies could be expected to achieve that goal. The fact that a multimillion dollar penalty prompted a change in policy sheds no light on the question whether a lesser deterrent would have adequately protected the interests of Alabama consumers. We are fully convinced that the grossly excessive award imposed in this case transcends the constitutional limit.

Justice SCALIA, with whom Justice THOMAS joins, dissenting.

Today we see the latest manifestation of this Court's recent and increasingly insistent "concern about punitive damages that 'run wild.'" Since the Constitution does not make that concern any of our business, the Court's activities in this area are an unjustified incursion into the province of state governments.

In earlier cases that were the prelude to this decision, I set forth my view that a state trial procedure that commits the decision whether to impose punitive damages, and the amount, to the discretion of the jury, subject to some judicial review for "reasonableness," furnishes a defendant with all the process that is "due." See TXO Production Corp. v. Alliance Resources Corp. (1993) (Scalia, J., concurring in judgment). I do not regard the Fourteenth Amendment's Due Process Clause as a secret repository of substantive guarantees against "unfairness" — neither the unfairness of an excessive civil compensatory award, nor the unfairness of an "unreasonable" punitive award. What the Fourteenth Amendment's procedural guarantee assures is an opportunity to contest the reasonableness of a damages judgment in state court; but there is no federal guarantee a damages award actually be reasonable. This view, which adheres to the text of the Due Process Clause, has not prevailed in our punitive damages cases. When, however, a constitutional doctrine adopted by the Court is not only mistaken but also insusceptible of principled application, I do not feel bound to give it stare decisis effect — indeed, I do not feel justified in doing so.

Our punitive damages jurisprudence compels such a response. The Constitution provides no warrant for federalizing yet another aspect of our Nation's legal culture (no matter how much in need of correction it may be), and the application of the Court's new rule of constitutional law is constrained by no principle other than the Justices' subjective assessment of the "reasonableness" of the award in relation to the conduct for which it was assessed.

That the issue has been framed in terms of a constitutional right against unreasonably excessive awards should not obscure the fact that the logical and necessary consequence of the Court's approach is the recognition of a constitutional right against unreasonably imposed awards as well. The elevation of "fairness" in punishment to a principle of "substantive due process" means that every punitive award unreasonably imposed is unconstitutional; such an award is by definition excessive, since it attaches a penalty to conduct undeserving of punishment. Indeed, if the Court is correct, it must be that every claim that a state jury's award of compensatory damages is "unreasonable" (because not supported by the evidence) amounts to an assertion of constitutional injury. And the same would be true for determinations of liability. By today's logic, every dispute as to evidentiary sufficiency in a state civil suit poses a question of constitutional moment, subject to review in this Court. That is a stupefying proposition.

STATE FARM MUTUAL AUTOMOBILE INSURANCE CO. v. CAMPBELL

538 U.S. 408 (2003)

Justice KENNEDY delivered the opinion of the Court.

We address once again the measure of punishment, by means of punitive damages, a State may impose upon a defendant in a civil case. The question is whether, in the circumstances we shall recount, an award of $145 million in punitive damages, where full compensatory damages are $1 million, is excessive and in violation of the Due Process Clause of the Fourteenth Amendment to the Constitution of the United States.

I

In 1981, Curtis Campbell (Campbell) was driving with his wife, Inez Preece Campbell, in Cache County, Utah. He decided to pass six vans traveling ahead of them on a two-lane highway. Todd Ospital was driving a small car approaching from the opposite direction. To avoid a head-on collision with Campbell, who by then was driving on the wrong side of the highway and toward oncoming traffic, Ospital swerved onto the shoulder, lost control of his automobile, and collided with a vehicle driven by Robert G. Slusher. Ospital was killed, and Slusher was rendered permanently disabled. The Campbells escaped unscathed.

In the ensuing wrongful death and tort action, Campbell insisted he was not at fault. Early investigations did support differing conclusions as to who caused the accident, but "a consensus was reached early on by the investigators and witnesses that Mr. Campbell's unsafe pass had indeed caused the crash." Campbell's insurance company, petitioner State Farm Mutual Automobile Insurance Company (State Farm), nonetheless decided to contest liability and declined offers by Slusher and Ospital's estate (Ospital) to settle the claims for the policy limit of $50,000 ($25,000 per claimant). State Farm also ignored the advice of one of its own investigators and took the case to trial, assuring the Campbells that "their assets were safe, that they had no liability for the accident, that [State Farm] would represent their interests, and that they did not need to procure separate counsel." To the contrary, a jury determined that Campbell was 100 percent at fault, and a judgment was returned for $185,849, far more than the amount offered in settlement.

At first State Farm refused to cover the $135,849 in excess liability. Its counsel made this clear to the Campbells: "'You may want to put for sale signs on your property to get things moving.'" Nor was State Farm willing to post a supersedeas bond to allow Campbell to appeal the judgment against him. Campbell obtained his own counsel to appeal the verdict. During the pendency of the appeal, in late 1984, Slusher, Ospital, and the Campbells reached an agreement whereby Slusher and Ospital agreed not to seek satisfaction of their claims against the Campbells. In exchange the Campbells agreed to pursue a bad faith action against State Farm and to be represented by Slusher's and Ospital's attorneys. The Campbells also agreed that Slusher and Ospital would have a right to play a part in all major decisions concerning the bad faith action. No settlement could be concluded without Slusher's and Ospital's approval, and Slusher and Ospital would receive 90 percent of any verdict against State Farm.

In 1989, the Utah Supreme Court denied Campbell's appeal in the wrongful death and tort actions. State Farm then paid the entire judgment, including the amounts in excess of the policy limits. The Campbells nonetheless filed a complaint against State Farm alleging bad faith, fraud, and intentional infliction of emotional distress. The jury awarded the Campbells $2.6 million in compensatory damages and $145 million in punitive damages, which the trial court reduced to $1 million and $25 million respectively. Both parties appealed. The Utah Supreme Court reinstated the $145 million punitive damages award.

II

We recognized in Cooper Industries, Inc. v. Leatherman Tool Group, Inc. (2001), that in our judicial system compensatory and punitive damages, although usually awarded at the same time by the same decisionmaker, serve different purposes. Compensatory damages "are intended to redress the concrete loss that the plaintiff has suffered by reason of the defendant's wrongful conduct." By contrast, punitive damages serve a broader function; they are aimed at deterrence and retribution. While States possess discretion over the imposition of punitive damages, it is well established that there are procedural and substantive constitutional limitations on these awards. The Due Process Clause of the Fourteenth Amendment prohibits the imposition of grossly excessive or arbitrary punishments on a tortfeasor. To the extent an award is grossly excessive, it furthers no legitimate purpose and constitutes an arbitrary deprivation of property. Although these awards serve the same purposes as criminal penalties, defendants subjected to punitive damages in civil cases have not been accorded the protections applicable in a criminal proceeding. This increases our concerns over the imprecise manner in which punitive damages systems are administered. We have admonished that "[p]unitive damages pose an acute danger of arbitrary deprivation of property."

In light of these concerns, in BMW v. Gore (1996) we instructed courts reviewing punitive damages to consider three guideposts: (1) the degree of reprehensibility of the defendant's misconduct; (2) the disparity between the actual or potential harm suffered by the plaintiff and the punitive damages award; and (3) the difference between the punitive damages awarded by the jury and the civil penalties authorized or imposed in comparable cases. We reiterated the importance of these three guideposts in *Cooper Industries* and mandated appellate courts to conduct de novo review of a trial court's application of them to the jury's award. Exacting appellate review ensures that an award of punitive damages is based upon an "'application of law, rather than a decisionmaker's caprice.'"

III

Under the principles outlined in BMW of North America, Inc. v. Gore, this case is neither close nor difficult. It was error to reinstate the jury's $145 million punitive damages award. We address each guidepost of *Gore* in some detail.

A

"[T]he most important indicium of the reasonableness of a punitive damages award is the degree of reprehensibility of the defendant's conduct." We have instructed courts to determine the reprehensibility of a defendant by considering whether: the harm caused was physical as opposed to economic; the tortious conduct evinced an indifference to or a reckless disregard of the health or safety of others; the target of the conduct had financial vulnerability; the conduct involved repeated actions or was an isolated incident; and the harm was the result of intentional malice, trickery, or deceit, or mere accident. The existence of any one of these factors weighing in favor of a plaintiff may not be sufficient to sustain a punitive damages award; and the absence of all of them renders any award suspect. It should be presumed a plaintiff has been made whole for his injuries by compensatory damages, so punitive damages should only be awarded if the defendant's culpability, after having paid compensatory damages, is so reprehensible as to warrant the imposition of further sanctions to achieve punishment or deterrence.

Applying these factors in the instant case, we must acknowledge that State Farm's handling of the claims against the Campbells merits no praise. The trial court found that State Farm's employees altered the company's records to make Campbell appear less culpable. State Farm disregarded the overwhelming likelihood of liability and the near-certain probability that, by taking the case to trial, a judgment in excess of the policy limits would be awarded. State Farm amplified the harm by at first assuring the Campbells their assets would be safe from any verdict and by later telling them, postjudgment, to put a for-sale sign on their house. While we do not suggest there was error in awarding punitive damages based upon State Farm's conduct toward the Campbells, a more modest punishment for this reprehensible conduct could have satisfied the State's legitimate objectives, and the Utah courts should have gone no further.

This case, instead, was used as a platform to expose, and punish, the perceived deficiencies of State Farm's operations throughout the country. The Utah Supreme Court's opinion makes explicit that State Farm was being condemned for its nationwide policies rather than for the conduct directed toward the Campbells. This was, as well, an explicit rationale of the trial court's decision in approving the award, though reduced from $145 million to $25 million.

A State cannot punish a defendant for conduct that may have been lawful where it occurred. Nor, as a general rule, does a State have a legitimate concern in imposing punitive damages to punish a defendant for unlawful acts committed outside of the State's jurisdiction. Any proper adjudication of conduct that occurred outside Utah to other persons would require their inclusion, and, to those parties, the Utah courts, in the usual case, would need to apply the laws of their relevant jurisdiction.

For a more fundamental reason, however, the Utah courts erred in relying upon this and other evidence: The courts awarded punitive damages to punish and deter conduct that bore no relation to the Campbells' harm. A defendant's dissimilar acts, independent from the acts upon which liability was premised, may not serve as the basis for punitive damages. A defendant should be punished for the conduct that harmed the plaintiff, not for being an unsavory individual or business. Due process does not permit courts, in the calculation of punitive damages, to adjudicate the merits of other parties' hypothetical claims against a defendant under the guise of the reprehensibility analysis, but we have no doubt the Utah Supreme Court did that here. Punishment on these bases creates the possibility of multiple punitive damages awards for the same conduct; for in the usual case non-parties are not bound by the judgment some other plaintiff obtains.

The same reasons lead us to conclude the Utah Supreme Court's decision cannot be justified on the grounds that State Farm was a recidivist. Although "[o]ur holdings that a recidivist may be punished more severely than a first offender recognize that repeated misconduct is more reprehensible than an individual instance of malfeasance," in the context of civil actions courts must ensure the conduct in question replicates the prior transgressions.

The Campbells have identified scant evidence of repeated misconduct of the sort that injured them. Nor does our review of the Utah courts' decisions convince us that State Farm was only punished for its actions toward the Campbells. Although evidence of other acts need not be identical to have relevance in the calculation of punitive damages, the Utah court erred here because evidence pertaining to claims that had nothing to do with a third-party lawsuit was introduced at length. For the reasons already stated, this argument is unconvincing. The reprehensibility guidepost does not permit courts to expand the scope of the case so that a defendant may be punished for any malfeasance, which in this case extended for a 20-year period. In this case, because the Campbells have shown no conduct by State Farm similar to that which harmed them, the conduct that harmed them is the only conduct relevant to the reprehensibility analysis.

B

Turning to the second *Gore* guidepost, we have been reluctant to identify concrete constitutional limits on the ratio between harm, or potential harm, to the plaintiff and the punitive damages award. We decline again to impose a bright-line ratio which a punitive damages award cannot exceed. Our jurisprudence and the principles it has now established demonstrate, however, that, in practice, few awards exceeding a single-digit ratio between punitive and compensatory damages, to a significant degree, will satisfy due process. While these ratios are not binding, they are instructive. They demonstrate what should be obvious: Single-digit multipliers are more likely to comport with due process, while still achieving the State's goals of deterrence and retribution, than awards with ratios in range of 500 to 1, or, in this case, of 145 to 1.

Nonetheless, because there are no rigid benchmarks that a punitive damages award may not surpass, ratios greater than those we have previously upheld may comport with due process where "a particularly egregious act has resulted in only a small amount of economic damages." The converse is also true, however. When compensatory damages are substantial, then a lesser ratio, perhaps only equal to compensatory damages, can reach the outermost limit of the due process guarantee. The precise award in any case, of course, must be based upon the facts and circumstances of the defendant's conduct and the harm to the plaintiff.

In sum, courts must ensure that the measure of punishment is both reasonable and proportionate to the amount of harm to the plaintiff and to the general damages recovered. In the context of this case, we have no doubt that there is a presumption against an award that has a 145-to-1 ratio. The compensatory award in this case was substantial; the Campbells were awarded $1 million for a year and a half of emotional distress. This was complete compensation. The harm arose from a transaction in the economic realm, not from some physical assault or trauma; there were no physical injuries; and State Farm paid the excess verdict before the complaint was filed, so the Campbells suffered only minor economic injuries for the 18-month period in which State Farm refused to resolve the claim against them. The compensatory damages for the injury suffered here, moreover, likely were based on a component which was duplicated in the punitive award. Much of the distress was caused by the outrage and humiliation the Campbells suffered at the actions of their insurer; and it is a major role of punitive damages to condemn such conduct. Compensatory damages, however, already contain this punitive element.

While States enjoy considerable discretion in deducing when punitive damages are warranted, each award must comport with the principles set forth in *Gore*. The wealth of a defendant cannot justify an otherwise unconstitutional punitive damages award. The principles set forth in *Gore* must be implemented with care, to ensure both reasonableness and proportionality.

C

The third guidepost in *Gore* is the disparity between the punitive damages award and the "civil penalties authorized or imposed in comparable cases." We note that, in the past, we have also looked to criminal penalties that could be imposed. The existence of a criminal penalty does have bearing on the seriousness with which a State views the wrongful action. When used to determine the dollar amount of the award, however, the criminal penalty has less utility. Great care must be taken to avoid use of the civil process to assess criminal penalties that can be imposed only after the heightened protections of a criminal trial have been observed, including, of course, its higher standards of proof. Punitive damages are not a substitute for the criminal process, and the remote possibility of a criminal sanction does not automatically sustain a punitive damages award.

Here, we need not dwell long on this guidepost. The most relevant civil sanction under Utah state law for the wrong done to the Campbells appears to be a $10,000 fine for an act of fraud, an amount dwarfed by the $145 million punitive damages award. The Supreme Court of Utah speculated about the loss of State Farm's business license, the disgorgement of profits, and possible imprisonment, but here again its references were to the broad fraudulent scheme drawn from evidence of out-of-state and dissimilar conduct. This analysis was insufficient to justify the award.

IV

An application of the *Gore* guideposts to the facts of this case, especially in light of the substantial compensatory damages awarded (a portion of which contained a punitive element), likely would justify a punitive damages award at or near the amount of compensatory damages. The punitive award of $145 million, therefore, was neither reasonable nor proportionate to the wrong committed, and it was an irrational and arbitrary deprivation of the property of the defendant. The proper calculation of punitive damages under the principles we have discussed should be resolved, in the first instance, by the Utah courts.

Justice SCALIA, dissenting.

I adhere to the view expressed in my dissenting opinion in BMW of North America, Inc. v. Gore (1996), that the Due Process Clause provides no substantive protections against "excessive" or "'unreasonable'" awards of punitive damages. I am also of the view that the punitive damages jurisprudence which has sprung forth from BMW v. Gore is insusceptible of principled application; accordingly, I do not feel justified in giving the case stare decisis effect. I would affirm the judgment of the Utah Supreme Court.

Justice THOMAS, dissenting.

I would affirm the judgment below because "I continue to believe that the Constitution does not constrain the size of punitive damages awards." Accordingly, I respectfully dissent.

Justice GINSBURG, dissenting.

Not long ago, this Court was hesitant to impose a federal check on state-court judgments awarding punitive damages. In *Gore*, I stated why I resisted the Court's foray into punitive damages "territory traditionally within the States' domain." I adhere to those views, and note again that, unlike federal habeas corpus review of state-court convictions under 28 U.S.C. §2254, the Court "work[s] at this business [of checking state courts] alone," unaided by the participation of federal district courts and courts of appeals. It was once recognized that "the laws of the particular State must suffice [to superintend punitive damages awards] until judges or legislators authorized to do so initiate system-wide change." I would adhere to that traditional view.

The large size of the award upheld by the Utah Supreme Court in this case indicates why damage-capping legislation may be altogether fitting and proper. Neither the amount of the award nor the trial record, however, justifies this Court's substitution of its judgment for that of Utah's competent decisionmakers. In this regard, I count it significant that, on the key criterion "reprehensibility," there is a good deal more to the story than the Court's abbreviated account tells.

Ample evidence allowed the jury to find that State Farm's treatment of the Campbells typified its "Performance, Planning and Review" (PP & R) program; implemented by top management in 1979, the program had "the explicit objective of using the claims-adjustment process as a profit center." "[T]he Campbells presented considerable evidence," the trial court noted, documenting "that the PP & R program . . . has functioned, and continues to function, as an unlawful scheme . . . to deny benefits owed consumers by paying out less than fair value in order to meet preset, arbitrary payout targets designed to enhance corporate profits."

The trial court further determined that the jury could find State Farm's policy "deliberately crafted" to prey on consumers who would be unlikely to defend themselves. In this regard, the trial court noted the testimony of several former State Farm employees affirming that they were trained to target "the weakest of the herd" — "the elderly, the poor, and other consumers who are least knowledgeable about their rights and thus most vulnerable to trickery or deceit, or who have little money and hence have no real alternative but to accept an inadequate offer to settle a claim at much less than fair value."

To further insulate itself from liability, trial evidence indicated, State Farm made "systematic" efforts to destroy internal company documents that might reveal its scheme, efforts that directly affected the Campbells. [W]hile the Campbells' case was pending, Janet Cammack, "an in-house attorney sent by top State Farm management, conducted a meeting . . . in Utah during which she instructed Utah claims management to search their offices and destroy a wide range of material of the sort that had proved damaging in bad-faith litigation in the past—in particular, old claim-handling manuals, memos, claim school notes, procedure guides and other similar documents."

State Farm's "policies and practices," the trial evidence thus bore out, were "responsible for the injuries suffered by the Campbells," and the means used to implement those policies could be found "callous, clandestine, fraudulent, and dishonest." The Utah Supreme Court, relying on the trial court's record-based recitations, understandably characterized State Farm's behavior as "egregious and malicious."

When the Court first ventured to override state-court punitive damages awards, it did so moderately. Today's decision exhibits no such respect and restraint. No longer content to accord state-court judgments "a strong presumption of validity," the Court announces that "few awards exceeding a single-digit ratio between punitive and compensatory damages, to a significant degree, will satisfy due process." Moreover, the Court adds, when compensatory damages are substantial, doubling those damages "can reach the outermost limit of the due process guarantee." In a legislative scheme or a state high court's design to cap punitive damages, the handiwork in setting single-digit and 1-to-1 benchmarks could hardly be questioned; in a judicial decree imposed on the States by this Court under the banner of substantive due process, the numerical controls today's decision installs seem to me boldly out of order.

I remain of the view that this Court has no warrant to reform state law governing awards of punitive damages. Even if I were prepared to accept the flexible guides prescribed in *Gore*, I would not join the Court's swift conversion of those guides into instructions that begin to resemble marching orders.

PHILIP MORRIS U.S.A. v. WILLIAMS

549 U.S. 346 (2007)

Justice Breyer delivered the opinion of the Court.

The question we address today concerns a large state-court punitive damages award. We are asked whether the Constitution's Due Process Clause permits a jury to base that award in part upon its desire to punish the defendant for harming persons who are not before the court (e.g., victims whom the parties do not represent). We hold that such an award would amount to a taking of "property" from the defendant without due process.

I

This lawsuit arises out of the death of Jesse Williams, a heavy cigarette smoker. Respondent, Williams' widow, represents his estate in this state lawsuit for negligence and deceit against Philip Morris, the manufacturer of Marlboro, the brand that Williams favored. A jury found that Williams' death was caused by smoking; that Williams smoked in significant part because he thought it was safe to do so; and that Philip Morris knowingly and falsely led him to believe that this was so. The jury ultimately found that Philip Morris was negligent (as was Williams) and that Philip Morris had engaged in deceit. In respect to deceit, the claim at issue here, it awarded compensatory damages of about $821,000 (about $21,000 economic and $800,000 noneconomic) along with $79.5 million in punitive damages.

Philip Morris made two arguments [on appeal to the Oregon Supreme Court] relevant here. First, it said that the trial court should have accepted, but did not accept, a proposed "punitive damages" instruction that specified the jury could not seek to punish Philip Morris for injury to other persons not before the court. In particular, Philip Morris pointed out that the plaintiff's attorney had told the jury to "think about how many other Jesse Williams in the last 40 years in the State of Oregon there have been. . . . In Oregon, how many people do we see outside, driving home . . . smoking cigarettes? . . . [C]igarettes . . . are going to kill ten [of every hundred]. [And] the market share of Marlboros [i.e., Philip Morris] is one-third [i.e., one of every three killed]." In light of this argument, Philip Morris asked the trial court to tell the jury that "you may consider the extent of harm suffered by others in determining what [the] reasonable relationship is" between any punitive award and "the harm caused to Jesse Williams" by Philip Morris' misconduct, "[but] you are not to punish the defendant for the impact of its alleged misconduct on other persons, who may bring lawsuits of their own in which other juries can resolve their claims. . . ." The judge rejected this proposal and instead told the jury that "[p]unitive damages are awarded against a defendant to punish misconduct and to deter misconduct," and "are not intended to compensate the plaintiff or anyone else for damages caused by the defendant's conduct." In Philip Morris' view, the result was a significant likelihood that a portion of the $79.5 million award represented punishment for its having harmed others, a punishment that the Due Process Clause would here forbid. Second, Philip Morris pointed to the roughly 100-to-1 ratio the $79.5 million punitive damages award bears to $821,000 in compensatory damages.

The Oregon Supreme Court rejected these and other Philip Morris arguments.

For reasons we shall set forth, we consider only the first of these questions. We vacate the Oregon Supreme Court's judgment, and we remand the case for further proceedings.

[II]

In our view, the Constitution's Due Process Clause forbids a State to use a punitive damages award to punish a defendant for injury that it inflicts upon nonparties or those whom they directly represent, i.e., injury that it inflicts upon those who are, essentially, strangers to the litigation. For one thing, the Due Process Clause prohibits a State from punishing an individual without first providing that individual with "an opportunity to present every available defense." Yet a defendant threatened with punishment for injuring a nonparty victim has no opportunity to defend against the charge, by showing, for example in a case such as this, that the other victim was not entitled to damages because he or she knew that smoking was dangerous or did not rely upon the defendant's statements to the contrary.

For another, to permit punishment for injuring a nonparty victim would add a near standardless dimension to the punitive damages equation. How many such victims are there? How seriously were they injured? Under what circumstances did injury occur? The trial will not likely answer such questions as to nonparty victims. The jury will be left to speculate. And the fundamental due process concerns to which our punitive damages cases refer—risks of arbitrariness, uncertainty and lack of notice—will be magnified.

Finally, we can find no authority supporting the use of punitive damages awards for the purpose of punishing a defendant for harming others. We have said that it may be appropriate to consider the reasonableness of a punitive damages award in light of the potential harm the defendant's conduct could have caused. But we have made clear that the potential harm at issue was harm potentially caused the plaintiff.

Respondent argues that she is free to show harm to other victims because it is relevant to a different part of the punitive damages constitutional equation, namely, reprehensibility. That is to say, harm to others shows more reprehensible conduct. Philip Morris, in turn, does not deny that a plaintiff may show harm to others in order to demonstrate reprehensibility. Nor do we. Evidence of actual harm to nonparties can help to show that the conduct that harmed the plaintiff also posed a substantial risk of harm to the general public, and so was particularly reprehensible—although counsel may argue in a particular case that conduct resulting in no harm to others nonetheless posed a grave risk to the public, or the converse. Yet for the reasons given above, a jury may not go further than this and use a punitive damages verdict to punish a defendant directly on account of harms it is alleged to have visited on nonparties.

Given the risks of unfairness that we have mentioned, it is constitutionally important for a court to provide assurance that the jury will ask the right question, not the wrong one. And given the risks of arbitrariness, the concern for adequate notice, and the risk that punitive damages awards can, in practice, impose one State's (or one jury's) policies (e.g., banning cigarettes) upon other States—all of which accompany awards that, today, may be many times the size of such awards in the 18th and 19th centuries[]—it is particularly important that States avoid procedure that unnecessarily deprives juries of proper legal guidance. We therefore conclude that the Due Process Clause requires States to provide assurance that juries are not asking the wrong question, i.e., seeking, not simply to determine reprehensibility, but also to punish for harm caused strangers.

[III]

As the preceding discussion makes clear, we believe that the Oregon Supreme Court applied the wrong constitutional standard when considering Philip

Morris' appeal. We remand this case so that the Oregon Supreme Court can apply the standard we have set forth. Because the application of this standard may lead to the need for a new trial, or a change in the level of the punitive damages award, we shall not consider whether the award is constitutionally "grossly excessive." We vacate the Oregon Supreme Court's judgment and remand the case for further proceedings not inconsistent with this opinion.

Justice STEVENS, dissenting.

Unlike the Court, I see no reason why an interest in punishing a wrongdoer "for harming persons who are not before the court[]" should not be taken into consideration when assessing the appropriate sanction for reprehensible conduct. Whereas compensatory damages are measured by the harm the defendant has caused the plaintiff, punitive damages are a sanction for the public harm the defendant's conduct has caused or threatened. There is little difference between the justification for a criminal sanction, such as a fine or a term of imprisonment, and an award of punitive damages. In our early history either type of sanction might have been imposed in litigation prosecuted by a private citizen. And while in neither context would the sanction typically include a pecuniary award measured by the harm that the conduct had caused to any third parties, in both contexts the harm to third parties would surely be a relevant factor to consider in evaluating the reprehensibility of the defendant's wrongdoing. We have never held otherwise.

In the case before us, evidence attesting to the possible harm the defendant's extensive deceitful conduct caused other Oregonians was properly presented to the jury. No evidence was offered to establish an appropriate measure of damages to compensate such third parties for their injuries, and no one argued that the punitive damages award would serve any such purpose. To award compensatory damages to remedy such third-party harm might well constitute a taking of property from the defendant without due process. But a punitive damages award, instead of serving a compensatory purpose, serves the entirely different purposes of retribution and deterrence that underlie every criminal sanction. This justification for punitive damages has even greater salience when, as in this case, the award is payable in whole or in part to the State rather than to the private litigant.

While apparently recognizing the novelty of its holding, the majority relies on a distinction between taking third-party harm into account in order to assess the reprehensibility of the defendant's conduct — which is permitted — from doing so in order to punish the defendant "directly" — which is forbidden. This nuance eludes me. When a jury increases a punitive damages award because injuries to third parties enhanced the reprehensibility of the defendant's conduct, the jury is by definition punishing the defendant — directly — for third-party harm. A murderer who kills his victim by throwing a bomb that injures dozens of bystanders should be punished more severely than one who harms no one other than his intended victim. Similarly, there is no reason why the measure of the appropriate punishment for engaging in a campaign of deceit in distributing a poisonous and addictive substance to thousands of cigarette smokers statewide should not include consideration of the harm to those "bystanders" as well as the harm to the individual plaintiff. The Court endorses a contrary conclusion without providing us with any reasoned justification.

It is far too late in the day to argue that the Due Process Clause merely guarantees fair procedure and imposes no substantive limits on a State's law-making power. It remains true, however, that the Court should be "reluctant to expand the concept of substantive due process because guideposts for responsible decisionmaking in this unchartered area are scarce and open-ended." Judicial restraint counsels us to "exercise the utmost care whenever we are asked to break new ground in this field." Today the majority ignores that sound advice when it announces its new rule of substantive law.

Justice THOMAS, dissenting.

I join Justice Ginsburg's dissent in full. I write separately to reiterate my view that "'the Constitution does not constrain the size of punitive damages awards.'" It matters not that the Court styles today's holding as "procedural" because the "procedural" rule is simply a confusing implementation of the substantive due process regime this Court has created for punitive damages. Today's opinion proves once again that this Court's punitive damages jurisprudence is "insusceptible of principled application."

Justice GINSBURG, with whom Justice SCALIA and Justice THOMAS join, dissenting.

The purpose of punitive damages, it can hardly be denied, is not to compensate, but to punish. Punish for what? Not for harm actually caused "strangers to the litigation," the Court states, but for the reprehensibility of defendant's conduct. "[C]onduct that risks harm to many," the Court observes, "is likely more reprehensible than conduct that risks harm to only a few." The Court thus conveys that, when punitive damages are at issue, a jury is properly instructed to consider the extent of harm suffered by others as a measure of reprehensibility, but not to mete out punishment for injuries in fact sustained by nonparties. The Oregon courts did not rule otherwise. They have endeavored to follow our decisions.

The right question regarding reprehensibility, the Court acknowledges, would train on "the harm that Philip Morris was prepared to inflict on the smoking public at large." The Court identifies no evidence introduced and no charge delivered inconsistent with that inquiry.

The Court ventures no opinion on the propriety of the charge proposed by Philip Morris, though Philip Morris preserved no other objection to the trial proceedings. Rather than addressing the one objection Philip Morris properly preserved, the Court reaches outside the bounds of the case as postured when the trial court entered its judgment. I would accord more respectful treatment to the proceedings and dispositions of state courts that sought diligently to adhere to our changing, less than crystalline precedent.

TOO MUCH DEFERENCE?

Notwithstanding the use of substantive due process in the punitive damage case presented above, not one law since 1937 has been declared unconstitutional by the Supreme Court as violating economic substantive due process. Ultimately, the question is whether this is appropriate judicial deference to legislative choices in regulating the economy, or whether this constitutes judicial abdication of an important role in protecting economic liberties. Are the decisions since 1937 an overreaction to the *Lochner*-era decisions? Or do the decisions reflect a properly limited judicial role in scrutinizing economic regulations?

Answering these normative questions requires consideration of whether there should be constitutional protection of economic rights, such as freedom of contract and a right to practice a trade or profession. Also, there must be consideration of the proper judicial role and whether there are reasons why the judiciary should be especially deferential to legislatures in this area.

The bottom line is that since 1937 economic substantive due process has been unavailable to challenge government economic and social welfare laws and regulations. Protection of economic rights, since 1937, such that it has been, has come under two specific constitutional provisions: the Contracts Clause of Article I, §10, and the Takings Clause of the Fifth Amendment.

C. THE CONTRACTS CLAUSE

1. *Introduction*

Article I, §10 provides that "[n]o State shall . . . pass any . . . Law impairing the Obligation of Contracts." It is firmly established that this provision applies only if a state or local law interferes with existing contracts. In other words, the Contracts Clause does not apply to the federal government; challenges to federal interference with contracts must be brought under the Due Process Clause where they will receive the deferential rational basis review described above. Also, the Contracts Clause does not limit the ability of the government to regulate the terms of future contracts; it applies only if the state or local government is interfering with performance of already existing contracts.[23]

The Contracts Clause seems to have been motivated by a desire to prevent states from adopting laws to help debtors at the expense of creditors.[24] The framers were concerned that in times of recession or depression, state legislatures might adopt laws to protect debtors who were unable to pay what was owed. The Contracts Clause was meant to stop such debtor relief legislation that had the effect of interfering with contractual rights. The goal was not only to protect creditors, but also to encourage credit by assuring lenders that they would be repaid.

In the first half of the nineteenth century, the Court aggressively used the Contracts Clause to invalidate state and local laws that interfered with rights under existing contracts. Although the Contracts Clause continued to be used by the Court in the latter half of the nineteenth century, by the twentieth century the Contracts Clause rarely was mentioned in Supreme Court decisions. During the *Lochner* era, from about 1897 until 1937, the Contracts Clause was made superfluous by the Court's protection of freedom of contract under the Due Process Clauses of the Fifth and Fourteenth Amendments. The freedom of

---

23. *See* Ogden v. Saunders, 25 U.S. (12 Wheat.) 213 (1827).
24. Benjamin Wright, *The Growth of American Constitutional Law* 41 (1967).

contract protected under these provisions limited both government regulation of future contracts and government interference with existing contracts. Because the Contracts Clause only applies to the latter, preventing impairment of existing contracts, the Court's use of due process to protect freedom of contract subsumed the content of the Contracts Clause.

2. The Modern Use of the Contracts Clause

The modern era of Contracts Clause law began in 1934, even before the end of economic substantive due process. In Home Building & Loan Assn. v. Blaisdell, below, the Supreme Court upheld a Minnesota law, enacted in response to the Depression, that prevented mortgage holders from foreclosing on mortgages for a two-year period.

HOME BUILDING & LOAN ASSOCIATION v. BLAISDELL
290 U.S. 398 (1934)

Chief Justice HUGHES delivered the opinion of the Court.

Appellant contests the validity of chapter 339 of the Laws of Minnesota of 1933, approved April 18, 1933, called the Minnesota Mortgage Moratorium Law, as being repugnant to the Contract Clause and the due process and Equal Protection Clauses of the Fourteenth Amendment of the Federal Constitution. The act provides that, during the emergency declared to exist, relief may be had through authorized judicial proceedings with respect to foreclosures of mortgages, and execution sales, of real estate; that sales may be postponed and periods of redemption may be extended. The act does not apply to mortgages subsequently made nor to those made previously which shall be extended for a period ending more than a year after the passage of the act.

We are here concerned with the provisions of part 1, authorizing the district court of the county to extend the period of redemption from foreclosure sales "for such additional time as the court may deem just and equitable," subject to the above-described limitation. The extension is to be made upon application to the court, on notice, for an order determining the reasonable value of the income on the property involved in the sale, or, if it has no income, then the reasonable rental value of the property, and directing the mortgagor "to pay all or a reasonable part of such income or rental value, in or toward the payment of taxes, insurance, interest, mortgage . . . indebtedness at such times and in such manner" as shall be determined by the court.

The statute does not affect the validity of the sale or the right of a mortgagee-purchaser to title in fee, or his right to obtain a deficiency judgment, if the mortgagor fails to redeem within the prescribed period. Aside from the extension of time, the other conditions of redemption are unaltered.

In determining whether the provision for this temporary and conditional relief exceeds the power of the state by reason of the clause in the Federal Constitution prohibiting impairment of the obligations of contracts, we must consider the relation of emergency to constitutional power, the historical setting of the contract clause, the development of the jurisprudence of this Court in the construction of that clause, and the principles of construction which we may consider to be established.

Emergency does not create power. Emergency does not increase granted power or remove or diminish the restrictions imposed upon power granted or reserved. The Constitution was adopted in a period of grave emergency. Its grants of power to the federal government and its limitations of the power of the States were determined in the light of emergency, and they are not altered by emergency. What power was thus granted and what limitations were thus imposed are questions which have always been, and always will be, the subject of close examination under our constitutional system.

While emergency does not create power, emergency may furnish the occasion for the exercise of power. "Although an emergency may not call into life a power which has never lived, nevertheless emergency may afford a reason for the exertion of a living power already enjoyed." The constitutional question presented in the light of an emergency is whether the power possessed embraces the particular exercise of it in response to particular conditions. Thus, the war power of the federal government is not created by the emergency of war, but it is a power given to meet that emergency.

In the construction of the Contract Clause, the debates in the Constitutional Convention are of little aid. But the reasons which led to the adoption of that clause, and of the other prohibitions of section 10 of article 1, are not left in doubt, and have frequently been described with eloquent emphasis. The widespread distress following the revolutionary period and the plight of debtors had called forth in the States an ignoble array of legislative schemes for the defeat of creditors and the invasion of contractual obligations. Legislative interferences had been so numerous and extreme that the confidence essential to prosperous trade had been undermined and the utter destruction of credit was threatened.

Not only is the constitutional provision qualified by the measure of control which the state retains over remedial processes, but the state also continues to possess authority to safeguard the vital interests of its people. It does not matter that legislation appropriate to that end "has the result of modifying or abrogating contracts already in effect." Not only are existing laws read into contracts in order to fix obligations as between the parties, but the reservation of essential attributes of sovereign power is also read into contracts as a postulate of the legal order. The policy of protecting contracts against impairment presupposes the maintenance of a government by virtue of which contractual relations are worth while, — a government which retains adequate authority to secure the peace and good order of society. This principle of harmonizing the constitutional prohibition with the necessary residuum of state power has had progressive recognition in the decisions of this Court. The economic interests of the state may justify the exercise of its continuing and dominant protective power notwithstanding interference with contracts.

Undoubtedly, whatever is reserved of state power must be consistent with the fair intent of the constitutional limitation of that power. The reserved power cannot be construed so as to destroy the limitation, nor is the limitation to be construed to destroy the reserved power in its essential aspects. They must be construed in harmony with each other. This principle precludes a construction which would permit the state to adopt as its policy the repudiation of debts or the destruction of contracts or the denial of means to enforce them. But it does not follow that conditions may not arise in which a temporary restraint of enforcement may be consistent with the spirit and purpose of the constitutional provision and thus be found to be within the range of the reserved power of the state to protect the vital interests of the community. It cannot be maintained that the constitutional prohibition should be so construed as to prevent limited and temporary interpositions with respect to the enforcement of contracts if made necessary by a great public calamity such as fire, flood, or earthquake.

The reservation of state power appropriate to such extraordinary conditions may be deemed to be as much a part of all contracts as is the reservation of state power to protect the public interest in the other situations to which we have referred. And, if state power exists to give temporary relief from the enforcement of contracts in the presence of disasters due to physical causes such as fire, flood, or earthquake, that power cannot be said to be nonexistent when the urgent public need demanding such relief is produced by other and economic causes.

It is no answer to say that this public need was not apprehended a century ago, or to insist that what the provision of the Constitution meant to the vision of that day it must mean to the vision of our time. If by the statement that what the Constitution meant at the time of its adoption it means today, it is intended to say that the great clauses of the Constitution must be confined to the interpretation which the framers, with the conditions and outlook of their time, would have placed upon them, the statement carries its own refutation. It was to guard against such a narrow conception that Chief Justice Marshall uttered the memorable warning — "We must never forget, that it is a *constitution* we are expounding" (McCulloch v. Maryland) — "a constitution intended to endure for ages to come, and, consequently, to be adapted to the various *crises* of human affairs." When we are dealing with the words of the Constitution, "we must realize that they have called into life a being the development of which could not have been foreseen completely by the most gifted of its begetters. . . . The case before us must be considered in the light of our whole experience and not merely in that of what was said a hundred years ago."

Applying the criteria established by our decisions, we conclude:

1. An emergency existed in Minnesota which furnished a proper occasion for the exercise of the reserved power of the state to protect the vital interests of the community. The declarations of the existence of this emergency by the Legislature and by the Supreme Court of Minnesota cannot be regarded as a subterfuge or as lacking in adequate basis.

2. The legislation was addressed to a legitimate end; that is, the legislation was not for the mere advantage of particular individuals but for the protection of a basic interest of society.

3. In view of the nature of the contracts in question — mortgages of unquestionable validity — the relief afforded and justified by the emergency, in order not to contravene the constitutional provision, could only be of a character appropriate to that emergency, and could be granted only upon reasonable conditions.

4. The conditions upon which the period of redemption is extended do not appear to be unreasonable. The initial extension of the time of redemption for thirty days from the approval of the act was obviously to give a reasonable opportunity for the authorized application to the court. As already noted, the integrity of the mortgage indebtedness is not impaired; interest continues to run; the validity of the sale and the right of a mortgagee-purchaser to title or to obtain a

deficiency judgment, if the mortgagor fails to redeem within the extended period, are maintained; and the conditions of redemption, if redemption there be, stand as they were under the prior law. The mortgagor during the extended period is not ousted from possession, but he must pay the rental value of the premises as ascertained in judicial proceedings and this amount is applied to the carrying of the property and to interest upon the indebtedness.

5. The legislation is temporary in operation. It is limited to the exigency which called it forth. While the postponement of the period of redemption from the foreclosure sale is to May 1, 1935, that period may be reduced by the order of the court under the statute, in case of a change in circumstances, and the operation of the statute itself could not validly outlast the emergency or be so extended as virtually to destroy the contracts.

We are of the opinion that the Minnesota statute as here applied does not violate the contract clause of the Federal Constitution. Whether the legislation is wise or unwise as a matter of policy is a question with which we are not concerned.

GOVERNMENT INTERFERENCE WITH PRIVATE CONTRACTS

The current law under the Contracts Clause distinguishes government interference with private contracts from government interference with its own contractual obligations. As to government interference with private contracts, the current test was articulated in Energy Reserves Group, Inc. v. Kansas Power & Light Co.

ENERGY RESERVES GROUP, INC. v. KANSAS POWER & LIGHT CO.
459 U.S. 400 (1983)

Justice BLACKMUN delivered the opinion of the Court.

This case concerns the regulation by the State of Kansas of the price of natural gas sold at wellhead in the intrastate market. It presents a federal Contract Clause issue. [A contract for natural gas provided that the price to be paid would be increased if government regulators fixed a higher price than that specified in the contract. Subsequently, Kansas adopted a law that provided that the price to be paid for natural gas under a contract could not be increased because of prices set by federal authorities. The state law prevented the natural gas producer from charging the higher prices that it was entitled to under the contract.]

Although the language of the Contract Clause is facially absolute, its prohibition must be accommodated to the inherent police power of the State "to safeguard the vital interests of its people." Home Bldg. & Loan Ass'n v. Blaisdell (1934).

The threshold inquiry is "whether the state law has, in fact, operated as a substantial impairment of a contractual relationship." Allied Structural Steel Co. v. Spannaus (1978). The severity of the impairment is said to increase the level of scrutiny to which the legislation will be subjected. Total destruction of contractual expectations is not necessary for a finding of substantial impairment. On the other hand, state regulation that restricts a party to gains it reasonably expected from the contract does not necessarily constitute a substantial impairment. In determining the extent of the impairment, we are to consider whether the industry the complaining party has entered has been regulated in the past. The Court long ago observed: "One whose rights, such as they are, are subject to state restriction, cannot remove them from the power of the State by making a contract about them." Hudson Water Co. v. McCarter (1908).

If the state regulation constitutes a substantial impairment, the State, in justification, must have a significant and legitimate public purpose behind the regulation, such as the remedying of a broad and general social or economic problem. Furthermore, since *Blaisdell*, the Court has indicated that the public purpose need not be addressed to an emergency or temporary situation. One legitimate state interest is the elimination of unforeseen windfall profits. The requirement of a legitimate public purpose guarantees that the State is exercising its police power, rather than providing a benefit to special interests.

Once a legitimate public purpose has been identified, the next inquiry is whether the adjustment of "the rights and responsibilities of contracting parties [is based] upon reasonable conditions and [is] of a character appropriate to the public purpose justifying [the legislation's] adoption." Unless the State itself is a contracting party, "[a]s is customary in reviewing economic and social regulation, . . . courts properly defer to legislative judgment as to the necessity and reasonableness of a particular measure."

The threshold determination is whether the Kansas Act has impaired substantially ERG's contractual rights. Significant here is the fact that the parties are operating in a heavily regulated industry. State authority to regulate natural gas prices is well established. At the time of the execution of these contracts, Kansas did not regulate natural gas prices specifically, but its supervision of the industry was extensive and intrusive.

It is in this context that the indefinite escalator clauses at issue here are to be viewed. In drafting each of the contracts, the parties included a statement of intent, which made clear that the escalator clause was designed to guarantee price increases consistent with anticipated increases in the value of ERG's gas. The very existence of the governmental price escalator clause and the price redetermination clause indicates that the contracts were structured against the background of regulated gas prices. If deregulation had not occurred, the contracts undoubtedly would have called for a much smaller price increase than that provided by the Kansas Act's adoption of the §109 ceiling.

Moreover, the contracts expressly recognize the existence of extensive regulation by providing that any contractual terms are subject to relevant present and future state and federal law. This latter provision could be interpreted to incorporate all future state price regulation, and thus dispose of the Contract Clause claim. Regardless of whether this interpretation is correct, the provision does suggest that ERG knew its contractual rights were subject to alteration by state price regulation. Price regulation existed and was foreseeable as the type of law that would alter contract obligations. Reading the Contract Clause as ERG does would mean that indefinite price escalator clauses could exempt ERG from any regulatory limitation of prices whatsoever. Such a result cannot be permitted. In short, ERG's reasonable expectations have not been impaired by the Kansas Act.

To the extent, if any, the Kansas Act impairs ERG's contractual interests, the Kansas Act rests on, and is prompted by, significant and legitimate state interests. Kansas has exercised its police power to protect consumers from the escalation of natural gas prices caused by deregulation. The State reasonably could find that higher gas prices have caused and will cause hardship among those who use gas heat but must exist on limited fixed incomes.

The State also has a legitimate interest in correcting the imbalance between the interstate and intrastate markets by permitting intrastate prices to rise only to the §109 level. By slowly deregulating interstate prices, the Act took the cap off intrastate prices as well. The Kansas Act attempts to coordinate the intrastate and interstate prices by supplementing the federal Act's regulation of intrastate gas. Congress specifically contemplated such action. Nor are the means chosen to implement these purposes deficient, particularly in light of the deference to which the Kansas Legislature's judgment is entitled.

In other words, when a state or local government interferes with existing private contracts, a three-part test is used: (1) Is there a substantial impairment of a contractual relationship? (2) If so, does it serve a significant and legitimate public purpose? (3) If so, is it reasonably related to achieving the goal? The test is very similar to traditional rational basis review.

As to the first part of the test, whether there is a substantial impairment of the contract, in General Motors v. Romein, 503 U.S. 181 (1992), the Court rejected a challenge to a state law that changed the workers' compensation program on the ground that it did not interfere with existing contracts. In 1981, the Michigan Supreme Court interpreted a recently adopted Michigan statute to allow employers to reduce workers' compensation payments to disabled employees who could receive compensation from other employer-funded sources. In 1987, the Michigan legislature overturned this ruling by statute and required that employers make retroactive payments. Employers sued and said that the change in the law constituted an impairment of the obligation of contracts. The U.S. Supreme Court rejected this challenge. It concluded that there was "no contractual agreement regarding the specific workers' compensation terms allegedly at issue." The Court explained, "The 1987 statute did not change the legal enforceability of the employment contracts here. . . . Moreover, petitioners' suggestion that we should read every workplace regulation into the private contracted arrangements of employers and employees would expand the definition of contract so far that the constitutional provision would lose its anchoring purpose . . . [and i]nstead, the Clause would protect against all changes in legislation."

As to the second and third prongs of the test, state and local laws are upheld, even if they interfere with contractual rights, as long as they meet a rational basis test. Not surprisingly, virtually all laws have been found to meet this deferential scrutiny. For example, in El Paso v. Simmons, 379 U.S. 497 (1965), the Supreme Court upheld a state law that clearly changed the terms of a contract. Under a 1910 contract, Texas sold public lands. The contract provided that if interest was not paid in a timely fashion, the state could terminate the contract and reclaim the land. However, the contract said that an owner could reinstate a claim to the land by paying the delinquent interest owed. In 1941, Texas adopted a law saying that reinstatement had to occur within five years after there was a forfeiture for nonpayment.

The Supreme Court upheld the Texas law, even though it obviously limited the rights of landowners to reclaim land that had been forfeited. The Court said that the law had a legitimate purpose in that it was intended "to restore confidence in the stability and integrity of land titles" and to end the "imbroglio over land titles in Texas." The Court found that the law was reasonably designed to achieve these goals and thus did not violate the Contracts Clause.

In Keystone Bituminous Coal Association v. DeBenedictis, 480 U.S. 470 (1987), the Court found that a state law limiting coal mining impaired existing contracts, but nonetheless upheld the law because it served a significant government interest. A state law prohibited coal mining that would cause subsidence damage to property. The coal mine companies frequently had entered into agreements with those owning the surface rights, whereby the companies were allowed to mine, even if it caused subsidence of the land. In other words, the law prevented exactly what the coal miners had bargained to be able to do. Although the Court recognized that the law interfered with contractual rights, it upheld the law because it was a reasonable way to prevent or repair environmental damage caused by coal mining.

There is only one case since 1934 where the Supreme Court has declared unconstitutional a state law that interfered with private contracts: Allied Structural Steel Co. v. Spannaus, 438 U.S. 234 (1978). An Illinois company operated an office in Minnesota and provided a pension plan for its employees. The terms of the plan provided that the company could, at any time, amend the plan or terminate the plan and distribute the assets to the employees. Employees were entitled to collect under the plan if they worked for the company until they reached age 65 and if the plan was in effect at that time. Minnesota adopted a Private Pension Benefits Protection Act that required employers to pay a "pension funding charge" if they terminated a pension plan or closed a Minnesota office. The charge was to ensure that pensions would be available for individuals when they reached retirement age. Allied Structural Steel closed its Minnesota facility and was assessed a $185,000 fee.

The Court found that the Minnesota law violated the Contracts Clause. Justice Potter Stewart, writing for the Court, began by declaring that the "Contract Clause remains part of the Constitution. It is not a dead letter." The Court found that the Minnesota statute was a substantial impairment of the obligation of contracts. The Court reasoned that the employer had a contract with its employees that permitted the termination of the contract at any point. The state, by forcing the company to make pension payments, was essentially abrogating this provision.

The Court said that the law was unconstitutional because it was not narrowly tailored emergency legislation like that in *Blaisdell*. Justice Stewart stated, "[T]his law can hardly be characterized, like the law at issue in the *Blaisdell* case, as one enacted to protect a broad society interest rather than a narrow class. This legislation, imposing a sudden, totally unanticipated, and substantial retroactive obligation upon the company to its employees, was not enacted to deal with a situation remotely approaching the broad and desperate economic conditions of the early 1930s. . . . [If] the Contract Clause means anything at all, it means that Minnesota could not constitutionally do what it tried to do to the company in this case."

Because *Allied Structural Steel* has not been followed by the Supreme Court in the last two decades, it is difficult to know whether it is an anomaly or whether it is a precedent that might someday be used to revitalize the Contracts Clause. Thus far, the Contracts Clause cases since *Allied Structural Steel* (presented and described above) — such as *Energy Reserves Group, Exxon,* and *Keystone Bituminous Coal* — have distinguished *Allied Structural Steel* and have refused to find a violation of the Contracts Clause.

GOVERNMENT INTERFERENCE WITH GOVERNMENT CONTRACTS

In United States Trust Co. v. New Jersey, the Supreme Court indicated that government interference with government contracts will be subjected to heightened scrutiny.

UNITED STATES TRUST CO. v. NEW JERSEY
431 U.S. 1 (1977)

[In 1962, New Jersey and New York adopted laws prohibiting the use of toll revenues from the Port Authority of New Jersey and New York from being used to subsidize railroad passenger service. The laws were meant to assure those holding Port Authority bonds that the toll funds would remain available to pay that debt. A decade later, during the energy crisis of the 1970s, the states adopted laws to repeal the earlier prohibition and to permit the use of toll funds to improve rail transit.]

Justice BLACKMUN delivered the opinion of the Court.

This case presents a challenge to a 1974 New Jersey statute as violative of the Contract Clause of the United States Constitution. That statute, together with a concurrent and parallel New York statute, repealed a statutory covenant made by the two States in 1962 that had limited the ability of The Port Authority of New York and New Jersey to subsidize rail passenger transportation from revenues and reserves.

We first examine appellant's general claim that repeal of the 1962 covenant impaired the obligation of the States' contract with the bondholders. It long has been established that the Contract Clause limits the power of the States to modify their own contracts as well as to regulate those between private parties. Fletcher v. Peck (1810); Dartmouth College v. Woodward (1819). Yet the Contract Clause does not prohibit the States from repealing or amending statutes generally, or from enacting legislation with retroactive effects. Thus, as a preliminary matter, appellant's claim requires a determination that the repeal has the effect of impairing a contractual obligation.

In this case the obligation was itself created by a statute, the 1962 legislative covenant. It is unnecessary, however, to dwell on the criteria for determining whether state legislation gives rise to a contractual obligation. The trial court found, and appellees do not deny, that the 1962 covenant constituted a contract between the two States and the holders of the Consolidated Bonds issued between 1962 and the 1973 prospective repeal. The intent to make a contract is clear from the statutory language: "The 2 States covenant and agree with each other and with the holders of any affected bonds. . . ." Moreover, as the chronology set forth above reveals, the purpose of the covenant was to invoke the constitutional protection of the Contract Clause as security against repeal. In return for their promise, the States received the benefit they bargained for: public marketability of Port Authority bonds to finance construction of the World Trade Center and acquisition of the Hudson & Manhattan Railroad. We therefore have no doubt that the 1962 covenant has been properly characterized as a contractual obligation of the two States.

It is not always unconstitutional, however, for changes in statutory remedies to affect pre-existing contracts. During the early years when the Contract Clause was regarded as an absolute bar to any impairment, this result was reached by treating remedies in a manner distinct from substantive contract obligations. Thus, for example, a State could abolish imprisonment for debt because elimination of this remedy did not impair the underlying obligation. Yet it was also recognized very early that the distinction between remedies and obligations was not absolute. Impairment of a remedy was held to be unconstitutional if it effectively reduced the value of substantive contract rights.

Although now largely an outdated formalism, the remedy/obligation distinction may be viewed as approximating the result of a more particularized inquiry into the legitimate expectations of the contracting parties. The parties may rely on the continued existence of adequate statutory remedies for enforcing their agreement, but they are unlikely to expect that state law will remain entirely static. Thus, a reasonable modification of statutes governing contract remedies is much less likely to upset expectations than a law adjusting the express terms of an agreement. In this respect, the repeal of the 1962 covenant is to be seen as a serious disruption of the bondholders' expectations.

The States must possess broad power to adopt general regulatory measures without being concerned that private contracts will be impaired, or even destroyed, as a result. Otherwise, one would be able to obtain immunity from the state regulation by making private contractual arrangements. Yet private contracts are not subject to unlimited modification under the police power. The Court in *Blaisdell* recognized that laws intended to regulate existing contractual relationships must serve a legitimate public purpose. A State could not "adopt as its policy the repudiation of debts or the destruction of contracts or the denial of means to enforce them." Legislation adjusting the rights and responsibilities of contracting parties must be upon reasonable conditions and of a character appropriate to the public purpose justifying its adoption. As is customary in reviewing economic and social regulation, however, courts properly defer to legislative judgment as to the necessity and reasonableness of a particular measure.

When a State impairs the obligation of its own contract, the reserved powers doctrine has a different basis. As with laws impairing the obligations of private contracts, an impairment may be constitutional if it is reasonable and necessary to serve an important public purpose. In applying this standard, however, complete deference to a legislative assessment of reasonableness and necessity is not appropriate because the State's self-interest is at stake. A governmental entity can always find a use for extra money, especially when taxes do not have to be raised. If a State could reduce its financial obligations whenever it wanted to spend the money for what it regarded as an important public purpose, the Contract Clause would provide no protection at all.

Mass transportation, energy conservation, and environmental protection are goals that are important and of legitimate public concern. Appellees contend that these goals are so important that any harm to bondholders from repeal of the 1962 covenant is greatly outweighed by the public benefit. We do not accept this invitation to engage in a utilitarian comparison of public benefit and private loss. [A] State cannot refuse to meet its legitimate financial obligations simply because it would prefer to spend the money to promote the public good rather than the private welfare of its creditors. We can only sustain the repeal of the 1962 covenant if that impairment was both reasonable and necessary to serve the admittedly important purposes claimed by the State.

The more specific justification offered for the repeal of the 1962 covenant was the States' plan for encouraging users of private automobiles to shift to public transportation. The States intended to discourage private automobile use by raising bridge and tunnel tolls and to use the extra revenue from those tolls to subsidize improved commuter railroad service. Appellees contend that repeal of the 1962 covenant was necessary to implement this plan because the new mass transit facilities could not possibly be self-supporting and the covenant's "permitted deficits" level had already been exceeded. We reject this justification because the repeal was neither necessary to achievement of the plan nor reasonable in light of the circumstances.

The determination of necessity can be considered on two levels. First, it cannot be said that total repeal of the covenant was essential; a less drastic modification would have permitted the contemplated plan without entirely removing the covenant's limitations on the use of Port Authority revenues and reserves to subsidize commuter railroads. Second, without modifying the covenant at all, the States could have adopted alternative means of achieving their twin goals of discouraging automobile use and improving mass transit. Appellees contend, however, that choosing among these alternatives is a matter for legislative discretion. But a State is not completely free to consider impairing the obligations of its own contracts on a par with other policy alternatives. Similarly, a State is not free to impose a drastic impairment when an evident and more moderate course would serve its purposes equally well.

We also cannot conclude that repeal of the covenant was reasonable in light of the surrounding circumstances. [I]n the instant case the need for mass transportation in the New York metropolitan area was not a new development, and the likelihood that publicly owned commuter railroads would produce substantial deficits was well known. As early as 1922, over a half century ago, there were pressures to involve the Port Authority in mass transit. It was with full knowledge of these concerns that the 1962 covenant was adopted. Indeed, the covenant was specifically intended to protect the pledged revenues and reserves against the possibility that such concerns would lead the Port Authority into greater involvement in deficit mass transit.

During the 12-year period between adoption of the covenant and its repeal, public perception of the importance of mass transit undoubtedly grew because of increased general concern with environmental protection and energy conservation. But these concerns were not unknown in 1962, and the subsequent changes were of degree and not of kind. We cannot say that these changes caused the covenant to have a substantially different impact in 1974 than when it was adopted in 1962. And we cannot conclude that the repeal was reasonable in the light of changed circumstances.

We therefore hold that the Contract Clause of the United States Constitution prohibits the retroactive repeal of the 1962 covenant.

Justice BRENNAN, with whom Justice WHITE and Justice MARSHALL join, dissenting.

Decisions of this Court for at least a century have construed the Contract Clause largely to be powerless in binding a State to contracts limiting the authority of successor legislatures to enact laws in furtherance of the health, safety, and similar collective interests of the polity. In short, those decisions established the principle that lawful exercises of a State's police powers stand paramount to private rights held under contract. Today's decision, in invalidating the New Jersey Legislature's 1974 repeal of its predecessor's 1962 covenant, rejects this previous understanding and remolds the Contract Clause into a potent instrument for overseeing important policy determinations of the state legislature. At the same time, by creating a constitutional safe haven for property rights embodied in a contract, the decision substantially distorts modern constitutional jurisprudence governing regulation of private economic interests. I might understand, though I could not accept, this revival of the Contract Clause were it in accordance with some coherent and constructive view of public policy. But elevation of the Clause to the status of regulator of the municipal bond market at the heavy price of frustration of sound legislative policymaking is as demonstrably unwise as it is unnecessary. The justification for today's decision, therefore, remains a mystery to me, and I respectfully dissent.

The Court's consideration of [the] actual background is, I believe, most unsatisfactory. The Court never explicitly takes issue with the core of New Jersey's defense of the repeal: that the State was faced with serious and growing environmental, energy, and transportation problems, and the covenant worked at cross-purposes with efforts at remedying these concerns. Indeed, the Court candidly concedes that the State's purposes in effectuating the 1974 repeal were "admittedly important." Instead, the Court's analysis focuses upon related, but peripheral, matters.

For example, several hypothetical alternative methods are proposed whereby New Jersey might hope to secure funding for public transportation, and these are made the basis for a holding that repeal of the covenant was not "necessary." Setting aside the propriety of this surprising legal standard, the Court's effort at fashioning its own legislative program for New York and New Jersey is notably unsuccessful. In fact, except for those proffered alternatives which also amount to a repeal or substantial modification of the 1962 covenant, none of the Court's suggestions is compatible with the basic antipollution and transportation-control strategies that are crucial to metropolitan New York.

Equally unconvincing is the Court's contention that repeal of the 1962 covenant was unreasonable because the environmental and energy concerns that prompted such action "were not unknown in 1962, and the subsequent changes were of degree and not of kind." Nowhere are we told why a state policy, no matter how responsive to the general welfare of its citizens, can be reasonable only if it confronts issues that previously were absolutely unforeseen.

The Court today dusts off the Contract Clause and thereby undermines the bipartisan policies of two States that manifestly seek to further the legitimate needs of their citizens. The Court's analysis, I submit, fundamentally misconceives the nature of the Contract Clause guarantee. One of the fundamental premises of our popular democracy is that each generation of representatives can and will remain responsive to the needs and desires of those whom they represent. Crucial to this end is the assurance that new legislators will not automatically be bound by the policies and undertakings of earlier days. In accordance with this philosophy, the framers of our Constitution conceived of the Contract Clause primarily as protection for economic transactions entered into by purely private parties, rather than obligations involving the State itself. The framers fully recognized that nothing would so jeopardize the legitimacy of a system of government that relies upon the ebbs and flows of politics to "clean out the rascals" than the possibility that those same rascals might perpetuate their policies simply by locking them into binding contracts.

This theme of judicial self-restraint and its underlying premise that a State always retains the sovereign authority to legislate in behalf of its people was commonly expressed by the doctrine that the Contract Clause will not even recognize efforts of a State to enter into contracts limiting the authority of succeeding legislators to enact laws in behalf of the health, safety, and similar collective interests of the polity; in short, that State's police power is inalienable by contract. I would not want to be read as suggesting that the States should blithely proceed down the path of repudiating their obligations, financial or otherwise. Their credibility in the credit market obviously is highly dependent on exercising their vast lawmaking powers with self-restraint and discipline, and I, for one, have little doubt that few, if any, jurisdictions would choose to use their authority "so foolish[ly] as to kill a goose that lays golden eggs for them." But in the final analysis, there is no reason to doubt that appellant's financial welfare is being adequately policed by the political processes and the bond marketplace itself. The role to be played by the Constitution is at most a limited one. For this Court should have learned long ago that the Constitution be it through the Contract or Due Process Clause can actively intrude into such economic and policy matters only if my Brethren are prepared to bear enormous institutional and social costs. Because I consider the potential dangers of such judicial interference to be intolerable, I dissent.

The dispute between the majority and the dissent in United States Trust v. New Jersey is over whether the Contracts Clause should apply to government contracts and, if so, the appropriate test to be used. Although the Court did not articulate a level of scrutiny, its use of least restrictive alternative analysis and the word "necessary" seem clearly indicative of heightened scrutiny. Because there has not been another Supreme Court case since *United States Trust* concerning government interference with government contracts, the precise test remains uncertain. Nonetheless, it is clear that laws impairing the government's obligations under its own contracts will be subjected to much more careful review than will laws interfering with private contracts.

D. THE TAKINGS CLAUSE

1. Introduction

Both the federal government and the states have the power of eminent domain; this is the authority to take private property when necessary for government activities. However, the Constitution contains an important limit on this power: The Fifth Amendment states, "[N]or shall private property be taken for public use without just compensation." This was the first provision of the Bill of Rights to be applied to the states.[25]

Analysis under the Takings Clause can be divided into four questions. First, is there a "taking"? As described below, there are two basic ways of finding a taking. A possessory taking occurs when the government confiscates or physically occupies property. Alternately, a regulatory taking is when government regulation leaves no reasonable economically viable use of property.

Second, is it "property"? Obviously, only if the object of the taking is "property" does the Fifth Amendment provision apply. Generally, the Court has relied on other sources of law, usually state law, in deciding whether there is a property interest.

Third, if there is a taking of property, the next question becomes: Is the taking for "public use"? If the taking is not for public use, the government must give the property back. However, as also is discussed below, the Court has very broadly defined public use so that almost any taking will meet the requirement. The Court has said that a taking is for public use as long as it is "rationally related to a conceivable public purpose";[26] in other words, a taking is for public use as long as it meets the rational basis test.

Fourth, assuming that it is a taking for public use, the final question becomes: Is "just compensation" paid? The key is that just compensation is measured in terms of the loss to the owner; the gain to the taker is irrelevant.

The Takings Clause is the most important protection of property rights in the Constitution. In part, the Takings Clause is about ensuring that the government does not confiscate the property of some to give it to others. Long ago, in Calder v. Bull, the Court condemned such a practice as violating the natural law principles on which the Constitution was founded.[27]

In part, too, the Takings Clause is about loss spreading. If the government takes away a person's property to benefit society, then society should pay. The Supreme Court has explained that a principal purpose of the Takings Clause is "to bar the Government from forcing some people alone to bear public burdens which, in all fairness and justice, should be borne by the public as a whole."[28]

Yet, as described below, very difficult questions arise in determining when the government incurs this obligation to pay just compensation. Almost any government regulation decreases the value of someone's property. The Court thus has long noted that "[g]overnment hardly could go on if to some extent values incident to property could not be diminished without paying for every such change in the general law."[29] No bright-line test ever has been, or likely ever will be, formulated to determine when government actions that decrease the value of property become a taking. Indeed, the Court has admitted that it "has been unable to develop any 'set formula' for determining when 'justice and fairness' require that economic injuries caused by public action be compensated by the government."[30] Rather, the Court has engaged in "ad hoc, factual

---

25. *See* Chicago, Burlington & Quincy Railroad v. Chicago, 166 U.S. 226 (1897).
26. Hawaii Housing Authority v. Midkiff, 467 U.S. 229 (1984).
27. 3 U.S. (3 Dall.) 386 (1798).
28. Armstrong v. United States, 364 U.S. 40, 49 (1960).
29. Pennsylvania Coal v. Mahon, 260 U.S. 393, 413 (1922).
30. Penn Central Transp. Co. v. New York City, 438 U.S. 104, 124 (1978).

inquiries" that turn "upon the particular circumstances in that case."[31] The result is a very large body of cases concerning the Takings Clause, but it often is difficult to find coherent principles to make sense of them.

2.   Is There a "Taking"?

The vast majority of litigation concerning the Takings Clause of the Fifth Amendment has focused on the question: What is a "taking"? It is the obvious threshold issue for Takings Clause analysis because the constitutional provision applies only if a court finds that a taking has occurred.

For the sake of clarity, two different types of takings can be identified, although the Supreme Court has not always used these categories and has not always consistently defined them. A "possessory" taking occurs when the government confiscates or physically occupies property. A "regulatory" taking occurs when the government's regulation leaves no reasonably economically viable use of the property.

POSSESSORY TAKINGS

The Supreme Court generally has found a taking when the government confiscates or physically occupies property: "When faced with a constitutional challenge to a permanent physical occupation of real property, this Court has invariably found a taking."[32] The following case is illustrative and discusses many of the most important Supreme Court decisions concerning possessory takings.

LORETTO v. TELEPROMPTER MANHATTAN CATV CORP.
458 U.S. 419 (1982)

Justice MARSHALL delivered the opinion of the Court.

This case presents the question whether a minor but permanent physical occupation of an owner's property authorized by government constitutes a "taking" of property for which just compensation is due under the Fifth and Fourteenth Amendments of the Constitution. New York law provides that a landlord must permit a cable television company to install its cable facilities upon his property. In this case, the cable installation occupied portions of appellant's roof and the side of her building. The New York Court of Appeals ruled that this appropriation does not amount to a taking. Because we conclude that such a physical occupation of property is a taking, we reverse.

Prior to 1973, Teleprompter routinely obtained authorization for its installations from property owners along the cable's route, compensating the owners at the standard rate of 5% of the gross revenues that Teleprompter realized from the particular property. To facilitate tenant access to CATV, the State of New York enacted §828 of the Executive Law, effective January 1, 1973. Section 828

---

31. *Id.* at 124 (citations omitted).
32. Loretto v. Teleprompter Manhattan CATV Corp., 458 U.S. 419, 427 (1982).

provides that a landlord may not "interfere with the installation of cable television facilities upon his property or premises," and may not demand payment from any tenant for permitting CATV, or demand payment from any CATV company "in excess of any amount which the [State Commission on Cable Television] shall, by regulation, determine to be reasonable." The landlord may, however, require the CATV company or the tenant to bear the cost of installation and to indemnify for any damage caused by the installation. Pursuant to §828(1)(b), the State Commission has ruled that a one-time $1 payment is the normal fee to which a landlord is entitled.

The Court of Appeals determined that §828 serves the legitimate public purpose of "rapid development of and maximum penetration by a means of communication which has important educational and community aspects," and thus is within the State's police power. We have no reason to question that determination. It is a separate question, however, whether an otherwise valid regulation so frustrates property rights that compensation must be paid.

We conclude that a permanent physical occupation authorized by government is a taking without regard to the public interests that it may serve. Our constitutional history confirms the rule, recent cases do not question it, and the purposes of the Takings Clause compel its retention.

[T]he Court has often upheld substantial regulation of an owner's use of his own property where deemed necessary to promote the public interest. At the same time, we have long considered a physical intrusion by government to be a property restriction of an unusually serious character for purposes of the Takings Clause. Our cases further establish that when the physical intrusion reaches the extreme form of a permanent physical occupation, a taking has occurred. In such a case, "the character of the government action" not only is an important factor in resolving whether the action works a taking but also is determinative.

When faced with a constitutional challenge to a permanent physical occupation of real property, this Court has invariably found a taking. As early as 1872, in Pumpelly v. Green Bay Co., this Court held that the defendant's construction, pursuant to state authority, of a dam which permanently flooded plaintiff's property constituted a taking. A unanimous Court stated, without qualification, that "where real estate is actually invaded by superinduced additions of water, earth, sand, or other material, or by having any artificial structure placed on it, so as to effectually destroy or impair its usefulness, it is a taking, within the meaning of the Constitution."

Professor Michelman has accurately summarized the case law concerning the role of the concept of physical invasions in the development of takings jurisprudence: "At one time it was commonly held that, in the absence of explicit expropriation, a compensable 'taking' could occur only through physical encroachment and occupation. The modern significance of physical occupation is that courts, while they sometimes do hold nontrespassory injuries compensable, never deny compensation for a physical takeover. The one incontestable case for compensation (short of formal expropriation) seems to occur when the government deliberately brings it about that its agents, or the public at large, 'regularly' use, or 'permanently' occupy, space or a thing which theretofore was understood to be under private ownership." Frank Michelman, Property, Utility, and Fairness: Comments on the Ethical Foundations of "Just Compensation" Law, 80 Harv. L. Rev. 1165, 1184 (1967).

More recent cases confirm the distinction between a permanent physical occupation, a physical invasion short of an occupation, and a regulation that merely restricts the use of property. In United States v. Causby (1946), the Court ruled that frequent flights immediately above a landowner's property constituted a taking, comparing such over flights to the quintessential form of a taking.

In short, when the "character of the governmental action," is a permanent physical occupation of property, our cases uniformly have found a taking to the extent of the occupation, without regard to whether the action achieves an important public benefit or has only minimal economic impact on the owner.

Finally, whether a permanent physical occupation has occurred presents relatively few problems of proof. The placement of a fixed structure on land or real property is an obvious fact that will rarely be subject to dispute. Once the fact of occupation is shown, of course, a court should consider the extent of the occupation as one relevant factor in determining the compensation due. For that reason, moreover, there is less need to consider the extent of the occupation in determining whether there is a taking in the first instance.

Teleprompter's cable installation on appellant's building constitutes a taking under the traditional test. The installation involved a direct physical attachment of plates, boxes, wires, bolts, and screws to the building, completely occupying space immediately above and upon the roof and along the building's exterior wall.

Justice BLACKMUN, with whom Justice BRENNAN and Justice WHITE join dissenting.

If the Court's decisions construing the Takings Clause state anything clearly, it is that "[t]here is no set formula to determine where regulation ends and taking begins." Goldblatt v. Town of Hempstead (1962). In a curiously anachronistic decision, the Court today acknowledges its historical disavowal of set formulae in almost the same breath as it constructs a rigid per se takings rule: "a permanent physical occupation authorized by government is a taking without regard to the public interests that it may serve." To sustain its rule against our recent precedents, the Court erects a strained and untenable distinction between "temporary physical invasions," whose constitutionality concededly "is subject to a balancing process," and "permanent physical occupations," which are "taking[s] without regard to other factors that a court might ordinarily examine."

In my view, the Court's approach "reduces the constitutional issue to a formalistic quibble" over whether property has been "permanently occupied" or "temporarily invaded." Sax, Takings and the Police Power, 74 Yale L.J. 36, 37 (1964). The Court's application of its formula to the facts of this case vividly illustrates that its approach is potentially dangerous as well as misguided. Despite its concession that "States have broad power to regulate . . . the land-lord-tenant relationship . . . without paying compensation for all economic injuries that such regulation entails," the Court uses its rule to undercut a carefully considered legislative judgment concerning landlord-tenant relationships. I therefore respectfully dissent.

REGULATORY TAKINGS

Assuming that the government has not confiscated or physically occupied property, under what circumstances may a taking be found because of government regulation? Government regulates property in countless ways, many of which diminish the value of property; which regulations are takings?

Traditionally, courts limited "takings" to situations where the government expropriated property or physically occupied it.[33] In the landmark case of Pennsylvania Coal Co. v. Mahon, the Court said that a taking also could be found if government regulation of the use of property went "too far."

PENNSYLVANIA COAL CO. v. MAHON
260 U.S. 393 (1922)

Justice HOLMES delivered the opinion of the Court.

This is a bill in equity brought by the defendants in error to prevent the Pennsylvania Coal Company from mining under their property in such way as to remove the supports and cause a subsidence of the surface and of their house. The bill sets out a deed executed by the Coal Company in 1878, under which the plaintiffs claim. The deed conveys the surface but in express terms reserves the right to remove all the coal under the same and the grantee takes the premises with the risk and waives all claim for damages that may arise from mining out the coal. But the plaintiffs say that whatever may have been the Coal Company's rights, they were taken away by an Act of Pennsylvania, approved May 27, 1921, commonly known there as the Kohler Act.

The statute forbids the mining of anthracite coal in such way as to cause the subsidence of, among other things, any structure used as a human habitation, with certain exceptions, including among them land where the surface is owned by the owner of the underlying coal and is distant more than one hundred and fifty feet from any improved property belonging to any other person. As applied to this case the statute is admitted to destroy previously existing rights of property and contract. The question is whether the police power can be stretched so far.

Government hardly could go on if to some extent values incident to property could not be diminished without paying for every such change in the general law. As long recognized some values are enjoyed under an implied limitation and must yield to the police power. But obviously the implied limitation must have its limits or the contract and Due Process Clauses are gone. One fact for consideration in determining such limits is the extent of the diminution. When it reaches a certain magnitude, in most if not in all cases there must be an exercise of eminent domain and compensation to sustain the act. So the question depends upon the particular facts. The greatest weight is given to the judgment of the legislature but it always is open to interested parties to contend that the legislature has gone beyond its constitutional power.

This is the case of a single private house. No doubt there is a public interest even in this, as there is in every purchase and sale and in all that happens within the commonwealth. Some existing rights may be modified even in such a case.

---

33. *See, e.g.,* Mugler v. Kansas, 123 U.S. 623, 668-669 (1887) (concluding that a state's prohibition of alcoholic beverages was not a taking and declaring that "a prohibition . . . upon the use of property for purposes that are declared, by valid legislation, to be injurious to the health, morals, or safety of the community, cannot, in any just sense, be deemed a taking or an appropriation of property for the public benefit").

But usually in ordinary private affairs the public interest does not warrant much of this kind of interference. A source of damage to such a house is not a public nuisance even if similar damage is inflicted on others in different places. The damage is not common or public.

The extent of the public interest is shown by the statute to be limited, since the statute ordinarily does not apply to land when the surface is owned by the owner of the coal. Furthermore, it is not justified as a protection of personal safety. That could be provided for by notice. Indeed the very foundation of this bill is that the defendant gave timely notice of its intent to mine under the house. On the other hand the extent of the taking is great. It purports to abolish what is recognized in Pennsylvania as an estate in land — a very valuable estate — and what is declared by the Court below to be a contract hitherto binding the plaintiffs.

It is our opinion that the act cannot be sustained as an exercise of the police power, so far as it affects the mining of coal under streets or cities in places where the right to mine such coal has been reserved. The rights of the public in a street purchased or laid out by eminent domain are those that it has paid for. If in any case its representatives have been so short sighted as to acquire only surface rights without the right of support we see no more authority for supplying the latter without compensation than there was for taking the right of way in the first place and refusing to pay for it because the public wanted it very much. The protection of private property in the Fifth Amendment presupposes that it is wanted for public use, but provides that it shall not be taken for such use without compensation.

The general rule at least is that while property may be regulated to a certain extent, if regulation goes too far it will be recognized as a taking. We are in danger of forgetting that a strong public desire to improve the public condition is not enough to warrant achieving the desire by a shorter cut than the constitutional way of paying for the change. As we already have said this is a question of degree — and therefore cannot be disposed of by general propositions. But we regard this as going beyond any of the cases decided by this Court.

We assume, of course, that the statute was passed upon the conviction that an exigency existed that would warrant it, and we assume that an exigency exists that would warrant the exercise of eminent domain. But the question at bottom is upon whom the loss of the changes desired should fall. So far as private persons or communities have seen fit to take the risk of acquiring only surface rights, we cannot see that the fact that their risk has become a danger warrants the giving to them greater rights than they bought.

Justice BRANDEIS dissenting.

The Kohler Act prohibits, under certain conditions, the mining of anthracite coal within the limits of a city in such a manner or to such an extent "as to cause the . . . subsidence of . . . any dwelling or other structure used as a human habitation, or any factory, store, or other industrial or mercantile establishment in which human labor is employed." Coal in place is land, and the right of the owner to use his land is not absolute. He may not so use it as to create a public nuisance, and uses, once harmless, may, owing to changed conditions, seriously threaten the public welfare. Whenever they do, the Legislature has power to prohibit such uses without paying compensation; and the power to prohibit extends alike to the manner, the character and the purpose of the use. Are we justified in declaring that the Legislature of Pennsylvania has, in restricting the right to mine anthracite, exercised this power so arbitrarily as to violate the Fourteenth Amendment?

Every restriction upon the use of property imposed in the exercise of the police power deprives the owner of some right theretofore enjoyed, and is, in that sense, an abridgment by the state of rights in property without making compensation. But restriction imposed to protect the public health, safety or morals from dangers threatened is not a taking. The restriction here in question is merely the prohibition of a noxious use. The property so restricted remains in the possession of its owner. The state does not appropriate it or make any use of it. The state merely prevents the owner from making a use which interferes with paramount rights of the public. Whenever the use prohibited ceases to be noxious — as it may because of further change in local or social conditions — the restriction will have to be removed and the owner will again be free to enjoy his property as heretofore.

The difficulty in deciding when government regulation constitutes a taking is illustrated by comparing Pennsylvania Coal v. Mahon to the following decision from a few years later, Miller v. Schoene, in which the Court found that a regulation was not a taking.

MILLER v. SCHOENE
276 U.S. 272 (1928)

Justice STONE delivered the opinion of the Court.

Acting under the Cedar Rust Act of Virginia, defendant in error, the state entomologist, ordered the plaintiffs in error to cut down a large number of ornamental red cedar trees growing on their property, as a means of preventing the communication of a rust or plant disease with which they were infected to the apple orchards in the vicinity. Neither the judgment of the court nor the statute as interpreted allows compensation for the value of the standing cedars or the decrease in the market value of the realty caused by their destruction whether considered as ornamental trees or otherwise. But they save to plaintiffs in error the privilege of using the trees when felled.

The Virginia statute presents a comprehensive scheme for the condemnation and destruction of red cedar trees infected by cedar rust. Cedar rust is an infectious plant disease in the form of a fungoid organism which is destructive of the fruit and foliage of the apple, but without effect on the value of the cedar. It is communicated by spores from one to the other over a radius of at least two miles. The only practicable method of controlling the disease and protecting apple trees from its ravages is the destruction of all red cedar trees, subject to the infection, located within two miles of apple orchards.

The red cedar, aside from its ornamental use, has occasional use and value as lumber. It is indigenous to Virginia, is not cultivated or dealt in commercially on any substantial scale, and its value throughout the state is shown to be small as compared with that of the apple orchards of the state. Apple growing is one of the principal agricultural pursuits in Virginia. The apple is used there and exported in large quantities. Many millions of dollars are invested in the orchards, which furnish employment for a large portion of the population, and have induced the development of attendant railroad and cold storage facilities.

On the evidence we may accept the conclusion of the Supreme Court of Appeals that the state was under the necessity of making a choice between the preservation of one class of property and that of the other wherever both existed in dangerous proximity. It would have been none the less a choice if, instead of enacting the present statute, the state, by doing nothing, had permitted serious injury to the apple orchards within its borders to go on unchecked. When forced to such a choice the state does not exceed its constitutional powers by deciding upon the destruction of one class of property in order to save another which, in the judgment of the legislature, is of greater value to the public. It will not do to say that the case is merely one of a conflict of two private interests and that the misfortune of apple growers may not be shifted to cedar owners by ordering the destruction of their property; for it is obvious that there may be, and that here there is, a preponderant public concern in the preservation of the one interest over the other. And where the public interest is involved preferment of that interest over the property interest of the individual, to the extent even of its destruction, is one of the distinguishing characteristics of every exercise of the police power which affects property.

For where, as here, the choice is unavoidable, we cannot say that its exercise, controlled by considerations of social policy which are not unreasonable, involves any denial of due process.

The issue of when government regulation constitutes a taking remains important and difficult to this day. No formula exists. But the Court has articulated general criteria that should be considered in evaluating whether a regulation is a taking. For example, in Connolly v. Pension Benefit Guaranty Corp., 475 U.S. 211 (1986), the Court said:

> [W]e have eschewed the development of any set formula for identifying a "taking" forbidden by the Fifth Amendment, and have relied instead on ad hoc, factual inquiries into the circumstances of each particular case. To aid in this determination, however, we have identified three factors which have "particular significance": (1) the economic impact of the regulation on the claimant; (2) the extent to which the regulation has interfered with investment-backed expectations; and (3) the character of the governmental action.

These criteria obviously accord courts a tremendous amount of discretion, and it is not surprising that cases concerning regulatory takings are often inconsistent and difficult to reconcile. As the criteria indicate, the Court especially focuses on the economic effect of the government regulations and the extent to which they interfere with the reasonable expectations of the property owner.

One important principle that emerges from the cases and that is crucial in judicial consideration of regulatory takings is that government regulation is a taking if it leaves no reasonable economically viable use of property; government regulation is not a taking simply because it decreases the value of a person's property, as long as it leaves reasonable economically viable uses.

Comparison of the following two Supreme Court cases illustrates this principle.

PENN CENTRAL TRANSPORTATION CO. v. NEW YORK CITY
438 U.S. 104 (1978)

Justice BRENNAN delivered the opinion of the Court.

The question presented is whether a city may, as part of a comprehensive program to preserve historic landmarks and historic districts, place restrictions on the development of individual historic landmarks—in addition to those imposed by applicable zoning ordinances—without effecting a "taking" requiring the payment of "just compensation." Specifically, we must decide whether the application of New York City's Landmarks Preservation Law to the parcel of land occupied by Grand Central Terminal has "taken" its owners' property in violation of the Fifth and Fourteenth Amendments.

I

A

Over the past 50 years, all 50 States and over 500 municipalities have enacted laws to encourage or require the preservation of buildings and areas with historic or aesthetic importance. These nationwide legislative efforts have been precipitated by two concerns. The first is recognition that, in recent years, large numbers of historic structures, landmarks, and areas have been destroyed without adequate consideration of either the values represented therein or the possibility of preserving the destroyed properties for use in economically productive ways. The second is a widely shared belief that structures with special historic, cultural, or architectural significance enhance the quality of life for all. Not only do these buildings and their workmanship represent the lessons of the past and embody precious features of our heritage, they serve as examples of quality for today. "[H]istoric conservation is but one aspect of the much larger problem, basically an environmental one, of enhancing—or perhaps developing for the first time—the quality of life for people."

B

This case involves the application of New York City's Landmarks Preservation Law to Grand Central Terminal (Terminal). The Terminal, which is owned by the Penn Central Transportation Co. and its affiliates (Penn Central), is one of New York City's most famous buildings. Opened in 1913, it is regarded not only as providing an ingenious engineering solution to the problems presented by urban railroad stations, but also as a magnificent example of the French beaux-arts style.

The Terminal is located in midtown Manhattan. Its south facade faces 42d Street and that street's intersection with Park Avenue. At street level, the Terminal is bounded on the west by Vanderbilt Avenue, on the east by the

Commodore Hotel, and on the north by the Pan-American Building. The Terminal itself is an eight-story structure which Penn Central uses as a railroad station and in which it rents space not needed for railroad purposes to a variety of commercial interests. The Terminal is one of a number of properties owned by appellant Penn Central in this area of midtown Manhattan. The others include the Barclay, Biltmore, Commodore, Roosevelt, and Waldorf-Astoria Hotels, the Pan-American Building and other office buildings along Park Avenue, and the Yale Club.

On January 22, 1968, appellant Penn Central, to increase its income, entered into a renewable 50-year lease and sublease agreement with appellant UGP Properties, Inc. (UGP), a wholly owned subsidiary of Union General Properties, Ltd., a United Kingdom corporation. Under the terms of the agreement, UGP was to construct a multistory office building above the Terminal. UGP promised to pay Penn Central $1 million annually during construction and at least $3 million annually thereafter. The rentals would be offset in part by a loss of some $700,000 to $1 million in net rentals presently received from concessionaires displaced by the new building.

Appellants UGP and Penn Central then applied to the Commission for permission to construct an office building atop the Terminal. After four days of hearings at which over 80 witnesses testified, the Commission denied this application as to [the] proposals.

II

Before considering appellants' specific contentions, it will be useful to review the factors that have shaped the jurisprudence of the Fifth Amendment injunction "nor shall private property be taken for public use, without just compensation." The question of what constitutes a "taking" for purposes of the Fifth Amendment has proved to be a problem of considerable difficulty. While this Court has recognized that the "Fifth Amendment's guarantee . . . [is] designed to bar Government from forcing some people alone to bear public burdens which, in all fairness and justice, should be borne by the public as a whole," this Court, quite simply, has been unable to develop any "set formula" for determining when "justice and fairness" require that economic injuries caused by public action be compensated by the government, rather than remain disproportionately concentrated on a few persons. Indeed, we have frequently observed that whether a particular restriction will be rendered invalid by the government's failure to pay for any losses proximately caused by it depends largely "upon the particular circumstances [in that] case."

In engaging in these essentially ad hoc, factual inquiries, the Court's decisions have identified several factors that have particular significance. The economic impact of the regulation on the claimant and, particularly, the extent to which the regulation has interfered with distinct investment-backed expectations are, of course, relevant considerations. So, too, is the character of the governmental action. A "taking" may more readily be found when the interference with property can be characterized as a physical invasion by government, than when interference arises from some public program adjusting the benefits and burdens of economic life to promote the common good.

More importantly for the present case, in instances in which a state tribunal reasonably concluded that "the health, safety, morals, or general welfare" would be promoted by prohibiting particular contemplated uses of land, this Court has upheld land-use regulations that destroyed or adversely affected recognized real property interests. Zoning laws are, of course, the classic example, see Euclid v. Ambler Realty Co. (1926) (prohibition of industrial use), which have been viewed as permissible governmental action even when prohibiting the most beneficial use of the property. Zoning laws generally do not affect existing uses of real property, but "taking" challenges have also been held to be without merit in a wide variety of situations when the challenged governmental actions prohibited a beneficial use to which individual parcels had previously been devoted and thus caused substantial individualized harm. Miller v. Schoene (1928).

In contending that the New York City law has "taken" their property in violation of the Fifth and Fourteenth Amendments, appellants make a series of arguments, which, while tailored to the facts of this case, essentially urge that any substantial restriction imposed pursuant to a landmark law must be accompanied by just compensation if it is to be constitutional. Before considering these, we emphasize what is not in dispute. Because this Court has recognized, in a number of settings, that States and cities may enact land-use restrictions or controls to enhance the quality of life by preserving the character and desirable aesthetic features of a city, appellants do not contest that New York City's objective of preserving structures and areas with special historic, architectural, or cultural significance is an entirely permissible governmental goal. They also do not dispute that the restrictions imposed on its parcel are appropriate means of securing the purposes of the New York City law.

[T]he submission that appellants may establish a "taking" simply by showing that they have been denied the ability to exploit a property interest that they heretofore had believed was available for development is quite simply untenable. [A]ppellants, focusing on the character and impact of the New York City law, argue that it effects a "taking" because its operation has significantly diminished the value of the Terminal site. Appellants concede that the decisions sustaining other land-use regulations, which, like the New York City law, are reasonably related to the promotion of the general welfare, uniformly reject the proposition that diminution in property value, standing alone, can establish a "taking," see Euclid v. Ambler Realty Co. (1926) (75% diminution in value caused by zoning law); Hadacheck v. Sebastian (1915) (871/2% diminution in value).

Stated baldly, appellants' position appears to be that the only means of ensuring that selected owners are not singled out to endure financial hardship for no reason is to hold that any restriction imposed on individual landmarks pursuant to the New York City scheme is a "taking" requiring the payment of "just compensation." Agreement with this argument would, of course, invalidate not just New York City's law, but all comparable landmark legislation in the Nation. We find no merit in it.

The New York City law does not interfere in any way with the present uses of the Terminal. Its designation as a landmark not only permits but contemplates that appellants may continue to use the property precisely as it has been used for the past 65 years: as a railroad terminal containing office space and concessions. So the law does not interfere with what must be regarded as Penn Central's primary expectation concerning the use of the parcel. More importantly, on this record, we must regard the New York City law as permitting Penn Central not only to profit from the Terminal but also to obtain a "reasonable return" on its investment.

Appellants, moreover, exaggerate the effect of the law on their ability to make use of the air rights above the Terminal in two respects. First, it simply cannot be maintained, on this record, that appellants have been prohibited from occupying any portion of the airspace above the Terminal. While the Commission's actions in denying applications to construct an office building in excess of 50 stories above the Terminal may indicate that it will refuse to issue a certificate of appropriateness for any comparably sized structure, nothing the Commission has said or done suggests an intention to prohibit any construction above the Terminal. Since appellants have not sought approval for the construction of a smaller structure, we do not know that appellants will be denied any use of any portion of the airspace above the Terminal.

On this record, we conclude that the application of New York City's Landmarks Law has not effected a "taking" of appellants' property. The restrictions imposed are substantially related to the promotion of the general welfare and not only permit reasonable beneficial use of the landmark site but also afford appellants opportunities further to enhance not only the Terminal site proper but also other properties.

Justice REHNQUIST, with whom the Chief Justice and Justice STEVENS join, dissenting.

Of the over one million buildings and structures in the city of New York, appellees have singled out 400 for designation as official landmarks. The owner of a building might initially be pleased that his property has been chosen by a distinguished committee of architects, historians, and city planners for such a singular distinction. But he may well discover, as appellant Penn Central Transportation Co. did here, that the landmark designation imposes upon him a substantial cost, with little or no offsetting benefit except for the honor of the designation. The question in this case is whether the cost associated with the city of New York's desire to preserve a limited number of "landmarks" within its borders must be borne by all of its taxpayers or whether it can instead be imposed entirely on the owners of the individual properties.

Over 50 years ago, Justice Holmes, speaking for the Court, warned that the courts were "in danger of forgetting that a strong public desire to improve the public condition is not enough to warrant achieving the desire by a shorter cut than the constitutional way of paying for the change." Pennsylvania Coal Co. v. Mahon. The Court's opinion in this case demonstrates that the danger thus foreseen has not abated.

The city of New York is in a precarious financial state, and some may believe that the costs of landmark preservation will be more easily borne by corporations such as Penn Central than the overburdened individual taxpayers of New York. But these concerns do not allow us to ignore past precedents construing the Eminent Domain Clause to the end that the desire to improve the public condition is, indeed, achieved by a shorter cut than the constitutional way of paying for the change.

LUCAS v. SOUTH CAROLINA COASTAL COUNCIL
505 U.S. 1003 (1992)

Justice SCALIA delivered the opinion of the Court.

In 1986, petitioner David H. Lucas paid $975,000 for two residential lots on the Isle of Palms in Charleston County, South Carolina, on which he intended to build single-family homes. In 1988, however, the South Carolina Legislature enacted the Beachfront Management Act, which had the direct effect of barring petitioner from erecting any permanent habitable structures on his two parcels. A state trial court found that this prohibition rendered Lucas's parcels "value-less." This case requires us to decide whether the Act's dramatic effect on the economic value of Lucas's lots accomplished a taking of private property under the Fifth and Fourteenth Amendments requiring the payment of "just compensation."

I

In the late 1970s, Lucas and others began extensive residential development of the Isle of Palms, a barrier island situated eastward of the city of Charleston. Toward the close of the development cycle for one residential subdivision known as "Beachwood East," Lucas in 1986 purchased the two lots at issue in this litigation for his own account. No portion of the lots, which were located approximately 300 feet from the beach, qualified as a "critical area" under the 1977 Act; accordingly, at the time Lucas acquired these parcels, he was not legally obliged to obtain a permit from the Council in advance of any development activity. His intention with respect to the lots was to do what the owners of the immediately adjacent parcels had already done: erect single-family residences. He commissioned architectural drawings for this purpose.

The Beachfront Management Act brought Lucas's plans to an abrupt end. [U]nder the Act construction of occupiable improvements was flatly prohibited seaward of a line drawn 20 feet landward of, and parallel to, the baseline. The Act provided no exceptions.

Lucas promptly filed suit in the South Carolina Court of Common Pleas, contending that the Beachfront Management Act's construction bar effected a taking of his property without just compensation. Lucas did not take issue with the validity of the Act as a lawful exercise of South Carolina's police power, but contended that the Act's complete extinguishment of his property's value entitled him to compensation regardless of whether the legislature had acted in furtherance of legitimate police power objectives.

[II]

Prior to Justice Holmes's exposition in Pennsylvania Coal Co. v. Mahon, it was generally thought that the Takings Clause reached only a "direct appropriation" of property, or the functional equivalent of a "practical ouster of [the owner's] possession." Justice Holmes recognized in *Mahon*, however, that if the protection against physical appropriations of private property was to be meaningfully enforced, the government's power to redefine the range of interests included in the ownership of property was necessarily constrained by constitutional limits. If, instead, the uses of private property were subject to unbridled, uncompensated qualification under the police power, "the natural tendency of human nature [would be] to extend the qualification more and more until at last private property disappear[ed]." These considerations gave birth in that case to the oft-cited maxim that, "while property may be regulated to a certain extent, if regulation goes too far it will be recognized as a taking."

Nevertheless, our decision in *Mahon* offered little insight into when, and under what circumstances, a given regulation would be seen as going "too far" for purposes of the Fifth Amendment. In 70-odd years of succeeding "regulatory takings" jurisprudence, we have generally eschewed any "'set formula'" for determining how far is too far, preferring to "engag[e] in . . . essentially ad hoc, factual inquiries." Penn Central Transportation Co. v. New York City (1978). We have, however, described at least two discrete categories of regulatory action as compensable without case-specific inquiry into the public interest advanced in support of the restraint. The first encompasses regulations that compel the property owner to suffer a physical "invasion" of his property. In general (at least with regard to permanent invasions), no matter how minute the intrusion, and no matter how weighty the public purpose behind it, we have required compensation. Loretto v. Teleprompter Manhattan CATV Corp. (1982).

The second situation in which we have found categorical treatment appropriate is where regulation denies all economically beneficial or productive use of land. As we have said on numerous occasions, the Fifth Amendment is violated when land-use regulation "does not substantially advance legitimate state interests or denies an owner economically viable use of his land."

We have never set forth the justification for this rule. Perhaps it is simply, as Justice Brennan suggested, that total deprivation of beneficial use is, from the landowner's point of view, the equivalent of a physical appropriation. Surely, at least, in the extraordinary circumstance when no productive or economically beneficial use of land is permitted, it is less realistic to indulge our usual assumption that the legislature is simply "adjusting the benefits and burdens of economic life," in a manner that secures an "average reciprocity of advantage" to everyone concerned. And the functional basis for permitting the government, by regulation, to affect property values without compensation — that "Government hardly could go on if to some extent values incident to property could not be diminished without paying for every such change in the general law," does not apply to the relatively rare situations where the government has deprived a landowner of all economically beneficial uses.

On the other side of the balance, affirmatively supporting a compensation requirement, is the fact that regulations that leave the owner of land without economically beneficial or productive options for its use — typically, as here, by requiring land to be left substantially in its natural state — carry with them a heightened risk that private property is being pressed into some form of public service under the guise of mitigating serious public harm.

We think, in short, that there are good reasons for our frequently expressed belief that when the owner of real property has been called upon to sacrifice all economically beneficial uses in the name of the common good, that is, to leave his property economically idle, he has suffered a taking.[34]

The trial court found Lucas's two beachfront lots to have been rendered value-less by respondent's enforcement of the coastal-zone construction ban. Under Lucas's theory of the case, which rested upon our "no economically viable use" statements, that finding entitled him to compensation.

Where the State seeks to sustain regulation that deprives land of all econom-ically beneficial use, we think it may resist compensation only if the logically antecedent inquiry into the nature of the owner's estate shows that the pro-scribed use interests were not part of his title to begin with. In light of our traditional resort to "existing rules or understandings that stem from an independent source such as state law" to define the range of interests that qualify for protection as "property" under the Fifth and Fourteenth Amend-ments, Board of Regents of State Colleges v. Roth (1972), this recognition that the Takings Clause does not require compensation when an owner is barred from putting land to a use that is proscribed by those "existing rules or under-standings" is surely unexceptional. When, however, a regulation that declares "off-limits" all economically productive or beneficial uses of land goes beyond what the relevant background principles would dictate, compensation must be paid to sustain it.

It seems unlikely that common-law principles would have prevented the erec-tion of any habitable or productive improvements on petitioner's land; they rarely support prohibition of the "essential use" of land. The question, however, is one of state law to be dealt with on remand. We emphasize that to win its case South Carolina must do more than proffer the legislature's declaration that the uses Lucas desires are inconsistent with the public interest, or the conclusory assertion that they violate a common-law maxim such as *sic utere tuo ut alienum non laedas*. As we have said, a "State, by ipse dixit, may not transform private property into public property without compensation. . . ." Webb's Fabulous Pharmacies, Inc. v. Beckwith (1980). Instead, as it would be required to do if it sought to restrain Lucas in a common-law action for public nuisance, South Carolina must identify background principles of nuisance and property law that prohibit the uses he now intends in the circumstances in which the property is presently found. Only on this showing can the State fairly claim that, in pro-scribing all such beneficial uses, the Beachfront Management Act is taking nothing.

---

34. Justice Stevens criticizes the "deprivation of all economically beneficial use" rule as "wholly arbitrary," in that "[the] landowner whose property is diminished in value 95% recovers nothing," while the landowner who suffers a complete elimination of value "recovers in land's full value." This analysis errs in its assumption that the landowner whose deprivation is one step short of complete is not entitled to compensation. Such an owner might not be able to claim the benefit of our categorical formulation, but, as we have acknowledged time and again, "[t]he economic impact of the regulation on the claimant and . . . the extent to which the regulation has interfered with distinct investment-backed expectations" are keenly relevant to takings analysis generally. Penn Central Transportation Co. v. New York City (1978). It is true that in at least some cases the landowner with 95% loss will get nothing, while the landowner with total loss will recover in full. But that occasional result is no more strange than the gross disparity between the landowner whose premises are taken for a highway (who recovers in full) and the landowner whose property is reduced to 5% of its former value by the highway (who recovers nothing). Takings law is full of these "all-or-nothing" situations. [Footnote by the Court.]

Justice BLACKMUN, dissenting.

Today the Court launches a missile to kill a mouse. The State of South Carolina prohibited petitioner Lucas from building a permanent structure on his property from 1988 to 1990. Relying on an unreviewed (and implausible) state trial court finding that this restriction left Lucas' property valueless, this Court granted review to determine whether compensation must be paid in cases where the State prohibits all economic use of real estate. According to the Court, such an occasion never has arisen in any of our prior cases, and the Court imagines that it will arise "relatively rarely" or only in "extraordinary circumstances." Almost certainly it did not happen in this case.

Nonetheless, the Court presses on to decide the issue, and as it does, it ignores its jurisdictional limits, remakes its traditional rules of review, and creates simultaneously a new categorical rule and an exception (neither of which is rooted in our prior case law, common law, or common sense). I protest not only the Court's decision, but each step taken to reach it. More fundamentally, I question the Court's wisdom in issuing sweeping new rules to decide such a narrow case.

The Court does not reject the South Carolina Supreme Court's decision simply on the basis of its disbelief and distrust of the legislature's findings. It also takes the opportunity to create a new scheme for regulations that eliminate all economic value. From now on, there is a categorical rule finding these regulations to be a taking unless the use they prohibit is a background common-law nuisance or property principle.

This Court repeatedly has recognized the ability of government, in certain circumstances, to regulate property without compensation no matter how adverse the financial effect on the owner may be. More than a century ago, the Court explicitly upheld the right of States to prohibit uses of property injurious to public health, safety, or welfare without paying compensation.

Ultimately even the Court cannot embrace the full implications of its per se rule: It eventually agrees that there cannot be a categorical rule for a taking based on economic value that wholly disregards the public need asserted. Instead, the Court decides that it will permit a State to regulate all economic value only if the State prohibits uses that would not be permitted under "background principles of nuisance and property law." Until today, the Court explicitly had rejected the contention that the government's power to act without paying compensation turns on whether the prohibited activity is a common-law nuisance.

The Court makes sweeping and, in my view, misguided and unsupported changes in our takings doctrine. While it limits these changes to the most narrow subset of government regulation — those that eliminate all economic value from land — these changes go far beyond what is necessary to secure petitioner Lucas' private benefit. One hopes they do not go beyond the narrow confines the Court assigns them to today.

I dissent.

An important area in which the Supreme Court frequently has considered regulatory takings is zoning ordinances. Zoning ordinances limit the way in which a person may use his or her property and therefore frequently have the effect of diminishing the property's economic value. Generally, though, the Court has refused to find a taking, concluding that the regulation does not eliminate all reasonable economically viable uses of the property.

Village of Euclid v. Amber Realty Co., 272 U.S. 365 (1926), was one of the first Supreme Court cases to consider a challenge to a zoning ordinance. A tract of vacant land was zoned for industrial uses and had a market value of about $10,000 per acre. The land was rezoned so that it could be used only for residential purposes, reducing its value to about $2,500 an acre. Nonetheless, the Supreme Court rejected a due process challenge to the revised zoning ordinance. The Court emphasized the government's strong police purpose in the zoning regulation. The Court said, "[T]he segregation of residential, business, and industrial buildings will make it easier to provide fire apparatus suitable for the character and intensity of the development in each section; that it will increase the safety and security of home life; greatly tend to prevent street accidents, especially to children, by reducing the traffic and resulting confusion in residential sections; decrease noise and other conditions which produce or intensify nervous disorders; preserve a more favorable environment in which to rear children."

Subsequent cases generally have followed this reasoning and have rejected takings challenges to zoning ordinances. For example, in Goldblatt v. Town of Hempstead, 369 U.S. 590 (1962), a city's zoning ordinance prevented further excavation of a stone and gravel quarry that had been in operation for over 30 years. The Court rejected the takings claim and noted that "[i]t is an oft-repeated truism that every regulation necessarily speaks as a prohibition. If this ordinance is otherwise a valid exercise of the town's police powers, the fact that it deprives the property of its most beneficial use does not render it unconstitutional." The Court said that the zoning ordinance was not a taking because "there is no evidence . . . which even remotely suggests that prohibition of further mining will reduce the value of the lot in question."

Similarly, in Agins v. City of Tiburon, 447 U.S. 255 (1980), the Supreme Court rejected a Takings Clause challenge to a zoning ordinance that required that property be used for single-family homes rather than multiple family dwellings. Whereas previously the owners might have constructed apartment or condominium buildings, the city of Tiburon adopted a zoning ordinance limiting construction to single-family homes. The effect of the ordinance was to substantially reduce the value of the property. But the Supreme Court concluded that there was not a taking because the owner still had reasonable economically viable use of the property and because of the government's important interest in "assuring careful and orderly development of residential property."

The Court has followed this reasoning in other cases where the government's regulation limits development or use of property. In Keystone Bituminous Coal Association v. DeBenedictis, 480 U.S. 470 (1987), the Court refused to find a taking when a Pennsylvania law prevented mining that could cause subsidence of buildings, and a Pennsylvania agency required that 50 percent of the coal be kept in the land underneath structures. The law and the agency's interpretation of it had the effect of preventing some mining, even in instances where the coal company had purchased surface rights. Nonetheless, the Supreme Court found that there was not a taking. The Court quoted *Agins* as establishing that "land use regulation can effect a taking if it does not substantially advance legitimate state interests . . . or denies an owner economically viable use of land."

The *Keystone* Court concluded that there was not a taking because the law served legitimate state interests and because it allowed economically viable development of the property. The Court explained that the legislature's goal was to protect public safety by preventing subsidence of land. The Court also observed that there was not a taking because the law did not eliminate all economically viable use of the property. The Court said, "When the coal that must remain beneath the ground is viewed in the context of any reasonable unit of petitioners' coal mining operations and financial-backed expectations, it is plain that petitioners have not come close to satisfying their burden of proving that they have been denied the economically viable use of that property."

All of these cases indicate that it is very difficult to persuade the Supreme Court that restrictions on the use of property, through zoning or other laws, constitute a taking. The Court only is willing to find a taking if the law prevents virtually all economically viable uses of the property, as was the situation in *Lucas*.

The above cases concerned the issue of when government prohibitions or restrictions on the use of property constitute a taking. By contrast, what if the government allows the development of property, but subjects it to specific conditions that the developer must meet? When are government conditions on development considered a taking?

In two decisions, the Supreme Court has announced that a condition on the development of property is a taking if the burden imposed by the condition is not roughly proportionate to the government's justification for regulating.

NOLLAN v. CALIFORNIA COASTAL COMMN., 483 U.S. 825 (1987): Justice SCALIA wrote the opinion for the Court. [The government had conditioned a permit for the development of beachfront property on the owners' granting the public an easement to cross the property for beach access.] Had California simply required the [appellants] to make an easement across their beachfront property available to the public on a permanent basis . . . we have no doubt that there would have been a taking. We think a "permanent physical occupation" has occurred . . . where individuals are given a permanent and continuous right to pass to and from, so that real property may continuously be traversed, even though no particular individual is permitted to station himself permanently upon the premises.

[The Court said that the police power allows the government to place a condition on development if it is rationally related to preventing harms caused by the new construction. For example, the government could put conditions on the development of beachfront property to protect the use of the beach from the effects of the new building. But the Court said that there is a taking if] the condition . . . utterly fails to further the end advanced as the justification. . . . In short, unless the permit condition serves the same governmental purposes as the development ban, the building restriction is not a valid regulation of land use but an out-and-out plan of extortion.

The Court clarified *Nollan* in a more recent case, Dolan v. City of Tigard.

DOLAN v. CITY OF TIGARD

512 U.S. 374 (1994)

Chief Justice REHNQUIST delivered the opinion of the Court.

Petitioner challenges the decision of the Oregon Supreme Court which held that the city of Tigard could condition the approval of her building permit on the dedication of a portion of her property for flood control and traffic improvements. We granted certiorari to resolve a question left open by our decision in Nollan v. California Coastal Comm'n (1987), of what is the required degree of connection between the exactions imposed by the city and the projected impacts of the proposed development.

I

The State of Oregon enacted a comprehensive land use management program in 1973. The program required all Oregon cities and counties to adopt new comprehensive land use plans that were consistent with the statewide planning goals. The plans are implemented by land use regulations which are part of an integrated hierarchy of legally binding goals, plans, and regulations. Pursuant to the State's requirements, the city of Tigard, a community of some 30,000 residents on the southwest edge of Portland, developed a comprehensive plan and codified it in its Community Development Code (CDC). The CDC requires property owners in the area zoned Central Business District to comply with a 15% open space and landscaping requirement, which limits total site coverage, including all structures and paved parking, to 85% of the parcel. After the completion of a transportation study that identified congestion in the Central Business District as a particular problem, the city adopted a plan for a pedestrian/bicycle pathway intended to encourage alternatives to automobile transportation for short trips. The CDC requires that new development facilitate this plan by dedicating land for pedestrian pathways where provided for in the pedestrian/bicycle pathway plan. The city also adopted a Master Drainage Plan (Drainage Plan). The Drainage Plan noted that flooding occurred in several areas along Fanno Creek, including areas near petitioner's property.

Petitioner Florence Dolan owns a plumbing and electric supply store located on Main Street in the Central Business District of the city. Petitioner applied to the city for a permit to redevelop the site. Her proposed plans called for nearly doubling the size of the store to 17,600 square feet and paving a 39-space parking lot.

The City Planning Commission (Commission) granted petitioner's permit application subject to conditions imposed by the city's CDC. [T]he Commission required that petitioner dedicate the portion of her property lying within the 100-year floodplain for improvement of a storm drainage system along Fanno Creek and that she dedicate an additional 15-foot strip of land adjacent to the floodplain as a pedestrian/bicycle pathway. The dedication required by that condition encompasses approximately 7,000 square feet, or roughly 10% of the property.

II

One of the principal purposes of the Takings Clause is "to bar Government from forcing some people alone to bear public burdens which, in all fairness and justice, should be borne by the public as a whole." Armstrong v. United States (1960). Without question, had the city simply required petitioner to dedicate a strip of land along Fanno Creek for public use, rather than conditioning the grant of her permit to redevelop her property on such a dedication, a taking would have occurred. Such public access would deprive petitioner of the right to exclude others, "one of the most essential sticks in the bundle of rights that are commonly characterized as property." Kaiser Aetna v. United States (1979).

On the other side of the ledger, the authority of state and local governments to engage in land use planning has been sustained against constitutional challenge as long ago as our decision in Village of Euclid v. Ambler Realty Co. (1926). "Government hardly could go on if to some extent values incident to property could not be diminished without paying for every such change in the general law." Pennsylvania Coal Co. v. Mahon (1922). A land use regulation does not effect a taking if it "substantially advance[s] legitimate state interests" and does not "den[y] an owner economically viable use of his land." Agins v. City of Tiburon (1980).

The sort of land use regulations discussed in the cases just cited, however, differ in two relevant particulars from the present case. First, they involved essentially legislative determinations classifying entire areas of the city, whereas here the city made an adjudicative decision to condition petitioner's application for a building permit on an individual parcel. Second, the conditions imposed were not simply a limitation on the use petitioner might make of her own parcel, but a requirement that she deed portions of the property to the city. In *Nollan*, we held that governmental authority to exact such a condition was circumscribed by the Fifth and Fourteenth Amendments. Under the well-settled doctrine of "unconstitutional conditions," the government may not require a person to give up a constitutional right — here the right to receive just compensation when property is taken for a public use — in exchange for a discretionary benefit conferred by the government where the benefit sought has little or no relationship to the property.

Petitioner contends that the city has forced her to choose between the building permit and her right under the Fifth Amendment to just compensation for the public easements. Petitioner does not quarrel with the city's authority to exact some forms of dedication as a condition for the grant of a building permit, but challenges the showing made by the city to justify these exactions.

III

In evaluating petitioner's claim, we must first determine whether the "essential nexus" exists between the "legitimate state interest" and the permit condition exacted by the city. *Nollan*. If we find that a nexus exists, we must then decide the required degree of connection between the exactions and the projected impact of the proposed development. We were not required to reach this question in *Nollan*, because we concluded that the connection did not meet even the loosest standard. Here, however, we must decide this question.

A

We addressed the essential nexus question in *Nollan*. The California Coastal Commission demanded a lateral public easement across the Nollans' beachfront lot in exchange for a permit to demolish an existing bungalow and replace it with a three-bedroom house. The public easement was designed to connect two public beaches that were separated by the Nollans' property. The Coastal Commission had asserted that the public easement condition was imposed to promote the legitimate state interest of diminishing the "blockage of the view of the ocean" caused by construction of the larger house.

We agreed that the Coastal Commission's concern with protecting visual access to the ocean constituted a legitimate public interest. We also agreed that the permit condition would have been constitutional "even if it consisted of the requirement that the Nollans provide a viewing spot on their property for passersby with whose sighting of the ocean their new house would interfere." We resolved, however, that the Coastal Commission's regulatory authority was set completely adrift from its constitutional moorings when it claimed that a nexus existed between visual access to the ocean and a permit condition requiring lateral public access along the Nollans' beachfront lot. How enhancing the public's ability to "traverse to and along the shorefront" served the same governmental purpose of "visual access to the ocean" from the roadway was beyond our ability to countenance. The absence of a nexus left the Coastal Commission in the position of simply trying to obtain an easement through gimmickry, which converted a valid regulation of land use into "'an out-and-out plan of extortion.'"

No such gimmicks are associated with the permit conditions imposed by the city in this case. Undoubtedly, the prevention of flooding along Fanno Creek and the reduction of traffic congestion in the Central Business District qualify as the type of legitimate public purposes we have upheld. It seems equally obvious that a nexus exists between preventing flooding along Fanno Creek and limiting development within the creek's 100-year floodplain. Petitioner proposes to double the size of her retail store and to pave her now-gravel parking lot, thereby expanding the impervious surface on the property and increasing the amount of storm water runoff into Fanno Creek.

The same may be said for the city's attempt to reduce traffic congestion by providing for alternative means of transportation. In theory, a pedestrian/bicycle pathway provides a useful alternative means of transportation for workers and shoppers.

B

The second part of our analysis requires us to determine whether the degree of the exactions demanded by the city's permit conditions bears the required relationship to the projected impact of petitioner's proposed development.

In some States, very generalized statements as to the necessary connection between the required dedication and the proposed development seem to suffice. We think this standard is too lax to adequately protect petitioner's right to just compensation if her property is taken for a public purpose.

Other state courts require a very exacting correspondence, described as the "specifi[c] and uniquely attributable" test. Under this standard, if the local government cannot demonstrate that its exaction is directly proportional to the specifically created need, the exaction becomes "a veiled exercise of the power of eminent domain and a confiscation of private property behind the defense of police regulations." We do not think the Federal Constitution requires such exacting scrutiny, given the nature of the interests involved.

A number of state courts have taken an intermediate position, requiring the municipality to show a "reasonable relationship" between the required dedication and the impact of the proposed development. Despite any semantical differences, general agreement exists among the courts "that the dedication should have some reasonable relationship to the needs created by the [development]."

We think the "reasonable relationship" test adopted by a majority of the state courts is closer to the federal constitutional norm than either of those previously discussed. But we do not adopt it as such, partly because the term "reasonable relationship" seems confusingly similar to the term "rational basis" which describes the minimal level of scrutiny under the Equal Protection Clause of the Fourteenth Amendment. We think a term such as "rough proportionality" best encapsulates what we hold to be the requirement of the Fifth Amendment. No precise mathematical calculation is required, but the city must make some sort of individualized determination that the required dedication is related both in nature and extent to the impact of the proposed development.

Cities have long engaged in the commendable task of land use planning, made necessary by increasing urbanization, particularly in metropolitan areas such as Portland. The city's goals of reducing flooding hazards and traffic congestion, and providing for public greenways, are laudable, but there are outer limits to how this may be done. "A strong public desire to improve the public condition [will not] warrant achieving the desire by a shorter cut than the constitutional way of paying for the change." [The Court remanded the case for the application of the standard that it announced.]

Justice STEVENS, with whom Justice BLACKMUN and Justice GINSBURG join, dissenting.

The record does not tell us the dollar value of petitioner Florence Dolan's interest in excluding the public from the greenway adjacent to her hardware business. The mountain of briefs that the case has generated nevertheless makes it obvious that the pecuniary value of her victory is far less important than the rule of law that this case has been used to establish. It is unquestionably an important case.

Certain propositions are not in dispute. The enlargement of the Tigard unit in Dolan's chain of hardware stores will have an adverse impact on the city's legitimate and substantial interests in controlling drainage in Fanno Creek and minimizing traffic congestion in Tigard's business district. That impact is sufficient to justify an outright denial of her application for approval of the expansion. The city has nevertheless agreed to grant Dolan's application if she will comply with two conditions, each of which admittedly will mitigate the adverse effects of her proposed development. The disputed question is whether the city has violated the Fourteenth Amendment to the Federal Constitution by refusing to allow Dolan's planned construction to proceed unless those conditions are met. The Court is correct in concluding that the city may not attach arbitrary conditions to a building permit or to a variance even when it can rightfully deny the application outright. Yet the Court's description of the doctrinal underpinnings of its decision, the phrasing of its fledgling test of "rough proportionality," and the application of that test to this case run contrary to the traditional treatment of these cases and break considerable and unpropitious new ground.

The exactions associated with the development of a retail business are a species of business regulation that heretofore warranted a strong presumption of constitutional validity. The city of Tigard has demonstrated that its plan is rational and impartial and that the conditions at issue are "conducive to fulfillment of authorized planning objectives." Dolan, on the other hand, has offered no evidence that her burden of compliance has any impact at all on the value or profitability of her planned development. Following the teaching of the cases on which it purports to rely, the Court should not isolate the burden associated with the loss of the power to exclude from an evaluation the benefit to be derived from the permit to enlarge the store and the parking lot.

The Court's assurances that its "rough proportionality" test leaves ample room for cities to pursue the "commendable task of land use planning," — even twice avowing that "[n]o precise mathematical calculation is required," — are wanting given the result that test compels here. Under the Court's approach, a city must not only "quantify its findings," and make "individualized determination[s]" with respect to the nature and the extent of the relationship between the conditions and the impact, but also demonstrate "proportionality." The correct inquiry should instead concentrate on whether the required nexus is present and venture beyond considerations of a condition's nature or germaneness only if the developer establishes that a concededly germane condition is so grossly disproportionate to the proposed development's adverse effects that it manifests motives other than land use regulation on the part of the city.

The Court has made a serious error by abandoning the traditional presumption of constitutionality and imposing a novel burden of proof on a city implementing an admittedly valid comprehensive land use plan. Even more consequential than its incorrect disposition of this case, however, is the Court's resurrection of a species of substantive due process analysis that it firmly rejected decades ago.

In our changing world one thing is certain: uncertainty will characterize predictions about the impact of new urban developments on the risks of floods, earthquakes, traffic congestion, or environmental harms. When there is doubt concerning the magnitude of those impacts, the public interest in averting them must outweigh the private interest of the commercial entrepreneur. If the government can demonstrate that the conditions it has imposed in a land use permit are rational, impartial and conducive to fulfilling the aims of a valid land use plan, a strong presumption of validity should attach to those conditions. The burden of demonstrating that those conditions have unreasonably impaired the economic value of the proposed improvement belongs squarely on the shoulders of the party challenging the state action's constitutionality. That allocation of burdens has served us well in the past. The Court has stumbled badly today by reversing it.

In subsequent years, the Supreme Court has considered two additional questions concerning regulatory takings. First, can a property owner bring a takings challenge to regulations that already were in place when the property was acquired? Palazzolo v. Rhode Island, below, addresses this question. Second, is temporarily denying an owner development of the property a taking? Tahoe-Sierra Preservation Council, Inc. v. Tahoe Regional Planning Agency, presented later, addresses this question.

PALAZZOLO v. RHODE ISLAND

533 U.S. 606 (2001)

Justice KENNEDY delivered the opinion of the Court.

Petitioner Anthony Palazzolo owns a waterfront parcel of land in the town of Westerly, Rhode Island. Almost all of the property is designated as coastal wetlands under Rhode Island law. After petitioner's development proposals were rejected by respondent Rhode Island Coastal Resources Management Council (Council), he sued in state court, asserting the Council's application of its wetlands regulations took the property without compensation in violation of the Takings Clause of the Fifth Amendment, binding upon the State through the Due Process Clause of the Fourteenth Amendment. Petitioner sought review in this Court, contending the Supreme Court of Rhode Island erred in rejecting his takings claim.

I

The town of Westerly is on an edge of the Rhode Island coastline. In 1959 petitioner, a lifelong Westerly resident, decided to invest in three undeveloped, adjoining parcels. To purchase and hold the property, petitioner and associates formed Shore Gardens, Inc. (SGI). After SGI purchased the property petitioner bought out his associates and became the sole shareholder. In the first decade of SGI's ownership of the property the corporation submitted a plat to the town subdividing the property into 80 lots; and it engaged in various transactions that left it with 74 lots, which together encompassed about 20 acres. During the same period SGI also made initial attempts to develop the property and submitted intermittent applications to state agencies to fill substantial portions of the parcel. Most of the property was then, as it is now, salt marsh subject to tidal flooding. The wet ground and permeable soil would require considerable fill — as much as six feet in some places — before significant structures could be built. SGI's proposal, submitted in 1962 to the Rhode Island Division of Harbors and Rivers (DHR), sought to dredge from Winnapaug Pond and fill the entire property. The application was denied for lack of essential information.

A second, similar proposal followed a year later. A third application, submitted in 1966 while the second application was pending, proposed more limited filling of the land for use as a private beach club. These latter two applications were referred to the Rhode Island Department of Natural Resources, which indicated initial assent. The agency later withdrew approval, however, citing adverse environmental impacts. SGI did not contest the ruling.

No further attempts to develop the property were made for over a decade. Two intervening events, however, become important to the issues presented. First, in 1971, Rhode Island enacted legislation creating the Council, an agency charged with the duty of protecting the State's coastal properties. Regulations promulgated by the Council designated salt marshes like those on SGI's property as protected "coastal wetlands." Second, in 1978 SGI's corporate charter was revoked for failure to pay corporate income taxes; and title to the property passed, by operation of state law, to petitioner as the corporation's sole shareholder.

In 1983 petitioner, now the owner, renewed the efforts to develop the property. An application to the Council, resembling the 1962 submission, requested permission to construct a wooden bulkhead along the shore of Winnapaug Pond and to fill the entire marsh land area. The Council rejected the application, noting it was "vague and inadequate for a project of this size and nature." The agency also found that "the proposed alteration . . . will conflict with the Coastal Resources Management Plan presently in effect." Petitioner did not appeal the agency's determination.

Petitioner went back to the drawing board, this time hiring counsel and preparing a more specific and limited proposal for use of the property. The new application, submitted to the Council in 1985, echoed the 1966 request to build a private beach club. The details do not tend to inspire the reader with an idyllic coastal image, for the proposal was to fill 11 acres of the property with gravel to accommodate "50 cars with boat trailers, a dumpster, port-a-johns, picnic tables, barbecue pits of concrete, and other trash receptacles."

The application fared no better with the Council than previous ones. In a short opinion the Council said the beach club proposal conflicted with the regulatory standard for a special exception. To secure a special exception the proposed activity must serve "a compelling public purpose which provides benefits to the public as a whole as opposed to individual or private interests." This time petitioner appealed the decision to the Rhode Island courts, challenging the Council's conclusion as contrary to principles of state administrative law. The Council's decision was affirmed.

Petitioner filed an inverse condemnation action in Rhode Island Superior Court, asserting that the State's wetlands regulations, as applied by the Council to his parcel, had taken the property without compensation in violation of the Fifth and Fourteenth Amendments. The suit alleged the Council's action deprived him of "all economically beneficial use" of his property, resulting in a total taking requiring compensation under Lucas v. South Carolina Coastal Council (1992). He sought damages in the amount of $3,150,000, a figure derived from an appraiser's estimate as to the value of a 74-lot residential subdivision. After a bench trial, a justice of the Superior Court ruled against petitioner, accepting some of the State's theories. The Rhode Island Supreme Court affirmed. Like the Superior Court, the State Supreme Court recited multiple grounds for rejecting petitioner's suit. The court held, first, that petitioner's takings claim was not ripe; second, that petitioner had no right to challenge regulations predating 1978, when he succeeded to legal ownership of the property from SGI; and third, that the claim of deprivation of all economically beneficial use was contradicted by undisputed evidence that he had $200,000 in development value remaining on an upland parcel of the property.

We disagree with the Supreme Court of Rhode Island as to the first two of these conclusions; and, we hold, the court was correct to conclude that the owner is not deprived of all economic use of his property because the value of upland portions is substantial. We remand for further consideration of the claim under the principles set forth in *Penn Central.*

II

The Takings Clause of the Fifth Amendment, applicable to the States through the Fourteenth Amendment, prohibits the government from taking private property for public use without just compensation. The clearest sort of taking occurs when the government encroaches upon or occupies private land for its own proposed use. Our cases establish that even a minimal "permanent physical occupation of real property" requires compensation under the Clause. Loretto v. Teleprompter Manhattan CATV Corp. (1982). In Pennsylvania Coal Co. v. Mahon (1922), the Court recognized that there will be instances when government actions do not encroach upon or occupy the property yet still affect and limit its use to such an extent that a taking occurs. In Justice Holmes' well-known, if less than self-defining, formulation, "while property may be regulated to a certain extent, if a regulation goes too far it will be recognized as a taking."

Since *Mahon*, we have given some, but not too specific, guidance to courts confronted with deciding whether a particular government action goes too far and effects a regulatory taking. First, we have observed, with certain qualifications, that a regulation which "denies all economically beneficial or productive use of land" will require compensation under the Takings Clause. Where a regulation places limitations on land that fall short of eliminating all economically beneficial use, a taking nonetheless may have occurred, depending on a complex of factors including the regulation's economic effect on the landowner, the extent to which the regulation interferes with reasonable investment-backed expectations, and the character of the government action. These inquiries are informed by the purpose of the Takings Clause, which is to prevent the government from "forcing some people alone to bear public burdens which, in all fairness and justice, should be borne by the public as a whole."

When the Council promulgated its wetlands regulations, the disputed parcel was owned not by petitioner but by the corporation of which he was sole shareholder. When title was transferred to petitioner by operation of law, the wetlands regulations were in force. The state court held the postregulation acquisition of title was fatal to the claim for deprivation of all economic use and to the *Penn Central* claim. [The state court's] holdings together amount to a single, sweeping, rule: A purchaser or a successive title holder like petitioner is deemed to have notice of an earlier-enacted restriction and is barred from claiming that it effects a taking.

The theory underlying the argument that postenactment purchasers cannot challenge a regulation under the Takings Clause seems to run on these lines: Property rights are created by the State. So, the argument goes, by prospective legislation the State can shape and define property rights and reasonable investment-backed expectations, and subsequent owners cannot claim any injury from lost value. After all, they purchased or took title with notice of the limitation.

The State may not put so potent a Hobbesian stick into the Lockean bundle. The right to improve property, of course, is subject to the reasonable exercise of state authority, including the enforcement of valid zoning and land-use restrictions. The Takings Clause, however, in certain circumstances allows a landowner to assert that a particular exercise of the State's regulatory power is so unreasonable or onerous as to compel compensation. Just as a prospective enactment, such as a new zoning ordinance, can limit the value of land without effecting a taking because it can be understood as reasonable by all concerned, other enactments are unreasonable and do not become less so through passage of time or title. Were we to accept the State's rule, the postenactment transfer of title would absolve the State of its obligation to defend any action restricting land use, no matter how extreme or unreasonable. A State would be allowed, in effect, to put an expiration date on the Takings Clause. This ought not to be the rule. Future generations, too, have a right to challenge unreasonable limitations on the use and value of land.

Nor does the justification of notice take into account the effect on owners at the time of enactment, who are prejudiced as well. Should an owner attempt to challenge a new regulation, but not survive the process of ripening his or her claim (which, as this case demonstrates, will often take years), under the proposed rule the right to compensation may not by asserted by an heir or successor, and so may not be asserted at all. The State's rule would work a critical alteration to the nature of property, as the newly regulated landowner is stripped of the ability to transfer the interest which was possessed prior to the regulation. The State may not by this means secure a windfall for itself. The proposed rule is, furthermore, capricious in effect. The young owner contrasted with the older owner, the owner with the resources to hold contrasted with the owner with the need to sell, would be in different positions. The Takings Clause is not so quixotic. A blanket rule that purchasers with notice have no compensation right when a claim becomes ripe is too blunt an instrument to accord with the duty to compensate for what is taken.

We have no occasion to consider the precise circumstances when a legislative enactment can be deemed a background principle of state law or whether those circumstances are present here. It suffices to say that a regulation that otherwise would be unconstitutional absent compensation is not transformed into a background principle of the State's law by mere virtue of the passage of title.

III

As the case is ripe, and as the date of transfer of title does not bar petitioner's takings claim, we have before us the alternative ground relied upon by the Rhode Island Supreme Court in ruling upon the merits of the takings claims. It held that all economically beneficial use was not deprived because the uplands portion of the property can still be improved. On this point, we agree with the court's decision. Petitioner accepts the Council's contention and the state trial court's finding that his parcel retains $200,000 in development value under the State's wetlands regulations. He asserts, nonetheless, that he has suffered a total taking and contends the Council cannot sidestep the holding in *Lucas* "by the simple expedient of leaving a landowner a few crumbs of value."

Assuming a taking is otherwise established, a State may not evade the duty to compensate on the premise that the landowner is left with a token interest. This is not the situation of the landowner in this case, however. A regulation permitting a landowner to build a substantial residence on an 18-acre parcel does not leave the property "economically idle."

Justice STEVENS, concurring in part and dissenting in part.

I

If a regulating body fails to adhere to its procedural or substantive obligations in developing land use restrictions, anyone adversely impacted by the restrictions may challenge their validity in an injunctive action if the application of such restriction to a property owner would cause her a "direct and substantial injury." It by no means follows, however, that, as the Court assumes, a succeeding owner may obtain compensation for a taking of property from her predecessor in interest. A taking is a discrete event, a governmental acquisition of private property for which the state is required to provide just compensation. Like other transfers of property, it occurs at a particular time, that time being the moment when the relevant property interest is alienated from its owner.

Precise specification of the moment a taking occurred and of the nature of the property interest taken is necessary in order to determine an appropriately compensatory remedy. For example, the amount of the award is measured by the value of the property at the time of taking, not the value at some later date. Similarly, interest on the award runs from that date. Most importantly for our purposes today, it is the person who owned the property at the time of the taking that is entitled to the recovery.

II

Much of the difficulty of this case stems from genuine confusion as to when the taking Palazzolo alleges actually occurred. If it is the regulations themselves of which petitioner complains, and if they did, in fact, diminish the value of his property, they did so when they were adopted. To the extent that the adoption of the regulations constitute the challenged taking, petitioner is simply the wrong party to be bringing this action. If the regulations imposed a compensable injury on anyone, it was on the owner of the property at the moment the regulations were adopted. Given the trial court's finding that petitioner did not own the property at that time, in my judgment it is pellucidly clear that he has no standing to claim that the promulgation of the regulations constituted a taking of any part of the property that he subsequently acquired. His lack of standing does not depend, as the Court seems to assume, on whether or not petitioner "is deemed to have notice of an earlier-enacted restriction." If those early regulations changed the character of the owner's title to the property, thereby diminishing its value, petitioner acquired only the net value that remained after that diminishment occurred.

Of course, if, as respondent contends, even the prior owner never had any right to fill wetlands, there never was a basis for the alleged takings claim in the first place. But accepting petitioner's theory of the case, he has no standing to complain that preacquisition events may have reduced the value of the property that he acquired. If the regulations are invalid, either because improper procedures were followed when they were adopted, or because they have somehow gone "too far," petitioner may seek to enjoin their enforcement, but he has no right to recover compensation for the value of property taken from someone else. A new owner may maintain an ejectment action against a trespasser who has lodged himself in the owner's orchard but surely could not recover damages for fruit a trespasser spirited from the orchard before he acquired the property.

When is a moratorium on development a taking?

TAHOE-SIERRA PRESERVATION COUNCIL, INC. v. TAHOE REGIONAL PLANNING AGENCY

535 U.S. 302 (2002)

Justice STEVENS delivered the opinion of the Court.

The question presented is whether a moratorium on development imposed during the process of devising a comprehensive land-use plan constitutes a per se taking of property requiring compensation under the Takings Clause of the United States Constitution. This case actually involves two moratoria ordered by respondent Tahoe Regional Planning Agency (TRPA) to maintain the status quo while studying the impact of development on Lake Tahoe and designing a strategy for environmentally sound growth. The first, Ordinance 81-5, was effective from August 24, 1981, until August 26, 1983, whereas the second more restrictive Resolution 83-21 was in effect from August 27, 1983, until April 25, 1984. As a result of these two directives, virtually all development on a substantial portion of the property subject to TRPA's jurisdiction was prohibited for a period of 32 months. Although the question we decide relates only to that 32-month period, a brief description of the events leading up to the moratoria and a comment on the two permanent plans that TRPA adopted thereafter will clarify the narrow scope of our holding.

I

The relevant facts are undisputed. All agree that Lake Tahoe is "uniquely beautiful," that President Clinton was right to call it a "'national treasure that must be protected and preserved,'" and that Mark Twain aptly described the clarity of its waters as "'not merely transparent, but dazzlingly, brilliantly so.'" Lake Tahoe's exceptional clarity is attributed to the absence of algae that obscures the waters of most other lakes. Historically, the lack of nitrogen and phosphorous, which nourish the growth of algae, has ensured the transparency of its waters. Unfortunately, the lake's pristine state has deteriorated rapidly over the past 40 years; increased land development in the Lake Tahoe Basin (Basin) has threatened the "'noble sheet of blue water'" beloved by Twain and countless others. As the District Court found, "[d]ramatic decreases in clarity first began to be noted in the 1950's/early 1960's, shortly after development at the lake began in earnest." The lake's unsurpassed beauty, it seems, is the wellspring of its undoing.

The upsurge of development in the area has caused "increased nutrient loading of the lake largely because of the increase in impervious coverage of land in the Basin resulting from that development." Given this trend, the District Court predicted that "unless the process is stopped, the lake will lose its clarity and its trademark blue color, becoming green and opaque for eternity."

Those areas in the Basin that have steeper slopes produce more runoff; therefore, they are usually considered "high hazard" lands. Moreover, certain areas near streams or wetlands known as "Stream Environment Zones" (SEZs) are especially vulnerable to the impact of development because, in their natural state, they act as filters for much of the debris that runoff carries. Because "[t]he most obvious response to this problem ... is to restrict development around the lake—especially in SEZ lands, as well as in areas already naturally prone to runoff," conservation efforts have focused on controlling growth in these high hazard areas.

In combination, Ordinance 81-5 and Resolution 83-21 effectively prohibited all construction on sensitive lands in California and on all SEZ lands in the entire Basin for 32 months, and on sensitive lands in Nevada (other than SEZ lands) for eight months. It is these two moratoria that are at issue in this case.

II

Approximately two months after the adoption of the 1984 Plan, petitioners filed parallel actions against TRPA and other defendants in federal courts in Nevada and California that were ultimately consolidated for trial in the District of Nevada. The petitioners include the Tahoe Sierra Preservation Council, a nonprofit membership corporation representing about 2,000 owners of both improved and unimproved parcels of real estate in the Lake Tahoe Basin, and a class of some 400 individual owners of vacant lots located either on SEZ lands or in other parts of districts 1, 2, or 3. Those individuals purchased their properties prior to the effective date of the 1980 Compact, primarily for the purpose of constructing "at a time of their choosing" a single-family home "to serve as a permanent, retirement or vacation residence." When they made those purchases, they did so with the understanding that such construction was authorized provided that "they complied with all reasonable requirements for building."

III

Petitioners make only a facial attack on Ordinance 81-5 and Resolution 83-21. They contend that the mere enactment of a temporary regulation that, while in effect, denies a property owner all viable economic use of her property gives rise to an unqualified constitutional obligation to compensate her for the value of its use during that period. Hence, they "face an uphill battle," Keystone Bituminous Coal Assn. v. DeBenedictis (1987), that is made especially steep by their desire for a categorical rule requiring compensation whenever the government imposes such a moratorium on development. Under their proposed rule, there is no need to evaluate the landowners' investment-backed expectations, the actual impact of the regulation on any individual, the importance of the public interest served by the regulation, or the reasons for imposing the temporary restriction. For petitioners, it is enough that a regulation imposes a temporary deprivation — no mater how brief — of all economically viable use to trigger a per se rule that a taking has occurred.

In our view the answer to the abstract question whether a temporary moratorium effects a taking is neither "yes, always" nor "no, never"; the answer depends upon the particular circumstances of the case. Resisting "[t]he temptation to adopt what amount to per se rules in either direction," we conclude that the circumstances in this case are best analyzed within the *Penn Central* framework.

IV

The text of the Fifth Amendment itself provides a basis for drawing a distinction between physical takings and regulatory takings. Its plain language requires the payment of compensation whenever the government acquires private property for a public purpose, whether the acquisition is the result of a condemnation proceeding or a physical appropriation. But the Constitution contains no comparable reference to regulations that prohibit a property owner from making certain uses of her private property. Our jurisprudence involving condemnations and physical takings is as old as the Republic and, for the most part, involves the straightforward application of per se rules. Our regulatory takings jurisprudence, in contrast, is of more recent vintage and is characterized by "essentially ad hoc, factual inquiries," designed to allow "careful examination and weighing of all the relevant circumstances."

When the government physically takes possession of an interest in property for some public purpose, it has a categorical duty to compensate the former owner, United States v. Pewee Coal Co. (1951), regardless of whether the interest that is taken constitutes an entire parcel or merely a part thereof. Thus, compensation is mandated when a leasehold is taken and the government occupies the property for its own purposes, even though that use is temporary. Similarly, when the government appropriates part of a rooftop in order to provide cable TV access for apartment tenants, Loretto v. Teleprompter Manhattan CATV Corp. (1982); or when its planes use private airspace to approach a government airport, United States v. Causby (1946), it is required to pay for that share no matter how small. But a government regulation that merely prohibits landlords from evicting tenants unwilling to pay a higher rent, Block v. Hirsh (1921); that bans certain private uses of a portion of an owner's property, Village of Euclid v. Ambler Realty Co., (1926); Keystone Bituminous Coal Assn. v. DeBenedictis (1987); or that forbids the private use of certain airspace, Penn Central Transp. Co. v. New York City (1978), does not constitute a categorical taking. "The first category of cases requires courts to apply a clear rule; the second necessarily entails complex factual assessments of the purposes and economic effects of government actions."

This longstanding distinction between acquisitions of property for public use, on the one hand, and regulations prohibiting private uses, on the other, makes it inappropriate to treat cases involving physical takings as controlling precedents for the evaluation of a claim that there has been a "regulatory taking," and vice versa. For the same reason that we do not ask whether a physical appropriation advances a substantial government interest or whether it deprives the owner of all economically valuable use, we do not apply our precedent from the physical takings context to regulatory takings claims. Land-use regulations are ubiquitous and most of them impact property values in some tangential way—often in completely unanticipated ways. Treating them all as per se takings would transform government regulation into a luxury few governments could afford. By contrast, physical appropriations are relatively rare, easily identified, and usually represent a greater affront to individual property rights.

"This case does not present the 'classi[c] taking' in which the government directly appropriates private property for its own use"; instead the interference with property rights "arises from some public program adjusting the benefits. . . ." Perhaps recognizing this fundamental distinction, petitioners wisely do not place all their emphasis on analogies to physical takings cases. Instead, they rely principally on our decision in Lucas v. South Carolina Coastal Council (1992) — a regulatory takings case that, nevertheless, applied a categorical rule — to argue that the *Penn Central* framework is inapplicable here.

[W]e have "generally eschewed" any set formula for determining how far is too far, choosing instead to engage in "'essentially ad hoc, factual inquiries.'" Indeed, we still resist the temptation to adopt per se rules in our cases involving partial regulatory takings, preferring to examine "a number of factors" rather than a simple "mathematically precise" formula. Justice Brennan's opinion for the Court in *Penn Central* did, however, make it clear that even though multiple factors are relevant in the analysis of regulatory takings claims, in such cases we must focus on "the parcel as a whole."

The categorical rule that we applied in *Lucas* states that compensation is required when a regulation deprives an owner of "all economically beneficial uses" of his land. Under that rule, a statute that "wholly eliminated the value" of Lucas' fee simple title clearly qualified as a taking. But our holding was limited to "the extraordinary circumstance when no productive or economically beneficial use of land is permitted." The emphasis on the word "no" in the text of the opinion was, in effect, reiterated in a footnote explaining that the categorical rule would not apply if the diminution in value were 95% instead of 100%. Anything less than a "complete elimination of value," or a "total loss," the Court acknowledged, would require the kind of analysis applied in *Penn Central*.

Certainly, our holding that the permanent "obliteration of the value" of a fee simple estate constitutes a categorical taking does not answer the question whether a regulation prohibiting any economic use of land for a 32-month period has the same legal effect. Petitioners seek to bring this case under the rule announced in *Lucas* by arguing that we can effectively sever a 32-month segment from the remainder of each landowner's fee simple estate, and then ask whether that segment has been taken in its entirety by the moratoria. Of course, defining the property interest taken in terms of the very regulation being challenged is circular. With property so divided, every delay would become a total ban; the moratorium and the normal permit process alike would constitute categorical takings. Petitioners' "conceptual severance" argument is unavailing because it ignores *Penn Central*'s admonition that in regulatory takings cases we must focus on "the parcel as a whole." We have consistently rejected such an approach to the "denominator" question.

An interest in real property is defined by the metes and bounds that describe its geographic dimensions and the term of years that describes the temporal aspect of the owner's interest. See Restatement of Property §§7-9 (1936). Both dimensions must be considered if the interest is to be viewed in its entirety. Hence, a permanent deprivation of the owner's use of the entire area is a taking of "the parcel as a whole," whereas a temporary restriction that merely causes a diminution in value is not. Logically, a fee simple estate cannot be rendered valueless by a temporary prohibition on economic use, because the property will recover value as soon as the prohibition is lifted.

V

[T]he ultimate constitutional question is whether the concepts of "fairness and justice" that underlie the Takings Clause will be better served by [a] categorical rule or by a *Penn Central* inquiry into all of the relevant circumstances in particular cases. From that perspective, the extreme categorical rule that any deprivation of all economic use, no matter how brief, constitutes a compensable taking surely cannot be sustained. Petitioners' broad submission would apply to numerous "normal delays in obtaining building permits, changes in zoning ordinances, variances, and the like," as well as to orders temporarily prohibiting access to crime scenes, businesses that violate health codes, fire-damaged buildings, or other areas that we cannot now foresee. Such a rule would undoubtedly require changes in numerous practices that have long been considered permissible exercises of the police power. As Justice Holmes warned in *Mahon*, "[g]overnment hardly could go on if to some extent values incident to property could not be diminished without paying for every such change in the general law." A rule that required compensation for every delay in the use of property would render routine government processes prohibitively expensive or encourage hasty decisionmaking. Such an important change in the law should be the product of legislative rulemaking rather than adjudication.

More importantly, we are persuaded that the better approach to claims that a regulation has effected a temporary taking "requires careful examination and weighing of all the relevant circumstances." Our polestar remains the principles set forth in *Penn Central* itself and our other cases that govern partial regulatory takings. Under these cases, interference with investment-backed expectations is one of a number of factors that a court must examine.

[W]e have eschewed "any 'set formula' for determining when 'justice and fairness' require that economic injuries caused by public action be compensated by the government, rather than remain disproportionately concentrated on a few persons." The outcome instead "depends largely 'upon the particular circumstances [in that] case.'"

The interest in facilitating informed decisionmaking by regulatory agencies counsels against adopting a per se rule that would impose such severe costs on their deliberations. Otherwise, the financial constraints of compensating property owners during a moratorium may force officials to rush through the planning process or to abandon the practice altogether. To the extent that communities are forced to abandon using moratoria, landowners will have incentives to develop their property quickly before a comprehensive plan can be enacted, thereby fostering inefficient and ill-conceived growth.

We would create a perverse system of incentives were we to hold that landowners must wait for a taking claim to ripen so that planners can make well-reasoned decisions while, at the same time, holding that those planners must compensate landowners for the delay. Indeed, the interest in protecting the decisional process is even stronger when an agency is developing a regional plan than when it is considering a permit for a single parcel. In the proceedings involving the Lake Tahoe Basin, for example, the moratoria enabled TRPA to obtain the benefit of comments and criticisms from interested parties, such as the petitioners, during its deliberations. Since a categorical rule tied to the length of deliberations would likely create added pressure on decisionmakers to reach a quick resolution of land-use questions, it would only serve to disadvantage those landowners and interest groups who are not as organized or familiar with the planning process. Moreover, with a temporary ban on development there is a lesser risk that individual landowners will be "singled out" to bear a special burden that should be shared by the public as a whole. At least with a moratorium there is a clear "reciprocity of advantage," because it protects the interests of all affected landowners against immediate construction that might be inconsistent with the provisions of the plan that is ultimately adopted. "While each of us is burdened somewhat by such restrictions, we, in turn, benefit greatly from the restrictions that are placed on others." In fact, there is reason to believe property values often will continue to increase despite a moratorium. Such an increase makes sense in this context because property values throughout the Basin can be expected to reflect the added assurance that Lake Tahoe will remain in its pristine state. Since in some cases a 1-year moratorium may not impose a burden at all, we should not adopt a rule that assumes moratoria always force individuals to bear a special burden that should be shared by the public as a whole.

It may well be true that any moratorium that lasts for more than one year should be viewed with special skepticism. But given the fact that the District Court found that the 32 months required by TRPA to formulate the 1984 Regional Plan was not unreasonable, we could not possibly conclude that every delay of over one year is constitutionally unacceptable. Formulating a general rule of this kind is a suitable task for state legislatures. In our view, the duration of the restriction is one of the important factors that a court must consider in the appraisal of a regulatory takings claim, but with respect to that factor as with respect to other factors, the "temptation to adopt what amount to per se rules in either direction must be resisted." There may be moratoria that last longer than one year which interfere with reasonable investment-backed expectations, but as the District Court's opinion illustrates, petitioners' proposed rule is simply "too blunt an instrument," for identifying those cases. We conclude, therefore, that the interest in "fairness and justice" will be best served by relying on the familiar *Penn Central* approach when deciding cases like this, rather than by attempting to craft a new categorical rule.

Chief Justice REHNQUIST, with whom Justice SCALIA and Justice THOMAS join, dissenting.

For over half a decade petitioners were prohibited from building homes, or any other structures, on their land. Because the Takings Clause requires the government to pay compensation when it deprives owners of all economically viable use of their land, see Lucas v. South Carolina Coastal Council (1992), and because a ban on all development lasting almost six years does not resemble any traditional land-use planning device, I dissent.

I

"A court cannot determine whether a regulation has gone 'too far' unless it knows how far the regulation goes." In failing to undertake this inquiry, the Court ignores much of the impact of respondent's conduct on petitioners. Instead, it relies on the flawed determination of the Court of Appeals that the relevant time period lasted only from August 1981 until April 1984. During that period, Ordinance 81-5 and Regulation 83-21 prohibited development pending the adoption of a new regional land-use plan. The adoption of the 1984 Regional Plan (hereinafter Plan or 1984 Plan) did not, however, change anything from the petitioners' standpoint. After the adoption of the 1984 Plan, petitioners still could make no use of their land. Because respondent caused petitioners' inability to use their land from 1981 through 1987, that is the appropriate period of time from which to consider their takings claim.

II

I now turn to determining whether a ban on all economic development lasting almost six years is a taking. *Lucas* reaffirmed our "frequently expressed" view that "when the owner of real property has been called upon to sacrifice all economically beneficial uses in the name of the common good, that is, to leave his property economically idle, he has suffered a taking." The District Court in this case held that the ordinances and resolutions in effect between August 24, 1981, and April 25, 1984, "did in fact deny the plaintiffs all economically viable use of their land." The Court of Appeals did not overturn this finding. And the 1984 injunction, issued because the environmental thresholds issued by respondent did not permit the development of single-family residences, forced petitioners to leave their land economically idle for at least another three years. The Court does not dispute that petitioners were forced to leave their land economically idle during this period. But the Court refuses to apply *Lucas* on the ground that the deprivation was "temporary."

Neither the Takings Clause nor our case law supports such a distinction. For one thing, a distinction between "temporary" and "permanent" prohibitions is tenuous. The "temporary" prohibition in this case that the Court finds is not a taking lasted almost six years. The "permanent" prohibition that the Court held to be a taking in *Lucas* lasted less than two years. Under the Court's decision today, the takings question turns entirely on the initial label given a regulation, a label that is often without much meaning. There is every incentive for government to simply label any prohibition on development "temporary," or to fix a set number of years. As in this case, this initial designation does not preclude the government from repeatedly extending the "temporary" prohibition into a long-term ban on all development. The Court now holds that such a designation by the government is conclusive even though in fact the moratorium greatly exceeds the time initially specified. Apparently, the Court would not view even a 10-year moratorium as a taking under *Lucas* because the moratorium is not "permanent."

More fundamentally, even if a practical distinction between temporary and permanent deprivations were plausible, to treat the two differently in terms of takings law would be at odds with the justification for the *Lucas* rule. The *Lucas* rule is derived from the fact that a "total deprivation of use is, from the landowner's point of view, the equivalent of a physical appropriation." The regulation in *Lucas* was the "practical equivalence" of a long-term physical appropriation, i.e., a condemnation, so the Fifth Amendment required compensation.

Lucas is implicated when the government deprives a landowner of "all economically beneficial or productive use of land." The District Court found, and the Court agrees, that the moratorium "temporarily" deprived petitioners of "'all economically viable use of their land.'" Because the rationale for the *Lucas* rule applies just as strongly in this case, the "temporary" denial of all viable use of land for six years is a taking.

III

The Court worries that applying *Lucas* here compels finding that an array of traditional, short-term, land-use planning devices are takings. But since the beginning of our regulatory takings jurisprudence, we have recognized that property rights "are enjoyed under an implied limitation." Thus, in *Lucas*, after holding that the regulation prohibiting all economically beneficial use of the coastal land came within our categorical takings rule, we nonetheless inquired into whether such a result "inhere[d] in the title itself, in the restrictions that background principles of the State's law of property and nuisance already place upon land ownership." Because the regulation at issue in *Lucas* purported to be permanent, or at least long term, we concluded that the only implied limitation of state property law that could achieve a similar long-term deprivation of all economic use would be something "achieved in the courts — by adjacent landowners (or other uniquely affected persons) under the State's law of private nuisance, or by the State under its complementary power to abate nuisances that affect the public generally, or otherwise."

When a regulation merely delays a final land use decision, we have recognized that there are other background principles of state property law that prevent the delay from being deemed a taking. We thus noted in *First English* that our discussion of temporary takings did not apply "in the case of normal delays in obtaining building permits, changes in zoning ordinances, variances, and the like." Thus, the short-term delays attendant to zoning and permit regimes are a longstanding feature of state property law and part of a landowner's reasonable investment-backed expectations.

But a moratorium prohibiting all economic use for a period of six years is not one of the longstanding, implied limitations of state property law. Moratoria are "interim controls on the use of land that seek to maintain the status quo with respect to land development in an area by either 'freezing' existing land uses or by allowing the issuance of building permits for only certain land uses that would not be inconsistent with a contemplated zoning plan or zoning change."

Because the prohibition on development of nearly six years in this case cannot be said to resemble any "implied limitation" of state property law, it is a taking that requires compensation.

Lake Tahoe is a national treasure and I do not doubt that respondent's efforts at preventing further degradation of the lake were made in good faith in furtherance of the public interest. But, as is the case with most governmental action that furthers the public interest, the Constitution requires that the costs and burdens be borne by the public at large, not by a few targeted citizens. Justice Holmes' admonition of 80 years ago again rings true: "We are in danger of forgetting that a strong public desire to improve the public condition is not enough to warrant achieving the desire by a shorter cut than the constitutional way of paying for the change."

3. Is It for "Public Use"?

The Fifth Amendment authorizes the government only to take private property for "public use." If the taking were deemed to be for private use, the taking would be invalidated and the government would have to return the power to the owner. The Supreme Court often has declared that "one person's property may not be taken for the benefit of another private person without a justifying public purpose, even though compensation be paid."[35] The framers' obvious concern was that the government might use its eminent domain power to play Robin Hood and take from some private owners and give to others.

However, the Supreme Court has expansively defined "public use" so that virtually any taking will meet the requirement. Two recent cases have held that a taking is for public use as long as the government reasonably believes that it will benefit the public. The first of these cases was unanimous and not controversial. The later, Kelo v. City of New London, is among the most controversial Supreme Court decisions in recent years.

HAWAII HOUSING AUTHORITY v. MIDKIFF
467 U.S. 229 (1984)

Justice O'CONNOR delivered the opinion of the Court.

The Fifth Amendment of the United States Constitution provides, in pertinent part, that "private property [shall not] be taken for public use, without just compensation." These cases present the question whether the Public Use Clause of that Amendment, made applicable to the States through the Fourteenth Amendment, prohibits the State of Hawaii from taking, with just compensation, title in real property from lessors and transferring it to lessees in order to reduce the concentration of ownership of fees simple in the State. We conclude that it does not.

I

The Hawaiian Islands were originally settled by Polynesian immigrants from the western Pacific. These settlers developed an economy around a feudal land tenure system in which one island high chief, the ali'i nui, controlled the land and assigned it for development to certain subchiefs. The subchiefs would then reassign the land to other lower ranking chiefs, who would administer the land and govern the farmers and other tenants working it. All land was held at the will of the ali'i nui and eventually had to be returned to his trust. There was no private ownership of land.

Beginning in the early 1800's, Hawaiian leaders and American settlers repeatedly attempted to divide the lands of the kingdom among the crown, the chiefs, and the common people. These efforts proved largely unsuccessful, however, and the land remained in the hands of a few. In the mid-1960's, after extensive

---

35. Thompson v. Consolidated Gas Corp., 300 U.S. 55, 80 (1937); *see also* Cincinnati v. Vester, 281 U.S. 439, 447 (1930); Missouri Pacific Railway Co. v. Nebraska, 164 U.S. 403, 416 (1896).

hearings, the Hawaii Legislature discovered that, while the State and Federal Governments owned almost 49% of the State's land, another 47% was in the hands of only 72 private landowners. The legislature further found that 18 land-holders, with tracts of 21,000 acres or more, owned more than 40% of this land and that on Oahu, the most urbanized of the islands, 22 landowners owned 72.5% of the fee simple titles. The legislature concluded that concentrated land ownership was responsible for skewing the State's residential fee simple market, inflating land prices, and injuring the public tranquility and welfare.

To redress these problems, the legislature decided to compel the large land-owners to break up their estates. The legislature considered requiring large landowners to sell lands which they were leasing to homeowners. However, the landowners strongly resisted this scheme, pointing out the significant federal tax liabilities they would incur. Indeed, the landowners claimed that the federal tax laws were the primary reason they previously had chosen to lease, and not sell, their lands. Therefore, to accommodate the needs of both lessors and lessees, the Hawaii Legislature enacted the Land Reform Act of 1967 (Act), which created a mechanism for condemning residential tracts and for transferring ownership of the condemned fees simple to existing lessees. By condemning the land in question, the Hawaii Legislature intended to make the land sales involuntary, thereby making the federal tax consequences less severe while still facilitating the redistribution of fees simple.

Under the Act's condemnation scheme, tenants living on single-family resi-dential lots within developmental tracts at least five acres in size are entitled to ask the Hawaii Housing Authority (HHA) to condemn the property on which they live. When 25 eligible tenants, or tenants on half the lots in the tract, whichever is less, file appropriate applications, the Act authorizes HHA to hold a public hearing to determine whether acquisition by the State of all or part of the tract will "effectuate the public purposes" of the Act. If HHA finds that these public purposes will be served, it is authorized to designate some or all of the lots in the tract for acquisition. It then acquires, at prices set either by condemnation trial or by negotiation between lessors and lessees, the former fee owners' full "right, title, and interest" in the land. In either case, compensation must equal the fair market value of the owner's leased fee interest. The adequacy of compensation is not before us.

After compensation has been set, HHA may sell the land titles to tenants who have applied for fee simple ownership. HHA is authorized to lend these tenants up to 90% of the purchase price, and it may condition final transfer on a right of first refusal for the first 10 years following sale. If HHA does not sell the lot to the tenant residing there, it may lease the lot or sell it to someone else, provided that public notice has been given. However, HHA may not sell to any one purchaser, or lease to any one tenant, more than one lot, and it may not operate for profit. In practice, funds to satisfy the condemnation awards have been supplied entirely by lessees.

[II]

The starting point for our analysis of the Act's constitutionality is the Court's decision in Berman v. Parker, (1954). In *Berman*, the Court held constitutional the District of Columbia Redevelopment Act of 1945. That Act provided both for the comprehensive use of the eminent domain power to redevelop slum areas and for the possible sale or lease of the condemned lands to private interests. In discussing whether the takings authorized by that Act were for a "public use," the Court stated: "We deal, in other words, with what traditionally has been known as the police power. An attempt to define its reach or trace its outer limits is fruitless, for each case must turn on its own facts. The definition is essentially the product of legislative determinations addressed to the purposes of government, purposes neither abstractly nor historically capable of complete definition. Subject to specific constitutional limitations, when the legislature has spoken, the public interest has been declared in terms well-nigh conclusive. In such cases the legislature, not the judiciary, is the main guardian of the public needs to be served by social legislation, whether it be Congress legislating concerning the District of Columbia . . . or the States legislating concerning local affairs. . . . This principle admits of no exception merely because the power of eminent domain is involved. . . ."

The "public use" requirement is thus coterminous with the scope of a sovereign's police powers. There is, of course, a role for courts to play in reviewing a legislature's judgment of what constitutes a public use, even when the eminent domain power is equated with the police power. But the Court in *Berman* made clear that it is "an extremely narrow" one.

To be sure, the Court's cases have repeatedly stated that "one person's property may not be taken for the benefit of another private person without a justifying public purpose, even though compensation be paid." But where the exercise of the eminent domain power is rationally related to a conceivable public purpose, the Court has never held a compensated taking to be proscribed by the Public Use Clause.

On this basis, we have no trouble concluding that the Hawaii Act is constitutional. The people of Hawaii have attempted, much as the settlers of the original 13 Colonies did, to reduce the perceived social and economic evils of a land oligopoly traceable to their monarchs. The land oligopoly has, according to the Hawaii Legislature, created artificial deterrents to the normal functioning of the State's residential land market and forced thousands of individual homeowners to lease, rather than buy, the land underneath their homes. Regulating oligopoly and the evils associated with it is a classic exercise of a State's police powers. We cannot disapprove of Hawaii's exercise of this power.

The State of Hawaii has never denied that the Constitution forbids even a compensated taking of property when executed for no reason other than to confer a private benefit on a particular private party. A purely private taking could not withstand the scrutiny of the public use requirement; it would serve no legitimate purpose of government and would thus be void. But no purely private taking is involved in these cases. The Hawaii Legislature enacted its Land Reform Act not to benefit a particular class of identifiable individuals but to attack certain perceived evils of concentrated property ownership in Hawaii — a legitimate public purpose. Use of the condemnation power to achieve this purpose is not irrational. Since we assume for purposes of these appeals that the weighty demand of just compensation has been met, the requirements of the Fifth and Fourteenth Amendments have been satisfied.

KELO v. CITY OF NEW LONDON

545 U.S. 469 (2005)

Justice STEVENS delivered the opinion of the Court.

In 2000, the city of New London approved a development plan that, in the words of the Supreme Court of Connecticut, was "projected to create in excess of 1,000 jobs, to increase tax and other revenues, and to revitalize an economically distressed city, including its downtown and waterfront areas." In assembling the land needed for this project, the city's development agent has purchased property from willing sellers and proposes to use the power of eminent domain to acquire the remainder of the property from unwilling owners in exchange for just compensation. The question presented is whether the city's proposed disposition of this property qualifies as a "public use" within the meaning of the Takings Clause of the Fifth Amendment to the Constitution.

I

The city of New London (hereinafter City) sits at the junction of the Thames River and the Long Island Sound in southeastern Connecticut. Decades of economic decline led a state agency in 1990 to designate the City a "distressed municipality." In 1996, the Federal Government closed the Naval Undersea Warfare Center, which had been located in the Fort Trumbull area of the City and had employed over 1,500 people. In 1998, the City's unemployment rate was nearly double that of the State, and its population of just under 24,000 residents was at its lowest since 1920.

These conditions prompted state and local officials to target New London, and particularly its Fort Trumbull area, for economic revitalization. To this end, respondent New London Development Corporation (NLDC), a private nonprofit entity established some years earlier to assist the City in planning economic development, was reactivated. In January 1998, the State authorized a $5.35 million bond issue to support the NLDC's planning activities and a $10 million bond issue toward the creation of a Fort Trumbull State Park. In February, the pharmaceutical company Pfizer Inc. announced that it would build a $300 million research facility on a site immediately adjacent to Fort Trumbull; local planners hoped that Pfizer would draw new business to the area, thereby serving as a catalyst to the area's rejuvenation. After receiving initial approval from the city council, the NLDC continued its planning activities and held a series of neighborhood meetings to educate the public about the process.

The city council approved the plan in January 2000, and designated the NLDC as its development agent in charge of implementation. The city council also authorized the NLDC to purchase property or to acquire property by exercising eminent domain in the City's name. The NLDC successfully negotiated the purchase of most of the real estate in the 90-acre area, but its negotiations with petitioners failed. As a consequence, in November 2000, the NLDC initiated the condemnation proceedings that gave rise to this case.

II

Petitioner Susette Kelo has lived in the Fort Trumbull area since 1997. She has made extensive improvements to her house, which she prizes for its water view. Petitioner Wilhelmina Dery was born in her Fort Trumbull house in 1918 and has lived there her entire life. Her husband Charles (also a petitioner) has lived in the house since they married some 60 years ago. In all, the nine petitioners own 15 properties in Fort Trumbull. There is no allegation that any of these properties is blighted or otherwise in poor condition; rather, they were condemned only because they happen to be located in the development area.

III

Two polar propositions are perfectly clear. On the one hand, it has long been accepted that the sovereign may not take the property of A for the sole purpose of transferring it to another private party B, even though A is paid just compensation. On the other hand, it is equally clear that a State may transfer property from one private party to another if future "use by the public" is the purpose of the taking; the condemnation of land for a railroad with common-carrier duties is a familiar example. Neither of these propositions, however, determines the disposition of this case.

As for the first proposition, the City would no doubt be forbidden from taking petitioners' land for the purpose of conferring a private benefit on a particular private party. Nor would the City be allowed to take property under the mere pretext of a public purpose, when its actual purpose was to bestow a private benefit. The takings before us, however, would be executed pursuant to a "carefully considered" development plan. The trial judge and all the members of the Supreme Court of Connecticut agreed that there was no evidence of an illegitimate purpose in this case.

On the other hand, this is not a case in which the City is planning to open the condemned land — at least not in its entirety — to use by the general public. Nor will the private lessees of the land in any sense be required to operate like common carriers, making their services available to all comers. But although such a projected use would be sufficient to satisfy the public use requirement, this "Court long ago rejected any literal requirement that condemned property be put into use for the general public." Indeed, while many state courts in the mid-19th century endorsed "use by the public" as the proper definition of public use, that narrow view steadily eroded over time. Not only was the "use by the public" test difficult to administer (e.g., what proportion of the public need have access to the property? at what price?), but it proved to be impractical given the diverse and always evolving needs of society. Accordingly, when this Court began applying the Fifth Amendment to the States at the close of the 19th century, it embraced the broader and more natural interpretation of public use as "public purpose."

The disposition of this case therefore turns on the question whether the City's development plan serves a "public purpose." Without exception, our cases have defined that concept broadly, reflecting our longstanding policy of deference to legislative judgments in this field.

In Berman v. Parker (1954), this Court upheld a redevelopment plan target-ing a blighted area of Washington, D.C., in which most of the housing for the area's 5,000 inhabitants was beyond repair. Under the plan, the area would be condemned and part of it utilized for the construction of streets, schools, and other public facilities. The remainder of the land would be leased or sold to private parties for the purpose of redevelopment, including the construction of low-cost housing. The owner of a department store located in the area chal-lenged the condemnation, pointing out that his store was not itself blighted and arguing that the creation of a "better balanced, more attractive community" was not a valid public use. Writing for a unanimous Court, Justice Douglas refused to evaluate this claim in isolation, deferring instead to the legislative and agency judgment that the area "must be planned as a whole" for the plan to be successful. The Court explained that "community redevelopment programs need not, by force of the Constitution, be on a piecemeal basis — lot by lot, building by building." The public use underlying the taking was unequivocally affirmed.

In Hawaii Housing Authority v. Midkiff (1984), the Court considered a Hawaii statute whereby fee title was taken from lessors and transferred to lessees (for just compensation) in order to reduce the concentration of land ownership. We unanimously upheld the statute and rejected the Ninth Circuit's view that it was "a naked attempt on the part of the state of Hawaii to take the property of A and transfer it to B solely for B's private use and benefit." Reaffirming *Berman*'s deferential approach to legislative judgments in this field, we con-cluded that the State's purpose of eliminating the "social and economic evils of a land oligopoly" qualified as a valid public use. Our opinion also rejected the contention that the mere fact that the State immediately transferred the prop-erties to private individuals upon condemnation somehow diminished the public character of the taking. "[I]t is only the taking's purpose, and not its mechanics," we explained, that matters in determining public use.

Viewed as a whole, our jurisprudence has recognized that the needs of society have varied between different parts of the Nation, just as they have evolved over time in response to changed circumstances. Our earliest cases in particular embodied a strong theme of federalism, emphasizing the "great respect" that we owe to state legislatures and state courts in discerning local public needs. For more than a century, our public use jurisprudence has wisely eschewed rigid formulas and intrusive scrutiny in favor of affording legislatures broad latitude in determining what public needs justify the use of the takings power.

IV

Those who govern the City were not confronted with the need to remove blight in the Fort Trumbull area, but their determination that the area was sufficiently distressed to justify a program of economic rejuvenation is entitled to our def-erence. The City has carefully formulated an economic development plan that it believes will provide appreciable benefits to the community, including — but by no means limited to — new jobs and increased tax revenue. As with other exer-cises in urban planning and development, the City is endeavoring to coordinate a variety of commercial, residential, and recreational uses of land, with the hope that they will form a whole greater than the sum of its parts. To effectuate this plan, the City has invoked a state statute that specifically authorizes the use of eminent domain to promote economic development. Given the comprehensive character of the plan, the thorough deliberation that preceded its adoption, and the limited scope of our review, it is appropriate for us, as it was in *Berman*, to resolve the challenges of the individual owners, not on a piecemeal basis, but rather in light of the entire plan. Because that plan unquestionably serves a public purpose, the takings challenged here satisfy the public use requirement of the Fifth Amendment.

To avoid this result, petitioners urge us to adopt a new bright-line rule that economic development does not qualify as a public use. Putting aside the unpersuasive suggestion that the City's plan will provide only purely economic benefits, neither precedent nor logic supports petitioners' proposal. Promoting economic development is a traditional and long accepted function of government. There is, moreover, no principled way of distinguishing economic development from the other public purposes that we have recognized. In our cases upholding takings that facilitated agriculture and mining, for example, we emphasized the importance of those industries to the welfare of the States in question. It would be incongruous to hold that the City's interest in the economic benefits to be derived from the development of the Fort Trumbull area has less of a public character than any of those other interests. Clearly, there is no basis for exempting economic development from our traditionally broad understanding of public purpose.

Petitioners contend that using eminent domain for economic development impermissibly blurs the boundary between public and private takings. Again, our cases foreclose this objection. Quite simply, the government's pursuit of a public purpose will often benefit individual private parties.

It is further argued that without a bright-line rule nothing would stop a city from transferring citizen A's property to citizen B for the sole reason that citizen B will put the property to a more productive use and thus pay more taxes. Such a one-to-one transfer of property, executed outside the confines of an integrated development plan, is not presented in this case. While such an unusual exercise of government power would certainly raise a suspicion that a private purpose was afoot, the hypothetical cases posited by petitioners can be confronted if and when they arise. They do not warrant the crafting of an artificial restriction on the concept of public use.

Alternatively, petitioners maintain that for takings of this kind we should require a "reasonable certainty" that the expected public benefits will actually accrue. Such a rule, however, would represent an even greater departure from our precedent. "When the legislature's purpose is legitimate and its means are not irrational, our cases make clear that empirical debates over the wisdom of takings — no less than debates over the wisdom of other kinds of socioeconomic legislation — are not to be carried out in the federal courts."

In affirming the City's authority to take petitioners' properties, we do not minimize the hardship that condemnations may entail, notwithstanding the payment of just compensation. We emphasize that nothing in our opinion precludes any State from placing further restrictions on its exercise of the takings power. Indeed, many States already impose "public use" requirements that are stricter than the federal baseline. Some of these requirements have been established as a matter of state constitutional law, while others are expressed in state eminent domain statutes that carefully limit the grounds upon which takings may be exercised. As the submissions of the parties and their amici make clear, the necessity and wisdom of using eminent domain to promote economic development are certainly matters of legitimate public debate. This Court's authority, however, extends only to determining whether the City's proposed condemnations are for a "public use" within the meaning of the Fifth Amendment to the Federal Constitution. Because over a century of our case law interpreting that provision dictates an affirmative answer to that question, we may not grant petitioners the relief that they seek.

Justice KENNEDY, concurring.

I join the opinion for the Court and add these further observations. This Court has declared that a taking should be upheld as consistent with the Public Use Clause, as long as it is "rationally related to a conceivable public purpose." Hawaii Housing Authority v. Midkiff (1984); see also Berman v. Parker (1954). This deferential standard of review echoes the rational-basis test used to review economic regulation under the Due Process and Equal Protection Clauses. The determination that a rational-basis standard of review is appropriate does not, however, alter the fact that transfers intended to confer benefits on particular, favored private entities, and with only incidental or pretextual public benefits, are forbidden by the Public Use Clause.

A court applying rational-basis review under the Public Use Clause should strike down a taking that, by a clear showing, is intended to favor a particular private party, with only incidental or pretextual public benefits, just as a court applying rational-basis review under the Equal Protection Clause must strike down a government classification that is clearly intended to injure a particular class of private parties, with only incidental or pretextual public justifications.

A court confronted with a plausible accusation of impermissible favoritism to private parties should treat the objection as a serious one and review the record to see if it has merit, though with the presumption that the government's actions were reasonable and intended to serve a public purpose. Here, the trial court conducted a careful and extensive inquiry.

My agreement with the Court that a presumption of invalidity is not warranted for economic development takings in general, or for the particular takings at issue in this case, does not foreclose the possibility that a more stringent standard of review than that announced in *Berman* and *Midkiff* might be appropriate for a more narrowly drawn category of takings. There may be private transfers in which the risk of undetected impermissible favoritism of private parties is so acute that a presumption (rebuttable or otherwise) of invalidity is warranted under the Public Use Clause. This demanding level of scrutiny, however, is not required simply because the purpose of the taking is economic development.

This is not the occasion for conjecture as to what sort of cases might justify a more demanding standard, but it is appropriate to underscore aspects of the instant case that convince me no departure from *Berman* and *Midkiff* is appropriate here. This taking occurred in the context of a comprehensive development plan meant to address a serious city-wide depression, and the projected economic benefits of the project cannot be characterized as *de minimis*. The identity of most of the private beneficiaries were unknown at the time the city formulated its plans. The city complied with elaborate procedural requirements that facilitate review of the record and inquiry into the city's purposes. In sum, while there may be categories of cases in which the transfers are so suspicious, or the procedures employed so prone to abuse, or the purported benefits are so trivial or implausible, that courts should presume an impermissible private purpose, no such circumstances are present in this case.

Justice O'CONNOR, with whom the Chief Justice, Justice SCALIA, and Justice THOMAS join, dissenting.

Over two centuries ago, just after the Bill of Rights was ratified, Justice Chase wrote: "An ACT of the Legislature (for I cannot call it a law) contrary to the great first principles of the social compact, cannot be considered a rightful exercise of legislative authority. . . . A few instances will suffice to explain what I mean. . . . [A] law that takes property from A. and gives it to B: It is against all reason and justice, for a people to entrust a Legislature with SUCH powers; and, therefore, it cannot be presumed that they have done it." Calder v. Bull (1798).

Today the Court abandons this long-held, basic limitation on government power. Under the banner of economic development, all private property is now vulnerable to being taken and transferred to another private owner, so long as it might be upgraded — i.e., given to an owner who will use it in a way that the legislature deems more beneficial to the public — in the process. To reason, as the Court does, that the incidental public benefits resulting from the subsequent ordinary use of private property render economic development takings "for public use" is to wash out any distinction between private and public use of property — and thereby effectively to delete the words "for public use" from the Takings Clause of the Fifth Amendment. Accordingly I respectfully dissent.

The public use requirement, in turn, imposes a more basic limitation, circumscribing the very scope of the eminent domain power: Government may compel an individual to forfeit her property for the public's use, but not for the benefit of another private person. This requirement promotes fairness as well as security. Where is the line between "public" and "private" property use? We give considerable deference to legislatures' determinations about what governmental activities will advantage the public. But were the political branches the sole arbiters of the public-private distinction, the Public Use Clause would amount to little more than hortatory fluff. An external, judicial check on how the public use requirement is interpreted, however limited, is necessary if this constraint on government power is to retain any meaning.

This case returns us for the first time in over 20 years to the hard question of when a purportedly "public purpose" taking meets the public use requirement. It presents an issue of first impression: Are economic development takings constitutional? I would hold that they are not.

Here New London does not claim that Susette Kelo's and Wilhelmina Dery's well-maintained homes are the source of any social harm. Indeed, it could not so claim without adopting the absurd argument that any single-family home that might be razed to make way for an apartment building, or any church that might be replaced with a retail store, or any small business that might be more lucrative if it were instead part of a national franchise, is inherently harmful to society and thus within the government's power to condemn.

In moving away from our decisions sanctioning the condemnation of harmful property use, the Court today significantly expands the meaning of public use. It holds that the sovereign may take private property currently put to ordinary private use, and give it over for new, ordinary private use, so long as the new use is predicted to generate some secondary benefit for the public — such as increased tax revenue, more jobs, maybe even aesthetic pleasure. But nearly any lawful use of real private property can be said to generate some incidental benefit to the public. Thus, if predicted (or even guaranteed) positive side-effects are enough to render transfer from one private party to another constitutional, then the words "for public use" do not realistically exclude any takings, and thus do not exert any constraint on the eminent domain power.

Even if there were a practical way to isolate the motives behind a given taking, the gesture toward a purpose test is theoretically flawed. If it is true that incidental public benefits from new private use are enough to ensure the "public purpose" in a taking, why should it matter, as far as the Fifth Amendment is concerned, what inspired the taking in the first place? How much the government does or does not desire to benefit a favored private party has no bearing on whether an economic development taking will or will not generate secondary benefit for the public. And whatever the reason for a given condemnation, the effect is the same from the constitutional perspective — private property is forcibly relinquished to new private ownership.

A second proposed limitation is implicit in the Court's opinion. The logic of today's decision is that eminent domain may only be used to upgrade — not downgrade — property. At best this makes the Public Use Clause redundant with the Due Process Clause, which already prohibits irrational government action. The Court rightfully admits, however, that the judiciary cannot get bogged down in predictive judgments about whether the public will actually be better off after a property transfer. In any event, this constraint has no realistic import. For who among us can say she already makes the most productive or attractive possible use of her property? The specter of condemnation hangs over all property. Nothing is to prevent the State from replacing any Motel 6 with a Ritz-Carlton, any home with a shopping mall, or any farm with a factory.

Any property may now be taken for the benefit of another private party, but the fallout from this decision will not be random. The beneficiaries are likely to be those citizens with disproportionate influence and power in the political process, including large corporations and development firms. As for the victims, the government now has license to transfer property from those with fewer resources to those with more. The Founders cannot have intended this perverse result. "[T]hat alone is a just government," wrote James Madison, "which impartially secures to every man, whatever is his own."

Justice THOMAS, dissenting.

Long ago, William Blackstone wrote that "the law of the land . . . postpone[s] even public necessity to the sacred and inviolable rights of private property." The Framers embodied that principle in the Constitution, allowing the government to take property not for "public necessity," but instead for "public use." Defying this understanding, the Court replaces the Public Use Clause with a "[P]ublic [P]urpose" Clause (or perhaps the "Diverse and Always Evolving Needs of Society" Clause), a restriction that is satisfied, the Court instructs, so long as the purpose is "legitimate" and the means "not irrational." This deferential shift in phraseology enables the Court to hold, against all common sense, that a costly urban-renewal project whose stated purpose is a vague promise of new jobs and increased tax revenue, but which is also suspiciously agreeable to the Pfizer Corporation, is for a "public use."

I cannot agree. If such "economic development" takings are for a "public use," any taking is, and the Court has erased the Public Use Clause from our Constitution, as Justice O'Connor powerfully argues in dissent. I do not believe that this Court can eliminate liberties expressly enumerated in the Constitution and therefore join her dissenting opinion.

Regrettably, however, the Court's error runs deeper than this. Today's decision is simply the latest in a string of our cases construing the Public Use Clause to be a virtual nullity, without the slightest nod to its original meaning. In my view, the Public Use Clause, originally understood, is a meaningful limit on the government's eminent domain power. Our cases have strayed from the Clause's original meaning, and I would reconsider them.

There is no justification, however, for affording almost insurmountable deference to legislative conclusions that a use serves a "public use." To begin with, a court owes no deference to a legislature's judgment concerning the quintessentially legal question of whether the government owns, or the public has a legal right to use, the taken property. Even under the "public purpose" interpretation, moreover, it is most implausible that the Framers intended to defer to legislatures as to what satisfies the Public Use Clause, uniquely among all the express provisions of the Bill of Rights. We would not defer to a legislature's determination of the various circumstances that establish, for example, when a search of a home would be reasonable, or when a convicted double-murderer may be shackled during a sentencing proceeding without on-the-record findings, or when state law creates a property interest protected by the Due Process Clause.

Still worse, it is backwards to adopt a searching standard of constitutional review for nontraditional property interests, such as welfare benefits, while deferring to the legislature's determination as to what constitutes a public use when it exercises the power of eminent domain, and thereby invades individuals' traditional rights in real property.

The consequences of today's decision are not difficult to predict, and promise to be harmful. So-called "urban renewal" programs provide some compensation for the properties they take, but no compensation is possible for the subjective value of these lands to the individuals displaced and the indignity inflicted by uprooting them from their homes. Allowing the government to take property solely for public purposes is bad enough, but extending the concept of public purpose to encompass any economically beneficial goal guarantees that these losses will fall disproportionately on poor communities. Those communities are not only systematically less likely to put their lands to the highest and best social use, but are also the least politically powerful. If ever there were justification for intrusive judicial review of constitutional provisions that protect "discrete and insular minorities," United States v. Carolene Products Co. (1938), surely that principle would apply with great force to the powerless groups and individuals the Public Use Clause protects. The deferential standard this Court has adopted for the Public Use Clause is therefore deeply perverse. It encourages "those citizens with disproportionate influence and power in the political process, including large corporations and development firms," to victimize the weak.

The Court relies almost exclusively on this Court's prior cases to derive today's far-reaching, and dangerous, result. But the principles this Court should employ to dispose of this case are found in the Public Use Clause itself, not in Justice Peckham's high opinion of reclamation laws. When faced with a clash of constitutional principle and a line of unreasoned cases wholly divorced from the text, history, and structure of our founding document, we should not hesitate to resolve the tension in favor of the Constitution's original meaning. For the reasons I have given, and for the reasons given in Justice O'Connor's dissent, the conflict of principle raised by this boundless use of the eminent domain power should be resolved in petitioners' favor. I would reverse the judgment of the Connecticut Supreme Court.

4. What Is the Requirement for "Just Compensation"?

The Constitution clearly envisions that the government will take private property for public use, but it requires that the government pay for it. The standard of payment is "just compensation."

The Supreme Court has consistently ruled that just compensation is measured in terms of the loss to the owner; the gain to the taker is irrelevant. Long ago, Justice Oliver Wendell Holmes declared that the measure is "what has the owner lost, not what has the taker gained."[36]

The Supreme Court has said that the loss should be valued in terms of the market value to the owner,[37] as of the time of the taking.[38] However, the government does not need to pay for an increase in the market value that occurred solely because of its plan to take the property.[39]

If there is a taking, the property owner can bring a legal action against the government to receive just compensation. One form of action is an "inverse condemnation suit," where an individual claims that a government action constitutes a taking. In First English Evangelical Lutheran Church of Glendale v. County of Los Angeles, 482 U.S. 304 (1987), the Supreme Court held that even if the government ceases its regulation in response to an inverse condemnation suit, the government nonetheless must pay damages for the time, however temporary, that it had taken the private property. In other words, the Court held that the government is required to pay just compensation for the entire time of its action, including the period before the judicial adjudication that it was a taking. The Court said that "[i]nvalidation of the ordinance . . . is not a sufficient remedy to meet the demands of the Just Compensation Clause." Rather, the government must pay just compensation when there is a taking, even if it is a temporary taking.

The Court recently decided an important case concerning how "just compensation" is determined.

---

36. Boston Chamber of Commerce v. Boston, 217 U.S. 189, 195 (1910).
37. *See, e.g.,* United States v. 564.54 Acres of Land, 441 U.S. 506 (1979).
38. *See* Kirby Forest Industries, Inc. v. United States, 467 U.S. 1 (1984).
39. *See, e.g.,* United States v. Fuller, 409 U.S. 488 (1973).

BROWN v. LEGAL FOUNDATION OF WASHINGTON

538 U.S. 216 (2003)

Justice STEVENS delivered the opinion of the Court.

The State of Washington, like every other State in the Union, uses interest on lawyers' trust accounts (IOLTA) to pay for legal services provided to the needy. Some IOLTA programs were created by statute, but in Washington, as in most other States, the IOLTA program was established by the State Supreme Court pursuant to its authority to regulate the practice of law. In Phillips v. Washington Legal Foundation (1998), a case involving the Texas IOLTA program, we held "that the interest income generated by funds held in IOLTA accounts is the 'private property' of the owner of the principal." We did not, however, express any opinion on the question whether the income had been "taken" by the State or "as to the amount of 'just compensation,' if any, due respondents." Ibid. We now confront those questions.

I

[I]n the course of their legal practice, attorneys are frequently required to hold clients' funds for various lengths of time. It has long been recognized that they have a professional and fiduciary obligation to avoid commingling their clients' money with their own, but it is not unethical to pool several clients' funds in a single trust account. Before 1980 client funds were typically held in non-interest-bearing federally insured checking accounts. Because federal banking regulations in effect since the Great Depression prohibited banks from paying interest on checking accounts, the value of the use of the clients' money in such accounts inured to the banking institutions. In 1980, Congress authorized federally insured banks to pay interest on a limited category of demand deposits referred to as "NOW accounts."

In response to the change in federal law, Florida adopted the first IOLTA program in 1981 authorizing the use of NOW accounts for the deposit of client funds, and providing that all of the interest on such accounts be used for charitable purposes. Every State in the Nation and the District of Columbia have followed Florida's lead and adopted an IOLTA program, either through their legislatures or their highest courts. The result is that, whereas before 1980 the banks retained the value of the use of the money deposited in non-interest-bearing client trust accounts, today, because of the adoption of IOLTA programs, that value is transferred to charitable entities providing legal services for the poor. The aggregate value of those contributions in 2001 apparently exceeded $200 million.

[The Washington] court described the four essential features of its IOLTA program: (a) the requirement that all client funds be deposited in interest-bearing trust accounts, (b) the requirement that funds that cannot earn net interest for the client be deposited in an IOLTA account, (c) the requirement that the lawyers direct the banks to pay the net interest on the IOLTA accounts to the Legal Foundation of Washington (Foundation), and (d) the requirement that the Foundation must use all funds received from

IOLTA accounts for tax-exempt law-related charitable and educational purposes.

The Fifth Amendment does not proscribe the taking of property; it proscribes taking without just compensation. [T]he "just compensation" required by the Fifth Amendment is measured by the property owner's loss rather than the government's gain. This conclusion is supported by consistent and unambiguous holdings in our cases. Most frequently cited is Justice Holmes' characteristically terse statement that "the question is what has the owner lost, not what has the taker gained." Boston Chamber of Commerce v. Boston (1910).

Applying the teaching of these cases to the question before us, it is clear that neither Brown nor Hayes is entitled to any compensation for the nonpecuniary consequences of the taking of the interest on his deposited funds, and that any pecuniary compensation must be measured by his net losses rather than the value of the public's gain. For that reason, both the majority and the dissenters on the Court of Appeals agreed that if petitioners' net loss was zero, the compensation that is due is also zero.[40]

The Rules adopted and administered by the Washington Supreme Court unambiguously require lawyers to deposit client funds in non-IOLTA accounts whenever those funds could generate net earnings for the client. Thus, if the [lawyers] deposited petitioners' money in IOLTA accounts could have generated net income, the [lawyers] violated the court's Rules. Any conceivable net loss to petitioners was the consequence of the [lawyers'] incorrect private decisions rather than any state action. Such mistakes may well give petitioners a valid claim against the [lawyers], but they would provide no support for a claim for compensation from the State, or from any of the respondents.

To recapitulate: It is neither unethical nor illegal for lawyers to deposit their clients' funds in a single bank account. A state law that requires client funds that could not otherwise generate net earnings for the client to be deposited in an IOLTA account is not a "regulatory taking." A law that requires that the interest on those funds be transferred to a different owner for a legitimate public use, however, could be a per se taking requiring the payment of "just compensation" to the client. Because that compensation is measured by the owner's pecuniary loss — which is zero whenever the Washington law is obeyed — there has been no violation of the Just Compensation Clause of the Fifth Amendment in this case.

Justice Scalia, with whom the Chief Justice, Justice Kennedy, and Justice Thomas join, dissenting.

The Court today concludes that the State of Washington may seize private property, without paying compensation, on the ground that the former owners suffered no "net loss" because their confiscated property was created by the beneficence of a state regulatory program. In so holding the Court creates a

---

40. Justice Scalia is mistaken in stating that we hold that just compensation is measured by the amount of interest "petitioners would have earned had their funds been deposited in non-IOLTA accounts." We hold (1) that just compensation is measured by the net value of the interest that was actually earned by petitioners and (2) that, by operation of the Washington IOLTA Rules, no net interest can be earned by the money that is placed in IOLTA accounts in Washington. See IOLTA Adoption Order (1984) ("IOLTA funds are only those funds that cannot, under any circumstances, earn net interest [after deducting transaction and administrative costs and bank fees] for the client"). [Footnote by the Court.]

novel exception to our oft-repeated rule that the just compensation owed to former owners of confiscated property is the fair market value of the property taken. What is more, the Court embraces a line of reasoning that we explicitly rejected in Phillips v. Washington Legal Foundation (1998). Our precedents compel the conclusion that petitioners are entitled to the fair market value of the interest generated by their funds held in interest on lawyers' trust accounts (IOLTA).

When a State has taken private property for a public use, the Fifth Amendment requires compensation in the amount of the market value of the property on the date it is appropriated. In holding that any just compensation that might be owed is zero, the Court neither pretends to ascertain the market value of the confiscated property nor asserts that the case falls within one of the two exceptions where market value need not be determined. Instead, the Court proclaims that just compensation is to be determined by the former property owner's "net loss," and endorses simultaneously two competing and irreconcilable theories of how that loss should be measured. The Court proclaims its agreement with the Ninth Circuit majority that just compensation is the interest petitioners would have earned had their funds been deposited in non-IOLTA accounts. At the same time, the Court approves the view of the Ninth Circuit dissenters that just compensation is the amount of interest actually earned in petitioners' IOLTA accounts, minus the amount that would have been lost in transaction costs had petitioners sought to keep the money for themselves. The Court cannot have it both ways — as the Ninth Circuit itself realized.

Under the Court's first theory, just compensation is zero because, under the State Supreme Court's Rules, the only funds placed in IOLTA accounts are those which could not have earned net interest for the client in a non-IOLTA savings account. This approach defines petitioners' "net loss" as the amount of interest they would have received had their funds been deposited in separate, non-IOLTA accounts. This definition of just compensation has no foundation in reason. Once interest is earned on petitioners' funds held in IOLTA accounts, that money is petitioners' property. It is at that point that the State appropriates the interest to fund LFW — after the interest has been generated in the pooled accounts — and it is at that point that just compensation for the taking must be assessed. It may very well be, as the Court asserts, that petitioners could not have earned money on their funds absent IOLTA's mandatory pooling arrangements, but just compensation is not to be measured by what would have happened in a hypothetical world in which the State's IOLTA program did not exist. When the State takes possession of petitioners' property — petitioners' money — and transfers it to LFW, the property obviously has value. The conclusion that it is devoid of value because of the circumstances giving rise to its creation is indefensible.

The Court's rival theory for explaining why just compensation is zero fares no better. Contrary to its aforementioned description of petitioners' "net loss" as the amount their funds would have earned in non-IOLTA accounts, the Court declares that just compensation is "the *net value* of the interest that was *actually earned* by petitioners," — net value consisting of the value of the funds, *less* "transaction and administrative costs and bank fees" that would be expended in extracting the funds from the IOLTA accounts. To support this concept of "net value," the Court cites nothing but the cases discussed earlier in its opinion, which establish that just compensation consists of the value the owner has lost rather than the value the government has gained. In this case, however, there is no difference between the two. Petitioners have lost the interest that Phillips says rightfully belongs to them — which is precisely what the government has gained. The Court's apparent fear that following the Constitution in this case will provide petitioners a "windfall" in the amount of transaction costs saved is based on the unfounded assumption that the State must return the interest directly to petitioners. The State could satisfy its obligation to pay just compensation by simply returning petitioners' money to the IOLTA account from which it was seized, leaving others to incur the accounting costs in the event petitioners seek to extract their interest from the account.

While the Court is correct that under the State's IOLTA rules, petitioners' funds could not have earned net interest in separate, that has no bearing on the transaction costs that petitioners would sustain in removing their earned interest from the IOLTA accounts. The Court today arbitrarily forecloses clients from recovering the "net interest" to which (even under the Court's definition of just compensation) they are entitled. What is more, there is no reason to believe that petitioners themselves do not fall within the class of clients whose funds, though unable to earn interest in non-IOLTA accounts, nevertheless generate "net interest" in IOLTA accounts. That is why the Ninth Circuit dissenters (who shared the Court's second theory of just compensation but not the first) voted to remand to the District Court for a factual determination of what the "net value" of petitioners' interest actually is.

Perhaps we are witnessing today the emergence of a whole new concept in Compensation Clause jurisprudence: the Robin Hood Taking, in which the government's extraction of wealth from those who own it is so cleverly achieved, and the object of the government's larcenous beneficence is so highly favored by the courts (taking from the rich to give to indigent defendants) that the normal rules of the Constitution protecting private property are suspended. One must hope that that is the case. For to extend to the entire run of Compensation Clause cases the rationale supporting today's judgment — what the government hath given, the government may freely take away — would be disastrous. The Court's judgment that petitioners are not entitled to the market value of their confiscated property has no basis in law.

CHAPTER
7

EQUAL PROTECTION

A. INTRODUCTION

1. Constitutional Provisions Concerning Equal Protection

The Constitution as originally drafted and ratified had no provisions assuring equal protection of the laws. This, of course, is not surprising for a document written for a society where blacks were enslaved and where women were routinely discriminated against. After the Civil War, widespread discrimination against former slaves led to the passage of the Fourteenth Amendment, which provides in part, "No state shall . . . deny to any person within its jurisdiction the equal protection of the laws."

The promise of this provision went unrealized for almost a century as the Supreme Court rarely found any state or local action to violate the Equal Protection Clause until the mid-1950s. Indeed, Justice Oliver Wendell Holmes derisively referred to the provision as "the last resort of constitutional arguments."[1] Holmes probably was referring to the possibility of challenging almost any law as discriminating against someone and to the Court's consistent reluctance to use the Equal Protection Clause to invalidate state or local laws.

Brown v. Board of Education, 347 U.S. 483 (1954), ushered in the modern era of equal protection jurisprudence. Since *Brown*, the Supreme Court has relied on the Equal Protection Clause as a key provision for combatting invidious discrimination and for safeguarding fundamental rights.

There remains no provision in the Constitution that says that the federal government cannot deny equal protection of the laws. However, in Bolling v. Sharpe, 347 U.S. 497 (1954), a companion case to Brown v. Board of Education that concerned the segregation of the District of Columbia public schools, the Court held that equal protection applies to the federal government through the Due Process Clause of the Fifth Amendment.

Obviously, it would be unacceptable to allow the federal government to discriminate based on race or gender in a manner prohibited the states by the Fourteenth Amendment. To avoid this embarrassment, the Court interpreted the Fifth Amendment as including an implicit requirement for equal

---

1. Buck v. Bell, 274 U.S. 200, 208 (1927).

protection. The Court simply declared that "discrimination may be so unjustifiable as to be violative of due process."

It is now well settled that the requirements of equal protection are the same whether the challenge is to the federal government under the Fifth Amendment or to state and local actions under the Fourteenth Amendment. The Supreme Court has expressly declared that "[e]qual protection analysis in the Fifth Amendment area is the same as that under the Fourteenth Amendment."[2] But technically, equal protection applies to the federal government through judicial interpretation of the Due Process Clause of the Fifth Amendment and to state and local governments through the Fourteenth Amendment.

2. A Framework for Equal Protection Analysis

All equal protection cases pose the same basic question: Is the government's classification justified by a sufficient purpose? Many government laws draw a distinction among people and thus are potentially susceptible to an equal protection challenge. For example, those under age 16 might claim to be discriminated against by the age requirement for obtaining a driver's license, and those denied government benefits might argue that they are discriminated against by eligibility guidelines. If these laws, or any government actions, are challenged based on equal protection, the issue is whether the government can identify a sufficiently important objective for its discrimination.

What constitutes a sufficient justification depends entirely on the type of discrimination. For instance, the Supreme Court has declared that it is extremely suspicious of race discrimination, and therefore the government may use racial classifications only if it proves that they are necessary to achieve a compelling government purpose. This is known as "strict scrutiny." In contrast, a 14-year-old who claimed that the denial of a driver's license violated equal protection would prevail only by proving that the law was not rationally related to a legitimate government purpose. This is known as "rational basis" review.

To be more specific, all equal protection issues can be broken down into three questions: What is the classification? What level of scrutiny should be applied? Does the particular government action meet the level of scrutiny?

QUESTION 1: WHAT IS THE CLASSIFICATION?

The first question is what is the government's classification? How is the government drawing a distinction among people? Equal protection analysis always must begin by identifying how the government is distinguishing among people. Sometimes this is clear; sometimes it is the focus of the litigation.

As described below, there are two basic ways of establishing a classification. One is where the classification exists on the face of the law — that is, where the law in its very terms draws a distinction among people based on a particular characteristic. For example, a law that prohibits blacks from serving on juries is

---

2. Buckley v. Valeo, 424 U.S. 1, 93 (1976).

an obvious facial racial classification.[3] Likewise, a law that says that only those 16 and older can have drivers' licenses is obviously a facial classification.

Alternatively, sometimes laws are facially neutral, but there is a discriminatory impact to the law or discriminatory effects from its administration. For instance, a law that requires that all police officers be at least 5'10" tall and 150 pounds is, on its face, only a height and weight classification. Statistics, however, show that 40 percent of men but only 2 percent of women will meet this requirement. The result is that the law has a discriminatory impact against women in hiring for the police force.

As described below, the Supreme Court has made it clear that discriminatory impact is insufficient to prove a racial or gender classification. If a law is facially neutral, demonstrating a race or gender classification requires proof that there is a discriminatory purpose behind the law.[4] Thus, women challenging the height and weight requirements for the police force must show that the government's purpose was to discriminate based on gender.

In other words, there are two alternative ways of proving the existence of a classification: showing that it exists on the face of the law or demonstrating that a facially neutral law has a discriminatory impact and a discriminatory purpose.

QUESTION 2: WHAT IS THE APPROPRIATE LEVEL OF SCRUTINY?

Once the classification is identified, the next step in analysis is to identify the level of scrutiny to be applied. The Supreme Court has made it clear that differing levels of scrutiny will be applied depending on the type of discrimination.

Discrimination based on race or national origin is subjected to strict scrutiny. Also, generally, discrimination against aliens is subjected to strict scrutiny, although there are several exceptions where less than strict scrutiny is used. Under strict scrutiny, a law is upheld if it is proven necessary to achieve a compelling government purpose. The government must have a truly significant reason for discriminating, and it must show that it cannot achieve its objective through any less discriminatory alternative. The government has the burden of proof under strict scrutiny and the law will be upheld only if the government persuades the court that it is necessary to achieve a compelling purpose. Strict scrutiny is usually fatal to the challenged law.[5]

Intermediate scrutiny is used for discrimination based on gender and for discrimination against nonmarital children. Under intermediate scrutiny, a law is upheld if it is substantially related to an important government purpose.[6] In other words, the Court need not find that the government's purpose is "compelling," but it must characterize the objective as "important." The means used need not be necessary, but must have a "substantial relationship" to the end

3. *See* Strauder v. West Virginia, 100 U.S. 303 (1879) (invalidating state law limiting jury service to "white male persons").

4. *See, e.g.,* Personnel Administrator of Massachusetts v. Feeney, 442 U.S. 256 (1979) (discriminatory impact is insufficient to prove a gender classification; there must be proof of discriminatory purpose); Washington v. Davis, 426 U.S. 229 (1976) (discriminatory impact is insufficient to prove a racial classification; there must be proof of discriminatory purpose).

5. Professor Gerald Gunther described it as "strict in theory and fatal in fact." *Foreword: In Search of Evolving Doctrine on a Changing Court: A Model for a Newer Equal Protection,* 86 Harv. L. Rev. 1, 8 (1972).

6. *See, e.g.,* Craig v. Boren, 429 U.S. 190, 197 (1976); Lehr v. Robertson, 463 U.S. 248, 266 (1983).

being sought. Under intermediate scrutiny, the government has the burden of proof. The Supreme Court recently explained that the "burden of justification is demanding and that it rests entirely on the state."[7]

Finally, there is the rational basis test. Rational basis review is the minimum level of scrutiny that all laws challenged under equal protection must meet. All laws not subjected to strict or intermediate scrutiny are evaluated under the rational basis test. Under rational basis review a law will be upheld if it is rationally related to a legitimate government purpose.[8] The government's objective need not be compelling or important, but just something that the government legitimately may do. The means chosen only need be a rational way to accomplish the end.

The challenger has the burden of proof under rational basis review. The rational basis test is enormously deferential to the government and only rarely have laws been declared unconstitutional for failing to meet this level of review.[9]

How has the Court decided which level of scrutiny to use for particular classifications? Although the Court has shown little willingness in the past two decades to subject additional classifications to strict or intermediate scrutiny, how will it evaluate such requests? Several criteria are applied in determining the level of scrutiny.

For example, the Court has emphasized that immutable characteristics — like race, national origin, gender, and the marital status of one's parents — warrant heightened scrutiny.[10] The notion is that it is unfair to penalize a person for characteristics that the person did not choose and that the individual cannot change.

The Court also considers the ability of the group to protect itself through the political process. Women, for example, are more than half the population, but traditionally have been severely underrepresented in political offices. Aliens do not have the ability to vote and thus the political process cannot be trusted to represent their interests.[11]

The history of discrimination against the group also is relevant to the Court in determining the level of scrutiny. A related issue is the Court's judgment concerning the likelihood that the classification reflects prejudice as opposed to a permissible government purpose.[12] For example, the Court's choice of strict scrutiny for racial classifications reflects its judgment that race is virtually never an acceptable justification for government action. In contrast, the Court's use of intermediate scrutiny for gender classifications reflects its view that the

---

7. *See* United States v. Virginia, 518 U.S. 515, 533 (1996).

8. *See, e.g.,* Pennell v. City of San Jose, 485 U.S. 1, 14 (1988); U.S. Railroad Retirement Board v. Fritz, 449 U.S. 166, 175, 177 (1980); Allied Stores of Ohio v. Bowers, 358 U.S. 522, 527 (1959).

9. *See, e.g.,* Romer v. Evans, 517 U.S. 620 (1996); City of Cleburne v. Cleburne Living Center, Inc., 473 U.S. 432 (1985); Zobel v. Williams, 457 U.S. 55 (1982); United States Department of Agriculture v. Moreno, 413 U.S. 528 (1973) (all discussed below).

10. *See, e.g.,* Fullilove v. Klutznick, 448 U.S. 448, 496 (1980); Kahn v. Shevin, 416 U.S. 351, 357 (1974) (Brennan, J., dissenting).

11. *See, e.g.,* Graham v. Richardson, 403 U.S. 365, 367 (1971).

12. *See* Cleburne v. Cleburne Living Center, 473 U.S. 432, 440 (1985) ("[W]hen a statute classifies by race, alienage, or national origin, [t]hese factors are so seldom relevant to the achievement of any legitimate state interest that laws grounded in such considerations are deemed to reflect prejudice and antipathy. . . . For these reasons and because such discrimination is unlikely to be soon rectified by legislative means, these laws are subjected to strict scrutiny and will be sustained only if they are suitably tailored to serve a compelling state interest.").

biological differences between men and women mean that there are more likely to be instances where sex is a justifiable basis for discrimination.

Although the levels of scrutiny are firmly established in constitutional law and especially in equal protection analysis, there are many who criticize the rigid tiers of review. For example, Justices Thurgood Marshall and John Paul Stevens, among others, have argued that there should be a sliding scale of review rather than the three levels of scrutiny.[13] They maintain that the Court should consider such factors as the constitutional and social importance of the interests adversely affected and the invidiousness of the basis on which the classification was drawn. They contend that under the rigid tiers of review the choice of the level of scrutiny is usually decisive and unduly limits the scope of judicial analysis. Those who favor a sliding scale believe that it would lead to more candid discussion of the competing interests and therefore provide overall better decision making.

Some critics suggest that although the Court speaks in terms of three tiers of review, in reality there is a spectrum of standards of review.[14] The claim is that in some cases where the Court says that it is using rational basis review, it is actually employing a test with more "bite" than the customarily deferential rational basis review. Similarly, it is argued that in some cases intermediate scrutiny is applied in a very deferential manner that is essentially rational basis review, while in other cases intermediate scrutiny seems indistinguishable from strict scrutiny. The argument is that although the Court articulates three tiers of review, the reality is a range of standards. In reading the cases below, it is useful to consider whether the Court's definitions and applications of the levels of scrutiny have been consistent, or whether the Court has varied in this regard to achieve the results it desires.

QUESTION 3: DOES THE GOVERNMENT ACTION MEET THE LEVEL OF SCRUTINY?

The level of scrutiny is the rule of law that is applied to the particular government action being challenged as denying equal protection. In evaluating the constitutionality of a law, the Court evaluates both the law's ends and its means. For strict scrutiny, the end must be deemed compelling for the law to be upheld; for intermediate scrutiny, the end has to be regarded as important; and for the rational basis test, there just has to be a legitimate purpose.

In evaluating the relationship of the means of the particular law to the end, the Supreme Court often focuses on the degree to which a law is underinclusive and/or overinclusive.[15] A law is underinclusive if it does not apply to individuals who are similar to those to whom the law applies. For example, a law that excludes those under age 16 from having drivers' licenses is somewhat

---

13. *See, e.g.,* Plyler v. Doe, 457 U.S. 202, 231 (1982) (Marshall, J., concurring); Craig v. Boren, 429 U.S. 190, 212 (1976) (Stevens, J., concurring); San Antonio Indep. School Dist. v. Rodriguez, 411 U.S. 1, 109, 110 (1973) (Marshall, J., dissenting).

14. *See* Jeffrey M. Shaman, *Cracks in the Structure: The Coming Breakdown of the Levels of Scrutiny,* 45 Ohio St. L.J. 161 (1984).

15. These concepts were articulated and explained in Joseph Tussman & Jacobus tenBroek, *The Equal Protection of the Laws,* 37 Cal. L. Rev. 341, 348-353 (1949).

overinclusive because some younger drivers undoubtedly have the physical ability and the emotional maturity to be effective drivers.

A law is overinclusive if it applies to those who need not be included in order for the government to achieve its purpose. In other words, the law unnecessarily applies to a group of people. For example, the government's decision to evacuate and intern all Japanese Americans on the West Coast during World War II was radically overinclusive.[16] Although the government's purported interest was in preventing espionage, individuals were evacuated and interned without any determination of their threat. Obviously, the law was enormously overinclusive because it harmed a large number of people unnecessarily.

A law can be both underinclusive and overinclusive. The decision to evacuate Japanese Americans during World War II was certainly both. If the goal was to isolate those who were a threat to security, interning only Japanese Americans was underinclusive in that it did not identify those of other races who posed a danger. At the same time, as explained above, the federal government's action was extremely overinclusive because few, if any, Japanese Americans posed any threat. In fact, not a single Japanese American during World War II was ever charged with espionage.[17]

The fact that a law is underinclusive and/or overinclusive does not mean that it is sure to be invalidated. Quite the contrary, virtually all laws are underinclusive, overinclusive, or both. The Court has recognized that laws often are underinclusive because the government may choose to proceed "one step at a time." But underinclusiveness and overinclusiveness are used by courts in evaluating the fit between the government's means and its ends. If strict scrutiny is used, a relatively close fit is required; in fact, the government will have to show that the means are necessary — the least restrictive alternative — to achieve the goal. Under intermediate scrutiny, a closer fit will be required and less underinclusiveness or overinclusiveness will be permitted than under the rational basis test.

Thus, equal protection analysis involves three questions: What is the classification? What level of scrutiny should be applied? Does the particular government action meet the level of scrutiny? Cases posing an equal protection issue always involve a dispute over one or more of these questions.[18]

THE PROTECTION OF FUNDAMENTAL RIGHTS UNDER EQUAL PROTECTION

Usually equal protection is used to analyze government actions that draw a distinction among people based on specific characteristics, such as race, gender, age, disability, or other traits. Sometimes, though, equal protection is used if the

---

16. *See* Korematsu v. United States, 323 U.S. 214 (1944), presented below.

17. *See* Nanette Dembitz, *Racial Discrimination and the Military Judgment: The Supreme Court's* Korematsu *and* Endo *Decisions*, 45 Colum. L. Rev. 175 (1945).

18. Although equal protection is usually thought of in terms of people suffering discrimination because of group characteristics, a person can bring an equal protection claim bases on a "class of one theory" — that he or she is singled out for different treatment than others similarly situated. Village of Willowbrook v. Olech, 528 U.S. 562 (2000). However, in Engquist v. Oregon Department of Agriculture, 553 U.S. 591 (2008), the Supreme Court ruled that government employees cannot bring class of one claims.

government discriminates among people as to the exercise of a fundamental right.

An early case using equal protection in this way was Skinner v. Oklahoma, 316 U.S. 535 (1942).[19] The Oklahoma Habitual Criminal Sterilization Act required surgical sterilization for individuals who had been convicted three or more times for crimes involving "moral turpitude." The Supreme Court declared the law unconstitutional as violating equal protection because it discriminated among people in their ability to exercise a fundamental liberty: the right to procreate. Justice William Douglas, writing for the Court, said, "We are dealing here with legislation which involves one of the basic civil rights of man. Marriage and procreation are fundamental to the very existence and survival of the race. The power to sterilize, if exercised, may have subtle, far-reaching and devastating effects." In other words, the Court found that the right to procreate was a fundamental right and essentially used strict scrutiny under the Equal Protection Clause to analyze the government's discrimination. The Court has used the Equal Protection Clause to protect other fundamental rights such as voting,[20] access to the judicial process,[21] and interstate travel.[22] The use of equal protection to safeguard these fundamental rights was, in part, based on the Supreme Court's desire to avoid substantive due process, which had all of the negative connotations of the *Lochner* era. However, the effect is the same whether a right is deemed fundamental under the Equal Protection Clause or under the Due Process Clause: Government infringements are subjected to strict scrutiny.

Chapter 8 discusses fundamental rights, including both those that the Court has protected under the Equal Protection Clause and those safeguarded under due process. This chapter focuses on the use of equal protection to analyze discrimination among people based on traits such as race, gender, alienage, legitimacy, age, disability, wealth, and sexual orientation.

B. THE RATIONAL BASIS TEST

1. Introduction

The rational basis test is the minimal level of scrutiny that all government actions challenged under equal protection must meet. In other words, unless the government action is a type of discrimination that warrants the application of intermediate or strict scrutiny, rational basis review is used. Although the Court has phrased the test in different ways over time,[23] the basic requirement is that a law meets rational basis review if it is rationally related to a legitimate government

---

19. *Skinner* is presented more fully in Chapter 8 in the discussion of the right to procreate.

20. *See, e.g.,* Harper v. Virginia Board of Elections, 383 U.S. 663 (1966); Reynolds v. Sims, 377 U.S. 533 (1964).

21. *See, e.g.,* Boddie v. Connecticut, 401 U.S. 371 (1971) (right to fee waiver for indigents in filing for divorce); Douglas v. California, 372 U.S. 353 (1963) (right to counsel on appeal for indigents); Griffin v. Illinois, 351 U.S. 12 (1956) (right to free transcripts on appeal for indigents).

22. *See, e.g.,* Shapiro v. Thompson, 394 U.S. 618 (1969) (declaring unconstitutional as violating the right to travel a state law creating a one-year residency requirement for receiving welfare).

23. *See, e.g.,* Lindsley v. National Carbonic Gas Co., 220 U.S. 61 (1911); Royston Guaro Co. v. Virginia, 253 U.S. 412 (1920).

purpose. For instance, in New Orleans v. Dukes, 427 U.S. 297 (1976), and in many other cases, the Court said that the Equal Protection Clause is satisfied as long as the classification is "rationally related to a legitimate state interest." Also, the Court has been consistent that the challenger has the burden of proof when rational basis review is applied. There is a strong presumption in favor of laws that are challenged under the rational basis test.[24]

The Supreme Court generally has been extremely deferential to the government when applying the rational basis test. As discussed below, the Court often has said that a law should be upheld if it is possible to conceive any legitimate purpose for the law, even if it was not the government's actual purpose. The result is that it is rare for the Supreme Court to find that a law fails the rational basis test.

This raises important questions. First, is this appropriate deference to the legislative process or undue judicial abdication? Since 1937, the Court has made it clear that it will defer to government economic and social regulations unless they infringe on a fundamental right or discriminate against a group that warrants special judicial protection.[25] This can be defended as proper judicial restraint, as the Court allows the more democratic branches of government to make decisions except in areas where there is reason for heightened judicial scrutiny.[26] Legislation often involves arbitrary choices favoring some over others, and judicial deference leaves these decisions to the political process.

But it also can be argued that the Court has gone too far in its deference under the rational basis test. Unfair laws are allowed to stand because a conceivable legitimate purpose can be identified for virtually any law. Frequently these are laws enacted to help a particular group with political clout at the expense of others who are less politically powerful.

Another underlying issue in considering the rational basis test is whether the Court has been consistent in applying it. Although in general the Court has been enormously deferential, there have been several cases where laws have been declared unconstitutional under rational basis review. For example, in City of Cleburne v. Cleburne Living Center, 473 U.S. 432 (1985), the Court used rational basis review to invalidate a zoning ordinance that prevented the operation of a home for the mentally disabled. In Romer v. Evans, 517 U.S. 620 (1996), the Court found that a voter initiative in Colorado that repealed laws prohibiting discrimination based on sexual orientation and that precluded the adoption of new protections failed rational basis review.

Many argue that the Court in these cases applied a different, more rigorous version of the rational basis test — one with "bite."[27] The claim is that there is

---

24. *See* McGowan v. Maryland, 366 U.S. 420, 425-426 (1961) ("State legislatures are presumed to have acted within their constitutional power despite the fact that, in practice, their laws result in some inequality.").

25. This, of course, was the philosophy articulated in the famous *Carolene Products* footnote 4. *See* United States v. Carolene Products Co., 304 U.S. 144, 152-153 n.4 (1938), presented in Chapter 6.

26. "Unless a statute employs a classification that is inherently invidious or that impinges on fundamental rights, areas in which the judiciary then has a duty to intervene in the democratic process, this Court properly exercises only a limited review power over Congress, the appropriate representative body through which the public makes democratic choices among alternative solutions to social and economic problems." Schweiker v. Wilson, 450 U.S. 221, 230 (1981).

27. *See* Jeffrey M. Shaman, *Cracks in the Structure: The Coming Breakdown of the Levels of Scrutiny*, 45 Ohio St. L.J. 161 (1984); Gerald Gunther, *Foreword: In Search of Evolving Doctrine on a Changing Court: A Model for a Newer Equal Protection*, 86 Harv. L. Rev. 1, 18-24 (1972).

not a singular rational basis test but one that varies between complete deference and substantial rigor. On the other hand, it might be argued that the test is consistent and that the Court is simply deciding that certain laws lack a legitimate purpose or are so arbitrary as to be unreasonable. In considering the cases below, it is important to assess whether there is a singular rational basis test or differences in the test applied by the Court depending on the results it wants to achieve.

In examining a law under rational basis review, there are two questions: Does the law have a legitimate purpose? Is the law rationally related to achieving it? Each of these issues is discussed in turn.

2.   Does the Law Have a Legitimate Purpose?

In assessing whether there is a legitimate purpose for a law, there are two interrelated questions. What constitutes a "legitimate" purpose? How should it be decided whether there is such a purpose present — must it be the actual purpose behind the law, or is it enough that such a purpose is conceivable?

WHAT CONSTITUTES A LEGITIMATE PURPOSE?

At the least, the government has a legitimate purpose if it advances a traditional "police" purpose: protecting safety, public health, or public morals. Public safety, public health, and public morals are legitimate government purposes, but they are not the only ones. Virtually any goal that is not forbidden by the Constitution will be deemed sufficient to meet the rational basis test. As the Supreme Court declared in Berman v. Parker, "Public safety, public health, morality, peace and quiet, law and order — these are some of the more conspicuous examples of the traditional application of the police power to municipal affairs. Yet they merely illustrate the scope of the power and do not delimit it."[28] For example, in New Orleans v. Dukes, 427 U.S. 297 (1976), the Supreme Court upheld an ordinance that banned all pushcart food vendors in the French Quarter, except those who had continuously operated there for eight or more years. The Court accepted the city's claim that "street peddlers and hawkers tend to interfere with the charm and beauty of a historic area and disturb tourists and disrupt their enjoyment of that charm and beauty, and that such vendors . . . might thus have a deleterious effect on the economy of the city." The Court said that the distinction among vendors based on their length of work in the French Quarter was legitimate because "[t]he city could reasonably decide that newer businesses were less likely to have built up substantial reliance interests in continued operation."

Only rarely has the Court found that a government purpose was not legitimate under the rational basis test. Romer v. Evans is likely the most important such decision.

28. 348 U.S. 26, 32 (1954).

ROMER v. EVANS
517 U.S. 620 (1996)

Justice KENNEDY delivered the opinion of the Court.

One century ago, the first Justice Harlan admonished this Court that the Constitution "neither knows nor tolerates classes among citizens." Plessy v. Ferguson (1896) (dissenting opinion). Unheeded then, those words now are understood to state a commitment to the law's neutrality where the rights of persons are at stake. The Equal Protection Clause enforces this principle and today requires us to hold invalid a provision of Colorado's Constitution.

I

The enactment challenged in this case is an amendment to the Constitution of the State of Colorado, adopted in a 1992 statewide referendum. The parties and the state courts refer to it as "Amendment 2," its designation when submitted to the voters. The impetus for the amendment and the contentious campaign that preceded its adoption came in large part from ordinances that had been passed in various Colorado municipalities. For example, the cities of Aspen and Boulder and the city and County of Denver each had enacted ordinances which banned discrimination based on sexual orientation in many transactions and activities, including housing, employment, education, public accommodations, and health and welfare services.

Yet Amendment 2, in explicit terms, does more than repeal or rescind these provisions. It prohibits all legislative, executive, or judicial action at any level of state or local government designed to protect the named class, a class we shall refer to as homosexual persons or gays and lesbians. The amendment reads:

> No Protected Status Based on Homosexual, Lesbian or Bisexual Orientation. Neither the State of Colorado, through any of its branches or departments, nor any of its agencies, political subdivisions, municipalities or school districts, shall enact, adopt or enforce any statute, regulation, ordinance or policy whereby homosexual, lesbian or bisexual orientation, conduct, practices or relationships shall constitute or otherwise be the basis of or entitle any person or class of persons to have or claim any minority status, quota preferences, protected status or claim of discrimination. This Section of the Constitution shall be in all respects self-executing.

II

The State's principal argument in defense of Amendment 2 is that it puts gays and lesbians in the same position as all other persons. So, the State says, the measure does no more than deny homosexuals special rights. This reading of the amendment's language is implausible. We rely not upon our own interpretation of the amendment but upon the authoritative construction of Colorado's Supreme Court. The critical discussion of the amendment is as follows:

> The immediate objective of Amendment 2 is, at a minimum, to repeal existing statutes, regulations, ordinances, and policies of state and local entities that barred

discrimination based on sexual orientation. . . . The "ultimate effect" of Amendment 2 is to prohibit any governmental entity from adopting similar, or more protective statutes, regulations, ordinances, or policies in the future unless the state constitution is first amended to permit such measures.

Sweeping and comprehensive is the change in legal status effected by this law. Homosexuals, by state decree, are put in a solitary class with respect to transactions and relations in both the private and governmental spheres. The amendment withdraws from homosexuals, but no others, specific legal protection from the injuries caused by discrimination, and it forbids reinstatement of these laws and policies.

The change Amendment 2 works in the legal status of gays and lesbians in the private sphere is far reaching, both on its own terms and when considered in light of the structure and operation of modern anti-discrimination laws. Amendment 2 bars homosexuals from securing protection against the injuries that public-accommodations laws address. That in itself is a severe consequence, but there is more. Amendment 2, in addition, nullifies specific legal protections for this targeted class in all transactions in housing, sale of real estate, insurance, health and welfare services, private education, and employment. Not confined to the private sphere, Amendment 2 also operates to repeal and forbid all laws or policies providing specific protection for gays or lesbians from discrimination by every level of Colorado government.

[T]he amendment imposes a special disability upon those persons alone. Homosexuals are forbidden the safeguards that others enjoy or may seek without constraint. They can obtain specific protection against discrimination only by enlisting the citizenry of Colorado to amend the State Constitution or perhaps, on the State's view, by trying to pass helpful laws of general applicability. This is so no matter how local or discrete the harm, no matter how public and widespread the injury. We find nothing special in the protections Amendment 2 withholds. These are protections taken for granted by most people either because they already have them or do not need them; these are protections against exclusion from an almost limitless number of transactions and endeavors that constitute ordinary civic life in a free society.

III

The Fourteenth Amendment's promise that no person shall be denied the equal protection of the laws must coexist with the practical necessity that most legislation classifies for one purpose or another, with resulting disadvantage to various groups or persons. We have attempted to reconcile the principle with the reality by stating that, if a law neither burdens a fundamental right nor targets a suspect class, we will uphold the legislative classification so long as it bears a rational relation to some legitimate end.

Amendment 2 fails, indeed defies, even this conventional inquiry. First, the amendment has the peculiar property of imposing a broad and undifferentiated disability on a single named group, an exceptional and, as we shall explain, invalid form of legislation. Second, its sheer breadth is so discontinuous with the reasons offered for it that the amendment seems inexplicable by anything but animus toward the class it affects; it lacks a rational relationship to legitimate state interests.

Taking the first point, even in the ordinary equal protection case calling for the most deferential of standards, we insist on knowing the relation between the classification adopted and the object to be attained. The search for the link between classification and objective gives substance to the Equal Protection Clause; it provides guidance and discipline for the legislature, which is entitled to know what sorts of laws it can pass; and it marks the limits of our own authority. In the ordinary case, a law will be sustained if it can be said to advance a legitimate government interest, even if the law seems unwise or works to the disadvantage of a particular group, or if the rationale for it seems tenuous. See New Orleans v. Dukes (1976) (tourism benefits justified classification favoring pushcart vendors of certain longevity). Williamson v. Lee Optical of Okla., Inc. (1955) (assumed health concerns justified law favoring optometrists over opticians). The laws challenged in the cases just cited were narrow enough in scope and grounded in a sufficient factual context for us to ascertain some relation between the classification and the purpose it served. By requiring that the classification bear a rational relationship to an independent and legitimate legislative end, we ensure that classifications are not drawn for the purpose of disadvantaging the group burdened by the law.

Amendment 2 confounds this normal process of judicial review. It is at once too narrow and too broad. It identifies persons by a single trait and then denies them protection across the board. The resulting disqualification of a class of persons from the right to seek specific protection from the law is unprecedented in our jurisprudence.

It is not within our constitutional tradition to enact laws of this sort. Central both to the idea of the rule of law and to our own Constitution's guarantee of equal protection is the principle that government and each of its parts remain open on impartial terms to all who seek its assistance. Respect for this principle explains why laws singling out a certain class of citizens for disfavored legal status or general hardships are rare. A law declaring that in general it shall be more difficult for one group of citizens than for all others to seek aid from the government is itself a denial of equal protection of the laws in the most literal sense.

A second and related point is that laws of the kind now before us raise the inevitable inference that the disadvantage imposed is born of animosity toward the class of persons affected. "[I]f the constitutional conception of 'equal protection of the laws' means anything, it must at the very least mean that a bare . . . desire to harm a politically unpopular group cannot constitute a legitimate governmental interest." Department of Agriculture v. Moreno (1973).

Amendment 2, however, in making a general announcement that gays and lesbians shall not have any particular protections from the law, inflicts on them immediate, continuing, and real injuries that outrun and belie any legitimate justifications that may be claimed for it. We conclude that, in addition to the far-reaching deficiencies of Amendment 2 that we have noted, the principles it offends, in another sense, are conventional and venerable; a law must bear a rational relationship to a legitimate governmental purpose, and Amendment 2 does not.

The primary rationale the State offers for Amendment 2 is respect for other citizens' freedom of association, and in particular the liberties of landlords or employers who have personal or religious objections to homosexuality.

Colorado also cites its interest in conserving resources to fight discrimination against other groups. The breadth of the amendment is so far removed from these particular justifications that we find it impossible to credit them. We cannot say that Amendment 2 is directed to any identifiable legitimate purpose or discrete objective. It is a status-based enactment divorced from any factual context from which we could discern a relationship to legitimate state interests; it is a classification of persons undertaken for its own sake, something the Equal Protection Clause does not permit. "[C]lass legislation . . . [is] obnoxious to the prohibitions of the Fourteenth Amendment. . . ." *Civil Rights Cases.*

We must conclude that Amendment 2 classifies homosexuals not to further a proper legislative end but to make them unequal to everyone else. This Colorado cannot do. A State cannot so deem a class of persons a stranger to its laws. Amendment 2 violates the Equal Protection Clause.

Justice SCALIA, with whom the Chief Justice and Justice THOMAS join, dissenting.

The Court has mistaken a Kulturkampf for a fit of spite. The constitutional amendment before us here is not the manifestation of a "'bare . . . desire to harm'" homosexuals, but is rather a modest attempt by seemingly tolerant Coloradans to preserve traditional sexual mores against the efforts of a politically powerful minority to revise those mores through use of the laws. That objective, and the means chosen to achieve it, are not only unimpeachable under any constitutional doctrine hitherto pronounced (hence the opinion's heavy reliance upon principles of righteousness rather than judicial holdings); they have been specifically approved by the Congress of the United States and by this Court.

In holding that homosexuality cannot be singled out for disfavorable treatment, the Court contradicts a decision, unchallenged here, pronounced only 10 years ago, see Bowers v. Hardwick (1986), and places the prestige of this institution behind the proposition that opposition to homosexuality is as reprehensible as racial or religious bias. Whether it is or not is precisely the cultural debate that gave rise to the Colorado constitutional amendment (and to the preferential laws against which the amendment was directed). Since the Constitution of the United States says nothing about this subject, it is left to be resolved by normal democratic means, including the democratic adoption of provisions in state constitutions. This Court has no business imposing upon all Americans the resolution favored by the elite class from which the Members of this institution are selected, pronouncing that "animosity" toward homosexuality, is evil. I vigorously dissent.

Despite all of its hand wringing about the potential effect of Amendment 2 on general antidiscrimination laws, the Court's opinion ultimately does not dispute all this, but assumes it to be true. The only denial of equal treatment it contends homosexuals have suffered is this: They may not obtain preferential treatment without amending the State Constitution. That is to say, the principle underlying the Court's opinion is that one who is accorded equal treatment under the laws, but cannot as readily as others obtain preferential treatment under the laws, has been denied equal protection of the laws. If merely stating this alleged "equal protection" violation does not suffice to refute it, our constitutional jurisprudence has achieved terminal silliness.

The central thesis of the Court's reasoning is that any group is denied equal protection when, to obtain advantage (or, presumably, to avoid disadvantage), it must have recourse to a more general and hence more difficult level of political decisionmaking than others. The world has never heard of such a principle, which is why the Court's opinion is so long on emotive utterance and so short on relevant legal citation. And it seems to me most unlikely that any multilevel democracy can function under such a principle. For *whenever* a disadvantage is imposed, or conferral of a benefit is prohibited, at one of the higher levels of democratic decisionmaking (i.e., by the state legislature rather than local government, or by the people at large in the state constitution rather than the legislature), the affected group has (under this theory) been denied equal protection. To take the simplest of examples, consider a state law prohibiting the award of municipal contracts to relatives of mayors or city councilmen. Once such a law is passed, the group composed of such relatives must, in order to get the benefit of city contracts, persuade the state legislature—unlike all other citizens, who need only persuade the municipality. It is ridiculous to consider this a denial of equal protection, which is why the Court's theory is unheard of.

I turn next to whether there was a legitimate rational basis for the substance of the constitutional amendment—for the prohibition of special protection for homosexuals. It is unsurprising that the Court avoids discussion of this question, since the answer is so obviously yes. The case most relevant to the issue before us today is not even mentioned in the Court's opinion: In Bowers v. Hardwick (1986), we held that the Constitution does not prohibit what virtually all States had done from the founding of the Republic until very recent years—making homosexual conduct a crime. That holding is unassailable, except by those who think that the Constitution changes to suit current fashions. If it is constitutionally permissible for a State to make homosexual conduct criminal, surely it is constitutionally permissible for a State to enact other laws merely disfavoring homosexual conduct. And a fortiori it is constitutionally permissible for a State to adopt a provision not even disfavoring homosexual conduct, but merely prohibiting all levels of state government from bestowing special protections upon homosexual conduct.

Today's opinion has no foundation in American constitutional law, and barely pretends to. The people of Colorado have adopted an entirely reasonable provision which does not even disfavor homosexuals in any substantive sense, but merely denies them preferential treatment. Amendment 2 is designed to prevent piecemeal deterioration of the sexual morality favored by a majority of Coloradans, and is not only an appropriate means to that legitimate end, but a means that Americans have employed before. Striking it down is an act, not of judicial judgment, but of political will. I dissent.

MUST IT BE THE ACTUAL PURPOSE, OR IS A CONCEIVABLE PURPOSE ENOUGH?

The Court's enormous judicial deference under the rational basis test is, in part, because of its willingness to accept any conceivable legitimate purpose as sufficient, even if it was not the government's actual purpose. In other words, a law will be upheld as long as the government's lawyer can identify some conceivable legitimate purpose, regardless of whether that was the government's actual motivation. The Court has declared that under rational basis review the actual purpose behind a law is irrelevant and the law must be upheld "if any state of facts reasonably may be conceived to justify" its discrimination.[29]

A key issue is whether any conceivable legitimate purpose should be sufficient or whether the courts should insist on a legitimate actual purpose. The Supreme Court has clearly held that under rational basis review the former, any conceivable legitimate purpose, is sufficient. An example of this is in U.S. Railroad Retirement Board v. Fritz, 449 U.S. 166 (1980), in which the Supreme Court upheld a federal law designed to prevent retired railroad workers from receiving benefits under both the Social Security system and the railroad retirement system. The law allowed those who were already retired and receiving dual benefits to continue to get them, but those who were still employed could not get dual benefits unless they had worked for the railroads for 25 years. The result was that a person who had worked 10 years for the railroads and was already retired could get dual benefits, but a person who had worked for 24 years and was still employed could not collect dual benefits.

In upholding the law, the Court said, "Where, as here, there are plausible reasons for Congress's action, our inquiry is at an end. It is, of course, constitutionally irrelevant whether this reasoning in fact underlies the legislative decision because this Court never has insisted that a legislative body articulate its reasons for enacting a statute. This is particularly true where the legislature must necessarily engage in a process of line drawing." The Court accepted the government's claim that the Congress could have believed that those who had acquired a statutory entitlement to dual benefits while still employed in the railroad industry "had a greater equitable claim to those benefits than [those] who were no longer in railroad employment when they became eligible for dual benefits."

Subsequently, in Federal Communications Commission v. Beach Communications, Inc., 508 U.S. 307 (1993), the Court reaffirmed that any conceivable legislative purpose is sufficient and even went so far as to say that "those attacking the rationality of the legislative classification have the burden to negate every conceivable basis which might support it." The case involved a challenge to a provision of the Federal Cable Communications Policy Act of 1984 that created an exemption to certain regulations for cable television facilities that serve one or more buildings under common ownership or operation. Justice Clarence Thomas, writing for the Court, said, "[B]ecause we never require a legislature to articulate its reasons for enacting a statute, it is entirely irrelevant for constitutional purposes whether the conceived reason for the challenged distinction actually motivated the legislature. . . . [A] legislative choice is not subject to courtroom factfinding and may be based on rational speculation unsupported by evidence or empirical data." Justice Stevens, in a concurring opinion, lamented that "[j]udicial review under the 'conceivable set of facts' test is tantamount to no review at all."

This issue—whether any conceivable legitimate purpose is sufficient or whether it must be the actual purpose—is crucial in determining the impact of rational basis review. If any conceivable purpose is sufficient, very few laws will fail the rational basis test. Government lawyers can invent some legitimate conceivable purpose for virtually every law. The critics argue that rational basis

---

29. McGowan v. Maryland, 366 U.S. 420, 426 (1961).

review is meaningful only if the Court limits itself to looking at the actual purpose for a law.

On the other hand, those who defend the Supreme Court point out that rarely is there a single, identifiable purpose for a law. Legislators might have radically different reasons for supporting a specific legislative act. Justice Rehnquist once remarked that actual purpose review "assumes that individual legislators are motivated by one discernable actual purpose, and ignores the fact that different legislators may vote for a single piece of legislation for widely different reasons."[30] Moreover, once a law is struck down for lack of an adequate actual purpose, Congress simply could reenact the law and assert a permissible goal.

Ultimately, the issue is over how much "bite" there should be in the rational basis test. Allowing any conceivable legitimate purpose to suffice makes the rational basis test a rule of almost complete deference to the government. Limiting the judiciary to considering only the actual purpose behind a law would dramatically increase the chance that laws would be struck down under rational basis review.

3.　The Requirement for a "Reasonable Relationship"

Under rational basis review, the Court also must decide "whether the classifications drawn in a statute are reasonable in light of its purpose."[31] However, the Court repeatedly has expressed that this is "the most relaxed and tolerant form of judicial scrutiny."[32] Thus, the Court has said that under the rational basis test, laws will be upheld unless the government's action is "clearly wrong, a display of arbitrary power, not an exercise of judgment."[33] As a result, under the rational basis test, the Court will allow laws that are both significantly underinclusive and overinclusive.

TOLERANCE FOR UNDERINCLUSIVENESS UNDER RATIONAL BASIS REVIEW

As described above, laws are underinclusive when they do not regulate all who are similarly situated. Underinclusive laws raise the concern that the government has enacted a law that targets a particular politically powerless group or that exempts those with more political clout. But the Supreme Court has said that when rational basis review is used, even substantial underinclusiveness is allowed, because the government "may take one step at a time, addressing itself to the phase of the problem which seems most acute to the legislative mind."[34] The following decision is a classic case used to illustrate the Court's willingness to tolerate underinclusiveness under rational basis review. Notice especially

---

30. Kassell v. Consolidated Freightways Corp., 450 U.S. 662, 702-703 (1981) (Rehnquist, J., dissenting).

31. McLaughlin v. Florida, 379 U.S. 184, 191 (1964).

32. Dallas v. Stanglin, 490 U.S. 19, 26 (1989).

33. Mathews v. DeCastro, 429 U.S. 181, 185 (1976), quoting Helvering v. Davis, 301 U.S. 619, 640 (1937).

34. Williamson v. Lee Optical, 348 U.S. 483, 489 (1955).

Justice Jackson's concurring opinion, which offers one of the clearest arguments for meaningful rational basis review under equal protection.

RAILWAY EXPRESS AGENCY, INC. v. NEW YORK
336 U.S. 106 (1949)

Justice Douglas delivered the opinion of the Court.

Section 124 of the Traffic Regulations of the City of New York promulgated by the Police Commissioner provides: "No person shall operate, or cause to be operated, in or upon any street an advertising vehicle; provided that nothing herein contained shall prevent the putting of business notices upon business delivery vehicles, so long as such vehicles are engaged in the usual business or regular work of the owner and not used merely or mainly for advertising."

Appellant is engaged in a nation-wide express business. It operates about 1,900 trucks in New York City and sells the space on the exterior sides of these trucks for advertising. That advertising is for the most part unconnected with its own business. It was convicted in the magistrates court and fined.

The question of equal protection of the laws is pressed strenuously on us. It is pointed out that the regulation draws the line between advertisements of products sold by the owner of the truck and general advertisements. It is argued that unequal treatment on the basis of such a distinction is not justified by the aim and purpose of the regulation. It is said, for example, that one of appellant's trucks carrying the advertisement of a commercial house would not cause any greater distraction of pedestrians and vehicle drivers than if the commercial house carried the same advertisement on its own truck. Yet the regulation allows the latter to do what the former is forbidden from doing. It is therefore contended that the classification which the regulation makes has no relation to the traffic problem since a violation turns not on what kind of advertisements are carried on trucks but on whose trucks they are carried.

That, however, is a superficial way of analyzing the problem, even if we assume that it is premised on the correct construction of the regulation. The local authorities may well have concluded that those who advertised their own wares on their trucks do not present the same traffic problem in view of the nature or extent of the advertising which they use. It would take a degree of omniscience which we lack to say that such is not the case. If that judgment is correct, the advertising displays that are exempt have less incidence on traffic than those of appellants.

We cannot say that that judgment is not an allowable one. Yet if it is, the classification has relation to the purpose for which it is made and does not contain the kind of discrimination against which the Equal Protection Clause affords protection. It is by such practical considerations based on experience rather than by theoretical inconsistencies that the question of equal protection is to be answered. And the fact that New York City sees fit to eliminate from traffic this kind of distraction but does not touch what may be even greater ones in a different category, such as the vivid displays on Times Square, is immaterial. It is no requirement of equal protection that all evils of the same genus be eradicated or none at all.

Justice JACKSON, concurring.

There are two clauses of the Fourteenth Amendment which this Court may invoke to invalidate ordinances by which municipal governments seek to solve their local problems. One says that no state shall "deprive any person of life, liberty, or property, without due process of law." The other declares that no state shall "deny to any person within its jurisdiction the equal protection of the laws."

My philosophy as to the relative readiness with which we should resort to these two clauses is almost diametrically opposed to the philosophy which prevails on this Court. While claims of denial of equal protection are frequently asserted, they are rarely sustained. But the Court frequently uses the Due Process Clause to strike down measures taken by municipalities to deal with activities in their streets and public places which the local authorities consider to create hazards, annoyances or discomforts to their inhabitants.

The burden should rest heavily upon one who would persuade us to use the Due Process Clause to strike down a substantive law or ordinance. Even its provident use against municipal regulations frequently disables all government — state, municipal and federal — from dealing with the conduct in question because the requirement of due process is also applicable to State and Federal Governments. Invalidation of a statute or an ordinance on due process grounds leaves ungoverned and ungovernable conduct which many people find objectionable.

Invocation of the Equal Protection Clause, on the other hand, does not disable any governmental body from dealing with the subject at hand. It merely means that the prohibition or regulation must have a broader impact. I regard it as a salutary doctrine that cities, states and the Federal Government must exercise their powers so as not to discriminate between their inhabitants except upon some reasonable differentiation fairly related to the object of regulation. This equality is not merely abstract justice. The framers of the Constitution knew, and we should not forget today, that there is no more effective practical guaranty against arbitrary and unreasonable government than to require that the principles of law which officials would impose upon a minority must be imposed generally. Conversely, nothing opens the door to arbitrary action so effectively as to allow those officials to pick and choose only a few to whom they will apply legislation and thus to escape the political retribution that might be visited upon them if larger numbers were affected. Courts can take no better measure to assure that laws will be just than to require that laws be equal in operation.

This case affords an illustration. Even casual observations from the sidewalks of New York will show that an ordinance which would forbid all advertising on vehicles would run into conflict with many interests, including some, if not all, of the great metropolitan newspapers, which use that advertising extensively. Their blandishment of the latest sensations is not less a cause of diverted attention and traffic hazard than the commonplace cigarette advertisement which this truck-owner is forbidden to display. But any regulation applicable to all such advertising would require much clearer justification in local conditions to enable its enactment than does some regulation applicable to a few. I do not mention this to criticize the motives of those who enacted this ordinance, but it dramatizes the point that we are much more likely to find arbitrariness in the regulation of the few than of the many. Hence, for my part, I am more receptive to attack on local ordinances for denial of equal protection than for denial of due process, while the Court has more often used the latter clause.

It is urged with considerable force that this local regulation does not comply with the Equal Protection Clause because it applies unequally upon classes whose differentiation is in no way relevant to the objects of the regulation. As a matter of principle and in view of my attitude toward the Equal Protection Clause, I do not think differences of treatment under law should be approved on classification because of differences unrelated to the legislative purpose. The Equal Protection Clause ceases to assure either equality or protection if it is avoided by any conceivable difference that can be pointed out between those bound and those left free.

TOLERANCE FOR OVERINCLUSIVENESS UNDER RATIONAL BASIS REVIEW

Likewise, even substantial overinclusiveness is tolerated under rational basis review. A law is overinclusive if it regulates individuals who are not similarly situated; that is, if it covers more people than it needs to in order to accomplish its purpose. Overinclusive laws are unfair to those who are unnecessarily regulated and they risk "burden[ing] a politically powerless group which would have been spared if it had enough clout to compel normal attention to the relevant costs and benefits."[35]

Nonetheless, the Supreme Court has indicated that even significant overinclusiveness is allowed under rational basis review. New York City Transit Authority v. Beazer is an important illustration in this regard. It also indicates that laws that are both significantly underinclusive and overinclusive often are upheld under rational basis review.

NEW YORK CITY TRANSIT AUTHORITY v. BEAZER
440 U.S. 568 (1979)

Justice STEVENS delivered the opinion of the Court.

The New York City Transit Authority refuses to employ persons who use methadone. The District Court found that this policy violates the Equal Protection Clause of the Fourteenth Amendment. We now reverse.

I

About 40,000 persons receive methadone maintenance treatment in New York City, of whom about 26,000 participate in the five major public or semipublic programs, and 14,000 are involved in about 25 private programs. The sole purpose of all these programs is to treat the addiction of persons who have been using heroin for at least two years.

---

35. Laurence H. Tribe, *American Constitutional Law* 1449 (2d ed. 1988).

The evidence indicates that methadone is an effective cure for the physical aspects of heroin addiction. The crucial indicator of successful methadone maintenance is the patient's abstinence from the illegal or excessive use of drugs and alcohol. The District Court found that the risk of reversion to drug or alcohol abuse declines dramatically after the first few months of treatment. Indeed, "the strong majority" of patients who have been on methadone maintenance for at least a year are free from illicit drug use. But a significant number are not. On this critical point, the evidence relied upon by the District Court reveals that even among participants with more than 12 months' tenure in methadone maintenance programs, the incidence of drug and alcohol abuse may often approach and even exceed 25%.

This litigation was brought by the four respondents as a class action on behalf of all persons who have been, or would in the future be, subject to discharge or rejection as employees of TA by reason of participation in a methadone maintenance program.

II

In this case, the Transit Authority's rule places a meaningful restriction on all of its employees and job applicants; in that sense the rule is one of general applicability and satisfies the equal protection principle without further inquiry. The District Court, however, interpreted the rule as applicable to the limited class of persons who regularly use narcotic drugs, including methadone. As so interpreted, we are necessarily confronted with the question whether the rule reflects an impermissible bias against a special class.

Respondents have never questioned the validity of a special rule for all users of narcotics. Rather, they originally contended that persons receiving methadone should not be covered by that rule; in other words, they should not be included within a class that is otherwise unobjectionable. Their constitutional claim was that methadone users are entitled to be treated like most other employees and applicants rather than like other users of narcotics. But the District Court's findings unequivocally establish that there are relevant differences between persons using methadone regularly and persons who use no narcotics of any kind.

In addition, a substantial percentage of persons taking methadone will not successfully complete the treatment program. The findings do not indicate with any precision the number who drop out, or the number who can fairly be classified as unemployable, but the evidence indicates that it may well be a majority of those taking methadone at any given time.

Respondents no longer question the need, or at least the justification, for special rules for methadone users. Indeed, they vigorously defend the District Court's opinion which expressly held that it would be permissible for the Transit Authority ["TA"] to have a special rule denying methadone users any employment unless they had been undergoing treatment for at least a year, and another special rule denying even the most senior and reliable methadone users any of the more dangerous jobs in the system.

But any special rule short of total exclusion that TA might adopt is likely to be less precise — and will assuredly be more costly — than the one that it currently enforces. If eligibility is marked at any intermediate point — whether after one year of treatment or later—the classification will inevitably discriminate between employees or applicants equally or almost equally apt to achieve full recovery. Even the District Court's opinion did not rigidly specify one year as a constitutionally mandated measure of the period of treatment that guarantees full recovery from drug addiction. The uncertainties associated with the rehabilitation of heroin addicts precluded it from identifying any bright line marking the point at which the risk of regression ends. By contrast, the "no drugs" policy now enforced by TA is supported by the legitimate inference that as long as a treatment program (or other drug use) continues, a degree of uncertainty persists. Accordingly, an employment policy that postpones eligibility until the treatment program has been completed, rather than accepting an intermediate point on an uncertain line, is rational. It is neither unprincipled nor invidious in the sense that it implies disrespect for the excluded subclass.

The dissent is therefore repeatedly mistaken in attributing to the District Court a finding that TA's "normal screening process without additional effort" would suffice in the absence of the "no drugs" rule. Aggravating this erroneous factual assumption is a mistaken legal proposition advanced by the dissent— that TA can be faulted for failing to prove the unemployability of "successfully maintained methadone users." Aside from the misallocation of the burden of proof that underlies this argument, it is important to note that TA did prove that 20% to 30% of the class afforded relief by the District Court are not "successfully maintained," and hence are assuredly not employable. Even assuming therefore that the percentage of employable persons in the remaining 70% is the same as that in the class of TA applicants who do not use methadone, it is respondents who must be faulted for failing to prove that the offending 30% could be excluded as cheaply and effectively in the absence of the rule.

At its simplest, the District Court's conclusion was that TA's rule is broader than necessary to exclude those methadone users who are not actually qualified to work for TA. We may assume not only that this conclusion is correct but also that it is probably unwise for a large employer like TA to rely on a general rule instead of individualized consideration of every job applicant. But these assumptions concern matters of personnel policy that do not implicate the principle safeguarded by the Equal Protection Clause. As the District Court recognized, the special classification created by TA's rule serves the general objectives of safety and efficiency. Moreover, the exclusionary line challenged by respondents "is not one which is directed 'against' any individual or category of persons, but rather it represents a policy choice . . . made by that branch of Government vested with the power to make such choices."

Because it does not circumscribe a class of persons characterized by some unpopular trait or affiliation, it does not create or reflect any special likelihood of bias on the part of the ruling majority. Under these circumstances, it is of no constitutional significance that the degree of rationality is not as great with respect to certain ill-defined subparts of the classification as it is with respect to the classification as a whole.

No matter how unwise it may be for TA to refuse employment to individual car cleaners, track repairmen, or bus drivers simply because they are receiving methadone treatment, the Constitution does not authorize a federal court to interfere in that policy decision.

Justice WHITE, with whom Justice MARSHALL joins, dissenting.

The District Court found that the evidence conclusively established that petitioners exclude from employment all persons who are successfully on methadone maintenance — that is, those who after one year are "free of the use of heroin, other illicit drugs, and problem drinking," those who have graduated from methadone programs and remain drug free for less than five years; that past or present successful methadone maintenance is not a meaningful predictor of poor performance or conduct in most job categories; that petitioners could use their normal employee-screening mechanisms to separate the successfully maintained users from the unsuccessful; and that petitioners do exactly that for other groups that common sense indicates might also be suspect employees. Petitioners did not challenge these factual conclusions in the Court of Appeals, but that court nonetheless reviewed the evidence and found that it overwhelmingly supported the District Court's findings.

It bears repeating, then, that both the District Court and the Court of Appeals found that those who have been maintained on methadone for at least a year and who are free from the use of illicit drugs and alcohol can easily be identified through normal personnel procedures and, for a great many jobs, are as employable as and present no more risk than applicants from the general population.

The question before us is the rationality of placing successfully maintained or recently cured persons in the same category as those just attempting to escape heroin addiction or who have failed to escape it, rather than in with the general population. The asserted justification for the challenged classification is the objective of a capable and reliable work force, and thus the characteristic in question is employability. "Employability," in this regard, does not mean that any particular applicant, much less every member of a given group of applicants, will turn out to be a model worker. Nor does it mean that no such applicant will ever become or be discovered to be a malingerer, thief, alcoholic, or even heroin addict. All employers take such risks. Employability, as the District Court used it in reference to successfully maintained methadone users, means only that the employer is no more likely to find a member of that group to be an unsatisfactory employee than he would an employee chosen from the general population.

Petitioners had every opportunity, but presented nothing to negative the employability of successfully maintained methadone users as distinguished from those who were unsuccessful. Instead, petitioners, like the Court, dwell on the methadone failures — those who quit the programs or who remain but turn to illicit drug use. The Court, for instance, makes much of the drug use of many of those in methadone programs, including those who have been in such programs for more than one year. But this has little force since those persons are not "successful," can be and have been identified as such, and, despite the Court's efforts to put them there, are not within the protection of the District Court's injunction. That 20% to 30% are unsuccessful after one year in a methadone program tells us nothing about the employability of the successful group, and it is the latter category of applicants that the District Court and the Court of Appeals held to be unconstitutionally burdened by the blanket rule disqualifying them from employment.

Finally, even were the District Court wrong, and even were successfully maintained persons marginally less employable than the average applicant, the blanket exclusion of only these people, when but a few are actually unemployable and when many other groups have varying numbers of unemployable members, is arbitrary and unconstitutional. Many persons now suffer from or may again suffer from some handicap related to employability. But petitioners have singled out respondents — unlike ex-offenders, former alcoholics and mental patients, diabetics, epileptics, and those currently using tranquilizers, for example — for sacrifice to this at best ethereal and likely nonexistent risk of increased unemployability. Such an arbitrary assignment of burdens among classes that are similarly situated with respect to the proffered objectives is the type of invidious choice forbidden by the Equal Protection Clause.

CASES IN WHICH LAWS ARE DEEMED ARBITRARY AND UNREASONABLE

Occasionally, the Supreme Court has found laws to be so arbitrary and unreasonable as to fail rational basis review. The following two decisions are examples of this. In examining these cases, consider whether the Court is applying the same deferential review as in the above decisions or whether it is a different rational basis test with more "bite."

U.S. DEPARTMENT OF AGRICULTURE v. MORENO
413 U.S. 528 (1973)

Justice BRENNAN delivered the opinion of the Court.

This case requires us to consider the constitutionality of §3(e) of the Food Stamp Act of 1964, which, with certain exceptions, excludes from participation in the food stamp program any household containing an individual who is unrelated to any other member of the household. In practical effect, §3(e) creates two classes of persons for food stamp purposes: one class is composed of those individuals who live in households all of whose members are related to one another, and the other class consists of those individuals who live in households containing one or more members who are unrelated to the rest. The latter class of persons is denied federal food assistance.

I

The federal food stamp program was established in 1964 in an effort to alleviate hunger and malnutrition among the more needy segments of our society. Eligibility for participation in the program is determined on a household rather than an individual basis. An eligible household purchases sufficient food stamps to provide that household with a nutritionally adequate diet. The household pays for the stamps at a reduced rate based upon its size and cumulative income. The food stamps are then used to purchase food at retail stores, and the Government redeems the stamps at face value, thereby paying the difference between the actual cost of the food and the amount paid by the household for the stamps.

As initially enacted, §3(e) defined a "household" as "a group of related or non-related individuals, who are not residents of an institution or boarding house, but are living as one economic unit sharing common cooking facilities and for whom food is customarily purchased in common." In January 1971, however Congress redefined the term "household" so as to include only groups of related individuals. Pursuant to this amendment, the Secretary of Agriculture promulgated regulations rendering ineligible for participation in the program any "household" whose members are not "all related to each other."

Appellees in this case consist of several groups of individuals who allege that, although they satisfy the income eligibility requirements for federal food assistance, they have nevertheless been excluded from the program solely because the persons in each group are not "all related to each other." Appellee Jacinta Moreno, for example is a 56-year-old diabetic who lives with Ermina Sanchez and the latter's three children. They share common living expenses, and Mrs. Sanchez helps to care for appellee. Appellee's monthly income, derived from public assistance, is $75; Mrs. Sanchez receives $133 per month from public assistance. The household pays $135 per month for rent, gas and electricity, of which appellee pays $50. Appellee spends $10 per month for transportation to a hospital for regular visits, and $5 per month for laundry. That leaves her $10 per month for food and other necessities. Despite her poverty, appellee has been denied federal food assistance solely because she is unrelated to the other members of her household. Moreover, although Mrs. Sanchez and her three children were permitted to purchase $108 worth of food stamps per month for $18, their participation in the program will be terminated if appellee Moreno continues to live with them.

II

Under traditional equal protection analysis, a legislative classification must be sustained, if the classification itself is rationally related to a legitimate governmental interest. The challenged statutory classification (households of related persons versus households containing one or more unrelated persons) is clearly irrelevant to the stated purposes of the Act. As the District Court recognized, "[t]he relationships among persons constituting one economic unit and sharing cooking facilities have nothing to do with their abilities to stimulate the agricultural economy by purchasing farm surpluses, or with their personal nutritional requirements."

Thus, if it is to be sustained, the challenged classification must rationally further some legitimate governmental interest other than those specifically stated in the congressional "declaration of policy." Regrettably, there is little legislative history to illuminate the purposes of the 1971 amendment of §3(e). The legislative history that does exist, however, indicates that that amendment was intended to prevent so-called "hippies" and "hippie communes" from participating in the food stamp program. See H.R. Conf. Rep. No. 91—1793, p. 8; 116 Cong. Rec. 44439 (1970) (Sen. Holland). The challenged classification clearly cannot be sustained by reference to this congressional purpose. For if the constitutional conception of "equal protection of the laws" means anything, it must at the very least mean that a bare congressional desire to harm a politically unpopular group cannot constitute a legitimate governmental interest. As a result, "[a] purpose to discriminate against hippies cannot, in and of itself and without reference to [some independent] considerations in the public interest, justify the 1971 amendment."

Although apparently conceding this point, the Government maintains that the challenged classification should nevertheless be upheld as rationally related to the clearly legitimate governmental interest in minimizing fraud in the administration of the food stamp program. In essence, the Government contends that, in adopting the 1971 amendment, Congress might rationally have thought (1) that households with one or more unrelated members are more likely than "fully related" households to contain individuals who abuse the program by fraudulently failing to report sources of income or by voluntarily remaining poor; and (2) that such households are "relatively unstable," thereby increasing the difficulty of detecting such abuses. But even if we were to accept as rational the Government's wholly unsubstantiated assumptions concerning the differences between "related" and "unrelated" households we still could not agree with the Government's conclusion that the denial of essential federal food assistance to all otherwise eligible households containing unrelated members constitutes a rational effort to deal with these concerns.

At the outset, it is important to note that the Food Stamp Act itself contains provisions, wholly independent of §3(e), aimed specifically at the problems of fraud and of the voluntarily poor. For example, with certain exceptions, the Act renders ineligible for assistance any household containing "an able-bodied adult person between the ages of eighteen and sixty-five" who fails to register for, and accept, offered employment. Similarly, [the Act] specifically impose[s] strict criminal penalties upon any individual who obtains or uses food stamps fraudulently. The existence of these provisions necessarily casts considerable doubt upon the proposition that the 1971 amendment could rationally have been intended to prevent those very same abuses.

Moreover, in practical effect, the challenged classification simply does not operate so as rationally to further the prevention of fraud. [I]n practical operation, the 1971 amendment excludes from participation in the food stamp program, not those persons who are "likely to abuse the program," but, rather, only those persons who are so desperately in need of aid that they cannot even afford to alter their living arrangements so as to retain their eligibility. Traditional equal protection analysis does not require that every classification be drawn with precise "mathematical nicety." But the classification here in issue is not only "imprecise," it is wholly without any rational basis.

Justice REHNQUIST, with whom the Chief Justice concurs, dissenting.

Here appellees challenged a provision in the Federal Food Stamp Act which limited food stamps to related people living in one "household." The result of this provision is that unrelated persons who live under the same roof and pool their resources may not obtain food stamps even though otherwise eligible.

The Court's opinion would make a very persuasive congressional committee report arguing against the adoption of the limitation in question. Undoubtedly, Congress attacked the problem with a rather blunt instrument and, just as undoubtedly, persuasive arguments may be made that what we conceive to be its purpose will not be significantly advanced by the enactment of the limitation. But questions such as this are for Congress, rather than for this Court; our role is limited to the determination of whether there is any rational basis on which Congress could decide that public funds made available under the food stamp program should not go to a household containing an individual who is unrelated to any other member of the household.

The limitation which Congress enacted could, in the judgment of reasonable men, conceivably deny food stamps to members of households which have been formed solely for the purpose of taking advantage of the food stamp program. Since the food stamp program is not intended to be a subsidy for every individual who desires low-cost food, this was a permissible congressional decision quite consistent with the underlying policy of the Act. The fact that the limitation will have unfortunate and perhaps unintended consequences beyond this does not make it unconstitutional.

CITY OF CLEBURNE, TEXAS v. CLEBURNE LIVING CENTER, INC.
473 U.S. 432 (1985)

Justice WHITE delivered the opinion of the Court.

A Texas city denied a special use permit for the operation of a group home for the mentally retarded, acting pursuant to a municipal zoning ordinance requiring permits for such homes. The Court of Appeals for the Fifth Circuit held that mental retardation is a "quasi-suspect" classification and that the ordinance violated the Equal Protection Clause because it did not substantially further an important governmental purpose. We hold that a lesser standard of scrutiny is appropriate, but conclude that under that standard the ordinance is invalid as applied in this case.

I

In July 1980, respondent Jan Hannah purchased a building at 201 Featherston Street in the city of Cleburne, Texas, with the intention of leasing it to Cleburne Living Center, Inc. (CLC), for the operation of a group home for the mentally retarded. It was anticipated that the home would house 13 retarded men and women, who would be under the constant supervision of CLC staff members. The house had four bedrooms and two baths, with a half bath to be added. CLC planned to comply with all applicable state and federal regulations.

The city informed CLC that a special use permit would be required for the operation of a group home at the site, and CLC accordingly submitted a permit application. After holding a public hearing on CLC's application, the City Council voted 3 to 1 to deny a special use permit.

II

[W]e conclude for several reasons that the Court of Appeals erred in holding mental retardation a quasi-suspect classification calling for a more exacting standard of judicial review than is normally accorded economic and social legislation. First, it is undeniable, and it is not argued otherwise here, that those who are mentally retarded have a reduced ability to cope with and function in the everyday world. Nor are they all cut from the same pattern: as the testimony in this record indicates, they range from those whose disability is not immediately evident to those who must be constantly cared for. They are thus different, immutably so, in relevant respects, and the States' interest in dealing with and providing for them is plainly a legitimate one. How this large and diversified group is to be treated under the law is a difficult and often a technical matter, very much a task for legislators guided by qualified professionals and not by the perhaps ill-informed opinions of the judiciary. Heightened scrutiny inevitably involves substantive judgments about legislative decisions, and we doubt that the predicate for such judicial oversight is present where the classification deals with mental retardation.

Second, the distinctive legislative response, both national and state, to the plight of those who are mentally retarded demonstrates not only that they have unique problems, but also that the lawmakers have been addressing their difficulties in a manner that belies a continuing antipathy or prejudice and a corresponding need for more intrusive oversight by the judiciary. Thus, the Federal Government has not only outlawed discrimination against the mentally retarded in federally funded programs, but it has also provided the retarded with the right to receive "appropriate treatment, services, and habilitation" in a setting that is "least restrictive of [their] personal liberty."

Such legislation thus singling out the retarded for special treatment reflects the real and undeniable differences between the retarded and others. That a civilized and decent society expects and approves such legislation indicates that governmental consideration of those differences in the vast majority of situations is not only legitimate but also desirable.

Even assuming that many of these laws could be shown to be substantially related to an important governmental purpose, merely requiring the legislature to justify its efforts in these terms may lead it to refrain from acting at all. Much recent legislation intended to benefit the retarded also assumes the need for measures that might be perceived to disadvantage them. The Education of the Handicapped Act, for example, requires an "appropriate" education, not one that is equal in all respects to the education of nonretarded children; clearly, admission to a class that exceeded the abilities of a retarded child would not be appropriate. Similarly, the Developmental Disabilities Assistance Act and the Texas Act give the retarded the right to live only in the "least restrictive setting" appropriate to their abilities, implicitly assuming the need for at least some restrictions that would not be imposed on others. Especially given the wide variation in the abilities and needs of the retarded themselves, governmental bodies must have a certain amount of flexibility and freedom from judicial oversight in shaping and limiting their remedial efforts.

Third, the legislative response, which could hardly have occurred and survived without public support, negates any claim that the mentally retarded are politically powerless in the sense that they have no ability to attract the attention of the lawmakers. Any minority can be said to be powerless to assert direct control over the legislature, but if that were a criterion for higher level scrutiny by the courts, much economic and social legislation would now be suspect.

Fourth, if the large and amorphous class of the mentally retarded were deemed quasi-suspect for the reasons given by the Court of Appeals, it would be difficult to find a principled way to distinguish a variety of other groups who have perhaps immutable disabilities setting them off from others, who cannot themselves mandate the desired legislative responses, and who can claim some degree of prejudice from at least part of the public at large. One need mention in this respect only the aging, the disabled, the mentally ill, and the infirm. We are reluctant to set out on that course, and we decline to do so.

Our refusal to recognize the retarded as a quasi-suspect class does not leave them entirely unprotected from invidious discrimination. To withstand equal protection review, legislation that distinguishes between the mentally retarded and others must be rationally related to a legitimate governmental purpose. This standard, we believe, affords government the latitude necessary both to pursue policies designed to assist the retarded in realizing their full potential, and to freely and efficiently engage in activities that burden the retarded in what is essentially an incidental manner. The State may not rely on a classification whose relationship to an asserted goal is so attenuated as to render the distinction arbitrary or irrational.

[III]

The constitutional issue is clearly posed. The city does not require a special use permit in an R-3 zone for apartment houses, multiple dwellings, boarding and lodging houses, fraternity or sorority houses, dormitories, apartment hotels, hospitals, sanitariums, nursing homes for convalescents or the aged (other than for the insane or feebleminded or alcoholics or drug addicts), private clubs or fraternal orders, and other specified uses. It does, however, insist on a special permit for the Featherston home, and it does so, as the District Court found, because it would be a facility for the mentally retarded. May the city require the permit for this facility when other care and multiple-dwelling facilities are freely permitted?

It is true, as already pointed out, that the mentally retarded as a group are indeed different from others not sharing their misfortune, and in this respect they may be different from those who would occupy other facilities that would be permitted in an R-3 zone without a special permit. But this difference is largely irrelevant unless the Featherston home and those who would occupy it would threaten legitimate interests of the city in a way that other permitted uses such as boarding houses and hospitals would not. Because in our view the record does not reveal any rational basis for believing that the Featherston home would pose any special threat to the city's legitimate interests, we affirm the judgment below insofar as it holds the ordinance invalid as applied in this case.

The District Court found that the City Council's insistence on the permit rested on several factors. First, the Council was concerned with the negative attitude of the majority of property owners located within 200 feet of the Featherston facility, as well as with the fears of elderly residents of the neighborhood. But mere negative attitudes, or fear, unsubstantiated by factors which are properly cognizable in a zoning proceeding, are not permissible bases for treating a home for the mentally retarded differently from apartment houses, multiple dwellings, and the like. It is plain that the electorate as a whole, whether by referendum or otherwise, could not order city action violative of the Equal Protection Clause, and the City may not avoid the strictures of that Clause by deferring to the wishes or objections of some fraction of the body politic. "Private biases may be outside the reach of the law, but the law cannot, directly or indirectly, give them effect."

Second, the Council had two objections to the location of the facility. It was concerned that the facility was across the street from a junior high school, and it feared that the students might harass the occupants of the Featherston home. But the school itself is attended by about 30 mentally retarded students, and denying a permit based on such vague, undifferentiated fears is again permitting some portion of the community to validate what would otherwise be an equal protection violation. The other objection to the home's location was that it was located on "a five hundred year flood plain." This concern with the possibility of a flood, however, can hardly be based on a distinction between the Featherston home and, for example, nursing homes, homes for convalescents or the aged, or sanitariums or hospitals, any of which could be located on the Featherston site without obtaining a special use permit. The same may be said of another concern of the Council — doubts about the legal responsibility for actions which the mentally retarded might take. If there is no concern about legal responsibility with respect to other uses that would be permitted in the area, such as boarding and fraternity houses, it is difficult to believe that the groups of mildly or moderately mentally retarded individuals who would live at 201 Featherston would present any different or special hazard.

Fourth, the Council was concerned with the size of the home and the number of people that would occupy it. The District Court found, and the Court of Appeals repeated, that "[i]f the potential residents of the Featherston Street home were not mentally retarded, but the home was the same in all other respects, its use would be permitted under the city's zoning ordinance." Given this finding, there would be no restrictions on the number of people who could occupy this home as a boarding house, nursing home, family dwelling, fraternity house, or dormitory. The question is whether it is rational to treat the mentally retarded differently. It is true that they suffer disability not shared by others; but why this difference warrants a density regulation that others need not observe is not at all apparent. At least this record does not clarify how, in this connection, the characteristics of the intended occupants of the Featherston home rationally justify denying to those occupants what would be permitted to groups occupying the same site for different purposes. Those who would live in the Featherston home are the type of individuals who, with supporting staff, satisfy federal and state standards for group housing in the community; and there is no dispute that the home would meet the federal square-footage-per-resident requirement for facilities of this type. In the words of the Court of Appeals, "[t]he City never justifies its apparent view that other people can live under such 'crowded' conditions when mentally retarded persons cannot."

In the courts below the city also urged that the ordinance is aimed at avoiding concentration of population and at lessening congestion of the streets. These concerns obviously fail to explain why apartment houses, fraternity and sorority houses, hospitals and the like, may freely locate in the area without a permit. So, too, the expressed worry about fire hazards, the serenity of the neighborhood, and the avoidance of danger to other residents fail rationally to justify singling out a home such as 201 Featherston for the special use permit, yet imposing no such restrictions on the many other uses freely permitted in the neighborhood.

The short of it is that requiring the permit in this case appears to us to rest on an irrational prejudice against the mentally retarded, including those who would occupy the Featherston facility and who would live under the closely supervised and highly regulated conditions expressly provided for by state and federal law.

C. CLASSIFICATIONS BASED ON RACE AND NATIONAL ORIGIN

Of all in the infinite array of distinctions drawn by American governments in the past 230 years, none has been more important than race discrimination. Some injustices are so enormous as to defy comprehension. Slavery, the apartheid that followed it in much of the country, and the systematic race discrimination that has existed throughout the nation are a profound embarrassment and a human tragedy of incalculable dimensions.

In discussing discrimination based on race and national origin, this section begins in subsection 1 by looking at race discrimination and slavery before the Civil War. Subsection 2 explains that strict scrutiny is used for evaluating race and national origin classifications.

Subsection 3 focuses on the question of how the existence of a race or national origin classification can be proven. There are two ways of proving such discrimination. One is where the classification exists on the face of the law; that is, the law in its very terms draws a distinction among people based on race or national origin. Alternatively, if a law is facially neutral, a racial classification can be proven by demonstrating that the law has a discriminatory purpose and a discriminatory impact. Each of these is discussed in turn.

No area of race discrimination has produced more litigation or has been more difficult for the courts than the problem of school segregation. Subsection 4 examines the issues surrounding remedies for school segregation.

Finally, subsection 5 discusses racial classifications that benefit minorities. This, of course, is the controversial issue of affirmative action that has produced a number of major Supreme Court decisions in recent years.

1. Race Discrimination and Slavery Before the Thirteenth and Fourteenth Amendments

Prior to the adoption of the Thirteenth Amendment in 1865, slavery was constitutional. Prior to the adoption of the Fourteenth Amendment in 1868, there was no constitutional assurance of equal protection and thus no limit on race discrimination. Despite the majestic words of the Declaration of Independence that "all men are created equal," blacks were anything but equal under the Constitution.

Several constitutional provisions expressly protected aspects of the institution of slavery. Article I, §2 requires apportionment of the House of Representatives based on the "whole Number of free Persons" and "three fifths of all other Persons." Article I, §9 prevented Congress from banning the importation of slaves until 1808 and Article V of the Constitution prohibited this provision from being altered by constitutional amendment. Article IV, §2 contains the Fugitive

Slave Clause, which provided, "No Person held to Service or Labour in one State, under the Laws thereof, escaping into another, shall, in Consequence of any Law or Regulation therein, be discharged from such Service or Labour, but shall be delivered up on Claim of the Party to whom such Service or Labour may be due."

Southern states simply would not have accepted a Constitution that abolished slavery. Additionally, many of the most influential drafters at the Constitutional Convention were slave owners. For example, such prominent framers as George Washington, James Madison, and John Rutledge all owned slaves.[36] The result was a Constitution that protected the institution of slavery.

The judiciary consistently enforced the institution of slavery by ruling in favor of slaveowners and against slaves.[37] For example, the Court enforced the Fugitive Slave Clause and prevented Northern states from protecting escaped slaves. In Prigg v. Pennsylvania, 41 U.S. (16 Pet.) 539 (1842), the Supreme Court declared unconstitutional a state law that prevented the use of force or violence to remove any person from the state to return the individual to slavery. The Fugitive Slave Act of 1793, adopted by the second Congress, required that judges return escaped slaves. In *Prigg*, the Supreme Court relied on this statute and the Fugitive Slave Clause to invalidate the Pennsylvania law. Justice Joseph Story, writing for the Court, held that the Constitution prohibited states from interfering with the return of fugitive slaves. The Court explained that the "object of this clause was to secure to the citizens of the slaveholding states the complete right and title of ownership in their slaves, as property, in every state in the Union into which they might escape from the state where they were held in servitude." Indeed, the Court said that the Fugitive Slave Clause "was so vital . . . that it cannot be doubted that it constituted a fundamental article, without the adoption of which the Union could not have been formed." Thus, the Court concluded that "we have not the slightest hesitation in holding, that, under and in virtue of the Constitution, the owner of a slave is clothed with entire authority, in every state in the Union, to seize and recapture his slave." Likewise, the Court also held that states could punish those who harbored fugitive slaves.

At no point prior to the Civil War did the Supreme Court significantly limit slavery or even raise serious questions about its constitutionality.[38] Nor were state courts, even in the North, a significant force in ending slavery. For example, in State v. Post, 20 N.J.L. 368 (1845), the Supreme Court of New Jersey rejected a claim that the state constitution abolished slavery. The Court said that "it has been often adjudged, both by the State and Federal courts, that slavery still exists; that the master's right of property in the slave has not been affected either by the declaration of independence, or the constitution of the United States."

The importance of slavery as a social and political issue during this time period cannot be overstated. Every discussion of the relationship between the federal and state governments was directly or indirectly about the

---

36. *See* Donald L. Robinson, *Slavery in the Structure of American Politics, 1765-1820*, 209-210 (1971).

37. For an excellent description of these cases and this history, *see* Robert M. Cover, *Justice Accused: Antislavery and the Judicial Process* (1975).

38. In *The Antelope*, 23 U.S. (10 Wheat.) 66 (1825), the Supreme Court suggested that slavery was inconsistent with national law and therefore had to be authorized by statute.

slavery question. It was the central dispute of the time and affected almost all other issues.

DRED SCOTT v. SANDFORD

In 1819, a major national controversy surrounded the admission of Missouri as a state and whether it, and other areas covered by the Louisiana Purchase, would be free or slave states. In a compromise that was intended to resolve the issue, known as the Missouri Compromise, Congress admitted Missouri as a slave state but prohibited slavery in the territories north of the latitude of 36°30′. Territories below this line could decide whether to allow slavery and could make that choice when admitted as states.

In Dred Scott v. Sandford, which follows, the Supreme Court declared the Missouri Compromise unconstitutional and broadly held that slaves were property, not citizens. Dred Scott, a slave owned in Missouri by John Emerson, was taken into Illinois, a free state. After Emerson died, John Sanford, a resident of New York, administered his estate.[39] Scott sued Sanford in federal court, basing jurisdiction on diversity of citizenship, and claimed that his residence in Illinois made him a free person.

The U.S. Supreme Court ruled against Scott in a decision that fills more than 200 pages in the United States Reports.

DRED SCOTT v. SANDFORD
60 U.S. (19 How.) 393 (1857)

Chief Justice TANEY delivered the opinion of the Court.

The question is simply this: Can a negro, whose ancestors were imported into this country, and sold as slaves, become a member of the political community formed and brought into existence by the Constitution of the United States, and as such become entitled to all the rights, and privileges, and immunities, guaranteed by that instrument to the citizen?

One of which rights is the privilege of suing in a court of the United States in the cases specified in the Constitution. The words "people of the United States" and "citizens" are synonymous terms, and mean the same thing. They both describe the political body who, according to our republican institutions, form the sovereignty, and who hold the power and conduct the Government through their representatives. They are what we familiarly call the "sovereign people," and every citizen is one of this people, and a constituent member of this sovereignty. The question before us is, whether the class of persons described in the plea in abatement compose a portion of this people, and are constituent members of this sovereignty? We think they are not, and that they are not included, and were not intended to be included, under the word "citizens" in the Constitution, and can therefore claim none of the rights and privileges which that instrument provides for and secures to citizens of the United States. On the contrary, they were at that time considered as a subordinate and

---

39. Sanford's name is misspelled in the United States Reports as "Sandford."

inferior class of beings, who had been subjugated by the dominant race, and, whether emancipated or not, had no rights or privileges but such as those who held the power and the Government might choose to grant them.

It is not the province of the court to decide upon the justice or injustice, the policy or impolicy, of these laws. The decision of that question belonged to the political or law-making power; to those who formed the sovereignty and framed the Constitution. The duty of the court is, to interpret the instrument they have framed, with the best lights we can obtain on the subject, and to administer it as we find it, according to its true intent and meaning when it was adopted.

In discussing this question, we must not confound the rights of citizenship which a State may confer within its own limits, and the rights of citizenship as a member of the Union. It does not by any means follow, because he has all the rights and privileges of a citizen of a State, that he must be a citizen of the United States. He may have all of the rights and privileges of the citizen of a State, and yet not be entitled to the rights and privileges of such courts, or rules that may have been laid down by common-law pleaders, can have no influence in the decision in this court. Because, under the Constitution and laws of the United States, the rules which govern the pleadings in its courts, in questions of juris-diction, stand on different principles and are regulated by different laws.

[T]he question to be decided is, whether the facts stated in the plea are sufficient to show that the plaintiff is not entitled to sue as a citizen in a court of the United States. This is certainly a very serious question, and one that now for the first time has been brought for decision before this court. But it is brought here by those who have a right to bring it, and it is our duty to meet it and decide it.

It will be observed, that the plea applies to that class of persons only whose ancestors were negroes of the African race, and imported into this country, and sold and held as slaves. The only matter in issue before the court, therefore, is, whether the descendants of such slaves, when they shall be emancipated, or who are born of parents who had become free before their birth, are citizens of a State, in the sense in which the word citizen is used in the Constitution of the United States. And this being the only matter in dispute on the pleadings, the court must be understood as speaking in this opinion of that class only, that is, of those persons who are the descendants of Africans who were imported into this country, and sold as slaves.

The situation of this population was altogether unlike that of the Indian race. The latter, it is true, formed no part of the colonial communities, and never amalgamated with them in social connections or in government. But although they were uncivilized, they were yet a free and independent people, associated together in nations or tribes, and governed by their own laws. Many of these political communities were situated in territories to which the white race claimed the ultimate right of dominion. But that claim was acknowledged to be subject to the right of the Indians to occupy it as long as they thought proper, and neither the English nor colonial Governments claimed or exercised any dominion over the tribe or nation by whom it was occupied, nor claimed the right to the possession of the territory, until the tribe or nation consented to cede it. These Indian Governments were regarded and treated as foreign Governments, as much so as if an ocean had separated the red man from the white; and their freedom has constantly been acknowledged, from the time of the first emigration to the English colonies to the present day, by the different

Governments which succeeded each other. Treaties have been negotiated with them, and their alliance sought for in war; and the people who compose these Indian political communities have always been treated as foreigners not living under our Government. It is true that the course of events has brought the Indian tribes within the limits of the United States under subjection to the white race; and it has been found necessary, for their sake as well as our own, to regard them as in a state of pupilage, and to legislate to a certain extent over them and the territory they occupy. But they may, without doubt, like the subjects of any other foreign Government, be naturalized by the authority of Congress, and become citizens of a State, and of the United States; and if an individual should leave his nation or tribe, and take up his abode among the white population, he would be entitled to all the rights and privileges which would belong to an emigrant from any other foreign people.

The language of the Declaration of Independence is equally conclusive: It . . . says: "We hold these truths to be self-evident: that all men are created equal; that they are endowed by their Creator with certain unalienable rights; that among them is life, liberty, and the pursuit of happiness; that to secure these rights, Governments are instituted, deriving their just powers from the consent of the governed." The general words above quoted would seem to embrace the whole human family, and if they were used in a similar instrument at this day would be so understood. But it is too clear for dispute, that the enslaved African race were not intended to be included, and formed no part of the people who framed and adopted this declaration; for if the language, as understood in that day, would embrace them, the conduct of the distinguished men who framed the Declaration of Independence would have been utterly and flagrantly inconsistent with the principles they asserted; and instead of the sympathy of mankind, to which they so confidently appealed, they would have deserved and received universal rebuke and reprobation.

The unhappy black race were separated from the white by indelible marks, and laws long before established, and were never thought of or spoken of except as property, and when the claims of the owner or the profit of the trader were supposed to need protection. And upon a full and careful consideration of the subject, the court is of opinion, that, upon the facts stated in the plea in abatement, Dred Scott was not a citizen of Missouri within the meaning of the Constitution of the United States, and not entitled as such to sue in its courts; and, consequently, that the Circuit Court had no jurisdiction of the case, and that the judgment on the plea in abatement is erroneous.

The act of Congress, upon which the plaintiff relies, declares that slavery and involuntary servitude, except as a punishment for crime, shall be forever prohibited in all that part of the territory ceded by France, under the name of Louisiana, which lies north of thirty-six degrees thirty minutes north latitude, and not included within the limits of Missouri. And the difficulty which meets us at the threshold of this part of the inquiry is, whether Congress was authorized to pass this law under any of the powers granted to it by the Constitution; for if the authority is not given by that instrument, it is the duty of this court to declare it void and inoperative, and incapable of conferring freedom upon any one who is held as a slave under the laws of any one of the States.

Now, as we have already said in an earlier part of this opinion, upon a different point, the right of property in a slave is distinctly and expressly affirmed in the Constitution. The right to traffic in it, like an ordinary article of merchandise and property, was guarantied to the citizens of the United States, in every State that might desire it, for twenty years. And the Government in express terms is pledged to protect it in all future time, if the slave escapes from his owner. This is done in plain words — too plain to be misunderstood. And no word can be found in the Constitution which gives Congress a greater power over slave property, or which entitles property of that kind to less protection than property of any other description. The only power conferred is the power coupled with the duty of guarding and protecting the owner in his rights.

Upon these considerations, it is the opinion of the court that the act of Congress which prohibited a citizen from holding and owning property of this kind in the territory of the United States north of the line therein mentioned, is not warranted by the Constitution, and is therefore void; and that neither Dred Scott himself, nor any of his family, were made free by being carried into this territory; even if they had been carried there by the owner, with the intention of becoming a permanent resident.

Although the Supreme Court undoubtedly thought that it was resolving the controversy over slavery in Dred Scott v. Sandford, the decision had exactly the opposite effect. The ruling became the focal point in the debate over slavery, and by striking down the Missouri Compromise, the decision helped to precipitate the Civil War.

Although Northern states generally did not allow slavery and often adopted laws to undermine that reprehensible institution, these states certainly did not provide equality for blacks before the Civil War. Laws in Northern states did not guarantee equal protection but, rather, institutionalized discrimination in diverse ways such as by prohibiting interracial marriage and requiring separation of the races in schools.[40]

THE POST-CIVIL WAR AMENDMENTS

As the Civil War was ending, in 1865, Congress enacted and the states ratified the Thirteenth Amendment, which prohibits slavery and involuntary servitude. Yet it was obvious that the Thirteenth Amendment would not by itself secure the rights of former slaves; Southern states systematically discriminated against blacks in every imaginable way. Congress therefore approved and the states ratified the Fourteenth Amendment in 1868.[41] Section 1 of the Fourteenth Amendment overrules the *Dred Scott* decision by declaring that all persons "born or naturalized in the United States . . . are citizens of the United States

---

40. *See* Roberts v. City of Boston, 59 Mass. (59 Cush.) 198 (1849) (upholding segregation in public education).

41. Initially, Southern states rejected the Fourteenth Amendment. These states approved the amendment only after Congress, in the Reconstruction Act, made ratification a condition for admission to the Union. By then, two Northern states rescinded their ratification. The Fourteenth Amendment was deemed ratified when three-fourths of the states — counting the Southern states that ratified under protest and the two states that had rescinded their ratification — had approved it. The history of the ratification of the Fourteenth Amendment is described in Erwin Chemerinsky, *Constitutional Law: Principles and Policies* (4th. ed. 2010) §1.3.

and of the State wherein they reside." Section 1 also guarantees that no state shall deprive any citizen of the privileges or immunities of citizenship, or deprive any person of life, liberty, or property without due process of law, or deny any person "equal protection of the laws."

2. Strict Scrutiny for Discrimination Based on Race and National Origin

It now is clearly established that racial classifications will be allowed only if the government can meet the heavy burden of demonstrating that the discrimination is necessary to achieve a compelling government purpose.[42] In other words, the government must show an extremely important reason for its action *and* it must demonstrate that the goal cannot be achieved through any less discriminatory alternative.[43] The Court has expressly declared that all racial classifications — whether disadvantaging or helping minorities — must meet strict scrutiny.[44]

Ironically, the Supreme Court first articulated the requirement for strict scrutiny for discrimination based on race and national origin in Korematsu v. United States, 323 U.S. 214 (1944) (presented below), which upheld the constitutionality of the relocation of Japanese Americans during World War II. The Court declared, "[A]ll legal restrictions which curtail the civil rights of a single racial group are immediately suspect. That is not to say that all such restrictions are unconstitutional. It is to say that courts must subject them to the most rigid scrutiny. Pressing public necessity may sometimes justify the existence of such restrictions; racial antagonism never can."

The Supreme Court has identified many reasons why strict scrutiny is appropriate for race and national origin classifications. These justifications are important both in understanding the Court's approach to racial discrimination and also in evaluating whether other types of discrimination warrant heightened scrutiny.

The Court long has recognized that the primary purpose of the Fourteenth Amendment was to protect African Americans; in fact, the initial Supreme Court decisions construing the Equal Protection Clause suggested that it could be used only to protect blacks.[45] The Court has emphasized that the long history of racial discrimination makes it likely that racial classifications will be based on stereotypes and prejudices. Chief Justice Warren Burger wrote, "A core purpose of the Fourteenth Amendment was to do away with all governmentally imposed discrimination based on race. Classifying persons according to their race is more likely to reflect racial prejudice than legitimate public concerns."[46]

Additionally, heightened scrutiny for government actions discriminating against racial and national origin minorities is justified because of the relative political powerlessness of these groups. In the famous *Carolene Products* footnote,

---

42. *See, e.g.,* Wygant v. Jackson Board of Education, 476 U.S. 267, 274 (1986); Palmore v. Sidoti, 466 U.S. 429, 432-433 (1984).

43. Wygant v. Jackson Board of Education, 476 U.S. 267, 280 n.6 (1986).

44. *See, e.g.,* Adarand Constructors, Inc. v. Pena, 515 U.S. 200 (1995) (federal affirmative action programs must meet strict scrutiny); Richmond v. J.A. Croson Co., 488 U.S. 469 (1989) (state and local affirmative action programs must meet strict scrutiny).

45. The *Slaughter-House Cases,* 83 U.S. 36, 81 (1872).

46. Palmore v. Sidoti, 466 U.S. 429, 432 (1984).

the Supreme Court indicated that "prejudice against discrete and insular minorities may be a special condition, which tends seriously to curtail the operation of those political processes ordinarily to be relied upon to protect minorities" and thus "may call for a correspondingly more searching judicial inquiry."[47] Prejudice and the history of discrimination make it less likely that racial and national origin minorities can protect themselves through the political process.

Also, the Court has emphasized that race is an immutable trait.[48] It is unfair to discriminate against people for a characteristic that is acquired at birth and cannot be changed.

For all of these reasons, it is firmly established that race and national origin classifications must meet the most exacting standard of judicial review. Such discrimination will be tolerated only if the government can prove that it is necessary to achieve a compelling government purpose.

3. Proving the Existence of a Race or National Origin Classification

There are two alternative ways of demonstrating the existence of a race or national origin classification. One is where the classification exists on the face of the law; that is, the text of the law draws a distinction among people based on race or national origin. Alternatively, if a law is facially neutral, a race or national origin classification might be proven by demonstrating discriminatory administration or discriminatory impact; however, the Supreme Court has held that this also requires proof of a discriminatory purpose. Subsection a looks at racial classifications on the face of the law, and subsection b considers facially neutral laws with a discriminatory impact or with discriminatory administration.

a. Race and National Origin Classifications on the Face of the Law

Facial race and national origin classifications exist when a law, in its very terms, draws a distinction among people based on those characteristics. There are three major types of such laws.

RACE-SPECIFIC CLASSIFICATIONS THAT DISADVANTAGE RACIAL MINORITIES

First, there are laws that expressly impose a burden or disadvantage on people because of their race or national origin. For example, in Strauder v. West Virginia, 100 U.S. (10 Otto) 303 (1879), the Supreme Court declared unconstitutional a West Virginia law that limited jury service to "white male persons who are twenty-one years of age and who are citizens of this State." The Court explained that the Fourteenth Amendment was "designed to assure to the colored race the enjoyment of all the civil rights that under the law are enjoyed

---

47. United States v. Carolene Products Co., 304 U.S. 144, 153 n.4 (1938), presented in Chapter 6.

48. See, e.g., Frontiero v. Richardson, 411 U.S. 677, 686 (1973); Lockhart v. McCree, 476 U.S. 162, 175 (1986).

by white persons, and to give to that race the protection of the general government, in that enjoyment, whenever it should be denied by the States." The Court
declared the law unconstitutional because it expressly "singled out" and disadvantaged blacks.

There is only one situation in which the Court expressly upheld under equal
protection racial classifications burdening minorities: the rulings affirming the
constitutionality of the evacuation of Japanese Americans during World War II.
During World War II, 110,000 Japanese Americans — adults and children, aliens
and citizens — were forcibly uprooted from their homes and placed in concentration camps. In some camps, they were housed in horse stalls and emprisoned
behind barbed wire.[49] The government's purported justification was national
security — a fear that Japanese Americans on the West Coast might aid an invading Japanese army or commit acts of espionage and sabotage. No evidence of a
specific threat was required to evacuate and intern a person. Race alone was used
to determine who would be uprooted and incarcerated and who would remain
free.

As you read Korematsu v. United States, consider whether the Court's
decision was appropriate judicial deference to the military during wartime or
unjustified judicial abdication in the face of racial prejudice and human rights
violations.

KOREMATSU v. UNITED STATES
323 U.S. 214 (1944)

Justice BLACK delivered the opinion of the Court.

The petitioner, an American citizen of Japanese descent, was convicted in a
federal district court for remaining in San Leandro, California, a "Military
Area," contrary to Civilian Exclusion Order No. 34 of the Commanding General
of the Western Command, U.S. Army, which directed that after May 9, 1942, all
persons of Japanese ancestry should be excluded from that area. No question
was raised as to petitioner's loyalty to the United States.

It should be noted, to begin with, that all legal restrictions which curtail the
civil rights of a single racial group are immediately suspect. That is not to say that
all such restrictions are unconstitutional. It is to say that courts must subject
them to the most rigid scrutiny. Pressing public necessity may sometimes justify
the existence of such restrictions; racial antagonism never can.

One of the series of orders and proclamations, a curfew order, which like the
exclusion order here was promulgated pursuant to Executive Order 9066, subjected all persons of Japanese ancestry in prescribed West Coast military areas to
remain in their residences from 8 p.m. to 6 a.m. As is the case with the exclusion
order here, that prior curfew order was designed as a "protection against espionage and against sabotage." In Kiyoshi Hirabayashi v. United States (1943), we
sustained a conviction obtained for violation of the curfew order. The Hirabayashi conviction and this one thus rest on the same 1942 Congressional Act and the

---

49. William Manchester, *The Glory and the Dream* 300-301 (1974) (describing the conditions in
internment camps).

same basic executive and military orders, all of which orders were aimed at the twin dangers of espionage and sabotage.

In the light of the principles we announced in the *Hirabayashi* case, we are unable to conclude that it was beyond the war power of Congress and the Executive to exclude those of Japanese ancestry from the West Coast war area at the time they did. True, exclusion from the area in which one's home is located is a far greater deprivation than constant confinement to the home from 8 p.m. to 6 a.m. Nothing short of apprehension by the proper military authorities of the gravest imminent danger to the public safety can constitutionally justify either. But exclusion from a threatened area, no less than curfew, has a definite and close relationship to the prevention of espionage and sabotage. The military authorities, charged with the primary responsibility of defending our shores, concluded that curfew provided inadequate protection and ordered exclusion. They did so, as pointed out in our *Hirabayashi* opinion, in accordance with Congressional authority to the military to say who should, and who should not, remain in the threatened areas.

Like curfew, exclusion of those of Japanese origin was deemed necessary because of the presence of an unascertained number of disloyal members of the group, most of whom we have no doubt were loyal to this country. It was because we could not reject the finding of the military authorities that it was impossible to bring about an immediate segregation of the disloyal from the loyal that we sustained the validity of the curfew order as applying to the whole group. In the instant case, temporary exclusion of the entire group was rested by the military on the same ground. The judgment that exclusion of the whole group was for the same reason a military imperative answers the contention that the exclusion was in the nature of group punishment based on antagonism to those of Japanese origin. That there were members of the group who retained loyalties to Japan has been confirmed by investigations made subsequent to the exclusion. Approximately five thousand American citizens of Japanese ancestry refused to swear unqualified allegiance to the United States and to renounce allegiance to the Japanese Emperor, and several thousand evacuees requested repatriation to Japan.

We uphold the exclusion order as of the time it was made and when the petitioner violated it. In doing so, we are not unmindful of the hardships imposed by it upon a large group of American citizens. But hardships are part of war, and war is an aggregation of hardships. All citizens alike, both in and out of uniform, feel the impact of war in greater or lesser measure. Citizenship has its responsibilities as well as its privileges, and in time of war the burden is always heavier. Compulsory exclusion of large groups of citizens from their homes, except under circumstances of direst emergency and peril, is inconsistent with our basic governmental institutions. But when under conditions of modern warfare our shores are threatened by hostile forces, the power to protect must be commensurate with the threatened danger.

To cast this case into outlines of racial prejudice, without reference to the real military dangers which were presented, merely confuses the issue. Korematsu was not excluded from the Military Area because of hostility to him or his race. He was excluded because we are at war with the Japanese Empire, because the properly constituted military authorities feared an invasion of our West Coast and felt constrained to take proper security measures, because they decided that the military urgency of the situation demanded that all citizens of Japanese ancestry be segregated from the West Coast temporarily, and finally, because Congress, reposing its confidence in this time of war in our military leaders — as inevitably it must — determined that they should have the power to do just this. There was evidence of disloyalty on the part of some, the military authorities considered that the need for action was great, and time was short. We cannot — by availing ourselves of the calm perspective of hindsight — now say that at that time these actions were unjustified.

Justice MURPHY, dissenting.

This exclusion of "all persons of Japanese ancestry, both alien and non-alien," from the Pacific Coast area on a plea of military necessity in the absence of martial law ought not to be approved. Such exclusion goes over "the very brink of constitutional power" and falls into the ugly abyss of racism.

In dealing with matters relating to the prosecution and progress of a war, we must accord great respect and consideration to the judgments of the military authorities who are on the scene and who have full knowledge of the military facts. The scope of their discretion must, as a matter of necessity and common sense, be wide. And their judgments ought not to be overruled lightly by those whose training and duties ill-equip them to deal intelligently with matters so vital to the physical security of the nation.

At the same time, however, it is essential that there be definite limits to military discretion, especially where martial law has not been declared. Individuals must not be left impoverished of their constitutional rights on a plea of military necessity that has neither substance nor support. Thus, like other claims conflicting with the asserted constitutional rights of the individual, the military claim must subject itself to the judicial process of having its reasonableness determined and its conflicts with other interests reconciled. "What are the allowable limits of military discretion, and whether or not they have been overstepped in a particular case, are judicial questions."

The judicial test of whether the Government, on a plea of military necessity, can validly deprive an individual of any of his constitutional rights is whether the deprivation is reasonably related to a public danger that is so "immediate, imminent, and impending" as not to admit of delay and not to permit the intervention of ordinary constitutional processes to alleviate the danger. Civilian Exclusion Order No. 34, banishing from a prescribed area of the Pacific Coast "all persons of Japanese ancestry, both alien and non-alien," clearly does not meet that test. Being an obvious racial discrimination, the order deprives all those within its scope of the equal protection of the laws as guaranteed by the Fifth Amendment. It further deprives these individuals of their constitutional rights to live and work where they will, to establish a home where they choose and to move about freely. In excommunicating them without benefit of hearings, this order also deprives them of all their constitutional rights to procedural due process. Yet no reasonable relation to an "immediate, imminent, and impending" public danger is evident to support this racial restriction which is one of the most sweeping and complete deprivations of constitutional rights in the history of this nation in the absence of martial law. The exclusion order necessarily must rely for its reasonableness upon the assumption that all persons of Japanese ancestry may have a dangerous tendency to commit sabotage and espionage and to aid our Japanese enemy in other ways. It is difficult to believe that reason, logic or experience could be marshalled in support of such an assumption.

That this forced exclusion was the result in good measure of this erroneous assumption of racial guilt rather than bona fide military necessity is evidenced by the Commanding General's Final Report on the evacuation from the Pacific Coast area. In it he refers to all individuals of Japanese descent as "subversive," as belonging to "an enemy race" whose "racial strains are undiluted," and as constituting "over 112,000 potential enemies . . . at large today" along the Pacific Coast. In support of this blanket condemnation of all persons of Japanese descent, however, no reliable evidence is cited to show that such individuals were generally disloyal, or had generally so conducted themselves in this area as to constitute a special menace to defense installations or war industries, or had otherwise by their behavior furnished reasonable ground for their exclusion as a group.

The main reasons relied upon by those responsible for the forced evacuation, therefore, do not prove a reasonable relation between the group characteristics of Japanese Americans and the dangers of invasion, sabotage and espionage. The reasons appear, instead, to be largely an accumulation of much of the misinformation, half-truths and insinuations that for years have been directed against Japanese Americans by people with racial and economic prejudices — the same people who have been among the foremost advocates of the evacuation. A military judgment based upon such racial and sociological considerations is not entitled to the great weight ordinarily given the judgments based upon strictly military considerations. Especially is this so when every charge relative to race, religion, culture, geographical location, and legal and economic status has been substantially discredited by independent studies made by experts in these matters.

The military necessity which is essential to the validity of the evacuation order thus resolves itself into a few intimations that certain individuals actively aided the enemy, from which it is inferred that the entire group of Japanese Americans could not be trusted to be or remain loyal to the United States. Moreover, this inference, which is at the very heart of the evacuation orders, has been used in support of the abhorrent and despicable treatment of minority groups by the dictatorial tyrannies which this nation is now pledged to destroy. To give constitutional sanction to that inference in this case, however well-intentioned may have been the military command on the Pacific Coast, is to adopt one of the cruelest of the rationales used by our enemies to destroy the dignity of the individual and to encourage and open the door to discriminatory actions against other minority groups in the passions of tomorrow. No adequate reason is given for the failure to treat these Japanese Americans on an individual basis by holding investigations and hearings to separate the loyal from the disloyal, as was done in the case of persons of German and Italian ancestry.

Moreover, there was no adequate proof that the Federal Bureau of Investigation and the military and naval intelligence services did not have the espionage and sabotage situation well in hand during this long period. Nor is there any denial of the fact that not one person of Japanese ancestry was accused or convicted of espionage or sabotage after Pearl Harbor while they were still free. It seems incredible that under these circumstances it would have been impossible to hold loyalty hearings for the mere 112,000 persons involved — or at least for the

70,000 American citizens—especially when a large part of this number represented children and elderly men and women. Any inconvenience that may have accompanied an attempt to conform to procedural due process cannot be said to justify violations of constitutional rights of individuals.

During a period of six months, the 112 alien tribunals or hearing boards set up by the British Government shortly after the outbreak of the present war summoned and examined approximately 74,000 German and Austrian aliens. These tribunals determined whether each individual enemy alien was a real enemy of the Allies or only a "friendly enemy." About 64,000 were freed from internment and from any special restrictions, and only 2,000 were interned. Kempner, "The Enemy Alien Problem in the Present War," 34 Amer. Journ. of Int. Law 443, 444-46; House Report No. 2124 (77th Cong., 2d Sess.), 280-1.

I dissent, therefore, from this legalization of racism. Racial discrimination in any form and in any degree has no justifiable part whatever in our democratic way of life. It is unattractive in any setting but it is utterly revolting among a free people who have embraced the principles set forth in the Constitution of the United States. All residents of this nation are kin in some way by blood or culture to a foreign land. Yet they are primarily and necessarily a part of the new and distinct civilization of the United States. They must accordingly be treated at all times as the heirs of the American experiment and as entitled to all the rights and freedoms guaranteed by the Constitution.

Mr. Justice JACKSON, dissenting.

Korematsu was born on our soil, of parents born in Japan. The Constitution makes him a citizen of the United States by nativity and a citizen of California by residence. No claim is made that he is not loyal to this country. There is no suggestion that apart from the matter involved here he is not law-abiding and well disposed. Korematsu, however, has been convicted of an act not commonly a crime. It consists merely of being present in the state whereof he is a citizen, near the place where he was born, and where all his life he has lived.

Even more unusual is the series of military orders which made this conduct a crime. They forbid such a one to remain, and they also forbid him to leave. They were so drawn that the only way Korematsu could avoid violation was to give himself up to the military authority. This meant submission to custody, examination, and transportation out of the territory, to be followed by indeterminate confinement in detention camps.

A citizen's presence in the locality, however, was made a crime only if his parents were of Japanese birth. Had Korematsu been one of four individuals—the others being, say, a German alien enemy, an Italian alien enemy, and a citizen of American-born ancestors, convicted of treason but out on parole—only Korematsu's presence would have violated the order. The difference between their innocence and his crime would result, not from anything he did, said, or thought, different than they, but only in that he was born of different racial stock.

My duties as a justice as I see them do not require me to make a military judgment as to whether General DeWitt's evacuation and detention program was a reasonable military necessity. I do not suggest that the courts should have attempted to interfere with the Army in carrying out its task. But I do not think they may be asked to execute a military expedient that has no place in law under the Constitution. I would reverse the judgment and discharge the prisoner.

In Ex parte Endo, 323 U.S. 283 (1944), decided the same day as *Korematsu,* the Supreme Court held that the continued detention of Japanese Americans was unwarranted.[50] The Court's holding was narrow, simply concluding that the executive orders that provided the authority for the evacuation of Japanese Americans did not expressly authorize the continued detention of loyal Japanese Americans. The Court did observe that "[a] citizen who is concededly loyal presents no problem of espionage or sabotage. Loyalty is a matter of the heart and mind, not of race, creed, or color."[51] Yet the Court never declared the evacuation and internment of Japanese Americans unconstitutional.

RACIAL CLASSIFICATIONS BURDENING BOTH WHITES AND MINORITIES

A second type of racial classification that can exist on the face of the law is government action that burdens both whites and minorities. For example, antimiscegenation laws — statutes that prohibit interracial cohabitation and marriage — apply to both whites and blacks. In fact, the Supreme Court initially upheld such laws on the ground that they did not discriminate; the Court saw them as treating blacks and whites equally. In Pace v. Alabama, 106 U.S. (16 Otto) 583 (1882), the Court upheld an Alabama law that provided for harsher penalties for adultery and fornication if the couple were composed of a white and a black than if the couple were both of the same race.

Subsequently, however, the Court recognized that such racial classifications are impermissible under the Equal Protection Clause because they are based on assumptions of the inferiority of blacks to whites. In McLaughlin v. Florida, 379 U.S. 184 (1964), the Supreme Court declared unconstitutional a Florida law that prohibited the habitual occupation of a room at night by unmarried interracial couples. The Court indicated that *Pace* "represents a limited view of the Equal Protection Clause which has not withstood analysis in the subsequent decisions of this Court." The Court emphasized that the state offered no acceptable justification for why a race-neutral law could not adequately serve its purposes of punishing premarital sexual relations.

In Loving v. Virginia, the Supreme Court considered the constitutionality of a state's miscegenation statute that made it a crime for a white person to marry outside the Caucasian race.[52]

---

50. For an excellent discussion of this case, *see* Patrick O. Gutridge, *Remember* Endo *?,* 116 Harv. L. Rev. 1933 (2003).

51. *Id.* at 302.

52. The Court in *Loving* also based its decision on the fundamental right to marry. This portion of the opinion is presented in Chapter 8.

LOVING v. VIRGINIA
388 U.S. 1 (1967)

Chief Justice WARREN delivered the opinion of the Court.

This case presents a constitutional question never addressed by this Court: whether a statutory scheme adopted by the State of Virginia to prevent marriages between persons solely on the basis of racial classifications violates the Equal Protection and Due Process Clauses of the Fourteenth Amendment. For reasons which seem to us to reflect the central meaning of those constitutional commands, we conclude that these statutes cannot stand consistently with the Fourteenth Amendment.

In June 1958, two residents of Virginia, Mildred Jeter, a Negro woman, and Richard Loving, a white man, were married in the District of Columbia pursuant to its laws. Shortly after their marriage, the Lovings returned to Virginia and established their marital abode in Caroline County. At the October Term, 1958, of the Circuit Court of Caroline County, a grand jury issued an indictment charging the Lovings with violating Virginia's ban on interracial marriages. On January 6, 1959, the Lovings pleaded guilty to the charge and were sentenced to one year in jail; however, the trial judge suspended the sentence for a period of 25 years on the condition that the Lovings leave the State and not return to Virginia together for 25 years. He stated in an opinion that:

> Almighty God created the races white, black, yellow, malay and red, and he placed them on separate continents. And but for the interference with his arrangement there would be no cause for such marriages. The fact that he separated the races shows that he did not intend for the races to mix.

After their convictions, the Lovings took up residence in the District of Columbia. On November 6, 1963, they filed a motion in the state trial court to vacate the judgment and set aside the sentence on the ground that the statutes which they had violated were repugnant to the Fourteenth Amendment. The Supreme Court of Appeals upheld the constitutionality of the anti-miscegenation statutes and, after modifying the sentence, affirmed the convictions.

Virginia is now one of 16 States which prohibit and punish marriages on the basis of racial classifications. Penalties for miscegenation arose as an incident to slavery and have been common in Virginia since the colonial period. The present statutory scheme dates from the adoption of the Racial Integrity Act of 1924, passed during the period of extreme nativism which followed the end of the First World War. The central features of this Act, and current Virginia law, are the absolute prohibition of a "white person" marrying other than another "white person," a prohibition against issuing marriage licenses until the issuing official is satisfied that the applicants' statements as to their race are correct, certificates of "racial composition" to be kept by both local and state registrars, and the carrying forward of earlier prohibitions against racial intermarriage. Over the past 15 years, 14 States have repealed laws outlawing interracial marriages: Arizona, California, Colorado, Idaho, Indiana, Maryland, Montana, Nebraska, Nevada, North Dakota, Oregon, South Dakota, Utah, and Wyoming.

In upholding the constitutionality of these provisions in the decision below, the Supreme Court of Appeals of Virginia referred to its 1955 decision in Naim v. Naim, as stating the reasons supporting the validity of these laws. In *Naim*, the state court concluded that the State's legitimate purposes were "to preserve the racial integrity of its citizens," and to prevent "the corruption of blood," "a mongrel breed of citizens," and "the obliteration of racial pride," obviously an endorsement of the doctrine of White Supremacy. The court also reasoned that marriage has traditionally been subject to state regulation without federal intervention, and, consequently, the regulation of marriage should be left to exclusive state control by the Tenth Amendment.

[T]he State argues that the meaning of the Equal Protection Clause, as illuminated by the statements of the framers, is only that state penal laws containing an interracial element as part of the definition of the offense must apply equally to whites and Negroes in the sense that members of each race are punished to the same degree. Thus, the State contends that, because its miscegenation statutes punish equally both the white and the Negro participants in an interracial marriage, these statutes, despite their reliance on racial classifications do not constitute an invidious discrimination based upon race.

[W]e reject the notion that the mere "equal application" of a statute containing racial classifications is enough to remove the classifications from the Fourteenth Amendment's proscription of all invidious racial discriminations.

There can be no question but that Virginia's miscegenation statutes rest solely upon distinctions drawn according to race. The statutes proscribe generally accepted conduct if engaged in by members of different races. Over the years, this Court has consistently repudiated "[d]istinctions between citizens solely because of their ancestry" as being "odious to a free people whose institutions are founded upon the doctrine of equality." At the very least, the Equal Protection Clause demands that racial classifications, especially suspect in criminal statutes, be subjected, to the "most rigid scrutiny," Korematsu v. United States (1944), and, if they are ever to be upheld, they must be shown to be necessary to the accomplishment of some permissible state objective, independent of the racial discrimination which it was the object of the Fourteenth Amendment to eliminate.

There is patently no legitimate overriding purpose independent of invidious racial discrimination which justifies this classification. The fact that Virginia prohibits only interracial marriages involving white persons demonstrates that the racial classifications must stand on their own justification, as measures designed to maintain White Supremacy. We have consistently denied the constitutionality of measures which restrict the rights of citizens on account of race. There can be no doubt that restricting the freedom to marry solely because of racial classifications violates the central meaning of the Equal Protection Clause.

The following case, in which a court used racial considerations to change a child custody order, also illustrates the "facial" use of race in a manner that could equally disadvantage whites or racial minorities.

PALMORE v. SIDOTI
466 U.S. 429 (1984)

Chief Justice BURGER delivered the opinion of the Court.

We granted certiorari to review a judgment of a state court divesting a natural mother of the custody of her infant child because of her remarriage to a person of a different race.

When petitioner Linda Sidoti Palmore and respondent Anthony J. Sidoti, both Caucasians, were divorced in May 1980 in Florida, the mother was awarded custody of their 3-year-old daughter. In September 1981 the father sought custody of the child by filing a petition to modify the prior judgment because of changed conditions. The change was that the child's mother was then cohabiting with a Negro, Clarence Palmore, Jr., whom she married two months later. Additionally, the father made several allegations of instances in which the mother had not properly cared for the child.

After hearing testimony from both parties and considering a court counselor's investigative report, the court noted that the father had made allegations about the child's care, but the court made no findings with respect to these allegations. On the contrary, the court made a finding that "there is no issue as to either party's devotion to the child, adequacy of housing facilities, or respectability of the new spouse of either parent."

[T]he court then noted the counselor's recommendation for a change in custody because "[t]he wife [petitioner] has chosen for herself and for her child, a life-style unacceptable to the father and to society. . . . The child . . . is, or at school age will be, subject to environmental pressures not of choice." The court then concluded that the best interests of the child would be served by awarding custody to the father. The court's rationale is contained in the following:

> The father's evident resentment of the mother's choice of a black partner is not sufficient to wrest custody from the mother. It is of some significance, however, that the mother did see fit to bring a man into her home and carry on a sexual relationship with him without being married to him. Such action tended to place gratification of her own desires ahead of her concern for the child's future welfare. This Court feels that despite the strides that have been made in bettering relations between the races in this country, it is inevitable that Melanie will, if allowed to remain in her present situation and attains school age and thus more vulnerable to peer pressures, suffer from the social stigmatization that is sure to come.

The judgment of a state court determining or reviewing a child custody decision is not ordinarily a likely candidate for review by this Court. However, the court's opinion, after stating that the "father's evident resentment of the mother's choice of a black partner is not sufficient" to deprive her of custody, then turns to what it regarded as the damaging impact on the child from remaining in a racially mixed household. This raises important federal concerns arising from the Constitution's commitment to eradicating discrimination based on race.

It would ignore reality to suggest that racial and ethnic prejudices do not exist or that all manifestations of those prejudices have been eliminated. There is a risk that a child living with a stepparent of a different race may be subject to a variety of pressures and stresses not present if the child were living with parents of the same racial or ethnic origin.

The question, however, is whether the reality of private biases and the possible injury they might inflict are permissible considerations for removal of an infant child from the custody of its natural mother. We have little difficulty concluding that they are not. The Constitution cannot control such prejudices but neither can it tolerate them. Private biases may be outside the reach of the law, but the law cannot, directly or indirectly, give them effect. "Public officials sworn to uphold the Constitution may not avoid a constitutional duty by bowing to the hypothetical effects of private racial prejudice that they assume to be both widely and deeply held." The effects of racial prejudice, however real, cannot justify a racial classification removing an infant child from the custody of its natural mother found to be an appropriate person to have such custody.

LAWS REQUIRING SEPARATION OF THE RACES

Statutes requiring separation of the races are a third type of racial classification that can exist on the face of the law. During the Reconstruction era that followed the Civil War, the South was under military rule and Congress enacted many laws to protect civil rights.[53] Substantial progress was made in protecting the rights of the former slaves.

By the 1880s, Reconstruction was over. In part, it ended through a compromise in 1877 to resolve a disputed presidential election. Although it appeared that Democrat Samuel Tilden won a majority of the popular vote, Democrats in Congress agreed to the election of Republican Rutherford Hayes in exchange for an end of military rule in the South. Also, in 1883, in the *Civil Rights Cases*, 109 U.S. 3 (1883), the Supreme Court declared unconstitutional the Civil Rights Act of 1875, which prohibited discrimination by places of public accommodations such as inns, theaters, and places of public amusement.[54] The Supreme Court broadly held that the Fourteenth Amendment only applies to government action, not to private conduct, and that therefore Congress acting under §5 of the Fourteenth Amendment can regulate only government actions.

As Reconstruction ended, many states, especially in the South, adopted laws that discriminated against blacks. Private violence against blacks increased dramatically — more than 3,000 lynchings were reported in the last two decades of the nineteenth century.[55] Every Southern state enacted statutes that required

---

53. For example, the Civil Rights Act of 1866 provided that blacks and whites should have the same rights to make and enforce contracts, sue, give evidence, and acquire property. These provisions now are codified at 42 U.S.C. §§1981 and 1982. In 1871, Congress adopted the Ku Klux Klan Act, which provided criminal penalties and civil liability for any person acting under color of state law who violates the Constitution or laws of the United States or who engages in a conspiracy to violate civil rights. These provisions are now codified as 18 U.S.C. §§241 and 242 (criminal provisions), 42 U.S.C. §1983 (civil liability), and 42 U.S.C. §1985 (civil liability for conspiracies). In 1875, Congress passed a law prohibiting discrimination by places of public accommodations such as inns, theaters, and places of public amusement. This law was declared unconstitutional in the *Civil Rights Cases*, 109 U.S. 3 (1883). This case is presented in Chapter 5.

54. This is presented in Chapter 5.

55. Daniel Farber, William N. Eskridge, Jr., & Philip P. Frickey, *Constitutional Law: Themes for the Constitution's Third Century* 37 (1993).

separation of the races in virtually every aspect of life. Called "Jim Crow laws," these statutes created a system of apartheid in which the government mandated segregation in public accommodations, transportation, schools, and almost everything else.[56]

PLESSY v. FERGUSON

Plessy v. Ferguson is the key case in which the Supreme Court considered and upheld laws requiring segregation of the races.

PLESSY v. FERGUSON
163 U.S. 537 (1896)

Justice BROWN delivered the opinion of the Court.

This case turns upon the constitutionality of an act of the general assembly of the state of Louisiana, passed in 1890, providing for separate railway carriages for the white and colored races. The first section of the statute enacts "that all railway companies carrying passengers in their coaches in this state, shall provide equal but separate accommodations for the white, and colored races, by providing two or more passenger coaches for each passenger train, or by dividing the passenger coaches by a partition so as to secure separate accommodations: provided, that this section shall not be construed to apply to street railroads. No person or persons shall be permitted to occupy seats in coaches, other than the ones assigned to them, on account of the race they belong to."

The petition for the writ of prohibition averred that petitioner was seven-eighths Caucasian and one-eighth African blood; that the mixture of colored blood was not discernible in him; and that he was entitled to every right, privilege, and immunity secured to citizens of the United States of the white race; and that, upon such theory, he took possession of a vacant seat in a coach where passengers of the white race were accommodated, and was ordered by the conductor to vacate said coach, and take a seat in another, assigned to persons of the colored race, and, having refused to comply with such demand, he was forcibly ejected, with the aid of a police officer, and imprisoned in the parish jail to answer a charge of having violated the above act.

The object of the [Fourteenth] amendment was undoubtedly to enforce the absolute equality of the two races before the law, but, in the nature of things, it could not have been intended to abolish distinctions based upon color, or to enforce social, as distinguished from political, equality, or a commingling of the two races upon terms unsatisfactory to either. Laws permitting, and even requiring, their separation, in places where they are liable to be brought into contact, do not necessarily imply the inferiority of either race to the other, and have been generally, if not universally, recognized as within the competency of the state legislatures in the exercise of their police power. The most common instance of this is connected with the establishment of separate schools for white and colored children, which have been held to be a valid exercise of the legislative

---

56. *See* C. Vann Woodward, *The Strange Career of Jim Crow* (1957).

power even by courts of states where the political rights of the colored race have been longest and most earnestly enforced. Laws forbidding the intermarriage of the two races may be said in a technical sense to interfere with the freedom of contract, and yet have been universally recognized as within the police power of the state.

We consider the underlying fallacy of the plaintiff's argument to consist in the assumption that the enforced separation of the two races stamps the colored race with a badge of inferiority. If this be so, it is not by reason of anything found in the act, but solely because the colored race chooses to put that construction upon it. The argument necessarily assumes that if, as has been more than once the case, and is not unlikely to be so again, the colored race should become the dominant power in the state legislature, and should enact a law in precisely similar terms, it would thereby relegate the white race to an inferior position. We imagine that the white race, at least, would not acquiesce in this assumption. The argument also assumes that social prejudices may be overcome by legislation, and that equal rights cannot be secured to the negro except by an enforced commingling of the two races. We cannot accept this proposition.

If the two races are to meet upon terms of social equality, it must be the result of natural affinities, a mutual appreciation of each other's merits, and a voluntary consent of individuals. Legislation is powerless to eradicate racial instincts, or to abolish distinctions based upon physical differences, and the attempt to do so can only result in accentuating the difficulties of the present situation. If the civil and political rights of both races be equal, one cannot be inferior to the other civilly or politically. If one race be inferior to the other socially, the constitution of the United States cannot put them upon the same plane.

Justice HARLAN dissenting.

In respect of civil rights, common to all citizens, the constitution of the United States does not, I think, permit any public authority to know the race of those entitled to be protected in the enjoyment of such rights. Every true man has pride of race, and under appropriate circumstances, when the rights of others, his equals before the law, are not to be affected, it is his privilege to express such pride and to take such action based upon it as to him seems proper. But I deny that any legislative body or judicial tribunal may have regard to the race of citizens when the civil rights of those citizens are involved. Indeed, such legislation as that here in question is inconsistent not only with that equality of rights which pertains to citizenship, national and state, but with the personal liberty enjoyed by every one within the United States.

It was said in argument that the statute of Louisiana does not discriminate against either race, but prescribes a rule applicable alike to white and colored citizens. But this argument does not meet the difficulty. Every one knows that the statute in question had its origin in the purpose, not so much to exclude white persons from railroad cars occupied by blacks, as to exclude colored people from coaches occupied by or assigned to white persons. Railroad corporations of Louisiana did not make discrimination among whites in the matter of accommodation for travelers. The thing to accomplish was, under the guise of giving equal accommodation for whites and blacks, to compel the latter to keep to themselves while traveling in railroad passenger coaches. No one would be so wanting in candor as to assert the contrary. If a white man and a black man choose to occupy the same public conveyance on a public highway, it is their right to do so; and no government, proceeding alone on grounds of race, can prevent it without infringing the personal liberty of each.

The white race deems itself to be the dominant race in this country. And so it is, in prestige, in achievements, in education, in wealth, and in power. So, I doubt not, it will continue to be for all time, if it remains true to its great heritage, and holds fast to the principles of constitutional liberty. But in view of the constitution, in the eye of the law, there is in this country no superior, dominant, ruling class of citizens. There is no caste here. Our constitution is color-blind, and neither knows nor tolerates classes among citizens. In respect of civil rights, all citizens are equal before the law. The humblest is the peer of the most powerful. The law regards man as man, and takes no account of his surroundings or of his color when his civil rights as guaranteed by the supreme law of the land are involved. It is therefore to be regretted that this high tribunal, the final expositor of the fundamental law of the land, has reached the conclusion that it is competent for a state to regulate the enjoyment by citizens of their civil rights solely upon the basis of race.

In my opinion, the judgment this day rendered will, in time, prove to be quite as pernicious as the decision made by this tribunal in the *Dred Scott case*. The arbitrary separation of citizens, on the basis of race, while they are on a public highway, is a badge of servitude wholly inconsistent with the civil freedom and the equality before the law established by the constitution. It cannot be justified upon any legal grounds. We boast of the freedom enjoyed by our people above all other peoples. But it is difficult to reconcile that boast with a state of the law which, practically, puts the brand of servitude and degradation upon a large class of our fellow-citizens, our equals before the law. The thin disguise of "equal" accommodations for passengers in railroad coaches will not mislead any one, nor atone for the wrong this day done. For the reason stated, I am constrained to withhold my assent from the opinion and judgment of the majority.

"Separate but equal" thus became the law of the land even though separate was anything but equal. In several subsequent cases, the Court reaffirmed Plessy v. Ferguson. "Separate but equal" was expressly approved in the realm of education. In Cumming v. Richmond County Board of Education, 175 U.S. 528 (1899), the Court upheld the government's operation of a high school open only for white students while none was available for blacks. The Court emphasized that local authorities were to be allowed great discretion in allocating funds between blacks and whites and that "any interference on the part of Federal authority with the management of such schools cannot be justified except in the case of a clear and unmistakable disregard of rights secured by the supreme law of the land."

In Berea College v. Kentucky, 211 U.S. 45 (1908), the Supreme Court affirmed the conviction of a private college that had violated a Kentucky law that required the separation of the races in education. Similarly, in Gong Lum v. Rice, 275 U.S. 78 (1927), the Supreme Court concluded that Mississippi could exclude a child of Chinese ancestry from attending schools reserved for whites. The Court said that the law was settled that racial segregation was permissible and that it did not "think that the question is any different or that any different result can be reached . . . where the issue is as between white pupils and the pupils of the yellow races."

THE INITIAL ATTACK ON "SEPARATE BUT EQUAL"

In several cases between 1938 and 1954, the Supreme Court found that states denied equal protection by failing to provide educational opportunities for blacks that were available to whites. Interestingly, most of these decisions involved the failure of states to provide equal opportunity for the legal education of blacks. The Court did not question the doctrine of separate but equal — instead it concluded that the lack of opportunities for blacks was unconstitutional.

In Missouri ex rel. Gaines v. Canada, 305 U.S. 337 (1938), the Supreme Court held that it was unconstitutional for Missouri to refuse to admit blacks to its law school, but instead to pay for blacks to attend out-of-state law schools. The Court explained that the "basic consideration is not as to what sort of opportunities other States provide, . . . but as to what opportunities Missouri itself furnishes to white students and denies to negroes solely upon the ground of color." In response, Missouri did not admit blacks to its law school, but instead created a new law school for blacks.

In Sweatt v. Painter, 339 U.S. 629 (1950), the Supreme Court for the first time ordered that a white university admit a black student. The University of Texas Law School had denied Heman Sweatt admission on the ground that he could attend the recently created Prairie View Law School. Although the Court was urged to reconsider Plessy v. Ferguson, it refused and instead found that the schools obviously were not equal. The University of Texas Law School had 16 full-time faculty members and substantial facilities. Prairie View Law School opened in 1947 with no full-time faculty and no library, though by the time the Court decided the case there were five full-time professors and a small library. The Court concluded, "[W]e cannot find substantial equality in the educational opportunities offered white and Negro law students by the State. . . . It is difficult to believe that one who had a free choice between these law schools would consider the question close."

In McLaurin v. Oklahoma State Regents, 339 U.S. 637 (1950), the Supreme Court held that once blacks were admitted to a previously all-white school, the university could not force them to sit in segregated areas of classrooms, libraries, and cafeterias. The Court ruled that such segregation hindered the student's "ability to study, to engage in discussions and exchange views with other students, and, in general, to learn his profession."

The reality, of course, was that the laws required racial separation but not equality. Only 1 of 41 law schools in the South was for blacks, and only 1 of 30 medical schools and none of 36 engineering schools admitted blacks.[57] Those facilities that existed for blacks were inferior by every measure.

---

57. Richard Kluger, *Simple Justice: The History of Brown v. Board of Education and Black America's Struggle for Equality* 257 (1977).

BROWN v. BOARD OF EDUCATION

In the 1952-1953 term, the Supreme Court granted review in five cases that challenged the doctrine of separate but equal in the context of elementary and high school education.[58] At the time, 17 states and the District of Columbia segregated public schools.[59] The school systems challenged in the five cases before the Supreme Court involved schools that were totally unequal. For example, one of the cases was a challenge to South Carolina's educational system.[60] The white schools had 1 teacher for every 28 pupils; the black schools had 1 teacher for every 47 students. The white schools were brick and stucco; the black schools were made of rotting wood. The white schools had indoor plumbing; the black schools had outhouses.[61]

The five cases were argued together during the 1952-1953 term. The justices could not agree as to a decision, and the cases were set for reargument for the following year. According to Justice William Douglas's autobiography, had the Supreme Court ruled in 1953, the decision would have been five to four to affirm Plessy v. Ferguson and the separate but equal doctrine:

> When the cases had been argued in December of 1952, only four of us — Minton, Burton, Black, and myself — felt that segregation was unconstitutional. . . . It was clear that if a decision had been reached in the 1952 Term, we would have had five saying that separate but equal schools were constitutional, that separate but unequal schools were not constitutional, and that the remedy was to give the states time to make the two systems of schools equal.[62]

The Supreme Court asked the parties to brief several questions that primarily focused on the intent of the framers of the Fourteenth Amendment. In the summer between the two Supreme Court terms, Chief Justice Fred Vinson died of a heart attack, and President Dwight Eisenhower appointed California governor Earl Warren to be the new chief justice. The cases were argued on October 13, 1953, and through intense effort, Chief Justice Warren persuaded all of the justices to join a unanimous decision holding that separate but equal was impermissible in the realm of public education.[63]

On May 17, 1954, the Supreme Court released its decision in Brown v. Board of Education.

BROWN v. BOARD OF EDUCATION

347 U.S. 483 (1954)

Chief Justice WARREN delivered the opinion of the Court.

These cases come to us from the States of Kansas, South Carolina, Virginia, and Delaware. They are premised on different facts and different local conditions, but a common legal question justifies their consideration together in this

---

58. For a superb discussion of this litigation and its history, *see* Kluger, *id.*
59. Kluger, *id.*, at 327.
60. Briggs v. Elliott, decided with Brown v. Board of Education, 347 U.S. 483 (1954).
61. Kluger, *supra* note 57, at 332.
62. William O. Douglas, *The Court Years: 1939-1975*, at 113 (1980).
63. *See* Kluger, *supra* note 57, at 694-699.

consolidated opinion. In each of the cases, minors of the Negro race, through their legal representatives, seek the aid of the courts in obtaining admission to the public schools of their community on a nonsegregated basis. In each instance, they have been denied admission to schools attended by white children under laws requiring or permitting segregation according to race. This segregation was alleged to deprive the plaintiffs of the equal protection of the laws under the Fourteenth Amendment.

The plaintiffs contend that segregated public schools are not "equal" and cannot be made "equal," and that hence they are deprived of the equal protection of the laws. Argument was heard in the 1952 Term, and reargument was heard this Term on certain questions propounded by the Court. Reargument was largely devoted to the circumstances surrounding the adoption of the Fourteenth Amendment in 1868. It covered exhaustively consideration of the Amendment in Congress, ratification by the states, then existing practices in racial segregation, and the views of proponents and opponents of the Amendment. This discussion and our own investigation convince us that, although these sources cast some light, it is not enough to resolve the problem with which we are faced. At best, they are inconclusive. The most avid proponents of the post-War Amendments undoubtedly intended them to remove all legal distinctions among "all persons born or naturalized in the United States." Their opponents, just as certainly, were antagonistic to both the letter and the spirit of the Amendments and wished them to have the most limited effect. What others in Congress and the state legislatures had in mind cannot be determined with any degree of certainty.

An additional reason for the inconclusive nature of the Amendment's history, with respect to segregated schools, is the status of public education at that time. In the South, the movement toward free common schools, supported by general taxation, had not yet taken hold. Education of white children was largely in the hands of private groups. Education of Negroes was almost nonexistent, and practically all of the race were illiterate. In fact, any education of Negroes was forbidden by law in some states. Today, in contrast, many Negroes have achieved outstanding success in the arts and sciences as well as in the business and professional world. It is true that public school education at the time of the Amendment had advanced further in the North, but the effect of the Amendment on Northern States was generally ignored in the congressional debates. Even in the North, the conditions of public education did not approximate those existing today. The curriculum was usually rudimentary; ungraded schools were common in rural areas; the school term was but three months a year in many states; and compulsory school attendance was virtually unknown. As a consequence, it is not surprising that there should be so little in the history of the Fourteenth Amendment relating to its intended effect on public education.

The words of the [Fourteenth] amendment, it is true, are prohibitory, but they contain a necessary implication of a positive immunity, or right, most valuable to the colored race, — the right to exemption from unfriendly legislation against them distinctively as colored, — exemption from legal discriminations, implying inferiority in civil society, lessening the security of their enjoyment of the rights which others enjoy, and discriminations which are steps towards reducing them to the condition of a subject race.

In the instant cases, that question is directly presented. Here, unlike Sweatt v. Painter, there are findings below that the Negro and white schools involved have been equalized, or are being equalized, with respect to buildings, curricula, qualifications and salaries of teachers, and other "tangible" factors. Our decision, therefore, cannot turn on merely a comparison of these tangible factors in the Negro and white schools involved in each of the cases. We must look instead to the effect of segregation itself on public education.

In approaching this problem, we cannot turn the clock back to 1868 when the Amendment was adopted, or even to 1896 when Plessy v. Ferguson was written. We must consider public education in the light of its full development and its present place in American life throughout the Nation. Only in this way can it be determined if segregation in public schools deprives these plaintiffs of the equal protection of the laws.

Today, education is perhaps the most important function of state and local governments. Compulsory school attendance laws and the great expenditures for education both demonstrate our recognition of the importance of education to our democratic society. It is required in the performance of our most basic public responsibilities, even service in the armed forces. It is the very foundation of good citizenship. Today it is a principal instrument in awakening the child to cultural values, in preparing him for later professional training, and in helping him to adjust normally to his environment. In these days, it is doubtful that any child may reasonably be expected to succeed in life if he is denied the opportunity of an education. Such an opportunity, where the state has undertaken to provide it, is a right which must be made available to all on equal terms.

We come then to the question presented: Does segregation of children in public schools solely on the basis of race, even though the physical facilities and other "tangible" factors may be equal, deprive the children of the minority group of equal educational opportunities? We believe that it does.

To separate [children] from others of similar age and qualifications solely because of their race generates a feeling of inferiority as to their status in the community that may affect their hearts and minds in a way unlikely ever to be undone. The effect of this separation on their educational opportunities was well stated by a finding in the Kansas case by a court which nevertheless felt compelled to rule against the Negro plaintiffs:

> Segregation of white and colored children in public schools has a detrimental effect upon the colored children. The impact is greater when it has the sanction of the law; for the policy of separating the races is usually interpreted as denoting the inferiority of the negro group. A sense of inferiority affects the motivation of a child to learn. Segregation with the sanction of law, therefore, has a tendency to [retard] the educational and mental development of Negro children and to deprive them of some of the benefits they would receive in a racial[ly] integrated school system.

Whatever may have been the extent of psychological knowledge at the time of Plessy v. Ferguson, this finding is amply supported by modern authority.[64] Any language in Plessy v. Ferguson contrary to this finding is rejected.

64. K.B. Clark, Effect of Prejudice and Discrimination on Personality Development (Midcentury White House Conference on Children and Youth, 1950); Witmer and Kotinsky, Personality in the Making (1952), c. VI; Deutscher and Chein, The Psychological Effects of Enforced Segregation: A Survey of Social Science Opinion, 26 J. Psychol. 259 (1948); Chein, What Are the Psychological Effects of Segregation Under Conditions of Equal Facilities?, 3 Int. J. Opinion and Attitude Res. 229 (1949); Brameld, Educational Costs, in Discrimination and National Welfare (MacIver, ed., 1949), 44-48; Frazier, The Negro in the United States (1949), 674-681. And see generally Myrdal, An American Dilemma (1944). [Footnote by the Court.]

We conclude that in the field of public education the doctrine of "separate but equal" has no place. Separate educational facilities are inherently unequal. Therefore, we hold that the plaintiffs and others similarly situated for whom the actions have been brought are, by reason of the segregation complained of, deprived of the equal protection of the laws guaranteed by the Fourteenth Amendment.

Because these are class actions, because of the wide applicability of this decision, and because of the great variety of local conditions, the formulation of decrees in these cases presents problems of considerable complexity. Cases ordered restored to docket for further argument on question of appropriate decrees.

In appraising *Brown*, it is important to consider the Court's emphasis on the harms of segregation in education, rather than providing an overall constitutional judgment about the impermissibility of government-mandated segregation. The Court supported its claim that separate can never be equal in education with citations to social science studies. This has been enormously controversial. Some argue that the Court erred by relying on social science studies to support its conclusion, rather than expressing a moral judgment that segregation was wrong.[65] Indeed, Professor Mark Yudof argued that "[v]irtually everyone who has examined the question now agrees that the Court erred" in relying on the social science data.[66] The concern is that the studies were "methodologically unsound"[67] and that reliance on them made the decision vulnerable if future research came to differing conclusions.

Yet others argue that Chief Justice Warren took the approach needed to secure a unanimous ruling from the Court, widely perceived as essential in light of the intense opposition to the decision. By focusing on the inherent inequality of racially segregated schools, and by supporting this claim with citations to social science research, Warren was able to secure a unanimous ruling.

The intense opposition to *Brown* and the Supreme Court's efforts to enforce it are discussed in the next section. A key question is whether the Court could have done more to achieve greater compliance with its desegregation mandate.

THE INVALIDATION OF SEGREGATION IN OTHER CONTEXTS

Others criticized *Brown* for focusing exclusively on education and thus failing to provide a basis for declaring segregation unconstitutional in other contexts.[68] Following *Brown*, in a series of *per curiam* opinions, the Supreme Court

---

65. *See, e.g.*, Edmond Cahn, *Jurisprudence*, 30 N.Y.U. L. Rev. 150 (1955).

66. Mark G. Yudof, *School Desegregation: Legal Realism, Reasoned Elaboration, and Social Science Research in the Supreme Court*, 42 Law & Contemp. Probs. 57, 70 (Autumn 1978).

67. *Id.*

68. Herbert Wechsler criticized *Brown* for lacking a sufficient "neutral principle" to justify its conclusion. *See* Herbert Wechsler, *Toward Neutral Principles of Constitutional Law*, 73 Harv. L. Rev. 1 (1959). For excellent responses to Wechsler, *see* Louis H. Pollak, *Racial Discrimination and Judicial Integrity: A Reply to Professor Wechsler*, 108 U. Pa. L. Rev. 1 (1959); Charles L. Black, Jr., *The Lawfulness of the Segregation Decisions*, 69 Yale L.J. 421 (1960).

affirmed lower court decisions declaring unconstitutional state laws requiring segregation in all of the remaining areas of Southern life. For example, in Mayor and City Council of Baltimore City v. Dawson, 350 U.S. 877 (1955), the Supreme Court, in a memorandum disposition without an opinion, affirmed a lower court decision declaring unconstitutional a law requiring segregation in the use of public beaches and bathhouses. The Court did the exact same thing in Holmes v. City of Atlanta, 350 U.S. 879 (1955), in declaring unconstitutional segregation of municipal golf courses; in Gayle v. Browder, 352 U.S. 903 (1956), in declaring unconstitutional the segregation of a municipal bus system; in Johnson v. Virginia, 373 U.S. 61 (1963), in declaring unconstitutional segregation of courtroom seating; and in Turner v. City of Memphis, 369 U.S. 350 (1962), in declaring unconstitutional segregation of public restaurants.

Although these decisions, of course, reached the necessary result, the Court can be criticized for deciding without any opinion. The decision in *Brown* was based on the importance of education and the harms of segregation in that area. The unconstitutionality of segregation in beaches, golf courses, or buses required a separate explanation, one that the Court never offered.

Nonetheless, it is clearly established that laws requiring separation of the races are racial classifications that will be allowed only if strict scrutiny is met. The Supreme Court recently reaffirmed this in the context of prisons. Although courts usually give great deference to prisons, the Supreme Court held that routine racial segregation of prisoners must meet strict scrutiny.

JOHNSON v. CALIFORNIA
543 U.S. 499 (2005)

Justice O'CONNOR delivered the opinion of the Court.

The California Department of Corrections (CDC) has an unwritten policy of racially segregating prisoners in double cells in reception centers for up to 60 days each time they enter a new correctional facility. We consider whether strict scrutiny is the proper standard of review for an equal protection challenge to that policy.

I

CDC institutions house all new male inmates and all male inmates transferred from other state facilities in reception centers for up to 60 days upon their arrival. During that time, prison officials evaluate the inmates to determine their ultimate placement. Double-cell assignments in the reception centers are based on a number of factors, predominantly race. In fact, the CDC has admitted that the chances of an inmate being assigned a cellmate of another race are "'[p]retty close'" to zero percent. The CDC further subdivides prisoners within each racial group. Thus, Japanese-Americans are housed separately from Chinese-Americans, and Northern California Hispanics are separated from Southern California Hispanics.

The CDC's asserted rationale for this practice is that it is necessary to prevent violence caused by racial gangs. It cites numerous incidents of racial violence in

CDC facilities and identifies five major prison gangs in the State: Mexican Mafia, Nuestra Familia, Black Guerrilla Family, Aryan Brotherhood, and Nazi Low Riders. The CDC also notes that prison-gang culture is violent and murderous. An associate warden testified that if race were not considered in making initial housing assignments, she is certain there would be racial conflict in the cells and in the yard. Other prison officials also expressed their belief that violence and conflict would result if prisoners were not segregated. The CDC claims that it must therefore segregate all inmates while it determines whether they pose a danger to others.

With the exception of the double cells in reception areas, the rest of the state prison facilities—dining areas, yards, and cells—are fully integrated. After the initial 60-day period, prisoners are allowed to choose their own cellmates. The CDC usually grants inmate requests to be housed together, unless there are security reasons for denying them.

Garrison Johnson is an African-American inmate in the custody of the CDC. He has been incarcerated since 1987 and, during that time, has been housed at a number of California prison facilities. Upon his arrival at Folsom prison in 1987, and each time he was transferred to a new facility thereafter, Johnson was double-celled with another African-American inmate.

II

A

We have held that "*all* racial classifications [imposed by government] . . . must be analyzed by a reviewing court under strict scrutiny." Adarand Constructors, Inc. v. Pena (1995) (emphasis added). Under strict scrutiny, the government has the burden of proving that racial classifications "are narrowly tailored measures that further compelling governmental interests." We have insisted on strict scrutiny in every context, even for so-called "benign" racial classifications, such as race-conscious university admissions policies, see Grutter v. Bollinger (2003), race-based preferences in government contracts, and race-based districting intended to improve minority representation, Shaw v. Reno (1993).

The reasons for strict scrutiny are familiar. Racial classifications raise special fears that they are motivated by an invidious purpose. Thus, we have admonished time and again that, "[a]bsent searching judicial inquiry into the justification for such race-based measures, there is simply no way of determining . . . what classifications are in fact motivated by illegitimate notions of racial inferiority or simple racial politics." Richmond v. J. A. Croson Co. (1989) (plurality opinion). We therefore apply strict scrutiny to all racial classifications to "'smoke out' illegitimate uses of race by assuring that [government] is pursuing a goal important enough to warrant use of a highly suspect tool."

The CDC claims that its policy should be exempt from our categorical rule because it is "neutral"—that is, it "neither benefits nor burdens one group or individual more than any other group or individual." In other words, strict scrutiny should not apply because all prisoners are "equally" segregated. The CDC's argument ignores our repeated command that "racial classifications receive close scrutiny even when they may be said to burden or benefit the races equally." Indeed, we rejected the notion that separate can ever be equal — or "neutral" — 50 years ago in Brown v. Board of Education (1954), and we refuse to resurrect it today.

The need for strict scrutiny is no less important here, where prison officials cite racial violence as the reason for their policy. As we have recognized in the past, racial classifications "threaten to stigmatize individuals by reason of their membership in a racial group and to incite racial hostility." Indeed, by insisting that inmates be housed only with other inmates of the same race, it is possible that prison officials will breed further hostility among prisoners and reinforce racial and ethnic divisions. By perpetuating the notion that race matters most, racial segregation of inmates "may exacerbate the very patterns of [violence that it is] said to counteract."

Because the CDC's policy is an express racial classification, it is "immediately suspect." We therefore hold that the Court of Appeals erred when it failed to apply strict scrutiny to the CDC's policy and to require the CDC to demonstrate that its policy is narrowly tailored to serve a compelling state interest.

B

The CDC invites us to make an exception to the rule that strict scrutiny applies to all racial classifications, and instead to apply the deferential standard of review articulated in Turner v. Safley (1987), because its segregation policy applies only in the prison context. We decline the invitation. In *Turner*, we considered a claim by Missouri prisoners that regulations restricting inmate marriages and inmate-to-inmate correspondence were unconstitutional. We rejected the prisoners' argument that the regulations should be subject to strict scrutiny, asking instead whether the regulation that burdened the prisoners' fundamental rights was "reasonably related" to "legitimate penological interests."

The right not to be discriminated against based on one's race is not susceptible to the logic of *Turner*. It is not a right that need necessarily be compromised for the sake of proper prison administration. On the contrary, compliance with the Fourteenth Amendment's ban on racial discrimination is not only consistent with proper prison administration, but also bolsters the legitimacy of the entire criminal justice system. Race discrimination is "especially pernicious in the administration of justice." And public respect for our system of justice is undermined when the system discriminates based on race. When government officials are permitted to use race as a proxy for gang membership and violence without demonstrating a compelling government interest and proving that their means are narrowly tailored, society as a whole suffers.

In the prison context, when the government's power is at its apex, we think that searching judicial review of racial classifications is necessary to guard against invidious discrimination. Granting the CDC an exemption from the rule that strict scrutiny applies to all racial classifications would undermine our "unceasing efforts to eradicate racial prejudice from our criminal justice system." McCleskey v. Kemp (1987).

The CDC argues that "[d]eference to the particular expertise of prison officials in the difficult task of managing daily prison operations" requires a more relaxed standard of review for its segregation policy. But we have refused to defer to state officials' judgments on race in other areas where those officials traditionally exercise substantial discretion. For example, we have held that, despite the broad discretion given to prosecutors when they use their peremptory challenges, using those challenges to strike jurors on the basis of their race is impermissible. Similarly, in the redistricting context, despite the traditional deference given to States when they design their electoral districts, we have subjected redistricting plans to strict scrutiny when States draw district lines based predominantly on race.

The CDC protests that strict scrutiny will handcuff prison administrators and render them unable to address legitimate problems of race-based violence in prisons. Not so. Strict scrutiny is not "strict in theory, but fatal in fact." Strict scrutiny does not preclude the ability of prison officials to address the compelling interest in prison safety. Prison administrators, however, will have to demonstrate that any race-based policies are narrowly tailored to that end.

The fact that strict scrutiny applies "says nothing about the ultimate validity of any particular law; that determination is the job of the court applying strict scrutiny." At this juncture, no such determination has been made. On remand, the CDC will have the burden of demonstrating that its policy is narrowly tailored with regard to new inmates as well as transferees. Prisons are dangerous places, and the special circumstances they present may justify racial classifications in some contexts. Such circumstances can be considered in applying strict scrutiny, which is designed to take relevant differences into account.

We do not decide whether the CDC's policy violates the Equal Protection Clause. We hold only that strict scrutiny is the proper standard of review and remand the case to allow the Court of Appeals for the Ninth Circuit, or the District Court, to apply it in the first instance.

Justice STEVENS, dissenting.

In my judgment a state policy of segregating prisoners by race during the first 60 days of their incarceration, as well as the first 60 days after their transfer from one facility to another, violates the Equal Protection Clause of the Fourteenth Amendment. The California Department of Corrections (CDC) has had an ample opportunity to justify its policy during the course of this litigation, but has utterly failed to do so whether judged under strict scrutiny or the more deferential standard set out in Turner v. Safley (1987). The CDC had no incentive in the proceedings below to withhold evidence supporting its policy; nor has the CDC made any offer of proof to suggest that a remand for further factual development would serve any purpose other than to postpone the inevitable. I therefore agree with the submission of the United States as amicus curiae that the Court should hold the policy unconstitutional on the current record.

The CDC's segregation policy is based on a conclusive presumption that housing inmates of different races together creates an unacceptable risk of racial violence. Under the policy's logic, an inmate's race is a proxy for gang membership, and gang membership is a proxy for violence. The CDC, however, has offered scant empirical evidence or expert opinion to justify this use of race under even a minimal level of constitutional scrutiny. The presumption underlying the policy is undoubtedly overbroad. The CDC has made no effort to prove what fraction of new or transferred inmates are members of race-based gangs, nor has it shown more generally that interracial violence is disproportionately greater than intraracial violence in its prisons.

Given the inherent indignity of segregation and its shameful historical connotations, one might assume that the CDC came to its policy only as a last resort. Distressingly, this is not so: There is no evidence that the CDC has ever experimented with, or even carefully considered, race-neutral methods of achieving its goals. That the policy is unwritten reflects, I think, the evident lack of deliberation that preceded its creation.

Specifically, the CDC has failed to explain why it could not, as an alternative to automatic segregation, rely on an individualized assessment of each inmate's risk of violence when assigning him to a cell in a reception center. The Federal Bureau of Prisons and other state systems do so without any apparent difficulty. For inmates who are being transferred from one facility to another — who represent approximately 85% of those subject to the segregation policy — the CDC can simply examine their prison records to determine if they have any known gang affiliations or if they have ever engaged in or threatened racial violence. For example, the CDC has had an opportunity to observe the petitioner for almost 20 years; surely the CDC could have determined his placement without subjecting him to a period of segregation. For new inmates, assignments can be based on their presentence reports, which contain information about offense conduct, criminal record, and personal history — including any available information about gang affiliations.

Justice THOMAS, with whom Justice SCALIA joins, dissenting.

The questions presented in this case require us to resolve two conflicting lines of precedent. On the one hand, as the Court stresses, this Court has said that "'all racial classifications reviewable under the Equal Protection Clause must be strictly scrutinized.'" Gratz v. Bollinger (2003). On the other, this Court has no less categorically said that "the [relaxed] standard of review we adopted in Turner [v. Safley (1987)] applies to *all* circumstances in which the needs of prison administration implicate constitutional rights." Washington v. Harper (1990) (emphasis added).

Emphasizing the former line of cases, the majority resolves the conflict in favor of strict scrutiny. I disagree. The Constitution has always demanded less within the prison walls. Time and again, even when faced with constitutional rights no less "fundamental" than the right to be free from state-sponsored racial discrimination, we have deferred to the reasonable judgments of officials experienced in running this Nation's prisons. There is good reason for such deference in this case. California oversees roughly 160,000 inmates, in prisons that have been a breeding ground for some of the most violent prison gangs in America — all of them organized along racial lines. In that atmosphere, California racially segregates a portion of its inmates, in a part of its prisons, for brief periods of up to 60 days, until the State can arrange permanent housing. The majority is concerned with sparing inmates the indignity and stigma of racial discrimination. California is concerned with their safety and saving their lives. I respectfully dissent.

The majority decides this case without addressing the problems that racial violence poses for wardens, guards, and inmates throughout the federal and state prison systems. But that is the core of California's justification for its policy: It maintains that, if it does not racially separate new cellmates thrown together in close confines during their initial admission or transfer, violence will erupt. The dangers California seeks to prevent are real.

The problem of prison gangs is not unique to California, but California has a history like no other. There are at least five major gangs in this country — the

Aryan Brotherhood, the Black Guerrilla Family, the Mexican Mafia, La Nuestra Familia, and the Texas Syndicate — all of which originated in California's prisons. Unsurprisingly, then, California has the largest number of gang-related inmates of any correctional system in the country, including the Federal Government.

As their very names suggest, prison gangs like the Aryan Brotherhood and the Black Guerrilla Family organize themselves along racial lines, and these gangs perpetuate hate and violence. Interracial murders and assaults among inmates perpetrated by these gangs are common. And, again, that brutality is particularly severe in California's prisons.

It is against this backdrop of pervasive racial violence that California racially segregates inmates in the reception centers' double cells, for brief periods of up to 60 days, until such time as the State can assign permanent housing. Viewed in that context and in light of the four factors enunciated in *Turner*, California's policy is constitutional: The CDC's policy is reasonably related to a legitimate penological interest; alternative means of exercising the restricted right remain open to inmates; racially integrating double cells might negatively impact prison inmates, staff, and administrators; and there are no obvious, easy alternatives to the CDC's policy.

In place of the Court's usual deference, the majority gives conclusive force to its own guesswork about "proper" prison administration. It hypothesizes that California's policy might incite, rather than diminish, racial hostility. The majority's speculations are implausible. New arrivals have a strong interest in promptly convincing other inmates of their willingness to use violent force. In any event, the majority's guesswork falls far short of the compelling showing needed to overcome the deference we owe to prison administrators.

b. Facially Neutral Laws with a Discriminatory Impact or with Discriminatory Administration

THE REQUIREMENT FOR PROOF OF A DISCRIMINATORY PURPOSE

If a racial classification appears on the face of the law, strict scrutiny is used. However, some laws that are facially race neutral are administered in a manner that discriminates against minorities or has a disproportionate impact against them. The Supreme Court has held that there must be proof of a discriminatory purpose for such laws to be treated as racial or national origin classifications.

Washington v. Davis was a key case articulating this requirement.

WASHINGTON v. DAVIS
426 U.S. 229 (1976)

Justice WHITE delivered the opinion of the Court.

This case involves the validity of a qualifying test administered to applicants for positions as police officers in the District of Columbia Metropolitan Police Department.

I

This action began on April 10, 1970, when two Negro police officers filed suit against the then Commissioner of the District of Columbia, the Chief of the District's Metropolitan Police Department, and the Commissioners of the United States Civil Service Commission. The respondents Harley and Sellers were permitted to intervene, their amended complaint asserting that their applications to become officers in the Department had been rejected, and that the Department's recruiting procedures discriminated on the basis of race against black applicants by a series of practices including, but not limited to, a written personnel test which excluded a disproportionately high number of Negro applicants. These practices were asserted to violate respondents' rights "under the due process clause of the Fifth Amendment to the United States Constitution."

According to the findings and conclusions of the District Court, to be accepted by the Department and to enter an intensive 17-week training program, the police recruit was required to satisfy certain physical and character standards, to be a high school graduate or its equivalent, and to receive a grade of at least 40 out of 80 on "Test 21," which is "an examination that is used generally throughout the federal service," which "was developed by the Civil Service Commission, not the Police Department," and which was "designed to test verbal ability, vocabulary, reading and comprehension."

The validity of Test 21 was the sole issue before the court on the motions for summary judgment. The District Court noted that there was no claim of "an intentional discrimination or purposeful discriminatory acts" but only a claim that Test 21 bore no relationship to job performance and "has a highly discriminatory impact in screening out black candidates." Respondents' evidence, the District Court said, warranted three conclusions: "(a) The number of black police officers, while substantial, is not proportionate to the population mix of the city. (b) A higher percentage of blacks fail the Test than whites. (c) The Test has not been validated to establish its reliability for measuring subsequent job performance." This showing was deemed sufficient to shift the burden of proof to the defendants in the action, petitioners here; but the court nevertheless concluded that on the undisputed facts respondents were not entitled to relief.

II

The central purpose of the Equal Protection Clause of the Fourteenth Amendment is the prevention of official conduct discriminating on the basis of race. But our cases have not embraced the proposition that a law or other official act, without regard to whether it reflects a racially discriminatory purpose, is unconstitutional solely because it has a racially disproportionate impact.

This is not to say that the necessary discriminatory racial purpose must be express or appear on the face of the statute, or that a law's disproportionate impact is irrelevant in cases involving Constitution-based claims of racial discrimination. A statute, otherwise neutral on its face, must not be applied so as invidiously to discriminate on the basis of race. Yick Wo v. Hopkins (1886).

Necessarily, an invidious discriminatory purpose may often be inferred from the totality of the relevant facts, including the fact, if it is true, that the law bears more heavily on one race than another. Nevertheless, we have not held that a law, neutral on its face and serving ends otherwise within the power of government to pursue, is invalid under the Equal Protection Clause simply because it may affect a greater proportion of one race than of another. Disproportionate impact is not irrelevant, but it is not the sole touchstone of an invidious racial discrimination forbidden by the Constitution. Standing alone, it does not trigger the rule, that racial classifications are to be subjected to the strictest scrutiny and are justifiable only by the weightiest of considerations.

There are some indications to the contrary in our cases. In Palmer v. Thompson (1971), the city of Jackson, Miss., following a court decree to this effect, desegregated all of its public facilities save five swimming pools which had been operated by the city and which, following the decree, were closed by ordinance pursuant to a determination by the city council that closure was necessary to preserve peace and order and that integrated pools could not be economically operated. Accepting the finding that the pools were closed to avoid violence and economic loss, this Court rejected the argument that the abandonment of this service was inconsistent with the outstanding desegregation decree and that the otherwise seemingly permissible ends served by the ordinance could be impeached by demonstrating that racially invidious motivations had prompted the city council's action. The holding was that the city was not overtly or covertly operating segregated pools and was extending identical treatment to both whites and Negroes. The opinion warned against grounding decision on legislative purpose or motivation, thereby lending support for the proposition that the operative effect of the law rather than its purpose is the paramount factor. But the holding of the case was that the legitimate purposes of the ordinance to preserve peace and avoid deficits were not open to impeachment by evidence that the councilmen were actually motivated by racial considerations. Whatever dicta the opinion may contain, the decision did not involve, much less invalidate, a statute or ordinance having neutral purposes but disproportionate racial consequences.

As an initial matter, we have difficulty understanding how a law establishing a racially neutral qualification for employment is nevertheless racially discriminatory and denies "any person . . . equal protection of the laws" simply because a greater proportion of Negroes fail to qualify than members of other racial or ethnic groups. Test 21, which is administered generally to prospective Government employees, concededly seeks to ascertain whether those who take it have acquired a particular level of verbal skill; and it is untenable that the Constitution prevents the Government from seeking modestly to upgrade the communicative abilities of its employees rather than to be satisfied with some lower level of competence, particularly where the job requires special ability to communicate orally and in writing. Respondents, as Negroes, could no more successfully claim that the test denied them equal protection than could white applicants who also failed. The conclusion would not be different in the face of proof that more Negroes than whites had been disqualified by Test 21. That other Negroes also failed to score well would, alone, not demonstrate that respondents individually were being denied equal protection of the laws by the application of an otherwise valid qualifying test being administered to prospective police recruits.

Nor on the facts of the case before us would the disproportionate impact of Test 21 warrant the conclusion that it is a purposeful device to discriminate against Negroes and hence an infringement of the constitutional rights of respondents as well as other black applicants. As we have said, the test is neutral on its face and rationally may be said to serve a purpose the Government is constitutionally empowered to pursue.

Under Title VII, Congress provided that when hiring and promotion practices disqualifying substantially disproportionate numbers of blacks are challenged, discriminatory purpose need not be proved, and that it is an insufficient response to demonstrate some rational basis for the challenged practices. It is necessary, in addition, that they be "validated" in terms of job performance in any one of several ways, perhaps by ascertaining the minimum skill, ability, or potential necessary for the position at issue and determining whether the qualifying tests are appropriate for the selection of qualified applicants for the job in question. We are not disposed to adopt this more rigorous standard for the purposes of applying the Fifth and the Fourteenth Amendments in cases such as this.

A rule that a statute designed to serve neutral ends is nevertheless invalid, absent compelling justification, if in practice it benefits or burdens one race more than another would be far-reaching and would raise serious questions about, and perhaps invalidate, a whole range of tax, welfare, public service, regulatory, and licensing statutes that may be more burdensome to the poor and to the average black than to the more affluent white.

Justice BRENNAN, with whom Justice MARSHALL joins, dissenting.

[I]t should be observed that every federal court, except the District Court in this case, presented with proof identical to that offered to validate Test 21 has reached a conclusion directly opposite to that of the Court today. Sound policy considerations support the view that, at a minimum, petitioners should have been required to prove that the police training examinations either measure job-related skills or predict job performance. Where employers try to validate written qualification tests by proving a correlation with written examinations in a training course, there is a substantial danger that people who have good verbal skills will achieve high scores on both tests due to verbal ability, rather than "job-specific ability." As a result, employers could validate any entrance examination that measures only verbal ability by giving another written test that measures verbal ability at the end of a training course. Any contention that the resulting correlation between examination scores would be evidence that the initial test is "job related" is plainly erroneous. It seems to me, however, that the Court's holding in this case can be read as endorsing this dubious proposition. Today's result will prove particularly unfortunate if it is extended to govern Title VII cases.

Although Washington v. Davis holds that equal protection requires proof of a discriminatory purpose in order to demonstrate that a facially neutral law constitutes a racial classification, civil rights statutes can, and often do, allow violations to be proven based on discriminatory impact without evidence of a discriminatory purpose. For example, Title VII of the 1964 Civil Rights Act allows employment discrimination to be established by proof of discriminatory impact.[69]

The Court has frequently applied Washington v. Davis to reject equal protection challenges to facially neutral laws that have a racially discriminatory impact. A particularly important example of this is McCleskey v. Kemp, in which the Court rejected an equal protection challenge to the administration of the death penalty.

McCLESKEY v. KEMP

481 U.S. 279 (1987)

Justice Powell delivered the opinion of the Court.

This case presents the question whether a complex statistical study that indicates a risk that racial considerations enter into capital sentencing determinations proves that petitioner McCleskey's capital sentence is unconstitutional under the Eighth or Fourteenth Amendment.

I

McCleskey, a black man, was convicted of two counts of armed robbery and one count of murder in the Superior Court of Fulton County, Georgia, on October 12, 1978. McCleskey's convictions arose out of the robbery of a furniture store and the killing of a white police officer during the course of the robbery. The evidence at trial indicated that McCleskey and three accomplices planned and carried out the robbery. All four were armed. McCleskey entered the front of the store while the other three entered the rear. McCleskey secured the front of the store by rounding up the customers and forcing them to lie face down on the floor. The other three rounded up the employees in the rear and tied them up with tape. The manager was forced at gunpoint to turn over the store receipts, his watch, and $6. During the course of the robbery, a police officer, answering a silent alarm, entered the store through the front door. As he was walking down the center aisle of the store, two shots were fired. Both struck the officer. One hit him in the face and killed him.

Several weeks later, McCleskey was arrested in connection with an unrelated offense. He confessed that he had participated in the furniture store robbery, but denied that he had shot the police officer. At trial, the State introduced evidence that at least one of the bullets that struck the officer was fired from a .38 caliber Rossi revolver. This description matched the description of the gun that McCleskey had carried during the robbery. The State also introduced the testimony of two witnesses who had heard McCleskey admit to the shooting.

The jury convicted McCleskey of murder. At the penalty hearing, the jury heard arguments as to the appropriate sentence. Under Georgia law, the jury

---

69. *See* Griggs v. Duke Power Co., 401 U.S. 424 (1971).

could not consider imposing the death penalty unless it found beyond a reasonable doubt that the murder was accompanied by one of the statutory aggravating circumstances. The jury in this case found two aggravating circumstances to exist beyond a reasonable doubt: the murder was committed during the course of an armed robbery, and the murder was committed upon a peace officer engaged in the performance of his duties. In making its decision whether to impose the death sentence, the jury considered the mitigating and aggravating circumstances of McCleskey's conduct. McCleskey offered no mitigating evidence. The jury recommended that he be sentenced to death on the murder charge and to consecutive life sentences on the armed robbery charges. The court followed the jury's recommendation and sentenced McCleskey to death.

McCleskey filed a petition for a writ of habeas corpus in the Federal District Court for the Northern District of Georgia. His petition raised 18 claims, one of which was that the Georgia capital sentencing process is administered in a racially discriminatory manner in violation of the Eighth and Fourteenth Amendments to the United States Constitution. In support of his claim, McCleskey proffered a statistical study performed by Professors David C. Baldus, Charles Pulaski, and George Woodworth, and (the Baldus study) that purports to show a disparity in the imposition of the death sentence in Georgia based on the race of the murder victim and, to a lesser extent, the race of the defendant. The Baldus study is actually two sophisticated statistical studies that examine over 2,000 murder cases that occurred in Georgia during the 1970's. The raw numbers collected by Professor Baldus indicate that defendants charged with killing white persons received the death penalty in 11% of the cases, but defendants charged with killing blacks received the death penalty in only 1% of the cases. The raw numbers also indicate a reverse racial disparity according to the race of the defendant: 4% of the black defendants received the death penalty, as opposed to 7% of the white defendants.

Baldus also divided the cases according to the combination of the race of the defendant and the race of the victim. He found that the death penalty was assessed in 22% of the cases involving black defendants and white victims; 8% of the cases involving white defendants and white victims; 1% of the cases involving black defendants and black victims; and 3% of the cases involving white defendants and black victims. Similarly, Baldus found that prosecutors sought the death penalty in 70% of the cases involving black defendants and white victims; 32% of the cases involving white defendants and white victims; 15% of the cases involving black defendants and black victims; and 19% of the cases involving white defendants and black victims.

Baldus subjected his data to an extensive analysis, taking account of 230 variables that could have explained the disparities on nonracial grounds. One of his models concludes that, even after taking account of 39 nonracial variables, defendants charged with killing white victims were 4.3 times as likely to receive a death sentence as defendants charged with killing blacks. According to this model, black defendants were 1.1 times as likely to receive a death sentence as other defendants. Thus, the Baldus study indicates that black defendants, such as McCleskey, who kill white victims have the greatest likelihood of receiving the death penalty.

II

McCleskey's first claim is that the Georgia capital punishment statute violates the Equal Protection Clause of the Fourteenth Amendment. He argues that race has infected the administration of Georgia's statute in two ways: persons who murder whites are more likely to be sentenced to death than persons who murder blacks, and black murderers are more likely to be sentenced to death than white murderers. As a black defendant who killed a white victim, McCleskey claims that the Baldus study demonstrates that he was discriminated against because of his race and because of the race of his victim. In its broadest form, McCleskey's claim of discrimination extends to every actor in the Georgia capital sentencing process, from the prosecutor who sought the death penalty and the jury that imposed the sentence, to the State itself that enacted the capital punishment statute and allows it to remain in effect despite its allegedly discriminatory application. We agree with the Court of Appeals, and every other court that has considered such a challenge, that this claim must fail.

A

Our analysis begins with the basic principle that a defendant who alleges an equal protection violation has the burden of proving "the existence of purposeful discrimination." A corollary to this principle is that a criminal defendant must prove that the purposeful discrimination "had a discriminatory effect" on him. Thus, to prevail under the Equal Protection Clause, McCleskey must prove that the decision-makers in his case acted with discriminatory purpose. He offers no evidence specific to his own case that would support an inference that racial considerations played a part in his sentence. Instead, he relies solely on the Baldus study. McCleskey argues that the Baldus study compels an inference that his sentence rests on purposeful discrimination. McCleskey's claim that these statistics are sufficient proof of discrimination, without regard to the facts of a particular case, would extend to all capital cases in Georgia, at least where the victim was white and the defendant is black.

[E]ach particular decision to impose the death penalty is made by a petit jury selected from a properly constituted venire. Each jury is unique in its composition, and the Constitution requires that its decision rest on consideration of innumerable factors that vary according to the characteristics of the individual defendant and the facts of the particular capital offense. Similarly, the policy considerations behind a prosecutor's traditionally "wide discretion" suggest the impropriety of our requiring prosecutors to defend their decisions to seek death penalties, "often years after they were made." Moreover, absent far stronger proof, it is unnecessary to seek such a rebuttal, because a legitimate and unchallenged explanation for the decision is apparent from the record: McCleskey committed an act for which the United States Constitution and Georgia laws permit imposition of the death penalty.

Finally, McCleskey's statistical proffer must be viewed in the context of his challenge. McCleskey challenges decisions at the heart of the State's criminal justice system. "[O]ne of society's most basic tasks is that of protecting the lives of its citizens and one of the most basic ways in which it achieves the task is through criminal laws against murder." Gregg v. Georgia (1976) (White, J., concurring). Implementation of these laws necessarily requires discretionary judgments. Because discretion is essential to the criminal justice process, we would demand exceptionally clear proof before we would infer that the discretion has been abused. The unique nature of the decisions at issue in this case also counsels against adopting such an inference from the disparities indicated by the Baldus study. Accordingly, we hold that the Baldus study is clearly insufficient to support an inference that any of the decision-makers in McCleskey's case acted with discriminatory purpose.

B

McCleskey also suggests that the Baldus study proves that the State as a whole has acted with a discriminatory purpose. He appears to argue that the State has violated the Equal Protection Clause by adopting the capital punishment statute and allowing it to remain in force despite its allegedly discriminatory application. But "'[d]iscriminatory purpose' . . . implies more than intent as volition or intent as awareness of consequences. It implies that the decisionmaker, in this case a state legislature, selected or reaffirmed a particular course of action at least in part 'because of,' not merely 'in spite of,' its adverse effects upon an identifiable group." Personnel Administrator of Massachusetts v. Feeney (1979). For this claim to prevail, McCleskey would have to prove that the Georgia Legislature enacted or maintained the death penalty statute because of an anticipated racially discriminatory effect. In Gregg v. Georgia, this Court found that the Georgia capital sentencing system could operate in a fair and neutral manner. There was no evidence then, and there is none now, that the Georgia Legislature enacted the capital punishment statute to further a racially discriminatory purpose.

Nor has McCleskey demonstrated that the legislature maintains the capital punishment statute because of the racially disproportionate impact suggested by the Baldus study. As legislatures necessarily have wide discretion in the choice of criminal laws and penalties, and as there were legitimate reasons for the Georgia Legislature to adopt and maintain capital punishment, we will not infer a discriminatory purpose on the part of the State of Georgia. Accordingly, we reject McCleskey's equal protection claims.

Justice BRENNAN, with whom Justice MARSHALL joins, and with whom Justice BLACKMUN and Justice STEVENS join, dissenting.

At some point in this case, Warren McCleskey doubtless asked his lawyer whether a jury was likely to sentence him to die. A candid reply to this question would have been disturbing. First, counsel would have to tell McCleskey that few of the details of the crime or of McCleskey's past criminal conduct were more important than the fact that his victim was white. Furthermore, counsel would feel bound to tell McCleskey that defendants charged with killing white victims in Georgia are 4.3 times as likely to be sentenced to death as defendants charged with killing blacks. In addition, frankness would compel the disclosure that it was more likely than not that the race of McCleskey's victim would determine whether he received a death sentence: 6 of every 11 defendants convicted of killing a white person would not have received the death penalty if their victims had been black, while, among defendants with aggravating and mitigating factors comparable to McCleskey's, 20 of every 34 would not have been sentenced to die if their victims had been black. Finally, the assessment would not be complete without the information that cases involving black defendants and white victims are more likely to result in a death sentence than cases featuring any other racial combination of defendant and victim. Ibid. The story could be told in a variety of ways, but McCleskey could not fail to grasp its essential narrative line: there was a significant chance that race would play a prominent role in determining if he lived or died.

Furthermore, even examination of the sentencing system as a whole, factoring in those cases in which the jury exercises little discretion, indicates the influence of race on capital sentencing. For the Georgia system as a whole, race accounts for a six percentage point difference in the rate at which capital punishment is imposed. Since death is imposed in 11% of all white-victim cases, the rate in comparably aggravated black-victim cases is 5%. The rate of capital sentencing in a white-victim case is thus 120% greater than the rate in a black-victim case. Put another way, over half — 55% — of defendants in white-victim crimes in Georgia would not have been sentenced to die if their victims had been black. Of the more than 200 variables potentially relevant to a sentencing decision, race of the victim is a powerful explanation for variation in death sentence rates — as powerful as non-racial aggravating factors such as a prior murder conviction or acting as the principal planner of the homicide.

These adjusted figures are only the most conservative indication of the risk that race will influence the death sentences of defendants in Georgia. Data unadjusted for the mitigating or aggravating effect of other factors show an even more pronounced disparity by race. The capital sentencing rate for all white-victim cases was almost 11 times greater than the rate for black-victim cases. Furthermore, blacks who kill whites are sentenced to death at nearly 22 times the rate of blacks who kill blacks, and more than 7 times the rate of whites who kill blacks. In addition, prosecutors seek the death penalty for 70% of black defendants with white victims, but for only 15% of black defendants with black victims, and only 19% of white defendants with black victims. Since our decision upholding the Georgia capital sentencing system in *Gregg*, the State has executed seven persons. All of the seven were convicted of killing whites, and six of the seven executed were black. Such execution figures are especially striking in light of the fact that, during the period encompassed by the Baldus study, only 9.2% of Georgia homicides involved black defendants and white victims, while 60.7% involved black victims.

The statistical evidence in this case thus relentlessly documents the risk that McCleskey's sentence was influenced by racial considerations. This evidence shows that there is a better than even chance in Georgia that race will influence the decision to impose the death penalty: a majority of defendants in white-victim crimes would not have been sentenced to die if their victims had been black.

Evaluation of McCleskey's evidence cannot rest solely on the numbers themselves. We must also ask whether the conclusion suggested by those numbers is consonant with our understanding of history and human experience. Georgia's legacy of a race-conscious criminal justice system, as well as this Court's own recognition of the persistent danger that racial attitudes may affect criminal proceedings, indicates that McCleskey's claim is not a fanciful product of mere statistical artifice.

For many years, Georgia operated openly and formally precisely the type of dual system the evidence shows is still effectively in place. The criminal law expressly differentiated between crimes committed by and against blacks and whites, distinctions whose lineage traced back to the time of slavery. During the colonial period, black slaves who killed whites in Georgia, regardless of whether in self-defense or in defense of another, were automatically executed. By the time of the Civil War, a dual system of crime and punishment was well established in Georgia.

This Court has invalidated portions of the Georgia capital sentencing system three times over the past 15 years. The specter of race discrimination was acknowledged by the Court in striking down the Georgia death penalty statute in Furman v. Georgia. Justice Douglas cited studies suggesting imposition of the death penalty in racially discriminatory fashion, and found the standardless statutes before the Court "pregnant with discrimination."

This historical review of Georgia criminal law is not intended as a bill of indictment calling the State to account for past transgressions. Citation of past practices does not justify the automatic condemnation of current ones. But it would be unrealistic to ignore the influence of history in assessing the plausible implications of McCleskey's evidence.

The discretion afforded prosecutors and jurors in the Georgia capital sentencing system creates such opportunities. No guidelines govern prosecutorial decisions to seek the death penalty, and Georgia provides juries with no list of aggravating and mitigating factors, nor any standard for balancing them against one another. Once a jury identifies one aggravating factor, it has complete discretion in choosing life or death, and need not articulate its basis for selecting life imprisonment. The Georgia sentencing system therefore provides considerable opportunity for racial considerations, however subtle and unconscious, to influence charging and sentencing decisions.

Warren McCleskey's evidence confronts us with the subtle and persistent influence of the past. His message is a disturbing one to a society that has formally repudiated racism, and a frustrating one to a Nation accustomed to regarding its destiny as the product of its own will. Nonetheless, we ignore him at our peril, for we remain imprisoned by the past as long as we deny its influence in the present.

It is tempting to pretend that minorities on death row share a fate in no way connected to our own, that our treatment of them sounds no echoes beyond the chambers in which they die. Such an illusion is ultimately corrosive, for the reverberations of injustice are not so easily confined. "The destinies of the two races in this country are indissolubly linked together," Plessy v. Ferguson (Harlan, J., dissenting), and the way in which we choose those who will die reveals the depth of moral commitment among the living.

The Court's decision today will not change what attorneys in Georgia tell other Warren McCleskeys about their chances of execution. Nothing will soften the harsh message they must convey, nor alter the prospect that race undoubtedly will continue to be a topic of discussion. McCleskey's evidence will not have obtained judicial acceptance, but that will not affect what is said on death row. However many criticisms of today's decision may be rendered, these painful conversations will serve as the most eloquent dissents of all.

Whether discrimination can be proven by showing a discriminatory impact is crucial in determining the reach of the Equal Protection Clause. Undoubtedly, there are many areas where a significant discriminatory impact can be proven, but there is not sufficient evidence of a discriminatory purpose. Current law means that the government need not offer a racially neutral explanation for these effects and, indeed, need do no more than meet a rational basis test.

On the one hand, this can be justified by the view that the Equal Protection Clause is concerned with stopping discriminatory acts by the government, not in bringing about equal results. Moreover, there is concern that countless laws might have some discriminatory impact given the enormous inequalities between whites and racial minorities that continue to exist. Also it is argued that there will be laws that have the impact of benefiting minorities and that these can counterbalance those that have a detrimental effect.

On the other hand, as discussed below, proving discriminatory purpose is very difficult; rarely will such a motivation be expressed and benign purposes can be articulated for most laws.[70] Therefore, many laws with both a discriminatory purpose and effect might be upheld simply because of evidentiary problems inherent in requiring proof of such a purpose. Scholars such as Professor Charles Lawrence argue that this is especially true because racism is often unconscious and such "unconscious racism . . . underlies much of the racially disproportionate impact of governmental policy."[71] In a society with a long history of discrimination, there can be a presumption that many laws with a discriminatory impact likely were motivated by a discriminatory purpose.[72]

Furthermore, it is argued that equal protection should be concerned with the results of government actions and not just their underlying motivations. Professor Lawrence Tribe explained, "The goal of the Equal Protection Clause is not to stamp out impure thoughts, but to guarantee a full measure of human dignity for all. . . . [M]inorities can also be injured when the government is 'only' indifferent to their suffering or 'merely' blind to how prior official discrimination contributed to it and how current official acts will perpetuate it."[73]

Ultimately, the issue of whether discriminatory purpose should be required, or whether discriminatory impact should be sufficient to prove an equal protection violation, turns on a determination of the fundamental mission of the Equal Protection Clause. Is the clause only about equal treatment by the government, or should it also be concerned with equal results?

The Supreme Court has extended the requirement for a discriminatory purpose to include the Fifteenth Amendment and its prohibition of race-based interference with the right to vote. Mobile v. Bolden is the key case.

CITY OF MOBILE v. BOLDEN

446 U.S. 55 (1980)

Justice STEWART announced the judgment of the Court and delivered an opinion, in which the Chief Justice, Justice POWELL, and Justice REHNQUIST joined.

---

70. *See* Daniel R. Ortiz, *The Myth of Intent in Equal Protection*, 41 Stan. L. Rev. 1105 (1989).

71. Charles R. Lawrence, III, *The Id, the Ego, and Equal Protection: Reckoning with Unconscious Racism*, 39 Stan. L. Rev. 317, 355 (1987).

72. *See* David A. Strauss, *Discriminatory Intent and the Taming of* Brown, 56 U. Chi. L. Rev. 935 (1989).

73. Laurence H. Tribe, *American Constitutional Law* 1516-1519 (2d ed. 1988).

The city of Mobile, Ala., has since 1911 been governed by a City Commission consisting of three members elected by the voters of the city at large. The question in this case is whether this at-large system of municipal elections violates the rights of Mobile's Negro voters in contravention of federal statutory or constitutional law.

I

In Alabama, the form of municipal government a city may adopt is governed by state law. Until 1911, cities not covered by specific legislation were limited to governing themselves through a mayor and city council. In that year, the Alabama Legislature authorized every large municipality to adopt a commission form of government. Mobile established its City Commission in the same year, and has maintained that basic system of municipal government ever since. The three Commissioners jointly exercise all legislative, executive and administrative power in the municipality. They are required after election to designate one of their number as Mayor, a largely ceremonial office, but no formal provision is made for allocating specific executive or administrative duties among the three. As required by the state law enacted in 1911, each candidate for the Mobile City Commission runs for election in the city at large for a term of four years in one of three numbered posts, and may be elected only by a majority of the total vote. This is the same basic electoral system that is followed by literally thousands of municipalities and other local governmental units throughout the Nation.

Our decisions, moreover, have made clear that action by a State that is racially neutral on its face violates the Fifteenth Amendment only if motivated by a discriminatory purpose. The Court's more recent decisions confirm the principle that racially discriminatory motivation is a necessary ingredient of a Fifteenth Amendment violation. In Gomillion v. Lightfoot the Court held that allegations of a racially motivated gerrymander of municipal boundaries stated a claim under the Fifteenth Amendment. The constitutional infirmity of the state law in that case, according to the allegations of the complaint, was that in drawing the municipal boundaries the legislature was "solely concerned with segregating white and colored voters by fencing Negro citizens out of town so as to deprive them of their pre-existing municipal vote." The Court made clear that in the absence of such an invidious purpose, a State is constitutionally free to redraw political boundaries in any manner it chooses. While other of the Court's Fifteenth Amendment decisions have dealt with different issues, none has questioned the necessity of showing purposeful discrimination in order to show a Fifteenth Amendment violation.

Despite repeated constitutional attacks upon multimember legislative districts, the Court has consistently held that they are not unconstitutional per se. We have recognized, however, that such legislative apportionments could violate the Fourteenth Amendment if their purpose were invidiously to minimize or cancel out the voting potential of racial or ethnic minorities. To prove such a purpose it is not enough to show that the group allegedly discriminated against has not elected representatives in proportion to its numbers. A plaintiff must prove that the disputed plan was "conceived or operated as [a] purposeful devic[e] to further racial . . . discrimination." This burden of proof is simply one aspect of the basic principle that only if there is purposeful discrimination can there be a violation of the Equal Protection Clause of the Fourteenth Amendment. See Washington v. Davis.

[T]he [district court and the court of appeals] found it highly significant that no Negro had been elected to the Mobile City Commission. From this fact they concluded that the processes leading to nomination and election were not open equally to Negroes. But the District Court's findings of fact, unquestioned on appeal, make clear that Negroes register and vote in Mobile "without hindrance," and that there are no official obstacles in the way of Negroes who wish to become candidates for election to the Commission. Indeed, it was undisputed that the only active "slating" organization in the city is comprised of Negroes. It may be that Negro candidates have been defeated but that fact alone does not work a constitutional deprivation.

Second, the District Court relied in part on its finding that the persons who were elected to the Commission discriminated against Negroes in municipal employment and in dispensing public services. If that is the case, those discriminated against may be entitled to relief under the Constitution, albeit of a sort quite different from that sought in the present case. But evidence of discrimination by white officials in Mobile is relevant only as the most tenuous and circumstantial evidence of the constitutional invalidity of the electoral system under which they attained their offices.

Third, the District Court and the Court of Appeals supported their conclusion by drawing upon the substantial history of official racial discrimination in Alabama. But past discrimination cannot, in the manner of original sin, condemn governmental action that is not itself unlawful. The ultimate question remains whether a discriminatory intent has been proved in a given case. More distant instances of official discrimination in other cases are of limited help in resolving that question.

Finally, the District Court and the Court of Appeals pointed to the mechanics of the at-large electoral system itself as proof that the votes of Negroes were being invidiously canceled out. But those features of that electoral system, such as the majority vote requirement, tend naturally to disadvantage any voting minority. They are far from proof that the at-large electoral scheme represents purposeful discrimination against Negro voters.

Justice WHITE, dissenting.

Both the District Court and the Court of Appeals properly found that an invidious discriminatory purpose could be inferred from the totality of facts in this case. The Court's cryptic rejection of their conclusions ignores the principles that an invidious discriminatory purpose can be inferred from objective factors and that the trial courts are in a special position to make such intensely local appraisals.

In the instant case the District Court and the Court of Appeals faithfully applied [constitutional] principles in assessing whether the maintenance of a system of at-large elections for the selection of Mobile City Commissioners denied Mobile Negroes their Fourteenth and Fifteenth Amendment rights. Scrupulously adhering to our admonition that "[t]he plaintiffs' burden is to produce evidence to support findings that the political processes leading to nomination and election were not equally open to participation by the group in question," the District Court conducted a detailed factual inquiry into the openness of the candidate selection process to blacks.

The court noted that "Mobile blacks were subjected to massive official and private racial discrimination until the Voting Rights Act of 1965" and that "[t]he pervasive effects of past discrimination still substantially affec[t] black political participation." Although the District Court noted that "[s]ince the Voting Rights Act of 1965, blacks register and vote without hindrance," the court found that "local political processes are not equally open" to blacks. Despite the fact that Negroes constitute more than 35% of the population of Mobile, no Negro has ever been elected to the Mobile City Commission. The plaintiffs introduced extensive evidence of severe racial polarization in voting patterns during the 1960s and 1970s with "white voting for white and black for black if a white is opposed to a black," resulting in the defeat of the black candidate or, if two whites are running, the defeat of the white candidate most identified with blacks. Nearly every active candidate for public office testified that because of racial polarization "it is highly unlikely that anytime in the foreseeable future, under the at-large system, . . . a black can be elected against a white." After single-member districts were created in Mobile County for state legislative elections, "three blacks of the present fourteen member Mobile County delegation have been elected." Based on the foregoing evidence, the District Court found "that the structure of the at-large election of city commissioners combined with strong racial polarization of Mobile's electorate continues to effectively discourage qualified black citizens from seeking office or being elected thereby denying blacks equal access to the slating or candidate selection process." Because I believe that the findings of the District Court amply support an inference of purposeful discrimination in violation of the Fourteenth and Fifteenth Amendments, I respectfully dissent.

Soon after *Mobile*, in Rogers v. Lodge, 458 U.S. 613 (1982), the Court found that an at-large election system was unconstitutional because there was sufficient proof of a discriminatory purpose behind the election system. *Rogers* involved a challenge to an at-large election scheme for a large rural county in Georgia. The district court found that the "at-large system in Burke County was being maintained for the invidious purpose of diluting the voting strength of the black population."

The Supreme Court upheld this factual finding, emphasizing that blacks were a substantial majority of the population in the county but a distinct minority of the registered voters. The Court also noted that no black ever had been elected to the county commission. The Court pointed to a long history of purposeful discrimination against blacks in voting in the county, including the use of poll taxes, literacy tests, and white primaries. Furthermore, schools within the county were racially segregated until 1969 and still remained largely segregated. The Court additionally observed that blacks had been excluded from participating in the political process, in party affairs, and in primary elections. All of these factors justified the conclusion that there was a discriminatory purpose behind the at-large election system.

Mobile v. Bolden and Rogers v. Lodge are consistent in that both clearly say that proof of a discriminatory purpose is required in order to challenge an at-large election scheme. But the key question is whether there is a meaningful factual distinction between the cases. Both involve Southern cities with a long history of overt racial discrimination, including in voting. In neither had a black ever been elected. But the Court saw a meaningful difference in the proof offered in the two cases and found only sufficient evidence of discriminatory purpose in the latter.

The 1982 Amendments to the Voting Rights Act of 1965 largely obviated the need to distinguish the two cases and to discern what sufficiently establishes discriminatory purpose.[74] The amendment was in response to Mobile v. Bolden and prohibits election systems that dilute the voting power of a racial minority. In other words, the 1982 Amendments eliminate the need for proof of discriminatory purpose in challenging an election system as being racially discriminatory.[75]

IS PROOF OF A DISCRIMINATORY EFFECT ALSO REQUIRED?

The cases discussed thus far involve situations where there is proof of a racially discriminatory impact of a facially neutral law. A distinct question that arises much less often is whether proof of discriminatory purpose is sufficient, by itself, to establish an equal protection violation or whether there must be both discriminatory impact and discriminatory purpose. This issue arises far less frequently because usually there is evidence of a discriminatory impact and the question is whether there is adequate proof of discriminatory purpose. Although the Supreme Court has never expressly addressed the question, it appears that both are required. Palmer v. Thompson is the case that indicates that discriminatory impact also must be shown; indeed, in Washington v. Davis, above, it was cited as standing for that proposition.

PALMER v. THOMPSON

403 U.S. 217 (1971)

Justice BLACK delivered the opinion of the Court.

In 1962 the city of Jackson, Mississippi, was maintaining five public parks along with swimming pools, golf links, and other facilities for use by the public on a racially segregated basis. Four of the swimming pools were used by whites only and one by Negroes only. Plaintiffs brought an action in the United States District Court seeking a declaratory judgment that this state-enforced segregation of the races was a violation of the Thirteenth and Fourteenth Amendments, and asking an injunction to forbid such practices. After hearings the District

---

74. 42 U.S.C. §1973.

75. *See* Johnson v. DeGrandy, 512 U.S. 997, 1096 (1994) (a court should find a violation only if the totality of the circumstances demonstrates that the challenged apportionment system was designed to suppress minority voting strength); Thornburg v. Gingles, 478 U.S. 30, 50-51 (1986) (articulating criteria that must be met in order to establish a prima facie case of vote dilution; (1) the minority must be sufficiently large and geographically compact as to be able to comprise a majority of a district; (2) the minority group must be shown to be "politically cohesive"; (3) racially polarized voting must be shown by demonstrating that it is likely that whites would vote as a bloc to defeat minority candidates).

In Bush v. Vera, 517 U.S. 952 (1996), Justice O'Connor, in a concurring opinion, said that she believed that compliance with §2 of the Voting Rights Act was a compelling interest sufficient to permit the use of race in districting.

Court entered a judgment declaring that enforced segregation denied equal protection of the laws but it declined to issue an injunction. The Court of Appeals affirmed, and we denied certiorari. The city proceeded to desegregate its public parks, auditoriums, golf courses, and the city zoo. However, the city council decided not to try to operate the public swimming pools on a desegregated basis. Acting in its legislative capacity, the council surrendered its lease on one pool and closed four which the city owned. A number of Negro citizens of Jackson then filed this suit to force the city to reopen the pools and operate them on a desegregated basis.

The question, however, is whether this closing of the pools is state action that denies "the equal protection of the laws" to Negroes. It should be noted first that neither the Fourteenth Amendment nor any Act of Congress purports to impose an affirmative duty on a State to begin to operate or to continue to operate swimming pools. Furthermore, this is not a case where whites are permitted to use public facilities while blacks are denied access. It is not a case where a city is maintaining different sets of facilities for blacks and whites and forcing the races to remain separate in recreational or educational activities.

Petitioners have also argued that respondents' action violates the Equal Protection Clause because the decision to close the pools was motivated by a desire to avoid integration of the races. But no case in this Court has held that a legislative act may violate equal protection solely because of the motivations of the men who voted for it.

First, it is extremely difficult for a court to ascertain the motivation, or collection of different motivations, that lie behind a legislative enactment. Here, for example, petitioners have argued that the Jackson pools were closed because of ideological opposition to racial integration in swimming pools. Some evidence in the record appears to support this argument. On the other hand the courts below found that the pools were closed because the city council felt they could not be operated safely and economically on an integrated basis. There is substantial evidence in the record to support this conclusion. It is difficult or impossible for any court to determine the "sole" or "dominant" motivation behind the choices of a group of legislators. Furthermore, there is an element of futility in a judicial attempt to invalidate a law because of the bad motives of its supporters. If the law is struck down for this reason, rather than because of its facial content or effect, it would presumably be valid as soon as the legislature or relevant governing body repassed it for different reasons.

Petitioners have argued strenuously that a city's possible motivations to ensure safety and save money cannot validate an otherwise impermissible state action. This proposition is, of course, true. Citizens may not be compelled to forgo their constitutional rights because officials fear public hostility or desire to save money. But the issue here is whether black citizens in Jackson are being denied their constitutional rights when the city has closed the public pools to black and white alike. Nothing in the history or the language of the Fourteenth Amendment nor in any of our prior cases persuades us that the closing of the Jackson swimming pools to all its citizens constitutes a denial of "the equal protection of the laws."

It has not been so many years since it was first deemed proper and lawful for cities to tax their citizens to build and operate swimming pools for the public. Probably few persons, prior to this case, would have imagined that cities could be forced by five lifetime judges to construct or refurbish swimming pools which they choose not to operate for any reason, sound or unsound. Should citizens of Jackson or any other city be able to establish in court that public, tax-supported swimming pools are being denied to one group because of color and supplied to another, they will be entitled to relief. But that is not the case here.

Justice DOUGLAS, dissenting.

May a State in order to avoid integration of the races abolish all of its public schools? That would dedicate the State to backwardness, ignorance, and existence in a new Dark Age. Yet is there anything in the Constitution that says that a State must have a public school system? Could a federal court enjoin the dismantling of a public school system? Could a federal court order a city to levy the taxes necessary to construct a public school system? Such supervision over municipal affairs by federal courts would be a vast undertaking, conceivably encompassing schools, parks, playgrounds, civic auditoriums, tennis courts, athletic fields, as well as swimming pools.

Closing of the pools probably works a greater hardship on the poor than on the rich; and it may work greater hardship on poor Negroes than on poor whites, a matter on which we have no light. Closing of the pools was at least in part racially motivated. And, as stated by the dissenters in the Court of Appeals:

> The closing of the City's pools has done more than deprive a few thousand Negroes of the pleasures of swimming. It has taught Jackson's Negroes a lesson: In Jackson the price of protest is high. Negroes there now know that they risk losing even segregated public facilities if they dare to protest segregation. Negroes will now think twice before protesting segregated public parks, segregated public libraries, or other segregated facilities. They must first decide whether they wish to risk living without the facility altogether, and at the same time engendering further animosity from a white community which has lost its public facilities also through the Negroes' attempts to desegregate these facilities.

I conclude that though a State may discontinue any of its municipal services — such as schools, parks, pools, athletic fields, and the like — it may not do so for the purpose of perpetuating or installing apartheid or because it finds life in a multiracial community difficult or unpleasant. If that is its reason, then abolition of a designated public service becomes a device for perpetuating a segregated way of life. That a State may not do.

HOW IS A DISCRIMINATORY PURPOSE PROVEN?

The crucial question then becomes: How can it be proven that a facially neutral law is motivated by a discriminatory purpose? The Supreme Court has made it clear that showing such a purpose requires proof that the government desired to discriminate; it is not enough to prove that the government took an action with knowledge that it would have discriminatory consequences. In Personnel Administrator of Massachusetts v. Feeney, a case dealing with gender discrimination, the Court chose a narrow definition of what constitutes discriminatory intent.

PERSONNEL ADMINISTRATOR OF MASSACHUSETTS v. FEENEY
442 U.S. 256 (1979)

Justice STEWART delivered the opinion of the Court.

This case presents a challenge to the constitutionality of the Massachusetts veterans' preference statute, on the ground that it discriminates against women in violation of the Equal Protection Clause of the Fourteenth Amendment. Under ch. 31, §23, all veterans who qualify for state civil service positions must be considered for appointment ahead of any qualifying nonveterans. The preference operates overwhelmingly to the advantage of males.

The District Court found that the absolute preference afforded by Massachusetts to veterans has a devastating impact upon the employment opportunities of women. Although it found that the goals of the preference were worthy and legitimate and that the legislation had not been enacted for the purpose of discriminating against women, the court reasoned that its exclusionary impact upon women was nonetheless so severe as to require the State to further its goals through a more limited form of preference. Finding that a more modest preference formula would readily accommodate the State's interest in aiding veterans, the court declared ch. 31, §23, unconstitutional and enjoined its operation.

The veterans' hiring preference in Massachusetts, as in other jurisdictions, has traditionally been justified as a measure designed to reward veterans for the sacrifice of military service, to ease the transition from military to civilian life, to encourage patriotic service, and to attract loyal and well-disciplined people to civil service occupations.

Notwithstanding the apparent attempts by Massachusetts to include as many military women as possible within the scope of the preference, the statute today benefits an overwhelmingly male class. This is attributable in some measure to the variety of federal statutes, regulations, and policies that have restricted the number of women who could enlist in the United States Armed Forces, and largely to the simple fact that women have never been subjected to a military draft. When this litigation was commenced, then, over 98% of the veterans in Massachusetts were male; only 1.8% were female. And over one-quarter of the Massachusetts population were veterans.

The dispositive question, then, is whether the appellee has shown that a gender-based discriminatory purpose has, at least in some measure, shaped the Massachusetts veterans' preference legislation. The appellee's ultimate argument rests upon the presumption, common to the criminal and civil law, that a person intends the natural and foreseeable consequences of his voluntary actions. Her position was well stated in the concurring opinion in the District Court:

> Conceding . . . that the goal here was to benefit the veteran, there is no reason to absolve the legislature from awareness that the means chosen to achieve this goal would freeze women out of all those state jobs actively sought by men. To be sure, the legislature did not wish to harm women. But the cutting-off of women's opportunities was an inevitable concomitant of the chosen scheme — as inevitable as the proposition that if tails is up, heads must be down. Where a law's consequences are that inevitable, can they meaningfully be described as unintended?

This rhetorical question implies that a negative answer is obvious, but it is not. The decision to grant a preference to veterans was of course "intentional." So, necessarily, did an adverse impact upon nonveterans follow from that decision. And it cannot seriously be argued that the Legislature of Massachusetts could have been unaware that most veterans are men. It would thus be disingenuous to say that the adverse consequences of this legislation for women were unintended, in the sense that they were not volitional or in the sense that they were not foreseeable.

"Discriminatory purpose," however, implies more than intent as volition or intent as awareness of consequences. It implies that the decisionmaker, in this case a state legislature, selected or reaffirmed a particular course of action at least in part "because of," not merely "in spite of," its adverse effects upon an identifiable group. Yet, nothing in the record demonstrates that this preference for veterans was originally devised or subsequently re-enacted because it would accomplish the collateral goal of keeping women in a stereotypic and predefined place in the Massachusetts Civil Service.

To the contrary, the statutory history shows that the benefit of the preference was consistently offered to "any person" who was a veteran. That benefit has been extended to women under a very broad statutory definition of the term veteran. When the totality of legislative actions establishing and extending the Massachusetts veterans' preference are considered, the law remains what it purports to be: a preference for veterans of either sex over nonveterans of either sex, not for men over women.

The issue, then, is how a plaintiff proves intent as defined in *Feeney*. In Village of Arlington Heights v. Metropolitan Housing Development Corp., the Supreme Court explained the different ways in which discriminatory purpose can be proven.

VILLAGE OF ARLINGTON HEIGHTS v. METROPOLITAN HOUSING DEVELOPMENT CORP.

429 U.S. 252 (1977)

Justice POWELL delivered the opinion of the Court.

In 1971 respondent Metropolitan Housing Development Corporation (MHDC) applied to petitioner, the Village of Arlington Heights, Ill., for the rezoning of a 15-acre parcel from single-family to multiple-family classification. Using federal financial assistance, MHDC planned to build 190 clustered townhouse units for low- and moderate-income tenants. The Village denied the rezoning request. MHDC, joined by other plaintiffs who are also respondents here, brought suit in the United States District Court for the Northern District of Illinois. They alleged that the denial was racially discriminatory and that it violated the Fourteenth Amendment and the Fair Housing Act of 1968.

Our decision last Term in Washington v. Davis (1976), made it clear that official action will not be held unconstitutional solely because it results in a racially disproportionate impact. "Disproportionate impact is not irrelevant, but it is not the sole touchstone of an invidious racial discrimination." Proof of racially discriminatory intent or purpose is required to show a violation of the Equal Protection Clause.

Davis does not require a plaintiff to prove that the challenged action rested solely on racially discriminatory purposes. Rarely can it be said that a legislature or administrative body operating under a broad mandate made a decision motivated solely by a single concern, or even that a particular purpose was the "dominant" or "primary" one. In fact, it is because legislators and administrators are properly concerned with balancing numerous competing considerations that courts refrain from reviewing the merits of their decisions, absent a showing of arbitrariness or irrationality. But racial discrimination is not just another competing consideration. When there is a proof that a discriminatory purpose has been a motivating factor in the decision, this judicial deference is no longer justified.

Determining whether invidious discriminatory purpose was a motivating factor demands a sensitive inquiry into such circumstantial and direct evidence of intent as may be available. The impact of the official action — whether it "bears more heavily on one race than another," Washington v. Davis — may provide an important starting point. Sometimes a clear pattern, unexplainable on grounds other than race, emerges from the effect of the state action even when the governing legislation appears neutral on its face. Yick Wo v. Hopkins (1886); Gomillion v. Lightfoot (1960).[76] The evidentiary inquiry is then relatively easy. But such cases are rare. Absent a pattern as stark as that in *Gomillion* or *Yick Wo*, impact alone is not determinative, and the Court must look to other evidence.

The historical background of the decision is one evidentiary source, particularly if it reveals a series of official actions taken for invidious purposes. The specific sequence of events leading up to the challenged decision also may shed some light on the decisionmaker's purposes. For example, if the property involved here always had been zoned R-5 but suddenly was changed to R-3 when the town learned of MHDC's plans to erect integrated housing, we would have a far different case. Departures from the normal procedural sequence also might afford evidence that improper purposes are playing a role. Substantive departures too may be relevant, particularly if the factors

---

76. In Yick Wo v. Hopkins, 118 U.S. 356 (1886), a city's ordinance required that laundries be located in brick or stone buildings unless a waiver was obtained from the board of supervisors. The plaintiff alleged that over 200 petitions by those of Chinese ancestry had been denied, although all but one of the petitions filed by non-Chinese individuals were granted. The Supreme Court unanimously reversed Yick Wo's conviction for violating the ordinance and explained, "[T]he facts shown establish an administration directed so exclusively against a particular class of persons as to warrant and require the conclusion, that, whatever may have been the intent of the ordinances as adopted, they are applied by the public authorities charged with the administration, and thus representing the State itself, with a mind so unequal and oppressive as to amount to a practical denial by the State of that equal protection of the laws."

Gomillion v. Lightfoot, 364 U.S. 339 (1960), involved a challenge to the government's redrawing of the city's boundaries to exclude blacks from participating in city elections. Tuskegee, Alabama, was transformed from a square shape into a 28-sided figure. All but 4 or 5 of the 400 blacks in the city were placed outside its boundaries, but no whites were excluded. The Court said that the "conclusion would be irresistible, tantamount for all practical purposes to a mathematical demonstration, that the legislation is solely concerned with segregating white and colored voters by fencing Negro citizens out of town so as to deprive them of their pre-existing municipal vote." [Footnote by casebook author.]

usually considered important by the decisionmaker strongly favor a decision contrary to the one reached.

The legislative or administrative history may be highly relevant, especially where there are contemporary statements by members of the decisionmaking body, minutes of its meetings, or reports. In some extraordinary instances the members might be called to the stand at trial to testify concerning the purpose of the official action, although even then such testimony frequently will be barred by privilege.

With these in mind, we now address the case before us. The impact of the Village's decision does arguably bear more heavily on racial minorities. Minorities constitute 18% of the Chicago area population, and 40% of the income groups said to be eligible for Lincoln Green. But there is little about the sequence of events leading up to the decision that would spark suspicion. The area around the Viatorian property has been zoned R-3 since 1959, the year when Arlington Heights first adopted a zoning map. Single-family homes surround the 80-acre site, and the Village is undeniably committed to single-family homes as its dominant residential land use. The rezoning request progressed according to the usual procedures. The Plan Commission even scheduled two additional hearings, at least in part to accommodate MHDC and permit it to supplement its presentation with answers to questions generated at the first hearing. In sum, Respondents simply failed to carry their burden of proving that discriminatory purpose was a motivating factor in the Village's decision.[77]

The Court applied the approach described in *Arlington Heights* in Hunter v. Underwood, 471 U.S. 222 (1985), which considered an Alabama law that permanently denied the right to vote to anyone convicted of a crime involving "moral turpitude." The Supreme Court held that it was unconstitutional race discrimination for the state to disenfranchise those convicted of misdemeanors. The Court reiterated the approach that it articulated in *Arlington Heights*: "Once racial discrimination is shown to have been a 'substantial' or 'motivating' factor behind enactment of the law, the burden shifts to the law's defenders to demonstrate that the law would have been enacted without this factor."

The evidence in the case indicated that excluding a misdemeanant from voting had a substantial discriminatory impact against blacks and that racial discrimination was a key purpose of the legislature when the law was adopted in 1901. The Court found no persuasive evidence that the law would have been adopted without this motivation and thus concluded that it was unconstitutional because "its original enactment was motivated by a desire to discriminate against

---

77. Proof that the decision by the Village was motivated in part by a racially discriminatory purpose would not necessarily have required invalidation of the challenged decision. Such proof would, however, have shifted to the Village the burden of establishing that the same decision would have resulted even had the impermissible purpose not been considered. If this were established, the complaining party in a case of this kind no longer fairly could attribute the injury complained of to improper consideration of a discriminatory purpose. In such circumstances, there would be no justification for judicial interference with the challenged decision. But in this case respondents failed to make the required threshold showing. See Mt. Healthy City School Dist. Bd. of Education v. Doyle (1977). [Footnote by the Court.]

blacks on account of race and the section continues to this day to have that effect."

APPLICATION: DISCRIMINATORY USE OF PEREMPTORY CHALLENGES

One of the most important areas where the Supreme Court has followed and applied this analysis is in holding unconstitutional the discriminatory use of peremptory challenges. Laws providing for peremptory challenges — the ability of attorneys to exclude prospective jurors without having to prove cause for excusing them — are facially race neutral. But peremptory challenges based on race or gender are motivated by a discriminatory intent and have a discriminatory impact. Thus, the Court has held that race- or gender-based peremptory challenges deny equal protection whether exercised by a prosecutor,[78] a criminal defendant,[79] or a civil litigant.[80]

Initially, in Swain v. Alabama, 380 U.S. 202 (1965), the Supreme Court held that racial discrimination by a prosecutor could be proven only by showing a pattern of discriminatory peremptory challenges over a series of cases. A defendant could not allege a denial of equal protection by the prosecution based on how peremptory challenges were exercised in that case; systematic discrimination had to be proven. In Batson v. Kentucky, the Supreme Court overruled Swain v. Alabama and explained that "[a] single invidiously discriminatory governmental act is not immunized by the absence of such discrimination in the making of other comparable decisions."

Batson thus holds that the discriminatory use of peremptory challenges by a prosecutor denies equal protection. *Batson* set forth a three-step process for determining whether there is impermissible discrimination in jury selection. First, the criminal defendant must set forth a prima facie case of discrimination by the prosecutor. The Supreme Court has not articulated precise standards for determining what is a prima facie case. In *Batson*, the Court said that "the defendant first must show that he is a member of a cognizable racial group, and that the prosecutor has exercised peremptory challenges to remove from the venire members of the defendant's race." But in practice what is enough for a prima facie case is unclear. The Court simply expressed "confidence that trial judges, experienced in supervising voir dire" would be able to "consider all relevant circumstances" and decide if there is a prima facie case of discrimination.

Second, once the defendant has presented a prima facie case of discrimination, the burden shifts to the prosecutor to offer a race-neutral explanation for the peremptory challenges. The Court said that the proponent of a strike "must give a 'clear and reasonably specific' explanation of his 'legitimate reasons' for exercising the challenges." Subsequently, in Purkett v. Elem, 514 U.S. 765 (1995), the Supreme Court said that "[t]he second step of this process does not demand an explanation that is persuasive, or even plausible. . . . It is not until the *third* step that the persuasiveness of the justification becomes relevant."

---

78. Batson v. Kentucky, 476 U.S. 79 (1986).
79. Georgia v. McCollum, 505 U.S. 42 (1992).
80. Edmonson v. Leesville Concrete Co., 500 U.S. 614 (1991).

In other words, the second step is simply the prosecutor offering the explanation; the third step is where the justification is evaluated.

In the third step, the trial court must decide whether the race-neutral explanation is persuasive or whether the "defendant has established purposeful discrimination." In two cases since *Batson*, the Supreme Court has elaborated this step and made it easier for courts to find a neutral explanation for the strikes of prospective jurors. In Hernandez v. New York, 500 U.S. 352 (1991), the Court found that there was a sufficient race-neutral explanation when a prosecutor said that he had struck two prospective Latino jurors because they spoke Spanish and therefore might not accept the translator's version of testimony from witnesses who were going to testify in Spanish.

More recently, in Purkett v. Elem, 514 U.S. 765 (1995), the Supreme Court said that "a 'legitimate reason' is not a reason that makes sense, but a reason that does not deny equal protection." *Purkett* did not elaborate; it is a short per curiam opinion, and there had been neither briefing nor oral arguments in the case. The Court upheld a trial court's conclusion that there was no discriminatory purpose when a prosecutor struck a prospective juror because of "long, unkempt hair, a mustache, and a beard." If any "legitimate reason," even one that does not make sense, is sufficient, *Batson* will be substantially weakened. It almost always will be possible for a prosecutor to articulate some race-neutral reason for a strike, such as the physical appearance of the prospective juror.

Although *Batson* involved only the issue of discriminatory peremptory strikes by prosecutors, the Court subsequently expanded it to apply to civil litigants and criminal defendants. In Edmonson v. Leesville Concrete Co., 500 U.S. 614 (1991), the Supreme Court ruled that *Batson* applies in private civil litigation. The Court explained that there is state action because peremptory challenges are authorized by state law and supervised by courts. In Georgia v. McCollum, 505 U.S. 42 (1992), the Supreme Court held that criminal defendants may not exercise peremptory challenges in a discriminatory manner. Although criminal defendants are the antithesis of the government, the Court followed its earlier rulings that prospective jurors have a right to be free from discrimination in jury selection[81] and that there is state action when a private party exercises peremptory challenges.

In J.E.B. v. Alabama ex rel. T.B., 511 U.S. 127 (1994), the Supreme Court extended *Batson* to apply to gender-based discrimination in the use of peremptory challenges. The Court, in an opinion by Justice Blackmun, stressed the long history of discrimination against women in the legal system and concluded that gender, like race, was an impermissible basis for peremptory challenges. The Court indicated, however, that *Batson* only would apply to types of discrimination that would receive heightened scrutiny under equal protection analysis. In addition to race and gender, this would include discrimination against nonmarital children and aliens; neither, however, is likely to be a basis for peremptory challenges, especially since aliens are usually not allowed to serve on juries. An unresolved issue is whether *Batson* will apply to peremptory challenges based on religion.

---

81. Powers v. Ohio, 499 U.S. 400 (1991).

4. Remedies: The Problem of School Segregation

INTRODUCTION: THE PROBLEM OF REMEDIES

If a court finds that there is an equal protection violation, it then must fashion a remedy. In some cases, the remedy is simply invalidating the discriminatory law. For example, in Strauder v. West Virginia, 100 U.S. 303 (1879), the remedy was declaring unconstitutional the law prohibiting blacks from serving on juries; in Loving v. Virginia, 388 U.S. 1 (1967), the remedy was invalidating the law prohibiting interracial marriage.

In some cases, the Court must go further and fashion an injunction. For example, in desegregation cases, the Court generally will issue an order prohibiting the offending conduct. If a state had a law requiring segregation of a park or a beach, the Court would declare the law unconstitutional and also issue an injunction preventing continued segregation of the facility.

Fashioning a remedy was most difficult, by far, in the area of school desegregation. In the area of schools, it was not sufficient simply to order removal of the "whites only" sign. Pupils and teachers had to be reassigned. Because schools tend to serve neighborhoods and residential segregation was prevalent, desegregating schools proved extremely difficult. Indeed, in Brown v. Board of Education, in 1954, the Supreme Court did not address the issue of remedies but instead set the case for reargument as to the issue of the appropriate remedies. This is the Court's short decision the next year on the question of remedies.

BROWN v. BOARD OF EDUCATION

349 U.S. 294 (1955)

Chief Justice WARREN delivered the opinion of the Court.

These cases were decided on May 17, 1954. The opinions of that date, declaring the fundamental principle that racial discrimination in public education is unconstitutional, are incorporated herein by reference. All provisions of federal, state, or local law requiring or permitting such discrimination must yield to this principle. There remains for consideration the manner in which relief is to be accorded.

Because these cases arose under different local conditions and their disposition will involve a variety of local problems, we requested further argument on the question of relief. These presentations were informative and helpful to the Court in its consideration of the complexities arising from the transition to a system of public education freed of racial discrimination. The presentations also demonstrated that substantial steps to eliminate racial discrimination in public schools have already been taken, not only in some of the communities in which these cases arose, but in some of the states appearing as amici curiae, and in other states as well. Substantial progress has been made in the District of Columbia and in the communities in Kansas and Delaware involved in this litigation. The defendants in the cases coming to us from South Carolina and Virginia are awaiting the decision of this Court concerning relief.

Full implementation of these constitutional principles may require solution of varied local school problems. School authorities have the primary responsibility for elucidating, assessing, and solving these problems; courts will have to consider whether the action of school authorities constitutes good faith implementation of the governing constitutional principles. Because of their proximity to local conditions and the possible need for further hearings, the courts which originally heard these cases can best perform this judicial appraisal. Accordingly, we believe it appropriate to remand the cases to those courts.

In fashioning and effectuating the decrees, the courts will be guided by equitable principles. Traditionally, equity has been characterized by a practical flexibility in shaping its remedies and by a facility for adjusting and reconciling public and private needs. These cases call for the exercise of these traditional attributes of equity power. At stake is the personal interest of the plaintiffs in admission to public schools as soon as practicable on a nondiscriminatory basis. To effectuate this interest may call for elimination of a variety of obstacles in making the transition to school systems operated in accordance with the constitutional principles set forth in our May 17, 1954, decision. Courts of equity may properly take into account the public interest in the elimination of such obstacles in a systematic and effective manner. But it should go without saying that the vitality of these constitutional principles cannot be allowed to yield simply because of disagreement with them.

While giving weight to these public and private considerations, the courts will require that the defendants make a prompt and reasonable start toward full compliance with our May 17, 1954, ruling. Once such a start has been made, the courts may find that additional time is necessary to carry out the ruling in an effective manner. The burden rests upon the defendants to establish that such time is necessary in the public interest and is consistent with good faith compliance at the earliest practicable date. To that end, the courts may consider problems related to administration, arising from the physical condition of the school plant, the school transportation system, personnel, revision of school districts and attendance areas into compact units to achieve a system of determining admission to the public schools on a nonracial basis, and revision of local laws and regulations which may be necessary in solving the foregoing problems. They will also consider the adequacy of any plans the defendants may propose to meet these problems and to effectuate a transition to a racially nondiscriminatory school system. During this period of transition, the courts will retain jurisdiction of these cases.

The judgments below are accordingly reversed and the cases are remanded to the District Courts to take such proceedings and enter such orders and decrees consistent with this opinion as are necessary and proper to admit to public schools on a racially nondiscriminatory basis with all deliberate speed the parties to these cases.

MASSIVE RESISTANCE

Southern states openly and aggressively resisted compliance with Brown v. Board of Education and the ordered end to school segregation. State legislatures adopted resolutions of "nullification" and "interposition" that declared that the Supreme Court's decisions were without effect.[82] State officials attempted to obstruct desegregation in every imaginable way.

The Supreme Court first responded to this in Cooper v. Aaron, 358 U.S. 1 (1958). The Little Rock school system was ordered desegregated during the 1957-1958 school year, but the governor called out the Arkansas National Guard to keep blacks out. Black students began attending the previously all-white high school only after President Dwight Eisenhower used federal troops to protect them. The Little Rock school system then asked for a stay of the integration plan. The U.S. Supreme Court responded with an unusual opinion that was signed by each of the nine justices. The Court began its opinion by declaring, "As this case reaches us it raises questions of the highest importance to the maintenance of our federal system of government. It necessarily involves a claim by the Governor and Legislature of a State that there is no duty on state officials to obey federal court orders resting on this Court's considered interpretation of the United States Constitution."

The Court declared that "[t]he constitutional rights of respondents are not to be sacrificed or yielded to the violence and disorder which have followed upon the actions of the Governor and Legislature." The Court invoked Marbury v. Madison to respond to the state's claim that it did not have to comply with the Supreme Court's decision. The Court said, "[*Marbury*] declared the basic principle that the federal judiciary is supreme in the exposition of the law of the Constitution, and that principle has ever since been respected by this Court and the Country as a permanent and indispensable feature of our constitutional system. It follows that the interpretation of the Fourteenth Amendment enunciated by this Court in the *Brown* case is the supreme law of the land. . . . No state legislator or executive or judicial officer can war against the Constitution without violating his undertaking to support it." The Court strongly reaffirmed *Brown* and said that it could not be nullified either "openly and directly by state legislators or state executive or judicial officers" or "indirectly by them through evasive schemes for segregation whether attempted 'ingeniously or ingenuously.'"

Cooper v. Aaron, however, did not end efforts by Southern states to circumvent *Brown* and prevent desegregation. Some areas attempted to close their public schools rather than desegregate.[83] Others sought to comply with *Brown* by creating voluntary transfer plans that allowed students to attend the school of their choice; segregation continued unabated under these plans.[84] Some school systems adopted "one grade a year" desegregation plans that would mean almost 20 years before a school system was fully desegregated.[85]

These and other state efforts succeeded in frustrating desegregation. In 1964, a decade after *Brown*, in the South, just 1.2 percent of black schoolchildren were attending school with whites.[86] In South Carolina, Alabama, and Mississippi, not one black child attended a public school with a white child in the 1962-1963

---

82. For a review of these laws, *see* Robert B. McKay, *"With All Deliberate Speed"—A Study of School Desegregation*, 31 N.Y.U. L. Rev. 991, 1039-1049 (1956).
83. *See* Griffin v. County School Board, 377 U.S. 218 (1964).
84. *See* Goss v. Board of Education, 373 U.S. 683 (1963).
85. *See* Rogers v. Paul, 382 U.S. 198 (1965).
86. Michael J. Klarman, Brown, *Racial Change, and the Civil Rights Movement*, 80 Va. L. Rev. 7, 9 (1994).

school year.[87] In North Carolina, only one-fifth of 1 percent — or 0.026 percent — of the black students attended desegregated schools in 1961, and the figure did not rise above 1 percent until 1965.[88] Similarly, in Virginia, in 1964, only 1.63 percent of blacks were attending desegregated schools.[89]

Except for Cooper v. Aaron, the Supreme Court did not hear a school desegregation case for almost a decade after *Brown*. In a series of cases in the mid- and late 1960s, the Court declared unconstitutional various obstructionist techniques used throughout the South. In 1963, in Goss v. Board of Education, 373 U.S. 683 (1963), the Supreme Court invalidated a Knoxville, Tennessee, law that allowed students who were assigned to new schools as part of desegregation to transfer from schools where they were a racial minority to ones where they would be in the racial majority. In other words, a white student who was placed in a predominately black school could transfer back to a white school, and a black student who was placed in a predominately white school could do the same. The Supreme Court declared this unconstitutional because "[i]t is readily apparent that the transfer system . . . lends itself to perpetuation of segregation."

In Griffin v. County School Bd., 377 U.S. 218 (1964), the Supreme Court declared it unconstitutional for school systems to close rather than desegregate. In 1959, Prince Edward County, Virginia, closed its school system rather than comply with a desegregation order. The Court ordered the schools reopened and explained that "[w]hatever nonracial grounds might support a State's allowing a county to abandon public schools, the object must be a constitutional one, and grounds of race and opposition to desegregation do not qualify as constitutional." The Court also expressed its frustration with the resistance to desegregation and declared that "[t]here has been entirely too much deliberation and not enough speed."

In 1969, in Green v. County School Board, 391 U.S. 430 (1968), the Supreme Court declared unconstitutional a "freedom of choice plan" that was a common approach used to frustrate desegregation. A school system in rural Virginia adopted a desegregation plan where students could choose which school to attend. Three years after it was enacted, no white student was attending a black school, and only 15 percent of black students were attending white schools. The Court said that "[i]t is incumbent upon the school board to establish that its proposed plan promises meaningful and immediate progress toward disestablishing state-imposed segregation. . . . Of course, the availability to the board of other more promising courses of action may indicate a lack of good faith; and at the least it places a heavy burden upon the board to explain its preference for an apparently less effective method." The Court emphatically declared that school boards have "the affirmative duty to take whatever steps might be necessary to convert to a unitary system in which racial discrimination would be eliminated root and branch."

These Supreme Court decisions ending obstruction to desegregation were accompanied by an important federal law: the Civil Rights Act of 1964. Title VI prohibited discrimination by schools receiving federal funds. This became especially significant when Congress enacted the Elementary and Secondary Education Act of 1965, which appropriated $2.5 billion for schools. Additionally, the

---

87. *Id.* at 9.
88. *Id.*
89. *Id.*

1964 Civil Rights Act authorized the U.S. attorney general to intervene in desegregation suits.

The combination of federal court action and the federal law had an effect in bringing about desegregation.[90] One by one the obstructionist techniques were defeated. Finally, by the mid-1960s, desegregation began to proceed. By 1968, the integration rate in the South rose to 32 percent, and by 1972-1973, 91.3 percent of Southern schools were desegregated.

Yet there is no doubt that despite over 40 years of judicial action, school segregation continues. Indeed, racial segregation in American schools has been increasing over the past decade. A study by the National School Boards Association found "a pattern in which impressive progress toward school integration among blacks and whites during the 1970s petered out in the 1980s."[91] A study by Harvard professor Gary Orfield found that in the South, "[f]rom 1988 to 1998, most of the progress from the previous two decades in increasing integration in the region was lost. The South is still more integrated than it was before the civil rights revolution, but it is moving backwards at an accelerating rate."[92]

In 1980, "63 percent of black students and 66 percent of Hispanics were in segregated schools, that is schools with more than half minority enrollment."[93] Today, it is much more than this. Professor Orfield's study shows that nationally the percentage of African American students attending schools with exclusively African American enrollment and schools where over 90 percent of the students are African American has increased dramatically over the past 15 years. A study by in 2012 by the Civil Rights Project at the University of California, Los Angeles, found that across the country, 43 percent of Latinos and 38 percent of blacks attend schools where fewer than 10 percent of their classmates are white. More than one in seven black and Latino students attend schools where fewer than 1 percent of their classmates are white.

The reality is that most children in the United States are educated only with children of their own race. A key question in light of this history is whether there is more that the Supreme Court could have done, in *Brown* or later, to desegregate American public schools.

JUDICIAL POWER TO IMPOSE REMEDIES IN SCHOOL DESEGREGATION CASES

In Swann v. Charlotte-Mecklenburg Board of Education, the Supreme Court addressed the issue of the federal courts' power to issue remedies in school desegregation cases.

---

90. An empirical study shows that Brown v. Board of Education had a substantial effect in changing decisions by federal district courts. *See* Francine Sanders, *Brown v. Board of Education: An Empirical Reexamination of Its Effects on Federal District Courts*, 29 L. & Soc. Rev. 731 (1995).

91. Larry Tye, *Social Racial Gaps Found Nationwide*, Boston Globe, Jan. 9, 1992, at 3.

92. Gary Orfield, *Schools More Separate: Consequences of a Decade of Resegregation* 2, The Civil Rights Project, Harvard Univ. (2001).

93. *Illinois Schools Most Segregated*, Chicago Sun Times, Sept. 5, 1982, at 6.

SWANN v. CHARLOTTE-MECKLENBURG BOARD OF EDUCATION
402 U.S. 1 (1971)

Chief Justice BURGER delivered the opinion of the Court.

We granted certiorari in this case to review important issues as to the duties of school authorities and the scope of powers of federal courts under this Court's mandates to eliminate racially separate public schools established and maintained by state action. Brown v. Board of Education (1954).

This case and those argued with it arose in States having a long history of maintaining two sets of schools in a single school system deliberately operated to carry out a governmental policy to separate pupils in schools solely on the basis of race. That was what Brown v. Board of Education was all about. These cases present us with the problem of defining in more precise terms than heretofore the scope of the duty of school authorities and district courts in implementing.

The objective today remains to eliminate from the public schools all vestiges of state-imposed segregation. Segregation was the evil struck down by *Brown I* as contrary to the equal protection guarantees of the Constitution. That was the violation sought to be corrected by the remedial measures of *Brown II*. If school authorities fail in their affirmative obligations under these holdings, judicial authority may be invoked. Once a right and a violation have been shown, the scope of a district court's equitable powers to remedy past wrongs is broad, for breadth and flexibility are inherent in equitable remedies.

In seeking to define even in broad and general terms how far this remedial power extends it is important to remember that judicial powers may be exercised only on the basis of a constitutional violation. Remedial judicial authority does not put judges automatically in the shoes of school authorities whose powers are plenary. Judicial authority enters only when local authority defaults.

In ascertaining the existence of legally imposed school segregation, the existence of a pattern of school construction and abandonment is thus a factor of great weight. In devising remedies where legally imposed segregation has been established, it is the responsibility of local authorities and district courts to see to it that future school construction and abandonment are not used and do not serve to perpetuate or re-establish the dual system. When necessary, district courts should retain jurisdiction to assure that these responsibilities are carried out.

The central issue in this case is that of student assignment, and there are essentially four problem areas:

(1)   to what extent racial balance or racial quotas may be used as an implement in a remedial order to correct a previously segregated system;

(2)   whether every all-Negro and all-white school must be eliminated as an indispensable part of a remedial process of desegregation;

(3)   what the limits are, if any, on the rearrangement of school districts and attendance zones, as a remedial measure; and

(4)   what the limits are, if any, on the use of transportation facilities to correct state-enforced racial school segregation.

(1)   RACIAL BALANCES OR RACIAL QUOTAS

In this case it is urged that the District Court has imposed a racial balance requirement of 71%-29% on individual schools. As the voluminous record in this case shows, the predicate for the District Court's use of the 71%-29% ratio was twofold: first, its express finding, approved by the Court of Appeals and not challenged here, that a dual school system had been maintained by the school authorities at least until 1969; second, its finding, also approved by the Court of Appeals, that the school board had totally defaulted in its acknowledged duty to come forward with an acceptable plan of its own, notwithstanding the patient efforts of the District Judge who, on at least three occasions, urged the board to submit plans.

We see therefore that the use made of mathematical ratios was no more than a starting point in the process of shaping a remedy, rather than an inflexible requirement. Awareness of the racial composition of the whole school system is likely to be a useful starting point in shaping a remedy to correct past constitutional violations. In sum, the very limited use made of mathematical ratios was within the equitable remedial discretion of the District Court.

(2)   ONE-RACE SCHOOLS

The record in this case reveals the familiar phenomenon that in metropolitan areas minority groups are often found concentrated in one part of the city. In some circumstances certain schools may remain all or largely of one race until new schools can be provided or neighborhood patterns change. Schools all or predominantly of one race in a district of mixed population will require close scrutiny to determine that school assignments are not part of state-enforced segregation.

In light of the above, it should be clear that the existence of some small number of one-race, or virtually one-race, schools within a district is not in and of itself the mark of a system that still practices segregation by law. The district judge or school authorities should make every effort to achieve the greatest possible degree of actual desegregation and will thus necessarily be concerned with the elimination of one-race schools. No per se rule can adequately embrace all the difficulties of reconciling the competing interests involved; but in a system with a history of segregation the need for remedial criteria of sufficient specificity to assure a school authority's compliance with its constitutional duty warrants a presumption against schools that are substantially disproportionate in their racial composition. Where the school authority's proposed plan for conversion from a dual to a unitary system contemplates the continued existence of some schools that are all or predominately of one race, they have the burden of showing that such school assignments are genuinely nondiscriminatory. The court should scrutinize such schools, and the burden upon the school authorities will be to satisfy the court that their racial composition is not the result of present or past discriminatory action on their part.

(3)   REMEDIAL ALTERING OF ATTENDANCE ZONES

The maps submitted in these cases graphically demonstrate that one of the principal tools employed by school planners and by courts to break up the dual school system has been a frank—and sometimes drastic—gerrymandering of school districts and attendance zones. As an interim corrective measure, this cannot be said to be beyond the broad remedial powers of a court.

The remedy for such segregation may be administratively awkward, inconvenient, and even bizarre in some situations and may impose burdens on some; but all awkwardness and inconvenience cannot be avoided in the interim period when remedial adjustments are being made to eliminate the dual school systems.

No fixed or even substantially fixed guidelines can be established as to how far a court can go, but it must be recognized that there are limits. The objective is to dismantle the dual school system. "Racially neutral" assignment plans proposed by school authorities to a district court may be inadequate; such plans may fail to counteract the continuing effects of past school segregation resulting from discriminatory location of school sites or distortion of school size in order to achieve or maintain an artificial racial separation. When school authorities present a district court with a "loaded game board," affirmative action in the form of remedial altering of attendance zones is proper to achieve truly nondiscriminatory assignments. In short, an assignment plan is not acceptable simply because it appears to be neutral. Conditions in different localities will vary so widely that no rigid rules can be laid down to govern all situations.

(4)   TRANSPORTATION OF STUDENTS

The scope of permissible transportation of students as an implement of a remedial decree has never been defined by this Court and by the very nature of the problem it cannot be defined with precision. No rigid guidelines as to student transportation can be given for application to the infinite variety of problems presented in thousands of situations. Bus transportation has been an integral part of the public education system for years, and was perhaps the single most important factor in the transition from the one-room schoolhouse to the consolidated school. Eighteen million of the Nation's public school children, approximately 39%, were transported to their schools by bus in 1969-1970 in all parts of the country.

The importance of bus transportation as a normal and accepted tool of educational policy is readily discernible. Charlotte school authorities did not purport to assign students on the basis of geographically drawn zones until 1965 and then they allowed almost unlimited transfer privileges. The District Court's conclusion that assignment of children to the school nearest their home serving their grade would not produce an effective dismantling of the dual system is supported by the record.

Thus the remedial techniques used in the District Court's order were within that court's power to provide equitable relief; implementation of the decree is well within the capacity of the school authority. The decree provided that the buses used to implement the plan would operate on direct routes. Students would be picked up at schools near their homes and transported to the schools they were to attend. The trips for elementary school pupils average about seven miles and the District Court found that they would take "not over 35 minutes at the most." This system compares favorably with the transportation plan previously operated in Charlotte under which each day 26,600 students on all grade levels were transported an average of 15 miles one way for an average trip requiring over an hour. In these circumstances, we find no basis for holding that the local school authorities may not be required to employ bus transportation as one tool of school desegregation. Desegregation plans cannot be limited to the walk-in school.

An objection to transportation of students may have validity when the time or distance of travel is so great as to either risk the health of the children or significantly impinge on the educational process. District courts must weigh the soundness of any transportation plan. It hardly needs stating that the limits on time of travel will vary with many factors, but probably with none more than the age of the students. The reconciliation of competing values in a desegregation case is, of course, a difficult task with many sensitive facets but fundamentally no more so than remedial measures courts of equity have traditionally employed.

At some point, these school authorities and others like them should have achieved full compliance with this Court's decision in *Brown I*. The systems would then be "unitary."

Although *Swann* broadly defined the remedial powers of federal courts, in Milliken v. Bradley the Supreme Court imposed a substantial limit on the courts' remedial powers in desegregation cases.

MILLIKEN v. BRADLEY
418 U.S. 717 (1974)

Chief Justice BURGER delivered the opinion of the Court.

We granted certiorari in these consolidated cases to determine whether a federal court may impose a multidistrict, areawide remedy to a single-district de jure segregation problem absent any finding that the other included school districts have failed to operate unitary school systems within their districts, absent any claim or finding that the boundary lines of any affected school district were established with the purpose of fostering racial segregation in public schools, absent any finding that the included districts committed acts which effected segregation within the other districts, and absent a meaningful opportunity for the included neighboring school districts to present evidence or be heard on the propriety of a multidistrict remedy or on the question of constitutional violations by those neighboring districts.

Viewing the record as a whole, it seems clear that the District Court and the Court of Appeals shifted the primary focus from a Detroit remedy to the metropolitan area only because of their conclusion that total desegregation of Detroit would not produce the racial balance which they perceived as desirable. Both courts proceeded on an assumption that the Detroit schools could not be truly desegregated — in their view of what constituted desegregation — unless the racial composition of the student body of each school substantially reflected the racial composition of the population of the metropolitan area as a whole. The metropolitan area was then defined as Detroit plus 53 of the outlying school districts.

The metropolitan remedy would require, in effect, consolidation of 54 independent school districts historically administered as separate units into a vast new super school district. Entirely apart from the logistical and other serious problems attending large-scale transportation of students, the consolidation would give rise to an array of other problems in financing and operating this new school system. Some of the more obvious questions would be: What would be the status and authority of the present popularly elected school boards? Would the children of Detroit be within the jurisdiction and operating control of a school board elected by the parents and residents of other districts? What board or boards would levy taxes for school operations in these 54 districts constituting the consolidated metropolitan area? What provisions could be made for assuring substantial equality in tax levies among the 54 districts, if this were deemed requisite? What provisions would be made for financing? Would the validity of long-term bonds be jeopardized unless approved by all of the component districts as well as the State? What body would determine that portion of the curricula now left to the discretion of local school boards? Who would establish attendance zones, purchase school equipment, locate and construct new schools, and indeed attend to all the myriad day-to-day decisions that are necessary to school operations affecting potentially more than three-quarters of a million pupils?

The controlling principle consistently expounded in our holdings is that the scope of the remedy is determined by the nature and extent of the constitutional violation. Before the boundaries of separate and autonomous school districts may be set aside by consolidating the separate units for remedial purposes or by imposing a cross-district remedy, it must first be shown that there has been a constitutional violation within one district that produces a significant segregative effect in another district. Specifically, it must be shown that racially discriminatory acts of the state or local school districts, or of a single school district have been a substantial cause of interdistrict segregation. Thus an interdistrict remedy might be in order where the racially discriminatory acts of one or more school districts caused racial segregation in an adjacent district, or where district lines have been deliberately drawn on the basis of race. In such circumstances an interdistrict remedy would be appropriate to eliminate the interdistrict segregation directly caused by the constitutional violation. Conversely, without an interdistrict violation and interdistrict effect, there is no constitutional wrong calling for an interdistrict remedy.

The record before us, voluminous as it is, contains evidence of de jute segregated conditions only in the Detroit schools; indeed, that was the theory on which the litigation was initially based and on which the District Court took evidence. With no showing of significant violation by the 53 outlying school districts and no evidence of any interdistrict violation or effect, the court went beyond the original theory of the case as framed by the pleadings and mandated a metropolitan area remedy. To approve the remedy ordered by the court would impose on the outlying districts, not shown to have committed any constitutional violation, a wholly impermissible remedy based on a standard not hinted at in *Brown I* and *II* or any holding of this Court.

Justice WHITE, with whom Justice DOUGLAS, Justice BRENNAN, and Justice MARSHALL join, dissenting.

The District Court and the Court of Appeals found that over a long period of years those in charge of the Michigan public schools engaged in various practices calculated to effect the segregation of the Detroit school system. The Court does not question these findings, nor could it reasonably do so. Neither does it question the obligation of the federal courts to devise a feasible and effective remedy. But it promptly cripples the ability of the judiciary to perform this task, which is of fundamental importance to our constitutional system, by fashioning a strict rule that remedies in school cases must stop at the school district line unless certain other conditions are met. As applied here, the remedy for unquestioned violations of the protection rights of Detroit's Negroes by the Detroit School Board and the State of Michigan must be totally confined to the limits of the school district and may not reach into adjoining or surrounding districts unless and until it is proved there has been some sort of "interdistrict violation" — unless unconstitutional actions of the Detroit School Board have had a segregative impact on other districts, or unless the segregated condition of the Detroit schools has itself been influenced by segregative practices in those surrounding districts into which it is proposed to extend the remedy.

The core of my disagreement is that deliberate acts of segregation and their consequences will go unremedied, not because a remedy would be infeasible or unreasonable in terms of the usual criteria governing school desegregation cases, but because an effective remedy would cause what the Court considers to be undue administrative inconvenience to the State. The result is that the State of Michigan, the entity at which the Fourteenth Amendment is directed, has successfully insulated itself from its duty to provide effective desegregation remedies by vesting sufficient power over its public schools in its local school districts. If this is the case in Michigan, it will be the case in most States.

Viewed in this light, remedies calling for school zoning, pairing, and pupil assignments, become more and more suspect as they require that schoolchildren spend more and more time in buses going to and from school and that more and more educational dollars be diverted to transportation systems. Manifestly, these considerations are of immediate and urgent concern when the issue is the desegregation of a city school system where residential patterns are predominantly segregated and the respective areas occupied by blacks and whites are heavily populated and geographically extensive. Thus, if one postulates a metropolitan school system covering a sufficiently large area, with the population evenly divided between whites and Negroes and with the races occupying identifiable residential areas, there will be very real practical limits on the extent to which racially identifiable schools can be eliminated within the school district. It is also apparent that the larger the proportion of Negroes in the area, the more difficult it would be to avoid having a substantial number of all-black or nearly all-black schools.

Milliken has a significant effect limiting the ability to achieve desegregation in many areas. In a number of major cities, inner-city school systems are substantially black and are surrounded by almost all-white suburbs. Desegregation obviously requires the ability to transfer students between the city and suburban schools. There simply are not enough white students in the city, or enough black students in the suburbs, to achieve desegregation without an interdistrict remedy. Yet *Milliken* precludes an interdistrict remedy unless there is proof of an interdistrict violation. In other words, a multidistrict remedy can be formulated for those districts whose own policies fostered discrimination or if a state law caused the interdistrict segregation. Otherwise, the remedy can include only those districts found to violate the Constitution. Such proof is often not available, although there have been some cases where the requirements of *Milliken* have been met.[94]

Milliken can be defended based on the traditional principle that a court has the authority to impose a remedy only after it is proven that the person or entity violated the law. But critics of *Milliken* argue that the segregated pattern in major metropolitan areas—blacks in the city and whites in the suburbs—did not occur by accident, but rather was the product of myriad government policies. Additionally, in many areas *Milliken* means no desegregation. Critics argue that together with San Antonio Independent School District v. Rodriguez[95]—which held that disparities in school funding do not violate equal protection—the result is separate and unequal schools: wealthy white suburban schools spending a great deal on education surrounding much poorer black city schools that spend much less on education.

WHEN SHOULD FEDERAL DESEGREGATION REMEDIES END?

In several cases, the Supreme Court has considered when a federal court desegregation order should be ended. The Court first addressed this issue in Pasadena City Board of Education v. Spangler, 427 U.S. 424 (1976). *Pasadena* involved a school system that had been segregated by law. A federal court order succeeded in desegregation: In 1970, no schools within the district were racially imbalanced. By 1974, five of the 32 schools in the district were over half black. The district court ordered that attendance lines be redrawn on an annual basis so that blacks would not be a majority in any school in the district. The Supreme Court deemed this improper. The Court noted that residential shifts were inevitable in cities and that they might alter the racial composition of the schools. The Court said that "having once implemented a racially neutral attendance pattern in order to remedy the perceived constitutional violations on the part of the defendants, the District Court had fully performed its function of providing the appropriate remedy for previous racially discriminatory attendance patterns."

In three cases in the 1990s, the Supreme Court hastened the end of federal court desegregation orders.

---

94. *See, e.g.,* United States v. Board of School Commrs., 456 F. Supp. 183 (S.D. Ind. 1978) *aff'd in part and vacated in part*, 637 F.2d 1101 (7th Cir.), *cert. denied*, 449 U.S. 838 (1980); Evans v. Buchanan, 416 F. Supp. 328 (D. Del. 1976) (approving interdistrict remedies); *see also* Hills v. Gautreaux, 425 U.S. 284 (1976) (approving an interdistrict remedy for housing discrimination).

95. 411 U.S. 1 (1973), presented in Chapter 8.

BOARD OF EDUCATION OF OKLAHOMA CITY PUBLIC SCHOOLS v. DOWELL

498 U.S. 237 (1991)

Chief Justice Rehnquist delivered the opinion of the Court.

Petitioner Board of Education of Oklahoma City sought dissolution of a decree entered by the District Court imposing a school desegregation plan.

This school desegregation litigation began almost 30 years ago. In 1961, respondents, black students and their parents, sued petitioners, the Board of Education of Oklahoma City (Board), to end de jure segregation in the public schools. In 1963, the District Court found that Oklahoma City had intentionally segregated both schools and housing in the past, and that Oklahoma City was operating a "dual" school system — one that was intentionally segregated by race. In 1965, the District Court found that the School Board's attempt to desegregate by using neighborhood zoning failed to remedy past segregation because residential segregation resulted in one-race schools. In 1972, finding that previous efforts had not been successful at eliminating state imposed segregation, the District Court ordered the Board to adopt the "Finger Plan," under which kindergarteners would be assigned to neighborhood schools unless their parents opted otherwise; children in grades 1-4 would attend formerly all white schools, and thus black children would be bused to those schools; children in grade 5 would attend formerly all black schools, and thus white children would be bused to those schools; students in the upper grades would be bused to various areas in order to maintain integrated schools; and in integrated neighborhoods there would be stand-alone schools for all grades.

The lower courts have been inconsistent in their use of the term "unitary." Some have used it to identify a school district that has completely remedied all vestiges of past discrimination. Under that interpretation of the word, a unitary school district is one that has met the mandate of Brown v. Board of Education. Other courts, however, have used "unitary" to describe any school district that has currently desegregated student assignments, whether or not that status is solely the result of a court-imposed desegregation plan. In other words, such a school district could be called unitary and nevertheless still contain vestiges of past discrimination.

The legal justification for displacement of local authority by an injunctive decree in a school desegregation case is a violation of the Constitution by the local authorities. Dissolving a desegregation decree after the local authorities have operated in compliance with it for a reasonable period of time properly recognizes that "necessary concern for the important values of local control of public school systems dictates that a federal court's regulatory control of such systems not extend beyond the time required to remedy the effects of past intentional discrimination."

Petitioner urges that we reinstate the decision of the District Court terminating the injunction, but we think that the preferable course is to remand the case to that court so that it may decide, in accordance with this opinion, whether the Board made a sufficient showing of constitutional compliance as of 1985, when the SRP was adopted, to allow the injunction to be dissolved. The District Court should address itself to whether the Board had complied in good faith with the desegregation decree since it was entered, and whether the vestiges of past discrimination had been eliminated to the extent practicable.

Justice MARSHALL, with whom Justice BLACKMUN and Justice STEVENS join, dissenting.

Oklahoma gained statehood in 1907. For the next 65 years, the Oklahoma City School Board maintained segregated schools — initially relying on laws requiring dual school systems; thereafter, by exploiting residential segregation that had been created by legally enforced restrictive covenants. In 1972 — 18 years after this Court first found segregated schools unconstitutional — a federal court finally interrupted this cycle, enjoining the Oklahoma City School Board to implement a specific plan for achieving actual desegregation of its schools.

The practical question now before us is whether, 13 years after that injunction was imposed, the same School Board should have been allowed to return many of its elementary schools to their former one-race status. The majority today suggests that 13 years of desegregation was enough. The Court remands the case for further evaluation of whether the purposes of the injunctive decree were achieved sufficient to justify the decree's dissolution. However, the inquiry it commends to the District Court fails to recognize explicitly the threatened reemergence of one-race schools as a relevant "vestige" of de jure segregation.

I believe a desegregation decree cannot be lifted so long as conditions likely to inflict the stigmatic injury condemned in *Brown I* persist and there remain feasible methods of eliminating such conditions. Because the record here shows, and the Court of Appeals found, that feasible steps could be taken to avoid one-race schools, it is clear that the purposes of the decree have not yet been achieved and the Court of Appeals' reinstatement of the decree should be affirmed.

It is undisputed that replacing the Finger Plan [the desegregation order] with a system of neighborhood school assignments for grades K-4 resulted in a system of racially identifiable schools. Under the SRP, over one-half of Oklahoma City's elementary schools now have student bodies that are either 90% Afro-American or 90% non-Afro-American.

Because this principal vestige of de jure segregation persists, lifting the decree would clearly be premature at this point. I therefore dissent.

In Freeman v. Pitts, 503 U.S. 467 (1992), the Supreme Court held that a federal court desegregation order should end when it is complied with, even if other desegregation orders for the same school system remain in place. A federal district court ordered desegregation of various aspects of a school system in Georgia that previously had been segregated by law. Part of the desegregation plan had been met; the school system had achieved desegregation in pupil assignment and in facilities. Another aspect of the desegregation order, concerning assignment of teachers, had not yet been fulfilled. The school system planned to construct a facility that likely would benefit whites more than blacks. Nonetheless, the Supreme Court held that the federal court could not review the discriminatory effects of the new construction because the part of the desegregation order concerning facilities had already been met. The Court said that once a portion of a desegregation order is met, the federal court should cease its efforts as to that part and remain involved only as to those aspects of the plan that have not been achieved.

Finally, in Missouri v. Jenkins, 515 U.S. 1139 (1995), the Supreme Court ordered an end to a school desegregation order for the Kansas City schools.[96] Missouri law once required the racial segregation of all public schools. It was not until 1977 that a federal district court ordered the desegregation of the Kansas City, Missouri, public schools. The federal court's desegregation effort made a difference. In 1983, 24 schools in the district had an African American enrollment of more than 90 percent or more. By 1993, no elementary-level student attended a school with an enrollment that was 90 percent or more African American. At the middle school and high school levels, the percentage of students attending schools with an African American enrollment of 90 percent or more declined from about 45 percent to 22 percent.

The Court, in an opinion by Chief Justice Rehnquist, ruled in favor of the state on every issue. There were three parts to the Court's holding. First, the Court ruled that the district court's order that attempted to attract nonminority students from outside the district was impermissible because there was no proof of an interdistrict violation. Chief Justice Rehnquist applied Milliken v. Bradley to conclude that the interdistrict remedy—incentives to attract students from outside the district into the Kansas City schools—was impermissible because there only was proof of an intradistrict violation.

Second, the Court ruled that the district court lacked authority to order an increase in teacher salaries. Although the district court believed that an across-the-board salary increase to attract teachers was essential for desegregation, the Supreme Court concluded that it was not necessary as a remedy.

Finally, the Court ruled that the continued disparity in student test scores did not justify continuance of the federal court's desegregation order. The Court concluded that the Constitution requires equal opportunity and not any result and that therefore disparities between African American and white students on standardized tests was not a sufficient basis for concluding that desegregation had not been achieved. The Supreme Court held that once a desegregation order is complied with, the federal court effort should be ended. Disparity in test scores is not a basis for continued federal court involvement.

In Oklahoma City v. Dowell, Freeman v. Pitts, and Missouri v. Jenkins, the Supreme Court is withdrawing federal courts from the fight against school segregation. Is this an unwarranted retreat or a desirable recognition that federal control over some local school systems must end?

The most recent Supreme Court decision concerning remedies for segregation involved whether school districts may choose to use race as a factor in assigning students to achieve racial diversity in schools. The Court, five to four, said no.

96. Earlier in Missouri v. Jenkins, 495 U.S. 33 (1990), the Supreme Court ruled that a federal district court could order that a local taxing body increase taxes to pay for compliance with a desegregation order, although the federal court should not itself order an increase in the taxes.

PARENTS INVOLVED IN COMMUNITY SCHOOLS v. SEATTLE SCHOOL DISTRICT NO. 1

555 U.S. 701 (2007)

Chief Justice ROBERTS announced the judgment of the Court, and delivered the opinion of the Court with respect to Parts I, II, III-A, and III-C, and an opinion with respect to Parts III-B and IV, in which Justices SCALIA, THOMAS, and ALITO join.

The school districts in these cases voluntarily adopted student assignment plans that rely upon race to determine which public schools certain children may attend. The Seattle school district classifies children as white or nonwhite; the Jefferson County school district as black or "other." In Seattle, this racial classification is used to allocate slots in oversubscribed high schools. In Jefferson County, it is used to make certain elementary school assignments and to rule on transfer requests. In each case, the school district relies upon an individual student's race in assigning that student to a particular school, so that the racial balance at the school falls within a predetermined range based on the racial composition of the school district as a whole. Parents of students denied assignment to particular schools under these plans solely because of their race brought suit, contending that allocating children to different public schools on the basis of race violated the Fourteenth Amendment guarantee of equal protection. The Courts of Appeals below upheld the plans. We granted certiorari, and now reverse.

I

Both cases present the same underlying legal question — whether a public school that had not operated legally segregated schools or has been found to be unitary may choose to classify students by race and rely upon that classification in making school assignments. Although we examine the plans under the same legal framework, the specifics of the two plans, and the circumstances surrounding their adoption, are in some respects quite different.

A

Seattle School District No. 1 operates 10 regular public high schools. In 1998, it adopted the plan at issue in this case for assigning students to these schools. The plan allows incoming ninth graders to choose from among any of the district's high schools, ranking however many schools they wish in order of preference.

Some schools are more popular than others. If too many students list the same school as their first choice, the district employs a series of "tiebreakers" to determine who will fill the open slots at the oversubscribed school. The first tiebreaker selects for admission students who have a sibling currently enrolled in the chosen school. The next tiebreaker depends upon the racial composition of the particular school and the race of the individual student. In the district's public schools approximately 41 percent of enrolled students are white; the remaining 59 percent, comprising all other racial groups, are classified by Seattle for assignment purposes as nonwhite. If an oversubscribed school is not within 10 percentage points of the district's overall white/nonwhite racial balance, it is what the district calls "integration positive," and the district employs a tiebreaker that selects for assignment students whose race "will serve to bring the school into balance." If it is still necessary to select students for the school after using the racial tiebreaker, the next tiebreaker is the geographic proximity of the school to the student's residence.

Seattle has never operated segregated schools — legally separate schools for students of different races — nor has it ever been subject to court-ordered desegregation. It nonetheless employs the racial tiebreaker in an attempt to address the effects of racially identifiable housing patterns on school assignments. Most white students live in the northern part of Seattle, most students of other racial backgrounds in the southern part.

B

Jefferson County Public Schools operates the public school system in metropolitan Louisville, Kentucky. In 1973 a federal court found that Jefferson County had maintained a segregated school system, and in 1975 the District Court entered a desegregation decree. Jefferson County operated under this decree until 2000, when the District Court dissolved the decree after finding that the district had achieved unitary status by eliminating "[t]o the greatest extent practicable" the vestiges of its prior policy of segregation.

In 2001, after the decree had been dissolved, Jefferson County adopted the voluntary student assignment plan at issue in this case. Approximately 34 percent of the district's 97,000 students are black; most of the remaining 66 percent are white. The plan requires all nonmagnet schools to maintain a minimum black enrollment of 15 percent, and a maximum black enrollment of 50 percent.

At the elementary school level, based on his or her address, each student is designated a "resides" school to which students within a specific geographic area are assigned; elementary resides schools are "grouped into clusters in order to facilitate integration." The district assigns students to nonmagnet schools in one of two ways: Parents of kindergartners, first-graders, and students new to the district may submit an application indicating a first and second choice among the schools within their cluster; students who do not submit such an application are assigned within the cluster by the district. "Decisions to assign students to schools within each cluster are based on available space within the schools and the racial guidelines in the District's current student assignment plan." If a school has reached the "extremes of the racial guidelines," a student whose race would contribute to the school's racial imbalance will not be assigned there. After assignment, students at all grade levels are permitted to apply to transfer between nonmagnet schools in the district. Transfers may be requested for any number of reasons, and may be denied because of lack of available space or on the basis of the racial guidelines.

II

[The Court found that the plaintiffs had standing because they alleged that individuals had been denied being able to attend schools because of their race. Chief Justice Roberts explained, "As we have held, one form of injury under the Equal Protection Clause is being forced to compete in a race-based system that may prejudice the plaintiff, an injury that the members of Parents Involved can validly claim on behalf of their children."]

III

A

It is well established that when the government distributes burdens or benefits on the basis of individual racial classifications, that action is reviewed under strict scrutiny. In order to satisfy this searching standard of review, the school districts must demonstrate that the use of individual racial classifications in the assignment plans here under review is "narrowly tailored" to achieve a "compelling" government interest.

Without attempting in these cases to set forth all the interests a school district might assert, it suffices to note that our prior cases, in evaluating the use of racial classifications in the school context, have recognized two interests that qualify as compelling. The first is the compelling interest of remedying the effects of past intentional discrimination. Yet the Seattle public schools have not shown that they were ever segregated by law, and were not subject to court-ordered desegregation decrees. The Jefferson County public schools were previously segregated by law and were subject to a desegregation decree entered in 1975. In 2000, the District Court that entered that decree dissolved it, finding that Jefferson County had "eliminated the vestiges associated with the former policy of segregation and its pernicious effects," and thus had achieved "unitary" status. Jefferson County accordingly does not rely upon an interest in remedying the effects of past intentional discrimination in defending its present use of race in assigning students.

Nor could it. We have emphasized that the harm being remedied by mandatory desegregation plans is the harm that is traceable to segregation, and that "the Constitution is not violated by racial imbalance in the schools, without more." Once Jefferson County achieved unitary status, it had remedied the constitutional wrong that allowed race-based assignments. Any continued use of race must be justified on some other basis.

The second government interest we have recognized as compelling for purposes of strict scrutiny is the interest in diversity in higher education upheld in *Grutter* [*v. Bollinger* (2003)]. The specific interest found compelling in *Grutter* was student body diversity "in the context of higher education." The diversity interest was not focused on race alone but encompassed "all factors that may contribute to student body diversity." The entire gist of the analysis in *Grutter* was that the admissions program at issue there focused on each applicant as an individual, and not simply as a member of a particular racial group. The classification of applicants by race upheld in *Grutter* was only as part of a highly individualized, holistic review.

In the present cases, by contrast, race is not considered as part of a broader effort to achieve "exposure to widely diverse people, cultures, ideas, and viewpoints"; race, for some students, is determinative standing alone. The districts argue that other factors, such as student preferences, affect assignment decisions under their plans, but under each plan when race comes into play, it is decisive by itself. It is not simply one factor weighed with others in reaching a decision, as in *Grutter*; it is *the* factor. Like the University of Michigan undergraduate plan struck down in *Gratz* [*v. Bollinger* (2003)], the plans here "do not provide for a meaningful individualized review of applicants" but instead rely on racial classifications in a "nonindividualized, mechanical" way.

Even when it comes to race, the plans here employ only a limited notion of diversity, viewing race exclusively in white/nonwhite terms in Seattle and black/ "other" terms in Jefferson County. The Seattle "Board Statement Reaffirming Diversity Rationale" speaks of the "inherent educational value" in "[p]roviding students the opportunity to attend schools with diverse student enrollment." But under the Seattle plan, a school with 50 percent Asian-American students and 50 percent white students but no African-American, Native-American, or Latino students would qualify as balanced, while a school with 30 percent Asian-American, 25 percent African-American, 25 percent Latino, and 20 percent white students would not. It is hard to understand how a plan that could allow these results can be viewed as being concerned with achieving enrollment that is "'broadly diverse.'"

In upholding the admissions plan in *Grutter*, though, this Court relied upon considerations unique to institutions of higher education, noting that in light of "the expansive freedoms of speech and thought associated with the university environment, universities occupy a special niche in our constitutional tradition." The Court explained that "[c]ontext matters" in applying strict scrutiny, and repeatedly noted that it was addressing the use of race "in the context of higher education." The Court in *Grutter* expressly articulated key limitations on its holding — defining a specific type of broad-based diversity and noting the unique context of higher education — but these limitations were largely disregarded by the lower courts in extending *Grutter* to uphold race-based assignments in elementary and secondary schools. The present cases are not governed by *Grutter*.

B

Perhaps recognizing that reliance on *Grutter* cannot sustain their plans, both school districts assert additional interests, distinct from the interest upheld in *Grutter*, to justify their race-based assignments. Each school district argues that educational and broader socialization benefits flow from a racially diverse learning environment, and each contends that because the diversity they seek is racial diversity — not the broader diversity at issue in *Grutter* — it makes sense to promote that interest directly by relying on race alone.

The parties and their amici dispute whether racial diversity in schools in fact has a marked impact on test scores and other objective yardsticks or achieves intangible socialization benefits. The debate is not one we need to resolve, however, because it is clear that the racial classifications employed by the districts are not narrowly tailored to the goal of achieving the educational and social benefits asserted to flow from racial diversity. In design and operation, the plans are directed only to racial balance, pure and simple, an objective this Court has repeatedly condemned as illegitimate.

The districts offer no evidence that the level of racial diversity necessary to achieve the asserted educational benefits happens to coincide with the racial demographics of the respective school districts — or rather the white/nonwhite or black/"other" balance of the districts, since that is the only diversity addressed by the plans. Indeed, in its brief Seattle simply assumes that the educational benefits track the racial breakdown of the district.

This working backward to achieve a particular type of racial balance, rather than working forward from some demonstration of the level of diversity that provides the purported benefits, is a fatal flaw under our existing precedent. We have many times over reaffirmed that "[r]acial balance is not to be achieved for its own sake."

Accepting racial balancing as a compelling state interest would justify the imposition of racial proportionality throughout American society, contrary to our repeated recognition that "[a]t the heart of the Constitution's guarantee of equal protection lies the simple command that the Government must treat citizens as individuals, not as simply components of a racial, religious, sexual or national class." Allowing racial balancing as a compelling end in itself would "effectively assur[e] that race will always be relevant in American life, and that the 'ultimate goal' of 'eliminating entirely from governmental decisionmaking such irrelevant factors as a human being's race' will never be achieved."

The principle that racial balancing is not permitted is one of substance, not semantics. Racial balancing is not transformed from "patently unconstitutional" to a compelling state interest simply by relabeling it "racial diversity." While the school districts use various verbal formulations to describe the interest they seek to promote — racial diversity, avoidance of racial isolation, racial integration — they offer no definition of the interest that suggests it differs from racial balance.

C

The districts assert, as they must, that the way in which they have employed individual racial classifications is necessary to achieve their stated ends. The minimal effect these classifications have on student assignments, however, suggests that other means would be effective. Seattle's racial tiebreaker results, in the end, only in shifting a small number of students between schools. Approximately 307 student assignments were affected by the racial tiebreaker in 2000-2001. In over one-third of the assignments affected by the racial tiebreaker the use of race in the end made no difference, and the district could identify only 52 students who were ultimately affected adversely by the racial tiebreaker in that it resulted in assignment to a school they had not listed as a preference and to which they would not otherwise have been assigned. Similarly, Jefferson County's use of racial classifications has only a minimal effect on the assignment of students.

While we do not suggest that greater use of race would be preferable, the minimal impact of the districts' racial classifications on school enrollment casts doubt on the necessity of using racial classifications. Classifying and assigning schoolchildren according to a binary conception of race is an extreme approach in light of our precedents and our Nation's history of using race in public schools, and requires more than such an amorphous end to justify it.

The districts have also failed to show that they considered methods other than explicit racial classifications to achieve their stated goals. Narrow tailoring requires "serious, good faith consideration of workable race-neutral alternatives," and yet in Seattle several alternative assignment plans — many of which would not have used express racial classifications — were rejected with little or no consideration. Jefferson County has failed to present any evidence that it considered alternatives, even though the district already claims that its goals are achieved primarily through means other than the racial classifications.

IV

Justice Breyer's dissent takes a different approach to these cases, one that fails to ground the result it would reach in law. Instead, it selectively relies on inapplicable precedent and even dicta while dismissing contrary holdings, alters and misapplies our well-established legal framework for assessing equal protection challenges to express racial classifications, and greatly exaggerates the consequences of today's decision.

Justice Breyer's position comes down to a familiar claim: The end justifies the means. He admits that "there is a cost in applying 'a state-mandated racial label,'" but he is confident that the cost is worth paying. Our established strict scrutiny test for racial classifications, however, insists on "detailed examination, both as to ends and as to means." Simply because the school districts may seek a worthy goal does not mean they are free to discriminate on the basis of race to achieve it, or that their racial classifications should be subject to less exacting scrutiny.

In keeping with his view that strict scrutiny should not apply, Justice Breyer repeatedly urges deference to local school boards on these issues. Such deference "is fundamentally at odds with our equal protection jurisprudence. We put the burden on state actors to demonstrate that their race-based policies are justified."

If the need for the racial classifications embraced by the school districts is unclear, even on the districts' own terms, the costs are undeniable. "[D]istinctions between citizens solely because of their ancestry are by their very nature odious to a free people whose institutions are founded upon the doctrine of equality." Government action dividing us by race is inherently suspect because such classifications promote "notions of racial inferiority and lead to a politics of racial hostility," "reinforce the belief, held by too many for too much of our history, that individuals should be judged by the color of their skin," and "endorse race-based reasoning and the conception of a Nation divided into racial blocs, thus contributing to an escalation of racial hostility and conflict."

All this is true enough in the contexts in which these statements were made — government contracting, voting districts, allocation of broadcast licenses, and electing state officers — but when it comes to using race to assign children to schools, history will be heard. In *Brown v. Board of Education* (1954) (*Brown I*), we held that segregation deprived black children of equal educational opportunities regardless of whether school facilities and other tangible factors were equal, because government classification and separation on grounds of race themselves denoted inferiority. The next Term, we accordingly stated that "full compliance" with *Brown I* required school districts "to achieve a system of determining admission to the public schools on a nonracial basis."

The parties and their amici debate which side is more faithful to the heritage of *Brown*, but the position of the plaintiffs in *Brown* was spelled out in their brief and could not have been clearer: "[T]he Fourteenth Amendment prevents states from according differential treatment to American children on the basis of their color or race." Brief for Appellants in Nos. 1, 2, and 4 and for Respondents in No. 10 on Reargument in *Brown I*, O.T.1953, p. 15 (Summary of Argument). What do the racial classifications at issue here do, if not accord differential treatment on the basis of race? As counsel who appeared before this Court for the plaintiffs in *Brown* put it: "We have one fundamental contention which we will seek to develop in the course of this argument, and that contention is that no State has any authority under the equal-protection clause of the Fourteenth Amendment to use race as a factor in affording educational opportunities among its citizens." Tr. of Oral Arg. in *Brown I*, p. 7 (Robert L. Carter, Dec. 9, 1952). There is no ambiguity in that statement. And it was that position that prevailed in this Court, which emphasized in its remedial opinion that what was "[a]t stake is the personal interest of the plaintiffs in admission to public schools as soon as practicable on a nondiscriminatory basis," and what was required was "determining admission to the public schools on a nonracial basis." *Brown II.* What do the racial classifications do in these cases, if not determine admission to a public school on a racial basis?

Before *Brown*, schoolchildren were told where they could and could not go to school based on the color of their skin. The school districts in these cases have not carried the heavy burden of demonstrating that we should allow this once again — even for very different reasons. For schools that never segregated on the basis of race, such as Seattle, or that have removed the vestiges of past segregation, such as Jefferson County, the way "to achieve a system of determining admission to the public schools on a nonracial basis," is to stop assigning students on a racial basis. The way to stop discrimination on the basis of race is to stop discriminating on the basis of race.

Justice THOMAS, concurring.

Today, the Court holds that state entities may not experiment with race-based means to achieve ends they deem socially desirable. I wholly concur in the Chief Justice's opinion. I write separately to address several of the contentions in Justice Breyer's dissent. Contrary to the dissent's arguments, resegregation is not occurring in Seattle or Louisville; these school boards have no present interest in remedying past segregation; and these race-based student-assignment programs do not serve any compelling state interest. Accordingly, the plans are unconstitutional. Disfavoring a color-blind interpretation of the Constitution, the dissent would give school boards a free hand to make decisions on the basis of race — an approach reminiscent of that advocated by the segregationists in *Brown v. Board of Education* (1954). This approach is just as wrong today as it was a half-century ago. The Constitution and our cases require us to be much more demanding before permitting local school boards to make decisions based on race.

The dissent repeatedly claims that the school districts are threatened with resegregation and that they will succumb to that threat if these plans are declared unconstitutional. It also argues that these plans can be justified as part of the school boards' attempts to "eradicat[e] earlier school segregation." Contrary to the dissent's rhetoric, neither of these school districts is threatened with resegregation, and neither is constitutionally compelled or permitted to undertake race-based remediation. Racial imbalance is not segregation, and the mere incantation of terms like resegregation and remediation cannot make up the difference.

Although there is arguably a danger of racial imbalance in schools in Seattle and Louisville, there is no danger of resegregation. No one contends that Seattle has established or that Louisville has reestablished a dual school system that separates students on the basis of race. The statistics cited in the dissent are not to the contrary. At most, those statistics show a national trend toward classroom racial imbalance. However, racial imbalance without intentional state action to separate the races does not amount to segregation. To raise the specter of resegregation to defend these programs is to ignore the meaning of the word and the nature of the cases before us.

The dissent asserts that racially balanced schools improve educational outcomes for black children. In support, the dissent unquestioningly cites certain social science research to support propositions that are hotly disputed among social scientists. In reality, it is far from apparent that coerced racial mixing has any educational benefits, much less that integration is necessary to black achievement.

Scholars have differing opinions as to whether educational benefits arise from racial balancing. Some have concluded that black students receive genuine educational benefits. Add to the inconclusive social science the fact of black achievement in "racially isolated" environments. Before *Brown*, the most prominent example of an exemplary black school was Dunbar High School. Dunbar is by no means an isolated example. Given this tenuous relationship between forced racial mixing and improved educational results for black children, the dissent cannot plausibly maintain that an educational element supports the integration interest, let alone makes it compelling.

It should escape no one that behind Justice Breyer's veil of judicial modesty hides an inflated role for the Federal Judiciary. The dissent's approach confers on judges the power to say what sorts of discrimination are benign and which are invidious. Having made that determination (based on no objective measure that I can detect), a judge following the dissent's approach will set the level of scrutiny to achieve the desired result. Only then must the judge defer to a democratic majority. In my view, to defer to one's preferred result is not to defer at all.

Most of the dissent's criticisms of today's result can be traced to its rejection of the color-blind Constitution. The dissent attempts to marginalize the notion of a color-blind Constitution by consigning it to me and Members of today's plurality. But I am quite comfortable in the company I keep. My view of the Constitution is Justice Harlan's view in *Plessy*: "Our Constitution is color-blind, and neither knows nor tolerates classes among citizens." And my view was the rallying cry for the lawyers who litigated *Brown*.

The plans before us base school assignment decisions on students' race. Because "[o]ur Constitution is color-blind, and neither knows nor tolerates classes among citizens," such race-based decisionmaking is unconstitutional. *Plessy* [*v. Ferguson* (1896)].

Justice KENNEDY, concurring in part and concurring in the judgment.

The Nation's schools strive to teach that our strength comes from people of different races, creeds, and cultures uniting in commitment to the freedom of all. In these cases two school districts in different parts of the country seek to teach that principle by having classrooms that reflect the racial makeup of the surrounding community. That the school districts consider these plans to be necessary should remind us our highest aspirations are yet unfulfilled. But the solutions mandated by these school districts must themselves be lawful. To make race matter now so that it might not matter later may entrench the very prejudices we seek to overcome. In my view the state-mandated racial classifications at issue, official labels proclaiming the race of all persons in a broad class of citizens — elementary school students in one case, high school students in another — are unconstitutional as the cases now come to us.

I

The dissent finds that the school districts have identified a compelling interest in increasing diversity, including for the purpose of avoiding racial isolation. The plurality, by contrast, does not acknowledge that the school districts have identified a compelling interest here. For this reason, among others, I do not join Parts III-B and IV. Diversity, depending on its meaning and definition, is a compelling educational goal a school district may pursue.

Our Nation from the inception has sought to preserve and expand the promise of liberty and equality on which it was founded. Today we enjoy a society that is remarkable in its openness and opportunity. Yet our tradition is to go beyond present achievements, however significant, and to recognize and confront the flaws and injustices that remain. This is especially true when we seek assurance that opportunity is not denied on account of race. The enduring hope is that race should not matter; the reality is that too often it does.

This is by way of preface to my respectful submission that parts of the opinion by the Chief Justice imply an all-too-unyielding insistence that race cannot be a factor in instances when, in my view, it may be taken into account. The plurality opinion is too dismissive of the legitimate interest government has in ensuring all people have equal opportunity regardless of their race. The plurality's postulate that "[t]he way to stop discrimination on the basis of race is to stop discriminating on the basis of race," is not sufficient to decide these cases. Fifty years of experience since *Brown v. Board of Education* (1954) should teach us that the problem before us defies so easy a solution. School districts can seek to reach *Brown*'s objective of equal educational opportunity. The plurality opinion is at least open to the interpretation that the Constitution requires school districts to ignore the problem of de facto resegregation in schooling. I cannot endorse that conclusion. To the extent the plurality opinion suggests the Constitution mandates that state and local school authorities must accept the status quo of racial isolation in schools, it is, in my view, profoundly mistaken.

The statement by Justice Harlan that "[o]ur Constitution is color-blind" was most certainly justified in the context of his dissent in *Plessy v. Ferguson* (1896). The Court's decision in that case was a grievous error it took far too long to overrule. *Plessy*, of course, concerned official classification by race applicable to all persons who sought to use railway carriages. And, as an aspiration, Justice Harlan's axiom must command our assent. In the real world, it is regrettable to say, it cannot be a universal constitutional principle.

In the administration of public schools by the state and local authorities it is permissible to consider the racial makeup of schools and to adopt general policies to encourage a diverse student body, one aspect of which is its racial composition. If school authorities are concerned that the student-body compositions of certain schools interfere with the objective of offering an equal educational opportunity to all of their students, they are free to devise race-conscious measures to address the problem in a general way and without treating each student in different fashion solely on the basis of a systematic, individual typing by race.

School boards may pursue the goal of bringing together students of diverse backgrounds and races through other means, including strategic site selection of new schools; drawing attendance zones with general recognition of the demographics of neighborhoods; allocating resources for special programs; recruiting students and faculty in a targeted fashion; and tracking enrollments, performance, and other statistics by race. These mechanisms are race conscious but do not lead to different treatment based on a classification that tells each student he or she is to be defined by race, so it is unlikely any of them would demand strict scrutiny to be found permissible. Executive and legislative branches, which for generations now have considered these types of policies and procedures, should be permitted to employ them with candor and with confidence that a constitutional violation does not occur whenever a decision-maker considers the impact a given approach might have on students of different races. Assigning to each student a personal designation according to a crude system of individual racial classifications is quite a different matter; and the legal analysis changes accordingly.

[II]

As to the dissent, the general conclusions upon which it relies have no principled limit and would result in the broad acceptance of governmental racial classifications in areas far afield from schooling. The dissent's permissive strict scrutiny (which bears more than a passing resemblance to rational-basis review) could invite widespread governmental deployment of racial classifications. There is every reason to think that, if the dissent's rationale were accepted, Congress, assuming an otherwise proper exercise of its spending authority or commerce power, could mandate either the Seattle or the Jefferson County plans nationwide. There seems to be no principled rule, moreover, to limit the dissent's rationale to the context of public schools.

To uphold these programs the Court is asked to brush aside two concepts of central importance for determining the validity of laws and decrees designed to alleviate the hurt and adverse consequences resulting from race discrimination. The first is the difference between de jure and de facto segregation; the second, the presumptive invalidity of a State's use of racial classifications to differentiate its treatment of individuals.

This Nation has a moral and ethical obligation to fulfill its historic commitment to creating an integrated society that ensures equal opportunity for all of its children. A compelling interest exists in avoiding racial isolation, an interest that a school district, in its discretion and expertise, may choose to pursue. Likewise, a district may consider it a compelling interest to achieve a diverse student population. Race may be one component of that diversity, but other demographic factors, plus special talents and needs, should also be considered. What the government is not permitted to do, absent a showing of necessity not made here, is to classify every student on the basis of race and to assign each of them to schools based on that classification. Crude measures of this sort threaten to reduce children to racial chits valued and traded according to one school's supply and another's demand.

The decision today should not prevent school districts from continuing the important work of bringing together students of different racial, ethnic, and economic backgrounds. Due to a variety of factors—some influenced by government, some not—neighborhoods in our communities do not reflect the diversity of our Nation as a whole. Those entrusted with directing our public schools can bring to bear the creativity of experts, parents, administrators, and other concerned citizens to find a way to achieve the compelling interests they face without resorting to widespread governmental allocation of benefits and burdens on the basis of racial classifications.

Justice STEVENS, dissenting.

There is a cruel irony in the Chief Justice's reliance on our decision in *Brown v. Board of Education* (1955). The first sentence in the concluding paragraph of his opinion states: "Before *Brown*, schoolchildren were told where they could and could not go to school based on the color of their skin." This sentence reminds me of Anatole France's observation: "[T]he majestic equality of the la[w], forbid[s] rich and poor alike to sleep under bridges, to beg in the streets, and to steal their bread." The Chief Justuce fails to note that it was only black schoolchildren who were so ordered; indeed, the history books do not tell stories of white children struggling to attend black schools. In this and other ways, the Chief Justice rewrites the history of one of this Court's most important decisions.

Justice BREYER, with whom Justice STEVENS, Justice SOUTER, and Justice GINSBURG join, dissenting.

These cases consider the longstanding efforts of two local school boards to integrate their public schools. The school board plans before us resemble many others adopted in the last 50 years by primary and secondary schools throughout the Nation. All of those plans represent local efforts to bring about the kind of racially integrated education that *Brown v. Board of Education* (1954) long ago promised—efforts that this Court has repeatedly required, permitted, and encouraged local authorities to undertake. This Court has recognized that the public interests at stake in such cases are "compelling." We have approved of "narrowly tailored" plans that are no less race-conscious than the plans before us. And we have understood that the Constitution permits local communities to adopt desegregation plans even where it does not require them to do so.

The plurality pays inadequate attention to this law, to past opinions' rationales, their language, and the contexts in which they arise. As a result, it reverses course and reaches the wrong conclusion. In doing so, it distorts precedent, it misapplies the relevant constitutional principles, it announces legal rules that will obstruct efforts by state and local governments to deal effectively with the growing resegregation of public schools, it threatens to substitute for present calm a disruptive round of race-related litigation, and it undermines *Brown*'s promise of integrated primary and secondary education that local communities have sought to make a reality. This cannot be justified in the name of the Equal Protection Clause.

I

Overall these efforts brought about considerable racial integration. More recently, however, progress has stalled. Between 1968 and 1980, the number of black children attending a school where minority children constituted more than half of the school fell from 77% to 63% in the Nation (from 81% to 57% in the South) but then reversed direction by the year 2000, rising from 63% to 72% in the Nation (from 57% to 69% in the South). Similarly, between 1968 and 1980, the number of black children attending schools that were more than 90% minority fell from 64% to 33% in the Nation (from 78% to 23% in the South), but that too reversed direction, rising by the year 2000 from 33% to 37% in the Nation (from 23% to 31% in the South). As of 2002, almost 2.4 million students, or over 5% of all public school enrollment, attended schools with a white population of less than 1%. Of these, 2.3 million were black and Latino students, and only 72,000 were white. Today, more than one in six black children attend a school that is 99-100% minority. In light of the evident risk of a return to school systems that are in fact (though not in law) resegregated, many school districts have felt a need to maintain or to extend their integration efforts.

The upshot is that myriad school districts operating in myriad circumstances have devised myriad plans, often with race-conscious elements, all for the sake of eradicating earlier school segregation, bringing about integration, or preventing retrogression. Seattle and Louisville are two such districts, and the histories of their present plans set forth typical school integration stories.

In both Seattle and Louisville, the local school districts began with schools that were highly segregated in fact. In both cities plaintiffs filed lawsuits claiming unconstitutional segregation. [Justice Breyer then described in detail the history of segregation in the Seattle and Louisville school systems.]

II

A longstanding and unbroken line of legal authority tells us that the Equal Protection Clause permits local school boards to use race-conscious criteria to achieve positive race-related goals, even when the Constitution does not compel it. Because of its importance, I shall repeat what this Court said about the matter in *Swann.* Chief Justice Burger, on behalf of a unanimous Court in a case of exceptional importance, wrote: "School authorities are traditionally charged with broad power to formulate and implement educational policy and might well conclude, for example, that in order to prepare students to live in a pluralistic society each school should have a prescribed ratio of Negro to white students reflecting the proportion for the district as a whole. To do this as an educational policy is within the broad discretionary powers of school authorities."

Courts are not alone in accepting as constitutionally valid the legal principle that *Swann* enunciated — i.e., that the government may voluntarily adopt race-conscious measures to improve conditions of race even when it is not under a constitutional obligation to do so. That principle has been accepted by every branch of government and is rooted in the history of the Equal Protection Clause itself.

There is reason to believe that those who drafted an Amendment with this basic purpose in mind would have understood the legal and practical difference between the use of race-conscious criteria in defiance of that purpose, namely to keep the races apart, and the use of race-conscious criteria to further that purpose, namely to bring the races together.

Here, the context is one in which school districts seek to advance or to maintain racial integration in primary and secondary schools. It is a context, as *Swann* makes clear, where history has required special administrative remedies. And it is a context in which the school boards' plans simply set race-conscious limits at the outer boundaries of a broad range.

This context is not a context that involves the use of race to decide who will receive goods or services that are normally distributed on the basis of merit and which are in short supply. It is not one in which race-conscious limits stigmatize or exclude; the limits at issue do not pit the races against each other or otherwise significantly exacerbate racial tensions. They do not impose burdens unfairly upon members of one race alone but instead seek benefits for members of all races alike. The context here is one of racial limits that seek, not to keep the races apart, but to bring them together.

In my view, this contextual approach to scrutiny is altogether fitting. I believe that the law requires application here of a standard of review that is not "strict" in the traditional sense of that word, although it does require the careful review I have just described.

III

A

Compelling Interest

The principal interest advanced in these cases to justify the use of race-based criteria goes by various names. Sometimes a court refers to it as an interest in achieving racial "diversity." Other times a court, like the plurality here, refers to it as an interest in racial "balancing." I have used more general terms to signify that interest, describing it, for example, as an interest in promoting or preserving greater racial "integration" of public schools. By this term, I mean the school districts' interest in eliminating school-by-school racial isolation and increasing the degree to which racial mixture characterizes each of the district's schools and each individual student's public school experience.

Regardless of its name, however, the interest at stake possesses three essential elements. First, there is a historical and remedial element: an interest in setting right the consequences of prior conditions of segregation. This refers back to a time when public schools were highly segregated, often as a result of legal or administrative policies that facilitated racial segregation in public schools. It is an interest in continuing to combat the remnants of segregation caused in whole or in part by these school-related policies, which have often affected not only schools, but also housing patterns, employment practices, economic conditions, and social attitudes. It is an interest in maintaining hard-won gains. And it has its roots in preventing what gradually may become the de facto resegregation of America's public schools.

Second, there is an educational element: an interest in overcoming the adverse educational effects produced by and associated with highly segregated schools. Studies suggest that children taken from those schools and placed in integrated settings often show positive academic gains. Other studies reach different conclusions. See, e.g., D. Armor, Forced Justice (1995). But the evidence supporting an educational interest in racially integrated schools is well established and strong enough to permit a democratically elected school board reasonably to determine that this interest is a compelling one.

Third, there is a democratic element: an interest in producing an educational environment that reflects the "pluralistic society" in which our children will live. It is an interest in helping our children learn to work and play together with children of different racial backgrounds. It is an interest in teaching children to engage in the kind of cooperation among Americans of all races that is necessary to make a land of three hundred million people one Nation.

If we are to insist upon unanimity in the social science literature before finding a compelling interest, we might never find one. I believe only that the Constitution allows democratically elected school boards to make up their own minds as to how best to include people of all races in one America.

B

Narrow Tailoring

I next ask whether the plans before us are "narrowly tailored" to achieve these "compelling" objectives. I shall not accept the school board's assurances on faith, and I shall subject the "tailoring" of their plans to "rigorous judicial review." Several factors, taken together, nonetheless lead me to conclude that the boards' use of race-conscious criteria in these plans passes even the strictest "tailoring" test.

First, the race-conscious criteria at issue only help set the outer bounds of broad ranges. They constitute but one part of plans that depend primarily upon other, nonracial elements. To use race in this way is not to set a forbidden "quota." In fact, the defining feature of both plans is greater emphasis upon student choice. In Seattle, for example, in more than 80% of all cases, that choice alone determines which high schools Seattle's ninth graders will attend.

Second, broad-range limits on voluntary school choice plans are less burdensome, and hence more narrowly tailored, than other race-conscious restrictions this Court has previously approved. Indeed, the plans before us are more narrowly tailored than the race-conscious admission plans that this Court approved in *Grutter*. Here, race becomes a factor only in a fraction of students' non-merit-based assignments—not in large numbers of students' merit-based applications. Moreover, the effect of applying race-conscious criteria here affects potentially disadvantaged students less severely, not more severely, than the criteria at issue in *Grutter*. Disappointed students are not rejected from a State's flagship graduate program; they simply attend a different one of the district's many public schools, which in aspiration and in fact are substantially equal. And, in Seattle, the disadvantaged student loses at most one year at the high school of his choice. One will search *Grutter* in vain for similarly persuasive evidence of narrow tailoring as the school districts have presented here.

Third, the manner in which the school boards developed these plans itself reflects "narrow tailoring." Each plan was devised to overcome a history of segregated public schools. Each plan embodies the results of local experience and community consultation. Each plan is the product of a process that has sought to enhance student choice, while diminishing the need for mandatory busing. And each plan's use of race-conscious elements is diminished compared to the use of race in preceding integration plans.

The school boards' widespread consultation, their experimentation with numerous other plans, indeed, the 40-year history that Part I sets forth, make clear that plans that are less explicitly race-based are unlikely to achieve the board's "compelling" objectives. The history of each school system reveals highly segregated schools, followed by remedial plans that involved forced busing, followed by efforts to attract or retain students through the use of plans that abandoned busing and replaced it with greater student choice. Both cities once tried to achieve more integrated schools by relying solely upon measures such as redrawn district boundaries, new school building construction, and unrestricted voluntary transfers. In neither city did these prior attempts prove sufficient to achieve the city's integration goals.

Moreover, giving some degree of weight to a local school board's knowledge, expertise, and concerns in these particular matters is not inconsistent with rigorous judicial scrutiny. It simply recognizes that judges are not well suited to act as school administrators. Indeed, in the context of school desegregation, this Court has repeatedly stressed the importance of acknowledging that local school boards better understand their own communities and have a better knowledge of what in practice will best meet the educational needs of their pupils.

Nor could the school districts have accomplished their desired aims (e.g., avoiding forced busing, countering white flight, maintaining racial diversity) by other means. Nothing in the extensive history of desegregation efforts over the past 50 years gives the districts, or this Court, any reason to believe that another method is possible to accomplish these goals. Nevertheless, Justice Kennedy suggests that school boards: "may pursue the goal of bringing together students of diverse backgrounds and races through other means, including strategic site selection of new schools; drawing attendance zones with general recognition of the demographics of neighborhoods; allocating resources for special programs; recruiting students and faculty in a targeted fashion; and tracking enrollments, performance, and other statistics by race."

But, as to "strategic site selection," Seattle has built one new high school in the last 44 years (and that specialized school serves only 300 students). As to "allocating resources for special programs," Seattle and Louisville have both experimented with this; indeed, these programs are often referred to as "magnet schools," but the limited desegregation effect of these efforts extends at most to those few schools to which additional resources are granted. In addition, there is no evidence from the experience of these school districts that it will make any meaningful impact. As to "recruiting faculty" on the basis of race, both cities have tried, but only as one part of a broader program. As to "tracking enrollments, performance and other statistics by race," tracking reveals the problem; it does not cure it.

[IV]

Consequences

The Founders meant the Constitution as a practical document that would transmit its basic values to future generations through principles that remained workable over time. Hence it is important to consider the potential consequences of the plurality's approach, as measured against the Constitution's objectives. To do so provides further reason to believe that the plurality's approach is legally unsound.

At a minimum, the plurality's views would threaten a surge of race-based litigation. Hundreds of state and federal statutes and regulations use racial classifications for educational or other purposes. In many such instances, the contentious force of legal challenges to these classifications, meritorious or not, would displace earlier calm.

As I have pointed out, supra, de facto resegregation is on the rise. It is reasonable to conclude that such resegregation can create serious educational, social, and civic problems. Given the conditions in which school boards work to set policy, they may need all of the means presently at their disposal to combat those problems. Yet the plurality would deprive them of at least one tool that some districts now consider vital — the limited use of broad race-conscious student population ranges.

I use the words "may need" here deliberately. The plurality, or at least those who follow Justice Thomas' "'color-blind'" approach, may feel confident that, to end invidious discrimination, one must end all governmental use of race-conscious criteria including those with inclusive objectives. By way of contrast, I do not claim to know how best to stop harmful discrimination; how best to create a society that includes all Americans; how best to overcome our serious problems of increasing de facto segregation, troubled inner city schooling, and poverty correlated with race. But, as a judge, I do know that the Constitution does not authorize judges to dictate solutions to these problems. Rather, the Constitution creates a democratic political system through which the people themselves must together find answers. And it is for them to debate how best to educate the Nation's children and how best to administer America's schools to achieve that aim. The Court should leave them to their work. And it is for them to decide, to quote the plurality's slogan, whether the best "way to stop discrimination on the basis of race is to stop discriminating on the basis of race." That is why the Equal Protection Clause outlaws invidious discrimination, but does not similarly forbid all use of race-conscious criteria.

Until today, this Court understood the Constitution as affording the people, acting through their elected representatives, freedom to select the use of "race-conscious" criteria from among their available options. Today, however, the Court restricts (and some Members would eliminate) that leeway. I fear the consequences of doing so for the law, for the schools, for the democratic process, and for America's efforts to create, out of its diversity, one Nation.

The last half-century has witnessed great strides toward racial equality, but we have not yet realized the promise of *Brown*. To invalidate the plans under review is to threaten the promise of *Brown*. The plurality's position, I fear, would break that promise. This is a decision that the Court and the Nation will come to regret.

5. *Racial Classifications Benefiting Minorities*

No topic in constitutional law is more controversial than affirmative action. In considering affirmative action, three questions are key: First, what level of scrutiny should be used for racial classifications benefiting minorities? Second, what purposes for affirmative action programs are sufficient to meet the level of scrutiny? Third, what techniques of affirmative action are sufficient to meet the level of scrutiny? In reading the cases concerning affirmative action, it is important to focus on how each decision answers these questions.

This section begins by presenting the initial cases concerning affirmative action, followed by those announcing strict scrutiny as the test for affirmative action programs. Then presented are the recent Supreme Court decisions concerning affirmative action in education and in drawing election district maps.

The Supreme Court first considered affirmative action in Regents of the University of California v. Bakke, 438 U.S. 265 (1978). The University of California-Davis Medical School had set aside 16 slots in an entering class of 100 for minority students. The Supreme Court, in a five-to-four decision, without a majority opinion, invalidated the set-aside but ruled that colleges and universities may use race as one factor in admissions decisions to benefit minorities and enhance diversity.

Justice Louis Powell, writing on his behalf, said that strict scrutiny should be used for racial classifications benefiting minorities. He concluded that the set-aside failed strict scrutiny but that colleges and universities have a compelling interest in having a diverse student body and that many consider race as one factor in admissions decisions to benefit minorities.

Justice William Brennan, joined by Justices White, Marshall, and Blackmun, argued that intermediate scrutiny should be used for racial classifications benefiting minorities. These justices would have upheld the set-aside, as well as the use of race as a factor in admissions decisions.

Justice Stevens, joined by Chief Justice Burger and Justices Stewart and Rehnquist, would have invalidated the set-aside and the use of race by colleges and universities as violating Title VI of the 1964 Civil Rights Act. Title VI prohibits recipients of federal funds from discriminating based on race.

Thus, there was no majority opinion as to the level of scrutiny for racial classifications benefiting minorities. Five justices voted to invalidate the set-aside, one on constitutional grounds and four on statutory grounds. Five justices approved colleges' and universities' pursuit of racial diversity by considering race as one factor in admissions decisions.

Two years after Bakke, in Fullilove v. Klutznick, 448 U.S. 448 (1980), the Supreme Court again considered an affirmative action program but did not produce a majority opinion concerning the appropriate level of scrutiny. The Court upheld a federal law that required that 10 percent of federal public works monies given to local governments be set aside for minority-owned businesses. Chief Justice Burger, in an opinion joined by Justices White and Powell, concluded that the affirmative action program was justified to remedy past discrimination but said that the "opinion does not adopt, either expressly or implicitly, the formulas of analysis articulated in cases such as University of California Regents v. Bakke."

Three justices — Marshall, Brennan, and Blackmun — concurred in the judgment to uphold the affirmative action program but argued again that intermediate scrutiny should be used for racial classifications serving a remedial purpose. Finally, three justices — Stewart, Rehnquist, and Stevens — dissented and said that strict scrutiny was the appropriate test. Justice Stewart, joined by Justice Rehnquist, wrote, "Under our Constitution, the government may never act to the detriment of a person solely because of that person's race. . . . The rule cannot be any different when the persons injured by a racially biased law are not members of a racial minority."

In United States v. Paradise, 480 U.S. 149 (1987), the Supreme Court upheld a federal court order that was designed to remedy proven intentional discrimination by the Alabama Department of Public Safety and mandated that a qualified black had to be hired or promoted every time a white was hired or promoted. Justice Brennan, writing for the plurality, found that "the relief ordered survives even strict scrutiny analysis"; "the race-conscious relief at issue here is justified by a compelling interest in remedying the discrimination."

In Wygant v. Jackson Board of Education, 476 U.S. 267 (1986), the Supreme Court declared unconstitutional a city's attempt to achieve faculty diversity in its schools by laying off white teachers with more seniority than black teachers who were retained. The Jackson, Michigan, school system, as part of a settlement to a discrimination suit, hired a number of African American teachers. When layoffs were required, the Board of Education decided that teachers with the most seniority would be retained, except that at no time would the percentage of minorities to be laid off exceed the percentage of minorities employed at the time of the layoffs. The result was that some white teachers were laid off even though they had more seniority than some of the black teachers who kept their jobs.

The Court rejected this as an acceptable means of affirmative action. The Court said that even if prior discrimination was proven, the layoff provision was not a constitutionally acceptable means of achieving even the compelling purpose of remedying prior discrimination. Justice Powell, writing for the plurality, said that "as a means of accomplishing purposes that otherwise may be legitimate, the Board's layoff plan is not sufficiently narrowly tailored. Other, less intrusive means of accomplishing similar purposes — such as the adoption of hiring goals — are available."

Justice Powell expressly rejected the government's justifications for affirmative action: remedying past discrimination and providing role models for students. He wrote, "This Court never has held that societal discrimination alone is sufficient to justify a racial classification. Rather, the Court has insisted upon some showing of prior discrimination by the governmental unit involved before allowing limited use of racial classifications in order to remedy such discrimination." Justice Powell also wrote, "The role model theory allows the Board to engage in discriminatory hiring and layoff practices long past the point required by any legitimate remedial purpose. . . . Moreover, because the role model theory does not necessarily bear a relationship to the harm caused by prior discriminatory hiring practices, it actually could be used to escape the obligation to remedy such practices by justifying the small percentage of black teachers by reference to the small percentage of black students."

THE EMERGENCE OF STRICT SCRUTINY AS THE TEST

It was not until 1989, in Richmond v. J.A. Croson Co., that a majority of the Court agreed on the level of scrutiny to use in evaluating government affirmative action programs.

RICHMOND v. J.A. CROSON CO.

488 U.S. 469 (1989)

Justice O'Connor announced the judgment of the Court and delivered the opinion of the Court with respect to Parts I, III-B, and IV, an opinion with respect to Part II, in which the Chief Justice and Justice White join, and an opinion with respect to Parts III-A and V, in which the Chief Justice, Justice White, and Justice Kennedy join.

In this case, we confront once again the tension between the Fourteenth Amendment's guarantee of equal treatment to all citizens, and the use of race-based measures to ameliorate the effects of past discrimination on the opportunities enjoyed by members of minority groups in our society.

I

On April 11, 1983, the Richmond City Council adopted the Minority Business Utilization Plan (the Plan). The Plan required prime contractors to whom the city awarded construction contracts to subcontract at least 30% of the dollar amount of the contract to one or more Minority Business Enterprises (MBE's). The 30% set-aside did not apply to city contracts awarded to minority-owned prime contractors. The Plan defined an MBE as "[a] business at least fifty-one (51) percent of which is owned and controlled . . . by minority group members." "Minority group members" were defined as "[c]itizens of the United States who are Blacks, Spanish-speaking, Orientals, Indians, Eskimos, or Aleuts." There was no geographic limit to the Plan; an otherwise qualified MBE from anywhere in the United States could avail itself of the 30% set-aside. The Plan declared that it was "remedial" in nature, and enacted "for the purpose of promoting wider participation by minority business enterprises in the construction of public projects." The Plan expired on June 30, 1988, and was in effect for approximately five years.

The Plan was adopted by the Richmond City Council after a public hearing. Proponents of the set-aside provision relied on a study which indicated that, while the general population of Richmond was 50% black, only 0.67% of the city's prime construction contracts had been awarded to minority businesses in the 5-year period from 1978 to 1983. It was also established that a variety of contractors' associations, whose representatives appeared in opposition to the ordinance, had virtually no minority businesses within their membership. There was no direct evidence of race discrimination on the part of the city in letting contracts or any evidence that the city's prime contractors had discriminated against minority-owned subcontractors.

II

It would seem clear that a state or local subdivision (if delegated the authority from the State) has the authority to eradicate the effects of private discrimination within its own legislative jurisdiction. This authority must, of course, be exercised within the constraints of §1 of the Fourteenth Amendment. As a matter of state law, the city of Richmond has legislative authority over its procurement policies, and can use its spending powers to remedy private discrimination, if it identifies that discrimination with the particularity required by the Fourteenth Amendment. Thus, if the city could show that it had essentially become a "passive participant" in a system of racial exclusion practiced by elements of the local construction industry, we think it clear that the city could take affirmative steps to dismantle such a system. It is beyond dispute that any public entity, state or federal, has a compelling interest in assuring that public dollars drawn from the tax contributions of all citizens, do not serve to finance the evil of private prejudice.

III

A

The Richmond Plan denies certain citizens the opportunity to compete for a fixed percentage of public contracts based solely upon their race. To whatever racial group these citizens belong, their "personal rights" to be treated with equal dignity and respect are implicated by a rigid rule erecting race as the sole criterion in an aspect of public decisionmaking.

Absent searching judicial inquiry into the justification for such race-based measures, there is simply no way of determining what classifications are "benign" or "remedial" and what classifications are in fact motivated by illegitimate notions of racial inferiority or simple racial politics. Indeed, the purpose of strict scrutiny is to "smoke out" illegitimate uses of race by assuring that the legislative body is pursuing a goal important enough to warrant use of a highly suspect tool. The test also ensures that the means chosen "fit" this compelling goal so closely that there is little or no possibility that the motive for the classification was illegitimate racial prejudice or stereotype. Classifications based on race carry a danger of stigmatic harm. Unless they are strictly reserved for remedial settings, they may in fact promote notions of racial inferiority and lead to a politics of racial hostility.

Even were we to accept a reading of the guarantee of equal protection under which the level of scrutiny varies according to the ability of different groups to defend their interests in the representative process, heightened scrutiny would still be appropriate in the circumstances of this case. One of the central arguments for applying a less exacting standard to "benign" racial classifications is that such measures essentially involve a choice made by dominant racial groups to disadvantage themselves. If one aspect of the judiciary's role under the Equal Protection Clause is to protect "discrete and insular minorities" from majoritarian prejudice or indifference, see United States v. Carolene Products Co. (1938), some maintain that these concerns are not implicated when the "white majority" places burdens upon itself. See J. Ely, Democracy and Distrust 170 (1980).

In this case, blacks constitute approximately 50% of the population of the city of Richmond. Five of the nine seats on the city council are held by blacks. The concern that a political majority will more easily act to the disadvantage of a minority based on unwarranted assumptions or incomplete facts would seem to militate for, not against, the application of heightened judicial scrutiny in this case.

B

The District Court found the city council's "findings sufficient to ensure that, in adopting the Plan, it was remedying the present effects of past discrimination in the construction industry." Like the "role model" theory employed in *Wygant,* a generalized assertion that there has been past discrimination in an entire industry provides no guidance for a legislative body to determine the precise scope of the injury it seeks to remedy. It "has no logical stopping point." "Relief" for such an ill-defined wrong could extend until the percentage of public contracts awarded to MBE's in Richmond mirrored the percentage of minorities in the population as a whole.

Appellant argues that it is attempting to remedy various forms of past discrimination that are alleged to be responsible for the small number of minority businesses in the local contracting industry. Among these the city cites the exclusion of blacks from skilled construction trade unions and training programs.

While there is no doubt that the sorry history of both private and public discrimination in this country has contributed to a lack of opportunities for black entrepreneurs, this observation, standing alone, cannot justify a rigid racial quota in the awarding of public contracts in Richmond, Virginia. Like the claim that discrimination in primary and secondary schooling justifies a rigid racial preference in medical school admissions, an amorphous claim that there has been past discrimination in a particular industry cannot justify the use of an unyielding racial quota.

It is sheer speculation how many minority firms there would be in Richmond absent past societal discrimination, just as it was sheer speculation how many minority medical students would have been admitted to the medical school at Davis absent past discrimination in educational opportunities. Defining these sorts of injuries as "identified discrimination" would give local governments license to create a patchwork of racial preferences based on statistical generalizations about any particular field of endeavor.

These defects are readily apparent in this case. The 30% quota cannot in any realistic sense be tied to any injury suffered by anyone. None of [the district court's] "findings," singly or together, provide the city of Richmond with a "strong basis in evidence for its conclusion that remedial action was necessary." There is nothing approaching a prima facie case of a constitutional or statutory violation by anyone in the Richmond construction industry.

The District Court accorded great weight to the fact that the city council designated the Plan as "remedial." But the mere recitation of a "benign" or legitimate purpose for a racial classification is entitled to little or no weight. Racial classifications are suspect, and that means that simple legislative assurances of good intention cannot suffice.

In sum, none of the evidence presented by the city points to any identified discrimination in the Richmond construction industry. We, therefore, hold that the city has failed to demonstrate a compelling interest in apportioning public contracting opportunities on the basis of race. To accept Richmond's claim that past societal discrimination alone can serve as the basis for rigid racial preferences would be to open the door to competing claims for "remedial relief" for every disadvantaged group. The dream of a Nation of equal citizens in a society where race is irrelevant to personal opportunity and achievement would be lost in a mosaic of shifting preferences based on inherently unmeasurable claims of past wrongs. "Courts would be asked to evaluate the extent of the prejudice and consequent harm suffered by various minority groups. Those whose societal injury is thought to exceed some arbitrary level of tolerability then would be entitled to preferential classifications. . . ." We think such a result would be contrary to both the letter and spirit of a constitutional provision whose central command is equality.

The foregoing analysis applies only to the inclusion of blacks within the Richmond set-aside program. There is absolutely no evidence of past discrimination against Spanish-speaking, Oriental, Indian, Eskimo, or Aleut persons in any aspect of the Richmond construction industry. It may well be that Richmond has never had an Aleut or Eskimo citizen. The random inclusion of racial groups that, as a practical matter, may never have suffered from discrimination in the construction industry in Richmond suggests that perhaps the city's purpose was not in fact to remedy past discrimination.

If a 30% set-aside was "narrowly tailored" to compensate black contractors for past discrimination, one may legitimately ask why they are forced to share this "remedial relief" with an Aleut citizen who moves to Richmond tomorrow? The gross overinclusiveness of Richmond's racial preference strongly impugns the city's claim of remedial motivation.

IV

As noted by the court below, it is almost impossible to assess whether the Richmond Plan is narrowly tailored to remedy prior discrimination since it is not linked to identified discrimination in any way. We limit ourselves to two observations in this regard.

First, there does not appear to have been any consideration of the use of race-neutral means to increase minority business participation in city contracting. Many of the barriers to minority participation in the construction industry relied upon by the city to justify a racial classification appear to be race neutral. If MBE's disproportionately lack capital or cannot meet bonding requirements, a race-neutral program of city financing for small firms would, a fortiori, lead to greater minority participation. There is no evidence in this record that the Richmond City Council has considered any alternatives to a race-based quota.

Second, the 30% quota cannot be said to be narrowly tailored to any goal, except perhaps outright racial balancing. It rests upon the "completely unrealistic" assumption that minorities will choose a particular trade in lockstep proportion to their representation in the local population. Since the city must already consider bids and waivers on a case-by-case basis, it is difficult to see the need for a rigid numerical quota.

V

Nothing we say today precludes a state or local entity from taking action to rectify the effects of identified discrimination within its jurisdiction. If the city of Richmond had evidence before it that nonminority contractors were systematically excluding minority businesses from subcontracting opportunities it could take action to end the discriminatory exclusion. Where there is a significant statistical disparity between the number of qualified minority contractors willing and able to perform a particular service and the number of such contractors actually engaged by the locality or the locality's prime contractors, an inference of discriminatory exclusion could arise. Under such circumstances, the city could act to dismantle the closed business system by taking appropriate measures against those who discriminate on the basis of race or other illegitimate criteria. In the extreme case, some form of narrowly tailored racial preference might be necessary to break down patterns of deliberate exclusion.

Even in the absence of evidence of discrimination, the city has at its disposal a whole array of race-neutral devices to increase the accessibility of city contracting opportunities to small entrepreneurs of all races. Simplification of bidding procedures, relaxation of bonding requirements, and training and financial aid for disadvantaged entrepreneurs of all races would open the public contracting market to all those who have suffered the effects of past societal discrimination or neglect. Many of the formal barriers to new entrants may be the product of bureaucratic inertia more than actual necessity, and may have a disproportionate effect on the opportunities open to new minority firms. Their elimination or modification would have little detrimental effect on the city's interests and would serve to increase the opportunities available to minority business without classifying individuals on the basis of race. The city may also act to prohibit discrimination in the provision of credit or bonding by local suppliers and banks. Business as usual should not mean business pursuant to the unthinking exclusion of certain members of our society from its rewards.

In the case at hand, the city has not ascertained how many minority enterprises are present in the local construction market nor the level of their participation in city construction projects. The city points to no evidence that qualified minority contractors have been passed over for city contracts or subcontracts, either as a group or in any individual case. Under such circumstances, it is simply impossible to say that the city has demonstrated "a strong basis in evidence for its conclusion that remedial action was necessary."

Proper findings in this regard are necessary to define both the scope of the injury and the extent of the remedy necessary to cure its effects. Such findings also serve to assure all citizens that the deviation from the norm of equal treatment of all racial and ethnic groups is a temporary matter, a measure taken in the service of the goal of equality itself. Absent such findings, there is a danger that a racial classification is merely the product of unthinking stereotypes or a form of racial politics. "[I]f there is no duty to attempt either to measure the recovery by the wrong or to distribute that recovery within the injured class in an evenhanded way, our history will adequately support a legislative preference for almost any ethnic, religious, or racial group with the political strength to negotiate 'a piece of the action' for its members." Because the city of Richmond has failed to identify the need for remedial action in the awarding of its public construction contracts, its treatment of its citizens on a racial basis violates the dictates of the Equal Protection Clause.

Justice SCALIA, concurring in the judgment.

I agree with much of the Court's opinion, and, in particular, with Justice O'Connor's conclusion that strict scrutiny must be applied to all governmental classification by race, whether or not its asserted purpose is "remedial" or "benign." I do not agree, however, with Justice O'Connor's dictum suggesting that, despite the Fourteenth Amendment, state and local governments may in some circumstances discriminate on the basis of race in order (in a broad sense) "to ameliorate the effects of past discrimination." The benign purpose of compensating for social disadvantages, whether they have been acquired by reason of prior discrimination or otherwise, can no more be pursued by the illegitimate means of racial discrimination than can other assertedly benign purposes we have repeatedly rejected.

I share the view expressed by Alexander Bickel that "[t]he lesson of the great decisions of the Supreme Court and the lesson of contemporary history have been the same for at least a generation: discrimination on the basis of race is illegal, immoral, unconstitutional, inherently wrong, and destructive of democratic society." A. Bickel, The Morality of Consent 133 (1975). At least where state or local action is at issue, only a social emergency rising to the level of imminent danger to life and limb — for example, a prison race riot, requiring temporary segregation of inmates, can justify an exception to the principle embodied in the Fourteenth Amendment that "[o]ur Constitution is colorblind, and neither knows nor tolerates classes among citizens."

In my view there is only one circumstance in which the States may act by race to "undo the effects of past discrimination": where that is necessary to eliminate their own maintenance of a system of unlawful racial classification. If, for example, a state agency has a discriminatory pay scale compensating black employees in all positions at 20% less than their nonblack counterparts, it may assuredly promulgate an order raising the salaries of "all black employees" to eliminate the differential. This distinction explains our school desegregation cases, in which we have made plain that States and localities sometimes have an obligation to adopt race-conscious remedies.

Since I believe that the appellee here had a constitutional right to have its bid succeed or fail under a decisionmaking process uninfected with racial bias, I concur in the judgment of the Court.

Justice MARSHALL, with whom Justice BRENNAN and Justice BLACKMUN join, dissenting.

It is a welcome symbol of racial progress when the former capital of the Confederacy acts forthrightly to confront the effects of racial discrimination in its midst. In my view, nothing in the Constitution can be construed to prevent Richmond, Virginia, from allocating a portion of its contracting dollars for businesses owned or controlled by members of minority groups. Indeed, Richmond's set-aside program is indistinguishable in all meaningful respects from — and in fact was patterned upon — the federal set-aside plan which this Court upheld in Fullilove v. Klutznick (1980).

A majority of this Court holds today, however, that the Equal Protection Clause of the Fourteenth Amendment blocks Richmond's initiative. The essence of the majority's position is that Richmond has failed to catalog adequate findings to prove that past discrimination has impeded minorities from joining or participating fully in Richmond's construction contracting industry. I find deep irony in second-guessing Richmond's judgment on this point. As much as any municipality in the United States, Richmond knows what racial discrimination is; a century of decisions by this and other federal courts has richly documented the city's disgraceful history of public and private racial discrimination. In any event, the Richmond City Council has supported its determination that minorities have been wrongly excluded from local construction contracting. Its proof includes statistics showing that minority-owned businesses have received virtually no city contracting dollars and rarely if ever belonged to area trade associations; testimony by municipal officials that discrimination has been widespread in the local construction industry; and the same exhaustive and widely publicized federal studies relied on in *Fullilove*, studies which showed that pervasive discrimination in the Nation's tight-knit construction industry had operated to exclude minorities from public contracting. These are precisely the types of statistical and testimonial evidence which, until today, this Court had credited in cases approving of race-conscious measures designed to remedy past discrimination.

More fundamentally, today's decision marks a deliberate and giant step backward in this Court's affirmative-action jurisprudence. Cynical of one municipality's attempt to redress the effects of past racial discrimination in a particular industry, the majority launches a grapeshot attack on race-conscious remedies in general. The majority's unnecessary pronouncements will inevitably discourage or prevent governmental entities, particularly States and localities, from acting to rectify the scourge of past discrimination. This is the harsh reality of the majority's decision, but it is not the Constitution's command.

Today, for the first time, a majority of this Court has adopted strict scrutiny as its standard of Equal Protection Clause review of race-conscious remedial measures. This is an unwelcome development. A profound difference separates governmental actions that themselves are racist, and governmental actions that seek to remedy the effects of prior racism or to prevent neutral governmental activity from perpetuating the effects of such racism. Racial classifications "drawn on the presumption that one race is inferior to another or because they put the weight of government behind racial hatred and separatism" warrant the strictest judicial scrutiny because of the very irrelevance of these rationales. By contrast, racial classifications drawn for the purpose of remedying the effects of discrimination that itself was race based have a highly pertinent basis: the tragic and indelible fact that discrimination against blacks and other racial minorities in this Nation has pervaded our Nation's history and continues to scar our society.

In concluding that remedial classifications warrant no different standard of review under the Constitution than the most brutal and repugnant forms of state-sponsored racism, a majority of this Court signals that it regards racial discrimination as largely a phenomenon of the past, and that government bodies need no longer preoccupy themselves with rectifying racial injustice. I, however, do not believe this Nation is anywhere close to eradicating racial discrimination or its vestiges. In constitutionalizing its wishful thinking, the majority today does a grave disservice not only to those victims of past and present racial discrimination in this Nation whom government has sought to assist, but also to this Court's long tradition of approaching issues of race with the utmost sensitivity.

A year after *Croson*, in Metro Broadcasting, Inc. v. Federal Communications Commission, 497 U.S. 547 (1990), the Supreme Court held that congressionally approved affirmative action programs only need to meet intermediate scrutiny.

The Supreme Court, in a five-to-four decision, upheld FCC policies that gave a preference to minority-owned businesses in broadcast licensing. The majority opinion expressly said, "We hold that benign race-conscious measures mandated by Congress — even if those measure are not 'remedial' in the sense of being designed to compensate victims of past governmental or societal discrimination — are constitutionally permissible to the extent that they serve important governmental objectives within the power of Congress and are substantially related to the achievement of those objectives."

The majority opinion in *Metro Broadcasting* was written by Justice Brennan and joined by Justices White, Marshall, Blackmun, and Stevens. The dissent comprised Justices O'Connor, Kennedy, Scalia, and Rehnquist. Between *Metro Broadcasting*, in 1990, and Adarand Constructors, Inc. v. Pena, 515 U.S. 200 (1995), four of the justices in the majority, but none of the justices in the dissent, resigned. In *Adarand*, the four dissenters from *Metro Broadcasting* were joined by Justice Thomas to create a majority that overruled *Metro Broadcasting*.

Justice O'Connor, writing for the Court, stated:

> Accordingly, we hold today that all racial classifications, imposed by whatever federal, state, or local governmental actor, must be analyzed by a reviewing court under strict scrutiny. In other words, such classifications are constitutional only if they are narrowly tailored measures that further compelling governmental interests. To the extent that *Metro Broadcasting* is inconsistent with that holding, it is overruled.
>
> Our action today makes explicit what Justice Powell thought implicit in the *Fullilove* lead opinion: Federal racial classifications, like those of a State, must serve a compelling governmental interest, and must be narrowly tailored to further that interest. Of course, it follows that to the extent (if any) that *Fullilove* held federal racial classifications to be subject to a less rigorous standard, it is no longer controlling. But we need not decide today whether the program upheld in *Fullilove* would survive strict scrutiny as our more recent cases have defined it.
>
> Finally, we wish to dispel the notion that strict scrutiny is "strict in theory, but fatal in fact." The unhappy persistence of both the practice and the lingering effects of racial discrimination against minority groups in this country is an unfortunate reality, and government is not disqualified from acting in response to it. As recently as 1987, for example, every Justice of this Court agreed that the Alabama Department of Public Safety's "pervasive, systematic, and obstinate discriminatory conduct" justified a narrowly tailored race-based remedy. See United States v. Paradise. When race-based action is necessary to further a compelling interest, such action is within constitutional constraints if it satisfies the "narrow tailoring" test this Court has set out in previous cases.

The Court remanded the case for the application of strict scrutiny. Justice Scalia wrote separately to express his view that remedying past discrimination can virtually never meet strict scrutiny:

> I join the opinion of the Court except insofar as it may be inconsistent with the following: In my view, government can never have a "compelling interest" in discriminating on the basis of race in order to "make up" for past racial discrimination in the opposite direction. Individuals who have been wronged by unlawful racial discrimination should be made whole; but under our Constitution there can be no such thing as either a creditor or a debtor race. That concept is alien to the Constitution's focus upon the individual. To pursue the concept of racial

entitlement — even for the most admirable and benign of purposes — is to reinforce and preserve for future mischief the way of thinking that produced race slavery, race privilege and race hatred. In the eyes of government, we are just one race here. It is American.

It is unlikely, if not impossible, that the challenged program would survive under this understanding of strict scrutiny, but I am content to leave that to be decided on remand.

Justice Thomas took a similar position:

I agree with the majority's conclusion that strict scrutiny applies to all government classifications based on race. I write separately, however, to express my disagreement with the premise underlying Justice Stevens's and Justice Ginsburg's dissents: that there is a racial paternalism exception to the principle of equal protection. I believe that there is a "moral [and] constitutional equivalence," between laws designed to subjugate a race and those that distribute benefits on the basis of race in order to foster some current notion of equality. Government cannot make us equal; it can only recognize, respect, and protect us as equal before the law.

That these programs may have been motivated, in part, by good intentions cannot provide refuge from the principle that under our Constitution, the government may not make distinctions on the basis of race. As far as the Constitution is concerned, it is irrelevant whether a government's racial classifications are drawn by those who wish to oppress a race or by those who have a sincere desire to help those thought to be disadvantaged. There can be no doubt that the paternalism that appears to lie at the heart of this program is at war with the principle of inherent equality that underlies and infuses our Constitution. See Declaration of Independence ("We hold these truths to be self-evident, that all men are created equal, that they are endowed by their Creator with certain unalienable Rights, that among these are Life, Liberty, and the pursuit of Happiness").

These programs not only raise grave constitutional questions, they also undermine the moral basis of the equal protection principle. Purchased at the price of immeasurable human suffering, the equal protection principle reflects our Nation's understanding that such classifications ultimately have a destructive impact on the individual and our society. Unquestionably, "[i]nvidious [racial] discrimination is an engine of oppression." It is also true that "[r]emedial" racial preferences may reflect "a desire to foster equality in society." But there can be no doubt that racial paternalism and its unintended consequences can be as poisonous and pernicious as any other form of discrimination. So-called "benign" discrimination teaches many that because of chronic and apparently immutable handicaps, minorities cannot compete with them without their patronizing indulgence. Inevitably, such programs engender attitudes of superiority or, alternatively, provoke resentment among those who believe that they have been wronged by the government's use of race. These programs stamp minorities with a badge of inferiority and may cause them to develop dependencies or to adopt an attitude that they are "entitled" to preferences.

In my mind, government-sponsored racial discrimination based on benign prejudice is just as noxious as discrimination inspired by malicious prejudice. In each instance, it is racial discrimination, plain and simple.

Justice Stevens wrote for the dissent:

Instead of deciding this case in accordance with controlling precedent, the Court today delivers a disconcerting lecture about the evils of governmental racial classifications. The Court's concept of "consistency" assumes that there is no significant difference between a decision by the majority to impose a special burden on the members of a minority race and a decision by the majority to provide a benefit to certain members of that minority notwithstanding its incidental burden on some members of the majority. In my opinion that assumption is untenable. There is no moral or constitutional equivalence between a policy that is designed to perpetuate a caste system and one that seeks to eradicate racial subordination. Invidious discrimination is an engine of oppression, subjugating a disfavored group to enhance or maintain the power of the majority. Remedial race-based preferences reflect the opposite impulse: a desire to foster equality in society. No sensible conception of the Government's constitutional obligation to "govern impartially," should ignore this distinction.

The consistency that the Court espouses would disregard the difference between a "No Trespassing" sign and a welcome mat. It would treat a Dixiecrat Senator's decision to vote against Thurgood Marshall's confirmation in order to keep African-Americans off the Supreme Court as on a par with President Johnson's evaluation of his nominee's race as a positive factor. It would equate a law that made black citizens ineligible for military service with a program aimed at recruiting black soldiers. An attempt by the majority to exclude members of a minority race from a regulated market is fundamentally different from a subsidy that enables a relatively small group of newcomers to enter that market. An interest in "consistency" does not justify treating differences as though they were similarities.

The Court's explanation for treating dissimilar race-based decisions as though they were equally objectionable is a supposed inability to differentiate between "invidious" and "benign" discrimination. But the term "affirmative action" is common and well understood. Its presence in everyday parlance shows that people understand the difference between good intentions and bad. As with any legal concept, some cases may be difficult to classify, but our equal protection jurisprudence has identified a critical difference between state action that imposes burdens on a disfavored few and state action that benefits the few "in spite of" its adverse effects on the many.

As a matter of constitutional and democratic principle, a decision by representatives of the majority to discriminate against the members of a minority race is fundamentally different from those same representatives' decision to impose incidental costs on the majority of their constituents in order to provide a benefit to a disadvantaged minority.

An additional reason for giving greater deference to the National Legislature than to a local lawmaking body is that federal affirmative-action programs represent the will of our entire Nation's elected representatives, whereas a state or local program may have an impact on nonresident entities who played no part in the decision to enact it. Thus, in the state or local context, individuals who were unable to vote for the local representatives who enacted a race-conscious program may nonetheless feel the effects of that program.

Ironically, after all of the time, effort, and paper this Court has expended in differentiating between federal and state affirmative action, the majority today virtually ignores the issue. It provides not a word of direct explanation for its sudden and enormous departure from the reasoning in past cases. Such silence, however, cannot erase the difference between Congress' institutional competence and constitutional authority to overcome historic racial subjugation and the States' lesser power to do so. In my judgment, the Court's novel doctrine of "congruence" is seriously misguided. Congressional deliberations about a matter as important as affirmative action should be accorded far greater deference than those of a State or municipality.

THE ARGUMENTS FOR AND AGAINST STRICT SCRUTINY

The debate over affirmative action is, in large part, as indicated in *Croson* and *Adarand*, about the level of scrutiny to be used. The reality is that the choice of the level of scrutiny is likely to be decisive in many cases in determining the fate of the affirmative action program.

Those who favor strict scrutiny for affirmative action programs argue that all racial classifications — whether invidious or benign — should be subjected to strict scrutiny. Justice Thomas, in *Adarand* above, espoused this view: "In my mind, government-sponsored racial discrimination based on benign prejudice is just as noxious as discrimination inspired by malicious prejudice. In each instance, it is racial discrimination, plain and simple." The view is that the Constitution requires that the government treat each person as an individual without regard to his or her race; strict scrutiny is used to ensure that this occurs.

Moreover, supporters of strict scrutiny for affirmative action argue that all racial classifications stigmatize and breed racial hostility, and therefore all should be subjected to strict scrutiny. Justice O'Connor, in *Croson*, stated, "Classifications based on race carry a danger of stigmatic harm. Unless they are strictly reserved for remedial settings, they may in fact promote notions of racial inferiority and lead to a politics of racial hostility." Professor Michael Perry made a similar point that affirmative action "inevitably foments racial resentment and thereby strains the effort to gain wider acceptance for the principle of the moral equality of the races."[97]

On the other side of the debate, supporters of affirmative action argue that there is a significant difference between the government using racial classifications to benefit minorities and the government using racial classifications to disadvantage minorities. There is a long history of racism and discrimination against minorities but no similar history of persecution of whites.[98] Those who argue for a lower level of scrutiny for judicial review of affirmative action programs also emphasize that achieving social equality requires affirmative action at this point in American history. The tremendous continuing disparities between blacks and whites in areas such as education, employment, and public contracting necessitate remedial action. Applying strict scrutiny would greatly impede such remedial efforts because relatively few affirmative action programs have survived this rigorous review.

Also it is argued that there is a major difference between a majority discriminating against a minority and the majority discriminating against itself. Professor John Hart Ely explained, "When the group that controls the decision making process classifies so as to advantage a minority and disadvantage itself, the reasons for being unusually suspicious, and consequently, employing a stringent brand of review are lacking. A White majority is unlikely to disadvantage itself for reasons of racial prejudice; nor is it likely to be tempted either to underestimate the needs and deserts of Whites relative to those of

---

97. Michael J. Perry, *Modern Equal Protection: A Conceptualization and Appraisal*, 79 Colum. L. Rev. 1023, 1048 (1979).

98. Richard Lempert, *The Force of Irony: On the Morality of Affirmative Action and United Steelworkers v. Weber*, 95 Ethics 86, 88-89 (1984).

others, or to overestimate the costs of devising an alternative classification that would extend to certain Whites the advantages generally extended to Blacks."[99]

THE USE OF RACE TO BENEFIT MINORITIES IN COLLEGE AND UNIVERSITY ADMISSIONS

In two cases, Grutter v. Bollinger and Gratz v. Bollinger, the Supreme Court considered the constitutionality of efforts by public colleges and universities to use racial classifications to benefit minorities and to enhance diversity. Simply put, in these cases, below, the Court held that colleges and universities may use race as one factor, among many, in admissions decisions, but it is not permissible to add a significant number of points to the admissions scores of minority students. In reading these important cases, it is important to consider how to draw the line between what is permissible and impermissible after these decisions. What types of efforts are likely to be allowed and which invalidated?

GRUTTER v. BOLLINGER

539 U.S. 306 (2003)

Justice O'CONNOR delivered the opinion of the Court.

This case requires us to decide whether the use of race as a factor in student admissions by the University of Michigan Law School (Law School) is unlawful.

I

A

The Law School ranks among the Nation's top law schools. It receives more than 3,500 applications each year for a class of around 350 students. Seeking to "admit a group of students who individually and collectively are among the most capable," the Law School looks for individuals with "substantial promise for success in law school" and "a strong likelihood of succeeding in the practice of law and contributing in diverse ways to the well-being of others." More broadly, the Law School seeks "a mix of students with varying backgrounds and experiences who will respect and learn from each other." In 1992, the dean of the Law School charged a faculty committee with crafting a written admissions policy to implement these goals. In particular, the Law School sought to ensure that its efforts to achieve student body diversity complied with this Court's most recent ruling on the use of race in university admissions. See Regents of Univ. of Cal. v. Bakke (1978). Upon the unanimous adoption of the committee's

---

99. John Hart Ely, *The Constitutionality of Reverse Racial Discrimination*, 41 U. Chi. L. Rev. 723, 735 (1974); *see also* Michel Rosenfeld, *Decoding* Richmond: *Affirmative Action and the Elusive Meaning of Constitutional Equality*, 87 Mich. L. Rev. 1729, 1774 (1989).

report by the Law School faculty, it became the Law School's official admissions policy.

The hallmark of that policy is its focus on academic ability coupled with a flexible assessment of applicants' talents, experiences, and potential "to contribute to the learning of those around them." The policy requires admissions officials to evaluate each applicant based on all the information available in the file, including a personal statement, letters of recommendation, and an essay describing the ways in which the applicant will contribute to the life and diversity of the Law School. In reviewing an applicant's file, admissions officials must consider the applicant's undergraduate grade point average (GPA) and Law School Admissions Test (LSAT) score because they are important (if imperfect) predictors of academic success in law school. The policy stresses that "no applicant should be admitted unless we expect that applicant to do well enough to graduate with no serious academic problems."

The policy makes clear, however, that even the highest possible score does not guarantee admission to the Law School. Nor does a low score automatically disqualify an applicant. Rather, the policy requires admissions officials to look beyond grades and test scores to other criteria that are important to the Law School's educational objectives. So-called "'soft' variables" such as "the enthusiasm of recommenders, the quality of the undergraduate institution, the quality of the applicant's essay, and the areas and difficulty of undergraduate course selection" are all brought to bear in assessing an "applicant's likely contributions to the intellectual and social life of the institution."

The policy aspires to "achieve that diversity which has the potential to enrich everyone's education and thus make a law school class stronger than the sum of its parts." The policy does not restrict the types of diversity contributions eligible for "substantial weight" in the admissions process, but instead recognizes "many possible bases for diversity admissions." The policy does, however, reaffirm the Law School's longstanding commitment to "one particular type of diversity," that is, "racial and ethnic diversity with special reference to the inclusion of students from groups which have been historically discriminated against, like African-Americans, Hispanics and Native Americans, who without this commitment might not be represented in our student body in meaningful numbers." By enrolling a "'critical mass' of [underrepresented] minority students," the Law School seeks to "ensur[e] their ability to make unique contributions to the character of the Law School."

The policy does not define diversity "solely in terms of racial and ethnic status." Nor is the policy "insensitive to the competition among all students for admission to the [L]aw [S]chool." Rather, the policy seeks to guide admissions officers in "producing classes both diverse and academically outstanding, classes made up of students who promise to continue the tradition of outstanding contribution by Michigan Graduates to the legal profession."

B

Petitioner Barbara Grutter is a white Michigan resident who applied to the Law School in 1996 with a 3.8 grade point average and 161 LSAT score. The Law School initially placed petitioner on a waiting list, but subsequently rejected her application. In December 1997, petitioner filed suit in the United States District Court for the Eastern District of Michigan.

II

A

We last addressed the use of race in public higher education over 25 years ago. In the landmark *Bakke* case, we reviewed a racial set-aside program that reserved 16 out of 100 seats in a medical school class for members of certain minority groups. The decision produced six separate opinions, none of which commanded a majority of the Court. Four Justices would have upheld the program against all attack on the ground that the government can use race to "remedy disadvantages cast on minorities by past racial prejudice." Four other Justices avoided the constitutional question altogether and struck down the program on statutory grounds. Justice Powell provided a fifth vote not only for invalidating the set-aside program, but also for reversing the state court's injunction against any use of race whatsoever. Since this Court's splintered decision in *Bakke*, Justice Powell's opinion announcing the judgment of the Court has served as the touchstone for constitutional analysis of race-conscious admissions policies. Public and private universities across the Nation have modeled their own admissions programs on Justice Powell's views on permissible race-conscious policies.

We do not find it necessary to decide whether Justice Powell's opinion is binding. More important, for the reasons set out below, today we endorse Justice Powell's view that student body diversity is a compelling state interest that can justify the use of race in university admissions.

B

The Equal Protection Clause provides that no State shall "deny to any person within its jurisdiction the equal protection of the laws." Because the Fourteenth Amendment "protect[s] persons, not groups," all "governmental action based on race — a group classification long recognized as in most circumstances irrelevant and therefore prohibited — should be subjected to detailed judicial inquiry to ensure that the personal right to equal protection of the laws has not been infringed." We have held that all racial classifications imposed by government "must be analyzed by a reviewing court under strict scrutiny." This means that such classifications are constitutional only if they are narrowly tailored to further compelling governmental interests. "Absent searching judicial inquiry into the justification for such race-based measures," we have no way to determine what "classifications are 'benign' or 'remedial' and what classifications are in fact motivated by illegitimate notions of racial inferiority or simple racial politics." We apply strict scrutiny to all racial classifications to "'smoke out' illegitimate uses of race by assuring that [government] is pursuing a goal important enough to warrant use of a highly suspect tool."

Strict scrutiny is not "strict in theory, but fatal in fact." Although all governmental uses of race are subject to strict scrutiny, not all are invalidated by it. When race-based action is necessary to further a compelling governmental interest, such action does not violate the constitutional guarantee of equal protection so long as the narrow-tailoring requirement is also satisfied.

III

A

With these principles in mind, we turn to the question whether the Law School's use of race is justified by a compelling state interest. Before this Court, as they have throughout this litigation, respondents assert only one justification for their use of race in the admissions process: obtaining "the educational benefits that flow from a diverse student body." In other words, the Law School asks us to recognize, in the context of higher education, a compelling state interest in student body diversity.

The Law School's educational judgment that such diversity is essential to its educational mission is one to which we defer. The Law School's assessment that diversity will, in fact, yield educational benefits is substantiated by respondents and their amici. Our scrutiny of the interest asserted by the Law School is no less strict for taking into account complex educational judgments in an area that lies primarily within the expertise of the university. Our holding today is in keeping with our tradition of giving a degree of deference to a university's academic decisions, within constitutionally prescribed limits. We have long recognized that, given the important purpose of public education and the expansive freedoms of speech and thought associated with the university environment, universities occupy a special niche in our constitutional tradition. In announcing the principle of student body diversity as a compelling state interest, Justice Powell invoked our cases recognizing a constitutional dimension, grounded in the First Amendment, of educational autonomy. Our conclusion that the Law School has a compelling interest in a diverse student body is informed by our view that attaining a diverse student body is at the heart of the Law School's proper institutional mission, and that "good faith" on the part of a university is "presumed" absent "a showing to the contrary."

As part of its goal of "assembling a class that is both exceptionally academically qualified and broadly diverse," the Law School seeks to "enroll a 'critical mass' of minority students." The Law School's interest is not simply "to assure within its student body some specified percentage of a particular group merely because of its race or ethnic origin." That would amount to outright racial balancing, which is patently unconstitutional. Rather, the Law School's concept of critical mass is defined by reference to the educational benefits that diversity is designed to produce.

These benefits are substantial. As the District Court emphasized, the Law School's admissions policy promotes "cross-racial understanding," helps to break down racial stereotypes, and "enables [students] to better understand persons of different races." These benefits are "important and laudable," because "classroom discussion is livelier, more spirited, and simply more enlightening and interesting" when the students have "the greatest possible variety of backgrounds."

The Law School's claim of a compelling interest is further bolstered by its amici, who point to the educational benefits that flow from student body diversity. In addition to the expert studies and reports entered into evidence at trial, numerous studies show that student body diversity promotes learning outcomes, and "better prepares students for an increasingly diverse workforce and society, and better prepares them as professionals." These benefits are not theoretical but real, as major American businesses have made clear that the skills needed in today's increasingly global marketplace can only be developed through exposure to widely diverse people, cultures, ideas, and viewpoints. What is more, high-ranking retired officers and civilian leaders of the United States military assert that, "[b]ased on [their] decades of experience," a "highly qualified, racially diverse officer corps . . . is essential to the military's ability to fulfill its principle mission to provide national security."

We have repeatedly acknowledged the overriding importance of preparing students for work and citizenship, describing education as pivotal to "sustaining our political and cultural heritage" with a fundamental role in maintaining the fabric of society. Plyler v. Doe (1982). This Court has long recognized that "education . . . is the very foundation of good citizenship." Brown v. Board of Education (1954). For this reason, the diffusion of knowledge and opportunity through public institutions of higher education must be accessible to all individuals regardless of race or ethnicity. The United States, as amicus curiae, affirms that "[e]nsuring that public institutions are open and available to all segments of American society, including people of all races and ethnicities, represents a paramount government objective." And, "[n]owhere is the importance of such openness more acute than in the context of higher education." Effective participation by members of all racial and ethnic groups in the civic life of our Nation is essential if the dream of one Nation, indivisible, is to be realized.

Moreover, universities, and in particular, law schools, represent the training ground for a large number of our Nation's leaders. Individuals with law degrees occupy roughly half the state governorships, more than half the seats in the United States Senate, and more than a third of the seats in the United States House of Representatives. The pattern is even more striking when it comes to highly selective law schools. A handful of these schools accounts for 25 of the 100 United States Senators, 74 United States Courts of Appeals judges, and nearly 200 of the more than 600 United States District Court judges.

In order to cultivate a set of leaders with legitimacy in the eyes of the citizenry, it is necessary that the path to leadership be visibly open to talented and qualified individuals of every race and ethnicity. Access to legal education (and thus the legal profession) must be inclusive of talented and qualified individuals of every race and ethnicity, so that all members of our heterogeneous society may participate in the educational institutions that provide the training and education necessary to succeed in America.

The Law School does not premise its need for critical mass on "any belief that minority students always (or even consistently) express some characteristic minority viewpoint on any issue." To the contrary, diminishing the force of such stereotypes is both a crucial part of the Law School's mission, and one that it cannot accomplish with only token numbers of minority students. Just as growing up in a particular region or having particular professional experiences is likely to affect an individual's views, so too is one's own, unique experience of being a racial minority in a society, like our own, in which race unfortunately still matters. The Law School has determined, based on its experience and expertise, that a "critical mass" of underrepresented minorities is necessary to further its compelling interest in securing the educational benefits of a diverse student body.

B

Even in the limited circumstance when drawing racial distinctions is permissible to further a compelling state interest, government is still "constrained in how it may pursue that end: [T]he means chosen to accomplish the [government's] asserted purpose must be specifically and narrowly framed to accomplish that purpose." The purpose of the narrow tailoring requirement is to ensure that "the means chosen 'fit' . . . th[e] compelling goal so closely that there is little or no possibility that the motive for the classification was illegitimate racial prejudice or stereotype."

Since *Bakke*, we have had no occasion to define the contours of the narrow-tailoring inquiry with respect to race-conscious university admissions programs. That inquiry must be calibrated to fit the distinct issues raised by the use of race to achieve student body diversity in public higher education. Contrary to Justice Kennedy's assertions, we do not "abandon[] strict scrutiny." Rather, as we have already explained, we adhere to *Adarand*'s teaching that the very purpose of strict scrutiny is to take such "relevant differences into account."

To be narrowly tailored, a race-conscious admissions program cannot use a quota system—it cannot "insulat[e] each category of applicants with certain desired qualifications from competition with all other applicants." Instead, a university may consider race or ethnicity only as a "'plus' in a particular applicant's file," without "insulat[ing] the individual from comparison with all other candidates for the available seats." In other words, an admissions program must be "flexible enough to consider all pertinent elements of diversity in light of the particular qualifications of each applicant, and to place them on the same footing for consideration, although not necessarily according them the same weight."

We find that the Law School's admissions program bears the hallmarks of a narrowly tailored plan. As Justice Powell made clear in *Bakke*, truly individualized consideration demands that race be used in a flexible, nonmechanical way. It follows from this mandate that universities cannot establish quotas for members of certain racial groups or put members of those groups on separate admissions tracks. Nor can universities insulate applicants who belong to certain racial or ethnic groups from the competition for admission. Universities can, however, consider race or ethnicity more flexibly as a "plus" factor in the context of individualized consideration of each and every applicant.

We are satisfied that the Law School's admissions program, like the Harvard plan described by Justice Powell, does not operate as a quota. Properly understood, a "quota" is a program in which a certain fixed number or proportion of opportunities are "reserved exclusively for certain minority groups." Quotas "'impose a fixed number or percentage which must be attained, or which cannot be exceeded,'" and "insulate the individual from comparison with all other candidates for the available seats." In contrast, "a permissible goal . . . require[s] only a good-faith effort . . . to come within a range demarcated by the goal itself," and permits consideration of race as a "plus" factor in any given case while still ensuring that each candidate "compete[s] with all other qualified applicants."

The Law School's goal of attaining a critical mass of underrepresented minority students does not transform its program into a quota. As the Harvard plan described by Justice Powell recognized, there is of course "some relationship between numbers and achieving the benefits to be derived from a diverse student body, and between numbers and providing a reasonable environment for those students admitted." "[S]ome attention to numbers," without more, does not transform a flexible admissions system into a rigid quota. Moreover, between 1993 and 2000, the number of African-American, Latino, and Native-American students in each class at the Law School varied from 13.5 to 20.1 percent, a range inconsistent with a quota.

We also find that, like the Harvard plan Justice Powell referenced in *Bakke*, the Law School's race-conscious admissions program adequately ensures that all factors that may contribute to student body diversity are meaningfully considered alongside race in admissions decisions. With respect to the use of race itself, all underrepresented minority students admitted by the Law School have been deemed qualified. By virtue of our Nation's struggle with racial inequality, such students are both likely to have experiences of particular importance to the Law School's mission, and less likely to be admitted in meaningful numbers on criteria that ignore those experiences.

The Law School does not, however, limit in any way the broad range of qualities and experiences that may be considered valuable contributions to student body diversity. To the contrary, the 1992 policy makes clear "[t]here are many possible bases for diversity admissions," and provides examples of admittees who have lived or traveled widely abroad, are fluent in several languages, have overcome personal adversity and family hardship, have exceptional records of extensive community service, and have had successful careers in other fields. The Law School seriously considers each "applicant's promise of making a notable contribution to the class by way of a particular strength, attainment, or characteristic — e.g., an unusual intellectual achievement, employment experience, nonacademic performance, or personal background." All applicants have the opportunity to highlight their own potential diversity contributions through the submission of a personal statement, letters of recommendation, and an essay describing the ways in which the applicant will contribute to the life and diversity of the Law School.

What is more, the Law School actually gives substantial weight to diversity factors besides race. The Law School frequently accepts nonminority applicants with grades and test scores lower than underrepresented minority applicants (and other nonminority applicants) who are rejected. This shows that the Law School seriously weighs many other diversity factors besides race that can make a real and dispositive difference for nonminority applicants as well. By this flexible approach, the Law School sufficiently takes into account, in practice as well as in theory, a wide variety of characteristics besides race and ethnicity that contribute to a diverse student body. Justice Kennedy speculates that "race is likely outcome determinative for many members of minority groups" who do not fall within the upper range of LSAT scores and grades. But the same could be said of the Harvard plan discussed approvingly by Justice Powell in *Bakke*, and indeed of any plan that uses race as one of many factors.

We agree with the Court of Appeals that the Law School sufficiently considered workable race-neutral alternatives. The District Court took the Law School to task for failing to consider race-neutral alternatives such as "using a lottery system" or "decreasing the emphasis for all applicants on undergraduate GPA and LSAT scores." But these alternatives would require a dramatic sacrifice of diversity, the academic quality of all admitted students, or both. The Law School's current admissions program considers race as one factor among many, in an effort to assemble a student body that is diverse in ways broader than race. Because a lottery would make that kind of nuanced judgment impossible, it would effectively sacrifice all other educational values, not to mention every other kind of diversity. So too with the suggestion that the Law School simply lower admissions standards for all students, a drastic remedy that would require the Law School to become a much different institution and sacrifice a vital component of its educational mission.

The United States advocates "percentage plans," recently adopted by public undergraduate institutions in Texas, Florida, and California to guarantee admission to all students above a certain class-rank threshold in every high school in the State. The United States does not, however, explain how such plans could work for graduate and professional schools. Moreover, even assuming such plans are race-neutral, they may preclude the university from conducting the individualized assessments necessary to assemble a student body that is not just racially diverse, but diverse along all the qualities valued by the university. We are satisfied that the Law School adequately considered race-neutral alternatives currently capable of producing a critical mass without forcing the Law School to abandon the academic selectivity that is the cornerstone of its educational mission.

As Justice Powell recognized in *Bakke*, so long as a race-conscious admissions program uses race as a "plus" factor in the context of individualized consideration, a rejected applicant "will not have been foreclosed from all consideration for that seat simply because he was not the right color or had the wrong surname. . . . His qualifications would have been weighed fairly and competitively, and he would have no basis to complain of unequal treatment under the Fourteenth Amendment." We agree that, in the context of its individualized inquiry into the possible diversity contributions of all applicants, the Law School's race-conscious admissions program does not unduly harm nonminority applicants.

We are mindful, however, that "[a] core purpose of the Fourteenth Amendment was to do away with all governmentally imposed discrimination based on race." Accordingly, race-conscious admissions policies must be limited in time. This requirement reflects that racial classifications, however compelling their goals, are potentially so dangerous that they may be employed no more broadly than the interest demands. Enshrining a permanent justification for racial preferences would offend this fundamental equal protection principle. We see no reason to exempt race-conscious admissions programs from the requirement that all governmental use of race must have a logical end point.

The requirement that all race-conscious admissions programs have a termination point "assure[s] all citizens that the deviation from the norm of equal treatment of all racial and ethnic groups is a temporary matter, a measure taken in the service of the goal of equality itself." It has been 25 years since Justice Powell first approved the use of race to further an interest in student body diversity in the context of public higher education. Since that time, the number of minority applicants with high grades and test scores has indeed increased. We expect that 25 years from now, the use of racial preferences will no longer be necessary to further the interest approved today.

IV

In summary, the Equal Protection Clause does not prohibit the Law School's narrowly tailored use of race in admissions decisions to further a compelling interest in obtaining the educational benefits that flow from a diverse student body.

Justice GINSBURG, with whom Justice BREYER joins, concurring.

It is well documented that conscious and unconscious race bias, even rank discrimination based on race, remain alive in our land, impeding realization of our highest values and ideals. As to public education, data for the years 2000-2001 show that 71.6% of African-American children and 76.3% of Hispanic children attended a school in which minorities made up a majority of the student body.

And schools in predominantly minority communities lag far behind others measured by the educational resources available to them.

However strong the public's desire for improved education systems may be, it remains the current reality that many minority students encounter markedly inadequate and unequal educational opportunities. Despite these inequalities, some minority students are able to meet the high threshold requirements set for admission to the country's finest undergraduate and graduate educational institutions. As lower school education in minority communities improves, an increase in the number of such students may be anticipated. From today's vantage point, one may hope, but not firmly forecast, that over the next generation's span, progress toward nondiscrimination and genuinely equal opportunity will make it safe to sunset affirmative action.

Justice SCALIA, with whom Justice THOMAS joins, concurring in part and dissenting in part.

I join the opinion of the Chief Justice. As he demonstrates, the University of Michigan Law School's mystical "critical mass" justification for its discrimination by race challenges even the most gullible mind. The admissions statistics show it to be a sham to cover a scheme of racially proportionate admissions. I also join Justice Thomas's opinion. I find particularly unanswerable his central point: that the allegedly "compelling state interest" at issue here is not the incremental "educational benefit" that emanates from the fabled "critical mass" of minority students, but rather Michigan's interest in maintaining a "prestige" law school whose normal admissions standards disproportionately exclude blacks and other minorities. If that is a compelling state interest, everything is.

I add the following: The "educational benefit" that the University of Michigan seeks to achieve by racial discrimination consists, according to the Court, of "'cross-racial understanding,'" and "'better prepar[ation of] students for an increasingly diverse workforce and society,'" all of which is necessary not only for work, but also for good "citizenship." This is not, of course, an "educational benefit" on which students will be graded on their Law School transcript (Works and Plays Well with Others: B+) or tested by the bar examiners (Q: Describe in 500 words or less your cross-racial understanding). For it is a lesson of life rather than law — essentially the same lesson taught to (or rather learned by, for it cannot be "taught" in the usual sense) people three feet shorter and twenty years younger than the full-grown adults at the University of Michigan Law School, in institutions ranging from Boy Scout troops to public-school kindergartens. If properly considered an "educational benefit" at all, it is surely not one that is either uniquely relevant to law school or uniquely "teachable" in a formal educational setting. And therefore: If it is appropriate for the University of Michigan Law School to use racial discrimination for the purpose of putting together a "critical mass" that will convey generic lessons in socialization and good citizenship, surely it is no less appropriate—indeed, particularly appropriate—for the civil service system of the State of Michigan to do so. There, also, those exposed to "critical masses" of certain races will presumably become better Americans, better Michiganders, better civil servants. And surely private employers cannot be criticized—indeed, should be praised—if they also "teach" good citizenship to their adult employees through a patriotic, all-American system of racial discrimination in hiring. The nonminority individuals who are deprived of a legal education, a civil service job, or any job at all by reason of their skin color will surely understand.

Unlike a clear constitutional holding that racial preferences in state educational institutions are impermissible, or even a clear anticonstitutional holding that racial preferences in state educational institutions are OK, today's *Grutter-Gratz* split double header seems perversely designed to prolong the controversy and the litigation.

Justice THOMAS, with whom Justice SCALIA joins, concurring in part and dissenting in part.

Frederick Douglass, speaking to a group of abolitionists almost 140 years ago, delivered a message lost on today's majority: "[I]n regard to the colored people, there is always more that is benevolent, I perceive, than just, manifested towards us. What I ask for the negro is not benevolence, not pity, not sympathy, but simply justice. The American people have always been anxious to know what they shall do with us. . . . I have had but one answer from the beginning. Do nothing with us! Your doing with us has already played the mischief with us. Do nothing with us! If the apples will not remain on the tree of their own strength, if they are worm-eaten at the core, if they are early ripe and disposed to fall, let them fall! . . . And if the negro cannot stand on his own legs, let him fall also. All I ask is, give him a chance to stand on his own legs! Let him alone! . . . [Y]our interference is doing him positive injury."

Like Douglass, I believe blacks can achieve in every avenue of American life without the meddling of university administrators. Because I wish to see all students succeed whatever their color, I share, in some respect, the sympathies of those who sponsor the type of discrimination advanced by the University of Michigan Law School (Law School). The Constitution does not, however, tolerate institutional devotion to the status quo in admissions policies when such devotion ripens into racial discrimination. Nor does the Constitution countenance the unprecedented deference the Court gives to the Law School, an approach inconsistent with the very concept of "strict scrutiny."

No one would argue that a university could set up a lower general admission standard and then impose heightened requirements only on black applicants. Similarly, a university may not maintain a high admission standard and grant exemptions to favored races. The Law School, of its own choosing, and for its own purposes, maintains an exclusionary admissions system that it knows produces racially disproportionate results. Racial discrimination is not a permissible solution to the self-inflicted wounds of this elitist admissions policy.

The majority upholds the Law School's racial discrimination not by interpreting the people's Constitution, but by responding to a faddish slogan of the cognoscenti. Nevertheless, I concur in part in the Court's opinion. First, I agree with the Court insofar as its decision, which approves of only one racial classification, confirms that further use of race in admissions remains unlawful. Second, I agree with the Court's holding that racial discrimination in higher education admissions will be illegal in 25 years. I respectfully dissent from the remainder of the Court's opinion and the judgment, however, because I believe that the Law School's current use of race violates the Equal Protection Clause and that the Constitution means the same thing today as it will in 300 months.

[I]

Unlike the majority, I seek to define with precision the interest being asserted by the Law School before determining whether that interest is so compelling as to justify racial discrimination. The Law School maintains that it wishes to obtain "educational benefits that flow from student body diversity." This statement must be evaluated carefully, because it implies that both "diversity" and "educational benefits" are components of the Law School's compelling state interest. Additionally, the Law School's refusal to entertain certain changes in its admissions process and status indicates that the compelling state interest it seeks to validate is actually broader than might appear at first glance.

Undoubtedly there are other ways to "better" the education of law students aside from ensuring that the student body contains a "critical mass" of underrepresented minority students. Attaining "diversity," whatever it means, is the mechanism by which the Law School obtains educational benefits, not an end of itself. The Law School, however, apparently believes that only a racially mixed student body can lead to the educational benefits it seeks. How, then, is the Law School's interest in these allegedly unique educational "benefits" not simply the forbidden interest in "racial balancing," that the majority expressly rejects?[100]

A distinction between these two ideas (unique educational benefits based on racial aesthetics and race for its own sake) is purely sophistic — so much so that the majority uses them interchangeably. The Law School's argument, as facile as it is, can only be understood in one way: Classroom aesthetics yields educational benefits, racially discriminatory admissions policies are required to achieve the right racial mix, and therefore the policies are required to achieve the educational benefits. It is the educational benefits that are the end, or allegedly compelling state interest, not "diversity." One must also consider the Law School's

---

100. "[D]iversity," for all of its devotees, is more a fashionable catchphrase than it is a useful term, especially when something as serious as racial discrimination is at issue. Because the Equal Protection Clause renders the color of one's skin constitutionally irrelevant to the Law School's mission, I refer to the Law School's interest as an "aesthetic." That is, the Law School wants to have a certain appearance, from the shape of the desks and tables in its classrooms to the color of the students sitting at them. I also use the term "aesthetic" because I believe it underlines the ineffectiveness of racially discriminatory admissions in actually helping those who are truly underprivileged. It must be remembered that the Law School's racial discrimination does nothing for those too poor or uneducated to participate in elite higher education and therefore presents only an illusory solution to the challenges facing our Nation. [Footnote by the Court.]

refusal to entertain changes to its current admissions system that might produce the same educational benefits. The Law School adamantly disclaims any race-neutral alternative that would reduce "academic selectivity," which would in turn "require the Law School to become a very different institution, and to sacrifice a core part of its educational mission." In other words, the Law School seeks to improve marginally the education it offers without sacrificing too much of its exclusivity and elite status.

The proffered interest that the majority vindicates today, then, is not simply "diversity." Instead the Court upholds the use of racial discrimination as a tool to advance the Law School's interest in offering a marginally superior education while maintaining an elite institution. Unless each constituent part of this state interest is of pressing public necessity, the Law School's use of race is unconstitutional. I find each of them to fall far short of this standard.

III

A close reading of the Court's opinion reveals that all of its legal work is done through one conclusory statement: The Law School has a "compelling interest in securing the educational benefits of a diverse student body." No serious effort is made to explain how these benefits fit with the state interests the Court has recognized (or rejected) as compelling, or to place any theoretical constraints on an enterprising court's desire to discover still more justifications for racial discrimination.

Under the proper standard, there is no pressing public necessity in maintaining a public law school at all and, it follows, certainly not an elite law school. Likewise, marginal improvements in legal education do not qualify as a compelling state interest.

While legal education at a public university may be good policy or otherwise laudable, it is obviously not a pressing public necessity when the correct legal standard is applied. Michigan has no compelling interest in having a law school at all, much less an elite one. Still, even assuming that a State may, under appropriate circumstances, demonstrate a cognizable interest in having an elite law school, Michigan has failed to do so here.

This Court has limited the scope of equal protection review to interests and activities that occur within that State's jurisdiction. The Law School today, however, does precious little training of those attorneys who will serve the citizens of Michigan. In 2002, graduates of the University of Michigan Law School made up less than 6% of applicants to the Michigan bar, even though the Law School's graduates constitute nearly 30% of all law students graduating in Michigan. Less than 16% of the Law School's graduating class elects to stay in Michigan after law school. Thus, while a mere 27% of the Law School's 2002 entering class are from Michigan, only half of these, it appears, will stay in Michigan. In sum, the Law School trains few Michigan residents and overwhelmingly serves students, who, as lawyers, leave the State of Michigan. By contrast, Michigan's other public law school, Wayne State University Law School, sends 88% of its graduates on to serve the people of Michigan. It does not take a social scientist to conclude that it is precisely the Law School's status as an elite institution that causes it to be a waystation for the rest of the country's lawyers, rather than a training ground for those who will remain in Michigan. The Law School's decision to be an elite institution does little to advance the welfare of the people of Michigan or any cognizable interest of the State of Michigan.

Finally, even if the Law School's racial tinkering produces tangible educational benefits, a marginal improvement in legal education cannot justify racial discrimination where the Law School has no compelling interest in either its existence or in its current educational and admissions policies.

IV

The interest in remaining elite and exclusive that the majority thinks so obviously critical requires the use of admissions "standards" that, in turn, create the Law School's "need" to discriminate on the basis of race. The Court validates these admissions standards by concluding that alternatives that would require "a dramatic sacrifice of . . . the academic quality of all admitted students," need not be considered before racial discrimination can be employed. In the majority's view, such methods are not required by the "narrow tailoring" prong of strict scrutiny because that inquiry demands, in this context, that any race-neutral alternative work "'about as well.'" The majority errs, however, because race-neutral alternatives must only be "workable," and do "about as well" in vindicating the compelling state interest. The Court never explicitly holds that the Law School's desire to retain the status quo in "academic selectivity" is itself a compelling state interest, and, as I have demonstrated, it is not. Therefore, the Law School should be forced to choose between its classroom aesthetic and its exclusionary admissions system — it cannot have it both ways.

With the adoption of different admissions methods, such as accepting all students who meet minimum qualifications, the Law School could achieve its vision of the racially aesthetic student body without the use of racial discrimination. The Law School concedes this, but the Court holds, implicitly and under the guise of narrow tailoring, that the Law School has a compelling state interest in doing what it wants to do. I cannot agree. First, under strict scrutiny, the Law School's assessment of the benefits of racial discrimination and devotion to the admissions status quo are not entitled to any sort of deference, grounded in the First Amendment or anywhere else. Second, even if its "academic selectivity" must be maintained at all costs along with racial discrimination, the Court ignores the fact that other top law schools have succeeded in meeting their aesthetic demands without racial discrimination.

The Court's deference to the Law School's conclusion that its racial experimentation leads to educational benefits will, if adhered to, have serious collateral consequences. The Court relies heavily on social science evidence to justify its deference. The Court never acknowledges, however, the growing evidence that racial (and other sorts) of heterogeneity actually impairs learning among black students. See, e.g., Flowers & Pascarella, Cognitive Effects of College Racial Composition on African American Students After 3 Years of College, 40 J. of College Student Development 669, 674 (1999) (concluding that black students experience superior cognitive development at Historically Black Colleges (HBCs) and that, even among blacks, "a substantial diversity moderates the cognitive effects of attending an HBC"); Allen, The Color of Success: African-American College Student Outcomes at Predominantly White and Historically Black Public Colleges and Universities, 62 Harv. Educ. Rev. 26, 35

(1992) (finding that black students attending HBCs report higher academic achievement than those attending predominantly white colleges).

The majority grants deference to the Law School's "assessment that diversity will, in fact, yield educational benefits." It follows, therefore, that an HBC's assessment that racial homogeneity will yield educational benefits would similarly be given deference. An HBC's rejection of white applicants in order to maintain racial homogeneity seems permissible, therefore, under the majority's view of the Equal Protection Clause. Contained within today's majority opinion is the seed of a new constitutional justification for a concept I thought long and rightly rejected — racial segregation.

V

Putting aside the absence of any legal support for the majority's reflexive deference, there is much to be said for the view that the use of tests and other measures to "predict" academic performance is a poor substitute for a system that gives every applicant a chance to prove he can succeed in the study of law. The rallying cry that in the absence of racial discrimination in admissions there would be a true meritocracy ignores the fact that the entire process is poisoned by numerous exceptions to "merit." For example, in the national debate on racial discrimination in higher education admissions, much has been made of the fact that elite institutions utilize a so-called "legacy" preference to give the children of alumni an advantage in admissions. This, and other, exceptions to a "true" meritocracy give the lie to protestations that merit admissions are in fact the order of the day at the Nation's universities. The Equal Protection Clause does not, however, prohibit the use of unseemly legacy preferences or many other kinds of arbitrary admissions procedures. What the Equal Protection Clause does prohibit are classifications made on the basis of race. So while legacy preferences can stand under the Constitution, racial discrimination cannot. I will not twist the Constitution to invalidate legacy preferences or otherwise impose my vision of higher education admissions on the Nation. The majority should similarly stay its impulse to validate faddish racial discrimination the Constitution clearly forbids.

VI

The absence of any articulated legal principle supporting the majority's principal holding suggests another rationale. I believe what lies beneath the Court's decision today are the benighted notions that one can tell when racial discrimination benefits (rather than hurts) minority groups, and that racial discrimination is necessary to remedy general societal ills. This Court's precedents supposedly settled both issues, but clearly the majority still cannot commit to the principle that racial classifications are per se harmful and that almost no amount of benefit in the eye of the beholder can justify such classifications.

Putting aside what I take to be the Court's implicit rejection of *Adarand*'s holding that beneficial and burdensome racial classifications are equally invalid, I must contest the notion that the Law School's discrimination benefits those admitted as a result of it. The Court spends considerable time discussing the impressive display of amicus support for the Law School in this case from all corners of society. But nowhere in any of the filings in this Court is any evidence that the purported "beneficiaries" of this racial discrimination prove themselves by performing at (or even near) the same level as those students who receive no preferences. Compare with Thernstrom & Thernstrom, Reflections on the Shape of the River, 46 UCLA L. Rev. 1583, 1605-1608 (1999) (discussing the failure of defenders of racial discrimination in admissions to consider the fact that its "beneficiaries" are underperforming in the classroom).

The Law School tantalizes unprepared students with the promise of a University of Michigan degree and all of the opportunities that it offers. These overmatched students take the bait, only to find that they cannot succeed in the cauldron of competition. And this mismatch crisis is not restricted to elite institutions. See T. Sowell, Race and Culture 176-177 (1994) ("Even if most minority students are able to meet the normal standards at the 'average' range of colleges and universities, the systematic mismatching of minority students begun at the top can mean that such students are generally overmatched throughout all levels of higher education"). Indeed, to cover the tracks of the aestheticists, this cruel farce of racial discrimination must continue — in selection for the Michigan Law Review, and in hiring at law firms and for judicial clerkships — until the "beneficiaries" are no longer tolerated. While these students may graduate with law degrees, there is no evidence that they have received a qualitatively better legal education (or become better lawyers) than if they had gone to a less "elite" law school for which they were better prepared. And the aestheticists will never address the real problems facing "underrepresented minorities," instead continuing their social experiments on other people's children.

Beyond the harm the Law School's racial discrimination visits upon its test subjects, no social science has disproved the notion that this discrimination "engender[s] attitudes of superiority or, alternatively, provoke[s] resentment among those who believe that they have been wronged by the government's use of race." "These programs stamp minorities with a badge of inferiority and may cause them to develop dependencies or to adopt an attitude that they are 'entitled' to preferences." It is uncontested that each year, the Law School admits a handful of blacks who would be admitted in the absence of racial discrimination. Who can differentiate between those who belong and those who do not? The majority of blacks are admitted to the Law School because of discrimination, and because of this policy all are tarred as undeserving. This problem of stigma does not depend on determinacy as to whether those stigmatized are actually the "beneficiaries" of racial discrimination. When blacks take positions in the highest places of government, industry, or academia, it is an open question today whether their skin color played a part in their advancement.

VII

The Court also holds that racial discrimination in admissions should be given another 25 years before it is deemed no longer narrowly tailored to the Law School's fabricated compelling state interest. While I agree that in 25 years the practices of the Law School will be illegal, they are, for the reasons I have given, illegal now. The majority does not and cannot rest its time limitation on any evidence that the gap in credentials between black and white students is shrinking or will be gone in that timeframe. In recent years there has been virtually no change, for example, in the proportion of law school applicants with LSAT scores of 165 and higher who are black. Nor is the Court's holding that racial discrimination will be unconstitutional in 25 years made contingent on the gap closing in that time. I therefore can understand the imposition of a 25-year time limit only as a holding that the deference the Court pays to the Law School's educational judgments and refusal to change its admissions policies will itself expire.

For the immediate future, however, the majority has placed its imprimatur on a practice that can only weaken the principle of equality embodied in the Declaration of Independence and the Equal Protection Clause. "Our Constitution is color-blind, and neither knows nor tolerates classes among citizens." Plessy v. Ferguson (1896) (Harlan, J., dissenting). It has been nearly 140 years since Frederick Douglass asked the intellectual ancestors of the Law School to "[d]o nothing with us!" and the Nation adopted the Fourteenth Amendment. Now we must wait another 25 years to see this principle of equality vindicated. I therefore respectfully dissent from the remainder of the Court's opinion and the judgment.

Chief Justice REHNQUIST, with whom Justice SCALIA, Justice KENNEDY, and Justice THOMAS join, dissenting.

I agree with the Court that, "in the limited circumstance when drawing racial distinctions is permissible," the government must ensure that its means are narrowly tailored to achieve a compelling state interest. I do not believe, however, that the University of Michigan Law School's (Law School) means are narrowly tailored to the interest it asserts. The Law School claims it must take the steps it does to achieve a "'critical mass'" of underrepresented minority students. But its actual program bears no relation to this asserted goal. Stripped of its "critical mass" veil, the Law School's program is revealed as a naked effort to achieve racial balancing.

In practice, the Law School's program bears little or no relation to its asserted goal of achieving "critical mass." Respondents explain that the Law School seeks to accumulate a "critical mass" of each underrepresented minority group. But the record demonstrates that the Law School's admissions practices with respect to these groups differ dramatically and cannot be defended under any consistent use of the term "critical mass." From 1995 through 2000, the Law School admitted between 1,130 and 1,310 students. Of those, between 13 and 19 were Native American, between 91 and 108 were African-Americans, and between 47 and 56 were Hispanic. If the Law School is admitting between 91 and 108 African-Americans in order to achieve "critical mass," thereby preventing African-American students from feeling "isolated or like spokespersons for their race," one would think that a number of the same order of magnitude would be necessary to accomplish the same purpose for Hispanics and Native Americans. Similarly, even if all of the Native American applicants admitted in a given year matriculate, which the record demonstrates is not at all the case, how can this possibly constitute a "critical mass" of Native Americans in a class of over 350 students? In order for this pattern of admission to be consistent with the Law School's explanation of "critical mass," one would have to believe that the objectives of "critical mass" offered by respondents are achieved with only half the number of Hispanics and one-sixth the number of Native Americans as compared to African-Americans. But respondents offer no race-specific reasons for such disparities. Instead, they simply emphasize the importance of achieving "critical mass," without any explanation of why that concept is applied differently among the three underrepresented minority groups.

The Court, in an unprecedented display of deference under our strict scrutiny analysis, upholds the Law School's program despite its obvious flaws. We have said that when it comes to the use of race, the connection between the ends and the means used to attain them must be precise. But here the flaw is deeper than that; it is not merely a question of "fit" between ends and means. Here the means actually used are forbidden by the Equal Protection Clause of the Constitution.

Justice KENNEDY, dissenting.

The separate opinion by Justice Powell in Regents of Univ. of Cal. v. Bakke is based on the principle that a university admissions program may take account of race as one, nonpredominant factor in a system designed to consider each applicant as an individual, provided the program can meet the test of strict scrutiny by the judiciary. This is a unitary formulation. If strict scrutiny is abandoned or manipulated to distort its real and accepted meaning, the Court lacks authority to approve the use of race even in this modest, limited way. The opinion by Justice Powell, in my view, states the correct rule for resolving this case. The Court, however, does not apply strict scrutiny. By trying to say otherwise, it undermines both the test and its own controlling precedents. Justice Powell's approval of the use of race in university admissions reflected a tradition, grounded in the First Amendment, of acknowledging a university's conception of its educational mission. Our precedents provide a basis for the Court's acceptance of a university's considered judgment that racial diversity among students can further its educational task, when supported by empirical evidence.

The Court, in a review that is nothing short of perfunctory, accepts the University of Michigan Law School's assurances that its admissions process meets with constitutional requirements. The majority fails to confront the reality of how the Law School's admissions policy is implemented. The dissenting opinion by The Chief Justice, which I join in full, demonstrates beyond question why the concept of critical mass is a delusion used by the Law School to mask its attempt to make race an automatic factor in most instances and to achieve numerical goals indistinguishable from quotas. An effort to achieve racial balance among the minorities the school seeks to attract is, by the Court's own admission, "patently unconstitutional."

To be constitutional, a university's compelling interest in a diverse student body must be achieved by a system where individual assessment is safeguarded through the entire process. There is no constitutional objection to the goal of considering race as one modest factor among many others to achieve diversity, but an educational institution must ensure, through sufficient procedures, that each applicant receives individual consideration and that race does not become a predominant factor in the admissions decisionmaking. The Law School failed to comply with this requirement, and by no means has it carried its burden to show otherwise by the test of strict scrutiny.

The Court's refusal to apply meaningful strict scrutiny will lead to serious consequences. By deferring to the law schools' choice of minority admissions programs, the courts will lose the talents and resources of the faculties and administrators in devising new and fairer ways to ensure individual consideration. Constant and rigorous judicial review forces the law school faculties to undertake their responsibilities as state employees in this most sensitive of areas with utmost fidelity to the mandate of the Constitution. Deference is antithetical to strict scrutiny, not consistent with it.

It is regrettable the Court's important holding allowing racial minorities to have their special circumstances considered in order to improve their educational opportunities is accompanied by a suspension of the strict scrutiny which was the predicate of allowing race to be considered in the first place. If the Court abdicates its constitutional duty to give strict scrutiny to the use of race in university admissions, it negates my authority to approve the use of race in pursuit of student diversity. The Constitution cannot confer the right to classify on the basis of race even in this special context absent searching judicial review. For these reasons, though I reiterate my approval of giving appropriate consideration to race in this one context, I must dissent in the present case.

GRATZ v. BOLLINGER

539 U.S. 244 (2003)

Chief Justice REHNQUIST delivered the opinion of the Court.

We granted certiorari in this case to decide whether "the University of Michigan's use of racial preferences in undergraduate admissions violate[s] the Equal Protection Clause of the Fourteenth Amendment, Title VI of the Civil Rights Act of 1964." Because we find that the manner in which the University considers the race of applicants in its undergraduate admissions guidelines violates these constitutional and statutory provisions, we reverse that portion of the District Court's decision upholding the guidelines.

I

A

Petitioners Jennifer Gratz and Patrick Hamacher both applied for admission to the University of Michigan's (University) College of Literature, Science, and the Arts (LSA) as residents of the State of Michigan. Both petitioners are Caucasian. Gratz, who applied for admission for the fall of 1995, was notified in April that the LSA was unable to offer her admission. She enrolled in the University of Michigan at Dearborn, from which she graduated in the spring of 1999. Hamacher applied for admission to the LSA for the fall of 1997 [and his] application was subsequently denied in April 1997, and he enrolled at Michigan State University.

In October 1997, Gratz and Hamacher filed a lawsuit in the United States District Court for the Eastern District of Michigan. Petitioners' complaint was a class-action suit [and] sought compensatory and punitive damages for past violations, declaratory relief finding that respondents violated petitioners' "rights to nondiscriminatory treatment," an injunction prohibiting respondents from "continuing to discriminate on the basis of race in violation of the Fourteenth

Amendment," and an order requiring the LSA to offer Hamacher admission as a transfer student.

B

The University has changed its admissions guidelines a number of times during the period relevant to this litigation, and we summarize the most significant of these changes briefly. The University's Office of Undergraduate Admissions (OUA) oversees the LSA admissions process. In order to promote consistency in the review of the large number of applications received, the OUA uses written guidelines for each academic year. Admissions counselors make admissions decisions in accordance with these guidelines.

OUA considers a number of factors in making admissions decisions, including high school grades, standardized test scores, high school quality, curriculum strength, geography, alumni relationships, and leadership. OUA also considers race. During all periods relevant to this litigation, the University has considered African-Americans, Hispanics, and Native Americans to be "underrepresented minorities," and it is undisputed that the University admits "virtually every qualified . . . applicant" from these groups.

During 1995 and 1996, OUA counselors evaluated applications according to grade point average combined with what were referred to as the "SCUGA" factors. These factors included the quality of an applicant's high school (S), the strength of an applicant's high school curriculum (C), an applicant's unusual circumstances (U), an applicant's geographical residence (G), and an applicant's alumni relationships (A). After these scores were combined to produce an applicant's "GPA 2" score, the reviewing admissions counselors referenced a set of "Guidelines" tables, which listed GPA 2 ranges on the vertical axis, and American College Test/Scholastic Aptitude Test (ACT/SAT) scores on the horizontal axis. Each table was divided into cells that included one or more courses of action to be taken, including admit, reject, delay for additional information, or postpone for reconsideration.

In both years, applicants with the same GPA 2 score and ACT/SAT score were subject to different admissions outcomes based upon their racial or ethnic status. For example, as a Caucasian in-state applicant, Gratz's GPA 2 score and ACT score placed her within a cell calling for a postponed decision on her application. An in-state or out-of-state minority applicant with Gratz's scores would have fallen within a cell calling for admission.

In 1997, the University modified its admissions procedure. Specifically, the formula for calculating an applicant's GPA 2 score was restructured to include additional point values under the "U" category in the SCUGA factors. Under this new system, applicants could receive points for underrepresented minority status, socioeconomic disadvantage, or attendance at a high school with a predominantly underrepresented minority population, or underrepresentation in the unit to which the student was applying (for example, men who sought to pursue a career in nursing). Under the 1997 procedures, Hamacher's GPA 2 score and ACT score placed him in a cell on the in-state applicant table calling for postponement of a final admissions decision. An underrepresented minority applicant placed in the same cell would generally have been admitted.

Beginning with the 1998 academic year, the OUA dispensed with the Guidelines tables and the SCUGA point system in favor of a "selection index," on which an applicant could score a maximum of 150 points. This index was divided linearly into ranges generally calling for admissions dispositions as follows: 100-150 (admit); 95-99 (admit or postpone); 90-94 (postpone or admit); 75-89 (delay or postpone); 74 and below (delay or reject). Each application received points based on high school grade point average, standardized test scores, academic quality of an applicant's high school, strength or weakness of high school curriculum, in-state residency, alumni relationship, personal essay, and personal achievement or leadership. Of particular significance here, under a "miscellaneous" category, an applicant was entitled to 20 points based upon his or her membership in an underrepresented racial or ethnic minority group. The University explained that the "'development of the selection index for admissions in 1998 changed only the mechanics, not the substance of how race and ethnicity were considered in admissions.'"

II

Petitioners argue that "diversity as a basis for employing racial preferences is simply too open-ended, ill-defined, and indefinite to constitute a compelling interest capable of supporting narrowly-tailored means." But for the reasons set forth today in Grutter v. Bollinger, the Court has rejected these arguments of petitioners.

It is by now well established that "all racial classifications reviewable under the Equal Protection Clause must be strictly scrutinized." This "'standard of review . . . is not dependent on the race of those burdened or benefited by a particular classification.'" To withstand our strict scrutiny analysis, respondents must demonstrate that the University's use of race in its current admission program employs "narrowly tailored measures that further compelling governmental interests." We find that the University's policy, which automatically distributes 20 points, or one-fifth of the points needed to guarantee admission, to every single "underrepresented minority" applicant solely because of race, is not narrowly tailored to achieve the interest in educational diversity that respondents claim justifies their program.

The current LSA policy does not provide such individualized consideration. The LSA's policy automatically distributes 20 points to every single applicant from an "underrepresented minority" group, as defined by the University. The only consideration that accompanies this distribution of points is a factual review of an application to determine whether an individual is a member of one of these minority groups. Moreover, unlike Justice Powell's example, where the race of a "particular black applicant" could be considered without being decisive, the LSA's automatic distribution of 20 points has the effect of making "the factor of race . . . decisive" for virtually every minimally qualified underrepresented minority applicant.

Respondents contend that "[t]he volume of applications and the presentation of applicant information make it impractical for [LSA] to use the . . . admissions system" upheld by the Court today in Grutter. But the fact that the implementation of a program capable of providing individualized consideration might present administrative challenges does not render constitutional an otherwise problematic system. Nothing in Justice Powell's opinion in Bakke signaled that a university may employ whatever means it desires to achieve the stated goal of diversity without regard to the limits imposed by our strict scrutiny analysis.

We conclude, therefore, that because the University's use of race in its current freshman admissions policy is not narrowly tailored to achieve respondents' asserted compelling interest in diversity, the admissions policy violates the Equal Protection Clause of the Fourteenth Amendment. We further find that the admissions policy also violates Title VI and 42 U.S.C. §1981.[101]

Justice O'CONNOR, concurring. Justice BREYER joins this opinion.

Unlike the law school admissions policy the Court upholds today in Grutter v. Bollinger, the procedures employed by the University of Michigan's (University) Office of Undergraduate Admissions do not provide for a meaningful individualized review of applicants. The law school considers the various diversity qualifications of each applicant, including race, on a case-by-case basis. By contrast, the Office of Undergraduate Admissions relies on the selection index to assign every underrepresented minority applicant the same, automatic 20-point bonus without consideration of the particular background, experiences, or qualities of each individual applicant. And this mechanized selection index score, by and large, automatically determines the admissions decision for each applicant. The selection index thus precludes admissions counselors from conducting the type of individualized consideration the Court's opinion in *Grutter* requires: consideration of each applicant's individualized qualifications, including the contribution each individual's race or ethnic identity will make to the diversity of the student body, taking into account diversity within and among all racial and ethnic groups.

Although the Office of Undergraduate Admissions does assign 20 points to some "soft" variables other than race, the points available for other diversity contributions, such as leadership and service, personal achievement, and geographic diversity, are capped at much lower levels. Even the most outstanding national high school leader could never receive more than five points for his or her accomplishments — a mere quarter of the points automatically assigned to an underrepresented minority solely based on the fact of his or her race. Of course, as Justice Powell made clear in *Bakke*, a university need not "necessarily accor[d]" all diversity factors "the same weight," and the "weight attributed to a particular quality may vary from year to year depending on the 'mix' both of the student body and the applicants for the incoming class." But the selection index, by setting up automatic, predetermined point allocations for the soft variables, ensures that the diversity contributions of applicants cannot be individually assessed. This policy stands in sharp contrast to the law school's admissions plan, which enables admissions officers to make nuanced judgments with respect to the contributions each applicant is likely to make to the diversity of the incoming class.

---

101. We have explained that discrimination that violates the Equal Protection Clause of the Fourteenth Amendment committed by an institution that accepts federal funds also constitutes a violation of Title VI. Likewise, with respect to §1981, we have explained that the provision was "meant, by its broad terms, to proscribe discrimination in the making or enforcement of contracts against, or in favor of, any race." Furthermore, we have explained that a contract for educational services is a "contract" for purposes of §1981. Finally, purposeful discrimination that violates the Equal Protection Clause of the Fourteenth Amendment will also violate §1981. [Footnote by the Court.]

For these reasons, the record before us does not support the conclusion that the University of Michigan's admissions program for its College of Literature, Science, and the Arts — to the extent that it considers race — provides the necessary individualized consideration. The University, of course, remains free to modify its system so that it does so. But the current system, as I understand it, is a nonindividualized, mechanical one. As a result, I join the Court's opinion reversing the decision of the District Court.

Justice GINSBURG, with whom Justice SOUTER joins, dissenting. Justice BREYER joins Part I of this opinion.

I

Educational institutions, the Court acknowledges, are not barred from any and all consideration of race when making admissions decisions. But the Court once again maintains that the same standard of review controls judicial inspection of all official race classifications. This insistence on "consistency" would be fitting were our Nation free of the vestiges of rank discrimination long reinforced by law, but we are not far distant from an overtly discriminatory past, and the effects of centuries of law-sanctioned inequality remain painfully evident in our communities and schools.

In the wake "of a system of racial caste only recently ended," large disparities endure. Unemployment, poverty, and access to health care vary disproportionately by race. Neighborhoods and schools remain racially divided. African-American and Hispanic children are all too often educated in poverty-stricken and underperforming institutions. Adult African-Americans and Hispanics generally earn less than whites with equivalent levels of education. Equally credentialed job applicants receive different receptions depending on their race. Irrational prejudice is still encountered in real estate markets and consumer transactions. "Bias both conscious and unconscious, reflecting traditional and unexamined habits of thought, keeps up barriers that must come down if equal opportunity and nondiscrimination are ever genuinely to become this country's law and practice."

The Constitution instructs all who act for the government that they may not "deny to any person . . . the equal protection of the laws." In implementing this equality instruction, as I see it, government decisionmakers may properly distinguish between policies of exclusion and inclusion. Actions designed to burden groups long denied full citizenship stature are not sensibly ranked with measures taken to hasten the day when entrenched discrimination and its after effects have been extirpated.

Our jurisprudence ranks race a "suspect" category, "not because [race] is inevitably an impermissible classification, but because it is one which usually, to our national shame, has been drawn for the purpose of maintaining racial inequality." But where race is considered "for the purpose of achieving equality," no automatic proscription is in order. For, as insightfully explained, "[t]he Constitution is both color blind and color conscious. To avoid conflict with the equal protection clause, a classification that denies a benefit, causes harm, or imposes a burden must not be based on race. In that sense, the Constitution is color blind. But the Constitution is color conscious to prevent discrimination being perpetuated and to undo the effects of past discrimination." Contemporary human rights documents draw just this line; they distinguish between policies of oppression and measures designed to accelerate de facto equality.

The mere assertion of a laudable governmental purpose, of course, should not immunize a race-conscious measure from careful judicial inspection. Close review is needed "to ferret out classifications in reality malign, but masquerading as benign," and to "ensure that preferences are not so large as to trammel unduly upon the opportunities of others or interfere too harshly with legitimate expectations of persons in once-preferred groups."

II

Examining in this light the admissions policy employed by the University of Michigan's College of Literature, Science, and the Arts (College), I see no constitutional infirmity. Like other top-ranking institutions, the College has many more applicants for admission than it can accommodate in an entering class. Every applicant admitted under the current plan, petitioners do not here dispute, is qualified to attend the College. The racial and ethnic groups to which the College accords special consideration (African-Americans, Hispanics, and Native-Americans) historically have been relegated to inferior status by law and social practice; their members continue to experience class-based discrimination to this day. There is no suggestion that the College adopted its current policy in order to limit or decrease enrollment by any particular racial or ethnic group, and no seats are reserved on the basis of race. Nor has there been any demonstration that the College's program unduly constricts admissions opportunities for students who do not receive special consideration based on race.[102]

The stain of generations of racial oppression is still visible in our society, and the determination to hasten its removal remains vital. One can reasonably anticipate, therefore, that colleges and universities will seek to maintain their minority enrollment—and the networks and opportunities thereby opened to minority graduates—whether or not they can do so in full candor through adoption of affirmative action plans of the kind here at issue. Without recourse to such plans, institutions of higher education may resort to camouflage. For example, schools may encourage applicants to write of their cultural traditions in the essays they submit, or to indicate whether English is their second language. Seeking to improve their chances for admission, applicants may high-

---

102. The United States points to the "percentage plans" used in California, Florida, and Texas as one example of a "race-neutral alternativ[e]" that would permit the College to enroll meaningful numbers of minority students. Calling such 10 or 20% plans "race-neutral" seems to me disingenuous, for they "unquestionably were adopted with the specific purpose of increasing representation of African-Americans and Hispanics in the public higher education system." Percentage plans depend for their effectiveness on continued racial segregation at the secondary school level: They can ensure significant minority enrollment in universities only if the majority-minority high school population is large enough to guarantee that, in many schools, most of the students in the top 10 or 20% are minorities. Moreover, because such plans link college admission to a single criterion—high school class rank—they create perverse incentives. They encourage parents to keep their children in low-performing segregated schools, and discourage students from taking challenging classes that might lower their grade point averages. And even if percentage plans could boost the sheer numbers of minority enrollees at the undergraduate level, they do not touch enrollment in graduate and professional schools. [Footnote by the Court.]

light the minority group associations to which they belong, or the Hispanic surnames of their mothers or grandparents. In turn, teachers' recommendations may emphasize who a student is as much as what he or she has accomplished. If honesty is the best policy, surely Michigan's accurately described, fully disclosed College affirmative action program is preferable to achieving similar numbers through winks, nods, and disguises.

DRAWING ELECTION DISTRICTS TO INCREASE MINORITY REPRESENTATION

One other form of affirmative action has received substantial attention from the Supreme Court: the use of race by the government to draw election districts so as to increase the likelihood that minority groups will be able to choose a representative. This might be done by grouping African Americans or Latinos together in a single district where they are the majority. Between 1993 and 1996, the Supreme Court decided four cases on the constitutionality of using race in districting to help racial minorities:[103] Shaw v. Reno, 509 U.S. 630 (1993), Miller v. Johnson, 515 U.S. 900 (1995), Shaw v. Hunt, 517 U.S. 899 (1996), and Bush v. Vera, 517 U.S. 952 (1996). In these cases, the Court addressed three major issues.

First, in each case, the Supreme Court ruled that the use of race in drawing election districts must meet strict scrutiny. Shaw v. Reno held, and each subsequent case reaffirmed, that the use of race in drawing election districts is permissible only if the government can show that it is necessary to achieve a compelling purpose. Although this is consistent with recent Supreme Court cases mandating strict scrutiny for government affirmative action efforts, the dissent made a strong argument that affirmative action in voting is different than affirmative action in areas such as employment or education. In the latter areas, racial classifications benefiting minorities arguably disadvantage a white individual who is not hired or admitted because of the affirmative action program. But in voting, every person still gets to vote and every vote is counted equally.[104]

Moreover, there is a long history of the government drawing district lines to keep racial and ethnic groups together. Justice Ginsburg, dissenting in Miller v. Johnson, observed, "To accommodate the reality of ethnic bonds, legislatures have long drawn voting districts along ethnic lines. Our Nation's cities are full of districts identified by their ethnic character — Chinese, Irish, Italian, Jewish, Polish, Russian, for example."[105]

Second, the Court indicated two ways in which it can be demonstrated that race was used in drawing election districts and thus strict scrutiny is to be applied. One is if a district has a "bizarre" shape that, in itself, makes clear that race was the basis for drawing the lines. Shaw v. Reno and Shaw v. Hunt

---

103. Also, in United States v. Hays, 515 U.S. 737 (1995), the Supreme Court held that only an individual who lives in the district where race allegedly was used in drawing election districts has standing to bring a challenge. This was reaffirmed in Shaw v. Hunt, 517 U.S. 899 (1996).

104. This is the point that Justice Souter emphasized in dissent in Shaw v. Reno, 509 U.S. at 681-682 (Souter, J., dissenting).

105. 515 U.S. at 944-945 (Ginsburg, J., dissenting).

involved an election district in North Carolina that had a quite unusual shape — it was very long and very narrow — and that had an African American majority. The Supreme Court said that it was apparent from the shape of the district that race had been used in drawing the district lines to create a majority black district.[106]

Alternatively, if the use of race in districting cannot be inferred from the shape of the district, strict scrutiny is justified if it is proven that race was a "predominant" factor in drawing the lines. In Miller v. Johnson, the Court considered an election district in Georgia that also had been created to provide a majority black district. Justice Kennedy, writing for the Court, said that if it is not obvious from the shape of the district that race was used in drawing its lines, the judiciary should use strict scrutiny if it is demonstrated that race was a "predominant" factor in districting.

Bush v. Vera, which involved congressional districts in Texas, reaffirmed this. Justice O'Connor, writing for a plurality, stated, "Strict scrutiny does not apply merely because redistricting is performed with consciousness of race. Nor does it apply to all cases of intentional creation of majority-minority districts. . . . For strict scrutiny to apply, the plaintiffs must prove that other, legitimate districting principles were 'subordinated' to race." The plurality concluded that strict scrutiny was appropriate in evaluating the Texas districts because the evidence demonstrated that racial motivations had a qualitatively greater influence on the drawing of district lines than political motivations.

Third, the Court considered what justifications are sufficient to meet strict scrutiny. For example, the Court held that §5 of the Voting Rights Act, which requires that the Justice Department approve changes in election systems in states where there has been a history of race discrimination with regard to voting, does not justify the use of race in districting.[107] The views of the Justice Department about the desirability of maximizing minority districts do not constitute a compelling interest sufficient to meet strict scrutiny.

The more difficult question is whether compliance with the 1982 Amendments to §2 of the Voting Rights Act is sufficient to meet strict scrutiny. Section two prohibits election systems, such as in districting, that have discriminatory effects against racial minorities. In Shaw v. Hunt and Bush v. Vera, the Court avoided the question of whether complying with this statutory provision is a compelling interest by finding that §2 would not have been violated by the failure to use race in districting in these cases.[108]

However, in *Bush*, Justice O'Connor wrote a separate opinion concurring in the judgment where she expressed the view that "compliance with the results test of §2 of the Voting Rights Act is a compelling state interest."[109] Thus, there are surely five votes on the current Court — O'Connor and the four dissenting justices (Stevens, Souter, Ginsburg, and Breyer) — who believe that race may be used in districting when it is necessary to achieve compliance with §2 of the Voting Rights Act.

---

106. 509 U.S. at 658. The Court reiterated this in Shaw v. Hunt, 517 U.S. at 905-906.
107. *See* Shaw v. Hunt, 517 U.S. at 913.
108. *Id.* at 915; Bush v. Vera, 517 U.S. at 978-979.
109. 517 U.S. at 990 (O'Connor, J., concurring). This opinion is particularly unusual because Justice O'Connor also wrote the plurality opinion; in other words, she wrote both the plurality opinion and a separate concurring opinion.

In its most recent decision concerning the use of race in districting, Easley v. Cromartie, the Court drew a distinction between race being used for political reasons (such as to create a majority Democratic district) as opposed to affirmative action reasons (to increase the likelihood of electing minority representatives). The former is permissible, but not the latter.

EASLEY v. CROMARTIE
532 U.S. 234 (2001)

Justice BREYER delivered the opinion of the Court.

In this appeal, we review a three-judge District Court's determination that North Carolina's legislature used race as the "predominant factor" in drawing its 12th Congressional District's 1997 boundaries. The court's findings, in our view, are clearly erroneous. We therefore reverse its conclusion that the State violated the Equal Protection Clause.

I

This "racial districting" litigation is before us for the fourth time. Our first two holdings addressed North Carolina's former Congressional District 12, one of two North Carolina congressional districts drawn in 1992 that contained a majority of African-American voters. See Shaw v. Reno (1993) (Shaw I); Shaw v. Hunt (1996) (Shaw II).

II

The issue in this case is evidentiary. We must determine whether there is adequate support for the District Court's key findings, particularly the ultimate finding that the legislature's motive was predominantly racial, not political. In making this determination, we are aware that, under *Shaw I* and later cases, the burden of proof on the plaintiffs (who attack the district) is a "demanding one." The Court has specified that those who claim that a legislature has improperly used race as a criterion, in order, for example, to create a majority-minority district, must show at a minimum that the "legislature subordinated traditional race-neutral districting principles . . . to racial considerations." Miller v. Johnson (1995). Race must not simply have been "a motivation for the drawing of a majority minority district," but "the 'predominant factor' motivating the legislature's districting decision." Plaintiffs must show that a facially neutral law "is unexplainable on grounds other than race."

The Court also has made clear that the underlying districting decision is one that ordinarily falls within a legislature's sphere of competence. Hence, the legislature "must have discretion to exercise the political judgment necessary to balance competing interests," and courts must "exercise extraordinary caution in adjudicating claims that a State has drawn district lines on the basis of race," especially appropriate in this case, where the State has articulated a legitimate political explanation for its districting decision, and the voting population is one in which race and political affiliation are highly correlated.

III

The critical District Court determination — the matter for which we remanded this litigation — consists of the finding that race rather than politics predominantly explains District 12's 1997 boundaries. That determination rests upon three findings (the district's shape, its splitting of towns and counties, and its high African-American voting population) that we previously found insufficient to support summary judgment. Given the undisputed evidence that racial identification is highly correlated with political affiliation in North Carolina, these facts in and of themselves cannot, as a matter of law, support the District Court's judgment. The District Court rested, however, upon new subsidiary findings to conclude that District 12's lines are the product of no "mer[e] correlat[ion]," but are instead a result of the predominance of race in the legislature's line-drawing process.

In considering each subsidiary finding, we have given weight to the fact that the District Court was familiar with this litigation, heard the testimony of each witness, and considered all the evidence with care. Nonetheless, we cannot accept the District Court's findings as adequate for reasons which we shall spell out in detail and which we can summarize as follows:

First, the primary evidence upon which the District Court relied for its "race, not politics," conclusion is evidence of voting registration, not voting behavior; and that is precisely the kind of evidence that we said was inadequate the last time this case was before us. Second, the additional evidence to which appellees' expert, Dr. Weber, pointed, and the statements made by Senator Cooper and Gerry Cohen, simply do not provide significant additional support for the District Court's conclusion. Third, the District Court, while not accepting the contrary conclusion of appellants' expert, Dr. Peterson, did not (and as far as the record reveals, could not) reject much of the significant supporting factual information he provided. Fourth, in any event, appellees themselves have provided us with charts summarizing evidence of voting behavior and those charts tend to refute the court's "race not politics" conclusion.

IV

We can put the matter more generally as follows: In a case such as this one where majority-minority districts (or the approximate equivalent) are at issue and where racial identification correlates highly with political affiliation, the party attacking the legislatively drawn boundaries must show at the least that the legislature could have achieved its legitimate political objectives in alternative ways that are comparably consistent with traditional districting principles. That party must also show that those districting alternatives would have brought about significantly greater racial balance. Appellees failed to make any such showing here. We conclude that the District Court's contrary findings are clearly erroneous.

Justice THOMAS, with whom the Chief Justice, Justice SCALIA, and Justice KENNEDY join, dissenting.

The issue for the District Court was whether racial considerations were predominant in the design of North Carolina's Congressional District 12. The issue for this Court is simply whether the District Court's factual finding — that racial considerations did predominate — was clearly erroneous. Because I do not believe the court below committed clear error, I respectfully dissent.

The District Court's conclusion that race was the predominant factor motivating the North Carolina Legislature is a factual finding. We are not permitted to reverse the court's finding "simply because [we are] convinced that [we] would have decided the case differently." "Where there are two permissible views of the evidence, the factfinder's choice between them cannot be clearly erroneous." We should upset the District Court's finding only if we are "'left with the definite and firm conviction that a mistake has been committed.'"

The Court does cite cases that address the correct standard of review, and does couch its conclusion in "clearly erroneous" terms. But these incantations of the correct standard are empty gestures, contradicted by the Court's conclusion that it must engage in "extensive review." In several ways, the Court ignores its role as a reviewing court and engages in its own factfinding enterprise. First, the Court suggests that there is some significance to the absence of an intermediate court in this action. This cannot be a legitimate consideration. If it were legitimate, we would have mentioned it in prior redistricting cases. After all, in *Miller* and *Shaw*, we also did not have the benefit of intermediate appellate review. Moreover, the implication of the Court's argument is that intermediate courts, because they are the first reviewers of the factfinder's conclusions, should engage in a level of review more rigorous than clear error review. This suggestion is not supported by law. Second, the Court appears to discount clear error review here because the trial was "not lengthy." Even if considerations such as the length of the trial were relevant in deciding how to review factual findings, an assumption about which I have my doubts, these considerations would not counsel against deference in this action. The trial was not "just a few hours" long, it lasted for three days in which the court heard the testimony of 12 witnesses. And quite apart from the total trial time, the District Court sifted through hundreds of pages of deposition testimony and expert analysis, including statistical analysis. It also should not be forgotten that one member of the panel has reviewed the iterations of District 12 since 1992. If one were to calibrate clear error review according to the trier of fact's familiarity with the case, there is simply no question that the court here gained a working knowledge of the facts of this litigation in myriad ways over a period far longer than three days.

Third, the Court downplays deference to the District Court's finding by highlighting that the key evidence was expert testimony requiring no traditional credibility determinations. As a factual matter, the Court overlooks the District Court's express assessment of the legislative redistricting leader's credibility. Although we have recognized that particular weight should be given to a trial court's credibility determinations, we have never held that factual findings based on documentary evidence and expert testimony justify "extensive review." On the contrary, we explained in *Anderson* that "[t]he rationale for deference . . . is not limited to the superiority of the trial judge's position to make determinations of credibility."

I do not doubt this Court's ability to sift through volumes of facts or to argue its interpretation of those facts persuasively. But I do doubt the wisdom, efficiency, increased accuracy, and legitimacy of an extensive review that is any more searching than clear error review.

D. GENDER CLASSIFICATIONS

There is a long history of discrimination against women in almost every aspect of society. Women were not accorded the right to vote until the Nineteenth Amendment was ratified in 1920. No woman ever has been elected president or vice president, and there have been only four women on the Supreme Court, all appointed since 1980. Over 95 percent of executive positions at the Fortune 500 companies still are held by men,[110] and overall, women's wages are 75 percent of the earnings of men.[111]

In examining gender discrimination under the Constitution, three issues are addressed. First, subsection 1 examines the level of scrutiny used for gender discrimination. Second, subsection 2 considers how gender discrimination can be proven. Finally, subsection 3 focuses on gender classifications benefiting women.

1. The Level of Scrutiny

It was not until 1971 that the Supreme Court first invalidated a gender classification.[112] This section begins by briefly reviewing the early cases approving gender discrimination and then considers the more recent cases holding that intermediate scrutiny is the appropriate test for evaluating gender classifications challenged under the Equal Protection Clause. The section concludes with United States v. Virginia, the most major recent Supreme Court decision concerning gender discrimination.

Throughout this section, the underlying question is what level of scrutiny should be used for gender classifications. Many of the factors that explain the use of strict scrutiny for racial classifications also apply to gender discrimination.[113] For example, there is a long history of discrimination against women in virtually every aspect of society. Ruth Bader Ginsburg, writing as a law professor, observed, "When the post-Civil War amendments were added to the Constitution, women were not accorded the vote. [Married] women in many states could not contract, hold property, litigate on their own behalf, or even control their own earnings. The fourteenth amendment left all that untouched."[114] As a

110. Larry Reynolds, *Translate Fury Into Action*, Management Rev. Mar. 1, 1992.

111. Anne B. Fisher, *When Will Women Get to the Top?*, Fortune, Sept. 21, 1992, at 45.

112. Reed v. Reed, 404 U.S. 71 (1971) (giving preference to men over women in administering estates), discussed below.

113. *See* Richard A. Wasserstrom, *Racism, Sexism, and Preferential Treatment: An Approach to the Topics*, 24 UCLA L. Rev. 581 (1977).

114. Ruth Bader Ginsburg, *Sexual Equality Under the Fourteenth and Equal Rights Amendments*, 1979 Wash. U. L.Q. 161, 162-163.

result, gender classifications, like race and national origin classifications, are usually based on stereotypes rather than important government interests. Many purported biological differences that are invoked to justify legal distinctions are in reality just stereotypes, such as in the cases reviewed below where women were kept from being licensed as bartenders or from being automatically considered for jury service.

Also, sex, like race and national origin, is an immutable characteristic. Strict scrutiny is advocated because of the need for a strong presumption against laws that discriminate against people based on traits that were not chosen and cannot be changed. Gender, like race, is an immediately visible characteristic. Moreover, women, like racial minorities, tend to be significantly underrepresented in the political process.

Those who argue for intermediate rather than strict scrutiny for gender classifications make several arguments. In part, the argument is historical: The framers of the Fourteenth Amendment meant to outlaw only race discrimination.[115] Also, it is argued that biological differences between men and women make it more likely that gender classifications will be justified and thus less than strict scrutiny is appropriate to increase the chances that desirable laws will be upheld.

Also, it is claimed that women are a political majority who are not isolated from men and thus cannot be considered a discrete and insular minority. Professor Ely remarked, "I may be wrong in supposing that because women now are in a position to protect themselves they will, that we are thus unlikely to see in the future the sort of official gender discrimination that has marked our past. But if women don't protect themselves from sex discrimination in the future, . . . [i]t will be because for one reason or another — substantive disagreement or more likely the assignment of a low priority to the issue — they don't choose to."[116]

The debate over whether strict or intermediate scrutiny should be used for gender classifications is complicated by the affirmative action debate. Many of those who previously favored strict scrutiny for gender classifications now are concerned that such review would make it much more difficult for the government to engage in affirmative action to benefit women.[117] Because intermediate scrutiny is generally successful in challenging invidious discrimination against women, there is concern that the primary effect of strict scrutiny might be to limit programs that help women. There, of course, are still many advocates of strict scrutiny for gender and many who continue to believe that intermediate scrutiny is the best approach.

EARLY CASES APPROVING GENDER DISCRIMINATION

The Supreme Court first addressed a gender discrimination issue in 1872 in Bradwell v. The State of Illinois, 83 U.S. (16 Wall.) 130 (1872), which upheld an

---

115. *See, e.g.*, Strauder v. West Virginia, 100 U.S. 303, 310 (1879); *Slaughter-House Cases*, 83 U.S. (16 Wall.) 36, 81 (1872) (declaring that the purpose of the Equal Protection Clause was to limit only racial discrimination).

116. John Hart Ely, *Democracy and Distrust* 169 (1980).

117. *See, e.g.*, Associated Gen. Contractors of Cal. v. San Francisco, 813 F.2d 922 (9th Cir. 1987) (upholding affirmative action program for women as meeting intermediate scrutiny, but declaring unconstitutional affirmative action program based on race as failing strict scrutiny).

Illinois law that prohibited women from being licensed to practice law. A very short majority opinion ruled against Myra Bradwell without considering gender discrimination. Justice Miller, writing for the Court, rejected the argument that practicing law was a "privilege" of citizenship protected under the Privileges or Immunities Clause of the Fourteenth Amendment.

However, Justice Bradley, in a concurring opinion, directly addressed the claim of sex discrimination and opined that the state was justified in excluding women from the practice of law: "The paramount destiny and mission of woman are to fulfil the noble and benign offices of wife and mother. This is the law of the Creator. And the rules of civil society must be adapted to the general constitution of things, and cannot be based on exceptional cases." He concluded that "in view of the peculiar characteristics, destiny, and mission of woman, it is within the province of the legislature to ordain what offices, positions, and callings shall be filled and discharged by men."

In several cases during the first third of the twentieth century, the Supreme Court upheld laws that expressly discriminated based on gender. During this period of constitutional history, often referred to as the *Lochner* era, the Supreme Court aggressively protected freedom of contract and invalidated many regulatory laws for violating that right.[118] However, the Court was much more willing to uphold such laws if women were being regulated. For example, although Lochner v. New York declared unconstitutional a maximum hours law for bakers,[119] three years later, in Muller v. Oregon, 208 U.S. 412 (1908), the Supreme Court upheld a maximum hours law for women employed in factories.[120] The Court in *Muller* said, "That woman's physical structure and the performance of maternal functions place her at a disadvantage in the struggle for subsistence is obvious. . . . Differentiated by these matters from the other sex, she is properly placed in a class by herself, and legislation designed for her protection may be sustained, even when like legislation is not necessary for men and could not be sustained."

Following this rationale, in Radice v. New York, 264 U.S. 292 (1924), the Court upheld a state law that prohibited women from being employed in restaurants between 10:00 P.M. and 6:00 A.M. However, the Court initially rejected a state law that created a minimum wage for women. In Adkins v. Children's Hospital, 261 U.S. 525 (1923), the Court said that "while the physical differences must be recognized in appropriate cases . . . women of mature age . . . may [not] be subjected to restrictions upon their liberty of contract which could not lawfully be imposed in the case of men under similar circumstances." The Court later overruled this holding and in West Coast Hotel Co. v. Parrish, 300 U.S. 379, 398 (1937) — a key case signaling the end of the *Lochner* era — upheld a minimum wage law for women, declaring, "What can be closer to the public interest than the health of women and their protection from unscrupulous and overreaching employers? And if the protection of women is a legitimate end of the exercise of state power, how can it be said that the requirement of the payment of a minimum wage fairly fixed in order to meet the very necessities of existence is not an admissible means to that end?"

118. These cases are presented in Chapter 6.
119. 198 U.S. 45 (1905).
120. This case is presented more fully in Chapter 6.

Even after World War II and the entrance of many women into the labor market, the Supreme Court continued to allow gender discrimination based on stereotypes. In Goesaert v. Cleary, 335 U.S. 464 (1948), the Supreme Court upheld a Michigan law that prevented the licensing of women as bartenders unless the woman was the wife or daughter of a male who owned the bar where she would work. Justice Frankfurter declared that "Michigan could, beyond question, forbid all women from working behind a bar." He said that "the vast changes in the social and legal position of women . . . [do] not preclude the States from drawing a sharp line between the sexes, certainly in such matters as the regulation of the liquor traffic." The Court said that the law's discrimination among women was permissible because "the line they have drawn is not without a basis in reason"; "the oversight assured through ownership of a bar by a barmaid's husband or father minimizes hazards that may confront a barmaid without such protecting oversight."

In 1961, in Hoyt v. Florida, 368 U.S. 57 (1961), the Court upheld a state law that made men eligible for jury service unless they requested and were granted an exception, whereas women were automatically exempted unless they waived it and expressed a desire to be included on the jury rolls. The Court applied the rational basis test and upheld the law. The Court said that "[d]espite the enlightened emancipation of women from the restrictions and protections of bygone years, and their entry into many parts of community life formerly considered to be reserved to men, woman is still regarded as the center of home and family life." Thus, a state could exempt women "from the civic duty of jury service unless she herself determines that such service is consistent with her own special responsibilities."

THE EMERGENCE OF INTERMEDIATE SCRUTINY

In Reed v. Reed, 404 U.S. 71 (1971), the Supreme Court for the first time invalidated a gender classification, but the Court professed to apply only rational basis review. An Idaho law specified the hierarchy of persons to be appointed as administrators of an estate when a person died intestate. Specifically, the law created eleven categories in rank order — parents were first, children second, and so on — and said that if there were two competing applicants in the same category, the male was to be preferred over the female.

The Court articulated the standard of review in traditional rational basis terms. It said, "A classification must be reasonable, not arbitrary, and must rest upon some ground of difference having a fair and substantial relation to the object of the legislation, so that all persons similarly circumstanced shall be treated alike." The Supreme Court said that the issue was whether gender had a rational relationship to the ability to administer the estate. Obviously, gender is irrelevant, and the Court held the law unconstitutional, concluding, "To give a mandatory preference to members of either sex over members of the other, merely to accomplish the elimination of hearings on the merits, is to make the very kind of arbitrary legislative choice forbidden by the Equal Protection Clause of the Fourteenth Amendment; and whatever may be said as to the positive values of avoiding intrafamily controversy, the choice in this context may not lawfully be mandated solely on the basis of sex."

Although the Court purported to be using just the rational basis test and did not express the view that gender was a suspect classification, its reasoning was not characteristic of rational basis review. If the law had said, "When there are two people in a category who are equally qualified, one will be chosen by random selection," that surely would have been permissible under rational basis review. Therefore, the use of gender had to have been regarded by the Court as worse than random selection and an inappropriate ground to use to simplify administration. In other words, the Court implicitly had to regard gender as an impermissible basis for government decisions.

In Frontiero v. Richardson, four justices took the position that gender classifications should be subjected to strict scrutiny.

FRONTIERO v. RICHARDSON
411 U.S. 677 (1973)

Justice BRENNAN announced the judgment of the Court in an opinion in which Justice DOUGLAS, Justice WHITE, and Justice MARSHALL join.

The question before us concerns the right of a female member of the uniformed services to claim her spouse as a "dependent" for the purposes of obtaining increased quarters allowances and medical and dental benefits on an equal footing with male members. Under these statutes, a serviceman may claim his wife as a "dependent" without regard to whether she is in fact dependent upon him for any part of her support. A servicewoman, on the other hand, may not claim her husband as a "dependent" under these programs unless he is in fact dependent upon her for over one-half of his support. Thus, the question for decision is whether this difference in treatment constitutes an unconstitutional discrimination against servicewomen in violation of the Due Process Clause of the Fifth Amendment.

Appellant Sharron Frontiero, a lieutenant in the United States Air Force, sought increased quarters allowances, and housing and medical benefits for her husband, appellant Joseph Frontiero, on the ground that he was her "dependent." Although such benefits would automatically have been granted with respect to the wife of a male member of the uniformed services, appellant's application was denied because she failed to demonstrate that her husband was dependent on her for more than one-half of his support.

At the outset, appellants contend that classifications based upon sex, like classifications based upon race, alienage, and national origin, are inherently suspect and must therefore be subjected to close judicial scrutiny. We agree and, indeed, find at least implicit support for such an approach in our unanimous decision only last Term in Reed v. Reed (1971).

There can be no doubt that our Nation has had a long and unfortunate history of sex discrimination. Traditionally, such discrimination was rationalized by an attitude of "romantic paternalism" which, in practical effect, put women, not on a pedestal, but in a cage.

As a result of notions such as these, our statute books gradually became laden with gross, stereotyped distinctions between the sexes and, indeed, throughout much of the 19th century the position of women in our society was, in many respects, comparable to that of blacks under the pre-Civil War slave codes.

Neither slaves nor women could hold office, serve on juries, or bring suit in their own names, and married women traditionally were denied the legal capacity to hold or convey property or to serve as legal guardians of their own children. And although blacks were guaranteed the right to vote in 1870, women were denied even that right — which is itself "preservative of other basic civil and political rights" — until adoption of the Nineteenth Amendment half a century later.

It is true, of course, that the position of women in America has improved markedly in recent decades. Nevertheless, it can hardly be doubted that, in part because of the high visibility of the sex characteristic, women still face pervasive, although at times more subtle, discrimination in our educational institutions, in the job market and, perhaps most conspicuously, in the political arena. Moreover, since sex, like race and national origin, is an immutable characteristic determined solely by the accident of birth, the imposition of special disabilities upon the members of a particular sex because of their sex would seem to violate "the basic concept of our system that legal burdens should bear some relationship to individual responsibility. . . ." And what differentiates sex from such non-suspect statuses as intelligence or physical disability, and aligns it with the recognized suspect criteria, is that the sex characteristic frequently bears no relation to ability to perform or contribute to society. As a result, statutory distinctions between the sexes often have the effect of invidiously relegating the entire class of females to inferior legal status without regard to the actual capabilities of its individual members.

With these considerations in mind, we can only conclude that classifications based upon sex, like classifications based upon race, alienage, or national origin, are inherently suspect, and must therefore be subjected to strict judicial scrutiny. Applying the analysis mandated by that stricter standard of review, it is clear that the statutory scheme now before us is constitutionally invalid.

The sole basis of the classification established in the challenged statutes is the sex of the individuals involved. Thus, under [federal law] a female member of the uniformed services seeking to obtain housing and medical benefits for her spouse must prove his dependency in fact, whereas no such burden is imposed upon male members.

Moreover, the Government concedes that the differential treatment accorded men and women under these statutes serves no purpose other than mere "administrative convenience." In essence, the Government maintains that, as an empirical matter, wives in our society frequently are dependent upon their husbands, while husbands rarely are dependent upon their wives.

The Government offers no concrete evidence, however, tending to support its view that such differential treatment in fact saves the Government any money. In order to satisfy the demands of strict judicial scrutiny, the Government must demonstrate, for example, that it is actually cheaper to grant increased benefits with respect to all male members, than it is to determine which male members are in fact entitled to such benefits and to grant increased benefits only to those members whose wives actually meet the dependency requirement.

In any case, our prior decisions make clear that, although efficacious administration of governmental programs is not without some importance, "the Constitution recognizes higher values than speed and efficiency." Stanley v. Illinois (1972). And when we enter the realm of "strict judicial scrutiny," there can be no doubt that "administrative convenience" is not a shibboleth, the mere recitation of which dictates constitutionality. We therefore conclude that, by according differential treatment to male and female members of the uniformed services for the sole purpose of achieving administrative convenience, the challenged statutes violate the Due Process Clause of the Fifth Amendment insofar as they require a female member to prove the dependency of her husband.

Justice STEWART concurs in the judgment, agreeing that the statutes before us work an invidious discrimination in violation of the Constitution.

Justice POWELL, with whom the Chief Justice and Justice BLACKMUN join, concurring in the judgment.

I agree that the challenged statutes constitute an unconstitutional discrimination against servicewomen in violation of the Due Process Clause of the Fifth Amendment, but I cannot join the opinion of Mr. Justice Brennan, which would hold that all classifications based upon sex, "like classifications based upon race, alienage, and national origin," are "inherently suspect and must therefore be subjected to close judicial scrutiny." It is unnecessary for the Court in this case to characterize sex as a suspect classification, with all of the far-reaching implications of such a holding. In my view, we can and should decide this case on the authority of *Reed* and reserve for the future any expansion of its rationale.

––––––––––––––––––

In Stanton v. Stanton, 421 U.S. 7 (1975), the Court declared unconstitutional a Utah law that required that parents support their female children until age 18 but that male children be supported until age 21. The Court said that the statute was based on "old notions" about social roles; "[no] longer is the female destined solely for the home and the rearing of the family, and only the male for the marketplace and the world of ideas. Women's activities and responsibilities are increasing and expanding." Again, the Court decided without a holding as to the level of scrutiny. In fact, the Court said that the law was unconstitutional "under any test — compelling state interest, or rational basis, or something in between."

Finally, in 1976, in Craig v. Boren, the Supreme Court agreed on intermediate scrutiny as the appropriate level of review for gender classifications.

CRAIG v. BOREN
429 U.S. 190 (1976)

Justice BRENNAN delivered the opinion of the Court.

The interaction of two sections of an Oklahoma statute, prohibits the sale of "nonintoxicating" 3.2% beer to males under the age of 21 and to females under the age of 18. The question to be decided is whether such a gender-based differential constitutes a denial to males 18-20 years of age of the equal protection of the laws in violation of the Fourteenth Amendment.

Analysis may appropriately begin with the reminder that *Reed* emphasized that statutory classifications that distinguish between males and females are "subject to scrutiny under the Equal Protection Clause." To withstand constitutional challenge, previous cases establish that classifications by gender must serve important governmental objectives and must be substantially related to achievement of those objectives.

We accept for purposes of discussion the District Court's identification of the objective underlying §§241 and 245 as the enhancement of traffic safety. Clearly, the protection of public health and safety represents an important function of state and local governments. However, appellees' statistics in our view cannot support the conclusion that the gender-based distinction closely serves to achieve that objective and therefore the distinction cannot under *Reed* withstand equal protection challenge.

The appellees introduced a variety of statistical surveys. First, an analysis of arrest statistics for 1973 demonstrated that 18- to 20-year-old male arrests for "driving under the influence" and "drunkenness" substantially exceeded female arrests for that same age period. Similarly, youths aged 17-21 were found to be overrepresented among those killed or injured in traffic accidents, with males again numerically exceeding females in this regard. Third, a random roadside survey in Oklahoma City revealed that young males were more inclined to drive and drink beer than were their female counterparts. Fourth, Federal Bureau of Investigation nationwide statistics exhibited a notable increase in arrests for "driving under the influence." Finally, statistical evidence gathered in other jurisdictions, particularly Minnesota and Michigan, was offered to corroborate Oklahoma's experience by indicating the pervasiveness of youthful participation in motor vehicle accidents following the imbibing of alcohol.

Even were this statistical evidence accepted as accurate, it nevertheless offers only a weak answer to the equal protection question presented here. The most focused and relevant of the statistical surveys, arrests of 18- to 20-year-olds for alcohol-related driving offenses, exemplifies the ultimate unpersuasiveness of this evidentiary record. Viewed in terms of the correlation between sex and the actual activity that Oklahoma seeks to regulate — driving while under the influence of alcohol — the statistics broadly establish that .18% of females and 2% of males in that age group were arrested for that offense. While such a disparity is not trivial in a statistical sense, it hardly can form the basis for employment of a gender line as a classifying device. Certainly if maleness is to serve as a proxy for drinking and driving, a correlation of 2% must be considered an unduly tenuous "fit." Indeed, prior cases have consistently rejected the use of sex as a decisionmaking factor even though the statutes in question certainly rested on far more predictive empirical relationships than this.

Moreover, the statistics exhibit a variety of other shortcomings that seriously impugn their value to equal protection analysis. Setting aside the obvious methodological problems, the surveys do not adequately justify the salient features of Oklahoma's gender-based traffic-safety law. None purports to measure the use and dangerousness of 3.2% beer as opposed to alcohol generally, a detail that is of particular importance since, in light of its low alcohol level, Oklahoma apparently considers the 3.2% beverage to be "nonintoxicating." Moreover, many of the studies, while graphically documenting the unfortunate increase in driving while under the influence of alcohol, make no effort to relate their findings to age-sex differentials as involved here. Indeed, the only survey that explicitly centered its attention upon young drivers and their use of beer, albeit apparently not of the diluted 3.2% variety, reached results that hardly can be viewed as impressive in justifying either a gender or age classification.

We conclude that the gender-based differential contained in [Oklahoma law] constitutes a denial of the equal protection of the laws to males aged 18-20.

Justice REHNQUST, dissenting.

The Court's disposition of this case is objectionable on two grounds. First is its conclusion that men challenging a gender-based statute which treats them less favorably than women may invoke a more stringent standard of judicial review than pertains to most other types of classifications. Second is the Court's enunciation of this standard, without citation to any source, as being that "classifications by gender must serve important governmental objectives and must be substantially related to achievement of those objectives."

The only redeeming feature of the Court's opinion, to my mind, is that it apparently signals a retreat by those who joined the plurality opinion in Frontiero v. Richardson (1973), from their view that sex is a "suspect" classification for purposes of equal protection analysis. I think the Oklahoma statute challenged here need pass only the "rational basis" equal protection analysis and I believe that it is constitutional under that analysis.

The Court's conclusion that a law which treats males less favorably than females "must serve important governmental objectives and must be substantially related to achievement of those objectives" apparently comes out of thin air. The Equal Protection Clause contains no such language, and none of our previous cases adopt that standard. I would think we have had enough difficulty with the two standards of review which our cases have recognized — the norm of "rational basis," and the "compelling state interest" required where a "suspect classification" is involved — so as to counsel weightily against the insertion of still another "standard" between those two. How is this Court to divine what objectives are important? How is it to determine whether a particular law is "substantially" related to the achievement of such objective, rather than related in some other way to its achievement? Both of the phrases used are so diaphanous and elastic as to invite subjective judicial preferences or prejudices relating to particular types of legislation, masquerading as judgments whether such legislation is directed at "important" objectives or, whether the relationship to those objectives is "substantial" enough.

One survey of arrest statistics assembled in 1973 indicated that males in the 18-20 age group were arrested for "driving under the influence" almost 18 times as often as their female counterparts, and for "drunkenness" in a ratio of almost 10 to 1. Accepting, as the Court does, appellants' comparison of the total figures with 1973 Oklahoma census data, this survey indicates a 2% arrest rate among males in the age group, as compared to a .18% rate among females.

Other surveys indicated (1) that over the five-year period from 1967 to 1972, nationwide arrests among those under 18 for drunken driving increased 138%, and that 93% of all persons arrested for drunken driving were male; (2) that youths in the 17-21 age group were overrepresented among those killed or injured in Oklahoma traffic accidents, that male casualties substantially exceeded female, and that deaths in this age group continued to rise while overall traffic deaths declined; (3) that over three-fourths of the drivers under 20 in the Oklahoma City area are males, and that each of them, on average, drives half again as many miles per year as their female counterparts; (4) that four-fifths of male drivers under 20 in the Oklahoma City area state a drink preference for beer, while about three-fifths of female drivers of that age state the same preference; and (5) that the percentage of male drivers under 20 admitting to drinking within two hours of driving was half again larger than the percentage for females, and that the percentage of male drivers of that age group with a blood alcohol content greater than .01% was almost half again larger than for female drivers.

The Court's criticism of the statistics relied on by the District Court conveys the impression that a legislature in enacting a new law is to be subjected to the judicial equivalent of a doctoral examination in statistics. Legislatures are not held to any rules of evidence such as those which may govern courts or other administrative bodies, and are entitled to draw factual conclusions on the basis of the determination of probable cause which an arrest by a police officer normally represents.

The Oklahoma Legislature could have believed that 18- to 20-year-old males drive substantially more, and tend more often to be intoxicated than their female counterparts; that they prefer beer and admit to drinking and driving at a higher rate than females; and that they suffer traffic injuries out of proportion to the part they make up of the population. Under the appropriate rational-basis test for equal protection, it is neither irrational nor arbitrary to bar them from making purchases of 3.2% beer, which purchases might in many cases be made by a young man who immediately returns to his vehicle with the beverage in his possession. There being no violation of either equal protection or due process, the statute should accordingly be upheld.

Since Craig v. Boren, the Supreme Court, on many occasions, has reaffirmed and applied intermediate scrutiny for gender classifications.[121] For example, in Kirchberg v. Feenstra, 450 U.S. 455 (1981), the Court expressly used intermediate scrutiny to invalidate a Louisiana law that gave a husband, as "head and master" of property jointly owned with his wife, the unilateral right to dispose of such property without his spouse's consent. Moreover, as described below in subsection 3, the Court has held that intermediate scrutiny is to be used both for gender classifications discriminating against women and those discriminating against men.

In United States v. Virginia, the Supreme Court used intermediate scrutiny in declaring unconstitutional the exclusion of women by the Virginia Military Institute (VMI). However, Justice Ginsburg's majority opinion also emphasized that there must be an "exceedingly persuasive justification" for gender classifications.

UNITED STATES v. VIRGINIA
518 U.S. 515 (1996)

Justice GINSBURG delivered the opinion of the Court.

Virginia's public institutions of higher learning include an incomparable military college, Virginia Military Institute (VMI). The United States maintains

---

121. *See, e.g.,* United States v. Virginia, 518 U.S. 515 (1996); Califano v. Westcott, 443 U.S. 76, 89 (1979); Caban v. Mohammed, 441 U.S. 380, 388 (1979); Orr v. Orr, 440 U.S. 268, 279 (1979); Califano v. Webster, 430 U.S. 313, 316-317 (1977).

that the Constitution's equal protection guarantee precludes Virginia from reserving exclusively to men the unique educational opportunities VMI affords. We agree.

I

Founded in 1839, VMI is today the sole single-sex school among Virginia's 15 public institutions of higher learning. VMI's distinctive mission is to produce "citizen-soldiers," men prepared for leadership in civilian life and in military service. VMI pursues this mission through pervasive training of a kind not available anywhere else in Virginia. Assigning prime place to character development, VMI uses an "adversative method" modeled on English public schools and once characteristic of military instruction. VMI constantly endeavors to instill physical and mental discipline in its cadets and impart to them a strong moral code. The school's graduates leave VMI with heightened comprehension of their capacity to deal with duress and stress, and a large sense of accomplishment for completing the hazardous course.

VMI has notably succeeded in its mission to produce leaders; among its alumni are military generals, Members of Congress, and business executives. The school's alumni overwhelmingly perceive that their VMI training helped them to realize their personal goals. VMI's endowment reflects the loyalty of its graduates; VMI has the largest per-student endowment of all public undergraduate institutions in the Nation.

Neither the goal of producing citizen-soldiers nor VMI's implementing methodology is inherently unsuitable to women. And the school's impressive record in producing leaders has made admission desirable to some women. Nevertheless, Virginia has elected to preserve exclusively for men the advantages and opportunities a VMI education affords.

II

In response to the Fourth Circuit's ruling [that Virginia had violated equal protection], Virginia proposed a parallel program for women: Virginia Women's Institute for Leadership (VWIL). The 4-year, state-sponsored undergraduate program would be located at Mary Baldwin College, a private liberal arts school for women, and would be open, initially, to about 25 to 30 students. Although VWIL would share VMI's mission — to produce "citizen-soldiers" — the VWIL program would differ, as does Mary Baldwin College, from VMI in academic offerings, methods of education, and financial resources.

The average combined SAT score of entrants at Mary Baldwin is about 100 points lower than the score for VMI freshmen. Mary Baldwin's faculty holds "significantly fewer Ph.D.'s than the faculty at VMI," and receives significantly lower salaries. While VMI offers degrees in liberal arts, the sciences, and engineering, Mary Baldwin, at the time of trial, offered only bachelor of arts degrees. A VWIL student seeking to earn an engineering degree could gain one, without public support, by attending Washington University in St. Louis, Missouri, for two years, paying the required private tuition.

III

The cross-petitions in this suit present two ultimate issues. First, does Virginia's exclusion of women from the educational opportunities provided by VMI — extraordinary opportunities for military training and civilian leadership development — deny to women "capable of all of the individual activities required of VMI cadets," the equal protection of the laws guaranteed by the Fourteenth Amendment? Second, if VMI's "unique" situation, as Virginia's sole single-sex public institution of higher education — offends the Constitution's equal protection principle, what is the remedial requirement?

IV

We note, once again, the core instruction of this Court's pathmarking decisions: Parties who seek to defend gender-based government action must demonstrate an "exceedingly persuasive justification" for that action. Today's skeptical scrutiny of official action denying rights or opportunities based on sex responds to volumes of history. As a plurality of this Court acknowledged a generation ago, "our Nation has had a long and unfortunate history of sex discrimination." Frontiero v. Richardson (1973). Through a century plus three decades and more of that history, women did not count among voters composing "We the People"; not until 1920 did women gain a constitutional right to the franchise. And for a half century thereafter, it remained the prevailing doctrine that government, both federal and state, could withhold from women opportunities accorded men so long as any "basis in reason" could be conceived for the discrimination.

The heightened review standard our precedent establishes does not make sex a proscribed classification. Supposed "inherent differences" are no longer accepted as a ground for race or national origin classifications. Physical differences between men and women, however, are enduring. "Inherent differences" between men and women, we have come to appreciate, remain cause for celebration, but not for denigration of the members of either sex or for artificial constraints on an individual's opportunity. Sex classifications may be used to compensate women "for particular economic disabilities [they have] suffered," Califano v. Webster (1977), to "promot[e] equal employment opportunity," to advance full development of the talent and capacities of our Nation's people. But such classifications may not be used, as they once were, to create or perpetuate the legal, social, and economic inferiority of women.

Measuring the record in this case against the review standard just described, we conclude that Virginia has shown no "exceedingly persuasive justification" for excluding all women from the citizen-soldier training afforded by VMI. Because the remedy proffered by Virginia — the Mary Baldwin VWIL program — does not cure the constitutional violation, i.e., it does not provide equal opportunity, we reverse the Fourth Circuit's final judgment in this case.

V

Virginia challenges and asserts two justifications in defense of VMI's exclusion of women. First, the Commonwealth contends, "single-sex education provides important educational benefits," and the option of single-sex education contributes to "diversity in educational approaches." Second, the Commonwealth argues, "the unique VMI method of character development and leadership training," the school's adversative approach, would have to be modified were VMI to admit women. We consider these two justifications in turn.

A

Single-sex education affords pedagogical benefits to at least some students, Virginia emphasizes, and that reality is uncontested in this litigation. Similarly, it is not disputed that diversity among public educational institutions can serve the public good. But Virginia has not shown that VMI was established, or has been maintained, with a view to diversifying, by its categorical exclusion of women, educational opportunities within the Commonwealth. In cases of this genre, our precedent instructs that "benign" justifications proffered in defense of categorical exclusions will not be accepted automatically; a tenable justification must describe actual state purposes, not rationalizations for actions in fact differently grounded.

B

Virginia next argues that VMI's adversative method of training provides educational benefits that cannot be made available, unmodified, to women. Alterations to accommodate women would necessarily be "radical," so "drastic," Virginia asserts, as to transform, indeed "destroy," VMI's program. Neither sex would be favored by the transformation, Virginia maintains: Men would be deprived of the unique opportunity currently available to them; women would not gain that opportunity because their participation would "eliminat[e] the very aspects of [the] program that distinguish [VMI] from . . . other institutions of higher education in Virginia."

It may be assumed, for purposes of this decision, that most women would not choose VMI's adversative method. As Fourth Circuit Judge Motz observed, however, in her dissent from the Court of Appeals' denial of rehearing en banc, it is also probable that "many men would not want to be educated in such an environment." Education, to be sure, is not a "one size fits all" business. The issue, however, is not whether "women — or men — should be forced to attend VMI"; rather, the question is whether the Commonwealth can constitutionally deny to women who have the will and capacity, the training and attendant opportunities that VMI uniquely affords.

The notion that admission of women would downgrade VMI's stature, destroy the adversative system and, with it, even the school, is a judgment hardly proved, a prediction hardly different from other "self-fulfilling prophec[ies]," once routinely used to deny rights or opportunities.

The Commonwealth's misunderstanding and, in turn, the District Court's, is apparent from VMI's mission: to produce "citizen-soldiers," individuals "'imbued with love of learning, confident in the functions and attitudes of leadership, possessing a high sense of public service, advocates of the American democracy and free enterprise system, and ready . . . to defend their country in time of national peril.'"

Surely that goal is great enough to accommodate women, who today count as citizens in our American democracy equal in stature to men. Just as surely, the Commonwealth's great goal is not substantially advanced by women's categorical exclusion, in total disregard of their individual merit, from the Commonwealth's premier "citizen-soldier" corps. Virginia, in sum, "has fallen far short of establishing the 'exceedingly persuasive justification,'" that must be the solid base for any gender-defined classification.

VI

In the second phase of the litigation, Virginia presented its remedial plan — maintain VMI as a male-only college and create VWIL as a separate program for women. The plan met District Court approval.

A remedial decree, this Court has said, must closely fit the constitutional violation; it must be shaped to place persons unconstitutionally denied an opportunity or advantage in "the position they would have occupied in the absence of [discrimination]." The constitutional violation in this suit is the categorical exclusion of women from an extraordinary educational opportunity afforded men. A proper remedy for an unconstitutional exclusion, we have explained, aims to "eliminate [so far as possible] the discriminatory effects of the past" and to "bar like discrimination in the future." Virginia chose not to eliminate, but to leave untouched, VMI's exclusionary policy.

The Task Force charged with developing the leadership program for women, drawn from the staff and faculty at Mary Baldwin College, "determined that a military model and, especially VMI's adversative method, would be wholly inappropriate for educating and training most women." As earlier stated, generalizations about "the way women are," estimates of what is appropriate for most women, no longer justify denying opportunity to women whose talent and capacity place them outside the average description. Notably, Virginia never asserted that VMI's method of education suits most men. It is also revealing that Virginia accounted for its failure to make the VWIL experience "the entirely militaristic experience of VMI" on the ground that VWIL "is planned for women who do not necessarily expect to pursue military careers." By that reasoning, VMI's "entirely militaristic" program would be inappropriate for men in general or as a group, for "[o]nly about 15% of VMI cadets enter career military service."

In contrast to the generalizations about women on which Virginia rests, we note again these dispositive realities: VMI's "implementing methodology" is not "inherently unsuitable to women," "some women . . . do well under [the] adversative model," "some women, at least, would want to attend [VMI] if they had the opportunity," "some women are capable of all of the individual activities required of VMI cadets," and "can meet the physical standards [VMI] now impose[s] on men." It is on behalf of these women that the United States has instituted this suit, and it is for them that a remedy must be crafted, a remedy that will end their exclusion from a state-supplied educational opportunity for which they are fit, a decree that will "bar like discrimination in the future."

Justice SCALIA, dissenting.

Today the Court shuts down an institution that has served the people of the Commonwealth of Virginia with pride and distinction for over a century and a half. To achieve that desired result, it rejects (contrary to our established practice) the factual findings of two courts below, sweeps aside the precedents of this Court, and ignores the history of our people. As to facts: It explicitly rejects the finding that there exist "gender-based developmental differences" supporting Virginia's restriction of the "adversative" method to only a men's institution, and the finding that the all-male composition of the Virginia Military Institute (VMI) is essential to that institution's character. As to precedent: It drastically revises our established standards for reviewing sex-based classifications. And as to history: It counts for nothing the long tradition, enduring down to the present, of men's military colleges supported by both States and the Federal Government.

Much of the Court's opinion is devoted to deprecating the closed-mindedness of our forebears with regard to women's education, and even with regard to the treatment of women in areas that have nothing to do with education. Closed-minded they were — as every age is, including our own, with regard to matters it cannot guess, because it simply does not consider them debatable. The virtue of a democratic system with a First Amendment is that it readily enables the people, over time, to be persuaded that what they took for granted is not so, and to change their laws accordingly. That system is destroyed if the smug assurances of each age are removed from the democratic process and written into the Constitution. So to counterbalance the Court's criticism of our ancestors, let me say a word in their praise: They left us free to change. The same cannot be said of this most illiberal Court, which has embarked on a course of inscribing one after another of the current preferences of the society (and in some cases only the counter-majoritarian preferences of the society's law-trained elite) into our Basic Law. Today it enshrines the notion that no substantial educational value is to be served by an all-men's military academy — so that the decision by the people of Virginia to maintain such an institution denies equal protection to women who cannot attend that institution but can attend others. Since it is entirely clear that the Constitution of the United States — the old one — takes no sides in this educational debate, I dissent.

2. Proving the Existence of a Gender Classification

There are two major ways of proving a gender classification; they are identical to the two methods of demonstrating a racial classification discussed above. First, the gender classification can exist on the face of the law; that is, the law in its very terms draws a distinction among people based on gender. All of the cases discussed thus far concerning gender discrimination are of this type. For example, Craig v. Boren involved a facial gender classification in that the Oklahoma law provided that women could buy low-alcohol beer at age 18, but men could not until age 21. Likewise, in United States v. Virginia, the Virginia policy that excluded women from attending the Virginia Military Institute was a classification on the face of the law.

Second, if a law is facially gender neutral, proving a gender classification requires demonstrating that there is both a discriminatory impact to the law and a discriminatory purpose behind it. In Personnel Administrator of Massachusetts v. Feeney, 442 U.S. 256 (1979), presented in section C, the Supreme Court upheld a state law that gave a preference in hiring to veterans even though it had a substantial discriminatory impact against women. Helen Feeney repeatedly took civil service exams for particular positions and received among the highest scores in the state, but was placed behind lists of veterans with lower scores. At the time the litigation was commenced, "over 98% of the veterans in Massachusetts were male; only 1.8% were female. And over one-quarter of the Massachusetts population were veterans."

Nonetheless, the Supreme Court rejected the claim of gender discrimination. The Court said that the law providing a preference for veterans was gender-neutral and that discriminatory impact is not sufficient to prove the existence of sex-based classification; there also must be proof of a discriminatory purpose. The Court concluded that "nothing in the record demonstrates that this preference for veterans was originally devised or subsequently re-enacted because it would accomplish the collateral goal of keeping women in a stereotypic and predefined place in the Massachusetts civil service." The ways of proving a discriminatory purpose based on gender are identical to the ways of proving a discriminatory racial purpose, described above.

WHEN IS IT "DISCRIMINATION"?

In Geduldig v. Aiello, the Court considered whether the law's failure to take into account biological differences between men and women constitutes gender discrimination.

GEDULDIG v. AIELLO
417 U.S. 484 (1974)

Justice STEWART delivered the opinion of the Court.

For almost 30 years California has administered a disability insurance system that pays benefits to persons in private employment who are temporarily unable to work because of disability not covered by workmen's compensation. The appellees brought this action to challenge the constitutionality of a provision of the California program that, in defining "disability," excludes from coverage certain disabilities resulting from pregnancy.

[Under California law] an individual is eligible for disability benefits if, during a one-year base period prior to his disability, he has contributed one percent of a minimum income of $300 to the Disability Fund. In the event he suffers a compensable disability, the individual can receive a "weekly benefit amount" of between $25 and $105, depending on the amount he earned during the highest quarter of the base period. In return for his one-percent contribution to the Disability Fund, the individual employee is insured against the risk of disability stemming from a substantial number of "mental or physical illness[es] and mental or physical injur[ies]."

It is not every disabling condition, however, that triggers the obligation to pay benefits under the program. As already noted, for example, any disability of less than eight days' duration is not compensable, except when the employee is hospitalized. Conversely, no benefits are payable for any single disability beyond 26 weeks. Further, disability is not compensable if it results from the individual's court commitment as a dipsomaniac, drug addict, or sexual psychopath. Finally, the Unemployment Insurance Code excludes from coverage certain disabilities that are attributable to pregnancy. It is this provision that is at issue in the present case.

It is clear that California intended to establish this benefit system as an insurance program that was to function essentially in accordance with insurance concepts. Since the program was instituted in 1946, it has been totally self-supporting, never drawing on general state revenues to finance disability or hospital benefits. The Disability Fund is wholly supported by the one percent of wages annually contributed by participating employees.

In ordering the State to pay benefits for disability accompanying normal pregnancy and delivery, the District Court acknowledged the State's contention "that coverage of these disabilities is so extraordinarily expensive that it would be impossible to maintain a program supported by employee contributions if these disabilities are included." There is considerable disagreement between the parties with respect to how great the increased costs would actually be, but they would clearly be substantial.

We cannot agree that the exclusion of this disability from coverage amounts to invidious discrimination under the Equal Protection Clause. California does not discriminate with respect to the persons or groups which are eligible for disability insurance protection under the program. The classification challenged in this case relates to the asserted underinclusiveness of the set of risks that the State has selected to insure. Although California has created a program to insure most risks of employment disability, it has not chosen to insure all such risks, and this decision is reflected in the level of annual contributions exacted from participating employees. This Court has held that, consistently with the Equal Protection Clause, a State "may take one step at a time, addressing itself to the phase of the problem which seems most acute to the legislative mind. . . . The legislature may select one phase of one field and apply a remedy there, neglecting the others. . . ." Williamson v. Lee Optical Co. (1955). Particularly with respect to social welfare programs, so long as the line drawn by the State is rationally supportable, the courts will not interpose their judgment as to the appropriate stopping point.

It is evident that a totally comprehensive program would be substantially more costly than the present program and would inevitably require state subsidy, a higher rate of employee contribution, a lower scale of benefits for those suffering insured disabilities, or some combination of these measures. There is nothing in the Constitution, however, that requires the State to subordinate or compromise its legitimate interests solely to create a more comprehensive social insurance program than it already has. The State has a legitimate interest in maintaining the self-supporting nature of its insurance program.

These policies provide an objective and wholly noninvidious basis for the State's decision not to create a more comprehensive insurance program than it has. There is no evidence in the record that the selection of the risks insured by the program worked to discriminate against any definable group or class in terms of the aggregate risk protection derived by that group or class from the program. There is no risk from which men are protected and women are not. Likewise, there is no risk from which women are protected and men are not.

The lack of identity between the excluded disability and gender as such under this insurance program becomes clear upon the most cursory analysis. The program divides potential recipients into two groups—pregnant women and non-pregnant persons. While the first group is exclusively female, the second includes members of both sexes. The fiscal and actuarial benefits of the program thus accrue to members of both sexes.

For the reasons we have stated, we hold that this contention is not a valid one under the Equal Protection Clause of the Fourteenth Amendment.

Justice BRENNAN, with whom Justice DOUGLAS and Justice MARSHALL join, dissenting.

Disabilities caused by pregnancy, however, like other physically disabling conditions covered by the Code, require medical care, often include hospitalization, anesthesia and surgical procedures, and may involve genuine risk to life. Moreover, the economic effects caused by pregnancy-related disabilities are functionally indistinguishable from the effects caused by any other disability: wages are lost due to a physical inability to work, and medical expenses are incurred for the delivery of the child and for postpartum care. In my view, by singling out for less favorable treatment a gender-linked disability peculiar to women, the State has created a double standard for disability compensation: a limitation is imposed upon the disabilities for which women workers may recover, while men receive full compensation for all disabilities suffered, including those that affect only or primarily their sex, such as prostatectomies, circumcision, hemophilia, and gout. In effect, one set of rules is applied to females and another to males. Such dissimilar treatment of men and women, on the basis of physical characteristics inextricably linked to one sex, inevitably constitutes sex discrimination.

Congress effectively overruled *Geduldig* by statute when it enacted the Pregnancy Discrimination Act, which defined sex discrimination to include pregnancy discrimination and which prohibits discrimination on that basis.[122] Although *Geduldig*'s impact has been negated in the area of pregnancy by the Pregnancy Discrimination Act, its reasoning is still applied by the Court in other contexts. In Bray v. Alexandria Women's Health Clinic, 506 U.S. 263 (1993), the Supreme Court considered whether those blocking access to abortion clinics were engaged in a form of gender discrimination in violation of federal civil rights statutes. The Supreme Court, in an opinion by Justice Scalia, expressly invoked *Geduldig* in rejecting the claim that there was a gender-based animus behind the protests. Scalia said that there were two categories of individuals: persons protesting and persons receiving abortions. The Court said that there was not gender discrimination because women were both in the former category, protestors, and in the latter category, those seeking abortions.

---

122. 42 U.S.C. §2000e(k).

3. Gender Classifications Benefiting Women

Interestingly, the majority of Supreme Court cases concerning gender discrimination have involved laws that benefit women and disadvantage men.[123] Two principles emerge from these decisions. First, gender classifications benefiting women based on role stereotypes generally will not be allowed. Second, gender classifications benefiting women designed to remedy past discrimination and differences in opportunity generally are permitted.

GENDER CLASSIFICATIONS BASED ON ROLE STEREOTYPES

The Supreme Court frequently has invalidated laws that benefit women and disadvantage men when the Court perceives the law as based on stereotypical assumptions about gender roles. Many of these laws were based on the stereotype of women being economically dependent on their husbands but men being economically independent of their wives.

ORR v. ORR
440 US. 268 (1979)

Justice Brennan delivered the opinion of the Court.

The question presented is the constitutionality of Alabama alimony statutes which provide that husbands, but not wives, may be required to pay alimony upon divorce.

In authorizing the imposition of alimony obligations on husbands, but not on wives, the Alabama statutory scheme "provides that different treatment be accorded . . . on the basis of . . . sex; it thus establishes a classification subject to scrutiny under the Equal Protection Clause." The fact that the classification expressly discriminates against men rather than women does not protect it from scrutiny. "To withstand scrutiny" under the Equal Protection Clause, "'classifications by gender must serve important governmental objectives and must be substantially related to achievement of those objectives.'"

Appellant views the Alabama alimony statutes as effectively announcing the State's preference for an allocation of family responsibilities under which the wife plays a dependent role, and as seeking for their objective the reinforcement of that model among the State's citizens. We agree, as he urges, that prior cases settle that this purpose cannot sustain the statutes.

The opinion of the Alabama Court of Civil Appeals suggests other purposes that the statute may serve. Its opinion states that the Alabama statutes were "designed" for "the wife of a broken marriage who needs financial assistance." This may be read as asserting either of two legislative objectives. One is a

---

123. There obviously also have been cases where women are discriminated against. *See, e.g.,* United States v. Virginia, 578 U.S. 515 (1996) (holding unconstitutional the exclusion of women from the Virginia Military Institute); Kirchberg v. Feenstra, 450 U.S. 455 (1981) (declaring unconstitutional a law that allows men, but not women, to dispose of property without their spouse's consent); Dothard v. Rawlinson, 433 U.S. 321 (1977) (upholding a law excluding women from "contact positions" in all male prisons).

legislative purpose to provide help for needy spouses, using sex as a proxy for need. The other is a goal of compensating women for past discrimination during marriage, which assertedly has left them unprepared to fend for themselves in the working world following divorce. We concede, of course, that assisting needy spouses is a legitimate and important governmental objective. We have also recognized "[r]eduction of the disparity in economic condition between men and women caused by the long history of discrimination against women . . . as . . . an important governmental objective." It only remains, therefore, to determine whether the classification at issue here is "substantially related to achievement of those objectives."

But in this case, even if sex were a reliable proxy for need, and even if the institution of marriage did discriminate against women, these factors still would "not adequately justify the salient features of" Alabama's statutory scheme. Under the statute, individualized hearings at which the parties' relative financial circumstances are considered already occur. There is no reason, therefore, to use sex as a proxy for need. Needy males could be helped along with needy females with little if any additional burden on the State. In such circumstances, not even an administrative-convenience rationale exists to justify operating by generalization or proxy. Similarly, since individualized hearings can determine which women were in fact discriminated against vis-a-vis their husbands, as well as which family units defied the stereotype and left the husband dependent on the wife, Alabama's alleged compensatory purpose may be effectuated without placing burdens solely on husbands. Progress toward fulfilling such a purpose would not be hampered, and it would cost the State nothing more, if it were to treat men and women equally by making alimony burdens independent of sex. "Thus, the gender-based distinction is gratuitous; without it, the statutory scheme would only provide benefits to those men who are in fact similarly situated to the women the statute aids," and the effort to help those women would not in any way be compromised.

Moreover, use of a gender classification actually produces perverse results in this case. As compared to a gender-neutral law placing alimony obligations on the spouse able to pay, the present Alabama statutes give an advantage only to the financially secure wife whose husband is in need. Although such a wife might have to pay alimony under a gender-neutral statute, the present statutes exempt her from that obligation.

Where, as here, the State's compensatory and ameliorative purposes are as well served by a gender-neutral classification as one that gender classifies and therefore carries with it the baggage of sexual stereotypes, the State cannot be permitted to classify on the basis of sex.

Similarly, the Supreme Court, on several occasions, has declared unconstitutional many laws that automatically allowed women economic benefits, such as when their husbands died, but permitted men the same benefits only if they proved dependence on their wives' income. In Weinberger v. Wiesenfeld, 420 U.S. 636 (1975), the Supreme Court deemed unconstitutional a provision of the Social Security Act that allowed a widowed mother, but not a widowed father, to receive benefits based on the earnings of the deceased spouse. The Court said that the law was based on the stereotype "that male workers' earnings are vital to the support of their families, while the earnings of female wage earners do not significantly contribute to their families' support."

The Court applied *Weinberger* in Califano v. Goldfarb, 430 U.S. 199 (1977), to hold unconstitutional a provision in the Federal Old-Age, Survivors, and Disability Insurance Benefits program, whereby a woman automatically would receive benefits based on the earnings of her husband, but a man would receive such benefits only if he could prove that he received at least half of his support from his wife. The Court declared the law unconstitutional because it was based, at least in part, on a "presumption that wives are usually dependent." The Court said that "such assumptions do not suffice to justify a gender-based discrimination in the distribution of employment-related benefits."

In Wengler v. Druggists Mutual Insurance Co., 446 U.S. 142 (1980), the Court applied the same principle to rule unconstitutional a state law that automatically allowed widows benefits, but only allowed widowers benefits if they proved that they were dependent on their wives' income or were physically incapacitated. In all of these cases — *Orr, Weinberger, Goldfarb,* and *Wengler* — the Court rejected laws that benefited women because they were based on the stereotype of economically dependent women and economically independent men.

Other stereotypes also have been rejected as a sufficient basis for gender classifications benefiting women. For example, in Mississippi University for Women v. Hogan, the Court declared unconstitutional a state policy of operating a nursing school that excluded men.

MISSISSIPPI UNIVERSITY FOR WOMEN v. HOGAN

458 U.S. 718 (1982)

Justice O'CONNOR delivered the opinion of the Court.

This case presents the narrow issue of whether a state statute that excludes males from enrolling in a state-supported professional nursing school violates the Equal Protection Clause of the Fourteenth Amendment.

I

The facts are not in dispute. In 1884, the Mississippi Legislature created the Mississippi Industrial Institute and College for the Education of White Girls of the State of Mississippi, now the oldest state-supported all-female college in the United States. The school, known today as Mississippi University for Women (MUW), has from its inception limited its enrollment to women. Mississippi maintains no other single-sex public university or college. Thus, we are not faced with the question of whether States can provide "separate but equal" undergraduate institutions for males and females.

Respondent, Joe Hogan, is a registered nurse but does not hold a baccalaureate degree in nursing. Since 1974, he has worked as a nursing supervisor in a medical center in Columbus, the city in which MUW is located. In 1979, Hogan applied for admission to the MUW School of Nursing's baccalaureate program. Although he was otherwise qualified, he was denied admission to the School of Nursing solely because of his sex.

II

Our decisions establish that the party seeking to uphold a statute that classifies individuals on the basis of their gender must carry the burden of showing an "exceedingly persuasive justification" for the classification. The burden is met only by showing at least that the classification serves "important governmental objectives and that the discriminatory means employed" are "substantially related to the achievement of those objectives."

Although the test for determining the validity of a gender-based classification is straightforward, it must be applied free of fixed notions concerning the roles and abilities of males and females. Care must be taken in ascertaining whether the statutory objective itself reflects archaic and stereotypic notions. Thus, if the statutory objective is to exclude or "protect" members of one gender because they are presumed to suffer from an inherent handicap or to be innately inferior, the objective itself is illegitimate.

The State's primary justification for maintaining the single-sex admissions policy of MUW's School of Nursing is that it compensates for discrimination against women and, therefore, constitutes educational affirmative action. In limited circumstances, a gender-based classification favoring one sex can be justified if it intentionally and directly assists members of the sex that is disproportionately burdened. However, we consistently have emphasized that "the mere recitation of a benign, compensatory purpose is not an automatic shield which protects against any inquiry into the actual purposes underlying a statutory scheme."

It is readily apparent that a State can evoke a compensatory purpose to justify an otherwise discriminatory classification only if members of the gender benefited by the classification actually suffer a disadvantage related to the classification. Mississippi has made no showing that women lacked opportunities to obtain training in the field of nursing or to attain positions of leadership in that field when the MUW School of Nursing opened its door or that women currently are deprived of such opportunities. In fact, in 1970, the year before the School of Nursing's first class enrolled, women earned 94 percent of the nursing baccalaureate degrees conferred in Mississippi and 98.6 percent of the degrees earned nationwide. As one would expect, the labor force reflects the same predominance of women in nursing. When MUW's School of Nursing began operation, nearly 98 percent of all employed registered nurses were female.

Rather than compensate for discriminatory barriers faced by women, MUW's policy of excluding males from admission to the School of Nursing tends to perpetuate the stereotyped view of nursing as an exclusively woman's job. By assuring that Mississippi allots more openings in its state-supported nursing schools to women than it does to men, MUW's admissions policy lends credibility to the old view that women, not men, should become nurses, and makes the assumption that nursing is a field for women a self-fulfilling prophecy. Thus, we conclude that, although the State recited a "benign, compensatory purpose," it failed to establish that the alleged objective is the actual purpose underlying the discriminatory classification.

The policy is invalid also because it fails the second part of the equal protection test, for the State has made no showing that the gender-based classification is substantially and directly related to its proposed compensatory objective. To the contrary, MUW's policy of permitting men to attend classes as auditors fatally undermines its claim that women, at least those in the School of Nursing, are adversely affected by the presence of men.

MUW permits men who audit to participate fully in classes. Additionally, both men and women take part in continuing education courses offered by the School of Nursing, in which regular nursing students also can enroll. The uncontroverted record reveals that admitting men to nursing classes does not affect teaching style, that the presence of men in the classroom would not affect the performance of the female nursing students, and that men in coeducational nursing schools do not dominate the classroom. In sum, the record in this case is flatly inconsistent with the claim that excluding men from the School of Nursing is necessary to reach any of MUW's educational goals.

Justice POWELL, with whom Justice REHNQUIST joins, dissenting.

The Court's opinion bows deeply to conformity. Left without honor — indeed, held unconstitutional — is an element of diversity that has characterized much of American education and enriched much of American life. The Court in effect holds today that no State now may provide even a single institution of higher learning open only to women students. It gives no heed to the efforts of the State of Mississippi to provide abundant opportunities for young men and young women to attend coeducational institutions, and none to the preferences of the more than 40,000 young women who over the years have evidenced their approval of an all-women's college by choosing Mississippi University for Women (MUW) over seven coeducational universities within the State.

Nor is respondent significantly disadvantaged by MUW's all-female tradition. His constitutional complaint is based upon a single asserted harm: that he must travel to attend the state-supported nursing schools that concededly are available to him. The Court characterizes this injury as one of "inconvenience." This description is fair and accurate, though somewhat embarrassed by the fact that there is, of course, no constitutional right to attend a state-supported university in one's home town. Thus the Court, to redress respondent's injury of inconvenience, must rest its invalidation of MUW's single-sex program on a mode of "sexual stereotype" reasoning that has no application whatever to the respondent or to the "wrong" of which he complains. At best this is anomalous. And ultimately the anomaly reveals legal error — that of applying a heightened equal protection standard, developed in cases of genuine sexual stereotyping, to a narrowly utilized state classification that provides an additional choice for women.

By applying heightened equal protection analysis to this case, the Court frustrates the liberating spirit of the Equal Protection Clause. It prohibits the States from providing women with an opportunity to choose the type of university they prefer. And yet it is these women whom the Court regards as the victims of an illegal, stereotyped perception of the role of women in our society. The Court reasons this way in a case in which no woman has complained, and the only complainant is a man who advances no claims on behalf of anyone else.

In sum, the practice of voluntarily chosen single-sex education is an honored tradition in our country, even if it now rarely exists in state colleges and universities. Mississippi's accommodation of such student choices is legitimate because it is completely consensual and is important because it permits students to decide for themselves the type of college education they think will benefit them most. Finally, Mississippi's policy is substantially related to its long-respected objective.

––––––––––––––

Thus, in all of these cases the Supreme Court invalidated laws benefiting women because they were based on stereotypes about women and their roles in the family and the economy. Yet in some cases the Court has upheld laws benefiting women even though they seem to be based on stereotypes. Michael M. v. Superior Court and Rostker v. Goldberg, which follow, both are cases in which the Court upheld gender classifications that appear to rest on stereotypes.

MICHAEL M. v. SUPERIOR COURT OF SONOMA COUNTY
450 US. 464 (1981)

Justice REHNQUIST announced the judgment of the Court and delivered an opinion, in which the Chief Justice, Justice STEWART, and Justice POWELL joined.

The question presented in this case is whether California's "statutory rape" law, §261.5 of the Cal. Penal Code Ann. violates the Equal Protection Clause of the Fourteenth Amendment. Section 261.5 defines unlawful sexual intercourse as "an act of sexual intercourse accomplished with a female not the wife of the perpetrator, where the female is under the age of 18 years." The statute thus makes men alone criminally liable for the act of sexual intercourse.

In July 1978, a complaint was filed in the Municipal Court of Sonoma County, Cal., alleging that petitioner, then a 17½-year-old male, had had unlawful sexual intercourse with a female under the age of 18, in violation of §261.5. The evidence, adduced at a preliminary hearing showed that at approximately midnight on June 3, 1978, petitioner and two friends approached Sharon, a 16½-year-old female, and her sister as they waited at a bus stop. Petitioner and Sharon, who had already been drinking, moved away from the others and began to kiss. After being struck in the face for rebuffing petitioner's initial advances, Sharon submitted to sexual intercourse with petitioner. Prior to trial, petitioner sought to set aside the information on both state and federal constitutional grounds, asserting that §261.5 unlawfully discriminated on the basis of gender. The trial court and the California Court of Appeal denied petitioner's request for relief and petitioner sought review in the Supreme Court of California. The Supreme Court held that "section 261.5 discriminates on the basis of sex because only females may be victims, and only males may violate the section."

[T]he fact that the California Legislature criminalized the act of illicit sexual intercourse with a minor female is a sure indication of its intent or purpose to discourage that conduct. Precisely why the legislature desired that result is of course somewhat less clear. This Court has long recognized that "[i]nquiries into congressional motives or purposes are a hazardous matter," United States v. O'Brien (1968), and the search for the "actual" or "primary" purpose of a statute is likely to be elusive. Here, for example, the individual legislators may have voted for the statute for a variety of reasons. Some legislators may have been concerned about preventing teenage pregnancies, others about protecting young females from physical injury or from the loss of "chastity," and still others about promoting various religious and moral attitudes towards premarital sex.

The justification for the statute offered by the State, and accepted by the Supreme Court of California, is that the legislature sought to prevent illegitimate teenage pregnancies. That finding, of course, is entitled to great deference. We are satisfied not only that the prevention of illegitimate pregnancy is at least one of the "purposes" of the statute, but also that the State has a strong interest in preventing such pregnancy. At the risk of stating the obvious, teenage pregnancies, which have increased dramatically over the last two decades, have significant social, medical, and economic consequences for both the mother and her child, and the State. Of particular concern to the State is that approximately half of all teenage pregnancies end in abortion. And of those children who are born, their illegitimacy makes them likely candidates to become wards of the State.

We need not be medical doctors to discern that young men and young women are not similarly situated with respect to the problems and the risks of sexual intercourse. Only women may become pregnant, and they suffer disproportionately the profound physical, emotional and psychological consequences of sexual activity. The statute at issue here protects women from sexual intercourse at an age when those consequences are particularly severe.

The question thus boils down to whether a State may attack the problem of sexual intercourse and teenage pregnancy directly by prohibiting a male from having sexual intercourse with a minor female. We hold that such a statute is sufficiently related to the State's objectives to pass constitutional muster. Because virtually all of the significant harmful and inescapably identifiable consequences of teenage pregnancy fall on the young female, a legislature acts well within its authority when it elects to punish only the participant who, by nature, suffers few of the consequences of his conduct. It is hardly unreasonable for a legislature acting to protect minor females to exclude them from punishment. Moreover, the risk of pregnancy itself constitutes a substantial deterrence to young females. No similar natural sanctions deter males. A criminal sanction imposed solely on males thus serves to roughly "equalize" the deterrents on the sexes.

In any event, we cannot say that a gender-neutral statute would be as effective as the statute California has chosen to enact. The State persuasively contends that a gender-neutral statute would frustrate its interest in effective enforcement. Its view is that a female is surely less likely to report violations of the statute if she herself would be subject to criminal prosecution. In an area already fraught with prosecutorial difficulties, we decline to hold that the Equal Protection Clause requires a legislature to enact a statute so broad that it may well be incapable of enforcement.

Contrary to the petitioner's assertions, the statute does not rest on the assumption that males are generally the aggressors. It is instead an attempt by a legislature to prevent illegitimate teenage pregnancy by providing an additional deterrent for men. The age of the man is irrelevant since young men are as capable as older men of inflicting the harm sought to be prevented.

Justice BRENNAN, with whom Justices WHITE and MARSHALL join, dissenting.

Applying the analytical framework provided by our precedents, I am convinced that there is only one proper resolution of this issue: the classification must be declared unconstitutional. I fear that the Court reaches the opposite result by placing too much emphasis on the desirability of achieving the State's asserted statutory goal—prevention of teenage pregnancy—and not enough emphasis on the fundamental question of whether the sex-based discrimination in the California statute is substantially related to the achievement of that goal.

The State of California vigorously asserts that the "important governmental objective" to be served by §261.5 is the prevention of teenage pregnancy. It claims that its statute furthers this goal by deterring sexual activity by males — the class of persons it considers more responsible for causing those pregnancies. But even assuming that prevention of teenage pregnancy is an important governmental objective and that it is in fact an objective of §261.5, California still has the burden of proving that there are fewer teenage pregnancies under its gender-based statutory rape law than there would be if the law were gender neutral. To meet this burden, the State must show that because its statutory rape law punishes only males, and not females, it more effectively deters minor females from having sexual intercourse.

However, a State's bare assertion that its gender-based statutory classification substantially furthers an important governmental interest is not enough to meet its burden of proof under Craig v. Boren. Rather, the State must produce evidence that will persuade the court that its assertion is true. The State has not produced such evidence in this case.

Moreover, there are at least two serious flaws in the State's assertion that law enforcement problems created by a gender-neutral statutory rape law would make such a statute less effective than a gender-based statute in deterring sexual activity. First, the experience of other jurisdictions, and California itself, belies the plurality's conclusion that a gender-neutral statutory rape law "may well be incapable of enforcement." There are now at least 37 States that have enacted gender-neutral statutory rape laws. Although most of these laws protect young persons (of either sex) from the sexual exploitation of older individuals, the laws of Arizona, Florida, and Illinois permit prosecution of both minor females and minor males for engaging in mutual sexual conduct. California has introduced no evidence that those States have been handicapped by the enforcement problems the plurality finds so persuasive. Surely, if those States could provide such evidence, we might expect that California would have introduced it.

The second flaw in the State's assertion is that even assuming that a gender-neutral statute would be more difficult to enforce, the State has still not shown that those enforcement problems would make such a statute less effective than a gender-based statute in deterring minor females from engaging in sexual intercourse. Common sense, however, suggests that a gender-neutral statutory rape law is potentially a greater deterrent of sexual activity than a gender-based law, for the simple reason that a gender-neutral law subjects both men and women to criminal sanctions and thus arguably has a deterrent effect on twice as many potential violators. Even if fewer persons were prosecuted under the gender-neutral law, as the State suggests, it would still be true that twice as many persons would be subject to arrest. The State's failure to prove that a gender-neutral law would be a less effective deterrent than a gender-based law, like the State's failure to prove that a gender-neutral law would be difficult to enforce, should have led this Court to invalidate §261.5.

Justice STEVENS, dissenting.

Local custom and belief—rather than statutory laws of venerable but doubtful ancestry—will determine the volume of sexual activity among unmarried teenagers. The empirical evidence cited by the plurality demonstrates the futility of the notion that a statutory prohibition will significantly affect the volume of that activity or provide a meaningful solution to the problems created by it.

I would have no doubt about the validity of a state law prohibiting all unmarried teenagers from engaging in sexual intercourse. The societal interests in reducing the incidence of venereal disease and teenage pregnancy are sufficient, in my judgment, to justify a prohibition of conduct that increases the risk of those harms. My conclusion that a nondiscriminatory prohibition would be constitutional does not help me answer the question whether a prohibition applicable to only half of the joint participants in the risk-creating conduct is also valid.

In my judgment, the fact that a class of persons is especially vulnerable to a risk that a statute is designed to avoid is a reason for making the statute applicable to that class. The argument that a special need for protection provides a rational explanation for an exemption is one I simply do not comprehend. In this case, the fact that a female confronts a greater risk of harm than a male is a reason for applying the prohibition to her — not a reason for granting her a license to use her own judgment on whether or not to assume the risk. Surely, if we examine the problem from the point of view of society's interest in preventing the risk-creating conduct from occurring at all, it is irrational to exempt 50% of the potential violators. And, if we view the government's interest as that of a parens patriae seeking to protect its subjects from harming themselves, the discrimination is actually perverse. Would a rational parent making rules for the conduct of twin children of opposite sex simultaneously forbid the son and authorize the daughter to engage in conduct that is especially harmful to the daughter? That is the effect of this statutory classification.

Finally, even if my logic is faulty and there actually is some speculative basis for treating equally guilty males and females differently, I still believe that any such speculative justification would be outweighed by the paramount interest in even-handed enforcement of the law. A rule that authorizes punishment of only one of two equally guilty wrongdoers violates the essence of the constitutional requirement that the sovereign must govern impartially.

ROSTKER v. GOLDBERG

453 U.S. 57 (1981)

Justice Rehnquist delivered the opinion of the Court.

The question presented is whether the Military Selective Service Act violates the Fifth Amendment to the United States Constitution in authorizing the President to require the registration of males and not females.

I

Congress is given the power under the Constitution "To raise and support Armies," "To provide and maintain a Navy," and "To make Rules for the Government and Regulation of the land and naval Forces." Pursuant to this grant of authority Congress has enacted the Military Selective Service Act. Section 3 of the Act, empowers the President, by proclamation, to require the registration of "every male citizen" and male resident aliens between the ages of 18 and 26. The purpose of this registration is to facilitate any eventual conscription: pursuant to §4(a) of the Act, those persons required to register are liable for training and service in the Armed Forces. The MSSA registration provision serves no other purpose beyond providing a pool for subsequent induction.

II

Whenever called upon to judge the constitutionality of an Act of Congress — "the gravest and most delicate duty that this Court is called upon to perform," Blodgett v. Holden (1927) (Holmes, J.) — the Court accords "great weight to the decisions of Congress." The Congress is a coequal branch of government whose Members take the same oath we do to uphold the Constitution of the United States. This is not, however, merely a case involving the customary deference accorded congressional decisions. The case arises in the context of Congress' authority over national defense and military affairs, and perhaps in no other area has the Court accorded Congress greater deference.

In Gilligan v. Morgan (1973), the Court noted: "[I]t is difficult to conceive of an area of governmental activity in which the courts have less competence. The complex, subtle, and professional decisions as to the composition, training, equipping, and control of a military force are essentially professional military judgments, subject always to civilian control of the Legislative and Executive Branches."

No one could deny that under the test of Craig v. Boren, supra, the Government's interest in raising and supporting armies is an "important governmental interest." Congress and its Committees carefully considered and debated two alternative means of furthering that interest: the first was to register only males for potential conscription, and the other was to register both sexes. Congress chose the former alternative. When that decision is challenged on equal protection grounds, the question a court must decide is not which alternative it would have chosen, had it been the primary decisionmaker, but whether that chosen by Congress denies equal protection of the laws.

III

This case is quite different from several of the gender-based discrimination cases we have considered in that, despite appellees' assertions, Congress did not act "unthinkingly" or "reflexively and not for any considered reason." The question of registering women for the draft not only received considerable national attention and was the subject of wide-ranging public debate, but also was extensively considered by Congress in hearings, floor debate, and in committee. Hearings held by both Houses of Congress in response to the President's request for authorization to register women adduced extensive testimony and evidence concerning the issue. These hearings built on other hearings held the previous year addressed to the same question. The House declined to provide for the registration of women when it passed the Joint Resolution allocating funds for the Selective Service System. When the Senate considered the Joint Resolution, it defeated, after extensive debate, an amendment which in effect would have authorized the registration of women. As noted earlier, Congress in H. J. Res. 521 only authorized funds sufficient to cover the registration of males. The foregoing clearly establishes that the decision to exempt women from registration was not the "accidental by-product of a traditional way of thinking about females."

The MSSA established a plan for maintaining "adequate armed strength . . . to insure the security of [the] Nation." Registration is the first step "in a united and continuous process designed to raise an army speedily and efficiently." Congress provided for the reactivation of registration in order to "provid[e] the means for the early delivery of inductees in an emergency." Any assessment of the congressional purpose and its chosen means must therefore consider the registration scheme as a prelude to a draft in a time of national emergency. Any other approach would not be testing the Act in light of the purposes Congress sought to achieve.

Congress determined that any future draft, which would be facilitated by the registration scheme, would be characterized by a need for combat troops. Women as a group, however, unlike men as a group, are not eligible for combat. The restrictions on the participation of women in combat in the Navy and Air Force are statutory. The Army and Marine Corps preclude the use of women in combat as a matter of established policy. Congress specifically recognized and endorsed the exclusion of women from combat in exempting women from registration.

The existence of the combat restrictions clearly indicates the basis for Congress's decision to exempt women from registration. The purpose of registration was to prepare for a draft of combat troops. Since women are excluded from combat, Congress concluded that they would not be needed in the event of a draft, and therefore decided not to register them. The Senate Report [stated]: "In the Committee's view, the starting point for any discussion of the appropriateness of registering women for the draft is the question of the proper role of women in combat. . . . The policy precluding the use of women in combat is, in the Committee's view, the most important reason, for not including women in a registration system."

The reason women are exempt from registration is not because military needs can be met by drafting men. This is not a case of Congress arbitrarily choosing to burden one of two similarly situated groups, such as would be the case with an all-black or all-white, or an all-Catholic or all-Lutheran, or an all-Republican or all-Democratic registration. Men and women, because of the combat restrictions on women, are simply not similarly situated for purposes of a draft or registration for a draft.

Congress's decision to authorize the registration of only men, therefore, does not violate the Due Process Clause. The exemption of women from registration is not only sufficiently but also closely related to Congress's purpose in authorizing registration. In light of the foregoing, we conclude that Congress acted well within its constitutional authority when it authorized the registration of men, and not women, under the Military Selective Service Act.

Justice WHITE, with whom Justice BRENNAN joins, dissenting.

I assume what has not been challenged in this case — that excluding women from combat positions does not offend the Constitution. Granting that, it is self-evident that if during mobilization for war, all noncombat military positions must be filled by combat-qualified personnel available to be moved into combat positions, there would be no occasion whatsoever to have any women in the Army, whether as volunteers or inductees. The Court appears to say, that Congress concluded as much and that we should accept that judgment even though the serious view of the Executive Branch, including the responsible military services, is to the contrary. The Court's position in this regard is most unpersuasive. I perceive little, if any, indication that Congress itself concluded that every position in the military, no matter how far removed from combat, must be filled, with combat-ready men. Common sense and experience in recent wars, where women volunteers were employed in substantial numbers, belie this view of reality. It should not be ascribed to Congress, particularly in the face of the testimony of military authorities, hereafter referred to, that there would be a substantial number of positions in the services that could be filled by women both in peacetime and during mobilization, even though they are ineligible for combat.

I would also have little difficulty agreeing to a reversal if all the women who could serve in wartime without adversely affecting combat readiness could predictably be obtained through volunteers. In that event, the equal protection component of the Fifth Amendment would not require the United States to go through, and a large segment of the population to be burdened with, the expensive and essentially useless procedure of registering women. But again I cannot agree with the Court, that Congress concluded or that the legislative record indicates that each of the services could rely on women volunteers to fill all the positions for which they might be eligible in the event of mobilization. On the contrary, the record as I understand it, supports the District Court's finding that the services would have to conscript at least 80,000 persons to fill positions for which combat-ready men would not be required. The consistent position of the Defense Department representatives was that their best estimate of the number of women draftees who could be used productively by the services in the event of a major mobilization would be approximately 80,000 over the first six months. Except for a single, unsupported, and ambiguous statement in the Senate Report to the effect that "women volunteers would fill the requirements for women," there is no indication that Congress rejected the Defense Department's figures or relied upon an alternative set of figures.

The Court also submits that because the primary purpose of registration and conscription is to supply combat troops and because the great majority of noncombat positions must be filled by combat-trained men ready to be rotated into combat, the absolute number of positions for which women would be eligible is so small as to be de minimis and of no moment for equal protection purposes, especially in light of the administrative burdens involved in registering all women of suitable age. There is some sense to this; but at least on the record before us, the number of women who could be used in the military without sacrificing combat readiness is not at all small or insubstantial, and administrative convenience has not been sufficient justification for the kind of outright gender-based discrimination involved in registering and conscripting men but no women at all.

As I understand the record, then, in order to secure the personnel it needs during mobilization, the Government cannot rely on volunteers and must register and draft not only to fill combat positions and those noncombat positions that must be filled by combat-trained men, but also to secure the personnel needed for jobs that can be performed by persons ineligible for combat without diminishing military effectiveness. The claim is that in providing for the latter category of positions, Congress is free to register and draft only men. I discern no adequate justification for this kind of discrimination between men and women. Accordingly, with all due respect, I dissent.

GENDER CLASSIFICATIONS BENEFITING WOMEN AS A REMEDY

The Court has indicated that gender classifications benefiting women will be allowed when they are designed to remedy past discrimination or differences in opportunity. Califano v. Webster is an example.

CALIFANO v. WEBSTER
430 U.S. 313 (1977)

PER CURIAM.

Under §215 of the Social Security Act, old-age insurance benefits are computed on the basis of the wage earner's "average monthly wage" earned during his "benefit computation years" which are the "elapsed years" (reduced by five) during which the wage earner's covered wages were highest. Until a 1972 amendment, "elapsed years" depended upon the sex of the wage earner. Section 215(b)(3) prescribed that the number of "elapsed years" for a male wage earner would be three higher than for an otherwise similarly situated female wage earner; for a male, the number of "elapsed years" equaled the number of years that elapsed after 1950 and before the year in which he attained age 65; for a female the number of "elapsed years" equaled the number of years that elapsed after 1950 and before the year in which she attained age 62. Thus, a male born in 1900 would have 14 "elapsed years" on retirement at age 65 but a female born in the same year would have only 11. Accordingly, a female wage earner could exclude from the computation of her "average monthly wage" three more lower earning years than a similarly situated male wage earner could exclude. This would result in a slightly higher "average monthly wage" and a correspondingly higher level of monthly old-age benefits for the retired female wage earner.

To withstand scrutiny under the equal protection component of the Fifth Amendment's Due Process Clause, "classifications by gender must serve important governmental objectives and must be substantially related to achievement of those objectives." Craig v. Boren (1976). Reduction of the disparity in economic condition between men and women caused by the long history of discrimination against women has been recognized as such an important governmental objective.

The more favorable treatment of the female wage earner enacted here was not a result of "archaic and overbroad generalizations" about women, or of "the roletyping society has long imposed" upon women, such as casual assumptions that women are "the weaker sex" or are more likely to be child-rearers or dependents. Rather, "the only discernible purpose of [§215's more favorable treatment is] the permissible one of redressing our society's longstanding disparate treatment of women."

The challenged statute operated directly to compensate women for past economic discrimination. Retirement benefits under the Act are based on past earnings. But as we have recognized: "Whether from overt discrimination or from the socialization process of a male-dominated culture, the job market is inhospitable to the woman seeking any but the lowest paid jobs." Thus, allowing women, who as such have been unfairly hindered from earning as much as men, to eliminate additional low-earning years from the calculation of their retirement benefits works directly to remedy some part of the effect of past discrimination.

———

Another example of the Court allowing gender classifications benefiting women to compensate for differences in opportunity is Schlesinger v. Ballard, 419 U.S. 498 (1975). In Schlesinger v. Ballard, the Court upheld a Navy regulation that required the discharge of male officers who had gone 9 years without a promotion but allowed women to remain 13 years without a promotion. The Court decided that this was constitutional because men had more opportunities for promotion than women. Justice Stewart, writing for the Court, explained, "Congress may quite rationally have believed that women line officers had less opportunity for promotion than did their male counterparts, and that a longer period of tenure for women officers would, therefore, be consistent with the goal to provide women officers with fair and equitable career advancement programs."

Thus far, the Court has not considered a constitutional challenge to an affirmative action program designed to benefit women. Although intermediate scrutiny is the test for all gender-based classifications, many of the same issues will arise as in the context of race-based affirmative action, including what interests justify affirmative action and what techniques are permissible.

CLASSIFICATIONS BENEFITING WOMEN BECAUSE OF BIOLOGICAL DIFFERENCES BETWEEN MEN AND WOMEN

In Nguyen v. Immigration & Naturalization Service, below, the Court allows a third type of gender classification: gender classifications benefiting women because of biological differences between men and women. The Court allows a difference in INS rules favoring mothers over fathers because of the greater certainty as to the identity of the mother as compared to the father and the greater opportunity that mothers have in establishing a relationship with their children.

Notice in reading the decision some of the key differences between the majority and the dissent: The majority articulates the test as intermediate scrutiny, whereas the dissent emphasizes that there also must be an "exceedingly persuasive justification" for the gender classification; the dissent emphasizes that only "actual" legislative purposes are sufficient, whereas the majority does not; and the majority and the dissent differ as to whether the law is based on stereotypes or biological differences between men and women.

NGUYEN v. IMMIGRATION & NATURALIZATION SERVICE
533 U.S. 53 (2001)

Justice KENNEDY delivered the opinion of the Court.

Title 8 U.S.C. §1409 governs the acquisition of United States citizenship by persons born to one United States citizen parent and one noncitizen parent when the parents are unmarried and the child is born outside of the United States or its possessions. The statute imposes different requirements for the child's acquisition of citizenship depending upon whether the citizen parent is the mother or the father. The question before us is whether the statutory distinction is consistent with the equal protection guarantee embedded in the Due Process Clause of the Fifth Amendment.

I

Petitioner Tuan Ahn Nguyen was born in Saigon, Vietnam, on September 11, 1969, to copetitioner Joseph Boulais and a Vietnamese citizen. Boulais and Nguyen's mother were not married. Boulais always has been a citizen of the United States, and he was in Vietnam under the employ of a corporation. After he and Nguyen's mother ended their relationship, Nguyen lived for a time with the family of Boulais' new Vietnamese girlfriend. In June 1975, Nguyen, then almost six years of age, came to the United States. He became a lawful permanent resident and was raised in Texas by Boulais.

In 1992, when Nguyen was 22, he pleaded guilty in a Texas state court to two counts of sexual assault on a child. He was sentenced to eight years in prison on each count. Three years later, the United States Immigration and Naturalization Service (INS) initiated deportation proceedings against Nguyen as an alien who had been convicted of two crimes involving moral turpitude, as well as an aggravated felony. Though later he would change his position and argue he was a United States citizen, Nguyen testified at his deportation hearing that he was a citizen of Vietnam. The Immigration Judge found him deportable.

Nguyen appealed to the Board of Immigration of Appeals and, in 1998, while the matter was pending, his father obtained an order of parentage from a state court, based on DNA testing. By this time, Nguyen was 28 years old. The Board dismissed Nguyen's appeal, rejecting his claim to United States citizenship because he had failed to establish compliance with 8 U.S.C. §1409(a), which sets forth the requirements for one who was born out of wedlock and abroad to a citizen father and a noncitizen mother.

Nguyen and Boulais appealed to the Court of Appeals for the Fifth Circuit, arguing that §1409 violates equal protection by providing different rules for attainment of citizenship by children born abroad and out of wedlock depending upon whether the one parent with American citizenship is the mother or the father. The court rejected the constitutional challenge.

We hold that §1409(a) is consistent with the constitutional guarantee of equal protection.

II

The general requirement for acquisition of citizenship by a child born outside the United States and its outlying possessions and to parents who are married, one of whom is a citizen and the other of whom is an alien, is set forth in 8 U.S.C. §1401(g). The statute provides that the child is also a citizen if, before the birth, the citizen parent had been physically present in the United States for a total of five years, at least two of which were after the parent turned 14 years of age.

As to an individual born under the same circumstances, save that the parents are unwed, §1409(a) sets forth the following requirements where the father is the citizen parent and the mother is an alien:

> (1) a blood relationship between the person and the father is established by clear and convincing evidence,
> (2) the father had the nationality of the United States at the time of the person's birth,
> (3) the father (unless deceased) has agreed in writing to provide financial support for the person until the person reaches the age of 18 years, and
> (4) while the person is under the age of 18 years —
>> (A) the person is legitimated under the law of the person's residence or domicile,
>> (B) the father acknowledges paternity of the person in writing under oath, or
>> (C) the paternity of the person is established by adjudication of a competent court.

When the citizen parent of the child born abroad and out of wedlock is the child's mother, the requirements for the transmittal of citizenship are described in §1409(c):

> (c) Notwithstanding the provision of subsection (a) of this section, a person born, after December 23, 1952, outside the United States and out of wedlock shall be held to have acquired at birth the nationality status of his mother, if the mother had the nationality of the United States at the time of such person's birth, and if the mother had previously been physically present in the United States or one of its outlying possessions for a continuous period of one year.

Section 1409(a) thus imposes a set of requirements on the children of citizen fathers born abroad and out of wedlock to a noncitizen mother that are not imposed under like circumstances when the citizen parent is the mother.

III

For a gender-based classification to withstand equal protection scrutiny, it must be established "at least that the [challenged] classification serves important governmental objectives and that the discriminatory means employed are substantially related to the achievement of those objectives." United States v. Virginia (1996). For reasons to follow, we conclude §1409 satisfies this standard. Given that determination, we need not decide whether some lesser degree of scrutiny pertains because the statute implicates Congress' immigration and naturalization power.

The statutory distinction relevant in this case, then, is that §1409(a)(4) requires one of three affirmative steps to be taken if the citizen parent is the father, but not if the citizen parent is the mother: legitimation; a declaration of paternity under oath by the father; or a court order of paternity. Congress' decision to impose requirements on unmarried fathers that differ from those on unmarried mothers is based on the significant difference between their respective relationships to the potential citizen at the time of birth. Specifically, the imposition of the requirement for a paternal relationship, but not a maternal one, is justified by two important governmental objectives. We discuss each in turn.

A

The first governmental interest to be served is the importance of assuring that a biological parent-child relationship exists. In the case of the mother, the relation is verifiable from the birth itself. The mother's status is documented in most instances by the birth certificate or hospital records and the witnesses who attest to her having given birth.

In the case of the father, the uncontestable fact is that he need not be present at the birth. If he is present, furthermore, that circumstance is not incontrovertible proof of fatherhood. Fathers and mothers are not similarly situated with regard to the proof of biological parenthood. The imposition of a different set of rules for making that legal determination with respect to fathers and mothers is neither surprising nor troublesome from a constitutional perspective. Section 1409(a)(4)'s provision of three options for a father seeking to establish paternity—legitimation, paternity oath, and court order of paternity—is designed to ensure an acceptable documentation of paternity.

Petitioners argue that the requirement of §1409(a)(1), that a father provide clear and convincing evidence of parentage, is sufficient to achieve the end of establishing paternity, given the sophistication of modern DNA tests. Section 1409(a)(1) does not actually mandate a DNA test, however. The Constitution, moreover, does not require that Congress elect one particular mechanism from among many possible methods of establishing paternity, even if that mechanism arguably might be the most scientifically advanced method. With respect to DNA testing, the expense, reliability, and availability of such testing in various parts of the world may have been of particular concern to Congress. The requirement of §1409(a)(4) represents a reasonable conclusion by the legislature that the satisfaction of one of several alternatives will suffice to establish the blood link between father and child required as a predicate to the child's acquisition of citizenship. Given the proof of motherhood that is inherent in birth itself, it is unremarkable that Congress did not require the same affirmative steps of mothers.

B

The second important governmental interest furthered in a substantial manner by §1409(a)(4) is the determination to ensure that the child and the citizen parent have some demonstrated opportunity or potential to develop not just a relationship that is recognized, as a formal matter, by the law, but one that consists of the real, everyday ties that provide a connection between child and citizen parent and, in turn, the United States. In the case of a citizen mother and a child born overseas, the opportunity for a meaningful relationship between citizen parent and child inheres in the very event of birth, an event so often critical to our constitutional and statutory understandings of citizenship. The mother knows that the child is in being and is hers and has an initial point of contact with him. There is at least an opportunity for mother and child to develop a real, meaningful relationship.

The same opportunity does not result from the event of birth, as a matter of biological inevitability, in the case of the unwed father. Given the 9-month interval between conception and birth, it is not always certain that a father will know that a child was conceived, nor is it always clear that even the mother will be sure of the father's identity. This fact takes on particular significance in the case of a child born overseas and out of wedlock. One concern in this context has always been with young people, men for the most part, who are on duty with the Armed Forces in foreign countries.

When we turn to the conditions which prevail today, we find that the passage of time has produced additional and even more substantial grounds to justify the statutory distinction. The ease of travel and the willingness of Americans to visit foreign countries have resulted in numbers of trips abroad that must be of real concern when we contemplate the prospect of accepting petitioners' argument, which would mandate, contrary to Congress' wishes, citizenship by male parentage subject to no condition save the father's previous length of residence in this country. In 1999 alone, Americans made almost 25 million trips abroad, excluding trips to Canada and Mexico. Visits to Canada and Mexico add to this figure almost 34 million additional visits. And the average American overseas traveler spent 15.1 nights out of the United States in 1999.

Principles of equal protection do not require Congress to ignore this reality. To the contrary, these facts demonstrate the critical importance of the Government's interest in ensuring some opportunity for a tie between citizen father and foreign born child which is a reasonable substitute for the opportunity manifest between mother and child at the time of birth. Indeed, especially in light of the number of Americans who take short sojourns abroad, the prospect that a father might not even know of the conception is a realistic possibility. Even if a father knows of the fact of conception, moreover, it does not follow that he will be present at the birth of the child. Thus, unlike the case of the mother, there is no assurance that the father and his biological child will ever meet. Without an initial point of contact with the child by a father who knows the child is his own, there is no opportunity for father and child to begin a relationship. Section 1409 takes the unremarkable step of ensuring that such an opportunity, inherent in the event of birth as to the mother-child relationship, exists between father and child before citizenship is conferred upon the latter.

The importance of the governmental interest at issue here is too profound to be satisfied merely by conducting a DNA test. The fact of paternity can be established even without the father's knowledge, not to say his presence. Paternity can be established by taking DNA samples even from a few strands of hair, years after the birth. Yet scientific proof of biological paternity does nothing, by itself, to ensure contact between father and child during the child's minority.

Congress is well within its authority in refusing, absent proof of at least the opportunity for the development of a relationship between citizen parent and child, to commit this country to embracing a child as a citizen entitled as of birth to the full protection of the United States, to the absolute right to enter its borders, and to full participation in the political process. If citizenship is to be conferred by the unwitting means petitioners urge, so that its acquisition abroad bears little relation to the realities of the child's own ties and allegiances, it is for Congress, not this Court, to make that determination. Congress has not taken that path but has instead chosen, by means of §1409, to ensure in the case of father and child the opportunity for a relationship to develop, an opportunity which the event of birth itself provides for the mother and child. It should be unobjectionable for Congress to require some evidence of a minimal opportunity for the development of a relationship with the child in terms the male can fulfill.

Petitioners and their amici argue in addition that, rather than fulfilling an important governmental interest, §1409 merely embodies a gender-based stereotype. Although the above discussion should illustrate that, contrary to petitioners' assertions, §1409 addresses an undeniable difference in the circumstance of the parents at the time a child is born, it should be noted, furthermore, that the difference does not result from some stereotype, defined as a frame of mind resulting from irrational or uncritical analysis. There is nothing irrational or improper in the recognition that at the moment of birth — a critical event in the statutory scheme and in the whole tradition of citizenship law — the mother's knowledge of the child and the fact of parenthood have been established in a way not guaranteed in the case of the unwed father. This is not a stereotype.

To fail to acknowledge even our most basic biological differences — such as the fact that a mother must be present at birth but the father need not be — risks making the guarantee of equal protection superficial, and so disserving it. Mechanistic classification of all our differences as stereotypes would operate to obscure those misconceptions and prejudices that are real. The distinction embodied in the statutory scheme here at issue is not marked by misconception and prejudice, nor does it show disrespect for either class. The difference between men and women in relation to the birth process is a real one, and the principle of equal protection does not forbid Congress to address the problem at hand in a manner specific to each gender.

Justice O'CONNOR, with whom Justice SOUTER, Justice GINSBURG, and Justice BREYER join, dissenting.

In a long line of cases spanning nearly three decades, this Court has applied heightened scrutiny to legislative classifications based on sex. The Court today confronts another statute that classifies individuals on the basis of their sex. While the Court invokes heightened scrutiny, the manner in which it explains and applies this standard is a stranger to our precedents. Because the Immigration and Naturalization Service (INS) has not shown an exceedingly persuasive justification for the sex-based classification embodied in 8 U.S.C. §1409(a)(4) — i.e., because it has failed to establish at least that the classification substantially relates to the achievement of important governmental objectives — I would reverse the judgment of the Court of Appeals.

I

Sex-based statutes, even when accurately reflecting the way most men or women behave, deny individuals opportunity. Such generalizations must be viewed not in isolation, but in the context of our Nation's "long and unfortunate history of sex discrimination." Sex-based generalizations both reflect and reinforce "fixed notions concerning the roles and abilities of males and females."

For these reasons, a party who seeks to defend a statute that classifies individuals on the basis of sex "must carry the burden of showing an 'exceedingly persuasive justification' for the classification." The defender of the classification meets this burden "only by showing at least that the classification serves 'important governmental objectives and that the discriminatory means employed' are 'substantially related to the achievement of those objectives.'"

Heightened scrutiny does not countenance justifications that "rely on overbroad generalizations about the different talents, capacities, or preferences of males and females." Rational basis review, by contrast, is much more tolerant of the use of broad generalizations about different classes of individuals, so long as the classification is not arbitrary or irrational. Moreover, overbroad sex-based generalizations are impermissible even when they enjoy empirical support.

The most important difference between heightened scrutiny and rational basis review, of course, is the required fit between the means employed and the ends served. Under heightened scrutiny, the discriminatory means must be "substantially related" to an actual and important governmental interest. Under rational basis scrutiny, the means need only be "rationally related" to a conceivable and legitimate state end. The fact that other means are better suited to the achievement of governmental ends therefore is of no moment under rational basis review. But because we require a much tighter fit between means and ends under heightened scrutiny, the availability of sex-neutral alternatives to a sex-based classification is often highly probative of the validity of the classification.

II

The Court recites the governing substantive standard for heightened scrutiny of sex-based classifications, but departs from the guidance of our precedents concerning such classifications in several ways.

For example, the majority hypothesizes about the interests served by the statute and fails adequately to inquire into the actual purposes of §1409(a)(4). The Court also does not always explain adequately the importance of the interests that it claims to be served by the provision. The majority also fails carefully to consider whether the sex-based classification is being used impermissibly "as a proxy for other, more germane bases of classification," and instead casually dismisses the relevance of available sex-neutral alternatives. And, contrary to the majority's conclusion, the fit between the means and ends of §1409(a)(4) is far too attenuated for the provision to survive heightened scrutiny. In all, the majority opinion represents far less than the rigorous application of heightened scrutiny that our precedents require.

A

According to the Court, "[t]he first governmental interest to be served is the importance of assuring that a biological parent-child relationship exists." The majority does not elaborate on the importance of this interest, which presumably lies in preventing fraudulent conveyances of citizenship. Nor does the majority demonstrate that this is one of the actual purposes of §1409(a)(4). Assuming that Congress actually had this purpose in mind in enacting parts of §1409(a)(4), the INS does not appear to rely on this interest in its effort to sustain §1409(a)(4)'s sex-based classification. In light of the reviewing court's duty to "determine whether the proffered justification is 'exceedingly persuasive,'" this disparity between the majority's defense of the statute and the INS' proffered justifications is striking, to say the least.

The gravest defect in the Court's reliance on this interest, however, is the insufficiency of the fit between §1409(a)(4)'s discriminatory means and the asserted end. Section 1409(c) imposes no particular burden of proof on mothers wishing to convey citizenship to their children. By contrast, §1409(a)(1), which petitioners do not challenge before this Court, requires that "a blood relationship between the person and the father [be] established by clear and convincing evidence." The virtual certainty of a biological link that modern DNA testing affords reinforces the sufficiency of §1409(a)(1).

If rational basis scrutiny were appropriate in this case, then the claim that "[t]he Constitution . . . does not require that Congress elect one particular mechanism from among many possible methods of establishing paternity[]" would have much greater force. But fidelity to the Constitution's pledge of equal protection demands more when a facially sex-based classification is at issue. This is not because we sit in judgment of the wisdom of laws in one instance but not the other, but rather because of the potential for "injury . . . to personal dignity" that inheres in or accompanies so many sex-based classifications.

B

The Court states that "[t]he second important governmental interest furthered in a substantial manner by §1409(a)(4) is the determination to ensure that the child and the citizen parent have some demonstrated opportunity or potential to develop not just a relationship that is recognized, as a formal matter, by the law, but one that consists of the real, everyday ties that provide a connection between child and citizen parent and, in turn, the United States." The Court again fails to demonstrate that this was Congress' actual purpose in enacting §1409(a)(4). The majority's focus on "some demonstrated opportunity or potential to develop . . . real, everyday ties," in fact appears to be the type of hypothesized rationale that is insufficient under heightened scrutiny.

Assuming, as the majority does, that Congress was actually concerned about ensuring a "demonstrated opportunity" for a relationship, it is questionable whether such an opportunity qualifies as an "important" governmental interest apart from the existence of an actual relationship. By focusing on "opportunity" rather than reality, the majority presumably improves the chances of a sufficient means-end fit. But in doing so, it dilutes significantly the weight of the interest. It is difficult to see how, in this citizenship-conferral context, anyone profits from a "demonstrated opportunity" for a relationship in the absence of the fruition of an actual tie. Children who have an "opportunity" for such a tie with a parent, of course, may never develop an actual relationship with that parent. If a child grows up in a foreign country without any postbirth contact with the citizen parent, then the child's never-realized "opportunity" for a relationship with the citizen seems singularly irrelevant to the appropriateness of granting citizenship to that child. Likewise, where there is an actual relationship, it is the actual relationship that does all the work in rendering appropriate a grant of citizenship, regardless of when and how the opportunity for that relationship arose.

Under the present law, the statute on its face accords different treatment to a mother who is by nature present at birth and a father who is by choice present at birth even though those two individuals are similarly situated with respect to the "opportunity" for a relationship. The mother can transmit her citizenship at birth, but the father cannot do so in the absence of at least one other affirmative act. The different statutory treatment is solely on account of the sex of the similarly situated individuals. This type of treatment is patently inconsistent with the promise of equal protection of the laws.

Indeed, the idea that a mother's presence at birth supplies adequate assurance of an opportunity to develop a relationship while a father's presence at birth does not would appear to rest only on an overbroad sex-based generalization. A mother may not have an opportunity for a relationship if the child is removed from his or her mother on account of alleged abuse or neglect, or if the child and mother are separated by tragedy, such as disaster or war, of the sort apparently present in this case. There is no reason, other than stereotype, to say that fathers who are present at birth lack an opportunity for a relationship on similar terms. The "[p]hysical differences between men and women[]" therefore do not justify §1409(a)(4)'s discrimination.

No one should mistake the majority's analysis for a careful application of this Court's equal protection jurisprudence concerning sex-based classifications. Today's decision instead represents a deviation from a line of cases in which we have vigilantly applied heightened scrutiny to such classifications to determine whether a constitutional violation has occurred. I trust that the depth and vitality of these precedents will ensure that today's error remains an aberration. I respectfully dissent.

E. ALIENAGE CLASSIFICATIONS

Alienage classifications refer to discrimination against noncitizens. This type of discrimination should be distinguished from national origin classifications that discriminate against individuals because of the country that a person, or his or her ancestors, came from.

Although America is very much a nation of immigrants, discrimination against aliens long has been widespread. Whether it is founded on economic protectionism, or xenophobia, or other motivations, aliens frequently have been denied benefits and privileges accorded to citizens. The issue is when such discrimination is a denial of equal protection of the laws.

Aliens are protected from discrimination because the Equal Protection Clause explicitly says that no "person" shall be denied equal protection of the laws. The clause does not mention the word "citizen," although it is used in the Privileges or Immunities Clause, which also is found in §1 of the Fourteenth Amendment. Long ago, in Yick Wo v. Hopkins, 118 U.S. 356 (1886), the U.S. Supreme Court declared, "The Fourteenth Amendment to the Constitution is not confined to the protection of citizens. . . . [Its] provisions are universal in their application, to all persons within the territorial jurisdiction, without regard to any differences of race, of color, or of nationality; and the equal protection of the laws is a pledge of the protection of equal laws."[124]

Often state and local laws that discriminate against aliens can be challenged on preemption grounds as well as for violating equal protection. The Supreme Court has held that federal immigration laws wholly occupy the field and preempt state efforts to regulate immigration.[125] For example, in Toll v. Moreno, 458 U.S. 1 (1982), the Supreme Court used preemption analysis to invalidate a state law denying resident aliens in-state tuition at the University of Maryland.

Sometimes state and local laws can be challenged both based on equal protection and on preemption analysis. In Graham v. Richardson, 403 U.S. 365 (1971), presented below, the Supreme Court declared unconstitutional a state law denying welfare benefits to aliens. The Court found both that it violated equal protection and that it was preempted by federal control over the field of immigration law.

As described below in subsection 1, the general rule is that strict scrutiny is used to evaluate discrimination against noncitizens. There are, however, several exceptions where less than strict scrutiny is used. Subsection 2 describes the case law establishing that alienage classifications related to self-government and the democratic process need only meet rational basis review. Subsection 3 discusses the use of rational basis review for federal laws that discriminate against aliens. The Supreme Court has recognized that Congress has plenary power to regulate immigration and thus has been deferential to federal statutes and presidential orders that discriminate against aliens. Finally, subsection 4 discusses the protection for undocumented aliens under equal protection.

1. Strict Scrutiny as the General Rule

The Supreme Court has held that generally alienage classifications must meet strict scrutiny.

---

124. *See also* Shaughnessy v. Mezei, 345 U.S. 206, 212 (1953); Wong Wing v. United States, 163 U.S. 228, 238 (1896).

125. *See, e.g.*, DeCanas v. Bica, 424 U.S. 351 (1976); Nyquist v. Mauclet, 432 U.S. 1 (1977); preemption is discussed in Chapter 4.

GRAHAM v. RICHARDSON
403 U.S. 365 (1971)

Justice BLACKMUN delivered the opinion of the Court.

These are welfare cases. The issue here is whether the Equal Protection Clause of the Fourteenth Amendment prevents a State from conditioning welfare benefits either (a) upon the beneficiary's possession of United States citizenship, or (b) if the beneficiary is an alien, upon his having resided in this country for a specified number of years. The facts are not in dispute.

This case, from Arizona, concerns the State's participation in federal categorical assistance programs. They are supported in part by federal grants-in-aid and are administered by the States under federal guidelines. Arizona Rev. Stat. Ann. §46233 reads: "A. No person shall be entitled to general assistance who does not meet and maintain the following requirements: 1. Is a citizen of the United States, or has resided in the United States a total of fifteen years. . . ."

Appellee Carmen Richardson, at the institution of this suit in July 1969, was 64 years of age. She is a lawfully admitted resident alien. She emigrated from Mexico in 1956 and since then has resided continuously in Arizona. She became permanently and totally disabled. She also met all other requirements for eligibility for APTD benefits except the 15-year residency specified for aliens. She applied for benefits but was denied relief solely because of the residency provision.

The appellants argue initially that the States, consistent with the Equal Protection Clause, may favor United States citizens over aliens in the distribution of welfare benefits. It is said that this distinction involves no "invidious discrimination" for the State is not discriminating with respect to race or nationality.

The Fourteenth Amendment provides, "[N]or shall any State deprive any person of life, liberty, or property, without due process of law; nor deny to any person within its jurisdiction the equal protection of the laws." It has long been settled, and it is not disputed here, that the term "person" in this context encompasses lawfully admitted resident aliens as well as citizens of the United States and entitles both citizens and aliens to the equal protection of the laws of the State in which they reside.

Under traditional equal protection principles, a State retains broad discretion to classify as long as its classification has a reasonable basis. This is so in "the area of economics and social welfare." But the Court's decisions have established that classifications based on alienage, like those based on nationality or race, are inherently suspect and subject to close judicial scrutiny. Aliens as a class are a prime example of a "discrete and insular" minority (see United States v. Carolene Products Co., n.4 (1938)) for whom such heightened judicial solicitude is appropriate.

Arizona seek[s] to justify [its] restrictions on the eligibility of aliens for public assistance solely on the basis of a State's "special public interest" in favoring its own citizens over aliens in the distribution of limited resources such as welfare benefits. It is true that this Court on occasion has upheld state statutes that treat citizens and noncitizens differently, the ground for distinction having been that such laws were necessary to protect special interests of the State or its citizens. [W]e conclude that a State's desire to preserve limited welfare benefits for its own citizens is inadequate to justify restricting benefits to citizens and longtime resident aliens.

[A]s the Court recognized in *Shapiro* [in declaring unconstitutional durational residency requirements for welfare]: "[A] State has a valid interest in preserving the fiscal integrity of its programs. It may legitimately attempt to limit its expenditures, whether for public assistance, public education, or any other program. But a State may not accomplish such a purpose by invidious distinctions between classes of its citizens. . . . The saving of welfare costs cannot justify an otherwise invidious classification." Since an alien as well as a citizen is a "person" for equal protection purposes, a concern for fiscal integrity is no more compelling a justification for the questioned classification in these cases than it was in *Shapiro*.

Accordingly, we hold that a state statute that denies welfare benefits to resident aliens and one that denies them to aliens who have not resided in the United States for a specified number of years violate the Equal Protection Clause.

The Court applied *Graham* in two cases decided in 1973: Sugarman v. Dougall, 413 U.S. 634 (1973), and In re Griffiths, 413 U.S. 717 (1973). In *Sugarman*, the Supreme Court declared unconstitutional a New York law that prevented aliens from holding civil service jobs. The Court said that excluding aliens denied equal protection and that a "flat ban on the employment of aliens in positions that have little, if any, relation to a State's legitimate interest, cannot withstand scrutiny under the Fourteenth Amendment."

In re Griffiths invalidated as violating equal protection a state law that excluded aliens from being licensed as attorneys. The Court reaffirmed that strict scrutiny was the appropriate test for discrimination against aliens and held that it was impermissible for states to require citizenship as a condition for practicing law.

The Court applied these decisions in later cases. In Examining Board of Engineers, Architects & Surveyors v. Flores de Otero, 426 U.S. 572 (1976), the Supreme Court declared unconstitutional a Puerto Rico statute that permitted only United States citizens to engage in the private practice of engineering. The Court said that the earlier decisions "establish that state classifications based on alienage are subject to strict judicial scrutiny." The Court said that excluding aliens from private practice as engineers has no "rational relationship to skill, competence, or financial responsibility."

Likewise, in Nyquist v. Mauclet, 432 U.S. 1 (1977), the Supreme Court used strict scrutiny to invalidate a New York law that limited financial aid for higher education to citizens, those who had applied for citizenship, and those who declared an intent to apply as soon as they were eligible. The Court emphasized the discriminatory nature of the statute, observing that the law "is directed at aliens and . . . only aliens are harmed by it."

2. Alienage Classifications Related to Self-Government and the Democratic Process

Although strict scrutiny is the general rule when the government discriminates against aliens, the Supreme Court has carved an important exception: Only rational basis review is used for alienage classifications related to self-government and the democratic process. The Supreme Court has said that "a democratic society is ruled by its people."[126] Hence, the Court has declared that a state may deny aliens the right to vote or hold political office[127] or serve on juries.[128]

Rather than use strict scrutiny and find these interests to be compelling, the Court has altered the level of scrutiny when the alienage classification relates to self-government and the democratic process.

FOLEY v. CONNELIE
435 U.S. 291 (1978)

Chief Justice BURGER delivered the opinion of the Court.

We noted probable jurisdiction in this case to consider whether a State may constitutionally limit the appointment of members of its police force to citizens of the United States. The appellant, Edmund Foley, is an alien eligible in due course to become a naturalized citizen, who is lawfully in this country as a permanent resident. He applied for appointment as a New York State trooper, a position which is filled on the basis of competitive examinations. Pursuant to a New York statute, state authorities refused to allow Foley to take the examination. The statute provides: "No person shall be appointed to the New York state police force unless he shall be a citizen of the United States."

Appellant claims that the relevant New York statute violates his rights under the Equal Protection Clause. The decisions of this Court with regard to the rights of aliens living in our society have reflected fine, and often difficult, questions of values. As a Nation we exhibit extraordinary hospitality to those who come to our country, which is not surprising for we have often been described as "a nation of immigrants." Indeed, aliens lawfully residing in this society have many rights which are accorded to noncitizens by few other countries. Our cases generally reflect a close scrutiny of restraints imposed by States on aliens.

But we have never suggested that such legislation is inherently invalid, nor have we held that all limitations on aliens are suspect.

It would be inappropriate, however, to require every statutory exclusion of aliens to clear the high hurdle of "strict scrutiny," because to do so would "obliterate all the distinctions between citizens and aliens, and thus depreciate the historic values of citizenship." The act of becoming a citizen is more than a ritual with no content beyond the fanfare of ceremony. A new citizen has become a member of a Nation, part of a people distinct from others. The individual, at that point, belongs to the polity and is entitled to participate in

---

126. Foley v. Connelie, 435 U.S. 291, 296 (1978).
127. Sugarman v. Dougall, 413 U.S. 634, 647 (1973).
128. Perkins v. Smith, 426 U.S. 913 (1976).

the processes of democratic decision-making. Accordingly, we have recognized "a State's historical power to exclude aliens from participation in its democratic political institutions," part of the sovereign's obligation "'to preserve the basic conception of a political community.'"

The practical consequence of this theory is that "our scrutiny will not be so demanding where we deal with matters firmly within a State's constitutional prerogatives." The State need only justify its classification by a showing of some rational relationship between the interest sought to be protected and the limiting classification. This is not intended to denigrate the valuable contribution of aliens who benefit from our traditional hospitality. It is no more than recognition of the fact that a democratic society is ruled by its people. Thus, it is clear that a State may deny aliens the right to vote, or to run for elective office, for these lie at the heart of our political institutions. Similar considerations support a legislative determination to exclude aliens from jury service. Likewise, we have recognized that citizenship may be a relevant qualification for fulfilling those "important nonelective executive, legislative, and judicial positions," held by "officers who participate directly in the formulation, execution, or review of broad public policy." This is not because our society seeks to reserve the better jobs to its members. Rather, it is because this country entrusts many of its most important policy responsibilities to these officers, the discretionary exercise of which can often more immediately affect the lives of citizens than even the ballot of a voter or the choice of a legislator. In sum, then, it represents the choice, and right, of the people to be governed by their citizen peers. To effectuate this result, we must necessarily examine each position in question to determine whether it involves discretionary decisionmaking, or execution of policy, which substantially affects members of the political community.

A discussion of the police function is essentially a description of one of the basic functions of government, especially in a complex modern society where police presence is pervasive. The police function fulfills a most fundamental obligation of government to its constituency. Police officers in the ranks do not formulate policy, per se, but they are clothed with authority to exercise an almost infinite variety of discretionary powers. The execution of the broad powers vested in them affects members of the public significantly and often in the most sensitive areas of daily life. Our Constitution, of course, provides safeguards to persons, homes and possessions, as well as guidance to police officers. And few countries, if any, provide more protection to individuals by limitations on the power and discretion of the police. Nonetheless, police may, in the exercise of their discretion, invade the privacy of an individual in public places. They may under some conditions break down a door to enter a dwelling or other building in the execution of a warrant, or without a formal warrant in very limited circumstances; they may stop vehicles traveling on public highways.

Clearly the exercise of police authority calls for a very high degree of judgment and discretion, the abuse or misuse of which can have serious impact on individuals. In short, it would be as anomalous to conclude that citizens may be subjected to the broad discretionary powers of noncitizen police officers as it would be to say that judicial officers and jurors with power to judge citizens can be aliens. It is not surprising, therefore, that most States expressly confine the employment of police officers to citizens, whom the State may reasonably presume to be more familiar with and sympathetic to American traditions. In the enforcement and execution of the laws the police function is one where citizenship bears a rational relationship to the special demands of the particular position. A State may, therefore, consonant with the Constitution, confine the performance of this important public responsibility to citizens of the United States.

Justice MARSHALL, with whom Justice BRENNAN and Justice STEVENS join, dissenting.

Today the Court upholds a law excluding aliens from public employment as state troopers. I do not agree with the Court that state troopers perform functions placing them within this "narro[w] . . . exception," to our usual rule that discrimination against aliens is presumptively unconstitutional. Accordingly I dissent.

In one sense, of course, it is true that state troopers participate in the execution of public policy. Just as firefighters execute the public policy that fires should be extinguished, and sanitation workers execute the public policy that streets should be kept clean, state troopers execute the public policy that persons believed to have committed crimes should be arrested. But this fact simply demonstrates that the exception, if read without regard to its context, "would swallow the rule."

Thus the phrase "execution of broad public policy" cannot be read to mean simply the carrying out of government programs, but rather must be interpreted to include responsibility for actually setting government policy pursuant to a delegation of substantial authority from the legislature. The head of an executive agency for example, charged with promulgating complex regulations under a statute, executes broad public policy in a sense that file clerks in the agency clearly do not. In short, those "elective or important nonelective" positions that involve broad policymaking responsibilities are the only state jobs from which aliens as a group may constitutionally be excluded. In my view, the job of state trooper is not one of those positions.

No one suggests that aliens as a class lack the intelligence or the courage to serve the public as police officers. The disqualifying characteristic is apparently a foreign allegiance which raises a doubt concerning trustworthiness and loyalty so pervasive that a flat ban against the employment of any alien in any law enforcement position is thought to be justified. But if the integrity of all aliens is suspect, why may not a State deny aliens the right to practice law? Are untrustworthy or disloyal lawyers more tolerable than untrustworthy or disloyal policemen? Or is the legal profession better able to detect such characteristics on an individual basis than is the police department? Unless the Court repudiates its holding in *In re Griffiths* it must reject any conclusive presumption that aliens, as a class, are disloyal or untrustworthy.

Even if the Court rejects this analysis, it should not uphold a statutory discrimination against aliens, as a class, without expressly identifying the group characteristic that justifies the discrimination. If the unarticulated characteristic is concern about possible disloyalty, it must equally disqualify aliens from the practice of law; yet the Court does not question the continuing vitality of its decision in *Griffiths*. Or if that characteristic is the fact that aliens do not participate in our democratic decisionmaking process, it is irrelevant to eligibility for this category of public service. If there is no group characteristic that explains the discrimination, one can only conclude that it is without any justification that has not already been rejected by the Court.

AMBACH v. NORWICK

441 U.S. 68 (1979)

Justice POWELL delivered the opinion of the Court.

This case presents the question whether a State, consistently with the Equal Protection Clause of the Fourteenth Amendment, may refuse to employ as elementary and secondary school teachers aliens who are eligible for United States citizenship but who refuse to seek naturalization. New York Education Law §3001(3) forbids certification as a public school teacher of any person who is not a citizen of the United States, unless that person has manifested an intention to apply for citizenship.

Appellee Norwick was born in Scotland and is a subject of Great Britain. She has resided in this country since 1965 and is married to a United States citizen. Appellee Dachinger is a Finnish subject who came to this country in 1966 and also is married to a United States citizen. Both Norwick and Dachinger currently meet all of the educational requirements New York has set for certification as a public school teacher, but they consistently have refused to seek citizenship in spite of their eligibility to do so. Norwick applied in 1973 for a teaching certificate covering nursery school through sixth grade, and Dachinger sought a certificate covering the same grades in 1975. Both applications were denied because of appellees' failure to meet the requirements of §3001(3).

The rule for governmental functions, which is an exception to the general standard applicable to classifications based on alienage, rests on important principles inherent in the Constitution. The distinction between citizens and aliens, though ordinarily irrelevant to private activity, is fundamental to the definition and government of a State. The Constitution itself refers to the distinction no less than 11 times, indicating that the status of citizenship was meant to have significance in the structure of our government. The assumption of that status, whether by birth or naturalization, denotes an association with the polity which, in a democratic republic, exercises the powers of governance. The form of this association is important: an oath of allegiance or similar ceremony cannot substitute for the unequivocal legal bond citizenship represents. It is because of this special significance of citizenship that governmental entities, when exercising the functions of government, have wider latitude in limiting the participation of noncitizens.

In determining whether, for purposes of equal protection analysis, teaching in public schools constitutes a governmental function, we look to the role of public education and to the degree of responsibility and discretion teachers possess in fulfilling that role. Each of these considerations supports the conclusion that public school teachers may be regarded as performing a task "that go[es] to the heart of representative government."

Public education, like the police function, "fulfills a most fundamental obligation of government to its constituency." The importance of public schools in the preparation of individuals for participation as citizens, and in the preservation of the values on which our society rests, long has been recognized by our decisions.

Within the public school system, teachers play a critical part in developing students' attitude toward government and understanding of the role of citizens in our society. Alone among employees of the system, teachers are in direct, day-to-day contact with students both in the classrooms and in the other varied activities of a modern school. In shaping the students' experience to achieve educational goals, teachers by necessity have wide discretion over the way the course material is communicated to students. They are responsible for presenting and explaining the subject matter in a way that is both comprehensible and inspiring. No amount of standardization of teaching materials or lesson plans can eliminate the personal qualities a teacher brings to bear in achieving these goals. Further, a teacher serves as a role model for his students, exerting a subtle but important influence over their perceptions and values. Thus, through both the presentation of course materials and the example he sets, a teacher has an opportunity to influence the attitudes of students toward government, the political process, and a citizen's social responsibilities. This influence is crucial to the continued good health of a democracy.

Furthermore, it is clear that all public school teachers, and not just those responsible for teaching the courses most directly related to government, history, and civic duties, should help fulfill the broader function of the public school system. Teachers, regardless of their specialty, may be called upon to teach other subjects, including those expressly dedicated to political and social subjects. More importantly, a State properly may regard all teachers as having an obligation to promote civic virtues and understanding in their classes, regardless of the subject taught.

Certainly a State also may take account of a teacher's function as an example for students, which exists independently of particular classroom subjects. In light of the foregoing considerations, we think it clear that public school teachers come well within the "governmental function" principle recognized in *Sugarman* and *Foley.* Accordingly, the Constitution requires only that a citizenship requirement applicable to teaching in the public schools bear a rational relationship to a legitimate state interest.

As the legitimacy of the State's interest in furthering the educational goals outlined above is undoubted, it remains only to consider whether §3001(3) bears a rational relationship to this interest. The restriction is carefully framed to serve its purpose, as it bars from teaching only those aliens who have demonstrated their unwillingness to obtain United States citizenship. Appellees, and aliens similarly situated, in effect have chosen to classify themselves. They prefer to retain citizenship in a foreign country with the obligations it entails of primary duty and loyalty. They have rejected the open invitation extended to qualify for eligibility to teach by applying for citizenship in this country. The people of New York, acting through their elected representatives, have made a judgment that citizenship should be a qualification for teaching the young of the State in the public schools, and §3001(3) furthers that judgment.

Justice BLACKMUN, with whom Justice BRENNAN, Justice MARSHALL, and Justice STEVENS join, dissenting.

Once again the Court is asked to rule upon the constitutionality of one of New York's many statutes that impose a requirement of citizenship upon a person before that person may earn his living in a specified occupation. These New York statutes, for the most part, have their origin in the frantic and overreactive days of the First World War when attitudes of parochialism and fear of the foreigner were the order of the day. We are concerned here with elementary and secondary education in the public schools of New York State. We are not concerned with teaching at the college or graduate levels. It seems constitution-ally absurd, to say the least, that in these lower levels of public education a Frenchman may not teach French or, indeed, an Englishwoman may not teach the grammar of the English language. The appellees, to be sure, are resident "aliens" in the technical sense, but there is not a word in the record that either appellee does not have roots in this country or is unqualified in anyway, other than the imposed requirement of citizenship, to teach. Both appellee Norwick and appellee Dachinger have been in this country for over 12 years. Each is married to a United States citizen. Each currently meets all the requirements, other than citizenship, that New York has specified for certifica-tion as a public school teacher. Each is willing, if required, to subscribe to an oath to support the Constitutions of the United States and of New York. Each lives in an American community, must obey its laws, and must pay all of the taxes citizens are obligated to pay.

[T]he New York classification is irrational. Is it better to employ a poor citizen teacher than an excellent resident alien teacher? Is it preferable to have a citizen who has never seen Spain or a Latin American country teach Spanish to eighth graders and to deny that opportunity to a resident alien who may have lived for 20 years in the culture of Spain or Latin America? The State will know how to select its teachers responsibly, wholly apart from citizenship, and can do so selectively and intelligently. That is the way to accomplish the desired result. An artificial citizenship bar is not a rational way. It is, instead, a stultifying provision. The route to "diverse and conflicting elements" and their being "brought together on a broad but common ground," which the Court so emphasizes, is hardly to be achieved by disregarding some of the diverse ele-ments that are available, competent, and contributory to the richness of our society and of the education it could provide.

In Cabell v. Chavez-Salido, 454 U.S. 432 (1982), the Supreme Court followed *Foley* and *Ambach* and held that a state may require citizenship for a person to be a probation officer. The Court said that probation officers serve both as law enforcement officers and also as teachers in the sense that they perform an educational function for those they supervise. The Court therefore used only the rational basis test and upheld the law.

But in Bernal v. Fainter, 467 U.S. 216 (1984), the Supreme Court refused to apply this exception to a state law that created a citizenship requirement for a person to be a notary public. The Court reaffirmed that "[a]s a general matter, a state law that discriminates on the basis of alienage can be sustained only if it can withstand strict judicial scrutiny." The Court emphasized that this is a "narrow" exception that applies only if it is specifically tailored to those who "participate directly in the formulation, execution, or review of broad public policy, and hence perform functions that go to the heart of representative government." The Court said that notary publics do not perform responsibilities that go to the heart of representative government. Therefore, strict scrutiny was applied and the state law was deemed to violate equal protection.

3. Congressionally Approved Discrimination

Another exception to the usual rule of strict scrutiny for alienage classifications is where the discrimination is a result of a federal law. The Supreme Court has ruled that the federal government's plenary power to control immigration requires judicial deference and that therefore only rational basis review is used if Congress has created the alienage classification or if it is the result of a presidential order.

In Mathews v. Diaz, 426 U.S. 67 (1976), the Supreme Court unanimously upheld a federal statute that denied Medicaid benefits to aliens unless they have been admitted for permanent residence and have resided for at least five years in the United States. The Court said that "the relationship between the United States and our alien visitors has been committed to the political branches of the Federal Government. Since decisions in these matters may implicate our relations with foreign powers, and since a wide variety of classifications must be defined in the light of changing political and economic circumstances, such decisions are frequently of a character more appropriate to either the Legislature or the Executive than to the Judiciary."

The Court thus drew a distinction between alienage classifications imposed by the federal government and those created by state and local governments. Strict scrutiny is used for the latter, but the Court said that the federal law was upheld because it was not "wholly irrational" and served the "legitimate" interests of the federal government in preserving the fiscal integrity of the program.

However, in Hamptom v. Wong, 426 U.S. 88 (1976), the Supreme Court clarified this and articulated a distinction between decisions by Congress or the president and those by federal administrative agencies; rational basis review is used only for the former. The Court invalidated a federal civil service regulation that denied employment to aliens. The Court said that "if the rule were expressly mandated by the Congress or the President, we might presume that any interest which might rationally be served by the rule did in fact give rise to its adoption." The Court therefore explained that if the civil service regulation had been adopted via a federal law or a presidential order, "it would be justified by the national interest in providing an incentive for aliens to become naturalized, or possibly even as providing the President with an expendable token for treaty negotiating purposes."

But the Civil Service Commission that adopted the regulation had no involvement in making decisions concerning immigration or foreign policy. Nor was there anything to "indicate that the Commission actually made any considered evaluation of the relative desirability of a simple exclusionary rule on the one hand, or the value . . . of enlarging the pool of eligible employees on the other." The Civil Service regulation was invalidated even though it would have been constitutional if adopted by other federal government institutions.

4. Undocumented Aliens and Equal Protection

Plyler v. Doe is the major Supreme Court decision concerning equal protection for undocumented aliens.

PLYLER v. DOE
457 U.S. 202 (1982)

Justice BRENNAN delivered the opinion of the Court.

The question presented by these cases is whether, consistent with the Equal Protection Clause of the Fourteenth Amendment, Texas may deny to undocumented school-age children the free public education that it provides to children who are citizens of the United States or legally admitted aliens.

[I]

The Fourteenth Amendment provides that "[n]o State shall . . . deprive any person of life, liberty, or property, without due process of law; nor deny to any person within its jurisdiction the equal protection of the laws." Appellants argue at the outset that undocumented aliens, because of their immigration status, are not "persons within the jurisdiction" of the State of Texas, and that they therefore have no right to the equal protection of Texas law. We reject this argument. Whatever his status under the immigration laws, an alien is surely a "person" in any ordinary sense of that term. Aliens, even aliens whose presence in this country is unlawful, have long been recognized as "persons" guaranteed due process of law by the Fifth and Fourteenth Amendments. Indeed, we have clearly held that the Fifth Amendment protects aliens whose presence in this country is unlawful from invidious discrimination by the Federal Government. Although the congressional debate concerning §1 of the Fourteenth Amendment was limited, that debate clearly confirms the understanding that the phrase "within its jurisdiction" was intended in a broad sense to offer the guarantee of equal protection to all within a State's boundaries, and to all upon whom the State would impose the obligations of its laws. Indeed, it appears from those debates that Congress, by using the phrase "person within its jurisdiction," sought expressly to ensure that the equal protection of the laws was provided to the alien population.

[II]

Sheer incapability or lax enforcement of the laws barring entry into this country, coupled with the failure to establish an effective bar to the employment of undocumented aliens, has resulted in the creation of a substantial "shadow population" of illegal migrants — numbering in the millions — within our borders. This situation raises the specter of a permanent caste of undocumented resident aliens, encouraged by some to remain here as a source of cheap labor, but nevertheless denied the benefits that our society makes available to citizens and lawful residents. The existence of such an underclass presents most difficult problems for a Nation that prides itself on adherence to principles of equality under law.

The children who are plaintiffs in these cases are special members of this underclass. Persuasive arguments support the view that a State may withhold its beneficence from those whose very presence within the United States is the product of their own unlawful conduct. These arguments do not apply with the same force to classifications imposing disabilities on the minor children of such illegal entrants. At the least, those who elect to enter our territory by stealth and in violation of our law should be prepared to bear the consequences, including, but not limited to, deportation. But the children of those illegal entrants are not comparably situated. Their "parents have the ability to conform their conduct to societal norms," and presumably the ability to remove themselves from the State's jurisdiction; but the children who are plaintiffs in these cases "can affect neither their parents' conduct nor their own status." Even if the State found it expedient to control the conduct of adults by acting against their children, legislation directing the onus of a parent's misconduct against his children does not comport with fundamental conceptions of justice.

Of course, undocumented status is not irrelevant to any proper legislative goal. Nor is undocumented status an absolutely immutable characteristic since it is the product of conscious, indeed unlawful, action. But §21.031 is directed against children, and imposes its discriminatory burden on the basis of a legal characteristic over which children can have little control. It is thus difficult to conceive of a rational justification for penalizing these children for their presence within the United States. Yet that appears to be precisely the effect of §21.031.

Public education is not a "right" granted to individuals by the Constitution. San Antonio Independent School Dist. v. Rodriguez (1973). But neither is it merely some governmental "benefit" indistinguishable from other forms of social welfare legislation. Both the importance of education in maintaining our basic institutions, and the lasting impact of its deprivation on the life of the child, mark the distinction. The "American people have always regarded education and [the] acquisition of knowledge as matters of supreme importance."

We have recognized "the public schools as a most vital civic institution for the preservation of a democratic system of government," and as the primary vehicle for transmitting "the values on which our society rests." "[A]s . . . pointed out early in our history, . . . some degree of education is necessary to prepare citizens to participate effectively and intelligently in our open political system if we are to preserve freedom and independence." And these historic "perceptions of the public schools as inculcating fundamental values necessary to the maintenance of a democratic political system have been confirmed by the observations of social scientists." In addition, education provides the basic tools by which individuals might lead economically productive lives to the benefit of us all. In sum, education has a fundamental role in maintaining the fabric of our society. We cannot ignore the significant social costs borne by our Nation when select groups are denied the means to absorb the values and skills upon which our social order rests.

In addition to the pivotal role of education in sustaining our political and cultural heritage, denial of education to some isolated group of children poses an affront to one of the goals of the Equal Protection Clause: the abolition of governmental barriers presenting unreasonable obstacles to advancement on the basis of individual merit. Paradoxically, by depriving the children of any disfavored group of an education, we foreclose the means by which that group might raise the level of esteem in which it is held by the majority. But more directly, "education prepares individuals to be self-reliant and self-sufficient participants in society." Illiteracy is an enduring disability. The inability to read and write will handicap the individual deprived of a basic education each and every day of his life. The inestimable toll of that deprivation on the social, economic, intellectual, and psychological well-being of the individual, and the obstacle it poses to individual achievement, make it most difficult to reconcile the cost or the principle of a status-based denial of basic education with the framework of equality embodied in the Equal Protection Clause.

B

These well-settled principles allow us to determine the proper level of deference to be afforded §21.031. Undocumented aliens cannot be treated as a suspect class because their presence in this country in violation of federal law is not a "constitutional irrelevancy." Nor is education a fundamental right; a State need not justify by compelling necessity every variation in the manner in which education is provided to its population. But more is involved in these cases than the abstract question whether §21.031 discriminates against a suspect class, or whether education is a fundamental right. Section 21.031 imposes a lifetime hardship on a discrete class of children not accountable for their disabling status. The stigma of illiteracy will mark them for the rest of their lives. By denying these children a basic education, we deny them the ability to live within the structure of our civic institutions, and foreclose any realistic possibility that they will contribute in even the smallest way to the progress of our Nation. In determining the rationality of §21.031, we may appropriately take into account its costs to the Nation and to the innocent children who are its victims. In light of these countervailing costs, the discrimination contained in §21.031 can hardly be considered rational unless it furthers some substantial goal of the State.

[III]

It is the State's principal argument, and apparently the view of the dissenting Justices, that the undocumented status of these children establishes a sufficient rational basis for denying them benefits that a State might choose to afford other residents. The State notes that while other aliens are admitted "on an equality of legal privileges with all citizens under non-discriminatory laws," the asserted right of these children to an education can claim no implicit congressional imprimatur. Indeed, in the State's view, Congress' apparent disapproval of the presence of these children within the United States, and the evasion of the federal regulatory program that is the mark of undocumented status, provides authority for its decision to impose upon them special disabilities.

To be sure, like all persons who have entered the United States unlawfully, these children are subject to deportation. But there is no assurance that a child subject to deportation will ever be deported. An illegal entrant might be granted federal permission to continue to reside in this country, or even to become a citizen. In light of the discretionary federal power to grant relief from deportation, a State cannot realistically determine that any particular undocumented child will in fact be deported until after deportation proceedings have been completed. It would of course be most difficult for the State to justify a denial of education to a child enjoying an inchoate federal permission to remain.

We are reluctant to impute to Congress the intention to withhold from these children, for so long as they are present in this country through no fault of their own, access to a basic education. In other contexts, undocumented status, coupled with some articulable federal policy, might enhance state authority with respect to the treatment of undocumented aliens. But in the area of special constitutional sensitivity presented by these cases, and in the absence of any contrary indication fairly discernible in the present legislative record, we perceive no national policy that supports the State in denying these children an elementary education. The State may borrow the federal classification. But to justify its use as a criterion for its own discriminatory policy, the State must demonstrate that the classification is reasonably adapted to "the purposes for which the state desires to use it."

Appellants argue that the classification at issue furthers an interest in the "preservation of the state's limited resources for the education of its lawful residents." Of course, a concern for the preservation of resources standing alone can hardly justify the classification used in allocating those resources. Graham v. Richardson (1971).

First, appellants appear to suggest that the State may seek to protect itself from an influx of illegal immigrants. While a State might have an interest in mitigating the potentially harsh economic effects of sudden shifts in population, §21.031 hardly offers an effective method of dealing with an urgent demographic or economic problem. There is no evidence in the record suggesting that illegal entrants impose any significant burden on the State's economy. To the contrary, the available evidence suggests that illegal aliens underutilize public services, while contributing their labor to the local economy and tax money to the state fisc. The dominant incentive for illegal entry into the State of Texas is the availability of employment; few if any illegal immigrants come to this country, or presumably to the State of Texas, in order to avail themselves of a free education.

Second, while it is apparent that a State may "not . . . reduce expenditures for education by barring [some arbitrarily chosen class of] children from its schools," appellants suggest that undocumented children are appropriately singled out for exclusion because of the special burdens they impose on the State's ability to provide high-quality public education. But the record in no way supports the claim that exclusion of undocumented children is likely to improve the overall quality of education in the State. As the District Court noted, the State failed to offer any "credible supporting evidence that a proportionately small diminution of the funds spent on each child [that might result from devoting some state funds to the education of the excluded group] will have a grave impact on the quality of education." And, after reviewing the State's school financing mechanism, the District Court concluded that barring undocumented children from local schools would not necessarily improve the quality of education provided in those schools. Of course, even if improvement in the quality of education were a likely result of barring some number of children from the schools of the State, the State must support its selection of this group as the appropriate target for exclusion. In terms of educational cost and need, however, undocumented children are "basically indistinguishable" from legally resident alien children.

Finally, appellants suggest that undocumented children are appropriately singled out because their unlawful presence within the United States renders them less likely than other children to remain within the boundaries of the State, and to put their education to productive social or political use within the State. Even assuming that such an interest is legitimate, it is an interest that is most difficult to quantify. The State has no assurance that any child, citizen or not, will employ the education provided by the State within the confines of the State's borders. In any event, the record is clear that many of the undocumented children disabled by this classification will remain in this country indefinitely, and that some will become lawful residents or citizens of the United States. It is difficult to understand precisely what the State hopes to achieve by promoting the creation and perpetuation of a subclass of illiterates within our boundaries, surely adding to the problems and costs of unemployment, welfare, and crime.

If the State is to deny a discrete group of innocent children the free public education that it offers to other children residing within its borders, that denial must be justified by a showing that it furthers some substantial state interest. No such showing was made here.

Chief Justice BURGER, with whom Justice WHITE, Justice REHNQIST, and Justice O'CONNOR join, dissenting.

Were it our business to set the Nation's social policy, I would agree without hesitation that it is senseless for an enlightened society to deprive any children—including illegal aliens—of an elementary education. I fully agree that it would be folly—and wrong—to tolerate creation of a segment of society made up of illiterate persons, many having a limited or no command of our language. However, the Constitution does not constitute us as "Platonic Guardians" nor does it vest in this Court the authority to strike down laws because they do not meet our standards of desirable social policy, "wisdom," or "common sense." We trespass on the assigned function of the political branches under our structure of limited and separated powers when we assume a policy-making role as the Court does today.

The Court's holding today manifests the justly criticized judicial tendency to attempt speedy and wholesale formulation of "remedies" for the failures—or simply the laggard pace—of the political processes of our system of government. The Court employs, and in my view abuses, the Fourteenth Amendment in an effort to become an omnipotent and omniscient problem solver. That the motives for doing so are noble and compassionate does not alter the fact that the Court distorts our constitutional function to make amends for the defaults of others.

The dispositive issue in these cases, simply put, is whether, for purpose of allocating its finite resources, a state has a legitimate reason to differentiate between persons who are lawfully within the state and those who are unlawfully there. The distinction the State of Texas has drawn—based not only upon its own legitimate interests but on classifications established by the Federal Government in its immigration laws and policies—is not unconstitutional.

The Court acknowledges that, except in those cases when state classifications disadvantage a "suspect class" or impinge upon a "fundamental right," the Equal Protection Clause permits a state "substantial latitude" in distinguishing between different groups of persons. Moreover, the Court expressly—and correctly—rejects any suggestion that illegal aliens are a suspect class, or that education is a fundamental right. Yet by patching together bits and pieces of what might be termed quasi-suspect-class and quasi-fundamental-rights analysis, the Court spins out a theory custom-tailored to the facts of these cases.

In the end, we are told little more than that the level of scrutiny employed to strike down the Texas law applies only when illegal alien children are deprived of a public education. If ever a court was guilty of an unabashedly result-oriented approach, this case is a prime example.

Once it is conceded — as the Court does — that illegal aliens are not a suspect class, and that education is not a fundamental right, our inquiry should focus on and be limited to whether the legislative classification at issue bears a rational relationship to a legitimate state purpose.

The State contends primarily that §21.031 serves to prevent undue depletion of its limited revenues available for education, and to preserve the fiscal integrity of the State's school-financing system against an ever-increasing flood of illegal aliens — aliens over whose entry or continued presence it has no control. Of course such fiscal concerns alone could not justify discrimination against a suspect class or an arbitrary and irrational denial of benefits to a particular group of persons. Yet I assume no Member of this Court would argue that prudent conservation of finite state revenues is per se an illegitimate goal. Indeed, the numerous classifications this Court has sustained in social welfare legislation were invariably related to the limited amount of revenues available to spend on any given program or set of programs.

Without laboring what will undoubtedly seem obvious to many, it simply is not "irrational" for a state to conclude that it does not have the same responsibility to provide benefits for persons whose very presence in the state and this country is illegal as it does to provide for persons lawfully present. By definition, illegal aliens have no right whatever to be here, and the state may reasonably, and constitutionally, elect not to provide them with governmental services at the expense of those who are lawfully in the state.

F. DISCRIMINATION AGAINST NONMARITAL CHILDREN

It is now clearly established that intermediate scrutiny is applied in evaluating laws that discriminate against nonmarital children — that is, children whose parents were not married. In Clark v. Jeter, 486 U.S. 456 (1988), the Supreme Court declared unconstitutional a state law that required a nonmarital child to establish paternity within six years of birth in order to seek support from his or her father. The Court expressly stated that intermediate scrutiny is used for discriminatory classifications based on illegitimacy. The Court felt that the six-year limitations period was impermissible because financial needs may not emerge until later and because it did not offer the child a sufficient opportunity to present his or her own claims.

Intermediate scrutiny is justified because of the unfairness of penalizing children because their parents were not married. The Supreme Court observed, "The status of illegitimacy has expressed through the ages society's condemnation of irresponsible liaisons beyond the bonds of marriage. But visiting this condemnation on the head of an infant is illogical and unjust. Moreover, imposing disabilities on the illegitimate child is contrary to the basic concept of our system that legal burdens should bear some relationship to individual responsibility or wrongdoing. Obviously, no child is responsible for his birth and penalizing the illegitimate child is ineffectual — as well as an unjust — way of deterring the parent."[129]

As with other classifications that receive heightened scrutiny, there is a long history of discrimination and it is immutable in the sense that there is nothing the individual can do to change his or her status.[130] As the Supreme Court noted, "[T]he legal status of illegitimacy, however defined, is, like race or national origin, a characteristic determined by causes not within the control of the illegitimate individual, and it bears no relation to the individual's ability to participate in and contribute to society."[131]

But the Court also has distinguished discrimination against nonmarital children from the types of classifications that receive strict scrutiny. Illegitimacy is different from race, which receives strict scrutiny, or gender, which receives intermediate scrutiny, in that "illegitimacy does not carry an obvious badge."[132] Additionally, the "discrimination against illegitimates has never approached the severity or pervasiveness of the historic legal and political discrimination against women and Negroes."[133]

In applying intermediate scrutiny in this area, two major principles emerge from the Court's decisions. First, laws that provide a benefit to all marital children, but no nonmarital children, always are declared unconstitutional. Second, laws that provide a benefit to some nonmarital children, while denying the benefit to other nonmarital children, are evaluated on a case-by-case basis under intermediate scrutiny.

LAWS DENYING BENEFITS TO ALL NONMARITAL CHILDREN

The Supreme Court consistently has invalidated laws that deny a benefit to all nonmarital children that is accorded to all marital children. In Levy v. Louisiana, 391 U.S. 68 (1968), the Supreme Court declared unconstitutional a state law that prevented nonmarital children from suing under a wrongful death statute for losses because of a mother's death. All marital children could sue but no nonmarital children. The Court found this unreasonable: "Legitimacy or illegitimacy of birth has no relation to the nature of the wrong allegedly inflicted on the mother. . . . [I]t is invidious to discriminate against [the children] when no action, conduct or demeanor of theirs is possibly relevant to the harm that was done the mother."

In a companion case, Glona v. American Guarantee & Liability Insurance Co., 391 U.S. 73 (1968), the Supreme Court declared unconstitutional a state law that prevented parents from suing for the wrongful death of their nonmarital children. The Court concluded that "[w]here the claimant is plainly the mother, the State denies equal protection of the laws to withhold relief merely because the child, wrongfully killed, was born to her out of wedlock."

---

129. Weber v. Aetna Casualty & Surety Co., 406 U.S. 164, 175 (1972).
130. *See* Harry D. Krause, *Equal Protection for the Illegitimate*, 65 Mich. L. Rev. 477, 498-499 (1967).
131. Mathews v. Lucas, 427 U.S. 495, 505 (1976).
132. *Id.* at 506.
133. *Id.*

Similarly, in New Jersey Welfare Rights Organization v. Cahill, 411 U.S. 619 (1973), the Supreme Court ruled unconstitutional a state law that discriminated against non-marital children in receiving public assistance. A New Jersey law limited receipt of benefits under the "Assistance to Families of the Working Poor" program to families where there were two married adults and a child. The Supreme Court said that allowing all marital children to receive these benefits, but no nonmarital children, violated equal protection.

In the same year that *Cahill* was decided, the Supreme Court also declared unconstitutional a Texas law that created a legal obligation for fathers to support their marital children but no similar duty with regard to nonmarital children. In Gomez v. Perez, 409 U.S. 535, 538 (1973), in concluding that the law violated equal protection, the Court stated, "[A] state may not invidiously discriminate against illegitimate children by denying them substantial benefits accorded children generally. We therefore hold that once a State posits a judicially enforceable right on behalf of children to needed support from their natural fathers there is no constitutionally sufficient justification for denying such an essential right to a child simply because its natural father has not married its mother."

In Trimble v. Gordon, 430 U.S. 762 (1977), the Supreme Court deemed unconstitutional a law that prevented nonmarital children from inheriting from fathers who died intestate (without a will). An Illinois law allowed marital children to inherit from either parent, but a nonmarital child only could inherit from his or her mother. Although the Court recognized the need to establish paternity for unwed fathers, it concluded that this did not justify the complete denial of benefits to all nonmarital children whose fathers died intestate.

In all of these cases, the laws in question allowed all marital children to receive a benefit that was denied to all nonmarital children. In each instance, the Supreme Court found that the discrimination violated equal protection.

LAWS THAT PROVIDE A BENEFIT TO SOME NONMARITAL CHILDREN

No similar bright-line rule exists when the law provides a benefit to some nonmarital children that it denies to other nonmarital children. In other words, rather than discriminating between marital and nonmarital children, these laws distinguish among nonmarital children. Such statutes are subjected to intermediate scrutiny and evaluated on a case-by-case basis with the courts determining whether there is an important interest served and whether the law is substantially related to that goal.

In Lalli v. Lalli, 439 U.S. 259 (1978), the Supreme Court upheld a state law that provided that a nonmarital child could inherit from his or her father only if paternity was established during the father's lifetime. In other words, some nonmarital children could inherit — those where paternity was established during the father's life, other nonmarital children could not inherit — where paternity was not so established. The Court said that the state had an important interest in preventing fraud and that requiring paternity to be established during the father's lifetime was substantially related to that objective.

In Labine v. Vincent, 401 U.S. 532 (1971), the Supreme Court upheld a state law that denied inheritance from a nonmarital father unless the child had been formally acknowledged by the father during the father's life. Although the Court does not expressly say so, it appears that in *Labine*, like in *Lalli*, the Court accepted the state's argument that requiring paternity to be established in this way is substantially related to the government's interest in preventing fraud.

Another case upholding a distinction among nonmarital children was Mathews v. Lucas, 427 U.S. 495 (1976). The Supreme Court sustained a provision of the Social Security Act that allowed children to receive survivors' benefits only if they could establish both paternity and that the father was providing financial support. The law created a presumption of dependency for all marital children and all nonmarital children who were entitled to inherit under state law. The law allowed other nonmarital children to inherit only if they could prove financial dependency on their fathers. The Court found that the distinction among nonmarital children was constitutional because it did not preclude any child from receiving benefits and because it allowed the government to reduce its administrative burdens. Requiring every child to prove dependency would have been a substantial additional burden on the government; allowing all children to inherit without having to prove dependency would have been a greater cost on the government that it was not constitutionally required to absorb.

However, not all laws discriminating among nonmarital children have been upheld. In Jiminez v. Weinberger, 417 U.S. 628 (1974), the Supreme Court invalidated a provision of the Social Security Act that allowed intestate inheritance of disability benefits by all marital children and by nonmarital children who had been "legitimated." Other nonmarital children could inherit benefits only if they proved that they were living with or being supported by the father at the time the disability began. In other words, nonmarital children who were neither living with the father nor being supported by him when the disability arose could not get benefits.

The Supreme Court said that this was unconstitutional and explained, "Assuming that the appellants are in fact dependent on the claimant, it would not serve the purposes of the Act to conclusively deny them an opportunity to establish their dependency and their right to insurance benefits, and it would discriminate between the two subclasses of afterborn illegitimates without any basis for the distinction since the potential for spurious claims is exactly the same as to both subclasses."

In other words, if the law's distinction is between marital and nonmarital children, the law is likely to be invalidated. But if the distinction is among nonmarital children, the Court will apply intermediate scrutiny in evaluating the law.

G. OTHER TYPES OF DISCRIMINATION: ONLY RATIONAL BASIS REVIEW

There is an infinite variety of ways that governments draw distinctions among people. For instance, laws that determine who can practice law, who can have a driver's license, who can receive welfare, who can be a police officer, and who can have a broadcast license all involve classifications. Any of these laws can be challenged as denying equal protection. Each, of course, would be subjected only to rational basis review, unless the discrimination was with regard to race, national origin, gender, alienage, or legitimacy. Thus far, these are the only types of discrimination for which the Supreme Court has approved either intermediate or strict scrutiny.[134]

The Supreme Court has expressly rejected heightened scrutiny for some other types of discrimination. Specifically, the Court has ruled that only rational basis review should be used for discrimination based on age, disability, wealth, and sexual orientation, even though these classifications share much in common with the types of discrimination for which heightened scrutiny is used.

1. Age Classifications

Many of the factors that justify heightened scrutiny for race, national origin, gender, alienage, and legitimacy classifications also exist with regard to age discrimination. There is a history of discrimination against the elderly with judgments often based on stereotypes. A person's age is immutable in the sense that a person cannot voluntarily change it and it is a characteristic that is visible. Yet the Supreme Court has expressly declared that only rational basis review should be used under equal protection analysis for age discrimination.

MASSACHUSETTS BOARD OF RETIREMENT v. MURGIA
427 U.S. 307 (1976)

Per Curiam.

This case presents the question whether the provision of Mass. Gen. Laws Ann., that a uniformed state police officer "shall be retired . . . upon his attaining age fifty," denies appellee police officer equal protection of the laws in violation of the Fourteenth Amendment.

Appellee Robert Murgia was an officer in the Uniformed Branch of the Massachusetts State Police. The Massachusetts Board of Retirement retired him upon his 50th birthday. Appellee brought this civil action in the United States District Court for the District of Massachusetts, alleging that the operation of [the law] denied him equal protection of the laws.

The primary function of the Uniformed Branch of the Massachusetts State Police is to protect persons and property and maintain law and order. Specifically, uniformed officers participate in controlling prison and civil disorders, respond to emergencies and natural disasters, patrol highways in marked cruisers, investigate crime, apprehend criminal suspects, and provide backup support for local law enforcement personnel. As the District Court observed, "service in this branch is, or can be, arduous." These considerations prompt the requirement that uniformed state officers pass a comprehensive physical examination biennially until age 40. After that, until mandatory retirement at

---

134. It also is likely that heightened scrutiny will be used for discrimination based on religion. *See, e.g.,* Griffin v. Illinois, 351 U.S. 12 (1956) (mentioning religion along with race and national origin as impermissible grounds for discrimination). However, such cases are likely to arise under the Free Exercise Clause of the First Amendment rather than under equal protection.

age 50, uniformed officers must pass annually a more rigorous examination, including an electrocardiogram and tests for gastro-intestinal bleeding. Appellee Murgia had passed such an examination four months before he was retired, and there is no dispute that, when he retired, his excellent physical and mental health still rendered him capable of performing the duties of a uniformed officer.

We need state only briefly our reasons for [concluding] that strict scrutiny is not the proper test for determining whether the mandatory retirement provision denies appellee equal protection. San Antonio School District v. Rodriguez (1973) reaffirmed that equal protection analysis requires strict scrutiny of a legislative classification only when the classification impermissibly interferes with the exercise of a fundamental right or operates to the peculiar disadvantage of a suspect class. Mandatory retirement at age 50 under the Massachusetts statute involves neither situation.

This Court's decisions give no support to the proposition that a right of governmental employment per se is fundamental. Nor does the class of uniformed state police officers over 50 constitute a suspect class for purposes of equal protection analysis.

While the treatment of the aged in this Nation has not been wholly free of discrimination, such persons, unlike, say, those who have been discriminated against on the basis of race or national origin, have not experienced a "history of purposeful unequal treatment" or been subjected to unique disabilities on the basis of stereotyped characteristics not truly indicative of their abilities. The class subject to the compulsory retirement feature of the Massachusetts statute consists of uniformed state police officers over the age of 50. It cannot be said to discriminate only against the elderly. Rather, it draws the line at a certain age in middle life. But even old age does not define a "discrete and insular" group, United States v. Carolene Products Co. (1938), in need of "extraordinary protection from the majoritarian political process." Instead, it marks a stage that each of us will reach if we live out our normal span. Even if the statute could be said to impose a penalty upon a class defined as the aged, it would not impose a distinction sufficiently akin to those classifications that we have found suspect to call for strict judicial scrutiny.

We turn then to examine this state classification under the rational-basis standard. In this case, the Massachusetts statute clearly meets the requirements of the Equal Protection Clause, for the State's classification rationally furthers the purpose identified by the State: Through mandatory retirement at age 50, the legislature seeks to protect the public by assuring physical preparedness of its uniformed police. Since physical ability generally declines with age, mandatory retirement at 50 serves to remove from police service those whose fitness for uniformed work presumptively has diminished with age. This clearly is rationally related to the State's objective. There is no indication that §26(3)(a) has the effect of excluding from service so few officers who are in fact unqualified as to render age 50 a criterion wholly unrelated to the objective of the statute.

We do not make light of the substantial economic and psychological effects premature and compulsory retirement can have on an individual; nor do we denigrate the ability of elderly citizens to continue to contribute to society. The problems of retirement have been well documented and are beyond serious dispute. But "[w]e do not decide today that the [Massachusetts statute] is wise, that it best fulfills the relevant social and economic objectives that [Massachusetts] might ideally espouse, or that a more just and humane system could not be revised." We decide only that the system enacted by the Massachusetts Legislature does not deny appellee equal protection of the laws.

Justice MARSHALL, dissenting.

Today the Court holds that it is permissible for the Commonwealth of Massachusetts to declare that members of its state police force who have been proved medically fit for service are nonetheless legislatively unfit to be policemen and must be involuntarily "retired" because they have reached the age of 50. Although we have called the right to work "of the very essence of the personal freedom and opportunity that it was the purpose of the [Fourteenth] Amendment to secure," Truax v. Raich (1915), the Court finds that the right to work is not a fundamental right. And, while agreeing that "the treatment of the aged in this Nation has not been wholly free of discrimination," the Court holds that the elderly are not a suspect class. Accordingly, the Court undertakes the scrutiny mandated by the bottom tier of its two-tier equal protection framework, finds the challenged legislation not to be "wholly unrelated" to its objective, and holds, therefore, that it survives equal protection attack. I respectfully dissent.

While depriving any government employee of his job is a significant deprivation, it is particularly burdensome when the person deprived is an older citizen. Once terminated, the elderly cannot readily find alternative employment. The lack of work is not only economically damaging, but emotionally and physically draining. Deprived of his status in the community and of the opportunity for meaningful activity, fearful of becoming dependent on others for his support, and lonely in his new-found isolation, the involuntarily retired person is susceptible to physical and emotional ailments as a direct consequence of his enforced idleness. Ample clinical evidence supports the conclusion that mandatory retirement poses a direct threat to the health and life expectancy of the retired person, and these consequences of termination for age are not disputed by appellants. Thus, an older person deprived of his job by the government loses not only his right to earn a living, but, too often, his health as well, in sad contradiction of Browning's promise: "The best is yet to be, The last of life, for which the first was made."

Not only are the elderly denied important benefits when they are terminated on the basis of age, but the classification of older workers is itself one that merits judicial attention. Whether older workers constitute a "suspect" class or not, it cannot be disputed that they constitute a class subject to repeated and arbitrary discrimination in employment.

Turning, then, to appellants' arguments, I agree that the purpose of the mandatory retirement law is legitimate, and indeed compelling[;] the Commonwealth has every reason to assure that its state police officers are of sufficient physical strength and health to perform their jobs. In my view, however, the means chosen, the forced retirement of officers at age 50, is so over-inclusive that it must fall.

[T]he Commonwealth is in the position of already individually testing its police officers for physical fitness, conceding that such testing is adequate to determine the physical ability of an officer to continue on the job, and conceding that that ability may continue after age 50. In these circumstances, I see no reason at all for automatically terminating those officers who reach the age of 50; indeed, that action seems the height of irrationality.

In Vance v. Bradley, 440 U.S. 93 (1979), the Supreme Court upheld a federal law that mandated retirement at age 60 for participants in the Foreign Service Retirement System. The statutory scheme drew a distinction between those covered by the Social Security system, where there was not a mandatory retirement age, and the Foreign Service Retirement System, which required retirement at age 60. The Court used the rational basis test and said that it upheld the law because the challengers failed "to demonstrate that Congress has no reasonable basis for believing that conditions overseas generally are more demanding than conditions in the United States and that at age 60 or before many persons begin something of a decline in mental and physical reliability." The Court said that the federal government had a legitimate interest in having a vigorous foreign service and that a mandatory retirement age was rationally related to that end.

2. Discrimination Based on Disability

The Supreme Court also has ruled that only rational basis review should be used for discrimination based on disability. City of Cleburne, Texas v. Cleburne Living Center, Inc., 473 U.S. 432 (1985), presented in section B, is the leading case. In *Cleburne*, the Supreme Court used the rational basis test to declare unconstitutional a city ordinance that required a special permit for the operation of a group home for the mentally disabled. The Court declared that "[t]o withstand equal protection review, legislation that distinguishes between the mentally retarded and others must be rationally related to a legitimate governmental purpose."

The Supreme Court has reaffirmed that only rational basis review is to be used for discrimination based on disability. In Heller v. Doe, 509 U.S. 312 (1993), the Supreme Court upheld a state law that allowed mentally retarded individuals to be civilly committed if there was clear and convincing evidence justifying institutionalization but required that there be proof beyond a reasonable doubt before an individual could be committed because of mental illness. In a five-to-four decision, the Supreme Court applied rational basis review and concluded that there were reasonable distinctions between the mentally retarded and the mentally ill.

The Court said that the state's law was constitutional because mental retardation is subject to more objective measures than mental illness. Also, the Court said that the "prevailing methods of treatment for [the] mentally retarded, as a general rule, are much less invasive than are those given the mentally ill."

Justice Blackmun dissented and argued for heightened scrutiny for laws that "discriminate against individuals with mental retardation." Justice Souter, joined by Justices O'Connor, Blackmun, and Stevens, contended that the law failed rational basis review. Souter said that proving mental retardation is not always easier than proving mental illness and that institutionalization and treatment of the mentally retarded also involves a substantial loss of freedom.

Although disability classifications receive only rational basis review under the Equal Protection Clause,[135] a federal statute broadly prohibits such discrimination: the Americans with Disabilities Act.[136]

3. Wealth Discrimination

For a time it appeared that the Court would use heightened scrutiny for laws discriminating against the poor. In Griffin v. Illinois, 351 U.S. 12 (1956), the Supreme Court held that it violated equal protection to deny free trial transcripts to indigent criminal defendants who were appealing their conviction. The Court said that "[i]n criminal trials a State can no more discriminate on account of poverty than on account of religion, race, or color." Likewise, in Harper v. Virginia Board of Elections, 383 U.S. 663 (1966), the Supreme Court declared unconstitutional a poll tax for state and local elections and said that "[l]ines drawn on the basis of wealth and property, like those of race, are traditionally disfavored."

Subsequently, however, the Supreme Court clearly held that only rational basis review should be used for wealth classifications. In Dandridge v. Williams, 397 U.S. 471 (1970), the Supreme Court upheld a state law that put a cap on welfare benefits to families regardless of their size. Children in larger families therefore received less per person than those in smaller families. The Supreme Court said that rational basis review was appropriate because the law related to "economics and social welfare." The Court thus accepted the state's interest in allocating scarce public benefits as sufficient to justify the law. The Court said that "the Constitution does not empower this Court to second-guess state officials charged with the difficult responsibility of allocating limited public welfare funds among the myriad of potential recipients."

In San Antonio Independent School District v. Rodriguez, 411 U.S. 1 (1973), presented in Chapter 8, the Supreme Court expressly held that poverty is not a suspect classification and that discrimination against the poor should only receive rational basis review. *Rodriguez* involved a challenge to Texas's system of relying heavily on local property taxes to pay for public education. The result was that poor areas taxed at high rates but still had little to spend on education. Wealthy areas could tax at low rates and had a great deal to spend on schooling. The plaintiffs argued, in part, that the disparity in funding discriminated against the poor in violation of the Equal Protection Clause.

The Supreme Court, in a five-to-four decision, held that discrimination against the poor does not warrant heightened scrutiny. The Court also rejected the claim that the law should be regarded as discriminating against the poor as a group. Justice Powell, writing for the Court, stated, "[A] cursory examination, however, demonstrates that neither of the two distinguishing characteristics of wealth classifications can be found here. First, in support of their charge that the system discriminates against the 'poor,' appellees have made no effort to

---

135. *See also* New York City Transit Authority v. Beazer, 440 U.S. 568 (1979) (using rational basis review for discrimination against methadone addicts), presented in section B.

136. 42 U.S.C. §§12101 *et seq.*

demonstrate that it operates to the peculiar disadvantage of any class fairly definable as indigent. . . . [T]here is no basis on the record in this case for assuming that the poorest people — defined by reference to any level of absolute impecunity — are concentrated in the poorest districts. Second, . . . lack of personal resources has not occasioned an absolute deprivation of the desired benefit."

A few years later, in Maher v. Roe, 432 U.S. 464 (1977), also presented in Chapter 8, the Supreme Court rejected an argument that the government violated equal protection when it refused to fund abortions, even though it was paying for childbirth and other medical care costs. The Court said that it "has never held that financial need alone identifies a suspect class for purposes of equal protection analysis."

On the one hand, the Court's refusal to find that poverty is a suspect classification can be justified by distinguishing that characteristic from those where heightened scrutiny is used. Poverty is not immutable, and most discrimination against the poor is a result of the effects of the law, rather than a product of intentional discrimination. Additionally, the Court clearly wanted to avoid creating a constitutional right to government benefits such as welfare, food, shelter, or medical care.

But the poor as a group do share many characteristics with groups that are protected by intermediate and strict scrutiny. The poor lack political power, especially in a political system where money is crucial for influence. Additionally, there is a long history of discrimination against the poor in many areas. Moreover, some prominent scholars have argued that there should be a right to minimum entitlements under the Constitution; every person should be assured of food, shelter, and medical care to survive.[137]

4. Discrimination Based on Sexual Orientation

In Romer v. Evans, 517 U.S. 620 (1996), presented in section B, the Supreme Court used the rational basis test to invalidate a Colorado initiative that encouraged discrimination based on sexual orientation. Colorado's Amendment 2 repealed all state and local laws that prohibited discrimination against gays, lesbians, and bisexuals. The popularly approved initiative also prevented future laws to protect these individuals. The Supreme Court found that Amendment 2 impermissibly discriminated based on sexual orientation. Justice Kennedy, writing for the Court, said, "Homosexuals, by state decree, are put in a solitary class with respect to transactions and relations in both the private and governmental spheres. The amendment withdraws from homosexuals, but no others, specific legal protection from the injuries caused by discrimination, and it forbids reinstatement of these laws and policies."

The Court said that the initiative failed even rational basis review. Justice Kennedy explained that "the amendment has the peculiar property of imposing a broad and undifferentiated disability on a single named group, an exceptional

---

137. *See, e.g.*, Charles L. Black, Jr., *Further Reflections on the Constitutional Justice of Livelihood*, 86 Colum. L. Rev. 1103 (1986); Peter Edelman, *The Next Century of Our Constitution: Rethinking Our Duty to the Poor*, 39 Hastings L.J. 1 (1987); Frank I. Michelman, *Foreword: On Protecting the Poor Through the Fourteenth Amendment*, 83 Harv. L. Rev. 7 (1969).

and . . . invalid form of legislation." The Court concluded that there was no legitimate purpose for denying gays, lesbians, and bisexuals the same use of the political process available to everyone else. Justice Kennedy observed that the only apparent purpose behind the law was "animosity toward the class of persons affected" and this fails even the rational basis test.

Romer v. Evans is significant because it is the first time the Court has invalidated discrimination based on sexual orientation. Although the Court used just rational basis review, the decision indicates at least some judicial willingness to protect gays, lesbians, and bisexuals from discrimination. *Romer* establishes that animus against gays and lesbians, even when presented as a purported "moral" basis for a law, is not sufficient to meet the rational basis test. Because *Romer* found the Colorado law unconstitutional under rational basis review, the Court had no need to consider whether heightened scrutiny is appropriate for discrimination based on sexual orientation.

In Lawrence v. Texas (2003), presented in the next chapter, the Court, relying on due process, struck down a state law prohibiting private consensual homosexual activity. The Court did not specify the level of scrutiny it was using.

CHAPTER

8

FUNDAMENTAL RIGHTS
UNDER DUE PROCESS AND
EQUAL PROTECTION

A. INTRODUCTION

THE CONCEPT OF FUNDAMENTAL RIGHTS

The Supreme Court has held that some liberties are so important that they are deemed to be "fundamental rights" and that generally the government cannot infringe them unless strict scrutiny is met; that is, the government's action must be necessary to achieve a compelling purpose. This chapter examines many of these liberties, including rights protecting family autonomy, procreation, sexual activity and sexual orientation, medical care decision making, travel, voting, and access to the courts. This chapter concludes by examining procedural due process. Freedom of speech and religious freedom also are deemed fundamental rights and are considered in Chapters 9 and 10, respectively. Criminal procedure protections — such as the Fourth Amendment's safeguard from unreasonable searches and seizure, the Fifth Amendment's protection from self-incrimination and double jeopardy, the Sixth Amendment's assurance of a speedy trial before an impartial jury, and the Eighth Amendment's right to bail and prohibition of cruel and unusual punishment — are beyond the scope of this book.

The relatively few claims of rights listed above trigger heightened scrutiny and require the government to meet strict scrutiny. Most claims of rights under equal protection or due process only receive minimal judicial scrutiny; that is, the government's action only has to meet the rational basis test and be shown to be rationally related to a legitimate government purpose. For example, as discussed in Chapter 6, claims of economic liberties under the Due Process Clause only receive rational basis review.

This chapter, though, examines those rights that are deemed fundamental. Of course, this chapter also will consider many examples where the Court has refused to recognize a particular right as fundamental and thus has used only rational basis review in upholding a law. The rights considered in this chapter share much in common. Almost all of these rights are not mentioned in the text of the Constitution.[1] Thus, as discussed hereafter, all raise the important issue of how the Court should decide whether a liberty should be regarded as a fundamental right. Also, for almost all of these rights, the Supreme Court has indicated that strict scrutiny should be used, which means that the government must justify its interference by proving that its action is necessary to achieve a compelling government purpose.

Almost all of these rights have been protected by the Court under the Due Process Clauses of the Fifth and Fourteenth Amendments and/or the Equal Protection Clause of the Fourteenth Amendment. Some of the rights have been protected solely under the Due Process Clause. For example, thus far, the Supreme Court has considered a constitutional right to refuse medical care as an aspect of the "liberty" protected in the Due Process Clause.[2] Other rights have so far been protected under the Equal Protection Clause. For example, the right to travel has been safeguarded under equal protection.[3] Also, the right to vote has been protected both under this clause and the Fifteenth Amendment that prohibits government racial discrimination concerning voting.[4]

Many of these rights, though, have been protected by the Court under both due process and equal protection. For example, the Court has invalidated state laws restricting access to contraceptives both as violating equal protection and as infringing the right to privacy.[5] In some cases, the justices disagree among themselves as to whether the right is protected under due process or equal protection. In Zablocki v. Redhail, 434 U.S. 374 (1978), presented below, the majority opinion found the right to marry to be a fundamental right protected under the Equal Protection Clause, but the concurring opinion used a due process approach.

Relatively little depends on whether the Court uses due process or equal protection as the basis for protecting a fundamental right. Under either provision, the Court must decide whether a claimed liberty is sufficiently important to be regarded as fundamental, even though it is not mentioned in the text of the Constitution. Also, once a right is deemed fundamental, under due process or equal protection, strict scrutiny is generally used.

The major difference between due process and equal protection as the basis for protecting fundamental rights is in how the constitutional arguments are

---

1. The only exception is the right to vote, which is protected by the Fifteenth Amendment. Additionally, however, the Supreme Court has said that the right to vote is a fundamental right protected under the Equal Protection Clause of the Fourteenth Amendment. *See, e.g.,* Harper v. Virginia State Bd. of Elections, 383 U.S. 663 (1966).

2. *See* Cruzan v. Director, Missouri Dept. of Health, 497 U.S. 261 (1990) (competent adults have the right, as part of liberty protected under the Due Process Clause, to refuse medical treatment) (discussed later).

3. *See, e.g.,* Shapiro v. Thompson, 394 U.S. 618 (1969) (residency requirements for receipt of welfare benefits violate the right to travel protected under the Equal Protection Clause). The right to travel is discussed later. It also has been recently protected under the Privileges or Immunities Clause of the Fourteenth Amendment. *See* Saenz v. Roe, 526 U.S. 489 (1999).

4. *See, e.g.,* Harper v. Virginia State Bd. of Elections, 383 U.S. 663 (1966) (poll taxes in state and local elections violate the Equal Protection Clause of the Fourteenth Amendment). The Twenty-Fourth Amendment outlaws poll taxes in federal elections.

5. Eisenstadt v. Baird, 405 U.S. 438 (1972) (finding that a law prohibiting distribution of contraceptives to unmarried individuals violated equal protection); Carey v. Population Services International, 431 U.S. 678 (1977) (declaring unconstitutional a law that provided that only a licensed pharmacist could provide contraceptives to persons over age 16 and that no one could provide them to those under age 16).

phrased. If a right is safeguarded under due process, the constitutional issue is whether the government's interference is justified by a sufficient purpose. But if the right is protected under equal protection, the issue is whether the government's discrimination as to who can exercise the right is justified by a sufficient purpose. Although the difference is generally just semantics and phrasing, there can be a real distinction: If a law denies the right to everyone, then due process would be the best grounds for analysis, but if a law denies a right to some, while allowing it to others, the discrimination can be challenged as offending equal protection or the violation of the right can be objected to under due process.

THE NINTH AMENDMENT

The Ninth Amendment is often mentioned in discussions of fundamental rights, especially rights not expressly mentioned in the text of the Constitution. The Ninth Amendment states: "The enumeration in the Constitution of certain rights, shall not be construed to disparage others retained by the people." The Supreme Court rarely has invoked the Ninth Amendment. A notable exception is Griswold v. Connecticut, 381 U.S. 479 (1965), presented below, in which Justice Goldberg, in a concurring opinion, reviewed the history of the Ninth Amendment and relied on it to justify invalidating a law prohibiting use of contraceptives.

The Ninth Amendment generally is not seen as the source of rights in that rights are not protected under it; there are no Ninth Amendment rights. Rather, the Ninth Amendment is used to provide a textual justification for the Court to protect nontextual rights, such as the right to privacy. From this perspective, the Ninth Amendment is not a repository of rights or even a provision that is itself interpreted but instead is a justification for the Court to safeguard unenumerated liberties.

PROCEDURAL DUE PROCESS

The existence of a right triggers two distinct burdens on the government. One is substantive; the government must justify an infringement by showing that its action is sufficiently related to an adequate justification. For example, when strict scrutiny is used, the substantive burden on the government is demonstrating that the law is necessary to achieve a compelling purpose. The other burden on the government is procedural. When the government takes away a person's life, liberty, or property, it must provide adequate procedures. Procedural due process is discussed in the final section of this chapter.

A simple example illustrates the concepts of substantive and procedural due process. As discussed below in section C, the Supreme Court has interpreted the word "liberty" in the Due Process Clause to mean that parents have a fundamental right to custody of their children. Substantive due process, as explained below, requires that the government show that terminating custody is necessary to achieve a compelling purpose. Procedural due process, as discussed in the final section, requires that the government provide notice and a hearing—procedures—before terminating custody.

Except for the final section on procedural due process, this chapter focuses on protection of substantive rights under due process and equal protection. In other words, the issue in all of these cases is whether the government adequately justifies its actions allegedly infringing fundamental rights.

B.   FRAMEWORK FOR ANALYZING FUNDAMENTAL RIGHTS

Litigation and judicial decision making in cases about individual rights can be understood as addressing one or more of four questions. First, is there a fundamental right? Second, is the right infringed? Third, is the government's action justified by a sufficient purpose? And fourth, are the means sufficiently related to the goal sought? These four questions arise in all areas concerning rights, including economic liberties discussed in Chapter 6 and First Amendment rights discussed in Chapters 9 and 10. Because these issues arise in cases throughout this chapter, the four questions are briefly examined here before consideration of particular rights.

FIRST ISSUE: IS THERE A FUNDAMENTAL RIGHT?

If a right is deemed fundamental, the government usually will be able to prevail only if it meets strict scrutiny, but if the right is not fundamental, generally only the rational basis test is applied. This is the framework for judicial review articulated in the famous *Carolene Products* more than a half century ago: The judiciary will defer to the legislature unless there is discrimination against a "discrete and insular" minority or infringement of a fundamental right.[6]

For example, in Washington v. Glucksberg, 521 U.S. 702 (1997), discussed hereafter, the crucial question was whether there was a fundamental right to physician-assisted suicide. If the Court had found such a right in the liberty of the Due Process Clause for terminally ill patients, a Washington law prohibiting aiding and abetting a suicide would have been upheld only if the state had met strict scrutiny. But the Court's refusal to find such a right meant that only rational basis review was used.

The constitutional interpretation debate, discussed in more detail in Chapter 1, has been primarily about how the Court should decide what rights are fundamental and particularly whether it should find fundamental rights that are not supported by the text or the clear intent of the framers. Many different theories have been advanced to explain when the Court should or shouldn't deem rights to be fundamental.

For example, originalists take the position that fundamental rights are limited to those liberties explicitly stated in the text or clearly intended by the framers. An originalist would say that the Court acts impermissibly and usurps the

---

6. United States v. Carolene Products Co., 304 U.S. 144, 152 n.4 (1938), discussed in detail in Chapter 6.

democratic process if it finds other rights to be fundamental. Nonoriginalism, in contrast, is the view that it is permissible for the Court to protect fundamental rights that are not enumerated in the Constitution or intended by its drafters.

Although, as described in Chapter 1, the debate often has been characterized as a dispute between originalists and nonoriginalists, many other theories also have been advanced for identifying fundamental rights. For example, in addition to strict originalism that limits the Court to rights stated in the text or intended by the framers, there also is moderate originalism, which is the view that the judiciary should implement the framers' general intent, but not necessarily their specific views.

Alternatively, at times, the Court often has looked to history and tradition in deciding what rights not mentioned in the text are fundamental. For instance, the Supreme Court has said that fundamental rights include those liberties that are "deeply rooted in this Nation's history and tradition."[7] In addition to the difficulty of deciding what counts as a sufficient tradition for recognizing a right as fundamental, there also is the question of the abstraction at which the right is stated. At a sufficiently general level of abstraction, any liberty can be justified as consistent with the nation's traditions. At a very specific level of abstraction, few nontextual rights would be justified.[8]

There are many other theories as well for deciding what is a fundamental right. Some argue that the Court's preeminent role is perfecting the processes of government and that the Court should only recognize nontextual rights that concern ensuring adequate representation and the effective operation of the political process.[9] Others argue that the Court should use natural law principles in deciding what rights to protect as fundamental.[10] Still other scholars maintain that the Court should recognize nontextual fundamental rights that are supported by a deeply embedded moral consensus that exists in society.[11]

These theories, and the arguments for and against them, are discussed in Chapter 1. Throughout this chapter an underlying question is whether a particular liberty should be deemed a fundamental right, and that raises the methodological question of how the Court should decide this issue. Inevitably, it provokes debate about the proper role of an unelected judiciary in a democratic society and also about what activities are so important that the courts should find a fundamental right to exist.

SECOND ISSUE: IS THE CONSTITUTIONAL RIGHT INFRINGED?

If there is a fundamental right, the next question must be: Has the government infringed the right? There, of course, is no doubt that a constitutional right is infringed and the government's action must be justified when the

---

7. Moore v. City of East Cleveland, 431 U.S. 494, 503 (1977).

8. Justice Scalia, for example, has argued that nontextual rights should be protected under the Due Process Clause only if there is a tradition, stated at the most specific level of abstraction, for protecting the rights. *See* Michael H. v. Gerald D., 491 U.S. 110, 127 n.6 (1989). For a powerful criticism of this view, *see* Laurence Tribe & Michael Dorf, *On Reading the Constitution* (1991).

9. *See, e.g.,* John Hart Ely, *Democracy and Distrust* (1980).

10. *See, e.g.,* Harry V. Jaffa, *Original Intent and the Framers of the Constitution* (1994).

11. *See, e.g.,* Harry H. Wellington, *Common Law Rules and Constitutional Double Standards: Some Notes on Adjudication,* 83 Yale L.J. 221, 284 (1973).

exercise of the right is prohibited. For example, if there is a fundamental right to purchase and use contraceptives, a law that outlaws all distribution and use of birth control obviously is an infringement. But when is burdening the exercise of a fundamental right also to be considered an infringement requiring the application of strict scrutiny?[12]

The Supreme Court has said that in evaluating whether there is a violation of a right it considers "[t]he directness and substantiality of the interference."[13] But there has been surprisingly little discussion of what constitutes a direct and substantial interference with a right.

Many cases, especially in the abortion context, have forced the Court to consider what constitutes an infringement of a right. Is denying public funding for abortions an infringement?[14] Is a waiting period for abortions or a requirement for spousal notification an infringement?[15] For any right the same basic issue can emerge: Under what circumstances is the government's action an infringement?

THIRD ISSUE: IS THERE A SUFFICIENT JUSTIFICATION FOR THE GOVERNMENT'S INFRINGEMENT OF A RIGHT?

If a right is deemed fundamental, the government must present a compelling interest to justify an infringement. Alternatively, if a right is not fundamental, only a legitimate purpose is required for the law to be sustained.

The Supreme Court never has articulated criteria for determining whether a claimed purpose is to be deemed "compelling." The most that can be said is that the government has the burden of persuading the Court that a truly vital interest is served by the law in question. For example, the Court has recognized as "compelling" interests such as winning a war[16] and assuring that children receive adequate care.[17]

FOURTH ISSUE: IS THE MEANS SUFFICIENTLY RELATED TO THE PURPOSE?

Under strict scrutiny it is not enough for the government to prove a compelling purpose behind a law; the government also must show that the law is *necessary* to achieve the objective. This requires that the government prove that it could not attain the goal through any means less restrictive of the right. In comparison, under rational basis review, the means only has to be a

12. For an excellent discussion of this issue, *see* Michael C. Dorf, *Incidental Burdens on Fundamental Rights*, 109 Harv. L. Rev. 1175 (1996).

13. Zablocki v. Redhail, 434 U.S. 374, 387 n.12 (1978), discussed later; Lyng v. Castillo, 477 U.S. 635, 638 (1986).

14. *See, e.g.*, Harris v. McRae, 448 U.S. 297 (1980); Maher v. Roe, 432 U.S. 464 (1977), discussed later.

15. *See* Planned Parenthood of Southern Pennsylvania v. Casey, 505 U.S. 833 (1992) (24-hour waiting period is constitutional; spousal notification requirements are unconstitutional).

16. *See* Korematsu v. United States, 323 U.S. 214 (1944) (justifying evacuation of Japanese Americans based on wartime necessity), discussed in Chapter 7.

17. *See, e.g.*, Zablocki v. Redhail, 434 U.S. 374 (1978) (accepting the need to protect children as a compelling interest), discussed later.

reasonable way to achieve the goal and the government is not required to use the least restrictive alternative.

There is no formula for deciding whether a means is necessary or whether a less restrictive means can suffice. The government's burden when there is an infringement of a fundamental right is to prove that no other alternative, less intrusive of the right, can work.

In some cases, all four of these issues are in controversy. In other cases, the focus might be on just one or two of the questions. Inevitably, all four require that the judiciary make value choices: What is important enough to be a fundamental right; what is intrusive enough to be deemed an invasion; what is significant enough to be regarded as a compelling interest; and what is narrowly tailored enough to be regarded as a necessary means? These four questions recur throughout the cases discussed in this chapter.

C. CONSTITUTIONAL PROTECTION FOR FAMILY AUTONOMY

1. *The Right to Marry*

The Supreme Court first recognized the right to marry as a fundamental right protected under the liberty of the Due Process Clause in Loving v. Virginia.

LOVING v. VIRGINIA, 388 U.S. 1 (1967): Chief Justice WARREN delivered the opinion of the Court.

This case presents a constitutional question never addressed by this Court: whether a statutory scheme adopted by the State of Virginia to prevent marriages between persons solely on the basis of racial classifications violates the Equal Protection and Due Process Clauses of the Fourteenth Amendment. For reasons which seem to us to reflect the central meaning of those constitutional commands, we conclude that these statutes cannot stand consistently with the Fourteenth Amendment.

In June 1958, two residents of Virginia, Mildred Jeter, a Negro woman, and Richard Loving, a white man, were married in the District of Columbia pursuant to its laws. Shortly after their marriage, the Lovings returned to Virginia and established their marital abode in Caroline County. At the October Term, 1958, of the Circuit Court of Caroline County, a grand jury issued an indictment charging the Lovings with violating Virginia's ban on interracial marriages. On January 6, 1959, the Lovings pleaded guilty to the charge and were sentenced to one year in jail; however, the trial judge suspended the sentence for a period of 25 years on the condition that the Lovings leave the State and not return to Virginia together for 25 years. He stated in an opinion that:

"Almighty God created the races white, black, yellow, malay and red, and he placed them on separate continents. And but for the interference with his arrangement there would be no cause for such marriages. The fact that he separated the races shows that he did not intend for the races to mix."

After their convictions, the Lovings took up residence in the District of Columbia. On November 6, 1963, they filed a motion in the state trial court to vacate the judgment and set aside the sentence on the ground that the statutes which they had violated were repugnant to the Fourteenth Amendment. The Supreme Court of Appeals upheld the constitutionality of the antimiscegenation statutes and, after modifying the sentence, affirmed the convictions.

Virginia is now one of 16 States which prohibit and punish marriages on the basis of racial classifications. Penalties for miscegenation arose as an incident to slavery and have been common in Virginia since the colonial period.

[The Supreme Court found that the Virginia law was impermissible race discrimination in violation of the Equal Protection Clause of the Fourteenth Amendment. This portion of the opinion is presented in Chapter 7.]

These statutes also deprive the Lovings of liberty without due process of law in violation of the Due Process Clause of the Fourteenth Amendment. The freedom to marry has long been recognized as one of the vital personal rights essential to the orderly pursuit of happiness by free men.

Marriage is one of the "basic civil rights of man," fundamental to our very existence and survival. Skinner v. State of Oklahoma (1942). To deny this fundamental freedom on so unsupportable a basis as the racial classifications embodied in these statutes, classifications so directly subversive of the principle of equality at the heart of the Fourteenth Amendment, is surely to deprive all the State's citizens of liberty without due process of law. The Fourteenth Amendment requires that the freedom of choice to marry not be restricted by invidious racial discriminations. Under our Constitution, the freedom to marry, or not marry, a person of another race resides with the individual and cannot be infringed by the State.

The most extended Supreme Court discussion of the right to marry is in Zablocki v. Redhail.

ZABLOCKI v. REDHAIL
434 U.S. 378 (1978)

Justice MARSHALL delivered the opinion of the Court.

At issue in this case is the constitutionality of a Wisconsin statute, §245.10, which provides that members of a certain class of Wisconsin residents may not marry, within the State or elsewhere, without first obtaining a court order granting permission to marry. The class is defined by the statute to include any "Wisconsin resident having minor issue not in his custody and which he is under obligation to support by any court order or judgment." The statute specifies that court permission cannot be granted unless the marriage applicant submits proof of compliance with the support obligation and, in addition, demonstrates that the children covered by the support order "are not then and are not likely thereafter to become public charges." No marriage license may lawfully be issued in Wisconsin to a person covered by the statute, except upon court order; any marriage entered into without compliance is declared void; and persons acquiring marriage licenses in violation of the section are subject to criminal penalties.

I

Appellee Redhail is a Wisconsin resident who, under the terms of §245.10, is unable to enter into a lawful marriage in Wisconsin or elsewhere so long as he maintains his Wisconsin residency. The facts, according to the stipulation filed by the parties in the District Court, are as follows. In January 1972, when appellee was a minor and a high school student, a paternity action was instituted against him in Milwaukee County Court, alleging that he was the father of a baby girl born out of wedlock on July 5, 1971. After he appeared and admitted that he was the child's father, the court entered an order on May 12, 1972, adjudging appellee the father and ordering him to pay $109 per month as support for the child until she reached 18 years of age. From May 1972 until August 1974, appellee was unemployed and indigent, and consequently was unable to make any support payments.

On September 27, 1974, appellee filed an application for a marriage license with appellant Zablocki, the County Clerk of Milwaukee County, and a few days later the application was denied on the sole ground that appellee had not obtained a court order granting him permission to marry, as required by §245.10. Although appellee did not petition a state court thereafter, it is stipulated that he would not have been able to satisfy either of the statutory prerequisites for an order granting permission to marry. First, he had not satisfied his support obligations to his illegitimate child, and as of December 1974 there was an arrearage in excess of $3,700. Second, the child had been a public charge since her birth, receiving benefits under the Aid to Families with Dependent Children program. It is stipulated that the child's benefit payments were such that she would have been a public charge even if appellee had been current in his support payments.

II

In evaluating §245.10 under the Equal Protection Clause, "we must first determine what burden of justification the classification created thereby must meet, by looking to the nature of the classification and the individual interests affected." Since our past decisions make clear that the right to marry is of fundamental importance, and since the classification at issue here significantly interferes with the exercise of that right, we believe that "critical examination" of the state interests advanced in support of the classification is required.

The leading decision of this Court on the right to marry is Loving v. Virginia (1967). Although *Loving* arose in the context of racial discrimination, prior and subsequent decisions of this Court confirm that the right to marry is of fundamental importance for all individuals. Long ago, in Maynard v. Hill (1888), the Court characterized marriage as "the most important relation in life," and as "the foundation of the family and of society, without which there would be neither civilization nor progress." In Meyer v. Nebraska (1923), the Court recognized that the right "to marry, establish a home and bring up children" is a central part of the liberty protected by the Due Process Clause, and in Skinner v. Oklahoma (1942), marriage was described as "fundamental to the very existence and survival of the race."

More recent decisions have established that the right to marry is part of the fundamental "right of privacy" implicit in the Fourteenth Amendment's Due Process Clause. In Griswold v. Connecticut (1965), the Court observed: "We deal with a right of privacy older than the Bill of Rights — older than our political parties, older than our school system. Marriage is a coming together for better or for worse, hopefully enduring, and intimate to the degree of being sacred. It is an association that promotes a way of life, not causes; a harmony in living, not political faiths; a bilateral loyalty, not commercial or social projects. Yet it is an association for as noble a purpose as any involved in our prior decisions." Cases subsequent to *Griswold* and *Loving* have routinely categorized the decision to marry as among the personal decisions protected by the right of privacy.

Further support for the fundamental importance of marriage is found in our decisions dealing with rights of access to courts in civil cases. In Boddie v. Connecticut (1971), we wrote that "marriage involves interests of basic importance in our society," and held that filing fees for divorce actions violated the due process rights of indigents unable to pay the fees.

It is not surprising that the decision to marry has been placed on the same level of importance as decisions relating to procreation, childbirth, child rearing, and family relationships. As the facts of this case illustrate, it would make little sense to recognize a right of privacy with respect to other matters of family life and not with respect to the decision to enter the relationship that is the foundation of the family in our society. The woman whom appellee desired to marry had a fundamental right to seek an abortion of their expected child, or to bring the child into life to suffer the myriad social, if not economic, disabilities that the status of illegitimacy brings. Surely, a decision to marry and raise the child in a traditional family setting must receive equivalent protection. And, if appellee's right to procreate means anything at all, it must imply some right to enter the only relationship in which the State of Wisconsin allows sexual relations legally to take place.

By reaffirming the fundamental character of the right to marry, we do not mean to suggest that every state regulation which relates in any way to the incidents of or prerequisites for marriage must be subjected to rigorous scrutiny. To the contrary, reasonable regulations that do not significantly interfere with decisions to enter into the marital relationship may legitimately be imposed. See Califano v. Jobst.

The statutory classification at issue here, however, clearly does interfere directly and substantially with the right to marry. Under the challenged statute, no Wisconsin resident in the affected class may marry in Wisconsin or elsewhere without a court order, and marriages contracted in violation of the statute are both void and punishable as criminal offenses. Some of those in the affected class, like appellee, will never be able to obtain the necessary court order, because they either lack the financial means to meet their support obligations or cannot prove that their children will not become public charges. These persons are absolutely prevented from getting married. Many others, able in theory to satisfy the statute's requirements, will be sufficiently burdened by having to do so that they will in effect be coerced into forgoing their right to marry. And even those who can be persuaded to meet the statute's requirements suffer a serious intrusion into their freedom of choice in an area in which we have held such freedom to be fundamental.

III

When a statutory classification significantly interferes with the exercise of a fundamental right, it cannot be upheld unless it is supported by sufficiently important state interests and is closely tailored to effectuate only those interests. Appellant asserts that two interests are served by the challenged statute: the permission-to-marry proceeding furnishes an opportunity to counsel the applicant as to the necessity of fulfilling his prior support obligations; and the welfare of the out-of-custody children is protected. We may accept for present purposes that these are legitimate and substantial interests, but, since the means selected by the State for achieving these interests unnecessarily impinge on the right to marry, the statute cannot be sustained.

There is evidence that the challenged statute, as originally introduced in the Wisconsin Legislature, was intended merely to establish a mechanism whereby persons with support obligations to children from prior marriages could be counseled before they entered into new marital relationships and incurred further support obligations. Court permission to marry was to be required, but apparently permission was automatically to be granted after counseling was completed. The statute actually enacted, however, does not expressly require or provide for any counseling whatsoever, nor for any automatic granting of permission to marry by the court, and thus it can hardly be justified as a means for ensuring counseling of the persons within its coverage. Even assuming that counseling does take place — a fact as to which there is no evidence in the record — this interest obviously cannot support the withholding of court permission to marry once counseling is completed.

[Nor does a] "collection device" rationale justify the statute's broad infringement on the right to marry. First, with respect to individuals who are unable to meet the statutory requirements, the statute merely prevents the applicant from getting married, without delivering any money at all into the hands of the applicant's prior children. More importantly, regardless of the applicant's ability or willingness to meet the statutory requirements, the State already has numerous other means for exacting compliance with support obligations, means that are at least as effective as the instant statute's and yet do not impinge upon the right to marry. Under Wisconsin law, whether the children are from a prior marriage or were born out of wedlock, court-determined support obligations may be enforced directly via wage assignments, civil contempt proceedings, and criminal penalties.

There is also some suggestion that §245.10 protects the ability of marriage applicants to meet support obligations to prior children by preventing the applicants from incurring new support obligations. But the challenged provisions of §245.10 are grossly underinclusive with respect to this purpose, since they do not limit in any way new financial commitments by the applicant other than those arising out of the contemplated marriage. The statutory classification is substantially overinclusive as well: Given the possibility that the new spouse will actually better the applicant's financial situation, by contributing income from a job or otherwise, the statute in many cases may prevent affected individuals from improving their ability to satisfy their prior support obligations.

The statutory classification created by §245.10 thus cannot be justified by the interests advanced in support of it.

Justice STEWART, concurring in the judgment.

I cannot join the opinion of the Court. To hold, as the Court does, that the Wisconsin statute violates the Equal Protection Clause seems to me to misconceive the meaning of that constitutional guarantee. The Equal Protection Clause deals not with substantive rights or freedoms but with invidiously discriminatory classifications. The problem in this case is not one of discriminatory classifications, but of unwarranted encroachment upon a constitutionally protected freedom. I think that the Wisconsin statute is unconstitutional because it exceeds the bounds of permissible state regulation of marriage, and invades the sphere of liberty protected by the Due Process Clause of the Fourteenth Amendment.

I do not agree with the Court that there is a "right to marry" in the constitutional sense. That right, or more accurately that privilege, is under our federal system peculiarly one to be defined and limited by state law. A State may not only "significantly interfere with decisions to enter into marital relationship," but may in many circumstances absolutely prohibit it. Surely, for example, a State may legitimately say that no one can marry his or her sibling, that no one can marry who is not at least 14 years old, that no one can marry without first passing an examination for venereal disease, or that no one can marry who has a living husband or wife. But, just as surely, in regulating the intimate human relationship of marriage, there is a limit beyond which a State may not constitutionally go.

The Constitution does not specifically mention freedom to marry, but it is settled that the "liberty" protected by the Due Process Clause of the Fourteenth Amendment embraces more than those freedoms expressly enumerated in the Bill of Rights. And the decisions of this Court have made clear that freedom of personal choice in matters of marriage and family life is one of the liberties so protected.

It is evident that the Wisconsin law now before us directly abridges that freedom. The question is whether the state interests that support the abridgment can overcome the substantive protections of the Constitution. The Wisconsin law makes permission to marry turn on the payment of money in support of one's children by a previous marriage or liaison. Those who cannot show both that they have kept up with their support obligations and that their children are not and will not become wards of the State are altogether prohibited from marrying.

The Wisconsin law makes no allowance for the truly indigent. The State flatly denies a marriage license to anyone who cannot afford to fulfill his support obligations and keep his children from becoming wards of the State. We may assume that the State has legitimate interests in collecting delinquent support payments and in reducing its welfare load. We may also assume that, as applied to those who can afford to meet the statute's financial requirements but choose not to do so, the law advances the State's objectives in ways superior to other means available to the State. The fact remains that some people simply cannot afford to meet the statute's financial requirements. To deny these people permission to marry penalizes them for failing to do that which they cannot do.

Insofar as it applies to indigents, the state law is an irrational means of achieving these objectives of the State.

Justice REHNQUIST, dissenting.

I reject the Court's conclusion that marriage is the sort of "fundamental right" which must invariably trigger the strictest judicial scrutiny. I would view this legislative judgment in the light of the traditional presumption of validity. I think that under the Equal Protection Clause the statute need pass only the "rational basis test," and that under the Due Process Clause it need only be shown that it bears a rational relation to a constitutionally permissible objective. Williamson v. Lee Optical Co. (1955).

The statute so viewed is a permissible exercise of the State's power to regulate family life and to assure the support of minor children, despite its possible imprecision in the extreme cases envisioned in the concurring opinions.

The opinions in *Zablocki* discuss two earlier cases, one of which, Boddie v. Connecticut, protected the right to marry, and the other, Califano v. Jobst, found that a state law did not interfere with that right. In Boddie v. Connecticut, 401 U.S. 371 (1971), the Court ruled that a state law requiring the payment of filing fees and court costs to receive a divorce violated indigent individuals' due process rights. At the outset of its analysis, the Supreme Court observed, "As this Court on more than one occasion has recognized, marriage involves interests of basic importance in our society." Obviously, preventing individuals from obtaining a divorce precludes them from exercising their right to marry someone else.

Not every law that impacts on the right to marry has been declared unconstitutional. As explained above, the Supreme Court has said that there must be a direct and substantial interference with the right in order to trigger heightened scrutiny. In Califano v. Jobst, 434 U.S. 47 (1977), the Court upheld the constitutionality of a provision of the Social Security Act that terminated benefits for disabled children, who were covered as dependents of wage earners, at the time they got married. The law had an exception if a child married a person who also was entitled to benefits under the act.

The Court acknowledged that the termination of benefits might have an impact on a person's desire to marry, but the Court said that a "general rule is not rendered invalid simply because some persons who might otherwise have married were deterred by the rule or because some who did marry were burdened thereby." The Court unanimously concluded that it was permissible for Congress to assume that "a married person is less likely to be dependent on his parents for support than one who is unmarried."

Similarly, in Bowen v. Owens, 476 U.S. 340 (1986), the Court rejected a challenge to another provision of the Social Security Act. The act provided survivor benefits from a wage earner's account to a widowed spouse who remarried after age 60 but denied such benefits to a similarly situated divorced widowed spouse. The law in essence created a divorce penalty allowing nondivorced widowed spouses to continue to receive benefits but denying continuing benefits to divorced spouses who remarried.

The Court said that "it was rational for Congress to assume that divorced widowed spouses are generally less dependent upon the resources of their former spouses than are widows and widowers." Thus, "[p]resumably Congress concluded that remarriage sufficiently reduced that lesser dependency to the point where it could conclude that benefits no longer were appropriate."

Califano v. Jobst and Bowen v. Owens reflect the principle that a right is not violated unless there has been a direct and substantial interference. Also, cases such as *Califano* and *Bowen* undoubtedly are, in part, about judicial deference to legislative decisions about how to allocate scarce funds in a program such as Social Security. Lines inevitably must be drawn, and the Court is understandably reluctant to second-guess the legislature unless there is discrimination against a suspect class or a clear infringement of a fundamental right. These cases, however, in no way deny that the right to marry is regarded as a fundamental right and that generally the government must meet strict scrutiny before interfering with this basic liberty.

The United States Supreme Court has not yet ruled as to whether the right to marry includes a right to same-sex marriage. A number of state supreme courts have found a right under their state constitutions, and several states adopted initiatives allowing marriage equality for gays and lesbians, while many states have amended their state constitutions to declare that marriage must be between a man and a woman. The Court is scheduled to hear two cases in early 2013 concerning marriage equality: United States v. Windsor, 699 F.3d 169 (2d Cir. October 18, 2012), *cert. granted*, 133 S. Ct. 786 (Dec. 7, 2012) (whether Section 3 of the Defense of Marriage Act—for purposes of federal benefits marriage must be between a man and a woman—is constitutional), and Hollingsworth v. Perry, 671 F.3d 1052 (9th Cir. 2012), *cert. granted*, 132 S. Ct.—(Dec. 7, 2012) (whether California's Proposition 8, which amended the California Constitution to declare that marriage in the state must be between a man and a woman, is constitutional).

2. The Right to Custody of One's Children

The Supreme Court has recognized that parents have a fundamental right to custody of their children. The Court has remarked that a "natural parent's desire for and right to the companionship, care, custody, and management of his or her children is an interest far more precious than any property right."[18] The Court has made it clear that there must be a very substantial reason before parental custody can be terminated. The Court observed, "We have little doubt that the Due Process Clause would be offended 'if a State were to attempt to force the breakup of a natural family, over the objection of the parents and their children, without some showing of unfitness and for the sole reason that to do so was thought to be in the children's best interest.'"[19]

STANLEY v. ILLINOIS, 405 U.S. 645 (1972): Justice WHITE delivered the opinion of the Court.

Joan Stanley lived with Peter Stanley intermittently for 18 years, during which time they had three children. When Joan Stanley died, Peter Stanley lost not

---

18. Santosky v. Kramer, 455 U.S. 745, 758-759 (1982) (citations omitted).
19. Quilloin v. Walcott, 434 U.S. 246, 255 (1978) (quoting Smith v. Organization of Foster Families, 431 U.S. 816, 862-863 (1977)) (Stewart, J., concurring in the judgment).

only her but also his children. Under Illinois law, the children of unwed fathers become wards of the State upon the death of the mother. Accordingly, upon Joan Stanley's death, in a dependency proceeding instituted by the State of Illinois, Stanley's children were declared wards of the State and placed with court-appointed guardians. Stanley appealed, claiming that he had never been shown to be an unfit parent and that since married fathers and unwed mothers could not be deprived of their children without such a showing, he had been deprived of the equal protection of the laws guaranteed him by the Fourteenth Amendment. The Illinois Supreme Court accepted the fact that Stanley's own unfitness had not been established but rejected the equal protection claim, holding that Stanley could properly be separated from his children upon proof of the single fact that he and the dead mother had not been married. Stanley's actual fitness as a father was irrelevant. Stanley presses his equal protection claim here. The State continues to respond that unwed fathers are presumed unfit to raise their children and that it is unnecessary to hold individualized hearings to determine whether particular fathers are in fact unfit parents before they are separated from their children.

The Court has frequently emphasized the importance of the family. The rights to conceive and to raise one's children have been deemed "essential," Meyer v. Nebraska (1923), "basic civil rights of man," Skinner v. Oklahoma (1942), and "(r)ights far more precious . . . than property rights," May v. Anderson (1953). "It is cardinal with us that the custody, care and nurture of the child reside first in the parents, whose primary function and freedom include preparation for obligations the state can neither supply nor hinder." Prince v. Massachusetts (1944). The integrity of the family unit has found protection in the Due Process Clause of the Fourteenth Amendment, the Equal Protection Clause of the Fourteenth Amendment, and the Ninth Amendment.

Nor has the law refused to recognize those family relationships unlegitimized by a marriage ceremony. The Court has declared unconstitutional a state statute denying natural, but illegitimate, children a wrongful-death action for the death of their mother, emphasizing that such children cannot be denied the right of other children because familial bonds in such cases were often as warm, enduring, and important as those arising within a more formally organized family unit. Levy v. Louisiana (1968). These authorities make it clear that, at the least, Stanley's interest in retaining custody of his children is cognizable and substantial.

We do not question the assertion that neglectful parents may be separated from their children. But we are here not asked to evaluate the legitimacy of the state ends, rather, to determine whether the means used to achieve these ends are constitutionally defensible. What is the state interest in separating children from fathers without a hearing designed to determine whether the father is unfit in a particular disputed case? We observe that the State registers no gain towards its declared goals when it separates children from the custody of fit parents. Indeed, if Stanley is a fit father, the State spites its own articulated goals when it needlessly separates him from his family.

It may be, as the State insists, that most unmarried fathers are unsuitable and neglectful parents. It may also be that Stanley is such a parent and that his children should be placed in other hands. But all unmarried fathers are not in this category; some are wholly suited to have custody of their children. This much the State readily concedes, and nothing in this record indicates that Stanley is or has been a neglectful father who has not cared for his children. Given the opportunity to make his case, Stanley may have been seen to be deserving of custody of his offspring. Had this been so, the State's statutory policy would have been furthered by leaving custody in him.

Procedure by presumption is always cheaper and easier than individualized determination. But when, as here, the procedure forecloses the determinative issues of competence and care, when it explicitly disdains present realities in deference to past formalities, it needlessly risks running roughshod over the important interests of both parent and child. It therefore cannot stand.

In other cases, however, the Supreme Court has ruled that the government can terminate the rights of unmarried fathers without being required to provide due process. Lehr v. Robertson, 463 U.S. 248 (1983), involved a nonmarital father who had not supported his two-year-old child and had not registered his interest in paternity in a putative father's registry maintained by the state. The Supreme Court held that the state could terminate the father's parental rights without providing notice or a hearing.

The Court distinguished *Stanley* because in that case the father had been actively involved in his children's lives. The Court observed, "When an unwed father demonstrates a full commitment to the responsibilities of parenthood by coming forward to participate in the rearing of his child, his interest in personal contact with his child acquires substantial protection under the due process clause. . . . But the mere existence of a biological link does not merit equivalent constitutional protection."

One of the most important cases limiting the rights of unmarried fathers, and one of the most significant recent Supreme Court decisions concerning substantive due process, is Michael H. v. Gerald D.

MICHAEL H. v. GERALD D.
491 U.S. 110 (1989)

Justice SCALIA announced the judgment of the Court and delivered an opinion, in which the Chief Justice joins, and in all but footnote 6 of which Justice O'CONNOR and Justice KENNEDY join.

Under California law, a child born to a married woman living with her husband is presumed to be a child of the marriage. The presumption of legitimacy may be rebutted only by the husband or wife, and then only in limited circumstances. The instant appeal presents the claim that this presumption infringes upon the due process rights of a man who wishes to establish his paternity of a child born to the wife of another man, and the claim that it infringes upon the constitutional right of the child to maintain a relationship with her natural father.

I

The facts of this case are, we must hope, extraordinary. On May 9, 1976, in Las Vegas, Nevada, Carole D., an international model, and Gerald D., a top executive in a French oil company, were married. The couple established a home in Playa del Rey, California, in which they resided as husband and wife when one or the other was not out of the country on business. In the summer of 1978, Carole became involved in an adulterous affair with a neighbor, Michael H. In September 1980, she conceived a child, Victoria D., who was born on May 11, 1981. Gerald was listed as father on the birth certificate and has always held Victoria out to the world as his daughter. Soon after delivery of the child, however, Carole informed Michael that she believed he might be the father.

In the first three years of her life, Victoria remained always with Carole, but found herself within a variety of quasi-family units. In October 1981, Gerald moved to New York City to pursue his business interests, but Carole chose to remain in California. At the end of that month, Carole and Michael had blood tests of themselves and Victoria, which showed a 98.07% probability that Michael was Victoria's father. In January 1982, Carole visited Michael in St. Thomas, where his primary business interests were based. There Michael held Victoria out as his child. In March, however, Carole left Michael and returned to California, where she took up residence with yet another man, Scott K. Later that spring, and again in the summer, Carole and Victoria spent time with Gerald in New York City, as well as on vacation in Europe. In the fall, they returned to Scott in California.

In November 1982, rebuffed in his attempts to visit Victoria, Michael filed a filiation action in California Superior Court to establish his paternity and right to visitation. In March 1983, the court appointed an attorney and guardian ad litem to represent Victoria's interests. Victoria then filed a cross-complaint asserting that if she had more than one psychological or de facto father, she was entitled to maintain her filial relationship, with all of the attendant rights, duties, and obligations, with both.

In May 1983, Carole filed a motion for summary judgment. During this period, from March through July 1983, Carole was again living with Gerald in New York. In August, however, she returned to California, became involved once again with Michael, and instructed her attorneys to remove the summary judgment motion from the calendar. For the ensuing eight months, when Michael was not in St. Thomas he lived with Carole and Victoria in Carole's apartment in Los Angeles and held Victoria out as his daughter. In April 1984, Carole and Michael signed a stipulation that Michael was Victoria's natural father. Carole left Michael the next month, however, and instructed her attorneys not to file the stipulation. In June 1984, Carole reconciled with Gerald and joined him in New York, where they now live with Victoria and two other children since born into the marriage.

In May 1984, Michael and Victoria, through her guardian ad litem, sought visitation rights for Michael. To assist in determining whether visitation would be in Victoria's best interests, the Superior Court appointed a psychologist to evaluate Victoria, Gerald, Michael, and Carole. The psychologist recommended that Carole retain sole custody, but that Michael be allowed continued contact with Victoria pursuant to a restricted visitation schedule.

On October 19, 1984, Gerald, who had intervened in the action, moved for summary judgment on the ground that under Cal. Evid. Code §621 there were no triable issues of fact as to Victoria's paternity. This law provides that "the issue of a wife cohabiting with her husband, who is not impotent or sterile, is conclusively presumed to be a child of the marriage." The presumption may be rebutted by blood tests, but only if a motion for such tests is made, within two years from the date of the child's birth, either by the husband or, if the natural father has filed an affidavit acknowledging paternity, by the wife.

On January 28, 1985, having found that affidavits submitted by Carole and Gerald sufficed to demonstrate that the two were cohabiting at conception and birth and that Gerald was neither sterile nor impotent, the Superior Court granted Gerald's motion for summary judgment, rejecting Michael's and Victoria's challenges to the constitutionality of §621. The court also denied their motions for continued visitation.

II

We address first the claims of Michael. At the outset, it is necessary to clarify what he sought and what he was denied. California law, like nature itself, makes no provision for dual fatherhood. Michael was seeking to be declared the father of Victoria. The immediate benefit he evidently sought to obtain from that status was visitation rights. But if Michael were successful in being declared the father, other rights would follow — most importantly, the right to be considered as the parent who should have custody, a status which "embrace[s] the sum of parental rights with respect to the rearing of a child, including the child's care; the right to the child's services and earnings; the right to direct the child's activities; the right to make decisions regarding the control, education, and health of the child; and the right, as well as the duty, to prepare the child for additional obligations, which includes the teaching of moral standards, religious beliefs, and elements of good citizenship."

Michael contends as a matter of substantive due process that, because he has established a parental relationship with Victoria, protection of Gerald's and Carole's marital union is an insufficient state interest to support termination of that relationship. This argument is, of course, predicated on the assertion that Michael has a constitutionally protected liberty interest in his relationship with Victoria.

It is an established part of our constitutional jurisprudence that the term "liberty" in the Due Process Clause extends beyond freedom from physical restraint. Without that core textual meaning as a limitation, defining the scope of the Due Process Clause "has at times been a treacherous field for this Court," giving "reason for concern lest the only limits to . . . judicial intervention become the predilections of those who happen at the time to be Members of this Court."

In an attempt to limit and guide interpretation of the Clause, we have insisted not merely that the interest denominated as a "liberty" be "fundamental" (a concept that, in isolation, is hard to objectify), but also that it be an interest traditionally protected by our society. As we have put it, the Due Process Clause affords only those protections "so rooted in the traditions and conscience of our people as to be ranked as fundamental." Snyder v. Massachusetts (1934) (Cardozo, J.). Our cases reflect "continual insistence upon respect for the teachings of history [and] solid recognition of the basic values that underlie our society. . . ." Griswold v. Connecticut (1965) (Harlan, J., concurring in judgment).

This insistence that the asserted liberty interest be rooted in history and tradition is evident, as elsewhere, in our cases according constitutional protection to certain parental rights. Michael reads the landmark case of Stanley v. Illinois (1972), and the subsequent cases as establishing that a liberty interest is created by biological fatherhood plus an established parental relationship—factors that exist in the present case as well. We think that distorts the rationale of those cases. As we view them, they rest not upon such isolated factors but upon the historic respect—indeed, sanctity would not be too strong a term—tradition-ally accorded to the relationships that develop within the unitary family.

Thus, the legal issue in the present case reduces to whether the relationship between persons in the situation of Michael and Victoria has been treated as a protected family unit under the historic practices of our society, or whether on any other basis it has been accorded special protection. We think it impossible to find that it has. In fact, quite to the contrary, our traditions have protected the marital family (Gerald, Carole, and the child they acknowledge to be theirs) against the sort of claim Michael asserts.

The presumption of legitimacy was a fundamental principle of the common law. H. Nicholas, Adulturine Bastardy 1 (1836). Traditionally, that presumption could be rebutted only by proof that a husband was incapable of procreation or had had no access to his wife during the relevant period. We have found nothing in the older sources, nor in the older cases, addressing specifically the power of the natural father to assert parental rights over a child born into a woman's existing marriage with another man.

What Michael asserts here is a right to have himself declared the natural father and thereby to obtain parental prerogatives. What he must establish, therefore, is not that our society has traditionally allowed a natural father in his circum-stances to establish paternity, but that it has traditionally accorded such a father parental rights, or at least has not traditionally denied them. Even if the law in all States had always been that the entire world could challenge the marital pre-sumption and obtain a declaration as to who was the natural father, that would not advance Michael's claim. Thus, it is ultimately irrelevant, even for purposes of determining current social attitudes towards the alleged substantive right Michael asserts, that the present law in a number of States appears to allow the natural father—including the natural father who has not established a relationship with the child—the theoretical power to rebut the marital pre-sumption. What counts is whether the States in fact award substantive parental rights to the natural father of a child conceived within, and born into, an extant marital union that wishes to embrace the child. We are not aware of a single case, old or new, that has done so. This is not the stuff of which fundamental rights qualifying as liberty interests are made.[20]

---

20. Justice Brennan criticizes our methodology in using historical traditions specifically relating to the rights of an adulterous natural father, rather than inquiring more generally "whether par-enthood is an interest that historically has received our attention and protection." We do not understand why, having rejected our focus upon the societal tradition regarding the natural father's rights vis-à-vis a child whose mother is married to another man, Justice Brennan would choose to focus instead upon "parenthood." Why should the relevant category not be even more general—perhaps "family relationships"; or "personal relationships"; or even "emotional attach-ments in general"? Though the dissent has no basis for the level of generality it would select, we do: We refer to the most specific level at which a relevant tradition protecting, or denying protection to, the asserted right can be identified. If, for example, there were no societal tradition, either way, regarding the rights of the natural father of a child adulterously conceived, we would have to consult, and (if possible) reason from, the traditions regarding natural fathers in general. But there is such a more specific tradition, and it unqualifiedly denies protection to such a parent.

We do not accept Justice Brennan's criticism that this result "squashes" the liberty that consists of "the freedom not to conform." It seems to us that reflects the erroneous view that there is only one side to this controversy—that one disposition can expand a "liberty" of sorts without contracting an equivalent "liberty" on the other side. Such a happy choice is rarely available. Here, to provide protection to an adulterous natural father is to deny protection to a marital father, and vice versa. If Michael has a "freedom not to conform" (whatever that means), Gerald must equivalently have a "freedom to conform." One of them will pay a price for asserting that "freedom"—Michael by being unable to act as father of the child he has adulterously begotten, or Gerald by being unable to preserve the integrity of the traditional family unit he and Victoria have established. Our disposition does not choose between these two "freedoms," but leaves that to the people of California. Justice Brennan's approach chooses one of them as the constitutional imperative, on no apparent basis except that the unconventional is to be preferred.

We have never had occasion to decide whether a child has a liberty interest, symmetrical with that of her parent, in maintaining her filial relationship. We need not do so here because, even assuming that such a right exists, Victoria's claim must fail. Victoria's due process challenge is, if anything, weaker than Michael's.

[W]hatever the merits of the guardian ad litem's belief that such an arrangement can be of great psychological benefit to a child, the claim that a State must recognize multiple fatherhood has no support in the history or traditions of this country. Moreover, even if we were to construe Victoria's argument as forwarding the lesser proposition that, whatever her status vis-à-vis Gerald, she has a liberty interest in maintaining a filial relationship with her natural father, Michael, we find that, at best, her claim is the obverse of Michael's and fails for the same reasons.

Justice BRENNAN, with whom Justice MARSHALL and Justice BLACKMUN join, dissenting.

Five Members of the Court refuse to foreclose "the possibility that a natural father might ever have a constitutionally protected interest in his relationship with a child whose mother was married to, and cohabiting with, another man at the time of the child's conception and birth."

Once we recognized that the "liberty" protected by the Due Process Clause of the Fourteenth Amendment encompasses more than freedom from bodily restraint, today's plurality opinion emphasizes, the concept was cut loose from one natural limitation on its meaning. This innovation paved the way, so the plurality hints, for judges to substitute their own preferences for those of elected officials. Dissatisfied with this supposedly unbridled and uncertain state of affairs, the plurality casts about for another limitation on the concept of liberty.

Because such general traditions provide such imprecise guidance, they permit judges to dictate rather than discern the society's views. The need, if arbitrary decisionmaking is to be avoided, to adopt the most specific tradition as the point of reference—or at least to announce, as Justice Brennan declines to do, some other criterion for selecting among the innumerable relevant traditions that could be consulted. Although assuredly having the virtue (if it be that) of leaving judges free to decide as they think best when the unanticipated occurs, a rule of law that binds neither by text nor by any particular, identifiable tradition is no rule of law at all. [Footnote by the Court.]

It finds this limitation in "tradition." Apparently oblivious to the fact that this concept can be as malleable and as elusive as "liberty" itself, the plurality pretends that tradition places a discernible border around the Constitution. The pretense is seductive; it would be comforting to believe that a search for "tradition" involves nothing more idiosyncratic or complicated than poring through dusty volumes on American history. Even if we could agree, moreover, on the content and significance of particular traditions, we still would be forced to identify the point at which a tradition becomes firm enough to be relevant to our definition of liberty and the moment at which it becomes too obsolete to be relevant any longer. The plurality supplies no objective means by which we might make these determinations.

It is ironic that an approach so utterly dependent on tradition is so indifferent to our precedents. Citing barely a handful of this Court's numerous decisions defining the scope of the liberty protected by the Due Process Clause to support its reliance on tradition, the plurality acts as though English legal treatises and the American Law Reports always have provided the sole source for our constitutional principles. They have not. Just as common-law notions no longer define the "property" that the Constitution protects, see Goldberg v. Kelly (1970), neither do they circumscribe the "liberty" that it guarantees.

Today's plurality, however, does not ask whether parenthood is an interest that historically has received our attention and protection; the answer to that question is too clear for dispute. Instead, the plurality asks whether the specific variety of parenthood under consideration—a natural father's relationship with a child whose mother is married to another man—has enjoyed such protection.

If we had looked to tradition with such specificity in past cases, many a decision would have reached a different result. Surely the use of contraceptives by unmarried couples, Eisenstadt v. Baird (1972), or even by married couples, Griswold v. Connecticut (1965); the freedom from corporal punishment in schools, Ingraham v. Wright (1977); the freedom from an arbitrary transfer from a prison to a psychiatric institution, Vitek v. Jones (1980); and even the right to raise one's natural but illegitimate children, Stanley v. Illinois (1972), were not "interest[s] traditionally protected by our society," at the time of their consideration by this Court. If we had asked, therefore, in *Eisenstadt, Griswold, Ingraham, Vitek*, or *Stanley* itself whether the specific interest under consideration had been traditionally protected, the answer would have been a resounding "no." That we did not ask this question in those cases highlights the novelty of the interpretive method that the plurality opinion employs today.

The plurality's interpretive method is more than novel; it is misguided. It ignores the good reasons for limiting the role of "tradition" in interpreting the Constitution's deliberately capacious language. In the plurality's constitutional universe, we may not take notice of the fact that the original reasons for the conclusive presumption of paternity are out of place in a world in which blood tests can prove virtually beyond a shadow of a doubt who sired a particular child and in which the fact of illegitimacy no longer plays the burdensome and stigmatizing role it once did. Moreover, by describing the decisive question as whether Michael's and Victoria's interest is one that has been "traditionally protected by our society," rather than one that society traditionally has thought important (with or without protecting it), and by suggesting that our sole function is to "discern the society's views," the plurality acts as if the only purpose of the Due Process Clause is to confirm the importance of interests already protected by a majority of the States. Transforming the protection afforded by the Due Process Clause into a redundancy mocks those who, with care and purpose, wrote the Fourteenth Amendment.

In construing the Fourteenth Amendment to offer shelter only to those interests specifically protected by historical practice, moreover, the plurality ignores the kind of society in which our Constitution exists. We are not an assimilative, homogeneous society, but a facilitative, pluralistic one, in which we must be willing to abide someone else's unfamiliar or even repellent practice because the same tolerant impulse protects our own idiosyncrasies. Even if we can agree, therefore, that "family" and "parenthood" are part of the good life, it is absurd to assume that we can agree on the content of those terms and destructive to pretend that we do. In a community such as ours, "liberty" must include the freedom not to conform. The plurality today squashes this freedom by requiring specific approval from history before protecting anything in the name of liberty.

The document that the plurality construes today is unfamiliar to me. It is not the living charter that I have taken to be our Constitution; it is instead a stagnant, archaic, hidebound document steeped in the prejudices and superstitions of a time long past. This Constitution does not recognize that times change, does not see that sometimes a practice or rule outlives its foundations. I cannot accept an interpretive method that does such violence to the charter that I am bound by oath to uphold.

Thus, to describe the issue in this case as whether the relationship existing between Michael and Victoria "has been treated as a protected family unit under the historic practices of our society, or whether on any other basis it has been accorded special protection," is to reinvent the wheel. On four prior occasions, we have considered whether unwed fathers have a constitutionally protected interest in their relationships with their children. Though different in factual and legal circumstances, these cases have produced a unifying theme: although an unwed father's biological link to his child does not, in and of itself, guarantee him a constitutional stake in his relationship with that child, such a link combined with a substantial parent-child relationship will do so. The evidence is undisputed that Michael, Victoria, and Carole did live together as a family; that is, they shared the same household, Victoria called Michael "Daddy," Michael contributed to Victoria's support, and he is eager to continue his relationship with her.

The atmosphere surrounding today's decision is one of make-believe. Beginning with the suggestion that the situation confronting us here does not repeat itself every day in every corner of the country, moving on to the claim that it is tradition alone that supplies the details of the liberty that the Constitution protects, and passing finally to the notion that the Court always has recognized a cramped vision of "the family," today's decision lets stand California's pronouncement that Michael — whom blood tests show to a 98 percent probability to be Victoria's father — is not Victoria's father. When and if the Court awakes to reality, it will find a world very different from the one it expects.

3. The Right to Keep the Family Together

The Supreme Court has recognized a fundamental right to keep the family together that includes an extended family. The key case was Moore v. City of East Cleveland.

MOORE v. CITY OF EAST CLEVELAND, OHIO
431 U.S. 494 (1977)

Justice POWELL announced the judgment of the Court, and delivered an opinion in which Justice BRENNAN, Justice MARSHALL, and Justice BLACKMUN joined.

East Cleveland's housing ordinance, like many throughout the country, limits occupancy of a dwelling unit to members of a single family. But the ordinance contains an unusual and complicated definitional section that recognizes as a "family" only a few categories of related individuals. Because her family, living together in her home, fits none of those categories, appellant stands convicted of a criminal offense. The question in this case is whether the ordinance violates the Due Process Clause of the Fourteenth Amendment.

I

Appellant, Mrs. Inez Moore, lives in her East Cleveland home together with her son, Dale Moore Sr., and her two grandsons, Dale, Jr., and John Moore, Jr. The two boys are first cousins rather than brothers; we are told that John came to live with his grandmother and with the elder and younger Dale Moores after his mother's death. In early 1973, Mrs. Moore received a notice of violation from the city, stating that John was an "illegal occupant" and directing her to comply with the ordinance. When she failed to remove him from her home, the city filed a criminal charge. Mrs. Moore moved to dismiss, claiming that the ordinance was constitutionally invalid on its face. Her motion was overruled, and upon conviction she was sentenced to five days in jail and a $25 fine.

II

The city argues that our decision in Village of Belle Terre v. Boraas (1974), requires us to sustain the ordinance attacked here. Belle Terre, like East Cleveland, imposed limits on the types of groups that could occupy a single dwelling unit. [W]e sustained the Belle Terre ordinance on the ground that it bore a rational relationship to permissible state objectives.

But one overriding factor sets this case apart from Belle Terre. The ordinance there affected only unrelated individuals. It expressly allowed all who were related by "blood, adoption, or marriage" to live together, and in sustaining the ordinance we were careful to note that it promoted "family needs" and "family values." East Cleveland, in contrast, has chosen to regulate the occupancy of its housing by slicing deeply into the family itself. This is no mere incidental result of the ordinance. On its face it selects certain categories of relatives who may live together and declares that others may not. In particular, it makes a crime of a grandmother's choice to live with her grandson in circumstances like those presented here.

When a city undertakes such intrusive regulation of the family, neither Belle Terre nor Euclid governs; the usual judicial deference to the legislature is inappropriate. "This Court has long recognized that freedom of personal choice in matters of marriage and family life is one of the liberties protected by the Due Process Clause of the Fourteenth Amendment." Of course, the family is not beyond regulation. But when the government intrudes on choices concerning family living arrangements, this Court must examine carefully the importance of the governmental interests advanced and the extent to which they are served by the challenged regulation.

When thus examined, this ordinance cannot survive. The city seeks to justify it as a means of preventing overcrowding, minimizing traffic and parking congestion, and avoiding an undue financial burden on East Cleveland's school system. Although these are legitimate goals, the ordinance before us serves them marginally, at best. For example, the ordinance permits any family consisting only of husband, wife, and unmarried children to live together, even if the family contains a half dozen licensed drivers, each with his or her own car. At the same time it forbids an adult brother and sister to share a household, even if both faithfully use public transportation. The ordinance would permit a grandmother to live with a single dependent son and children, even if his school-age children number a dozen, yet it forces Mrs. Moore to find another dwelling for her grandson John, simply because of the presence of his uncle and cousin in the same household. We need not labor the point. Section 1341.08 has but a tenuous relation to alleviation of the conditions mentioned by the city.

III

The city suggests that any constitutional right to live together as a family extends only to the nuclear family, essentially a couple and their dependent children. But unless we close our eyes to the basic reasons why certain rights associated with the family have been accorded shelter under the Fourteenth Amendment's Due Process Clause, we cannot avoid applying the force and rationale of these precedents to the family choice involved in this case.

Understanding those reasons requires careful attention to this Court's function under the Due Process Clause. Substantive due process has at times been a treacherous field for this Court. There are risks when the judicial branch gives enhanced protection to certain substantive liberties without the guidance of the more specific provisions of the Bill of Rights. As the history of the Lochner era demonstrates, there is reason for concern lest the only limits to such judicial intervention become the predilections of those who happen at the time to be Members of this Court. That history counsels caution and restraint. But it does not counsel abandonment, nor does it require what the city urges here: cutting off any protection of family rights at the first convenient, if arbitrary boundary — the boundary of the nuclear family.

Appropriate limits on substantive due process come not from drawing arbitrary lines but rather from careful "respect for the teachings of history [and], solid recognition of the basic values that underlie our society." Our decisions establish that the Constitution protects the sanctity of the family precisely because the institution of the family is deeply rooted in this Nation's history and tradition. It is through the family that we inculcate and pass down many of our most cherished values, moral and cultural.

Ours is by no means a tradition limited to respect for the bonds uniting the members of the nuclear family. The tradition of uncles, aunts, cousins, and especially grandparents sharing a household along with parents and children has roots equally venerable and equally deserving of constitutional recognition. Over the years millions of our citizens have grown up in just such an environment, and most, surely, have profited from it. Even if conditions of modern society have brought about a decline in extended family households, they have not erased the accumulated wisdom of civilization, gained over the centuries and honored throughout our history, that supports a larger conception of the family. Out of choice, necessity, or a sense of family responsibility, it has been common for close relatives to draw together and participate in the duties and the satisfactions of a common home. Especially in times of adversity, such as the death of a spouse or economic need, the broader family has tended to come together for mutual sustenance and to maintain or rebuild a secure home life. This is apparently what happened here.

Whether or not such a household is established because of personal tragedy, the choice of relatives in this degree of kinship to live together may not lightly be denied by the State. By the same token the Constitution prevents East Cleveland from standardizing its children and its adults by forcing all to live in certain narrowly defined family patterns.

Justice STEWART, with whom Justice REHNQUIST joins, dissenting.

In Village of Belle Terre v. Boraas, the Court considered a New York village ordinance that restricted land use within the village to single-family dwellings. That ordinance defined "family" to include all persons related by blood, adoption, or marriage who lived and cooked together as a single-housekeeping unit; it forbade occupancy by any group of three or more persons who were not so related. We held that the ordinance was a valid effort by the village government to promote the general community welfare, and that it did not violate the Fourteenth Amendment or infringe any other rights or freedoms protected by the Constitution.

To be sure, the ordinance involved in Belle Terre did not prevent blood relatives from occupying the same dwelling, and the Court's decision in that case does not, therefore, foreclose the appellant's arguments based specifically on the ties of kinship present in this case. Nonetheless, I would hold that the existence of those ties does not elevate either the appellant's claim of associational freedom or her claim of privacy to a level invoking constitutional protection.

Although the appellant's desire to share a single-dwelling unit also involves "private family life" in a sense, that desire can hardly be equated with any of the interests protected in the cases just cited. The ordinance about which the appellant complains did not impede her choice to have or not to have children, and it did not dictate to her how her own children were to be nurtured and reared. The ordinance clearly does not prevent parents from living together or living with their unemancipated offspring.

Obviously, East Cleveland might have as easily and perhaps as effectively hit upon a different definition of "family." The point is that any definition would produce hardships in some cases without materially advancing the legislative purpose. That this ordinance also does so is no reason to hold it unconstitutional, unless we are to use our power to interpret the United States Constitution as a sort of generalized authority to correct seeming inequity wherever it surfaces. It is not for us to rewrite the ordinance, or substitute our judgment for the discretion of the prosecutor who elected to initiate this litigation.

The Court has emphasized that individuals must be related to one another to be considered a family. For example, in *Moore*, the Court distinguished the earlier decision in Village of Belle Terre v. Boraas, 416 U.S. 1 (1974), where the Court had upheld a similar zoning ordinance that limited the number of unrelated people who could live together in one household. In *Belle Terre* a group of college students who wanted to share a house brought a constitutional challenge to the ordinance. The Court in *Moore* emphasized that *Belle Terre* had involved only "*unrelated* individuals" and, in fact, the zoning ordinance there had an exception for "all who were related by 'blood, adoption, or marriage.'"

The Court invoked the same distinction between relatives and non-relatives in Smith v. Organization of Foster Families for Equality and Reform, 431 U.S. 816 (1977), which concerned the rights of foster parents. The Supreme Court held that the state did not violate due process in providing preremoval hearings only to foster parents who had been with a child for 18 months or more. The Court observed that although its prior decisions had involved a biological relationship, "[n]o one would seriously dispute that a deeply loving and interdependent relationship between an adult and a child in his or her care may exist even in the absence of a blood relationship."

However, the Court also saw key differences between biological parents and foster parents. The Court said that "whatever emotional ties may develop between foster parent and foster child have their origins in an arrangement in which the State has been a partner from the outset." Also, the Court stressed that protecting a liberty interest for foster parents often would be at the expense of the liberty of natural parents.

———————————

The Court concluded that it did not need to resolve the nature of the liberty interest of foster parents because the state law provided adequate protections even assuming rights of foster parents. The Court said that due process did not require that there be a hearing every time a child was removed from a foster home and that it was sufficient for the government to provide preremoval due process for those foster parents who had been with a child for more than 18 months.

4. *The Right of Parents to Control the Upbringing of Their Children*

The first Supreme Court cases recognizing family autonomy involved the right of parents to control the upbringing of their children. It is notable that they were decided during the *Lochner* era and expressly use substantive due process to protect this right. Although economic substantive due process was abandoned in 1937, as discussed in Chapter 6, the Supreme Court's decisions of that era protecting parental decision making are very much still followed.

<u>MEYER v. NEBRASKA</u>

262 U.S. 390 (1923)

Justice McReynolds delivered the opinion of the Court.

Plaintiff in error was tried and convicted in the district court for Hamilton county, Nebraska, under an information which charged that on May 25, 1920, while an instructor in Zion Parochial School he unlawfully taught the subject of reading in the German language to Raymond Parpart, a child of 10 years. The information is based upon "An act relating to the teaching of foreign languages in the state of Nebraska," approved April 9, 1919, which follows:

> Section 1. No person, individually or as a teacher, shall, in any private, denominational, parochial or public school, teach any subject to any person in any language than the English language.
>
> Sec. 2. Languages, other than the English language, may be taught as languages only after a pupil shall have attained and successfully passed the eighth grade as evidenced by a certificate of graduation issued by the county superintendent of the county in which the child resides.
>
> Sec. 3. Any person who violates any of the provisions of this act shall be deemed guilty of a misdemeanor and upon conviction, shall be subject to a fine of not less than twenty-five dollars ($25), nor more than one hundred dollars ($100), or be confined in the county jail for any period not exceeding thirty days for each offense. The Supreme Court of the state affirmed the judgment of conviction.

While this court has not attempted to define with exactness the liberty thus guaranteed, the term has received much consideration and some of the included things have been definitely stated. Without doubt, it denotes not merely freedom from bodily restraint but also the right of the individual to contract, to engage in any of the common occupations of life, to acquire useful knowledge, to marry, establish a home and bring up children, to worship God according to the dictates of his own conscience, and generally to enjoy those privileges long recognized at common law as essential to the orderly pursuit of happiness by free men. The established doctrine is that this liberty may not be interfered with, under the guise of protecting the public interest, by legislative action which is arbitrary or without reasonable relation to some purpose within the competency of the state to effect. Determination by the Legislature of what constitutes proper exercise of police power is not final or conclusive but is subject to supervision by the courts.

Corresponding to the right of control, it is the natural duty of the parent to give his children education suitable to their station in life; and nearly all the states, including Nebraska, enforce this obligation by compulsory laws.

Mere knowledge of the German language cannot reasonably be regarded as harmful. Heretofore it has been commonly looked upon as helpful and desirable. Plaintiff in error taught this language in school as part of his occupation. His right thus to teach and the right of parents to engage him so to instruct their children, we think, are within the liberty of the amendment.

For the welfare of his Ideal Commonwealth, Plato suggested a law which should provide:

> That the wives of our guardians are to be common, and their children are to be common, and no parent is to know his own child, nor any child his parent. . . . The proper officers will take the offspring of the good parents to the pen or fold, and there they will deposit them with certain nurses who dwell in a separate quarter; but the offspring of the inferior, or of the better when they chance to be deformed, will be put away in some mysterious, unknown place, as they should be.

In order to submerge the individual and develop ideal citizens, Sparta assembled the males at seven into barracks and intrusted their subsequent education and training to official guardians. Although such measures have been deliberately approved by men of great genius, their ideas touching the relation between individual and state were wholly different from those upon which our institutions rest; and it hardly will be affirmed that any Legislature could impose such restrictions upon the people of a state without doing violence to both letter and spirit of the Constitution.

The desire of the Legislature to foster a homogeneous people with American ideals prepared readily to understand current discussions of civic matters is easy to appreciate. Unfortunate experiences during the late war and aversion toward every character of truculent adversaries were certainly enough to quicken that aspiration. But the means adopted, we think, exceed the limitations upon the power of the state and conflict with rights assured to plaintiff in error. The interference is plain enough and no adequate reason therefore in time of peace and domestic tranquility has been shown. It is well known that proficiency in a foreign language seldom comes to one not instructed at an early age, and experience shows that this is not injurious to the health, morals or understanding of the ordinary child.

PIERCE v. SOCIETY OF THE SISTERS OF THE HOLY NAMES OF JESUS & MARY, 268 U.S. 510 (1925): Justice McREYNOLDS delivered the opinion of the Court.

These appeals are from decrees, based upon undenied allegations, which granted preliminary orders restraining appellants from threatening or attempting to enforce the Compulsory Education Act adopted November 7, 1922, under the initiative provision of her Constitution by the voters of Oregon. The challenged act, effective September 1, 1926, requires every parent, guardian, or other person having control or charge or custody of a child between 8 and 16 years to send him "to a public school for the period of time a public school shall be held during the current year" in the district where the child resides; and failure so to do is declared a misdemeanor.

The inevitable practical result of enforcing the act under consideration would be destruction of appellees' primary schools, and perhaps all other private primary schools for normal children within the state of Oregon. Appellees are engaged in a kind of undertaking not inherently harmful, but long regarded as useful and meritorious. Certainly there is nothing in the present records to indicate that they have failed to discharge their obligations to patrons, students, or the state. And there are no peculiar circumstances or present emergencies which demand extraordinary measures relative to primary education.

Under the doctrine of Meyer v. Nebraska, we think it entirely plain that the Act of 1922 unreasonably interferes with the liberty of parents and guardians to direct the upbringing and education of children under their control. As often heretofore pointed out, rights guaranteed by the Constitution may not be abridged by legislation which has no reasonable relation to some purpose within the competency of the state. The fundamental theory of liberty upon which all governments in this Union repose excludes any general power of the state to standardize its children by forcing them to accept instruction from public teachers only. The child is not the mere creature of the state; those who nurture him and direct his destiny have the right, coupled with the high duty, to recognize and prepare him for additional obligations.

But the Court also has recognized that the right to make parenting decisions is not absolute and can be interfered with by the state if necessary to protect a child. For example, in Prince v. Massachusetts, 321 U.S. 158 (1944), the Court upheld the application of child labor laws to a nine-year-old girl who was soliciting for the Jehovah's Witnesses religion at the direction of her parents. The Court acknowledged that there is a "private realm of family life which the state cannot enter." But the Court said that "the family itself is not beyond regulation in the public interest. . . . Acting to guard the general interest in youth's well being, the state as parens patriae may restrict the parent's control by requiring school attendance, regulating or prohibiting the child's labor and in many other ways." The Court said that the need to protect children from being exploited and harmed justified upholding laws prohibiting child labor, even if the work was at the direction of the parents and even if it was undertaken for religious purposes.

In weighing the competing claims of parents and of the state on behalf of children, the Supreme Court has given great deference to parents.[21] In Wisconsin v. Yoder, 406 U.S. 205 (1972), the Supreme Court held that Amish parents had a constitutional right, based on their right to control the upbringing of their children and based on free exercise of religion, to exempt their 14- and 15-year-old children from a compulsory school attendance law. The Court said that "a State's interest in universal education, however highly we rank it, is not totally free from a balancing process when it impinges on fundamental rights and interests, such as those specifically protected by the Free Exercise Clause of the First Amendment, and the traditional interest of parents with respect to the religious upbringing of their children."

The Court gave great weight to the parents' claim that additional education would threaten their children's religious beliefs and to the uniquely insulated nature of the Amish culture. The Court accepted the argument that applying the mandatory schooling law to 14- and 15-year-old Amish children would interfere with free exercise of religion and with the ability of parents to make decisions concerning their children. The Court noted that there was no evidence of "any harm to the physical or mental health of the child or to the public safety, peace, order, or welfare." The Court thus concluded that "[u]nder the doctrine of

---

21. See James G. Dwyer, *Parents' Religion and Children's Welfare: Debunking the Doctrine of Parents' Rights*, 82 Cal. L. Rev. 1371 (1994).

Meyer v. Nebraska we think it entirely plain that the Act . . . interferes with the liberty of parents and guardians to direct the upbringing and education of children under their control."

The Court's substantial deference to parents also is reflected in Parham v. J.R., 442 U.S. 584 (1979). *Parham* presented the question of what type of procedural due process must be accorded to children when their parents commit them to an institution. The Supreme Court had earlier ruled that except in an emergency, before an adult can be committed to an institution there must be notice and a hearing.[22] But the Court said that the assumption must be that a parent is acting in the best interests of a child when making a commitment decision.

The Court recognized that some parents might abuse the power to institutionalize a child but said that this was not a sufficient basis for treating commitment of children like commitment of adults. Chief Justice Burger, writing for the Court, stated, "That some parents may at times be acting against the interests of their children . . . creates a basis for caution, but is hardly a reason to discard wholesale those pages of human experience that teach that parents generally do act in the child's best interests. The statist notion that governmental power should supersede parental authority in *all* cases because *some* parents abuse and neglect children is repugnant to American tradition."

Thus, the Court concluded that before a parent can institutionalize a child, there only need be a screening by a doctor or other neutral fact finder. A child, unlike an adult, did not have to be given notice and an evidentiary hearing. The dissenting opinion by Justice Brennan, joined by Justices Marshall and Stevens, emphasized the "massive curtailment of liberty" inherent to institutionalization and the need to protect children from the possibility of erroneous commitment. The dissent said that "[c]hildren incarcerated in public mental institutions are constitutionally entitled to a fair opportunity to contest the legitimacy of their confinement. They are entitled to some champion who can speak on their behalf and who stands ready to oppose a wrongful commitment. . . . And fairness demands that children abandoned by their supposed protectors to the rigors of institutional confinement be given the help of some separate voice."

The Court's most recent decision in this area strongly reaffirmed the constitutional right of parents to control the upbringing of their children.

TROXEL v. GRANVILLE

530 U.S. 57 (2000)

Justice O'CONNOR announced the judgment of the Court and delivered an opinion, in which the Chief Justice, Justice GINSBURG, and Justice BREYER join.

Section 26.10.160(3) of the Revised Code of Washington permits "[a]ny person" to petition a superior court for visitation rights "at any time," and authorizes that court to grant such visitation rights whenever "visitation may serve the best interest of the child." Petitioners Jenifer and Gary Troxel petitioned a Washington Superior Court for the right to visit their grandchildren, Isabelle and Natalie Troxel. Respondent Tommie Granville, the mother of Isabella and Natalie, opposed the petition. The case ultimately reached the

---

22. Addington v. Texas, 441 U.S. 418 (1979).

Washington Supreme Court, which held that §26.10.160(3) unconstitutionally interferes with the fundamental right of parents to rear their children.

I

Tommie Granville and Brad Troxel shared a relationship that ended in June 1991. The two never married, but they had two daughters, Isabelle and Natalie. Jenifer and Gary Troxel are Brad's parents, and thus the paternal grandparents of Isabelle and Natalie. After Tommie and Brad separated in 1991, Brad lived with his parents and regularly brought his daughters to his parents' home for weekend visitation. Brad committed suicide in May 1993. Although the Troxels at first continued to see Isabelle and Natalie on a regular basis after their son's death, Tommie Granville informed the Troxels in October 1993 that she wished to limit their visitation with her daughters to one short visit per month. In December 1993, the Troxels commenced the present action by filing, in the Washington Superior Court for Skagit County, a petition to obtain visitation rights with Isabelle and Natalie.

II

The demographic changes of the past century make it difficult to speak of an average American family. The composition of families varies greatly from household to household. While many children may have two married parents and grandparents who visit regularly, many other children are raised in single-parent households. In 1996, children living with only one parent accounted for 28 percent of all children under age 18 in the United States. Understandably, in these single-parent households, persons outside the nuclear family are called upon with increasing frequency to assist in the everyday tasks of child rearing. In many cases, grandparents play an important role. For example, in 1998, approximately 4 million children — or 5.6 percent of all children under age 18 — lived in the household of their grandparents.

The nationwide enactment of nonparental visitation statutes is assuredly due, in some part, to the States' recognition of these changing realities of the American family. Because grandparents and other relatives undertake duties of a parental nature in many households, States have sought to ensure the welfare of the children therein by protecting the relationships those children form with such third parties. The States' nonparental visitation statutes are further supported by a recognition, which varies from State to State, that children should have the opportunity to benefit from relationships with statutorily specified persons — for example, their grandparents. The extension of statutory rights in this area to persons other than a child's parents, however, comes with an obvious cost. For example, the State's recognition of an independent third-party interest in a child can place a substantial burden on the traditional parent-child relationship.

The liberty interest at issue in this case — the interest of parents in the care, custody, and control of their children — is perhaps the oldest of the fundamental liberty interests recognized by this Court. Section 26.10.160(3), as applied to Granville and her family in this case, unconstitutionally infringes on that fundamental parental right. The Washington nonparental visitation statute is breathtakingly broad. According to the statute's text, "[a]ny person may petition the court for visitation rights at any time," and the court may grant such visitation rights whenever "visitation may serve the best interest of the child."

That language effectively permits any third party seeking visitation to subject any decision by a parent concerning visitation of the parent's children to state-court review. Once the visitation petition has been filed in court and the matter is placed before a judge, a parent's decision that visitation would not be in the child's best interest is accorded no deference. Section 26.10.160(3) contains no requirement that a court accord the parent's decision any presumption of validity or any weight whatsoever. Instead, the Washington statute places the best-interest determination solely in the hands of the judge. Should the judge disagree with the parent's estimation of the child's best interests, the judge's view necessarily prevails. Thus, in practical effect, in the State of Washington a court can disregard and overturn any decision by a fit custodial parent concerning visitation whenever a third party affected by the decision files a visitation petition, based solely on the judge's determination of the child's best interests. The Washington Supreme Court had the opportunity to give §26.10.160(3) a narrower reading, but it declined to do so.

Turning to the facts of this case, the record reveals that the Superior Court's order was based on precisely the type of mere disagreement we have just described and nothing more. The Superior Court's order was not founded on any special factors that might justify the State's interference with Granville's fundamental right to make decisions concerning the rearing of her two daughters. To be sure, this case involves a visitation petition filed by grandparents soon after the death of their son — the father of Isabelle and Natalie — but the combination of several factors here compels our conclusion that §26.10.160(3), as applied, exceeded the bounds of the Due Process Clause.

First, the Troxels did not allege, and no court has found, that Granville was an unfit parent. That aspect of the case is important, for there is a presumption that fit parents act in the best interests of their children. [S]o long as a parent adequately cares for his or her children (i.e., is fit), there will normally be no reason for the State to inject itself into the private realm of the family to further question the ability of that parent to make the best decisions concerning the rearing of that parent's children.

The problem here is not that the Washington Superior Court intervened, but that when it did so, it gave no special weight at all to Granville's determination of her daughters' best interests. More importantly, it appears that the Superior Court applied exactly the opposite presumption. In an ideal world, parents might always seek to cultivate the bonds between grandparents and their grandchildren. Needless to say, however, our world is far from perfect, and in it the decision whether such an intergenerational relationship would be beneficial in any specific case is for the parent to make in the first instance. And, if a fit parent's decision of the kind at issue here becomes subject to judicial review, the court must accord at least some special weight to the parent's own determination.

Finally, we note that there is no allegation that Granville ever sought to cut off visitation entirely. Rather, the present dispute originated when Granville informed the Troxels that she would prefer to restrict their visitation with

Isabelle and Natalie to one short visit per month and special holidays[, w]hile the Troxels requested two weekends per month and two full weeks in the summer.

Considered together with the Superior Court's reasons for awarding visitation to the Troxels, the combination of these factors demonstrates that the visitation order in this case was an unconstitutional infringement on Granville's fundamental right to make decisions concerning the care, custody, and control of her two daughters. The Washington Superior Court failed to accord the determination of Granville, a fit custodial parent, any material weight.

Accordingly, we hold that §26.10.160(3), as applied in this case, is unconstitutional. Because we rest our decision on the sweeping breadth of §26.10.160(3) and the application of that broad, unlimited power in this case, we do not consider the primary constitutional question passed on by the Washington Supreme Court—whether the Due Process Clause requires all nonparental visitation statutes to include a showing of harm or potential harm to the child as a condition precedent to granting visitation. We do not, and need not, define today the precise scope of the parental due process right in the visitation context. In this respect, the constitutionality of any standard for awarding visitation turns on the specific manner in which that standard is applied and that the constitutional protections in this area are best "elaborated with care."

Justice SOUTER, concurring in the judgment.

I concur in the judgment affirming the decision of the Supreme Court of Washington, whose facial invalidation of its own state statute is consistent with this Court's prior cases addressing the substantive interests at stake. I would say no more. The issues that might well be presented by reviewing a decision addressing the specific application of the state statute by the trial court, are not before us and do not call for turning any fresh furrows in the "treacherous field" of substantive due process.

The Supreme Court of Washington invalidated its state statute based on the text of the statute alone, not its application to any particular case. Its ruling rested on two independently sufficient grounds: the failure of the statute to require harm to the child to justify a disputed visitation order, and the statute's authorization of "any person" at "any time" to petition and to receive visitation rights subject only to a free-ranging best-interests-of-the-child standard. I see no error in the second reason, that because the state statute authorizes any person at any time to request (and a judge to award) visitation rights, subject only to the State's particular best-interests standard, the state statute sweeps too broadly and is unconstitutional on its face. Consequently, there is no need to decide whether harm is required or to consider the precise scope of the parent's right or its necessary protections.

Justice THOMAS, concurring in the judgment.

I write separately to note that neither party has argued that our substantive due process cases were wrongly decided and that the original understanding of the Due Process Clause precludes judicial enforcement of unenumerated rights under that constitutional provision. As a result, I express no view on the merits of this matter, and I understand the plurality as well to leave the resolution of that issue for another day.

Consequently, I agree with the plurality that this Court's recognition of a fundamental right of parents to direct the upbringing of their children resolves this case. Our decision in Pierce v. Society of Sisters (1925) holds that parents have a fundamental constitutional right to rear their children, including the right to determine who shall educate and socialize them. The opinions of the plurality, Justice Kennedy, and Justice Souter recognize such a right, but curiously none of them articulates the appropriate standard of review. I would apply strict scrutiny to infringements of fundamental rights. Here, the State of Washington lacks even a legitimate governmental interest — to say nothing of a compelling one — in second-guessing a fit parent's decision regarding visitation with third parties. On this basis, I would affirm the judgment below.

Justice STEVENS, dissenting.

The Court today wisely declines to endorse either the holding or the reasoning of the Supreme Court of Washington. In my opinion, the Court would have been even wiser to deny certiorari. Given the problematic character of the trial court's decision and the uniqueness of the Washington statute, there was no pressing need to review a State Supreme Court decision that merely requires the state legislature to draft a better statute.

Having decided to address the merits, however, the Court should begin by recognizing that the State Supreme Court rendered a federal constitutional judgment holding a state law invalid on its face. In light of that judgment, I believe that we should confront the federal questions presented directly. For the Washington statute is not made facially invalid either because it may be invoked by too many hypothetical plaintiffs, or because it leaves open the possibility that someone may be permitted to sustain a relationship with a child without having to prove that serious harm to the child would otherwise result.

Justice SCALIA, dissenting.

In my view, a right of parents to direct the upbringing of their children is among the "unalienable Rights" with which the Declaration of Independence proclaims "all Men . . . are endowed by their Creator." And in my view that right is also among the "othe[r][rights] retained by the people" which the Ninth Amendment says the Constitution's enumeration of rights "shall not be construed to deny or disparage." The Declaration of Independence, however, is not a legal prescription conferring powers upon the courts; and the Constitution's refusal to "deny or disparage" other rights is far removed from affirming any one of them, and even farther removed from authorizing judges to identify what they might be, and to enforce the judges' list against laws duly enacted by the people. Consequently, while I would think it entirely compatible with the commitment to representative democracy set forth in the founding documents to argue, in legislative chambers or in electoral campaigns, that the state has no power to interfere with parents' authority over the rearing of their children, I do not believe that the power which the Constitution confers upon me as a judge entitles me to deny legal effect to laws that (in my view) infringe upon what is (in my view) that unenumerated right.

If we embrace this unenumerated right, I think it obvious — whether we affirm or reverse the judgment here, that we will be ushering in a new regime of judicially prescribed, and federally prescribed, family law. I have no reason to believe that federal judges will be better at this than state legislatures; and state legislatures have the great advantages of doing harm in a more circumscribed area, of being able to correct their mistakes in a flash, and of being removable by the people.

Justice KENNEDY, dissenting.

After acknowledging this statutory right to sue for visitation, the State Supreme Court invalidated the statute as violative of the United States Constitution, because it interfered with a parent's right to raise his or her child free from unwarranted interference.

The first flaw the State Supreme Court found in the statute is that it allows an award of visitation to a non-parent without a finding that harm to the child would result if visitation were withheld; and the second is that the statute allows any person to seek visitation at any time. In my view the first theory is too broad to be correct, as it appears to contemplate that the best interests of the child standard may not be applied in any visitation case. I acknowledge the distinct possibility that visitation cases may arise where, considering the absence of other protection for the parent under state laws and procedures, the best interests of the child standard would give insufficient protection to the parent's constitutional right to raise the child without undue intervention by the state; but it is quite a different matter to say, as I understand the Supreme Court of Washington to have said, that a harm to the child standard is required in every instance.

Given the error I see in the State Supreme Court's central conclusion that the best interests of the child standard is never appropriate in third-party visitation cases, that court should have the first opportunity to reconsider this case. I would remand the case to the state court for further proceedings. If it then found the statute has been applied in an unconstitutional manner because the best interests of the child standard gives insufficient protection to a parent under the circumstances of this case, or if it again declared the statute a nullity because the statute seems to allow any person at all to seek visitation at any time, the decision would present other issues which may or may not warrant further review in this Court. These include not only the protection the Constitution gives parents against state-ordered visitation but also the extent to which federal rules for facial challenges to statutes control in state courts. These matters, however, should await some further case. The judgment now under review should be vacated and remanded on the sole ground that the harm ruling that was so central to the Supreme Court of Washington's decision was error, given its broad formulation.

D. CONSTITUTIONAL PROTECTION FOR REPRODUCTIVE AUTONOMY

The Supreme Court has recognized three aspects of reproductive autonomy to be fundamental rights: the right to procreate, the right to purchase and use contraceptives, and the right to abortion.

1.   The Right to Procreate

The Supreme Court has held that the right to procreate is a fundamental right and therefore government-imposed involuntary sterilization must meet strict scrutiny. Initially, the Court rejected this position.

BUCK v. BELL, 274 U.S. 200 (1927): Justice HOLMES delivered the opinion of the Court.

This is a writ of error to review a judgment of the Supreme Court of Appeals of the State of Virginia, affirming a judgment of the Circuit Court of Amherst County, by which the defendant in error, the superintendent of the State Colony for Epileptics and Feeble Minded, was ordered to perform the operation of salpingectomy upon Carrie Buck, the plaintiff in error, for the purpose of making her sterile. The case comes here upon the contention that the statute authorizing the judgment is void under the Fourteenth Amendment as denying to the plaintiff in error due process of law and the equal protection of the laws.

Carrie Buck is a feeble-minded white woman who was committed to the State Colony above mentioned in due form. She is the daughter of a feeble-minded mother in the same institution, and the mother of an illegitimate feeble-minded child. She was eighteen years old at the time of the trial of her case in the Circuit Court in the latter part of 1924.

An Act of Virginia approved March 20, 1924 recites that the health of the patient and the welfare of society may be promoted in certain cases by the sterilization of mental defectives, under careful safeguard, etc.; that the sterilization may be effected in males by vasectomy and in females by salpingectomy, without serious pain or substantial danger to life; that the Commonwealth is supporting in various institutions many defective persons who if now discharged would become a menace but if incapable of procreating might be discharged with safety and become self-supporting with benefit to themselves and to society; and that experience has shown that heredity plays an important part in the transmission of insanity, imbecility, etc.

The judgment finds the facts that have been recited and that Carrie Buck "is the probable potential parent of socially inadequate offspring, likewise afflicted, that she may be sexually sterilized without detriment to her general health and that her welfare and that of society will be promoted by her sterilization," and thereupon makes the order. In view of the general declarations of the Legislature and the specific findings of the Court obviously we cannot say as matter of law that the grounds do not exist, and if they exist they justify the result. We have seen more than once that the public welfare may call upon the best citizens for their lives. It would be strange if it could not call upon those who already sap the strength of the State for these lesser sacrifices, often not felt to be such by those concerned, in order to prevent our being swamped with incompetence. It is better for all the world, if instead of waiting to execute degenerate offspring for crime, or to let them starve for their imbecility, society can prevent those who are manifestly unfit from continuing their kind. The principle that sustains compulsory vaccination is broad enough to cover cutting the Fallopian tubes. Three generations of imbeciles are enough.

The Court described Carrie Buck as a "feeble-minded white woman." In fact, in 1980, Carrie Buck was found to be alive and living with her sister, who also had been sterilized by the state. Carrie Buck was discovered to be a woman of normal intelligence.[23] She was one of almost 20,000 "forced eugenic sterilizations" that had been performed in the United States by 1935.[24]

The Supreme Court never has overruled Buck v. Bell or repudiated Justice Holmes's opinion, but Skinner v. Oklahoma, 15 years later, implicitly does so by recognizing a fundamental right to procreate. During the time between the two cases, the eugenics movement waned, certainly in large part after people saw the horrors of its implementation in Nazi Germany.

SKINNER v. OKLAHOMA

316 U.S. 535 (1942)

Justice DOUGLAS delivered the opinion of the Court.

This case touches a sensitive and important area of human rights. Oklahoma deprives certain individuals of a right which is basic to the perpetuation of a race — the right to have offspring. The statute involved is Oklahoma's Habitual Criminal Sterilization Act. That Act defines an "habitual criminal" as a person who, having been convicted two or more times for crimes "amounting to felonies involving moral turpitude" either in an Oklahoma court or in a court of any other State, is thereafter convicted of such a felony in Oklahoma and is sentenced to a term of imprisonment in an Oklahoma penal institution.

Petitioner was convicted in 1926 of the crime of stealing chickens and was sentenced to the Oklahoma State Reformatory. In 1929 he was convicted of the crime of robbery with firearms and was sentenced to the reformatory. In 1934 he was convicted again of robbery with firearms and was sentenced to the penitentiary. He was confined there in 1935 when the Act was passed. In 1936 the Attorney General instituted proceedings against him. Petitioner in his answer challenged the Act as unconstitutional by reason of the Fourteenth Amendment. A jury trial was had. The court instructed the jury that the crimes of which petitioner had been convicted were felonies involving moral turpitude and that the only question for the jury was whether the operation of vasectomy could be performed on petitioner without detriment to his general health. The jury found that it could be. A judgment directing that the operation of vasectomy be performed on petitioner was affirmed by the Supreme Court of Oklahoma by a five to four decision.

We are dealing here with legislation which involves one of the basic civil rights of man. Marriage and procreation are fundamental to the very existence and survival of the race. The power to sterilize, if exercised, may have subtle, far-reaching and devastating effects. In evil or reckless hands it can cause races or types which are inimical to the dominant group to wither and disappear. There is no redemption for the individual whom the law touches. Any experiment which the State conducts is to his irreparable injury. He is forever deprived of a basic liberty. We mention these matters not to reexamine the scope of the

23. *See* Stephen Jay Gould, *Carrie Buck's Daughter,* 2 Const. Comment. 331, 336 (1985).
24. *Id.* at 332.

police power of the States. We advert to them merely in emphasis of our view that strict scrutiny of the classification which a State makes in a sterilization law is essential, lest unwittingly or otherwise invidious discriminations are made against groups or types of individuals in violation of the constitutional guaranty of just and equal laws.

Sterilization of those who have thrice committed grand larceny with immunity for those who are embezzlers is a clear, pointed, unmistakable discrimination. Oklahoma makes no attempt to say that he who commits larceny by trespass or trick or fraud has biologically inheritable traits which he who commits embezzlement lacks. We have not the slightest basis for inferring that that line has any significance in eugenics nor that the inheritability of criminal traits follows the neat legal distinctions which the law has marked between those two offenses. In terms of fines and imprisonment the crimes of larceny and embezzlement rate the same under the Oklahoma code. Only when it comes to sterilization are the pains and penalties of the law different. The equal protection clause would indeed be a formula of empty words if such conspicuously artificial lines could be drawn.

Chief Justice STONE concurring.

I concur in the result, but I am not persuaded that we are aided in reaching it by recourse to the equal protection clause. If Oklahoma may resort generally to the sterilization of criminals on the assumption that their propensities are transmissible to future generations by inheritance, I seriously doubt that the equal protection clause requires it to apply the measure to all criminals in the first instance, or to none. And so I think the real question we have to consider is not one of equal protection, but whether the wholesale condemnation of a class to such an invasion of personal liberty, without opportunity to any individual to show that his is not the type of case which would justify resort to it, satisfies the demands of due process.

2.   The Right to Purchase and Use Contraceptives

A second aspect of reproductive freedom is the right to purchase and use contraceptives. Griswold v. Connecticut is the initial case here and an important decision in the debate over the proper method of constitutional interpretation.

GRISWOLD v. CONNECTICUT
381 U.S. 479 (1965)

Justice DOUGLAS delivered the opinion of the Court.

Appellant Griswold is Executive Director of the Planned Parenthood League of Connecticut. Appellant Buxton is a licensed physician and a professor at the Yale Medical School who served as Medical Director for the League at its Center in New Haven — a center open and operating from November 1 to November 10, 1961, when appellants were arrested.

They gave information, instruction, and medical advice to married persons as to the means of preventing conception. They examined the wife and prescribed the best contraceptive device or material for her use. Fees were usually charged, although some couples were serviced free.

The statutes whose constitutionality is involved in this appeal provide: "Any person who uses any drug, medicinal article or instrument for the purpose of preventing conception shall be fined not less than fifty dollars or imprisoned not less than sixty days nor more than one year or be both fined and imprisoned." "Any person who assists, abets, counsels, causes, hires or commands another to commit any offense may be prosecuted and punished as if he were the principal offender." The appellants were found guilty as accessories and fined $100 each.

[W]e are met with a wide range of questions that implicate the Due Process Clause of the Fourteenth Amendment. Overtones of some arguments suggest that Lochner v. State of New York should be our guide. But we decline that invitation as we did in West Coast Hotel Co. v. Parrish; Olsen v. State of Nebraska; Lincoln Federal Labor Union v. Northwestern Co.; Williamson v. Lee Optical Co. We do not sit as a super-legislature to determine the wisdom, need, and propriety of laws that touch economic problems, business affairs, or social conditions. This law, however, operates directly on an intimate relation of husband and wife and their physician's role in one aspect of that relation.

The association of people is not mentioned in the Constitution nor in the Bill of Rights. The right to educate a child in a school of the parents' choice — whether public or private or parochial — is also not mentioned. Nor is the right to study any particular subject or any foreign language. Yet the First Amendment has been construed to include certain of those rights.

By Pierce v. Society of Sisters, the right to educate one's children as one chooses is made applicable to the States by the force of the First and Fourteenth Amendments. By Meyer v. State of Nebraska, the same dignity is given the right to study the German language in a private school. In other words, the State may not, consistently with the spirit of the First Amendment, contract the spectrum of available knowledge.

The foregoing cases suggest that specific guarantees in the Bill of Rights have penumbras, formed by emanations from those guarantees that help give them life and substance. Various guarantees create zones of privacy. The right of association contained in the penumbra of the First Amendment is one, as we have seen. The Third Amendment in its prohibition against the quartering of soldiers "in any house" in time of peace without the consent of the owner is another facet of that privacy. The Fourth Amendment explicitly affirms the "right of the people to be secure in their persons, houses, papers, and effects, against unreasonable searches and seizures." The Fifth Amendment in its Self-Incrimination Clause enables the citizen to create a zone of privacy which government may not force him to surrender to his detriment. The Ninth Amendment provides: "The enumeration in the Constitution, of certain rights, shall not be construed to deny or disparage others retained by the people." We have had many controversies over these penumbral rights of "privacy and repose."

The present case, then, concerns a relationship lying within the zone of privacy created by several fundamental constitutional guarantees. And it concerns a law which, in forbidding the use of contraceptives rather than regulating their manufacture or sale, seeks to achieve its goals by means having a maximum destructive impact upon that relationship. Such a law cannot stand in light of the familiar principle, so often applied by this Court, that a "governmental purpose to control or prevent activities constitutionally subject to state regulation may not be achieved by means which sweep unnecessarily broadly and thereby invade the area of protected freedoms." Would we allow the police to search the sacred precincts of marital bedrooms for telltale signs of the use of contraceptives? The very idea is repulsive to the notions of privacy surrounding the marriage relationship.

We deal with a right of privacy older than the Bill of Rights — older than our political parties, older than our school system. Marriage is a coming together for better or for worse, hopefully enduring, and intimate to the degree of being sacred. It is an association that promotes a way of life, not causes; a harmony in living, not political faiths; a bilateral loyalty, not commercial or social projects. Yet it is an association for as noble a purpose as any involved in our prior decisions.

Justice GOLDBERG, whom the Chief Justice and Justice BRENNAN join, concurring.

I agree with the Court that Connecticut's birth-control law unconstitutionally intrudes upon the right of marital privacy, and I join in its opinion and judgment. My conclusion that the concept of liberty is not so restricted and that it embraces the right of marital privacy though that right is not mentioned explicitly in the Constitution is supported both by numerous decisions of this Court, referred to in the Court's opinion, and by the language and history of the Ninth Amendment. I add these words to emphasize the relevance of that Amendment to the Court's holding.

The Ninth Amendment reads, "The enumeration in the Constitution, of certain rights, shall not be construed to deny or disparage others retained by the people." The Amendment is almost entirely the work of James Madison. It was introduced in Congress by him and passed the House and Senate with little or no debate and virtually no change in language. It was proffered to quiet expressed fears that a bill of specifically enumerated rights could not be sufficiently broad to cover all essential rights and that the specific mention of certain rights would be interpreted as a denial that others were protected.

While this Court has had little occasion to interpret the Ninth Amendment, "[i]t cannot be presumed that any clause in the constitution is intended to be without effect." Marbury v. Madison. In interpreting the Constitution, "real effect should be given to all the words it uses." Myers v. United States. The Ninth Amendment to the Constitution may be regarded by some as a recent discovery and may be forgotten by others, but since 1791 it has been a basic part of the Constitution which we are sworn to uphold. To hold that a right so basic and fundamental and so deep-rooted in our society as the right of privacy in marriage may be infringed because that right is not guaranteed in so many words by the first eight amendments to the Constitution is to ignore the Ninth Amendment and to give it no effect whatsoever. Moreover, a judicial construction that this fundamental right is not protected by the Constitution because it is not mentioned in explicit terms by one of the first eight amendments or elsewhere in the Constitution would violate the Ninth Amendment, which specifically states that "[t]he enumeration in the Constitution, of certain rights shall not be construed to deny or disparage others retained by the people."

In sum, the Ninth Amendment simply lends strong support to the view that the "liberty" protected by the Fifth and Fourteenth Amendments from infringement by the Federal Government or the States is not restricted to rights specifically mentioned in the first eight amendments.

In determining which rights are fundamental, judges are not left at large to decide cases in light of their personal and private notions. Rather, they must look to the "traditions and [collective] conscience of our people" to determine whether a principle is "so rooted [there] . . . as to be ranked as fundamental." The inquiry is whether a right involved "is of such a character that it cannot be denied without violating those 'fundamental principles of liberty and justice which lie at the base of all our civil and political institutions.' . . ."

I agree fully with the Court that, applying these tests, the right of privacy is a fundamental personal right, emanating "from the totality of the constitutional scheme under which we live." While it may shock some of my Brethren that the Court today holds that the Constitution protects the right of marital privacy, in my view it is far more shocking to believe that the personal liberty guaranteed by the Constitution does not include protection against such totalitarian limitation of family size, which is at complete variance with our constitutional concepts. Yet, if upon a showing of a slender basis of rationality, a law outlawing voluntary birth control by married persons is valid, then, by the same reasoning, a law requiring compulsory birth control also would seem to be valid. In my view, however, both types of law would unjustifiably intrude upon rights of marital privacy which are constitutionally protected.

The State, at most, argues that there is some rational relation between this statute and what is admittedly a legitimate subject of state concern — the discouraging of extra-marital relations. It says that preventing the use of birth-control devices by married persons helps prevent the indulgence by some in such extra-marital relations. The rationality of this justification is dubious, particularly in light of the admitted widespread availability to all persons in the State of Connecticut, unmarried as well as married, of birth-control devices for the prevention of disease, as distinguished from the prevention of conception. But, in any event, it is clear that the state interest in safeguarding marital fidelity can be served by a more discriminately tailored statute, which does not, like the present one, sweep unnecessarily broadly, reaching far beyond the evil sought to be dealt with and intruding upon the privacy of all married couples. The State of Connecticut does have statutes, the constitutionality of which is beyond doubt, which prohibit adultery and fornication. These statutes demonstrate that means for achieving the same basic purpose of protecting marital fidelity are available to Connecticut without the need to "invade the area of protected freedoms."

Finally, it should be said of the Court's holding today that it in no way interferes with a State's proper regulation of sexual promiscuity or misconduct. As my Brother Harlan so well stated in his dissenting opinion in Poe v. Ullman, "Adultery, homosexuality and the like are sexual intimacies which the State forbids . . . but the intimacy of husband and wife is necessarily an essential and accepted feature of the institution of marriage, an institution which the State not only must allow, but which always and in every age it has fostered and protected. It is one thing when the State exerts its power either to forbid extra-marital sexuality . . . or to say who may marry, but it is quite another when, having acknowledged a marriage and the intimacies inherent in it, it undertakes to regulate by means of the criminal law the details of that intimacy."

In sum, I believe that the right of privacy in the marital relation is fundamental and basic — a personal right "retained by the people" within the meaning of the Ninth Amendment. Connecticut cannot constitutionally abridge this fundamental right, which is protected by the Fourteenth Amendment from infringement by the States. I agree with the Court that petitioners' convictions must therefore be reversed.

Justice HARLAN, concurring in the judgment.

In my view, the proper constitutional inquiry in this case is whether this Connecticut statute infringes the Due Process Clause of the Fourteenth Amendment because the enactment violates basic values "implicit in the concept of ordered liberty," Palko v. State of Connecticut. While the relevant inquiry may be aided by resort to one or more of the provisions of the Bill of Rights, it is not dependent on them or any of their radiations. The Due Process Clause of the Fourteenth Amendment stands, in my opinion, on its own bottom.

Judicial self-restraint will be achieved in this area, as in other constitutional areas, only by continual insistence upon respect for the teachings of history, solid recognition of the basic values that underlie our society, and wise appreciation of the great roles that the doctrines of federalism and separation of powers have played in establishing and preserving American freedoms. Adherence to these principles will not, of course, obviate all constitutional differences of opinion among judges, nor should it. Their continued recognition will, however, go farther toward keeping most judges from roaming at large in the constitutional field than will the interpolation into the Constitution of an artificial and largely illusory restriction on the content of the Due Process Clause.

Justice WHITE, concurring in the judgment.

In my view this Connecticut law as applied to married couples deprives them of "liberty" without due process of law, as that concept is used in the Fourteenth Amendment. There is no serious contention that Connecticut thinks the use of artificial or external methods of contraception immoral or unwise in itself, or that the anti-use statute is founded upon any policy of promoting population expansion. Rather, the statute is said to serve the State's policy against all forms of promiscuous or illicit sexual relationships, be they premarital or extramarital, concededly a permissible and legitimate legislative goal.

Without taking issue with the premise that the fear of conception operates as a deterrent to such relationships in addition to the criminal proscriptions Connecticut has against such conduct, I wholly fail to see how the ban on the use of contraceptives by married couples in any way reinforces the State's ban on illicit sexual relationships. Connecticut does not bar the importation or possession of contraceptive devices; they are not considered contraband material under state law, and their availability in that State is not seriously disputed. The only way Connecticut seeks to limit or control the availability of such devices is through its general aiding and abetting statute whose operation in this context has been quite obviously ineffective and whose most serious use has been against birth-control clinics rendering advice to married, rather than unmarried, persons. Moreover, it would appear that the sale of contraceptives to prevent disease is plainly legal under Connecticut law.

In these circumstances one is rather hard pressed to explain how the ban on use by married persons in any way prevents use of such devices by persons engaging in illicit sexual relations and thereby contributes to the State's policy against such relationships. Neither the state courts nor the State before the bar of this Court has tendered such an explanation. It is purely fanciful to believe that the broad proscription on use facilitates discovery of use by persons engaging in a prohibited relationship or for some other reason makes such use more unlikely and thus can be supported by any sort of administrative consideration.

I find nothing in this record justifying the sweeping scope of this statute, with its telling effect on the freedoms of married persons, and therefore conclude that it deprives such persons of liberty without due process of law.

Justice BLACK, with whom Justice STEWART joins, dissenting.

I do not to any extent whatever base my view that this Connecticut law is constitutional on a belief that the law is wise or that its policy is a good one. In order that there may be no room at all to doubt why I vote as I do, I feel constrained to add that the law is every bit as offensive to me as it is my Brethren of the majority.

The Court talks about a constitutional "right of privacy" as though there is some constitutional provision or provisions forbidding any law ever to be passed which might abridge the "privacy" of individuals. But there is not. There are, of course, guarantees in certain specific constitutional provisions which are designed in part to protect privacy at certain times and places with respect to certain activities. Such, for example, is the Fourth Amendment's guarantee against "unreasonable searches and seizures." But I think it belittles that Amendment to talk about it as though it protects nothing but "privacy." To treat it that way is to give it a niggardly interpretation, not the kind of liberal reading I think any Bill of Rights provision should be given.

For these reasons I get nowhere in this case by talk about a constitutional "right of privacy" as an emanation from one or more constitutional provisions. I like my privacy as well as the next one, but I am nevertheless compelled to admit that government has a right to invade it unless prohibited by some specific constitutional provision. For these reasons I cannot agree with the Court's judgment and the reasons it gives for holding this Connecticut law unconstitutional.

This brings me to the arguments made by my Brothers Harlan, White and Goldberg for invalidating the Connecticut law. I think that if properly construed neither the Due Process Clause nor the Ninth Amendment, nor both together, could under any circumstances be a proper basis for invalidating the Connecticut law. I discuss the due process and Ninth Amendment arguments together because on analysis they turn out to be the same thing — merely using different words to claim for this Court and the federal judiciary power to invalidate any legislative act which the judges find irrational, unreasonable or offensive.

My Brother Goldberg has adopted the recent discovery that the Ninth Amendment as well as the Due Process Clause can be used by this Court as authority to strike down all state legislation which this Court thinks violates "fundamental principles of liberty and justice," or is contrary to the "traditions and [collective] conscience of our people." He also states, without proof satisfactory to me, that in making decisions on this basis judges will not consider "their personal and private notions." One may ask how they can avoid considering them. Our Court certainly has no machinery with which to take a Gallup Poll. And the scientific miracles of this age have not yet produced a gadget which the Court can use to determine what traditions are rooted in the "[collective] conscience of our people." Moreover, one would certainly have to look far beyond the language of the Ninth Amendment to find that the framers vested in this Court any such awesome veto powers over lawmaking, either by the States or by the Congress. Nor does anything in the history of the Amendment offer any support for such a shocking doctrine. Use of any such broad, unbounded judicial authority would make of this Court's members a day-to-day constitutional convention.

I realize that many good and able men have eloquently spoken and written, sometimes in rhapsodical strains, about the duty of this Court to keep the Constitution in tune with the times. The idea is that the Constitution must be changed from time to time and that this Court is charged with a duty to make those changes. For myself, I must with all deference reject that philosophy.

The Constitution makers knew the need for change and provided for it. Amendments suggested by the people's elected representatives can be submitted to the people or their selected agents for ratification. That method of change was good for our Fathers, and being somewhat old-fashioned I must add it is good enough for me. And so, I cannot rely on the Due Process Clause or the Ninth Amendment or any mysterious and uncertain natural law concept as a reason for striking down this state law.

The late Judge Learned Hand, after emphasizing his view that judges should not use the due process formula suggested in the concurring opinions today or any other formula like it to invalidate legislation offensive to their "personal preferences," made the statement, with which I fully agree, that: "For myself it would be most irksome to be ruled by a bevy of Platonic Guardians, even if I knew how to choose them, which I assuredly do not."

Justice STEWART, whom Justice BLACK joins, dissenting.

Since 1879 Connecticut has had on its books a law which forbids the use of contraceptives by anyone. I think this is an uncommonly silly law. As a practical matter, the law is obviously unenforceable, except in the oblique context of the present case. As a philosophical matter, I believe the use of contraceptives in the relationship of marriage should be left to personal and private choice, based upon each individual's moral, ethical, and religious beliefs. As a matter of social policy, I think professional counsel about methods of birth control should be available to all, so that each individual's choice can be meaningfully made. But we are not asked in this case to say whether we think this law is unwise, or even asinine. We are asked to hold that it violates the United States Constitution. And that I cannot do.

It is the essence of judicial duty to subordinate our own personal views, our own ideas of what legislation is wise and what is not. If, as I should surely hope, the law before us does not reflect the standards of the people of Connecticut, the people of Connecticut can freely exercise their true Ninth and Tenth Amendment rights to persuade their elected representatives to repeal it. That is the constitutional way to take this law off the books.

The Court reaffirmed and extended *Griswold* in Eisenstadt v. Baird.

EISENSTADT v. BAIRD
405 U.S. 438 (1972)

Justice BRENNAN delivered the opinion of the Court.

Appellee William Baird was convicted at a bench trial in the Massachusetts Superior Court under Massachusetts General Laws Ann., first, for exhibiting contraceptive articles in the course of delivering a lecture on contraception to a group of students at Boston University and, second, for giving a young woman a package of Emko vaginal foam at the close of his address.

Massachusetts General Laws Ann. under which Baird was convicted, provides a maximum five-year term of imprisonment for "whoever . . . gives away . . . any drug, medicine, instrument or article whatever for the prevention of conception," except as authorized in §21A. Under §21A, "[a] registered physician may administer to or prescribe for any married person drugs or articles intended for the prevention of pregnancy or conception. [And a] registered pharmacist actually engaged in the business of pharmacy may furnish such drugs or articles to any married person presenting a prescription from a registered physician." As interpreted by the State Supreme Judicial Court, these provisions make it a felony for anyone, other than a registered physician or pharmacist acting in accordance with the terms of §21A, to dispense any article with the intention that it be used for the prevention of conception. The statutory scheme distinguishes among three distinct classes of distributees — first, married persons may obtain contraceptives to prevent pregnancy, but only from doctors or druggists on prescription; second, single persons may not obtain contraceptives from anyone to prevent pregnancy; and, third, married or single persons may obtain contraceptives from anyone to prevent, not pregnancy, but the spread of disease.

The question for our determination in this case is whether there is some ground of difference that rationally explains the different treatment accorded married and unmarried persons under Massachusetts laws. Section 21 stems from an 1879 statute, which prohibited without exception, distribution of articles intended to be used as contraceptives. In Commonwealth v. Allison (1917), the Massachusetts Supreme Judicial Court explained that the law's "plain purpose is to protect purity, to preserve chastity, to encourage continence and self restraint, to defend the sanctity of the home, and thus to engender in the State and nation a virile and virtuous race of men and women."

[W]e cannot agree that the deterrence of premarital sex may reasonably be regarded as the purpose of the Massachusetts law. It would be plainly unreasonable to assume that Massachusetts has prescribed pregnancy and the birth of an unwanted child as punishment for fornication, which is a misdemeanor under Massachusetts General Laws Ann. Aside from the scheme of values that assumption would attribute to the State, it is abundantly clear that the effect of the ban on distribution of contraceptives to unmarried persons has at best a marginal relation to the proffered objective.

If the Massachusetts statute cannot be upheld as a deterrent to fornication or as a health measure, may it, nevertheless, be sustained simply as a prohibition on contraception? Whatever the rights of the individual to access contraceptives may be, the rights must be the same for the unmarried and the married alike.

If under *Griswold* the distribution of contraceptives to married persons cannot be prohibited, a ban on distribution to unmarried persons would be equally impermissible. It is true that in *Griswold* the right of privacy in question inhered in the marital relationship. Yet the marital couple is not an independent entity with a mind and heart of its own, but an association of two individuals each with a separate intellectual and emotional makeup. If the right of privacy means anything, it is the right of the individual, married or single, to be free from unwarranted governmental intrusion into matters so fundamentally affecting a person as the decision whether to bear or beget a child.

[I]f *Griswold* is no bar to a prohibition on the distribution of contraceptives, the State could not, consistently with the Equal Protection Clause, outlaw distribution to unmarried but not to married persons. In each case the evil, as perceived by the State, would be identical, and the underinclusion would be invidious.

Chief Justice Burger, dissenting.

The judgment of the Supreme Judicial Court of Massachusetts in sustaining appellee's conviction for dispensing medicinal material without a license seems eminently correct to me and I would not disturb it. I see nothing in the Fourteenth Amendment or any other part of the Constitution that even vaguely suggests that these medicinal forms of contraceptives must be available in the open market. I do not challenge Griswold v. Connecticut despite its tenuous moorings to the text of the Constitution, but I cannot view it as controlling authority for this case. The Court was there confronted with a statute flatly prohibiting the use of contraceptives, not one regulating their distribution. I simply cannot believe that the limitation on the class of lawful distributors has significantly impaired the right to use contraceptives in Massachusetts. By relying on *Griswold* in the present context, the Court has passed beyond the penumbras of the specific guarantees into the uncircumscribed area of personal predilections.

The Court also protected the right to purchase and use contraceptives in Carey v. Population Services International, 431 U.S. 678 (1977). In *Carey*, the Court declared unconstitutional a New York law that made it a crime to sell or distribute contraceptives to minors under age 16, for anyone other than a licensed pharmacist to distribute contraceptives to persons over age 15, and for anyone to advertise or display contraceptives. The Court reviewed the cases concerning family and procreational autonomy and said that "[t]he decision whether or not to beget or bear a child is at the very heart of this cluster of constitutionally protected choices." The Court thus said that strict scrutiny must be met for the government to justify a law restricting access to contraceptives. Justice Brennan, writing for the Court, said, "'Compelling' is of course the key word; where a decision as fundamental as that whether to bear or beget a child is involved, regulations imposing a burden on it may be justified only by compelling state interests, and must be narrowly drawn to express only those interests."

Thus, the Court found that limiting distribution of contraceptives to licensed pharmacists unduly restricted access to birth control and infringed the right to control procreation. Additionally, the Court found that the law violated the rights of those under age 16 to have access to contraceptives. The Court explained, "Since the State may not impose a blanket prohibition, or even a blanket requirement of parental consent, on the choice of a minor to terminate her pregnancy, the constitutionality of a blanket prohibition of the distribution of contraceptives to a minor is a fortiori foreclosed." The Court doubted that prohibiting distribution of contraceptives would deter teenage sexual activity and, in any event, thought it irrational that the state would want an unwanted pregnancy to be the punishment for fornication.

3. The Right to Abortion

Few decisions in Supreme Court history have provoked the intense controversy that has surrounded the abortion rulings. The debate, in part, is over constitutional methodology. Should the Court protect such a right that is not mentioned in the text and was not clearly intended by the framers?[25] This, of course, is the same methodological question that can be asked about all of the unenumerated rights concerning family and reproductive autonomy protected by the Court. Also, the heated battle over abortion reflects the strong sentiments on both sides. There simply is no middle ground between those who believe that abortion is murder and those who reject that view and believe that a woman should not be forced by the state to be an incubator.

In examining the right to abortion, analysis is divided into five parts. The first subsection reviews the Supreme Court's conclusion that the Constitution protects the right of women to choose to terminate their pregnancies prior to viability. Roe v. Wade and Planned Parenthood v. Casey are presented in detail. The second subsection considers what types of state regulations of abortion are permissible and which are unconstitutional. The third subsection presents the decisions concerning laws that prohibit the use of government funds or facilities for performing abortions. The fourth subsection examines a particular type of government regulation that has been declared unconstitutional: spousal consent and spousal notification requirements for married women's abortions. Finally, the last subsection reviews the law concerning the ability of a state to require parental notice and/or consent for an unmarried minor's abortion.

a. The Recognition and Reaffirmation of the Right to Abortion

ROE v. WADE
410 U.S. 113 (1973)

Justice BLACKMUN delivered the opinion of the Court.

[I]

We forthwith acknowledge our awareness of the sensitive and emotional nature of the abortion controversy, of the vigorous opposing views, even among

---

25. For a criticism of *Roe* on this basis, *see* John Hart Ely, *The Wages of Crying Wolf: A Comment on Roe v. Wade*, 82 Yale L.J. 920, 947-949 (1973); for a defense of *Roe* on this basis, *see* Philip Heymann, *The Forest and the Trees: Roe v. Wade and Its Critics*, 53 B.U. L. Rev. 765, 772-774 (1973).

physicians, and of the deep and seemingly absolute convictions that the subject inspires. One's philosophy, one's experiences, one's exposure to the raw edges of human existence, one's religious training, one's attitudes toward life and family and their values, and the moral standards one establishes and seeks to observe, are all likely to influence and to color one's thinking and conclusions about abortion.

In addition, population growth, pollution, poverty, and racial overtones tend to complicate and not to simplify the problem. Our task, of course, is to resolve the issue by constitutional measurement, free of emotion and of predilection. We seek earnestly to do this, and, because we do, we have inquired into, and in this opinion place some emphasis upon, medical and medical-legal history and what that history reveals about man's attitudes toward the abortion procedure over the centuries.

[II]

It perhaps is not generally appreciated that the restrictive criminal abortion laws in effect in a majority of States today are of relatively recent vintage. Those laws, generally proscribing abortion or its attempt at any time during pregnancy except when necessary to preserve the pregnant woman's life, are not of ancient or even of common-law origin. Instead, they derive from statutory changes effected, for the most part, in the latter half of the 19th century.

1. Ancient attitudes. These are not capable of precise determination. We are told that at the time of the Persian Empire abortifacients were known and that criminal abortions were severely punished. We are also told, however, that abortion was practiced in Greek times as well as in the Roman Era, and that "it was resorted to without scruple." The Ephesian, Soranos, often described as the greatest of the ancient gynecologists, appears to have been generally opposed to Rome's prevailing free-abortion practices. He found it necessary to think first of the life of the mother, and he resorted to abortion when, upon this standard, he felt the procedure advisable. Greek and Roman law afforded little protection to the unborn. If abortion was prosecuted in some places, it seems to have been based on a concept of a violation of the father's right to his offspring. Ancient religion did not bar abortion.

2. The Hippocratic Oath. What then of the famous Oath that has stood so long as the ethical guide of the medical profession and that bears the name of the great Greek (460(§)-377(§) B.C.), who has been described as the Father of Medicine, the "wisest and the greatest practitioner of his art," and the "most important and most complete medical personality of antiquity," who dominated the medical schools of his time, and who typified the sum of the medical knowledge of the past? The Oath varies somewhat according to the particular translation, but in any translation the content is clear: "I will give no deadly medicine to anyone if asked, nor suggest any such counsel; and in like manner I will not give to a woman a pessary to produce abortion." Why did not the authority of Hippocrates dissuade abortion practice in his time and that of Rome? The late Dr. Edelstein provides us with a theory: The Oath was not uncontested even in Hippocrates' day; only the Pythagorean school of philosophers frowned upon the related act of suicide. Most Greek thinkers, on the other hand, commended abortion, at least prior to viability. Dr. Edelstein then concludes that the Oath

originated in a group representing only a small segment of Greek opinion and that it certainly was not accepted by all ancient physicians.

3. The common law. It is undisputed that at common law, abortion performed before "quickening" — the first recognizable movement of the fetus in utero, appearing usually from the 16th to the 18th week of pregnancy — was not an indictable offense. The absence of a common-law crime for pre-quickening abortion appears to have developed from a confluence of earlier philosophical, theological, and civil and canon law concepts of when life begins. Whether abortion of a quick fetus was a felony at common law, or even a lesser crime, is still disputed.

4. The American law. In this country, the law in effect in all but a few States until mid-19th century was the pre-existing English common law. Connecticut, the first State to enact abortion legislation, adopted in 1821 that part of Lord Ellenborough's Act that related to a woman "quick with child." The death penalty was not imposed. Abortion before quickening was made a crime in that State only in 1860. It was not until after the War Between the States that legislation began generally to replace the common law. Most of these initial statutes dealt severely with abortion after quickening but were lenient with it before quickening.

Gradually, in the middle and late 19th century the quickening distinction disappeared from the statutory law of most States and the degree of the offense and the penalties were increased. By the end of the 1950's a large majority of the jurisdictions banned abortion, however and whenever performed, unless done to save or preserve the life of the mother. In the past several years, however, a trend toward liberalization of abortion statutes has resulted in adoption, by about one-third of the States, of less stringent laws, most of them patterned after the ALI Model Penal Code. By the end of 1970, four other States had repealed criminal penalties for abortions performed in early pregnancy by a licensed physician, subject to stated procedural and health requirements.

It is thus apparent that at common law, at the time of the adoption of our Constitution, and throughout the major portion of the 19th century, abortion was viewed with less disfavor than under most American statutes currently in effect. Phrasing it another way, a woman enjoyed a substantially broader right to terminate a pregnancy than she does in most States today. At least with respect to the early stage of pregnancy, and very possibly without such a limitation, the opportunity to make this choice was present in this country well into the 19th century. Even later, the law continued for some time to treat less punitively an abortion procured in early pregnancy.

[III]

Three reasons have been advanced to explain historically the enactment of criminal abortion laws in the 19th century and to justify their continued existence. It has been argued occasionally that these laws were the product of a Victorian social concern to discourage illicit sexual conduct. Texas, however, does not advance this justification in the present case, and it appears that no court or commentator has taken the argument seriously.

A second reason is concerned with abortion as a medical procedure. When most criminal abortion laws were first enacted, the procedure was a hazardous one for the woman. This was particularly true prior to the development of antisepsis. Appellants and various amici refer to medical data indicating that abortion in early pregnancy, that is, prior to the end of the first trimester, although not without its risk, is now relatively safe. Mortality rates for women undergoing early abortions, where the procedure is legal, appear to be as low as or lower than the rates for normal childbirth. Consequently, any interest of the State in protecting the woman from an inherently hazardous procedure, except when it would be equally dangerous for her to forgo it, has largely disappeared. Of course, important state interests in the areas of health and medical standards do remain. The State has a legitimate interest in seeing to it that abortion, like any other medical procedure, is performed under circumstances that insure maximum safety for the patient. This interest obviously extends at least to the performing physician and his staff, to the facilities involved, to the availability of after-care, and to adequate provision for any complication or emergency that might arise. The prevalence of high mortality rates at illegal "abortion mills" strengthens, rather than weakens, the State's interest in regulating the conditions under which abortions are performed. Moreover, the risk to the woman increases as her pregnancy continues. Thus, the State retains a definite interest in protecting the woman's own health and safety when an abortion is proposed at a late stage of pregnancy.

The third reason is the State's interest — some phrase it in terms of duty — in protecting prenatal life. Some of the argument for this justification rests on the theory that a new human life is present from the moment of conception. The State's interest and general obligation to protect life then extends, it is argued, to prenatal life. Only when the life of the pregnant mother herself is at stake, balanced against the life she carries within her, should the interest of the embryo or fetus not prevail. Logically, of course, a legitimate state interest in this area need not stand or fall on acceptance of the belief that life begins at conception or at some other point prior to live birth. In assessing the State's interest, recognition may be given to the less rigid claim that as long as at least potential life is involved, the State may assert interests beyond the protection of the pregnant woman alone.

It is with these interests, and the weight to be attached to them, that this case is concerned.

[IV]

The Constitution does not explicitly mention any right of privacy. In a line of decisions, however, going back perhaps as far as Union Pacific R. Co. v. Botsford (1891), the Court has recognized that a right of personal privacy, or a guarantee of certain areas or zones of privacy, does exist under the Constitution. This right of privacy, whether it be founded in the Fourteenth Amendment's concept of personal liberty and restrictions upon state action, as we feel it is, or, as the District Court determined, in the Ninth Amendment's reservation of rights to the people, is broad enough to encompass a woman's decision whether or not to terminate her pregnancy. The detriment that the State would impose upon the pregnant woman by denying this choice altogether is apparent. Specific and direct harm medically diagnosable even in early pregnancy may be involved. Maternity, or additional offspring, may force upon the woman a distressful life and future. Psychological harm may be imminent. Mental and physical health may be taxed by child care. There is also the distress, for all concerned, associated with the unwanted child, and there is the problem of bringing a child into a family already unable, psychologically and otherwise, to care for it. In other cases, as in this one, the additional difficulties and continuing stigma of unwed motherhood may be involved. All these are factors the woman and her responsible physician necessarily will consider in consultation.

On the basis of elements such as these, appellant and some amici argue that the woman's right is absolute and that she is entitled to terminate her pregnancy at whatever time, in whatever way, and for whatever reason she alone chooses. With this we do not agree. Appellant's arguments that Texas either has no valid interest at all in regulating the abortion decision, or no interest strong enough to support any limitation upon the woman's sole determination, are unpersuasive. The Court's decisions recognizing a right of privacy also acknowledge that some state regulation in areas protected by that right is appropriate. As noted above, a State may properly assert important interests in safeguarding health, in maintaining medical standards, and in protecting potential life. At some point in pregnancy, these respective interests become sufficiently compelling to sustain regulation of the factors that govern the abortion decision. The privacy right involved, therefore, cannot be said to be absolute.

We, therefore, conclude that the right of personal privacy includes the abortion decision, but that this right is not unqualified and must be considered against important state interests in regulation.

Where certain "fundamental rights" are involved, the Court has held that regulation limiting these rights may be justified only by a "compelling state interest," and that legislative enactments must be narrowly drawn to express only the legitimate state interests at stake.

A. The appellee and certain amici argue that the fetus is a "person" within the language and meaning of the Fourteenth Amendment. In support of this, they outline at length and in detail the well-known facts of fetal development. If this suggestion of personhood is established, the appellant's case, of course, collapses, for the fetus' right to life would then be guaranteed specifically by the Amendment. The Constitution does not define "person" in so many words. [T]his, together with our observation, that throughout the major portion of the 19th century prevailing legal abortion practices were far freer than they are today, persuades us that the word "person," as used in the Fourteenth Amendment, does not include the unborn.

B. The pregnant woman cannot be isolated in her privacy. She carries an embryo and, later, a fetus, if one accepts the medical definitions of the developing young in the human uterus. The situation therefore is inherently different from marital intimacy, or bedroom possession of obscene material, or marriage, or procreation, or education, with which *Eisenstadt* and *Griswold*, *Stanley*, *Loving*, *Skinner* and *Pierce* and *Meyer* were respectively concerned. As we have intimated above, it is reasonable and appropriate for a State to decide that at some point in time another interest, that of health of the mother or that of potential human life, becomes significantly involved. The woman's privacy is no longer sole and any right of privacy she possesses must be measured accordingly.

Texas urges that, apart from the Fourteenth Amendment, life begins at conception and is present throughout pregnancy, and that, therefore, the State has a compelling interest in protecting that life from and after conception. We need not resolve the difficult question of when life begins. When those trained in the respective disciplines of medicine, philosophy, and theology are unable to arrive at any consensus, the judiciary, at this point in the development of man's knowledge, is not in a position to speculate as to the answer.

It should be sufficient to note briefly the wide divergence of thinking on this most sensitive and difficult question. There has always been strong support for the view that life does not begin until live birth. This was the belief of the Stoics. It appears to be the predominant, though not the unanimous, attitude of the Jewish faith. It may be taken to represent also the position of a large segment of the Protestant community, insofar as that can be ascertained; organized groups that have taken a formal position on the abortion issue have generally regarded abortion as a matter for the conscience of the individual and her family. As we have noted, the common law found greater significance in quickening. Physicians and their scientific colleagues have regarded that event with less interest and have tended to focus either upon conception, upon live birth, or upon the interim point at which the fetus becomes "viable," that is, potentially able to live outside the mother's womb, albeit with artificial aid. Viability is usually placed at about seven months (28 weeks) but may occur earlier, even at 24 weeks.

[T]hose in the [Catholic] Church would recognize the existence of life from the moment of conception. The latter is now, of course, the official belief of the Catholic Church. As one brief amicus discloses, this is a view strongly held by many non-Catholics as well, and by many physicians. Substantial problems for precise definition of this view are posed, however, by new embryological data that purport to indicate that conception is a "process" over time, rather than an event, and by new medical techniques such as menstrual extraction, the "morning-after" pill, implantation of embryos, artificial insemination, and even artificial wombs.

In view of all this, we do not agree that, by adopting one theory of life, Texas may override the rights of the pregnant woman that are at stake. We repeat, however, that the State does have an important and legitimate interest in preserving and protecting the health of the pregnant woman, whether she be a resident of the State or a non-resident who seeks medical consultation and treatment there, and that it has still another important and legitimate interest in protecting the potentiality of human life. These interests are separate and distinct. Each grows in substantiality as the woman approaches term and, at a point during pregnancy, each becomes "compelling."

With respect to the State's important and legitimate interest in the health of the mother, the "compelling" point, in the light of present medical knowledge, is at approximately the end of the first trimester. This is so because of the now-established medical fact, referred to above, that until the end of the first trimester mortality in abortion may be less than mortality in normal childbirth. It follows that, from and after this point, a State may regulate the abortion procedure to the extent that the regulation reasonably relates to the preservation and protection of maternal health. Examples of permissible state regulation in this area are requirements as to the qualifications of the person who is to perform the abortion; as to the licensure of that person; as to the facility in which the procedure is to be performed, that is, whether it must be a hospital or may be a clinic or some other place of less-than-hospital status; as to the licensing of the facility; and the like.

This means, on the other hand, that, for the period of pregnancy prior to this "compelling" point, the attending physician, in consultation with his patient, is free to determine, without regulation by the State, that, in his medical judgment, the patient's pregnancy should be terminated. If that decision is reached, the judgment may be effectuated by an abortion free of interference by the State.

With respect to the State's important and legitimate interest in potential life, the "compelling" point is at viability. This is so because the fetus then presumably has the capability of meaningful life outside the mother's womb. State regulation protective of fetal life after viability thus has both logical and biological justifications. If the State is interested in protecting fetal life after viability, it may go so far as to proscribe abortion during that period, except when it is necessary to preserve the life or health of the mother.

Measured against these standards, Art. 1196 of the Texas Penal Code, in restricting legal abortions to those "procured or attempted by medical advice for the purpose of saving the life of the mother," sweeps too broadly. The statute makes no distinction between abortions performed early in pregnancy and those performed later, and it limits to a single reason, "saving" the mother's life, the legal justification for the procedure. The statute, therefore, cannot survive the constitutional attack made upon it here.

[V]

To summarize and to repeat:

1. A state criminal abortion statute of the current Texas type, that excepts from criminality only a life-saving procedure on behalf of the mother, without regard to pregnancy stage and without recognition of the other interests involved, is violative of the Due Process Clause of the Fourteenth Amendment.

(a) For the stage prior to approximately the end of the first trimester, the abortion decision and its effectuation must be left to the medical judgment of the pregnant woman's attending physician.

(b) For the stage subsequent to approximately the end of the first trimester, the State, in promoting its interest in the health of the mother, may, if it chooses, regulate the abortion procedure in ways that are reasonably related to maternal health.

(c) For the stage subsequent to viability, the State in promoting its interest in the potentiality of human life may, if it chooses, regulate, and even proscribe, abortion except where it is necessary, in appropriate medical judgment, for the preservation of the life or health of the mother.

2. The State may define the term "physician" to mean only a physician currently licensed by the State, and may proscribe any abortion by a person who is not a physician as so defined.

Justice REHNQUIST, dissenting.

I have difficulty in concluding, as the Court does, that the right of "privacy" is involved in this case. Texas, by the statute here challenged, bars the performance of a medical abortion by a licensed physician on a plaintiff such as Roe. A transaction resulting in an operation such as this is not "private" in the ordinary usage of that word. Nor is the "privacy" that the Court finds here even a distant relative of the freedom from searches and seizures protected by the Fourth Amendment to the Constitution, which the Court has referred to as embodying a right to privacy. Katz v. United States (1967).

If the Court means by the term "privacy" no more than that the claim of a person to be free from unwanted state regulation of consensual transactions may be a form of "liberty" protected by the Fourteenth Amendment, there is no doubt that similar claims have been upheld in our earlier decisions on the basis of that liberty. But that liberty is not guaranteed absolutely against deprivation, only against deprivation without due process of law. The test traditionally applied in the area of social and economic legislation is whether or not a law such as that challenged has a rational relation to a valid state objective. Williamson v. Lee Optical Co. (1955). The Due Process Clause of the Fourteenth Amendment undoubtedly does place a limit, albeit a broad one, on legislative power to enact laws such as this. If the Texas statute were to prohibit an abortion even where the mother's life is in jeopardy, I have little doubt that such a statute would lack a rational relation to a valid state objective under the test stated in *Williamson*. But the Court's sweeping invalidation of any restrictions on abortion during the first trimester is impossible to justify under that standard, and the conscious weighing of competing factors that the Court's opinion apparently substitutes for the established test is far more appropriate to a legislative judgment than to a judicial one. The decision here to break pregnancy into three distinct terms and to outline the permissible restrictions the State may impose in each one, for example, partakes more of judicial legislation than it does of a determination of the intent of the drafters of the Fourteenth Amendment.

The fact that a majority of the States reflecting, after all the majority sentiment in those States, have had restrictions on abortions for at least a century is a strong indication, it seems to me, that the asserted right to an abortion is not "so rooted in the traditions and conscience of our people as to be ranked as fundamental," Snyder v. Massachusetts (1934). Even today, when society's views on abortion are changing, the very existence of the debate is evidence that the "right" to an abortion is not so universally accepted as the appellant would have us believe.

To reach its result, the Court necessarily has had to find within the scope of the Fourteenth Amendment a right that was apparently completely unknown to the drafters of the Amendment. As early as 1821, the first state law dealing directly with abortion was enacted by the Connecticut Legislature. By the time of the adoption of the Fourteenth Amendment in 1868, there were at least 36 laws enacted by state or territorial legislatures limiting abortion. While many States have amended or updated their laws, 21 of the laws on the books in 1868 remain in effect today. Indeed, the Texas statute struck down today was, as the majority notes, first enacted in 1857 and "has remained substantially unchanged to the present time."

There apparently was no question concerning the validity of this provision or of any of the other state statutes when the Fourteenth Amendment was adopted. The only conclusion possible from this history is that the drafters did not intend to have the Fourteenth Amendment withdraw from the States the power to legislate with respect to this matter.

For all of the foregoing reasons, I respectfully dissent.

By the 1990s, the change in the composition of the Supreme Court raised questions as to whether Roe v. Wade would be overruled. In 1989, in Webster v. Reproductive Health Services, 492 U.S. 490 (1989), four justices seemed poised to overrule *Roe*. A Missouri law declared the state's view that life begins at conception, prohibited the use of government funds or facilities from performing or "encouraging or counseling" a woman to have an abortion, and allowed abortions after 20 weeks of pregnancy only if a test was done to ensure that the fetus was not viable. The Supreme Court upheld the Missouri law, but without a majority opinion.

Chief Justice Rehnquist, in a plurality opinion joined by Justices White and Kennedy, strongly criticized *Roe*. Rehnquist attacked the trimester distinctions that were used by *Roe* to balance the rights of the mother and the state's interest in protecting the fetus. Rehnquist wrote, "[T]he rigid *Roe* framework is hardly consistent with the notion of a Constitution cast in general terms. . . . The key elements of the *Roe* framework—trimesters and viability—are not found in the text of the Constitution or in any place else one would expect to find a constitutional principle."

Even more important, Rehnquist said, "[W]e do not see why the State's interest in protecting potential human life should come into existence only at the point of viability, and that there should therefore be a rigid line allowing state regulation after viability, but prohibiting it before viability. . . . The State's interest, if compelling after viability, is equally compelling before viability." Although Rehnquist's opinion did not expressly urge the overruling of Roe v. Wade, that was the unmistakable implication of declaring that the state has a compelling interest in protecting fetal life from the moment of conception. Rehnquist and White were the two dissenters in *Roe*, and they had consistently argued for overruling it.[26]

Justice Scalia wrote a separate opinion concurring in part and concurring in the judgment. He said that the plurality opinion "effectively would overrule Roe v. Wade." He said, "I think that should be done, but would do it more explicitly." He argued that the failure to overrule *Roe* "needlessly . . . prolong[s] this Court's self-awarded sovereignty over a field where it has little proper business since the answers to most of the cruel questions posed are political and not juridical."

Justice O'Connor provided the fifth vote for the result in *Webster*, but she ruled only on the specifics of the Missouri law and did not opine on the question of whether *Roe* should be overruled. O'Connor noted that the Missouri law did not prohibit abortions and thus "there is no necessity to accept the state's invitation to reexamine the constitutional validity of *Roe*." She said that "[w]hen the constitutional invalidity of a State's abortion statute actually turns on the constitutional validity of Roe v. Wade, there will be time enough to reexamine *Roe*. And to do so carefully."

The dissent in *Webster* saw a Court on the verge of overruling *Roe*. Justice Blackmun, joined by Justices Brennan and Marshall, lamented, "Today, Roe v. Wade and the fundamental constitutional right of women to decide whether to terminate a pregnancy, survive but are not secure. . . . [T]he plurality discards a landmark case of the last generation and casts into darkness the hopes

---

26. *See, e.g.*, Thornburgh v. American College of Obstetricians & Gynecologists, 476 U.S. 747, 797 (1986) (White, J., dissenting).

and visions of every woman in this country who had come to believe that the Constitution guaranteed her right to exercise some control over her unique ability to bear children. . . . For today, at least, the law of abortion stands undisturbed. For today, the women of this Nation still retain the liberty to control their destinies. But the signs are evident and very ominous, and a chill wind blows."

PLANNED PARENTHOOD v. CASEY

Between 1989, when *Webster* was decided, and 1992, when Planned Parenthood v. Casey was before the Court, Justices Brennan and Marshall had resigned and were replaced, respectively, by Justices Souter and Thomas. It was thought that either of them, and particularly Justice Clarence Thomas, might cast the fifth vote to overrule Roe v. Wade. Indeed, the United States, through the solicitor general, urged the Court in *Casey* to use it as the occasion for overruling *Roe*. The Court, however, did not do so. But an unusual joint opinion by Justices O'Connor, Kennedy, and Souter overruled the trimester distinctions used in *Roe* and also the use of strict scrutiny for evaluating government regulation of abortions. *Casey* remains the major case articulating current protections and constitutional standards for the right to abortion. Below are excerpts from *Casey* that discuss whether *Roe* should be overruled and the standard to be used in evaluating abortion laws. The discussion in *Casey* of specific types of regulation — such as waiting periods, spousal notification, and parental consent — is presented below as each of those issues is considered.

PLANNED PARENTHOOD v. CASEY
505 U.S. 833 (1992)

Justice O'Connor, Justice Kennedy, and Justice Souter announced the judgment of the Court.

I

Liberty finds no refuge in a jurisprudence of doubt. Yet 19 years after our holding that the Constitution protects a woman's right to terminate her pregnancy in its early stages, Roe v. Wade (1973), that definition of liberty is still questioned. Joining the respondents as amicus curiae, the United States, as it has done in five other cases in the last decade, again asks us to overrule *Roe*.

At issue in these cases are five provisions of the Pennsylvania Abortion Control Act of 1982, as amended in 1988 and 1989. The Act requires that a woman seeking an abortion give her informed consent prior to the abortion procedure, and specifies that she be provided with certain information at least 24 hours before the abortion is performed. For a minor to obtain an abortion, the Act requires the informed consent of one of her parents, but provides for a judicial bypass option if the minor does not wish to or cannot obtain a parent's consent. Another provision of the Act requires that, unless certain exceptions apply, a married woman seeking an abortion must sign a statement indicating that she has notified her husband of her intended abortion. The Act exempts compliance with these three requirements in the event of a "medical emergency," which is defined in §3203 of the Act. In addition to the above provisions regulating the performance of abortions, the Act imposes certain reporting requirements on facilities that provide abortion services.

[W]e acknowledge that our decisions after *Roe* cast doubt upon the meaning and reach of its holding. Further, the Chief Justice admits that he would overrule the central holding of *Roe* and adopt the rational relationship test as the sole criterion of constitutionality. State and federal courts as well as legislatures throughout the Union must have guidance as they seek to address this subject in conformance with the Constitution. Given these premises, we find it imperative to review once more the principles that define the rights of the woman and the legitimate authority of the State respecting the termination of pregnancies by abortion procedures.

After considering the fundamental constitutional questions resolved by *Roe*, principles of institutional integrity, and the rule of stare decisis, we are led to conclude this: the essential holding of Roe v. Wade should be retained and once again reaffirmed.

It must be stated at the outset and with clarity that *Roe*'s essential holding, the holding we reaffirm, has three parts. First is a recognition of the right of the woman to choose to have an abortion before viability and to obtain it without undue interference from the State. Before viability, the State's interests are not strong enough to support a prohibition of abortion or the imposition of a substantial obstacle to the woman's effective right to elect the procedure. Second is a confirmation of the State's power to restrict abortions after fetal viability, if the law contains exceptions for pregnancies which endanger the woman's life or health. And third is the principle that the State has legitimate interests from the outset of the pregnancy in protecting the health of the woman and the life of the fetus that may become a child. These principles do not contradict one another; and we adhere to each.

II

Constitutional protection of the woman's decision to terminate her pregnancy derives from the Due Process Clause of the Fourteenth Amendment. The most familiar of the substantive liberties protected by the Fourteenth Amendment are those recognized by the Bill of Rights. We have held that the Due Process Clause of the Fourteenth Amendment incorporates most of the Bill of Rights against the States. It is tempting, as a means of curbing the discretion of federal judges, to suppose that liberty encompasses no more than those rights already guaranteed to the individual against federal interference by the express provisions of the first eight Amendments to the Constitution. But of course this Court has never accepted that view.

It is also tempting, for the same reason, to suppose that the Due Process Clause protects only those practices, defined at the most specific level, that were protected against government interference by other rules of law when the Fourteenth Amendment was ratified. But such a view would be inconsistent with our law. It is a promise of the Constitution that there is a realm of personal liberty which the government may not enter. We have vindicated this principle before. Marriage is mentioned nowhere in the Bill of Rights and interracial marriage was illegal in most States in the 19th century, but the Court was no doubt correct in finding it to be an aspect of liberty protected against state interference by the substantive component of the Due Process Clause in Loving v. Virginia (1967). Neither the Bill of Rights nor the specific practices of States at the time of the adoption of the Fourteenth Amendment marks the outer limits of the substantive sphere of liberty which the Fourteenth Amendment protects. The inescapable fact is that adjudication of substantive due process claims may call upon the Court in interpreting the Constitution to exercise that same capacity which by tradition courts always have exercised: reasoned judgment. Its boundaries are not susceptible of expression as a simple rule. That does not mean we are free to invalidate state policy choices with which we disagree; yet neither does it permit us to shrink from the duties of our office.

Men and women of good conscience can disagree, and we suppose some always shall disagree, about the profound moral and spiritual implications of terminating a pregnancy, even in its earliest stage. Some of us as individuals find abortion offensive to our most basic principles of morality, but that cannot control our decision. Our obligation is to define the liberty of all, not to mandate our own moral code. The underlying constitutional issue is whether the State can resolve these philosophic questions in such a definitive way that a woman lacks all choice in the matter, except perhaps in those rare circumstances in which the pregnancy is itself a danger to her own life or health, or is the result of rape or incest.

Our law affords constitutional protection to personal decisions relating to marriage, procreation, contraception, family relationships, child rearing, and education. Our cases recognize "the right of the individual, married or single, to be free from unwarranted governmental intrusion into matters so fundamentally affecting a person as the decision whether to bear or beget a child." Eisenstadt v. Baird. Our precedents "have respected the private realm of family life which the state cannot enter." These matters, involving the most intimate and personal choices a person may make in a lifetime, choices central to personal dignity and autonomy, are central to the liberty protected by the Fourteenth Amendment. At the heart of liberty is the right to define one's own concept of existence, of meaning, of the universe, and of the mystery of human life. Beliefs about these matters could not define the attributes of personhood were they formed under compulsion of the State.

While we appreciate the weight of the arguments made on behalf of the State in the cases before us, arguments which in their ultimate formulation conclude that *Roe* should be overruled, the reservations any of us may have in reaffirming the central holding of *Roe* are outweighed by the explication of individual liberty we have given combined with the force of stare decisis. We turn now to that doctrine.

III

The obligation to follow precedent begins with necessity, and a contrary necessity marks its outer limit. With Cardozo, we recognize that no judicial system could do society's work if it eyed each issue afresh in every case that raised it. See

B. Cardozo, *The Nature of the Judicial Process* 149 (1921). Indeed, the very concept of the rule of law underlying our own Constitution requires such continuity over time that a respect for precedent is, by definition, indispensable. At the other extreme, a different necessity would make itself felt if a prior judicial ruling should come to be seen so clearly as error that its enforcement was for that very reason doomed. Rather, when this Court reexamines a prior holding, its judgment is customarily informed by a series of prudential and pragmatic considerations designed to test the consistency of overruling a prior decision with the ideal of the rule of law, and to gauge the respective costs of reaffirming and overruling a prior case.

So in this case we may enquire whether *Roe*'s central rule has been found unworkable; whether the rule's limitation on state power could be removed without serious inequity to those who have relied upon it or significant damage to the stability of the society governed by it; whether the law's growth in the intervening years has left *Roe*'s central rule a doctrinal anachronism discounted by society; and whether *Roe*'s premises of fact have so far changed in the ensuing two decades as to render its central holding somehow irrelevant or unjustifiable in dealing with the issue it addressed.

Although *Roe* has engendered opposition, it has in no sense proven "unworkable," representing as it does a simple limitation beyond which a state law is unenforceable. While *Roe* has, of course, required judicial assessment of state laws affecting the exercise of the choice guaranteed against government infringement, and although the need for such review will remain as a consequence of today's decision, the required determinations fall within judicial competence.

The inquiry into reliance counts the cost of a rule's repudiation as it would fall on those who have relied reasonably on the rule's continued application. Abortion is customarily chosen as an unplanned response to the consequence of unplanned activity or to the failure of conventional birth control, and except on the assumption that no intercourse would have occurred but for *Roe*'s holding, such behavior may appear to justify no reliance claim. Even if reliance could be claimed on that unrealistic assumption, the argument might run, any reliance interest would be de minimis. This argument would be premised on the hypothesis that reproductive planning could take virtually immediate account of any sudden restoration of state authority to ban abortions. The Constitution serves human values, and while the effect of reliance on *Roe* cannot be exactly measured, neither can the certain cost of overruling *Roe* for people who have ordered their thinking and living around that case be dismissed.

To eliminate the issue of reliance that easily, however, one would need to limit cognizable reliance to specific instances of sexual activity. But to do this would be simply to refuse to face the fact that for two decades of economic and social developments, people have organized intimate relationships and made choices that define their views of themselves and their places in society, in reliance on the availability of abortion in the event that contraception should fail. The ability of women to participate equally in the economic and social life of the Nation has been facilitated by their ability to control their reproductive lives.

No evolution of legal principle has left *Roe*'s doctrinal footings weaker than they were in 1973. No development of constitutional law since the case was decided has implicitly or explicitly left *Roe* behind as a mere survivor of obsolete constitutional thinking.

We have seen how time has overtaken some of *Roe*'s factual assumptions: advances in maternal health care allow for abortions safe to the mother later in pregnancy than was true in 1973, and advances in neonatal care have advanced viability to a point somewhat earlier. But these facts go only to the scheme of time limits on the realization of competing interests, and the divergences from the factual premises of 1973 have no bearing on the validity of *Roe*'s central holding, that viability marks the earliest point at which the State's interest in fetal life is constitutionally adequate to justify a legislative ban on nontherapeutic abortions. The soundness or unsoundness of that constitutional judgment in no sense turns on whether viability occurs at approximately 28 weeks, as was usual at the time of *Roe*, at 23 to 24 weeks, as it sometimes does today, or at some moment even slightly earlier in pregnancy, as it may if fetal respiratory capacity can somehow be enhanced in the future. Whenever it may occur, the attainment of viability may continue to serve as the critical fact, just as it has done since *Roe* was decided; which is to say that no change in *Roe*'s factual underpinning has left its central holding obsolete, and none supports an argument for overruling it.

IV

From what we have said so far it follows that it is a constitutional liberty of the woman to have some freedom to terminate her pregnancy. We conclude that the basic decision in *Roe* was based on a constitutional analysis which we cannot now repudiate. The woman's liberty is not so unlimited, however, that from the outset the State cannot show its concern for the life of the unborn, and at a later point in fetal development the State's interest in life has sufficient force so that the right of the woman to terminate the pregnancy can be restricted.

That brings us, of course, to the point where much criticism has been directed at *Roe*, a criticism that always inheres when the Court draws a specific rule from what in the Constitution is but a general standard. We conclude, however, that the urgent claims of the woman to retain the ultimate control over her destiny and her body, claims implicit in the meaning of liberty, require us to perform that function. Liberty must not be extinguished for want of a line that is clear.

We conclude the line should be drawn at viability, so that before that time the woman has a right to choose to terminate her pregnancy. We adhere to this principle for two reasons. First, as we have said, is the doctrine of stare decisis. Any judicial act of line-drawing may seem somewhat arbitrary, but *Roe* was a reasoned statement, elaborated with great care. We have twice reaffirmed it in the face of great opposition.

The second reason is that the concept of viability, as we noted in *Roe*, is the time at which there is a realistic possibility of maintaining and nourishing a life outside the womb, so that the independent existence of the second life can in reason and all fairness be the object of state protection that now overrides the rights of the woman. Consistent with other constitutional norms, legislatures may draw lines which appear arbitrary without the necessity of offering a justification. But courts may not. We must justify the lines we draw. And there is no line other than viability which is more workable. The viability line also has, as a practical matter, an element of fairness. In some broad sense it might be said that a woman who fails to act before viability has consented to the State's intervention on behalf of the developing child. The woman's right to terminate her pregnancy before viability is the most central principle of Roe v. Wade. It is a rule of law and a component of liberty we cannot renounce.

On the other side of the equation is the interest of the State in the protection of potential life. The *Roe* Court recognized the State's "important and legitimate interest in protecting the potentiality of human life." The weight to be given this state interest, not the strength of the woman's interest, was the difficult question faced in *Roe*. We do not need to say whether each of us, had we been Members of the Court when the valuation of the state interest came before it as an original matter, would have concluded, as the *Roe* Court did, that its weight is insufficient to justify a ban on abortions prior to viability even when it is subject to certain exceptions. The matter is not before us in the first instance, and coming as it does after nearly 20 years of litigation in *Roe*'s wake we are satisfied that the immediate question is not the soundness of *Roe*'s resolution of the issue, but the precedential force that must be accorded to its holding. And we have concluded that the essential holding of *Roe* should be reaffirmed.

Roe established a trimester framework to govern abortion regulations. Under this elaborate but rigid construct, almost no regulation at all is permitted during the first trimester of pregnancy; regulations designed to protect the woman's health, but not to further the State's interest in potential life, are permitted during the second trimester; and during the third trimester, when the fetus is viable, prohibitions are permitted provided the life or health of the mother is not at stake.

The trimester framework no doubt was erected to ensure that the woman's right to choose not become so subordinate to the State's interest in promoting fetal life that her choice exists in theory but not in fact. We do not agree, however, that the trimester approach is necessary to accomplish this objective. A framework of this rigidity was unnecessary and in its later interpretation sometimes contradicted the State's permissible exercise of its powers.

Though the woman has a right to choose to terminate or continue her pregnancy before viability, it does not at all follow that the State is prohibited from taking steps to ensure that this choice is thoughtful and informed. Even in the earliest stages of pregnancy, the State may enact rules and regulations designed to encourage her to know that there are philosophic and social arguments of great weight that can be brought to bear in favor of continuing the pregnancy to full term and that there are procedures and institutions to allow adoption of unwanted children as well as a certain degree of state assistance if the mother chooses to raise the child herself. "'[T]he Constitution does not forbid a State or city, pursuant to democratic processes, from expressing a preference for normal childbirth.'" Webster v. Reproductive Health Services. It follows that States are free to enact laws to provide a reasonable framework for a woman to make a decision that has such profound and lasting meaning. This, too, we find consistent with *Roe*'s central premises, and indeed the inevitable consequence of our holding that the State has an interest in protecting the life of the unborn.

We reject the trimester framework, which we do not consider to be part of the essential holding of *Roe*. Measures aimed at ensuring that a woman's choice contemplates the consequences for the fetus do not necessarily interfere with the right recognized in *Roe*, although those measures have been found to be inconsistent with the rigid trimester framework announced in that case. A logical reading of the central holding in *Roe* itself, and a necessary reconciliation of the liberty of the woman and the interest of the State in promoting prenatal life, require, in our view, that we abandon the trimester framework as a rigid prohibition on all previability regulation aimed at the protection of fetal life. The trimester framework suffers from these basic flaws: in its formulation it misconceives the nature of the pregnant woman's interest; and in practice it undervalues the State's interest in potential life, as recognized in *Roe*.

As our jurisprudence relating to all liberties save perhaps abortion has recognized, not every law which makes a right more difficult to exercise is, ipso facto, an infringement of that right. An example clarifies the point. We have held that not every ballot access limitation amounts to an infringement of the right to vote. The abortion right is similar. Numerous forms of state regulation might have the incidental effect of increasing the cost or decreasing the availability of medical care, whether for abortion or any other medical procedure. The fact that a law which serves a valid purpose, one not designed to strike at the right itself, has the incidental effect of making it more difficult or more expensive to procure an abortion cannot be enough to invalidate it. Only where state regulation imposes an undue burden on a woman's ability to make this decision does the power of the State reach into the heart of the liberty protected by the Due Process Clause.

The very notion that the State has a substantial interest in potential life leads to the conclusion that not all regulations must be deemed unwarranted. Not all burdens on the right to decide whether to terminate a pregnancy will be undue. In our view, the undue burden standard is the appropriate means of reconciling the State's interest with the woman's constitutionally protected liberty.

A finding of an undue burden is a shorthand for the conclusion that a state regulation has the purpose or effect of placing a substantial obstacle in the path of a woman seeking an abortion of a nonviable fetus. A statute with this purpose is invalid because the means chosen by the State to further the interest in potential life must be calculated to inform the woman's free choice, not hinder it. And a statute which, while furthering the interest in potential life or some other valid state interest, has the effect of placing a substantial obstacle in the path of a woman's choice cannot be considered a permissible means of serving its legitimate ends.

Some guiding principles should emerge. What is at stake is the woman's right to make the ultimate decision, not a right to be insulated from all others in doing so. Regulations which do no more than create a structural mechanism by which the State, or the parent or guardian of a minor, may express profound respect for the life of the unborn are permitted, if they are not a substantial obstacle to the woman's exercise of the right to choose. Unless it has that effect on her right of choice, a state measure designed to persuade her to choose childbirth over abortion will be upheld if reasonably related to that goal. Regulations designed to foster the health of a woman seeking an abortion are valid if they do not constitute an undue burden.

We give this summary:

(a) To protect the central right recognized by Roe v. Wade while at the same time accommodating the State's profound interest in potential life, we will employ the undue burden analysis as explained in this opinion. An undue burden exists, and therefore a provision of law is invalid, if its purpose or effect is to place a substantial obstacle in the path of a woman seeking an abortion before the fetus attains viability.

(b) We reject the rigid trimester framework of Roe v. Wade. To promote the State's profound interest in potential life, throughout pregnancy the State may take measures to ensure that the woman's choice is informed, and measures designed to advance this interest will not be invalidated as long as their purpose is to persuade the woman to choose childbirth over abortion. These measures must not be an undue burden on the right.

(c) As with any medical procedure, the State may enact regulations to further the health or safety of a woman seeking an abortion. Unnecessary health regulations that have the purpose or effect of presenting a substantial obstacle to a woman seeking an abortion impose an undue burden on the right.

(d) Our adoption of the undue burden analysis does not disturb the central holding of Roe v. Wade, and we reaffirm that holding. Regardless of whether exceptions are made for particular circumstances, a State may not prohibit any woman from making the ultimate decision to terminate her pregnancy before viability.

(e) We also reaffirm *Roe*'s holding that "subsequent to viability, the State in promoting its interest in the potentiality of human life may, if it chooses, regulate, and even proscribe, abortion except where it is necessary, in appropriate medical judgment, for the preservation of the life or health of the mother."

Justice BLACKMUN, concurring in part, concurring in the judgment in part, and dissenting in part.

Three years ago, in Webster v. Reproductive Health Services (1989), four Members of this Court appeared poised to "cas[t] into darkness the hopes and visions of every woman in this country" who had come to believe that the Constitution guaranteed her the right to reproductive choice. All that remained between the promise of *Roe* and the darkness of the plurality was a single, flickering flame. But now, just when so many expected the darkness to fall, the flame has grown bright.

I do not underestimate the significance of today's joint opinion. Yet I remain steadfast in my belief that the right to reproductive choice is entitled to the full protection afforded by this Court before *Webster*. And I fear for the darkness as four Justices anxiously await the single vote necessary to extinguish the light.

Make no mistake, the joint opinion of Justices O'Connor, Kennedy, and Souter is an act of personal courage and constitutional principle. In contrast to previous decisions in which Justices O'Connor and Kennedy postponed reconsideration of Roe v. Wade, the authors of the joint opinion today join Justice Stevens and me in concluding that "the essential holding of Roe v. Wade should be retained and once again reaffirmed."

State restrictions on abortion violate a woman's right of privacy in two ways. First, compelled continuation of a pregnancy infringes upon a woman's right to bodily integrity by imposing substantial physical intrusions and significant risks of physical harm. During pregnancy, women experience dramatic physical changes and a wide range of health consequences. Labor and delivery pose additional health risks and physical demands. In short, restrictive abortion laws force women to endure physical invasions far more substantial than those this Court has held to violate the constitutional principle of bodily integrity in other contexts.

Further, when the State restricts a woman's right to terminate her pregnancy, it deprives a woman of the right to make her own decision about reproduction and family planning — critical life choices that this Court long has deemed central to the right to privacy. The decision to terminate or continue a pregnancy has no less an impact on a woman's life than decisions about contraception or marriage. Because motherhood has a dramatic impact on a woman's educational prospects, employment opportunities, and self-determination, restrictive abortion laws deprive her of basic control over her life. For these reasons, "the decision whether or not to beget or bear a child" lies at "the very heart of this cluster of constitutionally protected choices."

A State's restrictions on a woman's right to terminate her pregnancy also implicate constitutional guarantees of gender equality. State restrictions on abortion compel women to continue pregnancies they otherwise might terminate. By restricting the right to terminate pregnancies, the State conscripts women's bodies into its service, forcing women to continue their pregnancies, suffer the pains of childbirth, and in most instances, provide years of maternal care. The State does not compensate women for their services; instead, it assumes that they owe this duty as a matter of course. This assumption — that women can simply be forced to accept the "natural" status and incidents of motherhood — appears to rest upon a conception of women's role that has triggered the protection of the Equal Protection Clause. The joint opinion recognizes that these assumptions about women's place in society "are no longer consistent with our understanding of the family, the individual, or the Constitution."

The Court has held that limitations on the right of privacy are permissible only if they survive "strict" constitutional scrutiny — that is, only if the governmental entity imposing the restriction can demonstrate that the limitation is both necessary and narrowly tailored to serve a compelling governmental interest. We have applied this principle specifically in the context of abortion regulations.

In my view, application of this analytical framework is no less warranted than when it was approved by seven Members of this Court in *Roe*. Strict scrutiny of state limitations on reproductive choice still offers the most secure protection of the woman's right to make her own reproductive decisions, free from state coercion. No majority of this Court has ever agreed upon an alternative approach. The factual premises of the trimester framework have not been undermined, and the *Roe* framework is far more administrable, and far less manipulable, than the "undue burden" standard adopted by the joint opinion.

In sum, *Roe*'s requirement of strict scrutiny as implemented through a trimester framework should not be disturbed. No other approach has gained a majority, and no other is more protective of the woman's fundamental right. Lastly, no other approach properly accommodates the woman's constitutional right with the State's legitimate interests.

At long last, the Chief Justice and those who have joined him admit it. Gone are the contentions that the issue need not be (or has not been) considered. There, on the first page, for all to see, is what was expected: "We believe that *Roe* was wrongly decided, and that it can and should be overruled consistently with our traditional approach to stare decisis in constitutional cases." If there is much reason to applaud the advances made by the joint opinion today, there is far more to fear from the Chief Justice's opinion.

The Chief Justice's criticism of *Roe* follows from his stunted conception of individual liberty. While recognizing that the Due Process Clause protects more than simple physical liberty, he then goes on to construe this Court's personal-liberty cases as establishing only a laundry list of particular rights, rather than a principled account of how these particular rights are grounded in a more general right of privacy. This constricted view is reinforced by the Chief Justice's exclusive reliance on tradition as a source of fundamental rights. In the Chief Justice's world, a woman considering whether to terminate a pregnancy is entitled to no more protection than adulterers, murderers, and so-called "sexual deviates." Given the Chief Justice's exclusive reliance on tradition, people using contraceptives seem the next likely candidate for his list of outcasts.

Even more shocking than the Chief Justice's cramped notion of individual liberty is his complete omission of any discussion of the effects that compelled childbirth and motherhood have on women's lives. Nor does the Chief Justice give any serious consideration to the doctrine of stare decisis.

But, we are reassured, there is always the protection of the democratic process. While there is much to be praised about our democracy, our country since its founding has recognized that there are certain fundamental liberties that are not to be left to the whims of an election. A woman's right to reproductive choice is one of those fundamental liberties. Accordingly, that liberty need not seek refuge at the ballot box.

In one sense, the Court's approach is worlds apart from that of the Chief Justice and Justice Scalia. And yet, in another sense, the distance between the two approaches is short — the distance is but a single vote.

I am 83 years old. I cannot remain on this Court forever, and when I do step down, the confirmation process for my successor well may focus on the issue before us today. That, I regret, may be exactly where the choice between the two worlds will be made.

Chief Justice REHNQUIST, with whom Justice WHITE, Justice SCALIA, and Justice THOMAS join, concurring in the judgment in part and dissenting in part.

The joint opinion, following its newly minted variation on stare decisis, retains the outer shell of Roe v. Wade (1973), but beats a wholesale retreat from the substance of that case. We believe that *Roe* was wrongly decided, and that it can and should be overruled consistently with our traditional approach to stare decisis in constitutional cases.

In Roe v. Wade, the Court recognized a "guarantee of personal privacy" which "is broad enough to encompass a woman's decision whether or not to terminate her pregnancy." We are now of the view that, in terming this right fundamental, the Court in *Roe* read the earlier opinions upon which it based its decision much too broadly. Unlike marriage, procreation, and contraception, abortion "involves the purposeful termination of a potential life." The abortion decision must therefore "be recognized as sui generis, different in kind from the others that the Court has protected under the rubric of personal or family privacy and autonomy." One cannot ignore the fact that a woman is not isolated in her pregnancy, and that the decision to abort necessarily involves the destruction of a fetus.

Nor do the historical traditions of the American people support the view that the right to terminate one's pregnancy is "fundamental." The common law which we inherited from England made abortion after "quickening" an offense. At the time of the adoption of the Fourteenth Amendment, statutory prohibitions or restrictions on abortion were commonplace; in 1868, at least 28 of the then-37 States and 8 Territories had statutes banning or limiting abortion. J. Mohr, *Abortion in America* 200 (1978). By the turn of the century virtually every State had a law prohibiting or restricting abortion on its books. By the middle of the present century, a liberalization trend had set in. But 21 of the restrictive abortion laws in effect in 1868 were still in effect in 1973 when *Roe* was decided, and an overwhelming majority of the States prohibited abortion unless necessary to preserve the life or health of the mother. On this record, it can scarcely be said that any deeply rooted tradition of relatively unrestricted abortion in our history supported the classification of the right to abortion as "fundamental" under the Due Process Clause of the Fourteenth Amendment.

We think, therefore, both in view of this history and of our decided cases dealing with substantive liberty under the Due Process Clause, that the Court was mistaken in *Roe* when it classified a woman's decision to terminate her pregnancy as a "fundamental right" that could be abridged only in a manner which withstood "strict scrutiny."

Justice SCALIA, with whom the Chief Justice, Justice WHITE, and Justice THOMAS join, concurring in the judgment in part and dissenting in part.

My views on this matter are unchanged from those I set forth in my separate opinions in Webster v. Reproductive Health Services (1989). The States may, if they wish, permit abortion on demand, but the Constitution does not require them to do so. The permissibility of abortion, and the limitations upon it, are to be resolved like most important questions in our democracy: by citizens trying to persuade one another and then voting. As the Court acknowledges, "where reasonable people disagree the government can adopt one position or the other." A State's choice between two positions on which reasonable people can disagree is constitutional even when (as is often the case) it intrudes upon a "liberty" in the absolute sense. Laws against bigamy, for example — with which entire societies of reasonable people disagree — intrude upon men and women's liberty to marry and live with one another. But bigamy happens not to be a liberty specially "protected" by the Constitution.

That is, quite simply, the issue in these cases: not whether the power of a woman to abort her unborn child is a "liberty" in the absolute sense; or even whether it is a liberty of great importance to many women. Of course it is both. The issue is whether it is a liberty protected by the Constitution of the United States. I am sure it is not. I reach that conclusion not because of anything so exalted as my views concerning the "concept of existence, of meaning, of the universe, and of the mystery of human life." Rather, I reach it for the same reason I reach the conclusion that bigamy is not constitutionally protected — because of two simple facts: (1) the Constitution says absolutely nothing about it, and (2) the longstanding traditions of American society have permitted it to be legally proscribed.

The Court's description of the place of *Roe* in the social history of the United States is unrecognizable. Not only did *Roe* not, as the Court suggests, resolve the deeply divisive issue of abortion; it did more than anything else to nourish it, by elevating it to the national level where it is infinitely more difficult to resolve. National politics were not plagued by abortion protests, national abortion lobbying, or abortion marches on Congress before Roe v. Wade was decided. Profound disagreement existed among our citizens over the issue — as it does over other issues, such as the death penalty — but that disagreement was being worked out at the state level. As with many other issues, the division of sentiment within each State was not as closely balanced as it was among the population of the Nation as a whole, meaning not only that more people would be satisfied with the results of state-by-state resolution, but also that those results would be more stable. Pre-*Roe,* moreover, political compromise was possible.

Roe's mandate for abortion on demand destroyed the compromises of the past, rendered compromise impossible for the future, and required the entire issue to be resolved uniformly, at the national level. At the same time, *Roe* created a vast new class of abortion consumers and abortion proponents by eliminating the moral opprobrium that had attached to the act. ("If the Constitution guarantees abortion, how can it be bad?" — not an accurate line of thought, but a natural one.) Many favor all of those developments, and it is not for me to say that they are wrong. But to portray *Roe* as the statesmanlike "settlement" of a divisive issue, a jurisprudential Peace of Westphalia that is worth preserving, is nothing less than Orwellian. *Roe* fanned into life an issue that has inflamed our national politics in general, and has obscured with its smoke the selection of Justices to this Court in particular, ever since.

There is a poignant aspect to today's opinion. Its length, and what might be called its epic tone, suggest that its authors believe they are bringing to an end a troublesome era in the history of our Nation and of our Court. "It is the dimension" of authority, they say, to "cal[l] the contending sides of national controversy to end their national division by accepting a common mandate rooted in the Constitution."

There comes vividly to mind a portrait by Emanuel Leutze that hangs in the Harvard Law School: Roger Brooke Taney, painted in 1859, the 82d year of his life, the 24th of his Chief Justiceship, the second after his opinion in *Dred Scott.* He is all in black, sitting in a shadowed red armchair, left hand resting upon a pad of paper in his lap, right hand hanging limply, almost lifelessly, beside the inner arm of the chair. He sits facing the viewer and staring straight out. There seems to be on his face, and in his deep-set eyes, an expression of profound sadness and disillusionment. Perhaps he always looked that way, even when dwelling upon the happiest of thoughts. But those of us who know how the lustre of his great Chief Justiceship came to be eclipsed by *Dred Scott* cannot help believing that he had that case — its already apparent consequences for the Court and its soon-to-be-played-out consequences for the Nation — burning on his mind. I expect that two years earlier he, too, had thought himself "call [ing] the contending sides of national controversy to end their national division by accepting a common mandate rooted in the Constitution."

It is no more realistic for us in this litigation, than it was for him in that, to think that an issue of the sort they both involved — an issue involving life and death, freedom and subjugation — can be "speedily and finally settled" by the

Supreme Court, as President James Buchanan in his inaugural address said the issue of slavery in the territories would be. Quite to the contrary, by foreclosing all democratic outlet for the deep passions this issue arouses, by banishing the issue from the political forum that gives all participants, even the losers, the satisfaction of a fair hearing and an honest fight, by continuing the imposition of a rigid national rule instead of allowing for regional differences, the Court merely prolongs and intensifies the anguish. We should get out of this area, where we have no right to be, and where we do neither ourselves nor the country any good by remaining.

b. Government Regulation of Abortions

There are many different ways in which government can regulate the performance of abortions. After Planned Parenthood v. Casey, the government can regulate abortions performed prior to viability as long as there is not an undue burden on access to abortions. The Supreme Court has considered the constitutionality of a number of types of restrictions. The most recent Supreme Court decision considering a government regulation of abortion concerned a federal law banning the procedure termed "partial-birth abortion." In reading this decision, Gonzales v. Carhart, it is important to focus on the test the Court uses for deciding whether a regulation of previability abortions is an undue burden on the right to abortion.

In Stenberg v. Carhart, 530 U.S. 914 (2000), the Supreme Court, in a five-to-four decision, invalidated a Nebraska law prohibiting so-called partial-birth abortion. The law made it a crime to remove a living fetus or a substantial part of a living fetus with the intent of ending the fetus's life. The Court found the law unconstitutional because it lacked a health exception and because it would have prohibited many forms of abortions.

The federal Partial-Birth Abortion Ban Act of 2003 lacks a health exception and seems broader than what the Court said it would uphold in *Stenberg*. A crucial difference, of course, is that when the Court heard the *Gonzales* case, Justice O'Connor, a part of the majority in *Stenberg*, had been replaced by Justice Alito.

GONZALES v. CARHART

550 U.S. 124 (2007)

Justice KENNEDY delivered the opinion of the Court.

These cases require us to consider the validity of the Partial-Birth Abortion Ban Act of 2003, a federal statute regulating abortion procedures. In recitations preceding its operative provisions the Act refers to the Court's opinion in *Stenberg v. Carhart* (2000), which also addressed the subject of abortion procedures used in the later stages of pregnancy. Compared to the state statute at issue in *Stenberg*, the Act is more specific concerning the instances to which it applies and in this respect more precise in its coverage. We conclude the Act should be sustained against the objections lodged by the broad, facial attack brought against it.

The Act proscribes a particular manner of ending fetal life, so it is necessary here, as it was in *Stenberg*, to discuss abortion procedures in some detail. Abortion methods vary depending to some extent on the preferences of the physician and, of course, on the term of the pregnancy and the resulting stage of the unborn child's development. Between 85 and 90 percent of the approximately 1.3 million abortions performed each year in the United States take place in the first three months of pregnancy, which is to say in the first trimester. The most common first-trimester abortion method is vacuum aspiration (otherwise known as suction curettage) in which the physician vacuums out the embryonic tissue. Early in this trimester an alternative is to use medication, such as mifepristone (commonly known as RU-486), to terminate the pregnancy. The Act does not regulate these procedures.

Of the remaining abortions that take place each year, most occur in the second trimester. The surgical procedure referred to as "dilation and evacuation" or "D&E" is the usual abortion method in this trimester. Although individual techniques for performing D&E differ, the general steps are the same.

A doctor must first dilate the cervix at least to the extent needed to insert surgical instruments into the uterus and to maneuver them to evacuate the fetus. The steps taken to cause dilation differ by physician and gestational age of the fetus. After sufficient dilation the surgical operation can commence. The woman is placed under general anesthesia or conscious sedation. The doctor, often guided by ultrasound, inserts grasping forceps through the woman's cervix and into the uterus to grab the fetus. The doctor grips a fetal part with the forceps and pulls it back through the cervix and vagina, continuing to pull even after meeting resistance from the cervix. The friction causes the fetus to tear apart. For example, a leg might be ripped off the fetus as it is pulled through the cervix and out of the woman. The process of evacuating the fetus piece by piece continues until it has been completely removed. A doctor may make 10 to 15 passes with the forceps to evacuate the fetus in its entirety, though sometimes removal is completed with fewer passes. Once the fetus has been evacuated, the placenta and any remaining fetal material are suctioned or scraped out of the uterus. The doctor examines the different parts to ensure the entire fetal body has been removed.

Some doctors, especially later in the second trimester, may kill the fetus a day or two before performing the surgical evacuation. They inject digoxin or potassium chloride into the fetus, the umbilical cord, or the amniotic fluid. Fetal demise may cause contractions and make greater dilation possible. Once dead, moreover, the fetus' body will soften, and its removal will be easier. Other doctors refrain from injecting chemical agents, believing it adds risk with little or no medical benefit.

The abortion procedure that was the impetus for the numerous bans on "partial-birth abortion," including the Act, is a variation of this standard D&E. The medical community has not reached unanimity on the appropriate name for this D&E variation. It has been referred to as "intact D&E," "dilation and extraction" (D&X), and "intact D&X." For discussion purposes this D&E variation will be referred to as intact D&E. The main difference between the two procedures is that in intact D&E a doctor extracts the fetus intact or largely intact with only a few passes. There are no comprehensive statistics indicating what percentage of all D&Es are performed in this manner.

Intact D&E, like regular D&E, begins with dilation of the cervix. Sufficient dilation is essential for the procedure. In an intact D&E procedure the doctor extracts the fetus in a way conducive to pulling out its entire body, instead of ripping it apart. One doctor, for example, testified: "'[T]he surgeon then forces the scissors into the base of the skull or into the foramen magnum. Having safely entered the skull, he spreads the scissors to enlarge the opening. The surgeon removes the scissors and introduces a suction catheter into this hole and evacuates the skull contents. With the catheter still in place, he applies traction to the fetus, removing it completely from the patient.'"

This is an abortion doctor's clinical description. Dr. Haskell's approach is not the only method of killing the fetus once its head lodges in the cervix, and "the process has evolved" since his presentation. Another doctor, for example, squeezes the skull after it has been pierced "so that enough brain tissue exudes to allow the head to pass through." Still other physicians reach into the cervix with their forceps and crush the fetus' skull. Others continue to pull the fetus out of the woman until it disarticulates at the neck, in effect decapitating it. These doctors then grasp the head with forceps, crush it, and remove it.

D&E and intact D&E are not the only second-trimester abortion methods. Doctors also may abort a fetus through medical induction. The doctor medicates the woman to induce labor, and contractions occur to deliver the fetus. Induction, which unlike D&E should occur in a hospital, can last as little as 6 hours but can take longer than 48. It accounts for about five percent of second-trimester abortions before 20 weeks of gestation and 15 percent of those after 20 weeks. Doctors turn to two other methods of second-trimester abortion, hysterotomy and hysterectomy, only in emergency situations because they carry increased risk of complications. In a hysterotomy, as in a cesarean section, the doctor removes the fetus by making an incision through the abdomen and uterine wall to gain access to the uterine cavity. A hysterectomy requires the removal of the entire uterus. These two procedures represent about .07% of second-trimester abortions.

B

By the time of the *Stenberg* decision, about 30 States had enacted bans designed to prohibit the procedure. In 2003, after this Court's decision in *Stenberg*, Congress passed the Act at issue here.

The Act responded to *Stenberg* in two ways. First, Congress made factual findings. Congress found, among other things, that "[a] moral, medical, and ethical consensus exists that the practice of performing a partial-birth abortion . . . is a gruesome and inhumane procedure that is never medically necessary and should be prohibited."

Second, and more relevant here, the Act's language differs from that of the Nebraska statute struck down in *Stenberg*. The operative provisions of the Act provide in relevant part:

> (a) Any physician who, in or affecting interstate or foreign commerce, knowingly performs a partial-birth abortion and thereby kills a human fetus shall be fined under this title or imprisoned not more than 2 years, or both. This subsection does not apply to a partial-birth abortion that is necessary to

save the life of a mother whose life is endangered by a physical disorder, physical illness, or physical injury, including a life-endangering physical condition caused by or arising from the pregnancy itself. This subsection takes effect 1 day after the enactment.

(b) As used in this section —

(1) the term "partial-birth abortion" means an abortion in which the person performing the abortion —

(A) deliberately and intentionally vaginally delivers a living fetus until, in the case of a head-first presentation, the entire fetal head is outside the body of the mother, or, in the case of breech presentation, any part of the fetal trunk past the navel is outside the body of the mother, for the purpose of performing an overt act that the person knows will kill the partially delivered living fetus; and

(B) performs the overt act, other than completion of delivery, that kills the partially delivered living fetus.

(d)(1) A defendant accused of an offense under this section may seek a hearing before the State Medical Board on whether the physician's conduct was necessary to save the life of the mother whose life was endangered by a physical disorder, physical illness, or physical injury, including a life-endangering physical condition caused by or arising from the pregnancy itself.

(e) A woman upon whom a partial-birth abortion is performed may not be prosecuted under this section, for a conspiracy to violate this section, or for an offense under section 2, 3, or 4 of this title based on a violation of this section.

II

We assume the following principles for the purposes of this opinion. Before viability, a State "may not prohibit any woman from making the ultimate decision to terminate her pregnancy." It also may not impose upon this right an undue burden, which exists if a regulation's "purpose or effect is to place a substantial obstacle in the path of a woman seeking an abortion before the fetus attains viability." On the other hand, "[r]egulations which do no more than create a structural mechanism by which the State, or the parent or guardian of a minor, may express profound respect for the life of the unborn are permitted, if they are not a substantial obstacle to the woman's exercise of the right to choose." *Planned Parenthood v. Casey* (1992), in short, struck a balance. The balance was central to its holding. We now apply its standard to the cases at bar.

III

We conclude that the Act is not void for vagueness, does not impose an undue burden from any overbreadth, and is not invalid on its face.

A

The Act punishes "knowingly perform[ing]" a "partial-birth abortion." It defines the unlawful abortion in explicit terms. First, the person performing the abortion must "vaginally delive[r] a living fetus." The Act does not restrict an abortion procedure involving the delivery of an expired fetus. The Act, further-more, is inapplicable to abortions that do not involve vaginal delivery (for instance, hysterotomy or hysterectomy). The Act does apply both previability and postviability because, by common understanding and scientific terminol-ogy, a fetus is a living organism while within the womb, whether or not it is viable outside the womb.

Second, the Act's definition of partial-birth abortion requires the fetus to be delivered "until, in the case of a head-first presentation, the entire fetal head is outside the body of the mother, or, in the case of breech presentation, any part of the fetal trunk past the navel is outside the body of the mother." The Attorney General concedes, and we agree, that if an abortion procedure does not involve the delivery of a living fetus to one of these "anatomical 'landmarks'" — where, depending on the presentation, either the fetal head or the fetal trunk past the navel is outside the body of the mother — the prohibitions of the Act do not apply.

Third, to fall within the Act, a doctor must perform an "overt act, other than completion of delivery, that kills the partially delivered living fetus." For pur-poses of criminal liability, the overt act causing the fetus' death must be separate from delivery. And the overt act must occur after the delivery to an anatomical landmark.

Fourth, the Act contains scienter requirements concerning all the actions involved in the prohibited abortion. To begin with, the physician must have "deliberately and intentionally" delivered the fetus to one of the Act's anatom-ical landmarks. If a living fetus is delivered past the critical point by accident or inadvertence, the Act is inapplicable. In addition, the fetus must have been delivered "for the purpose of performing an overt act that the [doctor] knows will kill [it]." If either intent is absent, no crime has occurred. This follows from the general principle that where scienter is required no crime is committed absent the requisite state of mind.

B

Respondents contend the language described above is indeterminate, and they thus argue the Act is unconstitutionally vague on its face. "As generally stated, the void-for-vagueness doctrine requires that a penal statute define the criminal offense with sufficient definiteness that ordinary people can understand what conduct is prohibited and in a manner that does not encourage arbitrary and discriminatory enforcement." The Act satisfies both requirements.

The Act provides doctors "of ordinary intelligence a reasonable opportunity to know what is prohibited." Indeed, it sets forth "relatively clear guidelines as to prohibited conduct" and provides "objective criteria" to evaluate whether a doctor has performed a prohibited procedure. Unlike the statutory language in *Stenberg* that prohibited the delivery of a "'substantial portion'" of the fetus — where a doctor might question how much of the fetus is a substantial portion — the Act defines the line between potentially criminal conduct on the one hand and lawful abortion on the other. Doctors performing D&E will know that if they do not deliver a living fetus to an anatomical landmark they will not face criminal liability.

This conclusion is buttressed by the intent that must be proved to impose liability. The Court has made clear that scienter requirements alleviate vague-ness concerns. The Act requires the doctor deliberately to have delivered the fetus to an anatomical landmark. Because a doctor performing a D&E will not face criminal liability if he or she delivers a fetus beyond the prohibited point by mistake, the Act cannot be described as "a trap for those who act in good faith."

Respondents likewise have failed to show that the Act should be invalidated on its face because it encourages arbitrary or discriminatory enforcement. Just as the Act's anatomical landmarks provide doctors with objective standards, they also "establish minimal guidelines to govern law enforcement." The scienter requirements narrow the scope of the Act's prohibition and limit prosecutorial discretion. It cannot be said that the Act "vests virtually complete discretion in the hands of [law enforcement] to determine whether the [doctor] has satisfied [its provisions]." Respondents' arguments concerning arbitrary enforcement, furthermore, are somewhat speculative. This is a preenforcement challenge, where "no evidence has been, or could be, introduced to indicate whether the [Act] has been enforced in a discriminatory manner or with the aim of inhibiting [constitutionally protected conduct]." The Act is not vague.

C

We next determine whether the Act imposes an undue burden, as a facial matter, because its restrictions on second-trimester abortions are too broad. A review of the statutory text discloses the limits of its reach. The Act prohibits intact D&E; and, notwithstanding respondents' arguments, it does not prohibit the D&E procedure in which the fetus is removed in parts.

The Act prohibits a doctor from intentionally performing an intact D&E. The Act excludes most D&Es in which the fetus is removed in pieces, not intact. If the doctor intends to remove the fetus in parts from the outset, the doctor will not have the requisite intent to incur criminal liability. Removing the fetus in this manner does not violate the Act because the doctor will not have delivered the living fetus to one of the anatomical landmarks or committed an additional overt act that kills the fetus after partial delivery.

A comparison of the Act with the Nebraska statute struck down in *Stenberg* confirms this point. The statute in *Stenberg* prohibited "'deliberately and intentionally delivering into the vagina a living unborn child, or a substantial portion thereof, for the purpose of performing a procedure that the person performing such procedure knows will kill the unborn child and does kill the unborn child.'" The Court concluded that this statute encompassed D&E because "D&E will often involve a physician pulling a 'substantial portion' of a still living fetus, say, an arm or leg, into the vagina prior to the death of the fetus."

Congress, it is apparent, responded to these concerns because the Act departs in material ways from the statute in *Stenberg*. It adopts the phrase "delivers a living fetus," instead of "'delivering . . . a living unborn child, or a substantial portion thereof.'"

The identification of specific anatomical landmarks to which the fetus must be partially delivered also differentiates the Act from the statute at issue in *Stenberg*. The Court in *Stenberg* interpreted "'substantial portion'" of the fetus to include an arm or a leg. The Act's anatomical landmarks, by contrast, clarify that the removal of a small portion of the fetus is not prohibited. The landmarks also require the fetus to be delivered so that it is partially "outside the body of the mother." To come within the ambit of the Nebraska statute, on the other hand, a substantial portion of the fetus only had to be delivered into the vagina; no part of the fetus had to be outside the body of the mother before a doctor could face criminal sanctions.

By adding an overt-act requirement Congress sought further to meet the Court's objections to the state statute considered in *Stenberg*. The Act makes the distinction the Nebraska statute failed to draw (but the Nebraska Attorney General advanced) by differentiating between the overall partial-birth abortion and the distinct overt act that kills the fetus. The fatal overt act must occur after delivery to an anatomical landmark, and it must be something "other than [the] completion of delivery." This distinction matters because, unlike intact D&E, standard D&E does not involve a delivery followed by a fatal act.

IV

Under the principles accepted as controlling here, the Act, as we have interpreted it, would be unconstitutional "if its purpose or effect is to place a substantial obstacle in the path of a woman seeking an abortion before the fetus attains viability." The abortions affected by the Act's regulations take place both previability and postviability; so the quoted language and the undue burden analysis it relies upon are applicable. The question is whether the Act, measured by its text in this facial attack, imposes a substantial obstacle to late-term, but previability, abortions. The Act does not on its face impose a substantial obstacle, and we reject this further facial challenge to its validity.

A

The Act's purposes are set forth in recitals preceding its operative provisions. A description of the prohibited abortion procedure demonstrates the rationale for the congressional enactment. The Act proscribes a method of abortion in which a fetus is killed just inches before completion of the birth process. Congress stated as follows: "Implicitly approving such a brutal and inhumane procedure by choosing not to prohibit it will further coarsen society to the humanity of not only newborns, but all vulnerable and innocent human life, making it increasingly difficult to protect such life." The Act expresses respect for the dignity of human life.

The Act's ban on abortions that involve partial delivery of a living fetus furthers the Government's objectives. No one would dispute that, for many, D&E is a procedure itself laden with the power to devalue human life.

Respect for human life finds an ultimate expression in the bond of love the mother has for her child. The Act recognizes this reality as well. Whether to have an abortion requires a difficult and painful moral decision. While we find no reliable data to measure the phenomenon, it seems unexceptionable to conclude some women come to regret their choice to abort the infant life they once created and sustained. Severe depression and loss of esteem can follow.

The State has an interest in ensuring so grave a choice is well informed. It is self-evident that a mother who comes to regret her choice to abort must struggle with grief more anguished and sorrow more profound when she learns, only after the event, what she once did not know: that she allowed a doctor to pierce the skull and vacuum the fast-developing brain of her unborn child, a child assuming the human form.

It is a reasonable inference that a necessary effect of the regulation and the knowledge it conveys will be to encourage some women to carry the infant to full term, thus reducing the absolute number of late-term abortions. The medical profession, furthermore, may find different and less shocking methods to abort the fetus in the second trimester, thereby accommodating legislative demand. The State's interest in respect for life is advanced by the dialogue that better informs the political and legal systems, the medical profession, expectant mothers, and society as a whole of the consequences that follow from a decision to elect a late-term abortion.

It is objected that the standard D&E is in some respects as brutal, if not more, than the intact D&E, so that the legislation accomplishes little. What we have already said, however, shows ample justification for the regulation. Partial-birth abortion, as defined by the Act, differs from a standard D&E because the former occurs when the fetus is partially outside the mother to the point of one of the Act's anatomical landmarks. It was reasonable for Congress to think that partial-birth abortion, more than standard D&E, "undermines the public's perception of the appropriate role of a physician during the delivery process, and perverts a process during which life is brought into the world."

B

The Act's furtherance of legitimate government interests bears upon, but does not resolve, the next question: whether the Act has the effect of imposing an unconstitutional burden on the abortion right because it does not allow use of the barred procedure where "'necessary, in appropriate medical judgment, for [the] preservation of the . . . health of the mother.'" The prohibition in the Act would be unconstitutional, under precedents we here assume to be controlling, if it "subject[ed] [women] to significant health risks." [W]hether the Act creates significant health risks for women has been a contested factual question. The evidence presented in the trial courts and before Congress demonstrates both sides have medical support for their position.

Respondents presented evidence that intact D&E may be the safest method of abortion, for reasons similar to those adduced in *Stenberg*. Abortion doctors testified, for example, that intact D&E decreases the risk of cervical laceration or uterine perforation because it requires fewer passes into the uterus with surgical instruments and does not require the removal of bony fragments of the dismembered fetus, fragments that may be sharp. Respondents also presented evidence that intact D&E was safer both because it reduces the risks that fetal parts will remain in the uterus and because it takes less time to complete. Respondents, in addition, proffered evidence that intact D&E was safer for women with certain medical conditions or women with fetuses that had certain anomalies.

These contentions were contradicted by other doctors who testified in the District Courts and before Congress. They concluded that the alleged health advantages were based on speculation without scientific studies to support them. They considered D&E always to be a safe alternative.

There is documented medical disagreement whether the Act's prohibition would ever impose significant health risks on women.

The question becomes whether the Act can stand when this medical uncertainty persists. The Court's precedents instruct that the Act can survive this facial attack. The Court has given state and federal legislatures wide discretion to pass legislation in areas where there is medical and scientific uncertainty.

This traditional rule is consistent with *Casey*, which confirms the State's interest in promoting respect for human life at all stages in the pregnancy. Physicians are not entitled to ignore regulations that direct them to use reasonable alternative procedures. The law need not give abortion doctors unfettered choice in the course of their medical practice, nor should it elevate their status above other physicians in the medical community.

Medical uncertainty does not foreclose the exercise of legislative power in the abortion context any more than it does in other contexts. The medical uncertainty over whether the Act's prohibition creates significant health risks provides a sufficient basis to conclude in this facial attack that the Act does not impose an undue burden.

The conclusion that the Act does not impose an undue burden is supported by other considerations. Alternatives are available to the prohibited procedure. As we have noted, the Act does not proscribe D&E. If the intact D&E procedure is truly necessary in some circumstances, it appears likely an injection that kills the fetus is an alternative under the Act that allows the doctor to perform the procedure.

In reaching the conclusion the Act does not require a health exception we reject certain arguments made by the parties on both sides of these cases. On the one hand, the Attorney General urges us to uphold the Act on the basis of the congressional findings alone. Although we review congressional factfinding under a deferential standard, we do not in the circumstances here place dispositive weight on Congress' findings. The Court retains an independent constitutional duty to review factual findings where constitutional rights are at stake. As respondents have noted, and the District Courts recognized, some recitations in the Act are factually incorrect. Uncritical deference to Congress' factual findings in these cases is inappropriate.

On the other hand, relying on the Court's opinion in *Stenberg*, respondents contend that an abortion regulation must contain a health exception "if 'substantial medical authority supports the proposition that banning a particular procedure could endanger women's health.'" A zero tolerance policy would strike down legitimate abortion regulations, like the present one, if some part of the medical community were disinclined to follow the proscription. This is too exacting a standard to impose on the legislative power, exercised in this instance under the Commerce Clause, to regulate the medical profession. Considerations of marginal safety, including the balance of risks, are within the legislative competence when the regulation is rational and in pursuit of legitimate ends. When standard medical options are available, mere convenience does not suffice to displace them; and if some procedures have different risks than others, it does not follow that the State is altogether barred from imposing reasonable regulations. The Act is not invalid on its face where there is uncertainty over whether the barred procedure is ever necessary to preserve a woman's health, given the availability of other abortion procedures that are considered to be safe alternatives.

V

The considerations we have discussed support our further determination that these facial attacks should not have been entertained in the first instance. In these circumstances the proper means to consider exceptions is by as-applied challenge. This is the proper manner to protect the health of the woman if it can be shown that in discrete and well-defined instances a particular condition has or is likely to occur in which the procedure prohibited by the Act must be used. In an as-applied challenge the nature of the medical risk can be better quantified and balanced than in a facial attack.

As the previous sections of this opinion explain, respondents have not demonstrated that the Act would be unconstitutional in a large fraction of relevant cases. The Act is open to a proper as-applied challenge in a discrete case. No as-applied challenge need be brought if the prohibition in the Act threatens a woman's life because the Act already contains a life exception.

Justice THOMAS, with whom Justice SCALIA joins, concurring.

I join the Court's opinion because it accurately applies current jurisprudence, including *Planned Parenthood of Southeastern Pa. v. Casey* (1992). I write separately to reiterate my view that the Court's abortion jurisprudence, including *Casey* and *Roe v. Wade* (1973), has no basis in the Constitution. I also note that whether the Act constitutes a permissible exercise of Congress' power under the Commerce Clause is not before the Court. The parties did not raise or brief that issue; it is outside the question presented; and the lower courts did not address it.

Justice GINSBURG, with whom Justice STEVENS, Justice SOUTER, and Justice BREYER join, dissenting.

Today's decision is alarming. It refuses to take *Casey* and *Stenberg* seriously. It tolerates, indeed applauds, federal intervention to ban nationwide a procedure found necessary and proper in certain cases by the American College of Obstetricians and Gynecologists (ACOG). It blurs the line, firmly drawn in *Casey*, between previability and postviability abortions. And, for the first time since *Roe*, the Court blesses a prohibition with no exception safeguarding a woman's health.

I

A

As *Casey* comprehended, at stake in cases challenging abortion restrictions is a woman's "control over her [own] destiny." Their ability to realize their full potential, the Court recognized, is intimately connected to "their ability to control their reproductive lives." Thus, legal challenges to undue restrictions on abortion procedures do not seek to vindicate some generalized notion of privacy; rather, they center on a woman's autonomy to determine her life's course, and thus to enjoy equal citizenship stature.

In keeping with this comprehension of the right to reproductive choice, the Court has consistently required that laws regulating abortion, at any stage of pregnancy and in all cases, safeguard a woman's health. We have thus ruled that a State must avoid subjecting women to health risks not only where the pregnancy itself creates danger, but also where state regulation forces women to resort to less safe methods of abortion.

Adolescents and indigent women, research suggests, are more likely than other women to have difficulty obtaining an abortion during the first trimester of pregnancy. Minors may be unaware they are pregnant until relatively late in pregnancy, while poor women's financial constraints are an obstacle to timely receipt of services. Severe fetal anomalies and health problems confronting the pregnant woman are also causes of second-trimester abortions; many such conditions cannot be diagnosed or do not develop until the second trimester.

In *Stenberg*, we expressly held that a statute banning intact D&E was unconstitutional in part because it lacked a health exception. We noted that there existed a "division of medical opinion" about the relative safety of intact D&E, but we made clear that as long as "substantial medical authority supports the proposition that banning a particular abortion procedure could endanger women's health," a health exception is required.

B

In 2003, a few years after our ruling in *Stenberg*, Congress passed the Partial-Birth Abortion Ban Act—without an exception for women's health. The congressional findings on which the Partial-Birth Abortion Ban Act rests do not withstand inspection, as the lower courts have determined and this Court is obliged to concede. Many of the Act's recitations are incorrect. For example, Congress determined that no medical schools provide instruction on intact D&E. But in fact, numerous leading medical schools teach the procedure. More important, Congress claimed there was a medical consensus that the banned procedure is never necessary. But the evidence "very clearly demonstrate[d] the opposite."

Similarly, Congress found that "[t]here is no credible medical evidence that partial-birth abortions are safe or are safer than other abortion procedures." But the congressional record includes letters from numerous individual physicians stating that pregnant women's health would be jeopardized under the Act, as well as statements from nine professional associations, including ACOG, the American Public Health Association, and the California Medical Association, attesting that intact D&E carries meaningful safety advantages over other methods.

C

In contrast to Congress, the District Courts made findings after full trials at which all parties had the opportunity to present their best evidence. The courts had the benefit of "much more extensive medical and scientific evidence . . . concerning the safety and necessity of intact D&Es." During the District Court trials, "numerous" "extraordinarily accomplished" and "very experienced" medical experts explained that, in certain circumstances and for certain women, intact D&E is safer than alternative procedures and necessary to protect women's health.

According to the expert testimony plaintiffs introduced, the safety advantages of intact D&E are marked for women with certain medical conditions, for example, uterine scarring, bleeding disorders, heart disease, or compromised immune systems. Further, plaintiffs' experts testified that intact D&E is significantly safer for women with certain pregnancy-related conditions, such as placenta previa and accreta, and for women carrying fetuses with certain abnormalities, such as severe hydrocephalus.

Intact D&E, plaintiffs' experts explained, provides safety benefits over D&E by dismemberment for several reasons: First, intact D&E minimizes the number of times a physician must insert instruments through the cervix and into the uterus, and thereby reduces the risk of trauma to, and perforation of, the cervix and uterus—the most serious complication associated with nonintact D&E. Second, removing the fetus intact, instead of dismembering it in utero, decreases the likelihood that fetal tissue will be retained in the uterus, a condition that can cause infection, hemorrhage, and infertility. Third, intact D&E diminishes the chances of exposing the patient's tissues to sharp bony fragments sometimes resulting from dismemberment of the fetus. Fourth, intact D&E takes less operating time than D&E by dismemberment, and thus may reduce bleeding, the risk of infection, and complications relating to anesthesia.

Based on thoroughgoing review of the trial evidence and the congressional record, each of the District Courts to consider the issue rejected Congress' findings as unreasonable and not supported by the evidence. The trial courts concluded, in contrast to Congress' findings, that "significant medical authority supports the proposition that in some circumstances, [intact D&E] is the safest procedure." The District Courts' findings merit this Court's respect.

II

The Court offers flimsy and transparent justifications for upholding a nationwide ban on intact D&E sans any exception to safeguard a women's health. Today's ruling, the Court declares, advances "a premise central to [*Casey's*] conclusion"—i.e., the Government's "legitimate and substantial interest in preserving and promoting fetal life." But the Act scarcely furthers that interest: The law saves not a single fetus from destruction, for it targets only a method of performing abortion. And surely the statute was not designed to protect the lives or health of pregnant women. In short, the Court upholds a law that, while doing nothing to "preserv[e] . . . fetal life," bars a woman from choosing intact D&E although her doctor "reasonably believes [that procedure] will best protect [her]."

As another reason for upholding the ban, the Court emphasizes that the Act does not proscribe the nonintact D&E procedure. But why not, one might ask. Nonintact D&E could equally be characterized as "brutal," involving as it does "tear[ing] [a fetus] apart" and "ripp[ing] off" its limbs. "[T]he notion that either of these two equally gruesome procedures . . . is more akin to infanticide than the other, or that the State furthers any legitimate interest by banning one but not the other, is simply irrational."

Ultimately, the Court admits that "moral concerns" are at work, concerns that could yield prohibitions on any abortion. Notably, the concerns expressed are untethered to any ground genuinely serving the Government's interest in preserving life. By allowing such concerns to carry the day and case, overriding fundamental rights, the Court dishonors our precedent. Revealing in this regard, the Court invokes an antiabortion shibboleth for which it concededly has no reliable evidence: Women who have abortions come to regret their choices, and consequently suffer from "[s]evere depression and loss of esteem." Because of women's fragile emotional state and because of the "bond of love the mother has for her child," the Court worries, doctors may withhold information about the nature of the intact D&E procedure. The solution the Court approves, then, is not to require doctors to inform women, accurately and adequately, of the different procedures and their attendant risks. Instead, the Court deprives women of the right to make an autonomous choice, even at the expense of their safety.[27]

This way of thinking reflects ancient notions about women's place in the family and under the Constitution — ideas that have long since been discredited. Though today's majority may regard women's feelings on the matter as "self-evident," this Court has repeatedly confirmed that "[t]he destiny of the woman must be shaped . . . on her own conception of her spiritual imperatives and her place in society."

B

In cases on a "woman's liberty to determine whether to [continue] her pregnancy," this Court has identified viability as a critical consideration. "[T]here is no line [more workable] than viability," the Court explained in *Casey*, for viability is "the time at which there is a realistic possibility of maintaining and nourishing a life outside the womb, so that the independent existence of the second life can in reason and all fairness be the object of state protection that now overrides the rights of the woman. . . . In some broad sense it might be said that a woman who fails to act before viability has consented to the State's intervention on behalf of the developing child."

Today, the Court blurs that line, maintaining that "[t]he Act [legitimately] appl[ies] both previability and postviability because . . . a fetus is a living organism while within the womb, whether or not it is viable outside the womb." Instead of drawing the line at viability, the Court refers to Congress' purpose to differentiate "abortion and infanticide" based not on whether a fetus can survive outside the womb, but on where a fetus is anatomically located when a particular medical procedure is performed.

One wonders how long a line that saves no fetus from destruction will hold in face of the Court's "moral concerns." The Court's hostility to the right *Roe* and *Casey* secured is not concealed. Throughout, the opinion refers to obstetrician-gynecologists and surgeons who perform abortions not by the titles of their medical specialties, but by the pejorative label "abortion doctor." A fetus is described as an "unborn child," and as a "baby," second-trimester, previability abortions are referred to as "late-term," and the reasoned medical judgments of highly trained doctors are dismissed as "preferences" motivated by "mere convenience." Instead of the heightened scrutiny we have previously applied, the Court determines that a "rational" ground is enough to uphold the Act. And, most troubling, *Casey*'s principles, confirming the continuing vitality of "the essential holding of *Roe*," are merely "assume[d]" for the moment, rather than "retained" or "reaffirmed."

---

27. The Court is surely correct that, for most women, abortion is a painfully difficult decision. But "neither the weight of the scientific evidence to date nor the observable reality of 33 years of legal abortion in the United States comports with the idea that having an abortion is any more dangerous to a woman's long-term mental health than delivering and parenting a child that she did not intend to have. . . ." [Footnote by the Court.]

III

The Court further confuses our jurisprudence when it declares that "facial attacks" are not permissible in "these circumstances," i.e., where medical uncertainty exists. This holding is perplexing given that, in materially identical circumstances we held that a statute lacking a health exception was unconstitutional on its face.

Without attempting to distinguish *Stenberg* and earlier decisions, the majority asserts that the Act survives review because respondents have not shown that the ban on intact D&E would be unconstitutional "in a large fraction of relevant cases." But *Casey* makes clear that, in determining whether any restriction poses an undue burden on a "large fraction" of women, the relevant class is not "all women," nor "all pregnant women," nor even all women "seeking abortions." Rather, a provision restricting access to abortion, "must be judged by reference to those [women] for whom it is an actual rather than an irrelevant restriction." Thus the absence of a health exception burdens all women for whom it is relevant — women who, in the judgment of their doctors, require an intact D&E because other procedures would place their health at risk. It makes no sense to conclude that this facial challenge fails because respondents have not shown that a health exception is necessary for a large fraction of second-trimester abortions, including those for which a health exception is unnecessary: The very purpose of a health *exception* is to protect women in *exceptional* cases.

If there is anything at all redemptive to be said of today's opinion, it is that the Court is not willing to foreclose entirely a constitutional challenge to the Act. "The Act is open," the Court states, "to a proper as-applied challenge in a discrete case." Surely the Court cannot mean that no suit may be brought until a woman's health is immediately jeopardized by the ban on intact D&E. A woman "suffer[ing] from medical complications[]" needs access to the medical procedure at once and cannot wait for the judicial process to unfold.

The Court appears, then, to contemplate another lawsuit by the initiators of the instant actions. In such a second round, the Court suggests, the challengers could succeed upon demonstrating that "in discrete and well-defined instances a particular condition has or is likely to occur in which the procedure prohibited by the Act must be used." One may anticipate that such a preenforcement challenge will be mounted swiftly, to ward off serious, sometimes irremediable harm, to women whose health would be endangered by the intact D&E prohibition.

The Court's allowance only of an "as-applied challenge in a discrete case," jeopardizes women's health and places doctors in an untenable position. Even if courts were able to carve-out exceptions through piecemeal litigation for "discrete and well-defined instances," women whose circumstances have not been anticipated by prior litigation could well be left unprotected. In treating those women, physicians would risk criminal prosecution, conviction, and imprisonment if they exercise their best judgment as to the safest medical procedure for their patients. The Court is thus gravely mistaken to conclude that narrow as-applied challenges are "the proper manner to protect the health of the woman."

In sum, the notion that the Partial-Birth Abortion Ban Act furthers any legitimate governmental interest is, quite simply, irrational. The Court's defense of the statute provides no saving explanation. In candor, the Act, and the Court's defense of it, cannot be understood as anything other than an effort to chip away at a right declared again and again by this Court—and with increasing comprehension of its centrality to women's lives. When "a statute burdens constitutional rights and all that can be said on its behalf is that it is the vehicle that legislators have chosen for expressing their hostility to those rights, the burden is undue."

Another type of government regulation of abortion is waiting periods. Prior to *Casey*, the Supreme Court had invalidated waiting periods for adult women's abortions. In City of Akron v. Akron Center for Reproductive Health, Inc., 462 U.S. 416 (1983), the Court declared unconstitutional a part of a city ordinance that prohibited a physician from performing an abortion until 24 hours after the pregnant woman signed a consent form. Justice Powell, writing for the Court, explained that the city had "failed to demonstrate that any legitimate state interest is furthered by an arbitrary and inflexible waiting period. There is no evidence suggesting that the abortion procedure will be performed more safely. Nor are we convinced that the State's legitimate concern that the woman's decision be informed is reasonably served by requiring a 24-hour delay as a matter of course."

However, in Planned Parenthood v. Casey, the Supreme Court used the undue burden test, rather than strict scrutiny as in *Akron*, and upheld the constitutionality of a waiting period. In fact, the joint opinion in *Casey* reviewed the invalidation of the waiting period in *Akron* and declared, "We consider that conclusion to be wrong. The idea that important decisions will be more informed and deliberate if they follow some period of reflection does not strike us as unreasonable, particularly where the statute directs that important information become part of the background of the decision."

The joint opinion in *Casey* argued that a waiting period is not an undue burden on access to abortion. The joint opinion acknowledged that the district court had found that because of travel and scheduling problems there often would be more than a day's delay before an abortion could be received and thus that waiting periods would increase the cost and risks of abortions. But the joint opinion concluded that 24-hour waiting periods are constitutional. It declared, "Yet, as we have stated, under the undue burden standard a State is permitted to enact persuasive measures which favor childbirth over abortion, even if those measures do not further a health interest. And while the waiting period does limit a physician's discretion, that is not, standing alone, a reason to invalidate it." The four justices who favored overruling *Roe*—Rehnquist, White, Scalia, and Thomas—provided the other votes necessary to uphold the waiting period requirement.

Yet another type of government regulation of abortion are so-called informed consent requirements. The Supreme Court has had several occasions to consider "informed consent" requirements—laws that require that women be advised about the fetus and its characteristics at that stage of pregnancy. Again, prior to *Casey*, the Supreme Court had consistently invalidated these requirements, but after *Casey* they are much more likely to be upheld.

In Akron v. Akron Center for Reproductive Health, cited above, the Supreme Court also declared unconstitutional a part of a city ordinance that required that physicians inform women seeking abortions about the development of her fetus, that the "unborn child is a human life from the moment of conception," the date of possible viability, and the physical and emotional consequences that may result from an abortion. The Court said that "much of the information required is designed not to inform the woman's consent but rather to persuade her to withhold it altogether. . . . By insisting upon recitation of a lengthy and inflexible list of information, Akron unreasonably has placed obstacles in the path of the doctor upon whom the woman is entitled to rely for advice in connection with her decision."

Similarly, in Thornburgh v. American College of Obstetricians & Gynecologists (1986), the Court invalidated a Pennsylvania law that required, in part, that women be given seven different kinds of information at least 24 hours before they give consent for abortions. These included telling the woman that there may be unforeseeable detrimental physical and psychological effects to having an abortion, the possible availability of prenatal and childbirth medical care, and the father's liability to pay child support. Also, the physician had to inform the woman of the availability of printed materials that describe the anatomical and physiological characteristics of the "unborn child" at two-week gestational increments. The Court said that, as in *Akron*, the Pennsylvania law was unconstitutional because it was motivated by a desire to discourage women from having abortions and because it imposed a rigid requirement that a specific body of information be communicated regardless of the needs of the patient or the judgment of the physician.

In *Casey*, however, the Court upheld a provision virtually identical to that invalidated in *Thornburgh*, and the joint opinion said, "To the extent *Akron I* and *Thornburgh* find a constitutional violation where the government requires . . . the giving of truthful, nonmisleading information about the nature of the abortion procedure, the attendant health risks and those of childbirth, and the 'probable gestational age' of the fetus, those cases are inconsistent with *Roe*'s acknowledgment of an important interest in potential life, and are overruled." Specifically, the Court upheld a section of the statute that required that women be told information and that they be informed of the availability of other materials that describe the fetus, provide information about medical care for childbirth, and that list adoption providers.

The shift from *Akron* and *Thornburgh* to *Casey* reflects the Court's abandoning the position that the state may not regulate abortions in a way to encourage childbirth. The issue that *Casey* leaves unresolved is how far the government can go in this direction in the form of informed consent laws. For example, do *Akron* and *Thornburgh* remain good law in that the government could not require that women be given detailed descriptions of the fetus, or shown photographs, or told that human life begins at conception? There is a strong argument that all of these go much further than the Pennsylvania law in *Casey* and thus that the Court might find them to be an undue burden on access to abortion.

c. Government Restrictions on Funds and Facilities for Abortions

The Supreme Court repeatedly has held that the government is not constitutionally required to subsidize abortions even if it is paying for childbirth. In 1977, the Court upheld the ability of the government to deny funding for "nontherapeutic abortions" — that is, abortions that were not performed to protect the life or health of the mother.

MAHER v. ROE

432 U.S. 464 (1977)

Justice POWELL delivered the opinion of the Court.

A regulation of the Connecticut Welfare Department limits state Medicaid benefits for first trimester abortions to those that are "medically necessary," a term defined to include psychiatric necessity. In this case, we must decide whether the Constitution requires a participating State to pay for nontherapeutic abortions when it pays for childbirth.

The Constitution imposes no obligation on the States to pay the pregnancy-related medical expenses of indigent women, or indeed to pay any of the medical expenses of indigents. But when a State decides to alleviate some of the hardships of poverty by providing medical care, the manner in which it dispenses benefits is subject to constitutional limitations. Appellees' claim is that Connecticut must accord equal treatment to both abortion and childbirth, and may not evidence a policy preference by funding only the medical expenses incident to childbirth. This challenge to the classifications established by the Connecticut regulation presents a question arising under the Equal Protection Clause of the Fourteenth Amendment.

This case involves no discrimination against a suspect class. An indigent woman desiring an abortion does not come within the limited category of disadvantaged classes so recognized by our cases. Nor does the fact that the impact of the regulation falls upon those who cannot pay lead to a different conclusion. In a sense, every denial of welfare to an indigent creates a wealth classification as compared to nonindigents who are able to pay for the desired goods or services. But this Court has never held that financial need alone identifies a suspect class for purposes of equal protection analysis. Accordingly, the central question in this case is whether the regulation "impinges upon a fundamental right explicitly or implicitly protected by the Constitution."

Roe v. Wade can be understood only by considering both the woman's interest and the nature of the State's interference with it. *Roe* did not declare an unqualified "constitutional right to an abortion," as the District Court seemed to think. Rather, the right protects the woman from unduly burdensome interference with her freedom to decide whether to terminate her pregnancy. It implies no limitation on the authority of a State to make a value judgment favoring childbirth over abortion, and to implement that judgment by the allocation of public funds.

The Connecticut regulation before us is different in kind from the laws invalidated in our previous abortion decisions. The Connecticut regulation places no obstacles absolute or otherwise in the pregnant woman's path to an abortion. An indigent woman who desires an abortion suffers no disadvantage as a consequence of Connecticut's decision to fund childbirth; she continues as before to be dependent on private sources for the service she desires. The State may have made childbirth a more attractive alternative, thereby influencing the woman's decision, but it has imposed no restriction on access to abortions that was not already there. The indigency that may make it difficult and in some cases, perhaps, impossible for some women to have abortions is neither created nor in any way affected by the Connecticut regulation. We conclude that the Connecticut regulation does not impinge upon the fundamental right recognized in *Roe*. Our conclusion signals no retreat from *Roe* or the cases applying it. There is a basic difference between direct state interference with a protected activity and state encouragement of an alternative activity consonant with legislative policy.

We certainly are not unsympathetic to the plight of an indigent woman who desires an abortion, but "the Constitution does not provide judicial remedies for every social and economic ill." Our cases uniformly have accorded the States a wider latitude in choosing among competing demands for limited public funds.

The decision whether to expend state funds for nontherapeutic abortion is fraught with judgments of policy and value over which opinions are sharply divided. Our conclusion that the Connecticut regulation is constitutional is not based on a weighing of its wisdom or social desirability, for this Court does not strike down state laws "because they may be unwise, improvident, or out of harmony with a particular school of thought." Indeed, when an issue involves policy choices as sensitive as those implicated by public funding of nontherapeutic abortions, the appropriate forum for their resolution in a democracy is the legislature. We should not forget that "legislatures are ultimate guardians of the liberties and welfare of the people in quite as great a degree as the courts."

Justice BRENNAN, with whom Justice MARSHALL and Justice BLACKMUN join, dissenting.

A distressing insensitivity to the plight of impoverished pregnant women is inherent in the Court's analysis. The stark reality for too many, not just "some," indigent pregnant women is that indigency makes access to competent licensed physicians not merely "difficult" but "impossible." As a practical matter, many indigent women will feel they have no choice but to carry their pregnancies to term because the State will pay for the associated medical services, even though they would have chosen to have abortions if the State had also provided funds for that procedure, or indeed if the State had provided funds for neither procedure. This disparity in funding by the State clearly operates to coerce indigent pregnant women to bear children they would not otherwise choose to have, and just as clearly, this coercion can only operate upon the poor, who are uniquely the victims of this form of financial pressure. Mr. Justice Frankfurter's words are apt: "To sanction such a ruthless consequence, inevitably resulting from a money hurdle erected by the State, would justify a latter-day Anatole France to add one more item to his ironic comments on the 'majestic equality' of the law. 'The law, in its majestic equality, forbids the rich as well as the poor to sleep under bridges, to beg in the streets, and to steal bread.' . . ." Griffin v. Illinois (1956) (concurring opinion).

In two companion cases to *Maher*, the Court upheld other restrictions on funding for nontherapeutic abortions. In Beal v. Doe, 432 U.S. 438 (1977), the Supreme Court held that the federal Medicaid Act did not require that states fund nontherapeutic first-trimester abortions as part of participating in the joint federal-state program. In Poelker v. Doe, 432 U.S. 519 (1977), the Court found that it was constitutional for a city to refuse to pay for nontherapeutic first-trimester abortions in its public hospital.

In 1980, the Supreme Court went further and upheld the constitutionality of laws that denied public funding for medically necessary abortions except where necessary to save the life of the mother.

HARRIS v. McRAE, 448 U.S. 297 (1980): Justice STEWART delivered the opinion of the Court.

This case presents constitutional questions concerning the public funding of abortions under Title XIX of the Social Security Act, commonly known as the "Medicaid Act," and recent annual Appropriations Acts containing the so-called "Hyde Amendment." The constitutional question is whether the Hyde Amendment, by denying public funding for certain medically necessary abortions, contravenes the liberty or equal protection guarantees of the Due Process Clause of the Fifth Amendment.

Since September 1976, Congress has prohibited — either by an amendment to the annual appropriations bill for the Department of Health, Education, and Welfare or by a joint resolution — the use of any federal funds to reimburse the cost of abortions under the Medicaid program except under certain specified circumstances. This funding restriction is commonly known as the "Hyde Amendment," after its original congressional sponsor, Representative Hyde. The current version of the Hyde Amendment, applicable for fiscal year 1980, provides: "[N]one of the funds provided by this joint resolution shall be used to perform abortions except where the life of the mother would be endangered if the fetus were carried to term; or except for such medical procedures necessary for the victims of rape or incest when such rape or incest has been reported promptly to a law enforcement agency or public health service."

We address first the appellees' argument that the Hyde Amendment, by restricting the availability of certain medically necessary abortions under Medicaid, impinges on the "liberty" protected by the Due Process Clause as recognized in Roe v. Wade, and its progeny. But the Court in *Wade* also recognized that a State has legitimate interests during a pregnancy in both ensuring the health of the mother and protecting potential human life. These state interests, which were found to be "separate and distinct" and to "gro[w] in substantiality as the woman approaches term," pose a conflict with a woman's untrammeled freedom of choice.

The Hyde Amendment, like the Connecticut welfare regulation at issue in *Maher*, places no governmental obstacle in the path of a woman who chooses to terminate her pregnancy, but rather, by means of unequal subsidization of abortion and other medical services, encourages alternative activity deemed in the public interest. The present case does differ factually from *Maher* insofar as that case involved a failure to fund nontherapeutic abortions, whereas the Hyde Amendment withholds funding of certain medically necessary abortions. Accordingly, the appellees argue that because the Hyde Amendment affects a significant interest not present or asserted in *Maher* — the interest of a woman in protecting her health during pregnancy — and because that interest lies at the core of the personal constitutional freedom recognized in *Wade*, the present case is constitutionally different from *Maher*.

But, regardless of whether the freedom of a woman to choose to terminate her pregnancy for health reasons lies at the core or the periphery of the due process liberty recognized in *Wade*, it simply does not follow that a woman's freedom of choice carries with it a constitutional entitlement to the financial resources to avail herself of the full range of protected choices. The reason why was explained in *Maher*: although government may not place obstacles in the path of a woman's exercise of her freedom of choice, it need not remove those not of its own creation. Indigency falls in the latter category. The financial constraints that restrict an indigent woman's ability to enjoy the full range of constitutionally protected freedom of choice are the product not of governmental restrictions on access to abortions, but rather of her indigency. Although Congress has opted to subsidize medically necessary services generally, but not certain medically necessary abortions, the fact remains that the Hyde Amendment leaves an indigent woman with at least the same range of choice in deciding whether to obtain a medically necessary abortion as she would have had if Congress had chosen to subsidize no health care costs at all. We are thus not persuaded that the Hyde Amendment impinges on the constitutionally protected freedom of choice recognized in *Wade*. A refusal to fund protected activity, without more, cannot be equated with the imposition of a "penalty" on that activity.

Although the liberty protected by the Due Process Clause affords protection against unwarranted government interference with freedom of choice in the context of certain personal decisions, it does not confer an entitlement to such funds as may be necessary to realize all the advantages of that freedom. To hold otherwise would mark a drastic change in our understanding of the Constitution. It cannot be that because government may not prohibit the use of contraceptives, Griswold v. Connecticut, or prevent parents from sending their child to a private school, Pierce v. Society of Sisters, government, therefore, has an affirmative constitutional obligation to ensure that all persons have the financial resources to obtain contraceptives or send their children to private schools. To translate the limitation on governmental power implicit in the Due Process Clause into an affirmative funding obligation would require Congress to subsidize the medically necessary abortion of an indigent woman even if Congress had not enacted a Medicaid program to subsidize other medically necessary services. Nothing in the Due Process Clause supports such an extraordinary result. Whether freedom of choice that is constitutionally protected warrants federal subsidization is a question for Congress to answer, not a matter of constitutional entitlement. Accordingly, we conclude that the Hyde Amendment does not impinge on the due process liberty recognized in *Wade*.

d. Spousal Consent and Notice Requirements

The Supreme Court has held that the government cannot require either spousal consent or spousal notification as a prerequisite for a married woman's obtaining an abortion.

PLANNED PARENTHOOD v. DANFORTH, 428 U.S. 52 (1976): Justice BLACKMUN delivered the opinion of the Court.

[Missouri law] requires the prior written consent of the spouse of the woman seeking an abortion during the first 12 weeks of pregnancy, unless "the abortion is certified by a licensed physician to be necessary in order to preserve the life of the mother."

The appellees defend [the law] on the ground that it was enacted in the light of the General Assembly's "perception of marriage as an institution," and that any major change in family status is a decision to be made jointly by the marriage partners. Reference is made to an abortion's possible effect on the woman's child bearing potential. It is said that marriage always has entailed some legislatively imposed limitations: Reference is made to adultery and bigamy as criminal offenses; to Missouri's general requirement that for an adoption of a child born in wedlock the consent of both parents is necessary; to similar joint-consent requirements imposed by a number of States with respect to artificial insemination and the legitimacy of children so conceived; to the laws of two States requiring spousal consent for voluntary sterilization; and to the long-established requirement of spousal consent for the effective disposition of an interest in real property.

We now hold that the State may not constitutionally require the consent of the spouse, as is specified under the Missouri Act, as a condition for abortion during the first 12 weeks of pregnancy. We thus agree with the dissenting judge in the present case that the State cannot "delegate to a spouse a veto power which the state itself is absolutely and totally prohibited from exercising during the first trimester of pregnancy." Clearly, since the State cannot regulate or proscribe abortion during the first stage, when the physician and his patient make that decision, the State cannot delegate authority to any particular person, even the spouse, to prevent abortion during that same period.

We are not unaware of the deep and proper concern and interest that a devoted and protective husband has in his wife's pregnancy and in the growth and development of the fetus she is carrying. Neither has this Court failed to appreciate the importance of the marital relationship in our society. See, e.g., Griswold v. Connecticut (1965). Moreover, we recognize that the decision whether to undergo or to forego an abortion may have profound effects on the future of any marriage, effects that are both physical and mental, and possibly deleterious. Notwithstanding these factors, we cannot hold that the State has the constitutional authority to give the spouse unilaterally the ability to prohibit the wife from terminating her pregnancy, when the State itself lacks that right.

This section does much more than insure that the husband participate in the decision whether his wife should have an abortion. The State, instead, has determined that the husband's interest in continuing the pregnancy of his wife always outweighs any interest on her part in terminating it irrespective of the condition of their marriage. The State, accordingly, has granted him the right to prevent unilaterally, and for whatever reason, the effectuation of his wife's and her physician's decision to terminate her pregnancy. This state determination not only may discourage the consultation that might normally be expected to precede a major decision affecting the marital couple but also, and more importantly, the State has interposed an absolute obstacle to a woman's decision that *Roe* held to be constitutionally protected from such interference.

It seems manifest that, ideally, the decision to terminate a pregnancy should be one concurred in by both the wife and her husband. No marriage may be viewed as harmonious or successful if the marriage partners are fundamentally divided on so important and vital an issue. But it is difficult to believe that the goal of fostering mutuality and trust in a marriage, and of strengthening the marital relationship and the marriage institution, will be achieved by giving the husband a veto power exercisable for any reason whatsoever or for no reason at all. Even if the State had the ability to delegate to the husband a power it itself could not exercise, it is not at all likely that such action would further, as the District Court majority phrased it, the "interest of the state in protecting the mutuality of decisions vital to the marriage relationship."

We recognize, of course, that when a woman, with the approval of her physician but without the approval of her husband, decides to terminate her pregnancy, it could be said that she is acting unilaterally. The obvious fact is that when the wife and the husband disagree on this decision, the view of only one of the two marriage partners can prevail. Inasmuch as it is the woman who physically bears the child and who is the more directly and immediately affected by the pregnancy, as between the two, the balance weighs in her favor.

We conclude that the Missouri Act is inconsistent with the standards enunciated in Roe v. Wade and is unconstitutional.

The Supreme Court invalidated a spousal notification requirement in Planned Parenthood v. Casey. The portion of *Casey* describing the general test for abortion is presented above. Justices O'Connor, Kennedy, and Souter issued a joint opinion in which they said that government regulation of abortions before viability would be allowed as long as there was not an undue burden on the right. They applied this test to strike down Pennsylvania's spousal notification requirement. Justices Blackmun and Stevens concurred in this part of the judgment and used strict scrutiny to strike down this requirement. Chief Justice Rehnquist and Justices White, Scalia, and Thomas dissented.

PLANNED PARENTHOOD v. CASEY
505 U.S. 833 (1992)

Justice O'Connor, Justice Kennedy, and Justice Souter announced the judgment of the Court.

Section 3209 of Pennsylvania's abortion law provides, except in cases of medical emergency, that no physician shall perform an abortion on a married woman without receiving a signed statement from the woman that she has notified her spouse that she is about to undergo an abortion. The woman has the option of providing an alternative signed statement certifying that her husband is not the man who impregnated her; that her husband could not be located; that the pregnancy is the result of spousal sexual assault which she has reported; or that the woman believes that notifying her husband will cause him or someone else to inflict bodily injury upon her. A physician who performs an abortion on a married woman without receiving the appropriate signed statement will have his or her license revoked, and is liable to the husband for damages.

The limited research that has been conducted with respect to notifying one's husband about an abortion, although involving samples too small to be representative, supports the District Court's findings of fact. The vast majority of women notify their male partners of their decision to obtain an abortion. In many cases in which married women do not notify their husbands, the pregnancy is the result of an extramarital affair. Where the husband is the father, the primary reason women do not notify their husbands is that the husband and wife are experiencing marital difficulties, often accompanied by incidents of violence. Ryan & Plutzer, When Married Women Have Abortions: Spousal Notification and Marital Interaction, 51 J. Marriage & the Family 41, 44 (1989).

These findings are supported by studies of domestic violence. The American Medical Association (AMA) has published a summary of the recent research in this field, which indicates that in an average 12-month period in this country, approximately two million women are the victims of severe assaults by their male partners. In a 1985 survey, women reported that nearly one of every eight husbands had assaulted their wives during the past year. The AMA views these figures as "marked underestimates," because the nature of these incidents discourages women from reporting them, and because surveys typically exclude the very poor, those who do not speak English well, and women who are homeless or in institutions or hospitals when the survey is conducted. According to the AMA, "[r]esearchers on family violence agree that the true incidence of partner violence is probably *double* the above estimates; or four million severely assaulted women per year. Studies on prevalence suggest that from one-fifth to one-third of all women will be physically assaulted by a partner or ex-partner during their lifetime." AMA Council on Scientific Affairs, Violence Against Women 7 (1991) (emphasis in original). Thus on an average day in the United States, nearly 11,000 women are severely assaulted by their male partners. Many of these incidents involve sexual assault.

Other studies fill in the rest of this troubling picture. Physical violence is only the most visible form of abuse. Psychological abuse, particularly forced social and economic isolation of women, is also common. L. Walker, The Battered Woman Syndrome 27-28 (1984). Many victims of domestic violence remain with their abusers, perhaps because they perceive no superior alternative. Many abused women who find temporary refuge in shelters return to their husbands, in large part because they have no other source of income. Returning to one's abuser can be dangerous. Recent Federal Bureau of Investigation statistics disclose that 8.8 percent of all homicide victims in the United States are killed by their spouses. Thirty percent of female homicide victims are killed by their male partners.

This information and the District Court's findings reinforce what common sense would suggest. In well-functioning marriages, spouses discuss important intimate decisions such as whether to bear a child. But there are millions of women in this country who are the victims of regular physical and psychological abuse at the hands of their husbands. Should these women become pregnant, they may have very good reasons for not wishing to inform their husbands of their decision to obtain an abortion. Many may have justifiable fears of physical abuse, but may be no less fearful of the consequences of reporting prior abuse to the Commonwealth of Pennsylvania. Many may have a reasonable fear that notifying their husbands will provoke further instances of child abuse; these women are not exempt from §3209's notification requirement. Many may fear devastating forms of psychological abuse from their husbands, including verbal harassment, threats of future violence, the destruction of possessions, physical confinement to the home, the withdrawal of financial support, or the disclosure of the abortion to family and friends. These methods of psychological abuse may act as even more of a deterrent to notification than the possibility of physical violence, but women who are the victims of the abuse are not exempt from §3209's notification requirement. And many women who are pregnant as a result of sexual assaults by their husbands will be unable to avail themselves of the exception for spousal sexual assault, §3209(b)(3), because the exception requires that the woman have notified law enforcement authorities within 90 days of the assault, and her husband will be notified of her report once an investigation begins, §3128(c). If anything in this field is certain, it is that victims of spousal sexual assault are extremely reluctant to report the abuse to the government; hence, a great many spousal rape victims will not be exempt from the notification requirement imposed by §3209.

The spousal notification requirement is thus likely to prevent a significant number of women from obtaining an abortion. It does not merely make abortions a little more difficult or expensive to obtain; for many women, it will impose a substantial obstacle. We must not blind ourselves to the fact that the significant number of women who fear for their safety and the safety of their children are likely to be deterred from procuring an abortion as surely as if the Commonwealth had outlawed abortion in all cases.

Respondents attempt to avoid the conclusion that §3209 is invalid by pointing out that it imposes almost no burden at all for the vast majority of women seeking abortions. They begin by noting that only about 20 percent of the women who obtain abortions are married. They then note that of these women about 95 percent notify their husbands of their own volition. Thus, respondents argue, the effects of §3209 are felt by only one percent of the women who obtain abortions. Respondents argue that since some of these women will be able to notify their husbands without adverse consequences or will qualify for one of the exceptions, the statute affects fewer than one percent of women seeking abortions. For this reason, it is asserted, the statute cannot be invalid on its face. We disagree with respondents' basic method of analysis.

The analysis does not end with the one percent of women upon whom the statute operates; it begins there. Legislation is measured for consistency with the Constitution by its impact on those whose conduct it affects. For example, we would not say that a law which requires a newspaper to print a candidate's reply to an unfavorable editorial is valid on its face because most newspapers would adopt the policy even absent the law. See Miami Herald Publishing Co. v. Tornillo (1974). The proper focus of constitutional inquiry is the group for whom the law is a restriction, not the group for whom the law is irrelevant.

This conclusion is in no way inconsistent with our decisions upholding parental notification or consent requirements. Those enactments, and our judgment that they are constitutional, are based on the quite reasonable assumption that minors will benefit from consultation with their parents and that children will often not realize that their parents have their best interests at heart. We cannot adopt a parallel assumption about adult women.

We recognize that a husband has a "deep and proper concern and interest . . . in his wife's pregnancy and in the growth and development of the fetus she is carrying." With regard to the children he has fathered and raised, the Court has recognized his "cognizable and substantial" interest in their custody. If these cases concerned a State's ability to require the mother to notify the father before taking some action with respect to a living child raised by both, therefore, it would be reasonable to conclude as a general matter that the father's interest in the welfare of the child and the mother's interest are equal.

Before birth, however, the issue takes on a very different cast. It is an inescapable biological fact that state regulation with respect to the child a woman is carrying will have a far greater impact on the mother's liberty than on the father's. The effect of state regulation on a woman's protected liberty is doubly deserving of scrutiny in such a case, as the State has touched not only upon the private sphere of the family but upon the very bodily integrity of the pregnant woman. The Court has held that "when the wife and the husband disagree on this decision, the view of only one of the two marriage partners can prevail. Inasmuch as it is the woman who physically bears the child and who is the more directly and immediately affected by the pregnancy, as between the two, the balance weighs in her favor." This conclusion rests upon the basic nature of marriage and the nature of our Constitution: "[T]he marital couple is not an independent entity with a mind and heart of its own, but an association of two individuals each with a separate intellectual and emotional makeup. If the right of privacy means anything, it is the right of the individual, married or single, to be free from unwarranted governmental intrusion into matters so fundamentally affecting a person as the decision whether to bear or beget a child." Eisenstadt v. Baird. The Constitution protects individuals, men and women alike, from unjustified state interference, even when that interference is enacted into law for the benefit of their spouses.

There was a time, not so long ago, when a different understanding of the family and of the Constitution prevailed. In keeping with our rejection of the common-law understanding of a woman's role within the family, the Court held in *Danforth* that the Constitution does not permit a State to require a married woman to obtain her husband's consent before undergoing an abortion. The principles that guided the Court in *Danforth* should be our guides today. For the great many women who are victims of abuse inflicted by their husbands, or whose children are the victims of such abuse, a spousal notice requirement enables the husband to wield an effective veto over his wife's decision. Whether the prospect of notification itself deters such women from seeking abortions, or whether the husband, through physical force or psychological pressure or economic coercion, prevents his wife from obtaining an abortion until it is too late, the notice requirement will often be tantamount to the veto found unconstitutional in *Danforth*. The women most affected by this law—those who most reasonably fear the consequences of notifying their husbands that they are pregnant—are in the gravest danger.

The husband's interest in the life of the child his wife is carrying does not permit the State to empower him with this troubling degree of authority over his wife. The contrary view leads to consequences reminiscent of the common law. A husband has no enforceable right to require a wife to advise him before she exercises her personal choices. If a husband's interest in the potential life of the child outweighs a wife's liberty, the State could require a married woman to notify her husband before she uses a postfertilization contraceptive. Perhaps next in line would be a statute requiring pregnant married women to notify their husbands before engaging in conduct causing risks to the fetus. After all, if the husband's interest in the fetus' safety is a sufficient predicate for state regulation, the State could reasonably conclude that pregnant wives should notify their husbands before drinking alcohol or smoking. Perhaps married women should notify their husbands before using contraceptives or before undergoing any type of surgery that may have complications affecting the husband's interest in his wife's reproductive organs. And if a husband's interest justifies notice in any of these cases, one might reasonably argue that it justifies exactly what the *Danforth* Court held it did not justify—a requirement of the husband's consent as well. A State may not give to a man the kind of dominion over his wife that parents exercise over their children.

Section 3209 embodies a view of marriage consonant with the common-law status of married women but repugnant to our present understanding of marriage and of the nature of the rights secured by the Constitution. Women do not lose their constitutionally protected liberty when they marry. The Constitution protects all individuals, male or female, married or unmarried, from the abuse of governmental power, even where that power is employed for the supposed benefit of a member of the individual's family. These considerations confirm our conclusion that §3209 is invalid.

Chief Justice REHNQUIST, with whom Justice WHITE, Justice SCALIA, and Justice THOMAS join, concurring in the judgment in part and dissenting in part.

The State itself has legitimate interests both in protecting these interests of the father and in protecting the potential life of the fetus, and the spousal notification requirement is reasonably related to advancing those state interests. By providing that a husband will usually know of his spouse's intent to have an abortion, the provision makes it more likely that the husband will participate in deciding the fate of his unborn child, a possibility that might otherwise have been denied him. This participation might in some cases result in a decision to proceed with the pregnancy. As Judge Alito observed in his dissent below, "[t]he Pennsylvania legislature could have rationally believed that some married women are initially inclined to obtain an abortion without their husbands' knowledge because of perceived problems—such as economic constraints, future plans, or the husbands' previously expressed opposition—that may be obviated by discussion prior to the abortion."

The State also has a legitimate interest in promoting "the integrity of the marital relationship." This Court has previously recognized "the importance of the marital relationship in our society." In our view, the spousal notice requirement is a rational attempt by the State to improve truthful communication between spouses and encourage collaborative decisionmaking, and thereby fosters marital integrity.

Petitioners argue that the notification requirement does not further any such interest; they assert that the majority of wives already notify their husbands of their abortion decisions, and the remainder have excellent reasons for keeping their decisions a secret. In the first case, they argue, the law is unnecessary, and in the second case it will only serve to foster marital discord and threats of harm. Thus, petitioners see the law as a totally irrational means of furthering whatever legitimate interest the State might have. But, in our view, it is unrealistic to assume that every husband-wife relationship is either (1) so perfect that this type of truthful and important communication will take place as a matter of course, or (2) so imperfect that, upon notice, the husband will react selfishly, violently, or contrary to the best interests of his wife.

The spousal notice provision will admittedly be unnecessary in some circumstances, and possibly harmful in others, but "the existence of particular cases in which a feature of a statute performs no function (or is even counterproductive) ordinarily does not render the statute unconstitutional or even constitutionally suspect." The Pennsylvania Legislature was in a position to weigh the likely benefits of the provision against its likely adverse effects, and presumably concluded, on balance, that the provision would be beneficial. Whether this was a wise decision or not, we cannot say that it was irrational. We therefore conclude that the spousal notice provision comports with the Constitution.

e. Parental Notice and Consent Requirements

The Supreme Court has held that a state may require parental notice and/or consent for an unmarried minor's abortion but only if it creates an alternative procedure by which a minor can obtain an abortion by going before a judge who can approve the abortion by finding that it would be in the minor's best interest or by concluding that the minor is mature enough to decide for herself.

BELLOTTI v. BAIRD

443 U.S. 622 (1979)

Justice Powell announced the judgment of the Court and delivered an opinion, in which the Chief Justice, Mr. Justice Stewart, and Mr. Justice Rehnquist joined.

These appeals present a challenge to the constitutionality of a state statute regulating the access of minors to abortions.

[Massachusetts law] provides in part: "If the mother is less than eighteen years of age and has not married, the consent of both the mother and her parents [to an abortion to be performed on the mother] is required. If one or both of the mother's parents refuse such consent, consent may be obtained by order of a judge of the superior court for good cause shown, after such hearing as he deems necessary. Such a hearing will not require the appointment of a guardian for the mother. If one of the parents has died or has deserted his or her family, consent by the remaining parent is sufficient. If both parents have died or have deserted their family, consent of the mother's guardian or other person having duties similar to a guardian, or any person who had assumed the care and custody of the mother is sufficient." Physicians performing abortions in the absence of the consent required by §12S are subject to injunctions and criminal penalties.

A child, merely on account of his minority, is not beyond the protection of the Constitution. As the Court said in In re Gault (1967), "whatever may be their precise impact, neither the Fourteenth Amendment nor the Bill of Rights is for adults alone." This observation, of course, is but the beginning of the analysis. The Court long has recognized that the status of minors under the law is unique in many respects.

The unique role in our society of the family, the institution by which "we inculcate and pass down many of our most cherished values, moral and cultural," Moore v. East Cleveland (1977), requires that constitutional principles be applied with sensitivity and flexibility to the special needs of parents and children. We have recognized three reasons justifying the conclusion that the constitutional rights of children cannot be equated with those of adults: the peculiar vulnerability of children; their inability to make critical decisions in an informed, mature manner; and the importance of the parental role in child rearing.

Unquestionably, there are many competing theories about the most effective way for parents to fulfill their central role in assisting their children on the way to responsible adulthood. While we do not pretend any special wisdom on this subject, we cannot ignore that central to many of these theories, and deeply rooted in our Nation's history and tradition, is the belief that the parental role implies a substantial measure of authority over one's children. Indeed, "constitutional interpretation has consistently recognized that the parents' claim to authority in their own household to direct the rearing of their children is basic in the structure of our society."

With these principles in mind, we consider the specific constitutional questions presented by these appeals. In §12S, Massachusetts has attempted to reconcile the constitutional right of a woman, in consultation with her physician, to choose to terminate her pregnancy as established by Roe v. Wade (1973), with the special interest of the State in encouraging an unmarried pregnant minor to seek the advice of her parents in making the important decision whether or not to bear a child.

We previously had held in Planned Parenthood of Central Missouri v. Danforth (1976) that a State could not lawfully authorize an absolute parental veto over the decision of a minor to terminate her pregnancy. Appellees and intervenors contend that even as interpreted by the Supreme Judicial Court of Massachusetts, §12S does unduly burden this right. They suggest, for example, that the mere requirement of parental notice constitutes such a burden. [H]owever, parental notice and consent are qualifications that typically may be imposed by the State on a minor's right to make important decisions. As immature minors often lack the ability to make fully informed choices that take account of both immediate and long-range consequences, a State reasonably may determine that parental consultation often is desirable and in the best interest of the minor. It may further determine, as a general proposition, that such consultation is particularly desirable with respect to the abortion decision — one that for some people raises profound moral and religious concerns.

In Roe v. Wade, we emphasized the importance of the role of the attending physician. Those cases involved adult women presumably capable of selecting and obtaining a competent physician. In this case, however, we are concerned only with minors who, according to the record, may range in age from children of 12 years to 17-year-old teenagers. Even the latter are less likely than adults to know or be able to recognize ethical, qualified physicians, or to have the means to engage such professionals. Many minors who bypass their parents probably will resort to an abortion clinic, without being able to distinguish the competent and ethical from those that are incompetent or unethical.

But we are concerned here with a constitutional right to seek an abortion. The abortion decision differs in important ways from other decisions that may be made during minority. The need to preserve the constitutional right and the unique nature of the abortion decision, especially when made by a minor, require a State to act with particular sensitivity when it legislates to foster parental involvement in this matter.

The pregnant minor's options are much different from those facing a minor in other situations, such as deciding whether to marry. A minor not permitted to marry before the age of majority is required simply to postpone her decision. She and her intended spouse may preserve the opportunity for later marriage should they continue to desire it. A pregnant adolescent, however, cannot preserve for long the possibility of aborting, which effectively expires in a matter of weeks from the onset of pregnancy.

Moreover, the potentially severe detriment facing a pregnant woman is not mitigated by her minority. Indeed, considering her probable education, employment skills, financial resources, and emotional maturity, unwanted motherhood may be exceptionally burdensome for a minor. In addition, the fact of having a child brings with it adult legal responsibility, for parenthood, like attainment of the age of majority, is one of the traditional criteria for the termination of the legal disabilities of minority. In sum, there are few situations in which denying a minor the right to make an important decision will have consequences so grave and indelible.

Yet, an abortion may not be the best choice for the minor. The circumstances in which this issue arises will vary widely. In a given case, alternatives to abortion, such as marriage to the father of the child, arranging for its adoption, or assuming the responsibilities of motherhood with the assured support of family, may be feasible and relevant to the minor's best interests. Nonetheless, the abortion decision is one that simply cannot be postponed, or it will be made by default with far-reaching consequences.

For these reasons, as we held in Planned Parenthood of Central Missouri v. Danforth, "the State may not impose a blanket provision . . . requiring the consent of a parent or person in loco parentis as a condition for abortion of an unmarried minor during the first 12 weeks of her pregnancy." Although such deference to parents may be permissible with respect to other choices facing a minor, the unique nature and consequences of the abortion decision make it inappropriate "to give a third party an absolute, and possibly arbitrary, veto over the decision of the physician and his patient to terminate the patient's pregnancy, regardless of the reason for withholding the consent." We therefore conclude that if the State decides to require a pregnant minor to obtain one or both parents' consent to an abortion, it also must provide an alternative procedure whereby authorization for the abortion can be obtained.

A pregnant minor is entitled in such a proceeding to show either: (1) that she is mature enough and well enough informed to make her abortion decision, in consultation with her physician, independently of her parents' wishes; or (2) that even if she is not able to make this decision independently, the desired abortion would be in her best interests. The proceeding in which this showing is made must assure that a resolution of the issue, and any appeals that may follow, will be completed with anonymity and sufficient expedition to provide an effective opportunity for an abortion to be obtained. In sum, the procedure must ensure that the provision requiring parental consent does not in fact amount to the "absolute, and possibly arbitrary, veto" that was found impermissible in *Danforth*.

We conclude, therefore, that under state regulation such as that undertaken by Massachusetts, every minor must have the opportunity — if she so desires — to go directly to a court without first consulting or notifying her parents. If she satisfies the court that she is mature and well enough informed to make intelligently the abortion decision on her own, the court must authorize her to act without parental consultation or consent. If she fails to satisfy the court that she is competent to make this decision independently, she must be permitted to show that an abortion nevertheless would be in her best interests. If the court is persuaded that it is, the court must authorize the abortion. If, however, the court is not persuaded by the minor that she is mature or that the abortion would be in her best interests, it may decline to sanction the operation.

Justice STEVENS, with whom Justice BRENNAN, Justice MARSHALL, and Justice BLACKMUN join, concurring in the judgment.

Massachusetts requires the consent of both of the woman's parents. It does, of course, provide an alternative in the form of a suit initiated by the woman in superior court. But in that proceeding, the judge is afforded an absolute veto over the minor's decisions, based on his judgment of her best interests. In Massachusetts, then, the State has imposed an "absolute limitation on the minor's right to obtain an abortion," applicable to every pregnant minor in the State who has not married.

The provision of an absolute veto to a judge — or, potentially, to an appointed administrator — is to me particularly troubling. The constitutional right to make the abortion decision affords protection to both of the privacy interests recognized in this Court's cases: "One is the individual interest in avoiding disclosure of personal matters, and another is the interest in independence in making certain kinds of important decisions." It is inherent in the right to make the abortion decision that the right may be exercised without public scrutiny and in defiance of the contrary opinion of the sovereign or other third parties. In Massachusetts, however, every minor who cannot secure the consent of both her parents — which under *Danforth* cannot be an absolute prerequisite to an abortion — is required to secure the consent of the sovereign. As a practical matter, I would suppose that the need to commence judicial proceedings in order to obtain a legal abortion would impose a burden at least as great as, and probably greater than, that imposed on the minor child by the need to obtain the consent of a parent. Moreover, once this burden is met, the only standard provided for the judge's decision is the best interest of the minor. That standard provides little real guidance to the judge, and his decision must necessarily reflect personal and societal values and mores whose enforcement upon the minor — particularly when contrary to her own informed and reasonable decision — is fundamentally at odds with privacy interests underlying the constitutional protection afforded to her decision.

———————————

In H.L. v. Matheson, 450 U.S. 398 (1981), the Supreme Court upheld a Utah law that required that a physician "[n]otify, if possible, the parents or guardian of the woman upon whom the abortion is to be performed, if she is a minor." The Court said that although "a state may not constitutionally legislate a blanket, unreviewable veto power of parents to veto their daughter's abortion, a statute setting out a 'mere requirement of parental notice' does not violate the constitutional rights of an immature, dependent minor." The Court emphasized that parents have a constitutional right to raise their children and that therefore the state has an important interest in making sure that parents are notified prior to an abortion on a teenage girl. The Court also stressed that the "Utah statute gives neither parents nor the judges a veto power over the minor's abortion decision." The Court said that the fact that the notice requirement might "inhibit some minors from seeking abortions is not a valid basis to void the statute."

Subsequently, the Supreme Court upheld parental notification requirements as long as they have the judicial bypass procedures outlined in *Bellotti*. In Ohio v. Akron Center for Reproductive Health, 497 U.S. 502 (1990), the Court upheld a law that required that notice be given to at least one parent of an unmarried minor before an abortion could be performed. The law allowed an abortion without such notification if a judge approved it either by finding it would be in the minor's best interests or by concluding that she is mature enough to decide for herself.

In Hodgson v. Minnesota, 497 U.S. 417 (1990), the Supreme Court upheld the constitutionality of an even more burdensome law that required that notice be given to both of a minor's parents before an abortion could be performed. The Court specifically ruled that a two-parent notification requirement without a judicial bypass procedure was unconstitutional but that such a requirement is permissible as long as there is a mechanism for judicial bypass.

E. CONSTITUTIONAL PROTECTION FOR MEDICAL CARE DECISIONS

Another major area where the Supreme Court has considered the existence of a fundamental right is with regard to medical care decisions. Specifically, two major issues considered by the courts are whether there is a constitutional right to refuse treatment and whether there is a constitutional right to physician-assisted suicide.

RIGHT TO REFUSE TREATMENT

Generally, there is a constitutional right of individuals to refuse medical treatment, but it certainly is not absolute and can be regulated by the state. For example, in Jacobson v. Massachusetts, 197 U.S. 11 (1905), the Supreme Court upheld a Massachusetts law that required vaccinations. The Court allowed the law because of the government's compelling interest in stopping the spread of communicable diseases.

In Washington v. Harper, 494 U.S. 210 (1990), the Court said that prisoners had the right to be free from the involuntary administration of antipsychotic drugs. The Court observed that prisoners possess "a significant liberty interest in avoiding the unwanted administration of antipsychotic drugs under the Due Process Clause of the Fourteenth Amendment." The Court therefore said that "[t]he forcible injection of medication into a nonconsenting person's body represents a substantial interference with that person's liberty." However, the Court said that this interest was adequately protected by providing an inmate with notice and a hearing before a tribunal of medical and prison personnel at which the inmate could challenge the decision to administer the drugs.

The most important case, thus far, concerning a right to refuse medical care is Cruzan v. Director, Missouri Department of Health.

CRUZAN v. DIRECTOR, MISSOURI DEPARTMENT OF HEALTH
497 U.S. 261 (1990)

Chief Justice REHNQUIST delivered the opinion of the Court.

Petitioner Nancy Beth Cruzan was rendered incompetent as a result of severe injuries sustained during an automobile accident. Copetitioners Lester and Joyce Cruzan, Nancy's parents and coguardians, sought a court order directing the withdrawal of their daughter's artificial feeding and hydration equipment after it became apparent that she had virtually no chance of recovering her cognitive faculties. The Supreme Court of Missouri held that because there was no clear and convincing evidence of Nancy's desire to have life-sustaining treatment withdrawn under such circumstances, her parents lacked authority to effectuate such a request. We granted certiorari, and now affirm.

On the night of January 11, 1983, Nancy Cruzan lost control of her car as she traveled down Elm Road in Jasper County, Missouri. The vehicle overturned, and Cruzan was discovered lying face down in a ditch without detectable respiratory or cardiac function. Paramedics were able to restore her breathing and heartbeat at the accident site, and she was transported to a hospital in an unconscious state. An attending neurosurgeon diagnosed her as having sustained probable cerebral contusions compounded by significant anoxia (lack of oxygen). The Missouri trial court in this case found that permanent brain damage generally results after 6 minutes in an anoxic state; it was estimated that Cruzan was deprived of oxygen from 12 to 14 minutes. She remained in a coma for approximately three weeks and then progressed to an unconscious state in which she was able to orally ingest some nutrition. In order to ease feeding and further the recovery, surgeons implanted a gastrostomy feeding and hydration tube in Cruzan with the consent of her then husband. Subsequent rehabilitative efforts proved unavailing. She now lies in a Missouri state hospital in what is commonly referred to as a persistent vegetative state: generally, a condition in which a person exhibits motor reflexes but evinces no indications of significant cognitive function. The State of Missouri is bearing the cost of her care.

After it had become apparent that Nancy Cruzan had virtually no chance of regaining her mental faculties, her parents asked hospital employees to terminate the artificial nutrition and hydration procedures. All agree that such a removal would cause her death. The employees refused to honor the request without court approval. The parents then sought and received authorization from the state trial court for termination. The court found that a person in Nancy's condition had a fundamental right under the State and Federal Constitutions to refuse or direct the withdrawal of "death prolonging procedures." The court also found that Nancy's "expressed thoughts at age twenty-five in somewhat serious conversation with a housemate friend that if sick or injured she would not wish to continue her life unless she could live at least halfway normally suggests that given her present condition she would not wish to continue on with her nutrition and hydration." The Supreme Court of Missouri reversed by a divided vote.

We granted certiorari to consider the question whether Cruzan has a right under the United States Constitution which would require the hospital to withdraw life-sustaining treatment from her under these circumstances.

At common law, even the touching of one person by another without consent and without legal justification was a battery. This notion of bodily integrity has been embodied in the requirement that informed consent is generally required for medical treatment. The informed consent doctrine has become firmly entrenched in American tort law. The logical corollary of the doctrine of informed consent is that the patient generally possesses the right not to consent, that is, to refuse treatment.

The principle that a competent person has a constitutionally protected liberty interest in refusing unwanted medical treatment may be inferred from our prior decisions. In Jacobson v. Massachusetts (1905), for instance, the Court balanced an individual's liberty interest in declining an unwanted smallpox vaccine against the State's interest in preventing disease. Just this Term, in the course of holding that a State's procedures for administering antipsychotic medication to prisoners were sufficient to satisfy due process concerns, we recognized that prisoners possess "a significant liberty interest in avoiding the unwanted administration of antipsychotic drugs under the Due Process Clause of the Fourteenth Amendment." Washington v. Harper (1990).

But determining that a person has a "liberty interest" under the Due Process Clause does not end the inquiry; "whether respondent's constitutional rights have been violated must be determined by balancing his liberty interests against the relevant state interests." Petitioners insist that under the general holdings of our cases, the forced administration of life-sustaining medical treatment, and even of artificially delivered food and water essential to life, would implicate a competent person's liberty interest. Although we think the logic of the cases discussed above would embrace such a liberty interest, the dramatic consequences involved in refusal of such treatment would inform the inquiry as to whether the deprivation of that interest is constitutionally permissible. But for purposes of this case, we assume that the United States Constitution would grant a competent person a constitutionally protected right to refuse lifesaving hydration and nutrition.

Petitioners insist that under the general holdings of our cases, the forced administration of life-sustaining medical treatment, and even of artificially delivered food and water essential to life, would implicate a competent person's liberty interest. The difficulty with petitioners' claim is that in a sense it begs the question: An incompetent person is not able to make an informed and voluntary choice to exercise a hypothetical right to refuse treatment or any other right. Such a "right" must be exercised for her, if at all, by some sort of surrogate. Here, Missouri has in effect recognized that under certain circumstances a surrogate may act for the patient in electing to have hydration and nutrition withdrawn in such a way as to cause death, but it has established a procedural safeguard to assure that the action of the surrogate conforms as best it may to the wishes expressed by the patient while competent. Missouri requires that evidence of the incompetent's wishes as to the withdrawal of treatment be proved by clear and convincing evidence. The question, then, is whether the

United States Constitution forbids the establishment of this procedural requirement by the State. We hold that it does not.

Whether or not Missouri's clear and convincing evidence requirement comports with the United States Constitution depends in part on what interests the State may properly seek to protect in this situation. Missouri relies on its interest in the protection and preservation of human life, and there can be no gainsaying this interest. As a general matter, the States — indeed, all civilized nations — demonstrate their commitment to life by treating homicide as a serious crime. Moreover, the majority of States in this country have laws imposing criminal penalties on one who assists another to commit suicide. We do not think a State is required to remain neutral in the face of an informed and voluntary decision by a physically able adult to starve to death.

But in the context presented here, a State has more particular interests at stake. The choice between life and death is a deeply personal decision of obvious and overwhelming finality. We believe Missouri may legitimately seek to safeguard the personal element of this choice through the imposition of heightened evidentiary requirements. It cannot be disputed that the Due Process Clause protects an interest in life as well as an interest in refusing life-sustaining medical treatment. Not all incompetent patients will have loved ones available to serve as surrogate decision-makers. And even where family members are present, "[t]here will, of course, be some unfortunate situations in which family members will not act to protect a patient." A State is entitled to guard against potential abuses in such situations. Similarly, a State is entitled to consider that a judicial proceeding to make a determination regarding an incompetent's wishes may very well not be an adversarial one, with the added guarantee of accurate factfinding that the adversary process brings with it. Finally, we think a State may properly decline to make judgments about the "quality" of life that a particular individual may enjoy.

In our view, Missouri has permissibly sought to advance these interests through the adoption of a "clear and convincing" standard of proof to govern such proceedings. "This Court has mandated an intermediate standard of proof — 'clear and convincing evidence' — when the individual interests at stake in a state proceeding are both 'particularly important' and 'more substantial than mere loss of money.'" Santosky v. Kramer (1982). Thus, such a standard has been required in deportation proceedings, in denaturalization proceedings, in civil commitment proceedings, and in proceedings for the termination of parental rights.

We think it self-evident that the interests at stake in the instant proceedings are more substantial, both on an individual and societal level, than those involved in a run-of-the-mill civil dispute. But not only does the standard of proof reflect the importance of a particular adjudication, it also serves as "a societal judgment about how the risk of error should be distributed between the litigants." The more stringent the burden of proof a party must bear, the more that party bears the risk of an erroneous decision. We believe that Missouri may permissibly place an increased risk of an erroneous decision on those seeking to terminate an incompetent individual's life-sustaining treatment. An erroneous decision not to terminate results in a maintenance of the status quo; the possibility of subsequent developments such as advancements in medical science, the discovery of new evidence regarding the patient's intent, changes in the law, or simply the unexpected death of the patient despite the administration of life-sustaining treatment at least create the potential that a wrong decision will eventually be corrected or its impact mitigated. An erroneous decision to withdraw life-sustaining treatment, however, is not susceptible of correction.

In sum, we conclude that a State may apply a clear and convincing evidence standard in proceedings where a guardian seeks to discontinue nutrition and hydration of a person diagnosed to be in a persistent vegetative state.

The Supreme Court of Missouri held that in this case the testimony adduced at trial did not amount to clear and convincing proof of the patient's desire to have hydration and nutrition withdrawn. In so doing, it reversed a decision of the Missouri trial court which had found that the evidence "suggest[ed]" Nancy Cruzan would not have desired to continue such measures, but which had not adopted the standard of "clear and convincing evidence" enunciated by the Supreme Court. The testimony adduced at trial consisted primarily of Nancy Cruzan's statements made to a housemate about a year before her accident that she would not want to live should she face life as a "vegetable," and other observations to the same effect. The observations did not deal in terms with withdrawal of medical treatment or of hydration and nutrition. We cannot say that the Supreme Court of Missouri committed constitutional error in reaching the conclusion that it did.

Petitioners alternatively contend that Missouri must accept the "substituted judgment" of close family members even in the absence of substantial proof that their views reflect the views of the patient. No doubt is engendered by anything in this record but that Nancy Cruzan's mother and father are loving and caring parents. If the State were required by the United States Constitution to repose a right of "substituted judgment" with anyone, the Cruzans would surely qualify. But we do not think the Due Process Clause requires the State to repose judgment on these matters with anyone but the patient herself. Close family members may have a strong feeling — a feeling not at all ignoble or unworthy, but not entirely disinterested, either — that they do not wish to witness the continuation of the life of a loved one which they regard as hopeless, meaningless, and even degrading. But there is no automatic assurance that the view of close family members will necessarily be the same as the patient's would have been had she been confronted with the prospect of her situation while competent. All of the reasons previously discussed for allowing Missouri to require clear and convincing evidence of the patient's wishes lead us to conclude that the State may choose to defer only to those wishes, rather than confide the decision to close family members.[28]

Justice O'CONNOR, concurring.

I agree that a protected liberty interest in refusing unwanted medical treatment may be inferred from our prior decisions, and that the refusal of artificially delivered food and water is encompassed within that liberty interest. I write separately to clarify why I believe this to be so.

---

28. We are not faced in this case with the question whether a State might be required to defer to the decision of a surrogate if competent and probative evidence established that the patient herself had expressed a desire that the decision to terminate life-sustaining treatment be made for her by that individual. [Footnote by the Court.]

As the Court notes, the liberty interest in refusing medical treatment flows from decisions involving the State's invasions into the body. Because our notions of liberty are inextricably entwined with our idea of physical freedom and self-determination, the Court has often deemed state incursions into the body repugnant to the interests protected by the Due Process Clause. See, e.g., Rochin v. California (1952) ("Illegally breaking into the privacy of the petitioner, the struggle to open his mouth and remove what was there, the forcible extraction of his stomach's contents . . . is bound to offend even hardened sensibilities"). Our Fourth Amendment jurisprudence has echoed this same concern. See Schmerber v. California (1966) ("The integrity of an individual's person is a cherished value of our society"); Winston v. Lee (1985) ("A compelled surgical intrusion into an individual's body for evidence . . . implicates expectations of privacy and security of such magnitude that the intrusion may be 'unreasonable' even if likely to produce evidence of a crime"). The State's imposition of medical treatment on an unwilling competent adult necessarily involves some form of restraint and intrusion. A seriously ill or dying patient whose wishes are not honored may feel a captive of the machinery required for life-sustaining measures or other medical interventions. Such forced treatment may burden that individual's liberty interests as much as any state coercion.

The State's artificial provision of nutrition and hydration implicates identical concerns. Artificial feeding cannot readily be distinguished from other forms of medical treatment. Whether or not the techniques used to pass food and water into the patient's alimentary tract are termed "medical treatment," it is clear they all involve some degree of intrusion and restraint. Feeding a patient by means of a nasogastric tube requires a physician to pass a long flexible tube through the patient's nose, throat, and esophagus and into the stomach. Because of the discomfort such a tube causes, "[m]any patients need to be restrained forcibly and their hands put into large mittens to prevent them from removing the tube." A gastrostomy tube (as was used to provide food and water to Nancy Cruzan) must be surgically implanted into the stomach or small intestine. Requiring a competent adult to endure such procedures against her will burdens the patient's liberty, dignity, and freedom to determine the course of her own treatment. Accordingly, the liberty guaranteed by the Due Process Clause must protect, if it protects anything, an individual's deeply personal decision to reject medical treatment, including the artificial delivery of food and water.

I also write separately to emphasize that the Court does not today decide the issue whether a State must also give effect to the decisions of a surrogate decisionmaker. In my view, such a duty may well be constitutionally required to protect the patient's liberty interest in refusing medical treatment. Few individuals provide explicit oral or written instructions regarding their intent to refuse medical treatment should they become incompetent. States which decline to consider any evidence other than such instructions may frequently fail to honor a patient's intent. Such failures might be avoided if the State considered an equally probative source of evidence: the patient's appointment of a proxy to make health care decisions on her behalf. Delegating the authority to make medical decisions to a family member or friend is becoming a common method of planning for the future. Several States have recognized the practical wisdom of such a procedure by enacting durable power of attorney statutes that specifically authorize an individual to appoint a surrogate to make medical treatment decisions. Some state courts have suggested that an agent appointed pursuant to a general durable power of attorney statute would also be empowered to make health care decisions on behalf of the patient. Other States allow an individual to designate a proxy to carry out the intent of a living will. These procedures for surrogate decisionmaking, which appear to be rapidly gaining in acceptance, may be a valuable additional safeguard of the patient's interest in directing his medical care. Moreover, as patients are likely to select a family member as a surrogate, giving effect to a proxy's decisions may also protect the "freedom of personal choice in matters of . . . family life."

Today's decision, holding only that the Constitution permits a State to require clear and convincing evidence of Nancy Cruzan's desire to have artificial hydration and nutrition withdrawn, does not preclude a future determination that the Constitution requires the States to implement the decisions of a patient's duly appointed surrogate. Nor does it prevent States from developing other approaches for protecting an incompetent individual's liberty interest in refusing medical treatment. As is evident from the Court's survey of state court decisions, no national consensus has yet emerged on the best solution for this difficult and sensitive problem. Today we decide only that one State's practice does not violate the Constitution; the more challenging task of crafting appropriate procedures for safeguarding incompetents' liberty interests is entrusted to the "laboratory" of the States in the first instance.

Justice SCALIA, concurring.

The various opinions in this case portray quite clearly the difficult, indeed agonizing, questions that are presented by the constantly increasing power of science to keep the human body alive for longer than any reasonable person would want to inhabit it. The States have begun to grapple with these problems through legislation. I am concerned, from the tenor of today's opinions, that we are poised to confuse that enterprise as successfully as we have confused the enterprise of legislating concerning abortion — requiring it to be conducted against a background of federal constitutional imperatives that are unknown because they are being newly crafted from Term to Term. That would be a great misfortune.

While I agree with the Court's analysis today, and therefore join in its opinion, I would have preferred that we announce, clearly and promptly, that the federal courts have no business in this field; that American law has always accorded the State the power to prevent, by force if necessary, suicide — including suicide by refusing to take appropriate measures necessary to preserve one's life; that the point at which life becomes "worthless," and the point at which the means necessary to preserve it become "extraordinary" or "inappropriate," are neither set forth in the Constitution nor known to the nine Justices of this Court any better than they are known to nine people picked at random from the Kansas City telephone directory; and hence, that even when it is demonstrated by clear and convincing evidence that a patient no longer wishes certain measures to be taken to preserve his or her life, it is up to the citizens of Missouri to decide, through their elected representatives, whether that wish will be honored. It is quite impossible (because the Constitution says nothing about the matter) that those citizens will decide upon a line less lawful than the one we would choose;

and it is unlikely (because we know no more about "life and death" than they do) that they will decide upon a line less reasonable.

Justice BRENNAN, with whom Justice MARSHALL and Justice BLACKMUN join, dissenting.

"Medical technology has effectively created a twilight zone of suspended animation where death commences while life, in some form, continues. Some patients, however, want no part of a life sustained only by medical technology. Instead, they prefer a plan of medical treatment that allows nature to take its course and permits them to die with dignity."

Nancy Cruzan has dwelt in that twilight zone for six years. She is oblivious to her surroundings and will remain so. Her body twitches only reflexively, without consciousness. The areas of her brain that once thought, felt, and experienced sensations have degenerated badly and are continuing to do so. The "'cerebral cortical atrophy is irreversible, permanent, progressive and ongoing.'" "Nancy will never interact meaningfully with her environment again. She will remain in a persistent vegetative state until her death." Because she cannot swallow, her nutrition and hydration are delivered through a tube surgically implanted in her stomach.

A grown woman at the time of the accident, Nancy had previously expressed her wish to forgo continuing medical care under circumstances such as these. Her family and her friends are convinced that this is what she would want. A guardian ad litem appointed by the trial court is also convinced that this is what Nancy would want. Yet the Missouri Supreme Court, alone among state courts deciding such a question, has determined that an irreversibly vegetative patient will remain a passive prisoner of medical technology—for Nancy, perhaps for the next 30 years.

Today the Court, while tentatively accepting that there is some degree of constitutionally protected liberty interest in avoiding unwanted medical treatment, including life-sustaining medical treatment such as artificial nutrition and hydration, affirms the decision of the Missouri Supreme Court. The majority opinion, as I read it, would affirm that decision on the ground that a State may require "clear and convincing" evidence of Nancy Cruzan's prior decision to forgo life-sustaining treatment under circumstances such as hers in order to ensure that her actual wishes are honored. Because I believe that Nancy Cruzan has a fundamental right to be free of unwanted artificial nutrition and hydration, which right is not outweighed by any interests of the State, and because I find that the improperly biased procedural obstacles imposed by the Missouri Supreme Court impermissibly burden that right, I respectfully dissent. Nancy Cruzan is entitled to choose to die with dignity.

Although the right to be free of unwanted medical intervention, like other constitutionally protected interests, may not be absolute, no state interest could outweigh the rights of an individual in Nancy Cruzan's position. Whatever a State's possible interests in mandating life-support treatment under other circumstances, there is no good to be obtained here by Missouri's insistence that Nancy Cruzan remain on life-support systems if it is indeed her wish not to do so. Missouri does not claim, nor could it, that society as a whole will be benefited by Nancy's receiving medical treatment. No third party's situation will be improved and no harm to others will be averted.

The only state interest asserted here is a general interest in the preservation of life. But the State has no legitimate general interest in someone's life, completely abstracted from the interest of the person living that life, that could outweigh the person's choice to avoid medical treatment. Thus, the State's general interest in life must accede to Nancy Cruzan's particularized and intense interest in self-determination in her choice of medical treatment. There is simply nothing legitimately within the State's purview to be gained by superseding her decision.

Cruzan leaves many questions unanswered about the right to refuse treatment. Chief Justice Rehnquist's majority opinion assumes that there is a right to refuse treatment, and five justices—Justice O'Connor and the four dissenters—expressly recognize this right. Yet the Court never indicates the level of scrutiny to be used for this liberty interest. Also, the Court approves a state's requiring clear and convincing evidence that a person wanted treatment terminated before it is ended. But the Court does not consider whether a state may go even further in protecting life and require proof beyond a reasonable doubt. Nor does the Court indicate what type of evidence, such as living wills, might be sufficient to meet this proof requirement.

RIGHT TO PHYSICIAN-ASSISTED DEATH

The Court has not returned to the issue of the right to refuse treatment since *Cruzan*, but it has considered a closely related question: whether there is a constitutional right to physician-assisted suicide.

WASHINGTON v. GLUCKSBERG

521 U.S. 702 (1997)

Chief Justice REHNQUIST delivered the opinion of the Court.

The question presented in this case is whether Washington's prohibition against "caus[ing]" or "aid[ing]" a suicide offends the Fourteenth Amendment to the United States Constitution. We hold that it does not.

It has always been a crime to assist a suicide in the State of Washington. In 1854, Washington's first Territorial Legislature outlawed "assisting another in the commission of self-murder." Today, Washington law provides: "A person is guilty of promoting a suicide attempt when he knowingly causes or aids another person to attempt suicide." "Promoting a suicide attempt" is a felony, punishable by up to five years' imprisonment and up to a $10,000 fine.

Petitioners in this case are the State of Washington and its Attorney General. Respondents Harold Glucksberg, M.D., Abigail Halperin, M.D., Thomas A. Preston, M.D., and Peter Shalit, M.D., are physicians who practice in Washington. These doctors occasionally treat terminally ill, suffering patients, and declare that they would assist these patients in ending their lives if not for Washington's assisted-suicide ban. In January 1994, respondents, along with three gravely ill, pseudonymous plaintiffs who have since died and Compassion in Dying, a nonprofit organization that counsels people considering physician-assisted suicide, sued in the United States District Court, seeking a declaration that the Washington law is, on its face, unconstitutional.

The plaintiffs asserted "the existence of a liberty interest protected by the Fourteenth Amendment which extends to a personal choice by a mentally competent, terminally ill adult to commit physician-assisted suicide." We begin, as we do in all due process cases, by examining our Nation's history, legal traditions, and practices. In almost every State — indeed, in almost every western democracy — it is a crime to assist a suicide. The States' assisted-suicide bans are not innovations. Rather, they are longstanding expressions of the States' commitment to the protection and preservation of all human life. Indeed, opposition to and condemnation of suicide — and, therefore, of assisting suicide — are consistent and enduring themes of our philosophical, legal, and cultural heritages. That suicide remained a grievous, though nonfelonious, wrong is confirmed by the fact that colonial and early state legislatures and courts did not retreat from prohibiting assisting suicide.

Though deeply rooted, the States' assisted-suicide bans have in recent years been reexamined and, generally, reaffirmed. Because of advances in medicine and technology, Americans today are increasingly likely to die in institutions, from chronic illnesses. Public concern and democratic action are therefore sharply focused on how best to protect dignity and independence at the end of life, with the result that there have been many significant changes in state laws and in the attitudes these laws reflect. Many States, for example, now permit "living wills," surrogate health-care decisionmaking, and the withdrawal or refusal of life-sustaining medical treatment. At the same time, however, voters and legislators continue for the most part to reaffirm their States' prohibitions on assisting suicide.

[W]e "ha[ve] always been reluctant to expand the concept of substantive due process because guideposts for responsible decisionmaking in this unchartered area are scarce and open-ended." By extending constitutional protection to an asserted right or liberty interest, we, to a great extent, place the matter outside the arena of public debate and legislative action. We must therefore "exercise the utmost care whenever we are asked to break new ground in this field," lest the liberty protected by the Due Process Clause be subtly transformed into the policy preferences of the Members of this Court.

Our established method of substantive-due-process analysis has two primary features: First, we have regularly observed that the Due Process Clause specially protects those fundamental rights and liberties which are, objectively, "deeply rooted in this Nation's history and tradition," and "implicit in the concept of ordered liberty," such that "neither liberty nor justice would exist if they were sacrificed." Second, we have required in substantive-due-process cases a "careful description" of the asserted fundamental liberty interest. Our Nation's history, legal traditions, and practices thus provide the crucial "guideposts for responsible decisionmaking," that direct and restrain our exposition of the Due Process Clause. We now inquire whether this asserted right has any place in our Nation's traditions. Here, we are confronted with a consistent and almost universal tradition that has long rejected the asserted right, and continues explicitly to reject it today, even for terminally ill, mentally competent adults.

To hold for respondents, we would have to reverse centuries of legal doctrine and practice, and strike down the considered policy choice of almost every State.

Respondents contend that in *Cruzan* we "acknowledged that competent, dying persons have the right to direct the removal of life-sustaining medical treatment and thus hasten death," and that "the constitutional principle behind recognizing the patient's liberty to direct the withdrawal of artificial life support applies at least as strongly to the choice to hasten impending death by consuming lethal medication." The right assumed in *Cruzan*, however, was not simply deduced from abstract concepts of personal autonomy. Given the common-law rule that forced medication was a battery, and the long legal tradition protecting the decision to refuse unwanted medical treatment, our assumption was entirely consistent with this Nation's history and constitutional traditions. The decision to commit suicide with the assistance of another may be just as personal and profound as the decision to refuse unwanted medical treatment, but it has never enjoyed similar legal protection. Indeed, the two acts are widely and reasonably regarded as quite distinct.

The history of the law's treatment of assisted suicide in this country has been and continues to be one of the rejection of nearly all efforts to permit it. That being the case, our decisions lead us to conclude that the asserted "right" to assistance in committing suicide is not a fundamental liberty interest protected by the Due Process Clause.

The Constitution also requires, however, that Washington's assisted-suicide ban be rationally related to legitimate government interests. This requirement is unquestionably met here. As the court below recognized, Washington's assisted-suicide ban implicates a number of state interests.

First, Washington has an "unqualified interest in the preservation of human life." The State's prohibition on assisted suicide, like all homicide laws, both reflects and advances its commitment to this interest. Those who attempt suicide—terminally ill or not—often suffer from depression or other mental disorders. See New York Task Force (more than 95% of those who commit suicide had a major psychiatric illness at the time of death; among the terminally ill, uncontrolled pain is a "risk factor" because it contributes to depression). Research indicates, however, that many people who request physician-assisted suicide withdraw that request if their depression and pain are treated. The State also has an interest in protecting the integrity and ethics of the medical profession. And physician-assisted suicide could, it is argued, undermine the trust that is essential to the doctor-patient relationship by blurring the time-honored line between healing and harming.

Next, the State has an interest in protecting vulnerable groups—including the poor, the elderly, and disabled persons—from abuse, neglect, and mistakes. If physician-assisted suicide were permitted, many might resort to it to spare their families the substantial financial burden of end-of-life health-care costs. The State's interest here goes beyond protecting the vulnerable from coercion; it extends to protecting disabled and terminally ill people from prejudice, negative and inaccurate stereotypes, and "societal indifference."

Finally, the State may fear that permitting assisted suicide will start it down the path to voluntary and perhaps even involuntary euthanasia. Thus, it turns out that what is couched as a limited right to "physician-assisted suicide" is likely, in effect, a much broader license, which could prove extremely difficult to police and contain. Washington's ban on assisting suicide prevents such erosion.

This concern is further supported by evidence about the practice of euthanasia in the Netherlands. The Dutch government's own study revealed that in 1990, there were 2,300 cases of voluntary euthanasia (defined as "the deliberate termination of another's life at his request"), 400 cases of assisted suicide, and more than 1,000 cases of euthanasia without an explicit request. In addition to these latter 1,000 cases, the study found an additional 4,941 cases where physicians administered lethal morphine overdoses without the patients' explicit consent. This study suggests that, despite the existence of various reporting procedures, euthanasia in the Netherlands has not been limited to competent, terminally ill adults who are enduring physical suffering, and that regulation of the practice may not have prevented abuses in cases involving vulnerable persons, including severely disabled neonates and elderly persons suffering from dementia. The New York Task Force, citing the Dutch experience, observed that "assisted suicide and euthanasia are closely linked," and concluded that the "risk of . . . abuse is neither speculative nor distant." Washington, like most other States, reasonably ensures against this risk by banning, rather than regulating, assisting suicide.

We need not weigh exactly the relative strengths of these various interests. They are unquestionably important and legitimate, and Washington's ban on assisted suicide is at least reasonably related to their promotion and protection. Throughout the Nation, Americans are engaged in an earnest and profound debate about the morality, legality, and practicality of physician-assisted suicide. Our holding permits this debate to continue, as it should in a democratic society.

Justice O'CONNOR, concurring. Justice GINSBURG concurs in the Court's judgments substantially for the reasons stated in this opinion. Justice BREYER joins this opinion except insofar as it joins the opinions of the Court.

Death will be different for each of us. For many, the last days will be spent in physical pain and perhaps the despair that accompanies physical deterioration and a loss of control of basic bodily and mental functions. Some will seek medication to alleviate that pain and other symptoms.

The Court frames the issue in Washington v. Glucksberg as whether the Due Process Clause of the Constitution protects a "right to commit suicide which itself includes a right to assistance in doing so," and concludes that our Nation's history, legal traditions, and practices do not support the existence of such a right. I join the Court's opinions because I agree that there is no generalized right to "commit suicide." But respondents urge us to address the narrower question whether a mentally competent person who is experiencing great suffering has a constitutionally cognizable interest in controlling the circumstances of his or her imminent death. I see no need to reach that question in the context of the facial challenges to the New York and Washington laws at issue here.

The parties and amici agree that in these States a patient who is suffering from a terminal illness and who is experiencing great pain has no legal barriers to obtaining medication, from qualified physicians, to alleviate that suffering, even to the point of causing unconsciousness and hastening death. In this light, even assuming that we would recognize such an interest, I agree that the State's interests in protecting those who are not truly competent or facing imminent death, or those whose decisions to hasten death would not truly be voluntary, are sufficiently weighty to justify a prohibition against physician-assisted suicide.

Every one of us at some point may be affected by our own or a family member's terminal illness. There is no reason to think the democratic process will not strike the proper balance between the interests of terminally ill, mentally competent individuals who would seek to end their suffering and the State's interests in protecting those who might seek to end life mistakenly or under pressure. As the Court recognizes, States are presently undertaking extensive and serious evaluation of physician-assisted suicide and other related issues. In such circumstances, "the . . . challenging task of crafting appropriate procedures for safeguarding . . . liberty interests is entrusted to the 'laboratory' of the States . . . in the first instance."

In sum, there is no need to address the question whether suffering patients have a constitutionally cognizable interest in obtaining relief from the suffering that they may experience in the last days of their lives. There is no dispute that dying patients in Washington and New York can obtain palliative care, even when doing so would hasten their deaths. The difficulty in defining terminal illness and the risk that a dying patient's request for assistance in ending his or her life might not be truly voluntary justifies the prohibitions on assisted suicide we uphold here.

Justice STEVENS, concurring in the judgments.

The Court ends its opinion with the important observation that our holding today is fully consistent with a continuation of the vigorous debate about the "morality, legality, and practicality of physician-assisted suicide" in a democratic society. I write separately to make it clear that there is also room for further debate about the limits that the Constitution places on the power of the States to punish the practice.

Today, the Court decides that Washington's statute prohibiting assisted suicide is not invalid "on its face," that is to say, in all or most cases in which it might be applied. That holding, however, does not foreclose the possibility that some applications of the statute might well be invalid.

As the Court's opinion demonstrates, Washington's statute prohibiting assisted suicide has a "plainly legitimate sweep." While that demonstration provides a sufficient justification for rejecting respondents' facial challenge, it does not mean that every application of the statute should or will be upheld.

History and tradition provide ample support for refusing to recognize an open-ended constitutional right to commit suicide. Much more than the State's paternalistic interest in protecting the individual from the irrevocable consequences of an ill-advised decision motivated by temporary concerns is at stake. There is truth in John Donne's observation that "No man is an island." The State has an interest in preserving and fostering the benefits that every human being may provide to the community—a community that thrives on the exchange of ideas, expressions of affection, shared memories, and humorous incidents, as well as on the material contributions that its members create and support. The value to others of a person's life is far too precious to allow the individual to claim a constitutional entitlement to complete autonomy in making a decision to end that life. Thus, I fully agree with the Court that the "liberty" protected by the Due Process Clause does not include a categorical "right to commit suicide which itself includes a right to assistance in doing so."

But just as our conclusion that capital punishment is not always unconstitutional did not preclude later decisions holding that it is sometimes impermissibly cruel, so is it equally clear that a decision upholding a general statutory prohibition of assisted suicide does not mean that every possible application of the statute would be valid. A State, like Washington, that has authorized the death penalty, and thereby has concluded that the sanctity of human life does not require that it always be preserved, must acknowledge that there are situations in which an interest in hastening death is legitimate. Indeed, not only is that interest sometimes legitimate, I am also convinced that there are times when it is entitled to constitutional protection.

Justice BREYER, concurring in the judgments.

I agree with the Court that the critical question in both of the cases before us is whether "the 'liberty' specially protected by the Due Process Clause includes a right" of the sort that the respondents assert. I do not agree, however, with the Court's formulation of that claimed "liberty" interest. The Court describes it as a "right to commit suicide with another's assistance." But I would not reject the respondents' claim without considering a different formulation, for which our legal tradition may provide greater support. That formulation would use words roughly like a "right to die with dignity." But irrespective of the exact words used, at its core would lie personal control over the manner of death, professional medical assistance, and the avoidance of unnecessary and severe physical suffering — combined.

The respondents here argue that one can find a "right to die with dignity" by examining the protection the law has provided for related, but not identical, interests relating to personal dignity, medical treatment, and freedom from state-inflicted pain. I do not believe, however, that this Court need or now should decide whether or a not such a right is "fundamental." That is because, in my view, the avoidance of severe physical pain (connected with death) would have to constitute an essential part of any successful claim and because, as Justice O'Connor points out, the laws before us do not force a dying person to undergo that kind of pain. Rather, the laws of New York and of Washington do not prohibit doctors from providing patients with drugs sufficient to control pain despite the risk that those drugs themselves will kill. And under these circumstances the laws of New York and Washington would overcome any remaining significant interests and would be justified, regardless.

Medical technology, we are repeatedly told, makes the administration of pain-relieving drugs sufficient, except for a very few individuals for whom the ineffectiveness of pain control medicines can mean not pain, but the need for sedation which can end in a coma. We are also told that there are many instances in which patients do not receive the palliative care that, in principle, is available, but that is so for institutional reasons or inadequacies or obstacles, which would seem possible to overcome, and which do not include a prohibitive set of laws. This legal circumstance means that the state laws before us do not infringe directly upon the (assumed) central interest (what I have called the core of the interest in dying with dignity) as, by way of contrast, the state anticontraceptive laws did interfere with the central interest there at stake — by bringing the State's police powers to bear upon the marital bedroom.

Were the legal circumstances different — for example, were state law to prevent the provision of palliative care, including the administration of drugs as needed to avoid pain at the end of life — then the law's impact upon serious and otherwise unavoidable physical pain (accompanying death) would be more directly at issue. And as Justice O'Connor suggests, the Court might have to revisit its conclusions in these cases.

The companion case to Washington v. Glucksberg, decided the same day, was Vacco v. Quill. *Vacco* involved a challenge by terminally ill patients to the New York law that prohibited aiding or abetting a suicide. The U.S. Court of Appeals for the Second Circuit declared the law unconstitutional on equal protection grounds. The Second Circuit said that the New York law discriminated in that those on life support had a right to physician-assisted suicide because *Cruzan* recognized a right to refuse treatment. But those not on life support had no such right and thus were discriminated against. The Supreme Court rejected this claim.

VACCO v. QUILL, 521 U.S. 793 (1997): Chief Justice Rehnquist delivered the opinion of the Court.

In New York, as in most States, it is a crime to aid another to commit or attempt suicide, but patients may refuse even lifesaving medical treatment. The question presented by this case is whether New York's prohibition on assisting suicide therefore violates the Equal Protection Clause of the Fourteenth Amendment. We hold that it does not.

The Court of Appeals for the Second Circuit determined that, despite the assisted-suicide ban's apparent general applicability, "New York law does not treat equally all competent persons who are in the final stages of fatal illness and wish to hasten their deaths," because "those in the final stages of terminal illness who are on life-support systems are allowed to hasten their deaths by directing the removal of such systems; but those who are similarly situated, except for the previous attachment of life-sustaining equipment, are not allowed to hasten death by self-administering prescribed drugs."

The Equal Protection Clause commands that no State shall "deny to any person within its jurisdiction the equal protection of the laws." This provision creates no substantive rights. Instead, it embodies a general rule that States must treat like cases alike but may treat unlike cases accordingly.

New York's statutes outlawing assisting suicide affect and address matters of profound significance to all New Yorkers alike. They neither infringe fundamental rights nor involve suspect classifications. These laws are therefore entitled to a "strong presumption of validity." On their faces, neither New York's ban on assisting suicide nor its statutes permitting patients to refuse medical treatment treat anyone differently from anyone else or draw any distinctions between persons. Everyone, regardless of physical condition, is entitled, if competent, to refuse unwanted lifesaving medical treatment; no one is permitted to assist a suicide. Generally speaking, laws that apply evenhandedly to all "unquestionably comply" with the Equal Protection Clause.

The Court of Appeals, however, concluded that some terminally ill people — those who are on life-support systems — are treated differently from those who are not, in that the former may "hasten death" by ending treatment, but the latter may not "hasten death" through physician-assisted suicide. This conclusion depends on the submission that ending or refusing lifesaving medical treatment "is nothing more nor less than assisted suicide." Unlike the Court of Appeals, we think the distinction between assisting suicide and withdrawing life-sustaining treatment, a distinction widely recognized and endorsed in the medical profession and in our legal traditions, is both important and logical; it is certainly rational.

The distinction comports with fundamental legal principles of causation and intent. First, when a patient refuses life-sustaining medical treatment, he dies from an underlying fatal disease or pathology; but if a patient ingests lethal medication prescribed by a physician, he is killed by that medication. Furthermore, a physician who withdraws, or honors a patient's refusal to begin, life-sustaining medical treatment purposefully intends, or may so intend, only to respect his patient's wishes and "to cease doing useless and futile or degrading things to the patient when [the patient] no longer stands to benefit from them." The same is true when a doctor provides aggressive palliative care; in some cases, painkilling drugs may hasten a patient's death, but the physician's purpose and intent is, or may be, only to ease his patient's pain. A doctor who assists a suicide, however, "must, necessarily and indubitably, intend primarily that the patient be made dead." Similarly, a patient who commits suicide with a doctor's aid necessarily has the specific intent to end his or her own life, while a patient who refuses or discontinues treatment might not. The law has long used actors' intent or purpose to distinguish between two acts that may have the same result.

Similarly, the overwhelming majority of state legislatures have drawn a clear line between assisting suicide and withdrawing or permitting the refusal of unwanted lifesaving medical treatment by prohibiting the former and permitting the latter. And "nearly all states expressly disapprove of suicide and assisted suicide either in statutes dealing with durable powers of attorney in health-care situations, or in 'living will' statutes." Thus, even as the States move to protect and promote patients' dignity at the end of life, they remain opposed to physician-assisted suicide.

New York's reasons for recognizing and acting on this distinction — including prohibiting intentional killing and preserving life; preventing suicide; maintaining physicians' role as their patients' healers; protecting vulnerable people from indifference, prejudice, and psychological and financial pressure to end their lives; and avoiding a possible slide towards euthanasia — are discussed in greater detail in our opinion in *Glucksberg*. These valid and important public interests easily satisfy the constitutional requirement that a legislative classification bear a rational relation to some legitimate end.

All nine justices voted to uphold the Washington and New York laws in Washington v. Glucksberg and Vacco v. Quill. However, it is notable that five justices — O'Connor, Stevens, Souter, Ginsburg, and Breyer — indicated that they may be willing to find these laws unconstitutional as applied in particular instances. None of the opinions was explicit about the circumstances in which laws prohibiting physician-assisted suicide would be declared unconstitutional as applied. But especially the opinions by Justices O'Connor and Breyer indicated that the state does not have an interest in prolonging suffering and that the result may be different in a situation where no alternative to eliminating suffering exists. The question, though, remains as to the circumstances, if any, in which the Court will find laws prohibiting physician-assisted suicide to be unconstitutional as applied.

F. CONSTITUTIONAL PROTECTION FOR SEXUAL ORIENTATION AND SEXUAL ACTIVITY

In Bowers v. Hardwick, 478 U.S. 186 (1986), the Supreme Court held that the right to privacy does not protect a right to engage in private consensual homosexual activity. In a five-to-four decision, the Court upheld a Georgia law that prohibited oral-genital or anal-genital contact. Although the statute applied to both heterosexual and homosexual activity, the Court's opinion focused exclusively on the constitutionality of states' prohibiting homosexual activity. The Court said that such a right did not exist because it was not supported by the Constitution's text, the framers' intent, or tradition.

In Lawrence v. Texas, the Court expressly overruled Bowers v. Hardwick and held that the right to privacy protects a right to engage in private consensual homosexual activity.[29] In reading this important decision, consider: What level of scrutiny is the majority using and does it matter? Does the decision have implications for whether there is a constitutional right to same-sex marriage or whether other laws regulating private consensual sexual activity (i.e., adultery laws or prostitution laws) are unconstitutional?

LAWRENCE v. TEXAS
539 U.S. 558 (2003)

Justice KENNEDY delivered the opinion of the Court.

Liberty protects the person from unwarranted government intrusions into a dwelling or other private places. In our tradition the State is not omnipresent in the home. And there are other spheres of our lives and existence, outside the home, where the State should not be a dominant presence. Freedom extends beyond spatial bounds. Liberty presumes an autonomy of self that includes freedom of thought, belief, expression, and certain intimate conduct. The instant case involves liberty of the person both in its spatial and more transcendent dimensions.

I

The question before the Court is the validity of a Texas statute making it a crime for two persons of the same sex to engage in certain intimate sexual conduct. In

---

29. For an excellent description of the facts and history of the *Lawrence* litigation, *see* Dale Carpenter, *Flagrant Conduct: The Story of Lawrence v. Texas: How a Bedroom Arrest Decriminalized Gay Americans* (2012).

Houston, Texas, officers of the Harris County Police Department were dispatched to a private residence in response to a reported weapons disturbance. They entered an apartment where one of the petitioners, John Geddes Lawrence, resided. The right of the police to enter does not seem to have been questioned. The officers observed Lawrence and another man, Tyron Garner, engaging in a sexual act. The two petitioners were arrested, held in custody over night, and charged and convicted before a Justice of the Peace.

The complaints described their crime as "deviate sexual intercourse, namely anal sex, with a member of the same sex (man)." The applicable state law is Tex. Penal Code Ann. §21.06(a) (2003). It provides: "A person commits an offense if he engages in deviate sexual intercourse with another individual of the same sex." The statute defines "[d]eviate sexual intercourse" as follows: "(A) any contact between any part of the genitals of one person and the mouth or anus of another person"; or "(B) the penetration of the genitals or the anus of another person with an object." §21.01(1).

II

We conclude the case should be resolved by determining whether the petitioners were free as adults to engage in the private conduct in the exercise of their liberty under the Due Process Clause of the Fourteenth Amendment to the Constitution. For this inquiry we deem it necessary to reconsider the Court's holding in *Bowers*.

The facts in *Bowers* had some similarities to the instant case. A police officer, whose right to enter seems not to have been in question, observed Hardwick, in his own bedroom, engaging in intimate sexual conduct with another adult male. The conduct was in violation of a Georgia statute making it a criminal offense to engage in sodomy. One difference between the two cases is that the Georgia statute prohibited the conduct whether or not the participants were of the same sex, while the Texas statute, as we have seen, applies only to participants of the same sex. Hardwick was not prosecuted, but he brought an action in federal court to declare the state statute invalid. He alleged he was a practicing homosexual and that the criminal prohibition violated rights guaranteed to him by the Constitution. The Court, in an opinion by Justice White, sustained the Georgia law. Chief Justice Burger and Justice Powell joined the opinion of the Court and filed separate, concurring opinions.

The Court began its substantive discussion in *Bowers* as follows: "The issue presented is whether the Federal Constitution confers a fundamental right upon homosexuals to engage in sodomy and hence invalidates the laws of the many States that still make such conduct illegal and have done so for a very long time." That statement, we now conclude, discloses the Court's own failure to appreciate the extent of the liberty at stake. To say that the issue in *Bowers* was simply the right to engage in certain sexual conduct demeans the claim the individual put forward, just as it would demean a married couple were it to be said marriage is simply about the right to have sexual intercourse. The laws involved in *Bowers* and here are, to be sure, statutes that purport to do no more than prohibit a particular sexual act. Their penalties and purposes, though, have more far-reaching consequences, touching upon the most private human conduct, sexual behavior, and in the most private of places, the home.

The statutes do seek to control a personal relationship that, whether or not entitled to formal recognition in the law, is within the liberty of persons to choose without being punished as criminals.

This, as a general rule, should counsel against attempts by the State, or a court, to define the meaning of the relationship or to set its boundaries absent injury to a person or abuse of an institution the law protects. It suffices for us to acknowledge that adults may choose to enter upon this relationship in the confines of their homes and their own private lives and still retain their dignity as free persons. When sexuality finds overt expression in intimate conduct with another person, the conduct can be but one element in a personal bond that is more enduring. The liberty protected by the Constitution allows homosexual persons the right to make this choice.

Having misapprehended the claim of liberty there presented to it, and thus stating the claim to be whether there is a fundamental right to engage in consensual sodomy, the *Bowers* Court said: "Proscriptions against that conduct have ancient roots." At the outset it should be noted that there is no longstanding history in this country of laws directed at homosexual conduct as a distinct matter. Beginning in colonial times there were prohibitions of sodomy derived from the English criminal laws passed in the first instance by the Reformation Parliament of 1533. The English prohibition was understood to include relations between men and women as well as relations between men and men. Nineteenth-century commentators similarly read American sodomy, buggery, and crime-against-nature statutes as criminalizing certain relations between men and women and between men and men. The absence of legal prohibitions focusing on homosexual conduct may be explained in part by noting that according to some scholars the concept of the homosexual as a distinct category of person did not emerge until the late 19th century. Thus early American sodomy laws were not directed at homosexuals as such but instead sought to prohibit nonprocreative sexual activity more generally. This does not suggest approval of homosexual conduct. It does tend to show that this particular form of conduct was not thought of as a separate category from like conduct between heterosexual persons.

Laws prohibiting sodomy do not seem to have been enforced against consenting adults acting in private. A substantial number of sodomy prosecutions and convictions for which there are surviving records were for predatory acts against those who could not or did not consent, as in the case of a minor or the victim of an assault. As to these, one purpose for the prohibitions was to ensure there would be no lack of coverage if a predator committed a sexual assault that did not constitute rape as defined by the criminal law. Thus the model sodomy indictments presented in a 19th-century treatise, addressed the predatory acts of an adult man against a minor girl or minor boy. Instead of targeting relations between consenting adults in private, 19th-century sodomy prosecutions typically involved relations between men and minor girls or minor boys, relations between adults involving force, relations between adults implicating disparity in status, or relations between men and animals.

In all events that infrequency makes it difficult to say that society approved of a rigorous and systematic punishment of the consensual acts committed in private and by adults. The longstanding criminal prohibition of homosexual sodomy upon which the *Bowers* decision placed such reliance is as consistent with a general condemnation of nonprocreative sex as it is with an established tradition of prosecuting acts because of their homosexual character.

The policy of punishing consenting adults for private acts was not much discussed in the early legal literature. We can infer that one reason for this was the very private nature of the conduct. Despite the absence of prosecutions, there may have been periods in which there was public criticism of homosexuals as such and an insistence that the criminal laws be enforced to discourage their practices. But far from possessing "ancient roots," American laws targeting same-sex couples did not develop until the last third of the 20th century. The reported decisions concerning the prosecution of consensual, homosexual sodomy between adults for the years 1880-1995 are not always clear in the details, but a significant number involved conduct in a public place. It was not until the 1970's that any State singled out same-sex relations for criminal prosecution, and only nine States have done so. Post-*Bowers* even some of these States did not adhere to the policy of suppressing homosexual conduct. Over the course of the last decades, States with same-sex prohibitions have moved toward abolishing them. In summary, the historical grounds relied upon in *Bowers* are more complex than the majority opinion and the concurring opinion by Chief Justice Burger indicate. Their historical premises are not without doubt and, at the very least, are overstated.

It must be acknowledged, of course, that the Court in *Bowers* was making the broader point that for centuries there have been powerful voices to condemn homosexual conduct as immoral. The condemnation has been shaped by religious beliefs, conceptions of right and acceptable behavior, and respect for the traditional family. For many persons these are not trivial concerns but profound and deep convictions accepted as ethical and moral principles to which they aspire and which thus determine the course of their lives. These considerations do not answer the question before us, however. The issue is whether the majority may use the power of the State to enforce these views on the whole society through operation of the criminal law. "Our obligation is to define the liberty of all, not to mandate our own moral code." Planned Parenthood of Southeastern Pa. v. Casey (1992).

Chief Justice Burger joined the opinion for the Court in *Bowers* and further explained his views as follows: "Decisions of individuals relating to homosexual conduct have been subject to state intervention throughout the history of Western civilization. Condemnation of those practices is firmly rooted in Judeo-Christian moral and ethical standards." In all events we think that our laws and traditions in the past half century are of most relevance here. These references show an emerging awareness that liberty gives substantial protection to adult persons in deciding how to conduct their private lives in matters pertaining to sex. "[H]istory and tradition are the starting point but not in all cases the ending point of the substantive due process inquiry."

In *Bowers* the Court referred to the fact that before 1961 all 50 States had outlawed sodomy, and that at the time of the Court's decision 24 States and the District of Columbia had sodomy laws. Justice Powell pointed out that these prohibitions often were being ignored, however. Georgia, for instance, had not sought to enforce its law for decades.

In our own constitutional system the deficiencies in *Bowers* became even more apparent in the years following its announcement. The 25 States with laws prohibiting the relevant conduct referenced in the *Bowers* decision are reduced now to 13, of which 4 enforce their laws only against homosexual conduct. In those States where sodomy is still proscribed, whether for same-sex or heterosexual conduct, there is a pattern of nonenforcement with respect to consenting adults acting in private. The State of Texas admitted in 1994 that as of that date it had not prosecuted anyone under those circumstances.

Two principal cases decided after *Bowers* cast its holding into even more doubt. In Planned Parenthood of Southeastern Pa. v. Casey (1992), the Court reaffirmed the substantive force of the liberty protected by the Due Process Clause. The *Casey* decision again confirmed that our laws and tradition afford constitutional protection to personal decisions relating to marriage, procreation, contraception, family relationships, child rearing, and education. In explaining the respect the Constitution demands for the autonomy of the person in making these choices, we stated as follows: "These matters, involving the most intimate and personal choices a person may make in a lifetime, choices central to personal dignity and autonomy, are central to the liberty protected by the Fourteenth Amendment. At the heart of liberty is the right to define one's own concept of existence, of meaning, of the universe, and of the mystery of human life. Beliefs about these matters could not define the attributes of personhood were they formed under compulsion of the State." Persons in a homosexual relationship may seek autonomy for these purposes, just as heterosexual persons do. The decision in *Bowers* would deny them this right.

The second post-*Bowers* case of principal relevance is Romer v. Evans (1996). There the Court struck down class-based legislation directed at homosexuals as a violation of the Equal Protection Clause. *Romer* invalidated an amendment to Colorado's constitution which named as a solitary class persons who were homosexuals, lesbians, or bisexual either by "orientation, conduct, practices or relationships," and deprived them of protection under state antidiscrimination laws. We concluded that the provision was "born of animosity toward the class of persons affected" and further that it had no rational relation to a legitimate governmental purpose.

As an alternative argument in this case, counsel for the petitioners and some amici contend that *Romer* provides the basis for declaring the Texas statute invalid under the Equal Protection Clause. That is a tenable argument, but we conclude the instant case requires us to address whether *Bowers* itself has continuing validity. Were we to hold the statute invalid under the Equal Protection Clause some might question whether a prohibition would be valid if drawn differently, say, to prohibit the conduct both between same-sex and different-sex participants.

The central holding of *Bowers* has been brought in question by this case, and it should be addressed. Its continuance as precedent demeans the lives of homosexual persons. The stigma this criminal statute imposes, moreover, is not trivial. The offense, to be sure, is but a class C misdemeanor, a minor offense in the Texas legal system. Still, it remains a criminal offense with all that imports for the dignity of the persons charged. The petitioners will bear on their record the history of their criminal convictions.

Bowers was not correct when it was decided, and it is not correct today. It ought not to remain binding precedent. Bowers v. Hardwick should be and now is overruled.

The present case does not involve minors. It does not involve persons who might be injured or coerced or who are situated in relationships where consent might not easily be refused. It does not involve public conduct or prostitution. It does not involve whether the government must give formal recognition to any relationship that homosexual persons seek to enter. The case does involve two adults who, with full and mutual consent from each other, engaged in sexual practices common to a homosexual lifestyle. The petitioners are entitled to respect for their private lives. The State cannot demean their existence or control their destiny by making their private sexual conduct a crime. Their right to liberty under the Due Process Clause gives them the full right to engage in their conduct without intervention of the government. "It is a promise of the Constitution that there is a realm of personal liberty which the government may not enter." The Texas statute furthers no legitimate state interest which can justify its intrusion into the personal and private life of the individual.

Had those who drew and ratified the Due Process Clauses of the Fifth Amendment or the Fourteenth Amendment known the components of liberty in its manifold possibilities, they might have been more specific. They did not presume to have this insight. They knew times can blind us to certain truths and later generations can see that laws once thought necessary and proper in fact serve only to oppress. As the Constitution endures, persons in every generation can invoke its principles in their own search for greater freedom.

Justice O'CONNOR, concurring in the judgment.

The Court today overrules Bowers v. Hardwick (1986). I joined *Bowers*, and do not join the Court in overruling it. Nevertheless, I agree with the Court that Texas' statute banning same-sex sodomy is unconstitutional. Rather than relying on the substantive component of the Fourteenth Amendment's Due Process Clause, as the Court does, I base my conclusion on the Fourteenth Amendment's Equal Protection Clause.

The Equal Protection Clause of the Fourteenth Amendment "is essentially a direction that all persons similarly situated should be treated alike." Under our rational basis standard of review, "legislation is presumed to be valid and will be sustained if the classification drawn by the statute is rationally related to a legitimate state interest." Laws such as economic or tax legislation that are scrutinized under rational basis review normally pass constitutional muster, since "the Constitution presumes that even improvident decisions will eventually be rectified by the democratic processes." We have consistently held, however, that some objectives, such as "a bare . . . desire to harm a politically unpopular group," are not legitimate state interests. When a law exhibits such a desire to harm a politically unpopular group, we have applied a more searching form of rational basis review to strike down such laws under the Equal Protection Clause.

We have been most likely to apply rational basis review to hold a law unconstitutional under the Equal Protection Clause where, as here, the challenged legislation inhibits personal relationships. The statute at issue here makes sodomy a crime only if a person "engages in deviate sexual intercourse with another individual of the same sex." Sodomy between opposite-sex partners, however, is not a crime in Texas. That is, Texas treats the same conduct differently based solely on the participants. Those harmed by this law are people who have a same-sex sexual orientation and thus are more likely to engage in behavior prohibited by §21.06.

The Texas statute makes homosexuals unequal in the eyes of the law by making particular conduct — and only that conduct — subject to criminal sanction. It appears that prosecutions under Texas' sodomy law are rare. This case shows, however, that prosecutions under §21.06 do occur. And while the penalty imposed on petitioners in this case was relatively minor, the consequences of conviction are not. And the effect of Texas' sodomy law is not just limited to the threat of prosecution or consequence of conviction. Texas' sodomy law brands all homosexuals as criminals, thereby making it more difficult for homosexuals to be treated in the same manner as everyone else. Indeed, Texas itself has previously acknowledged the collateral effects of the law, stipulating in a prior challenge to this action that the law "legally sanctions discrimination against [homosexuals] in a variety of ways unrelated to the criminal law," including in the areas of "employment, family issues, and housing."

Texas attempts to justify its law, and the effects of the law, by arguing that the statute satisfies rational basis review because it furthers the legitimate governmental interest of the promotion of morality. In *Bowers*, we held that a state law criminalizing sodomy as applied to homosexual couples did not violate substantive due process. We rejected the argument that no rational basis existed to justify the law, pointing to the government's interest in promoting morality. The only question in front of the Court in *Bowers* was whether the substantive component of the Due Process Clause protected a right to engage in homosexual sodomy. *Bowers* did not hold that moral disapproval of a group is a rational basis under the Equal Protection Clause to criminalize homosexual sodomy when heterosexual sodomy is not punished.

This case raises a different issue than *Bowers*: whether, under the Equal Protection Clause, moral disapproval is a legitimate state interest to justify by itself a statute that bans homosexual sodomy, but not heterosexual sodomy. It is not. Moral disapproval of this group, like a bare desire to harm the group, is an interest that is insufficient to satisfy rational basis review under the Equal Protection Clause. Indeed, we have never held that moral disapproval, without any other asserted state interest, is a sufficient rationale under the Equal Protection Clause to justify a law that discriminates among groups of persons.

Moral disapproval of a group cannot be a legitimate governmental interest under the Equal Protection Clause because legal classifications must not be "drawn for the purpose of disadvantaging the group burdened by the law." Texas' invocation of moral disapproval as a legitimate state interest proves nothing more than Texas' desire to criminalize homosexual sodomy. But the Equal Protection Clause prevents a State from creating "a classification of persons undertaken for its own sake." And because Texas so rarely enforces its sodomy law as applied to private, consensual acts, the law serves more as a statement of dislike and disapproval against homosexuals than as a tool to stop criminal behavior. The Texas sodomy law "raise[s] the inevitable inference that the disadvantage imposed is born of animosity toward the class of persons affected."

Texas argues, however, that the sodomy law does not discriminate against homosexual persons. Instead, the State maintains that the law discriminates only against homosexual conduct. While it is true that the law applies only to conduct, the conduct targeted by this law is conduct that is closely correlated with being homosexual. Under such circumstances, Texas' sodomy law is targeted at more than conduct. It is instead directed toward gay persons as a class.

But the State cannot single out one identifiable class of citizens for punishment that does not apply to everyone else, with moral disapproval as the only asserted state interest for the law. The Texas sodomy statute subjects homosexuals to "a lifelong penalty and stigma. A legislative classification that threatens the creation of an underclass . . . cannot be reconciled with" the Equal Protection Clause. Whether a sodomy law that is neutral both in effect and application, would violate the substantive component of the Due Process Clause is an issue that need not be decided today. I am confident, however, that so long as the Equal Protection Clause requires a sodomy law to apply equally to the private consensual conduct of homosexuals and heterosexuals alike, such a law would not long stand in our democratic society.

That this law as applied to private, consensual conduct is unconstitutional under the Equal Protection Clause does not mean that other laws distinguishing between heterosexuals and homosexuals would similarly fail under rational basis review. Texas cannot assert any legitimate state interest here, such as national security or preserving the traditional institution of marriage. Unlike the moral disapproval of same-sex relations — the asserted state interest in this case — other reasons exist to promote the institution of marriage beyond mere moral disapproval of an excluded group.

A law branding one class of persons as criminal solely based on the State's moral disapproval of that class and the conduct associated with that class runs contrary to the values of the Constitution and the Equal Protection Clause, under any standard of review. I therefore concur in the Court's judgment that Texas' sodomy law banning "deviate sexual intercourse" between consenting adults of the same sex, but not between consenting adults of different sexes, is unconstitutional.

Justice SCALIA, with whom the Chief Justice and Justice THOMAS join, dissenting.

"Liberty finds no refuge in a jurisprudence of doubt." Planned Parenthood of Southeastern Pa. v. Casey (1992). That was the Court's sententious response, barely more than a decade ago, to those seeking to overrule Roe v. Wade (1973). The Court's response today, to those who have engaged in a 17-year crusade to overrule Bowers v. Hardwick (1986), is very different. The need for stability and certainty presents no barrier.

Most of the rest of today's opinion has no relevance to its actual holding — that the Texas statute "furthers no legitimate state interest which can justify" its application to petitioners under rational-basis review. Though there is discussion of "fundamental proposition[s]," and "fundamental decisions," nowhere does the Court's opinion declare that homosexual sodomy is a "fundamental right" under the Due Process Clause; nor does it subject the Texas law to the standard of review that would be appropriate (strict scrutiny) if homosexual sodomy were a "fundamental right." Thus, while overruling the outcome of *Bowers*, the Court leaves strangely untouched its central legal conclusion: "[R]espondent would have us announce . . . a fundamental right to engage in homosexual sodomy. This we are quite unwilling to do." Instead the Court simply describes petitioners' conduct as "an exercise of their liberty" — which it undoubtedly is — and proceeds to apply an unheard-of form of rational-basis review that will have far-reaching implications beyond this case.

I

I begin with the Court's surprising readiness to reconsider a decision rendered a mere 17 years ago in Bowers v. Hardwick. I do not myself believe in rigid adherence to stare decisis in constitutional cases; but I do believe that we should be consistent rather than manipulative in invoking the doctrine. Today's opinions in support of reversal do not bother to distinguish — or indeed, even bother to mention — the paean to stare decisis coauthored by three Members of today's majority in Planned Parenthood v. Casey. There, when stare decisis meant preservation of judicially invented abortion rights, the widespread criticism of *Roe* was strong reason to reaffirm it. Today, however, the widespread opposition to *Bowers*, a decision resolving an issue as "intensely divisive" as the issue in *Roe*, is offered as a reason in favor of overruling it. Gone, too, is any "enquiry" (of the sort conducted in *Casey*) into whether the decision sought to be overruled has "proven unworkable."

Today's approach to stare decisis invites us to overrule an erroneously decided precedent (including an "intensely divisive" decision) if: (1) its foundations have been "eroded" by subsequent decisions, (2) it has been subject to "substantial and continuing" criticism, and (3) it has not induced "individual or societal reliance" that counsels against overturning. The problem is that *Roe* itself — which today's majority surely has no disposition to overrule — satisfies these conditions to at least the same degree as *Bowers*.

State laws against bigamy, same-sex marriage, adult incest, prostitution, masturbation, adultery, fornication, bestiality, and obscenity are likewise sustainable only in light of *Bowers'* validation of laws based on moral choices. Every single one of these laws is called into question by today's decision; the Court makes no effort to cabin the scope of its decision to exclude them from its holding. The impossibility of distinguishing homosexuality from other traditional "morals" offenses is precisely why *Bowers* rejected the rational-basis challenge. "The law," it said, "is constantly based on notions of morality, and if all laws representing essentially moral choices are to be invalidated under the Due Process Clause, the courts will be very busy indeed."

What a massive disruption of the current social order, therefore, the overruling of *Bowers* entails. Not so the overruling of *Roe*, which would simply have restored the regime that existed for centuries before 1973, in which the permissibility of and restrictions upon abortion were determined legislatively State-by-State.

II

Having decided that it need not adhere to stare decisis, the Court still must establish that *Bowers* was wrongly decided and that the Texas statute, as applied to petitioners, is unconstitutional. Texas Penal Code Ann. §21.06(a) (2003) undoubtedly imposes constraints on liberty. So do laws prohibiting prostitution, recreational use of heroin, and, for that matter, working more than 60 hours per week in a bakery. But there is no right to "liberty" under the Due Process Clause, though today's opinion repeatedly makes that claim. The Fourteenth Amendment expressly allows States to deprive their citizens of "liberty," so long as "due process of law" is provided. Our opinions applying the doctrine known as "substantive due process" hold that the Due Process Clause prohibits States from infringing fundamental liberty interests, unless the infringement is narrowly tailored to serve a compelling state interest. Washington v. Glucksberg (1997). We have held repeatedly, in cases the Court today does not overrule, that only fundamental rights qualify for this so-called "heightened scrutiny" protection — that is, rights which are "deeply rooted in this Nation's history and tradition." All other liberty interests may be abridged or abrogated pursuant to a validly enacted state law if that law is rationally related to a legitimate state interest.

Bowers held, first, that criminal prohibitions of homosexual sodomy are not subject to heightened scrutiny because they do not implicate a "fundamental right" under the Due Process Clause. The Court today does not overrule this holding. Not once does it describe homosexual sodomy as a "fundamental right" or a "fundamental liberty interest," nor does it subject the Texas statute to strict scrutiny.

III

The Court's description of "the state of the law" at the time of Bowers only confirms that Bowers was right. After discussing the history of antisodomy laws, the Court proclaims that, "it should be noted that there is no longstanding history in this country of laws directed at homosexual conduct as a distinct matter." This observation in no way casts into doubt the "definitive [historical] conclusion," on which Bowers relied: that our Nation has a longstanding history of laws prohibiting sodomy in general — regardless of whether it was performed by same-sex or opposite-sex couples: "It is obvious to us that neither of these formulations would extend a fundamental right to homosexuals to engage in acts of consensual sodomy. Proscriptions against that conduct have ancient roots. Sodomy was a criminal offense at common law and was forbidden by the laws of the original 13 States when they ratified the Bill of Rights. In 1868, when the Fourteenth Amendment was ratified, all but 5 of the 37 States in the Union had criminal sodomy laws. In fact, until 1961, all 50 States outlawed sodomy, and today, 24 States and the District of Columbia continue to provide criminal penalties for sodomy performed in private and between consenting adults. Against this background, to claim that a right to engage in such conduct is 'deeply rooted in this Nation's history and tradition' or 'implicit in the concept of ordered liberty' is, at best, facetious." Whether homosexual sodomy was prohibited by a law targeted at same-sex sexual relations or by a more general law prohibiting both homosexual and heterosexual sodomy, the only relevant point is that it was criminalized — which suffices to establish that homosexual sodomy is not a right "deeply rooted in our Nation's history and tradition." The Court today agrees that homosexual sodomy was criminalized and thus does not dispute the facts on which Bowers actually relied.

Next the Court makes the claim, again unsupported by any citations, that "[l]aws prohibiting sodomy do not seem to have been enforced against consenting adults acting in private." The key qualifier here is "acting in private" — since the Court admits that sodomy laws were enforced against consenting adults. I do not know what "acting in private" means; surely consensual sodomy, like heterosexual intercourse, is rarely performed on stage. If all the Court means by "acting in private" is "on private premises, with the doors closed and windows covered," it is entirely unsurprising that evidence of enforcement would be hard to come by. (Imagine the circumstances that would enable a search warrant to be obtained for a residence on the ground that there was probable cause to believe that consensual sodomy was then and there occurring.) Surely that lack of evidence would not sustain the proposition that consensual sodomy on private premises with the doors closed and windows covered was regarded as a "fundamental right," even though all other consensual sodomy was criminalized. There are 203 prosecutions for consensual, adult homosexual sodomy reported in the West Reporting system and official state reporters from the years 1880-1995. There are also records of 20 sodomy prosecutions and 4 executions during the colonial period. *Bowers'* conclusion that homosexual sodomy is not a fundamental right "deeply rooted in this Nation's history and tradition" is utterly unassailable.

In any event, an "emerging awareness" is by definition not "deeply rooted in this Nation's history and tradition[s]," as we have said "fundamental right" status requires. Constitutional entitlements do not spring into existence because some States choose to lessen or eliminate criminal sanctions on certain behavior. Much less do they spring into existence, as the Court seems to believe, because foreign nations decriminalize conduct.

IV

I turn now to the ground on which the Court squarely rests its holding: the contention that there is no rational basis for the law here under attack. This proposition is so out of accord with our jurisprudence — indeed, with the jurisprudence of any society we know — that it requires little discussion.

The Texas statute undeniably seeks to further the belief of its citizens that certain forms of sexual behavior are "immoral and unacceptable," — the same interest furthered by criminal laws against fornication, bigamy, adultery, adult incest, bestiality, and obscenity. *Bowers* held that this was a legitimate state interest. The Court today reaches the opposite conclusion. The Texas statute, it says, "furthers no legitimate state interest which can justify its intrusion into the personal and private life of the individual." The Court embraces instead Justice Stevens' declaration in his *Bowers* dissent, that "the fact that the governing majority in a State has traditionally viewed a particular practice as immoral is not a sufficient reason for upholding a law prohibiting the practice." This effectively decrees the end of all morals legislation. If, as the Court asserts, the promotion of majoritarian sexual morality is not even a legitimate state interest, none of the above-mentioned laws can survive rational-basis review.

V

Finally, I turn to petitioners' equal-protection challenge, which no Member of the Court, save Justice O'Connor, embraces: On its face §21.06(a) applies equally to all persons. Men and women, heterosexuals and homosexuals, are all subject to its prohibition of deviate sexual intercourse with someone of the same sex. To be sure, §21.06 does distinguish between the sexes insofar as concerns the partner with whom the sexual acts are performed: men can violate the law only with other men, and women only with other women. But this cannot itself be a denial of equal protection, since it is precisely the same distinction regarding partner that is drawn in state laws prohibiting marriage with someone of the same sex while permitting marriage with someone of the opposite sex. Even if the Texas law does deny equal protection to "homosexuals as a class," that denial still does not need to be justified by anything more than a rational basis, which our cases show is satisfied by the enforcement of traditional notions of sexual morality.

Today's opinion is the product of a Court, which is the product of a law-profession culture, that has largely signed on to the so-called homosexual agenda, by which I mean the agenda promoted by some homosexual activists directed at eliminating the moral opprobrium that has traditionally attached to homosexual conduct. One of the most revealing statements in today's opinion is the Court's grim warning that the criminalization of homosexual conduct is "an invitation to subject homosexual persons to discrimination both in the public and in the private spheres." It is clear from this that the Court has taken sides in the culture war, departing from its role of assuring, as neutral observer, that the democratic rules of engagement are observed. Many Americans do not want persons who openly engage in homosexual conduct as partners in their business, as scoutmasters for their children, as teachers in their children's schools, or as boarders in their home. They view this as protecting themselves and their families from a lifestyle that they believe to be immoral and destructive. The Court views it as "discrimination" which it is the function of our judgments to deter. So imbued is the Court with the law profession's anti-anti-homosexual culture, that it is seemingly unaware that the attitudes of that culture are not obviously "mainstream"; that in most States what the Court calls "discrimination" against those who engage in homosexual acts is perfectly legal; that proposals to ban such "discrimination" under Title VII have repeatedly been rejected by Congress; that in some cases such "discrimination" is mandated by federal statute, see 10 U.S.C. §654(b)(1) (mandating discharge from the armed forces of any service member who engages in or intends to engage in homosexual acts); and that in some cases such "discrimination" is a constitutional right, see Boy Scouts of America v. Dale (2000).

Let me be clear that I have nothing against homosexuals, or any other group, promoting their agenda through normal democratic means. Social perceptions of sexual and other morality change over time, and every group has the right to persuade its fellow citizens that its view of such matters is the best. That homosexuals have achieved some success in that enterprise is attested to by the fact that Texas is one of the few remaining States that criminalize private, consensual homosexual acts. But persuading one's fellow citizens is one thing, and imposing one's views in absence of democratic majority will is something else. I would no more require a State to criminalize homosexual acts — or, for that matter, display any moral disapprobation of them — than I would forbid it to do so. What Texas has chosen to do is well within the range of traditional democratic action, and its hand should not be stayed through the invention of a brand-new "constitutional right" by a Court that is impatient of democratic change.

One of the benefits of leaving regulation of this matter to the people rather than to the courts is that the people, unlike judges, need not carry things to their logical conclusion. The people may feel that their disapprobation of homosexual conduct is strong enough to disallow homosexual marriage, but not strong enough to criminalize private homosexual acts—and may legislate accordingly. The Court today pretends that it possesses a similar freedom of action, so that that we need not fear judicial imposition of homosexual marriage, as has recently occurred in Canada (in a decision that the Canadian Government has chosen not to appeal). See Halpern v. Toronto (Ontario Ct. App. 2003).

Today's opinion dismantles the structure of constitutional law that has permitted a distinction to be made between heterosexual and homosexual unions, insofar as formal recognition in marriage is concerned. If moral disapprobation of homosexual conduct is "no legitimate state interest" for purposes of proscribing that conduct, what justification could there possibly be for denying the benefits of marriage to homosexual couples exercising "[t]he liberty protected by the Constitution"? Surely not the encouragement of procreation, since the sterile and the elderly are allowed to marry. This case "does not involve" the issue of homosexual marriage only if one entertains the belief that principle and logic have nothing to do with the decisions of this Court. Many will hope that, as the Court comfortingly assures us, this is so. The matters appropriate for this Court's resolution are only three: Texas's prohibition of sodomy neither infringes a "fundamental right" (which the Court does not dispute), nor is unsupported by a rational relation to what the Constitution considers a legitimate state interest, nor denies the equal protection of the laws. I dissent.

Justice Thomas, dissenting.

I join Justice Scalia's dissenting opinion. I write separately to note that the law before the Court today "is . . . uncommonly silly." Griswold v. Connecticut (1965) (Stewart, J., dissenting). If I were a member of the Texas Legislature, I would vote to repeal it. Punishing someone for expressing his sexual preference through noncommercial consensual conduct with another adult does not appear to be a worthy way to expend valuable law enforcement resources.

Notwithstanding this, I recognize that as a member of this Court I am not empowered to help petitioners and others similarly situated. My duty, rather, is to "decide cases 'agreeably to the Constitution and laws of the United States.'" And, just like Justice Stewart, I "can find [neither in the Bill of Rights nor any other part of the Constitution a] general right of privacy," or as the Court terms it today, the "liberty of the person both in its spatial and more transcendent dimensions."

G. CONSTITUTIONAL PROTECTION FOR CONTROL OVER INFORMATION

A basic aspect of privacy is the ability of people to control information about themselves. In an era of computer data banks, the existence and scope of this right is of obvious importance. Surprisingly, though, thus far the Court has rarely addressed this issue directly. Whalen v. Roe is the primary Supreme Court case concerning constitutional protection for control over information.

WHALEN v. ROE
429 U.S. 589 (1977)

Justice STEVENS delivered the opinion of the Court.

The constitutional question presented is whether the State of New York may record, in a centralized computer file, the names and addresses of all persons who have obtained, pursuant to a doctor's prescription, certain drugs for which there is both a lawful and an unlawful market.

Many drugs have both legitimate and illegitimate uses. In response to a concern that such drugs were being diverted into unlawful channels, in 1970 the New York Legislature created a special commission to evaluate the State's drug-control laws. The commission found the existing laws deficient in several respects. There was no effective way to prevent the use of stolen or revised prescriptions, to prevent unscrupulous pharmacists from repeatedly refilling prescriptions, to prevent users from obtaining prescriptions from more than one doctor, or to prevent doctors from over-prescribing, either by authorizing an excessive amount in one prescription or by giving one patient multiple prescriptions. In drafting new legislation to correct such defects, the commission consulted with enforcement officials in California and Illinois where central reporting systems were being used effectively.

The new New York statute classified potentially harmful drugs in five schedules. Drugs, such as heroin, which are highly abused and have no recognized medical use, are in Schedule I; they cannot be prescribed. Schedules II through V include drugs which have a progressively lower potential for abuse but also have a recognized medical use. Our concern is limited to Schedule II which includes the most dangerous of the legitimate drugs.

With an exception for emergencies, the Act requires that all prescriptions for Schedule II drugs be prepared by the physician in triplicate on an official form. The completed form identifies the prescribing physician; the dispensing pharmacy; the drug and dosage; and the name, address, and age of the patient. One copy of the form is retained by the physician, the second by the pharmacist, and the third is forwarded to the New York State Department of Health in Albany. A prescription made on an official form may not exceed a 30-day supply, and may not be refilled.

The District Court found that about 100,000 Schedule II prescription forms are delivered to a receiving room at the Department of Health in Albany each month. They are sorted, coded, and logged and then taken to another room where the data on the forms is recorded on magnetic tapes for processing by a computer. Thereafter, the forms are returned to the receiving room to be retained in a vault for a five-year period and then destroyed as required by the statute. The receiving room is surrounded by a locked wire fence and protected by an alarm system. The computer tapes containing the prescription data are kept in a locked cabinet. When the tapes are used, the computer is run "off-line," which means that no terminal outside of the computer room can read or record any information. Public disclosure of the identity of patients is expressly prohibited by the statute and by a Department of Health regulation. Willful violation of these prohibitions is a crime punishable by up to one year in prison and a $2,000 fine. At the time of trial there were 17 Department of Health employees with access to the files; in addition, there were 24 investigators with authority to investigate cases of overdispensing which might be identified by the computer. Twenty months after the effective date of the Act, the computerized data had only been used in two investigations involving alleged overuse by specific patients.

State legislation which has some effect on individual liberty or privacy may not be held unconstitutional simply because a court finds it unnecessary, in whole or in part. For we have frequently recognized that individual States have broad latitude in experimenting with possible solutions to problems of vital local concern.

The New York statute challenged in this case represents a considered attempt to deal with such a problem. It is manifestly the product of an orderly and rational legislative decision. It was recommended by a specially appointed commission which held extensive hearings on the proposed legislation, and drew on experience with similar programs in other States. There surely was nothing unreasonable in the assumption that the patient-identification requirement might aid in the enforcement of laws designed to minimize the misuse of dangerous drugs. For the requirement could reasonably be expected to have a deterrent effect on potential violators as well as to aid in the detection or investigation of specific instances of apparent abuse.

Appellees contend that the statute invades a constitutionally protected "zone of privacy." The cases sometimes characterized as protecting "privacy" have in fact involved at least two different kinds of interests. One is the individual interest in avoiding disclosure of personal matters, and another is the interest in independence in making certain kinds of important decisions.

We are persuaded, however, that the New York program does not, on its face, pose a sufficiently grievous threat to either interest to establish a constitutional violation. Public disclosure of patient information can come about in three ways. Health Department employees may violate the statute by failing, either deliberately or negligently, to maintain proper security. A patient or a doctor may be accused of a violation and the stored data may be offered in evidence in a judicial proceeding. Or, thirdly, a doctor, a pharmacist, or the patient may voluntarily reveal information on a prescription form.

The third possibility existed under the prior law and is entirely unrelated to the existence of the computerized data bank. Neither of the other two possibilities provides a proper ground for attacking the statute as invalid on its face. There is no support in the record, or in the experience of the two States that New York has emulated, for an assumption that the security provisions of the statute will be administered improperly. And the remote possibility that judicial supervision of the evidentiary use of particular items of stored information will provide inadequate protection against unwarranted disclosures is surely not a sufficient reason for invalidating the entire patient-identification program.

Even without public disclosure, it is, of course, true that private information must be disclosed to the authorized employees of the New York Department of Health. Such disclosures, however, are not significantly different from those that were required under the prior law. Nor are they meaningfully distinguishable from a host of other unpleasant invasions of privacy that are associated with many facets of health care. Unquestionably, some individuals' concern for their own privacy may lead them to avoid or to postpone needed medical attention. Nevertheless, disclosures of private medical information to doctors, to hospital personnel, to insurance companies, and to public health agencies are often an essential part of modern medical practice even when the disclosure may reflect unfavorably on the character of the patient. Requiring such disclosures to representatives of the State having responsibility for the health of the community, does not automatically amount to an impermissible invasion of privacy.

We hold that neither the immediate nor the threatened impact of the patient-identification requirements in the New York State Controlled Substances Act of 1972 on either the reputation or the independence of patients for whom Schedule II drugs are medically indicated is sufficient to constitute an invasion of any right or liberty protected by the Fourteenth Amendment.

A final word about issues we have not decided. We are not unaware of the threat to privacy implicit in the accumulation of vast amounts of personal information in computerized data banks or other massive government files. The collection of taxes, the distribution of welfare and social security benefits, the supervision of public health, the direction of our Armed Forces, and the enforcement of the criminal laws all require the orderly preservation of great quantities of information, much of which is personal in character and potentially embarrassing or harmful if disclosed. The right to collect and use such data for public purposes is typically accompanied by a concomitant statutory or regulatory duty to avoid unwarranted disclosures. Recognizing that in some circumstances that duty arguably has its roots in the Constitution, nevertheless New York's statutory scheme, and its implementing administrative procedures, evidence a proper concern with, and protection of, the individual's interest in privacy. We therefore need not, and do not, decide any question which might be presented by the unwarranted disclosure of accumulated private data whether intentional or unintentional or by a system that did not contain comparable security provisions. We simply hold that this record does not establish an invasion of any right or liberty protected by the Fourteenth Amendment.

The Court also has upheld reporting requirements in other areas even though they pose some risk to privacy. For example, in California Bankers Association v. Schultz, 416 U.S. 21 (1974), the Court upheld the constitutionality of the Bank Secrecy Act of 1970, which required banks to maintain records of financial transactions and to report certain domestic and foreign transactions. The Court rejected claims based on the Fourth and Fifth Amendments and concluded that the law was constitutional because of the government's need to monitor financial transactions and to prevent fraudulent conduct.

In National Aeronautics and Space Administration v. Nelson, 131 S. Ct. 746 (2011), the Court upheld a requirement for background checks for employees of government contractors working with NASA. The Court said, "We assume, without deciding, that the Constitution protects a privacy right. We hold, however, that the challenged portions of the Government's background check do not violate this right in the present case." Justice Scalia, joined by Justice Thomas, concurred in the judgment and declared, "A federal constitutional right to 'informational privacy' does not exist."

Thus, although there is a strong argument that the Constitution should be interpreted to protect a right to control information, there is thus far little support for such a right from the Supreme Court.

H. CONSTITUTIONAL PROTECTION FOR TRAVEL

The Supreme Court has held that there is a fundamental right to travel and to interstate migration within the United States. Therefore, laws that prohibit or burden travel within the United States must meet strict scrutiny. Although the text of the Constitution does not mention a right to travel, it long has been recognized by the Supreme Court. For example, in the *Passenger Cases*, Smith v. Turner 48 U.S. (7 How.) 283 (1849), the Supreme Court declared unconstitutional a state law imposing a tax on aliens arriving from foreign ports. Even the dissenting justices in the case acknowledged a basic right to interstate travel. Chief Justice Taney, in dissent, remarked, "We are all citizens of the United States; and, as members of the same community, must have the right to pass and repass through every part of it without interruption, as freely as in our own States. And a tax imposed by a State for entering its territories or harbours, is inconsistent with the rights which belong to the citizens of other States as members of the Union, and with the objects which that Union was intended to attain."

In Saenz v. Roe, in 1999, below, the Court comprehensively reviewed prior decisions concerning the right to travel.

SAENZ v. ROE
526 U.S. 489 (1999)

Justice STEVENS delivered the opinion of the Court.

In 1992, California enacted a statute limiting the maximum welfare benefits available to newly arrived residents. The scheme limits the amount payable to a family that has resided in the State for less than 12 months to the amount payable by the State of the family's prior residence. The questions presented by this case are whether the 1992 statute was constitutional when it was enacted and, if not, whether an amendment to the Social Security Act enacted by Congress in 1996 affects that determination.

I

California is not only one of the largest, most populated, and most beautiful States in the Nation; it is also one of the most generous. Like all other States, California has participated in several welfare programs authorized by the Social Security Act and partially funded by the Federal Government. Its programs, however, provide a higher level of benefits and serve more needy citizens than those of most other States. In one year the most expensive of those programs, Aid to Families with Dependent Children (AFDC), which was replaced in 1996 with Temporary Assistance to Needy Families (TANF), provided benefits for an average of 2,645,814 persons per month at an annual cost to the State of $2.9 billion. In California the cash benefit for a family of two—a mother and one child—is $456 a month, but in the neighboring State of Arizona, for example, it is only $275.

In 1992, in order to make a relatively modest reduction in its vast welfare budget, the California Legislature enacted §11450.03 of the state Welfare and Institutions Code. That section sought to change the California AFDC program by limiting new residents, for the first year they live in California, to the benefits they would have received in the State of their prior residence.

[II]

The word "travel" is not found in the text of the Constitution. Yet the "constitutional right to travel from one State to another" is firmly embedded in our jurisprudence. Indeed, as Justice Stewart reminded us in Shapiro v. Thompson (1969), the right is so important that it is "assertable against private interference as well as governmental action . . . a virtually unconditional personal right, guaranteed by the Constitution to us all."

In *Shapiro*, we reviewed the constitutionality of three statutory provisions that denied welfare assistance to residents of Connecticut, the District of Columbia, and Pennsylvania, who had resided within those respective jurisdictions less than one year immediately preceding their applications for assistance. Without pausing to identify the specific source of the right, we began by noting that the Court had long "recognized that the nature of our Federal Union and our constitutional concepts of personal liberty unite to require that all citizens be free to travel throughout the length and breadth of our land uninhibited by statutes, rules, or regulations which unreasonably burden or restrict this movement." We squarely held that it was "constitutionally impermissible" for a State to enact durational residency requirements for the purpose of inhibiting the migration by needy persons into the State. We further held that a classification that had the effect of imposing a penalty on the exercise of the right to travel violated the Equal Protection Clause "unless shown to be necessary to promote a compelling governmental interest," and that no such showing had been made.

The "right to travel" discussed in our cases embraces at least three different components. It protects the right of a citizen of one State to enter and to leave another State, the right to be treated as a welcome visitor rather than an unfriendly alien when temporarily present in the second State, and, for those travelers who elect to become permanent residents, the right to be treated like other citizens of that State.

It was the right to go from one place to another, including the right to cross state borders while en route, that was vindicated in Edwards v. California (1941), which invalidated a state law that impeded the free interstate passage of the indigent. We reaffirmed that right in United States v. Guest (1966), which afforded protection to the "'right to travel freely to and from the State of Georgia and to use highway facilities and other instrumentalities of interstate commerce within the State of Georgia.'" Given that §11450.03 imposed no obstacle to respondents' entry into California, we think the State is correct when it argues that the statute does not directly impair the exercise of the right to free interstate movement. For the purposes of this case, therefore, we need not identify the source of that particular right in the text of the Constitution. The right of "free ingress and regress to and from" neighboring States, which was expressly mentioned in the text of the Articles of Confederation, may simply have been "conceived from the beginning to be a necessary concomitant of the stronger Union the Constitution created."

The second component of the right to travel is, however, expressly protected by the text of the Constitution. The first sentence of Article IV, §2, provides: "The Citizens of each State shall be entitled to all Privileges and Immunities of Citizens in the several States."[30] Thus, by virtue of a person's state citizenship, a citizen of one State who travels in other States, intending to return home at the end of his journey, is entitled to enjoy the "Privileges and Immunities of Citizens in the several States" that he visits. This provision removes "from the citizens of each State the disabilities of alienage in the other States." Those protections are not "absolute," but the Clause "does bar discrimination against citizens of other States where there is no substantial reason for the discrimination beyond the mere fact that they are citizens of other States."

What is at issue in this case, then, is a third aspect of the right to travel — the right of the newly arrived citizen to the same privileges and immunities enjoyed by other citizens of the same State. That right is protected not only by the new arrival's status as a state citizen, but also by her status as a citizen of the United States. That additional source of protection is plainly identified in the opening words of the Fourteenth Amendment: "All persons born or naturalized in the United States, and subject to the jurisdiction thereof, are citizens of the United States and of the State wherein they reside. No State shall make or enforce any law which shall abridge the privileges or immunities of citizens of the United States; . . ." Despite fundamentally differing views concerning the coverage of the Privileges or Immunities Clause of the Fourteenth Amendment, most notably expressed in the majority and dissenting opinions in the *Slaughter-House Cases* (1872), it has always been common ground that this Clause protects the third component of the right to travel.

That newly arrived citizens "have two political capacities, one state and one federal," adds special force to their claim that they have the same rights as others who share their citizenship. Neither mere rationality nor some intermediate standard of review should be used to judge the constitutionality of a state rule that discriminates against some of its citizens because they have been domiciled in the State for less than a year. The appropriate standard may be more categorical than that articulated in *Shapiro*, but it is surely no less strict.

Because this case involves discrimination against citizens who have completed their interstate travel, the State's argument that its welfare scheme affects the right to travel only "incidentally" is beside the point. Were we concerned solely with actual deterrence to migration, we might be persuaded that a partial withholding of benefits constitutes a lesser incursion on the right to travel than an outright denial of all benefits. But since the right to travel embraces the citizen's right to be treated equally in her new State of residence, the discriminatory classification is itself a penalty.

It is undisputed that respondents and the members of the class that they represent are citizens of California and that their need for welfare benefits is unrelated to the length of time that they have resided in California. We thus have no occasion to consider what weight might be given to a citizen's length of residence if the bona fides of her claim to state citizenship were questioned.

---

30. The Privileges and Immunities Clause of Article IV, §2 is discussed in Chapter 4 of this book. [Footnote by casebook author.]

Moreover, because whatever benefits they receive will be consumed while they remain in California, there is no danger that recognition of their claim will encourage citizens of other States to establish residency for just long enough to acquire some readily portable benefit, such as a divorce or a college education, that will be enjoyed after they return to their original domicile.

The classifications challenged in this case — and there are many — are defined entirely by (a) the period of residency in California and (b) the location of the prior residences of the disfavored class members. But since the right to travel embraces the citizen's right to be treated equally in her new State of residence, the discriminatory classification is itself a penalty.

Disavowing any desire to fence out the indigent, California has instead advanced an entirely fiscal justification for its multitiered scheme. The enforcement of §11450.03 will save the State approximately $10.9 million a year. The question is not whether such saving is a legitimate purpose but whether the State may accomplish that end by the discriminatory means it has chosen. An even-handed, across-the-board reduction of about 72 cents per month for every beneficiary would produce the same result. But our negative answer to the question does not rest on the weakness of the State's purported fiscal justification. It rests on the fact that the Citizenship Clause of the Fourteenth Amendment expressly equates citizenship with residence: "That Clause does not provide for, and does not allow for, degrees of citizenship based on length of residence." It is equally clear that the Clause does not tolerate a hierarchy of 45 subclasses of similarly situated citizens based on the location of their prior residence. Neither the duration of respondents' California residence, nor the identity of their prior States of residence, has any relevance to their need for benefits. Nor do those factors bear any relationship to the State's interest in making an equitable allocation of the funds to be distributed among its needy citizens.

The question that remains is whether congressional approval of durational residency requirements in the 1996 amendment to the Social Security Act somehow resuscitates the constitutionality of §11450.03. That question is readily answered, for we have consistently held that Congress may not authorize the States to violate the Fourteenth Amendment. Moreover, the protection afforded to the citizen by the Citizenship Clause of that Amendment is a limitation on the powers of the National Government as well as the States.

Chief Justice REHNQUIST, with whom Justice THOMAS joins, dissenting.

The Court today breathes new life into the previously dormant Privileges or Immunities Clause of the Fourteenth Amendment — a Clause relied upon by this Court in only one other decision, Colgate v. Harvey (1935), overruled five years later by Madden v. Kentucky (1940). It uses this Clause to strike down what I believe is a reasonable measure falling under the head of a "good-faith residency requirement." Because I do not think any provision of the Constitution — and surely not a provision relied upon for only the second time since its enactment 130 years ago — requires this result, I dissent.

Much of the Court's opinion is unremarkable and sound. The right to travel clearly embraces the right to go from one place to another, and prohibits States from impeding the free interstate passage of citizens. The state law in Edwards v. California (1941), which prohibited the transport of any indigent person into California, was a classic barrier to travel or migration and the Court rightly struck it down. Indeed, for most of this country's history, what the Court today calls the first "component" of the right to travel, was the entirety of this right.

But I cannot see how the right to become a citizen of another State is a necessary "component" of the right to travel, or why the Court tries to marry these separate and distinct rights. A person is no longer "traveling" in any sense of the word when he finishes his journey to a State which he plans to make his home. Indeed, under the Court's logic, the protections of the Privileges or Immunities Clause recognized in this case come into play only when an individual stops traveling with the intent to remain and become a citizen of a new State. The right to travel and the right to become a citizen are distinct, their relationship is not reciprocal, and one is not a "component" of the other.

In unearthing from its tomb the right to become a state citizen and to be treated equally in the new State of residence, however, the Court ignores a State's need to assure that only persons who establish a bona fide residence receive the benefits provided to current residents of the State. While the physical presence element of a bona fide residence is easy to police, the subjective intent element is not. It is simply unworkable and futile to require States to inquire into each new resident's subjective intent to remain. Hence, States employ objective criteria such as durational residence requirements to test a new resident's resolve to remain before these new citizens can enjoy certain in-state benefits. Recognizing the practical appeal of such criteria, this Court has repeatedly sanctioned the State's use of durational residence requirements before new residents receive in-state tuition rates at state universities. Starns v. Malkerson (1971) (upholding 1-year residence requirement for in-state tuition). The Court has declared: "The State can establish such reasonable criteria for in-state status as to make virtually certain that students who are not, in fact, bona fide residents of the State, but have come there solely for educational purposes, cannot take advantage of the in-state rates." Vlandis v. Kline (1973). The Court has done the same in upholding a 1-year residence requirement for eligibility to obtain a divorce in state courts, see Sosna v. Iowa (1975), and in upholding political party registration restrictions that amounted to a durational residency requirement for voting in primary elections, see Rosario v. Rockefeller (1973).

If States can require individuals to reside in-state for a year before exercising the right to educational benefits, the right to terminate a marriage, or the right to vote in primary elections that all other state citizens enjoy, then States may surely do the same for welfare benefits. Indeed, there is no material difference between a 1-year residence requirement applied to the level of welfare benefits given out by a State, and the same requirement applied to the level of tuition subsidies at a state university. The welfare payment here and in-state tuition rates are cash subsidies provided to a limited class of people, and California's standard of living and higher education system make both subsidies quite attractive.

I therefore believe that the durational residence requirement challenged here is a permissible exercise of the State's power to "assur[e] that services provided for its residents are enjoyed only by residents." The 1-year period established in §11450.03 is the same period this Court approved in *Starns* and *Sosna*. The requirement does not deprive welfare recipients of all benefits; indeed, the limitation has no effect whatsoever on a recipient's ability to enjoy the full 5-year period of welfare eligibility; to enjoy the full range of employment, training, and accompanying supportive services; or to take full advantage of health care benefits under Medicaid. This waiting period does not preclude new residents from all cash payments, but merely limits them to what they received in their prior State of residence.

Saenz reviews the major prior decisions concerning the right to travel. For example, in Edwards v. California, 314 U.S. 160 (1941), the Court invalidated a California law that made it a crime to bring a nonresident into the state knowing the individual to be "an indigent person." The majority opinion, written by Justice Byrne, declared the law unconstitutional as violating the Commerce Clause and did not address the right to travel. However, in concurring opinions, Justices Douglas, Black, Murphy, and Jackson argued that the right to travel is a fundamental right protected under the Privileges or Immunities Clause of the Fourteenth Amendment. Justice Douglas declared, "[T]he right of persons to move freely from State to State . . . is so fundamental. . . . The right to move freely from State to State is an incident of *national* citizenship protected by the privileges and immunities clause of the Fourteenth Amendment against state interference."

The Supreme Court has articulated and applied the right to travel primarily in evaluating laws that impose durational residency requirements. A durational residency requirement is where a person must live in the jurisdiction for a specified amount of time in order to receive a benefit. Prominent examples involve waiting periods required for receipt of welfare benefits, voting, and divorces. The Supreme Court has recognized that durational residency requirements discourage interstate travel, and especially migration. The Court, therefore, has said that strict scrutiny should be applied in this area.

The seminal decision was Shapiro v. Thompson, 394 U.S. 618 (1969), which declared unconstitutional laws that imposed a one-year residency requirement in the state as a prerequisite for eligibility for welfare. The Court said that "[s]ince the classification here touches on the fundamental right of interstate movement, its constitutionality must be judged by the stricter standard of whether it promotes a compelling state interest. Under this standard, the waiting-period requirement clearly violates the Equal Protection Clause." The Court reviewed the justifications proffered by the states for the waiting period and found that none was sufficient to meet strict scrutiny.

In subsequent cases, the Court applied *Shapiro* to invalidate other durational residency requirements. For instance, in Memorial Hospital v. Maricopa County, 415 U.S. 250 (1974), the Court declared unconstitutional a government rule that required a year's residency in the county as condition to receiving non-emergency hospitalization or medical care at the county's expense. The Court reviewed the prior decisions in this area and said that they "stand for the proposition that a classification which operates to penalize those persons . . . who have exercised their constitutional right of interstate migration, must be justified by a compelling state interest."

The Supreme Court followed this reasoning in invalidating and limiting the length of durational residency requirements for voting. In Dunn v. Blumstein, 405 U.S. 330 (1972), the Court declared unconstitutional a state law that created a one-year residency requirement for voting eligibility. Vanderbilt law professor James Blumstein challenged Tennessee's waiting period in order to register to vote. The Court noted that the state law drew a distinction among residents solely on the basis of their recent migration and travel.

The Court said that it was thus clear that "the durational residence requirement directly impinges on the exercise of a . . . fundamental personal right, the right to travel." The Court explained that "it is clear that the freedom to travel includes the 'freedom to enter and abide in any State in the Union.' Obviously durational residence laws single out the class of bona fide state and county residents who have recently exercised this constitutionally protected right, and penalize such travelers directly."

The Court rejected each of the state's justifications and invalidated the law. For example, the state said that the durational residency requirement was justified by the state's desire to have knowledgeable voters. The Court ruled that a state cannot exclude residents from voting based on an assessment of their knowledge, sophistication with local issues, or how they might vote.

Subsequently, the Supreme Court has qualified Dunn v. Blumstein and has allowed some residency requirements for voting. The Court has permitted durational residency requirements of up to 50 days for voting to give the government time to check election rolls, prevent fraud, and administer the electoral system.[31]

One area where the Court has upheld durational residency requirements is for divorces within a state. In Sosna v. Iowa, 419 U.S. 393 (1975), the Court upheld the constitutionality of a state law that required one year of residency in the state before a person could obtain a divorce. The Court distinguished earlier cases invalidating durational residency requirements for receipt of government benefits, such as *Shapiro* and *Maricopa County*. The Court said, "But none of those cases intimated that the States might never impose durational residency requirements, and such a proposition was in fact expressly disclaimed. What those cases had in common was that the durational residency requirements they struck down were justified on the basis of budgetary or record-keeping considerations which were held insufficient to outweigh the constitutional claims of the individuals." The Court felt that the state's durational residency requirement was "of a different stripe." The Court said that the difference was that a person moving into the state "would eventually qualify" for eligibility for divorce and "could ultimately have obtained the same opportunity for adjudication which she asserts ought to have been hers at an earlier point in time."

RESTRICTIONS ON FOREIGN TRAVEL

However, the Supreme Court has held that there is not a fundamental right to international travel and that therefore only a rational basis test will be used in evaluating restrictions on foreign travel. The Supreme Court's initial decisions in this area had broad dicta that suggested such a right, but more recent cases have clearly held that the Court does not recognize a fundamental right to foreign travel.

For example, in Califano v. Aznavorian, 439 U.S. 170 (1978), the Court upheld a provision of the Social Security Act that caused a person to lose

---

31. Marston v. Lewis, 410 U.S. 679 (1973).

Supplemental Security Income benefits for any month during all of which the individual was out of the United States and until the person had been back in the country for 30 consecutive days. The Court expressly distinguished the right to interstate travel from the right to foreign travel; only the former is deemed fundamental. The Court stated, "The constitutional right of interstate travel is virtually unqualified. By contrast, the 'right' of international travel has been considered to be no more than an aspect of the 'liberty' protected by the Due Process Clause of the Fifth Amendment. . . . Thus, legislation which is said to infringe the freedom to travel abroad is not to be judged by the same standard applied to laws that penalize the right of interstate travel, such as durational residency requirements imposed by the States."

The use of the rational basis test for restrictions on foreign travel was reaffirmed in later cases. In Haig v. Agee, 453 U.S. 280 (1981), the Court upheld the authority of the Secretary of State to revoke the passport of a former CIA agent who had threatened to identify CIA officers and agents and to take measures to drive them out of countries where they were operating. The Court emphasized the ability of the government to regulate international travel to further its foreign policy objectives. Chief Justice Burger, writing for the Court, said, "Revocation of a passport undeniably curtails travel, but the freedom to travel abroad . . . is subordinate to national security and foreign policy considerations; as such, it is subject to reasonable governmental regulation. The Court has made it plain that the freedom to travel outside the United States must be distinguished from the right to travel within the United States."

Similarly, in Regan v. Wald, 468 U.S. 222 (1984), the Court used the rational basis test to uphold a federal regulation that prevented travel to Cuba. Justice Rehnquist, writing for the Court, said, "Matters relating 'to the conduct of foreign relations . . . are so exclusively entrusted to the political branches of government as to be largely immune from judicial inquiry or interference.'"

I. THE RIGHT TO VOTE

1. The Right to Vote as a Fundamental Right

Many of the amendments to the Constitution concern the right to vote. The Fifteenth Amendment says, "The right of citizens of the United States to vote shall not be denied or abridged by the United States or by any State on account of race, color, or previous condition of servitude." The Nineteenth Amendment, adopted in 1920, extended the right to vote to women and says that the "right of citizens of the United States to vote shall not be denied or abridged by the United States or by any State on account of sex."

The Twenty-Fourth Amendment, ratified in 1964, prohibits poll taxes in elections for federal office. Specifically, it provides, "The right of citizens of the United States to vote in any primary or other election for President or Vice President, for electors for President or Vice President, or for Senator or Representative in Congress, shall not be denied or abridged by the United States or any State by reason of failure to pay any poll tax or other tax."

The Twenty-Sixth Amendment, adopted in 1971, extends the right to vote to all citizens who are 18 years of age or older. It says, "The right of citizens of the United States, who are eighteen years of age or older, to vote shall not be denied or abridged by the United States or by any State on account of age."

In addition to these textual provisions, the Supreme Court repeatedly has declared that the right to vote is a fundamental right protected under equal protection.[32] The right to vote is regarded as fundamental because it is essential in a democratic society; it is obviously through voting that the people choose their government and hold it accountable. The Court has explained that "[t]he right to vote freely for the candidate of one's choice is of the essence of a democratic society, and any restrictions on that right strike at the heart of representative government."[33] Hence, "any unjustified discrimination in determining who may participate in political affairs or in the selection of public officials undermines the legitimacy of representative government."[34]

Indeed, the Court long has said that the right to vote is a "fundamental political right" because it is "preservative of all rights."[35] Voting is itself a form of expression, but it also is the way in which people choose a government that will safeguard all of their liberties and interests. As the Court observed, "No right is more precious in a free country than that of having a voice in the election of those who make the laws under which, as good citizens, we must live. Other rights, even the most basic, are illusory if the right to vote is undermined."[36]

Thus, it is clearly established that laws infringing the right to vote must meet strict scrutiny. The Court has explained that "[e]specially since the right to exercise the franchise in a free and unimpaired manner is preservative of other basic civil and political rights, any alleged infringement of the right of citizens to vote must be carefully and meticulously scrutinized."[37]

Two major issues concerning the right to vote are discussed below: laws that deny some citizens the right to vote and laws that dilute the voting power of some citizens. The Court has said that "the right of suffrage can be denied by a debasement or dilution of the weight of a citizen's vote just as effectively as by wholly prohibiting the free exercise of the franchise."[38] Other issues concerning voting are discussed in other chapters. For example, race discrimination in election systems is discussed in connection with equal protection in Chapter 7. Issues related to government regulation of political parties and the political process are discussed in Chapter 9.

2. Restrictions on the Ability to Vote

Laws that deny or limit the ability of citizens to vote must meet strict scrutiny. For example, as described below, the Supreme Court has used strict scrutiny in evaluating poll taxes, property ownership requirements for voting, and dura-

32. *See, e.g.,* Kramer v. Union Free School District, 395 U.S. 621, 626 (1969); Harper v. Virginia State Board of Elections, 383 U.S. 663, 666 (1966); Reynolds v. Sims, 377 U.S. 533, 555 (1964).
33. Reynolds v. Sims, 377 U.S. at 555.
34. Kramer v. Union Free School Dist., 395 U.S. at 626.
35. Yick Wo v. Hopkins, 118 U.S. 356, 370 (1886).
36. Wesberry v. Sanders, 376 U.S. 1, 17 (1964).
37. Harper v. Virginia State Bd. of Elections, 383 U.S. at 667.
38. Reynolds v. Sims, 377 U.S. at 555.

tional residency requirements. However, there are some areas where the Court did not use strict scrutiny and upheld restrictions on voting: literacy tests, laws preventing those convicted of felonies from voting, and a requirement for photo identification for voting. Each of these areas is discussed in turn.

POLL TAXES

Poll taxes — the requirement that people pay a fee in order to vote — likely will keep some citizens from voting. The Twenty-Fourth Amendment prohibits poll taxes in elections for federal offices. Additionally, the Supreme Court in Harper v. Virginia State Board of Elections held that poll taxes are unconstitutional as a denial of equal protection for all other elections.

HARPER v. VIRGINIA STATE BOARD OF ELECTIONS
383 U.S. 663 (1966)

Justice DOUGLAS delivered the opinion of the Court.

These are suits by Virginia residents to have declared unconstitutional Virginia's poll tax. Section 173 of Virginia's Constitution directs the General Assembly to levy an annual poll tax not exceeding $1.50 on every resident of the State 21 years of age and over (with exceptions not relevant here). One dollar of the tax is to be used by state officials "exclusively in aid of the public free schools" and the remainder is to be returned to the counties for general purposes. Section 18 of the Constitution includes payment of poll taxes as a precondition for voting.

While the right to vote in federal elections is conferred by Art. I, §2, of the Constitution, the right to vote in state elections is nowhere expressly mentioned. It is argued that the right to vote in state elections is implicit, particularly by reason of the First Amendment and that it may not constitutionally be conditioned upon the payment of a tax or fee. We do not stop to canvass the relation between voting and political expression. For it is enough to say that once the franchise is granted to the electorate, lines may not be drawn which are inconsistent with the Equal Protection Clause of the Fourteenth Amendment.

We conclude that a State violates the Equal Protection Clause of the Fourteenth Amendment whenever it makes the affluence of the voter or payment of any fee an electoral standard. Voter qualifications have no relation to wealth nor to paying or not paying this or any other tax. Our cases demonstrate that the Equal Protection Clause of the Fourteenth Amendment restrains the States from fixing voter qualifications which invidiously discriminate.

We say the same whether the citizen, otherwise qualified to vote, has $1.50 in his pocket or nothing at all, pays the fee or fails to pay it. The principle that denies the State the right to dilute a citizen's vote on account of his economic status or other such factors by analogy bars a system which excludes those unable to pay a fee to vote or who fail to pay.

It is argued that a State may exact fees from citizens for many different kinds of licenses; that if it can demand from all an equal fee for a driver's license, it can demand from all an equal poll tax for voting. But we must remember that the interest of the State, when it comes to voting, is limited to the power to fix qualifications. Wealth, like race, creed, or color, is not germane to one's ability to participate intelligently in the electoral process. Lines drawn on the basis of wealth or property, like those of race, are traditionally disfavored. To introduce wealth or payment of a fee as a measure of a voter's qualifications is to introduce a capricious or irrelevant factor. The degree of the discrimination is irrelevant. In this context — that is, as a condition of obtaining a ballot — the requirement of fee paying causes an "invidious" discrimination that runs afoul of the Equal Protection Clause.

We have long been mindful that where fundamental rights and liberties are asserted under the Equal Protection Clause, classifications which might invade or restrain them must be closely scrutinized and carefully confined. Those principles apply here. For to repeat, wealth or fee paying has, in our view, no relation to voting qualifications; the right to vote is too precious, too fundamental to be so burdened or conditioned.

PROPERTY OWNERSHIP REQUIREMENTS

Laws requiring property ownership as a requirement for voting seem to run afoul of *Harper*'s forceful declaration that wealth cannot be a basis for denying individuals the ability to vote. Yet the Court's record in dealing with such property ownership requirements is mixed. Kramer v. Union Free School District seems to broadly invalidate property ownership requirements for voting, but later cases have approved them in very narrow circumstances.

KRAMER v. UNION FREE SCHOOL DISTRICT

395 U.S. 621 (1969)

Chief Justice WARREN delivered the opinion of the Court.

In this case we are called on to determine whether §2012 of the New York Education Law is constitutional. The legislation provides that in certain New York school districts residents who are otherwise eligible to vote in state and federal elections may vote in the school district election only if they (1) own (or lease) taxable real property within the district, or (2) are parents (or have custody of) children enrolled in the local public schools. Appellant, a bachelor who neither owns nor leases taxable real property, filed suit in federal court claiming that §2012 denied him equal protection of the laws in violation of the Fourteenth Amendment.

Appellant is a 31-year-old college-educated stockbroker who lives in his parents' home in the Union Free School District No. 15, a district to which §2012 applies. He is a citizen of the United States and has voted in federal and state elections since 1959. However, since he has no children and neither owns nor leases taxable real property, appellant's attempts to register for and vote in the local school district elections have been unsuccessful.

Besides appellant and others who similarly live in their parents' homes, the statute also disenfranchises the following persons (unless they are parents or guardians of children enrolled in the district public school): senior citizens and others living with children or relatives; clergy, military personnel, and others who live on tax-exempt property; boarders and lodgers; parents who neither own nor lease qualifying property and whose children are too young to attend school; parents who neither own nor lease qualifying property and whose children attend private schools.

We turn therefore to question whether the exclusion is necessary to promote a compelling state interest. First appellees argue that the State has a legitimate interest in limiting the franchise in school district elections to "members of the community of interest" — those "primarily interested in such elections." Second, appellees urge that the State may reasonably and permissibly conclude that "property taxpayers" (including lessees of taxable property who share the tax burden through rent payments) and parents of the children enrolled in the district's schools are those "primarily interested" in school affairs.

We do not understand appellees to argue that the State is attempting to limit the franchise to those "subjectively concerned" about school matters. Rather, they appear to argue that the State's legitimate interest is in restricting a voice in school matters to those "directly affected" by such decisions. The State apparently reasons that since the schools are financed in part by local property taxes, persons whose out-of-pocket expenses are "directly" affected by property tax changes should be allowed to vote. Similarly, parents of children in school are thought to have a "direct" stake in school affairs and are given a vote.

Appellees argue that it is necessary to limit the franchise to those "primarily interested" in school affairs because "the ever increasing complexity of the many interacting phases of the school system and structure make it extremely difficult for the electorate fully to understand the whys and wherefores of the detailed operations of the school system." We need express no opinion as to whether the State in some circumstances might limit the exercise of the franchise to those "primarily interested" or "primarily affected." Of course, we therefore do not reach the issue of whether these particular elections are of the type in which the franchise may be so limited. For, assuming, arguendo, that New York legitimately might limit the franchise in these school district elections to those "primarily interested in school affairs," close scrutiny of the §2012 classifications demonstrates that they do not accomplish this purpose with sufficient precision to justify denying appellant the franchise.

Whether classifications allegedly limiting the franchise to those resident citizens "primarily interested" deny those excluded equal protection of the laws depends, on whether all those excluded are in fact substantially less interested or affected than those the statute includes. In other words, the classifications must be tailored so that the exclusion of appellant and members of his class is necessary to achieve the articulated state goal. Section 2012 does not meet the exacting standard of precision we require of statutes which selectively distribute the franchise. The classifications in §2012 permit inclusion of many persons who have, at best, a remote and indirect interest, in school affairs and, on the other hand, exclude others who have a distinct and direct interest in the school meeting decisions.

Nor do appellees offer any justification for the exclusion of seemingly interested and informed residents — other than to argue that the §2012 classifications include those "whom the State could understandably deem to be the most intimately interested in actions taken by the school board." But the issue is not whether the legislative judgments are rational. A more exacting standard obtains. The issue is whether the §2012 requirements do in fact sufficiently further a compelling state interest to justify denying the franchise to appellant and members of his class. The requirements of §2012 are not sufficiently tailored to limiting the franchise to those "primarily interested" in school affairs to justify the denial of the franchise to appellant and members of his class.

Justice STEWART, with whom Justice BLACK, and Justice HARLAN join, dissenting.

In Lassiter v. Northampton County Election Bd. this Court upheld against constitutional attack a literacy requirement, applicable to voters in all state and federal elections, imposed by the State of North Carolina. Writing for a unanimous Court, Mr. Justice Douglas said: "The States have long been held to have broad powers to determine the conditions under which the right of suffrage may be exercised, absent of course the discrimination which the Constitution condemns."

Believing that the appellant in this case is not the victim of any "discrimination which the Constitution condemns," I would affirm the judgment of the District Court. Although at times variously phrased, the traditional test of a statute's validity under the Equal Protection Clause is a familiar one: a legislative classification is invalid only "if it rest[s] on grounds wholly irrelevant to achievement of the regulation's objectives." It was under just such a test that the literacy requirement involved in *Lassiter* was upheld. The premise of our decision in that case was that a State may constitutionally impose upon its citizens voting requirements reasonably "designed to promote intelligent use of the ballot." A similar premise underlies the proposition, consistently endorsed by this Court, that a State may exclude nonresidents from participation in its elections. Such residence requirements, designed to help ensure that voters have a substantial stake in the outcome of elections and an opportunity to become familiar with the candidates and issues voted upon, are entirely permissible exercises of state authority.

Thus judged, the statutory classification involved here seems to me clearly to be valid. New York has made the judgment that local educational policy is best left to those persons who have certain direct and definable interests in that policy: those who are either immediately involved as parents of school children or who, as owners or lessees of taxable property are burdened with the local cost of funding school district operations. True, persons outside those classes may be genuinely interested in the conduct of a school district's business — just as commuters from New Jersey may be genuinely interested in the outcome of a New York City election. But unless this Court is to claim a monopoly of wisdom regarding the sound operation of school systems in the 50 States, I see no way to justify the conclusion that the legislative classification involved here is not rationally related to a legitimate legislative purpose. "There is no group more interested in the operation and management of the public schools than the taxpayers who support them and the parents whose children attend them."

In any event, it seems to me that under any equal protection standard, short of a doctrinaire insistence that universal suffrage is somehow mandated by the Constitution, the appellant's claim must be rejected. [I]t must be emphasized — despite the Court's undifferentiated references to what it terms "the franchise" — that we are dealing here, not with a general election, but with a limited, special-purpose election. The appellant is eligible to vote in all state, local, and federal elections in which general governmental policy is determined.

He is fully able, therefore, to participate not only in the processes by which the requirements for school district voting may be changed, but also in those by which the levels of state and federal financial assistance to the District are determined. He clearly is not locked into any self-perpetuating status of exclusion from the electoral process.

However, *Kramer* does not mean that all property ownership requirements for voting are invalid. In Salyer Land Co. v. Tulare Lake Basin Water Storage Dist., 410 U.S. 719 (1973), the Supreme Court upheld state laws that limited voting in water storage district elections to property owners and that apportioned votes according to assessed valuation of land within the districts. The Court emphasized that landowners had a far greater interest in the outcome of the election than other citizens. The Court explained, "Landowners as a class were to bear the entire burden of the district's costs, and the State could rationally conclude that they, to the exclusion of residents, should be charged with responsibility for its operation."[39] The Court also noted that although the water district has some governmental authority, it does not provide general public services ordinarily attributed to a governing body. Thus, it concluded "that nothing in the Equal Protection Clause precluded California from limiting the voting for directors of appellee district by totally excluding those who merely reside within the district."

The Court followed and applied *Salyer* in Ball v. James, 451 U.S. 355 (1981). *Ball*, like *Salyer*, involved a water district election. In *Ball*, votes were allocated based on property ownership: The basic rule was one acre, one vote. Unlike in *Salyer*, decisions by the governing body in *Ball* had a wide impact. The district was a major supplier of hydroelectric power, and about 40 percent of its water went to urban areas for nonagricultural uses.

Nonetheless, the Court found that the property ownership requirement for voting was justified. The Court explained that only the landowners were subject to the acreage-based taxing power of the water district. The Court did not deny that others had an interest in and were affected by the decisions of the district. But the Court said that "[t]he *Salyer* opinion did not say that the selected class of voters for a special public entity must be the only parties at all affected by the operation of the entity, or that their entire economic well-being must depend on that entity. Rather, the question was whether the effect of the entity's operations on them was disproportionately greater than the effect on those seeking the vote."

LITERACY TESTS

The Supreme Court has concluded that literacy tests are constitutionally permissible as a qualification for voting, although they have been outlawed by federal statutes. The Court first confronted literacy tests in Guinn v. United States, 238 U.S. 347 (1915), and the Court upheld the ability of states to require

39. *Id.* at 731.

passing a literacy test as a condition for voting. However, in *Guinn* the Court invalidated a "grandfather clause" that exempted from the literacy test anyone, or their lineal descendants, who could have voted on January 1, 1866. Obviously, the effect was to deny the vote to blacks who were ineligible to vote at the end of the Civil War. But apart from the grandfather clause, the Court was explicit that literacy tests are permissible: "No time need be spent on the question of the validity of the literacy test, considered alone, since, as we have seen, its establishment was but the exercise by the state of a lawful power vested in it, not subject to our supervision, and, indeed, its validity is admitted."

More recently, in 1959 in Lassiter v. Northampton County Board of Elections, 360 U.S. 45 (1959), the Court upheld a North Carolina statute that conditioned voting eligibility on a person's ability to read and write any section of the Constitution in the English language. Justice Douglas, writing for the Court, emphasized that "[t]he States have long been held to have broad powers to determine the conditions under which the right of suffrage may be exercised, absent of course discrimination which the Constitution condemns."

Thus the Court concluded that literacy tests may be used because the ability to read and write is relevant to the ability to exercise the franchise intelligently. Justice Douglas wrote, "The ability to read and write likewise has some relation to standards designed to promote intelligent use of the ballot. Literacy and illiteracy are neutral on race, creed, color, and sex, as reports around the world show. Literacy and intelligence are obviously not synonymous. Illiterate people may be intelligent voters. Yet in our society where newspapers, periodicals, books, and other printed matter canvass and debate campaign issues, a State may conclude that only those who are literate should exercise the franchise."

However, although literacy tests are constitutional, they have been outlawed by federal statute. Congress initially limited literacy tests and then amended the Voting Rights Act to completely prohibit them.[40] The Supreme Court upheld these laws as a valid exercise of Congress's powers under §5 of the Fourteenth Amendment even though they had the effect of overturning an earlier Court decision.[41]

PRISONERS' AND CONVICTED CRIMINALS' RIGHT TO VOTE

Many cases have concerned the ability of the state to restrict voting by those held in prison or those convicted of crimes. To summarize the cases described below, states cannot deny the right to vote to those being held waiting for trial and, in fact, must provide them absentee ballots if they have no other way of voting. However, once a person has been convicted of a felony, a state may permanently disenfranchise the individual. But at least where there was evidence of a racially discriminatory purpose behind the law, a state was prevented from permanently denying the right to vote to those convicted of crimes involving moral turpitude.

In a series of cases, the Court considered the duty of the government to provide absentee ballots to those held in jail while waiting for trial. In

---

40. Oregon v. Mitchell, 400 U.S. 112 (1970).
41. *See, e.g.*, Katzenbach v. Morgan, 384 U.S. 641 (1966), presented in Chapter 2.

O'Brien v. Skinner, 414 U.S. 524 (1974), the Court held that the government must provide absentee ballots to jail inmates where it is proven that they have no other way of voting. In *O'Brien*, the record demonstrated that the state refused to provide jail inmates absentee ballots and did not create polling places at jails or transport inmates outside to vote. Actually, the state law was even more irrational: Inmates being held outside their county of residence could receive an absentee ballot, but those in jail within their home county could not obtain an absentee ballot.

However, once a person has been convicted of a felony, a state may permanently deny the individual the right to vote. In Richardson v. Ramirez, 418 U.S. 24 (1974), the Court relied on the language of §2 of the Fourteenth Amendment to uphold the ability of states to disenfranchise felons and ex-felons. Section 2, in part, says that "[r]epresentatives shall be apportioned among the several states according to their respective numbers, counting the whole number of persons in each State, excluding Indians not taxed." However, the provision says that representation shall be decreased if a state denies the right to vote to any male citizens, 21 years of age or older, "except for participation in rebellion, or other crimes." In other words, the provision says that there would be no penalty in terms of representation in the House of Representatives if a state denied the right to vote to those who participated in rebellion or other crimes.

The Court, in an opinion by Justice Rehnquist, reviewed the legislative history of this provision and also noted that at the time the Fourteenth Amendment was ratified, "29 States had provisions in their constitutions which prohibited, or authorized the legislature to prohibit, exercise of the franchise by persons convicted of felonies or infamous crimes." The Court also relied on earlier decisions, from the late nineteenth century, that denied bigamists and polygamists the right to vote in territorial Utah and Idaho. The Court concluded that a state may deny the right to vote to those convicted of felonies, even if they had completed their sentences and paroles.

However, in Hunter v. Underwood, 471 U.S. 222 (1985), the Court invalidated an Alabama law that denied the right to vote to those who had been convicted of crimes involving moral turpitude. A federal district court found that the provision had been adopted with the purpose of disenfranchising blacks and that it had that effect. The Supreme Court accepted these findings and said, "Without deciding whether [the law] would be valid if enacted today without any impermissible motivation, we simply observe that its original enactment was motivated by a desire to discriminate against blacks on account of race and the section continues to this day to have that effect."

REQUIREMENT FOR PHOTO IDENTIFICATION FOR VOTING

In Crawford v. Marion County Election Board, the Supreme Court considered the constitutionality of a requirement for photo identification for voting, an issue that remains controversial. There was no majority opinion for the Court as there was a three-to-three-to-three split among the justices, with six voting to allow the regulation. In reading the case, it is important to focus on what test each group of justices would use. Also, it is important to consider whether this case can be reconciled with other decisions concerning the right to vote, such as those striking down poll taxes and property ownership requirements for voting.

CRAWFORD v. MARION COUNTY ELECTION BOARD
553 U.S. 181 (2008)

Justice Stevens announced the judgment of the Court and delivered an opinion in which the Chief Justice and Justice Kennedy join.

At issue in these cases is the constitutionality of an Indiana statute requiring citizens voting in person on election day, or casting a ballot in person at the office of the circuit court clerk prior to election day, to present photo identification issued by the government.

Referred to as either the "Voter ID Law," or SEA 483, the statute applies to in-person voting at both primary and general elections.

The requirement does not apply to absentee ballots submitted by mail, and the statute contains an exception for persons living and voting in a state-licensed facility such as a nursing home. A voter who is indigent or has a religious objection to being photographed may cast a provisional ballot that will be counted only if she executes an appropriate affidavit before the circuit court clerk within 10 days following the election. A voter who has photo identification but is unable to present that identification on election day may file a provisional ballot that will be counted if she brings her photo identification to the circuit county clerk's office within 10 days. No photo identification is required in order to register to vote, and the State offers free photo identification to qualified voters able to establish their residence and identity.

I

In Harper v. Virginia Bd. of Elections (1966), the Court held that Virginia could not condition the right to vote in a state election on the payment of a poll tax of $1.50. We rejected the dissenters' argument that the interest in promoting civic responsibility by weeding out those voters who did not care enough about public affairs to pay a small sum for the privilege of voting provided a rational basis for the tax. Applying a stricter standard, we concluded that a State "violates the Equal Protection Clause of the Fourteenth Amendment whenever it makes the affluence of the voter or payment of any fee an electoral standard." We used the term "invidiously discriminate" to describe conduct prohibited under that standard, noting that we had previously held that while a State may obviously impose "reasonable residence restrictions on the availability of the ballot," it "may not deny the opportunity to vote to a bona fide resident merely because he is a member of the armed services." Although the State's justification for the tax was rational, it was invidious because it was irrelevant to the voter's qualifications.

Thus, under the standard applied in *Harper*, even rational restrictions on the right to vote are invidious if they are unrelated to voter qualifications. In Anderson v. Celebrezze (1983), however, we confirmed the general rule that "evenhanded restrictions that protect the integrity and reliability of the electoral process itself" are not invidious and satisfy the standard set forth in *Harper*. Rather than applying any "litmus test" that would neatly separate valid from invalid restrictions, we concluded that a court must identify and evaluate the interests put forward by the State as justifications for the burden imposed by its rule, and then make the "hard judgment" that our adversary system demands.

II

The State has identified several state interests that arguably justify the burdens that SEA 483 imposes on voters and potential voters. While petitioners argue that the statute was actually motivated by partisan concerns and dispute both the significance of the State's interests and the magnitude of any real threat to those interests, they do not question the legitimacy of the interests the State has identified. Each is unquestionably relevant to the State's interest in protecting the integrity and reliability of the electoral process.

The first is the interest in deterring and detecting voter fraud. The State has a valid interest in participating in a nationwide effort to improve and modernize election procedures that have been criticized as antiquated and inefficient. The State also argues that it has a particular interest in preventing voter fraud in response to a problem that is in part the product of its own maladministration — namely, that Indiana's voter registration rolls include a large number of names of persons who are either deceased or no longer live in Indiana. Finally, the State relies on its interest in safeguarding voter confidence. Each of these interests merits separate comment.

ELECTION MODERNIZATION

Two recently enacted federal statutes have made it necessary for States to reexamine their election procedures. Both contain provisions consistent with a State's choice to use government-issued photo identification as a relevant source of information concerning a citizen's eligibility to vote.

In the National Voter Registration Act of 1993 (NVRA), Congress established procedures that would both increase the number of registered voters and protect the integrity of the electoral process. The statute requires state motor vehicle driver's license applications to serve as voter registration applications. While that requirement has increased the number of registered voters, the statute also contains a provision restricting States' ability to remove names from the lists of registered voters. These protections have been partly responsible for inflated lists of registered voters. For example, evidence credited by Judge Barker estimated that as of 2004 Indiana's voter rolls were inflated by as much as 41.4%, and data collected by the Election Assistance Committee in 2004 indicated that 19 of 92 Indiana counties had registration totals exceeding 100% of the 2004 voting-age population.

In HAVA, Congress required every State to create and maintain a computerized statewide list of all registered voters. HAVA also requires the States to verify voter information contained in a voter registration application and specifies either an "applicant's driver's license number" or "the last 4 digits of the applicant's social security number" as acceptable verifications.

HAVA also imposes new identification requirements for individuals registering to vote for the first time who submit their applications by mail. If the voter is casting his ballot in person, he must present local election officials with written identification, which may be either "a current and valid photo identification" or another form of documentation such as a bank statement or paycheck. If the voter is voting by mail, he must include a copy of the identification with his ballot. A voter may also include a copy of the documentation with his application or provide his driver's license number or Social Security number for verification. Finally, in a provision entitled "Fail-safe voting," HAVA authorizes the casting of provisional ballots by challenged voters. Of course, neither HAVA nor NVRA required Indiana to enact SEA 483, but they do indicate that Congress believes that photo identification is one effective method of establishing a voter's qualification to vote and that the integrity of elections is enhanced through improved technology. That conclusion is also supported by a report issued shortly after the enactment of SEA 483 by the Commission on Federal Election Reform chaired by former President Jimmy Carter and former Secretary of State James A. Baker III, which is a part of the record in these cases.

VOTER FRAUD

The only kind of voter fraud that SEA 483 addresses is in-person voter impersonation at polling places. The record contains no evidence of any such fraud actually occurring in Indiana at any time in its history. Moreover, petitioners argue that provisions of the Indiana Criminal Code punishing such conduct as a felony provide adequate protection against the risk that such conduct will occur in the future. It remains true, however, that flagrant examples of such fraud in other parts of the country have been documented throughout this Nation's history by respected historians and journalists, that occasional examples have surfaced in recent years, and that Indiana's own experience with fraudulent voting in the 2003 Democratic primary for East Chicago Mayor — though perpetrated using absentee ballots and not in-person fraud — demonstrate that not only is the risk of voter fraud real but that it could affect the outcome of a close election.

There is no question about the legitimacy or importance of the State's interest in counting only the votes of eligible voters. Moreover, the interest in orderly administration and accurate recordkeeping provides a sufficient justification for carefully identifying all voters participating in the election process. While the most effective method of preventing election fraud may well be debatable, the propriety of doing so is perfectly clear.

Finally, the State contends that it has an interest in protecting public confidence "in the integrity and legitimacy of representative government." While that interest is closely related to the State's interest in preventing voter fraud, public confidence in the integrity of the electoral process has independent significance, because it encourages citizen participation in the democratic process. As the Carter-Baker Report observed, the "electoral system cannot inspire public confidence if no safeguards exist to deter or detect fraud or to confirm the identity of voters."

III

States employ different methods of identifying eligible voters at the polls. Some merely check off the names of registered voters who identify themselves; others require voters to present registration cards or other documentation before they can vote; some require voters to sign their names so their signatures can be compared with those on file; and in recent years an increasing number of States have relied primarily on photo identification. A photo identification requirement imposes some burdens on voters that other methods of identification do not share. For example, a voter may lose his photo identification, may have his wallet stolen on the way to the polls, or may not resemble the photo in the identification because he recently grew a beard. Burdens of that sort arising from life's vagaries, however, are neither so serious nor so frequent as to raise any question about the constitutionality of SEA 483; the availability of the right to cast a provisional ballot provides an adequate remedy for problems of that character.

The burdens that are relevant to the issue before us are those imposed on persons who are eligible to vote but do not possess a current photo identification that complies with the requirements of SEA 483. The fact that most voters already possess a valid driver's license, or some other form of acceptable identification, would not save the statute under our reasoning in *Harper*, if the State required voters to pay a tax or a fee to obtain a new photo identification. But just as other States provide free voter registration cards, the photo identification cards issued by Indiana's BMV are also free. For most voters who need them, the inconvenience of making a trip to the BMV, gathering the required documents, and posing for a photograph surely does not qualify as a substantial burden on the right to vote, or even represent a significant increase over the usual burdens of voting.

Both evidence in the record and facts of which we may take judicial notice, however, indicate that a somewhat heavier burden may be placed on a limited number of persons. They include elderly persons born out-of-state, who may have difficulty obtaining a birth certificate; persons who because of economic or other personal limitations may find it difficult either to secure a copy of their birth certificate or to assemble the other required documentation to obtain a state-issued identification; homeless persons; and persons with a religious objection to being photographed. If we assume, as the evidence suggests, that some members of these classes were registered voters when SEA 483 was enacted, the new identification requirement may have imposed a special burden on their right to vote.

The severity of that burden is, of course, mitigated by the fact that, if eligible, voters without photo identification may cast provisional ballots that will ultimately be counted. To do so, however, they must travel to the circuit court clerk's office within 10 days to execute the required affidavit. It is unlikely that such a requirement would pose a constitutional problem unless it is wholly unjustified. And even assuming that the burden may not be justified as to a few voters, that conclusion is by no means sufficient to establish petitioners' right to the relief they seek in this litigation.

IV

Given the fact that petitioners have advanced a broad attack on the constitutionality of SEA 483, seeking relief that would invalidate the statute in all its applications, they bear a heavy burden of persuasion. Petitioners ask this Court, in effect, to perform a unique balancing analysis that looks specifically at a small number of voters who may experience a special burden under the statute and weighs their burdens against the State's broad interests in protecting election integrity. Petitioners urge us to ask whether the State's interests justify the burden imposed on voters who cannot afford or obtain a birth certificate and who must make a second trip to the circuit court clerk's office after voting. But on the basis of the evidence in the record it is not possible to quantify either the magnitude of the burden on this narrow class of voters or the portion of the burden imposed on them that is fully justified.

First, the evidence in the record does not provide us with the number of registered voters without photo identification; Judge Barker found petitioners' expert's report to be "utterly incredible and unreliable." Much of the argument about the numbers of such voters comes from extrarecord, postjudgment studies, the accuracy of which has not been tested in the trial court. The record says virtually nothing about the difficulties faced by either indigent voters or voters with religious objections to being photographed.

In sum, on the basis of the record that has been made in this litigation, we cannot conclude that the statute imposes "excessively burdensome requirements" on any class of voters. When we consider only the statute's broad application to all Indiana voters we conclude that it "imposes only a limited burden on voters' rights." The "precise interests" advanced by the State are therefore sufficient to defeat petitioners' facial challenge to SEA 483.

Finally we note that petitioners have not demonstrated that the proper remedy—even assuming an unjustified burden on some voters—would be to invalidate the entire statute. When evaluating a neutral, nondiscriminatory regulation of voting procedure, "[w]e must keep in mind that '[a] ruling of unconstitutionality frustrates the intent of the elected representatives of the people.'"

V

In their briefs, petitioners stress the fact that all of the Republicans in the General Assembly voted in favor of SEA 483 and the Democrats were unanimous in opposing it. It is fair to infer that partisan considerations may have played a significant role in the decision to enact SEA 483. If such considerations had provided the only justification for a photo identification requirement, we may also assume that SEA 483 would suffer the same fate as the poll tax at issue in *Harper*.

But if a nondiscriminatory law is supported by valid neutral justifications, those justifications should not be disregarded simply because partisan interests may have provided one motivation for the votes of individual legislators. The state interests identified as justifications for SEA 483 are both neutral and sufficiently strong to require us to reject petitioners' facial attack on the statute. The application of the statute to the vast majority of Indiana voters is amply justified by the valid interest in protecting "the integrity and reliability of the electoral process."

Justice SCALIA, with whom Justice THOMAS and Justice ALITO join, concurring in the judgment.

The lead opinion assumes petitioners' premise that the voter-identification law "may have imposed a special burden on" some voters, but holds that petitioners have not assembled evidence to show that the special burden is severe enough to warrant strict scrutiny. That is true enough, but for the sake of clarity and finality (as well as adherence to precedent), I prefer to decide these cases on the grounds that petitioners' premise is irrelevant and that the burden at issue is minimal and justified.

To vote in person in Indiana, everyone must have and present a photo identification that can be obtained for free. The State draws no classifications, let alone discriminatory ones, except to establish optional absentee and provisional balloting for certain poor, elderly, and institutionalized voters and for religious objectors. Nor are voters who already have photo identifications exempted from the burden, since those voters must maintain the accuracy of the information displayed on the identifications, renew them before they expire, and replace them if they are lost.

The Indiana photo-identification law is a generally applicable, nondiscriminatory voting regulation, and our precedents refute the view that individual impacts are relevant to determining the severity of the burden it imposes. Insofar as our election-regulation cases rest upon the requirements of the Fourteenth Amendment, weighing the burden of a nondiscriminatory voting law upon each voter and concomitantly requiring exceptions for vulnerable voters would effectively turn back decades of equal-protection jurisprudence. A voter complaining about such a law's effect on him has no valid equal-protection claim because, without proof of discriminatory intent, a generally applicable law with disparate impact is not unconstitutional. See, e.g., Washington v. Davis (1976). The Fourteenth Amendment does not regard neutral laws as invidious ones, *even when their burdens purportedly fall disproportionately on a protected class. A fortiori* it does not do so when, as here, the classes complaining of disparate impact are not even protected.[42]

Even if I thought that stare decisis did not foreclose adopting an individual-focused approach, I would reject it as an original matter. This is an area where the dos and don'ts need to be known in advance of the election, and voter-by-voter examination of the burdens of voting regulations would prove especially disruptive. A case-by-case approach naturally encourages constant litigation. Very few new election regulations improve everyone's lot, so the potential allegations of severe burden are endless. A State reducing the number of polling places would be open to the complaint it has violated the rights of disabled voters who live near the closed stations. Indeed, it may even be the case that some laws already on the books are especially burdensome for some voters, and one can predict lawsuits demanding that a State adopt voting over the Internet or expand absentee balloting.

That sort of detailed judicial supervision of the election process would flout the Constitution's express commitment of the task to the States. See Art. I, §4. It

---

42. A number of our early right-to-vote decisions, purporting to rely upon the Equal Protection Clause, strictly scrutinized nondiscriminatory voting laws requiring the payment of fees. See, *e.g.*, Harper v. Virginia Bd. of Elections (1966) (poll tax); Bullock v. Carter (1972) (ballot-access fee); Lubin v. Panish (1974) (ballot-access fee). To the extent those decisions continue to stand for a principle that Burdick v. Takushi (1992) does not already encompass, it suffices to note that we have never held that legislatures must calibrate all election laws, even those totally unrelated to money, for their impacts on poor voters or must otherwise accommodate wealth disparities. [Footnote by the Court.]

is for state legislatures to weigh the costs and benefits of possible changes to their election codes, and their judgment must prevail unless it imposes a severe and unjustified overall burden upon the right to vote, or is intended to disadvantage a particular class. Judicial review of their handiwork must apply an objective, uniform standard that will enable them to determine, ex ante, whether the burden they impose is too severe.

The lead opinion's record-based resolution of these cases, which neither rejects nor embraces the rule of our precedents, provides no certainty, and will embolden litigants who surmise that our precedents have been abandoned. There is no good reason to prefer that course.

The universally applicable requirements of Indiana's voter-identification law are eminently reasonable. The burden of acquiring, possessing, and showing a free photo identification is simply not severe, because it does not "even represent a significant increase over the usual burdens of voting." And the State's interests are sufficient to sustain that minimal burden. That should end the matter. That the State accommodates some voters by permitting (not requiring) the casting of absentee or provisional ballots, is an indulgence — not a constitutional imperative that falls short of what is required.

Justice SOUTER, with whom Justice GINSBURG joins, dissenting.

Indiana's "Voter ID Law" threatens to impose nontrivial burdens on the voting right of tens of thousands of the State's citizens, and a significant percentage of those individuals are likely to be deterred from voting. The statute is unconstitutional under the balancing standard of Burdick v. Takushi (1992): a State may not burden the right to vote merely by invoking abstract interests, be they legitimate, or even compelling, but must make a particular, factual showing that threats to its interests outweigh the particular impediments it has imposed. The State has made no such justification here, and as to some aspects of its law, it has hardly even tried. I therefore respectfully dissent from the Court's judgment sustaining the statute.

I

Voting-rights cases raise two competing interests, the one side being the fundamental right to vote. The Judiciary is obliged to train a skeptical eye on any qualification of that right.

Given the legitimacy of interests on both sides, we have avoided pre-set levels of scrutiny in favor of a sliding-scale balancing analysis: the scrutiny varies with the effect of the regulation at issue. And whatever the claim, the Court has long made a careful, ground-level appraisal both of the practical burdens on the right to vote and of the State's reasons for imposing those precise burdens. The lead opinion does not disavow these basic principles. But I think it does not insist enough on the hard facts that our standard of review demands.

II

Under *Burdick*, "the rigorousness of our inquiry into the propriety of a state election law depends upon the extent to which a challenged regulation burdens

First and Fourteenth Amendment rights," upon an assessment of the "character and magnitude of the asserted [threatened] injury," and an estimate of the number of voters likely to be affected.

A

The first set of burdens shown in these cases is the travel costs and fees necessary to get one of the limited variety of federal or state photo identifications needed to cast a regular ballot under the Voter ID Law. The travel is required for the personal visit to a license branch of the Indiana Bureau of Motor Vehicles (BMV), which is demanded of anyone applying for a driver's license or non-driver photo identification. The need to travel to a BMV branch will affect voters according to their circumstances, with the average person probably viewing it as nothing more than an inconvenience. Poor, old, and disabled voters who do not drive a car, however, may find the trip prohibitive, witness the fact that the BMV has far fewer license branches in each county than there are voting precincts.

The burden of traveling to a more distant BMV office rather than a conveniently located polling place is probably serious for many of the individuals who lack photo identification, and public transportation in Indiana is fairly limited. According to a report published by Indiana's Department of Transportation in August 2007, 21 of Indiana's 92 counties have no public transportation system at all, and as of 2000, nearly 1 in every 10 voters lived within 1 of these 21 counties. State officials recognize the effect that travel costs can have on voter turnout, as in Marion County, for example, where efforts have been made to "establis[h] most polling places in locations even more convenient than the statutory minimum," in order to "provid[e] for neighborhood voting." Although making voters travel farther than what is convenient for most and possible for some does not amount to a "severe" burden under *Burdick*, that is no reason to ignore the burden altogether. It translates into an obvious economic cost (whether in work time lost, or getting and paying for transportation) that an Indiana voter must bear to obtain an ID.

For those voters who can afford the roundtrip, a second financial hurdle appears: in order to get photo identification for the first time, they need to present "'a birth certificate, a certificate of naturalization, U.S. veterans photo identification, U.S. military photo identification, or a U.S. passport.'" As the lead opinion says, the two most common of these documents come at a price: Indiana counties charge anywhere from $3 to $12 for a birth certificate (and in some other States the fee is significantly higher), and that same price must usually be paid for a first-time passport, since a birth certificate is required to prove U.S. citizenship by birth. The total fees for a passport, moreover, are up to about $100. So most voters must pay at least one fee to get the ID necessary to cast a regular ballot. As with the travel costs, these fees are far from shocking on their face, but in the *Burdick* analysis it matters that both the travel costs and the fees are disproportionately heavy for, and thus disproportionately likely to deter, the poor, the old, and the immobile.

B

To be sure, Indiana has a provisional-ballot exception to the ID requirement for individuals the State considers "indigent" as well as those with religious objections to being photographed, and this sort of exception could in theory provide a way around the costs of procuring an ID. But Indiana's chosen exception does not amount to much relief.

The law allows these voters who lack the necessary ID to sign the poll book and cast a provisional ballot. As the lead opinion recognizes, though, that is only the first step; to have the provisional ballot counted, a voter must then appear in person before the circuit court clerk or county election board within 10 days of the election, to sign an affidavit attesting to indigency or religious objection to being photographed (or to present an ID at that point). Unlike the trip to the BMV (which, assuming things go smoothly, needs to be made only once every four years for renewal of nondriver photo identification), this one must be taken every time a poor person or religious objector wishes to vote, because the State does not allow an affidavit to count in successive elections. And unlike the trip to the BMV (which at least has a handful of license branches in the more populous counties), a county has only one county seat. Forcing these people to travel to the county seat every time they try to vote is particularly onerous for the reason noted already, that most counties in Indiana either lack public transportation or offer only limited coverage.

That the need to travel to the county seat each election amounts to a high hurdle is shown in the results of the 2007 municipal elections in Marion County, to which Indiana's Voter ID Law applied. Thirty-four provisional ballots were cast, but only two provisional voters made it to the County Clerk's Office within the 10 days.

All of this suggests that provisional ballots do not obviate the burdens of getting photo identification. And even if that were not so, the provisional-ballot option would be inadequate for a further reason: the indigency exception by definition offers no relief to those voters who do not consider themselves (or would not be considered) indigent but as a practical matter would find it hard, for nonfinancial reasons, to get the required ID (most obviously the disabled).

C

Indiana's Voter ID Law thus threatens to impose serious burdens on the voting right, even if not "severe" ones, and the next question under *Burdick* is whether the number of individuals likely to be affected is significant as well. Record evidence and facts open to judicial notice answer yes.

Although the District Court found that petitioners failed to offer any reliable empirical study of numbers of voters affected, we may accept that court's rough calculation that 43,000 voting-age residents lack the kind of identification card required by Indiana's law. The District Court made that estimate by comparing BMV records reproduced in petitioners' statistician's report with U.S. Census Bureau figures for Indiana's voting-age population in 2004, and the State does not argue that these raw data are unreliable.

So a fair reading of the data supports the District Court's finding that around 43,000 Indiana residents lack the needed identification, and will bear the burdens the law imposes. To be sure, the 43,000 figure has to be discounted to some extent, residents of certain nursing homes being exempted from the photo identification requirement. But the State does not suggest that this narrow exception could possibly reduce 43,000 to an insubstantial number.

The upshot is this. Tens of thousands of voting-age residents lack the necessary photo identification. A large proportion of them are likely to be in bad shape economically. The Voter ID Law places hurdles in the way of either getting an ID or of voting provisionally, and they translate into nontrivial economic costs. There is accordingly no reason to doubt that a significant number of state residents will be discouraged or disabled from voting.[43]

Petitioners, to be sure, failed to nail down precisely how great the cohort of discouraged and totally deterred voters will be, but empirical precision beyond the foregoing numbers has never been demanded for raising a voting-rights claim. While of course it would greatly aid a plaintiff to establish his claims beyond mathematical doubt, he does enough to show that serious burdens are likely.

III

Because the lead opinion finds only "limited" burdens on the right to vote, it avoids a hard look at the State's claimed interests. But having found the Voter ID Law burdens far from trivial, I have to make a rigorous assessment of "'the precise interests put forward by the State as justifications for the burden imposed by its rule,' [and] 'the extent to which those interests make it necessary to burden the plaintiff's rights.'"

As the lead opinion sees it, the State has offered four related concerns that suffice to justify the Voter ID Law: modernizing election procedures, combating voter fraud, addressing the consequences of the State's bloated voter rolls, and protecting public confidence in the integrity of the electoral process. On closer look, however, it appears that the first two (which are really just one) can claim modest weight at best, and the latter two if anything weaken the State's case.

The lead opinion's discussion of the State's reasons begins with the State's asserted interests in "election modernization," and in combating voter fraud. Although these are given separate headings, any line drawn between them is unconvincing; as I understand it, the "effort to modernize elections[]" is not for modernity's sake, but to reach certain practical (or political) objectives. The State says that it adopted the ID law principally to combat voter fraud, and it is this claim, not the slogan of "election modernization," that warrants attention.

There is no denying the abstract importance, the compelling nature, of combating voter fraud. But it takes several steps to get beyond the level of abstraction here.

To begin with, requiring a voter to show photo identification before casting a regular ballot addresses only one form of voter fraud: in-person voter impersonation. The photo ID requirement leaves untouched the problems of absentee-ballot fraud, which (unlike in-person voter impersonation) is a documented problem in Indiana); of registered voters voting more than once (but maintaining their own identities) in different counties or in different States; of felons and

---

43. Studies in other States suggest that the burdens of an ID requirement may also fall disproportionately upon racial minorities. See Overton, Voter Identification, 105 Mich. L. Rev. 631, 659 (2007) ("In 1994, the U.S. Department of Justice found that African-Americans in Louisiana were four to five times less likely than white residents to have government sanctioned photo identification"; describing June 2005 study by the Employment and Training Institute at the University of Wisconsin Milwaukee, which found that while 17% of voting age whites lacked a valid driver's license, 55% of black males and 49% of black females were unlicensed, and 46% of Latino males and 59% of Latino females were similarly unlicensed). [Footnote by the Court.]

other disqualified individuals voting in their own names; of vote buying; or, for that matter, of ballot-stuffing, ballot miscounting, voter intimidation, or any other type of corruption on the part of officials administering elections.

And even the State's interest in deterring a voter from showing up at the polls and claiming to be someone he is not must, in turn, be discounted for the fact that the State has not come across a single instance of in-person voter impersonation fraud in all of Indiana's history. Neither the District Court nor the Indiana General Assembly that passed the Voter ID Law was given any evidence whatsoever of in-person voter impersonation fraud in the State.

The State responds to the want of evidence with the assertion that in-person voter impersonation fraud is hard to detect. But this is like saying the "man who wasn't there" is hard to spot, and to know whether difficulty in detection accounts for the lack of evidence one at least has to ask whether in-person voter impersonation is (or would be) relatively harder to ferret out than other kinds of fraud (e.g., by absentee ballot) which the State has had no trouble documenting. The answer seems to be no; there is reason to think that "impersonation of voters is . . . the most likely type of fraud to be discovered." This is in part because an individual who impersonates another at the polls commits his fraud in the open, under the scrutiny of local poll workers who may well recognize a fraudulent voter when they hear who he claims to be.

The relative ease of discovering in-person voter impersonation is also owing to the odds that any such fraud will be committed by "organized groups such as campaigns or political parties" rather than by individuals acting alone. It simply is not worth it for individuals acting alone to commit in-person voter impersonation, which is relatively ineffectual for the foolish few who may commit it. If an imposter gets caught, he is subject to severe criminal penalties.

In sum, fraud by individuals acting alone, however difficult to detect, is unlikely. And while there may be greater incentives for organized groups to engage in broad-gauged in-person voter impersonation fraud, it is also far more difficult to conceal larger enterprises of this sort. The State's argument about the difficulty of detecting the fraud lacks real force.

What is left of the State's claim must be downgraded further for one final reason: regardless of the interest the State may have in adopting a photo identification requirement as a general matter, that interest in no way necessitates the particular burdens the Voter ID Law imposes on poor people and religious objectors. Individuals unable to get photo identification are forced to travel to the county seat every time they wish to exercise the franchise, and they have to get there within 10 days of the election. Nothing about the State's interest in fighting voter fraud justifies this requirement of a post-election trip to the county seat instead of some verification process at the polling places.

The State's final justification, its interest in safeguarding voter confidence, similarly collapses. The problem with claiming this interest lies in its connection to the bloated voter rolls; the State has come up with nothing to suggest that its citizens doubt the integrity of the State's electoral process, except its own failure to maintain its rolls. The answer to this problem is not to burden the right to vote, but to end the official negligence.

Without a shred of evidence that in-person voter impersonation is a problem in the State, much less a crisis, Indiana has adopted one of the most restrictive photo identification requirements in the country. The State recognizes that tens of thousands of qualified voters lack the necessary federally issued or state-issued identification, but it insists on implementing the requirement immediately, without allowing a transition period for targeted efforts to distribute the required identification to individuals who need it. The State hardly even tries to explain its decision to force indigents or religious objectors to travel all the way to their county seats every time they wish to vote, and if there is any waning of confidence in the administration of elections it probably owes more to the State's violation of federal election law than to any imposters at the polling places. It is impossible to say, on this record, that the State's interest in adopting its signally inhibiting photo identification requirement has been shown to outweigh the serious burdens it imposes on the right to vote.

The Indiana Voter ID Law is thus unconstitutional: the state interests fail to justify the practical limitations placed on the right to vote, and the law imposes an unreasonable and irrelevant burden on voters who are poor and old. I would vacate the judgment of the Seventh Circuit, and remand for further proceedings.

3. Dilution of the Right to Vote

Prior to the 1960s, many state legislatures were badly malapportioned. One district for the legislature often would be far more populous than another district for the same body. Likewise, districts within a state for electing members of the House of Representatives often were significantly malapportioned. Malapportionment in many areas was a result of population shifts to urban areas. Districts often were not redrawn after urban migration, causing cities to be underrepresented compared with more rural areas. Legislators who benefited from the malapportionment were unlikely to change the districting.

Initially, the Supreme Court ruled that challenges to malapportionment posed a nonjusticiable political question.[44] However, in Baker v. Carr, 369 U.S. 186 (1962), the Court concluded that equal protection challenges to malapportionment were justiciable.[45] Soon after, the Court articulated the rule of one person, one vote; that is, for any legislative body, all districts must be about the same in population size.

The first case to announce this principle was Gray v. Sanders, 372 U.S. 368 (1963). *Gray* involved a challenge to the Georgia system of selecting representatives for the Georgia House of the General Assembly on a county basis. An inequality resulted because counties varied widely in population size. Justice Douglas, writing for the Court, explained why this is unconstitutional: "How then can one person be given twice or 10 times the voting power of another person in a statewide election merely because he lives in a rural area or because he lives in the smallest rural county? Once the geographical unit for which a representative is to be chosen is designated, all who participate in the election are to have an equal vote — whatever their race, whatever their sex, wherever their occupation, whatever their income, and whatever their home may be in that geographic unit. This is required by the Equal Protection Clause of the Fourteenth Amendment."

---

44. Colegrove v. Green, 328 U.S. 549 (1946), discussed in Chapter 1.
45. The political question doctrine, and Baker v. Carr's discussion of it, is presented in Chapter 1.

The Court's most famous and most elaborate discussion of the one-person, one-vote rule was in Reynolds v. Sims.

REYNOLDS v. SIMS
377 U.S. 533 (1964)

Plaintiffs below alleged that the last apportionment of the Alabama Legislature was based on the 1900 federal census, despite the requirement of the State Constitution that the legislature be reapportioned decennially. They asserted that, since the population growth in the State from 1900 to 1960 had been uneven, Jefferson and other counties were now victims of serious discrimination with respect to the allocation of legislative representation. As a result of the failure of the legislature to reapportion itself, plaintiffs asserted, they were denied "equal suffrage in free and equal elections . . . and the equal protection of the laws" in violation of the Alabama Constitution and the Fourteenth Amendment to the Federal Constitution.

On July 21, 1962, the District Court held that the inequality of the existing representation in the Alabama Legislature violated the Equal Protection Clause of the Fourteenth Amendment, a finding which the Court noted had been "generally conceded" by the parties to the litigation, since population growth and shifts had converted the 1901 scheme, as perpetuated some 60 years later, into an invidiously discriminatory plan completely lacking in rationality. Under the existing provisions, applying 1960 census figures, only 25.1% of the State's total population resided in districts represented by a majority of the members of the Senate, and only 25.7% lived in counties which could elect a majority of the members of the House of Representatives. Population-variance ratios of up to about 41-to-1 existed in the Senate, and up to about 16-to-1 in the House. Bullock County, with a population of only 13,462, and Henry County, with a population of only 15,286, each were allocated two seats in the Alabama House, whereas Mobile County, with a population of 314,301, was given only three seats, and Jefferson County, with 634,864 people, had only seven representatives. With respect to senatorial apportionment, since the pertinent Alabama constitutional provisions had been consistently construed as prohibiting the giving of more than one Senate seat to any one county, Jefferson County, with over 600,000 people, was given only one senator, as was Lowndes County, with a 1960 population of only 15,417, and Wilcox County, with only 18,739 people.

No effective political remedy to obtain relief against the alleged malapportionment of the Alabama Legislature appears to have been available. No initiative procedure exists under Alabama law. Amendment of the State Constitution can be achieved only after a proposal is adopted by three-fifths of the members of both houses of the legislature and is approved by a majority of the people, or as a result of a constitutional convention convened after approval by the people of a convention call initiated by a majority of both houses of the Alabama Legislature.

Undeniably the Constitution of the United States protects the right of all qualified citizens to vote, in state as well as in federal elections. A consistent line of decisions by this Court in cases involving attempts to deny or restrict the right of suffrage has made this indelibly clear. It has been repeatedly recognized that all qualified voters have a constitutionally protected right to vote, and to have their votes counted. Undoubtedly, the right of suffrage is a fundamental matter in a free and democratic society. Especially since the right to exercise the franchise in a free and unimpaired manner is preservative of other basic civil and political rights, any alleged infringement of the right of citizens to vote must be carefully and meticulously scrutinized.

Legislators represent people, not trees or acres. Legislators are elected by voters, not farms or cities or economic interests. As long as ours is a representative form of government, and our legislatures are those instruments of government elected directly by and directly representative of the people, the right to elect legislators in a free and unimpaired fashion is a bedrock of our political system. It could hardly be gainsaid that a constitutional claim had been asserted by an allegation that certain otherwise qualified voters had been entirely prohibited from voting for members of their state legislature. And, if a State should provide that the votes of citizens in one part of the State should be given two times, or five times, or 10 times the weight of votes of citizens in another part of the State, it could hardly be contended that the right to vote of those residing in the disfavored areas had not been effectively diluted. It would appear extraordinary to suggest that a State could be constitutionally permitted to enact a law providing that certain of the State's voters could vote two, five, or 10 times for their legislative representatives, while voters living elsewhere could vote only once. And it is inconceivable that a state law to the effect that, in counting votes for legislators, the votes of citizens in one part of the State would be multiplied by two, five, or 10, while the votes of persons in another area would be counted only at face value, could be constitutionally sustainable. Of course, the effect of state legislative districting schemes which give the same number of representatives to unequal numbers of constituents is identical.

Overweighting and overvaluation of the votes of those living here has the certain effect of dilution and undervaluation of the votes of those living there. The resulting discrimination against those individual voters living in disfavored areas is easily demonstrable mathematically. Their right to vote is simply not the same right to vote as that of those living in a favored part of the State. Two, five, or 10 of them must vote before the effect of their voting is equivalent to that of their favored neighbor. Weighting the votes of citizens differently, by any method or means, merely because of where they happen to reside, hardly seems justifiable. One must be ever aware that the Constitution forbids "sophisticated as well as simpleminded modes of discrimination."

State legislatures are, historically, the fountainhead of representative government in this country. A number of them have their roots in colonial times, and substantially antedate the creation of our Nation and our Federal Government. Full and effective participation by all citizens in state government requires, therefore, that each citizen have an equally effective voice in the election of members of his state legislature. Modern and viable state government needs, and the Constitution demands, no less.

With respect to the allocation of legislative representation, all voters, as citizens of a State, stand in the same relation regardless of where they live. Any suggested criteria for the differentiation of citizens are insufficient to justify any discrimination, as to the weight of their votes, unless relevant to the permissible purposes of legislative apportionment. Since the achieving of fair and effective representation for all citizens is concededly the basic aim of legislative apportionment, we conclude that the Equal Protection Clause guarantees the opportunity for equal participation by all voters in the election of state legislators. Diluting the weight of votes because of place of residence impairs basic constitutional rights under the Fourteenth Amendment just as much as invidious discriminations based upon factors such as race or economic status.

We are advised that States can rationally consider factors other than population in apportioning legislative representation. We are admonished not to restrict the power of the States to impose differing views as to political philosophy on their citizens. We are cautioned about the dangers of entering into political thickets and mathematical quagmires. Our answer is this: a denial of constitutionally protected rights demands judicial protection; our oath and our office require no less of us.

To the extent that a citizen's right to vote is debased, he is that much less a citizen. The fact that an individual lives here or there is not a legitimate reason for overweighting or diluting the efficacy of his vote. The complexions of societies and civilizations change, often with amazing rapidity. A nation once primarily rural in character becomes predominantly urban. Representation schemes once fair and equitable become archaic and outdated. But the basic principle of representative government remains, and must remain, unchanged — the weight of a citizen's vote cannot be made to depend on where he lives. Population is, of necessity, the starting point for consideration and the controlling criterion for judgment in legislative apportionment controversies. A citizen, a qualified voter, is no more nor no less so because he lives in the city or on the farm. This is the clear and strong command of our Constitution's Equal Protection Clause. This is an essential part of the concept of a government of laws and not men. This is at the heart of Lincoln's vision of "government of the people, by the people, [and] for the people." The Equal Protection Clause demands no less than substantially equal state legislative representation for all citizens, of all places as well as of all races.

We hold that, as a basic constitutional standard, the Equal Protection Clause requires that the seats in both houses of a bicameral state legislature must be apportioned on a population basis. Simply stated, an individual's right to vote for state legislators is unconstitutionally impaired when its weight is in a substantial fashion diluted when compared with votes of citizens living in other parts of the State.

Since neither of the houses of the Alabama Legislature, under any of the three plans considered by the District Court, was apportioned on a population basis, we would be justified in proceeding no further. However, one of the proposed plans, that contained in the so-called 67-Senator Amendment, at least superficially resembles the scheme of legislative representation followed in the Federal Congress. Under this plan, each of Alabama's 67 counties is allotted one senator, and no counties are given more than one Senate seat. Arguably, this is analogous to the allocation of two Senate seats, in the Federal Congress, to each of the 50 States, regardless of population.

The system of representation in the two Houses of the Federal Congress is one ingrained in our Constitution, as part of the law of the land. It is one conceived out of compromise and concession indispensable to the establishment of our federal republic. Arising from unique historical circumstances, it is based on the consideration that in establishing our type of federalism a group of formerly

independent States bound themselves together under one national government. Admittedly, the original 13 States surrendered some of their sovereignty
in agreeing to join together "to form a more perfect Union." But at the heart of
our constitutional system remains the concept of separate and distinct governmental entities which have delegated some, but not all, of their formerly held
powers to the single national government.

Political subdivisions of States — counties, cities, or whatever — never were
and never have been considered as sovereign entities. Rather, they have been
traditionally regarded as subordinate governmental instrumentalities created by
the State to assist in the carrying out of state governmental functions. Thus, we
conclude that the plan contained in the 67-Senator Amendment for apportioning seats in the Alabama Legislature cannot be sustained by recourse to the so-
called federal analogy.

By holding that as a federal constitutional requisite both houses of a state
legislature must be apportioned on a population basis, we mean that the Equal
Protection Clause requires that a State make an honest and good faith effort to
construct districts, in both houses of its legislature, as nearly of equal population
as is practicable. We realize that it is a practical impossibility to arrange legislative
districts so that each one has an identical number of residents, or citizens, or
voters. Mathematical exactness or precision is hardly a workable constitutional
requirement.

Justice HARLAN, dissenting.

In these cases the Court holds that seats in the legislatures of six States are
apportioned in ways that violate the Federal Constitution. Under the Court's
ruling it is bound to follow that the legislatures in all but a few of the other 44
States will meet the same fate. These decisions have the effect of placing basic
aspects of state political systems under the pervasive overlordship of the federal
judiciary. I must register my protest.

Today's holding is that the Equal Protection Clause of the Fourteenth Amendment requires every State to structure its legislature so that all the members of
each house represent substantially the same number of people; other factors
may be given play only to the extent that they do not significantly encroach on
this basic "population" principle. Whatever may be thought of this holding as a
piece of political ideology — and even on that score the political history and
practices of this country from its earliest beginnings leave wide room for
debate — I think it demonstrable that the Fourteenth Amendment does not
impose this political tenet on the States or authorize this Court to do so.

Had the Court paused to probe more deeply into the matter, it would have
found that the Equal Protection Clause was never intended to inhibit the States
in choosing any democratic method they pleased for the apportionment of their
legislatures. This is shown by the language of the Fourteenth Amendment taken
as a whole, by the understanding of those who proposed and ratified it, and by
the political practices of the States at the time the Amendment was adopted. It is
confirmed by numerous state and congressional actions since the adoption of
the Fourteenth Amendment, and by the common understanding of the Amendment as evidenced by subsequent constitutional amendments and decisions of
this Court before Baker v. Carr made an abrupt break with the past in 1962.

The failure of the Court to consider any of these matters cannot be excused or
explained by any concept of "developing" constitutionalism. It is meaningless to

speak of constitutional "development" when both the language and history of the controlling provisions of the Constitution are wholly ignored. Since it can, I think, be shown beyond doubt that state legislative apportionments, as such, are wholly free of constitutional limitations, save such as may be imposed by the Republican Form of Government Clause (Const., Art. IV, §4), the Court's action now bringing them within the purview of the Fourteenth Amendment amounts to nothing less than an exercise of the amending power by this Court. So far as the Federal Constitution is concerned, the complaints in these cases should all have been dismissed below for failure to state a cause of action, because what has been alleged or proved shows no violation of any constitutional right.

The Supreme Court followed the principle of one person, one vote as applied to elections for the U.S. House of Representatives in Wesberry v. Sanders.

WESBERRY v. SANDERS, 376 U.S. 1 (1964): Justice BLACK delivered the opinion of the Court.

Appellants are citizens and qualified voters of Fulton County, Georgia, and as such are entitled to vote in congressional elections in Georgia's Fifth Congressional District. That district, one of ten created by a 1931 Georgia statute, includes Fulton, DeKalb, and Rockdale Counties and has a population according to the 1960 census of 823,680. The average population of the ten districts is 394,312, less than half that of the Fifth. One district, the Ninth, has only 272,154 people, less than one-third as many as the Fifth. Since there is only one Congressman for each district, this inequality of population means that the Fifth District's Congressman has to represent from two to three times as many people as do Congressmen from some of the other Georgia districts. Claiming that these population disparities deprived them and voters similarly situated of a right under the Federal Constitution to have their votes for Congressmen given the same weight as the votes of other Georgians, the appellants brought this action.

We hold that, construed in its historical context, the command of Art. I, §2, that Representatives be chosen "by the People of the several States" means that as nearly as is practicable one man's vote in a congressional election is to be worth as much as another's. To say that a vote is worth more in one district than in another would not only run counter to our fundamental ideas of democratic government, it would cast aside the principle of a House of Representatives elected "by the People," a principle tenaciously fought for and established at the Constitutional Convention. The history of the Constitution, particularly that part of it relating to the adoption of Art. I, §2, reveals that those who framed the Constitution meant that, no matter what the mechanics of an election, whether statewide or by districts, it was population which was to be the basis of the House of Representatives.

It would defeat the principle solemnly embodied in the Great Compromise — equal representation in the House for equal numbers of people — for us to hold that, within the States, legislatures may draw the lines of congressional districts in such a way as to give some voters a greater voice in choosing a Congressman than others. The House of Representatives, the Convention agreed, was to represent the people as individuals, and on a basis of complete equality for each voter. The delegates were quite aware of what Madison called the "vicious representation" in Great Britain whereby "rotten boroughs" with few inhabitants were represented in Parliament on or almost on a par with cities of greater population. Wilson urged that people must be represented as individuals, so that America would escape the evils of the English system under which one man could send two members of Parliament to represent the borough of Old Sarum while London's million people sent but four. The delegates referred to rotten borough apportionments in some of the state legislatures as the kind of objectionable governmental action that the Constitution should not tolerate in the election of congressional representatives.

It is in the light of such history that we must construe Art. I, §2, of the Constitution, which, carrying out the ideas of Madison and those of like views, provides that Representatives shall be chosen "by the People of the several States" and shall be "apportioned among the several States . . . according to their respective Numbers." No right is more precious in a free country than that of having a voice in the election of those who make the laws under which, as good citizens, we must live. Other rights, even the most basic, are illusory if the right to vote is undermined. Our Constitution leaves no room for classification of people in a way that unnecessarily abridges this right. While it may not be possible to draw congressional districts with mathematical precision, that is no excuse for ignoring our Constitution's plain objective of making equal representation for equal numbers of people the fundamental goal for the House of Representatives. That is the high standard of justice and common sense which the Founders set for us.

In a companion case to *Reynolds,* Lucas v. Forty-Fourth General Assembly, 377 U.S. 713 (1964), the Court said that it was irrelevant that voters, by initiative, had approved the malapportionment. The Court explained that one person, one vote is a constitutional mandate and that voter approval does not justify a violation, any more than voter approval would permit the violation of any other constitutional right. The Court observed that "[a]n individual's constitutionally protected right to cast an equally weighted vote cannot be denied even by a vote of a majority of a State's electorate."

The principle of one person, one vote has been extended to all forms of local governments. In Avery v. Midland County, 390 U.S. 474, 485 (1968), the Court said that one person, one vote applied to county commissioners who had "general government powers over the entire geographic area served by the body." In Hadley v. Junior College District, 397 U.S. 50 (1970), the principle was applied to an elected body with limited governing authority: a junior college district. The elected body had the authority to tax, to employ teachers, and to manage the educational program. The Court rejected earlier attempts to distinguish legislative officials from administrative ones. The Court said that all elected officials must be selected in a manner that avoids vote dilution. The Court stated, "[A]s a general rule, whenever a state or local government decides to select persons by popular election to perform governmental functions, [equal protection] requires that each qualified voter must be given an equal opportunity to participate in that election, and when members of an elected body are chosen from separate districts, each district must be established on a basis that will insure, as far as practicable, that equal numbers of voters can vote for proportionately equal numbers of officials."

The rule of one person, one vote does not require mathematical exactness in the size of districts, but only relatively small deviations are tolerated. More latitude is given to deviations in districting for state and local offices than for districts for the U.S. House of Representatives. In Kirkpatrick v. Preisler, 394 U.S. 526 (1969), the Court invalidated districting for the House of Representatives where the "most populous district was 3.13% above the mathematical ideal, and the least populous was 2.84% below." The Court emphasized that the government must "make a good-faith effort to achieve precise mathematical equality." In White v. Weiser, 412 U.S. 783 (1973), the Court declared unconstitutional even smaller deviations in districts for the House of Representatives. The Court repeatedly has emphasized that, especially with regard to elections for federal offices, any deviation must be justified. For example, in Karcher v. Daggett, 462 U.S. 725 (1983), the Court declared unconstitutional districting for the House of Representatives where the deviation between them was 0.7 percent. This deviation was impermissible because the state could offer no justification as to why it was needed.

The Court, though, has allowed more deviation in districts for electing state and local officials. In Mahan v. Howell, 410 U.S. 315 (1973), the Court expressly said that "broader latitude has been afforded the States under the Equal Protection Clause in state legislative redistricting." For example, in *Mahan*, the Court allowed deviations where the overrepresented districts exceeded the ideal by 6.8 percent and the underrepresented districts were 9.6 percent away from the target. Similarly, in Gaffney v. Cummings, 412 U.S. 735 (1973), the Court upheld a legislative apportionment where the maximum deviation was 7.83 percent and concluded that the differences were insignificant. In White v. Regester, 412 U.S. 755 (1973), the Court allowed an apportionment scheme where the total variation between the largest and the smallest district was 9.9 percent, though the Court indicated that this was near the maximum allowable deviation.[46]

There is no doubt that the reapportionment decisions have had an enormous effect on American government. Although they were extremely controversial in the 1960s, they are now seen as a paradigm of the judiciary acting to perfect the political process and reinforce democracy.[47] Reapportionment was very unlikely to occur without judicial action because officeholders were not likely to give up their seats voluntarily. The decisions dramatically changed the composition of state legislatures and thus undoubtedly affected the laws adopted.

Yet some still criticize the cases as being excessive judicial activism because there was no authority in the text or the framers' intent for the rule of one person, one vote.[48] The critics see the decisions as improper judicial interference, unsupported by the text of the Constitution or the framers' intent, with the political process.

---

46. *See also* Brown v. Thomson, 462 U.S. 835 (1983) (allowing a maximum deviation of 8.9 percent in drawing congressional districts).

47. *See* John Ely, *Democracy and Distrust* 101-102 (1980).

48. Robert Bork, *The Tempting of America* 87 (1990) (criticizing the decisions on the ground that the "Warren majority's new constitutional doctrine was supported by nothing").

4. Counting "Uncounted" Votes in a Presidential Election: Bush v. Gore

On December 12, 2000, for the first time in American history, the Supreme Court essentially decided who would be the next president of the United States.

THE EVENTS LEADING TO BUSH v. GORE

The presidential election of Tuesday, November 7, 2000, was one of the closest in American history. By early Wednesday morning, it was clear that the Democratic candidate, Vice President Albert Gore, had won the national popular vote, but the outcome of the electoral vote was uncertain. The presidency turned on Florida and its 25 electoral votes. Early on election night, the television networks called Gore the winner in Florida, only to retract their prediction later in the evening. In the early hours of Wednesday, November 8, the networks declared George W. Bush the winner of Florida and the presidency, only to recant a short time later and conclude that the outcome in Florida, and thus of the national election, was too close to call.

On November 8, the Florida Division of Elections reported that Bush had received 2,909,135 votes and Gore had received 2,907,351 votes. Florida law provides for a recount of votes if the election is decided by less than one-half of 1 percent of the votes cast.[49] Because the difference in votes between the two candidates was less than one-half of 1 percent, Gore immediately asked for a machine recount of the tally of votes in four counties: Volusia, Palm Beach, Broward, and Miami-Dade. On November 9, Florida Secretary of State Katherine Harris declined to extend the statutory deadline for county vote totals beyond November 14. By this point, the machine recount had narrowed Bush's lead to a mere 327 votes.

Upon learning of the close margin between him and Bush, Gore petitioned and received permission to conduct a hand recount in the four counties in question. On Saturday, November 11, Bush sued in federal district court to block the manual recount, but this request was denied.

However, Secretary of State Harris emphasized that she would enforce the November 14 deadline and would not accept late recounts from counties in Florida. She said that the Florida election statute required counties to report their votes within one week of the election, unless one of the statutory exceptions was met. These included "proof of fraud that affects the outcome of the election, substantial noncompliance with statutory election procedures, and a reasonable doubt exist[ing] as to whether the certified results expressed the will of the voters," or where compliance with the deadline is "prevented as a result of an act of God, or extenuating circumstances beyond control."

The four counties submitted their responses and requested acceptance of late completion of totals; Harris denied each one. A suit was brought against Harris

---

49. The Florida statute, §102.141(4), provides:

> (4) If the returns for any office reflect that a candidate was defeated or eliminated by one-half of a percent or less of the votes cast for such office . . . the board responsible for certifying the results of the vote on such race or measure shall order a recount of the votes cast with respect to such office or measure.

in Florida state court to compel her to accept the time for the reporting of the results. On Friday, November 17, the Florida state trial court ruled in favor of Harris. On Monday, November 20, the Florida Supreme Court held a nationally televised hearing. On Tuesday night, November 21, the Florida Supreme Court unanimously reversed the trial court and ordered that the secretary of state accept hand recounts from the four counties if they were completed by Sunday, November 26, at 5:00 P.M., or Monday morning, if the secretary of state's office was not open for business on Sunday afternoon.

The Florida Supreme Court ruled that Florida's secretary of state abused her discretion in refusing to extend the deadline for certifying elections so as to provide the time needed for the recounts. The Court said it was confronted with a conflict between two statutes. One statute, Fla. Stat. §102.111, provides that local election canvassing boards must provide their results "by 5:00 of the seventh day following an election." This law was amended in 1989 by §102.112, which provides that election results may be ignored and board members shall be fined if these deadlines are not met.

However, another statute, Fla. Stat. §102.166(4)(a), specifically allows any candidate to request a manual recount. This provision states, "[A]ny candidate whose name appeared on the ballot . . . or any political party whose candidate's name appeared on the ballot may file a written request with the county canvassing board for a manual recount." The law provides that the written request may be made prior to the time the board certifies the returns or within 72 hours after the election—whichever occurs later.

The Florida Supreme Court expressly noted that these statutes "conflict." The court relied on "traditional rules of statutory construction"—such as that specific laws prevail over general ones and the more recently enacted law takes precedence over the older one—and concluded that Harris erred in denying the extension of time for the counting.

The Florida Supreme Court also said that "a statutory provision will not be construed in such a way that renders meaningless or absurd any other statutory provision." In order to effectuate the law allowing recounts, the court concluded that time must be allowed in which to conduct the recount. The court said that the secretary of state's refusal to accept hand recounts was wrong because it completely negated the statute that expressly provided for this.

On Friday, November 24, the day after Thanksgiving, the Supreme Court granted certiorari in this case and scheduled oral argument for the following Friday, December 1. In an unprecedented order, the Court permitted the broadcasting of the oral argument immediately after it was finished. A few days later, in Bush v. Palm Beach County Canvassing Bd., 531 U.S. 70 (2000), the Supreme Court remanded the case back to the Florida Supreme Court for clarification of its earlier decision. The U.S. Supreme Court, in a *per curiam* opinion, said it was unclear whether the Florida court's decision was based on its interpretation of the Florida Constitution or Florida statutes. The former apparently would be an impermissible basis for decision, while the latter would be acceptable, based on the U.S. Supreme Court's interpretation of federal election laws. On Monday, December 11—the same day the Supreme Court held oral argument in Bush v. Gore—the Florida Supreme Court issued a decision saying its decision was based on interpreting Florida's statutes, not its constitution.

Meanwhile, on Sunday, November 26, some counties asked for additional time to complete their counting. For example, Palm Beach County asked for two additional hours beyond the Sunday 5:00 P.M. deadline set by the Florida Supreme Court, particularly because the state Supreme Court expressly had allowed the secretary of state to wait until Monday morning before receiving the recount totals. The secretary of state refused all requests for extensions. On Sunday night, November 26, the Florida Elections Canvassing Commission certified the election results: Bush was determined to be the winner of Florida by 537 votes and thus the winner of Florida's 25 electoral votes.

On Monday, November 27, Gore filed suit in Florida under the Florida law providing for "contests" of election results.[50] This provision, §102.168(3)(c), provides that "[r]eceipt of a number of illegal votes or rejection of a number of legal votes sufficient to change or place in doubt the result of the election" shall be grounds for a contest. The statute authorizes a court, if it finds there are successful grounds for a contest, to "provide any relief appropriate under such circumstances." Fla. Stat. §102.168(8).

On Saturday and Sunday, December 2 and 3, a Florida state trial court held a hearing as to whether Gore had met the statutory requirements for a successful contest. On Monday, December 4, the Florida trial court ruled against Gore on the grounds that Gore failed to prove a "reasonable probability" that the election would have turned out differently if not for problems counting ballots.

The Florida Supreme Court granted review and scheduled oral arguments for Thursday, December 7. On Friday afternoon, December 8, the Florida Supreme Court, by a four-to-three decision, reversed the trial court. The Florida Supreme Court ruled that the trial court had used the wrong standard in insisting that Gore demonstrate a "reasonable probability" that the election would have been decided differently. The Florida Supreme Court said the statute requires only a showing of "[r]eceipt of a number of illegal votes or rejection of a number of legal votes sufficient to change or place in doubt the result of the election."

The Florida Supreme Court ordered "the Supervisor of Elections and the Canvassing Boards, as well as the necessary public officials, in all counties that have not conducted a manual recount or tabulation of the undervotes . . . to do so forthwith, said tabulation to take place in the individual counties where the ballots are located." The Florida Supreme Court also determined that Palm Beach County and Miami-Dade County, in their earlier manual recounts, had identified a net gain of 215 and 168 legal votes for Vice President Gore and that these should be included in the vote total even though they were reported after the deadline of Sunday, November 26.

Just hours after the Florida Supreme Court's decision, on Friday night, December 8, a Florida trial court judge ordered that the counting of the uncounted votes commence the next morning and that it be completed by Sunday afternoon, December 10, at 2:00 P.M. The judge said that he would resolve any disputes.

---

50. It should be noted that other lawsuits, unrelated to the specific issues in Bush v. Gore, were proceeding simultaneously. For example, voters in Palm Beach County brought a lawsuit seeking a new election there based on the so-called butterfly ballot, which they claimed violated Florida law and caused several thousand votes intended for Gore to be mistakenly cast for Pat Buchanan. The Florida trial court concluded that it lacked the constitutional authority to order a new election and the Florida Supreme Court denied review. Also, lawsuits were filed in two counties claiming that election officials had illegally filled in missing information on requests for absentee ballots. Both Florida trial court judges held this was not a basis for refusing to count the absentee ballots because the actions of election officials did not in any way taint the ballots themselves.

On Saturday morning, counting commenced as ordered. At the same time, Bush asked the U.S. Supreme Court to stay the counting and grant certiorari in the case. In the early afternoon on Saturday, the Supreme Court, in a five-to-four ruling, stayed the counting of the votes in Florida. Justice Stevens dissented on grounds there was not an irreparable injury, which is a requirement for such a stay. Justice Scalia wrote a short opinion, not joined by any other justice, in which he said the requirements for a stay were met. He said that Bush had shown a likelihood of prevailing on the merits and also irreparable injury. Justice Scalia said there were two such harms: First, there would be a cloud over the legitimacy of a Bush presidency if the counting showed Gore ahead, but the counting was disallowed by the Supreme Court. Second, handling of the ballots would lead to their degradation and prevent a more accurate counting later if that were ordered by the Court.

On Monday, December 11, the Supreme Court held oral arguments. Again, they were broadcast immediately after their completion. On Tuesday night, December 12, at approximately 10:00 P.M. eastern time, the Court released its opinion in Bush v. Gore.

THE DECISION

BUSH v. GORE
531 U.S. 98 (2000)

Per Curiam.

I

On December 8, 2000, the Supreme Court of Florida ordered that the Circuit Court of Leon County tabulate by hand 9,000 ballots in Miami-Dade County. It also ordered the inclusion in the certified vote totals of 215 votes identified in Palm Beach County and 168 votes identified in Miami-Dade County for Vice President Albert Gore, Jr., and Senator Joseph Lieberman, Democratic Candidates for President and Vice President. The Supreme Court noted that petitioner, Governor George W. Bush, asserted that the net gain for Vice President Gore in Palm Beach County was 176 votes, and directed the Circuit Court to resolve that dispute on remand.

The court further held that relief would require manual recounts in all Florida counties where so-called undervotes had not been subject to manual tabulation. The court ordered all manual recounts to begin at once. Governor Bush and Richard Cheney, Republican Candidates for the Presidency and Vice Presidency, filed an emergency application for a stay of this mandate. On December 9, we granted the application, treated the application as a petition for a writ of certiorari, and granted certiorari.

On November 8, 2000, the day following the Presidential election, the Florida Division of Elections reported that petitioner, Governor Bush, had received 2,909,135 votes, and respondent, Vice President Gore, had received 2,907,351 votes, a margin of 1,784 for Governor Bush. Because Governor Bush's margin of victory was less than "one-half of a percent . . . of the votes cast," an automatic machine recount was conducted under §102.141(4) of the election code, the results of which showed Governor Bush still winning the race but by a diminished margin. Vice President Gore then sought manual recounts in Volusia, Palm Beach, Broward, and Miami-Dade Counties, pursuant to Florida's election protest provisions. Fla. Stat. §102.166 (2000). A dispute arose concerning the deadline for local county canvassing boards to submit their returns to the Secretary of State (Secretary). The Secretary declined to waive the November 14 deadline imposed by statute. The Florida Supreme Court, however, set the deadline at November 26. We granted certiorari and vacated the Florida Supreme Court's decision, finding considerable uncertainty as to the grounds on which it was based. Bush v. Palm Beach County Canvassing Bd. (2000) (per curiam). On December 11, the Florida Supreme Court issued a decision on remand reinstating that date.

On November 26, the Florida Elections Canvassing Commission certified the results of the election and declared Governor Bush the winner of Florida's 25 electoral votes. On November 27, Vice President Gore, pursuant to Florida's contest provisions, filed a complaint in Leon County Circuit Court contesting the certification. He sought relief pursuant to §102.168(3)(c), which provides that "[r]eceipt of a number of illegal votes or rejection of a number of legal votes sufficient to change or place in doubt the result of the election" shall be grounds for a contest. The Circuit Court denied relief, stating that Vice President Gore failed to meet his burden of proof. He appealed to the First District Court of Appeal, which certified the matter to the Florida Supreme Court.

Accepting jurisdiction, the Florida Supreme Court affirmed in part and reversed in part. The court held that the Circuit Court had been correct to reject Vice President Gore's challenge to the results certified in Nassau County and his challenge to the Palm Beach County Canvassing Board's determination that 3,300 ballots cast in that county were not, in the statutory phrase, "legal votes."

The Supreme Court held that Vice President Gore had satisfied his burden of proof under §102.168(3)(c) with respect to his challenge to Miami-Dade County's failure to tabulate, by manual count, 9,000 ballots on which the machines had failed to detect a vote for President ("undervotes"). Noting the closeness of the election, the Court explained that "[o]n this record, there can be no question that there are legal votes within the 9,000 uncounted votes sufficient to place the results of this election in doubt." A "legal vote," as determined by the Supreme Court, is "one in which there is a 'clear indication of the intent of the voter.'" The court therefore ordered a hand recount of the 9,000 ballots in Miami-Dade County. Observing that the contest provisions vest broad discretion in the circuit judge to "provide any relief appropriate under such circumstances," Fla. Stat. §102.168(8) (2000), the Supreme Court further held that the Circuit Court could order "the Supervisor of Elections and the Canvassing Boards, as well as the necessary public officials, in all counties that have not conducted a manual recount or tabulation of the undervotes . . . to do so forthwith, said tabulation to take place in the individual counties where the ballots are located."

The Supreme Court also determined that both Palm Beach County and Miami-Dade County, in their earlier manual recounts, had identified a net gain of 215 and 168 legal votes for Vice President Gore. Rejecting the Circuit Court's conclusion that Palm Beach County lacked the authority to include the 215 net votes submitted past the November 26 deadline, the Supreme Court explained that the deadline was not intended to exclude votes identified after that date through ongoing manual recounts. As to Miami-Dade County, the Court concluded that although the 168 votes identified were the result of a partial recount, they were "legal votes [that] could change the outcome of the election." The Supreme Court therefore directed the Circuit Court to include those totals in the certified results, subject to resolution of the actual vote total from the Miami-Dade partial recount.

The petition presents the following questions: whether the Florida Supreme Court established new standards for resolving Presidential election contests, thereby violating Art. II, §1, cl. 2, of the United States Constitution and failing to comply with 3 U.S.C. §5, and whether the use of standardless manual recounts violates the Equal Protection and Due Process Clauses. With respect to the equal protection question, we find a violation of the Equal Protection Clause.

II

A

The closeness of this election, and the multitude of legal challenges which have followed in its wake, have brought into sharp focus a common, if heretofore unnoticed, phenomenon. Nationwide statistics reveal that an estimated 2% of ballots cast do not register a vote for President for whatever reason, including deliberately choosing no candidate at all or some voter error, such as voting for two candidates or insufficiently marking a ballot. In certifying election results, the votes eligible for inclusion in the certification are the votes meeting the properly established legal requirements.

This case has shown that punch card balloting machines can produce an unfortunate number of ballots which are not punched in a clean, complete way by the voter. After the current counting, it is likely legislative bodies nationwide will examine ways to improve the mechanisms and machinery for voting.

B

The individual citizen has no federal constitutional right to vote for electors for the President of the United States unless and until the state legislature chooses a statewide election as the means to implement its power to appoint members of the Electoral College. U.S. Const., Art. II, §l. This is the source for the statement in McPherson v. Blacker (1892), that the State legislature's power to select the manner for appointing electors is plenary; it may, if it so chooses, select the electors itself, which indeed was the manner used by State legislatures in several States for many years after the Framing of our Constitution. History has now favored the voter, and in each of the several States the citizens themselves vote for Presidential electors. When the state legislature vests the right to vote for President in its people, the right to vote as the legislature has prescribed is fundamental; and one source of its fundamental nature lies in the equal weight accorded to each vote and the equal dignity owed to each voter.

The right to vote is protected in more than the initial allocation of the franchise. Equal protection applies as well to the manner of its exercise. Having once granted the right to vote on equal terms, the State may not, by later arbitrary and disparate treatment, value one person's vote over that of another. See, e.g., Harper v. Virginia Bd. of Elections (1966) ("[O]nce the franchise is granted to the electorate, lines may not be drawn which are inconsistent with the Equal Protection Clause of the Fourteenth Amendment"). It must be remembered that "the right of suffrage can be denied by a debasement or dilution of the weight of a citizen's vote just as effectively as by wholly prohibiting the free exercise of the franchise." Reynolds v. Sims (1964).

There is no difference between the two sides of the present controversy on these basic propositions. Respondents say that the very purpose of vindicating the right to vote justifies the recount procedures now at issue. The question before us, however, is whether the recount procedures the Florida Supreme Court has adopted are consistent with its obligation to avoid arbitrary and disparate treatment of the members of its electorate.

Much of the controversy seems to revolve around ballot cards designed to be perforated by a stylus but which, either through error or deliberate omission, have not been perforated with sufficient precision for a machine to count them. In some cases a piece of the card — a chad — is hanging, say by two corners. In other cases there is no separation at all, just an indentation.

The Florida Supreme Court has ordered that the intent of the voter be discerned from such ballots. For purposes of resolving the equal protection challenge, it is not necessary to decide whether the Florida Supreme Court had the authority under the legislative scheme for resolving election disputes to define what a legal vote is and to mandate a manual recount implementing that definition. The recount mechanisms implemented in response to the decisions of the Florida Supreme Court do not satisfy the minimum requirement for non-arbitrary treatment of voters necessary to secure the fundamental right. Florida's basic command for the count of legally cast votes is to consider the "intent of the voter." This is unobjectionable as an abstract proposition and a starting principle. The problem inheres in the absence of specific standards to ensure its equal application. The formulation of uniform rules to determine intent based on these recurring circumstances is practicable and, we conclude, necessary.

The law does not refrain from searching for the intent of the actor in a multitude of circumstances; and in some cases the general command to ascertain intent is not susceptible to much further refinement. In this instance, however, the question is not whether to believe a witness but how to interpret the marks or holes or scratches on an inanimate object, a piece of cardboard or paper which, it is said, might not have registered as a vote during the machine count. The factfinder confronts a thing, not a person. The search for intent can be confined by specific rules designed to ensure uniform treatment.

The want of those rules here has led to unequal evaluation of ballots in various respects. As seems to have been acknowledged at oral argument, the standards for accepting or rejecting contested ballots might vary not only from county to county but indeed within a single county from one recount team to another.

The record provides some examples. A monitor in Miami-Dade County testified at trial that he observed that three members of the county canvassing board applied different standards in defining a legal vote. And testimony at trial also revealed that at least one county changed its evaluative standards during the counting process. Palm Beach County, for example, began the process with a 1990 guideline which precluded counting completely attached chads, switched to a rule that considered a vote to be legal if any light could be seen through a chad, changed back to the 1990 rule, and then abandoned any pretense of a per se rule, only to have a court order that the county consider dimpled chads legal. This is not a process with sufficient guarantees of equal treatment.

An early case in our one person, one vote jurisprudence arose when a State accorded arbitrary and disparate treatment to voters in its different counties. Gray v. Sanders (1963). The Court found a constitutional violation. We relied on these principles in the context of the Presidential selection process in Moore v. Ogilvie (1969), where we invalidated a county-based procedure that diluted the influence of citizens in larger counties in the nominating process. There we observed that "[t]he idea that one group can be granted greater voting strength than another is hostile to the one man, one vote basis of our representative government."

The State Supreme Court ratified this uneven treatment. It mandated that the recount totals from two counties, Miami-Dade and Palm Beach, be included in the certified total. The court also appeared to hold sub silentio that the recount totals from Broward County, which were not completed until after the original November 14 certification by the Secretary of State, were to be considered part of the new certified vote totals even though the county certification was not contested by Vice President Gore. Yet each of the counties used varying standards to determine what was a legal vote. Broward County used a more forgiving standard than Palm Beach County, and uncovered almost three times as many new votes, a result markedly disproportionate to the difference in population between the counties.

In addition, the recounts in these three counties were not limited to so-called undervotes but extended to all of the ballots. The distinction has real consequences. A manual recount of all ballots identifies not only those ballots which show no vote but also those which contain more than one, the so-called overvotes. Neither category will be counted by the machine. This is not a trivial concern. At oral argument, respondents estimated there are as many as 110,000 overvotes statewide. As a result, the citizen whose ballot was not read by a machine because he failed to vote for a candidate in a way readable by a machine may still have his vote counted in a manual recount; on the other hand, the citizen who marks two candidates in a way discernable by the machine will not have the same opportunity to have his vote count, even if a manual examination of the ballot would reveal the requisite indicia of intent. Furthermore, the citizen who marks two candidates, only one of which is discernable by the machine, will have his vote counted even though it should have been read as an invalid ballot. The State Supreme Court's inclusion of vote counts based on these variant standards exemplifies concerns with the remedial processes that were under way.

That brings the analysis to yet a further equal protection problem. The votes certified by the court included a partial total from one county, Miami-Dade. The Florida Supreme Court's decision thus gives no assurance that the recounts included in a final certification must be complete. This accommodation no doubt results from the truncated contest period established by the Florida Supreme Court, at respondents' own urging. The press of time does not diminish the constitutional concern. A desire for speed is not a general excuse for ignoring equal protection guarantees.

In addition to these difficulties the actual process by which the votes were to be counted under the Florida Supreme Court's decision raises further concerns. That order did not specify who would recount the ballots. The county canvassing boards were forced to pull together ad hoc teams comprised of judges from various Circuits who had no previous training in handling and interpreting ballots. Furthermore, while others were permitted to observe, they were prohibited from objecting during the recount.

The recount process, in its features here described, is inconsistent with the minimum procedures necessary to protect the fundamental right of each voter in the special instance of a statewide recount under the authority of a single state judicial officer. Our consideration is limited to the present circumstances, for the problem of equal protection in election processes generally presents many complexities.

The question before the Court is not whether local entities, in the exercise of their expertise, may develop different systems for implementing elections. Instead, we are presented with a situation where a state court with the power to assure uniformity has ordered a statewide recount with minimal procedural safeguards. When a court orders a statewide remedy, there must be at least some assurance that the rudimentary requirements of equal treatment and fundamental fairness are satisfied.

Given the Court's assessment that the recount process underway was probably being conducted in an unconstitutional manner, the Court stayed the order directing the recount so it could hear this case and render an expedited decision. The contest provision, as it was mandated by the State Supreme Court, is not well calculated to sustain the confidence that all citizens must have in the outcome of elections. The State has not shown that its procedures include the necessary safeguards. The problem, for instance, of the estimated 110,000 overvotes has not been addressed.

Upon due consideration of the difficulties identified to this point, it is obvious that the recount cannot be conducted in compliance with the requirements of equal protection and due process without substantial additional work. It would require not only the adoption (after opportunity for argument) of adequate statewide standards for determining what is a legal vote, and practicable procedures to implement them, but also orderly judicial review of any disputed matters that might arise. In addition, the Secretary of State has advised that the recount of only a portion of the ballots requires that the vote tabulation equipment be used to screen out undervotes, a function for which the machines were not designed. If a recount of overvotes were also required, perhaps even a second screening would be necessary. Use of the equipment for this purpose, and any new software developed for it, would have to be evaluated for accuracy by the Secretary of State, as required by [Florida law].

The Supreme Court of Florida has said that the legislature intended the State's electors to "participat[e] fully in the federal electoral process," as provided in 3 U.S.C. §5. That statute, in turn, requires that any controversy or contest that is designed to lead to a conclusive selection of electors be completed by December 12. That date is upon us, and there is no recount procedure in place under the State Supreme Court's order that comports with minimal constitutional standards. Because it is evident that any recount seeking to meet the December 12 date will be unconstitutional for the reasons we have discussed, we reverse the judgment of the Supreme Court of Florida ordering a recount to proceed.

Seven Justices of the Court agree that there are constitutional problems with the recount ordered by the Florida Supreme Court that demand a remedy. The only disagreement is as to the remedy. Because the Florida Supreme Court has said that the Florida Legislature intended to obtain the safe-harbor benefits of 3 U.S.C. §5, Justice Breyer's proposed remedy — remanding to the Florida Supreme Court for its ordering of a constitutionally proper contest until December 18 — contemplates action in violation of the Florida election code, and hence could not be part of an "appropriate" order authorized by Fla. Stat. §102.168(8) (2000).

None are more conscious of the vital limits on judicial authority than are the members of this Court, and none stand more in admiration of the Constitution's design to leave the selection of the President to the people, through their legislatures, and to the political sphere. When contending parties invoke the process of the courts, however, it becomes our unsought responsibility to resolve the federal and constitutional issues the judicial system has been forced to confront.

The judgment of the Supreme Court of Florida is reversed, and the case is remanded for further proceedings not inconsistent with this opinion.

Chief Justice REHNQUIST, with whom Justice SCALIA and Justice THOMAS join, concurring.

We join the per curiam opinion. We write separately because we believe there are additional grounds that require us to reverse the Florida Supreme Court's decision.

I

We deal here not with an ordinary election, but with an election for the President of the United States. In most cases, comity and respect for federalism compel us to defer to the decisions of state courts on issues of state law. That practice reflects our understanding that the decisions of state courts are definitive pronouncements of the will of the States as sovereigns. Of course, in ordinary cases, the distribution of powers among the branches of a State's government raises no questions of federal constitutional law, subject to the requirement that the government be republican in character. But there are a few exceptional cases in which the Constitution imposes a duty or confers a power on a particular branch of a State's government. This is one of them. Article II, §1, cl. 2, provides that "[e]ach State shall appoint, in such Manner as the Legislature thereof may direct," electors for President and Vice President. Thus, the text of the election law itself, and not just its interpretation by the courts of the States, takes on independent significance.

3 U.S.C. §5 informs our application of Art. II, §1, cl. 2, to the Florida statutory scheme, which, as the Florida Supreme Court acknowledged, took that statute into account. Section 5 provides that the State's selection of electors "shall be conclusive, and shall govern in the counting of the electoral votes" if the electors are chosen under laws enacted prior to election day, and if the selection process

is completed six days prior to the meeting of the electoral college. As we noted in Bush v. Palm Beach County Canvassing Bd. (2000), "Since §5 contains a principle of federal law that would assure finality of the State's determination if made pursuant to a state law in effect before the election, a legislative wish to take advantage of the 'safe harbor' would counsel against any construction of the Election Code that Congress might deem to be a change in the law."

If we are to respect the legislature's Article II powers, therefore, we must ensure that postelection state-court actions do not frustrate the legislative desire to attain the "safe harbor" provided by §5. In Florida, the legislature has chosen to hold statewide elections to appoint the State's 25 electors. Importantly, the legislature has delegated the authority to run the elections and to oversee election disputes to the Secretary of State, and to state circuit courts. Isolated sections of the code may well admit of more than one interpretation, but the general coherence of the legislative scheme may not be altered by judicial interpretation so as to wholly change the statutorily provided apportionment of responsibility among these various bodies. In any election but a Presidential election, the Florida Supreme Court can give as little or as much deference to Florida's executives as it chooses, so far as Article II is concerned, and this Court will have no cause to question the court's actions. But, with respect to a Presidential election, the court must be both mindful of the legislature's role under Article II in choosing the manner of appointing electors and deferential to those bodies expressly empowered by the legislature to carry out its constitutional mandate.

In order to determine whether a state court has infringed upon the legislature's authority, we necessarily must examine the law of the State as it existed prior to the action of the court. Though we generally defer to state courts on the interpretation of state law, there are of course areas in which the Constitution requires this Court to undertake an independent, if still deferential, analysis of state law.

This inquiry does not imply a disrespect for state courts but rather a respect for the constitutionally prescribed role of state legislatures. To attach definitive weight to the pronouncement of a state court, when the very question at issue is whether the court has actually departed from the statutory meaning, would be to abdicate our responsibility to enforce the explicit requirements of Article II.

II

Acting pursuant to its constitutional grant of authority, the Florida Legislature has created a detailed, if not perfectly crafted, statutory scheme that provides for appointment of Presidential electors by direct election.

In its latest opinion, however, the court empties certification of [election results as prescribed by Florida law of] virtually all legal consequence during the contest, and in doing so departs from the provisions enacted by the Florida Legislature. The court determined that canvassing boards' decisions regarding whether to recount ballots past the certification deadline are to be reviewed de novo, although the election code clearly vests discretion whether to recount in the boards, and sets strict deadlines subject to the Secretary's rejection of late tallies and monetary fines for tardiness. Moreover, the Florida court held that all late vote tallies arriving during the contest period should be automatically included in the certification regardless of the certification deadline, thus virtually eliminating both the deadline and the Secretary's discretion to disregard recounts that violate it.

Moreover, the court's interpretation of "legal vote," and hence its decision to order a contest-period recount, plainly departed from the legislative scheme. Florida statutory law cannot reasonably be thought to require the counting of improperly marked ballots. Each Florida precinct before election day provides instructions on how properly to cast a vote; each polling place on election day contains a working model of the voting machine it uses; and each voting booth contains a sample ballot. In precincts using punch-card ballots, voters are instructed to punch out the ballot cleanly:

AFTER VOTING, CHECK YOUR BALLOT CARD TO BE SURE YOUR VOTING SELECTIONS ARE CLEARLY
AND CLEANLY PUNCHED AND THERE ARE NO CHIPS LEFT HANGING ON THE BACK OF THE CARD.

No reasonable person would call it "an error in the vote tabulation," Fla. Stat. §102.166(5), or a "rejection of legal votes," Fla. Stat. §102.168(3)(c), when electronic or electromechanical equipment performs precisely in the manner designed, and fails to count those ballots that are not marked in the manner that these voting instructions explicitly and prominently specify. The scheme that the Florida Supreme Court's opinion attributes to the legislature is one in which machines are required to be "capable of correctly counting votes," but which nonetheless regularly produces elections in which legal votes are predictably not tabulated, so that in close elections manual recounts are regularly required. This is of course absurd. The Secretary of State, who is authorized by law to issue binding interpretations of the election code, rejected this peculiar reading of the statutes. The Florida Supreme Court, although it must defer to the Secretary's interpretations, see Krivanek v. Take Back Tampa Political Committee (Fla. 1993), rejected her reasonable interpretation and embraced the peculiar one.

But as we indicated in our remand of the earlier case, in a Presidential election the clearly expressed intent of the legislature must prevail. And there is no basis for reading the Florida statutes as requiring the counting of improperly marked ballots, as an examination of the Florida Supreme Court's textual analysis shows. For the court to step away from this established practice, prescribed by the Secretary of State, the state official charged by the legislature with "responsibility to . . . [o]btain and maintain uniformity in the application, operation, and interpretation of the election laws," §97.012(1), was to depart from the legislative scheme.

III

The scope and nature of the remedy ordered by the Florida Supreme Court jeopardizes the "legislative wish" to take advantage of the safe harbor provided by 3 U.S.C. §5. December 12, 2000, is the last date for a final determination of the Florida electors that will satisfy §5. Yet in the late afternoon of December 8th — four days before this deadline — the Supreme Court of Florida ordered recounts of tens of thousands of so-called "undervotes" spread through 64 of the State's 67 counties. This was done in a search for elusive — perhaps delusive — certainty as to the exact count of 6 million votes. But no one claims that these ballots have not previously been tabulated; they were initially read by voting machines at the time of the election, and thereafter reread by virtue of Florida's automatic recount provision. No one claims there was any fraud in the election. The Supreme Court of Florida ordered this additional recount under the provision of the election code giving the circuit judge the authority to provide relief that is "appropriate under such circumstances."

Surely when the Florida Legislature empowered the courts of the State to grant "appropriate" relief, it must have meant relief that would have become final by the cut-off date of 3 U.S.C. §5. In light of the inevitable legal challenges and ensuing appeals to the Supreme Court of Florida and petitions for certiorari to this Court, the entire recounting process could not possibly be completed by that date.

Given all these factors, and in light of the legislative intent identified by the Florida Supreme Court to bring Florida within the "safe harbor" provision of 3 U.S.C. §5, the remedy prescribed by the Supreme Court of Florida cannot be deemed an "appropriate" one as of December 8. It significantly departed from the statutory framework in place on November 7, and authorized open-ended further proceedings which could not be completed by December 12, thereby preventing a final determination by that date. For these reasons, in addition to those given in the per curiam, we would reverse.

Justice STEVENS, with whom Justice GINSBURG and Justice BREYER join, dissenting.

The Constitution assigns to the States the primary responsibility for determining the manner of selecting the Presidential electors. When questions arise about the meaning of state laws, including election laws, it is our settled practice to accept the opinions of the highest courts of the States as providing the final answers. On rare occasions, however, either federal statutes or the Federal Constitution may require federal judicial intervention in state elections. This is not such an occasion.

The federal questions that ultimately emerged in this case are not substantial. Article II provides that "[e]ach State shall appoint, in such Manner as the Legislature thereof may direct, a Number of Electors." It does not create state legislatures out of whole cloth, but rather takes them as they come — as creatures born of, and constrained by, their state constitutions. The legislative power in Florida is subject to judicial review pursuant to Article V of the Florida Constitution, and nothing in Article II of the Federal Constitution frees the state legislature from the constraints in the state constitution that created it. Moreover, the Florida Legislature's own decision to employ a unitary code for all elections indicates that it intended the Florida Supreme Court to play the same role in Presidential elections that it has historically played in resolving electoral disputes. The Florida Supreme Court's exercise of appellate jurisdiction therefore was wholly consistent with, and indeed contemplated by, the grant of authority in Article II.

It hardly needs stating that Congress, pursuant to 3 U.S.C. §5, did not impose any affirmative duties upon the States that their governmental branches could "violate." Rather, §5 provides a safe harbor for States to select electors in contested elections "by judicial or other methods" established by laws prior to the election day. Section 5, like Article II, assumes the involvement of the state judiciary in interpreting state election laws and resolving election disputes under those laws. Neither §5 nor Article II grants federal judges any special authority to substitute their views for those of the state judiciary on matters of state law.

Nor are petitioners correct in asserting that the failure of the Florida Supreme Court to specify in detail the precise manner in which the "intent of the voter" is to be determined rises to the level of a constitutional violation. We found such a violation when individual votes within the same State were weighted unequally, see, e.g., Reynolds v. Sims (1964), but we have never before called into question the substantive standard by which a State determines that a vote has been legally cast. And there is no reason to think that the guidance provided to the factfind-ers, specifically the various canvassing boards, by the "intent of the voter" standard is any less sufficient — or will lead to results any less uniform — than, for example, the "beyond a reasonable doubt" standard employed every-day by ordinary citizens in courtrooms across this country.

Admittedly, the use of differing substandards for determining voter intent in different counties employing similar voting systems may raise serious concerns. Those concerns are alleviated — if not eliminated — by the fact that a single impartial magistrate will ultimately adjudicate all objections arising from the recount process. Of course, as a general matter, "[t]he interpretation of constitutional principles must not be too literal. We must remember that the machinery of government would not work if it were not allowed a little play in its joints." Bain Peanut Co. of Tex. v. Pinson (1931) (Holmes, J.). If it were otherwise, Florida's decision to leave to each county the determination of what balloting system to employ — despite enormous differences in accuracy — might run afoul of equal protection. So, too, might the similar decisions of the vast majority of state legislatures to delegate to local authorities certain decisions with respect to voting systems and ballot design.[51]

Even assuming that aspects of the remedial scheme might ultimately be found to violate the Equal Protection Clause, I could not subscribe to the majority's disposition of the case. As the majority explicitly holds, once a state legislature determines to select electors through a popular vote, the right to have one's vote counted is of constitutional stature. As the majority further acknowledges, Florida law holds that all ballots that reveal the intent of the voter constitute valid votes. Recognizing these principles, the majority nonetheless orders the termination of the contest proceeding before all such votes have been tabulated. Under their own reasoning, the appropriate course of action would be to remand to allow more specific procedures for implementing the legislature's uniform general standard to be established.

In the interest of finality, however, the majority effectively orders the disen-franchisement of an unknown number of voters whose ballots reveal their intent — and are therefore legal votes under state law — but were for some reason rejected by ballot-counting machines. It does so on the basis of the dead-lines set forth in Title 3 of the United States Code. But, as I have already noted,

---

51. The percentage of nonvotes in this election in counties using a punch-card system was 3.92%; in contrast, the rate of error under the more modern optical-scan systems was only 1.43%. Put in other terms, for every 10,000 votes cast, punch-card systems result in 250 more nonvotes than optical-scan systems. A total of 3,718,305 votes were cast under punch-card systems, and 2,353,811 votes were cast under optical-scan systems. [Footnote by the Court.]

those provisions merely provide rules of decision for Congress to follow when selecting among conflicting slates of electors. They do not prohibit a State from counting what the majority concedes to be legal votes until a bona fide winner is determined. Indeed, in 1960, Hawaii appointed two slates of electors and Congress chose to count the one appointed on January 4, 1961, well after the Title 3 deadlines. Thus, nothing prevents the majority, even if it properly found an equal protection violation, from ordering relief appropriate to remedy that violation without depriving Florida voters of their right to have their votes counted. As the majority notes, "[a] desire for speed is not a general excuse for ignoring equal protection guarantees."

Finally, neither in this case, nor in its earlier opinion in Palm Beach County Canvassing Bd. v. Harris, did the Florida Supreme Court make any substantive change in Florida electoral law. Its decisions were rooted in long-established precedent and were consistent with the relevant statutory provisions, taken as a whole. It did what courts do—it decided the case before it in light of the legislature's intent to leave no legally cast vote uncounted. In so doing, it relied on the sufficiency of the general "intent of the voter" standard articulated by the state legislature, coupled with a procedure for ultimate review by an impartial judge, to resolve the concern about disparate evaluations of contested ballots. If we assume—as I do—that the members of that court and the judges who would have carried out its mandate are impartial, its decision does not even raise a colorable federal question.

What must underlie petitioners' entire federal assault on the Florida election procedures is an unstated lack of confidence in the impartiality and capacity of the state judges who would make the critical decisions if the vote count were to proceed. Otherwise, their position is wholly without merit. The endorsement of that position by the majority of this Court can only lend credence to the most cynical appraisal of the work of judges throughout the land. It is confidence in the men and women who administer the judicial system that is the true backbone of the rule of law. Time will one day heal the wound to that confidence that will be inflicted by today's decision. One thing, however, is certain. Although we may never know with complete certainty the identity of the winner of this year's Presidential election, the identity of the loser is perfectly clear. It is the Nation's confidence in the judge as an impartial guardian of the rule of law. I respectfully dissent.

Justice SOUTER, with whom Justice BREYER joins and with whom Justice STEVENS and Justice GINSBURG join with regard to all but Part C, dissenting.

As will be clear, I am in substantial agreement with the dissenting opinions of Justice Stevens, Justice Ginsburg, and Justice Breyer. I write separately only to say how straightforward the issues before us really are. There are three issues: whether the State Supreme Court's interpretation of the statute providing for a contest of the state election results somehow violates 3 U.S.C. §5; whether that court's construction of the state statutory provisions governing contests impermissibly changes a state law from what the State's legislature has provided, in violation of Article II, §1, cl. 2, of the national Constitution; and whether the manner of interpreting markings on disputed ballots failing to cause machines to register votes for President (the undervote ballots) violates the equal protection or due process guaranteed by the Fourteenth Amendment. None of these issues is difficult to describe or to resolve.

A

The 3 U.S.C. §5 issue is not serious. That provision sets certain conditions for treating a State's certification of Presidential electors as conclusive in the event that a dispute over recognizing those electors must be resolved in the Congress under 3 U.S.C. §15. Conclusiveness requires selection under a legal scheme in place before the election, with results determined at least six days before the date set for casting electoral votes. But no State is required to conform to §5 if it cannot do that (for whatever reason); the sanction for failing to satisfy the conditions of §5 is simply loss of what has been called its "safe harbor." And even that determination is to be made, if made anywhere, in the Congress.

B

The second matter here goes to the State Supreme Court's interpretation of certain terms in the state statute governing election "contests." The issue is whether the judgment of the State Supreme Court has displaced the state legislature's provisions for election contests: is the law as declared by the court different from the provisions made by the legislature, to which the national Constitution commits responsibility for determining how each State's Presidential electors are chosen? Bush does not, of course, claim that any judicial act interpreting a statute of uncertain meaning is enough to displace the legislative provision and violate Article II; statutes require interpretation, which does not without more affect the legislative character of a statute within the meaning of the Constitution. What Bush does argue, as I understand the contention, is that the interpretation of §102.168 was so unreasonable as to transcend the accepted bounds of statutory interpretation, to the point of being a nonjudicial act and producing new law untethered to the legislative act in question.

The starting point for evaluating the claim that the Florida Supreme Court's interpretation effectively re-wrote §102.168 must be the language of the provision on which Gore relies to show his right to raise this contest: that the previously certified result in Bush's favor was produced by "rejection of a number of legal votes sufficient to change or place in doubt the result of the election." Fla. Stat. §102.168(3)(c) (2000). None of the state court's interpretations is unreasonable to the point of displacing the legislative enactment quoted.

1. The statute does not define a "legal vote," the rejection of which may affect the election. The State Supreme Court was therefore required to define it, and in doing that the court looked to another election statute, §101.5614(5), dealing with damaged or defective ballots, which contains a provision that no vote shall be disregarded "if there is a clear indication of the intent of the voter as determined by a canvassing board." The court read that objective of looking to the voter's intent as indicating that the legislature probably meant "legal vote" to mean a vote recorded on a ballot indicating what the voter intended. It is perfectly true that the majority might have chosen a different reading. But even so, there is no constitutional violation in following the majority view; Article II is unconcerned with mere disagreements about interpretive merits.

2. The Florida court next interpreted "rejection" to determine what act in the counting process may be attacked in a contest. Again, the statute does not define the term. The court majority read the word to mean simply a failure to count. That reading is certainly within the bounds of common sense, given the objective to give effect to a voter's intent if that can be determined. A different

reading, of course, is possible. The majority might have concluded that "rejection" should refer to machine malfunction, or that a ballot should not be treated as "reject[ed]" in the absence of wrongdoing by election officials, lest contests be so easy to claim that every election will end up in one. There is, however, nothing nonjudicial in the Florida majority's more hospitable reading.

3. The same is true about the court majority's understanding of the phrase "votes sufficient to change or place in doubt" the result of the election in Florida. The court held that if the uncounted ballots were so numerous that it was reasonably possible that they contained enough "legal" votes to swing the election, this contest would be authorized by the statute. While the majority might have thought (as the trial judge did) that a probability, not a possibility, should be necessary to justify a contest, that reading is not required by the statute's text, which says nothing about probability. Whatever people of good will and good sense may argue about the merits of the Florida court's reading, there is no warrant for saying that it transcends the limits of reasonable statutory interpretation to the point of supplanting the statute enacted by the "legislature" within the meaning of Article II.

In sum, the interpretations by the Florida court raise no substantial question under Article II. That court engaged in permissible construction in determining that Gore had instituted a contest authorized by the state statute, and it proceeded to direct the trial judge to deal with that contest in the exercise of the discretionary powers generously conferred by Fla. Stat. §102.168(8) (2000), to "fashion such orders as he or she deems necessary to ensure that each allegation in the complaint is investigated, examined, or checked, to prevent or correct any alleged wrong, and to provide any relief appropriate under such circumstances."

C

It is only on the third issue before us that there is a meritorious argument for relief, as this Court's Per Curiam opinion recognizes. It is an issue that might well have been dealt with adequately by the Florida courts if the state proceedings had not been interrupted, and if not disposed of at the state level it could have been considered by the Congress in any electoral vote dispute. But because the course of state proceedings has been interrupted, time is short, and the issue is before us, I think it sensible for the Court to address it.

Petitioners have raised an equal protection claim in the charge that unjustifiably disparate standards are applied in different electoral jurisdictions to otherwise identical facts. It is true that the Equal Protection Clause does not forbid the use of a variety of voting mechanisms within a jurisdiction, even though different mechanisms will have different levels of effectiveness in recording voters' intentions; local variety can be justified by concerns about cost, the potential value of innovation, and so on. But evidence in the record here suggests that a different order of disparity obtains under rules for determining a voter's intent that have been applied (and could continue to be applied) to identical types of ballots used in identical brands of machines and exhibiting identical physical characteristics (such as "hanging" or "dimpled" chads). I can conceive of no legitimate state interest served by these differing treatments of the expressions of voters' fundamental rights. The differences appear wholly arbitrary.

In deciding what to do about this, we should take account of the fact that electoral votes are due to be cast in six days. I would therefore remand the case to the courts of Florida with instructions to establish uniform standards for evaluating the several types of ballots that have prompted differing treatments, to be applied within and among counties when passing on such identical ballots in any further recounting (or successive recounting) that the courts might order.

Unlike the majority, I see no warrant for this Court to assume that Florida could not possibly comply with this requirement before the date set for the meeting of electors, December 18. To recount these manually would be a tall order, but before this Court stayed the effort to do that the courts of Florida were ready to do their best to get that job done. There is no justification for denying the State the opportunity to try to count all disputed ballots now. I respectfully dissent.

Justice GINSBURG, with whom Justice STEVENS joins, and with whom Justice SOUTER and Justice BREYER join as to Part I, dissenting.

I

The Chief Justice acknowledges that provisions of Florida's Election Code "may well admit of more than one interpretation." But instead of respecting the state high court's province to say what the State's Election Code means, the Chief Justice maintains that Florida's Supreme Court has veered so far from the ordinary practice of judicial review that what it did cannot properly be called judging. My colleagues have offered a reasonable construction of Florida's law. Their construction coincides with the view of one of Florida's seven Supreme Court justices. I might join the Chief Justice were it my commission to interpret Florida law. But disagreement with the Florida court's interpretation of its own State's law does not warrant the conclusion that the justices of that court have legislated. There is no cause here to believe that the members of Florida's high court have done less than "their mortal best to discharge their oath of office," and no cause to upset their reasoned interpretation of Florida law.

No doubt there are cases in which the proper application of federal law may hinge on interpretations of state law. Unavoidably, this Court must sometimes examine state law in order to protect federal rights. But we have dealt with such cases ever mindful of the full measure of respect we owe to interpretations of state law by a State's highest court.

In deferring to state courts on matters of state law, we appropriately recognize that this Court acts as an "'outside[r]' lacking the common exposure to local law which comes from sitting in the jurisdiction." That recognition has sometimes prompted us to resolve doubts about the meaning of state law by certifying issues to a State's highest court, even when federal rights are at stake. Notwithstanding our authority to decide issues of state law underlying federal claims, we have used the certification device to afford state high courts an opportunity to inform us on matters of their own State's law because such restraint "helps build a cooperative judicial federalism." I would have thought the "cautious approach" we counsel when federal courts address matters of state law, and our commitment to "build[ing] cooperative judicial federalism," demanded greater restraint.

Rarely has this Court rejected outright an interpretation of state law by a state high court. As Justice Breyer convincingly explains, this case involves nothing close to the kind of recalcitrance by a state high court that warrants extraordinary action by this Court. The Florida Supreme Court concluded that counting every legal vote was the overriding concern of the Florida Legislature when it enacted the State's Election Code. The court surely should not be bracketed with state high courts of the Jim Crow South.

The extraordinary setting of this case has obscured the ordinary principle that dictates its proper resolution: Federal courts defer to state high courts' interpretations of their state's own law. This principle reflects the core of federalism, on which all agree. The Chief Justice's solicitude for the Florida Legislature comes at the expense of the more fundamental solicitude we owe to the legislature's sovereign. Were the other members of this Court as mindful as they generally are of our system of dual sovereignty, they would affirm the judgment of the Florida Supreme Court.

II

I agree with Justice Stevens that petitioners have not presented a substantial equal protection claim. Ideally, perfection would be the appropriate standard for judging the recount. But we live in an imperfect world, one in which thousands of votes have not been counted. I cannot agree that the recount adopted by the Florida court, flawed as it may be, would yield a result any less fair or precise than the certification that preceded that recount.

Even if there were an equal protection violation, I would agree with Justice Stevens, Justice Souter, and Justice Breyer that the Court's concern about "the December 12 deadline," is misplaced. Time is short in part because of the Court's entry of a stay on December 9, several hours after an able circuit judge in Leon County had begun to superintend the recount process. More fundamentally, the Court's reluctance to let the recount go forward—despite its suggestion that "[t]he search for intent can be confined by specific rules designed to ensure uniform treatment[]"—ultimately turns on its own judgment about the practical realities of implementing a recount, not the judgment of those much closer to the process.

Equally important, as Justice Breyer explains, the December 12 "deadline" for bringing Florida's electoral votes into 3 U.S.C. §5's safe harbor lacks the significance the Court assigns it. Were that date to pass, Florida would still be entitled to deliver electoral votes Congress must count unless both Houses find that the votes "ha[d] not been . . . regularly given." 3 U.S.C. §15. The statute identifies other significant dates. See, e.g., §7 (specifying December 18 as the date electors "shall meet and give their votes"); §12 (specifying "the fourth Wednesday in December"—this year, December 27—as the date on which Congress, if it has not received a State's electoral votes, shall request the state secretary of state to send a certified return immediately). But none of these dates has ultimate significance in light of Congress's detailed provisions for determining, on "the sixth day of January," the validity of electoral votes.

The Court assumes that time will not permit "orderly judicial review of any disputed matters that might arise." But no one has doubted the good faith and diligence with which Florida election officials, attorneys for all sides of this controversy, and the courts of law have performed their duties. Notably, the Florida Supreme Court has produced two substantial opinions within 29 hours of oral argument. In sum, the Court's conclusion that a constitutionally adequate recount is impractical is a prophecy the Court's own judgment will not allow to be tested. Such an untested prophecy should not decide the Presidency of the United States. I dissent.

Justice BREYER, with whom Justice STEVENS and Justice GINSBURG join except as to Part I-A-1, and with whom Justice SOUTER joins as to Part I, dissenting.

The Court was wrong to take this case. It was wrong to grant a stay. It should now vacate that stay and permit the Florida Supreme Court to decide whether the recount should resume.

I

The political implications of this case for the country are momentous. But the federal legal questions presented, with one exception, are insubstantial.

The majority raises three Equal Protection problems with the Florida Supreme Court's recount order: first, the failure to include overvotes in the manual recount; second, the fact that all ballots, rather than simply the undervotes, were recounted in some, but not all, counties; and third, the absence of a uniform, specific standard to guide the recounts. As far as the first issue is concerned, petitioners presented no evidence, to this Court or to any Florida court, that a manual recount of overvotes would identify additional legal votes. The same is true of the second, and, in addition, the majority's reasoning would seem to invalidate any state provision for a manual recount of individual counties in a statewide election.

The majority's third concern does implicate principles of fundamental fairness. The majority concludes that the Equal Protection Clause requires that a manual recount be governed not only by the uniform general standard of the "clear intent of the voter," but also by uniform subsidiary standards (for example, a uniform determination whether indented, but not perforated, "undervotes" should count). The opinion points out that the Florida Supreme Court ordered the inclusion of Broward County's undercounted "legal votes" even though those votes included ballots that were not perforated but simply "dimpled," while newly recounted ballots from other counties will likely include only votes determined to be "legal" on the basis of a stricter standard. In light of our previous remand, the Florida Supreme Court may have been reluctant to adopt a more specific standard than that provided for by the legislature for fear of exceeding its authority under Article II. However, since the use of different standards could favor one or the other of the candidates, since time was, and is, too short to permit the lower courts to iron out significant differences through ordinary judicial review, and since the relevant distinction was embodied in the order of the State's highest court, I agree that, in these very special circumstances, basic principles of fairness may well have counseled the adoption of a uniform standard to address the problem. In light of the majority's disposition, I need not decide whether, or the extent to which, as a remedial matter, the Constitution would place limits upon the content of the uniform standard.

Nonetheless, there is no justification for the majority's remedy, which is simply to reverse the lower court and halt the recount entirely. An appropriate remedy would be, instead, to remand this case with instructions that, even at this late date, would permit the Florida Supreme Court to require recounting all under-counted votes in Florida, including those from Broward, Volusia, Palm Beach, and Miami-Dade Counties, whether or not previously recounted prior to the end of the protest period, and to do so in accordance with a single-uniform substandard.

The majority justifies stopping the recount entirely on the ground that there is no more time. In particular, the majority relies on the lack of time for the Secretary to review and approve equipment needed to separate undervotes. But the majority reaches this conclusion in the absence of any record evidence that the recount could not have been completed in the time allowed by the Florida Supreme Court. The majority finds facts outside of the record on matters that state courts are in a far better position to address. Of course, it is too late for any such recount to take place by December 12, the date by which election disputes must be decided if a State is to take advantage of the safe harbor provisions of 3 U.S.C. §5. Whether there is time to conduct a recount prior to December 18, when the electors are scheduled to meet, is a matter for the state courts to determine. And whether, under Florida law, Florida could or could not take further action is obviously a matter for Florida courts, not this Court, to decide.

By halting the manual recount, and thus ensuring that the uncounted legal votes will not be counted under any standard, this Court crafts a remedy out of proportion to the asserted harm. And that remedy harms the very fairness interests the Court is attempting to protect. The manual recount would itself redress a problem of unequal treatment of ballots. As Justice STEVENS points out, the ballots of voters in counties that use punch-card systems are more likely to be disqualified than those in counties using optical-scanning systems. According to recent news reports, variations in the undervote rate are even more pronounced. See Fessenden, No-Vote Rates Higher in Punch Card Count, N.Y. Times, Dec. 1, 2000, p. A29 (reporting that 0.3% of ballots cast in 30 Florida counties using optical-scanning systems registered no Presidential vote, in comparison to 1.53% in the 15 counties using Votomatic punch card ballots). Thus, in a system that allows counties to use different types of voting systems, voters already arrive at the polls with an unequal chance that their votes will be counted. I do not see how the fact that this results from counties' selection of different voting machines rather than a court order makes the outcome any more fair. Nor do I understand why the Florida Supreme Court's recount order, which helps to redress this inequity, must be entirely prohibited based on a deficiency that could easily be remedied.

II

Despite the reminder that this case involves "an election for the President of the United States," no preeminent legal concern, or practical concern related to legal questions, required this Court to hear this case, let alone to issue a stay that stopped Florida's recount process in its tracks. With one exception, petitioners' claims do not ask us to vindicate a constitutional provision designed to protect a basic human right. Petitioners invoke fundamental fairness, namely, the need for procedural fairness, including finality. But with the one "equal protection" exception, they rely upon law that focuses, not upon that basic need, but upon the constitutional allocation of power. Respondents invoke a competing fundamental consideration — the need to determine the voter's true intent. But they look to state law, not to federal constitutional law, to protect that interest. Neither side claims electoral fraud, dishonesty, or the like. And the more fundamental equal protection claim might have been left to the state court to resolve if and when it was discovered to have mattered. It could still be resolved through a remand conditioned upon issuance of a uniform standard; it does not require reversing the Florida Supreme Court.

Of course, the selection of the President is of fundamental national importance. But that importance is political, not legal. And this Court should resist the temptation unnecessarily to resolve tangential legal disputes, where doing so threatens to determine the outcome of the election.

The Constitution and federal statutes themselves make clear that restraint is appropriate. They set forth a road map of how to resolve disputes about electors, even after an election as close as this one. That road map foresees resolution of electoral disputes by state courts. But it nowhere provides for involvement by the United States Supreme Court.

To the contrary, the Twelfth Amendment commits to Congress the authority and responsibility to count electoral votes. A federal statute, the Electoral Count Act, enacted after the close 1876 Hayes-Tilden Presidential election, specifies that, after States have tried to resolve disputes (through "judicial" or other means), Congress is the body primarily authorized to resolve remaining disputes. The legislative history of the Act makes clear its intent to commit the power to resolve such disputes to Congress, rather than the courts.

Those who caution judicial restraint in resolving political disputes have described the quintessential case for that restraint as a case marked, among other things, by the "strangeness of the issue," its "intractability to principled resolution," its "sheer momentousness, . . . which tends to unbalance judicial judgment," and "the inner vulnerability, the self-doubt of an institution which is electorally irresponsible and has no earth to draw strength from." Alexander Bickel, The Least Dangerous Branch (1962). Those characteristics mark this case.

At the same time, as I have said, the Court is not acting to vindicate a fundamental constitutional principle, such as the need to protect a basic human liberty. No other strong reason to act is present. Congressional statutes tend to obviate the need. And, above all, in this highly politicized matter, the appearance of a split decision runs the risk of undermining the public's confidence in the Court itself. That confidence is a public treasure. It has been built slowly over many years, some of which were marked by a Civil War and the tragedy of segregation. It is a vitally necessary ingredient of any successful effort to protect basic liberty and, indeed, the rule of law itself. We run no risk of returning to the days when a President (responding to this Court's efforts to protect the Cherokee Indians) might have said, "John Marshall has made his decision; now let him enforce it!" But we do risk a self-inflicted wound — a wound that may harm not just the Court, but the Nation.

I fear that in order to bring this agonizingly long election process to a definitive conclusion, we have not adequately attended to that necessary "check upon our own exercise of power," "our own sense of self-restraint." United States v. Butler (1936) (Stone, J., dissenting). Justice Brandeis once said of the Court, "The most important thing we do is not doing." What it does today, the Court should have left undone. I would repair the damage done as best we now can, by permitting the Florida recount to continue under uniform standards. I respectfully dissent.

ISSUES TO CONSIDER CONCERNING BUSH v. GORE

There are many issues to consider regarding Bush v. Gore. First, was the case justiciable? Gore did not raise justiciability issues in his briefs or at oral argument. Yet justiciability is jurisdictional; the Court must raise it on its own. The question is whether Bush had standing to raise the equal protection claims of the Florida voters. Also, was the case ripe for review at the time it was decided by the U.S. Supreme Court? Should the Court have found that the matter was a political question and left it to Congress to resolve?

Second, was the Court correct in finding a denial of equal protection? Seven of the justices expressed concern over a denial of equal protection from counting votes without uniform standards. However, it is notable that Justices Souter and Breyer, who shared this concern with the majority, did not file opinions "concurring in part and dissenting in part" but rather just dissented. How, exactly, was equal protection denied?

Third, was the Court justified in ending the counting in Florida? The Court, in its *per curiam* opinion, said that the Florida Supreme Court had indicated that it wanted to follow the December 12 deadline set by the federal "safe harbor" statute. Because it was December 12, the Supreme Court ordered an end to the counting. But because it was an issue of Florida state law, should the Supreme Court have remanded the case for the Florida Supreme Court to decide the content of Florida law under the unprecedented circumstances?

On December 13, 2000, the day after Bush v. Gore was decided, Al Gore conceded the election to George W. Bush. Rightly or wrongly, for the first time in history, the Supreme Court decided a presidential election.

J. CONSTITUTIONAL PROTECTION FOR ACCESS TO COURTS

The Supreme Court has spoken of "the fundamental constitutional right of access to the courts."[52] The Court long has said that the right to be heard in court is an essential aspect of due process. For example, in Windsor v. McVeigh, 93 U.S. 274 (1876), the Court spoke of the right to be heard as a principle that "lies at the foundation of all well-ordered systems of jurisprudence" and is "founded in the first principles of natural justice."

---

52. Bounds v. Smith, 430 U.S. 817, 828 (1977).

Additionally, the Court has held that discrimination among people as to access to the courts is subjected to strict scrutiny under equal protection. The Court has quoted the Magna Charta, "To no one will we sell, to no one will we refuse, or delay, right or justice. . . . No free man shall be taken or imprisoned, . . . but by the lawful judgment of his peers or by the law of the land."[53] The Court has said that "[i]n this tradition, our own constitutional guaranties of due process and equal protection both call for procedures in criminal trials which allow no invidious discriminations between persons and different groups of persons."

Access to the courts also is protected by specific guarantees in the Bill of Rights, most notably by the Sixth Amendment's guarantee of the right to counsel in criminal cases. In Gideon v. Wainwright, 372 U.S. 335 (1963), the Supreme Court held that this right applies to the state and subsequently the Court clarified that states are constitutionally required to provide indigent defendants an attorney in all criminal cases where there is a punishment of imprisonment. In *Gideon*, the Court forcefully declared that "reason and reflection require us to recognize that in our adversary system of criminal justice, any person haled into court, who is too poor to hire a lawyer, cannot be assured a fair trial unless counsel is provided for him."

For example, the Court has held that wealth inequalities with regard to the appellate process unconstitutionally violate the right of access to the courts. Neither the text of the Constitution nor the Bill of Rights mentions a right to appeal. Nor has the Supreme Court held that due process requires appellate review of criminal convictions or civil judgments.[54] But the Court has ruled that when appeals are made available, the government cannot discriminate or create barriers that limit the ability of indigents to exercise this right. In Griffin v. Illinois, 351 U.S. 12 (1956), the Supreme Court concluded that the government must provide transcripts on appeal for indigent criminal defendants. Illinois law created a right to appeal criminal convictions, but direct appellate review was available only if the defendant provided the appellate court with a bill of exceptions or a report of the trial proceedings certified by the trial judge. It sometimes was impossible to prepare such documents without a stenographic transcript of the trial proceedings. Under state law these were provided free of charge only to defendants who had been sentenced to death. *Griffin* involved a defendant who had been sentenced for armed robbery and was kept from appealing solely because he lacked the funds to pay for a transcript.

The Supreme Court did not hold that there is a constitutional right to appeal, but did say that if state law creates such a right, the state may not "den[y] the poor an adequate appellate review accorded to all who have enough money to pay the costs in advance." The Court concluded that the state must purchase a stenographic transcript if the defendant could not afford one.

The Court also has found that the government must provide a free attorney to indigent defendants for their appeals, but the Court has limited this to first appeals where courts must review the case and has not extended the right

---

53. Griffin v. Illinois, 351 U.S. 12, 16-17 (1956).
54. *See* McKane v. Durston, 153 U.S. 684 (1894) (state is not obligated to provide an appeal for all criminal defendants).

to second, discretionary appeals or to collateral attacks on convictions. In Douglas v. California, 372 U.S. 353 (1963), decided the same day as Gideon v. Wainwright, the Court ruled that the government must provide indigent criminal defendants free counsel on appeal, at least for their initial appeal, which state law requires the courts of appeals to hear. The Court explained, "There is lacking that equality demanded by the Fourteenth Amendment where the rich man, who appeals as of right, enjoys the benefit of counsel's examination into the record, research of the law, and marshalling of arguments on his behalf, while the indigent, already burdened by a preliminary declaration that his case is without merit, is forced to shift for himself. The indigent, where the record is unclear or the errors are hidden, has only the right to a meaningless ritual, while the rich man has a meaningful appeal."

However, the Court subsequently limited this right to initial appeals that are created as a matter of right by state law; that is, appeals that state appellate courts are obligated to hear and decide. In Ross v. Moffitt, 417 U.S. 600 (1974), the Court held that the government is not required to appoint counsel for an indigent defendant's discretionary appeal to the highest state court or to the U.S. Supreme Court. *Ross* involved a criminal defendant who was provided with an attorney for his initial appeal to the state court of appeals, but was denied an attorney to seek discretionary review in the North Carolina Supreme Court or to file a petition for writ of certiorari in the U.S. Supreme Court.

The Supreme Court acknowledged that the lack of an attorney is a significant disadvantage in seeking such review, but it nonetheless found no constitutional violation in the government's refusing to pay for a lawyer at these stages for indigent defendants. The Court explained, "The duty of the State under our cases is not to duplicate the legal arsenal that may be privately retained by a criminal defendant in a continuing effort to reverse his conviction, but only to assure the indigent defendant an adequate opportunity to present his claims fairly in the context of State's appellate process. We think respondent was given that opportunity under the existing North Carolina system."

Similarly, the Court has held that the government is not required to provide free counsel to indigent defendants to bring collateral attacks on their convictions, such as through writs of habeas corpus. In Pennsylvania v. Finley, 481 U.S. 551 (1987), the Court said, "We have never held that prisoners have a constitutional right to counsel when mounting collateral attacks upon their convictions and we decline to so hold today. Our cases establish that the right to appointed counsel extends to the first appeal as of right, and no further." In Murray v. Giarratano, 492 U.S. 1 (1989), the Court went even further and held that the government is not required to provide indigent defendants sentenced to death with free counsel to pursue collateral attacks on their convictions and sentences. The Court reiterated that the government has the constitutional duty to provide counsel to indigent defendants only for their first appeal as of right and not for discretionary appeals or for collateral attacks. The Court expressly rejected the argument that a defendant facing a death sentence is entitled to special protection on appeal.

Two important areas in which the Court has considered the right of access to the courts are the constitutionality of filing fees and the ability of prisoners to use the judicial process.

FILING FEES

Despite strong statements of a right of equal access to the courts for rich and poor, the Court has been very inconsistent as to whether the government is constitutionally obligated to waive filing fees for indigent individuals in civil proceedings. In fact, generally, the Court has refused to find that filing fees impermissibly violate equal protection or due process. The leading case that found a filing fee requirement unconstitutional is Boddie v. Connecticut.

BODDIE v. CONNECTICUT
401 U.S. 371 (1971)

Justice HARLAN delivered the opinion of the Court.

Appellants, welfare recipients residing in the State of Connecticut, brought this action on behalf of themselves and others similarly situated, challenging, as applied to them, certain state procedures for the commencement of litigation, including requirements for payment of court fees and costs for service of process, that restrict their access to the courts in their effort to bring an action for divorce.

It appears from the briefs and oral argument that the average cost to a litigant for bringing an action for divorce is $60. There is no dispute as to the inability of the named appellants in the present case to pay either the court fees required by statute or the cost incurred for the service of process. The affidavits in the record establish that appellants' welfare income in each instance barely suffices to meet the costs of the daily essentials of life and includes no allotment that could be budgeted for the expense to gain access to the courts in order to obtain a divorce. Also undisputed is appellants' "good faith" in seeking a divorce.

Our conclusion is that, given the basic position of the marriage relationship in this society's hierarchy of values and the concomitant state monopolization of the means for legally dissolving this relationship, due process does prohibit a State from denying, solely because of inability to pay, access to its courts to individuals who seek judicial dissolution of their marriages.

As this Court on more than one occasion has recognized, marriage involves interests of basic importance in our society. See, e.g., Loving v. Virginia (1967). It is not surprising, then, that the States have seen fit to oversee many aspects of that institution. Without a prior judicial imprimatur, individuals may freely enter into and rescind commercial contracts, for example, but we are unaware of any jurisdiction where private citizens may covenant for or dissolve marriages without state approval. Even where all substantive requirements are concededly met, we know of no instance where two consenting adults may divorce and mutually liberate themselves from the constraints of legal obligations that go with marriage, and more fundamentally the prohibition against remarriage, without invoking the State's judicial machinery.

Thus, although they assert here due process rights as would-be plaintiffs, we think appellants' plight, because resort to the state courts is the only avenue to dissolution of their marriages, is akin to that of defendants faced with exclusion from the only forum effectively empowered to settle their disputes. Resort to the judicial process by these plaintiffs is no more voluntary in a realistic sense than that of the defendant called upon to defend his interests in court. For both groups this process is not only the paramount dispute-settlement technique, but, in fact, the only available one. In this posture we think that this appeal is properly to be resolved in light of the principles enunciated in our due process decisions that delimit rights of defendants compelled to litigate their differences in the judicial forum.

These due process decisions, representing over a hundred years of effort by this Court to give concrete embodiment to this concept, provide, we think, complete vindication for appellants' contentions. Prior cases establish that due process requires, at a minimum, that absent a countervailing state interest of overriding significance, persons forced to settle their claims of right and duty through the judicial process must be given a meaningful opportunity to be heard. Drawing upon [this] principle, we conclude that the State's refusal to admit these appellants to its courts, the sole means in Connecticut for obtaining a divorce, must be regarded as the equivalent of denying them an opportunity to be heard upon their claimed right to a dissolution of their marriages, and, in the absence of a sufficient countervailing justification for the State's action, a denial of due process.

The arguments for this kind of fee and cost requirement are that the State's interest in the prevention of frivolous litigation is substantial, its use of court fees and process costs to allocate scarce resources is rational, and its balance between the defendant's right to notice and the plaintiff's right to access is reasonable. In our opinion, none of these considerations is sufficient to override the interest of these plaintiff-appellants in having access to the only avenue open for dissolving their allegedly untenable marriages. Not only is there no necessary connection between a litigant's assets and the seriousness of his motives in bringing suit, but it is here beyond present dispute that appellants bring these actions in good faith. Moreover, other alternatives exist to fees and cost requirements as a means for conserving the time of courts and protecting parties from frivolous litigation, such as penalties for false pleadings or affidavits, and actions for malicious prosecution or abuse of process, to mention only a few. In the same vein we think that reliable alternatives exist to service of process by a state-paid sheriff if the State is unwilling to assume the cost of official service. This is perforce true of service by publication which is the method of notice least calculated to bring to a potential defendant's attention the pendency of judicial proceedings. We think in this case service at defendant's last known address by mail and posted notice is equally effective as publication in a newspaper.

We are thus left to evaluate the State's asserted interest in its fee and cost requirements as a mechanism of resource allocation or cost recoupment. Such a justification was offered and rejected in Griffin v. Illinois (1956). In *Griffin* it was the requirement of a transcript beyond the means of the indigent that blocked access to the judicial process. While in *Griffin* the transcript could be waived as a convenient but not necessary predicate to court access, here the State invariably imposes the costs as a measure of allocating its judicial resources. Surely, then, the rationale of *Griffin* covers this case.

In concluding that the Due Process Clause of the Fourteenth Amendment requires that these appellants be afforded an opportunity to go into court to obtain a divorce, we wish to re-emphasize that we go no further than necessary to dispose of the case before us, a case where the bona fides of both appellants' indigency and desire for divorce are here beyond dispute. We do not decide that access for all individuals to the courts is a right that is, in all circumstances, guaranteed by the Due Process Clause of the Fourteenth Amendment so that its exercise may not be placed beyond the reach of any individual, for, as we have already noted, in the case before us this right is the exclusive precondition to the adjustment of a fundamental human relationship. The requirement that these appellants resort to the judicial process is entirely a state-created matter. Thus we hold only that a State may not, consistent with the obligations imposed on it by the Due Process Clause of the Fourteenth Amendment, pre-empt the right to dissolve this legal relationship without affording all citizens access to the means it has prescribed for doing so.

Justice BLACK, dissenting.

This is a strange case and a strange holding. Absent some specific federal constitutional or statutory provision, marriage in this country is completely under state control, and so is divorce. When the first settlers arrived here the power to grant divorces in Great Britain was not vested in that country's courts but in its Parliament. And as recently as 1888 this Court, in Maynard v. Hill, upheld a divorce granted by the Legislature of the Territory of Oregon. Since that time the power of state legislatures to grant divorces or vest that power in their courts seems not to have been questioned. It is not by accident that marriage and divorce have always been considered to be under state control. The institution of marriage is of peculiar importance to the people of the States. It is within the States that they live and vote and rear their children under laws passed by their elected representatives. The States provide for the stability of their social order, for the good morals of all their citizens, and for the needs of children from broken homes. The States, therefore, have particular interests in the kinds of laws regulating their citizens when they enter into, maintain, and dissolve marriages. The power of the States over marriage and divorce is complete except as limited by specific constitutional provisions.

The Court here holds, however, that the State of Connecticut has so little control over marriages and divorces of its own citizens that it is without power to charge them practically nominal initial court costs when they are without ready money to put up those costs. The Court holds that the state law requiring payment of costs is barred by the Due Process Clause of the Fourteenth Amendment of the Federal Constitution. Two members of the majority believe that the Equal Protection Clause also applies. I think the Connecticut court costs law is barred by neither of those clauses.

Civil lawsuits are not like government prosecutions for crime. Civil courts are set up by government to give people who have quarrels with their neighbors the chance to use a neutral governmental agency to adjust their differences. In such cases the government is not usually involved as a party, and there is no deprivation of life, liberty, or property as punishment for crime. Our Federal Constitution, therefore, does not place such private disputes on the same high level as it places criminal trials and punishment. There is consequently no necessity, no reason, why government should in civil trials be hampered or handicapped by the strict and rigid due process rules the Constitution has provided to protect people charged with crime.

One more thought about the Due Process and Equal Protection Clauses: neither, in my judgment, justifies judges in trying to make our Constitution fit the times, or hold laws constitutional or not on the basis of a judge's sense of fairness. The rules set out in the Constitution itself provide what is governmentally fair and what is not. Neither due process nor equal protection permits state laws to be invalidated on any such nonconstitutional standard as a judge's personal view of fairness. The people and their elected representatives, not judges, are constitutionally vested with the power to amend the Constitution. Judges should not usurp that power in order to put over their own views.

However, in subsequent cases not involving constitutional rights, the Court refused to extend *Boddie* to require a waiver of filing fees in other civil proceedings. Compare United States v. Kras, and consider whether the Court's distinctions of *Boddie* are persuasive.

UNITED STATES v. KRAS
409 U.S. 434 (1973)

Justice BLACKMUN delivered the opinion of the Court.

The Bankruptcy Act and one of this Court's complementary Orders in Bankruptcy impose fees and make the payment of those fees a condition to a discharge in voluntary bankruptcy. Appellee Kras, an indigent petitioner in bankruptcy, challenged the fees on Fifth Amendment grounds.

Robert William Kras presented his voluntary petition in bankruptcy to the United States District Court for the Eastern District of New York on May 28, 1971. The petition was accompanied by Kras' motion for leave to file and proceed in bankruptcy without payment of any of the filing fees as a condition precedent to discharge. The motion was supported by Kras' affidavit containing the following allegations that have not been controverted by the Government:

1. Kras resides in a 2½-room apartment with his wife, two children, ages 5 years and 8 months, his mother, and his mother's 6-year-old daughter. His younger child suffers from cystic fibrosis and is undergoing treatment in a medical center.

2. Kras has been unemployed since May 1969 except for odd jobs producing about $300 in 1969 and a like amount in 1970. His last steady job was as an insurance agent with Metropolitan Life Insurance Company. He was discharged by Metropolitan in 1969 when premiums he had collected were stolen from his home and he was unable to make up the amount to his employer. Metropolitan's claim against him has increased to over $1,000 and is one of the debts listed in his bankruptcy petition. He has diligently sought steady employment in New York City, but, because of unfavorable references from Metropolitan, he has been unsuccessful. Mrs. Kras was employed until March 1970, when she was forced to stop because of pregnancy. All her attention now will be devoted to caring for the younger child who is coming out of the hospital soon.

3. The Kras household subsists entirely on $210 per month public assistance received for Kras' own family and $156 per month public

assistance received for his mother and her daughter. These benefits are all expended for rent and day-to-day necessities. The rent is $102 per month. Kras owns no automobile and no asset that is non-exempt under the bankruptcy law. He receives no unemployment or disability benefit. His sole assets are wearing apparel and $50 worth of essential household goods. He has a couch of negligible value in storage on which a $6 payment is due monthly.

4. Because of his poverty, Kras is wholly unable to pay or promise to pay the bankruptcy fees, even in small installments. He has been unable to borrow money. The New York City Department of Social Services refuses to allot money for payment of the fees. He has no prospect of immediate employment.

5. Kras seeks a discharge in bankruptcy of $6,428.69 in total indebtedness in order to relieve himself and his family of the distress of financial insolvency and creditor harassment and in order to make a new start in life. It is especially important that he obtain a discharge of his debt to Metropolitan soon "because until that is cleared up Metropolitan will continue to falsely charge me with fraud and give me bad references which prevent my getting employment."

Kras contends that his case falls squarely within *Boddie*. The Government, on the other hand, stresses the differences between divorce (with which *Boddie* was concerned) and bankruptcy, and claims that *Boddie* is not controlling and that the fee requirements constitute a reasonable exercise of Congress's plenary power over bankruptcy.

We agree with the Government that our decision in *Boddie* does not control the disposition of this case and that the District Court's reliance upon *Boddie* is misplaced.

A. *Boddie* was based on the notion that a State cannot deny access, simply because of one's poverty, to a "judicial proceeding [that is] the only effective means of resolving the dispute at hand." Throughout the opinion there is constant and recurring reference to Connecticut's exclusive control over the establishment, enforcement, and dissolution of the marital relationship. The Court emphasized that "marriage involves interests of basic importance in our society," and spoke of "state monopolization of the means for legally dissolving this relationship." "[R]esort to the state courts [was] the only avenue to dissolution of . . . marriages," which was "not only the paramount dispute-settlement technique, but, in fact, the only available one." The Court acknowledged that it knew "of no instance where two consenting adults may divorce and mutually liberate themselves from the constraints of legal obligations that go with marriage, and more fundamentally the prohibition against remarriage, without invoking the State's judicial machinery." In the light of all this, we concluded that resort to the judicial process was "no more voluntary in a realistic sense than that of the defendant called upon to defend his interests in court" and we resolved the case "in light of the principles enunciated in our due process decisions that delimit rights of defendants compelled to litigate their differences in the judicial forum."

B. The appellants in *Boddie*, on the one hand, and Robert Kras, on the other, stand in materially different postures. The denial of access to the judicial forum in *Boddie* touched directly, as has been noted, on the marital relationship and on the associational interests that surround the establishment and dissolution of that relationship. On many occasions we have recognized the fundamental importance of these interests under our Constitution. The *Boddie* appellants' inability to dissolve their marriages seriously impaired their freedom to pursue other protected associational activities. Kras' alleged interest in the elimination of his debt burden, and in obtaining his desired new start in life, although important and so recognized by the enactment of the Bankruptcy Act, does not rise to the same constitutional level. If Kras is not discharged in bankruptcy, his position will not be materially altered in any constitutional sense. Gaining or not gaining a discharge will effect no change with respect to basic necessities. We see no fundamental interest that is gained or lost depending on the availability of a discharge in bankruptcy.

C. Nor is the Government's control over the establishment, enforcement, or dissolution of debts nearly so exclusive as Connecticut's control over the marriage relationship in *Boddie*. In contrast with divorce, bankruptcy is not the only method available to a debtor for the adjustment of his legal relationship with his creditors. The utter exclusiveness of court access and court remedy, as has been noted, was a potent factor in *Boddie*. But "[w]ithout a prior judicial imprimatur, individuals may freely enter into and rescind commercial contracts. . . ."

However unrealistic the remedy may be in a particular situation, a debtor, in theory, and often in actuality, may adjust his debts by negotiated agreement with his creditors. At times the happy passage of the applicable limitation period, or other acceptable creditor arrangement, will provide the answer. Government's role with respect to the private commercial relationship is qualitatively and quantitatively different from its role in the establishment, enforcement, and dissolution of marriage. Resort to the court, therefore, is not Kras' sole path to relief. *Boddie*'s emphasis on exclusivity finds no counterpart in the bankrupt's situation.

[D.] There is no constitutional right to obtain a discharge of one's debts in bankruptcy. The Constitution, Art. I, §8, cl. 4, merely authorizes the Congress to "establish . . . uniform Laws on the subject of Bankruptcies throughout the United States." The rational basis for the fee requirement is readily apparent. Congressional power over bankruptcy, of course, is plenary and exclusive.

[E.] If the $50 filing fees are paid in installments over six months as General Order No. 35(4) permits on a proper showing, the required average weekly payment is $1.92. If the payment period is extended for the additional three months as the Order permits, the average weekly payment is lowered to $1.28. This is a sum less than the payments Kras makes on his couch of negligible value in storage, and less than the price of a movie and little more than the cost of a pack or two of cigarettes. If, as Kras alleges in his affidavit, a discharge in bankruptcy will afford him that new start he so desires, and the Metropolitan then no longer will charge him with fraud and give him bad references, and if he really needs and desires that discharge, this much available revenue should be within his able-bodied reach when the adjudication in bankruptcy has stayed collection and has brought to a halt whatever harassment, if any, he may have sustained from creditors.

We decline to extend the principle of *Boddie* to the no-asset bankruptcy proceeding. That relief, if it is to be forthcoming, should originate with Congress.

Justice STEWART, with whom Mr. Justice DOUGLAS, Mr. Justice BRENNAN, and Mr. Justice MARSHALL join, dissenting.

On May 28, 1971, Robert Kras, the appellee, sought to file a voluntary petition in bankruptcy. In an accompanying affidavit, he described his economic plight. He resided in a 2½-room apartment with his wife, his two young children, his mother, and her child. His eight-month-old son had cystic fibrosis and at the time of the affidavit was undergoing hospital treatment. Unemployed since May 1969, except for odd jobs, he supported his household on a total public assistance allotment of $366 per month — all of which was consumed on rent and the most basic necessities of life. His sole assets consisted of $50 worth of clothing and essential household goods.

Boddie held that a Connecticut statute requiring the payment of an average $60 fee as a prerequisite to a divorce action was unconstitutional under the Due Process Clause of the Fourteenth Amendment, as applied to indigents unable to pay the fee. The violation of due process seems to me equally clear in the present case. It is undisputed that Kras is making a good-faith attempt to obtain a discharge in bankruptcy, and that he is in fact indigent. As was true in *Boddie*, the "welfare income . . . barely suffices to meet the costs of the daily essentials of life and includes no allotment that could be budgeted for the expense to gain access to the courts. . . ."

Similarly, the debtor, like the married plaintiffs in *Boddie*, originally entered into his contract freely and voluntarily. But it is the Government nevertheless that continues to enforce that obligation, and under our "legal system" that debt is effective only because the judicial machinery is there to collect it. The bankrupt is bankrupt precisely for the reason that the State stands ready to exact all of his debts through garnishment, attachment, and the panoply of other creditor remedies. The appellee can be pursued and harassed by his creditors since they hold his legally enforceable debts.

And in the unique situation of the indigent bankrupt, the Government provides the only effective means of his ever being free of these Government-imposed obligations. As in *Boddie*, there are no "recognized, effective alternatives." While the creditors of a bankrupt with assets might well desire to reach a compromise settlement, that possibility is foreclosed to the truly indigent bankrupt. With no funds and not even a sufficient prospect of income to be able to promise the payment of a $50 fee in weekly installments of $1.28, the assetless bankrupt has absolutely nothing to offer his creditors. And his creditors have nothing to gain by allowing him to escape or reduce his debts; their only hope is that eventually he might make enough income for them to attach. Unless the Government provides him access to the bankruptcy court, Kras will remain in the totally hopeless situation he now finds himself. The Government has thus truly pre-empted the only means for the indigent bankrupt to get out from under a lifetime burden of debt.

Justice MARSHALL, dissenting.

The dissent of Justice Stewart, in which I have joined, makes clear the majority's failure to distinguish this case from Boddie v. Connecticut (1971). I add only some comments on the extraordinary route by which the majority reaches its conclusion.

The majority notes that the minimum amount that appellee Kras must pay each week if he is permitted to pay the filing fees in installments is only $1.28. It says that "this much available revenue should be within his able-bodied reach." Appellee submitted an affidavit in which he claimed that he was "unable to pay or promise to pay the filing fees, even in small installments." This claim was supported by detailed statements of his financial condition.

I cannot agree with the majority that it is so easy for the desperately poor to save $1.92 each week over the course of six months. The 1970 Census found that over 800,000 families in the Nation had annual incomes of less than $1,000 or $19.23 a week. I see no reason to require that families in such straits sacrifice over 5% of their annual income as a prerequisite to getting a discharge in bankruptcy.

It may be easy for some people to think that weekly savings of less than $2 are no burden. But no one who has had close contact with poor people can fail to understand how close to the margin of survival many of them are. A sudden illness, for example, may destroy whatever savings they may have accumulated, and by eliminating a sense of security may destroy the incentive to save in the future. A pack or two of cigarettes may be, for them, not a routine purchase but a luxury indulged in only rarely. The desperately poor almost never go to see a movie, which the majority seems to believe is an almost weekly activity. They have more important things to do with what little money they have — like attempting to provide some comforts for a gravely ill child, as Kras must do.

It is perfectly proper for judges to disagree about what the Constitution requires. But it is disgraceful for an interpretation of the Constitution to be premised upon unfounded assumptions about how people live.

In Ortwein v. Schwab, 410 U.S. 656 (1973), the Court followed the reasoning in *Kras* and held that the government was not obligated to waive filing fees for judicial review of adverse welfare decisions. An individual sought judicial review of a reduction in his welfare benefits, but he could not afford the $25 filing fee. The Supreme Court found no violation of due process or equal protection in precluding judicial review because of the inability to pay the fee. The Court relied on *Kras* and again distinguished *Boddie* on the ground that a denial or reduction in welfare benefits did not implicate constitutional rights. Interestingly, in *Ortwein*, as in *Boddie*, the state had a monopoly for resolving disputes: Only judicial review could reverse the denial of welfare benefits. Nonetheless, the Court found no constitutional violation in denying judicial review because of an inability to pay the filing fee.

Although *Boddie* and *Ortwein* make it very difficult to challenge filing fee requirements, it is still possible in areas where fundamental rights are at issue and where the state has a monopoly in providing redress. In M.L.B. v. S.L.J., 519 U.S. 102 (1996), the Supreme Court declared unconstitutional a state requirement that parents pay a fee for preparation of the trial record in order to appeal a termination of custody. A Mississippi court entered an order permanently terminating a mother's custody of her child. The mother sought to appeal from the termination decree, but Mississippi required that she pay in advance record preparation fees estimated at $2,352.36. Because she lacked funds to pay the fees, her appeal was dismissed.

The Court, in an opinion by Justice Ginsburg, found this constitutional. Justice Ginsburg began by stressing the fundamental rights involved: "Choices about marriage, family life, and the upbringing of children are among associational rights this Court has ranked as 'of basic importance in our society,' rights sheltered by the Fourteenth Amendment against the State's unwarranted usurpation, disregard, or disrespect."

The Court noted that access to the courts, as reflected in prior decisions, embodied "both equal protection and due process concerns." The Court said that generally access fees only have to meet rational basis review but that there is an exception in that "access to judicial processes in cases criminal or 'quasi criminal in nature,' [may not] turn on ability to pay." The Court said that proceedings to permanently terminate parental custody fit into the latter category because "termination adjudications involve the awesome authority of the State 'to destroy permanently all legal recognition of the parental relationship.'" Thus, the imposition of costs for the record preparation was declared unconstitutional.

PRISONERS' RIGHT OF ACCESS TO THE COURTS

One area where, until recently, the Court has been protective of a right of access to the courts is for prisoners. In Ex parte Hull, 312 U.S. 546 (1941), the Court said that "the state and its officers may not abridge or impair petitioner's right to apply to a federal court for a writ of habeas corpus." In *Hull*, the Court declared unconstitutional actions by prison officials in repeatedly seizing and destroying habeas corpus petitions prepared by a prison inmate.

In Johnson v. Avery, 393 U.S. 483 (1969), the Supreme Court declared unconstitutional a state prison regulation that provided that no inmate could advise or assist another inmate in preparing writs or giving legal assistance. The Court said that unless the state provides reasonable alternatives in assisting inmates with post-conviction proceedings, it may not enforce a regulation that bars inmates from assisting other prisoners. The Court said that because "the basic purpose of the writ is to enable those unlawfully incarcerated to obtain their freedom, it is fundamental that access of prisoners to the courts for the purpose of presenting their complaints may not be denied or obstructed."

The Court followed this reasoning in Procunier v. Martinez, 416 U.S. 396 (1974), and declared unconstitutional a prison regulation that prevented law students and paralegals from conducting attorney-client interviews with clients. The Court said that "[t]he constitutional guarantee of due process of law has as a corollary the requirement that prisoners be afforded access to the courts in order to challenge unlawful convictions and to seek redress for violations of their opportunity to seek and receive the assistance of attorneys." The Court concluded that the state had no interest in barring all law students and paralegals from the prison.

In Bounds v. Smith, 430 U.S. 817 (1977), the Court extended this reasoning and held that prisons were obligated to provide law library facilities and appropriate supplies to inmates. *Bounds* is particularly important because of its declaration of a fundamental right of access to the courts and its protection of this for prisoners.

BOUNDS v. SMITH, 430 U.S. 817 (1977): Justice MARSHALL delivered the opinion of the Court.

The issue in this case is whether States must protect the right of prisoners to access to the courts by providing them with law libraries or alternative sources of legal knowledge. Respondents are inmates incarcerated in correctional facilities of the Division of Prisons of the North Carolina Department of Correction. Respondents alleged, in pertinent part, that they were denied access to the courts in violation of their Fourteenth Amendment rights by the State's failure to provide legal research facilities.

It is now established beyond doubt that prisoners have a constitutional right of access to the courts. More recent decisions have struck down restrictions and required remedial measures to insure that inmate access to the courts is adequate, effective, and meaningful. Moreover, our decisions have consistently required States to shoulder affirmative obligations to assure all prisoners meaningful access to the courts. It is indisputable that indigent inmates must be provided at state expense with paper and pen to draft legal documents, with notarial services to authenticate them, and with stamps to mail them. States must forgo collection of docket fees otherwise payable to the treasury and expend funds for transcripts. State expenditures are necessary to pay lawyers for indigent defendants at trial, Gideon v. Wainwright (1963), and in appeals as of right, Douglas v. California (1963). This is not to say that economic factors may not be considered, for example, in choosing the methods used to provide meaningful access. But the cost of protecting a constitutional right cannot justify its total denial. Thus, neither the availability of jailhouse lawyers nor the necessity for affirmative state action is dispositive of respondents' claims. The inquiry is rather whether law libraries or other forms of legal assistance are needed to give prisoners a reasonably adequate opportunity to present claimed violations of fundamental constitutional rights to the courts.

Although it is essentially true, as petitioners argue, that a habeas corpus petition or civil rights complaint need only set forth facts giving rise to the cause of action, it hardly follows that a law library or other legal assistance is not essential to frame such documents. It would verge on incompetence for a lawyer to file an initial pleading without researching such issues as jurisdiction, venue, standing, exhaustion of remedies, proper parties plaintiff and defendant, and types of relief available. Most importantly, of course, a lawyer must know what the law is in order to determine whether a colorable claim exists, and if so, what facts are necessary to state a cause of action.

If a lawyer must perform such preliminary research, it is no less vital for a pro se prisoner. Indeed, despite the "less stringent standards" by which a pro se pleading is judged, it is often more important that a prisoner complaint set forth a nonfrivolous claim meeting all procedural prerequisites, since the court may pass on the complaint's sufficiency before allowing filing in forma pauperis and may dismiss the case if it is deemed frivolous. Moreover, if the State files a response to a pro se pleading, it will undoubtedly contain seemingly authoritative citations. Without a library, an inmate will be unable to rebut the State's argument. It is not enough to answer that the court will evaluate the facts pleaded in light of the relevant law. Even the most dedicated trial judges are bound to overlook meritorious cases without the benefit of an adversary presentation.

We hold, therefore, that the fundamental constitutional right of access to the courts requires prison authorities to assist inmates in the preparation and filing of meaningful legal papers by providing prisoners with adequate law libraries or adequate assistance from persons trained in the law.

Justice STEWART, with whom the Chief Justice joins, dissenting.

Despite the Court's valiant efforts, I find its reasoning unpersuasive. More than 20 years of experience with pro se habeas corpus petitions as a Member of this Court and as a Circuit Judge have convinced me that "meaningful access" to the federal courts can seldom be realistically advanced by the device of making law libraries available to prison inmates untutored in their use. In the vast majority of cases, access to a law library will, I am convinced, simply result in the filing of pleadings heavily larded with irrelevant legalisms possessing the veneer but lacking the substance of professional competence.

Justice REHNQUIST, with whom the Chief Justice joins, dissenting.

The Court's reasoning today appears to be that we have long held that prisoners have a "right of access" to the courts in order to file petitions for habeas corpus, and that subsequent decisions have expanded this concept into what the Court today describes as a "meaningful right of access." So, we are told, the right of a convicted prisoner to "meaningful access" extends to requiring the State to furnish such prisoners law libraries to aid them in piecing together complaints to be filed in the courts. This analysis places questions of prisoner access on a "slippery slope," and I would reject it because I believe that the early cases upon which the Court relies have a totally different rationale from that which underlies the present holding. There is nothing in the United States Constitution which requires that a convict serving a term of imprisonment in a state penal institution pursuant to a final judgment of a court of competent jurisdiction have a "right of access" to the federal courts in order to attack his sentence.

In Lewis v. Casey, the Supreme Court greatly limited, and perhaps overruled, Bounds v. Smith both by limiting situations in which prisoners will have standing to enforce it and in expressly adopting a rational basis test for prison policies with regard to libraries and legal assistance. In reading *Lewis*, it is important to consider what an inmate now must show in order to have standing to bring a challenge and what circumstances, if any, would justify a court finding a prison library to be inadequate.

LEWIS v. CASEY
518 U.S. 343 (1996)

Justice SCALIA delivered the opinion of the Court.

Respondents are 22 inmates of various prisons operated by the Arizona Department of Corrections. In January 1990, they filed this class action "on behalf of all adult prisoners who are or will be incarcerated by the State of Arizona Department of Corrections," alleging that petitioners were "depriving [respondents] of their rights of access to the courts and counsel protected by the First, Sixth, and Fourteenth Amendments." The court identified a variety of shortcomings of the ADOC system, in matters ranging from the training of library staff, to the updating of legal materials, to the availability of photocopying services. In addition to these general findings, the court found that two groups of inmates were particularly affected by the system's inadequacies: "[l]ockdown prisoners" (inmates segregated from the general prison population for disciplinary or security reasons), who "are routinely denied physical access to the law library" and "experience severe interference with their access to the courts"; and illiterate or non-English-speaking inmates, who do not receive adequate legal assistance.

The requirement that an inmate alleging a violation of *Bounds* must show actual injury derives ultimately from the doctrine of standing, a constitutional principle that prevents courts of law from undertaking tasks assigned to the political branches. It is the role of courts to provide relief to claimants, in individual or class actions, who have suffered, or will imminently suffer, actual harm; it is not the role of courts, but that of the political branches, to shape the institutions of government in such fashion as to comply with the laws and the Constitution. In the context of the present case: It is for the courts to remedy past or imminent official interference with individual inmates' presentation of claims to the courts; it is for the political branches of the State and Federal Governments to manage prisons in such fashion that official interference with the presentation of claims will not occur.

The foregoing analysis would not be pertinent here if, as respondents seem to assume, the right at issue — the right to which the actual or threatened harm must pertain — were the right to a law library or to legal assistance. But *Bounds* established no such right. The right that *Bounds* acknowledged was the (already well-established) right of access to the courts.

In other words, prison law libraries and legal assistance programs are not ends in themselves, but only the means for ensuring "a reasonably adequate opportunity to present claimed violations of fundamental constitutional rights to the courts." Because *Bounds* did not create an abstract, freestanding right to a law library or legal assistance, an inmate cannot establish relevant actual injury simply by establishing that his prison's law library or legal assistance program is subpar in some theoretical sense. That would be the precise analog of the healthy inmate claiming constitutional violation because of the inadequacy of the prison infirmary. Insofar as the right vindicated by *Bounds* is concerned, "meaningful access to the courts is the touchstone," and the inmate therefore must go one step further and demonstrate that the alleged shortcomings in the library or legal assistance program hindered his efforts to pursue a legal claim. He might show, for example, that a complaint he prepared was dismissed for failure to satisfy some technical requirement which, because of deficiencies in the prison's legal assistance facilities, he could not have known. Or that he had suffered arguably actionable harm that he wished to bring before the courts, but was so stymied by inadequacies of the law library that he was unable even to file a complaint.

Although *Bounds* itself made no mention of an actual-injury requirement, it can hardly be thought to have eliminated that constitutional prerequisite. And actual injury is apparent on the face of almost all the opinions in the 35-year line of access-to-courts cases on which *Bounds* relied. It must be acknowledged that several statements in *Bounds* went beyond the right of access recognized in the earlier cases on which it relied, which was a right to bring to court a grievance that the inmate wished to present. These statements appear to suggest that the State must enable the prisoner to discover grievances, and to litigate effectively once in court. These elaborations upon the right of access to the courts have no antecedent in our pre-*Bounds* cases, and we now disclaim them. To demand the conferral of such sophisticated legal capabilities upon a mostly uneducated and indeed largely illiterate prison population is effectively to demand permanent provision of counsel, which we do not believe the Constitution requires.

Finally, we must observe that the injury requirement is not satisfied by just any type of frustrated legal claim. Nearly all of the access-to-courts cases in the *Bounds* line involved attempts by inmates to pursue direct appeals from the convictions for which they were incarcerated. In other words, *Bounds* does not guarantee inmates the wherewithal to transform themselves into litigating engines capable of filing everything from shareholder derivative actions to slip-and-fall claims. The tools it requires to be provided are those that the inmates need in order to attack their sentences, directly or collaterally, and in order to challenge the conditions of their confinement. Impairment of any other litigating capacity is simply one of the incidental (and perfectly constitutional) consequences of conviction and incarceration.

There are further reasons why the order here cannot stand. We held in Turner v. Safley (1987) that a prison regulation impinging on inmates' constitutional rights "is valid if it is reasonably related to legitimate penological interests." Such a deferential standard is necessary, we explained, "if 'prison administrators . . . , and not the courts, [are] to make the difficult judgments concerning institutional operations.' Subjecting the day-to-day judgments of prison officials to an inflexible strict scrutiny analysis would seriously hamper their ability to anticipate security problems and to adopt innovative solutions to the intractable problems of prison administration."

Justice THOMAS, concurring.

The Constitution charges federal judges with deciding cases and controversies, not with running state prisons. Yet, too frequently, federal district courts in the name of the Constitution effect wholesale takeovers of state correctional facilities and run them by judicial decree. This case is a textbook example. Dissatisfied with the quality of the law libraries and the legal assistance at Arizona's correctional institutions, the District Court imposed a statewide decree on the Arizona Department of Corrections (ADOC), dictating in excruciatingly minute detail a program to assist inmates in the filing of lawsuits — right down to permissible noise levels in library reading rooms. Such gross overreaching by a federal district court simply cannot be tolerated in our federal system. Principles of federalism and separation of powers dictate that exclusive responsibility for administering state prisons resides with the State and its officials.

In Bounds v. Smith (1977), we recognized as part of the State's constitutional obligations a duty to provide prison inmates with law libraries or other legal assistance at state expense, an obligation we described as part of a loosely defined "right of access to the courts" enjoyed by prisoners. While the Constitution may guarantee state inmates an opportunity to bring suit to vindicate their federal constitutional rights, I find no basis in the Constitution — and *Bounds* cited none — for the right to have the government finance the endeavor.

Justice STEVENS, dissenting.

The Fourteenth Amendment prohibits the States from depriving any person of life, liberty, or property without due process of law. While at least one 19th-century court characterized the prison inmate as a mere "slave of the State," Ruffin v. Commonwealth, 62 Va. 790 (1871), in recent decades this Court has repeatedly held that the convicted felon's loss of liberty is not total. See Turner v. Safley (1987). "Prison walls do not . . . separat[e] . . . inmates from the protections of the Constitution," and even convicted criminals retain some of the liberties enjoyed by all who live outside those walls in communities to which most prisoners will someday return.

The "well-established" right of access to the courts is one of these aspects of liberty that States must affirmatively protect. The right to claim a violation of a constitutional provision in a manner that will be recognized by the courts is also embedded in those rights recognized by the Constitution's text and our interpretations of it. Without the ability to access the courts and draw their attention to constitutionally improper behavior, all of us—prisoners and free citizens alike—would be deprived of the first—and often the only—"line of defense" against constitutional violations.

Even if we had reason to delve into standing requirements in this case, the Court's view of those requirements is excessively strict. I think it perfectly clear that the prisoners had standing, even absent the specific examples of failed complaints. There is a constitutional right to effective access, and if a prisoner alleges that he personally has been denied that right, he has standing to sue.

K. CONSTITUTIONAL PROTECTION FOR A RIGHT TO EDUCATION

The Supreme Court has refused to recognize a fundamental right to education. San Antonio Independent School District v. Rodriguez is the key case.

SAN ANTONIO INDEPENDENT SCHOOL DISTRICT v. RODRIGUEZ
411 U.S. 1 (1973)

Justice POWELL delivered the opinion of the Court.

This suit attacking the Texas system of financing public education was initiated by Mexican-American parents whose children attend the elementary and secondary schools in the Edgewood Independent School District, an urban school district in San Antonio, Texas. They brought a class action on behalf of schoolchildren throughout the State who are members of minority groups or who are poor and reside in school districts having a low property tax base.

I

The first Texas State Constitution, promulgated upon Texas' entry into the Union in 1845, provided for the establishment of a system of free schools.

Until recent times, Texas was a predominantly rural State and its population and property wealth were spread relatively evenly across the State. Sizable differences in the value of assessable property between local school districts became increasingly evident as the State became more industrialized and as rural-to-urban population shifts became more pronounced. The location of commercial and industrial property began to play a significant role in determining the amount of tax resources available to each school district. These growing disparities in population and taxable property between districts were responsible in part for increasingly notable differences in levels of local expenditure for education.

Recognizing the need for increased state funding to help offset disparities in local spending and to meet Texas' changing educational requirements, the state legislature in the late 1940s undertook a thorough evaluation of public education with an eye toward major reform. [T]he Texas Minimum Foundation School Program [was adopted and t]oday this Program accounts for approximately half of the total educational expenditures in Texas. The Program calls for state and local contributions to a fund earmarked specifically for teacher salaries, operating expenses, and transportation costs. The State, supplying funds from its general revenues, finances approximately 80% of the Program, and the school districts are responsible — as a unit — for providing the remaining 20%. Today every school district does impose a property tax from which it derives locally expendable funds in excess of the amount necessary to satisfy its Local Fund Assignment under the Foundation Program.

The school district in which appellees reside, the Edgewood Independent School District, has been compared throughout this litigation with the Alamo Heights Independent School District. This comparison between the least and most affluent districts in the San Antonio area serves to illustrate the manner in which the dual system of finance operates and to indicate the extent to which substantial disparities exist despite the State's impressive progress in recent years. Edgewood is one of seven public school districts in the metropolitan area. Approximately 22,000 students are enrolled in its 25 elementary and secondary schools. The district is situated in the core-city sector of San Antonio in a residential neighborhood that has little commercial or industrial property. The residents are predominantly of Mexican-American descent: approximately 90% of the student population is Mexican-American and over 6% is Negro. The average assessed property value per pupil is $5,960 — the lowest in the metropolitan area — and the median family income ($4,686) is also the lowest. At an equalized tax rate of $1.05 per $100 of assessed property — the highest in the metropolitan area — the district contributed $26 to the education of each child for the 1967-1968 school year above its Local Fund Assignment for the Minimum Foundation Program. The Foundation Program contributed $222 per pupil for a state-local total of $248. Federal funds added another $108 for a total of $356 per pupil.

Alamo Heights is the most affluent school district in San Antonio. Its six schools, housing approximately 5,000 students, are situated in a residential community quite unlike the Edgewood District. The school population is predominantly "Anglo," having only 18% Mexican-Americans and less than 1% Negroes. The assessed property value per pupil exceeds $49,000, and the median family income is $8,001. In 1967-1968 the local tax rate of $.85 per $100 of valuation yielded $333 per pupil over and above its contribution to the Foundation Program. Coupled with the $225 provided from that Program, the district was able to supply $558 per student. Supplemented by a $36 per-pupil grant from federal sources, Alamo Heights spent $594 per pupil.

This, then, establishes the framework for our analysis. We must decide, first, whether the Texas system of financing public education operates to the disadvantage of some suspect class or impinges upon a fundamental right explicitly or implicitly protected by the Constitution, thereby requiring strict judicial scrutiny. If not, the Texas scheme must still be examined to determine whether it rationally furthers some legitimate, articulated state purpose and therefore does not constitute an invidious discrimination in violation of the Equal Protection Clause of the Fourteenth Amendment.

II

[A]ppellees assert that the State's system impermissibly interferes with the exercise of a "fundamental" right and that accordingly the prior decisions of this Court require the application of the strict standard of judicial review.[55] It is this question—whether education is a fundamental right, in the sense that it is among the rights and liberties protected by the Constitution—which has so consumed the attention of courts and commentators in recent years. Nothing this Court holds today in any way detracts from our historic dedication to public education. But the importance of a service performed by the State does not determine whether it must be regarded as fundamental for purposes of examination under the Equal Protection Clause. It is not the province of this Court to create substantive constitutional rights in the name of guaranteeing equal protection of the laws. Thus, the key to discovering whether education is "fundamental" is not to be found in comparisons of the relative societal significance of education as opposed to subsistence or housing. Nor is it to be found by weighing whether education is as important as the right to travel. Rather, the answer lies in assessing whether there is a right to education explicitly or implicitly guaranteed by the Constitution.

Education, of course, is not among the rights afforded explicit protection under our Federal Constitution. Nor do we find any basis for saying it is implicitly so protected. As we have said, the undisputed importance of education will not alone cause this Court to depart from the usual standard for reviewing a State's social and economic legislation. It is appellees' contention, however, that education is distinguishable from other services and benefits provided by the State because it bears a peculiarly close relationship to other rights and liberties accorded protection under the Constitution. Specifically, they insist that education is itself a fundamental personal right because it is essential to the effective exercise of First Amendment freedoms and to intelligent utilization of the right to vote.

---

55. The Court also considered and rejected the claim that the Texas system for funding public schools was unconstitutional because it discriminated against the poor. For example, the Court concluded, "For these reasons—the absence of any evidence that the financing system discriminates against any definable category of 'poor' people or that it results in the absolute deprivation of education—the disadvantaged class is not susceptible of identification in traditional terms." This aspect of the case and of the use of equal protection to safeguard the poor from discrimination is discussed in Chapter 7. [Footnote by casebook author.]

Even if it were conceded that some identifiable quantum of education is a constitutionally protected prerequisite to the meaningful exercise of either right, we have no indication that the present levels of educational expenditures in Texas provide an education that falls short. Whatever merit appellees' argument might have if a State's financing system occasioned an absolute denial of educational opportunities to any of its children, that argument provides no basis for finding an interference with fundamental rights where only relative differences in spending levels are involved and where — as is true in the present case — no charge fairly could be made that the system fails to provide each child with an opportunity to acquire the basic minimal skills necessary for the enjoyment of the rights of speech and of full participation in the political process.

Furthermore, the logical limitations on appellees' nexus theory are difficult to perceive. How, for instance, is education to be distinguished from the significant personal interests in the basics of decent food and shelter? Empirical examination might well buttress an assumption that the ill-fed, ill-clothed, and ill-housed are among the most ineffective participants in the political process, and that they derive the least enjoyment from the benefits of the First Amendment.

It should be clear, for the reasons stated above and in accord with the prior decisions of this Court, that this is not a case in which the challenged state action must be subjected to the searching judicial scrutiny reserved for laws that create suspect classifications or impinge upon constitutionally protected rights. We need not rest our decision, however, solely on the inappropriateness of the strict-scrutiny test. A century of Supreme Court adjudication under the Equal Protection Clause affirmatively supports the application of the traditional standard of review, which requires only that the State's system be shown to bear some rational relationship to legitimate state purposes.

[W]e are urged to direct the States either to alter drastically the present system or to throw out the property tax altogether in favor of some other form of taxation. No scheme of taxation, whether the tax is imposed on property, income, or purchases of goods and services, has yet been devised which is free of all discriminatory impact. In such a complex arena in which no perfect alternatives exist, the Court does well not to impose too rigorous a standard of scrutiny lest all local fiscal schemes become subjects of criticism under the Equal Protection Clause.

In addition to matters of fiscal policy, this case also involves the most persistent and difficult questions of educational policy, another area in which this Court's lack of specialized knowledge and experience counsels against premature interference with the informed judgments made at the state and local levels. Education, perhaps even more than welfare assistance, presents a myriad of "intractable economic, social, and even philosophical problems." In such circumstances, the judiciary is well advised to refrain from imposing on the States inflexible constitutional restraints that could circumscribe or handicap the continued research and experimentation so vital to finding even partial solutions to educational problems and to keeping abreast of ever-changing conditions.

It must be remembered, also, that every claim arising under the Equal Protection Clause has implications for the relationship between national and state power under our federal system. Questions of federalism are always inherent in the process of determining whether a State's laws are to be accorded the traditional presumption of constitutionality, or are to be subjected instead to rigorous judicial scrutiny. While "[t]he maintenance of the principles of federalism is a foremost consideration in interpreting any of the pertinent constitutional provisions under which this Court examines state action," it would be difficult to imagine a case having a greater potential impact on our federal system than the one now before us, in which we are urged to abrogate systems of financing public education presently in existence in virtually every State.

Justice BRENNAN, dissenting.

Although I agree with my Brother WHITE that the Texas statutory scheme is devoid of any rational basis, and for that reason is violative of the Equal Protection Clause, I also record my disagreement with the Court's rather distressing assertion that a right may be deemed "fundamental" for the purposes of equal protection analysis only if it is "explicitly or implicitly guaranteed by the Constitution." As my Brother MARSHALL convincingly demonstrates, our prior cases stand for the proposition that "fundamentality" is, in large measure, a function of the right's importance in terms of the effectuation of those rights which are in fact constitutionally guaranteed. Thus, "[a]s the nexus between the specific constitutional guarantee and the nonconstitutional interest draws closer, the nonconstitutional interest becomes more fundamental and the degree of judicial scrutiny applied when the interest is infringed on a discriminatory basis must be adjusted accordingly."

Here, there can be no doubt that education is inextricably linked to the right to participate in the electoral process and to the rights of free speech and association guaranteed by the First Amendment. This being so, any classification affecting education must be subjected to strict judicial scrutiny, and since even the State concedes that the statutory scheme now before us cannot pass constitutional muster under this stricter standard of review, I can only conclude that the Texas school-financing scheme is constitutionally invalid.

Mr. Justice MARSHALL, with whom Mr. Justice DOUGLAS concurs, dissenting.

The Court today decides, in effect, that a State may constitutionally vary the quality of education which it offers its children in accordance with the amount of taxable wealth located in the school districts within which they reside. The majority's decision represents an abrupt departure from the mainstream of recent state and federal court decisions concerning the unconstitutionality of state educational financing schemes dependent upon taxable local wealth. More unfortunately, though, the majority's holding can only be seen as a retreat from our historic commitment to equality of educational opportunity and as unsupportable acquiescence in a system which deprives children in their earliest years of the chance to reach their full potential as citizens. The Court does this despite the absence of any substantial justification for a scheme which arbitrarily channels educational resources in accordance with the fortuity of the amount of taxable wealth within each district.

In my judgment, the right of every American to an equal start in life, so far as the provision of a state service as important as education is concerned, is far too vital to permit state discrimination on grounds as tenuous as those presented by this record. Nor can I accept the notion that it is sufficient to remit these appellees to the vagaries of the political process which, contrary to the majority's suggestion, has proved singularly unsuited to the task of providing a remedy for this discrimination. I, for one, am unsatisfied with the hope of an ultimate "political" solution sometime in the indefinite future while, in the meantime, countless children unjustifiably receive inferior educations that may "affect their hearts and minds in a way unlikely ever to be undone." Brown v. Board of Education (1954). I must therefore respectfully dissent.

The majority is, of course, correct when it suggests that the process of determining which interests are fundamental is a difficult one. But I do not think the problem is insurmountable. And I certainly do not accept the view that the process need necessarily degenerate into an unprincipled, subjective "picking-and-choosing" between various interests or that it must involve this Court in creating "substantive constitutional rights in the name of guaranteeing equal protection of the laws." Although not all fundamental interests are constitutionally guaranteed, the determination of which interests are fundamental should be firmly rooted in the text of the Constitution. The task in every case should be to determine the extent to which constitutionally guaranteed rights are dependent on interests not mentioned in the Constitution. As the nexus between the specific constitutional guarantee and the nonconstitutional interest draws closer, the nonconstitutional interest becomes more fundamental and the degree of judicial scrutiny applied when the interest is infringed on a discriminatory basis must be adjusted accordingly.

Thus, it cannot be denied that interests such as procreation, the exercise of the state franchise, and access to criminal appellate processes are not fully guaranteed to the citizen by our Constitution. But these interests have nonetheless been afforded special judicial consideration in the face of discrimination because they are, to some extent, interrelated with constitutional guarantees. Procreation is now understood to be important because of its interaction with the established constitutional right of privacy. The exercise of the state franchise is closely tied to basic civil and political rights inherent in the First Amendment. And access to criminal appellate processes enhances the integrity of the range of rights implicit in the Fourteenth Amendment guarantee of due process of law. Only if we closely protect the related interests from state discrimination do we ultimately ensure the integrity of the constitutional guarantee itself. This is the real lesson that must be taken from our previous decisions involving interests deemed to be fundamental.

Since the Court now suggests that only interests guaranteed by the Constitution are fundamental for purposes of equal protection analysis, and since it rejects the contention that public education is fundamental, it follows that the Court concludes that public education is not constitutionally guaranteed. It is true that this Court has never deemed the provision of free public education to be required by the Constitution. Nevertheless, the fundamental importance of education is amply indicated by the prior decisions of this Court, by the unique status accorded public education by our society, and by the close relationship between education and some of our most basic constitutional values.

Education directly affects the ability of a child to exercise his First Amendment rights, both as a source and as a receiver of information and ideas, whatever interests he may pursue in life. The opportunity for formal education may not necessarily be the essential determinant of an individual's ability to enjoy throughout his life the rights of free speech and association guaranteed to him by the First Amendment. But such an opportunity may enhance the individual's enjoyment of those rights, not only during but also following school attendance. Thus, in the final analysis, "the pivotal position of education to success in American society and its essential role in opening up to the individual the central experiences of our culture lend it an importance that is undeniable."

Of particular importance is the relationship between education and the political process. "Americans regard the public schools as a most vital civic institution for the preservation of a democratic system of government." Education serves the essential function of instilling in our young an understanding of and appreciation for the principles and operation of our governmental processes. Education may instill the interest and provide the tools necessary for political discourse and debate. Indeed, it has frequently been suggested that education is the dominant factor affecting political consciousness and participation. But of most immediate and direct concern must be the demonstrated effect of education on the exercise of the franchise by the electorate.

Appellees do not now seek the best education Texas might provide. They do seek, however, an end to state discrimination resulting from the unequal distribution of taxable district property wealth that directly impairs the ability of some districts to provide the same educational opportunity that other districts can provide with the same or even substantially less tax effort. The issue is, in other words, one of discrimination that affects the quality of the education which Texas has chosen to provide its children; and, the precise question here is what importance should attach to education for purposes of equal protection analysis of that discrimination. As this Court held in Brown v. Board of Education, the opportunity of education, "where the state has undertaken to provide it, is a right which must be made available to all on equal terms." The factors just considered, including the relationship between education and the social and political interests enshrined within the Constitution, compel us to recognize the fundamentality of education and to scrutinize with appropriate care the bases for state discrimination affecting equality of educational opportunity in Texas' school districts.

The Court seeks solace for its action today in the possibility of legislative reform. The Court's suggestions of legislative redress and experimentation will doubtless be of great comfort to the schoolchildren of Texas' disadvantaged districts, but considering the vested interests of wealthy school districts in the preservation of the status quo, they are worth little more. The possibility of legislative action is, in all events, no answer to this Court's duty under the Constitution to eliminate unjustified state discrimination. In this case we have been presented with an instance of such discrimination, in a particularly invidious form, against an individual interest of large constitutional and practical importance. To support the demonstrated discrimination in the provision of educational opportunity the State has offered a justification which, on analysis, takes on at best an ephemeral character. Thus, I believe that the wide disparities in taxable district property wealth inherent in the local property tax element of the Texas financing scheme render that scheme violative of the Equal Protection Clause.

In Kadrmas v. Dickinson Public Schools, 487 U.S. 450 (1988), the Court reaffirmed that education is not a fundamental right under the Equal Protection

Clause. *Kadrmas* involved a challenge brought by a poor family to a state law authorizing local school systems to charge a fee for use of school buses. The Court again reiterated that poverty is not a suspect classification and that discrimination against the poor has to meet only rational basis review. The Court said that education was not denied because the fee did not preclude the student from attending school. Hence, the Court said that rational basis review was appropriate and concluded that the plaintiffs "failed to carry the 'heavy burden' of demonstrating the challenged statute is both arbitrary and irrational."

Although the Court never has held that there is a fundamental right to education, the Court has recognized education's importance. In Plyler v. Doe, 457 U.S. 202 (1982), the Supreme Court declared unconstitutional a Texas law that provided a free public education to citizens and to children of documented immigrants but required undocumented immigrants to pay for their public education.[56] The Court ruled that the law denied equal protection and, in part, based this conclusion on the importance of education. Justice Brennan, writing for the Court, stated, "Public education is not a 'right' granted to individuals by the Constitution. But neither is it merely some governmental 'benefit' indistinguishable from other forms of social welfare legislation. Both the importance of education in maintaining our basic institutions, and the lasting impact of its deprivation on the life of the child, mark the distinction. . . . [E]ducation provides the basic tools by which individuals might lead economically productive lives to the benefit of us all. In sum, education has a fundamental role in maintaining the fabric of our society."

The Court emphasized the great harms to children if they are denied an education. The Court also stressed the unfairness of penalizing children because of the choices made by their parents. Thus, without declaring education to be a fundamental right or using strict scrutiny, the Court invalidated the Texas law.

The Court's refusal to find a fundamental right to education is consistent with its general unwillingness to hold that there are constitutional rights to affirmative services provided by the government. But there is a strong argument that education is different; education is essential for the exercise of constitutional rights, for economic opportunity, and ultimately for achieving equality. In fact, several state courts—including the Texas Supreme Court—have found a fundamental right to education under their state constitutions and have concluded that inequities in school funding are impermissible as a matter of state constitutional law.[57]

L. PROCEDURAL DUE PROCESS

Thus far, this chapter has focused on the protection of fundamental rights under due process and equal protection. The Due Process Clause also is used

---

56. *Plyler* is presented in detail in Chapter 7, in discussing equal protection for aliens.

57. *See, e.g.,* Serrano v. Priest, 557 P.2d 929 (Cal. 1977); Abbott v. Burke, 575 A.2d 359 (N.J. 1990); Tennessee Small School Systems v. McWherter, 851 S.W.2d 139 (Tenn. 1993); McDuffy v. Secretary of Education, 615 N.E.2d 516 (Mass. 1993); Rose v. Council for Better Education, 790 S.W.2d 186 (Ky. 1989); Edgewood Indep. School Dist. v. Kirby, 777 S.W.2d 391 (Tex. 1989).

in another way: to impose procedures on government when it takes away a person's life, liberty, or property. This is referred to as "procedural due process."

Procedural due process, as the phrase implies, refers to the procedures that the government must follow before it deprives a person of life, liberty, or property. Classic procedural due process issues concern what kind of notice and what form of hearing the government must provide when it takes a particular action.

"Substantive due process," as that phrase connotes, asks whether the government has an adequate reason for taking away a person's life, liberty, or property. In other words, substantive due process looks to whether there is sufficient justification for the government's action. Whether there is such justification depends very much on the level of scrutiny used. For example, if a law addresses an area where only rational basis review is applied, substantive due process is met as long as the law is rationally related to a legitimate government purpose. But if it concerns an area where strict scrutiny is used, such as for protecting fundamental rights, then the government will meet substantive due process only if it can prove that the law is necessary to achieve a compelling government purpose.

An illustration of the distinction between procedural and substantive due process can be found in the constitutional right of parents to custody of their children. The Supreme Court has held that parents have a liberty interest in the custody of their children.[58] Therefore, procedural due process requires that the government provide notice and a hearing, and that there be clear and convincing evidence of a need to terminate custody, before parental rights are permanently ended.[59] Because the right to custody is deemed a fundamental right, substantive due process requires that the government prove that terminating custody is necessary to achieve a compelling purpose, such as the need to prevent abuse or neglect of the child.[60]

Thus, it is possible to distinguish procedural and substantive due process based on the remedy sought. If the plaintiff is seeking to have a government action declared unconstitutional as violating a constitutional right, substantive due process is involved. But when a person or a group is seeking to have a government action declared unconstitutional because of the lack of adequate safeguards, such as notice and a hearing, procedural due process is the issue.

Procedural and substantive due process can involve some of the same questions. For example, for both, it often is necessary to define what is "liberty" or "property." If there is not a denial of life, liberty, or property, then the government does not have to provide procedural or substantive due process.

Procedural due process can be broken down into three basic questions: (1) Has there been a "deprivation"? (2) Is it of "life, liberty, or property"? (3) Is it without "due process of law"? Thus, subsection 1 of this section looks at what is a deprivation; subsection 2 considers whether it is of life, liberty, or property; and subsection 3 focuses on what procedures are required.

---

58. *See, e.g.,* Santosky v. Kramer, 455 U.S. 745 (1982); Little v. Streater, 452 U.S. 1 (1981); Stanley v. Illinois, 405 U.S. 645 (1972). The substantive due process aspect of this right is discussed above in this chapter.

59. *See* Santosky v. Kramer, 455 U.S. 745 (1982).

60. *See, e.g.,* Stanley v. Illinois, 405 U.S. 645 (1972) (rights of unmarried fathers); *but see* Michael H. v. Gerald D., 491 U.S. 110 (1989) (denying rights to unmarried fathers where the mother was married to another man at the time of the birth of the child), presented above.

1. *What Is a "Deprivation"?*

The text of the Due Process Clause prohibits the government from depriving a person of life, liberty, or property without due process of law. A crucial question, therefore, concerns the meaning of "deprive." Two main issues are discussed below: First, is government negligence sufficient to create a deprivation, or must there be a reckless or intentional government action? Second, when is the government's failure to protect a person from privately inflicted harms a deprivation?[61]

IS NEGLIGENCE SUFFICIENT TO CONSTITUTE A DEPRIVATION?

What mental state of the government actors is sufficient for there to be a "deprivation" by the government? In Daniels v. Williams, the Court held that government negligence is insufficient to state a claim under the Due Process Clause.

DANIELS v. WILLIAMS
474 U.S. 327 (1986)

Justice Rehnquist delivered the opinion of the Court.

We conclude that the Due Process Clause is simply not implicated by a negligent act of an official causing unintended loss of or injury to life, liberty, or property.

In this §1983 action, petitioner seeks to recover damages for back and ankle injuries allegedly sustained when he fell on a prison stairway. He claims that, while an inmate at the city jail in Richmond, Virginia, he slipped on a pillow negligently left on the stairs by respondent, a correctional deputy stationed at the jail. Respondent's negligence, the argument runs, "deprived" petitioner of his "liberty" interest in freedom from bodily injury, see Ingraham v. Wright (1977); because respondent maintains that he is entitled to the defense of sovereign immunity in a state tort suit, petitioner is without an "adequate" state remedy. Accordingly, the deprivation of liberty was without "due process of law."

The Due Process Clause of the Fourteenth Amendment provides: "[N]or shall any State deprive any person of life, liberty, or property, without due process of law." Historically, this guarantee of due process has been applied to deliberate decisions of government officials to deprive a person of life, liberty, or property. This history reflects the traditional and common-sense notion that the Due Process Clause, like its forebear in the Magna Carta, was "'intended to secure the individual from the arbitrary exercise of the powers of government.'" By requiring the government to follow appropriate procedures when its agents decide to "deprive any person of life, liberty, or property," the Due Process

---

61. These cases concerning what constitutes a deprivation also concern substantive due process. They are placed here because for procedural due process, as for substantive due process, the issue arises as to what is sufficient to constitute a deprivation.

Clause promotes fairness in such decisions. And by barring certain government actions regardless of the fairness of the procedures used to implement them, it serves to prevent governmental power from being "used for purposes of oppression."

We think that the actions of prison custodians in leaving a pillow on the prison stairs, or mislaying an inmate's property, are quite remote from the concerns just discussed. Far from an abuse of power, lack of due care suggests no more than a failure to measure up to the conduct of a reasonable person. To hold that injury caused by such conduct is a deprivation within the meaning of the Fourteenth Amendment would trivialize the centuries-old principle of due process of law.

Our Constitution deals with the large concerns of the governors and the governed, but it does not purport to supplant traditional tort law in laying down rules of conduct to regulate liability for injuries that attend living together in society. We have previously rejected reasoning that "'would make of the Fourteenth Amendment a font of tort law to be superimposed upon whatever systems may already be administered by the States.'"

That injuries inflicted by governmental negligence are not addressed by the United States Constitution is not to say that they may not raise significant legal concerns and lead to the creation of protectible legal interests. The enactment of tort claim statutes, for example, reflects the view that injuries caused by such negligence should generally be redressed. It is no reflection on either the breadth of the United States Constitution or the importance of traditional tort law to say that they do not address the same concerns. Where a government official's act causing injury to life, liberty, or property is merely negligent, "no procedure for compensation is constitutionally required."

Davidson v. Cannon, 474 U.S. 344 (1986), was a companion case to *Daniels*, decided the same day. In *Davidson*, a prisoner claimed that prison authorities violated his due process rights by failing to protect him from attack by another prisoner. The prisoner had been threatened and had informed prison authorities, but they inadvertently forgot about the message and the prisoner was subsequently seriously injured by the attack. Under New Jersey law, the prisoner could not bring an action to recover for the injuries against the guards or prison officials in state court.[62] The Court ruled, as in *Daniels*, that the allegation of government negligence was insufficient to state a claim under the Due Process Clause.

Lower courts have found that allegations of government recklessness or deliberate indifference, as well as claims of intentional wrongdoing, are sufficient to state a claim under the Due Process Clause. However, in County of Sacramento v. Lewis, the Supreme Court held that in emergency situations a standard much more protective of the government should be used.

---

62. N.J. Stat. Ann. §59:5-2(b)(4) ("Neither a public entity nor a public employee is liable for . . . any injury caused by a prisoner to any other prisoner.").

COUNTY OF SACRAMENTO v. LEWIS

523 U.S. 833 (1998)

Justice Souter delivered the opinion of the Court.

The issue in this case is whether a police officer violates the Fourteenth Amendment's guarantee of substantive due process by causing death through deliberate or reckless indifference to life in a high-speed automobile chase aimed at apprehending a suspected offender. We answer no, and hold that in such circumstances only a purpose to cause harm unrelated to the legitimate object of arrest will satisfy the element of arbitrary conduct shocking to the conscience, necessary for a due process violation.

I

On May 22, 1990, at approximately 8:30 p.m., petitioner James Everett Smith, a Sacramento County sheriff's deputy, along with another officer, Murray Stapp, responded to a call to break up a fight. Upon returning to his patrol car, Stapp saw a motorcycle approaching at high speed. It was operated by 18-year-old Brian Willard and carried Philip Lewis, respondents' 16-year-old decedent, as a passenger. Neither boy had anything to do with the fight that prompted the call to the police.

Stapp turned on his overhead rotating lights, yelled to the boys to stop, and pulled his patrol car closer to Smith's, attempting to pen the motorcycle in. Instead of pulling over in response to Stapp's warning lights and commands, Willard slowly maneuvered the cycle between the two police cars and sped off. Smith immediately switched on his own emergency lights and siren, made a quick turn, and began pursuit at high speed. For 75 seconds over a course of 1.3 miles in a residential neighborhood, the motorcycle wove in and out of oncoming traffic, forcing two cars and a bicycle to swerve off of the road. The motorcycle and patrol car reached speeds up to 100 miles an hour, with Smith following at a distance as short as 100 feet; at that speed, his car would have required 650 feet to stop.

The chase ended after the motorcycle tipped over as Willard tried a sharp left turn. By the time Smith slammed on his brakes, Willard was out of the way, but Lewis was not. The patrol car skidded into him at 40 miles an hour, propelling him some 70 feet down the road and inflicting massive injuries. Lewis was pronounced dead at the scene.

Since the time of our early explanations of due process, we have understood the core of the concept to be protection against arbitrary action. We have emphasized time and again that "[t]he touchstone of due process is protection of the individual against arbitrary action of government," whether the fault lies in a denial of fundamental procedural fairness, or in the exercise of power without any reasonable justification in the service of a legitimate governmental objective. While due process protection in the substantive sense limits what the government may do in both its legislative, and its executive capacities, criteria to identify what is fatally arbitrary differ depending on whether it is legislation or a specific act of a governmental officer that is at issue.

Our cases dealing with abusive executive action have repeatedly emphasized that only the most egregious official conduct can be said to be "arbitrary in the constitutional sense," thereby recognizing the point made in different circumstances by Chief Justice Marshall, "that it is a constitution we are expounding." To this end, for half a century now we have spoken of the cognizable level of executive abuse of power as that which shocks the conscience. We first put the test this way in Rochin v. California, where we found the forced pumping of a suspect's stomach enough to offend due process as conduct "that shocks the conscience" and violates the "decencies of civilized conduct." In the intervening years we have repeatedly adhered to *Rochin's* benchmark. While the measure of what is conscience-shocking is no calibrated yardstick, it does, as Judge Friendly put it, point[] the way."

It should not be surprising that the constitutional concept of conscience-shocking duplicates no traditional category of common-law fault, but rather points clearly away from liability, or clearly toward it, only at the ends of the tort law's spectrum of culpability. Thus, we have made it clear that the due process guarantee does not entail a body of constitutional law imposing liability whenever someone cloaked with state authority causes harm.

We have accordingly rejected the lowest common denominator of customary tort liability as any mark of sufficiently shocking conduct, and have held that the Constitution does not guarantee due care on the part of state officials; liability for negligently inflicted harm is categorically beneath the threshold of constitutional due process. See Daniels v. Williams. It is, on the contrary, behavior at the other end of the culpability spectrum that would most probably support a substantive due process claim; conduct intended to injure in some way unjustifiable by any government interest is the sort of official action most likely to rise to the conscience-shocking level.

As the very term "deliberate indifference" implies, the standard is sensibly employed only when actual deliberation is practical, and in the custodial situation of a prison, forethought about an inmate's welfare is not only feasible but obligatory under a regime that incapacitates a prisoner to exercise ordinary responsibility for his own welfare.

Like prison officials facing a riot, the police on an occasion calling for fast action have obligations that tend to tug against each other. Their duty is to restore and maintain lawful order, while not exacerbating disorder more than necessary to do their jobs. They are supposed to act decisively and to show restraint at the same moment, and their decisions have to be made "in haste, under pressure, and frequently without the luxury of a second chance." A police officer deciding whether to give chase must balance on one hand the need to stop a suspect and show that flight from the law is no way to freedom, and, on the other, the high-speed threat to everyone within stopping range, be they suspects, their passengers, other drivers, or bystanders.

To recognize a substantive due process violation in these circumstances when only mid-level fault has been shown would be to forget that liability for deliberate indifference to inmate welfare rests upon the luxury enjoyed by prison officials of having time to make unhurried judgments, upon the chance for repeated reflection, largely uncomplicated by the pulls of competing obligations. When such extended opportunities to do better are teamed with protracted failure even to care, indifference is truly shocking. But when unforeseen circumstances demand an officer's instant judgment, even precipitate recklessness fails to inch close enough to harmful purpose to spark the shock that implicates "the large concerns of the governors and the governed." Just as a purpose to cause harm is needed for Eighth Amendment liability in a riot case, so it ought to be needed for Due Process liability in a pursuit case. Accordingly, we hold that high-speed chases with no intent to harm suspects physically or to worsen their legal plight do not give rise to liability under the Fourteenth Amendment, redressible by an action under §1983.

The fault claimed on Smith's part in this case accordingly fails to meet the shocks-the-conscience test. The summary judgment proceedings revealed that the height of the fault actually claimed was "conscious disregard," the malice allegation having been made in aid of a request for punitive damages, but unsupported either in allegations of specific conduct or in any affidavit of fact offered on the motions for summary judgment.

Smith was faced with a course of lawless behavior for which the police were not to blame. They had done nothing to cause Willard's high-speed driving in the first place, nothing to excuse his flouting of the commonly understood law enforcement authority to control traffic, and nothing (beyond a refusal to call off the chase) to encourage him to race through traffic at breakneck speed forcing other drivers out of their travel lanes. Willard's outrageous behavior was practically instantaneous, and so was Smith's instinctive response. While prudence would have repressed the reaction, the officer's instinct was to do his job as a law enforcement officer, not to induce Willard's lawlessness, or to terrorize, cause harm, or kill. Prudence, that is, was subject to countervailing enforcement considerations, and while Smith exaggerated their demands, there is no reason to believe that they were tainted by an improper or malicious motive on his part.

Regardless whether Smith's behavior offended the reasonableness held up by tort law or the balance struck in law enforcement's own codes of sound practice, it does not shock the conscience, and petitioners are not called upon to answer for it under §1983.

WHEN IS THE GOVERNMENT'S FAILURE TO PROTECT A PERSON FROM PRIVATELY INFLICTED HARMS A DEPRIVATION?

In DeShaney v. Winnebago County Department of Social Services, the Supreme Court considered the government's duty under the Due Process Clause to protect individuals from privately inflicted harms.

DeSHANEY v. WINNEBAGO COUNTY DEPARTMENT OF SOCIAL SERVICES

489 U.S. 189 (1989)

Chief Justice REHNQUIST delivered the opinion of the Court.

Petitioner is a boy who was beaten and permanently injured by his father, with whom he lived. Respondents are social workers and other local officials who received complaints that petitioner was being abused by his father and had reason to believe that this was the case, but nonetheless did not act to remove petitioner from his father's custody. Petitioner sued respondents claiming that their failure to act deprived him of his liberty in violation of the Due Process Clause of the Fourteenth Amendment to the United States Constitution. We hold that it did not.

I

The facts of this case are undeniably tragic. Petitioner Joshua DeShaney was born in 1979. In 1980, a Wyoming court granted his parents a divorce and awarded custody of Joshua to his father, Randy DeShaney. The father shortly thereafter moved to Neenah, a city located in Winnebago County, Wisconsin, taking the infant Joshua with him. There he entered into a second marriage, which also ended in divorce.

The Winnebago County authorities first learned that Joshua DeShaney might be a victim of child abuse in January 1982, when his father's second wife complained to the police, at the time of their divorce, that he had previously "hit the boy causing marks and [was] a prime case for child abuse." The Winnebago County Department of Social Services (DSS) interviewed the father, but he denied the accusations, and DSS did not pursue them further. In January 1983, Joshua was admitted to a local hospital with multiple bruises and abrasions. The examining physician suspected child abuse and notified DSS, which immediately obtained an order from a Wisconsin juvenile court placing Joshua in the temporary custody of the hospital. Three days later, the county convened an ad hoc "Child Protection Team"—consisting of a pediatrician, a psychologist, a police detective, the county's lawyer, several DSS caseworkers, and various hospital personnel—to consider Joshua's situation. At this meeting, the Team decided that there was insufficient evidence of child abuse to retain Joshua in the custody of the court. The Team did, however, decide to recommend several measures to protect Joshua, including enrolling him in a preschool program, providing his father with certain counselling services, and encouraging his father's girlfriend to move out of the home. Randy DeShaney entered into a voluntary agreement with DSS in which he promised to cooperate with them in accomplishing these goals.

Based on the recommendation of the Child Protection Team, the juvenile court dismissed the child protection case and returned Joshua to the custody of his father. A month later, emergency room personnel called the DSS caseworker handling Joshua's case to report that he had once again been treated for suspicious injuries. The caseworker concluded that there was no basis for action. For the next six months, the caseworker made monthly visits to the DeShaney home, during which she observed a number of suspicious injuries on Joshua's head; she also noticed that he had not been enrolled in school, and that the girlfriend had not moved out. The caseworker dutifully recorded these incidents in her files, along with her continuing suspicions that someone in the DeShaney household was physically abusing Joshua, but she did nothing more. In November 1983, the emergency room notified DSS that Joshua had been treated once again for injuries that they believed to be caused by child abuse. On the caseworker's next two visits to the DeShaney home, she was told that Joshua was too ill to see her. Still DSS took no action.

In March 1984, Randy DeShaney beat 4-year-old Joshua so severely that he fell into a life-threatening coma. Emergency brain surgery revealed a series of hemorrhages caused by traumatic injuries to the head inflicted over a long period of time. Joshua did not die, but he suffered brain damage so severe that he is expected to spend the rest of his life confined to an institution for the profoundly retarded. Randy DeShaney was subsequently tried and convicted of child abuse.

Joshua and his mother brought this action under 42 U.S.C. §1983 in the United States District Court for the Eastern District of Wisconsin against respondents Winnebago County, DSS, and various individual employees of DSS. The complaint alleged that respondents had deprived Joshua of his liberty without due process of law, in violation of his rights under the Fourteenth Amendment, by failing to intervene to protect him against a risk of violence at his father's hands of which they knew or should have known.

Petitioners contend that the State deprived Joshua of his liberty interest in "free[dom] from . . . unjustified intrusions on personal security," see Ingraham v. Wright (1977), by failing to provide him with adequate protection against his father's violence. But nothing in the language of the Due Process Clause itself requires the State to protect the life, liberty, and property of its citizens against invasion by private actors. The Clause is phrased as a limitation on the State's power to act, not as a guarantee of certain minimal levels of safety and security. It forbids the State itself to deprive individuals of life, liberty, or property without "due process of law," but its language cannot fairly be extended to impose an affirmative obligation on the State to ensure that those interests do not come to harm through other means. Nor does history support such an expansive reading of the constitutional text. Like its counterpart in the Fifth Amendment, the Due Process Clause of the Fourteenth Amendment was intended to prevent government "from abusing [its] power, or employing it as an instrument of oppression." Its purpose was to protect the people from the State, not to ensure that the State protected them from each other. The framers were content to leave the extent of governmental obligation in the latter area to the democratic political processes.

Consistent with these principles, our cases have recognized that the Due Process Clauses generally confer no affirmative right to governmental aid, even where such aid may be necessary to secure life, liberty, or property interests of which the government itself may not deprive the individual. If the Due Process Clause does not require the State to provide its citizens with particular protective services, it follows that the State cannot be held liable under the Clause for injuries that could have been averted had it chosen to provide them. As a general matter, then, we conclude that a State's failure to protect an individual against private violence simply does not constitute a violation of the Due Process Clause.

Petitioners contend, however, that even if the Due Process Clause imposes no affirmative obligation on the State to provide the general public with adequate protective services, such a duty may arise out of certain "special relationships" created or assumed by the State with respect to particular individuals. Petitioners argue that such a "special relationship" existed here because the State knew that Joshua faced a special danger of abuse at his father's hands, and specifically proclaimed, by word and by deed, its intention to protect him against that danger. Having actually undertaken to protect

Joshua from this danger—which petitioners concede the State played no part in creating—the State acquired an affirmative "duty," enforceable through the Due Process Clause, to do so in a reasonably competent fashion. Its failure to discharge that duty, so the argument goes, was an abuse of governmental power that so "shocks the conscience," Rochin v. California (1952), as to constitute a substantive due process violation.

We reject this argument. It is true that in certain limited circumstances the Constitution imposes upon the State affirmative duties of care and protection with respect to particular individuals. In Estelle v. Gamble (1976), we recognized that the Eighth Amendment's prohibition against cruel and unusual punishment, made applicable to the States through the Fourteenth Amendment's Due Process Clause, requires the State to provide adequate medical care to incarcerated prisoners. We reasoned that because the prisoner is unable "by reason of the deprivation of his liberty [to] care for himself," it is only "just" that the State be required to care for him.

But these cases afford petitioners no help. Taken together, they stand only for the proposition that when the State takes a person into its custody and holds him there against his will, the Constitution imposes upon it a corresponding duty to assume some responsibility for his safety and general well-being. The rationale for this principle is simple enough: when the State by the affirmative exercise of its power so restrains an individual's liberty that it renders him unable to care for himself, and at the same time fails to provide for his basic human needs—e.g., food, clothing, shelter, medical care, and reasonable safety—it transgresses the substantive limits on state action set by the Eighth Amendment and the Due Process Clause. The affirmative duty to protect arises not from the State's knowledge of the individual's predicament or from its expressions of intent to help him, but from the limitation which it has imposed on his freedom to act on his own behalf.

Petitioners concede that the harms Joshua suffered occurred not while he was in the State's custody, but while he was in the custody of his natural father, who was in no sense a state actor. While the State may have been aware of the dangers that Joshua faced in the free world, it played no part in their creation, nor did it do anything to render him any more vulnerable to them. That the State once took temporary custody of Joshua does not alter the analysis, for when it returned him to his father's custody, it placed him in no worse position than that in which he would have been had it not acted at all; the State does not become the permanent guarantor of an individual's safety by having once offered him shelter. Under these circumstances, the State had no constitutional duty to protect Joshua. Because, as explained above, the State had no constitutional duty to protect Joshua against his father's violence, its failure to do so—though calamitous in hindsight—simply does not constitute a violation of the Due Process Clause.

The people of Wisconsin may well prefer a system of liability which would place upon the State and its officials the responsibility for failure to act in situations such as the present one. They may create such a system, if they do not have it already, by changing the tort law of the State in accordance with the regular lawmaking process. But they should not have it thrust upon them by this Court's expansion of the Due Process Clause of the Fourteenth Amendment.

Justice BRENNAN, with whom Justice MARSHALL and Justice BLACKMUN join, dissenting.

"The most that can be said of the state functionaries in this case," the Court today concludes, "is that they stood by and did nothing when suspicious circumstances dictated a more active role for them." Because I believe that this description of respondents' conduct tells only part of the story and that, accordingly, the Constitution itself "dictated a more active role" for respondents in the circumstances presented here, I cannot agree that respondents had no constitutional duty to help Joshua DeShaney.

It may well be, as the Court decides, that the Due Process Clause as construed by our prior cases creates no general right to basic governmental services. That, however, is not the question presented here; indeed, that question was not raised in the complaint, urged on appeal, presented in the petition for certiorari, or addressed in the briefs on the merits. No one, in short, has asked the Court to proclaim that, as a general matter, the Constitution safeguards positive as well as negative liberties.

It simply belies reality, therefore, to contend that the State "stood by and did nothing" with respect to Joshua. Through its child-protection program, the State actively intervened in Joshua's life and, by virtue of this intervention, acquired ever more certain knowledge that Joshua was in grave danger.

The Court's baseline is the absence of positive rights in the Constitution and a concomitant suspicion of any claim that seems to depend on such rights. From this perspective, the DeShaneys' claim is first and foremost about inaction (the failure, here, of respondents to take steps to protect Joshua), and only tangentially about action (the establishment of a state program specifically designed to help children like Joshua). And from this perspective, holding these Wisconsin officials liable — where the only difference between this case and one involving a general claim to protective services is Wisconsin's establishment and operation of a program to protect children — would seem to punish an effort that we should seek to promote.

I would begin from the opposite direction. I would focus first on the action that Wisconsin has taken with respect to Joshua and children like him, rather than on the actions that the State failed to take. I would recognize, as the Court apparently cannot, that "the State's knowledge of [an] individual's predicament [and] its expressions of intent to help him" can amount to a "limitation . . . on his freedom to act on his own behalf" or to obtain help from others.

Wisconsin has established a child-welfare system specifically designed to help children like Joshua. Wisconsin law places upon the local departments of social services such as respondent (DSS or Department) a duty to investigate reported instances of child abuse. See Wis. Stat. §48.981(3) (1987-1988). While other governmental bodies and private persons are largely responsible for the reporting of possible eases of child abuse, see §48.981(2), Wisconsin law channels all such reports to the local departments of social services for evaluation and, if necessary, further action. §48.981(3). Even when it is the sheriff's office or police department that receives a report of suspected child abuse, that report is referred to local social services departments for action, see §48.981(3)(a); the only exception to this occurs when the reporter fears for the child's immediate safety. §48.981(3)(b). The specific facts before us bear out this view of Wisconsin's system of protecting children. Each time someone voiced a suspicion that Joshua was being abused, that information was relayed to the Department for investigation and possible action.

In these circumstances, a private citizen, or even a person working in a government agency other than DSS, would doubtless feel that her job was done as soon as she had reported her suspicions of child abuse to DSS. Through its child-welfare program, in other words, the State of Wisconsin has relieved ordinary citizens and governmental bodies other than the Department of any sense of obligation to do anything more than report their suspicions of child abuse to DSS. If DSS ignores or dismisses these suspicions, no one will step in to fill the gap. Wisconsin's child-protection program thus effectively confined Joshua DeShaney within the walls of Randy DeShaney's violent home until such time as DSS took action to remove him. Conceivably, then, children like Joshua are made worse off by the existence of this program when the persons and entities charged with carrying it out fail to do their jobs.

As the Court today reminds us, "the Due Process Clause of the Fourteenth Amendment was intended to prevent government 'from abusing [its] power, or employing it as an instrument of oppression.'" My disagreement with the Court arises from its failure to see that inaction can be every bit as abusive of power as action, that oppression can result when a State undertakes a vital duty and then ignores it. Today's opinion construes the Due Process Clause to permit a State to displace private sources of protection and then, at the critical moment, to shrug its shoulders and turn away from the harm that it has promised to try to prevent. Because I cannot agree that our Constitution is indifferent to such indifference, I respectfully dissent.

Justice BLACKMUN, dissenting.

Today, the Court purports to be the dispassionate oracle of the law, unmoved by "natural sympathy." But, in this pretense, the Court itself retreats into a sterile formalism which prevents it from recognizing either the facts of the case before it or the legal norms that should apply to those facts. As Justice Brennan demonstrates, the facts here involve not mere passivity, but active state intervention in the life of Joshua DeShaney — intervention that triggered a fundamental duty to aid the boy once the State learned of the severe danger to which he was exposed.

The Court fails to recognize this duty because it attempts to draw a sharp and rigid line between action and inaction. But such formalistic reasoning has no place in the interpretation of the broad and stirring Clauses of the Fourteenth Amendment. Like the antebellum judges who denied relief to fugitive slaves, the Court today claims that its decision, however harsh, is compelled by existing legal doctrine. On the contrary, the question presented by this case is an open one, and our Fourteenth Amendment precedents may be read more broadly or narrowly depending upon how one chooses to read them. Faced with the choice, I would adopt a "sympathetic" reading, one which comports with dictates of fundamental justice and recognizes that compassion need not be exiled from the province of judging.

Poor Joshua! Victim of repeated attacks by an irresponsible, bullying, cowardly, and intemperate father, and abandoned by respondents who placed him in a dangerous predicament and who knew or learned what was going on, and yet did essentially nothing except, as the Court revealingly observes, "dutifully recorded these incidents in [their] files." It is a sad commentary upon American life, and constitutional principles — so full of late of patriotic fervor and proud proclamations about "liberty and justice for all" — that this child, Joshua DeShaney, now is assigned to live out the remainder of his life profoundly retarded. Joshua and his mother, as petitioners here, deserve — but now are denied by this Court — the opportunity to have the facts of their case considered in the light of the constitutional protection that 42 U.S.C. §1983 is meant to provide.

In Town of Castle Rock v. Gonzales, 545 U.S. 748 (2005), the Court concluded that there was no duty to provide protection even if state law required police to enforce restraining orders.

TOWN OF CASTLE ROCK v. GONZALES
545 U.S. 748 (2005)

Justice SCALIA delivered the opinion of the Court.

We decide in this case whether an individual who has obtained a state-law restraining order has a constitutionally protected property interest in having the police enforce the restraining order when they have probable cause to believe it has been violated.

I

The horrible facts of this case are contained in the complaint that respondent Jessica Gonzales filed in Federal District Court. (Because the case comes to us on appeal from a dismissal of the complaint, we assume its allegations are true.) Respondent alleges that petitioner, the town of Castle Rock, Colorado, violated the Due Process Clause of the Fourteenth Amendment to the United States Constitution when its police officers, acting pursuant to official policy or custom, failed to respond properly to her repeated reports that her estranged husband was violating the terms of a restraining order.

The restraining order had been issued by a state trial court several weeks earlier in conjunction with respondent's divorce proceedings. The original form order, issued on May 21, 1999, and served on respondent's husband on June 4, 1999, commanded him not to "molest or disturb the peace of [respondent] or of any child," and to remain at least 100 yards from the family home at all times. The bottom of the preprinted form noted that the reverse side contained "IMPORTANT NOTICES FOR RESTRAINED PARTIES AND LAW ENFORCEMENT OFFICIALS." the preprinted text on the back of the form included the following "WARNING":

> A KNOWING VIOLATION OF A RESTRAINING ORDER IS A CRIME. . . . A VIOLATION WILL ALSO CONSTITUTE CONTEMPT OF COURT. YOU MAY BE ARRESTED WITHOUT NOTICE IF A LAW ENFORCEMENT OFFICER HAS PROBABLE CAUSE TO BELIEVE THAT YOU HAVE KNOWINGLY VIOLATED THIS ORDER.

The preprinted text on the back of the form also included a "NOTICE TO LAW ENFORCEMENT OFFICIALS," which read in part:

YOU SHALL USE EVERY REASONABLE MEANS TO ENFORCE THIS RESTRAINING ORDER. YOU SHALL ARREST, OR, IF AN ARREST WOULD BE IMPRACTICAL UNDER THE CIRCUMSTANCES, SEEK A WARRANT FOR THE ARREST OF THE RESTRAINED PERSON WHEN YOU HAVE INFORMA-TION AMOUNTING TO PROBABLE CAUSE THAT THE RESTRAINED PERSON HAS VIOLATED OR ATTEMPTED TO VIOLATE ANY PROVISION OF THIS ORDER AND THE RESTRAINED PERSON HAS BEEN PROPERLY SERVED WITH A COPY OF THIS ORDER OR HAS RECEIVED ACTUAL NOTICE OF THE EXISTENCE OF THIS ORDER.

On June 4, 1999, the state trial court modified the terms of the restraining order and made it permanent. The modified order gave respondent's husband the right to spend time with his three daughters (ages 10, 9, and 7) on alternate weekends, for two weeks during the summer, and, "'upon reasonable notice,'" for a midweek dinner visit "'arranged by the parties'"; the modified order also allowed him to visit the home to collect the children for such "parenting time."

According to the complaint, at about 5 or 5:30 p.m. on Tuesday, June 22, 1999, respondent's husband took the three daughters while they were playing outside the family home. No advance arrangements had been made for him to see the daughters that evening. When respondent noticed the children were missing, she suspected her husband had taken them. At about 7:30 p.m., she called the Castle Rock Police Department, which dispatched two officers. The complaint continues: "When [the officers] arrived . . . , she showed them a copy of the TRO and requested that it be enforced and the three children be returned to her immediately. [The officers] stated that there was nothing they could do about the TRO and suggested that [respondent] call the Police Department again if the three children did not return home by 10:00 p.m."

At approximately 8:30 p.m., respondent talked to her husband on his cellular telephone. He told her "he had the three children [at an] amusement park in Denver." She called the police again and asked them to "have someone check for" her husband or his vehicle at the amusement park and "put out an [all points bulletin]" for her husband, but the officer with whom she spoke "refused to do so," again telling her to "wait until 10:00 p.m. and see if" her husband returned the girls.

At approximately 10:10 p.m., respondent called the police and said her chil-dren were still missing, but she was now told to wait until midnight. She called at midnight and told the dispatcher her children were still missing. She went to her husband's apartment and, finding nobody there, called the police at 12:10 a.m.; she was told to wait for an officer to arrive. When none came, she went to the police station at 12:50 a.m. and submitted an incident report. The officer who took the report "made no reasonable effort to enforce the TRO or locate the three children. Instead, he went to dinner."

At approximately 3:20 a.m., respondent's husband arrived at the police station and opened fire with a semiautomatic handgun he had purchased earlier that evening. Police shot back, killing him. Inside the cab of his pickup truck, they found the bodies of all three daughters, whom he had already murdered.

On the basis of the foregoing factual allegations, respondent brought an action claiming that the town violated the Due Process Clause because its police department had "an official policy or custom of failing to respond properly to complaints of restraining order violations" and "tolerate[d] the non-enforcement of restraining orders by its police officers." The complaint also alleged that the town's actions "were taken either willfully, recklessly or with such gross negligence as to indicate wanton disregard and deliberate indifference to" respondent's civil rights.

II

The Fourteenth Amendment to the United States Constitution provides that a State shall not "deprive any person of life, liberty, or property, without due process of law." Amdt. 14, §1. In 42 U.S.C. §1983, Congress has created a federal cause of action for "the deprivation of any rights, privileges, or immunities secured by the Constitution and laws." Respondent claims the benefit of this provision on the ground that she had a property interest in police enforcement of the restraining order against her husband; and that the town deprived her of this property without due process by having a policy that tolerated non-enforcement of restraining orders.

As the Court of Appeals recognized, we left a similar question unanswered in DeShaney v. Winnebago County Dept. of Social Servs. (1989), another case with "undeniably tragic" facts: Local child-protection officials had failed to protect a young boy from beatings by his father that left him severely brain damaged. We held that the so-called "substantive" component of the Due Process Clause does not "requir[e] the State to protect the life, liberty, and property of its citizens against invasion by private actors."

The procedural component of the Due Process Clause does not protect everything that might be described as a "benefit": "To have a property interest in a benefit, a person clearly must have more than an abstract need or desire" and "more than a unilateral expectation of it. He must, instead, have a legitimate claim of entitlement to it." Board of Regents of State Colleges v. Roth (1972). Such entitlements are, "'of course, . . . not created by the Constitution. Rather, they are created and their dimensions are defined by existing rules or understandings that stem from an independent source such as state law.'" Paul v. Davis (1976).

Our cases recognize that a benefit is not a protected entitlement if government officials may grant or deny it in their discretion. The Court of Appeals in this case determined that Colorado law created an entitlement to enforcement of the restraining order because the "court-issued restraining order . . . specifically dictated that its terms must be enforced" and a "state statute command[ed]" enforcement of the order when certain objective conditions were met (probable cause to believe that the order had been violated and that the object of the order had received notice of its existence).

B

The critical language in the restraining order came not from any part of the order itself (which was signed by the state-court trial judge and directed to the restrained party, respondent's husband), but from the preprinted notice to law-enforcement personnel that appeared on the back of the order. That notice effectively restated the statutory provision describing "peace officers' duties" related to the crime of violation of a restraining order. We do not believe that these provisions of Colorado law truly made enforcement of restraining orders mandatory. A well established tradition of police discretion has long coexisted with apparently mandatory arrest statutes.

"In each and every state there are long-standing statutes that, by their terms, seem to preclude nonenforcement by the police. . . . However, for a number of reasons, including their legislative history, insufficient resources, and sheer physical impossibility, it has been recognized that such statutes cannot be interpreted literally. . . . [T]hey clearly do not mean that a police officer may not lawfully decline to make an arrest. As to third parties in these states, the full-enforcement statutes simply have no effect, and their significance is further diminished." 1 ABA Standards for Criminal Justice (2d ed. 1980).

The deep-rooted nature of law-enforcement discretion, even in the presence of seemingly mandatory legislative commands, is illustrated by Chicago v. Morales (1999), which involved an ordinance that said a police officer "'shall order'" persons to disperse in certain circumstances. This Court rejected out of hand the possibility that "the mandatory language of the ordinance . . . afford[ed] the police no discretion." It is, the Court proclaimed, simply "common sense that all police officers must use some discretion in deciding when and where to enforce city ordinances."

Against that backdrop, a true mandate of police action would require some stronger indication from the Colorado Legislature than "shall use every reasonable means to enforce a restraining order" (or even "shall arrest . . . or . . . seek a warrant"). That language is not perceptibly more mandatory than the Colorado statute which has long told municipal chiefs of police that they "shall pursue and arrest any person fleeing from justice in any part of the state" and that they "shall apprehend any person in the act of committing any offense . . . and, forthwith and without any warrant, bring such person before a . . . competent authority for examination and trial." It is hard to imagine that a Colorado peace officer would not have some discretion to determine that—despite probable cause to believe a restraining order has been violated—the circumstances of the violation or the competing duties of that officer or his agency counsel decisively against enforcement in a particular instance. The practical necessity for discretion is particularly apparent in a case such as this one, where the suspected violator is not actually present and his whereabouts are unknown.

The dissent correctly points out that, in the specific context of domestic violence, mandatory-arrest statutes have been found in some States to be more mandatory than traditional mandatory-arrest statutes. Even in the domestic-violence context, however, it is unclear how the mandatory-arrest paradigm applies to cases in which the offender is not present to be arrested.

Even if we were to think otherwise concerning the creation of an entitlement by Colorado, it is by no means clear that an individual entitlement to enforcement of a restraining order could constitute a "property" interest for purposes of the Due Process Clause. Such a right would not, of course, resemble any traditional conception of property. Although that alone does not disqualify it from due process protection, as *Roth* and its progeny show, the right to have a restraining order enforced does not "have some ascertainable monetary value," as even our "*Roth*-type property-as-entitlement" cases have implicitly required. Perhaps most radically, the alleged property interest here arises incidentally, not out of some new species of government benefit or service, but out of a function that government actors have always performed — to wit, arresting people who they have probable cause to believe have committed a criminal offense.

III

We conclude, therefore, that respondent did not, for purposes of the Due Process Clause, have a property interest in police enforcement of the restraining order against her husband. In light of today's decision and that in *DeShaney*, the benefit that a third party may receive from having someone else arrested for a crime generally does not trigger protections under the Due Process Clause, neither in its procedural nor in its "substantive" manifestations. This result reflects our continuing reluctance to treat the Fourteenth Amendment as "'a font of tort law,'" Parratt v. Taylor (1981), but it does not mean States are powerless to provide victims with personally enforceable remedies. Although the framers of the Fourteenth Amendment and the Civil Rights Act of 1871 did not create a system by which police departments are generally held financially accountable for crimes that better policing might have prevented, the people of Colorado are free to craft such a system under state law.

Justice STEVENS, with whom Justice GINSBURG joins, dissenting.

The issue presented to us is much narrower than is suggested by the far-ranging arguments of the parties and their amici. Neither the tragic facts of the case, nor the importance of according proper deference to law enforcement professionals, should divert our attention from that issue. That issue is whether the restraining order entered by the Colorado trial court on June 4, 1999, created a "property" interest that is protected from arbitrary deprivation by the Due Process Clause of the Fourteenth Amendment.

The central question in this case is therefore whether, as a matter of Colorado law, respondent had a right to police assistance comparable to the right she would have possessed to any other service the government or a private firm might have undertaken to provide.

Even if the Court had good reason to doubt the Court of Appeals' determination of state law, it would, in my judgment, be a far wiser course to certify the question to the Colorado Supreme Court. Powerful considerations support certification in this case. First, principles of federalism and comity favor giving a State's high court the opportunity to answer important questions of state law, particularly when those questions implicate uniquely local matters such as law enforcement and might well require the weighing of policy considerations for their correct resolution. Second, by certifying a potentially dispositive state-law issue, the Court would adhere to its wise policy of avoiding the unnecessary adjudication of difficult questions of constitutional law. Third, certification would promote both judicial economy and fairness to the parties. After all, the Colorado Supreme Court is the ultimate authority on the meaning of Colorado law, and if in later litigation it should disagree with this Court's provisional state-law holding, our efforts will have been wasted and respondent will have been deprived of the opportunity to have her claims heard under the authoritative view of Colorado law. The unique facts of this case only serve to emphasize the importance of employing a procedure that will provide the correct answer to the central question of state law.

Three flaws in the Court's rather superficial analysis of the merits highlight the unwisdom of its decision to answer the state-law question de novo. First, the Court places undue weight on the various statutes throughout the country that seemingly mandate police enforcement but are generally understood to preserve police discretion. As a result, the Court gives short shrift to the unique case of "mandatory arrest" statutes in the domestic violence context; States passed a wave of these statutes in the 1980's and 1990's with the unmistakable goal of eliminating police discretion in this area. Second, the Court's formalistic analysis fails to take seriously the fact that the Colorado statute at issue in this case was enacted for the benefit of the narrow class of persons who are beneficiaries of domestic restraining orders, and that the order at issue in this case was specifically intended to provide protection to respondent and her children. Finally, the Court is simply wrong to assert that a citizen's interest in the government's commitment to provide police enforcement in certain defined circumstances does not resemble any "traditional conception of property"; in fact, a citizen's property interest in such a commitment is just as concrete and worthy of protection as her interest in any other important service the government or a private firm has undertaken to provide.

Given that Colorado law has quite clearly eliminated the police's discretion to deny enforcement, respondent is correct that she had much more than a "unilateral expectation" that the restraining order would be enforced; rather, she had a "legitimate claim of entitlement" to enforcement. Recognizing respondent's property interest in the enforcement of her restraining order is fully consistent with our precedent. This Court has "made clear that the property interests protected by procedural due process extend well beyond actual ownership of real estate, chattels, or money." The "types of interests protected as 'property' are varied and, as often as not, intangible, 'relating to the whole domain of social and economic fact.'" Police enforcement of a restraining order is a government service that is no less concrete and no less valuable than other government services, such as education.

The relative novelty of recognizing this type of property interest is explained by the relative novelty of the domestic violence statutes creating a mandatory arrest duty; before this innovation, the unfettered discretion that characterized police enforcement defeated any citizen's "legitimate claim of entitlement" to this service. Novel or not, respondent's claim finds strong support in the principles that underlie our due process jurisprudence. In this case, Colorado law guaranteed the provision of a certain service, in certain defined circumstances, to a certain class of beneficiaries, and respondent reasonably relied on that guarantee. As we observed in *Roth*, "[i]t is a purpose of the ancient institution of property to protect those claims upon which people rely in their daily lives, reliance that must not be arbitrarily undermined." Surely, if respondent had contracted with a private security firm to provide her and her daughters with protection from her husband, it would be apparent that she possessed a property interest in such a contract. Here, Colorado undertook a comparable obligation, and respondent—with restraining order in hand—justifiably relied on that undertaking. Respondent's claim of entitlement to this promised service is no less legitimate than the other claims our cases have upheld, and no less concrete than a hypothetical agreement with a private firm. The fact that it is based on a statutory enactment and a judicial order entered for her special protection, rather than on a formal contract, does not provide a principled basis for refusing to consider it "property" worthy of constitutional protection.

Because respondent had a property interest in the enforcement of the restraining order, state officials could not deprive her of that interest without observing fair procedures. Her description of the police behavior in this case and the department's callous policy of failing to respond properly to reports of restraining order violations clearly alleges a due process violation. At the very least, due process requires that the relevant state decisionmaker listen to the claimant and then apply the relevant criteria in reaching his decision.

2. Is It a Deprivation of "Life, Liberty, or Property"?

THE "RIGHTS-PRIVILEGES" DISTINCTION AND ITS DEMISE

The government is required to provide due process only if there has been a deprivation of life, liberty, or property. Until the past thirty years, the Supreme Court narrowly defined what constitutes a liberty or property interest. The Court repeatedly held that there was a liberty or a property interest only if there was a "right." A government-bestowed "privilege" was not a basis for requiring due process.

A classic articulation of the rights-privileges distinction was in the ruling of then-State Court Justice Oliver Wendell Holmes that the government did not have to provide due process before firing a police officer for his political activities: The petitioner may have a constitutional right to talk politics, but he has no constitutional right to be a policeman.[63] Under this view, the government was not required to provide due process if a person was fired from a government job,[64] or terminated government benefits,[65] or revoked an occupational license.[66] All of these were regarded as privileges, not rights, so that no due process was required if the government made the decision to remove them.

By the 1960s, there was substantial criticism of the rights-privileges distinction as a basis for determining whether there was an interest requiring due process. In a classic article, Professor Charles Reich argued that the rights-privileges distinction is an anachronism in an era where people depend on government for so much that is essential for survival.[67] Government benefits such as education, welfare, Social Security, licenses, and jobs are relied on by people and thus hold the same place in a person's life as property traditionally occupied.

Thus, Reich argued there is the same need to prevent arbitrary government action. He wrote, "Society today is built around entitlements. . . . Many of the most important of these entitlements now flow from government. . . . Such sources of security, whether private or public, are no longer regarded as luxuries

---

63. McAuliffe v. New Bedford, 155 Mass. 216, 29 N.E. 517, 517 (1892).
64. *See, e.g.,* Bailey v. Richardson, 182 F.2d 46 (D.C.C. 1950), *aff'd by an equally divided Court,* 341 U.S. 918 (1951).
65. Flemming v. Nestor, 363 U.S. 603 (1960).
66. *See, e.g.,* Barsky v. Board of Regents of University, 347 U.S. 442, 451 (1954).
67. Charles A. Reich, *The New Property,* 73 Yale L.J. 733 (1964); *see also* Charles A. Reich, *Individual Rights and Social Welfare: The Emerging Legal Issues,* 74 Yale L.J. 1245 (1965).

or gratuities; to the recipients they are essentials, fully deserved, and in no sense a form of charity."[68] Reich contended that the rights-privileges distinction should be discarded and that due process should be provided when the government terminates the "new property."

By the end of the 1960s, this view was accepted by a majority of the Supreme Court. Goldberg v. Kelly was the key case in this regard.

GOLDBERG v. KELLY
397 U.S. 254 (1970)

Justice BRENNAN delivered the opinion of the Court.

The question for decision is whether a State that terminates public assistance payments to a particular recipient without affording him the opportunity for an evidentiary hearing prior to termination denies the recipient procedural due process in violation of the Due Process Clause of the Fourteenth Amendment.

This action was brought in the District Court for the Southern District of New York by residents of New York City receiving financial aid under the federally assisted program of Aid to Families with Dependent Children (AFDC) or under New York State's general Home Relief program. Their complaint alleged that the New York State and New York City officials administering these programs terminated, or were about to terminate, such aid without prior notice and hearing, thereby denying them due process of law. At the time the suits were filed there was no requirement of prior notice or hearing of any kind before termination of financial aid.

I

The constitutional issue to be decided, therefore, is the narrow one whether the Due Process Clause requires that the recipient be afforded an evidentiary hearing before the termination of benefits.

Appellant does not contend that procedural due process is not applicable to the termination of welfare benefits. Such benefits are a matter of statutory entitlement for persons qualified to receive them. Their termination involves state action that adjudicates important rights. The constitutional challenge cannot be answered by an argument that public assistance benefits are a "privilege" and not a "right." Relevant constitutional restraints apply as much to the withdrawal of public assistance benefits as to disqualification for unemployment compensation; or to denial of a tax exemption; or to discharge from public employment. The extent to which procedural due process must be afforded the recipient is influenced by the extent to which he may be "condemned to suffer grievous loss," and depends upon whether the recipient's interest in avoiding that loss outweighs the governmental interest in summary adjudication. Accordingly, "consideration of what procedures due process may require under any given set of circumstances must begin with a determination of the precise nature of

---

68. Reich, *id.*, *Individual Rights and Social Welfare*, 74 Yale L.J. at 1255.

the government function involved as well as of the private interest that has been affected by governmental action.[69]

It is true, of course, that some governmental benefits may be administratively terminated without affording the recipient a pre-termination evidentiary hearing. But we agree with the District Court that when welfare is discontinued, only a pre-termination evidentiary hearing provides the recipient with procedural due process. For qualified recipients, welfare provides the means to obtain essential food, clothing, housing, and medical care. Thus the crucial factor in this context—a factor not present in the case of the blacklisted government contractor, the discharged government employee, the taxpayer denied a tax exemption, or virtually anyone else whose governmental entitlements are ended—is that termination of aid pending resolution of a controversy over eligibility may deprive an eligible recipient of the very means by which to live while he waits. Since he lacks independent resources, his situation becomes immediately desperate. His need to concentrate upon finding the means for daily subsistence, in turn, adversely affects his ability to seek redress from the welfare bureaucracy.

Moreover, important governmental interests are promoted by affording recipients a pre-termination evidentiary hearing. From its founding the Nation's basic commitment has been to foster the dignity and well-being of all persons within its borders. We have come to recognize that forces not within the control of the poor contribute to their poverty.

Public assistance, then, is not mere charity, but a means to "promote the general Welfare, and secure the Blessings of Liberty to ourselves and our Posterity." The same governmental interests that counsel the provision of welfare, counsel as well its uninterrupted provision to those eligible to receive it; pre-termination evidentiary hearings are indispensable to that end.

Appellant does not challenge the force of these considerations but argues that they are outweighed by countervailing governmental interests in conserving fiscal and administrative resources. These interests, the argument goes, justify the delay of any evidentiary hearing until after discontinuance of the grants. Summary adjudication protects the public fisc by stopping payments promptly upon discovery of reason to believe that a recipient is no longer eligible. Since most terminations are accepted without challenge, summary adjudication also conserves both the fisc and administrative time and energy by reducing the number of evidentiary hearings actually held.

---

69. It may be realistic today to regard welfare entitlements as more like "property" than a "gratuity." Much of the existing wealth in this country takes the form of rights that do not fall within traditional common-law concepts of property. It has been aptly noted that "[s]ociety today is built around entitlement. The automobile dealer has his franchise, the doctor and lawyer their professional licenses, the worker his union membership, contract, and pension rights, the executive his contract and stock options; all are devices to aid security and independence. Many of the most important of these entitlements now flow from government: subsidies to farmers and businessmen, routes for airlines and channels for television stations; long-term contracts for defense, space, and education; Social Security pensions for individuals. Such sources of security, whether private or public, are no longer regarded as luxuries or gratuities; to the recipients they are essentials, fully deserved, and in no sense a form of charity. It is only the poor whose entitlements, although recognized by public policy, have not been effectively enforced." Reich, Individual Rights and Social Welfare: The Emerging Legal Issues, 74 Yale L.J. 1245, 1255 (1965). See also Reich, The New Property, 73 Yale L.J. 733 (1964). [Footnote by the Court.]

We agree with the District Court, however, that these governmental interests are not overriding in the welfare context. The requirement of a prior hearing doubtless involves some greater expense, and the benefits paid to ineligible recipients pending decision at the hearing probably cannot be recouped, since these recipients are likely to be judgment-proof. But the State is not without weapons to minimize these increased costs. Much of the drain on fiscal and administrative resources can be reduced by developing procedures for prompt pre-termination hearings and by skillful use of personnel and facilities. Indeed, the very provision for a post-termination evidentiary hearing in New York's Home Relief program is itself cogent evidence that the State recognizes the primacy of the public interest in correct eligibility determinations and therefore in the provision of procedural safeguards. Thus, the interest of the eligible recipient in uninterrupted receipt of public assistance, coupled with the State's interest that his payments not be erroneously terminated, clearly outweighs the State's competing concern to prevent any increase in its fiscal and administrative burdens. As the District Court correctly concluded, "[t]he stakes are simply too high for the welfare recipient, and the possibility for honest error or irritable misjudgment too great, to allow termination of aid without giving the recipient a chance, if he so desires, to be fully informed of the case against him so that he may contest its basis and produce evidence in rebuttal."

II

We also agree with the District Court, however, that the pre-termination hearing need not take the form of a judicial or quasi-judicial trial. We bear in mind that the statutory "fair hearing" will provide the recipient with a full administrative review. Accordingly, the pre-termination hearing has one function only: to produce an initial determination of the validity of the welfare department's grounds for discontinuance of payments in order to protect a recipient against an erroneous termination of his benefits. Thus, a complete record and a comprehensive opinion, which would serve primarily to facilitate judicial review and to guide future decisions, need not be provided at the pre-termination stage. We recognize, too, that both welfare authorities and recipients have an interest in relatively speedy resolution of questions of eligibility, that they are used to dealing with one another informally, and that some welfare departments have very burdensome caseloads. These considerations justify the limitation of the pre-termination hearing to minimum procedural safeguards, adapted to the particular characteristics of welfare recipients, and to the limited nature of the controversies to be resolved. We wish to add that we, no less than the dissenters, recognize the importance of not imposing upon the States or the Federal Government in this developing field of law any procedural requirements beyond those demanded by rudimentary due process.

"The fundamental requisite of due process of law is the opportunity to be heard." The hearing must be "at a meaningful time and in a meaningful manner." In the present context these principles require that a recipient have timely and adequate notice detailing the reasons for a proposed termination, and an effective opportunity to defend by confronting any adverse witnesses and by presenting his own arguments and evidence orally.

Justice BLACK, dissenting.

In the last half century the United States, along with many, perhaps most, other nations of the world, has moved far toward becoming a welfare state, that is, a nation that for one reason or another taxes its most affluent people to help support, feed, clothe, and shelter its less fortunate citizens. The result is that today more than nine million men, women, and children in the United States receive some kind of state or federally financed public assistance in the form of allowances or gratuities, generally paid them periodically, usually by the week, month, or quarter. Since these gratuities are paid on the basis of need, the list of recipients is not static, and some people go off the lists and others are added from time to time. These ever-changing lists put a constant administrative burden on government and it certainly could not have reasonably anticipated that this burden would include the additional procedural expense imposed by the Court today.

The more than a million names on the relief rolls in New York, and the more than nine million names on the rolls of all the 50 States were not put there at random. The names are there because state welfare officials believed that those people were eligible for assistance. Probably in the officials' haste to make out the lists many names were put there erroneously in order to alleviate immediate suffering, and undoubtedly some people are drawing relief who are not entitled under the law to do so. Doubtless some draw relief checks from time to time who know they are not eligible, either because they are not actually in need or for some other reason. Many of those who thus draw undeserved gratuities are without sufficient property to enable the government to collect back from them any money they wrongfully receive. But the Court today holds that it would violate the Due Process Clause of the Fourteenth Amendment to stop paying those people weekly or monthly allowances unless the government first affords them a full "evidentiary hearing" even though welfare officials are persuaded that the recipients are not rightfully entitled to receive a penny under the law. In other words, although some recipients might be on the lists for payment wholly because of deliberate fraud on their part, the Court holds that the government is helpless and must continue, until after an evidentiary hearing, to pay money that it does not owe, never has owed, and never could owe. I do not believe there is any provision in our Constitution that should thus paralyze the government's efforts to protect itself against making payments to people who are not entitled to them.

The Court apparently feels that this decision will benefit the poor and needy. In my judgment the eventual result will be just the opposite. [T]oday's decision requires only the opportunity to have the benefit of counsel at the administrative hearing, but it is difficult to believe that the same reasoning process would not require the appointment of counsel, for otherwise the right to counsel is a meaningless one since these people are too poor to hire their own advocates. Thus the end result of today's decision may well be that the government, once it decides to give welfare benefits, cannot reverse that decision until the recipient has had the benefits of full administrative and judicial review, including, of course, the opportunity to present his case to this Court. Since this process will usually entail a delay of several years, the inevitable result of such a consti-tutionally imposed burden will be that the government will not put a claimant on the rolls initially until it has made an exhaustive investigation to determine his eligibility. While this Court will perhaps have insured that no needy person will be taken off the rolls without a full "due process" proceeding, it will also have insured that many will never get on the rolls, or at least that they will remain destitute during the lengthy proceedings followed to determine initial eligibility.

For the foregoing reasons I dissent from the Court's holding. The operation of a welfare state is a new experiment for our Nation. For this reason, among others, I feel that new experiments in carrying out a welfare program should not be frozen into our constitutional structure. They should be left, as are other legislative determinations, to the Congress and the legislatures that the people elect to make our laws.

After the Court recognized that welfare benefits, once bestowed, become property requiring due process before termination, the rights-privileges distinction obviously had been discarded. The question then becomes, if the rights-privileges distinction is not to be used in defining "liberty" and "property," how is the Court to decide if such an interest is present? This is examined in the following sections. The constant question is whether the Court has resurrected the rights-privileges distinction not expressly but in the way in which it has defined property and liberty.

WHAT IS A DEPRIVATION OF PROPERTY?

There never has been doubt that the government must provide due process before it deprives a person of real or personal property. After the demise of the rights-privileges distinction, the question becomes when are government benefits, such as jobs or payments, to be considered property?

Goldberg v. Kelly strongly suggests that the importance of the interest to the individual — welfare, for example, being deemed essential for life — determines whether there is a property interest. In Board of Regents v. Roth, just a few years later, the Court reaffirmed the demise of the rights-privileges distinction but used a different approach for determining if there is a property interest.

BOARD OF REGENTS v. ROTH
408 U.S. 564 (1972)

Justice STEWART delivered the opinion of the Court.

In 1968 the respondent, David Roth, was hired for his first teaching job as assistant professor of political science at Wisconsin State University-Oshkosh. He was hired for a fixed term of one academic year. The notice of his faculty appointment specified that his employment would begin on September 1, 1968, and would end on June 30, 1969. The respondent completed that term. But he was informed that he would not be rehired for the next academic year.

The respondent had no tenure rights to continued employment. Under Wisconsin statutory law a state university teacher can acquire tenure as a "permanent" employee only after four years of year-to-year employment.

Having acquired tenure, a teacher is entitled to continued employment "during efficiency and good behavior." A relatively new teacher without tenure, however, is under Wisconsin law entitled to nothing beyond his one-year appointment. There are no statutory or administrative standards defining eligibility for re-employment. State law thus clearly leaves the decision whether to rehire a non-tenured teacher for another year to the unfettered discretion of university officials.

In conformance with these Rules, the President of Wisconsin State University-Oshkosh informed the respondent before February 1, 1969, that he would not be rehired for the 1969-1970 academic year. He gave the respondent no reason for the decision and no opportunity to challenge it at any sort of hearing.

The respondent then brought this action in Federal District Court alleging that the decision not to rehire him for the next year infringed his Fourteenth Amendment rights.

I

The requirements of procedural due process apply only to the deprivation of interests encompassed by the Fourteenth Amendment's protection of liberty and property. When protected interests are implicated, the right to some kind of prior hearing is paramount. But the range of interests protected by procedural due process is not infinite.

"Liberty" and "property" are broad and majestic terms. They are among the "[g]reat [constitutional] concepts . . . purposely left to gather meaning from experience. . . . [T]hey relate to the whole domain of social and economic fact, and the statesmen who founded this Nation knew too well that only a stagnant society remains unchanged." For that reason, the Court has fully and finally rejected the wooden distinction between "rights" and "privileges" that once seemed to govern the applicability of procedural due process rights. The Court has also made clear that the property interests protected by procedural due process extend well beyond actual ownership of real estate, chattels, or money. By the same token, the Court has required due process protection for deprivations of liberty beyond the sort of formal constraints imposed by the criminal process.

II

"While this court has not attempted to define with exactness the liberty . . . guaranteed [by the Fourteenth Amendment], the term has received much consideration and some of the included things have been definitely stated. Without doubt, it denotes not merely freedom from bodily restraint but also the right of the individual to contract, to engage in any of the common occupations of life, to acquire useful knowledge, to marry, establish a home and bring up children, to worship God according to the dictates of his own conscience, and generally to enjoy those privileges long recognized . . . as essential to the orderly pursuit of happiness by free men." Meyer v. Nebraska. In a Constitution for a free people, there can be no doubt that the meaning of "liberty" must be broad indeed.

There might be cases in which a State refused to re-employ a person under such circumstances that interests in liberty would be implicated. But this is not such a case.

The State, in declining to rehire the respondent, did not make any charge against him that might seriously damage his standing and associations in his community. It did not base the nonrenewal of his contract on a charge, for example, that he had been guilty of dishonesty, or immorality. Had it done so, this would be a different case. In such a case, due process would accord an opportunity to refute the charge before University officials. In the present case, however, there is no suggestion whatever that the respondent's "good name, reputation, honor, or integrity" is at stake.

Similarly, there is no suggestion that the State, in declining to re-employ the respondent, imposed on him a stigma or other disability that foreclosed his freedom to take advantage of other employment opportunities. The State, for example, did not invoke any regulations to bar the respondent from all other public employment in state universities. Had it done so, this, again, would be a different case.

Hence, on the record before us, all that clearly appears is that the respondent was not rehired for one year at one university. It stretches the concept too far to suggest that a person is deprived of "liberty" when he simply is not rehired in one job but remains as free as before to seek another.

III

The Fourteenth Amendment's procedural protection of property is a safeguard of the security of interests that a person has already acquired in specific benefits. These interests — property interests — may take many forms. Certain attributes of "property" interests protected by procedural due process emerge from these decisions. To have a property interest in a benefit, a person clearly must have more than an abstract need or desire for it. He must have more than a unilateral expectation of it. He must, instead, have a legitimate claim of entitlement to it. It is a purpose of the ancient institution of property to protect those claims upon which people rely in their daily lives, reliance that must not be arbitrarily undermined. It is a purpose of the constitutional right to a hearing to provide an opportunity for a person to vindicate those claims.

Property interests, of course, are not created by the Constitution. Rather they are created and their dimensions are defined by existing rules or understandings that stem from an independent source such as state law — rules or understandings that secure certain benefits and that support claims of entitlement to those benefits.

Just as the welfare recipients' "property" interest in welfare payments was created and defined by statutory terms, so the respondent's "property" interest in employment at Wisconsin State University-Oshkosh was created and defined by the terms of his appointment. Those terms secured his interest in employment up to June 30, 1969. But the important fact in this case is that they specifically provided that the respondent's employment was to terminate on June 30. They did not provide for contract renewal absent "sufficient cause." Indeed, they made no provision for renewal whatsoever.

Thus, the terms of the respondent's appointment secured absolutely no interest in re-employment for the next year. They supported absolutely no possible claim of entitlement to re-employment. Nor, significantly, was there any state statute or University rule or policy that secured his interest in re-employment or that created any legitimate claim to it. In these circumstances, the respondent surely had an abstract concern in being rehired, but he did not have a property interest sufficient to require the University authorities to give him a hearing when they declined to renew his contract of employment.

Justice MARSHALL, dissenting.

Respondent was hired as an assistant professor of political science at Wisconsin State University-Oshkosh for the 1968-1969 academic year. During the course of that year he was told that he would not be rehired for the next academic term, but he was never told why. In this case, he asserts that the Due Process Clause of the Fourteenth Amendment to the United States Constitution entitled him to a statement of reasons and a hearing on the University's decision not to rehire him for another year.

I would go further than the Court does in defining the terms "liberty" and "property." The prior decisions of this Court, discussed at length in the opinion of the Court, establish a principle that is as obvious as it is compelling—i.e., federal and state governments and governmental agencies are restrained by the Constitution from acting arbitrarily with respect to employment opportunities that they either offer or control. Hence, it is now firmly established that whether or not a private employer is free to act capriciously or unreasonably with respect to employment practices, at least absent statutory or contractual controls, a government employer is different. The government may only act fairly and reasonably.

This Court has long maintained that "the right to work for a living in the common occupations of the community is of the very essence of the personal freedom and opportunity that it was the purpose of the [Fourteenth] Amendment to secure." Truax v. Raich (1915). It has also established that the fact that an employee has no contract guaranteeing work for a specific future period does not mean that as the result of action by the government he may be "discharged at any time, for any reason or for no reason."

In my view, every citizen who applies for a government job is entitled to it unless the government can establish some reason for denying the employment. This is the "property" right that I believe is protected by the Fourteenth Amendment and that cannot be denied "without due process of law." And it is also liberty—liberty to work—which is the "very essence of the personal freedom and opportunity" secured by the Fourteenth Amendment.

It may be argued that to provide procedural due process to all public employees or prospective employees would place an intolerable burden on the machinery of government. Cf. Goldberg v. Kelly, supra. The short answer to that argument is that it is not burdensome to give reasons when reasons exist. Whenever an application for employment is denied, an employee is discharged, or a decision not to rehire an employee is made, there should be some reason for the decision. It can scarcely be argued that government would be crippled by a requirement that the reason be communicated to the person most directly affected by the government's action.

Goldberg v. Kelly and Board of Regents v. Roth reflect very different approaches in defining whether there is a property interest. One approach to defining entitlement would find a property interest if there is an important benefit regardless of the content of the state law. An alternative definition, however, would find a property interest only if the state law creates a reasonable expectation to receipt of a benefit, regardless of the importance of the interest.

Each definition has problems. If the existence of property is determined solely by the importance of the benefit, there seems no principled way to decide which government benefits are sufficiently significant to constitute property. The government provides a vast array of services and programs that people rely on. How is the Court to decide which are important enough to constitute property and require due process when they are ended?

Defining property based on whether the law creates a reasonable expectation to continued receipt of a benefit solves this problem because it provides a basis for deciding what constitutes property apart from the importance of the interest. But it creates a different major difficulty: Could the state simply deny the existence of property by expressly stating that individuals should have no expectation to continued receipt? In other words, if property is defined by expectations, the state can defeat property interests by making it clear that people should have no expectations. In essence, the rights-privileges distinction is recreated under a different label; the state could deny a property interest merely by making it clear that the benefit or program was something that the government could terminate at any point. Indeed, the more arbitrary the government is, the less there can be reasonable expectations to continued receipt of the benefit and the less likely there will be a requirement for due process.

To this day, the Court has not resolved this tension. The Court generally has adopted the second approach to defining property—that is, as a reasonable expectation to continued receipt of a benefit. Yet the Court has been inconsistent in its willingness to embrace the consequence that the government then can deny a property interest merely by informing people that they should not expect the benefit to continue.

The primary area where the Court has struggled with defining property is in the context of deciding when government employment constitutes an entitlement. *Roth*, itself, involved this issue. In a companion case to *Roth*, Perry v. Sindermann, 408 U.S. 593 (1972), the Court made it clear that it was defining property based on a reasonable expectation to continued receipt of a benefit. Sinderman was a professor at Odessa Junior College, and although the college did not have a tenure system, its faculty guide stated that it "wishes the faculty member to feel that he has permanent tenure as long as his teaching services are satisfactory and as long as he displays a cooperative attitude." The Court said that the absence of a formal tenure system was not dispositive in deciding whether there was a property interest. The Court explained that the teacher had raised "a genuine issue as to his interest in continued employment, [which] though not secured by a formal contractual tenure provision, was secured by a no less binding understanding fostered by the college administration."

But, as described above, does this approach mean that the government can prevent there from being a property interest in a government job simply by making it clear to the employees that they should have no expectation of the job continuing? Justice Rehnquist suggested this in Arnett v. Kennedy, 416 U.S. 134 (1974). The issue in *Arnett* was whether the government could fire a nonprobationary employee without a pretermination hearing. There was no majority opinion by the Court, but six of the justices recognized that there was a property interest in the job. The ruling was that there was not a denial of due process because the government provided a pretermination review and a post-termination hearing.

However, Justice Rehnquist, joined by Chief Justice Burger and Justice Stewart, would not have found a property interest requiring due process. Rehnquist emphasized that the property interest in the job is only that which the statute provides. He also wrote that "where the grant of a substantive right is inextricably intertwined with the limitations on the procedures which are to be employed in determining that right, a litigant in the position of appellee must take the bitter with the sweet." The other six justices appeared to reject this and objected that the Rehnquist "view misconceives the origin of the right to procedural due process. That right is conferred, not by legislative grace, but by constitutional guarantee."

This view appeared to attract support from a majority of the Supreme Court in Bishop v. Wood, 426 U.S. 341 (1976). The plaintiff, a city police officer, was considered a "permanent employee" under state law. Nonetheless, the federal district court found that as a matter of state law, the police officer "held his position at the will and pleasure of the city." Therefore, the Court concluded that he did not have a property interest in his job and that he was not entitled to due process with regard to his termination. This means that the government can prevent there from being a property interest simply by making it clear that it retains the right to fire the individual at will. As such, it seems little different from the rights-privileges distinction that the Court so expressly repudiated in cases like *Goldberg* and *Roth.*

Subsequent to *Bishop,* the Court has clarified that if there is a property right, the issue of what procedures are required is a matter of federal constitutional law to be decided by the courts. In Cleveland Board of Education v. Loudermill, 470 U.S. 532 (1985), the Supreme Court considered a state civil service law that provided that employees were entitled only to post-termination administrative review. There was no dispute that the law created a property interest in that it required that employees only be terminated if there was "cause." The Court then said that due process required a predischarge opportunity to be heard and that state law could not alter this requirement. The Court said that it was "settled that the bitter with the sweet approach misconceives the constitutional guarantee" and that when there is a property interest, the Constitution — and not the state law — determines the procedures to be followed.

Loudermill, however, only addresses the question of what procedures are required when there has been a deprivation of life, liberty, or property, which is addressed below. *Loudermill* does not overrule or change *Bishop*'s holding: In deciding if there is a property interest in a government job, the relevant inquiry is the expectations created by the law and customs surrounding the position.

WHAT IS A DEPRIVATION OF LIBERTY?

There is, of course, no doubt that constitutional rights are a liberty interest. The difficult question arises as to what other interests fit under the rubric of liberty and require due process. Again, there are two different ways for the Court to approach this and define liberty. One would be for the Court to determine what is "liberty" based on the importance of the interest at stake. The other way would be for the Court to determine whether there is a liberty interest based on the expectations engendered by state law. Again, both are present in the case law. Two examples illustrate this: (1) Are harms to reputation a liberty interest? (2) When do prisoners have liberty interests?

REPUTATION AS A LIBERTY INTEREST

When, if at all, is harm to reputation a deprivation of liberty? In Goss v. Lopez, the Court indicated that reputation is a liberty interest and also found a property interest in students attending school.

GOSS v. LOPEZ
419 U.S. 565 (1975)

Justice WHITE delivered the opinion of the Court.

This appeal by various administrators of the Columbus, Ohio, Public School System (CPSS) challenges the judgment of a three-judge federal court, declaring that appellees—various high school students in the CPSS—were denied due process of law contrary to the command of the Fourteenth Amendment in that they were temporarily suspended from their high schools without a hearing either prior to suspension or within a reasonable time thereafter, and enjoining the administrators to remove all references to such suspensions from the students' records.

I

Ohio law, Rev. Code Ann. §3313.64 (1972), provides for free education to all children between the ages of six and 21. Section 3313.66 of the Code empowers the principal of an Ohio public school to suspend a pupil for misconduct for up to 10 days or to expel him. In either case, he must notify the student's parents within 24 hours and state the reasons for his action. A pupil who is expelled, or his parents, may appeal the decision to the Board of Education and in connection therewith shall be permitted to be heard at the board meeting. The Board may reinstate the pupil following the hearing. No similar procedure is provided in §3313.66 or any other provision of state law for a suspended student. Aside from a regulation tracking the statute, at the time of the imposition of the suspensions in this case the CPSS itself had not issued any written procedure applicable to suspensions. Nor, so far as the record reflects, had any of the individual high schools involved in this case. Each, however, had formally or informally described the conduct for which suspension could be imposed.

The nine named appellees, each of whom alleged that he or she had been suspended from public high school in Columbus for up to 10 days without a hearing pursuant to §3313.66, filed an action under 42 U.S.C. §1983 against the Columbus Board of Education and various administrators of the CPSS.

II

At the outset, appellants contend that because there is no constitutional right to an education at public expense, the Due Process Clause does not protect against expulsions from the public school system. This position misconceives the nature of the issue and is refuted by prior decisions. The Fourteenth Amendment forbids the State to deprive any person of life, liberty, or property without due process of law. Protected interests in property are normally "not created by the Constitution. Rather, they are created and their dimensions are defined" by an independent source such as state statutes or rules entitling the citizen to certain benefits. Board of Regents v. Roth (1972).

Here, on the basis of state law, appellees plainly had legitimate claims of entitlement to a public education. Ohio Rev. Code Ann. §§3313.48 and 3313.64 direct local authorities to provide a free education to all residents between five and 21 years of age, and a compulsory-attendance law requires attendance for a school year of not less than 32 weeks. It is true that §3313.66 of the Code permits school principals to suspend students for up to 10 days; but suspensions may not be imposed without any grounds whatsoever. All of the schools had their own rules specifying the grounds for expulsion or suspension. Having chosen to extend the right to an education to people of appellees' class generally, Ohio may not withdraw that right on grounds of misconduct absent fundamentally fair procedures to determine whether the misconduct has occurred. [T]he State is constrained to recognize a student's legitimate entitlement to a public education as a property interest which is protected by the Due Process Clause and which may not be taken away for misconduct without adherence to the minimum procedures required by that Clause.

The Due Process Clause also forbids arbitrary deprivations of liberty. "Where a person's good name, reputation, honor, or integrity is at stake because of what the government is doing to him," the minimal requirements of the Clause must be satisfied. Wisconsin v. Constantineau (1971). School authorities here suspended appellees from school for periods of up to 10 days based on charges of misconduct. If sustained and recorded, those charges could seriously damage the students' standing with their fellow pupils and their teachers as well as interfere with later opportunities for higher education and employment. It is apparent that the claimed right of the State to determine unilaterally and without process whether that misconduct has occurred immediately collides with the requirements of the Constitution.

A short suspension is, of course, a far milder deprivation than expulsion. But, "education is perhaps the most important function of state and local governments," Brown v. Board of Education (1954), and the total exclusion from the educational process for more than a trivial period, and certainly if the suspension is for 10 days, is a serious event in the life of the suspended child. Neither the property interest in educational benefits temporarily denied nor the liberty interest in reputation, which is also implicated, is so insubstantial that suspensions may constitutionally be imposed by any procedure the school chooses, no matter how arbitrary.

III

"Once it is determined that due process applies, the question remains what process is due." The difficulty is that our schools are vast and complex. Some modicum of discipline and order is essential if the educational function is to be performed. Events calling for discipline are frequent occurrences and sometimes require immediate, effective action. Suspension is considered not only to be a necessary tool to maintain order but a valuable educational device. The prospect of imposing elaborate hearing requirements in every suspension case is viewed with great concern, and many school authorities may well prefer the untrammeled power to act unilaterally, unhampered by rules about notice and hearing. But it would be a strange disciplinary system in an educational institution if no communication was sought by the disciplinarian with the student in an effort to inform him of his dereliction and to let him tell his side of the story in order to make sure that an injustice is not done. "[F]airness can rarely be obtained by secret, one-sided determination of facts decisive of rights. . . ." "Secrecy is not congenial to truth-seeking and self-righteousness gives too slender an assurance of tightness. No better instrument has been devised for arriving at truth than to give a person in jeopardy of serious loss notice of the case against him and opportunity to meet it."

We do not believe that school authorities must be totally free from notice and hearing requirements if their schools are to operate with acceptable efficiency. Students facing temporary suspension have interests qualifying for protection of the Due Process Clause, and due process requires, in connection with a suspension of 10 days or less, that the student be given oral or written notice of the charges against him and, if he denies them, an explanation of the evidence the authorities have and an opportunity to present his side of the story. The Clause requires at least these rudimentary precautions against unfair or mistaken findings of misconduct and arbitrary exclusion from school.

In holding as we do, we do not believe that we have imposed procedures on school disciplinarians which are inappropriate in a classroom setting. Instead we have imposed requirements which are, if anything, less than a fair-minded school principal would impose upon himself in order to avoid unfair suspensions.

Justice POWELL, with whom the Chief Justice, Justice BLACKMUN, and Justice REHNQUIST join, dissenting.

The Court today invalidates an Ohio statute that permits student suspensions from school without a hearing "for not more than ten days." The decision unnecessarily opens avenues for judicial intervention in the operation of our public schools that may affect adv ersely the quality of education. The Court holds for the first time that the federal courts, rather than educational officials and state legislatures, have the authority to determine the rules applicable to routine classroom discipline of children and teenagers in the public schools. It justifies this unprecedented intrusion into the process of elementary and secondary education by identifying a new constitutional right: the right of a student not to be suspended for as much as a single day without notice and a due process hearing either before or promptly following the suspension. In my view, a student's interest in education is not infringed by a suspension within the limited period prescribed by Ohio law. Moreover, to the extent that there may be some arguable infringement, it is too speculative, transitory, and insubstantial to justify imposition of a constitutional rule.

Goss expressly speaks of a student's liberty interest in his or her reputation. But in Paul v. Davis, the Court rejected such a liberty interest.

PAUL v. DAVIS
424 U.S. 693 (1976)

Justice Rehnquist delivered the opinion of the Court.

We granted certiorari in this case to consider whether respondent's charge that petitioners' defamation of him, standing alone and apart from any other governmental action with respect to him, stated a claim for relief under 42 U.S.C. §1983 and the Fourteenth Amendment. For the reasons hereinafter stated, we conclude that it does not.

Petitioner Paul is the Chief of Police of the Louisville, Ky., Division of Police, while petitioner McDaniel occupies the same position in the Jefferson County, Ky., Division of Police. In late 1972 they agreed to combine their efforts for the purpose of alerting local area merchants to possible shoplifters who might be operating during the Christmas season. In early December petitioners distributed to approximately 800 merchants in the Louisville metropolitan area a "flyer," which began as follows:

> To: Business Men in the Metropolitan Area
>
> The Chiefs of The Jefferson County and City of Louisville Police Departments, in an effort to keep their officers advised on shoplifting activity, have approved the attached alphabetically arranged flyer of subjects known to be active in this criminal field.
>
> This flyer is being distributed to you, the business man, so that you may inform your security personnel to watch for these subjects. These persons have been arrested during 1971 and 1972 or have been active in various criminal fields in high density shopping areas.

The flyer consisted of five pages of "mug shot" photos, arranged alphabetically. Each page was headed: November 1972 City of Louisville Jefferson [and] County Police Departments' Active Shoplifters. In approximately the center of page 2 there appeared photos and the name of the respondent, Edward Charles Davis III.

Respondent appeared on the flyer because on June 14, 1971, he had been arrested in Louisville on a charge of shoplifting. He had been arraigned on this charge in September 1971, and, upon his plea of not guilty, the charge had been "filed away with leave [to reinstate]," a disposition which left the charge outstanding. Thus, at the time petitioners caused the flyer to be prepared and circulated respondent had been charged with shoplifting but his guilt or innocence of that offense had never been resolved. Shortly after circulation of the flyer the charge against respondent was finally dismissed by a judge of the Louisville Police Court.

Respondent's due process claim is grounded upon his assertion that the flyer, and in particular the phrase "Active Shoplifters" appearing at the head of the page upon which his name and photograph appear, impermissibly deprived him of some "liberty" protected by the Fourteenth Amendment. His complaint asserted that the "active shoplifter" designation would inhibit him from entering business establishments for fear of being suspected of shoplifting and possibly apprehended, and would seriously impair his future employment opportunities.

The words "liberty" and "property" as used in the Fourteenth Amendment do not in terms single out reputation as a candidate for special protection over and above other interests that may be protected by state law. While we have in a number of our prior cases pointed out the frequently drastic effect of the "stigma" which may result from defamation by the government in a variety of contexts, this line of cases does not establish the proposition that reputation alone, apart from some more tangible interests such as employment, is either "liberty" or "property" by itself sufficient to invoke the procedural protection of the Due Process Clause.

This conclusion is quite consistent with our most recent holding in this area, Goss v. Lopez (1975), that suspension from school based upon charges of misconduct could trigger the procedural guarantees of the Fourteenth Amendment. While the Court noted that charges of misconduct could seriously damage the student's reputation, it also took care to point out that Ohio law conferred a right upon all children to attend school, and that the act of the school officials suspending the student there involved resulted in a denial or deprivation of that right.

Kentucky law does not extend to respondent any legal guarantee of present enjoyment of reputation which has been altered as a result of petitioners' actions. Rather his interest in reputation is simply one of a number which the State may protect against injury by virtue of its tort law, providing a forum for vindication of those interests by means of damages actions. And any harm or injury to that interest, even where as here inflicted by an officer of the State, does not result in a deprivation of any "liberty" or "property" recognized by state or federal law, nor has it worked any change of respondent's status as theretofore recognized under the State's laws. For these reasons we hold that the interest in reputation asserted in this case is neither "liberty" nor "property" guaranteed against state deprivation without due process of law.

Respondent in this case cannot assert denial of any right vouchsafed to him by the State and thereby protected under the Fourteenth Amendment. That being the case, petitioners' defamatory publications, however seriously they may have harmed respondent's reputation, did not deprive him of any "liberty" or "property" interests protected by the Due Process Clause.

Justice BRENNAN, with whom Justice MARSHALL concurs and Justice WHITE concurs in part, dissenting.

I dissent. The Court today holds that police officials, acting in their official capacities as law enforcers, may on their own initiative and without trial constitutionally condemn innocent individuals as criminals and thereby brand them with one of the most stigmatizing and debilitating labels in our society. If there are no constitutional restraints on such oppressive behavior, the safeguards constitutionally accorded an accused in a criminal trial are rendered a sham, and no individual can feel secure that he will not be arbitrarily singled out for similar Ex parte punishment by those primarily charged with fair enforcement of the law. The Court accomplishes this result by excluding a person's interest in his good name and reputation from all constitutional protection, regardless of the character of or necessity for the government's actions. The result, which is demonstrably inconsistent with our prior case law and unduly restrictive in its construction of our precious Bill of Rights, is one in which I cannot concur.

The Court now implicitly repudiates a substantial body of case law and finds no such constitutionally cognizable interest in a person's reputation, thus foreclosing any inquiry into the procedural protections accorded that interest in a given situation.

I have always thought that one of this Court's most important roles is to provide a formidable bulwark against governmental violation of the constitutional safeguards securing in our free society the legitimate expectations of every person to innate human dignity and sense of worth. It is a regrettable abdication of that role and a saddening denigration of our majestic Bill of Rights when the Court tolerates arbitrary and capricious official conduct branding an individual as a criminal without compliance with constitutional procedures designed to ensure the fair and impartial ascertainment of criminal culpability. Today's decision must surely be a shortlived aberration.

LIBERTY INTEREST FOR PRISONERS

In defining "liberty," the Court has struggled most with cases involving prisoners. Over the past quarter of a century, the Court has shifted its approach several times. Initially, the Court indicated that prisoners have a liberty interest when an important matter is at stake. The Court, however, later moved away from this approach and repeatedly held that liberty interests for prisoners are a function of statutes and regulations; prisoners have liberty interests when the relevant statutes and regulations create them. However, most recently in Sandin v. Conner, the Supreme Court backed away from this approach and held that regardless of the content of statutes and regulations, there is a liberty interest only if there is a significant deprivation of freedom that is atypical to the usual conditions of confinement.

In Morrissey v. Brewer, 408 U.S. 471 (1972), the Supreme Court held that revocation of parole is a deprivation of liberty that requires the provision of due process. The Court emphasized the importance of the interest to the individual. When out on parole, an individual can be "gainfully employed and is free to be with family and friends and to form the other enduring attachments of normal life." This, of course, is taken away if parole is revoked, and the Supreme Court found that there was a liberty interest in remaining on parole because ending parole "inflicts a grievous loss on the parolee and often on others." In other words, *Morrissey* found a liberty interest based on the significance of the interest to the parolee, rather than focusing on the specifics of the state law involved.

Likewise, a year later, in Gagnon v. Scarpelli, 411 U.S. 778 (1973), the Supreme Court ruled that the revocation of probation is a deprivation of liberty requiring due process. The Court explained that "revocation of probation . . . is constitutionally indistinguishable from the revocation of parole."

Soon after these cases, however, the Court shifted its approach and based its determination of whether there is a liberty interest on the content of the statutes or rules, rather than on the importance of the interest to the individual. For example, in Wolff v. McDonnell, 418 U.S. 539 (1974), the Supreme Court held that prisoners have a liberty interest in "good time credits" awarded under state law. The Court explained that although a state need not give prisoners good time credits, "the State having created the right to good time . . . , the prisoner's interest has real substance and is sufficiently embraced within Fourteenth Amendment liberty to entitle him to those minimum procedures . . . required by the Due Process Clause to insure that the state-created right is not arbitrarily abrogated." The Court said that a "person's liberty is equally protected, even when the liberty itself is a statutory creation of the state." In other words, *Wolff* found a liberty interest based on the expectations created by state law, rather than based on the significance of the credits for the individual prisoner.

The Court applied *Wolff* in Meachum v. Fano, 427 U.S. 215 (1976), where the Supreme Court held that prisoners do not have a liberty interest in remaining in a minimum-security facility, as opposed to a maximum-security facility, unless the state or federal law clearly creates such an expectation. A prisoner argued that a transfer from a minimum-security facility to a maximum-security facility obviously meant that he had less liberty. The Court disagreed and declared, "We reject at the outset the notion that any grievous loss visited upon a person by the State is sufficient to invoke the procedural protections of the Due Process Clause. . . . That life in one prison is much more disagreeable than in another does not in itself signify that a Fourteenth Amendment liberty interest is implicated."

In dissent, Justice Stevens, joined by Justices Brennan and Marshall, disagreed and argued that "neither the Bill of Rights nor the laws of sovereign States create the liberty which the Due Process Clause protects. . . . It is . . . basic freedom which the Due Process Clause protects, rather than the particular rights or privileges conferred by specific laws or regulations." The conflict between the dissent and the majority was over how to determine when a prisoner has a liberty interest. For the dissent, a deprivation of liberty occurs when a prisoner is denied important freedoms regardless of the content of statutes or regulations. For the majority, a deprivation of liberty occurs if there is the removal of a freedom created by a statute or regulation.

After *Wolff* and *Meachum,* the question becomes what statutes and rules create liberty interests? The Supreme Court focused on whether a law or rule was sufficiently mandatory so as to create a reasonable expectation on the part of the prisoner. For example, in Greenholtz v. Inmates of Nebraska Penal & Correctional Complex, 442 U.S. 1 (1979), the Supreme Court held that the existence of a parole system is not enough to create a liberty interest in parole; rather, there must be specific requirements in the law that transform parole from a mere hope to an entitlement under particular circumstances. The Court found that Nebraska created a liberty interest in parole because state law allowed the denial of parole only under specific statutorily defined reasons and because the law allowed denial only if there were specific findings to support the decision. The Court emphasized that the word "shall" in the state law created a legitimate expectation to release on parole unless one of the statute's exceptions was met.

The contrast in approach between Morrissey v. Brewster and *Greenholtz* is striking. *Morrissey* found a liberty interest in parole because it determines a person's freedom. *Greenholtz* held that there is a liberty interest in parole only if the state law makes it one by its mandatory language.

The *Greenholtz* approach was followed in a series of cases spanning over two decades. For example, the Supreme Court has held that a prisoner has a liberty interest in not being placed in disciplinary segregation or being transferred to another, more restrictive facility, only if state law creates such an expectation. In Hewitt v. Helms, 459 U.S. 460 (1983), the Supreme Court found that a prison had to provide due process before placing a prisoner in administrative segregation because state law had created such a liberty interest. The Court explained that generally prisoners have no liberty interest in being confined in one place as opposed to another. But the Court said that the state had done more than issue procedural guidelines; it had used "language of an unmistakably mandatory character" and made it clear that a prisoner would not be placed in administrative segregation "absent specific substantive predicates."

Similarly, in Connecticut Board of Pardons v. Dumschat, 452 U.S. 458 (1981), the Supreme Court found that a prisoner did not have a liberty interest in having a review of a request for commutation of a life sentence. The Court explained that state law did not create an expectation that sentences would be commuted, even though in practice the review board commuted most of the life sentences in the cases it considered. The Court said that the Connecticut law governing commutation of sentences did not provide "particularized standards or criteria [to] guide the State's decisionmakers."

In other words, in deciding whether a prisoner has a liberty interest, the Court would examine the statutes and regulations governing the prison. If they were written in mandatory language and created a legitimate expectation of a benefit, then the Court would find a liberty interest. The Court expressly stated this in Kentucky Department of Corrections v. Thompson, 490 U.S. 454, 463 (1989), where it declared, "We have . . . articulated a requirement . . . that the regulations contain explicitly mandatory language, i.e., specific directives to the decision maker that if the regulations' substantive predicates are present, a particular outcome must follow, in order to create a liberty interest." In *Thompson*, the Supreme Court held that prisoners in Kentucky did not have a liberty interest in visitation, even visitation from family members, because the regulations "lack the requisite relevant mandatory language."

Although in all of these cases the Court emphasized the content of the laws and regulations, there were some cases that did not fit this pattern and where the Court found a liberty interest primarily based on the importance of the interest to the prisoner. For example, in Vitek v. Jones, 445 U.S. 480 (1980), the Court held that a prisoner is deprived of liberty when transferred from a prison to a mental hospital. The Court, in part, focused on the content of the state's prison regulations and concluded that they created an expectation that the inmate would be kept in prison facilities and not moved to a mental hospital without a proven need for treatment. But the Court also emphasized that there was a loss of liberty because confinement to a mental hospital likely would mean the imposition of mandatory treatment and also a realistic possibility of stigma. The clear implication of *Vitek* is that prisoners have a liberty interest in not being transferred to a mental hospital regardless of the content of the specific laws or regulations for that prison.

Also, in Washington v. Harper, 494 U.S. 210 (1990), the Supreme Court recognized that prisoners have a liberty interest in avoiding the involuntary administration of antipsychotic medications. The Court made it clear that independent of any state law or regulation, prisoners have a liberty interest in being free from the involuntary administration of psychotropic drugs. The Court found that the state's law met the requirements for procedural and substantive due process before the administration of these drugs. Prison regulations required that the prisoner be given at least 24 hours' notice before the administration of this medication, and it provided the opportunity for a hearing before health professionals and prison officials. The Court found that this was procedurally adequate to meet the requirements of due process.

Thus, up until June 1995, a liberty interest for prisoners could be found either if the prison statutes and regulations were written in mandatory language and created such an interest or if the interest was so important that the Court would deem it to be a part of liberty regardless of the content of the statutes or regulations. In Sandin v. Conner, however, the Court called into question the approach of finding liberty interests based on the content of statutes and regulations and shifted back to an approach that determines liberty interests based on the importance of the interest involved.

SANDIN v. CONNER, 515 U.S. 472 (1995): Chief Justice REHNQUIST delivered the opinion of the Court.

We granted certiorari to reexamine the circumstances under which state prison regulations afford inmates a liberty interest protected by the Due Process Clause.

I

DeMont Conner was convicted of numerous state crimes, including murder, kidnaping, robbery, and burglary, for which he is currently serving an indeterminate sentence of 30 years to life in a Hawaii prison. He was confined in the Halawa Correctional Facility, a maximum security prison in central Oahu. In August 1987, a prison officer escorted him from his cell to the module program area. The officer subjected Conner to a strip search, complete with an inspection of the rectal area. Conner retorted with angry and foul language directed at the officer. Eleven days later he received notice that he had been charged with disciplinary infractions. The notice charged Conner with "high misconduct" for using physical interference to impair a correctional function, and "low moderate misconduct" for using abusive or obscene language and for harassing employees.

Conner appeared before an adjustment committee on August 28, 1987. The committee refused Conner's request to present witnesses at the hearing, stating that "[w]itnesses were unavailable due to move [sic] to the medium facility and being short staffed on the modules." At the conclusion of proceedings, the committee determined that Conner was guilty of the alleged misconduct. It sentenced him to 30 days' disciplinary segregation in the Special Holding Unit. The Court of Appeals for the Ninth Circuit reversed the judgment. It concluded that Conner had a liberty interest in remaining free from disciplinary segregation and that there was a disputed question of fact with respect to whether Conner received all of the process due under this Court's pronounce-ment in Wolff v. McDonnell. The Court of Appeals based its conclusion on a prison regulation that instructs the committee to find guilt when a charge of misconduct is supported by substantial evidence.

II

[The Court reviewed the shift from cases looking at the importance of the interest for the prisoner to those considering the content of the prison regula-tions and stated:] no longer did inmates need to rely on a showing that they had suffered a "grievous loss" of liberty retained even after sentenced to terms of imprisonment. For the Court had ceased to examine the "nature" of the interest with respect to interests allegedly created by the State. In a series of cases since *Hewitt*, the Court has wrestled with the language of intricate, often rather routine prison guidelines to determine whether mandatory language and substantive predicates created an enforceable expectation that the State would produce a particular outcome with respect to the prisoner's conditions of confinement.

By shifting the focus of the liberty interest inquiry to one based on the lan-guage of a particular regulation, and not the nature of the deprivation, the Court encouraged prisoners to comb regulations in search of mandatory lan-guage on which to base entitlements to various state-conferred privileges. Such a conclusion may be entirely sensible in the ordinary task of construing a statute defining rights and remedies available to the general public. It is a good deal less sensible in the case of a prison regulation primarily designed to guide correc-tional officials in the administration of a prison. Not only are such regulations not designed to confer rights on inmates, but the result of the negative impli-cation jurisprudence is not to require the prison officials to follow the negative implication drawn from the regulation, but is instead to attach procedural pro-tections that may be of quite a different nature.

Hewitt has produced at least two undesirable effects. First, it creates disincen-tives for States to codify prison management procedures in the interest of uniform treatment. Prison administrators need be concerned with the safety of the staff and inmate population. Ensuring that welfare often leads prison administrators to curb the discretion of staff on the front line who daily encounter prisoners hostile to the authoritarian structure of the prison environ-ment. Such guidelines are not set forth solely to benefit the prisoner. They also aspire to instruct subordinate employees how to exercise discretion vested by the State in the warden, and to confine the authority of prison personnel in order to avoid widely different treatment of similar incidents. The approach embraced by *Hewitt* discourages this desirable development: States may avoid creation of "liberty" interests by having scarcely any regulations, or by conferring standard-less discretion on correctional personnel.

Second, the *Hewitt* approach has led to the involvement of federal courts in the day-to-day management of prisons, often squandering judicial resources with little offsetting benefit to anyone. In so doing, it has run counter to the view expressed in several of our cases that federal courts ought to afford appro-priate deference and flexibility to state officials trying to manage a volatile environment. Such flexibility is especially warranted in the fine-tuning of the ordinary incidents of prison life, a common subject of prisoner claims since *Hewitt*. See, e.g., Klos v. Haskell (CA2 1995) (claiming liberty interest in right to participate in "shock program"—a type of boot camp for inmates); Segal v. Biller (CA9 1994) (unpublished) (claiming liberty interest in a waiver of the travel limit imposed on prison furloughs); Burgin v. Nix (CA8 1990) (claiming liberty interest in receiving a tray lunch rather than a sack lunch); Spruytte v. Walters (CA6 1985) (finding liberty interest in receiving a paperback dictionary due to a rule that states a prisoner "may receive any book . . . which does not present a threat to the order or security of the institution").

In light of the above discussion, we believe that the search for a negative implication from mandatory language in prisoner regulations has strayed from the real concerns undergirding the liberty protected by the Due Process Clause. The time has come to return to the due process principles we believe were correctly established and applied in *Wolff* and *Meachum*. This case, though concededly punitive, does not present a dramatic departure from the basic conditions of Conner's indeterminate sentence. Conner's confinement did not exceed similar, but totally discretionary, confinement in either duration or degree of restriction. Indeed, the conditions at Halawa involve significant amounts of "lockdown time" even for inmates in the general population. Based on a comparison between inmates inside and outside disciplinary segregation, the State's actions in placing him there for 30 days did not work a major disruption in his environment.

Justice BREYER, with whom Justice SOUTER joins, dissenting.

The specific question in this case is whether a particular punishment that, among other things, segregates an inmate from the general prison population for violating a disciplinary rule deprives the inmate of "liberty" within the terms of the Fourteenth Amendment's Due Process Clause. The majority, asking whether that punishment "imposes atypical and significant hardship on the inmate in relation to the ordinary incidents of prison life," concludes that it does not do so. The majority's reasoning, however, particularly when read in light of this Court's precedents, seems to me to lead to the opposite conclusion. And, for that reason, I dissent.

If we apply these pre-existing principles to the relevant facts before us, it seems fairly clear, as the Ninth Circuit found, that the prison punishment here at issue deprived Conner of constitutionally protected "liberty." For one thing, the punishment worked a fairly major change in Conner's conditions. In the absence of the punishment, Conner, like other inmates in Halawa's general prison population, would have left his cell and worked, taken classes, or mingled with others for eight hours each day. As a result of disciplinary segregation, however, Conner, for 30 days, had to spend his entire time alone in his cell (with the exception of 50 minutes each day on average for brief exercise and shower periods, during which he nonetheless remained isolated from other inmates and was constrained by leg irons and waist chains).

In Wilkinson v. Austin, 545 U.S. 209 (2005), the Court held, using the test from Sandin v. Conner, that placing a prisoner in a "super max" facility that includes solitary confinement for 23 hours per day is a deprivation of liberty. But the Court found that the state's procedures were sufficient to meet due process.

3. What Procedures Are Required?

When the government must provide due process, it must always supply certain basic safeguards such as notice of the charges or issue,[70] the opportunity for a meaningful hearing,[71] and an impartial decision maker.[72] These long have been regarded as the core elements of due process. In Mullane v. Central Hanover Bank & Trust Co., 339 U.S. 306 (1950), the Court declared the much-quoted words, "Many controversies have raged about the cryptic and abstract words of the Due Process Clause but there can be no doubt that at a minimum they require that deprivation of life, liberty, or property by adjudication be proceeded by notice and opportunity for hearing appropriate to the nature of the case."

Yet even when notice and a hearing are required, there are a multitude of ways of providing them. For example, what type of notice is required—must it be notice that is personally served, or is notice by posting or even by publication sufficient? What type of a hearing must be supplied—is a full trial-type, adversarial hearing required, or is a much more informal proceeding sufficient? What procedural safeguards must be accorded at the hearing? Must the government provide the right to be represented by an attorney at the hearing, and if so, is the government required to provide indigents with a free lawyer if they cannot afford one? When must the hearing occur—must it be before the deprivation can occur, or is a post-deprivation hearing sufficient? What is the standard of proof, and who has the burden of proof? Who is a permissible decision maker—must it be a judge or can others suffice? And these are just some of the choices that must be made in deciding what due process requires.

In Mathews v. Eldridge, the Court articulated a balancing test for deciding what procedures are required when there has been a deprivation of life, liberty, or property and due process is required. The Supreme Court has applied it repeatedly in deciding what process is due.

MATHEWS v. ELDRIDGE

424 U.S. 319 (1976)

Justice POWELL delivered the opinion of the Court.

The issue in this case is whether the Due Process Clause of the Fifth Amendment requires that prior to the termination of Social Security disability benefit payments the recipient be afforded an opportunity for an evidentiary hearing.

---

70. *See, e.g.,* Mullane v. Central Hanover Bank & Trust Co., 339 U.S. 306 (1950) (discussing notice as a requirement of due process).

71. *See, e.g.,* Goldberg v. Kelly, 397 U.S. 254 (1970) (hearing required before termination of welfare benefits).

72. *See, e.g.,* Gibson v. Berryhill, 411 U.S. 564 (1973) (unconstitutional to have decision makers who potentially would personally gain from their decisions). *See also* Caperton v. A.T. Massey Coal Co., 556 U.S. 868 (2009) (concluding that due process was denied for lack of an impartial decision maker when the officials of Massey Coal spent $3 million to get their candidate of choice elected to the Supreme Court and he then participated in a decision to overrule a $50 million judgment against Massey Coal).

I

Cash benefits are provided to workers during periods in which they are completely disabled under the disability insurance benefits program created by the 1956 amendments to Title II of the Social Security Act. Respondent Eldridge was first awarded benefits in June 1968. In March 1972, he received a questionnaire from the state agency charged with monitoring his medical condition. Eldridge completed the questionnaire, indicating that his condition had not improved and identifying the medical sources, including physicians, from whom he had received treatment recently. The state agency then obtained reports from his physician and a psychiatric consultant. After considering these reports and other information in his file the agency informed Eldridge by letter that it had made a tentative determination that his disability had ceased in May 1972. The letter included a statement of reasons for the proposed termination of benefits, and advised Eldridge that he might request reasonable time in which to obtain and submit additional information pertaining to his condition.

In his written response, Eldridge disputed one characterization of his medical condition and indicated that the agency already had enough evidence to establish his disability. The state agency then made its final determination that he had ceased to be disabled in May 1972. This determination was accepted by the Social Security Administration (SSA), which notified Eldridge in July that his benefits would terminate after that month. The notification also advised him of his right to seek reconsideration by the state agency of this initial determination within six months.

Instead of requesting reconsideration Eldridge commenced this action challenging the constitutional validity of the administrative procedures established by the Secretary of Health, Education, and Welfare for assessing whether there exists a continuing disability. He sought an immediate reinstatement of benefits pending a hearing on the issue of his disability.

II

A

Procedural due process imposes constraints on governmental decisions which deprive individuals of "liberty" or "property" interests within the meaning of the Due Process Clause of the Fifth or Fourteenth Amendment. The Secretary does not contend that procedural due process is inapplicable to terminations of Social Security disability benefits. He recognizes, as has been implicit in our prior decisions, that the interest of an individual in continued receipt of these benefits is a statutorily created "property" interest protected by the Fifth Amendment. Rather, the Secretary contends that the existing administrative procedures, detailed below, provide all the process that is constitutionally due before a recipient can be deprived of that interest.

This Court consistently has held that some form of hearing is required before an individual is finally deprived of a property interest. The "right to be heard before being condemned to suffer grievous loss of any kind, even though it may not involve the stigma and hardships of a criminal conviction, is a principle basic to our society." The fundamental requirement of due process is the opportunity to be heard "at a meaningful time and in a meaningful manner." Eldridge agrees that the review procedures available to a claimant before the initial determination of ineligibility becomes final would be adequate if disability benefits were not terminated until after the evidentiary hearing stage of the administrative process. The dispute centers upon what process is due prior to the initial termination of benefits, pending review.

[R]esolution of the issue whether the administrative procedures provided here are constitutionally sufficient requires analysis of the governmental and private interests that are affected. [O]ur prior decisions indicate that identification of the specific dictates of due process generally requires consideration of three distinct factors: First, the private interest that will be affected by the official action; second, the risk of an erroneous deprivation of such interest through the procedures used, and the probable value, if any, of additional or substitute procedural safeguards; and finally, the Government's interest, including the function involved and the fiscal and administrative burdens that the additional or substitute procedural requirement would entail.

Since a recipient whose benefits are terminated is awarded full retroactive relief if he ultimately prevails, his sole interest is in the uninterrupted receipt of this source of income pending final administrative decision on his claim. His potential injury is thus similar in nature to that of the welfare recipient in *Goldberg*. Only in *Goldberg* has the Court held that due process requires an evidentiary hearing prior to a temporary deprivation. It was emphasized there that welfare assistance is given to persons on the very margin of subsistence. Eligibility for disability benefits, in contrast, is not based upon financial need. Indeed, it is wholly unrelated to the worker's income or support from any other sources.

As *Goldberg* illustrates, the degree of potential deprivation that may be created by a particular decision is a factor to be considered in assessing the validity of any administrative decisionmaking process. The potential deprivation here is generally likely to be less than in *Goldberg*, although the degree of difference can be overstated. In view of the torpidity of this administrative review process, and the typically modest resources of the family unit of the physically disabled worker, the hardship imposed upon the erroneously terminated disability recipient may be significant. Still, the disabled worker's need is likely to be less than that of a welfare recipient. In addition to the possibility of access to private resources, other forms of government assistance will become available where the termination of disability benefits places a worker or his family below the subsistence level. In view of these potential sources of temporary income, there is less reason here than in *Goldberg* to depart from the ordinary principle, established by our decisions, that something less than an evidentiary hearing is sufficient prior to adverse administrative action.

An additional factor to be considered here is the fairness and reliability of the existing pretermination procedures, and the probable value, if any, of additional procedural safeguards. Central to the evaluation of any administrative process is the nature of the relevant inquiry.

In order to remain eligible for benefits the disabled worker must demonstrate by means of "medically acceptable clinical and laboratory diagnostic techniques," that he is unable "to engage in any substantial gainful activity by reason of any medically determinable physical or mental impairment. . . ." In short, a medical assessment of the worker's physical or mental condition is required. This is a more sharply focused and easily documented decision than the typical determination of welfare entitlement. In the latter case, a wide variety of information may be deemed relevant, and issues of witness credibility and veracity often are critical to the decisionmaking process. *Goldberg* noted that in such circumstances "written submissions are a wholly unsatisfactory basis for decision." By contrast, the decision whether to discontinue disability benefits will turn, in most cases, upon "routine, standard, and unbiased medical reports by physician specialists." To be sure, credibility and veracity may be a factor in the ultimate disability assessment in some cases. But procedural due process rules are shaped by the risk of error inherent in the truthfinding process as applied to the generality of cases, not the rare exceptions. The potential value of an evidentiary hearing, or even oral presentation to the decisionmaker, is substantially less in this context than in *Goldberg*.

A further safeguard against mistake is the policy of allowing the disability recipient's representative full access to all information relied upon by the state agency. In addition, prior to the cutoff of benefits the agency informs the recipient of its tentative assessment, the reasons therefore, and provides a summary of the evidence that it considers most relevant. Opportunity is then afforded the recipient to submit additional evidence or arguments, enabling him to challenge directly the accuracy of information in his file as well as the correctness of the agency's tentative conclusions. These procedures, again as contrasted with those before the Court in *Goldberg*, enable the recipient to "mold" his argument to respond to the precise issues which the decisionmaker regards as crucial.

In striking the appropriate due process balance the final factor to be assessed is the public interest. This includes the administrative burden and other societal costs that would be associated with requiring, as a matter of constitutional right, an evidentiary hearing upon demand in all cases prior to the termination of disability benefits. The most visible burden would be the incremental cost resulting from the increased number of hearings and the expense of providing benefits to ineligible recipients pending decision. No one can predict the extent of the increase, but the fact that full benefits would continue until after such hearings would assure the exhaustion in most cases of this attractive option.

Financial cost alone is not a controlling weight in determining whether due process requires a particular procedural safeguard prior to some administrative decision. But the Government's interest, and hence that of the public, in conserving scarce fiscal and administrative resources is a factor that must be weighed. At some point the benefit of an additional safeguard to the individual affected by the administrative action and to society in terms of increased assurance that the action is just, may be outweighed by the cost.

The ultimate balance involves a determination as to when, under our constitutional system, judicial-type procedures must be imposed upon administrative action to assure fairness. In assessing what process is due in this case, substantial weight must be given to the good-faith judgments of the individuals charged by Congress with the administration of social welfare programs that the procedures they have provided assure fair consideration of the entitlement claims of individuals. This is especially so where, as here, the prescribed procedures not only provide the claimant with an effective process for asserting his claim prior to any administrative action, but also assure a right to an evidentiary hearing, as well as to subsequent judicial review, before the denial of his claim becomes final. We conclude that an evidentiary hearing is not required prior to the termination of disability benefits and that the present administrative proce-dures fully comport with due process.

Justice BRENNAN, with whom Justice MARSHALL concurs, dissenting.

I agree with the District Court and the Court of Appeals that, prior to termi-nation of benefits, Eldridge must be afforded an evidentiary hearing of the type required for welfare beneficiaries. See Goldberg v. Kelly (1970). I would add that the Court's consideration that a discontinuance of disability benefits may cause the recipient to suffer only a limited deprivation is no argument. It is speculative. Moreover, the very legislative determination to provide disability benefits, without any prerequisite determination of need in fact, presumes a need by the recipient which is not this Court's function to denigrate. Indeed, in the present case, it is indicated that because disability benefits were terminated there was a foreclosure upon the Eldridge home and the family's furniture was repossessed, forcing Eldridge, his wife, and their children to sleep in one bed. Finally, it is also no argument that a worker, who has been placed in the untenable position of having been denied disability benefits, may still seek other forms of public assistance.

The *Mathews* test has been praised because it focuses a court's attention on what seem to be the right questions in deciding the nature of the procedural protections. *Mathews* requires courts to balance the importance of the interest involved, the degree to which the procedure will make a difference, and the cost to the government. An expensive trial-type hearing would be out of place for a minor interest in a situation where there is little likelihood of a factual dispute.[73] But an adversarial hearing is essential, despite its expense, if there is a fundamental right at stake, such as the right of parents to the custody of their children.

Yet *Mathews* also can be criticized for failing to provide any real guidance as to how courts should balance the competing interests. The reality is that courts have enormous discretion in evaluating each of the three factors and especially how to balance them. Such multipart balancing inherently provides little con-straint on judicial decisions. Indeed, Justice Rehnquist once remarked that under *Mathews*, "[t]he balance is simply an ad hoc weighing which depends to a great extent upon how the Court subjectively views the underlying interests at stake."[74]

Moreover, the *Mathews* test has been criticized for giving insufficient weight to the intrinsic benefits of procedural protections and for giving disproportionate weight to quantifiable variables such as cost.[75] Due process, it is argued, is important not only to enhance the accuracy of decision makers but to treat individuals fairly and with dignity when important decisions are made about their lives. *Mathews* can be criticized for failing to recognize these values.

---

73. *See, e.g.*, Henry J. Friendly, *Some Kind of Hearing*, 123 U. Pa. L. Rev. 1267, 1276 (1975).

74. Cleveland Bd. of Educ. v. Loudermill, 470 U.S. 532, 562 (1985) (Rehnquist, J., dissenting).

75. *See, e.g.*, Jerry Mashaw, *The Supreme Court's Due Process Calculus for Administrative Adjudication in Mathews v. Eldridge: Three Factors in Search of a Theory of Value*, 44 U. Chi. L. Rev. 28 (1976).

Nonetheless, it is firmly established that in deciding what procedures are required, the Court employs the *Mathews* three-part balancing test. Two examples are presented below: government employment and parents' rights.

GOVERNMENT EMPLOYMENT

In Arnett v. Kennedy, 416 U.S. 134 (1974), the Supreme Court, without a majority opinion, ruled that the government could fire a public employee for misconduct without a full hearing prior to termination. The Court said that it was sufficient that there was the opportunity for a pretermination review within the department followed by a post-termination hearing.

The Court reaffirmed this in Cleveland Board of Education v. Loudermill, 470 U.S. 532 (1985), where it expressly applied the *Mathews* balancing test. In *Loudermill*, the Court concluded that due process was satisfied if the government provided a fired employee both an informal pretermination proceeding where it was possible to respond to charges and then a later post-termination hearing.

As to the first aspect of the *Mathews* balancing test, the Court found that continued employment by the government is a "significant" interest for the individual. As to the second part of the balancing test, the Court concluded that an informal pretermination proceeding was essential to avoid erroneous terminations. As to the third prong of the test, the Court recognized that any pretermination proceeding would entail costs to the government. But the Court said that the importance of the interest to the individual and the need to avoid errors justified requiring an informal pretermination proceeding despite these costs. The Court emphasized that "the pre-termination hearing, though necessary, need not be elaborate."

Arnett, and especially *Loudermill*, provide the type of compromise that *Mathews* envisioned. The Court recognizes the importance of providing a pretermination hearing to employees but also acknowledges the costs to the government of doing this. So the Court strikes a compromise: an informal pretermination proceeding to be followed, if necessary, by a formal post-termination hearing.

FAMILY RIGHTS

The Supreme Court has been inconsistent in the degree of due process it has required in cases concerning parental rights. On the one hand, there have been cases where the Court has stressed the importance of the interest and has required substantial procedural protections. For example, the Supreme Court has held that a state must prove, by "clear and convincing evidence," the need to terminate parental rights at a hearing before such rights are terminated.[76]

The Court also has recognized the right of an individual to deny paternity. In Little v. Streater, 452 U.S. 1 (1981), the Court held that the government must pay for blood tests for indigent defendants in paternity cases. The Court explained that a defendant unable to afford the cost of the blood tests would

---

76. Santosky v. Kramer, 455 U.S. 745, 769 (1982).

lack a "meaningful opportunity to be heard" because there was no other way to refute the allegation of paternity. The Court explained that "a cost requirement, valid on its face, may offend due process because it operates to foreclose a particular party's opportunity to be heard."

But on the other hand, the Court has held that the government need not automatically provide an attorney to indigent parents at parental termination proceedings. In Lassiter v. Department of Social Services, 452 U.S. 18 (1981), the Court explicitly applied the *Mathews* test and concluded that the obligation to provide counsel depends on the circumstances of the particular case and is not required in all instances where the government seeks to end parental rights. The Court said that it had recognized an automatic right to government-appointed counsel for indigents "only where the litigant may lose his physical liberty if he loses the litigation."

The Court recognized that a "parent's desire for and right to the companionship, care, custody, and management of his or her children is an undeniably important interest that undeniably warrants deference." The Court said that "the State has an urgent interest in the welfare of the child" that also is served by ensuring accurate and just results at parental termination hearings.

Nonetheless, the Court did not find that due process always requires the provision of counsel for indigent parents at such proceedings. The Court said that sometimes the presence of an attorney would matter little in the outcome of the proceedings. The Court declared that "the presence of counsel for Ms. Lassiter could not have made a determinative difference." The Court said that "Ms. Lassiter had expressly declined to appear at the 1975 child custody hearing, . . . had not even bothered to speak to her retained lawyer after being notified of the termination hearing, . . . [and failed] to make an effort to contest the termination proceeding."

The Court said that "wise public policy" may cause states to provide an attorney for all indigent parents at termination proceedings and those concerning neglect or dependency. The Court also recognized that in some instances the government would be required to appoint counsel where "the parent's interests were at their strongest, the State's interests were at their weakest, and the risks of errors were at their peak." But the Court concluded that the Constitution does not "require the appointment of counsel in every parental termination proceeding."

The likelihood of error without the appointment of counsel was the decisive factor for the majority in *Lassiter*. The dissent, written by Justice Blackmun and joined by Justices Brennan and Marshall, argued that attorneys always should be provided to prevent errors. Often parents will not know enough about their rights and the procedures to make a showing as to how an attorney would make a difference. In some cases, it would take an attorney to make the argument as to why an attorney is necessary, but no lawyer is provided until after such a showing. Justice Blackmun thus lamented that "[b]y intimidation, inarticulateness, or confusion, a parent can lose forever all contact and involvement with his or her offspring."

In a separate dissenting opinion, Justice Stevens questioned the application of the *Mathews* balancing test to a fundamental liberty interest outside the property context. He argued that the utilitarian calculus employed under *Mathews* is ill suited for cases involving basic freedoms. He said that even if the costs to the state were great, procedural protections such as the right to counsel in termination proceedings are essential because "protecting our liberty from deprivation by the State without due process of law is priceless."

SUBSTANTIVE AND PROCEDURAL DUE PROCESS: THE RELATIONSHIP

Cases generally present substantive or procedural due process issues, but certainly the same case could involve both. For example, as explained above, the Court has said that under the liberty of the due process clause, parents have a right to custody of their children. Substantive due process requires that the government show a compelling reason for terminating custody; procedural due process requires notice and a hearing before termination of custody. Both could arise in the same case. The case below presents an example of substantive and procedural due process arising in the same case as a convicted criminal defendant argued that both provided him the right to have DNA testing done (at his own expense), which could have exonerated him of the crime for which he was convicted. The Supreme Court rejected both claims and ruled in favor of the government.

DISTRICT ATTORNEY'S OFFICE FOR THE THIRD JUDICIAL DISTRICT v. OSBORNE

557 U.S. 52 (2009)

Chief Justice ROBERTS delivered the opinion of the Court.

DNA testing has an unparalleled ability both to exonerate the wrongly convicted and to identify the guilty. It has the potential to significantly improve both the criminal justice system and police investigative practices. The Federal Government and the States have recognized this, and have developed special approaches to ensure that this evidentiary tool can be effectively incorporated into established criminal procedure — usually but not always through legislation.

Against this prompt and considered response, the respondent, William Osborne, proposes a different approach: the recognition of a freestanding and far-reaching constitutional right of access to this new type of evidence. This approach would take the development of rules and procedures in this area out of the hands of legislatures and state courts shaping policy in a focused manner and turn it over to federal courts applying the broad parameters of the Due Process Clause. There is no reason to constitutionalize the issue in this way. Because the decision below would do just that, we reverse.

I

This lawsuit arose out of a violent crime committed 16 years ago, which has resulted in a long string of litigation in the state and federal courts. On the evening of March 22, 1993, two men driving through Anchorage, Alaska, solicited sex from a female prostitute, K.G. She agreed to perform fellatio on both men for $100 and got in their car. The three spent some time looking for a place to stop and ended up in a deserted area near Earthquake Park. When K.G. demanded payment in advance, the two men pulled out a gun and forced her to perform fellatio on the driver while the passenger penetrated her vaginally, using a blue condom she had brought. The passenger then ordered K.G. out of the car and told her to lie face-down in the snow. Fearing for her life, she refused, and the two men choked her and beat her with the gun. When K.G. tried to flee, the passenger beat her with a wooden axe handle and shot her in the head while she lay on the ground. They kicked some snow on top of her and left her for dead.

K.G. did not die; the bullet had only grazed her head. Once the two men left, she found her way back to the road, and flagged down a passing car to take her home. Ultimately, she received medical care and spoke to the police. At the scene of the crime, the police recovered a spent shell casing, the axe handle, some of K.G.'s clothing stained with blood, and the blue condom.

Six days later, two military police officers at Fort Richardson pulled over Dexter Jackson for flashing his headlights at another vehicle. In his car they discovered a gun (which matched the shell casing), as well as several items K.G. had been carrying the night of the attack. The car also matched the description K.G. had given to the police. Jackson admitted that he had been the driver during the rape and assault, and told the police that William Osborne had been his passenger. Other evidence also implicated Osborne. K.G. picked out his photograph (with some uncertainty) and at trial she identified Osborne as her attacker. Other witnesses testified that shortly before the crime, Osborne had called Jackson from an arcade, and then driven off with him. An axe handle similar to the one at the scene of the crime was found in Osborne's room on the military base where he lived.

The State also performed DQ Alpha testing on sperm found in the blue condom. DQ Alpha testing is a relatively inexact form of DNA testing that can clear some wrongly accused individuals, but generally cannot narrow the perpetrator down to less than 5% of the population. The semen found on the condom had a genotype that matched a blood sample taken from Osborne, but not ones from Jackson, K.G., or a third suspect named James Hunter. Osborne is black, and approximately 16% of black individuals have such a genotype. App. 117-119. In other words, the testing ruled out Jackson and Hunter as possible sources of the semen, and also ruled out over 80% of other black individuals. The State also examined some pubic hairs found at the scene of the crime, which were not susceptible to DQ Alpha testing, but which state witnesses attested to be similar to Osborne's.

Osborne and Jackson were convicted by an Alaska jury of kidnapping, assault, and sexual assault. They were acquitted of an additional count of sexual assault and of attempted murder. Finding it "nearly miraculous" that K.G. had survived, the trial judge sentenced Osborne to 26 years in prison, with 5 suspended. His conviction and sentence were affirmed on appeal. Osborne then sought post-conviction relief in Alaska state court. He claimed that he had asked his attorney, Sidney Billingslea, to seek more discriminating restriction-fragment-length-polymorphism (RFLP) DNA testing during trial, and argued that she was constitutionally ineffective for not doing so. In two decisions, the Alaska Court of Appeals concluded that Osborne had no right to the RFLP test. The court relied heavily on the fact that Osborne had confessed to some of his crimes in a 2004 application for parole — in which it is a crime to lie. In this statement, Osborne acknowledged forcing K.G. to have sex at gunpoint, as well as beating her and covering her with snow. He repeated this confession before the parole board.

II

Modern DNA testing can provide powerful new evidence unlike anything known before. Since its first use in criminal investigations in the mid-1980s, there have been several major advances in DNA technology, culminating in STR technology. It is now often possible to determine whether a biological tissue matches a suspect with near certainty. While of course many criminal trials proceed without any forensic and scientific testing at all, there is no technology comparable to DNA testing for matching tissues when such evidence is at issue. DNA testing has exonerated wrongly convicted people, and has confirmed the convictions of many others.

At the same time, DNA testing alone does not always resolve a case. Where there is enough other incriminating evidence and an explanation for the DNA result, science alone cannot prove a prisoner innocent. The availability of technologies not available at trial cannot mean that every criminal conviction, or even every criminal conviction involving biological evidence, is suddenly in doubt. The dilemma is how to harness DNA's power to prove innocence without unnecessarily overthrowing the established system of criminal justice.

That task belongs primarily to the legislature. "[T]he States are currently engaged in serious, thoughtful examinations," of how to ensure the fair and effective use of this testing within the existing criminal justice framework. Forty-six States have already enacted statutes dealing specifically with access to DNA evidence. The State of Alaska itself is considering joining them. The Federal Government has also passed the Innocence Protection Act of 2004, which allows federal prisoners to move for court-ordered DNA testing under certain specified conditions.

These laws recognize the value of DNA evidence but also the need for certain conditions on access to the State's evidence. A requirement of demonstrating materiality is common, but it is not the only one. The federal statute, for example, requires a sworn statement that the applicant is innocent. This requirement is replicated in several state statutes. States also impose a range of diligence requirements. Several require the requested testing to "have been technologically impossible at trial." Others deny testing to those who declined testing at trial for tactical reasons.

Alaska is one of a handful of States yet to enact legislation specifically addressing the issue of evidence requested for DNA testing. But that does not mean that such evidence is unavailable for those seeking to prove their innocence. Instead, Alaska courts are addressing how to apply existing laws for discovery and postconviction relief to this novel technology. [T]he Alaska Court of Appeals has invoked a widely accepted three-part test to govern additional rights to DNA access under the State Constitution. Drawing on the experience with DNA evidence of State Supreme Courts around the country, the Court of Appeals explained that it was "reluctant to hold that Alaska law offers no remedy to defendants who could prove their factual innocence." It was "prepared to hold, however, that a defendant who seeks post-conviction DNA testing . . . must show (1) that the conviction rested primarily on eyewitness identification evidence, (2) that there was a demonstrable doubt concerning the defendant's identification as the perpetrator, and (3) that scientific testing would likely be conclusive on this issue." Thus, the Alaska courts have suggested that even those who do not get discovery under the State's criminal rules have available to them a safety valve under the State Constitution.

[III]

"No State shall . . . deprive any person of life, liberty, or property, without due process of law." This Clause imposes procedural limitations on a State's power to take away protected entitlements. Osborne argues that access to the State's evidence is a "process" needed to vindicate his right to prove himself innocent and get out of jail. Process is not an end in itself, so a necessary premise of this argument is that he has an entitlement (what our precedents call a "liberty interest") to prove his innocence even after a fair trial has proved otherwise. We must first examine this asserted liberty interest to determine what process (if any) is due.

In identifying his potential liberty interest, Osborne first attempts to rely on the Governor's constitutional authority to "grant pardons, commutations, and reprieves." That claim can be readily disposed of. We have held that noncapital defendants do not have a liberty interest in traditional state executive clemency, to which no particular claimant is *entitled* as a matter of state law. Osborne therefore cannot challenge the constitutionality of any procedures available to vindicate an interest in state clemency.

Osborne does, however, have a liberty interest in demonstrating his innocence with new evidence under state law. As explained, Alaska law provides that those who use "newly discovered evidence" to "establis[h] by clear and convincing evidence that [they are] innocent" may obtain "vacation of [their] conviction or sentence in the interest of justice." This "state-created right can, in some circumstances, beget yet other rights to procedures essential to the realization of the parent right."

A criminal defendant proved guilty after a fair trial does not have the same liberty interests as a free man. At trial, the defendant is presumed innocent and may demand that the government prove its case beyond reasonable doubt. But "[o]nce a defendant has been afforded a fair trial and convicted of the offense for which he was charged, the presumption of innocence disappears." "Given a valid conviction, the criminal defendant has been constitutionally deprived of his liberty."

The State accordingly has more flexibility in deciding what procedures are needed in the context of postconviction relief. "[W]hen a State chooses to offer help to those seeking relief from convictions," due process does not "dictat[e] the exact form such assistance must assume." Osborne's right to due process is not parallel to a trial right, but rather must be analyzed in light of the fact that he has already been found guilty at a fair trial, and has only a limited interest in postconviction relief.

Instead, the question is whether consideration of Osborne's claim within the framework of the State's procedures for postconviction relief "offends some principle of justice so rooted in the traditions and conscience of our people as to be ranked as fundamental," or "transgresses any recognized principle of fundamental fairness in operation."

We see nothing inadequate about the procedures Alaska has provided to vindicate its state right to postconviction relief in general, and nothing inadequate about how those procedures apply to those who seek access to DNA evidence. Alaska provides a substantive right to be released on a sufficiently compelling showing of new evidence that establishes innocence. It exempts such claims from otherwise applicable time limits. The State provides for discovery in postconviction proceedings, and has — through judicial decision — specified that this discovery procedure is available to those seeking access to DNA evidence. These procedures are not without limits. The evidence must indeed be newly available to qualify under Alaska's statute, must have been diligently pursued, and must also be sufficiently material. These procedures are similar to those provided for DNA evidence by federal law and the law of other States and they are not inconsistent with the "traditions and conscience of our people" or with "any recognized principle of fundamental fairness." And there is more. While the Alaska courts have not had occasion to conclusively decide the question, the Alaska Court of Appeals has suggested that the State Constitution provides an additional right of access to DNA. In expressing its "reluctan[ce] to hold that Alaska law offers no remedy" to those who belatedly seek DNA testing, and in invoking the three-part test used by other state courts, the court indicated that in an appropriate case the State Constitution may provide a failsafe even for those who cannot satisfy the statutory requirements under general postconviction procedures.

The Court of Appeals below relied only on procedural due process, but Osborne seeks to defend the judgment on the basis of substantive due process as well. He asks that we recognize a freestanding right to DNA evidence untethered from the liberty interests he hopes to vindicate with it. We reject the invitation and conclude, in the circumstances of this case, that there is no such substantive due process right. "As a general matter, the Court has always been reluctant to expand the concept of substantive due process because guideposts for responsible decisionmaking in this unchartered area are scarce and open-ended." Osborne seeks access to state evidence so that he can apply new DNA-testing technology that might prove him innocent. There is no long history of such a right, and "[t]he mere novelty of such a claim is reason enough to doubt that 'substantive due process' sustains it."

And there are further reasons to doubt. The elected governments of the States are actively confronting the challenges DNA technology poses to our criminal justice systems and our traditional notions of finality, as well as the opportunities it affords. To suddenly constitutionalize this area would short-circuit what looks to be a prompt and considered legislative response. The first DNA testing statutes were passed in 1994 and 1997. In the past decade, 44 States and the Federal Government have followed suit, reflecting the increased availability of DNA testing. As noted, Alaska itself is considering such legislation. "By extending constitutional protection to an asserted right or liberty interest, we, to a great extent, place the matter outside the arena of public debate and legislative action. We must therefore exercise the utmost care whenever we are asked to break new ground in this field." "[J]udicial imposition of a categorical remedy . . . might pretermit other responsible solutions being considered in Congress and state legislatures." If we extended substantive due process to this area, we would cast these statutes into constitutional doubt and be forced to take over the issue of DNA access ourselves. We are reluctant to enlist the Federal Judiciary in creating a new constitutional code of rules for handling DNA.

Establishing a freestanding right to access DNA evidence for testing would force us to act as policymakers, and our substantive-due-process rulemaking authority would not only have to cover the right of access but a myriad of other issues. We would soon have to decide if there is a constitutional obligation to preserve forensic evidence that might later be tested. If so, for how long? Would it be different for different types of evidence? Would the State also have some obligation to gather such evidence in the first place? How much, and when? No doubt there would be a miscellany of other minor directives.

DNA evidence will undoubtedly lead to changes in the criminal justice system. It has done so already. The question is whether further change will primarily be made by legislative revision and judicial interpretation of the existing system, or whether the Federal Judiciary must leap ahead — revising (or even discarding) the system by creating a new constitutional right and taking over responsibility for refining it.

Federal courts should not presume that state criminal procedures will be inadequate to deal with technological change. The criminal justice system has historically accommodated new types of evidence, and is a time-tested means of carrying out society's interest in convicting the guilty while respecting individual rights. That system, like any human endeavor, cannot be perfect. DNA evidence shows that it has not been. But there is no basis for Osborne's approach of assuming that because DNA has shown that these procedures are not flawless, DNA evidence must be treated as categorically outside the process, rather than within it.

Justice STEVENS, with whom Justice GINSBURG and Justice BREYER join, and with whom Justice SOUTER joins as to Part I, dissenting.

The State of Alaska possesses physical evidence that, if tested, will conclusively establish whether respondent William Osborne committed rape and attempted murder. If he did, justice has been served by his conviction and sentence. If not, Osborne has needlessly spent decades behind bars while the true culprit has not been brought to justice. The DNA test Osborne seeks is a simple one, its cost modest, and its results uniquely precise. Yet for reasons the State has been unable or unwilling to articulate, it refuses to allow Osborne to test the evidence at his own expense and to thereby ascertain the truth once and for all.

Because I am convinced that Osborne has a constitutional right of access to the evidence he wishes to test and that, on the facts of this case, he has made a sufficient showing of entitlement to that evidence, I would affirm the decision of the Court of Appeals.

Osborne asserts a right to access the State's evidence that derives from the Due Process Clause itself. Whether framed as a "substantive liberty interest . . . protected through a procedural due process right" to have evidence made available for testing, or as a substantive due process right to be free of arbitrary government action, the result is the same: On the record now before us, Osborne has established his entitlement to test the State's evidence.

The liberty protected by the Due Process Clause is not a creation of the Bill of Rights. Indeed, our Nation has long recognized that the liberty safeguarded by the Constitution has far deeper roots.

Although a valid criminal conviction justifies punitive detention, it does not entirely eliminate the liberty interests of convicted persons. For while a prisoner's "rights may be diminished by the needs and exigencies of the institutional environment[,] . . . [t]here is no iron curtain drawn between the Constitution and the prisons of this country." It is therefore far too late in the day to question the basic proposition that convicted persons such as Osborne retain a constitutionally protected measure of interest in liberty, including the fundamental liberty of freedom from physical restraint.

Recognition of this right draws strength from the fact that 46 States and the Federal Government have passed statutes providing access to evidence for DNA testing, and 3 additional states (including Alaska) provide similar access through court-made rules alone. These legislative developments are consistent with recent trends in legal ethics recognizing that prosecutors are obliged to disclose all forms of exculpatory evidence that come into their possession following conviction. The fact that nearly all the States have now recognized some postconviction right to DNA evidence makes it more, not less, appropriate to recognize a limited federal right to such evidence in cases where litigants are unfairly barred from obtaining relief in state court.

Recent scientific advances in DNA analysis have made "it literally possible to confirm guilt or innocence beyond any question whatsoever, at least in some categories of cases." As the Court recognizes today, the powerful new evidence that modern DNA testing can provide is "unlike anything known before."

If the right Osborne seeks to vindicate is framed as purely substantive, the proper result is no less clear. "The touchstone of due process is protection of the individual against arbitrary action of government." When government action is so lacking in justification that it "can properly be characterized as arbitrary, or conscience shocking, in a constitutional sense," it violates the Due Process Clause. In my view, the State's refusal to provide Osborne with access to evidence for DNA testing qualifies as arbitrary.

Throughout the course of state and federal litigation, the State has failed to provide any concrete reason for denying Osborne the DNA testing he seeks, and none is apparent. Because Osborne has offered to pay for the tests, cost is not a factor. And as the State now concedes, there is no reason to doubt that such testing would provide conclusive confirmation of Osborne's guilt or revelation of his innocence. In the courts below, the State refused to provide an explanation for its refusal to permit testing of the evidence, and in this Court, its explanation has been, at best, unclear. Insofar as the State has articulated any reason at all, it appears to be a generalized interest in protecting the finality of the judgment of conviction from any possible future attacks.

While we have long recognized that States have an interest in securing the finality of their judgments, finality is not a stand-alone value that trumps a State's overriding interest in ensuring that justice is done in its courts and secured to its citizens. Indeed, when absolute proof of innocence is readily at hand, a State should not shrink from the possibility that error may have occurred. Rather, our system of justice is strengthened by "recogniz[ing] the need for, and imperative of, a safety valve in those rare instances where objective proof that the convicted actually did not commit the offense later becomes available through the progress of science."

This conclusion draws strength from the powerful state interests that offset the State's purported interest in finality *per se*. When a person is convicted for a crime he did not commit, the true culprit escapes punishment. DNA testing may lead to his identification. Crime victims, the law enforcement profession, and society at large share a strong interest in identifying and apprehending the actual perpetrators of vicious crimes, such as the rape and attempted murder that gave rise to this case.

The arbitrariness of the State's conduct is highlighted by comparison to the private interests it denies. It seems to me obvious that if a wrongly convicted person were to produce proof of his actual innocence, no state interest would be sufficient to justify his continued punitive detention. If such proof can be readily obtained without imposing a significant burden on the State, a refusal to provide access to such evidence is wholly unjustified.

In sum, an individual's interest in his physical liberty is one of constitutional significance. That interest would be vindicated by providing postconviction access to DNA evidence, as would the State's interest in ensuring that it punishes the true perpetrator of a crime. In this case, the State has suggested no counter-vailing interest that justifies its refusal to allow Osborne to test the evidence in its possession and has not provided any other nonarbitrary explanation for its conduct. Consequently, I am left to conclude that the State's failure to provide Osborne access to the evidence constitutes arbitrary action that offends basic principles of due process.

CHAPTER
9

FIRST AMENDMENT: FREEDOM OF EXPRESSION

A. INTRODUCTION

The First Amendment states, "Congress shall make no law respecting an establishment of religion, or prohibiting the free exercise thereof; or abridging the freedom of speech, or of the press; or the right of the people peaceably to assemble, and to petition the Government for a redress of grievances." The next chapter, Chapter 10, considers the Religion Clauses. This chapter focuses on the other provisions of the First Amendment, all of which concern aspects of freedom of expression.

1. Historical Background

The First Amendment undoubtedly was a reaction against the suppression of speech and of the press that existed in English society. Until 1694, there was an elaborate system of licensing in England, and no publication was allowed without a government-granted license. Blackstone, in his famous commentaries on the law, remarked that "[t]he liberty of the press consists in laying no *previous* restraints upon publications, and not in freedom from censure for criminal matter when published. . . . [To] subject the press to the restrictive power of a licenser . . . is to subject all freedom of sentiment to the prejudices of one man, and make him the arbitrary and infallible judge of all controverted points in learning, religion, and government."[1] It is widely accepted that the First Amendment was meant, at the very least, to abolish such prior restraints on publication.

Speech in England also was restricted by the law of seditious libel that made criticizing the government a crime.[2] The English Court of the Star Chamber announced the principle that the king was above public criticism and that, therefore, statements critical of the government were forbidden. Chief Justice

---

1. 4 William Blackstone, *Commentaries on the Laws of England,* 151-152 (1769) (emphasis in original).
2. A classic history of the First Amendment, which reviews this background, is Zechariah Chaffee, Jr., *Free Speech in the United States* (1941).

Holt, writing in 1704, explained the perceived need for the prohibition of seditious libel: "If people should not be called to account for possessing the people with an ill opinion of the government, no government can subsist. For it is very necessary for all governments that the people should have a good opinion of it."[3] Truth was not a defense to the crime because the goal was to prevent and punish all criticism of the government; if anything, true speech was perceived as worse because it might do more to damage the image and reputation of the government. Professor Zechariah Chaffee said that "the First Amendment was . . . intended to wipe out the common law of sedition, and make further prosecutions for criticism of the government, without any incitement to law-breaking, forever impossible in the United States of America."[4]

The record for protection of freedom of speech in the colonies was mixed. There were fewer prosecutions for seditious libel than in England during the time period, but there were other controls, formal and informal, over dissident speech. Professor Leonard Levy said that each community "tended to be a tight little island clutching its own respective orthodoxy and . . . eager to banish or extralegally punish unwelcome dissidents."[5]

Of the prosecutions that occurred for seditious libel, the most famous was the trial of John Peter Zenger in 1735 for publishing criticisms of the governor of New York. Zenger's lawyer argued that truth should be a defense to the crime of seditious libel. Although the court rejected this argument, the jury was persuaded to disregard the law and to acquit Zenger.[6]

There is thus little doubt that the First Amendment was meant to prohibit licensing of publication such as existed in England and to forbid punishment for seditious libel. Beyond this, though, there is little indication of what the framers intended. Certainly nothing in the historical record sheds light on most of the free speech issues that face society and the courts in the early twenty-first century. Professor Rodney Smolla remarked that "[o]ne can keep going round and round on the original meaning of the First Amendment, but no clear, consistent vision of what the framers meant by freedom of speech will ever emerge."[7]

In fact, ascertaining the framers' intent is made more difficult by the fact that Congress in 1798—with many of the Constitution's drafters and ratifiers participating—adopted the Alien and Sedition Acts of 1798.[8] The law prohibited the publication of "false, scandalous, and malicious writing or writings against the government of the United States, or either house of the Congress of the United States, or the President of the United States, with intent to defame . . . ; or to bring them . . . into contempt or disrepute; or to excite against them . . . hatred of the good people of the United States, or to stir up sedition within the United States, or to excite any unlawful combinations therein, for opposing or resisting any law of the United States, or any act of the President of the United States." The law did allow truth as a defense and required proof of malicious intent.

The Federalists under President John Adams aggressively used the law against their rivals, the Republicans. The Alien and Sedition Act was a major political

---

3. 14 Thomas Howell, *A Collection of State Trials* 1095, 1128 (1704).
4. Chaffee, *supra* note 2, at 21.
5. Leonard W. Levy, *The Emergence of a Free Press* 16 (1985).
6. *See* Vincent Buranelli, *The Trial of Peter Zenger* (1957).
7. Rodney A. Smolla, *Smolla and Nimmer on Freedom of Speech* at 1-18 (1996).
8. 1 Stat. 596, Act of July 14, 1798.

issue in the election of 1800, and after he was elected president, Thomas Jefferson pardoned those who had been convicted under the law. The Alien and Sedition Act was repealed, and the Supreme Court never ruled on its constitutionality. However, in New York Times v. Sullivan, in 1964, the Court declared, "Although the Sedition Act was never tested in this Court, the attack upon its validity has carried the day in the court of history."[9]

Not surprisingly, then, Supreme Court cases dealing with freedom of expression focus less on the framers' intent than do cases involving many other constitutional provisions. There is relatively little that can be discerned as to the drafters' views other than their desire to prohibit prior restraints, such as the licensing scheme, and their rejection of the crime of seditious libel.

2. Why Should Freedom of Speech Be a Fundamental Right?

Inevitably, the courts must decide what speech is protected by the First Amendment and what can be regulated by the government. Although the First Amendment is written in absolute language that Congress shall make "no law," the Supreme Court never has accepted the view that the First Amendment prohibits all government regulation of expression. Justice Hugo Black took the absolutist view of the First Amendment,[10] but he is virtually alone among Supreme Court justices.[11] Indeed, the Court expressly declared that it "reject[ed] the view that freedom of speech and association, . . . as protected by the First and Fourteenth Amendments, are absolutes."[12]

No matter how appealing the absolute position may be to the First Amendment's staunchest supporters, it is simply untenable. Even one example of an instance where government must be able to punish speech is sufficient to refute the desirability of an absolutist approach. For example, perjury laws or laws that prohibit quid pro quo sexual harassment ("sleep with me or you are fired") both punish speech, but no one would deny that such statutes are imperative.

Line drawing is inevitable as to what speech will be protected under the First Amendment and what can be proscribed or limited. Moreover, lines must be drawn as to where and when speech will be allowed. Even an absolutist view surely would not permit spectators to yell out while a court is in session and prevent the judge from hearing the proceeding. Lines also must be drawn in defining what is speech. Justice Black attempted to make his view plausible by distinguishing between speech and conduct, allowing the government to regulate the latter, but not the former. This distinction, too, requires line drawing as to when nonverbal communication should be regarded as speech.

Because even for originalists there is little guidance from history or the framers' intent as to the meaning of the First Amendment, the Supreme Court inescapably must make value choices as to what speech is protected, under what

---

9. 376 U.S. 254, 276 (1964).

10. *See, e.g.,* Hugo Black, *The Bill of Rights*, 35 N.Y.U. L. Rev. 865, 874, 879 (1960) ("The phrase 'Congress shall make no law' is composed of plain words, easily understood. The language is absolute. . . . [T]he framers themselves did this balancing when they wrote the [First Amendment]. . . . Courts have neither the right nor the power to make a different judgment.").

11. Justice William O. Douglas also took this view at times. Konigsberg v. State Bar of California, 366 U.S. 36, 56 (1961) (Black, J., dissenting, joined by Douglas, J.).

12. Konigsberg v. State Bar of California, 366 U.S. at 49.

circumstances, and when and how the government may regulate. Such analysis is possible only with reference to the goals that freedom of speech is meant to achieve.

There thus is a voluminous literature debating why freedom of speech should be regarded as a fundamental right. The issue is important in general in understanding freedom of expression, but is also crucial in appraising specific First Amendment issues and how they have been handled by the Supreme Court.

There is not a single, universally accepted theory of the First Amendment, but rather, several different views as to why freedom of speech should be regarded as a fundamental right. To a large extent, the theories are not mutually exclusive, although the choice of a theory can influence views on many specific issues. The four major theories, reviewed below, are that freedom of speech is protected to further self-governance, to aid the discovery of truth via the marketplace of ideas, to promote autonomy, and to foster tolerance. Justice Louis Brandeis offered an eloquent explanation for why freedom of speech is protected that includes all of these rationales. He wrote:

> Those who won our independence believed that the final end of the state was to make men free to develop their faculties, and that in its government the deliberative forces should prevail over the arbitrary. They valued liberty both as an end and as a means. They believed liberty to be the secret of happiness and courage to be the secret of liberty. They believed that freedom to think as you will and to speak as you think are means indispensable to the discovery and spread of political truth; that without free speech and assembly discussion would be futile; that with them, discussion affords ordinarily adequate protection against the dissemination of noxious doctrine; that the greatest menace to freedom is an inert people; that public discussion is a political duty; and that this should be a fundamental principle of American government. They recognized the risks to which all human institutions are subject. But they knew that order cannot be secured merely through fear of punishment for its infraction; that it is hazardous to discourage thought, hope, and imagination; that fear breeds repression; that repression breeds hate; that hate menaces stable government; that the path of safety lies in the opportunity to discuss freely supposed grievances and proposed remedies; and that the fitting remedy for evil counsels is good ones.[13]

a. Self-Governance

Freedom of speech is crucial in a democracy: Open discussion of candidates is essential for voters to make informed selections in elections; it is through speech that people can influence their government's choice of policies; public officials are held accountable through criticisms that can pave the way for their replacement. Alexander Meiklejohn wrote that freedom of speech "is a deduction from the basic American agreement that public issues shall be decided by universal suffrage."[14] He argued that "[s]elf-government can exist only insofar as the voters acquire the intelligence, integrity, sensitivity, and generous devotion to the general welfare that, in theory, casting a ballot is assumed to express."[15]

---

13. Whitney v. California, 274 U.S. 357, 375 (1927) (Brandeis, J., concurring).
14. Alexander Meiklejohn, *Free Speech and Its Relation to Self-Government* 27 (1948).
15. Alexander Meiklejohn, *The First Amendment Is an Absolute*, 1961 Sup. Ct. Rev. 245, 255.

Professor Vincent Blasi argued that freedom of speech serves an essential "checking value" on government.[16] He wrote of the value that free speech serves in checking the abuse of power by public officials and said that through speech voters retain "a veto power to be employed when the decisions of officials pass certain bounds."[17]

There is little disagreement that political speech is at the core of that protected by the First Amendment. The Supreme Court has spoken of the ability to criticize government and government officers as "the central meaning of the First Amendment."[18] Some commentators have argued that political speech should be the *only* speech protected by the First Amendment. Robert Bork is perhaps the foremost advocate of this position and argued that the "notion that all valuable types of speech must be protected by the first amendment confuses the constitutionality of laws with their wisdom. Freedom of nonpolitical speech rests, as does freedom for other valuable forms of behavior, upon the enlightenment of society and its elected representatives."[19]

The Supreme Court never has accepted this view that the First Amendment protects only political speech. Indeed, the Court has declared that the "guarantees for speech and press are not the preserve of political expression or comment upon public affairs, essential as those are to healthy government."[20] In part, this is probably because of the difficulty of defining what is political speech. Virtually everything from comic strips to commercial advertisements to even pornography can have a political dimension. In part, too, the refusal to narrowly limit the First Amendment in this way reflects the importance of freedom of speech about other topics ranging from scientific debates to accurate commercial information in the marketplace.

b. Discovering Truth

Another classic argument for protecting freedom of speech as a fundamental right is that it is essential for the discovery of truth. Justice Oliver Wendell Holmes invoked the powerful metaphor of the "marketplace of ideas" and wrote that "the best test of truth is the power of the thought to get itself accepted in the competition of the market, and that truth is the only ground upon which their wishes safely can be carried out."[21] The argument is that truth is most likely to emerge from the clash of ideas.

John Stuart Mill expressed this view when he wrote that the "peculiar evil of silencing the expression of an opinion is that it is robbing the human race, posterity as well as the existing generation — those who dissent from the opinion, still more than those who hold it."[22] He said that an opinion may be true and may be wrongly suppressed by those in power, or a view may be false and people are informed by its refutation. Justice Brandeis embraced this view when he said that the "fitting remedy for evil counsels is good ones" and that "[i]f

---

16. Vincent Blasi, *The Checking Value in First Amendment Theory*, 1977 Am. B. Found. Res. J. 523.
17. *Id.* at 542.
18. New York Times v. Sullivan, 376 U.S. 254, 273 (1964).
19. Robert Bork, *Neutral Principles and Some First Amendment Problems*, 47 Ind. L.J. 1, 28 (1971).
20. Time, Inc. v. Hill, 385 U.S. 374, 388 (1967).
21. Abrams v. United States, 250 U.S. 616, 630 (1919) (Holmes, J., dissenting).
22. John Stuart Mill, *On Liberty* 76 (1859).

there be time to expose through discussion the falsehood and fallacies, to avert the evil by the processes of education, the remedy to be applied is more speech, not enforced silence."[23]

The marketplace of ideas rationale for freedom of speech has been subjected to powerful criticism by scholars.[24] Critics argue that it is wrong to assume that all ideas will enter the marketplace of ideas and even if they do, some may drown out others because some have more resources to have their voices heard. Professor Laurence Tribe observed that "[e]specially when the wealthy have more access to the most potent media of communication than the poor, how sure can we be that 'free trade in ideas' is likely to generate truth?"[25] Professor Jerome Barron said that "if ever there were a self-operating marketplace of ideas, it has long ceased to exist."[26]

Moreover, critics of the marketplace metaphor argue that it is wrong to assume that truth necessarily will triumph over falsehood; history shows that people may be swayed by emotion more than reason. Professor Edwin Baker argued that "the belief that the marketplace leads to truth, or even to the best or most desirable decision, is implausible."[27] He said that it assumes that people will use "their rational capabilities in order to eliminate distortion caused by the form and frequency of message presentation. . . . This [assumption] cannot be accepted. . . . People consistently respond to emotional or irrational appeals."[28] Moreover, even if truth ultimately prevails, enormous harms can occur in the interim. Professor Harry Wellington powerfully made this point when he wrote: "In the long run, true ideas do tend to drive out false ones. The problem is that the short run may be very long, that one short run follows hard upon another, and that we may become overwhelmed by the inexhaustible supply of freshly minted, often very seductive, false ideas. . . . [M]ost of us do believe that the book is closed on some issues. Genocide is an example. . . . Truth may win, and in the long run it may almost always win, but millions of Jews were deliberately and systematically murdered in a very short period of time. . . . Before those murders occurred, many individuals must have come 'to have false beliefs.'"[29]

However, the response to these criticisms is to concede the problems with the marketplace of ideas, but to argue that the alternative — government determination of truth and censorship of falsehoods — is worse. The marketplace of ideas may be terribly flawed, but allowing the government to decide what is true and right and suppress all else is much worse. Inevitably, government will censor to serve its own ends, such as by silencing its critics, and even a benevolent government will make mistakes as to what is true and false. Professor Nimmer thus remarked that "[i]f acceptance of an idea in the competition of the market is not the 'best test,' [what] is the alternative? It can only be acceptance of an idea by some individual or group narrower than that of the public at large."[30]

---

23. Whitney v. California, 274 U.S. at 375, 377 (Brandeis, J., concurring).
24. *See, e.g.,* C. Edwin Baker, *Human Liberty and Freedom of Speech* (1989); Stanley Ingber, *The Marketplace of Ideas: A Legitimizing Myth,* 1984 Duke L.J. 1.
25. Laurence H. Tribe, *American Constitutional Law* 786 (2d ed. 1988).
26. Jerome Barron, *Access to the Press — A New First Amendment Right,* 80 Harv. L. Rev. 1641, 1641 (1967).
27. Baker, *supra* note 24, at 12.
28. *Id.*
29. Harry Wellington, *On Freedom of Expression,* 88 Yale L.J. 1105, 1130, 1132 (1979).
30. Melville Nimmer, *Nimmer on Freedom of Speech* 1-12 (1984).

c. Advancing Autonomy

A third major rationale often expressed for protecting freedom of speech as a fundamental right is that it is an essential aspect of personhood and autonomy. Professor Baker said that "[t]o engage voluntarily in a speech act is to engage in self-definition of expression. A Vietnam war protestor may explain that when she chants 'Stop This War Now' at a demonstration, she does so without any expectation that her speech will affect continuance of the war . . . ; rather, she participates and chants in order to *define* herself publicly in opposition to the war. This war protestor provides a dramatic illustration of the importance of this self-expressive use of speech, independent of any effective communication to others, for self-fulfillment or self-realization."[31]

Protecting speech because it aids the political process or furthers the search for truth emphasizes the instrumental values of expression. Protecting speech because it is a crucial aspect of autonomy sees expression as intrinsically important.[32] Justice Thurgood Marshall observed that "[t]he First Amendment serves not only the needs of the polity but also those of the human spirit — a spirit that demands self-expression."[33]

This view, too, has been criticized. Robert Bork, for example, argued that there is no inherent reason to find speech to be a fundamental right compared with countless other activities that might be regarded as a part of autonomy or that could advance self-fulfillment. Bork said that the self-fulfillment/autonomy rationale does "not distinguish speech from any other human activity. An individual may develop his faculties or derive pleasure from trading on the stock market, working as a barmaid, engaging in sexual activity, or in any of thousands of other endeavors. Speech can be preferred to other activities only by ranking forms of personal gratification. One cannot, on neutral grounds, choose to protect speech on this basis more than one protects any other claimed freedom."[34]

Moreover, critics of this view maintain that it ignores the ways in which protecting freedom of speech for some can undermine the autonomy and self-fulfillment of others. In recent years, some have argued for restricting hate speech or pornography because of how such expression demeans and injures others.[35]

d. Promoting Tolerance

Another explanation for protecting freedom of speech as a fundamental right that has received substantial attention in recent years is that it is integral to

---

31. C. Edwin Baker, *Scope of the First Amendment Freedom of Speech*, 25 UCLA L. Rev. 964, 994 (1978).

32. *See, e.g.,* Martin Redish, *The Value of Free Speech*, 130 U. Pa. L. Rev. 591 (1982) (arguing that self-realization should be regarded as the exclusive value of the First Amendment).

33. Procunier v. Martinez, 416 U.S. 396, 427 (1974) (Marshall, J., concurring).

34. Bork, *supra* note 19, at 25.

35. *See, e.g.,* Mari Matsuda, *Public to Racist Speech: Considering the Victim's Story*, 87, Mich. L. Rev. 2320 (1989); Richard Delgado, *Words that Wound: A Tort Action for Racial Insults, Epithets, and Name-Calling*, 17 Harv. C.R.-C.L. L. Rev. 133 (1982) (arguing for restriction of hate speech); Catharine MacKinnon *Feminism Unmodified* 146-213 (1987) (arguing for restriction of pornography because of its harmful effects on women). Hate speech is discussed below.

tolerance, which should be a basic value in our society. Professor Lee Bollinger is a primary advocate of this view, and he argued, "[W]hile free speech theory has traditionally focused on the value of the activity protected (speech), [an alternative approach] seeks a justification by looking at the disvalue of the [frequently intolerant] response to that activity. . . . [The free speech principle] involves a special act of carving out one area of social interaction for extraordinary self-restraint, the purpose of which is to develop and demonstrate a social capacity to control feelings evoked by a host of social encounters."[36] The free speech principle is thus concerned with nothing less than helping to shape "the intellectual character of the society."[37]

The claim is that tolerance is a desirable, if not essential, value and that protecting unpopular or distasteful speech is itself an act of tolerance. Moreover, such tolerance serves as a model that encourages more tolerance throughout society. But critics question why tolerance should be regarded as a basic value.[38] For example, critics argue that society need not be tolerant of the intolerance of others, such as those who advocate great harm, even genocide. Preventing such harms is claimed to be much more important than being tolerant of those who argue for them.

e. Conclusion

These four theories are not mutually exclusive.[39] None is sufficient to explain all of the cases, and none is without problems.[40] Yet all are important in understanding why freedom of speech is protected, in considering what expression should be safeguarded and what can be regulated, and in appraising the Supreme Court's decisions in this area.

3. The Issues in Free Expression Analysis

In examining the First Amendment's protection of freedom of expression, analysis is divided into five sections. First, section B examines ways of evaluating any government action restricting freedom of speech. For example, any law can be reviewed to determine whether it is content-based or content-neutral, a distinction that the Court has said is crucial in determining whether strict scrutiny or intermediate scrutiny should be used.[41] Also, any law regulating speech is unconstitutional if it is unduly vague or overbroad. The Court additionally has said that prior restraints of speech are strongly disfavored and thus any

---

36. Lee Bollinger, *The Tolerant Society: Freedom of Speech and Extremist Speech in America* 9-10 (1986).
37. *Id.* at 120.
38. *See* David Strauss, *Why Be Tolerant?*, 53 U. Chi. L. Rev. 1485 (1986).
39. *See* Rodney A. Smolla, *Free Speech in an Open Society* 14-17 (1992) (arguing for "multiple justifications" for freedom of speech); Steven Shiffrin, *The First Amendment and Economic Regulation: Away from a General Theory of the First Amendment*, 78 Nw. U. L. Rev. 1212 (1983) (many values underlie the First Amendment; no need to reduce the First Amendment to a single theory).
40. *See* Ronald Cass, *The Perils of Positive Thinking: Constitutional Interpretation and Negative First Amendment Theory*, 34 UCLA L. Rev. 1405 (1987) (criticizing the foundational theories of the First Amendment).
41. Turner Broadcasting v. FCC, 512 U.S. 622 (1994).

government action restricting speech can be challenged if it constitutes a prior restraint. Finally, there is the basic question in evaluating any law as to whether it constitutes a restriction of speech; what government actions sufficiently burden expression as to trigger First Amendment analysis?

Second, section C focuses on types of speech that are unprotected by the First Amendment or less protected. The Supreme Court has declared that some types of expression are unprotected so that they may be prohibited and punished. There are other categories of speech that are deemed less protected so that the government has more latitude in regulating them. These categories include incitement of illegal activity, fighting words and provocation of hostile audiences, obscenity and sexually oriented speech, defamatory speech, conduct that communicates, and commercial speech.

Third, section D considers the places that are available for speech. Many First Amendment cases involve a claim of a right of access to government-owned property for speech purposes or present a challenge to restrictions on the use of public property for expression. The Supreme Court has drawn distinctions among types of government properties and has articulated rules as to when the government may regulate speech in each.

Fourth, section E examines freedom of association. Although association is not expressly mentioned in the First Amendment, the Supreme Court has held that it is a fundamental right because of its close relationship to speech and assembly.[42]

Finally, section F focuses on freedom of the press. Many issues concerning press freedom are discussed throughout the chapter. For example, prior restraint of the press — a crucial aspect of the Constitution's protection of the media — is discussed in section B. Section F considers the extent to which the First Amendment is a shield that protects the press from government regulation, such as from being taxed or forced to disclose information or being required to allow others to use it. The section also considers whether and when freedom of the press creates a right for the press to have access to government papers, activities, and facilities.

Part of what makes First Amendment analysis difficult is that many of these issues can be present in the same case, and there is no prescribed order for analysis. For instance, if the government were to prohibit sexually explicit displays in public parks, the law might be challenged as vague and overbroad; it might be analyzed as to whether it is obscenity unprotected by the First Amendment; and it might be considered as to whether it is a permissible restriction of speech in a public forum. All these issues and others are presented. There is no reason why one question should inherently precede the others. Simply put, it is not possible to comprehensively flowchart the First Amendment as a defined series of questions in a required sequential order. There are many ways of approaching and evaluating government actions restricting expression.

---

42. *See, e.g.*, NAACP v. Alabama, 357 U.S. 449 (1958).

B. FREE SPEECH METHODOLOGY

This section considers doctrines that can be used to evaluate any government restrictions of speech. Subsection 1 describes the distinction between content-based and content-neutral laws regulating speech and the significance of this difference. Subsection 2 considers the vagueness and overbreadth doctrines: Even in regulating unprotected speech, laws are unconstitutional if they are unduly vague or overbroad. Subsection 3 examines the strong presumption against prior restraints and especially focuses on classic forms of prior restraints such as court orders suppressing speech and licensing systems. Finally, subsection 4 discusses the basic question of what constitutes an infringement of speech.

1. The Distinction Between Content-Based and Content-Neutral Laws

The Supreme Court frequently has declared that the very core of the First Amendment is that the government cannot regulate speech based on its content. The Court stated, "[A]bove all else, the First Amendment means that government has no power to restrict expression because of its message, its ideas, its subject matter or its content."[43] The Court has declared that "[c]ontent-based regulations are presumptively invalid."[44] In countless First Amendment cases, involving many of the issues discussed throughout this chapter, the Court has invoked the content-based/content-neutral distinction as the basis for its decisions.

The material in this part begins by discussing the importance of the distinction, including the Court's dictate that strict scrutiny is generally used for content-based restrictions, while intermediate scrutiny is used for content-neutral laws. Considered next is the question of how it is determined whether a law is content-based. Finally, problems in applying the distinction between content-based and content-neutral laws are discussed.

a. The Importance of the Distinction

In Turner Broadcasting System v. Federal Communications Commn., the Court discussed the importance of the distinction in terms of the level of scrutiny used.

TURNER BROADCASTING SYSTEM, INC. v. FEDERAL COMMUNICATIONS COMMISSION
512 U.S. 622 (1994)

Justice KENNEDY delivered the opinion of the Court.

Sections 4 and 5 of the Cable Television Consumer Protection and Competition Act of 1992 require cable television systems to devote a portion of their

---

43. Police Deparment of Chicago v. Mosley, 408 U.S. 92, 95-96 (1972).
44. R.A.V. v. City of St. Paul, 505 U.S. 377, 382 (1992).

channels to the transmission of local broadcast television stations. This case presents the question whether these provisions abridge the freedom of speech or of the press, in violation of the First Amendment. At issue in this case is the constitutionality of the so-called must-carry provisions, which require cable operators to carry the signals of a specified number of local broadcast television stations.

By requiring cable systems to set aside a portion of their channels for local broadcasters, the must-carry rules regulate cable speech in two respects: The rules reduce the number of channels over which cable operators exercise unfettered control, and they render it more difficult for cable programmers to compete for carriage on the limited channels remaining.

Nevertheless, because not every interference with speech triggers the same degree of scrutiny under the First Amendment, we must decide at the outset the level of scrutiny applicable to the must-carry provisions.

At the heart of the First Amendment lies the principle that each person should decide for himself or herself the ideas and beliefs deserving of expression, consideration, and adherence. Our political system and cultural life rest upon this ideal. Government action that stifles speech on account of its message, or that requires the utterance of a particular message favored by the Government, contravenes this essential right. Laws of this sort pose the inherent risk that the Government seeks not to advance a legitimate regulatory goal, but to suppress unpopular ideas or information or manipulate the public debate through coercion rather than persuasion. These restrictions "rais[e] the specter that the Government may effectively drive certain ideas or viewpoints from the marketplace."

For these reasons, the First Amendment, subject only to narrow and well-understood exceptions, does not countenance governmental control over the content of messages expressed by private individuals. Our precedents thus apply the most exacting scrutiny to regulations that suppress, disadvantage, or impose differential burdens upon speech because of its content. Laws that compel speakers to utter or distribute speech bearing a particular message are subject to the same rigorous scrutiny. In contrast, regulations that are unrelated to the content of speech are subject to an intermediate level of scrutiny because in most cases they pose a less substantial risk of excising certain ideas or viewpoints from the public dialogue.

Deciding whether a particular regulation is content based or content neutral is not always a simple task. We have said that the "principal inquiry in determining content neutrality . . . is whether the government has adopted a regulation of speech because of [agreement or] disagreement with the message it conveys." The purpose, or justification, of a regulation will often be evident on its face. But while a content-based purpose may be sufficient in certain circumstances to show that a regulation is content based, it is not necessary to such a showing in all cases. Nor will the mere assertion of a content-neutral purpose be enough to save a law which, on its face, discriminates based on content.

As a general rule, laws that by their terms distinguish favored speech from disfavored speech on the basis of the ideas or views expressed are content based. Insofar as they pertain to the carriage of full-power broadcasters, the must-carry rules, on their face, impose burdens and confer benefits without reference to the content of speech. Although the provisions interfere with cable operators' editorial discretion by compelling them to offer carriage to a certain minimum number of broadcast stations, the extent of the interference does not depend upon the content of the cable operators' programming. Nothing in the Act imposes a restriction, penalty, or burden by reason of the views, programs, or stations the cable operator has selected or will select. The number of channels a cable operator must set aside depends only on the operator's channel capacity; hence, an operator cannot avoid or mitigate its obligations under the Act by altering the programming it offers to subscribers.

The must-carry provisions also burden cable programmers by reducing the number of channels for which they can compete. But, again, this burden is unrelated to content, for it extends to all cable programmers irrespective of the programming they choose to offer viewers. And finally, the privileges conferred by the must-carry provisions are also unrelated to content. The rules benefit all full power broadcasters who request carriage — be they commercial or noncommercial, independent or network affiliated, English or Spanish language, religious or secular. The aggregate effect of the rules is thus to make every full power commercial and noncommercial broadcaster eligible for must-carry, provided only that the broadcaster operates within the same television market as a cable system.

Justice O'CONNOR, with whom Justice SCALIA and Justice GINSBURG join, and with whom Justice THOMAS joins in part, concurring in part and dissenting in part.

There are only so many channels that any cable system can carry. If there are fewer channels than programmers who want to use the system, some programmers will have to be dropped. In the must-carry provisions of the Cable Television Consumer Protection and Competition Act of 1992, Congress made a choice: By reserving a little over one-third of the channels on a cable system for broadcasters, it ensured that in most cases it will be a cable programmer who is dropped and a broadcaster who is retained.

I agree with the Court that some speaker-based restrictions — those genuinely justified without reference to content — need not be subject to strict scrutiny. But looking at the statute at issue, I cannot avoid the conclusion that its preference for broadcasters over cable programmers is justified with reference to content. The findings, enacted by Congress as §2 of the Act, and which I must assume state the justifications for the law, make this clear. "There is a substantial governmental and First Amendment interest in promoting a diversity of views provided through multiple technology media. [P]ublic television provides educational and informational programming to the Nation's citizens, thereby advancing the Government's compelling interest in educating its citizens. A primary objective and benefit of our Nation's system of regulation of television broadcasting is the local origination of programming. There is a substantial governmental interest in ensuring its continuation. Broadcast television stations continue to be an important source of local news and public affairs programming and other local broadcast services critical to an informed electorate."

Similar justifications are reflected in the operative provisions of the Act. In determining whether a broadcast station should be eligible for must-carry in a particular market, the Federal Communications Commission (FCC) must "afford particular attention to the value of localism by taking into account such factors as . . . whether any other [eligible station] provides news coverage of issues of concern to such community or provides carriage or coverage of sporting and other events of interest to the community."

Preferences for diversity of viewpoints, for localism, for educational programming, and for news and public affairs all make reference to content. They may not reflect hostility to particular points of view, or a desire to suppress certain subjects because they are controversial or offensive. They may be quite benignly motivated. But benign motivation, we have consistently held, is not enough to avoid the need for strict scrutiny of content-based justifications. The First Amendment does more than just bar government from intentionally suppressing speech of which it disapproves. It also generally prohibits the government from excepting certain kinds of speech from regulation because it thinks the speech is especially valuable.

This is why the Court is mistaken in concluding that the interest in diversity — in "access to a multiplicity" of "diverse and antagonistic sources[]" — is content-neutral. Indeed, the interest is not "related to the suppression of free expression," but that is not enough for content neutrality. The interest in giving a tax break to religious, sports, or professional magazines is not related to the suppression of speech; the interest in giving labor picketers an exemption from a general picketing ban is not related to the suppression of speech. But they are both related to the content of speech — to its communicative impact. The interest in ensuring access to a multiplicity of diverse and antagonistic sources of information, no matter how praiseworthy, is directly tied to the content of what the speakers will likely say.

The Court did not decide the constitutionality of the must-carry provision, but instead remanded the case for the application of intermediate scrutiny by the lower courts. The case then came back to the Supreme Court in Turner Broadcasting System, Inc. v. Federal Communications Commn., 520 U.S. 180 (1997). The Court, in a five-to-four decision, upheld the constitutionality of the must-carry provision, concluding that it met intermediate scrutiny.

The Court, in an opinion by Justice Kennedy, reaffirmed that "[a] content-neutral regulation will be sustained under the First Amendment if it advances important governmental interests unrelated to the suppression of free speech and does not burden substantially more speech than necessary to further those interests." The Court said that must-carry was designed to serve "three interrelated interests: (1) preserving the benefits of free, over-the-air local broadcast television; (2) promoting the widespread dissemination of information from a multiplicity of sources; and (3) promoting fair competition in the market for television programming." The Court concluded "that each of those is an important governmental interest." The Court also concluded that "[b]ecause the burden imposed by must-carry is congruent to the benefits it affords, we conclude must-carry is narrowly tailored to preserve a multiplicity of broadcast stations for the 40 percent of American households without cable."

A more recent example of the Court stressing the need for heightened scrutiny of content-based regulation of speech is United States v. Alvarez, 132 S. Ct. 2537 (2012). The federal Stolen Valor Act makes it a crime for a person to falsely claim to have received military honors or decorations. Xavier Alvarez was a member of a local government water district commission and lied about having won the Congressional Medal of Honor. (Justice Kennedy begins his opinion by saying of Alvarez, "Lying was his habit.")

The Court, in a six-to-three decision, without a majority opinion, declared the Stolen Valor Act unconstitutional. Justice Kennedy wrote a plurality opinion, joined by Chief Justice Roberts and Justices Ginsburg and Sotomayor, saying that the act was a content-based restriction on speech and "[w]hen content-based speech regulation is in question, exacting scrutiny is required." Justice Kennedy said that the government failed to prove sufficient harms from people lying about military honors to justify the law and also that Congress could achieve its goals in narrower ways, such as publishing lists of those who have received military honors so that liars could be quickly exposed.

Justice Breyer wrote an opinion concurring in the judgment, joined by Justice Kagan, and said that "intermediate scrutiny" was the appropriate test. Justice Breyer concluded that the law failed intermediate scrutiny because the government could achieve its goal through a narrower means, such as prohibiting people from lying about military honors if they were seeking a tangible benefit.

Justice Alito wrote a dissent, joined by Justices Scalia and Thomas, and argued that the law was constitutional because of the government's crucial interest in protecting the integrity of military honors and the absence of any less restrictive alternative. He emphasized that false speech should not be protected by the First Amendment: "By holding that the First Amendment nevertheless shields these lies, the Court breaks sharply from a long line of cases recognizing that the right to free speech does not protect false factual statements that inflict real harm and serve no legitimate interest."

Some categories of speech are unprotected or less protected by the First Amendment, such as incitement of illegal activity, obscenity, and defamation. These categories, by definition, are content-based. These categories, discussed in section C, are exceptions to the usual rule of strict scrutiny for content-based regulations. It also might be said that the Supreme Court essentially has found that there is a compelling interest in excluding speech such as incitement or obscenity from First Amendment protection. But apart from these categories, content-based discrimination must meet strict scrutiny, and the Court has indicated that content-based distinctions within these categories also must pass strict scrutiny.[45]

Why is there so much concern about content neutrality?[46] Obviously, the fear is that the government will target particular messages and attempt to control thoughts on a topic by regulating speech.[47] As the Court said in *Turner Broadcasting*, "Laws of this sort pose the inherent risk that the Government seeks not to advance a legitimate regulatory goal, but to suppress unpopular ideas or information or to manipulate the public debate through coercion rather than persuasion."[48]

A viewpoint restriction does this directly. The government could try to control dissent and advance its own interests by stopping speech that expresses criticism

---

45. *See* R.A.V. v. City of St. Paul, 505 U.S. 377 (1992), discussed below in Section C.

46. For an excellent explanation of the basis for the content-based/content-neutral distinction, *see* Geoffrey Stone, *Content-Neutral Restrictions*, 54 U. Chi. L. Rev. 46 (1987); for an excellent argument that the Court has given undue weight to this distinction, *see* Martin Redish, *The Content Distinction in First Amendment Analysis*, 34 Stan. L. Rev. 113 (1981) (arguing, in part, that content-based restrictions limit less speech than content-neutral ones).

47. As the Court noted, "[such restrictions] raise the specter that the government may effectively drive certain ideas or viewpoints from the marketplace." Simon & Schuster, Inc. v. Members of the New York St. Crime Victims Board, 502 U.S. 105, 116 (1991).

48. Turner Broadcast System v. Federal Communication Commn., 512 U.S. at 641.

of government policy, while allowing praise. A subject-matter restriction on speech can accomplish the same goal. In the 1960s, a law prohibiting speech about the war in Vietnam — a subject-matter restriction — obviously would have had a far greater impact on antiwar speech. The Court has explained that "[t]o allow a government the choice of permissible subjects for public debate would be to allow the government control over the search for political truth."[49]

b. How Is It Determined Whether a Law Is Content-Based?

The requirement that the government be content-neutral in its regulation of speech means that the government must be both viewpoint-neutral and subject-matter-neutral.[50] In other words, a law will be found to be content-based and must meet strict scrutiny if it is either a viewpoint or a subject-matter restriction. Viewpoint-neutral means that the government cannot regulate speech based on the ideology of the message.[51] For example, it would be clearly unconstitutional for the government to say that pro-choice demonstrations are allowed in the park but antiabortion demonstrations are not allowed. In Boos v. Barry, the Court considered whether a law was viewpoint-based. In reading this decision, consider why the Court found that the law was viewpoint-neutral, although subject-matter-based, and whether you agree with this conclusion.

BOOS v. BARRY
485 U.S. 312 (1988)

Justice O'Connor delivered the opinion of the Court.

The question presented in this case is whether a provision of the District of Columbia Code violates the First Amendment. This section prohibits the display of any sign within 500 feet of a foreign embassy if that sign tends to bring that foreign government into "public odium" or "public disrepute." Petitioners are three individuals who wish to carry signs critical of the Governments of the Soviet Union and Nicaragua on the public sidewalks within 500 feet of the embassies of those Governments in Washington, D.C. Petitioners Bridget M. Brooker and Michael Boos, for example, wish to display signs stating "RELEASE SAKHAROV" and "SOLIDARITY" in front of the Soviet Embassy. Petitioner J. Michael Waller wishes to display a sign reading "STOP THE KILLING" within 500 feet of the Nicaraguan Embassy.

[T]he display clause operates at the core of the First Amendment by prohibiting petitioners from engaging in classically political speech. We have recognized that the First Amendment reflects a "profound national commitment" to the principle that "debate on public issues should be uninhibited, robust, and wide-open," New York Times Co. v. Sullivan (1964), and have consistently commented on the central importance of protecting speech on public issues.

---

49. Consolidated Edison Co. of N.Y., Inc. v. Public Service Commn., 447 U.S. 530, 538 (1980).
50. *See, e.g.,* Perry Education Assn. V. Perry Local Educators' Assn., 460 U.S. 37, 45 (1983).
51. *See* Amy Sabrin, *Thinking About Content: Can It Play an Appropriate Role in Government Funding of the Arts?*, 102 Yale L.J. 1209, 1220 (1993).

[The display clause] is content-based. Whether individuals may picket in front of a foreign embassy depends entirely upon whether their picket signs are critical of the foreign government or not. One category of speech has been completely prohibited within 500 feet of embassies. Other categories of speech, however, such as favorable speech about a foreign government or speech concerning a labor dispute with a foreign government, are permitted.

Both respondents and the United States contend that the statute is not content-based because the government is not itself selecting between viewpoints; the permissible message on a picket sign is determined solely by the policies of a foreign government.

We reject this contention, although we agree the provision is not viewpoint-based. The display clause determines which viewpoint is acceptable in a neutral fashion by looking to the policies of foreign governments. While this prevents the display clause from being directly viewpoint-based, a label with potential First Amendment ramifications of its own, it does not render the statute content-neutral. Rather, we have held that a regulation that "does not favor either side of a political controversy" is nonetheless impermissible because the "First Amendment's hostility to content-based regulation extends . . . to prohibition of public discussion of an entire topic." Here the government has determined that an entire category of speech — signs or displays critical of foreign governments — is not to be permitted. Because the display clause regulates speech due to its potential primary impact, we conclude it must be considered content-based.

Our cases indicate that as a content-based restriction on political speech in a public forum, [this law] must be subjected to the most exacting scrutiny. Thus, we have required the State to show that the "regulation is necessary to serve a compelling state interest and that it is narrowly drawn to achieve that end." We consider whether the display clause serves a compelling governmental interest in protecting the dignity of foreign diplomatic personnel. Since the dignity of foreign officials will be affronted by signs critical of their governments or governmental policies, we are told, these foreign diplomats must be shielded from such insults in order to fulfill our country's obligations under international law.

As a general matter, we have indicated that in public debate our own citizens must tolerate insulting, and even outrageous, speech in order to provide "adequate 'breathing space' to the freedoms protected by the First Amendment." A "dignity" standard, like the "outrageousness" standard that we rejected in *Hustler,* is so inherently subjective that it would be inconsistent with "our long-standing refusal to [punish speech] because the speech in question may have an adverse emotional impact on the audience." We are not persuaded that the differences between foreign officials and American citizens require us to deviate from these principles here.

"Subject-matter-neutral" means that the government cannot regulate speech based on the topic of the speech. Carey v. Brown, 447 U.S. 455 (1980), is illustrative. Chicago adopted an ordinance prohibiting all picketing in residential neighborhoods unless it was labor picketing connected to a place of employment. The Supreme Court held this regulation unconstitutional. The Court explained that the law allowed speech if it was about the subject of labor, but not otherwise. The Court said that whenever the government attempts to regulate speech in public places it must be subject-matter-neutral.

Simon & Schuster, Inc. v. Members of the New York State Crime Victims Board, 502 U.S. 105 (1991), is another example of a case in which the Court found a law to be a subject-matter restriction. The case concerned a state law that prevented those accused or convicted of a crime from profiting from the crime; any funds derived from description of the crime were to be placed in an escrow account used to compensate crime victims. The Court unanimously invalidated the law, finding that it was content-based. Justice O'Connor, delivering the opinion of the Court, wrote:

> The Son of Sam law is such a content-based statute. It singles out income derived from expressive activity for a burden the State places on no other income, and it is directed only at works with a specified content. Whether the First Amendment "speaker" is considered to be [the author] whose income the statute places in escrow because of the story he has told, or [the publisher] which can publish books about crime with the assistance of only those criminals willing to forgo remuneration for at least five years, the statute plainly imposes a financial disincentive only on speech of a particular content.

The Court concluded, "The State's interest in compensating victims from the fruits of crime is a compelling one, but the Son of Sam law is not narrowly tailored to advance that objective. As a result, the statute is inconsistent with the First Amendment." The Court said there were alternative ways to ensure compensation of crime victims.

In Republican Party of Minnesota v. White, the Court focused on what justifications are sufficient to permit content-based restrictions on political speech.

REPUBLICAN PARTY OF MINNESOTA v. WHITE

536 U.S. 765 (2002)

Justice Scalia delivered the opinion of the Court.

The question presented in this case is whether the First Amendment permits the Minnesota Supreme Court to prohibit candidates for judicial election in that State from announcing their views on disputed legal and political issues.

I

Since Minnesota's admission to the Union in 1858, the State's Constitution has provided for the selection of all state judges by popular election. Since 1912, those elections have been nonpartisan. Since 1974, they have been subject to a legal restriction which states that a "candidate for a judicial office, including an incumbent judge," shall not "announce his or her views on disputed legal or political issues." Minn. Code of Judicial Conduct, Canon 5(A)(3)(d)(i) (2000). This prohibition, promulgated by the Minnesota Supreme Court and based on Canon 7(B) of the 1972 American Bar Association (ABA) Model Code of Judicial Conduct, is known as the "announce clause." Incumbent judges who violate it are subject to discipline, including removal, censure, civil penalties, and suspension without pay. Lawyers who run for judicial office also must comply with the announce clause. Those who violate it are subject to, inter alia, disbarment, suspension, and probation. Rule 8.4(a); Minn. Rules on Lawyers Professional Responsibility 8-14, 15(a) (2002).

In 1996, one of the petitioners, Gregory Wersal, ran for associate justice of the Minnesota Supreme Court. In the course of the campaign, he distributed literature criticizing several Minnesota Supreme Court decisions on issues such as crime, welfare, and abortion. A complaint against Wersal challenging, among other things, the propriety of this literature was filed with the Office of Lawyers Professional Responsibility, the agency which, under the direction of the Minnesota Lawyers Professional Responsibility Board, investigates and prosecutes ethical violations of lawyer candidates for judicial office. The Lawyers Board dismissed the complaint; with regard to the charges that his campaign materials violated the announce clause, it expressed doubt whether the clause could constitutionally be enforced. Nonetheless, fearing that further ethical complaints would jeopardize his ability to practice law, Wersal withdrew from the election. In 1998, Wersal ran again for the same office. Early in that race, he sought an advisory opinion from the Lawyers Board with regard to whether it planned to enforce the announce clause. The Lawyers Board responded equivocally, stating that, although it had significant doubts about the constitutionality of the provision, it was unable to answer his question because he had not submitted a list of the announcements he wished to make. Shortly thereafter, Wersal filed this lawsuit in Federal District Court against respondents, seeking a declaration that the announce clause violates the First Amendment and an injunction against its enforcement.

II

Before considering the constitutionality of the announce clause, we must be clear about its meaning. Its text says that a candidate for judicial office shall not "announce his or her views on disputed legal or political issues." Minn. Code of Judicial Conduct, Canon 5(A)(3)(d)(i) (2002). We know that "announcing] . . . views" on an issue covers much more than promising to decide an issue a particular way. The prohibition extends to the candidate's mere statement of his current position, even if he does not bind himself to maintain that position after election. All the parties agree this is the case, because the Minnesota Code contains a so-called "pledges or promises" clause, which separately prohibits judicial candidates from making "pledges or promises of conduct in office other than the faithful and impartial performance of the duties of the office[]"—a prohibition that is not challenged here and on which we express no view.

In any event, it is clear that the announce clause prohibits a judicial candidate from stating his views on any specific nonfanciful legal question within the province of the court for which he is running, except in the context of discussing past decisions—and in the latter context as well, if he expresses the view that he is not bound by stare decisis.

Respondents contend that this still leaves plenty of topics for discussion on the campaign trail. These include a candidate's "character," "education," "work habits," and "how [he] would handle administrative duties if elected." Indeed, the Judicial Board has printed a list of preapproved questions which judicial candidates are allowed to answer. These include how the candidate feels about cameras in the courtroom, how he would go about reducing the caseload, how the costs of judicial administration can be reduced, and how he proposes to ensure that minorities and women are treated more fairly by the court system. Whether this list of preapproved subjects, and other topics not prohibited by the announce clause, adequately fulfill the First Amendment's guarantee of freedom of speech is the question to which we now turn.

III

As the Court of Appeals recognized, the announce clause both prohibits speech on the basis of its content and burdens a category of speech that is "at the core of our First Amendment freedoms" — speech about the qualifications of candidates for public office. The Court of Appeals concluded that the proper test to be applied to determine the constitutionality of such a restriction is what our cases have called strict scrutiny. The parties do not dispute that this is correct. Under the strict-scrutiny test, respondents have the burden to prove that the announce clause is (1) narrowly tailored, to serve (2) a compelling state interest. In order for respondents to show that the announce clause is narrowly tailored, they must demonstrate that it does not "unnecessarily circumscrib[e] protected expression." Brown v. Hartlage (1982).

The Court of Appeals concluded that respondents had established two interests as sufficiently compelling to justify the announce clause: preserving the impartiality of the state judiciary and preserving the appearance of the impartiality of the state judiciary. Respondents reassert these two interests before us, arguing that the first is compelling because it protects the due process rights of litigants, and that the second is compelling because it preserves public confidence in the judiciary. Respondents are rather vague, however, about what they mean by "impartiality." Indeed, although the term is used throughout the Eighth Circuit's opinion, the briefs, the Minnesota Code of Judicial Conduct, and the ABA Codes of Judicial Conduct, none of these sources bothers to define it. Clarity on this point is essential before we can decide whether impartiality is indeed a compelling state interest, and, if so, whether the announce clause is narrowly tailored to achieve it.

A

One meaning of "impartiality" in the judicial context — and of course its root meaning — is the lack of bias for or against either party to the proceeding. Impartiality in this sense assures equal application of the law. That is, it guarantees a party that the judge who hears his case will apply the law to him in the same way he applies it to any other party. This is the traditional sense in which the term is used. It is also the sense in which it is used in the cases cited by respondents and amici for the proposition that an impartial judge is essential to due process.

We think it plain that the announce clause is not narrowly tailored to serve impartiality (or the appearance of impartiality) in this sense. Indeed, the clause is barely tailored to serve that interest at all, inasmuch as it does not restrict speech for or against particular parties, but rather speech for or against particular issues. To be sure, when a case arises that turns on a legal issue on which the judge (as a candidate) had taken a particular stand, the party taking the opposite stand is likely to lose. But not because of any bias against that party, or favoritism toward the other party. Any party taking that position is just as likely to lose. The judge is applying the law (as he sees it) evenhandedly.

B

It is perhaps possible to use the term "impartiality" in the judicial context (though this is certainly not a common usage) to mean lack of preconception in favor of or against a particular legal view. This sort of impartiality would be concerned, not with guaranteeing litigants equal application of the law, but rather with guaranteeing them an equal chance to persuade the court on the legal points in their case. Impartiality in this sense may well be an interest served by the announce clause, but it is not a compelling state interest, as strict scrutiny requires. A judge's lack of predisposition regarding the relevant legal issues in a case has never been thought a necessary component of equal justice, and with good reason. For one thing, it is virtually impossible to find a judge who does not have preconceptions about the law. As then-Justice Rehnquist observed of our own Court: "Since most Justices come to this bench no earlier than their middle years, it would be unusual if they had not by that time formulated at least some tentative notions that would influence them in their interpretation of the sweeping clauses of the Constitution and their interaction with one another. It would be not merely unusual, but extraordinary, if they had not at least given opinions as to constitutional issues in their previous legal careers." Laird v. Tatum (1972). Indeed, even if it were possible to select judges who did not have preconceived views on legal issues, it would hardly be desirable to do so. "Proof that a Justice's mind at the time he joined the Court was a complete tabula rasa in the area of constitutional adjudication would be evidence of lack of qualification, not lack of bias." The Minnesota Constitution positively forbids the selection to courts of general jurisdiction of judges who are impartial in the sense of having no views on the law. Minn. Const., Art. VI, §5 ("Judges of the supreme court, the court of appeals and the district court shall be learned in the law"). And since avoiding judicial preconceptions on legal issues is neither possible nor desirable, pretending otherwise by attempting to preserve the "appearance" of that type of impartiality can hardly be a compelling state interest either.

C

A third possible meaning of "impartiality" (again not a common one) might be described as openmindedness. This quality in a judge demands, not that he have no preconceptions on legal issues, but that he be willing to consider views that oppose his preconceptions, and remain open to persuasion, when the issues arise in a pending case. This sort of impartiality seeks to guarantee each litigant, not an equal chance to win the legal points in the case, but at least some chance of doing so. It may well be that impartiality in this sense, and the appearance of it, are desirable in the judiciary, but we need not pursue that inquiry, since we do not believe the Minnesota Supreme Court adopted the announce clause for that purpose.

Respondents argue that the announce clause serves the interest in openmindedness, or at least in the appearance of openmindedness, because it relieves a judge from pressure to rule a certain way in order to maintain consistency with statements the judge has previously made. The problem is, however, that statements in election campaigns are such an infinitesimal portion of the public commitments to legal positions that judges (or judges-to-be) undertake, that this object of the prohibition is implausible. Before they arrive on the bench (whether by election or otherwise) judges have often committed themselves on legal issues that they must later rule upon.

More common still is a judge's confronting a legal issue on which he has expressed an opinion while on the bench. Most frequently, of course, that prior expression will have occurred in ruling on an earlier case. But judges often state their views on disputed legal issues outside the context of adjudication—in classes that they conduct, and in books and speeches. Like the ABA Codes of Judicial Conduct, the Minnesota Code not only permits but encourages this. See Minn. Code of Judicial Conduct, Canon 4(B) (2002) ("A judge may write, lecture, teach, speak and participate in other extra-judicial activities concerning the law . . ."); Minn. Code of Judicial Conduct, Canon 4(B), Comment (2002) ("To the extent that time permits, a judge is encouraged to do so . . ."). That is quite incompatible with the notion that the need for openmindedness (or for the appearance of openmindedness) lies behind the prohibition at issue here.

The short of the matter is this: In Minnesota, a candidate for judicial office may not say "I think it is constitutional for the legislature to prohibit same-sex marriages." He may say the very same thing, however, up until the very day before he declares himself a candidate, and may say it repeatedly (until litigation is pending) after he is elected. As a means of pursuing the objective of openmindedness that respondents now articulate, the announce clause is so woefully under-inclusive as to render belief in that purpose a challenge to the credulous.

Moreover, the notion that the special context of electioneering justifies an abridgment of the right to speak out on disputed issues sets our First Amendment jurisprudence on its head. "[D]ebate on the qualifications of candidates" is "at the core of our electoral process and of the First Amendment freedoms," not at the edges. "The role that elected officials play in our society makes it all the more imperative that they be allowed freely to express themselves on matters of current public importance." Wood v. Georgia (1962). "It is simply not the function of government to select which issues are worth discussing or debating in the course of a political campaign." We have never allowed the government to prohibit candidates from communicating relevant information to voters during an election.

The Minnesota Supreme Court's canon of judicial conduct prohibiting candidates for judicial election from announcing their views on disputed legal and political issues violates the First Amendment. Accordingly, we reverse the grant of summary judgment to respondents and remand the case for proceedings consistent with this opinion.

Justice O'CONNOR, concurring.

I join the opinion of the Court but write separately to express my concerns about judicial elections generally. Respondents claim that "[t]he Announce Clause is necessary . . . to protect the State's compelling governmental interes[t] in an actual and perceived . . . impartial judiciary." I am concerned that, even aside from what judicial candidates may say while campaigning, the very practice of electing judges undermines this interest.

We of course want judges to be impartial, in the sense of being free from any personal stake in the outcome of the cases to which they are assigned. But if judges are subject to regular elections they are likely to feel that they have at least some personal stake in the outcome of every publicized case. Elected judges cannot help being aware that if the public is not satisfied with the outcome of a particular case, it could hurt their reelection prospects. See Eule, Crocodiles in the Bathtub: State Courts, Voter Initiatives and the Threat of Electoral Reprisal, 65 U. Colo. L. Rev. 733, 739 (1994) (quoting former California Supreme Court Justice Otto Kaus' statement that ignoring the political consequences of visible decisions is "like ignoring a crocodile in your bathtub"); Bright & Keenan, Judges and the Politics of Death: Deciding Between the Bill of Rights and the Next Election in Capital Cases, 75 B.U. L. Rev. 759, 793-794 (1995) (citing statistics indicating that judges who face elections are far more likely to override jury sentences of life without parole and impose the death penalty than are judges who do not run for election). Even if judges were able to suppress their awareness of the potential electoral consequences of their decisions and refrain from acting on it, the public's confidence in the judiciary could be undermined simply by the possibility that judges would be unable to do so.

Moreover, contested elections generally entail campaigning. And campaigning for a judicial post today can require substantial funds. Unless the pool of judicial candidates is limited to those wealthy enough to independently fund their campaigns, a limitation unrelated to judicial skill, the cost of campaigning requires judicial candidates to engage in fundraising. Yet relying on campaign donations may leave judges feeling indebted to certain parties or interest groups. See Thomas, National L.J., Mar. 16, 1998, p. A8, col. 1 (reporting that a study by the public interest group Texans for Public Justice found that 40 percent of the $9,200,000 in contributions of $100 or more raised by seven of Texas' nine Supreme Court justices for their 1994 and 1996 elections "came from parties and lawyers with cases before the court or contributors closely linked to these parties"). Even if judges were able to refrain from favoring donors, the mere possibility that judges' decisions may be motivated by the desire to repay campaign contributors is likely to undermine the public's confidence in the judiciary.

Minnesota has chosen to select its judges through contested popular elections instead of through an appointment system or a combined appointment and retention election system along the lines of the Missouri Plan. In doing so the State has voluntarily taken on the risks to judicial bias described above. As a result, the State's claim that it needs to significantly restrict judges' speech in order to protect judicial impartiality is particularly troubling. If the State has a problem with judicial impartiality, it is largely one the State brought upon itself by continuing the practice of popularly electing judges.

Justice KENNEDY, concurring.

I agree with the Court that Minnesota's prohibition on judicial candidates' announcing their legal views is an unconstitutional abridgment of the freedom of speech. There is authority for the Court to apply strict scrutiny analysis to resolve some First Amendment cases, and the Court explains in clear and forceful terms why the Minnesota regulatory scheme fails that test. So I join its opinion.

I adhere to my view, however, that content-based speech restrictions that do not fall within any traditional exception should be invalidated without inquiry into narrow tailoring or compelling government interests. The speech at issue here does not come within any of the exceptions to the First Amendment recognized by the Court. "Here, a law is directed to speech alone where the speech in question is not obscene, not defamatory, not words tantamount to an act otherwise criminal, not an impairment of some other constitutional right, not an incitement to lawless action, and not calculated or likely to bring about imminent harm the State has the substantive power to prevent. No further inquiry is necessary to reject the State's argument that the statute should be upheld."

The political speech of candidates is at the heart of the First Amendment, and direct restrictions on the content of candidate speech are simply beyond the power of government to impose. Here, Minnesota has sought to justify its speech restriction as one necessary to maintain the integrity of its judiciary. Nothing in the Court's opinion should be read to cast doubt on the vital importance of this state interest. Courts, in our system, elaborate principles of law in the course of resolving disputes. The power and the prerogative of a court to perform this function rest, in the end, upon the respect accorded to its judgments. The citizen's respect for judgments depends in turn upon the issuing court's absolute probity. Judicial integrity is, in consequence, a state interest of the highest order.

Minnesota may choose to have an elected judiciary. It may strive to define those characteristics that exemplify judicial excellence. It may enshrine its definitions in a code of judicial conduct. It may adopt recusal standards more rigorous than due process requires, and censure judges who violate these standards. What Minnesota may not do, however, is censor what the people hear as they undertake to decide for themselves which candidate is most likely to be an exemplary judicial officer. Deciding the relevance of candidate speech is the right of the voters, not the State. See Brown v. Hartlage (1982). The law in question here contradicts the principle that unabridged speech is the foundation of political freedom.

Justice GINSBURG, with whom Justice STEVENS, Justice SOUTER, and Justice BREYER join, dissenting.

Whether state or federal, elected or appointed, judges perform a function fundamentally different from that of the people's elected representatives. Legislative and executive officials act on behalf of the voters who placed them in office; "judge[s] represen[t] the Law." Unlike their counterparts in the political branches, judges are expected to refrain from catering to particular constituencies or committing themselves on controversial issues in advance of adversarial presentation. Their mission is to decide "individual cases and controversies" on individual records, neutrally applying legal principles, and, when necessary, "stand[ing] up to what is generally supreme in a democracy: the popular will." A judiciary capable of performing this function, owing fidelity to no person or party, is a "longstanding Anglo-American tradition," an essential bulwark of constitutional government, a constant guardian of the rule of law. The guarantee of an independent, impartial judiciary enables society to "withdraw certain subjects from the vicissitudes of political controversy, to place them beyond the reach of majorities and officials and to establish them as legal principles to be applied by the courts." West Virginia Bd. of Ed. v. Barnette (1943). "Without this, all the reservations of particular rights or privileges would amount to nothing." The Federalist No. 78, p. 466 (C. Rossiter ed. 1961).

The ability of the judiciary to discharge its unique role rests to a large degree on the manner in which judges are selected. The Framers of the Federal Constitution sought to advance the judicial function through the structural protections of Article III, which provide for the selection of judges by the President on the advice and consent of the Senate, generally for lifetime terms. Through its own Constitution, Minnesota, in common with most other States, has decided to allow its citizens to choose judges directly in periodic elections. But Minnesota has not thereby opted to install a corps of political actors on the bench; rather, it has endeavored to preserve the integrity of its judiciary by other means. Recognizing that the influence of political parties is incompatible with the judge's role, for example, Minnesota has designated all judicial elections nonpartisan. And it has adopted a provision, here called the Announce Clause, designed to prevent candidates for judicial office from "publicly making known how they would decide issues likely to come before them as judges."

I

The speech restriction must fail, in the Court's view, because an electoral process is at stake; if Minnesota opts to elect its judges, the Court asserts, the State may not rein in what candidates may say.

I do not agree with this unilocular, "an election is an election," approach. Instead, I would differentiate elections for political offices, in which the First Amendment holds full sway, from elections designed to select those whose office it is to administer justice without respect to persons. Minnesota's choice to elect its judges, I am persuaded, does not preclude the State from installing an election process geared to the judicial office.

Legislative and executive officials serve in representative capacities. They are agents of the people; their primary function is to advance the interests of their constituencies. Candidates for political offices, in keeping with their representative role, must be left free to inform the electorate of their positions on specific issues. Armed with such information, the individual voter will be equipped to cast her ballot intelligently, to vote for the candidate committed to positions the voter approves. Campaign statements committing the candidate to take sides on contentious issues are therefore not only appropriate in political elections, they are "at the core of our electoral process," for they "enhance the accountability of government officials to the people whom they represent."

Judges, however, are not political actors. They do not sit as representatives of particular persons, communities, or parties; they serve no faction or constituency. "[I]t is the business of judges to be indifferent to popularity." They must strive to do what is legally right, all the more so when the result is not the one "the home crowd" wants. Even when they develop common law or give concrete meaning to constitutional text, judges act only in the context of individual cases, the outcome of which cannot depend on the will of the public.

Thus, the rationale underlying unconstrained speech in elections for political office — that representative government depends on the public's ability to choose agents who will act at its behest — does not carry over to campaigns for the bench. As to persons aiming to occupy the seat of judgment, the Court's unrelenting reliance on decisions involving contests for legislative and executive posts is manifestly out of place. In view of the magisterial role judges must fill in a system of justice, a role that removes them from the partisan fray, States may limit judicial campaign speech by measures impermissible in elections for political office.[52]

II

Proper resolution of this case requires correction of the Court's distorted construction of the provision before us for review. According to the Court, the Announce Clause "prohibits a judicial candidate from stating his views on any specific nonfanciful legal question within the province of the court for which he is running, except in the context of discussing past decisions — and in the latter context as well, if he expresses the view that he is not bound by stare decisis."

First and most important, the Court ignores a crucial limiting construction placed on the Announce Clause by the courts below. The provision does not bar a candidate from generally "stating [her] views" on legal questions; it prevents her from "publicly making known how [she] would decide" disputed issues. That limitation places beyond the scope of the Announce Clause a wide range of comments that may be highly informative to voters. Consistent with the Eighth Circuit's construction, such comments may include, for example, statements of historical fact ("As a prosecutor, I obtained 15 drunk driving convictions"); qualified statements ("Judges should use sparingly their discretion to grant lenient sentences to drunk drivers"); and statements framed at a sufficient level of generality ("Drunk drivers are a threat to the safety of every driver"). What remains within the Announce Clause is the category of statements that essentially commit the candidate to a position on a specific issue, such as "I think all drunk drivers should receive the maximum sentence permitted by law."

Second, the Court misportrays the scope of the Clause as applied to a candidate's discussion of past decisions. The Court concludes that "statements critical of past judicial decisions are not permissible if the candidate also states that he is against stare decisis." That conclusion, however, draws no force from the meaning attributed to the Announce Clause by the Eighth Circuit. In line with the Minnesota Board on Judicial Standards, the Court of Appeals stated

---

52. The author of the Court's opinion declined on precisely these grounds to tell the Senate whether he would overrule a particular case:

> Let us assume that I have People arguing before me to do it or not to do it. I think it is quite a thing to be arguing to somebody who you know has made a representation in the course of his confirmation hearings, and that is, by way of condition to his being confirmed, that he will do this or do that. I think I would be in a very bad position to adjudicate the case without being accused of having a less than impartial view of the matter. 13 R. Mersky & J. Jacobstein, The Supreme Court of the United States: Hearings and Reports on Successful and Unsuccessful Nominations of Supreme Court Justices by the Senate Judiciary Committee, 1916-1986, 131 (1989) (hearings before the Senate Judiciary Committee on the nomination of then-Judge Scalia). [Footnote by the Court.]

without qualification that the Clause "does not prohibit candidates from discussing appellate court decisions."

The Announce Clause is thus more tightly bounded, and campaigns conducted under that provision more robust, than the Court acknowledges.

For more than three-quarters of a century, States like Minnesota have endeavored, through experiment tested by experience, to balance the constitutional interests in judicial integrity and free expression within the unique setting of an elected judiciary. The Announce Clause, borne of this long effort, "comes to this Court bearing a weighty title of respect." I would uphold it as an essential component in Minnesota's accommodation of the complex and competing concerns in this sensitive area.

These cases show that a law is content-based if it is either a subject-matter or a viewpoint restriction. In contrast, a law regulating speech is content-neutral if it applies to all speech regardless of the message. For example, a law prohibiting the posting of all signs on public utility poles would be content-neutral because it would apply to every sign regardless of its subject matter or viewpoint.[53] In Turner Broadcasting v. FCC, the Supreme Court found that a federal law requiring cable companies to carry local broadcast stations was content-neutral because the companies were required to include all stations, whatever their programming. A law might also be content-neutral if it regulates conduct and it has an effect on speech without regard to its content. For example, a sales tax applicable to all purchases, including purchases of reading material, might have a significant incidental effect on speech, but it is content-neutral.[54]

c. Problems in Applying the Distinction Between Content-Based and Content-Neutral Laws

Three important problems arise in applying the distinction between content-based and content-neutral laws. First, does a permissible purpose for a law prevent it from being deemed content-based, even if a content restriction is on the face of the law? In Turner Broadcasting v. FCC (preceding), the Court said, "Nor will the mere assertion of a content-neutral purpose be enough to save a law which, on its face, discriminates based on content." However, in other cases, the Supreme Court has indicated that a facial content-based restriction will be deemed content-neutral if it is motivated by a permissible content-neutral purpose. The Court articulated this rule in City of Renton v. Playtime Theatres, Inc.

---

53. *See* Members of the City Council of Los Angeles v. Taxpayers for Vincent, 466 U.S. 789 (1984).

54. *See, e.g.*, Leathers v. Medlock, 499 U.S. 439 (1991), upholding the application of a general sales tax to cable television that was not applicable to the print media, because it did not suppress ideas and did not target a small group of speakers.

CITY OF RENTON v. PLAYTIME THEATRES, INC.

475 U.S. 41 (1986)

Justice REHNQUIST delivered the opinion of the Court.

This case involves a constitutional challenge to a zoning ordinance, enacted by appellant city of Renton, Washington, that prohibits adult motion picture theaters from locating within 1,000 feet of any residential zone, single- or multiple-family dwelling, church, park, or school.

I

In May 1980, the Mayor of Renton, a city of approximately 32,000 people located just south of Seattle, suggested to the Renton City Council that it consider the advisability of enacting zoning legislation dealing with adult entertainment uses. No such uses existed in the city at that time. In April 1981, acting on the basis of the Planning and Development Committee's recommendation, the City Council enacted Ordinance No. 3526. The ordinance prohibited any "adult motion picture theater" from locating within 1,000 feet of any residential zone, single- or multiple-family dwelling, church, or park, and within one mile of any school. The term "adult motion picture theater" was defined as "[a]n enclosed building used for presenting motion picture films, video cassettes, cable television, or any other such visual media, distinguished or characteri[zed] by an emphasis on matter depicting, describing or relating to 'specified sexual activities' or 'specified anatomical areas' . . . for observation by patrons therein."

The Renton ordinance does not ban adult theaters altogether, but merely provides that such theaters may not be located within 1,000 feet of any residential zone, single- or multiple-family dwelling, church, park, or school. The ordinance is therefore properly analyzed as a form of time, place, and manner regulation. This Court has long held that regulations enacted for the purpose of restraining speech on the basis of its content presumptively violate the First Amendment. On the other hand, so-called "content-neutral" time, place, and manner regulations are acceptable so long as they are designed to serve a substantial governmental interest and do not unreasonably limit alternative avenues of communication.

At first glance, the Renton ordinance does not appear to fit neatly into either the "content-based" or the "content-neutral" category. To be sure, the ordinance treats theaters that specialize in adult films differently from other kinds of theaters. Nevertheless, as the District Court concluded, the Renton ordinance is aimed not at the content of the films shown at "adult motion picture theatres," but rather at the secondary effects of such theaters on the surrounding community. The District Court found that the City Council's "predominate concerns" were with the secondary effects of adult theaters, and not with the content of adult films themselves.

The appropriate inquiry in this case, then, is whether the Renton ordinance is designed to serve a substantial governmental interest and allows for reasonable alternative avenues of communication. It is clear that the ordinance meets such a standard. As a majority of this Court recognized in Young v. American Mini Theatres (1976), a city's "interest in attempting to preserve the quality of urban life is one that must be accorded high respect." Exactly the same vital governmental interests are at stake here.

Justice BRENNAN, with whom Justice MARSHALL joins, dissenting.

Renton's zoning ordinance selectively imposes limitations on the location of a movie theater based exclusively on the content of the films shown there. The constitutionality of the ordinance is therefore not correctly analyzed under standards applied to content-neutral time, place, and manner restrictions. But even assuming that the ordinance may fairly be characterized as content neutral, it is plainly unconstitutional under the standards established by the decisions of this Court. Although the Court's analysis is limited to cases involving "businesses that purvey sexually explicit materials," and thus does not affect our holdings in cases involving state regulation of other kinds of speech, I dissent.

"[A] constitutionally permissible time, place, or manner restriction may not be based upon either the content or subject matter of speech." Consolidated Edison Co. v. Public Service Commn. of N.Y. (1980). The Court asserts that the ordinance is "aimed not at the content of the films shown at 'adult motion picture theatres,' but rather at the secondary effects of such theaters on the surrounding community," and thus is simply a time, place, and manner regulation. This analysis is misguided.

The fact that adult movie theaters may cause harmful "secondary" land-use effects may arguably give Renton a compelling reason to regulate such establishments; it does not mean, however, that such regulations are content neutral. Because the ordinance imposes special restrictions on certain kinds of speech on the basis of content, I cannot simply accept, as the Court does, Renton's claim that the ordinance was not designed to suppress the content of adult movies.

The ordinance discriminates on its face against certain forms of speech based on content. Movie theaters specializing in "adult motion pictures" may not be located within 1,000 feet of any residential zone, single- or multiple-family dwelling, church, park, or school. Other motion picture theaters, and other forms of "adult entertainment," such as bars, massage parlors, and adult bookstores, are not subject to the same restrictions. This selective treatment strongly suggests that Renton was interested not in controlling the "secondary effects" associated with adult businesses, but in discriminating against adult theaters based on the content of the films they exhibit. The Court ignores this discriminatory treatment, declaring that Renton is free "to address the potential problems created by one particular kind of adult business," and to amend the ordinance in the future to include other adult enterprises. However, because of the First Amendment interests at stake here, this one-step-at-a-time analysis is wholly inappropriate. In this case, the city has not justified treating adult movie theaters differently from other adult entertainment businesses. The ordinance's underinclusiveness is cogent evidence that it was aimed at the content of the films shown in adult movie theaters.

Applying this standard to the facts of this case, the ordinance is patently unconstitutional. Renton has not shown that locating adult movie theaters in proximity to its churches, schools, parks, and residences will necessarily result in undesirable "secondary effects," or that these problems could not be effectively addressed by less intrusive restrictions.

Renton has been strongly criticized by commentators.[55] Critics argue that *Renton* "permits an end run around the First Amendment: The government can always point to some neutral, nonspeech justification for its actions."[56] Justice Brennan expressed his "continued disagreement with the proposition that an otherwise content-based restriction on speech can be recast as 'content-neutral' if the restriction 'aims' at 'secondary-effects' of the speech. . . . [S]uch secondary effects offer countless excuses for content-based suppression of political speech."[57]

The argument is that the *Renton* approach seems to confuse whether a law is content-based or content-neutral with the question of whether a law is justified by a sufficient purpose. The law may have been properly upheld as needed to combat crime and the secondary effects of adult theaters, but it nonetheless was clearly content-based: It applied only to theaters showing films with sexually explicit content.

The Court has been inconsistent in applying *Renton*. In some cases, the Court has distinguished *Renton* and rejected the argument that the goal of preventing secondary effects prevents a law from being deemed content-based. For example, in Boos v. Barry, presented earlier, the government argued that the restriction of speech critical of foreign governments near their embassies was justified based on an international law obligation to shield diplomats from speech that offends their dignity. Justice O'Connor, writing for the plurality in declaring this part of the law unconstitutional, distinguished *Renton* because the ordinance restricting speech near embassies was "justified *only* by reference to the content of the speech. Respondents and the United States do not point to the 'secondary effects' of picket signs in front of embassies. They do not point to congestion, to interference with ingress or egress, to visual clutter, or to the need to protect the security of embassies. Rather, they rely on the need to protect the dignity of foreign diplomatic personnel by shielding them from speech that is critical of their governments. This justification focuses *only* on the content of the speech and the direct impact that speech has on its listeners."

The Court also distinguished *Renton* in City of Cincinnati v. Discovery Network, Inc., 507 U.S. 410 (1993), where the Court declared unconstitutional a prohibition on the use of newsracks on public property for the distribution of commercial handbills. The city argued that the ordinance was justified by concern over the secondary effects of such newsracks with regard to safety and aesthetics. The Court rejected this argument and characterized the ordinance as content-based. Justice Stevens, writing for the Court, said, "The argument is unpersuasive because the very basis for the regulation is the difference in content between ordinary newspapers and commercial speech. . . . Under the city's newsrack policy, whether any particular newsrack falls within the ban is determined by the content of the publication resting inside that newsrack. Thus, by any commonsense understanding of the term, the ban is 'content-based.'" Justice Stevens expressly distinguished *Renton* and said that the city's "reliance on *Renton* is misplaced." He said that "[i]n contrast to the speech at issue in

55. For an excellent summary of these criticisms, *see* Marcy Strauss, *From Witness to Riches: The Constitutionality of Restricting Witness Speech*, 38 Ariz. L. Rev. 291 (1996).
56. *Id.* at 317.
57. Boos v. Barry, 485 U.S. at 334-335 (Brennan, J., concurring in part and concurring in the judgment).

Renton, there are no secondary effects attributable to . . . newsracks [containing commercial handbills] that distinguish them from the newsracks Cincinnati permits to remain on its sidewalks."[58]

In contrast, in City of Erie v. Pap's AM (2000), the Court upheld a city's public nudity law and its application to prevent nude dancing on the ground that the ordinance was content-neutral. Justice O'Connor's plurality opinion expressly applied *Renton* and concluded that the city's goal of preventing the secondary effects of nude dancing were sufficient to make the law content-neutral.

Thus, at this point, it appears that a law that on its face regulates speech based on its viewpoint or message will be presumed to be content-based, but the government can refute this by persuading a court that the regulation is justified by a content-neutral desire to avoid undesirable secondary effects of the speech. The content-neutral justification must be truly unrelated to the desire to suppress speech and it must be unique to the speech suppressed as compared to the speech allowed.

A second problem in applying the content-based/content-neutral distinction concerns situations in which the government must make content-based choices. There are some instances when the government inescapably must make content choices. For instance, if the government is choosing to subsidize speech, there is no way that it can avoid content considerations in deciding what to finance. Many situations like this are discussed in this chapter, such as when the government runs a theater or a concert hall and is choosing programs, or when a public library is deciding what books to buy, or when a public university is evaluating a professor's writings for purposes of tenure and promotion. The government simply cannot ignore content in these situations. The Court indicated that in such circumstances the government must be viewpoint-neutral but otherwise can consider content. In reading this case, consider whether the Court was correct in finding the federal law to be viewpoint-neutral.

NATIONAL ENDOWMENT FOR THE ARTS v. FINLEY
524 U.S. 569 (1998)

Justice O'CONNOR delivered the opinion of the Court.

The National Foundation on the Arts and Humanities Act, as amended in 1990, requires the Chairperson of the National Endowment for the Arts (NEA) to ensure that "artistic excellence and artistic merit are the criteria by which [grant] applications are judged, taking into consideration general standards of decency and respect for the diverse beliefs and values of the American public." We conclude that [the law] is facially valid, as it neither inherently interferes with First Amendment rights nor violates constitutional vagueness principles.

I

With the establishment of the NEA in 1965, Congress embarked on a "broadly conceived national policy of support for the . . . arts in the United States," pledging federal funds to "help create and sustain not only a climate en-

---

58. *City of Cincinnati,* 507 U.S. at 430.

couraging freedom of thought, imagination, and inquiry but also the material conditions facilitating the release of . . . creative talent." The enabling statute vests the NEA with substantial discretion to award grants; it identifies only the broadest funding priorities, including "artistic and cultural significance, giving emphasis to American creativity and cultural diversity," "professional excellence," and the encouragement of "public knowledge, education, understanding, and appreciation of the arts."

Applications for NEA funding are initially reviewed by advisory panels composed of experts in the relevant field of the arts. Under the 1990 Amendments to the enabling statute, those panels must reflect "diverse artistic and cultural points of view" and include "wide geographic, ethnic, and minority representation," as well as "lay individuals who are knowledgeable about the arts." The panels report to the 26-member National Council on the Arts (Council), which, in turn, advises the NEA Chairperson. The Chairperson has the ultimate authority to award grants but may not approve an application as to which the Council has made a negative recommendation.

Since 1965, the NEA has distributed over three billion dollars in grants to individuals and organizations, funding that has served as a catalyst for increased state, corporate, and foundation support for the arts. Throughout the NEA's history, only a handful of the agency's roughly 100,000 awards have generated formal complaints about misapplied funds or abuse of the public's trust. Two provocative works, however, prompted public controversy in 1989 and led to congressional revaluation of the NEA's funding priorities and efforts to increase oversight of its grant-making procedures. The Institute of Contemporary Art at the University of Pennsylvania had used $30,000 of a visual arts grant it received from the NEA to fund a 1989 retrospective of photographer Robert Mapplethorpe's work. The exhibit, entitled The Perfect Moment, included homoerotic photographs that several Members of Congress condemned as pornographic. Members also denounced artist Andres Serrano's work Piss Christ, a photograph of a crucifix immersed in urine. Serrano had been awarded a $15,000 grant from the Southeast Center for Contemporary Art, an organization that received NEA support.

Ultimately, Congress adopted [a law] which directs the Chairperson, in establishing procedures to judge the artistic merit of grant applications, to "tak[e] into consideration general standards of decency and respect for the diverse beliefs and values of the American public."

The four individual respondents in this case, Karen Finley, John Fleck, Holly Hughes, and Tim Miller, are performance artists who applied for NEA grants. An advisory panel recommended approval of respondents' projects, both initially and after receiving [NEA Chairman John] Frohnmayer's request to reconsider three of the applications. A majority of the Council subsequently recommended disapproval, and in June 1990, the NEA informed respondents that they had been denied funding. Respondents filed suit, alleging that the NEA had violated their First Amendment rights.

II

Respondents raise a facial constitutional challenge to [the law] and consequently they confront "a heavy burden" in advancing their claim. Facial invalidation "is, manifestly, strong medicine" that "has been employed by the Court sparingly and only as a last resort." To prevail, respondents must demonstrate a substantial risk that application of the provision will lead to the suppression of speech.

Respondents argue that the provision is a paradigmatic example of viewpoint discrimination because it rejects any artistic speech that either fails to respect mainstream values or offends standards of decency. The NEA, however, reads the provision as merely hortatory, and contends that it stops well short of an absolute restriction. Section 954(d)(1) adds "considerations" to the grant-making process; it does not preclude awards to projects that might be deemed "indecent" or "disrespectful," nor place conditions on grants, or even specify that those factors must be given any particular weight in reviewing an application.

That §954(d)(1) admonishes the NEA merely to take "decency and respect" into consideration, and that the legislation was aimed at reforming procedures rather than precluding speech, undercut respondents' argument that the provision inevitably will be utilized as a tool for invidious viewpoint discrimination. In cases where we have struck down legislation as facially unconstitutional, the dangers were both more evident and more substantial.

Any content-based considerations that may be taken into account in the grant-making process are a consequence of the nature of arts funding. The NEA has limited resources and it must deny the majority of the grant applications that it receives, including many that propose "artistically excellent" projects. The agency may decide to fund particular projects for a wide variety of reasons, "such as the technical proficiency of the artist, the creativity of the work, the anticipated public interest in or appreciation of the work, the work's contemporary relevance, its educational value, its suitability for or appeal to special audiences (such as children or the disabled), its service to a rural or isolated community, or even simply that the work could increase public knowledge of an art form." As the dissent below noted, it would be "impossible to have a highly selective grant program without denying money to a large amount of constitutionally protected expression." The "very assumption" of the NEA is that grants will be awarded according to the "artistic worth of competing applications," and absolute neutrality is simply "inconceivable." In the context of arts funding, in contrast to many other subsidies, the Government does not indiscriminately "encourage a diversity of views from private speakers." The NEA's mandate is to make aesthetic judgments, and the inherently content-based "excellence" threshold for NEA support sets it apart [from other situations]. Respondents do not allege discrimination in any particular funding decision. Thus, we have no occasion here to address an as-applied challenge in a situation where the denial of a grant may be shown to be the product of invidious viewpoint discrimination.

If the NEA were to leverage its power to award subsidies on the basis of subjective criteria into a penalty on disfavored viewpoints, then we would confront a different case. We have stated that, even in the provision of subsidies, the Government may not "ai[m] at the suppression of dangerous ideas," and if a subsidy were "manipulated" to have a "coercive effect," then relief could be appropriate. In addition, as the NEA itself concedes, a more pressing constitutional question would arise if government funding resulted in the imposition of a disproportionate burden calculated to drive "certain ideas or viewpoints from the marketplace." Unless and until §954(d)(1) is applied in a manner that raises concern about the suppression of disfavored viewpoints, however, we uphold the constitutionality of the provision.

Finally, although the First Amendment certainly has application in the subsidy context, we note that the Government may allocate competitive funding according to criteria that would be impermissible were direct regulation of speech or a criminal penalty at stake. So long as legislation does not infringe on other constitutionally protected rights, Congress has wide latitude to set spending priorities. Congress may "selectively fund a program to encourage certain activities it believes to be in the public interest, without at the same time funding an alternative program which seeks to deal with the problem in another way." In doing so, "the Government has not discriminated on the basis of viewpoint; it has merely chosen to fund one activity to the exclusion of the other."

Justice SOUTER, dissenting.

The question here is whether this statute is unconstitutional on its face: "artistic excellence and artistic merit are the criteria by which applications [for grants from the National Endowment for the Arts] are judged, taking into consideration general standards of decency and respect for the diverse beliefs and values of the American public." The decency and respect proviso mandates viewpoint-based decisions in the disbursement of government subsidies, and the Government has wholly failed to explain why the statute should be afforded an exemption from the fundamental rule of the First Amendment that viewpoint discrimination in the exercise of public authority over expressive activity is unconstitutional. The Court's conclusions that the proviso is not viewpoint based, that it is not a regulation, and that the NEA may permissibly engage in viewpoint-based discrimination, are all patently mistaken.

"If there is a bedrock principle underlying the First Amendment, it is that the government may not prohibit the expression of an idea simply because society finds the idea itself offensive or disagreeable." Texas v. Johnson (1989). Because this principle applies not only to affirmative suppression of speech, but also to disqualification for government favors, Congress is generally not permitted to pivot discrimination against otherwise protected speech on the offensiveness or unacceptability of the views it expresses.

[A] statute disfavoring speech that fails to respect America's "diverse beliefs and values" is the very model of viewpoint discrimination; it penalizes any view disrespectful to any belief or value espoused by someone in the American populace. Boiled down to its practical essence, the limitation obviously means that art that disrespects the ideology, opinions, or convictions of a significant segment of the American public is to be disfavored, whereas art that reinforces those values is not. After all, the whole point of the proviso was to make sure that works like Serrano's ostensibly blasphemous portrayal of Jesus would not be funded, while a reverent treatment, conventionally respectful of Christian sensibilities, would not run afoul of the law. Nothing could be more viewpoint-based than that. The fact that the statute disfavors art insufficiently respectful of America's "diverse" beliefs and values alters this conclusion not one whit: the First Amendment does not validate the ambition to disqualify many disrespectful viewpoints instead of merely one.

In United States v. American Library Association, 539 U.S. 194 (2003), the Court, without a majority opinion, upheld a federal law requiring libraries receiving federal funds to install filters to block sexually explicit material. Chief Justice Rehnquist's plurality opinion stressed that libraries need not buy all materials or allow access to all materials on the Internet. Thus, it is constitutional for Congress to condition federal funds on a requirement that local libraries place filters on their computers which are available to users. Justices Kennedy and Breyer, concurring in the judgment, emphasized that under the law, patrons may request librarians to lift filters. They said that since none of the plaintiffs in the suit had been denied access to any materials, it was premature to consider the constitutional issue.

A third problem with applying the distinction between content-based and content-neutral regulations is the Court's holding that the First Amendment does not apply at all of if the government is the speaker or even adopts private speech as its own. The question is how much this opens the door to the government circumventing the Constitution by being able to adopt private messages as government speech. Although the following case was unanimous, some of the justices in their concurring opinions raise exactly this question.

PLEASANT GROVE CITY, UTAH v. SUMMUM

555 U.S. 460 (2009)

Justice Alito delivered the opinion of the Court.

This case presents the question whether the Free Speech Clause of the First Amendment entitles a private group to insist that a municipality permit it to place a permanent monument in a city park in which other donated monuments were previously erected. The Court of Appeals held that the municipality was required to accept the monument because a public park is a traditional public forum. We conclude, however, that although a park is a traditional public forum for speeches and other transitory expressive acts, the display of a permanent monument in a public park is not a form of expression to which forum analysis applies. Instead, the placement of a permanent monument in a public park is best viewed as a form of government speech and is therefore not subject to scrutiny under the Free Speech Clause.

I

Pioneer Park (or Park) is a 2.5 acre public park located in the Historic District of Pleasant Grove City (or City) in Utah. The Park currently contains 15 permanent displays, at least 11 of which were donated by private groups or individuals. These include an historic granary, a wishing well, the City's first fire station, a September 11 monument, and a Ten Commandments monument donated by the Fraternal Order of Eagles in 1971.

Respondent Summum is a religious organization founded in 1975 and headquartered in Salt Lake City, Utah. On two separate occasions in 2003, Summum's president wrote a letter to the City's mayor requesting permission to erect a "stone monument," which would contain "the Seven Aphorisms of

SUMMUM" and be similar in size and nature to the Ten Commandments monument. The City denied the requests.

In May 2005, respondent's president again wrote to the mayor asking to erect a monument, but the letter did not describe the monument, its historical significance, or Summum's connection to the community. The city council rejected this request.

In 2005, respondent filed this action against the City and various local officials (petitioners), asserting, among other claims, that petitioners had violated the Free Speech Clause of the First Amendment by accepting the Ten Commandments monument but rejecting the proposed Seven Aphorisms monument.

II

No prior decision of this Court has addressed the application of the Free Speech Clause to a government entity's acceptance of privately donated, permanent monuments for installation in a public park, and the parties disagree sharply about the line of precedents that governs this situation. The parties' fundamental disagreement thus centers on the nature of petitioners' conduct when they permitted privately donated monuments to be erected in Pioneer Park. Were petitioners engaging in their own expressive conduct? Or were they providing a forum for private speech?

If petitioners were engaging in their own expressive conduct, then the Free Speech Clause has no application. The Free Speech Clause restricts government regulation of private speech; it does not regulate government speech. Indeed, it is not easy to imagine how government could function if it lacked this freedom. "If every citizen were to have a right to insist that no one paid by public funds express a view with which he disagreed, debate over issues of great concern to the public would be limited to those in the private sector, and the process of government as we know it radically transformed."

A government entity may exercise this same freedom to express its views when it receives assistance from private sources for the purpose of delivering a government-controlled message.

This does not mean that there are no restraints on government speech. For example, government speech must comport with the Establishment Clause. The involvement of public officials in advocacy may be limited by law, regulation, or practice. And of course, a government entity is ultimately "accountable to the electorate and the political process for its advocacy."

While government speech is not restricted by the Free Speech Clause, the government does not have a free hand to regulate private speech on government property. This Court long ago recognized that members of the public retain strong free speech rights when they venture into public streets and parks, "which 'have immemorially been held in trust for the use of the public and, time out of mind, have been used for purposes of assembly, communicating thoughts between citizens, and discussing public questions.'" In order to preserve this freedom, government entities are strictly limited in their ability to regulate private speech in such "traditional public fora." Reasonable time, place, and manner restrictions are allowed, but any restriction based on the content of the speech must satisfy strict scrutiny, that is, the restriction must be narrowly tailored to serve a compelling government interest, and restrictions based on viewpoint are prohibited.

III

There may be situations in which it is difficult to tell whether a government entity is speaking on its own behalf or is providing a forum for private speech, but this case does not present such a situation. Permanent monuments displayed on public property typically represent government speech.

Governments have long used monuments to speak to the public. Since ancient times, kings, emperors, and other rulers have erected statues of themselves to remind their subjects of their authority and power. Triumphal arches, columns, and other monuments have been built to commemorate military victories and sacrifices and other events of civic importance. A monument, by definition, is a structure that is designed as a means of expression. When a government entity arranges for the construction of a monument, it does so because it wishes to convey some thought or instill some feeling in those who see the structure. Neither the Court of Appeals nor respondent disputes the obvious proposition that a monument that is commissioned and financed by a government body for placement on public land constitutes government speech.

Just as government-commissioned and government-financed monuments speak for the government, so do privately financed and donated monuments that the government accepts and displays to the public on government land. It certainly is not common for property owners to open up their property for the installation of permanent monuments that convey a message with which they do not wish to be associated. And because property owners typically do not permit the construction of such monuments on their land, persons who observe donated monuments routinely — and reasonably — interpret them as conveying some message on the property owner's behalf. In this context, there is little chance that observers will fail to appreciate the identity of the speaker. This is true whether the monument is located on private property or on public property, such as national, state, or city park land.

Public parks are often closely identified in the public mind with the government unit that owns the land. City parks ranging from those in small towns, like Pioneer Park in Pleasant Grove City, to those in major metropolises, like Central Park in New York City — commonly play an important role in defining the identity that a city projects to its own residents and to the outside world. Accordingly, cities and other jurisdictions take some care in accepting donated monuments. Government decisionmakers select the monuments that portray what they view as appropriate for the place in question, taking into account such content-based factors as esthetics, history, and local culture. The monuments that are accepted, therefore, are meant to convey and have the effect of conveying a government message, and they thus constitute government speech.

IV

In this case, it is clear that the monuments in Pleasant Grove's Pioneer Park represent government speech. Although many of the monuments were not designed or built by the City and were donated in completed form by private entities, the City decided to accept those donations and to display them in the Park. Respondent does not claim that the City ever opened up the Park for the placement of whatever permanent monuments might be offered by private donors. Rather, the City has "effectively controlled" the messages sent by the monuments in the Park by exercising "final approval authority" over their selection. The City has selected those monuments that it wants to display for the purpose of presenting the image of the City that it wishes to project to all who frequent the Park; it has taken ownership of most of the monuments in the Park, including the Ten Commandments monument that is the focus of respondent's concern; and the City has now expressly set forth the criteria it will use in making future selections.

Respondent voices the legitimate concern that the government speech doctrine not be used as a subterfuge for favoring certain private speakers over others based on viewpoint. Respondent's suggested solution is to require a government entity accepting a privately donated monument to go through a formal process of adopting a resolution publicly embracing "the message" that the monument conveys.

We see no reason for imposing a requirement of this sort. The parks of this country contain thousands of donated monuments that government entities have used for their own expressive purposes, usually without producing the sort of formal documentation that respondent now says is required to escape Free Speech Clause restrictions. Requiring all of these jurisdictions to go back and proclaim formally that they adopt all of these monuments as their own expressive vehicles would be a pointless exercise that the Constitution does not mandate.

Contrary to respondent's apparent belief, it frequently is not possible to identify a single "message" that is conveyed by an object or structure, and consequently, the thoughts or sentiments expressed by a government entity that accepts and displays such an object may be quite different from those of either its creator or its donor. By accepting a privately donated monument and placing it on city property, a city engages in expressive conduct, but the intended and perceived significance of that conduct may not coincide with the thinking of the monument's donor or creator. Indeed, when a privately donated memorial is funded by many small donations, the donors themselves may differ in their interpretation of the monument's significance. By accepting such a monument, a government entity does not necessarily endorse the specific meaning that any particular donor sees in the monument.

By contrast, public parks can accommodate only a limited number of permanent monuments. Public parks have been used, "'time out of mind, . . . for purposes of assembly, communicating thoughts between citizens, and discussing public questions,'" but "one would be hard pressed to find a 'long tradition' of allowing people to permanently occupy public space with any manner of monuments."

Speakers, no matter how long-winded, eventually come to the end of their remarks; persons distributing leaflets and carrying signs at some point tire and go home; monuments, however, endure. They monopolize the use of the land on which they stand and interfere permanently with other uses of public space. A public park, over the years, can provide a soapbox for a very large number of orators — often, for all who want to speak — but it is hard to imagine how a public park could be opened up for the installation of permanent monuments by every person or group wishing to engage in that form of expression.

If government entities must maintain viewpoint neutrality in their selection of donated monuments, they must either "brace themselves for an influx of clutter" or face the pressure to remove longstanding and cherished monuments. Every jurisdiction that has accepted a donated war memorial may be asked to provide equal treatment for a donated monument questioning the cause for which the veterans fought. New York City, having accepted a donated statue of one heroic dog (Balto, the sled dog who brought medicine to Nome, Alaska, during a diphtheria epidemic) may be pressed to accept monuments for other dogs who are claimed to be equally worthy of commemoration. The obvious truth of the matter is that if public parks were considered to be traditional public forums for the purpose of erecting privately donated monuments, most parks would have little choice but to refuse all such donations. And where the application of forum analysis would lead almost inexorably to closing of the forum, it is obvious that forum analysis is out of place.

To be sure, there are limited circumstances in which the forum doctrine might properly be applied to a permanent monument — for example, if a town created a monument on which all of its residents (or all those meeting some other criterion) could place the name of a person to be honored or some other private message. But as a general matter, forum analysis simply does not apply to the installation of permanent monuments on public property.

V

In sum, we hold that the City's decision to accept certain privately donated monuments while rejecting respondent's is best viewed as a form of government speech. As a result, the City's decision is not subject to the Free Speech Clause, and the Court of Appeals erred in holding otherwise. We therefore reverse.

Justice STEVENS, with whom Justice GINSBURG joins, concurring.

This case involves a property owner's rejection of an offer to place a permanent display on its land. While I join the Court's persuasive opinion, I think the reasons justifying the city's refusal would have been equally valid if its acceptance of the monument, instead of being characterized as "government speech," had merely been deemed an implicit endorsement of the donor's message. To date, our decisions relying on the recently minted government speech doctrine to uphold government action have been few and, in my view, of doubtful merit. The Court's opinion in this case signals no expansion of that doctrine. And by joining the Court's opinion, I do not mean to indicate agreement with our earlier decisions. Nor is it likely, given the near certainty that observers will associate permanent displays with the governmental property owner, that the government will be able to avoid political accountability for the views that it endorses or expresses through this means. Finally, recognizing permanent displays on public property as government speech will not give the government free license to communicate offensive or partisan messages. For even if the Free Speech Clause neither restricts nor protects government speech, government speakers are bound by the Constitution's other proscriptions, including those supplied by the Establishment and Equal Protection Clauses. Together with the checks imposed by our democratic processes, these constitutional safeguards ensure that the effect of today's decision will be limited.

Justice SOUTER, concurring in the judgment.

I agree with the Court that the Ten Commandments monument is government speech, that is, an expression of a government's position on the moral and religious issues raised by the subject of the monument. And although the government should lose when the character of the speech is at issue and its governmental nature has not been made clear, I also agree with the Court that the city need not satisfy the particular formality urged by Summum as a condition of recognizing that the expression here falls within the public category. I have qualms, however, about accepting the position that public monuments are government speech categorically.

Because the government speech doctrine is "recently minted," it would do well for us to go slow in setting its bounds, which will affect existing doctrine in ways not yet explored.

The case shows that it may not be easy to work out. After today's decision, whenever a government maintains a monument it will presumably be understood to be engaging in government speech. If the monument has some religious character, the specter of violating the Establishment Clause will behoove it to take care to avoid the appearance of a flat-out establishment of religion, in the sense of the government's adoption of the tenets expressed or symbolized. In such an instance, there will be safety in numbers, and it will be in the interest of a careful government to accept other monuments to stand nearby, to dilute the appearance of adopting whatever particular religious position the single example alone might stand for. As mementoes and testimonials pile up, however, the chatter may well make it less intuitively obvious that the government is speaking in its own right simply by maintaining the monuments.

To avoid relying on a *per se* rule to say when speech is governmental, the best approach that occurs to me is to ask whether a reasonable and fully informed observer would understand the expression to be government speech, as distinct from private speech the government chooses to oblige by allowing the monument to be placed on public land. This reasonable observer test for governmental character is of a piece with the one for spotting forbidden governmental endorsement of religion in the Establishment Clause cases. The adoption of it would thus serve coherence within Establishment Clause law, and it would make sense of our common understanding that some monuments on public land display religious symbolism that clearly does not express a government's chosen views.

Application of this observer test provides the reason I find the monument here to be government expression.

2. Vagueness and Overbreadth

Laws that regulate speech can be challenged as facially unconstitutional on the grounds that they are unduly vague and overbroad. A successful facial challenge usually means that the law is entirely invalidated, as opposed to being declared unconstitutional as to certain applications. Vagueness and overbreadth are thus powerful doctrines that can be used to challenge any law regulating speech, including by a person whose speech is unprotected by the First Amendment. This section looks first at vagueness, then it considers overbreadth, and finally it discusses the relationship between the two doctrines.

a. Vagueness

A law is unconstitutionally vague if a reasonable person cannot tell what speech is prohibited and what is permitted.[59] It is important to emphasize that unduly vague laws violate due process whether or not speech is regulated.[60] For example, in Kolender v. Lawson, the Court declared unconstitutional California's loitering law and declared that "the void-for-vagueness doctrine requires that a penal statute define the criminal offense with sufficient definiteness that ordinary people can understand what conduct is prohibited and in a manner that does not encourage arbitrary and discriminatory enforcement."[61]

In part, the vagueness doctrine is about fairness; it is unjust to punish a person without providing clear notice as to what conduct was prohibited. Vague laws also risk selective prosecution; under vague statutes and ordinances the government can choose who to prosecute based on their views or politics. Justice O'Connor said that "[t]he more important aspect of the vagueness doctrine 'is not actual notice, but the other principal element of the doctrine — the requirement that a legislature establish minimal guidelines to govern law enforcement.' Where the legislature fails to provide such minimal guidelines, a criminal statute may permit 'a standardless sweep [that] allows policemen, prosecutors, and juries to pursue their personal predilections.'"[62]

Although all laws regulating conduct can be challenged under the due process vagueness doctrine, courts are particularly troubled about vague laws restricting speech out of concern that they will chill constitutionally protected speech. The Court has observed that freedom of speech is "delicate and vulnerable, as well as supremely precious in our society . . . [and] the threat of sanctions may deter their exercise almost as potently as the actual application of sanctions."[63] Thus, the Supreme Court has declared laws regulating speech to be void on vagueness grounds when they are so ambiguous that the reasonable person cannot tell what expression is forbidden and what is allowed. Coates v. City of Cincinnati is illustrative.

COATES v. CITY OF CINCINNATI, 402 U.S. 611 (1971): Justice STEWART delivered the opinion of the Court.

A Cincinnati, Ohio, ordinance makes criminal offense for "three or more persons to assemble . . . on any of the sidewalks . . . and there conduct themselves in a manner annoying to persons passing by. . . ." The issue before us is whether this ordinance is unconstitutional on its face.

The record brought before the reviewing courts tells us no more than that the appellant Coates was a student involved in a demonstration and the other appellants were pickets involved in a labor dispute. For throughout this litigation it

---

59. *See, e.g.*, Connally v. General Construction Co., 269 U.S. 385, 391 (1926) (a law is unconstitutionally vague when people "of common intelligence must necessarily guess at its meaning").
60. *See, e.g.*, Papachristou v. Jacksonville, 405 U.S. 156 (1972) (declaring vagrancy law unconstitutional).
61. 461 U.S. 352, 357 (1983).
62. *Id.* at 358.
63. NAACP v. Button, 371 U.S. 415, 433 (1963).

has been the appellants' position that the ordinance on its face violates the First and Fourteenth Amendments of the Constitution.

We are thus relegated, at best, to the words of the ordinance itself. If three or more people meet together on a sidewalk or street corner, they must conduct themselves so as not to annoy any police officer or other person who should happen to pass by. In our opinion this ordinance is unconstitutionally vague because it subjects the exercise of the right of assembly to an unascertainable standard, and unconstitutionally broad because it authorizes the punishment of constitutionally protected conduct.

Conduct that annoys some people does not annoy others. Thus, the ordinance is vague, not in the sense that it requires a person to conform his conduct to an imprecise but comprehensible normative standard, but rather in the sense that no standard of conduct is specified at all. As a result, "men of common intelligence must necessarily guess at its meaning."

It is said that the ordinance is broad enough to encompass many types of conduct clearly within the city's constitutional power to prohibit. And so, indeed, it is. The city is free to prevent people from blocking sidewalks, obstructing traffic, littering streets, committing assaults, or engaging in countless other forms of antisocial conduct. It can do so through the enactment and enforcement of ordinances directed with reasonable specificity toward the conduct to be prohibited. It cannot constitutionally do so through the enactment and enforcement of an ordinance whose violation may entirely depend upon whether or not a policeman is annoyed.

The ordinance also violates the constitutional right of free assembly and association. The First and Fourteenth Amendments do not permit a State to make criminal the exercise of the right of assembly simply because its exercise may be "annoying" to some people. If this were not the rule, the right of the people to gather in public places for social or political purposes would be continually subject to summary suspension through the good-faith enforcement of a prohibition against annoying conduct.

The ordinance before us makes a crime out of what under the Constitution cannot be a crime. It is aimed directly at activity protected by the Constitution.

Similarly, in Baggett v. Bullitt, 377 U.S. 360 (1964), the Court declared unconstitutional a state's loyalty oath that, among other things, prevented any "subversive person" from being employed in the state and required a person to swear that he or she was not such an individual or a part of any subversive organization. The Court found "the oath requirements and the statutory provisions on which they are based . . . invalid on their face because their language is unduly vague, uncertain, and broad." The Court stressed that the ambiguities inherent in the term "subversive" and in the language of the statute gave individuals little guidance as to what speech and associational activities were proscribed.

There is not and never will be a litmus test for evaluating when a law is too vague and thus offends the Constitution. Ambiguity is inherent in language and all laws will have some vagueness. But the Court has made it clear that greater precision is required when laws regulate speech, and statutes will be invalidated if a judge concludes that they provide inadequate notice as to what speech is prohibited and what is allowed. The void-for-vagueness doctrine is thus a powerful tool in First Amendment litigation because it allows facial challenges to laws even by those whose speech otherwise would be unprotected by the First Amendment.

b. Overbreadth

A law is unconstitutionally overbroad if it regulates substantially more speech than the Constitution allows to be regulated, and a person to whom the law constitutionally can be applied can argue that it would be unconstitutional as applied to others. In other words, in an area where the government can regulate speech, such as obscenity, a law that regulates much more expression than the Constitution allows to be restricted will be declared unconstitutional on overbreadth grounds. An individual whose speech is unprotected by the First Amendment and who could constitutionally be punished under a more narrow statute may argue that the law is unconstitutional because of how it might be applied to third parties not before the Court. Schad v. Borough of Mount Ephraim is illustrative.

SCHAD v. BOROUGH OF MOUNT EPHRAIM, 452 U.S. 61 (1981): Justice WHITE delivered the opinion of the Court.

In 1973, appellants began operating an adult bookstore in the commercial zone in the Borough of Mount Ephraim in Camden County, N.J. The store sold adult books, magazines, and films. Amusement licenses shortly issued permitting the store to install coin-operated devices by virtue of which a customer could sit in a booth, insert a coin, and watch an adult film. In 1976, the store introduced an additional coin-operated mechanism permitting the customer to watch a live dancer, usually nude, performing behind a glass panel.

Appellants appealed to this Court. Their principal claim is that the imposition of criminal penalties under an ordinance prohibiting all live entertainment, including nonobscene, nude dancing, violated their rights of free expression guaranteed by the First and Fourteenth Amendments of the United States Constitution. By excluding live entertainment throughout the Borough, the Mount Ephraim ordinance prohibits a wide range of expression that has long been held to be within the protections of the First and Fourteenth Amendments. Entertainment, as well as political and ideological speech, is protected; motion pictures, programs broadcast by radio and television, and live entertainment, such as musical and dramatic works fall within the First Amendment guarantee.

Whatever First Amendment protection should be extended to nude dancing, live or on film, however, the Mount Ephraim ordinance prohibits all live entertainment in the Borough: no property in the Borough may be principally used for the commercial production of plays, concerts, musicals, dance, or any other form of live entertainment. Because appellants' claims are rooted in the First Amendment, they are entitled to rely on the impact of the ordinance on the expressive activities of others as well as their own. Because overbroad laws, like vague ones, deter privileged activit[ies], our cases firmly establish appellant's standing to raise an overbreadth challenge.

There are thus two major aspects to the overbreadth doctrine. First, a law must be substantially overbroad; that is, it must restrict significantly more speech than the Constitution allows to be controlled. In Broadrick v. Oklahoma, 413 U.S. 601 (1973), the Court said that "particularly where conduct and not merely speech is involved, we believe that the overbreadth of a statute must not only be real, but substantial as well, judged in relation to the statute's plainly legitimate sweep." In *Broadrick*, the Court upheld the constitutionality of an Oklahoma law that prohibited political activities by government employees. The challengers argued that the law was overbroad because it prohibited constitutionally protected activity such as the wearing of political buttons or the displaying of bumper stickers. The Supreme Court acknowledged some overbreadth, but upheld the law because it was "not substantially overbroad and whatever overbreadth may exist should be cured through case-by-case analysis of the fact situations to which its sanctions, assertedly, may not be applied." In other words, the Court said that the law should not be declared unconstitutional on its face because it was not substantially overbroad, but that particular applications of the law could be declared unconstitutional in future cases.

In subsequent cases, the Court made it clear that the requirement for substantial overbreadth applies in all cases, whether the law regulates conduct that communicates or "pure speech."[64] The Court has declared that "[a] statute may be invalidated on its face . . . only if the overbreadth is substantial."[65] In City Council v. Taxpayers for Vincent, 466 U.S. 789 (1984), the Court upheld a municipal ordinance that prohibited the posting of signs on public property and emphasized that "substantial overbreadth" was required in order for a law to be invalidated.

In *Vincent*, the Court also addressed the question of what is "substantial overbreadth." The Court said that "[t]he concept of substantial overbreadth is not readily reduced to an exact definition. It is clear, however, that the mere fact that one can conceive of some impermissible applications of a statute is not sufficient to render it susceptible to an overbreadth challenge. . . . In short, there must be a realistic danger that the statute itself will significantly compromise recognized First Amendment protections of parties not before the Court for it to be facially challenged on overbreadth grounds."

It appears, then, that substantial overbreadth might be demonstrated by showing a significant number of situations where a law could be applied to prohibit constitutionally protected speech. For example, in Houston v. Hill, 482 U.S. 451 (1987), the Court declared unconstitutional an ordinance that made it unlawful to interrupt police officers in the performance of their duties. An individual was convicted of violating the law for shouting at police officers to divert their attention from arresting his friend. The Court declared the law unconstitutional and said that the "ordinance criminalizes a substantial amount of constitutionally protected speech, and accords the police unconstitutional discretion in enforcement. The ordinance's plain language is admittedly violated scores of times daily . . . , yet only some individuals—those chosen by the police in their unguided discretion—are arrested. Far from providing the 'breathing space'

---

64. *See, e.g.*, City Council of Los Angeles v. Taxpayers for Vincent, 466 U.S. 789, 800 (1984); New York v. Ferber, 458 U.S. 747, 772 (1982).

65. Board of Airport Commissioners of Los Angeles v. Jews for Jesus, Inc., 482 U.S. 569, 574 (1987).

that 'First Amendment freedoms need to survive,' the ordinance is susceptible of regular application to protected expression. We conclude that the statute is substantially overbroad."

In contrast, if the Court believes that the law will apply to relatively few situations where speech is constitutionally protected, it will not be declared overbroad. For example, in New York v. Ferber, 458 U.S. 747 (1982), the Court upheld a state law prohibiting child pornography, although it acknowledged that the statute could be applied to material with serious literary, scientific, or educational value. The Court said that the law was constitutional because these applications of the statute would not "amount to more than a tiny fraction of the materials within the statute's reach." These applications thus could be dealt with on a case-by-case basis if prosecutions arose, rather than by declaring the entire law unconstitutional.

The second major aspect of the overbreadth doctrine is that a person to whom the law constitutionally may be applied can argue that it would be unconstitutional as applied to others. The usual rule of standing is "that a person to whom a statute may constitutionally be applied will not be heard to challenge that statute on the ground that it may conceivably be applied unconstitutionally to others, in other situations not before the Court."[66] But overbreadth is an exception to this general standing principle that requires people to assert only their own rights.

Secretary of State v. J. H. Munson Co., 467 U.S. 947 (1984), illustrates this aspect of the overbreadth doctrine. A Maryland statute prohibited charitable organizations from soliciting funds unless at least 75 percent of their revenue was used for "charitable purposes." The law was challenged by a professional fundraiser who raised the First Amendment rights of his clients, charities who were not parties to the lawsuit. The Supreme Court permitted the fundraiser standing to argue the constitutional claims of charitable organizations. The Court said that "where the claim is that a statute is overly broad in violation of the First Amendment, the Court has allowed a party to assert the rights of another without regard to the ability of the other to assert his own claims and with no requirement that the person making the attack demonstrate that his own conduct could not be regulated by a statute drawn with the requisite narrow specificity."

The Supreme Court thus regards the overbreadth doctrine as "strong medicine"[67] because it involves the facial invalidation of a law and because it permits individuals standing to raise the claims of others not before the Court. Individuals who otherwise could be constitutionally punished are allowed to go free. The Court has justified the overbreadth doctrine because the "First Amendment needs breathing space."[68] The concerns are that overbroad laws will chill significant constitutionally protected speech and that individuals to whom the law is unconstitutional may refrain from expression rather than bring a challenge to the statute. Justice Brennan explained that the overbreadth doctrine is "necessary because persons whose expression is constitutionally protected may well refrain from exercising their rights for fear of criminal sanctions provided by a statute susceptible of application to protected expression."[69]

---

66. Broadrick v. Oklahoma, 413 U.S. at 610. The prohibition against such "third party" standing is discussed in Chapter 1.

67. *Id.* at 613.

68. *Id.* at 611.

69. Gooding v. Wilson, 405 U.S. 518, 521 (1972).

This rationale for the overbreadth doctrine is illustrated by the Court's holding that it does not apply in challenges to laws regulating commercial speech.[70] The Court believes that the incentive to engage in advertising is sufficiently strong as to lessen any worries that such speech will be chilled.

Because the overbreadth doctrine is perceived as "strong medicine," the Court has said that it will avoid invalidating laws by allowing courts to construe statutes narrowly and thus avoid overbreadth. In Osborne v. Ohio, 495 U.S. 103 (1990), the Court used this approach to avoid declaring a child pornography law unconstitutional on overbreadth grounds. The law prohibited private possession of child pornography and, by its terms, outlawed possession of nude photographs. The Supreme Court has long recognized that nudity, by itself, is not enough to place pictures outside the scope of the First Amendment. The Ohio Supreme Court adopted a narrowing construction of the law so that it applied only to "the possession or viewing of material or performance of a minor who is in a state of nudity, where such nudity constitutes a lewd exhibition or involves a graphic focus on the genitals, and where the person depicted is neither the child nor the ward of the person charged." The U.S. Supreme Court accepted this narrowing construction as avoiding "penalizing persons for viewing or possessing innocuous photographs of naked children." The Court thus found that the law was not impermissibly overbroad.

In contrast, in Gooding v. Wilson, 405 U.S. 518 (1972), the absence of narrowing constructions by state courts led to a law prohibiting fighting words being invalidated on overbreadth grounds. A Georgia law made it a crime for "[a]ny person who shall, without provocation, use to or of another, and in his presence opprobrious words or abusive language, tending to cause a breach of the peace." The Court said that the law could be upheld under the First Amendment "only if, as authoritatively construed by the Georgia courts, it is not susceptible of application to speech, although vulgar or offensive, that is protected by the First and Fourteenth Amendments." The Court reviewed Georgia court decisions and, finding no such limiting construction, declared the law unconstitutionally overbroad.

c. Relationship Between Vagueness and Overbreadth

The concepts of vagueness and overbreadth are closely related; laws often are challenged under both of these doctrines simultaneously. Both vagueness and overbreadth involve facial challenges to laws. But these concepts are best understood as overlapping, not identical. Sometimes a law might be overbroad but not vague. Board of Airport Commissioners of Los Angeles v. Jews for Jesus, Inc., illustrates this.

BOARD OF AIRPORT COMMISSIONERS OF THE CITY OF LOS ANGELES v. JEWS FOR JESUS, INC., 482 U.S. 569 (1987): Justice O'Connor delivered the opinion of the Court.

The issue presented in this case is whether a resolution banning all "First Amendment activities" at Los Angeles International Airport (LAX) violates

---

70. *See, e.g.*, Village of Hoffman Estates v. Flipside, Hoffman Estate, Inc., 455 U.S. 489, 497 (1982) ("the overbreadth doctrine does not apply to commercial speech").

the First Amendment. On July 13, 1983, the Board of Airport Commissioners (Board) adopted Resolution No. 13787, which provides in pertinent part:

> NOW, THEREFORE, BE IT RESOLVED by the Board of Airport Commissioners that the Central Terminal Area at Los Angeles International Airport is not open for First Amendment activities by any individual and/or entity.

Respondent Jews for Jesus, Inc., is a nonprofit religious corporation. On July 6, 1984, Alan Howard Snyder, a minister of the Gospel for Jews for Jesus, was stopped by a Department of Airports peace officer while distributing free religious literature on a pedestrian walkway in the Central Terminal Area at LAX. Snyder stopped distributing the leaflets and left the airport terminal. Jews for Jesus and Snyder then filed this action in the District Court for the Central District of California, challenging the constitutionality of the resolution.

Under the First Amendment overbreadth doctrine, an individual whose own speech or conduct may be prohibited is permitted to challenge a statute on its face "because it also threatens others not before the court—those who desire to engage in legally protected expression but who may refrain from doing so rather than risk prosecution or undertake to have the law declared partially invalid." A statute may be invalidated on its face, however, only if the overbreadth is "substantial." The requirement that the overbreadth be substantial arose from our recognition that application of the overbreadth doctrine is, "manifestly, strong medicine," and that "there must be a realistic danger that the statute itself will significantly compromise recognized First Amendment protections of parties not before the Court for it to be facially challenged on overbreadth grounds."

On its face, the resolution at issue in this case reaches the universe of expressive activity, and, by prohibiting all protected expression, purports to create a virtual "First Amendment Free Zone" at LAX. The resolution does not merely regulate expressive activity in the Central Terminal Area that might create problems such as congestion or the disruption of the activities of those who use LAX. Instead, the resolution expansively states that LAX "is not open for First Amendment activities by any individual and/or entity." The resolution therefore does not merely reach the activity of respondents at LAX; it prohibits even talking and reading, or the wearing of campaign buttons or symbolic clothing. Under such a sweeping ban, virtually every individual who enters LAX may be found to violate the resolution by engaging in some "First Amendment activit[y]." We think it obvious that such a ban cannot be justified even if LAX were a nonpublic forum because no conceivable governmental interest would justify such an absolute prohibition of speech.

Sometimes a law can be vague but not overbroad. For example, if the Los Angeles ordinance declared unconstitutional in *Board of Airport Commissioners* was rewritten to prohibit all speech not protected by the First Amendment, it would, by definition, not be overbroad. It would forbid only expression that by law could be regulated. But the law would be vague because a reasonable person could not know what was outlawed and what was permitted.

Often, however, laws that are vulnerable to vagueness challenges also can be objected to on overbreadth grounds. For instance, in Coates v. Cincinnati, above, the Court declared unconstitutional an ordinance that made it a criminal offense for "three or more persons to assemble . . . on any of the sidewalks . . . and there conduct themselves in a manner annoying to persons passing by." The Court said that the law "is unconstitutionally vague because it subjects the exercise of the right of assembly to an unascertainable standard, and unconstitutionally broad because it authorizes the punishment of constitutionally protected conduct."

3. *Prior Restraints*

a. What Is a Prior Restraint?

The Supreme Court has declared that "prior restraints on speech and publication are the most serious and least tolerable infringement on First Amendment rights."[71] The Supreme Court frequently has said that "[a]ny system of prior restraints of expression comes to this Court bearing a heavy presumption against its constitutional validity."[72] As explained above, the First Amendment was, in part, a reaction against the licensing requirements for publication that had existed in England. It was this legacy that prompted Blackstone to declare that "the liberty of the press is, indeed, essential to the nature of a free state; but this consists in laying no previous restraints upon publication, and not in freedom from censure for criminal matter when published."[73] Although it is clear that "the prohibition of laws abridging the freedom of speech is not confined to previous restraints,"[74] there is no doubt that prior restraints are regarded as a particularly undesirable way of regulating speech.

Yet a clear definition of "prior restraint" is elusive. It is too broad to say that a prior restraint is a government action that prevents speech from occurring. All laws outlawing speech would constitute prior restraints by this definition. Nor is the traditional distinction between censorship before speech and after-the-fact punishments sufficient. All punishment for speech—whether under prior restraints or other laws—occurs after the expression takes place. All government actions regulating speech—whether prior restraints or not—exist before the speech occurs.

The clearest definition of prior restraint is as an administrative system or a judicial order that prevents speech from occurring. For example, in Alexander v. United States, 509 U.S. 444 (1993), the Court said that "[t]he term prior restraint is used 'to describe administrative and judicial orders forbidding certain communications when issued in advance of the time that such communication are to occur.'" As Professor Rodney Smolla has observed, "[i]n practice, most prior restraints involve either an administrative rule requiring some form of license or permit before one may engage in expression, or a judicial order directing an individual not to engage in expression, on pain of contempt."[75]

71. Nebraska Press Association v. Stuart, 427 U.S. 539, 559 (1976).
72. New York Times v. United States, 403 U.S. 713, 714 (1971).
73. 4 William Blackstone, *Commentaries*, 151-152 (1769).
74. Schenck v. United States, 249 U.S. 47, 51 (1919).
75. Rodney Smolla, *Smolla and Nimmer on Freedom of Speech*, 8-4 (1996).

While court injunctions stopping speech and licensing systems are classic forms of prior restraints, they are not the only types of government actions that constitute prior restraints.[76] For example, a prior restraint clearly would exist if the government were to seize every copy of a particular newspaper.

b. Are Prior Restraints Really So Bad?

The Supreme Court repeatedly has found that prior restraints are the worst form of government regulation of speech and that there is a strong presumption against prior restraints. But why are prior restraints so bad? After-the-fact punishments, if large enough, can prevent speech just as much as any prior restraint.[77] Also, prior restraints have the virtue that they are usually specific in the form of a court order stopping particular speech or the denial of a license for certain expression.[78] There usually is some due process in the form of a judicial or administrative hearing before the prior restraint.

A classic argument as to why prior restraints are the worst form of speech regulations was advanced by noted First Amendment scholar Thomas Emerson: "A system of prior restraint is in many ways more inhibiting than a system of subsequent punishment: It is likely to bring under government scrutiny a far wider range of expression; it shuts off communication before it takes place; suppression by a stroke of the pen is more likely to be applied than suppression through a criminal process; the procedures do not require attention to the safeguards of the criminal process; the system allows less opportunity for public appraisal and criticism; the dynamics of the system drive toward excesses, as the history of all censorship shows."[79]

Prior restraints prevent speech from ever occurring. The Court explained that "[b]ehind the distinction is a theory deeply etched in our law: a free society prefers to punish the few who abuse rights of speech *after* they break the law than to throttle them and all others beforehand."[80] Inevitably, prior restraints could be imposed based on predictions of danger that would not actually materialize and thus would not be the basis for subsequent punishments.[81]

Perhaps the most persuasive argument as to why prior restraints are worse than other ways of regulating speech is the collateral bar rule: A person violating an unconstitutional law may not be punished, but a person violating an unconstitutional prior restraint generally may be punished. Specifically, the collateral bar rule provides that "a court order must be obeyed until it is set aside, and that persons subject to the order who disobey it may not defend against the ensuing

---

76. *See, e.g.,* Bantam Books, Inc. v. Sullivan, 372 U.S. 58 (1963), finding that there was a prior restraint when the Rhode Island Commission to Encourage Morality in Youth encouraged booksellers not to sell certain materials that it deemed objectionable. Although there was no court or administrative order preventing the sale of the books, the Court found sufficient coercive pressure to constitute a prior restraint.

77. *See, e.g.,* John C. Jeffries, Jr., *Rethinking Prior Restraint,* 92 Yale L.J. 409 (1983) (questioning the usefulness and desirability of the prior restraint doctrine).

78. *See, e.g.,* William T. Mayton, *Toward a Theory of First Amendment Process: Injunctions of Speech, Subsequent Punishment, and the Costs of the Prior Restraint Doctrine,* 67 Cornell L. Rev. 245 (1982).

79. Thomas Emerson, *The System of Freedom of Expression* 506 (1970).

80. Southeastern Promotions, Ltd. v. Conrad, 420 U.S. 546, 559 (1975).

81. *See, e.g.,* Vincent Blasi, *Toward a Theory of Prior Restraint: The Central Linkage,* 66 Minn. L. Rev. 11, 49-54 (1981).

charge of criminal contempt on the ground that the order was erroneous or even unconstitutional."[82]

For example, in Walker v. City of Birmingham, 388 U.S. 307 (1967), the Court upheld the contempt convictions of defendants, civil rights protestors, who had violated a court order preventing them from engaging in demonstrations on city streets without a permit. The Court ruled that the protestors — Dr. Martin Luther King and seven other African American ministers — were barred from challenging the constitutionality of the court order because they had violated it. The Court said, "This Court cannot hold that the petitioners were constitutionally free to ignore all the procedures of the law and carry their battle to the streets. . . . [R]espect for judicial process is a small price to pay for the civilizing hand of law, which alone can give abiding meaning to constitutional freedom." The Court indicated that the collateral bar rule precluded challenges to punishment for violating a court order, unless the injunction was "transparently invalid or had only a frivolous pretense to validity."

The collateral bar rule explains why prior restraints are worse than after-the-fact punishments. A law prohibiting expression and imposing punishments for violations always can be challenged as unconstitutional. But an unconstitutional court order cannot be challenged if it has been violated. The collateral bar rule is justified as necessary to protect respect for the judiciary and compliance with its orders. Yet it seems unjust to punish a person for constitutionally protected speech.

The Court, at times, has applied the collateral bar rule to licensing schemes as well as to court orders. In Poulos v. New Hampshire, 345 U.S. 395 (1953), the Court affirmed an individual's conviction for conducting a religious service in a public park without the required license. The Court said that the defendant could not challenge the denial of a license as arbitrary and unconstitutional when the licensing system is valid on its face and when he proceeded without a license rather than challenge its denial. The Court said, "The valid requirements of license are for the good of the applicants and the public. . . . Delay is unfortunate but the expense and annoyance of litigation is a price citizens must pay for life in an orderly society. . . . Nor can we say that a state's requirement that redress must be sought through appropriate judicial procedure violates due process."

But in Shuttlesworth v. City of Birmingham, 394 U.S. 147 (1969), the Court overturned the convictions of civil rights protestors who violated a city's ordinance by having a demonstration without the required permit. The Court found the permit law unconstitutional because it gave city officials unfettered discretion in granting and denying permits. The Court refused to apply the collateral bar rule and prevent a challenge. In fact, the Court said that "a person faced with such an unconstitutional licensing law may ignore it and engage with impunity in the exercise of the right of free expression for which the law purports to require a license."

The difference between *Poulos* and *Shuttlesworth* is that the former involved a law that was valid on its face because it contained adequate standards and safeguards, whereas the latter case concerned a law that was facially invalid because of the absence of criteria to limit administrative discretion. *Shuttlesworth* establishes that courts will not preclude a person who failed to apply for a license from challenging a licensing law as facially unconstitutional, such as in giving too much discretion to

---

82. Stephen Barnett, *The Puzzle of Prior Restraint*, 29 Stan. L. Rev. 539, 552 (1977).

government officials in awarding licenses. But *Poulos* likely remains good law in that a licensing law that is valid on its face must be complied with; a failure to follow the procedures or to challenge the denial of a permit through available administrative and judicial challenges will preclude later assertion that the speech was protected by the First Amendment. Yet, even here, the justification for the collateral bar rule in preserving respect for courts and in ensuring compliance with judicial orders is absent in administrative licensing systems.

i.   Court Orders as a Prior Restraint

One classic form of prior restraint is a court order stopping speech from occurring. This subsection begins by presenting Near v. Minnesota, a key case recognizing court orders as a prior restraint. The subsection then considers court orders in three areas: to protect national security, to safeguard a defendant's right to a fair trial, and to seize the assets of businesses convicted of obscenity law violations.

NEAR v. STATE OF MINNESOTA ex rel. OLSON
283 U.S. 697 (1931)

Chief Justice HUGHES delivered the opinion of the Court.

Chapter 285 of the Session Laws of Minnesota for the year 1925 provides for the abatement, as a public nuisance, of a "malicious, scandalous and defamatory newspaper, magazine or other periodical." [The law provides]: "Any person who, as an individual, or as a member or employee of a firm, or association or organization, shall be engaged in the business of regularly or customarily producing, publishing or circulating, having in possession, selling or giving away (a) an obscene, lewd and lascivious newspaper, magazine, or other periodical, or (b) a malicious, scandalous and defamatory newspaper, magazine or other periodical[] — is guilty of a nuisance, and all persons guilty of such nuisance may be enjoined." The court is empowered, as in other cases of contempt, to punish disobedience to a temporary or permanent injunction by fine of not more than $1,000 or by imprisonment in the county jail for not more than twelve months.

Under this statute, the county attorney of Hennepin County brought this action to enjoin the publication of what was described as a "malicious, scandalous and defamatory newspaper, magazine or other periodical," known as The Saturday Press, published by the defendants in the city of Minneapolis. The complaint alleged that the defendants, on September 24, 1927, and on eight subsequent dates in October and November, 1927, published and circulated editions of that periodical which were "largely devoted to malicious, scandalous and defamatory articles." Without attempting to summarize the contents of the voluminous exhibits attached to the complaint, we deem it sufficient to say that the articles charged, in substance, that a Jewish gangster was in control of gambling, bootlegging, and racketeering in Minneapolis, and that law enforcing officers and agencies were not energetically performing their duties.

Judgment was entered adjudging that "the newspaper, magazine and periodical known as The Saturday Press," as a public nuisance, "be and is hereby abated." The judgment perpetually enjoined the defendants "from producing, editing, publishing, circulating, having in their possession, selling or giving away any publication whatsoever which is a malicious, scandalous or defamatory newspaper, as defined by law," and also "from further conducting said nuisance under the name and title of said The Saturday Press or any other name or title."

This statute, for the suppression as a public nuisance of a newspaper or periodical, is unusual, if not unique, and raises questions of grave importance transcending the local interests involved in the particular action. The object of the statute is not punishment, in the ordinary sense, but suppression of the offending newspaper or periodical. The reason for the enactment, as the state court has said, is that prosecutions to enforce penal statutes for libel do not result in "efficient repression or suppression of the evils of scandal."

The statute not only operates to suppress the offending newspaper or periodical, but to put the publisher under an effective censorship. When a newspaper or periodical is found to be "malicious, scandalous and defamatory," and is suppressed as such, resumption of publication is punishable as a contempt of court by fine or imprisonment. Thus, where a newspaper or periodical has been suppressed because of the circulation of charges against public officers of official misconduct, it would seem to be clear that the renewal of the publication of such charges would constitute a contempt, and that the judgment would lay a permanent restraint upon the publisher, to escape which he must satisfy the court as to the character of a new publication. Whether he would be permitted again to publish matter deemed to be derogatory to the same or other public officers would depend upon the court's ruling. In the present instance the judgment restrained the defendants from "publishing, circulating, having in their possession, selling or giving away any publication whatsoever which is malicious, scandalous or defamatory."

The question is whether a statute authorizing such proceedings in restraint of publication is consistent with the conception of the liberty of the press as historically conceived and guaranteed. In determining the extent of the constitutional protection, it has been generally, if not universally, considered that it is the chief purpose of the guaranty to prevent previous restraints upon publication. The struggle in England, directed against the legislative power of the licenser, resulted in renunciation of the censorship of the press. The liberty deemed to be established was thus described by Blackstone: "The liberty of the press is indeed essential to the nature of a free state; but this consists in laying no previous restraints upon publications, and not in freedom from censure for criminal matter when published."

The objection has been made that the principle as to immunity from previous restraint is stated too broadly, if every such restraint is deemed to be prohibited. That is undoubtedly true; the protection even as to previous restraint is not absolutely unlimited. But the limitation has been recognized only in exceptional cases. "When a nation is at war many things that might be said in time of peace are such a hindrance to its effort that their utterance will not be endured so long as men fight and that no Court could regard them as protected by any constitutional right." Schenck v. United States (1919). No one would question but that a government might prevent actual obstruction to its recruiting service or the publication of the sailing dates of transports or the number and location of troops. On similar grounds, the primary requirements of decency may be enforced against obscene publications. The security of the community life may be protected against incitements to acts of violence and the overthrow by force of orderly government. The constitutional guaranty of free speech does not "protect a man from an injunction against uttering words that may have all the effect of force." These limitations are not applicable here. Nor are we now concerned with questions as to the extent of authority to prevent publications in order to protect private rights according to the principles governing the exercise of the jurisdiction of courts of equity.

The statute in question cannot be justified by reason of the fact that the publisher is permitted to show, before injunction issues, that the matter published is true and is published with good motives and for justifiable ends. If such a statute, authorizing suppression and injunction on such a basis, is constitutionally valid, it would be equally permissible for the Legislature to provide that at any time the publisher of any newspaper could be brought before a court, or even an administrative officer (as the constitutional protection may not be regarded as resting on mere procedural details), and required to produce proof of the truth of his publication, or of what he intended to publish and of his motives, or stand enjoined. If this can be done, the Legislature may provide machinery for determining in the complete exercise of its discretion what are justifiable ends and restrain publication accordingly. And it would be but a step to a complete system of censorship. The recognition of authority to impose previous restraint upon publication in order to protect the community against the circulation of charges of misconduct, and especially of official misconduct, necessarily would carry with it the admission of the authority of the censor against which the constitutional barrier was erected.

For these reasons we hold the statute to be an infringement of the liberty of the press guaranteed by the Fourteenth Amendment.

ii. Court Orders to Protect National Security

Near spoke of national security — such as to prevent publication of the details of when and where a military action would occur — as justifying prior restraints. New York Times v. United States, the Pentagon Papers case, is the primary decision thus far considering national security as the basis for a court order stopping speech. The New York Times, and then the Washington Post, published excerpts from a top secret Defense Department history of the Vietnam War. The United States government sought federal court injunctions precluding publication on national security grounds. The federal district courts refused to issue such orders. The District of Columbia Circuit affirmed, while the Second Circuit reversed and approved the injunction. The case proceeded quickly: Just 18 days elapsed from the first article in the New York Times until the decision in the Supreme Court.

NEW YORK TIMES CO. v. UNITED STATES

403 U.S. 713 (1971)

PER CURIAM.

We granted certiorari, in these cases in which the United States seeks to enjoin the New York Times and the Washington Post from publishing the contents of a classified study entitled "History of U.S. Decision-Making Process on Viet Nam Policy."

"Any system of prior restraints of expression comes to this Court bearing a heavy presumption against its constitutional validity." The Government "thus carries a heavy burden of showing justification for the imposition of such a restraint." The District Court for the Southern District of New York in the New York Times case, and the District Court for the District of Columbia and the Court of Appeals for the District of Columbia Circuit, in the Washington Post case held that the Government had not met that burden. We agree.

Justice BLACK, with whom Justice DOUGLAS joins, concurring.

I adhere to the view that the Government's case against the Washington Post should have been dismissed and that the injunction against the New York Times should have been vacated without oral argument when the cases were first presented to this Court. I believe that every moment's continuance of the injunctions against these newspapers amounts to a flagrant, indefensible, and continuing violation of the First Amendment. In my view it is unfortunate that some of my Brethren are apparently willing to hold that the publication of news may sometimes be enjoined. Such a holding would make a shambles of the First Amendment.

Our Government was launched in 1789 with the adoption of the Constitution. The Bill of Rights, including the First Amendment, followed in 1791. Now, for the first time in the 182 years since the founding of the Republic, the federal courts are asked to hold that the First Amendment does not mean what it says, but rather means that the Government can halt the publication of current news of vital importance to the people of this country.

In seeking injunctions against these newspapers and in its presentation to the Court, the Executive Branch seems to have forgotten the essential purpose and history of the First Amendment. [T]he Solicitor General argues and some members of the Court appear to agree that the general powers of the Government adopted in the original Constitution should be interpreted to limit and restrict the specific and emphatic guarantees of the Bill of Rights adopted later. I can imagine no greater perversion of history. Madison and the other framers of the First Amendment, able men that they were, wrote in language they earnestly believed could never be misunderstood: "Congress shall make no law . . . abridging the freedom . . . of the press. . . ." Both the history and language of the First Amendment support the view that the press must be left free to publish news, whatever the source, without censorship, injunctions, or prior restraints.

Justice DOUGLAS, with whom Justice BLACK joins, concurring.

It should be noted at the outset that the First Amendment provides that "Congress shall make no law . . . abridging the freedom of speech, or of the press." That leaves, in my view, no room for governmental restraint on the press. There is, moreover, no statute barring the publication by the press of the material which the Times and the Post seek to use.

The dominant purpose of the First Amendment was to prohibit the widespread practice of governmental suppression of embarrassing information. It is common knowledge that the First Amendment was adopted against the widespread use of the common law of seditious libel to punish the dissemination of material that is embarrassing to the powers-that-be. The present cases will, I think, go down in history as the most dramatic illustration of that principle. A debate of large proportions goes on in the Nation over our posture in

Vietnam. That debate antedated the disclosure of the contents of the present documents. The latter are highly relevant to the debate in progress.

Secrecy in government is fundamentally anti-democratic, perpetuating bureaucratic errors. Open debate and discussion of public issues are vital to our national health. On public questions there should be "uninhibited, robust, and wide-open" debate.

The stays is these cases that have been in effect for more than a week constitute a flouting of the principles of the First Amendment as interpreted in Near v. Minnesota ex rel. Olson.

Justice BRENNAN, concurring.

The error that has pervaded these cases from the outset was the granting of any injunctive relief whatsoever, interim or otherwise. The entire thrust of the Government's claim throughout these cases has been that publication of the material sought to be enjoined "could," or "might," or "may" prejudice the national interest in various ways. But the First Amendment tolerates absolutely no prior judicial restraints of the press predicated upon surmise or conjecture that untoward consequences may result. Our cases, it is true, have indicated that there is a single, extremely narrow class of cases in which the First Amendment's ban on prior judicial restraint may be overridden. Our cases have thus far indicated that such cases may arise only when the Nation "is at war," Schenck v. United States (1919), during which times "[n]o one would question but that a government might prevent actual obstruction to its recruiting service or the publication of the sailing dates of transports or the number and location of troops." Near v. Minnesota ex rel. Olson (1931).

Even if the present world situation were assumed to be tantamount to a time of war, or if the power of presently available armaments would justify even in peacetime the suppression of information that would set in motion a nuclear holocaust, in neither of these actions has the Government presented or even alleged that publication of items from or based upon the material at issue would cause the happening of an event of that nature. "[T]he chief purpose of [the First Amendment's] guaranty [is] to prevent previous restraints upon publication." Near v. Minnesota ex rel.

Thus, only governmental allegation and proof that publication must inevitably, directly, and immediately cause the occurrence of an event kindred to imperiling the safety of a transport already at sea can support even the issuance of an interim restraining order. In no event may mere conclusions be sufficient: for if the Executive Branch seeks judicial aid in preventing publication, it must inevitably submit the basis upon which that aid is sought to scrutiny by the judiciary. And therefore, every restraint issued in this case, whatever its form, has violated the First Amendment — and not less so because that restraint was justified as necessary to afford the courts an opportunity to examine the claim more thoroughly. Unless and until the Government has clearly made out its case, the First Amendment commands that no injunction may issue.

Justice STEWART, with whom Justice WHITE joins, concurring.

In the governmental structure created by our Constitution, the Executive is endowed with enormous power in the two related areas of national defense and international relations. This power, largely unchecked by the Legislative and Judicial branches, has been pressed to the very hilt since the advent of the nuclear missile age. For better or for worse, the simple fact is that a President of the United States possesses vastly greater constitutional independence in these two vital areas of power than does, say, a prime minister of a country with a parliamentary form of government.

[It] is elementary that the successful conduct of international diplomacy and the maintenance of an effective national defense require both confidentiality and secrecy. Other nations can hardly deal with this Nation in an atmosphere of mutual trust unless they can be assured that their confidences will be kept. And within our own executive departments, the development of considered and intelligent international policies would be impossible if those charged with their formulation could not communicate with each other freely, frankly, and in confidence. In the area of basic national defense the frequent need for absolute secrecy is, of course, self-evident.

I think there can be but one answer to this dilemma, if dilemma it be. The responsibility must be where the power is. If the Constitution gives the Executive a large degree of unshared power in the conduct of foreign affairs and the maintenance of our national defense, then under the Constitution the Executive must have the largely unshared duty to determine and preserve the degree of internal security necessary to exercise that power successfully. It is an awesome responsibility, requiring judgment and wisdom of a high order.

We are asked, quite simply, to prevent the publication by two newspapers of material that the Executive Branch insists should not, in the national interest, be published. I am convinced that the Executive is correct with respect to some of the documents involved. But I cannot say that disclosure of any of them will surely result in direct, immediate, and irreparable damage to our Nation or its people. That being so, there can under the First Amendment be but one judicial resolution of the issues before us. I join the judgments of the Court.

Justice WHITE, with whom Justice STEWART joins, concurring.

I concur in today's judgments, but only because of the concededly extraordinary protection against prior restraints enjoyed by the press under our constitutional system. I do not say that in no circumstances would the First Amendment permit an injunction against publishing information about government plans or operations. Nor, after examining the materials the Government characterizes as the most sensitive and destructive, can I deny that revelation of these documents will do substantial damage to public interests. Indeed, I am confident that their disclosure will have that result. But I nevertheless agree that the United States has not satisfied the very heavy burden that it must meet to warrant an injunction against publication in these cases, at least in the absence of express and appropriately limited congressional authorization for prior restraints in circumstances such as these.

The Government's position is simply stated: The responsibility of the Executive for the conduct of the foreign affairs and for the security of the Nation is so basic that the President is entitled to an injunction against publication of a newspaper story whenever he can convince a court that the information to be revealed threatens "grave and irreparable" injury to the public interest; and the injunction should issue whether or not the material to be published is classified, whether or not publication would be lawful under relevant criminal statutes enacted by Congress, and regardless of the circumstances by which the newspaper came into possession of the information.

At least in the absence of legislation by Congress, based on its own investigations and findings, I am quite unable to agree that the inherent powers of the Executive and the courts reach so far as to authorize remedies having such sweeping potential for inhibiting publications by the press. Indeed, even today where we hold that the United States has not met its burden, the material remains sealed in court records and it is properly not discussed in today's opinions. Moreover, because the material poses substantial dangers to national interests and because of the hazards of criminal sanctions, a responsible press may choose never to publish the more sensitive materials. To sustain the Government in these cases would start the courts down a long and hazardous road that I am not willing to travel, at least without congressional guidance and direction.

Justice MARSHALL, concurring.

The Government contends that the only issue in these cases is whether in a suit by the United States, "the First Amendment bars a court from prohibiting a newspaper from publishing material whose disclosure would pose a 'grave and immediate danger to the security of the United States.'" With all due respect, I believe the ultimate issue in this case is even more basic than the one posed by the Solicitor General. The issue is whether this Court or the Congress has the power to make law.

The problem here is whether in these particular cases the Executive Branch has authority to invoke the equity jurisdiction of the courts to protect what it believes to be the national interest. It would be utterly inconsistent with the concept of separation of powers for this Court to use its power of contempt to prevent behavior that Congress has specifically declined to prohibit. There would be a similar damage to the basic concept of these co-equal branches of Government if when the Executive Branch has adequate authority granted by Congress to protect "national security" it can choose instead to invoke the contempt power of a court to enjoin the threatened conduct. The Constitution provides that Congress shall make laws, the President execute laws, and courts interpret laws. It did not provide for government by injunction in which the courts and the Executive Branch can "make law" without regard to the action of Congress. It may be more convenient for the Executive Branch if it need only convince a judge to prohibit conduct rather than ask the Congress to pass a law, and it may be more convenient to enforce a contempt order than to seek a criminal conviction in a jury trial. Moreover, it may be considered politically wise to get a court to share the responsibility for arresting those who the Executive Branch has probable cause to believe are violating the law. But convenience and political considerations of the moment do not justify a basic departure from the principles of our system of government.

Chief Justice BURGER, dissenting.

So clear are the constitutional limitations on prior restraint against expression, that we have had little occasion to be concerned with cases involving prior restraints against news reporting on matters of public interest. There is, therefore, little variation among the members of the Court in terms of resistance to prior restraints against publication. Adherence to this basic constitutional principle, however, does not make these cases simple ones. In these cases, the imperative of a free and unfettered press comes into collision with another imperative, the effective functioning of a complex modern government and specifically the effective exercise of certain constitutional powers of the Executive. Only those who view the First Amendment as an absolute in all circumstances — a view I respect, but reject — can find such cases as these to be simple or easy.

These cases are not simple for another and more immediate reason. We do not know the facts of the cases. No District Judge knew all the facts. No Court of Appeals Judge knew all the facts. No member of this Court knows all the facts. Why are we in this posture, in which only those judges to whom the First Amendment is absolute and permits of no restraint in any circumstances or for any reason, are really in a position to act?

I suggest we are in this posture because these cases have been conducted in unseemly haste. The prompt settling of these cases reflects our universal abhorrence of prior restraint. But prompt judicial action does not mean unjudicial haste.

Here, moreover, the frenetic haste is due in large part to the manner in which the Times proceeded from the date it obtained the purloined documents. It seems reasonably clear now that the haste precluded reasonable and deliberate judicial treatment of these cases and was not warranted. The precipitate action of this Court aborting trials not yet completed is not the kind of judicial conduct that ought to attend the disposition of a great issue.

An issue of this importance should be tried and heard in a judicial atmosphere conducive to thoughtful, reflective deliberation, especially when haste, in terms of hours, is unwarranted in light of the long period the Times, by its own choice, deferred publication. It is not disputed that the Times has had unauthorized possession of the documents for three to four months, during which it has had its expert analysts studying them, presumably digesting them and preparing the material for publication. During all of this time, the Times, presumably in its capacity as trustee of the public's "right to know," has held up publication for purposes it considered proper and thus public knowledge was delayed. No doubt this was for a good reason; the analysis of 7,000 pages of complex material drawn from a vastly greater volume of material would inevitably take time and the writing of good news stories takes time. But why should the United States Government, from whom this information was illegally acquired by someone, along with all the counsel, trial judges, and appellate judges be placed under needless pressure? After these months of deferral, the alleged "right to know" has somehow and suddenly become a right that must be vindicated instanter.

Would it have been unreasonable, since the newspaper could anticipate the Government's objections to release of secret material, to give the Government an opportunity to review the entire collection and determine whether agreement could be reached on publication? Stolen or not, if security was not in fact jeopardized, much of the material could no doubt have been declassified, since it spans a period ending in 1968. With such an approach — one that great newspapers have in the past practiced and stated editorially to be the duty of an honorable press — the newspapers and Government might well have narrowed the area of disagreement as to what was and was not publishable, leaving the remainder to be resolved in orderly litigation, if necessary. To me it is hardly believable that a newspaper long regarded as a great institution in American life would fail to perform one of the basic and simple duties of every citizen with respect to the discovery or possession of stolen property or secret government documents. That duty, I had thought — perhaps naively — was to report forthwith, to responsible public officers. This duty rests on taxi drivers, Justices, and the New York Times. The course followed by the Times, whether so calculated or not, removed any possibility of orderly litigation of the issues. If the action of the judges up to now has been correct, that result is sheer happenstance.

The consequence of all this melancholy series of events is that we literally do not know what we are acting on. As I see it, we have been forced to deal with litigation concerning rights of great magnitude without an adequate record, and surely without time for adequate treatment either in the prior proceedings or in this Court. I would affirm the Court of Appeals for the Second Circuit and allow the District Court to complete the trial aborted by our grant of certiorari, meanwhile preserving the status quo in the post case.

Justice HARLAN, with whom the Chief Justice and Justice BLACKMUN join, dissenting.

With all respect, I consider that the Court has been almost irresponsibly feverish in dealing with these cases. Both the Court of Appeals for the Second Circuit and the Court of Appeals for the District of Columbia Circuit rendered judgment on June 23. The New York Times' petition for certiorari, its motion for accelerated consideration thereof, and its application for interim relief were filed in this Court on June 24 at about 11 A.M. The application of the United States for interim relief in the Post case was also filed here on June 24 at about 7:15 P.M. This Court's order setting a hearing before us on June 26 at 11 A.M., a course which I joined only to avoid the possibility of even more peremptory action by the Court, was issued less than 24 hours before. The record in the Post case was filed with the Clerk shortly before 1 P.M. on June 25; the record in the Times case did not arrive until 7 or 8 o'clock that same night. The briefs of the parties were received less than two hours before argument on June 26.

This frenzied train of events took place in the name of the presumption against prior restraints created by the First Amendment. Due regard for the extraordinarily important and difficult questions involved in these litigations should have led the Court to shun such a precipitate timetable.

There are difficult questions of fact, of law, and of judgment; the potential consequences of erroneous decision are enormous. The time which has been available to us, to the lower courts, and to the parties has been wholly inadequate for giving these cases the kind of consideration they deserve. It is a reflection on the stability of the judicial process that these great issues — as important as any that have arisen during my time on the Court — should have been decided under the pressures engendered by the torrent of publicity that has attended these litigations from their inception.

Forced as I am to reach the merits of these cases, I dissent from the opinion and judgments of the Court. Pending further hearings in each case conducted under the appropriate ground rules, I would continue the restraints on publication. I cannot believe that the doctrine prohibiting prior restraints reaches to the point of preventing courts from maintaining the status quo long enough to act responsibly in matters of such national importance as those involved here.

Justice BLACKMUN, dissenting.

The First Amendment, after all, is only one part of an entire Constitution. Article II of the great document vests in the Executive Branch primary power over the conduct of foreign affairs and places in that branch the responsibility for the Nation's safety. Each provision of the Constitution is important, and I cannot subscribe to a doctrine of unlimited absolutism for the First Amendment at the cost of downgrading other provisions. First Amendment absolutism has never commanded a majority of this Court.

What is needed here is a weighing, upon properly developed standards, of the broad right of the press to print and of the very narrow right of the Government to prevent. Such standards are not yet developed. The parties here are in disagreement as to what those standards should be. But even the newspapers concede that there are situations where restraint is in order and is constitutional.

I strongly urge, and sincerely hope, that these two newspapers will be fully aware of their ultimate responsibilities to the United States of America. Judge Wilkey, dissenting in the District of Columbia case, after a review of only the affidavits before his court (the basic papers had not then been made available by either party), concluded that there were a number of examples of documents that, if in the possession of the Post, and if published, "could clearly result in great harm to the nation," and he defined "harm" to mean "the death of soldiers, the destruction of alliances, the greatly increased difficulty of negotiation with our enemies, the inability of our diplomats to negotiate. . . ." I, for one, have now been able to give at least some cursory study not only to the affidavits, but to the material itself. I regret to say that from this examination I fear that Judge Wilkey's statements have possible foundation. I therefore share his concern. I hope that damage has not already been done. If, however, damage has been done, and if, with the Court's action today, these newspapers proceed to publish the critical documents and there results therefrom "the death of soldiers, the destruction of alliances, the greatly increased difficulty of negotiation with our enemies, the inability of our diplomats to negotiate," to which list I might add the factors of prolongation of the war and of further delay in the freeing of United States prisoners, then the Nation's people will know where the responsibility for these sad consequences rests.

New York Times leaves two major questions open. First, what circumstances, if any, would justify a court order preventing publication so as to protect national security? Second, what difference, if any, would it make if there was a statute authorizing a prior restraint?

No Supreme Court case has dealt with these issues since the Pentagon Papers case. One case that might have presented these questions was resolved before it reached the Supreme Court. In United States v. Progressive, Inc., 467 F. Supp. 990 (W.D. Wis. 1979), a federal district court issued an injunction to keep a magazine from publishing an article on how to build a hydrogen bomb. Unlike the Pentagon Papers case, there was a provision in the Atomic Energy Act that appeared to authorize the injunction and the government claimed that preventing nuclear proliferation was a justification sufficient to warrant the prior restraint. The case, however, was dismissed while on appeal because others published the same information in other places.

iii.   Court Orders to Protect Fair Trials

Another major area where the Court has considered court orders as prior restraints is in injunctions against pretrial coverage of legal proceedings so as to enhance a criminal defendant's ability to receive a fair trial. In Nebraska Press Assn. v. Stuart, the Supreme Court ruled that the strong presumption against prior restraints means that such gag orders on the press will be allowed only in the rarest of circumstances, if at all.

NEBRASKA PRESS ASSOCIATION v. STUART
427 U.S. 539 (1976)

Chief Justice BURGER delivered the opinion of the Court.

The respondent State District Judge entered an order restraining the petitioners from publishing or broadcasting accounts of confessions or admission made by the accused or facts "strongly implicative" of the accused in a widely reported murder of six persons. We granted certiorari to decide whether the entry of such an order on the showing made before the state court violated the constitutional guarantee of freedom of the press.

I

On the evening of October 18, 1975, local police found the six members of the Henry Kellie family murdered in their home in Sutherland, Neb., a town of about 850 people. Police released the description of a suspect, Erwin Charles Simants, to the reporters who had hastened to the scene of the crime. Simants was arrested and arraigned in Lincoln County Court the following morning, ending a tense night for this small rural community.

The crime immediately attracted widespread news coverage, by local, regional, and national newspapers, radio and television stations. Three days after the crime, the County Attorney and Simants' attorney joined in asking the County Court to enter a restrictive order relating to "matters that may or may not be publicly reported or disclosed to the public," because of the "mass coverage by news media" and the "reasonable likelihood of prejudicial news which would make difficult, if not impossible, the impaneling of an impartial jury and tend to prevent a fair trial." The County Court heard oral argument but took no evidence; no attorney for members of the press appeared at this stage. The County Court granted the prosecutor's motion for a restrictive order and entered it the next day, October 22. The order prohibited everyone in attendance from "releas[ing] or authoriz[ing] the release for public dissemination in any form or manner whatsoever any testimony given or evidence adduced"; the order also required members of the press to observe the Nebraska Bar-Press Guidelines.

Petitioners several press and broadcast associations, publishers, and individual reporters moved on October 23 for leave to intervene in the District Court, asking that the restrictive order imposed by the County Court be vacated. The judge found "because of the nature of the crimes charged in the complaint that there is a clear and present danger that pre-trial publicity could impinge upon the defendant's right to a fair trial." The order applied only until the jury was impaneled, and specifically prohibited petitioners from reporting five subjects: (1) the existence or contents of a confession Simants had made to law enforcement officers, which had been introduced in open court at arraignment; (2) the fact or nature of statements Simants had made to other persons; (3) the contents of a note he had written the night of the crime; (4) certain aspects of the medical testimony at the preliminary hearing; and (5) the identity of the victims of the alleged sexual assault and the nature of the assault. It also prohibited reporting the exact nature of the restrictive order itself.

II

The problems presented by this case are almost as old as the Republic. Neither in the Constitution nor in contemporaneous writings do we find that the conflict between these two important rights was anticipated, yet it is inconceivable that the authors of the Constitution were unaware of the potential conflicts between the right to an unbiased jury and the guarantee of freedom of the press. The Sixth Amendment in terms guarantees "trial, by an impartial jury . . ." in federal criminal prosecutions. Because "trial by jury in criminal cases is fundamental to the American scheme of justice," the Due Process Clause of the Fourteenth Amendment guarantees the same right in state criminal prosecutions.

[But] pretrial publicity even pervasive, adverse publicity does not inevitably lead to an unfair trial. The capacity of the jury eventually impaneled to decide the case fairly is influenced by the tone and extent of the publicity, which is in part, and often in large part, shaped by what attorneys, police, and other officials do to precipitate news coverage. The trial judge has a major responsibility. What the judge says about a case, in or out of the courtroom, is likely to appear in newspapers and broadcasts. More important, the measures a judge takes or fails to take to mitigate the effects of pretrial publicity may well determine whether the defendant receives a trial consistent with the requirements of due process.

The costs of failure to afford a fair trial are high. In the most extreme cases, like *Sheppard* and *Estes*, the risk of injustice was avoided when the convictions were reversed. But a reversal means that justice has been delayed for both the defendant and the State; in some cases, because of lapse of time retrial is impossible or further prosecution is gravely handicapped. Moreover, in borderline cases in which the conviction is not reversed, there is some possibility of an injustice unredressed.

III

The First Amendment provides that "Congress shall make no law . . . abridging the freedom . . . of the press," and it is "no longer open to doubt that the liberty of the press and of speech, is within the liberty safeguarded by the due process clause of the Fourteenth Amendment from invasion by state action." Near v. Minnesota ex rel. Olson (1931). The Court has interpreted these guarantees to afford special protection against orders that prohibit the publication or broadcast of particular information or commentary orders that impose a "previous" or "prior" restraint on speech.

"Any prior restraint on expression comes to this Court with a 'heavy presumption' against its constitutional validity." [P]rior restraints on speech and publication are the most serious and the least tolerable infringement on First Amendment rights. The damage can be particularly great when the prior restraint falls upon the communication of news and commentary on current events. Truthful reports of public judicial proceedings have been afforded special protection against subsequent punishment. For the same reasons the protection against prior restraint should have particular force as applied to reporting of criminal proceedings, whether the crime in question is a single isolated act or a pattern of criminal conduct.

The authors of the Bill of Rights did not undertake to assign priorities as between First Amendment and Sixth Amendment rights, ranking one as superior to the other. In this case, the petitioners would have us declare the right of an accused subordinate to their right to publish in all circumstances. But if the authors of these guarantees, fully aware of the potential conflicts between them, were unwilling or unable to resolve the issue by assigning to one priority over the other, it is not for us to rewrite the Constitution by undertaking what they declined to do. It is unnecessary, after nearly two centuries, to establish a priority applicable in all circumstances. Yet it is nonetheless clear that the barriers to prior restraint remain high unless we are to abandon what the Court has said for nearly a quarter of our national existence and implied throughout all of it.

IV

We turn now to the record in this case to determine whether, as [Chief Judge] Learned Hand put it, "the gravity of the 'evil,' discounted by its improbability, justifies such invasion of free speech as is necessary to avoid the danger." To do so, we must examine the evidence before the trial judge when the order was entered to determine (a) the nature and extent of pretrial news coverage; (b) whether other measures would be likely to mitigate the effects of unrestrained pretrial publicity; and (c) how effectively a restraining order would operate to prevent the threatened danger. The precise terms of the restraining order are also important. We must then consider whether the record supports the entry of a prior restraint on publication, one of the most extraordinary remedies known to our jurisprudence.

A

In assessing the probable extent of publicity, the trial judge had before him newspapers demonstrating that the crime had already drawn intensive news coverage, and the testimony of the County Judge, who had entered the initial restraining order based on the local and national attention the case had attracted. The District Judge was required to assess the probable publicity that would be given these shocking crimes prior to the time a jury was selected and sequestered. He then had to examine the probable nature of the publicity and determine how it would affect prospective jurors.

Our review of the pretrial record persuades us that the trial judge was justified in concluding that there would be intense and pervasive pretrial publicity concerning this case. He could also reasonably conclude, based on common man experience, that publicity might impair the defendant's right to a fair trial. He did not purport to say more, for he found only "a clear and present danger that pre-trial publicity could impinge upon the defendant's right to a fair trial." His conclusion as to the impact of such publicity on prospective jurors was of necessity speculative, dealing as he was with factors unknown and unknowable.

B

We find little in the record that goes to another aspect of our task, determining whether measures short of an order restraining all publication would have insured the defendant a fair trial. Although the entry of the order might be read as a judicial determination that other measures would not suffice, the trial court made no express findings to that effect. [A]lternatives to prior restraint of publication in these circumstances [include]: (a) change of trial venue to a place less exposed to the intense publicity that seemed imminent in Lincoln County; (b) postponement of the trial to allow public attention to subside; (c) searching questioning of prospective jurors to screen out those with fixed opinions as to guilt or innocence; (d) the use of emphatic and clear instructions on the sworn duty of each juror to decide the issues only on evidence presented in open court. Sequestration of jurors is, of course, always available. Although that measure insulates jurors only after they are sworn, it also enhances the likelihood of dissipating the impact of pretrial publicity and emphasizes the elements of the jurors' oaths. This Court has outlined other measures short of prior restraints on publication tending to blunt the impact of pretrial publicity. Professional studies have filled out these suggestions, recommending that trial courts in appropriate cases limit what the contending lawyers, the police, and witnesses may say to anyone.

We have noted earlier that pretrial publicity, even if pervasive and concentrated, cannot be regarded as leading automatically and in every kind of criminal case to an unfair trial. The decided cases "cannot be made to stand for the proposition that juror exposure to information about a state defendant's prior convictions or to news accounts of the crime with which he is charged alone presumptively deprives the defendant of due process."

We have therefore examined this record to determine the probable efficacy of the measures short of prior restraint on the press and speech. There is no finding that alternative measures would not have protected Simants' rights, and the Nebraska Supreme Court did no more than imply that such measures might not be adequate. Moreover, the record is lacking in evidence to support such a finding.

C

We must also assess the probable efficacy of prior restraint on publication as a workable method of protecting Simants' right to a fair trial, and we cannot ignore the reality of the problems of managing and enforcing pretrial restraining orders. The territorial jurisdiction of the issuing court is limited by concepts of sovereignty. Finally, we note that the events disclosed by the record took place in a community of 850 people. It is reasonable to assume that, without any news accounts being printed or broadcast, rumors would travel swiftly by word of mouth. One can only speculate on the accuracy of such reports, given the generative propensities of rumors; they could well be more damaging than reasonably accurate news accounts. But plainly a whole community cannot be restrained from discussing a subject intimately affecting life within it. Given these practical problems, it is far from clear that prior restraint on publication would have protected Simants' rights.

Of necessity our holding is confined to the record before us. But our conclusion is not simply a result of assessing the adequacy of the showing made in this case; it results in part from the problems inherent in meeting the heavy burden of demonstrating, in advance of trial, that without prior restraint a fair trial will be denied. The practical problems of managing and enforcing restrictive orders will always be present. In this sense, the record now before us is illustrative rather than exceptional. It is significant that when this Court has reversed a state conviction, because of prejudicial publicity, it has carefully noted that some course of action short of prior restraint would have made a critical difference.

However difficult it may be, we need not rule out the possibility of showing the kind of threat to fair trial rights that would possess the requisite degree of certainty to justify restraint. This Court has frequently denied that First Amendment rights are absolute and has consistently rejected the proposition that a prior restraint can never be employed.

We hold that, with respect to the order entered in this case prohibiting reporting or commentary on judicial proceedings held in public, the barriers have not been overcome; to the extent that this order restrained publication of such material, it is clearly invalid.

————————————

The Court in *Nebraska Press* said that it was not creating an absolute ban on prior restraints to protect a defendant's right to a fair trial, but from a practical perspective, the Court did just that.[83] It is hard to imagine a case where all three requirements can be met. Even assuming that extensive pretrial publicity threatens a defendant's right to a fair trial, it is difficult to see how a court could conclude that all alternatives to a gag order would fail or that a prior restraint would be successful in keeping prospective jurors from receiving information. Indeed, as Professor Rodney Smolla observed, "[l]ower courts have treated *Nebraska Press* as tantamount to an absolute prohibition on such prior restraints, consistently refusing to permit orders limiting press coverage of judicial proceedings."[84]

Nor has the Supreme Court approved a prior restraint to protect a defendant's right to a fair trial since *Nebraska Press*. In Oklahoma Publishing Co. v. District Court, 430 U.S. 308 (1977), the Court declared unconstitutional a

---

83. It should be noted that three justices, Brennan, Stewart, and Marshall, took the position that prior restraints would never be justified to protect a defendant's right to a fair trial, and a fourth, Justice White, expressed "grave doubt" that such a prior restraint would ever be justified.

84. Smolla, *supra* note 39, at 8-41. *See id.* at n.12 (collecting cases rejecting such prior restraints). One of the few cases where a lower court imposed a prior restraint was in United States v. Noriega, 752 F. Supp. 1032 (S.D. Fla.), *aff'd*, United States v. Noriega, 917 F.2d 1543 (11th Cir.), *cert. denied*, Cable News Network, Inc. v. Noriega, 498 U.S. 976 (1990), where a federal district court enjoined CNN from broadcasting tapes of conversations between deposed Panamanian dictator Manuel Noriega and his attorneys.

judge's order enjoining the news media from publishing, broadcasting, or disseminating the name or picture of an 11-year-old boy who was accused of murder. In a brief *per curiam* opinion, the Court said that the media had lawfully obtained the information and thus there could be no injunction to prevent its truthful reporting.

The Supreme Court has never addressed the question of when it is permissible for courts to impose gag orders on attorneys and other trial participants. Such restrictions are increasingly common and there are lower court cases both invalidating and upholding such orders. Professor Smolla notes that the law in this area is in "significant disarray" and that "[a]ppellate courts tend to reverse such gag orders when they do not pose serious and imminent threats to the fairness of the proceedings. When the order is narrowly tailored to eliminate serious and imminent threats, however, appellate courts are inclined to sustain such orders."[85]

On the one hand, attorneys are officers of the Court, and the Supreme Court has approved greater restrictions on attorney speech than for others in society.[86] Restricting the speech of trial participants seems less restrictive than an injunction on the press. But on the other hand, a gag order on lawyers is a prior restraint and should have to overcome the same strong presumption as other prior restraints. Moreover, limiting speech by trial participants effectively restricts the media's ability to cover proceedings with complete and accurate information.

iv. Court Orders Seizing the Assets of Businesses Convicted of Obscenity Violations

In *Near*, *New York Times*, and *Nebraska Press*, the Supreme Court found court orders suppressing speech to be a prior restraint. In contrast, in Alexander v. United States, the Court rejected the argument that there is a prior restraint when the court seizes the assets of a business convicted of obscenity law violations.

ALEXANDER v. UNITED STATES

509 U.S. 544 (1993)

Chief Justice REHNQUIST delivered the opinion of the Court.

Petitioner was in the so-called "adult entertainment" business for more than 30 years, selling pornographic magazines and sexual paraphernalia, showing sexually explicit movies, and eventually selling and renting videotapes of a similar nature. He received shipments of these materials at a warehouse in Minneapolis, Minnesota, where they were wrapped in plastic, priced, and boxed. He then sold his products through some 13 retail stores in several different Minnesota cities, generating millions of dollars in annual revenues.

After a full criminal trial, petitioner Ferris J. Alexander, owner of more than a dozen stores and theaters dealing in sexually explicit materials, was convicted on 17 obscenity counts and 3 counts of violating the Racketeer Influenced and Corrupt Organizations Act (RICO). The obscenity convictions, based on the jury's findings that four magazines and three videotapes sold at several of

---

85. Smolla, *supra* note 39, at 8-67.
86. *See* Gentile v. State Bar of Nevada, 501 U.S. 1030 (1991).

petitioner's stores were obscene, served as the predicates for his three RICO convictions. Petitioner was sentenced to a total of six years in prison, fined $100,000, and ordered to pay the cost of prosecution, incarceration, and supervised release.

In addition to imposing a prison term and fine, the District Court ordered petitioner to forfeit certain assets that were directly related to his racketeering activity as punishment for his RICO violations. The court ultimately ordered petitioner to forfeit his wholesale and retail businesses (including all the assets of those businesses) and almost $9 million in moneys acquired through racketeering activity. Not wishing to go into the business of selling pornographic materials—regardless of whether they were legally obscene—the Government decided that it would be better to destroy the forfeited expressive materials than sell them to members of the public. Petitioner argues that this forfeiture violated the First and Eighth Amendments to the Constitution. We reject petitioner's claims under the First Amendment but remand for reconsideration of his Eighth Amendment challenge.

Petitioner first contends that the forfeiture in this case, which effectively shut down his adult entertainment business, constituted an unconstitutional prior restraint on speech, rather than a permissible criminal punishment. According to petitioner, forfeiture of expressive materials and the assets of businesses engaged in expressive activity, when predicated solely upon previous obscenity violations, operates as a prior restraint because it prohibits future presumptively protected expression in retaliation for prior unprotected speech. Practically speaking, petitioner argues, the effect of the RICO forfeiture order here was no different from the injunction prohibiting the publication of expressive material found to be a prior restraint in Near v. Minnesota ex rel. Olson (1931).

We disagree. By lumping the forfeiture imposed in this case after a full criminal trial with an injunction enjoining future speech, petitioner stretches the term "prior restraint" well beyond the limits established by our cases. To accept petitioner's argument would virtually obliterate the distinction, solidly grounded in our cases, between prior restraints and subsequent punishments.

The term prior restraint is used "to describe administrative and judicial orders forbidding certain communications when issued in advance of the time that such communications are to occur." Temporary restraining orders and permanent injunctions—i.e., court orders that actually forbid speech activities—are classic examples of prior restraints. This understanding of what constitutes a prior restraint is borne out by our cases, even those on which petitioner relies.

By contrast, the RICO forfeiture order in this case does not forbid petitioner from engaging in any expressive activities in the future, nor does it require him to obtain prior approval for any expressive activities. It only deprives him of specific assets that were found to be related to his previous racketeering violations. Assuming, of course, that he has sufficient untainted assets to open new stores, restock his inventory, and hire staff, petitioner can go back into the adult entertainment business tomorrow, and sell as many sexually explicit magazines and videotapes as he likes, without any risk of being held in contempt for violating a court order. [T]he forfeiture order in this case imposes no legal impediment to—no prior restraint on—petitioner's ability to engage in any expressive activity he chooses. He is perfectly free to open an adult bookstore or otherwise engage in the production and distribution of erotic materials; he just cannot finance these enterprises with assets derived from his prior racketeering offenses.

In this case, however, the assets in question were ordered forfeited not because they were believed to be obscene, but because they were directly related to petitioner's past racketeering violations. The RICO forfeiture statute calls for the forfeiture of assets because of the financial role they play in the operation of the racketeering enterprise. The statute is oblivious to the expressive or non-expressive nature of the assets forfeited; books, sports cars, narcotics, and cash are all forfeitable alike under RICO. Indeed, a contrary scheme would be disastrous from a policy standpoint, enabling racketeers to evade forfeiture by investing the proceeds of their crimes in businesses engaging in expressive activity. Nor were the assets in question ordered forfeited without according petitioner the requisite procedural safeguards, another recurring theme in our prior restraint cases.

Justice KENNEDY, with whom Justice BLACKMUN and Justice STEVENS join, and with whom Justice SOUTER joins, dissenting.

The Court today embraces a rule that would find no affront to the First Amendment in the Government's destruction of a book and film business and its entire inventory of legitimate expression as punishment for a single past speech offense. Until now I had thought one could browse through any book or film store in the United States without fear that the proprietor had chosen each item to avoid risk to the whole inventory and indeed to the business itself. This ominous, onerous threat undermines free speech and press principles essential to our personal freedom.

What is at work in this case is not the power to punish an individual for his past transgressions but the authority to suppress a particular class of disfavored speech. The forfeiture provisions accomplish this in a direct way by seizing speech presumed to be protected along with the instruments of its dissemination, and in an indirect way by threatening all who engage in the business of distributing adult or sexually explicit materials with the same disabling measures.

Obscenity laws would not work unless an offender could be arrested and imprisoned despite the resulting chill on his own further speech. But, at least before today, we have understood state action directed at protected books or other expressive works themselves to raise distinct constitutional concerns. [T]he destruction of books and films that were not obscene and not adjudged to be so is a remedy with no parallel in our cases. The Court's decision is a grave repudiation of First Amendment principles, and with respect I dissent.

c. Licensing as a Prior Restraint

Another form of prior restraint — in fact, the classic type of prior restraint — is where the government requires a license or permit in order for speech to occur. Lovell v. City of Griffin is an early case declaring a licensing system to be an impermissible prior restraint.

LOVELL v. CITY OF GRIFFIN, GA., 303 U.S. 444 (1938): Chief Justice HUGHES delivered the opinion of the Court.

Appellant, Alma Lovell, was convicted in the recorder's court of the City of Griffin, Ga., of the violation of a city ordinance and was sentenced to imprisonment for fifty days in default of the payment of a fine of $50. The ordinance in question is as follows:

> Section 1. That the practice of distributing, either by hand or otherwise, circulars, handbooks, advertising, or literature of any kind, whether said articles are being delivered free, or whether same are being sold, within the limits of the City of Griffin, without first obtaining written permission from the City Manager of the City of Griffin, such practice shall be deemed a nuisance, and punishable as an offense against the City of Griffin.
>
> Section 2. The Chief of Police of the City of Griffin and the police force of the City of Griffin are hereby required and directed to suppress the same and to abate any nuisance as is described in the first section of this ordinance.

The violation, which is not denied, consisted of the distribution without the required permission of a pamphlet and magazine in the nature of religious tracts, setting forth the gospel of the "Kingdom of Jehovah." Appellant did not apply for a permit, as she regarded herself as sent "by Jehovah to do His work" and that such an application would have been "an act of disobedience to His commandment."

The ordinance is comprehensive with respect to the method of distribution. It covers every sort of circulation "either by hand or otherwise." There is thus no restriction in its application with respect to time or place. It is not limited to ways which might be regarded as inconsistent with the maintenance of public order, or as involving disorderly conduct, the molestation of the inhabitants, or the misuse or littering of the streets. The ordinance prohibits the distribution of literature of any kind at any time, at any place, and in any manner without a permit from the city manager.

We think that the ordinance is invalid on its face. Whatever the motive which induced its adoption, its character is such that it strikes at the very foundation of the freedom of the press by subjecting it to license and censorship. The struggle for the freedom of the press was primarily directed against the power of the licensor. It was against that power that John Milton directed his assault by his "Appeal for the Liberty of Unlicensed Printing." And the liberty of the press became initially a right to publish "without a license what formerly could be published only with one." While this freedom from previous restraint upon publication cannot be regarded as exhausting the guaranty of liberty, the prevention of that restraint was a leading purpose in the adoption of the constitutional provision. Legislation of the type of the ordinance in question would restore the system of license and censorship in its baldest form.

The ordinance cannot be saved because it relates to distribution and not to publication. "Liberty of circulating is as essential to that freedom as liberty of publishing; indeed, without the circulation, the publication would be of little value."

As the ordinance is void on its face, it was not necessary for appellant to seek a permit under it. She was entitled to contest its validity in answer to the charge against her.

Watchtower Bible & Tract Society of New York, Inc. v. Village of Stratton is a more recent example of the Court's invalidating a licensing system.

WATCHTOWER BIBLE & TRACT SOCIETY OF NEW YORK, INC. v. VILLAGE OF STRATTON

536 U.S. 150 (2002)

Justice STEVENS delivered the opinion of the Court.

Petitioners contend that a village ordinance making it a misdemeanor to engage in door-to-door advocacy without first registering with the mayor and receiving a permit violates the First Amendment. Through this facial challenge, we consider the door-to-door canvassing regulation not only as it applies to religious proselytizing, but also to anonymous political speech and the distribution of handbills.

I

Petitioner Watchtower Bible and Tract Society of New York, Inc., coordinates the preaching activities of Jehovah's Witnesses throughout the United States and publishes Bibles and religious periodicals that are widely distributed. Petitioner Wellsville, Ohio, Congregation of Jehovah's Witnesses, Inc., supervises the activities of approximately 59 members in a part of Ohio that includes the Village of Stratton (Village). Petitioners offer religious literature without cost to anyone interested in reading it. They allege that they do not solicit contributions or orders for the sale of merchandise or services, but they do accept donations.

Section 116.01 prohibits "canvassers" and others from "going in and upon" private residential property for the purpose of promoting any "cause" without first having obtained a permit pursuant to §116.03. That section provides that any canvasser who intends to go on private property to promote a cause, must obtain a "Solicitation Permit" from the office of the mayor; there is no charge for the permit, and apparently one is issued routinely after an applicant fills out a fairly detailed "Solicitor's Registration Form." The canvasser is then authorized to go upon premises that he listed on the registration form, but he must carry the permit upon his person and exhibit it whenever requested to do so by a police officer or by a resident. The ordinance sets forth grounds for the denial or revocation of a permit, but the record before us does not show that any application has been denied or that any permit has been revoked. Petitioners did not apply for a permit.

A section of the ordinance that petitioners do not challenge establishes a procedure by which a resident may prohibit solicitation even by holders of permits. If the resident files a "No Solicitation Registration Form" with the mayor, and also posts a "No Solicitation" sign on his property, no uninvited canvassers may enter his property, unless they are specifically authorized to do so in the "No Solicitation Registration Form" itself. Only 32 of the Village's 278 residents filed such forms.

II

For over 50 years, the Court has invalidated restrictions on door-to-door canvassing and pamphleteering. It is more than historical accident that most of these cases involved First Amendment challenges brought by Jehovah's Witnesses, because door-to-door canvassing is mandated by their religion. Moreover, because they lack significant financial resources, the ability of the Witnesses to proselytize is seriously diminished by regulations that burden their efforts to canvass door-to-door.

Although our past cases involving Jehovah's Witnesses, most of which were decided shortly before and during World War II, do not directly control the question we confront today, they provide both a historical and analytical backdrop for consideration of petitioners' First Amendment claim that the breadth of the Village's ordinance offends the First Amendment. From these decisions, several themes emerge that guide our consideration of the ordinance at issue here.

The cases emphasize the value of the speech involved. For example, in Murdock v. Pennsylvania, the Court noted that "hand distribution of religious tracts is an age-old form of missionary evangelism — as old as the history of printing presses. It has been a potent force in various religious movements down through the years. . . . This form of religious activity occupies the same high estate under the First Amendment as do worship in the churches and preaching from the pulpits. It has the same claim to protection as the more orthodox and conventional exercises of religion. It also has the same claim as the others to the guarantees of freedom of speech and freedom of the press." In addition, the cases discuss extensively the historical importance of door-to-door canvassing and pamphleteering as vehicles for the dissemination of ideas.

Despite the emphasis on the important role that door-to-door canvassing and pamphleteering has played in our constitutional tradition of free and open discussion, these early cases also recognized the interests a town may have in some form of regulation, particularly when the solicitation of money is involved. Despite recognition of these interests as legitimate, our precedent is clear that there must be a balance between these interests and the effect of the regulations on First Amendment rights. We "must 'be astute to examine the effect of the challenged legislation' and must 'weigh the circumstances and . . . appraise the substantiality of the reasons advanced in support of the regulation.'"

Finally, the cases demonstrate that efforts of the Jehovah's Witnesses to resist speech regulation have not been a struggle for their rights alone. In *Martin*, after cataloging the many groups that rely extensively upon this method of communication, the Court summarized that "[d]oor to door distribution of circulars is essential to the poorly financed causes of little people."

III

The Village argues that three interests are served by its ordinance: the prevention of fraud, the prevention of crime, and the protection of residents' privacy. We have no difficulty concluding, in light of our precedent, that these are important interests that the Village may seek to safeguard through some form of regulation of solicitation activity. We must also look, however, to the amount of speech covered by the ordinance and whether there is an appropriate balance between the affected speech and the governmental interests that the ordinance purports to serve.

The text of the Village's ordinance prohibits "canvassers" from going on private property for the purpose of explaining or promoting any "cause," unless they receive a permit and the residents visited have not opted for a "no solicitation" sign. Had this provision been construed to apply only to commercial activities and the solicitation of funds, arguably the ordinance would have been tailored to the Village's interest in protecting the privacy of its residents and preventing fraud. Yet, even though the Village has explained that the ordinance was adopted to serve those interests, it has never contended that it should be so narrowly interpreted. To the contrary, the Village's administration of its ordinance unquestionably demonstrates that the provisions apply to a significant number of noncommercial "canvassers" promoting a wide variety of "causes." Indeed, on the "No Solicitation Forms" provided to the residents, the canvassers include "Camp Fire Girls," "Jehovah's Witnesses," "Political Candidates," "Trick or Treaters during Halloween Season," and "Persons Affiliated with Stratton Church." The ordinance unquestionably applies, not only to religious causes, but to political activity as well. It would seem to extend to "residents casually soliciting the votes of neighbors," or ringing doorbells to enlist support for employing a more efficient garbage collector.

The mere fact that the ordinance covers so much speech raises constitutional concerns. It is offensive — not only to the values protected by the First Amendment, but to the very notion of a free society — that in the context of everyday public discourse a citizen must first inform the government of her desire to speak to her neighbors and then obtain a permit to do so. Even if the issuance of permits by the mayor's office is a ministerial task that is performed promptly and at no cost to the applicant, a law requiring a permit to engage in such speech constitutes a dramatic departure from our national heritage and constitutional tradition.

Three obvious examples illustrate the pernicious effect of such a permit requirement. First, as our cases involving distribution of unsigned handbills demonstrate, there are a significant number of persons who support causes anonymously. "The decision to favor anonymity may be motivated by fear of economic or official retaliation, by concern about social ostracism, or merely by a desire to preserve as much of one's privacy as possible." McIntyre v. Ohio Elections Comm'n (1995). The requirement that a canvasser must be identified in a permit application filed in the mayor's office and available for public inspection necessarily results in a surrender of that anonymity.

Second, requiring a permit as a prior condition on the exercise of the right to speak imposes an objective burden on some speech of citizens holding religious or patriotic views. As our World War II-era cases dramatically demonstrate, there are a significant number of persons whose religious scruples will prevent them from applying for such a license. There are no doubt other patriotic citizens, who have such firm convictions about their constitutional right to engage in uninhibited debate in the context of door-to-door advocacy, that they would prefer silence to speech licensed by a petty official.

Third, there is a significant amount of spontaneous speech that is effectively banned by the ordinance. A person who made a decision on a holiday or a weekend to take an active part in a political campaign could not begin to pass out handbills until after he or she obtained the required permit. Even a spontaneous decision to go across the street and urge a neighbor to vote against the mayor could not lawfully be implemented without first obtaining the mayor's permission.

The Village, however, argues that the ordinance is nonetheless valid because it serves the two additional interests of protecting the privacy of the resident and the prevention of crime.

With respect to the former, it seems clear that §107 of the ordinance, which provides for the posting of "No Solicitation" signs and which is not challenged in this case, coupled with the resident's unquestioned right to refuse to engage in conversation with unwelcome visitors, provides ample protection for the unwilling listener. The annoyance caused by an uninvited knock on the front door is the same whether or not the visitor is armed with a permit.

With respect to the latter, it seems unlikely that the absence of a permit would preclude criminals from knocking on doors and engaging in conversations not covered by the ordinance. They might, for example, ask for directions or permission to use the telephone, or pose as surveyors or census takers. Or they might register under a false name with impunity because the ordinance contains no provision for verifying an applicant's identity or organizational credentials. Moreover, the Village did not assert an interest in crime prevention below, and there is an absence of any evidence of a special crime problem related to door-to-door solicitation in the record before us.

The rhetoric used in the World War II-era opinions that repeatedly saved petitioners' coreligionists from petty prosecutions reflected the Court's evaluation of the First Amendment freedoms that are implicated in this case. The value judgment that then motivated a united democratic people fighting to defend those very freedoms from totalitarian attack is unchanged. It motivates our decision today.

Chief Justice REHNQUIST, dissenting.

More than half a century ago we recognized that canvassers, "whether selling pots or distributing leaflets, may lessen the peaceful enjoyment of a home," and that "burglars frequently pose as canvassers, either in order that they may have a pretense to discover whether a house is empty and hence ripe for burglary, or for the purpose of spying out the premises in order that they may return later." Martin v. City of Struthers (1943). These problems continue to be associated with door-to-door canvassing, as are even graver ones.

A recent double murder in Hanover, New Hampshire, a town of approximately 7,500 that would appear tranquil to most Americans but would probably seem like a bustling town of Dartmouth College students to Stratton residents, illustrates these dangers. Two teenagers murdered a married couple of Dartmouth College professors, Half and Susanne Zantop, in the Zantop's home. Investigators have concluded, based on the confession of one of the teenagers, that the teenagers went door-to-door intent on stealing access numbers to bank debit cards and then killing their owners. See Dartmouth Professors Called Random Targets, Washington Post, Feb. 20, 2002, p. A2. Their modus operandi was to tell residents that they were conducting an environmental survey for school. They canvassed a few homes where no one answered. At another, the resident did not allow them in to conduct the "survey." They were allowed into the Zantop home. After conducting the phony environmental survey, they stabbed the Zantops to death.

In order to reduce these very grave risks associated with canvassing, the 278 "little people" of Stratton, who, unlike petitioners, do not have a team of attorneys at their ready disposal, enacted the ordinance at issue here. The residents did not prohibit door-to-door communication, they simply required that canvassers obtain a permit before going door-to-door. And the village does not have the discretion to reject an applicant who completes the application.

The town had little reason to suspect that the negligible burden of having to obtain a permit runs afoul of the First Amendment. For over 60 years, we have categorically stated that a permit requirement for door-to-door canvassers, which gives no discretion to the issuing authority, is constitutional. The Court today, however, abruptly changes course and invalidates the ordinance.

The Stratton ordinance does not prohibit door-to-door canvassing; it merely requires that canvassers fill out a form and receive a permit. The mayor does not exercise any discretion in deciding who receives a permit; approval of the permit is automatic upon proper completion of the form. And petitioners do not contend in this Court that the ordinance is vague.

There is no support in our case law for applying anything more stringent than intermediate scrutiny to the ordinance. The ordinance is content-neutral and does not bar anyone from going door-to-door in Stratton. It merely regulates the manner in which one must canvass: A canvasser must first obtain a permit. The Stratton regulation is aimed at three significant governmental interests: the prevention of fraud, the prevention of crime, and the protection of privacy.

The ordinance prevents and detects serious crime by making it a crime not to register. Take the Hanover double murder discussed earlier. The murderers did not achieve their objective until they visited their fifth home over a period of seven months. If Hanover had a permit requirement, the teens may have been stopped before they achieved their objective. One of the residents they visited may have informed the police that there were two canvassers who lacked a permit. Such neighborly vigilance, though perhaps foreign to those residing in modern day cities, is not uncommon in small towns. Or the police on their own may have discovered that two canvassers were violating the ordinance. Apprehension for violating the permit requirement may well have frustrated the teenagers' objectives; it certainly would have assisted in solving the murders had the teenagers gone ahead with their plan.

Of course, the Stratton ordinance does not guarantee that no canvasser will ever commit a burglary or violent crime. The Court seems to think this dooms the ordinance, erecting an insurmountable hurdle that a law must provide a fool-proof method of preventing crime. In order to survive intermediate scrutiny, however, a law need not solve the crime problem, it need only further the interest in preventing crime. Some deterrence of serious criminal activity is more than enough to survive intermediate scrutiny.

The final requirement of intermediate scrutiny is that a regulation leave open ample alternatives for expression. Undoubtedly, ample alternatives exist here. Most obviously, canvassers are free to go door-to-door after filling out the permit application. And those without permits may communicate on public sidewalks, on street corners, through the mail, or through the telephone.

Ironically, however, today's decision may result in less of the door-to-door communication that the Court extols. As the Court recognizes, any homeowner may place a "No Solicitation" sign on his or her property, and it is a crime to violate that sign. In light of today's decision depriving Stratton residents of the degree of accountability and safety that the permit requirement provides, more and more residents may decide to place these signs in their yards and cut off door-to-door communication altogether.

The Supreme Court has held that licensing or permit laws are allowed only if the government has an important reason for licensing and only if there are clear criteria leaving almost no discretion to the licensing authority. In addition, there must be procedural safeguards, such as a requirement for prompt determinations as to license requests and judicial review of license denials. Each requirement is discussed in turn.

i. *Important Reason for Licensing*

First, there must be an important reason for licensing. For example, in Cox v. New Hampshire, 312 U.S. 569 (1941), the Court upheld an ordinance that required that those wishing to hold a parade or demonstration obtain a permit. The ordinance allowed a permit to be denied only if the area already was in use by another group. The Court emphasized that the city had an important reason for licensing: to receive notice of demonstrations to be able to "afford opportunity for proper policing" and to preserve order by ensuring only one parade at a particular place at a specific time. The Court stressed that the "licensing board was not vested with arbitrary power or an unfettered discretion."

ii. *Clear Standards Leaving Almost No Discretion to the Government*

Second, there must be clear standards leaving almost no discretion to the licensing authority. The Court is very concerned that discretion could be used for content-based censorship; the government could grant permits to speech that it liked but deny licenses to disfavored expression.

CITY OF LAKEWOOD v. PLAIN DEALER PUBLISHING CO., 486 U.S. 750 (1988): Justice BRENNAN delivered the opinion of the Court.

The city of Lakewood, a suburban community bordering Cleveland, Ohio, appeals a judgment of the Court of Appeals for the Sixth Circuit enjoining enforcement of its local ordinance regulating the placement of newsracks. The court's decision was based in part on its conclusion that the ordinance vests the mayor with unbridled discretion over which publishers may place newsracks on public property and where.

Prior to 1983, the city of Lakewood absolutely prohibited the private placement of any structure on public property. On the strength of that law, the city denied the Plain Dealer Publishing Company (Newspaper) permission to place its coin-operated newspaper dispensing devices on city sidewalks. The District Court adjudged the absolute prohibition unconstitutional. Although the city could have appealed the District Court's judgment, it decided instead to adopt two ordinances permitting the placement of structures on city property under certain conditions. One of those ordinances specifically concerns newsracks.

That ordinance gives the mayor the authority to grant or deny applications for annual newsrack permits. If the mayor denies an application, he is required to "stat[e] the reasons for such denial."

Recognizing the explicit protection accorded speech and the press in the text of the First Amendment, our cases have long held that when a licensing statute allegedly vests unbridled discretion in a government official over whether to permit or deny expressive activity, one who is subject to the law may challenge it facially without the necessity of first applying for, and being denied, a license. At the root of this long line of precedent is the time-tested knowledge that in the area of free expression a licensing statute placing unbridled discretion in the hands of a government official or agency constitutes a prior restraint and may result in censorship.

First, the mere existence of the licensor's unfettered discretion, coupled with the power of prior restraint, intimidates parties into censoring their own speech, even if the discretion and power are never actually abused. It is not difficult to visualize a newspaper that relies to a substantial degree on single issue sales feeling significant pressure to endorse the incumbent mayor in an upcoming election, or to refrain from criticizing him, in order to receive a favorable and speedy disposition on its permit application. Only standards limiting the licensor's discretion will eliminate this danger by adding an element of certainty fatal to self-censorship.

Second, the absence of express standards makes it difficult to distinguish, "as applied," between a licensor's legitimate denial of a permit and its illegitimate abuse of censorial power. Standards provide the guideposts that check the licensor and allow courts quickly and easily to determine whether the licensor is discriminating against disfavored speech. Without these guideposts, post hoc rationalizations by the licensing official and the use of shifting or illegitimate criteria are far too easy, making it difficult for courts to determine in any particular case whether the licensor is permitting favorable, and suppressing unfavorable, expression.

It is apparent that the face of the ordinance itself contains no explicit limits on the mayor's discretion. Indeed, nothing in the law as written requires the mayor to do more than make the statement "it is not in the public interest" when denying a permit application. Similarly, the mayor could grant the application, but require the newsrack to be placed in an inaccessible location without providing any explanation whatever. To allow these illusory "constraints" to constitute the standards necessary to bound a licensor's discretion renders the guarantee against censorship little more than a high-sounding ideal.

In Saia v. New York, 334 U.S. 558 (1948), the Supreme Court declared unconstitutional an ordinance that required a permit in order to use a sound amplification system on a motor vehicle. Although the Court has upheld restrictions on such sound trucks, an ordinance that gives unfettered discretion to government officials to decide who can use such vehicles violates the First Amendment. Similarly, in Kunz v. New York, 340 U.S. 290 (1951), the Court declared unconstitutional an ordinance that prohibited the holding of a religious meeting on a public street without a permit. The Court said that the government "cannot vest restraining control over the right to speak . . . in an administrative official where there are no appropriate standards to guide his action."

In Forsyth County, Georgia v. Nationalist Movement, 505 U.S. 123 (1992), the Court followed the same reasoning in declaring unconstitutional an ordinance that required a permit in order for a demonstration to occur and that vested discretion in the government to set the amount of the fee up to $1,000. The Court found that the licensing law was impermissible because "[t]here are no articulated standards either in the ordinance or in the county's established practice. The administrator is not required to rely on any objective factors. He need not provide any explanation for his decision, and that decision is unreviewable." The Court concluded that "[n]othing in the law or its application prevents the official from encouraging some views and discouraging others through the arbitrary application of the fees. The First Amendment prohibits the vesting of such unbridled discretion in a government official."

iii. Procedural Safeguards

Finally, in order for a licensing or permit system to be constitutional, there must be procedural safeguards. Any system of prior restraints must have a prompt decision made by the government as to whether the speech will be allowed;[87] there must be a full and fair hearing before speech is prevented;[88] and there must be a prompt and final judicial determination of the validity of any preclusion of speech.[89]

In Freedman v. Maryland, 380 U.S. 51 (1965), the Court unanimously declared unconstitutional a Maryland law that made it unlawful to exhibit a motion picture without having first obtained a license. The Court noted that such a licensing system presents grave dangers for freedom of speech. The Court said that such a system would be allowed "only if it takes place under procedural safeguards designed to obviate the dangers of . . . censorship." The "burden of proving that the film is unprotected expression must rest on the censor." There must be a requirement for a prompt determination by the government whether to issue or deny the license request. Also, prompt judicial review must be available for all permit denials. The Court said that "only a judicial determination in an adversary proceeding ensures the necessary sensitivity to freedom of expression."

The Court repeatedly has held that such procedural safeguards are required for government actions that operate like licensing systems, such as postal stop orders for obscene materials[90] and customs seizures of obscene materials.[91] In FW/PBS, Inc. v. City of Dallas, 493 U.S. 215 (1990), the Court declared uncon-

---

87. *See, e.g.*, Teitel Film Corp. v. Cusack, 390 U.S. 139 (1968) (a 50-day delay before seeking an injunction, during which time the speech could not be disseminated, violated the First Amendment).

88. *See, e.g.*, Carroll v. President & Commissioners of Princess Anne County, 393 U.S. 175 (1968) (ex parte court orders are impermissible in restraining speech because of the lack of adversarial presentation).

89. *See* National Socialist Party of America v. Village of Skokie, 432 U.S. 43 (1977) (improper to leave an injunction in place pending an appeal that could take up to a year; either the injunction had to be lifted or the appeal had to be expedited).

90. Blount v. Rizzi, 400 U.S. 410 (1971).

91. United States v. Thirty-Seven Photographs, 402 U.S. 363 (1971).

stitutional a city ordinance that required licensing of "sexually oriented businesses" because of the absence of the procedural safeguards prescribed in *Freedman*. The Court noted that the law failed to require prompt determination of license requests or to provide for judicial review of license denials.

However, in its most recent cases, the Court has not adhered to *Freedman* and has relaxed the procedural safeguards. For example, in Thomas and Windy City Hemp Development Board v. Chicago Park District, 534 U.S. 316 (2002), the Court rejected the application of some of the procedural safeguards from *Freedman* to requirements for obtaining a license in order to use a park. Specifically, the Court rejected that the "Park District, like the Board of Censors in *Freedman*, must initiate litigation every time it denies a permit and that the ordinance must specify a deadline for judicial review of a challenge to a permit denial." The Court explained that it never has "required that a content-neutral permit scheme regulating speech in a public forum must adhere to the procedural requirements set forth in *Freedman*."

In City of Littleton, Colorado v. Z.J. Gifts D-4, L.L.C., 541 U.S. 774 (2004), the Court also dealt with the application of the *Freedman* procedural requirements to a licensing system. The Court reaffirmed that a city's licensing of adult businesses must comply with the First Amendment and that this must include judicial review of license denials. However, the Court said that the ordinance itself need not specify the availability of prompt judicial review as long as timely judicial review is available.

4. What Is an Infringement of Freedom of Speech?

A threshold question in many cases is whether the government has infringed freedom of speech and therefore whether First Amendment analysis is applicable. Often, it is clear that a law infringes freedom of speech and is susceptible to First Amendment challenge. For example, a statute that prohibits speech and authorizes criminal punishments obviously has to meet constitutional scrutiny. Section C, below, reviews many of these laws, such as those prohibiting speech that incites illegal conduct, obscenity, and false advertising. Although these are categories of unprotected speech and regulation is allowed, there is no doubt that the laws interfere with expression and must meet First Amendment standards.

Also, there is no doubt that prior restraints, discussed above, are infringements of expression and must meet First Amendment standards. Court orders preventing speech and licensing systems precluding speech without a permit thus always are subject to review on constitutional grounds.

But what types of government actions, apart from prohibitions via laws, court orders, or licensing systems, are infringements of speech triggering First Amendment analysis? A wide variety of government actions sufficiently burden speech so as to be considered an infringement and thus be subjected to First Amendment scrutiny. A finding that a law substantially burdens or infringes speech does not, of course, mean that it is automatically unconstitutional, but it does mean that the law will have to meet heightened scrutiny unless it regulates a category of unprotected speech. As explained above, the general rule is that content-based regulations of speech must meet strict scrutiny, while content-neutral regulation must meet intermediate scrutiny.

Laws that significantly burden speech are ones that allow civil liability for expression; that prevent compensation for speech; that compel expression; that condition a benefit on a person's foregoing speech; and that pressure individuals not to speak. These are discussed, in turn, in the following subsections. Additionally, laws that regulate conduct might have an incidental effect on speech because of the communicative content of behavior. First Amendment analysis of such conduct that communicates is discussed in section C.

CIVIL LIABILITY AND DENIAL OF COMPENSATION FOR SPEECH

The Court repeatedly has held that civil liability for speech, even in the context of private civil litigation, is an interference with speech and therefore must meet First Amendment scrutiny. In New York Times v. Sullivan, 376 U.S. 254 (1964), the Court held that state defamation law was limited by the First Amendment. New York Times v. Sullivan, presented in detail in section C below, involved a defamation suit brought by the Montgomery, Alabama, police commissioner against the *New York Times* and four black clergymen for an advertisement criticizing the handling of demonstrations. A jury awarded the plaintiff $500,000 under Alabama's defamation law.

The Supreme Court expressly held that the First Amendment applied. Justice Brennan, writing one of the most famous and important free speech cases in history, declared, "What a State may not constitutionally bring about by means of a criminal statute is likewise beyond the reach of its civil law of libel. The fear of damage awards under a rule such as that invoked by the Alabama courts here may be markedly more inhibiting than the fear of prosecution under a criminal statute." The Court noted that the "judgment awarded in this case — without the need for any proof of actual pecuniary loss — was one thousand times greater than the maximum fine provided by the Alabama criminal [libel law], and one hundred times greater than that provided by the Sedition Act. . . . Whether or not a newspaper can survive a succession of such judgments, the pall of fear and timidity imposed upon those who would give voice to public criticism is an atmosphere in which the First Amendment freedoms cannot survive."

The Supreme Court has followed this and held that liability for such torts as invasion of privacy,[92] false light,[93] and intentional infliction of emotional distress[94] must be consistent with the First Amendment. These torts, and the applicable First Amendment limits, are discussed in section C.

Although it is litigation between two private parties, there is clearly state action in such tort litigation. It is the state's law — whether statutory or common law — that is the basis for liability and recovery. The courts oversee the judicial proceedings and ultimately impose any judgment. In Shelley v. Kraemer, 334 U.S. 1 (1948), the Supreme Court held that judges cannot enforce racially restrictive covenants because court action is a form of state action.[95] Similarly, court action in private civil litigation is state action and thus any civil liability must comport with First Amendment standards.

---

92. Florida Star v. B.J.F., 491 U.S. 524 (1989).
93. Time, Inc. v. Hill, 385 U.S. 374 (1967).
94. Hustler Magazine v. Falwell, 485 U.S. 46 (1988).
95. The case is presented in Chapter 5.

PROHIBITIONS ON COMPENSATION

The Supreme Court has clearly indicated that another way in which the government can infringe freedom of speech is by prohibiting individuals from being paid for their expression. In Simon & Schuster v. Members of the New York State Crime Victims Board, 502 U.S. 105 (1991), referenced above, the Court declared unconstitutional a state law that prevented an accused or convicted criminal from profiting from selling the story of his or her crime to any media. The New York law did not prohibit any speech; it only prevented individuals from keeping profits from selling the tales of their criminal activity. Nonetheless, the Supreme Court found the law to violate the First Amendment. The Court said that "[a] statute is presumptively inconsistent with the First Amendment if it imposes a financial burden on speakers because of the content of their speech."

United States v. National Treasury Employees Union reaffirms that prohibitions on compensation for speech infringe the First Amendment.

UNITED STATES v. NATIONAL TREASURY EMPLOYEES UNION
513 U.S. 454 (1995)

Justice STEVENS delivered the opinion of the Court.

In 1989 Congress enacted a law that broadly prohibits federal employees from accepting any compensation for making speeches or writing articles. The prohibition applies even when neither the subject of the speech or article nor the person or group paying for it has any connection with the employee's official duties.

Federal employees who write for publication in their spare time have made significant contributions to the marketplace of ideas. They include literary giants like Nathaniel Hawthorne and Herman Melville, who were employed by the Customs Service; Walt Whitman, who worked for the Departments of Justice and Interior; and Bret Harte, an employee of the Mint.

Even though respondents work for the Government, they have not relinquished "the First Amendment rights they would otherwise enjoy as citizens to comment on matters of public interest." They seek compensation for their expressive activities in their capacity as citizens, not as Government employees. They claim their employment status has no more bearing on the quality or market value of their literary output than it did on that of Hawthorne or Melville. With few exceptions, the content of respondents' messages has nothing to do with their jobs and does not even arguably have any adverse impact on the efficiency of the offices in which they work. They do not address audiences composed of co-workers or supervisors; instead, they write or speak for segments of the general public. Neither the character of the authors, the subject matter of their expression, the effect of the content of their expression on their official duties, nor the kind of audiences they address has any relevance to their employment.

Although [the law] neither prohibits any speech nor discriminates among speakers based on the content or viewpoint of their messages, its prohibition on compensation unquestionably imposes a significant burden on expressive activity. Publishers compensate authors because compensation provides a significant incentive toward more expression. By denying respondents that incentive, the honoraria ban induces them to curtail their expression if they wish to continue working for the Government.

The ban imposes a far more significant burden on respondents than on the relatively small group of lawmakers whose past receipt of honoraria motivated its enactment. The absorbing and time-consuming responsibilities of legislators and policymaking executives leave them little opportunity for research or creative expression on subjects unrelated to their official responsibilities. Such officials often receive invitations to appear and talk about subjects related to their work because of their official identities. In contrast, invitations to rank-and-file employees usually depend only on the market value of their messages. The honoraria ban is unlikely to reduce significantly the number of appearances by high-ranking officials as long as travel expense reimbursement for the speaker and one relative is available as an alternative form of remuneration. In contrast, the denial of compensation for lower paid, nonpolicymaking employees will inevitably diminish their expressive output.

The large-scale disincentive to Government employees' expression also imposes a significant burden on the public's right to read and hear what the employees would otherwise have written and said. We have no way to measure the true cost of that burden, but we cannot ignore the risk that it might deprive us of the work of a future Melville or Hawthorne. The honoraria ban imposes the kind of burden that abridges speech under the First Amendment.

Chief Justice REHNQUIST, with whom Justice SCALIA and Justice THOMAS join, dissenting.

I believe that the Court's opinion is seriously flawed in two respects. First, its application of the First Amendment understates the weight that should be accorded to the governmental justifications for the honoraria ban and overstates the amount of speech that actually will be deterred. Second, its discussion of the impact of the statute that it strikes down is carefully limited to only a handful of the most appealing individual situations, but when it deals with the remedy it suddenly shifts gears and strikes down the statute as applied to the entire class of Executive Branch employees below grade GS-16. I therefore dissent.

The Court concedes that in light of the abuses of honoraria by its Members, Congress could reasonably assume that "payments of honoraria to judges or high-ranking officials in the Executive Branch might generate a similar appearance of improper influence," but it concludes that Congress could not extend this presumption to federal employees below grade GS-16. The theory underlying the Court's distinction — that federal employees below grade GS-16 have negligible power to confer favors on those who might pay to hear them speak or to read their articles — is seriously flawed. Tax examiners, bank examiners, enforcement officials, or any number of federal employees have substantial power to confer favors even though their compensation level is below grade GS-16.

I believe that a proper application of the [law] to this content-neutral restriction on the receipt of compensation compels the conclusion that the honoraria ban is consistent with the First Amendment.

COMPELLED SPEECH

The cases reviewed thus far concerning what constitutes an infringement of speech all have involved the government prohibiting or penalizing speech — criminally, civilly, or by withholding compensation. The government also can infringe the First Amendment by compelling speech. Just as there is a right to speak, so, it is clear, there is a right to be silent and refrain from speaking.

The classic case in this regard was West Virginia State Board of Education v. Barnette.

WEST VIRGINIA STATE BOARD OF EDUCATION v. BARNETTE
319 U.S. 624 (1943)

Justice JACKSON delivered the opinion of the Court.

The Board of Education on January 9, 1942, adopted a resolution ordering that the salute to the flag become "a regular part of the program of activities in the public schools," that all teachers and pupils "shall be required to participate in the salute honoring the Nation represented by the Flag; provided, however, that refusal to salute the Flag be regarded as an Act of insubordination, and shall be dealt with accordingly." What is now required is the "stiff-arm" salute, the saluter to keep the right hand raised with palm turned up while the following is repeated: "I pledge allegiance to the Flag of the United States of America and to the Republic for which it stands; one Nation, indivisible, with liberty and justice for all."

Failure to conform is "insubordination" dealt with by expulsion. Readmission is denied by statute until compliance. Meanwhile the expelled child is "unlawfully absent" and may be proceeded against as a delinquent. His parents or guardians are liable to prosecution, and if convicted are subject to fine not exceeding $50 and jail term not exceeding thirty days.

Appellees, citizens of the United States and of West Virginia, brought suit in the United States District Court for themselves and others similarly situated asking its injunction to restrain enforcement of these laws and regulations against Jehovah's Witnesses. The Witnesses' religious beliefs include a literal version of Exodus, Chapter 20, verses 4 and 5, which says: "Thou shalt not make unto thee any graven image, or any likeness of anything that is in heaven above, or that is in the earth beneath, or that is in the water under the earth; thou shalt not bow down thyself to them nor serve them." They consider that the flag is an "image" within this command. For this reason they refuse to salute it.

Children of this faith have been expelled from school and are threatened with exclusion for no other cause. Officials threaten to send them to reformatories maintained for criminally inclined juveniles. Parents of such children have been prosecuted and are threatened with prosecutions for causing delinquency.

There is no doubt that, in connection with the pledges, the flag salute is a form of utterance. Symbolism is a primitive but effective way of communicating ideas. The use of an emblem or flag to symbolize some system, idea, institution, or personality, is a short cut from mind to mind.

It is also to be noted that the compulsory flag salute and pledge requires affirmation of a belief and an attitude of mind. It is not clear whether the regulation contemplates that pupils forego any contrary convictions of their own and become unwilling converts to the prescribed ceremony or whether it will be acceptable if they simulate assent by words without belief and by a gesture barren of meaning. It is now a commonplace that censorship or suppression of expression of opinion is tolerated by our Constitution only when the expression presents a clear and present danger of action of a kind the State is empowered to prevent and punish. It would seem that involuntary affirmation could be commanded only on even more immediate and urgent grounds than silence. But here the power of compulsion is invoked without any allegation that remaining passive during a flag salute ritual creates a clear and present danger that would justify an effort even to muffle expression. To sustain the compulsory flag salute we are required to say that a Bill of Rights which guards the individual's right to speak his own mind, left it open to public authorities to compel him to utter what is not in his mind.

The Fourteenth Amendment, as now applied to the States, protects the citizen against the State itself and all of its creatures—Boards of Education not excepted. These have, of course, important, delicate, and highly discretionary functions, but none that they may not perform within the limits of the Bill of Rights. Such Boards are numerous and their territorial jurisdiction often small. But small and local authority may feel less sense of responsibility to the Constitution, and agencies of publicity may be less vigilent in calling it to account.

The very purpose of a Bill of Rights was to withdraw certain subjects from the vicissitudes of political controversy, to place them beyond the reach of majorities and officials and to establish them as legal principles to be applied by the courts. One's right to life, liberty, and property, to free speech, a free press, freedom of worship and assembly, and other fundamental rights may not be submitted to vote; they depend on the outcome of no elections.

The case is made difficult not because the principles of its decision are obscure but because the flag involved is our own. Nevertheless, we apply the limitations of the Constitution with no fear that freedom to be intellectually and spiritually diverse or even contrary will disintegrate the social organization. To believe that patriotism will not flourish if patriotic ceremonies are voluntary and spontaneous instead of a compulsory routine is to make an unflattering estimate of the appeal of our institutions to free minds. We can have intellectual individualism and the rich cultural diversities that we owe to exceptional minds only at the price of occasional eccentricity and abnormal attitudes. When they are so harmless to others or to the State as those we deal with here, the price is not too great. But freedom to differ is not limited to things that do not matter much. That would be a mere shadow of freedom. The test of its substance is the right to differ as to things that touch the heart of the existing order.

If there is any fixed star in our constitutional constellation, it is that no official, high or petty, can prescribe what shall be orthodox in politics, nationalism, religion, or other matters of opinion or force citizens to confess by word or act their faith therein. If there are any circumstances which permit an exception, they do not now occur to us. We think the action of the local authorities in compelling the flag salute and pledge transcends constitutional limitations on their power and invades the sphere of intellect and spirit which it is the purpose of the First Amendment to our Constitution to reserve from all official control.

Justice FRANKFURTER, dissenting.

One who belongs to the most vilified and persecuted minority in history is not likely to be insensible to the freedoms guaranteed by our Constitution. Were my purely personal attitude relevant I should whole-heartedly associate myself with the general libertarian views in the Court's opinion, representing as they do the thought and action of a lifetime. But as judges we are neither Jew nor Gentile, neither Catholic nor agnostic. We owe equal attachment to the Constitution and are equally bound by our judicial obligations whether we derive our citizenship from the earliest or the latest immigrants to these shores. As a member of this Court I am not justified in writing my private notions of policy into the Constitution, no matter how deeply I may cherish them or how mischievous I may deem their disregard. The duty of a judge who must decide which of two claims before the Court shall prevail, that of a State to enact and enforce laws within its general competence or that of an individual to refuse obedience because of the demands of his conscience, is not that of the ordinary person.

It can never be emphasized too much that one's own opinion about the wisdom or evil of a law should be excluded altogether when one is doing one's duty on the bench. The only opinion of our own even looking in that direction that is material is our opinion whether legislators could in reason have enacted such a law. In the light of all the circumstances, including the history of this question in this Court, it would require more daring than I possess to deny that reasonable legislators could have taken the action which is before us for review.

Most unwillingly, therefore, I must differ from my brethren with regard to legislation like this. I cannot bring my mind to believe that the "liberty" secured by the Due Process Clause gives this Court authority to deny to the State of West Virginia the attainment of that which we all recognize as a legitimate legislative end, namely, the promotion of good citizenship, by employment of the means here chosen.

The Court followed this principle in other cases, such as in Wooley v. Maynard, 430 U.S. 705 (1977), where it ruled that an individual could not be punished for blocking out the portion of his automobile license plate that contained the New Hampshire state motto, "Live Free or Die." The Court said that "the right of freedom of thought protected by the First Amendment . . . includes both the right to speak freely and the right to refrain from speaking at all. The right to speak and the right to refrain from speaking are complementary components of the broader concept of 'individual freedom of mind.'"

But in other cases, the Court has been more willing to allow compelled speech. In Johannes v. Livestock Marketing Assn., 544 U.S. 550 (2005), the Court upheld a $1 per head assessment on livestock to fund a generic ad campaign encouraging beef consumption. The Court stressed that the government may impose taxes, including on specific items, to engage in speech. The Court noted that livestock producers were not themselves forced to engage in any speech.

More dramatically, in Rumsfeld v. Forum for Academic & Institutional Rights, the Court upheld a provision of federal law that requires that law schools allow the military to recruit on their premises.

RUMSFELD v. FORUM FOR ACADEMIC &
INSTITUTIONAL RIGHTS, INC.

547 U.S. 47 (2006)

Chief Justice ROBERTS delivered the opinion of the Court.

When law schools began restricting the access of military recruiters to their students because of disagreement with the Government's policy on homosexuals in the military, Congress responded by enacting the Solomon Amendment. See 10 U.S.C.A. §983. That provision specifies that if any part of an institution of higher education denies military recruiters access equal to that provided other recruiters, the entire institution would lose certain federal funds. The law schools responded by suing, alleging that the Solomon Amendment infringed their First Amendment freedoms of speech and association. The District Court disagreed but was reversed by a divided panel of the Court of Appeals for the Third Circuit, which ordered the District Court to enter a preliminary injunction against enforcement of the Solomon Amendment.

I

Respondent Forum for Academic and Institutional Rights, Inc. (FAIR), is an association of law schools and law faculties. They would like to restrict military recruiting on their campuses because they object to the policy Congress has adopted with respect to homosexuals in the military. See 10 U.S.C. §654.[96] The Solomon Amendment, however, forces institutions to choose between enforcing their nondiscrimination policy against military recruiters in this way and continuing to receive specified federal funding.

II

The Solomon Amendment denies federal funding to an institution of higher education that "has a policy or practice . . . that either prohibits, or in effect prevents" the military "from gaining access to campuses, or access to students . . . on campuses, for purposes of military recruiting in a manner that is at least equal in quality and scope to the access to campuses and to students that is provided to any other employer." 10 U.S.C.A. §983(b). The statute provides an exception for an institution with "a longstanding policy of pacifism based on historical religious affiliation." The Government and FAIR agree on what this statute requires: In order for a law school and its university to receive federal funding, the law school must offer military recruiters the same access to its campus and students that it provides to the nonmilitary recruiter receiving the most favorable access.

---

96. Under this policy, a person generally may not serve in the Armed Forces if he has engaged in homosexual acts, stated that he is a homosexual, or married a person of the same sex. Respondents do not challenge that policy in this litigation. [Footnote by the Court.]

III

The Constitution grants Congress the power to "provide for the common Defence," "[t]o raise and support Armies," and "[t]o provide and maintain a Navy." Art. I, §8, cls. 1, 12-13. Congress' power in this area "is broad and sweeping," and there is no dispute in this case that it includes the authority to require campus access for military recruiters. That is, of course, unless Congress exceeds constitutional limitations on its power in enacting such legislation. But the fact that legislation that raises armies is subject to First Amendment constraints does not mean that we ignore the purpose of this legislation when determining its constitutionality; as we [have] recognized "judicial deference . . . is at its apogee" when Congress legislates under its authority to raise and support armies.

Although Congress has broad authority to legislate on matters of military recruiting, it nonetheless chose to secure campus access for military recruiters indirectly, through its Spending Clause power. The Solomon Amendment gives universities a choice: Either allow military recruiters the same access to students afforded any other recruiter or forgo certain federal funds. Congress' decision to proceed indirectly does not reduce the deference given to Congress in the area of military affairs. Congress' choice to promote its goal by creating a funding condition deserves at least as deferential treatment as if Congress had imposed a mandate on universities.

This case does not require us to determine when a condition placed on university funding goes beyond the "reasonable" choice and becomes an unconstitutional condition. It is clear that a funding condition cannot be unconstitutional if it could be constitutionally imposed directly. Because the First Amendment would not prevent Congress from directly imposing the Solomon Amendment's access requirement, the statute does not place an unconstitutional condition on the receipt of federal funds.

A

The Solomon Amendment neither limits what law schools may say nor requires them to say anything. Law schools remain free under the statute to express whatever views they may have on the military's congressionally mandated employment policy, all the while retaining eligibility for federal funds. As a general matter, the Solomon Amendment regulates conduct, not speech. It affects what law schools must do — afford equal access to military recruiters — not what they may or may not say.

Nevertheless, the Third Circuit concluded that the Solomon Amendment violates law schools' freedom of speech in a number of ways. First, in assisting military recruiters, law schools provide some services, such as sending e-mails and distributing flyers, that clearly involve speech. The Court of Appeals held that in supplying these services law schools are unconstitutionally compelled to speak the Government's message. Second, military recruiters are, to some extent, speaking while they are on campus. The Court of Appeals held that, by forcing law schools to permit the military on campus to express its message, the Solomon Amendment unconstitutionally requires law schools to host or accommodate the military's speech. Third, although the Court of Appeals thought that the Solomon Amendment regulated speech, it held in the alternative that, if the statute regulates conduct, this conduct is expressive and regulating it unconstitutionally infringes law schools' right to engage in expressive conduct. We consider each issue in turn.

1

Some of this Court's leading First Amendment precedents have established the principle that freedom of speech prohibits the government from telling people what they must say. In *West Virginia Bd. of Ed. v. Barnette* (1943), we held unconstitutional a state law requiring schoolchildren to recite the Pledge of Allegiance and to salute the flag. And in *Wooley v. Maynard* (1977), we held unconstitutional another that required New Hampshire motorists to display the state motto — "Live Free or Die" — on their license plates.

The Solomon Amendment does not require any similar expression by law schools. Nonetheless, recruiting assistance provided by the schools often includes elements of speech. For example, schools may send e-mails or post notices on bulletin boards on an employer's behalf. Law schools offering such services to other recruiters must also send e-mails and post notices on behalf of the military to comply with the Solomon Amendment. As FAIR points out, these compelled statements of fact ("The U.S. Army recruiter will meet interested students in Room 123 at 11 a.m."), like compelled statements of opinion, are subject to First Amendment scrutiny.

This sort of recruiting assistance, however, is a far cry from the compelled speech in *Barnette* and *Wooley*. The Solomon Amendment, unlike the laws at issue in those cases, does not dictate the content of the speech at all, which is only "compelled" if, and to the extent, the school provides such speech for other recruiters. There is nothing in this case approaching a government-mandated pledge or motto that the school must endorse.

The compelled speech to which the law schools point is plainly incidental to the Solomon Amendment's regulation of conduct, and "it has never been deemed an abridgment of freedom of speech or press to make a course of conduct illegal merely because the conduct was in part initiated, evidenced, or carried out by means of language, either spoken, written, or printed." Congress, for example, can prohibit employers from discriminating in hiring on the basis of race. The fact that this will require an employer to take down a sign reading "White Applicants Only" hardly means that the law should be analyzed as one regulating the employer's speech rather than conduct. Compelling a law school that sends scheduling e-mails for other recruiters to send one for a military recruiter is simply not the same as forcing a student to pledge allegiance, or forcing a Jehovah's Witness to display the motto "Live Free or Die," and it trivializes the freedom protected in *Barnette* and *Wooley* to suggest that it is.

2

Our compelled-speech cases are not limited to the situation in which an individual must personally speak the government's message. We have also in a number of instances limited the government's ability to force one speaker to host or accommodate another speaker's message. See *Hurley v. Irish-American Gay, Lesbian and Bisexual Group of Boston, Inc.* (1995) (state law cannot require a parade to include a group whose message the parade's organizer does not wish to send); *Pacific Gas & Elec. Co. v. Public Util. Comm'n of Cal.* (1986) (state agency cannot require a utility company to include a third-party newsletter in its billing envelope); *Miami Herald Publishing Co. v. Tornillo* (right-of-reply statute violates editors' right to determine the content of their newspapers). Relying on these precedents, the Third Circuit concluded that the Solomon Amendment unconstitutionally compels law schools to accommodate the military's message "[b]y requiring schools to include military recruiters in the interviews and recruiting receptions the schools arrange."

The compelled-speech violation in each of our prior cases, however, resulted from the fact that the complaining speaker's own message was affected by the speech it was forced to accommodate. The expressive nature of a parade was central to our holding in *Hurley*. We concluded that because "every participating unit affects the message conveyed by the [parade's] private organizers," a law dictating that a particular group must be included in the parade "alter[s] the expressive content of th[e] parade." As a result, we held that the State's public accommodation law, as applied to a private parade, "violates the fundamental rule of protection under the First Amendment, that a speaker has the autonomy to choose the content of his own message."

In this case, accommodating the military's message does not affect the law schools' speech, because the schools are not speaking when they host interviews and recruiting receptions. Unlike a parade organizer's choice of parade contingents, a law school's decision to allow recruiters on campus is not inherently expressive. Law schools facilitate recruiting to assist their students in obtaining jobs. A law school's recruiting services lack the expressive quality of a parade, a newsletter, or the editorial page of a newspaper; its accommodation of a military recruiter's message is not compelled speech because the accommodation does not sufficiently interfere with any message of the school.

The schools respond that if they treat military and nonmilitary recruiters alike in order to comply with the Solomon Amendment, they could be viewed as sending the message that they see nothing wrong with the military's policies, when they do. We rejected a similar argument in *PruneYard Shopping Center v. Robins* (1980). In that case, we upheld a state law requiring a shopping center owner to allow certain expressive activities by others on its property. We explained that there was little likelihood that the views of those engaging in the expressive activities would be identified with the owner, who remained free to disassociate himself from those views and who was "not . . . being compelled to affirm [a] belief in any governmentally prescribed position or view."

The same is true here. Nothing about recruiting suggests that law schools agree with any speech by recruiters, and nothing in the Solomon Amendment restricts what the law schools may say about the military's policies.

3

Having rejected the view that the Solomon Amendment impermissibly regulates speech, we must still consider whether the expressive nature of the conduct regulated by the statute brings that conduct within the First Amendment's protection. [W]e have extended First Amendment protection only to conduct that is inherently expressive. In *Texas v. Johnson* (1989), for example, we held that burning the American flag was sufficiently expressive to warrant First Amendment protection.

Unlike flag burning, the conduct regulated by the Solomon Amendment is not inherently expressive. Prior to the adoption of the Solomon Amendment's equal-access requirement, law schools "expressed" their disagreement with the military by treating military recruiters differently from other recruiters. But these actions were expressive only because the law schools accompanied their conduct with speech explaining it. For example, the point of requiring military interviews to be conducted on the undergraduate campus is not "overwhelmingly apparent." An observer who sees military recruiters interviewing away from the law school has no way of knowing whether the law school is expressing its disapproval of the military, all the law school's interview rooms are full, or the military recruiters decided for reasons of their own that they would rather interview someplace else. The expressive component of a law school's actions is not created by the conduct itself but by the speech that accompanies it. The fact that such explanatory speech is necessary is strong evidence that the conduct at issue here is not so inherently expressive that it warrants protection. If combining speech and conduct were enough to create expressive conduct, a regulated party could always transform conduct into "speech" simply by talking about it.

B

The Solomon Amendment does not violate law schools' freedom of speech, but the First Amendment's protection extends beyond the right to speak. We have recognized a First Amendment right to associate for the purpose of speaking, which we have termed a "right of expressive association." See, e.g., *Boy Scouts of America v. Dale* (2000). The reason we have extended First Amendment protection in this way is clear: The right to speak is often exercised most effectively by combining one's voice with the voices of others. If the government were free to restrict individuals' ability to join together and speak, it could essentially silence views that the First Amendment is intended to protect.

FAIR argues that the Solomon Amendment violates law schools' freedom of expressive association. According to FAIR, law schools' ability to express their message that discrimination on the basis of sexual orientation is wrong is significantly affected by the presence of military recruiters on campus and the schools' obligation to assist them.

The Solomon Amendment, however, does not similarly affect a law school's associational rights. To comply with the statute, law schools must allow military recruiters on campus and assist them in whatever way the school chooses to assist other employers. Law schools therefore "associate" with military recruiters in the sense that they interact with them. But recruiters are not part of the law school. Recruiters are, by definition, outsiders who come onto campus for the limited purpose of trying to hire students—not to become members of the school's expressive association. This distinction is critical. Unlike the public accommodations law in *Dale*, the Solomon Amendment does not force a law school "to accept members it does not desire." The law schools say that allowing military recruiters equal access impairs their own expression by requiring them to associate with the recruiters, but just as saying conduct is undertaken for expressive purposes cannot make it symbolic speech, so too a speaker cannot "erect a shield" against laws requiring access "simply by asserting" that mere association "would impair its message."

The Solomon Amendment has no similar effect on a law school's associational rights. Students and faculty are free to associate to voice their disapproval of the military's message; nothing about the statute affects the composition of the group by making group membership less desirable. The Solomon Amendment therefore does not violate a law school's First Amendment rights. A military recruiter's mere presence on campus does not violate a law school's right to associate, regardless of how repugnant the law school considers the recruiter's message.

The right to not speak includes a right to not disclose one's identity when speaking. In Talley v. California, 362 U.S. 60 (1960), the Supreme Court declared unconstitutional a ban on anonymous handbills. The Court observed that the "obnoxious press licensing law of England, which was also enforced on the Colonies was due in part to the knowledge that exposure of the names of printers, writers and distributors would lessen the circulation of literature critical of the government." Justice Black, writing for the Court, said that "[p]ersecuted groups and sects from time to time throughout history have been able to criticize oppressive practices and laws either anonymously or not at all."

In McIntyre v. Ohio Elections Commn., the Court declared unconstitutional a law that prohibited the distribution of anonymous campaign literature.

McINTYRE v. OHIO ELECTIONS COMMISSION
514 U.S. 334 (1995)

Justice STEVENS delivered the opinion of the Court.

The question presented is whether an Ohio statute that prohibits the distribution of anonymous campaign literature is a "law . . . abridging the freedom of speech" within the meaning of the First Amendment.

I

On April 27, 1988, Margaret McIntyre distributed leaflets to persons attending a public meeting at the Blendon Middle School in Westerville, Ohio. At this meeting, the superintendent of schools planned to discuss an imminent referendum on a proposed school tax levy. The leaflets expressed Mrs. McIntyre's opposition to the levy. There is no suggestion that the text of her message was false, misleading, or libelous. She had composed and printed it on her home computer and had paid a professional printer to make additional copies. Some of the handbills identified her as the author; others merely purported to express the views of "CONCERNED PARENTS AND TAX PAYERS." Except for the help provided by her son and a friend, who placed some of the leaflets on car windshields in the school parking lot, Mrs. McIntyre acted independently. While Mrs. McIntyre distributed her handbills, an official of the school district, who supported the tax proposal, advised her that the unsigned leaflets did not conform to the Ohio election laws. Undeterred, Mrs. McIntyre appeared at another meeting on the next evening and handed out more of the handbills.

[T]he same school official filed a complaint with the Ohio Elections Commission charging that Mrs. McIntyre's distribution of unsigned leaflets violated the Ohio Code [which prohibits the distribution of anonymous material in connection with any election]. The commission agreed and imposed a fine of $100. [The Ohio law] provides: "No person shall write, print, post, or distribute, or cause to be written, printed, posted, or distributed, a notice, placard, dodger, advertisement, sample ballot, or any other form of general publication which is designed to promote the nomination or election or defeat of a candidate, or to promote the adoption or defeat of any issue, or to influence the voters in any election . . . unless there appears on such form of publication in a conspicuous place or is contained within said statement the name and residence or business address of the chairman, treasurer, or secretary of the organization issuing the same, or the person who issues, makes, or is responsible therefor."

II

"Anonymous pamphlets, leaflets, brochures and even books have played an important role in the progress of mankind." Talley v. California. Great works of literature have frequently been produced by authors writing under assumed names.[97] Despite readers' curiosity and the public's interest in identifying the creator of a work of art, an author generally is free to decide whether or not to disclose his or her true identity. The decision in favor of anonymity may be motivated by fear of economic or official retaliation, by concern about social ostracism, or merely by a desire to preserve as much of one's privacy as possible. Whatever the motivation may be, at least in the field of literary endeavor, the interest in having anonymous works enter the marketplace of ideas unquestionably outweighs any public interest in requiring disclosure as a condition of entry. Accordingly, an author's decision to remain anonymous, like other decisions concerning omissions or additions to the content of a publication, is an aspect of the freedom of speech protected by the First Amendment.

The freedom to publish anonymously extends beyond the literary realm. On occasion, quite apart from any threat of persecution, an advocate may believe her ideas will be more persuasive if her readers are unaware of her identity. Anonymity thereby provides a way for a writer who may be personally unpopular to ensure that readers will not prejudge her message simply because they do not like its proponent. Thus, even in the field of political rhetoric, where "the identity of the speaker is an important component of many attempts to persuade," the most effective advocates have sometimes opted for anonymity.

Indeed, the speech in which Mrs. McIntyre engaged — handing out leaflets in the advocacy of a politically controversial viewpoint — is the essence of First Amendment expression. That this advocacy occurred in the heat of a controversial referendum vote only strengthens the protection afforded to Mrs. McIntyre's expression: Urgent, important, and effective speech can be no less protected than impotent speech, lest the right to speak be relegated to those instances when it is least needed. No form of speech is entitled to greater constitutional protection than Mrs. McIntyre's.

97. American names such as Mark Twain (Samuel Langhorne Clemens) and O. Henry (William Sydney Porter) come readily to mind. Benjamin Franklin employed numerous different pseudonyms. Distinguished French authors such as Voltaire (Francois Marie Arouet) and George Sand (Amandine Aurore Lucie Dupin), and British authors such as George Eliot (Mary Ann Evans), Charles Lamb (sometimes wrote as "Elia"), and Charles Dickens (sometimes wrote as "Boz"), also published under assumed names. Indeed, some believe the works of Shakespeare were actually written by the Earl of Oxford rather than by William Shakespeare of Stratford-on-Avon. [Footnote by the Court.]

When a law burdens core political speech, we apply "exacting scrutiny," and we uphold the restriction only if it is narrowly tailored to serve an overriding state interest.

IV

Nevertheless, the State argues that, even under the strictest standard of review, the disclosure requirement is justified by two important and legitimate state interests. Ohio judges its interest in preventing fraudulent and libelous statements and its interest in providing the electorate with relevant information to be sufficiently compelling to justify the anonymous speech ban. These two interests necessarily overlap to some extent, but it is useful to discuss them separately.

Insofar as the interest in informing the electorate means nothing more than the provision of additional information that may either buttress or undermine the argument in a document, we think the identity of the speaker is no different from other components of the document's content that the author is free to include or exclude.

The state interest in preventing fraud and libel stands on a different footing. We agree with Ohio's submission that this interest carries special weight during election campaigns when false statements, if credited, may have serious adverse consequences for the public at large.

Ohio's prohibition of anonymous leaflets plainly is not its principal weapon against fraud. Rather, it serves as an aid to enforcement of the specific prohibitions and as a deterrent to the making of false statements by unscrupulous prevaricators. As this case demonstrates, the prohibition encompasses documents that are not even arguably false or misleading. It applies not only to the activities of candidates and their organized supporters, but also to individuals acting independently and using only their own modest resources. It applies not only to elections of public officers, but also to ballot issues that present neither a substantial risk of libel nor any potential appearance of corrupt advantage. It applies not only to leaflets distributed on the eve of an election, when the opportunity for reply is limited, but also to those distributed months in advance. It applies no matter what the character or strength of the author's interest in anonymity. Moreover, as this case also demonstrates, the absence of the author's name on a document does not necessarily protect either that person or a distributor of a forbidden document from being held responsible for compliance with the Election Code. Nor has the State explained why it can more easily enforce the direct bans on disseminating false documents against anonymous authors and distributors than against wrongdoers who might use false names and addresses in an attempt to avoid detection. We recognize that a State's enforcement interest might justify a more limited identification requirement, but Ohio has shown scant cause for inhibiting the leafletting at issue here.

VI

Under our Constitution, anonymous pamphleteering is not a pernicious, fraudulent practice, but an honorable tradition of advocacy and of dissent. Anonymity is a shield from the tyranny of the majority. It thus exemplifies the purpose behind the Bill of Rights, and of the First Amendment in particular: to protect unpopular individuals from retaliation — and their ideas from suppression — at the hand of an intolerant society. The right to remain anonymous may be abused when it shields fraudulent conduct. But political speech by its nature will sometimes have unpalatable consequences, and, in general, our society accords greater weight to the value of free speech than to the dangers of its misuse.

Justice THOMAS, concurring in the judgment.

I agree with the majority's conclusion that Ohio's election law is inconsistent with the First Amendment. I would apply, however, a different methodology to this case. Instead of asking whether "an honorable tradition" of anonymous speech has existed throughout American history, or what the "value" of anonymous speech might be, we should determine whether the phrase "freedom of speech, or of the press," as originally understood, protected anonymous political leafletting. I believe that it did.

When interpreting the Free Speech and Press Clauses, we must be guided by their original meaning, for "[t]he Constitution is a written instrument. As such its meaning does not alter. That which it meant when adopted, it means now." South Carolina v. United States (1905). We have long recognized that the meaning of the Constitution "must necessarily depend on the words of the constitution [and] the meaning and intention of the convention which framed and proposed it for adoption and ratification to the conventions . . . in the several states." Rhode Island v. Massachusetts (1838). We should seek the original understanding when we interpret the Speech and Press Clauses. When the framers did not discuss the precise question at issue, we have turned to "what history reveals was the contemporaneous understanding of [the Establishment Clause's] guarantees."

Unfortunately, we have no record of discussions of anonymous political expression either in the First Congress, which drafted the Bill of Rights, or in the state ratifying conventions. Thus, our analysis must focus on the practices and beliefs held by the Founders concerning anonymous political articles and pamphlets. There is little doubt that the framers engaged in anonymous political writing. The essays in the Federalist Papers, published under the pseudonym of "Publius," are only the most famous example of the outpouring of anonymous political writing that occurred during the ratification of the Constitution.

[T]he historical evidence indicates that Founding-era Americans opposed attempts to require that anonymous authors reveal their identities on the ground that forced disclosure violated the "freedom of the press." For example, the earliest and most famous American experience with freedom of the press, the 1735 *Zenger* trial, centered around anonymous political pamphlets. The case involved a printer, John Peter Zenger, who refused to reveal the anonymous authors of published attacks on the Crown Governor of New York. When the Governor and his council could not discover the identity of the authors, they prosecuted Zenger himself for seditious libel.

This evidence leads me to agree with the majority's result, but not its reasoning. The majority fails to seek the original understanding of the First Amendment. I cannot join the majority's analysis because it deviates from our settled approach to interpreting the Constitution and because it superimposes its modern theories concerning expression upon the constitutional text.

Justice SCALIA, with whom the Chief Justice joins, dissenting.

At a time when both political branches of Government and both political parties reflect a popular desire to leave more decisionmaking authority to the States, today's decision moves in the opposite direction, adding to the legacy of inflexible central mandates (irrevocable even by Congress) imposed by this Court's constitutional jurisprudence. [T]he Court invalidates a species of protection for the election process that exists, in a variety of forms, in every State except California, and that has a pedigree dating back to the end of the 19th century. Preferring the views of the English utilitarian philosopher John Stuart Mill to the considered judgment of the American people's elected representatives from coast to coast, the Court discovers a hitherto unknown right-to-be-unknown while engaging in electoral politics. I dissent from this imposition of free-speech imperatives that are demonstrably not those of the American people today, and that there is inadequate reason to believe were those of the society that begat the First Amendment or the Fourteenth.

I do not know where the Court derives its perception that "anonymous pamphleteering is not a pernicious, fraudulent practice, but an honorable tradition of advocacy and of dissent." I can imagine no reason why an anonymous leaflet is any more honorable, as a general matter, than an anonymous phone call or an anonymous letter. It facilitates wrong by eliminating accountability, which is ordinarily the very purpose of the anonymity. There are of course exceptions, and where anonymity is needed to avoid "threats, harassment, or reprisals" the First Amendment will require an exemption from the Ohio law. But to strike down the Ohio law in its general application — and similar laws of 49 other States and the Federal Government — on the ground that all anonymous communication is in our society traditionally sacrosanct, seems to me a distortion of the past that will lead to a coarsening of the future. I respectfully dissent.

Similarly, in Buckley v. American Constitutional Law Foundation, Inc., 525 U.S. 182 (1999), the Court invalidated a law that regulated those gathering signatures for ballot initiatives in Colorado and imposed (1) the requirement that they wear an identification badge bearing the circulator's name and (2) the requirement that proponents of an initiative report the names and addresses of all paid circulators and the amount paid to each circulator.

The Court said that "the restraint on speech in this case is more severe than was the restraint in *McIntyre.* Petition circulation is the less fleeting encounter, for the circulator must endeavor to persuade electors to sign the petition. The injury to speech is heightened for the petition circulator because the badge requirement compels personal name identification at the precise moment when the circulator's interest in anonymity is greatest."

But in a more recent case, John Doe No. 1 v. Reed, 130 S. Ct. 2811 (2010), the Court held that it does not inherently violate the First Amendment for a state to disclose who signed petitions in support of a referendum. The Washington state legislature adopted a law expanding benefits for domestic partners. The process of qualifying a referendum for the ballot requires gathering a specified number of signatures, and individuals must disclose their names and addresses.

A request was made under the Washington Public Records Act for the names and addresses of those who signed the petitions.

The Supreme Court focused solely on whether disclosure inherently would violate the First Amendment. The Court, in an opinion by Chief Justice Roberts, recognized that disclosure burdens freedom of speech and said, "We have a series of precedents considering First Amendment challenges to disclosure requirements in the electoral context. These precedents have reviewed such challenges under what has been termed 'exacting scrutiny.' That standard 'requires a "substantial relation" between the disclosure requirement and a "sufficiently important" governmental interest.' To withstand this scrutiny, 'the strength of the governmental interest must reflect the seriousness of the actual burden on First Amendment rights.'"

The Court found that the government's interest in "(1) preserving the integrity of the electoral process by combating fraud, detecting invalid signatures, and fostering government transparency and accountability" was sufficient to "to justify the burdens of compelled disclosure under the PRA on First Amendment rights." The Court explained, "Public disclosure thus helps ensure that the only signatures counted are those that should be, and that the only referenda placed on the ballot are those that garner enough valid signatures. Public disclosure also promotes transparency and accountability in the electoral process to an extent other measures cannot. In light of the foregoing, we reject plaintiffs' argument and conclude that public disclosure of referendum petitions in general is substantially related to the important interest of preserving the integrity of the electoral process." The Court left open the possibility that there could be a challenge in a particular case, including this one, that disclosure would so burden speech (i.e., signing petitions) as to violate the First Amendment, but it concluded that in general disclosing the signers of petitions does not infringe freedom of speech.

UNCONSTITUTIONAL CONDITIONS

The unconstitutional condition doctrine is the principle that the government cannot condition a benefit on the requirement that a person forgo a constitutional right. The corollary is that the "government may not deny a benefit to a person because he exercises a constitutional right."[98] Unfortunately, the Supreme Court's decisions in this area appear quite inconsistent in the application of the doctrine. In reading the cases that have applied and that have refused to apply the unconstitutional condition doctrine, it is important to consider whether there is a consistent principle being followed.

Speiser v. Randall is a classic example of the application of the unconstitutional condition doctrine.

SPEISER v. RANDALL, 357 U.S. 513 (1958): Justice BRENNAN delivered the opinion of the Court.

The appellants are honorably discharged veterans of World War II who claimed the veterans' property-tax exemption provided by the California Con-

---

98. Regan v. Taxation with Representation of Washington, 461 U.S. 540, 545 (1983), quoting Perry v. Sindermann, 408 U.S. 593, 597 (1972).

stitution. Under California law applicants for such exemption must annually complete a standard form of application and file it with the local assessor. The form was revised in 1954 to add an oath by the applicant: "I do not advocate the overthrow of the Government of the United States or of the State of California by force or violence or other unlawful means, nor advocate the support of a foreign Government against the United States in event of hostilities." Each refused to subscribe [to] the oath and struck it from the form which he executed and filed for the tax year 1954-1955. Each contended that the exaction of the oath as a condition of obtaining a tax exemption was forbidden by the Federal Constitution. The respective assessors denied the exemption solely for the refusal to execute the oath.

To deny an exemption to claimants who engage in certain forms of speech is in effect to penalize them for such speech. Its deterrent effect is the same as if the State were to fine them for this speech. The appellees are plainly mistaken in their argument that, because a tax exemption is a "privilege" or "bounty," its denial may not infringe speech. So here, the denial of a tax exemption for engaging in certain speech necessarily will have the effect of coercing the claimants to refrain from the proscribed speech.

The doctrine was followed in Federal Communications Commn. v. League of Women Voters of California, 468 U.S. 364 (1984). The Supreme Court declared unconstitutional a federal statute that prohibited any noncommercial educational broadcasting station that received a grant from the Corporation for Public Broadcasting from engaging in editorializing. The Court said that the government could not condition funds on a requirement that the stations relinquish their right to editorialize.

Yet other cases have allowed the government to condition a benefit on individuals' forgoing their First Amendment rights. In Regan v. Taxation with Representation of Washington, 461 U.S. 540 (1983), the Court upheld a provision of the federal tax law that conditioned tax-exempt status on the requirement that the organization not participate in lobbying or partisan political activities. The Court said, "Congress has not infringed any First Amendment rights or regulated any First Amendment activity. Congress has simply chosen not to pay for TWR's lobbying." The Court said that it found "no indication that the statute was intended to suppress any ideas or any demonstration that it has had that effect." The *Regan* Court concluded, "We have held in several contexts that a legislature's decision not to subsidize the exercise of a fundamental right does not infringe the right, and thus is not subject to strict scrutiny." In other words, the Court rejected the unconstitutional conditions argument even though the government was conditioning a very valuable tax benefit on the requirement that the recipient forgo engaging in First Amendment protected speech.

Two cases applied the unconstitutional conditions doctrine and came to opposite conclusions. In Rust v. Sullivan, the Court upheld a federal law restricting recipients of federal funds from engaging in abortion-related activities. In Legal Services Corp. v. Velazquez, the Court invalidated a restriction on federal legal services funds recipients challenge of welfare laws. In reading these cases, consider whether there is a meaningful distinction between them.

RUST v. SULLIVAN
500 U.S. 173 (1991)

Chief Justice REHNQUIST delivered the opinion of the Court.

These cases concern a facial challenge to Department of Health and Human Services (HHS) regulations which limit the ability of Title X fund recipients to engage in abortion-related activities.

I

In 1970, Congress enacted Title X of the Public Health Service Act (Act), which provides federal funding for family-planning services. The Act authorizes the Secretary to "make grants to and enter into contracts with public or nonprofit private entities to assist in the establishment and operation of voluntary family planning projects which shall offer a broad range of acceptable and effective family planning methods and services." Grants and contracts under Title X must "be made in accordance with such regulations as the Secretary may promulgate." Section 1008 of the Act, however, provides that "[n]one of the funds appropriated under this subchapter shall be used in programs where abortion is a method of family planning." That restriction was intended to ensure that Title X funds would "be used only to support preventive family planning services, population research, infertility services, and other related medical, informational, and educational activities."

In 1988, the Secretary promulgated new regulations designed to provide "'clear and operational guidance' to grantees about how to preserve the distinction between Title X programs and abortion as a method of family planning." The regulations attach three principal conditions on the grant of federal funds for Title X projects. First, the regulations specify that a "Title X project may not provide counseling concerning the use of abortion as a method of family planning or provide referral for abortion as a method of family planning." The Title X project is expressly prohibited from referring a pregnant woman to an abortion provider, even upon specific request. One permissible response to such an inquiry is that "the project does not consider abortion an appropriate method of family planning and therefore does not counsel or refer for abortion."

Second, the regulations broadly prohibit a Title X project from engaging in activities that "encourage, promote or advocate abortion as a method of family planning." Forbidden activities include lobbying for legislation that would increase the availability of abortion as a method of family planning, developing or disseminating materials advocating abortion as a method of family planning, providing speakers to promote abortion as a method of family planning, using legal action to make abortion available in any way as a method of family planning, and paying dues to any group that advocates abortion as a method of family planning as a substantial part of its activities.

Third, the regulations require that Title X projects be organized so that they are "physically and financially separate" from prohibited abortion activities. To be deemed physically and financially separate, "a Title X project must have an objective integrity and independence from prohibited activities. Mere bookkeeping separation of Title X funds from other monies is not sufficient."

II

Petitioners contend that the regulations violate the First Amendment by impermissibly discriminating based on viewpoint because they prohibit "all discussion about abortion as a lawful option—including counseling, referral, and the provision of neutral and accurate information about ending a pregnancy—while compelling the clinic or counselor to provide information that promotes continuing a pregnancy to term." They assert that the regulations violate the "free speech rights of private health care organizations that receive Title X funds, of their staff, and of their patients" by impermissibly imposing "viewpoint-discriminatory conditions on government subsidies" and thus "penaliz[e] speech funded with non-Title X monies." Because "Title X continues to fund speech ancillary to pregnancy testing in a manner that is not evenhanded with respect to views and information about abortion, it invidiously discriminates on the basis of viewpoint."

There is no question but that the statutory prohibition is constitutional. In Maher v. Roe (1977), we upheld a state welfare regulation under which Medicaid recipients received payments for services related to childbirth, but not for nontherapeutic abortions. The Court rejected the claim that this unequal subsidization worked a violation of the Constitution. We held that the government may "make a value judgment favoring childbirth over abortion, and . . . implement that judgment by the allocation of public funds."

The Government can, without violating the Constitution, selectively fund a program to encourage certain activities it believes to be in the public interest, without at the same time funding an alternative program which seeks to deal with the problem in another way. In so doing, the Government has not discriminated on the basis of viewpoint; it has merely chosen to fund one activity to the exclusion of the other. "[A] legislature's decision not to subsidize the exercise of a fundamental right does not infringe the right." A refusal to fund protected activity, without more, cannot be equated with the imposition of a "penalty" on that activity. "There is a basic difference between direct state interference with a protected activity and state encouragement of an alternative activity consonant with legislative policy."

The challenged regulations implement the statutory prohibition by prohibiting counseling, referral, and the provision of information regarding abortion as a method of family planning. They are designed to ensure that the limits of the federal program are observed. The Title X program is designed not for prenatal care, but to encourage family planning. A doctor who wished to offer prenatal care to a project patient who became pregnant could properly be prohibited from doing so because such service is outside the scope of the federally funded program. The regulations prohibiting abortion counseling and referral are of the same ilk; "no funds appropriated for the project may be used in programs where abortion is a method of family planning," and a doctor employed by the project may be prohibited in the course of his project duties from counseling abortion or referring for abortion. This is not a case of the Government "suppressing a dangerous idea," but of a prohibition on a project grantee or its employees from engaging in activities outside of the project's scope.

To hold that the Government unconstitutionally discriminates on the basis of viewpoint when it chooses to fund a program dedicated to advance certain permissible goals, because the program in advancing those goals necessarily discourages alternative goals, would render numerous Government programs constitutionally suspect. When Congress established a National Endowment for Democracy to encourage other countries to adopt democratic principles, it was not constitutionally required to fund a program to encourage competing lines of political philosophy such as communism and fascism. Petitioners' assertions ultimately boil down to the position that if the government chooses to subsidize one protected right, it must subsidize analogous counterpart rights. But the Court has soundly rejected that proposition. Within far broader limits than petitioners are willing to concede, when the Government appropriates public funds to establish a program it is entitled to define the limits of that program.

Petitioners also contend that the restrictions on the subsidization of abortion-related speech contained in the regulations are impermissible because they condition the receipt of a benefit, in these cases Title X funding, on the relinquishment of a constitutional right, the right to engage in abortion advocacy and counseling. Petitioners' reliance on these cases is unavailing, however, because here the Government is not denying a benefit to anyone, but is instead simply insisting that public funds be spent for the purposes for which they were authorized. The Secretary's regulations do not force the Title X grantee to give up abortion-related speech; they merely require that the grantee keep such activities separate and distinct from Title X activities. The grantee receives Title X funds, however, for the specific and limited purpose of establishing and operating a Title X project. The regulations govern the scope of the Title X project's activities, and leave the grantee unfettered in its other activities. The Title X grantee can continue to perform abortions, provide abortion-related services, and engage in abortion advocacy; it simply is required to conduct those activities through programs that are separate and independent from the project that receives Title X funds.

In contrast, our "unconstitutional conditions" cases involve situations in which the Government has placed a condition on the recipient of the subsidy rather than on a particular program or service, thus effectively prohibiting the recipient from engaging in the protected conduct outside the scope of the federally funded program.

The condition that federal funds will be used only to further the purposes of a grant does not violate constitutional rights. "Congress could, for example, grant funds to an organization dedicated to combating teenage drug abuse, but condition the grant by providing that none of the money received from Congress should be used to lobby state legislatures." By requiring that the Title X grantee engage in abortion-related activity separately from activity receiving federal funding, Congress has, consistent with our teachings in *League of Women Voters* and *Regan*, not denied it the right to engage in abortion-related activities. Congress has merely refused to fund such activities out of the public fisc, and the Secretary has simply required a certain degree of separation from the Title X project in order to ensure the integrity of the federally funded program.

The same principles apply to petitioners' claim that the regulations abridge the free speech rights of the grantee's staff. Individuals who are voluntarily employed for a Title X project must perform their duties in accordance with the regulation's restrictions on abortion counseling and referral. The employees remain free, however, to pursue abortion-related activities when they are not acting under the auspices of the Title X project. The regulations, which govern solely the scope of the Title X project's activities, do not in any way restrict the activities of those persons acting as private individuals. The employees' freedom of expression is limited during the time that they actually work for the project; but this limitation is a consequence of their decision to accept employment in a project, the scope of which is permissibly restricted by the funding authority.

Justice BLACKMUN, with whom Justice MARSHALL and Justice STEVENS join dissenting.

[T]he Court, for the first time, upholds viewpoint-based suppression of speech solely because it is imposed on those dependent upon the Government for economic support. Under essentially the same rationale, the majority upholds direct regulation of dialogue between a pregnant woman and her physician when that regulation has both the purpose and the effect of manipulating her decision as to the continuance of her pregnancy. I conclude that the Secretary's regulation of referral, advocacy, and counseling activities exceeds his statutory authority, and, also, that the regulations violate the First and Fifth Amendments of our Constitution.

Until today, the Court never has upheld viewpoint-based suppression of speech simply because that suppression was a condition upon the acceptance of public funds. Whatever may be the Government's power to condition the receipt of its largess upon the relinquishment of constitutional rights, it surely does not extend to a condition that suppresses the recipient's cherished freedom of speech based solely upon the content or viewpoint of that speech.

It cannot seriously be disputed that the counseling and referral provisions at issue in the present cases constitute content-based regulation of speech. Title X grantees may provide counseling and referral regarding any of a wide range of family planning and other topics, save abortion. The regulations are also clearly viewpoint based. While suppressing speech favorable to abortion with one hand, the Secretary compels antiabortion speech with the other. For example, the Department of Health and Human Services' own description of the regulations makes plain that "Title X projects are required to facilitate access to prenatal care and social services, including adoption services, that might be needed by the pregnant client to promote her well-being and that of her child, while making it abundantly clear that the project is not permitted to promote abortion by facilitating access to abortion through the referral process." 53 Fed. Reg. 2927 (1988). The regulations pertaining to "advocacy" are even more explicitly viewpoint based. These provide: "A Title X project may not encourage, promote or advocate abortion as a method of family planning."

Remarkably, the majority concludes that "the Government has not discriminated on the basis of viewpoint; it has merely chosen to fund one activity to the exclusion of the other." But the majority's claim that the regulations merely limit a Title X project's speech to preventive or preconceptional services, rings hollow in light of the broad range of nonpreventive services that the regulations authorize Title X projects to provide. By refusing to fund those family-planning projects that advocate abortion because they advocate abortion, the Government plainly has targeted a particular viewpoint. The majority's reliance on the fact that the regulations pertain solely to funding decisions simply begs the question. Clearly, there are some bases upon which government may not rest its decision to fund or not to fund. For example, the Members of the majority surely would agree that government may not base its decision to support an activity upon considerations of race. As demonstrated above, our cases make clear that ideological viewpoint is a similarly repugnant ground upon which to base funding decisions.

LEGAL SERVICES CORP. v. VELAZQUEZ
531 U.S. 533 (2001)

Justice KENNEDY delivered the opinion of the Court.

In 1974, Congress enacted the Legal Services Corporation Act. The Act establishes the Legal Services Corporation (LSC) as a District of Columbia nonprofit corporation. LSC's mission is to distribute funds appropriated by Congress to eligible local grantee organizations "for the purpose of providing financial support for legal assistance in noncriminal proceedings or matters to persons financially unable to afford legal assistance."

LSC grantees consist of hundreds of local organizations governed, in the typical case, by local boards of directors. In many instances the grantees are funded by a combination of LSC funds and other public or private sources. The grantee organizations hire and supervise lawyers to provide free legal assistance to indigent clients. Each year LSC appropriates funds to grantees or recipients that hire and supervise lawyers for various professional activities, including representation of indigent clients seeking welfare benefits.

This suit requires us to decide whether one of the conditions imposed by Congress on the use of LSC funds violates the First Amendment rights of LSC grantees and their clients. For purposes of our decision, the restriction, to be quoted in further detail, prohibits legal representation funded by recipients of LSC moneys if the representation involves an effort to amend or otherwise challenge existing welfare law. As interpreted by the LSC and by the Government, the restriction prevents an attorney from arguing to a court that a state statute conflicts with a federal statute or that either a state or federal statute by its terms or in its application is violative of the United States Constitution.

I

From the inception of the LSC, Congress has placed restrictions on its use of funds. For instance, the LSC Act prohibits recipients from making available LSC funds, program personnel, or equipment to any political party, to any political campaign, or for use in "advocating or opposing any ballot measures." The Act further proscribes use of funds in most criminal proceedings and in litigation involving nontherapeutic abortions, secondary school desegregation, military desertion, or violations of the Selective Service statute. Fund recipients are barred from bringing class-action suits unless express approval is obtained from LSC.

The relevant portion of §504(a)(16) prohibits funding of any organization "that initiates legal representation or participates in any other way, in litigation, lobbying, or rulemaking, involving an effort to reform a Federal or State welfare system, except that this paragraph shall not be construed to preclude a recipient from representing an individual eligible client who is seeking specific relief from a welfare agency if such relief does not involve an effort to amend or otherwise challenge existing law in effect on the date of the initiation of the representation."

The prohibitions apply to all of the activities of an LSC grantee, including those paid for by non-LSC funds. We are concerned with the statutory provision which excludes LSC representation in cases which "involve an effort to amend or otherwise challenge existing law in effect on the date of the initiation of the representation."

In 1997, LSC adopted final regulations clarifying §504(a)(16). LSC interpreted the statutory provision to allow indigent clients to challenge welfare agency determinations of benefit ineligibility under interpretations of existing law. For example, an LSC grantee could represent a welfare claimant who argued that an agency made an erroneous factual determination or that an agency misread or misapplied a term contained in an existing welfare statute. According to LSC, a grantee in that position could argue as well that an agency policy violated existing law. Under LSC's interpretation, however, grantees could not accept representations designed to change welfare laws, much less argue against the constitutionality or statutory validity of those laws. Even in cases where constitutional or statutory challenges became apparent after representation was well under way, LSC advised that its attorneys must withdraw.

II

The United States and LSC rely on Rust v. Sullivan (1991) as support for the LSC program restrictions. In *Rust*, Congress established program clinics to provide subsidies for doctors to advise patients on a variety of family planning topics. Congress did not consider abortion to be within its family planning objectives, however, and it forbade doctors employed by the program from discussing abortion with their patients. Recipients of funds under Title X of the Public Health Service Act, challenged the Act's restriction that provided that none of the Title X funds appropriated for family planning services could "be used in programs where abortion is a method of family planning." The recipients argued that the regulations constituted impermissible viewpoint discrimination favoring an antiabortion position over a proabortion approach in the sphere of family planning. They asserted as well that Congress had imposed an unconstitutional condition on recipients of federal funds by requiring them to relinquish their right to engage in abortion advocacy and counseling in exchange for the subsidy.

We upheld the law, reasoning that Congress had not discriminated against viewpoints on abortion, but had "merely chosen to fund one activity to the exclusion of the other." The restrictions were considered necessary "to ensure that the limits of the federal program [were] observed." Title X did not single out a particular idea for suppression because it was dangerous or disfavored; rather, Congress prohibited Title X doctors from counseling that was outside the scope of the project.

The Court in *Rust* did not place explicit reliance on the rationale that the counseling activities of the doctors under Title X amounted to governmental speech; when interpreting the holding in later cases, however, we have explained *Rust* on this understanding. We have said that viewpoint-based funding decisions can be sustained in instances in which the government is itself the speaker, see Board of Regents of Univ. of Wis. System v. Southworth (2000), or instances, like *Rust,* in which the government "used private speakers to transmit information pertaining to its own program." Rosenberger v. Rector and Visitors of Univ. of Va. (1995). As we said in *Rosenberger,* "[w]hen the government disburses public funds to private entities to convey a governmental message, it may take legitimate and appropriate steps to ensure that its message is neither garbled nor distorted by the grantee." The latitude which may exist for restrictions on speech where the government's own message is being delivered flows in part from our observation that, "[w]hen the government speaks, for instance to promote its own policies or to advance a particular idea, it is, in the end, accountable to the electorate and the political process for its advocacy. If the citizenry objects, newly elected officials later could espouse some different or contrary position."

Neither the latitude for government speech nor its rationale applies to subsidies for private speech in every instance, however. As we have pointed out, "[i]t does not follow . . . that viewpoint-based restrictions are proper when the [government] does not itself speak or subsidize transmittal of a message it favors but instead expends funds to encourage a diversity of views from private speakers."

Although the LSC program differs from the program at issue in *Rosenberger* in that its purpose is not to "encourage a diversity of views," the salient point is that, like the program in *Rosenberger,* the LSC program was designed to facilitate private speech, not to promote a governmental message. Congress funded LSC grantees to provide attorneys to represent the interests of indigent clients. In the specific context of §504(a)(16) suits for benefits, an LSC-funded attorney speaks on the behalf of the client in a claim against the government for welfare benefits. The lawyer is not the government's speaker. The attorney defending the decision to deny benefits will deliver the government's message in the litigation. The LSC lawyer, however, speaks on the behalf of his or her private, indigent client.

The Government has designed this program to use the legal profession and the established Judiciary of the States and the Federal Government to accomplish its end of assisting welfare claimants in determination or receipt of their benefits. The advice from the attorney to the client and the advocacy by the attorney to the courts cannot be classified as governmental speech even under a generous understanding of the concept. In this vital respect this suit is distinguishable from *Rust.*

The private nature of the speech involved here, and the extent of LSC's regulation of private expression, are indicated further by the circumstance that the Government seeks to use an existing medium of expression and to control it, in a class of cases, in ways which distort its usual functioning. Where the government uses or attempts to regulate a particular medium, we have been informed by its accepted usage in determining whether a particular restriction on speech is necessary for the program's purposes and limitations.

When the government creates a limited forum for speech, certain restrictions may be necessary to define the limits and purposes of the program. The same is true when the government establishes a subsidy for specified ends. Here the program presumes that private, nongovernmental speech is necessary, and a substantial restriction is placed upon that speech. At oral argument and in its briefs the LSC advised us that lawyers funded in the Government program may not undertake representation in suits for benefits if they must advise clients respecting the questionable validity of a statute which defines benefit eligibility and the payment structure. The limitation forecloses advice or legal assistance to question the validity of statutes under the Constitution of the United States. It extends further, it must be noted, so that state statutes inconsistent with federal law under the Supremacy Clause may be neither challenged nor questioned.

By providing subsidies to LSC, the Government seeks to facilitate suits for benefits by using the State and Federal courts and the independent bar on which those courts depend for the proper performance of their duties and responsibilities. Restricting LSC attorneys in advising their clients and in presenting arguments and analyses to the courts distorts the legal system by altering the traditional role of the attorneys in much the same way broadcast systems or student publication networks were changed in the limited forum cases we have cited. Just as government in those cases could not elect to use a broadcasting network or a college publication structure in a regime which prohibits speech necessary to the proper functioning of those systems, it may not design a subsidy to effect this serious and fundamental restriction on advocacy of attorneys and the functioning of the judiciary.

LSC has advised us, furthermore, that upon determining a question of statutory validity is present in any anticipated or pending case or controversy, the LSC-funded attorney must cease the representation at once. This is true whether the validity issue becomes apparent during initial attorney-client consultations or in the midst of litigation proceedings.

Interpretation of the law and the Constitution is the primary mission of the judiciary when it acts within the sphere of its authority to resolve a case or controversy. Marbury v. Madison (1803). An informed, independent judiciary presumes an informed, independent bar. Under §504(a)(16), however, cases would be presented by LSC attorneys who could not advise the courts of serious questions of statutory validity. The disability is inconsistent with the proposition that attorneys should present all the reasonable and well-grounded arguments necessary for proper resolution of the case. By seeking to prohibit the analysis of certain legal issues and to truncate presentation to the courts, the enactment under review prohibits speech and expression upon which courts must depend for the proper exercise of the judicial power. Congress cannot wrest the law from the Constitution which is its source.

The restriction imposed by the statute here threatens severe impairment of the judicial function. Section 504(a)(16) sifts out cases presenting constitutional challenges in order to insulate the Government's laws from judicial inquiry. If the restriction on speech and legal advice were to stand, the result would be two tiers of cases. In cases where LSC counsel were attorneys of record, there would be lingering doubt whether the truncated representation had resulted in complete analysis of the case, full advice to the client, and proper presentation to the court. The courts and the public would come to question the adequacy and fairness of professional representations when the attorney, either consciously to comply with this statute or unconsciously to continue the representation despite the statute, avoided all reference to questions of statutory validity and constitutional authority. A scheme so inconsistent with accepted separation-of-powers principles is an insufficient basis to sustain or uphold the restriction on speech.

It is no answer to say the restriction on speech is harmless because, under LSC's interpretation of the Act, its attorneys can withdraw. This misses the point. The statute is an attempt to draw lines around the LSC program to exclude from litigation those arguments and theories Congress finds unacceptable but which by their nature are within the province of the courts to consider.

The restriction on speech is even more problematic because in cases where the attorney withdraws from a representation, the client is unlikely to find other counsel. The explicit premise for providing LSC attorneys is the necessity to make available representation "to persons financially unable to afford legal assistance." There often will be no alternative source for the client to receive vital information respecting constitutional and statutory rights bearing upon claimed benefits. Thus, with respect to the litigation services Congress has funded, there is no alternative channel for expression of the advocacy Congress seeks to restrict. This is in stark contrast to *Rust*. There, a patient could receive the approved Title X family planning counseling funded by the Government and later could consult an affiliate or independent organization to receive abortion counseling. Unlike indigent clients who seek LSC representation, the patient in *Rust* was not required to forfeit the Government-funded advice when she also received abortion counseling through alternative channels. Because LSC attorneys must withdraw whenever a question of a welfare statute's validity arises, an individual could not obtain joint representation so that the constitutional challenge would be presented by a non-LSC attorney, and other, permitted, arguments advanced by LSC counsel.

Congress was not required to fund an LSC attorney to represent indigent clients; and when it did so, it was not required to fund the whole range of legal representations or relationships. The LSC and the United States, however, in effect ask us to permit Congress to define the scope of the litigation it funds to exclude certain vital theories and ideas. The attempted restriction is designed to insulate the Government's interpretation of the Constitution from judicial challenge. The Constitution does not permit the Government to confine litigants and their attorneys in this manner. We must be vigilant when Congress imposes rules and conditions which in effect insulate its own laws from legitimate judicial challenge. Where private speech is involved, even Congress' antecedent funding decision cannot be aimed at the suppression of ideas thought inimical to the Government's own interest. For the reasons we have set forth, the funding condition is invalid.

Justice SCALIA, with whom the Chief Justice, Justice O'CONNOR, and Justice THOMAS join, dissenting.

Section 504(a)(16) of the Omnibus Consolidated Rescissions and Appropriations Act of 1996 (Appropriations Act) defines the scope of a federal spending program. It does not directly regulate speech, and it neither establishes a public forum nor discriminates on the basis of viewpoint. The Court agrees with all this, yet applies a novel and unsupportable interpretation of our public-forum precedents to declare §504(a)(16) facially unconstitutional. This holding not only has no foundation in our jurisprudence; it is flatly contradicted by a recent decision that is on all fours with the present case.

The LSC Act is a federal subsidy program, not a federal regulatory program, and "[t]here is a basic difference between [the two]." Maher v. Roe (1977). Regulations directly restrict speech; subsidies do not. Subsidies, it is true, may indirectly abridge speech, but only if the funding scheme is "'manipulated' to have a 'coercive effect'" on those who do not hold the subsidized position. National Endowment for Arts v. Finley (1998). Proving unconstitutional coercion is difficult enough when the spending program has universal coverage and excludes only certain speech — such as a tax exemption scheme excluding lobbying expenses. The Court has found such programs unconstitutional only when the exclusion was "aimed at the suppression of dangerous ideas." Speiser v. Randall (1958). Proving the requisite coercion is harder still when a spending program is not universal but limited, providing benefits to a restricted number of recipients, see Rust v. Sullivan (1991). The Court has found such selective spending unconstitutionally coercive only once, when the government created a public forum with the spending program but then discriminated in distributing funding within the forum on the basis of viewpoint. See Rosenberger v. Rector and Visitors of Univ. of Va. (1995). When the limited spending program does not create a public forum, proving coercion is virtually impossible, because simply denying a subsidy "does not 'coerce' belief," and because the criterion of unconstitutionality is whether denial of the subsidy threatens "to drive certain ideas or viewpoints from the marketplace." Absent such a threat, "the Government may allocate . . . funding according to criteria that would be impermissible were direct regulation of speech or a criminal penalty at stake."

In Rust v. Sullivan, the Court applied these principles to a statutory scheme that is in all relevant respects indistinguishable from §504(a)(16). The statute in *Rust* authorized grants for the provision of family planning services, but provided that "[n]one of the funds . . . shall be used in programs where abortion is a method of family planning." Valid regulations implementing the statute required funding recipients to refer pregnant clients "for appropriate prenatal . . . services by furnishing a list of available providers that promote the welfare of mother and unborn child," but forbade them to refer a pregnant woman specifically to an abortion provider, even upon request. We rejected a First Amendment free-speech challenge to the funding scheme, explaining that "[t]he Government can, without violating the Constitution, selectively fund a program to encourage certain activities it believes to be in the public interest, without at the same time funding an alternative program which seeks to deal with the problem another way." This was not, we said, the type of "discriminate[ion] on the basis of viewpoint" that triggers strict scrutiny, because the "decision not to subsidize the exercise of a fundamental right does not infringe the right."

The same is true here. The LSC Act, like the scheme in *Rust*, does not create a public forum. Far from encouraging a diversity of views, it has always, as the Court accurately states, "placed restrictions on its use of funds." Nor does §504(a)(16) discriminate on the basis of viewpoint, since it funds neither challenges to nor defenses of existing welfare law. The provision simply declines to subsidize a certain class of litigation, and under *Rust* that decision "does not infringe the right" to bring such litigation. The Court's repeated claims that §504(a)(16) "restricts" and "prohibits" speech, and "insulates" laws from judicial review, are simply baseless. No litigant who, in the absence of LSC funding, would bring a suit challenging existing welfare law is deterred from doing so by §504(a)(16). *Rust* thus controls these cases and compels the conclusion that §504(a)(16) is constitutional.

The Court contends that *Rust* is different because the program at issue sub-sidized government speech, while the LSC funds private speech. This is so unpersuasive it hardly needs response. If the private doctors' confidential advice to their patients at issue in *Rust* constituted "government speech," it is hard to imagine what subsidized speech would not be government speech. Moreover, the majority's contention that the subsidized speech in these cases is not gov-ernment speech because the lawyers have a professional obligation to represent the interests of their clients founders on the reality that the doctors in *Rust* had a professional obligation to serve the interests of their patients, which at the time of *Rust* we had held to be highly relevant to the permissible scope of federal regulation. Even respondents agree that "the true speaker in *Rust* was not the government, but a doctor."

The Court further asserts that these cases are different from *Rust* because the welfare funding restriction "seeks to use an existing medium of expression and to control it . . . in ways which distort its usual functioning." This is wrong on both the facts and the law. It is wrong on the law because there is utterly no precedent for the novel and facially implausible proposition that the First Amendment has anything to do with government funding that — though it does not actually abridge anyone's speech — "distorts an existing medium of expression." None of the three cases cited by the Court mentions such an odd principle.

Finally, the Court is troubled "because in cases where the attorney withdraws from a representation, the client is unlikely to find other counsel." That is surely irrelevant, since it leaves the welfare recipient in no worse condition than he would have been in had the LSC program never been enacted. Respondents properly concede that even if welfare claimants cannot obtain a lawyer anywhere else, the Government is not required to provide one. It is hard to see how providing free legal services to some welfare claimants (those whose claims do not challenge the applicable statutes) while not providing it to others is beyond the range of legitimate legislative choice. *Rust* rejected a similar argument.

This has been a very long discussion to make a point that is embarrassingly simple: The LSC subsidy neither prevents anyone from speaking nor coerces anyone to change speech, and is indistinguishable in all relevant respects from the subsidy upheld in Rust v. Sullivan. There is no legitimate basis for declaring §504(a)(16) facially unconstitutional.

GOVERNMENT PRESSURES

Is it an infringement of speech if the government places pressure on individ-uals or entities to refrain from First Amendment behavior without actually pro-hibiting or in any way penalizing speech? The cases are mixed in dealing with this issue. In Bantam Books, Inc. v. Sullivan, 372 U.S. 58 (1963), the Court held that it was unconstitutional for the Rhode Island Commission to Encourage Morality in Youth to identify "objectionable" books because they were unsuit-able for children and to write to sellers urging them to stop having them avail-able. The letter also informed the recipient that the Commission recommended obscenity prosecutions to prosecutors and turned its list of distributors of objec-tionable books over to local police. In fact, a police officer often followed up and visited the recipient of a letter to see what actions had been taken. The Supreme Court found that such pressure constituted an unconstitutional prior restraint of speech, even though no books were actually banned and no prosecutions were undertaken.

However, other cases point in the opposite direction. In Meese v. Keene, 481 U.S. 465 (1987), the Court held that the government could label a film without violating the First Amendment. Pursuant to the Foreign Agents Registration Act, the federal government identified some Canadian films as political propaganda. One, titled *If You Love This Planet*, won the Academy Award for Best Short Documentary in 1982 and depicted an anti-nuclear weapons speech given by the president of the U.S.-based group Physicians for Social Responsibility. A second film, *Acid Rain: Requiem or Recovery?*, also produced by the National Film Board of Canada, focused on the harms from acid rain.

By labeling the films as propaganda under the Foreign Agents Registration Act, the exhibitors of the movies were required to place the words "political propaganda" at the beginning of the films. Additionally, the producer, the National Film Board of Canada, was required to provide the government with a list of all major distributors of the films and all the groups that had requested the films for viewing.

The government's actions, as in *Bantam Books*, did not prohibit any speech but created obvious pressure against showing such movies. However, the Court found no violation of the First Amendment. The Court emphasized that "[t]he statute itself neither prohibits nor censors the dissemination of advocacy materials by agents of foreign principles. . . . The term 'political propaganda' does nothing to place regulated expressive material 'beyond the pale of legitimate discourse.' . . . To the contrary, Congress simply required the disseminators of such material to make additional disclosures that would better enable the public to evaluate the import of the propaganda."

The underlying issue in these cases concerns when the government's own speech should be regarded as impermissible pressure and thus an infringement of the First Amendment. Would a government-imposed rating system for records or television programs simply be, in the words of *Meese*, "additional disclosures that would better enable the public to evaluate" the speech? Or would it be a form of pressure to self-censorship as in *Bantam Books*? Are letters from government agencies or commissions pressuring stores not to sell certain adult-oriented magazines simply the government expressing its views or is it an infringement of the First Amendment because of the government's prosecutorial powers?[99] Are speeches by high-level political officials condemning certain speech, such as rap lyrics, an exercise of the officials' expressive rights, or are they impermissible pressure in light of *Bantam Books*? Cases such as *Bantam Books* and *Meese* point in opposite directions. Ultimately, the task for courts is to evaluate the degree of pressure against speech. If the pressure is more than minimal, cases such as *Bantam Books* suggest that First Amendment scrutiny is required. Meese v. Keene might be distinguished on the ground that the Court saw little adverse effect on speech by the government labeling material as political propaganda.

---

99. Penthouse International, Ltd. v. Meese, 939 F.2d 1011 (D.C. Cir. 1991) (finding that letters sent from a government commission to stores accusing them of selling obscene materials did not violate the First Amendment).

C. TYPES OF UNPROTECTED
AND LESS PROTECTED SPEECH

The Supreme Court has identified some categories of unprotected speech that the government can prohibit and punish. Incitement of illegal activity, fighting words, and obscenity are examples of such categories of unprotected speech. Additionally, there are categories of less-protected speech where the government has more latitude to regulate than usual under the First Amendment. For instance, government generally can regulate commercial speech if intermediate scrutiny is met. Also, the Court has indicated that some types of sexually oriented speech, although protected by the First Amendment, are deemed to be of "low value" and thus are more susceptible to government regulation.

These categories are defined based on the subject matter of the speech and thus represent an exception to the usual rule that content-based regulation must meet strict scrutiny. It was traditionally thought that the government had broad latitude to prohibit and regulate speech within the categories of unprotected expression. The conventional view was that laws in these areas would be upheld as long as they met the rational basis test that all government actions must satisfy. However, in R.A.V. v. City of St. Paul, 505 U.S. 377 (1992), discussed below, the Court indicated that generally content-based distinctions within categories of unprotected speech must meet strict scrutiny. In *R.A.V.*, the Court declared unconstitutional a city's ordinance that prohibited hate speech based on race, color, religion, or gender that was likely to "anger, alarm, or cause resentment." The Court said that even though fighting words are a category of unprotected speech, the law impermissibly drew content-based distinctions among fighting words, such as prohibiting expression of hate based on race, but not based on political affiliation. It is unclear after *R.A.V.* how much its reasoning will limit the ability of government to regulate within the categories of unprotected speech.

The categories of unprotected and less protected speech reflect value judgments by the Supreme Court that the justifications for regulating such speech outweigh the value of the expression. For each of the categories discussed below, the Court's judgment can be questioned. For example, is the Court correct that obscenity is "utterly without redeeming social importance" and therefore is unprotected by the First Amendment?[100] Is the Court right that commercial speech is less important than other types of speech and therefore worthy only of intermediate scrutiny? Also, it is important to consider whether other categories of unprotected speech should be recognized because of the harms of such speech relative to its benefits.

Moreover, the categorical approach requires careful attention to how the types of unprotected speech are defined. For instance, the definitions of "incitement" or "obscenity" are enormously important because they determine whether the government can punish the speech or whether the expression is safeguarded by the First Amendment. A recurring theme throughout this

---

100. Roth v. United States, 354 U.S. 476, 484 (1957).

section is whether the Court's definitions of the categories are sufficiently specific and a desirable way of separating protected from unprotected speech.

Also, there is the question of whether new categories of unprotected speech should be recognized. After the presentation below of the categories of unprotected speech — incitement, fighting words, obscenity — there is the question recently addressed by the Supreme Court of whether violent speech should be recognized as a new category of unprotected speech.

1. Incitement of Illegal Activity

The topic of incitement is important for many reasons. It was the first area that produced a large body of Supreme Court cases. Thus, the doctrines articulated in this area — such as the clear and present danger test — have been carried over to many other areas of First Amendment law.

The issue of incitement also is important because it poses a basic value question: How should society balance its need for social order against its desire to protect freedom of speech? When, if at all, may speech that advocates criminal activity or the overthrow of the government be stopped to promote order and security?

Some commentators have argued that all such advocacy of illegal conduct should be deemed unprotected by the First Amendment. Robert Bork, for example, contended that "[a]dvocacy of law violation is a call to set aside the results that political speech has produced. The process of the 'discovery and spread of political truth' is damaged or destroyed if the outcome is defeated by a minority that makes law enforcement, and hence the putting of political truth into practice, impossible or less effective. There should, therefore, be no constitutional protection for any speech advocating violation of law."[101]

The Supreme Court never has taken this view. Justice Brandeis explained that "even advocacy of [law] violation, however reprehensible morally, is not a justification for denying free speech where the advocacy falls short of incitement and there is nothing to indicate that the advocacy would be immediately acted on."[102] The strong presumption in favor of protecting speech is viewed as justifying safeguarding even advocacy of illegality unless there is a substantial likelihood of imminent harm. Also, advocacy of law violation, or even civil disobedience, is seen as a powerful way of expressing a message. But the Court also never has taken the position that such speech is completely protected by the First Amendment, and the government is limited to punishing the criminal acts themselves.

Thus, the Court has been confronted with the task of defining when advocacy of illegality constitutes unprotected incitement and when it is safeguarded by the First Amendment.[103] Over the course of this century, the Supreme Court has used at least four major different approaches in this area. Interestingly, often the later tests have replaced earlier ones without overruling them or even acknowledging their differences.

---

101. Robert Bork, *Neutral Priniciples and Some First Amendment Problems*, 47 Ind. L.J. 1, 31 (1971).
102. Whitney v. California, 274 U.S. 357, 376 (1927) (Brandeis, J., concurring).
103. For an excellent in-depth discussion of the law in this area, *see* Kent Greenawalt, *Speech, Crime, and the Uses of Language* (1989).

During World War I and the years immediately following it, the Supreme Court articulated and applied the "clear and present danger test." During the 1920s and 1930s, the Court did not often use this formulation, but instead used a "reasonableness test" that allowed the government to punish advocacy of illegality as long as it was reasonable to do so. The reasonableness test is the one approach that has been expressly repudiated by later Court decisions. In the 1950s, during the McCarthy era, the Court reformulated the clear and present danger test as a risk formula; whether speech was protected depended on the gravity of the evil compared with its likelihood. Most recently, since the late 1960s, the Court has narrowly defined incitement to maximize protection of speech. Under this approach, advocacy can be punished only if there is a likelihood of imminent illegal conduct and the speech is directed to causing imminent illegality. These four approaches are discussed in turn. In reading the cases from each era, it is important to consider whether the Court was creating a new test or using an old one and also, most important, whether the Court struck an appropriate balance between protecting freedom of speech and society's need for law and order.

a. The "Clear and Present Danger" Test

There was substantial criticism within the country of American involvement in World War I.[104] There was significant opposition to the draft, and it is estimated that there were more than 350,000 draft evaders or delinquents during the war.[105] At about the same time, the success of the Bolshevik revolution in Russia led to fears of a leftist uprising in this country.

In response to all of this, two months after America's entry into World War I, Congress enacted the Espionage Act of 1917. The law, in part, made it a crime when the nation was at war for any person willfully to "make or convey false reports or false statements with intent to interfere" with the military success or "to promote the success of its enemies."[106] The law also made it a crime to willfully "obstruct the recruiting or enlistment service of the United States."[107] Convictions could be punished by sentences of up to 20 years of imprisonment and fines of up to $10,000.

In 1918, Congress adopted a law even more restrictive of speech. The Sedition Act of 1918 prohibited individuals from saying anything with the intent to obstruct the sale of war bonds; to "utter, print, write, or publish any disloyal, profane, scurrilous, or abusive language" intended to cause contempt or scorn for the form of the government of the United States, the Constitution, or the flag; to urge the curtailment of production of war materials with the intent of hindering the war effort; or to utter any words supporting the cause of any country at war with the United States or opposing the cause of the United States.[108]

---

104. *See* David Rabban, *The First Amendment in Its Forgotten Years*, 90 Yale L.J. at 581-582; Zechariah Chaffee, *Free Speech in the United States* 108-111 (1941).
105. Robert J. Goldstein, *Political Repression in Modern America from 1870 to the Present* 105 (1978).
106. Act of June 15, 1917, ch. 30, tit. I, §3, 40 Stat. 219.
107. *Id.*
108. Act of May 16, 1918, 40 Stat. 553.

In a series of cases, the Supreme Court upheld the constitutionality of both the laws and their application to speech that, in hindsight, was mild and ineffectual.[109] The Court articulated the clear and present danger test and found it was met in the cases before it.[110] The first cases—Schenck v. United States, Frohwerk v. United States, and Debs v. United States—involved the 1917 Act. In each of these cases, the Court upheld convictions.

SCHENCK v. UNITED STATES

249 U.S. 47 (1919)

Justice HOLMES delivered the opinion of the Court.

This is an indictment [that] charges a conspiracy to violate the Espionage Act of June 15, 1917, by causing and attempting to cause insubordination in the military and naval forces of the United States, and to obstruct the recruiting and enlistment service of the United States, when the United States was at war with the German Empire, to-wit, that the defendant wilfully conspired to have printed and circulated to men who had been called and accepted for military service a document set forth and alleged to be calculated to cause such insubordination and obstruction. The count alleges overt acts in pursuance of the conspiracy, ending in the distribution of the document set forth. The defendants were found guilty.

The document in question upon its first printed side recited the first section of the Thirteenth Amendment, said that the idea embodied in it was violated by the conscription act and that a conscript is little better than a convict. In impassioned language it intimated that conscription was despotism in its worst form and a monstrous wrong against humanity in the interest of Wall Street's chosen few. It said, "Do not submit to intimidation," but in form at least confined itself to peaceful measures such as a petition for the repeal of the act. The other and later printed side of the sheet was headed "Assert Your Rights." It stated reasons for alleging that any one violated the Constitution when he refused to recognize "your right to assert your opposition to the draft," and went on, "If you do not assert and support your rights, you are helping to deny or disparage rights which it is the solemn duty of all citizens and residents of the United States to retain." It described the arguments on the other side as coming from cunning politicians and a mercenary capitalist press, and even silent consent to the conscription law as helping to support an infamous conspiracy. It denied the power to send our citizens away to foreign shores to shoot up the people of other lands, and added that words could not express

---

109. In additional to Supreme Court rulings, there were notable decisions by lower federal courts concerning the acts. For example, in Masses Publishing Co. v. Patten, 244 F. 535 (S.D.N.Y. 1917), *rev'd*, 246 F. 24 (2d Cir. 1917), Judge Learned Hand attempted to draw a clear distinction between incitement and discussion. He wrote that one "may not counsel or advise others to violate the law as it stands. Words are not only the keys of persuasion, but the triggers of action." Criticism of the law is constitutionally protected; advocacy of its violation is not.

In Shaffer v. United States, 255 F. 886 (9th Cir. 1919), the court upheld the application of the Espionage Act of 1917 against a book critical of American involvement in World War I. The court said that the test is "whether the natural and probable tendency and effect of [the publication] are such as are calculated to produce the result condemned by statute."

110. For a thorough review of these cases, *see* Zechariah Chaffee, Jr., *Free Speech in the United States* (1941).

the condemnation such cold-blooded ruthlessness deserves, winding up, "You must do your share to maintain, support and uphold the rights of the people of this country." Of course the document would not have been sent unless it had been intended to have some effect, and we do not see what effect it could be expected to have upon persons subject to the draft except to influence them to obstruct the carrying of it out.

But it is said, suppose that that was the tendency of this circular, it is protected by the First Amendment to the Constitution. It well may be that the prohibition of laws abridging the freedom of speech is not confined to previous restraints, although to prevent them may have been the main purpose. We admit that in many places and in ordinary times the defendants in saying all that was said in the circular would have been within their constitutional rights. But the character of every act depends upon the circumstances in which it is done. The most stringent protection of free speech would not protect a man in falsely shouting fire in a theatre and causing a panic.

The question in every case is whether the words used are used in such circumstances and are of such a nature as to create a clear and present danger that they will bring about the substantive evils that Congress has a right to prevent. It is a question of proximity and degree. When a nation is at war many things that might be said in time of peace are such a hindrance to its effort that their utterance will not be endured so long as men fight and that no Court could regard them as protected by any constitutional right. It seems to be admitted that if an actual obstruction of the recruiting service were proved, liability for words that produced that effect might be enforced. The statute of 1917 in section 4 punishes conspiracies to obstruct as well as actual obstruction. If the act, (speaking, or circulating a paper,) its tendency and the intent with which it is done are the same, we perceive no ground for saying that success alone warrants making the act a crime.

FROHWERK v. UNITED STATES

249 U.S. 204 (1919)

Justice HOLMES delivered the opinion of the Court.

This is an indictment in thirteen counts. The [indictment alleges] a conspiracy between the plaintiff in error and one Carl Gleeser, they then being engaged in the preparation and publication of a newspaper, the Missouri Staats Zeitung, to violate the Espionage Act of June 15, 1917. It alleges as overt acts the preparation and circulation of twelve articles in the said newspaper at different dates from July 6, 1917, to December 7 of the same year. The other counts allege attempts to cause disloyalty, mutiny and refusal of duty in the military and naval forces of the United States, by the same publications, each count being confined to the publication of a single date. There was a trial and Frohwerk was found guilty on all the counts except the seventh, which needs no further mention. He was sentenced to a fine and to ten years imprisonment on each count, the imprisonment on the later counts to run concurrently with that on the first.

The first [article] begins by declaring it a monumental and inexcusable mistake to send our soldiers to France, says that it comes no doubt from the great trusts, and later that it appears to be outright murder without serving anything practical; speaks of the unconquerable spirit and undiminished strength of the German nation, and characterizes its own discourse as words of warning to the American people. Later, on August 3, came discussion of the causes of the war, laying it to the administration and saying "that a few men and corporations might amass unprecedented fortunes we sold our honor, our very soul" with the usual repetition that we went to war to protect the loans of Wall Street. Later, after more similar discourse, comes "We say therefore, cease firing."

It may be that all this might be said or written even in time of war in circumstances that would not make it a crime. We do not lose our right to condemn either measures or men because the country is at war. It does not appear that there was any special effort to reach men who were subject to the draft.

But we must take the case on the record as it is, and on that record it is impossible to say that it might not have been found that the circulation of the paper was in quarters where a little breath would be enough to kindle a flame and that the fact was known and relied upon by those who sent the paper out. Small compensation would not exonerate the defendant if it were found that he expected the result, even if pay were his chief desire. When we consider that we do not know how strong the Government's evidence may have been we find ourselves unable to say that the articles could not furnish a basis for a conviction upon the first count at least.

DEBS v. UNITED STATES

249 U.S. 211 (1919)

Justice HOLMES delivered the opinion of the Court.

This is an indictment under the Espionage Act of June 15, 1917. It has been cut down to two counts, originally the third and fourth. The former of these alleges that on or about June 16, 1918, at Canton, Ohio, the defendant caused and incited and attempted to cause and incite insubordination, disloyalty, mutiny and refusal of duty in the military and naval forces of the United States and with intent so to do delivered, to an assembly of people, a public speech, set forth. The fourth count alleges that he obstructed and attempted to obstruct the recruiting and enlistment service of the United States and to that end and with that intent delivered the same speech, again set forth. The defendant was found guilty and was sentenced to ten years' imprisonment on each of the two counts, the punishment to run concurrently on both.

The main theme of the speech was Socialism, its growth, and a prophecy of its ultimate success. With that we have nothing to do, but if a part or the manifest intent of the more general utterances was to encourage those present to obstruct the recruiting service and if in passages such encouragement was directly given, the immunity of the general theme may not be enough to protect the speech. The speaker began by saying that he had just returned from a visit to the workhouse in the neighborhood where three of their most loyal comrades were paying the penalty for their devotion to the working class — these being Wagenknecht, Baker and Ruthenberg, who had been convicted of aiding and abetting another in failing to register for the draft. He said that he had to be prudent and might not be able to say all that he thought, thus intimating to his hearers that they might infer that he meant more, but he did say that those persons were paying the penalty for standing erect and for seeking to pave the way to better conditions for all mankind. Later he added further eulogies and said that he was proud of them. He then expressed opposition to Prussian militarism in a way that naturally might have been thought to be intended to include the mode of proceeding in the United States. There followed personal experiences and illustrations of the growth of Socialism, a glorification of minorities, and a prophecy of the success of the international Socialist crusade, with the interjection that "you need to know that you are fit for something better than slavery and cannon fodder."

Without going into further particulars we are of opinion that the verdict on the fourth count, for obstructing and attempting to obstruct the recruiting service of the United States, must be sustained. Therefore it is less important to consider whether that upon the third count, for causing and attempting to cause insubordination in the military and naval forces, is equally impregnable. The jury were instructed that for the purposes of the statute the persons designated by the Act of May 18, 1917, registered and enrolled under it, and thus subject to be called into the active service, were a part of the military forces of the United States. The Government presents a strong argument from the history of the statutes that the instruction was correct and in accordance with established legislative usage. We see no sufficient reason for differing from the conclusion but think it unnecessary to discuss the question in detail.

Interestingly, later in the year in which these cases were decided, Justice Holmes, joined by Justice Brandeis, dissented in the case of Abrams v. United States, in which the Supreme Court upheld convictions for violating the 1918 Act. In reading *Abrams*, consider whether there is a meaningful distinction between it and the earlier cases, *Schenck*, *Debs*, and *Frohwerk*, in which Holmes wrote the majority opinions. Notice Justice Holmes's eloquent dissent in *Abrams* in which he articulated the marketplace of ideas metaphor for the First Amendment.

ABRAMS v. UNITED STATES
250 U.S. 616 (1919)

Justice Clarke delivered the opinion of the Court.

On a single indictment, containing four counts, the five plaintiffs in error, hereinafter designated the defendants, were convicted of conspiring to violate provisions of the Espionage Act of Congress of 1917 as amended by Act of 1918. Each of the first three counts charged the defendants with conspiring, when the United States was at war with the Imperial Government of Germany, to unlawfully utter, print, write and publish: In the first count, "disloyal, scurrilous and abusive language about the form of government of the United States;" in the second count, language "intended to bring the form of government of the United States into contempt, scorn, contumely, and disrepute;" and in the third count, language "intended to incite, provoke and encourage resistance to the United States in said war." The charge in the fourth count was that the defendants conspired "when the United States was at war with the Imperial German Government, . . . unlawfully and willfully, by utterance, writing, printing and publication to urge, incite and advocate curtailment of production of things and products, to wit, ordnance and ammunition, necessary and essential to the prosecution of the war."

It was charged in each count of the indictment that it was a part of the conspiracy that the defendants would attempt to accomplish their unlawful purpose by printing, writing and distributing in the city of New York many copies of a leaflet or circular, printed in the English language, and of another printed in the Yiddish language, copies of which, properly identified, were attached to the indictment. All of the five defendants were born in Russia. They were intelligent, had considerable schooling, and at the time they were arrested they had lived in the United States terms varying from five to ten years, but none of them had applied for naturalization. Four of them testified as witnesses in their own behalf, and of these three frankly avowed that they were "rebels," "revolutionists," "anarchists," that they did not believe in government in any form, and they declared that they had no interest whatever in the government of the United States.

It was admitted on the trial that the defendants had united to print and distribute the described circulars and that 5,000 of them had been printed and distributed about the 22d day of August, 1918. The circulars were distributed, some by throwing them from a window of a building where one of the defendants was employed and others secretly, in New York City.

On the record thus described it is argued, somewhat faintly, that the acts charged against the defendants were not unlawful because within the protection of that freedom of speech and of the press which is guaranteed by the First Amendment to the Constitution of the United States, and that the entire Espionage Act is unconstitutional because in conflict with that amendment. This contention is sufficiently discussed and is definitely negatived in Schenck v. United States and in Frohwerk v. United States.

Justice HOLMES, dissenting.

This indictment is founded wholly upon the publication of two leaflets. The first of these leaflets says that the President's cowardly silence about the intervention in Russia reveals the hypocrisy of the plutocratic gang in Washington. It intimates that "German militarism combined with allied capitalism to crush the Russian revolution" — goes on that the tyrants of the world fight each other until they see a common enemy — working class enlightenment, when they combine to crush it; and that now militarism and capitalism combined, though not openly, to crush the Russian revolution. It says that there is only one enemy of the workers of the world and that is capitalism; that it is a crime for workers of America, etc., to fight the workers' republic of Russia, and ends "Awake! Awake, you workers of the world! Revolutionists." A note adds "It is absurd to call us pro-German. We hate and despise German militarism more than do you hypocritical tyrants. We have more reason for denouncing German militarism than has the coward of the White House."

The other leaflet, headed "Workers — Wake Up," with abusive language says that America together with the Allies will march for Russia to help the Czecko-Slovaks in their struggle against the Bolsheviki, and that this time the hypocrites shall not fool the Russian emigrants and friends of Russia in America. It tells the Russian emigrants that they now must spit in the face of the false military propaganda by which their sympathy and help to the prosecution of the war have been called forth and says that with the money they have lent or are going to lend "they will make bullets not only for the Germans but also for the Workers Soviets of Russia," and further, "Workers in the ammunition factories, you are producing bullets, bayonets, cannon to murder not only the Germans, but also your dearest, best, who are in Russia fighting for freedom."

No argument seems to be necessary to show that these pronunciamentos in no way attack the form of government of the United States. [I]t seems too plain to be denied that the suggestion to workers in the ammunition factories that they are producing bullets to murder their dearest, and the further advocacy of a general strike, both in the second leaflet, do urge curtailment of production of things necessary to the prosecution of the war within the meaning of the Act of May 16, 1918. But to make the conduct criminal that statute requires that it should be "with intent by such curtailment to cripple or hinder the United States in the prosecution of the war." It seems to me that no such intent is proved.

I never have seen any reason to doubt that the questions of law that alone were before this Court in the Cases of *Schenck*, *Frohwerk*, and *Debs* were rightly decided. I do not doubt for a moment that by the same reasoning that would justify punishing persuasion to murder, the United States constitutionally may punish speech that produces or is intended to produce a clear and imminent danger that it will bring about forthwith certain substantive evils that the United States constitutionally may seek to prevent. The power undoubtedly is greater in time of war than in time of peace because war opens dangers that do not exist at other times.

But as against dangers peculiar to war, as against others, the principle of the right to free speech is always the same. It is only the present danger of immediate evil or an intent to bring it about that warrants Congress in setting a limit to the expression of opinion where private rights are not concerned. Congress certainly cannot forbid all effort to change the mind of the country. Now nobody can suppose that the surreptitious publishing of a silly leaflet by an unknown man, without more, would present any immediate danger that its opinions would hinder the success of the government arms or have any appreciable tendency to do so. Publishing those opinions for the very purpose of obstructing, however, might indicate a greater danger and at any rate would have the quality of an attempt.

I do not see how anyone can find the intent required by the statute in any of the defendant's words. [I]t is evident from the beginning to the end that the only object of the paper is to help Russia and stop American intervention there against the popular government — not to impede the United States in the war that it was carrying on. In this case sentences of twenty years imprisonment have been imposed for the publishing of two leaflets that I believe the defendants had as much right to publish as the Government has to publish the Constitution of the United States now vainly invoked by them.

Persecution for the expression of opinions seems to me perfectly logical. If you have no doubt of your premises or your power and want a certain result with all your heart you naturally express your wishes in law and sweep away all opposition. To allow opposition by speech seems to indicate that you think the speech impotent, as when a man says that he has squared the circle, or that you do not care whole heartedly for the result, or that you doubt either your power or your premises. But when men have realized that time has upset many fighting faiths, they may come to believe even more than they believe the very foundations of their own conduct that the ultimate good desired is better reached by free trade in ideas — that the best test of truth is the power of the thought to get itself accepted in the competition of the market, and that truth is the only ground upon which their wishes safely can be carried out. That at any rate is the theory of our Constitution. It is an experiment, as all life is an experiment. Every year if not every day we have to wager our salvation upon some prophecy based upon imperfect knowledge. While that experiment is part of our system I think that we should be eternally vigilant against attempts to check the expression of opinions that we loathe and believe to be fraught with death, unless they so imminently threaten immediate interference with the lawful and pressing purposes of the law that an immediate check is required to save the country.

b. The Reasonableness Approach

During the 1920s and the 1930s, the Court decided a series of cases involving criminal syndicalism laws, statutes that made it a crime to advocate the overthrow of the U.S. government or industrial organization by force or violence. The Court decided these cases without invoking the clear and present danger test. Rather, the Court appeared to use a reasonableness approach; it upheld the laws and their applications as long as the government's law and prosecution were reasonable.

Gitlow v. New York, the first case that indicated that the First Amendment applied to the states through its incorporation into the Due Process Clause of the Fourteenth Amendment, upheld a conviction under the New York criminal anarchy statute.

GITLOW v. NEW YORK

268 U.S. 652 (1925)

Justice SANFORD delivered the opinion of the Court.

Benjamin Gitlow was indicted in the Supreme Court of New York, with three others, for the statutory crime of criminal anarchy. Its material provisions are: "Sec. 160. Criminal Anarchy Defined. Criminal anarchy is the doctrine that organized government should be overthrown by force or violence, or by assassination of the executive head or of any of the executive officials of government, or by any unlawful means. The advocacy of such doctrine either by word of mouth or writing is a felony." He was separately tried, convicted, and sentenced to imprisonment.

The following facts were established on the trial by undisputed evidence and admissions: The defendant is a member of the Left Wing Section of the Socialist Party, a dissenting branch or faction of that party formed in opposition to its dominant policy of "moderate Socialism." Membership in both is open to aliens as well as citizens. The Left Wing Section was organized nationally at a conference in New York City in June, 1919, attended by ninety delegates from twenty different States. The conference elected a National Council, of which the defendant was a member, and left to it the adoption of a "Manifesto." This was published in The Revolutionary Age, the official organ of the Left Wing. The defendant was on the board of managers of the paper and was its business manager. He arranged for the printing of the paper and took to the printer the manuscript of the first issue which contained the Left Wing Manifesto, and also a Communist Program and a Program of the Left Wing that had been adopted by the conference. Coupled with a review of the rise of Socialism, it condemned the dominant "moderate Socialism" for its recognition of the necessity of the democratic parliamentary state; repudiated its policy of introducing Socialism by legislative measures; and advocated, in plain and unequivocal language, the necessity of accomplishing the "Communist Revolution" by a militant and "revolutionary Socialism," based on "the class struggle" and mobilizing the "power of the proletariat in action," through mass industrial revolts developing into mass political strikes and "revolutionary mass action," for the purpose of conquering and destroying the parliamentary state and establishing in its place, through a "revolutionary dictatorship of the proletariat," the system of Communist Socialism. Sixteen thousand copies were printed, which were delivered at the premises in New York City used as the office of the Revolutionary Age and the head quarters of the Left Wing, and occupied by the defendant and other officials.

The precise question presented is whether the statute, as construed and applied in this case, by the State courts, deprived the defendant of his liberty of expression in violation of the due process clause of the Fourteenth Amendment. For present purposes we may and do assume that freedom of speech and of the press — which are protected by the First Amendment from abridgment by Congress — are among the fundamental personal rights and "liberties" protected by the due process clause of the Fourteenth Amendment from impairment by the States.

The statute does not penalize the utterance or publication of abstract "doctrine" or academic discussion having no quality of incitement to any concrete action. It is not aimed against mere historical or philosophical essays. It does not restrain the advocacy of changes in the form of government by constitutional and lawful means. What it prohibits is language advocating, advising or teaching the overthrow of organized government by unlawful means. These words imply urging to action.

It is a fundamental principle, long established, that the freedom of speech and of the press which is secured by the Constitution, does not confer an absolute right to speak or publish, without responsibility, whatever one may choose, or an unrestricted and unbridled license that gives immunity for every possible use of language and prevents the punishment of those who abuse this freedom. That a State in the exercise of its police power may punish those who abuse this freedom by utterances inimical to the public welfare, tending to corrupt public morals, incite to crime, or disturb the public peace, is not open to question. In short this freedom does not deprive a State of the primary and essential right of self preservation; which, so long as human governments endure, they cannot be denied.

By enacting the present statute the State has determined, through its legislative body, that utterances advocating the overthrow of organized government by force, violence and unlawful means, are so inimical to the general welfare and involve such danger of substantive evil that they may be penalized in the exercise of its police power. That determination must be given great weight. Every presumption is to be indulged in favor of the validity of the statute. And the case is to be considered "in the light of the principle that the State is primarily the judge of regulations required in the interest of public safety and welfare"; and that its police "statutes may only be declared unconstitutional where they are arbitrary or unreasonable attempts to exercise authority vested in the State in the public interest."

That utterances inciting to the overthrow of organized government by unlawful means, present a sufficient danger of substantive evil to bring their punishment within the range of legislative discretion, is clear. Such utterances, by their very nature, involve danger to the public peace and to the security of the State. They threaten breaches of the peace and ultimate revolution. And the immediate danger is none the less real and substantial, because the effect of a given utterance cannot be accurately foreseen. The State cannot reasonably be required to measure the danger from every such utterance in the nice balance of a jeweler's scale. A single revolutionary spark may kindle a fire that, smoldering for a time, may burst into a sweeping and destructive conflagration. It cannot be said that the State is acting arbitrarily or unreasonably when in the exercise of its judgment as to the measures necessary to protect the public peace and safety, it seeks to extinguish the spark without waiting until it has enkindled the flame or blazed into the conflagration. It cannot reasonably be required to defer the adoption of measures for its own peace and safety until the revolutionary utterances lead to actual disturbances of the public peace or imminent and immediate danger of its own destruction; but it may, in the exercise of its judgment, suppress the threatened danger in its incipiency.

We cannot hold that the present statute is an arbitrary or unreasonable exercise of the police power of the State unwarrantably infringing the freedom of speech or press; and we must and do sustain its constitutionality.

Justice HOLMES (dissenting).

Justice Brandeis and I are of opinion that this judgment should be reversed. If I am right then I think that the criterion sanctioned by the full Court in Schenck v. United States applies: "The question in every case is whether the words used are used in such circumstances and are of such a nature as to create a clear and present danger that they will bring about the substantive evils that [the State] has a right to prevent."

If what I think the correct test is applied it is manifest that there was no present danger of an attempt to overthrow the government by force on the part of the admittedly small minority who shared the defendant's views. It is said that this manifesto was more than a theory, that it was an incitement. Every idea is an incitement. It offers itself for belief and if believed it is acted on unless some other belief outweighs it or some failure of energy stifles the movement at its birth. The only difference between the expression of an opinion and an incitement in the narrower sense is the speaker's enthusiasm for the result. Eloquence may set fire to reason. But whatever may be thought of the redundant discourse before us it had no chance of starting a present conflagration. If in the long run the beliefs expressed in proletarian dictatorship are destined to be accepted by the dominant forces of the community, the only meaning of free speech is that they should be given their chance and have their way.

Similarly, the Court used a reasonableness approach to uphold a conviction for criminal syndicalism in Whitney v. California. *Whitney* is perhaps most famous for Justice Brandeis's eloquent opinion defending the importance of freedom of speech. Ironically, Brandeis's opinion is a concurrence to a majority opinion upholding the conviction.

WHITNEY v. CALIFORNIA
274 U.S. 357 (1927)

Justice SANFORD delivered the opinion of the Court.

By a criminal information filed in the Superior Court of Alameda County, California, the plaintiff in error was charged, in five counts, with violations of the Criminal Syndicalism Act of that State. The pertinent provisions of the Criminal Syndicalism Act are: "Section 1. The term 'criminal syndicalism' as used in this act is hereby defined as any doctrine or precept advocating, teaching or aiding and abetting the commission of crime, sabotage (which word is hereby defined as meaning willful and malicious physical damage or injury to physical property), or unlawful acts of force and violence or unlawful methods of terrorism as a means of accomplishing a change in industrial ownership or control or effecting any political change." She was tried, convicted on the first count, and sentenced to imprisonment.

The following facts, among many others, were established on the trial by undisputed evidence: The defendant, a resident of Oakland, in Alameda County, California, had been a member of the Local Oakland branch of the Socialist Party. This Local sent delegates to the national convention of the Socialist Party held in Chicago in 1919, which resulted in a split between the "radical" group and the old-wing Socialists. The "radicals" — to whom the Oakland delegates adhered — being ejected, went to another hall, and formed the Communist Labor Party of America. Shortly thereafter the Local Oakland withdrew from the Socialist Party, and sent accredited delegates, including the defendant, to a convention held in Oakland in November 1919, for the purpose of organizing a California branch of the Communist Labor Party. The defendant, after taking out a temporary membership in the Communist Labor Party, attended this convention as a delegate and took an active part in its proceedings. She also testified that it was not her intention that the Communist Labor Party of California should be an instrument of terrorism or violence, and that it was not her purpose or that of the Convention to violate any known law.

That the freedom of speech which is secured by the Constitution does not confer an absolute right to speak, without responsibility, whatever one may choose, or an unrestricted and unbridled license giving immunity for every possible use of language and preventing the punishment of those who abuse this freedom; and that a State in the exercise of its police power may punish those who abuse this freedom by utterances inimical to the public welfare, tending to incite to crime, disturb the public peace, or endanger the foundations of organized government and threaten its overthrow by unlawful means, is not open to question.

By enacting the provisions of the Syndicalism Act the State has declared, through its legislative body, that to knowingly be or become a member of or assist in organizing an association to advocate, teach or aid and abet the commission of crimes or unlawful acts of force, violence or terrorism as a means of accomplishing industrial or political changes, involves such danger to the public peace and the security of the State, that these acts should be penalized in the exercise of its police power. That determination must be given great weight. Every presumption is to be indulged in favor of the validity of the statute, and it may not be declared unconstitutional unless it is an arbitrary or unreasonable attempt to exercise the authority vested in the State in the public interest.

The essence of the offense denounced by the Act is the combining with others in an association for the accomplishment of the desired ends through the advocacy and use of criminal and unlawful methods. It partakes of the nature of a criminal conspiracy. That such united and joint action involves even greater danger to the public peace and security than the isolated utterances and acts of individuals is clear. We cannot hold that, as here applied, the Act is an unreasonable or arbitrary exercise of the police power of the State, unwarrantably infringing any right of free speech, assembly or association, or that those persons are protected from punishment by the due process clause who abuse such rights by joining and furthering an organization thus menacing the peace and welfare of the State.

Justice BRANDEIS (concurring).

The right of free speech, the right to teach and the right of assembly are, of course, fundamental rights. These may not be denied or abridged. But, although the rights of free speech and assembly are fundamental, they are not in their nature absolute. Their exercise is subject to restriction, if the particular restriction proposed is required in order to protect the state from destruction or from serious injury, political, economic or moral. That the necessity which is essential to a valid restriction does not exist unless speech would produce, or is intended to produce, a clear and imminent danger of some substantive evil which the state constitutionally may seek to prevent has been settled.

This court has not yet fixed the standard by which to determine when a danger shall be deemed clear; how remote the danger may be and yet be deemed present; and what degree of evil shall be deemed sufficiently substantial to justify resort to abridgment of free speech and assembly as the means of protection.

Those who won our independence believed that the final end of the state was to make men free to develop their faculties, and that in its government the deliberative forces should prevail over the arbitrary. They valued liberty both as an end and as a means. They believed liberty to [be] the secret of happiness and courage to be the secret of liberty. They believed that freedom to think as you will and to speak as you think are means indispensable to the discovery and spread of political truth; that without free speech and assembly discussion would be futile; that with them, discussion affords ordinarily adequate protection against the dissemination of noxious doctrine; that the greatest menace to freedom is an inert people; that public discussion is a political duty; and that this should be a fundamental principle of the American government. They recognized the risks to which all human institutions are subject. But they knew that order cannot be secured merely through fear of punishment for its infraction; that it is hazardous to discourage thought, hope and imagination; that fear breeds repression; that repression breeds hate; that hate menaces stable government; that the path of safety lies in the opportunity to discuss freely supposed grievances and proposed remedies; and that the fitting remedy for evil counsels is good ones. Believing in the power of reason as applied through public discussion, they eschewed silence coerced by law — the argument of force in its worst form. Recognizing the occasional tyrannies of governing majorities, they amended the Constitution so that free speech and assembly should be guaranteed.

Fear of serious injury cannot alone justify suppression of free speech and assembly. Men feared witches and burnt women. It is the function of speech to free men from the bondage of irrational fears. To justify suppression of free speech there must be reasonable ground to fear that serious evil will result if free speech is practiced. There must be reasonable ground to believe that the danger apprehended is imminent. There must be reasonable ground to believe that the evil to be prevented is a serious one. Every denunciation of existing law tends in some measure to increase the probability that there will be violation of it. Condonation of a breach enhances the probability. Expressions of approval add to the probability. Propagation of the criminal state of mind by teaching syndicalism increases it. Advocacy of lawbreaking heightens it still further. But even advocacy of violation, however reprehensible morally, is not a justification for denying free speech where the advocacy falls short of incitement and there is nothing to indicate that the advocacy would be immediately acted on. The wide difference between advocacy and incitement, between preparation and attempt, between assembling and conspiracy, must be borne in mind. In order to support a finding of clear and present danger it must be shown either that immediate serious violence was to be expected or was advocated, or that the past conduct furnished reason to believe that such advocacy was then contemplated.

Those who won our independence by revolution were not cowards. They did not fear political change. They did not exalt order at the cost of liberty. To courageous, self-reliant men, with confidence in the power of free and fearless reasoning applied through the processes of popular government, no danger flowing from speech can be deemed clear and present, unless the incidence of the evil apprehended is so imminent that it may befall before there is opportunity for full discussion. If there be time to expose through discussion the falsehood and fallacies, to avert the evil by the processes of education, the remedy to be applied is more speech, not enforced silence. Only an emergency can justify repression. Such must be the rule if authority is to be reconciled with freedom. Such, in my opinion, is the command of the Constitution. It is therefore always open to Americans to challenge a law abridging free speech and assembly by showing that there was no emergency justifying it.

Moreover, even imminent danger cannot justify resort to prohibition of these functions essential to effective democracy, unless the evil apprehended is relatively serious. Prohibition of free speech and assembly is a measure so stringent that it would be inappropriate as the means for averting a relatively trivial harm to society. A police measure may be unconstitutional merely because the remedy, although effective as means of protection, is unduly harsh or oppressive. The fact that speech is likely to result in some violence or in destruction of property is not enough to justify its suppression. There must be the probability of serious injury to the State. Among free men, the deterrents ordinarily to be applied to prevent crime are education and punishment for violations of the law, not abridgment of the rights of free speech and assembly.

I am unable to assent to the suggestion in the opinion of the court that assembling with a political party, formed to advocate the desirability of a proletarian revolution by mass action at some date necessarily far in the future, is not a right within the protection of the Fourteenth Amendment. In the present case, however, there was other testimony which tended to establish the existence of a conspiracy, on the part of members of the International Workers of the World, to commit present serious crimes, and likewise to show that such a conspiracy would be furthered by the activity of the society of which Miss Whitney was a member. Under these circumstances the judgment of the State court cannot be disturbed.

In several cases after *Gitlow* and *Whitney*, the Supreme Court overturned convictions under criminal syndicalism laws. In each, the Court still did not use the clear and present danger test, but rather, found the convictions unreasonable. In Fiske v. Kansas, 274 U.S. 380 (1927), the Supreme Court for the first time overturned a state court conviction as violating the First Amendment as applied to the states through the Fourteenth Amendment. In *Fiske*, the Court concluded that there was no evidence of criminal syndicalism because there were no declarations by the defendant, or his organization, urging unlawful acts. The Court said that the conviction was "an arbitrary and unreasonable exercise of the police power of the State."

Similarly, in DeJonge v. Oregon, 299 U.S. 353 (1937), the Court overturned a conviction for holding a meeting of the Communist Party. Again, the Court emphasized that no one at the meeting advocated illegal acts or the overthrow of the government. The Court said that "peaceable assembly for lawful discussion cannot be made a crime. The holding of meetings for peaceable political action cannot be proscribed."

The majority in all of these cases used an approach that now would be termed rational basis review. None applied the clear and present danger test or anything akin to heightened scrutiny.[111] Thus, the reasonableness approach is inconsistent with the now firmly established heightened scrutiny for fundamental rights. Indeed, the Supreme Court has declared that "*Whitney* has been thoroughly discredited by later decisions."[112]

---

111. Interestingly, in other areas, not involving advocacy of illegal activity, the Court during the 1930s and 1940s expressly used the clear and present danger test. *See, e.g.*, Bridges v. California, 314 U.S. 252 (1941) (speech critical of courts could be held in contempt only if there was a clear and present danger); Cantwell v. Connecticut, 310 U.S. 296 (1940) (speech that provokes a hostile audience can be punished only if there is a clear and present danger).

112. Brandenburg v. Ohio, 395 U.S. 444, 447 (1969).

c. The Risk Formula Approach

During the late 1940s and early 1950s, Senator Joseph McCarthy led a crusade to identify and exclude communists in government. It was the age of suspicion, a time when merely being suspected of being part of a communist or radical group was enough to cause a person to lose a job or appear on a blacklist.[113]

Amid this, in 1951, the Supreme Court decided Dennis v. United States.

DENNIS v. UNITED STATES
341 U.S. 494 (1951)

Chief Justice VINSON announced the judgment of the Court and an opinion in which Mr. Justice REED, Mr. Justice BURTON, and Mr. Justice MINTON join.

Petitioners were indicted in July, 1948, for violation of the conspiracy provisions of the Smith Act during the period of April, 1945, to July, 1948. Sections 2 and 3 of the Smith Act, provide as follows: "Sec. 2. (a) It shall be unlawful for any person — (1) to knowingly or willfully advocate, abet, advise, or teach the duty, necessity, desirability, or propriety of overthrowing or destroying any government in the United States by force or violence, or by the assassination of any officer of any such government; (2) with intent to cause the overthrow or destruction of any government in the United States, to print, publish, edit, issue, circulate, sell, distribute, or publicly display any written or printed matter advocating, advising, or teaching the duty, necessity, desirability, or propriety of overthrowing or destroying any government in the United States by force or violence; (3) to organize or help to organize any society, group, or assembly of persons who teach, advocate, or encourage the overthrow or destruction of any government in the United States by force or violence; or to be or become a member of, or affiliate with, any such society, group, or assembly of persons, knowing the purposes thereof. Sec. 3. It shall be unlawful for any person to attempt to commit, or to conspire to commit, any of the acts prohibited by the provisions of . . . this title."

The indictment charged the petitioners with wilfully and knowingly conspiring (1) to organize as the Communist Party of the United States of America a society, group and assembly of persons who teach and advocate the overthrow and destruction of the Government of the United States by force and violence, and (2) knowingly and wilfully to advocate and teach the duty and necessity of overthrowing and destroying the Government of the United States by force and violence.

The obvious purpose of the statute is to protect existing Government, not from change by peaceable, lawful and constitutional means, but from change by violence, revolution and terrorism. That it is within the power of the Congress to protect the Government of the United States from armed rebellion is a proposition which requires little discussion. Whatever theoretical merit there may be to the argument that there is a "right" to rebellion against dictatorial governments is without force where the existing structure of the government provides for peaceful and orderly change. We reject any principle of governmental helplessness in the face of preparation for revolution, which principle,

---

113. *See* Victor Navasky, *Naming Names* (1980).

carried to its logical conclusion, must lead to anarchy. No one could conceive that it is not within the power of Congress to prohibit acts intended to overthrow the Government by force and violence.

In this case we are squarely presented with the application of the "clear and present danger" test, and must decide what that phrase imports. Overthrow of the Government by force and violence is certainly a substantial enough interest for the Government to limit speech. Indeed, this is the ultimate value of any society, for if a society cannot protect its very structure from armed internal attack, it must follow that no subordinate value can be protected. If, then, this interest may be protected, the literal problem which is presented is what has been meant by the use of the phrase "clear and present danger" of the utterances bringing about the evil within the power of Congress to punish.

Obviously, the words cannot mean that before the Government may act, it must wait until the putsch is about to be executed, the plans have been laid and the signal is awaited. If Government is aware that a group aiming at its overthrow is attempting to indoctrinate its members and to commit them to a course whereby they will strike when the leaders feel the circumstances permit, action by the Government is required. The argument that there is no need for Government to concern itself, for Government is strong, it possesses ample powers to put down a rebellion, it may defeat the revolution with ease needs no answer. For that is not the question. Certainly an attempt to overthrow the Government by force, even though doomed from the outset because of inadequate numbers or power of the revolutionists, is a sufficient evil for Congress to prevent. The damage which such attempts create both physically and politically to a nation makes it impossible to measure the validity in terms of the probability of success, or the immediacy of a successful attempt. In the instant case the trial judge charged the jury that they could not convict unless they found that petitioners intended to overthrow the Government as speedily as circumstances would permit. This does not mean, and could not properly mean, that they would not strike until there was certainty of success. What was meant was that the revolutionists would strike when they thought the time was ripe. We must therefore reject the contention that success or probability of success is the criterion.

Chief Judge Learned Hand, writing for the majority below, interpreted the phrase as follows: "In each case [courts] must ask whether the gravity of the 'evil,' discounted by its improbability, justifies such invasion of free speech as is necessary to avoid the danger." We adopt this statement of the rule. As articulated by Chief Judge Hand, it is as succinct and inclusive as any other we might devise at this time. It takes into consideration those factors which we deem relevant, and relates their significances. More we cannot expect from words. The mere fact that from the period 1945 to 1948 petitioners' activities did not result in an attempt to overthrow the Government by force and violence is of course no answer to the fact that there was a group that was ready to make the attempt. The formation by petitioners of such a highly organized conspiracy, with rigidly disciplined members subject to call when the leaders, these petitioners, felt that the time had come for action, coupled with the inflammable nature of world conditions, similar uprisings in other countries, and the touch-and-go nature of our relations with countries with whom petitioners were in the very least ideologically attuned, convince us that their convictions were justified on this score. And this analysis disposes of the contention that a conspiracy to advocate, as distinguished from the advocacy itself, cannot be constitutionally restrained, because it comprises only the preparation. It is the existence of the conspiracy which creates the danger. If the ingredients of the reaction are present, we cannot bind the Government to wait until the catalyst is added.

We hold that the Smith Act [does] not inherently, or as construed or applied in the instant case, violate the First Amendment and other provisions of the Bill of Rights, or the First and Fifth Amendments because of indefiniteness. Petitioners intended to overthrow the Government of the United States as speedily as the circumstances would permit. Their conspiracy to organize the Communist Party and to teach and advocate the overthrow of the Government of the United States by force and violence created a "clear and present danger" of an attempt to overthrow the Government by force and violence. They were properly and constitutionally convicted for violation of the Smith Act. The judgments of conviction are affirmed.

Justice FRANKFURTER, concurring in affirmance of the judgment.

In enacting a statute which makes it a crime for the defendants to conspire to do what they have been found to have conspired to do, did Congress exceed its constitutional power? Few questions of comparable import have come before this Court in recent years. The appellants maintain that they have a right to advocate a political theory, so long, at least, as their advocacy does not create an immediate danger of obvious magnitude to the very existence of our present scheme of society. On the other hand, the Government asserts the right to safeguard the security of the Nation by such a measure as the Smith Act. Our judgment is thus solicited on a conflict of interests of the utmost concern to the well-being of the country.

But how are competing interests to be assessed? Since they are not subject to quantitative ascertainment, the issue necessarily resolves itself into asking, who is to make the adjustment?—who is to balance the relevant factors and ascertain which interest is in the circumstances to prevail? Full responsibility for the choice cannot be given to the courts. Courts are not representative bodies. They are not designed to be a good reflex of a democratic society. Their judgment is best informed, and therefore most dependable, within narrow limits. Their essential quality is detachment, founded on independence. History teaches that the independence of the judiciary is jeopardized when courts become embroiled in the passions of the day and assume primary responsibility in choosing between competing political, economic and social pressures.

Primary responsibility for adjusting the interests which compete in the situation before us of necessity belongs to the Congress. The nature of the power to be exercised by this Court has been delineated in decisions not charged with the emotional appeal of situations such as that now before us. We are to set aside the judgment of those whose duty it is to legislate only if there is no reasonable basis for it. We are to determine whether a statute is sufficiently definite to meet the constitutional requirements of due process, and whether it respects the safeguards against undue concentration of authority secured by separation of power. Above all we must remember that this Court's power of judicial review is not "an exercise of the powers of a super-Legislature."

Civil liberties draw at best only limited strength from legal guaranties. Preoccupation by our people with the constitutionality, instead of with the wisdom, of legislation or of executive action is preoccupation with a false value. Even those who would most freely use the judicial brake on the democratic process by invalidating legislation that goes deeply against their grain, acknowledge, at least by paying lip service, that constitutionality does not exact a sense of proportion or the sanity of humor or an absence of fear. Focusing attention on constitutionality tends to make constitutionality synonymous with wisdom. When legislation touches freedom of thought and freedom of speech, such a tendency is a formidable enemy of the free spirit. Much that should be rejected as illiberal, because repressive and envenoming, may well be not unconstitutional. The ultimate reliance for the deepest needs of civilization must be found outside their vindication in courts of law.

Justice BLACK, dissenting.

At the outset I want to emphasize what the crime involved in this case is, and what it is not. These petitioners were not charged with an attempt to overthrow the Government. They were not charged with overt acts of any kind designed to overthrow the Government. They were not even charged with saying anything or writing anything designed to overthrow the Government. The charge was that they agreed to assemble and to talk and publish certain ideas at a later date: The indictment is that they conspired to organize the Communist Party and to use speech or newspapers and other publications in the future to teach and advocate the forcible overthrow of the Government. No matter how it is worded, this is a virulent form of prior censorship of speech and press, which I believe the First Amendment forbids.

But let us assume, contrary to all constitutional ideas of fair criminal procedure, that petitioners although not indicted for the crime of actual advocacy, maybe punished for it. Even on this radical assumption, the other opinions in this case show that the only way to affirm these convictions is to repudiate directly or indirectly the established "clear and present danger" rule. This the Court does in a way which greatly restricts the protections afforded by the First Amendment. The opinions for affirmance indicate that the chief reason for jettisoning the rule is the expressed fear that advocacy of Communist doctrine endangers the safety of the Republic. Undoubtedly, a governmental policy of unfettered communication of ideas does entail dangers. To the Founders of this Nation, however, the benefits derived from free expression were worth the risk. I have always believed that the First Amendment is the keystone of our Government, that the freedoms it guarantees provide the best insurance against destruction of all freedom. At least as to speech in the realm of public matters, I believe that the "clear and present danger" test does not "mark the furthermost constitutional boundaries of protected expression" but does "no more than recognize a minimum compulsion of the Bill of Rights."

So long as this Court exercises the power of judicial review of legislation, I cannot agree that the First Amendment permits us to sustain laws suppressing freedom of speech and press on the basis of Congress' or our own notions of mere "reasonableness." Such a doctrine waters down the First Amendment so that it amounts to little more than an admonition to Congress. The Amendment as so construed is not likely to protect any but those "safe" or orthodox views which rarely need its protection.

Justice DOUGLAS, dissenting.

If this were a case where those who claimed protection under the First Amendment were teaching the techniques of sabotage, the assassination of the

President, the filching of documents from public files, the planting of bombs, the art of street warfare, and the like, I would have no doubts. The freedom to speak is not absolute; the teaching of methods of terror and other seditious conduct should be beyond the pale along with obscenity and immorality. This case was argued as if those were the facts.

The argument imported much seditious conduct into the record. That is easy and it has popular appeal, for the activities of Communists in plotting and scheming against the free world are common knowledge. But the fact is that no such evidence was introduced at the trial. There is a statute which makes a seditious conspiracy unlawful. Petitioners, however, were not charged with a "conspiracy to overthrow" the Government. They were charged with a conspiracy to form a party and groups and assemblies of people who teach and advocate the overthrow of our Government by force or violence and with a conspiracy to advocate and teach its overthrow by force and violence. It may well be that indoctrination in the techniques of terror to destroy the Government would be indictable under either statute. But the teaching which is condemned here is of a different character.

So far as the present record is concerned, what petitioners did was to organize people to teach and themselves teach the Marxist-Leninist doctrine contained chiefly in four books: Foundations of Leninism by Stalin (1924); The Communist Manifesto by Marx and Engels (1848); State and Revolution by Lenin (1917); History of the Communist Party of the Soviet Union (B.) (1939).

Those books are to Soviet Communism what Mein Kampf was to Nazism. If they are understood, the ugliness of Communism is revealed, its deceit and cunning are exposed, the nature of its activities becomes apparent, and the chances of its success less likely.

The opinion of the Court does not outlaw these texts nor condemn them to the fire, as the Communists do literature offensive to their creed. But if the books themselves are not outlawed, if they can lawfully remain on library shelves, by what reasoning does their use in a classroom become a crime?

If we are to take judicial notice of the threat of Communists within the nation, it should not be difficult to conclude that as a political party they are of little consequence. Communists in this country have never made a respectable or serious showing in any election. I would doubt that there is a village, let alone a city or county or state, which the Communists could carry. Communism in the world scene is no bogey-man; but Communism as a political faction or party in this country plainly is. Communism has been so thoroughly exposed in this country that it has been crippled as a political force. Free speech has destroyed it as an effective political party. [T]he people know Soviet Communism; the doctrine of Soviet revolution is exposed in all of its ugliness and the American people want none of it.

How it can be said that there is a clear and present danger that this advocacy will succeed is, therefore, a mystery. Some nations less resilient than the United States, where illiteracy is high and where democratic traditions are only budding, might have to take drastic steps and jail these men for merely speaking their creed. But in America they are miserable merchants of unwanted ideas; their wares remain unsold. The fact that their ideas are abhorrent does not make them powerful.

Neither prejudice nor hate nor senseless fear should be the basis of this solemn act. Free speech — the glory of our system of government — should not be sacrificed on anything less than plain and objective proof of danger that the evil advocated is imminent. On this record no one can say that petitioners and their converts are in such a strategic position as to have even the slightest chance of achieving their aims.

———————

In the years following *Dennis*, the Supreme Court decided several cases under the Smith Act. In Yates v. United States, 354 U.S. 298 (1957), the Court overturned the convictions of several individuals for conspiracy to violate the Smith Act. The Court emphasized that there was a crucial "distinction between advocacy of abstract doctrine and advocacy directed at promoting unlawful action." The Court did not overrule *Dennis*, but distinguished it. Justice Harlan, writing for the Court, said that *Dennis* held that "the indoctrination of a group in preparation for future violent action, as well as exhortation to immediate action . . . is not constitutionally protected when the group is of sufficient size and cohesiveness, is sufficiently oriented towards action, and other circumstances are such as reasonably to justify the apprehension that action will occur." But the Court said that was not present in *Yates*. Justice Harlan explained that the "essential distinction is that those to whom the advocacy is addressed must be urged to *do* something, now or in the future, rather than merely to *believe* in something."

The problem, of course, is deciding whether speech is advocacy of doctrine or advocacy to action. In many instances, this is likely to be an ephemeral distinction based entirely on how a judge chooses to characterize the speech. As Justice Holmes said, "Every idea is an incitement."[114]

Yates did not mark the end of the Court's willingness to uphold convictions under the Smith Act. For example, in Scales v. United States, 367 U.S. 203 (1961), the Court upheld a conviction for being a member of an organization that advocates the overthrow of the government. The Court stressed that for the government to punish such association there must be proof that an individual actively affiliated with a group, knowing of its illegal objectives and with the specific intent of furthering those goals. The Court concluded that there was sufficient evidence in the record "to make a case for the jury on the issue of illegal Party advocacy." In contrast, in Noto v. United States, 367 U.S. 290 (1961), the Court reversed a conviction under the Smith Act for conspiracy because of inadequate evidence to meet these requirements.

d.   The *Brandenburg* Test

By the mid-1960s, the Court appeared to be much more protective of speech. In Bond v. Floyd, 385 U.S. 116 (1966), the Court held that the Georgia General Assembly could not refuse to seat Representative Julian Bond because of his support for a statement strongly critical of the Vietnam War and the draft. The Court invoked Yates v. United States (1957) and concluded that Bond's statements were advocacy of ideas protected by the First Amendment.

———————

114. Gitlow v. New York, 268 U.S. (1925), at 673.

Also, in Watts v. United States, 394 U.S. 705 (1969), the Court reversed the conviction of an individual for violating the law that made it a crime to "knowingly and willfully . . . [threaten] to take the life of or to inflict bodily harm upon the President." An individual was convicted under this law for saying, "If they ever make me carry a rifle the first man I want to get in my sights is L.B.J. They are not going to make me kill my black brothers." The Court said that Watts's statement was "political hyperbole," not a real threat, and thus was protected by the First Amendment.

The key case defining when the government may punish advocacy of illegality is Brandenburg v. Ohio.

BRANDENBURG v. OHIO

395 U.S. 444 (1969)

Per Curiam.

The appellant, a leader of a Ku Klux Klan group, was convicted under the Ohio Criminal Syndicalism statute for "advocate[ing] . . . the duty, necessity, or propriety of crime, sabotage, violence, or unlawful methods of terrorism as a means of accomplishing industrial or political reform" and for "voluntarily assembl[ing] with any society, group, or assemblage of persons formed to teach or advocate the doctrines of criminal syndicalism." He was fined $1,000 and sentenced to one to 10 years' imprisonment.

The record shows that a man, identified at trial as the appellant, telephoned an announcer-reporter on the staff of a Cincinnati television station and invited him to come to a Ku Klux Klan "rally" to be held at a farm in Hamilton County. With the cooperation of the organizers, the reporter and a cameraman attended the meeting and filmed the events. The prosecution's case rested on the films and on testimony identifying the appellant as the person who communicated with the reporter and who spoke at the rally. The State also introduced into evidence several articles appearing in the film, including a pistol, a rifle, a shotgun, ammunition, a Bible, and a red hood worn by the speaker in the films.

One film showed 12 hooded figures, some of whom carried firearms. They were gathered around a large wooden cross, which they burned. No one was present other than the participants and the newsmen who made the film. Most of the words uttered during the scene were incomprehensible when the film was projected, but scattered phrases could be understood that were derogatory of Negroes and, in one instance, of Jews. Another scene on the same film showed the appellant, in Klan regalia, making a speech.

The second film showed six hooded figures one of whom, later identified as the appellant, repeated a speech very similar to that recorded on the first film. The reference to the possibility of "revengeance" was omitted, and one sentence was added: "Personally, I believe the nigger should be returned to Africa, the Jew returned to Israel." Though some of the figures in the films carried weapons, the speaker did not.

The Ohio Criminal Syndicalism Statute was enacted in 1919. From 1917 to 1920, identical or quite similar laws were adopted by 20 States and two territories. In 1927, this Court sustained the constitutionality of California's Criminal Syndicalism Act, the text of which is quite similar to that of the laws of Ohio. Whitney v. California (1927). But *Whitney* has been thoroughly discredited by later decisions. See Dennis v. United States (1951). These later decisions have fashioned the principle that the constitutional guarantees of free speech and free press do not permit a State to forbid or proscribe advocacy of the use of force or of law violation except where such advocacy is directed to inciting or producing imminent lawless action and is likely to incite or produce such action.

As we said in Noto v. United States (1961), "the mere abstract teaching . . . of the moral propriety or even moral necessity for a resort to force and violence, is not the same as preparing a group for violent action and steeling it to such action." A statute which fails to draw this distinction impermissibly intrudes upon the freedoms guaranteed by the First and Fourteenth Amendments. It sweeps within its condemnation speech which our Constitution has immunized from governmental control.

Measured by this test, Ohio's Criminal Syndicalism Act cannot be sustained. The Act punishes persons who "advocate or teach the duty, necessity, or propriety" of violence "as a means of accomplishing industrial or political reform"; or who publish or circulate or display any book or paper containing such advocacy; or who "justify" the commission of violent acts "with intent to exemplify, spread or advocate the propriety of the doctrines of criminal syndicalism"; or who "voluntarily assemble" with a group formed "to teach or advocate the doctrines of criminal syndicalism." Neither the indictment nor the trial judge's instructions to the jury in any way refined the statute's bald definition of the crime in terms of mere advocacy not distinguished from incitement to imminent lawless action.

Accordingly, we are here confronted with a statute which, by its own words and as applied, purports to punish mere advocacy and to forbid, on pain of criminal punishment, assembly with others merely to advocate the described type of action. Such a statute falls within the condemnation of the First and Fourteenth Amendments. The contrary teaching of Whitney v. California, cannot be supported, and that decision is therefore overruled.

Brandenburg is the Supreme Court's most speech-protective formulation of an incitement test. A conviction for incitement under *Brandenburg* is constitutional only if several requirements are met: imminent harm, a likelihood of producing illegal action, and an intent to cause imminent illegality. None of the earlier tests had contained an intent requirement. Also, none ever had so clearly stated a requirement for a likelihood of imminent harm.

Therefore, on a doctrinal level, it is puzzling that the Court presented the *Brandenburg* test as if it followed from the *Dennis* formulation, rather than as a substantial expansion in the protection of speech. In *Dennis*, the Court expressly denied that there was a requirement for proof of an imminent danger of likely harm.

Brandenburg does not answer, however, how imminence and likelihood are to be appraised. Are these requirements to be assessed relative to the harms to be prevented, so that the more serious the danger, the less in the way of imminence or likelihood that will be required? Or is some showing of imminence and likelihood necessary no matter how great the harm? If imminence and likelihood are judged relative to the nature of the danger, then *Brandenburg* in essence creates a risk formula like the *Dennis* test, even though one is not expressly stated in the *Brandenburg* formulation. Nor does the Court in *Brandenburg* elaborate as to the intent requirement and what must be proven to satisfy it.

There have been few Supreme Court cases in the decades since *Brandenburg* applying or explaining its standard. Hess v. Indiana, 414 U.S. 105 (1973), involved an individual who was convicted of disorderly conduct for declaring, "We'll take the fucking street later," after the police had cleared a demonstration from the street. The Court said that the speech was protected by the First Amendment. The Court explained that "at best . . . , the statement could be taken as counsel for present moderation; at worst, it amounted to nothing more than advocacy of illegal action at some indefinite future time." The Court said that this was insufficient to meet the *Brandenburg* test because there was "no evidence . . . that his words were intended to produce, and likely to produce, *imminent* disorder."

In NAACP v. Claiborne Hardware Co., 458 U.S. 886 (1982), the Court overturned a judgment against the NAACP for a boycott of white-owned businesses that it alleged engaged in racial discrimination. In part, the trial court had based the liability of the NAACP for damages from the boycott on a speech by an NAACP official that included the statement, "If we catch any of you going in any of them racist stores, we're gonna break your damn neck." The Court held that this speech was protected by the First Amendment under the *Brandenburg* test and thus could not be the basis for liability. The Court explained, "In the passionate atmosphere in which the speeches were delivered, they might have been understood as inviting an unlawful form of discipline or, at least, intending to create a fear of violence whether or not improper discipline was specifically intended. . . . This Court has made clear, however, that mere *advocacy* of the use of force or violence does not remove speech from the protection of the First Amendment. . . . The emotionally charged rhetoric of Charles Evers' speeches did not transcend the bounds of protected speech set forth in *Brandenburg*."

Brandenburg, Hess, and *NAACP* indicate that the Court has redefined the test for incitement in much more speech-protective terms. Under this law, an individual can be convicted for incitement only if it is proven that there was a likelihood of imminent illegal conduct and if the speech was directed at causing imminent illegal conduct. Yet perhaps the major difference between these cases and such earlier decisions as *Schenck, Gitlow, Whitney,* and *Dennis* is the social climate. The prior cases all were issued in tense times where there were strong pressures to suppress speech. Only in the unfortunate event that such times occur again will it be possible to know if the *Brandenburg* test better succeeds in protecting dissent in times of crisis.

In a recent case, the Supreme Court held that the government could punish speech that materially assists a terrorist organization. It is notable that the majority upheld the law without reference to *Brandenburg* or any of the cases in this area. Justice Breyer's dissent, however, argues that *Brandenburg* should have been applied and was not met here.

HOLDER v. HUMANITARIAN LAW PROJECT

130 S. Ct. 2705 (2010)

Chief Justice ROBERTS delivered the opinion of the Court. Congress has prohibited the provision of "material support or resources" to certain foreign organizations that engage in terrorist activity. 18 U.S.C. §2339B(a)(1). That prohibition is based on a finding that the specified organizations "are so tainted by their criminal conduct that any contribution to such an organization facilitates that conduct." The plaintiffs in this litigation seek to provide support to two such organizations. Plaintiffs claim that they seek to facilitate only the lawful, nonviolent purposes of those groups, and that applying the material-support law to prevent them from doing so violates the Constitution. In particular, they claim that the statute is too vague, in violation of the Fifth Amendment, and that it infringes their rights to freedom of speech and association, in violation of the First Amendment. We conclude that the material-support statute is constitutional as applied to the particular activities plaintiffs have told us they wish to pursue. We do not, however, address the resolution of more difficult cases that may arise under the statute in the future.

I

This litigation concerns 18 U.S.C. §2339B, which makes it a federal crime to "knowingly provid[e] material support or resources to a foreign terrorist organization." Congress has amended the definition of "material support or resources" periodically, but at present it is defined as follows: "[T]he term 'material support or resources' means any property, tangible or intangible, or service, including currency or monetary instruments or financial securities, financial services, lodging, training, expert advice or assistance, safehouses, false documentation or identification, communications equipment, facilities, weapons, lethal substances, explosives, personnel (1 or more individuals who may be or include oneself), and transportation, except medicine or religious materials."

The authority to designate an entity a "foreign terrorist organization" rests with the Secretary of State. She may, in consultation with the Secretary of the Treasury and the Attorney General, so designate an organization upon finding that it is foreign, engages in "terrorist activity" or "terrorism," and thereby "threatens the security of United States nationals or the national security of the United States." "'[N]ational security' means the national defense, foreign relations, or economic interests of the United States." §1189(d)(2). An entity designated a foreign terrorist organization may seek review of that designation before the D.C. Circuit within 30 days of that designation.

In 1997, the Secretary of State designated 30 groups as foreign terrorist organizations. Two of those groups are the Kurdistan Workers' Party (also known as the Partiya Karkeran Kurdistan, or PKK) and the Liberation Tigers of Tamil Eelam (LTTE). The PKK is an organization founded in 1974 with the aim of establishing an independent Kurdish state in southeastern Turkey. The LTTE is an organization founded in 1976 for the purpose of creating an independent Tamil state in Sri Lanka. The District Court in this action found that the PKK and the LTTE engage in political and humanitarian activities. The Government has presented evidence that both groups have also committed numerous terrorist attacks, some of which have harmed American citizens. The LTTE sought judicial review of its designation as a foreign terrorist organization; the D.C. Circuit upheld that designation. The PKK did not challenge its designation.

Plaintiffs in this litigation are two U.S. citizens and six domestic organizations.

II

Given the complicated 12-year history of this litigation, we pause to clarify the questions before us. Plaintiffs challenge §2339B's prohibition on four types of material support-"training," "expert advice or assistance," "service," and "personnel."

Plaintiffs do not challenge the above statutory terms in all their applications. Rather, plaintiffs claim that §2339B is invalid to the extent it prohibits them from engaging in certain specified activities. With respect to the HLP, those activities are: (1) "train[ing] members of [the] PKK on how to use humanitarian and international law to peacefully resolve disputes"; (2) "engag[ing] in political advocacy on behalf of Kurds who live in Turkey"; and (3) "teach[ing] PKK members how to petition various representative bodies such as the United Nations for relief." With respect to the other plaintiffs, those activities are: (1) "train[ing] members of [the] LTTE to present claims for tsunami-related aid to mediators and international bodies"; (2) "offer[ing] their legal expertise in negotiating peace agreements between the LTTE and the Sri Lankan government"; and (3) "engag[ing] in political advocacy on behalf of Tamils who live in Sri Lanka."

[III]

A

We next consider whether the material-support statute, as applied to plaintiffs, violates the freedom of speech guaranteed by the First Amendment.[115] Both plaintiffs and the Government take extreme positions on this question. Plaintiffs claim that Congress has banned their "pure political speech." It has not. Under the material-support statute, plaintiffs may say anything they wish on any topic. They may speak and write freely about the PKK and LTTE, the governments of Turkey and Sri Lanka, human rights, and international law. They may advocate before the United Nations. As the Government states: "The statute does not prohibit independent advocacy or expression of any kind." Section 2339B also "does not prevent [plaintiffs] from becoming members of the PKK and LTTE or impose any sanction on them for doing so." Congress has not, therefore, sought to suppress ideas or opinions in the form of "pure political speech." Rather, Congress has prohibited "material support," which most often does not take the form of speech at all. And when it does, the statute is carefully drawn to cover only a narrow category of speech to, under the direction of, or in coordination with foreign groups that the speaker knows to be terrorist organizations.

For its part, the Government takes the foregoing too far, claiming that the only thing truly at issue in this litigation is conduct, not speech. Section 2339B is directed at the fact of plaintiffs' interaction with the PKK and LTTE, the Government contends, and only incidentally burdens their expression. The Government is wrong that the only thing actually at issue in this litigation is conduct, and therefore wrong to argue that [intermediate scrutiny is] the correct standard of review. §2339B regulates speech on the basis of its content. Plaintiffs

---

115. The Court also rejected the argument that the terms of the statute "training," "expert advice or assistance," "service," and "personnel" were so vague as to violate the First Amendment. [Footnote by casebook author.]

want to speak to the PKK and the LTTE, and whether they may do so under §2339B depends on what they say. If plaintiffs' speech to those groups imparts a "specific skill" or communicates advice derived from "specialized knowledge"—for example, training on the use of international law or advice on petitioning the United Nations—then it is barred. On the other hand, plaintiffs' speech is not barred if it imparts only general or unspecialized knowledge.

B

The First Amendment issue before us is more refined than either plaintiffs or the Government would have it. It is not whether the Government may prohibit pure political speech, or may prohibit material support in the form of conduct. It is instead whether the Government may prohibit what plaintiffs want to do—provide material support to the PKK and LTTE in the form of speech.

Everyone agrees that the Government's interest in combating terrorism is an urgent objective of the highest order. The objective of combating terrorism does not justify prohibiting their speech, plaintiffs argue, because their support will advance only the legitimate activities of the designated terrorist organizations, not their terrorism.

Whether foreign terrorist organizations meaningfully segregate support of their legitimate activities from support of terrorism is an empirical question. When it enacted §2339B in 1996, Congress made specific findings regarding the serious threat posed by international terrorism. One of those findings explicitly rejects plaintiffs' contention that their support would not further the terrorist activities of the PKK and LTTE: "[F]oreign organizations that engage in terrorist activity are so tainted by their criminal conduct that *any contribution to such an organization* facilitates that conduct."

Plaintiffs argue that the reference to "any contribution" in this finding meant only monetary support. There is no reason to read the finding to be so limited, particularly because Congress expressly prohibited so much more than monetary support in §2339B. Congress's use of the term "contribution" is best read to reflect a determination that any form of material support furnished "to" a foreign terrorist organization should be barred, which is precisely what the material-support statute does.

The PKK and the LTTE are deadly groups. "The PKK's insurgency has claimed more than 22,000 lives." The LTTE has engaged in extensive suicide bombings and political assassinations, including killings of the Sri Lankan President, Security Minister, and Deputy Defense Minister. "On January 31, 1996, the LTTE exploded a truck bomb filled with an estimated 1,000 pounds of explosives at the Central Bank in Colombo, killing 100 people and injuring more than 1,400. This bombing was the most deadly terrorist incident in the world in 1996." It is not difficult to conclude as Congress did that the "tain[t]" of such violent activities is so great that working in coordination with or at the command of the PKK and LTTE serves to legitimize and further their terrorist means.

Material support meant to "promot[e] peaceable, lawful conduct," can further terrorism by foreign groups in multiple ways. "Material support" is a valuable resource by definition. Such support frees up other resources within the organization that may be put to violent ends. It also importantly helps lend legitimacy to foreign terrorist groups—legitimacy that makes it easier for those groups to persist, to recruit members, and to raise funds—all of which facilitate more terrorist attacks. "Terrorist organizations do not maintain *organizational* 'fire-walls' that would prevent or deter . . . sharing and commingling of support and benefits." "[I]nvestigators have revealed how terrorist groups systematically conceal their activities behind charitable, social, and political fronts." "Indeed, some designated foreign terrorist organizations use social and political components to recruit personnel to carry out terrorist operations, and to provide support to criminal terrorists and their families in aid of such operations."

Money is fungible, and "[w]hen foreign terrorist organizations that have a dual structure raise funds, they highlight the civilian and humanitarian ends to which such moneys could be put." But "there is reason to believe that foreign terrorist organizations do not maintain legitimate *financial* firewalls between those funds raised for civil, nonviolent activities, and those ultimately used to support violent, terrorist operations." Thus, "[f]unds raised ostensibly for charitable purposes have in the past been redirected by some terrorist groups to fund the purchase of arms and explosives."

The dissent argues that there is "no natural stopping place" for the proposition that aiding a foreign terrorist organization's lawful activity promotes the terrorist organization as a whole. But Congress has settled on just such a natural stopping place: The statute reaches only material support coordinated with or under the direction of a designated foreign terrorist organization. Independent advocacy that might be viewed as promoting the group's legitimacy is not covered.

Providing foreign terrorist groups with material support in any form also furthers terrorism by straining the United States' relationships with its allies and undermining cooperative efforts between nations to prevent terrorist attacks. We see no reason to question Congress's finding that "international cooperation is required for an effective response to terrorism, as demonstrated by the numerous multilateral conventions in force providing universal prosecutive jurisdiction over persons involved in a variety of terrorist acts, including hostage taking, murder of an internationally protected person, and aircraft piracy and sabotage." The material-support statute furthers this international effort by prohibiting aid for foreign terrorist groups that harm the United States' partners abroad.

C

In analyzing whether it is possible in practice to distinguish material support for a foreign terrorist group's violent activities and its nonviolent activities, we do not rely exclusively on our own inferences drawn from the record evidence. We have before us an affidavit stating the Executive Branch's conclusion on that question. The State Department informs us that "[t]he experience and analysis of the U.S. government agencies charged with combating terrorism strongly suppor[t]" Congress's finding that all contributions to foreign terrorist organizations further their terrorism.

That evaluation of the facts by the Executive, like Congress's assessment, is entitled to deference. This litigation implicates sensitive and weighty interests of national security and foreign affairs. The PKK and the LTTE have committed terrorist acts against American citizens abroad, and the material-support statute addresses acute foreign policy concerns involving relationships with our Nation's allies.

Our precedents, old and new, make clear that concerns of national security and foreign relations do not warrant abdication of the judicial role. We do not defer to the Government's reading of the First Amendment, even when such interests are at stake. But when it comes to collecting evidence and drawing factual inferences in this area, "the lack of competence on the part of the courts is marked," and respect for the Government's conclusions is appropriate.

At bottom, plaintiffs simply disagree with the considered judgment of Congress and the Executive that providing material support to a designated foreign terrorist organization — even seemingly benign support — bolsters the terrorist activities of that organization. That judgment, however, is entitled to significant weight, and we have persuasive evidence before us to sustain it. Given the sensitive interests in national security and foreign affairs at stake, the political branches have adequately substantiated their determination that, to serve the Government's interest in preventing terrorism, it was necessary to prohibit providing material support in the form of training, expert advice, personnel, and services to foreign terrorist groups, even if the supporters meant to promote only the groups' nonviolent ends.

We turn to the particular speech plaintiffs propose to undertake. First, plaintiffs propose to "train members of [the] PKK on how to use humanitarian and international law to peacefully resolve disputes." Congress can, consistent with the First Amendment, prohibit this direct training. It is wholly foreseeable that the PKK could use the "specific skill[s]" that plaintiffs propose to impart, as part of a broader strategy to promote terrorism. The PKK could, for example, pursue peaceful negotiation as a means of buying time to recover from short-term setbacks, lulling opponents into complacency, and ultimately preparing for renewed attacks. A foreign terrorist organization introduced to the structures of the international legal system might use the information to threaten, manipulate, and disrupt. This possibility is real, not remote.

Second, plaintiffs propose to "teach PKK members how to petition various representative bodies such as the United Nations for relief." The Government acts within First Amendment strictures in banning this proposed speech because it teaches the organization how to acquire "relief," which plaintiffs never define with any specificity, and which could readily include monetary aid. Indeed, earlier in this litigation, plaintiffs sought to teach the LTTE "to present claims for tsunami-related aid to mediators and international bodies," which naturally included monetary relief. Money is fungible and Congress logically concluded that money a terrorist group such as the PKK obtains using the techniques plaintiffs propose to teach could be redirected to funding the group's violent activities.

Finally, plaintiffs propose to "engage in political advocacy on behalf of Kurds who live in Turkey," and "engage in political advocacy on behalf of Tamils who live in Sri Lanka." As explained above, plaintiffs do not specify their expected level of coordination with the PKK or LTTE or suggest what exactly their "advocacy" would consist of. Plaintiffs' proposals are phrased at such a high level of generality that they cannot prevail in this preenforcement challenge.

All this is not to say that any future applications of the material-support statute to speech or advocacy will survive First Amendment scrutiny. It is also not to say that any other statute relating to speech and terrorism would satisfy the First Amendment. In particular, we in no way suggest that a regulation of independent speech would pass constitutional muster, even if the Government were to show that such speech benefits foreign terrorist organizations. We also do not suggest that Congress could extend the same prohibition on material support at issue here to domestic organizations. We simply hold that, in prohibiting the particular forms of support that plaintiffs seek to provide to foreign terrorist groups, §2339B does not violate the freedom of speech.

The Preamble to the Constitution proclaims that the people of the United States ordained and established that charter of government in part to "provide for the common defence." As Madison explained, "[s]ecurity against foreign danger is . . . an avowed and essential object of the American Union." We hold that, in regulating the particular forms of support that plaintiffs seek to provide to foreign terrorist organizations, Congress has pursued that objective consistent with the limitations of the First and Fifth Amendments.

Justice BREYER, with whom Justices GINSBURG, and SOTOMAYOR join, dissenting.

Like the Court, and substantially for the reasons it gives, I do not think this statute is unconstitutionally vague. But I cannot agree with the Court's conclusion that the Constitution permits the Government to prosecute the plaintiffs criminally for engaging in coordinated teaching and advocacy furthering the designated organizations' lawful political objectives. In my view, the Government has not met its burden of showing that an interpretation of the statute that would prohibit this speech- and association-related activity serves the Government's compelling interest in combating terrorism. And I would interpret the statute as normally placing activity of this kind outside its scope.

The plaintiffs, all United States citizens or associations, now seek an injunction and declaration providing that, without violating the statute, they can (1) "train members of [the] PKK on how to use humanitarian and international law to peacefully resolve disputes"; (2) "engage in political advocacy on behalf of Kurds who live in Turkey"; (3) "teach PKK members how to petition various representative bodies such as the United Nations for relief"; and (4) "engage in political advocacy on behalf of Tamils who live in Sri Lanka." All these activities are of a kind that the First Amendment ordinarily protects.

In my view, the Government has not made the strong showing necessary to justify under the First Amendment the criminal prosecution of those who engage in these activities. All the activities involve the communication and advocacy of political ideas and lawful means of achieving political ends. Even the subjects the plaintiffs wish to teach — using international law to resolve disputes peacefully or petitioning the United Nations, for instance — concern political speech. We cannot avoid the constitutional significance of these facts on the basis that some of this speech takes place outside the United States and is directed at foreign governments, for the activities also involve advocacy in *this* country directed to *our* government and *its* policies. The plaintiffs, for example, wish to write and distribute publications and to speak before the United States Congress.

That this speech and association for political purposes is the *kind* of activity to which the First Amendment ordinarily offers its strongest protection is elementary. Although in the Court's view the statute applies only where the PKK helps to coordinate a defendant's activities, the simple fact of "coordination" alone cannot readily remove protection that the First Amendment would otherwise grant. That amendment, after all, also protects the freedom of association. "Coordination" with a political group, like membership, involves association.

"Coordination" with a group that engages in unlawful activity also does not deprive the plaintiffs of the First Amendment's protection under any traditional "categorical" exception to its protection. The plaintiffs do not propose to solicit a crime. They will not engage in fraud or defamation or circulate obscenity. And the First Amendment protects advocacy even of *unlawful* action so long as that advocacy is not "directed to inciting or producing *imminent lawless action* and . . . *likely to incite or produce* such action." Here the plaintiffs seek to advocate peaceful, *lawful* action to secure *political* ends; and they seek to teach others how to do the same. No one contends that the plaintiffs' speech to these organizations can be prohibited as incitement. Moreover, the Court has previously held that a person who associates with a group that uses unlawful means to achieve its ends does not thereby necessarily forfeit the First Amendment's protection for freedom of association.

Not even the "serious and deadly problem" of international terrorism can require *automatic* forfeiture of First Amendment rights. After all, this Court has recognized that not "[e]ven the war power . . . remove[s] constitutional limitations safeguarding essential liberties." Thus, there is no general First Amendment exception that applies here. If the statute is constitutional in this context, it would have to come with a strong justification attached.

The Government does identify a compelling countervailing interest, namely, the interest in protecting the security of the United States and its nationals from the threats that foreign terrorist organizations pose by denying those organizations financial and other fungible resources. I do not dispute the importance of this interest. But I do dispute whether the interest can justify the statute's criminal prohibition. To put the matter more specifically, precisely how does application of the statute to the protected activities before us *help achieve* that important security-related end?

The Government makes two efforts to answer this question. *First,* the Government says that the plaintiffs' support for these organizations is "fungible" in the same sense as other forms of banned support. Being fungible, the plaintiffs' support could, for example, free up other resources, which the organization might put to terrorist ends. The proposition that the two very different kinds of "support" are "fungible," however, is not *obviously* true. There is no *obvious* way in which undertaking advocacy for political change through peaceful means or teaching the PKK and LTTE, say, how to petition the United Nations for political change is fungible with other resources that might be put to more sinister ends in the way that donations of money, food, or computer training are fungible. It is far from obvious that these advocacy activities can themselves be redirected, or will free other resources that can be directed, towards terrorist ends.

Second, the Government says that the plaintiffs' proposed activities will "bolste[r] a terrorist organization's efficacy and strength in a community" and "undermin[e] this nation's efforts to *delegitimize and weaken* those groups." In the Court's view, too, the Constitution permits application of the statute to activities of the kind at issue in part because those activities could provide a group that engages in terrorism with "legitimacy." The Court suggests that, armed with this greater "legitimacy," these organizations will more readily be able to obtain material support of the kinds Congress plainly intended to ban — money, arms, lodging, and the like.

Yet the Government does not claim that the statute forbids *any* speech "legitimating" a terrorist group. Rather, it reads the statute as permitting

(1) membership in terrorist organizations, (2) "peaceably assembling with members of the PKK and LTTE for lawful discussion," or (3) "independent advocacy" on behalf of these organizations. The Court, too, emphasizes that activities not "*coordinated with*" the terrorist groups are not banned.

But this "legitimacy" justification cannot by itself warrant suppression of political speech, advocacy, and association. Speech, association, and related activities on behalf of a group will often, perhaps always, help to legitimate that group. Thus, were the law to accept a "legitimating" effect, in and of itself and without qualification, as providing sufficient grounds for imposing such a ban, the First Amendment battle would be lost in untold instances where it should be won. Once one accepts this argument, there is no natural stopping place.

Nor can the Government overcome these considerations simply by narrowing the covered activities to those that involve *coordinated*, rather than *independent*, advocacy. Conversations, discussions, or logistical arrangements might well prove necessary to carry out the speech-related activities here at issue (just as conversations and discussions are a necessary part of *membership* in any organization). The Government does not distinguish this kind of "coordination" from any other. I am not aware of any form of words that might be used to describe "coordination" that would not, at a minimum, seriously chill not only the kind of activities the plaintiffs raise before us, but also the "independent advocacy" the Government purports to permit. And, as for the Government's willingness to distinguish *independent* advocacy from *coordinated* advocacy, the former is *more* likely, not *less* likely, to confer legitimacy than the latter. Thus, other things being equal, the distinction "coordination" makes is arbitrary in respect to furthering the statute's purposes. And a rule of law that finds the "legitimacy" argument adequate in respect to the latter would have a hard time distinguishing a statute that sought to attack the former.

Throughout, the majority emphasizes that it would defer strongly to Congress' "informed judgment." But here, there is no evidence that Congress has made such a judgment regarding the specific activities at issue in these cases. I concede that the Government's expertise in foreign affairs may warrant deference in respect to many matters, *e.g.*, our relations with Turkey. But it remains for this Court to decide whether the Government has shown that such an interest justifies criminalizing speech activity otherwise protected by the First Amendment. And the fact that other nations may like us less for granting that protection cannot in and of itself carry the day.

For the reasons I have set forth, I believe application of the statute as the Government interprets it would gravely and without adequate justification injure interests of the kind the First Amendment protects. Thus, there is "a serious doubt" as to the statute's constitutionality. And where that is so, we must "ascertain whether a construction of the statute is fairly possible by which the question may be avoided."

I believe that a construction that would avoid the constitutional problem is "fairly possible." In particular, I would read the statute as criminalizing First-Amendment-protected pure speech and association only when the defendant knows or intends that those activities will assist the organization's unlawful terrorist actions. Under this reading, the Government would have to show, at a minimum, that such defendants provided support that they knew was significantly likely to help the organization pursue its unlawful terrorist aims.

This reading of the statute protects those who engage in pure speech and association ordinarily protected by the First Amendment. But it does not protect that activity where a defendant purposefully intends it to help terrorism or where a defendant knows (or willfully blinds himself to the fact) that the activity is significantly likely to assist terrorism. Where the activity fits into these categories of purposefully or knowingly supporting terrorist ends, the act of providing material support to a known terrorist organization bears a close enough relation to terrorist acts that, in my view, it likely can be prohibited notwithstanding any First Amendment interest. At the same time, this reading does not require the Government to undertake the difficult task of proving which, as between peaceful and nonpeaceful purposes, a defendant specifically preferred; knowledge is enough. This reading is consistent with the statute's text. The statute prohibits "*knowingly* provid[ing] *material* support or resources to a foreign terrorist organization."

Having interpreted the statute to impose the *mens rea* requirement just described, I would remand the cases so that the lower courts could consider more specifically the precise activities in which the plaintiffs still wish to engage and determine whether and to what extent a grant of declaratory and injunctive relief were warranted.

In sum, these cases require us to consider how to apply the First Amendment where national security interests are at stake. When deciding such cases, courts are aware and must respect the fact that the Constitution entrusts to the Executive and Legislative Branches the power to provide for the national defense, and that it grants particular authority to the President in matters of foreign affairs. Nonetheless, this Court has also made clear that authority and expertise in these matters do not automatically trump the Court's own obligation to secure the protection that the Constitution grants to individuals. In these cases, for the reasons I have stated, I believe the Court has failed to examine the Government's justifications with sufficient care. It has failed to insist upon specific evidence, rather than general assertion. It has failed to require tailoring of means to fit compelling ends. And ultimately it deprives the individuals before us of the protection that the First Amendment demands.

2. Fighting Words, the Hostile Audience, and the Problem of Racist Speech

The preceding section focuses on when speech can be punished because it advocates illegal acts or the overthrow of the government. This section considers a related, though distinct, question: When may speech be punished because of the risk that it may provoke an audience into using illegal force against the speaker? In other words, the former cases involve concern that an audience may follow the speaker into lawlessness; these cases concern the danger that the audience may be lawless in its reaction against the speaker.

The Court has formulated two doctrines that deal with this issue. One is the Court's holding that "fighting words" — speech that is directed at another and likely to provoke a violent response — are unprotected by the First Amendment. The other is a series of cases concerning when a speaker may be punished because of the reaction of the audience. These doctrines are discussed in turn below in subsections a and b.

Closely related to these topics, but again distinct, is the question of whether and when the government may prohibit and punish expression of hate. This topic, which has attracted a great deal of attention over the last couple of decades because of the development of hate speech codes at campuses across the country, is discussed in subsection c.

a. Fighting Words

In Chaplinsky v. New Hampshire, in 1942, the Supreme Court expressly held that "fighting words" are a category of speech unprotected by the First Amendment.

CHAPLINSKY v. NEW HAMPSHIRE
315 U.S. 568 (1942)

Appellant, a member of the sect known as Jehovah's Witnesses, was convicted in the municipal court of Rochester, New Hampshire, for violation of the Public Laws of New Hampshire: "No person shall address any offensive, derisive or annoying word to any other person who is lawfully in any street or other public place, nor call him by any offensive or derisive name, nor make any noise or exclamation in his presence and hearing with intent to deride, offend or annoy him, or to prevent him from pursuing his lawful business or occupation."

The complaint charged that appellant "with force and arms, in a certain public place in said city of Rochester, to wit, on the public sidewalk on the easterly side of Wakefield Street, near unto the entrance of the City Hall, did unlawfully repeat, the words following, addressed to the complainant, that is to say, 'You are a God damned racketeer' and 'a damned Fascist and the whole government of Rochester are Fascists or agents of Fascists' the same being offensive, derisive and annoying words and names."

There is no substantial dispute over the facts. Chaplinsky was distributing the literature of his sect on the streets of Rochester on a busy Saturday afternoon. Members of the local citizenry complained to the City Marshal, Bowering, that Chaplinsky was denouncing all religion as a "racket." Bowering told them that Chaplinsky was lawfully engaged, and then warned Chaplinsky that the crowd was getting restless. Some time later a disturbance occurred and the traffic officer on duty at the busy intersection started with Chaplinsky for the police station, but did not inform him that he was under arrest or that he was going to be arrested. On the way they encountered Marshal Bowering who had been advised that a riot was under way and was therefore hurrying to the scene. Bowering repeated his earlier warning to Chaplinsky who then addressed to Bowering the words set forth in the complaint.

Chaplinsky's version of the affair was slightly different. He testified that when he met Bowering, he asked him to arrest the ones responsible for the disturbance. In reply Bowering cursed him and told him to come along. Appellant admitted that he said the words charged in the complaint with the exception of the name of the Deity.

Allowing the broadest scope to the language and purpose of the Fourteenth Amendment, it is well understood that the right of free speech is not absolute at all times and under all circumstances. There are certain well-defined and narrowly limited classes of speech, the prevention and punishment of which has never been thought to raise any Constitutional problem. These include the lewd and obscene, the profane, the libelous, and the insulting or "fighting" words — those which by their very utterance inflict injury or tend to incite an immediate breach of the peace. It has been well observed that such utterances are no essential part of any exposition of ideas, and are of such slight social value as a step to truth that any benefit that may be derived from them is clearly outweighed by the social interest in order and morality. "Resort to epithets or personal abuse is not in any proper sense communication of information or opinion safeguarded by the Constitution, and its punishment as a criminal act would raise no question under that instrument."

On the authority of its earlier decisions, the state court declared that the statute's purpose was to preserve the public peace, no words being "forbidden except such as have a direct tendency to cause acts of violence by the person to whom, individually, the remark is addressed." The statute, as construed, does no more than prohibit the face-to-face words plainly likely to cause a breach of the peace by the addressee, words whose speaking constitute a breach of the peace by the speaker — including "classical fighting words," words in current use less "classical" but equally likely to cause violence, and other disorderly words, including profanity, obscenity and threats.

We are unable to say that the limited scope of the statute as thus construed contravenes the constitutional right of free expression. It is a statute narrowly drawn and limited to define and punish specific conduct lying within the domain of state power, the use in a public place of words likely to cause a breach of the peace.

Nor can we say that the application of the statute to the facts disclosed by the record substantially or unreasonably impinges upon the privilege of free speech. Argument is unnecessary to demonstrate that the appellations "damn racketeer" and "damn Fascist" are epithets likely to provoke the average person to retaliation, and thereby cause a breach of the peace.

Chaplinsky appears to recognize two situations where speech constitutes fighting words: Where it is likely to cause a violent response against the speaker and where it is an insult likely to inflict immediate emotional harm. Each aspect raises questions about whether such speech should be outside the protection of the First Amendment. As to the former, the danger that the listener will be provoked to fight, the issue is whether the appropriate response is to punish the speaker or rather to punish the person who actually resorts to violence. As to the latter, speech that inflicts an emotional injury, the question — which is key in the discussion of hate speech considered below — is whether speech should be punished because it is upsetting or deeply offensive to an audience.

The Supreme Court never has overturned *Chaplinsky*; fighting words remains a category of speech unprotected by the First Amendment. But in the more than 70 years since *Chaplinsky*, the Court has never again upheld a fighting words conviction. Every time the Court has reviewed a case involving fighting words, the Court has reversed the conviction, but without overruling *Chaplinsky.*

The Court has used three techniques in overturning these convictions. First, the Court has narrowed the scope of the fighting words doctrine by ruling that it applies only to speech directed at another person that is likely to produce a violent response. Second, the Court frequently has found laws prohibiting fighting words to be unconstitutionally vague or overbroad. Third, the Court has found laws that prohibit some fighting words — such as expression of hate based on race or gender — to be impermissible content-based restrictions of speech.

Each of these techniques is discussed below. The cumulative impact of these decisions is to make it unlikely that a fighting words law could survive. If the law is narrow, then it likely would be deemed an impermissible content-based restriction because it outlaws some fighting words, but not others, based on the content of the speech. If the law is broad, then it probably would be invalidated on vagueness or overbreadth grounds.

i. Narrowing the Fighting Words Doctrine

In Street v. New York, 394 U.S. 576 (1969), the Supreme Court said that there is a "small class of 'fighting words' which are 'likely to provoke the average person to retaliation, and thereby cause a breach of the peace.'" In *Street,* the Court reversed the conviction of an individual who had burned an American flag after learning that James Meredith had been shot. He declared, "We don't need no damn flag. . . . If they let that happen to Meredith we don't need an American flag." The Court said that while some may have found the speech inherently inflammatory, it was not fighting words unprotected by the First Amendment.

This was further clarified in Cohen v. California, 403 U.S. 15 (1971), presented below in the discussion of symbolic speech, where the Court held that unprotected fighting words occur only if the speech is directed to a specific person and likely to provoke violent response. Cohen was convicted for disturbing the peace for having in a courthouse a jacket that had on its back the words, "Fuck the Draft." The state argued, in part, that the inscription on the jacket constituted fighting words because of the possible violent response from people who saw and were angered by the message. The Court, in an opinion by Justice Harlan, rejected this and stated: "While the four-letter word displayed by Cohen in relation to the draft is not uncommonly employed in a personally provocative fashion, in this instance it was clearly not directed to the person of the hearer. No individual actually or likely to be present could reasonably have regarded the words on appellant's jacket as a direct personal insult."

The Court applied this requirement in Texas v. Johnson, 491 U.S. 397 (1989), presented in detail below, where it held that flag burning was a form of speech protected by the First Amendment. As in *Street,* one argument made by the government was that the flag destruction was likely to provoke a violent response from the audience and thus was a form of fighting words. The Court rejected this contention for the reason given in *Cohen:* The speech was not directed at a particular person. Justice Brennan, writing for the Court, said, "[N]o reasonable onlooker would have regarded [the] generalized expression of dissatisfaction with the policies of the Federal Government as a direct personal insult or an invitation to exchange fisticuffs."

ii. *Fighting Words Laws Invalidated as Vague and Overbroad*

In most cases since Chaplinsky involving fighting words, the Court has reversed the convictions by declaring the laws to be unconstitutionally vague and overbroad. Gooding v. Wilson is illustrative.

GOODING v. WILSON
405 U.S. 518 (1972)

Justice BRENNAN delivered the opinion of the Court.

Appellee was convicted in Superior Court, Fulton County, Georgia, on two counts of using opprobrious words and abusive language in violation of Georgia Code, §26-6303, which provides: "Any person who shall, without provocation, use to or of another, and in his presence . . . opprobrious words or abusive language, tending to cause a breach of the peace . . . shall be guilty of a misdemeanor."

Count 3 of the indictment alleged that the accused "did without provocation use to and of M.G. Redding and in his presence, the following abusive language and opprobrious words, tending to cause a breach of the peace: 'White son of a bitch, I'll kill you.' 'You son of a bitch, I'll choke you to death.'" Count 4 alleged that the defendant "did without provocation use to and of T.L. Raborn, and in his presence, the following abusive language and opprobrious words, tending to cause a breach of the peace: 'You son of a bitch, if you ever put your hands on me again, I'll cut you all to pieces.'"

Section 26-6303 punishes only spoken words. It can therefore withstand appellee's attack upon its facial constitutionality only if, as authoritatively construed by the Georgia courts, it is not susceptible of application to speech, although vulgar or offensive, that is protected by the First and Fourteenth Amendments. It matters not that the words appellee used might have been constitutionally prohibited under a narrowly and precisely drawn statute.

The constitutional guarantees of freedom of speech forbid the States to punish the use of words or language not within "narrowly limited classes of speech." Chaplinsky v. New Hampshire (1942). Even as to such a class, however, because "the line between speech unconditionally guaranteed and speech which may legitimately be regulated, suppressed, or punished is finely drawn," "[i]n every case the power to regulate must be so exercised as not, in attaining a permissible end, unduly to infringe the protected freedom." In other words, the statute must be carefully drawn or be authoritatively construed to punish only unprotected speech and not be susceptible of application to protected expression. "Because First Amendment freedoms need breathing space to survive, government may regulate in the area only with narrow specificity." Appellant does not challenge these principles but contends that the Georgia statute is narrowly drawn to apply only to a constitutionally unprotected class of words — "fighting" words — "those which by their very utterance inflict injury or tend to incite an immediate breach of the peace." Chaplinsky v. New Hampshire. Appellant argues that the Georgia appellate courts have by construction limited the proscription of §26-6303 to "fighting" words, as the New Hampshire Supreme Court limited the New Hampshire statute.

The dictionary definitions of "opprobrious" and "abusive" give them greater reach than "fighting" words. Webster's Third New International Dictionary (1961) defined "opprobrious" as "conveying or intended to convey disgrace," and "abusive" as including "harsh insulting language." Georgia appellate decisions have construed §26-6303 to apply to utterances that, although within these definitions, are not "fighting" words as *Chaplinsky* defines them. In Lyons v. State, 94 Ga. App. 570 (1956), a conviction under the statute was sustained for awakening 10 women scout leaders on a camp-out by shouting, "Boys, this is where we are going to spend the night." "Get the G—d— bed rolls out . . . let's see how close we can come to the G—d— tents." Again, in Fish v. State, 124 Ga. 416 (1905), the Georgia Supreme Court held that a jury question was presented by the remark, "You swore a lie." Georgia appellate decisions construing the reach of "tending to cause a breach of the peace" underscore that §26-6303 is not limited, as appellant argues, to words that "naturally tend to provoke violent resentment." Unlike the construction of the New Hampshire statute by the New Hampshire Supreme Court, the Georgia appellate courts have not construed §26-6303 "so as to avoid all constitutional difficulties."

Justice BLACKMUN, with whom the Chief Justice joins, dissenting.

It seems strange, indeed, that in this day a man may say to a police officer, who is attempting to restore access to a public building, "White son of a bitch, I'll kill you" and "You son of a bitch, I'll choke you to death," and say to an accompanying officer, "You son of a bitch, if you ever put your hands on me again, I'll cut you all to pieces," and yet constitutionally cannot be prosecuted and convicted under a state statute that makes it a misdemeanor to "use to or of another, and in his presence . . . opprobrious words or abusive language, tending to cause a breach of the peace. . . ." This, however, is precisely what the Court pronounces as the law today.

The Supreme Court of Georgia, when the conviction was appealed, unanimously held the other way. Surely any adult who can read — and I do not exclude this appellee-defendant from that category — should reasonably expect no other conclusion. The words of Georgia Code §26-6303 are clear. They are also concise. They are not, in my view, overbroad or incapable of being understood. Except perhaps for the "big" word "opprobrious" — and no point is made of its bigness — any Georgia schoolboy would expect that this defendant's fighting and provocative words to the officers were covered by §26-6303. Common sense permits no other conclusion. This is demonstrated by the fact that the appellee, and this Court, attack the statute, not as it applies to the appellee, but as it conceivably might apply to others who might utter other words.

In three other cases also decided in 1972 — Rosenfeld v. New Jersey, 408 U.S. 901 (1972), Lewis v. City of New Orleans, 408 U.S. 913 (1972), and Brown v. Oklahoma, 408 U.S. 914 (1972) — the Court overturned fighting words laws by finding them to be impermissibly vague and overbroad. *Rosenfeld, Lewis,* and

Brown all involved the angry use of profanity in a manner likely to provoke an audience. In each case, the Court overturned a fighting words conviction and vacated in light of Gooding v. Wilson. In *Rosenfeld*, the defendant, speaking at a school board meeting, repeatedly used the word "motherfucker" in describing teachers and school board members. In *Lewis*, a woman called the police, who were arresting her son, "goddamn motherfucker police." In *Brown*, an individual in a speech referred to police officers as "motherfucking fascist pig cops" and spoke of one particular officer as a "black motherfucking pig." In each of the instances, the Court reversed the convictions, making it clear that speech is protected even if it uttered in anger, filled with profanities, and likely to anger the audience.

In City of Houston v. Hill, 482 U.S. 451 (1987), the Court overturned a city ordinance that made it a crime for a person to "oppose, molest, abuse, or interrupt any policeman in the execution of his duty." The Court explained that the "ordinance's plain language is admittedly violated scores of times daily. . . . It is not limited to fighting words nor even to obscene or opprobrious language, but prohibits speech that 'in any manner . . . interrupt[s] an officer.' The Constitution does not allow such speech to be made a crime."

These cases indicate that a fighting words law will be upheld only if it is specific and narrowly tailored to apply just to speech that is not protected by the First Amendment. Otherwise, the statute or ordinance will be deemed void on vagueness grounds or invalidated as being impermissibly overbroad.

iii. Narrow Fighting Words Laws as Content-Based Restrictions

However, a very narrow fighting words law likely will be declared unconstitutional as impermissibly drawing content-based distinctions as to what speech is prohibited and what is allowed. This was the result in R.A.V. v. City of St. Paul, the Supreme Court's most recent fighting words decision.

R.A.V. v. CITY OF ST. PAUL, MINNESOTA

505 U.S. 377 (1992)

Justice SCALIA delivered the opinion of the Court.

In the predawn hours of June 21, 1990, petitioner and several other teenagers allegedly assembled a crudely made cross by taping together broken chair legs. They then allegedly burned the cross inside the fenced yard of a black family that lived across the street from the house where petitioner was staying. Although this conduct could have been punished under any of a number of laws, one of the two provisions under which respondent city of St. Paul chose to charge petitioner (then a juvenile) was the St. Paul Bias-Motivated Crime Ordinance, St. Paul, Minn., Legis. Code §292.02 (1990), which provides: "Whoever places on public or private property a symbol, object, appellation, characterization or graffiti, including, but not limited to, a burning cross or Nazi swastika, which one knows or has reasonable grounds to know arouses anger, alarm or resentment in others on the basis of race, color, creed, religion or gender commits disorderly conduct and shall be guilty of a misdemeanor."

Petitioner moved to dismiss this count on the ground that the St. Paul ordinance was substantially overbroad and impermissibly content based and therefore facially invalid under the First Amendment. The trial court granted this motion, but the Minnesota Supreme Court reversed. That court rejected petitioner's overbreadth claim because, as construed in prior Minnesota cases, the modifying phrase "arouses anger, alarm or resentment in others" limited the reach of the ordinance to conduct that amounts to "fighting words," i.e., "conduct that itself inflicts injury or tends to incite immediate violence . . . ," and therefore the ordinance reached only expression "that the first amendment does not protect." The court also concluded that the ordinance was not impermissibly content based because, in its view, "the ordinance is a narrowly tailored means toward accomplishing the compelling governmental interest in protecting the community against bias-motivated threats to public safety and order."

I

In construing the St. Paul ordinance, we are bound by the construction given to it by the Minnesota court. Accordingly, we accept the Minnesota Supreme Court's authoritative statement that the ordinance reaches only those expressions that constitute "fighting words" within the meaning of *Chaplinsky*. Petitioner and his amici urge us to modify the scope of the *Chaplinsky* formulation, thereby invalidating the ordinance as "substantially overbroad." We find it unnecessary to consider this issue. Assuming, arguendo, that all of the expression reached by the ordinance is proscribable under the "fighting words" doctrine, we nonetheless conclude that the ordinance is facially unconstitutional in that it prohibits otherwise permitted speech solely on the basis of the subjects the speech addresses.

The First Amendment generally prevents government from proscribing speech, because of disapproval of the ideas expressed. Content-based regulations are presumptively invalid. From 1791 to the present, however, our society, like other free but civilized societies, has permitted restrictions upon the content of speech in a few limited areas, which are "of such slight social value as a step to truth that any benefit that may be derived from them is clearly outweighed by the social interest in order and morality."

We have sometimes said that these categories of expression are "not within the area of constitutionally protected speech," or that the "protection of the First Amendment does not extend" to them. Such statements must be taken in context, however, and are no more literally true than is the occasionally repeated shorthand characterizing obscenity "as not being speech at all." What they mean is that these areas of speech can, consistently with the First Amendment, be regulated because of their constitutionally proscribable content (obscenity, defamation, etc.) — not that they are categories of speech entirely invisible to the Constitution, so that they may be made the vehicles for content discrimination unrelated to their distinctively proscribable content. Thus, the government may proscribe libel; but it may not make the further content discrimination of proscribing only libel critical of the government.

Our cases surely do not establish the proposition that the First Amendment imposes no obstacle whatsoever to regulation of particular instances of such proscribable expression, so that the government "may regulate [them] freely."

That would mean that a city council could enact an ordinance prohibiting only those legally obscene works that contain criticism of the city government or, indeed, that do not include endorsement of the city government. Such a simplistic, all-or-nothing-at-all approach to First Amendment protection is at odds with common sense and with our jurisprudence as well. It is not true that "fighting words" have at most a "de minimis" expressive content, or that their content is in all respects "worthless and undeserving of constitutional protection," sometimes they are quite expressive indeed. We have not said that they constitute "no part of the expression of ideas," but only that they constitute "no essential part of any exposition of ideas." Chaplinsky v. New Hampshire.

The proposition that a particular instance of speech can be proscribable on the basis of one feature (e.g., obscenity) but not on the basis of another (e.g., opposition to the city government) is commonplace and has found application in many contexts. We have long held, for example, that nonverbal expressive activity can be banned because of the action it entails, but not because of the ideas it expresses — so that burning a flag in violation of an ordinance against outdoor fires could be punishable, whereas burning a flag in violation of an ordinance against dishonoring the flag is not.

And just as the power to proscribe particular speech on the basis of a noncontent element (e.g., noise) does not entail the power to proscribe the same speech on the basis of a content element; so also, the power to proscribe it on the basis of one content element (e.g., obscenity) does not entail the power to proscribe it on the basis of other content elements.

In other words, the exclusion of "fighting words" from the scope of the First Amendment simply means that, for purposes of that Amendment, the unprotected features of the words are, despite their verbal character, essentially a "nonspeech" element of communication. Fighting words are thus analogous to a noisy sound truck: Each is, as Justice Frankfurter recognized, a "mode of speech," both can be used to convey an idea; but neither has, in and of itself, a claim upon the First Amendment. As with the sound truck, however, so also with fighting words: The government may not regulate use based on hostility — or favoritism — towards the underlying message expressed.

When the basis for the content discrimination consists entirely of the very reason the entire class of speech at issue is proscribable, no significant danger of idea or viewpoint discrimination exists. Such a reason, having been adjudged neutral enough to support exclusion of the entire class of speech from First Amendment protection, is also neutral enough to form the basis of distinction within the class. To illustrate: A State might choose to prohibit only that obscenity which is the most patently offensive in its prurience — i.e., that which involves the most lascivious displays of sexual activity. But it may not prohibit, for example, only that obscenity which includes offensive political messages. And the Federal Government can criminalize only those threats of violence that are directed against the President, see 18 U.S.C. §871 — since the reasons why threats of violence are outside the First Amendment (protecting individuals from the fear of violence, from the disruption that fear engenders, and from the possibility that the threatened violence will occur) have special force when applied to the person of the President.

Another valid basis for according differential treatment to even a content-defined subclass of proscribable speech is that the subclass happens to be associated with particular "secondary effects" of the speech, so that the regulation is "justified without reference to the content of the . . . speech," Renton v. Playtime Theatres, Inc. (1986). A State could, for example, permit all obscene live performances except those involving minors. Moreover, since words can in some circumstances violate laws directed not against speech but against conduct (a law against treason, for example, is violated by telling the enemy the Nation's defense secrets), a particular content-based subcategory of a proscribable class of speech can be swept up incidentally within the reach of a statute directed at conduct rather than speech. Thus, for example, sexually derogatory "fighting words," among other words, may produce a violation of Title VII's general prohibition against sexual discrimination in employment practices. Where the government does not target conduct on the basis of its expressive content, acts are not shielded from regulation merely because they express a discriminatory idea or philosophy.

These bases for distinction refute the proposition that the selectivity of the restriction is "even arguably conditioned upon the sovereign's agreement with what a speaker may intend to say." There may be other such bases as well. Indeed, to validate such selectivity (where totally proscribable speech is at issue) it may not even be necessary to identify any particular "neutral" basis, so long as the nature of the content discrimination is such that there is no realistic possibility that official suppression of ideas is afoot. (We cannot think of any First Amendment interest that would stand in the way of a State's prohibiting only those obscene motion pictures with blue-eyed actresses.) Save for that limitation, the regulation of "fighting words," like the regulation of noisy speech, may address some offensive instances and leave other, equally offensive, instances alone.

II

Applying these principles to the St. Paul ordinance, we conclude that, even as narrowly construed by the Minnesota Supreme Court, the ordinance is facially unconstitutional. Although the phrase in the ordinance, "arouses anger, alarm or resentment in others," has been limited by the Minnesota Supreme Court's construction to reach only those symbols or displays that amount to "fighting words," the remaining, unmodified terms make clear that the ordinance applies only to "fighting words" that insult, or provoke violence, "on the basis of race, color, creed, religion or gender." Displays containing abusive invective, no matter how vicious or severe, are permissible unless they are addressed to one of the specified disfavored topics. Those who wish to use "fighting words" in connection with other ideas—to express hostility, for example, on the basis of political affiliation, union membership, or homosexuality—are not covered. The First Amendment does not permit St. Paul to impose special prohibitions on those speakers who express views on disfavored subjects.

In its practical operation, moreover, the ordinance goes even beyond mere content discrimination, to actual viewpoint discrimination. Displays containing some words—odious racial epithets, for example—would be prohibited to proponents of all views. But "fighting words" that do not themselves invoke race, color, creed, religion, or gender—aspersions upon a person's mother, for example—would seemingly be usable ad libitum in the placards of those arguing in favor of racial, color, etc., tolerance and equality, but could not be used by those speakers' opponents. One could hold up a sign saying, for example, that all "anti-Catholic bigots" are misbegotten; but not that all "papists" are, for that would insult and provoke violence "on the basis of religion." St. Paul has no such authority to license one side of a debate to fight freestyle, while requiring the other to follow Marquis of Queensberry rules.

The content-based discrimination reflected in the St. Paul ordinance comes within neither any of the specific exceptions to the First Amendment prohibition we discussed earlier nor a more general exception for content discrimination that does not threaten censorship of ideas. It assuredly does not fall within the exception for content discrimination based on the very reasons why the particular class of speech at issue (here, fighting words) is proscribable.

Let there be no mistake about our belief that burning a cross in someone's front yard is reprehensible. But St. Paul has sufficient means at its disposal to prevent such behavior without adding the First Amendment to the fire.

Justice WHITE, with whom Justice BLACKMUN and Justice O'CONNOR join, and with whom Justice STEVENS joins concurring in the judgment.

I agree with the majority that the judgment of the Minnesota Supreme Court should be reversed. However, our agreement ends there. This case could easily be decided within the contours of established First Amendment law by holding, as petitioner argues, that the St. Paul ordinance is fatally overbroad because it criminalizes not only unprotected expression but expression protected by the First Amendment.

This Court's decisions have plainly stated that expression falling within certain limited categories so lacks the values the First Amendment was designed to protect that the Constitution affords no protection to that expression. Chaplinsky v. New Hampshire (1942). For instance, the Court has held that the individual who falsely shouts "fire" in a crowded theater may not claim the protection of the First Amendment. Schenck v. United States (1919). The Court has concluded that neither child pornography nor obscenity is protected by the First Amendment. New York v. Ferber (1982); Miller v. California (1973). And the Court has observed that, "[l]eaving aside the special considerations when public officials [and public figures] are the target, a libelous publication is not protected by the Constitution."

All of these categories are content based. But the Court has held that the First Amendment does not apply to them because their expressive content is worthless or of de minimis value to society. This categorical approach has provided a principled and narrowly focused means for distinguishing between expression that the government may regulate freely and that which it may regulate on the basis of content only upon a showing of compelling need.

Today, however, the Court announces that earlier Courts did not mean their repeated statements that certain categories of expression are "not within the area of constitutionally protected speech." The present Court submits that such clear statements "must be taken in context" and are not "literally true." To the contrary, those statements meant precisely what they said: The categorical approach is a firmly entrenched part of our First Amendment jurisprudence.

Nevertheless, the majority holds that the First Amendment protects those narrow categories of expression long held to be undeserving of First Amendment protection — at least to the extent that lawmakers may not regulate some fighting words more strictly than others because of their content. The Court announces that such content-based distinctions violate the First Amendment because "[t]he government may not regulate use based on hostility — or favoritism — towards the underlying message expressed." Should the government want to criminalize certain fighting words, the Court now requires it to criminalize all fighting words.

To borrow a phrase: "Such a simplistic, all-or-nothing-at-all approach to First Amendment protection is at odds with common sense and with our jurisprudence as well." It is inconsistent to hold that the government may proscribe an entire category of speech because the content of that speech is evil, but that the government may not treat a subset of that category differently without violating the First Amendment; the content of the subset is by definition worthless and undeserving of constitutional protection.

In a second break with precedent, the Court refuses to sustain the ordinance even though it would survive under the strict scrutiny applicable to other protected expression. Assuming, arguendo, that the St. Paul ordinance is a content-based regulation of protected expression, it nevertheless would pass First Amendment review under settled law upon a showing that the regulation "is necessary to serve a compelling state interest and is narrowly drawn to achieve that end."

St. Paul has urged that its ordinance, in the words of the majority, "helps to ensure the basic human rights of members of groups that have historically been subjected to discrimination. . . ." The Court expressly concedes that this interest is compelling and is promoted by the ordinance. Nevertheless, the Court treats strict scrutiny analysis as irrelevant to the constitutionality of the legislation. Under the majority's view, a narrowly drawn, content-based ordinance could never pass constitutional muster if the object of that legislation could be accomplished by banning a wider category of speech. This appears to be a general renunciation of strict scrutiny review, a fundamental tool of First Amendment analysis.

Although I disagree with the Court's analysis, I do agree with its conclusion: The St. Paul ordinance is unconstitutional. However, I would decide the case on overbreadth grounds. Although the ordinance as construed reaches categories of speech that are constitutionally unprotected, it also criminalizes a substantial amount of expression that — however repugnant — is shielded by the First Amendment.

Justice BLACKMUN, concurring in the judgment.

I regret what the Court has done in this case. The majority opinion signals one of two possibilities: It will serve as precedent for future cases, or it will not. Either result is disheartening.

In the first instance, by deciding that a State cannot regulate speech that causes great harm unless it also regulates speech that does not (setting law and logic on their heads), the Court seems to abandon the categorical approach, and inevitably to relax the level of scrutiny applicable to content-based laws. This weakens the traditional protections of speech. If all expressive activity must be accorded the same protection, that protection will be scant. The simple reality is that the Court will never provide child pornography or cigarette advertising the level of protection customarily granted political speech. If we are forbidden to categorize, as the Court has done here, we shall reduce protection across the board. It is sad that in its effort to reach a satisfying result in this case, the Court is willing to weaken First Amendment protections.

In the second instance is the possibility that this case will not significantly alter First Amendment jurisprudence but, instead, will be regarded as an aberration — a case where the Court manipulated doctrine to strike down an ordinance whose premise it opposed, namely, that racial threats and verbal assaults are of greater harm than other fighting words. I fear that the Court has been distracted from its proper mission by the temptation to decide the issue over "politically correct speech" and "cultural diversity," neither of which is presented here. If this is the meaning of today's opinion, it is perhaps even more regrettable.

I see no First Amendment values that are compromised by a law that prohibits hoodlums from driving minorities out of their homes by burning crosses on their lawns, but I see great harm in preventing the people of Saint Paul from specifically punishing the race-based fighting words that so prejudice their community.

I concur in the judgment, however, because I agree with Justice WHITE that this particular ordinance reaches beyond fighting words to speech protected by the First Amendment.

R.A.V. can be appraised on many levels. First, it can be analyzed in terms of what it means for the fighting words doctrine. *R.A.V.* means that a fighting words law will be upheld only if does not draw content-based distinctions among types of speech, such as by prohibiting fighting words based on race, but not based on political affiliation. The problem, though, is that it will be extremely difficult for legislation to meet this requirement without being so broad that the law will be invalidated on vagueness or overbreadth grounds.

Second, *R.A.V.* can be analyzed in terms of the Court's holding that there is a strong presumption against content-based discrimination within categories of unprotected speech. This was the issue that most divided the justices in the majority from those concurring in the judgment. On the one hand, Justice Scalia makes a powerful argument that the government should not be able to prohibit only obscenity or fighting words that contain messages critical of the government. But on the other hand, the concurring justices make a persuasive point that inevitably in regulating categories of unprotected speech, the government will not forbid all such speech but draw lines. Such lines are vulnerable after *R.A.V.*

Finally, in examining *R.A.V.*, there is the question of whether the case should have been found to meet the exceptions that Justice Scalia recognized where content-based discrimination is allowed. Justice Scalia's majority opinion indicated two circumstances where content-based distinctions within categories of unprotected speech would be allowed. One instance where Justice Scalia would allow content discrimination is where the distinction advances the reason why the category is unprotected. Yet there is a strong argument that this was true with regard to the St. Paul ordinance; the law seemingly was based on a judgment that fighting words based on race, religion, or gender are most likely to cause the harms that the fighting words doctrine means to prevent.

The other exception is where the restriction of speech is meant to prevent secondary effects. The St. Paul ordinance is written specifically in terms of secondary effects; it proscribes speech that would "anger, alarm, or cause resentment." The problem is in deciding whether these are "secondary effects" or a content-based justification for regulating speech.

b. The Hostile Audience Cases

In some cases, especially in the 1940s and the 1950s, the Supreme Court applied the clear and present danger test in dealing with the issue of when the government may punish individuals for speech that provokes a hostile audience reaction. For example, in Terminiello v. Chicago, 337 U.S. 1 (1949), the Court overturned a conviction for disturbing the peace because it was not shown that the speech posed a clear and present danger of lawlessness. Terminiello was convicted for disturbing the peace because of a speech that he gave in which he attacked his opponents as "slimy scum," "snakes," and "bedbugs." Despite the presence of many police officers, disturbances broke out. The trial court's instructions to the jury said that the defendant could be convicted for speech that "stirs the public to anger, invites dispute, brings about a condition of unrest, or creates a disturbance."

The Court overturned the conviction and found that the jury instruction was not sufficiently protective of speech. The Court declared: "A function of free speech under our system is to invite dispute. It may indeed best serve its high purpose when it induces a condition of unrest, creates dissatisfaction with conditions as they are, or even stirs people to anger. [That] is why freedom of speech, though not absolute, [is] nevertheless protected against censorship or punishment, *unless shown likely to produce a clear and present danger of a serious substantive evil that rises far above public inconvenience, annoyance or unrest.*"

Similarly, in Cantwell v. Connecticut, 310 U.S. 296 (1940), the Supreme Court overturned a conviction for disturbing the peace because of the absence of proof of a clear and present danger. Jesse Cantwell, a Jehovah's Witness, was prosecuted for playing a phonograph record on a street corner that attacked the Roman Catholic religion. The Court said that "[w]hen clear and present danger of riot, disorder, interference with traffic upon the public streets, or other immediate threat to public safety, peace, or order, appears, the power of the State to prevent or punish is obvious. Equally obvious is it that a State may not unduly suppress free communication of views, religious or otherwise, under the guise of conserving desirable conditions." The Court overturned the conviction because the speech posed "no such clear and present menace to public peace and order."

Although in *Terminiello* and *Cantwell* the Court applied the clear and present danger test to protect speech, in Feiner v. New York the test was used to uphold a conviction.

FEINER v. NEW YORK
340 U.S. 315 (1951)

Chief Justice VINSON delivered the opinion of the Court.

Petitioner was convicted of the offense of disorderly conduct, a misdemeanor under the New York penal laws. On the evening of March 8, 1949, petitioner Irving Feiner was addressing an open-air meeting at the corner of South McBride and Harrison Streets in the City of Syracuse. At approximately 6:30 P.M., the police received a telephone complaint concerning the meeting, and two officers were detailed to investigate. One of these officers went to the scene immediately, the other arriving some twelve minutes later. They found a crowd of about seventy-five or eighty people, both Negro and white, filling the sidewalk and spreading out into the street. Petitioner, standing on a large wooden box on the sidewalk, was addressing the crowd through a loud-speaker system attached to an automobile. Although the purpose of his speech was to urge his listeners to attend a meeting to be held that night in the Syracuse Hotel, in its course he was making derogatory remarks concerning President Truman, the American Legion, the Mayor of Syracuse, and other local political officials.

The police officers made no effort to interfere with petitioner's speech, but were first concerned with the effect of the crowd on both pedestrian and vehicular traffic. Since traffic was passing at the time, the officers attempted to get the people listening to petitioner back on the sidewalk. The crowd was restless and there was some pushing, shoving and milling around. At this time, petitioner was speaking in a "loud, high-pitched voice." He gave the impression that he was endeavoring to arouse the Negro people against the whites, urging that they rise up in arms and fight for equal rights.

Some of the onlookers made remarks to the police about their inability to handle the crowd and at least one threatened violence if the police did not act. There were others who appeared to be favoring petitioner's arguments. Because of the feeling that existed in the crowd both for and against the speaker, the officers finally "stepped in to prevent it from resulting in a fight." One of the officers approached the petitioner, not for the purpose of arresting him, but to get him to break up the crowd. He asked petitioner to get down off the box, but the latter refused to accede to his request and continued talking. The officer waited for a minute and then demanded that he cease talking. Although the officer had thus twice requested petitioner to stop over the course of several minutes, petitioner not only ignored him but continued talking. During all this time, the crowd was pressing closer around petitioner and the officer. Finally, the officer told petitioner he was under arrest and ordered him to get down from the box, reaching up to grab him. Petitioner stepped down, announcing over the microphone that "the law has arrived, and I suppose they will take over now." In all, the officer had asked petitioner to get down off the box three times over a space of four or five minutes. Petitioner had been speaking for over a half hour.

We are well aware that the ordinary murmurings and objections of a hostile audience cannot be allowed to silence a speaker, and are also mindful of the possible danger of giving overzealous police officials complete discretion to break up otherwise lawful public meetings. But we are not faced here with such a situation. It is one thing to say that the police cannot be used as an instrument for the suppression of unpopular views, and another to say that, when as here the speaker passes the bounds of argument or persuasion and undertakes incitement to riot, they are powerless to prevent a breach of the peace. Nor in this case can we condemn the considered judgment of three New York courts approving the means which the police, faced with a crisis, used in the exercise of their power and duty to preserve peace and order. The findings of the state courts as to the existing situation and the imminence of greater disorder coupled with petitioner's deliberate defiance of the police officers convince us that we should not reverse this conviction in the name of free speech.

Justice BLACK, dissenting.

The record before us convinces me that petitioner, a young college student, has been sentenced to the penitentiary for the unpopular views he expressed on matters of public interest while lawfully making a street-corner speech in Syracuse, New York. Even accepting every "finding of fact" below, I think this conviction makes a mockery of the free speech guarantees of the First and Fourteenth Amendments. The end result of the affirmance here is to approve a simple and readily available technique by which cities and states can with impunity subject all speeches, political or otherwise, on streets or elsewhere, to the supervision and censorship of the local police. I will have no part or parcel in this holding which I view as a long step toward totalitarian authority.

The Court's opinion apparently rests on this reasoning: The policeman, under the circumstances detailed, could reasonably conclude that serious fighting or even riot was imminent; therefore he could stop petitioner's speech to prevent a breach of peace; accordingly, it was "disorderly conduct" for petitioner to continue speaking in disobedience of the officer's request. As to the existence of a dangerous situation on the street corner, it seems farfetched to suggest that the "facts" show any imminent threat of riot or uncontrollable disorder. It is neither unusual nor unexpected that some people at public street meetings mutter, mill about, push, shove, or disagree, even violently, with the speaker. Indeed, it is rare where controversial topics are discussed that an outdoor crowd does not do some or all of these things. Nor does one isolated threat to assault the speaker forebode disorder.

Moreover, assuming that the "facts" did indicate a critical situation, I reject the implication of the Court's opinion that the police had no obligation to protect petitioner's constitutional right to talk. The police of course have power to prevent breaches of the peace. But if, in the name of preserving order, they ever can interfere with a lawful public speaker, they first must make all reasonable efforts to protect him. Here the policemen did not even pretend to try to protect petitioner. Their duty was to protect petitioner's right to talk, even to the extent of arresting the man who threatened to interfere. Instead, they shirked that duty and acted only to suppress the right to speak.

In my judgment, today's holding means that as a practical matter, minority speakers can be silenced in any city. Hereafter, despite the First and Fourteenth Amendments, the policeman's club can take heavy toll of a current administration's public critics. Criticism of public officials will be too dangerous for all but the most courageous.

In later cases, the Supreme Court appeared to follow the approach articulated in Justice Black's dissent in *Feiner*, although the Court never has overruled *Feiner* or the earlier cases using the clear and present danger test. For example, in Edwards v. South Carolina, 372 U.S. 229 (1963), the Court overturned a conviction for civil rights protestors who had staged a march to the South Carolina capitol. A significant hostile crowd gathered, although there was no violence or threat of violence. The speakers were arrested after they ignored a police order to disperse. The Court emphasized that "police protection at the scene was at all times sufficient to meet any foreseeable possibility of disorder." The Court distinguished *Feiner* based on the absence of any violence or threat of violence in the march to the state capitol.

In Cox v. Louisiana, 379 U.S. 536 (1965), an individual was convicted for giving a speech objecting to the racial segregation of lunch counters and urging a sit-in. Some members of the audience found the speech inflammatory and the speaker was arrested a day after the demonstration. The Court overturned the conviction and again emphasized the ability of the police to control the crowd. The Court stated, "It is virtually undisputed, however, that the students themselves were not violent and threatened no violence. The fear of violence seems to have been based upon the reaction of the groups of white citizens looking on from across the street. . . . There is no indication, however, that any member of the white group threatened violence. . . . [A police officer testified that] they could have handled the crowd."

Similarly, in Gregory v. City of Chicago, 394 U.S. 111 (1969), the Court unanimously overturned convictions for disturbing the peace for a group of civil rights demonstrators who had been arrested when an angry group threatened the marchers. The civil rights protestors were marching to the mayor's house when some members of an opposing group reacted angrily, made threats against the demonstrators, and threw rocks at them. The Court overturned the conviction because the law did not limit convictions to instances where there was a threat of imminent violence, where the police made all reasonable efforts to protect the demonstrators, and where the police requested that the demonstration be stopped.

Perhaps these cases can be read as applications of the clear and present danger test with the Court concluding that there was not sufficient evidence under the circumstances to justify a conclusion of imminent threat to a breach of the peace. But an alternative way of reading the cases is as being more speech-protective than the clear and present danger test; that is, as being much closer to Justice Black's approach in *Feiner* than to its majority opinion. From this perspective, the First Amendment requires that the police try to control the audience that is threatening violence and stop the speaker only if crowd control is impossible and a threat to breach of the peace is imminent.[116]

THE PROBLEM OF RACIST SPEECH

Over the past few decades, there has been an important debate among scholars as to whether, and when, the government may punish racist speech.[117] Over

116. One of the more highly publicized instances concerning the ability of the government to prevent speech because of a possible violent audience reaction was in Skokie, Illinois, where the city attempted to stop the Nazi party from marching because of threats from the community. The United States Court of Appeals for the Seventh Circuit held that the Nazis had a right to speak and declared unconstitutional ways in which Skokie tried to stop them. Collin v. Smith, 578 F.2d 1197 (7th Cir. 1978). The Supreme Court refused to issue a stay of the Seventh Circuit's ruling, Smith v. Collin, 436 U.S. 953 (1978).

117. *See, e.g.,* Charles R. Lawrence, III, *If He Hollers Let Him Go: Regulating Racist Speech on Campus,* 1990 Duke L.J. 431; Mari Matsuda, *Public Response to Racist Speech: Considering the Victim's Story,* 87 Mich. L. Rev. 2320 (1989); David Kretzmer, *Freedom of Speech and Racism,* 8 Cardozo L. Rev. 445 (1987); Richard Delgado, *Words That Wound: A Tort Action for Racial Insults, Epithets, and Name-Calling,* 17 Harv. Civ. Rts.-Civ. Lib. L. Rev. 133 (1982) (all favoring restrictions on hate speech); *see also* Lee Bollinger, *The Tolerant Society* (1986); Marjorie Heins, *Banning Words: A Comment on "Words That Wound,"* 18 Harv. Civ. Rts.-Civ. Lib. L. Rev. 585 (1983) (arguing for tolerance for expessions of hate).

200 colleges and universities have adopted hate speech codes of various types. Additionally, many governments have adopted laws prohibiting racist speech.

Those who favor restrictions on hate speech emphasize how racist hate speech undermines the constitutional value of equality. For example, in the context of colleges and universities, hate speech makes traditionally underrepresented minorities feel unwelcome and perpetuates their exclusion. Moreover, it is argued that hate speech is a form of verbal assault that the law should punish.

But those who oppose such hate speech restrictions maintain that it is wrong to stop speech because it is distasteful and offensive. Additionally, opponents argue that it is impossible to formulate a definition of racist speech that is not unconstitutionally vague and overbroad. Furthermore, opponents of hate speech codes argue that practical experience indicates that they are most likely to be used against minorities. The opponents maintain that unless the speech meets the traditional definition of an assault, racist speech, however vile, is protected by the First Amendment.

The Supreme Court has not directly addressed this debate, but several decisions are relevant to it. Almost a half century ago, the Supreme Court held that group libel is not protected by the First Amendment.

BEAUHARNAIS v. ILLINOIS
343 U.S. 250 (1952)

Justice FRANKFURTER delivered the opinion of the Court.

The petitioner was convicted upon information in the Municipal Court of Chicago of violating the Illinois Criminal Code. The section provides:

> It shall be unlawful for any person, firm or corporation to manufacture, sell, or offer for sale, advertise or publish, present or exhibit in any public place in this state any lithograph, moving picture, play, drama or sketch, which publication or exhibition portrays depravity, criminality, unchastity, or lack of virtue of a class of citizens, of any race, color, creed or religion which said publication or exhibition exposes the citizens of any race, color, creed or religion to contempt, derision, or obloquy or which is productive of breach of the peace or riots. . . .

The information, cast generally in the terms of the statute, charged that Beauharnais "did unlawfully . . . exhibit in public places lithographs, which publications portray depravity, criminality, unchastity or lack of virtue of citizens of Negro race and color and which exposes [sic] citizens of Illinois of the Negro race and color to contempt, derision, or obloquy. . . ." The lithograph complained of was a leaflet setting forth a petition calling on the Mayor and City Council of Chicago "to halt the further encroachment, harassment and invasion of white people, their property, neighborhoods and persons, by the Negro. . . ." Below was a call for "One million self respecting white people in Chicago to unite. . . ." with the statement added that "If persuasion and the need to prevent the white race from becoming mongrelized by the negro will not unite us, then the aggressions . . . rapes, robberies, knives, guns and marijuana of the negro, surely will." This, with more language, similar if not so violent, concluded with an attached application for membership in the White Circle League of America, Inc.

The statute before us is not a catchall enactment left at large by the State court which applied it. It is a law specifically directed at a defined evil, its language drawing from history and practice in Illinois and in more than a score of other jurisdictions a meaning confirmed by the Supreme Court of that State in upholding this conviction.

The precise question before us, then, is whether the protection of "liberty" in the Due Process Clause of the Fourteenth Amendment prevents a State from punishing such libels — as criminal libel has been defined, limited and constitutionally recognized time out of mind — directed at designated collectivities and flagrantly disseminated.

But if an utterance directed at an individual may be the object of criminal sanctions, we cannot deny to a State power to punish the same utterance directed at a defined group, unless we can say that this a wilful and purposeless restriction unrelated to the peace and well-being of the State.

Illinois did not have to look beyond her own borders or await the tragic experience of the last three decades to conclude that wilful purveyors of falsehood concerning racial and religious groups promote strife and tend powerfully to obstruct the manifold adjustments required for free, ordered life in a metropolitan, polyglot community. From the murder of the abolitionist Lovejoy in 1837 to the Cicero riots of 1951, Illinois has been the scene of exacerbated tension between races, often flaring into violence and destruction. In many of these outbreaks, utterances of the character here in question, so the Illinois legislature could conclude, played a significant part. The law was passed on June 29, 1917, at a time when the State was struggling to assimilate vast numbers of new inhabitants, as yet concentrated in discrete racial or national or religious groups — foreign-born brought to it by the crest of the great wave of immigration, and Negroes attracted by jobs in war plants and the allurements of northern claims. Nine years earlier, in the very city where the legislature sat, what is said to be the first northern race riot had cost the lives of six people, left hundreds of Negroes homeless and shocked citizens into action far beyond the borders of the State. Less than a month before the bill was enacted, East St. Louis had seen a day's rioting, prelude to an out-break, only four days after the bill became law, so bloody that it led to Congressional investigation. A series of bombings had begun which was to culminate two years later in the awful race riot which held Chicago in its grip for seven days in the summer of 1919. Nor has tension and violence between the groups defined in the statute been limited in Illinois to clashes between whites and Negroes.

In the face of this history and its frequent obligato of extreme racial and religious propaganda, we would deny experience to say that the Illinois legislature was without reason in seeking ways to curb false or malicious defamation of racial and religious groups, made in public places and by means calculated to have a powerful emotional impact on those to whom it was presented. "There are limits to the exercise of these liberties [of speech and of the press]. The danger in these times from the coercive activities of those who in the delusion of racial or religious conceit would incite violence and breaches of the peace in order to deprive others of their equal right to the exercise of their liberties, is emphasized by events familiar to all. These and other transgressions of those limits the states appropriately may punish."

The scope of the statute before us, as construed by the Illinois court, disposes of the contention that the conduct prohibited by the law is so ill-defined that judges and juries in applying the statute and men in acting cannot draw from it adequate standards to guide them. Nor, thus construed and limited, is the act so broad that the general verdict of guilty on an indictment drawn in the statutory language might have been predicated on constitutionally protected conduct.

Libelous utterances not being within the area of constitutionally protected speech, it is unnecessary, either for us or for the State courts, to consider the issues behind the phrase "clear and present danger." Certainly no one would contend that obscene speech, for example, may be punished only upon a showing of such circumstances. Libel, as we have seen, is in the same class.

Justice BLACK, with whom Justice DOUGLAS concurs, dissenting.

This case is here because Illinois inflicted criminal punishment on Beauharnais for causing the distribution of leaflets in the city of Chicago. The conviction rests on the leaflet's contents, not on the time, manner or place of distribution. Beauharnais is head of an organization that opposes amalgamation and favors segregation of white and colored people.

Today's case degrades First Amendment freedoms to the "rational basis" level. It is now a certainty that the new "due process" coverall offers far less protection to liberty than would adherence to our former cases compelling states to abide by the unequivocal First Amendment command that its defined freedoms shall not be abridged.

My own belief is that no legislature is charged with the duty or vested with the power to decide what public issues Americans can discuss. In a free country that is the individual's choice, not the state's. State experimentation in curbing freedom of expression is startling and frightening doctrine in a country dedicated to self-government by its people. I reject the holding that either state or nation can punish people for having their say in matters of public concern.

Unless I misread history the majority is giving libel a more expansive scope and more respectable status than it was ever accorded even in the Star Chamber. For here it is held to be punishable to give publicity to any picture, moving picture, play, drama or sketch, or any printed matter which a judge may find unduly offensive to any race, color, creed or religion. In other words, in arguing for or against the enactment of laws that may differently affect huge groups, it is now very dangerous indeed to say something critical of one of the groups.

If there be minority groups who hail this holding as their victory, they might consider the possible relevancy of this ancient remark: "Another such victory and I am undone."

Beauharnais is the strongest authority for the government to regulate racist speech, and it never has been overruled. Yet for many reasons it is questionable whether *Beuharnais* is still good law.[118] *Beauharnais* is based on the assumption that defamation liability is unlimited by the First Amendment, a premise expressly rejected by the Supreme Court a decade later in New York Times v.

---

118. Indeed, the U.S. Court of Appeals for the Seventh Circuit has expressly said it does not believe that *Beauharnais* survives and is no longer good law. American Booksellers Association v. Hudnut, 771 F.2d 323 (7th Cir. 1985); Collin v. Smith, 578 F.2d 1197, 1204-1205 (7th Cir. 1978).

Sullivan.[119] The speech that led to the conviction in *Beauharnais*, however vile, was political speech, and it is doubtful that the Court would allow punishment of individuals for expressing opinions about racial groups or calling for government actions. The Court's decision in R.A.V. v. St. Paul, described above, strongly indicates that expression of hate is not a category of speech entirely outside First Amendment protection. Moreover, the Illinois statute upheld in *Beauharnais* almost certainly would be declared unconstitutional today based on vagueness and overbreadth grounds.

A reflection of the unwillingness of courts to follow *Beauharnais* is reflected in the protection of the ability of Nazis to stage a march in the predominantly Jewish suburb of Skokie, Illinois. In 1977, the leaders of the Nationalist Socialist Party of America announced that it planned to hold a peaceful demonstration in Skokie, a town where there were many survivors of Nazi concentration camps.

A trial court issued an injunction preventing the marchers from wearing Nazi uniforms, displaying swastikas, or expressing hatred of Jewish people. The court relied in part on testimony concerning a large counterdemonstration and the fear of a violent confrontation between the two groups. Although the state appellate courts upheld this injunction, the U.S. Supreme Court granted certiorari and summarily reversed the state courts.[120] The Court emphasized that appellate review of the trial court's injunction could take a year or more to complete and said that a stay was required unless there was immediate appellate review. On remand, the Illinois Court of Appeals modified the injunction so that it only prohibited display of the swastika. The Illinois Supreme Court reversed and vacated the entire injunction as violating the First Amendment.[121]

Meanwhile, Skokie adopted several ordinances that were intended to prevent the Nazis from speaking there. For example, the laws required applicants for parade permits to purchase a substantial amount of insurance, prohibited dissemination of material that "promotes and incites hatred" based on race or religion, and outlawed wearing military-style uniforms in demonstrations. The U.S. Court of Appeals for the Seventh Circuit declared these ordinances unconstitutional and expressly said that it no longer regarded *Beauharnais* as good law.[122] After winning in the courts, the Nazi party cancelled its rally in Skokie and held a small protest march in Chicago.

The Skokie controversy reflects many basic First Amendment principles. Expression of hate is protected speech, and the government may not outlaw symbols of hate such as swastikas. Moreover, the government cannot suppress a speaker because of the reaction of the audience. Skokie was not allowed to prevent the Nazis from marching because their demonstration would deeply offend and upset Holocaust survivors or might even provoke a violent response.[123]

---

119. 376 U.S. 254 (1964), presented below.

120. Nationalist Socialist Party of America v. Village of Skokie, 432 U.S. 43, 44 (1977).

121. 69 Ill. 2d 605, 373 N.E.2d 21 (1978).

122. Collin v. Smith, 578 F.2d 1197 (7th Cir. 1978). The Supreme Court denied a stay of this decision. Smith v. Collin, 436 U.S. 953 (1978).

123. The Supreme Court, however, has held that the government may provide for penalty enhancements for hate-motivated crimes. In Wisconsin v. Mitchell, 508 U.S. 476 (1993), the Court upheld a state law that imposed greater punishments if it could be proven that a victim was chosen because of his or her race. The Supreme Court emphasized that such penalty enhancements are directed at conduct, not at speech. The Court said that greater punishment for hate-motivated crimes was justified because of their harms to society. Chief Justice Rehnquist, writing for a unanimous Court, explained that the law "singles out for enhancement bias-inspired conduct

The Supreme Court most recently addressed the issue of racist speech in Virginia v. Black, where it considered the constitutionality of a law criminally prohibiting cross burning.

VIRGINIA v. BLACK
538 U.S. 343 (2003)

Justice O'CONNOR announced the judgment of the Court and delivered the opinion of the Court with respect to Parts I, II, and III, and an opinion with respect to Parts IV and V, in which the Chief Justice, Justice STEVENS, and Justice BREYER join.

In this case we consider whether the Commonwealth of Virginia's statute banning cross burning with "an intent to intimidate a person or group of persons" violates the First Amendment. We conclude that while a State, consistent with the First Amendment, may ban cross burning carried out with the intent to intimidate, the provision in the Virginia statute treating any cross burning as prima facie evidence of intent to intimidate renders the statute unconstitutional in its current form.

I

Respondents Barry Black, Richard Elliott, and Jonathan O'Mara were convicted separately of violating Virginia's cross-burning statute. That statute provides: "It shall be unlawful for any person or persons, with the intent of intimidating any person or group of persons, to burn, or cause to be burned, a cross on the property of another, a highway or other public place. Any person who shall violate any provision of this section shall be guilty of a Class 6 felony." "Any such burning of a cross shall be prima facie evidence of an intent to intimidate a person or group of persons."

On August 22, 1998, Barry Black led a Ku Klux Klan rally in Carroll County, Virginia. Twenty-five to thirty people attended this gathering, which occurred on private property with the permission of the owner, who was in attendance. The property was located on an open field just off Brushy Fork Road (State Highway 690) in Cana, Virginia. When the sheriff of Carroll County learned that a Klan rally was occurring in his county, he went to observe it from the side of the road. During the approximately one hour that the sheriff was present, about 40 to 50 cars passed the site, a "few" of which stopped to ask the sheriff what was happening on the property. Eight to ten houses were located in the vicinity of the rally. Rebecca Sechrist, who was related to the owner of the property where the rally took place, "sat and watched to see wha[t was] going on" from the lawn of her in-laws' house. She looked on

---

because this conduct is thought to inflict greater individual and societal harm. For example, . . . bias-motivated crimes are more likely to provoke retaliatory crimes, inflict distinct emotional harms on their victims, and incite community unrest. The State's desire to redress these perceived harms provides an adequate explanation for its penalty enhancement provision over and above mere disagreement with offenders' beliefs or biases."

as the Klan prepared for the gathering and subsequently conducted the rally itself.

During the rally, Sechrist heard Klan members speak about "what they were" and "what they believed in." The speakers "talked real bad about the blacks and the Mexicans." One speaker told the assembled gathering that "he would love to take a .30/.30 and just random[ly] shoot the blacks." The speakers also talked about "President Clinton and Hillary Clinton," and about how their tax money "goes to . . . the black people." Sechrist testified that this language made her "very . . . scared."

At the conclusion of the rally, the crowd circled around a 25- to 30-foot cross. The cross was between 300 and 350 yards away from the road. According to the sheriff, the cross "then all of a sudden . . . went up in a flame." As the cross burned, the Klan played Amazing Grace over the loudspeakers. Sechrist stated that the cross burning made her feel "awful" and "terrible."

When the sheriff observed the cross burning, he informed his deputy that they needed to "find out who's responsible and explain to them that they cannot do this in the State of Virginia." The sheriff then went down the driveway, entered the rally, and asked "who was responsible for burning the cross." Black responded, "I guess I am because I'm the head of the rally." The sheriff then told Black, "[T]here's a law in the State of Virginia that you cannot burn a cross and I'll have to place you under arrest for this."

Black was charged with burning a cross with the intent of intimidating a person or group of persons, in violation of §18.2-423. At his trial, the jury was instructed that "intent to intimidate means the motivation to intentionally put a person or a group of persons in fear of bodily harm. Such fear must arise from the willful conduct of the accused rather than from some mere temperamental timidity of the victim." The trial court also instructed the jury that "the burning of a cross by itself is sufficient evidence from which you may infer the required intent."

On May 2, 1998, respondents Richard Elliott and Jonathan O'Mara, as well as a third individual, attempted to burn a cross on the yard of James Jubilee. Jubilee, an African-American, was Elliott's next-door neighbor in Virginia Beach, Virginia. Four months prior to the incident, Jubilee and his family had moved from California to Virginia Beach. Before the cross burning, Jubilee spoke to Elliott's mother to inquire about shots being fired from behind the Elliott home. Elliott's mother explained to Jubilee that her son shot firearms as a hobby, and that he used the backyard as a firing range. On the night of May 2, respondents drove a truck onto Jubilee's property, planted a cross, and set it on fire. Their apparent motive was to "get back" at Jubilee for complaining about the shooting in the backyard. Respondents were not affiliated with the Klan. The next morning, as Jubilee was pulling his car out of the driveway, he noticed the partially burned cross approximately 20 feet from his house. Elliott and O'Mara were charged with attempted cross burning and conspiracy to commit cross burning. O'Mara pleaded guilty to both counts, reserving the right to challenge the constitutionality of the cross-burning statute. The judge sentenced O'Mara to 90 days in jail and fined him $2,500. The judge also suspended 45 days of the sentence and $1,000 of the fine.

The jury found Elliott guilty of attempted cross burning and acquitted him of conspiracy to commit cross burning. It sentenced Elliott to 90 days in jail and a $2,500 fine.

II

Cross burning originated in the 14th century as a means for Scottish tribes to signal each other. Sir Walter Scott used cross burnings for dramatic effect in The Lady of the Lake, where the burning cross signified both a summons and a call to arms. Cross burning in this country, however, long ago became unmoored from its Scottish ancestry. Burning a cross in the United States is inextricably intertwined with the history of the Ku Klux Klan.

The first Ku Klux Klan began in Pulaski, Tennessee, in the spring of 1866. Although the Ku Klux Klan started as a social club, it soon changed into something far different. The Klan fought Reconstruction and the corresponding drive to allow freed blacks to participate in the political process. Soon the Klan imposed "a veritable reign of terror" throughout the South. The Klan employed tactics such as whipping, threatening to burn people at the stake, and murder. The Klan's victims included blacks, southern whites who disagreed with the Klan, and "carpetbagger" northern whites.

From [early in the 20th century], cross burnings have been used to communicate both threats of violence and messages of shared ideology. The first initiation ceremony occurred on Stone Mountain near Atlanta, Georgia. While a 40-foot cross burned on the mountain, the Klan members took their oaths of loyalty. This cross burning was the second recorded instance in the United States. The first known cross burning in the country had occurred a little over one month before the Klan initiation, when a Georgia mob celebrated the lynching of Leo Frank by burning a "gigantic cross" on Stone Mountain that was "visible throughout" Atlanta.

Throughout the history of the Klan, cross burnings have also remained potent symbols of shared group identity and ideology. The burning cross became a symbol of the Klan itself and a central feature of Klan gatherings. According to the Klan constitution (called the kloran), the "fiery cross" was the "emblem of that sincere, unselfish devotedness of all klansmen to the sacred purpose and principles we have espoused." And the Klan has often published its newsletters and magazines under the name The Fiery Cross. At Klan gatherings across the country, cross burning became the climax of the rally or the initiation. Posters advertising an upcoming Klan rally often featured a Klan member holding a cross.

In short, a burning cross has remained a symbol of Klan ideology and of Klan unity. To this day, regardless of whether the message is a political one or whether the message is also meant to intimidate, the burning of a cross is a "symbol of hate." And while cross burning sometimes carries no intimidating message, at other times the intimidating message is the only message conveyed. For example, when a cross burning is directed at a particular person not affiliated with the Klan, the burning cross often serves as a message of intimidation, designed to inspire in the victim a fear of bodily harm. Moreover, the history of violence associated with the Klan shows that the possibility of injury or death is not just hypothetical. The person who burns a cross directed at a particular person often is making a serious threat, meant to coerce the victim to comply with the Klan's wishes unless the victim is willing to risk the wrath of the Klan. Indeed, as the cases of respondents Elliott and O'Mara indicate, individuals without Klan affiliation who wish to threaten or menace another person sometimes use cross burning because of this association between a burning cross and violence.

In sum, while a burning cross does not inevitably convey a message of intimidation, often the cross burner intends that the recipients of the message fear for their lives. And when a cross burning is used to intimidate, few if any messages are more powerful.

III

A

The hallmark of the protection of free speech is to allow "free trade in ideas" — even ideas that the overwhelming majority of people might find distasteful or discomforting. Thus, the First Amendment "ordinarily" denies a State "the power to prohibit dissemination of social, economic and political doctrine which a vast majority of its citizens believes to be false and fraught with evil consequence." The protections afforded by the First Amendment, however, are not absolute, and we have long recognized that the government may regulate certain categories of expression consistent with the Constitution. The First Amendment permits "restrictions upon the content of speech in a few limited areas, which are 'of such slight social value as a step to truth that any benefit that may be derived from them is clearly outweighed by the social interest in order and morality.'"

Thus, for example, a State may punish those words "which by their very utterance inflict injury or tend to incite an immediate breach of the peace." We have consequently held that fighting words — "those personally abusive epithets which, when addressed to the ordinary citizen, are, as a matter of common knowledge, inherently likely to provoke violent reaction" — are generally proscribable under the First Amendment. Furthermore, "the constitutional guarantees of free speech and free press do not permit a State to forbid or proscribe advocacy of the use of force or of law violation except where such advocacy is directed to inciting or producing imminent lawless action and is likely to incite or produce such action." Brandenburg v. Ohio (1969). And the First Amendment also permits a State to ban a "true threat." Watts v. United States (1969).

"True threats" encompass those statements where the speaker means to communicate a serious expression of an intent to commit an act of unlawful violence to a particular individual or group of individuals. The speaker need not actually intend to carry out the threat. Rather, a prohibition on true threats "protect[s] individuals from the fear of violence" and "from the disruption that fear engenders," in addition to protecting people "from the possibility that the threatened violence will occur." Intimidation in the constitutionally proscribable sense of the word is a type of true threat, where a speaker directs a threat to a person or group of persons with the intent of placing the victim in fear of bodily harm or death. Respondents do not contest that some cross burnings fit within this meaning of intimidating speech, and rightly so. As noted in Part II, supra, the history of cross burning in this country shows that cross burning is often intimidating, intended to create a pervasive fear in victims that they are a target of violence.

B

It is true, as the Supreme Court of Virginia held, that the burning of a cross is symbolic expression. The reason why the Klan burns a cross at its rallies, or individuals place a burning cross on someone else's lawn, is that the burning cross represents the message that the speaker wishes to communicate. Individuals burn crosses as opposed to other because cross burning carries a message in an effective and dramatic manner.[124]

The fact that cross burning is symbolic expression, however, does not resolve the constitutional question. In R.A.V. v. St. Paul (1992), we held that a local ordinance that banned certain symbolic conduct, including cross burning, when done with the knowledge that such conduct would "arouse anger, alarm or resentment in others on the basis of race, color, creed, religion or gender" was unconstitutional. We held that the ordinance did not pass constitutional muster because it discriminated on the basis of content by targeting only those individuals who "provoke violence" on a basis specified in the law. The ordinance did not cover "[t]hose who wish to use 'fighting words' in connection with other ideas — to express hostility, for example, on the basis of political affiliation, union membership, or homosexuality." This content-based discrimination was unconstitutional because it allowed the city "to impose special prohibitions on those speakers who express views on disfavored subjects."

We did not hold in R.A.V. that the First Amendment prohibits all forms of content-based discrimination within a proscribable area of speech. Rather, we specifically stated that some types of content discrimination did not violate the First Amendment. Indeed, we noted that it would be constitutional to ban only a particular type of threat: "[T]he Federal Government can criminalize only those threats of violence that are directed against the President . . . since the reasons why threats of violence are outside the First Amendment . . . have special force when applied to the person of the President." And a State may "choose to prohibit only that obscenity which is the most patently offensive in its prurience — i.e., that which involves the most lascivious displays of sexual activity." Unlike the statute at issue in R.A.V., the Virginia statute does not single out for opprobrium only that speech directed toward "one of the specified disfavored topics." It does not matter whether an individual burns a cross with intent to intimidate because of the victim's race, gender, or religion, or because of the victim's "political affiliation, union membership, or homosexuality." Moreover, as a factual matter it is not true that cross burners direct their intimidating conduct solely to racial or religious minorities.

The First Amendment permits Virginia to outlaw cross burnings done with the intent to intimidate because burning a cross is a particularly virulent form of intimidation. Instead of prohibiting all intimidating messages, Virginia may choose to regulate this subset of intimidating messages in light of cross burning's long and pernicious history as a signal of impending violence. Thus, just as a State may regulate only that obscenity which is the most obscene due to its prurient content, so too may a State choose to prohibit only those forms of intimidation that are most likely to inspire fear of bodily harm. A ban on cross burning carried out with the intent to intimidate is fully consistent with our holding in R.A.V. and is proscribable under the First Amendment.

---

124. Justice Thomas argues in dissent that cross burning is "conduct, not expression." While it is of course true that burning a cross is conduct, it is equally true that the First Amendment protects symbolic conduct as well as pure speech. As Justice Thomas has previously recognized, a burning cross is a "symbol of hate," and "a symbol of white supremacy." [Footnote by the Court.]

IV

The Supreme Court of Virginia ruled in the alternative that Virginia's cross-burning statute was unconstitutionally overbroad due to its provision stating that "[a]ny such burning of a cross shall be prima facie evidence of an intent to intimidate a person or group of persons." The Commonwealth added the prima facie provision to the statute in 1968. The court below did not reach whether this provision is severable from the rest of the cross-burning statute under Virginia law. The Supreme Court of Virginia has not ruled on the meaning of the prima facie evidence provision. It has, however, stated that "the act of burning a cross alone, with no evidence of intent to intimidate, will nonetheless suffice for arrest and prosecution and will insulate the Commonwealth from a motion to strike the evidence at the end of its case-in-chief."

The prima facie evidence provision, as interpreted by the jury instruction, renders the statute unconstitutional. As construed by the jury instruction, the prima facie provision strips away the very reason why a State may ban cross burning with the intent to intimidate. The prima facie evidence provision permits a jury to convict in every cross-burning case in which defendants exercise their constitutional right not to put on a defense. And even where a defendant like Black presents a defense, the prima facie evidence provision makes it more likely that the jury will find an intent to intimidate regardless of the particular facts of the case. The provision permits the Commonwealth to arrest, prosecute, and convict a person based solely on the fact of cross burning itself.

It is apparent that the provision as so interpreted "would create an unacceptable risk of the suppression of ideas." The act of burning a cross may mean that a person is engaging in constitutionally proscribable intimidation. But that same act may mean only that the person is engaged in core political speech. The prima facie evidence provision in this statute blurs the line between these two meanings of a burning cross. As interpreted by the jury instruction, the provision chills constitutionally protected political speech because of the possibility that a State will prosecute — and potentially convict — somebody engaging only in lawful political speech at the core of what the First Amendment is designed to protect.

As the history of cross burning indicates, a burning cross is not always intended to intimidate. Rather, sometimes the cross burning is a statement of ideology, a symbol of group solidarity. It is a ritual used at Klan gatherings, and it is used to represent the Klan itself. Thus, "[b]urning a cross at a political rally would almost certainly be protected expression." Indeed, occasionally a person who burns a cross does not intend to express either a statement of ideology or intimidation. Cross burnings have appeared in movies such as Mississippi Burning, and in plays such as the stage adaptation of Sir Walter Scott's The Lady of the Lake.

The prima facie provision makes no effort to distinguish among these different types of cross burnings. It does not distinguish between a cross burning done with the purpose of creating anger or resentment and a cross burning done with the purpose of threatening or intimidating a victim. It does not distinguish between a cross burning at a public rally or a cross burning on a neighbor's lawn. It does not treat the cross burning directed at an individual differently from the cross burning directed at a group of like-minded believers. It allows a jury to treat a cross burning on the property of another with the owner's acquiescence in the same manner as a cross burning on the property of another without the owner's permission.

It may be true that a cross burning, even at a political rally, arouses a sense of anger or hatred among the vast majority of citizens who see a burning cross. But this sense of anger or hatred is not sufficient to ban all cross burnings. The prima facie evidence provision in this case ignores all of the contextual factors that are necessary to decide whether a particular cross burning is intended to intimidate. The First Amendment does not permit such a shortcut.

For these reasons, the prima facie evidence provision, as interpreted through the jury instruction and as applied in Barry Black's case, is unconstitutional on its face.

V

With respect to Barry Black, we agree with the Supreme Court of Virginia that his conviction cannot stand, and we affirm the judgment of the Supreme Court of Virginia. With respect to Elliott and O'Mara, we vacate the judgment of the Supreme Court of Virginia, and remand the case for further proceedings.

Justice THOMAS, dissenting.

In every culture, certain things acquire meaning well beyond what outsiders can comprehend. That goes for both the sacred, and the profane. I believe that cross burning is the paradigmatic example of the latter.

I

Although I agree with the majority's conclusion that it is constitutionally permissible to "ban . . . cross burning carried out with intent to intimidate," I believe that the majority errs in imputing an expressive component to the activity in question. In my view, whatever expressive value cross burning has, the legislature simply wrote it out by banning only intimidating conduct undertaken by a particular means. A conclusion that the statute prohibiting cross burning with intent to intimidate sweeps beyond a prohibition on certain conduct into the zone of expression overlooks not only the words of the statute but also reality.

"In holding [the ban on cross burning with intent to intimidate] unconstitutional, the Court ignores Justice Holmes' familiar aphorism that 'a page of history is worth a volume of logic.'" "The world's oldest, most persistent terrorist organization is not European or even Middle Eastern in origin. Fifty years before the Irish Republican Army was organized, a century before Al Fatah declared its holy war on Israel, the Ku Klux Klan was actively harassing, torturing and murdering in the United States. Today . . . its members remain fanatically committed to a course of violent opposition to social progress and racial equality in the United States." M. Newton & J. Newton, The Ku Klux Klan: An Encyclopedia vii (1991).

To me, the majority's brief history of the Ku Klux Klan only reinforces this common understanding of the Klan as a terrorist organization, which, in its endeavor to intimidate, or even eliminate those it dislikes, uses the most brutal of methods. Such methods typically include cross burning—"a tool for the intimidation and harassment of racial minorities, Catholics, Jews, Communists, and any other groups hated by the Klan." For those not easily frightened, cross burning has been followed by more extreme measures, such as beatings and murder. As the Solicitor General points out, the association between acts of intimidating cross burning and violence is well documented in recent American history. In our culture, cross burning has almost invariably meant lawlessness and understandably instills in its victims well-grounded fear of physical violence.

Virginia's experience has been no exception. In Virginia, though facing widespread opposition in the 1920s, the KKK developed localized strength in the southeastern part of the State, where there were reports of scattered raids and floggings. Although the KKK was disbanded at the national level in 1944, a series of cross burnings in Virginia took place between 1949 and 1952.

It strains credulity to suggest that a state legislature that adopted a litany of segregationist laws self-contradictorily intended to squelch the segregationist message. Even for segregationists, violent and terroristic conduct, the Siamese twin of cross burning, was intolerable. The ban on cross burning with intent to intimidate demonstrates that even segregationists understood the difference between intimidating and terroristic conduct and racist expression. It is simply beyond belief that, in passing the statute now under review, the Virginia legislature was concerned with anything but penalizing conduct it must have viewed as particularly vicious.

Accordingly, this statute prohibits only conduct, not expression. And, just as one cannot burn down someone's house to make a political point and then seek refuge in the First Amendment, those who hate cannot terrorize and intimidate to make their point. In light of my conclusion that the statute here addresses only conduct, there is no need to analyze it under any of our First Amendment tests.

II

Even assuming that the statute implicates the First Amendment, in my view, the fact that the statute permits a jury to draw an inference of intent to intimidate from the cross burning itself presents no constitutional problems. Therein lies my primary disagreement with the plurality.

The plurality is troubled by the presumption because this is a First Amendment case. The plurality laments the fate of an innocent cross-burner who burns a cross, but does so without an intent to intimidate. The plurality fears the chill on expression because, according to the plurality, the inference permits "the Commonwealth to arrest, prosecute and convict a person based solely on the fact of cross burning itself." First, it is, at the very least, unclear that the inference comes into play during arrest and initiation of a prosecution, that is, prior to the instructions stage of an actual trial. Second, the inference is rebuttable and, as the jury instructions given in this case demonstrate, Virginia law still requires the jury to find the existence of each element, including intent to intimidate, beyond a reasonable doubt.

3. Sexually Oriented Speech

A major topic in First Amendment law is the ability of the government to regulate sexually oriented speech. First, the Supreme Court has held that obscenity is a category of speech unprotected by the First Amendment and has struggled to define what is "obscene." These cases are discussed in subsection a. This section also considers whether obscenity should be a category of unprotected speech and the proposals that some have advanced that pornography should be banned as a form of discrimination against women.

Second, the Court has indicated that child pornography is not protected by the First Amendment, even if it does not fit within the definition of obscenity. This is considered in subsection b.

Third, the Court has indicated the government has more latitude to regulate sexually oriented speech, even if it is not obscenity or child pornography that is unprotected by the First Amendment. For example, the Court has allowed the use of zoning ordinances to limit the locations of adult bookstores and movie theaters and permitted the government to ban nude dancing. These cases are discussed in subsection c.

Subsection d examines the techniques that the government may and may not use in regulating sexually oriented materials. Governments have tried many techniques ranging from licensing schemes to prohibition of private possession to seizing assets of businesses convicted of violating obscenity laws.

Finally, subsection e considers the related question of the constitutional protection for profane language and indecent speech. The Supreme Court generally has held that profane and indecent speech are protected by the First Amendment, although there are exceptions where limits are allowed, notably over the broadcast media and in schools.

a. Obscenity

i. Supreme Court Decisions Finding Obscenity Unprotected

In Roth v. United States, the Supreme Court held that obscenity is a category of speech unprotected by the First Amendment.

ROTH v. UNITED STATES
354 U.S. 476 (1957)

Justice BRENNAN delivered the opinion of the Court.

The constitutionality of a criminal obscenity statute is the question. In *Roth*, the primary constitutional question is whether the federal obscenity statute violates the provision of the First Amendment. The federal obscenity statute prohibited the mailing of: "Every obscene, lewd, lascivious, or filthy book, pamphlet, picture, paper, letter, writing, print, or other publication of an indecent character."

The dispositive question is whether obscenity is utterance within the area of protected speech and press. Although this is the first time the question has been squarely presented to this Court, either under the First Amendment or under the Fourteenth Amendment, expressions found in numerous opinions indicate that this Court has always assumed that obscenity is not protected by the freedoms of speech and press.

The guaranties of freedom of expression in effect in 10 of the 14 States which by 1792 had ratified the Constitution, gave no absolute protection for every utterance. Thirteen of the 14 States provided for the prosecution of libel, and all of those States made either blasphemy or profanity, or both, statutory crimes. As early as 1712, Massachusetts made it criminal to publish "any filthy, obscene, or profane song, pamphlet, libel or mock sermon" in imitation or mimicking of religious services.

In light of this history, it is apparent that the unconditional phrasing of the First Amendment was not intended to protect every utterance. At the time of the adoption of the First Amendment, obscenity law was not as fully developed as libel law, but there is sufficiently contemporaneous evidence to show that obscenity, too, was outside the protection intended for speech and press.

The protection given speech and press was fashioned to assure unfettered interchange of ideas for the bringing about of political and social changes desired by the people. All ideas having even the slightest redeeming social importance—unorthodox ideas, controversial ideas, even ideas hateful to the prevailing climate of opinion—have the full protection of the guaranties, unless excludable because they encroach upon the limited area of more important interests. But implicit in the history of the First Amendment is the rejection of obscenity as utterly without redeeming social importance. This rejection for that reason is mirrored in the universal judgment that obscenity should be restrained, reflected in the international agreement of over 50 nations, in the obscenity laws of all of the 48 States, and in the 20 obscenity laws enacted by the Congress from 1842 to 1856.

However, sex and obscenity are not synonymous. Obscene material is material which deals with sex in a manner appealing to prurient interest.[125] The portrayal of sex, e.g., in art, literature and scientific works, is not itself sufficient reason to deny material the constitutional protection of freedom of speech and press. Sex, a great and mysterious motive force in human life, has indisputably been a subject of absorbing interest to mankind through the ages; it is one of the vital problems of human interest and public concern. Many decisions have recognized that these terms of obscenity statutes are not precise. This Court, however, has consistently held that lack of precision is not itself offensive to the requirements of due process.

In summary, then, we hold that these statutes, applied according to the proper standard for judging obscenity, do not offend constitutional safeguards against convictions based upon protected material, or fail to give mean in acting adequate notice of what is prohibited.

Justice DOUGLAS, with whom Mr. Justice BLACK concurs, dissenting.

When we sustain these convictions, we make the legality of a publication turn on the purity of thought which a book or tract instills in the mind of the reader. I do not think we can approve that standard and be faithful to the command of

---

125. [This is], material having a tendency to excite lustful thoughts. Webster's New International Dictionary (Unabridged, 2d ed., 1949) defines prurient, in pertinent part, as follows: ". . . Itching; longing; uneasy with desire or longing; of persons, having itching, morbid, or lascivious longings; of desire, curiosity, or propensity, lewd . . ." Pruriency is defined, in pertinent part, as follows: ". . . Quality of being prurient; lascivious desire or thought." We perceive no significant difference between the meaning of obscenity developed in the case law and the definition of the A.L.I., Model Penal Code, ". . . A thing is obscene if, considered as a whole, its predominant appeal is to prurient interest, i.e., a shameful or morbid interest in nudity, sex, or exertion, and if it goes substantially beyond customary limits of candor in description or representation of such matters." [Footnote by the Court.]

the First Amendment, which by its terms is a restraint on Congress and which by the Fourteenth is a restraint on the States.

In the *Roth* case the trial judge charged the jury that the statutory words "obscene, lewd and lascivious" describe "that form of immorality which has relation to sexual impurity and has a tendency to excite lustful thoughts." By these standards punishment is inflicted for thoughts provoked, not for overt acts nor antisocial conduct. This test cannot be squared with our decisions under the First Amendment.

The tests by which these convictions were obtained require only the arousing of sexual thoughts. Yet the arousing of sexual thoughts and desires happens every day in normal life in dozens of ways. The test of obscenity the Court endorses today gives the censor free range over a vast domain. To allow the State to step in and punish mere speech or publication that the judge or the jury thinks has an undesirable impact on thoughts but that is not shown to be a part of unlawful action is drastically to curtail the First Amendment.

In the years after *Roth*, the Court struggled to formulate a definition of obscenity.[126] The difficulty of these efforts was expressed by Justice Potter Stewart when he declared in Jacobellis v. Ohio, 378 U.S. 184 (1964) (Stewart, J., concurring): "I shall not today attempt further to define the kinds of material I understand to be embraced within that shorthand description; and perhaps I could never succeed in intelligibly doing so. But I know it when I see it, and the motion picture involved in this case is not that." Beginning in 1967, in Redrup v. New York, 386 U.S. 767 (1967), the Court overturned obscenity convictions in *per curiam* decisions without an opinion, something that the Court did more than 30 times in obscenity cases in the next six years.

In two five-to-four decisions in 1973, Paris Adult Theatre v. Slaton and Miller v. California, the Court reaffirmed that obscene "material is not protected by the First Amendment" and formulated the test for obscenity that continues to be used. The opinion in *Paris Adult Theatre* focuses primarily on justifying the continued exclusion of obscenity from First Amendment protection. Miller v. California articulated the definition of obscenity used to this day.

PARIS ADULT THEATRE I v. SLATON

413 U.S. 49 (1973)

Chief Justice BURGER delivered the opinion of the Court.

Petitioners are two Atlanta, Georgia, movie theaters and their owners and managers, operating in the style of "adult" theaters. On December 28, 1970, respondents, the local state district attorney and the solicitor for the local state trial court, filed civil complaints in that court alleging that petitioners were exhibiting to the public for paid admission two allegedly obscene films, contrary to Georgia Code Ann. The two films in question, "Magic Mirror" and "It All

---

126. *See, e.g.*, Mishkin v. New York, 383 U.S. 502 (1966); Ginzburg v. United States, 383 U.S. 463 (1966); Memoirs v. Massachusetts, 383 U.S. 413 (1966).

Comes Out in the End," depict sexual conduct characterized by the Georgia Supreme Court as "hard core pornography" leaving "little to the imagination." Paris Adult Theatre I and Paris Adult Theatre II [had] a conventional, inoffensive theater entrance, without any pictures, but with signs indicating that the theaters exhibit "Atlanta's Finest Mature Feature Films." On the door itself is a sign saying: "Adult Theatre — You must be 21 and able to prove it. If viewing the nude body offends you, Please Do Not Enter."

I

It should be clear from the outset that we do not undertake to tell the States what they must do, but rather to define the area in which they may chart their own course in dealing with obscene material. This Court has consistently held that obscene material is not protected by the First Amendment as a limitation on the state police power by virtue of the Fourteenth Amendment.

We categorically disapprove the theory, apparently adopted by the trial judge, that obscene, pornographic films acquire constitutional immunity from state regulation simply because they are exhibited for consenting adults only. This holding was properly rejected by the Georgia Supreme Court. Although we have often pointedly recognized the high importance of the state interest in regulating the exposure of obscene materials to juveniles and unconsenting adults, this Court has never declared these to be the only legitimate state interests permitting regulation of obscene material. The States have a long-recognized legitimate interest in regulating the use of obscene material in local commerce and in all places of public accommodation, as long as these regulations do not run afoul of specific constitutional prohibitions. "In an unbroken series of cases extending over a long stretch of this Court's history it has been accepted as a postulate that 'the primary requirements of decency may be enforced against obscene publications.'"

In particular, we hold that there are legitimate state interests at stake in stemming the tide of commercialized obscenity, even assuming it is feasible to enforce effective safeguards against exposure to juveniles and to passersby. These include the interest of the public in the quality of life and the total community environment, the tone of commerce in the great city centers, and, possibly, the public safety itself. The Hill-Link Minority Report of the Commission on Obscenity and Pornography indicates that there is at least an arguable correlation between obscene material and crime. As Chief Justice Warren stated, there is a "right of the Nation and of the States to maintain a decent society."

If we accept the unprovable assumption that a complete education requires the reading of certain books, and the well nigh universal belief that good books, plays, and art lift the spirit, improve the mind, enrich the human personality, and develop character, can we then say that a state legislature may not act on the corollary assumption that commerce in obscene books, or public exhibitions focused on obscene conduct, have a tendency to exert a corrupting and debasing impact leading to antisocial behavior? "Many of these effects may be intangible and indistinct, but they are nonetheless real."

To summarize, we have today reaffirmed the basic holding of Roth v. United States that obscene material has no protection under the First Amendment. We have directed our holdings, not at thoughts or speech, but at depiction and description of specifically defined sexual conduct that States may regulate within limits designed to prevent infringement of First Amendment rights. We have also reaffirmed that commerce in obscene material is unprotected by any constitutional doctrine of privacy. In this case we hold that the States have a legitimate interest in regulating commerce in obscene material and in regulating exhibition of obscene material in places of public accommodation, including so-called "adult" theaters from which minors are excluded. In light of these holdings, nothing precludes the State of Georgia from the regulation of the allegedly obscene material exhibited in Paris Adult Theatre I or II, provided that the applicable Georgia law, as written or authoritatively interpreted by the Georgia courts, meets the First Amendment standards set forth in Miller v. California.

Justice BRENNAN, with whom Justice STEWART and Justice MARSHALL join, dissenting.

This case requires the Court to confront once again the vexing problem of reconciling state efforts to suppress sexually oriented expression with the protections of the First Amendment, as applied to the States through the Fourteenth Amendment. No other aspect of the First Amendment has, in recent years, demanded so substantial a commitment of our time, generated such disharmony of views, and remained so resistant to the formulation of stable and manageable standards. I am convinced that the approach initiated 16 years ago in Roth v. United States (1957), and culminating in the Court's decision today, cannot bring stability to this area of the law without jeopardizing fundamental First Amendment values, and I have concluded that the time has come to make a significant departure from that approach.

In Roth v. United States, the Court held that obscenity, although expression, falls outside the area of speech or press constitutionally protected under the First and Fourteenth Amendments against state or federal infringement. Yet our efforts to implement that approach demonstrate that agreement on the existence of something called "obscenity" is still a long and painful step from agreement on a workable definition of the term. The essence of our problem in the obscenity area is that we have been unable to provide "sensitive tools" to separate obscenity from other sexually oriented but constitutionally protected speech, so that efforts to suppress the former do not spill over into the suppression of the latter.

Of course, the vagueness problem would be largely of our own creation if it stemmed primarily from our failure to reach a consensus on any one standard. But after 16 years of experimentation and debate I am reluctantly forced to the conclusion that none of the available formulas, including the one announced today, can reduce the vagueness to a tolerable level while at the same time striking an acceptable balance between the protections of the First and Fourteenth Amendments, on the one hand, and on the other the asserted state interest in regulating the dissemination of certain sexually oriented materials. Any effort to draw a constitutionally acceptable boundary on state power must resort to such indefinite concepts as "prurient interest," "patent offensiveness," "serious literary value," and the like. The meaning of these concepts necessarily varies with the experience, outlook, and even idiosyncrasies of the person defining them. Although we have assumed that obscenity does exist and that we "know it when [we] see it," Jacobellis v. Ohio (Stewart, J., concurring), we are manifestly unable to describe it in advance except by reference to concepts so elusive that they fail to distinguish clearly between protected and unprotected speech.

Our experience since *Roth* requires us not only to abandon the effort to pick out obscene material on a case-by-case basis, but also to reconsider a fundamental postulate of *Roth*: that there exists a definable class of sexually oriented expression that may be totally suppressed by the Federal and State Governments. Assuming that such a class of expression does in fact exist, I am forced to conclude that the concept of "obscenity" cannot be defined with sufficient specificity and clarity to provide fair notice to persons who create and distribute sexually oriented materials, to prevent substantial erosion of protected speech as a byproduct of the attempt to suppress unprotected speech, and to avoid very costly institutional harms.

Like the proscription of abortions, the effort to suppress obscenity is predicated on unprovable, although strongly held, assumptions about human behavior, morality, sex, and religion. The existence of these assumptions cannot validate a statute that substantially undermines the guarantees of the First Amendment, any more than the existence of similar assumptions on the issue of abortion can validate a statute that infringes the constitutionally protected privacy interests of a pregnant woman.

In short, while I cannot say that the interests of the State — apart from the question of juveniles and unconsenting adults — are trivial or nonexistent, I am compelled to conclude that these interests cannot justify the substantial damage to constitutional rights and to this Nation's judicial machinery that inevitably results from state efforts to bar the distribution even of unprotected material to consenting adults.

Justice Douglas, dissenting.

My Brother Brennan is to be commended for seeking a new path through the thicket which the Court entered when it undertook to sustain the constitutionality of obscenity laws and to place limits on their application. I have expressed on numerous occasions my disagreement with the basic decision that held that "obscenity" was not protected by the First Amendment. I disagreed also with the definitions that evolved. Art and literature reflect tastes; and tastes, like musical appreciation, are hardly reducible to precise definitions. That is one reason I have always felt that "obscenity" was not an exception to the First Amendment. For matters of taste, like matters of belief, turn on the idiosyncrasies of individuals.

I am sure I would find offensive most of the books and movies charged with being obscene. But in a life that has not been short, I have yet to be trapped into seeing or reading something that would offend me. I never read or see the materials coming to the Court under charges of "obscenity," because I have thought the First Amendment made it unconstitutional for me to act as a censor.

When man was first in the jungle he took care of himself. When he entered a societal group, controls were necessarily imposed. But our society — unlike most in the world — presupposes that freedom and liberty are in a frame of reference that makes the individual, not government, the keeper of his tastes, beliefs, and ideas. That is the philosophy of the First Amendment; and it is the article of faith that sets us apart from most nations in the world.

MILLER v. CALIFORNIA

413 U.S. 15 (1973)

Chief Justice BURGER delivered the opinion of the Court.

This is one of a group of "obscenity-pornography" cases being reviewed by the Court in a re-examination of standards enunciated in earlier cases involving what Mr. Justice Harlan called "the intractable obscenity problem." Appellant conducted a mass mailing campaign to advertise the sale of illustrated books, euphemistically called "adult" material. After a jury trial, he was convicted of violating California Penal Code, a misdemeanor, by knowingly distributing obscene matter.

This case involves the application of a State's criminal obscenity statute to a situation in which sexually explicit materials have been thrust by aggressive sales action upon unwilling recipients who had in no way indicated any desire to receive such materials. This Court has recognized that the States have a legitimate interest in prohibiting dissemination or exhibition of obscene material when the mode of dissemination carries with it a significant danger of offending the sensibilities of unwilling recipients or of exposure to juveniles.

It is in this context that we are called on to define the standards which must be used to identify obscene material that a State may regulate without infringing on the First Amendment as applicable to the States through the Fourteenth Amendment. Apart from the initial formulation in the *Roth* case, no majority of the Court has at any given time been able to agree on a standard to determine what constitutes obscene, pornographic material subject to regulation under the States' police power.

This much has been categorically settled by the Court, that obscene material is unprotected by the First Amendment. We acknowledge, however, the inherent dangers of undertaking to regulate any form of expression. State statutes designed to regulate obscene materials must be carefully limited. As a result, we now confine the permissible scope of such regulation to works which depict or describe sexual conduct. That conduct must be specifically defined by the applicable state law, as written or authoritatively construed. A state offense must also be limited to works which, taken as a whole, appeal to the prurient interest in sex, which portray sexual conduct in a patently offensive way, and which, taken as a whole, do not have serious literary, artistic, political, or scientific value.

The basic guidelines for the trier of fact must be: (a) whether "the average person, applying contemporary community standards" would find that the work, taken as a whole, appeals to the prurient interest; (b) whether the work depicts or describes, in a patently offensive way, sexual conduct specifically defined by the applicable state law; and (c) whether the work, taken as a whole, lacks serious literary, artistic, political, or scientific value. We do not adopt as a constitutional standard the "utterly without redeeming social value" test of Memoirs v. Massachusetts; that concept has never commanded the adherence of more than three Justices at one time.

We emphasize that it is not our function to propose regulatory schemes for the States. That must await their concrete legislative efforts. It is possible, however, to give a few plain examples of what a state statute could define for regulation under part (b) of the standard announced in this opinion; (a) Patently offensive representations or descriptions of ultimate sexual acts, normal or perverted, actual or simulated; (b) Patently offensive representation or descriptions of masturbation, excretory functions, and lewd exhibition of the genitals.

Sex and nudity may not be exploited without limit by films or pictures exhibited or sold in places of public accommodation any more than live sex and nudity can be exhibited or sold without limit in such public places. At a minimum, prurient, patently offensive depiction or description of sexual conduct must have serious literary, artistic, political, or scientific value to merit First Amendment protection. Under the holdings announced today, no one will be subject to prosecution for the sale or exposure of obscene materials unless these materials depict or describe patently offensive "hard core" sexual conduct specifically defined by the regulating state law, as written or construed. We are satisfied that these specific prerequisites will provide fair notice to a dealer in such materials that his public and commercial activities may bring prosecution.

Since *Miller*, the Court has adhered to the test articulated in that case. First, the Court has followed *Miller*'s, holding that the material must appeal to prurient interest and that is to be decided by a community standard. For example, the Court has ruled that juries applying federal obscenity laws define prurient interest from a community perspective. The Court said that "[t]he fact that distributors of allegedly obscene materials may be subjected to varying community standards in the various federal judicial districts does not render a federal statute unconstitutional because of the failure of application of uniform national standards of obscenity."[127]

Second, in order for material to be obscene it must be patently offensive under the law prohibiting obscenity. In Ward v. Illinois, 431 U.S. 767 (1977), the Supreme Court held that the law did not need to provide an "exhaustive list of the sexual conduct" that would be patently offensive. The Court said that it was sufficient that a law included the examples included in *Miller*.

However, in Jenkins v. Georgia, 418 U.S. 153 (1974), the Court ruled that there are limits on what a state may deem to be patently offensive. In *Jenkins*, the Court concluded that the mainstream movie "Carnal Knowledge," with actors including Jack Nicholson and Ann Margaret, could not be found obscene because "[t]here is no exhibition whatever of the actors' genitals, lewd or otherwise. . . . There are occasional scenes of nudity, but nudity alone is not enough to make material legally obscene under the *Miller* standards." The Court stated that "the film could not, as a matter of constitutional law, be found to depict sexual content in a patently offensive way, and is therefore not outside the protection of the First and Fourteenth Amendments because it is obscene."

Finally, in order for material to be obscene, it must, taken as a whole, lack serious redeeming artistic, literary, political, or scientific value. In Pope v. Illinois, 481 U.S. 497 (1987), the Court held that social value is to be determined by a national standard — how the work would be appraised across the country — and not a community standard. The Court said that "the value of [a] work [does not] vary from community to community. . . . The proper inquiry [is] whether a reasonable person would find such value in the material."

---

127. Hamling v. United States, 418 U.S. 87, 106 (1974).

ii.   Should Obscenity Be a Category of Unprotected Speech?

Many disagree with the Court that obscenity should be deemed a category of unprotected speech.[128] They argue that the very definition of obscenity used in *Roth* focuses on controlling thoughts, something that should be beyond the reach of the government.

Those who favor allowing the government to prohibit obscenity make several arguments. One is that a community should be able to determine its moral environment. In Paris Adult Theatre I v. Slaton, the Court accepted this justification for regulating obscenity and spoke of "the interest of the public in the quality of life and the total community environment [and] the tone of commerce in the great city centers." Henry Clor argued that the "ethical convictions of social man do not simply rest upon his explicit opinions. They rest also upon a delicate network of moral and aesthetic feelings, sensibilities, tastes. These 'finer feelings' could be blunted and eroded by a steady stream of impressions which assault them. Men whose sensibilities are frequently assaulted by prurient and lurid impressions may become desensitized. . . . This is what is meant by 'an erosion of the moral fabric.'"[129]

However, those who oppose a First Amendment exception for obscenity argue that the government should not be able to decide what is moral and suppress speech that does not advance that conception. In fact, the Supreme Court has held in other contexts that the government may not prohibit speech simply because it advances ideas that the government deems immoral. For example, in Kingsley International Pictures Corp. v. Regents, 360 U.S. 684 (1959), the Court held that a state could not prohibit the film *Lady Chatterly's Lover*, because it shows adultery and thus "portrays acts of sexual immorality [as] desirable, acceptable or proper patterns of behavior." The Court said that what the state "has done, [is] to prevent the exhibition of a motion picture because that picture advocates an idea — that adultery under certain circumstances may be proper behavior. Yet the First Amendment's basic guarantee is of freedom to advocate ideas. The State, quite simply, has thus struck at the very heart of constitutionally protected liberty." It is not for the government to stop speech to advance any particular idea of what is moral.

A second major argument for excluding obscenity from First Amendment protection is that it causes antisocial behavior, particularly violence against women. In Paris Adult Theatre I v. Slaton, Chief Justice Burger, writing for the Court, said that obscenity "possibly [endangers] the public safety itself. The Hill-Link Minority Report of the Commission on Obscenity and Pornography indicates that there is at least an arguable correlation between obscene material and crime." Professor Catharine MacKinnon, who advocates creating a new categorical exception for pornography as a form of discrimination against women, argued that "[r]ecent experimental research on pornography shows that . . . exposure to [it] increases normal men's immediately subsequent willingness to aggress against women under laboratory conditions. . . . It also

128. *See, e.g.*, David Cole, *Playing by Pornography's Rules: The Regulation of Sexual Expression*, 143 U. Pa. L. Rev. 111 (1994); David A.J. Richards, *Free Speech and Obscenity Law: Toward a Moral Theory of the First Amendment*, 123 U. Pa. L. Rev. 45 (1974).
129. Henry Clor, *Obsenity and Public Morality* at 170-171 (1969).

significantly increases attitudinal measures known to correlate with rape."[130] The Meese Commission on Pornography believed that experimental studies found that exposure to violent pornography increased a willingness to be violent in laboratory experiments.[131]

But others challenge these studies and whether they establish that obscenity increases the likelihood of antisocial behavior. The Report of the Commission on Obscenity and Pornography, a commission appointed by President Richard Nixon, reviewed the empirical literature and concluded that there was no evidence that "exposure to explicit sexual materials plays a significant role in the causation of delinquent or criminal behavior."[132] Moreover, it is questioned whether the laboratory experiments that measure aggression in laboratory settings or conduct on mock juries indicates anything about whether obscenity causes antisocial behavior in society. Also, it is argued that these studies show, at most, that depictions of violence — whether erotic or not — correlate with more violence in laboratory experiments; they maintain that there is no evidence that nonviolent sexual depictions increase aggressive or violent behavior.[133]

A third argument made for excluding obscenity from First Amendment protection is that it should be regarded as a sex aid, not as speech. Professor Fred Schauer argued that "hardcore pornography is designed to produce a purely physical effect. [It is] essentially a physical rather than a mental stimulus. . . . The pornographic item is in a real sense a sexual surrogate. . . . Consider further rubber, plastic, or leather sex aids. It is hard to find any free speech aspects in their sale or use. . . . The mere fact that in pornography the stimulating experience is initiated by visual rather than tactile means is irrelevant. Neither means constitutes communication in the cognitive sense."[134]

Yet in response it is argued that other forms of speech produce physical reactions. A movie or book is not deprived of First Amendment protection because it provokes tears. A beautiful symphony is not unprotected because of the physical reactions it evokes. Moreover, it is argued that sexual material does have a cognitive dimension. Professor David Cole observed that the argument that sexual speech is "noncognitive" because it is designed to produce a physical effect is predicated on an impoverished view of sexuality. He wrote, "[Sexual] expression, like human sexuality itself, cannot be 'purely physical.' Rather, it is deeply and inextricably interwoven with our identities, our upbringing, our emotions, our relationships to other human beings, and the ever-changing narratives and images that our community finds stimulating."[135]

130. Catharine R. MacKinnon, *Pornography, Civil Rights, and Speech*, 20 Harv. C.R.-C.L. L. Rev. 1, 52, 54 (1985); *see also* Catharine R. MacKinnon, *Only Words* (1994).

131. Report of the Attorney General's Commission on Pornography (1986).

132. Report of the Commission on Obscenity and Pornography 26-27 (1970).

133. *See* Deana Pollard, *Regulating Violent Pornography*, 43 Vand. L. Rev. 125, 128-129 (1990) (reviewing social science studies on the effects of pornography).

134. Frederick Schauer, *Speech and "Speech" — Obscenity and "Obscenity": An Exercise in the Interpretation of Constitutional Language*, 67 Geo. L.J. 899, 922-923 (1979).

135. Cole, *supra* note 128, at 127.

iii.   Should There Be a New Exception for Pornography?

Some commentators, most notably Catharine MacKinnon and Andrea Dworkin, have argued that a new exception should be created to the First Amendment that excludes pornography as a form of sex discrimination against women. They argue that pornography is "the graphic sexually explicit subordination of women through pictures and/or words."[136] They propose an ordinance that would outlaw such depictions if, for example, "[w]omen are presented as sexual objects who enjoy pain or humiliation; or . . . [w]omen are presented as sexual objects who experience sexual pleasure in being raped; or . . . women are presented as sexual objects for domination, conquest, violation, exploitation, possession, or use, or through postures or positions of servility or submission or display."[137]

MacKinnon argues that pornography causes harmful attitudes and actions toward women in society.[138] She maintains that restrictions on pornography are justified to advance equality for women. She argues furthermore that women are coerced into the making of pornography and that the prohibition of pornography is necessary to provide protection. She contends that obscenity is inadequate as an approach to sexually oriented material because it requires that the work be looked at as a whole and because of its focus on the prurient interest.[139]

Critics of the MacKinnon approach argue that it is vague and extremely broad in terms of what it would deem to be pornography unprotected by the First Amendment. Professor Thomas Emerson argued that "[t]he sweep of the [MacKinnon] ordinance is breathtaking. It would subject to governmental ban virtually all depictions of rape, verbal or pictoral, and a substantial proportion of other sexual encounters. More specifically, it would outlaw such works of literature as the *Arabian Nights*, Henry Miller's *Tropic of Cancer*, John Cleland's *Fanny Hill*, William Faulkner's *Sanctuary*, and Norman Mailer's *Ancient Evenings*, to name a few."[140]

The U.S. Court of Appeals for the Seventh Circuit, in American Booksellers Assn. v. Hudnut, 771 F.2d 323 (7th Cir. 1985), declared unconstitutional a version of the MacKinnon ordinance that had been enacted in Indianapolis. The court found that the ordinance was impermissible viewpoint discrimination because it attempted to outlaw depictions of certain images of women. The court said: "The ordinance discriminates on the ground of the content of the speech. Speech treating women in the approved way . . . is lawful no matter how sexually explicit. Speech treating women in the disapproved way — as submissive in matters sexual or as enjoying humiliation — is unlawful no matter how significant the literary, artistic, or political qualities of the work taken as a whole. The state may not ordain preferred viewpoints in this way."

---

136. *See* American Booksellers Assn., Inc. v. Hudnut, 771 F.2d 323 (7th Cir. 1985) (describing Indianapolis ordinance based on MacKinnon-Dworkin proposal).
137. *Id.* at 324.
138. *See, e.g.,* Catharine MacKinnon, *Only Words* (1994); Catharine MacKinnon, *Feminism Unmodified* (1987); Catharine MacKinnon, *Pornography, Civil Rights and Speech*, 20 Harv. C.R.-C.L. L. Rev. 1, 18-20 (1985).
139. MacKinnon, *Feminism Unmodified* at 152-158.
140. Thomas Emerson, *Pornography and the First Amendment: A Reply to Professor MacKinnon*, 3 Yale L. & Pol. Rev. 130, 131-132 (1985).

The debate over pornography raises basic questions about the First Amendment. May the government restrict some speech in an attempt to advance equality by controlling how a group is treated or portrayed? How much proof of harm from speech such as pornography must there be in order to justify regulation?

b. Child Pornography

In New York v. Ferber, the Supreme Court held that the government may prohibit the exhibition, sale, or distribution of child pornography even if it does not meet the test for obscenity. However, in Ashcroft v. Free Speech Coalition, the Court made it clear that for material to be considered child pornography, children must be used in its production.

NEW YORK v. FERBER

458 U.S. 747 (1982)

Justice WHITE delivered the opinion of the Court.

At issue in this case is the constitutionality of a New York criminal statute which prohibits persons from knowingly promoting sexual performances by children under the age of 16 by distributing material which depicts such performances.

I

In recent years, the exploitive use of children in the production of pornography has become a serious national problem. The Federal Government and 47 States have sought to combat the problem with statutes specifically directed at the production of child pornography. At least half of such statutes do not require that the materials produced be legally obscene. Thirty-five States and the United States Congress have also passed legislation prohibiting the distribution of such materials; 20 States prohibit the distribution of material depicting children engaged in sexual conduct without requiring that the material be legally obscene.

Like obscenity statutes, laws directed at the dissemination of child pornography run the risk of suppressing protected expression by allowing the hand of the censor to become unduly heavy. For the following reasons, however, we are persuaded that the States are entitled to greater leeway in the regulation of pornographic depictions of children.

First. It is evident beyond the need for elaboration that a State's interest in "safeguarding the physical and psychological well-being of a minor" is "compelling." "A democratic society rests, for its continuance, upon the healthy, well-rounded growth of young people into full maturity as citizens." Prince v. Massachusetts (1944). Accordingly, we have sustained legislation aimed at protecting the physical and emotional well-being of youth even when the laws have operated in the sensitive area of constitutionally protected rights. The prevention of sexual exploitation and abuse of children constitutes a government objective of surpassing importance. The legislative findings accompanying passage of the New York laws reflect this concern. The legislative judgment, as well as the judgment found in the relevant literature, is that the use of children as subjects of pornographic materials is harmful to the physiological, emotional, and mental health of the child. That judgment, we think, easily passes muster under the First Amendment.

Second. The distribution of photographs and films depicting sexual activity by juveniles is intrinsically related to the sexual abuse of children in at least two ways. First, the materials produced are a permanent record of the children's participation and the harm to the child is exacerbated by their circulation. Second, the distribution network for child pornography must be closed if the production of material which requires the sexual exploitation of children is to be effectively controlled. Indeed, there is no serious contention that the legislature was unjustified in believing that it is difficult, if not impossible, to halt the exploitation of children by pursuing only those who produce the photographs and movies. While the production of pornographic materials is a low-profile, clandestine industry, the need to market the resulting products requires a visible apparatus of distribution. The most expeditious if not the only practical method of law enforcement may be to dry up the market for this material by imposing severe criminal penalties on persons selling, advertising, or otherwise promoting the product. Thirty-five States and Congress have concluded that restraints on the distribution of pornographic materials are required in order to effectively combat the problem, and there is a body of literature and testimony to support these legislative conclusions.

The *Miller* standard, like all general definitions of what may be banned as obscene, does not reflect the State's particular and more compelling interest in prosecuting those who promote the sexual exploitation of children. Thus, the question under the *Miller* test of whether a work, taken as a whole, appeals to the prurient interest of the average person bears no connection to the issue of whether a child has been physically or psychologically harmed in the production of the work. Similarly, a sexually explicit depiction need not be "patently offensive" in order to have required the sexual exploitation of a child for its production. In addition, a work which, taken on the whole, contains serious literary, artistic, political, or scientific value may nevertheless embody the hardest core of child pornography. "It is irrelevant to the child [who has been abused] whether or not the material . . . has a literary, artistic, political or social value." We therefore cannot conclude that the *Miller* standard is a satisfactory solution to the child pornography problem.

Third. The advertising and selling of child pornography provide an economic motive for and are thus an integral part of the production of such materials, an activity illegal throughout the Nation. "It rarely has been suggested that the constitutional freedom for speech and press extends its immunity to speech or writing used as an integral part of conduct in violation of a valid criminal statute." We note that were the statutes outlawing the employment of children in these films and photographs fully effective, and the constitutionality of these laws has not been questioned, the First Amendment implications would be no greater than that presented by laws against distribution: enforceable production laws would leave no child pornography to be marketed.

Fourth. The value of permitting live performances and photographic reproductions of children engaged in lewd sexual conduct is exceedingly modest, if not de minimis. We consider it unlikely that visual depictions of children performing sexual acts or lewdly exhibiting their genitals would often constitute an important and necessary part of a literary performance or scientific or educational work. As a state judge in this case observed, if it were necessary for literary or artistic value, a person over the statutory age who perhaps looked younger could be utilized. Simulation outside of the prohibition of the statute could provide another alternative. Nor is there any question here of censoring a particular literary theme or portrayal of sexual activity.

Fifth. Recognizing and classifying child pornography as a category of material outside the protection of the First Amendment is not incompatible with our earlier decisions. Thus, it is not rare that a content-based classification of speech has been accepted because it may be appropriately generalized that within the confines of the given classification, the evil to be restricted so overwhelmingly outweighs the expressive interests, if any, at stake, that no process of case-by-case adjudication is required. When a definable class of material, such as that covered by §263.15, bears so heavily and pervasively on the welfare of children engaged in its production, we think the balance of competing interests is clearly struck and that it is permissible to consider these materials as without the protection of the First Amendment.

There are, of course, limits on the category of child pornography which, like obscenity, is unprotected by the First Amendment. As with all legislation in this sensitive area, the conduct to be prohibited must be adequately defined by the applicable state law, as written or authoritatively construed. Here the nature of the harm to be combated requires that the state offense be limited to works that visually depict sexual conduct by children below a specified age. The category of "sexual conduct" proscribed must also be suitably limited and described.

The test for child pornography is separate from the obscenity standard enunciated in *Miller*, but may be compared to it for the purpose of clarity. The *Miller* formulation is adjusted in the following respects: A trier of fact need not find that the material appeals to the prurient interest of the average person; it is not required that sexual conduct portrayed be done so in a patently offensive manner; and the material at issue need not be considered as a whole. We note that the distribution of descriptions or other depictions of sexual conduct, not otherwise obscene, which do not involve live performance or photographic or other visual reproduction of live performances, retains First Amendment protection. As with obscenity laws, criminal responsibility may not be imposed without some element of scienter on the part of the defendant.

Justice BRENNAN, with whom Justice MARSHALL joins, concurring in the judgment.

I agree with much of what is said in the Court's opinion. [T]he State has a special interest in protecting the well-being of its youth. This special and compelling interest, and the particular vulnerability of children, afford the State the leeway to regulate pornographic material, the promotion of which is harmful to children, even though the State does not have such leeway when it seeks only to protect consenting adults from exposure to such material.

But in my view application of §263.15 or any similar statute to depictions of children that in themselves do have serious literary, artistic, scientific, or medical value, would violate the First Amendment. As the Court recognizes, the limited classes of speech, the suppression of which does not raise serious First

Amendment concerns, have two attributes. They are of exceedingly "slight social value," and the State has a compelling interest in their regulation. The First Amendment value of depictions of children that are in themselves serious contributions to art, literature, or science, is, by definition, simply not "de minimis." At the same time, the State's interest in suppression of such materials is likely to be far less compelling. In short, it is inconceivable how a depiction of a child that is itself a serious contribution to the world of art or literature or science can be deemed "material outside the protection of the First Amendment." With this understanding, I concur in the Court's judgment in this case.

ASHCROFT v. FREE SPEECH COALITION

535 U.S. 234 (2002)

Justice KENNEDY delivered the opinion of the Court.

We consider in this case whether the Child Pornography Prevention Act of 1996 (CPPA), abridges the freedom of speech. The CPPA extends the federal prohibition against child pornography to sexually explicit images that appear to depict minors but were produced without using any real children. The statute prohibits, in specific circumstances, possessing or distributing these images, which may be created by using adults who look like minors or by using computer imaging. The new technology, according to Congress, makes it possible to create realistic images of children who do not exist.

By prohibiting child pornography that does not depict an actual child, the statute goes beyond New York v. Ferber (1982), which distinguished child pornography from other sexually explicit speech because of the State's interest in protecting the children exploited by the production process. As a general rule, pornography can be banned only if obscene, but under *Ferber*, pornography showing minors can be proscribed whether or not the images are obscene under the definition set forth in Miller v. California (1973). *Ferber* recognized that "[t]he *Miller* standard, like all general definitions of what may be banned as obscene, does not reflect the State's particular and more compelling interest in prosecuting those who promote the sexual exploitation of children."

The CPPA, however, is not directed at speech that is obscene; Congress has proscribed those materials through a separate statute. 18 U.S.C. §§1460-1466. Like the law in *Ferber*, the CPPA seeks to reach beyond obscenity, and it makes no attempt to conform to the *Miller* standard. For instance, the statute would reach visual depictions, such as movies, even if they have redeeming social value.

The principal question to be resolved, then, is whether the CPPA is constitutional where it proscribes a significant universe of speech that is neither obscene under *Miller* nor child pornography under *Ferber*.

I

Before 1996, Congress defined child pornography as the type of depictions at issue in *Ferber*, images made using actual minors. The CPPA retains that prohibition and adds three other prohibited categories of speech, of which the first, §2256(8)(B), and the third, §2256(8)(D), are at issue in this case. Section 2256(8)(B) prohibits "any visual depiction, including any photograph, film, video, picture, or computer or computer-generated image or picture" that "is, or appears to be, of a minor engaging in sexually explicit conduct." The prohibition on "any visual depiction" does not depend at all on how the image is produced. The section captures a range of depictions, sometimes called "virtual child pornography," which include computer-generated images, as well as images produced by more traditional means. For instance, the literal terms of the statute embrace a Renaissance painting depicting a scene from classical mythology, a "picture" that "appears to be, of a minor engaging in sexually explicit conduct." The statute also prohibits Hollywood movies, filmed without any child actors, if a jury believes an actor "appears to be" a minor engaging in "actual or simulated . . . sexual intercourse."

These images do not involve, let alone harm, any children in the production process; but Congress decided the materials threaten children in other, less direct, ways. Pedophiles might use the materials to encourage children to participate in sexual activity. "[A] child who is reluctant to engage in sexual activity with an adult, or to pose for sexually explicit photographs, can sometimes be convinced by viewing depictions of other children 'having fun' participating in such activity." Furthermore, pedophiles might "whet their own sexual appetites" with the pornographic images, "thereby increasing the creation and distribution of child pornography and the sexual abuse and exploitation of actual children." Under these rationales, harm flows from the content of the images, not from the means of their production. In addition, Congress identified another problem created by computer-generated images: Their existence can make it harder to prosecute pornographers who do use real minors. As imaging technology improves, Congress found, it becomes more difficult to prove that a particular picture was produced using actual children. To ensure that defendants possessing child pornography using real minors cannot evade prosecution, Congress extended the ban to virtual child pornography.

Section 2256(8)(C) prohibits a more common and lower tech means of creating virtual images, known as computer morphing. Rather than creating original images, pornographers can alter innocent pictures of real children so that the children appear to be engaged in sexual activity. Although morphed images may fall within the definition of virtual child pornography, they implicate the interests of real children and are in that sense closer to the images in *Ferber*. Respondents do not challenge this provision, and we do not consider it.

Respondents do challenge §2256(8)(D). Like the text of the "appears to be" provision, the sweep of this provision is quite broad. Section 2256(8)(D) defines child pornography to include any sexually explicit image that was "advertised, promoted, presented, described, or distributed in such a manner that conveys the impression" it depicts "a minor engaging in sexually explicit conduct." The statute is not so limited in its reach, however, as it punishes even those possessors who took no part in pandering. Once a work has been described as child pornography, the taint remains on the speech in the hands of subsequent possessors, making possession unlawful even though the content otherwise would not be objectionable.

II

[A] law imposing criminal penalties on protected speech is a stark example of speech suppression. The CPPA's penalties are indeed severe. A first offender may be imprisoned for 15 years. §2252A(b)(1). A repeat offender faces a prison sentence of not less than 5 years and not more than 30 years in prison. While even minor punishments can chill protected speech, see Wooley v. Maynard (1977), this case provides a textbook example of why we permit facial challenges to statutes that burden expression. With these severe penalties in force, few legitimate movie producers or book publishers, or few other speakers in any capacity, would risk distributing images in or near the uncertain reach of this law. The Constitution gives significant protection from overbroad laws that chill speech within the First Amendment's vast and privileged sphere. Under this principle, the CPPA is unconstitutional on its face if it prohibits a substantial amount of protected expression.

The CPPA prohibits speech despite its serious literary, artistic, political, or scientific value. The statute proscribes the visual depiction of an idea — that of teenagers engaging in sexual activity — that is a fact of modern society and has been a theme in art and literature throughout the ages. Under the CPPA, images are prohibited so long as the persons appear to be under 18 years of age. This is higher than the legal age for marriage in many States, as well as the age at which persons may consent to sexual relations. See §2243(a) (age of consent in the federal maritime and territorial jurisdiction is 16); U.S. National Survey of State Laws 384-388 (R. Leiter ed., 3d ed. 1999) (48 States permit 16-year-olds to marry with parental consent); W. Eskridge & N. Hunter, Sexuality, Gender, and the Law 1021-1022 (1997) (in 39 States and the District of Columbia, the age of consent is 16 or younger).

Both themes — teenage sexual activity and the sexual abuse of children — have inspired countless literary works. William Shakespeare created the most famous pair of teenage lovers, one of whom is just 13 years of age. See Romeo and Juliet, act I, sc. 2, 1. 9 ("She hath not seen the change of fourteen years"). In the drama, Shakespeare portrays the relationship as something splendid and innocent, but not juvenile. The work has inspired no less than 40 motion pictures, some of which suggest that the teenagers consummated their relationship. Shakespeare may not have written sexually explicit scenes for the Elizabethan audience, but were modern directors to adopt a less conventional approach, that fact alone would not compel the conclusion that the work was obscene.

Contemporary movies pursue similar themes. Last year's Academy Awards featured the movie, Traffic, which was nominated for Best Picture. The film portrays a teenager, identified as a 16-year-old, who becomes addicted to drugs. The viewer sees the degradation of her addiction, which in the end leads her to a filthy room to trade sex for drugs. The year before, American Beauty won the Academy Award for Best Picture. In the course of the movie, a teenage girl engages in sexual relations with her teenage boyfriend, and another yields herself to the gratification of a middle-aged man. The film also contains a scene where, although the movie audience understands the act is not taking place, one character believes he is watching a teenage boy performing a sexual act on an older man.

Our society, like other cultures, has empathy and enduring fascination with the lives and destinies of the young. Art and literature express the vital interest we all have in the formative years we ourselves once knew, when wounds can be so grievous, disappointment so profound, and mistaken choices so tragic, but when moral acts and self-fulfillment are still in reach. Whether or not the films we mention violate the CPPA, they explore themes within the wide sweep of the statute's prohibitions. If these films, or hundreds of others of lesser note that explore those subjects, contain a single graphic depiction of sexual activity within the statutory definition, the possessor of the film would be subject to severe punishment without inquiry into the work's redeeming value. This is inconsistent with an essential First Amendment rule: The artistic merit of a work does not depend on the presence of a single explicit scene.

The Government seeks to address this deficiency by arguing that speech prohibited by the CPPA is virtually indistinguishable from child pornography, which may be banned without regard to whether it depicts works of value. Where the images are themselves the product of child sexual abuse, *Ferber* recognized that the State had an interest in stamping it out without regard to any judgment about its content. The production of the work, not its content, was the target of the statute.

The Government says these indirect harms are sufficient because, as *Ferber* acknowledged, child pornography rarely can be valuable speech. This argument, however, suffers from two flaws. First, *Ferber*'s judgment about child pornography was based upon how it was made, not on what it communicated. The second flaw in the Government's position is that *Ferber* did not hold that child pornography is by definition without value. On the contrary, the Court recognized some works in this category might have significant value, but relied on virtual images — the very images prohibited by the CPPA — as an alternative and permissible means of expression: "[I]f it were necessary for literary or artistic value, a person over the statutory age who perhaps looked younger could be utilized. Simulation outside of the prohibition of the statute could provide another alternative." *Ferber*, then, not only referred to the distinction between actual and virtual child pornography, it relied on it as a reason supporting its holding. *Ferber* provides no support for a statute that eliminates the distinction and makes the alternative mode criminal as well.

III

The CPPA, for reasons we have explored, is inconsistent with *Miller* and finds no support in *Ferber*. The Government seeks to justify its prohibitions in other ways. It argues that the CPPA is necessary because pedophiles may use virtual child pornography to seduce children. There are many things innocent in themselves, however, such as cartoons, video games, and candy, that might be used for immoral purposes, yet we would not expect those to be prohibited because they can be misused. The Government, of course, may punish adults who provide unsuitable materials to children, and it may enforce criminal penalties for unlawful solicitation. The precedents establish, however, that speech within the rights of adults to hear may not be silenced completely in an attempt to shield children from it.

Here, the Government wants to keep speech from children not to protect them from its content but to protect them from those who would commit other crimes. The principle, however, remains the same: The Government cannot ban speech fit for adults simply because it may fall into the hands of children. The evil in question depends upon the actor's unlawful conduct, conduct defined as criminal quite apart from any link to the speech in question. This establishes that the speech ban is not narrowly drawn. The objective is to prohibit illegal conduct, but this restriction goes well beyond that interest by restricting the speech available to law-abiding adults.

The Government submits further that virtual child pornography whets the appetites of pedophiles and encourages them to engage in illegal conduct. This rationale cannot sustain the provision in question. The mere tendency of speech to encourage unlawful acts is not a sufficient reason for banning it. The government "cannot constitutionally premise legislation on the desirability of controlling a person's private thoughts." First Amendment freedoms are most in danger when the government seeks to control thought or to justify its laws for that impermissible end. The right to think is the beginning of freedom, and speech must be protected from the government because speech is the beginning of thought.

The Government has shown no more than a remote connection between speech that might encourage thoughts or impulses and any resulting child abuse. Without a significantly stronger, more direct connection, the Government may not prohibit speech on the ground that it may encourage pedophiles to engage in illegal conduct.

The Government next argues that its objective of eliminating the market for pornography produced using real children necessitates a prohibition on virtual images as well. Virtual images, the Government contends, are indistinguishable from real ones; they are part of the same market and are often exchanged. In this way, it is said, virtual images promote the trafficking in works produced through the exploitation of real children. The hypothesis is somewhat implausible. If virtual images were identical to illegal child pornography, the illegal images would be driven from the market by the indistinguishable substitutes. Few pornographers would risk prosecution by abusing real children if fictional, computerized images would suffice. In the case of the material covered by *Ferber*, the creation of the speech is itself the crime of child abuse; the prohibition deters the crime by removing the profit motive.

Finally, the Government says that the possibility of producing images by using computer imaging makes it very difficult for it to prosecute those who produce pornography by using real children. Experts, we are told, may have difficulty in saying whether the pictures were made by using real children or by using computer imaging. The necessary solution, the argument runs, is to prohibit both kinds of images. The argument, in essence, is that protected speech may be banned as a means to ban unprotected speech. This analysis turns the First Amendment upside down.

The Government may not suppress lawful speech as the means to suppress unlawful speech. Protected speech does not become unprotected merely because it resembles the latter. The Constitution requires the reverse. "[T]he possible harm to society in permitting some unprotected speech to go unpunished is outweighed by the possibility that protected speech of others may be muted. . . ." Broadrick v. Oklahoma. The overbreadth doctrine prohibits the Government from banning unprotected speech if a substantial amount of protected speech is prohibited or chilled in the process.

In sum, §2256(8)(B) covers materials beyond the categories recognized in *Ferber* and *Miller*, and the reasons the Government offers in support of limiting the freedom of speech have no justification in our precedents or in the law of the First Amendment. The provision abridges the freedom to engage in a substantial amount of lawful speech. For this reason, it is overbroad and unconstitutional.

Justice O'CONNOR, with whom the Chief Justice and Justice SCALIA join as to Part II, concurring in the judgment in part and dissenting in part.

The Court has long recognized that the Government has a compelling interest in protecting our Nation's children. This interest is promoted by efforts directed against sexual offenders and actual-child pornography. These efforts, in turn, are supported by the CPPA's ban on virtual-child pornography. Such images whet the appetites of child molesters, who may use the images to seduce young children. Of even more serious concern is the prospect that defendants indicted for the production, distribution, or possession of actual-child pornography may evade liability by claiming that the images attributed to them are in fact computer-generated. Respondents may be correct that no defendant has successfully employed this tactic. But, given the rapid pace of advances in computer-graphics technology, the Government's concern is reasonable.

Respondents argue that, even if the Government has a compelling interest to justify banning virtual-child pornography, the "appears to be . . . of a minor" language is not narrowly tailored to serve that interest. They assert that the CPPA would capture even cartoon-sketches or statues of children that were sexually suggestive. Such images surely could not be used, for instance, to seduce children. I agree. A better interpretation of "appears to be . . . of" is "virtually indistinguishable from" — an interpretation that would not cover the examples respondents provide. Not only does the text of the statute comfortably bear this narrowing interpretation, the interpretation comports with the language that Congress repeatedly used in its findings of fact.

Reading the statute only to bar images that are virtually indistinguishable from actual children would not only assure that the ban on virtual-child pornography is narrowly tailored, but would also assuage any fears that the "appears to be . . . of a minor" language is vague. The narrow reading greatly limits any risks from "discriminatory enforcement." Respondents maintain that the "virtually indistinguishable from" language is also vague because it begs the question: from whose perspective? This problem is exaggerated. This Court has never required "mathematical certainty" or "meticulous specificity" from the language of a statute.

The Court concludes that the CPPA's ban on virtual-child pornography is overbroad. The basis for this holding is unclear. Although a content-based regulation may serve a compelling state interest, and be as narrowly tailored as possible while substantially serving that interest, the regulation may unintentionally ensnare speech that has serious literary, artistic, political, or scientific value or that does not threaten the harms sought to be combated by the Government. If so, litigants may challenge the regulation on its face as overbroad, but in doing so they bear the heavy burden of demonstrating that the regulation forbids a substantial amount of valuable or harmless speech. Respondents have not made such a demonstration. Respondents provide no examples of films or other materials that are wholly computer-generated and contain images that "appea[r] to be . . . of minors" engaging in indecent conduct, but that have serious value or do not facilitate child abuse. Their overbreadth challenge therefore fails.

Although in my view the CPPA's ban on youthful-adult pornography appears to violate the First Amendment, the ban on virtual-child pornography does not. Heeding this caution, I would strike the "appears to be" provision only insofar as it is applied to the subset of cases involving youthful-adult pornography.

In sum, I would strike down the CPPA's ban on material that "conveys the impression" that it contains actual-child pornography, but uphold the ban on pornographic depictions that "appea[r] to be" of minors so long as it is not applied to youthful-adult pornography.

Chief Justice Rehnquist, with whom Justice Scalia joins in part, dissenting.

I agree with Part II of Justice O'Connor's opinion concurring in the judgment in part and dissenting in part. Congress has a compelling interest in ensuring the ability to enforce prohibitions of actual child pornography, and we should defer to its findings that rapidly advancing technology soon will make it all but impossible to do so.

I also agree with Justice O'Connor that serious First Amendment concerns would arise were the Government ever to prosecute someone for simple distribution or possession of a film with literary or artistic value, such as "Traffic" or "American Beauty." I write separately, however, because the Child Pornography Prevention Act of 1996 (CPPA) need not be construed to reach such materials.

We normally do not strike down a statute on First Amendment grounds "when a limiting instruction has been or could be placed on the challenged statute."

Indeed, we should be loath to construe a statute as banning film portrayals of Shakespearean tragedies, without some indication — from text or legislative history — that such a result was intended. In fact, Congress explicitly instructed that such a reading of the CPPA would be wholly unwarranted.

This narrow reading of "sexually explicit conduct" not only accords with the text of the CPPA and the intentions of Congress; it is exactly how the phrase was understood prior to the broadening gloss the Court gives it today. Indeed, had "sexually explicit conduct" been thought to reach the sort of material the Court says it does, then films such as "Traffic" and "American Beauty" would not have been made the way they were. "Traffic" won its Academy Award in 2001. "American Beauty" won its Academy Award in 2000. But the CPPA has been on the books, and has been enforced, since 1996. The chill felt by the Court, has apparently never been felt by those who actually make movies.

To the extent the CPPA prohibits possession or distribution of materials that "convey the impression" of a child engaged in sexually explicit conduct, that prohibition can and should be limited to reach "the sordid business of pandering" which lies outside the bounds of First Amendment protection. Ginzburg v. United States (1966).

Following Ashcroft v. Free Speech Coalition, Congress adopted the Prosecutorial Remedies and Other Tools to End the Exploitation of Children Today (PROTECT) Act, 18 U.S.C. §2252A. In United States v. Williams, 553 U.S. 285 (2008), the Supreme Court upheld the Act. The Court emphasized that the law required that the material could be deemed child pornography only if children were actually used in its production. The Court concluded that the law was constitutional in providing punishment for those who solicit or offer material reasonably believing that it is child pornography even if it isn't.

c. Protected but Low-Value Sexual Speech

The Supreme Court has indicated there is a category of sexual speech that does not meet the test for obscenity and thus is protected by the First Amendment, but is deemed to be speech of low value, and thus the government has latitude to regulate such expression. The Court never has defined the contours of this category, but it clearly involves sexually explicit material.

i. Zoning Ordinances

The Court has upheld the ability of local governments to use zoning ordinances to regulate the location of adult bookstores and movie theaters. In Young v. American Mini Theatres, Inc., the Supreme Court upheld a city's ordinance that limited the number of adult theaters that could be on any block and prevented such enterprises from operating in residential areas.

YOUNG v. AMERICAN MINI THEATRES, INC.
427 U.S. 50 (1976)

Justice STEVENS delivered the opinion of the Court.

Zoning ordinances adopted by the city of Detroit differentiate between motion picture theaters which exhibit sexually explicit "adult" movies and those which do not. The principal question presented by this case is whether that statutory classification is unconstitutional because it is based on the content of communication protected by the First Amendment.

Effective November 2, 1972, Detroit adopted the ordinances challenged in this litigation. Instead of concentrating "adult" theaters in limited zones, these ordinances require that such theaters be dispersed. Specifically, an adult theater may not be located within 1,000 feet of any two other "regulated uses" or within 500 feet of a residential area. The term "regulated uses" includes 10 different kinds of establishments in addition to adult theaters.

The classification of a theater as "adult" is expressly predicated on the character of the motion pictures which it exhibits. If the theater is used to present "material distinguished or characterized by an emphasis on matter depicting, describing or relating to 'Specified Sexual Activities' or 'Specified Anatomical Areas,'" it is an adult establishment. These terms are defined as follows: "For the purpose of this Section, 'Specified Sexual Activities' is defined as: 1. Human Genitals in a state of sexual stimulation or arousal; 2. Acts of human masturbation, sexual intercourse or sodomy; 3. Fondling or other erotic touching of human genitals, pubic region, buttock or female breast." And "Specified Anatomical Areas" is defined as: "1. Less than completely and opaquely covered: (a) human genitals, pubic region, (b) buttock, and (c) female breast below a point immediately above the top of the areola; and 2. Human male genitals in a discernibly turgid state, even if completely and opaquely covered."

We are not persuaded that the Detroit zoning ordinances will have a significant deterrent effect on the exhibition of films protected by the First Amendment. [T]he only vagueness in the ordinances relates to the amount of sexually explicit activity that may be portrayed before the material can be said to "characterized by an emphasis" on such matter. For most films the question will be readily answerable; to the extent that an area of doubt exists, we see no reason why the ordinances are not "readily subject to a narrowing construction by the state courts." [T]here is surely a less vital interest in the uninhibited exhibition of material that is on the borderline between pornography and artistic expression than in the free dissemination of ideas of social and political significance.

The ordinances are not challenged on the ground that they impose a limit on the total number of adult theaters which may operate in the city of Detroit. There is no claim that distributors or exhibitors of adult films are denied access to the market or, conversely, that the viewing public is unable to satisfy its appetite for sexually explicit fare. Viewed as an entity, the market for this commodity is essentially unrestrained.

It is true, however, that adult films may only be exhibited commercially in licensed theaters. But that is also true of all motion pictures. The city's general zoning laws require all motion picture theaters to satisfy certain locational as well as other requirements; we have no doubt that the municipality may control the location of theaters as well as the location of other commercial establishments, either by confining them to certain specified commercial zones or by requiring that they be dispersed throughout the city.

Putting to one side for the moment the fact that adult motion picture theaters must satisfy a locational restriction not applicable to other theaters, we are also persuaded that the 1,000-foot restriction does not, in itself, create an impermissible restraint on protected communication. The city's interest in planning and regulating the use of property for commercial purposes is clearly adequate to support that kind of restriction applicable to all theaters within the city limits.

The question whether speech is, or is not, protected by the First Amendment often depends on the content of the speech. Thus, the line between permissible advocacy and impermissible incitation to crime or violence depends, not merely on the setting in which the speech occurs, but also on exactly what the speaker had to say. Similarly, it is the content of the utterance that determines whether it is a protected epithet or an unprotected "fighting comment."

Even within the area of protected speech, a difference in content may require a different governmental response. Moreover, even though we recognize that the First Amendment will not tolerate the total suppression of erotic materials that have some arguably artistic value, it is manifest that society's interest in protecting this type of expression is of a wholly different, and lesser, magnitude than the interest in untrammeled political debate that inspired Voltaire's immortal comment. Whether political oratory or philosophical discussion moves us to applaud or to despise what is said, every schoolchild can understand why our duty to defend the right to speak remains the same. But few of us would march our sons and daughters off to war to preserve the citizen's right to see "Specified Sexual Activities" exhibited in the theaters of our choice. Even though the First Amendment protects communication in this area from total suppression, we hold that the State may legitimately use the content of these materials as the basis for placing them in a different classification from other motion pictures.

The remaining question is whether the line drawn by these ordinances is justified by the city's interest in preserving the character of its neighborhoods. The record disclosed a factual basis for the Common Council's conclusion that this kind of restriction will have the desired effect. It is not our function to appraise the wisdom of its decision to require adult theaters to be separated rather than concentrated in the same areas. In either event, the city's interest in attempting to preserve the quality of urban life is one that must be accorded high respect. Moreover, the city must be allowed a reasonable opportunity to experiment with solutions to admittedly serious problems.

Since what is ultimately at stake is nothing more than a limitation on the place where adult films may be exhibited, even though the determination of whether a particular film fits that characterization turns on the nature of its content, we conclude that the city's interest in the present and future character of its neighborhoods adequately supports its classification of motion pictures.

Justice STEWART, with whom Justice BRENNAN, Justice MARSHALL, and Justice BLACKMUN join, dissenting.

The Court today holds that the First and Fourteenth Amendments do not prevent the city of Detroit from using a system of prior restraints and criminal sanctions to enforce content-based restrictions on the geographic location of motion picture theaters that exhibit nonobscene but sexually oriented films. I dissent from this drastic departure from established principles of First Amendment law.

This case does not involve a simple zoning ordinance, or a content-neutral time, place, and manner restriction, or a regulation of obscene expression or other speech that is entitled to less than the full protection of the First Amendment. The kind of expression at issue here is no doubt objectionable to some, but that fact does not diminish its protected status.

What this case does involve is the constitutional permissibility of selective interference with protected speech whose content is thought to produce distasteful effects. It is elementary that a prime function of the First Amendment is to guard against just such interference. By refusing to invalidate Detroit's ordinance the Court rides roughshod over cardinal principles of First Amendment law, which require that time, place, and manner regulations that affect protected expression be content neutral except in the limited context of a captive or juvenile audience. In place of these principles the Court invokes a concept wholly alien to the First Amendment. Since "few of us would march our sons and daughters off to war to preserve the citizen's right to see 'Specified Sexual Activities' exhibited in the theaters of our choice," the Court implies that these films are not entitled to the full protection of the Constitution. This stands "Voltaire's immortal comment[]" on its head. For if the guarantees of the First Amendment were reserved for expression that more than a "few of us" would take up arms to defend, then the right of free expression would be defined and circumscribed by current popular opinion. The guarantees of the Bill of Rights were designed to protect against precisely such majoritarian limitations on individual liberty.

I can only interpret today's decision as an aberration. The Court is undoubtedly sympathetic, as am I, to the well-intentioned efforts of Detroit to "clean up" its streets and prevent the proliferation of "skid rows." But it is in those instances where protected speech grates most unpleasantly against the sensibilities that judicial vigilance must be at its height.

Likewise, in City of Renton v. Playtime Theatres, Inc., presented above in section B of this chapter, the Supreme Court relied on *Young* to uphold a zoning ordinance that excluded adult motion picture theaters from operating within 1,000 feet of any residential zone, church, park, or school. The effect was to exclude such theaters from about 95 percent of the land in the city. Of the remaining land, a substantial part was occupied by a sewage disposal and treatment plant, a horse racing track, a warehouse and manufacturing facility, an oil tank farm, and a shopping center. Nonetheless, the Supreme Court upheld the ordinance, saying that the result was "largely dictated by our decision in *Young.*"

However, unlike *Young*, in which the Court acknowledged the regulation as content-based, the Court in *Renton* described the ordinance as being content-neutral because the "City Council's '*predominate* concerns' were with the secondary effects of adult theaters, and not with the content of adult films themselves." The Court said that the ordinance was designed to "prevent crime, protect the city's retail trade, maintain property values, and generally protect and preserve the quality of the city's neighborhoods, commercial districts, and the quality of urban life, not to suppress the expression of unpopular views." In other words, the Court defined content neutrality not by the terms of the law, but rather, by the legislature's predominant purpose.

Most recently, in City of Los Angeles v. Alameda Books, Inc., 535 U.S. 425 (2002), the Supreme Court upheld a Los Angeles ordinance that prohibits "the establishment or maintenance of more than one adult entertainment business in the same building, structure, or portion thereof." The Court said that the city could rely on a study from 1977 showing that a concentration of adult business increases crime.

ii. Nude Dancing

Another example of the Court's treatment of sexually oriented speech as being of "low value" is its willingness to allow the government to prohibit nude dancing.

In Barnes v. Glen Theatre, Inc., 501 U.S. 560 (1991), the Supreme Court held that the government may completely ban nude dancing. Specifically, the Court ruled that an Indiana statute prohibiting public nudity could be used to require that female dancers must, at a minimum, wear pasties and a G-string when they dance. There was no majority opinion for the Court in its five-to-four decision. Chief Justice Rehnquist wrote the plurality opinion joined by Justices O'Connor and Kennedy and initially noted that "nude dancing of the kind sought to be performed here is expressive conduct within the outer perimeters of the First Amendment, though we view it as only marginally so."

The plurality saw nude dancing as a form of conduct that communicates and applied the test used for regulating symbolic speech: "[A] government regulation is sufficiently justified if it is within the constitutional power of the Government; if it furthers an important or substantial governmental interest; if the governmental interest is unrelated to the suppression of free expression; and if the incidental restriction on alleged First Amendment freedoms is no greater than is essential to the furtherance of that interest."[141] The plurality upheld the prohibition of nude dancing because it served the goal of "protecting societal order and morality."[142]

Justice Scalia, concurring in the judgment, took a different approach. He argued, "[T]he challenged regulation must be upheld, not because it survives some lower level of First Amendment scrutiny, but because as a general law regulating conduct and not specifically directed at expression, it is not subject to First Amendment scrutiny at all." In other cases, as well, Justice Scalia has advanced the view that the First Amendment's protections of speech and religion are not violated by neutral laws of general applicability that burden these rights.[143] Justice Scalia also expressly rejected the dissent's argument that public nudity laws exist only to protect unwilling viewers from offense. He wrote, "The purpose of Indiana's nudity law would be violated, I think, if 60,000 fully consenting adults crowded into the Hoosier Dome to display their genitals to one another, even if there were not an offended innocent in the crowd. Our society prohibits, and all human societies have prohibited, certain activities not because they harm others, but because they are considered, in the traditional phrase, . . . immoral."

Justice Souter also concurred in the judgment and focused on the secondary effects of nude dancing. He said "that legislation seeking to combat the secondary effects of adult entertainment need not await localized proof of those effects [and that] the State of Indiana could reasonably conclude that forbidding nude entertainment of the type offered at the Kitty Kat Lounge [furthers] its interest in preventing prostitution, sexual assault, and associated crimes."

Justice White wrote a dissenting opinion joined by Justices Brennan, Marshall, and Blackmun and emphasized that stopping nude dancing was suppressing a message. Justice White said, "[T]he nudity of the dancer is an integral part of the emotions and thoughts that a nude dancing performance evokes. The sight of a fully clothed, or even a partially clothed, dancer generally will have a far different impact on a spectator than that of a nude dancer, even if the same dance is performed. The nudity itself is an expressive component of the dance, not merely incidental 'conduct.'"

In 2000, in City of Erie v. Pap's A.M., the Court reaffirmed *Barnes*. Justice O'Connor's plurality opinion also reaffirmed *Renton*'s holding that the government's interest in preventing secondary effects is sufficient to make the law content-neutral and to uphold the closing of nude dancing establishments.

---

141. The topic of symbolic speech is discussed in detail below.
142. *Barnes*, 501 U.S. *Id.* at 568.
143. *See, e.g.*, Cohen v. Cowles Media Co., 501 U.S. 663 (1991); Employment Division v. Smith, 494 U.S. 872 (1990).

CITY OF ERIE v. PAP'S A.M.

529 U.S. 277 (2000)

Justice O'CONNOR announced the judgment of the Court and delivered an opinion in which the Chief Justice, Justice KENNEDY, and Justice BREYER join.

The city of Erie, Pennsylvania, enacted an ordinance banning public nudity. Respondent Pap's A.M. (hereinafter Pap's), which operated a nude dancing establishment in Erie, challenged the constitutionality of the ordinance and sought a permanent injunction against its enforcement. The Pennsylvania Supreme Court, although noting that this Court in Barnes v. Glen Theatre, Inc. (1991), had upheld an Indiana ordinance that was "strikingly similar" to Erie's, found that the public nudity sections of the ordinance violated respondent's right to freedom of expression under the United States Constitution. This case raises the question whether the Pennsylvania Supreme Court properly evaluated the ordinance's constitutionality under the First Amendment. We hold that Erie's ordinance is a content-neutral regulation that satisfies the [First Amendment].

I

On September 28, 1994, the city council for the city of Erie, Pennsylvania, enacted a public indecency ordinance that makes it a summary offense to knowingly or intentionally appear in public in a "state of nudity." Respondent Pap's, a Pennsylvania corporation, operated an establishment in Erie known as "Kandyland" that featured totally nude erotic dancing performed by women. To comply with the ordinance, these dancers must wear, at a minimum, "pasties" and a "G-string." On October 14, 1994, two days after the ordinance went into effect, Pap's filed a complaint against the city of Erie, the mayor of the city, and members of the city council, seeking declaratory relief and a permanent injunction against the enforcement of the ordinance.

[II]

Being "in a state of nudity" is not an inherently expressive condition. As we explained in *Barnes*, however, nude dancing of the type at issue here is expressive conduct, although we think that it falls only within the outer ambit of the First Amendment's protection.

To determine what level of scrutiny applies to the ordinance at issue here, we must decide "whether the State's regulation is related to the suppression of expression." If the governmental purpose in enacting the regulation is unrelated to the suppression of expression, then the regulation need only satisfy the "less stringent" standard. If the government interest is related to the content of the expression, however, then the regulation must be justified under a more demanding standard.

The ordinance here, like the statute in *Barnes*, is on its face a general prohibition on public nudity. By its terms, the ordinance regulates conduct alone. It does not target nudity that contains an erotic message; rather, it bans all public nudity, regardless of whether that nudity is accompanied by expressive activity.

Respondent and Justice Stevens contend nonetheless that the ordinance is related to the suppression of expression because language in the ordinance's preamble suggests that its actual purpose is to prohibit erotic dancing of the type performed at Kandyland. That is not how the Pennsylvania Supreme Court interpreted that language, however. The Pennsylvania Supreme Court construed [the legislative history] to mean that one purpose of the ordinance was "to combat negative secondary effects."

As Justice Souter noted in *Barnes*, "on its face, the governmental interest in combating prostitution and other criminal activity is not at all inherently related to expression." So too here, the ordinance prohibiting public nudity is aimed at combating crime and other negative secondary effects caused by the presence of adult entertainment establishments like Kandyland and not at suppressing the erotic message conveyed by this type of nude dancing. Put another way, the ordinance does not attempt to regulate the primary effects of the expression, i.e., the effect on the audience of watching nude erotic dancing, but rather the secondary effects, such as the impacts on public health, safety, and welfare, which we have previously recognized are "caused by the presence of even one such" establishment. Renton v. Playtime Theatres, Inc. (1986).

[E]ven if Erie's public nudity ban has some minimal effect on the erotic message by muting that portion of the expression that occurs when the last stitch is dropped, the dancers at Kandyland and other such establishments are free to perform wearing pasties and G-strings. Any effect on the overall expression is de minimis. And as Justice Stevens eloquently stated for the plurality in Young v. American Mini Theatres, Inc. (1976), "even though we recognize that the First Amendment will not tolerate the total suppression of erotic materials that have some arguably artistic value, it is manifest that society's interest in protecting this type of expression is of a wholly different, and lesser, magnitude than the interest in untrammeled political debate," and "few of us would march our sons or daughters off to war to preserve the citizen's right to see" specified anatomical areas exhibited at establishments like Kandyland. If States are to be able to regulate secondary effects, then de minimis intrusions on expression such as those at issue here cannot be sufficient to render the ordinance content based.

We conclude that Erie's asserted interest in combating the negative secondary effects associated with adult entertainment establishments like Kandyland is unrelated to the suppression of the erotic message conveyed by nude dancing. The asserted interests of regulating conduct through a public nudity ban and of combating the harmful secondary effects associated with nude dancing are undeniably important. And in terms of demonstrating that such secondary effects pose a threat, the city need not "conduct new studies or produce evidence independent of that already generated by other cities" to demonstrate the problem of secondary effects, "so long as whatever evidence the city relies upon is reasonably believed to be relevant to the problem that the city addresses." Renton v. Playtime Theatres, Inc. Because the nude dancing at Kandyland is of the same character as the adult entertainment at issue in *Renton* and Young v. American Mini Theatres, Inc. (1976), it was reasonable for Erie to conclude that such nude dancing was likely to produce the same secondary effects. In any event, Erie also relied on its own findings. The city council members, familiar with commercial downtown Erie, are the individuals who would likely have had first-hand knowledge of what took place at and around nude dancing establishments in Erie, and can make particularized, expert judgments about the resulting harmful secondary effects. We hold, therefore, that Erie's ordinance is a content-neutral regulation that is valid under *O'Brien*.

Justice Scalia, with whom Justice Thomas joins, concurring in the judgment.

[E]ven were I to conclude that the city of Erie had specifically singled out the activity of nude dancing, I still would not find that this regulation violated the First Amendment unless I could be persuaded (as on this record I cannot) that it was the communicative character of nude dancing that prompted the ban. When conduct other than speech itself is regulated, it is my view that the First Amendment is violated only "[w]here the government prohibits conduct precisely because of its Communicative attributes." Here, even if one hypothesizes that the city's object was to suppress only nude dancing, that would not establish an intent to suppress what (if anything) nude dancing communicates. I do not feel the need, as the Court does, to identify some "secondary effects" associated with nude dancing that the city could properly seek to eliminate. (I am highly skeptical, to tell the truth, that the addition of pasties and G-strings will at all reduce the tendency of establishments such as Kandyland to attract crime and prostitution, and hence to foster sexually transmitted disease.) The traditional power of government to foster good morals, and the acceptability of the traditional judgment (if Erie wishes to endorse it) that nude public dancing itself is immoral, have not been repealed by the First Amendment.

Justice Souter, dissenting in part.

I do not believe, however, that the current record allows us to say that the city has made a sufficient evidentiary showing to sustain its regulation, and I would therefore vacate the decision of the Pennsylvania Supreme Court and remand the case for further proceedings.

In several recent cases, we have confronted the need for factual justifications to satisfy intermediate scrutiny under the First Amendment. Those cases do not identify with any specificity a particular quantum of evidence, nor do I seek to do so in this brief concurrence. What the cases do make plain, however, is that application of an intermediate scrutiny test to a government's asserted rationale for regulation of expressive activity demands some factual justification to connect that rationale with the regulation in issue.

[T]he record before us today is deficient in its failure to reveal any evidence on which Erie may have relied, either for the seriousness of the threatened harm or for the efficacy of its chosen remedy. The plurality does the best it can with the materials to hand, but the pickings are slim. [T]he recitation does not get beyond conclusions on a subject usually fraught with some emotionalism. Nor does the invocation of Barnes v. Glen Theatre, Inc. (1991), in one paragraph of the preamble to Erie's ordinance suffice. The plurality opinion in *Barnes* made no mention of evidentiary showings at all, and though my separate opinion did make a pass at the issue, I did not demand reliance on germane evidentiary demonstrations, whether specific to the statute in question or developed elsewhere. To invoke *Barnes*, therefore, does not indicate that the issue of evidence has been addressed.

The proposition that the presence of nude dancing establishments increases the incidence of prostitution and violence is amenable to empirical treatment, and the city councilors who enacted Erie's ordinance are in a position to look to the facts of their own community's experience as well as to experiences elsewhere. Their failure to do so is made all the clearer by one of the amicus briefs, largely devoted to the argument that scientifically sound studies show no such correlation. See Brief for First Amendment Lawyers Association as Amicus Curiae.

The record before us now does not permit the conclusion that Erie's ordinance is reasonably designed to mitigate real harms. This does not mean that the required showing cannot be made, only that, on this record, Erie has not made it. I would remand to give it the opportunity to do so.

Justice STEVENS, with whom Justice GINSBURG joins, dissenting.

Far more important than the question whether nude dancing is entitled to the protection of the First Amendment are the dramatic changes in legal doctrine that the Court endorses today. Until now, the "secondary effects" of commercial enterprises featuring indecent entertainment have justified only the regulation of their location. For the first time, the Court has now held that such effects may justify the total suppression of protected speech.

The Court relies on the so-called "secondary effects" test to defend the ordinance. The present use of that rationale, however, finds no support whatsoever in our precedents. Never before have we approved the use of that doctrine to justify a total ban on protected First Amendment expression. On the contrary, we have been quite clear that the doctrine would not support that end.

[T]he city of Erie has not in fact pointed to any study by anyone suggesting that the adverse secondary effects of commercial enterprises featuring erotic dancing depends in the slightest on the precise costume worn by the performers — it merely assumes it to be so. If the city is permitted simply to assume that a slight addition to the dancers' costumes will sufficiently decrease secondary effects, then presumably the city can require more and more clothing as long as any danger of adverse effects remains.

The reason we have limited our secondary effects cases to zoning and declined to extend their reasoning to total bans is clear and straightforward: A dispersal that simply limits the places where speech may occur is a minimal imposition whereas a total ban is the most exacting of restrictions. The State's interest in fighting presumed secondary effects is sufficiently strong to justify the former, but far too weak to support the latter, more severe burden. Yet it is perfectly clear that in the present case the city of Erie has totally silenced a message the dancers at Kandyland want to convey. The fact that this censorship may have a laudable ulterior purpose cannot mean that censorship is not censorship. The Court's use of the secondary effects rationale to permit a total ban has grave implications for basic free speech principles.

iii. Should There Be Such a Category as Low-Value Sexual Speech?

Ultimately, cases like *Young, Renton, Barnes,* and *Erie* raise the question of whether there should be a category of minimally protected sexually oriented speech. Answering this inquiry turns on the general question of whether there should be a hierarchy of protected speech, and on the specific question of whether sexually oriented speech that is not obscene should be regarded as low in value. The cases above do not specify the level of scrutiny used, but it obviously is far less than strict scrutiny and appears to be little more than rational basis review. But in two recent cases presented below, Ashcroft v. ACLU and United States v. Playboy Entertainment Group, the Court used strict scrutiny for content-based regulation of sexual speech. There is an obvious tension in the earlier cases using little more than rational basis review.

There is also the crucial issue of what justifications are sufficient to warrant regulation of this speech. *Young, Renton,* and especially Justice O'Connor's plurality opinion in *Erie* all focus on the need to regulate speech to stop secondary effects. But almost all speech has some secondary effects; parades and demonstrations, for example, cause litter. These cases also raise the question of whether a state's interest in advancing a certain moral vision is sufficient to warrant restriction of the speech.

Finally, it must be noted that the Court has never defined the content of this category of low-value sexually oriented speech. The Court has made it clear that nudity, alone, is not enough to place speech in this category. In Erznoznik v. City of Jacksonville, 422 U.S. 205 (1975), the Court declared unconstitutional an ordinance that declared it a public nuisance for any drive-in movie theater to exhibit any motion picture "in which the human male or female bare buttocks, human female bare breasts, or human bare pubic areas are shown, if such motion picture [is] visible from any public street or public place." The Court noted that the law "sweepingly forbids display of all films containing *any* uncovered buttocks or breasts, irrespective of context or pervasiveness. . . . [A]ll nudity cannot be deemed obscene even as to minors." Nudity alone, therefore, is not enough to make speech less protected. The contours of the category of less protected sexual speech never have been defined.

d. Government Techniques for Controlling Obscenity and Child Pornography

The Supreme Court has made it clear that the government can prohibit the sale, distribution, and exhibition of obscene materials even to willing recipients. In Paris Adult Theatre I v. Slaton, presented above, the Court said that "[t]he States have the power to make a morally neutral judgment that public exhibition of obscene material, or commerce in such material, has a tendency to injure the community as a whole, to endanger the public safety, or to jeopardize . . . the States' 'right to maintain a decent society.'"

However, the Court also has held that the government cannot prohibit or punish the private possession of obscene material, although it may outlaw the private possession of child pornography.

STANLEY v. GEORGIA
394 U.S. 557 (1969)

Justice MARSHALL delivered the opinion of the Court.

An investigation of appellant's alleged bookmaking activities led to the issuance of a search warrant for appellant's home. Under authority of this warrant, federal and state agents secured entrance. They found very little evidence of bookmaking activity, but while looking through a desk drawer in an upstairs bedroom, one of the federal agents, accompanied by a state officer, found three reels of eight-millimeter film. Using a projector and screen found in an upstairs living room, they viewed the films. The state officer concluded that they were obscene and seized them. Since a further examination of the bedroom indicated that appellant occupied it, he was charged with possession of obscene matter and placed under arrest. He was later [convicted] for "knowingly hav[ing] possession of . . . obscene matter" in violation of Georgia law.

Appellant argues that the Georgia obscenity statute, insofar as it punishes mere private possession of obscene matter, violates the First Amendment, as made applicable to the States by the Fourteenth Amendment. [W]e agree that the mere private possession of obscene matter cannot constitutionally be made a crime.

[W]e do not believe that this case can be decided simply by citing *Roth. Roth* and its progeny certainly do mean that the First and Fourteenth Amendments recognize a valid governmental interest in dealing with the problem of obscenity. But the assertion of that interest cannot, in every context, be insulated from all constitutional protections. Neither *Roth* nor any other decision of this Court reaches that far.

It is now well established that the Constitution protects the right to receive information and ideas. This right to receive information and ideas, regardless of their social worth, is fundamental to our free society. Moreover, in the context of this case a prosecution for mere possession of printed or filmed matter in the privacy of a person's own home that right takes on an added dimension. For also fundamental is the right to be free, except in very limited circumstances, from unwanted governmental intrusions into one's privacy.

These are the rights that appellant is asserting in the case before us. He is asserting the right to read or observe what he pleases — the right to satisfy his intellectual and emotional needs in the privacy of his own home. He is asserting the right to be free from state inquiry into the contents of his library. Whatever may be the justifications for other statutes regulating obscenity, we do not think they reach into the privacy of one's own home. If the First Amendment means anything, it means that a State has no business telling a man, sitting alone in his own house, what books he may read or what films he may watch. Our whole constitutional heritage rebels at the thought of giving government the power to control men's minds.

Perhaps recognizing this, Georgia asserts that exposure to obscene materials may lead to deviant sexual behavior or crimes of sexual violence. There appears to be little empirical basis for that assertion. Given the present state of knowledge, the State may no more prohibit mere possession of obscene matter on the ground that it may lead to antisocial conduct than it may prohibit possession of chemistry books on the ground that they may lead to the manufacture of homemade spirits. We hold that the First and Fourteenth Amendments prohibit making mere private possession of obscene material a crime.

Although *Stanley* never has been overruled, the Court has been consistently unwilling to extend it. For example, in United States v. Reidel, 402 U.S. 351 (1971), the Court held that *Stanley* did not protect a right to receive obscene materials. A federal law prohibits the shipment of obscene materials in the mail. The defendant argued that the right to possess such material as recognized in *Stanley* means that there must be a right to receive it. The Supreme Court disagreed and held that the government may prohibit shipment of such materials. The Court expressly distinguished *Stanley* and said that the defendant was "in a wholly different position . . . [because he] has no complaints about governmental violations of his private thoughts or fantasies, but stands squarely on a claimed First Amendment right to do business in obscenity and use the mails in the process. . . . *Stanley* did not overrule *Roth* and we decline to do so now."

Even more significantly, the Court in Osborne v. Ohio held that the government may prohibit and punish the private possession of child pornography.

OSBORNE v. OHIO, 495 U.S. 103 (1990): Justice WHITE delivered the opinion of the Court.

Petitioner, Clyde Osborne, was convicted and sentenced to six months in prison, after the Columbus, Ohio, police, pursuant to a valid search, found four photographs in Osborne's home. Each photograph depicts a nude male adolescent posed in a sexually explicit position.

The threshold question in this case is whether Ohio may constitutionally proscribe the possession and viewing of child pornography or whether, as Osborne argues, our decision in Stanley v. Georgia (1969), compels the contrary result. *Stanley* should not be read too broadly. We have previously noted that *Stanley* was a narrow holding, and, since the decision in that case, the value of permitting child pornography has been characterized as "exceedingly modest, if not de minimis." New York v. Ferber (1982).

But assuming, for the sake of argument, that Osborne has a First Amendment interest in viewing and possessing child pornography, we nonetheless find this case distinct from *Stanley* because the interests underlying child pornography prohibitions far exceed the interests justifying the Georgia law at issue in *Stanley*. Every court to address the issue has so concluded. The difference here is obvious: The State does not rely on a paternalistic interest in regulating Osborne's mind. Rather, Ohio has enacted [its law] in order to protect the victims of child pornography; it hopes to destroy a market for the exploitative use of children. It is also surely reasonable for the State to conclude that it will decrease the production of child pornography if it penalizes those who possess and view the product, thereby decreasing demand.

Given the importance of the State's interest in protecting the victims of child pornography, we cannot fault Ohio for attempting to stamp out this vice at all levels in the distribution chain. According to the State, since the time of our decision in *Ferber*, much of the child pornography market has been driven underground; as a result, it is now difficult, if not impossible, to solve the child pornography problem by only attacking production and distribution. Indeed, 19 States have found it necessary to proscribe the possession of this material. Given the gravity of the State's interests in this context, we find that Ohio may constitutionally proscribe the possession and viewing of child pornography.

e. Profanity and "Indecent" Speech

Although profanity and "indecent" speech are not obscene, government often has tried to punish them. The Supreme Court has held that such language is generally protected by the First Amendment, but there are notable exceptions. This subsection begins by presenting Cohen v. California, which is the strongest declaration of First Amendment protection for such speech. The subsection then considers how the Court has treated government regulation of indecent speech over various media. The Court has expressly adopted a medium-by-medium approach, considering indecent speech over the broadcast media (television and radio), over telephones, over the Internet, and over cable television. Each of these areas is considered below.

COHEN v. CALIFORNIA

403 U.S. 15 (1971)

Justice HARLAN delivered the opinion of the Court.

This case may seem at first blush too inconsequential to find its way into our books, but the issue it presents is of no small constitutional significance. Appellant Paul Robert Cohen was convicted in the Los Angeles Municipal Court of violating that part of California Penal Code which prohibits "maliciously and willfully disturb[ing] the peace or quiet of any neighborhood or person . . . by . . . offensive conduct. . . ." He was given 30 days' imprisonment.

On April 26, 1968, the defendant was observed in the Los Angeles County Court house in the corridor of the municipal court wearing a jacket bearing the words "Fuck the Draft" which were plainly visible. There were women and children present in the corridor. The defendant was arrested. The defendant testified that he wore the jacket knowing that the words were on the jacket as a means of informing the public of the depth of his feelings against the Vietnam War and the draft.

The defendant did not engage in, nor threaten to engage in, nor did anyone as the result of his conduct in fact commit or threaten to commit any act of violence. The defendant did not make any loud or unusual noise, nor was there any evidence that he uttered any sound prior to his arrest.

I

In order to lay hands on the precise issue which this case involves, it is useful first to canvass various matters which this record does not present. The conviction quite clearly rests upon the asserted offensiveness of the words Cohen used to convey his message to the public. The only "conduct" which the State sought to punish is the fact of communication. Thus, we deal here with a conviction resting solely upon "speech."

[T]his case cannot be said to fall within those relatively few categories of instances where prior decisions have established the power of government to deal more comprehensively with certain forms of individual expression simply upon a showing that such a form was employed. This is not, for example, an obscenity case. Whatever else may be necessary to give rise to the States' broader power to prohibit obscene expression, such expression must be, in some significant way, erotic. It cannot plausibly be maintained that this vulgar allusion to the Selective Service System would conjure up such psychic stimulation in anyone likely to be confronted with Cohen's crudely defaced jacket.

This Court has also held that the States are free to ban the simple use, without a demonstration of additional justifying circumstances, of so-called "fighting words," those personally abusive epithets which, when addressed to the ordinary citizen, are, as a matter of common knowledge, inherently likely to provoke violent reaction. While the four-letter word displayed by Cohen in relation to the draft is not uncommonly employed in a personally provocative fashion, in this instance it was clearly not "directed to the person of the hearer." No individual actually or likely to be present could reasonably have regarded the words on appellant's jacket as a direct personal insult. Nor do we have here an instance of the exercise of the State's police power to prevent a speaker from intentionally provoking a given group to hostile reaction. There is, as noted above, no showing that anyone who saw Cohen was in fact violently aroused or that appellant intended such a result.

Finally, in arguments before this Court much has been made of the claim that Cohen's distasteful mode of expression was thrust upon unwilling or unsuspecting viewers, and that the State might therefore legitimately act as it did in order to protect the sensitive from otherwise unavoidable exposure to appellant's crude form of protest. Of course, the mere presumed presence of unwitting listeners or viewers does not serve automatically to justify curtailing all speech capable of giving offense. While this Court has recognized that government may properly act in many situations to prohibit intrusion into the privacy of the home of unwelcome views and ideas which cannot be totally banned from the public dialogue, we have at the same time consistently stressed that "we are often 'captives' outside the sanctuary of the home and subject to objectionable speech." The ability of government, consonant with the Constitution, to shut off discourse solely to protect others from hearing it is, in other words, dependent upon a showing that substantial privacy interests are being invaded in an essentially intolerable manner. Any broader view of this authority would effectively empower a majority to silence dissidents simply as a matter of personal predilections.

In this regard, persons confronted with Cohen's jacket were in a quite different posture than, say, those subjected to the raucous emissions of sound trucks blaring outside their residences. Those in the Los Angeles courthouse could effectively avoid further bombardment of their sensibilities simply by averting their eyes. And, while it may be that one has a more substantial claim to a recognizable privacy interest when walking through a courthouse corridor than, for example, strolling through Central Park, surely it is nothing like the interest in being free from unwanted expression in the confines of one's own home. Given the subtlety and complexity of the factors involved, if Cohen's "speech" was otherwise entitled to constitutional protection, we do not think the fact that some unwilling "listeners" in a public building may have been briefly exposed to it can serve to justify this breach of the peace conviction where, as here, there was no evidence that persons powerless to avoid appellant's conduct did in fact object to it.

II

Against this background, the issue flushed by this case stands out in bold relief. It is whether California can excise, as "offensive conduct," one particular scurrilous epithet from the public discourse.

The constitutional right of free expression is powerful medicine in a society as diverse and populous as ours. It is designed and intended to remove governmental restraints from the arena of public discussion, putting the decision as to what views shall be voiced largely into the hands of each of us, in the hope that use of such freedom will ultimately produce a more capable citizenry and more perfect polity and in the belief that no other approach would comport with the premise of individual dignity and choice upon which our political system rests. To many, the immediate consequence of this freedom may often appear to be only verbal tumult, discord, and even offensive utterance. These are, however, within established limits, in truth necessary side effects of the broader enduring values which the process of open debate permits us to achieve. That the air may at times seem filled with verbal cacophony is, in this sense not a sign of weakness but of strength. We cannot lose sight of the fact that, in what otherwise might seem a trifling and annoying instance of individual distasteful abuse of a privilege, these fundamental societal values are truly implicated.

Against this perception of the constitutional policies involved, we discern certain more particularized considerations that peculiarly call for reversal of this conviction. First, the principle contended for by the State seems inherently boundless. How is one to distinguish this from any other offensive word? Surely the State has no right to cleanse public debate to the point where it is grammatically palatable to the most squeamish among us. Yet no readily ascertainable general principle exists for stopping short of that result were we to affirm the judgment below. For, while the particular four-letter word being litigated here is perhaps more distasteful than most others of its genre, it is nevertheless often true that one man's vulgarity is another's lyric. Indeed, we think it is largely because governmental officials cannot make principled distinctions in this area that the Constitution leaves matters of taste and style so largely to the individual.

Additionally, we cannot overlook the fact, because it is well illustrated by the episode involved here, that much linguistic expression serves a dual communicative function: it conveys not only ideas capable of relatively precise, detached explication, but otherwise inexpressible emotions as well. In fact, words are often chosen as much for their emotive as their cognitive force. We cannot sanction the view that the Constitution, while solicitous of the cognitive content of individual speech has little or no regard for that emotive function which practically speaking, may often be the more important element of the overall message sought to be communicated.

Finally, and in the same vein, we cannot indulge the facile assumption that one can forbid particular words without also running a substantial risk of suppressing ideas in the process. Indeed, governments might soon seize upon the censorship of particular words as a convenient guise for banning the expression of unpopular views. We have been able, as noted above, to discern little social benefit that might result from running the risk of opening the door to such grave results.

It is, in sum, our judgment that, absent a more particularized and compelling reason for its actions, the State may not, consistently with the First and Fourteenth Amendments, make the simple public display here involved of this single four-letter expletive a criminal offense.

Justice BLACKMUN, with whom the Chief Justice and Justice BLACK join.

I dissent. Cohen's absurd and immature antic, in my view, was mainly conduct and little speech. Further, the case appears to me to be well within the sphere of Chaplinsky v. New Hampshire (1942), where Justice Murphy, a known champion of First Amendment freedoms, wrote for a unanimous bench. As a consequence, this Court's agonizing over First Amendment values seem misplaced and unnecessary.

Since *Cohen*, the Court has considered government regulation of indecent speech in a variety of media—the broadcast media (television and radio), telephones, the Internet, and cable television. Indeed, at times, in the cases below, the Court has expressly said that it has followed a medium-by-medium approach. In reading these cases, it is important to consider whether there is a meaningful distinction among them. For instance, the Court has upheld regulation of indecent speech over the broadcast medium, but not over the telephone or the Internet. Also, it is important to consider the desirability of the medium-by-medium approach. As increasingly all of these media, and even newspapers, are likely to be received through a single cable or phone line, does the different treatment of separate media still make sense?

i.   The Broadcast Media

Cohen's strong declaration that profane and indecent language are protected by the First Amendment can be contrasted with its decision in FCC v. Pacifica Foundation, which upheld the prohibition of indecent speech over television and radio.

FEDERAL COMMUNICATIONS COMMISSION v. PACIFICA FOUNDATION

438 U.S. 726 (1978)

Justice STEVENS delivered the opinion of the Court and an opinion in which the Chief Justice and Mr. Justice REHNQUIST joined (Parts IV-A and IV-B).

This case requires that we decide whether the Federal Communications Commission has any power to regulate a radio broadcast that is indecent but not obscene.

A satiric humorist named George Carlin recorded a 12-minute monologue entitled "Filthy Words" before a live audience in a California theater. He began by referring to his thoughts about "the words you couldn't say on the public, ah, airwaves, um, the ones you definitely wouldn't say, ever." He proceeded to list those words and repeat them over and over again in a variety of colloquialisms.

The transcript of the recording, which is appended to this opinion, indicates frequent laughter from the audience.

At about 2 o'clock in the afternoon on Tuesday, October 30, 1973, a New York radio station, owned by respondent Pacifica Foundation, broadcast the "Filthy Words" monologue. A few weeks later a man, who stated that he had heard the broadcast while driving with his young son, wrote a letter complaining to the Commission.

The complaint was forwarded to the station for comment. In its response, Pacifica explained that the monologue had been played during a program about contemporary society's attitude toward language and that, immediately before its broadcast, listeners had been advised that it included "sensitive language which might be regarded as offensive to some." Pacifica characterized George Carlin as "a significant social satirist" who "like Twain and Sahl before him, examines the language of ordinary people. . . . Carlin is not mouthing obscenities, he is merely using words to satirize as harmless and essentially silly our attitudes towards those words." Pacifica stated that it was not aware of any other complaints about the broadcast.

On February 21, 1975, the Commission issued a declaratory order granting the complaint and holding that Pacifica "could have been the subject of administrative sanctions." The Commission did not impose formal sanctions, but it did state that the order would be "associated with the station's license file, and in the event that subsequent complaints are received, the Commission will then decide whether it should utilize any of the available sanctions it has been granted by Congress." [T]he Commission found a power to regulate indecent broadcasting in two statutes: 18 U.S.C. §1464, which forbids the use of "any obscene, indecent, or profane language by means of radio communications," and 47 U.S.C. §303(g), which requires the Commission to "encourage the larger and more effective use of radio in the public interest."

IV

Pacifica makes two constitutional attacks on the Commission's order. First, it argues that the Commission's construction of the statutory language broadly encompasses so much constitutionally protected speech that reversal is required even if Pacifica's broadcast of the "Filthy Words" monologue is not itself protected by the First Amendment. Second, Pacifica argues that inasmuch as the recording is not obscene, the Constitution forbids any abridgment of the right to broadcast it on the radio.

A

The first argument fails because our review is limited to the question whether the Commission has the authority to proscribe this particular broadcast. As the Commission itself emphasized, its order was "issued in a specific factual context."

It is true that the Commission's order may lead some broadcasters to censor themselves. At most, however, the Commission's definition of indecency will deter only the broadcasting of patently offensive references to excretory and sexual organs and activities. While some of these references may be protected, they surely lie at the periphery of First Amendment concern.

B

When the issue is narrowed to the facts of this case, the question is whether the First Amendment denies government any power to restrict the public broadcast of indecent language in any circumstances. For if the government has any such power, this was an appropriate occasion for its exercise.

The question in this case is whether a broadcast of patently offensive words dealing with sex and excretion may be regulated because of its content. Obscene materials have been denied the protection of the First Amendment because their content is so offensive to contemporary moral standards. But the fact that society may find speech offensive is not a sufficient reason for suppressing it. Indeed, if it is the speaker's opinion that gives offense, that consequence is a reason for according it constitutional protection. For it is a central tenet of the First Amendment that the government must remain neutral in the marketplace of ideas. If there were any reason to believe that the Commission's characterization of the Carlin monologue as offensive could be traced to its political content — or even to the fact that it satirized contemporary attitudes about four-letter words — First Amendment protection might be required. But that is simply not this case. These words offend for the same reasons that obscenity offends. Their place in the hierarchy of First Amendment values was aptly sketched by Mr. Justice Murphy when he said: "Such utterances are no essential part of any exposition of ideas, and are of such slight social value as a step to truth that any benefit that may be derived from them is clearly outweighed by the social interest in order and morality." Chaplinsky v. New Hampshire.

Although these words ordinarily lack literary, political, or scientific value, they are not entirely outside the protection of the First Amendment. Some uses of even the most offensive words are unquestionably protected. Indeed, we may assume, arguendo, that this monologue would be protected in other contexts. Nonetheless, the constitutional protection accorded to a communication containing such patently offensive sexual and excretory language need not be the same in every context. It is a characteristic of speech such as this that both its capacity to offend and its "social value," to use Mr. Justice Murphy's term, vary with the circumstances. Words that are commonplace in one setting are shocking in another. To paraphrase Justice Harlan, one occasion's lyric is another's vulgarity.

In this case it is undisputed that the content of Pacifica's broadcast was "vulgar," "offensive," and "shocking." We have long recognized that each medium of expression presents special First Amendment problems. And of all forms of communication, it is broadcasting that has received the most limited First Amendment protection. First, the broadcast media have established a uniquely pervasive presence in the lives of all Americans. Patently offensive, indecent material presented over the airwaves confronts the citizen, not only in public, but also in the privacy of the home, where the individual's right to be left alone plainly outweighs the First Amendment rights of an intruder. Because the broadcast audience is constantly tuning in and out, prior warnings cannot completely protect the listener or viewer from unexpected program content. To say that one may avoid further offense by turning off the radio when he hears indecent language is like saying that the remedy for an assault is to run away after the first blow. One may hang up on an indecent phone call, but that option does not give the caller a constitutional immunity or avoid a harm that has already taken place.

Second, broadcasting is uniquely accessible to children, even those too young to read. Although Cohen's written message might have been incomprehensible to a first grader, Pacifica's broadcast could have enlarged a child's vocabulary in an instant. Other forms of offensive expression may be withheld from the young without restricting the expression at its source. Bookstores and motion picture theaters, for example, may be prohibited from making indecent material available to children.

It is appropriate, in conclusion, to emphasize the narrowness of our holding. This case does not involve a two-way radio conversation between a cab driver and a dispatcher, or a telecast of an Elizabethan comedy. We have not decided that an occasional expletive in either setting would justify any sanction or, indeed, that this broadcast would justify a criminal prosecution. The Commission's decision rested entirely on a nuisance rationale under which context is all-important. The concept requires consideration of a host of variables. The time of day was emphasized by the Commission. The content of the program in which the language is used will also affect the composition of the audience, and differences between radio, television, and perhaps closed-circuit transmissions, may also be relevant. As Justice Sutherland wrote a "nuisance may be merely a right thing in the wrong place, — like a pig in the parlor instead of the barnyard." Euclid v. Ambler Realty Co. We simply hold that when the Commission finds that a pig has entered the parlor, the exercise of its regulatory power does not depend on proof that the pig is obscene.

After *Pacifica*, the FCC adopted a policy that it would not punish a "fleeting expletive," a single use of a profanity primarily as an adjective. In a few instances in 2002 and 2003, primarily at music awards shows, profanities were used, and the FCC found that even though these were "fleeting expletives," they could be punished. In FCC v. Fox Television Stations, Inc., 132 S. Ct. 2307 (2012), the Court found that such punishment violated due process because the television stations did not have advance warning, "fair notice" that fleeting profanities or fleeting nudity could be punished. The Court stressed that because it "resolves these cases on fair notice grounds under the Due Process Clause, it need not address the First Amendment implications of the Commission's indecency policy." The issue remains open as to whether it violates the First Amendment for the government to punish a fleeting expletive.

ii. Telephones

In Sable Communications v. FCC, 492 U.S. 115 (1989), the Court declared unconstitutional a federal statute designed to eliminate the "dial-a-porn" industry; the law prohibited obscene or indecent telephone conversations. The Supreme Court drew a distinction between the "obscene" and the "indecent." The Court said that while the law was constitutional in prohibiting obscene speech, it was unconstitutional in prohibiting indecent speech.

The Court emphasized that the government could not ban speech simply because it was "indecent." The Court noted that there is no "captive audience" problem here; callers will generally not be unwilling listeners. Moreover, the

Court said that Congress's goal of protecting children could be achieved through means less restrictive of speech. Justice White, writing for the Court, said that the "Congressional record contains no legislative findings that would justify us in concluding that there is no constitutionally acceptable less restrictive means, short of a total ban, to achieve the Government's interest in protecting minors."

Thus, the Supreme Court in *Sable Communications* drew a distinction between the "obscene" and the "indecent." The difficulty, of course, is how to draw this distinction. It would seem exceedingly difficult for an attorney for a company like Sable Communications to advise it as to what its employees could say (the "indecent"), as opposed to what they must not say (the "obscene").

iii. The Internet

The Supreme Court's first major decision concerning the Internet, Reno v. American Civil Liberties Union, involved the same distinction between obscene and indecent speech in a federal law regulating the Internet. The Court declared unconstitutional the regulation of indecent speech over the Internet.

RENO v. AMERICAN CIVIL LIBERTIES UNION
521 U.S. 844 (1997)

Justice STEVENS delivered the opinion of the Court.

At issue is the constitutionality of two statutory provisions enacted to protect minors from "indecent" and "patently offensive" communications on the Internet. Notwithstanding the legitimacy and importance of the congressional goal of protecting children from harmful materials, we agree with the three-judge District Court that the statute abridges "the freedom of speech" protected by the First Amendment.

I

The District Court made extensive findings of fact, most of which were based on a detailed stipulation prepared by the parties. The findings describe the character and the dimensions of the Internet, the availability of sexually explicit material in that medium, and the problems confronting age verification for recipients of Internet communications. Because those findings provide the underpinnings for the legal issues, we begin with a summary of the undisputed facts.

THE INTERNET

The Internet is an international network of interconnected computers. It is the outgrowth of what began in 1969 as a military program called "ARPANET," which was designed to enable computers operated by the military, defense contractors, and universities conducting defense-related research to communicate with one another by redundant channels even if some portions of the network were damaged in a war. While the ARPANET no longer exists, it provided an example for the development of a number of civilian networks that, eventually linking with each other, now enable tens of millions of people to communicate with one another and to access vast amounts of information from around the world. The Internet is "a unique and wholly new medium of worldwide human communication."

The Internet has experienced "extraordinary growth." The number of "host" computers — those that store information and relay communications — increased from about 300 in 1981 to approximately 9,400,000 by the time of the trial in 1996. Roughly 60% of these hosts are located in the United States. About 40 million people used the Internet at the time of trial, a number that is expected to mushroom to 200 million by 1999.

II

The Telecommunications Act of 1996 was an unusually important legislative enactment. As stated on the first of its 103 pages, its primary purpose was to reduce regulation and encourage "the rapid deployment of new telecommunications technologies." The major components of the statute have nothing to do with the Internet; they were designed to promote competition in the local telephone service market, the multichannel video market, and the market for over-the-air broadcasting. The Act includes seven Titles, six of which are the product of extensive committee hearings and the subject of discussion in Reports prepared by Committees of the Senate and the House of Representatives. By contrast, Title V — known as the "Communications Decency Act of 1996" (CDA) — contains provisions that were either added in executive committee after the hearings were concluded or as amendments offered during floor debate on the legislation. An amendment offered in the Senate was the source of the two statutory provisions challenged in this case. They are informally described as the "indecent transmission" provision and the "patently offensive display" provision.

The first, §223(a), prohibits the knowing transmission of obscene or indecent messages to any recipient under 18 years of age. The second provision, §223(d), prohibits the knowing sending or displaying of patently offensive messages in a manner that is available to a person under 18 years of age. The breadth of these prohibitions is qualified by two affirmative defenses. One covers those who take "good faith, reasonable, effective, and appropriate actions" to restrict access by minors to the prohibited communications. The other covers those who restrict access to covered material by requiring certain designated forms of age proof, such as a verified credit card or an adult identification number or code.

III

[T]here are significant differences between the order upheld in FCC v. Pacifica Foundation and the CDA. First, the order in *Pacifica*, issued by an agency that had been regulating radio stations for decades, targeted a specific broadcast that represented a rather dramatic departure from traditional program content in order to designate when — rather than whether — it would be permissible to air

such a program in that particular medium. The CDA's broad categorical prohibitions are not limited to particular times and are not dependent on any
evaluation by an agency familiar with the unique characteristics of the Internet.
Second, unlike the CDA, the Commission's declaratory order was not punitive;
we expressly refused to decide whether the indecent broadcast "would justify a
criminal prosecution." Finally, the Commission's order applied to a medium
which as a matter of history had "received the most limited First Amendment
protection," in large part because warnings could not adequately protect the
listener from unexpected program content. The Internet, however, has no comparable history. Moreover, the District Court found that the risk of encountering
indecent material by accident is remote because a series of affirmative steps is
required to access specific material.

According to the Government, the CDA is constitutional because it constitutes a sort of "cyberzoning" on the Internet. But the CDA applies broadly to the
entire universe of cyberspace. And the purpose of the CDA is to protect children
from the primary effects of "indecent" and "patently offensive" speech, rather
than any "secondary" effect of such speech. Thus, the CDA is a content-based
blanket restriction on speech, and, as such, cannot be "properly analyzed as a
form of time, place, and manner regulation."

[IV]

In Southeastern Promotions, Ltd. v. Conrad (1975), we observed that "[e]ach
medium of expression . . . may present its own problems." Thus, some of our
cases have recognized special justifications for regulation of the broadcast media
that are not applicable to other speakers. Those factors are not present in
cyberspace. Neither before nor after the enactment of the CDA have the vast
democratic forums of the Internet been subject to the type of government supervision and regulation that has attended the broadcast industry. Moreover, the
Internet is not as "invasive" as radio or television. The District Court specifically
found that "[c]ommunications over the Internet do not 'invade' an individual's
home or appear on one's computer screen unbidden. Users seldom encounter
content 'by accident.'" It also found that "[a]lmost all sexually explicit images
are preceded by warnings as to the content," and cited testimony that "'odds
are slim' that a user would come across a sexually explicit sight by accident."

[V]

Regardless of whether the CDA is so vague that it violates the Fifth Amendment,
the many ambiguities concerning the scope of its coverage render it problematic
for purposes of the First Amendment. For instance, each of the two parts of the
CDA uses a different linguistic form. The first uses the word "indecent," while
the second speaks of material that "in context, depicts or describes, in terms
patently offensive as measured by contemporary community standards, sexual
or excretory activities or organs." Given the absence of a definition of either
term, this difference in language will provoke uncertainty among speakers about
how the two standards relate to each other and just what they mean. Could a
speaker confidently assume that a serious discussion about birth control prac-

tices, homosexuality, or the consequences of prison rape would not violate the CDA? This uncertainty undermines the likelihood that the CDA has been carefully tailored to the congressional goal of protecting minors from potentially harmful materials.

The vagueness of the CDA is a matter of special concern for two reasons. First, the CDA is a content-based regulation of speech. The vagueness of such a regulation raises special First Amendment concerns because of its obvious chilling effect on free speech. Second, the CDA is a criminal statute. In addition to the opprobrium and stigma of a criminal conviction, the CDA threatens violators with penalties including up to two years in prison for each act of violation. The severity of criminal sanctions may well cause speakers to remain silent rather than communicate even arguably unlawful words, ideas, and images.

[VI]

We are persuaded that the CDA lacks the precision that the First Amendment requires when a statute regulates the content of speech. In order to deny minors access to potentially harmful speech, the CDA effectively suppresses a large amount of speech that adults have a constitutional right to receive and to address to one another. That burden on adult speech is unacceptable if less restrictive alternatives would be at least as effective in achieving the legitimate purpose that the Statute was enacted to serve.

In evaluating the free speech rights of adults, we have made it perfectly clear that "[s]exual expression which is indecent but not obscene is protected by the First Amendment." It is true that we have repeatedly recognized the governmental interest in protecting children from harmful materials. But that interest does not justify an unnecessarily broad suppression of speech addressed to adults. As we have explained, the Government may not "reduc[e] the adult population . . . to . . . only what is fit for children."

The breadth of the CDA's coverage is wholly unprecedented. Unlike the regulations upheld in *Ginsberg* and *Pacifica*, the scope of the CDA is not limited to commercial speech or commercial entities. Its open-ended prohibitions embrace all nonprofit entities and individuals posting indecent messages or displaying them on their own computers in the presence of minors. The general, undefined terms "indecent" and "patently offensive" cover large amounts of nonpornographic material with serious educational or other value.

The Court followed the same reasoning in its subsequent decision in *Ashcroft v. American Civil Liberties Union*, 542 U.S. 656 (2004). The case involved the constitutionality of the Child On-Line Protection Act, a federal law that regulated sexually oriented commercial websites. The statute applied only to commercial websites that included material that appealed to the prurient interest and would be offensive to contemporary community standards. The law required that such websites verify users' ages and provided several ways in which they could do so.

A federal district court issued a preliminary injunction, and the U.S. Court of Appeals for the Third Circuit affirmed. The Supreme Court also upheld the preliminary injunction. The majority opinion was written by Justice Anthony Kennedy and joined by Justices Stevens, Souter, Ginsburg, and Thomas.

Justice Kennedy's opinion said that the law is a content-based restriction of speech, applying only to sexual speech, and that it therefore must meet strict scrutiny. The Court said that the preliminary injunction was upheld because there was a substantial likelihood that the plaintiffs would prevail in their argument that the law does not meet strict scrutiny. Justice Kennedy explained that filtering devices, which are installed on individual computers, likely are a less restrictive alternative for protecting children from exposure to sexually explicit material. The Court remanded the case to the federal district court for a determination of whether such filtering devices are a less restrictive alternative. On remand, the Third Circuit declared the law unconstitutional and issued a permanent injunction.

iv. Cable Television

A final medium considered by the Court is cable television. There have been two decisions concerning federal laws regulating sexual speech over this medium. The first was Denver Area Educational Telecommunications Consortium, Inc. v. FCC, 518 U.S. 727 (1996). The case involved First Amendment challenges to three provisions of the Cable Television Consumer Protection and Competition Act of 1992 that regulate the broadcasting of "patently offensive" sexually oriented material on cable television. One provision permits a cable system operator to prohibit the broadcasting of programming that "depicts sexual or excretory activities or organs in a patently offensive manner." A second challenged section requires that cable systems allowing such material segregate it on a single channel and block the channel from viewer access unless the viewer requests it in writing. The final provision allows cable systems to prohibit sexually oriented material on "public, educational, or governmental channels."

Without a majority opinion, the Court upheld the first provision but invalidated the latter two sections. As to the first clause, which allowed cable systems to refuse to carry sexually explicit broadcasting, Justice Breyer wrote a plurality opinion that was joined by Justices Stevens, O'Connor, and Souter. Justice Breyer explicitly eschewed choosing or applying a level of scrutiny, saying it was "unwise and unnecessary" to do so. Nonetheless, the plurality said that the first provision is constitutional because it serves "an extremely important justification, one that this Court has often found compelling—the need to protect children from exposure to patently offensive sex-related material." The plurality opinion expressly analogized to *Pacifica* and said that the Cable Act was even less restrictive of speech than what the Court had upheld in the earlier case; the Cable Act permits but does not require cable systems to prohibit sexually explicit material. The plurality also rejected the argument that the law was impermissibly vague.

Justice Thomas, in an opinion joined by Chief Justice Rehnquist and Justice Scalia, concurred in the judgment and said that cable system operators have the First Amendment right to decide what programming to broadcast. Accordingly, the First Amendment is not violated by allowing cable companies to refuse to carry sexually explicit material.

Justice Kennedy, joined by Justice Ginsburg, dissented as to this part of the opinion. Justice Kennedy criticized the plurality's refusal to adopt a level of scrutiny and argued that strict scrutiny was the appropriate test: "When the government identifies certain speech on the basis of its content as vulnerable to exclusion from a common carrier or public forum, strict scrutiny applies. These laws cannot survive that exacting review."

As to the second part of the act, Justice Breyer wrote a majority opinion — joined by Justices Stevens, O'Connor, Kennedy, Souter, and Ginsburg — declaring unconstitutional the requirement that sexual material be segregated and available only on request. Justice Breyer explained that this part of the act was mandatory on cable companies carrying sexual material and imposed substantial restrictions on access. For example, there could be a 30-day delay before receiving such material and "the written notice requirement will further restrict viewing by subscribers who fear for their reputations should the operator, advertently or inadvertently, disclose the list of those who wish to watch the 'patently offensive' channel." Moreover, the Court said that less restrictive alternatives could protect children, such as a system where parents could request blocking by telephone or employ lockboxes.

Justice Thomas, joined again by Justices Rehnquist and Scalia, dissented on the ground that the provision was "narrowly tailored to achieve [a] well-established compelling interest. . . . [G]overnment may support parental authority to direct the moral upbringing of their children by imposing a blocking requirement as a default position."

Finally, as to the third provision, Justice Breyer wrote a plurality opinion, joined by Justices Stevens and Souter, finding unconstitutional the provision of the Cable Act that permitted cable systems to prohibit sexually explicit material over public access channels. The plurality distinguished leased channels, where the authority to prohibit such material was upheld, from public access channels, where it was declared unconstitutional. The plurality found that there was not proof of "a compelling need, nationally, to protect children from significantly harmful material" on these channels. Justice Kennedy, again joined by Justice Ginsburg, concurred in the judgment and argued that the public access channels are public forums and that the content-based restriction on speech failed strict scrutiny. Justice Thomas, once more joined by Chief Justice Rehnquist and Justice Scalia, dissented on the ground that cable system operators have a First Amendment right to decide what programming to include or exclude.

In light of the fragmented Court,[144] it is difficult to draw generalizations from the *Denver Area* decision. The plurality's express refusal to adopt a level of scrutiny makes it even harder to assess the impact of the case. The Court's second and more recent decision concerning cable television did produce a majority opinion choosing a level of scrutiny, albeit by a five-to-four margin.

The Court returned to the issue of government regulation of sexual speech over cable television in United States v. Playboy Entertainment Group, 529 U.S. 803 (2000), in which the Court considered a challenge to §505 of the Telecommunications Act of 1996. Section 505 requires cable television operators who provide channels "primarily dedicated to sexually-oriented programming"

---

144. Justices Stevens, Souter, and O'Connor also wrote separate opinions.

either to "fully scramble or otherwise fully block" those channels or to limit their transmission to hours when children are unlikely to be viewing, set by administrative regulation as the hours between 10 P.M. and 6 A.M.

To comply with the statute, the majority of cable operators adopted the second, or "time channeling," approach. The effect of the widespread adoption of time channeling was to eliminate altogether the transmission of the targeted programming outside the safe harbor period in affected cable service areas.

The Supreme Court, in an opinion by Justice Kennedy, declared this unconstitutional. The Court stressed that strict scrutiny was to be used because the law was content-based; it applied to sexual content, but not to other material. The Court concluded that the law failed strict scrutiny because less restrictive alternatives existed: Individuals who did not want such channels could have them blocked.

4. A New Exception for Violent Speech?

In two recent cases, in very different contexts, the Court considered whether there should be a new exception for violent speech. In both, the Court rejected such an exception and made clear its reluctance to create new categories of unprotected speech.

UNITED STATES v. STEVENS
130 S. Ct. 1577 (2010)

Chief Justice ROBERTS delivered the opinion of the Court.

Congress enacted 18 U.S.C. §48 to criminalize the commercial creation, sale, or possession of certain depictions of animal cruelty. The statute does not address underlying acts harmful to animals, but only portrayals of such conduct. The question presented is whether the prohibition in the statute is consistent with the freedom of speech guaranteed by the First Amendment.

I

Section 48 establishes a criminal penalty of up to five years in prison for anyone who knowingly "creates, sells, or possesses a depiction of animal cruelty," if done "for commercial gain" in interstate or foreign commerce. A depiction of "animal cruelty" is defined as one "in which a living animal is intentionally maimed, mutilated, tortured, wounded, or killed," if that conduct violates federal or state law where "the creation, sale, or possession takes place." In what is referred to as the "exceptions clause," the law exempts from prohibition any depiction "that has serious religious, political, scientific, educational, journalistic, historical, or artistic value."

The legislative background of §48 focused primarily on the interstate market for "crush videos." According to the House Committee Report on the bill, such videos feature the intentional torture and killing of helpless animals, including cats, dogs, monkeys, mice, and hamsters. Crush videos often depict women slowly crushing animals to death "with their bare feet or while wearing high heeled shoes," sometimes while "talking to the animals in a kind of dominatrix patter" over "[t]he cries and squeals of the animals, obviously in great pain." Apparently these depictions "appeal to persons with a very specific sexual fetish who find them sexually arousing or otherwise exciting." The acts depicted in crush videos are typically prohibited by the animal cruelty laws enacted by all 50 States and the District of Columbia. But crush videos rarely disclose the participants' identities, inhibiting prosecution of the underlying conduct.

This case, however, involves an application of §48 to depictions of animal fighting. Dogfighting, for example, is unlawful in all 50 States and the District of Columbia, and has been restricted by federal law since 1976. Respondent Robert J. Stevens ran a business, "Dogs of Velvet and Steel," and an associated Web site, through which he sold videos of pit bulls engaging in dogfights and attacking other animals.

Stevens moved to dismiss the indictment, arguing that §48 is facially invalid under the First Amendment. The District Court denied the motion. It held that the depictions subject to §48, like obscenity or child pornography, are categorically unprotected by the First Amendment. The jury convicted Stevens on all counts, and the District Court sentenced him to three concurrent sentences of 37 months' imprisonment, followed by three years of supervised release. The en banc Third Circuit, over a three-judge dissent, declared §48 facially unconstitutional and vacated Stevens's conviction.

II

The Government's primary submission is that §48 necessarily complies with the Constitution because the banned depictions of animal cruelty, as a class, are categorically unprotected by the First Amendment. We disagree.

"[A]s a general matter, the First Amendment means that government has no power to restrict expression because of its message, its ideas, its subject matter, or its content." Section 48 explicitly regulates expression based on content: The statute restricts "visual [and] auditory depiction[s]," such as photographs, videos, or sound recordings, depending on whether they depict conduct in which a living animal is intentionally harmed. As such, §48 is "'presumptively invalid,' and the Government bears the burden to rebut that presumption."

"From 1791 to the present," however, the First Amendment has "permitted restrictions upon the content of speech in a few limited areas," and has never "include[d] a freedom to disregard these traditional limitations." These "historic and traditional categories long familiar to the bar," including obscenity, defamation, fraud, incitement, and speech integral to criminal conduct, are "well-defined and narrowly limited classes of speech, the prevention and punishment of which have never been thought to raise any Constitutional problem."

The Government argues that "depictions of animal cruelty" should be added to the list. It contends that depictions of "illegal acts of animal cruelty" that are "made, sold, or possessed for commercial gain" necessarily "lack expressive value," and may accordingly "be regulated as *unprotected* speech." The claim is not just that Congress may regulate depictions of animal cruelty subject to the First Amendment, but that these depictions are outside the reach of that Amendment altogether-that they fall into a "'First Amendment Free Zone.'"

As the Government notes, the prohibition of animal cruelty itself has a long history in American law, starting with the early settlement of the Colonies. But we are unaware of any similar tradition excluding *depictions* of animal cruelty from "the freedom of speech" codified in the First Amendment, and the Government points us to none.

The Government contends that "historical evidence" about the reach of the First Amendment is not "a necessary prerequisite for regulation today," and that categories of speech may be exempted from the First Amendment's protection without any long-settled tradition of subjecting that speech to regulation. Instead, the Government points to Congress's "'legislative judgment that . . . depictions of animals being intentionally tortured and killed [are] of such minimal redeeming value as to render [them] unworthy of First Amendment protection,'" and asks the Court to uphold the ban on the same basis. The Government thus proposes that a claim of categorical exclusion should be considered under a simple balancing test: "Whether a given category of speech enjoys First Amendment protection depends upon a categorical balancing of the value of the speech against its societal costs."

As a free-floating test for First Amendment coverage, that sentence is startling and dangerous. The First Amendment's guarantee of free speech does not extend only to categories of speech that survive an ad hoc balancing of relative social costs and benefits. The First Amendment itself reflects a judgment by the American people that the benefits of its restrictions on the Government outweigh the costs. Our Constitution forecloses any attempt to revise that judgment simply on the basis that some speech is not worth it.

When we have identified categories of speech as fully outside the protection of the First Amendment, it has not been on the basis of a simple cost-benefit analysis. In [New York v.] Ferber, for example, we classified child pornography as such a category. We noted that the State of New York had a compelling interest in protecting children from abuse, and that the value of using children in these works (as opposed to simulated conduct or adult actors) was *de minimis*. But our decision did not rest on this "balance of competing interests" alone. We made clear that *Ferber* presented a special case: The market for child pornography was "intrinsically related" to the underlying abuse, and was therefore "an integral part of the production of such materials, an activity illegal throughout the Nation." *Ferber* thus grounded its analysis in a previously recognized, long-established category of unprotected speech, and our subsequent decisions have shared this understanding.

Our decisions in *Ferber* and other cases cannot be taken as establishing a freewheeling authority to declare new categories of speech outside the scope of the First Amendment. Maybe there are some categories of speech that have been historically unprotected, but have not yet been specifically identified or discussed as such in our case law. But if so, there is no evidence that "depictions of animal cruelty" is among them. We need not foreclose the future recognition of such additional categories to reject the Government's highly manipulable balancing test as a means of identifying them.

III

Because we decline to carve out from the First Amendment any novel exception for §48, we review Stevens's First Amendment challenge under our existing doctrine.

Stevens challenged §48 on its face, arguing that any conviction secured under the statute would be unconstitutional. The court below decided the case on that basis.

To succeed in a typical facial attack, Stevens would have to establish "that no set of circumstances exists under which [§48] would be valid," or that the statute lacks any "plainly legitimate sweep." In the First Amendment context, however, this Court recognizes "a second type of facial challenge," whereby a law may be invalidated as overbroad if "a substantial number of its applications are uncon-stitutional, judged in relation to the statute's plainly legitimate sweep." Stevens argues that §48 applies to common depictions of ordinary and lawful activities, and that these depictions constitute the vast majority of materials subject to the statute. The Government makes no effort to defend such a broad ban as constitutional. Instead, the Government's entire defense of §48 rests on inter-preting the statute as narrowly limited to specific types of "extreme" material. As the parties have presented the issue, therefore, the constitutionality of §48 hinges on how broadly it is construed. It is to that question that we now turn.

As we explained two Terms ago, "[t]he first step in overbreadth analysis is to construe the challenged statute; it is impossible to determine whether a statute reaches too far without first knowing what the statute covers." We read §48 to create a criminal prohibition of alarming breadth. To begin with, the text of the statute's ban on a "depiction of animal cruelty" nowhere requires that the depicted conduct be cruel. That text applies to "any . . . depiction" in which "a living animal is intentionally maimed, mutilated, tortured, wounded, or killed." "[M]aimed, mutilated, [and] tortured" convey cruelty, but "wounded" or "killed" do not suggest any such limitation.

The Government contends that the terms in the definition should be read to require the additional element of "accompanying acts of cruelty." But the phrase "wounded . . . or killed" at issue here contains little ambiguity. We agree that "wounded" and "killed" should be read according to their ordinary meaning. Nothing about that meaning requires cruelty.

While not requiring cruelty, §48 does require that the depicted conduct be "illegal." But this requirement does not limit §48 along the lines the Govern-ment suggests. There are myriad federal and state laws concerning the proper treatment of animals, but many of them are not designed to guard against animal cruelty.

What is more, the application of §48 to depictions of illegal conduct extends to conduct that is illegal in only a single jurisdiction. Under subsection (c)(1), the depicted conduct need only be illegal in "the State in which the creation, sale, or possession takes place, regardless of whether the . . . wounding . . . or killing took place in [that] State." A depiction of entirely lawful conduct runs afoul of the ban if that depiction later finds its way into another State where the same conduct is unlawful. This provision greatly expands the scope of §48, because although there may be "a broad societal consensus" against cruelty to animals, there is substantial disagreement on what types of conduct are properly regarded as cruel. Both views about cruelty to animals and regulations having no connection to cruelty vary widely from place to place.

In the District of Columbia, for example, all hunting is unlawful. Other jurisdictions permit or encourage hunting, and there is an enormous national market for hunting-related depictions in which a living animal is intentionally killed. Hunting periodicals have circulations in the hundreds of thousands or millions, and hunting television programs, videos, and Web sites are equally popular. The demand for hunting depictions exceeds the estimated demand for crush videos or animal fighting depictions by several orders of magnitude.

Those seeking to comply with the law thus face a bewildering maze of regulations from at least 56 separate jurisdictions. Some States permit hunting with crossbows, while others forbid it, or restrict it only to the disabled. Missouri allows the "canned" hunting of ungulates held in captivity, but Montana restricts such hunting to certain bird species. The sharp-tailed grouse may be hunted in Idaho, but not in Washington. The disagreements among the States — and the "commonwealth[s], territor[ies], or possession[s] of the United States," — extend well beyond hunting. State agricultural regulations permit different methods of livestock slaughter in different places or as applied to different animals.

The only thing standing between defendants who sell such depictions and five years in federal prison-other than the mercy of a prosecutor-is the statute's exceptions clause. Subsection (b) exempts from prohibition "any depiction that has serious religious, political, scientific, educational, journalistic, historical, or artistic value."

The Government's attempt to narrow the statutory ban, however, requires an unrealistically broad reading of the exceptions clause. But the text says "serious" value, and "serious" should be taken seriously. We decline the Government's invitation — advanced for the first time in this Court — to regard as "serious" anything that is not "scant."

Quite apart from the requirement of "serious" value in §48(b), the excepted speech must also fall within one of the enumerated categories. Much speech does not. Most hunting videos, for example, are not obviously instructional in nature, except in the sense that all life is a lesson.

The Government explains that the language of §48(b) was largely drawn from our opinion in Miller v. California (1973), which excepted from its definition of obscenity any material with "serious literary, artistic, political, or scientific value." According to the Government, this incorporation of the *Miller* standard into §48 is therefore surely enough to answer any First Amendment objection.

We did not, however, determine that serious value could be used as a general precondition to protecting *other* types of speech in the first place. *Most* of what we say to one another lacks "religious, political, scientific, educational, journalistic, historical, or artistic value" (let alone serious value), but it is still sheltered from government regulation. Even "'[w]holly neutral futilities . . . come under the protection of free speech as fully as do Keats' poems or Donne's sermons.'" Thus, the protection of the First Amendment presumptively extends to many forms of speech that do not qualify for the serious-value exception of §48(b), but nonetheless fall within the broad reach of §48(c).

Not to worry, the Government says: The Executive Branch construes §48 to reach only "extreme" cruelty, and it "neither has brought nor will bring a prosecution for anything less." The Government hits this theme hard, invoking its prosecutorial discretion several times. But the First Amendment protects against the Government; it does not leave us at the mercy of *noblesse oblige.* We would not uphold an unconstitutional statute merely because the Government promised to use it responsibly.

Nor does the Government seriously contest that the presumptively impermissible applications of §48 (properly construed) far outnumber any permissible ones. However "growing" and "lucrative" the markets for crush videos and dogfighting depictions might be, they are dwarfed by the market for other depictions, such as hunting magazines and videos, that we have determined to be within the scope of §48. We therefore need not and do not decide whether a statute limited to crush videos or other depictions of extreme animal cruelty would be constitutional. We hold only that §48 is not so limited but is instead substantially overbroad, and therefore invalid under the First Amendment.

Justice ALITO, dissenting.

The Court strikes down in its entirety a valuable statute, 18 U.S.C. §48, that was enacted not to suppress speech, but to prevent horrific acts of animal cruelty — in particular, the creation and commercial exploitation of "crush videos," a form of depraved entertainment that has no social value. The Court's approach, which has the practical effect of legalizing the sale of such videos and is thus likely to spur a resumption of their production, is unwarranted. Respondent was convicted under §48 for selling videos depicting dogfights. On appeal, he argued, among other things, that §48 is unconstitutional as applied to the facts of this case, and he highlighted features of those videos that might distinguish them from other dogfight videos brought to our attention.

In determining whether a statute's overbreadth is substantial, we consider a statute's application to real-world conduct, not fanciful hypotheticals. Accordingly, we have repeatedly emphasized that an over-breadth claimant bears the burden of demonstrating, "from the text of [the law] *and from actual fact,*" that substantial overbreadth exists. Similarly, "there must be a *realistic danger* that the statute itself will significantly compromise recognized First Amendment protections of parties not before the Court for it to be facially challenged on over-breadth grounds."

In holding that §48 violates the overbreadth rule, the Court declines to decide whether, as the Government maintains, §48 is constitutional as applied to two broad categories of depictions that exist in the real world: crush videos and depictions of deadly animal fights. Instead, the Court tacitly assumes for the sake of argument that §48 is valid as applied to these depictions, but the Court concludes that §48 reaches too much protected speech to survive. The Court relies primarily on depictions of hunters killing or wounding game and depictions of animals being slaughtered for food.

The Court's interpretation is seriously flawed. "When a federal court is dealing with a federal statute challenged as overbroad, it should, of course, construe the statute to avoid constitutional problems, if the statute is subject to such a limiting construction." Applying this canon, I would hold that §48 does not apply to depictions of hunting. First, because §48 targets depictions of "animal cruelty," I would interpret that term to apply only to depictions involving acts of animal cruelty as defined by applicable state or federal law, not to depictions of acts that happen to be illegal for reasons having nothing to do with the prevention of animal cruelty.

Second, even if the hunting of wild animals were otherwise covered by §48(a), I would hold that hunting depictions fall within the exception in §48(b) for depictions that have "serious" (i.e., not "trifling") "scientific," "educational," or "historical" value. While there are certainly those who find hunting objectionable, the predominant view in this country has long been that hunting serves many important values, and it is clear that Congress shares that view. I do not have the slightest doubt that Congress, in enacting §48, had no intention of restricting the creation, sale, or possession of depictions of hunting. Proponents of the law made this point clearly.

In sum, we have a duty to interpret §48 so as to avoid serious constitutional concerns, and §48 may reasonably be construed not to reach almost all, if not all, of the depictions that the Court finds constitutionally protected. Thus, §48 does not appear to have a large number of unconstitutional applications. Invalidation for overbreadth is appropriate only if the challenged statute suffers from *substantial* overbreadth—judged not just in absolute terms, but in relation to the statute's "plainly legitimate sweep."

IV

It is undisputed that the *conduct* depicted in crush videos may constitutionally be prohibited. All 50 States and the District of Columbia have enacted statutes prohibiting animal cruelty. But before the enactment of §48, the underlying conduct depicted in crush videos was nearly impossible to prosecute. These videos, which "often appeal to persons with a very specific sexual fetish," were made in secret, generally without a live audience, and "the faces of the women inflicting the torture in the material often were not shown, nor could the location of the place where the cruelty was being inflicted or the date of the activity be ascertained from the depiction." Thus, law enforcement authorities often were not able to identify the parties responsible for the torture.

In light of the practical problems thwarting the prosecution of the creators of crush videos under state animal cruelty laws, Congress concluded that the only effective way of stopping the underlying criminal conduct was to prohibit the commercial exploitation of the videos of that conduct. And Congress' strategy appears to have been vindicated. We are told that "[b]y 2007, sponsors of §48 declared the crush video industry dead. Even overseas Websites shut down in the wake of §48. Now, after the Third Circuit's decision [facially invalidating the statute], crush videos are already back online."

The First Amendment protects freedom of speech, but it most certainly does not protect violent criminal conduct, even if engaged in for expressive purposes. Crush videos present a highly unusual free speech issue because they are so closely linked with violent criminal conduct. The videos record the commission of violent criminal acts, and it appears that these crimes are committed for the sole purpose of creating the videos. In addition, as noted above, Congress was presented with compelling evidence that the only way of preventing these crimes was to target the sale of the videos. Under these circumstances, I cannot believe that the First Amendment commands Congress to step aside and allow the underlying crimes to continue.

The most relevant of our prior decisions is Ferber v. New York (1982), which concerned child pornography. The Court there held that child pornography is not protected speech, and I believe that *Ferber*'s reasoning dictates a similar conclusion here.

It must be acknowledged that §48 differs from a child pornography law in an important respect: preventing the abuse of children is certainly much more important than preventing the torture of the animals used in crush videos. But while protecting children is unquestionably *more* important than protecting animals, the Government also has a compelling interest in preventing the torture depicted in crush videos.

The animals used in crush videos are living creatures that experience excruciating pain. Our society has long banned such cruelty, which is illegal throughout the country. In *Ferber*, the Court noted that "virtually all of the States and the United States have passed legislation proscribing the production of or otherwise combating 'child pornography,'" and the Court declined to "second-guess [that] legislative judgment."

In sum, §48 may validly be applied to at least two broad real-world categories of expression covered by the statute: crush videos and dogfighting videos. Thus, the statute has a substantial core of constitutionally permissible applications. Moreover, for the reasons set forth above, the record does not show that §48, properly interpreted, bans a substantial amount of protected speech in absolute terms. *A fortiori*, respondent has not met his burden of demonstrating that any impermissible applications of the statute are "substantial" in relation to its "plainly legitimate sweep." Accordingly, I would reject respondent's claim that §48 is facially unconstitutional under the overbreadth doctrine.[145]

BROWN v. ENTERTAINMENT MERCHANTS ASSOCIATION

131 S. Ct. (2011)

Justice SCALIA delivered the opinion of the Court.

We consider whether a California law imposing restrictions on violent video games comports with the First Amendment.

I

California Assembly Bill 1179 (2005) prohibits the sale or rental of "violent video games" to minors, and requires their packaging to be labeled "18." The Act covers games "in which the range of options available to a player includes killing, maiming, dismembering, or sexually assaulting an image of a human being, if those acts are depicted" in a manner that "[a] reasonable person, considering the game as a whole, would find appeals to a deviant or morbid interest of minors," that is "patently offensive to prevailing standards in the community as to what is suitable for minors," and that "causes the game, as a whole, to lack serious literary, artistic, political, or scientific value for minors." Violation of the Act is punishable by a civil fine of up to $1,000.

---

145. After the Court's decision in *Stevens*, Congress enacted a new version of §48, which is much narrower and focuses just on "crush videos." [Footnote by casebook author.]

II

California correctly acknowledges that video games qualify for First Amendment protection. The Free Speech Clause exists principally to protect discourse on public matters, but we have long recognized that it is difficult to distinguish politics from entertainment, and dangerous to try. "Everyone is familiar with instances of propaganda through fiction. What is one man's amusement, teaches another's doctrine." Winters v. New York, 333 U.S. 507, 510, 68 S. Ct. 665, 92 L. Ed. 840 (1948). Like the protected books, plays, and movies that preceded them, video games communicate ideas — and even social messages — through many familiar literary devices (such as characters, dialogue, plot, and music) and through features distinctive to the medium (such as the player's interaction with the virtual world). That suffices to confer First Amendment protection. Under our Constitution, "esthetic and moral judgments about art and literature . . . are for the individual to make, not for the Government to decree, even with the mandate or approval of a majority." And whatever the challenges of applying the Constitution to ever-advancing technology, "the basic principles of freedom of speech and the press, like the First Amendment's command, do not vary" when a new and different medium for communication appears.

The most basic of those principles is this: "[A]s a general matter, . . . government has no power to restrict expression because of its message, its ideas, its subject matter, or its content." There are of course exceptions.

Last Term, in [United States v.] Stevens, we held that new categories of unprotected speech may not be added to the list by a legislature that concludes certain speech is too harmful to be tolerated. As in *Stevens*, California has tried to make violent-speech regulation look like obscenity regulation by appending a saving clause required for the latter. That does not suffice. Our cases have been clear that the obscenity exception to the First Amendment does not cover whatever a legislature finds shocking, but only depictions of "sexual conduct."

Because speech about violence is not obscene, it is of no consequence that California's statute mimics the New York statute regulating obscenity-for-minors that we upheld in Ginsberg v. New York (1968). That case approved a prohibition on the sale to minors of *sexual* material that would be obscene from the perspective of a child.

The California Act is something else entirely. It does not adjust the boundaries of an existing category of unprotected speech to ensure that a definition designed for adults is not uncritically applied to children. California does not argue that it is empowered to prohibit selling offensively violent works *to adults* — and it is wise not to, since that is but a hair's breadth from the argument rejected in *Stevens*. Instead, it wishes to create a wholly new category of content-based regulation that is permissible only for speech directed at children.

That is unprecedented and mistaken. "[M]inors are entitled to a significant measure of First Amendment protection, and only in relatively narrow and well-defined circumstances may government bar public dissemination of protected materials to them." No doubt a State possesses legitimate power to protect children from harm, but that does not include a free-floating power to restrict the ideas to which children may be exposed. "Speech that is neither obscene as to youths nor subject to some other legitimate proscription cannot be suppressed solely to protect the young from ideas or images that a legislative body thinks unsuitable for them."

California's argument would fare better if there were a longstanding tradition in this country of specially restricting children's access to depictions of violence, but there is none. Certainly the *books* we give children to read — or read to them when they are younger — contain no shortage of gore. Grimm's Fairy Tales, for example, are grim indeed. As her just deserts for trying to poison Snow White, the wicked queen is made to dance in red hot slippers "till she fell dead on the floor, a sad example of envy and jealousy." Cinderella's evil stepsisters have their eyes pecked out by doves. And Hansel and Gretel (children!) kill their captor by baking her in an oven.

California claims that video games present special problems because they are "interactive," in that the player participates in the violent action on screen and determines its outcome. The latter feature is nothing new: Since at least the publication of *The Adventures of You: Sugarcane Island* in 1969, young readers of choose-your-own-adventure stories have been able to make decisions that determine the plot by following instructions about which page to turn to. As for the argument that video games enable participation in the violent action, that seems to us more a matter of degree than of kind. As Judge Posner has observed, all literature is interactive. "[T]he better it is, the more interactive. Literature when it is successful draws the reader into the story, makes him identify with the characters, invites him to judge them and quarrel with them, to experience their joys and sufferings as the reader's own."

III

Because the Act imposes a restriction on the content of protected speech, it is invalid unless California can demonstrate that it passes strict scrutiny — that is, unless it is justified by a compelling government interest and is narrowly drawn to serve that interest. "It is rare that a regulation restricting speech because of its content will ever be permissible."

California cannot meet that standard. At the outset, it acknowledges that it cannot show a direct causal link between violent video games and harm to minors. The State's evidence is not compelling. California relies primarily on the research of Dr. Craig Anderson and a few other research psychologists whose studies purport to show a connection between exposure to violent video games and harmful effects on children. These studies have been rejected by every court to consider them, and with good reason: They do not prove that violent video games *cause* minors to *act* aggressively (which would at least be a beginning). Instead, "[n]early all of the research is based on correlation, not evidence of causation, and most of the studies suffer from significant, admitted flaws in methodology." They show at best some correlation between exposure to violent entertainment and minuscule real-world effects, such as children's feeling more aggressive or making louder noises in the few minutes after playing a violent game than after playing a nonviolent game.

Even taking for granted Dr. Anderson's conclusions that violent video games produce some effect on children's feelings of aggression, those effects are both small and indistinguishable from effects produced by other media. And he admits that the *same* effects have been found when children watch cartoons starring Bugs Bunny or the Road Runner, *id.,* at 1304, or when they play video games like Sonic the Hedgehog that are rated "E" (appropriate for all ages), or even when they "vie[w] a picture of a gun."

Of course, California has (wisely) declined to restrict Saturday morning cartoons, the sale of games rated for young children, or the distribution of pictures of guns. The consequence is that its regulation is wildly underinclusive when judged against its asserted justification, which in our view is alone enough to defeat it. Underinclusiveness raises serious doubts about whether the government is in fact pursuing the interest it invokes, rather than disfavoring a particular speaker or viewpoint. Here, California has singled out the purveyors of video games for disfavored treatment — at least when compared to booksellers, cartoonists, and movie producers — and has given no persuasive reason why.

The Act is also seriously underinclusive in another respect — and a respect that renders irrelevant the contentions of the concurrence and the dissents that video games are qualitatively different from other portrayals of violence. The California Legislature is perfectly willing to leave this dangerous, mind-altering material in the hands of children so long as one parent (or even an aunt or uncle) says it's OK. And there are not even any requirements as to how this parental or avuncular relationship is to be verified; apparently the child's or putative parent's, aunt's, or uncle's say-so suffices. That is not how one addresses a serious social problem.

California claims that the Act is justified in aid of parental authority: By requiring that the purchase of violent video games can be made only by adults, the Act ensures that parents can decide what games are appropriate. At the outset, we note our doubts that punishing third parties for conveying protected speech to children *just in case* their parents disapprove of that speech is a proper governmental means of aiding parental authority.

But leaving that aside, California cannot show that the Act's restrictions meet a substantial need of parents who wish to restrict their children's access to violent video games but cannot do so. The video-game industry has in place a voluntary rating system designed to inform consumers about the content of games. The system, implemented by the Entertainment Software Rating Board (ESRB), assigns age-specific ratings to each video game submitted: EC (Early Childhood); E (Everyone); E10þ (Everyone 10 and older); T (Teens); M (17 and older); and AO (Adults Only — 18 and older).

And finally, the Act's purported aid to parental authority is vastly overinclusive. Not all of the children who are forbidden to purchase violent video games on their own have parents who *care* whether they purchase violent video games. While some of the legislation's effect may indeed be in support of what some parents of the restricted children actually want, its entire effect is only in support of what the State thinks parents *ought* to want. This is not the narrow tailoring to "assisting parents" that restriction of First Amendment rights requires.

California's legislation straddles the fence between (1) addressing a serious social problem and (2) helping concerned parents control their children. Both ends are legitimate, but when they affect First Amendment rights they must be pursued by means that are neither seriously underinclusive nor seriously overinclusive. As a means of protecting children from portrayals of violence, the legislation is seriously under-inclusive, not only because it excludes portrayals other than video games, but also because it permits a parental or avuncular veto. And as a means of assisting concerned parents it is seriously overinclusive because it abridges the First Amendment rights of young people whose parents (and aunts and uncles) think violent video games are a harmless pastime. And the overbreadth in achieving one goal is not cured by the underbreadth in achieving the other. Legislation such as this, which is neither fish nor fowl, cannot survive strict scrutiny.

Justice ALITO, with whom THE CHIEF JUSTICE joins, concurring in the judgment.

The California statute that is before us in this case represents a pioneering effort to address what the state legislature and others regard as a potentially serious social problem: the effect of exceptionally violent video games on impressionable minors, who often spend countless hours immersed in the alternative worlds that these games create. Although the California statute is well intentioned, its terms are not framed with the precision that the Constitution demands, and I therefore agree with the Court that this particular law cannot be sustained.

I disagree, however, with the approach taken in the Court's opinion. In considering the application of unchanging constitutional principles to new and rapidly evolving technology, this Court should proceed with caution. We should make every effort to understand the new technology.

We should take into account the possibility that developing technology may have important societal implications that will become apparent only with time. We should not jump to the conclusion that new technology is fundamentally the same as some older thing with which we are familiar. And we should not hastily dismiss the judgment of legislators, who may be in a better position than we are to assess the implications of new technology. The opinion of the Court exhibits none of this caution.

In the view of the Court, all those concerned about the effects of violent video games — federal and state legislators, educators, social scientists, and parents — are unduly fearful, for violent video games really present no serious problem. Spending hour upon hour controlling the actions of a character who guns down scores of innocent victims is not different in "kind" from reading a description of violence in a work of literature.

The Court is sure of this; I am not. There are reasons to suspect that the experience of playing violent video games just might be very different from reading a book, listening to the radio, or watching a movie or a television show.

Here, the California law does not define "violent video games" with the "narrow specificity" that the Constitution demands. I conclude that the California violent video game law fails to provide the fair notice that the Constitution requires. And I would go no further. I would not express any view on whether a properly drawn statute would or would not survive First Amendment scrutiny. We should address that question only if and when it is necessary to do so.

Justice THOMAS, dissenting.

The Court's decision today does not comport with the original public understanding of the First Amendment. The majority strikes down, as facially unconstitutional, a state law that prohibits the direct sale or rental of certain video games to minors because the law "abridg[es] the freedom of speech." But I do not think the First Amendment stretches that far. The practices and beliefs of the founding generation establish that "the freedom of speech," as originally understood, does not include a right to speak to minors (or a right of minors to access speech) without going through the minors' parents or guardians. I would hold that the law at issue is not facially unconstitutional under the First Amendment, and reverse and remand for further proceedings.

When interpreting a constitutional provision, "the goal is to discern the most likely public understanding of [that] provision at the time it was adopted." Because the Constitution is a written instrument, "its meaning does not alter." "That which it meant when adopted, it means now."

In my view, the "practices and beliefs held by the Founders" reveal another category of excluded speech: speech to minor children bypassing their parents. The historical evidence shows that the founding generation believed parents had absolute authority over their minor children and expected parents to use that authority to direct the proper development of their children. It would be absurd to suggest that such a society understood "the freedom of speech" to include a right to speak to minors (or a corresponding right of minors to access speech) without going through the minors' parents. The founding generation would not have considered it an abridgment of "the freedom of speech" to support parental authority by restricting speech that bypasses minors' parents.

"The freedom of speech," as originally understood, does not include a right to speak to minors without going through the minors' parents or guardians. Therefore, I cannot agree that the statute at issue is facially unconstitutional under the First Amendment.

Justice BREYER, dissenting.

Applying traditional First Amendment analysis, I would uphold the statute as constitutional on its face and would consequently reject the industries' facial challenge.

In determining whether the statute is unconstitutional, I would apply both this Court's "vagueness" precedents and a strict form of First Amendment scrutiny. In doing so, the special First Amendment category I find relevant is not (as the Court claims) the category of "depictions of violence," but rather the category of "protection of children." This Court has held that the "power of the state to control the conduct of children reaches beyond the scope of its authority over adults." And the "'regulatio[n] of communication addressed to [children] need not conform to the requirements of the [F]irst [A]mendment in the same way as those applicable to adults.'" Ginsberg v. New York (1968).

Comparing the language of California's statute with the language of New York's statute, it is difficult to find any vagueness-related difference. Why are the words "kill," "maim," and "dismember" any more difficult to understand than the word "nudity?" All that is required for vagueness purposes is that the terms "kill," "maim," and "dismember" give fair notice as to what they cover, which they do.

The remainder of California's definition copies, almost word for word, the language this Court used in Miller v. California (1973), in permitting a *total ban* on material that satisfied its definition (one enforced with *criminal* penalties).

What, then, is the difference between *Ginsberg* and *Miller* on the one hand and the California law on the other? It will often be easy to pick out cases at which California's statute directly aims, involving, say, a character who shoots out a police officer's knee, douses him with gasoline, lights him on fire, urinates on his burning body, and finally kills him with a gunshot to the head. (Footage of one such game sequence has been submitted in the record.) As in *Miller* and *Ginsberg*, the California law clearly *protects* even the most violent games that possess serious literary, artistic, political, or scientific value. And it is easier here than in *Miller* or *Ginsberg* to separate the sheep from the goats at the statute's border. That is because here the industry itself has promulgated standards and created a review process, in which adults who "typically have experience with children" assess what games are inappropriate for minors.

There is, of course, one obvious difference: The *Ginsberg* statute concerned depictions of "nudity," while California's statute concerns extremely violent video games. But for purposes of vagueness, why should that matter?

Thus, I can find no meaningful vagueness-related differences between California's law and the New York law upheld in *Ginsberg*. And if there remain any vagueness problems, the state courts can cure them through interpretation.

III

Like the majority, I believe that the California law must be "narrowly tailored" to further a "compelling interest," without there being a "less restrictive" alternative that would be "at least as effective." I would evaluate the degree to which the statute injures speech-related interests, the nature of the potentially-justifying "compelling interests," the degree to which the statute furthers that interest, the nature and effectiveness of possible alternatives, and, in light of this evaluation, whether, overall, "the statute works speech-related harm . . . out of proportion to the benefits that the statute seeks to provide."

California's law imposes no more than a modest restriction on expression. The statute prevents no one from playing a video game, it prevents no adult from buying a video game, and it prevents no child or adolescent from obtaining a game provided a parent is willing to help. All it prevents is a child or adolescent from buying, without a parent's assistance, a gruesomely violent video game of a kind that the industry *itself* tells us it wants to keep out of the hands of those under the age of 17.

Nor is the statute, if upheld, likely to create a precedent that would adversely affect other media, say films, or videos, or books. A typical video game involves a significant amount of physical activity. And pushing buttons that achieve an interactive, virtual form of target practice (using images of human beings as targets), while containing an expressive component, is not just like watching a typical movie.

The interest that California advances in support of the statute is compelling. As this Court has previously described that interest, it consists of both (1) the "basic" parental claim "to authority in their own household to direct the rearing of their children," which makes it proper to enact "laws designed to aid discharge of [parental] responsibility," and (2) the State's "independent interest in the well-being of its youth." And where these interests work in tandem, it is not fatally "under-inclusive" for a State to advance its interests in protecting children against the special harms present in an interactive video game medium through a default rule that still allows parents to provide their children with what their parents wish.

At the same time, there is considerable evidence that California's statute significantly furthers this compelling interest. That is, in part, because video games are excellent teaching tools.

In particular, extremely violent games can harm children by rewarding them for being violently aggressive in play, and thereby often teaching them to be violently aggressive in life. And video games can cause more harm in this respect than can typically passive media, such as books or films or television programs.

There are many scientific studies that support California's views. Social scientists, for example, have found *causal* evidence that playing these games results in harm. Longitudinal studies, which measure changes over time, have found that increased exposure to violent video games causes an increase in aggression over the same period. Experimental studies in laboratories have found that subjects randomly assigned to play a violent video game subsequently displayed more characteristics of aggression than those who played nonviolent games. Surveys of 8th and 9th grade students have found a correlation between playing violent video games and aggression. Cutting-edge neuroscience has shown that "virtual violence in video game playing results in those neural patterns that are considered characteristic for aggressive cognition and behavior." And "meta-analyses," *i.e.*, studies of all the studies, have concluded that exposure to violent video games "was positively associated with aggressive behavior, aggressive cognition, and aggressive affect," and that "playing violent video games is a *causal* risk factor for long-term harmful outcomes."

Experts debate the conclusions of all these studies. Like many, perhaps most, studies of human behavior, each study has its critics, and some of those critics have produced studies of their own in which they reach different conclusions. (I list both sets of research in the appendixes.) I, like most judges, lack the social science expertise to say definitively who is right. But associations of public health professionals who do possess that expertise have reviewed many of these studies and found a significant risk that violent video games, when compared with more passive media, are particularly likely to cause children harm.

I can find no "less restrictive" alternative to California's law that would be "at least as effective." The majority points to a voluntary alternative: The industry tries to prevent those under 17 from buying extremely violent games by labeling those games with an "M" (Mature) and encouraging retailers to restrict their sales to those 17 and older. But this voluntary system has serious enforcement gaps. When California enacted its law, a Federal Trade Commission (FTC) study had found that nearly 70% of unaccompanied 13- to 16-year-olds were able to buy M-rated video games. Subsequently the voluntary program has become more effective. But as of the FTC's most recent update to Congress, 20% of those under 17 are still able to buy M-rated video games, and, breaking down sales by store, one finds that this number rises to nearly 50% in the case of one large national chain.

IV

The upshot is that California's statute, as applied to its heartland of applications (*i.e.*, buyers under 17; extremely violent, realistic video games), imposes a restriction on speech that is modest at most. That restriction is justified by a compelling interest (supplementing parents' efforts to prevent their children from purchasing potentially harmful violent, interactive material). And there is no equally effective, less restrictive alternative. California's statute is consequently constitutional on its face — though litigants remain free to challenge the statute as applied in particular instances, including any effort by the State to apply it to minors aged 17.

I add that the majority's different conclusion creates a serious anomaly in First Amendment law. *Ginsberg* makes clear that a State can prohibit the sale to minors of depictions of nudity; today the Court makes clear that a State cannot prohibit the sale to minors of the most violent interactive video games. But what sense does it make to forbid selling to a 13-year-old boy a magazine with an image of a nude woman, while protecting a sale to that 13-year-old of an interactive video game in which he actively, but virtually, binds and gags the woman, then tortures and kills her? What kind of First Amendment would permit the government to protect children by restricting sales of that extremely violent video game *only* when the woman — bound, gagged, tortured, and killed — is also topless?

This anomaly is not compelled by the First Amendment. It disappears once one recognizes that extreme violence, where interactive, and *without literary, artistic, or similar justification,* can prove at least as, if not more, harmful to children as photographs of nudity. And the record here is more than adequate to support such a view. That is why I believe that *Ginsberg* controls the outcome here *a fortiori.* And it is why I believe California's law is constitutional on its face.

This case is ultimately less about censorship than it is about education. Our Constitution cannot succeed in securing the liberties it seeks to protect unless we can raise future generations committed cooperatively to making our system of government work. Education, however, is about choices. Sometimes, children need to learn by making choices for themselves. Other times, choices are made for children — by their parents, by their teachers, and by the people acting democratically through their governments. In my view, the First Amendment does not disable government from helping parents make such a choice here — a choice not to have their children buy extremely violent, interactive video games, which they more than reasonably fear pose only the risk of harm to those children.

5. *Commercial Speech*

a. **Constitutional Protection for Commercial Speech**

In 1942 in Valentine v. Christensen, 316 U.S. 52 (1942), the Supreme Court held that commercial speech was not protected by the First Amendment. A city's ordinance prohibited the distribution of any "handbill [or] other advertising matter [in] or upon any street." An individual was prosecuted for circulating an advertisement to visit a submarine that was being exhibited. Without analysis or explanation, the Supreme Court stated, "We are equally clear that the Constitution imposes no restraint on government as respects purely commercial advertising."

Commercial speech remained unprotected by the First Amendment until 1975 when the Court decided Bigelow v. Virginia, 421 U.S. 809 (1975). The Court in *Bigelow* declared unconstitutional a state law that made it a crime to encourage or prompt the provision of abortion services; specifically, the Court held that advertisements for abortion services in newspapers are protected by the First Amendment. The Court said that "speech is not stripped of First Amendment protection merely because it appears" as a commercial advertisement. The Court said that "[t]he fact that the particular advertisement in appellant's newspaper had commercial aspects or reflected the advertiser's commercial interests did not negate all First Amendment guarantees." The Court expressly said that the state court had erred in its conclusion "that advertising, as such, was entitled to no First Amendment protection."

A year later, in Virginia State Board of Pharmacy v. Virginia Citizens Consumer Council, Inc., the Court made it even clearer that commercial speech is protected by the First Amendment and that Valentine v. Christensen no longer was the law.

VIRGINIA STATE BOARD OF PHARMACY v. VIRGINIA CITIZENS CONSUMER COUNCIL, INC.

425 U.S. 748 (1976)

Justice BLACKMUN delivered the opinion of the Court.

The plaintiff-appellees in this case attack, as violative of the First and Fourteenth Amendments, that portion of [Virginia law] which provides that a pharmacist licensed in Virginia is guilty of unprofessional conduct if he "publishes, advertises or promotes, directly or indirectly, in any manner whatsoever, any amount price, fee, premium, discount, rebate or credit terms . . . for any drugs which may be dispensed only by prescription."

Inasmuch as only a licensed pharmacist may dispense prescription drugs in Virginia, advertising or other affirmative dissemination of prescription drug price information is effectively forbidden in the State. Some pharmacies refuse even to quote prescription drug prices over the telephone. Certainly that information may be of value. Drug prices in Virginia, for both prescription and nonprescription items, strikingly vary from outlet to outlet even within the same locality. It is stipulated, for example, that in Richmond "the cost of 40 Achromycin tablets ranges from $2.59 to $6.00, a difference of 140% [sic]," and that in the Newport News-Hampton area the cost of tetracycline ranges from $1.20 to $9.00, a difference of 650%.

The appellants contend that the advertisement of prescription drug prices is outside the protection of the First Amendment because it is "commercial speech." There can be no question that in past decisions the Court has given some indication that commercial speech is unprotected. In Valentine v. Christensen, [t]he Court concluded that, although the First Amendment would forbid the banning of all communication by handbill in the public thoroughfares, it imposed "no such restraint on government as respects purely commercial advertising."

Last Term, in Bigelow v. Virginia, the notion of unprotected "commercial speech" all but passed from the scene. We reversed a conviction for violation of a Virginia statute that made the circulation of any publication to encourage or promote the processing of an abortion in Virginia a misdemeanor. We rejected the contention that the publication was unprotected because it was commercial. Some fragment of hope for the continuing validity of a "commercial speech" exception arguably might have persisted because of the subject matter of the advertisement in *Bigelow*. We noted that in announcing the availability of legal abortions in New York, the advertisement "did more than simply propose a commercial transaction. It contained factual material of clear 'public interest.'" And, of course, the advertisement related to activity with which, at least in some respects, the State could not interfere.

Here, in contrast, the question whether there is a First Amendment exception for "commercial speech" is squarely before us. Our pharmacist does not wish to editorialize on any subject, cultural, philosophical, or political. He does not wish to report any particularly newsworthy fact, or to make generalized observations even about commercial matters. The "idea" he wishes to communicate is simply this: "I will sell you the X prescription drug at the Y price." Our question, then, is whether this communication is wholly outside the protection of the First Amendment.

We begin with several propositions that already are settled or beyond serious dispute. It is clear, for example, that speech does not lose its First Amendment protection because money is spent to project it, as in a paid advertisement of one form or another. If there is a kind of commercial speech that lacks all First Amendment protection, therefore, it must be distinguished by its content. Yet the speech whose content deprives it of protection cannot simply be speech on a commercial subject. No one would contend that our pharmacist may be prevented from being heard on the subject of whether, in general, pharmaceutical prices should be regulated, or their advertisement forbidden. Nor can it be dispositive that a commercial advertisement is noneditorial, and merely reports a fact. Purely factual matter of public interest may claim protection.

Focusing first on the individual parties to the transaction that is proposed in the commercial advertisement, we may assume that the advertiser's interest is a purely economic one. That hardly disqualifies him from protection under the First Amendment. The interests of the contestants in a labor dispute are primarily economic, but it has long been settled that both the employee and the employer are protected by the First Amendment when they express themselves on the merits of the dispute in order to influence its outcome.

As to the particular consumer's interest in the free flow of commercial information, that interest may be as keen, if not keener by far, than his interest in the day's most urgent political debate. Those whom the suppression of prescription drug price information hits the hardest are the poor, the sick, and particularly the aged. A disproportionate amount of their income tends to be spent on prescription drugs; yet they are the least able to learn, by shopping from pharmacist to pharmacist, where their scarce dollars are best spent. When drug prices vary as strikingly they do, information as to who is charging what becomes more than a convenience. It could mean the alleviation of physical pain or the enjoyment of basic necessities.

Generalizing, society also may have a strong interest in the free flow of commercial information. Even an individual advertisement, though entirely "commercial," may be of general public interest. The facts of decided cases furnish illustrations: advertisements stating that referral services for legal abortions are available; that a manufacturer of artificial furs promotes his product as an alternative to the extinction by his competitors of fur-bearing mammals; and that a domestic producer advertises his product as an alternative to imports that tend to deprive American residents of their jobs. Obviously, not all commercial messages contain the same or even a very great public interest element. There are few to which such an element, however, could not be added. Our pharmacist, for example, could cast himself as a commentator on store-to-store disparities in drug prices, giving his own and those of a competitor as proof. We see little point in requiring him to do so, and little difference if he does not.

Moreover, there is another consideration that suggests that no line between publicly "interesting" or "important" commercial advertising and the opposite kind could ever be drawn. Advertising, however tasteless and excessive it sometimes may seem, is nonetheless dissemination of information as to who is producing and selling what product, for what reason, and at what price. So long as we preserve a predominantly free enterprise economy, the allocation of our resources in large measure will be made through numerous private economic decisions. It is a matter of public interest that those decisions, in the aggregate, be intelligent and well informed. To this end, the free flow of commercial information is indispensable. And if it is indispensable to the proper allocation of resources in a free enterprise system, it is also indispensable to the formation of intelligent opinions as to how that system ought to be regulated or altered. Therefore, even if the First Amendment were thought to be primarily an instrument to enlighten public decisionmaking in a democracy, we could not say that the free flow of information does not serve that goal.

Arrayed against these substantial individual and societal interests are a number of justifications for the advertising ban. These have to do principally with maintaining a high degree of professionalism on the part of licensed pharmacists. Indisputably, the State has a strong interest in maintaining that professionalism. Price advertising, it is argued, will place in jeopardy the pharmacist's expertise and, with it, the customer's health. It is claimed that the aggressive price competition that will result from unlimited advertising will make it impossible for the pharmacist to supply professional services in the compounding, handling, and dispensing of prescription drugs.

The strength of these proffered justifications is greatly undermined by the fact that high professional standards, to a substantial extent, are guaranteed by the close regulation to which pharmacists in Virginia are subject. And this case concerns the retail sale by the pharmacist more than it does his professional standards. Surely, any pharmacist guilty of professional dereliction that actually endangers his customer will promptly lose his license.

The advertising ban does not directly affect professional standards one way or the other. It affects them only through the reactions it is assumed people will have to the free flow of drug price information. There is no claim that the advertising ban in any way prevents the cutting of corners by the pharmacist who is so inclined. That pharmacist is likely to cut corners in any event. The only effect the advertising ban has on him is to insulate him from price competition and to open the way for him to make a substantial, and perhaps even excessive, profit in addition to providing an inferior service. The more painstaking pharmacist is also protected but, again, it is a protection based in large part on public ignorance.

In concluding that commercial speech, like other varieties, is protected, we of course do not hold that it can never be regulated in any way. Some forms of commercial speech regulation are surely permissible. We mention a few only to make clear that they are not before us and therefore are not fore-closed by this case. There is no claim that prescription drug price advertise-ments are forbidden because they are false or misleading in any way. Untruth-ful speech, commercial or otherwise, has never been protected for its own sake. Obviously, much commercial speech is not provably false, or even wholly false, but only deceptive or misleading. We foresee no obstacle to a State's dealing effectively with this problem. The First Amendment, as we construe it today does not prohibit the State from insuring that the stream of commercial infor-mation flow cleanly as well as freely. Also, there is no claim that the transac-tions proposed in the forbidden advertisements are themselves illegal in any way.

What is at issue is whether a State may completely suppress the dissemination of concededly truthful information about entirely lawful activity, fearful of that information's effect upon its disseminators and its recipients. Reserving other questions, we conclude that the answer to this one is in the negative.

Justice REHNQUIST, dissenting.

The logical consequences of the Court's decision in this case, a decision which elevates commercial intercourse between a seller hawking his wares and a buyer seeking to strike a bargain to the same plane as has been previously reserved for the free marketplace of ideas, are far reaching indeed. Under the Court's opin-ion the way will be open not only for dissemination of price information but for active promotion of prescription drugs, liquor, cigarettes, and other products the use of which it has previously been thought desirable to discourage. Now, however, such promotion is protected by the First Amendment so long as it is not misleading or does not promote an illegal product or enterprise. In coming to this conclusion, the Court has overruled a legislative determination that such advertising should not be allowed and has done so on behalf of a consumer group which is not directly disadvantaged by the statute in question.

The Court insists that the rule it lays down is consistent even with the view that the First Amendment is "primarily an instrument to enlighten public decision-making in a democracy." I had understood this view to relate to public decision-making as to political, social, and other public issues, rather than the decision of a particular individual as to whether to purchase one or another kind of shampoo. It is undoubtedly arguable that many people in the country regard the choice of shampoo as just as important as who may be elected to local, state, or national political office, but that does not automatically bring information about compet-ing shampoos within the protection of the First Amendment. It is one thing to say that the line between strictly ideological and political commentaries and other kinds of commentary is difficult to draw, and that the mere fact that the former may have in it an element of commercialism does not strip it of First Amendment protection.

In the case of "our" hypothetical pharmacist, he may now presumably adver-tise not only the prices of prescription drugs, but may attempt to energetically promote their sale so long as he does so truthfully. Quite consistently with Virginia law requiring prescription drugs to be available only through a physician, "our" pharmacist might run any of the following representative advertisements in a local newspaper:

"Pain getting you down? Insist that your physician prescribe Demerol. You pay a little more than for aspirin, but you get a lot more relief."

"Can't shake the flu? Get a prescription for Tetracycline from your doctor today."

"Don't spend another sleepless night. Ask your doctor to prescribe Seconal without delay."

Unless the State can show that these advertisements are either actually untruthful or misleading, it presumably is not free to restrict in any way commercial efforts on the part of those who profit from the sale of prescription drugs to put them in the widest possible circulation. But such a line simply makes no allowance whatever for what appears to have been a considered legislative judgment in most States that while prescription drugs are a necessary and vital part of medical care and treatment, there are sufficient dangers attending their widespread use that they simply may not be promoted in the same manner as hair creams, deodorants, and toothpaste. The very real dangers that general advertising for such drugs might create in terms of encouraging, even though not sanctioning, illicit use of them by individuals for whom they have not been prescribed, or by generating patient pressure upon physicians to prescribe them, are simply not dealt with in the Court's opinion. If prescription drugs may be advertised, they may be advertised on television during family viewing time. Nothing we know about the acquisitive instincts of those who inhabit every business and profession to a greater or lesser extent gives any reason to think that such persons will not do everything they can to generate demand for these products in much the same manner and to much the same degree as demand for other commodities has been generated. I do not believe that the First Amendment mandates the Court's "open door policy" toward such commercial advertising.

Since 1976, the Supreme Court has decided a large number of cases involving commercial speech. The Court, however, has never wavered from the basic holding of *Virginia State Board of Pharmacy*: Commercial speech is protected by the First Amendment. The issue thus arises as to whether such speech should be safeguarded.

Critics of the protection of commercial speech argue, in part, that the expression is not worthy of protection because it does not directly concern the political process and self-government.[146] Moreover, critics argue that the deference to government economic regulation since 1937 should include deference to government restrictions of commercial speech. Professors Thomas Jackson and John Jeffries argue that "in terms of relevance to political decisionmaking, advertising is neither more nor less significant than a host of other market activities that legislatures concededly may regulate. . . . The decisive point is the absence of any principled distinction between commercial soliciting and other aspects of economic activity. . . . [E]conomic due process is resurrected, clothed in the ill-fitting garb of the first amendment."[147]

146. *See* Vincent Blasi, *The Pathological Perspective and the First Amendment*, 85 Colum. L. Rev. 449, 486 (1985); Edwin P. Baker, *Commercial Speech: A Problem, in the Theory of Freedom*, 62 Iowa L. Rev. 1 (1976).
147. Thomas H. Jackson & John C. Jeffries, Jr., *Commercial Speech: Economic Due Process and the First Amendment*, 65 Va. L. Rev. 1, 18, 30 (1979).

But defenders of the constitutional protection of commercial speech argue that the First Amendment is not limited to protecting speech about the political process.[148] Moreover, it is argued that, as Justice Blackmun concluded, commercial speech is important to individuals and thus worthy of First Amendment protection. Professor Martin Redish, for example, argued that "[i]f the individual is to achieve the maximum degree of material satisfaction permitted by his resources, he must be presented with as much information as possible concerning the relative merits of competing products."[149]

OVERVIEW OF THE SECTION

Once the Court decided that commercial speech is protected by the First Amendment, the issue inevitably arises as to what is "commercial speech." This is discussed in subsection b. Beginning with Central Hudson Gas v. Public Service Commn. of New York (1980), the Court has formulated and refined a test for when the government can regulate commercial speech. This test, which is essentially a form of intermediate scrutiny, is reviewed in subsection c.

Under the *Central Hudson* test, four types of government regulations of commercial speech can be identified. First are laws that outlaw advertising of illegal activities. The Court consistently has held that such advertising is not protected by the First Amendment. Second is the prohibition of false and deceptive advertising. The Court also has always held that such ads are not protected by the First Amendment. Third, the Court has indicated that the government may prohibit true advertising that inherently risks becoming false or deceptive. For example, as discussed below, the government can prohibit professionals from advertising and practicing under trade names and can forbid attorneys from engaging in in-person solicitation of clients for profit. In both instances the Court stressed the inherent danger of deception in such speech. Fourth are laws that limit commercial advertising to achieve other goals, such as enhancing the image of lawyers, decreasing consumption of alcohol or tobacco products, preventing panic selling of houses in neighborhoods, or decreasing gambling. The largest number of cases fit into this category and do not follow a consistent path. These four types of government regulation of commercial speech are discussed in subsection d.

b. What Is Commercial Speech?

In *Virginia State Board of Pharmacy*, the Court said that commercial speech was expression that "propose[s] a commercial transaction." No one, of course, would disagree that advertising of prices for products is a form of commercial speech. The issue arises, though, as to what other speech, besides price advertising, should be regarded as commercial speech. Defining commercial speech as advertising is both overinclusive and underinclusive. Advertising can be pure

---

148. *See* Sylvia A. Law, *Addiction, Autonomy, and Advertising,* 77 Iowa L. Rev. 909, 932 (1992).

149. Martin H. Redish, *The First Amendment in the Marketplace: Commercial Speech and the Values of Free Expression,* 39 Geo. Wash. L. Rev. 429, 433 (1971).

political speech, such as in the advertisement that was the basis for New York Times v. Sullivan, 376 U.S. 254 (1964), presented below, which criticized the government's handling of civil rights demonstrations. But defining commercial speech as advertising is also underinclusive because the commercial speech may take forms other than advertising, such as in attorneys' direct solicitations of prospective clients.

In Central Hudson Gas & Electric Corp. v. Public Service Commn., presented below, the Court said that commercial speech was "expression related solely to the economic interests of the speaker and its audience." But this definition, too, is difficult to apply. A book publisher or a broadcast station may be motivated solely by economic interests in deciding what to publish or broadcast. Yet those decisions, even if related solely to economic considerations, are obviously protected by the First Amendment.

Bolger v. Youngs Drug Products Corp. is the major Supreme Court case to address directly the question of what is commercial speech.

BOLGER v. YOUNGS DRUG PRODUCTS CORP.

463 U.S. 60 (1983)

Justice Marshall delivered the opinion of the Court.

Title 39 U.S.C. §3001(e)(2) prohibits the mailing of unsolicited advertisements for contraceptives. Appellee Youngs Drug Products Corporation (Youngs) is engaged in the manufacture, sale and distribution of contraceptives. Youngs markets its products primarily through sales to chain warehouses and wholesale distributors, who in turn sell contraceptives to retail pharmacists, who then sell those products to individual customers. Appellee publicizes the availability and desirability of its products by various methods. This litigation resulted from Youngs' decision to undertake a campaign of unsolicited mass mailings to members of the public. In conjunction with its wholesalers and retailers, Youngs seeks to mail to the public on an unsolicited basis three types of materials:

- multi-page, multi-item flyers promoting a large variety of products available at a drug store, including prophylactics;
- flyers exclusively or substantially devoted to promoting prophylactics;
- informational pamphlets discussing the desirability and availability of prophylactics in general or Youngs' products in particular.

Because the degree of protection afforded by the First Amendment depends on whether the activity sought to be regulated constitutes commercial or non-commercial speech, we must first determine the proper classification of the mailings at issue here. Most of appellee's mailings fall within the core notion of commercial speech — "speech which does 'no more than propose a commercial transaction.'" Youngs' informational pamphlets, however, cannot be characterized merely as proposals to engage in commercial transactions. Their proper classification as commercial or non-commercial speech thus presents a closer question. The mere fact that these pamphlets are conceded to be advertisements clearly does not compel the conclusion that they are commercial speech. Similarly, the reference to a specific product does not by itself render the pamphlets commercial speech. Finally, the fact that Youngs has an economic motivation for mailing the pamphlets would clearly be insufficient by itself to turn the materials into commercial speech.

The combination of all these characteristics, however, provides strong support for the District Court's conclusion that the informational pamphlets are properly characterized as commercial speech. The mailings constitute commercial speech notwithstanding the fact that they contain discussions of important public issues such as venereal disease and family planning. We have made clear that advertising which "links a product to a current public debate" is not thereby entitled to the constitutional protection afforded non-commercial speech. A company has the full panoply of protections available to its direct comments on public issues, so there is no reason for providing similar constitutional protection when such statements are made in the context of commercial transactions. Advertisers should not be permitted to immunize false or misleading product information from government regulation simply by including references to public issues.

We conclude, therefore, that all of the mailings in this case are entitled to the qualified but nonetheless substantial protection accorded to commercial speech. [After reviewing the government's argument for the law, the Court concluded:] We thus conclude that the justifications offered by the Government are insufficient to warrant the sweeping prohibition on the mailing of unsolicited contraceptive advertisements.

The definition of commercial speech in *Bolger*, while seemingly specific, leaves many questions unanswered. For example, are "image advertisements" meant to enhance the public's perception of a business or a particular product a form of commercial speech? If tobacco companies produce advertisements that discuss scientific studies about the harms of smoking, is that commercial speech? These are unanswered questions because, as Professor Steven Shriffin observed, "[t]he Court has yet to fully focus on the question of what speech outside advertising is to count as commercial speech."[150]

c. The Test for Evaluating Regulation of Commercial Speech

In Central Hudson Gas v. Public Service Commn., the Supreme Court articulated a test, often invoked in subsequent cases, for when the government may regulate commercial speech.

CENTRAL HUDSON GAS & ELECTRIC CORP. v.
PUBLIC SERVICE COMMISSION OF NEW YORK

447 U.S. 557 (1980)

Justice POWELL delivered the opinion of the Court.

This case presents the question whether a regulation of the Public Service Commission of the State of New York violates the First and Fourteenth

---

150. Steven Shiffrin, *The First Amendment and Economic Regulation: Away from a General Theory of the First Amendment*, 78 Nw. U. L. Rev. 1212, 1223 (1983).

Amendments because it completely bans promotional advertising by an electrical utility.

I

In December 1973, the Commission, appellee here, ordered electric utilities in New York State to cease all advertising that "promot[es] the use of electricity." The order was based on the Commission's finding that "the interconnected utility system in New York State does not have sufficient fuel stocks or sources of supply to continue furnishing all customer demands for the 1973-1974 winter." Three years later, when the fuel shortage had eased, the Commission requested comments from the public on its proposal to continue the ban on promotional advertising. Central Hudson Gas & Electric Corp., the appellant in this case, opposed the ban on First Amendment grounds. After reviewing the public comments, the Commission extended the prohibition in a Policy Statement issued on February 25, 1977.

II

The Commission's order restricts only commercial speech, that is, expression related solely to the economic interests of the speaker and its audience. The First Amendment, as applied to the States through the Fourteenth Amendment, protects commercial speech from unwarranted governmental regulation. Commercial expression not only serves the economic interest of the speaker, but also assists consumers and furthers the societal interest in the fullest possible dissemination of information. In applying the First Amendment to this area, we have rejected the "highly paternalistic" view that government has complete power to suppress or regulate commercial speech. "[P]eople will perceive their own best interests if only they are well enough informed, and . . . the best means to that end is to open the channels of communication rather than to close them. . . ." Even when advertising communicates only an incomplete version of the relevant facts, the First Amendment presumes that some accurate information is better than no information at all.

Nevertheless, our decisions have recognized "the 'commonsense' distinction between speech proposing a commercial transaction, which occurs in an area traditionally subject to government regulation, and other varieties of speech." The Constitution therefore accords a lesser protection to commercial speech than to other constitutionally guaranteed expression. The protection available for particular commercial expression turns on the nature both of the expression and of the governmental interests served by its regulation.

The First Amendment's concern for commercial speech is based on the informational function of advertising. Consequently, there can be no constitutional objection to the suppression of commercial messages that do not accurately inform the public about lawful activity. The government may ban forms of communication more likely to deceive the public than to inform it. If the communication is neither misleading nor related to unlawful activity, the government's power is more circumscribed. The State must assert a substantial interest to be achieved by restrictions on commercial speech. Moreover, the regulatory technique must be in proportion to that interest. The limitation on expression must be designed carefully to achieve the State's goal. Compliance with this requirement may be measured by two criteria. First, the restriction must directly advance the state interest involved; the regulation may not be sustained if it provides only ineffective or remote support for the government's purpose. Second, if the governmental interest could be served as well by a more limited restriction on commercial speech, the excessive restrictions cannot survive.

Under the first criterion, the Court has declined to uphold regulations that only indirectly advance the state interest involved. In both Bates v. Arizona State Bar and *Virginia Pharmacy Board*, the Court concluded that an advertising ban could not be imposed to protect the ethical or performance standards of a profession. The second criterion recognizes that the First Amendment mandates that speech restrictions be "narrowly drawn." The regulatory technique may extend only as far as the interest it serves. The State cannot regulate speech that poses no danger to the asserted state interest, nor can it completely suppress information when narrower restrictions on expression would serve its interest as well.

In commercial speech cases, then, a four-part analysis has developed. At the outset, we must determine whether the expression is protected by the First Amendment. For commercial speech to come within that provision, it at least must concern lawful activity and not be misleading. Next, we ask whether the asserted governmental interest is substantial. If both inquiries yield positive answers, we must determine whether the regulation directly advances the governmental interest asserted, and whether it is not more extensive than is necessary to serve that interest.

III

We now apply this four-step analysis for commercial speech to the Commission's arguments in support of its ban on promotional advertising. The Commission does not claim that the expression at issue either is inaccurate or relates to unlawful activity. Even in monopoly markets, the suppression of advertising reduces the information available for consumer decisions and thereby defeats the purpose of the First Amendment. Most businesses — even regulated monopolies — are unlikely to underwrite promotional advertising that is of no interest or use to consumers. Indeed, a monopoly enterprise legitimately may wish to inform the public that it has developed new services or terms of doing business. A consumer may need information to aid his decision whether or not to use the monopoly service at all, or how much of the service he should purchase.

The Commission offers as [a] justification for the ban on promotional advertising energy conservation. Any increase in demand for electricity — during peak or off-peak periods — means greater consumption of energy. In view of our country's dependence on energy resources beyond our control, no one can doubt the importance of energy conservation. Plainly, therefore, the state interest asserted is substantial. [T]he State's interest in energy conservation is directly advanced by the Commission order at issue here. There is an immediate connection between advertising and demand for electricity.

We come finally to the critical inquiry in this case: whether the Commission's complete suppression of speech ordinarily protected by the First Amendment is no more extensive than necessary to further the State's interest in energy conservation. The Commission's order reaches all promotional advertising, regardless of the impact of the touted service on overall energy use. But the energy conservation rationale, as important as it is, cannot justify suppressing information about electric devices or services that would cause no net increase in total energy use. In addition, no showing has been made that a more limited restriction on the content of promotional advertising would not serve adequately the State's interests.

Thus, the *Central Hudson* test for commercial speech is: (1) Does the speech advertise illegal activities or constitute false or deceptive advertising that is unprotected by the First Amendment? (2) Is the government's restriction justified by a substantial government interest? (3) Does the law directly advance the government's interest? (4) Is the regulation of speech no more extensive than necessary to achieve the government's interest?

Hence, the test is similar, if not identical, to intermediate scrutiny in evaluating government regulation of truthful advertising for legal activities. In fact, the Court has expressly said that "we engage in 'intermediate' scrutiny of restrictions on commercial speech."[151]

The Court has ruled that the government has the burden of proof to demonstrate that the *Central Hudson* test is met in order to justify a restriction on commercial speech. The Court repeatedly has said that "[t]he party seeking to uphold a restriction on commercial speech carries the burden of justifying it."[152]

IS LEAST RESTRICTIVE ALTERNATIVE ANALYSIS APPLICABLE?

The Court has consistently invoked and applied the *Central Hudson* test in dealing with commercial speech issues. However, the Court has modified the fourth part of the test, the requirement that the regulation be no more extensive than necessary to achieve the government's purpose. In Board of Trustees of the State University of New York v. Fox, 492 U.S. 469 (1989), the Court held that government regulation of commercial speech need not use the least restrictive alternative. *Fox* concerned a state regulation that prohibited commercial solicitations on state university campuses.

The Court, in an opinion by Justice Scalia, expressly rejected the least restrictive alternative test for commercial speech. The Court said, "Our jurisprudence has emphasized that commercial speech enjoys a limited measure of protection, commensurate with its subordinate position in the scale of First Amendment values, and is subject to modes of regulation that might be impermissible in the realm of noncommercial expression. The ample scope of reg-

---

151. Florida Bar v. Went for It, Inc., 515 U.S. 618, 623 (1995).

152. Bolger v. Youngs Drugs Products Corp., 463 U.S. at 71; Edenfield v. Fane, 507 U.S. 761, 770 (1993).

ulatory authority suggested by such statements would be illusory if it were subject to a least-restrictive-means requirement, which imposes a heavy burden on the State." The Court said that while the government need not use the least restrictive alternative, it must use "a means narrowly tailored to achieve the desired objective."

Although *Fox* expressly rejected least restrictive alternative analysis for commercial speech cases, in Rubin v. Coors Brewing Co., 514 U.S. 476 (1995), the Court comes close to reinstituting it. *Rubin* involved a challenge to a provision of the Federal Alcohol Administration Act that prohibited the statement of alcohol content on beer labels. Interestingly, both sides in the case and the Court accepted that this constituted commercial speech. It, of course, is different from usual commercial speech, which is advertising for a particular product or service. Statements on labels about the alcohol content of beer are commercial speech in the sense that they may affect purchasers in deciding whether to buy a particular product.

The Court said that government regulation of commercial speech must advance the government's interest "in a direct and material way," and "[t]hat burden 'is not satisfied by mere speculation or conjecture; rather, a governmental body seeking to sustain a restriction on commercial speech must demonstrate that the harms it recites are real and that its restriction will in fact alleviate them to a material degree.'" The Court found that the government failed to meet this burden because of the "irrationality" of the regulatory scheme; the government did not prohibit listing of the alcohol content in advertisements for products, just on labels. The Court also found that there were a number of alternative ways of preventing strength wars and that these options "could advance the Government's asserted interest in a manner less intrusive to respondent's First Amendment rights." The Court said that this indicates that the law "is more extensive than necessary." Indeed, the Court concluded its opinion by emphasizing "the availability of alternatives that would prove less intrusive to the First Amendment's protections for commercial speech."

It is very difficult, if not impossible, to reconcile the language in *Rubin* with *Fox*. Where *Fox* says that government regulation of commercial speech need not use the least restrictive alternative, the *Rubin* Court says that a regulation of commercial speech is unconstitutional because less intrusive alternatives would suffice. Even more troubling is that Justice Thomas's opinion for the Court does not even cite *Fox*, let alone attempt to reconcile this inconsistency.[153]

Nor did the Court's decision in 44 Liquormart, Inc. v. Rhode Island, 517 U.S. 484 (1996), clarify this confusion. In *44 Liquormart*, the Supreme Court declared unconstitutional a state law that prohibited advertisement of liquor prices. The plurality opinion, written by Justice Stevens and joined by Justices Kennedy, Souter, and Ginsburg, said: "The State also cannot satisfy the requirement that its restriction on speech be no more extensive than necessary. It is perfectly obvious that alternative forms of regulation that would not involve any restriction on speech would be more likely to achieve the State's goal of promoting temperance." This is clearly the language of least restrictive alternative analysis. In the next paragraph, Justice Stevens invoked *Fox* and said that "even under the

---

153. The result in *Rubin* was unanimous. Justice Stevens concurred in the judgment and challenged the premise that commercial speech is entitled to less protection than other types of expression.

less than strict standard that generally applies in commercial speech cases, the State has failed to establish a 'reasonable fit' between its abridgement of speech and its temperance goal."

Nor do the other opinions in *Rubin* clarify this confusion. Justice Thomas's opinion concurring in the judgment argued that the government should not be able to regulate truthful commercial speech based on the premise that people will be better off with less information. Justice Scalia wrote a short opinion expressing doubts about the *Central Hudson* test and agreeing with Justice Thomas's analysis. Justice O'Connor wrote an opinion concurring in the judgment, joined by Chief Justice Rehnquist and Justices Souter and Breyer, that expressly invoked *Fox* and said that "[w]hile the State need not employ the least restrictive means to accomplish its goal, the fit between means and ends must be 'narrowly tailored.'" Justice O'Connor concluded that the Rhode Island law failed this test.

The Court's most recent commercial speech case to address this issue, Greater New Orleans Broadcasting Association v. United States, 527 U.S. 173 (1999), declared unconstitutional a federal law that prohibited advertising by casinos. The Court expressly relied on the *Central Hudson* test, declaring that "*Central Hudson*, as applied in our more recent commercial speech cases, provides an adequate basis for decision." The Court said that "[t]he fourth part of the test complements the direct-advancement inquiry of the third, asking whether the speech restriction is not more extensive than necessary to serve the interests that support it. The Government is not required to employ the least restrictive means conceivable, but it must demonstrate narrow tailoring of the challenged regulation to the asserted interest—'a fit that is not necessarily perfect, but reasonable; that represents not necessarily the single best disposition but one whose scope is in proportion to the interest served.'" The Court cited *Fox* as establishing this proposition. The Court then concluded that the federal law prohibiting casino advertising was not substantially related to achieving the objective of decreasing gambling because of the many exceptions in the law, such as in allowing advertising by Native American tribes and by state-run lotteries.

Thus, Fox, as reaffirmed in *Greater New Orleans Broadcasting*, rejects the use of least restrictive alternative analysis, but requires that any government regulation of commercial speech be narrowly tailored to achieving its objective.

d. Advertising of Illegal Activities

The Court consistently has held that advertising of illegality is not protected by the First Amendment.[154] The Court always has stated this as an axiom and offered little explanation. In some ways, it is a curious proposition. One would think that the government would welcome advertising of illegal activity; such ads, if they occurred, could help law enforcement. Moreover, speech that advocates illegal conduct is protected by the First Amendment unless it meets the test for incitement. Yet advertising of illegality is unprotected by the First Amendment without any need to meet the test for incitement.

---

154. *See, e.g.*, Central Hudson Gas v. Public Service Commn., 447 U.S. at 563-564.

The only Supreme Court case to consider advertising of illegality, Pittsburgh Press Co. v. Pittsburgh Commn. on Human Relations, 413 U.S. 376 (1973), was actually decided before the Supreme Court held that commercial speech is protected by the First Amendment. The Court upheld a decision by the Pittsburgh Commission on Human Relations that a newspaper violated the city's Human Relations Ordinance by placing help-wanted advertisements in columns captioned "Jobs-Male Interest," "Jobs-Female Interest," and "Male-Female."

The Court emphasized that "[d]iscrimination in employment is not only commercial activity, it is *illegal* commercial activity under the Ordinance. We have no doubt that a newspaper constitutionally could be forbidden to publish a want ad proposing a sale of narcotics or soliciting prostitutes. . . . The illegality in this case may be less overt, but we see no difference in principle here."

Pittsburgh Press is constantly cited with approval as establishing that advertising of illegal activities is not protected by the First Amendment. Thus, such advertisements can be prohibited, punished, and the basis for civil liability.

e.   False and Deceptive Advertising

It also is clearly established that false and deceptive advertisements are unprotected by the First Amendment. The Court frequently has declared that only truthful commercial speech is constitutionally protected.[155] The Supreme Court, however, has never decided a First Amendment case concerning false and deceptive ads.

False and deceptive advertisements do not contribute to the marketplace of ideas or the commercial marketplace in any useful way. In fact, false and deceptive advertisements distort those markets and thus are undeserving of First Amendment protection. Yet in contexts outside the commercial speech realm, it is clear that false speech is often protected. In New York Times v. Sullivan, 376 U.S. 254 (1964), the Court said that "erroneous statement is inevitable in free debate, [and] it must be protected if the freedoms of expression are to have the breathing space that they need to survive." The absence of protection for false commercial speech seems based on a judgment that such speech is more harmful, less likely to be chilled because of the profit motive, and more easily verified than most other types of expression.

f.   Advertising That Inherently Risks Deception

The Supreme Court has held that even true advertisements that inherently risk deception are unprotected by the First Amendment. The Court has considered this in two areas: laws that prohibit professionals from advertising or practicing under trade names, and restrictions on the ability of professionals to solicit prospective clients.

---

155. *See, e.g.,* Central Hudson Gas v. Public Service Commn., 447 U.S. at 566.

RESTRICTIONS ON TRADE NAMES

In Friedman v. Rogers, the Supreme Court upheld a state law that prohibited optometrists from advertising and practicing under trade names.

FRIEDMAN v. ROGERS
────────────────
440 U.S. 1 (1979)

Justice POWELL delivered the opinion of the Court.

Texas law prohibits the practice of optometry under a trade name. Once a trade name has been in use for some time, it may serve to identify an optometrical practice and also to convey information about the type, price, and quality of services offered for sale in that practice. In each role, the trade name is used as part of a proposal of a commercial transaction. Like the pharmacist who desired to advertise his prices in Virginia Pharmacy, the optometrist who uses a trade name "does not wish to editorialize on any subject, cultural, philosophical, or political. He does not wish to report any particularly newsworthy fact, or to make generalized observations even about commercial matters." His purpose is strictly business. The use of trade names in connection with optometrical practice, then, is a form of commercial speech and nothing more.

A trade name is, however, a significantly different form of commercial speech from that considered in *Virginia Pharmacy* and *Bates*. In those cases, the State had proscribed advertising by pharmacists and lawyers that contained statements about the products or services offered and their prices. These statements were self-contained and self-explanatory. Here, we are concerned with a form of commercial speech that has no intrinsic meaning. A trade name conveys no information about the price and nature of the services offered by an optometrist until it acquires meaning over a period of time by associations formed in the minds of the public between the name and some standard of price or quality. Because these ill-defined associations of trade names with price and quality information can be manipulated by the users of trade names, there is a significant possibility that trade names will be used to mislead the public.

The possibilities for deception are numerous. The trade name of an optometrical practice can remain unchanged despite changes in the staff of optometrists upon whose skill and care the public depends when it patronizes the practice. Thus, the public may be attracted by a trade name that reflects the reputation of an optometrist no longer associated with the practice. A trade name frees an optometrist from dependence on his personal reputation to attract clients, and even allows him to assume a new trade name if negligence or misconduct casts a shadow over the old one. By using different trade names at shops under his common ownership, an optometrist can give the public the false impression of competition among the shops. The use of a trade name also facilitates the advertising essential to large-scale commercial practices with numerous branch offices, conduct the State rationally may wish to discourage while not prohibiting commercial optometrical practice altogether.

The concerns of the Texas Legislature about the deceptive and misleading uses of optometrical trade names were not speculative or hypothetical, but were based on experience in Texas with which the legislature was familiar when in

1969 it enacted §5.13(d). It is clear that the State's interest in protecting the public from the deceptive and misleading use of optometrical trade names is substantial and well demonstrated. We are convinced that §5.13(d) is a constitutionally permissible state regulation in furtherance of this interest.

ATTORNEY SOLICITATION OF PROSPECTIVE CLIENTS

The Supreme Court has ruled that the government may not prohibit attorneys from engaging in truthful, nondeceptive advertising of their services.[156] However, the Supreme Court has held that the government may prohibit attorney in-person solicitation of prospective clients for profit. The underlying rationale is that such speech inherently risks becoming deceptive and thus even truthful solicitations can be forbidden when they are conducted in person and where the attorney would profit from the representation.

This rule emerged from a series of Supreme Court cases. In Ohralik v. Ohio State Bar Assn., 436 U.S. 447 (1978), the Court found no violation of the First Amendment when a lawyer was punished for impermissible solicitation for approaching an automobile accident victim in her hospital room and offering to represent her on a contingency fee basis. The Court noted that the government has a "compelling interest in preventing those aspects of solicitation that involve fraud, undue influence, intimidation, overreaching, and other forms of vexatious conduct." The Court stressed that face-to-face solicitation inherently risks deception and pressure because no one is there to monitor the communications. Because of this inherent danger, the Court said that it is not "violative of the Constitution for a State to respond with what in effect is a prophylactic rule."

However, in another case decided the same day, In re Primus, 436 U.S. 412 (1978), the Supreme Court held that solicitations are protected by the First Amendment when the lawyer offers to represent a client without charge. An attorney affiliated with the American Civil Liberties Union in South Carolina was disciplined for impermissible solicitation for offering to represent women for free after the welfare department told the women that they had to be sterilized in order to continue to receive public medical assistance. The Supreme Court, however, held that the lawyer's speech was protected by the First Amendment.

The Court noted that "[t]he ACLU engages in litigation as a vehicle for effective political expression and association, as well as a means of communicating useful information to the public." Thus, the Court said that South Carolina's action punishing the lawyer for offering free representation "must withstand the exacting scrutiny applicable to limitations on core First Amendment rights." The Court expressly distinguished Ohralik on the ground that the attorney in Primus was not seeking to profit directly from the client. This was important for the Court both in enhancing the importance of the speech as a form of political activity and in lessening the likelihood of deceptive practices by the attorney. The Court said that it was irrelevant that the ACLU attorney would seek attorney's fees from the state if the plaintiff prevailed in the case.

In Shapero v. Kentucky Bar Assn., 486 U.S. 466 (1988), the Court declared unconstitutional a state law that prohibited targeted direct-mail solicitation by

---

156. *See* Bates v. State Bar of Arizona, 433 U.S. 350 (1977).

lawyers for pecuniary gain. The Court explained that letter solicitation does not have the same risk of abuse as face-to-face solicitation. There is less risk of deception because there is a written record of the communication compared to face-to-face solicitation where no one is present to monitor the conversations. There is less risk of pressure or undue influence because people are accustomed to throwing away mail that is not of interest. The Court explained that "[l]ike print advertising, . . . letter[s] — and targeted, direct-mail solicitation generally — pose[] much less risk of overreaching or undue influence than does in-person solicitation."

Thus, *Orhralik*, *Primus*, and *Shapero* taken together establish the proposition that states may prohibit attorney in-person solicitation of clients for profit. Conversely, solicitation where the attorney would not profit directly from the client or solicitation by mail is generally protected by the First Amendment.

The Court, however, has carved one exception where mail solicitation by lawyers can be regulated. In Florida Bar v. Went for It, Inc., 515 U.S. 618 (1995), the Supreme Court upheld a Florida law that prohibited attorneys from soliciting personal injury or wrongful death clients for 30 days after an accident. The Court said that the "purpose of the 30-day targeted direct-mail ban is to forestall the outrage and irritation with the state-licensed legal profession that the practice of direct solicitation only days after accidents has engendered." The Court, in its 5-4 decision, concluded that the regulation was justified to protect accident victims and their estates from "invasive conduct by lawyers and in preventing the erosion of confidence in the profession that such repeated invasions have engendered."

Justice Kennedy wrote a dissenting opinion, joined by Justices Stevens, Souter, and Ginsburg. The dissent questioned whether letter solicitations are invasive and explained that they are important in informing people of their right to sue. The state did not limit the ability of claims adjusters or insurance companies to settle claims during this 30-day period; restricting such communications from plaintiffs' attorneys could harm accident victims and their estates by denying them needed information. Moreover, the Court consistently had rejected the argument that attorney advertising could be restricted because of its negative impact on the image of the profession.

SOLICITATION BY ACCOUNTANTS

The Supreme Court has held that the government may not prohibit accountants from engaging in in-person solicitation of clients for profit. In Edenfield v. Fane, 507 U.S. 761 (1993), the Court declared unconstitutional a state law that prohibited certified public accountants from engaging in in-person solicitations. The Court said that there was no evidence that accountants were engaged in abusive solicitations. The Court expressly distinguished *Ohralik*, which had upheld an identical rule for lawyers. Justice Kennedy, writing for the Court, said, "The solicitation here poses none of the same dangers. Unlike a lawyer, a CPA is not a professional trained in the art of persuasion. A CPA's training emphasizes independence and objectivity, not advocacy. The typical client of a CPA is far less susceptible to manipulation than the young accident victim in *Ohralik*."

This distinction between attorneys and accountants seems questionable. Attorneys and accountants obviously are both capable of trying to pressure prospective clients. The Court in *Ohralik* upheld all prohibitions on in-person solicitation of clients, regardless of their sophistication; the Court in *Edenfield* invalidated all prohibitions of in-person solicitation by accountants, regardless of the client's lack of sophistication. As Justice O'Connor said in dissent, "[t]he attorney's rhetorical power derives not only from his specific training in the art of persuasion, but more generally from his professional expertise." Nonetheless, the current law is that the government may prohibit attorney in-person solicitation for profit, but it may not prohibit accountants from engaging in such solicitation.

g. Regulating Commercial Speech to Achieve Other Goals

Perhaps the most difficult issue in the area of commercial speech concerns the ability of the government to regulate truthful, nondeceptive advertising of legal activities to achieve other goals. For example, may the government regulate commercial advertising to reduce sales of houses to preserve the racial balance in a neighborhood, to decrease consumption of alcohol or tobacco products, to lessen gambling, or to enhance the image of attorneys? In all of these areas, the restriction on commercial speech is based on a premise that seems at odds with the very core of the First Amendment: that people will be better off with less information. Justice Thomas, in a recent concurring opinion, rejected the notion that the government should be able to restrict commercial speech based on the assumption that people will be better off if they are kept in the dark about particular information.[157]

For the most part, the Supreme Court's commercial speech cases are consistent with this view as the Court generally has rejected state laws limiting commercial speech based on the belief that people will be better off with less information. The primary exception has been in the area of gambling advertisements where the Court has allowed restrictions of commercial speech to achieve the goal of decreasing gambling.[158]

This section reviews these cases, focusing in turn on the Court's treatment of the regulation of commercial speech concerning the sales of houses, alcohol products, gambling, and lawyers' and other professionals' services. In all of these cases, the issue is when the government may regulate truthful advertising of legal activities so as to achieve other objectives.

i. *"For Sale" Signs on Houses*

In Linmark Associates v. Township of Willingboro, the Supreme Court considered an ordinance that prohibited the display of "For Sale" or "Sold" signs.

---

157. 44 Liquormart, Inc. v. Rhode Island, 517 U.S. at 525-526.
158. United States v. Edge Broadcasting Co., 509 U.S. 418 (1993); Posadas de Puerto Rico Associates v. Tourism Co. of P.R., 478 U.S. 328 (1986).

LINMARK ASSOCIATES, INC. v. TOWNSHIP OF WILLINGBORO
431 U.S. 85 (1977)

Justice MARSHALL delivered the opinion of the Court.

This case presents the question whether the First Amendment permits a municipality to prohibit the posting of "For Sale" or "Sold" signs when the municipality acts to stem what it perceives as the flight of white homeowners from a racially integrated community.

If the Willingboro law is to be treated differently from those invalidated in *Bigelow* and *Virginia Pharmacy Bd.*, it cannot be because the speakers or listeners have a lesser First Amendment interest in the subject matter of the speech that is regulated here. Persons desiring to sell their homes are just as interested in communicating that fact as are sellers of other goods and services. Similarly, would-be purchasers of realty are no less interested in receiving information about available property than are purchasers of other commodities in receiving like information about those commodities. And the societal interest in "the free flow of commercial information," is in no way lessened by the fact that the subject of the commercial information here is realty rather than abortions or drugs.

Respondents do seek to distinguish *Bigelow* and *Virginia Pharmacy Bd.* by relying on the vital goal this ordinance serves: namely, promoting stable, racially integrated housing. There can be no question about the importance of achieving this goal. This Court has expressly recognized that substantial benefits flow to both whites and blacks from interracial association and that Congress has made a strong national commitment to promote integrated housing.

The record here demonstrates that respondents failed to establish that this ordinance is needed to assure that Willingboro remains an integrated community. As the District Court concluded, the evidence does not support the Council's apparent fears that Willingboro was experiencing a substantial incidence of panic selling by white homeowners. A fortiori, the evidence does not establish that "For Sale" signs in front of 2% of Willingboro homes were a major cause of panic selling. And the record does not confirm the township's assumption that proscribing such signs will reduce public awareness of realty sales and thereby decrease public concern over selling.

The constitutional defect in this ordinance, however, is far more basic. The Township Council here, like the Virginia Assembly in *Virginia Pharmacy Bd.*, acted to prevent its residents from obtaining certain information. That information, which pertains to sales activity in Willingboro, is of vital interest to Willingboro residents, since it may bear on one of the most important decisions they have a right to make: where to live and raise their families. The Council has sought to restrict the free flow of these data because it fears that otherwise homeowners will make decisions inimical to what the Council views as the homeowners' self-interest and the corporate interest of the township: they will choose to leave town. The Council's concern, then, was not with any commercial aspect of "For Sale" signs with offerors communicating offers to offerees but with the substance of the information communicated to Willingboro citizens. If dissemination of this information can be restricted, then every locality in the country can suppress any facts that reflect poorly on the locality, so long as a plausible claim can be made that disclosure would cause the recipients of the information to act "irrationally." *Virginia Pharmacy Bd.* denies government such sweeping powers. As we said there in rejecting Virginia's claim that the only way it could enable its citizens to find their self-interest was to deny them information that is neither false nor misleading: "There is . . . an alternative to this highly paternalistic approach. That alternative is to assume that this information is not in itself harmful, that people will perceive their own best interests if only they are well enough informed, and that the best means to that end is to open the channels of communication rather than to close them. . . . But the choice among these alternative approaches is not ours to make or the Virginia General Assembly's. It is precisely this kind of choice, between the dangers of suppressing information, and the dangers of its misuse if it is freely available, that the First Amendment makes for us."

ii. Alcohol Products

The Court has refused to allow the government to limit the advertising of alcohol products based on its goal of decreasing consumption. For example, in Rubin v. Coors Brewing Co., 514 U.S. 476 (1995), the Court declared unconstitutional a federal law that prohibited stating on beer labels the alcohol content of the product. The Court accepted that the government had a substantial interest in preventing strength wars among malt beverage products. The Court said that the government has a "significant interest in protecting the health, safety, and welfare of its citizens by preventing brewers from competing on the basis of alcohol strength, which could lead to greater alcoholism and its attendant social costs."

However, the Court declared the federal law unconstitutional because the government could achieve this goal "in a manner less intrusive to respondent's First Amendment rights." The Court identified "several alternatives, such as directly limiting the alcohol content of beers, prohibiting marketing efforts emphasizing high alcohol strength (which is apparently the policy in some other western nations), or limiting the labeling ban only to malt liquors, which is the segment of the market that allegedly is threatened with a strength war."

Subsequently, in 44 Liquormart, Inc. v. Rhode Island, the Supreme Court declared unconstitutional a state law that prohibited price advertising of alcoholic beverages.

44 LIQUORMART, INC. v. RHODE ISLAND
517 U.S. 484 (1996)

Justice STEVENS announced the judgment of the Court.

Last Term we held that a federal law abridging a brewer's right to provide the public with accurate information about the alcoholic content of malt beverages is unconstitutional. Rubin v. Coors Brewing Co. (1995). We now hold that Rhode Island's statutory prohibition against advertisements that provide the public with accurate information about retail prices of alcoholic beverages is also invalid. Our holding rests on the conclusion that such an advertising ban is an abridgment of speech protected by the First Amendment and that it is not shielded from constitutional scrutiny by the Twenty-first Amendment.

In 1956, the Rhode Island Legislature enacted two separate prohibitions against advertising the retail price of alcoholic beverages. The first applies to vendors licensed in Rhode Island as well as to out-of-state manufacturers, wholesalers, and shippers. The second statute applies to the Rhode Island news media. It contains a categorical prohibition against the publication or broadcast of any advertisements — even those referring to sales in other States — that "make reference to the price of any alcoholic beverages."

It is the State's interest in protecting consumers from "commercial harms" that provides "the typical reason why commercial speech can be subject to greater governmental regulation than noncommercial speech." Yet bans that target truthful, nonmisleading commercial messages rarely protect consumers from such harms. Instead, such bans often serve only to obscure an "underlying governmental policy" that could be implemented without regulating speech. In this way, these commercial speech bans not only hinder consumer choice, but also impede debate over central issues of public policy.

Precisely because bans against truthful, nonmisleading commercial speech rarely seek to protect consumers from either deception or overreaching, they usually rest solely on the offensive assumption that the public will respond "irrationally" to the truth. The First Amendment directs us to be especially skeptical of regulations that seek to keep people in the dark for what the government perceives to be their own good. That teaching applies equally to state attempts to deprive consumers of accurate information about their chosen products.

In this case, there is no question that Rhode Island's price advertising ban constitutes a blanket prohibition against truthful, nonmisleading speech about a lawful product. There is also no question that the ban serves an end unrelated to consumer protection. Accordingly, we must review the price advertising ban with "special care," mindful that speech prohibitions of this type rarely survive constitutional review.

The State argues that the price advertising prohibition should nevertheless be upheld because it directly advances the State's substantial interest in promoting temperance, and because it is no more extensive than necessary. Although there is some confusion as to what Rhode Island means by temperance, we assume that the State asserts an interest in reducing alcohol consumption.

In evaluating the ban's effectiveness in advancing the State's interest, we note that a commercial speech regulation "may not be sustained if it provides only ineffective or remote support for the government's purpose." For that reason, the State bears the burden of showing not merely that its regulation will advance its interest, but also that it will do so "to a material degree." The need for the State to make such a showing is particularly great given the drastic nature of its chosen means — the wholesale suppression of truthful, nonmisleading information. Accordingly, we must determine whether the State has shown that the price advertising ban will significantly reduce alcohol consumption.

We can agree that common sense supports the conclusion that a prohibition against price advertising, like a collusive agreement among competitors to refrain from such advertising, will tend to mitigate competition and maintain prices at a higher level than would prevail in a completely free market. Despite the absence of proof on the point, we can even agree with the State's contention that it is reasonable to assume that demand, and hence consumption throughout the market, is somewhat lower whenever a higher, noncompetitive price level prevails. However, without any findings of fact, or indeed any evidentiary support whatsoever, we cannot agree with the assertion that the price advertising ban will significantly advance the State's interest in promoting temperance.

Although the record suggests that the price advertising ban may have some impact on the purchasing patterns of temperate drinkers of modest means, the State has presented no evidence to suggest that its speech prohibition will significantly reduce marketwide consumption. Indeed, the District Court's considered and uncontradicted finding on this point is directly to the contrary. The State also cannot satisfy the requirement that its restriction on speech be no more extensive than necessary. It is perfectly obvious that alternative forms of regulation that would not involve any restriction on speech would be more likely to achieve the State's goal of promoting temperance. As the State's own expert conceded, higher prices can be maintained either by direct regulation or by increased taxation.

As a result, even under the less than strict standard that generally applies in commercial speech cases, the State has failed to establish a "reasonable fit" between its abridgment of speech and its temperance goal. Board of Trustees of State Univ. of N.Y. v. Fox (1989).

Justice THOMAS concurring in the judgment.

In cases such as this, in which the government's asserted interest is to keep legal users of a product or service ignorant in order to manipulate their choices in the marketplace, the balancing test adopted in Central Hudson Gas & Elec. Corp. v. Public Serv. Comm'n of N.Y. (1980) should not be applied, in my view. Rather, such an "interest" is per se illegitimate and can no more justify regulation of "commercial" speech than it can justify regulation of "noncommercial" speech. I do not join the principal opinion's application of the *Central Hudson* balancing test because I do not believe that such a test should be applied to a restriction of "commercial" speech, at least when, as here, the asserted interest is one that is to be achieved through keeping would-be recipients of the speech in the dark.

Justice O'CONNOR, with whom the Chief Justice, Justice SOUTER, and Justice BREYER join, concurring in the judgment.

Rhode Island prohibits advertisement of the retail price of alcoholic beverages, except at the place of sale. The State's only asserted justification for this ban is that it promotes temperance by increasing the cost of alcoholic beverages. I agree with the Court that Rhode Island's price-advertising ban is invalid. I would resolve this case more narrowly, however, by applying our established *Central Hudson* test to determine whether this commercial speech regulation survives First Amendment scrutiny.

Under that test, we first determine whether the speech at issue concerns lawful activity and is not misleading, and whether the asserted governmental interest is substantial. If both these conditions are met, we must decide whether the regulation "directly advances the governmental interest asserted, and whether it is not more extensive than is necessary to serve that interest."

Given the means by which this regulation purportedly serves the State's interest, our conclusion is plain: Rhode Island's regulation fails First Amendment scrutiny. Both parties agree that the first two prongs of the *Central Hudson* test are met. Even if we assume, arguendo, that Rhode Island's regulation also satisfies the requirement that it directly advance the governmental interest, Rhode Island's regulation fails the final prong; that is, its ban is more extensive than necessary to serve the State's interest.

As we have explained, in order for a speech restriction to pass muster under the final prong, there must be a fit between the legislature's goal and method, "a fit that is not necessarily perfect, but reasonable; that represents not necessarily the single best disposition but one whose scope is in proportion to the interest served." Board of Trustees of State Univ. of N.Y. v. Fox (1989). The availability of less burdensome alternatives to reach the stated goal signals that the fit between the legislature's ends and the means chosen to accomplish those ends may be too imprecise to withstand First Amendment scrutiny.

The fit between Rhode Island's method and this particular goal is not reasonable. If the target is simply higher prices generally to discourage consumption, the regulation imposes too great, and unnecessary, a prohibition on speech in order to achieve it. The State has other methods at its disposal — methods that would more directly accomplish this stated goal without intruding on sellers' ability to provide truthful, nonmisleading information to customers. Indeed, Rhode Island's own expert conceded that "the objective of lowering consumption of alcohol by banning price advertising could be accomplished by establishing minimum prices and/or by increasing sales taxes on alcoholic beverages." A tax, for example, is not normally very difficult to administer and would have a far more certain and direct effect on prices, without any restriction on speech. The ready availability of such alternatives — at least some of which would far more effectively achieve Rhode Island's only professed goal, at comparatively small additional administrative cost — demonstrates that the fit between ends and means is not narrowly tailored.

iii. Tobacco Products

In Lorillard Tobacco Co. v. Reilly, the Supreme Court considered the constitutionality of Massachusetts's regulation of tobacco advertising. The most significant aspects of the regulations prevented advertising of tobacco products within 1,000 feet of a school or playground and required that places selling tobacco products place ads for these items at least five feet off the ground to avoid being at eye level for children. The Supreme Court declared these regulations of cigarette advertising to be preempted by federal law. This aspect of the decision, and the dissent concerning it, is presented in Chapter 4. The federal law, however, only concerns cigarettes and not cigars or smokeless tobacco. Therefore, the Court considered whether the restrictions on advertising of these products violated the First Amendment.

The case seems particularly important in reaffirming that *Central Hudson*'s four-part test is used in evaluating government regulation of commercial speech. The decision also is significant in limiting the ability of the government to regulate advertising so as to discourage harmful behavior.

LORILLARD TOBACCO CO. v. REILLY
533 U.S. 525 (2001)

O'CONNOR, J., delivered the opinion of the Court, Parts III-A, III-C, and III-D of which were joined by REHNQUIST, C.J., and SCALIA, KENNEDY, SOUTER, and THOMAS,

JJ.; Part III-B-1 of which was joined by Rehnquist, C.J., and Stevens, Souter, Ginsburg, and Breyer, JJ.; and Parts III-B-2 of which was joined by Rehnquist, C.J., and Scalia, Kennedy, and Thomas, JJ.

[I]

By its terms, the FCLAA's pre-emption provision only applies to cigarettes. Accordingly, we must evaluate the smokeless tobacco and cigar petitioners' First Amendment challenges to the State's outdoor and point-of-sale advertising regulations.

A

For over 25 years, the Court has recognized that commercial speech does not fall outside the purview of the First Amendment. Instead, the Court has afforded commercial speech a measure of First Amendment protection "commensurate" with its position in relation to other constitutionally guaranteed expression. In recognition of the "distinction between speech proposing a commercial trans-action, which occurs in an area traditionally subject to government regulation, and other varieties of speech," we developed a framework for analyzing regula-tions of commercial speech that is "substantially similar" to the test for time, place, and manner restrictions. The analysis contains four elements:

> At the outset, we must determine whether the expression is protected by the First Amendment. For commercial speech to come within that provision, it at least must concern lawful activity and not be misleading. Next, we ask whether the asserted governmental interest is substantial. If both inquiries yield positive answers, we must determine whether the regulation directly advances the governmental interest asserted, and whether it is not more extensive than is necessary to serve that interest. Central Hudson Gas & Electric Corp. v. Public Service Commission of New York (1980).

Petitioners urge us to reject the *Central Hudson* analysis and apply strict scru-tiny. They are not the first litigants to do so. Admittedly, several Members of the Court have expressed doubts about the *Central Hudson* analysis and whether it should apply in particular cases. But we see "no need to break new ground. *Central Hudson*, as applied in our more recent commercial speech cases, provides an adequate basis for decision."

Only the last two steps of *Central Hudson*'s four-part analysis are at issue here. The Attorney General has assumed for purposes of summary judgment that petitioners' speech is entitled to First Amendment protection. With respect to the second step, none of the petitioners contests the importance of the State's interest in preventing the use of tobacco products by minors.

The third step of *Central Hudson* concerns the relationship between the harm that underlies the State's interest and the means identified by the State to advance that interest. It requires that "the speech restriction directly and mate-rially advanc[e] the asserted governmental interest. 'This burden is not satisfied by mere speculation or conjecture; rather, a governmental body seeking to sustain a restriction on commercial speech must demonstrate that the harms it recites are real and that its restriction will in fact alleviate them to a material degree.'"

We do not, however, require that "empirical data come . . . accompanied by a surfeit of background information. . . . [W]e have permitted litigants to justify speech restrictions by reference to studies and anecdotes pertaining to different locales altogether, or even, in a case applying strict scrutiny, to justify restrictions based solely on history, consensus, and 'simple common sense.'" Florida Bar v. Went For It, Inc. (1995).

The last step of the *Central Hudson* analysis "complements" the third step, "asking whether the speech restriction is not more extensive than necessary to serve the interests that support it." We have made it clear that "the least restrictive means" is not the standard; instead, the case law requires a reasonable "fit between the legislature's ends and the means chosen to accomplish those ends, . . . a means narrowly tailored to achieve the desired objective." Focusing on the third and fourth steps of the *Central Hudson* analysis, we first address the outdoor advertising and point-of-sale advertising regulations for smokeless tobacco and cigars. We then address the sales practices regulations for all tobacco products.

B

The outdoor advertising regulations prohibit smokeless tobacco or cigar advertising within a 1,000-foot radius of a school or playground. The District Court and Court of Appeals concluded that the Attorney General had identified a real problem with underage use of tobacco products, that limiting youth exposure to advertising would combat that problem, and that the regulations burdened no more speech than necessary to accomplish the State's goal. The smokeless tobacco and cigar petitioners take issue with all of these conclusions.

1

The smokeless tobacco and cigar petitioners contend that the Attorney General's regulations do not satisfy *Central Hudson*'s third step. They maintain that although the Attorney General may have identified a problem with underage cigarette smoking, he has not identified an equally severe problem with respect to underage use of smokeless tobacco or cigars. The smokeless tobacco petitioner emphasizes the "lack of parity" between cigarettes and smokeless tobacco. The cigar petitioners catalogue a list of differences between cigars and other tobacco products, including the characteristics of the products and marketing strategies. The petitioners finally contend that the Attorney General cannot prove that advertising has a causal link to tobacco use such that limiting advertising will materially alleviate any problem of underage use of their products.

In previous cases, we have acknowledged the theory that product advertising stimulates demand for products, while suppressed advertising may have the opposite effect. The Attorney General cites numerous studies to support this theory in the case of tobacco products. The Attorney General relies in part on evidence gathered by the Food and Drug Administration (FDA) in its attempt to regulate the advertising of cigarettes and smokeless tobacco. The FDA made specific findings with respect to smokeless tobacco. The FDA concluded that "[t]he recent and very large increase in the use of smokeless tobacco products by young people and the addictive nature of these products has persuaded the agency that these products must be included in any regulatory approach that is designed to help prevent future generations of young people from becoming addicted to nicotine-containing tobacco products." Researchers tracked a dramatic shift in patterns of smokeless tobacco use from older to younger users over the past 30 years. Another study documented the targeting of youth through smokeless tobacco sales and advertising techniques.

The Attorney General presents different evidence with respect to cigars. There was no data on underage cigar use prior to 1996 because the behavior was considered "uncommon enough not to be worthy of examination." More recently, however, data on youth cigar use has emerged. The National Cancer Institute concluded in its 1998 Monograph that the rate of cigar use by minors is increasing and that, in some States, the cigar use rates are higher than the smokeless tobacco use rates for minors. Studies have also demonstrated a link between advertising and demand for cigars. After Congress recognized the power of images in advertising and banned cigarette advertising in electronic media, television advertising of small cigars "increased dramatically in 1972 and 1973, filled the void left by cigarette advertisers," and "sales . . . soared."

Our review of the record reveals that the Attorney General has provided ample documentation of the problem with underage use of smokeless tobacco and cigars. In addition, we disagree with petitioners' claim that there is no evidence that preventing targeted campaigns and limiting youth exposure to advertising will decrease underage use of smokeless tobacco and cigars. On this record and in the posture of summary judgment, we are unable to conclude that the Attorney General's decision to regulate advertising of smokeless tobacco and cigars in an effort to combat the use of tobacco products by minors was based on mere "speculation [and] conjecture."

2

Whatever the strength of the Attorney General's evidence to justify the outdoor advertising regulations, however, we conclude that the regulations do not satisfy the fourth step of the *Central Hudson* analysis. The final step of the *Central Hudson* analysis, the "critical inquiry in this case," requires a reasonable fit between the means and ends of the regulatory scheme. The Attorney General's regulations do not meet this standard. The broad sweep of the regulations indicates that the Attorney General did not "carefully calcula[te] the costs and benefits associated with the burden on speech imposed" by the regulations.

The outdoor advertising regulations prohibit any smokeless tobacco or cigar advertising within 1,000 feet of schools or playgrounds. In the District Court, petitioners maintained that this prohibition would prevent advertising in 87% to 91% of Boston, Worcester, and Springfield, Massachusetts. The 87% to 91% figure appears to include not only the effect of the regulations, but also the limitations imposed by other generally applicable zoning restrictions. The Attorney General disputed petitioners' figures but "concede[d] that the reach of the regulations is substantial." Thus, the Court of Appeals concluded that the regulations prohibit advertising in a substantial portion of the major metropolitan areas of Massachusetts.

The substantial geographical reach of the Attorney General's outdoor advertising regulations is compounded by other factors. "Outdoor" advertising includes not only advertising located outside an establishment, but also advertising inside a store if that advertising is visible from outside the store. The regulations restrict advertisements of any size and the term advertisement also includes oral statements.

In some geographical areas, these regulations would constitute nearly a complete ban on the communication of truthful information about smokeless tobacco and cigars to adult consumers. The breadth and scope of the regulations, and the process by which the Attorney General adopted the regulations, do not demonstrate a careful calculation of the speech interests involved.

The State's interest in preventing underage tobacco use is substantial, and ever compelling, but it is no less true that the sale and use of tobacco products by adults is a legal activity. We must consider that tobacco retailers and manufacturers have an interest in conveying truthful information about their products to adults, and adults have a corresponding interest in receiving truthful information about tobacco products. In a case involving indecent speech on the Internet we explained that "the governmental interest in protecting children from harmful materials . . . does not justify an unnecessarily broad suppression of speech addressed to adults." Reno v. American Civil Liberties Union (1997).

In some instances, Massachusetts' outdoor advertising regulations would impose particularly onerous burdens on speech. For example, we disagree with the Court of Appeals' conclusion that because cigar manufacturers and retailers conduct a limited amount of advertising in comparison to other tobacco products, "the relative lack of cigar advertising also means that the burden imposed on cigar advertisers is correspondingly small." If some retailers have relatively small advertising budgets, and use few avenues of communication, then the Attorney General's outdoor advertising regulations potentially place a greater, not lesser, burden on those retailers' speech. Furthermore, to the extent that cigar products and cigar advertising differ from that of other tobacco products, that difference should inform the inquiry into what speech restrictions are necessary.

In addition, a retailer in Massachusetts may have no means of communicating to passersby on the street that it sells tobacco products because alternative forms of advertisement, like newspapers, do not allow that retailer to propose an instant transaction in the way that onsite advertising does. The ban on any indoor advertising that is visible from the outside also presents problems in establishments like convenience stores, which have unique security concerns that counsel in favor of full visibility of the store from the outside. It is these sorts of considerations that the Attorney General failed to incorporate into the regulatory scheme.

We conclude that the Attorney General has failed to show that the outdoor advertising regulations for smokeless tobacco and cigars are not more extensive than necessary to advance the State's substantial interest in preventing underage tobacco use.

C

Massachusetts has also restricted indoor, point-of-sale advertising for smokeless tobacco and cigars. Advertising cannot be "placed lower than five feet from the floor of any retail establishment which is located within a one thousand foot radius of" any school or playground. We conclude that the point-of-sale advertising regulations fail both the third and fourth steps of the *Central Hudson* analysis. A regulation cannot be sustained if it "provides only ineffective or remote support for the government's purpose," or if there is "little chance" that the restriction will advance the State's goal. As outlined above, the State's goal is to prevent minors from using tobacco products and to curb demand for that activity by limiting youth exposure to advertising. The 5-foot rule does not seem to advance that goal. Not all children are less than 5 feet tall, and those who are certainly have the ability to look up and take in their surroundings.

Massachusetts may wish to target tobacco advertisements and displays that entice children, much like floor-level candy displays in a convenience store, but the blanket height restriction does not constitute a reasonable fit with that goal. The Court of Appeals recognized that the efficacy of the regulation was questionable, but decided that "[i]n any event, the burden on speech imposed by the provision is very limited." There is no de minimis exception for a speech restriction that lacks sufficient tailoring or justification. We conclude that the restriction on the height of indoor advertising is invalid under *Central Hudson*'s third and fourth prongs.

Justice THOMAS, concurring in part and concurring in the judgment.

I join the opinion of the court, [but] I continue to believe that when the government seeks to restrict truthful speech in order to suppress the ideas it conveys, strict scrutiny is appropriate, whether or not the speech in question may be characterized as "commercial." I would subject all of the advertising restrictions to strict scrutiny and would hold that they violate the First Amendment.

Whatever power the State may have to regulate commercial speech, it may not use that power to limit the content of commercial speech, as it has done here, "for reasons unrelated to the preservation of a fair bargaining process." Such content-discriminatory regulation — like all other content-based regulation of speech — must be subjected to strict scrutiny.

Under strict scrutiny, the advertising ban may be saved only if it is narrowly tailored to promote a compelling government interest. If that interest could be served by an alternative that is less restrictive of speech, then the State must use that alternative instead. Applying this standard, the regulations here must fail.

Underlying many of the arguments of respondents and their amici is the idea that tobacco is in some sense sui generis — that it is so special, so unlike any other object of regulation, that application of normal First Amendment principles should be suspended. Smoking poses serious health risks, and advertising may induce children (who lack the judgment to make an intelligent decision about whether to smoke) to begin smoking, which can lead to addiction. The State's assessment of the urgency of the problem posed by tobacco is a policy judgment, and it is not this Court's place to second-guess it. Nevertheless, it seems appropriate to point out that to uphold the Massachusetts tobacco regulations would be to accept a line of reasoning that would permit restrictions on advertising for a host of other products.

Tobacco use is, we are told, "the single leading cause of preventable death in the United States." The second largest contributor to mortality rates in the United States is obesity. It is associated with increased incidence of diabetes, hypertension, and coronary artery disease, and it represents a public health problem that is rapidly growing worse. Although the growth of obesity over the last few decades has had many causes, a significant factor has been the increased availability of large quantities of high-calorie, high-fat foods. Such foods, of course, have been aggressively marketed and promoted by fast food companies.

Respondents say that tobacco companies are covertly targeting children in their advertising. Fast food companies do so openly. Moreover, there is considerable evidence that they have been successful in changing children's eating behavior. The effect of advertising on children's eating habits is significant for two reasons. First, childhood obesity is a serious health problem in its own right. Second, eating preferences formed in childhood tend to persist in adulthood. So even though fast food is not addictive in the same way tobacco is, children's exposure to fast food advertising can have deleterious consequences that are difficult to reverse.

To take another example, the third largest cause of preventable deaths in the United States is alcohol. Alcohol use is associated with tens of thousands of deaths each year from cancers and digestive diseases. And the victims of alcohol use are not limited to those who drink alcohol. In 1996, over 17,000 people were killed, and over 321,000 people were injured, in alcohol-related car accidents. Each year, alcohol is involved in several million violent crimes, including almost 200,000 sexual assaults.

Although every State prohibits the sale of alcohol to those under age 21, much alcohol advertising is viewed by children. Not surprisingly, there is considerable evidence that exposure to alcohol advertising is associated with underage drinking. Like underage tobacco use, underage drinking has effects that cannot be undone later in life. Those who begin drinking early are much more likely to become dependent on alcohol. Indeed, the probability of lifetime alcohol dependence decreases approximately 14 percent with each additional year of age at which alcohol is first used. And obviously the effects of underage drinking are irreversible for the nearly 1,700 Americans killed each year by teenage drunk drivers.

Respondents have identified no principle of law or logic that would preclude the imposition of restrictions on fast food and alcohol advertising similar to those they seek to impose on tobacco advertising. In effect, they seek a "vice" exception to the First Amendment. No such exception exists. If it did, it would have almost no limit, for "any product that poses some threat to public health or public morals might reasonably be characterized by a state legislature as relating to 'vice activity.'" That is why "a 'vice' label that is unaccompanied by a corresponding prohibition against the commercial behavior at issue fails to provide a principled justification for the regulation of commercial speech about that activity."

No legislature has ever sought to restrict speech about an activity it regarded as harmless and inoffensive. Calls for limits on expression always are made when the specter of some threatened harm is looming. The identity of the harm may vary. People will be inspired by totalitarian dogmas and subvert the Republic. They will be inflamed by racial demagoguery and embrace hatred and bigotry. Or they will be enticed by cigarette advertisements and choose to smoke, risking disease. It is therefore no answer for the State to say that the makers of cigarettes are doing harm: perhaps they are. But in that respect they are no different from the purveyors of other harmful products, or the advocates of harmful ideas. When the State seeks to silence them, they are all entitled to the protection of the First Amendment.

Justice STEVENS, concurring in part and dissenting in part, joined by Justices GINSBURG and BREYER.

I would, however, reach different dispositions as to the 1,000-foot rule and the height restrictions for indoor advertising, and my evaluation of the sales practice restrictions differs from the Court's.

THE 1,000-FOOT RULE

I am in complete accord with the Court's analysis of the importance of the interests served by the advertising restrictions. As the Court lucidly explains, few interests are more "compelling[]" than ensuring that minors do not become addicted to a dangerous drug before they are able to make a mature and informed decision as to the health risks associated with that substance. Unlike other products sold for human consumption, tobacco products are addictive and ultimately lethal for many long-term users. When that interest is combined with the State's concomitant concern for the effective enforcement of its laws regarding the sale of tobacco to minors, it becomes clear that Massachusetts' regulations serve interests of the highest order and are, therefore, immune from any ends-based challenge, whatever level of scrutiny one chooses to employ.

Nevertheless, noble ends do not save a speech-restricting statute whose means are poorly tailored. Such statutes may be invalid for two different reasons. First, the means chosen may be insufficiently related to the ends they purportedly serve. Alternatively, the statute may be so broadly drawn that, while effectively achieving its ends, it unduly restricts communications that are unrelated to its policy aims. The second difficulty is most frequently encountered when government adopts measures for the protection of children that impose substantial restrictions on the ability of adults to communicate with one another.

To my mind, the 1,000-foot rule does not present a tailoring problem of the first type. For reasons cogently explained in our prior opinions and in the opinion of the Court, we may fairly assume that advertising stimulates consumption and, therefore, that regulations limiting advertising will facilitate efforts to stem consumption.

However, I share the majority's concern as to whether the 1,000-foot rule unduly restricts the ability of cigarette manufacturers to convey lawful information to adult consumers. This, of course, is a question of line-drawing. While a ban on all communications about a given subject would be the most effective way to prevent children from exposure to such material, the state cannot by fiat reduce the level of discourse to that which is "fit for children."

Finding the appropriate balance is no easy matter. Though many factors plausibly enter the equation when calculating whether a child-directed location restriction goes too far in regulating adult speech, one crucial question is whether the regulatory scheme leaves available sufficient "alternative avenues of communication." Because I do not think the record contains sufficient information to enable us to answer that question, I would vacate the award of summary judgment upholding the 1,000-foot rule and remand for trial on that issue.

iv. Gambling

In sharp contrast to the Court's unwillingness to allow the government to regulate advertisements for alcohol products based on the desire to decrease consumption, the Court has permitted the government to prohibit gambling advertisements in order to attempt to reduce gambling. In Posadas de Puerto Rico Associates v. Tourism Co., 478 U.S. 328 (1986), the Supreme Court upheld a Puerto Rico law that prohibited advertising by casino gambling establishments. The Court accepted Puerto Rico's argument that the government has an important interest in discouraging gambling and said that it had "no difficulty in concluding that the Puerto Rico Legislature's interest in the health, safety, and welfare of its citizens constitutes a 'substantial' governmental interest."

The Court said that prohibiting casino advertising was sufficiently narrowly tailored to achieve this goal so as to meet the requirements of the First Amendment. The Court said that the law was not unconstitutional because it targeted advertising for casino gambling, but left advertising for other forms of gambling unregulated. The Court said that the "legislature felt that for Puerto Ricans the risks associated with casino gambling were significantly greater than those associated with the more traditional kinds of gambling in Puerto Rico."

The Court also noted that the government could have banned all casino gambling. It concluded that it therefore could take the lesser step of only prohibiting advertisements. The Court said, "Here, on the other hand, the Puerto Rico legislature surely could have prohibited casino gambling by the residents of Puerto Rico altogether. In our view, the greater power to completely ban casino gambling necessarily includes the lesser power to ban advertising of casino gambling."

The Court followed the *Posadas* case in United States v. Edge Broadcasting Co., 509 U.S. 418 (1993), where it upheld a federal law that prohibited lottery advertising by radio stations located in states that did not operate lotteries. A radio station in North Carolina wished to broadcast advertisements for the Virginia lottery. Evidence demonstrated that over 92 percent of the broadcast station's audience resided in Virginia, where lotteries were legal. However, the federal law prohibited the radio station from broadcasting such advertisements because the station was located in North Carolina, which did not have a lottery. Again, the Court upheld the law based on the government's substantial interest in discouraging gambling by limiting advertisements for it. The Court also stressed that the federal law served to effectuate the desires of each state by permitting advertising where states choose to have lotteries and prohibiting it where they do not.

But in its most recent commercial speech case, Greater New Orleans Broadcasting Association, Inc. v. United States, 527 U.S. 173 (1999), the Supreme Court invalidated a federal law that prohibited advertising by casinos. The Court invoked the *Central Hudson* test and held that the many exceptions permitted in the federal law—such as allowing advertising on Native American reservations and by state-run lotteries—meant that the law could not be deemed narrowly tailored to achieving its goal of discouraging gambling.

v. Advertising by Lawyers and Other Professionals

One of the most frequent topics of commercial speech before the Supreme Court has been state attempts to restrict advertising by lawyers and other professionals. The ability of states to regulate solicitation by attorneys and accountants is discussed above. Additionally, states have attempted to prohibit attorneys and other professionals from advertising and to restrict the content of the ads that are produced. The Supreme Court repeatedly has made it clear that such advertisements are protected by the First Amendment as long as they are truthful and not deceptive.

The Court initially ruled that states cannot prohibit lawyers from advertising in Bates v. State Bar of Arizona, 433 U.S. 350 (1977). A lawyer had been disciplined by the bar for an advertisement that stated prices for routine legal services such as uncontested divorces, name changes, and simple nonbusiness bankruptcies. The state presented a number of justifications for prohibiting and punishing the advertisement. It argued, for example, that such advertisements cause a negative public impression of attorneys; that they foment litigation; and that they are inherently deceptive because inevitably legal services involve complications that cannot be foreseen. The Court rejected all of these justifications for prohibiting lawyer advertisements. The Court explained that it was far too tenuous and speculative to believe that lawyer advertising would have any of these ill effects.

As in *Virginia Board of Pharmacy*, the Court stressed the value to consumers of receiving truthful information about prices and availability of services. Justice Blackmun, writing for the Court, said that the state's justifications were impermissibly "based on the benefits of public ignorance." Justice Blackmun explained that the First Amendment precludes the state from acting on the premise that "the public is best kept in ignorance than trusted with correct but incomplete information."

Repeatedly since *Bates* the Supreme Court has reiterated that truthful, non-deceptive advertisements by professionals are protected by the First Amendment. Many of these cases involved other efforts by states to restrict lawyer advertisements. For example, in In re R.M.J., 455 U.S. 191 (1982), a lawyer was disciplined for not following state rules regulating lawyer advertising. The attorney, for instance, listed his specialty as "real estate" and not "property" as prescribed in the rule. He also sent announcement cards to persons other than "lawyers, clients, former clients, personal friends and relatives." The Court held that the lawyer's speech and activities were protected by the First Amendment because the expression was true and not deceptive. The Court emphasized that the state could achieve all of its goals through means less restrictive of speech. In a unanimous decision, the Court said that "although the States may regulate commercial speech, the First and Fourteenth Amendments require that they do so with care and in a manner no more extensive than reasonably necessary to further substantial state interests."

In Zauderer v. Office of Disciplinary Counsel of the Supreme Court of Ohio, 471 U.S. 626 (1985), the Supreme Court again held that truthful advertisements are protected by the First Amendment, but the government can punish deception including that which occurs through omission. An attorney published advertisements offering to represent women who were injured by the Dalkon Shield intrauterine device (a contraceptive device). The lawyer was punished for three reasons. First, he was disciplined for violating a rule that prohibited advertisements containing advice or information about a specific legal problem. Second, he was punished because his advertisement included an illustration, a drawing of a Dalkon Shield. Third, he was disciplined for deception; the advertisement stated that he would provide representation on a contingency fee basis and that the client would not have to pay any fee if the case was not won. The ad did not disclose that the clients were liable for litigation costs.

The Supreme Court rejected the first two grounds for discipline, but accepted the third. The Court said that a state could not prohibit advertisements that targeted a particular audience or a group of clients with a specific legal problem. The Court emphasized the difference from in-person solicitations, in that "[p]rint advertising . . . lack[s] the coercive force of the personal presence of a trained advocate." Moreover, the Court said that illustrations were allowed in ads unless there was proof in a specific case that they were deceptive or misleading.

But the Court said that the omission of a statement about the client's liability for litigation costs could be the basis for discipline because its absence was deceptive. The Court rejected any claim that the lawyer had a First Amendment right to not include the information. The Court said, "Because the extension of First Amendment protection to commercial speech is justified principally by the value to consumers of the information such speech provides, appellant's constitutionally protected interest in *not* providing any particular factual information in his advertising is minimal."

In Peel v. Attorney Registration and Disciplinary Commission of Illinois, 496 U.S. 91 (1990), the Court invalidated a state law that limited the ability of attorneys to advertise specialties. A lawyer had been disciplined for advertising himself as a trial specialist, as this was prohibited by a state bar rule. The plurality opinion by Justice Stevens emphasized that the statement on the attorney's letterhead about the receipt of a certificate of specialty was accurate and truthful. The plurality said that the state failed to meet its "heavy burden of justifying a categorical prohibition against the dissemination of accurate factual information to the public."

The Court followed the same reasoning in Ibanez v. Florida Department of Business and Professional Regulation, 512 U.S. 136 (1994). An attorney was disciplined for an advertisement listing that she also is a certified public accountant and a certified financial planner. The Court held that the information was accurate and thus could not be the basis for discipline.

Thus, the case law in this area is clear: Truthful, nondeceptive advertisements by lawyers are protected by the First Amendment. The Court refuses to allow the government to regulate attorney advertisements to improve the public's image of the bar, or out of fear that advertisements will foment litigation, or out of unsupported fear that the public will not understand their content and will thereby be deceived.

6. *Reputation, Privacy, Publicity, and the First Amendment: Torts and the First Amendment*

Many tort claims seek to impose liability for speech. For example, the tort of defamation — libel and slander — is liability for speech injurious to reputation. Similarly, the "false light" tort is liability for speech that creates a false impression about a person and his or her activities. Speech can be the basis for a claim for the intentional infliction of emotional distress. Also, speech that discloses private information or exploits the commercial likeness of another may be the basis for a tort for invasion of privacy or for violating the right of publicity. This section considers in turn each of these torts and the First Amendment limits upon them.

In New York Times v. Sullivan, below, the Supreme Court expressly held that the First Amendment limits the ability of the government to impose tort liability. Although tort litigation is generally between two private parties, there is state action in that it is the state's law, whether statutory or common law, that allows recovery. Besides, it is a branch of the government, the judiciary, that is imposing liability for the speech. The Court in New York Times v. Sullivan declared that "[w]hat a State may not constitutionally bring about by means of a criminal statute is likewise beyond the reach of its civil law. . . . The fear of damage awards . . . may be markedly more inhibiting than the fear of prosecution under a criminal statute."

a. Defamation

In New York Times v. Sullivan, the Court held that recovery for defamation — libel and slander — is limited by the First Amendment. The challenge for the Court in this area is to balance the need to protect reputation, the obvious central concern of defamation law, with the desire to safeguard expression, which can be chilled and limited by tort liability.

Since *New York Times*, the Supreme Court has attempted to strike this balance by developing a complex series of rules that depend on the identity of the plaintiff and the nature of the subject matter. As described below, there are four major categories of situations: where the plaintiff is a public official or running for public office; where the plaintiff is a public figure; where the plaintiff is a private figure and the matter is of public concern; and where the plaintiff is a private figure and the matter is not of public concern.

i. *Public Officials as Defamation Plaintiffs*

If the plaintiff is a public official or running for public office, the plaintiff can recover for defamation only by proving with clear and convincing evidence the falsity of the statements and actual malice. Actual malice means that the defendant knew that the statement was false or acted with reckless disregard of the truth. New York Times Co. v. Sullivan is the seminal case in this area.

NEW YORK TIMES CO. v. SULLIVAN

376 U.S. 254 (1964)

Justice BRENNAN delivered the opinion of the Court.

We are required in this case to determine for the first time the extent to which the constitutional protections for speech and press limit a State's power to award damages in a libel action brought by a public official against critics of his official conduct.

Respondent L. B. Sullivan is one of the three elected Commissioners of the City of Montgomery, Alabama. He testified that he was "Commissioner of Public Affairs and the duties are supervision of the Police Department, Fire Department, Department of Cemetery and Department of Scales." He brought this civil libel action against the four individual petitioners, who are Negroes and Alabama clergymen, and against petitioner the New York Times Company, a New York corporation which publishes the New York Times, a daily newspaper. A jury in the Circuit Court of Montgomery County awarded him damages of $500,000, the full amount claimed, against all the petitioners, and the Supreme Court of Alabama affirmed.

Respondent's complaint alleged that he had been libeled by statements in a full-page advertisement that was carried in the New York Times on March 29, 1960. Entitled "Heed Their Rising Voices," the advertisement began by stating that "As the whole world knows by now, thousands of Southern Negro students are engaged in widespread non-violent demonstrations in positive affirmation of the right to live in human dignity as guaranteed by the U.S. Constitution and the Bill of Rights." It went on to charge that "in their efforts to uphold these guarantees, they are being met by an unprecedented wave of terror by those who would deny and negate that document which the whole world looks upon as setting the pattern for modern freedom." Succeeding paragraphs purported to illustrate the "wave of terror" by describing certain alleged events. The text concluded with an appeal for funds.

Of the 10 paragraphs of text in the advertisement, the third and a portion of the sixth were the basis of respondent's claim of libel. They read as follows: Third paragraph: "In Montgomery, Alabama, after students sang 'My Country, 'Tis of Thee' on the State Capitol steps, their leaders were expelled from school, and truckloads of police armed with shotguns and tear-gas ringed the Alabama State College Campus. When the entire student body protested to state authorities by refusing to re-register, their dining hall was padlocked in an attempt to starve them into submission." Sixth paragraph: "Again and again the Southern violators have answered Dr. King's peaceful protests with intimidation and violence. They have bombed his home almost killing his wife and child. They have assaulted his person. They have arrested him seven times — for 'speeding,' 'loitering' and similar 'offenses.'"

It is uncontroverted that some of the statements contained in the two paragraphs were not accurate descriptions of events which occurred in Montgomery. Although Negro students staged a demonstration on the State Capitol steps, they sang the National Anthem and not "My Country, 'Tis of Thee." Although nine students were expelled by the State Board of Education, this was not for leading the demonstration at the Capitol, but for demanding service at a lunch counter in the Montgomery County Courthouse on another day. Not the entire student body, but most of it, had protested the expulsion, not by refusing to register, but by boycotting classes on a single day; virtually all the students did register for the ensuing semester. The campus dining hall was not padlocked on any occasion, and the only students who may have been barred from eating there were the few who had neither signed a preregistration application nor requested temporary meal tickets. Although the police were deployed near the campus in large numbers on three occasions, they did not at any time "ring" the campus, and they were not called to the campus in connection with the demonstration on the State Capitol steps, as the third paragraph implied. Dr. King had not been arrested seven times, but only four; and although he claimed to have been assaulted some years earlier in connection with his arrest for loitering outside a courtroom, one of the officers who made the arrest denied that there was such an assault.

The trial judge submitted the case to the jury under instructions that the statements in the advertisement were "libelous per se" and were not privileged, so that petitioners might be held liable if the jury found that they had published the advertisement and that the statements were made "of and concerning" respondent. The jury was instructed that, because the statements were libelous per se, "the law . . . implies legal injury from the bare fact of publication itself," "falsity and malice are presumed," "general damages need not be alleged or proved but are presumed," and "punitive damages may be awarded by the jury even though the amount of actual damages is neither found nor shown." In affirming the judgment, the Supreme Court of Alabama sustained the trial judge's rulings and instructions in all respects.

We hold that the rule of law applied by the Alabama courts is constitutionally deficient for failure to provide the safeguards for freedom of speech and of the press that are required by the First and Fourteenth Amendments in a libel action brought by a public official against critics of his official conduct. We further hold that under the proper safeguards the evidence presented in this case is constitutionally insufficient to support the judgment for respondent.

The question before us is whether this rule of liability, as applied to an action brought by a public official against critics of his official conduct, abridges the freedom of speech and of the press that is guaranteed by the First and Fourteenth Amendments. The general proposition that freedom of expression upon public questions is secured by the First Amendment has long been settled by our decisions. The constitutional safeguard, we have said, "was fashioned to assure unfettered interchange of ideas for the bringing about of political and social changes desired by the people." Thus we consider this case against the background of a profound national commitment to the principle that debate on public issues should be uninhibited, robust, and wide-open, and that it may well include vehement, caustic, and sometimes unpleasantly sharp attacks on government and public officials. The present advertisement, as an expression of grievance and protest on one of the major public issues of our time, would seem clearly to qualify for the constitutional protection. The question is whether it forfeits that protection by the falsity of some of its factual statements and by its alleged defamation of respondent.

Authoritative interpretations of the First Amendment guarantees have consistently refused to recognize an exception for any test of truth—whether administered by judges, juries, or administrative officials—and especially one that puts the burden of proving truth on the speaker. The constitutional protection does not turn upon "the truth, popularity, or social utility of the ideas and beliefs which are offered." As Madison said, "Some degree of abuse is inseparable from the proper use of every thing; and in no instance is this more true than in that of the press." [E]rroneous statement is inevitable in free debate, and that it must be protected if the freedoms of expression are to have the "breathing space" that they "need . . . to survive." Criticism of their official conduct does not lose its constitutional protection merely because it is effective criticism and hence diminishes their official reputations.

If neither factual error nor defamatory content suffices to remove the constitutional shield from criticism of official conduct, the combination of the two elements is no less inadequate. This is the lesson to be drawn from the great controversy over the Sedition Act of 1798, which first crystallized a national awareness of the central meaning of the First Amendment. That statute made it a crime, punishable by a $5,000 fine and five years in prison, "if any person shall write, print, utter or publish . . . any false, scandalous and malicious writing or writings against the government of the United States, or either house of the Congress . . . , or the President . . . , with intent to defame . . . or to bring them, or either of them, into contempt or disrepute; or to excite against them, or either or any of them, the hatred of the good people of the United States." The Act allowed the defendant the defense of truth, and provided that the jury were to be judges both of the law and the facts. Despite these qualifications, the Act was vigorously condemned as unconstitutional in an attack joined in by Jefferson and Madison.

Although the Sedition Act was never tested in this Court, the attack upon its validity has carried the day in the court of history. Fines levied in its prosecution were repaid by Act of Congress on the ground that it was unconstitutional. Calhoun, reporting to the Senate on February 4, 1836, assumed that its invalidity was a matter "which no one now doubts." Jefferson, as President, pardoned those who had been convicted and sentenced under the Act and remitted their fines.

The state rule of law is not saved by its allowance of the defense of truth. A rule compelling the critic of official conduct to guarantee the truth of all his factual assertions—and to do so on pain of libel judgments virtually unlimited in amount—leads to a comparable "self-censorship." Allowance of the defense of truth, with the burden of proving it on the defendant, does not mean that only false speech will be deterred. Under such a rule, would-be critics of official conduct may be deterred from voicing their criticism, even though it is believed to be true and even though it is in fact true, because of doubt whether it can be proved in court or fear of the expense of having to do so. They tend to make only statements which "steer far wider of the unlawful zone." The rule thus dampens the vigor and limits the variety of public debate. It is inconsistent with the First and Fourteenth Amendments.

The constitutional guarantees require, we think, a federal rule that prohibits a public official from recovering damages for a defamatory falsehood relating to his official conduct unless he proves that the statement was made with "actual malice"—that is, with knowledge that it was false or with reckless disregard of whether it was false or not.

Applying these standards, we consider that the proof presented to show actual malice lacks the convincing clarity which the constitutional standard demands, and hence that it would not constitutionally sustain the judgment for respondent under the proper rule of law. The case of the individual petitioners requires little discussion. Even assuming that they could constitutionally be found to have authorized the use of their names on the advertisement, there was no evidence whatever that they were aware of any erroneous statements or were in any way reckless in that regard. The judgment against them is thus without constitutional support. As to the Times, we similarly conclude that the facts do not support a finding of actual malice.

Under *New York Times*, there are four requirements in this category: (1) The plaintiff must be a public official or running for public office; (2) the plaintiff must prove his or her case with clear and convincing evidence; (3) the plaintiff must prove falsity of the statement; and (4) the plaintiff must prove actual malice — that the defendant knew the statement was false or acted with reckless disregard of the truth. Each is discussed in turn.

First, the plaintiff must be a public official or running for public office for the case to fit within this category. Although *New York Times* involved a plaintiff who was a government official, the Court extended this to those running for public office.[159] For example, the Court has said that *New York Times* applies to "anything which might touch on an official's fitness for office."[160]

The Supreme Court never has held that all government employees are to be considered public officials under *New York Times*, but nor has the Court formulated a precise test for determining which public employees are public officials. In *New York Times*, in a footnote, the Court said that it had "no occasion here to determine how far down into the lower ranks of government employees the 'public official' designation would extend."

The primary Supreme Court decision clarifying who is a "public official" was Rosenblatt v. Baer, 383 U.S. 75 (1966). In *Rosenblatt*, the plaintiff was a fired supervisor of a county-owned ski resort. The Court said that "public officials" are "at the very least . . . those among the hierarchy of government employees who have, or appear to the public to have, substantial responsibility for or control over the conduct of governmental affairs." The Court said that public officials are those who hold positions of such "apparent importance that the public has an independent interest in the qualifications and performance of the person who holds it."

It is certainly possible to imagine government employees who do not fit this definition. Yet, for any government employee, even at the lowest rung of the hierarchy, it is possible that issues could arise concerning their performance on the job and thus be of importance to the public. Thus, no clear definition exists as to who is a public official for purposes of the *New York Times* test.[161]

Second, the plaintiff in this category must prove his or her case with clear and convincing evidence; preponderance of the evidence, the usual standard in civil cases, is not enough. In New York Times v. Sullivan, the Court said that the

---

159. *See* Monitor Patriot Co. v. Roy, 401 U.S. 265 (1971) (defamation of a candidate for public office covered by the *New York Times* standard).

160. Garrison v. Louisiana, 379 U.S. 64, 77 (1964).

161. Generally, lower courts have found government officials of all sorts to be public officials. *See, e.g.*, Crane v. Arizona Republic, 972 F.2d 1511 (9th Cir. 1992) (prosecutor is a public official); Stevens v. Tillman, 855 F.2d 394 (7th Cir. 1988) (elementary school principal is a public official); McKinley v. Baden, 777 F.2d 1017 (5th Cir. 1985) (police officer is a public official).

plaintiff had the burden of proving falsity of the statement and actual malice with "convincing clarity." The Court subsequently equated this standard with a requirement for "clear and convincing evidence."[162]

To ensure that this requirement is met, appellate courts are required to conduct an independent review to ensure that there is clear and convincing evidence that defendant uttered false statements with actual malice. In Bose Corp. v. Consumers Union of United States, Inc., 466 U.S. 485 (1984), the Court said that under the "actual malice" standard of *New York Times*, "[a]ppellate judges in such a case must exercise independent judgment and determine whether the record establishes actual malice with convincing clarity."

Third, the plaintiff must prove the falsity of the statements. At the very least, this means that the defendant in this category cannot be forced to prove truth of the statements. A difficult issue arises here in drawing a distinction between expression of opinion and false statements of fact. In Gertz v. Welch, below, the Court observed that "[u]nder the First Amendment there is no such thing as a false idea. However pernicious an opinion may seem, we depend for its correction not on the conscience of judges and juries but on the competition of other ideas. But there is no constitutional value in false statements of fact."

However, separating opinion from fact is inherently difficult. Is calling a public official "stupid" a statement of fact, because IQ can be measured, or of opinion? Is calling a person a "crook" fact or opinion? The Supreme Court addressed the fact/opinion distinction in Milkovich v. Lorain Journal Co., 497 U.S. 1 (1990). Michael Milkovich was the wrestling coach at a public high school and prevailed in a lawsuit overturning sanctions that had been imposed on him and the school because of an altercation that occurred at a match. A column in a local newspaper said that the school had prevailed with "the big lie," implying that Milkovich had lied under oath.

The Court in *Milkovich* said that the language in *Gertz*, quoted above, was not "intended to create a wholesale defamation exemption for anything that might be labeled 'opinion.'" However, the Court also made it clear that only false statements of fact could be the basis for defamation liability. Chief Justice Rehnquist, writing for the Court, said "a statement on matters of public concern must be provable as false before there can be liability under state defamation law. . . . [A] statement of opinion relating to matters of public concern which does not contain a provably false factual connotation will receive full constitutional protection."

Therefore, the focus is not on whether a statement is opinion, but whether it contains, directly or by clear implication, factual statements. False statements of fact are a prerequisite for defamation liability. Yet, this still leaves unresolved the key question: When are statements "rhetorical hyperbole" protected by the First Amendment and when are they factual statements that can be the basis for defamation actions? All *Milkovich* holds is that labeling a statement as opinion is not sufficient, by itself, to preclude defamation liability.

Fourth and finally in this category, there must be proof of actual malice; that is, the defendant knew that the statement was false or acted with reckless disregard of the truth. The Court has explained that this requires proof that the statements were made with "the high degree of awareness of their probable

---

162. Gertz v. Welch, 418 U.S. 323, 331-332 (1974).

falsity."[163] The Court has said that actual malice is a "term of art denoting deliberate or reckless falsification."[164]

In St. Amant v. Thompson, 390 U.S. 727 (1968), the Supreme Court said that actual malice requires that the defendant "in fact entertained serious doubts as to the truth of his publication." In *St. Amant*, a candidate for public office made highly critical statements about the conduct of the sheriff. The Supreme Court overturned defamation liability and emphasized that actual malice could not be proven by showing that the defendant failed to verify the accuracy of facts or even that the defendant acted recklessly. Actual malice requires that the defendant have a subjective awareness of probable falsity; there must be proof that the defendant had serious doubts about the accuracy of the statements before making them.

The Court has held that even the intentional fabrication of quotations is not enough, by itself, to prove actual malice if the statements were substantially accurate in reflecting what was said. Masson v. New Yorker, 501 U.S. 496 (1991), concerned a defamation suit brought by Jeffrey Masson, a psychoanalyst, against Janet Malcolm, a writer for *New Yorker* magazine. Although the case did not involve a public official, it did involve a plaintiff who was a public figure, and as described below, this meant that the *New York Times* test applied. The article was based on more than 40 hours of interviews and contained many quotations; none of the quotes, however, was an actual statement made during the interviews.

The Court, in an opinion by Justice Kennedy, said that quotation marks do not convey that what is within them is a word-for-word transcription of an actual statement. Rather, the Court said that a quotation implies a substantially accurate representation of a person's statement. The issue, therefore, is not whether the quotation published is a verbatim reflection of what was said, but whether it is substantially accurate. Falsely attributing a statement to a person can be the basis for defamation liability, but there has to be proof that the statements substantially changed the meaning of what was said.

Thus, actual malice is a difficult standard to meet. It is a subjective standard that requires that the plaintiff prove that defendant knew that the statement was false or acted with serious doubts about its truth.

ii. Public Figures as Plaintiffs

The Supreme Court has held that the same rules apply in defamation suits brought by public figures. The Court initially applied the *New York Times* test to public figures in Curtis Publishing Co. v. Butts, 388 U.S. 130 (1967), and Associated Press v. Walker, 388 U.S. 130 (1967). Both of these cases involved plaintiffs who did not hold public office, but were very prominent in their communities. *Butts* involved game-fixing allegations directed at a football coach at a state university who actually was employed by a private corporation that administered the school's athletic programs. *Walker* involved a former army general accused of leading an angry crowd that obstructed federal marshals who were facilitating

---

163. Garrison v. Louisiana, 379 U.S. 64, 74 (1964).
164. Masson v. New Yorker Magazine, Inc., 501 U.S. 496, 499 (1991).

the enrollment of James Meredith, an African-American student, and the desegregation of the University of Mississippi.

There was not a majority opinion in either case. Justice Harlan, writing for the plurality, said that although the plaintiffs were not public officials, "the public interest in the circulation of the materials here involved, and the publisher's interest in circulating them, is not less than that involved in *New York Times*." While the plurality would have allowed public figures to recover with less than proof of actual malice, a majority of the Justices rejected that view. Chief Justice Warren said that "differentiation between 'public figures' and 'public officials' and adoption of separate standards of proof for each have no basis in law, logic, or First Amendment policy." Justices Brennan and White agreed that actual malice should be required when public figures are defamation plaintiffs, and Justices Black and Douglas took an absolutist position that would have barred any defamation liability. Thus, five justices said that public figures cannot recover for defamation with less than proof of actual malice.

In Rosenbloom v. Metromedia, Inc., 403 U.S. 29 (1971), a plurality of the Court went even further and held that the actual malice test should be used as long as the matter is of public concern, even if the plaintiff was neither a public official nor a public figure. Justice Brennan, writing for the plurality, said that "[i]f a matter is a subject of public or general interest, it cannot suddenly become less so merely because a private individual is involved, or because in some sense the individual did not 'voluntarily' choose to become involved."

However, a majority of the Court never accepted this view, and in fact, it was expressly rejected in Gertz v. Welch, where the Court expressly drew the distinction between public and private figures. *Gertz* remains a key case in establishing that the *New York Times* standard applies to defamation suits by public figures and also with regard to the standard for recovery by private figures.

GERTZ v. WELCH
_____
418 U.S. 323 (1974)

Justice POWELL delivered the opinion of the Court.

This Court has struggled for nearly a decade to define the proper accommodation between the law of defamation and the freedoms of speech and press protected by the First Amendment. We granted certiorari to reconsider the extent of a publisher's constitutional privilege against liability for defamation of a private citizen.

I

In 1968 a Chicago policeman named Nuccio shot and killed a youth named Nelson. The state authorities prosecuted Nuccio for the homicide and ultimately obtained a conviction for murder in the second degree. The Nelson family retained petitioner Elmer Gertz, a reputable attorney, to represent them in civil litigation against Nuccio.

Respondent publishes American Opinion, a monthly outlet for the views of the John Birch Society. Early in the 1960s the magazine began to warn of a nationwide conspiracy to discredit local law enforcement agencies and create in their stead a national police force capable of supporting a Communist dictatorship. In March 1969 respondent published the resulting article under the title "FRAME-UP: Richard Nuccio and the War on Police." The article purports to demonstrate that the testimony against Nuccio at his criminal trial was false and that his prosecution was part of the Communist campaign against the police.

In his capacity as counsel for the Nelson family in the civil litigation, petitioner attended the coroner's inquest into the boy's death and initiated actions for damages, but he neither discussed Officer Nuccio with the press nor played any part in the criminal proceeding. Notwithstanding petitioner's remote connection with the prosecution of Nuccio, respondent's magazine portrayed him as an architect of the "frame-up." The article stated that petitioner had been an official of the "Marxist League for Industrial Democracy, originally known as the Intercollegiate Socialist Society, which has advocated the violent seizure of our government." It labeled Gertz a "Leninist" and a "Communist-fronter." It also stated that Gertz had been an officer of the National Lawyers Guild, described as a Communist organization that "probably did more than any other outfit to plan the Communist attack on the Chicago police during the 1968 Democratic Convention."

These statements contained serious inaccuracies. The implication that petitioner had a criminal record was false. Petitioner had been a member and officer of the National Lawyers Guild some 15 years earlier, but there was no evidence that he or that organization had taken any part in planning the 1968 demonstrations in Chicago. There was also no basis for the charge that petitioner was a "Leninist" or a "Communist-fronter." And he had never been a member of the "Marxist League for Industrial Democracy" or the "Intercollegiate Socialist Society." The managing editor of American Opinion made no effort to verify or substantiate the charges against petitioner.

II

The principal issue in this case is whether a newspaper or broadcaster that publishes defamatory falsehoods about an individual who is neither a public official nor a public figure may claim a constitutional privilege against liability for the injury inflicted by those statements.

We begin with the common ground. Under the First Amendment there is no such thing as a false idea. However pernicious an opinion may seem, we depend for its correction not on the conscience of judges and juries but on the competition of other ideas. But there is no constitutional value in false statements of fact. Neither the intentional lie nor the careless error materially advances society's interest in "uninhibited, robust, and wide-open" debate on public issues. They belong to that category of utterances which "are no essential part of any exposition of ideas, and are of such slight social value as a step to truth that any benefit that may be derived from them is clearly outweighed by the social interest in order and morality."

Although the erroneous statement of fact is not worthy of constitutional protection, it is nevertheless inevitable in free debate. And punishment of error runs the risk of inducing a cautious and restrictive exercise of the constitutionally guaranteed freedoms of speech and press. Our decisions recognize that a rule of strict liability that compels a publisher or broadcaster to guarantee the accuracy of his factual assertions may lead to intolerable self-censorship.

The need to avoid self-censorship by the news media is, however, not the only societal value at issue. If it were, this Court would have embraced long ago the view that publishers and broadcasters enjoy an unconditional and indefeasible immunity from liability for defamation. The legitimate state interest underlying the law of libel is the compensation of individuals for the harm inflicted on them by defamatory falsehood. We would not lightly require the State to abandon this purpose. [T]he individual's right to the protection of his own good name "reflects no more than our basic concept of the essential dignity and worth of every human being — a concept at the root of any decent system of ordered liberty."

Some tension necessarily exists between the need for a vigorous and uninhibited press and the legitimate interest in redressing wrongful injury. In our continuing effort to define the proper accommodation between these competing concerns, we have been especially anxious to assure to the freedoms of speech and press that "breathing space" essential to their fruitful exercise. To that end this Court has extended a measure of strategic protection to defamatory falsehood.

The *New York Times* standard defines the level of constitutional protection appropriate to the context of defamation of a public person. Those who, by reason of the notoriety of their achievements or the vigor and success with which they seek the public's attention, are properly classed as public figures and those who hold governmental office may recover for injury to reputation only on clear and convincing proof that the defamatory falsehood was made with knowledge of its falsity or with reckless disregard for the truth.

This standard administers an extremely powerful antidote to the inducement to media self-censorship of the common-law rule of strict liability for libel and slander. And it exacts a correspondingly high price from the victims of defamatory falsehood. Plainly many deserving plaintiffs, including some intentionally subjected to injury, will be unable to surmount the barrier of the *New York Times* test. Despite this substantial abridgment of the state law right to compensation for wrongful hurt to one's reputation, the Court has concluded that the protection of the *New York Times* privilege should be available to publishers and broadcasters of defamatory falsehood concerning public officials and public figures.

[W]e have no difficulty in distinguishing among defamation plaintiffs. The first remedy of any victim of defamation is self-help — using available opportunities to contradict the lie or correct the error and thereby to minimize its adverse impact on reputation. Public officials and public figures usually enjoy significantly greater access to the channels of effective communication and hence have a more realistic opportunity to counteract false statements than private individuals normally enjoy. Private individuals are therefore more vulnerable to injury, and the state interest in protecting them is correspondingly greater.

More important than the likelihood that private individuals will lack effective opportunities for rebuttal, there is a compelling normative consideration underlying the distinction between public and private defamation plaintiffs. An individual who decides to seek governmental office must accept certain necessary consequences of that involvement in public affairs. He runs the risk of closer public scrutiny than might otherwise be the case.

Those classed as public figures stand in a similar position. Hypothetically, it may be possible for someone to become a public figure through no purposeful action of his own, but the instances of truly involuntary public figures must be exceedingly rare. For the most part those who attain this status have assumed roles of especial prominence in the affairs of society. Some occupy positions of such persuasive power and influence that they are deemed public figures for all purposes. More commonly, those classed as public figures have thrust themselves to the forefront of particular public controversies in order to influence the resolution of the issues involved. In either event, they invite attention and comment.

Even if the foregoing generalities do not obtain in every instance, the communications media are entitled to act on the assumption that public officials and public figures have voluntarily exposed themselves to increased risk of injury from defamatory falsehood concerning them. No such assumption is justified with respect to a private individual. He has not accepted public office or assumed an "influential role in ordering society." He has relinquished no part of his interest in the protection of his own good name, and consequently he has a more compelling call on the courts for redress of injury inflicted by defamatory falsehood. Thus, private individuals are not only more vulnerable to injury than public officials and public figures; they are also more deserving of recovery.

For these reasons we conclude that the States should retain substantial latitude in their efforts to enforce a legal remedy for defamatory falsehood injurious to the reputation of a private individual. The extension of the *New York Times* test proposed by the *Rosenbloom* plurality would abridge this legitimate state interest to a degree that we find unacceptable. And it would occasion the additional difficulty of forcing state and federal judges to decide on an ad hoc basis which publications address issues of "general or public interest" and which do not. We doubt the wisdom of committing this task to the conscience of judges.

We hold that, so long as they do not impose liability without fault, the States may define for themselves the appropriate standard of liability for a publisher or broadcaster of defamatory falsehood injurious to a private individual. This approach provides a more equitable boundary between the competing concerns involved here. It recognizes the strength of the legitimate state interest in compensating private individuals for wrongful injury to reputation, yet shields the press and broadcast media from the rigors of strict liability for defamation.

Our accommodation of the competing values at stake in defamation suits by private individuals allows the States to impose liability on the publisher or broadcaster of defamatory falsehood on a less demanding showing than that required by *New York Times*. But this countervailing state interest extends no further than compensation for actual injury. For the reasons stated below, we hold that the States may not permit recovery of presumed or punitive damages, at least when liability is not based on a showing of knowledge of falsity or reckless disregard for the truth.

Respondent's characterization of petitioner as a public figure raises a different question. Petitioner has long been active in community and professional affairs. He has served as an officer of local civic groups and of various professional organizations, and he has published several books and articles on legal subjects. Although petitioner was consequently well known in some circles, he had achieved no general fame or notoriety in the community.

None of the prospective jurors called at the trial had ever heard of petitioner prior to this litigation, and respondent offered no proof that this response was atypical of the local population. In this context it is plain that petitioner was not a public figure. He plainly did not thrust himself into the vortex of this public issue, nor did he engage the public's attention in an attempt to influence its outcome.

Justice BRENNAN, dissenting.

I cannot agree, however, that free and robust debate — so essential to the proper functioning of our system of government — is permitted adequate "breathing space," when, as the Court holds, the States may impose all but strict liability for defamation if the defamed party is a private person and "the substance of the defamatory statement" makes substantial danger to reputation apparent." I adhere to my view expressed in Rosenbloom v. Metromedia, Inc., that we strike the proper accommodation between avoidance of media self-censorship and protection of individual reputations only when we require States to apply the New York Times Co. v. Sullivan (1964), knowing-or-reckless-falsity standard in civil libel actions concerning media reports of the involvement of private individuals in events of public or general interest.

Justice WHITE, dissenting.

For some 200 years — from the very founding of the Nation — the law of defamation and right of the ordinary citizen to recover for false publication injurious to his reputation have been almost exclusively the business of state courts and legislatures. Under typical state defamation law, the defamed private citizen had to prove only a false publication that would subject him to hatred, contempt, or ridicule. Given such publication, general damage to reputation was presumed, while punitive damages required proof of additional facts. The law governing the defamation of private citizens remained untouched by the First Amendment because until relatively recently, the consistent view of the Court was that libelous words constitute a class of speech wholly unprotected by the First Amendment, subject only to limited exceptions carved out since 1964.

But now, using that Amendment as the chosen instrument, the Court, in a few printed pages, has federalized major aspects of libel law by declaring unconstitutional in important respects the prevailing defamation law in all or most of the 50 States. That result is accomplished by requiring the plaintiff in each and every defamation action to prove not only the defendant's culpability beyond his act of publishing defamatory material but also actual damage to reputation resulting from the publication. Moreover, punitive damages may not be recovered by showing malice in the traditional sense of ill will; knowing falsehood or reckless disregard of the truth will not be required.

I assume these sweeping changes will be popular with the press, but this is not the road to salvation for a court of law. As I see it, there are wholly insufficient grounds for scuttling the libel laws of the States in such wholesale fashion, to say nothing of deprecating the reputation interest of ordinary citizens and rendering them powerless to protect themselves. I do not suggest that the decision is illegitimate or beyond the bounds of judicial review, but it is an ill-considered exercise of the power entrusted to this Court, particularly when the Court has not had the benefit of briefs and argument addressed to most of the major issues which the Court now decides. I respectfully dissent.

No subsequent Supreme Court case has formulated a precise definition of who is a public figure. The later cases all indicate, however, that in order to be a public figure a person must voluntarily, affirmatively thrust himself or herself into the limelight. For example, in Time v. Firestone, 424 U.S. 448 (1976), the Court held that Mary Alice Firestone, the wife of a member of the wealthy Firestone family, was a private figure. Firestone was prominent in social circles and often in the newspapers; she even hired a clipping service to keep track of publicity about her. *Time* magazine wrongly reported that her divorce was granted on grounds of adultery and was sued for defamation. The Court held that Firestone was a private figure because she "did not assume any role of especial prominence in the affairs of society, other than perhaps Palm Beach society, and she did not thrust herself to the forefront of any particular public controversy in order to influence the resolution of the issues involved in it."

Similarly, in Wolston v. Reader's Digest Association, 443 U.S. 157 (1979), the Court found that an individual was a private figure even though he had been convicted of contempt for his refusal to appear before a grand jury investigating espionage by the Soviet Union. An article, published 16 years after the conviction, described Wolston as a Soviet agent. The Supreme Court said that Wolston was neither a general public figure nor even a limited public figure even though there had been extensive publicity about his refusal to testify before the grand jury. The Court said that the plaintiff had not "engaged the attention of the public in an attempt to influence the resolution of the issues involved." As in Time v. Firestone, the Court stressed that the plaintiff did not "voluntarily thrust" or "inject . . . himself into the forefront."

In Hutchinson v. Proxmire, 443 U.S. 111 (1979), the Court ruled that an individual who received a "Golden Fleece of the Month Award" from Senator William Proxmire was a private figure. Ronald Hutchinson received substantial federal funding for research into aggressive monkey behavior. Senator Proxmire ridiculed the grant with his "Golden Fleece Award." The Court said that Hutchinson could sue Senator Proxmire for defamation because the statement was not protected by the "Speech or Debate Clause." The Court also ruled that Hutchinson was a private figure because he "at no time assumed any role of public prominence." The Court said that "[n]either his applications for federal grants nor his publications in professional journals can be said to have invited that degree of public attention and comment on his receipt of federal grants essential to meet the public figure level."

These cases do not offer a clear definition of who is a public figure. They do indicate a restrictive view of who is a public figure, as they require that a person take voluntary, affirmative steps to thrust himself or herself into the limelight. At the very least, they make it difficult for anyone to be found an involuntary public figure.

iii. Private Figures, Matters of Public Concern

In Gertz v. Welch, above, the Court articulated the standard for defamation recovery by private figures. If the plaintiff is a private figure and the matter is of public concern, a state can allow a plaintiff to recover compensatory damages if there is proof that the statements were false and of negligence by the defendant. However, proof of presumed or punitive damages requires proof of actual malice. "Private figures" are obviously plaintiffs who are not public officials or public figures. "Matter of public concern" has never been defined, but generally it refers to issues in which the public has a legitimate interest.

In Dun & Bradstreet, Inc. v. Greenmoss Builders, Inc., the Supreme Court said that a distinction must be drawn in suits against private figures between speech that involves matters of public concern and that which does not.

DUN & BRADSTREET, INC. v. GREENMOSS BUILDERS, INC.

472 U.S. 749 (1985)

Justice POWELL announced the judgment of the Court.

In Gertz v. Robert Welch, Inc. (1974), we held that the First Amendment restricted the damages that a private individual could obtain from a publisher for a libel that involved a matter of public concern. More specifically, we held that in these circumstances the First Amendment prohibited awards of presumed and punitive damages for false and defamatory statements unless the plaintiff shows "actual malice," that is, knowledge of falsity or reckless disregard for the truth. The question presented in this case is whether this rule of *Gertz* applies when the false and defamatory statements do not involve matters of public concern.

I

Petitioner Dun & Bradstreet, a credit reporting agency, provides subscribers with financial and related information about businesses. All the information is confidential; under the terms of the subscription agreement the subscribers may not reveal it to anyone else. On July 26, 1976, petitioner sent a report to five subscribers indicating that respondent, a construction contractor, had filed a voluntary petition for bankruptcy. This report was false and grossly misrepresented respondent's assets and liabilities. That same day, while discussing the possibility of future financing with its bank, respondent's president was told that the bank had received the defamatory report. He immediately called petitioner's regional office, explained the error, and asked for a correction. In addition, he requested the names of the firms that had received the false report in order to assure them that the company was solvent. Petitioner promised to look into the matter but refused to divulge the names of those who had received the report.

After determining that its report was indeed false, petitioner issued a corrective notice on or about August 3, 1976, to the five subscribers who had received the initial report. The notice stated that one of respondent's former employees, not respondent itself, had filed for bankruptcy and that respondent "continued in business as usual."

After trial, the jury returned a verdict in favor of respondent and awarded $50,000 in compensatory or presumed damages and $300,000 in punitive damages.

II

We have never considered whether the *Gertz* balance obtains when the defamatory statements involve no issue of public concern. To make this determination, we must employ the approach approved in *Gertz* and balance the State's interest in compensating private individuals for injury to their reputation against the First Amendment interest in protecting this type of expression. This state interest is identical to the one weighed in *Gertz*.

The First Amendment interest, on the other hand, is less important than the one weighed in *Gertz*. We have long recognized that not all speech is of equal First Amendment importance. It is speech on "matters of public concern" that is "at the heart of the First Amendment's protection." In contrast, speech on matters of purely private concern is of less First Amendment concern.

In *Gertz*, we found that the state interest in awarding presumed and punitive damages was not "substantial" in view of their effect on speech at the core of First Amendment concern. This interest, however, is "substantial" relative to the incidental effect these remedies may have on speech of significantly less constitutional interest. The rationale of the common-law rules has been the experience and judgment of history that "proof of actual damage will be impossible in a great many cases where, from the character of the defamatory words and the circumstances of publication, it is all but certain that serious harm has resulted in fact." As a result, courts for centuries have allowed juries to presume that some damage occurred from many defamatory utterances and publications. This rule furthers the state interest in providing remedies for defamation by ensuring that those remedies are effective. In light of the reduced constitutional value of speech involving no matters of public concern, we hold that the state interest adequately supports awards of presumed and punitive damages — even absent a showing of "actual malice."

The only remaining issue is whether petitioner's credit report involved a matter of public concern. [P]etitioner's credit report concerns no public issue. It was speech solely in the individual interest of the speaker and its specific business audience. Moreover, since the credit report was made available to only five subscribers, who, under the terms of the subscription agreement, could not disseminate it further, it cannot be said that the report involves any "strong interest in the free flow of commercial information."

We conclude that permitting recovery of presumed and punitive damages in defamation cases absent a showing of "actual malice" does not violate the First Amendment when the defamatory statements do not involve matters of public concern.

Justice BRENNAN, with whom Justice MARSHALL, Justice BLACKMUN, and Justice STEVENS join, dissenting.

The question presented here is narrow. Neither the parties nor the courts below have suggested that respondent Greenmoss Builders should be required to show actual malice to obtain a judgment and actual compensatory damages. Nor do the parties question the requirement of *Gertz* that respondent must show fault to obtain a judgment and actual damages. The only question presented is whether a jury award of presumed and punitive damages based on less than a showing of actual malice is constitutionally permissible. *Gertz* provides a forthright negative answer.

Even accepting the notion that a distinction can and should be drawn between matters of public concern and matters of purely private concern, however, the analys[is] presented by Justice Powell fail[s] on [its] own terms. [He] propose[s] an impoverished definition of "matters of public concern" that is irreconcilable with First Amendment principles. The credit reporting at issue here surely involves a subject matter of sufficient public concern to require the comprehensive protections of *Gertz*. Were this speech appropriately characterized as a matter of only private concern, moreover, the elimination of the *Gertz* restrictions on presumed and punitive damages would still violate basic First Amendment requirements.

Thus, it is established that if the plaintiff is a private figure and the matter is of public concern, a state can allow recovery of compensatory damages if the plaintiff proves falsity of the statement and negligence by the speaker. But presumed or punitive damages require proof of actual malice. The Court has expressly ruled that the plaintiff must bear the burden of proof in this category, just as when the plaintiff is a public official or a public figure. In Philadelphia Newspapers, Inc. v. Hepps, 475 U.S. 767 (1986), the Court held that the First Amendment requires that the plaintiff prove falsity of the statement. A newspaper ran a series of articles linking the owner of a chain of stores to organized crime. The state court had ruled that the defendant had the burden of proving truth of the statements because the plaintiff was neither a public official nor a public figure. The Court said that "[t]o ensure that true speech on matters of public concern is not deterred, we hold that the common-law presumption that defamatory speech is false cannot stand when a plaintiff seeks damages against a media defendant for speech of public concern."

Philadelphia Newspapers, Inc. v. Hepps articulates a rule for when there is a media defendant. The Court has never elaborated on the distinction between media and nonmedia defendants. On the one hand, the media obviously play a crucial role in informing the public and can claim special protection as the "press" under the First Amendment. On the other hand, defining the "media" is likely to be extremely difficult; nonmedia individuals and entities also can play an important role in informing the public. As discussed below, the Court generally has been reluctant to provide any special rights for the institutional press. In Dun & Bradstreet v. Greenmoss Builders, five justices — though in separate opinions — expressly rejected any distinction between media and nonmedia defendants for purposes of defamation liability. Justice White, in an opinion concurring in the judgment, said that he agreed with the four dissenters "that the First Amendment gives no more protection to the press in defamation suits than it does to others exercising their freedom of speech."

iv. Private Figures, Matters Not of Public Concern

There only has been one case, Dun & Bradstreet v. Greenmoss Builders, above, that thus far has considered the category of private figures and speech that is not of public concern. In *Dun & Bradstreet*, the Court ruled that in this category presumed and punitive damages do not require proof of actual malice.

The Supreme Court never has considered what should be the standard of liability or even who must bear the burden of proof when a private figure is the plaintiff and the matter is not of public concern. The Court only has ruled that in this category presumed or punitive damages do not require proof of actual malice.

v. Conclusion

This law of defamation has been criticized on many grounds. The categories at times seem arbitrary and ill-defined; a great deal depends on whether a plaintiff is classified as a public figure or whether a matter is deemed a matter of public concern. Some argue that the Court's approach has provided too much protection for speech and not enough for reputation.[165] Others argue that the approach does not provide enough protection for speech and that the current law chills speech and, indeed, "perpetuates a system of censorship by libel lawyers — a system in which the relevant question is not whether a story is libelous, but whether the subject is likely to sue, and if so, how much it will cost to defend."[166]

But the current approach also can be defended as drawing sensible compromises between the important values of speech and reputation. The categories obviously try to strike a balance: They give more weight to speech that is relevant to the political process and of public interest; they give more weight to reputation when a person has not voluntarily entered the public domain and when the matter is not of public concern.

b. Intentional Infliction of Emotional Distress

In Hustler Magazine v. Falwell, the Supreme Court held that recovery for the tort of intentional infliction of emotional distress had to meet the *New York Times* standards. In Snyder v. Phelps, the Court went further and held that there cannot be liability for intentional infliction of emotional distress for speech that is otherwise protected by the First Amendment.

---

165. *See* Dun & Bradstreet v. Greenmoss Builders, 472 U.S. at 771 (White, J., concurring in the judgment).

166. David Anderson, *Libel and Press Self-Censorship*, 53 Tex. L. Rev. 422, 424-425 (1975); *see also* Rodney A. Smolla, *Let the Author Beware: The Rejuvenation of the American Law of Libel*, 132 U. Pa. L. Rev. 1 (1983).

HUSTLER MAGAZINE v. FALWELL

485 U.S. 46 (1988)

Chief Justice REHNQUIST delivered the opinion of the Court.

Petitioner Hustler Magazine, Inc., is a magazine of nationwide circulation. Respondent Jerry Falwell, a nationally known minister who has been active as a commentator on politics and public affairs, sued petitioner and its publisher, petitioner Larry Flynt, to recover damages for invasion of privacy, libel, and intentional infliction of emotional distress.

The inside front cover of the November 1983 issue of Hustler Magazine featured a "parody" of an advertisement for Campari Liqueur that contained the name and picture of respondent and was entitled "Jerry Falwell talks about his first time." This parody was modeled after actual Campari ads that included interviews with various celebrities about their "first times." Although it was apparent by the end of each interview that this meant the first time they sampled Campari, the ads clearly played on the sexual double entendre of the general subject of "first times." Copying the form and layout of these Campari ads, Hustler's editors chose respondent as the featured celebrity and drafted an alleged "interview" with him in which he states that his "first time" was during a drunken incestuous rendezvous with his mother in an outhouse. The Hustler parody portrays respondent and his mother as drunk and immoral, and suggests that respondent is a hypocrite who preaches only when he is drunk. In small print at the bottom of the page, the ad contains the disclaimer, "ad parody — not to be taken seriously." The magazine's table of contents also lists the ad as "Fiction; Ad and Personality Parody."

Soon after the November issue of Hustler became available to the public, respondent brought this diversity action. Respondent stated in his complaint that publication of the ad parody in Hustler entitled him to recover damages for libel, invasion of privacy, and intentional infliction of emotional distress. The case proceeded to trial. The jury then found against respondent on the libel claim, specifically finding that the ad parody could not "reasonably be understood as describing actual facts about [respondent] or actual events in which [he] participated." The jury ruled for respondent on the intentional infliction of emotional distress claim, however, and stated that he should be awarded $100,000 in compensatory damages, as well as $50,000 each in punitive damages from petitioners.

This case presents us with a novel question involving First Amendment limitations upon a State's authority to protect its citizens from the intentional infliction of emotional distress. We must decide whether a public figure may recover damages for emotional harm caused by the publication of an ad parody offensive to him, and doubtless gross and repugnant in the eyes of most. Respondent would have us find that a State's interest in protecting public figures from emotional distress is sufficient to deny First Amendment protection to speech that is patently offensive and is intended to inflict emotional injury, even when that speech could not reasonably have been interpreted as stating actual facts about the public figure involved. This we decline to do.

One of the prerogatives of American citizenship is the right to criticize public men and measures. Such criticism, inevitably, will not always be reasoned or moderate; public figures as well as public officials will be subject to "vehement, caustic, and sometimes unpleasantly sharp attacks."

Generally speaking the law does not regard the intent to inflict emotional distress as one which should receive much solicitude, and it is quite understandable that most if not all jurisdictions have chosen to make it civilly culpable where the conduct in question is sufficiently "outrageous." But in the world of debate about public affairs, many things done with motives that are less than admirable are protected by the First Amendment.

Thus while such a bad motive may be deemed controlling for purposes of tort liability in other areas of the law, we think the First Amendment prohibits such a result in the area of public debate about public figures. Were we to hold otherwise, there can be little doubt that political cartoonists and satirists would be subjected to damages awards without any showing that their work falsely defamed its subject. Webster's defines a caricature as "the deliberately distorted picturing or imitating of a person, literary style, etc. by exaggerating features or mannerisms for satirical effect." The appeal of the political cartoon or caricature is often based on exploitation of unfortunate physical traits or politically embarrassing events—an exploitation often calculated to injure the feelings of the subject of the portrayal. The art of the cartoonist is often not reasoned or evenhanded, but slashing and one-sided. One cartoonist expressed the nature of the art in these words: "The political cartoon is a weapon of attack, of scorn and ridicule and satire; it is least effective when it tries to pat some politician on the back. It is usually as welcome as a bee sting and is always controversial in some quarters." Long, The Political Cartoon: Journalism's Strongest Weapon, The Quill 56, 57 (Nov. 1962).

Respondent contends, however, that the caricature in question here was so "outrageous" as to distinguish it from more traditional political cartoons. There is no doubt that the caricature of respondent and his mother published in Hustler is at best a distant cousin of the political cartoons described above, and a rather poor relation at that. If it were possible by laying down a principled standard to separate the one from the other, public discourse would probably suffer little or no harm. But we doubt that there is any such standard, and we are quite sure that the pejorative description "outrageous" does not supply one. "Outrageousness" in the area of political and social discourse has an inherent subjectiveness about it which would allow a jury to impose liability on the basis of the jurors' tastes or views, or perhaps on the basis of their dislike of a particular expression. An "outrageousness" standard thus runs afoul of our longstanding refusal to allow damages to be awarded because the speech in question may have an adverse emotional impact on the audience.

We conclude that public figures and public officials may not recover for the tort of intentional infliction of emotional distress by reason of publications such as the one here at issue without showing in addition that the publication contains a false statement of fact which was made with "actual malice," i.e., with knowledge that the statement was false or with reckless disregard as to whether or not it was true. This is not merely a "blind application" of the *New York Times* standard, it reflects our considered judgment that such a standard is necessary to give adequate "breathing space" to the freedoms protected by the First Amendment.

SNYDER v. PHELPS

131 S. Ct. 1207 (2011)

Chief Justice ROBERTS delivered the opinion of the Court.

A jury held members of the Westboro Baptist Church liable for millions of dollars in damages for picketing near a soldier's funeral service. The picket signs reflected the church's view that the United States is overly tolerant of sin and that God kills American soldiers as punishment. The question presented is whether the First Amendment shields the church members from tort liability for their speech in this case.

I

Fred Phelps founded the Westboro Baptist Church in Topeka, Kansas, in 1955. The church's congregation believes that God hates and punishes the United States for its tolerance of homosexuality, particularly in America's military. The church frequently communicates its views by picketing, often at military funerals. In the more than 20 years that the members of Westboro Baptist have publicized their message, they have picketed nearly 600 funerals.

Marine Lance Corporal Matthew Snyder was killed in Iraq in the line of duty. Lance Corporal Snyder's father selected the Catholic church in the Snyders' hometown of Westminster, Maryland, as the site for his son's funeral. Local newspapers provided notice of the time and location of the service.

Phelps became aware of Matthew Snyder's funeral and decided to travel to Maryland with six other Westboro Baptist parishioners (two of his daughters and four of his grandchildren) to picket. On the day of the memorial service, the Westboro congregation members picketed on public land adjacent to public streets near the Maryland State House, the United States Naval Academy, and Matthew Snyder's funeral. The Westboro picketers carried signs that were largely the same at all three locations. They stated, for instance: "God Hates the USA/ Thank God for 9/11," "America is Doomed," "Don't Pray for the USA," "Thank God for IEDs," "Thank God for Dead Soldiers," "Pope in Hell," "Priests Rape Boys," "God Hates Fags," "You're Going to Hell," and "God Hates You."

The church had notified the authorities in advance of its intent to picket at the time of the funeral, and the picketers complied with police instructions in staging their demonstration. The picketing took place within a 10-by-25-foot plot of public land adjacent to a public street, behind a temporary fence. That plot was approximately 1,000 feet from the church where the funeral was held. Several buildings separated the picket site from the church. The Westboro picketers displayed their signs for about 30 minutes before the funeral began and sang hymns and recited Bible verses. None of the picketers entered church property or went to the cemetery. They did not yell or use profanity, and there was no violence associated with the picketing.

The funeral procession passed within 200 to 300 feet of the picket site. Although Snyder testified that he could see the tops of the picket signs as he drove to the funeral, he did not see what was written on the signs until later that night, while watching a news broadcast covering the event.

Snyder filed suit against Phelps, Phelps's daughters, and the Westboro Baptist Church (collectively Westboro or the church). A jury found for Snyder on the intentional infliction of emotional distress, intrusion upon seclusion, and civil conspiracy claims, and held Westboro liable for $2.9 million in compensatory damages and $8 million in punitive damages. The District Court remitted the punitive damages award to $2.1 million, but left the jury verdict otherwise intact.

Whether the First Amendment prohibits holding Westboro liable for its speech in this case turns largely on whether that speech is of public or private concern, as determined by all the circumstances of the case. "[S]peech on 'matters of public concern' . . . is 'at the heart of the First Amendment's protection.'" The First Amendment reflects "a profound national commitment to the principle that debate on public issues should be uninhibited, robust, and wide-open." New York Times Co. v. Sullivan (1964). That is because "speech concerning public affairs is more than self-expression; it is the essence of self-government." Accordingly, "speech on public issues occupies the highest rung of the hierarchy of First Amendment values, and is entitled to special protection."

"[N]ot all speech is of equal First Amendment importance," however, and where matters of purely private significance are at issue, First Amendment protections are often less rigorous. That is because restricting speech on purely private matters does not implicate the same constitutional concerns as limiting speech on matters of public interest: "[T]here is no threat to the free and robust debate of public issues; there is no potential interference with a meaningful dialogue of ideas"; and the "threat of liability" does not pose the risk of "a reaction of self-censorship" on matters of public import.

We noted a short time ago, in considering whether public employee speech addressed a matter of public concern, that "the boundaries of the public concern test are not well defined." Although that remains true today, we have articulated some guiding principles, principles that accord broad protection to speech to ensure that courts themselves do not become inadvertent censors.

Speech deals with matters of public concern when it can "be fairly considered as relating to any matter of political, social, or other concern to the community," or when it "is a subject of legitimate news interest; that is, a subject of general interest and of value and concern to the public."

The "content" of Westboro's signs plainly relates to broad issues of interest to society at large, rather than matters of "purely private concern." The placards read "God Hates the USA/Thank God for 9/11," "America is Doomed," "Don't Pray for the USA," "Thank God for IEDs," "Fag Troops," "Semper Fi Fags," "God Hates Fags," "Maryland Taliban," "Fags Doom Nations," "Not Blessed Just Cursed," "Thank God for Dead Soldiers," "Pope in Hell," "Priests Rape Boys," "You're Going to Hell," and "God Hates You." While these messages may fall short of refined social or political commentary, the issues they highlight — the political and moral conduct of the United States and its citizens, the fate of our Nation, homosexuality in the military, and scandals involving the Catholic clergy — are matters of public import. The signs certainly convey Westboro's position on those issues, in a manner designed to reach as broad a public audience as possible.

Apart from the content of Westboro's signs, Snyder contends that the "context" of the speech — its connection with his son's funeral — makes the speech a matter of private rather than public concern. The fact that Westboro spoke in connection with a funeral, however, cannot by itself transform the nature of

Westboro's speech. Westboro's signs, displayed on public land next to a public street, reflect the fact that the church finds much to condemn in modern society. Its speech is "fairly characterized as constituting speech on a matter of public concern" and the funeral setting does not alter that conclusion.

Westboro's choice to convey its views in conjunction with Matthew Snyder's funeral made the expression of those views particularly hurtful to many, especially to Matthew's father. The record makes clear that the applicable legal term — "emotional distress" — fails to capture fully the anguish Westboro's choice added to Mr. Snyder's already incalculable grief. But Westboro conducted its picketing peacefully on matters of public concern at a public place adjacent to a public street. Such space occupies a "special position in terms of First Amendment protection." "[W]e have repeatedly referred to public streets as the archetype of a traditional public forum," noting that "'[t]ime out of mind' public streets and sidewalks have been used for public assembly and debate."

That said, "[e]ven protected speech is not equally permissible in all places and at all times." Westboro's choice of where and when to conduct its picketing is not beyond the Government's regulatory reach — it is "subject to reasonable time, place, or manner restrictions" that are consistent with the standards announced in this Court's precedents. Maryland now has a law imposing restrictions on funeral picketing. To the extent these laws are content neutral, they raise very different questions from the tort verdict at issue in this case. Maryland's law, however, was not in effect at the time of the events at issue here, so we have no occasion to consider how it might apply to facts such as those before us, or whether it or other similar regulations are constitutional.

Simply put, the church members had the right to be where they were. Westboro alerted local authorities to its funeral protest and fully complied with police guidance on where the picketing could be staged. The picketing was conducted under police supervision some 1,000 feet from the church, out of the sight of those at the church. The protest was not unruly; there was no shouting, profanity, or violence.

The record confirms that any distress occasioned by Westboro's picketing turned on the content and viewpoint of the message conveyed, rather than any interference with the funeral itself. A group of parishioners standing at the very spot where Westboro stood, holding signs that said "God Bless America" and "God Loves You," would not have been subjected to liability. It was what Westboro said that exposed it to tort damages.

Given that Westboro's speech was at a public place on a matter of public concern, that speech is entitled to "special protection" under the First Amendment. Such speech cannot be restricted simply because it is upsetting or arouses contempt. "If there is a bedrock principle underlying the First Amendment, it is that the government may not prohibit the expression of an idea simply because society finds the idea itself offensive or disagreeable." Indeed, "the point of all speech protection . . . is to shield just those choices of content that in someone's eyes are misguided, or even hurtful."

The jury here was instructed that it could hold Westboro liable for intentional infliction of emotional distress based on a finding that Westboro's picketing was "outrageous." "Outrageousness," however, is a highly malleable standard with "an inherent subjectiveness about it which would allow a jury to impose liability on the basis of the jurors' tastes or views, or perhaps on the basis of their dislike of a particular expression." In a case such as this, a jury is "unlikely to be neutral with respect to the content of [the] speech," posing "a real danger of becoming an instrument for the suppression of . . . 'vehement, caustic, and sometimes unpleasan[t]'" expression. Such a risk is unacceptable; "in public debate [we] must tolerate insulting, and even outrageous, speech in order to provide adequate 'breathing space' to the freedoms protected by the First Amendment." What Westboro said, in the whole context of how and where it chose to say it, is entitled to "special protection" under the First Amendment, and that protection cannot be overcome by a jury finding that the picketing was outrageous.

For all these reasons, the jury verdict imposing tort liability on Westboro for intentional infliction of emotional distress must be set aside.

Our holding today is narrow. We are required in First Amendment cases to carefully review the record, and the reach of our opinion here is limited by the particular facts before us. Westboro believes that America is morally flawed; many Americans might feel the same about Westboro. Westboro's funeral picketing is certainly hurtful and its contribution to public discourse may be negligible. But Westboro addressed matters of public import on public property, in a peaceful manner, in full compliance with the guidance of local officials. The speech was indeed planned to coincide with Matthew Snyder's funeral, but did not itself disrupt that funeral, and Westboro's choice to conduct its picketing at that time and place did not alter the nature of its speech.

Speech is powerful. It can stir people to action, move them to tears of both joy and sorrow, and — as it did here — inflict great pain. On the facts before us, we cannot react to that pain by punishing the speaker. As a Nation we have chosen a different course — to protect even hurtful speech on public issues to ensure that we do not stifle public debate. That choice requires that we shield Westboro from tort liability for its picketing in this case.

Justice Alito, dissenting.

Our profound national commitment to free and open debate is not a license for the vicious verbal assault that occurred in this case.

Petitioner Albert Snyder is not a public figure. He is simply a parent whose son, Marine Lance Corporal Matthew Snyder, was killed in Iraq. Mr. Snyder wanted what is surely the right of any parent who experiences such an incalculable loss: to bury his son in peace. But respondents, members of the Westboro Baptist Church, deprived him of that elementary right. They first issued a press release and thus turned Matthew's funeral into a tumultuous media event. They then appeared at the church, approached as closely as they could without trespassing, and launched a malevolent verbal attack on Matthew and his family at a time of acute emotional vulnerability. As a result, Albert Snyder suffered severe and lasting emotional injury. The Court now holds that the First Amendment protected respondents' right to brutalize Mr. Snyder. I cannot agree.

Respondents and other members of their church have strong opinions on certain moral, religious, and political issues, and the First Amendment ensures that they have almost limitless opportunities to express their views. They may write and distribute books, articles, and other texts; they may create and disseminate video and audio recordings; they may circulate petitions; they may speak to individuals and groups in public forums and in any private venue that wishes to accommodate them; they may picket peacefully in countless locations; they may appear on television and speak on the radio; they may post messages on the Internet and send out e-mails. And they may express their views in terms that are "uninhibited," "vehement," and "caustic."

It does not follow, however, that they may intentionally inflict severe emotional injury on private persons at a time of intense emotional sensitivity by launching vicious verbal attacks that make no contribution to public debate. To protect against such injury, "most if not all jurisdictions" permit recovery in tort for the intentional infliction of emotional distress (or IIED). This is a very narrow tort with requirements that "are rigorous, and difficult to satisfy."

This Court has recognized that words may "by their very utterance inflict injury" and that the First Amendment does not shield utterances that form "no essential part of any exposition of ideas, and are of such slight social value as a step to truth that any benefit that may be derived from them is clearly outweighed by the social interest in order and morality." When grave injury is intentionally inflicted by means of an attack like the one at issue here, the First Amendment should not interfere with recovery.

In this case, respondents brutally attacked Matthew Snyder, and this attack, which was almost certain to inflict injury, was central to respondents' well-practiced strategy for attracting public attention.

On the morning of Matthew Snyder's funeral, respondents could have chosen to stage their protest at countless locations. They could have picketed the United States Capitol, the White House, the Supreme Court, the Pentagon, or any of the more than 5,600 military recruiting stations in this country. They could have returned to the Maryland State House or the United States Naval Academy, where they had been the day before. They could have selected any public road where pedestrians are allowed. They could have staged their protest in a public park. They could have chosen any Catholic church where no funeral was taking place. But of course, a small group picketing at any of these locations would have probably gone unnoticed.

One final comment about the opinion of the Court is in order. The Court suggests that the wounds inflicted by vicious verbal assaults at funerals will be prevented or at least mitigated in the future by new laws that restrict picketing within a specified distance of a funeral. It is apparent, however, that the enactment of these laws is no substitute for the protection provided by the established IIED tort; according to the Court, the verbal attacks that severely wounded petitioner in this case complied with the new Maryland law regulating funeral picketing. And there is absolutely nothing to suggest that Congress and the state legislatures, in enacting these laws, intended them to displace the protection provided by the well-established IIED tort.

Respondents' outrageous conduct caused petitioner great injury, and the Court now compounds that injury by depriving petitioner of a judgment that acknowledges the wrong he suffered.

In order to have a society in which public issues can be openly and vigorously debated, it is not necessary to allow the brutalization of innocent victims like petitioner. I therefore respectfully dissent.

c. Public Disclosure of Private Facts

The tort of public disclosure of private facts, a tort for invasion of privacy, exists if there is publication of nonpublic information that is not "of legitimate concern to the public" and that the reasonable person would find offensive to have published.[167] Unlike defamation where the information is false and a retraction conceivably could lessen the harm to reputation, the tort of public disclosure of private facts involves the publication of true information, and the harm is done once publication occurs.

The Supreme Court has held that the First Amendment prevents liability for public disclosure of private facts if the information was lawfully obtained from public records and is truthfully reported.

COX BROADCASTING CORP. v. COHN

420 U.S. 469 (1975)

Justice WHITE delivered the opinion of the Court.

The issue before us in this case is whether, consistently with the First and Fourteenth Amendments, a State may extend a cause of action for damages for invasion of privacy caused by the publication of the name of a deceased rape victim which was publicly revealed in connection with the prosecution of the crime.

I

In August 1971, appellee's 17-year-old daughter was the victim of a rape and did not survive the incident. Six youths were soon indicted for murder and rape. Although there was substantial press coverage of the crime and of subsequent developments, the identity of the victim was not disclosed pending trial, perhaps because of Ga. Code Ann. §26-9901 which makes it a misdemeanor to publish or broadcast the name or identity of a rape victim. In April 1972, some eight months later, the six defendants appeared in court. Five pleaded guilty to rape or attempted rape, the charge of murder having been dropped. The guilty pleas were accepted by the court, and the trial of the defendant pleading not guilty was set for a later date.

In the course of the proceedings that day, appellant Wasell, a reporter covering the incident for his employer, learned the name of the victim from an examination of the indictments which were made available for his inspection in the courtroom. That the name of the victim appears in the indictments and that the indictments were public records available for inspection are not disputed. Later that day, Wassell broadcast over the facilities of station WSB-TV, a television station owned by appellant Cox Broadcasting Corp., a news report concerning the court proceedings. The report named the victim of the crime and was repeated the following day. In May 1972, appellee brought an action for money damages against appellants, relying on §26-9901 and claiming that his right to privacy had been invaded by the television broadcasts giving the name of his deceased daughter.

---

167. Restatement (Second) of Torts §652(D) (1977).

II

Georgia stoutly defends both §26-9901 and the State's common-law privacy action challenged here. Its claims are not without force, for powerful arguments can be made, and have been made, that however it may be ultimately defined, there is a zone of privacy surrounding every individual, a zone within which the State may protect him from intrusion by the press, with all its attendant publicity. Indeed, the central thesis of the root article by Warren and Brandeis, The Right to Privacy, 4 Harv. L. Rev. 193 (1890), was that the press was overstepping its prerogatives by publishing essentially private information and that there should be a remedy for the alleged abuses.

In this sphere of collision between claims of privacy and those of the free press, the interests on both sides are plainly rooted in the traditions and significant concerns of our society. Rather than address the broader question whether truthful publications may ever be subjected to civil or criminal liability consistently with the First and Fourteenth Amendments, or to put it another way, whether the State may ever define and protect an area of privacy free from unwanted publicity in the press, it is appropriate to focus on the narrower interface between press and privacy that this case presents, namely, whether the State may impose sanctions on the accurate publication of the name of a rape victim obtained from public records — more specifically, from judicial records which are maintained in connection with a public prosecution and which themselves are open to public inspection. We are convinced that the State may not do so. In the first place, in a society in which each individual has but limited time and resources with which to observe at first hand the operations of his government, he relies necessarily upon the press to bring to him in convenient form the facts of those operations. Great responsibility is accordingly placed upon the news media to report fully and accurately the proceedings of government, and official records and documents open to the public are the basic data of governmental operations. Without the information provided by the press most of us and many of our representatives would be unable to vote intelligently or to register opinions on the administration of government generally. With respect to judicial proceedings in particular, the function of the press serves to guarantee the fairness of trials and to bring to bear the beneficial effects of public scrutiny upon the administration of justice.

The special protected nature of accurate reports of judicial proceedings has repeatedly been recognized. This Court, in an opinion written by Justice Douglas, has said: "A trial is a public event. What transpires in the court room is public property. There is no special perquisite of the judiciary which enables it, as distinguished from other institutions of democratic government, to suppress, edit, or censor events which transpire in proceedings before it."

By placing the information in the public domain on official court records, the State must be presumed to have concluded that the public interest was thereby being served. Public records by their very nature are of interest to those concerned with the administration of government, and a public benefit is performed by the reporting of the true contents of the records by the media. The freedom of the press to publish that information appears to us to be of critical importance to our type of government in which the citizenry is the final judge of the proper conduct of public business. In preserving that form of government the First and Fourteenth Amendments command nothing less than that the

States may not impose sanctions on the publication of truthful information contained in official court records open to public inspection.

We are reluctant to embark on a course that would make public records generally available to the media but forbid their publication if offensive to the sensibilities of the supposed reasonable man. Such a rule would make it very difficult for the media to inform citizens about the public business and yet stay within the law. The rule would invite timidity and self-censorship and very likely lead to the suppression of many items that would otherwise be published and that should be made available to the public. At the very least, the First and Fourteenth Amendments will not allow exposing the press to liability for truthfully publishing information released to the public in official court records. Once true information is disclosed in public court documents open to public inspection, the press cannot be sanctioned for publishing it. In this instance as in others reliance must rest upon the judgment of those who decide what to publish or broadcast.

In Florida Star v. B.J.F., 491 U.S. 524 (1989), the Court applied *Cox Broadcasting* and *Smith* to hold that there cannot be liability for invasion of privacy when there is the truthful reporting of information lawfully obtained from public records, at least unless there is a state interest of the highest order justifying liability. A newspaper reporter obtained a rape victim's name from publicly released police records. The name was published in the newspaper, even though Florida law prohibited the publication of the name of a victim of a sexual offense. A jury awarded the victim $75,000 in compensatory damages and $25,000 in punitive damages.

The Supreme Court overturned this liability. The Court began by refusing to hold that "truthful publication may never be punished consistent with the First Amendment." But the Court said that liability for the truthful reporting of information lawfully obtained from public records and concerning a matter of public significance would be allowed only if there was an interest of the highest order. The Court explained that the rape victim's name was lawfully obtained from police records and was truthfully communicated. The Court rejected the claim that protecting the privacy of rape victims was a sufficient interest to justify liability. The Court emphasized the failings of the Florida law that created liability for publishing a rape victim's identity, including that it allowed liability where the information was released by the government, that it permitted liability without any scienter requirement, and that it applied only to actions of the mass media.

The Court stressed that its "holding . . . is limited." The Court said, "We do not hold that truthful publication is automatically constitutionally protected, or that there is no zone of personal privacy within which the State may protect the individual from intrusion by the press, or even that a State may never punish publication of the name of a victim of a sexual offense. We hold only that where a newspaper publishes truthful information which it has lawfully obtained, punishment may lawfully be imposed, if at all, only when narrowly tailored to a state interest of the highest order."

The principle protecting publication of material gained from public records has been followed in other cases as well. In Landmark Communications, Inc. v. Virginia, 435 U.S. 829 (1978), the Supreme Court held unconstitutional a state statute that created criminal liability for divulging or publishing truthful information regarding confidential proceedings of a judicial inquiry board. A newspaper was convicted for violating this statute for accurately reporting that the Virginia Judicial Inquiry and Review Commission was initiating an investigation of a state court judge. The Court said that "the publication Virginia seeks to punish under its statute lies near the core of the First Amendment, and the Commonwealth's interests advanced by the imposition of criminal sanctions are insufficient to justify the actual and potential encroachments on freedom of speech and of the press which follow therefrom." The Court said that the "Commonwealth has offered little more than assertion and conjecture to support its claim that without criminal sanctions the objectives of the statutory scheme would be seriously undermined."

INFORMATION FROM NONGOVERNMENT SOURCES

All of these cases involve the truthful publication of information gained from the government. In Bartnicki v. Vopper, 532 U.S. 514 (2001), the Court considered privacy claims when the information was illegally obtained from nongovernment sources.

Gloria Bartnicki worked for the Pennsylvania Educators' Association and helped local teachers' unions as they negotiated new contracts with school boards. She was in Wyoming, Pennsylvania, and while on her cellular telephone had a conversation with the president of the local teachers' union. They clearly thought that they were having a private conversation, but unknown to them, it was illegally intercepted and recorded. A tape of the phone conversation was given to the president of a local taxpayers' union that was opposing a pay raise for the teachers. The tape was given to a local radio talk show host, Fred Vopper, who played it twice on his program. Bartnicki sued the radio station and Vopper on various state and federal claims.

The Supreme Court, in a six-to-three decision, with Justice Stevens writing the majority, concluded that allowing liability in these circumstances would violate the First Amendment. Justice Stevens repeatedly emphasized the narrowness of the Court's holding. He said that the press was protected here because it did not participate in the illegal interception and recording and because the tape concerned a matter of public importance. Justice Stevens concluded, "In this case, privacy concerns give way when balanced against the interest in publishing matters of public importance. . . . One of the costs associated with participation in public affairs is an attendant loss of privacy. We think it clear that a stranger's illegal conduct does not suffice to remove the First Amendment shield from speech about a matter of public concern."

Justice Breyer wrote a concurring opinion, joined by Justice O'Connor, to stress the narrowness of the Court's holding. He said, "I join the Court's opinion because I agree with its 'narrow' holding, limited to the special circumstances present here: (1) the radio broadcasters acted lawfully (up to the time of final public disclosure); and (2) the information publicized involved a matter of unusual public concern, namely a threat of potential physical harm to others." The latter refers to a statement made during the conversation by the president of the local teachers' union that if the school board did not agree to their demands, they would have to go "blow away the porch" of the school board president's house. Although this clearly seems to be hyperbole in a private conversation, it was given great weight by Justice Breyer.

Chief Justice Rehnquist wrote a dissenting opinion, joined by Justices Scalia and Thomas, in which he stressed the chilling effect that the ruling would have on speech. He said that people would be less likely to use cell phones for communication once they learned that illegally intercepted calls could be broadcast as long as the media did not participate in the interception or recording.

Although both the majority and concurring opinions repeatedly emphasize the narrowness of the decision, it seems broader in its significance than they acknowledge. This is the first time that the Court has considered a privacy claim when the information comes from nongovernment sources. Also, it is the first time that the Court has dealt with information that was illegally obtained. Nonetheless, the Court found that freedom of speech and press outweigh the privacy interests involved.

d. Right of Publicity

The right of publicity protects the ability of a person to control the commercial value of his or her name, likeness, or performance. In Zacchini v. Scripps-Howard Broadcasting Co., 433 U.S. 562 (1977), the Court held that a state may allow liability for invasion of this right when a television station broadcast a tape of an entire performance without the performer's authorization. A television station broadcast a 15-second tape of a circus act featuring a "human cannonball" shot from a cannon into a net. The Supreme Court held that the broadcast station could be held liable because it broadcast the entire performance without authorization. The Court noted, however, that the plaintiff would have to prove damages and noted that it was quite possible that "respondent's news broadcast increased the value of petitioner's performance by stimulating the public's interest in seeing the act live." The *Zacchini* Court emphasized that "the State's interest is closely analogous to the goals of patent and copyright law, focusing on the right of the individual to reap the reward of his endeavors."

7. *Conduct That Communicates*

a. What Is Speech?

People often communicate through symbols other than words. Marches, picketing, armbands, and peace signs are just a few examples of obviously expressive conduct. To deny First Amendment protection for such forms of communication would mean a loss of some of the most effective means of communicating messages. Also, words are obviously symbols and there is no reason why the First Amendment should be limited to protecting just these symbols to the exclusion of all others.

Thus, the Supreme Court long has protected conduct that communicates under the First Amendment. For example, in Stromberg v. California, 283 U.S. 359 (1931), the Court declared unconstitutional a state law that prohibited the display of a "red flag." In West Virginia State Board of Education v. Barnette, above in section B, the Supreme Court invalidated a law that required that students salute the flag. The Court found that the state statute impermissibly compelled expression and emphasized that saluting, or not saluting, a flag is a form of speech. The Court explained that "[s]ymbolism is a primitive but effective way of communicating ideas. The use of an emblem or flag to symbolize some system, idea, institution, or personality, is a shortcut from mind to mind."

Conduct of all sorts can convey a message. Yet, if taken to the extreme, it would mean that virtually every criminal law would have to meet strict scrutiny because any criminal defendant could argue that his or her conduct was meant to communicate a message. Two interrelated questions thus emerge: When should conduct be analyzed under the First Amendment? And what should be the test for analyzing whether conduct that communicates is protected by the First Amendment?

b. When Is Conduct Communicative?

The Supreme Court observed that "[i]t is possible to find some kernel of expression in almost every activity a person undertakes — for example, walking down the street or meeting one's friends at a shopping mall — but such a kernel is not sufficient to bring the activity within the protection of the First Amendment."[168] In Spence v. Washington, 418 U.S. 405 (1974), the Court considered the issue of when conduct should be regarded as communicative.

An individual who taped a peace sign on an American flag after the killing of students at Kent State was convicted of violating a state law prohibiting flag desecration. The Supreme Court, in a *per curiam* opinion, reversed the conviction and found that the act was speech protected by the First Amendment. The Court said that "this was not an act of mindless nihilism. Rather, it was a pointed expression of anguish by appellant about the then-current domestic and foreign affairs of his government." The Court emphasized two factors in concluding that the conduct was communicative: "An intent to convey a particularized message was present, and in the surrounding circumstances the likelihood was great that the message would be understood by those who viewed it."

In other words, under this approach, conduct is analyzed as speech under the First Amendment if, first, there is the intent to convey a specific message, and second, there is a substantial likelihood that the message would be understood by those receiving it. Problems in applying this test are inevitable. How is it to be decided whether a person intended an act to communicate a message? Is it subjective, in which case a person always can claim such an intent in a hope to avoid punishment, or is it objective from the perspective of the reasonable listener, in which case it collapses the first part of the test into the second? How is it to be decided whether the message is sufficiently understood by the audience? Moreover, why should protection of speech depend on the sophistication and perceptiveness of the audience? For example, there may be great works of art whose message people fail to comprehend.

There are many examples of conduct that the Supreme Court has properly recognized as communicative.[169] For example, in Tinker v. Des Moines Inde-

---

168. City of Dallas v. Stanglin, 490 U.S. 19, 25 (1989).

169. *See also* Schacht v. United States, 398 U.S. 58 (1970), declaring unconstitutional a federal law that allowed wearing a military uniform only "if the portrayal does not tend to discredit" the armed forces. This law obviously was content-based: The symbol of the uniform could be used to express a pro-military view, but not an antimilitary sentiment.

pendent Community School District, 393 U.S. 503 (1969), presented below in section D, the Court held that wearing a black armband to protest the Vietnam War was speech protected by the First Amendment. The Court explained that "the wearing of an armband for the purpose of expressing certain views is the type of symbolic act that is within the First Amendment. . . . It [is] closely akin to 'pure speech.'" In terms of the *Spence* test, there is little doubt that the armband was worn to communicate a message and that those seeing it, in the context of the times, would understand it as a symbol of protest against the Vietnam War.

c. When May the Government Regulate Conduct That Communicates?

i. *The* O'Brien *Test*

Finding that conduct communicates does not mean that it is immune from government regulation. The question then arises as to whether the government has sufficient justification for regulating the conduct. In United States v. O'Brien, the Court formulated a test for evaluating the constitutional protection for conduct that communicates.

UNITED STATES v. O'BRIEN
391 U.S. 367 (1968)

Chief Justice WARREN delivered the opinion of the Court.

On the morning of March 31, 1966, David Paul O'Brien and three companions burned their Selective Service registration certificates on the steps of the South Boston Courthouse. A sizable crowd, including several agents of the Federal Bureau of Investigation, witnessed the event. For this act, O'Brien was indicted, tried, convicted, and sentenced in the United States District Court for the District of Massachusetts.

The indictment upon which he was tried charged that he "willfully and knowingly did mutilate, destroy, and change by burning . . . [his] Registration Certificate (Selective Service System Form No. 2); in violation of Title 50, App., United States Code, Section 462(b)." Section 462(b) is part of the Universal Military Training and Service Act of 1948. Section 462(b)(3) was amended by Congress in 1965, so that at the time O'Brien burned his certificate an offense was committed by any person, "who forges, alters, knowingly destroys, knowingly mutilates, or in any manner changes any such certificate. . . ." We hold that the 1965 Amendment is constitutional both as enacted and as applied.

I

When a male reaches the age of 18, he is required by the Universal Military Training and Service Act to register with a local draft board. He is assigned a Selective Service number, and within five days he is issued a registration certificate (SSS Form No. 2). Subsequently, and based on a questionnaire completed by the registrant, he is assigned a classification denoting his eligibility for induction, and "[a]s soon as practicable" thereafter he is issued a Notice of Classification (SSS Form No. 110).

Both the registration and classification certificates are small white cards, approximately 2 by 3 inches. The registration certificate specifies the name of the registrant, the date of registration, and the number and address of the local board with which he is registered. Also inscribed upon it are the date and place of the registrant's birth, his residence at registration, his physical description, his signature, and his Selective Service number.

The classification certificate shows the registrant's name, Selective Service number, signature, and eligibility classification. It specifies whether he was so classified by his local board, an appeal board, or the President. It contains the address of his local board and the date the certificate was mailed.

Both the registration and classification certificates bear notices that the registrant must notify his local board in writing of every change in address, physical condition, and occupational, marital, family, dependency, and military status, and of any other fact which might change his classification. Both also contain a notice that the registrant's Selective Service number should appear on all communications to his local board.

By the 1965 Amendment, Congress added to §12(b)(3) of the 1948 Act the provision here at issue, subjecting to criminal liability not only one who "forges, alters, or in any manner changes" but also one who "knowingly destroys [or] knowingly mutilates" a certificate. We note at the outset that the 1965 Amendment plainly does not abridge free speech on its face, and we do not understand O'Brien to argue otherwise. Amended §12(b)(3) on its face deals with conduct having no connection with speech. It prohibits the knowing destruction of certificates issued by the Selective Service System, and there is nothing necessarily expressive about such conduct.

O'Brien nonetheless argues that the 1965 Amendment is unconstitutional in its application to him, and is unconstitutional as enacted because what he calls the "purpose" of Congress was "to suppress freedom of speech." We consider these arguments separately.

II

O'Brien first argues that the 1965 Amendment is unconstitutional as applied to him because his act of burning his registration certificate was protected "symbolic speech" within the First Amendment. His argument is that the freedom of expression which the First Amendment guarantees includes all modes of "communication of ideas by conduct," and that his conduct is within this definition because he did it in "demonstration against the war and against the draft."

We cannot accept the view that an apparently limitless variety of conduct can be labeled "speech" whenever the person engaging in the conduct intends thereby to express an idea. However, even on the assumption that the alleged communicative element in O'Brien's conduct is sufficient to bring into play the First Amendment, it does not necessarily follow that the destruction of a registration certificate is constitutionally protected activity. This Court has held that when "speech" and "nonspeech" elements are combined in the same course of conduct, a sufficiently important governmental interest in regulating the non-speech element can justify incidental limitations on First Amendment freedoms.

[W]e think it clear that a government regulation is sufficiently justified if it is within the constitutional power of the Government; if it furthers an important or substantial governmental interest; if the governmental interest is unrelated to the suppression of free expression; and if the incidental restriction on alleged First Amendment freedoms is no greater than is essential to the furtherance of that interest. We find that the 1965 Amendment to the Universal Military Training and Service Act meets all of these requirements, and consequently that O'Brien can be constitutionally convicted for violating it.

The power of Congress to classify and conscript manpower for military service is "beyond question." The issuance of certificates indicating the registration and eligibility classification of individuals is a legitimate and substantial administrative aid in the functioning of this system. And legislation to insure the continuing availability of issued certificates serves a legitimate and substantial purpose in the system's administration.

Many of these purposes would be defeated by the certificates' destruction or mutilation. Among these are:

1. The registration certificate serves as proof that the individual described thereon has registered for the draft. The classification certificate shows the eligibility classification of a named but undescribed individual. Voluntarily displaying the two certificates is an easy and painless way for a young man to dispel a question as to whether he might be delinquent in his Selective Service obligations. Further, since both certificates are in the nature of "receipts" attesting that the registrant has done what the law requires, it is in the interest of the just and efficient administration of the system that they be continually available, in the event, for example, of a mix-up in the registrant's file. Additionally, in a time of national crisis, reasonable availability to each registrant of the two small cards assures a rapid and uncomplicated means for determining his fitness for immediate induction, no matter how distant in our mobile society he may be from his local board.

2. The information supplied on the certificates facilitates communication between registrants and local boards, simplifying the system and benefiting all concerned. To begin with, each certificate bears the address of the registrant's local board, an item unlikely to be committed to memory. Further, each card bears the registrant's Selective Service number, and a registrant who has his number readily available so that he can communicate it to his local board when he supplies or requests information can make simpler the board's task in locating his file. Finally, a registrant's inquiry, particularly through a local board other than his own, concerning his eligibility status is frequently answerable simply on the basis of his classification certificate; whereas, if the certificate were not reasonably available and the registrant were uncertain of his classification, the task of answering his questions would be considerably complicated.

3. Both certificates carry continual reminders that the registrant must notify his local board of any change of address, and other specified changes in his status. The smooth functioning of the system requires that local boards be continually aware of the status and whereabouts of registrants, and the destruction of certificates deprives the system of a potentially useful notice device.

4. The regulatory scheme involving Selective Service certificates includes clearly valid prohibitions against the alteration, forgery, or similar deceptive misuse of certificates. The destruction or mutilation of certificates obviously increases the difficulty of detecting and tracing abuses such as these. Further, a mutilated certificate might itself be used for deceptive purposes.

The many functions performed by Selective Service certificates establish beyond doubt that Congress has a legitimate and substantial interest in preventing their wanton and unrestrained destruction and assuring their continuing availability by punishing people who knowingly and wilfully destroy or mutilate them.

In conclusion, we find that because of the Government's substantial interest in assuring the continuing availability of issued Selective Service certificates, because amended §462(b) is an appropriately narrow means of protecting this interest and condemns only the independent noncommunicative impact of conduct within its reach, and because the noncommunicative impact of O'Brien's act of burning his registration certificate frustrated the Government's interest, a sufficient governmental interest has been shown to justify O'Brien's conviction.

III

O'Brien finally argues that the 1965 Amendment is unconstitutional as enacted because what he calls the "purpose" of Congress was "to suppress freedom of speech." We reject this argument because under settled principles the purpose of Congress, as O'Brien uses that term, is not a basis for declaring this legislation unconstitutional.

It is a familiar principle of constitutional law that this Court will not strike down an otherwise constitutional statute on the basis of an alleged illicit legislative motive. Inquiries into congressional motives or purposes are a hazardous matter. When the issue is simply the interpretation of legislation, the Court will look to statements by legislators for guidance as to the purpose of the legislature, because the benefit to sound decision-making in this circumstance is thought sufficient to risk the possibility of misreading Congress' purpose. It is entirely a different matter when we are asked to void a statute that is, under well-settled criteria, constitutional on its face, on the basis of what fewer than a handful of Congressmen said about it. What motivates one legislator to make a speech about a statute is not necessarily what motivates scores of others to enact it, and the stakes are sufficiently high for us to eschew guesswork. We decline to void essentially on the ground that it is unwise legislation which Congress had the undoubted power to enact and which could be reenacted in its exact form if the same or another legislator made a "wiser" speech about it.

ii. Flag Desecration

A major area where the Supreme Court has applied the *O'Brien* test is with regard to flag burning and flag desecration laws. After initial cases that protected flag desecration on narrow grounds, but without resolving the issue, the Court in

1989 and again in 1990 made it clear that flag burning is a constitutionally protected form of speech.

In Street v. New York, 394 U.S. 576 (1969), the Court overturned a conviction of an individual who burned a flag in anger after learning that James Meredith had been shot. The individual exclaimed, "We don't need no damn flag. [If] they let that happen to Meredith we don't need an American flag." The Court said that the law was unconstitutional because it allowed the individual to be punished solely for speaking contemptuously about the flag; indeed, it was impossible to tell in *Street* whether the punishment was for the speech about the flag or for its destruction.

In Smith v. Goguen, 415 U.S. 566 (1974), the Court declared unconstitutional on vagueness grounds a state law that made it a crime when any individual "publicly mutilates, tramples upon, defaces or treats contemptuously the flag of the United States." An individual was convicted for sewing to the seat of his pants a small cloth replica of the flag. The Court found that the state law was void on vagueness grounds because of the inherent ambiguity in deciding what is "contemptuous" treatment of the flag.

In Spence v. Washington, described above, the Court found that the First Amendment protected the right of an individual to tape a peace symbol to a flag. The Court emphasized that the protestor's "message was direct, likely to be understood, and within the contours of the First Amendment."

The Court went even further in 1989 in Texas v. Johnson.

TEXAS v. JOHNSON
491 U.S. 397 (1989)

Justice BRENNAN delivered the opinion of the Court.

After publicly burning an American flag as a means of political protest, Gregory Lee Johnson was convicted of desecrating a flag in violation of Texas law. This case presents the question whether his conviction is consistent with the First Amendment. We hold that it is not.

I

While the Republican National Convention was taking place in Dallas in 1984, respondent Johnson participated in a political demonstration dubbed the "Republican War Chest Tour." As explained in literature distributed by the demonstrators and in speeches made by them, the purpose of this event was to protest the policies of the Reagan administration and of certain Dallas-based corporations. The demonstrators marched through the Dallas streets, chanting political slogans and stopping at several corporate locations to stage "die-ins" intended to dramatize the consequences of nuclear war. On several occasions they spray-painted the walls of buildings and overturned potted plants, but Johnson himself took no part in such activities. He did, however, accept an American flag handed to him by a fellow protestor who had taken it from a flagpole outside one of the targeted buildings.

The demonstration ended in front of Dallas City Hall, where Johnson unfurled the American flag, doused it with kerosene, and set it on fire. While the flag burned, the protestors chanted: "America, the red, white, and blue, we spit on you." After the demonstrators dispersed, a witness to the flag burning collected the flag's remains and buried them in his backyard. No one was physically injured or threatened with injury, though several witnesses testified that they had been seriously offended by the flag burning.

Of the approximately 100 demonstrators, Johnson alone was charged with a crime. The only criminal offense with which he was charged was the desecration of a venerated object in violation of Tex. Penal Code Ann. §42.09(a)(3). After a trial, he was convicted, sentenced to one year in prison, and fined $2,000.

II

Johnson was convicted of flag desecration for burning the flag rather than for uttering insulting words. This fact somewhat complicates our consideration of his conviction under the First Amendment. We must first determine whether Johnson's burning of the flag constituted expressive conduct, permitting him to invoke the First Amendment in challenging his conviction. See, e.g., Spence v. Washington (1974). If his conduct was expressive, we next decide whether the State's regulation is related to the suppression of free expression. See, e.g., United States v. O'Brien (1968). If the State's regulation is not related to expression, then the less stringent standard we announced in United States v. O'Brien for regulations of noncommunicative conduct controls. If it is, then we are outside of *O'Brien*'s test, and we must ask whether this interest justifies Johnson's conviction under a more demanding standard.

In order to decide whether *O'Brien*'s test applies here, therefore, we must decide whether Texas has asserted an interest in support of Johnson's conviction that is unrelated to the suppression of expression. The State offers two separate interests to justify this conviction: preventing breaches of the peace and preserving the flag as a symbol of nationhood and national unity. We hold that the first interest is not implicated on this record and that the second is related to the suppression of expression.

A

Texas claims that its interest in preventing breaches of the peace justifies Johnson's conviction for flag desecration. However, no disturbance of the peace actually occurred or threatened to occur because of Johnson's burning of the flag. Although the State stresses the disruptive behavior of the protestors during their march toward City Hall, it admits that "no actual breach of the peace occurred at the time of the flagburning or in response to the flagburning." The State's emphasis on the protestors' disorderly actions prior to arriving at City Hall is not only somewhat surprising given that no charges were brought on the basis of this conduct, but it also fails to show that a disturbance of the peace was a likely reaction to Johnson's conduct.

B

The State also asserts an interest in preserving the flag as a symbol of nationhood and national unity. We are persuaded that this interest is related to expression in the case of Johnson's burning of the flag. The State, apparently, is concerned that such conduct will lead people to believe either that the flag does not stand for nationhood and national unity, but instead reflects other, less positive concepts, or that the concepts reflected in the flag do not in fact exist, that is, that we do not enjoy unity as a Nation. These concerns blossom only when a person's treatment of the flag communicates some message, and thus are related "to the suppression of free expression" within the meaning of *O'Brien*. We are thus outside of *O'Brien's* test altogether.

IV

It remains to consider whether the State's interest in preserving the flag as a symbol of nationhood and national unity justifies Johnson's conviction. Johnson was not, we add, prosecuted for the expression of just any idea; he was prosecuted for his expression of dissatisfaction with the policies of this country, expression situated at the core of our First Amendment values. If he had burned the flag as a means of disposing of it because it was dirty or torn, he would not have been convicted of flag desecration under this Texas law. The Texas law is thus not aimed at protecting the physical integrity of the flag in all circumstances, but is designed instead to protect it only against impairments that would cause serious offense to others. Whether Johnson's treatment of the flag violated Texas law thus depended on the likely communicative impact of his expressive conduct. Johnson's political expression was restricted because of the content of the message he conveyed. We must therefore subject the State's asserted interest in preserving the special symbolic character of the flag to "the most exacting scrutiny."

Texas argues that its interest in preserving the flag as a symbol of nationhood and national unity survives this close analysis. If there is a bedrock principle underlying the First Amendment, it is that the government may not prohibit the expression of an idea simply because society finds the idea itself offensive or disagreeable. We have not recognized an exception to this principle even where our flag has been involved. In short, nothing in our precedents suggests that a State may foster its own view of the flag by prohibiting expressive conduct relating to it.

Texas' focus on the precise nature of Johnson's expression, moreover, misses the point of our prior decisions: their enduring lesson, that the government may not prohibit expression simply because it disagrees with its message, is not dependent on the particular mode in which one chooses to express an idea. If we were to hold that a State may forbid flag burning wherever it is likely to endanger the flag's symbolic role, but allow it wherever burning a flag promotes that role — as where, for example, a person ceremoniously burns a dirty flag — we would be saying that when it comes to impairing the flag's physical integrity, the flag itself may be used as a symbol — as a substitute for the written or spoken word or a "short cut from mind to mind" — only in one direction. We would be permitting a State to "prescribe what shall be orthodox" by saying that one may burn the flag to convey one's attitude toward it and its referents only if one does not endanger the flag's representation of nationhood and national unity. We never before have held that the Government may ensure that a symbol be used to express only one view of that symbol or its referents.

To conclude that the government may permit designated symbols to be used to communicate only a limited set of messages would be to enter territory having no discernible or defensible boundaries. Could the government, on this theory, prohibit the burning of state flags? Of copies of the Presidential seal? Of the Constitution? In evaluating these choices under the First Amendment, how would we decide which symbols were sufficiently special to warrant this unique status? To do so, we would be forced to consult our own political preferences, and impose them on the citizenry, in the very way that the First Amendment forbids us to do.

We are fortified in today's conclusion by our conviction that forbidding criminal punishment for conduct such as Johnson's will not endanger the special role played by our flag or the feelings it inspires. To paraphrase Justice Holmes, we submit that nobody can suppose that this one gesture of an unknown man will change our Nation's attitude towards its flag. We are tempted to say, in fact, that the flag's deservedly cherished place in our community will be strengthened, not weakened, by our holding today. Our decision is a reaffirmation of the principles of freedom and inclusiveness that the flag best reflects, and of the conviction that our toleration of criticism such as Johnson's is a sign and source of our strength.

The way to preserve the flag's special role is not to punish those who feel differently about these matters. It is to persuade them that they are wrong. We can imagine no more appropriate response to burning a flag than waving one's own, no better way to counter a flag burner's message than by saluting the flag that burns, no surer means of preserving the dignity even of the flag that burned than by—as one witness here did—according its remains a respectful burial. We do not consecrate the flag by punishing its desecration, for in doing so we dilute the freedom that this cherished emblem represents.

Chief Justice REHNQUIST, with whom Justice WHITE and Justice O'CONNOR join, dissenting.

For more than 200 years, the American flag has occupied a unique position as the symbol of our Nation, a uniqueness that justifies a governmental prohibition against flag burning in the way respondent Johnson did here. The flag symbolizes the Nation in peace as well as in war. It signifies our national presence on battleships, airplanes, military installations, and public buildings from the United States Capitol to the thousands of county courthouses and city halls throughout the country. Two flags are prominently placed in our courtroom.

No other American symbol has been as universally honored as the flag. In 1931, Congress declared "The Star-Spangled Banner" to be our national anthem. In 1949, Congress declared June 14th to be Flag Day. In 1987, John Philip Sousa's "The Stars and Stripes Forever" was designated as the national march. Congress has also established "The Pledge of Allegiance to the Flag" and the manner of its deliverance.

The American flag, then, throughout more than 200 years of our history, has come to be the visible symbol embodying our Nation. It does not represent the views of any particular political party, and it does not represent any particular political philosophy. The flag is not simply another "idea" or "point of view" competing for recognition in the marketplace of ideas. Millions and millions of Americans regard it with an almost mystical reverence regardless of what sort of social, political, or philosophical beliefs they may have. I cannot agree that the First Amendment invalidates the Act of Congress, and the laws of 48 of the 50 States, which make criminal the public burning of the flag.

Here it may be said that the public burning of the American flag by Johnson was no essential part of any exposition of ideas, and at the same time it had a tendency to incite a breach of the peace. Johnson was free to make any verbal denunciation of the flag that he wished; indeed, he was free to burn the flag in private. He could publicly burn other symbols of the Government or effigies of political leaders. The result of the Texas statute is obviously to deny one in Johnson's frame of mind one of many means of "symbolic speech." Far from being a case of "one picture being worth a thousand words," flag burning is the equivalent of an inarticulate grunt or roar that, it seems fair to say, is most likely to be indulged in not to express any particular idea, but to antagonize others.

The Texas statute deprived Johnson of only one rather inarticulate symbolic form of protest—a form of protest that was profoundly offensive to many—and left him with a full panoply of other symbols and every conceivable form of verbal expression to express his deep disapproval of national policy. Thus, in no way can it be said that Texas is punishing him because his hearers—or any other group of people—were profoundly opposed to the message that he sought to convey. Such opposition is no proper basis for restricting speech or expression under the First Amendment. It was Johnson's use of this particular symbol, and not the idea that he sought to convey by it or by his many other expressions, for which he was punished.

Justice STEVENS, dissenting.

As the Court analyzes this case, it presents the question whether the State of Texas, or indeed the Federal Government, has the power to prohibit the public desecration of the American flag. The question is unique. In my judgment rules that apply to a host of other symbols, such as state flags, armbands, or various privately promoted emblems of political or commercial identity, are not necessarily controlling. Even if flag burning could be considered just another species of symbolic speech under the logical application of the rules that the Court has developed in its interpretation of the First Amendment in other contexts, this case has an intangible dimension that makes those rules inapplicable.

A country's flag is a symbol of more than "nationhood and national unity." It also signifies the ideas that characterize the society that has chosen that emblem as well as the special history that has animated the growth and power of those ideas. The message conveyed by some flags—the swastika, for example—may survive long after it has outlived its usefulness as a symbol of regimented unity in a particular nation.

So it is with the American flag. It is more than a proud symbol of the courage, the determination, and the gifts of nature that transformed 13 fledgling Colonies into a world power. It is a symbol of freedom, of equal opportunity, of religious tolerance, and of good will for other peoples who share our aspirations. The symbol carries its message to dissidents both at home and abroad who may have no interest at all in our national unity or survival.

The value of the flag as a symbol cannot be measured. Even so, I have no doubt that the interest in preserving that value for the future is both significant and legitimate. Conceivably that value will be enhanced by the Court's conclusion that our national commitment to free expression is so strong that even the United States as ultimate guarantor of that freedom is without power to prohibit the desecration of its unique symbol. But I am unpersuaded. The creation of a federal right to post bulletin boards and graffiti on the Washington Monument might enlarge the market for free expression, but at a cost I would not pay. Similarly, in my considered judgment, sanctioning the public desecration of the flag will tarnish its value — both for those who cherish the ideas for which it waves and for those who desire to don the robes of martyrdom by burning it. That tarnish is not justified by the trivial burden on free expression occasioned by requiring that an available, alternative mode of expression — including uttering words critical of the flag — be employed.

The ideas of liberty and equality have been an irresistible force in motivating leaders like Patrick Henry, Susan B. Anthony, and Abraham Lincoln, schoolteachers like Nathan Hale and Booker T. Washington, the Philippine Scouts who fought at Bataan, and the soldiers who scaled the bluff at Omaha Beach. If those ideas are worth fighting for — and our history demonstrates that they are — it cannot be true that the flag that uniquely symbolizes their power is not itself worthy of protection from unnecessary desecration. I respectfully dissent.

Texas v. Johnson produced an enormous amount of controversy and proposals to amend the Constitution to prohibit flag burning. In an effort to avoid such an amendment, Congress adopted the Flag Protection Act of 1989 that made it a crime for any person to knowingly mutilate, deface, defile, burn, or trample upon the flag. Unlike the Texas law, the reach of the Flag Protection Act was not limited to situations where the conduct would offend another. In United States v. Eichman, 496 U.S. 310 (1990), the Supreme Court declared this law unconstitutional. The Court's split was identical to that in Texas v. Johnson: Brennan, Marshall, Blackmun, Scalia, and Kennedy were in the majority; Rehnquist, White, Stevens, and O'Connor dissented. Justice Brennan again wrote the opinion for the Court and said that the statute had the "same fundamental flaw" as the Texas law that had been invalidated a year earlier. The law's primary purpose was to keep the flag from being used to communicate protest or dissent. The Court said that this was a purpose directly focused on the message and that strict scrutiny was therefore the appropriate test.

iii. Spending Money as Political Speech

One of the most important areas in which the Court has considered conduct that communicates is in evaluating government laws regulating the spending of money in political campaigns. The seminal case addressing this issue was Buckley v. Valeo.

BUCKLEY v. VALEO

424 U.S. 1 (1976)

Per Curiam.

These appeals present constitutional challenges to the key provisions of the Federal Election Campaign Act of 1971 (Act), as amended in 1974. The statutes at issue summarized in broad terms, contain the following provisions: (a) individual political contributions are limited to $1,000 to any single candidate per election, with an overall annual limitation of $25,000 by any contributor; independent expenditures by individuals and groups "relative to a clearly identified candidate" are limited to $1,000 a year; campaign spending by candidates for various federal offices and spending for national conventions by political parties are subject to prescribed limits; (b) contributions and expenditures above certain threshold levels must be reported and publicly disclosed; (c) a system for public funding of Presidential campaign activities is established by Subtitle H of the Internal Revenue Code; and (d) a Federal Election Commission is established to administer and enforce the legislation.

I. Contribution and Expenditure Limitations

The intricate statutory scheme adopted by Congress to regulate federal election campaigns includes restrictions on political contributions and expenditures that apply broadly to all phases of and all participants in the election process. The major contribution and expenditure limitations in the Act prohibit individuals from contributing more than $25,000 in a single year or more than $1,000 to any single candidate for an election campaign and from spending more than $1,000 a year "relative to a clearly identified candidate." Other provisions restrict a candidate's use of personal and family resources in his campaign and limit the overall amount that can be spent by a candidate in campaigning for federal office.

A. GENERAL PRINCIPLES

The Act's contribution and expenditure limitations operate in an area of the most fundamental First Amendment activities. Discussion of public issues and debate on the qualifications of candidates are integral to the operation of the system of government established by our Constitution. The First Amendment affords the broadest protection to such political expression in order "to assure [the] unfettered interchange of ideas for the bringing about of political and social changes desired by the people." The First Amendment protects political association as well as political expression.

It is with these principles in mind that we consider the primary contentions of the parties with respect to the Act's limitations upon the giving and spending of money in political campaigns. Those conflicting contentions could not more sharply define the basic issues before us. Appellees contend that what the Act regulates is conduct, and that its effect on speech and association is incidental at most. Appellants respond that contributions and expenditures are at the very core of political speech, and that the Act's limitations thus constitute restraints on First Amendment liberty that are both gross and direct.

In upholding the constitutional validity of the Act's contribution and expenditure provisions on the ground that those provisions should be viewed as regulating conduct, not speech, the Court of Appeals relied upon United States v. O'Brien (1968). We cannot share the view that the present Act's contribution and expenditure limitations are comparable to the restrictions on conduct upheld in *O'Brien*. The expenditure of money simply cannot be equated with such conduct as destruction of a draft card. Some forms of communication made possible by the giving and spending of money involve speech alone, some involve conduct primarily, and some involve a combination of the two. Yet this Court has never suggested that the dependence of a communication on the expenditure of money operates itself to introduce a nonspeech element or to reduce the exacting scrutiny required by the First Amendment.

Even if the categorization of the expenditure of money as conduct were accepted, the limitations challenged here would not meet the *O'Brien* test because the governmental interests advanced in support of the Act involve "suppressing communication." The interests served by the Act include restricting the voices of people and interest groups who have money to spend and reducing the overall scope of federal election campaigns. Although the Act does not focus on the ideas expressed by persons or groups subject to its regulations, it is aimed in part at equalizing the relative ability of all voters to affect electoral outcomes by placing a ceiling on expenditures for political expression by citizens and groups. Unlike *O'Brien*, where the Selective Service System's administrative interest in the preservation of draft cards was wholly unrelated to their use as a means of communication, it is beyond dispute that the interest in regulating the alleged "conduct" of giving or spending money "arises in some measure because the communication allegedly integral to the conduct is itself thought to be harmful."

A restriction on the amount of money a person or group can spend on political communication during a campaign necessarily reduces the quantity of expression by restricting the number of issues discussed, the depth of their exploration, and the size of the audience reached. This is because virtually every means of communicating ideas in today's mass society requires the expenditure of money. The distribution of the humblest handbill or leaflet entails printing, paper, and circulation costs. Speeches and rallies generally necessitate hiring a hall and publicizing the event. The electorate's increasing dependence on television, radio, and other mass media for news and information has made these expensive modes of communication indispensable instruments of effective political speech.

The expenditure limitations contained in the Act represent substantial rather than merely theoretical restraints on the quantity and diversity of political speech. The $1,000 ceiling on spending "relative to a clearly identified candidate," would appear to exclude all citizens and groups except candidates, political parties, and the institutional press from any significant use of the most effective modes of communication. Although the Act's limitations on expenditures by campaign organizations and political parties provide substantially greater room for discussion and debate, they would have required restrictions in the scope of a number of past congressional and Presidential campaigns and would operate to constrain campaigning by candidates who raise sums in excess of the spending ceiling.

By contrast with a limitation upon expenditures for political expression, a limitation upon the amount that any one person or group may contribute to a candidate or political committee entails only a marginal restriction upon the contributor's ability to engage in free communication. A contribution serves as a general expression of support for the candidate and his views, but does not communicate the underlying basis for the support. The quantity of communication by the contributor does not increase perceptibly with the size of his contribution, since the expression rests solely on the undifferentiated, symbolic act of contributing. At most, the size of the contribution provides a very rough index of the intensity of the contributor's support for the candidate. A limitation on the amount of money a person may give to a candidate or campaign organization thus involves little direct restraint on his political communication, for it permits the symbolic expression of support evidenced by a contribution but does not in any way infringe the contributor's freedom to discuss candidates and issues. While contributions may result in political expression if spent by a candidate or an association to present views to the voters, the transformation of contributions into political debate involves speech by someone other than the contributor.

Given the important role of contributions in financing political campaigns, contribution restrictions could have a severe impact on political dialogue if the limitations prevented candidates and political committees from amassing the resources necessary for effective advocacy. There is no indication, however, that the contribution limitations imposed by the Act would have any dramatic adverse effect on the funding of campaigns and political associations. The overall effect of the Act's contribution ceilings is merely to require candidates and political committees to raise funds from a greater number of persons and to compel people who would otherwise contribute amounts greater than the statutory limits to expend such funds on direct political expression, rather than to reduce the total amount of money potentially available to promote political expression.

In sum, although the Act's contribution and expenditure limitations both implicate fundamental First Amendment interests, its expenditure ceilings impose significantly more severe restrictions on protected freedoms of political expression and association than do its limitations on financial contributions.

B. CONTRIBUTION LIMITATIONS

Section 608(b) provides, with certain limited exceptions, that "no person shall make contributions to any candidate with respect to any election for Federal office which, in the aggregate, exceed $1,000." According to the parties and amici, the primary interest served by the limitations and, indeed, by the Act as a whole, is the prevention of corruption and the appearance of corruption spawned by the real or imagined coercive influence of large financial contributions on candidates' positions and on their actions if elected to office. Two "ancillary" interests underlying the Act are also allegedly furthered by the $1,000 limits on contributions. First, the limits serve to mute the voices of affluent persons and groups in the election process and thereby to equalize the relative ability of all citizens to affect the outcome of elections. Second, it is argued, the ceilings may to some extent act as a brake on the skyrocketing cost of political campaigns and thereby serve to open the political system more widely to candidates without access to sources of large amounts of money.

It is unnecessary to look beyond the Act's primary purpose to limit the actuality and appearance of corruption resulting from large individual financial contributions in order to find a constitutionally sufficient justification for the $1,000 contribution limitation. To the extent that large contributions are given to secure a political quid pro quo from current and potential office holders, the integrity of our system of representative democracy is undermined. Although the scope of such pernicious practices can never be reliably ascertained, the deeply disturbing examples surfacing after the 1972 election demonstrate that the problem is not an illusory one. Of almost equal concern as the danger of actual quid pro quo arrangements is the impact of the appearance of corruption stemming from public awareness of the opportunities for abuse inherent in a regime of large individual financial contributions.

The Act's $1,000 contribution limitation focuses precisely on the problem of large campaign contributions[—]the narrow aspect of political association where the actuality and potential for corruption have been identified while leaving persons free to engage in independent political expression, to associate actively through volunteering their services, and to assist to a limited but nonetheless substantial extent in supporting candidates and committees with financial resources. Significantly, the Act's contribution limitations in themselves do not undermine to any material degree the potential for robust and effective discussion of candidates and campaign issues by individual citizens, associations, the institutional press, candidates, and political parties.

We find that, under the rigorous standard of review established by our prior decisions, the weighty interests served by restricting the size of financial contributions to political candidates are sufficient to justify the limited effect upon First Amendment freedoms caused by the $1,000 contribution ceiling.

C. EXPENDITURE LIMITATIONS

The Act's expenditure ceilings impose direct and substantial restraints on the quantity of political speech. The most drastic of the limitations restricts individuals and groups, including political parties that fail to place a candidate on the ballot, to an expenditure of $1,000 "relative to a clearly identified candidate during a calendar year." Other expenditure ceilings limit spending by candidates, their campaigns, and political parties in connection with election campaigns. It is clear that a primary effect of these expenditure limitations is to restrict the quantity of campaign speech by individuals, groups, and candidates. The restrictions, while neutral as to the ideas expressed, limit political expression "at the core of our electoral process and of the First Amendment freedoms."

1. The $1,000 Limitation on Expenditures "Relative to a Clearly Identified Candidate"

Section 608(e)(1) provides that "[n]o person may make any expenditure . . . relative to a clearly identified candidate during a calendar year which, when added to all other expenditures made by such person during the year advocating the election or defeat of such candidate, exceeds $1,000." The plain effect is to prohibit all individuals, who are neither candidates nor owners of institutional press facilities, and all groups, except political parties and campaign organizations, from voicing their views "relative to a clearly identified candidate" through means that entail aggregate expenditures of more than $1,000 during a calendar year. The provision, for example, would make it a federal criminal offense for a person or association to place a single one-quarter page advertisement "relative to a clearly identified candidate" in a major metropolitan newspaper.

We find that the governmental interest in preventing corruption and the appearance of corruption is inadequate to justify §608(e)(1)'s ceiling on independent expenditures. First, assuming, arguendo, that large independent expenditures pose the same dangers of actual or apparent quid pro quo arrangements as do large contributions, §608(e)(1) does not provide an answer that sufficiently relates to the elimination of those dangers. Unlike the contribution limitations' total ban on the giving of large amounts of money to candidates, §608(e)(1) prevents only some large expenditures. So long as persons and groups eschew expenditures that in express terms advocate the election or defeat of a clearly identified candidate, they are free to spend as much as they want to promote the candidate and his views. The exacting interpretation of the statutory language necessary to avoid unconstitutional vagueness thus undermines the limitation's effectiveness as a loophole-closing provision by facilitating circumvention by those seeking to exert improper influence upon a candidate or office-holder. It would naively underestimate the ingenuity and resourcefulness of persons and groups desiring to buy influence to believe that they would have much difficulty devising expenditures that skirted the restriction on express advocacy of election or defeat but nevertheless benefited the candidate's campaign. Yet no substantial societal interest would be served by a loophole-closing provision designed to check corruption that permitted unscrupulous persons and organizations to expend unlimited sums of money in order to obtain improper influence over candidates for elective office.

Second, quite apart from the shortcomings of §608(e)(1) in preventing any abuses generated by large independent expenditures, the independent advocacy restricted by the provision does not presently appear to pose dangers of real or apparent corruption comparable to those identified with large campaign contributions. The parties defending §608(e)(1) contend that it is necessary to prevent would-be contributors from avoiding the contribution limitations by the simple expedient of paying directly for media advertisements or for other portions of the candidate's campaign activities. They argue that expenditures controlled by or coordinated with the candidate and his campaign might well have virtually the same value to the candidate as a contribution and would pose similar dangers of abuse. Yet such controlled or coordinated expenditures are treated as contributions rather than expenditures under the Act. Section 608(b)'s contribution ceilings rather than §608(e)(1)'s independent expenditure limitation prevent attempts to circumvent the Act through prearranged or coordinated expenditures amounting to disguised contributions. By contrast, §608(e)(1) limits expenditures for express advocacy of candidates made totally independently of the candidate and his campaign. Unlike contributions, such independent expenditures may well provide little assistance to the candidate's campaign and indeed may prove counterproductive. The absence of prearrangement and coordination of an expenditure with the candidate or his agent not only undermines the value of the expenditure to the candidate, but also alleviates the danger that expenditures will be given as a quid pro quo for improper commitments from the candidate. Rather than preventing circumvention of the contribution limitations, §608(e)(1) severely restricts all independent advocacy despite its substantially diminished potential for abuse.

While the independent expenditure ceiling thus fails to serve any substantial governmental interest in stemming the reality or appearance of corruption in the electoral process, it heavily burdens core First Amendment expression. For the First Amendment right to "speak one's mind . . . on all public institutions" includes the right to engage in "'vigorous advocacy' no less than 'abstract discussion.'" Advocacy of the election or defeat of candidates for federal office is no less entitled to protection under the First Amendment than the discussion of political policy generally or advocacy of the passage or defeat of legislation.

It is argued, however, that the ancillary governmental interest in equalizing the relative ability of individuals and groups to influence the outcome of elections serves to justify the limitation on express advocacy of the election or defeat of candidates imposed by §608(e)(1)'s expenditure ceiling. But the concept that government may restrict the speech of some elements of our society in order to enhance the relative voice of others is wholly foreign to the First Amendment, which was designed "to secure 'the widest possible dissemination of information from diverse and antagonistic sources,'" and "to assure unfettered interchange of ideas for the bringing about of political and social changes desired by the people."

2. *Limitation on Expenditures by Candidates from Personal or Family Resources*

The Act also sets limits on expenditures by a candidate "from his personal funds, or the personal funds of his immediate family, in connection with his campaigns during any calendar year." §608(a)(1). These ceilings vary from $50,000 for Presidential or Vice Presidential candidates to $35,000 for senatorial candidates, and $25,000 for most candidates for the House of Representatives.

The ceiling on personal expenditures by candidates on their own behalf, like the limitations on independent expenditures contained in §608(e)(1), imposes a substantial restraint on the ability of persons to engage in protected First Amendment expression. The candidate, no less than any other person, has a First Amendment right to engage in the discussion of public issues and vigorously and tirelessly to advocate his own election and the election of other candidates. Indeed, it is of particular importance that candidates have the unfettered opportunity to make their views known so that the electorate may intelligently evaluate the candidates' personal qualities and their positions on vital public issues before choosing among them on election day. Section 608(a)'s ceiling on personal expenditures by a candidate in furtherance of his own candidacy thus clearly and directly interferes with constitutionally protected freedoms.

The primary governmental interest served by the Act the prevention of actual and apparent corruption of the political process does not support the limitation on the candidate's expenditure of his own personal funds. Indeed, the use of personal funds reduces the candidate's dependence on outside contributions and thereby counteracts the coercive pressures and attendant risks of abuse to which the Act's contribution limitations are directed.

The ancillary interest in equalizing the relative financial resources of candidates competing for elective office, therefore, provides the sole relevant rationale for §608(a)'s expenditure ceiling. That interest is clearly not sufficient to justify the provision's infringement of fundamental First Amendment rights.

[T]he First Amendment simply cannot tolerate §608(a)'s restriction upon the freedom of a candidate to speak without legislative limit on behalf of his own candidacy. We therefore hold that §608(a)'s restriction on a candidate's personal expenditures is unconstitutional.

3. Limitations on Campaign Expenditures

Section 608(c) places limitations on overall campaign expenditures by candidates seeking nomination for election and election to federal office. Presidential candidates may spend $10,000,000 in seeking nomination for office and an additional $20,000,000 in the general election campaign. The ceiling on senatorial campaigns is pegged to the size of the voting-age population of the State with minimum dollar amounts applicable to campaigns in States with small populations. The Act imposes blanket $70,000 limitations on both primary campaigns and general election campaigns for the House of Representatives with the exception that the senatorial ceiling applies to campaigns in States entitled to only one Representative.

No governmental interest that has been suggested is sufficient to justify the restriction on the quantity of political expression imposed by §608(c)'s campaign expenditure limitations. The major evil associated with rapidly increasing campaign expenditures is the danger of candidate dependence on large contributions. The interest in alleviating the corrupting influence of large contributions is served by the Act's contribution limitations and disclosure provisions rather than by §608(c)'s campaign expenditure ceilings.

The campaign expenditure ceilings appear to be designed primarily to serve the governmental interests in reducing the allegedly skyrocketing costs of political campaigns. [T]he mere growth in the cost of federal election campaigns in and of itself provides no basis for governmental restrictions on the quantity of campaign spending and the resulting limitation on the scope of federal campaigns. The First Amendment denies government the power to determine that spending to promote one's political views is wasteful, excessive, or unwise. In the free society ordained by our Constitution it is not the government, but the people individually as citizens and candidates and collectively as associations and political committees who must retain control over the quantity and range of debate on public issues in a political campaign.

In sum, the provisions of the Act that impose a $1,000 limitation on contributions to a single candidate, a $5,000 limitation on contributions by a political committee to a single candidate, and a $25,000 limitation on total contributions by an individual during any calendar year, are constitutionally valid. These limitations, along with the disclosure provisions, constitute the Act's primary weapons against the reality or appearance of improper influence stemming from the dependence of candidates on large campaign contributions. The contribution ceilings thus serve the basic governmental interest in safeguarding the integrity of the electoral process without directly impinging upon the rights of individual citizens and candidates to engage in political debate and discussion. By contrast, the First Amendment requires the invalidation of the Act's independent expenditure ceiling, its limitation on a candidate's expenditures from his own personal funds, and its ceilings on overall campaign expenditures. These provisions place substantial and direct restrictions on the ability of candidates, citizens, and associations to engage in protected political expression, restrictions that the First Amendment cannot tolerate.

Buckley also upheld the disclosure requirements imposed by the law because they provide important information to the electorate about candidates, they "deter actual corruption and avoid the appearance of corruption," and they provide crucial information for enforcing the contribution limits in the law. The Court noted, however, that there may be instances involving minor or dissident parties "where the threat to the exercise of First Amendment rights is so serious and the state interest furthered by disclosure so insubstantial that the Act's requirements cannot be constitutionally applied." The Court said that there was no proof of such an impact in the case before it.

Finally, the Court upheld the provision of the law that provided for public funding of presidential elections. The Court said that such government financing does not restrict speech, but rather increases expression in connection with election campaigns. The Court said that the provision is a "congressional effort, not to abridge, restrict, or censor speech, but rather to use public money to facilitate and enlarge public discussion and participation in the electoral process, goals vital to a self-governing people." The Court said that expenditure limits were permissible as a condition for receipt of such federal money because "acceptance of federal funding entails voluntary acceptance of an expenditure ceiling."

CRITICISMS OF BUCKLEY

Buckley v. Valeo had an enormous practical impact on the nature of political campaigns. The Court's invalidation of expenditure limits led to the proliferation of political action committees and the continued skyrocketing of the costs of election campaigns. There is widespread criticism that this leads to enormous inequalities in political influence and directly affects who can run for office and who can get elected.

Buckley has been criticized on many levels. First, the Court's treatment of spending money as speech, rather than as conduct that communicates, has been questioned.[170] Spending money may facilitate speech and it is a way of expressing support for a candidate, but it is arguably distinguishable from "pure" speech. The argument is that the less protective *O'Brien* test should have been applied instead of the strict scrutiny test used by the Court.

Second, the Court's distinction between expenditure and contribution limits has been questioned.[171] Elected officials can be influenced by who spends money on their behalf, just as they can be influenced by who directly contributes money to them. The perception of corruption may be generated by large expenditures for a candidate, just as it can be caused by large contributions.

---

170. *See, e.g.,* J. Skelly Wright, *Politics and the Constitution: Is Money Speech?,* 85 Yale L.J., 1001 (1976).

171. *See, e.g.,* Lillian R. BeVier, *Money and Politics: A Perspective on the First Amendment and Campaign Finance Reform,* 73 Cal. L. Rev. 1045 (1985).

Third, many have criticized the Court for giving inadequate weight to the value of equality of influence in political campaigns.[172] Allowing unlimited expenditures allows the wealthy to drown out the voices of those with less money. It thus permits those with money to have much more influence in election campaigns and ultimately with elected officials. Critics argue that equality is a compelling interest that justified the limits on expenditures that the Court invalidated.

THE CONTINUING DISTINCTION BETWEEN CONTRIBUTIONS AND EXPENDITURES

Since *Buckley*, the Court has adhered to the distinction between contributions and expenditures. For example, in California Medical Assn. v. FEC, 453 U.S. 182 (1981), the Supreme Court upheld a provision of the Federal Election Campaign Act that limited the amount that individuals and associations could contribute to a political action committee. The Court followed the same reasoning as in *Buckley*, concluding that restricting the amount of contributions does not significantly limit speech. The Court said that the speech value of contributions to political action committees is even less than when the money is given to candidates; the money is used for political expression only when spent by the political action committee.

In contrast, in FEC v. National Conservative PAC, 470 U.S. 480 (1985), the Court declared unconstitutional expenditure limits imposed on political action committees by the Presidential Election Campaign Fund Act. The law said that a political action committee could not spend more than $1,000 on behalf of a presidential candidate who accepted public financing. As in *Buckley*, the Court stressed that restrictions on expenditures limited speech; the ability of political action committees to speak in campaigns was restricted by the laws. The Court noted that political action committees allow people to pool their resources to express themselves. The Court concluded, as in *Buckley*, that the expenditure limits violated the First Amendment.

WHEN ARE CONTRIBUTION LIMITS TOO LOW?

An issue concerning contribution limits is when they are so low as to violate the First Amendment. In Nixon v. Shrink Missouri Government PAC, described above, the Court considered a Missouri law that set contribution limits for candidates to state government office. The statute set limits ranging from $1,075 for candidates to statewide office, such as the governor or attorney general, to $275 for candidates for state representative or for any office for which there are fewer than 100,000 people represented.

The Supreme Court, by a six-to-three margin, upheld the Missouri law. Justice Souter wrote the opinion for the Court and said that the Missouri contribution limits were constitutional for the same reasons that the contribution limits were upheld in *Buckley*; large contributions risk corruption and the appearance of

---

172. *See, e.g.*, Marlene Arnold Nicholson, *Buckley v. Valeo: The Constitutionality of the Federal Election Campaign Act Amendments of 1974*, 1977 Wis. L. Rev. 323, 336.

corruption. The Court acknowledged that there may be laws where the judiciary will need to examine whether there is sufficient evidence of a problem to justify the restrictions, but the Court said that "this case does not present a close call requiring further definition of whatever the State evidentiary obligation may be."

Nor was the Court willing to consider whether inflation since *Buckley* makes contribution limits of the sort approved there too low now. Although the challengers pressed this argument, the Court understandably was reluctant to try and calibrate what specific contribution limits are appropriate for particular states or times.

But in Randall v. Sorrell, the Court for the first time found that contribution limits were so low as to violate the First Amendment.

RANDALL v. SORRELL
548 U.S. 230 (2006)

Justice BREYER announced the judgment of the Court, and delivered an opinion in which the Chief Justice joins, and in which Justice ALITO joins except as to Parts II-B-1 and II-B-2.

We here consider the constitutionality of a Vermont campaign finance statute that limits both (1) the amounts that candidates for state office may spend on their campaigns (expenditure limitations) and (2) the amounts that individuals, organizations, and political parties may contribute to those campaigns (contribution limitations). We hold that both sets of limitations are inconsistent with the First Amendment. Well-established precedent makes clear that the expenditure limits violate the First Amendment. Buckley v. Valeo (1976) (per curiam). The contribution limits are unconstitutional because in their specific details (involving low maximum levels and other restrictions) they fail to satisfy the First Amendment's requirement of careful tailoring. That is to say, they impose burdens upon First Amendment interests that (when viewed in light of the statute's legitimate objectives) are disproportionately severe.

I

Prior to 1997, Vermont's campaign finance law imposed no limit upon the amount a candidate for state office could spend. It did, however, impose limits upon the amounts that individuals, corporations, and political committees could contribute to the campaign of such a candidate.

In 1997, Vermont enacted a more stringent campaign finance law, Pub. Act No. 64, the statute at issue here. Act 64, which took effect immediately after the 1998 elections, imposes mandatory expenditure limits on the total amount a candidate for state office can spend during a "two-year general election cycle," i.e., the primary plus the general election, in approximately the following amounts: governor, $300,000; lieutenant governor, $100,000; other statewide offices, $45,000; state senator, $4,000 (plus an additional $2,500 for each additional seat in the district); state representative (two-member district), $3,000; and state representative (single member district), $2,000. These limits are adjusted for inflation in odd-numbered years based on the Consumer Price Index.

Incumbents seeking reelection to statewide office may spend no more than 85% of the above amounts, and incumbents seeking reelection to the State Senate or House may spend no more than 90% of the above amounts. The Act defines "[e]xpenditure" broadly to mean the "payment, disbursement, distribution, advance, deposit, loan or gift of money or anything of value, paid or promised to be paid, for the purpose of influencing an election, advocating a position on a public question, or supporting or opposing one or more candidates."

Act 64 also imposes strict contribution limits. The amount any single individual can contribute to the campaign of a candidate for state office during a "two-year general election cycle" is limited as follows: governor, lieutenant governor, and other statewide offices, $400; state senator, $300; and state representative, $200. §2805(a). Unlike its expenditure limits, Act 64's contribution limits are not indexed for inflation.

A political committee is subject to these same limits. So is a political party, defined broadly to include "any subsidiary, branch or local unit" of a party, as well as any "national or regional affiliates" of a party (taken separately or together). Thus, for example, the statute treats the local, state, and national affiliates of the Democratic Party as if they were a single entity and limits their total contribution to a single candidate's campaign for governor (during the primary and the general election together) to $400.

The Act also imposes a limit of $2,000 upon the amount any individual can give to a political party during a 2-year general election cycle. The Act defines "contribution" broadly in approximately the same way it defines "expenditure."

II

We turn first to the Act's expenditure limits. Do those limits violate the First Amendment's free speech guarantees? In Buckley v. Valeo, the Court considered the constitutionality of the Federal Election Campaign Act of 1971 (FECA), a statute that, much like the Act before us, imposed both expenditure and contribution limitations on campaigns for public office. The Court, while upholding FECA's contribution limitations as constitutional, held that the statute's expenditure limitations violated the First Amendment. Over the last 30 years, in considering the constitutionality of a host of different campaign finance statutes, this Court has repeatedly adhered to *Buckley*'s constraints, including those on expenditure limits. [The Court invalidated the expenditure limits as violating the First Amendment.]

III

We turn now to a more complex question, namely, the constitutionality of Act 64's contribution limits. The parties, while accepting *Buckley*'s approach, dispute whether, despite *Buckley*'s general approval of statutes that limit campaign contributions, Act 64's contribution limits are so severe that in the circumstances its particular limits violate the First Amendment.

Following *Buckley*, we must determine whether Act 64's contribution limits prevent candidates from "amassing the resources necessary for effective [campaign] advocacy," whether they magnify the advantages of incumbency to the point where they put challengers to a significant disadvantage; in a word, whether they are too low and too strict to survive First Amendment scrutiny. In answering these questions, we recognize, as *Buckley* stated, that we have "no scalpel to probe" each possible contribution level. We cannot determine with any degree of exactitude the precise restriction necessary to carry out the statute's legitimate objectives. In practice, the legislature is better equipped to make such empirical judgments, as legislators have "particular expertise" in matters related to the costs and nature of running for office. Thus ordinarily we have deferred to the legislature's determination of such matters.

Nonetheless, as *Buckley* acknowledged, we must recognize the existence of some lower bound. At some point the constitutional risks to the democratic electoral process become too great. After all, the interests underlying contribution limits, preventing corruption and the appearance of corruption, "directly implicate the integrity of our electoral process." Yet that rationale does not simply mean "the lower the limit, the better." That is because contribution limits that are too low can also harm the electoral process by preventing challengers from mounting effective campaigns against incumbent officeholders, thereby reducing democratic accountability. Thus, we see no alternative to the exercise of independent judicial judgment as a statute reaches those outer limits. And, where there is strong indication in a particular case, i.e., danger signs, that such risks exist (both present in kind and likely serious in degree), courts, including appellate courts, must review the record independently and carefully with an eye toward assessing the statute's "tailoring," that is, toward assessing the proportionality of the restrictions.

We find those danger signs present here. As compared with the contribution limits upheld by the Court in the past, and with those in force in other States, Act 64's limits are sufficiently low as to generate suspicion that they are not closely drawn. The Act sets its limits per election cycle, which includes both a primary and a general election. Thus, in a gubernatorial race with both primary and final election contests, the Act's contribution limit amounts to $200 per election per candidate (with significantly lower limits for contributions to candidates for State Senate and House of Representatives). These limits apply both to contributions from individuals and to contributions from political parties, whether made in cash or in expenditures coordinated (or presumed to be coordinated) with the candidate.

In sum, Act 64's contribution limits are substantially lower than both the limits we have previously upheld and comparable limits in other States. These are danger signs that Act 64's contribution limits may fall outside tolerable First Amendment limits. We consequently must examine the record independently and carefully to determine whether Act 64's contribution limits are "closely drawn" to match the State's interests.

C

Our examination of the record convinces us that, from a constitutional perspective, Act 64's contribution limits are too restrictive. We reach this conclusion based not merely on the low dollar amounts of the limits themselves, but also on the statute's effect on political parties and on volunteer activity in Vermont elections. Taken together, Act 64's substantial restrictions on the ability of candidates to raise the funds necessary to run a competitive election, on the ability of political parties to help their candidates get elected, and on the ability of individual citizens to volunteer their time to campaigns show that the

Act is not closely drawn to meet its objectives. In particular, five factors together lead us to this decision.

First, the record suggests, though it does not conclusively prove, that Act 64's contribution limits will significantly restrict the amount of funding available for challengers to run competitive campaigns.

Second, Act 64's insistence that political parties abide by exactly the same low contribution limits that apply to other contributors threatens harm to a particularly important political right, the right to associate in a political party.

Third, the Act's treatment of volunteer services aggravates the problem. Like its federal statutory counterpart, the Act excludes from its definition of "contribution" all "services provided without compensation by individuals volunteering their time on behalf of a candidate." But the Act does not exclude the expenses those volunteers incur, such as travel expenses, in the course of campaign activities. The Act's broad definitions would seem to count those expenses against the volunteer's contribution limit, at least where the spending was facilitated or approved by campaign officials. The absence of some such exception may matter in the present context, where contribution limits are very low.

Fourth, unlike the contribution limits we upheld in *Shrink*, Act 64's contribution limits are not adjusted for inflation. Its limits decline in real value each year.

Fifth, we have found nowhere in the record any special justification that might warrant a contribution limit so low or so restrictive as to bring about the serious associational and expressive problems that we have described. Rather, the basic justifications the State has advanced in support of such limits are those present in *Buckley*. The record contains no indication that, for example, corruption (or its appearance) in Vermont is significantly more serious a matter than elsewhere.

Justice THOMAS, with whom Justice SCALIA joins, concurring in the judgment.

Although I agree with the plurality that Act 64 is unconstitutional, I disagree with its rationale for striking down that statute. I continue to believe that *Buckley* provides insufficient protection to political speech, the core of the First Amendment. The illegitimacy of *Buckley* is further underscored by the continuing inability of the Court (and the plurality here) to apply *Buckley* in a coherent and principled fashion. As a result, stare decisis should pose no bar to overruling *Buckley* and replacing it with a standard faithful to the First Amendment. Accordingly, I concur only in the judgment.

I adhere to my view that this Court erred in *Buckley* when it distinguished between contribution and expenditure limits, finding the former to be a less severe infringement on First Amendment rights. Likewise, *Buckley*'s suggestion that contribution caps only marginally restrict speech, because "[a] contribution serves as a general expression of support for the candidate and his views, but does not communicate the underlying basis for the support," even if descriptively accurate, does not support restrictions on contributions.

Today's newly minted, multifactor test, particularly when read in combination with the Court's decision in *Shrink*, places this Court in the position of addressing the propriety of regulations of political speech based upon little more than its impression of the appropriate limits.

Given that these contribution limits severely impinge on the ability of candidates to run campaigns and on the ability of citizens to contribute to campaigns, and do so without any demonstrable need to avoid corruption, they cannot possibly satisfy even *Buckley*'s ambiguous level of scrutiny.

Justice STEVENS, dissenting.

I am convinced that *Buckley*'s holding on expenditure limits is wrong, and that the time has come to overrule it. I have not reached this conclusion lightly. As Justice Breyer correctly observes, stare decisis is a principle of "fundamental importance." But it is not an inexorable command, and several factors, taken together, provide special justification for revisiting the constitutionality of statutory limits on candidate expenditures.

To begin with, *Buckley*'s holding on expenditure limits itself upset a long-established practice. For the preceding 65 years, congressional races had been subject to statutory limits on both expenditures and contributions. There are further reasons for reexamining *Buckley*'s holding on candidate expenditure limits that do not apply to its holding on candidate contribution limits.

The interest in freeing candidates from the fundraising straitjacket is even more compelling. Without expenditure limits, fundraising devours the time and attention of political leaders, leaving them too busy to handle their public responsibilities effectively.

Additionally, there is no convincing evidence that these important interests favoring expenditure limits are fronts for incumbency protection. And only by "permit[ting] States nationwide to experiment with these critically needed reforms" — as 18 States urge us to do — will we enable further research on how expenditure limits relate to our incumbent reelection rates. In the meantime, a legislative judgment that "enough is enough" should command the greatest possible deference from judges interpreting a constitutional provision that, at best, has an indirect relationship to activity that affects the quantity — rather than the quality or the content — of repetitive speech in the marketplace of ideas.

Justice SOUTER, with whom Justice GINSBURG joins, and with whom Justice STEVENS joins, dissenting.

Although I would defer judgment on the merits of the expenditure limitations, I believe the Court of Appeals correctly rejected the challenge to the contribution limits. Low though they are, one cannot say that "the contribution limitation[s are] so radical in effect as to render political association ineffective, drive the sound of a candidate's voice below the level of notice, and render contributions pointless."

The limits set by Vermont are not remarkable departures either from those previously upheld by this Court or from those lately adopted by other States.

Still, our cases do not say deference should be absolute. We can all imagine dollar limits that would be laughable, and per capita comparisons that would be meaningless because aggregated donations simply could not sustain effective campaigns. The plurality thinks that point has been reached in Vermont, and in particular that the low contribution limits threaten the ability of challengers to run effective races against incumbents. Thus, the plurality's limit of deference is substantially a function of suspicion that political incumbents in the legislature set low contribution limits because their public recognition and easy access to free publicity will effectively augment their own spending power beyond anything a challenger can muster. The suspicion is, in other words, that incumbents cannot be trusted to set fair limits, because facially neutral limits do not in fact give challengers an even break. But this received suspicion is itself a proper subject of suspicion. The petitioners offered, and the plurality invokes, no evidence that the risk of a pro-incumbent advantage has been realized; in fact, the record evidence runs the other way, as the plurality concedes.

Because I would not pass upon the constitutionality of Vermont's expenditure limits prior to further enquiry into their fit with the problem of fundraising demands on candidates, and because I do not see the contribution limits as depressed to the level of political inaudibility, I respectfully dissent.

ARE CORPORATE EXPENDITURES PROTECTED SPEECH?

In First National Bank v. Bellotti, the Supreme Court for the first time held that corporate spending is speech protected by the First Amendment. The Court declared unconstitutional a Massachusetts law that prohibited banks or businesses from making contributions or expenditures in connection with ballot initiatives and referenda.

FIRST NATIONAL BANK OF BOSTON v. BELLOTTI

435 U.S. 765 (1978)

Justice POWELL delivered the opinion of the Court.

In sustaining a state criminal statute that forbids certain expenditures by banks and business corporations for the purpose of influencing the vote on referendum proposals, the Massachusetts Supreme Judicial Court held that the First Amendment rights of a corporation are limited to issues that materially affect its business, property, or assets. The court rejected appellants' claim that the statute abridges freedom of speech in violation of the First and Fourteenth Amendments. The issue presented in this context is one of first impression in this Court. We now reverse.

I

The statute at issue, prohibits appellants, two national banking associations and three business corporations, from making contributions or expenditures "for the purpose of . . . influencing or affecting the vote on any question submitted to the voters, other than one materially affecting any of the property, business or assets of the corporation." The statute further specifies that "[n]o question submitted to the voters solely concerning the taxation of the income, property or transactions of individuals shall be deemed materially to affect the property, business or assets of the corporation." A corporation that violates [this law] may receive a maximum fine of $50,000; a corporate officer, director, or agent who violates the section may receive a maximum fine of $10,000 or imprisonment for up to one year, or both.

Appellants wanted to spend money to publicize their views on a proposed constitutional amendment that was to be submitted to the voters as a ballot question at a general election on November 2, 1976. The amendment would have permitted the legislature to impose a graduated tax on the income of individuals.

II

The court below framed the principal question in this case as whether and to what extent corporations have First Amendment rights. We believe that the court posed the wrong question. The Constitution often protects interests broader than those of the party seeking their vindication. The First Amendment, in particular, serves significant societal interests. The proper question therefore is not whether corporations "have" First Amendment rights and, if so, whether they are coextensive with those of natural persons. Instead, the question must be whether [this law] abridges expression that the First Amendment was meant to protect. We hold that it does.

The speech proposed by appellants is at the heart of the First Amendment's protection. As the Court said in Mills v. Alabama (1966), "there is practically universal agreement that a major purpose of [the First] Amendment was to protect the free discussion of governmental affairs." If the speakers here were not corporations, no one would suggest that the State could silence their proposed speech. It is the type of speech indispensable to decisionmaking in a democracy, and this is no less true because the speech comes from a corporation rather than an individual. The inherent worth of the speech in terms of its capacity for informing the public does not depend upon the identity of its source, whether corporation, association, union, or individual.

The court below nevertheless held that corporate speech is protected by the First Amendment only when it pertains directly to the corporation's business interests. The question in this case, simply put, is whether the corporate identity of the speaker deprives this proposed speech of what otherwise would be its clear entitlement to protection.

We find no support in the First or Fourteenth Amendment, or in the decisions of this Court, for the proposition that speech that otherwise would be within the protection of the First Amendment loses that protection simply because its source is a corporation that cannot prove, to the satisfaction of a court, a material effect on its business or property. The "materially affecting" requirement is not an identification of the boundaries of corporate speech etched by the Constitution itself. Rather, it amounts to an impermissible legislative prohibition of speech based on the identity of the interests that spokesmen may represent in public debate over controversial issues and a requirement that the speaker have a sufficiently great interest in the subject to justify communication.

[The law] permits a corporation to communicate to the public its views on certain referendum subjects — those materially affecting its business — but not others. In the realm of protected speech, the legislature is constitutionally disqualified from dictating the subjects about which persons may speak and the speakers who may address a public issue.

Appellee advances a number of arguments in support of his view that these interests are endangered by corporate participation in discussion of a referendum issue. They hinge upon the assumption that such participation would exert an undue influence on the outcome of a referendum vote, and—in the end—destroy the confidence of the people in the democratic process and the integrity of government. According to appellee, corporations are wealthy and powerful and their views may drown out other points of view. If appellee's arguments were supported by record or legislative findings that corporate advocacy threatened imminently to undermine democratic processes, thereby denigrating rather than serving First Amendment interests, these arguments would merit our consideration. But there has been no showing that the relative voice of corporations has been overwhelming or even significant in influencing referenda in Massachusetts, or that there has been any threat to the confidence of the citizenry in government.

Nor are appellee's arguments inherently persuasive or supported by the precedents of this Court. Referenda are held on issues, not candidates for public office. The risk of corruption perceived in cases involving candidate elections, simply is not present in a popular vote on a public issue. To be sure, corporate advertising may influence the outcome of the vote; this would be its purpose. But the fact that advocacy may persuade the electorate is hardly a reason to suppress it: The Constitution "protects expression which is eloquent no less than that which is unconvincing."

Finally, appellee argues that [the law] protects corporate shareholders, an interest that is both legitimate and traditionally within the province of state law. The statute is said to serve this interest by preventing the use of corporate resources in furtherance of views with which some shareholders may disagree. This purpose is belied, however, by the provisions of the statute, which are both underinclusive and overinclusive.

The underinclusiveness of the statute is self-evident. Corporate expenditures with respect to a referendum are prohibited, while corporate activity with respect to the passage or defeat of legislation is permitted, even though corporations may engage in lobbying more often than they take positions on ballot questions submitted to the voters. Nor does [the law] prohibit a corporation from expressing its views, by the expenditure of corporate funds, on any public issue until it becomes the subject of a referendum, though the displeasure of disapproving shareholders is unlikely to be any less.

The overinclusiveness of the statute is demonstrated by the fact that [the law] would prohibit a corporation from supporting or opposing a referendum proposal even if its shareholders unanimously authorized the contribution or expenditure. Ultimately shareholders may decide, through the procedures of corporate democracy, whether their corporation should engage in debate on public issues. Acting through their power to elect the board of directors or to insist upon protective provisions in the corporation's charter, shareholders normally are presumed competent to protect their own interests. In addition to intracorporate remedies, minority shareholders generally have access to the judicial remedy of a derivative suit to challenge corporate disbursements alleged to have been made for improper corporate purposes or merely to further the personal interests of management.

Justice WHITE, with whom Justice BRENNAN and Justice MARSHALL join, dissenting.

The Court invalidates the Massachusetts statute and holds that the First Amendment guarantees corporate managers the right to use not only their personal funds, but also those of the corporation, to circulate fact and opinion irrelevant to the business placed in their charge and necessarily representing their own personal or collective views about political and social questions. I do not suggest for a moment that the First Amendment requires a State to forbid such use of corporate funds, but I do strongly disagree that the First Amendment forbids state interference with managerial decisions of this kind.

By holding that Massachusetts may not prohibit corporate expenditures or contributions made in connection with referenda involving issues having no material connection with the corporate business, the Court not only invalidates a statute which has been on the books in one form or another for many years, but also casts considerable doubt upon the constitutionality of legislation passed by some 31 States restricting corporate political activity, as well as upon the Federal Corrupt Practices Act.

The Court's fundamental error is its failure to realize that the state regulatory interests in terms of which the alleged curtailment of First Amendment rights accomplished by the statute must be evaluated are themselves derived from the First Amendment. The question posed by this case, as approached by the Court, is whether the State has struck the best possible balance, i.e., the one which it would have chosen, between competing First Amendment interests. Although in my view the choice made by the State would survive even the most exacting scrutiny, perhaps a rational argument might be made to the contrary. What is inexplicable, is for the Court to substitute its judgment as to the proper balance for that of Massachusetts where the State has passed legislation reasonably designed to further First Amendment interests in the context of the political arena where the expertise of legislators is at its peak and that of judges is at its very lowest. Moreover, the result reached today in critical respects marks a drastic departure from the Court's prior decisions which have protected against governmental infringement the very First Amendment interests which the Court now deems inadequate to justify the Massachusetts statute.

Bellotti has been sharply criticized by many commentators. The primary objection is that the Court gave inadequate weight to the value of equality and how corporate speech can distort the marketplace of ideas because of corporate wealth and resources.[173] Professor Mark Tushnet, for example, declared, "The first amendment has replaced the due process clause as the primary guarantor of the privileged. Indeed, it protects the privileged more perniciously than the due process clause ever did. . . . Today, the First Amendment stands as a general obstruction to all progressive legislative efforts. . . . Under *Buckley* and *Bellotti*, their investments in politics — or politicians — cannot be regulated significantly."[174]

---

173. *See* Daniel H. Lowenstein, *Campaign Spending and Ballot Propositions: Recent Experience, Public Choice Theory and the First Amendment*, 29 UCLA L. Rev. 505 (1982).

174. Mark Tushnet, *An Essay on Rights*, 62 Texas L. Rev. 1363, 1387 (1984).

In subsequent cases, the Court upheld the constitutionality of restrictions on corporate expenditures in election campaigns. In Austin v. Michigan State Chamber of Commerce, 494 U.S. 652 (1990), the Court upheld a restriction on corporate contributions or expenditures and spoke of the ability of the state to limit corporate speech so as to limit the distortions caused by corporate wealth. A Michigan law prohibited corporations from using their revenues to contribute to candidates or to make expenditures for or against candidates. The corporations, however, could create a separate fund to solicit contributions and could spend money from this segregated fund. Justice Marshall said that the Michigan law was directed at "the corrosive and distorting effects of immense aggregations of wealth that are accumulated with the help of the corporate form and that have little or no correlation to the public's support for the corporation's political ideas. The Act does not attempt to equalize the relative influence of speakers on elections; rather, it ensures that expenditures reflect actual public support for the political ideas espoused by corporations." The Court was explicit in accepting the argument that "[c]orporate wealth can unfairly influence elections."

In McConnell v. Federal Election Commission, 540 U.S. 93 (2003), the Court followed this reasoning and upheld a provision of the Bipartisan Campaign Finance Reform Act, which prohibited corporate expenditures for electronic advertising on behalf of an identifiable candidate 30 days before a primary election and 60 days before a general election. *McConnell*, though, was overruled in Citizens United v. Federal Election Commission.

CITIZENS UNITED v. FEDERAL ELECTION COMMISSION

130 S. Ct. 876 (2010)

Justice KENNEDY delivered the opinion of the Court.

Federal law prohibits corporations and unions from using their general treasury funds to make independent expenditures for speech defined as an "electioneering communication" or for speech expressly advocating the election or defeat of a candidate. Limits on electioneering communications were upheld in McConnell v. Federal Election Comm'n (2003). The holding of *McConnell* rested to a large extent on an earlier case, Austin v. Michigan Chamber of Commerce (1990). *Austin* had held that political speech may be banned based on the speaker's corporate identity.

In this case we are asked to reconsider *Austin* and, in effect, *McConnell.* It has been noted that "*Austin* was a significant departure from ancient First Amendment principles." We agree with that conclusion and hold that *stare decisis* does not compel the continued acceptance of *Austin.* The Government may regulate corporate political speech through disclaimer and disclosure requirements, but it may not suppress that speech altogether. We turn to the case now before us.

I

Citizens United is a nonprofit corporation. Citizens United has an annual budget of about $12 million. Most of its funds are from donations by individuals; but, in addition, it accepts a small portion of its funds from for-profit corporations.

In January 2008, Citizens United released a film entitled *Hillary: The Movie*. It is a 90-minute documentary about then-Senator Hillary Clinton, who was a candidate in the Democratic Party's 2008 Presidential primary elections. *Hillary* mentions Senator Clinton by name and depicts interviews with political commentators and other persons, most of them quite critical of Senator Clinton. *Hillary* was released in theaters and on DVD, but Citizens United wanted to increase distribution by making it available through video-on-demand.

Video-on-demand allows digital cable subscribers to select programming from various menus, including movies, television shows, sports, news, and music. The viewer can watch the program at any time and can elect to rewind or pause the program. In December 2007, a cable company offered, for a payment of $1.2 million, to make *Hillary* available on a video-on-demand channel called "Elections '08." Some video-on-demand services require viewers to pay a small fee to view a selected program, but here the proposal was to make *Hillary* available to viewers free of charge.

To implement the proposal, Citizens United was prepared to pay for the video-on-demand; and to promote the film, it produced two 10-second ads and one 30-second ad for *Hillary*. Each ad includes a short (and, in our view, pejorative) statement about Senator Clinton, followed by the name of the movie and the movie's Website address. Citizens United desired to promote the video-on-demand offering by running advertisements on broadcast and cable television.

Before the Bipartisan Campaign Reform Act of 2002 (BCRA), federal law prohibited — and still does prohibit — corporations and unions from using general treasury funds to make direct contributions to candidates or independent expenditures that expressly advocate the election or defeat of a candidate, through any form of media, in connection with certain qualified federal elections. BCRA §203 amended §441b to prohibit any "electioneering communication" as well. An electioneering communication is defined as "any broadcast, cable, or satellite communication" that "refers to a clearly identified candidate for Federal office" and is made within 30 days of a primary or 60 days of a general election. The Federal Election Commission's (FEC) regulations further define an electioneering communication as a communication that is "publicly distributed." Corporations and unions are barred from using their general treasury funds for express advocacy or electioneering communications. They may establish, however, a "separate segregated fund" (known as a political action committee, or PAC) for these purposes. The moneys received by the segregated fund are limited to donations from stockholders and employees of the corporation or, in the case of unions, members of the union.

In December 2007, Citizens United sought declaratory and injunctive relief against the FEC.

[II]

The First Amendment provides that "Congress shall make no law . . . abridging the freedom of speech." Laws enacted to control or suppress speech may operate at different points in the speech process. The following are just a few examples of restrictions that have been attempted at different stages of the speech process-all laws found to be invalid: restrictions requiring a permit at the outset, Watchtower Bible & Tract Soc. of N.Y., Inc. v. Village of Stratton (2002); imposing a burden by impounding proceeds on receipts or royalties, Simon & Schuster, Inc. v. Members of N.Y. State Crime Victims Bd.; seeking to exact a cost after the speech occurs, New York Times Co. v. Sullivan (1964); and subjecting the speaker to criminal penalties, Brandenburg v. Ohio (1969) (*per curiam*).

The law before us is an outright ban, backed by criminal sanctions. Section 441b makes it a felony for all corporations — including nonprofit advocacy corporations — either to expressly advocate the election or defeat of candidates or to broadcast electioneering communications within 30 days of a primary election and 60 days of a general election. Thus, the following acts would all be felonies under §441b: The Sierra Club runs an ad, within the crucial phase of 60 days before the general election, that exhorts the public to disapprove of a Congressman who favors logging in national forests; the National Rifle Association publishes a book urging the public to vote for the challenger because the incumbent U.S. Senator supports a handgun ban; and the American Civil Liberties Union creates a Web site telling the public to vote for a Presidential candidate in light of that candidate's defense of free speech. These prohibitions are classic examples of censorship.

Section 441b is a ban on corporate speech notwithstanding the fact that a PAC created by a corporation can still speak. A PAC is a separate association from the corporation. Even if a PAC could somehow allow a corporation to speak-and it does not-the option to form PACs does not alleviate the First Amendment problems with §441b. PACs are burdensome alternatives; they are expensive to administer and subject to extensive regulations.

Section 441b's prohibition on corporate independent expenditures is thus a ban on speech. As a "restriction on the amount of money a person or group can spend on political communication during a campaign," that statute "necessarily reduces the quantity of expression by restricting the number of issues discussed, the depth of their exploration, and the size of the audience reached." Buckley v. Valeo (1976) (*per curiam*). Were the Court to uphold these restrictions, the Government could repress speech by silencing certain voices at any of the various points in the speech process. If §441b applied to individuals, no one would believe that it is merely a time, place, or manner restriction on speech. Its purpose and effect are to silence entities whose voices the Government deems to be suspect.

Speech is an essential mechanism of democracy, for it is the means to hold officials accountable to the people. The right of citizens to inquire, to hear, to speak, and to use information to reach consensus is a precondition to enlightened self-government and a necessary means to protect it. The First Amendment "'has its fullest and most urgent application' to speech uttered during a campaign for political office."

For these reasons, political speech must prevail against laws that would suppress it, whether by design or inadvertence. Laws that burden political speech are "subject to strict scrutiny," which requires the Government to prove that the restriction "furthers a compelling interest and is narrowly tailored to achieve that interest."

Premised on mistrust of governmental power, the First Amendment stands against attempts to disfavor certain subjects or viewpoints. Prohibited, too, are restrictions distinguishing among different speakers, allowing speech by some but not others. As instruments to censor, these categories are interrelated: Speech restrictions based on the identity of the speaker are all too often simply a means to control content.

Quite apart from the purpose or effect of regulating content, moreover, the Government may commit a constitutional wrong when by law it identifies certain preferred speakers. By taking the right to speak from some and giving it to others, the Government deprives the disadvantaged person or class of the right to use speech to strive to establish worth, standing, and respect for the speaker's voice. The Government may not by these means deprive the public of the right and privilege to determine for itself what speech and speakers are worthy of consideration. The First Amendment protects speech and speaker, and the ideas that flow from each.

We find no basis for the proposition that, in the context of political speech, the Government may impose restrictions on certain disfavored speakers. Both history and logic lead us to this conclusion.

A

The Court has recognized that First Amendment protection extends to corporations. This protection has been extended by explicit holdings to the context of political speech. Under the rationale of these precedents, political speech does not lose First Amendment protection "simply because its source is a corporation." The Court has thus rejected the argument that political speech of corporations or other associations should be treated differently under the First Amendment simply because such associations are not "natural persons."

Thus the law stood until *Austin*. *Austin* "uph[eld] a direct restriction on the independent expenditure of funds for political speech for the first time in [this Court's] history." There, the Michigan Chamber of Commerce sought to use general treasury funds to run a newspaper ad supporting a specific candidate. Michigan law, however, prohibited corporate independent expenditures that supported or opposed any candidate for state office. A violation of the law was punishable as a felony. The Court sustained the speech prohibition.

To bypass *Buckley* and *Bellotti*, the *Austin* Court identified a new governmental interest in limiting political speech: an antidistortion interest. *Austin* found a compelling governmental interest in preventing "the corrosive and distorting effects of immense aggregations of wealth that are accumulated with the help of the corporate form and that have little or no correlation to the public's support for the corporation's political ideas."

B

The Court is thus confronted with conflicting lines of precedent: a pre-*Austin* line that forbids restrictions on political speech based on the speaker's corporate identity and a post-*Austin* line that permits them. No case before *Austin* had held that Congress could prohibit independent expenditures for political speech based on the speaker's corporate identity. Before *Austin* Congress had enacted legislation for this purpose, and the Government urged the same proposition before this Court.

As for *Austin*'s antidistortion rationale, the Government does little to defend it. And with good reason, for the rationale cannot support §441b. If the First Amendment has any force, it prohibits Congress from fining or jailing citizens, or associations of citizens, for simply engaging in political speech. If the antidistortion rationale were to be accepted, however, it would permit Government to ban political speech simply because the speaker is an association that has taken on the corporate form. The Government contends that *Austin* permits it to ban corporate expenditures for almost all forms of communication stemming from a corporation. If *Austin* were correct, the Government could prohibit a corporation from expressing political views in media beyond those presented here, such as by printing books. The Government responds "that the FEC has never applied this statute to a book," and if it did, "there would be quite [a] good as-applied challenge." This troubling assertion of brooding governmental power cannot be reconciled with the confidence and stability in civic discourse that the First Amendment must secure.

Political speech is "indispensable to decisionmaking in a democracy, and this is no less true because the speech comes from a corporation rather than an individual." This protection for speech is inconsistent with *Austin*'s antidistortion rationale. *Austin* sought to defend the antidistortion rationale as a means to prevent corporations from obtaining "'an unfair advantage in the political marketplace'" by using "'resources amassed in the economic marketplace.'"

Either as support for its antidistortion rationale or as a further argument, the *Austin* majority undertook to distinguish wealthy individuals from corporations on the ground that "[s]tate law grants corporations special advantages-such as limited liability, perpetual life, and favorable treatment of the accumulation and distribution of assets." This does not suffice, however, to allow laws prohibiting speech. "It is rudimentary that the State cannot exact as the price of those special advantages the forfeiture of First Amendment rights."

It is irrelevant for purposes of the First Amendment that corporate funds may "have little or no correlation to the public's support for the corporation's political ideas." All speakers, including individuals and the media, use money amassed from the economic marketplace to fund their speech. The First Amendment protects the resulting speech, even if it was enabled by economic transactions with persons or entities who disagree with the speaker's ideas.

Austin's antidistortion rationale would produce the dangerous, and unacceptable, consequence that Congress could ban political speech of media corporations. Media corporations are now exempt from §441b's ban on corporate expenditures. Yet media corporations accumulate wealth with the help of the corporate form, the largest media corporations have "immense aggregations of wealth," and the views expressed by media corporations often "have little or no correlation to the public's support" for those views. Thus, under the Government's reasoning, wealthy media corporations could have their voices diminished to put them on par with other media entities. There is no precedent for permitting this under the First Amendment.

The media exemption discloses further difficulties with the law now under consideration. There is no precedent supporting laws that attempt to distinguish between corporations which are deemed to be exempt as media corporations and those which are not. "We have consistently rejected the proposition that the institutional press has any constitutional privilege beyond that of other speakers." With the advent of the Internet and the decline of print and broadcast media, moreover, the line between the media and others who wish to comment on political and social issues becomes far more blurred.

The law's exception for media corporations is, on its own terms, all but an admission of the invalidity of the antidistortion rationale. And the exemption results in a further, separate reason for finding this law invalid: Again by its own terms, the law exempts some corporations but covers others, even though both have the need or the motive to communicate their views. The exemption applies to media corporations owned or controlled by corporations that have diverse and substantial investments and participate in endeavors other than news. So even assuming the most doubtful proposition that a news organization has a right to speak when others do not, the exemption would allow a conglomerate that owns both a media business and an unrelated business to influence or control the media in order to advance its overall business interest. At the same time, some other corporation, with an identical business interest but no media outlet in its ownership structure, would be forbidden to speak or inform the public about the same issue. This differential treatment cannot be squared with the First Amendment.

There is simply no support for the view that the First Amendment, as originally understood, would permit the suppression of political speech by media corporations. The Framers may not have anticipated modern business and media corporations. Yet television networks and major newspapers owned by media corporations have become the most important means of mass communication in modern times. The First Amendment was certainly not understood to condone the suppression of political speech in society's most salient media. It was understood as a response to the repression of speech and the press that had existed in England and the heavy taxes on the press that were imposed in the colonies.

Austin interferes with the "open marketplace" of ideas protected by the First Amendment. It permits the Government to ban the political speech of millions of associations of citizens.

The censorship we now confront is vast in its reach. The Government has "muffle[d] the voices that best represent the most significant segments of the economy." And "the electorate [has been] deprived of information, knowledge and opinion vital to its function." By suppressing the speech of manifold corporations, both for-profit and nonprofit, the Government prevents their voices and viewpoints from reaching the public and advising voters on which persons or entities are hostile to their interests.

The purpose and effect of this law is to prevent corporations, including small and nonprofit corporations, from presenting both facts and opinions to the public. When Government seeks to use its full power, including the criminal law, to command where a person may get his or her information or what distrusted source he or she may not hear, it uses censorship to control thought. This is unlawful. The First Amendment confirms the freedom to think for ourselves.

What we have said also shows the invalidity of other arguments made by the Government. For the most part relinquishing the antidistortion rationale, the Government falls back on the argument that corporate political speech can be banned in order to prevent corruption or its appearance. In *Buckley*, the Court found this interest "sufficiently important" to allow limits on contributions but did not extend that reasoning to expenditure limits. When *Buckley* examined an expenditure ban, it found "that the governmental interest in preventing corruption and the appearance of corruption [was] inadequate to justify [the ban] on independent expenditures."

A single footnote in *Bellotti* purported to leave open the possibility that corporate independent expenditures could be shown to cause corruption. For the reasons explained above, we now conclude that independent expenditures, including those made by corporations, do not give rise to corruption or the appearance of corruption.

When *Buckley* identified a sufficiently important governmental interest in preventing corruption or the appearance of corruption, that interest was limited to *quid pro quo* corruption. The fact that speakers may have influence over or access to elected officials does not mean that these officials are corrupt. The appearance of influence or access, furthermore, will not cause the electorate to lose faith in our democracy. By definition, an independent expenditure is political speech presented to the electorate that is not coordinated with a candidate. The fact that a corporation, or any other speaker, is willing to spend money to try to persuade voters presupposes that the people have the ultimate influence over elected officials.

The Government contends further that corporate independent expenditures can be limited because of its interest in protecting dissenting shareholders from being compelled to fund corporate political speech. This asserted interest, like *Austin*'s antidistortion rationale, would allow the Government to ban the political speech even of media corporations. Assume, for example, that a shareholder of a corporation that owns a newspaper disagrees with the political views the newspaper expresses. Under the Government's view, that potential disagreement could give the Government the authority to restrict the media corporation's political speech. The First Amendment does not allow that power. There is, furthermore, little evidence of abuse that cannot be corrected by shareholders "through the procedures of corporate democracy."

We need not reach the question whether the Government has a compelling interest in preventing foreign individuals or associations from influencing our Nation's political process. Section 441b is not limited to corporations or associations that were created in foreign countries or funded predominately by foreign shareholders.

c

Our precedent is to be respected unless the most convincing of reasons demonstrates that adherence to it puts us on a course that is sure error. For the reasons above, it must be concluded that *Austin* was not well reasoned. The Government defends *Austin*, relying almost entirely on "the quid pro quo interest, the corruption interest or the shareholder interest," and not *Austin*'s expressed antidistortion rationale. When neither party defends the reasoning of a precedent, the principle of adhering to that precedent through *stare decisis* is diminished.

Austin is undermined by experience since its announcement. Political speech is so ingrained in our culture that speakers find ways to circumvent campaign finance laws. Our Nation's speech dynamic is changing, and informative voices should not have to circumvent onerous restrictions to exercise their First Amendment rights. Speakers have become adept at presenting citizens with sound bites, talking points, and scripted messages that dominate the 24-hour news cycle. Corporations, like individuals, do not have monolithic views. On certain topics corporations may possess valuable expertise, leaving them the best equipped to point out errors or fallacies in speech of all sorts, including the speech of candidates and elected officials.

Due consideration leads to this conclusion: *Austin* should be and now is overruled. We return to the principle established in *Buckley* and *Bellotti* that the Government may not suppress political speech on the basis of the speaker's corporate identity. No sufficient governmental interest justifies limits on the political speech of nonprofit or for-profit corporations.

Given our conclusion we are further required to overrule the part of *McConnell* that upheld BCRA §203's extension of §441b's restrictions on corporate independent expenditures. The *McConnell* Court relied on the antidistortion interest recognized in *Austin* to uphold a greater restriction on speech than the restriction upheld in *Austin* and we have found this interest unconvincing and insufficient. This part of *McConnell* is now overruled.

[IV]

When word concerning the plot of the movie *Mr. Smith Goes to Washington* reached the circles of Government, some officials sought, by persuasion, to discourage its distribution. Under *Austin,* though, officials could have done more than discourage its distribution-they could have banned the film. After all, it, like *Hillary,* was speech funded by a corporation that was critical of Members of Congress. *Mr. Smith Goes to Washington* may be fiction and caricature; but fiction and caricature can be a powerful force.

Some members of the public might consider *Hillary* to be insightful and instructive; some might find it to be neither high art nor a fair discussion on how to set the Nation's course; still others simply might suspend judgment on these points but decide to think more about issues and candidates. Those choices and assessments, however, are not for the Government to make. "The First Amendment underwrites the freedom to experiment and to create in the realm of thought and speech. Citizens must be free to use new forms, and new forums, for the expression of ideas. The civic discourse belongs to the people, and the Government may not prescribe the means used to conduct it."

Justice SCALIA, with whom Justice ALITO joins, and with whom Justice THOMAS joins in part, concurring.

I join the opinion of the Court. I write separately to address Justice Stevens' discussion of "*Original Understandings.*" This section of the dissent purports to show that today's decision is not supported by the original understanding of the First Amendment. The dissent attempts this demonstration, however, in splendid isolation from the text of the First Amendment. It never shows why "the freedom of speech" that was the right of Englishmen did not include the freedom to speak in association with other individuals, including association in the corporate form. To be sure, in 1791 (as now) corporations could pursue only the objectives set forth in their charters; but the dissent provides no evidence that their speech in the pursuit of those objectives could be censored.

Instead of taking this straightforward approach to determining the Amendment's meaning, the dissent embarks on a detailed exploration of the Framers' views about the "role of corporations in society." The Framers didn't like corporations, the dissent concludes, and therefore it follows (as night the day) that corporations had no rights of free speech. Of course the Framers' personal affection or disaffection for corporations is relevant only insofar as it can be thought to be reflected in the understood meaning of the text they enacted — not, as the dissent suggests, as a freestanding substitute for that text. But the dissent's distortion of proper analysis is even worse than that. Though faced with a constitutional text that makes no distinction between types of speakers, the dissent feels no necessity to provide even an isolated statement from the founding era to the effect that corporations are *not* covered, but places the burden on petitioners to bring forward statements showing that they *are*.

Despite the corporation-hating quotations the dissent has dredged up, it is far from clear that by the end of the 18th century corporations were despised. If so, how came there to be so many of them? The dissent's statement that there were few business corporations during the eighteenth century — "only a few hundred during all of the 18th century" — is misleading. There were approximately 335 charters issued to business corporations in the United States by the end of the 18th century.

Even if we thought it proper to apply the dissent's approach of excluding from First Amendment coverage what the Founders disliked, and even if we agreed that the Founders disliked founding-era corporations; modern corporations might not qualify for exclusion. Most of the Founders' resentment towards corporations was directed at the state-granted monopoly privileges that individually chartered corporations enjoyed. Modern corporations do not have such privileges, and would probably have been favored by most of our enterprising Founders — excluding, perhaps, Thomas Jefferson and others favoring perpetuation of an agrarian society. Moreover, if the Founders' specific intent with respect to corporations is what matters, why does the dissent ignore the Founders' views about other legal entities that have more in common with modern business corporations than the founding-era corporations? At the time of the founding, religious, educational, and literary corporations were incorporated under general incorporation statutes, much as business corporations are today. Were all of these silently excluded from the protections of the First Amendment?

The lack of a textual exception for speech by corporations cannot be explained on the ground that such organizations did not exist or did not speak. To the contrary, colleges, towns and cities, religious institutions, and guilds had long been organized as corporations at common law and under the King's charter, and as I have discussed, the practice of incorporation only expanded in the United States. Both corporations and voluntary associations actively petitioned the Government and expressed their views in newspapers and pamphlets.

Historical evidence relating to the textually similar clause "the freedom of . . . the press" also provides no support for the proposition that the First Amendment excludes conduct of artificial legal entities from the scope of its protection. The freedom of "the press" was widely understood to protect the publishing activities of individual editors and printers. But these individuals often acted through newspapers, which (much like corporations) had their own names, outlived the individuals who had founded them, could be bought and sold, were sometimes owned by more than one person, and were operated for profit. Their activities were not stripped of First Amendment protection simply because they were carried out under the banner of an artificial legal entity. And the notion which follows from the dissent's view, that modern newspapers, since they are incorporated, have free-speech rights only at the sufferance of Congress, boggles the mind.

The dissent says that when the Framers "constitutionalized the right to free speech in the First Amendment, it was the free speech of individual Americans that they had in mind." That is no doubt true. All the provisions of the Bill of Rights set forth the rights of individual men and women — not, for example, of trees or polar bears. But the individual person's right to speak includes the right to speak *in association with other individual persons.* Surely the dissent does not believe that speech by the Republican Party or the Democratic Party can be censored because it is not the speech of "an individual American." It is the speech of many individual Americans, who have associated in a common cause, giving the leadership of the party the right to speak on their behalf. The association of individuals in a business corporation is no different — or at least it cannot be denied the right to speak on the simplistic ground that it is not "an individual American."

But to return to, and summarize, my principal point, which is the conformity of today's opinion with the original meaning of the First Amendment. The Amendment is written in terms of "speech," not speakers. Its text offers no foothold for excluding any category of speaker, from single individuals to partnerships of individuals, to unincorporated associations of individuals, to incorporated associations of individuals — and the dissent offers no evidence about the original meaning of the text to support any such exclusion. We are therefore simply left with the question whether the speech at issue in this case is "speech" covered by the First Amendment. No one says otherwise. A documentary film critical of a potential Presidential candidate is core political speech, and its nature as such does not change simply because it was funded by a corporation. Nor does the character of that funding produce any reduction whatever in the "inherent worth of the speech" and "its capacity for informing the public," First Nat. Bank of Boston v. Bellotti (1978). Indeed, to exclude or impede corporate speech is to muzzle the principal agents of the modern free economy. We should celebrate rather than condemn the addition of this speech to the public debate.

Justice STEVENS, with whom Justice GINSBURG, Justice BREYER, and Justice SOTOMAYOR join, concurring in part and dissenting in part.

The real issue in this case concerns how, not if, the appellant may finance its electioneering. Citizens United is a wealthy nonprofit corporation that runs a political action committee (PAC) with millions of dollars in assets. Under the Bipartisan Campaign Reform Act of 2002 (BCRA), it could have used those assets to televise and promote *Hillary: The Movie* wherever and whenever it wanted to. It also could have spent unrestricted sums to broadcast *Hillary* at any time other than the 30 days before the last primary election. Neither Citizens United's nor any other corporation's speech has been "banned." All that the parties dispute is whether Citizens United had a right to use the funds in its general treasury to pay for broadcasts during the 30-day period. The notion that the First Amendment dictates an affirmative answer to that question is, in my judgment, profoundly misguided. Even more misguided is the notion that the Court must rewrite the law relating to campaign expenditures by *for-profit* corporations and unions to decide this case.

The basic premise underlying the Court's ruling is its iteration, and constant reiteration, of the proposition that the First Amendment bars regulatory distinctions based on a speaker's identity, including its "identity" as a corporation. While that glittering generality has rhetorical appeal, it is not a correct statement of the law. Nor does it tell us when a corporation may engage in electioneering that some of its shareholders oppose. It does not even resolve the specific question whether Citizens United may be required to finance some of its messages with the money in its PAC. The conceit that corporations must be treated identically to natural persons in the political sphere is not only inaccurate but also inadequate to justify the Court's disposition of this case.

In the context of election to public office, the distinction between corporate and human speakers is significant. Although they make enormous contributions to our society, corporations are not actually members of it. They cannot vote or run for office. Because they may be managed and controlled by nonresidents, their interests may conflict in fundamental respects with the interests of eligible voters. The financial resources, legal structure, and instrumental orientation of corporations raise legitimate concerns about their role in the electoral process. Our lawmakers have a compelling constitutional basis, if not also a democratic duty, to take measures designed to guard against the potentially deleterious effects of corporate spending in local and national races.

The majority's approach to corporate electioneering marks a dramatic break from our past. Congress has placed special limitations on campaign spending by corporations ever since the passage of the Tillman Act in 1907. We have unanimously concluded that this "reflects a permissible assessment of the dangers posed by those entities to the electoral process," FEC v. National Right to Work Comm. (1982) (*NRWC*), and have accepted the "legislative judgment that the special characteristics of the corporate structure require particularly careful regulation." The Court today rejects a century of history when it treats the distinction between corporate and individual campaign spending as an invidious novelty born of Austin v. Michigan Chamber of Commerce (1990). Relying largely on individual dissenting opinions, the majority blazes through our precedents, overruling or disavowing a body of case law.

Although I concur in the Court's decision to sustain BCRA's disclosure provisions and join Part IV of its opinion, I emphatically dissent from its principal holding.

I

The Court's ruling threatens to undermine the integrity of elected institutions across the Nation. The path it has taken to reach its outcome will, I fear, do damage to this institution. Before turning to the question whether to overrule *Austin* and part of *McConnell*, it is important to explain why the Court should not be deciding that question. [Justice Stevens then argued that the case should have been decided as an "as applied" rather than a facial challenge and also that it should have been decided on narrower grounds.]

II

The final principle of judicial process that the majority violates is the most transparent: *stare decisis*. I am not an absolutist when it comes to *stare decisis*, in the campaign finance area or in any other. No one is. But if this principle is to do any meaningful work in supporting the rule of law, it must at least demand a significant justification, beyond the preferences of five Justices, for overturning settled doctrine. "[A] decision to overrule should rest on some special reason over and above the belief that a prior case was wrongly decided." Planned Parenthood of Southeastern Pa. v. Casey (1992). No such justification exists in this case, and to the contrary there are powerful prudential reasons to keep faith with our precedents.

The Court's central argument for why *stare decisis* ought to be trumped is that it does not like *Austin*. The opinion "was not well reasoned," our colleagues assert, and it conflicts with First Amendment principles. This, of course, is the Court's merits argument, the many defects in which we will soon consider. I am perfectly willing to concede that if one of our precedents were dead wrong in its reasoning or irreconcilable with the rest of our doctrine, there would be a compelling basis for revisiting it. But neither is true of *Austin,* and restating a merits argument with additional vigor does not give it extra weight in the *stare decisis* calculus.

We have recognized that "*[s]tare decisis* has special force when legislators or citizens 'have acted in reliance on a previous decision, for in this instance overruling the decision would dislodge settled rights and expectations or require an extensive legislative response.'" *Stare decisis* protects not only personal rights involving property or contract but also the ability of the elected branches to shape their laws in an effective and coherent fashion. Today's decision takes away a power that we have long permitted these branches to exercise. State legislatures have relied on their authority to regulate corporate electioneering, confirmed in *Austin*, for more than a century. The Federal Congress has relied on this authority for a comparable stretch of time, and it specifically relied on *Austin* throughout the years it spent developing and debating BCRA. The total record it compiled was *100,000 pages* long. Pulling out the rug beneath Congress after affirming the constitutionality of §203 six years ago shows great disrespect for a coequal branch.

In the end, the Court's rejection of *Austin* and *McConnell* comes down to nothing more than its disagreement with their results. Virtually every one of its arguments was made and rejected in those cases, and the majority opinion is essentially an amalgamation of resuscitated dissents. The only relevant thing that has changed since *Austin* and *McConnell* is the composition of this Court. Today's ruling thus strikes at the vitals of *stare decisis*, "the means by which we ensure that the law will not merely change erratically, but will develop in a principled and intelligible fashion" that "permits society to presume that bedrock principles are founded in the law rather than in the proclivities of individuals."

III

The novelty of the Court's procedural dereliction and its approach to *stare decisis* is matched by the novelty of its ruling on the merits. The ruling rests on several premises. First, the Court claims that *Austin* and *McConnell* have "banned" corporate speech. Second, it claims that the First Amendment precludes regulatory distinctions based on speaker identity, including the speaker's identity as a corporation. Third, it claims that *Austin* and *McConnell* were radical outliers in our First Amendment tradition and our campaign finance jurisprudence. Each of these claims is wrong.

THE SO-CALLED "BAN"

Pervading the Court's analysis is the ominous image of a "categorical ba[n]" on corporate speech. Indeed, the majority invokes the specter of a "ban" on nearly every page of its opinion. This characterization is highly misleading, and needs to be corrected.

In fact it already has been. Our cases have repeatedly pointed out that, "[c]ontrary to the [majority's] critical assumptions," the statutes upheld in *Austin* and *McConnell* do "not impose an *absolute* ban on all forms of corporate political spending." For starters, both statutes provide exemptions for PACs, separate segregated funds established by a corporation for political purposes. "The ability to form and administer separate segregated funds," we observed in *McConnell*, "has provided corporations and unions with a constitutionally sufficient opportunity to engage in express advocacy. That has been this Court's unanimous view."

Under BCRA, any corporation's "stockholders and their families and its executive or administrative personnel and their families" can pool their resources to finance electioneering communications. A significant and growing number of corporations avail themselves of this option; during the most recent election cycle, corporate and union PACs raised nearly a billion dollars. Administering a PAC entails some administrative burden, but so does complying with the disclaimer, disclosure, and reporting requirements that the Court today upholds, and no one has suggested that the burden is severe for a sophisticated for-profit corporation. To the extent the majority is worried about this issue, it is important to keep in mind that we have no record to show how substantial the burden really is, just the majority's own unsupported factfinding. Like all other natural persons, every shareholder of every corporation remains entirely free under *Austin* and *McConnell* to do however much electioneering she pleases outside of the corporate form. The owners of a "mom & pop" store can simply place ads in their own names, rather than the store's.

So let us be clear: Neither *Austin* nor *McConnell* held or implied that corporations may be silenced; the FEC is not a "censor"; and in the years since these cases were decided, corporations have continued to play a major role in the national dialogue. Laws such as §203 target a class of communications that is especially likely to corrupt the political process, that is at least one degree removed from the views of individual citizens, and that may not even reflect the views of those who pay for it. Such laws burden political speech, and that is always a serious matter, demanding careful scrutiny. But the majority's incessant talk of a "ban" aims at a straw man.

IDENTITY-BASED DISTINCTIONS

The second pillar of the Court's opinion is its assertion that "the Government cannot restrict political speech based on the speaker's . . . identity." The case on which it relies for this proposition is *First Nat. Bank of Boston v. Bellotti* (1978). As I shall explain, the holding in that case was far narrower than the Court implies.

[I]n a variety of contexts, we have held that speech can be regulated differentially on account of the speaker's identity, when identity is understood in categorical or institutional terms. The Government routinely places special restrictions on the speech rights of students, prisoners, members of the Armed Forces, foreigners, and its own employees. When such restrictions are justified by a legitimate governmental interest, they do not necessarily raise constitutional problems. In contrast to the blanket rule that the majority espouses, our cases recognize that the Government's interests may be more or less compelling with respect to different classes of speakers, and that the constitutional rights of certain categories of speakers, in certain contexts, "are not automatically coextensive with the rights" that are normally accorded to members of our society.

The election context is distinctive in many ways, and the Court, of course, is right that the First Amendment closely guards political speech. But in this context, too, the authority of legislatures to enact viewpoint-neutral regulations based on content and identity is well settled. We have, for example, allowed state-run broadcasters to exclude independent candidates from televised debates. Arkansas Ed. Television Comm'n v Forbes (1998). We have upheld statutes that prohibit the distribution or display of campaign materials near a polling place. Burson v. Freeman, (1992). Although we have not reviewed them directly, we have never cast doubt on laws that place special restrictions on campaign spending by foreign nationals. And we have consistently approved laws that bar Government employees, but not others, from contributing to or participating in political activities.

The same logic applies to this case with additional force because it is the identity of corporations, rather than individuals, that the Legislature has taken into account. As we have unanimously observed, legislatures are entitled to decide "that the special characteristics of the corporate structure require particularly careful regulation" in an electoral context. Not only has the distinctive potential of corporations to corrupt the electoral process long been recognized, but within the area of campaign finance, corporate spending is also "furthest from the core of political expression, since corporations' First Amendment speech and association interests are derived largely from those of their members and of the public in receiving information," Campaign finance distinctions based on corporate identity tend to be less worrisome, in other words, because the "speakers" are not natural persons, much less members of our political community, and the governmental interests are of the highest order. Furthermore, when corporations, as a class, are distinguished from noncorporations, as a class, there is a lesser risk that regulatory distinctions will reflect invidious discrimination or political favoritism.

If taken seriously, our colleagues' assumption that the identity of a speaker has *no* relevance to the Government's ability to regulate political speech would lead to some remarkable conclusions. Such an assumption would have accorded the propaganda broadcasts to our troops by "Tokyo Rose" during World War II the same protection as speech by Allied commanders. More pertinently, it would appear to afford the same protection to multinational corporations controlled by foreigners as to individual Americans. Under the majority's view, I suppose it may be a First Amendment problem that corporations are not permitted to vote, given that voting is, among other things, a form of speech.

OUR FIRST AMENDMENT TRADITION

A third fulcrum of the Court's opinion is the idea that *Austin* and *McConnell* are radical outliers, "aberration[s]," in our First Amendment tradition. The Court has it exactly backwards. It is today's holding that is the radical departure from what had been settled First Amendment law. To see why, it is useful to take a long view.

Let us start from the beginning. The Court invokes "ancient First Amendment principles," and original understandings, to defend today's ruling, yet it makes only a perfunctory attempt to ground its analysis in the principles or understandings of those who drafted and ratified the Amendment. Perhaps this is because there is not a scintilla of evidence to support the notion that anyone believed it would preclude regulatory distinctions based on the corporate form. To the extent that the Framers' views are discernible and relevant to the disposition of this case, they would appear to cut strongly against the majority's position.

This is not only because the Framers and their contemporaries conceived of speech more narrowly than we now think of it, but also because they held very different views about the nature of the First Amendment right and the role of corporations in society. Those few corporations that existed at the founding were authorized by grant of a special legislative charter. The individualized charter mode of incorporation reflected the "cloud of disfavor under which corporations labored" in the early years of this Nation.

The Framers thus took it as a given that corporations could be comprehensively regulated in the service of the public welfare. Unlike our colleagues, they had little trouble distinguishing corporations from human beings, and when they constitutionalized the right to free speech in the First Amendment, it was the free speech of individual Americans that they had in mind. While individuals might join together to exercise their speech rights, business corporations, at least, were plainly not seen as facilitating such associational or expressive ends. In light of these background practices and understandings, it seems to me implausible that the Framers believed "the freedom of speech" would extend equally to all corporate speakers, much less that it would preclude legislatures from taking limited measures to guard against corporate capture of elections.

A century of more recent history puts to rest any notion that today's ruling is faithful to our First Amendment tradition. At the federal level, the express distinction between corporate and individual political spending on elections stretches back to 1907, when Congress passed the Tillman Act, banning all corporate contributions to candidates.

In sum, over the course of the past century Congress has demonstrated a recurrent need to regulate corporate participation in candidate elections to "[p]reserv[e] the integrity of the electoral process, preven[t] corruption, . . . sustai[n] the active, alert responsibility of the individual citizen," protect the expressive interests of shareholders, and "[p]reserv[e] . . . the individual citizen's confidence in government." Time and again, we have recognized these realities in approving measures that Congress and the States have taken. None of the cases the majority cites is to the contrary. The only thing new about *Austin* was the dissent, with its stunning failure to appreciate the legitimacy of interests recognized in the name of democratic integrity since the days of the Progressives.

IV

Having explained why this is not an appropriate case in which to revisit *Austin* and *McConnell* and why these decisions sit perfectly well with "First Amendment principles," I come at last to the interests that are at stake. The majority recognizes that *Austin* and *McConnell* may be defended on anticorruption, antidistortion, and shareholder protection rationales. It badly errs both in explaining the nature of these rationales, which overlap and complement each other, and in applying them to the case at hand.

THE ANTICORRUPTION INTEREST

Undergirding the majority's approach to the merits is the claim that the only "sufficiently important governmental interest in preventing corruption or the appearance of corruption" is one that is "limited to *quid pro quo* corruption." While it is true that we have not always spoken about corruption in a clear or consistent voice, the approach taken by the majority cannot be right, in my judgment. It disregards our constitutional history and the fundamental demands of a democratic society.

On numerous occasions we have recognized Congress' legitimate interest in preventing the money that is spent on elections from exerting an "undue influence on an officeholder's judgment" and from creating "the appearance of such influence," beyond the sphere of *quid pro quo* relationships. Corruption can take many forms. Bribery may be the paradigm case. But the difference between selling a vote and selling access is a matter of degree, not kind. And selling access is not qualitatively different from giving special preference to those who spent money on one's behalf. Corruption operates along a spectrum, and the majority's apparent belief that *quid pro quo* arrangements can be neatly demarcated from other improper influences does not accord with the theory or reality of politics. It certainly does not accord with the record Congress developed in passing BCRA, a record that stands as a remarkable testament to the energy and ingenuity with which corporations, unions, lobbyists, and politicians may go about scratching each other's backs — and which amply supported Congress' determination to target a limited set of especially destructive practices.

The cluster of interrelated interests threatened by such undue influence and its appearance has been well captured under the rubric of "democratic integrity." This value has underlined a century of state and federal efforts to regulate the role of corporations in the electoral process.

ANTIDISTORTION

The fact that corporations are different from human beings might seem to need no elaboration, except that the majority opinion almost completely elides it. *Austin* set forth some of the basic differences. Unlike natural persons, corporations have "limited liability" for their owners and managers, "perpetual life," separation of ownership and control, "and favorable treatment of the accumulation and distribution of assets . . . that enhance their ability to attract capital and to deploy their resources in ways that maximize the return on their share-holders' investments." Unlike voters in U.S. elections, corporations may be foreign controlled. Unlike other interest groups, business corporations have been "effectively delegated responsibility for ensuring society's economic wel-fare"; they inescapably structure the life of every citizen. "[T]he resources in the treasury of a business corporation," furthermore, "are not an indication of popular support for the corporation's political ideas." "They reflect instead the economically motivated decisions of investors and customers. The availabil-ity of these resources may make a corporation a formidable political presence, even though the power of the corporation may be no reflection of the power of its ideas."

It might also be added that corporations have no consciences, no beliefs, no feelings, no thoughts, no desires. Corporations help structure and facilitate the activities of human beings, to be sure, and their "personhood" often serves as a useful legal fiction. But they are not themselves members of "We the People" by whom and for whom our Constitution was established.

These basic points help explain why corporate electioneering is not only more likely to impair compelling governmental interests, but also why restric-tions on that electioneering are less likely to encroach upon First Amendment freedoms. One fundamental concern of the First Amendment is to "protec[t] the individual's interest in self-expression." Freedom of speech helps "make men free to develop their faculties," it respects their "dignity and choice," and it facilitates the value of "individual self-realization." Corporate speech, however, is derivative speech, speech by proxy. A regulation such as BCRA §203 may affect the way in which individuals disseminate certain messages through the corporate form, but it does not prevent anyone from speaking in his or her own voice. "Within the realm of [campaign spending] generally," corporate spending is "furthest from the core of political expression."

None of this is to suggest that corporations can or should be denied an opportunity to participate in election campaigns or in any other public forum (much less that a work of art such as *Mr. Smith Goes to Washington* may be banned), or to deny that some corporate speech may contribute significantly to public debate. What it shows, however, is that *Austin's* "concern about corporate domination of the political process," reflects more than a concern to protect governmental interests outside of the First Amendment. It also reflects a concern to *facilitate* First Amendment values by preserving some breathing room around the electoral "marketplace" of ideas, the marketplace in which the actual people of this Nation determine how they will govern themselves. The majority seems oblivious to the simple truth that laws such as §203 do not merely pit the anticorruption interest against the First Amend-ment, but also pit competing First Amendment values against each other. There are, to be sure, serious concerns with any effort to balance the First Amendment rights of speakers against the First Amendment rights of listen-ers. But when the speakers in question are not real people and when the appeal to "First Amendment principles" depends almost entirely on the lis-teners' perspective, it becomes necessary to consider how listeners will actually be affected.

In critiquing *Austin's* antidistortion rationale and campaign finance regula-tion more generally, our colleagues place tremendous weight on the example of media corporations. Yet it is not at all clear that *Austin* would permit §203 to be applied to them. The press plays a unique role not only in the text, history, and structure of the First Amendment but also in facilitating public discourse; as the *Austin* Court explained, "media corporations differ significantly from other corporations in that their resources are devoted to the collection of information and its dissemination to the public." Our colleagues have raised some interesting and difficult questions about Congress' authority to regulate electioneering by the press, and about how to define what constitutes the press. *But that is not the case before us.* Section 203 does not apply to media corporations, and even if it did, Citizens United is not a media corporation. There would be absolutely no reason to consider the issue of media corporations if the majority did not, first, transform Citizens United's as-applied challenge into a facial challenge and, second, invent the theory that legislatures must eschew all "identity"-based distinctions and treat a local nonprofit news outlet exactly the same as General Motors.

SHAREHOLDER PROTECTION

There is yet another way in which laws such as §203 can serve First Amendment values. Interwoven with *Austin*'s concern to protect the integrity of the electoral process is a concern to protect the rights of shareholders from a kind of coerced speech: electioneering expenditures that do not "reflec[t] [their] support." When corporations use general treasury funds to praise or attack a particular candidate for office, it is the shareholders, as the residual claimants, who are effectively footing the bill. Those shareholders who disagree with the corporation's electoral message may find their financial investments being used to undermine their political convictions.

The PAC mechanism, by contrast, helps assure that those who pay for an electioneering communication actually support its content and that managers do not use general treasuries to advance personal agendas. It "allows corporate political participation without the temptation to use corporate funds for political influence, quite possibly at odds with the sentiments of some shareholders or members."

V

In a democratic society, the longstanding consensus on the need to limit corporate campaign spending should outweigh the wooden application of judge-made rules. The majority's rejection of this principle "elevate[s] corporations to a level of deference which has not been seen at least since the days when substantive due process was regularly used to invalidate regulatory legislation thought to unfairly impinge upon established economic interests." At bottom, the Court's opinion is thus a rejection of the common sense of the American people, who have recognized a need to prevent corporations from undermining self-government since the founding, and who have fought against the distinctive corrupting potential of corporate electioneering since the days of Theodore Roosevelt. It is a strange time to repudiate that common sense. While American democracy is imperfect, few outside the majority of this Court would have thought its flaws included a dearth of corporate money in politics.

THE CONSTITUTIONALITY OF PUBLIC FINANCING OF ELECTIONS

One frequently discussed approach to decreasing the undesirable effects of large campaign expenditures has been to have public financing of elections. Buckley v. Valeo holds that it is to limit a candidate's expenditures as a condition for receiving public funding for a campaign, though no candidate can be required to accept public funds. In Arizona Free Enterprise Club's Freedom Club PAC v. Bennett, the Court declared unconstitutional a public funding system that increased the contribution and spending limits for those not taking public money based on the amount spent by opponents.

ARIZONA FREE ENTERPRISE CLUB'S FREEDOM CLUB PAC v. BENNETT

131 S. Ct. (2011)

Chief Justice ROBERTS delivered the opinion of the Court. Under Arizona law, candidates for state office who accept public financing can receive additional money from the State in direct response to the campaign activities of privately financed candidates and independent expenditure groups. Once a set spending limit is exceeded, a publicly financed candidate receives roughly one dollar for every dollar spent by an opposing privately financed candidate. The publicly financed candidate also receives roughly one dollar for every dollar spent by independent expenditure groups to support the privately financed candidate, or to oppose the publicly financed candidate. We hold that Arizona's matching funds scheme substantially burdens protected political speech without serving a compelling state interest and therefore violates the First Amendment.

I

The Arizona Citizens Clean Elections Act, passed by initiative in 1998, created a voluntary public financing system to fund the primary and general election campaigns of candidates for state office. All eligible candidates for Governor, secretary of state, attorney general, treasurer, superintendent of public instruction, the corporation commission, mine inspector, and the state legislature (both the House and Senate) may opt to receive public funding. Eligibility is contingent on the collection of a specified number of five-dollar contributions from Arizona voters, and the acceptance of certain campaign restrictions and obligations. Publicly funded candidates must agree, among other things, to limit their expenditure of personal funds to $500; participate in at least one public debate; adhere to an overall expenditure cap; and return all unspent public moneys to the State.

In exchange for accepting these conditions, participating candidates are granted public funds to conduct their campaigns. In many cases, this initial allotment may be the whole of the State's financial backing of a publicly funded candidate. But when certain conditions are met, publicly funded candidates are granted additional "equalizing" or matching funds.

Matching funds are available in both primary and general elections. In a primary, matching funds are triggered when a privately financed candidate's expenditures, combined with the expenditures of independent groups made in support of the privately financed candidate or in opposition to a publicly financed candidate, exceed the primary election allotment of state funds to the publicly financed candidate. During the general election, matching funds are triggered when the amount of money a privately financed candidate receives in contributions, combined with the expenditures of independent groups made in support of the privately financed candidate or in opposition to a publicly financed candidate, exceed the general election allotment of state funds to the publicly financed candidate. A privately financed candidate's expenditures of his personal funds are counted as contributions for purposes of calculating matching funds during a general election. Once matching funds are triggered, each additional dollar that a privately financed candidate spends during the primary results in one dollar in additional state funding to his publicly financed opponent (less a 6% reduction meant to account for fundraising expenses). During a general election, every dollar that a candidate receives in contributions — which includes any money of his own that a candidate spends on his campaign — results in roughly one dollar in additional state funding to his publicly financed opponent. In an election where a privately funded candidate faces multiple publicly financed candidates, one dollar raised or spent by the privately financed candidate results in an almost one dollar increase in public funding to each of the publicly financed candidates.

Once the public financing cap is exceeded, additional expenditures by independent groups can result in dollar-for-dollar matching funds as well. Spending by independent groups on behalf of a privately funded candidate, or in opposition to a publicly funded candidate, results in matching funds. Independent expenditures made in support of a publicly financed candidate can result in matching funds for other publicly financed candidates in a race. The matching funds provision is not activated, however, when independent expenditures are made in opposition to a privately financed candidate. Matching funds top out at two times the initial authorized grant of public funding to the publicly financed candidate.

Under Arizona law, a privately financed candidate may raise and spend unlimited funds, subject to state-imposed contribution limits and disclosure requirements. Contributions to candidates for statewide office are limited to $840 per contributor per election cycle and contributions to legislative candidates are limited to $410 per contributor per election cycle.

II

"Discussion of public issues and debate on the qualifications of candidates are integral to the operation" of our system of government. As a result, the First Amendment "'has its fullest and most urgent application' to speech uttered during a campaign for political office." "Laws that burden political speech are" accordingly "subject to strict scrutiny, which requires the Government to prove that the restriction furthers a compelling interest and is narrowly tailored to achieve that interest."

Although the speech of the candidates and independent expenditure groups that brought this suit is not directly capped by Arizona's matching funds provision, those parties contend that their political speech is substantially burdened by the state law in the same way that speech was burdened by the law we recently found invalid in Davis v. Federal Election Comm'n (2008). In *Davis*, we considered a First Amendment challenge to the so-called "Millionaire's Amendment" of the Bipartisan Campaign Reform Act of 2002. Under that Amendment, if a candidate for the United States House of Representatives spent more than $350,000 of his personal funds, "a new, asymmetrical regulatory scheme [came] into play." The opponent of the candidate who exceeded that limit was permitted to collect individual contributions up to $6,900 per contributor — three times the normal contribution limit of $2,300. The candidate who spent more than the personal funds limit remained subject to the original contribution cap. Davis argued that this scheme "burden[ed] his exercise of his First Amendment right to make unlimited expenditures of his personal funds because" doing so had "the effect of enabling his opponent to raise more money and to use that money to finance speech that counteract[ed] and thus diminishe[d] the effectiveness of Davis' own speech."

The logic of *Davis* largely controls our approach to this case. Much like the burden placed on speech in *Davis*, the matching funds provision "imposes an unprecedented penalty on any candidate who robustly exercises [his] First Amendment right[s]." Under that provision, "the vigorous exercise of the right to use personal funds to finance campaign speech" leads to "advantages for opponents in the competitive context of electoral politics."

Once a privately financed candidate has raised or spent more than the State's initial grant to a publicly financed candidate, each personal dollar spent by the privately financed candidate results in an award of almost one additional dollar to his opponent. That plainly forces the privately financed candidate to "shoulder a special and potentially significant burden" when choosing to exercise his First Amendment right to spend funds on behalf of his candidacy. If the law at issue in *Davis* imposed a burden on candidate speech, the Arizona law unquestionably does so as well.

The burdens that this regime places on independent expenditure groups are akin to those imposed on the privately financed candidates themselves. Just as with the candidate the independent group supports, the more money spent on that candidate's behalf or in opposition to a publicly funded candidate, the more money the publicly funded candidate receives from the State. And just as with the privately financed candidate, the effect of a dollar spent on election speech is a guaranteed financial payout to the publicly funded candidate the group opposes. Moreover, spending one dollar can result in the flow of dollars to multiple candidates the group disapproves of, dollars directly controlled by the publicly funded candidate or candidates.

In some ways, the burden the Arizona law imposes on independent expenditure groups is worse than the burden it imposes on privately financed candidates, and thus substantially worse than the burden we found constitutionally impermissible in *Davis*. If a candidate contemplating an electoral run in Arizona surveys the campaign landscape and decides that the burdens imposed by the matching funds regime make a privately funded campaign unattractive, he at least has the option of taking public financing. Independent expenditure groups, of course, do not.

Once the spending cap is reached, an independent expenditure group that wants to support a particular candidate — because of that candidate's stand on an issue of concern to the group — can only avoid triggering matching funds in one of two ways. The group can either opt to change its message from one addressing the merits of the candidates to one addressing the merits of an issue, or refrain from speaking altogether. Presenting independent expenditure groups with such a choice makes the matching funds provision particularly burdensome to those groups. And forcing that choice — trigger matching funds, change your message, or do not speak — certainly contravenes "the fundamental rule of protection under the First Amendment, that a speaker has the autonomy to choose the content of his own message."

The State argues that the matching funds provision actually results in more speech by "increas[ing] debate about issues of public concern" in Arizona elections and "promot[ing] the free and open debate that the First Amendment was intended to foster." In the State's view, this promotion of First Amendment ideals offsets any burden the law might impose on some speakers.

Not so. Any increase in speech resulting from the Arizona law is of one kind and one kind only — that of publicly financed candidates. The burden imposed on privately financed candidates and independent expenditure groups reduces their speech; "restriction[s] on the amount of money a person or group can spend on political communication during a campaign necessarily reduces the quantity of expression." Thus, even if the matching funds provision did result in more speech by publicly financed candidates and more speech in general, it would do so at the expense of impermissibly burdening (and thus reducing) the speech of privately financed candidates and independent expenditure groups. This sort of "beggar thy neighbor" approach to free speech — "restrict[ing] the speech of some elements of our society in order to enhance the relative voice of others" — is "wholly foreign to the First Amendment."

Arizona asserts that no "candidate or independent expenditure group is 'obliged personally to express a message he disagrees with'" or "required by the government to subsidize a message he disagrees with." True enough. But that does not mean that the matching funds provision does not burden speech. The direct result of the speech of privately financed candidates and independent expenditure groups is a state-provided monetary subsidy to a political rival. That cash subsidy, conferred in response to political speech, penalizes speech to a greater extent and more directly than the Millionaire's Amendment in *Davis*. The fact that this may result in more speech by the other candidates is no more adequate a justification here than it was in *Davis*.

Because the Arizona matching funds provision imposes a substantial burden on the speech of privately financed candidates and independent expenditure groups, "that provision cannot stand unless it is 'justified by a compelling state interest.'"

There is a debate between the parties in this case as to what state interest is served by the matching funds provision. The privately financed candidates and independent expenditure groups contend that the provision works to "level[] electoral opportunities" by equalizing candidate "resources and influence." The State and the Clean Elections Institute counter that the provision "furthers Arizona's interest in preventing corruption and the appearance of corruption."

There is ample support for the argument that the matching funds provision seeks to "level the playing field" in terms of candidate resources. We have repeatedly rejected the argument that the government has a compelling state interest in "leveling the playing field" that can justify undue burdens on political speech. "Leveling electoral opportunities means making and implementing judgments about which strengths should be permitted to contribute to the outcome of an election,"—a dangerous enterprise and one that cannot justify burdening protected speech. The dissent essentially dismisses this concern, but it needs to be taken seriously; we have, as noted, held that it is not legitimate for the government to attempt to equalize electoral opportunities in this manner. And such basic intrusion by the government into the debate over who should govern goes to the heart of First Amendment values.

"Leveling the playing field" can sound like a good thing. But in a democracy, campaigning for office is not a game. It is a critically important form of speech. The First Amendment embodies our choice as a Nation that, when it comes to such speech, the guiding principle is freedom — the "unfettered interchange of ideas"—not whatever the State may view as fair.

As already noted, the State and the Clean Elections Institute disavow any interest in "leveling the playing field." They instead assert that the "Equal funding of candidates" provision, serves the State's compelling interest in combating corruption and the appearance of corruption. But even if the ultimate objective of the matching funds provision is to combat corruption—and not "level the playing field"—the burdens that the matching funds provision imposes on protected political speech are not justified.

Burdening a candidate's expenditure of his own funds on his own campaign does not further the State's anticorruption interest. Indeed, we have said that "reliance on personal funds *reduces* the threat of corruption" and that "discouraging [the] use of personal funds[ ] disserves the anticorruption interest." That is because "the use of personal funds reduces the candidate's dependence on outside contributions and thereby counteracts the coercive pressures and attendant risks of abuse" of money in politics. The matching funds provision counts a candidate's expenditures of his own money on his own campaign as contributions, and to that extent cannot be supported by any anticorruption interest.

We have also held that "independent expenditures . . . do not give rise to corruption or the appearance of corruption." "By definition, an independent expenditure is political speech presented to the electorate that is not coordinated with a candidate." The candidate-funding circuit is broken. The separation between candidates and independent expenditure groups negates the possibility that independent expenditures will result in the sort of *quid pro quo* corruption with which our case law is concerned.

III

We do not today call into question the wisdom of public financing as a means of funding political candidacy. That is not our business. But determining whether laws governing campaign finance violate the First Amendment is very much our business. In carrying out that responsibility over the past 35 years, we have upheld some restrictions on speech and struck down others.

We have said that governments "may engage in public financing of election campaigns" and that doing so can further "significant governmental interest[s]," such as the state interest in preventing corruption. But the goal of creating a viable public financing scheme can only be pursued in a manner consistent with the First Amendment.

"[T]here is practically universal agreement that a major purpose of" the First Amendment "was to protect the free discussion of governmental affairs," "includ[ing] discussions of candidates." That agreement "reflects our 'profound national commitment to the principle that debate on public issues should be uninhibited, robust, and wide-open.'" True when we said it and true today. Laws like Arizona's matching funds provision that inhibit robust and wide-open political debate without sufficient justification cannot stand.

Justice KAGAN, with whom Justice GINSBURG, Justice BREYER, and Justice SOTO-MAYOR join, dissenting.

Imagine two States, each plagued by a corrupt political system. In both States, candidates for public office accept large campaign contributions in exchange for the promise that, after assuming office, they will rank the donors' interests ahead of all others. As a result of these bargains, politicians ignore the public interest, sound public policy languishes, and the citizens lose confidence in their government.

Recognizing the cancerous effect of this corruption, voters of the first State, acting through referendum, enact several campaign finance measures previously approved by this Court. They cap campaign contributions; require disclosure of substantial donations; and create an optional public financing program that gives candidates a fixed public subsidy if they refrain from private fundraising. But these measures do not work. Individuals who "bundle" campaign contributions become indispensable to candidates in need of money. Simple disclosure fails to prevent shady dealing. And candidates choose not to participate in the public financing system because the sums provided do not make them competitive with their privately financed opponents. So the State remains afflicted with corruption.

Voters of the second State, having witnessed this failure, take an ever-so-slightly different tack to cleaning up their political system. They too enact contribution limits and disclosure requirements. But they believe that the greatest hope of eliminating corruption lies in creating an effective public financing program, which will break candidates' dependence on large donors and bundlers. These voters realize, based on the first State's experience, that such a program will not work unless candidates agree to participate in it. And candidates will participate only if they know that they will receive sufficient funding to run competitive races. So the voters enact a program that carefully adjusts the money given to would-be officeholders, through the use of a matching funds mechanism, in order to provide this assurance. The program does not discriminate against any candidate or point of view, and it does not restrict any person's ability to speak. In fact, by providing resources to many candidates, the program creates more speech and thereby broadens public debate. And just as the voters had hoped, the program accomplishes its mission of restoring integrity to the political system. The second State rids itself of corruption.

A person familiar with our country's core values—our devotion to democratic self-governance, as well as to "uninhibited, robust, and wide-open" debate—might expect this Court to celebrate, or at least not to interfere with, the second State's success. But today, the majority holds that the second State's system—the system that produces honest government, working on behalf of all the people—clashes with our Constitution. The First Amendment, the majority insists, requires us all to rely on the measures employed in the first State, even when they have failed to break the stranglehold of special interests on elected officials.

I disagree. The First Amendment's core purpose is to foster a healthy, vibrant political system full of robust discussion and debate. Nothing in Arizona's anti-corruption statute, the Arizona Citizens Clean Elections Act, violates this constitutional protection. To the contrary, the Act promotes the values underlying both the First Amendment and our entire Constitution by enhancing the "opportunity for free political discussion to the end that government may be responsive to the will of the people." I therefore respectfully dissent.

I

Campaign finance reform over the last century has focused on one key question: how to prevent massive pools of private money from corrupting our political system. If an officeholder owes his election to wealthy contributors, he may act for their benefit alone, rather than on behalf of all the people. As we recognized in Buckley v. Valeo (1976) our seminal campaign finance case, large private contributions may result in "political *quid pro quo[s]*," which undermine the integrity of our democracy. And even if these contributions are not converted into corrupt bargains, they still may weaken confidence in our political system because the public perceives "the opportunities for abuse[s]." To prevent both corruption and the appearance of corruption—and so to protect our democratic system of governance—citizens have implemented reforms designed to curb the power of special interests.

Among these measures, public financing of elections has emerged as a potentially potent mechanism to preserve elected officials' independence. By supplanting private cash in elections, public financing eliminates the source of political corruption. For this reason, public financing systems today dot the national landscape. Almost one-third of the States have adopted some form of public financing, and so too has the Federal Government for presidential elections.

But [the] model which distributes a lump-sum grant at the beginning of an election cycle has a significant weakness: It lacks a mechanism for setting the subsidy at a level that will give candidates sufficient incentive to participate, while also conserving public resources. Public financing can achieve its goals only if a meaningful number of candidates receive the state subsidy, rather than raise private funds. And candidates will choose to sign up only if the subsidy provided enables them to run competitive races.

The difficulty, then, is in finding the Goldilocks solution—not too large, not too small, but just right. And this in a world of countless variables—where the amount of money needed to run a viable campaign against a privately funded candidate depends on, among other things, the district, the office, and the election cycle.

II

Arizona's statute does not impose a "restriction," or "substantia[l] burde[n]," on expression. The law has quite the opposite effect: It subsidizes and so produces *more* political speech. We recognized in *Buckley* that, for this reason, public financing of elections "facilitate[s] and enlarge[s] public discussion," in support of First Amendment values. And what we said then is just as true today. Except in a world gone topsy-turvy, additional campaign speech and electoral competition is not a First Amendment injury.

At every turn, the majority tries to convey the impression that Arizona's matching fund statute is of a piece with laws prohibiting electoral speech. The majority invokes the language of "limits," "bar[s]," and "restraints." It equates the law to a "restrictio[n] on the amount of money a person or group can spend on political communication during a campaign." It insists that the statute "restrict[s] the speech of some elements of our society" to enhance the speech of others. And it concludes by reminding us that the point of the First Amendment is to protect "against unjustified government restrictions on speech."

There is just one problem. Arizona's matching funds provision does not restrict, but instead subsidizes, speech. The law "impose[s] no ceiling on [speech] and do[es] not prevent anyone from speaking." The statute does not tell candidates or their supporters how much money they can spend to convey their message, when they can spend it, or what they can spend it on. Rather, the Arizona law, like the public financing statute in *Buckley*, provides funding for political speech, thus "facilitat[ing] communication by candidates with the electorate." By enabling participating candidates to respond to their opponents' expression, the statute expands public debate, in adherence to "our tradition that more speech, not less, is the governing rule." What the law does — all the law does — is fund more speech.

This case arose because Arizonans wanted their government to work on behalf of all the State's people. On the heels of a political scandal involving the near-routine purchase of legislators' votes, Arizonans passed a law designed to sever political candidates' dependence on large contributors. They wished, as many of their fellow Americans wish, to stop corrupt dealing — to ensure that their representatives serve the public, and not just the wealthy donors who helped put them in office. The legislation that Arizona's voters enacted was the product of deep thought and care. It put into effect a public financing system that attracted large numbers of candidates at a sustainable cost to the State's taxpayers. The system discriminated against no ideas and prevented no speech. Indeed, by increasing electoral competition and enabling a wide range of candidates to express their views, the system "further[ed] . . . First Amendment values." Less corruption, more speech. Robust campaigns leading to the election of representatives not beholden to the few, but accountable to the many. The people of Arizona might have expected a decent respect for those objectives.

Today, they do not get it. No precedent compels the Court to take this step; to the contrary, today's decision is in tension with broad swaths of our First Amendment doctrine. No fundamental principle of our Constitution backs the Court's ruling; to the contrary, it is the law struck down today that fostered both the vigorous competition of ideas and its ultimate object — a government responsive to the will of the people. Arizonans deserve better. Like citizens across this country, Arizonans deserve a government that represents and serves them all. And no less, Arizonans deserve the chance to reform their electoral system so as to attain that most American of goals.

Truly, democracy is not a game. I respectfully dissent.

D. WHAT PLACES ARE AVAILABLE FOR SPEECH?

Speech often requires a place for it to occur. Most people lack access to the mass media — television, radio, newspapers — to express their message. They need to have a place to distribute leaflets or a corner to place a soapbox. Moreover, some types of expression require a larger area than a private person is likely to own. A protest rally or demonstration is an important way of attracting public attention and communicating that a large group shares a sentiment. Indeed, such activity is a form of "assembly" expressly protected by the First Amendment.

Thus, the issue arises as to what property is available for speech. Most of these cases involve claims of a right to use government property for speech purposes. The Court has dealt with this issue by identifying different types of government property — public forums, limited public forums (synonymously termed "designated public forums"), and nonpublic forums — and by articulating different rules as to when the government can regulate each. These cases are discussed in subsection 1.

There have been claims of a right to use private property for speech, especially privately owned shopping centers. After an initial decision in the other direction, it is now clearly established that there generally is no right to use private property for speech purposes. Because such property is privately owned, there is no state action, and the Constitution does not apply. These cases are presented in Chapter 5 in connection with the state action doctrine and are briefly reviewed in subsection 2 below.

Finally, the identity of the places is sometimes relevant in another sense. The Supreme Court has treated speech in some government places differently based on the need for greater government control. These are authoritarian environments such as the military, prisons, and schools. Although the juxtaposition of these three places may seem odd, in each the Court has expressed a need for great deference to the government based on a need for deference to authority. These cases are discussed in subsection 3.

1. Government Properties and Speech

a. Initial Rejection and Subsequent Recognition of a Right to Use Government Property for Speech

Initially, the courts rejected any claim of a right to use government property for speech purposes. In Davis v. Massachusetts, 167 U.S. 43 (1897), the Supreme Court upheld a Boston ordinance that prohibited "any public address" on publicly owned property "except in accordance with a permit from the mayor." The Supreme Court affirmed a decision of the Massachusetts Supreme Judicial Court that found the ordinance constitutional. Oliver Wendell Holmes, then a justice on the Massachusetts Court, concluded that the law was permissible because the government has the right to control the use of its property. Holmes wrote that for "the Legislature absolutely or conditionally to forbid public speaking in a highway or public park is no more an infringement of the rights of a member of the public than for the owner of a private house to forbid it in his house."

The U.S. Supreme Court affirmed and also spoke broadly of the government's ability to restrict the use of its property. The Court explained that the government's "right to exclude all right to use, necessarily includes the authority to determine under what circumstances such use may be availed of, as the greater power contains the lesser." The Court refused to recognize any First Amendment right to use government property for speech purposes.

Although occasionally the Supreme Court still speaks in terms of the government's ability to control its property however it wishes, including by prohibiting speech,[175] for the last half century the Court has recognized a right to use at least some government property under some circumstances for speech. Hague v. CIO and Schneider v. State, both decided in 1939, were crucial in recognizing this right.

HAGUE v. COMMITTEE FOR INDUSTRIAL ORGANIZATION
307 U.S. 496 (1939)

Justice ROBERTS delivered an opinion.

After trial upon the merits the District Court entered findings of fact and conclusions of law and a decree in favor of respondents. In brief, the court found that the purposes of respondents, were the organization of unorganized workers into labor unions, causing such unions to exercise the normal and legal functions of labor organizations, such as collective bargaining with respect to the betterment of wages, hours of work and other terms and conditions of employment, and that these purposes were lawful; that the petitioners, acting in their official capacities, have adopted and enforced the deliberate policy of excluding and removing from Jersey City the agents of the respondents; have interfered with their right of passage upon the streets and access to the parks of the city; that these ends have been accomplished by force and violence despite the fact that the persons affected were acting in an orderly and peaceful manner; that exclusion, removal, personal restraint and interference, by force and violence, is accomplished without authority of law and without promptly bringing the persons taken into custody before a judicial officer for hearing.

The court further found that the petitioners, as officials, acting in reliance on the ordinance dealing with the subject, have adopted and enforced a deliberate policy of preventing the respondents, and their associates, from distributing circulars, leaflets, or handbills in Jersey City; that this has been done by policemen acting forcibly and violently; that the petitioners propose to continue to enforce the policy of such prevention; that the circulars and handbills, distribution of which has been prevented, were not offensive to public morals, and did not advocate unlawful conduct, but were germane to the purposes alleged in the bill, and that their distribution was being carried out in a way consistent with public order and without molestation of individuals or misuse or littering of the

---

175. *See, e.g.*, Adderley v. Florida, 385 U.S. 39 (1966) ("The State, no less than a private owner of property, has power to preserve the property under its control for the use to which it is lawfully dedicated.").

streets. Similar findings were made with respect to the prevention of the distribution of placards.

We have no occasion to determine whether, on the facts disclosed, Davis v. Massachusetts was rightly decided, but we cannot agree that it rules the instant case. Wherever the title of streets and parks may rest, they have immemorially been held in trust for the use of the public and, time out of mind, have been used for purposes of assembly, communicating thoughts between citizens, and discussing public questions. Such use of the streets and public places has, from ancient times, been a part of the privileges, immunities, rights, and liberties of citizens. The privilege of a citizen of the United States to use the streets and parks for communication of views on national questions may be regulated in the interest of all; it is not absolute, but relative, and must be exercised in subordination to the general comfort and convenience, and in consonance with peace and good order; but it must not, in the guise of regulation, be abridged or denied.

We think the court below was right in holding the ordinance void upon its face. It does not make comfort or convenience in the use of streets or parks the standard of official action. It enables the Director of Safety to refuse a permit on his mere opinion that such refusal will prevent "riots, disturbances or disorderly assemblage." It can thus, as the record discloses, be made the instrument of arbitrary suppression of free expression of views on national affairs for the prohibition of all speaking will undoubtedly "prevent" such eventualities. But uncontrolled official suppression of the privilege cannot be made a substitute for the duty to maintain order in connection with the exercise of the right.

SCHNEIDER v. NEW JERSEY

308 U.S. 147 (1939)

Justice ROBERTS delivered the opinion of the Court.

The Municipal Code of the City of Los Angeles, 1936, provides: "Sec. 28.00. 'Hand-Bill' shall mean any hand-bill, dodger, commercial advertising circular, folder, booklet, letter, card, pamphlet, sheet, poster, sticker, banner, notice or other written, printed or painted matter calculated to attract attention of the public." "Sec. 2801. No person shall distribute any hand-bill to or among pedestrians along or upon any street, sidewalk or park, or to passengers on any street car, or throw, place or attach any hand-bill in, to or upon any automobile or other vehicle." The handbill which the appellant was distributing bore a notice of a meeting to be held under the auspices of "Friends Lincoln Brigade" at which speakers would discuss the war in Spain.

An ordinance of the City of Milwaukee, Wisconsin, provides: "It is hereby made unlawful for any person . . . to . . . throw . . . paper . . . or to circulate or distribute any circular, hand-bills, cards, posters, dodgers, or other printed or advertising matter . . . in or upon any sidewalk, street, alley, wharf, boat landing, dock or other public place, park or ground within the City of Milwaukee." The petitioner, who was acting as a picket, stood in the street in front of a meat market and distributed to passing pedestrians hand-bills which pertained to a labor dispute with the meat market, set forth the position of organized labor with respect to the market, and asked citizens to refrain from patronizing it.

Some of the bills were thrown in the street by the persons to whom they were given and it resulted that many of the papers lay in the gutter and in the street. The police officers who arrested the petitioner and charged him with a violation of the ordinance did not arrest any of those who received the bills and threw them away.

An ordinance of the Town of Irvington, New Jersey, provides: "No person except as in this ordinance provided shall canvass, solicit, distribute circulars, or other matter, or call from house to house in the Town of Irvington without first having reported to and received a written permit from the Chief of Police or the officer in charge of Police Headquarters." The petitioner was arrested and charged with canvassing without a permit. The proofs show that she is a member of the Watch Tower Bible and Tract Society and, as such, certified by the society to be one of "Jehovah's Witnesses." In this capacity she called from house to house in the town at all hours of the day and night and showed to the occupants a so called testimony and identification card signed by the society. The petitioner was convicted in the Recorder's Court.

Although a municipality may enact regulations in the interest of the public safety, health, welfare or convenience, these may not abridge the individual liberties secured by the Constitution to those who wish to speak, write, print or circulate information or opinion. Municipal authorities, as trustees for the public, have the duty to keep their communities' streets open and available for movement of people and property, the primary purpose to which the streets are dedicated. So long as legislation to this end does not abridge the constitutional liberty of one rightfully upon the street to impart information through speech or the distribution of literature, it may lawfully regulate the conduct of those using the streets. For example, a person could not exercise this liberty by taking his stand in the middle of a crowded street, contrary to traffic regulations, and maintain his position to the stoppage of all traffic; a group of distributors could not insist upon a constitutional right to form a cordon across the street and to allow no pedestrian to pass who did not accept a tendered leaflet; nor does the guarantee of freedom of speech or of the press deprive a municipality of power to enact regulations against throwing literature broadcast in the streets. Prohibition of such conduct would not abridge the constitutional liberty since such activity bears no necessary relationship to the freedom to speak, write, print or distribute information or opinion.

This court has characterized the freedom of speech and that of the press as fundamental personal rights and liberties. The phrase is not an empty one and was not lightly used. It reflects the belief of the framers of the Constitution that exercise of the rights lies at the foundation of free government by free men. It stresses, as do many opinions of this court, the importance of preventing the restriction of enjoyment of these liberties.

The motive of the legislation under attack is held by the courts below to be the prevention of littering of the streets and, although the alleged offenders were not charged with themselves scattering paper in the streets, their convictions were sustained upon the theory that distribution by them encouraged or resulted in such littering. We are of opinion that the purpose to keep the streets clean and of good appearance is insufficient to justify an ordinance which prohibits a person rightfully on a public street from handing literature to one willing to receive it. Any burden imposed upon the city authorities in cleaning and caring for the streets as an indirect consequence of such distribution results from the constitutional protection of the freedom of speech and press. This constitutional protection does not deprive a city of all power to prevent street littering. There are obvious methods of preventing littering. Amongst these is the punishment of those who actually throw papers on the streets.

We are not to be taken as holding that commercial soliciting and canvassing may not be subjected to such regulation as the ordinance requires. Nor do we hold that the town may not fix reasonable hours when canvassing may be done by persons having such objects as the petitioner. Doubtless there are other features of such activities which may be regulated in the public interest without prior licensing or other invasion of constitutional liberty. We do hold, however, that the ordinance in question, as applied to the petitioner's conduct, is void.

b. What Government Property and Under What Circumstances?

Once a right to use government property for speech is recognized, the issue inevitably arises: What publicly owned property must be made available for speech and under what circumstances?[176] For example, while *Hague* and *Schneider* recognize a presumptive right to use the sidewalks and the parks for speech purposes, there obviously would be problems with allowing speech in the middle of a courtroom during a trial or on the runways of a publicly owned airport or in the middle of a highway during rush hour.

The Court has dealt with this issue by classifying different types of government property and articulating varying rules for when speech in each can be regulated. A clear statement of these categories and the rules applied for each is in Perry Education Association v. Perry Local Educators' Association, 460 U.S. 37 (1983). The issue was whether it was permissible for a school to give the teachers' collective bargaining representative exclusive use of an interschool mail system in the district. A rival union wished to use the mail system and pointed to the fact that it was available to community groups, teachers, and the administration. The Court upheld the exclusion of the rival union from using the postal system and in doing so identified types of government property:

> The existence of a right of access to public property and the standard by which limitations upon such a right must be evaluated differ depending on the character of the property at issue. . . . In places which by long tradition or by government fiat have been devoted to assembly and debate, the rights of the state to limit expressive activity are sharply circumscribed . . . [such as] streets and parks. . . . In these quintessential public forums, the government may not prohibit all communicative activity. For the state to enforce a content-based exclusion it must show that its regulation is necessary to serve a compelling state interest and is narrowly drawn to achieve that end. . . . A second category consists of public property which the state has voluntarily opened for use by the public as a place for expressive activity. . . . Although a state is not required to indefinitely retain the open character of the facility, as long as it does so it is bound by the same standards as apply in a traditional public forum. . . . Public

---

176. Excellent scholarship on this topic includes Lillian BeVier, *Rehabilitating Public Forum Doctrine: In Defense of Categories*, 1993 Sup. Ct. Rev. 79; Robert Post, *Between Governance and Management: The History and Theory of the Public Forum*, 34 UCLA L. Rev. 1713 (1987); Geoffrey Stone, *Fora Americana: Speech in Public Places*, 1974 Sup. Ct. Rev. 233; Harry Kalven, *The Concept of the Public Forum: Cox v. Louisiana*, 1965 Sup. Ct. Rev. 1.

property which is not by tradition or designation a forum for public communication is governed by different standards. . . . [T]he state may reserve the forum for its intended purposes, communicative or otherwise, as long as the regulation on speech is reasonable and not an effort to suppress expression merely because public officials oppose the speakers' views.[177]

Thus, under *Perry* the constitutionality of a regulation of speech depends on the place and the nature of the government's action. In its most recent formulation, in Christian Legal Society v. Martinez, 130 S. Ct. 2971 (2010), the Court also defined these categories. In a footnote, Justice Ginsburg, writing for the Court, stated:

In conducting forum analysis, our decisions have sorted government property into three categories. First, in traditional public forums, such as public streets and parks, "any restriction based on the content of . . . speech must satisfy strict scrutiny, that is, the restriction must be narrowly tailored to serve a compelling government interest." Second, governmental entities create designated public forums when "government property that has not traditionally been regarded as a public forum is intentionally opened up for that purpose"; speech restrictions in such a forum "are subject to the same strict scrutiny as restrictions in a traditional public forum." Third, governmental entities establish limited public forums by opening property "limited to use by certain groups or dedicated solely to the discussion of certain subjects." As noted in text, "[i]n such a forum, a governmental entity may impose restrictions on speech that are reasonable and viewpoint-neutral."[178]

Interestingly, although prior cases speak of "nonpublic forums," government properties that the government can and does close to speech, this formulation does not mention them. All of the types of forums mentioned by Justice Ginsburg are opened for at least some speech activities. It is possible that the Court has collapsed nonpublic forums into the category of limited public forums since the test for both would be the same: Government regulation is allowed if it is reasonable and viewpoint neutral. Or it is possible that this was simply an omission because the Court in Christian Legal Society v. Martinez was dealing with what the Court deemed a "limited public forum" and did not have any occasion to consider nonpublic forums.

The presentation below focuses on the three types of forums identified by Justice Ginsburg — public forums, designated public forums, and limited public forums — and assumes that nonpublic forums remain a category as well. The constitutionality of a regulation of speech depends on the place and the nature of the government's action. The law concerning each of these types of forums is reviewed in turn below.

c. Public Forums

Public forums are government property that the government is constitutionally obligated to make available for speech. Sidewalks and parks are paradigm

---

177. The Court found that the school mail system was a nonpublic forum and that the regulation was constitutional because it was reasonable and viewpoint neutral.

178. *Id.* at 2984 n.11 (citations omitted).

examples of the public forum. The government may regulate speech in public forums only if certain requirements are met. First, the regulation must be content-neutral unless the government can justify a content-based restriction by meeting strict scrutiny. Second, it must be a reasonable time, place, or manner restriction that serves an important government interest and leaves open adequate alternative places for speech. Third, a licensing or permit system for the use of public forums must serve an important purpose, give clear criteria to the licensing authority that leaves almost no discretion, and provide procedural safeguards such as a requirement for prompt determination of license requests and judicial review of license denials. Finally, the Court has ruled that government regulation of speech in public forums need not use the least restrictive alternative, although they must be narrowly tailored to achieve the government's purpose. Each of these requirements is discussed in turn.

i. Content Neutrality

The general requirement that the government be content-neutral when regulating speech is discussed above in section B of this chapter. The Court has specifically ruled, as in *Perry* quoted above, that government regulation of speech in public forums must be content-neutral. At a minimum, this means that the government cannot regulate speech based on its viewpoint or its subject matter unless strict scrutiny is met.[179]

POLICE DEPARTMENT OF THE CITY OF CHICAGO v. MOSLEY
408 U.S. 92 (1972)

Justice MARSHALL delivered the opinion of the Court.

The city of Chicago exempts peaceful labor picketing from its general prohibition on picketing next to a school. The question we consider here is whether this selective exclusion from a public place is permitted. Our answer is "No."

The suit was brought by Earl Mosley, a federal postal employee, who for seven months prior to the enactment of the ordinance had frequently picketed Jones Commercial High School in Chicago. During school hours and usually by himself, Mosley would walk the public sidewalk adjoining the school, carrying a sign that read: "Jones High School practices black discrimination. Jones High School has a black quota." His lonely crusade was always peaceful, orderly, and quiet, and was conceded to be so by the city of Chicago.

Because Chicago treats some picketing differently from others, we analyze this ordinance in terms of the Equal Protection Clause of the Fourteenth Amendment. Of course, the equal protection claim in this case is closely intertwined with First Amendment interests; the Chicago ordinance affects picketing, which is expressive conduct; moreover, it does so by classifications formulated in terms of the subject of the picketing.

---

179. *See, e.g.*, Niemotko v. Maryland, 340 U.S. 268 (1951) (declaring it unconstitutional for a city to deny Jehovah's Witnesses a permit to use a city park when other religious and political groups were able to do so).

The central problem with Chicago's ordinance is that it describes permissible picketing in terms of its subject matter. Peaceful picketing on the subject of a school's labor-management dispute is permitted, but all other peaceful picketing is prohibited. The operative distinction is the message on a picket sign. But, above all else, the First Amendment means that government has no power to restrict expression because of its message, its ideas, its subject matter, or its content.

To permit the continued building of our politics and culture, and to assure self-fulfillment for each individual, our people are guaranteed the right to express any thought, free from government censorship. The essence of this forbidden censorship is content control. Any restriction on expressive activity because of its content would completely undercut the "profound national commitment to the principle that debate on public issues should be uninhibited, robust, and wide-open."

Necessarily, then, under the Equal Protection Clause, not to mention the First Amendment itself, government may not grant the use of a forum to people whose views it finds acceptable, but deny use to those wishing to express less favored or more controversial views. And it may not select which issues are worth discussing or debating in public facilities. Once a forum is opened up to assembly or speaking by some groups, government may not prohibit others from assembling or speaking on the basis of what they intend to say. Selective exclusions from a public forum may not be based on content alone, and may not be justified by reference to content alone.

This is not to say that all picketing must always be allowed. We have continually recognized that reasonable "time, place and manner" regulations of picketing may be necessary to further significant governmental interests. Similarly, under an equal protection analysis, there may be sufficient regulatory interests justifying selective exclusions or distinctions among pickets. Conflicting demands on the same place may compel the State to make choices among potential users and uses. And the State may have a legitimate interest in prohibiting some picketing to protect public order. But these justifications for selective exclusions from a public forum must be carefully scrutinized. Because picketing plainly involves expressive conduct within the protection of the First Amendment, discriminations among pickets must be tailored to serve a substantial governmental interest.

In this case, the ordinance itself describes impermissible picketing not in terms of time, place, and manner, but in terms of subject matter. The regulation "thus slip[s] from the neutrality of time, place, and circumstance into a concern about content." This is never permitted.

Similarly, in Carey v. Brown, 447 U.S. 455 (1980), the Supreme Court declared unconstitutional an Illinois statute that prohibited picketing or demonstrations in or around a person's residence unless the dwelling is used as a place of business or is a place of employment involved in a labor dispute. In other words, under the law, picketing in residential neighborhoods was allowed if it was a labor dispute connected to a place of employment, but otherwise generally speech was prohibited. The Court again applied equal protection and found the law unconstitutional. The Court applied *Mosley* and concluded, "[The] Act accords preferential treatment to the expression of views on one particular subject; information about labor disputes may be freely disseminated, but discussion of all other issues is restricted. When government discriminates among speech-related activities in a public forum, the Equal Protection Clause mandates that the legislation be finely tailored to serve substantial interests, and the justifications offered for and distinctions its draws must be carefully scrutinized."

In contrast, the Court has upheld ordinances that prohibited focused picketing at persons' homes when the laws are completely subject-matter-neutral. In Frisby v. Schultz, 487 U.S. 474 (1988), the Court upheld an ordinance that prohibited picketing "before or about" any residence. Although the law was adopted in response to targeted picketing by anti-abortion protestors of a doctor's home, the Court concluded that the law was permissible because it was content-neutral and it was narrowly tailored to protect people's tranquility and repose in their homes. The Court stressed that the ordinance allowed picketing in the area and even on the street, but just not targeted at one person's home. Justice O'Connor, writing for the Court, said that "[t]he First Amendment permits the government to prohibit offensive speech as intrusive when the 'captive' audience cannot avoid the objectionable speech. The target of the focused picketing banned by the . . . ordinance is just such a 'captive.' The resident is figuratively, and perhaps literally, trapped within the home."

Whether the analysis is under equal protection or solely under the First Amendment does not matter. The government cannot regulate speech in a public forum based on the viewpoint or subject matter of the speech unless it meets strict scrutiny. Although history shows that strict scrutiny is rarely met, occasionally the Court finds that the test is satisfied. For example, in Burson v. Freeman, 504 U.S. 191 (1992), the Court found that there was a content-based regulation, used strict scrutiny, and upheld a federal law that prohibited distribution of campaign literature within 100 feet of the entrance of a polling place. The Court said that the history of campaign workers intimidating voters around polling places created a compelling interest sufficient to justify content-based restrictions of speech.

ii. Time, Place, and Manner Restrictions

The concept of "time, place, and manner restrictions" is often uttered in connection with the First Amendment. It refers to the ability of the government to regulate speech in a public forum in a manner that minimizes disruption of a public place while still protecting freedom of speech. In Heffron v. International Society for Krishna Consciousness, 452 U.S. 640 (1981), the Court said that it had often approved reasonable time, place, and manner restrictions "provided that they are justified without regard to the content of the regulated speech, that they serve a significant government interest, and that they leave open ample alternative channels for communication of the information."

In Heffron, the Supreme Court upheld a regulation of speech at the Minnesota State Fair that prohibited the distribution of literature or the soliciting of funds except at booths. Booths were available on a first-come, first-served basis. The Court said that the regulation was content-neutral because it applied to all literature and solicitations regardless of the speaker, viewpoint, or subject matter.

The Court accepted the state's argument that the regulation was justified by an important interest: regulating the flow of pedestrian traffic through the state fair grounds. The Court said the need for crowd control was "sufficient to satisfy the requirement that a place or manner restriction must serve a substantial state interest." The Court also observed that the Krishna had other ways of reaching the audience, both off the fair grounds and at booths within the grounds.

A recent, important case upholding a time, place, and manner restriction is Hill et al. v. Colorado. The case also is important for its discussion and the disagreement between the majority and the dissent over whether the law is content-neutral.

HILL v. COLORADO

530 U.S. 703 (2000)

Justice STEVENS delivered the opinion of the Court.

At issue is the constitutionality of a 1993 Colorado statute that regulates speech-related conduct within 100 feet of the entrance to any health care facility. The specific section of the statute that is challenged, makes it unlawful within the regulated areas for any person to "knowingly approach" within eight feet of another person, without that person's consent, "for the purpose of passing a leaflet or handbill to, displaying a sign to, or engaging in oral protest, education, or counseling with such other person. . . ." Although the statute prohibits speakers from approaching unwilling listeners, it does not require a standing speaker to move away from anyone passing by. Nor does it place any restriction on the content of any message that anyone may wish to communicate to anyone else, either inside or outside the regulated areas. It does, however, make it more difficult to give unwanted advice, particularly in the form of a handbill or leaflet, to persons entering or leaving medical facilities.

The question is whether the First Amendment rights of the speaker are abridged by the protection the statute provides for the unwilling listener.

I

Five months after the statute was enacted, petitioners filed a complaint in the District Court for Jefferson County, Colorado, praying for a declaration that §18-9-122(3) was facially invalid and seeking an injunction against its enforcement. They stated that prior to the enactment of the statute, they had engaged in "sidewalk counseling" on the public ways and sidewalks within 100 feet of the entrances to facilities where human abortion is practiced or where medical personnel refer women to other facilities for abortions. "Sidewalk counseling" consists of efforts "to educate, counsel, persuade, or inform passersby about abortion and abortion alternatives by means of verbal or written speech, including conversation and/or display of signs and/or distribution of literature." They further alleged that such activities frequently entail being within eight feet of other persons and that their fear of prosecution under the new statute caused them "to be chilled in the exercise of fundamental constitutional rights."

II

Before confronting the question whether the Colorado statute reflects an acceptable balance between the constitutionally protected rights of law-abiding speakers and the interests of unwilling listeners, it is appropriate to examine the competing interests at stake.

The First Amendment interests of petitioners are clear and undisputed. [T]hey correctly state that their leafletting, sign displays, and oral communications are protected by the First Amendment. The fact that the messages conveyed by those communications may be offensive to their recipients does not deprive them of constitutional protection. [T]he public sidewalks, streets, and ways affected by the statute are "quintessential" public forums for free speech. [A]lthough there is debate about the magnitude of the statutory impediment to their ability to communicate effectively with persons in the regulated zones, that ability, particularly the ability to distribute leaflets, is unquestionably lessened by this statute.

On the other hand, petitioners do not challenge the legitimacy of the state interests that the statute is intended to serve. It is a traditional exercise of the States' "police powers to protect the health and safety of their citizens." That interest may justify a special focus on unimpeded access to health care facilities and the avoidance of potential trauma to patients associated with confrontational protests. See Madsen v. Women's Health Center, Inc. (1994). It is also important when conducting this interest analysis to recognize the significant difference between state restrictions on a speaker's right to address a willing audience and those that protect listeners from unwanted communication. This statute deals only with the latter. The right to free speech, of course, includes the right to attempt to persuade others to change their views, and may not be curtailed simply because the speaker's message may be offensive to his audience. But the protection afforded to offensive messages does not always embrace offensive speech that is so intrusive that the unwilling audience cannot avoid it. Frisby v. Schultz (1988). The unwilling listener's interest in avoiding unwanted communication has been repeatedly identified in our cases. It is an aspect of the broader "right to be let alone" that one of our wisest Justices characterized as "the most comprehensive of rights and the right most valued by civilized men." Olmstead v. United States (1928) (Brandeis, J., dissenting).

III

All four of the state court opinions upholding the validity of this statute concluded that it is a content-neutral time, place, and manner regulation. It is therefore appropriate to comment on the "content neutrality" of the statute. The Colorado statute passes that test for three independent reasons. First, it is not a "regulation of speech." Rather, it is a regulation of the places where some speech may occur. Second, it was not adopted "because of disagreement with the message it conveys." This conclusion is supported not just by the Colorado courts' interpretation of legislative history, but more importantly by the State Supreme Court's unequivocal holding that the statute's "restrictions apply equally to all demonstrators, regardless of viewpoint, and the statutory language makes no reference to the content of the speech." Third, the State's interests in protecting access and privacy, and providing the police with clear guidelines, are unrelated to the content of the demonstrators' speech. As we have repeatedly explained, government regulation of expressive activity is "content neutral" if it is justified without reference to the content of regulated speech.

The Colorado statute's regulation of the location of protests, education, and counseling places no restrictions on — and clearly does not prohibit — either a particular viewpoint or any subject matter that may be discussed by a speaker. Rather, it simply establishes a minor place restriction on an extremely broad category of communications with unwilling listeners. Instead of drawing distinctions based on the subject that the approaching speaker may wish to address, the statute applies equally to used car salesmen, animal rights activists, fundraisers, environmentalists, and missionaries. Each can attempt to educate unwilling listeners on any subject, but without consent may not approach within eight feet to do so.

We also agree with the state courts' conclusion that [the law] is a valid time, place, and manner regulation. The three types of communication regulated by §18-9-122(3) are the display of signs, leafletting, and oral speech. The 8-foot separation between the speaker and the audience should not have any adverse impact on the readers' ability to read signs displayed by demonstrators. In fact, the separation might actually aid the pedestrians' ability to see the signs by preventing others from surrounding them and impeding their view. Furthermore, the statute places no limitations on the number, size, text, or images of the placards.

With respect to oral statements, the distance certainly can make it more difficult for a speaker to be heard, particularly if the level of background noise is high and other speakers are competing for the pedestrian's attention. Notably, the statute places no limitation on the number of speakers or the noise level, including the use of amplification equipment, although we have upheld such restrictions in past cases. [T]his 8-foot zone allows the speaker to communicate at a "normal conversational distance." Additionally, the statute allows the speaker to remain in one place, and other individuals can pass within eight feet of the protester without causing the protester to violate the statute. Finally, here there is a "knowing" requirement that protects speakers "who thought they were keeping pace with the targeted individual" at the proscribed distance from inadvertently violating the statute.

The burden on the ability to distribute handbills is more serious because it seems possible that an 8-foot interval could hinder the ability of a leafletter to deliver handbills to some unwilling recipients. The statute does not, however, prevent a leafletter from simply standing near the path of oncoming pedestrians and proffering his or her material, which the pedestrians can easily accept. And, as in all leafletting situations, pedestrians continue to be free to decline the tender.

Finally, in determining whether a statute is narrowly tailored, we have noted that "[w]e must, of course, take account of the place to which the regulations apply in determining whether these restrictions burden more speech than necessary." States and municipalities plainly have a substantial interest in controlling the activity around certain public and private places. For example, we have recognized the special governmental interests surrounding schools, courthouses, polling places, and private homes. Additionally, we previously have noted the unique concerns that surround health care facilities. Persons who are attempting to enter health care facilities—for any purpose—are often in particularly vulnerable physical and emotional conditions. The State of Colorado has responded to its substantial and legitimate interest in protecting these persons from unwanted encounters, confrontations, and even assaults by enacting an exceedingly modest restriction on the speakers' ability to approach. This restriction is thus reasonable and narrowly tailored.

Justice SCALIA, with whom Justice THOMAS joins, dissenting.

What is before us is a speech regulation directed against the opponents of abortion, and it therefore enjoys the benefit of the "ad hoc nullification machine" that the Court has set in motion to push aside whatever doctrines of constitutional law stand in the way of that highly favored practice. Having deprived abortion opponents of the political right to persuade the electorate that abortion should be restricted by law, the Court today continues and expands its assault upon their individual right to persuade women contemplating abortion that what they are doing is wrong. Because, like the rest of our abortion jurisprudence, today's decision is in stark contradiction of the constitutional principles we apply in all other contexts, I dissent.

I have no doubt that this regulation would be deemed content-based in an instant if the case before us involved antiwar protesters, or union members seeking to "educate" the public about the reasons for their strike. "[I]t is," we would say, "the content of the speech that determines whether it is within or without the statute's blunt prohibition," Carey v. Brown (1980). But the jurisprudence of this Court has a way of changing when abortion is involved.

The Court asserts that this statute is not content-based for purposes of our First Amendment analysis because it neither (1) discriminates among viewpoints nor (2) places restrictions on "any subject matter that may be discussed by a speaker." But we have never held that the universe of content-based regulations is limited to those two categories, and such a holding would be absurd. Imagine, for instance, special place-and-manner restrictions on all speech except that which "conveys a sense of contentment or happiness." This "happy speech" limitation would not be "viewpoint-based"—citizens would be able to express their joy in equal measure at either the rise or fall of the NASDAQ, at either the success or the failure of the Republican Party—and would not discriminate on the basis of subject matter, since gratification could be expressed about anything at all. Or consider a law restricting the writing or recitation of poetry—neither viewpoint-based nor limited to any particular subject matter. Surely this Court would consider such regulations to be "content-based" and deserving of the most exacting scrutiny.

A restriction that operates only on speech that communicates a message of protest, education, or counseling presents exactly this risk. When applied, as it is here, at the entrance to medical facilities, it is a means of impeding speech against abortion. The Court's confident assurance that the statute poses no special threat to First Amendment freedoms because it applies alike to "used car salesmen, animal rights activists, fundraisers, environmentalists, and missionaries," is a wonderful replication (except for its lack of sarcasm) of Anatole France's observation that "[t]he law, in its majestic equality, forbids the rich as well as the poor to sleep under bridges. . . ." This Colorado law is no more targeted at used car salesmen, animal rights activists, fund raisers, environmentalists, and missionaries than French vagrancy law was targeted at the rich. We know what the Colorado legislators, by their careful selection of content ("protest, education, and counseling"), were taking aim at, for they set it forth in the statute itself: the "right to protest or counsel against certain medical procedures" on the sidewalks and streets surrounding health care facilities.

In sum, it blinks reality to regard this statute, in its application to oral communications, as anything other than a content-based restriction upon speech in the public forum. As such, it must survive that stringent mode of constitutional analysis our cases refer to as "strict scrutiny," which requires that the restriction be narrowly tailored to serve a compelling state interest. Since the Court does not even attempt to support the regulation under this standard, I shall discuss it only briefly. Suffice it to say that if protecting people from unwelcome communications (the governmental interest the Court posits) is a compelling state interest, the First Amendment is a dead letter. And if forbidding peaceful, nonthreatening, but uninvited speech from a distance closer than eight feet is a "narrowly tailored" means of preventing the obstruction of entrance to medical facilities (the governmental interest the State asserts) narrow tailoring must refer not to the standards of Versace, but to those of Omar the tentmaker. In the last analysis all of this does not matter, however, since as I proceed to discuss neither the restrictions upon oral communications nor those upon handbilling can withstand a proper application of even the less demanding scrutiny we apply to truly content-neutral regulations of speech in a traditional public forum.

Does the deck seem stacked? You bet. As I have suggested throughout this opinion, today's decision is not an isolated distortion of our traditional constitutional principles, but is one of many aggressively proabortion novelties announced by the Court in recent years. Today's distortions, however, are particularly blatant. Restrictive views of the First Amendment that have been in dissent since the 1930's suddenly find themselves in the majority. "Uninhibited, robust, and wide open" debate is replaced by the power of the state to protect an unheard-of "right to be let alone" on the public streets. I dissent.

Justice KENNEDY, dissenting.

The Court's holding contradicts more than a half century of well-established First Amendment principles. For the first time, the Court approves a law which bars a private citizen from passing a message, in a peaceful manner and on a profound moral issue, to a fellow citizen on a public sidewalk. If from this time forward the Court repeats its grave errors of analysis, we shall have no longer the proud tradition of free and open discourse in a public forum.

The statute is content based: It restricts speech on particular topics. Of course, the enactment restricts "oral protest, education, or counselling" on any subject; but a statute of broad application is not content neutral if its terms control the substance of a speaker's message. If oral protest, education, or counseling on every subject within an 8-foot zone present a danger to the public, the statute should apply to every building entrance in the State. It does not. It applies only to a special class of locations: entrances to buildings with health care facilities. We would close our eyes to reality were we to deny that "oral protest, education, or counseling" outside the entrances to medical facilities concern a narrow range of topics—indeed, one topic in particular. By confining the law's application to the specific locations where the prohibited discourse occurs, the State has made a content-based determination. The Court ought to so acknowledge. Clever content-based restrictions are no less offensive than censoring on the basis of content. If, just a few decades ago, a State with a history of enforcing racial discrimination had enacted a statute like this one, regulating "oral protest, education, or counseling" within 100 feet of the entrance to any lunch counter, our predecessors would not have hesitated to hold it was content based or viewpoint based. It should be a profound disappointment to defenders of the First Amendment that the Court today refuses to apply the same structural analysis when the speech involved is less palatable to it.

Colorado's scheme of disfavored-speech zones on public streets and sidewalks, and the Court's opinion validating them, are antithetical to our entire First Amendment tradition. To say that one citizen can approach another to ask the time or the weather forecast or the directions to Main Street but not to initiate discussion on one of the most basic moral and political issues in all of contemporary discourse, a question touching profound ideas in philosophy and theology, is an astonishing view of the First Amendment. For the majority to examine the statute under rules applicable to content-neutral regulations is an affront to First Amendment teachings.

In many other cases, the Court also upheld government restrictions of speech in public forums as permissible time, place, and manner restrictions. In Kovacs v. Cooper, 336 U.S. 77 (1949), the Court upheld a restriction on the use of sound amplification devices, such as loudspeakers on trucks. The Court emphasized that the law did not prohibit all such devices, but rather was a reasonable time, place, and manner restriction. In Grayned v. Rockford, 408 U.S. 104 (1972), the Court upheld a city's ordinance that prohibited any "person, while on public or private grounds adjacent to any building in which a school or any class thereof is in session, to make any noise or diversion which disturbs or tends to disturb the peace or good order of such school." The Court found that the restriction was a reasonable time, place, and manner restriction and affirmed a conviction for violating it. The Court said that the "crucial question is whether the manner of expression is basically incompatible with the normal activity of a particular place at a particular time." The Court said that the ordinance was constitutional because it prohibited speech disruptive of schools and that was permissible based on the city's important interest in ensuring order sufficient for schooling.

In Clark v. Community for Creative Non-Violence, 468 U.S. 288 (1984), the Court upheld a federal regulation and Park Service decision to keep a group protesting the plight of the homeless from sleeping in the park. The National Park Service allowed the Community for Creative Non-Violence to erect a tent city in Lafayette Park and the Mall in Washington, D.C., as a symbolic protest, but refused to allow the demonstrators to sleep in the tents because of a regulation prohibiting camping in these parks. The Supreme Court accepted arguendo the contention that overnight sleeping as a part of this protest was a form of expressive conduct, but the Court upheld the regulation as a reasonable time, place, and manner restriction. The Court emphasized that the restriction was content-neutral, that it served the important purpose of preserving the attractiveness of the parks, and that it left adequate alternative ways of expressing the message. For example, the demonstrators could "feign" sleep in the tents, just not actually sleep there.

While in *Hejfron, Hill, Kovacs, Grayned,* and *Clark* the Court upheld the regulations as permissible time, place, and manner restrictions, in other cases the Court has ruled against the government using this test. For instance, in Brown v. Louisiana, 383 U.S. 131 (1966), the Court reversed the conviction of a group of African Americans who had conducted a silent sit-in as a protest at a racially segregated public library. The plurality opinion stressed that it was a silent protest that did not interfere with the operation of the library. The plurality also was undoubtedly influenced by the importance of the protest. The plurality said that the First Amendment protected "the right in a peaceful and orderly manner to protest by silent and reproachful presence, in a place where the protestant has every right to be, the unconstitutional segregation of public facilities."

In United States v. Grace, 461 U.S. 171 (1983), the Court declared unconstitutional a broad restriction of speech on the public sidewalks surrounding the Supreme Court's building. In part, the regulation prohibited the display of "any flag, banner, or device designed to bring into public notice any party, organization, or movement." The Court found that the rule was not a reasonable time, place, and manner restriction because a total ban on all speech was unnecessary to preserve order and prevent disruption of Supreme Court proceedings. Silent protests never would interfere with the Court, and the Court rejected the argument that protests could be prohibited to prevent the public from inferring that decisions were influenced by the demonstrators.

Looked at together, all of these cases indicate that the determination of whether a regulation is a reasonable time, place, and manner restriction is entirely contextual. In each instance, the Court has to assess whether it serves an important interest and whether it leaves open adequate alternative places for expression.

iii. Licensing and Permit Systems

As described in section B above, a licensing or permit system is a classic form of prior restraint. The Court has made it clear that the government can require a license for speech in public forums only if there is an important reason for licensing, there are clear criteria leaving almost no discretion to the licensing authority, and there are procedural safeguards such as a requirement for prompt determination of license requests and judicial review of license denials.

A permit system that meets all of these requirements will be allowed. For instance, in Cox v. New Hampshire, 312 U.S. 569 (1941), the Court upheld an ordinance that required that those wishing to hold a parade or demonstration obtain a permit and that allowed a permit to be denied only if the area already was in use by another group. The Court found that the government had an important interest in requiring a permit for speech so as to make sure that there was only one demonstration in a place at a time. Professor Harry Kalven referred to this as "Robert's Rules of Order" for use of the public forum.[180] The Court emphasized that the "licensing board was not vested with arbitrary power or unfettered discretion."

---

180. Harry Kalven, *The Concept of the Public Forum: Cox v. Louisiana,* 1965 S. Ct. Rev. 1, 26, 28-29.

In contrast, permit systems that leave significant discretion to the licensing authority are declared unconstitutional because they risk the government's granting permits to favored speech and denying them to unpopular expression. In Lovell v. Griffin, 303 U.S. 444 (1938), presented above, the Court declared unconstitutional a city's ordinance that prohibited the distribution of leaflets, literature, or advertising without the written permission of the city manager. The Court explained that the regulation was a prior restraint that "strikes at the very foundation of the freedom of the press by subjecting it to license and censorship. The struggle for freedom of the press was primarily directed against the power of the licensor." The Court said that "[l]egislation of the type of the ordinance in question would restore the system of license and censorship in its baldest form."

Likewise, the Court has held that the government cannot require a permit fee for demonstrations if government officials have discretion in setting the amount of the charge. In Forsyth County, Georgia v. Nationalist Movement, 505 U.S. 123 (1992), the Court declared unconstitutional an ordinance that required a permit in order for a demonstration to occur and that allowed government officials to charge a permit fee of up to $1,000. The Court found that the licensing law was impermissible because "[t]here are no articulated standards either in the ordinance or in the county's established practice. The administrator is not required to rely on any objective factors. He need not provide any explanation for his decision, and that decision is unreviewable." The Court concluded that "nothing in the law or its application prevents the official from encouraging some views and discouraging others through the arbitrary application of the fees. The First Amendment prohibits the vesting of such unbridled discretion in a government official."

Nationalist Movement did not declare unconstitutional all permit fee requirements; it simply held that such charges are unconstitutional if government officials have discretion as to the amount. In Cox v. New Hampshire, described above, the Court upheld a licensing system that allowed the government to charge a permit fee of up to $300. Although the discretion under this ordinance likely would make it unconstitutional under *Nationalist Movement*, the Court never has overruled its conclusion that the government can charge "a nominal fee imposed . . . to defray the expenses of policing the activities in question." But nor has the Court ever clarified what fees are permissible under what circumstances.

On the one hand, there is a strong argument that all charges for the use of public property for speech should be declared unconstitutional.[181] Any fee might keep some from speaking, and the loss is not just to the speaker's First Amendment rights, but to the rights of all who are denied hearing the message. If the government can charge demonstrators for use of public property or for police protection, that often will have the same effect as a complete ban on the speech. On the other hand, the government is almost never required to subsidize the exercise of constitutional rights. A prohibition of all permit fees would be forcing the government to subsidize the use of the public forum for speech purposes.

181. For an excellent development of this argument, *see* David Goldberger, *A Reconsideration of Cox v. New Hampshire: Can Demonstrators Be Required to Pay the Costs of Using America's Public Forums?*, 62 Tex. L. Rev. 403 (1983).

iv.   No Requirement for Use of the Least Restrictive Alternative

Finally, in Ward v. Rock Against Racism, the Court has held that when the government regulates speech in the public forum, it need not use the least restrictive alternative, although any regulation must be narrowly tailored.

WARD v. ROCK AGAINST RACISM
491 U.S. 781 (1989)

Justice KENNEDY delivered the opinion of the Court.

In the southeast portion of New York City's Central Park, about 10 blocks upward from the park's beginning point at 59th Street, there is an amphitheater and stage structure known as the Naumberg Acoustic Bandshell. The bandshell faces west across the remaining width of the park. In close proximity to the bandshell, and lying within the directional path of its sound, is a grassy open area called the Sheep Meadow. The city has designated the Sheep Meadow as a quiet area for passive recreations like reclining, walking, and reading. Just beyond the park, and also within the potential sound range of the bandshell, are the apartments and residences of Central Park West.

This case arises from the city's attempt to regulate the volume of amplified music at the bandshell so the performances are satisfactory to the audience without intruding upon those who use the Sheep Meadow or live on Central Park West and in its vicinity. The city's regulation requires bandshell performers to use sound-amplification equipment and a sound technician provided by the city. The challenge to this volume control technique comes from the sponsor of a rock concert.

Music is one of the oldest forms of human expression. From Plato's discourse in the Republic to the totalitarian state in our own times, rulers have known its capacity to appeal to the intellect and to the emotions, and have censored musical compositions to serve the needs of the state.

The principal justification for the sound-amplification guideline is the city's desire to control noise levels at bandshell events, in order to retain the character of the Sheep Meadow and its more sedate activities, and to avoid undue intrusion into residential areas and other areas of the park. This justification for the guideline "ha[s] nothing to do with content," and it satisfies the requirement that time, place, or manner regulations be content neutral.

The city's regulation is also "narrowly tailored to serve a significant governmental interest." Despite respondent's protestations to the contrary, it can no longer be doubted that government "ha[s] a substantial interest in protecting its citizens from unwelcome noise." Lest any confusion on the point remain, we reaffirm today that a regulation of the time, place, or manner of protected speech must be narrowly tailored to serve the government's legitimate, content-neutral interests but that it need not be the least restrictive or least intrusive means of doing so. Rather, the requirement of narrow tailoring is satisfied "so long as the . . . regulation promotes a substantial government interest that would be achieved less effectively absent the regulation."

To be sure, this standard does not mean that a time, place, or manner regulation may burden substantially more speech than is necessary to further the government's legitimate interests. Government may not regulate expression in such a manner that a substantial portion of the burden on speech does not serve to advance its goals. So long as the means chosen are not substantially broader than necessary to achieve the government's interest, however, the regulation will not be invalid simply because a court concludes that the government's interest could be adequately served by some less-speech-restrictive alternative. While time, place, or manner regulations must also be "narrowly tailored" in order to survive First Amendment challenge, we have never applied strict scrutiny in this context. As a result, the same degree of tailoring is not required of these regulations, and least-restrictive-alternative analysis is wholly out of place.

It is undeniable that the city's substantial interest in limiting sound volume is served in a direct and effective way by the requirement that the city's sound technician control the mixing board during performances. Absent this requirement, the city's interest would have been served less well, as is evidenced by the complaints about excessive volume generated by respondent's past concerts.

The final requirement, that the guideline leave open ample alternative channels of communication, is easily met. Indeed, in this respect the guideline is far less restrictive than regulations we have upheld in other cases, for it does not attempt to ban any particular manner or type of expression at a given place or time. Rather, the guideline continues to permit expressive activity in the bandshell, and has no effect on the quantity or content of that expression beyond regulating the extent of amplification.

Justice MARSHALL, with whom Justice BRENNAN and Justice STEVENS join, dissenting.

No one can doubt that government has a substantial interest in regulating the barrage of excessive sound that can plague urban life. Unfortunately, the majority plays to our shared impatience with loud noise to obscure the damage that it does to our First Amendment rights. Until today, a key safeguard of free speech has been government's obligation to adopt the least intrusive restriction necessary to achieve its goals. By abandoning the requirement that time, place, and manner regulations must be narrowly tailored, the majority replaces constitutional scrutiny with mandatory deference. The majority's willingness to give government officials a free hand in achieving their policy ends extends so far as to permit, in this case, government control of speech in advance of its dissemination. Because New York City's Use Guidelines (Guidelines) are not narrowly tailored to serve its interest in regulating loud noise, and because they constitute an impermissible prior restraint, I dissent.

d. Designated Public Forums

In Christian Legal Society v. Martinez, quoted above, the Supreme Court said that "designated public forums [exist] when 'government property that has not traditionally been regarded as a public forum is intentionally opened up for that purpose'; speech restrictions in such a forum 'are subject to the same strict scrutiny as restrictions in a traditional public forum.'"

For example, the Court has held that if the public schools and universities open their property for use by student and community groups, they cannot exclude religious groups. In Widmar v. Vincent, 454 U.S. 263 (1981), the Court ruled that a university that allowed student groups to use school buildings could not exclude religious student groups from access. Similarly, in Lamb's Chapel v. Center Moriches Union Free School Dist., 508 U.S. 384 (1993), the Court held that once a school district allowed community groups to use facilities during evenings and weekends, religious groups could not be excluded. It is very unlikely that these school facilities would be considered a public forum; the government likely could exclude all use by student or community groups. But once the government chose to open these places to speech, it had to comply with all of the same rules as in public forums, including refraining from content-based discrimination.

In Good News Club v. Milford Central School, 533 U.S. 98 (2001), the Court considered the constitutionality of an elementary school's exclusion of a group's using school property after school for religious activities including prayer and Bible study.

There were two parts to the Court's holding. First, the Court ruled that excluding the group violated the Speech Clause of the First Amendment. The Court said that the parties in the case had accepted that by opening its facilities the school had created a "limited public forum." The Court said that "[w]hen the State establishes a limited public forum, the State is not required to and does not allow persons to engage in every type of speech. The State may be justified 'in reserving [its forum] for certain groups or for the discussion of certain topics.' The State's power to restrict speech, however, is not without limits. The restriction must not discriminate against speech on the basis of viewpoint, and the restriction must be 'reasonable in light of the purpose served by the forum.'" The Court found that excluding the religious speech was impermissible viewpoint discrimination. Second, the Court concluded that allowing the religious group to use the property on the same terms as other community groups would not violate the Establishment Clause of the First Amendment. The latter aspect of the case is discussed in Chapter 10.

e. Limited Public Forums

In Christian Legal Society v. Martinez, quoted above, the Supreme Court said that "governmental entities establish limited public forums by opening property 'limited to use by certain groups or dedicated solely to the discussion of certain subjects.' In such a forum, a governmental entity may impose restrictions on speech that are reasonable and viewpoint-neutral."[182] The Court, however, did not clarify how it is to be determined whether the government has created a "designated public forum," where subject-matter restrictions are not allowed, or a "limited public forum," where subject-matter restrictions are permitted.

In Christian Legal Society v. Martinez, the Court upheld the constitutionality of a law school at a public university requiring student groups to accept all

---

182. An example of this from an earlier case would be Lehman v. Shaker Heights, 418 U.S. 298 (1974). A city allowed commercial but not political advertisements on city buses, and the Supreme Court upheld this as constitutional. Under current tests, the Court essentially said that this was a limited public forum — a place being opened just to some topics — and it was allowed because the regulation was reasonable and viewpoint neutral.

members and denying recognition to student groups that discriminated based on religion and sexual orientation. The majority opinion, by Justice Ginsburg, found that the university had created a limited public forum and that the regulation was allowed because it was reasonable and viewpoint neutral.

CHRISTIAN LEGAL SOCIETY CHAPTER OF THE UNIVERSITY OF CALIFORNIA, HASTINGS COLLEGE OF THE LAW v. MARTINEZ
130 S. Ct. 2971 (2010)

Justice GINSBURG delivered the opinion of the Court.

In a series of decisions, this Court has emphasized that the First Amendment generally precludes public universities from denying student organizations access to student activities at public universities. May a public law school condition its official recognition of a student group — and the attendant use of school funds and facilities — on the organization's agreement to open eligibility for membership and leadership to all students?

In the view of petitioner Christian Legal Society (CLS), an accept-all-comers policy impairs its First Amendment rights to free speech, expressive association, and free exercise of religion by prompting it, on pain of relinquishing the advantages of recognition, to accept members who do not share the organization's core beliefs about religion and sexual orientation. From the perspective of respondent Hastings College of the Law (Hastings or the Law School), CLS seeks special dispensation from an across-the-board open-access requirement designed to further the reasonable educational purposes underpinning the school's student-organization program.

In accord with the District Court and the Court of Appeals, we reject CLS's First Amendment challenge. Compliance with Hastings' all-comers policy, we conclude, is a reasonable, viewpoint-neutral condition on access to the student-organization forum. In requiring CLS — in common with all other student organizations — to choose between welcoming all students and forgoing the benefits of official recognition, we hold, Hastings did not transgress constitutional limitations. CLS, it bears emphasis, seeks not parity with other organizations, but a preferential exemption from Hastings' policy. The First Amendment shields CLS against state prohibition of the organization's expressive activity, however exclusionary that activity may be. But CLS enjoys no constitutional right to state subvention of its selectivity.

I

Through its "Registered Student Organization" (RSO) program, Hastings extends official recognition to student groups. Several benefits attend this school-approved status. RSOs are eligible to seek financial assistance from the Law School, which subsidizes their events using funds from a mandatory student-activity fee imposed on all students. RSOs may also use Law-School channels to communicate with students: They may place announcements in a weekly Office-of-Student-Services newsletter, advertise events on designated bulletin boards, send e-mails using a Hastings-organization address, and participate in an annual Student Organizations Fair designed to advance recruitment efforts. In addition, RSOs may apply for permission to use the Law School's facilities for meetings and office space. Finally, Hastings allows officially recognized groups to use its name and logo.

In exchange for these benefits, RSOs must abide by certain conditions. Only a "non-commercial organization whose membership is limited to Hastings students may become [an RSO]." A prospective RSO must submit its bylaws to Hastings for approval, and if it intends to use the Law School's name or logo, it must sign a license agreement. Critical here, all RSOs must undertake to comply with Hastings' "Policies and Regulations Applying to College Activities, Organizations and Students."

The Law School's Policy on Nondiscrimination (Nondiscrimination Policy), which binds RSOs, states:

> [Hastings] is committed to a policy against legally impermissible, arbitrary or unreasonable discriminatory practices. All groups, including administration, faculty, student governments, [Hastings]-owned student residence facilities and programs sponsored by [Hastings], are governed by this policy of nondiscrimination. [Hasting's] policy on nondiscrimination is to comply fully with applicable law.
>
> [Hastings] shall not discriminate unlawfully on the basis of race, color, religion, national origin, ancestry, disability, age, sex or sexual orientation. This nondiscrimination policy covers admission, access and treatment in Hastings-sponsored programs and activities.

Hastings interprets the Nondiscrimination Policy, as it relates to the RSO program, to mandate acceptance of all comers: School-approved groups must "allow any student to participate, become a member, or seek leadership positions in the organization, regardless of [her] status or beliefs." Other law schools have adopted similar all-comers policies. From Hastings' adoption of its Nondiscrimination Policy in 1990 until the events stirring this litigation, "no student organization at Hastings . . . ever sought an exemption from the Policy." In 2004, CLS became the first student group to do so. At the beginning of the academic year, the leaders of a predecessor Christian organization—which had been an RSO at Hastings for a decade—formed CLS by affiliating with the national Christian Legal Society (CLS-National). CLS-National, an association of Christian lawyers and law students, charters student chapters at law schools throughout the country. CLS chapters must adopt bylaws that require members and officers to sign a "Statement of Faith" and to conduct their lives in accord with prescribed principles. Among those tenets is the belief that sexual activity should not occur outside of marriage between a man and a woman; CLS thus interprets its bylaws to exclude from affiliation anyone who engages in "unrepentant homosexual conduct." CLS also excludes students who hold religious convictions different from those in the Statement of Faith.

On September 17, 2004, CLS submitted to Hastings an application for RSO status, accompanied by all required documents, including the set of bylaws mandated by CLS-National. Several days later, the Law School rejected the application; CLS's bylaws, Hastings explained, did not comply with the Nondiscrimination Policy because CLS barred students based on religion and sexual orientation.

CLS formally requested an exemption from the Nondiscrimination Policy, but Hastings declined to grant one. "[T]o be one of our student-recognized organizations," Hastings reiterated, "CLS must open its membership to all students irrespective of their religious beliefs or sexual orientation." If CLS instead chose to operate outside the RSO program, Hastings stated, the school "would be pleased to provide [CLS] the use of Hastings facilities for its meetings and activities." CLS would also have access to chalkboards and generally available campus bulletin boards to announce its events. In other words, Hastings would do nothing to suppress CLS's endeavors, but neither would it lend RSO-level support for them.

Refusing to alter its bylaws, CLS did not obtain RSO status. It did, however, operate independently during the 2004-2005 academic year. CLS held weekly Bible-study meetings and invited Hastings students to Good Friday and Easter Sunday church services. It also hosted a beach barbeque, Thanksgiving dinner, campus lecture on the Christian faith and the legal practice, several fellowship dinners, an end-of-year banquet, and other informal social activities. On October 22, 2004, CLS filed suit against various Hastings officers and administrators under 42 U.S.C. §1983.

II

Before considering the merits of CLS's constitutional arguments, we must resolve a preliminary issue: CLS urges us to review the Nondiscrimination Policy as written — prohibiting discrimination on several enumerated bases, including religion and sexual orientation — and not as a requirement that all RSOs accept all comers. The written terms of the Nondiscrimination Policy, CLS contends, "targe[t] solely those groups whose beliefs are based on religion or that disapprove of a particular kind of sexual behavior," and leave other associations free to limit membership and leadership to individuals committed to the group's ideology. For example, "[a] political . . . group can insist that its leaders support its purposes and beliefs," CLS alleges, but "a religious group cannot."

CLS's assertion runs headlong into the stipulation of facts it jointly submitted with Hastings at the summary-judgment stage. In that filing, the parties specified: "Hastings requires that registered student organizations allow *any* student to participate, become a member, or seek leadership positions in the organization, regardless of [her] status or beliefs. Thus, for example, the Hastings Democratic Caucus cannot bar students holding Republican political beliefs from becoming members or seeking leadership positions in the organization."

"[Factual stipulations are] binding and conclusive . . . , and the facts stated are not subject to subsequent variation. So, the parties will not be permitted to deny the truth of the facts stated, . . . or to maintain a contention contrary to the agreed statement, . . . or to suggest, on appeal, that the facts were other than as stipulated or that any material fact was omitted." This Court has accordingly refused to consider a party's argument that contradicted a joint "stipulation [entered] at the outset of th[e] litigation." Time and again, the dissent races away from the facts to which CLS stipulated. But factual stipulations are "formal concessions . . . that have the effect of withdrawing a fact from issue and dispensing wholly with the need for proof of the fact. Thus, a judicial admission . . . is conclusive in the case."

In light of the joint stipulation, both the District Court and the Ninth Circuit trained their attention on the constitutionality of the all-comers requirement, as described in the parties' accord. We reject CLS's unseemly attempt to escape from the stipulation and shift its target to Hastings' policy as written. This opinion, therefore, considers only whether conditioning access to a student-organization forum on compliance with an all-comers policy violates the Constitution.

III

A

In support of the argument that Hastings' all-comers policy treads on its First Amendment rights to free speech and expressive association, CLS draws on two lines of decisions. First, in a progression of cases, this Court has employed forum analysis to determine when a governmental entity, in regulating property in its charge, may place limitations on speech. Recognizing a State's right "to preserve the property under its control for the use to which it is lawfully dedicated," the Court has permitted restrictions on access to a limited public forum, like the RSO program here, with this key caveat: Any access barrier must be reasonable and viewpoint neutral. Second, as evidenced by another set of decisions, this Court has rigorously reviewed laws and regulations that constrain associational freedom. In the context of public accommodations, we have subjected restrictions on that freedom to close scrutiny; such restrictions are permitted only if they serve "compelling state interests" that are "unrelated to the suppression of ideas" — interests that cannot be advanced "through . . . significantly less restrictive [means]." "Freedom of association," we have recognized, "plainly presupposes a freedom not to associate." Insisting that an organization embrace unwelcome members, we have therefore concluded, "directly and immediately affects associational rights."

CLS would have us engage each line of cases independently, but its expressive-association and free-speech arguments merge: *Who* speaks on its behalf, CLS reasons, colors *what* concept is conveyed. It therefore makes little sense to treat CLS's speech and association claims as discrete. Instead, three observations lead us to conclude that our limited-public-forum precedents supply the appropriate framework for assessing both CLS's speech and association rights.

First, the same considerations that have led us to apply a less restrictive level of scrutiny to speech in limited public forums as compared to other environments, apply with equal force to expressive association occurring in limited public forums. As just noted, speech and expressive-association rights are closely linked.

Second, and closely related, the strict scrutiny we have applied in some settings to laws that burden expressive association would, in practical effect, invalidate a defining characteristic of limited public forums-the State may "reserv[e] [them] for certain groups."

Third, this case fits comfortably within the limited-public-forum category, for CLS, in seeking what is effectively a state subsidy, faces only indirect pressure to modify its membership policies; CLS may exclude any person for any reason if it forgoes the benefits of official recognition. The expressive-association precedents on which CLS relies, in contrast, involved regulations that *compelled* a group to include unwanted members, with no choice to opt out. In diverse contexts, our decisions have distinguished between policies that require action and those that withhold benefits.

In sum, we are persuaded that our limited-public-forum precedents adequately respect both CLS's speech and expressive-association rights, and fairly balance those rights against Hastings' interests as property owner and educational institution. We turn to the merits of the instant dispute, therefore, with the limited-public-forum decisions as our guide.

[B]

We first consider whether Hastings' policy is reasonable taking into account the RSO forum's function and "all the surrounding circumstances."

Our inquiry is shaped by the educational context in which it arises: "First Amendment rights," we have observed, "must be analyzed in light of the special characteristics of the school environment." This Court is the final arbiter of the question whether a public university has exceeded constitutional constraints, and we owe no deference to universities when we consider that question. Cognizant that judges lack the on-the-ground expertise and experience of school administrators, however, we have cautioned courts in various contexts to resist "substitut[ing] their own notions of sound educational policy for those of the school authorities which they review."

A college's commission—and its concomitant license to choose among pedagogical approaches—is not confined to the classroom, for extracurricular programs are, today, essential parts of the educational process. Schools, we have emphasized, enjoy "a significant measure of authority over the type of officially recognized activities in which their students participate." We therefore "approach our task with special caution," mindful that Hastings' decisions about the character of its student-group program are due decent respect.

With appropriate regard for school administrators' judgment, we review the justifications Hastings offers in defense of its all-comers requirement. First, the open-access policy "ensures that the leadership, educational, and social opportunities afforded by [RSOs] are available to all students." Just as "Hastings does not allow its professors to host classes open only to those students with a certain status or belief," so the Law School may decide, reasonably in our view, "that the . . . educational experience is best promoted when all participants in the forum must provide equal access to all students." RSOs, we count it significant, are eligible for financial assistance drawn from mandatory student-activity fees; the all-comers policy ensures that no Hastings student is forced to fund a group that would reject her as a member.

Second, the all-comers requirement helps Hastings police the written terms of its Nondiscrimination Policy without inquiring into an RSO's motivation for membership restrictions. To bring the RSO program within CLS's view of the Constitution's limits, CLS proposes that Hastings permit exclusion because of *belief* but forbid discrimination due to *status*. But that proposal would impose on Hastings a daunting labor. How should the Law School go about determining whether a student organization cloaked prohibited status exclusion in belief-based garb? If a hypothetical Male-Superiority Club barred a female student from running for its presidency, for example, how could the Law

School tell whether the group rejected her bid because of her sex or because, by seeking to lead the club, she manifested a lack of belief in its fundamental philosophy?

Third, the Law School reasonably adheres to the view that an all-comers policy, to the extent it brings together individuals with diverse backgrounds and beliefs, "encourages tolerance, cooperation, and learning among students." And if the policy sometimes produces discord, Hastings can rationally rank among RSO-program goals development of conflict-resolution skills, toleration, and readiness to find common ground.

Fourth, Hastings' policy, which incorporates — in fact, subsumes — state-law proscriptions on discrimination, conveys the Law School's decision "to decline to subsidize with public monies and benefits conduct of which the people of California disapprove."

In sum, the several justifications Hastings asserts in support of its all-comers requirement are surely reasonable in light of the RSO forum's purposes.

The Law School's policy is all the more creditworthy in view of the "substantial alternative channels that remain open for [CLS-student] communication to take place." If restrictions on access to a limited public forum are viewpoint discriminatory, the ability of a group to exist outside the forum would not cure the constitutional shortcoming. But when access barriers are viewpoint neutral, our decisions have counted it significant that other available avenues for the group to exercise its First Amendment rights lessen the burden created by those barriers.

In this case, Hastings offered CLS access to school facilities to conduct meetings and the use of chalkboards and generally available bulletin boards to advertise events. Although CLS could not take advantage of RSO-specific methods of communication, the advent of electronic media and social-networking sites reduces the importance of those channels.

Private groups, from fraternities and sororities to social clubs and secret societies, commonly maintain a presence at universities without official school affiliation. Based on the record before us, CLS was similarly situated: It hosted a variety of activities the year after Hastings denied it recognition, and the number of students attending those meetings and events doubled. "The variety and type of alternative modes of access present here," in short, "compare favorably with those in other [limited public] forum cases where we have upheld restrictions on access."

CLS also assails the reasonableness of the all-comers policy in light of the RSO forum's function by forecasting that the policy will facilitate hostile takeovers; if organizations must open their arms to all, CLS contends, saboteurs will infiltrate groups to subvert their mission and message. This supposition strikes us as more hypothetical than real. CLS points to no history or prospect of RSO-hijackings at Hastings. Students tend to self-sort and presumably will not endeavor en masse to join — let alone seek leadership positions in — groups pursuing missions wholly at odds with their personal beliefs. And if a rogue student intent on sabotaging an organization's objectives nevertheless attempted a takeover, the members of that group would not likely elect her as an officer. RSOs, moreover, in harmony with the all-comers policy, may condition eligibility for membership and leadership on attendance, the payment of dues, or other neutral requirements designed to ensure that students join because of their commitment to a group's vitality, not its demise.

Hastings, furthermore, could reasonably expect more from its law students than the disruptive behavior CLS hypothesizes — and to build this expectation into its educational approach. A reasonable policy need not anticipate and preemptively close off every opportunity for avoidance or manipulation. If students begin to exploit an all-comers policy by hijacking organizations to distort or destroy their missions, Hastings presumably would revisit and revise its policy.

[C]

We next consider whether Hastings' all-comers policy is viewpoint neutral. Although this aspect of limited-public-forum analysis has been the constitutional sticking point in our prior decisions, as earlier recounted, we need not dwell on it here. It is, after all, hard to imagine a more viewpoint-neutral policy than one requiring *all* student groups to accept *all* comers.

Conceding that Hastings' all-comers policy is "nominally neutral," CLS attacks the regulation by pointing to its effect: The policy is vulnerable to constitutional assault, CLS contends, because "it systematically and predictably burdens most heavily those groups whose viewpoints are out of favor with the campus mainstream." Even if a regulation has a differential impact on groups wishing to enforce exclusionary membership policies, "[w]here the [State] does not target conduct on the basis of its expressive content, acts are not shielded from regulation merely because they express a discriminatory idea or philosophy."

Hastings' requirement that student groups accept all comers, we are satisfied, "is justified without reference to the content [or viewpoint] of the regulated speech." The Law School's policy aims at the *act* of rejecting would-be group members without reference to the reasons motivating that behavior: Hastings' "desire to redress th[e] perceived harms" of exclusionary membership policies "provides an adequate explanation for its [all-comers condition] over and above mere disagreement with [any student group's] beliefs or biases." CLS's conduct — not its Christian perspective — is, from Hastings' vantage point, what stands between the group and RSO status.

Finding Hastings' open-access condition on RSO status reasonable and viewpoint neutral, we reject CLS' free-speech and expressive-association claims.

Justice KENNEDY, concurring.

An objection might be that the all-comers policy, even if not so designed or intended, in fact makes it difficult for certain groups to express their views in a manner essential to their message. A group that can limit membership to those who agree in full with its aims and purposes may be more effective in delivering its message or furthering its expressive objectives; and the Court has recognized that this interest can be protected against governmental interference or regulation. By allowing like-minded students to form groups around shared identities, a school creates room for self-expression and personal development.

In the instant case, however, if the membership qualification were enforced, it would contradict a legitimate purpose for having created the limited forum in the first place. Many educational institutions, including respondent Hastings College of Law, have recognized that the process of learning occurs both formally in a classroom setting and informally outside of it. Students may be shaped as profoundly by their peers as by their teachers. Extracurricular activities, such as those in the Hastings "Registered Student Organization" program, facilitate interactions between students, enabling them to explore new points of view, to develop interests and talents, and to nurture a growing sense of self. The Hasting program is designed to allow all students to interact with their colleagues across a broad, seemingly unlimited range of ideas, views, and activities.

In addition to a circumstance, already noted, in which it could be demonstrated that a school has adopted or enforced its policy with the intent or purpose of discriminating or disadvantaging a group on account of its views, petitioner also would have a substantial case on the merits if it were shown that the all-comers policy was either designed or used to infiltrate the group or challenge its leadership in order to stifle its views. But that has not been shown to be so likely or self-evident as a matter of group dynamics in this setting that the Court can declare the school policy void without more facts; and if there were a showing that in a particular case the purpose or effect of the policy was to stifle speech or make it ineffective, that, too, would present a case different from the one before us.

Justice ALITO, with whom The CHIEF JUSTICE, Justice SCALIA, and Justice THOMAS join, dissenting.

The proudest boast of our free speech jurisprudence is that we protect the freedom to express "the thought that we hate." Today's decision rests on a very different principle: no freedom for expression that offends prevailing standards of political correctness in our country's institutions of higher learning.

The Hastings College of the Law, a state institution, permits student organizations to register with the law school and severely burdens speech by unregistered groups. Hastings currently has more than 60 registered groups and, in all its history, has denied registration to exactly one: the Christian Legal Society (CLS). CLS claims that Hastings refused to register the group because the law school administration disapproves of the group's viewpoint and thus violated the group's free speech rights.

The Court's treatment of this case is deeply disappointing. The Court does not address the constitutionality of the very different policy that Hastings invoked when it denied CLS's application for registration. Nor does the Court address the constitutionality of the policy that Hastings now purports to follow. And the Court ignores strong evidence that the accept-all-comers policy is not viewpoint neutral because it was announced as a pretext to justify viewpoint discrimination. Brushing aside inconvenient precedent, the Court arms public educational institutions with a handy weapon for suppressing the speech of unpopular groups-groups to which, as Hastings candidly puts it, these institutions "do not wish to . . . lend their name[s]."

I

The Court provides a misleading portrayal of this case. I begin by correcting the picture.

The Court bases all of its analysis on the proposition that the relevant Hastings' policy is the so-called accept-all-comers policy. This frees the Court from the difficult task of defending the constitutionality of either the policy that Hastings actually—and repeatedly—invoked when it denied registration, *i.e.,* the school's written Nondiscrimination Policy, or the policy that Hastings belatedly unveiled when it filed its brief in this Court. Overwhelming evidence, however, shows that Hastings denied CLS's application pursuant to the Non-discrimination Policy and that the accept-all-comers policy was nowhere to be found until it was mentioned by a former dean in a deposition taken well after this case began.

During the 2004-2005 school year, Hastings had more than 60 registered groups, including political groups (*e.g.,* the Hastings Democratic Caucus and the Hastings Republicans), religious groups (*e.g.,* the Hastings Jewish Law Students Association and the Hastings Association of Muslim Law Students), groups that promote social causes (*e.g.,* both pro-choice and pro-life groups), groups organized around racial or ethnic identity (*e.g.,* the Black Law Students Association, the Korean American Law Society, La Raza Law Students Association, and the Middle Eastern Law Students Association), and groups that focus on gender or sexuality (*e.g.,* the Clara Foltz Feminist Association and Students Raising Consciousness at Hastings).

Not surprisingly many of these registered groups were and are dedicated to expressing a message. For example, Silenced Right, a pro-life group, taught that "all human life from the moment of conception until natural death is sacred and has inherent dignity," while Law Students for Choice aimed to "defend and expand reproductive rights."

Hastings claims that this accept-all-comers policy has existed since 1990 but points to no evidence that the policy was ever put in writing or brought to the attention of members of the law school community prior to the dean's deposition. Indeed, Hastings has adduced no evidence of the policy's existence before that date.

[T]he record is replete with evidence that, at least until Dean Kane unveiled the accept-all-comers policy in July 2005, Hastings routinely registered student groups with bylaws limiting membership and leadership positions to those who agreed with the groups' viewpoints. For example, the bylaws of the Hastings Democratic Caucus provided that "any full-time student at Hastings may become a member of HDC *so long as they do not exhibit a consistent disregard and lack of respect for the objective of the organization* as stated in Article 3, Section 1." The constitution of the Association of Trial Lawyers of America at Hastings provided that every member must "adhere to the objectives of the Student Chapter as well as the mission of ATLA." A student could become a member of the Vietnamese American Law Society so long as the student did not "exhibit a consistent disregard and lack of respect for the objective of the organization," which centers on a "celebrat[ion] [of] Vietnamese culture." Silenced Right limited voting membership to students who "are committed" to the group's "mission" of "spread[ing] the pro-life message." La Raza limited voting membership to "students of Raza background." Since Hastings requires any student group applying for registration to submit a copy of its bylaws, Hastings cannot claim that it was unaware of such provisions.

Like the majority of this Court, the Ninth Circuit relied on the following Joint Stipulation. I agree that the parties must be held to their Joint Stipulation, but the terms of the stipulation should be respected. What was admitted in the Joint Stipulation filed in December 2005 is that Hastings had an accept-all-comers policy. CLS did not stipulate that its application had been denied more than a year earlier pursuant to such a policy. On the contrary, the Joint Stipulation notes that the reason repeatedly given by Hasting at that time was that the CLS bylaws did not comply with *the Nondiscrimination Policy*. Indeed, the parties did not even stipulate that the accept-all-comers policy existed in the fall of 2004. In addition, Hastings itself is now attempting to walk away from this stipulation by disclosing that its real policy is an accept-some-comers policy.

The Court also distorts the record with respect to the effect on CLS of Hastings' decision to deny registration. The Court quotes a letter written by Hastings' general counsel in which she stated that Hastings "would be pleased to provide [CLS] the use of Hastings facilities for its meetings and activities." Later in its opinion, the Court reiterates that "Hastings offered CLS access to school facilities to conduct meetings," but the majority does not mention that this offer was subject to important qualifications. As Hastings' attorney put it in the District Court, Hastings told CLS: "'Hastings allows community groups to some degree to use its facilities, sometimes on a pay basis, I understand, if they're available after priority is given to registered organizations'. We offered that."

Other statements in the majority opinion make it seem as if the denial of registration did not hurt CLS at all. The Court notes that CLS was able to hold Bible-study meetings and other events. And "[a]lthough CLS could not take advantage of RSO-specific methods of communication," the Court states, "the advent of electronic media and social-networking sites reduces the importance of those channels." At the beginning of the 2005 school year, the Hastings CLS group had seven members, so there can be no suggestion that the group flourished. And since one of CLS's principal claims is that it was subjected to discrimination based on its viewpoint, the majority's emphasis on CLS's ability to endure that discrimination — by using private facilities and means of communication — is quite amazing.

This Court does not customarily brush aside a claim of unlawful discrimination with the observation that the effects of the discrimination were really not so bad. We have never before taken the view that a little viewpoint discrimination is acceptable. Nor have we taken this approach in other discrimination cases.

[II]

In this case, the forum consists of the RSO program. Once a public university opens a limited public forum, it "must respect the lawful boundaries it has itself set." The university "may not exclude speech where its distinction is not 'reasonable in light of the purpose served by the forum.'" And the university must maintain strict viewpoint neutrality.

This requirement of viewpoint neutrality extends to the expression of religious viewpoints. In an unbroken line of decisions analyzing private religious speech in limited public forums, we have made it perfectly clear that "[r]eligion is [a] viewpoint from which ideas are conveyed."

Analyzed under this framework, Hastings' refusal to register CLS pursuant to its Nondiscrimination Policy plainly fails. As previously noted, when Hastings refused to register CLS, it claimed that the CLS bylaws impermissibly discriminated on the basis of religion and sexual orientation. As interpreted by Hastings and applied to CLS, both of these grounds constituted viewpoint discrimination.

As Hastings stated in its answer, the Nondiscrimination Policy "permit[ted] political, social, and cultural student organizations to select officers and members who are dedicated to a particular set of ideals or beliefs." But the policy singled out one category of expressive associations for disfavored treatment: groups formed to express a religious message. Only religious groups were required to admit students who did not share their views. An environmentalist group was not required to admit students who rejected global warming. An animal rights group was not obligated to accept students who supported the use of animals to test cosmetics. But CLS was required to admit avowed atheists. This was patent viewpoint discrimination. "By the very terms of the [Nondiscrimination Policy], the University . . . select[ed] for disfavored treatment those student [groups] with religious . . . viewpoints." It is no wonder that the Court makes no attempt to defend the constitutionality of the Nondiscrimination Policy.

The Hastings Nondiscrimination Policy, as interpreted by the law school, also discriminated on the basis of viewpoint regarding sexual morality. CLS has a particular viewpoint on this subject, namely, that sexual conduct outside marriage between a man and a woman is wrongful. Hastings would not allow CLS to express this viewpoint by limiting membership to persons willing to express a sincere agreement with CLS's views. By contrast, nothing in the Nondiscrimination Policy prohibited a group from expressing a contrary viewpoint by limiting membership to persons willing to endorse that group's beliefs. A Free Love Club could require members to affirm that they reject the traditional view of sexual morality to which CLS adheres. It is hard to see how this can be viewed as anything other than viewpoint discrimination.

The Court is also wrong in holding that the accept-all-comers policy is viewpoint neutral. The Court proclaims that it would be "hard to imagine a more viewpoint-neutral policy," but I would not be so quick to jump to this conclusion. Even if it is assumed that the policy is viewpoint neutral on its face, there is strong evidence in the record that the policy was announced as a pretext.

Here, CLS has made a strong showing that Hastings' sudden adoption and selective application of its accept-all-comers policy was a pretext for the law school's unlawful denial of CLS's registration application under the Nondiscrimination Policy.

Here, Hastings claims that it has had an accept-all-comers policy since 1990, but it has not produced a single written document memorializing that policy. Nor has it cited a single occasion prior to the dean's deposition when this putative policy was orally disclosed to either student groups interested in applying for registration or to the Office of Student Services, which was charged with reviewing the bylaws of applicant groups to ensure that they were in compliance with the law school's policies.

Since it appears that no one was told about the accept-all-comers policy before July 2005, it is not surprising that the policy was not enforced. The record is replete with evidence that Hastings made no effort to enforce the all-comers policy until after it was proclaimed by the former dean.

[III]

One final aspect of the Court's decision warrants comment. In response to the argument that the accept-all-comers-policy would permit a small and unpopular group to be taken over by students who wish to silence its message, the Court states that the policy would permit a registered group to impose membership requirements "designed to ensure that students join because of their commitment to a group's vitality, not its demise." With this concession, the Court tacitly recognizes that Hastings does not really have an accept-all-comers policy — it has an accept-some-dissident-comers policy — and the line between members who merely seek to change a group's message (who apparently must be admitted) and those who seek a group's "demise" (who may be kept out) is hopelessly vague.

Justice Kennedy takes a similarly mistaken tack. He contends that CLS "would have a substantial case on the merits if it were shown that the all-comers policy was . . . used to infiltrate the group or challenge its leadership in order to stifle its views," but he does not explain on what ground such a claim could succeed. The Court holds that the accept-all-comers policy is viewpoint neutral and reasonable in light of the purposes of the RSO forum. How could those characteristics be altered by a change in the membership of one of the forum's registered groups? No explanation is apparent.

In the end, the Court refuses to acknowledge the consequences of its holding. A true accept-all-comers policy permits small unpopular groups to be taken over by students who wish to change the views that the group expresses. Rules requiring that members attend meetings, pay dues, and behave politely, would not eliminate this threat.

The possibility of such takeovers, however, is by no means the most important effect of the Court's holding. There are religious groups that cannot in good conscience agree in their bylaws that they will admit persons who do not share their faith, and for these groups, the consequence of an accept-all-comers policy is marginalization. This is where the Court's decision leads.

I do not think it is an exaggeration to say that today's decision is a serious setback for freedom of expression in this country. Our First Amendment reflects a "profound national commitment to the principle that debate on public issues should be uninhibited, robust, and wide-open." Even if the United States is the only Nation that shares this commitment to the same extent, I would not change our law to conform to the international norm. I fear that the Court's decision marks a turn in that direction. Even those who find CLS's views objectionable should be concerned about the way the group has been treated-by Hastings, the Court of Appeals, and now this Court. I can only hope that this decision will turn out to be an aberration.

f. Nonpublic Forums

Nonpublic forums are government properties that the government can close to all speech activities. The government may prohibit or restrict speech in nonpublic forums as long as the regulation is reasonable and viewpoint neutral. The Court has found many different types of government property to be nonpublic forums.

For example, in Adderly v. Florida, 385 U.S. 39 (1966), the Court held that the government could prohibit speech in the areas outside prisons and jails. Civil rights demonstrators held a rally outside a jail after a group of their colleagues had been arrested for engaging in a civil rights protest. The Court, in an opinion by Justice Black, upheld the convictions of those protesting at the jail who did not disperse in response to an order from the sheriff. Although the Court emphasized the government's security interests, it also spoke very broadly about the government's ability to restrict speech in public places. Justice Black declared, "The State, no less than a private owner of property, has the power to preserve the property under its control for the use to which it is lawfully dedicated. . . . The United States Constitution does not forbid a State to control the use of its own property for its own lawful nondiscriminatory purpose."

Justice Douglas wrote for the four dissenters and stressed the importance of the jail as a place for protest. He said, "The jailhouse, like an executive mansion, a legislative chamber, a courthouse, or the statehouse itself is one of the seats of government, whether it be the Tower of London, the Bastille, or a small county jail. And when it houses political prisoners or those who many think are unjustly held, it is an obvious center for protest."

In Greer v. Spock, 424 U.S. 828 (1976), the Court held that military bases, even parts of bases usually open to the public, are a nonpublic forum. Although civilians were allowed free access to nonrestricted areas of Fort Dix, a regulation prohibited "demonstrations, picketing, sit-ins, protest marches, [and] political speeches." The Supreme Court upheld this regulation and said that it is the business of a military installation like Fort Dix to train soldiers, not to provide a public forum. The Court said that the government could exclude such speech to insulate the military from political activities.

In United States v. Kokinda, 497 U.S. 720 (1990), the Court upheld a restriction on solicitations on post office properties. Sidewalks, of course, are the paradigm public forum. But the plurality opinion of Justice O'Connor said that sidewalks on post office property were a nonpublic forum. The plurality of four justices concluded that a postal sidewalk does not "have the characteristics of public sidewalks traditionally open to expressive activity." Justice O'Connor said that the "postal sidewalk was constructed solely to provide for the passage of individuals engaged in postal business." Although others had been allowed to use the postal property for speaking, leafleting, and picketing, the plurality concluded that this was not enough to transform it into a designated public forum because it did not add up to the dedication of postal property to speech activities.

Justice Kennedy, the fifth vote for upholding the regulation, wrote an opinion concurring in the judgment and said that there were strong grounds for applying the standards for public forums because of the wide array of activities allowed on the sidewalks. Justice Kennedy, however, said that the issue of how to characterize the forum did not need be resolved because the regulation was a reasonable time, place, and manner restriction.

In International Society for Krishna Consciousness, Inc. v. Lee, the Court applies these cases in considering whether airports are a nonpublic forum.

INTERNATIONAL SOCIETY FOR KRISHNA CONSCIOUSNESS, INC. v. LEE

505 U.S. 672 (1992)

Chief Justice REHNQUIST delivered the opinion of the Court.

In this case we consider whether an airport terminal operated by a public authority is a public forum and whether a regulation prohibiting solicitation in the interior of an airport terminal violates the First Amendment.

The relevant facts in this case are not in dispute. Petitioner International Society for Krishna Consciousness, Inc. (ISKCON), is a not-for-profit religious corporation whose members perform a ritual known as sankirtan. The ritual consists of "going into public places, disseminating religious literature and soliciting funds to support the religion." The primary purpose of this ritual is raising funds for the movement.

Respondent Walter Lee, now deceased, was the police superintendent of the Port Authority of New York and New Jersey and was charged with enforcing the regulation at issue. The Port Authority has adopted a regulation forbidding within the terminals the repetitive solicitation of money or distribution of literature.

It is uncontested that the solicitation at issue in this case is a form of speech protected under the First Amendment. But it is also well settled that the government need not permit all forms of speech on property that it owns and controls. Where the government is acting as a proprietor, managing its internal operations, rather than acting as lawmaker with the power to regulate or license, its action will not be subjected to the heightened review to which its actions as a lawmaker may be subject.

The parties [disagree about] whether the airport terminals are public fora or nonpublic fora. They also disagree whether the regulation survives the "reasonableness" review governing nonpublic fora, should that prove the appropriate category. Like the Court of Appeals, we conclude that the terminals are nonpublic fora and that the regulation reasonably limits solicitation.

Our recent cases provide guidance on the characteristics of a public forum. [W]e have noted that a traditional public forum is property that has as "a principal purpose . . . the free exchange of ideas." Moreover, consistent with the notion that the government—like other property owners—"has power to preserve the property under its control for the use to which it is lawfully dedicated," the government does not create a public forum by inaction. Nor is a public forum created "whenever members of the public are permitted freely to visit a place owned or operated by the Government." The decision to create a public forum must instead be made "by intentionally opening a nontraditional forum for public discourse." Finally, we have recognized that the location of property also has bearing because separation from acknowledged public areas may serve to indicate that the separated property is a special enclave, subject to greater restriction.

These precedents foreclose the conclusion that airport terminals are public fora. Reflecting the general growth of the air travel industry, airport terminals have only recently achieved their contemporary size and character. But given the lateness with which the modern air terminal has made its appearance, it hardly qualifies for the description of having "immemorially . . . time out of mind" been held in the public trust and used for purposes of expressive activity. Moreover, even within the rather short history of air transport, it is only "[i]n recent years [that] it has become a common practice for various religious and nonprofit organizations to use commercial airports as a forum for the distribution of literature, the solicitation of funds, the proselytizing of new members, and other similar activities." Thus, the tradition of airport activity does not demonstrate that airports have historically been made available for speech activity. Nor can we say that these particular terminals, or airport terminals generally, have been intentionally opened by their operators to such activity; the frequent and continuing litigation evidencing the operators' objections belies any such claim. In short, there can be no argument that society's time-tested judgment, expressed through acquiescence in a continuing practice, has resolved the issue in petitioners' favor.

Petitioners attempt to circumvent the history and practice governing airport activity by pointing our attention to the variety of speech activity that they claim historically occurred at various "transportation nodes" such as rail stations, bus stations, wharves, and Ellis Island. [T]he relevant unit for our inquiry is an airport, not "transportation nodes" generally. When new methods of transportation develop, new methods for accommodating that transportation are also likely to be needed. And with each new step, it therefore will be a new inquiry whether the transportation necessities are compatible with various kinds of expressive activity. To make a category of "transportation nodes," therefore, would unjustifiably elide what may prove to be critical differences of which we should rightfully take account.

Although many airports have expanded their function beyond merely contributing to efficient air travel, few have included among their purposes the designation of a forum for solicitation and distribution activities. Thus, we think that neither by tradition nor purpose can the terminals be described as satisfying the standards we have previously set out for identifying a public forum. We have no doubt that under this standard the prohibition on solicitation passes muster.

We have on many prior occasions noted the disruptive effect that solicitation may have on business. The restrictions here challenged, therefore, need only satisfy a requirement of reasonableness. We have no doubt that under this standard the prohibition on solicitation passes muster. We have on many prior occasions noted the disruptive effect that solicitation may have on business.

Passengers who wish to avoid the solicitor may have to alter their paths, slowing both themselves and those around them. The result is that the normal flow of traffic is impeded. This is especially so in an airport, where "[a]ir travelers, who are often weighted down by cumbersome baggage . . . may be hurrying to catch a plane or to arrange ground transportation." Delays may be particularly costly in this setting, as a flight missed by only a few minutes can result in hours worth of subsequent inconvenience.

In addition, face-to-face solicitation presents risks of duress that are an appropriate target of regulation. The skillful, and unprincipled, solicitor can target the most vulnerable, including those accompanying children or those suffering physical impairment and who cannot easily avoid the solicitation. Compounding this problem is the fact that, in an airport, the targets of such activity frequently are on tight schedules. This in turn makes such visitors unlikely to stop and formally complain to airport authorities. As a result, the airport faces considerable difficulty in achieving its legitimate interest in monitoring solicitation activity to assure that travelers are not interfered with unduly. As a result, we conclude that the solicitation ban is reasonable.

————————————

But the Court in *Lee* also ruled by a five-to-four margin that the prohibition of the distribution of literature in airports was unconstitutional. Justice O'Connor, who voted with the majority in finding that airports are nonpublic forums and in upholding the ban on solicitation, joined with the four dissenters on those issues to create a majority to overturn the ban on distribution of literature. She concluded that the ban on leafleting was not reasonable and thus was impermissible even though the airport was a nonpublic forum.

Subsequent to International Society for Krishna Consciousness v. Lee, in Arkansas Educational Television Commission v. Forbes, 523 U.S. 666 (1998), the Court held that a candidate debate sponsored by a government-owned television station is a nonpublic forum and that the exclusion of minor party candidates is not viewpoint discrimination. The state of Arkansas owns and operates a public television station that held a debate among candidates for a congressional seat. Only the Democratic and Republican candidates, and not the third-party candidates, were invited. A challenge was brought arguing that by holding the debate, the government created a limited public forum, and at the very least, excluding minor-party candidates was a form of viewpoint discrimination that is impermissible even in nonpublic forums.

In an opinion by Justice Kennedy, the Court rejected both of these contentions and ruled in favor of the public television station. Justice Kennedy said that "[h]aving first arisen in the context of streets and parks, the public forum doctrine should not be extended in a mechanical way to the very different context of public television broadcasting. . . . In the case of television broadcasting, however, broad rights of access for outside speakers would be antithetical, as a general rule, to the discretion that stations and their editorial staff must exercise to fulfill their journalistic purpose and statutory obligations." Indeed, the Court said that a broadcaster's choice of content and selection of speakers is itself expressive activity protected by the First Amendment.

Nor was the Court persuaded that the government, by holding the debate, had created a limited public forum. Justice Kennedy explained, "[The] debate was not a designated public forum. To create a forum of this type, the government must intend to make the property 'generally available.' A designated public forum is not created when the government allows selective access for individual speakers rather than general access for a class of speakers. . . . [The] cases illustrate the distinction between 'general access,' which indicates the property is a designated public forum, and 'selective access,' which indicates the property is a nonpublic forum." The Court was concerned that forcing the station to allow all candidates to participate could result in its choosing not to hold the debate at all.

The Court also rejected the claim that selecting major-party candidates and rejecting those from third parties was viewpoint discrimination. Justice Kennedy said that the selection was based on the level of popular support and thus the likely viability of the candidacy and not the viewpoint expressed. He concluded, "There is no substance to Forbes' suggestion that he was excluded because his views were unpopular or out of the mainstream. His own objective lack of support, not his platform, was the criterion. . . . The broadcaster's decision to exclude Forbes was a reasonable, viewpoint-neutral exercise of journalistic discretion consistent with the First Amendment."

Justice Stevens, in a dissenting opinion joined by Justices Souter and Ginsburg, expressed concern over the lack of standards in the government's decision-making process. The most troubling aspect of Forbes is whether the choice to include the Democratic and Republican candidates, while excluding third-party candidates, is viewpoint neutral. The Court said that the difference is in their degree of support, not their viewpoint. But the problem with this argument is that the less popular viewpoint is exactly the reason they are third-party candidates. Perhaps the case can be best understood as reflecting the majority's expressed judgment that candidate debates are extremely important and its concern that they will decrease if government-owned stations have to include every minor candidate.

The Supreme Court never has articulated clear criteria for deciding whether a place is a public forum, a designated public forum, or a nonpublic forum. Several criteria are implicit in the cases. Unfortunately, especially as applied in recent cases like *Kokinda*, *Lee*, and *Forbes*, it will be very difficult to find that any government property is a public or limited public forum.

One factor the Court considers is the tradition of availability of the place for speech. Sidewalks and parks, the classic public forums, are regarded as having been long available for speech purposes. But in recent cases, the Court's analysis has focused on whether the particular place has been open to speech. In *Kokinda*, for instance, the Court focused not on sidewalks generally, but on sidewalks on post office property; in *Lee*, the Court refused to consider places of transportation generally, but looked just at airports. Even as to airports, the Court said that because they are relatively new in American history, albeit decades old, they could not be regarded as places traditionally open to speech. This narrow focus makes it difficult to find that a place is a public forum based on a tradition of openness to speech.

Second, the Court considers the extent to which speech is incompatible with the usual functioning of the place. The greater the incompatibility, the more likely that the Court will find the place to be a nonpublic forum. For instance, in *Adderley*, the Court relied on security concerns to justify deeming areas outside prisons and jails to be a nonpublic forum. However, the cases indicate that the Court requires little proof that speech actually will interfere with the functioning of the place. For instance, in *Adderley*, there was no evidence that the peaceful protest on a grassy area outside the jail was a security threat. In *Greer*, there was no proof that speech on the military base would interfere with its functioning or cause the appearance of political entanglement with the military.

Third, the Court considers whether the primary purpose of the place is for speech. In *Lee*, the Court observed that this obviously is not the primary purpose of airports. In *Kokinda*, the plurality said that sidewalks on post office property were not even limited public forums because they had not been dedicated to speech activities. By this criteria, virtually no property ever would be a public forum or a limited public forum. Except for speakers corner in Hyde Park in London, virtually no government property was created for the purpose of speech or has been dedicated to speech activities. Sidewalks are constructed primarily for pedestrian traffic, and parks are built for recreation.

Although these recent cases indicate a strong presumption for finding government property to be a nonpublic forum, the criteria can be applied in a more speech-protective manner to safeguard expression in public property. Courts can find a tradition of availability to speech based on the general availability of that type of property for expressive purposes. Even some incompatibility with the usual functioning of a place can be tolerated so as to accommodate First Amendment values. For example, in *Schneider*, the Court held that the government could not prohibit leafletting even though it had an important interest in preventing litter and in preserving aesthetics. Although a place's primary purpose may not be for speech, it should be found to be a limited public forum if the government has opened it to some speech. A place should be found to be a public forum, even though it obviously has other uses, if it is an important place for the communication of messages.

2. *Private Property and Speech*

The cases described above all involve claims of a right to use *government* property for speech purposes. There is not a right to use private property owned by others for speech. Because it is private property, the Constitution does not apply. The requirement for state action and its application to the use of private property for speech is discussed in Chapter 5.

Most of the cases involving a right to use private property for speech have concerned claims of a right to use privately owned shopping centers for expression. Initially, the Supreme Court recognized such a right and then later limited it and ultimately overruled it. In Amalgamated Food Employees Union v. Logan Valley Plaza, 391 U.S. 308 (1968), the Supreme Court held that a privately owned shopping center could not exclude striking laborers from picketing a store within it. The Court relied on an earlier decision, Marsh v. Alabama, 326 U.S. 501 (1946), which held that a company-owned town could not exclude Jehovah's Witnesses that wished to distribute literature. The Court in *Logan Valley* expressly analogized to *Marsh* and said that "[t]he similarities between the business block in *Marsh* and the shopping center . . . are striking. . . . The shopping center here is clearly the functional equivalent of the business district of Chickasaw involved in *Marsh*." The Court stressed that the shopping center was an important gathering place that served as the commercial center of town.

Four years later, in Lloyd Corp. v. Tanner, 407 U.S. 551 (1972), the Supreme Court held that a privately owned shopping center could exclude anti-Vietnam War protestors from distributing literature on its premises. The Court explained that *Logan Valley* involved a labor protest related to the functioning of a store in the shopping center, whereas the speech in *Lloyd* was an antiwar protest unrelated to the conduct of the business. The problem with this distinction is that it is a content-based distinction among speech. Under *Lloyd*, speech in shopping centers is constitutionally protected and cannot be the basis for a trespassing conviction only if its content concerns the functioning of the shopping centers. This runs afoul of the basic principle described at the beginning of this chapter that speech cannot be regulated based on its content.

In Hudgens v. National Labor Relations Board, 424 U.S. 507 (1976), the Court recognized these problems and expressly overruled *Logan Valley*. The Court said that "the reasoning of the Court's opinion in *Lloyd* cannot be squared with the reasoning of the Court's opinion in *Logan Valley*." The Court explained that if the First Amendment applies to privately owned shopping centers, then the law cannot permit a distinction based on the content of the speech. The Court concluded that the First Amendment does not create a right to use privately owned shopping centers for speech.

Subsequent to *Hudgens*, in PruneYard Shopping Center v. Robins, 447 U.S. 74 (1980), the Supreme Court held that a state could create a state constitutional right of access to shopping centers for speech purposes. The shopping center appealed to the Supreme Court and contended that forcing it to allow speakers violated its First Amendment rights and constituted a taking of its property without just compensation. The United States Supreme Court rejected both of these arguments and held that states could recognize a state constitutional right of access to shopping centers.

3. Speech in Authoritarian Environments: Military, Prisons, and Schools

The place where speech occurs is relevant in another sense: The Court has held that some government-operated places are environments where great deference is required to regulations of speech. Specifically, the Court generally has sided with the government when regulating expression in the military, in prisons, and in schools. Although there are obvious differences between these contexts, there also are similarities. All involve places where people often are involuntarily present. All are authoritarian environments that do not operate internally in a democratic fashion. In each, the Court has proclaimed a need for deference to authority and to the expertise of those managing the place.

The underlying issue as to each is whether the restrictions on speech upheld by the Court are appropriate or show excessive deference. The Court has presumed that aggressive judicial review and significant protection of speech is inconsistent with the functioning of such authoritarian environments. But, on the other hand, there is a strong argument that court protection of rights such as freedom of speech is essential in such places precisely because of the lack of political oversight and responsiveness to those in these places. The Court's decisions, described below, can be criticized as overly deferential in that they allowed restrictions of speech without any proof that the expression actually would interfere with the functioning of the institution.

a. Military

The Supreme Court generally has been extremely deferential to the military in its ability to restrict constitutional rights; this also has been true for First Amendment freedoms. Parker v. Levy is illustrative.

PARKER v. LEVY
417 U.S. 733 (1974)

Justice REHNQUIST delivered the opinion of the Court.

Appellee Howard Levy, a physician, was a captain in the Army stationed at Fort Jackson, South Carolina. From the time he entered on active duty in July 1965 until his trial by court-martial, he was assigned as Chief of the Dermatological Service of the United States Army Hospital at Fort Jackson. On June 2, 1967, appellee was convicted by a general court-martial of violations of Arts. 90, 133, and 134 of the Uniform Code of Military Justice, and sentenced to dismissal from the service, forfeiture of all pay and allowances, and confinement for three years at hard labor.

The facts upon which his conviction rests are virtually undisputed. [A]ppellee made several public statements to enlisted personnel at the post, of which the following is representative: "The United States is wrong in being involved in the Viet Nam War. I would refuse to go to Viet Nam if ordered to do so. I don't see why any colored soldier would go to Viet Nam: they should refuse to go to Viet Nam and if sent should refuse to fight because they are discriminated against and denied their freedom in the United States, and they are sacrificed and discriminated against in Viet Nam by being given all the hazardous duty and they are suffering the majority of casualties. If I were a colored soldier I would refuse to go to Viet Nam and if I were a colored soldier and were sent I would refuse to fight. Special Forces personnel are liars and thieves and killers of peasants and murderers of women and children." Appellee's military superiors originally contemplated nonjudicial proceedings against him under Art. 15 of the Uniform Code of Military Justice, 10 U.S.C. §815, but later determined that courtmartial proceedings were appropriate.

This Court has long recognized that the military is, by necessity, a specialized society separate from civilian society. We have also recognized that the military has, again by necessity, developed laws and traditions of its own during its long history. The differences between the military and civilian communities result from the fact that "it is the primary business of armies and navies to fight or [be] ready to fight wars should the occasion arise."

While the members of the military are not excluded from the protection granted by the First Amendment, the different character of the military community and of the military mission requires a different application of those protections. The fundamental necessity for obedience, and the consequent necessity for imposition of discipline, may render permissible within the military that which would be constitutionally impermissible outside it. Doctrines of First Amendment overbreadth asserted in support of challenges to imprecise language like that contained in Arts. 133 and 134 are not exempt from the operation of these principles.

The Uniform Code of Military Justice applies a series of sanctions, varying from severe criminal penalties to administratively imposed minor sanctions, upon members of the military. However, for the reasons dictating a different application of First Amendment principles in the military context described above, we think that the "weighty countervailing policies," which permit the extension of standing in First Amendment cases involving civilian society, must be accorded a good deal less weight in the military context.

There is a wide range of the conduct of military personnel to which Arts. 133 and 134 may be applied without infringement of the First Amendment. While there may lurk at the fringes of the articles, even in the light of their narrowing construction by the United States Court of Military Appeals, some possibility that conduct which would be ultimately held to be protected by the First Amendment could be included within their prohibition, we deem this insufficient to invalidate either of them at the behest of appellee. His conduct, that of a commissioned officer publicly urging enlisted personnel to refuse to obey orders which might send them into combat, was unprotected under the most expansive notions of the First Amendment.

Justice DOUGLAS, dissenting.

This is the first case that presents to us a question of what protection, if any, the First Amendment gives people in the Armed Services. On its face there are no exceptions — no preferred classes for whose benefit the First Amendment extends, no exempt classes. The military by tradition and by necessity demands discipline; and those necessities require obedience in training and in action. A command is speech brigaded with action, and permissible commands may not be disobeyed. There may be a borderland or penumbra that in time can be established by litigated cases.

I cannot imagine, however, that Congress would think it had the power to authorize the military to curtail the reading list of books, plays, poems, periodicals, papers, and the like which a person in the Armed Services may read. Nor can I believe Congress would assume authority to empower the military to suppress conversations at a bar, ban discussions of public affairs, prevent enlisted men or women or draftees from meeting in discussion groups at times and places and for such periods of time that do not interfere with the performance of military duties.

Justice STEWART, with whom Justice DOUGLAS and Justice BRENNAN join, dissenting.

I cannot conclude that the statutory language clearly warned the appellee that his speech was illegal. It may have been, of course, that Dr. Levy had a subjective feeling that his conduct violated some military law. But that is not enough. [T]he general articles are unconstitutionally vague under the standards normally and repeatedly applied by this Court. It may be that military necessity justifies the promulgation of substantive rules of law that are wholly foreign to civilian life, but I fail to perceive how any legitimate military goal is served by enshrouding these rules in language so vague and uncertain as to be incomprehensible to the servicemen who are to be governed by them. Indeed, I should suppose that vague laws, with their serious capacity for arbitrary and discriminatory enforcement, can in the end only hamper the military's objectives of high morale and esprit de corps.

In Brown v. Glines, 444 U.S. 348 (1980), the Court went even further in exempting the military from the application of the First Amendment. *Brown* involved an Air Force regulation prohibiting members of the Air Force from posting or distributing printed materials at an Air Force installation without the permission of the commander. This, of course, is the most blatant form of prior restraint: a government licensing system for speech. Unlike Parker v. Levy, this was not punishment for specific speech that threatened the military's operation. Yet the Court upheld the prior restraint and concluded that "since a commander is charged with maintaining morale, discipline, and readiness, he must have authority over the distribution of materials that could affect adversely these essential attributes of an effective military." Again, the underlying issue is whether this is necessary deference to military authority or excessive deference by allowing a system of prior restraint that would be permitted in virtually no other situation.

b. Prisons

The Court has held that the general test is that the government may restrict and punish the speech of prisoners if the action is reasonably related to a legitimate penological interest.[183] The Court has said that "[i]n a prison context, an inmate does not retain those First Amendment rights that are inconsistent with his status as a prisoner or with the legitimate penological objectives of the corrections system."[184] Thornburgh v. Abbott is illustrative.

THORNBURGH v. ABBOTT
490 U.S. 401 (1989)

Justice BLACKMUN delivered the opinion of the Court.

Regulations promulgated by the Federal Bureau of Prisons broadly permit federal prisoners to receive publications from the "outside," but authorize prison officials to reject incoming publications found to be detrimental to institutional security. The warden may reject it "only if it is determined detrimental to the security, good order, or discipline of the institution or if it might facilitate criminal activity." The warden, however, may not reject a publication "solely because its content is religious, philosophical, political, social or sexual, or because its content is unpopular or repugnant."

There is little doubt that the kind of censorship just described would raise grave First Amendment concerns outside the prison context. It is equally certain that "[p]rison walls do not form a barrier separating prison inmates from the protections of the Constitution," nor do they bar free citizens from exercising their own constitutional rights by reaching out to those on the "inside." We have recognized, however, that these rights must be exercised with due regard for the "inordinately difficult undertaking" that is modern prison administration. Acknowledging the expertise of these officials and that the judiciary is "ill equipped" to deal with the difficult and delicate problems of prison management, this Court has afforded considerable deference to the determinations of prison administrators who, in the interest of security, regulate the relations between prisoners and the outside world.

We deal here with incoming publications, material requested by an individual inmate but targeted to a general audience. Once in the prison, material of this kind reasonably may be expected to circulate among prisoners, with the concomitant potential for coordinated disruptive conduct. Furthermore, prisoners may observe particular material in the possession of a fellow prisoner, draw inferences about their fellow's beliefs, sexual orientation, or gang affiliations from that material, and cause disorder by acting accordingly.

The Court in Turner v. Safly identified several factors that are relevant to, and that serve to channel, the reasonableness inquiry. [W]e must determine whether the governmental objective underlying the regulations at issue is legitimate and neutral, and that the regulations are rationally related to that objective. We agree with the District Court that this requirement has been met.

The legitimacy of the Government's purpose in promulgating these regulations is beyond question. The regulations are expressly aimed at protecting prison security, a purpose this Court has said is "central to all other corrections goals." We also conclude that the broad discretion accorded prison wardens by

183. Turner v. Safly, 482 U.S. 78 (1987).
184. Jones v. North Carolina Prisoners' Union, 433 U.S. 119 (1977).

the regulations here at issue is rationally related to security interests. We reach this conclusion for two reasons. The first has to do with the kind of security risk presented by incoming publications. Second, we are comforted by the individualized nature of the determinations required by the regulation. Under the regulations, no publication may be excluded unless the warden himself makes the determination that it is "detrimental to the security, good order, or discipline of the institution or . . . might facilitate criminal activity."

In sum, we hold that *Turner's* reasonableness standard is to be applied to the regulations at issue in this case, and that those regulations are facially valid under that standard.

Justice STEVENS, with whom Justice BRENNAN and Justice MARSHALL join, concurring in part and dissenting in part.

An article in Labyrinth, a magazine published by the Committee for Prisoner Humanity & Justice, began as follows:

> In January 1975, William Lowe, a black prisoner at the United States Penitentiary at Terre Haute, Indiana died of asthma. . . . In August 1975, Joseph (Yusef) Jones, Jr., a black prisoner at the U.S. Penitentiary, Terre Haute, IN. died of asthma.
> . . . The prison infirmary at that time had only one respirator[,] known to be inoperative in January 1975 when William Lowe died. It was still broken in August 1975 when Joseph Jones needed it.
> On the day of his death Jones was suffering an acute asthma attack; he was gasping for breath in the stale, hot, humid air in the cell. He requested medical aid of the guards. After several hours of unheeded pleading, accompanied by complaints to the guards from fellow prisoners in the cell block, Jones became frantic. Each breath was painful; each breath brought him closer to suffocation. Finally, guards called the PA (physician's assistant) . . . , who brought with him the broken respirator. Finding the equipment unusable, the PA gave Jones an injection of the tranquilizer, thorazine, to calm him. Treatment with a tranquilizer was unquestionably contraindicated by Jones' medical condition. Twenty minutes later, Jones was dead.
> Conclusion: Jones, who was convicted of bank robbery and sentenced to 10 years in prison, was in fact, sentenced to death and was murdered by neglect.

Labyrinth's efforts to disseminate the article to its subscribers at Marion Federal Penitentiary met Government resistance. Marion officials, acting within Federal Bureau of Prisons (Bureau) regulations, returned the magazine on the ground that "the article entitled 'Medical Murder' would be detrimental to the good order and discipline of this institution. . . . [T]his type of philosophy could guide inmates in this institution into situations which could cause themselves and other inmates problems with the Medical Staff." Two years after publication a Marion official testified that he believed the article had posed no threat. Nonetheless, the District Court below found the suppression of this and 45 other publications "reasonable," and thus sustained the rejections wholesale.

I cannot agree with either [the majority's] holding that another finding of "reasonableness" will justify censorship or its premature approval of the Bureau's regulations. These latter determinations upset precedent in a headlong rush to strip inmates of all but a vestige of free communication with the world beyond the prison gate.

———————————

Most regulations of prisoner speech have been upheld under the reasonableness test. Procunier v. Martinez, 416 U.S. 396 (1974), is the exception; the Court declared unconstitutional a prison regulation that restricted the types of letters that prisoners can write. The regulation said that prisoners could not write letters that would "magnify grievances" or that were "lewd, obscene, defamatory, or otherwise inappropriate." The Court held that this restriction on the ability of prisoners to communicate with those outside the prison was unnecessary for the maintenance of order and discipline among prisoners. The prison had no legitimate interest in stopping prisoners from expressing their grievances to those outside the prison or in censoring the content of prisoner correspondence.

Yet Procunier v. Martinez is exceptional, even in the area of prisoner speech to those outside the prison. In other cases, the Court has allowed restrictions on prisoner correspondence and expression to others outside the prison. In Turner v. Safly, 482 U.S. 78 (1987), the Court upheld a prison regulation that prohibited correspondence between inmates at other prisons. The Court accepted the government's claim that correspondence among prisoners could lead to comparisons that could provoke dissatisfaction and unrest. The Court also accepted the government's concern that unrest could spread among institutions through such correspondence.

In several cases, the Court upheld the ability of prisons to restrict the ability of the press to interview prisoners or have access to prisons. In Pell v. Procunier, 417 U.S. 817 (1974), and Saxbe v. Washington Post Co., 417 U.S. 843 (1974), the Court upheld prison regulations that prevented the media from interviewing particular prisoners. The Court said that the regulations were justified because "press attention concentrated on a relatively small number of inmates who, as a result, became virtual 'public figures' within the prison society and gained a disproportionate degree of notoriety and influence among their fellow inmates . . . and became the source of severe disciplinary problems."

In Houchins v. KQED, 438 U.S. 1 (1978), the Court, in a plurality opinion, held that the press did not have a right of access to prisons to observe conditions. The media was allowed only monthly tours, without cameras or tape recorders, of the Greystone portion of the Santa Rita jail. The Court upheld the restriction, in part, based on the lack of any special First Amendment rights for the press to gather information and, in part, based on the need for government control over prisons.

The Court not only has restricted the ability of prisoners to communicate with those outside, but also has limited the ability of prisoners to receive information. In Bell v. Wolfish, 441 U.S. 520 (1979), the Court upheld a regulation that prevented jail inmates from receiving hardcover books except when mailed from publishers or bookstores. The Court accepted the prison's concern that books could contain contraband and that the need for security required limiting the source for such books. The Court rejected the argument that searching the books prior to delivery to the inmates could satisfy the security concern.

In Beard v. Banks, 548 U.S. 521 (2006), the Court upheld a Pennsylvania law denying newspapers, magazines, and photographs to certain prison inmates. The Court again stressed the need for deference to prison officials.

Finally, in addition to restricting speech from and to prisoners, the Court also has limited speech among inmates in a prison. In Jones v. North Carolina Prisoners' Union, 433 U.S. 119 (1977), the Court upheld a prison regulation that prohibited prisoners from forming a union and that specifically forbade inmates from soliciting others to join the union and outlawed union meetings. The Court expressed the need for great deference to prison authorities: "Because the realities of running a penal institution are complex and difficult, we have long recognized the wide-ranging deference to be accorded the decisions of prison administrators." The Court upheld the prohibition of the prison union because of the prison's claim that it threatened discipline and order within the institution. The Court said that the "prison officials concluded that the presence, perhaps even the objectives, of a prisoners' labor union would be detrimental to order and security; it is enough to say that they have not been conclusively shown to be wrong in this view."

In Shaw v. Murphy, 532 U.S. 223 (2001), a prisoner sent a letter containing legal advice to an inmate at another institution. Prison authorities intercepted it and did not deliver it. A suit was brought under the First Amendment.

The Supreme Court, in an opinion by Justice Thomas, unanimously held that there was no violation of the First Amendment rights of the prisoners. Justice Thomas reaffirmed that Turner v. Saffly states the appropriate test: Prisoner speech may be regulated if it is rationally related to a legitimate penological interest. Justice Thomas stressed that this test is to be applied with great deference to prison authorities. He stated, "[U]nder *Turner* and its predecessors, prison officials are to remain the primary arbiters of the problems that arise in prison management. If courts were permitted to enhance constitutional protection based on their assessments of the content of the particular communications, courts would be in a position to assume a greater role in decisions affecting prison administration."

Although the letter contained legal advice, the *Court* accepted the claim that such speech has sufficient risks to justify the prison's refusal to deliver it. Justice Thomas wrote, "Although supervised inmate legal assistance programs may serve valuable ends, it is 'indisputable' that inmate law clerks 'are sometimes a menace to prison discipline' and that prisoners have an 'acknowledged propensity . . . to abuse both the giving and the seeking of [legal] assistance.' Prisoners have used legal correspondence as a means for passing contraband and communicating instructions on how to manufacture drugs or weapons."

In Overton v. Bazzetta, 539 U.S. 126 (2003), the Supreme Court, in an opinion by Justice Kennedy, upheld a law that regulated visits to prisoners. Michigan's prison regulations prevented inmates from having noncontact family visits with minor nieces, nephews, and children to whom parental rights had been terminated; prohibited inmates from visiting with former inmates; required children to be accompanied by a family member or legal guardian; and subjected inmates with two substance-abuse violations to a ban of at least two years on future visitation. The Court held that these restrictions were constitutional because they were rationally related to legitimate penological objectives and did not violate the substantive due process or free association guarantees of the First Amendment. Also, the Court held that a two-year ban on visitation for inmates with two substance-abuse violations did not violate the constitutional prohibition against cruel and unusual punishment. The Court emphasized the need for judicial deference to prison officials and that prison regulations should be upheld as long as they are rationally related to legitimate interests.

Most recently, in Beard v. Banks, 548 U.S. 521 (2006), the Court upheld a Pennsylvania prison regulation that prevented some prison inmates from having access to newspapers, magazines, or photographs. The Court used the Turner v. Saffly test, allowing regulations that are reasonably related to a legitimate penological interest, and found that it was met. Justice Breyer, writing for the Court in a six-to-three decision, said, "The Secretary in his motion set forth several justifications for the prison's policy, including the need to motivate better behavior on the part of particularly difficult prisoners, the need to minimize the amount of property they control in their cells, and the need to ensure prison safety, by, for example, diminishing the amount of material a prisoner might use to start a cell fire. We need go no further than the first justification, that of providing increased incentives for better prison behavior. Applying the well-established substantive and procedural standards . . . we find, on the basis of the record before us, that the Secretary's justification is adequate."

c. Schools

Schools, of course, are in many ways different from prisons and the military. An important function of schools is in teaching constitutional principles, such as the importance of freedom of speech. Restrictions of expression within schools is counter to that teaching. Also, although there is a need for discipline and order in schools, it is quite different in this regard from prisons or the military. On the other hand, courts tend to defer to the expertise of school officials and their need to make decisions about education and how to preserve discipline and order within the schools.

Some Supreme Court decisions have been very protective of student speech. In West Virginia Board of Education v. Barnette, 319 U.S. 624 (1943), discussed above in section B, the Court declared unconstitutional a state law that required that students salute the flag at the beginning of the school day. Although the Court focused on the First Amendment's prohibition against compelled expression, the decision obviously accepted the protection of First Amendment rights in schools.

Tinker v. Des Moines School District is the most important Supreme Court decision finding First Amendment protection for student speech.

TINKER v. DES MOINES INDEPENDENT COMMUNITY SCHOOL DISTRICT

393 U.S. 503 (1969)

Justice FORTAS delivered the opinion of the Court.

Petitioner John F. Tinker, 15 years old, and petitioner Christopher Eckhardt, 16 years old, attended high schools in Des Moines, Iowa. Petitioner Mary Beth Tinker, John's sister, was a 13-year-old student in junior high school. In December 1965, a group of adults and students in Des Moines held a meeting at the Eckhardt home. The group determined to publicize their objections to the hostilities in Vietnam and their support for a truce by wearing black armbands during the holiday season and by fasting on December 16 and New Year's Eve.

On December 16, Mary Beth and Christopher wore black armbands to their schools. John Tinker wore his armband the next day. They were all sent home and suspended from school until they would come back without their armbands. They did not return to school until after the planned period for wearing armbands had expired — that is, until after New Year's Day.

I

First Amendment rights, applied in light of the special characteristics of the school environment, are available to teachers and students. It can hardly be argued that either students or teachers shed their constitutional rights to freedom of speech or expression at the schoolhouse gate. This has been the unmistakable holding of this Court for almost 50 years. On the other hand, the Court has repeatedly emphasized the need for affirming the comprehensive authority of the States and of school officials, consistent with fundamental constitutional safeguards, to prescribe and control conduct in the schools.

II

The problem posed by the present case does not relate to regulation of the length of skirts or the type of clothing, to hair style, or deportment. It does not concern aggressive, disruptive action or even group demonstrations. Our problem involves direct, primary First Amendment rights akin to "pure speech." The school officials banned and sought to punish petitioners for a silent, passive expression of opinion, unaccompanied by any disorder or disturbance on the part of petitioners. There is here no evidence whatever of petitioners' interference, actual or nascent, with the schools' work or of collision with the rights of other students to be secure and to be let alone. Accordingly, this case does not concern speech or action that intrudes upon the work of the schools or the rights of other students. Only a few of the 18,000 students in the school system wore the black armbands. Only five students were suspended for wearing them. There is no indication that the work of the schools or any class was disrupted. Outside the classrooms, a few students made hostile remarks to the children wearing armbands, but there were no threats or acts of violence on school premises.

The District Court concluded that the action of the school authorities was reasonable because it was based upon their fear of a disturbance from the wearing of the armbands. But, in our system, undifferentiated fear or apprehension of disturbance is not enough to overcome the right to freedom of expression. Any departure from absolute regimentation may cause trouble. Any variation from the majority's opinion may inspire fear. Any word spoken, in class, in the lunchroom, or on the campus, that deviates from the views of another person may start an argument or cause a disturbance. But our Constitution says we must take this risk, and our history says that it is this sort of hazardous freedom — this kind of openness — that is the basis of our national strength and of the independence and vigor of Americans who grow up and live in this relatively permissive, often disputatious, society.

In order for the State in the person of school officials to justify prohibition of a particular expression of opinion, it must be able to show that its action was caused by something more than a mere desire to avoid the discomfort and unpleasantness that always accompany an unpopular viewpoint. Certainly where there is no finding and no showing that engaging in the forbidden conduct would "materially and substantially interfere with the requirements of appropriate discipline in the operation of the school," the prohibition cannot be sustained.

In the present case, the District Court made no such finding, and our independent examination of the record fails to yield evidence that the school authorities had reason to anticipate that the wearing of the armbands would substantially interfere with the work of the school or impinge upon the rights of other students. Even an official memorandum prepared after the suspension that listed the reasons for the ban on wearing the armbands made no reference to the anticipation of such disruption.

It is also relevant that the school authorities did not purport to prohibit the wearing of all symbols of political or controversial significance. The record shows that students in some of the schools wore buttons relating to national political campaigns, and some even wore the Iron Cross, traditionally a symbol of Nazism. The order prohibiting the wearing of armbands did not extend to these. Instead, a particular symbol — black armbands worn to exhibit opposition to this Nation's involvement in Vietnam — was singled out for prohibition. Clearly, the prohibition of expression of one particular opinion, at least without evidence that it is necessary to avoid material and substantial interference with schoolwork or discipline, is not constitutionally permissible.

In our system, state-operated schools may not be enclaves of totalitarianism. School officials do not possess absolute authority over their students. Students in school as well as out of school are "persons" under our Constitution. They are possessed of fundamental rights which the State must respect, just as they themselves must respect their obligations to the State. In our system, students may not be regarded as closed-circuit recipients of only that which the State chooses to communicate. They may not be confined to the expression of those sentiments that are officially approved. In the absence of a specific showing of constitutionally valid reasons to regulate their speech, students are entitled to freedom of expression of their views.

Justice BLACK, dissenting.

The Court's holding in this case ushers in what I deem to be an entirely new era in which the power to control pupils by the elected "officials of state supported public schools" in the United States is in ultimate effect transferred to the Supreme Court.

While the record does not show that any of these armband students shouted, used profane language, or were violent in any manner, detailed testimony by some of them shows their armbands caused comments, warnings by other students, the poking of fun at them, and a warning by an older football player that other, nonprotesting students had better let them alone. There is also evidence that a teacher of mathematics had his lesson period practically "wrecked" chiefly by disputes with Mary Beth Tinker, who wore her armband for her "demonstration."

Even a casual reading of the record shows that this armband did divert students' minds from their regular lessons, and that talk, comments, etc., made John Tinker "self-conscious" in attending school with his armband. While the absence of obscene remarks or boisterous and loud disorder perhaps justifies the Court's statement that the few armband students did not actually "disrupt" the classwork, I think the record overwhelmingly shows that the armbands did exactly what the elected school officials and principals foresaw they would, that is, took the students' minds off their classwork and diverted them to thoughts about the highly emotional subject of the Vietnam war. And I repeat that if the time has come when pupils of state-supported schools, kindergartens, grammar schools, or high schools, can defy and flout orders of school officials to keep their minds on their own schoolwork, it is the beginning of a new revolutionary era of permissiveness in this country fostered by the judiciary. The next logical step, it appears to me, would be to hold unconstitutional laws that bar pupils under 21 or 18 from voting, or from being elected members of the boards of education.

Nor are public school students sent to the schools at public expense to broadcast political or any other views to educate and inform the public. The original idea of schools, which I do not believe is yet abandoned as worthless or not of date, was that children had not yet reached the point of experience and wisdom which enabled them to teach all of their elders. It may be that the Nation has outworn the old-fashioned slogan that "children are to be seen not heard," but one may, I hope, be permitted to harbor the thought that taxpayers send children to school on the premise that at their age they need to learn, not teach.

This case, therefore, wholly without constitutional reasons in my judgment, subjects all the public schools in the country to the whims and caprices of their loudest-mouthed, but maybe not their brightest, students. I, for one, am not fully persuaded that school pupils are wise enough, even with this Court's expert help from Washington, to run the 23,390 public school systems in our 50 States. I wish, therefore, wholly to disclaim any purpose on my part to hold that the Federal Constitution compels the teachers, parents, and elected school officials to surrender control of the American public school system to public school students. I dissent.

The Court applied *Tinker* to the college context in Papish v. Board of Curators of the University of Missouri, 410 U.S. 667 (1973), where it held that a student could not be expelled for a political cartoon in a newspaper. A student drew a cartoon for publication in an off-campus underground newspaper, which depicted a police officer raping the Statue of Liberty. Also, the student wrote an article that used the word "motherfucker." The Court held that expelling the student for this speech violated the First Amendment: It was political speech; it appeared in an off-campus newspaper; it occurred at a university; and there was no showing of any disruption of the school's activities.

In more recent years, however, the Court has been much less protective of speech in school environments and much more deferential to school authorities. In Bethel School District No. 403 v. Fraser, Hazelwood School District v. Kuhlmeier, and Morse v. Frederick, the Court rejected student speech claims and sided with school authorities. While reading these cases, consider whether they are a significant departure from *Tinker* or whether they can be distinguished from *Tinker*.

BETHEL SCHOOL DISTRICT NO. 403 v. FRASER

478 U.S. 675 (1986)

Chief Justice BURGER delivered the opinion of the Court.

We granted certiorari to decide whether the First Amendment prevents a school district from disciplining a high school student for giving a lewd speech at a school assembly.

I

On April 26, 1983, respondent Matthew N. Fraser, a student at Bethel High School in Pierce County, Washington, delivered a speech nominating a fellow student for student elective office. Approximately 600 high school students, many of whom were 14-year-olds, attended the assembly. Students were required to attend the assembly or to report to the study hall. The assembly was part of a school-sponsored educational program in self-government. Students who elected not to attend the assembly were required to report to study hall.

During the entire speech, Fraser referred to his candidate in terms of an elaborate, graphic, and explicit sexual metaphor. Two of Fraser's teachers, with whom he discussed the contents of his speech in advance, informed him that the speech was "inappropriate and that he probably should not deliver it," and that his delivery of the speech might have "severe consequences." A Bethel High School disciplinary rule prohibits the use of obscene language in the school.

During Fraser's delivery of the speech, a school counselor observed the reaction of students to the speech. Some students hooted and yelled; some by gestures graphically simulated the sexual activities pointedly alluded to in respondent's speech. Other students appeared to be bewildered and embarrassed by the speech. One teacher reported that on the day following the speech, she found it necessary to forgo a portion of the scheduled class lesson in order to discuss the speech with the class.

The morning after the assembly, the Assistant Principal called Fraser into her office and notified him that the school considered his speech to have been a violation of this rule. Fraser was then informed that he would be suspended for three days, and that his name would be removed from the list of candidates for graduation speaker at the school's commencement exercises.

II

This Court acknowledged in Tinker v. Des Moines Independent Community School Dist., that students do not "shed their constitutional rights to freedom of speech or expression at the schoolhouse gate." The marked distinction between the political "message" of the armbands in *Tinker* and the sexual content of respondent's speech in this case seems to have been given little weight by the Court of Appeals. In upholding the students' right to engage in a nondisruptive, passive expression of a political viewpoint in *Tinker*, this Court was careful to note that the case did "not concern speech or action that intrudes upon the work of the schools or the rights of other students."

Surely it is a highly appropriate function of public school education to prohibit the use of vulgar and offensive terms in public discourse. Indeed, the "fundamental values necessary to the maintenance of a democratic political system" disfavor the use of terms of debate highly offensive or highly threatening to others. Nothing in the Constitution prohibits the states from insisting that certain modes of expression are inappropriate and subject to sanctions. The inculcation of these values is truly the "work of the schools." The determination of what manner of speech in the classroom or in school assembly is inappropriate properly rests with the school board.

The process of educating our youth for citizenship in public schools is not confined to books, the curriculum, and the civics class; schools must teach by example the shared values of a civilized social order. Consciously or otherwise, teachers — and indeed the older students — demonstrate the appropriate form of civil discourse and political expression by their conduct and deportment in and out of class. Inescapably, like parents, they are role models. The schools, as instruments of the state, may determine that the essential lessons of civil, mature conduct cannot be conveyed in a school that tolerates lewd, indecent, or offensive speech and conduct such as that indulged in by this confused boy.

The pervasive sexual innuendo in Fraser's speech was plainly offensive to both teachers and students — indeed to any mature person. By glorifying male sexuality, and in its verbal content, the speech was acutely insulting to teenage girl students. The speech could well be seriously damaging to its less mature audience, many of whom were only 14 years old and on the threshold of awareness of human sexuality. Some students were reported as bewildered by the speech and the reaction of mimicry it provoked.

We hold that petitioner School District acted entirely within its permissible authority in imposing sanctions upon Fraser in response to his offensively lewd and indecent speech. Unlike the sanctions imposed on the students wearing armbands in *Tinker*, the penalties imposed in this case were unrelated to any political viewpoint. The First Amendment does not prevent the school officials from determining that to permit a vulgar and lewd speech such as respondent's would undermine the school's basic educational mission. A high school assembly or classroom is no place for a sexually explicit monologue directed towards an unsuspecting audience of teenage students.

Justice BRENNAN, concurring in the judgment.

Respondent gave the following speech at a high school assembly in support of a candidate for student government office: "I know a man who is firm — he's firm in his pants, he's firm in his shirt, his character is firm — but most . . . of all, his belief in you, the students of Bethel, is firm. Jeff Kuhlman is a man who takes his point and pounds it in. If necessary, he'll take an issue and nail it to the wall. He doesn't attack things in spurts — he drives hard, pushing and pushing until finally — he succeeds. Jeff is a man who will go to the very end — even the climax, for each and every one of you. So vote for Jeff for A.S.B. vice-president — he'll never come between you and the best our high school can be."

The Court, referring to these remarks as "obscene," "vulgar," "lewd," and "offensively lewd," concludes that school officials properly punished respondent for uttering the speech. Having read the full text of respondent's remarks, I find it difficult to believe that it is the same speech the Court describes. To my mind, the most that can be said about respondent's speech — and all that need be said—is that in light of the discretion school officials have to teach high school students how to conduct civil and effective public discourse, and to prevent disruption of school educational activities, it was not unconstitutional for school officials to conclude, under the circumstances of this case, that respondent's remarks exceeded permissible limits.

Justice MARSHALL, dissenting.

I dissent from the Court's decision, however, because in my view the School District failed to demonstrate that respondent's remarks were indeed disruptive. The District Court and Court of Appeals conscientiously applied Tinker v. Des Moines Independent Community School Dist. (1969), and concluded that the School District had not demonstrated any disruption of the educational process. I recognize that the school administration must be given wide latitude to determine what forms of conduct are inconsistent with the school's educational mission; nevertheless, where speech is involved, we may not unquestioningly accept a teacher's or administrator's assertion that certain pure speech interfered with education. Here the School District, despite a clear opportunity to do so, failed to bring in evidence sufficient to convince either of the two lower courts that education at Bethel School was disrupted by respondent's speech. I therefore see no reason to disturb the Court of Appeals' judgment.

HAZELWOOD SCHOOL DISTRICT v. KUHLMEIER

484 U.S. 260 (1988)

Justice WHITE delivered the opinion of the Court.

This case concerns the extent to which educators may exercise editorial control over the contents of a high school newspaper produced as part of the school's journalism curriculum.

I

Petitioners are the Hazelwood School District in St. Louis County, Missouri and various school officials. Respondents are three former Hazelwood East students who were staff members of Spectrum, the school newspaper. They contend that school officials violated their First Amendment rights by deleting two pages of articles from the May 13, 1983, issue of Spectrum.

Spectrum was written and edited by the Journalism II class at Hazelwood East. The newspaper was published every three weeks or so during the 1982-1983 school year. More than 4,500 copies of the newspaper were distributed during that year to students, school personnel, and members of the community. The Board of Education allocated funds from its annual budget for the printing of Spectrum. These funds were supplemented by proceeds from sales of the newspaper.

The practice at Hazelwood East during the spring 1983 semester was for the journalism teacher to submit page proofs of each Spectrum issue to Principal Reynolds for his review prior to publication. On May 10, [the journalism teacher] delivered the proofs of the May 13 edition to Reynolds, who objected to two of the articles scheduled to appear in that edition. One of the stories described three Hazelwood East students' experiences with pregnancy; the other discussed the impact of divorce on students at the school.

Reynolds was concerned that, although the pregnancy story used false names "to keep the identity of these girls a secret," the pregnant students still might be identifiable from the text. He also believed that the article's references to sexual activity and birth control were inappropriate for some of the younger students at the school. In addition, Reynolds was concerned that a student identified by name in the divorce story had complained that her father "wasn't spending enough time with my mom, my sister and I" prior to the divorce, "was always out of town on business or out late playing cards with the guys," and "always argued about everything" with her mother. Reynolds believed that the student's parents should have been given an opportunity to respond to these remarks or to consent to their publication. He was unaware that [journalism teacher] Emerson had deleted the student's name from the final version of the article.

Reynolds believed that there was no time to make the necessary changes in the stories before the scheduled press run and that the newspaper would not appear before the end of the school year if printing were delayed to any significant extent. He concluded that his only options under the circumstances were to publish a four-page newspaper instead of the planned six-page newspaper, eliminating the two pages on which the offending stories appeared, or to publish no newspaper at all. Accordingly, he directed Emerson to withhold from publication the two pages containing the stories on pregnancy and divorce. He informed his superiors of the decision, and they concurred.

II

Students in the public schools do not "shed their constitutional rights to freedom of speech or expression at the schoolhouse gate." They cannot be punished merely for expressing their personal views on the school premises — whether "in the cafeteria, or on the playing field, or on the campus during the authorized hours," unless school authorities have reason to believe that such expression will "substantially interfere with the work of the school or impinge upon the rights of other students." We have nonetheless recognized that the First Amendment rights of students in the public schools "are not automatically coextensive with the rights of adults in other settings," and must be "applied in light of the special characteristics of the school environment." A school need not tolerate student speech that is inconsistent with its "basic educational mission," even though the government could not censor similar speech outside the school. We thus [have] recognized that "[t]he determination of what manner of speech in the classroom or in school assembly is inappropriate properly rests with the school board," rather than with the federal courts. It is in this context that respondents' First Amendment claims must be considered.

We deal first with the question whether Spectrum may appropriately be characterized as a forum for public expression. The public schools do not possess all of the attributes of streets, parks, and other traditional public forums that "time out of mind, have been used for purposes of assembly, communicating thoughts between citizens, and discussing public questions."

The policy of school officials toward Spectrum was reflected in Hazelwood School Board Policy and the Hazelwood East Curriculum Guide. Board Policy provided that "[s]chool sponsored publications are developed within the adopted curriculum and its educational implications in regular classroom activities." The Hazelwood East Curriculum Guide described the Journalism II course as a "laboratory situation in which the students publish the school newspaper applying skills they have learned in Journalism I." Journalism II was taught by a faculty member during regular class hours. Students received grades and academic credit for their performance in the course. School officials did not deviate in practice from their policy that production of Spectrum was to be part of the educational curriculum and a "regular classroom activit[y]."

The question whether the First Amendment requires a school to tolerate particular student speech—the question that we addressed in *Tinker*—is different from the question whether the First Amendment requires a school affirmatively to promote particular student speech. The former question addresses educators' ability to silence a student's personal expression that happens to occur on the school premises. The latter question concerns educators' authority over school-sponsored publications, theatrical productions, and other expressive activities that students, parents, and members of the public might reasonably perceive to bear the imprimatur of the school. These activities may fairly be characterized as part of the school curriculum, whether or not they occur in a traditional classroom setting, so long as they are supervised by faculty members and designed to impart particular knowledge or skills to student participants and audiences.

Educators are entitled to exercise greater control over this second form of student expression to assure that participants learn whatever lessons the activity is designed to teach, that readers or listeners are not exposed to material that may be inappropriate for their level of maturity, and that the views of the individual speaker are not erroneously attributed to the school. Hence, a school may in its capacity as publisher of a school newspaper or producer of a school play "disassociate itself," not only from speech that would "substantially interfere with [its] work . . . or impinge upon the rights of other students," but also from speech that is, for example, ungrammatical, poorly written, inadequately researched, biased or prejudiced, vulgar or profane, or unsuitable for immature audiences. A school must be able to set high standards for the student speech that is disseminated under its auspices—standards that may be higher than those demanded by some newspaper publishers or theatrical producers in the "real" world—and may refuse to disseminate student speech that does not meet those standards.

In addition, a school must be able to take into account the emotional maturity of the intended audience in determining whether to disseminate student speech on potentially sensitive topics, which might range from the existence of Santa Claus in an elementary school setting to the particulars of teenage sexual activity in a high school setting. A school must also retain the authority to refuse to sponsor student speech that might reasonably be perceived to advocate drug or alcohol use, irresponsible sex, or conduct otherwise inconsistent with "the shared values of a civilized social order," or to associate the school with any position other than neutrality on matters of political controversy. Accordingly, we conclude that the standard articulated in *Tinker* for determining when a school may punish student expression need not also be the standard for determining when a school may refuse to lend its name and resources to the dissemination of student expression. Instead, we hold that educators do not offend the First Amendment by exercising editorial control over the style and content of student speech in school-sponsored expressive activities so long as their actions are reasonably related to legitimate pedagogical concerns.

This standard is consistent with our oft-expressed view that the education of the Nation's youth is primarily the responsibility of parents, teachers, and state and local school officials, and not of federal judges. It is only when the decision to censor a school-sponsored publication, theatrical production, or other vehicle of student expression has no valid educational purpose that the First Amendment is so "directly and sharply implicate[d]," as to require judicial intervention to protect students' constitutional rights.

We also conclude that Principal Reynolds acted reasonably in requiring the deletion from the May 13 issue of Spectrum of the pregnancy article, the divorce article, and the remaining articles that were to appear on the same pages of the newspaper. The initial paragraph of the pregnancy article declared that "[a]ll names have been changed to keep the identity of these girls a secret." The principal concluded that the students' anonymity was not adequately protected, however, given the other identifying information in the article and the small number of pregnant students at the school. In addition, he could reasonably have been concerned that the article was not sufficiently sensitive to the privacy interests of the students' boyfriends and parents, who were discussed in the article but who were given no opportunity to consent to its publication or to offer a response. The article did not contain graphic accounts of sexual activity. The girls did comment in the article, however, concerning their sexual histories and their use or nonuse of birth control. It was not unreasonable for the principal to have concluded that such frank talk was inappropriate in a school-sponsored publication distributed to 14-year-old freshmen and presumably taken home to be read by students' even younger brothers and sisters.

The student who was quoted by name in the version of the divorce article seen by Principal Reynolds made comments sharply critical of her father. The principal could reasonably have concluded that an individual publicly identified as an inattentive parent — indeed, as one who chose "playing cards with the guys" over home and family — was entitled to an opportunity to defend himself as a matter of journalistic fairness. In sum, we cannot reject as unreasonable Principal Reynolds' conclusion that neither the pregnancy article nor the divorce article was suitable for publication in Spectrum.

Justice BRENNAN, with whom Justice MARSHALL and Justice BLACKMUN join, dissenting.

When the young men and women of Hazelwood East High School registered for Journalism II, they expected a civics lesson. The school board itself affirmatively guaranteed the students of Journalism II an atmosphere conducive to fostering such an appreciation and exercising the full panoply of rights associated with a free student press. "School sponsored student publications," it vowed, "will not restrict free expression or diverse viewpoints within the rules of responsible journalism."

This case arose when the Hazelwood East administration breached its own promise, dashing its students' expectations. The school principal, without prior consultation or explanation, excised six articles — comprising two full pages — of the May 13, 1983, issue of Spectrum. He did so not because any of the articles would "materially and substantially interfere with the requirements of appropriate discipline," but simply because he considered two of the six "inappropriate, personal, sensitive, and unsuitable" for student consumption.

In my view the principal broke more than just a promise. He violated the First Amendment's prohibitions against censorship of any student expression that neither disrupts classwork nor invades the rights of others, and against any censorship that is not narrowly tailored to serve its purpose.

Since the censorship served no legitimate pedagogical purpose, it cannot by any stretch of the imagination have been designed to prevent "materia[l] disrup[tion of] classwork." Nor did the censorship fall within the category that *Tinker* described as necessary to prevent student expression from "inva[ding] the rights of others." If that term is to have any content, it must be limited to rights that are protected by law. "Any yardstick less exacting than [that] could result in school officials curtailing speech at the slightest fear of disturbance," a prospect that would be completely at odds with this Court's pronouncement that the "undifferentiated fear or apprehension of disturbance is not enough [even in the public school context] to overcome the right to freedom of expression." And, as the Court of Appeals correctly reasoned, whatever journalistic impropriety these articles may have contained, they could not conceivably be tortious, much less criminal.

Finally, even if the majority were correct that the principal could constitutionally have censored the objectionable material, I would emphatically object to the brutal manner in which he did so. Where "[t]he separation of legitimate from illegitimate speech calls for more sensitive tools," the principal used a paper shredder. He objected to some material in two articles, but excised six entire articles. He did not so much as inquire into obvious alternatives, such as precise deletions or additions (one of which had already been made), rearranging the layout, or delaying publication. Such unthinking contempt for individual rights is intolerable from any state official. It is particularly insidious from one to whom the public entrusts the task of inculcating in its youth an appreciation for the cherished democratic liberties that our Constitution guarantees. The young men and women of Hazelwood East expected a civics lesson, but not the one the Court teaches them today.

MORSE v. FREDERICK
_____
551 U.S. 393 (2007)

Chief Justice ROBERTS delivered the opinion of the Court.

At a school-sanctioned and school-supervised event, a high school principal saw some of her students unfurl a large banner conveying a message she reasonably regarded as promoting illegal drug use. Consistent with established school policy prohibiting such messages at school events, the principal directed the students to take down the banner. One student — among those who had brought the banner to the event — refused to do so. The principal confiscated the banner and later suspended the student.

Our cases make clear that students do not "shed their constitutional rights to freedom of speech or expression at the schoolhouse gate." *Tinker v. Des Moines*

Independent Community School Dist. (1969). At the same time, we have held that "the constitutional rights of students in public school are not automatically coextensive with the rights of adults in other settings," *Bethel School Dist. No. 403 v. Fraser* (1986), and that the rights of students "must be 'applied in light of the special characteristics of the school environment.'" *Hazelwood School Dist. v. Kuhlmeier* (1988). Consistent with these principles, we hold that schools may take steps to safeguard those entrusted to their care from speech that can reasonably be regarded as encouraging illegal drug use. We conclude that the school officials in this case did not violate the First Amendment by confiscating the pro-drug banner and suspending the student responsible for it.

I

On January 24, 2002, the Olympic Torch Relay passed through Juneau, Alaska, on its way to the winter games in Salt Lake City, Utah. The torchbearers were to proceed along a street in front of Juneau-Douglas High School (JDHS) while school was in session. Petitioner Deborah Morse, the school principal, decided to permit staff and students to participate in the Torch Relay as an approved social event or class trip. Students were allowed to leave class to observe the relay from either side of the street. Teachers and administrative officials monitored the students' actions.

Respondent Joseph Frederick, a JDHS senior, was late to school that day. When he arrived, he joined his friends (all but one of whom were JDHS students) across the street from the school to watch the event. Not all the students waited patiently. Some became rambunctious, throwing plastic cola bottles and snowballs and scuffling with their classmates. As the torchbearers and camera crews passed by, Frederick and his friends unfurled a 14-foot banner bearing the phrase: "BONG HiTS 4 JESUS." The large banner was easily readable by the students on the other side of the street.

Principal Morse immediately crossed the street and demanded that the banner be taken down. Everyone but Frederick complied. Morse confiscated the banner and told Frederick to report to her office, where she suspended him for 10 days. Morse later explained that she told Frederick to take the banner down because she thought it encouraged illegal drug use, in violation of established school policy. Juneau School Board Policy No. 5520 states: "The Board specifically prohibits any assembly or public expression that . . . advocates the use of substances that are illegal to minors. . . ." In addition, Juneau School Board Policy No. 5850 subjects "[p]upils who participate in approved social events and class trips" to the same student conduct rules that apply during the regular school program.

Frederick administratively appealed his suspension, but the Juneau School District Superintendent upheld it, limiting it to time served (8 days). In a memorandum setting forth his reasons, the superintendent determined that Frederick had displayed his banner "in the midst of his fellow students, during school hours, at a school-sanctioned activity." He further explained that Frederick "was not disciplined because the principal of the school 'disagreed' with his message, but because his speech appeared to advocate the use of illegal drugs."

The superintendent continued:

> The common-sense understanding of the phrase "bong hits" is that it is a reference to a means of smoking marijuana. Given [Frederick's] inability or unwillingness to express any other credible meaning for the phrase, I can only agree with the principal and countless others who saw the banner as advocating the use of illegal drugs. [Frederick's] speech was not political. He was not advocating the legalization of marijuana or promoting a religious belief. He was displaying a fairly silly message promoting illegal drug usage in the midst of a school activity, for the benefit of television cameras covering the Torch Relay. [Frederick's] speech was potentially disruptive to the event and clearly disruptive of and inconsistent with the school's educational mission to educate students about the dangers of illegal drugs and to discourage their use.

Frederick then filed suit under 42 U.S.C. §1983, alleging that the school board and Morse had violated his First Amendment rights. He sought declaratory and injunctive relief, unspecified compensatory damages, punitive damages, and attorney's fees.

II

At the outset, we reject Frederick's argument that this is not a school speech case. The event occurred during normal school hours. It was sanctioned by Principal Morse "as an approved social event or class trip," and the school district's rules expressly provide that pupils in "approved social events and class trips are subject to district rules for student conduct." Teachers and administrators were interspersed among the students and charged with supervising them. The high school band and cheerleaders performed. Frederick, standing among other JDHS students across the street from the school, directed his banner toward the school, making it plainly visible to most students. Under these circumstances, we agree with the superintendent that Frederick cannot "stand in the midst of his fellow students, during school hours, at a school-sanctioned activity and claim he is not at school."

III

The message on Frederick's banner is cryptic. It is no doubt offensive to some, perhaps amusing to others. To still others, it probably means nothing at all. Frederick himself claimed "that the words were just nonsense meant to attract television cameras." But Principal Morse thought the banner would be interpreted by those viewing it as promoting illegal drug use, and that interpretation is plainly a reasonable one.

As Morse later explained in a declaration, when she saw the sign, she thought that "the reference to a 'bong hit' would be widely understood by high school students and others as referring to smoking marijuana." She further believed that "display of the banner would be construed by students, District personnel, parents and others witnessing the display of the banner, as advocating or promoting illegal drug use" — in violation of school policy.

We agree with Morse. At least two interpretations of the words on the banner demonstrate that the sign advocated the use of illegal drugs. First, the phrase could be interpreted as an imperative: "[Take] bong hits . . ." — a message equivalent, as Morse explained in her declaration, to "smoke marijuana" or "use an illegal drug." Alternatively, the phrase could be viewed as celebrating drug use — "bong hits [are a good thing]," or "[we take] bong hits" — and we discern no meaningful distinction between celebrating illegal drug use in the midst of fellow students and outright advocacy or promotion.

Elsewhere in its opinion, the dissent emphasizes the importance of political speech and the need to foster "national debate about a serious issue," as if to suggest that the banner is political speech. But not even Frederick argues that the banner conveys any sort of political or religious message. Contrary to the dissent's suggestion, this is plainly not a case about political debate over the criminalization of drug use or possession.

IV

The question thus becomes whether a principal may, consistent with the First Amendment, restrict student speech at a school event, when that speech is reasonably viewed as promoting illegal drug use. We hold that she may.

In *Tinker*, this Court made clear that "First Amendment rights, applied in light of the special characteristics of the school environment, are available to teachers and students." *Tinker* involved a group of high school students who decided to wear black armbands to protest the Vietnam War. School officials learned of the plan and then adopted a policy prohibiting students from wearing armbands. When several students nonetheless wore armbands to school, they were suspended. The students sued, claiming that their First Amendment rights had been violated, and this Court agreed.

Tinker held that student expression may not be suppressed unless school officials reasonably conclude that it will "materially and substantially disrupt the work and discipline of the school."

This Court's next student speech case was *Fraser*. Matthew Fraser was suspended for delivering a speech before a high school assembly in which he employed what this Court called "an elaborate, graphic, and explicit sexual metaphor." Analyzing the case under *Tinker*, the District Court and Court of Appeals found no disruption, and therefore no basis for disciplining Fraser. This Court reversed, holding that the "School District acted entirely within its permissible authority in imposing sanctions upon Fraser in response to his offensively lewd and indecent speech."

The mode of analysis employed in *Fraser* is not entirely clear. The Court was plainly attuned to the content of Fraser's speech, citing the "marked distinction between the political 'message' of the armbands in *Tinker* and the sexual content of [Fraser's] speech." But the Court also reasoned that school boards have the authority to determine "what manner of speech in the classroom or in school assembly is inappropriate."

We need not resolve this debate to decide this case. For present purposes, it is enough to distill from *Fraser* two basic principles. First, *Fraser*'s holding demonstrates that "the constitutional rights of students in public school are not automatically coextensive with the rights of adults in other settings." Had Fraser delivered the same speech in a public forum outside the school context, it would have been protected. In school, however, Fraser's First Amendment rights were circumscribed "in light of the special characteristics of the school environment." Second, *Fraser* established that the mode of analysis set forth in *Tinker* is not absolute. Whatever approach *Fraser* employed, it certainly did not conduct the "substantial disruption" analysis prescribed by *Tinker*.

Drawing on the principles applied in our student speech cases, we have held in the Fourth Amendment context that "while children assuredly do not 'shed their constitutional rights . . . at the schoolhouse gate,' . . . the nature of those rights is what is appropriate for children in school."

Even more to the point, these cases also recognize that deterring drug use by schoolchildren is an "important—indeed, perhaps compelling" interest. Drug abuse can cause severe and permanent damage to the health and well-being of young people. The problem remains serious today. See generally 1 National Institute on Drug Abuse, National Institutes of Health, Monitoring the Future: National Survey Results on Drug Use, 1975-2005, Secondary School Students (2006). About half of American 12th graders have used an illicit drug, as have more than a third of 10th graders and about one-fifth of 8th graders. Nearly one in four 12th graders has used an illicit drug in the past month. Some 25% of high schoolers say that they have been offered, sold, or given an illegal drug on school property within the past year.

The "special characteristics of the school environment," and the governmental interest in stopping student drug abuse—reflected in the policies of Congress and myriad school boards[]—allow schools to restrict student expression that they reasonably regard as promoting illegal drug use. Tinker warned that schools may not prohibit student speech because of "undifferentiated fear or apprehension of disturbance" or "a mere desire to avoid the discomfort and unpleasantness that always accompany an unpopular viewpoint." The danger here is far more serious and palpable. The particular concern to prevent student drug abuse at issue here, embodied in established school policy, extends well beyond an abstract desire to avoid controversy.

School principals have a difficult job, and a vitally important one. When Frederick suddenly and unexpectedly unfurled his banner, Morse had to decide to act—or not act—on the spot. It was reasonable for her to conclude that the banner promoted illegal drug use—in violation of established school policy—and that failing to act would send a powerful message to the students in her charge, including Frederick, about how serious the school was about the dangers of illegal drug use. The First Amendment does not require schools to tolerate at school events student expression that contributes to those dangers.

Justice THOMAS, concurring.

The Court today decides that a public school may prohibit speech advocating illegal drug use. I agree and therefore join its opinion in full. I write separately to state my view that the standard set forth in *Tinker v. Des Moines Independent Community School Dist.* (1969) is without basis in the Constitution.

In my view, the history of public education suggests that the First Amendment, as originally understood, does not protect student speech in public schools. Although colonial schools were exclusively private, public education proliferated in the early 1800's. By the time the States ratified the Fourteenth Amendment, public schools had become relatively common. If students in public schools were originally understood as having free-speech rights, one would have expected 19th-century public schools to have respected those rights and courts to have enforced them. They did not.

Teachers instilled these values not only by presenting ideas but also through strict discipline. Schools punished students for behavior the school considered disrespectful or wrong. Rules of etiquette were enforced, and courteous behavior was demanded. To meet their educational objectives, schools required absolute obedience. In short, in the earliest public schools, teachers taught, and students listened. Teachers commanded, and students obeyed. Teachers did not rely solely on the power of ideas to persuade; they relied on discipline to maintain order.

Through the legal doctrine of in loco parentis, courts upheld the right of schools to discipline students, to enforce rules, and to maintain order. Applying in loco parentis, the judiciary was reluctant to interfere in the routine business of school administration, allowing schools and teachers to set and enforce rules and to maintain order. Thus, in the early years of public schooling, schools and teachers had considerable discretion in disciplinary matters.

Tinker effected a sea change in students' speech rights, extending them well beyond traditional bounds. *Tinker*'s reasoning conflicted with the traditional understanding of the judiciary's role in relation to public schooling, a role limited by in loco parentis.

Today, the Court creates another exception. In doing so, we continue to distance ourselves from *Tinker*, but we neither overrule it nor offer an explanation of when it operates and when it does not. I am afraid that our jurisprudence now says that students have a right to speak in schools except when they don't — a standard continuously developed through litigation against local schools and their administrators. In my view, petitioners could prevail for a much simpler reason: As originally understood, the Constitution does not afford students a right to free speech in public schools.

I join the Court's opinion because it erodes *Tinker*'s hold in the realm of student speech, even though it does so by adding to the patchwork of exceptions to the *Tinker* standard. I think the better approach is to dispense with *Tinker* altogether, and given the opportunity, I would do so.

Justice Alito, with whom Justice Kennedy joins, concurring.

I join the opinion of the Court on the understanding that (a) it goes no further than to hold that a public school may restrict speech that a reasonable observer would interpret as advocating illegal drug use and (b) it provides no support for any restriction of speech that can plausibly be interpreted as commenting on any political or social issue, including speech on issues such as "the wisdom of the war on drugs or of legalizing marijuana for medicinal use."

The opinion of the Court correctly reaffirms the recognition in *Tinker v. Des Moines Independent Community School Dist.* (1969) of the fundamental principle that students do not "shed their constitutional rights to freedom of speech or expression at the schoolhouse gate." The Court is also correct in noting that *Tinker*, which permits the regulation of student speech that threatens a concrete and "substantial disruption," does not set out the only ground on which in-school student speech may be regulated by state actors in a way that would not be constitutional in other settings.

But I do not read the opinion to mean that there are necessarily any grounds for such regulation that are not already recognized in the holdings of this Court. In addition to *Tinker*, the decision in the present case allows the restriction of speech advocating illegal drug use; *Bethel School Dist. No. 403 v. Fraser* (1986) permits the regulation of speech that is delivered in a lewd or vulgar manner as part of a middle school program; and *Hazelwood School Dist. v. Kuhlmeier* (1988) allows a school to regulate what is in essence the school's own speech, that is, articles that appear in a publication that is an official school organ. I join the opinion of the Court on the understanding that the opinion does not hold that the special characteristics of the public schools necessarily justify any other speech restrictions.

In most settings, the First Amendment strongly limits the government's ability to suppress speech on the ground that it presents a threat of violence. But due to the special features of the school environment, school officials must have greater authority to intervene before speech leads to violence. And, in most cases, *Tinker*'s "substantial disruption" standard permits school officials to step in before actual violence erupts.

Speech advocating illegal drug use poses a threat to student safety that is just as serious, if not always as immediately obvious. As we have recognized in the past and as the opinion of the Court today details, illegal drug use presents a grave and in many ways unique threat to the physical safety of students. I therefore conclude that the public schools may ban speech advocating illegal drug use. But I regard such regulation as standing at the far reaches of what the First Amendment permits. I join the opinion of the Court with the understanding that the opinion does not endorse any further extension.

Justice STEVENS, with whom Justice SOUTER and Justice GINSBURG join, dissenting.

A significant fact barely mentioned by the Court sheds a revelatory light on the motives of both the students and the principal of Juneau-Douglas High School (JDHS). On January 24, 2002, the Olympic Torch Relay gave those Alaska residents a rare chance to appear on national television. As Joseph Frederick repeatedly explained, he did not address the curious message — "BONG HiTS 4 JESUS" — to his fellow students. He just wanted to get the camera crews' attention. Moreover, concern about a nationwide evaluation of the conduct of the JDHS student body would have justified the principal's decision to remove an attention-grabbing 14-foot banner, even if it had merely proclaimed "Glaciers Melt!"

I agree with the Court that the principal should not be held liable for pulling down Frederick's banner [because of qualified immunity]. I would hold, however, that the school's interest in protecting its students from exposure to speech "reasonably regarded as promoting illegal drug use[]" cannot justify disciplining Frederick for his attempt to make an ambiguous statement to a television audience simply because it contained an oblique reference to drugs. The First Amendment demands more, indeed, much more.

The Court holds otherwise only after laboring to establish two uncontroversial propositions: first, that the constitutional rights of students in school settings are not coextensive with the rights of adults; and second, that deterring drug use by schoolchildren is a valid and terribly important interest. As to the first, I take the Court's point that the message on Frederick's banner is not necessarily protected speech, even though it unquestionably would have been had the banner been unfurled elsewhere. As to the second, I am willing to assume that the Court is correct that the pressing need to deter drug use supports JDHS's rule prohibiting willful conduct that expressly "advocates the use of substances that are illegal to minors." But it is a gross non sequitur to draw from these two unremarkable propositions the remarkable conclusion that the school may suppress student speech that was never meant to persuade anyone to do anything.

In my judgment, the First Amendment protects student speech if the message itself neither violates a permissible rule nor expressly advocates conduct that is illegal and harmful to students. This nonsense banner does neither, and the Court does serious violence to the First Amendment in upholding—indeed, lauding—a school's decision to punish Frederick for expressing a view with which it disagreed.

I

In December 1965, we were engaged in a controversial war, a war that "divided this country as few other issues ever have." *Tinker v. Des Moines Independent Community School Dist.* (1969) (Black, J., dissenting). Two cardinal First Amendment principles animate both the Court's opinion in *Tinker* and Justice Harlan's dissent. First, censorship based on the content of speech, particularly censorship that depends on the viewpoint of the speaker, is subject to the most rigorous burden of justification. Second, punishing someone for advocating illegal conduct is constitutional only when the advocacy is likely to provoke the harm that the government seeks to avoid. See *Brandenburg v. Ohio* (1969) (per curiam).

Yet today the Court fashions a test that trivializes the two cardinal principles upon which *Tinker* rests. The Court's test invites stark viewpoint discrimination. In this case, for example, the principal has unabashedly acknowledged that she disciplined Frederick because she disagreed with the pro-drug viewpoint she ascribed to the message on the banner. It is also perfectly clear that "promoting illegal drug use[]" comes nowhere close to proscribable "incitement to imminent lawless action." Encouraging drug use might well increase the likelihood that a listener will try an illegal drug, but that hardly justifies censorship[.]

No one seriously maintains that drug advocacy (much less Frederick's ridiculous sign) comes within the vanishingly small category of speech that can be prohibited because of its feared consequences. Such advocacy, to borrow from Justice Holmes, "ha[s] no chance of starting a present conflagration."

II

The Court rejects outright these twin foundations of *Tinker* because, in its view, the unusual importance of protecting children from the scourge of drugs supports a ban on all speech in the school environment that promotes drug use. Whether or not such a rule is sensible as a matter of policy, carving out pro-drug speech for uniquely harsh treatment finds no support in our case law and is inimical to the values protected by the First Amendment.

I will nevertheless assume for the sake of argument that the school's concededly powerful interest in protecting its students adequately supports its restriction on "any assembly or public expression that . . . advocates the use of substances that are illegal to minors. . . ." But it is one thing to restrict speech that advocates drug use. It is another thing entirely to prohibit an obscure message with a drug theme that a third party subjectively—and not very reasonably—thinks is tantamount to express advocacy.

There is absolutely no evidence that Frederick's banner's reference to drug paraphernalia "willful[ly]" infringed on anyone's rights or interfered with any of the school's educational programs. Therefore, just as we insisted in *Tinker* that the school establish some likely connection between the armbands and their feared consequences, so too JDHS must show that Frederick's supposed advocacy stands a meaningful chance of making otherwise-abstemious students try marijuana.

But instead of demanding that the school make such a showing, the Court punts. To the extent the Court independently finds that "BONG HiTS 4 JESUS" objectively amounts to the advocacy of illegal drug use—in other words, that it can most reasonably be interpreted as such—that conclusion practically refutes itself. This is a nonsense message, not advocacy. The Court's feeble effort to divine its hidden meaning is strong evidence of that (positing that the banner might mean, alternatively, "'[Take] bong hits,'" "'bong hits [are a good thing],'" or "'[we take] bong hits'"). Admittedly, some high school students (including those who use drugs) are dumb. Most students, however, do not shed their brains at the schoolhouse gate, and most students know dumb advocacy when they see it. The notion that the message on this banner would actually persuade either the average student or even the dumbest one to change his or her behavior is most implausible. That the Court believes such a silly message can be proscribed as advocacy underscores the novelty of its position, and suggests that the principle it articulates has no stopping point.

Among other things, the Court's ham-handed, categorical approach is deaf to the constitutional imperative to permit unfettered debate, even among high-school students, about the wisdom of the war on drugs or of legalizing marijuana for medicinal use. If Frederick's stupid reference to marijuana can in the Court's view justify censorship, then high school students everywhere could be forgiven for zipping their mouths about drugs at school lest some "reasonable" observer censor and then punish them for promoting drugs.

Although this case began with a silly, nonsensical banner, it ends with the Court inventing out of whole cloth a special First Amendment rule permitting the censorship of any student speech that mentions drugs, at least so long as someone could perceive that speech to contain a latent pro-drug message.

Even in high school, a rule that permits only one point of view to be expressed is less likely to produce correct answers than the open discussion of countervailing views. In the national debate about a serious issue, it is the expression of the minority's viewpoint that most demands the protection of the First Amendment. Whatever the better policy may be, a full and frank discussion of the costs and benefits of the attempt to prohibit the use of marijuana is far wiser than suppression of speech because it is unpopular.

———————————

Although *Barnette*, *Tinker*, *Papish*, *Bethel*, *Hazelwood*, and *Morse* all focused on student speech, other First Amendment issues arise in schools as well. For example, in Board of Education, Island Trees Union Free School District v. Pico, 457 U.S. 853 (1982), the Court considered the ability of a school library to remove books because they were deemed "objectionable." The books included writings of authors such as Kurt Vonnegut, Desmond Morris, Langston Hughes, and Eldridge Cleaver. The Court said that the "First Amendment rights of students may be directly and sharply implicated by the removal of the books from a school library." The Court explained that the First Amendment protects a right to receive information and that the "special characteristics of the school *library* make that environment especially appropriate for the recognition of the First Amendment rights of students."

The Court observed that it would clearly violate the First Amendment if a Republican school board removed all books by Democratic authors or if the government removed all books written by blacks or arguing for racial equality. The Court said that "[o]ur Constitution does not permit the official suppression of ideas." The Court concluded that whether the "removal of the books from their school libraries [violated the] First Amendment depends upon the motivation behind [the government's] action. If petitioners *intended* by their removal decision to deny respondents access to ideas with which petitioners disagreed, and if this intent was the decisive factor in petitioners' decision, then petitioners exercised their discretion in violation of the Constitution. On the other hand, an unconstitutional motivation would *not* be demonstrated if it were shown that petitioners had decided to remove the books at issue because those books were pervasively vulgar." The Court remanded the case for a determination of this issue.

No school library can buy every book, and obtaining new volumes often means discarding old ones. Inherently, these choices are made based on the content of the books. Yet the Court also is obviously correct that a school board could not make these choices based on the political party affiliation or ideology of the authors. The problem is in courts striking the balance between deferring to the schools' inevitable choices and preventing school censorship of ideas or forms of expression that are unpopular, especially with some school board members. *Pico* attempts to do this by focusing on the motivation behind the decisions. Inevitably, this will turn on the content of the speech. It is difficult to imagine any permissible justification for a school library to remove from its shelves books by authors such as Kurt Vonnegut, Desmond Morris, Langston Hughes, or Eldridge Cleaver. On the other hand, no court would require that an elementary school library purchase *Hustler* magazine. As much as the prohibition of content-based discrimination is at the core of the First Amendment, this is an area where content-based choices are inevitable.

d.   The Speech Rights of Government Employees

The Supreme Court has held that the government may not punish the speech of public employees if it involves matters of public concern unless the state can prove that the needs of the government outweigh the speech rights of the employee. In other words, speech by public employees is clearly less protected than other speech; First Amendment protection does not exist unless the expression is about public concern, and even then, the employee can be disciplined or fired if the government can show, on balance, that the efficient operation of the office justified the action. *See, e.g.,* Pickering v. Board of Education, 391 U.S. 563 (1968).

In Garcetti v. Ceballos, below, the Court imposed a significant new limit on constitutional protection for the speech of government employees. The Court held that such speech is not protected if it is by a government employee while on the job and as part of his or her duties.

GARCETTI v. CEBALLOS

547 U.S. 410 (2006)

Justice KENNEDY delivered the opinion of the Court.

It is well settled that "a State cannot condition public employment on a basis that infringes the employee's constitutionally protected interest in freedom of expression." *Connick v. Myers* (1983). The question presented by the instant case is whether the First Amendment protects a government employee from discipline based on speech made pursuant to the employee's official duties.

I

Respondent Richard Ceballos has been employed since 1989 as a deputy district attorney for the Los Angeles County District Attorney's Office. During the period relevant to this case, Ceballos was a calendar deputy in the office's Pomona branch, and in this capacity he exercised certain supervisory responsibilities over other lawyers. In February 2000, a defense attorney contacted Ceballos about a pending criminal case. The defense attorney said there were inaccuracies in an affidavit used to obtain a critical search warrant. The attorney informed Ceballos that he had filed a motion to traverse, or challenge, the warrant, but he also wanted Ceballos to review the case. According to Ceballos, it was not unusual for defense attorneys to ask calendar deputies to investigate aspects of pending cases. After examining the affidavit and visiting the location it described, Ceballos determined the affidavit contained serious misrepresentations. The affidavit called a long driveway what Ceballos thought should have been referred to as a separate roadway. Ceballos also questioned the affidavit's statement that tire tracks led from a stripped-down truck to the premises covered by the warrant. His doubts arose from his conclusion that the roadway's composition in some places made it difficult or impossible to leave visible tire tracks.

Ceballos spoke on the telephone to the warrant affiant, a deputy sheriff from the Los Angeles County Sheriff's Department, but he did not receive a satisfactory explanation for the perceived inaccuracies. He relayed his findings to his supervisors, petitioners Carol Najera and Frank Sundstedt, and followed up by preparing a disposition memorandum. The memo explained Ceballos' concerns and recommended dismissal of the case.

Despite Ceballos' concerns, Sundstedt decided to proceed with the prosecution, pending disposition of the defense motion to traverse. The trial court held a hearing on the motion. Ceballos was called by the defense and recounted his observations about the affidavit, but the trial court rejected the challenge to the warrant.

Ceballos claims that in the aftermath of these events he was subjected to a series of retaliatory employment actions. The actions included reassignment from his calendar deputy position to a trial deputy position, transfer to another courthouse, and denial of a promotion. 25 S.Ct. 1395, 161 L.Ed.2d 188 (2005), and we now reverse.

II

As the Court's decisions have noted, for many years "the unchallenged dogma was that a public employee had no right to object to conditions placed upon the terms of employment—including those which restricted the exercise of constitutional rights." That dogma has been qualified in important respects. The Court has made clear that public employees do not surrender all their First Amendment rights by reason of their employment. Rather, the First Amendment protects a public employee's right, in certain circumstances, to speak as a citizen addressing matters of public concern.

Pickering and the cases decided in its wake identify two inquiries to guide interpretation of the constitutional protections accorded to public employee speech. The first requires determining whether the employee spoke as a citizen on a matter of public concern. If the answer is no, the employee has no First Amendment cause of action based on his or her employer's reaction to the speech. If the answer is yes, then the possibility of a First Amendment claim arises. The question becomes whether the relevant government entity had an adequate justification for treating the employee differently from any other member of the general public. This consideration reflects the importance of the relationship between the speaker's expressions and employment. A government entity has broader discretion to restrict speech when it acts in its role as employer, but the restrictions it imposes must be directed at speech that has some potential to affect the entity's operations.

When a citizen enters government service, the citizen by necessity must accept certain limitations on his or her freedom. Government employers, like private employers, need a significant degree of control over their employees' words and actions; without it, there would be little chance for the efficient provision of public services. Public employees, moreover, often occupy trusted positions in society. When they speak out, they can express views that contravene governmental policies or impair the proper performance of governmental functions.

At the same time, the Court has recognized that a citizen who works for the government is nonetheless a citizen. The First Amendment limits the ability of a public employer to leverage the employment relationship to restrict, incidentally or intentionally, the liberties employees enjoy in their capacities as private citizens. So long as employees are speaking as citizens about matters of public concern, they must face only those speech restrictions that are necessary for their employers to operate efficiently and effectively.

III

With these principles in mind we turn to the instant case. Respondent Ceballos believed the affidavit used to obtain a search warrant contained serious misrepresentations. He conveyed his opinion and recommendation in a memo to his supervisor. That Ceballos expressed his views inside his office, rather than publicly, is not dispositive. Employees in some cases may receive First Amendment protection for expressions made at work. Many citizens do much of their talking inside their respective workplaces, and it would not serve the goal of treating public employees like "any member of the general public[]" to hold that all speech within the office is automatically exposed to restriction.

The memo concerned the subject matter of Ceballos' employment, but this, too, is nondispositive. The First Amendment protects some expressions related to the speaker's job.

The controlling factor in Ceballos' case is that his expressions were made pursuant to his duties as a calendar deputy. That consideration — the fact that Ceballos spoke as a prosecutor fulfilling a responsibility to advise his supervisor about how best to proceed with a pending case — distinguishes Ceballos' case from those in which the First Amendment provides protection against discipline. We hold that when public employees make statements pursuant to their official duties, the employees are not speaking as citizens for First Amendment purposes, and the Constitution does not insulate their communications from employer discipline. Ceballos wrote his disposition memo because that is part of what he, as a calendar deputy, was employed to do. It is immaterial whether he experienced some personal gratification from writing the memo; his First Amendment rights do not depend on his job satisfaction. The significant point is that the memo was written pursuant to Ceballos' official duties. Restricting speech that owes its existence to a public employee's professional responsibilities does not infringe any liberties the employee might have enjoyed as a private citizen. It simply reflects the exercise of employer control over what the employer itself has commissioned or created.

Ceballos did not act as a citizen when he went about conducting his daily professional activities, such as supervising attorneys, investigating charges, and preparing filings. In the same way he did not speak as a citizen by writing a memo that addressed the proper disposition of a pending criminal case. When he went to work and performed the tasks he was paid to perform, Ceballos acted as a government employee. The fact that his duties sometimes required him to speak or write does not mean his supervisors were prohibited from evaluating his performance.

This result is consistent with our precedents' attention to the potential societal value of employee speech. Our holding likewise is supported by the emphasis of our precedents on affording government employers sufficient discretion to manage their operations. Employers have heightened interests in controlling speech made by an employee in his or her professional capacity. Official communications have official consequences, creating a need for substantive consistency and clarity. Supervisors must ensure that their employees' official communications are accurate, demonstrate sound judgment, and promote the employer's mission. Ceballos' memo is illustrative. It demanded the attention of his supervisors and led to a heated meeting with employees from the sheriff's department. If Ceballos' superiors thought his memo was inflammatory or misguided, they had the authority to take proper corrective action.

Ceballos' proposed contrary rule, adopted by the Court of Appeals, would commit state and federal courts to a new, permanent, and intrusive role, mandating judicial oversight of communications between and among government employees and their superiors in the course of official business. This displacement of managerial discretion by judicial supervision finds no support in our precedents. When an employee speaks as a citizen addressing a matter of public concern, the First Amendment requires a delicate balancing of the competing interests surrounding the speech and its consequences. When, however, the employee is simply performing his or her job duties, there is no warrant for a similar degree of scrutiny. To hold otherwise would be to demand permanent judicial intervention in the conduct of governmental operations to a degree inconsistent with sound principles of federalism and the separation of powers.

Exposing governmental inefficiency and misconduct is a matter of considerable significance. As the Court noted in *Connick*, public employers should, "as a matter of good judgment," be "receptive to constructive criticism offered by their employees." The dictates of sound judgment are reinforced by the powerful network of legislative enactments — such as whistle-blower protection laws and labor codes — available to those who seek to expose wrongdoing. Cases involving government attorneys implicate additional safeguards in the form of, for example, rules of conduct and constitutional obligations apart from the First Amendment. These imperatives, as well as obligations arising from any other applicable constitutional provisions and mandates of the criminal and civil laws, protect employees and provide checks on supervisors who would order unlawful or otherwise inappropriate actions.

We reject, however, the notion that the First Amendment shields from discipline the expressions employees make pursuant to their professional duties. Our precedents do not support the existence of a constitutional cause of action behind every statement a public employee makes in the course of doing his or her job.

Justice STEVENS, dissenting.

The proper answer to the question "whether the First Amendment protects a government employee from discipline based on speech made pursuant to the employee's official duties[]," is "Sometimes," not "Never." Of course a supervisor may take corrective action when such speech is "inflammatory or misguided." But what if it is just unwelcome speech because it reveals facts that the supervisor would rather not have anyone else discover?

As Justice Souter explains, public employees are still citizens while they are in the office. The notion that there is a categorical difference between speaking as a citizen and speaking in the course of one's employment is quite wrong. Over a quarter of a century has passed since then-Justice Rehnquist, writing for a unanimous Court, rejected "the conclusion that a public employee forfeits his protection against governmental abridgment of freedom of speech if he decides to express his views privately rather than publicly." *Givhan v. Western Line Consol. School Dist.* (1979). We had no difficulty recognizing that the First Amendment applied when Bessie Givhan, an English teacher, raised concerns about the school's racist employment practices to the principal. Our silence as to whether or not her speech was made pursuant to her job duties demonstrates that the point was immaterial. That is equally true today, for it is senseless to let constitutional protection for exactly the same words hinge on whether they fall within a job description. Moreover, it seems perverse to fashion a new rule that provides employees with an incentive to voice their concerns publicly before talking frankly to their superiors.

Justice SOUTER, with whom Justice STEVENS and Justice GINSBURG join, dissenting.

The Court holds that "when public employees make statements pursuant to their official duties, the employees are not speaking as citizens for First Amendment purposes, and the Constitution does not insulate their communications from employer discipline." I respectfully dissent. I agree with the majority that a government employer has substantial interests in effectuating its chosen policy and objectives, and in demanding competence, honesty, and judgment from employees who speak for it in doing their work. But I would hold that private and public interests in addressing official wrongdoing and threats to health and safety can outweigh the government's stake in the efficient implementation of policy, and when they do public employees who speak on these matters in the course of their duties should be eligible to claim First Amendment protection.

Open speech by a private citizen on a matter of public importance lies at the heart of expression subject to protection by the First Amendment. At the other extreme, a statement by a government employee complaining about nothing beyond treatment under personnel rules raises no greater claim to constitutional protection against retaliatory response than the remarks of a private employee. In between these points lies a public employee's speech unwelcome to the government but on a significant public issue. Such an employee speaking as a citizen, that is, with a citizen's interest, is protected from reprisal unless the statements are too damaging to the government's capacity to conduct public business to be justified by any individual or public benefit thought to flow from the statements. *Pickering v. Board of Ed. of Township High School Dist. 205, Will Cty.* (1968). Entitlement to protection is thus not absolute.

This significant, albeit qualified, protection of public employees who irritate the government is understood to flow from the First Amendment, in part, because a government paycheck does nothing to eliminate the value to an individual of speaking on public matters, and there is no good reason for categorically discounting a speaker's interest in commenting on a matter of public concern just because the government employs him. Still, the First Amendment safeguard rests on something more, being the value to the public of receiving the opinions and information that a public employee may disclose. "Government employees are often in the best position to know what ails the agencies for which they work." The reason that protection of employee speech is qualified is that it can distract co-workers and supervisors from their tasks at hand and thwart the implementation of legitimate policy, the risks of which grow greater the closer the employee's speech gets to commenting on his own workplace and responsibilities. It is one thing for an office clerk to say there is waste in government and quite another to charge that his own department pays full-time salaries to part-time workers. Even so, we have regarded eligibility for protection

by *Pickering* balancing as the proper approach when an employee speaks critically about the administration of his own government employer.

Nothing, then, accountable on the individual and public side of the *Pickering*
balance changes when an employee speaks "pursuant" to public duties. On the
side of the government employer, however, something is different, and to this
extent, I agree with the majority of the Court. The majority is rightly concerned
that the employee who speaks out on matters subject to comment in doing his
own work has the greater leverage to create office uproars and fracture the
government's authority to set policy to be carried out coherently through the
ranks. "Official communications have official consequences, creating a need for
substantive consistency and clarity. Supervisors must ensure that their employees' official communications are accurate, demonstrate sound judgment, and
promote the employer's mission." Up to a point, then, the majority makes good
points: government needs civility in the workplace, consistency in policy, and
honesty and competence in public service.

But why do the majority's concerns, which we all share, require categorical
exclusion of First Amendment protection against any official retaliation for
things said on the job? Is it not possible to respect the unchallenged individual
and public interests in the speech through a *Pickering* balance without drawing
the strange line I mentioned before? This is, to be sure, a matter of judgment,
but the judgment has to account for the undoubted value of speech to those,
and by those, whose specific public job responsibilities bring them face to face
with wrongdoing and incompetence in government, who refuse to avert their
eyes and shut their mouths. And it has to account for the need actually to disrupt
government if its officials are corrupt or dangerously incompetent. It is thus no
adequate justification for the suppression of potentially valuable information
simply to recognize that the government has a huge interest in managing its
employees and preventing the occasionally irresponsible one from turning his
job into a bully pulpit. Even there, the lesson of *Pickering* (and the object of most
constitutional adjudication) is still to the point: when constitutionally significant
interests clash, resist the demand for winner-take-all; try to make adjustments
that serve all of the values at stake.

Justice BREYER, dissenting.

This case asks whether the First Amendment protects public employees when
they engage in speech that both (1) involves matters of public concern and
(2) takes place in the ordinary course of performing the duties of a government
job. The majority answers the question by holding that "when public employees
make statements pursuant to their official duties, the employees are not speaking as citizens for First Amendment purposes, and the Constitution does not
insulate their communications from employer discipline." In a word, the
majority says, "never." That word, in my view, is too absolute.

Like the majority, I understand the need to "affor[d] government employers
sufficient discretion to manage their operations." And I agree that the Constitution does not seek to "displac[e] . . . managerial discretion by judicial supervision." Nonetheless, there may well be circumstances with special demand for
constitutional protection of the speech at issue, where governmental justifications may be limited, and where administrable standards seem readily available — to the point where the majority's fears of department management by
lawsuit are misplaced. In such an instance, I believe that courts should apply the

Pickering standard, even though the government employee speaks upon matters of public concern in the course of his ordinary duties.

This is such a case. The respondent, a government lawyer, complained of retaliation, in part, on the basis of speech contained in his disposition memorandum that he says fell within the scope of his obligations under *Brady v. Maryland* (1963). The facts present two special circumstances that together justify First Amendment review.

First, the speech at issue is professional speech — the speech of a lawyer. Such speech is subject to independent regulation by canons of the profession. Those canons provide an obligation to speak in certain instances. And where that is so, the government's own interest in forbidding that speech is diminished.

Second, the Constitution itself here imposes speech obligations upon the government's professional employee. A prosecutor has a constitutional obligation to learn of, to preserve, and to communicate with the defense about exculpatory and impeachment evidence in the government's possession. Hence, I would find that the Constitution mandates special protection of employee speech in such circumstances. Thus I would apply the *Pickering* balancing test here.

I conclude that the First Amendment sometimes does authorize judicial actions based upon a government employee's speech that both (1) involves a matter of public concern and also (2) takes place in the course of ordinary job-related duties. But it does so only in the presence of augmented need for constitutional protection and diminished risk of undue judicial interference with governmental management of the public's affairs. In my view, these conditions are met in this case and *Pickering* balancing is consequently appropriate.

E.　FREEDOM OF ASSOCIATION

The Supreme Court has expressly held that freedom of association is a fundamental right protected by the First Amendment. Although "association" is not listed among those freedoms enumerated in the Amendment, the Court has nonetheless declared that "freedom to engage in association for the advancement of beliefs and ideas is an inseparable aspect of the 'liberty' assured by the Due Process Clause of the Fourteenth Amendment, which embraces freedom of speech."[185]

Freedom of association is regarded as integral to the speech and assembly protected by the First Amendment. The Supreme Court explained that "[e]ffective advocacy of both public and private points of view, particularly controversial ones, is undeniably enhanced by group association."[186] Groups have resources — in human capital and money — that a single person lacks. The Court has observed that an "individual's freedom to speak and to petition the Government for the redress of grievances could not be vigorously protected unless a correlative freedom to engage in group effort for those ends were not

---

185. NAACP v. Alabama ex rel. Patterson, 357 U.S. 449 (1958).
186. *Id.* at 460.

also guaranteed."[187] Additionally, the very existence of group support for an idea conveys a message. Association is also important as people benefit from being with others in many ways.[188]

This section considers four issues concerning freedom of association. Subsection 1 considers when the government may prohibit or punish membership in a group. Subsection 2 focuses on when the government may require disclosure of membership, particularly where disclosure will chill association. Subection 3 focuses on when the government may "force" association, such as by requiring contributions. Finally, subsection 4 looks at when freedom of association protects a right of groups to discriminate.

1.   *Laws Prohibiting and Punishing Membership*

Obviously, freedom of association is most directly infringed if the government outlaws and punishes membership in a group. The Court has held that the government may punish membership only if it proves that a person actively affiliated with a group, knowing of its illegal objectives, and with the specific intent to further those objectives. For example, in Scales v. United States, 367 U.S. 203 (1961), the Court affirmed the conviction of the chairman of the North Carolina and South Carolina Districts of the Communist Party under the "membership clause" of the Smith Act that made a felony "the acquisition or holding of knowing membership in any organization which advocates the overthrow of the Government by force or violence." The Court said that earlier precedents had established that "the advocacy with which we are here concerned is not constitutionally protected speech, and it was further established that a combination to promote such advocacy, albeit under the aegis of what purports to be a political party, is not such association as is protected by the First Amendment."

Justice Harlan, writing for the Court, said that the government's ability to prohibit such speech meant that it also had the authority to forbid associations to further these ideas and activities. Justice Harlan wrote, "We can discern no reason why membership, when it constitutes a purposeful form of complicity in a group engaging in this same forbidden advocacy, should receive any greater degree of protection from the guarantees of that Amendment." The Court emphasized that Scales was being punished for his active affiliation with the Communist Party, with knowledge of its illegal objectives and with proof that he "specifically intends to accomplish the aims of the party by resort to violence."

In contrast, in Noto v. United States, 367 U.S. 290 (1961), decided the same day, the Court reversed a conviction for membership in the Communist Party because of the absence of "illegal advocacy." The Court stressed that the speech was advocacy of abstract ideas and that there was not proof that the individual had the specific intent to further any illegal activities.

---

187. Roberts v. Jaycees, 468 U.S. 609, 622 (1984).
188. The Court, however, generally has been unwilling to extend protection of freedom of association outside situations where it relates to First Amendment purpose. For instance, in City of Dallas v. Stanglin, 490 U.S. 19 (1989), the Court upheld a city ordinance that limited the ability of adults to gain access to teenage dance halls. The Court rejected a challenge based on freedom of association and emphasized that the restriction did not limit association for expressive purposes.

The court has applied this test for punishing association in many contexts.[189] For example, the Court has held that the government may deny public employment to an individual based on group affiliation, or require that an individual take an oath concerning group affiliation, only if it is limited to situations where the individual actively affiliated with the group, knowing of its illegal activities, and with the specific intent to further those illegal goals.

In Elfbrandt v. Russell, 384 U.S. 11 (1966), the Court declared unconstitutional a state's loyalty oath and law that prohibited anyone from holding office who was a member of a group such as the Communist Party. The Court explained that "[n]othing in the oath, the statutory gloss, or the construction of the oath and statutes given by the Arizona Supreme Court, purports to exclude association by one who does not subscribe to the organization's unlawful ends." The Court applied the *Scales* test and said that it was impermissible for the government to punish individuals for being members of a group without proof that the individual joined the organization knowing of its illegal objectives and with the specific intent to further them. The Court said that the law was unconstitutional because it "threatens the cherished freedom of association protected by the First Amendment."

Similarly, in Keyishian v. Board of Regents, 385 U.S. 589 (1967), the Court declared unconstitutional a state law that denied employment as teachers to those who were part of organizations that advocated the overthrow of the government. The Court emphasized that the law punished mere membership in a "subversive" group, without any requirement for proof that the individual knew of the illegal objectives or intended to further them.

The same standards have been applied with regard to the ability of states to deny bar membership to individuals based on their group affiliations. In Konigsberg v. State Bar, 366 U.S. 36 (1961), the Court held that the government could deny bar membership to an individual who refused to answer questions concerning membership in the Communist Party.[190] But a decade later, the Court said that the government may require individuals to answer such questions only if they are narrowly focused on whether the individual actively affiliated with a group, knowing of its illegal objectives, and with the specific intent to further those goals.

In Baird v. State Bar, 401 U.S. 1 (1971), and In re Stollar, 401 U.S. 23 (1971), the Court invalidated bar questions that asked whether a person was or had ever been a member of the Communist Party or any organization that advocated the overthrow of the government by force or violence. In contrast, in a companion case, Law Students Civil Rights Research Council v. Wadmond, 401 U.S. 154 (1971), the Court upheld a bar question that asked whether a person ever had joined a group knowing that its objective was the overthrow of the government by force or violence, and if so, whether the individual had the specific intent to advance those goals. The difference among these cases is obviously the specificity of the questions; the inquiry is allowed only if it is narrowly focused on whether a person actively affiliated with a group that advocated the overthrow of

---

189. *See, e.g.,* Communist Party of Indiana v. Whitcomb, 414 U.S. 441 (1974) (declaring unconstitutional a state law that said that political parties could not be listed on the ballot unless they filed an affidavit that they did not advocate the overthrow of the government by force or violence); Aptheker v. Secretary of State, 378 U.S. 500 (1964) (declaring unconstitutional the law barring the use of a passport by a member of the Communist organization).

190. *See also* In re Anastaplo, 366 U.S. 82 (1961).

the government, knowing of its goals, and with the specific intent to further them.

2. Laws Requiring Disclosure of Membership

The Supreme Court has held that the government may require disclosure of membership, where disclosure will chill association, only if it meets strict scrutiny. NAACP v. Alabama ex rel. Patterson articulates this principle.

NAACP v. STATE OF ALABAMA ex rel. PATTERSON

357 U.S. 449 (1958)

Justice HARLAN delivered the opinion of the Court.

We review from the standpoint of its validity under the Federal Constitution a judgment of civil contempt entered against petitioner, the National Association for the Advancement of Colored People, in the courts of Alabama. The question presented is whether Alabama, consistently with the Due Process Clause of the Fourteenth Amendment, can compel petitioner to reveal to the State's Attorney General the names and addresses of all its Alabama members and agents, without regard to their positions or functions in the Association. The judgment of contempt was based upon petitioner's refusal to comply fully with a court order requiring in part the production of membership lists. Petitioner's claim is that the order, in the circumstances shown by this record, violated rights assured to petitioner and its members under the Constitution.

The Association both urges that it is constitutionally entitled to resist official inquiry into its membership lists, and that it may assert, on behalf of its members, a right personal to them to be protected from compelled disclosure by the State of their affiliation with the Association as revealed by the membership lists. Petitioner argues that in view of the facts and circumstances shown in the record, the effect of compelled disclosure of the membership lists will be to abridge the rights of its rank-and-file members to engage in lawful association in support of their common beliefs. It contends that governmental action which, although not directly suppressing association, nevertheless carries this consequence, can be justified only upon some overriding valid interest of the State.

Effective advocacy of both public and private points of view, particularly controversial ones, is undeniably enhanced by group association, as this Court has more than once recognized by remarking upon the close nexus between the freedoms of speech and assembly. It is beyond debate that freedom to engage in association for the advancement of beliefs and ideas is an inseparable aspect of the "liberty" assured by the Due Process Clause of the Fourteenth Amendment, which embraces freedom of speech.

Of course, it is immaterial whether the beliefs sought to be advanced by association pertain to political, economic, religious or cultural matters, and state action which may have the effect of curtailing the freedom to associate is subject to the closest scrutiny. It is hardly a novel perception that compelled disclosure of affiliation with groups engaged in advocacy may constitute as effective a restraint on freedom of association as the forms of governmental action in the cases above were thought likely to produce upon the particular constitutional rights there involved. This Court has recognized the vital relationship between freedom to associate and privacy in one's associations. Inviolability of privacy in group association may in many circumstances be indispensable to preservation of freedom of association, particularly where a group espouses dissident beliefs.

We think that the production order, in the respects here drawn in question, must be regarded as entailing the likelihood of a substantial restraint upon the exercise by petitioner's members of their right to freedom of association. Petitioner has made an uncontroverted showing that on past occasions revelation of the identity of its rank-and-file members has exposed these members to economic reprisal, loss of employment, threat of physical coercion, and other manifestations of public hostility. Under these circumstances, we think it apparent that compelled disclosure of petitioner's Alabama membership is likely to affect adversely the ability of petitioner and its members to pursue their collective effort to foster beliefs which they admittedly have the right to advocate, in that it may induce members to withdraw from the Association and dissuade others from joining it because of fear of exposure of their beliefs shown through their associations and of the consequences of this exposure.

We turn to the final question whether Alabama has demonstrated an interest in obtaining the disclosures it seeks from petitioner which is sufficient to justify the deterrent effect which we have concluded these disclosures may well have on the free exercise by petitioner's members of their constitutionally protected right of association. It is important to bear in mind that petitioner asserts no right to absolute immunity from state investigation, and no right to disregard Alabama's laws. As shown by its substantial compliance with the production order, petitioner does not deny Alabama's right to obtain from it such information as the State desires concerning the purposes of the Association and its activities within the State. Petitioner has not objected to divulging the identity of its members who are employed by or hold official positions with it. It has urged the rights solely of its ordinary rank-and-file members. This is therefore not analogous to a case involving the interest of a State in protecting its citizens in their dealings with paid solicitors or agents of foreign corporations by requiring identifications.

We hold that the immunity from state scrutiny of membership lists which the Association claims on behalf of its members is here so related to the right of the members to pursue their lawful private interests privately and to associate freely with others in so doing as to come within the protection of the Fourteenth Amendment. And we conclude that Alabama has fallen short of showing a controlling justification for the deterrent effect on the free enjoyment of the right to associate which disclosure of membership lists is likely to have.

Similarly, in Shelton v. Tucker, 364 U.S. 479 (1960), the Court declared unconstitutional a state law that required that all teachers disclose their group memberships on an annual basis. The Court again stressed the impact of such disclosures in chilling constitutionally protected association. The Court explained, "[To] compel a teacher to disclose his every associational tie is to impair that teacher's right of free association. [The] statute does not provide that the information it requires be kept confidential. Even if there were no disclosure to the general public, the pressure upon a teacher to avoid any ties which might displease those who control his professional destiny would be constant and heavy." Although the Court recognized the government's important interest in having competent teachers, it concluded that the state cannot pursue the goal "by means that broadly stifle fundamental personal liberties when the end can be more narrowly achieved."

CAMPAIGN FINANCE DISCLOSURE

A crucial aspect of many campaign finance laws is a requirement that candidates disclose their contributors. Such disclosures may chill contributions. Nonetheless, the Court generally has upheld such requirements because of the government's compelling interest in stopping corruption, except where there is reason to believe that the disclosure will chill contributions to a minor party or candidate.

In Buckley v. Valeo, 424 U.S. 1 (1976), the Court upheld a provision in the Federal Election Campaign Act of 1971 that required that every political candidate and political committee keep records of the names and addresses of all who contributed more than $10. These records were required to be available to the Federal Election Commission and for public inspection and copying. There is no doubt that in some contexts people might be chilled from making a contribution because of the disclosure requirement. But the Court found that the requirement served significant government interests. The Court said that "disclosure provides the electorate with information as to where political campaign money comes from in order to aid the voters in evaluating those who seek federal office." The Court also observed that the disclosure requirements discourage corruption and the appearance of corruption because of the "light of publicity." Finally, the Court explained that such "requirements are an essential means of gathering the data necessary to detect violations of the contribution limits."

The Court in *Buckley* recognized that disclosure might have a particularly harmful to the point where the movement cannot survive. The Court said that for a minor party there was much less need for disclosure to prevent corruption "for it is far less likely that the candidate will be victorious."

Although no such parties were involved in *Buckley*, in Brown v. Socialist Workers '74 Campaign Committee, 459 U.S. 87 (1982), the Court held that it was unconstitutional to require the Socialist Workers Party to comply with a state campaign disclosure law. The Court applied its dicta from *Buckley* and concluded that the Socialist Workers Party was a minor party that was historically unpopular so that disclosure requirements would serve little purpose and would likely chill contributions and associational activity.

In its most recent campaign finance case concerning disclosure requirements, Citizens United v. Federal Election Commission, 130 S. Ct. 876 (2010), the Court invalidated restrictions on independent expenditures by corporations and unions (the opinion is earlier in this chapter), but once more upheld disclosure requirements. The Court explained "that disclosure is a less restrictive alternative to more comprehensive regulations of speech. . . . The First Amendment protects political speech; and disclosure permits citizens and shareholders to react to the speech of corporate entities in a proper way. This transparency enables the electorate to make informed decisions and give proper weight to different speakers and messages."

3.   Compelled Association

In Abood v. Detroit Board of Education, 431 U.S. 209 (1977), the Court considered a state law that required all local government employees to pay a union service charge. Union members paid this amount as their dues; nonmembers were required to pay a charge of the same amount. The Court said that the nonmembers could be forced to pay a charge to subsidize the collective bargaining activities of the union. The Court explained that nonmembers would benefit from the gains of collective bargaining and would be "free riders" if not required to pay for these activities. Although nonmembers may disagree with the union's labor-related activities, or even to the existence of the union, the Court found no violation of the First Amendment in forcing nonmembers to pay for the union's collective bargaining conduct.

But the Court said that it violated the First Amendment to force the nonmembers to pay for ideological causes with which they disagreed. The Court explained that it was unconstitutional to use the mandatory service charges "to contribute to political candidates and to express political views unrelated to its duties as exclusive bargaining representative." The Court said that the "heart of the First Amendment is the notion that an individual should be free to believe as he will, and that in a free society one's beliefs should be shaped by his mind and his conscience rather than coerced by the State."

The union was free to use its members' dues or collect voluntary contributions for its ideological activities. The Court said that "the Constitution requires only that expenditures be financed from charges . . . paid by employees who do not object to advancing those ideas and who are not coerced into doing so against their will by the threat of loss of governmental employment."

The Court reaffirmed and applied *Abood* in Keller v. State Bar of California, 496 U.S. 1 (1990). The Court said that compulsory bar dues could be used only if "reasonably incurred for the purpose of regulating the legal profession or improving the quality of the legal service available to the people of the State." The Court explained that bar dues could be collected from all members to pay for bar-related activities. But the Court said that "[c]ompulsory dues may not be expended to endorse or advance a gun control or nuclear weapons freeze initiative; at the other end of the spectrum petitioners have no valid constitutional objection to their compulsory dues being spent for activities connected with disciplining members of the bar or proposing ethical codes for the profession."

After *Abood*, the Court approved a system in which nonunion members could "opt out" of paying the portion of union dues that went to political activities. However, in Knox v. Service Employees International Union, Local 1000, 132 S. Ct. 2277 (2012), the Court indicated that an "opt-out" choice is not sufficient; nonmembers must affirmatively "opt in" to supporting the political activities of unions. The issue arose in the context of a special assessment imposed by a union, the SEIU, to oppose ballot initiatives in California that would have decreased the political influence of public employees' unions. (Ironically, one of them would have required that nonmembers be required to opt in to supporting political activities of unions.) The issue presented to the Court was whether a special notice had to be given to nonmembers of their ability to opt out. But the majority, in an opinion by Justice Alito, said that opt-in was constitutionally required to avoid unconstitutionally compelled speech. The Court stated, "Similarly, requiring objecting nonmembers to opt out of paying the nonchargeable portion of union dues — as opposed to exempting them from making such payments unless they opt in — represents a remarkable boon for unions. Courts "do not presume acquiescence in the loss of fundamental rights. To respect the limits of the First Amendment, the union should have sent out a new notice allowing nonmembers to opt in to the special fee rather than requiring them to opt out."

Justices Sotomayor and Ginsburg concurred in the judgment (they would have required the union send a new notice to nonmembers regarding their ability to opt out), and Justices Breyer and Kagan dissented. These four justices objected to the Court deciding an issue that had not been raised by the parties and expressed concern that opting in will now be the requirement not just for special assessments but also whenever a nonunion member's money will be spent for political activities.

It is interesting and important to contrast these cases concerning compelled speech with the following decision, which upholds the constitutionality of mandatory student activities fees.

BOARD OF REGENTS OF THE UNIVERSITY OF WISCONSIN SYSTEM v. SOUTHWORTH

529 U.S. 217 (2000)

Justice KENNEDY delivered the opinion of the Court.

Respondents are a group of students at the University of Wisconsin. They brought a First Amendment challenge to a mandatory student activity fee imposed by petitioner Board of Regents of the University of Wisconsin and used in part by the University to support student organizations engaging in political or ideological speech. Respondents object to the speech and expression of some of the student organizations. Relying upon our precedents which protect members of unions and bar associations from being required to pay fees used for speech the members find objectionable, both the District Court and the Court of Appeals invalidated the University's student fee program. The University contends that its mandatory student activity fee and the speech which it supports are appropriate to further its educational mission.

We reverse. The First Amendment permits a public university to charge its students an activity fee used to fund a program to facilitate extracurricular student speech if the program is viewpoint neutral. We do not sustain, however, the student referendum mechanism of the University's program, which appears to permit the exaction of fees in violation of the viewpoint neutrality principle. As to that aspect of the program, we remand for further proceedings.

I

It seems that since its founding the University has required full-time students enrolled at its Madison campus to pay a nonrefundable activity fee. For the 1995-1996 academic year, when this suit was commenced, the activity fee amounted to $331.50 per year. The fee is segregated from the University's tuition charge. Once collected, the activity fees are deposited by the University into the accounts of the State of Wisconsin. The fees are drawn upon by the University to support various campus services and extracurricular student activities. In the University's view, the activity fees "enhance the educational experience" of its students by "promot[ing] extracurricular activities," "stimulating advocacy and debate on diverse points of view," enabling "participa[tion] in political activity," "promot[ing] student participa[tion] in campus administrative activity," and providing "opportunities to develop social skills," all consistent with the University's mission.

The board of regents classifies the segregated fee into allocable and nonallocable portions. The nonallocable portion approximates 80% of the total fee and covers expenses such as student health services, intramural sports, debt service, and the upkeep and operations of the student union facilities. Respondents did not challenge the purposes to which the University commits the nonallocable portion of the segregated fee.

The allocable portion of the fee supports extracurricular endeavors pursued by the University's registered student organizations or RSOs. To qualify for RSO status students must organize as a not-for-profit group, limit membership primarily to students, and agree to undertake activities related to student life on campus. During the 1995-1996 school year, 623 groups had RSO status on the Madison campus. To name but a few, RSOs included the Future Financial Gurus of America; the International Socialist Organization; the College Democrats; the College Republicans; and the American Civil Liberties Union Campus Chapter. As one would expect, the expressive activities undertaken by RSOs are diverse in range and content, from displaying posters and circulating newsletters throughout the campus, to hosting campus debates and guest speakers, and to what can best be described as political lobbying.

RSOs may obtain a portion of the allocable fees in one of three ways. Most do so by seeking funding from the Student Government Activity Fund (SGAF), administered by the ASM. SGAF moneys may be issued to support an RSO's operations and events, as well as travel expenses "central to the purpose of the organization." As an alternative, an RSO can apply for funding from the General Student Services Fund (GSSF), administered through the ASM's finance committee. A student referendum provides a third means for an RSO to obtain funding. While the record is sparse on this feature of the University's program, the parties inform us that the student body can vote either to approve or to disapprove an assessment for a particular RSO. One referendum resulted in an allocation of $45,000 to WISPIRG during the 1995-1996 academic year.

II

It is inevitable that government will adopt and pursue programs and policies within its constitutional powers but which nevertheless are contrary to the profound beliefs and sincere convictions of some of its citizens. The government, as a general rule, may support valid programs and policies by taxes or other exactions binding on protesting parties. Within this broader principle it seems inevitable that funds raised by the government will be spent for speech and other expression to advocate and defend its own policies. The case we decide here, however, does not raise the issue of the government's right, or, to be more specific, the state-controlled University's right, to use its own funds to advance a particular message. The University's whole justification for fostering the challenged expression is that it springs from the initiative of the students, who alone give it purpose and content in the course of their extracurricular endeavors.

The University of Wisconsin exacts the fee at issue for the sole purpose of facilitating the free and open exchange of ideas by, and among, its students. We conclude the objecting students may insist upon certain safeguards with respect to the expressive activities which they are required to support. Our public forum cases are instructive here by close analogy. This is true even though the student activities fund is not a public forum in the traditional sense of the term and despite the circumstance that those cases most often involve a demand for access, not a claim to be exempt from supporting speech. The standard of viewpoint neutrality found in the public forum cases provides the standard we find controlling. We decide that the viewpoint neutrality requirement of the University program is in general sufficient to protect the rights of the objecting students. The student referendum aspect of the program for funding speech and expressive activities, however, appears to be inconsistent with the viewpoint neutrality requirement.

We must begin by recognizing that the complaining students are being required to pay fees which are subsidies for speech they find objectionable, even offensive. The *Abood* and *Keller* cases, then, provide the beginning point for our analysis. While those precedents identify the interests of the protesting students, the means of implementing First Amendment protections adopted in those decisions are neither applicable nor workable in the context of extracurricular student speech at a university.

The proposition that students who attend the University cannot be required to pay subsidies for the speech of other students without some First Amendment protection follows from the *Abood* and *Keller* cases. Students enroll in public universities to seek fulfillment of their personal aspirations and of their own potential. If the University conditions the opportunity to receive a college education, an opportunity comparable in importance to joining a labor union or bar association, on an agreement to support objectionable, extracurricular expression by other students, the rights acknowledged in *Abood* and *Keller* become implicated. It infringes on the speech and beliefs of the individual to be required, by this mandatory student activity fee program, to pay subsidies for the objectionable speech of others without any recognition of the State's corresponding duty to him or her. Yet recognition must be given as well to the important and substantial purposes of the University, which seeks to facilitate a wide range of speech.

In *Abood* and *Keller* the constitutional rule took the form of limiting the required subsidy to speech germane to the purposes of the union or bar association. The standard of germane speech as applied to student speech at a university is unworkable, however, and gives insufficient protection both to the objecting students and to the University program itself. Even in the context of a labor union, whose functions are, or so we might have thought, well known and understood by the law and the courts after a long history of government regulation and judicial involvement, we have encountered difficulties in deciding what is germane and what is not.

The speech the University seeks to encourage in the program before us is distinguished not by discernible limits but by its vast, unexplored bounds. To insist upon asking what speech is germane would be contrary to the very goal the University seeks to pursue. It is not for the Court to say what is or is not germane to the ideas to be pursued in an institution of higher learning.

Just as the vast extent of permitted expression makes the test of germane speech inappropriate for intervention, so too does it underscore the high potential for intrusion on the First Amendment rights of the objecting students. It is all but inevitable that the fees will result in subsidies to speech which some students find objectionable and offensive to their personal beliefs. If the standard of germane speech is inapplicable, then, it might be argued the remedy is to allow each student to list those causes which he or she will or will not support. If a university decided that its students' First Amendment interests were better protected by some type of optional or refund system it would be free to do so. We decline to impose a system of that sort as a constitutional requirement, however. The restriction could be so disruptive and expensive that the program to support extracurricular speech would be ineffective. The First Amendment does not require the University to put the program at risk.

The University may determine that its mission is well served if students have the means to engage in dynamic discussions of philosophical, religious, scientific, social, and political subjects in their extracurricular campus life outside the lecture hall. If the University reaches this conclusion, it is entitled to impose a mandatory fee to sustain an open dialogue to these ends.

The University must provide some protection to its students' First Amendment interests, however. The proper measure, and the principal standard of protection for objecting students, we conclude, is the requirement of viewpoint neutrality in the allocation of funding support. The parties have stipulated that the program the University has developed to stimulate extracurricular student expression respects the principle of viewpoint neutrality. If the stipulation is to continue to control the case, the University's program in its basic structure must be found consistent with the First Amendment.

It remains to discuss the referendum aspect of the University's program. While the record is not well developed on the point, it appears that by majority vote of the student body a given RSO may be funded or defunded. It is unclear to us what protection, if any, there is for viewpoint neutrality in this part of the process. To the extent the referendum substitutes majority determinations for viewpoint neutrality it would undermine the constitutional protection the program requires. The whole theory of viewpoint neutrality is that minority views are treated with the same respect as are majority views. Access to a public forum, for instance, does not depend upon majoritarian consent. That principle is controlling here. A remand is necessary and appropriate to resolve this point; and the case in all events must be reexamined in light of the principles we have discussed.

4. Laws Prohibiting Discrimination

Many state and local governments have adopted laws that prohibit discrimination by private groups and clubs. Frequently, those wishing to discriminate bring challenges to these laws; the claim is that freedom of association protects their right to discriminate and exclude whomever they want from their group. The Supreme Court has held that the compelling interest in stopping discrimination justifies interfering with such associational freedoms. The Court has indicated that freedom of association would protect a right to discriminate only if it is intimate association or where the discrimination is integral to express activity. Roberts v. United States Jaycees is the leading case articulating this test.

ROBERTS v. UNITED STATES JAYCEES
468 U.S. 609 (1984)

Justice BRENNAN delivered the opinion of the Court.

This case requires us to address a conflict between a State's efforts to eliminate gender-based discrimination against its citizens and the constitutional freedom of association asserted by members of a private organization. In the decision under review, the Court of Appeals for the Eighth Circuit concluded that, by requiring the United States Jaycees to admit women as full voting members, the Minnesota Human Rights Act violates the First and Fourteenth Amendment rights of the organization's members. We now reverse.

I

The United States Jaycees (Jaycees), founded in 1920 as the Junior Chamber of Commerce, is a nonprofit membership corporation, incorporated in Missouri with national headquarters in Tulsa, Okla. The objective of the Jaycees, as set out in its bylaws, is to pursue "such educational and charitable purposes as will promote and foster the growth and development of young men's civic organizations in the United States, designed to inculcate in the individual membership of such organization a spirit of genuine Americanism and civic interest, and as a supplementary education institution to provide them with opportunity for personal development and achievement and an avenue for intelligent participation by young men in the affairs of their community, state and nation, and to develop true friendship and understanding among young men of all nations." Regular membership is limited to young men between the ages of 18 and 35, while associate membership is available to individuals or groups ineligible for regular membership, principally women and older men. An associate member, whose dues are somewhat lower than those charged regular members, may not vote, hold local or national office, or participate in certain leadership training and awards programs.

The bylaws define a local chapter as "[a]ny young men's organization of good repute existing in any community within the United States, organized for purposes similar to and consistent with those" of the national organization. The ultimate policymaking authority of the Jaycees rests with an annual national convention, consisting of delegates from each local chapter, with a national president and board of directors. At the time of trial in August 1981, the Jaycees had approximately 295,000 members in 7,400 local chapters affiliated with 51 state organizations. There were at that time about 11,915 associate members. The national organization's executive vice president estimated at trial that women associate members make up about two percent of the Jaycees' total membership.

In 1974 and 1975, respectively, the Minneapolis and St. Paul chapters of the Jaycees began admitting women as regular members. Currently, the memberships and boards of directors of both chapters include a substantial proportion of women. As a result, the two chapters have been in violation of the national organization's bylaws for about 10 years. The national organization has imposed a number of sanctions on the Minneapolis and St. Paul chapters for violating the bylaws, including denying their members eligibility for state or national office or awards programs, and refusing to count their membership in computing votes at national conventions.

In December 1978, the president of the national organization advised both chapters that a motion to revoke their charters would be considered at a forthcoming meeting of the national board of directors in Tulsa. Shortly after receiving this notification, members of both chapters filed charges of discrimination with the Minnesota Department of Human Rights. The complaints alleged that the exclusion of women from full membership required by the national organization's bylaws violated the Minnesota Human Rights Act (Act), which provides in part: "It is an unfair discriminatory practice: To deny any person the full and equal enjoyment of the goods, services, facilities, privileges, advantages, and accommodations of a place of public accommodation because of race, color, creed, religion, disability, national origin or sex." The term "place of public accommodation" is defined in the Act as "a business, accommodation, refreshment, entertainment, recreation, or transportation facility of any kind, whether licensed or not, whose goods, services, facilities, privileges, advantages or accommodations are extended, offered, sold, or otherwise made available to the public."

II

Our decisions have referred to constitutionally protected "freedom of association" in two distinct senses. In one line of decisions, the Court has concluded that choices to enter into and maintain certain intimate human relationships must be secured against undue intrusion by the State because of the role of such relationships in safeguarding the individual freedom that is central to our constitutional scheme. In this respect, freedom of association receives protection as a fundamental element of personal liberty. In another set of decisions, the Court has recognized a right to associate for the purpose of engaging in those activities protected by the First Amendment — speech, assembly, petition for the redress of grievances, and the exercise of religion. The Constitution guarantees freedom of association of this kind as an indispensable means of preserving other individual liberties.

The intrinsic and instrumental features of constitutionally protected association may, of course, coincide. In particular, when the State interferes with individuals' selection of those with whom they wish to join in a common endeavor, freedom of association in both of its forms may be implicated. The Jaycees contend that this is such a case. Still, the nature and degree of constitutional protection afforded freedom of association may vary depending on the extent to which one or the other aspect of the constitutionally protected liberty is at stake in a given case. We therefore find it useful to consider separately the effect of applying the Minnesota statute to the Jaycees on what could be called its members' freedom of intimate association and their freedom of expressive association.

A

The Court has long recognized that, because the Bill of Rights is designed to secure individual liberty, it must afford the formation and preservation of certain kinds of highly personal relationships a substantial measure of sanctuary from unjustified interference by the State. The personal affiliations that exemplify these considerations, and that therefore suggest some relevant limitations on the relationships that might be entitled to this sort of constitutional protection, are those that attend the creation and sustenance of a family — marriage, childbirth, the raising and education of children, and cohabitation with one's relatives. Among other things, therefore, they are distinguished by such attributes as relative smallness, a high degree of selectivity in decisions to begin and maintain the affiliation, and seclusion from others in critical aspects of the relationship. As a general matter, only relationships with these sorts of qualities are likely to reflect the considerations that have led to an understanding of freedom of association as an intrinsic element of personal liberty. Conversely, an association lacking these qualities — such as a large business enterprise — seems remote from the concerns giving rise to this constitutional protection. Accordingly, the Constitution undoubtedly imposes constraints on the State's power to control the selection of one's spouse that would not apply to regulations affecting the choice of one's fellow employees.

Between these poles, of course, lies a broad range of human relationships that may make greater or lesser claims to constitutional protection from particular incursions by the State. Determining the limits of state authority over an individual's freedom to enter into a particular association therefore unavoidably entails a careful assessment of where that relationship's objective characteristics locate it on a spectrum from the most intimate to the most attenuated of personal attachments. We need not mark the potentially significant points on this terrain with any precision. We note only that factors that may be relevant include size, purpose, policies, selectivity, congeniality, and other characteristics that in a particular case may be pertinent. In this case, however, several features of the Jaycees clearly place the organization outside of the category of relationships worthy of this kind of constitutional protection.

The undisputed facts reveal that the local chapters of the Jaycees are large and basically unselective groups. At the time of the state administrative hearing, the Minneapolis chapter had approximately 430 members, while the St. Paul chapter had about 400. Apart from age and sex, neither the national organization nor the local chapters employ any criteria for judging applicants for membership, and new members are routinely recruited and admitted with no inquiry into their backgrounds. In fact, a local officer testified that he could recall no instance in which an applicant had been denied membership on any basis other than age or sex. In short, the local chapters of the Jaycees are neither small nor selective. Moreover, much of the activity central to the formation and maintenance of the association involves the participation of strangers to that relationship. Accordingly, we conclude that the Jaycees chapters lack the distinctive characteristics that might afford constitutional protection to the decision of its members to exclude women.

B

An individual's freedom to speak, to worship, and to petition the government for the redress of grievances could not be vigorously protected from interference by the State unless a correlative freedom to engage in group effort toward those ends were not also guaranteed. According protection to collective effort on behalf of shared goals is especially important in preserving political and cultural diversity and in shielding dissident expression from suppression by the majority. Consequently, we have long understood as implicit in the right to engage in activities protected by the First Amendment a corresponding right to associate with others in pursuit of a wide variety of political, social, economic, educational, religious, and cultural ends.

Government actions that may unconstitutionally infringe upon this freedom can take a number of forms. Among other things, government may seek to impose penalties or withhold benefits from individuals because of their membership in a disfavored group; it may attempt to require disclosure of the fact of membership in a group seeking anonymity; and it may try to interfere with the internal organization or affairs of the group. By requiring the Jaycees to admit women as full voting members, the Minnesota Act works an infringement of the last type. There can be no clearer example of an intrusion into the internal structure or affairs of an association than a regulation that forces the group to accept members it does not desire. Such a regulation may impair the ability of the original members to express only those views that brought them together. Freedom of association therefore plainly presupposes a freedom not to associate.

The right to associate for expressive purposes is not, however, absolute. Infringements on that right may be justified by regulations adopted to serve compelling state interests, unrelated to the suppression of ideas, that cannot be achieved through means significantly less restrictive of associational freedoms.

We are persuaded that Minnesota's compelling interest in eradicating discrimination against its female citizens justifies the impact that application of the statute to the Jaycees may have on the male members' associational freedoms. On its face, the Minnesota Act does not aim at the suppression of speech, does not distinguish between prohibited and permitted activity on the basis of viewpoint, and does not license enforcement authorities to administer the statute on the basis of such constitutionally impermissible criteria. Instead, as the Minnesota Supreme Court explained, the Act reflects the State's strong historical commitment to eliminating discrimination and assuring its citizens equal access to publicly available goods and services. That goal, which is unrelated to the suppression of expression, plainly serves compelling state interests of the highest order.

In applying the Act to the Jaycees, the State has advanced those interests through the least restrictive means of achieving its ends. Indeed, the Jaycees has failed to demonstrate that the Act imposes any serious burdens on the male members' freedom of expressive association.

There is, however, no basis in the record for concluding that admission of women as full voting members will impede the organization's ability to engage in these protected activities or to disseminate its preferred views. The Act requires no change in the Jaycees' creed of promoting the interests of young men, and it imposes no restrictions on the organization's ability to exclude individuals with ideologies or philosophies different from those of its existing members. Moreover, the Jaycees already invites women to share the group's views and philosophy and to participate in much of its training and community activities. Accordingly, any claim that admission of women as full voting members will impair a symbolic message conveyed by the very fact that women are not permitted to vote is attenuated at best.

It is similarly arguable that, insofar as the Jaycees is organized to promote the views of young men whatever those views happen to be, admission of women as voting members will change the message communicated by the group's speech because of the gender-based assumptions of the audience. Neither supposition, however, is supported by the record. In claiming that women might have a different attitude about such issues as the federal budget, school prayer, voting rights, and foreign relations, or that the organization's public positions would have a different effect if the group were not "a purely young men's association," the Jaycees relies solely on unsupported generalizations about the relative interests and perspectives of men and women. Although such generalizations may or may not have a statistical basis in fact with respect to particular positions adopted by the Jaycees, we have repeatedly condemned legal decisionmaking that relies uncritically on such assumptions. In the absence of a showing far more substantial than that attempted by the Jaycees, we decline to indulge in the sexual stereotyping that underlies appellee's contention that, by allowing women to vote, application of the Minnesota Act will change the content or impact of the organization's speech. In any event, even if enforcement of the Act causes some incidental abridgment of the Jaycees' protected speech, that effect is no greater than is necessary to accomplish the State's legitimate purposes.

Similarly, in Board of Directors of Rotary International v. Rotary Club of Duarte, 481 U.S. 537 (1987), the Court held that it did not violate the First Amendment rights of the Rotary Club to force them to admit women in compliance with a California law that prohibited private business establishments from discriminating based on characteristics such as gender.

In *Roberts* and *Rotary Club*, the Court recognized that freedom of association would protect a right to discriminate in limited circumstances. For instance, if the activity is "intimate association"—a small private gathering—freedom of association would protect a right to discriminate. Also, freedom of association would protect a right to discriminate where discrimination is integral to expressive activity. For example, the Klan likely could exclude African Americans or the Nazi party could exclude Jews because discrimination is a key aspect of their message.

In Hurley v. Irish-American Gay, Lesbian, and Bisexual Group of Boston, 515 U.S. 557 (1995), the Court found that freedom of association and freedom of speech allowed a group to discriminate. Every St. Patrick's Day, the Veterans Council, a private group, organizes a parade in Boston. The Veterans Council refused to allow the Irish-American Gay, Lesbian, and Bisexual Group of Boston to participate in its parade. The Irish-American Gay, Lesbian, and Bisexual Group sued in Massachusetts state court based on the state's public accommodations law that prohibited discrimination by business establishments based on sexual orientation. The Massachusetts Supreme Judicial Court sided with the Irish-American Gay, Lesbian, and Bisexual Group.

The U.S. Supreme Court unanimously reversed. The Court, in an opinion by Justice Souter, said that organizing a parade is inherently expressive activity and that it violated the First Amendment to force the organizers to include messages that they find inimical. Justice Souter explained that compelling the Veterans Council to include the Irish-American Gay, Lesbian, and Bisexual Group "violates the fundamental rule . . . under the First Amendment, that a speaker has the autonomy to choose the content of his own message."

The Court expressly invoked the principle that there is a First Amendment right not to speak. Justice Souter wrote that "the Council clearly decided to exclude a message it did not like from the communication it chose to make, and that is enough to invoke its right as a private speaker to shape its expression by speaking on one subject while remaining silent on another."

The most important Supreme Court case concerning a right to exclude based on freedom of association is Boy Scouts of America v. Dale.

BOY SCOUTS OF AMERICA v. DALE
530 U.S. 640 (2000)

Chief Justice Rehnquist delivered the opinion of the Court.

Petitioners are the Boy Scouts of America and the Monmouth Council, a division of the Boy Scouts of America (collectively, Boy Scouts). The Boy Scouts is a private, not-for-profit organization engaged in instilling its system of values in young people. The Boy Scouts asserts that homosexual conduct is inconsistent with the values it seeks to instill. Respondent is James Dale, a former Eagle Scout whose adult membership in the Boy Scouts was revoked when the Boy Scouts learned that he is an avowed homosexual and gay rights activist. The New Jersey Supreme Court held that New Jersey's public accommodations law requires that the Boy Scouts admit Dale. This case presents the question whether applying New Jersey's public accommodations law in this way violates the Boy Scouts' First Amendment right of expressive association. We hold that it does.

I

James Dale entered scouting in 1978 at the age of eight by joining Monmouth Council's Cub Scout Pack 142. Dale became a Boy Scout in 1981 and remained a Scout until he turned 18. By all accounts, Dale was an exemplary Scout. In 1988, he achieved the rank of Eagle Scout, one of Scouting's highest honors. Dale applied for adult membership in the Boy Scouts in 1989. The Boy Scouts approved his application for the position of assistant scoutmaster of Troop 73.

Around the same time, Dale left home to attend Rutgers University. After arriving at Rutgers, Dale first acknowledged to himself and others that he is gay. He quickly became involved with, and eventually became the copresident of, the Rutgers University Lesbian/Gay Alliance. In 1990, Dale attended a seminar addressing the psychological and health needs of lesbian and gay teenagers. A newspaper covering the event interviewed Dale about his advocacy of homosexual teenagers' need for gay role models. In early July 1990, the newspaper published the interview and Dale's photograph over a caption identifying him as the copresident of the Lesbian/Gay Alliance.

Later that month, Dale received a letter from Monmouth Council Executive James Kay revoking his adult membership. Dale wrote to Kay requesting the reason for Monmouth Council's decision. Kay responded by letter that the Boy Scouts "specifically forbid membership to homosexuals." In 1992, Dale filed a complaint against the Boy Scouts in the New Jersey Superior Court. The complaint alleged that the Boy Scouts had violated New Jersey's public accommodations statute and its common law by revoking Dale's membership based solely on his sexual orientation. New Jersey's public accommodations statute prohibits, among other things, discrimination on the basis of sexual orientation in places of public accommodation. The New Jersey Supreme Court held that the Boy Scouts was a place of public accommodation subject to the public accommodations law, that the organization was not exempt from the law under any of its express exceptions, and that the Boy Scouts violated the law by revoking Dale's membership based on his avowed homosexuality.

II

The forced inclusion of an unwanted person in a group infringes the group's freedom of expressive association if the presence of that person affects in a significant way the group's ability to advocate public or private viewpoints. But the freedom of expressive association, like many freedoms, is not absolute. We have held that the freedom could be overridden "by regulations adopted to serve compelling state interests, unrelated to the suppression of ideas, that cannot be achieved through means significantly less restrictive of associational freedoms."

To determine whether a group is protected by the First Amendment's expressive associational right, we must determine whether the group engages in "expressive association." The First Amendment's protection of expressive association is not reserved for advocacy groups. But to come within its ambit, a group must engage in some form of expression, whether it be public or private.

The Boy Scouts is a private, nonprofit organization. According to its mission statement: "It is the mission of the Boy Scouts of America to serve others by helping to instill values in young people and, in other ways, to prepare them to make ethical choices over their lifetime in achieving their full potential. The values we strive to instill are based on those found in the Scout Oath and Law: On my honor I will do my best to do my duty to God and my country and to obey the Scout Law; To help other people at all times; To keep myself physically strong, mentally awake, and morally straight."

Thus, the general mission of the Boy Scouts is clear: "[T]o instill values in young people." The Boy Scouts seeks to instill these values by having its adult leaders spend time with the youth members, instructing and engaging them in activities like camping, archery, and fishing. During the time spent with the youth members, the scoutmasters and assistant scoutmasters inculcate them with the Boy Scouts' values — both expressly and by example. It seems indisputable that an association that seeks to transmit such a system of values engages in expressive activity. Given that the Boy Scouts engages in expressive activity, we must determine whether the forced inclusion of Dale as an assistant scoutmaster would significantly affect the Boy Scouts' ability to advocate public or private viewpoints. This inquiry necessarily requires us first to explore, to a limited extent, the nature of the Boy Scouts' view of homosexuality.

The values the Boy Scouts seeks to instill are "based on" those listed in the Scout Oath and Law. The Boy Scouts explains that the Scout Oath and Law provide "a positive moral code for living; they are a list of 'do's' rather than 'don'ts.'" The Boy Scouts asserts that homosexual conduct is inconsistent with the values embodied in the Scout Oath and Law, particularly with the values represented by the terms "morally straight" and "clean."

Obviously, the Scout Oath and Law do not expressly mention sexuality or sexual orientation. And the terms "morally straight" and "clean" are by no means self-defining. Different people would attribute to those terms very different meanings. For example, some people may believe that engaging in homosexual conduct is not at odds with being "morally straight" and "clean." And others may believe that engaging in homosexual conduct is contrary to being "morally straight" and "clean." The Boy Scouts says it falls within the latter category.

The Boy Scouts publicly expressed its views with respect to homosexual conduct by its assertions in prior litigation. For example, throughout a California case with similar facts filed in the early 1980's, the Boy Scouts consistently asserted the same position with respect to homosexuality that it asserts today. We cannot doubt that the Boy Scouts sincerely holds this view.

We must then determine whether Dale's presence as an assistant scoutmaster would significantly burden the Boy Scouts' desire to not "promote homosexual conduct as a legitimate form of behavior." As we give deference to an association's assertions regarding the nature of its expression, we must also give deference to an association's view of what would impair its expression. That is not to say that an expressive association can erect a shield against antidiscrimination laws simply by asserting that mere acceptance of a member from a particular group would impair its message. But here Dale, by his own admission, is one of a group of gay Scouts who have "become leaders in their community and are open and honest about their sexual orientation." Dale was the copresident of a gay and lesbian organization at college and remains a gay rights activist. Dale's presence in the Boy Scouts would, at the very least, force the organization to send a message, both to the youth members and the world, that the Boy Scouts accepts homosexual conduct as a legitimate form of behavior.

Having determined that the Boy Scouts is an expressive association and that the forced inclusion of Dale would significantly affect its expression, we inquire whether the application of New Jersey's public accommodations law to require that the Boy Scouts accept Dale as an assistant scoutmaster runs afoul of the Scouts' freedom of expressive association. We conclude that it does. We are not, as we must not be, guided by our views of whether the Boy Scouts' teachings with respect to homosexual conduct are right or wrong; public or judicial disapproval of a tenet of an organization's expression does not justify the State's effort to compel the organization to accept members where such acceptance would derogate from the organization's expressive message. "While the law is free to promote all sorts of conduct in place of harmful behavior, it is not free to interfere with speech for no better reason than promoting an approved message or discouraging a disfavored one, however enlightened either purpose may strike the government."

Justice STEVENS, with whom Justice SOUTER, Justice GINSBURG and Justice BREYER join, dissenting.

New Jersey "prides itself on judging each individual by his or her merits" and on being "in the vanguard in the fight to eradicate the cancer of unlawful discrimination of all types from our society." The New Jersey Supreme Court's construction of the statutory definition of a "place of public accommodation" has given its statute a more expansive coverage than most similar state statutes. The question in this case is whether that expansive construction trenches on the federal constitutional rights of the Boy Scouts of America (BSA).

In this case, Boy Scouts of America contends that it teaches the young boys who are Scouts that homosexuality is immoral. Consequently, it argues, it would violate its right to associate to force it to admit homosexuals as members, as doing so would be at odds with its own shared goals and values. This contention, quite plainly, requires us to look at what, exactly, are the values that BSA actually teaches.

BSA's mission statement reads as follows: "It is the mission of the Boy Scouts of America to serve others by helping to instill values in young people and, in other ways, to prepare them to make ethical choices over their lifetime in achieving their full potential." Its federal charter declares its purpose is "to promote, through organization, and cooperation with other agencies, the ability of boys to do things for themselves and others, to train them in scoutcraft, and to teach them patriotism, courage, self-reliance, and kindred values." BSA describes itself as having a "representative membership," which it defines as "boy membership [that] reflects proportionately the characteristics of the boy population of its service area." In particular, the group emphasizes that "[n]either the charter nor the bylaws of the Boy Scouts of America permits the exclusion of any boy. . . . To meet these responsibilities we have made a commitment that our membership shall be representative of all the population in every community, district, and council."

To bolster its claim that its shared goals include teaching that homosexuality is wrong, BSA directs our attention to two terms appearing in the Scout Oath and Law. The first is the phrase "morally straight," which appears in the Oath ("On my honor I will do my best . . . To keep myself . . . morally straight"); the second term is the word "clean," which appears in a list of 12 characteristics together comprising the Scout Law.

The Boy Scout Handbook defines "morally straight," as such: "To be a person of strong character, guide your life with honesty, purity, and justice. Respect and defend the rights of all people. Your relationships with others should be honest and open. Be clean in your speech and actions, and faithful in your religious beliefs. The values you follow as a Scout will help you become virtuous and self-reliant." As for the term "clean," the Boy Scout Handbook offers the following: "A Scout is CLEAN. A Scout keeps his body and mind fit and clean. He chooses the company of those who live by these same ideals. He helps keep his home and community clean." "You never need to be ashamed of dirt that will wash off. If you play hard and work hard you can't help getting dirty. But when the game is over or the work is done, that kind of dirt disappears with soap and water. There's another kind of dirt that won't come off by washing. It is the kind that shows up in foul language and harmful thoughts. Swear words, profanity, and dirty stories are weapons that ridicule other people and hurt their feelings. The same is true of racial slurs and jokes making fun of ethnic groups or people with physical or mental limitations. A Scout knows there is no kindness or honor in such mean-spirited behavior. He avoids it in his own words and deeds. He defends those who are targets of insults."

It is plain as the light of day that neither one of these principles — "morally straight" and "clean" — says the slightest thing about homosexuality. Indeed, neither term in the Boy Scouts' Law and Oath expresses any position whatsoever on sexual matters.

BSA's published guidance on that topic underscores this point. Scouts, for example, are directed to receive their sex education at home or in school, but not from the organization: "Your parents or guardian or a sex education teacher should give you the facts about sex that you must know." Boy Scout Handbook (1992). Moreover, Scoutmasters are specifically directed to steer curious adolescents to other sources of information: "If Scouts ask for information regarding . . . sexual activity, answer honestly and factually, but stay within your realm of expertise and comfort. If a Scout has serious concerns that you cannot answer, refer him to his family, religious leader, doctor, or other professional."

In light of BSA's self-proclaimed ecumenism, furthermore, it is even more difficult to discern any shared goals or common moral stance on homosexuality. Insofar as religious matters are concerned, BSA's bylaws state that it is "absolutely nonsectarian in its attitude toward . . . religious training." Because a number of religious groups do not view homosexuality as immoral or wrong and reject discrimination against homosexuals, it is exceedingly difficult to believe that BSA nonetheless adopts a single particular religious or moral philosophy when it comes to sexual orientation. BSA surely is aware that some religions do not teach that homosexuality is wrong.

[I]n *Jaycees*, we asked whether Minnesota's Human Rights Law requiring the admission of women "impose[d] any serious burdens" on the group's "collective effort on behalf of [its] shared goals." Notwithstanding the group's obvious publicly stated exclusionary policy, we did not view the inclusion of women as a "serious burden" on the Jaycees' ability to engage in the protected speech of its choice. Similarly, in *Rotary Club*, we asked whether California's law would "affect in any significant way the existing members' ability" to engage in their protected speech, or whether the law would require the clubs "to abandon their basic goals." The relevant question is whether the mere inclusion of the person at issue would "impose any serious burden," "affect in any significant way," or be "a substantial restraint upon" the organization's "shared goals," "basic goals," or "collective effort to foster beliefs."

The evidence before this Court makes it exceptionally clear that BSA has, at most, simply adopted an exclusionary membership policy and has no shared goal of disapproving of homosexuality. BSA's mission statement and federal charter say nothing on the matter; its official membership policy is silent; its

Scout Oath and Law—and accompanying definitions—are devoid of any view on the topic; its guidance for Scouts and Scoutmasters on sexuality declare that such matters are "not construed to be Scouting's proper area," but are the province of a Scout's parents and pastor; and BSA's posture respecting religion tolerates a wide variety of views on the issue of homosexuality. Moreover, there is simply no evidence that BSA otherwise teaches anything in this area, or that it instructs Scouts on matters involving homosexuality in ways not conveyed in the Boy Scout or Scoutmaster Handbooks. In short, Boy Scouts of America is simply silent on homosexuality. There is no shared goal or collective effort to foster a belief about homosexuality at all—let alone one that is significantly burdened by admitting homosexuals. As in *Jaycees*, there is "no basis in the record for concluding that admission of [homosexuals] will impede the [Boy Scouts'] ability to engage in [its] protected activities or to disseminate its preferred views" and New Jersey's law "requires no change in [BSA's] creed." It is entirely clear that BSA in fact expresses no clear, unequivocal message burdened by New Jersey's law.

Unfavorable opinions about homosexuals "have ancient roots." Like equally atavistic opinions about certain racial groups, those roots have been nourished by sectarian doctrine. That such prejudices are still prevalent and that they have caused serious and tangible harm to countless members of the class New Jersey seeks to protect are established matters of fact that neither the Boy Scouts nor the Court disputes. That harm can only be aggravated by the creation of a constitutional shield for a policy that is itself the product of a habitual way of thinking about strangers. As Justice Brandeis so wisely advised, "we must be ever on our guard, lest we erect our prejudices into legal principles." If we would guide by the light of reason, we must let our minds be bold. I respectfully dissent.

F.   FREEDOM OF THE PRESS

1.   *Introduction: Are There Special Rights for the Press?*

Although the First Amendment expressly protects "freedom of the press," most of the issues concerning press freedom have been covered throughout this chapter. For example, the basic methodological issues concerning the First Amendment—such as the distinction between content-based and content-neutral laws, the requirement that laws not be vague or overbroad, and especially the prohibition of prior restraints—all apply to the press. Indeed, many of these cases, particularly those concerning prior restraints, arose in the context of actions against newspapers. Similarly, the categories of unprotected and less protected speech apply to all speakers, including the press.

This section focuses on issues that uniquely apply to the press. The underlying question is whether the press is entitled to any protections greater than others under the First Amendment. For example, does freedom of the press provide the media with an exemption from general government laws? Does it protect a right to news gathering and thus give the media special access to government places and papers?

On the one hand, freedom of the press is enumerated as a distinct right from freedom of speech. This arguably reflects the important and unique role of informing the public and thereby checking government.[191] Sometimes the failure to protect the press as an institution will mean that the people will be denied significant information. For instance, arguably the failure to allow reporters to keep their sources confidential will mean the loss of information that might have been available if secrecy could have been promised.

But others argue that the press is entitled to no special protections under the First Amendment.[192] In part, the argument against special status for the press is based on the framers' intent and the view that they used the words "speech" and "press" synonymously. Also, those who oppose special protections for the press argue that defining the press poses insurmountable obstacles. For example, if reporters can keep their sources confidential, is anyone who purports to be writing a story entitled to the privilege? Any distinctions could raise serious First Amendment and equal protection issues.[193] Opposition to special protections for the press also reflects a long-standing hostility to the media in American society. Some fear that special protection would unduly enlarge the power of the press.

The Supreme Court generally has taken the latter view that the press is not entitled to any special rights or protections under the First Amendment. The issue remains, though, as to whether this is a desirable interpretation of the First Amendment and whether it adequately protects the need of the people to be informed.

Two major types of issues arise concerning freedom of the press. First, does freedom of the press provide the media a shield that it can use to immunize itself from government regulation? Subsection 2 focuses on this issue and considers many specific issues. When do taxes on the press violate the First Amendment? Does freedom of the press exempt it from the application of general regulatory laws? Does the press have a constitutional right to keep its sources secret? Does the First Amendment protect the press from laws that create a right to use it to reply to attacks?

A second major set of issues concerns whether freedom of the press can be used as a "sword" to gain access to government places and papers. There are two interrelated issues here: Does the First Amendment create a right of access for anyone to government places and papers; and does the press have a preferred right of access or any rights greater than the general population? As discussed in subsection 3, the Court has found a First Amendment right for people to attend judicial proceedings but otherwise has refused to find such a First Amendment right of access and has thus far failed to create greater rights for the press than for others in society.

---

191. *See, e.g.*, David A. Anderson, *The Origins of the Press Clause*, 30 UCLA L. Rev. 455 (1983); Potter Stewart, *Or of the Press*, 26 Hastings L.J. 631 (1975).

192. *See, e.g.*, Leonard Levy, *Legacy of Suppression* 174 (1960); *see also* First National Bank of Boston v. Bellotti, 435 U.S. 765, 767-801 (1978) (Burger, C.J., concurring).

193. It should be noted, though, that many states have adopted reporter shield laws that define who is entitled to protection under them.

2.   Freedom of the Press as a Shield to Protect the Press from the Government

a.   Taxes on the Press

The Supreme Court consistently has held that taxes that single out the press are unconstitutional, but the press can be required to pay general taxes applicable to all businesses. The obvious concern is that the government could use taxes to punish the press for aggressive reporting or pointed criticism. The fear of such taxes could chill the press. For example, in Grosjean v. American Press Co., 297 U.S. 233 (1936), the Court declared unconstitutional a state statute imposing a license tax on advertisements in publications having a circulation of more than 20,000 copies a week. The Court reviewed the history of the First Amendment and concluded that the framers clearly intended to prohibit taxes directed at the press because of fear that they could cripple or at least chill the press. The Court said that although the First Amendment did not exempt the press from ordinary taxation, it did provide immunity from taxes directed solely at them. Although the Court did not discuss the circumstances that caused Louisiana to adopt its tax on the press, it likely was influenced by the fact that Governor Huey Long initiated the tax as retaliation against newspapers that had opposed him.

More recently, the Court applied *Grosjean* in Minneapolis Star & Tribune Co. v. Minnesota Commissioner of Revenue and declared unconstitutional a print and ink tax.

MINNEAPOLIS STAR & TRIBUNE CO. v. MINNESOTA COMMISSIONER OF REVENUE

460 U.S. 575 (1983)

Justice O'CONNOR delivered the opinion of the Court.

This case presents the question of a State's power to impose a special tax on the press and, by enacting exemptions, to limit its effect to only a few newspapers.

I

Since 1967, Minnesota has imposed a sales tax on most sales of goods for a price in excess of a nominal sum. The appellant, Minneapolis Star and Tribune Company ("Star Tribune") is the publisher of a morning newspaper and an evening newspaper in Minneapolis. From 1967 until 1971, it enjoyed an exemption from the sales and use tax provided by Minnesota for periodic publications. In 1971, however, while leaving the exemption from the sales tax in place, the legislature amended the scheme to impose a "use tax" on the cost of paper and ink products consumed in the production of a publication. In 1974, the legislature again amended the statute, this time to exempt the first $100,000 worth of ink and paper consumed by a publication in any calendar year, in effect giving each publication an annual tax credit of $4,000. After the enactment of the $100,000 exemption, 11 publishers, producing 14 of the 388 paid circulation newspapers in the State, incurred a tax liability in 1974. Star Tribune was one of the 11, and, of the $893,355 collected, it paid $608,634, or roughly two-thirds of the total revenue raised by the tax. In 1975, 13 publishers, producing 16 out of 374 paid circulation papers, paid a tax. That year, Star Tribune again bore roughly two-thirds of the total receipts from the use tax on ink and paper.

II

Star Tribune argues that we must strike this tax on the authority of Grosjean v. American Press Co., Inc. (1936). Although there are similarities between the two cases, we agree with the State that *Grosjean* is not controlling. We think that the result in *Grosjean* may have been attributable in part to the perception on the part of the Court that the state imposed the tax with an intent to penalize a selected group of newspapers. In the case currently before us, however, there is no legislative history and no indication, apart from the structure of the tax itself, of any impermissible or censorial motive on the part of the legislature. We cannot resolve the case by simple citation to *Grosjean*. Instead, we must analyze the problem anew under the general principles of the First Amendment.

III

Clearly, the First Amendment does not prohibit all regulation of the press. It is beyond dispute that the States and the Federal Government can subject newspapers to generally applicable economic regulations without creating constitutional problems. Minnesota, however, has not chosen to apply its general sales and use tax to newspapers. Instead, it has created a special tax that applies only to certain publications protected by the First Amendment. Although the State argues now that the tax on paper and ink is part of the general scheme of taxation, the use tax provision is facially discriminatory, singling out publications for treatment that is, to our knowledge, unique in Minnesota tax law.

By creating this special use tax, which, to our knowledge, is without parallel in the State's tax scheme, Minnesota has singled out the press for special treatment. We then must determine whether the First Amendment permits such special taxation. A tax that burdens rights protected by the First Amendment cannot stand unless the burden is necessary to achieve an overriding governmental interest.

There is substantial evidence that differential taxation of the press would have troubled the framers of the First Amendment. A power to tax differentially, as opposed to a power to tax generally, gives a government a powerful weapon against the taxpayer selected. When the State singles out the press, though, the political constraints that prevent a legislature from passing crippling taxes of general applicability are weakened, and the threat of burdensome taxes becomes acute. That threat can operate as effectively as a censor to check critical comment by the press, undercutting the basic assumption of our political system that the press will often serve as an important restraint on government.

Further, differential treatment, unless justified by some special characteristic of the press, suggests that the goal of the regulation is not unrelated to suppression of expression, and such a goal is presumptively unconstitutional. Differential taxation of the press, then, places such a burden on the interests protected by the First Amendment that we cannot countenance such treatment unless the State asserts a counterbalancing interest of compelling importance that it cannot achieve without differential taxation.

The main interest asserted by Minnesota in this case is the raising of revenue. Of course that interest is critical to any government. Standing alone, however, it cannot justify the special treatment of the press, for an alternative means of achieving the same interest without raising concerns under the First Amendment is clearly available: the State could raise the revenue by taxing businesses generally, avoiding the censorial threat implicit in a tax that singles out the press.

Addressing the concern with differential treatment, Minnesota invites us to look beyond the form of the tax to its substance. The tax is, according to the State, merely a substitute for the sales tax, which, as a generally applicable tax, would be constitutional as applied to the press. There are two fatal flaws in this reasoning. First, the State has offered no explanation of why it chose to use a substitute for the sales tax rather than the sales tax itself. Further, even assuming that the legislature did have valid reasons for substituting another tax for the sales tax, we are not persuaded that this tax does serve as a substitute. The State asserts that this scheme actually favors the press over other businesses, because the same rate of tax is applied, but, for the press, the rate applies to the cost of components rather than to the sales price. We would be hesitant to fashion a rule that automatically allowed the State to single out the press for a different method of taxation as long as the effective burden was no different from that on other taxpayers or the burden on the press was lighter than that on other businesses. One reason for this reluctance is that the very selection of the press for special treatment threatens the press not only with the current differential treatment, but with the possibility of subsequent differentially more burdensome treatment. Thus, even without actually imposing an extra burden on the press, the government might be able to achieve censorial effects, for "[t]he threat of sanctions may deter [the] exercise of [First Amendment] rights almost as potently as the actual application of sanctions." [C]ourts as institutions are poorly equipped to evaluate with precision the relative burdens of various methods of taxation.

Minnesota's ink and paper tax violates the First Amendment not only because it singles out the press, but also because it targets a small group of newspapers. The effect of the $100,000 exemption enacted in 1974 is that only a handful of publishers pay any tax at all, and even fewer pay any significant amount of tax. [W]hen the exemption selects such a narrowly defined group to bear the full burden of the tax, the tax begins to resemble more a penalty for a few of the largest newspapers than an attempt to favor struggling smaller enterprises. Since Minnesota has offered no satisfactory justification for its tax on the use of ink and paper, the tax violates the First Amendment.

Justice REHNQUIST, dissenting.

Today we learn from the Court that a State runs afoul of the First Amendment proscription of laws "abridging the freedom of speech, or of the press" where the State structures its taxing system to the advantage of newspapers. This seems very much akin to protecting something so overzealously that in the end it is smothered. While the Court purports to rely on the intent of the "framers of the First Amendment," I believe it safe to assume that in 1791 "abridge" meant the same thing it means today: to diminish or curtail. Not until the Court's decision in this case, nearly two centuries after adoption of the First Amendment has it been read to prohibit activities which in no way diminish or curtail the freedoms it protects.

The Court recognizes in several parts of its opinion that the State of Minnesota could avoid constitutional problems by imposing on newspapers the 4% sales tax that it imposes on other retailers. Rather than impose such a tax, however, the Minnesota legislature decided to provide newspapers with an exemption from the sales tax and impose a 4% use tax on ink and paper; thus, while both taxes are part of one "system of sales and use taxes," newspapers are classified differently within that system. The problem the Court finds too difficult to deal with is whether this difference in treatment results in a significant burden on newspapers.

The record reveals that in 1974 the Minneapolis Star & Tribune had an average daily circulation of 489,345 copies. Using the price we were informed of at argument of 25 cents per copy, gross sales revenue for the year would be $38,168,910. The Sunday circulation for 1974 was 640,756; even assuming that it did not sell for more than the daily paper, gross sales revenue for the year would be at least $8,329,828. Thus, total sales revenues in 1974 would be $46,498,738. Had a 4% sales tax been imposed, the Minneapolis Star & Tribune would have been liable for $1,859,950 in 1974. The same "complexities of factual economic proof" can be analyzed for 1975. Daily circulation was 481,789; at 25 cents per copy, gross sales revenue for the year would be $37,579,542. The Sunday circulation for 1975 was 619,154; at 25 cents per copy, gross sales revenue for the year would be $8,049,002. Total sales revenues in 1975 would be $45,628,544; at a 4% rate, the sales tax for 1975 would be $1,825,142. Therefore, had the sales tax been imposed, as the Court agrees would have been permissible, the Minneapolis Star & Tribune's liability for 1974 and 1975 would have been $3,685,092.

The record further indicates that the Minneapolis Star & Tribune paid $608,634 in use taxes in 1974 and $636,113 in 1975—a total liability of $1,244,747. We need no expert testimony from modern day Euclids or Einsteins to determine that the $1,224,747 paid in use taxes is significantly less burdensome than the $3,685,092 that could have been levied by a sales tax. A fortiori, the Minnesota taxing scheme which singles out newspapers for "differential treatment" has benefited, not burdened, the "freedom of speech, [and] of the press."

Where the State devises classifications that infringe on the fundamental guaranties protected by the Constitution the Court has demanded more of the State in justifying its action. But there is no infringement, and thus the Court has never required more, unless the State's classifications significantly burden these specially protected rights.

In *Grosjean* and *Minneapolis Star*, the tax both singled out the press and had a discriminatory effect among newspapers; larger papers would be taxed much more than small ones. In Arkansas Writers' Project, Inc. v. Ragland, 481 U.S. 221 (1987), the Court ruled that the government cannot discriminate among types of publications. A state exempted from its sales tax special interest publications such as religious, professional, trade, and sports journals, but did not exempt general interest magazines. The Court emphasized that any differential taxation of the press — either at the press as opposed to others in society or at particular parts of the press — risked chilling reporting. The Arkansas law also was found unconstitutional on more basic grounds: It was content-based. The application of the tax turned entirely on the content of the publication and thus ran afoul of the fundamental prohibition against content-based discrimination except where necessary to serve a compelling purpose.

However, in Leathers v. Medlock, 499 U.S. 439 (1991), the Court did uphold a tax that treated media differently from each other. *Leathers* involved a state law that exempted newspapers and magazines from a state gross receipts tax, but did not exempt cable television. Although the tax singled out a particular branch of the media, the Court found it constitutional. The Court said that unlike *Grosjean* and *Minneapolis Star*, the tax did not single out the press and unlike the tax in *Ragland* it was not content-based. The Court said that because the tax was not discriminatory on either of these grounds, it was constitutional. Justice O'Connor, who also wrote the opinion for the Court in *Minneapolis Star*, stated for the majority that the "extension of [a state's] generally applicable sales tax to cable television, while exempting the print media, does not violate the First Amendment."

The cases can be reconciled by seeing the earlier decisions only as prohibiting the government from having a tax that is directed solely at the press or that distinguishes among branches of the press. *Leathers* does not involve either of these features and thus the tax was upheld. But if the earlier cases are seen as establishing the broader principle that the government should not be able to discriminate among parts of the press, then *Leathers* cannot be reconciled with the earlier precedents. The concern is that the government could retaliate against a particular branch of the press by a tax directed at it or by denying it an exemption granted to other parts of the press.

b. Application of General Regulatory Laws

The Supreme Court consistently has refused to find that the protection of freedom of the press entitles it to exemptions from general regulatory laws. For example, attempts by the press to receive constitutionally based exemptions to antitrust statutes, labor laws, and liability under state contract law have been expressly rejected.

In Associated Press v. United States, 326 U.S. 1 (1945), the Court expressly rejected the claim that the First Amendment entitled the press to an exemption from federal antitrust laws. An action was brought against an alleged monopoly in the dissemination of news through an association of member newspapers where nonmembers were denied access to the association's news and membership was restricted. Justice Black, writing for the Court, flatly rejected the claim that the First Amendment protected the press from antitrust liability. He said, "Freedom to publish is guaranteed by the Constitution, but freedom to combine to keep others from publishing is not. Freedom of the press from governmental interference under the First Amendment does not sanction repression of that freedom by private interests. The First Amendment offers not the slightest support for the contention that a combination to restrain trade in news and views has any constitutional immunity." Indeed, the Court said that First Amendment values were served by the application of antitrust laws so as to ensure the widest possible dissemination of news.

The Court followed *Associated Press* in Citizens Publishing Co. v. United States, 394 U.S. 131 (1969), which again rejected the claim of a First Amendment exemption to antitrust laws. *Citizens Publishing* involved an antitrust action against two newspapers in Tucson, Arizona, that formed a joint operating agreement that involved price fixing, profit pooling, and market controls. The Court upheld a finding of antitrust violations by the papers and noted that "[n]either news gathering nor news dissemination is being regulated by the present decree." The Court invoked *Associated Press* for the proposition that antitrust laws enhance, not hinder, First Amendment values by encouraging diverse sources of information and news.

Likewise, the Court has rejected claims by the press that the First Amendment entitles it to exemptions from federal labor laws. In Associated Press v. NLRB, 301 U.S. 103 (1937), the Court rejected the argument that freedom of the press provided it an exemption from the National Labor Relations Act, which secures for employees the right to organize and bargain collectively. The Court explained, "The business of the Associated Press is not immune from regulation because it is an agency of the press. The publisher of a newspaper has no special immunity from the application of general laws. He has no special privilege to invade the rights and liberties of others. He must answer for libel. He may be punished for contempt of court. He is subject to anti-trust laws. Like others he must pay equitable and nondiscriminatory taxes. The regulation here in question has no relation whatsoever to the impartial distribution of news."

In Oklahoma Press Publishing Co. v. Walling, 327 U.S. 186 (1946), the Court held that the First Amendment does not exempt the press from the Fair Labor Standards Act, which requires payment of the minimum wage and sets maximum hours limits for employees. The Court said that *Associated Press* established that there was no merit to the claim that it violated the First Amendment to apply labor laws to the press. The Court said, "If Congress can remove obstructions to commerce by requiring publishers to bargain collectively with employees and refrain from interfering with their rights of self-organization, matters closely related to eliminating low wages and long hours, Congress likewise may strike directly at those evils when they adversely affect commerce."

The strongest statement that the press is not exempt from general laws was in Cohen v. Cowles Media Co.

COHEN v. COWLES MEDIA CO.

501 U.S. 663 (1991)

Justice WHITE delivered the opinion of the Court.

The question before us is whether the First Amendment prohibits a plaintiff from recovering damages, under state promissory estoppel law, for a newspaper's breach of a promise of confidentiality given to the plaintiff in exchange for information. We hold that it does not.

During the closing days of the 1982 Minnesota gubernatorial race, Dan Co-hen, an active Republican associated with Wheelock Whitney's Independent-Republican gubernatorial campaign, approached reporters from the St. Paul Pioneer Press Dispatch (Pioneer Press) and the Minneapolis Star and Tribune (Star Tribune) and offered to provide documents relating to a candidate in the upcoming election. Cohen made clear to the reporters that he would provide the information only if he was given a promise of confidentiality. Reporters from both papers promised to keep Cohen's identity anonymous and Cohen turned over copies of two public court records concerning Marlene Johnson, the Democratic-Farmer-Labor candidate for Lieutenant Governor. The first record indicated that Johnson had been charged in 1969 with three counts of unlawful assembly, and the second that she had been convicted in 1970 of petit theft. Both newspapers interviewed Johnson for her explanation and one reporter tracked down the person who had found the records for Cohen. As it turned out, the unlawful assembly charges arose out of Johnson's participa-tion in a protest of an alleged failure to hire minority workers on municipal construction projects, and the charges were eventually dismissed. The petit theft conviction was for leaving a store without paying for $6 worth of sewing materials. The incident apparently occurred at a time during which Johnson was emotionally distraught, and the conviction was later vacated.

After consultation and debate, the editorial staffs of the two newspapers inde-pendently decided to publish Cohen's name as part of their stories concerning Johnson. In their stories, both papers identified Cohen as the source of the court records, indicated his connection to the Whitney campaign, and included denials by Whitney campaign officials of any role in the matter. The same day the stories appeared, Cohen was fired by his employer.

Respondents rely on the proposition that "if a newspaper lawfully obtains truthful information about a matter of public significance then state officials may not constitutionally punish publication of the information, absent a need to further a state interest of the highest order." This case, however, is not con-trolled by this line of cases but, rather, by the equally well-established line of decisions holding that generally applicable laws do not offend the First Amend-ment simply because their enforcement against the press has incidental effects on its ability to gather and report the news. As the cases relied on by respondents recognize, the truthful information sought to be published must have been lawfully acquired. The press may not with impunity break and enter an office or dwelling to gather news. Neither does the First Amendment relieve a newspaper reporter of the obligation shared by all citizens to respond to a grand jury subpoena and answer questions relevant to a criminal investigation, even though the reporter might be required to reveal a confidential source. [E]nforcement of such general laws against the press is not subject to stricter scrutiny than would be applied to enforcement against other persons or organizations.

There can be little doubt that the Minnesota doctrine of promissory estoppel is a law of general applicability. It does not target or single out the press. Rather, insofar as we are advised, the doctrine is generally applicable to the daily trans-actions of all the citizens of Minnesota. The First Amendment does not forbid its application to the press.

Respondents and amici argue that permitting Cohen to maintain a cause of action for promissory estoppel will inhibit truthful reporting because news organizations will have legal incentives not to disclose a confidential source's identity even when that person's identity is itself newsworthy. But if this is the case, it is no more than the incidental, and constitutionally insignificant, consequence of applying to the press a generally applicable law that requires those who make certain kinds of promises to keep them.

Justice SOUTER, with whom Justice MARSHALL, Justice BLACKMUN, and Justice O'CONNOR join, dissenting.

"[T]here is nothing talismanic about neutral laws of general applicability," for such laws may restrict First Amendment rights just as effectively as those directed specifically at speech itself. Because I do not believe the fact of general applicability to be dispositive, I find it necessary to articulate, measure, and compare the competing interests involved in any given case to determine the legitimacy of burdening constitutional interests, and such has been the Court's recent practice in publication cases. Nor can I accept the majority's position that we may dispense with balancing because the burden on publication is in a sense "self-imposed" by the newspaper's voluntary promise of confidentiality.

[F]reedom of the press is ultimately founded on the value of enhancing such discourse for the sake of a citizenry better informed and thus more prudently self-governed. The importance of this public interest is integral to the balance that should be struck in this case. There can be no doubt that the fact of Cohen's identity expanded the universe of information relevant to the choice faced by Minnesota voters in that State's 1982 gubernatorial election, the publication of which was thus of the sort quintessentially subject to strict First Amendment protection. The propriety of his leak to respondents could be taken to reflect on his character, which in turn could be taken to reflect on the character of the candidate who had retained him as an adviser. An election could turn on just such a factor; if it should, I am ready to assume that it would be to the greater public good, at least over the long run.

This is not to say that the breach of such a promise of confidentiality could never give rise to liability. One can conceive of situations in which the injured party is a private individual, whose identity is of less public concern than that of petitioner; liability there might not be constitutionally prohibited. Nor do I mean to imply that the circumstances of acquisition are irrelevant to the balance, although they may go only to what balances against, and not to diminish, the First Amendment value of any particular piece of information.

Because I believe the State's interest in enforcing a newspaper's promise of confidentiality insufficient to outweigh the interest in unfettered publication of the information revealed in this case, I respectfully dissent.

c. Keeping Reporters' Sources and Secrets Confidential

Confidential sources are often crucial to the media's gathering of information and being able to inform the public. Individuals may be willing to disclose important information to reporters only with a promise that their identity will be kept confidential. "Deep Throat" — the confidential source who provided the basis for many of the key stories by *Washington Post* reporters Carl Bernstein and Bob Woodward — was instrumental in helping to expose the criminal acts surrounding the Watergate cover-up and actions of the Campaign to Reelect President Nixon.

Thus, the press has claimed that the First Amendment gives it a right to resist subpoenas that require it to disclose the identity of sources. The Supreme Court, however, rejected this position in Branzburg v. Hayes.

BRANZBURG v. HAYES
408 U.S. 665 (1972)

Opinion of the Court by Mr. Justice WHITE.

The issue in these cases is whether requiring newsmen to appear and testify before state or federal grand juries abridges the freedom of speech and press guaranteed by the First Amendment. We hold that it does not.

I

The writ of certiorari in Branzburg v. Hayes and *Meigs*, brings before us two judgments of the Kentucky Court of Appeals, both involving petitioner Branzburg, a staff reporter for the Courier-Journal, a daily newspaper published in Louisville, Kentucky. On November 15, 1969, the Courier-Journal carried a story under petitioner's byline describing in detail his observations of two young residents of Jefferson County synthesizing hashish from marihuana, an activity which, they asserted, earned them about $5,000 in three weeks. The article included a photograph of a pair of hands working above a laboratory table on which was a substance identified by the caption as hashish. The article stated that petitioner had promised not to reveal the identity of the two hashish makers. Petitioner was shortly subpoenaed by the Jefferson County grand jury; he appeared, but refused to identify the individuals he had seen possessing marihuana or the persons he had seen making hashish from marihuana. A state trial court judge ordered petitioner to answer these questions and rejected his contention that the Kentucky reporters' privilege statute, the First Amendment of the United States Constitution, or the Kentucky Constitution authorized his refusal to answer.

In re Pappas originated when petitioner Pappas, a television newsman-photographer working out of the Providence, Rhode Island, office of a New Bedford, Massachusetts, television station, was called to New Bedford on July 30, 1970, to report on civil disorders there which involved fires and other turmoil. He intended to cover a Black Panther news conference at that group's headquarters in a boarded-up store. Petitioner found the streets around the store barricaded, but he ultimately gained entrance to the area and recorded and photographed a prepared statement read by one of the Black Panther leaders at about 3 P.M. He then asked for and received permission to re-enter the area. Returning at about 9 o'clock, he was allowed to enter and remain inside Panther headquarters. As a condition of entry, Pappas agreed not to disclose anything he saw or heard inside the store except an anticipated police raid, which Pappas, "on his own," was free to photograph and report as he wished. Pappas stayed inside the headquarters for about three hours, but there was no police raid, and petitioner wrote no story and did not otherwise reveal what had occurred in the store while he was there. Two months later, petitioner was summoned before the Bristol County Grand Jury and appeared, answered questions as to his name, address, employment, and what he had seen and heard outside Panther headquarters, but refused to answer any questions about what had taken place inside headquarters while he was there, claiming that the First Amendment afforded him a privilege to protect confidential informants and their information.

United States v. Caldwell arose from subpoenas issued by a federal grand jury in the Northern District of California to respondent Earl Caldwell, a reporter for the New York Times assigned to cover the Black Panther Party and other black militant groups. A subpoena duces tecum was served on respondent on February 2, 1970, ordering him to appear before the grand jury to testify and to bring with him notes and tape recordings of interviews given him for publication by officers and spokesmen of the Black Panther Party concerning the aims, purposes, and activities of that organization.

II

Petitioners Branzburg and Pappas and respondent Caldwell press First Amendment claims that may be simply put: that to gather news it is often necessary to agree either not to identify the source of information published or to publish only part of the facts revealed, or both; that if the reporter is nevertheless forced to reveal these confidences to a grand jury, the source so identified and other confidential sources of other reporters will be measurably deterred from furnishing publishable information, all to the detriment of the free flow of information protected by the First Amendment. Although the newsmen in these cases do not claim an absolute privilege against official interrogation in all circumstances, they assert that the reporter should not be forced either to appear or to testify before a grand jury or at trial until and unless sufficient grounds are shown for believing that the reporter possesses information relevant to a crime the grand jury is investigating, that the information the reporter has is unavailable from other sources, and that the need for the information is sufficiently compelling to override the claimed invasion of First Amendment interests occasioned by the disclosure.

We do not question the significance of free speech, press, or assembly to the country's welfare. Nor is it suggested that news gathering does not qualify for First Amendment protection; without some protection for seeking out the news, freedom of the press could be eviscerated. But these cases involve no intrusions upon speech or assembly, no prior restraint or restriction on what the press may publish, and no express or implied command that the press publish what it prefers to withhold. No exaction or tax for the privilege of publishing, and no penalty, civil or criminal, related to the content of published material is at issue here. The use of confidential sources by the press is not forbidden or restricted; reporters remain free to seek news from any source by means within the law. No attempt is made to require the press to publish its sources of information or indiscriminately to disclose them on request.

The sole issue before us is the obligation of reporters to respond to grand jury subpoenas as other citizens do and to answer questions relevant to an investigation into the commission of crime. Citizens generally are not constitutionally immune from grand jury subpoenas; and neither the First Amendment nor any other constitutional provision protects the average citizen from disclosing to a grand jury information that he has received in confidence. The claim is, however, that reporters are exempt from these obligations because if forced to respond to subpoenas and identify their sources or disclose other confidences, their informants will refuse or be reluctant to furnish newsworthy information in the future. This asserted burden on news gathering is said to make compelled testimony from newsmen constitutionally suspect and to require a privileged position for them.

It is clear that the First Amendment does not invalidate every incidental burdening of the press that may result from the enforcement of civil or criminal statutes of general applicability. Under prior cases, otherwise valid laws serving substantial public interests may be enforced against the press as against others, despite the possible burden that may be imposed. The Court has emphasized that "[t]he publisher of a newspaper has no special immunity from the application of general laws. He has no special privilege to invade the rights and liberties of others." Associated Press v. NLRB (1937).

It has generally been held that the First Amendment does not guarantee the press a constitutional right of special access to information not available to the public generally. Despite the fact that news gathering may be hampered, the press is regularly excluded from grand jury proceedings, our own conferences, the meetings of other official bodies gathered in executive session, and the meetings of private organizations. Newsmen have no constitutional right of access to the scenes of crime or disaster when the general public is excluded, and they may be prohibited from attending or publishing information about trials if such restrictions are necessary to assure a defendant a fair trial before an impartial tribunal.

It is thus not surprising that the great weight of authority is that newsmen are not exempt from the normal duty of appearing before a grand jury and answering questions relevant to a criminal investigation. At common law, courts consistently refused to recognize the existence of any privilege authorizing a newsman to refuse to reveal confidential information to a grand jury.

A number of States have provided newsmen a statutory privilege of varying breadth, but the majority have not done so, and none has been provided by federal statute. Until now the only testimonial privilege for unofficial witnesses that is rooted in the Federal Constitution is the Fifth Amendment privilege against compelled self-incrimination. We are asked to create another by interpreting the First Amendment to grant newsmen a testimonial privilege that other citizens do not enjoy. This we decline to do.

On the records now before us, we perceive no basis for holding that the public interest in law enforcement and in ensuring effective grand jury proceedings is insufficient to override the consequential, but uncertain, burden on news gathering that is said to result from insisting that reporters, like other citizens, respond to relevant questions put to them in the course of a valid grand jury investigation or criminal trial.

This conclusion itself involves no restraint on what newspapers may publish or on the type or quality of information reporters may seek to acquire, nor does it threaten the vast bulk of confidential relationships between reporters and their sources. Grand juries address themselves to the issues of whether crimes have been committed and who committed them. Only where news sources themselves are implicated in crime or possess information relevant to the grand jury's task need they or the reporter be concerned about grand jury subpoenas. Nothing before us indicates that a large number or percentage of all confidential news sources falls into either category and would in any way be deterred by our holding that the Constitution does not, as it never has, exempt the newsman from performing the citizen's normal duty of appearing and furnishing information relevant to the grand jury's task.

Thus, we cannot seriously entertain the notion that the First Amendment protects a newsman's agreement to conceal the criminal conduct of his source, or evidence thereof, on the theory that it is better to write about crime than to do something about it. Insofar as any reporter in these cases undertook not to reveal or testify about the crime he witnessed, his claim of privilege under the First Amendment presents no substantial question. The crimes of news sources are no less reprehensible and threatening to the public interest when witnessed by a reporter than when they are not.

There remain those situations where a source is not engaged in criminal conduct but has information suggesting illegal conduct by others. Newsmen frequently receive information from such sources pursuant to a tacit or express agreement to withhold the source's name and suppress any information that the source wishes not published. Such informants presumably desire anonymity in order to avoid being entangled as a witness in a criminal trial or grand jury investigation. They may fear that disclosure will threaten their job security or personal safety or that it will simply result in dishonor or embarrassment.

The argument that the flow of news will be diminished by compelling reporters to aid the grand jury in a criminal investigation is not irrational, nor are the records before us silent on the matter. But we remain unclear how often and to what extent informers are actually deterred from furnishing information when newsmen are forced to testify before a grand jury.

Moreover, grand juries characteristically conduct secret proceedings, and law enforcement officers are themselves experienced in dealing with informers, and have their own methods for protecting them without interference with the effective administration of justice. There is little before us indicating that informants whose interest in avoiding exposure is that it may threaten job security, personal safety, or peace of mind, would in fact be in a worse position, or would think they would be, if they risked placing their trust in public officials as well as reporters. We doubt if the informer who prefers anonymity but is sincerely interested in furnishing evidence of crime will always or very often be deterred by the prospect of dealing with those public authorities characteristically charged with the duty to protect the public interest as well as his.

Neither are we now convinced that a virtually impenetrable constitutional shield, beyond legislative or judicial control, should be forged to protect a private system of informers operated by the press to report on criminal conduct, a system that would be unaccountable to the public, would pose a threat to the citizen's justifiable expectations of privacy, and would equally protect well-intentioned informants and those who for pay or otherwise betray their trust to their employer or associates.

We are unwilling to embark the judiciary on a long and difficult journey to such an uncertain destination. The administration of a constitutional newsman's privilege would present practical and conceptual difficulties of a high order. Sooner or later, it would be necessary to define those categories of newsmen who qualified for the privilege, a questionable procedure in light of the traditional doctrine that liberty of the press is the right of the lonely pamphleteer who uses carbon paper or a mimeograph just as much as of the large metropolitan publisher who utilizes the latest photocomposition methods. The informative function asserted by representatives of the organized press in the present cases is also performed by lecturers, political pollsters, novelists, academic researchers, and dramatists. Almost any author may quite accurately assert that he is contributing to the flow of information to the public, that he relies on confidential sources of information, and that these sources will be silenced if he is forced to make disclosures before a grand jury.

At the federal level, Congress has freedom to determine whether a statutory newsman's privilege is necessary and desirable and to fashion standards and rules as narrow or broad as deemed necessary to deal with the evil discerned and, equally important, to refashion those rules as experience from time to time may dictate. There is also merit in leaving state legislatures free, within First Amendment limits, to fashion their own standards in light of the conditions and problems with respect to the relations between law enforcement officials and press in their own areas. It goes without saying, of course, that we are powerless to bar state courts from responding in their own way and construing their own constitutions so as to recognize a newsman's privilege, either qualified or absolute.

Justice POWELL, concurring.

I add this brief statement to emphasize what seems to me to be the limited nature of the Court's holding. The Court does not hold that newsmen, subpoenaed to testify before a grand jury, are without constitutional rights with respect to the gathering of news or in safeguarding their sources. [T]he Court states that no harassment of newsmen will be tolerated. If a newsman believes that the grand jury investigation is not being conducted in good faith he is not without remedy. Indeed, if the newsman is called upon to give information bearing only a remote and tenuous relationship to the subject of the investigation, or if he has some other reason to believe that his testimony implicates confidential source relationship without a legitimate need of law enforcement, he will have access to the court on a motion to quash and an appropriate protective order may be entered. The asserted claim to privilege should be judged on its facts by the striking of a proper balance between freedom of the press and the obligation of all citizens to give relevant testimony with respect to criminal conduct. The balance of these vital constitutional and societal interests on a case-by-case basis accords with the tried and traditional way of adjudicating such questions. In short, the courts will be available to newsmen under circumstances where legitimate First Amendment interests require protection.

Justice STEWART, with whom Justice BRENNAN and Justice MARSHALL join, dissenting.

The Court's crabbed view of the First Amendment reflects a disturbing insensitivity to the critical role of an independent press in our society. The question whether a reporter has a constitutional right to a confidential relationship with his source is of first impression here, but the principles that should guide our decision are as basic as any to be found in the Constitution. While Mr. Justice

Powell's enigmatic concurring opinion gives some hope of a more flexible view in the future, the Court in these cases holds that a newsman has no First Amendment right to protect his sources when called before a grand jury. The Court thus invites state and federal authorities to undermine the historic independence of the press by attempting to annex the journalistic profession as an investigative arm of government. Not only will this decision impair performance of the press' constitutionally protected functions, but it will, I am convinced, in the long run, harm rather than help the administration of justice. I respectfully dissent.

The reporter's constitutional right to a confidential relationship with his source stems from the broad societal interest in a full and free flow of information to the public. It is this basic concern that underlies the Constitution's protection of a free press. Enlightened choice by an informed citizenry is the basic ideal upon which an open society is premised, and a free press is thus indispensable to a free society.

A corollary of the right to publish must be the right to gather news. The full flow of information to the public protected by the free-press guarantee would be severely curtailed if no protection whatever were afforded to the process by which news is assembled and disseminated. No less important to the news dissemination process is the gathering of information. News must not be unnecessarily cut off at its source, for without freedom to acquire information the right to publish would be impermissibly compromised.

The right to gather news implies, in turn, a right to a confidential relationship between a reporter and his source. This proposition follows as a matter of simple logic once three factual predicates are recognized: (1) newsmen require informants to gather news; (2) confidentiality—the promise or understanding that names or certain aspects of communications will be kept off the record—is essential to the creation and maintenance of a news-gathering relationship with informants; and (3) an unbridled subpoena power—the absence of a constitutional right protecting, in *any* way, a confidential relationship from compulsory process—will either deter sources from divulging information or deter reporters from gathering and publishing information.

After today's decision, the potential informant can never be sure that his identity or off-the-record communications will not subsequently be revealed through the compelled testimony of a newsman. A public-spirited person inside government, who is not implicated in any crime, will now be fearful of revealing corruption or other governmental wrongdoing, because he will now know he can subsequently be identified by use of compulsory process. The potential source must, therefore, choose between risking exposure by giving information or avoiding the risk by remaining silent.

The impairment of the flow of news cannot, of course, be proved with scientific precision, as the Court seems to demand. Obviously, not every news-gathering relationship requires confidentiality. And it is difficult to pinpoint precisely how many relationship[s] do require a promise or understanding of nondisclosure. But we have never before demanded that First Amendment rights rest on elaborate empirical studies demonstrating beyond any conceivable doubt that deterrent effects exist; we have never before required proof of the exact number of people potentially affected by governmental action, who would actually be dissuaded from engaging in First Amendment activity.

To require any greater burden of proof is to shirk our duty to protect values securely embedded in the Constitution. We cannot await an unequivocal — and therefore unattainable — imprimatur from empirical studies. We can and must accept the evidence developed in the record, and elsewhere, that overwhelmingly supports the premise that deterrence will occur with regularity in important types of news-gathering relationships.

Thus, we cannot escape the conclusion that when neither the reporter nor his source can rely on the shield of confidentiality against unrestrained use of the grand jury's subpoena power, valuable information will not be published and the public dialogue will inevitably be impoverished.

The Supreme Court has followed *Branzburg* in other cases in refusing to find First Amendment exemption for the press in court proceedings and law enforcement actions. In Zurcher v. Stanford Daily, 436 U.S. 547 (1978), the Court upheld the ability of the police to search press newsrooms to gather information to aid criminal investigations. A student newspaper published stories about a violent confrontation between students and the police at a demonstration. The police then obtained a warrant to search the newspaper's offices for negatives, films, and pictures that would help to identify the demonstrators. The search was conducted, though it did not yield any information that had not already been punished.

The newspaper then sued the police for violating the First Amendment. The Court held that the First Amendment did not protect the press from valid searches pursuant to valid warrants. Justice White again wrote the opinion for the Court and once more rejected the claim of any special protection for the press under the First Amendment. He said, "Properly administered the preconditions for a warrant — probable cause, specificity with respect to the place to be searched and the things to be seized, and overall reasonableness — should afford sufficient protection against the harms that are assertedly threatened by warrants for searching newspaper offices. . . . [Nor] are we convinced, any more than we were in *Branzburg* that confidential sources will disappear."

Almost immediately after *Zurcher*, Congress enacted the Privacy Protection Act of 1980 to protect the press from searches of newsrooms.[194] The law prohibits law enforcement from searches of those reasonably believed to be engaged in disseminating information to the public unless there is probable cause to believe that the person committed a crime or that giving notice by subpoena likely would result in the loss of evidence.

d.   Laws Requiring That the Media Make Access Available

The issues described above focus on the application of general laws and law enforcement procedures to the press. A distinct issue arises concerning laws that attempt to regulate the press and require that it allow others to use it. Can the government require that the media make newspaper space or broadcast time

---

194. 42 U.S.C. §2000a.

available to respond to personal attacks? Arguably, such access laws enhance First Amendment values; they expand the voices that the public can hear. But the laws also infringe the First Amendment value of press autonomy; the ability of the media to control what it publishes or broadcasts is compromised when the government mandates access.

Interestingly, the Court has found that the First Amendment is not violated by such requirements as applied to the broadcast media, but has invalidated these laws when applied to the print media. In Red Lion Broadcasting Co. v. FCC, the Court unanimously upheld the constitutionality of the fairness doctrine that required that broadcast stations present balanced discussion on public issues.

RED LION BROADCASTING CO. v. FEDERAL COMMUNICATIONS COMMISSION

395 U.S. 367 (1969)

Justice WHITE delivered the opinion of the Court.

The Federal Communications Commission has for many years imposed on radio and television broadcasters the requirement that discussion of public issues be presented on broadcast stations, and that each side of those issues must be given fair coverage. This is known as the fairness doctrine, which originated very early in the history of broadcasting and has maintained its present outlines for some time. It is an obligation whose content has been defined in a long series of FCC rulings in particular cases, and which is distinct from the statutory requirement of §315 of the Communications Act that equal time be allotted all qualified candidates for public office. Two aspects of the fairness doctrine, relating to personal attacks in the context of controversial public issues and to political editorializing, were codified more precisely in the form of FCC regulations in 1967. The two cases before us now, which were decided separately below, challenge the constitutional and statutory bases of the doctrine and component rules. Red Lion involves the application of the fairness doctrine to a particular broadcast, and RTNDA arises as an action to review the FCC's 1967 promulgation of the personal attack and political editorializing regulations, which were laid down after the *Red Lion* litigation had begun.

I

The Red Lion Broadcasting Company is licensed to operate a Pennsylvania radio station, WGCB. On November 27, 1964, WGCB carried a 15-minute broadcast by the Reverend Billy James Hargis as part of a "Christian Crusade" series. A book by Fred J. Cook entitled "Goldwater — Extremist on the Right" was discussed by Hargis, who said that Cook had been fired by a newspaper for making false charges against city officials; that Cook had then worked for a Communist-affiliated publication; that he had defended Alger Hiss and attacked J. Edgar Hoover and the Central Intelligence Agency; and that he had now written a "book to smear and destroy Barry Goldwater." When Cook heard of the broadcast he concluded that he had been personally attacked and demanded free reply time, which the station refused. After an exchange of letters among

Cook, Red Lion, and the FCC, the FCC declared that the Hargis broadcast constituted a personal attack on Cook; that Red Lion had failed to meet its obligation under the fairness doctrine to send a tape, transcript, or summary of the broadcast to Cook and offer him reply time; and that the station must provide reply time whether or not Cook would pay for it.

Not long after the *Red Lion* litigation was begun, the FCC issued a Notice of Proposed Rule Making, with an eye to making the personal attack aspect of the fairness doctrine more precise and more readily enforceable, and to specifying its rules relating to political editorials.

Believing that the specific application of the fairness doctrine in *Red Lion*, and the promulgation of the regulations in RTNDA, are both authorized by Congress and enhance rather than abridge the freedoms of speech and press protected by the First Amendment, we hold them valid and constitutional.

II

The history of the emergence of the fairness doctrine and of the related legislation shows that the Commission's action in the *Red Lion* case did not exceed its authority, and that in adopting the new regulations the Commission was implementing congressional policy rather than embarking on a frolic of its own.

Before 1927, the allocation of frequencies was left entirely to the private sector, and the result was chaos. It quickly became apparent that broadcast frequencies constituted a scarce resource whose use could be regulated and rationalized only by the Government. Without government control, the medium would be of little use because of the cacophony of competing voices, none of which could be clearly and predictably heard. Consequently, the Federal Radio Commission was established to allocate frequencies among competing applicants in a manner responsive to the public "convenience, interest, or necessity."

Very shortly thereafter the Commission expressed its view that the "public interest requires ample play for the free and fair competition of opposing views, and the commission believes that the principle applies to all discussions of issues of importance to the public." This doctrine was applied through denial of license renewals or construction permits.

There is a twofold duty laid down by the FCC's decisions. The broadcaster must give adequate coverage to public issues, and coverage must be fair in that it accurately reflects the opposing views. When a personal attack has been made on a figure involved in a public issue both the doctrine of cases and also the 1967 regulations at issue in RTNDA require that the individual attacked himself be offered an opportunity to respond.

III

The broadcasters challenge the fairness doctrine and its specific manifestations in the personal attack and political editorial rules on conventional First Amendment grounds, alleging that the rules abridge their freedom of speech and press. Their contention is that the First Amendment protects their desire to use their allotted frequencies continuously to broadcast whatever they choose, and to exclude whomever they choose from ever using that frequency. No man may be prevented from saying or publishing what he thinks, or from refusing in his speech or other utterances to give equal weight to the views of his opponents. This right, they say, applies equally to broadcasters.

Although broadcasting is clearly a medium affected by a First Amendment interest, differences in the characteristics of new media justify differences in the First Amendment standards applied to them. [B]ecause the frequencies reserved for public broadcasting were limited in number, it was essential for the Government to tell some applicants that they could not broadcast at all because there was room for only a few. Where there are substantially more individuals who want to broadcast than there are frequencies to allocate, it is idle to posit an unbridgeable First Amendment right to broadcast comparable to the right of every individual to speak, write, or publish. If 100 persons want broadcast licenses but there are only 10 frequencies to allocate, all of them may have the same "right" to a license; but if there is to be any effective communication by radio, only a few can be licensed and the rest must be barred from the airwaves. No one has a First Amendment right to a license or to monopolize a radio frequency; to deny a station license because "the public interest" requires it "is not a denial of free speech."

By the same token, as far as the First Amendment is concerned those who are licensed stand no better than those to whom licenses are refused. A license permits broadcasting, but the licensee has no constitutional right to be the one who holds the license or to monopolize a radio frequency to the exclusion of his fellow citizens. There is nothing in the First Amendment which prevents the Government from requiring a licensee to share his frequency with others and to conduct himself as a proxy or fiduciary with obligations to present those views and voices which are representative of his community and which would otherwise, by necessity, be barred from the airwaves.

This is not to say that the First Amendment is irrelevant to public broadcasting. On the contrary, it has a major role to play as the Congress itself recognized, which forbids FCC interference with "the right of free speech by means of radio communication." Because of the scarcity of radio frequencies, the Government is permitted to put restraints on licensees in favor of others whose views should be expressed on this unique medium. But the people as a whole retain their interest in free speech by radio and their collective right to have the medium function consistently with the ends and purposes of the First Amendment. It is the right of the viewers and listeners, not the right of the broadcasters, which is paramount. It is the purpose of the First Amendment to preserve an uninhibited marketplace of ideas in which truth will ultimately prevail, rather than to countenance monopolization of that market, whether it be by the Government itself or a private licensee. It is the right of the public to receive suitable access to social, political, esthetic, moral, and other ideas and experiences which is crucial here.

Rather than confer frequency monopolies on a relatively small number of licensees, in a Nation of 200,000,000, the Government could surely have decreed that each frequency should be shared among all or some of those who wish to use it, each being assigned a portion of the broadcast day or the broadcast week. The ruling and regulations at issue here do not go quite so far. They assert that under specified circumstances, a licensee must offer to make available a reasonable amount of broadcast time to those who have a view different from that which has already been expressed on his station. The expression of a political endorsement, or of a personal attack while dealing with a controversial public issue, simply triggers this time sharing. As we have said, the First Amendment confers no right on licensees to prevent others from broadcasting on "their" frequencies and no right to an unconditional monopoly of a scarce resource which the Government has denied others the right to use.

Nor can we say that it is inconsistent with the First Amendment goal of producing an informed public capable of conducting its own affairs to require a broadcaster to permit answers to personal attacks occurring in the course of discussing controversial issues, or to require that the political opponents of those endorsed by the station be given a chance to communicate with the public. Otherwise, station owners and a few networks would have unfettered power to make time available only to the highest bidders, to communicate only their own views on public issues, people and candidates, and to permit on the air only those with whom they agreed. There is no sanctuary in the First Amendment for unlimited private censorship operating in a medium not open to all. "Freedom of the press from governmental interference under the First Amendment does not sanction repression of that freedom by private interests."

It is strenuously argued, however, that if political editorials or personal attacks will trigger an obligation in broadcasters to afford the opportunity for expression to speakers who need not pay for time and whose views are unpalatable to the licensees, then broadcasters will be irresistibly forced to self-censorship and their coverage of controversial public issues will be eliminated or at least rendered wholly ineffective. Such a result would indeed be a serious matter, for should licensees actually eliminate their coverage of controversial issues, the purposes of the doctrine would be stifled.

At this point, however, as the Federal Communications Commission has indicated, that possibility is at best speculative. The communications industry, and in particular the networks, have taken pains to present controversial issues in the past, and even now they do not assert that they intend to abandon their efforts in this regard. It would be better if the FCC's encouragement were never necessary to induce the broadcasters to meet their responsibility. And if experience with the administration of those doctrines indicates that they have the net effect of reducing rather than enhancing the volume and quality of coverage, there will be time enough to reconsider the constitutional implications. The fairness doctrine in the past has had no such overall effect.

That this will occur now seems unlikely, however, since if present licensees should suddenly prove timorous, the Commission is not powerless to insist that they give adequate and fair attention to public issues. It does not violate the First Amendment to treat licensees given the privilege of using scarce radio frequencies as proxies for the entire community, obligated to give suitable time and attention to matters of great public concern.

In view of the scarcity of broadcast frequencies, the Government's role in allocating those frequencies, and the legitimate claims of those unable without governmental assistance to gain access to those frequencies for expression of their views, we hold the regulations and ruling at issue here are both authorized by statute and constitutional.

However, just five years later, in Miami Herald v. Tornillo, the Court unanimously declared unconstitutional a right-to-reply law as applied to newspapers.

MIAMI HERALD v. TORNILLO
418 U.S. 241 (1974)

Chief Justice BURGER delivered the opinion of the Court.

The issue in this case is whether a state statute granting a political candidate a right to equal space to reply to criticism and attacks on his record by a newspaper violates the guarantees of a free press.

I

In the fall of 1972, appellee, Executive Director of the Classroom Teachers Association, apparently a teachers' collective-bargaining agent, was a candidate for the Florida House of Representatives. On September 20, 1972, and again on September 29, 1972, appellant printed editorials critical of appellee's candidacy. In response to these editorials appellee demanded that appellant print verbatim his replies, defending the role of the Classroom Teachers Association and the organization's accomplishments for the citizens of Dade County. Appellant declined to print the appellee's replies and appellee brought suit in Circuit Court, Dade County, seeking declaratory and injunctive relief and actual and punitive damages in excess of $5,000. The action was premised on Florida Statute §104.38, a "right of reply" statute which provides that if a candidate for nomination or election is assailed regarding his personal character or official record by any newspaper, the candidate has the right to demand that the newspaper print, free of cost to the candidate, any reply the candidate may make to the newspaper's charges. The reply must appear in as conspicuous a place and in the same kind of type as the charges which prompted the reply, provided it does not take up more space than the charges. Failure to comply with the statute constitutes a first-degree misdemeanor.

II

The challenged statute creates a right to reply to press criticism of a candidate for nomination or election. The statute was enacted in 1913, and this is only the second recorded case decided under its provisions.

The appellee and supporting advocates of an enforceable right of access to the press vigorously argue that government has an obligation to ensure that a wide variety of views reach the public. Access advocates submit that although newspapers of the present are superficially similar to those of 1791 the press of today is in reality very different from that known in the early years of our national existence. The elimination of competing newspapers in most of our large cities, and the concentration of control of media that results from the only newspaper's being owned by the same interests which own a television station and a radio station, are important components of this trend toward concentration of control of outlets to inform the public. The result of these vast changes has been to place in a few hands the power to inform the American people and shape public opinion. The monopoly of the means of communication allows for little or no critical analysis of the media except in professional journals of very limited readership.

The obvious solution, which was available to dissidents at an earlier time when entry into publishing was relatively inexpensive, today would be to have additional newspapers. But the same economic factors which have caused the disappearance of vast numbers of metropolitan newspapers, have made entry into the marketplace of ideas served by the print media almost impossible. However much validity may be found in these arguments, at each point the implementation of a remedy such as an enforceable right of access necessarily calls for some mechanism, either governmental or consensual. If it is governmental coercion, this at once brings about a confrontation with the express provisions of the First Amendment and the judicial gloss on that Amendment developed over the years.

[T]he Court has expressed sensitivity as to whether a restriction or requirement constituted the compulsion exerted by government on a newspaper to print that which it would not otherwise print. The clear implication has been that any such compulsion to publish that which "'reason' tells them should not be published" is unconstitutional. A responsible press is an undoubtedly desirable goal, but press responsibility is not mandated by the Constitution and like many other virtues it cannot be legislated.

Appellee's argument that the Florida statute does not amount to a restriction of appellant's right to speak because "the statute in question here has not prevented the Miami Herald from saying anything it wished" begs the core question. Compelling editors or publishers to publish that which "'reason' tells them should not be published" is what is at issue in this case. The Florida statute operates as a command in the same sense as a statue or regulation forbidding appellant to publish specified matter. Governmental restraint on publishing need not fall into familiar or traditional patterns to be subject to constitutional limitations on governmental powers.

The Florida statute exacts a penalty on the basis of the content of a newspaper. The first phase of the penalty resulting from the compelled printing of a reply is exacted in terms of the cost in printing and composing time and materials and in taking up space that could be devoted to other material the newspaper may have preferred to print. It is correct, as appellee contends, that a newspaper is not subject to the finite technological limitations of time that confront a broadcaster but it is not correct to say that, as an economic reality, a newspaper can proceed to infinite expansion of its column space to accommodate the replies that a government agency determines or a statute commands the readers should have available.

Faced with the penalties that would accrue to any newspaper that published news or commentary arguably within the reach of the right-of-access statute, editors might well conclude that the safe course is to avoid controversy. Therefore, under the operation of the Florida statute, political and electoral coverage would be blunted or reduced. Government-enforced right of access inescapably "dampens the vigor and limits the variety of public debate."

Even if a newspaper would face no additional costs to comply with a compulsory access law and would not be forced to forgo publication of news or opinion by the inclusion of a reply, the Florida statute fails to clear the barriers of the First Amendment because of its intrusion into the function of editors. A newspaper is more than a passive receptacle or conduit for news, comment, and advertising. The choice of material to go into a newspaper, and the decisions made as to limitations on the size and content of the paper, and treatment of public issues and public officials — whether fair or unfair — constitute the exercise of editorial control and judgment. It has yet to be demonstrated how governmental regulation of this crucial process can be exercised consistent with First Amendment guarantees of a free press as they have evolved to this time.

There is an obvious tension between *Red Lion* and *Tornillo*. Right-to-reply laws are allowed as to the broadcast media, but not the print media. In *Tornillo*, the Court emphasized the danger that such laws will chill coverage; yet in *Red Lion* the Court rejected exactly this argument as unsupported conjecture. The distinction between *Red Lion* and *Tornillo* seems to be based on the inherent scarcity of the broadcast media.[195] Broadcast frequencies are inherently limited. But economics mean that the number of newspapers is also likely to be scarce, and it is unclear why technological scarcity deserves more weight in First Amendment analysis than economically induced scarcity. In every city, there are far more television and radio stations than newspapers. Indeed, the development of cable television and direct broadcast satellites undermines the claim that broadcast space is scarcer than print space, even if that was ever true. In fact, in 1987, the Federal Communications Commission repealed the fairness doctrine, although there have been repeated attempts to have it reinstituted by statute.

If the distinction between the print and broadcast media is rejected,[196] the issue then becomes whether it would be better to apply the *Red Lion* or the *Tornillo* approach to both media. Allowing right-to-reply laws has the benefit of enhancing the viewpoints that are heard.[197] But such laws also intrude on a crucial First Amendment value: press autonomy to decide what to publish.[198]

3. Freedom of the Press as a Sword: A First Amendment Right of Access to Government Places and Papers?

The previous section considered the extent to which the First Amendment provides the press with a shield that protects it from government regulation.

---

195. The Court had relied on the scarcity of the broadcast media as the justification for licensing stations and regulating them. *See* National Broadcasting Co. v. United States, 319 U.S. 190 (1943); *see also* FCC v. National Citizens Committee for Broadcasting, 436 U.S. 775 (1978) (upholding federal regulations that prevented common ownership of a broadcast station and a daily newspaper in the same area).

196. Professor Lee Bollinger has defended the distinction not on grounds of scarcity, but on grounds of the desirability of having one medium largely unregulated while the other is subjected to more government regulation. *See* Lee Bollinger, *Freedom of the Press and Public Access: Toward a Theory of Partial Regulation of the Mass Media*, 75 Mich. L. Rev. 1, 26-36 (1976).

197. For an excellent development of this argument, *see* Jerome A. Barron, *Access to the Press — A New First Amendment Right*, 80 Harv. L. Rev. 1641 (1967).

198. The Court has rejected the claim that there is a First Amendment right of access to use the broadcast media apart from statutes creating such a right. In Columbia Broadcasting System v. Democratic National Committee, 412 U.S. 94 (1973), the Court said that there was no obligation of the broadcast media to accept editorial advertisements apart from that created by the fairness doctrine.

A distinct issue is whether the First Amendment provides the press a "sword" that it can use to gain access to government proceedings and papers. Actually, there are two interrelated subquestions here: First, does the First Amendment provide anyone such a right of access, and second, if so, does the press have a preferred right of access?

Thus far, the Supreme Court has not answered either question in general terms, but rather, has dealt with the issues in two specific contexts. The Court has held that the public has a right of access to court proceedings, but has not recognized a preferred right of access for the press. In contrast, the Court has ruled that the public does not have a right of access to prison inmates and facilities, and the Court expressly has rejected any special right of access for the press.

On the one hand, without a right of access to government papers and places, the people will be denied information that is crucial in monitoring government and holding it accountable. The press obviously plays a crucial role in this regard. While it is not realistic to open a prison to all observers, the press can be the eyes and ears of the public. On the other hand, creating a right of access to government places and papers may be better accomplished through statutes, such as freedom of information acts and open meeting laws, which can be drawn with specificity and can balance competing interests. Additionally, any special rights for the press will raise the issues, described earlier, of defining who is entitled to the privileges.

a. Access to Judicial Proceedings

The Court has recognized a broad First Amendment right for people to attend judicial proceedings. Initially, the Court rejected such a right, at least for pretrial proceedings. In Gannett v. DePasquale, 443 U.S. 368 (1979), the Court held that the press could be excluded from a pretrial proceeding that considered the suppression of a confession. The prosecution and defense both consented to closing the courtroom for the hearing, and the trial judge had found a "reasonable probability of prejudice" to the defendant if the confession was deemed inadmissible but reported on in the press. The Court also emphasized that no one, including the press, had initially objected to the closure and that a transcript was made available once the proceedings were completed.

Yet it is questionable whether *Gannett* remains good law because the Court subsequently has consistently recognized a First Amendment right of access to court proceedings. Richmond Newspapers v. Virginia is the key case in the area.

RICHMOND NEWSPAPERS v. VIRGINIA
448 U.S. 555 (1980)

Chief Justice BURGER announced the judgment of the Court and delivered an opinion, in which Justice WHITE and Justice STEVENS joined.

The narrow question presented in this case is whether the right of the public and press to attend criminal trials is guaranteed under the United States Constitution.

I

In March 1976, one Stevenson was indicted for the murder of a hotel manager who had been found stabbed to death on December 2, 1975. Tried promptly in July 1976, Stevenson was convicted of second-degree murder in the Circuit Court of Hanover County, Va. The Virginia Supreme Court reversed the conviction in October 1977, holding that a bloodstained shirt purportedly belonging to Stevenson had been improperly admitted into evidence. Stevenson was retried in the same court. This second trial ended in a mistrial on May 30, 1978, when a juror asked to be excused after trial had begun and no alternate was available. A third trial, which began in the same court on June 6, 1978, also ended in a mistrial. It appears that the mistrial may have been declared because a prospective juror had read about Stevenson's previous trials in a newspaper and had told other prospective jurors about the case before the retrial began.

Stevenson was tried in the same court for a fourth time beginning on September 11, 1978. Present in the courtroom when the case was called were appellants Wheeler and McCarthy, reporters for appellant Richmond Newspapers, Inc. Before the trial began, counsel for the defendant moved that it be closed to the public. The trial judge, who had presided over two of the three previous trials, asked if the prosecution had any objection to clearing the courtroom. The prosecutor stated he had no objection and would leave it to the discretion of the court.

II

We begin consideration of this case by noting that the precise issue presented here has not previously been before this Court for decision. In Gannett Co. v. DePasquale, the Court was not required to decide whether a right of access to trials, as distinguished from hearings on pretrial motions, was constitutionally guaranteed. The Court held that the Sixth Amendment's guarantee to the accused of a public trial gave neither the public nor the press an enforceable right of access to a pretrial suppression hearing.

In prior cases the Court has treated questions involving conflicts between publicity and a defendant's right to a fair trial; as we observed in Nebraska Press Assn. v. Stuart, "[t]he problems presented by this [conflict] are almost as old as the Republic." But here for the first time the Court is asked to decide whether a criminal trial itself may be closed to the public upon the unopposed request of a defendant, without any demonstration that closure is required to protect the defendant's superior right to a fair trial, or that some other overriding consideration requires closure.

The origins of the proceeding which has become the modern criminal trial in Anglo-American justice can be traced back beyond reliable historical records. We need not here review all details of its development, but a summary of that history is instructive. What is significant for present purposes is that throughout its evolution, the trial has been open to all who care to observe. From these early times, although great changes in courts and procedures took place, one thing remained constant: the public character of the trial at which guilt or innocence was decided. We have found nothing to suggest that the presumptive openness of the trial, which English courts were later to call "one of the essential qualities of a court of justice," was not also an attribute of the judicial systems of colonial America.

[T]he historical evidence demonstrates conclusively that at the time when our organic laws were adopted, criminal trials both here and in England had long been presumptively open. This is no quirk of history; rather, it has long been recognized as an indispensable attribute of an Anglo-American trial. Both Hale in the 17th century and Blackstone in the 18th saw the importance of openness to the proper functioning of a trial; it gave assurance that the proceedings were conducted fairly to all concerned, and it discouraged perjury, the misconduct of participants, and decisions based on secret bias or partiality.

The early history of open trials in part reflects the widespread acknowledgment, long before there were behavioral scientists, that public trials had significant community therapeutic value. Even without such experts to frame the concept in words, people sensed from experience and observation that, especially in the administration of criminal justice, the means used to achieve justice must have the support derived from public acceptance of both the process and its results.

When a shocking crime occurs, a community reaction of outrage and public protest often follows. Thereafter the open processes of justice serve an important prophylactic purpose, providing an outlet for community concern, hostility, and emotion. Without an awareness that society's responses to criminal conduct are underway, natural human reactions of outrage and protest are frustrated and may manifest themselves in some form of vengeful "self-help," as indeed they did regularly in the activities of vigilante "committees" on our frontiers.

Civilized societies withdraw both from the victim and the vigilante the enforcement of criminal laws, but they cannot erase from people's consciousness the fundamental, natural yearning to see justice done — or even the urge for retribution. The crucial prophylactic aspects of the administration of justice cannot function in the dark; no community catharsis can occur if justice is "done in a corner [or] in any covert manner." A result considered untoward may undermine public confidence, and where the trial has been concealed from public view an unexpected outcome can cause a reaction that the system at best has failed and at worst has been corrupted. To work effectively, it is important that society's criminal process "satisfy the appearance of justice," and the appearance of justice can best be provided by allowing people to observe it.

Looking back, we see that when the ancient "town meeting" form of trial became too cumbersome, 12 members of the community were delegated to act as its surrogates, but the community did not surrender its right to observe the conduct of trials. The people retained a "right of visitation" which enabled them to satisfy themselves that justice was in fact being done.

People in an open society do not demand infallibility from their institutions, but it is difficult for them to accept what they are prohibited from observing. When a criminal trial is conducted in the open, there is at least an opportunity both for understanding the system in general and its workings in a particular case.

From this unbroken, uncontradicted history, supported by reasons as valid today as in centuries past, we are bound to conclude that a presumption of openness inheres in the very nature of a criminal trial under our system of justice. This conclusion is hardly novel; without a direct holding on the issue, the Court has voiced its recognition of it in a variety of contexts over the years.

III

The Bill of Rights was enacted against the backdrop of the long history of trials being presumptively open. Public access to trials was then regarded as an important aspect of the process itself; the conduct of trials "before as many of the people as chuse to attend" was regarded as one of "the inestimable advantages of a free English constitution of government." In guaranteeing freedoms such as those of speech and press, the First Amendment can be read as protecting the right of everyone to attend trials so as to give meaning to those explicit guarantees. "[T]he First Amendment goes beyond protection of the press and the self-expression of individuals to prohibit government from limiting the stock of information from which members of the public may draw." Free speech carries with it some freedom to listen. "In a variety of contexts this Court has referred to a First Amendment right to 'receive information and ideas.'" What this means in the context of trials is that the First Amendment guarantees of speech and press, standing alone, prohibit government from summarily closing courtroom doors which had long been open to the public at the time that Amendment was adopted. "For the First Amendment does not speak equivocally. . . . It must be taken as a command of the broadest scope that explicit language, read in the context of a liberty-loving society, will allow."

It is not crucial whether we describe this right to attend criminal trials to hear, see, and communicate observations concerning them as a "right of access," or a "right to gather information," for we have recognized that "without some protection for seeking out the news, freedom of the press could be eviscerated." The explicit, guaranteed rights to speak and to publish concerning what takes place at a trial would lose much meaning if access to observe the trial could, as it was here, be foreclosed arbitrarily.

The right of access to places traditionally open to the public, as criminal trials have long been, may be seen as assured by the amalgam of the First Amendment guarantees of speech and press; and their affinity to the right of assembly is not without relevance. From the outset, the right of assembly was regarded not only as an independent right but also as a catalyst to augment the free exercise of the other First Amendment rights with which it was deliberately linked by the draftsmen.

The State argues that the Constitution nowhere spells out a guarantee for the right of the public to attend trials, and that accordingly no such right is protected. But arguments such as the State makes have not precluded recognition of important rights not enumerated. Notwithstanding the appropriate caution against reading into the Constitution rights not explicitly defined, the Court has acknowledged that certain unarticulated rights are implicit in enumerated guarantees. For example, the rights of association and of privacy, the right to be presumed innocent, and the right to be judged by a standard of proof beyond a reasonable doubt in a criminal trial, as well as the right to travel, appear nowhere in the Constitution or Bill of Rights. Yet these important but unarticulated rights have nonetheless been found to share constitutional protection in common with explicit guarantees.

We hold that the right to attend criminal trials is implicit in the guarantees of the First Amendment; without the freedom to attend such trials, which people have exercised for centuries, important aspects of freedom of speech and "of the press could be eviscerated."[199] Absent an overriding interest articulated in find-ings, the trial of a criminal case must be open to the public.

Justice BRENNAN, with whom Justice MARSHALL joins, concurring in the judgment.

Gannett Co. v. DePasquale (1979) held that the Sixth Amendment right to a public trial was personal to the accused, conferring no right of access to pretrial proceedings that is separately enforceable by the public or the press. The instant case raises the question whether the First Amendment, of its own force and as applied to the States through the Fourteenth Amendment, secures the public an independent right of access to trial proceedings. Because I believe that the First Amendment — of itself and as applied to the States through the Fourteenth Amendment — secures such a public right of access, I agree with those of my Brethren who hold that, without more, agreement of the trial judge and the parties cannot constitutionally close a trial to the public.

First, the case for a right of access has special force when drawn from an enduring and vital tradition of public entree to particular proceedings or infor-mation. Such a tradition commands respect in part because the Constitution carries the gloss of history. More importantly, a tradition of accessibility implies the favorable judgment of experience. Second, the value of access must be measured in specifics. Analysis is not advanced by rhetorical statements that all information bears upon public issues; what is crucial in individual cases is whether access to a particular government process is important in terms of that very process.

Tradition, contemporaneous state practice, and this Court's own decisions manifest a common understanding that "[a] trial is a public event. What tran-spires in the court room is public property." Craig v. Harney (1947). As a matter of law and virtually immemorial custom, public trials have been the essentially unwavering rule in ancestral England and in our own Nation.

Publicity serves to advance several of the particular purposes of the trial (and, indeed, the judicial) process. Open trials play a fundamental role in furthering the efforts of our judicial system to assure the criminal defendant a fair and accurate adjudication of guilt or innocence. But, as a feature of our governing system of justice, the trial process serves other, broadly political, interests, and public access advances these objectives as well. To that extent, trial access pos-sesses specific structural significance.

The trial is a means of meeting "the notion, deeply rooted in the common law, that 'justice must satisfy the appearance of justice.'" Secrecy is profoundly inim-ical to this demonstrative purpose of the trial process. Open trials assure the public that procedural rights are respected, and that justice is afforded equally. Closed trials breed suspicion of prejudice and arbitrariness, which in turn spawns disrespect for law. Public access is essential, therefore, if trial adjudica-tion is to achieve the objective of maintaining public confidence in the admin-istration of justice.

But the trial is more than a demonstrably just method of adjudicating disputes and protecting rights. It plays a pivotal role in the entire judicial process, and, by

199. Whether the public has a right to attend trials of civil cases is a question not raised by this case, but we note that historically both civil and criminal trials have been presumptively open. [Footnote by the Court.]

extension, in our form of government. Under our system, judges are not mere umpires, but, in their own sphere, lawmakers — a coordinate branch of government. It follows that the conduct of the trial is pre-eminently a matter of public interest.

As previously noted, resolution of First Amendment public access claims in individual cases must be strongly influenced by the weight of historical practice and by an assessment of the specific structural value of public access in the circumstances. With regard to the case at hand, our ingrained tradition of public trials and the importance of public access to the broader purposes of the trial process, tip the balance strongly toward the rule that trials be open. What countervailing interests might be sufficiently compelling to reverse this presumption of openness need not concern us now, for the statute at stake here authorizes trial closures at the unfettered discretion of the judge and parties.

Justice REHNQUIST, dissenting.

In the Gilbert and Sullivan operetta "Iolanthe," the Lord Chancellor recites: "The Law is the true embodiment of everything that's excellent, It has no kind of fault or flaw, And I, my Lords, embody the Law."

It is difficult not to derive more than a little of this flavor from the various opinions supporting the judgment in this case. I do not believe that either the First or Sixth Amendment, as made applicable to the States by the Fourteenth, requires that a State's reasons for denying public access to a trial, where both the prosecuting attorney and the defendant have consented to an order of closure approved by the judge, are subject to any additional constitutional review at our hands.

We have at present 50 state judicial systems and one federal judicial system in the United States, and our authority to reverse a decision by the highest court of the State is limited to only those occasions when the state decision violates some provision of the United States Constitution. And that authority should be exercised with a full sense that the judges whose decisions we review are making the same effort as we to uphold the Constitution.

The issue here is not whether the "right" to freedom of the press conferred by the First Amendment to the Constitution overrides the defendant's "right" to a fair trial conferred by other Amendments to the Constitution; it is instead whether any provision in the Constitution may fairly be read to prohibit what the trial judge in the Virginia state-court system did in this case. Being unable to find any such prohibition in the First, Sixth, Ninth, or any other Amendment to the United States Constitution, or in the Constitution itself, I dissent.

In several subsequent cases, the Court applied *Richmond Newspapers* and declared unconstitutional the closure of judicial proceedings. In Globe Newspaper Co. v. Superior Court, 457 U.S. 596 (1982), the Court declared unconstitutional a Massachusetts law that allowed trial courts to exclude the press and the public from hearing the testimony of witnesses under age 18 who allegedly were the victims of sex crimes. The Court said that *Richmond Newspapers* "firmly established . . . that the press and general public have a constitutional right of access to criminal trials." The Court said, therefore, that closing court proceedings would be allowed only if it was demonstrated to be "necessitated by a compelling governmental interest, and is narrowly tailored to serve that interest." The Court accepted that protecting minor victims was a compelling interest, but concluded that the state law that required closure in all cases was not sufficiently narrowly tailored; a case-by-case approach would adequately serve the state's interests.

In Press-Enterprise Co. v. Superior Court, 464 U.S. 501 (1984), the Court held that it violated the First Amendment for a court to close voir dire proceedings to the public and the press. The Court explained that voir dire proceedings are a key phase of the trial. The Court said that the "presumption of openness may be overcome only by an overriding interest based on findings that closure is essential to preserve the higher values and narrowly tailored to serve that interest." The Court acknowledged that in some instances closure might be justified, where questioning of prospective jurors would pertain to "deeply personal matters." But even then closure should be regarded as a last resort because of the importance of the public monitoring what occurs during the crucial phase of jury selection. For example, during the O.J. Simpson murder case, there were claims that the prosecution was treating prospective African American jurors differently from white jurors during voir dire. This raised an important issue concerning the conduct of a government officer and required that the press and public be present to observe and report on what occurred.

Although these cases emphatically recognize a First Amendment right of access to court proceedings, they leave many questions unanswered. Is *Gannett* still good law; can a court close pretrial proceedings involving the suppression of evidence? Arguably, press reporting on suppressed evidence could jeopardize the defendant's right to a fair trial. But suppression hearings are of great interest to the public: They concern the conduct of police and decisions by judges as to what evidence will be admitted.[200]

Another unanswered question is whether the press has a preferred right of access to judicial proceedings. If there are only a limited number of seats in a courtroom, must some of them be reserved for reporters? The values underlying the First Amendment would seem to require this because the public only can learn about what occurred in court if the press is present to observe and report. But the Court has not yet recognized a preferred right for the press and, as discussed throughout this section, has generally rejected any special rights for the press.

In fact, in Seattle Times Co. v. Rhinehart, 467 U.S. 20 (1984), the Court held that the press did not have a right of access to information produced in discovery in a civil suit that was covered by a protective order. Specifically, the press wanted to obtain a list of contributors to a controversial religious organization. The Court unanimously ruled against the newspaper and said that the press was not entitled to the information because the public would not have had a right to it. The Court concluded that "where a protective order is entered on a showing of good cause as required by Rule 26(c), is limited to the context of pretrial civil discovery, and does not restrict the dissemination of information if gained from other sources, it does not offend the First Amendment."

---

200. *See also* Press Enterpise Co. v. Superior Court, 478 U.S. 1 (1986) (recognizing a First Amendment right to transcripts of a preliminary hearing).

b. Prisons

The other context where the Supreme Court has considered a First Amendment right of access is with regard to prisons. Here the Court has expressly rejected such a right and has specifically ruled that the press is not entitled to any greater rights than the general public. In several cases, the Court upheld the ability of prisons to restrict the ability of the press to interview prisoners or have access to prisons. In Pell v. Procunier, 417 U.S. 817 (1974), and Saxbe v. Washington Post Co., 417 U.S. 843 (1974), the Court sustained prison regulations that prevented the media from interviewing particular prisoners. The Court said that the regulations were justified because "press attention . . . concentrated on a relatively small number of inmates who, as a result, became virtual 'public figures' within the prison society and gained a disproportionate degree of notoriety and influence among their fellow inmates . . . and became the source of severe disciplinary problems."

The Court followed this reasoning in Houchins v. KQED, in which the press sought access to the Greystone facility in the Santa Rita jail.

HOUCHINS v. KQED
438 U.S. 1 (1978)

Chief Justice BURGER announced the judgment of the Court and delivered an opinion, in which Justice WHITE and Justice REHNQUIST joined.

The question presented is whether the news media have a constitutional right of access to a county jail, over and above that of other persons, to interview inmates and make sound recordings, films, and photographs for publication and broadcasting by newspapers, radio, and television.

I

Petitioner Houchins, as Sheriff of Alameda County, Cal., controls all access to the Alameda County Jail at Santa Rita. Respondent KQED operates licensed television and radio broadcasting stations which have frequently reported newsworthy events relating to penal institutions in the San Francisco Bay Area. On March 31, 1975, KQED reported the suicide of a prisoner in the Greystone portion of the Santa Rita jail. The report included a statement by a psychiatrist that the conditions at the Greystone facility were responsible for the illnesses of his patient-prisoners there, and a statement from petitioner denying that prison conditions were responsible for the prisoners' illnesses.

KQED requested permission to inspect and take pictures within the Greystone facility. After permission was refused, KQED and the Alameda and Oakland branches of the National Association for the Advancement of Colored People (NAACP) filed suit. They alleged that petitioner had violated the First Amendment by refusing to permit media access and failing to provide any effective means by which the public could be informed of conditions prevailing in the Greystone facility or learn of the prisoners' grievances. Public access to such information was essential, they asserted, in order for NAACP members to participate in the public debate on jail conditions in Alameda County. They further asserted that television coverage of the conditions in the cells and facilities was the most effective way of informing the public of prison conditions.

On June 17, 1975, when the complaint was filed, there appears to have been no formal policy regarding public access to the Santa Rita jail. However, according to petitioner, he had been in the process of planning a program of regular monthly tours since he took office six months earlier. On July 8, 1975, he announced the program and invited all interested persons to make arrangements for the regular public tours. News media were given notice in advance of the public and presumably could have made early reservations. Six monthly tours were planned and funded by the county at an estimated cost of $1,800. Each tour was limited to 25 persons and permitted only limited access to the jail. The tours did not include the disciplinary cells or the portions of the jail known as "Little Greystone," the scene of alleged rapes, beatings, and adverse physical conditions. Photographs of some parts of the jail were made available, but no cameras or tape recorders were allowed on the tours. Those on the tours were not permitted to interview inmates, and inmates were generally removed from view.

II

Notwithstanding our holding in Pell v. Procunier, respondents assert that the right recognized by the Court of Appeals flows logically from our decisions construing the First Amendment. They argue that there is a constitutionally guaranteed right to gather news. From the right to gather news and the right to receive information, they argue for an implied special right of access to government-controlled sources of information.

We can agree with many of the respondents' generalized assertions; conditions in jails and prisons are clearly matters "of great public importance." Penal facilities are public institutions which require large amounts of public funds, and their mission is crucial in our criminal justice system. It is equally true that with greater information, the public can more intelligently form opinions about prison conditions. Beyond question, the role of the media is important; acting as the "eyes and ears" of the public, they can be a powerful and constructive force, contributing to remedial action in the conduct of public business. They have served that function since the beginning of the Republic, but like all other components of our society media representatives are subject to limits.

The media are not a substitute for or an adjunct of government and, like the courts, they are "ill equipped" to deal with problems of prison administration. The public importance of conditions in penal facilities and the media's role of providing information afford no basis for reading into the Constitution a right of the public or the media to enter these institutions, with camera equipment, and take moving and still pictures of inmates for broadcast purposes. This Court has never intimated a First Amendment guarantee of a right of access to all sources of information within government control.

The right to receive ideas and information is not the issue in this case. The issue is a claimed special privilege of access which the Court rejected in Pell and Saxbe, a right which is not essential to guarantee the freedom to communicate or publish.

The respondents' argument is flawed, not only because it lacks precedential support and is contrary to statements in this Court's opinions, but also because it invites the Court to involve itself in what is clearly a legislative task which the Constitution has left to the political processes. Whether the government should open penal institutions in the manner sought by respondents is a question of policy which a legislative body might appropriately resolve one way or the other.

A number of alternatives are available to prevent problems in penal facilities from escaping public attention. The early penal reform movements in this country and England gained impetus as a result of reports from citizens and visiting committees who volunteered or received commissions to visit penal institutions and make reports. Petitioner cannot prevent respondents from learning about jail conditions in a variety of ways, albeit not as conveniently as they might prefer. Respondents have a First Amendment right to receive letters from inmates criticizing jail officials and reporting on conditions. Respondents are free to interview those who render the legal assistance to which inmates are entitled. They are also free to seek out former inmates, visitors to the prison, public officials, and institutional personnel, as they sought out the complaining psychiatrist here.

Neither the First Amendment nor the Fourteenth Amendment mandates a right of access to government information or sources of information within the government's control. [U]ntil the political branches decree otherwise, as they are free to do, the media have no special right of access to the Alameda County Jail different from or greater than that accorded the public generally.

Justice Stewart, concurring in the judgment.

In my view, however, KQED was entitled to injunctive relief of more limited scope. The First and Fourteenth Amendments do not guarantee the public a right of access to information generated or controlled by government, nor do they guarantee the press any basic right of access superior to that of the public generally. The Constitution does no more than assure the public and the press equal access once government has opened its doors. Accordingly, I agree substantially with what the opinion of The Chief Justice has to say on that score.

We part company, however, in applying these abstractions to the facts of this case. Whereas he appears to view "equal access" as meaning access that is identical in all respects, I believe that the concept of equal access must be accorded more flexibility in order to accommodate the practical distinctions between the press and the general public. When on assignment, a journalist does not tour a jail simply for his own edification. He is there to gather information to be passed on to others, and his mission is protected by the Constitution for very specific reasons.

That the First Amendment speaks separately of freedom of speech and freedom of the press is no constitutional accident, but an acknowledgment of the critical role played by the press in American society. The Constitution requires sensitivity to that role, and to the special needs of the press in performing it effectively. A person touring Santa Rita jail can grasp its reality with his own eyes and ears. But if a television reporter is to convey the jail's sights and sounds to those who cannot personally visit the place, he must use cameras and sound equipment. In short, terms of access that are reasonably imposed on individual members of the public may, if they impede effective reporting without sufficient justification, be unreasonable as applied to journalists who are there to convey to the general public what the visitors see.

Under these principles, KQED was clearly entitled to some form of preliminary injunctive relief. At the time of the District Court's decision, members of the public were permitted to visit most parts of the Santa Rita jail, and the First and Fourteenth Amendments required the Sheriff to give members of the press effective access to the same areas. The Sheriff evidently assumed that he could fulfill this obligation simply by allowing reporters to sign up for tours on the same terms as the public. I think he was mistaken in this assumption, as a matter of constitutional law.

Justice STEVENS, with whom Justice BRENNAN and Justice POWELL join, dissenting.

Respondent KQED, Inc., has televised a number of programs about prison conditions and prison inmates, and its reporters have been granted access to various correctional facilities in the San Francisco Bay area, including San Quentin State Prison, Soledad Prison, and the San Francisco County Jails at San Bruno and San Francisco, to prepare program material. They have taken their cameras and recording equipment inside the walls of those institutions and interviewed inmates. No disturbances or other problems have occurred on those occasions.

Here, the broad restraints on access to information regarding operation of the jail that prevailed on the date this suit was instituted are plainly disclosed by the record. The public and the press had consistently been denied any access to those portions of the Santa Rita facility where inmates were confined and there had been excessive censorship of inmate correspondence. Petitioner's no-access policy, modified only in the wake of respondents' resort to the courts, could survive constitutional scrutiny only if the Constitution affords no protection to the public's right to be informed about conditions within those public institutions where some of its members are confined because they have been charged with or found guilty of criminal offenses.

The preservation of a full and free flow of information to the general public has long been recognized as a core objective of the First Amendment to the Constitution. It is for this reason that the First Amendment protects not only the dissemination but also the receipt of information and ideas. In addition to safeguarding the right of one individual to receive what another elects to communicate, the First Amendment serves an essential societal function. Our system of self-government assumes the existence of an informed citizenry.

It is not sufficient, therefore, that the channels of communication be free of governmental restraints. Without some protection for the acquisition of information about the operation of public institutions such as prisons by the public at large, the process of self-governance contemplated by the framers would be stripped of its substance.

For that reason information gathering is entitled to some measure of constitutional protection. As this Court's decisions clearly indicate, however, this protection is not for the private benefit of those who might qualify as representatives of the "press" but to insure that the citizens are fully informed regarding matters of public interest and importance.

In this case, "[r]espondents do not assert a right to force disclosure of confidential information or to invade in any way the decisionmaking processes of governmental officials." They simply seek an end to petitioner's policy of concealing prison conditions from the public. Those conditions are wholly without claim to confidentiality. While prison officials have an interest in the time and manner of public acquisition of information about the institutions they administer, there is no legitimate penological justification for concealing from citizens the conditions in which their fellow citizens are being confined.

The reasons which militate in favor of providing special protection to the flow of information to the public about prisons relate to the unique function they perform in a democratic society. Not only are they public institutions, financed with public funds and administered by public servants, they are an integral component of the criminal justice system.

In this case, the record demonstrates that both the public and the press had been consistently denied any access to the inner portions of the Santa Rita jail, that there had been excessive censorship of inmate correspondence, and that there was no valid justification for these broad restraints on the flow of information. An affirmative answer to the question whether respondents established a likelihood of prevailing on the merits did not depend, in final analysis, on any right of the press to special treatment beyond that accorded the public at large. Rather, the probable existence of a constitutional violation rested upon the special importance of allowing a democratic community access to knowledge about how its servants were treating some of its members who have been committed to their custody. An official prison policy of concealing such knowledge from the public by arbitrarily cutting off the flow of information at its source abridges the freedom of speech and of the press protected by the First and Fourteenth Amendments to the Constitution.

CHAPTER
10

FIRST AMENDMENT: RELIGION

A. INTRODUCTION

1. *Constitutional Provisions Concerning Religion and the Tension Between Them*

The First Amendment begins with the words "Congress shall make no law respecting an establishment of religion, or prohibiting the free exercise thereof." These two clauses are commonly referred to, respectively, as the "Establishment Clause" and the "Free Exercise Clause." The Free Exercise Clause was first applied to the states through its incorporation into the Due Process Clause of the Fourteenth Amendment in Cantwell v. Connecticut, 310 U.S. 296 (1940). The Establishment Clause was first found to be incorporated and applied to the states in Everson v. Board of Education, 330 U.S. 1 (1947).[1] The incorporation of the Establishment Clause is more controversial than the incorporation of the Free Exercise Clause because the latter clearly safeguards individual liberty while the former seems directed at the government. The Supreme Court, however, has explained that the Establishment Clause, too, protects liberty. Justice Brennan, concurring in Abington School District v. Schempp, 374 U.S. 203 (1963), explained that "the Establishment Clause [is] a co-guarantor, with the Free Exercise Clause, of religious liberty. The framers did not entrust the liberty of religious beliefs to either clause alone." As the Court declared in Lee v. Weisman, 505 U.S. 577 (1992), "A state-created orthodoxy puts at grave risk that freedom of belief and conscience which are the sole assurance that religious faith is real, not imposed."

To a large extent, the Establishment and Free Exercise Clauses are complementary. Both protect freedom of religious belief and actions. Many government

---

1. In addition to the provisions of the First Amendment, the text of the Constitution contains one other provision concerning religion. Article VI, Clause 3, says, "The Senators and Representatives before mentioned, and the Members of the several State Legislatures, and all executive and judicial Officers, both of the United States and of the several States, shall be bound by Oath or Affirmation, to support this Constitution; but no religious Test shall ever be required as a Qualification to any Office or public Trust under the United States." Although the provision did not protect religious freedom for the general public, it did assure that the government could not establish a religion as a condition for holding federal office or infringe free exercise of religion for these individuals. This provision was applied to the states in Torcaso v. Watkins, 367 U.S. 488 (1961).

actions would simultaneously violate both of these provisions. For example, if the state were to create a religion and compel participation, it obviously would be establishing religion and, at the same time, denying free exercise to those who did not want to participate in religion or who wished to choose a different faith. Mandatory school prayers likewise involve both the government establishing religion and interfering with free exercise of religious beliefs for those who do not believe in the prayers. In a recent case, presented below, Hosana-Tabor Evangelical Lutheran Church and School v. EEOC, 132 S. Ct. 694 (2012), the Court held that it violated both the Establishment and the Free Exercise Clauses to hold a religious institution liable for discrimination in the choices it makes as to who will be its ministers. The case involved a religious elementary school where many of the teachers were designated as ministers. A teacher who lost her job after an illness and then was fired sued under the Americans with Disabilities Act. The Court unanimously ruled that it would infringe both the Establishment Clause and the Free Exercise Clause to hold a religious institution liable for the choices it makes as to who will be its ministers.

Yet there also is often tension between the Establishment and Free Exercise Clauses. Government actions to facilitate free exercise might be challenged as impermissible establishments, and government efforts to refrain from establishing religion might be objected to as denying the free exercise of religion. For instance, if the government pays for and provides ministers for those in the armed services, it arguably is establishing religion, but if the government refuses to do so on these grounds, it arguably is denying free exercise of religion.

Indeed, the primary test used for the Establishment Clause — articulated in Lemon v. Kurtzman, 403 U.S. 602 (1971), and reviewed in detail below in section C — makes this tension inevitable. Under the *Lemon* test, the government violates the Establishment Clause if the government's primary purpose is to advance religion, or if the principal effect is to aid or inhibit religion, or if there is excessive government entanglement with religion. Yet any time the government acts to protect free exercise of religion, its primary purpose is to advance religion; any time the principal effect is to facilitate free exercise, the government is aiding religion. For example, if the government creates an exemption to a law solely for religion, it arguably violates the Establishment Clause; if the government fails to create such an exemption for religion, it arguably infringes free exercise.[2]

The Court has recognized that this tension is inherent in the First Amendment and has noted the difficulty of finding "a neutral course between the two Religion Clauses, both of which are cast in absolute terms, and either of which, if expanded to a logical extreme, would tend to clash with the other."[3] Additionally, there is a tension between the First Amendment's protection of speech and its prohibition against establishment of religion. For example, allowing government financial aid to student religious groups[4] or permitting religious groups to

---

2. *See* Suzanna Sherry, *Lee v. Weisman: Paradox Redux*, 1992 Sup. Ct. Rev. 123 (arguing that the tension between the Establishment and Free Exercise Clauses is inherent and difficult to reconcile).

3. Walz v. Tax Commission, 397 U.S. 664, 668-669 (1970).

4. *See* Rosenberger v. Rector & Visitors of the University of Virginia, 515 U.S. 819 (1995), discussed in section C below.

use school facilities[5] arguably violates the Establishment Clause; but denying funds or facilities because of the religious content of the expression seems to infringe the First Amendment's protection of freedom of speech. This tension between the Establishment Clause and freedom of speech has received a great deal of attention from the Supreme Court in recent years and is discussed below.

2. History in Interpreting the Religion Clauses

As with all constitutional provisions, some look to history as a guide to the meaning of the Religion Clauses. This is particularly difficult for these provisions because there is no apparent agreement among the framers as to what they meant. Justice Brennan expressed this well when he stated: "A too literal quest for the advice of the Founding Fathers upon the issues of these cases seems to me futile and misdirected for several reasons. . . . [T]he historical record is at best ambiguous, and statements can readily be found to support either side of the proposition."[6] Yet justices on all sides of the issue continue to invoke history and the original understanding of that text to support their position. Chief Justice Rehnquist has remarked that "[t]he true meaning of Establishment Clause can only be seen in its history."[7] In Rosenberger v. Rector & Visitors of the University of Virginia, 515 U.S. 819 (1995), which concerned whether a public university could deny student activity funds to a religious group, both Justice Thomas, in a concurring opinion, and Justice Souter, dissenting, focused at length on James Madison's views of religious freedom.[8]

As Professor Laurence Tribe has cogently summarized, there were at least three main views of religion among key framers.[9]

> [A]t least three distinct schools of thought . . . influenced the drafters of the Bill of Rights: first, the evangelical view (associated primarily with Roger Williams) that "worldly corruptions . . . might consume the churches if sturdy fences against the wilderness were not maintained"; second, the Jeffersonian view that the church should be walled off from the state in order to safeguard secular interests (public and private) "against ecclesiastical depredations and incursions"; and, third, the Madisonian view that religious and secular interests alike would be advanced best by diffusing and decentralizing power so as to assure competition among sects rather than dominance by any one.[10]

These are quite distinct views of the proper relationship between religion and the government. Roger Williams was primarily concerned that government involvement with religion would corrupt and undermine religion, whereas Thomas Jefferson had the opposite fear that religion would corrupt and undermine the government. James Madison saw religion as one among many types of

---

5. *See, e.g.,* Lamb's Chapel v. Center Moriches Union Free School District, 508 U.S. 384 (1993), discussed below in section C.

6. Abington School Dist. v. Schempp, 374 U.S. at 237.

7. Wallace v. Jaffree, 472 U.S. 38, 113 (1985) (Rehnquist, J., dissenting).

8. James Madison issued his famous *Remonstrance* in arguing against a Virginia decision to renew a tax to support the church. This is reviewed in detail in Everson v. Board of Education, 330 U.S. 1, 12 (1947); *id.* at 31-34 (Rutledge, J., dissenting).

9. Laurence H. Tribe, *American Constitutional Law* 1158-1160 (2d ed. 1988).

10. *Id.* at 1158-1159 (citations omitted).

factions that existed. He wrote that "[i]n a free government the security for civil rights must be the same as that for religious rights. It consists in the one case in the multiplicity of interests, and the other in the multiplicity of sects. The degree of security in both cases will depend on the number of interests and sects."[11]

The problem of using history in interpreting the Religion Clauses is compounded by the enormous changes in the country since the First Amendment was adopted. The country is much more religiously diverse today than it was in 1791. Justice Brennan observed that "our religious composition makes us a vastly more diverse people than were our forefathers. They knew differences chiefly among Protestant sects. Today the nation is far more heterogeneous religiously, including as it does substantial minorities not only of Catholics and Jews but as well of those who worship according to no version of the Bible and those who worship no God at all."[12]

Also, as discussed below, a significant number of cases involving the Establishment Clause have arisen in the context of religious activities in connection with schools. But public education, as it exists now, did not exist when the Bill of Rights was ratified, and it is inherently difficult to apply the framers' views to situations that they could not have imagined. Justice Brennan also remarked that "the structure of American education has greatly changed since the First Amendment was adopted. In the context of our modern emphasis upon public education available to all citizens, any views of the eighteenth century as to whether the exercises at bar are an 'establishment' offer little aid to decision."[13]

Nonetheless, debates about history and the framers' intent are likely to remain a key aspect of decisions concerning the Religion Clauses. Members of the Supreme Court who follow an originalist philosophy of constitutional interpretation believe that the Constitution's meaning is to be ascertained solely from its text and from its framers' intent. Also, the divergence of views among the framers, and the abstractness with which they were stated, makes it possible for those on all sides of the debate to invoke history in support of their positions.

3. What Is Religion?

Under both the Establishment and the Free Exercise Clauses, the issue can arise as to what is "religion." Yet, not surprisingly, the Court has avoided trying to formulate a definition. It seems impossible to formulate a definition of religion that encompasses the vast array of spiritual beliefs and practices that are present in the United States.[14] As one commentator noted, "[T]here is no single characteristic or set of characteristics that all religions have in common that makes them religions."[15] Moreover, any attempt to define religion raises concern that choosing a single definition is itself an establishment of religion.

---

11. James Madison, Federalist No. 51, *The Federalist Papers* 322 (C. Rossiter ed. 1961).

12. Abington School Dist. v. Schempp, 374 U.S. at 240 (Brennan, J., concurring).

13. *Id.* at 238.

14. There is a rich literature focusing on the question of the definition of religion. *See, e.g.,* Stanley Ingber, *Religion or Ideology: A Needed Clarification of the Religion Clauses,* 41 Stan. L. Rev. 233 (1989); Jesse Choper, *Defining "Religion" in the First Amendment,* 1982 U. Ill. L. Rev. 579; Note, *Toward a Constitutional Definition of Religion,* 91 Harv. L. Rev. 1056 (1978).

15. George C. Freeman, *The Misguided Search for the Constitutional Definition of "Religion,"* 71 Geo. L.J. 1519, 1548 (1983).

Additionally, there is a desire for a broad definition of religion for purposes of the Free Exercise Clause so as to maximize protection for religious conduct but a narrow definition of religion for Establishment Clause analysis so as to limit the constraints on government. For instance, the issue has arisen in the lower courts as to whether a school's course in transcendental meditation violates the Establishment Clause.[16] Safeguarding the right of people to engage in transcendental meditation leads to the desire for a broad definition of religion that includes this practice, but wanting to allow schools to offer such a course causes a desire for a narrow definition of religion that excludes it.

Although some commentators have argued for separate definitions of religion for the Establishment and the Free Exercise Clauses, the Supreme Court never has accepted this position. In fact, Justice Rutledge expressly rejected this approach in his opinion in Everson v. Board of Education: "'Religion' appears only once in the Amendment. But the word governs two prohibitions and governs them alike. It does not have two meanings, one narrow to forbid 'an establishment' and another, much broader, for 'securing' the free exercise thereof."

While the Supreme Court never has formulated a definition of religion, it has considered the issue in three contexts. First, in cases under the Selective Service Act, the Court struggled to define religion for purposes of the conscientious objector exemption. Second, the Court has said that a court can inquire as to whether a religious belief is sincerely held in deciding whether it is protected under the Constitution. Finally, the Court has made it clear that an individual's sincerely held religious belief is protected by the First Amendment even if it is not the dogma or dominant view within the religion. Each of these concepts is discussed in turn.

THE ATTEMPT TO DEFINE RELIGION UNDER THE SELECTIVE SERVICE ACT

The primary effort by the Supreme Court to define religion has not been in First Amendment cases, but rather in decisions concerning the scope of a religious exemption to the Selective Service Act, which authorized the military draft. In other words, these cases involved statutory construction, rather than constitutional interpretation. Yet these cases are important as the only decisions to attempt to define religion.

UNITED STATES v. SEEGER

380 U.S. 163 (1965)

Justice CLARK delivered the opinion of the court.

These cases involve claims of conscientious objectors under §6(j) of the Universal Military Training and Service Act, which exempts from combatant training and service in the armed forces of the United States those persons who by reason of their religious training and belief are conscientiously opposed

---

16. *See* Malnak v. Yogi, 592 F.2d 197 (3d Cir. 1979) (finding that a course in transcendental meditation violates the Establishment Clause).

to participation in war in any form. The parties raise the basic question of the constitutionality of the section which defines the term "religious training and belief," as used in the Act, as "an individual's belief in a relation to a Supreme Being involving duties superior to those arising from any human relation, but (not including) essentially political, sociological, or philosophical views or a merely personal moral code."

Seeger was convicted in the District Court for the Southern District of New York of having refused to submit to induction in the armed forces. He was originally classified 1-A in 1953 by his local board, but this classification was changed in 1955 to 2-S (student) and he remained in this status until 1958 when he was reclassified 1-A. He first claimed exemption as a conscientious objector in 1957 after successive annual renewals of his student classification. Although he did not adopt verbatim the printed Selective Service System form, he declared that he was conscientiously opposed to participation in war in any form by reason of his "religious" belief; that he preferred to leave the question as to his belief in a Supreme Being open, "rather than answer 'yes' or 'no'"; that his "skepticism or disbelief in the existence of God" did "not necessarily mean lack of faith in anything whatsoever"; that his was a "belief in and devotion to goodness and virtue for their own sakes, and a religious faith in a purely ethical creed." He cited such personages as Plato, Aristotle and Spinoza for support of his ethical belief in intellectual and moral integrity "without belief in God, except in the remotest sense."

His belief was found to be sincere, honest, and made in good faith; and his conscientious objection to be based upon individual training and belief, both of which included research in religious and cultural fields. Seeger's claim, however, was denied solely because it was not based upon a "belief in a relation to a Supreme Being" as required by §6(j) of the Act.

Few would quarrel, we think, with the proposition that in no field of human endeavor has the tool of language proved so inadequate in the communication of ideas as it has in dealing with the fundamental questions of man's predicament in life, in death or in final judgment and retribution. This fact makes the task of discerning the intent of Congress in using the phrase "Supreme Being" a complex one. Nor is it made the easier by the richness and variety of spiritual life in our country. Over 250 sects inhabit our land. Some believe in a purely personal God, some in a supernatural deity; others think of religion as a way of life envisioning as its ultimate goal the day when all men can live together in perfect understanding and peace. There are those who think of God as the depth of our being; others, such as the Buddhists, strive for a state of lasting rest through self-denial and inner purification; in Hindu philosophy, the Supreme Being is the transcendental reality which is truth, knowledge and bliss. Even those religious groups which have traditionally opposed war in every form have splintered into various denominations. This vast panoply of beliefs reveals the magnitude of the problem which faced the Congress when it set about providing an exemption from armed service. It also emphasizes the care that Congress realized was necessary in the fashioning of an exemption which would be in keeping with its long-established policy of not picking and choosing among religious beliefs.

We have concluded that Congress, in using the expression "Supreme Being" rather than the designation "God," was merely clarifying the meaning of religious training and belief so as to embrace all religions and to exclude essentially political, sociological, or philosophical views. We believe that under this construction, the test of belief "in a relation to a Supreme Being" is whether a given belief that is sincere and meaningful occupies a place in the life of its possessor parallel to that filled by the orthodox belief in God of one who clearly qualifies for the exemption. Where such beliefs have parallel positions in the lives of their respective holders we cannot say that one is "in a relation to Supreme Being" and the other is not. We have concluded that the beliefs of the objectors in these cases meet these criteria.

The Court in *Seeger*, however, offered no criteria for assessing whether a particular view is religious under this definition. Nor did the Court do so in the subsequent case of Welsh v. United States, 398 U.S. 333 (1970). *Welsh*, like *Seeger*, involved a person seeking an exemption from the draft on religious grounds. Welsh actually crossed out the words "religious training" on his form. The plurality opinion by Justice Black said that his situation was indistinguishable from Seeger's: "[B]oth Seeger and Welsh affirmed on those applications that they held deep conscientious scruples against taking part in wars where people were killed. Both strongly believed that killing in war was wrong, unethical, and immoral, and their consciences forbade them to take part in such an evil practice." Again, the Court said that the crucial inquiry "in determining whether the registrant's beliefs are religious is whether these beliefs play the role of a religion and function as a religion in the registrant's life."

The plurality explained that belief in God is characteristic of most religions, but not a prerequisite for religion. Justice Black wrote, "Most of the great religions of today and of the past have embodied the idea of a Supreme Being or a Supreme Reality—a God—who communicates to man in some way a consciousness of what is right and should be done, of what is wrong and therefore should be shunned. If an individual deeply and sincerely holds beliefs that are purely ethical or moral in source and content but that nevertheless impose upon him a duty of conscience to refrain from participating in any war at any time, those beliefs certainly occupy in the life of that individual 'a place parallel to that filled by . . . God' in traditionally religious persons." The Court concluded that the statute "exempts from military service all those whose consciences, spurred by deeply held moral, ethical, or religious beliefs, would give them no rest or peace if they allowed themselves to become a part of an instrument of war." The Court concluded that Welsh's moral opposition to war fit within this definition of religion.

Although *Seeger* and *Welsh* involved the Court's interpreting a statutory provision and not the First Amendment, they likely would be the starting points for any cases that required the Court to define religion under the Establishment and Free Exercise Clauses. On the one hand, these cases can be praised for broadening the definition of religion to include nontheistic views. Many religions reject the idea of a Supreme Being, and *Seeger* and *Welsh* adopt an approach that allows these faiths to be protected by the First Amendment. Moreover, the broad definitions employed allow moral judgments to be protected whether they are based on religion or philosophy. This is desirable because it does not give special status to religious moral judgments over secular ones and thereby avoids an Establishment Clause problem.[17]

On other hand, these cases can be criticized because of the lack of guidance they provide in defining what is a religious belief. A judge in a future case has little guidance in deciding what is a belief that is "sincere and meaningful [and] occupies a place in the life of its possessor parallel to that filled by the orthodox belief in God of one who clearly qualifies for the exemption."

REQUIREMENT FOR SINCERELY HELD BELIEFS

The need to define "religion" might arise in the context of an individual who is seeking an exemption from a law because of views that he or she terms religious. How is a court to decide if they are "religious" beliefs? The Supreme Court has indicated that the judiciary can determine only whether they are sincerely held views, not whether they are true or false. The court drew this distinction in United States v. Ballard.

UNITED STATES v. BALLARD
322 U.S. 78 (1944)

Mr. Justice DOUGLAS delivered the opinion of the Court.

Respondents were indicted and convicted for using, and conspiring to use, the mails to defraud. The indictment was in twelve counts. It charged a scheme to defraud by organizing and promoting the I Am movement through the use of the mails. The charge was that certain designated corporations were formed, literature distributed and sold, funds solicited, and memberships in the I Am movement sought "by means of false and fraudulent representations, pretenses and promises." It is sufficient at this point to say that they covered respondents' alleged religious doctrines or beliefs. [The indictment charged] "that Guy W. Ballard, during his lifetime, and Edna W. Ballard and Donald Ballard had, by reason of supernatural attainments, the power to heal persons of ailments and diseases and to make well persons afflicted with any diseases, injuries, or ailments, and did falsely represent to persons intended to be defrauded that the three designated persons had the ability and power to cure persons of those diseases normally classified as curable and also of diseases which are ordinarily classified by the medical profession as being incurable diseases; and did further represent that the three designated persons had in fact cured either by the activity of one, either, or all of said persons, hundreds of persons afflicted with diseases and ailments." Each of the representations enumerated in the indictment was followed by the charge that respondents "well knew" it was false.

[W]e do not agree that the truth or verity of respondents' religious doctrines or beliefs should have been submitted to the jury. Whatever this particular indictment might require, the First Amendment precludes such a course, as the United States seems to concede. "The law knows no heresy, and is

---

17. However, the Court also has said that "[t]here is no doubt that 'only beliefs rooted in religion are protected by the Free Exercise Clause.' Purely secular views do not suffice." Frazee v. Illinois Employment Security Department, 489 U.S. 829, 833 (1989) (citation omitted).

committed to the support of no dogma, the establishment of no sect." The First Amendment has a dual aspect. It not only "forestalls compulsion by law of the acceptance of any creed or the practice of any form of worship" but also "safeguards the free exercise of the chosen form of religion."

Thus the Amendment embraces two concepts — freedom to believe and freedom to act. The first is absolute but, in the nature of things, the second cannot be. Freedom of thought, which includes freedom of religious belief, is basic in a society of free men. It embraces the right to maintain theories of life and of death and of the hereafter which are rank heresy to followers of the orthodox faiths. Heresy trials are foreign to our Constitution. Men may believe what they cannot prove. They may not be put to the proof of their religious doctrines or beliefs. Religious experiences which are as real as life to some may be incomprehensible to others. Yet the fact that they may be beyond the ken of mortals does not mean that they can be made suspect before the law.

Many take their gospel from the New Testament. But it would hardly be supposed that they could be tried before a jury charged with the duty of determining whether those teachings contained false representations. The miracles of the New Testament, the Divinity of Christ, life after death, the power of prayer are deep in the religious convictions of many. If one could be sent to jail because a jury in a hostile environment found those teachings false, little indeed would be left of religious freedom. The Fathers of the Constitution were not unaware of the varied and extreme views of religious sects, of the violence of disagreement among them, and of the lack of any one religious creed on which all men would agree. They fashioned a charter of government which envisaged the widest possible toleration of conflicting views. Man's relation to his God was made no concern of the state. He was granted the right to worship as he pleased and to answer to no man for the verity of his religious views.

The religious views espoused by respondents might seem incredible, if not preposterous, to most people. But if those doctrines are subject to trial before a jury charged with finding their truth or falsity, then the same can be done with the religious beliefs of any sect. When the triers of fact undertake that task, they enter a forbidden domain. The First Amendment does not select any one group or any one type of religion for preferred treatment. It puts them all in that position. So we conclude that the District Court ruled properly when it withheld from the jury all questions concerning the truth or falsity of the religious beliefs or doctrines of respondents.

Justice JACKSON, dissenting.

I should say the defendants have done just that for which they are indicted. If I might agree to their conviction without creating a precedent, I cheerfully would do so. I can see in their teachings nothing but humbug, untainted by any trace of truth. But that does not dispose of the constitutional question whether misrepresentation of religious experience or belief is prosecutable; it rather emphasizes the danger of such prosecutions.

The Ballard family claimed miraculous communication with the spirit world and supernatural power to heal the sick. They were brought to trial for mail fraud on an indictment which charged that their representations were false and that they "well knew" they were false. The trial judge, obviously troubled, ruled that the court could not try whether the statements were untrue, but could inquire whether the defendants knew them to be untrue; and, if so, they could be convicted.

I find it difficult to reconcile this conclusion with our traditional religious freedoms. In the first place, as a matter of either practice or philosophy I do not see how we can separate an issue as to what is believed from considerations as to what is believable. The most convincing proof that one believes his statements is to show that they have been true in his experience.

Likewise, that one knowingly falsified is best proved by showing that what he said happened never did happen. How can the Government prove these persons knew something to be false which it cannot prove to be false? If we try religious sincerity severed from religious verity, we isolate the dispute from the very considerations which in common experience provide its most reliable answer.

In the second place, any inquiry into intellectual honesty in religion raises profound psychological problems. William James, who wrote on these matters as a scientist, reminds us that it is not theology and ceremonies which keep religion going. Its vitality is in the religious experiences of many people. "If you ask what these experiences are, they are conversations with the unseen, voices and visions, responses to prayer, changes of heart, deliverances from fear, inflowings of help, assurances of support, whenever certain persons set their own internal attitude in certain appropriate ways." If religious liberty includes, as it must, the right to communicate such experiences to others, it seems to me an impossible task for juries to separate fancied ones from real ones, dreams from happenings, and hallucinations from true clairvoyance. Such experiences, like some tones and colors, have existence for one, but none at all for another. They cannot be verified to the minds of those whose field of consciousness does not include religious insight. When one comes to trial which turns on any aspect of religious belief or representation, unbelievers among his judges are likely not to understand and are almost certain not to believe him.

There appear to be persons—let us hope not many—who find refreshment and courage in the teachings of the "I Am" cult. If the members of the sect get comfort from the celestial guidance of their "Saint Germain," however doubtful it seems to me, it is hard to say that they do not get what they pay for. Scores of sects flourish in this country by teaching what to me are queer notions. It is plain that there is wide variety in American religious taste. The Ballards are not alone in catering to it with a pretty dubious product.

Prosecutions of this character easily could degenerate into religious persecution. I do not doubt that religious leaders may be convicted of fraud for making false representations on matters other than faith or experience, as for example if one represents that funds are being used to construct a church when in fact they are being used for personal purposes. But that is not this case, which reaches into wholly dangerous ground. When does less than full belief in a professed credo become actionable fraud if one is soliciting gifts or legacies? Such inquiries may discomfort orthodox as well as unconventional religious teachers, for even the most regular of them are sometimes accused of taking their orthodoxy with a grain of salt.

I would dismiss the indictment and have done with this business of judicial examining other people's faiths.

THE RELEVANCE OF RELIGIOUS DOGMA AND SHARED BELIEFS

One way to assess the sincerity of a religious belief is with reference to the prevailing doctrines, if any, of that religion. In other words, what do others of that faith think with regard to the particular question? The problem, however, is that religion is inherently personal, as well as often group-based, and an individual may have a sincere religious belief that departs from the dogma of his or her religion. In fact, for this reason, the Court has said that the dominant views in a faith are not determinative in assessing whether a particular belief is religious.

In Thomas v. Review Board of the Indiana Employment Security Division, 450 U.S. 707 (1981), the Court ruled that an individual could claim a religious belief even though it was inconsistent with the doctrines of his or her religion. A person who was a member of Jehovah's Witnesses quit his job rather than be transferred to a department that produced turrets for military tanks. He claimed that producing armaments was contrary to his religious beliefs. The state denied him unemployment benefits because he had voluntarily left his job, but he sued under a line of cases holding that a state may not deny benefits to people who quit their jobs for religious reasons.

The state argued that the Jehovah's Witnesses' faith did not prevent an individual from working in the armaments plant. The state pointed to others from that religion who worked on tank turrets and to testimony that such work was "scripturally" acceptable. The Court said, however, that this was irrelevant and declared, "[T]he guarantee of free exercise is not limited to beliefs which are shared by all of the members of a religious sect. Particularly in this sensitive area, it is not within the judicial function and judicial competence to inquire whether the petitioner or his fellow worker more correctly perceived the commands of their common faith. Courts are not arbiters of scriptural interpretation."

Similarly, in Frazee v. Illinois Employment Security Department, 489 U.S. 829 (1989), the Court allowed an individual to claim a religious basis for refusing to work on Sundays even though others of his and similar religions did not have such a proscription. The Court said, "Undoubtedly, membership in an organized religious denomination, especially one with a specific tenet forbidding members to work on Sunday, would simplify the problem of identifying sincerely held religious beliefs, but we reject the notion that to claim the protection of the Free Exercise Clause, one must be responding to the commands of a particular religious organization." Thus, the inquiry must be whether a particular individual holds a sincere religious belief.

B. THE FREE EXERCISE CLAUSE

1. Introduction: Free Exercise Clause Issues

The Supreme Court repeatedly has stated that the government may not compel or punish religious beliefs; people may think and believe anything that they want.

In Reynolds v. United States, 98 U.S. 145, 164 (1878), the first case to construe the Free Exercise Clause, Chief Justice Waite wrote that "Congress was deprived of all legislative power over mere opinion, but was left free to reach actions." Likewise, in Braunfeld v. Brown, 366 U.S. 599, 603 (1961), Chief Justice Warren declared that "[t]he freedom to hold religious beliefs and opinions is absolute."

The Free Exercise Clause, however, obviously does not provide absolute protection for religiously motivated conduct. The Court has thus said that the Free Exercise Clause "embraces two concepts—freedom to believe and freedom to act. The first is absolute but, in the nature of things, the second cannot be."[18] Similarly, the Court spoke of the "distinction between the absolute constitutional protection against governmental regulation of religious beliefs on the one hand, and the qualified protection against the regulation of religiously motivated conduct."[19]

Governments, though, do not adopt laws prohibiting or requiring thoughts; statutes invariably regulate conduct. Thus, the Free Exercise Clause is invoked in several situations. One is when the government prohibits behavior that a person's religion requires. For example, in Reynolds v. United States, the Supreme Court upheld the constitutionality of a law forbidding polygamy even though Mormons said that it was required by their religion.

The Free Exercise Clause also is invoked when the government requires conduct that a person's religion prohibits. For instance, the Court rejected a challenge by Amish individuals who said that the requirement that they obtain Social Security numbers and pay Social Security taxes violated their religious beliefs.[20]

Additionally, the Free Exercise Clause is invoked when individuals claim that laws burden or make more difficult religious observances. An illustration of this is the many cases where the Court held that the government impermissibly burdens religion if it denies benefits to individuals who quit their jobs for religious reasons.[21]

2.   The Current Test

In Employment Division v. Smith, in 1990, the Court substantially changed the law regarding the Free Exercise Clause and articulated the test that is used today. Following *Smith*, earlier case law is reviewed and the application of the *Smith* test is discussed.

EMPLOYMENT DIVISION, DEPARTMENT OF HUMAN
RESOURCES OF OREGON v. SMITH

494 U.S. 875 (1990)

Justice Scalia delivered the opinion of the Court.

This case requires us to decide whether the Free Exercise Clause of the First Amendment permits the State of Oregon to include religiously inspired peyote

---

18. Cantwell v. Connecticut, 310 U.S. 296, 303-304 (1940).
19. Employment Division v. Smith, 494 U.S. 872, 670 n.13 (1990).
20. United States v. Lee, 455 U.S. 252 (1982).
21. *See, e.g.,* Thomas v. Review Board, 450 U.S. 707 (1981); Sherbert v. Verner, 374 U.S. 398 (1963).

use within the reach of its general criminal prohibition on use of that drug, and thus permits the State to deny unemployment benefits to persons dismissed from their jobs because of such religiously inspired use.

I

Oregon law prohibits the knowing or intentional possession of a "controlled substance" unless the substance has been prescribed by a medical practitioner. Persons who violate this provision by possessing a controlled substance listed on Schedule I are "guilty of a Class B felony." As compiled by the State Board of Pharmacy under its statutory authority, Schedule I contains the drug peyote, a hallucinogen.

Respondents Alfred Smith and Galen Black (hereinafter respondents) were fired from their jobs with a private drug rehabilitation organization because they ingested peyote for sacramental purposes at a ceremony of the Native American Church, of which both are members. When respondents applied to petitioner Employment Division (hereinafter petitioner) for unemployment compensation, they were determined to be ineligible for benefits because they had been discharged for work-related "misconduct." The Oregon Supreme Court held that respondents' religiously inspired use of peyote [was protected by the] Free Exercise Clause.

II

The free exercise of religion means, first and foremost, the right to believe and profess whatever religious doctrine one desires. Thus, the First Amendment obviously excludes all "governmental regulation of religious beliefs as such." The government may not compel affirmation of religious belief, punish the expression of religious doctrines it believes to be false, impose special disabilities on the basis of religious views or religious status, or lend its power to one or the other side in controversies over religious authority or dogma.

But the "exercise of religion" often involves not only belief and profession but the performance of (or abstention from) physical acts: assembling with others for a worship service, participating in sacramental use of bread and wine, proselytizing, abstaining from certain foods or certain modes of transportation. It would be true, we think (though no case of ours has involved the point), that a State would be "prohibiting the free exercise [of religion]" if it sought to ban such acts or abstentions only when they are engaged in for religious reasons, or only because of the religious belief that they display. It would doubtless be unconstitutional, for example, to ban the casting of "statues that are to be used for worship purposes," or to prohibit bowing down before a golden calf.

Respondents in the present case, however, seek to carry the meaning of "prohibiting the free exercise [of religion]" one large step further. They contend that their religious motivation for using peyote places them beyond the reach of a criminal law that is not specifically directed at their religious practice, and that is concededly constitutional as applied to those who use the drug for other reasons. They assert, in other words, that "prohibiting the free exercise [of religion]" includes requiring any individual to observe a generally applicable law that requires (or forbids) the performance of an act that his religious belief forbids (or requires). As a textual matter, we do not think the words must be given that meaning.

We have never held that an individual's religious beliefs excuse him from compliance with an otherwise valid law prohibiting conduct that the State is free to regulate. On the contrary, the record of more than a century of our free exercise jurisprudence contradicts that proposition. [D]ecisions have consistently held that the right of free exercise does not relieve an individual of the obligation to comply with a "valid and neutral law of general applicability on the ground that the law proscribes (or prescribes) conduct that his religion prescribes (or proscribes)."

Our most recent decision involving a neutral, generally applicable regulatory law that compelled activity forbidden by an individual's religion was United States v. Lee. There an Amish employer, on behalf of himself and his employees, sought exemption from collection and payment of Social Security taxes on the ground that the Amish faith prohibited participation in governmental support programs. We rejected the claim that an exemption was constitutionally required. There would be no way, we observed, to distinguish the Amish believer's objection to Social Security taxes from the religious objections that others might have to the collection or use of other taxes. "If, for example, a religious adherent believes war is a sin, and if a certain percentage of the federal budget can be identified as devoted to war-related activities, such individuals would have a similarly valid claim to be exempt from paying that percentage of the income tax. The tax system could not function if denominations were allowed to challenge the tax system because tax payments were spent in a manner that violates their religious belief."

The only decisions in which we have held that the First Amendment bars application of a neutral, generally applicable law to religiously motivated action have involved not the Free Exercise Clause alone, but the Free Exercise Clause in conjunction with other constitutional protections, such as freedom of speech and of the press, see Cantwell v. Connecticut [1940] (invalidating a licensing system for religious and charitable solicitations under which the administrator had discretion to deny a license to any cause he deemed nonreligious); Murdock v. Pennsylvania (1943) (invalidating a flat tax on solicitation as applied to the dissemination of religious ideas); or the right of parents, acknowledged in Pierce v. Society of Sisters (1925), to direct the education of their children, see Wisconsin v. Yoder (1972) (invalidating compulsory school-attendance laws as applied to Amish parents who refused on religious grounds to send their children to school).

The present case does not present such a hybrid situation, but a free exercise claim unconnected with any communicative activity or parental right. Respondents urge us to hold, quite simply, that when otherwise prohibitable conduct is accompanied by religious convictions, not only the convictions but the conduct itself must be free from governmental regulation. We have never held that, and decline to do so now. There being no contention that Oregon's drug law represents an attempt to regulate religious beliefs, the communication of religious beliefs, or the raising of one's children in those beliefs, the rule to which we have adhered ever since *Reynolds* plainly controls.

Respondents argue that even though exemption from generally applicable criminal laws need not automatically be extended to religiously motivated actors, at least the claim for a religious exemption must be evaluated under the balancing test set forth in Sherbert v. Verner (1963). Under the *Sherbert* test, governmental actions that substantially burden a religious practice must be justified by a compelling governmental interest. Applying that test we have, on three occasions, invalidated state unemployment compensation rules that conditioned the availability of benefits upon an applicant's willingness to work under conditions forbidden by his religion. We have never invalidated any governmental action on the basis of the *Sherbert* test except the denial of unemployment compensation. Although we have sometimes purported to apply the *Sherbert* test in contexts other than that, we have always found the test satisfied.

In recent years we have abstained from applying the *Sherbert* test (outside the unemployment compensation field) at all. In Bowen v. Roy (1986), we declined to apply *Sherbert* analysis to a federal statutory scheme that required benefit applicants and recipients to provide their Social Security numbers. The plaintiffs in that case asserted that it would violate their religious beliefs to obtain and provide a Social Security number for their daughter. We held the statute's application to the plaintiffs valid regardless of whether it was necessary to effectuate a compelling interest.

In Lyng v. Northwest Indian Cemetery Protective Assn. (1988), we declined to apply *Sherbert* analysis to the Government's logging and road construction activities on lands used for religious purposes by several Native American Tribes, even though it was undisputed that the activities "could have devastating effects on traditional Indian religious practices." In Goldman v. Weinberger (1986), we rejected application of the *Sherbert* test to military dress regulations that forbade the wearing of yarmulkes.

Even if we were inclined to breathe into *Sherbert* some life beyond the unemployment compensation field, we would not apply it to require exemptions from a generally applicable criminal law. The *Sherbert* test, it must be recalled, was developed in a context that lent itself to individualized governmental assessment of the reasons for the relevant conduct. As a plurality of the Court noted in *Roy*, a distinctive feature of unemployment compensation programs is that their eligibility criteria invite consideration of the particular circumstances behind an applicant's unemployment. Whether or not the decisions are that limited, they at least have nothing to do with an across-the-board criminal prohibition on a particular form of conduct.

The government's ability to enforce generally applicable prohibitions of socially harmful conduct, like its ability to carry out other aspects of public policy, "cannot depend on measuring the effects of a governmental action on a religious objector's spiritual development." To make an individual's obligation to obey such a law contingent upon the law's coincidence with his religious beliefs, except where the State's interest is "compelling" — permitting him, by virtue of his beliefs, "to become a law unto himself" — contradicts both constitutional tradition and common sense.

The "compelling government interest" requirement seems benign, because it is familiar from other fields. But using it as the standard that must be met before the government may accord different treatment on the basis of race, or before the government may regulate the content of speech, is not remotely comparable to using it for the purpose asserted here. What it produces in those other fields — equality of treatment and an unrestricted flow of contending speech — are constitutional norms; what it would produce here — a private right to ignore generally applicable laws — is a constitutional anomaly.

Nor is it possible to limit the impact of respondents' proposal by requiring a "compelling state interest" only when the conduct prohibited is "central" to the individual's religion. It is no more appropriate for judges to determine the "centrality" of religious beliefs before applying a "compelling interest" test in the free exercise field, than it would be for them to determine the "importance" of ideas before applying the "compelling interest" test in the free speech field. What principle of law or logic can be brought to bear to contradict a believer's assertion that a particular act is "central" to his personal faith? Judging the centrality of different religious practices is akin to the unacceptable "business of evaluating the relative merits of differing religious claims."

If the "compelling interest" test is to be applied at all, then, it must be applied across the board, to all actions thought to be religiously commanded. Moreover, if "compelling interest" really means what it says (and watering it down here would subvert its rigor in the other fields where it is applied), many laws will not meet the test. Any society adopting such a system would be courting anarchy, but that danger increases in direct proportion to the society's diversity of religious beliefs, and its determination to coerce or suppress none of them. Precisely because "we are a cosmopolitan nation made up of people of almost every conceivable religious preference," and precisely because we value and protect that religious divergence, we cannot afford the luxury of deeming presumptively invalid, as applied to the religious objector, every regulation of conduct that does not protect an interest of the highest order. The rule respondents favor would open the prospect of constitutionally required religious exemptions from civic obligations of almost every conceivable kind — ranging from compulsory military service to the payment of taxes, to health and safety regulation such as manslaughter and child neglect laws, compulsory vaccination laws, drug laws, and traffic laws, to social welfare legislation such as minimum wage laws, child labor laws, animal cruelty laws, environmental protection laws, and laws providing for equality of opportunity for the races. The First Amendment's protection of religious liberty does not require this.

Values that are protected against government interference through enshrinement in the Bill of Rights are not thereby banished from the political process. Just as a society that believes in the negative protection accorded to the press by the First Amendment is likely to enact laws that affirmatively foster the dissemination of the printed word, so also a society that believes in the negative protection accorded to religious belief can be expected to be solicitous of that value in its legislation as well. It is therefore not surprising that a number of States have made an exception to their drug laws for sacramental peyote use.

But to say that a nondiscriminatory religious-practice exemption is permitted, or even that it is desirable, is not to say that it is constitutionally required, and that the appropriate occasions for its creation can be discerned by the courts. It may fairly be said that leaving accommodation to the political process will place at a relative disadvantage those religious practices that are not widely engaged in; but that unavoidable consequence of democratic government must be preferred to a system in which each conscience is a law unto itself or in which judges weigh the social importance of all laws against the centrality of all religious beliefs.

Because respondents' ingestion of peyote was prohibited under Oregon law, and because that prohibition is constitutional, Oregon may, consistent with the Free Exercise Clause, deny respondents unemployment compensation when their dismissal results from use of the drug.

Justice O'Connor, with whom Justice Brennan, Justice Marshall, and Justice Blackmun join as to Parts I and II, concurring in the judgment.

Although I agree with the result the Court reaches in this case, I cannot join its opinion. In my view, today's holding dramatically departs from well-settled First Amendment jurisprudence, appears unnecessary to resolve the question presented, and is incompatible with our Nation's fundamental commitment to individual religious liberty.

I

At the outset, I note that I agree with the Court's implicit determination that the constitutional question upon which we granted review—whether the Free Exercise Clause protects a person's religiously motivated use of peyote from the reach of a State's general criminal law prohibition—is properly presented in this case. As the Court recounts, respondents Alfred Smith and Galen Black (hereinafter respondents) were denied unemployment compensation benefits because their sacramental use of peyote constituted work-related "misconduct," not because they violated Oregon's general criminal prohibition against possession of peyote.

II

The Court today extracts from our long history of free exercise precedents the single categorical rule that "if prohibiting the exercise of religion . . . is . . . merely the incidental effect of a generally applicable and otherwise valid provision, the First Amendment has not been offended." Indeed, the Court holds that where the law is a generally applicable criminal prohibition, our usual free exercise jurisprudence does not even apply. To reach this sweeping result, however, the Court must not only give a strained reading of the First Amendment but must also disregard our consistent application of free exercise doctrine to cases involving generally applicable regulations that burden religious conduct.

The Court today interprets the Clause to permit the government to prohibit, without justification, conduct mandated by an individual's religious beliefs, so long as that prohibition is generally applicable. But a law that prohibits certain conduct—conduct that happens to be an act of worship for someone—manifestly does prohibit that person's free exercise of his religion. A person who is barred from engaging in religiously motivated conduct is barred from freely exercising his religion. Moreover, that person is barred from freely exercising his religion regardless of whether the law prohibits the conduct only when engaged in for religious reasons, only by members of that religion, or by all persons. It is difficult to deny that a law that prohibits religiously motivated conduct, even if the law is generally applicable, does not at least implicate First Amendment concerns.

The Court responds that generally applicable laws are "one large step" removed from laws aimed at specific religious practices. The First Amendment, however, does not distinguish between laws that are generally applicable and laws that target particular religious practices. Indeed, few States would be so naïve as to enact a law directly prohibiting or burdening a religious practice as such. Our free exercise cases have all concerned generally applicable laws that had the effect of significantly burdening a religious practice. If the First Amendment is to have any vitality, it ought not be construed to cover only the extreme and hypothetical situation in which a State directly targets a religious practice. As we have noted in a slightly different context, "[s]uch a test has no basis in precedent and relegates a serious First Amendment value to the barest level of minimum scrutiny that the Equal Protection Clause already provides."

To say that a person's right to free excise has been burdened, of course, does not mean that he has an absolute right to engage in the conduct. Under our established First Amendment jurisprudence, we have recognized that the freedom to act, unlike the freedom to believe, cannot be absolute. Instead, we have respected both the First Amendment's express textual mandate and the governmental interest in regulation of conduct by requiring the government to justify any substantial burden on religiously motivated conduct by a compelling state interest and by means narrowly tailored to achieve that interest.

The compelling interest test effectuates the First Amendment's command that religious liberty is an independent liberty, that it occupies a preferred position, and that the Court will not permit encroachments upon this liberty, whether direct or indirect, unless required by clear and compelling governmental interests "of the highest order." "Only an especially important governmental interest pursued by narrowly tailored means can justify exacting a sacrifice of First Amendments freedoms as the price for an equal share of the rights, benefits, and privileges enjoyed by other citizens."

The Court attempts to support its narrow reading of the Clause by claiming that "[w]e have never held that an individual's religious beliefs excuse him from compliance with an otherwise valid law prohibiting conduct that the State is free to regulate." But as the Court later notes, as it must, in cases such as *Cantwell* and *Yoder* we have in fact interpreted the Free Exercise Clause to forbid application of a generally applicable prohibition to religiously motivated conduct.

Moreover, in each of the other cases cited by the Court to support its categorical rule, we rejected the particular constitutional claims before us only after carefully weighing the competing interests. That we rejected the free exercise claims in those cases hardly calls into question the applicability of First Amendment doctrine in the first place. Indeed, it is surely unusual to judge the vitality of a constitutional doctrine by looking to the win-loss record of the plaintiffs who happen to come before us.

In my view, however, the essence of a free exercise claim is relief from a burden imposed by government on religious practices or beliefs, whether the burden is imposed directly through laws that prohibit or compel specific religious practices, or indirectly through laws that, in effect, make abandonment of one's own religion or conformity to the religious beliefs of others the price of an equal place in the civil community.

Once it has been shown that a government regulation or criminal prohibition burdens the free exercise of religion, we have consistently asked the government to demonstrate that unbending application of its regulation to the religious objector "is essential to accomplish an overriding governmental interest," or represents "the least restrictive means of achieving some compelling state interest."

To me, the sounder approach — the approach more consistent with our role as judges to decide each case on its individual merits — is to apply this test in each case to determine whether the burden on the specific plaintiffs before us is constitutionally significant and whether the particular criminal interest asserted by the State before us is compelling. Even if, as an empirical matter, a government's criminal laws might usually serve a compelling interest in health, safety, or public order, the First Amendment at least requires a case-by-case determination of the question, sensitive to the facts of each particular claim. Given the range of conduct that a State might legitimately make criminal, we cannot assume, merely because a law carries criminal sanctions and is generally applicable, that the First Amendment never requires the State to grant a limited exemption for religiously motivated conduct.

The Court today gives no convincing reason to depart from settled First Amendment jurisprudence. There is nothing talismanic about neutral law of general applicability or general criminal prohibitions, for laws neutral toward religion can coerce a person to violate his religious conscience or intrude upon his religious duties just as effectively as laws aimed at religion. Although the Court suggests that the compelling interest test, as applied to generally applicable laws, would result in a "constitutional anomaly," the First Amendment unequivocally makes freedom of religion, like freedom from race discrimination and freedom of speech a "constitutional nor[m]," not an "anomaly." Nor would application of our established free exercise doctrine to this case necessarily be incompatible with our equal protection cases. As the language of the Clauses itself makes clear, an individual's free exercise of religion is a preferred constitutional activity. A law that makes criminal such an activity therefore triggers constitutional concern — and heightened judicial scrutiny — even if it does not target the particular religious conduct at issue. Our free speech cases similarly recognize that neutral regulations that affect free speech values are subject to a balancing, rather than categorical, approach. The Court's parade of horribles not only fails as a reason for discarding the compelling interest test, it instead demonstrates just the opposite: that courts have been quite capable of applying our free exercise jurisprudence to strike sensible balances between religious liberty and competing state interests.

Finally, the Court today suggests that the disfavoring of minority religions is an "unavoidable consequence" under our system of government and that accommodation of such religions must be left to the political process. In my view, however, the First Amendment was enacted precisely to protect the rights of those whose religious practices are not shared by the majority and may be viewed with hostility. The history of our free exercise doctrine amply demonstrates the harsh impact majoritarian rule has had on unpopular or emerging religious groups such as the Jehovah's Witnesses and the Amish. Indeed, the words of Justice Jackson in West Virginia State Bd. of Ed. v. Barnette (1940) are apt:

> The very purpose of a Bill of Rights was to withdraw certain subjects from the vicissitudes of political controversy, to place them beyond the reach of majorities and officials and to establish them as legal principles to be applied by the courts. One's right to life, liberty, and property, to free speech, a free press, freedom of worship and assembly, and other fundamental rights may not be submitted to vote; they depend on the outcome of no elections.

The compelling interest test reflects the First Amendment's mandate of preserving religious liberty to the fullest extent possible in a pluralistic society. For the Court to deem this command a "luxury[]," is to denigrate "[t]he very purpose of a Bill of Rights."

III

The Court's holding today not only misreads settled First Amendment precedent; it appears to be unnecessary to this case. I would reach the same result applying our established free exercise jurisprudence. There is no dispute that Oregon's criminal prohibition of peyote places a severe burden on the ability of respondents to freely exercise their religion. Peyote is a sacrament of the Native American Church and is regarded as vital to respondents' ability to practice their religion. There is also no dispute that Oregon has a significant interest in enforcing laws that control the possession and use of controlled substances by its citizens. As we recently noted, drug abuse is "one of the greatest problems affecting the health and welfare of our population" and thus "one of the most serious problems confronting our society today." Oregon has a compelling interest in prohibiting the possession of peyote by its citizens. Although the question is close, I would conclude that uniform application of Oregon's criminal prohibition is "essential to accomplish[]," its overriding interest in preventing the physical harm caused by the use of a Schedule I controlled substance. Oregon's criminal prohibition represents that State's judgment that the possession and use of controlled substances, even by only one person, is inherently harmful and dangerous. Because the health effects caused by the use of controlled substances exist regardless of the motivation of the user, the use of such substances, even for religious purposes, violates the very purpose of the laws that prohibit them. Moreover, in view of the societal interest in preventing trafficking in controlled substances, uniform application of the criminal prohibition at issue is essential to the effectiveness of Oregon's stated interest in preventing any possession of peyote.

For these reasons, I believe that granting a selective exemption in this case would seriously impair Oregon's compelling interest in prohibiting possession of peyote by its citizens. Under such circumstances, the Free Exercise Clause does not require the State to accommodate respondents' religiously motivated conduct. I would therefore adhere to our established free exercise jurisprudence and hold that the State in this case has a compelling interest in regulating peyote use by its citizens and that accommodating respondents' religiously motivated conduct "will unduly interfere with fulfillment of the government interest."

Justice BLACKMUN, with whom Justice BRENNAN and Justice MARSHALL join, dissenting.

This Court over the years painstakingly has developed a consistent and exacting standard to test the constitutionality of a state statute that burdens the free exercise of religion. Such a statute may stand only if the law in general, and the State's refusal to allow a religious exemption in particular, are justified by a compelling interest that cannot be served by less restrictive means. Until today, I thought this was a settled and inviolate principle of this Court's First Amendment jurisprudence. The majority, however, perfunctorily dismisses it as a "constitutional anomaly."

In short, it effectuates a wholesale overturning of settled law concerning the Religion Clauses of our Constitution. One hopes that the Court is aware of the consequences, and that its result is not a product of overreaction to the serious problems the country's drug crisis has generated. This distorted view of our precedents leads the majority to conclude that strict scrutiny of a state law burdening the free exercise of religion is a "luxury" that a well-ordered society cannot afford, and that the repression of minority religions is an "unavoidable consequence of democratic government." I do not believe the Founders thought their dearly bought freedom from religious persecution a "luxury," but an essential element of liberty — and they could not have thought religious intolerance "unavoidable," for they drafted the Religion Clauses precisely in order to avoid that intolerance.

The State proclaims an interest in protecting the health and safety of its citizens from the dangers of unlawful drugs. It offers, however, no evidence that the religious use of peyote has ever harmed anyone. The carefully circumscribed ritual context in which respondents used peyote is far removed from the irresponsible and unrestricted recreational use of unlawful drugs. The Native American Church's internal restrictions on, and supervision of, its members' use of peyote substantially obviate the State's health and safety concerns.

For these reasons, I conclude that Oregon's interest in enforcing its drug laws against religious use of peyote is not sufficiently compelling to outweigh respondents' right to the free exercise of their religion. The State could not constitutionally enforce its criminal prohibition against respondents, the interests underlying the State's drug laws cannot justify its denial of unemployment benefits.

THE LAW BEFORE EMPLOYMENT DIVISION v. SMITH

The majority and the dissent in *Smith* obviously disagree as to the proper characterization of the law before *Smith.* Understanding *Smith* and assessing its impact require consideration of the law of the Free Exercise Clause before 1990. After this review, post-*Smith* developments are reviewed.

The Supreme Court's earliest treatment of free exercise of religion was in Reynolds v. United States, 98 U.S. (8 Otto) 145 (1878). A federal law prohibited polygamy in the territories and a defendant argued that his Mormon religion required that he have multiple wives. The Supreme Court rejected the Free Exercise Clause argument and the claim that the constitutional provision required an exemption from otherwise valid criminal laws. Chief Justice Waite wrote, "[A]s a law of the organization of society under the exclusive dominion of the United States, it is provided that plural marriages shall not be allowed. Can a man excuse his practices to the contrary because of his religious belief? To permit this would be to make the professed doctrines of religious belief superior to the law of the land, and in effect to permit every citizen to become a law unto himself. Government could exist only in name under such circumstances."

The Court thus drew a distinction between beliefs and action; the Free Exercise Clause limited government regulation of the former, but not the latter. Chief Justice Waite said, "Congress was deprived of all legislative power over mere opinion, but was left free to reach actions which were in violation of social duties or subversive of good order."

The Supreme Court's initial explicit protection of free exercise of religion occurred in a series of cases that involved laws restricting religious groups from soliciting funds. For example, Cantwell v. Connecticut, 310 U.S. 296 (1940), overturned the convictions of several Jehovah's Witnesses who were convicted of soliciting money without a license. Although the Court recognized that freedom of religious conduct was not absolute, it said that "[i]n every case the power to regulate must be so exercised as not, in attaining a permissible end, unduly to infringe the protected freedom." The Court said that a licensing system for religious solicitations violated both the Free Exercise and Free Speech Clauses of the First Amendment.

In Sherbert v. Verner, the Supreme Court expressly held that strict scrutiny was the appropriate test in evaluating government laws burdening religious freedom. *Sherbert* is discussed by both the majority and the dissent in *Smith*; the majority distinguishes it so that despite *Smith*'s narrowing of the Free Exercise Clause, *Sherbert* remains good law.

SHERBERT v. VERNER

374 U.S. 398 (1963)

Justice BRENNAN delivered the opinion of the Court.

Appellant, a member of the Seventh-day Adventist Church was discharged by her South Carolina employer because she would not work on Saturday, the Sabbath Day of her faith. When she was unable to obtain other employment because from conscientious scruples she would not take Saturday work, she filed a claim for unemployment compensation benefits under the South Carolina Unemployment Compensation Act. The appellee Employment Security Commission, in administrative proceedings under the statute, found that appellant's restriction upon her availability for Saturday work brought her within the provision disqualifying for benefits insured workers who fail, without good cause, to accept "suitable work when offered . . . by the employment office or the employer. . . . "

I

The door of the Free Exercise Clause stands tightly closed against any governmental regulation of religious beliefs. As such Government may neither compel affirmation of a repugnant belief, nor penalize or discriminate against individuals or groups because they hold religious views abhorrent to the authorities, nor employ the taxing power to inhibit the dissemination of particular religious views. On the other hand, the Court has rejected challenges under the Free Exercise Clause to governmental regulation of certain overt acts promoted by religious beliefs or principles, for "even when the action is in accord with one's religious convictions, [it] is not totally free from legislative restrictions." The conduct or actions so regulated have invariably posed some substantial threat to public safety, peace or order.

Plainly enough, appellant's conscientious objection to Saturday work constitutes no conduct prompted by religious principles of a kind within the reach of state legislation. If, therefore, the decision of the South Carolina Supreme Court is to withstand appellant's constitutional challenge, it must be either because her disqualification as a beneficiary represents no infringement by the State of her constitutional rights of free exercise, or because any incidental burden on the free exercise of appellant's religion may be justified by a "compelling state interest in the regulation of a subject within the State's constitutional power to regulate."

II

We turn first to the question whether the disqualification for benefits imposes any burden on the free exercise of appellant's religion. We think it is clear that it does. In a sense the consequences of such a disqualification to religious principles and practices may be only an indirect result of welfare legislation within the State's general competence to enact; it is true that no criminal sanctions directly compel appellant to work a six-day week. But this is only the beginning, not the end, of our inquiry.

Here not only is it apparent that appellant's declared ineligibility for benefits derives solely from the practice of her religion, but the pressure upon her to forego that practice is unmistakable. The ruling forces her to choose between following the precepts of her religion and forfeiting benefits, on the one hand, and abandoning one of the precepts of her religion in order to accept work, on the other hand. Governmental imposition of such a choice puts the same kind of burden upon the free exercise of religion as would a fine imposed against appellant for her Saturday worship.

We must next consider whether some compelling state interest enforced in the eligibility provisions of the South Carolina statute justifies the substantial infringement of appellant's First Amendment right. It is basic that no showing merely of a rational relationship to some colorable state interest would suffice; in this highly sensitive constitutional area, even if the possibility of spurious claims did threaten to dilute the fund and disrupt the scheduling of work, it would plainly be incumbent upon the appellees to demonstrate that no alternative forms of regulation would combat such abuses without infringing First Amendment rights.

Justice HARLAN, whom Justice WHITE joins, dissenting.

Today's decision is disturbing both in its rejection of existing precedent and in its implications for the future. What the Court is holding is that if the State chooses to condition unemployment compensation on the applicant's availability for work, it is constitutionally compelled to carve out an exception — and to provide benefits — for those whose unavailability is due to their religious convictions.

[T]he implications of the present decision are far more troublesome than its apparently narrow dimensions would indicate at first glance. The meaning of today's holding, as already noted, it that the State must furnish unemployment benefits to one who is unavailable for work if the unavailability stems from the exercise of religious convictions. The State, in other words, must single out for financial assistance those whose identical behavior (in this case, inability to work on Saturdays) is not religiously motivated.

It has been suggested that such singling out of religious conduct for special treatment may violate the constitutional limitations on state action. I cannot subscribe to the conclusion that the State is constitutionally compelled to carve out an exception to its general rule of eligibility in the present case. Those situations in which the Constitution may require special treatment on account of religion are, in my view, few and far between, and this view is amply supported by the course of constitutional litigation in this area. Such compulsion in the present case is particularly inappropriate in light of the indirect, remote, and insubstantial effect of the decision below on the exercise of appellant's religion and in light of the direct financial assistance to religion that today's decision requires.

Although *Sherbert* clearly stated that strict scrutiny was to be used in evaluating laws infringing free exercise of religion, following *Sherbert* the Court rarely struck down laws on this basis. In fact, there were only two areas where the Court invalidated laws for violating free exercise: laws, like the statute in *Sherbert*, that denied benefits to those who quit their jobs for religious reasons; and the application of a compulsory school law to the Amish. In all other Free Exercise Clause cases between 1960 and 1990, the Court upheld the laws.

a.   Government Benefit Cases

In several later cases, the Court reaffirmed its holding in Sherbert v. Verner that the government could not deny benefits to individuals who left their jobs because of religious reasons. For example, in Thomas v. Review Board, 450 U.S. 707 (1981), the Court held that the government could not deny unemployment benefits to an individual who quit his job rather than accept a transfer to work in the armaments section of a factory. The individual said that he was quitting for religious reasons, and the Court said it accepted this explanation even though others of his faith saw no problem in working in that part of the factory. The Court said that it was not for the judiciary to evaluate the proper content of religious doctrines and said it was "clear that Thomas terminated his employment for religious reasons."[22]

---

22. *Thomas*, 450 U.S. at 716.

In Hobbie v. Unemployment Appeals Commission of Florida, 480 U.S. 136 (1987), the Court applied *Sherbert* and *Thomas* and held that the state was required to provide unemployment benefits to a woman who was fired when she refused to work on her Saturday Sabbath. Similarly, in Frazee v. Illinois Department of Income Security, 489 U.S. 829 (1989), the Court found that a state law that required unemployed individuals to be available for work seven days a week infringed free exercise when it was applied to deny benefits to an individual who refused to work on his Sunday Sabbath. The Court said it was immaterial that the individual was not a member of an organized church, sect, or denomination. His sincere religious belief was impermissibly burdened by the denial of benefits.

b. Compulsory Schooling

The only other case where the Court found a violation of the Free Exercise Clause during this time was in Wisconsin v. Yoder, 406 U.S. 205 (1972), where the Court held that free exercise of religion required that Amish parents be granted an exemption from compulsory school laws for their 14- and 15-year-old children. The Court noted that the "Amish objection to formal education beyond the eighth grade is firmly grounded in these central religious concepts. They object to the high school, and higher education generally, because the values they teach are in marked variance with Amish values and the Amish way of life; they view secondary school education as an impermissible exposure of their children to a 'worldly' influence in conflict with their beliefs." The Court said that "[a] regulation neutral on its face may, in its application, nonetheless offend the constitutional requirement for governmental neutrality if it unduly burdens the free exercise of religion."

The Court accepted this argument and found that requiring 14- and 15-year-old Amish children to attend school violated the Free Exercise Clause and also infringed the right of parents to control the upbringing of their children. Chief Justice Burger, writing for the Court, said that "the record in this case abundantly supports the claim that the traditional way of life of the Amish is not merely a matter of personal preference, but one of deep religious conviction, shared by an organized group, and intimately related to daily living." The Court concluded that "[t]he impact of the compulsory-attendance law on respondents' practice of the Amish religion is not only severe, but inescapable, for the Wisconsin law affirmatively compels them, under threat of criminal sanction, to perform acts undeniably at odds with . . . their religious beliefs. . . . [E]nforcement of the State's requirement of compulsory formal education after the eighth grade would gravely endanger if not destroy the free exercise of respondents' religious beliefs."

The Court concluded that the "self-sufficient" nature of Amish society made education for 14- and 15-year-old children unnecessary. The Court said that the lack of "two additional years of compulsory education will not impair the physical or mental health of the child, or result in an inability to be self-supporting or to discharge the duties and responsibilities of citizenship, or in any other way materially detract from the welfare of society." In *Smith*, the Court distinguished *Yoder* as involving "hybrid" rights, specifically the right of parents to control the upbringing of their children.

c.   Cases Rejecting Exemptions Based on the Free Exercise Clause

Other than the employment compensation cases and *Yoder*, the Court during this period found no other law to violate the Free Exercise Clause. The Court was asked in many cases to allow an exemption to a law based on free exercise.[23] In each the Court rejected the constitutional claim.

The cases rejecting free exercise challenges occurred in a wide variety of contexts. For example, two years before *Sherbert*, in Braunfeld v. Brown, 366 U.S. 599 (1961), the Supreme Court rejected a Free Exercise Clause challenge to Sunday closing laws. Orthodox Jews argued that their religion required that their businesses be closed on Saturdays and that it was difficult for them to adhere to their religion if they also had to be closed Sundays. Chief Justice Warren, writing for the plurality, rejected this argument and said, "[T]he statute before us does not make criminal the holding of any religious belief or opinion, nor does it force anyone to embrace any religious belief. . . . To strike down legislation which imposes only an indirect burden on the exercise of religion would radically restrict the operating latitude of the legislature." The Court accepted the state's argument that Sunday closing laws served the important government interest of providing a uniform day of rest.

In many cases during this time period, the Court rejected challenges to tax laws based on free exercise of religion. In United States v. Lee, 455 U.S. 252 (1982), the Court rejected a claim by an Amish individual that the requirement for paying Social Security taxes violated the Free Exercise Clause. The argument was that "the Amish believe it sinful not to provide for their own elderly and therefore are religiously opposed to the national social security system." The Court found, however, that this restriction on religious freedom was "essential to accomplish an overriding governmental interest." The Court concluded that mandatory participation in the Social Security system was "indispensable to [its] fiscal vitality."

In Bob Jones University v. United States, 461 U.S. 574 (1983), where the Court held that the denial of tax exempt status to private schools that racially discriminated because of sincere religious beliefs did not violate the Free Exercise Clause. The Court, in an opinion by Chief Justice Burger, explained, "[T]he Government has a fundamental, overriding interest in eradicating racial discrimination in education [which] substantially outweighs whatever burden denial of tax benefits places on petitioners' exercise of their religious beliefs." The Court found that eliminating discrimination was a compelling government interest and that "no less restrictive means are available to achieve the government interest."

In Bowen v. Roy, 476 U.S. 693 (1986), the Court rejected the claim for a religious exemption to the requirement that individuals provide Social Security numbers in order to receive welfare benefits. Individuals argued that their religion was violated by the requirement for Social Security numbers. The Court denied this claim and declared, "Never to our knowledge has the Court

---

23. There is rich scholarly literature reviewing the framers' intent behind the Free Exercise Clause and debating the extent to which it was meant to be a basis for exemptions from laws. *See, e.g.*, Michael W. McConnell, *The Origins and Historical Understanding of Free Exercise of Religion*, 103 Harv. L. Rev. 1409 (1990); Ira C. Lupu, *Where Rights Begin: The Problem of Burdens on the Free Exercise of Religion*, 102 Harv. L. Rev. 933 (1989).

interpreted the First Amendment to require the Government *itself* to behave in ways that the individual believes will further his or her spiritual development. . . . [The] Free Exercise Clause affords an individual protection from certain forms of governmental compulsion; it does not afford an individual a right to dictate the conduct of the Government's internal procedures."

The Court rejected a free exercise challenge to the military in Goldman v. Weinberger, 475 U.S. 503 (1986), where the Court, by a five-to-four margin, denied the claim of an Orthodox Jewish doctor in the Air Force who said that his religion required that he wear a yarmulke in violation of the dress code. Simcha Goldman, a clinical psychologist in the Air Force, was an Orthodox Jew and an ordained rabbi. He was ordered not to wear his yarmulke on duty because it was inconsistent with the Air Force dress code.

The Court proclaimed the need for deference to the military and said that "[o]ur review of military regulations challenged on First Amendment grounds is far more deferential than constitutional review of similar laws or regulations designed for civilian society." The Court said that "to accomplish its mission the military must foster instinctive obedience, unity, commitment and espirit de corps. The essence of military service is the subordination of the desires and interests of the individual to the needs of the service." The Court concluded that it accepted the "considered professional judgment of the Air Force . . . that the traditional outfitting of personnel in standardized uniforms encourages the subordination of personal preferences and identities in favor of the overall group mission." Justice Rehnquist, writing for the Court, concluded that the "First Amendment does not require the military to accommodate such practices in the face of its view that they would detract from the uniformity sought by the dress regulations."

In these cases, the Courts refused to uphold free exercise challenges to specific laws. In Lyng v. Northwest Indian Cemetery Protective Association, 485 U.S. 439 (1988), the Court made this even more explicit and rejected a Free Exercise Clause challenge to the federal government's building a road and allowing timber harvesting in a national forest that contained sacred Indian burial grounds. The Court recognized that the construction would "virtually . . . destroy the Indians' ability to practice their religion" because it would irreparably damage "sacred areas which are an integral and necessary part of their belief systems." Nonetheless, the Court said that "[t]he Free Exercise Clause simply cannot be understood to require the Government to conduct its own internal affairs in ways that comport with the religious beliefs of particular citizens. . . . [The] Free Exercise Clause affords an individual protection from certain forms of government compulsion; it does not afford an individual a right to dictate the conduct of the Government's internal procedures."

Twice since *Smith* has the Supreme Court found a violation of the Free Exercise Clause. In Church of the Lukumi Babalu Aye, Inc. v. Hialeah, 508 U.S. 520 (1993), the Court struck down a law that prohibited ritual sacrifice of animals on the ground that it was not a neutral law of general applicability. The Santeria religion uses animal sacrifice as one of its principal forms of worship. Animals are killed and then cooked and eaten in accord with Santeria rituals. After practitioners of Santeria announced plans to establish a house of worship, a school, a cultural center, and a museum in Hialeah, Florida, the city adopted an ordinance prohibiting ritual sacrifice of animals. The law defined "sacrifice" as killing animals "not for the primary purpose of food consumption." The law applied only to an individual or group that "kills, slaughters, or sacrifices animals for any type of ritual, regardless of whether or not the flesh or blood of the animal is to be consumed."

All of the justices agreed the law was unconstitutional, with Justice Kennedy writing the opinion for the Court. At the outset, Justice Kennedy reaffirmed the *Smith* test and declared that "our cases establish the general proposition that a law that is neutral and of general applicability need not be justified by a compelling governmental interest even if the law has the incidental effect of burdening a particular religious practice." Kennedy said, however, that "[a] law failing to satisfy these requirements must be justified by a compelling interest and must be narrowly tailored to advance that interest."

The Court decided that the Hialeah law was not neutral because its clear object was to prohibit a religious practice. Justice Kennedy's majority opinion noted that the text of the law spoke of "sacrifice" and "ritual" and that its purpose was clearly to prohibit the practice of the Santeria religion. The Court also focused on the exceptions to the law that allowed killing of animals by other religions, such as in kosher slaughtering of animals, and that allowed killing of animals for nonreligious purposes. The Court said that this further indicated the lack of neutrality of the law. The Court concluded that "the neutrality inquiry leads to one conclusion: The ordinances had as their object the suppression of religion."

The Court also said that the law was not one of "general applicability." The Court again noted that "[d]espite the city's proffered interest in preventing cruelty to animals, the ordinances are drafted with care to forbid few killings but those occasioned by religious sacrifice. Many types of animal deaths or kills are either not prohibited or approved by express provision."

Because it concluded that the ordinance was neither neutral nor of general applicability, the Court applied strict scrutiny. The Court found the law unconstitutional because the government could achieve the goals of safe and sanitary disposal of animal remains without targeting the Santeria religion.

Justice Scalia, in an opinion concurring in part and concurring in the judgment and joined by Chief Justice Rehnquist, wrote separately to argue that the purpose behind a law should not be relevant in determining whether it is neutral and of general applicability. Justice Souter also wrote an opinion concurring in part and concurring in the judgment. He argued that the Court should reconsider and overrule *Smith.* Justice Blackmun concurred in the judgment, in an opinion joined by Justice O'Connor, and "emphasize[d] that the First Amendment's protection of religion extends beyond those rare occasions on which the government explicitly targets religion (or a particular religion) for disfavored treatment."

The other and more recent instance in which the Court found a violation of the Establishment Clause was Hosanna-Tabor Evangelical Lutheran Church and School v. EEOC, 132 S. Ct. 694 (2012). The Court held that it would violate the Free Exercise Clause, as well as the Establishment Clause, to hold a religious institution liable under an antidiscrimination law for the choices it makes as to who will be its ministers. The case involved a teacher at a religious elementary school who was fired for insubordination when the school thought she might sue them under the Americans with Disability Act after she lost her job when she developed a serious illness.

The Court found that holding the religious institution liable for choices it makes as to who will be its ministers infringes the Free Exercise Clause. Chief Justice Roberts, writing for a unanimous Court, distinguished Employment Division v. Smith:

> By imposing an unwanted minister, the state infringes the Free Exercise Clause, which protects a religious group's right to shape its own faith and mission through its appointments.
>
> The [Equal Employment Opportunity Commission and the teacher] also contend that our decision in Employment Div., Dept. of Human Resources of Ore. v. Smith (1990), precludes recognition of a ministerial exception. It is true that the ADA's prohibition on retaliation, like Oregon's prohibition on peyote use, is a valid and neutral law of general applicability. But a church's selection of its ministers is unlike an individual's ingestion of peyote. *Smith* involved government regulation of only outward physical acts. The present case, in contrast, concerns government interference with an internal church decision that affects the faith and mission of the church itself. The contention that *Smith* forecloses recognition of a ministerial exception rooted in the Religion Clauses has no merit.

STATUTORY PROTECTION OF RELIGIOUS FREEDOM

The Religious Freedom Restoration Act (RFRA) of 1993, 42 U.S.C. §2000bb, was adopted to negate the *Smith* test and require strict scrutiny for Free Exercise Clause claims. The act declares that its purpose is "to restore the compelling interest test as set forth in Sherbert v. Verner and Wisconsin v. Yoder, and to guarantee its application in all cases where free exercise of religion is substantially burdened; and to provide a claim or defense to persons whose religious exercise is substantially burdened by government." In City of Boerne v. Flores, 521 U.S. 507 (1997), the Supreme Court declared the law unconstitutional as applied to state and local governments. Boerne, which is presented in Chapter 2, held that Congress lacked the authority under §5 of the Fourteenth Amendment to expand the scope of rights and that RFRA was thus unconstitutional as applied to state and local governments.

The Supreme Court has never expressly upheld the constitutionality of RFRA as applied to the federal government. However, in Gonzales v. O Centro Espirita Beneficente Unia Do, 546 U.S. 418 (2006), the Supreme Court applied the Religious Freedom Restoration Act to the federal government. Although the Court did not expressly address the issue of whether the statute is constitutional as applied to the federal government, the Court did use the act to rule in favor of a religion and against the federal government. The case involved a small religion, with relatively few adherents in the United States, whose members receive communion by drinking hoasca, a tea brewed from plants unique to the Amazon rainforest that contains a hallucinogen regulated under Schedule I of the Controlled Substances Act. Members of the religion brought a suit seeking a declaratory judgment that their use of the tea was protected by the Religious Freedom Restoration Act.

Chief Justice Roberts wrote for a unanimous Court and ruled in favor of the religion. In response to the government's claim of a need to stop the availability of hallucinogenic drugs, the Court stated, "RFRA requires the Government to demonstrate that the compelling interest test is satisfied through application of the challenged law 'to the person'—the particular claimant whose sincere exercise of religion is being substantially burdened. RFRA expressly adopted the compelling interest test 'as set forth in Sherbert v. Verner (1963) and Wisconsin v. Yoder (1972).' In each of those cases, this Court looked beyond broadly formulated interests justifying the general applicability of government mandates and scrutinized the asserted harm of granting specific exemptions to particular religious claimants."

Applying this test, the Court concluded, "Under the more focused inquiry required by RFRA and the compelling interest test, the Government's mere invocation of the general characteristics of Schedule I substances, as set forth in the Controlled Substances Act, cannot carry the day. It is true, of course, that Schedule I substances are exceptionally dangerous. Nevertheless, there is no indication that Congress considered the harms posed by the particular use at issue here — the circumscribed, sacramental use of hoasca by [this religion]."

The case indicates that RFRA is applicable to the federal government and that the Court approves a rigorous application of strict scrutiny under the statute.

After RFRA was declared unconstitutional as applied to state and local governments, Congress enacted the Religious Land Use and Institutionalized Persons Act (RLUIPA), 42 U.S.C. §2001cc-1, which says the government land use decisions and treatment of prisoners that significantly burden religion must meet strict scrutiny.

In Cutter v. Wilkinson, the Court considered whether this law violates the Establishment Clause.

CUTTER v. WILKINSON
544 U.S. 709 (2005)

Justice GINSBURG delivered the opinion of the Court.

Section 3 of the Religious Land Use and Institutionalized Persons Act of 2000 (RLUIPA) provides in part: "No government shall impose a substantial burden on the religious exercise of a person residing in or confined to an institution," unless the burden furthers "a compelling governmental interest," and does so by "the least restrictive means." Plaintiffs below, petitioners here, are current and former inmates of institutions operated by the Ohio Department of Rehabilitation and Correction and assert that they are adherents of "nonmainstream" religions: the Satanist, Wicca, and Asatru religions, and the Church of Jesus Christ Christian. They complain that Ohio prison officials (respondents here), in violation of RLUIPA, have failed to accommodate their religious exercise "in a variety of different ways, including retaliating and discriminating against them for exercising their nontraditional faiths, denying them access to religious literature, denying them the same opportunities for group worship that are granted to adherents of mainstream religions, forbidding them to adhere to the dress and appearance mandates of their religions, withholding religious ceremonial items that are substantially identical to those that the adherents of mainstream religions are permitted, and failing to provide a chaplain trained in their faith."

In response to petitioners' complaints, respondent prison officials have mounted a facial challenge to the institutionalized-persons provision of RLUIPA; respondents contend that the Act improperly advances religion in violation of the First Amendment's Establishment Clause.

"This Court has long recognized that the government may . . . accommodate religious practices . . . without violating the Establishment Clause." Just last Term, in Locke v. Davey (2004), the Court reaffirmed that "there is room for play in the joints between" the Free Exercise and Establishment Clauses, allowing the government to accommodate religion beyond free exercise requirements, without offense to the Establishment Clause. "At some point, accommodation may devolve into an unlawful fostering of religion." But §3 of RLUIPA, we hold, does not, on its face, exceed the limits of permissible government accommodation of religious practices.

Our decisions recognize that "there is room for play in the joints" between the Clauses, some space for legislative action neither compelled by the Free Exercise Clause nor prohibited by the Establishment Clause. In accord with the majority of Courts of Appeals that have ruled on the question, we hold that §3 of RLUIPA fits within the corridor between the Religion Clauses: On its face, the Act qualifies as a permissible legislative accommodation of religion that is not barred by the Establishment Clause.

Foremost, we find RLUIPA's institutionalized-persons provision compatible with the Establishment Clause because it alleviates exceptional government-created burdens on private religious exercise. Furthermore, the Act on its face does not founder on shoals our prior decisions have identified: Properly applying RLUIPA, courts must take adequate account of the burdens a requested accommodation may impose on nonbeneficiaries, and they must be satisfied that the Act's prescriptions are and will be administered neutrally among different faiths.

"[T]he 'exercise of religion' often involves not only belief and profession but the performance of . . . physical acts [such as] assembling with others for a worship service [or] participating in sacramental use of bread and wine. . . ." Section 3 covers state-run institutions—mental hospitals, prisons, and the like—in which the government exerts a degree of control unparalleled in civilian society and severely disabling to private religious exercise. RLUIPA thus protects institutionalized persons who are unable freely to attend to their religious needs and are therefore dependent on the government's permission and accommodation for exercise of their religion.

We do not read RLUIPA to elevate accommodation of religious observances over an institution's need to maintain order and safety. Our decisions indicate that an accommodation must be measured so that it does not override other significant interests. We have no cause to believe that RLUIPA would not be applied in an appropriately balanced way, with particular sensitivity to security concerns. While the Act adopts a "compelling governmental interest" standard, "[c]ontext matters" in the application of that standard. Lawmakers supporting RLUIPA were mindful of the urgency of discipline, order, safety, and security in penal institutions. They anticipated that courts would apply the Act's standard with "due deference to the experience and expertise of prison and jail administrators in establishing necessary regulations and procedures to maintain good order, security and discipline, consistent with consideration of costs and limited resources."

Finally, RLUIPA does not differentiate among bona fide faiths. RLUIPA presents no such defect. It confers no privileged status on any particular religious sect, and singles out no bona fide faith for disadvantageous treatment.

The Sixth Circuit misread our precedents to require invalidation of RLUIPA as "impermissibly advancing religion by giving greater protection to religious rights than to other constitutionally protected rights." Were the Court of Appeals' view the correct reading of our decisions, all manner of religious accommodations would fall. Congressional permission for members of the military to wear religious apparel while in uniform would fail, as would accommodations Ohio itself makes. Ohio could not, as it now does, accommodate "traditionally recognized" religions. The State provides inmates with chaplains "but not with publicists or political consultants," and allows "prisoners to assemble for worship, but not for political rallies."

In upholding RLUIPA's institutionalized-persons provision, we emphasize that respondents "have raised a facial challenge to [the Act's] constitutionality, and have not contended that under the facts of any of [petitioners'] specific cases . . . [that] applying RLUIPA would produce unconstitutional results." Should inmate requests for religious accommodations become excessive, impose unjustified burdens on other institutionalized persons, or jeopardize the effective functioning of an institution, the facility would be free to resist the imposition. In that event, adjudication in as-applied challenges would be in order.

3. Is Denial of Funding for Religious Education a Violation of Free Exercise of Religion?

The discussion below concerning the Establishment Clause shows that in recent years the Supreme Court has been more permissive in allowing government aid to religious education. Locke v. Davey, below, presents the question of whether the denial of funding for religious education violates free exercise of religion. The case involved a scholarship program for college students in Washington state. Students could not use the scholarships if they were pursuing "devotional" studies to be ordained a minister. The Supreme Court, in a seven-to-two decision, rejected the argument that the state's refusal to fund such religious education violated the Free Exercise Clause of the First Amendment.

LOCKE v. DAVEY

540 U.S. 714 (2004)

Chief Justice REHNQUIST delivered the opinion of the Court.

The State of Washington established the Promise Scholarship Program to assist academically gifted students with postsecondary education expenses. In accordance with the State Constitution, students may not use the scholarship at an institution where they are pursuing a degree in devotional theology. We hold that such an exclusion from an otherwise inclusive aid program does not violate the Free Exercise Clause of the First Amendment.

To be eligible for the scholarship, a student must meet academic, income, and enrollment requirements. The student must enroll "at least half time in an eligible postsecondary institution in the state of Washington," and may not pursue a degree in theology at that institution while receiving the scholarship.

Private institutions, including those religiously affiliated, qualify as "eligible postsecondary institution[s]" if they are accredited by a nationally recognized accrediting body. A "degree in theology" is not defined in the statute, but, as both parties concede, the statute simply codifies the State's constitutional prohibition on providing funds to students to pursue degrees that are "devotional in nature or designed to induce religious faith."

Respondent, Joshua Davey, was awarded a Promise Scholarship, and chose to attend Northwest College. Northwest is a private, Christian college affiliated with the Assemblies of God denomination, and is an eligible institution under the Promise Scholarship Program. Davey had "planned for many years to attend a Bible college and to prepare [himself] through that college training for a lifetime of ministry, specifically as a church pastor." To that end, when he enrolled in Northwest College, he decided to pursue a double major in pastoral ministries and business management/administration. There is no dispute that the pastoral ministries degree is devotional and therefore excluded under the Promise Scholarship Program.

At the beginning of the 1999-2000 academic year, Davey met with Northwest's director of financial aid. He learned for the first time at this meeting that he could not use his scholarship to pursue a devotional theology degree. He was informed that to receive the funds appropriated for his use, he must certify in writing that he was not pursuing such a degree at Northwest. He refused to sign the form and did not receive any scholarship funds.

The Religion Clauses of the First Amendment provide: "Congress shall make no law respecting an establishment of religion, or prohibiting the free exercise thereof." These two Clauses, the Establishment Clause and the Free Exercise Clause, are frequently in tension. Yet we have long said that "there is room for play in the joints" between them. Walz v. Tax Comm'n of City of New York (1970). In other words, there are some state actions permitted by the Establishment Clause but not required by the Free Exercise Clause.

This case involves that "play in the joints" described above. Under our Establishment Clause precedent, the link between government funds and religious training is broken by the independent and private choice of recipients. See Zelman v. Simmons-Harris (2002). As such, there is no doubt that the State could, consistent with the Federal Constitution, permit Promise Scholars to pursue a degree in devotional theology, and the State does not contend otherwise. The question before us, however, is whether Washington, pursuant to its own constitutions,[24] which has been authoritatively interpreted as prohibiting even indirectly funding religious instruction that will prepare students for the ministry, can deny them such funding without violating the Free Exercise Clause.

Even though the differently worded Washington Constitution draws a more stringent line than that drawn by the United States Constitution, the interest it seeks to further is scarcely novel. In fact, we can think of few areas in which a

---

24. The relevant provision of the Washington Constitution, Art. I, §11, states: "Religious Freedom, Absolute freedom of conscience in all matters of religious sentiment, belief and worship, shall be guaranteed to every individual, and no one shall be molested or disturbed in person or property on account of religion; but the liberty of conscience hereby secured shall not be so construed as to excuse acts of licentiousness or justify practices inconsistent with the peace and safety of the state. No public money or property shall be appropriated for or applied to any religious worship, exercise or instruction, or the support of any religious establishment." [Footnote by the Court.]

State's antiestablishment interests come more into play. Since the founding of our country, there have been popular uprisings against procuring taxpayer funds to support church leaders, which was one of the hallmarks of an "established" religion. Most States that sought to avoid an establishment of religion around the time of the founding placed in their constitutions formal prohibitions against using tax funds to support the ministry.[25]

Far from evincing the hostility toward religion which was manifest in *Lukumi*, we believe that the entirety of the Promise Scholarship Program goes a long way toward including religion in its benefits. The program permits students to attend pervasively religious schools, so long as they are accredited. And under the Promise Scholarship Program's current guidelines, students are still eligible to take devotional theology courses. Davey notes all students at Northwest are required to take at least four devotional courses, and some students may have additional religious requirements as part of their majors.

In short, we find neither in the history or text of Article I, §11 of the Washington Constitution, nor in the operation of the Promise Scholarship Program, anything that suggests animus towards religion. Given the historic and substantial state interest at issue, we therefore cannot conclude that the denial of funding for vocational religious instruction alone is inherently constitutionally suspect.

Without a presumption of unconstitutionality, Davey's claim must fail. The State's interest in not funding the pursuit of devotional degrees is substantial and the exclusion of such funding places a relatively minor burden on Promise Scholars. If any room exists between the two Religion Clauses, it must be here. We need not venture further into this difficult area in order to uphold the Promise Scholarship Program as currently operated by the State of Washington.

Justice SCALIA, with whom Justice THOMAS joins, dissenting.

In Church of Lukumi Babalu Aye, Inc. v. Hialeah (1993), the majority opinion held that "[a] law burdening religious practice that is not neutral . . . must undergo the most rigorous of scrutiny," and that "the minimum requirement of neutrality is that a law not discriminate on its face." The concurrence of two Justices stated that "[w]hen a law discriminates against religion as such, . . . it automatically will fail strict scrutiny." (Blackmun, J., joined by O'Connor, J., concurring in judgment.) And the concurrence of a third Justice endorsed the "noncontroversial principle" that "formal neutrality" is a "necessary conditio[n] for free-exercise constitutionality." (Souter, J., concurring in part and concurring in judgment.) These opinions are irreconcilable with today's decision, which sustains a public benefits program that facially discriminates against religion.

When the State makes a public benefit generally available, that benefit becomes part of the baseline against which burdens on religion are measured; and when the State withholds that benefit from some individuals solely on the basis of religion, it violates the Free Exercise Clause no less than if it had

25. The amici contend that Washington's Constitution was born of religious bigotry because it contains a so-called Blaine Amendment, which has been linked with anti-Catholicism. As the State notes and Davey does not dispute, however, the provision in question is not a Blaine Amendment. Neither Davey nor amici has established a credible connection between the Blaine Amendment and Article I, §11, the relevant constitutional provision. Accordingly, the Blaine Amendment's history is simply not before us. [Footnote by the Court.]

imposed a special tax. That is precisely what the State of Washington has done here. It has created a generally available public benefit, whose receipt is conditioned only on academic performance, income, and attendance at an accredited school. It has then carved out a solitary course of study for exclusion: theology. No field of study but religion is singled out for disfavor in this fashion. Davey is not asking for a special benefit to which others are not entitled. He seeks only equal treatment—the right to direct his scholarship to his chosen course of study, a right every other Promise Scholar enjoys.

The Court does not dispute that the Free Exercise Clause places some constraints on public benefits programs, but finds none here, based on a principle of "play in the joints." I use the term "principle" loosely, for that is not so much a legal principle as a refusal to apply any principle when faced with competing constitutional directives. There is nothing anomalous about constitutional commands that abut. A municipality hiring public contractors may not discriminate against blacks or in favor of them; it cannot discriminate a little bit each way and then plead "play in the joints" when haled into court. If the Religion Clauses demand neutrality, we must enforce them, in hard cases as well as easy ones.

Even if "play in the joints" were a valid legal principle, surely it would apply only when it was a close call whether complying with one of the Religion Clauses would violate the other. But that is not the case here. It is not just that "the State could, consistent with the Federal Constitution, permit Promise Scholars to pursue a degree in devotional theology." The establishment question would not even be close, as is evident from the fact that this Court's decision in Witters v. Washington Dept. of Servs. for Blind (1986), was unanimous. Perhaps some formally neutral public benefits programs are so gerrymandered and devoid of plausible secular purpose that they might raise specters of state aid to religion, but an even-handed Promise Scholarship Program is not among them.

In any case, the State already has all the play in the joints it needs. There are any number of ways it could respect both its unusually sensitive concern for the conscience of its taxpayers and the Federal Free Exercise Clause. It could make the scholarships redeemable only at public universities (where it sets the curriculum), or only for select courses of study. Either option would replace a program that facially discriminates against religion with one that just happens not to subsidize it. The State could also simply abandon the scholarship program altogether. If that seems a dear price to pay for freedom of conscience, it is only because the State has defined that freedom so broadly that it would be offended by a program with such an incidental, indirect religious effect.

What is the nature of the State's asserted interest here? It cannot be protecting the pocketbooks of its citizens; given the tiny fraction of Promise Scholars who would pursue theology degrees, the amount of any citizen's tax bill at stake is de minimis. It cannot be preventing mistaken appearance of endorsement; where a State merely declines to penalize students for selecting a religious major, "[n]o reasonable observer is likely to draw . . . an inference that the State itself is endorsing a religious practice or belief." Nor can Washington's exclusion be defended as a means of assuring that the State will neither favor nor disfavor Davey in his religious calling. Davey will throughout his life contribute to the public fisc through sales taxes on personal puchases, property taxes on his home, and so on; and nothing in the Court's opinion turns on whether Davey winds up a net winner or loser in the State's tax-and-spend scheme.

No, the interest to which the Court defers is not fear of a conceivable Establishment Clause violation, budget constraints, avoidance of endorsement, or substantive neutrality—none of these. It is a pure philosophical preference: the State's opinion that it would violate taxpayers' freedom of conscience not to discriminate against candidates for the ministry. This sort of protection of "freedom of conscience" has no logical limit and can justify the singling out of religion for exclusion from public programs in virtually any context. The Court never says whether it deems this interest compelling (the opinion is devoid of any mention of standard of review) but, self-evidently, it is not.

C.   THE ESTABLISHMENT CLAUSE

1.   *Competing Theories of the Establishment Clause*

There are three major competing approaches to the Establishment Clause.[26] Each has adherents on the Court, and each is supported by a body of scholarly literature. The theory chosen determines the approach used and often the result.

a.   Strict Separation

The first theory often is termed "strict separation." This approach says that to the greatest extent possible, government and religion should be separated. The government should be, as much as possible, secular; religion should be entirely in the private realm of society. This theory is perhaps best described by Thomas Jefferson's metaphor that there should be a wall separating church and state.[27] As the Supreme Court declared in Everson v. Board of Education, 330 U.S. 1 (1947), "The First Amendment has erected a wall between church and state. That wall must be kept high and impregnable."

Jefferson's famous words were uttered, as was Madison's Remonstrance, as part of a campaign against Virginia's renewing its tax to support the church. In *Everson*, Justice Rutledge reviewed this history in describing the philosophy underlying the Establishment Clause: "The Amendment's purpose was not to strike merely at the official establishment of a single sect, creed or religion, outlawing only a formal relation such as had prevailed in England and some of the colonies. Necessarily it was to uproot all such relationships. But the object was broader than separating church and state in this narrow sense. It was to create a complete and permanent separation of the spheres of religious activity and civil authority by comprehensively forbidding every form of public aid or support for religion."

---

26. Although these theories have been presented and discussed most by the justices and commentators in the context of the Establishment Clause, they also can be used in Free Exercise Clause analysis. Also, these three theories are not exhaustive of all views, and there are variants of each.

27. Thomas Jefferson, Letter to Messrs. Nehemiah Dodge and Others, a Committee of the Danbury Baptist Assoc., *Writings* 510 (1984).

A strict separation of church and state is seen as necessary to protect religious liberty.[28] When religion becomes a part of government, separationists argue, there is inevitable coercion to participate in that faith. Those of different faiths and those who profess no religious beliefs are made to feel excluded and unwelcome when government and religion become intertwined. Moreover, government involvement with religion is inherently divisive in a country with so many different religions and many people who claim no religion at all.[29]

There are problems with the strict separation approach, as there are with all of the theories. A complete prohibition of all government assistance to religion would threaten the free exercise of religion. For example, a refusal by the government to provide police, fire, or sanitation services obviously would seemingly infringe free exercise. Thus, a total wall separating church and state is impossible, and the issue becomes how to draw the appropriate line. Moreover, religion has traditionally been a part of many government activities, from the phrase "In God We Trust" on coins to the invocation before Supreme Court session, "God save this honorable Court."

b.   Neutrality Theory

A second major approach to the Establishment Clause says that the government must be neutral on religion; that is, the government cannot favor religion over secularism or one religion over others. Professor Philip Kurland, a key exponent of this approach to the Religion Clauses, wrote that "the clauses should be read as stating a single precept: that government cannot utilize religion as a standard for action or inaction because these clauses, read together as they should be, prohibit classification in terms of religion either to confer a benefit or to impose a burden."[30] Professor Douglas Laycock has said that substantive neutrality means that "the religion clauses require government to minimize the extent to which it either encourages or discourages religious belief or disbelief, practice or nonpractice, observance or nonobservance."[31]

Several Supreme Court justices have advanced an "endorsement" test in evaluating the neutrality of a government's action. Under this approach, the government violates the Establishment Clause if it symbolically endorses a

---

28. *See* Alan Schwarz, *No Imposition of Religion: The Establishment Clause Value*, 77 Yale L.J. 692, 708 (1968).

29. Justice Brennan has articulated these purposes behind the Establishment Clause:

> The first, which is most closely related to the more general conceptions of liberty found in the remainder of the First Amendment, is to guarantee the individual right to conscience. . . . The second purpose of separation and neutrality is to keep the state from interfering in the essential autonomy of religious life, either by taking upon itself the decision of religious issues, or by unduly involving itself in the supervision of religious institutions or officials. The third purpose of separation and neutrality is to prevent the trivialization and degradation of religion by too close an attachment to the organs of government. . . . Finally, the principles of separation and neutrality help assure that essentially religious issues, precisely because of their importance and sensitivity, not become the occasion for battle in the political arena.

Marsh v. Chambers, 463 U.S. 783, 803-805 (1983) (Brennan, J., dissenting) (citations omitted).

30. Philip Kurland, *Of Church and State and the Supreme Court*, 29 U. Chi. L. Rev. 1, 96 (1961).

31. Douglas Laycock, *Formal, Substantive and Disaggregated Neutrality Toward Religion*, 39 DePaul L. Rev. 993, 1001 (1990).

particular religion or if it generally endorses either religion or secularism. For example, Justice O'Connor has written that "[e]very government practice must be judged in its unique circumstances to determine whether it constitutes an endorsement or disapproval of religion."[32]

Justice O'Connor explained the importance of such government neutrality: "As a theoretical matter, the endorsement test captures the essential command of the Establishment Clause, namely, that government must not make a person's religious beliefs relevant to his or her standing in the political community by conveying a message 'that religion or a particular religious belief is favored or preferred.' . . . If government is to be neutral in matters of religion, rather than showing either favoritism or disapproval towards citizens based on their personal religious choices, government cannot endorse the religious practices and beliefs of some citizens without sending a clear message to nonadherents that they are outsiders or less than full members of the political community."[33]

The difficulty is in determining what government actions constitute an "endorsement" of religion. Several justices discussed this in Capitol Square Review & Advisory Board v. Pinette, 515 U.S. 753 (1995). The issue in *Pinette* was whether it was unconstitutional for the government to preclude the Ku Klux Klan from erecting a large Latin cross in the park across from the Ohio Statehouse. Although there was no majority opinion for the Court, seven justices voted that excluding the cross violated the Klan's free speech rights and that allowing it to be present would not violate the Establishment Clause. In the course of the Establishment Clause discussion, several of the justices addressed what constitutes a symbolic endorsement.

Justice O'Connor, in an opinion concurring in the judgment joined by Justices Souter and Breyer, concluded that the cross should be allowed because the reasonable observer would not perceive it as an endorsement of religion. O'Connor said that "[w]here the government's operation of a public forum has the effect of endorsing religion, even if the governmental actor neither intends nor actively encourages that result, the Establishment Clause is violated." Justice O'Connor said that a reasonable observer would not likely perceive the cross as being endorsed by the government because there was "a sign disclaiming government sponsorship or endorsement" and this would "remove doubt about State approval of [the] religious message."

O'Connor said that the endorsement test is applied "from the perspective of a hypothetical observer who is presumed to possess a certain level of information that all citizens might not share." She said that the reasonable observer "must be deemed aware of the history and content of the community and forum in which the religious display appears [and] the general history of the place in which the cross is displayed. [An] informed observer will know how the public space in question has been used in the past."

Justices Stevens and Ginsburg dissented and argued that endorsement exists if a reasonable person passing by would perceive government support for religion. Justice Stevens wrote, "If a reasonable person could perceive a government endorsement of religion from a private display, then the State may not allow its property to be used as a forum for that display. No less strin-

---

32. Lynch v. Donnelly, 465 U.S. 668, 694 (1984).
33. County of Allegheny v. Greater Pittsburgh ACLU, 492 U.S. 573, 627 (1989) (O'Connor, J., concurring in part and concurring in the judgment) (citations omitted).

gent rule can adequately protect non-adherents from a well-grounded perception that their sovereign supports a faith to which they do not subscribe." Justice Stevens argued that Justice O'Connor's "'reasonable person' comes off as a well-schooled jurist, a being finer than the tort-law model. . . . [T]his enhanced tort-law standard is singularly out of place in the Establishment Clause context. It strips of constitutional protection every person whose knowledge happens to fall below some 'ideal' standard."

Thus, three different approaches to the endorsement test were expressed in *Pinette*. Justice Scalia, writing for the plurality, rejected using the test at all where the issue is private speech on government property. Justice O'Connor, writing for herself and Justices Souter and Breyer, said that the symbolic endorsement test should be applied from the perspective of the perceptions of a well-educated and well-informed observer. Justice Stevens, dissenting and joined by Justice Ginsburg, said that the symbolic endorsement test should look to the perceptions of the reasonable passerby.

The endorsement test is defended as a desirable approach to the Establishment Clause because it is a way of determining whether the government is neutral or whether it is favoring religion. A key purpose of the Establishment Clause is to prevent the government from making those who are not a part of the favored religion from feeling unwelcome. The symbolic endorsement test is seen as a way of assessing the likely perceptions of and reactions to government conduct.[34]

Those who criticize the endorsement test often focus on its ambiguity and indeterminancy.[35] People will perceive symbols in widely varying ways. The Court inevitably is left to make a subjective choice as to how people will perceive a particular symbol. Moreover, judges who are part of the dominant religion may be insensitive to how those of minority religions perceive particular symbols. At the same time, some argue that the endorsement test is too restrictive of government involvement with religion. Justice Kennedy, for example, said, "Either the endorsement test must invalidate scores of traditional practices recognizing the place religion holds in our culture, or it must be twisted and stretched to avoid inconsistency with practices we know to have been permitted in the past, while condemning similar practices with no greater endorsement effect simply by reason of their lack of historical antecedent. Neither result is acceptable."[36]

c. Accommodation

A third major theory is termed an "accommodation" approach. Under this view, the Court should interpret the Establishment Clause to recognize the importance

---

34. For a defense of the symbolic endorsement test, *see* Jesse Choper, *Securing Religious Liberty: Principles for Judicial Interpretation of the Religion Clauses* 28-29 (1995); Arnold H. Loewy, *Rethinking Government Neutrality Towards Religion Under the Establishment Clause: The Untapped Potential of Justice O'Connor's Insight*, 64 N.C. L. Rev. 1049 (1986).

35. *See, e.g.*, William Marshall, *"We Know It When We See It," the Supreme Court and the Establishment Clause*, 59 So. Cal. L. Rev. 495, 537 (1986); Steven D. Smith, *Symbols, Perceptions, and Doctrinal Illusions: Establishment Neutrality and the "No Endorsement" Test*, 86 Mich. L. Rev. 266, 283 (1987) (identifying this and other problems with the symbolic endorsement test).

36. County of Allegheny v. Greater Pittsburgh ACLU, 492 U.S. at 674.

of religion in society and accommodate its presence in government. Specifically, under the accommodation approach the government violates the Establishment Clause only if it literally establishes a church or coerces religious participation. Justice Kennedy, for example, has said that "the Establishment Clause . . . guarantees at a minimum that a government may not coerce anyone to support or participate in religion or its exercise, or otherwise act in a way which establishes a [state] religion or religious faith, or tends to do so."[37] In fact, wrote Justice Kennedy, "[b]arring all attempts to aid religion through government coercion goes far toward the attainment of [the] object [of the Establishment Clause]."[38]

The key question under this approach concerns what constitutes government "coercion." Several justices discussed this in Lee v. Weisman, 505 U.S. 577 (1992), presented below, where the Court declared unconstitutional clergy-delivered prayers at public school graduations. Justice Kennedy, writing for the Court, found that such prayers are inherently coercive because there is great pressure on students to attend their graduation ceremonies and to not leave during the prayers.

Justice Blackmun, in an opinion joined by Justices Stevens and O'Connor, wrote to emphasize that the Establishment Clause can be violated even without coercion. He remarked that it "is not enough that the government refrain from compelling religious practices; it must not engage in them either." Likewise, Justice Souter, joined by Justices Stevens and O'Connor, wrote separately to stress that coercion is sufficient for a finding of Establishment Clause violation, but it is not necessary; Establishment Clause violations exist without coercion if there is symbolic government endorsement of religion.

The dissenting opinion by Justice Scalia, joined by Chief Justice Rehnquist and Justices White and Thomas, advocated the accommodation approach, but defined coercion much more narrowly than Justice Kennedy. Justice Scalia said that "[t]he coercion that was a hallmark of historical establishments of religion was coercion of religious orthodoxy and of financial support by force of law and threat of penalty."

In other words, for the dissenters in *Lee,* coercion exists only if the law requires and punishes the failure to engage in religious practices. For Justice Kennedy, coercion can be found by more indirect pressures to engage in religious activity. The other justices in *Lee* reject the accommodation approach that coercion is a prerequisite for finding an Establishment Clause violation.

Those who defend the accommodation approach argue that it best reflects the importance and prevalence of religion in American society. Professor Michael McConnell, an advocate of this view, said that it is desirable because it makes "religion . . . a welcome element in the mix of beliefs and associations present in the community. Under this view, the emphasis is placed on freedom of choice and diversity among religious opinion. The nation is understood not as secular but as pluralistic. Religion is under no special disability in public life; indeed, it is at least as protected and encouraged as any other form of belief and association — in some ways more so."[39] Anything less than accommodation, it is argued, is unacceptable hostility to religion.

---

37. Lee v. Weisman, 505 U.S. 577 (1992).
38. County of Allegheny v. Greater Pittsburgh ACLU, 492 U.S. at 660 (Kennedy, J., concurring in the judgment in part and dissenting in part).
39. Michael W. McConnell, *Accommodation of Religion,* 1985 Sup. Ct. Rev. 1, 14.

Opponents of the accommodation approach argue that, especially as defined by Justice Scalia, little ever will violate the Establishment Clause.[40] Nothing except the government creating its own church or by force of law requiring religious practices or discriminating among religions will offend the provision. Those disagreeing with this theory argue that the Establishment Clause also should serve to prevent the government from making those of other religions feel unwelcome and to keep the government from using its power and influence to advance religion or a particular religion. Justice O'Connor expressed this view when she wrote, "An Establishment Clause standard that prohibits only 'coercive' practices or overt efforts at government proselytization, but fails to take account of the numerous more subtle ways that government can show favoritism to particular beliefs or convey a message of disapproval to others, would not, in my view, adequately protect the religious liberty or respect the religious diversity of the members of our pluralistic political community. Thus, this Court has never relied on coercion alone as the touchstone of Establishment Clause analysis."

d. The Theories Applied: An Example

The importance of these three theories in determining the inquiry and the results in Establishment Clause cases is reflected in Allegheny County v. Greater Pittsburgh ACLU.

COUNTY OF ALLEGHENY v. AMERICAN CIVIL LIBERTIES UNION, GREATER PITTSBURGH CHAPTER

492 U.S. 573 (1989)

Justice BLACKMUN announced the judgment of the Court.

This litigation concerns the constitutionality of two recurring holiday displays located on public property in downtown Pittsburgh. The first is a creche placed on the Grand Staircase of the Allegheny County Courthouse. The second is a Chanukah menorah placed just outside the City-County Building, next to a Christmas tree and a sign saluting liberty. The Court of Appeals for the Third Circuit ruled that each display violates the Establishment Clause of the First Amendment because each has the impermissible effect of endorsing religion. We agree that the creche display has that unconstitutional effect but reverse the Court of Appeals' judgment regarding the menorah display.

In the course of adjudicating specific cases, this Court has come to understand the Establishment Clause to mean that government may not promote or affiliate itself with any religious doctrine or organization, may not discriminate among persons on the basis of their religious beliefs and practices, may not delegate a governmental power to a religious institution, and may not involve itself too deeply in such an institution's affairs. Our subsequent decisions further have refined the definition of governmental action that unconstitutionally advances

---

40. Professor Sherry argues that the coercion test "makes the Establishment Clause redundant. Any government action that coerces religious belief violates the Free Exercise Clause." Suzanna Sherry, *Lee v. Weisman: Paradox Redux*, 1992 Sup. Ct. Rev. 123, 134.

religion. In recent years, we have paid particularly close attention to whether the challenged governmental practice either has the purpose or effect of "endorsing" religion, a concern that has long had a place in our Establishment Clause jurisprudence. Of course, the word "endorsement" is not self-defining. Rather, it derives its meaning from other words that this Court has found useful over the years in interpreting the Establishment Clause. Thus, it has been noted that the prohibition against governmental endorsement of religion "preclude[s] government from conveying or attempting to convey a message that religion or a particular religious belief is favored or preferred." Whether the key word is "endorsement," "favoritism," or "promotion," the essential principle remains the same.

We have had occasion in the past to apply Establishment Clause principles to the government's display of objects with religious significance. In Lynch v. Donnelly, we considered whether the city of Pawtucket, R.I., had violated the Establishment Clause by including a creche in its annual Christmas display, located in a private park within the downtown shopping district. By a 5-to-4 decision in that difficult case, the Court upheld inclusion of the creche in the Pawtucket display, holding that the inclusion of the creche did not have the impermissible effect of advancing or promoting religion. The five Justices in concurrence and dissent in *Lynch* agreed upon the relevant constitutional principles: the government's use of religious symbolism is unconstitutional if it has the effect of endorsing religious beliefs, and the effect of the government's use of religious symbolism depends upon its context. These general principles are sound, and have been adopted by the Court in subsequent cases. Since *Lynch*, the Court has made clear that, when evaluating the effect of government conduct under the Establishment Clause, we must ascertain whether "the challenged governmental action is sufficiently likely to be perceived by adherents of the controlling denominations as an endorsement, and by the nonadherents as a disapproval, of their individual religious choices."

We turn first to the county's creche display. There is no doubt, of course, that the creche itself is capable of communicating a religious message. Under the Court's holding in *Lynch*, the effect of a creche display turns on its setting. Here, unlike in *Lynch*, nothing in the context of the display detracts from the creche's religious message. The *Lynch* display composed a series of figures and objects, each group of which had its own focal point. Santa's house and his reindeer were objects of attention separate from the creche, and had their specific visual story to tell. Similarly, whatever a "talking" wishing well may be, it obviously was a center of attention separate from the creche. Here, in contrast, the creche stands alone: it is the single element of the display on the Grand Staircase.

The display of the Chanukah menorah in front of the City-County Building may well present a closer constitutional question. The menorah, one must recognize, is a religious symbol: it serves to commemorate the miracle of the oil as described in the Talmud. But the menorah's message is not exclusively religious. The menorah is the primary visual symbol for a holiday that, like Christmas, has both religious and secular dimensions.

[T]he menorah here stands next to a Christmas tree and a sign saluting liberty. While no challenge has been made here to the display of the tree and the sign, their presence is obviously relevant in determining the effect of the menorah's display. The necessary result of placing a menorah next to a Christmas tree is to create an "overall holiday setting" that represents both Christmas and Chanukah — two holidays, not one. The mere fact that Pittsburgh displays symbols of both Christmas and Chanukah does not end the constitutional inquiry. If the city celebrates both Christmas and Chanukah as religious holidays, then it violates the Establishment Clause. The simultaneous endorsement of Judaism and Christianity is no less constitutionally infirm than the endorsement of Christianity alone.

Accordingly, the relevant question for Establishment Clause purposes is whether the combined display of the tree, the sign, and the menorah has the effect of endorsing both Christian and Jewish faiths, or rather simply recognizes that both Christmas and Chanukah are part of the same winter-holiday season, which has attained a secular status in our society. Of the two interpretations of this particular display, the latter seems far more plausible and is also in line with *Lynch*.

Justice O'CONNOR concurring in part and concurring in the judgment.

I agree that the creche displayed on the Grand Staircase of the Allegheny County Courthouse, the seat of county government, conveys a message to non-adherents of Christianity that they are not full members of the political community, and a corresponding message to Christians that they are favored members of the political community. In contrast to the creche in *Lynch*, which was displayed in a private park in the city's commercial district as part of a broader display of traditional secular symbols of the holiday season, this creche stands alone in the county courthouse. The display of religious symbols in public areas of core government buildings runs a special risk of "mak[ing] religion relevant, in reality or public perception, to status in the political community." The Court correctly concludes that placement of the central religious symbol of the Christmas holiday season at the Allegheny County Courthouse has the unconstitutional effect of conveying a government endorsement of Christianity.

For reasons which differ somewhat from those set forth in Justice Blackmun's opinion, I also conclude that the city of Pittsburgh's combined holiday display of a Chanukah menorah, a Christmas tree, and a sign saluting liberty does not have the effect of conveying an endorsement of religion. In my view, the relevant question for Establishment Clause purposes is whether the city of Pittsburgh's display of the menorah, the religious symbol of a religious holiday, next to a Christmas tree and a sign saluting liberty sends a message of government endorsement of Judaism or whether it sends a message of pluralism and freedom to choose one's own beliefs. The message of pluralism conveyed by the city's combined holiday display is not a message that endorses religion over nonreligion.

Justice BRENNAN, with whom Justice MARSHALL and Justice STEVENS join, concurring in part and dissenting in part.

I continue to believe that the display of an object that "retains a specifically Christian [or other] religious meaning" is incompatible with the separation of church and state demanded by our Constitution. I therefore agree with the Court that Allegheny County's display of a creche at the county courthouse signals an endorsement of the Christian faith in violation of the Establishment Clause. Court's opinion. I cannot agree, however, that the city's display of a 45-foot Christmas tree and an 18-foot Chanukah menorah at the entrance to the building housing the mayor's office shows no favoritism towards Christianity, Judaism, or both. Indeed, I should have thought that the answer as to the first display supplied the answer to the second.

Justice STEVENS, with whom Justice BRENNAN and Justice MARSHALL join, concurring in part and dissenting in part.

In my opinion the Establishment Clause should be construed to create a strong presumption against the display of religious symbols on public property. There is always a risk that such symbols will offend nonmembers of the faith being advertised as well as adherents who consider the particular advertisement disrespectful. Some devout Christians believe that the creche should be placed only in reverential settings, such as a church or perhaps a private home; they do not countenance its use as an aid to commercialization of Christ's birthday. In this very suit, members of the Jewish faith firmly opposed the use to which the menorah was put by the particular sect that sponsored the display at Pittsburgh's City-County Building. Even though "[p]assersby who disagree with the message conveyed by these displays are free to ignore them, or even to turn their backs," displays of this kind inevitably have a greater tendency to emphasize sincere and deeply felt differences among individuals than to achieve an ecumenical goal. The Establishment Clause does not allow public bodies to foment such disagreement.

Justice KENNEDY, with whom the Chief Justice, Justice WHITE, and Justice SCALIA join, concurring in the judgment in part and dissenting in part.

The majority holds that the County of Allegheny violated the Establishment Clause by displaying a creche in the county courthouse, because the "principal or primary effect" of the display is to advance religion. This view of the Establishment Clause reflects an unjustified hostility toward religion, a hostility inconsistent with our history and our precedents, and I dissent from this holding. The creche display is constitutional, and, for the same reasons, the display of a menorah by the city of Pittsburgh is permissible as well. On this latter point, I concur in the result, but not the reasoning, of Justice Blackmun's opinion.

Rather than requiring government to avoid any action that acknowledges or aids religion, the Establishment Clause permits government some latitude in recognizing and accommodating the central role religion plays in our society. Any approach less sensitive to our heritage would border on latent hostility toward religion, as it would require government in all its multifaceted roles to acknowledge only the secular, to the exclusion and so to the detriment of the religious. A categorical approach would install federal courts as jealous guardians of an absolute "wall of separation," sending a clear message of disapproval. In this century, as the modern administrative state expands to touch the lives of its citizens in such diverse ways and redirects their financial choices through programs of its own, it is difficult to maintain the fiction that requiring government to avoid all assistance to religion can in fairness be viewed as serving the goal of neutrality.

The ability of the organized community to recognize and accommodate religion in a society with a pervasive public sector requires diligent observance of the border between accommodation and establishment. Our cases disclose two limiting principles: government may not coerce anyone to support or participate in any religion or its exercise; and it may not, in the guise of avoiding hostility or callous indifference, give direct benefits to religion in such a degree that it in fact "establishes a [state] religion or religious faith, or tends to do so."

These principles are not difficult to apply to the facts of the cases before us. In permitting the displays on government property of the menorah and the creche, the city and county sought to do no more than "celebrate the season," and to acknowledge, along with many of their citizens, the historical background and the religious, as well as secular, nature of the Chanukah and Christmas holidays. This interest falls well within the tradition of government accommodation and acknowledgment of religion that has marked our history from the beginning. It cannot be disputed that government, if it chooses, may participate in sharing with its citizens the joy of the holiday season, by declaring public holidays, installing or permitting festive displays, sponsoring celebrations and parades, and providing holiday vacations for its employees. All levels of our government do precisely that. As we said in *Lynch*, "Government has long recognized — indeed it has subsidized — holidays with religious significance."

If government is to participate in its citizens' celebration of a holiday that contains both a secular and a religious component, enforced recognition of only the secular aspect would signify the callous indifference toward religious faith that our cases and traditions do not require; for by commemorating the holiday only as it is celebrated by nonadherents, the government would be refusing to acknowledge the plain fact, and the historical reality, that many of its citizens celebrate its religious aspects as well. Judicial invalidation of government's attempts to recognize the religious underpinnings of the holiday would signal not neutrality but a pervasive intent to insulate government from all things religious. The Religion Clauses do not require government to acknowledge these holidays or their religious component; but our strong tradition of government accommodation and acknowledgment permits government to do so.

There is no suggestion here that the government's power to coerce has been used to further the interests of Christianity or Judaism in any way. No one was compelled to observe or participate in any religious ceremony or activity. Neither the city nor the county contributed significant amounts of tax money to serve the cause of one religious faith. The creche and the menorah are purely passive symbols of religious holidays. Passersby who disagree with the message conveyed by these displays are free to ignore them, or even to turn their backs, just as they are free to do when they disagree with any other form of government speech.

2.   *Government Discrimination Among Religions*

It is firmly established that the government violates the Establishment Clause if it discriminates among religious groups. Such discrimination will be allowed only if strict scrutiny is met. If there is not discrimination, the case is discussed under the *Lemon* test described in the next subsection. In Hernandez v. Commissioner, 490 U.S. 680 (1989), the Court explained, "[W]hen it is claimed that a denominational preference exists, the initial inquiry is whether the law facially differentiates among religions. If no such facial preference exists, we proceed to apply the customary three-pronged Establishment Clause inquiry derived from Lemon v. Kurtzman."

Larson v. Valente, 456 U.S. 228 (1982), applied this principle to declare unconstitutional a Minnesota law that imposed registration and reporting requirements on charitable organizations but exempted religious institutions that received more than half of their financial support from members' contributions.

The Court said that the "history and logic of the Establishment Clause [mean] that no State can 'pass laws which aid one religion' or that 'prefer one religion over another.'" The Court concluded that the 50 percent requirement "clearly grants denominational preferences of the sort consistently and firmly deprecated in our precedents" and thus could not be allowed unless strict scrutiny was met. Religions that met the requirement, such as the Catholic Church, had the great benefit of being exempt from the burdens of the statute; religions that did not meet the requirement, such as the "Moonies," would have to comply with the law. The Court found that there was no compelling interest to justify the discrimination and thus concluded that the "fifty percent rule sets up precisely the sort of official denominational preference that the Framers of the First Amendment forbade."

The Court also applied this neutrality principle in Board of Education of Kiryas Joel Village School District v. Grumet, 512 U.S. 687 (1994), to declare unconstitutional a state law that created a separate school district for a small village that was inhabited by Hasidic Jews. The Village of Kiryas Joel was created by a sect known as Satmar Hasidim. They maintained two parochial schools, one for boys and one for girls. However, they did not have any services available for children with disabilities. Until the Supreme Court declared it unconstitutional in 1985, the government provided special education for such children within the parochial schools.[41] In response to these Supreme Court decisions, the State of New York adopted a law that created a public school district with boundaries identical to those of the Village of Kiryas Joel. The school board for the village was like all other school boards, except that all of its elected members were part of the Satmar Hasidic sect.

Justice Souter, writing for the Court, declared the New York law unconstitutional as impermissible preference for one religion over others. The government created a school district specifically to help one religion so that it could provide special education without its children having to attend school with those outside the faith. Justice Souter explained that "the fundamental source of constitutional concern here is that the legislature itself may fail to exercise governmental authority in a religiously neutral way."

In a part of the opinion that was joined only by a plurality, Justice Souter also said that the law violated the Establishment Clause because the government was impermissibly delegating government authority to a religious entity. He said that creating a government entity contiguous with a religious community and thereby allowing the religion to control its political process was an impermissible "fusion of governmental and religious functions."

Thus, cases such as Larson and Kiryas Joel establish that a government action violates the Establishment Clause if it prefers one religion or sect over others. In such instances, the Court invalidates the law without reaching the Lemon test, discussed below. Yet the neutrality approach taken in cases such as Larson and

---

41. Grand Rapids School District v. Ball, 473 U.S. 373 (1985); Aguilar v. Felton, 473 U.S. 402 (1985). As indicated below, Aguilar was overruled in Agostini v. Felton, 521 U.S. 203 (1997).

Kiryas Joel is remarkably similar to the analysis under the first two prongs of the *Lemon* test: If the government is favoring one religion, it is acting with the purpose, and there is the effect of fostering that religion.

3. The **Lemon** *Test for the Establishment Clause*

If a law is not discriminatory, the Supreme Court says that a court should apply the three-part test articulated in Lemon v. Kurtzman.

LEMON v. KURTZMAN
403 U.S. 602 (1971)

Chief Justice BURGER delivered the opinion of the Court.

These two appeals raise questions as to Pennsylvania and Rhode Island statutes providing state aid to church-related elementary and secondary schools. Pennsylvania has adopted a statutory program that provides financial support to nonpublic elementary and secondary schools by way of reimbursement for the cost of teachers' salaries, textbooks, and instructional materials in specified secular subjects. Rhode Island has adopted a statute under which the State pays directly to teachers in nonpublic elementary schools a supplement of 15% of their annual salary. Under each statute state aid has been given to church-related educational institutions. We hold that both statutes are unconstitutional.

The language of the Religion Clauses of the First Amendment is at best opaque, particularly when compared with other portions of the Amendment. Its authors did not simply prohibit the establishment of a state church or a state religion, an area history shows they regarded as very important and fraught with great dangers. Instead they commanded that there should be "no law respecting an establishment of religion." A law may be one "respecting" the forbidden objective while falling short of its total realization. A law "respecting" the proscribed result, that is, the establishment of religion, is not always easily identifiable as one violative of the Clause. A given law might not establish a state religion but nevertheless be one "respecting" that end in the sense of being a step that could lead to such establishment and hence offend the First Amendment.

In the absence of precisely stated constitutional prohibitions. we must draw lines with reference to the three main evils against which the Establishment Clause was intended to afford protection: "sponsorship, financial support, and active involvement of the sovereign in religious activity."

Every analysis in this area must begin with consideration of the cumulative criteria developed by the Court over many years. Three such tests may be gleaned from our cases. First, the statute must have a secular legislative purpose; second, its principal or primary effect must be one that neither advances nor inhibits religion; finally, the statute must not foster "an excessive government entanglement with religion."

Inquiry into the legislative purposes of the Pennsylvania and Rhode Island statutes affords no basis for a conclusion that the legislative intent was to advance religion. On the contrary, the statutes themselves clearly state that they are intended to enhance the quality of the secular education in all schools covered by the compulsory attendance laws. There is no reason to believe the legislatures meant anything else. [However,] we conclude that the cumulative impact of the entire relationship arising under the statutes in each State involves excessive entanglement between government and religion. In order to determine whether the government entanglement with religion is excessive, we must examine the character and purposes of the institutions that are benefited, the nature of the aid that the State provides, and the resulting relationship between the government and the religious authority. Mr. Justice Harlan echoed the classic warning as to "programs whose very nature is apt to entangle the state in details of administration." Here we find that both statutes foster an impermissible degree of entanglement.

Although there have been many cases where the Court decided Establishment Clause cases without applying the *Lemon* test,[42] it has been frequently used. While several justices have criticized the test and called for it to be overruled, this has not occurred.[43] Indeed, Justice Scalia, the primary advocate for overruling the *Lemon* test, colorfully lamented its survival and analogized it to "a ghoul in a late-night horror movie that repeatedly sits up in its grave and shuffles abroad, after being repeatedly killed and buried. [It] is there to scare us [when] we wish it to do so, but we can command it to return to the tomb at will. When we wish to strike down a practice it forbids, we invoke it, when we wish to uphold a practice it forbids, we ignore it entirely."[44]

The *Lemon* test is favored and used by justices taking the strict separationist approach to the Establishment Clause. It also is used by justices taking the neutrality approach, although they emphasize whether the purpose or effect is to symbolically endorse religion.[45] Justices favoring the accommodationist approach urge the overruling of the *Lemon* test.

The current and future role of the *Lemon* test is uncertain. The test has not been expressly overruled or discarded, and it has been invoked in recent years. For example, in one of the most recent Establishment Clause cases, McCreary County v. American Civil Liberties Union of Kentucky, 545 U.S. 844 (2005), below, the Court used the *Lemon* test in invalidating a court's requirement for posting the Ten Commandments. Yet a majority of the justices on the current Court have expressed dissatisfaction with the test and have advocated

---

42. *See, e.g.*, Board of Education of Kiryas Joel Village School Dist. v. Grumet, 512 U.S. 687 (1994) (finding favoritism for one religion by creating a school district contiguous with a religious community violates the Establishment Clause); Lynch v. Donnelly, 465 U.S. 668 (1984) (allowing nativity scene on government property); Marsh v. Chambers, 463 U.S. 783 (1983) (allowing government payment of a legislative chaplain because of history of the practice).

43. *See* Lamb's Chapel v. Center Moriches Union Free School District, 508 U.S. 384 (1993) (applying the *Lemon* test and concluding that the Establishment Clause was not violated by allowing religious groups to use school facilities during evenings and weekends).

44. Lamb's Chapel v. Center Moriches Union Free School Dist., 508 U.S, at 398-399 (Scalia, J., dissenting).

45. *See, e.g.*, Lynch v. Donnelly, 465 U.S. at 690 (O'Connor, J., concurring) ("The purpose prong of the *Lemon* test asks whether government's actual purpose is to endorse or disapprove of religion. The effect prong asks whether, irrespective of government's actual purpose, the practice under review in fact conveys a message of endorsement or disapproval. An affirmative answer to either question should render the challenged practice invalid.").

alternatives, such as focusing on whether government action symbolically endorses religion or on deference to the government unless it creates a church or coerces religious participation.

THE REQUIREMENT FOR A SECULAR PURPOSE

The first prong of the *Lemon* test is the requirement that there be a secular purpose for a law. For example, in Stone v. Graham, 449 U.S. 39 (1980), the Supreme Court declared unconstitutional a state law that required the Ten Commandments to be posted on the walls of every public school classroom. The Court concluded that the law "has no secular legislative purpose" and therefore violated the Establishment Clause. Similarly, in Wallace v. Jaffree, 472 U.S. 38 (1985), the Court invalidated a state law that authorized public school teachers to hold a one-minute period of silence for meditation or voluntary prayer. The Court found that the purpose behind the law was to reintroduce prayer into public schools and deemed the law unconstitutional because it "was not motivated by any clearly secular purpose — indeed, the statute had *no* secular purpose."

In Edwards v. Aguillard, 482 U.S. 578 (1987), the Court followed this reasoning and ruled unconstitutional a state law that required that public schools that teach evolution also teach "creation science." Since "creation science" is a religious theory explaining the origin of human life, the Court concluded, "Because the primary purpose of the Creationism Act is to endorse a particular religious doctrine, the Act furthers religion in violation of the establishment clause."

In contrast, in McGowan v. Maryland, 366 U.S. 420 (1961), the Supreme Court upheld the constitutionality of state laws requiring businesses to be closed on Sunday. The Court acknowledged "the strongly religious origin of these laws." Nonetheless, the Court found the laws permissible because "[t]he present purpose and effect of most of them is to provide a uniform day of rest for all citizens; the fact that this day is Sunday, a day of particular significance for the dominant Christian sects, does not bar the State from achieving its secular goals."

Several of the justices — especially Chief Justice Rehnquist and Justice Scalia — have criticized the first prong of the *Lemon* test. Rehnquist has argued that the requirement for a secular purpose "is a constitutional theory [that] has no basis in the history of the amendment it seeks to interpret, is difficult to apply and yields unprincipled results."[46] Scalia contended, "[D]iscerning the subjective motivation of those enacting the statue is, to be honest, almost always an impossible task. The number of possible motivations ... is not binary, or indeed even finite. ... To look for *the sole purpose* of even a single legislator is probably to look for something that does not exist."[47]

On the other hand, the Court considers legislative purpose, despite the difficulty in ascertaining it, in other areas of constitutional law, such as in the requirement for proof of a discriminatory purpose to prove a race or gender classification when there is a facially neutral law.[48] The rationale for the first

---

46. Wallace v. Jaffree, 472 U.S. at 112 (Rehnquist, J., dissenting).
47. Edwards v. Aguillard, 482 U.S. at 636-637 (Scalia, J., dissenting).
48. *See, e.g.*, Washington v. Davis, 426 U.S. 229 (1976), discussed in Chapter 7.

prong of the *Lemon* test is that the very essence of the Establishment Clause is to keep the government from acting to advance religion.

THE REQUIREMENT FOR A SECULAR EFFECT

The second prong of the *Lemon* test requires that the principal or primary effect of a law must be one that neither advances nor inhibits religion. In recent years, this often has been expressed in terms of symbolic endorsement: The government's action must not symbolically endorse religion or a particular religion.[49]

Estate of Thornton v. Caldor, 472 U.S. 703 (1985), is an example where the Court used the second part of the *Lemon* test to invalidate a law. A Connecticut statute provided that no person may be required by an employer to work on his or her Sabbath. The Supreme Court declared the law unconstitutional and emphasized that the law created an absolute and unqualified right for individuals to not work for religious reasons and thus favored religion over all other interests. The Court concluded that "the statute goes beyond having an incidental or remote effect of advancing religion. The statute has a primary effect that impermissibly advances a particular religious practice."

However, in other cases, the Court has upheld exemptions from laws for religion. In Corporation of the Presiding Bishop of the Church of Jesus Christ of Latter-Day Saints v. Amos, 483 U.S. 327 (1987), the Court found constitutional an exemption for religious organizations from Title VII's prohibition against discrimination in employment based on religion. The Court concluded that the exemption met the first prong of the *Lemon* test because it was a permissible purpose "to alleviate significant government interference with the ability of religious organizations to define and carry out their religious missions."

More significantly, the Court found that the exemption was not inconsistent with the second part of the *Lemon* test. Justice White, writing for the majority, said that "[a] law is not unconstitutional simply because it *allows* churches to advance religion, which is their very purpose. For a law to have forbidden 'effects' under *Lemon*, it must be fair to say that the *government itself* has advanced religion through its own activities and influence."

The difference between *Thornton* and *Amos* is that the latter involved an exemption in a statute for religion, whereas the former concerned a law that provided a benefit solely for religion. The Court found that the latter was permissible, but that the former was the government advancing religion through its own activities and influence. Yet the distinction is difficult because both laws provided a preference for religion alone.

THE PROHIBITION OF EXCESSIVE ENTANGLEMENT

The final prong of the *Lemon* test forbids government actions that cause excessive entanglement with religion. The Court has said that a law violates

---

49. *See, e.g.*, Board of Education of Westside Community Schools v. Mergens, 496 U.S. 226, 249-253 (1990) (plurality opinion) (using the symbolic endorsement test to determine whether the effect of a government action was to advance religion impermissibly).

the Establishment Clause when it requires a "comprehensive, discriminating, and continuing state survieillance."[50] The Court also has said that "apart from any specific entanglement of the State in particular religious programs, assistance . . . [violates the Establishment Clause if it] carries the [grave] potential for entanglement in the broader sense of continuing political strife over aid to religion."[51]

For example, the Supreme Court has held that the government cannot pay teacher salaries in parochial schools, even for teachers of secular subjects.[52] If the government paid such salaries, it would need to monitor whether the teachers were teaching secular or religious material. Any such monitoring would be excessive government entanglement with religion.

In Agostini v. Felton, 521 U.S. 203 (1997), however, the Court held that it was permissible for public schoolteachers to provide remedial education in parochial schools. In doing so, the Court case doubt as to whether the "entanglement prong" remains a separate prong of the analysis. The Court said, "Thus, it is simplest to recognize why entanglement is significant and treat it as an aspect of the inquiry into a statute's effect." But the Court also reiterated that "excessive entanglement" violates the Establishment Clause: "Not all entanglements, of course, have the effect of advancing or inhibiting religion. Interaction between church and state is inevitable, and we have always tolerated some level of involvement between the two. Entanglement must be 'excessive' before it runs afoul of the Establishment Clause." Subsequently, Justice O'Connor observed, "In Agostini v. Felton (1997), we folded the entanglement inquiry into the primary effect inquiry."[53]

4.   Religious Speech and the First Amendment

In recent years, a significant number of cases concerning the Establishment Clause have involved free speech claims. Specifically, these cases concern situations where the government chooses to restrict private religious speech on government property or with government funds because of a desire to avoid violating the Establishment Clause. The Supreme Court consistently has held that excluding such religious speech violates the First Amendment's protection of freedom of speech because it is an impermissible content-based restriction of expression.

These cases mark a significant development in Establishment Clause jurisprudence that changes the way many cases will be litigated and decided. If a government action can be characterized as a restriction of private religious speech, it can be challenged as violating the First Amendment's protection of freedom of speech, and the challenger has a strong likelihood of prevailing; no longer will such cases be seen as exclusively or even predominantly involving the Establishment Clause.

---

50. Lemon v. Kurtzman, 403 U.S. at 619.
51. Committee for Public Education v. Nyquist, 413 U.S. 756, 794 (1973).
52. *See, e.g.,* Grand Rapids v. Ball, 473 U.S. 373 (1985).
53. Zelman v. Simmons-Harris, 536 U.S. 639 (2002).

a. Religious Group Access to School Facilities

The initial Supreme Court cases in this area concerned efforts by the government to restrict religious groups from using school facilities so as to avoid violating the Establishment Clause. In Widmar v. Vincent, 454 U.S. 263 (1981), the Supreme Court declared unconstitutional a state university's policy of preventing student groups from using school facilities for religious worship or religious discussion. The University of Missouri at Kansas City allowed registered student groups to use its facilities, but forbade their use "for purposes of religious worship or religious teaching."

The Court said that the university "discriminated against student groups and speakers based on their desire to use a generally open forum to engage in religious worship and discussion. These are forms of speech and association protected by the First Amendment." The Court expressly rejected the dissent's argument that religious worship is not speech protected by the free speech guarantee of the First Amendment. The Court said that the university had created a public forum by opening these places to speech and said that "[i]n order to justify discriminatory exclusion from a public forum based on the religious content of a group's intended speech, the University must therefore satisfy the standard of review appropriate to content-based exclusions. It must show that its regulation is necessary to serve a compelling state interest and that it is narrowly drawn to achieve that end."

The Court then concluded that excluding religious speech was not necessary in order to be consistent with the Establishment Clause. The Court applied the *Lemon* test and said that opening school facilities to all groups served the secular purpose of providing a forum for student meetings. The Court said that any effect in advancing religion would be "incidental." The Court concluded that allowing religious groups to use school facilities was not excessive entanglement with religion; no state monitoring would be necessary if the university allowed secular and religious groups to use the facilities.

The Court followed similar reasoning in Board of Education of Westside Community Schools v. Mergens, 496 U.S. 226 (1990). *Mergens* involved a constitutional challenge to the federal Equal Access Act, which applies to any public school that receives federal financial assistance. The Equal Access Act says that any such school that opens its facilities to noncurricular student groups may not deny equal access to any students who wish to conduct meetings on similar terms because of the religious, political, philosophical, or other content of their speech.

Justice O'Connor, writing for the plurality, said that "the logic of *Widmar* applies." Justice O'Connor used the *Lemon* test and concluded that preventing discrimination against speech because of its religious, political, or philosophical content was a legitimate secular purpose. She said that the effect was not to advance religion because allowing religious groups to use school facilities was not likely to be perceived as a symbolic government endorsement of religion. Justice O'Connor wrote that "secondary school students are mature enough and are likely to understand that a school does not endorse or support student speech that it merely permits on a nondiscriminatory basis." She said that "there is a crucial difference between government speech endorsing religion, which the Establishment Clause forbids, and private speech endorsing religion, which the Free Speech and Free Exercise Clauses protect." Finally, Justice O'Conner concluded that there was not excessive entanglement with religion because faculty sponsors were not allowed to participate actively in religious groups' meetings.

Justices Brennan and Marshall concurred in the judgment and emphasized that schools had the consitutional duty to make it clear that the government was not endorsing the views or activities of the religious groups. Justices Kennedy and Scalia also concurred in the judgment, though they used an accommodationist approach rather than the *Lemon* test. They said that the only relevant inquiries were whether the government aid was so extensive as to have a clear tendency to establish a state religion or whether the government was coercing student religious participation. They concluded that the Establishment Clause was not violated because there was neither the establishment of a state religion nor coercion of religious activities.

In Lamb's Chapel v. Center Moriches Union Free School District, 508 U.S. 384 (1993), the Court followed this reasoning and declared unconstitutional a school district's policy of excluding religious groups from using school facilities during evenings and weekends. Pursuant to state law, a school district opened its facilities to community and civic groups during evenings and weekends, but said that "school premises shall not be used by any group for religious purposes."

The Court expressly followed the reasoning in *Widmar* and said that once the government chose to open its facilities to community groups it could not discriminate against those engaging in religious speech unless strict scrutiny was met. The Court again rejected the claim that avoiding violation of the Establishment Clause provided such a compelling interest. The Court said: "We have no more trouble than did the *Widmar* Court in disposing of the claimed defense on the ground that the posited fears of an Establishment Clause violation are unfounded. The showing of this film series would not have been during school hours, would not have been sponsored by the school, and would have been open to the public, not just to church members." The Court concluded that "[a]s in *Widmar,* permitting District property to be used . . . would not have been an establishment of religion under the three-part test articulated in Lemon v. Kurtzman. The challenged governmental action has a secular purpose, does not have the principal or primary effect of advancing or inhibiting religion, and does not foster an excessive entanglement with religion."

In Good News Club v. Milford Central School, 533 U.S. 98 (2001), the Supreme Court declared unconstitutional a school policy that allowed community groups to conduct after-school programs for students, but excluded a religious group that was essentially conducting workshop sessions, including Bible study. The Court, in an opinion by Justice Thomas, found that excluding the group was an impermissible content-based restriction on speech because it was denied access solely because of the religious content of its speech. The Court also found that allowing the group use of the facilities did not violate the Establishment Clause as long as religious and nonreligious groups were treated equally.

b.   Student Religious Groups' Receipt of Government Funds

The court applied these cases in Rosenberger v. Rector & Visitors of the University of Virginia to declare unconstitutional a state university's refusal to give student activity funds to a Christian group that published an expressly religious magazine.

ROSENBERGER v. RECTOR & VISITORS
OF THE UNIVERSITY OF VIRGINIA

515 U.S. 819 (1995)

Justice KENNEDY delivered the opinion of the Court.

The University of Virginia, an instrumentality of the Commonwealth for which it is named and thus bound by the First and Fourteenth Amendments, authorizes the payment of outside contractors for the printing costs of a variety of student publications. It withheld any authorization for payments on behalf of petitioners for the sole reason that their student paper "primarily promotes or manifests a particular belie[f] in or about a deity or an ultimate reality." That the paper did promote or manifest views within the defined exclusion seems plain enough. The challenge is to the University's regulation and its denial of authorization, the case raising issues under the Speech and Establishment Clauses of the First Amendment.

I

The public corporation we refer to as the "University" is denominated by state law as "the Rector and Visitors of the University of Virginia," and it is responsible for governing the school. Founded by Thomas Jefferson in 1819, and ranked by him, together with the authorship of the Declaration of Independence and of the Virginia Act for Religious Freedom, as one of his proudest achievements, the University is among the Nation's oldest and most respected seats of higher learning. It has more than 11,000 undergraduate students, and 6,000 graduate and professional students.

Before a student group is eligible to submit bills from its outside contractors for payment by the fund described below, it must become a "Contracted Independent Organization" (CIO). CIO status is available to any group the majority of whose members are students, whose managing officers are fulltime students, and that complies with certain procedural requirements.

All CIO's may exist and operate at the University, but some are also entitled to apply for funds from the Student Activities Fund (SAF). Established and governed by University Guidelines, the purpose of the SAF is to support a broad range of extracurricular student activities that "are related to the educational purpose of the University." The SAF is based on the University's "recogni[tion] that the availability of a wide range of opportunities" for its students "tends to enhance the University environment." The Guidelines require that it be administered "in a manner consistent with the educational purpose of the University as well as with state and federal law." The SAF receives its money from a mandatory fee of $14 per semester assessed to each full-time student. The Student Council, elected by the students, has the initial authority to disburse the funds, but its actions are subject to review by a faculty body chaired by a designee of the Vice President for Student Affairs.

The student activities that are excluded from SAF support are religious activities, philanthropic contributions and activities, political activities, activities that would jeopardize the University's tax-exempt status, those which involve payment of honoraria or similar fees, or social entertainment or related expenses. The prohibition on "political activities" is defined so that it is limited to electioneering and lobbying. The Guidelines provide that "[t]hese restrictions on funding political activities are not intended to preclude funding of any otherwise eligible student organization which . . . espouses particular positions or ideological viewpoints, including those that may be unpopular or are not generally accepted." A "religious activity," by contrast, is defined as any activity that "primarily promotes or manifests a particular belie[f] in or about a deity or an ultimate reality."

During the 1990-1991 academic year, 343 student groups qualified as CIO's. One hundred thirty-five of them applied for support from the SAF, and 118 received funding.

Petitioners' organization, Wide Awake Productions (WAP), qualified as a CIO. Formed by petitioner Ronald Rosenberger and other undergraduates in 1990, WAP was established "[t]o publish a magazine of philosophical and religious expression, [t]o facilitate discussion which fosters an atmosphere of sensitivity to and tolerance of Christian viewpoints, and [t]o provide a unifying focus for Christians of multicultural backgrounds." WAP publishes Wide Awake: A Christian Perspective at the University of Virginia. The paper's Christian viewpoint was evident from the first issue, in which its editors wrote that the journal "offers a Christian perspective on both personal and community issues, especially those relevant to college students at the University of Virginia." The editors committed the paper to a two-fold mission: "to challenge Christians to live, in word and deed, according to the faith they proclaim and to encourage students to consider what a personal relationship with Jesus Christ means." The first issue had articles about racism, crisis pregnancy, stress, prayer, C.S. Lewis' ideas about evil and free will, and reviews of religious music. In the next two issues, Wide Awake featured stories about homosexuality, Christian missionary work, and eating disorders, as well as music reviews and interviews with University professors. Each page of Wide Awake, and the end of each article or review, is marked by a cross. The advertisements carried in Wide Awake also reveal the Christian perspective of the journal. For the most part, the advertisers are churches, centers for Christian study, or Christian bookstores. By June 1992, WAP had distributed about 5,000 copies of Wide Awake to University students, free of charge.

WAP had acquired CIO status soon after it was organized. This is an important consideration in this case, for had it been a "religious organization," WAP would not have been accorded CIO status. As defined by the Guidelines, a "[r]eligious [o]rganization" is "an organization whose purpose is to practice a devotion to an acknowledged ultimate reality or deity." At no stage in this controversy has the University contended that WAP is such an organization.

A few months after being given CIO status, WAP requested the SAF to pay its printer $5,862 for the costs of printing its newspaper. The Appropriations Committee of the Student Council denied WAP's request on the ground that Wide Awake was a "religious activity" within the meaning of the Guidelines, i.e., that the newspaper "promote[d] or manifest[ed] a particular belie[f] in or about a deity or an ultimate reality." It made its determination after examining the first issue. WAP appealed the denial to the full Student Council, contending that WAP met all the applicable Guidelines and that denial of SAF support on the basis of the magazine's religious perspective violated the Constitution. The appeal was denied without further comment, and WAP appealed to the next level, the Student Activities Committee. In a letter signed by the Dean of Students, the committee sustained the denial of funding.

Having no further recourse within the University structure, WAP, Wide Awake, and three of its editors and members filed suit in the United States District Court for the Western District of Virginia.

II

It is axiomatic that the government may not regulate speech based on its substantive content or the message it conveys. Other principles follow from this precept. In the realm of private speech or expression, government regulation may not favor one speaker over another. Discrimination against speech because of its message is presumed to be unconstitutional. These rules informed our determination that the government offends the First Amendment when it imposes financial burdens on certain speakers based on the content of their expression. When the government targets not subject matter, but particular views taken by speakers on a subject, the violation of the First Amendment is all the more blatant. Viewpoint discrimination is thus an egregious form of content discrimination. The government must abstain from regulating speech when the specific motivating ideology or the opinion or perspective of the speaker in the rationale for the restriction.

These principles provide the framework forbidding the State to exercise viewpoint discrimination, even when the limited public forum is one of its own creation. In a case involving a school district's provision of school facilities for private uses, we declared that "[t]here is no question that the District, like the private owner of property, may legally preserve the property under its control for the use to which it is dedicated." Once it has opened a limited forum, however, the State must respect the lawful boundaries it has itself set. The State may not exclude speech where its distinction is not "reasonable in light of the purpose served by the forum," nor may it discriminate against speech on the basis of its viewpoint. Thus, in determining whether the State is acting to preserve the limits of the forum it has created so that the exclusion of a class of speech is legitimate, we have observed a distinction between, on the one hand, content discrimination, which may be permissible if it preserves the purposes of that limited forum, and, on the other hand, viewpoint discrimination, which is presumed impermissible when directed against speech otherwise within the forum's limitations.

The SAF is a forum more in a metaphysical than in a spatial or geographic sense, but the same principles are applicable. The most recent and most apposite case is our decision in *Lamb's Chapel*. There, a school district had opened school facilities for use after school hours by community groups for a wide variety of social, civic, and recreational purposes. The district, however, had enacted a formal policy against opening facilities to groups for religious purposes. Invoking its policy, the district rejected a request from a group desiring to show a film series addressing various child-rearing questions from a "Christian perspective." There was no indication in the record in *Lamb's Chapel* that the request to use the school facilities was "denied, for any reason other than the fact that the presentation would have been from a religious perspective." Our conclusion was unanimous: "[I]t discriminates on the basis of viewpoint to permit school property to be used for the presentation of all views about family issues and childrearing except those dealing with the subject matter from a religious standpoint."

The University does acknowledge (as it must in light of our precedents) that "ideologically driven attempts to suppress a particular point of view are presumptively unconstitutional in funding as in other contexts," but insists that this case does not present that issue because the Guidelines draw lines based on content, not viewpoint. As we have noted, discrimination against one set of views or ideas is but a subset or particular instance of the more general phenomenon of content discrimination. And, it must be acknowledged, the distinction is not a precise one. We conclude, nonetheless, that here, as in *Lamb's Chapel*, viewpoint discrimination is the proper way to interpret the University's objections to Wide Awake. By the very terms of the SAF prohibition, the University does not exclude religion as a subject matter but selects for disfavored treatment those student journalistic efforts with religious editorial viewpoints. Religion may be a vast area of inquiry, but it also provides, as it did here, a specific premise, a perspective, a standpoint from which a variety of subjects may be discussed and considered. The prohibited perspective, not the general subject matter, resulted in the refusal to make third-party payments, for the subjects discussed were otherwise within the approved category of publications.

The University denial of WAP's request for third-party payments in the present case is based upon viewpoint discrimination not unlike the discrimination the school district relied upon in *Lamb's Chapel* and that we found invalid. The church group in *Lamb's Chapel* would have been qualified as a social or civic organization, save for its religious purposes. Furthermore, just as the social district in *Lamb's Chapel* pointed to nothing but the religious views of the groups as the rationale for excluding its message, so in this case the University justifies its denial of SAF participation of WAP on the ground that the contents of Wide Awake reveal an avowed religious perspective.

The University tries to escape the consequences of our holding in *Lamb's Chapel* by urging that this case involves the provision of funds rather than access to facilities. The University begins with the unremarkable proposition that the State must have substantial discretion in determining how to allocate scare resources to accomplish its educational mission. Citing our decisions in Rust v. Sullivan (1991), Regan v. Taxation with Representation of Wash. (1983), and Widmar v. Vincent (1981), the University argues that content-based funding decisions are both inevitable and lawful. Were the reasoning of *Lamb's Chapel* to apply to funding decisions as well as to those involving access to facilities, it is urged, its holding "would become a judicial juggernaut, constitutionalizing the ubiquitous content-based decisions that schools, colleges, and other government entities routinely make in the allocation of public funds."

It does not follow, however, and we did not suggest in *Widmar*, that viewpoint-based restrictions are proper when the University does not itself speak or subsidize transmittal of a message it favors but instead expends funds to encourage a diversity of views from private speakers. A holding that the University may not discriminate based on the viewpoint of private persons whose speech it facilitates does not restrict the University's own speech, which is controlled by different principles. For that reason, the University's reliance on Regan v. Taxation with Representation of Wash. is inapposite as well. *Regan* involved a challenge to Congress' choice to grant tax deductions for contributions made to veterans' groups engaged in lobbying, while denying that favorable status to other charities which pursued lobbying efforts. Although acknowledging that the Government is not required to subsidize the exercise of fundamental rights, we reaffirmed the requirement of viewpoint neutrality in the Government's provision of financial benefits by observing that "[t]he case would be different if Congress were to discriminate invidiously in its subsidies in such a way as to ai[m] at the suppression of dangerous ideas."

Justice Kennedy concluded that providing funds to the religious group would not violate the Establishment Clause. He emphasized that "[t]he governmental program here is neutral toward religion." The government was acting with the purpose and effect of helping student groups and fostering a wide array of activities and viewpoints on campus. Justice Kennedy cited to *Widmar, Mergens,* and *Lamb's Chapel* and said that "[t]here is no difference in logic or principle, and no difference of constitutional significance, between a school using its funds to operate a facility to which students have access, and a school paying a third-party contractor to operate the facility on its behalf." Justice Kennedy's majority opinion concluded, "There is no Establishment Clause violation in the University's honoring its duties under the Free Speech Clause."

Justice Souter dissented and was joined by Justices Stevens, Ginsburg, and Breyer. He emphasized that this was the first time that the Court ever had allowed, let alone required, direct government financial subsidies to a religious group. Souter stated that "[u]sing public funds for the direct subsidization of preaching the word is categorically forbidden under the Establishment Clause, and if the Clause was meant to accomplish nothing else, it was meant to bar this use of public money." He concluded that "[t]he principle against direct funding with public money is patently violated by the contested use of today's student activity fee."

c. Student-Delivered Prayers

The Court also has considered the relationship between free speech and the Establishment Clause is the context of student-delivered prayers in public schools. As discussed below, the Court has consistently prohibited school-sponsored prayers in public schools. The issue in *Doe* was whether prohibiting student-delivered prayers at public high school football games, on the facts presented, would be an impermissible content-based restriction of the students' speech.

SANTA FE INDEPENDENT SCHOOL DISTRICT v. DOE
530 U.S. 290 (2000)

Justice STEVENS delivered the opinion of the Court.

Prior to 1995, the Santa Fe High School student who occupied the school's elective office of student council chaplain delivered a prayer over the public address system before each varsity football game for the entire season. This practice, along with others, was challenged in District Court as a violation of the Establishment Clause of the First Amendment. While these proceedings were pending in the District Court, the school district adopted a different policy that permits, but does not require, prayer initiated and led by a student at all home games. The District Court entered an order modifying that policy to permit only nonsectarian, nonproselytizing prayer. The Court of Appeals held that, even as modified by the District Court, the football prayer policy was invalid.

I

The Santa Fe Independent School District (District) is a political subdivision of the State of Texas, responsible for the education of more than 4,000 students in a small community in the southern part of the State. The District includes the Santa Fe High School, two primary schools, an intermediate school and the junior high school. Respondents are two sets of current or former students and their respective mothers. One family is Mormon and the other is Catholic. The District Court permitted respondents (Does) to litigate anonymously to protect them from intimidation or harassment.

[The school's policy evolved over time.] The August policy was titled "Prayer at Football Games." It authorized two student elections, the first to determine whether "invocations" should be delivered, and the second to select the spokesperson to deliver them. Like the July policy, it contained two parts, an initial statement that omitted any requirement that the content of the invocation be "nonsectarian and nonproselytising," and a fallback provision that automatically added that limitation if the preferred policy should be enjoined. On August 31, 1995, according to the parties' stipulation, "the district's high school students voted to determine whether a student would deliver prayer at varsity football games. . . . The students chose to allow a student to say a prayer at football games." A week later, in a separate election, they selected a student "to deliver the prayer at varsity football games."

The final policy (October policy) is essentially the same as the August policy, though it omits the word "prayer" from its title, and refers to "messages" and "statements" as well as "invocations." It is the validity of that policy that is before us.

We granted the District's petition for certiorari, limited to the following question: "Whether petitioner's policy permitting student-led, student-initiated prayer at football games violates the Establishment Clause." We conclude, as did the Court of Appeals, that it does.

II

In Lee v. Weisman (1992), we held that a prayer delivered by a rabbi at a middle school graduation ceremony violated that Clause. Although this case involves student prayer at a different type of school function, our analysis is properly guided by the principles that we endorsed in *Lee.*

In this case the District first argues that this principle is inapplicable to its October policy because the messages are private student speech, not public speech. It reminds us that there is a crucial difference between *government* speech endorsing religion, which the Establishment Clause forbids, and *private* speech endorsing religion, which the Free Speech and Free Exercise Clauses protect.

We certainly agree with that distinction, but we are not persuaded that the pregame invocations should be regarded as "private speech." These invocations are authorized by a government policy and take place on government property at government-sponsored school-related events. Of course, not every message delivered under such circumstances is the government's own. We have held, for example, that an individual's contribution to a government-created forum was not government speech. See Rosenberger v. Rector and Visitors of Univ. of Va. (1995). Although the District relies heavily on *Rosenberger* and similar cases involving such forums, it is clear that the pregame ceremony is not the type of forum discussed in those cases. The Santa Fe school officials simply do not "evince either 'by policy or by practice,' any intent to open the [pregame ceremony] to 'indiscriminate use,' . . . by the student body generally." Rather, the school allows only one student, the same student for the entire season, to give the invocation. The statement or invocation, moreover, is subject to particular regulations that confine the content and topic of the student's message.

Granting only one student access to the stage at a time does not, of course, necessarily preclude a finding that a school has created a limited public forum. Here, however, Santa Fe's student election system ensures that only those messages deemed "appropriate" under the District's policy may be delivered. That is, the majoritarian process implemented by the District guarantees, by definition, that minority candidates will never prevail and that their views will be effectively silenced.

In *Lee*, the school district made the related argument that its policy of endorsing only "civic or nonsectarian" prayer was acceptable because it minimized the intrusion on the audience as a whole. We rejected that claim by explaining that such a majoritarian policy "does not lessen the offense or isolation to the objectors. At best it narrows their number, at worst increases their sense of isolation and affront." Similarly, while Santa Fe's majoritarian election might ensure that most of the students are represented, it does nothing to protect the minority; indeed, it likely serves to intensify their offense.

Moreover, the District has failed to divorce itself from the religious content in the invocations. It has not succeeded in doing so, either by claiming that its policy is "'one of neutrality rather than endorsement'" or by characterizing the individual student as the "circuit-breaker" in the process. Contrary to the District's repeated assertions that it has adopted a "hands-off" approach to the pregame invocation, the realities of the situation plainly reveal that its policy involves both perceived and actual endorsement of religion. In this case, as we found in *Lee*, the "degree of school involvement" makes it clear that the pregame prayers bear "the imprint of the State and thus put school-age children who objected in an untenable position."

The District has attempted to disentangle itself from the religious messages by developing the two-step student election process. The text of the October policy, however, exposes the extent of the school's entanglement. The elections take place at all only because the school "board has chosen to permit students to deliver a brief invocation and/or message." The elections thus "shall" be conducted "by the high school student council" and "[u]pon advice and direction of the high school principal." The decision whether to deliver a message is first made by majority vote of the entire student body, followed by a choice of the speaker in a separate, similar majority election. Even though the particular words used by the speaker are not determined by those votes, the policy mandates that the "statement or invocation" be "consistent with the goals and purposes of this policy," which are "to solemnize the event, to promote good sportsmanship and student safety, and to establish the appropriate environment for the competition."

In addition to involving the school in the selection of the speaker, the policy, by its terms, invites and encourages religious messages. The policy itself states that the purpose of the message is "to solemnize the event." A religious message is the most obvious method of solemnizing an event. Moreover, the requirements that the message "promote good citizenship" and "establish the appropriate environment for competition" further narrow the types of message deemed appropriate, suggesting that a solemn, yet nonreligious, message, such as commentary on United States foreign policy, would be prohibited. Indeed, the only type of message that is expressly endorsed in the text is an "invocation" — a term that primarily described an appeal for divine assistance. In fact, as used in the past at Santa Fe High School, an "invocation" has always entailed a focused religious message. Thus, the expressed purposes of the policy encourage the selection of a religious message, and that is precisely how the students understand the policy. The results of the elections described in the parties' stipulation make it clear that the students understood that the central question before them was whether prayer should be a part of the pregame ceremony. We recognize the important role that public worship plays in many communities, as well as the sincere desire to include public prayer as a part of various occasions so as to mark those occasions' significance. But such religious activity in public schools, as elsewhere, must comport with the First Amendment.

The actual or perceived endorsement of the message, moreover, is established by factors beyond just the text of the policy. Once the student speaker is selected and the message composed, the invocation is then delivered to a large audience assembled as part of a regularly scheduled, school-sponsored function conducted on school property. The message is broadcast over the school's public address system, which remains subject to the control of school officials. It is fair to assume that the pregame ceremony is clothed in the traditional indicia of school sporting events, which generally include not just the team, but also cheerleaders and band members dressed in uniforms sporting the school name and mascot. The school's name is likely written in large print across the field and on banners and flags. The crowd will certainly include many who display the school colors and insignia on their school T-shirts, jackets, or hats and who may also be waving signs displaying the school name. It is in a setting such as this that "[t]he board has chosen to permit" the elected student to rise and give the "statement or invocation."

In this context the members of the listening audience must perceive the pregame message as a public expression of the views of the majority of the student body delivered with the approval of the school administration. In cases involving state participation in a religious activity, one of the relevant questions is "whether an objective observer, acquainted with the text, legislative history, and implementation of the statute, would perceive it as a state endorsement of prayer in public schools." Regardless of the listener's support for, or objection to, the message, an objective Santa Fe High School student will unquestionably perceive the inevitable pregame prayer as stamped with her school's seal of approval.

School sponsorship of religious message is impermissible because it sends the ancillary message to members of the audience who are nonadherents "that they are outsiders, not full members of the political community, and an accompanying message to adherents that they are insiders, favored members of the political community." The delivery of such a message — over the school's public address system, by a speaker representing the student body, under the supervision of school faculty, and pursuant to a school policy that explicitly and implicitly encourages public prayer — is not properly characterized as "private" speech.

The District next argues that its football policy is distinguishable from the graduation prayer in *Lee* because it does not coerce students to participate in religious observances. Attendance at a high school football game, unlike showing up for class, is certainly not required in order to receive a diploma. Moreover, we may assume that the District is correct in arguing that the informal pressure to attend an athletic event is not as strong as a senior's desire to attend her own graduation ceremony. There are some students, however, such as cheerleaders, members of the band, and, of course, the team members themselves, for whom seasonal commitments mandate their attendance, sometimes for class credit. The District also minimizes the importance to many students of attending and participating in extracurricular activities as part of a complete educational experience.

High school home football games are traditional gatherings of a school community; they bring together students and faculty as well as friends and family from years present and past to root for a common cause. Undoubtedly, the games are not important to some students, and they voluntarily choose not to attend. For many others, however, the choice between whether to attend these games or to risk facing a personally offensive religious ritual is in no practical sense an easy one. The Constitution, moreover, demands that the school may not force this difficult choice upon these students for "[i]t is a tenet of the First Amendment that the State cannot require one of its citizens to forfeit his or her rights and benefits as the price of resisting conformance to state-sponsored religious practice."

Even if we regard every high school student's decision to attend a home football game as purely voluntary, we are nevertheless persuaded that the delivery of a pregame prayer has the improper effect of coercing those present to participate in an act of religious worship. For "the government may no more use social pressure to enforce orthodoxy than it may use more direct means."

Chief Justic REHNQUIST, with whom Justice SCALIA and Justice THOMAS join, dissenting.

The Court distorts existing precedent to conclude that the school district's student-message program is invalid on its face under the Establishment Clause. But even more disturbing than its holding is the tone of the Court's opinion; it bristles with hostility to all things religious in public life. Neither the holding nor the tone of the opinion is faithful to the meaning of the Establishment Clause, when it is recalled that George Washington himself, at the request of the very Congress which passed the Bill of Rights, proclaimed a day of "public thanksgiving and prayer, to be observed by acknowledging with grateful hearts the many and signal favors of Almighty God."

The Court, venturing into the realm of prophesy, decides that it "need not wait for the inevitable" and invalidates the district's policy on its face. To do so, it applies the most rigid version of the oft-criticized test of Lemon v. Kurtzman (1971). Even if it were appropriate to apply the *Lemon* test here, the district's student-message policy should not be invalidated on its face.

[W]ith respect to the policy's purpose, the Court holds that "the simple enactment of this policy, with the purpose and perception of school endorsement of student prayer, was a constitutional violation." But the policy itself has plausible secular purposes: "[T]o solemnize the event, to promote good sportsmanship and student safety, and to establish the appropriate environment for the competition." Where a governmental body "expresses a plausible secular purpose" for an enactment, "courts should generally defer to that stated intent." Under the Court's logic, a public school that sponsors the singing of the national anthem before football games violates the Establishment Clause. Although the Court apparently believes that solemnizing football games is an illegitimate purpose, the voters in the school district seem to disagree. Nothing in the Establishment Clause prevents them from making this choice.

d. Religious Symbols on Government Property

In *Allegheny County*, above, the Court considered the constitutionality of a nativity scene and a menorah on government property. More recently, in two cases, the Court considered the constitutionality of Ten Commandments displays on government property.

The court declared the display in *McCreary County* unconstitutional, but upheld the display in *Van Orden*. In reading the decisions, consider whether there is a meaningful distinction between these cases. Also, it is important to consider what lower courts should do, in light of these decisions, if they are confronted with cases involving Ten Commandments monuments or other religious symbols.

McCREARY COUNTY v. AMERICAN CIVIL LIBERTIES UNION OF KENTUCKY

545 U.S. 844 (2005)

Justice SOUTER delivered the opinion of the Court.

Executives of two counties posted a version of the Ten Commandments on the walls of their courthouses. After suits were filed charging violations of the Establishment Clause, the legislative body of each county adopted a resolution calling for a more extensive exhibit meant to show that the Commandments are Kentucky's "precedent legal code." The result in each instance was a modified display of the Commandments surrounded by texts containing religious references as their sole common element. After changing counsel, the counties revised the exhibits again by eliminating some documents, expanding the text set out in another, and adding some new ones.

The issues are whether a determination of the counties' purpose is a sound basis for ruling on the Establishment Clause complaints, and whether evaluation of the counties' claim of secular purpose for the ultimate displays may take their evolution into account. We hold that the counties' manifest objective may be dispositive of the constitutional enquiry, and that the development of the presentation should be considered when determining its purpose.

I

In the summer of 1999, petitioners McCreary County and Pulaski County, Kentucky (hereinafter Counties), put up in their respective courthouses large, gold-framed copies of an abridged text of the King James version of the Ten Commandments, including a citation to the Book of Exodus. In McCreary County, the placement of the Commandments responded to an order of the county legislative body requiring "the display [to] be posted in 'a very high traffic area' of the courthouse." In Pulaski County, amidst reported controversy over the propriety of the display, the Commandments were hung in a ceremony presided over by the county Judge-Executive, who called them "good rules to live by" and who recounted the story of an astronaut who became convinced "there must be a divine God" after viewing the Earth from the moon.

In November 1999, respondents American Civil Liberties Union of Kentucky et al. sued the Counties in Federal District Court and sought a preliminary injunction against maintaining the displays, which the ACLU charged were violations of the prohibition of religious establishment included in the First Amendment of the Constitution. Within a month, and before the District Court had responded to the request for injunction, the legislative body of each County authorized a second, expanded display, by nearly identical resolutions reciting that the Ten Commandments are "the precedent legal code upon which the civil and criminal codes of . . . Kentucky are founded," and stating several grounds for taking that position: that "the Ten Commandments are codified in Kentucky's civil and criminal laws"; that the Kentucky House of Representatives had in 1993 "voted unanimously . . . to adjourn . . . 'in remembrance and honor of Jesus Christ, the Prince of Ethics'"; that the "County Judge and . . . magistrates agree with the arguments set out by Judge [Roy] Moore" in defense of his "display [of] the Ten Commandments in his courtroom"; and that the "Founding Father[s] [had an] explicit understanding of the duty of elected officials to publicly acknowledge God as the source of America's strength and direction."

As directed by the resolutions, the Counties expanded the displays of the Ten Commandments in their locations, presumably along with copies of the resolution, which instructed that it, too, be posted. In addition to the first display's large framed copy of the edited King James version of the Commandments, the second included eight other documents in smaller frames, each either having a religious theme or excerpted to highlight a religious element. The documents were the "endowed by their Creator" passage from the Declaration of Independence; the Preamble to the Constitution of Kentucky; the national motto, "In God We Trust"; a page from the Congressional Record of February 2, 1983, proclaiming the Year of the Bible and including a statement of the Ten Commandments; a proclamation by President Abraham Lincoln designating April 30, 1863, a National Day of Prayer and Humiliation; an excerpt from President Lincoln's "Reply to Loyal Colored People of Baltimore upon Presentation of a

Bible," reading that "[t]he Bible is the best gift God has ever given to man"; a proclamation by President Reagan marking 1983 the Year of the Bible; and the Mayflower Compact.

II

Twenty-five years ago in a case prompted by posting the Ten Commandments in Kentucky's public schools, this Court recognized that the Commandments "are undeniably a sacred text in the Jewish and Christian faiths" and held that their display in public classrooms violated the First Amendment's bar against establishment of religion. Stone v. Graham (1980). *Stone* found a predominantly religious purpose in the government's posting of the Commandments, given their prominence as "'an instrument of religion.'" The Counties ask for a different approach here by arguing that official purpose is unknowable and the search for it inherently vain.

A

Ever since Lemon v. Kurtzman (1971) summarized the three familiar considerations for evaluating Establishment Clause claims, looking to whether government action has "a secular legislative purpose" has been a common, albeit seldom dispositive, element of our cases. Though we have found government action motivated by an illegitimate purpose only four times since *Lemon*, and "the secular purpose requirement alone may rarely be determinative . . . , it nevertheless serves an important function."

The touchstone for our analysis is the principle that the "First Amendment mandates governmental neutrality between religion and religion, and between religion and nonreligion." When the government acts with the ostensible and predominant purpose of advancing religion, it violates that central Establishment Clause value of official religious neutrality, there being no neutrality when the government's ostensible object is to take sides. Manifesting a purpose to favor one faith over another, or adherence to religion generally, clashes with the "understanding, reached . . . after decades of religious war, that liberty and social stability demand a religious tolerance that respects the religious views of all citizens. . . ." By showing a purpose to favor religion, the government "sends the . . . message to . . . nonadherents 'that they are outsiders, not full members of the political community, and an accompanying message to adherents that they are insiders, favored members. . . .'"

B

Despite the intuitive importance of official purpose to the realization of Establishment Clause values, the Counties ask us to abandon *Lemon*'s purpose test, or at least to truncate any enquiry into purpose here. Their first argument is that the very consideration of purpose is deceptive: according to them, true "purpose" is unknowable, and its search merely an excuse for courts to act selectively and unpredictably in picking out evidence of subjective intent. The assertions are as seismic as they are unconvincing.

Examination of purpose is a staple of statutory interpretation that makes up the daily fare of every appellate court in the country, and governmental purpose is a key element of a good deal of constitutional doctrine, e.g., Washington v. Davis (1976) (discriminatory purpose required for Equal Protection violation); Hunt v. Washington State Apple Advertising Comm'n (1977) (discriminatory purpose relevant to dormant Commerce Clause claim); Church of Lukumi Babalu Aye, Inc. v. Hialeah (1993) (discriminatory purpose raises level of scrutiny required by free exercise claim). With enquiries into purpose this common, if they were nothing but hunts for mares' nests deflecting attention from bare judicial will, the whole notion of purpose in law would have dropped into disrepute long ago.

But scrutinizing purpose does make practical sense, as in Establishment Clause analysis, where an understanding of official objective emerges from readily discoverable fact, without any judicial psychoanalysis of a drafter's heart of hearts. The eyes that look to purpose belong to an "objective observer," one who takes account of the traditional external signs that show up in the "text, legislative history, and implementation of the statute," or comparable official act. There is, then, nothing hinting at an unpredictable or disingenuous exercise when a court enquires into purpose after a claim is raised under the Establishment Clause.

Nor is there any indication that the enquiry is rigged in practice to finding a religious purpose dominant every time a case is filed. In the past, the test has not been fatal very often, presumably because government does not generally act unconstitutionally, with the predominant purpose of advancing religion. That said, one consequence of the corollary that Establishment Clause analysis does not look to the veiled psyche of government officers could be that in some of the cases in which establishment complaints failed, savvy officials had disguised their religious intent so cleverly that the objective observer just missed it. But that is no reason for great constitutional concern. If someone in the government hides religious motive so well that the "objective observer, acquainted with the text, legislative history, and implementation of the statute[]," cannot see it, then without something more the government does not make a divisive announcement that in itself amounts to taking religious sides. A secret motive stirs up no strife and does nothing to make outsiders of nonadherents, and it suffices to wait and see whether such government action turns out to have (as it may even be likely to have) the illegitimate effect of advancing religion.

C

After declining the invitation to abandon concern with purpose wholesale, we also have to avoid the Counties' alternative tack of trivializing the enquiry into it. The Counties would read the cases as if the purpose enquiry were so naive that any transparent claim to secularity would satisfy it, and they would cut context out of the enquiry, to the point of ignoring history, no matter what bearing it actually had on the significance of current circumstances. There is no precedent for the Counties' arguments, or reason supporting them.

Lemon said that government action must have "a secular . . . purpose," and after a host of cases it is fair to add that although a legislature's stated reasons will generally get deference, the secular purpose required has to be genuine, not a sham, and not merely secondary to a religious objective.

The Counties' second proffered limitation can be dispatched quickly. They argue that purpose in a case like this one should be inferred, if at all, only from the latest news about the last in a series of governmental actions, however close they may all be in time and subject. But the world is not made brand new every morning, and the Counties are simply asking us to ignore perfectly probative evidence; they want an absentminded objective observer, not one presumed to be familiar with the history of the government's actions and competent to learn what history has to show. The Counties' position just bucks common sense: reasonable observers have reasonable memories, and our precedents sensibly forbid an observer "to turn a blind eye to the context in which [the] policy arose."

III

We take *Stone* as the initial legal benchmark, our only case dealing with the constitutionality of displaying the Commandments. *Stone* recognized that the Commandments are an "instrument of religion" and that, at least on the facts before it, the display of their text could presumptively be understood as meant to advance religion: although state law specifically required their posting in public school classrooms, their isolated exhibition did not leave room even for an argument that secular education explained their being there. But *Stone* did not purport to decide the constitutionality of every possible way the Commandments might be set out by the government, and under the Establishment Clause detail is key. Hence, we look to the record of evidence showing the progression leading up to the third display of the Commandments.

The display rejected in *Stone* had two obvious similarities to the first one in the sequence here: both set out a text of the Commandments as distinct from any traditionally symbolic representation, and each stood alone, not part of an arguably secular display. *Stone* stressed the significance of integrating the Commandments into a secular scheme to forestall the broadcast of an otherwise clearly religious message, and for good reason, the Commandments being a central point of reference in the religious and moral history of Jews and Christians. They proclaim the existence of a monotheistic god (no other gods). They regulate details of religious obligation (no graven images, no sabbath breaking, no vain oath swearing). And they unmistakably rest even the universally accepted prohibitions (as against murder, theft, and the like) on the sanction of the divinity proclaimed at the beginning of the text. Displaying that text is thus different from a symbolic depiction, like tablets with 10 roman numerals, which could be seen as alluding to a general notion of law, not a sectarian conception of faith. Where the text is set out, the insistence of the religious message is hard to avoid in the absence of a context plausibly suggesting a message going beyond an excuse to promote the religious point of view. The display in *Stone* had no context that might have indicated an object beyond the religious character of the text, and the Counties' solo exhibit here did nothing more to counter the sectarian implication than the postings at issue in *Stone*. Actually, the posting by the Counties lacked even the *Stone* display's implausible disclaimer that the Commandments were set out to show their effect on the civil law. What is more, at the ceremony for posting the framed Commandments in Pulaski County, the county executive was accompanied by his pastor, who testified to the certainty of the existence of God. The reasonable observer could only think that the Counties meant to emphasize and celebrate the Commandments' religious message.

This is not to deny that the Commandments have had influence on civil or secular law; a major text of a majority religion is bound to be felt. The point is simply that the original text viewed in its entirety is an unmistakably religious statement dealing with religious obligations and with morality subject to religious sanction. When the government initiates an effort to place this statement alone in public view, a religious object is unmistakable.

Once the Counties were sued, they modified the exhibits and invited additional insight into their purpose in a display that hung for about six months. This new one was the product of forthright and nearly identical Pulaski and McCreary County resolutions listing a series of American historical documents with theistic and Christian references, which were to be posted in order to furnish a setting for displaying the Ten Commandments and any "other Kentucky and American historical documen[t]" without raising concern about "any Christian or religious references" in them. As mentioned, the resolutions expressed support for an Alabama judge who posted the Commandments in his courtroom, and cited the fact the Kentucky Legislature once adjourned a session in honor of "Jesus Christ, Prince of Ethics."

In this second display, unlike the first, the Commandments were not hung in isolation, merely leaving the Counties' purpose to emerge from the pervasively religious text of the Commandments themselves. Instead, the second version was required to include the statement of the government's purpose expressly set out in the county resolutions, and underscored it by juxtaposing the Commandments to other documents with highlighted references to God as their sole common element. The display's unstinting focus was on religious passages, showing that the Counties were posting the Commandments precisely because of their sectarian content. That demonstration of the government's objective was enhanced by serial religious references and the accompanying resolution's claim about the embodiment of ethics in Christ. Together, the display and resolution presented an indisputable, and undisputed, showing of an impermissible purpose.

Today, the Counties make no attempt to defend their undeniable objective, but instead hopefully describe version two as "dead and buried." Their refusal to defend the second display is understandable, but the reasonable observer could not forget it.

After the Counties changed lawyers, they mounted a third display, without a new resolution or repeal of the old one. The result was the "Foundations of American Law and Government" exhibit, which placed the Commandments in the company of other documents the Counties thought especially significant in the historical foundation of American government.

These new statements of purpose were presented only as a litigating position, there being no further authorizing action by the Counties' governing boards. And although repeal of the earlier county authorizations would not have erased them from the record of evidence bearing on current purpose, the extraordinary resolutions for the second display passed just months earlier were not repealed or otherwise repudiated. Indeed, the sectarian spirit of the common resolution found enhanced expression in the third display, which quoted more of the purely religious language of the Commandments than the first two displays had done. No reasonable observer could swallow the claim that the Counties had cast off the objective so unmistakable in the earlier displays.

In holding the preliminary injunction adequately supported by evidence that the Counties' purpose had not changed at the third stage, we do not decide that the Counties' past actions forever taint any effort on their part to deal with the subject matter. We hold only that purpose needs to be taken seriously under the

Establishment Clause and needs to be understood in light of context; an implausible claim that governmental purpose has changed should not carry the day in a court of law any more than in a head with common sense. It is enough to say here that district courts are fully capable of adjusting preliminary relief to take account of genuine changes in constitutionally significant conditions.

Nor do we have occasion here to hold that a sacred text can never be integrated constitutionally into a governmental display on the subject of law, or American history. We do not forget, and in this litigation have frequently been reminded, that our own courtroom frieze was deliberately designed in the exercise of governmental authority so as to include the figure of Moses holding tablets exhibiting a portion of the Hebrew text of the later, secularly phrased Commandments; in the company of 17 other lawgivers, most of them secular figures, there is no risk that Moses would strike an observer as evidence that the National Government was violating neutrality in religion.

IV

The dissent, however, puts forward a limitation on the application of the neutrality principle, with citations to historical evidence said to show that the Framers understood the ban on establishment of religion as sufficiently narrow to allow the government to espouse submission to the divine will. The dissent identifies God as the God of monotheism, all of whose three principal strains (Jewish, Christian, and Muslim) acknowledge the religious importance of the Ten Commandments. On the dissent's view, it apparently follows that even rigorous espousal of a common element of this common monotheism is consistent with the establishment ban.

But the dissent's argument for the original understanding is flawed from the outset by its failure to consider the full range of evidence showing what the Framers believed. The dissent is certainly correct in putting forward evidence that some of the Framers thought some endorsement of religion was compatible with the establishment ban.

But the fact is that we do have more to go on, for there is also evidence supporting the proposition that the Framers intended the Establishment Clause to require governmental neutrality in matters of religion, including neutrality in statements acknowledging religion. The very language of the Establishment Clause represented a significant departure from early drafts that merely prohibited a single national religion, and the final language instead "extended [the] prohibition to state support for 'religion' in general."

The historical record, moreover, is complicated beyond the dissent's account by the writings and practices of figures no less influential than Thomas Jefferson and James Madison. Jefferson, for example, refused to issue Thanksgiving Proclamations because he believed that they violated the Constitution. And Madison, whom the dissent claims as supporting its thesis, criticized Virginia's general assessment tax not just because it required people to donate "three pence" to religion, but because "it is itself a signal of persecution. It degrades from the equal rank of Citizens all those whose opinions in Religion do not bend to those of the Legislative authority."

The fair inference is that there was no common understanding about the limits of the establishment prohibition, and the dissent's conclusion that its narrower view was the original understanding stretches the evidence beyond tensile capacity. What the evidence does show is a group of statesmen, like others before and after them, who proposed a guarantee with contours not wholly worked out, leaving the Establishment Clause with edges still to be determined. And none the worse for that. Indeterminate edges are the kind to have in a constitution meant to endure, and to meet "exigencies which, if foreseen at all, must have been seen dimly, and which can be best provided for as they occur."

While the dissent fails to show a consistent original understanding from which to argue that the neutrality principle should be rejected, it does manage to deliver a surprise. As mentioned, the dissent says that the deity the Framers had in mind was the God of monotheism, with the consequence that government may espouse a tenet of traditional monotheism. This is truly a remarkable view. Today's dissent, however, apparently means that government should be free to approve the core beliefs of a favored religion over the tenets of others, a view that should trouble anyone who prizes religious liberty. Certainly history cannot justify it; on the contrary, history shows that the religion of concern to the Framers was not that of the monotheistic faiths generally, but Christianity in particular, a fact that no member of this Court takes as a premise for construing the Religion Clauses.

Historical evidence thus supports no solid argument for changing course (whatever force the argument might have when directed at the existing precedent), whereas public discourse at the present time certainly raises no doubt about the value of the interpretative approach invoked for 60 years now. We are centuries away from the St. Bartholomew's Day massacre and the treatment of heretics in early Massachusetts, but the divisiveness of religion in current public life is inescapable. This is no time to deny the prudence of understanding the Establishment Clause to require the Government to stay neutral on religious belief, which is reserved for the conscience of the individual.

Justice O'CONNOR, concurring.

I join in the Court's opinion. The First Amendment expresses our Nation's fundamental commitment to religious liberty by means of two provisions—one protecting the free exercise of religion, the other barring establishment of religion. They were written by the descendents of people who had come to this land precisely so that they could practice their religion freely. Together with the other First Amendment guarantees—of free speech, a free press, and the rights to assemble and petition—the Religion Clauses were designed to safeguard the freedom of conscience and belief that those immigrants had sought. They embody an idea that was once considered radical: Free people are entitled to free and diverse thoughts, which government ought neither to constrain nor to direct.

Reasonable minds can disagree about how to apply the Religion Clauses in a given case. But the goal of the Clauses is clear: to carry out the Founders' plan of preserving religious liberty to the fullest extent possible in a pluralistic society.

By enforcing the Clauses, we have kept religion a matter for the individual conscience, not for the prosecutor or bureaucrat. At a time when we see around the world the violent consequences of the assumption of religious authority by government, Americans may count themselves fortunate: Our regard for constitutional boundaries has protected us from similar travails, while allowing private religious exercise to flourish. The well-known statement that "[w]e are a religious people" has proved true. Americans attend their places of worship more often than do citizens of other developed nations, and describe religion as playing an especially important role in their lives. Those who would renegotiate the boundaries between church and state must therefore answer a difficult question: Why would we trade a system that has served us so well for one that has served others so poorly?

When we enforce these restrictions, we do so for the same reason that guided the Framers — respect for religion's special role in society. Our Founders conceived of a Republic receptive to voluntary religious expression, and provided for the possibility of judicial intervention when government action threatens or impedes such expression. Voluntary religious belief and expression may be as threatened when government takes the mantle of religion upon itself as when government directly interferes with private religious practices. When the government associates one set of religious beliefs with the state and identifies nonadherents as outsiders, it encroaches upon the individual's decision about whether and how to worship. In the marketplace of ideas, the government has vast resources and special status. Government religious expression therefore risks crowding out private observance and distorting the natural interplay between competing beliefs. Allowing government to be a potential mouthpiece for competing religious ideas risks the sort of division that might easily spill over into suppression of rival beliefs. Tying secular and religious authority together poses risks to both.

Given the history of this particular display of the Ten Commandments, the Court correctly finds an Establishment Clause violation. The purpose behind the counties' display is relevant because it conveys an unmistakable message of endorsement to the reasonable observer. It is true that many Americans find the Commandments in accord with their personal beliefs. But we do not count heads before enforcing the First Amendment. Nor can we accept the theory that Americans who do not accept the Commandments' validity are outside the First Amendment's protections. There is no list of approved and disapproved beliefs appended to the First Amendment — and the Amendment's broad terms do not admit of such a cramped reading.

It is true that the Framers lived at a time when our national religious diversity was neither as robust nor as well recognized as it is now. They may not have foreseen the variety of religions for which this Nation would eventually provide a home. They surely could not have predicted new religions, some of them born in this country. But they did know that line-drawing between religions is an enterprise that, once begun, has no logical stopping point. They worried that "the same authority which can establish Christianity, in exclusion of all other Religions, may establish with the same ease any particular sect of Christians, in exclusion of all other Sects." The Religion Clauses, as a result, protect adherents of all religions, as well as those who believe in no religion at all.

We owe our First Amendment to a generation with a profound commitment to religion and a profound commitment to religious liberty — visionaries who held their faith "with enough confidence to believe that what should be rendered to God does not need to be decided and collected by Caesar." In my opinion, the display at issue was an establishment of religion in violation of our Constitution. For the reasons given above, I join in the Court's opinion.

Justice SCALIA, with whom the Chief Justice and Justice THOMAS join, and with whom Justice KENNEDY joins as to Parts II and III, dissenting.

I would uphold McCreary County and Pulaski County, Kentucky's (hereinafter Counties) displays of the Ten Commandments. I shall discuss, first, why the Court's oft repeated assertion that the government cannot favor religious practice is false; second, why today's opinion extends the scope of that falsehood even beyond prior cases; and third, why even on the basis of the Court's false assumptions the judgment here is wrong.

I

A

On September 11, 2001, I was attending in Rome, Italy, an international conference of judges and lawyers, principally from Europe and the United States. That night and the next morning virtually all of the participants watched, in their hotel rooms, the address to the Nation by the President of the United States concerning the murderous attacks upon the Twin Towers and the Pentagon, in which thousands of Americans had been killed. The address ended, as Presidential addresses often do, with the prayer "God bless America." The next afternoon I was approached by one of the judges from a European country, who, after extending his profound condolences for my country's loss, sadly observed: "How I wish that the Head of State of my country, at a similar time of national tragedy and distress, could conclude his address 'God bless _____.' It is of course absolutely forbidden."

That is one model of the relationship between church and state — a model spread across Europe by the armies of Napoleon, and reflected in the Constitution of France, which begins "France is [a] . . . secular . . . Republic." France Const., Art. 1. Religion is to be strictly excluded from the public forum. This is not, and never was, the model adopted by America. George Washington added to the form of Presidential oath prescribed by Art. II, §1, cl. 8, of the Constitution, the concluding words "so help me God." The Supreme Court under John Marshall opened its sessions with the prayer, "God save the United States and this Honorable Court." The First Congress instituted the practice of beginning its legislative sessions with a prayer. The same week that Congress submitted the Establishment Clause as part of the Bill of Rights for ratification by the States, it enacted legislation providing for paid chaplains in the House and Senate. The day after the First Amendment was proposed, the same Congress that had proposed it requested the President to proclaim "a day of public thanksgiving and prayer, to be observed, by acknowledging, with grateful hearts, the many and signal favours of Almighty God." President Washington offered the first Thanksgiving Proclamation shortly thereafter, devoting November 26, 1789, on behalf of the American people "'to the service of that great and glorious Being who is the beneficent author of all the good that is, that was, or that will be,'" thus beginning a tradition of offering gratitude to God that continues today. The same Congress also reenacted the Northwest Territory Ordinance of 1787, Article III of which provided: "Religion, morality, and knowledge, being necessary to good government and the happiness of mankind, schools and the means of education shall forever be encouraged." And of course the First

Amendment itself accords religion (and no other manner of belief) special constitutional protection.

These actions of our First President and Congress and the Marshall Court were not idiosyncratic; they reflected the beliefs of the period. Those who wrote the Constitution believed that morality was essential to the well-being of society and that encouragement of religion was the best way to foster morality. The "fact that the Founding Fathers believed devotedly that there was a God and that the unalienable rights of man were rooted in Him is clearly evidenced in their writings, from the Mayflower Compact to the Constitution itself."

Nor have the views of our people on this matter significantly changed. Presidents continue to conclude the Presidential oath with the words "so help me God." Our legislatures, state and national, continue to open their sessions with prayer led by official chaplains. The sessions of this Court continue to open with the prayer "God save the United States and this Honorable Court." Invocation of the Almighty by our public figures, at all levels of government, remains commonplace. Our coinage bears the motto "IN GOD WE TRUST." And our Pledge of Allegiance contains the acknowledgment that we are a Nation "under God." As one of our Supreme Court opinions rightly observed, "We are a religious people whose institutions presuppose a Supreme Being." Zorach v. Clauson (1952).

With all of this reality (and much more) staring it in the face, how can the Court possibly assert that "the First Amendment mandates governmental neutrality between . . . religion and nonreligion," and that "[m]anifesting a purpose to favor . . . adherence to religion generally," is unconstitutional? Who says so? Surely not the words of the Constitution. Surely not the history and traditions that reflect our society's constant understanding of those words. Surely not even the current sense of our society, recently reflected in an Act of Congress adopted unanimously by the Senate and with only 5 nays in the House of Representatives, criticizing a Court of Appeals opinion that had held "under God" in the Pledge of Allegiance unconstitutional. Nothing stands behind the Court's assertion that governmental affirmation of the society's belief in God is unconstitutional except the Court's own say-so, citing as support only the unsubstantiated say-so of earlier Courts going back no farther than the mid-20th century. And it is, moreover, a thoroughly discredited say-so. It is discredited, to begin with, because a majority of the Justices on the current Court (including at least one Member of today's majority) have, in separate opinions, repudiated the brain-spun "Lemon test" that embodies the supposed principle of neutrality between religion and irreligion. And it is discredited because the Court has not had the courage (or the foolhardiness) to apply the neutrality principle consistently.

What distinguishes the rule of law from the dictatorship of a shifting Supreme Court majority is the absolutely indispensable requirement that judicial opinions be grounded in consistently applied principle. That is what prevents judges from ruling now this way, now that — thumbs up or thumbs down — as their personal preferences dictate.

Besides appealing to the demonstrably false principle that the government cannot favor religion over irreligion, today's opinion suggests that the posting of the Ten Commandments violates the principle that the government cannot favor one religion over another. That is indeed a valid principle where public aid or assistance to religion is concerned, or where the free exercise of religion is at issue, but it necessarily applies in a more limited sense to public acknowledgment of the Creator. If religion in the public forum had to be entirely nondenominational, there could be no religion in the public forum at all. One cannot say the word "God," or "the Almighty," one cannot offer public supplication or thanksgiving, without contradicting the beliefs of some people that there are many gods, or that God or the gods pay no attention to human affairs. With respect to public acknowledgment of religious belief, it is entirely clear from our Nation's historical practices that the Establishment Clause permits this disregard of polytheists and believers in unconcerned deities, just as it permits the disregard of devout atheists. The Thanksgiving Proclamation issued by George Washington at the instance of the First Congress was scrupulously nondenominational — but it was monotheistic. In Marsh v. Chambers (1983), we said that the fact the particular prayers offered in the Nebraska Legislature were "in the Judeo-Christian tradition" posed no additional problem, because "there is no indication that the prayer opportunity has been exploited to proselytize or advance any one, or to disparage any other, faith or belief."

Historical practices thus demonstrate that there is a distance between the acknowledgment of a single Creator and the establishment of a religion. The former is, as Marsh v. Chambers put it, "a tolerable acknowledgment of beliefs widely held among the people of this country." The three most popular religions in the United States, Christianity, Judaism, and Islam — which combined account for 97.7% of all believers — are monotheistic. All of them, moreover (Islam included), believe that the Ten Commandments were given by God to Moses, and are divine prescriptions for a virtuous life. Publicly honoring the Ten Commandments is thus indistinguishable, insofar as discriminating against other religions is concerned, from publicly honoring God. Both practices are recognized across such a broad and diverse range of the population — from Christians to Muslims — that they cannot be reasonably understood as a government endorsement of a particular religious viewpoint.

B

I must respond to Justice Stevens' assertion that I would "marginaliz[e] the belief systems of more than 7 million Americans" who adhere to religions that are not monotheistic. Surely that is a gross exaggeration. The beliefs of those citizens are entirely protected by the Free Exercise Clause, and by those aspects of the Establishment Clause that do not relate to government acknowledgment of the Creator. Invocation of God despite their beliefs is permitted not because nonmonotheistic religions cease to be religions recognized by the religion clauses of the First Amendment, but because governmental invocation of God is not an establishment. Justice Stevens fails to recognize that in the context of public acknowledgments of God there are legitimate competing interests: On the one hand, the interest of that minority in not feeling "excluded"; but on the other, the interest of the overwhelming majority of religious believers in being able to give God thanks and supplication as a people, and with respect to our national endeavors. Our national tradition has resolved that conflict in favor of the majority. It is not for this Court to change a disposition that accounts, many Americans think, for the phenomenon remarked upon in a quotation attributed to various authors, including Bismarck, but which I prefer to associate with Charles de Gaulle: "God watches over little children, drunkards, and the United States of America."

II

As bad as the *Lemon* test is, it is worse for the fact that, since its inception, its seemingly simple mandates have been manipulated to fit whatever result the Court aimed to achieve. Today's opinion is no different. In two respects it modifies *Lemon* to ratchet up the Court's hostility to religion. First, the Court justifies inquiry into legislative purpose, not as an end itself, but as a means to ascertain the appearance of the government action to an "'objective observer.'" Because in the Court's view the true danger to be guarded against is that the objective observer would feel like an "outside[r]" or "not [a] full membe[r] of the political community," its inquiry focuses not on the actual purpose of government action, but the "purpose apparent from government action." Under this approach, even if a government could show that its actual purpose was not to advance religion, it would presumably violate the Constitution as long as the Court's objective observer would think otherwise.

I have remarked before that it is an odd jurisprudence that bases the unconstitutionality of a government practice that does not actually advance religion on the hopes of the government that it would do so. But that oddity pales in comparison to the one invited by today's analysis: the legitimacy of a government action with a wholly secular effect would turn on the misperception of an imaginary observer that the government officials behind the action had the intent to advance religion.

Second, the Court replaces *Lemon*'s requirement that the government have "a secular . . . purpose" with the heightened requirement that the secular purpose "predominate" over any purpose to advance religion. The Court treats this extension as a natural outgrowth of the longstanding requirement that the government's secular purpose not be a sham, but simple logic shows the two to be unrelated. If the government's proffered secular purpose is not genuine, then the government has no secular purpose at all. The new demand that secular purpose predominate contradicts *Lemon*'s more limited requirement, and finds no support in our cases.

I have urged that *Lemon*'s purpose prong be abandoned, because (as I have discussed in Part I) even an exclusive purpose to foster or assist religious practice is not necessarily invalidating. But today's extension makes things even worse. By shifting the focus of *Lemon*'s purpose prong from the search for a genuine, secular motivation to the hunt for a predominantly religious purpose, the Court converts what has in the past been a fairly limited inquiry into a rigorous review of the full record. Those responsible for the adoption of the Religion Clauses would surely regard it as a bitter irony that the religious values they designed those Clauses to protect have now become so distasteful to this Court that if they constitute anything more than a subordinate motive for government action they will invalidate it.

III

Even accepting the Court's *Lemon*-based premises, the displays at issue here were constitutional. To any person who happened to walk down the hallway of the McCreary or Pulaski County Courthouse during the roughly nine months when the Foundations Displays were exhibited, the displays must have seemed unremarkable—if indeed they were noticed at all. The walls of both court-houses were already lined with historical documents and other assorted por-traits; each Foundations Display was exhibited in the same format as these other displays and nothing in the record suggests that either County took steps to give it greater prominence. On its face, the Foundations Displays manifested the purely secular purpose that the Counties asserted before the District Court: "to display documents that played a significant role in the foundation of our system of law and government." That the Displays included the Ten Command-ments did not transform their apparent secular purpose into one of impermis-sible advocacy for Judeo-Christian beliefs.

Acknowledgment of the contribution that religion has made to our Nation's legal and governmental heritage partakes of a centuries-old tradition. Display of the Ten Commandments is well within the mainstream of this practice of acknowledgment. Federal, State, and local governments across the Nation have engaged in such display. The Supreme Court Building itself includes depic-tions of Moses with the Ten Commandments in the Courtroom and on the east pediment of the building, and symbols of the Ten Commandments "adorn the metal gates lining the north and south sides of the Courtroom as well as the doors leading into the Courtroom." Similar depictions of the Decalogue appear on public buildings and monuments throughout our Nation's Capital. The frequency of these displays testifies to the popular understanding that the Ten Commandments are a foundation of the rule of law, and a symbol of the role that religion played, and continues to play, in our system of government.

VAN ORDEN v. PERRY

545 U.S. 677 (2005)

Chief Justice REHNQUIST announced the judgment of the Court and delivered an opinion, in which Justice SCALIA, Justice KENNEDY, and Justice THOMAS join.

The question here is whether the Establishment Clause of the First Amend-ment allows the display of a monument inscribed with the Ten Commandments on the Texas State Capitol grounds. We hold that it does.

The 22 acres surrounding the Texas State Capitol contain 17 monuments and 21 historical markers commemorating the "people, ideals, and events that com-pose Texan identity." The monolith challenged here stands 6-feet high and 3½ feet wide. It is located to the north of the Capitol building, between the Capitol and the Supreme Court building. Its primary content is the text of the Ten Commandments. An eagle grasping the American flag, an eye inside of a pyramid, and two small tablets with what appears to be an ancient script are carved above the text of the Ten Commandments. Below the text are two Stars of David and the superimposed Greek letters Chi and Rho, which represent Christ. The bottom of the monument bears the inscription "PRESENTED TO THE PEOPLE AND YOUTH OF TEXAS BY THE FRATERNAL ORDER OF EAGLES OF TEXAS 1961."

The legislative record surrounding the State's acceptance of the monument from the Eagles—a national social, civic, and patriotic organization—is limited to legislative journal entries. After the monument was accepted, the State selected a site for the monument based on the recommendation of the state organization responsible for maintaining the Capitol grounds. The Eagles paid the cost of erecting the monument, the dedication of which was presided over by two state legislators.

Petitioner Thomas Van Orden is a native Texan and a resident of Austin. At one time he was a licensed lawyer, having graduated from Southern Methodist Law School. Van Orden testified that, since 1995, he has encountered the Ten Commandments monument during his frequent visits to the Capitol grounds. Forty years after the monument's erection and six years after Van Orden began to encounter the monument frequently, he sued numerous state officials in their official capacities seeking both a declaration that the monument's placement violates the Establishment Clause and an injunction requiring its removal.

Our cases, Januslike, point in two directions in applying the Establishment Clause. One face looks toward the strong role played by religion and religious traditions throughout our Nation's history. The other face looks toward the principle that governmental intervention in religious matters can itself endanger religious freedom.

This case, like all Establishment Clause challenges, presents us with the difficulty of respecting both faces. Our institutions presuppose a Supreme Being, yet these institutions must not press religious observances upon their citizens. One face looks to the past in acknowledgment of our Nation's heritage, while the other looks to the present in demanding a separation between church and state. Reconciling these two faces requires that we neither abdicate our responsibility to maintain a division between church and state nor evince a hostility to religion by disabling the government from in some ways recognizing our religious heritage.

These two faces are evident in representative cases both upholding and invalidating laws under the Establishment Clause. Over the last 25 years, we have sometimes pointed to Lemon v. Kurtzman (1971) as providing the governing test in Establishment Clause challenges. Whatever may be the fate of the *Lemon* test in the larger scheme of Establishment Clause jurisprudence, we think it not useful in dealing with the sort of passive monument that Texas has erected on its Capitol grounds. Instead, our analysis is driven both by the nature of the monument and by our Nation's history.

As we explained in Lynch v. Donnelly (1984): "There is an unbroken history of official acknowledgment by all three branches of government of the role of religion in American life from at least 1789." For example, both Houses passed resolutions in 1789 asking President George Washington to issue a Thanksgiving Day Proclamation to "recommend to the people of the United States a day of public thanksgiving and prayer, to be observed by acknowledging, with grateful hearts, the many and signal favors of Almighty God." President Washington's proclamation directly attributed to the Supreme Being the foundations and successes of our young Nation.

Recognition of the role of God in our Nation's heritage has also been reflected in our decisions. We have acknowledged, for example, that "religion has been closely identified with our history and government," and that "[t]he history of man is inseparable from the history of religion." This recognition has led us to hold that the Establishment Clause permits a state legislature to open its daily sessions with a prayer by a chaplain paid by the State. Marsh v. Chambers (1982). With similar reasoning, we have upheld laws, which originated from one of the Ten Commandments, that prohibited the sale of merchandise on Sunday. McGowan v. Maryland (1961).

In this case we are faced with a display of the Ten Commandments on government property outside the Texas State Capitol. Such acknowledgments of the role played by the Ten Commandments in our Nation's heritage are common throughout America. We need only look within our own Courtroom. Since 1935, Moses has stood, holding two tablets that reveal portions of the Ten Commandments written in Hebrew, among other lawgivers in the south frieze. Representations of the Ten Commandments adorn the metal gates lining the north and south sides of the Courtroom as well as the doors leading into the Courtroom. Moses also sits on the exterior east facade of the building holding the Ten Commandments tablets.

Similar acknowledgments can be seen throughout a visitor's tour of our Nation's Capital. For example, a large statue of Moses holding the Ten Commandments, alongside a statue of the Apostle Paul, has overlooked the rotunda of the Library of Congress' Jefferson Building since 1897. And the Jefferson Building's Great Reading Room contains a sculpture of a woman beside the Ten Commandments with a quote above her from the Old Testament (Micah 6:8). A medallion with two tablets depicting the Ten Commandments decorates the floor of the National Archives. Inside the Department of Justice, a statue entitled "The Spirit of Law" has two tablets representing the Ten Commandments lying at its feet. In front of the Ronald Reagan Building is another sculpture that includes a depiction of the Ten Commandments. So too a 24-foot-tall sculpture, depicting, among other things, the Ten Commandments and a cross, stands outside the federal courthouse that houses both the Court of Appeals and the District Court for the District of Columbia. Moses is also prominently featured in the Chamber of the United States House of Representatives.

Of course, the Ten Commandments are religious—they were so viewed at their inception and so remain. The monument, therefore, has religious significance. According to Judeo-Christian belief, the Ten Commandments were given to Moses by God on Mt. Sinai. But Moses was a lawgiver as well as a religious leader. And the Ten Commandments have an undeniable historical meaning, as the foregoing examples demonstrate. Simply having religious content or promoting a message consistent with a religious doctrine does not run afoul of the Establishment Clause.

There are, of course, limits to the display of religious messages or symbols. For example, we held unconstitutional a Kentucky statute requiring the posting of the Ten Commandments in every public schoolroom. Stone v. Graham (1980) (per curiam). In the classroom context, we found that the Kentucky statute had an improper and plainly religious purpose.

The placement of the Ten Commandments monument on the Texas State Capitol grounds is a far more passive use of those texts than was the case in *Stone,* where the text confronted elementary school students every day. Indeed, Van Orden, the petitioner here, apparently walked by the monument for a number of years before bringing this lawsuit. Texas has treated her Capitol grounds monuments as representing the several strands in the State's political and legal history. The inclusion of the Ten Commandments monument in this group has a dual significance, partaking of both religion and government. We cannot say that Texas' display of this monument violates the Establishment Clause of the First Amendment.

Justice THOMAS, concurring.

This case would be easy if the Court were willing to abandon the inconsistent guideposts it has adopted for addressing Establishment Clause challenges, and return to the original meaning of the Clause. I have previously suggested that the Clause's text and history "resis[t] incorporation" against the States. If the Establishment Clause does not restrain the States, then it has no application here, where only state action is at issue.

Even if the Clause is incorporated, or if the Free Exercise Clause limits the power of States to establish religions, our task would be far simpler if we returned to the original meaning of the word "establishment" than it is under the various approaches this Court now uses. The Framers understood an establishment "necessarily [to] involve actual legal coercion." "In other words, establishment at the founding involved, for example, mandatory observance or mandatory payment of taxes supporting ministers." And "government practices that have nothing to do with creating or maintaining . . . coercive state establishments" simply do not "implicate the possible liberty interest of being free from coercive state establishments."

There is no question that, based on the original meaning of the Establishment Clause, the Ten Commandments display at issue here is constitutional. In no sense does Texas compel petitioner Van Orden to do anything. The only injury to him is that he takes offense at seeing the monument as he passes it on his way to the Texas Supreme Court Library. He need not stop to read it or even to look at it, let alone to express support for it or adopt the Commandments as guides for his life. The mere presence of the monument along his path involves no coercion and thus does not violate the Establishment Clause.

Returning to the original meaning would do more than simplify our task. It also would avoid the pitfalls present in the Court's current approach to such challenges. This Court's precedent elevates the trivial to the proverbial "federal case," by making benign signs and postings subject to challenge. Even worse, the incoherence of the Court's decisions in this area renders the Establishment Clause impenetrable and incapable of consistent application. All told, this Court's jurisprudence leaves courts, governments, and believers and non-believers alike confused — an observation that is hardly new.

Finally, the very "flexibility" of this Court's Establishment Clause precedent leaves it incapable of consistent application. The inconsistency between the decisions the Court reaches today in this case and in McCreary County v. American Civil Liberties Union of Ky. (2005) only compounds the confusion.

Much, if not all, of this would be avoided if the Court would return to the views of the Framers and adopt coercion as the touchstone for our Establishment Clause inquiry. Every acknowledgment of religion would not give rise to an Establishment Clause claim. Courts would not act as theological commissions, judging the meaning of religious matters. Most important, our precedent would be capable of consistent and coherent application. While the Court correctly rejects the challenge to the Ten Commandments monument on the Texas Capitol grounds, a more fundamental rethinking of our Establishment Clause jurisprudence remains in order.

Justice BREYER, concurring in the judgment.

In School Dist. of Abington Township v. Schempp (1963), Justice Goldberg, joined by Justice Harlan, wrote, in respect to the First Amendment's Religion Clauses, that there is "no simple and clear measure which by precise application can readily and invariably demark the permissible from the impermissible." One must refer instead to the basic purposes of those Clauses. They seek to "assure the fullest possible scope of religious liberty and tolerance for all." They seek to avoid that divisiveness based upon religion that promotes social conflict, sapping the strength of government and religion alike. They seek to maintain that "separation of church and state" that has long been critical to the "peaceful dominion that religion exercises in [this] country," where the "spirit of religion" and the "spirit of freedom" are productively "united," "reign[ing] together" but in separate spheres "on the same soil."

The Court has made clear, as Justices Goldberg and Harlan noted, that the realization of these goals means that government must "neither engage in nor compel religious practices," that it must "effect no favoritism among sects or between religion and nonreligion," and that it must "work deterrence of no religious belief." The government must avoid excessive interference with, or promotion of, religion. But the Establishment Clause does not compel the government to purge from the public sphere all that in any way partakes of the religious. Such absolutism is not only inconsistent with our national traditions, but would also tend to promote the kind of social conflict the Establishment Clause seeks to avoid.

The case before us is a borderline case. It concerns a large granite monument bearing the text of the Ten Commandments located on the grounds of the Texas State Capitol. On the one hand, the Commandments' text undeniably has a religious message, invoking, indeed emphasizing, the Deity. On the other hand, focusing on the text of the Commandments alone cannot conclusively resolve this case. Rather, to determine the message that the text here conveys, we must examine how the text is used. And that inquiry requires us to consider the context of the display.

In certain contexts, a display of the tablets of the Ten Commandments can convey not simply a religious message but also a secular moral message (about proper standards of social conduct). And in certain contexts, a display of the tablets can also convey a historical message (about a historic relation between those standards and the law) — a fact that helps to explain the display of those tablets in dozens of courthouses throughout the Nation, including the Supreme Court of the United States.

Here the tablets have been used as part of a display that communicates not simply a religious message, but a secular message as well. The circumstances surrounding the display's placement on the capitol grounds and its physical setting suggest that the State itself intended the latter, nonreligious aspects of the tablets' message to predominate. And the monument's 40-year history on the Texas state grounds indicates that that has been its effect.

The group that donated the monument, the Fraternal Order of Eagles, a private civic (and primarily secular) organization, while interested in the religious aspect of the Ten Commandments, sought to highlight the Commandments' role in shaping civic morality as part of that organization's efforts to combat juvenile delinquency. The Eagles' consultation with a committee composed of members of several faiths in order to find a nonsectarian text underscores the group's ethics-based motives. The tablets, as displayed on the monument, prominently acknowledge that the Eagles donated the display, a factor which, though not sufficient, thereby further distances the State itself from the religious aspect of the Commandments' message.

The physical setting of the monument, moreover, suggests little or nothing of the sacred. The monument sits in a large park containing 17 monuments and 21 historical markers, all designed to illustrate the "ideals" of those who settled in Texas and of those who have lived there since that time. The setting does not readily lend itself to meditation or any other religious activity. But it does provide a context of history and moral ideals. It (together with the display's inscription about its origin) communicates to visitors that the State sought to reflect moral principles, illustrating a relation between ethics and law that the State's citizens, historically speaking, have endorsed.

If these factors provide a strong, but not conclusive, indication that the Commandments' text on this monument conveys a predominantly secular message, a further factor is determinative here. As far as I can tell, 40 years passed in which the presence of this monument, legally speaking, went unchallenged (until the single legal objection raised by petitioner). And I am not aware of any evidence suggesting that this was due to a climate of intimidation. Those 40 years suggest that the public visiting the capitol grounds has considered the religious aspect of the tablets' message as part of what is a broader moral and historical message reflective of a cultural heritage.

This case, moreover, is distinguishable from instances where the Court has found Ten Commandments displays impermissible. The display is not on the grounds of a public school, where, given the impressionability of the young, government must exercise particular care in separating church and state. This case also differs from *McCreary County*, where the short (and stormy) history of the courthouse Commandments' displays demonstrates the substantially religious objectives of those who mounted them, and the effect of this readily apparent objective upon those who view them. That history there indicates a governmental effort substantially to promote religion, not simply an effort primarily to reflect, historically, the secular impact of a religiously inspired document. And, in today's world, in a Nation of so many different religious and comparable nonreligious fundamental beliefs, a more contemporary state effort to focus attention upon a religious text is certainly likely to prove divisive in a way that this longstanding, pre-existing monument has not.

For these reasons, I believe that the Texas display—serving a mixed but primarily nonreligious purpose, not primarily "advanc[ing]" or "inhibit[ing] religion," and not creating an "excessive government entanglement with religion"—might satisfy this Court's more formal Establishment Clause tests. But, as I have said, in reaching the conclusion that the Texas display falls on the permissible side of the constitutional line, I rely less upon a literal application of any particular test than upon consideration of the basic purposes of the First Amendment's Religion Clauses themselves. This display has stood apparently uncontested for nearly two generations. That experience helps us understand that as a practical matter of degree this display is unlikely to prove divisive. And this matter of degree is, I believe, critical in a borderline case such as this one.

At the same time, to reach a contrary conclusion here, based primarily on the religious nature of the tablets' text would, I fear, lead the law to exhibit a hostility toward religion that has no place in our Establishment Clause traditions. Such a holding might well encourage disputes concerning the removal of longstanding depictions of the Ten Commandments from public buildings across the Nation. And it could thereby create the very kind of religiously based divisiveness that the Establishment Clause seeks to avoid.

Justice STEVENS, with whom Justice GINSBURG joins, dissenting.

The sole function of the monument on the grounds of Texas' State Capitol is to display the full text of one version of the Ten Commandments. The monument is not a work of art and does not refer to any event in the history of the State. Viewed on its face, Texas' display has no purported connection to God's role in the formation of Texas or the founding of our Nation; nor does it provide the reasonable observer with any basis to guess that it was erected to honor any individual or organization. The message transmitted by Texas' chosen display is quite plain: This State endorses the divine code of the "Judeo-Christian" God.

For those of us who learned to recite the King James version of the text long before we understood the meaning of some of its words, God's Commandments may seem like wise counsel. The question before this Court, however, is whether it is counsel that the State of Texas may proclaim without violating the Establishment Clause of the Constitution. If any fragment of Jefferson's metaphorical "wall of separation between church and State" is to be preserved — if there remains any meaning to the "wholesome 'neutrality' of which this Court's [Establishment Clause] cases speak" — a negative answer to that question is mandatory.

I

In my judgment, at the very least, the Establishment Clause has created a strong presumption against the display of religious symbols on public property. The adornment of our public spaces with displays of religious symbols and messages undoubtedly provides comfort, even inspiration, to many individuals who subscribe to particular faiths. Unfortunately, the practice also runs the risk of "offend[ing] nonmembers of the faith being advertised as well as adherents who consider the particular advertisement disrespectful." Government's obligation to avoid divisiveness and exclusion in the religious sphere is compelled by the Establishment and Free Exercise Clauses, which together erect a wall of separation between church and state.

This metaphorical wall protects principles long recognized and often recited in this Court's cases. The first and most fundamental of these principles, one that a majority of this Court today affirms, is that the Establishment Clause demands religious neutrality — government may not exercise a preference for one religious faith over another. This essential command, however, is not merely a prohibition against the government's differentiation among religious sects. We have repeatedly reaffirmed that neither a State nor the Federal Government "can constitutionally pass laws or impose requirements which aid all religions as against non-believers, and neither can aid those religions based on a belief in the existence of God as against those religions founded on different beliefs." This principle is based on the straightforward notion that governmental promotion of orthodoxy is not saved by the aggregation of several orthodoxies under the State's banner.

This case, however, is not about historic preservation or the mere recognition of religion. The issue is obfuscated rather than clarified by simplistic commentary on the various ways in which religion has played a role in American life, and by the recitation of the many extant governmental "acknowledgments" of the role the Ten Commandments played in our Nation's heritage. Surely, the mere compilation of religious symbols, none of which includes the full text of the Commandments and all of which are exhibited in different settings, has only marginal relevance to the question presented in this case.

The monolith displayed on Texas Capitol grounds cannot be discounted as a passive acknowledgment of religion, nor can the State's refusal to remove it upon objection be explained as a simple desire to preserve a historic relic. This Nation's resolute commitment to neutrality with respect to religion is flatly inconsistent with the plurality's wholehearted validation of an official state endorsement of the message that there is one, and only one, God.

II

When the Ten Commandments monument was donated to the State of Texas in 1961, it was not for the purpose of commemorating a noteworthy event in Texas history, signifying the Commandments' influence on the development of secular law, or even denoting the religious beliefs of Texans at that time. To the contrary, the donation was only one of over a hundred largely identical monoliths, and of over a thousand paper replicas, distributed to state and local governments throughout the Nation over the course of several decades. This ambitious project was the work of the Fraternal Order of Eagles, a well-respected benevolent organization whose good works have earned the praise of several Presidents.

As the story goes, the program was initiated by the late Judge E. J. Ruegemer, a Minnesota juvenile court judge and then-Chairman of the Eagles National Commission on Youth Guidance. Inspired by a juvenile offender who had never heard of the Ten Commandments, the judge approached the Minnesota Eagles with the idea of distributing paper copies of the Commandments to be posted in courthouses nationwide. The State's Aerie undertook this project and its popularity spread. When Cecil B. DeMille, who at that time was filming the movie *The Ten Commandments*, heard of the judge's endeavor, he teamed up with the Eagles to produce the type of granite monolith now displayed in front of the Texas Capitol and at courthouse squares, city halls, and public parks throughout the Nation. Granite was reportedly chosen over DeMille's original suggestion of bronze plaques to better replicate the original Ten Commandments. The donors were motivated by a desire to "inspire the youth" and curb juvenile delinquency by providing children with a "code of conduct or standards by which to govern their actions."

It is the Eagles' belief that disseminating the message conveyed by the Ten Commandments will help to persuade young men and women to observe civilized standards of behavior, and will lead to more productive lives.

The desire to combat juvenile delinquency by providing guidance to youths is both admirable and unquestionably secular. But achieving that goal through biblical teachings injects a religious purpose into an otherwise secular endeavor. By spreading the word of God and converting heathens to Christianity, missionaries expect to enlighten their converts, enhance their satisfaction with life, and improve their behavior. Similarly, by disseminating the "law of God" — directing fidelity to God and proscribing murder, theft, and adultery — the Eagles hope that this divine guidance will help wayward youths conform their behavior and improve their lives. In my judgment, the significant secular by-products that are intended consequences of religious instruction — indeed, of the establishment of most religions — are not the type of "secular" purposes that justify government promulgation of sacred religious messages.

Though the State of Texas may genuinely wish to combat juvenile delin-quency, and may rightly want to honor the Eagles for their efforts, it cannot effectuate these admirable purposes through an explicitly religious medium. The reason this message stands apart is that the Decalogue is a venerable religious text. As we held 25 years ago, it is beyond dispute that "[t]he Ten Commandments are undeniably a sacred text in the Jewish and Christian faiths." For many followers, the Commandments represent the literal word of God as spoken to Moses and repeated to his followers after descending from Mount Sinai. Attempts to secularize what is unquestionably a sacred text defy credibility and disserve people of faith.

The profoundly sacred message embodied by the text inscribed on the Texas monument is emphasized by the especially large letters that identify its author: "I AM the LORD thy God." It commands present worship of Him and no other deity. It directs us to be guided by His teaching in the current and future con-duct of all of our affairs. It instructs us to follow a code of divine law, some of which has informed and been integrated into our secular legal code ("Thou shalt not kill"), but much of which has not ("Thou shalt not make to thyself any graven images. . . . Thou shalt not covet").

Moreover, despite the Eagles' best efforts to choose a benign nondenomina-tional text, the Ten Commandments display projects not just a religious, but an inherently sectarian message. There are many distinctive versions of the Deca-logue, ascribed to by different religions and even different denominations within a particular faith; to a pious and learned observer, these differences may be of enormous religious significance. In choosing to display this version of the Commandments, Texas tells the observer that the State supports this side of the doctrinal religious debate.

Even if, however, the message of the monument, despite the inscribed text, fairly could be said to represent the belief system of all Judeo-Christians, it would still run afoul of the Establishment Clause by prescribing a compelled code of conduct from one God, namely a Judeo-Christian God, that is rejected by prom-inent polytheistic sects, such as Hinduism, as well as nontheistic religions, such as Buddhism. And, at the very least, the text of the Ten Commandments imper-missibly commands a preference for religion over irreligion. Any of those bases, in my judgment, would be sufficient to conclude that the message should not be proclaimed by the State of Texas on a permanent monument at the seat of its government.

III

The plurality relies heavily on the fact that our Republic was founded, and has been governed since its nascence, by leaders who spoke then (and speak still) in plainly religious rhetoric. The speeches and rhetoric characteristic of the founding era, however, do not answer the question before us. I have already explained why Texas' display of the full text of the Ten Commandments, given the content of the actual display and the context in which it is situated, sets this case apart from the countless examples of benign government recognitions of religion. But there is another crucial difference. Our leaders, when delivering public addresses, often express their blessings simultaneously in the service of God and their constituents. Thus, when public officials deliver public speeches, we recognize that their words are not exclusively a transmission from the government because those oratories have embedded within them the inherently personal views of the speaker as an individual member of the polity. The permanent placement of a textual religious display on state property is different in kind; it amalgamates otherwise discordant individual views into a collective statement of government approval. Moreover, the message never ceases to transmit itself to objecting viewers whose only choices are to accept the message or to ignore the offense by averting their gaze. In this sense, although Thanksgiving Day proclamations and inaugural speeches undoubtedly seem official, in most circumstances they will not constitute the sort of governmental endorsement of religion at which the separation of church and state is aimed.

The plurality's reliance on early religious statements and proclamations made by the Founders is also problematic because those views were not espoused at the Constitutional Convention in 1787 nor enshrined in the Constitution's text. Thus, the presentation of these religious statements as a unified historical narrative is bound to paint a misleading picture. Ardent separationists aside, there is another critical nuance lost in the plurality's portrayal of history. Simply put, many of the Founders who are often cited as authoritative expositors of the Constitution's original meaning understood the Establishment Clause to stand for a narrower proposition than the plurality, for whatever reason, is willing to accept. Namely, many of the Framers understood the word "religion" in the Establishment Clause to encompass only the various sects of Christianity.

The original understanding of the type of "religion" that qualified for constitutional protection under the Establishment Clause likely did not include those followers of Judaism and Islam who are among the preferred "monotheistic" religions Justice Scalia has embraced in his *McCreary County* opinion. Given the original understanding of the men who championed our "Christian nation" — men who had no cause to view anti-Semitism or contempt for atheists as problems worthy of civic concern — one must ask whether Justice Scalia "has not had the courage (or the foolhardiness) to apply [his originalism] principle consistently."

Indeed, to constrict narrowly the reach of the Establishment Clause to the views of the Founders would lead to more than this unpalatable result; it would also leave us with an unincorporated constitutional provision — in other words, one that limits only the federal establishment of "a national religion." Under this view, not only could a State constitutionally adorn all of its public spaces with crucifixes or passages from the New Testament, it would also have full authority to prescribe the teachings of Martin Luther or Joseph Smith as the official state religion. Only the Federal Government would be prohibited from taking sides (and only then as between Christian sects).

A reading of the First Amendment dependent on either of the purported original meanings expressed above would eviscerate the heart of the

Establishment Clause. It would replace Jefferson's "wall of separation" with a perverse wall of exclusion — Christians inside, non-Christians out. It would permit States to construct walls of their own choosing — Baptists inside, Mormons out; Jewish Orthodox inside, Jewish Reform out. A Clause so understood might be faithful to the expectations of some of our Founders, but it is plainly not worthy of a society whose enviable hallmark over the course of two centuries has been the continuing expansion of religious pluralism and tolerance.

It is our duty, therefore, to interpret the First Amendment's command that "Congress shall make no law respecting an establishment of religion" not by merely asking what those words meant to observers at the time of the founding, but instead by deriving from the Clause's text and history the broad principles that remain valid today. The principle that guides my analysis is neutrality. The basis for that principle is firmly rooted in our Nation's history and our Constitution's text. I recognize that the requirement that government must remain neutral between religion and irreligion would have seemed foreign to some of the Framers; so too would a requirement of neutrality between Jews and Christians. The evil of discriminating today against atheists, "polytheists[,] and believers in unconcerned deities," is in my view a direct descendent of the evil of discriminating among Christian sects. The Establishment Clause thus forbids it and, in turn, forbids Texas from displaying the Ten Commandments monument the plurality so casually affirms.

IV

The Eagles may donate as many monuments as they choose to be displayed in front of Protestant churches, benevolent organizations' meeting places, or on the front lawns of private citizens. The expurgated text of the King James version of the Ten Commandments that they have crafted is unlikely to be accepted by Catholic parishes, Jewish synagogues, or even some Protestant denominations, but the message they seek to convey is surely more compatible with church property than with property that is located on the government side of the metaphorical wall.

The judgment of the Court in this case stands for the proposition that the Constitution permits governmental displays of sacred religious texts. This makes a mockery of the constitutional ideal that government must remain neutral between religion and irreligion. If a State may endorse a particular deity's command to "have no other gods before me," it is difficult to conceive of any textual display that would run afoul of the Establishment Clause.

The disconnect between this Court's approval of Texas's monument and the constitutional prohibition against preferring religion to irreligion cannot be reduced to the exercise of plotting two adjacent locations on a slippery slope. Rather, it is the difference between the shelter of a fortress and exposure to "the winds that would blow" if the wall were allowed to crumble.

Justice SOUTER, with whom Justice STEVENS and Justice GINSBURG join, dissenting.

Although the First Amendment's Religion Clauses have not been read to mandate absolute governmental neutrality toward religion, the Establishment Clause requires neutrality as a general rule, and thus expresses Madison's condemnation of "employ[ing] Religion as an engine of Civil policy." A governmental display of an obviously religious text cannot be squared with neutrality, except in a setting that plausibly indicates that the statement is not placed in view with a predominant purpose on the part of government either to adopt the religious message or to urge its acceptance by others.

Until today, only one of our cases addressed the constitutionality of posting the Ten Commandments, Stone v. Graham (1980). A Kentucky statute required posting the Commandments on the walls of public school classrooms. [The Court stated:]

> The pre-eminent purpose for posting the Ten Commandments on schoolroom walls is plainly religious in nature. The Ten Commandments are undeniably a sacred text in the Jewish and Christian faiths, and no legislative recitation of a supposed secular purpose can blind us to that fact. The Commandments do not confine themselves to arguably secular matters, such as honoring one's parents, killing or murder, adultery, stealing, false witness, and covetousness. Rather, the first part of the Commandments concerns the religious duties of believers: worshipping the Lord God alone, avoiding idolatry, not using the Lord's name in vain, and observing the Sabbath Day.

What these observations underscore are the simple realities that the Ten Commandments constitute a religious statement, that their message is inherently religious, and that the purpose of singling them out in a display is clearly the same.

To drive the religious point home, and identify the message as religious to any viewer who failed to read the text, the engraved quotation is framed by religious symbols: two tablets with what appears to be ancient script on them, two Stars of David, and the superimposed Greek letters Chi and Rho as the familiar monogram of Christ. Nothing on the monument, in fact, detracts from its religious nature, and the plurality does not suggest otherwise. It would therefore be difficult to miss the point that the government of Texas is telling everyone who sees the monument to live up to a moral code because God requires it, with both code and conception of God being rightly understood as the inheritances specifically of Jews and Christians. And it is likewise unsurprising that the District Court expressly rejected Texas's argument that the State's purpose in placing the monument on the capitol grounds was related to the Commandments' role as "part of the foundation of modern secular law in Texas and elsewhere."

The monument's presentation of the Commandments with religious text emphasized and enhanced stands in contrast to any number of perfectly constitutional depictions of them, the frieze of our own Courtroom providing a good example, where the figure of Moses stands among history's great lawgivers. While Moses holds the tablets of the Commandments showing some Hebrew text, no one looking at the lines of figures in marble relief is likely to see a religious purpose behind the assemblage or take away a religious message from it. Only one other depiction represents a religious leader, and the historical personages are mixed with symbols of moral and intellectual abstractions like Equity and Authority. Since Moses enjoys no especial prominence on the frieze, viewers can readily take him to be there as a lawgiver in the company of other lawgivers; and the viewers may just as naturally see the tablets of the Commandments (showing the later ones, forbidding things like killing and theft, but without the divine preface) as background from which the concept of law emerged, ultimately having a secular influence in the history of the Nation. Government may, of course, constitutionally call attention to this influence, and may post displays or erect monuments recounting this aspect of our history no less than any other, so long as there is a context and that context is historical. Hence, a display of the Commandments accompanied by an exposition of how they have influenced modern law would most likely be constitutionally unobjectionable. And the Decalogue could, as *Stone* suggested, be integrated constitutionally into a course of study in public schools.

Texas seeks to take advantage of the recognition that visual symbol and written text can manifest a secular purpose in secular company, when it argues that its monument (like Moses in the frieze) is not alone and ought to be viewed as only 1 among 17 placed on the 22 acres surrounding the state capitol. Texas, indeed, says that the Capitol grounds are like a museum for a collection of exhibits, the kind of setting that several Members of the Court have said can render the exhibition of religious artifacts permissible, even though in other circumstances their display would be seen as meant to convey a religious message forbidden to the State.

But 17 monuments with no common appearance, history, or esthetic role scattered over 22 acres is not a museum, and anyone strolling around the lawn would surely take each memorial on its own terms without any dawning sense that some purpose held the miscellany together more coherently than fortuity and the edge of the grass. One monument expresses admiration for pioneer women. One pays respect to the fighters of World War II. And one quotes the God of Abraham whose command is the sanction for moral law. The themes are individual grit, patriotic courage, and God as the source of Jewish and Christian morality; there is no common denominator. In like circumstances, we rejected an argument similar to the State's, noting in *County of Allegheny* that "[t]he presence of Santas or other Christmas decorations elsewhere in the . . . [c]ourthouse, and of the nearby gallery forum, fail to negate the [crèche's] endorsement effect. . . . The record demonstrates . . . that the crèche, with its floral frame, was its own display distinct from any other decorations or exhibitions in the building."

Nor can the plurality deflect *Stone* by calling the Texas monument "a far more passive use of [the Decalogue] than was the case in *Stone*, where the text confronted elementary school students every day." Placing a monument on the ground is not more "passive" than hanging a sheet of paper on a wall when both contain the same text to be read by anyone who looks at it. The problem in *Stone* was simply that the State was putting the Commandments there to be seen, just as the monument's inscription is there for those who walk by it.

The monument in this case sits on the grounds of the Texas State Capitol. There is something significant in the common term "statehouse" to refer to a state capitol building: it is the civic home of every one of the State's citizens. If neutrality in religion means something, any citizen should be able to visit that civic home without having to confront religious expressions clearly meant to convey an official religious position that may be at odds with his own religion, or with rejection of religion.

5.   When Can Religion Become a Part of Government Activities?

Many cases under the Establishment Clause have involved issues of when, if at all, religion can become a part of government activities. For example, a large number of decisions have concerned the question of when religion impermissibly becomes a part of public school education. The Court has considered this topic in evaluating laws that allow children to be released from school for religious education, in considering prayers in public schools, and in evaluating curricular decisions made for religious reasons. In contrast to this area in which the Court has been very restrictive of religious presence in government activities, the Court has upheld the constitutionality of the government's employment of a chaplain for the legislature. These cases are discussed in turn.

a.   Religion as a Part of Government Activities: Schools

RELEASE TIME

The first Supreme Court cases to consider religion as a part of public school activities concerned policies that allowed students to be released from classes to receive religious instruction. The Court said that this was impermissible if the religious teaching occurred on school premises, but allowed if the students were released to receive religious training elsewhere.

In McCollum v. Board of Education, 333 U.S. 203 (1948), the Court declared unconstitutional a school's policy of allowing students to be released, with parental permission, to religious instruction classes conducted during regular school hours in the school building by outside teachers. The superintendent of schools approved the religious teachers, and attendance records were kept and reported to school authorities in the same way as for other classes. Students not attending the religion classes were left in a study hall; Justice Jackson referred to turning the school into a temporary jail for those who did not go to church.

The Court, in an opinion by Justice Black, found the law unconstitutional as violating the "wall of separation between church and state." Justice Black explained, "Here not only are the state's tax-supported public school buildings used for the dissemination of religious doctrines. The State also affords sectarian groups an invaluable aid in that it helps to provide pupils for their religious classes through use of the State's compulsory public school machinery. This is not separation of Church and State."

A few years later, in Zorach v. Clauson, 343 U.S. 306 (1952), the Supreme Court upheld a school board policy that allowed students to be released, during the school day, for religious instruction outside the school. Although Justice Douglas, writing for the Court, said that "[t]here cannot be the slightest doubt that the First Amendment reflects the philosophy that Church and State should be separated." He also said, "We are a religious people whose institutions presuppose a Supreme Being." The Court concluded that allowing students to receive religious instruction during school hours was simply accommodating religion and not a violation of the Establishment Clause since government funds and facilities were not used. Douglas wrote, "We would have to press the concept of separation of Church and State to these extremes to condemn the present law on constitutional grounds. . . . When the state encourages religious instruction or cooperates with religious authorities by adjusting the schedule of public events to sectarian needs, it follows the best of our traditions. For it then respects the religious nature of our people and accommodates the public service to their spiritual needs."

The Court distinguished *McCollum* because there "the classrooms were used for religious instruction and the force of the public school was used to promote that instruction." In contrast, in *Zorach*, all of the religious education occurred off school premises.

SCHOOL PRAYERS AND BIBLE READING

Few Supreme Court decisions have been as controversial as those that declared unconstitutional prayers and Bible readings in public schools. The Supreme Court has invalidated prayer in public schools, including voluntary prayers led by instructors and a government-mandated moment of "silent prayer." The Court also has followed this reasoning to invalidate clergy-delivered prayers at public school graduations. The Court, however, has not yet ruled as to whether a government-mandated moment of silent reflection would be allowed; nor has it decided the constitutionality of student-delivered prayers at public school graduations.

Engel v. Vitale was the initial Supreme Court case holding prayers in public schools to be unconstitutional.

ENGEL v. VITALE
370 U.S. 421 (1962)

Justice BLACK delivered the opinion of the Court.

The respondent Board of Education of Union Free School District No. 9, New Hyde Park, New York, acting in its official capacity under state law, directed the School District's principal to cause the following prayer to be said aloud by each class in the presence of a teacher at the beginning of each school day: "Almighty God, we acknowledge our dependence upon Thee, and we beg Thy blessings upon us, our parents, our teachers and our Country."

This daily procedure was adopted on the recommendation of the State Board of Regents, a governmental agency created by the State Constitution to which the New York Legislature has granted broad supervisory, executive, and legislative powers over the State's public school system. These state officials composed the prayer which they recommended and published as a part of their "Statement on Moral and Spiritual Training in the Schools," saying: "We believe that this Statement will be subscribed to by all men and women of good will, and we call upon all of them to aid in giving life to our program."

We think that by using its public school system to encourage recitation of the Regents' prayer, the State of New York has adopted a practice wholly inconsistent with the Establishment Clause. There can, of course, be no doubt that New York's program of daily classroom invocation of God's blessings as prescribed in the Regents' prayer is a religious activity. It is a solemn avowal of divine faith and supplication for the blessings of the Almighty. The nature of such a prayer has always been religious, none of the respondents has denied this and the trial court expressly so found.

The petitioners contend among other things that the state laws requiring or permitting use of the Regents' prayer must be struck down as a violation of the Establishment Clause because that prayer was composed by governmental officials as a part of a governmental program to further religious beliefs. For this reason, petitioners argue, the State's use of the Regents' prayer in its public school system breaches the constitutional wall of separation between Church and State. We agree with that contention since we think that the constitutional prohibition against laws respecting an establishment of religion must at least mean that in this country it is no part of the business of government to compose official prayers for any group of the American people to recite as a part of a religious program carried on by government.

It is a matter of history that this very practice of establishing governmentally composed prayers for religious services was one of the reasons which caused many of our early colonists to leave England and seek religious freedom in America. The Book of Common Prayer, which was created under governmental direction and which was approved by Acts of Parliament in 1548 and 1549, set out in minute detail the accepted form and content of prayer and other religious ceremonies to be used in the established, tax-supported Church of England. The controversies over the Book and what should be its content repeatedly threatened to disrupt the peace of that country as the accepted forms of prayer in the established church changed with the views of the particular ruler that happened to be in control at the time. Powerful groups representing some of the varying religious views of the people struggled among themselves to impress their particular views upon the Government and obtain amendments of the Book more suitable to their respective notions of how religious services should be conducted in order that the official religious establishment would advance their particular religious beliefs. Other groups, lacking the necessary political power to influence the Government on the matter, decided to leave England and its established church and seek freedom in America from England's governmentally ordained and supported religion.

There can be no doubt that New York's state prayer program officially establishes the religious beliefs embodied in the Regents' prayer. The respondents' argument to the contrary, which is largely based upon the contention that the Regents' prayer is "nondenominational" and the fact that the program, as modified and approved by state courts, does not require all pupils to recite the prayer but permits those who wish to do so to remain silent or be excused from the room, ignores the essential nature of the program's constitutional defects. Neither the fact that the prayer may be denominationally neutral nor the fact that its observance on the part of the students is voluntary can serve to free it from the limitations of the Establishment Clause.

It has been argued that to apply the Constitution in such a way as to prohibit state laws respecting an establishment of religious services in public schools is to indicate a hostility toward religion or toward prayer. Nothing, of course, could be more wrong. It is neither sacrilegious nor antireligious to say that each separate government in this country should stay out of the business of writing or sanctioning official prayers and leave that purely religious function to the people themselves and to those the people choose to look to for religious guidance.

Justice STEWART, dissenting.

A local school board in New York has provided that those pupils who wish to do so may join in a brief prayer at the beginning of each school day, acknowledging their dependence upon God and asking His blessing upon them and upon their parents, their teachers, and their country. The Court today decides that in permitting this brief non-denominational prayer the school board has violated the Constitution of the United States. I think this decision is wrong.

With all respect, I think the Court has misapplied a great constitutional principle. I cannot see how an "official religion" is established by letting those who want to say a prayer say it. On the contrary, I think that to deny the wish of these school children to join in reciting this prayer is to deny them the opportunity of sharing in the spiritual heritage of our Nation.

At the opening of each day's Session of this Court we stand, while one of our officials invokes the protection of God. Since the days of John Marshall our Crier has said, "God save the United States and this Honorable Court." Both the Senate and the House of Representatives open their daily Sessions with prayer. Each of our Presidents, from George Washington to John F. Kennedy, has upon assuming his Office asked the protection and help of God.

Countless similar examples could be listed, but there is no need to belabor the obvious. It was all summed up by this Court just ten years ago in a single sentence: "We are a religious people whose institutions presuppose a Supreme Being." Zorach v. Clauson. I do not believe that this Court, or the Congress, or the President has by the actions and practices I have mentioned established an "official religion" in violation of the Constitution. And I do not believe the State of New York has done so in this case. What each has done has been to recognize and to follow the deeply entrenched and highly cherished spiritual traditions of our Nation — traditions which come down to us from those who almost two hundred years ago avowed their "firm Reliance on the Protection of divine Providence" when they proclaimed the freedom and independence of this brave new world.

A year later, in Abington School District v. Schempp, 374 U.S. 203 (1963), the Court declared unconstitutional a state's law and a city's rule that required the reading, without comment, at the beginning of each school day of verses from the Bible and the recitation of the Lord's Prayer by students in unison. Although *Schempp*, unlike *Engel*, did not involve a state-composed prayer, the laws requiring Bible reading and reciting of the Lord's Prayer were deemed to violate the Establishment Clause. The Court emphasized that these religious exercises were prescribed as part of the curricular activities of students, conducted in school buildings, and supervised by teachers.

The Court distinguished studying the Bible in a literature or comparative religion course, which would be permissible. The Court said that "the exercises here do not fall into those categories. They are religious exercises, required by the States in violation of the command of the First Amendment that the Government maintain strict neutrality, neither aiding nor opposing religion."

In Wallace v. Jaffree, 472 U.S. 38 (1985), the Court followed *Engel* and *Schempp* and declared unconstitutional an Alabama law that authorized a moment of silence in public schools for "meditation or voluntary prayer." The legislative history of the law was clear that its purpose was to reintroduce prayer into the public schools. The Court said that the record was "unambiguous" that the law "was not motivated by any clearly secular purpose — indeed, the statute had *no* secular purpose."

The Court did not resolve the question of whether a moment of "silent reflection" would be permissible absent legislative history that indicated that its purpose was to reintroduce prayer into public schools. For some people, there seems little objectionable about teachers asking students to be silent for a moment at the beginning of the school day to collect their thoughts and mentally prepare for learning. But for others, government-mandated moments of silent reflection and prayer seem unnecessary; students surely have been saying silent prayers as long as teachers have been giving tests.

In Lee v. Weisman, which is discussed in the *Doe* case above, the Court declared unconstitutional clergy-delivered prayers at public school graduations. The competing theories of the Establishment Clause, discussed earlier in this chapter, are very much in evidence in the opinions in *Lee*.

LEE v. WEISMAN
505 U.S. 577 (1992)

Justice KENNEDY delivered the opinion of the Court.

School principals in the public school system of the city of Providence, Rhode Island, are permitted to invite members of the clergy to offer invocation and benediction prayers as part of the formal graduation ceremonies for middle schools and for high schools. The question before us is whether including clerical members who offer prayers as part of the official school graduation ceremony is consistent with the Religion Clauses of the First Amendment, provisions the Fourteenth Amendment makes applicable with full force to the States and their school districts.

I

Deborah Weisman graduated from Nathan Bishop Middle School, a public school in Providence, at a formal ceremony in June 1989. She was about 14 years old. For many years it has been the policy of the Providence School Committee and the Superintendent of Schools to permit principals to invite members of the clergy to give invocations and benedictions at middle school and high school graduations. Many, but not all, of the principals elected to include prayers as part of the graduation ceremonies. Acting for himself and his daughter, Deborah's father, Daniel Weisman, objected to any prayers at Deborah's middle school graduation, but to no avail. The school principal, petitioner Robert E. Lee, invited a rabbi to deliver prayers at the graduation exercise for Deborah's class. Rabbi Leslie Gutterman, of the Temple Beth El in Providence, accepted.

It has been the custom of Providence school officials to provide invited clergy with a pamphlet entitled "Guidelines for Civic Occasions," prepared by the National Conference of Christians and Jews. The guidelines recommend that public prayers at nonsectarian civic ceremonies be composed with "inclusiveness and sensitivity," though they acknowledge that "[p]rayer of any kind may be inappropriate on some civic occasions." The principal gave Rabbi Gutterman the pamphlet before the graduation and advised him the invocation and benediction should be nonsectarian.

Rabbi Gutterman's prayers were as follows:

INVOCATION

God of the Free, Hope of the Brave:

For the legacy of America where diversity is celebrated and the rights of minorities are protected, we thank You. May these young men and women grow up to enrich it.

For the liberty of America, we thank You. May these new graduates grow up to guard it.

For the political process of America in which all its citizens may participate, for its court system where all may seek justice we thank You. May those we honor this morning always turn to it in trust.

For the destiny of America we thank You. May the graduates of Nathan Bishop Middle School so live that they might help to share it.

May our aspirations for our country and for these young people, who are our hope for the future, be richly fulfilled.

AMEN

BENEDICTION

O God, we are grateful to You for having endowed us with the capacity for learning which we have celebrated on this joyous commencement.

Happy families give thanks for seeing their children achieve an important milestone. Send Your blessings upon the teachers and administrators who helped prepare them.

The graduates now need strength and guidance for the future, help them to understand that we are not complete with academic knowledge alone. We must each strive to fulfill what You require of us all: To do justly, to love mercy, to walk humbly.

We give thanks to You, Lord, for keeping us alive, sustaining us and allowing us to reach this special, happy occasion.

AMEN

The record in this case is sparse in many respects, and we are unfamiliar with any fixed custom or practice at middle school graduations, referred to by the school district as "promotional exercise." We are not so constrained with reference to high schools, however. High school graduations are such an integral part of Amercian cultural life we can with confidence describe their customary features.

II

These dominant facts mark and control the confines of our decision. State officials direct the performance of a formal religious exercise at promotional and graduation ceremonies for secondary schools. Even for those students who object to the religious exercise, their attendance and participation in the state-sponsored religious activity are in a fair and real sense obligatory, though the school district does not require attendance as a condition for receipt of the diploma.

[T]he controlling precedents as they relate to prayer and religious exercise in primary and secondary public schools compel the holding here that the policy of the city of Providence is an unconstitutional one. We can decide the case without reconsidering the general constitutional framework by which public schools' efforts to accommodate religion are measured. Thus we do not accept the invitation of petitioners and amicus the United States to reconsider our decision in Lemon v. Kurtzman.

The government involvement with religious activity in this case is pervasive, to the point of creating a state-sponsored and state-directed religious exercise in a public school. Conducting this formal religious observance conflicts with settled rules pertaining to prayer exercise for students, and that suffices to determine the question before us.

The principle that government may accommodate the free exercise of religion does not supersede the fundamental limitations imposed by the Establishment Clause. It is beyond dispute that, at a minimum, the Constitution guarantees that government may not coerce anyone to support or participate in religion or its exercise, or otherwise act in a way which "establishes a [state] religion or religious faith, or tends to do so." The State's involvement in the school prayers challenged today violates these central principles.

That involvement is as troubling as it is undenied. A school official, the principal, decided that an invocation and a benediction should be given; this is a choice attributable to the State, and from a constitutional perspective it is as if a state statute decreed that the prayers must occur. The principal chose the religious participant, here a rabbi, and that choice is also attributable to the State.

The State's role did not end with the decision to include a prayer and with the choice of a clergyman. Principal Lee provided Rabbi Gutterman with a copy of the "Guidelines for Civic Occasion," and advised him that his prayers should be nonsectarian. Through these means the principal directed and controlled the content of the prayers. Even if the only sanction for ignoring the instructions were that the rabbi would not be invited back, we think no religious representative who valued his or her continued reputation and effectiveness in the community would incur the State's displeasure in this regard. It is a cornerstone principle of our Establishment Clause jurisprudence that "it is no part of the business of government to compose official prayers for any group of the Amercian people to recite as a part of a religious program carried on by government," Engel v. Vitale (1962), and that is what the school officials attempted to do.

The First Amendment's Religion Clauses mean that religious beliefs and religious expression are too precious to be either proscribed or prescribed by the State. The design of the Constitution is that preservation and transmission of religious beliefs and worship is a responsibility and a choice committed to the private sphere, which itself is promised freedom to pursue that mission.

We turn our attention now to consider the position of the students, both those who desired the prayer and she who did not. As we have observed before, there are heightened concerns with protecting freedom of conscience from subtle coercive pressure in the elementary and secondary public schools. What to most believers may seem nothing more than a reasonable request that the nonbeliever respect their religious practices, in a school context may appear to the nonbeliever or dissenter to be an attempt to employ the machinery of the State of enforce a religious orthodoxy.

We need not look beyond the circumstances of this case to see the phenomenon at work. The undeniable fact is that the school district's supervision and control of a high school graduation ceremony places public pressure, as well as peer pressure, on attending students to stand as a group or, at least, maintain respectful silence during the invocation and benediction. This pressure, though subtle and indirect, can be as real as any overt compulsion. Of course, in our culture standing or remaining silent can signify adherence to a view or simple respect for the views of others. And no doubt some persons who have no desire to join a prayer have little objection to standing as a sign of respect for those who do. But for the dissenter of high school age, who has a reasonable perception that she is being forced by the State to pray in a manner her conscience will not allow, the injury is no less real. There can be no doubt that for many, if not most, of the students at the graduation, the act of standing or remaining silent was an expression of participation in the rabbi's prayer. That was the very point of the religious exercise. It is of little comfort to a dissenter, then, to be told that for her the act of standing or remaining in silence signifies mere respect, rather than participation. What matters is that, given our social conventions, a reasonable dissenter in this milieu could believe that the group exercise signified her own participation or approval of it.

The injury caused by the government's action, and the reason why Daniel and Deborah Weisman object to it, is that the State, in a school setting, in effect required participation in a religious exercise. There was a stipulation in the District Court that attendance at graduation and promotional ceremonies is voluntary. Petitioners and the United States, as amicus, made this a center point of the case, arguing that the option of not attending the graduation excuses any inducement or coercion in the ceremony itself. The argument lacks all persuasion. Law reaches past formalism. And to say a teenage student has a real choice not to attend her high school graduation is formalistic in the extreme. True, Deborah could elect not to attend commencement without renouncing her diploma; but we shall not allow the case to turn on this point. Everyone knows that in our society and in our culture high school graduation is one of life's most significant occasions. A school rule which excuses attendance is beside the point. Attendance may not be required by official decree, yet it is apparent that a student is not free to absent herself from the graduation exercise in any real sense of the term "voluntary," for absence would require forfeiture of those intangible benefits which have motivated the student through youth and all her high school years. Graduation is a time for family and those closest to the student to celebrate success and express mutual wishes of gratitude and respect, all to the end of impressing upon the young person the role that it is his or her right and duty to assume in the community and all of its diverse parts.

The Government's argument gives insufficient recognition to the real conflict of conscience faced by the young student. The essence of the Government's position is that with regard to a civic, social occasion of this importance it is the objector, not the majority, who must take unilateral and private action to avoid compromising religious scruples, hereby electing to miss the graduation exercise. This turns conventional First Amendment analysis on its head. It is a tenet of the First Amendment that the State cannot require one of its citizens to forfeit his or her rights and benefits as the price of resisting conformance to state-sponsored religious practice. To say that a student must remain apart from the ceremony at the opening invocation and closing benediction is to risk compelling conformity in an environment analogous to the classroom setting, where we have said the risk of compulsion is especially high.

The sole question presented is whether a religious exercise may be conducted at a graduation ceremony in circumstances where, as we have found, young graduates who object are induced to conform. No holding by this Court suggests that a school can persuade or compel a student to participate in a religious exercise. That is being done here, and it is forbidden by the Establishment Clause of the First Amendment.

Justice BLACKMUN, with whom Justice STEVENS and Justice O'CONNOR join, concurring.

Nearly half a century of review and refinement of Establishment Clause jurisprudence has distilled one clear understanding: Government may neither promote not affiliate itself with any religious doctrine or organization, nor may it obtrude itself in the internal affairs of any religious institution. The application of these principles to the present case mandates the decision reached today by the Court.

I join the Court's opinion today because I find nothing in it inconsistent with the essential precepts of the Establishment Clause developed in our precedents. The Court holds that the graduation prayer is unconstitutional because the State "in effect required participation in a religious exercise." Although our precedents make clear that proof of government coercion is not necessary to prove an Establishment Clause violation, it is sufficient. Government pressure to participate in a religious activity is an obvious indication that the government is endorsing or promoting religion.

But it is not enough that the government restrain from compelling religious practices: It must not engage in them either. The Court repeatedly has recognized that a violation of the Establishment Clause is not predicated on coercion. The Establishment Clause proscribes public schools from "conveying or attempting to convey a message that religion or a particular religious belief is favored or preferred," even if the schools do not actually "impos[e] pressure upon a student to participate in a religious activity."

We have believed that religious freedom cannot exist in the absence of a free democratic government, and that such a government cannot endure when there is fusion between religion and the political regime. We have believed that religious freedom cannot thrive in the absence of a vibrant religious community and that such a community cannot prosper when it is bound to the secular. And we have believed that these were the animating principles behind the adoption of the Establishment Clause. To that end, our cases have prohibited government endorsement of religion, its sponsorship, and active involvement in religion, whether or not citizens were coerced to conform.

[Justice Souter also concurred, saying that coercion is sufficient, though not necessary, for a violation of the Establishment Clause.]

Justice S_CALIA_, with whom the Chief Justice, Justice W_HITE_, and Justice T_HOMAS_ join, dissenting.

Three Terms ago, I joined an opinion recognizing that the Establishment Clause must be construed in light of the "[g]overnment policies of accommodation, acknowledgement, and support for religion [that] are an accepted part of our political and cultural heritage." That opinion affirmed that "the meaning of the Clause is to be determined by reference to historical practices and understandings." County of Allegheny v. American Civil Liberties Union, Greater Pittsburgh Chapter (1989) (Kennedy, J., concurring in judgment in part and dissenting in part).

These views of course prevent me from joining today's opinion, which is conspicuously bereft of any reference to history. In holding that the Establishment Clause prohibits invocations and benedictions at public-school graduation ceremonies, the Court—with nary a mention that it is doing so—lays waste a tradition that is as old as public-school graduation ceremonies themselves, and that is a component of an even more longstanding American tradition of nonsectarian prayer to God at public celebrations generally. As its instrument of destruction, the bulldozer of its social engineering, the Court invents a boundless, and boundlessly manipulable, test of psychological coercion.

Justice Holmes' aphorism that "a page of history is worth a volume of logic," applies with particular force to our Establishment Clause jurisprudence. The history and tradition of our Nation are replete with public ceremonies featuring prayers of thanksgiving and petition. From our Nation's origin, prayer has been a prominent part of governmental ceremonies and proclamations. The Declaration of Independence, the document marking our birth as a separate people, "appeal[ed] to the Supreme Judge of the world for the rectitude of our intentions" and avowed "a firm reliance on the protection of divine providence." In his first inaugural address, after swearing his oath of office on a Bible, George Washington deliberately made a prayer a part of his first official act as President.

The Court presumably would separate graduation invocations and benedictions from other instances of public "preservation and transmission of religious beliefs" on the ground that they involve "psychological coercion." I find it a sufficient embarrassment that our Establishment Clause jurisprudence regarding holiday displays, see County of Allegheny v. American Civil Liberties Union, Greater Pittsburgh Chapter (1989), has come to "requir[e] scrutiny more commonly associated with interior decorators than with the judiciary." But interior decorating is a rock-hard science compared to psychology practiced by amateurs. A few citations of "[r]esearch in psychology" that have no particular bearing upon the precise issue here, cannot disguise that fact that the Court has gone beyond the realm where judges know what they are doing. The Court's argument that state officials have "coerced" students to take part in the invocation and benediction at graduation ceremonies is, not to put too fine a point on it, incoherent.

The Court declares that students' "attendance and participation in the [invocation and benediction] are in a fair and real sense obligatory." But what exactly is this "fair and real sense"? According to the Court, students at graduation who want "to avoid the fact or appearance of participation," in the invocation and benediction are psychologically obligated by "public pressure, as well as peer pressure, . . . to stand as a group or, at least, maintain respectful silence" during those prayers. This assertion—the very linchpin of the Court's opinion—is almost as intriguing for what it does not say as for what it says. It does not say, for example, that students are psychologically coerced to bow their heads, place their hands in a Durer-like prayer position, pay attention to the prayers, utter "Amen," or in fact pray. (Perhaps further intensive psychological research remains to be done on these matters.) It claims only that students are psychologically coerced "to stand . . . or, at least, maintain respectful silence."

To begin with the latter: The Court's notion that a student who simply sits in "respectful silence" during the invocations and benediction (when all others are standing) has somehow joined — or would somehow be perceived as having joined — in the prayers is nothing short of ludicrous. We indeed live in a vulgar age. But surely "our social conventions," have not coarsened to the point that anyone who does not stand on his chair and shout obscenities can reasonably be deemed to have assented to everything said in his presence. Since the Court does not dispute that students exposed to prayer at graduation ceremonies retain (despite "subtle coercive pressures") the free will to sit, there is absolutely no basis for the Court's decision. It is fanciful enough to say that "a reasonable dissenter," standing head erect in a class of bowed heads, "could believe that the group exercise signified her own participation or approval of it." It is beyond the absurd to say that she could entertain such a belief while pointedly declining to rise.

But let us assume the very worst, that the nonparticipating graduate is "subtly coerced" . . . to stand! Even that half of the disjunctive does not remotely establish a "participation" (or an "appearance of participation") in a religious exercise. I may add, moreover, that maintaining respect for the religious observances of others is a fundamental civic virtue that government (including the public schools) can and should cultivate — so that even if it were the case that the displaying of such respect might be mistaken for taking part in the prayer, I would deny that the dissenter's interest in avoiding even the false appearance of participation constitutionally trumps the government's interest in fostering respect for religion generally.

The opinion manifests that the Court itself has not given careful consideration to its test of psychological coercion. For if it had, how could it observe, with no hint of concern or disapproval, that students stood for the Pledge of Allegiance, which immediately preceded Rabbi Gutterman's invocation? The government can, of course, no more coerce political orthodoxy than religious orthodoxy.

I also find it odd that the Court concludes that high school graduates may not be subject to this supposed psychological coercion, yet refrains from addressing whether "mature adults" may. I had though that the reason graduation from high school is regarded as so significant an event is that it is generally associated with transition from adolescence to young adulthood. Many graduating seniors, of course, are old enough to vote. Why then, does the Court treat them as though they were first-graders? Will we soon have a jurisprudence that distinguishes between mature and immature adults?

The deeper flaw in the Court's opinion does not lie in its wrong answer to the question whether there was state-induced "peer-pressure" coercion; it lies, rather, in the Court's making violation of the Establishment Clause hinge on such a precious question. The coercion that was a hallmark of historical establishments of religion was coercion of religious orthodoxy and of financial support by force of law and threat of penalty. The Establishment Clause was adopted to prohibit such an establishment of religion at the federal level (and to protect state establishments of religion from federal interference).

Thus, while I have no quarrel with the Court's general proposition that the Establishment Clause "guarantees that government may not coerce anyone to support or participate in religion or its exercise," I see no warrant for expanding the concept of coercion beyond acts backed by threat of penalty — a brand of coercion that, happily, is readily discernible to those of us who have made a career of reading the disciples of Blackstone rather than of Freud. The framers were indeed opposed to coercion of religious worship by the National Government; but, as their own sponsorship of nonsectarian prayer in public events demonstrates, they understood that "[s]peech is not coercive; the listener may do as he likes."

The reader has been told much in this case about the personal interest of Mr. Weisman and his daughter, and very little about the personal interests on the other side. They are not inconsequential. Church and state would not be such a difficult subject if religion were, as the Court apparently thinks it to be, some purely personal avocation that can be indulged entirely in secret, like pornography, in the privacy of one's room. For most believers it is not that, and has never been. Religious men and women of almost all denominations have felt it necessary to acknowledge and beseech the blessing of God as a people, and not just as individuals, because they believe in the "protection of divine Providence," as the Declaration of Independence put it, not just for individuals but for societies; because they believe God to be, as Washington's first Thanksgiving Proclamation put it, the "Great Lord and Ruler of Nations." One can believe in the effectiveness of such public worship, or one can deprecate and deride it. But the longstanding Amercian tradition of prayer at official ceremonies displays with unmistakable clarity that the Establishment Clause does not forbid the government to accommodate it.

I must add one final observation: The Founders of our Republic knew the fearsome potential of sectarian religious belief to generate civil dissension and civil strife. And they also knew that nothing, absolutely nothing, is so inclined to foster among religious believers of various faith a toleration — no, an affection — for one another than voluntarily joining in prayer together, to the God whom they all worship and seek. Needless to say, no one should be compelled to do that, but it is a shame to deprive our public culture of the opportunity, and indeed the encouragement, for people to do it voluntarily. The Baptist or Catholic who heard and joined in the simple and inspiring prayers of Rabbi Gutterman on this official and patriotic occasion was inoculated from religious bigotry and prejudice in a manner that cannot be replicated. To deprive our society of that important unifying mechanism, in order to spare the nonbeliever what seems to me the minimal inconvenience of standing or even sitting in respectful nonparticipation, is as senseless in policy as it in unsupported in law.

———————————

The Court's most recent decision concerning prayer in public schools, Santa Fe Independent School District v. Doe, is presented earlier in this chapter. In *Doe*, the Court followed Lee v. Weisman and declared unconstitutional student-delivered prayers at public school football games.

CURRICULAR DECISIONS

The Supreme Court has declared unconstitutional government decisions concerning the curriculum that were motivated by religious purpose. These cases primarily have concerned state law prohibiting the teaching of evolution or requiring the teaching of "creationism" when evolution is taught.

In Epperson v. Arkansas, 393 U.S. 97 (1968), the Court declared unconstitutional an Arkansas law that made it unlawful for a teacher in a state-supported school or university "to teach the theory or doctrine that mankind ascended or descended from a lower order of animals" or "to adopt or use in any such institution a textbook that teaches" this theory. The Court held that the law prohibiting teaching of evolution was motivated by a religious purpose and thus violated the Establishment Clause. The Court explained, "The overriding fact is that Arkansas' law selects from the body of knowledge a particular segment which it proscribes for the sole reason that it is deemed to conflict with a particular religious doctrine; that is, with a particular interpretation of the Book of Genesis by a particular religious group." The Court observed that "[t]here is and can be no doubt that the First Amendment does not permit the State to require that teaching and learning must be tailored to the principles or prohibitions of any religious sect or dogma." The Arkansas law did exactly that: preclude teaching of evolution because it was a theory opposed by some religions.

In Edwards v. Aguillard, 482 U.S. 578 (1987), the Court followed this same reasoning and declared unconstitutional a Louisiana law that prohibited the teaching of the theory of evolution in public schools unless accompanied by instruction in "creation science." The Court noted that, as in *Epperson*, the "same historic and contemporaneous antagonisms between the teachings of certain religious denominations and the teaching of evolution are present in this case." The Court said that the law's "primary purpose was to change the science curriculum of public schools in order to provide persuasive advantage to a particular religious doctrine that rejects the factual basis of evolution in its entirety." The Court thus concluded, "Because the primary purpose of the Creationism Act is to advance a particular religious belief, the Act endorses religion in violation of the First Amendment."

b. Religion as a Part of Government Activities: Legislative Chaplains

In contrast to the prohibition of religion in public school activities, in Marsh v. Chambers, the Court upheld the constitutionality of the state's employment of a minister to begin legislative sessions with a prayer.

MARSH v. CHAMBERS, 463 U.S. 783 (1983): Chief Justice BURGER delivered the opinion of the Court.

[The issue was the constitutionality of a state legislature employing a Presbyterian minister for 18 years to begin each session with a prayer. The Nebraska legislature had employed Robert E. Palmer, a Presbyterian minister, since 1965 to open each legislative day with a prayer.]

The opening of sessions of legislative and other deliberative public bodies with prayer is deeply embedded in the history and tradition of this country.

From colonial times through the founding of the Republic and ever since, the practice of legislative prayer has coexisted with the principles of disestablishment and religious freedom. This unique history leads us to accept the interpretation of the First Amendment draftsmen who saw no real threat to the Establishment Clause arising from a practice of prayer similar to that now challenged.

In light of the unambiguous and unbroken history of more than 200 years, there can be no doubt that the practice of opening legislative sessions with prayer has become part of the fabric of our society. Nor is the compensation of the chaplain from public funds a reason to invalidate the Nebraska Legislature's chaplaincy: remuneration is grounded in historic practice initiated by the same Congress that drafted the Establishment Clause of the First Amendment.

It is notable that in *Marsh* the Court did not apply the *Lemon* test. Instead, the Court stressed history in upholding the legislative chaplain and legislative prayer.

6. When Can Government Give Aid to Religion?

Many Establishment Clause cases have involved the issue of government assistance to religion. Decisions in this area are numerous but often difficult to reconcile. The Court inevitably is involved in line drawing. Total government subsidy of churches or parochial schools undoubtedly would violate the Establishment Clause. Indeed, James Madison's *Memorial and Remonstrance Against Religious Assessments* was made in the context of opposing a state tax to aid the church.[54] But it also would be clearly unconstitutional if the government provided no public services — no police or fire protection, no sanitation services — to religious institutions. Such discrimination surely would violate equal protection and infringe free exercise of religion.[55]

Therefore, the Court must draw a line between aid that is permissible and that which is forbidden. No bright line test exists or likely ever will be developed. Any aid provided to a religious institution or a parochial school frees resources that can be used to further its religious mission.[56] The dominant approach for the past quarter of a century has been to apply the test from Lemon v. Kurtzman, presented above, and to ask whether there is a secular purpose for the assistance, whether the aid has the effect of advancing religion, and whether the particular

---

54. Madison's *Remonstrance* is reprinted in Everson v. Board of Education, 330 U.S. 1, 63 (1947).

55. *See, e.g.*, Lemon v. Kurtzman, 403 U.S. at 614 ("Fire inspections, building and zoning regulations, and state requirements under compulsory school attendance laws are examples of necessary and permissible contacts.").

56. In the initial case concerning government aid to parochial schools, Everson v. Board of Education, 330 U.S. 1 (1947), the Court upheld the constitutionality of the government reimbursing parents for the costs of bus transportation to and from parochial school. The Court recognized that "[t]here is even a possibility that some of the children might not be sent to the church schools if the parents were compelled . . . to pay their children's bus fares out of their own pockets . . . when transportation to a public school would have been paid for by the State."

form of assistance causes excessive government entanglement with religion. But not every case has used the *Lemon* test.

There have been four major areas where the Court has considered government aid to religion: assistance to parochial elementary and secondary schools; tax exemptions for religious institutions; aid to religious colleges and universities; and assistance to religious institutions other than schools. Each of these is considered below in turn. By far, most cases have concerned aid to religious elementary and secondary schools, and it thus receives the most attention.

AID TO PAROCHIAL ELEMENTARY AND SECONDARY SCHOOLS

The Court has considered the constitutionality of a vast array of different types of assistance, ranging from tuition tax credits to textbooks to audiovisual equipment to medical diagnostic tests to many other kinds of aid. The decisions often seem difficult to reconcile. For example, the Court has upheld the government providing buses to take children to and from parochial schools,[57] but not buses to take parochial school students on field trips.[58] The Court has forbidden the government from paying teacher salaries in parochial schools, even for teachers of secular subjects;[59] but the Court allowed the government to provide a sign language interpreter for hearing-impaired students in parochial schools.[60] The Court has permitted the government to pay for administering standardized tests in parochial schools,[61] but not for essay exams assessing writing achievement.[62]

In 1997, the Court signaled a likely shift to its approach to the Establishment Clause. In Agostini v. Felton, 521 U.S. 203 (1997), the Court held that public school remedial education teachers may provide instruction in private schools. In doing so, the Court overruled a decision from a decade earlier, Aguilar v. Felton, 473 U.S. 402 (1985), which held that such instruction violates the Establishment Clause. *Agostini* was a five-to-four decision, and the majority opinion was written by Justice O'Connor and joined by Chief Justice Rehnquist and Justices Scalia, Kennedy, and Thomas.

At the end of the majority opinion, Justice O'Connor appeared to state a new test for the Establishment Clause: "To summarize, New York City's Title I program does not run afoul of any of the three primary criteria we currently use to evaluate whether government aid has the effect of advancing religion: it does not result in government indoctrination; define its recipient by reference to religion; or create an excessive entanglement." Justice O'Connor presents this as if it is restating existing law, and yet this seems to articulate a new approach that aid to parochial schools is unconstitutional only if the government participates in indoctrinating religion, or if the government discriminates among religions, or if there is excessive government entanglement with religion.

In Mitchell v. Helms, several of the opinions discuss this aspect of Justice O'Connor's opinion in *Agostini*. In *Mitchell*, the Supreme Court reconsidered

---

57. Everson v. Board of Education, 330 U.S. 1 (1947).
58. Wolman v. Walter, 433 U.S. 229 (1977).
59. Grand Rapids School Dist. v. Ball, 473 U.S. 373 (1985); Aguilar v. Felton, 473 U.S. 402 (1985); Lemon v. Kurtzman, 403 U.S. 602 (1971).
60. Zobrest v. Catalina Foothills School Dist., 509 U.S. 1 (1993).
61. Committee for Public Education & Religious Liberty v. Regan, 444 U.S. 646 (1980).
62. Levitt v. Community for Public Education, 413 U.S. 472 (1973).

whether the government violates the Establishment Clause when it provides instructional equipment to parochial schools. Earlier, in Meek v. Pittenger, 421 U.S. 349 (1975), the Court declared unconstitutional a state law that provided instructional materials, including audiovisual equipment, to parochial schools. In reconsidering this issue, the justices expressed their views as to the more general issue: What aid to parochial school violates the Establishment Clause?

MITCHELL v. HELMS
530 U.S. 793 (2000)

Justice THOMAS announced the judgment of the Court and delivered an opinion, in which the Chief Justice, Justice SCALIA, and Justice KENNEDY join.

As part of a longstanding school aid program known as Chapter 2, the Federal Government distributes funds to state and local governmental agencies, which in turn lend educational materials and equipment to public and private schools, with the enrollment of each participating school determining the amount of aid that it receives. The question is whether Chapter 2, as applied in Jefferson Parish, Louisiana, is a law respecting an establishment of religion, because many of the private schools receiving Chapter 2 aid in that parish are religiously affiliated. We hold that Chapter 2 is not such a law.

I

Chapter 2 of the Education Consolidation and Improvement Act of 1981, has its origins in the Elementary and Secondary Education Act of 1965 (ESEA), and is a close cousin of the provision of the ESEA that we recently considered in Agostini v. Felton (1997). Like the provision at issue in *Agostini*, Chapter 2 channels federal funds to local educational agencies (LEA's), which are usually public school districts, via state educational agencies (SEA's), to implement programs to assist children in elementary and secondary schools. Among other things, Chapter 2 provides aid "for the acquisition and use of instructional and educational materials, including library services and materials (including media materials), assessments, reference materials, computer software and hardware for instructional use, and other curricular materials."

Several restrictions apply to aid to private schools. Most significantly, the "services, materials, and equipment" provided to private schools must be "secular, neutral, and nonideological." In addition, private schools may not acquire control of Chapter 2 funds or title to Chapter 2 materials, equipment, or property. A private school receives the materials and equipment by submitting to the LEA an application detailing which items the school seeks and how it will use them; the LEA, if it approves the application, purchases those items from the school's allocation of funds, and then lends them to that school.

In Jefferson Parish (the Louisiana governmental unit at issue in this case), as in Louisiana as a whole, private schools have primarily used their allocations for nonrecurring expenses, usually materials and equipment. In the 1986-1987 fiscal year, for example, 44% of the money budgeted for private schools in Jefferson Parish was spent by LEA's for acquiring library and media materials, and 48% for instructional equipment. Among the materials and equipment provided have been library books, computers, and computer software, and also slide and movie projectors, overhead projectors, television sets, tape recorders, VCR's, projection screens, laboratory equipment, maps, globes, filmstrips, slides, and cassette recordings.

It appears that, in an average year, about 30% of Chapter 2 funds spent in Jefferson Parish are allocated for private schools. For the 1985-1986 fiscal year, 41 private schools participated in Chapter 2. For the following year, 46 participated, and the participation level has remained relatively constant since then. Of these 46, 34 were Roman Catholic; 7 were otherwise religiously affiliated; and 5 were not religiously affiliated.

II

The Establishment Clause of the First Amendment dictates that "Congress shall make no law respecting an establishment of religion." In the over 50 years since *Everson*, we have consistently struggled to apply these simple words in the context of governmental aid to religious schools.

In *Agostini*, however, we brought some clarity to our case law, by overruling two anomalous precedents and by consolidating some of our previously disparate considerations under a revised test. Whereas in *Lemon* we had considered whether a statute (1) has a secular purpose, (2) has a primary effect of advancing or inhibiting religion, or (3) creates an excessive entanglement between government and religion, in *Agostini* we modified *Lemon* for purposes of evaluating aid to schools and examined only the first and second factors. We acknowledged that our cases discussing excessive entanglement had applied many of the same considerations as had our cases discussing primary effect, and we therefore recast *Lemon*'s entanglement inquiry as simply one criterion relevant to determining a statute's effect. We also acknowledged that our cases had pared somewhat the factors that could justify a finding of excessive entanglement.

We then set out revised criteria for determining the effect of a statute: "To summarize, New York City's Title I program does not run afoul of any of three primary criteria we currently use to evaluate whether government aid has the effect of advancing religion: It does not result in governmental indoctrination; define its recipients by reference to religion; or create an excessive entanglement."

In this case, our inquiry under *Agostini*'s purpose and effect test is a narrow one. Because respondents do not challenge the District Court's holding that Chapter 2 has a secular purpose, and because the Fifth Circuit also did not question that holding, we will consider only Chapter 2's effect. Further, in determining that effect, we will consider only the first two *Agostini* criteria, since neither respondents nor the Fifth Circuit has questioned the District Court's holding, that Chapter 2 does not create an excessive entanglement. Considering Chapter 2 in light of our more recent case law, we conclude that it neither results in religious indoctrination by the government nor defines its recipients by reference to religion. We therefore hold that Chapter 2 is not a "law respecting an establishment of religion." In so holding, we acknowledge what both the Ninth and Fifth Circuits saw was inescapable — *Meek* and *Wolman* are anomalies in our case law. We therefore conclude that they are no longer good law.

A

As we indicated in *Agostini,* and have indicated elsewhere, the question whether governmental aid to religious schools results in governmental indoctrination is ultimately a question whether any religious indoctrination that occurs in those schools could reasonably be attributed to governmental action. We have also indicated that the answer to the question of indoctrination will resolve the question whether a program of educational aid "subsidizes" religion, as our religion cases use that term.

In distinguishing between indoctrination that is attributable to the State and indoctrination that is not, we have consistently turned to the principle of neutrality, upholding aid that is offered to a broad range of groups or persons without regard to their religion. If the religious, irreligious, and areligious are all alike eligible for governmental aid, no one would conclude that any indoctrination that any particular recipient conducts has been done at the behest of the government. For attribution of indoctrination is a relative question. If the government is offering assistance to recipients who provide, so to speak, a broad range of indoctrination, the government itself is not thought responsible for any particular indoctrination. To put the point differently, if the government, seeking to further some legitimate secular purpose, offers aid on the same terms, without regard to religion, to all who adequately further that purpose, then it is fair to say that any aid going to a religious recipient only has the effect of furthering that secular purpose. The government, in crafting such an aid program, has had to conclude that a given level of aid is necessary to further that purpose among secular recipients and has provided no more than that same level to religious recipients.

As a way of assuring neutrality, we have repeatedly considered whether any governmental aid that goes to a religious institution does so "only as a result of the genuinely independent and private choices of individuals." We have viewed as significant whether the "private choices of individual parents," as opposed to the "unmediated" will of government, determine what schools ultimately benefit from the governmental aid, and how much. For if numerous private choices, rather than the single choice of a government, determine the distribution of aid pursuant to neutral eligibility criteria, then a government cannot, or at least cannot easily, grant special favors that might lead to a religious establishment. Private choice also helps guarantee neutrality by mitigating the preference for pre-existing recipients that is arguably inherent in any governmental aid program, and that could lead to a program inadvertently favoring one religion or favoring religious private schools in general over nonreligious ones.

Witters and *Mueller* employed similar reasoning. In *Witters,* we held that the Establishment Clause did not bar a State from including within a neutral program providing tuition payments for vocational rehabilitation a blind person studying at a Christian college to become a pastor, missionary, or youth director.

The tax deduction for educational expenses that we upheld in *Mueller* was, in these respects, the same as the tuition grant in *Witters.* We upheld it chiefly because it "neutrally provides state assistance to a broad spectrum of citizens," and because "numerous, private choices of individual parents of school-age children," determined which schools would benefit from the deductions. We explained that "[w]here, as here, aid to parochial schools is available only as a result of decisions of individual parents no 'imprimatur of state approval' can be deemed to have been conferred on any particular religion, or on religion generally."

We hasten to add, what should be obvious from the rule itself, that simply because an aid program offers private schools, and thus religious schools, a benefit that they did not previously receive does not mean that the program, by reducing the cost of securing a religious education, creates, under *Agostini's* second criterion, an "incentive" for parents to choose such an education for their children. For any aid will have some such effect.

B

1

Respondents offer two rules that they contend should govern our determination of whether Chapter 2 has the effect of advancing religion. They argue first, and chiefly, that "direct, nonincidental" aid to the primary educational mission of religious schools is always impermissible. Second, they argue that provision to religious schools of aid that is divertible to religious use is similarly impermissible. Respondents' arguments are inconsistent with our more recent case law and we therefore reject them.

Although some of our earlier cases did emphasize the distinction between direct and indirect aid, the purpose of this distinction was merely to prevent "subsidization" of religion. As even the dissent all but admits, our more recent cases address this purpose not through the direct/indirect distinction but rather through the principle of private choice, as incorporated in the first *Agostini* criterion (i.e., whether any indoctrination could be attributed to the government). If aid to schools, even "direct aid," is neutrally available and, before reaching or benefiting any religious school, first passes through the hands (literally or figuratively) of numerous private citizens who are free to direct the aid elsewhere, the government has not provided any "support of religion." Although the presence of private choice is easier to see when aid literally passes through the hands of individuals — which is why we have mentioned directness in the same breath with private choice, there is no reason why the Establishment Clause requires such a form.

Further, respondents' formalistic line breaks down in the application to real-world programs. In Allen v. Board of Education, for example, although we did recognize that students themselves received and owned the textbooks, we also noted that the books provided were those that the private schools required for courses, that the schools could collect students' requests for books and submit them to the board of education, that the schools could store the textbooks, and that the textbooks were essential to the schools' teaching of secular subjects.

Of course, we have seen "special Establishment Clause dangers," when money is given to religious schools or entities directly rather than, as in *Witters* and *Mueller*, indirectly. But direct payments of money are not at issue in this case, and we refuse to allow a "special" case to create a rule for all cases.

2

Respondents also contend that the Establishment Clause requires that aid to religious schools not be impermissibly religious in nature or be divertible to religious use. We agree with the first part of this argument but not the second. Respondents' "no divertibility" rule is inconsistent with our more recent case law and is unworkable. So long as the governmental aid is not itself "unsuitable for use in the public schools because of religious content," and eligibility for aid is determined in a constitutionally permissible manner, any use of that aid to indoctrinate cannot be attributed to the government and is thus not of constitutional concern. And, of course, the use to which the aid is put does not affect the criteria governing the aid's allocation and thus does not create any impermissible incentive under *Agostini*'s second criterion.

The issue is not divertibility of aid but rather whether the aid itself has an impermissible content. Where the aid would be suitable for use in a public school, it is also suitable for use in any private school. Similarly, the prohibition against the government providing impermissible content resolves the Establishment Clause concerns that exist if aid is actually diverted to religious uses.

A concern for divertibility, as opposed to improper content, is misplaced not only because it fails to explain why the sort of aid that we have allowed is permissible, but also because it is boundless — enveloping all aid, no matter how trivial — and thus has only the most attenuated (if any) link to any realistic concern for preventing an "establishment of religion." Presumably, for example, government-provided lecterns, chalk, crayons, pens, paper, and paintbrushes would have to be excluded from religious schools under respondents' proposed rule. But we fail to see how indoctrination by means of (i.e., diversion of) such aid could be attributed to the government. In fact, the risk of improper attribution is less when the aid lacks content, for there is no risk (as there is with books), of the government inadvertently providing improper content. Finally, any aid, with or without content, is "divertible" in the sense that it allows schools to "divert" resources. Yet we have "not accepted the recurrent argument that all aid is forbidden because aid to one aspect of an institution frees it to spend its other resources on religious ends."

It is perhaps conceivable that courts could take upon themselves the task of distinguishing among the myriad kinds of possible aid based on the ease of diverting each kind. But it escapes us how a court might coherently draw any such line. It not only is far more workable, but also is actually related to real concerns about preventing advancement of religion by government, simply to require that a program of aid to schools not provide improper content and that it determine eligibility and allocate the aid on a permissible basis.

One of the dissent's factors deserves special mention: whether a school that receives aid (or whose students receive aid) is pervasively sectarian. The dissent is correct that there was a period when this factor mattered, particularly if the pervasively sectarian school was a primary or secondary school. But that period is one that the Court should regret, and it is thankfully long past.

There are numerous reasons to formally dispense with this factor. First, its relevance in our precedents is in sharp decline. Although our case law has consistently mentioned it even in recent years, we have not struck down an aid program in reliance on this factor since 1985.

Second, the religious nature of a recipient should not matter to the constitutional analysis, so long as the recipient adequately furthers the government's secular purpose. If a program offers permissible aid to the religious (including the pervasively sectarian), the areligious, and the irreligious, it is a mystery which view of religion the government has established, and thus a mystery what the constitutional violation would be. The pervasively sectarian recipient has not received any special favor, and it is most bizarre that the

Court would, as the dissent seemingly does, reserve special hostility for those who take their religion seriously, who think that their religion should affect the whole of their lives, or who make the mistake of being effective in transmitting their views to children.

Third, the inquiry into the recipient's religious views required by a focus on whether a school is pervasively sectarian is not only unnecessary but also offensive. It is well established, in numerous other contexts, that courts should refrain from trolling through a person's or institution's religious beliefs.

Finally, hostility to aid to pervasively sectarian schools has a shameful pedigree that we do not hesitate to disavow. Although the dissent professes concern for "the implied exclusion of the less favored," the exclusion of pervasively sectarian schools from government-aid programs is just that, particularly given the history of such exclusion. Opposition to aid to "sectarian" schools acquired prominence in the 1870's with Congress's consideration (and near passage) of the Blaine Amendment, which would have amended the Constitution to bar any aid to sectarian institutions. Consideration of the amendment arose at a time of pervasive hostility to the Catholic Church and to Catholics in general, and it was an open secret that "sectarian" was code for "Catholic." Notwithstanding its history, of course, "sectarian" could, on its face, describe the school of any religious sect, but the Court eliminated this possibility of confusion when it coined the term "pervasively sectarian" — a term which, at that time, could be applied almost exclusively to Catholic parochial schools and which even today's dissent exemplifies chiefly by reference to such schools.

In short, nothing in the Establishment Clause requires the exclusion of pervasively sectarian schools from otherwise permissible aid programs, and other doctrines of this Court bar it. This doctrine, born of bigotry should be buried now.

Applying the two relevant *Agostini* criteria, we see no basis for concluding that Jefferson Parish's Chapter 2 program "has the effect of advancing religion." Chapter 2 does not result in governmental indoctrination, because it determines eligibility for aid neutrally, allocates that aid based on the private choices of the parents of schoolchildren, and does not provide aid that has an impermissible content. Nor does Chapter 2 define its recipients by reference to religion.

Justice O'CONNOR, with whom Justice BREYER joins, concurring in the judgment.

In 1965, Congress passed the Elementary and Secondary Education Act. Under Title I, Congress provided monetary grants to States to address the needs of educationally deprived children of low-income families. Under Title II, Congress provided further monetary grants to States for the acquisition of library resources, textbooks, and other instructional materials for use by children and teachers in public and private elementary and secondary schools. Since 1965, Congress has reauthorized the Title I and Title II programs several times. I believe that *Agostini* likewise controls the constitutional inquiry respecting Title II presented here, and requires the reversal of the Court of Appeals' judgment that the program is unconstitutional as applied in Jefferson Parish, Louisiana. To the extent our decisions in Meek v. Pittenger (1975), and Wolman v. Walter (1977), are inconsistent with the Courts judgment today, I agree that those decisions should be overruled. I therefore concur in the judgment.

I write separately because, in my view, the plurality announces a rule of unprecedented breadth for the evaluation of Establishment Clause challenges to government school-aid programs. Reduced to its essentials, the plurality's rule states that government aid to religious schools does not have the effect of advancing religion so long as the aid is offered on a neutral basis and the aid is secular in content. The plurality also rejects the distinction between direct and indirect aid, and holds that the actual diversion of secular aid by a religious school to the advancement of its religious mission is permissible. Although the expansive scope of the plurality's rule is troubling, two specific aspects of the opinion compel me to write separately. First, the plurality's treatment of neutrality comes close to assigning that factor singular importance in the future adjudication of Establishment Clause challenges to government school-aid programs. Second, the plurality's approval of actual diversion of government aid to religious indoctrination is in tension with our precedents and, in any event, unnecessary to decide the instant case.

I agree with Justice Souter that the plurality, by taking such a stance, "appears to take evenhanded neutrality and in practical terms promote it to a single and sufficient test for the establishment of the constitutionality of school aid." I do not quarrel with the plurality's recognition that neutrality is an important reason for upholding government-aid programs against Establishment Clause challenges. Nevertheless, we have never held that a government-aid program passes constitutional muster solely because of the neutral criteria it employs as a basis for distributing aid. I also disagree with the plurality's conclusion that actual diversion of government aid to religious indoctrination is consistent with the Establishment Clause.

I believe the distinction between a per-capita school-aid program and a true private-choice program is significant for purposes of endorsement. In terms of public perception, a government program of direct aid to religious schools based on the number of students attending each school differs meaningfully from the government distributing aid directly to individual students who, in turn, decide to use the aid at the same religious schools.

In the former example, if the religious school uses the aid to inculcate religion in its students, it is reasonable to say that the government has communicated a message of endorsement. Because the religious indoctrination is supported by government assistance, the reasonable observer would naturally perceive the aid program as government support for the advancement of religion. That the amount of aid received by the school is based on the school's enrollment does not separate the government from the endorsement of the religious message. The aid formula does not — and could not — indicate to a reasonable observer that the inculcation of religion is endorsed only by the individuals attending the religious school, who each affirmatively choose to direct the secular government aid to the school and its religious mission. No such choices have been made. In contrast, when government aid supports a school's religious mission only because of independent decisions made by numerous individuals to guide their secular aid to that school, "[n]o reasonable observer is likely to draw from the facts . . . an inference that the State itself is endorsing a religious practice or belief."

Finally, the distinction between a per-capita-aid program and a true private-choice program is important when considering aid that consists of direct monetary subsidies. This Court has "recognized special Establishment Clause dangers where the government makes direct money payments to sectarian institutions." If, as the plurality contends, a per-capita-aid program is identical in relevant constitutional respects to a true private-choice program, then there is no reason that, under the plurality's reasoning, the government should be precluded from providing direct money payments to religious organizations (including churches) based on the number of persons belonging to each organization. And, because actual diversion is permissible under the plurality's holding, the participating religious organizations (including churches) could use that aid to support religious indoctrination. To be sure, the plurality does not actually hold that its theory extends to direct money payments. That omission, however, is of little comfort. In its logic — as well as its specific advisory language — the plurality opinion foreshadows the approval of direct monetary subsidies to religious organizations, even when they use the money to advance their religious objectives.

Because divertibility fails to explain the distinction our cases have drawn between textbooks and instructional materials and equipment, there remains the question of which of the two irreconcilable strands of our Establishment Clause jurisprudence we should now follow. Between the two, I would adhere to the rule that we have applied in the context of textbook lending programs: To establish a First Amendment violation, plaintiffs must prove that the aid in question actually is, or has been, used for religious purposes.

Because I believe that the Court should abandon the presumption adopted in *Meek* and *Wolman* respecting the use of instructional materials and equipment by religious-school teachers, I see no constitutional need for pervasive monitoring under the Chapter 2 program. The safeguards employed by the program are constitutionally sufficient. At the federal level, the statute limits aid to "secular, neutral, and nonideological services, materials; and equipment"; requires that the aid only supplement and not supplant funds from non-Federal sources; and prohibits "any payment . . . for religious worship or instruction." At the state level, the Louisiana Department of Education (the relevant SEA for Louisiana) requires all nonpublic schools to submit signed assurances that they will use Chapter 2 aid only to supplement and not to supplant non-Federal funds, and that the instructional materials and equipment "will only be used for secular, neutral and nonideological purposes." The evidence proffered by respondents concerning actual diversion of Chapter 2 aid in Jefferson Parish is de minimis.

Justice SOUTER, with whom Justice STEVENS and Justice GINSBURG join, dissenting.

The First Amendment's Establishment Clause prohibits Congress (and, by incorporation, the States) from making any law respecting an establishment of religion. It has been held to prohibit not only the institution of an official church, but any government act favoring religion, a particular religion, or for that matter irreligion. Thus it bars the use of public funds for religious aid.

The establishment prohibition of government religious funding serves more than one end. It is meant to guarantee the right of individual conscience against compulsion, to protect the integrity of religion against the corrosion of secular support, and to preserve the unity of political society against the implied exclusion of the less favored and the antagonism of controversy over public support for religious causes.

These objectives are always in some jeopardy since the substantive principle of no aid to religion is not the only limitation on government action toward religion. Because the First Amendment also bars any prohibition of individual free exercise of religion, and because religious organizations cannot be isolated from the basic government functions that create the civil environment, it is as much necessary as it is difficult to draw lines between forbidden aid and lawful benefit. For more than 50 years, this Court has been attempting to draw these lines. Owing to the variety of factual circumstances in which the lines must be drawn, not all of the points creating the boundary have enjoyed self-evidence.

So far as the line drawn has addressed government aid to education, a few fundamental generalizations are nonetheless possible. There may be no aid supporting a sectarian school's religious exercise or the discharge of its religious mission, while aid of a secular character with no discernible benefit to such a sectarian objective is allowable. Because the religious and secular spheres largely overlap in the life of many such schools, the Court has tried to identify some facts likely to reveal the relative religious or secular intent or effect of the government benefits in particular circumstances. We have asked whether the government is acting neutrally in distributing its money, and about the form of the aid itself, its path from government to religious institution, its divertibility to religious nurture, its potential for reducing traditional expenditures of religious institutions, and its relative importance to the recipient, among other things.

In all the years of its effort, the Court has isolated no single test of constitutional sufficiency, and the question in every case addresses the substantive principle of no aid: what reasons are there to characterize this benefit as aid to the sectarian school in discharging its religious mission? Particular factual circumstances control, and the answer is a matter of judgment.

At least three concerns have been expressed since the founding and run throughout our First Amendment jurisprudence. First, compelling an individual to support religion violates the fundamental principle of freedom of conscience. Madison's and Jefferson's now familiar words establish clearly that liberty of personal conviction requires freedom from coercion to support religion, and this means that the government can compel no aid to fund it. Madison put it simply: "[T]he same authority which can force a citizen to contribute three pence only of his property for the support of any one establishment, may force him to conform to any other establishment."

Second, government aid corrupts religion. Madison argued that establishment of religion weakened the beliefs of adherents so favored, strengthened their opponents, and generated "pride and indolence in the Clergy; ignorance and servility in the laity; [and] in both, superstition, bigotry and persecution." In a variant of Madison's concern, we have repeatedly noted that a government's favor to a particular religion or sect threatens to taint it with "corrosive secularism."

Third, government establishment of religion is inextricably linked with conflict. In our own history, the turmoil thus produced has led to a rejection of the idea that government should subsidize religious education, a position that illustrates the Court's understanding that any implicit endorsement of religion is unconstitutional.

The insufficiency of evenhandedness neutrality as a stand-alone criterion of constitutional intent or effect has been clear from the beginning of our interpretative efforts, for an obvious reason. Evenhandedness in distributing a benefit approaches the equivalence of constitutionality in this area only when the term refers to such universality of distribution that it makes no sense to think of the benefit as going to any discrete group. Conversely, when evenhandedness refers to distribution to limited groups within society, like groups of schools or schoolchildren, it does make sense to regard the benefit as aid to the recipients. Hence, if we looked no further than evenhandedness, and failed to ask what activities the aid might support, or in fact did support, religious schools could be blessed with government funding as massive as expenditures made for the benefit of their public school counterparts, and religious missions would thrive on public money. This is why the consideration of less than universal neutrality has never been recognized as dispositive and has always been teamed with attention to other facts bearing on the substantive prohibition of support for a school's religious objective.

[O]ne point [is] clear beyond peradventure: together with James Madison we have consistently understood the Establishment Clause to impose a substantive prohibition against public aid to religion and, hence, to the religious mission of sectarian schools. Evenhandedness neutrality is one, nondispositive pointer toward an intent and (to a lesser degree) probable effect on the permissible side of the line between forbidden aid and general public welfare benefit. Other pointers are facts about the religious mission and education level of benefited schools and their pupils, the pathway by which a benefit travels from public treasury to educational effect, the form and content of the aid, its adaptability to religious ends, and its effects on school budgets. The object of all enquiries into such matters is the same whatever the particular circumstances: is the benefit intended to aid in providing the religious element of the education and is it likely to do so?

The facts most obviously relevant to the Chapter 2 scheme in Jefferson Parish are those showing divertibility and actual diversion in the circumstance of pervasively sectarian religious schools. The type of aid, the structure of the program, and the lack of effective safeguards clearly demonstrate the divertibility of the aid. While little is known about its use, owing to the anemic enforcement system in the parish, even the thin record before us reveals that actual diversion occurred.

The aid that the government provided was highly susceptible to unconstitutional use. Much of the equipment provided under Chapter 2 was not of the type provided for individual students, but included "slide projectors, movie projectors, overhead projectors, television sets, tape recorders, projection screens, maps, globes, filmstrips, cassettes, computers," and computer software and peripherals, as well as library books and materials. The videocassette players, overhead projectors, and other instructional aids were of the sort that we have found can easily be used by religious teachers for religious purposes. The same was true of the computers, which were as readily employable for religious teaching as the other equipment, and presumably as immune to any countervailing safeguard.

The divertibility thus inherent in the forms of Chapter 2 aid was enhanced by lie structure of the program in Jefferson Parish. Requests for specific items under Chapter 2 came not from secular officials, but from officials of the religious schools (and even parents of religious school pupils). The sectarian schools decided what they wanted and often ordered the supplies, to be forwarded directly to themselves. It was easy to select whatever instructional materials and library books the schools wanted, just as it was easy to employ computers for the support of the religious content of the curriculum infused with religious instruction.

The plurality nonetheless condemns any enquiry into the pervasiveness of doctrinal content as a remnant of anti-Catholic bigotry (as if evangelical Protestant schools and Orthodox Jewish yeshivas were never pervasively sectarian), and it equates a refusal to aid religious schools with hostility to religion (as if aid to religious teaching were not opposed in this very case by at least one religious respondent and numerous religious amici curiae in a tradition claiming descent from Roger Williams). My concern with these arguments goes not so much to their details as it does to the fact that the plurality's choice to employ imputations of bigotry and irreligion as terms in the Court's debate makes one point clear: that in rejecting the principle of no aid to a school's religious mission the plurality is attacking the most fundamental assumption underlying the Establishment Clause, that government can in fact operate with neutrality in its relation to religion. I believe that it can, and so respectfully dissent.

———————————

Prior to Mitchell v. Helms, it was possible to explain most of the cases by seeing them as applying three criteria. First, the aid must be available to all students enrolled in public and parochial schools; aid that is available only to parochial school students is sure to be invalidated. Second, the aid is more likely to be allowed if it is provided directly to the students than if it is provided to the schools. Third, the aid will be permitted if it is a type that likely cannot be used for religions instruction, but it will be invalidated if it can be easily used for religious education. After *Mitchell*, the first two criteria still seem to be followed by a majority of the justices, but the third criterion seems no longer used.

The first factor is whether the aid is available to all students. Aid that is available only to parochial school students is sure to be invalidated, but that same assistance is likely to be allowed if it is given to public school students as well and meets the other criteria. For example, in Committee for Public Education v. Nyquist, 413 U.S. 756 (1973), and Sloan v. Lemon, 413 U.S. 825 (1973), the Court declared unconstitutional state laws that provided reimbursement and tax credits to students attending nonpublic schools. In *Nyquist*, a New York statute provided for reimbursement and tax credits for costs of nonpublic school elementary and secondary education for up to one-half of the costs of tuition for low- and middle-income students. Specifically, the law provided for reimbursement payments to families with incomes below $15,000 and tax credits for families with incomes below $25,000. *Sloan* involved a Pennsylvania law that provided funds to reimburse parents for a portion of tuition expenses incurred in sending their children to nonpublic schools. Unlike the New York law in *Nyquist*, the Pennsylvania statute allowed families of all incomes to receive funds.

The Supreme Court declared both of these laws unconstitutional even though the aid went directly to the families rather than the schools. The Court emphasized that the aid was available only to nonpublic school students. The Court concluded that the aid "has a 'primary effect' that advances religion' and offends the constitutional prohibition 'respecting an establishment of religion.'"

In contrast, in Mueller v. Allen, 463 U.S. 388 (1983), discussed by all of the justices in *Mitchell*, the Court upheld a program of tax credits that were available to all students at both public and parochial schools. A Minnesota law allowed taxpayers to deduct certain expenses incurred in providing education to their children from their state income taxes. The deduction was limited to actual expenses for tuition, textbooks, and transportation and could not exceed $500 per dependent for grades kindergarten through six and $700 per student in grades seven through twelve.

By a five-to-four decision, the Court applied the *Lemon* test and upheld the income tax credits as constitutional. As to the first part of the *Lemon* test, the Court said that "[a] State's decision to defray the cost of educational expenses incurred by parents — regardless of the type of schools their children attend — evidences a purpose that is both secular and understandable. An educated populace is essential to the political and economic health of any community, and a State's efforts to assist parents in meeting the rising cost of educational expenses plainly serves this secular purpose of ensuring that the State's citizenry is well educated."

In applying the second prong of the *Lemon* test, the Court emphasized that the tax credits were one of many deductions available and were limited in size. The Court said that the "[l]egislature's judgment that a deduction for educational expenses fairly equalizes the tax burden of its citizens and encourages desirable expenditures for educational purposes is entitled to substantial deference." Most importantly, the Court stressed that the "deduction is available for educational expenses incurred by *all* parents, including those whose children attend public schools and those whose children attend nonsectarian private schools or sectarian private schools." The Court saw this as the key distinction with *Nyquist* where the aid was available only to students attending nonpublic schools.

Finally, the Court concluded that allowing the tax credits did not entail government entanglement with religion. No government monitoring was involved in the program; the government was not required by the law to oversee any aspect of the parochial schools.

Justice Marshall dissented and was joined by Justices Brennan, Blackmun, and Stevens. Justice Marshall contended that the Establishment Clause prohibits the government from subsidizing parochial schools, even if it is providing the same assistance to public schools students. Justice Marshall said, "The Establishment Clause of the First Amendment prohibits a State from subsidizing religious education, whether it does so directly or indirectly. In my view, this principle of neutrality forbids not only the tax benefits struck down in Committee for Public Education v. Nyquist, but any tax benefit, including the tax deduction at issue here, which subsidizes tuition payments to sectarian schools."

The Court appeared to resolve this tension in Zelman v. Simmons-Harris, where the Court, by a five-to-four margin, upheld a voucher program through which aid could be used for parochial schools.

ZELMAN v. SIMMONS-HARRIS

536 U.S. 639 (2002)

Chief Justice REHNQUIST delivered the opinion of the Court.

The State of Ohio has established a pilot program designed to provide educational choices to families with children who reside in the Cleveland City School District. The question presented is whether this program offends the Establishment Clause of the United States Constitution. We hold that it does not.

There are more than 75,000 children enrolled in the Cleveland City School District. The majority of these children are from low-income and minority families. Few of these families enjoy the means to send their children to any school other than an inner-city public school. For more than a generation, however, Cleveland's public schools have been among the worst performing public schools in the Nation. In 1995, a Federal District Court declared a "crisis of magnitude" and placed the entire Cleveland school district under state control. Shortly thereafter, the state auditor found that Cleveland's public schools were in the midst of a "crisis that is perhaps unprecedented in the history of American education." The district had failed to meet any of the 18 state standards for minimal acceptable performance. Only 1 in 10 ninth graders could pass a basic proficiency examination, and students at all levels performed at a dismal rate compared with students in other Ohio public schools. More than two-thirds of high school students either dropped or failed out before graduation. Of those students who managed to reach their senior year, one of every four still failed to graduate. Of those students who did graduate, few could read, write, or compute at levels comparable to their counterparts in other cities.

It is against this backdrop that Ohio enacted, among other initiatives, its Pilot Project Scholarship Program. The program provides financial assistance to families in any Ohio school district that is or has been "under federal court order requiring supervision and operational management of the district by the state superintendent." Cleveland is the only Ohio school district to fall within that category.

The program provides two basic kinds of assistance to parents of children in a covered district. First, the program provides tuition aid for students in kindergarten through third grade, expanding each year through eighth grade, to attend a participating public or private school of their parent's choosing. Second, the program provides tutorial aid for students who choose to remain enrolled in public school.

The tuition aid portion of the program is designed to provide educational choices to parents who reside in a covered district. Any private school, whether religious or nonreligious, may participate in the program and accept program students so long as the school is located within the boundaries of a covered district and meets statewide educational standards. Participating private schools must agree not to discriminate on the basis of race, religion, or ethnic background, or to "advocate or foster unlawful behavior or teach hatred of any person or group on the basis of race, ethnicity, national origin, or religion." Any public school located in a school district adjacent to the covered district may also participate in the program. Adjacent public schools are eligible to receive a $2,250 tuition grant for each program student accepted in addition to the full amount of per-pupil state funding attributable to each additional student. All participating schools, whether public or private, are required to accept students in accordance with rules and procedures established by the state superintendent.

Tuition aid is distributed to parents according to financial need. Families with incomes below 200% of the poverty line are given priority and are eligible to receive 90% of private school tuition up to $2,250. For these lowest-income families, participating private schools may not charge a parental co-payment greater than $250. For all other families, the program pays 75% of tuition costs, up to $1,875, with no co-payment cap. These families receive tuition aid only if the number of available scholarships exceeds the number of low-income children who choose to participate. Where tuition aid is spent depends solely upon where parents who receive tuition aid choose to enroll their child. If parents choose a private school, checks are made payable to the parents who then endorse the checks over to the chosen school.

The tutorial aid portion of the program provides tutorial assistance through grants to any student in a covered district who chooses to remain in public school. Parents arrange for registered tutors to provide assistance to their children and then submit bills for those services to the State for payment. Students from low-income families receive 90% of the amount charged for such assistance up to $360. All other students receive 75% of that amount. The number of tutorial assistance grants offered to students in a covered district must equal the number of tuition aid scholarships provided to students enrolled at participating private or adjacent public schools.

The program has been in operation within the Cleveland City School District since the 1996-1997 school year. In the 1999-2000 school year, 56 private schools participated in the program, 46 (or 82%) of which had a religious affiliation. None of the public schools in districts adjacent to Cleveland have elected to participate. More than 3,700 students participated in the scholarship program, most of whom (96%) enrolled in religiously affiliated schools. Sixty percent of these students were from families at or below the poverty line. In the 1998-1999 school year, approximately 1,400 Cleveland public school students received tutorial aid. This number was expected to double during the 1999-2000 school year.

The program is part of a broader undertaking by the State to enhance the educational options of Cleveland's schoolchildren in response to the 1995 takeover. That undertaking includes programs governing community and magnet schools. Community schools are funded under state law but are run by their own school boards, not by local school districts. These schools enjoy academic independence to hire their own teachers and to determine their own curriculum. They can have no religious affiliation and are required to accept students by lottery. During the 1999-2000 school year, there were 10 start-up community schools in the Cleveland City School District with more than 1,900 students enrolled. For each child enrolled in a community school, the school receives state funding of $4,518, twice the funding a participating program school may receive.

Magnet schools are public schools operated by a local school board that emphasize a particular subject area, teaching method, or service to students. For each student enrolled in a magnet school, the school district receives $7,746, including state funding of $4,167, the same amount received per student enrolled at a traditional public school. As of 1999, parents in Cleveland were able to choose from among 23 magnet schools, which together enrolled more than 13,000 students in kindergarten through eighth grade. These schools provide specialized teaching methods, such as Montessori, or a particularized curriculum focus, such as foreign language, computers, or the arts.

The Establishment Clause of the First Amendment, applied to the States through the Fourteenth Amendment, prevents a State from enacting laws that have the "purpose" or "effect" of advancing or inhibiting religion.

There is no dispute that the program challenged here was enacted for the valid secular purpose of providing educational assistance to poor children in a demonstrably failing public school system. Thus, the question presented is whether the Ohio program nonetheless has the forbidden "effect" of advancing or inhibiting religion.

To answer that question, our decisions have drawn a consistent distinction between government programs that provide aid directly to religious schools, Mitchell v. Helms (2000), and programs of true private choice, in which government aid reaches religious schools only as a result of the genuine and independent choices of private individuals, Mueller v. Allen (1983); Witters v. Washington Dept. of Servs. for Blind (1986); Zobrest v. Catalina Foothills School Dist. (1993). While our jurisprudence with respect to the constitutionality of direct aid programs has "changed significantly" over the past two decades, our jurisprudence with respect to true private choice programs has remained consistent and unbroken. Three times we have confronted Establishment Clause challenges to neutral government programs that provide aid directly to a broad class of individuals, who, in turn, direct the aid to religious schools or institutions of their own choosing. Three times we have rejected such challenges.

In *Mueller*, we rejected an Establishment Clause challenge to a Minnesota program authorizing tax deductions for various educational expenses, including private school tuition costs, even though the great majority of the program's beneficiaries (96%) were parents of children in religious schools. We began by focusing on the class of beneficiaries, finding that because the class included "all parents," including parents with "children [who] attend nonsectarian private schools or sectarian private schools," the program was "not readily subject to challenge under the Establishment Clause." Then, viewing the program as a whole, we emphasized the principle of private choice, noting that public funds were made available to religious schools "only as a result of numerous, private choices of individual parents of school-age children." This, we said, ensured that "'no imprimatur of state approval' can be deemed to have been conferred on any particular religion, or on religion generally." We thus found it irrelevant to the constitutional inquiry that the vast majority of beneficiaries were parents of children in religious schools, saying: "We would be loath to adopt a rule grounding the constitutionality of a facially neutral law on annual reports reciting the extent to which various classes of private citizens claimed benefits under the law." That the program was one of true private choice, with no evidence that the State deliberately skewed incentives toward religious schools, was sufficient for the program to survive scrutiny under the Establishment Clause.

In *Witters*, we used identical reasoning to reject an Establishment Clause challenge to a vocational scholarship program that provided tuition aid to a student studying at a religious institution to become a pastor. Looking at the program as a whole, we observed that "[a]ny aid . . . that ultimately flows to religious institutions does so only as a result of the genuinely independent and private choices of aid recipients." We further remarked that, as in *Mueller*, "[the] program is made available generally without regard to the sectarian-nonsectarian, or public-nonpublic nature of the institution benefited." In light of these factors, we held that the program was not inconsistent with the Establishment Clause. Five Members of the Court, in separate opinions, emphasized the general rule from *Mueller* that the amount of government aid channeled to religious institutions by individual aid recipients was not relevant to the constitutional inquiry. Our holding thus rested not on whether few or many recipients chose to expend government aid at a religious school but, rather, on whether recipients generally were empowered to direct the aid to schools or institutions of their own choosing.

Finally, in *Zobrest*, we applied *Mueller* and *Witters* to reject an Establishment Clause challenge to a federal program that permitted sign-language interpreters to assist deaf children enrolled in religious schools. Reviewing our earlier decisions, we stated that "government programs that neutrally provide benefits to a broad class of citizens defined without reference to religion are not readily subject to an Establishment Clause challenge." Looking once again to the challenged program as a whole, we observed that the program "distributes benefits neutrally to any child qualifying as 'disabled.'" Its "primary beneficiaries," we said, were "disabled children, not sectarian schools." We further observed that "[b]y according parents freedom to select a school of their choice, the statute ensures that a government-paid interpreter will be present in a sectarian school only as a result of the private decision of individual parents." Our focus again was on neutrality and the principle of private choice, not on the number of program beneficiaries attending religious schools. Because the program ensured that parents were the ones to select a religious school as the best learning environment for their handicapped child, the circuit between government and religion was broken, and the Establishment Clause was not implicated.

Mueller, Witters, and *Zobrest* thus make clear that where a government aid program is neutral with respect to religion, and provides assistance directly to a broad class of citizens who, in turn, direct government aid to religious schools wholly as a result of their own genuine and independent private choice, the program is not readily subject to challenge under the Establishment Clause. A program that shares these features permits government aid to reach religious institutions only by way of the deliberate choices of numerous individual recipients. The incidental advancement of a religious mission, or the perceived endorsement of a religious message, is reasonably attributable to the individual recipient, not to the government, whose role ends with the disbursement of benefits. As a plurality of this Court recently observed: "[I]f numerous private choices, rather than the single choice of a government, determine the distribution of aid, pursuant to neutral eligibility criteria, then a government cannot, or at least cannot easily, grant special favors that might lead to a religious establishment." Mitchell v. Helms (2000).

We believe that the program challenged here is a program of true private choice, consistent with *Mueller, Witters,* and *Zobrest,* and thus constitutional. As was true in those cases, the Ohio program is neutral in all respects toward religion. It is part of a general and multifaceted undertaking by the State of Ohio to provide educational opportunities to the children of a failed school district. It confers educational assistance directly to a broad class of individuals defined without reference to religion, i.e., any parent of a school-age child who resides in the Cleveland City School District. The program permits the participation of all schools within the district, religious or nonreligious. Adjacent public schools also may participate and have a financial incentive to do so. Program benefits are available to participating families on neutral terms, with no reference to religion. The only preference stated anywhere in the program is a preference for low-income families, who receive greater assistance and are given priority for admission at participating schools.

There are no "financial incentive[s]" that "ske[w]" the program toward religious schools. Such incentives "[are] not present . . . where the aid is allocated on the basis of neutral, secular criteria that neither favor nor disfavor religion, and is made available to both religious and secular beneficiaries on a nondiscriminatory basis." The program here in fact creates financial disincentives for religious schools, with private schools receiving only half the government assistance given to community schools and one-third the assistance given to magnet schools. Adjacent public schools, should any choose to accept program students, are also eligible to receive two to three times the state funding of a private religious school. Families too have a financial disincentive to choose a private religious school over other schools. Parents that choose to participate in the scholarship program and then to enroll their children in a private school (religious or nonreligious) must copay a portion of the school's tuition. Families that choose a community school, magnet school, or traditional public school pay nothing. Although such features of the program are not necessary to its constitutionality, they clearly dispel the claim that the program "creates . . . financial incentive[s] for parents to choose a sectarian school."

Respondents suggest that even without a financial incentive for parents to choose a religious school, the program creates a "public perception that the State is endorsing religious practices and beliefs." But we have repeatedly recognized that no reasonable observer would think a neutral program of private choice, where state aid reaches religious schools solely as a result of the numerous independent decisions of private individuals, carries with it the imprimatur of government endorsement. The argument is particularly misplaced here since "the reasonable observer in the endorsement inquiry must be deemed aware" of the "history and context" underlying a challenged program.

There also is no evidence that the program fails to provide genuine opportunities for Cleveland parents to select secular educational options for their school-age children. Cleveland schoolchildren enjoy a range of educational choices: They may remain in public school as before, remain in public school with publicly funded tutoring aid, obtain a scholarship and choose a religious school, obtain a scholarship and choose a nonreligious private school, enroll in a community school, or enroll in a magnet school. That 46 of the 56 private schools now participating in the program are religious schools does not condemn it as a violation of the Establishment Clause. The Establishment Clause question is whether Ohio is coercing parents into sending their children to religious schools, and that question must be answered by evaluating all options Ohio provides Cleveland schoolchildren, only one of which is to obtain a program scholarship and then choose a religious school.

Justice Souter speculates that because more private religious schools currently participate in the program, the program itself must somehow discourage the participation of private nonreligious schools. But Cleveland's preponderance of religiously affiliated private schools certainly did not arise as a result of the program; it is a phenomenon common to many American cities. Indeed, by all accounts the program has captured a remarkable cross-section of private schools, religious and nonreligious. It is true that 82% of Cleveland's participating private schools are religious schools, but it is also true that 81% of private schools in Ohio are religious schools. To attribute constitutional significance to this figure, moreover, would lead to the absurd result that a neutral school-choice program might be permissible in some parts of Ohio, such as Columbus, where a lower percentage of private schools are religious schools, but not in inner-city Cleveland, where Ohio has deemed such programs most sorely needed, but where the preponderance of religious schools happens to be greater. Likewise, an identical private choice program might be constitutional in some States, such as Maine or Utah, where less that 45% of private schools are religious schools, but not in other States, such as Nebraska or Kansas, where over 90% of private schools are religious schools.

Respondents and Justice Souter claim that even if we do not focus on the number of participating schools that are religious schools, we should attach constitutional significance to the fact that 96% of scholarship recipients have enrolled in religious schools. They claim that this alone proves parents lack genuine choice, even if one parent has ever said so. We need not consider this argument in detail, since it was flatly rejected in *Mueller*, where we found it irrelevant that 96% of parents taking deductions for tuition expenses paid tuition at religious schools. Indeed, we have recently found it irrelevant even to the constitutionality of a direct aid program that a vast majority of program benefits went to religious schools. The constitutionality of a neutral educational aid program simply does not turn on whether and why, in a particular area, at a particular time, most private schools are run by religious organizations, or most recipients choose to use the aid at a religious school. As we said in *Mueller*, "[s]uch an approach would scarcely provide the certainty that this field stands in need of, nor can we perceive principled standards by which such statistical evidence might be evaluated."

This point is aptly illustrated here. The 96% figure upon which respondents and Justice Souter rely discounts entirely (1) the more than 1,900 Cleveland children enrolled in alternative community schools, (2) the more than 13,000 children enrolled in alternative magnet schools, and (3) the more than 1,400 children enrolled in traditional public schools with tutorial assistance. Including some or all of these children in the denominator of children enrolled in nontraditional schools during the 1999-2000 school year drops the percentage enrolled in religious schools from 96% to under 20%. The 96% figure also represents but a snapshot of one particular school year. In the 1997-1998 school year, by contrast, only 78% of scholarship recipients attended religious schools.

In sum, the Ohio program is entirely neutral with respect to religion. It provides benefits directly to a wide spectrum of individuals, defined only by financial need and residence in a particular school district. It permits such individuals to exercise genuine choice among options public and private, secular and religious. The program is therefore a program of true private choice. In keeping with an unbroken line of decisions rejecting challenges to similar programs, we hold that the program does not offend the Establishment Clause.

Justice O'Connor, concurring.

There is little question in my mind that the Cleveland voucher program is neutral as between religious schools and nonreligious schools. Justice Souter rejects the Court's notion of neutrality, proposing that the neutrality of a program should be gauged not by the opportunities it presents but rather by its effects. But Justice Souter's notion of neutrality is inconsistent with that in our case law. As we put it in *Agostini*, government aid must be "made available to both religious and secular beneficiaries on a nondiscriminatory basis."

I do not agree that the nonreligious schools have failed to provide Cleveland parents reasonable alternatives to religious schools in the voucher program. For nonreligious schools to qualify as genuine options for parents, they need not be superior to religious schools in every respect. They need only be adequate substitutes for religious schools in the eyes of parents. The District Court record demonstrates that nonreligious schools were able to compete effectively with Catholic and other religious schools in the Cleveland voucher program. The best evidence of this is that many parents with vouchers selected nonreligious private schools over religious alternatives and an even larger number of parents send their children to community and magnet schools rather than seeking vouchers at all. Moreover, there is no record evidence that any voucher-eligible student was turned away from a nonreligious private school in the voucher program, let alone a community or magnet school.

I find the Court's answer to the question whether parents of students eligible for vouchers have a genuine choice between religious and nonreligious schools persuasive. In looking at the voucher program, all the choices available to potential beneficiaries of the government program should be considered.

Considering all the educational options available to parents whose children are eligible for vouchers, including community and magnet schools, the Court finds that parents in the Cleveland schools have an array of nonreligious options.

Based on the reasoning in the Court's opinion, which is consistent with the realities of the Cleveland educational system, I am persuaded that the Cleveland voucher program affords parents of eligible children genuine nonreligious options and is consistent with the Establishment Clause.

Justice THOMAS, concurring.

Frederick Douglass once said that "[e]ducation . . . means emancipation. It means light and liberty. It means the uplifting of the soul of man into the glorious light of truth, the light by which men can only be made free." Today many of our inner-city public schools deny emancipation to urban minority students. Despite this Court's observation nearly 50 years ago in Brown v. Board of Education, that "it is doubtful that any child may reasonably be expected to succeed in life if he is denied the opportunity of an education," urban children have been forced into a system that continually fails them. These cases present an example of such failures. Besieged by escalating financial problems and declining academic achievement, the Cleveland City School District was in the midst of an academic emergency when Ohio enacted its scholarship program.

The dissents and respondents wish to invoke the Establishment Clause of the First Amendment, as incorporated through the Fourteenth, to constrain a State's neutral efforts to provide greater educational opportunity for underprivileged minority students. Today's decision properly upholds the program as constitutional, and I join it in full.

I

I agree with the Court that Ohio's program easily passes muster under our stringent test, but, as a matter of first principles, I question whether this test should be applied to the States. The Establishment Clause of the First Amendment states that "Congress shall make no law respecting an establishment of religion." On its face, this provision places no limit on the States with regard to religion. The Establishment Clause originally protected States, and by extension their citizens, from the imposition of an established religion by the Federal Government. Whether and how this Clause should constrain state action under the Fourteenth Amendment is a more difficult question.

Thus, while the Federal Government may "make no law respecting an establishment of religion," the States may pass laws that include or touch on religious matters so long as these laws do not impede free exercise rights or any other individual religious liberty interest. By considering the particular religious liberty right alleged to be invaded by a State, federal courts can strike a proper balance between the demands of the Fourteenth Amendment on the one hand and the federalism prerogatives of States on the other.

Whatever the textual and historical merits of incorporating the Establishment Clause, I can accept that the Fourteenth Amendment protects religious liberty rights. But I cannot accept its use to oppose neutral programs of school choice through the incorporation of the Establishment Clause. There would be a tragic irony in converting the Fourteenth Amendment's guarantee of individual liberty into a prohibition on the exercise of educational choice.

II

The wisdom of allowing States greater latitude in dealing with matters of religion and education can be easily appreciated in this context. Respondents advocate using the Fourteenth Amendment to handcuff the State's ability to experiment with education. But without education one can hardly exercise the civic, political, and personal freedoms conferred by the Fourteenth Amendment. Faced with a severe educational crisis, the State of Ohio enacted wide-ranging educational reform that allows voluntary participation of private and religious schools in educating poor urban children otherwise condemned to failing public schools. The program does not force any individual to submit to religious indoctrination or education. It simply gives parents a greater choice as to where and in what manner to educate their children. This is a choice that those with greater means have routinely exercised.

In addition to expanding the reach of the scholarship program, the inclusion of religious schools makes sense given Ohio's purpose of increasing educational performance and opportunities. Religious schools, like other private schools, achieve far better educational results than their public counterparts. For example, the students at Cleveland's Catholic schools score significantly higher on Ohio proficiency tests than students at Cleveland public schools. Of Cleveland eighth graders taking the 1999 Ohio proficiency test, 95 percent in Catholic schools passed the reading test, whereas only 57 percent in public schools passed. And 75 percent of Catholic school students passed the math proficiency test, compared to only 22 percent of public school students. But the success of religious and private schools is in the end beside the point, because the State has a constitutional right to experiment with a variety of different programs to promote educational opportunity. That Ohio's program includes successful schools simply indicates that such reform can in fact provide improved education to underprivileged urban children.

Although one of the purposes of public schools was to promote democracy and a more egalitarian culture, failing urban public schools disproportionately affect minority children most in need of educational opportunity. At the time of Reconstruction, blacks considered public education "a matter of personal liberation and a necessary function of a free society." Today, however, the promise of public school education has failed poor inner-city blacks. While in theory providing education to everyone, the quality of public schools varies significantly across districts. Just as blacks supported public education during Reconstruction, many blacks and other minorities now support school choice programs because they provide the greatest educational opportunities for their children in struggling communities. Opponents of the program raise formalistic concerns about the Establishment Clause but ignore the core purposes of the Fourteenth Amendment.[63]

While the romanticized ideal of universal public education resonates with the cognoscenti who oppose vouchers, poor urban families just want the best education for their children, who will certainly need it to function in our high-tech and advanced society. As Thomas Sowell noted 30 years ago: "Most black people have faced too many grim, concrete problems to be romantics. They want and need certain tangible results, which can be achieved only by developing certain specific abilities." The same is true today. An individual's life prospects increase dramatically with each successfully completed phase of education. For instance, a black high school dropout earns just over $13,500, but with a high school degree the average income is almost $21,000. Blacks with a bachelor's degree have an average annual income of about $37,500, and $75,500 with a professional degree. Staying in school and earning a degree generates real and tangible financial benefits, whereas failure to obtain even a high school degree essentially relegates students to a life of poverty and, all too often, of crime. The failure to provide education to poor urban children perpetuates a vicious cycle of poverty, dependence, criminality, and alienation that continues for the remainder of their lives. If society cannot end racial discrimination, at least it can arm minorities with the education to defend themselves from some of discrimination's effects.

Ten States have enacted some form of publicly funded private school choice as one means of raising the quality of education provided to underprivileged urban children. These programs address the root of the problem with failing urban public schools that disproportionately affect minority students. Society's other solution to these educational failures is often to provide racial preferences in higher education. Such preferences, however, run afoul of the Fourteenth Amendment's prohibition against distinctions based on race. By contrast, school

---

63. Minority and low-income parents express the greatest support for parental choice and are most interested in placing their children in private schools. "[T]he appeal of private schools is especially strong among parents who are low in income, minority, and live in low-performing districts: precisely the parents who are the most disadvantaged under the current system." T. Moe, Schools, Special Vouchers, and the American Public 164 (2001). Nearly three-fourths of all public school parents with an annual income less than $20,000 support vouchers, compared to 57 percent of public school parents with an annual income of over $60,000. In addition, 75 percent of black public school parents support vouchers, as do 71 percent of Hispanic public school parents. [Footnote by the Court.]

choice programs that involve religious schools appear unconstitutional only to those who would twist the Fourteenth Amendment against itself by expansively incorporating the Establishment Clause. Converting the Fourteenth Amendment from a guarantee of opportunity to an obstacle against education reform distorts our constitutional values and disserves those in the greatest need. As Frederick Douglass poignantly noted "no greater benefit can be bestowed upon a long benighted people, than giving to them, as we are here earnestly this day endeavoring to do, the means of an education."

Justice STEVENS, dissenting.

Is a law that authorizes the use of public funds to pay for the indoctrination of thousands of grammar school children in particular religious faiths a "law respecting an establishment of religion" within the meaning of the First Amendment? In answering that question, I think we should ignore three factual matters that are discussed at length by my colleagues.

First, the severe educational crisis that confronted the Cleveland City School District when Ohio enacted its voucher program is not a matter that should affect our appraisal of its constitutionality. In the 1999-2000 school year, that program provided relief to less than five percent of the students enrolled in the district's schools. The solution to the disastrous conditions that prevented over 90 percent of the student body from meeting basic proficiency standards obviously required massive improvements unrelated to the voucher program. Of course, the emergency may have given some families a powerful motivation to leave the public school system and accept religious indoctrination that they would otherwise have avoided, but that is not a valid reason for upholding the program.

Second, the wide range of choices that have been made available to students within the public school system has no bearing on the question whether the State may pay the tuition for students who wish to reject public education entirely and attend private schools that will provide them with a sectarian education. The fact that the vast majority of the voucher recipients who have entirely rejected public education receive religious indoctrination at state expense does, however, support the claim that the law is one "respecting an establishment of religion." The State may choose to divide up its public schools into a dozen different options and label them magnet schools, community schools, or whatever else it decides to call them, but the State is still required to provide a public education and it is the State's decision to fund private school education over and above its traditional obligation that is at issue in these cases.

Third, the voluntary character of the private choice to prefer a parochial education over an education in the public school system seems to me quite irrelevant to the question whether the government's choice to pay for religious indoctrination is constitutionally permissible. Today, however, the Court seems to have decided that the mere fact that a family that cannot afford a private education wants its children educated in a parochial school is a sufficient justification for this use of public funds.

For the reasons stated by Justice Souter and Justice Breyer, I am convinced that the Court's decision is profoundly misguided. Admittedly, in reaching that conclusion I have been influenced by my understanding of the impact of religious strife on the decisions of our forbears to migrate to this continent, and on the decisions of neighbors in the Balkans, Northern Ireland, and the

Middle East to mistrust one another. Whenever we remove a brick from the wall that was designed to separate religion and government, we increase the risk of religious strife and weaken the foundation of our democracy.

Justice Souter with whom Justice Stevens, Justice Ginsburg, and Justice Breyer join, dissenting.

The Court's majority holds that the Establishment Clause is no bar to Ohio's payment of tuition at private religious elementary and middle schools under a scheme that systematically provides tax money to support the schools' religious missions. The occasion for the legislation thus upheld is the condition of public education in the city of Cleveland. The record indicates that the schools are failing to serve their objective, and the vouchers in issue here are said to be needed to provide adequate alternatives to them. If there were an excuse for giving short shrift to the Establishment Clause, it would probably apply here. But there is no excuse. Constitutional limitations are placed on government to preserve constitutional values in hard cases, like these.

Today, however, the majority holds that the Establishment Clause is not offended by Ohio's Pilot Project Scholarship Program, under which students may be eligible to receive as much as $2,250 in the form of tuition vouchers transferable to religious schools. In the city of Cleveland the overwhelming proportion of large appropriations for voucher money must be spent on religious schools if it is to be spent at all, and will be spent in amounts that cover almost all of tuition. The money will thus pay for eligible students' instruction not only in secular subjects but in religion as well, in schools that can fairly be characterized as founded to teach religious doctrine and to imbue teaching in all subjects with a religious dimension. Public tax money will pay at a systemic level for teaching the covenant with Israel and Mosaic law in Jewish schools, the primacy of the Apostle Peter and the Papacy in Catholic schools, the truth of reformed Christianity in Protestant schools, and the revelation to the Prophet in Muslim schools, to speak only of major religious groupings in the Republic.

II

Although it has taken half a century since *Everson* to reach the majority's twin standards of neutrality and free choice, the facts show that, in the majority's hands, even these criteria cannot convincingly legitimize the Ohio scheme.

A

Consider first the criterion of neutrality. As recently as two Terms ago, a majority of the Court recognized that neutrality conceived of as evenhandedness toward aid recipients had never been treated as alone sufficient to satisfy the Establishment Clause. Today, however, the majority employs the neutrality criterion in a way that renders it impossible to understand.

In order to apply the neutrality test, then, it makes sense to focus on a category of aid that may be directed to religious as well as secular schools, and ask whether the scheme favors a religious direction. Here, one would ask whether the voucher provisions, allowing for as much as $2,250 toward private school tuition (or a grant to a public school in an adjacent district), were written in a way that skewed the scheme toward benefiting religious schools. This, however, is not what the majority asks. The majority looks not to the provisions for tuition vouchers, but to every provision for educational opportunity.

The illogic is patent. If regular, public schools (which can get no voucher payments) "participate" in a voucher scheme with schools that can, and public expenditure is still predominantly on public schools, then the majority's reasoning would find neutrality in a scheme of vouchers available for private tuition in districts with no secular private schools at all. "Neutrality" as the majority employs the term is, literally, verbal and nothing more. This, indeed, is the only way the majority can gloss over the very nonneutral feature of the total scheme covering "all schools": public tutors may receive from the State no more than $324 per child to support extra tutoring (that is, the State's 90% of a total amount of $360), whereas the tuition voucher schools (which turn out to be mostly religious) can receive up to $2,250.

Why the majority does not simply accept the fact that the challenge here is to the more generous voucher scheme and judge its neutrality in relation to religious use of voucher money seems very odd. It seems odd, that is, until one recognizes that comparable schools for applying the criterion of neutrality are also the comparable schools for applying the other majority criterion, whether the immediate recipients of voucher aid have a genuinely free choice of religious and secular schools to receive the voucher money. And in applying this second criterion, the consideration of "all schools" is ostensibly helpful to the majority position.

B

The majority addresses the issue of choice the same way it addresses neutrality, by asking whether recipients or potential recipients of voucher aid have a choice of public schools among secular alternatives to religious schools. Again, however, the majority asks the wrong question and misapplies the criterion. The majority has confused choice in spending scholarships with choice from the entire menu of possible educational placements, most of them open to anyone willing to attend a public school. I say "confused" because the majority's new use of the choice criterion, which it frames negatively as "whether Ohio is coercing parents into sending their children to religious schools," ignores the reason for having a private choice enquiry in the first place. Cases since *Mueller* have found private choice relevant under a rule that aid to religious schools can be permissible so long as it first passes through the hands of students or parents. The majority's view that all educational choices are comparable for purposes of choice thus ignores the whole point of the choice test: it is a criterion for deciding whether indirect aid to a religious school is legitimate because it passes through private hands that can spend or use the aid in a secular school. The question is whether the private hand is genuinely free to send the money in either a secular direction or a religious one. The majority now has transformed this question about private choice in channeling aid into a question about selecting from examples of state spending (on education) including direct spending on magnet and community public schools that goes through no private hands and could never reach a religious school under any circumstance. When the choice test is transformed from where to spend the money to where to go to school, it is cut loose from its very purpose.

If, contrary to the majority, we ask the right question about genuine choice to use the vouchers, the answer shows that something is influencing choices in a way that aims the money in a religious direction: of 56 private schools in the district participating in the voucher program (only 53 of which accepted voucher students in 1999-2000); 46 of them are religious; 96.6% of all voucher recipients go to religious schools, only 3.4% to nonreligious ones. Unfortunately for the majority position, there is no explanation for this that suggests the religious direction results simply from free choices by parents. One answer to these statistics, for example, which would be consistent with the genuine choice claimed to be operating, might be that 96.6% of families choosing to avail themselves of vouchers choose to educate their children in schools of their own religion. This would not, in my view, render the scheme constitutional, but it would speak to the majority's choice criterion. Evidence shows, however, that almost two out of three families using vouchers to send their children to religious schools did not embrace the religion of those schools. The families made it clear they had not chosen the schools because they wished their children to be proselytized in a religion not their own, or in any religion, but because of educational opportunity.

Even so, the fact that some 2,270 students chose to apply their vouchers to schools of other religions, might be consistent with true choice if the students "chose" their religious schools over a wide array of private nonreligious options, or if it could be shown generally that Ohio's program had no effect on educational choices and thus no impermissible effect of advancing religious education. But both possibilities are contrary to fact. First, even if all existing nonreligious private schools in Cleveland were willing to accept large numbers of voucher students, only a few more than the 129 currently enrolled in such schools would be able to attend, as the total enrollment at all nonreligious private schools in Cleveland for kindergarten through eighth grade is only 510 children, and there is no indication that these schools have many open seats. Second, the $2,500 cap that the program places on tuition for participating low-income pupils has the effect of curtailing the participation of nonreligious schools: "nonreligious schools with higher tuition (about $4,000) stated that they could afford to accommodate just a few voucher students." By comparison, the average tuition at participating Catholic schools in Cleveland in 1999-2000 was $1,592, almost $1,000 below the cap.

There is, in any case, no way to interpret the 96.6% of current voucher money going to religious schools as reflecting a free and genuine choice by the families that apply for vouchers. The 96.6% reflects, instead, the fact that too few nonreligious school desks are available and few but religious schools can afford to accept more than a handful of voucher students. And contrary to the majority's assertion, public schools in adjacent districts hardly have a financial incentive to participate in the Ohio voucher program, and none has. For the overwhelming number of children in the voucher scheme, the only alternative to the public schools is religious. And it is entirely irrelevant that the State did not deliberately design the network of private schools for the sake of channeling money into religious institutions. The criterion is one of genuinely free choice on the part of the private individuals who choose, and a Hobson's choice is not a choice, whatever the reason for being Hobsonian.

III

I do not dissent merely because the majority has misapplied its own law, for even if I assumed arguendo that the majority's formal criteria were satisfied on the facts, today's conclusion would be profoundly at odds with the Constitution. Proof of this is clear on two levels.

The scale of the aid to religious schools approved today is unprecedented, both in the number of dollars and in the proportion of systemic school expenditure supported. As we said in *Meek*, "it would simply ignore reality to attempt to separate secular educational functions from the predominantly religious role" as the object of aid that comes in "substantial amounts."

It is virtually superfluous to point out that every objective underlying the prohibition of religious establishment is betrayed by this scheme, but something has to be said about the enormity of the violation. I anticipated these objectives earlier, the first being respect for freedom of conscience. Jefferson described it as the idea that no one "shall be compelled to . . . support any religious worship, place, or ministry whatsoever," even a "teacher of his own religious persuasion," and Madison thought it violated by any "'authority which can force a citizen to contribute three pence . . . of his property for the support of any . . . establishment.'" Memorial and Remonstrance ¶ 3. "Any tax to establish religion is antithetical to the command that the minds of men always be wholly free." Madison's objection to three pence has simply been lost in the majority's formalism.

As for the second objective, to save religion from its own corruption, Madison wrote of the "'experience . . . that ecclesiastical establishments, instead of maintaining the purity and efficacy of Religion, have had a contrary operation.'" Memorial and Remonstrance ¶ 7. In Madison's time, the manifestations were "pride and indolence in the Clergy; ignorance and servility in the laity[,] in both, superstition, bigotry and persecution"; in the 21st century, the risk is one of "corrosive secularism" to religious schools, and the specific threat is to the primacy of the schools' mission to educate the children of the faithful according to the unaltered precepts of their faith. Even "[t]he favored religion may be compromised as political figures reshape the religion's beliefs for their own purposes; it may be reformed as government largesse brings government regulation." The risk is already being realized. In Ohio, for example, a condition of receiving government money under the program is that participating religious schools may not "discriminate on the basis of . . . religion," which means the school may not give admission preferences to children who are members of the patron faith; children of a parish are generally consigned to the same admission lotteries as non-believers. For perspective on this foot-in-the-door of religious regulation, it is well to remember that the money had barely begun to flow.

If the divisiveness permitted by today's majority is to be avoided in the short term, it will be avoided only by action of the political branches at the state and national levels. Legislatures not driven to desperation by the problems of public education may be able to see the threat in vouchers negotiable in sectarian schools. Perhaps even cities with problems like Cleveland's will perceive the danger, now that they know a federal court will not save them from it.

My own course as judge on the Court cannot, however, simply be to hope that the political branches will save us from the consequences of the majority's decision. *Everson*'s statement is still the touchstone of sound law, even though the reality is that in the matter of educational aid the Establishment Clause has largely been read away. True, the majority has not approved vouchers for religious schools alone, or aid earmarked for religious instruction. But no scheme so clumsy will ever get before us, and in the cases that we may see, like these, the Establishment Clause is largely silenced. I do not have the option to leave it silent, and I hope that a future Court will reconsider today's dramatic departure from basic Establishment Clause principle.

Justice BREYER, with whom Justice STEVENS and Justice SOUTER join, dissenting.

I write separately, however, to emphasize the risk that publicly financed voucher programs pose in terms of religiously based social conflict. I do so because I believe that the Establishment Clause concern for protecting the Nation's social fabric from religious conflict poses an overriding obstacle to the implementation of this well-intentioned school voucher program. And by explaining the nature of the concern, I hope to demonstrate why, in my view, "parental choice" cannot significantly alleviate the constitutional problem.

With respect to government aid to private education, did not history show that efforts to obtain equivalent funding for the private education of children whose parents did not hold popular religious beliefs only exacerbated religious strife? As Justice Rutledge recognized: "Public money devoted to payment of religious costs, educational or other, brings the quest for more. It brings too the struggle of sect against sect for the larger share or for any. Here one [religious sect] by numbers [of adherents] alone will benefit most, there another. This is precisely the history of societies which have had an established religion and dissident groups." Everson v. Board of Ed. of Ewing (1947) (dissenting opinion).

The upshot is the development of constitutional doctrine that reads the Establishment Clause as avoiding religious strife, not by providing every religion with an equal opportunity (say, to secure state funding or to pray in the public schools), but by drawing fairly clear lines of separation between church and state — at least where the heartland of religious belief, such as primary religious education, is at issue.

The principle underlying these cases — avoiding religiously based social conflict — remains of great concern. As religiously diverse as America had become when the Court decided its major 20th century Establishment Clause cases, we are exponentially more diverse today. America boasts more than 55 different religious groups and subgroups with a significant number of members.

Under these modern-day circumstances, how is the "equal opportunity" principle to work — without risking the "struggle of sect against sect" against which Justice Rutledge warned? School voucher programs finance the religious education of the young. And, if widely adopted, they may well provide billions of dollars that will do so. Why will different religions not become concerned about, and seek to influence, the criteria used to channel this money to religious schools? Why will they not want to examine the implementation of the programs that provide this money — to determine, for example, whether implementation has biased a program toward or against particular sects, or whether recipient religious schools are adequately fulfilling a program's criteria? If so, just how is the State to resolve the resulting controversies without provoking legitimate fears of the kinds of religious controversies without provoking legitimate fears of the kinds of religious favoritism that, in so religiously diverse a Nation, threaten social dissension?

Consider the voucher program here at issue. That program insists that the religious school accept students of all religions. Does that criterion treat fairly groups whose religion forbids them to do so? The program also insists that no participating school "advocate or foster unlawful behavior or teach hatred of any person or group on the basis of race, ethnicity, national origin, or religion." And it requires the State to "revoke the registration of any school if, after a hearing, the superintendent determines that the school is in violation" of the program's rules. As one amicus argues, "it is difficult to imagine a more divisive activity" than the appointment of state officials as referees to determine whether a particular religious doctrine "teaches hatred or advocates lawlessness." Brief for National Committee For Public Education And Religious Liberty as Amicus Curiae 23.

How are state officials to adjudicate claims that one religion or another is advocating, for example, civil disobedience in response to unjust laws, the use of illegal drugs in a religious ceremony, or resort to force to call attention to what it views as an immoral social practice? What kind of public hearing will there be in response to claims that one religion or another is continuing to teach a view of history that casts members of other religions in the worst possible light? How will the public react to government funding for schools that take controversial religious positions on topics that are of current popular interest — say, the conflict in the Middle East or the war on terrorism? Yet any major funding program for primary religious education will require criteria. And the selection of those criteria, as well as their application, inevitably pose problems that are divisive. Efforts to respond to these problems not only will seriously entangle church and state, but also will promote division among religious groups, as one group or another fears (often legitimately) that it will receive unfair treatment at the hands of the government.

I recognize that other nations, for example Great Britain and France, have in the past reconciled religious school funding and religious freedom without creating serious strife. Yet British and French societies are religiously more homogeneous — and it bears noting that recent waves of immigration have begun to create problems of social division there as well. See, e.g., the Muslims of France, 75 Foreign Affairs 78 (1996) (describing increased religious strife in France, as exemplified by expulsion of teenage girls from school for wearing traditional Muslim scarves); Ahmed, Extreme Prejudice; Muslims in Britain, The Times of London, May 2, 1992, p. 10 (describing religious strife in connection with increased Muslim immigration in Great Britain).

In a society as religiously diverse as ours, the Court has recognized that we must rely on the Religion Clauses of the First Amendment to protect against religious strife, particularly when what is at issue is an area as central to religious belief as the shaping, through primary education, of the next generation's minds and spirits.

The Court, in effect, turns the clock back. It adopts, under the name of "neutrality," an interpretation of the Establishment Clause that this Court rejected more than half a century ago. In its view, the parental choice that offers each religious group a kind of equal opportunity to secure government funding overcomes the Establishment Clause concern for social concord. An earlier

Court found that "equal opportunity" principle insufficient; it read the Clause as insisting upon greater separation of church and state, at least in respect to primary education. In a society composed of many different religious creeds, I fear that this present departure form the Court's earlier understanding risks creating a form of religiously based conflict potentially harmful to the Nation's social fabric. Because I believe the Establishment Clause was written in part to avoid this kind of conflict, I respectfully dissent.

TAX EXEMPTIONS FOR RELIGIOUS ORGANIZATIONS

Tax exemptions that benefit only religion are unconstitutional, but those that benefit other groups along with religion, such as charitable and educational institutions, are permissible. In Walz v. Tax Commission, 397 U.S. 664 (1970), the Court upheld a state law that provided property tax exemptions for real or personal property used exclusively for religious, educational, or charitable purposes. The plaintiffs argued that the Establishment Clause was violated by the tax exemption for religious property that was used solely for religious worship. The Supreme Court disagreed and emphasized that the government "granted exemption to all houses of religious worship within a broad class of property owned by nonprofit, quasi-public corporations which include hospitals, libraries, playgrounds, scientific, professional, historical, and patriotic groups."

The Court said that "[t]he legislative purpose of a property tax exemption is neither the advancement nor the inhibition of religion; it is neither sponsorship nor hostility." Rather, the goal is to help nonprofit institutions that the government regards as important to the community. The Court also concluded that granting the tax exemption did not entail excessive government involvement with religion. In fact, the Court said that "[e]limination of exemption would tend to expand the involvement of government by giving rise to tax valuation of church property, tax liens, tax foreclosures, and the direct confrontations and conflicts that follow in the train of those legal processes."

In contrast, in Texas Monthly, Inc. v. Bullock, 489 U.S. 1 (1989), the Court declared unconstitutional a tax exemption that was available only for religious organizations. A Texas law provided an exemption from the state sales and use tax for periodicals that were published or distributed by a religious faith and that consisted solely of writings promulgating the teaching of the faith and for books that consisted wholly of writings sacred to a religions faith. The plurality opinion by Justice Brennan, and joined by Justices Marshall and Stevens, emphasized that *Walz* was distinguishable because there "the benefits derived by religious organizations flowed to a large number of nonreligious groups as well." Justice Brennan explained, "Insofar as that subsidy is conferred upon a wide array of nonsectarian groups as well as religious organizations . . . , the fact that religious groups benefit incidentally does not deprive the subsidy of the secular purpose and primary effect mandated by the Establishment Clause. However, when government directs a subsidy exclusively to religious organizations that is not required by the Free Exercise Clause . . . , it provide[s] unjustifiable awards of assistance to religious organizations and cannot but 'convey a message of endorsement' to slighted members of the community."

Justice Scalia dissented and was joined by Chief Justice Rehnquist and Justice Kennedy. Scalia objected in strong language claiming that "[a]s a judicial demolition project today's decision is impressive," and that the "decision introduces a new strain of irrationality in our Religion Clause jurisprudence." Scalia lamented that laws, like Texas's, that existed in 15 states were declared unconstitutional. For the dissent, the tax exemption for religious publications was a permissible accommodation of religion and did not have the purpose or effect of advancing religion or entail excessive government entanglement with religion.

Thus, *Walz* and *Texas Monthly* together indicate that states may give tax exemptions to religious groups only if nonreligious charitable organizations also are beneficiaries. A tax exemption solely for religious groups violates the Establishment Clause.[64]

AID TO RELIGIOUS COLLEGES AND UNIVERSITIES

The Court has been more lenient in allowing government assistance to religious colleges and universities. The Court has distinguished colleges and universities on the grounds that they are not likely to be as permeated with religious doctrine and dogma as are elementary and secondary schools. Also, the Court has emphasized the difference in the age of the students and their ability to understand that government assistance is not endorsement of religion. Additionally, the Court has stressed that aid to colleges and universities is much less likely to produce the political divisiveness that seems inherent to assistance to parochial elementary and secondary schools.

In Tilton v. Richardson, 403 U.S. 672 (1971), the Court upheld the constitutionality of religious colleges and universities receiving federal money for the construction of facilities that would not be used for religious instruction. *Tilton* concerned Title I of the Higher Education Facilities Act of 1963, which provided construction grants for buildings and facilities used exclusively for secular purposes. The Court applied the *Lemon* test and concluded that it was permissible for religious schools to receive the assistance. The Court concluded that the purpose of the aid was to expand facilities in colleges and universities to "accommodate rapidly growing numbers of youth who aspire to a higher education." The Court said that this is a "legitimate secular objective entirely appropriate for governmental action."

Moreover, the Court found that the aid did not have the effect of advancing religion because the law "was carefully drafted to ensure that the federally subsidized facilities would be devoted to the secular and not the religious function of the recipient institutions. It authorizes grants and loans only for academic facilities that will be used for defined secular purposes and expressly prohibits their use for religious instruction, training or worship." The Court, however, invalidated a part of the act that allowed the facilities to be used for religious purposes after 20 years. The Court said that allowing the building to be converted to religious use at that time would impermissibly have the "effect of advancing religion."

---

64. However, the Court upheld an exemption solely for religious groups from Title VII's prohibition of employment discrimination based on religion. *See* Corporation of the Presiding Bishop of the Church of Jesus Christ of Latter-Day Saints v. Amos, 483 U.S. 327 (1987).

Finally, the Court concluded that allowing the aid would not cause excessive government entanglement with religion. The Court said that "[t]here are generally significant differences between the religious aspects of church-related institutions of higher learning and parochial elementary and secondary schools. . . . [C]ollege students are less impressionable and less susceptible to religious indoctrination. . . . Since religious indoctrination is not a substantial purpose or activity of these church-related colleges and universities, there is less likelihood than in primary and secondary schools that religion will permeate the area of secular education."

Justices Douglas, Black, Marshall, and Brennan dissented. They argued that direct government financial aid to religious institutions, including at the college and university level, violates the Establishment Clause. Justice Douglas said that "even a small amount coming out of the pocket of taxpayers and going into the coffers of a church was not in keeping with our constitutional ideal."

In Hunt v. McNair, 413 U.S. 734 (1973), the Court followed the same reasoning as in *Tilton* and allowed the use of state revenue bonds for religious colleges and universities. A state's Educational Facilities Authority issued bonds to finance the construction of facilities in colleges and universities in the state. Beneficiaries included religious schools, but they were not allowed to use the funds for the construction of facilities to be used for religious activities and the bonds had to be repaid by the schools. The Court relied on *Tilton* to uphold the aid, again emphasizing that the use of the funds was restricted, that the money was available to secular and religious schools, and that the institution was not permeated with religious instruction in the same way as an elementary or secondary school.

In Roemer v. Board of Public Works, 426 U.S. 736 (1976), the distinction between colleges and universities as compared to elementary and secondary schools was even clearer as the Court upheld a program of direct state financial aid to religious colleges and universities. Maryland created a program whereby it provided for grants to private colleges and universities for students and universities. The aid was calculated at 15 percent of the amount per student that the state spent in the public college system. Religious schools, except for seminaries, were allowed to receive the aid. The Court, by a five-to-four margin, but without a majority opinion, upheld the program.

Justice Blackmun's plurality opinion invoked *Tilton* and *Hunt* and found that the requirements of the *Lemon* test were met. Justice Blackmun said that the "purpose of Maryland's aid program is the secular one of supporting private higher education generally, as an economic alternative to a wholly public system." Moreover, he said that the "institutions are not so permeated by religion that the secular side cannot be separated from the sectarian."[65] Therefore, the effect was not to advance religion because the state law required that "state funds not be used to support specifically religious activity."[66] Finally, the plurality opinion concluded that there was not excessive entanglement because there was minimal state oversight required and because "the danger of political divisiveness is substantially less when the aided institution is not an elementary or secondary school, but a college, whose student constituency is not local but diverse and widely dispersed." Justices White and Rehnquist concurred in the judgment and criticized the *Lemon* test but agreed that this aid was not motivated by a religious purpose and did not have a primary effect of advancing religion.

AID TO RELIGIOUS INSTITUTIONS OTHER THAN SCHOOLS

Relatively few cases have involved attempts by the government to give assistance to religious institutions other than schools. The decisions thus far indicate that the Court is more likely to be deferential to the government — as in reviewing aid to colleges and universities — than it is to be more vigilant in its review — as it is concerning aid to elementary and secondary schools.

In Bradfield v. Roberts, 175 U.S. 291 (1899), the Court upheld the constitutionality of the government building a new facility for a church-affiliated hospital. The Court allowed the government aid to a hospital operated by members of the Roman Catholic Church under the auspices of the Church. The Court noted that the hospital did not discriminate based on religion and said that it was "wholly immaterial" that a religious group ran the hospital.

More recently, in Bowen v. Kendrick, 487 U.S. 549 (1988), the Court deemed constitutional the Adolescent Family Life Act, which provided for grants to organizations to provide counseling and care to pregnant adolescents and their parents, and also to provide counseling to prevent adolescent sexual activity. The law specifically authorized receipt of grants by religious, as well as non-religious, organizations. The law prohibited the use of any federal funds for family planning services, for abortion counseling, or for abortions.

Chief Justice Rehnquist wrote for the majority in the five-to-four decision and applied the *Lemon* test to uphold the law. Rehnquist said that the law "was motivated primarily, if not entirely, by a legitimate secular purpose — the elimination or reduction of social and economic problems caused by teenage sexuality, pregnancy, and parenthood."

The Court also said that the law did not have an impermissible effect of advancing religion, even though it specifically encouraged organizations to allow religious groups to play a role. The Court concluded that the law did not favor or disfavor religious groups compared to secular ones and thus was permissible. Rehnquist stressed that the statute was successful in its "maintenance of a course of neutrality among religions and between religion and nonreligion." The Court said that it was "important that the aid is made available regardless of whether it will ultimately flow to a secular or sectarian institution." In fact, the Court invoked Bradfield v. Roberts as establishing the proposition that "religious institutions are [not] disabled by the First Amendment from participating in publicly sponsored social welfare programs."

Finally, the Court said that there was not excessive entanglement with religion. Although the law did not require monitoring by the government, the Court said that most of the cases that had applied the entanglement test had involved elementary and secondary schools that "were pervasively sectarian and had as a substantial purpose the inculcation of religious values." The Court said that "[h]ere, by contrast, there is no reason to assume that the religious organizations which may receive grants are pervasively sectarian in the same sense as the Court has held parochial schools to be."

Justice Blackmun wrote a dissenting opinion joined by Justices Brennan, Marshall, and Stevens. Blackmun focused on the act's subsidizing religious teaching. He said that the "statute encouraged the use of public funds for such instruction, by giving religious groups a central pedagogical and counseling role without imposing any restraints on the sectarian quality of the participation." Blackmun particularly objected to the Court's claim that the groups were not pervasively sectarian; he questioned both the relevance of this factor and the characterization of the particular groups that would receive funds. Blackmun argued that the law clearly had the effect of advancing religion: "Government funds are paying for religious organizations to teach and counsel impressionable adolescents on a highly sensitive subject of considerable religious significance, often on the premises of a church or parochial school and without any effort to remove religious symbols from the sites."

Bowen is a relatively narrow decision. What types of aid the government can provide to religious institutions and under what circumstance remain to be resolved.

TABLE OF CASES

INDEX